Cheri Brown
MA 271
236-4058

A DICTIONARY-OIE WOWAPI WAN of TETON SIOUX

LAKOTA - ENGLISH : ENGLISH - LAKOTA

LAKOTA - IESKA : IESKA - LAKOTA

(With consideration given to Yankton and Santee dialects)

Compiled by

Rev. Eugene Buechel, S.J.

Edited by

Rev. Paul Manhart, S.J.

In cooperation with the

Institute of Indian Studies
University of South Dakota
Vermillion, South Dakota

●

Red Cloud Indian School, Inc.
Holy Rosary Mission
Pine Ridge, South Dakota

1983

Red Cloud Indian School, Inc.
Pine Ridge, South Dakota 57770

Library of Congress Catalogue Number: 74-114669.

In grateful acknowledgement of the

Louis W. and Maud Hill Family Foundation
St. Paul, Minnesota

and the

William H. Donner Foundation, Inc.
New York, New York

Hau kola!
Pilaunyayapi ca napeunniyuzapelo.

Corrections, suggestions, criticisms, questions, etc. may be sent to the editor at Pine Ridge, South Dakota./ Dakota wicaṡa na tuwe ke c'eyaṡ yaecetupi kin iyuha editor ekta wahokiya yo, Pine Ridge, South Dakota 57770 k'el.

Waŋbli Sapa

Wakaŋtaŋka Okolakiciye Tawa wacekiya wicaśa na ogligle waŋ

Black Eagle

Reverend Eugene Buechel, S.J.

priest and missionary of God's Church

T A B L E   O F   C O N T E N T S

P R E F A C E

In the fall of the year 1954 when Father Eugene Buechel, S.J. died, Rev. John F. Bryde, S.J., gathered the entire collection of words and sources Buechel had been erecting into his Teton Dictionary. Bryde was then the only white man fluent in the speaking of Lakota, and so he was granted leave to move the manuscript etc. from St. Francis Mission in St. Francis, S. D., to Holy Rosary Mission in Pine Ridge, S. D.. There he eventually became totally involved in the work of education at the Mission school. Thus it was in the summer of 1958 that Father Bryde presented me with the opportunity to work on the manuscript in view of publishing. From then on until the summer of 1968, very little was accomplished except for a few pages prepared and typed in some sort of systematic form.

It was all through those years, even preceding 1958, that those of us who worked among the Sioux were unimpressed with the need for thorough study of these people. It is true even today people ask: What is the difference between Sioux and Lakota? And even that is a rather advanced type of question compared with: Are there any Sioux left?

But, thanks to many deeper understandings of human values and experience, and perhaps even because of the present sharp awareness of cultural traits and values that demand concern and rightful ordering in American society, peoples can hope to live and bring up their children in a more balanced society which respects the wholesome and varied contributions to life that men require for their own well-being and sanity. These realizations, as a propitious cloud, brought the favorable climate and opportunity and desire that this dictionary be brought forth. Young men anxious to learn the language thoroughly, teachers concerned over their effectiveness in teaching Indian children of a distinct milieu and often as if English were their mother tongue, missionaries young and old wishing to enter more closely into the spirit of this great people, and even Siouan people themselves hoping to attain a more thorough and accurate grasp upon their spoken tongue---people from private and public life have expressed a desire for Buechel's work to be completed.

For all this, Holy Rosary Mission granted me leave of one year to perform the task. So, on September 11, 1968, I arrived at a quiet place in the Jesuit Seminary at St. Bonifacius, Minnesota, where the work was programmed and executed in a first edition. The task was to produce in type what Buechel had scrawled on approximately 30,000 file cards. This was done, with some editing. Many things he wrote will, we would hope, afford others in the future an opportunity to perfect. Examples in the use of words are abundant and often without direct translation. Synonyms and other like words are in need of sharper distinction. And, in general, the perfecting and making consistent the entries as to format etc. leaves much to be done. This is not, however, to imply that the dictionary is lacking in a high degree of utility.

In fact, it was the desire in many requests that a further degree of usefulness be extended in the preparation of the dictionary, not just the presentation of a Lakota-English section which Buechel had in his notes, but also an English-Lakota section which had to be erected from his notes. This took a considerable amount of time and effort. But in the end, it was most helpful, chiefly because it gave an added opportunity to try to present the language the way Buechel understood it in its morpheme units. Moreover, in order to present a broader perspective of the language through a grammar and brief history of the Sioux people, we have hoped other questions too might be answered.

This extra work drew to the interest of the dictionary Rev. Mr. George P. Casey, S.J., who prepared the brief grammar from Buechel's Grammar of Lakota. It is concise and should prove useful to beginners in the language. I feel highly indebted to him and his collegues who participated with him in the writing. Moreover, a large contribution was made, thanks to Mrs. Dorothy Gilroy, in the brief story of the Sioux which was written and left in manuscript by her late husband Leo P. Gilroy in 1967 and then made available to us by the University of South Dakota in Vermillion from the L. P. Gilroy Collection. It is perhaps the finest and more balanced survey of the history of the Dakota people. My hope was that by including this section people's many questions would be attempted to be answered by reading. I cannot help but feel a deep sense of gratitude to Mrs. Gilroy for the kind interest she has shown in seeking to have her husband's study put to a practical use.

There are many whose interest and encouragement have been indispensable in this long and painstaking work. I want especially to mention Rev. Richard Jones, S.J., Mission Superior of St. Francis Mission, who graced this project from the start with his kind concern and interest. Also, the kind interest of Rev. Joseph Karol, S.J., brought to us the story of Buechel's life. Many thanks to Rev. Paul B. Steinmetz, S.J., for his help in approaching Foundations for help in publication. And grateful am I too to Rev. Earl Kurth, S.J., who encouraged the undertaking an immediate publication of Buechel's work in view of the general needs of education and the ministry. There are indeed others, many others, whose help has been given ungrudgingly to help make this work a success. This also includes the team of Indian people who helped by their encouragement and by providing definitions for over 900 words Buechel left without definitions. Particular and special mention is made of these splendid persons in that section on Lately Defined Word List. Here, then, I wish to extend my hand in greeting to each and every one who has by word or work assisted in making this dictionary possible and come to print.

Pilamayayapi yelo. Wakaŋtaŋka oŋśimala ye.

P.M.SJ

LIFE OF FATHER EUGENE BUECHEL, S.J.

If it were a warm summer afternoon, you would have found him sitting on the green bench under the trees behind the faculty building of St. Francis Mission, St. Francis, South Dakota. He would be chatting in Lakota with those patriarchs of the Brule Sioux, Black Spotted Horse, German Good Breast, and George Horse Looking. He was Black Eagle, Waŋbli Sapa,--a stooped but thick-set man of 80, dressed in a black cassock, with gray, close-cropped hair and beard, and blue eyes sparkling with animation behind thick-lensed, black-rimmed glasses. Smiling and laughing as he talked, Black Eagle may have been reminiscing about the happenings he and his cronies had been part of since his arrival at St. Francis in 1902. But more than likely he was quizzing his Indian friends about some obscure Lakota word. For this was Father Eugene Buechel, S.J., missionary to the Dakota, builder of a Sioux museum, writer of a Lakota grammar, Bible History, and dictionary, and authority on the Lakota language, customs and culture.

The green benches were empty after September 15th. Father Buechel lay sick. On the previous Sunday, he went to his mission station at Two Strike and preached his usual 45-minute sermon in Lakota. Then that week he suffered a stroke. He died on October 27, 1954.

Although the cold wind pelted them with sleet, hundreds of Indians and white people from miles around came to St. Francis for the funeral rites, in the church Buechel himself had built. As the crowd left the church and turned east, they crossed the walk to a small, one-room, cream-colored building of concrete block. It is a memorial to Father Buechel's love of the Dakota--a museum of Sioux artifacts, completed shortly before his death.

In 1908, while Buechel was pastor of the church in Pine Ridge, South Dakota, about 100 miles west of St. Francis on the Oglala reservation, The chief Red Cloud was living just east of the agency town. The chief died in 1909 and was buried with a very lonely ceremony, Buechel later recalled. Only twelve Indian police were in attendance at the burial on that cold, white winter day.

Perhaps it was the death of Red Cloud that started the missionary on his artifact collection, in 1912 while he was superior of Holy Rosary Mission four miles north of Red Cloud's home. If he admired some object in an Indian home, often enough the family would give it to him. And if he could not beg an item, he would buy it. His collection got a great boost in 1914 when a group of Oglala gave him hundreds of valuable items.

He brought the collection to St. Francis when he was appointed superior of the Mission there in 1916. He continued adding items during his term of office ending in 1923, and then especially through the years after as he travelled his circuit of chapels and homes among the Brule of the Rosebud. The collection finally outgrew the room set aside for it at the mission. So in 1947, as a present on his 50th anniversary as a Jesuit, Brother Joseph Schwart, S.J. built the present building for his museum.

Father Buechel was born in Schleida, Thuringia, Germany, on October 20, 1874. He attended schools, Volkschule and Gymnasium, in Fulda, Germany, from 1881 to 1896. In 1896 and 1897 he studied in a Clerical seminary in Fulda. In October, 1897, he entered the Jesuit Order in Blyenback, Holland. And in the year 1900 he came to the United States where in 1906 he received ordination.

But the museum was only one memorial to a busy life spent with the Dakota. In his book-cluttered missionary office where he met the many people who came to him was a large filing case containing over 25,000 carefully catalogued Lakota words with their English meanings. This was the raw material for the Lakota-English dictionary he had been working on since 1910. It was to be the largest and most complete collection of its kind in the world.

Buechel kept cataloguing new words he had learned from his backyard conversations with his Indian cronies right up to the day he suffered the fatal stroke.

Although failure to finish the dictionary saddened him, he had some consolation thumbing through two Lakota works he had published, a Bible History in 1923 and a 378-page Grammar of Lakota in 1939. Both of these books grew out of a study of Lakota that began three weeks after his arrival first in St. Francis as a 28-year-old student for the priesthood and wearing the fine black beard that was to give him the name of Black Eagle. He squeezed his study of the language between his work as teacher and disciplinarian of the Indian boys, continued it during 1904-06, while he finished his studies at St. Louis University, and during the two summer of 1904 and 1905. Then, after ordination, he returned to the missions to spend his vacation working and studying with the pioneer missionaries.

His language study continued as well in 1907 at Holy Rosary Mission as at St. Francis until 1923. In that year he began the work that occupied his full time until his death, namely that of a field man, conducting prayer meetings in chapels and visiting in the homes. He used Lakota constantly, in several hundred sermons and instructions annually.

He loved the Dakota with a Christian love because he was their priest, and with a family love because he was their brother. His love was also based on the cold facts of history. He was always ready with an impassioned defense of the people based on those facts--whiskey, rationing, poor food, land, unjust or violated treaties, and the many other factors that so bewildered a people unused to the white man's legalistic and complicated civilization. It can be said that he became of a people proud and sensitive to a heritage as lords of the plains.

Buechel's favorite argument was that no people in history had risen so swiftly from a primitive life to meet a strange civilization as had the Sioux. Whereas the English, Irish, German and other European barbaric peoples had become civilized gradually over the centuries. The Indian had been whirled into a confrontation. And yet in about 75 years they had made a marvelous adaptation. In fact during his 49 years of work among the Dakota, he witnessed and helped bring about that meeting in perhaps the most telling way.

May 1, 1969. Rev. Joseph Karol, S.J.

The SIOUX

1. Sioux is a name composed by the French, putting together two words from Algonquin, nadowe (snake) and sioux (little), and applied by the Buanag or Ojibwa (Chippewa) to especially the Dakota people. The hard inner core of Siouan people consists of the groups distinguished first by closely allied dialects that are spoken: the Dakota, the Nakota and the Lakota, a title meaning "allies". And in the second place, they are distinguished by certain traits: the Santee, the Yankton and the Teton respectively; the eastern, central and western groups. The Santee (Isáŋti) seem to have received this name from the fact that they were used to camping long periods of time in the place they collected stone for the making of knives (isáŋ). The Yankton were the people from the villages far towards the extremeties of the nation. And the Teton were known as the people encamped upon the prairie. These three principal groups of the Sioux formed a loosely knit confederacy of seven sub-tribes:

The Santee

1- Mdewakaŋtoŋwaŋ (Mde-wakaŋtoŋ, the People of Spirit Lake).
2- Waḣpekute (The Leaf Shooters).
3- Waḣpetoŋwaŋ or Waḣpetoŋ (the People on Lake Traverse).
4- Sisitoŋwaŋ (Sissetoŋ, People of the Marsh).

The Yankton

5- Ihaŋktoŋwaŋ (Yankton, People of the End).
6- Ihaŋktoŋwaŋna (Yanktonai, The Little Yaŋkton).

The Teton

7- Titoŋwaŋ (Teton, an American-Canadian corruption of the word, People of the Prairie).

	RESERVATIONS
Oglala	(The Pine Ridge)
Brule	(The Rosebud)
Huŋkpapa	(The Standing Rock)
Miniconju	(The Cheyenne River)
Sans Arc	(The Cheyenne River)
Two Kettle	(The Cheyenne River)

We must not pass over those other tribes that are cognate tribes of the confederacy:

Assiniboin (a seceded Yankton tribe)
Blackfoot Sioux (Rocky Mountain Sioux)
Stone (Rocky Mountain Sioux)
Absaroka (Crow)
Gros Ventre: Hidatsa or Minitaree, Minitare
Mandan
Winnebego
Iowa
Omaha
Ponca
Oto
Missouri
Kaw

Osage
Quapaw
Catawba
Biloxi
Ocanechee
Tuteh

These cognate tribes are related through the so-called stock Siouan language. We should note that the term "People", or village, in the above names does not indicate a fixed abode, but rather a nomadic band that moved from site to site at intervals with all their property. "Camp" would be more proper a term. Moreover, "toŋwaŋ" can mean people, village, or band, the latter in the sense of a group of people--a community.

2. Territory. Sioux tribes, about 1200 A.D., occupied central Virginia, North Carolina and South Carolina. Then the majority, excepting the Catawba and several other tribes, moved west to the head waters of the Mississippi River in Minnesota. They made their way thither, pushing before them a number of other tribes who were forced north and south, as well as westward during that movement. They took territory extending from Wisconsin north to about 46 degrees 30 minutes North latitude, or one day's march from Lake Superior, and west into the Dakotas, Wyoming, Montana, Nebraska, and south to Texas, and from Montana and North Dakota into the Canadian provinces of Alberta and Saskatchewan. They occupied the country across the Mississippi from about Bemidji (Leech Lake) to Bayfield, Wisconsin, on Lake Superior, south to central Wisconsin and northwest Iowa. Minnesota was held by various Santee bands; eastern Dakotas to the Missouri River and northwestern Iowa by the Yankton and Yanktonai. The west Missouri country was held by Tetons, the latter comprising three-fifths of the nation. The Omaha held lands south of the Niobrara River and along the Missouri in the vicinity of Omaha and Council Bluffs. Poncas were in Nebraska west and south of the Omahas into central Kansas. The Assiniboin held lands in North Dakota and Montana and southern Canada about the Assiniboin River and in Saskatchewan to southeastern Alberta. The Crows held land in central Montana, northeastern Dakota and north central Wyoming. The Mandans were in central Dakota along the Missouri River. And the Winnebego were scattered in Wisconsin and Minnesota.

But in time, pressure by the Ojibwa caused them to move their western boundary across the upper Red River and Minnesota River. They retained southern Minnesota, part of Wisconsin and northern Iowa, as well as all land west of the Red River at the Canadian border to the North Platte River and west beyond the Black Hills into eastern Wyoming, eastern Montana and northern Nebraska

In the latter part of the 19th century, three Sioux chiefs stood out in the public mind: Pananapapi (Strikes the Ree) from the Yanktons; Maȟpiya Luta (Red Cloud) an Oglala among the Teton; and Siŋte Gleśka (Spotted Tail) a Brule also of the Teton.

3. The Assiniboin separated from the Yankton prior to 1640. When Europeans first came into contact with the Sioux about 1650, the latter centered about Mille Lac and Leech Lake toward the head of the Mississippi River in central Minnesota. Their eastern frontier was about a day's march from Lake Superior. They were gradually forced back from positions further east by the Ojibwa (Chippewa) who had obtained fire arms from the whites. And from that point of their eastern frontier where they were first met by whites they were later driven back by the Ojibwa, from about the confluence of the Chippewa and Red Cedar Rivers in Wisconsin (about 45 degrees North and 92 degrees West) along a northwesterly line through Minnesota (north of St. Paul) to a point west of present-day Fargo at about 47 degrees North and 98 degrees West; from that point on a northwesterly line circling Stump Lake, Devils Lake and Sweetwater Lake to the loop of the Souris River, northwest of Devils Lake; thence southward on to Bismark; thence westward to the vicinity of the Montana line at about the Little Missouri River; southwesterly to the Platte River, west of the Black Hills and along the headwaters of the Powder, Belle Fourche and the Dry Fork of the Cheyenne Rivers to the Platte River at the northern ranges of the Laramie Mountains; thence easterly along the Platte River into Nebraska to the confluence of the Blue River; thence northeasterly to the Keyapaha River west of Turtle Butte; thence easterly along the left bank of the Keyapaha to the Niobrara River and along the left bank of the Niobrara to it confluence with the Missouri River; thence along the left bank of the Missouri to Sioux City, Iowa; thence northeasterly to the Minnesota-Wisconsin line. The pressure of the Ojibwa in turn caused pressure by the Sioux upon the Cheyenne, Omaha, Crow, Arapahoe, Blackfoot (Siksika), as they advanced. The Teton or Lakota bore the brunt of the advance fighting, holding both the north and south wings. They were stopped by the Crow (Absaroka) at their western limits and southern line in Wyoming, and by the Pawnee at the Platte in Nebraska. This was accomplished about 1750. Bitter enmity against those two tribes prevails since that time.

When the pressure of the Ojibwa began, the Sioux were "canoe" Indians. When they crossed the Missouri, they learned the value of horses and raided far south and west among tribes in those areas clear into Texas and into Montana and Idaho to obtain them, the Blackfoot horses being especially prized. Those were the famous appelousa spotted horses. After obtaining horses, the Sioux really "went to town" and became the "finest light cavalry in the world" as has often been said. The Teton, or Prairie Bands, were the ones to obtain the horses and to develope military tactics in the use of cavalry.

4. The name Nadowesioux was used by Father Paul LeJeune in 1640 on information of Jean Nicolet who visited the Sioux country of Wisconsin about 1634 or 1635.

About 1655-56, the Sioux were sheltering a band of Hurons who had fled from the Iroquois. The surrounding tribes at that time rated the Sioux as having 30 villages or bands and as being a terror to them by reason of their numbers and prowess, although they were reputed to be less cruel than others. Father Marquette caused them to make peace with one another. It was a peace that lasted from 1665 until 1671 when the Sioux, provoked by insults from the eastern tribes, returned Marquette's presents and declared war on their hereditary foes the Ojibwa, Sac, Fox, Illinois and others. That state lasted until 1674 when they sent a delegation to Sault Sainte Marie to arrange peace. While the delegation sat there in council in the mission church, they were attacked by the Ojibwa. A desparate encounter ensued. The Ojibwa set fire to the church to dislodge the Sioux. That all furthered the state of war. But the Sioux stayed friandly to the French traders.

In 1680, a band of Isaⁿti captured Father Hennepin whom they met on the Mississippi that spring while on their way south to attack the Illinois tribes. They kept him prisoner until fall, and then they turned him over to Pierre DuLuth who traded with them.

By 1695, after Nicholas Perrot established a post at the lower end of Lake Pepin on the Minnesota side in Wabasha County, and Pierre LeSueur had established one near present Red Wing, Minnesota, the Sioux had obtained a number of guns and began to push further to the west, driving the Cheyenne, Omaha and Oto down upon the Missouri and pushing out onto the buffalo plains of the present Dakotas.

About 1698, the French assisted the Sioux in a war against the Fox and got themselves involved in a conflict that lasted 40 years. Before its end, the Sioux turned against the French and gave refuge to the defeated Fox who by that time were ruined as a tribe.

In 1736, the Sioux massacred Verendrye the younger and all of his party of 20 at the Lake of the Woods in Canada just north of the Minnesota-Manitoba border, deep in Ojibwa territory.

In 1745-46, the Fox having been completely crushed the French made peace with the Sioux and between the Sioux and Ojibwa.

On the fall of Canada to the English in 1763, the Sioux went to the English post at Green Bay with proffers of friendship and asked that traders come into their territory. Two thousand of the Sioux warriors now had guns, while the others and larger portion still depended on the bow in the use of which they excelled all others. The commander at Green Bay described them as the largest and greatest nation of Indians yet found, and said that they held all other Indians to be their slaves or dogs.

In the winter of 1766-67, Jonathan Carver, an American, spent several months with the Isaⁿti, visited their sacred burial grounds in a sacred cave near St. Paul, saw burial ceremonies in which the bereaved gashed themselves in frenzied grief.

Soon after that time the Sioux abandoned the Mille Lac and Leech Lake area to the Ojibwa, with whom the hereditary war was still going on. The final engagement in that area occurred in 1768 when the Ojibwa ambushed a Santee canoe fleet with a crew of 500 warriors near the confluence of the Mississippi and Crow Wing Rivers west of Brainerd, with a much smaller number of men, and entirely defeated them, practically eliminating the Santee as a fighting force for some time.

In 1775 peace was established between the two tribes, due to English efforts to do so in the face of the coming Revolution. The peace lasted until the close of the Revolution in which both tribes furnished contingents against the American frontier. But afterwards the warriors returned home and the old war broke out again.

In the meantime, between 1634-35 and 1696, the Teton or Lakota tribes were pushing westward on a broad front, pushing the Arikara up the Missouri, engulfing them and the Mandan finally. About 1796 French traders and trappers from St. Louis began coming into the Yankton and Teton territory which later became part of the Louisiana Purchase. And after that purchase Manuel Lisa, a Spaniard from St. Louis, founded the American Fur Company and established his headquarters at Cedar Island in the Missouri below Pierre, South Dakota, later moving it down to the site of present Chamberlain.

Lewis and Clark travelled up the Missouri, holding councils with the Yankton and Teton tribes, as well as with the Mandan and Arikara (Ree), and were given descriptions, land marks, water courses and climatic information of the land to the west, in addition to the names of the tribes whose territory they would pass through en route to the Pacific. They made their return in 1806.

This led to the first Sioux, a Yankton delegation, visiting Washington, D. C. This marked the beginning of the U. S. Government giving the Sioux the Great White Father business, which has cost them dear since, with a few credits on their side now and then.

In the meantime, 1805-06, Lt. Zebulon M. Pike visited the Santee and other tribes along the upper Mississippi and negotiated the first treaty with the Sioux, in the vicinity of present St. Paul, Minnesota. On September 23, 1805, a treaty with the Santee and other tribes of that region was signed for the establishment of military posts (Ft. Snelling principally), and the Santee gave up their British flags and medals and accepted American ones.

Prior to 1805, from time immemorial and for some time later, the Sioux Allies--Dakota, Lakota and Nakota--who at the latter date were diverging rapidly to the west and south had met in an annual council on the lower James River in present South Dakota.

In 1807 Manuel Lisa established his trading post and headquarters, as has been mentioned, on Cedar Island and later moved it to the vicinity of Chamberlain. He operated several other trading posts among the Teton, Yankton and Omaha. He taught the tribes how to plant gardens and tend to cattle and hogs, set up blacksmith shops for their benefit without charge, and cared for their aged and helpless. It has been said in his time that he was the best liked white man in his time, and today he is still remembered fondly by them. He was intensely American in feeling--he was creole Spa nish--and was appointed the first U. S. Government Agent for the upper Missouri tribes. By his great influence with them he held them friendly to the U. S. during the war of 1812. Later, in 1820 he died. Notwithstanding that, most of the Santee, through the efforts of Tecumseh the Shawnee chief and Robert Dickson a British trader declared war for England and furnished a contingent against Fort Meigs. They besieged the fort unsuccessfully from May 1st to May 9th, 1813, and then they left Ohio and the Maumee River.

5. At the close of the War of 1812, a council was held at Portage des Sioux, Missouri, just above St. Louis, with the various Sioux bands . At that time the Santee again made peace with the U. S., and with the other Sioux tribes acknowledging the sovereignty of the U. S. Other hostile tribes who participated with the British made peace at the same time. This was a great and vast gathering of the Middle West tribes and marks the beginning of their modern history.

In 1820, Fort Snelling was built at present Minneapolis at a spot overlooking the Minnesota River, so as to control the Santee and Ojibwa.

In 1825, another council met at Prairie du Chien, Wisconsin, to draw up a treaty for the deliniation of tribal boundaries, to put an end to all tribal wars and clear the way for future land cessions. At that time and for many years later the Sioux led all other tribes in volume, in the fur trade, consisting principally in buffalo and beaver skins.

In 1834 regular missions were established among the Sioux by the Congregational Church. It was among the Santee at Lake Calhoun in Minneapolis; the following year they established others at Lake Harriet and Lac qui Parle, Minnesota. In 1837 Lutherans established a mission at Red Wing, Minnesota. In 1841, the Catholics began mission work among the Sioux at present St. Paul. In 1837 and again in 1848 and 1850, Catholic missionaries started work among the various Teton and Yankton bands, principally the Brule. In 1851 an inter-tribal council met at Fort Laramie, Wyoming in the Teton Oglala country.

It was in 1837 that the Sioux sold all their territory east of the Mississippi River. In the winter of 1837-38 smallpox, alleged to have been introduced from a passing steamer, swept through all the tribes of the upper Missouri River. An estimated 30,000 Indians died, a large proportion being Sioux. At the same time war with the Chippewa again flared on the eastern (Santee) frontier. In a battle at the site of present Stillwater, during June 1839, some 50 Chippewa were killed, and later one of the camps was raided while the Chippewa warriors were away. 91 Chippewa scalps of women, children, aged and cripples, wounded etc. were taken. In 1851 the Santee sold all their lands in Minnesota and Iowa, except a 20-mile strip on the upper Minnesota River.

Although there were four missions among the Santee, they were reported to have an inveterate hatred of Christianity. In 1851 then, they attacked, under the leadership of Inkpaduta, the scattered white settlements about Spirit Lake on the Iowa-Minnesota border, killing 50 and burning many houses. They captured four white women, two of whom were killed later, and two who were rescued by Christian Indians. Inkpaduta participated in all the Indian warfare for the next twenty years, until 1877.

In 1858 the Yankton sold all their lands in South Dakota except the Yankton Reservation (Agency). The famous quarry at Pipe Stone, Minnesota, was also permanently reserved for Indian uses. And in 1860 the Reverend Samuel Henman opened a mission of the Episcopal Church among the Santee.

In 1862 there occurred the so-called "Minnesota Outbreak", involving nearly all the Santee bands and caused by the government confiscating a large proportion of treaty funds to satisfy traders' claims and aggravating them by long delay in an annuity issue. The weakening of garrisons and general upset of conditions were owing to the Civil War and so encouraged the revolt. Trouble began on August 2, 1862 with an attack upon the agency at Redwood, Minnesota where 5,000 Indians were waiting distribution of supplies. The troops were overpowered and the commissary goods seized. No other damage was done. On August 17, 1862 a party of hunters, after being refused food at a settler's cabin, massacred the family and fled with the news to the camp of Little Crow where a general attack on all whites and Christian Indians was resolved upon. Within a week almost every farm cabin and small settlement in southern Minnesota was wiped out and most of the inhabitants massacred, except a few who escaped to Fort Ridgely at the lower end of the reservation. The latter were mainly Christians and their white missionaries.

Fort Ridgely was then attacked on August 20-21, New Ulm on August 22, both being unsuccessful assaults and the Indians were finally repulsed. On September 2, 1862, 1,500 regular and volunteer soldiers defeated the Santee at Birch Coulee and on September 23 again defeated them at Wood Lake. This broke the uprising. Most of the hostiles surrendered and the rest fled in small bands to the west and north. 300 prisoners were condemned to death by a court martial, but the number was cut to 38 by Presidential Order. Those 38 were hanged at Mankato on December 23, 1862. On September 24, 1863, one part of the fugitives trying to escape into the Yanktonai country was overtaken and defeated with great loss by the troops near Big Mound, North Dakota. The survivors fled to the Teton beyond the Missouri River and others into Canada where they still live. Two months after the outbreak Congress declared the Santee treaties abrogated. On September 3, 1863, troops attacked the main Santee camp under Inkpaduta at Whitestone Hill near Ellendale, North Dakota, killed 300 and captured nearly as many more. On July 28, 1864, the final blow was delivered to a combined force of Santee together with some northern Teton and Yanktonai at Killdeer Mountain in North Dakota. The prisoners taken and others of the lately hostile bands were settled on two reservations established for the Lower Yanktonai at Crow Creek, South Dakota and for the Santee at Santee in northeastern Nebraska. They are still on those reserves. The outbreak cost lives of whites---nearly 700 in the first few days of fighting---and the lives of almost twice as many Santee, Northern Teton and Yanktonai.

The chief of the 3,000 Yankton, Pananapapi, refused to join the fight, as did the Brule and Oglala of the Tetons---13,000 strong. Thus, in October 1865 at old Fort Sully, near Pierre, South Dakota, a general treaty of peace was made with the Santee, Yankton, Yanktonai and one Teton band, the Lower Brule, who all agreed to go on reservations. The great body of the Tetons refused to take part. That included all west of the Missouri River.

6. After the discovery of <u>gold in California</u> in 1849 and the opening of the emigrant trail along the North Platte River and across the Rocky Mountains, the Indians along the route became alarmed at the disturbance of the buffalo herds, upon which they depended practically entirely for food, clothing and shelter. The Brule and Oglala Sioux were the principal complainants. For protection of the trail, in 1849 the Government bought the trading post of Fort Laramie and garrisoned it on the upper North Platte River in Wyoming (which is not to be confused with the present city of Laramie). The Fort was located in Goshen County about 18 miles west of the Wyoming-Nebraska line and northwest of Scotts Bluff, Nebraska at the confluence of the Laramie and North Platte Rivers.

In 1851 a council of nearly all tribes and bands of the northern plains was held there with Government agents and army officers, during which a treaty was negotiated by which they agreed in regard to rival territorial claims, pledged peace---among the tribes themselves and with the whites---and promised not to disturb the trail upon consideration of stipulated annual payments to them by the Federal Government. That treaty was not ratified by the officials in Washington who declined to do so. Thus, on August 17, 1854 while the tribes were assembled about it, there occurred the famed Fort Laramie massacre, in which Lt. Grattan and a detachment of 29 soldiers were killed while trying to arrest some Brule who had killed and eaten an emigrant's cow. The attitude and indiscretion of Lt. Grattan, which all available evidence indicated, caused the outbreak. After the affray the Brule and other bands took forcible possession of the annuity goods and left without making any attempt against the post and its garrison.

The Brule were thereupon declared hostile and General Harney was sent against them with 1,200 men. On September 3, 1854, he came upon them at Ash Hollow in western Nebraska, and while pretending to parley with them on their offer to surrender, suddenly attacked and killed 136 of them and destroyed all of their tepees and camp equipment.

Late in 1863 the Oglala under their chief Maȟpiya Luta, and the Brule under Spotted Tail, Siŋtegleśka, became actively hostile, being inflamed by reports of the Santee outbreak and the Civil War in the South. They were joined by the Cheyenne and for two years all travel across the plains was virtually suspended.

In march 1865, aroused to desperation by the proclamation that two new roads were to be opened through their best hunting grounds to the newly opened Montana goldfields, they notified the Government that under Red Cloud's leadership they would allow no new roads or garrison posts to be established in their country. Thereafter, they opened and carried on war with such determination that the Government asked for a peace parley and sent a peace commission in April-May of 1868. They signed a treaty which provided that the Montana Road which had been opened north from the town of Laramie and three posts that had been established to protect it be all abandoned. However, Red Cloud refused to sign until after the troops were withdrawn. The treaty left the territory south of the North Platte open to road building and recognized all the country north of the North Platte and east of the Big Horn Mountains as unceded Indian territory, and thus established the Great Sioux Reservation, nearly equivalent to all of South Dakota west of the Missouri River. Provision was made for an agency on that River and the inauguration of regular governmental civilizing work. In consideration of those promises and their giving up their old freedom, the Indians were promised free aid of blacksmiths, doctors, a sawmill, and a complete suit of clothing yearly for 30 years to every individual of the bands concerned, based on the actual yearly census. Among the officials witnessing were the Reverend Henman, an Episcopalian missionary, and Father Pierre DeSmet, a Catholic missionary. That treaty brought all three of the Sioux allies comprising the Sioux Nation under agency restriction, when its ratification in February 1869 brought the five years of war to a close. In that war Red Cloud had been the principal leader, as Spotted Tail had been won to friendship earlier by the kindness of some of the officers at Fort Laramie when his daughter died and was buried there with Christian rites.

During that war, the Cheyenne and Northern Arapahoe also acted with the Teton. The chief fighting was centered around Fort Kearney which Red Cloud held under repeated siege and near which on December 21,

1866, occurred the Fetterman Massacre when 80 men under Captain (Lt.) Fetterman were completely exterminated by an overwhelming force of Indians.

7. By <u>treaties</u> made in 1867 the reservations were established at Lake Traverse, South Dakota, and Fort Totten, North Dakota, for the Sisseton and Wahpeton Santee and the Cutmeat Yanktonai, most of whom had been concerned in the Minnesota outbreak. In 1870 a part of the Christian Santee separated from their bands in Nebraska and moved to Flandreau, South Dakota, and became citizens.

In 1871, despite protests of Red Cloud and other leading chiefs, the Northern Pacific Railroad was constructed along the south bank of the Yellowstone River and several new posts were built for its protection. And so war was on again with the Teton, Northern Cheyenne and Northern Arapahoe. Several skirmishes took place, and in 1873 General Custer was ordered to Dakota. The following year he made an exploratory march into the Black Hills in southern South Dakota (which Hills are square in the middle of the Teton Reservation of that day). He reported there was gold in the Black Hills, as some former miners in the 7th Cavalry had found "color" along the streams. Despite a treaty the gold rush began, with miners from all quarters wading in with the usual accompaniment of camp followers. The Indians refused to sell the Hills, Paha Sapa to them, on any terms offered. The military patrol which had been sent in and which expelled all the miners etc. whom the could find was then withdrawn, and mining towns sprang up all over the Hills, a ten thousand square mile area. Indians who were in hunting camps in the general area with permits from the Indian agents at the various agencies were ordered to report to their agencies by January 31, 1876 or be considered hostile. But even the runners who carried the messages were unable to return because of the heavy snows and severity of the weather, until after war had been declared by the Government.

That war is known as the Custer War from its central event of June 25, 1876 when Custer and a squadron of the 7th Cavalry numbering 204 men vaingloriously attacked the main camp of about 2,500 warriors of the Sioux and Cheyenne on the Little Big Horn River in southeastern Montana. All were killed who were present. There was a trumpeter who had left in the late hours of the previous night or early hours of the morning (and who incidentally got his Purple Heart decoration some 67 or 68 years later when in his 90's). Also, there was a Crow scout called Curley who managed to make his way out of the melee at the opening of the fight when he saw the strength of the hostile encampment. The only escapee was a horse owned by Captain Tom Custer, a brother to the general. That horse, called Commanche, lived for many years after at Fort Robinson, Nebraska.

On June 26, 1876, and the following day, in the same vicinity other units under Reno and Benteen had fierce encounters with the Sioux and Cheyenne, in which 60 men were killed. Upon the approach of Generals Terry and Gibbons from the north, the hostiles withdrew under Crazy Horse, Taśuᵑka Witko, and Gall, Pizi, in good order with their families and horse herds, the latter augmented by some of Custer's mounts. Sitting Bull, Tataᵑka Iyotaka, of the Huᵑkpapa, was present but not in command. Red Cloud and Spotted Tail had remained at their agencies. Several minor engagements occurred later that year, which resulted in the surrender and return of most of the late hostiles to their agencies, while Sitting Bull and Gall escaped later in June 1877 to Canada. By a series of treaties made September 23, 1876, and October 27, 1876, the Teton surrendered the entire Black Hills country and the western outlet in consideration of certain promises of the Government, which were never kept.

On September 7, 1877, Crazy Horse, who had come in with his band of Oglala some months before, was killed by a guard at the Fort Robinson guardhouse. That same month the last of the hostiles surrendered.

Soon after the treaty a large delegation of Tetons visited Washington and as a result the Red Cloud (Oglala) agency was established at Pine Ridge, South Dakota, and the Spotted Tail (Brule) agency at Rosebud, South Dakota, in 1878. That marked the beginning of the civilization of those two bands.

In 1881 all of the late hostiles in Canada came in and surrendered. Sitting Bull and his band of Huŋkpapa, after being held in confinement for two years, were permitted to return to their homes on the Standing Rock Reservation in South Dakota. On August 5, 1881, Spotted Tail was killed by a rival chief. On July 29, 1888 Pananapapi the famous Yankton died at 84 years of age.

8. In 1887 Father Francis M. J. <u>Croft</u> organized a Catholic sisterhood, many of whose members served as nurses in Cuba in 1898 during the Spanish-American War, and prior to that time they worked among the confederated Grosventre, Arikara and Mandan, nursing the sick and teaching the women nursing, and instructing them all in sanitation, first at Standing Rock in South Dakota and later at Fort Berthold, Montana.

In 1889 the Great Sioux Reservation, after long and persistent objections on the part of their chiefs, was cut in two and reduced by about one half of what remained after the loss of the Black Hills area. In this latter instance, they lost all territory between the White and Cheyenne Rivers in South Dakota and all north of the Cheyenne River west of 102 degrees longitude. The following spring those lands were homesteaded by whites. In the meantime payment for those lands was delayed, the annuity goods failed to arrive until winter was nearly over, crops had failed that year through lack of tending while the tribes were at the councils of the preceding spring. Epidemic diseases were in all the villages, and as a final straw Congress, despite previous promises, cut down the beef ration by over 4,000,000 pounds on the ground of stipulated money payments, which however did not arrive.

In 1889 rumors also reached the tribes in the Dakotas of a new Indian messiah beyond the Rocky Mountains. They sent two delegations to see him in western Nevada. Both confirmed the truth of the report. Thus in the spring of 1890 the Ghost Dance intended to fulfil the prophecy and was inaugurated at Pine Ridge among the Oglala. From there it spread to all the other Teton reservations until the tribes were in a frenzy of religious ecstasy. A newly appointed tender-foot agent got spooked, so the story goes, and clamored for troops, thus precipitating the 1890 Teton outbreak. By December 1st there were 3,000 troops disposed in the neighborhood of the Pine Ridge in southwestern South Dakota and northwestern Nebraska. Under orders of Gen. Nelson A. Miles orders were issued to the Indian police at the Standing Rock Reservation to arrest Sitting Bull of the Huŋkpapa.

When they tried to do so, he and his son and six police were killed as he resisted, on December 15th, at Sitting Bull's camp on the Grand River west of present Mobridge, South Dakota. At the time, Sitting Bull's band from the Standing Rock and others from there and the Cheyenne River agency were in flight to the Bad Lands of western South Dakota. There they had joined other refugee hostiles from Pine Ridge and Rosebud.

On December 29, 1890, Big Foot, Sitaⁿka, and his band who had surrendered were at Wounded Knee Creek about 20 miles northwest of Pine Ridge, South Dakota. A party from the group hiding out in the Bad Lands came to Big Foot's camp the night before. But some of their scouts found the area surrounded and they made their getaway. At dawn the 7th Cavalry under Col. Forsythe attacked Big Foot's camp, and after a short fight the entire band was practically decimated---men, women and children.

On January 16, 1891, the hostiles came to Pine Ridge and surrendered.

9. From then on the story of the <u>Sioux Nation</u> is one of decline. Under a law passed in 1887, their reservations were gradually reduced, negotiations being carried on with one band at a time, until at present practically all Sioux are individual owners of small parcels of land in their old territory which by degrees was thrown open to white homesteaders. Indian dress and adornment are obsolete except for celebrations and other gatherings. Most are stockmen and farmers on a small scale on lands upon which, according to the old timers of South Dakota "you can't even raise hell with a jug of whiskey and two six-shooters". Many of them have served and are serving in the various armed services from 1898 through the Spanish-American War, in the Phillipine Islands, in the Mexican border troubles, World War I and II, and in Korea. Many have left their old hunting grounds and are mixed among the general population of the country. Some have done very well among the whites, in many lines of endeavor from the lowly to the high.

Of those Sioux who fled to Canada and remained, about 1,500 or perhaps more, many are at the Standing Buffalo Reservation in Saskatchewan near Fort Qu'Appelle.

10. <u>The Sioux</u> were not a compact nation with centralized government and a supreme head chief, but they were a loose confederacy of sub-tribes speaking the Sioux language in a number of dialects. The Teton or <u>Lakota</u> was the largest dialectical group, numbering about 60 per-cent of the entire nation, and the principal tribe among the allies. The Santee or <u>Dakota</u> was second among the dialectical groups and second in importance among the allies. The Yankton or <u>Nakota</u> was third. The Omaha, Iowa, Ponca, Oto, Missouri, Kaw, Osage and Quapaw spoke a language (each with a dialectical difference with variations of that of the allies) called Dhegiha which is a Sioux language. The Assiniboin speak the Yankton dialect, just as do the Siksika or Blackfoot; they were not among the allies. The Winnebago speak a dialect of the Santee but were not among the allies. The Crow or Absaroka, the Hidatsa or Minitari, and the Mandan speak a variant of Teton, but none were among the allies. The Catawba of North and South Carolina spoke a Sioux language which is not identified with certainty as part of any particular group of those in the west. The Biloxi of Mississippi and Louisiana spoke a Sioux language not identified with any of the other groups.

It is curious to note that, whereas it has been said that Waȟpetoŋ (title of one of the allies from among the Santee) means Village of or in the Leaves, this seems rather inane. The name does indicate that they are the Petun or Tobacco Nation, a band of the Wyandat or Ouendat (Huron) who fled to protection with the Santee from the Iroquois.

Among the Santee chieftainship was more or less hereditary, but not positively so. The council usually named the son to succeed the father (much as in some of our backward segments of government today). The Teton and Yankton chief, as was done also among those cognate tribes west of the Mississippi , was selected in council on the basis of proven ability, prowess in war as well as in parley.

In the period prior to the coming of the whites, and before obtaining horses from the western and southern tribes, the Sioux subsisted chiefly on wild rice, berries, fish, venison, bear and small game. They were "canoe Indians" and experts with them---making forays along the lakes and rivers into enemy country. In some instances they came down the Mississippi and Missouri to the Ohio and up the Ohio into its headwaters to war on the Iroquois. Other forays were made on Lake Superior and Lakes Michigan, Huron and Ontario, as well as on Lakes Winnipeg, Winnipegosis and Lake of the Woods. Their westward trek from the Atlantic seaboard was principally by water, either through the Cumberland Gap or down the Kanawha, Tennessee or Cumberland Rivers to the Ohio. The Miami first sighted the Omaha on the Ohio. The probabilities are that all three routes were used. But whether it was a slow advance of a number of years or a mass migration or general pursuit of enemies will probably never be known. Still, it appears the movement was on a broad front with the Biloxi at the extreme south and the Santee at the extreme north. To the east of the Red River of the north, they lived in birch bark lodges; to the west they lived in buffalo hide tipis. Their dead were placed in coffins or wrappings on platforms on the plains, in trees in the east. Sometimes the coffin was placed on the ground, which was usually an emergency. Food and valuables were left with the corpse. Relatives cut their bodies with knives and cut off their hair to show grief for the deceased. Besides the knife, bow and arrow the war club was used in the east. The "horse tribes" used the lance and shield. After the coming of the whites, the club was often replaced by steel hand axes.

Polygamy was recognized. There was no clan system. To them the earth was a great island surrounded by an ocean. To the west was the spirit world where the spirits of men who died went after their burial. There were said to be two souls (some said more), one of which remained in the vicinity of the grave or corpse if it was not formally buried, while the other went on the spirit world road to the west, or became in some instances a wandering and dangerous ghost.

In the west also was a magic house on top of a high mountain guarded by four sentinels (animals) at the four doorways. Wakiŋyaŋ (Thunder) lived there. These four sentinels were the greatest of the "gods" and enemies of the subterranean earth spirits and water spirits. The sun was also a great "god". There was no "Great Spirit" or Supreme Being, as has been almost universally supposed by whites. They had not ethical code (as we know it from Western tradition) to their supernaturalism; no heaven or hell. In their spirit world, among animals the buffalo was highly "venerated". Fairies and strange monsters, both of whom were either good or bad, were everywhere, usually invisible, but sometimes revealing themselves in warning portents. Dreams were held as direct revelations of the supernatural. Taboos, fasting, sacrifice including voluntary torture were frequent.

Among the great ceremonials, the annual Sundance was most important. The principal performers danced at short intervals for four days and nights, without food, drink, or sleep, undergoing at the same time painful body lacerations. It is not certain whether this was done as a propitiation for some wrong done or in thanksgiving for or fulfilment of a vow.

There were several warrior societies and an unknown number of secret societies, each of which had special dances.

There was a puberty ceremony for girls.

In physique, intellect, morality and general manliness they ranked high, being among the finest of the plains tribes. Their valor was noteworthy, especially in that one of their duels was to death, each striving for a single knife. They were great tacticians and took no foolhardy chances, each move in battle being planned, and in event of failure there was no "enfant perdu" or last stand business. The reserve force covered for the disengagement, then the withdrawls were in small groups under a predetermined plan and route to a specified rendevouz in preparation for another strike.

The Sioux had an abundant mass of history and legend, much of which has been recorded. They had no material record except a few signs and symbols, and certain sacred or holy objects. There was also a small amount of pictography mostly decorative.

Population numbers prior to 1849 are in no way reliable. At that time they were estimated at 20,000 by one estimate. Others said 40,000 or more. In 1851 a missionary in Minnesota estimated them at 25,000 but underestimated the Teton bands who were ever on the move and having no fixed abode. In 1910 an official census among the allies 28,618 including all mixed bloods. Inter-marriage with neighboring tribes and with captives and whites was not uncommon. In the latter instances, a loss to the tribe generally resulted as the women usually left with their white husbands and many of their descendants are scattered from the middle U. S. and adjoining Canada through Michigan, Minnesota, Wisconsin, Iowa, Nebraska, the Dakota, Wyoming, Montana, Colorado, Kansas and Oklahoma where they are incorporated among the whites, as well as in Ontario, Manitoba, Saskatchewan and Alberta. Between 1850 and 1910 the loss of life among them due to disease, principally smallpox and tuberculosis was high. Many died also from malnutrition after the buffalo herds were decimated. Wars took many more. Among the cognate tribes who were not part of the alliance, the story is the same.

Leo P. Gilroy

INTRODUCTION

1. Dakota Siouan tongue. The Dakota language may be conveniently divided into three dialects, with a fourth sister dialect in the Assiniboin. The latter is not treated here because it is spoken by Dakota bands not so near at hand living to the north and northwest mostly within Canada. In this sense, then, we are thinking of the Dakota tongue in three dialects: the Lakota, Yankton and Dakota. The Lakota dialect is spoken by the western group of the Dakota; the Yankton by the central and northern group; and the Dakota by the eastern. This eastern group carries also the name Santee; the western also is distinguished by the title Teton.

Sometime ago in 1911, Franz Boas published some notes which fairly well distinguished the Ponca and Winnebago Siouan languages from the Dakota. (Bur. of Amer. Ethnol., Bull. 41 Part 1) There yet remains the task of setting forth a clearer line of distinction between the Dakota dialects themselves. However, what seems to be the suggestion left us by Boas and Deloria especially is that the Dakota dialects have a broad but common groundwork in both grammar and vocabulary. The depth of this common ground will determine the extent to which we can draw together into one a clear and detailed study. (Dakota Grammar, Deloria; U.S.G. Print. Off., 1941)

Buechel, in 1939, gave us perhaps the most useful and detailed study of the Teton dialect. From it we clearly see the broad lines of word structure and syntax which run through the other two dialects. As to vocabulary, there are evidently words, especially conjunctions, that are particular to each dialect. Thus, it cannot be said that a person will err in saying that he has begun well his study of Dakota with the study of one of the dialects. Therefore, to help students of the language to begin the bridging between Lakota and both Yankton and Santee, we are presenting a skeme that will be quite useful.

2. Orthographic Interchange. When we write from one Dakota dialect into another, we are guided by two considerations: 1) consonant clusters, and 2) single consonants. Generally speaking, vowels remain constant, for the most part.

I. Single Consonant Interchange: (from Teton to Yankton and Santee)

A. Initial* l becomes d. Except: l becomes n , lila nina.
laka naka

B. Final* l becomes n. Thus: terminal l becomes n .
la diminutive becomes na or daŋ.
ŋla becomes ŋna.
lya becomes nya.

* syllable or letter of that syllable (prefixes excluded).

C. Final b becomes m . Terminal p(T) becomes b(Y).
Prefix pa becomes ba. Terminal k(T) becomes g(Y).
Prefix wo becomes bo. Terminal l(T) becomes d(Y) in the
Final wé becomes bé or yé. contraction of -ta.

Terminal ta, ca become: l(T), d(Y), n(S).

II. STUDY TABLE of DAKOTA Orthography to ASSIST WRITING.

Teton (T), Yankton (Y), Santee (S)

Initial Consonant	Second Consonant of the Cluster: p	t	k	s	ś	c	l / d	n	b / w	m	
p	-	pt	-	ps	pś	pc	pl				(T)
							(bd)				(Y)
							(md)				(S)
t (S)	tp	-	tk	-	-	-					
k (T)	kp	kt	-	ks	kś	kc					
							kd	kn	kb	km	(Y)
h							hd	hn	hb	hm	(S)
g							gl	gn	gb	gm	(T)
b							(bd)				(Y)
m							md				(Y)(S)
							bl				(T)
s	sp	st	sk	-	-	sc	sd	sn	sb	sm	(Y)(S)
							sl	sn	sw	sm	(T)
ś	śp	śt	śk	-	-	śc	śd	śn	śb	śm	(Y)(S)
							śl	śn	św--	śm	(T)
ȟ	ȟp	ȟt	ȟk	-	-	ȟc	ȟd	ȟn	ȟb	ȟm	(Y)(S)
							ȟl	ȟn	ȟw	ȟm	(T)

Notes: Clusters whose second consonant is drawn from the group (l, d, n, b, w, m, and p) alone involve a cluster interchange. Indentations are used to indicate the members of the group in which an interchange exists. Clusters within parentheses ( ) form part of a group, except (bd) which is not contained in the group (md, bl).

Some Vowel Interchanges used:

(T) Initial	(T) Final	(Y) Initial	(Y) Final	(S) Initial	(S) Final
la*				(na)*	
				ni*	
na*				ni*	
waη*				wiη*	
i**		i**		u(η)**	
hiη		hiη		huη	
niη		niη		nuη	
	iη		iη		uη
	ni		ni(na)		na
uη***		i(η)***		i(η)***	

* non-prefix.
** uη followed by y, or kt, gl(hd), gn(hn).
*** iη followed by w.
N.B. uη(T) is most often used, where, within a word, it does not confuse itself with the verb "to be". Otherwise, we may use oη(T) pronounced identically.

3. Phonetics. There will be some concern over certain particular sounds in Lakota. The concern arises partly because of the differences in dialect, and partly because earlier notations seem to have distinguished the k p t and c sounds (excluding the glottal stops) narrowly. Buechel, it seems, wanted to maintain a further distinction in the k p t so as to account for accurate pronunciation and in turn to sharpen the dialect differences. Thus, in dropping the d from the Lakota alphabet, just as Riggs had done, we have had a perfect symmetry of four pairs: k k̔ , p p̔ , t t̔ , c c̔ These present a two-fold distinction for each sound, in Deloria's terminology the medial and the aspirate, the first being surd. But, Buechel in striving to be faithful to his accurate observation and use of the Lakota presents also the sonant as k̇ ṗ ṫ which are a kind of merger of k and g , p and b , t and d . Our symmetry does change to three triads of the k p t ; but then we can associate the c pair with the three pairs of spirants z j ġ . Moreover, he would drop aspirate c̔ and reduce it to a kind of surd c , yet retaining the ch sound as in "chair". Then there would be some explanation for his introducing ċ , which might be thought of as in the order of sonant. To illustrate:

k̇ as g in give: k̇iŋháŋ, If.
k as k in kill: kíŋja, To whine. kaŋhé, To shell.
k̔ as k in kill*(but gutturalized): k̔áta, Hot.

ṗ as b in bill: ṗa, To urge; prefix.
p as p in pat: pa, Bitter; head. páta, To cut.
p̔ as p in pill:* p̔e, Top of the head; sharp.

ṫ as d in day: ṫaku, Something.
t as t in take: tápa, Ball. takója, Grandchild.
t̔ as t in tall:* t̔aŋni, Old.

ċ as g in gentle: ċík'ala, Small. ċóċo, Soft.
c as ch in chair: caŋ, Tree. ciŋcá, Child.

4. Common English Typewriter. It may be useful to some to have a guide to consistency when one is typing Dakota dialects on a common English typewriter, without all the diacritical marks. Following are rules of a sort.

Drop all diacritical marks except the following:

ḣ followed by a vowel mark h̲ .
(h followed by a consonant or stop (') and final h, understand ḣ*)

ŋ followed by a vowel type n̲ .
(n followed by a consonant and final n , understand ŋ .)

ś always mark s̲ .

* Except in the cluster "hw" in the particle hwo.

GUIDE TO THE USE OF THE DICTIONARY

I. LAKOTA to ENGLISH.

A. Entry Words and Their Arrangement.

1. All entries, including proper nouns, contractions, abbreviations, prefixes, suffixes, and words compounded into phrases are listed in alphabetical order. This order is identical to that of English where English and Lakota have common letters. Lakota, however, drops six letters, d f q r v x . Thus, the Lakota alphabet, with consonants and vowels peculiar to itself, is as follows: d (Y)(S)

a aŋ b c c' e g g' h ȟ ȟ' i iŋ j k k' l l' m n ŋ o oŋ

p p' s s' ś ś' t t' u uŋ w y z z'

2. An entry occurs

   1) against the left margin;
   2) after a given entry and immediately after the sign -- ;
   3) against the left margin, but immediately after the previous entry, without an intervening blank line being introduced.

These are three types of entries. Type 1) is of equal value with types 2) and 3). Types 2) and 3) are used this way so as to help the reader to associate words through their roots or derivatives and to take note of the typical building of words through prefixes, suffixes and inserted syllables, each and every part having meaningful value. Note that there are some 2) type entries that assume the 1) type entry or a previous 2) or 3) type entry, so that after the sign (--) an entry word does not occur explicitly, but rather the previous entry word is assumed. Thus, such entries begin immediately with the part of speech. The rule of entry is that in 2) type entries that lack an entry word, the entry word is the most proximate preceding entry in its exact representation.

3. Some entries may have an almost equivalent spelling, and on occasion these will follow immediately after the entry word of any type. At other times even a similar word, just as other alternative words suggested, will follow the definition of the entry. As a further help, there will frequently be cross-reference words indicated by Cf. Moreover, when specially helpful will be a synonym(s), it will follow immediately Syn.-

4. There are many Lakota verbs that can be used in their indefinite form as nouns. Where this double office occurs, frequently the noun will be defined under the same entry verb and simply noted as a noun. Similarly, where the verb can be used as adverb, it will be so noted.

5. Certain words are nuclei of other words, and they may permit often an elaborate list of distinct words. These series will be variously entered:

   a. A listing simply by way of illustration, in a column where each word starts with a capital letter.

b. A listing also as an illustration, but with the original root entry indicated by the sign (-). This sign always, when used to indicate the insertion of the original or previous entry word, is preceded and followed by one full space.

6. Prefixes and suffixes, as well as inserted syllables, are given as though they were full word entries. Indeed, it was Buechel's contention that Dakota ought so to be written as to show clearly its syllabic development when it is written in a dictionary layout. Every syllable carries its meaning. And so he hoped to relieve the language of the burden of unsounded and useless lettering, an understood phenomenon in English. In this he was truly following Riggs and Deloria. One should note that we have entered words without breaking them into syllables, except for the break for the insertion of the accent at the end of the syllable accented. This does help to identify a syllable. But for the learning of the language, it would seem only necessary to know that a syllable is formed by an initial consonant or consonant cluster (two successive consonants; three is very unusual) and a vowel. Sometimes, at the end of a word, a terminal consonant is said to belong to the previous syllable. Initial vowels and successive vowels are sounded separately.

7. Foreign words are currently in use in the spoken language. These consist chiefly of business and scientific terms. And since these are familiar and distinct, there has been no attempt to incorporate them into this collection.

B. Pronunciation.

1. Since the lexicographer is not the law-maker, but rather the recorder of the living law of custom currently apparent among cultivated speakers of a language, he then assumes the existence of variations in the spoken language. The point is even stressed by the fact that custom has led to a distinction among many Siouan languages, to say nothing of the dialects among the Dakota. In a very true sense, then, we can say that language does not submit to a categorical and water-tight division. Moreover, in typical English fashion, the Dakota take up foreign words bodily and incorporate them into their vocabulary. We can say that both English and Dakota opt for this, as will become evident after a brief study of the grammar and vocabulary. This book attempts to depict as clearly as possible the Lakota dialect of the Dakota. In the Introduction one can find skemes by which one may write words from one dialect to the other.

2. This collection of Lakota words rests upon extensive and thorough sources. Chief among these are Riggs' Dakota-English dictionary, Deloria's Dakota Texts, Buechel's Bible History and his unpublished manuscript stories (MS) which numbers 583 pages. For many other live sources, see Word Sources. Surely we realize how indispensable are the personal living sources. The actual sounding of words is incomplete except in the spoken word. We must, then, assume that the learner, in the beginning and without, perhaps, the help of hearing will have difficulties at least in acquiring the sense of a good utterance of the language. Exact pronunciation has always been the concern of lexicographers, and that is the primary concern in systems of diacritical marks which are used to help one distinguish sounds and emphasis and lead to

some security in a fuller knowledge of the tongue. Riggs' system was limited to lettering, syllabification and accent. Deloria, in her Texts and Grammar, seemed to move forward toward a more developed diacritical system. She is thorough in the use of the stop ('), the aspirate (ᶜ), and all nasal vowels have a subscript (꜀). Moreover, she employs the guttural ȟ and the surd ś, as well as the sonant ġ, just as Riggs. However, she seemed to be struggling with the vowel stop, as distinguished from the consonant stop; and by superscript vowels she tries to provide for the sounding of gl gn gm by writing them g.l g.n g.m in most places, but in others with a suitable letter superscript. This, of course was to indicate how the two consonants are melded together smoothly with the use of a soft vowel interjected. Also in superscript she uses a letter with the stop, as in the case of writing śke'; in this case, a vowel stop with a superscript. Here is where complication does seem to set in. As to accent, she employs both primary and secondary, the latter being back slanted.

Buechel tries to be as brief, adding to Riggs only what would seem to avoid a cumbersome system. All subscripts are removed, the sign of the nasal ƞ is preserved and all superscripts are reduced to non-letter signs, as : k̇ k k̑ k' i' ś gl . For details of this system see below. His superscript for k̇ was g; for k, h; for k̑, k; for ṗ, b; for p, h; for p̑, p; for ṫ, d; for t, h; t̑, t.

Letter	Manuscript Superscripts			As appears in Dictionary			Stops
k	g	h	k	k̇	k	k̑	k'
p	b	h	p	ṗ	p	p̑	p'
t	d	h	t	ṫ	t	t̑	t'
c	j			ċ			c'
g				ġ			g'
h					ȟ		ȟ'
					h		
s					ś		ś'
					s		s'
l							l'
e							e'
i							i'

ƞ is the sign of the nasal of vowels a i o u .
<u>aƞ iƞ oƞ uƞ</u>

3. Key to Pronunciation.

SYMBOL	SOUND as	ENGLISH KEY WORD	LAKOTA KEY WORD	NOTES
a	a	fa̲ther	a̲té	
ă	a	a̲rm	ska̲	
ā	a	fār	caη	
aη	an	bl̄anc (french)	áηpo	
b	b	rib	bubú	
ċ	j	joy	c̲íscila	
c	ch	chair	séc̲a	
c'	ch*	ch-air	ic'ú	*Consonant is pronounced alone without the aid of a vowel; called a glottal stop. A vowel stop is the vowel lightly repeated.
e	a	hate	cépa	
ĕ	e	elk	até̲	
ē	e	they	ble	
g	g	rig	ogna	
ġ	ch	machen (german)	káġa	
g'	g *	g-o	śuηg'íte	
h	h	hip	ha	
ḣ	h **	hog	ḣe	**Gutturalized.
ḣ'	h ** *	h-og	naḣ'óη	
i	e	be	ilé	
ĭ	i	mill	naġí	
ī	i	machine	ité	
iη	in	ink	kiη	
j	s	fusion	jiηca	
k̇	g	give	k̇iη	
k	k	kill	kíηja	
ḱ	k **	kill	ḱáta	
k'	k *	k-ettle	k'u	
l	l	love	ilála	
l'	l *	sol-stice	lol'	
m	m	man	máni	
n	n	name	ni	
η	n	ink	íηkpa	η is sign of the nasal vowel preceding. It also is accustomed to be noted as n.
o	o	smoke	hoġáη	
ŏ	o	obey	kóla	
ō	o	old	óta	
oη	oo η	soon	óηśila	
ṗ	b	bill	ṗahá	
p	p	pink	pa (head)	
p̂	p **	pill	p̂ejí	
p'	p *	p-ay	p'o	
s	s	say	siηté	
s'	s *	s-ay	s'e	
ś	sh	ship	śi	
ś'	sh *	sh-ock	waś'aka	
ṫ	d	day	waśṫé	
t	t	take	tápa	
t̂	t **	tar	taηni	
t'	t *	t-ar	t'a	
u	oo	boot	úta	
ŭ	u	put	ojúla	
ū	u	rule	u	
uη	oo η	soon	uη	
w	w	way	wakáη	
y	y	yonder	yaηká	
z	z	zero	waziyata	
z'	z *	z-ink	maz'ípame	

Note: All vowels, when they terminate a statement of fact, are stopped, being indicated thus: śka', haη', śke', keyapi', etc. Cf. * .

II. ENGLISH to LAKOTA.

A. Entries. The order of entries is somewhat the same as in the Lakota-English section. But, in general, entry words are given in a contextual pattern, somewhat by way of genus; as animals are all under that title mainly, a very few exceptions being made. So too, birds are under that title, etc. Where a separate entry would best be made it is done so. In one way or another, all that is in the Lakota section is in the English.

1. Each entry is first assumed to be generic in nature. Hence, the part of speech following the entry word may apply to the entry word, or to the Lakota word that follows; but in this latter case, the part of speech is often placed later and closer following the actual word it identifies. What occurs in parentheses are contextual indicators of genus being specified by words that follow. Parentheses always indicate context. Because contextual entries can become rather distended, frequently a definition will begin with a word or root which will recur in words immediately following. This intention is indicated immediately after the word or root by a full-colon. Thereafter, until the sentence period is reached, the word or root, when repeated, will be indicated only by the sign (-). Most often when a word precedes this full-colon, the word will first be followed by its part of speech. A semi-colon will often follow to indicate some break in a series of definitions. The period is used to indicate a new line of definitions. As the sign (-) indicates the insertion of the word or root immediately before the full-colon, so too the same sign, when an English specification is used and where the original entry is to be inserted, is set in its proper place. Note that specific definitions will have the part of speech indicated generally after the word of definition. English specific definitions, when given, always begin with a capital letter.

2. Word lists. Quite a number of lists of specific words occur. So one will have to keep this in mind as he uses this section of the dictionary. By considering this well, a person will more readily grasp the system of roots employed in Lakota.

B. Omissions. In order to avoid undue duplication, and yet to help the reader to find words and to formulate a clear notion of the basic structure of words and syllabic meanings, certain Lakota words are omitted in the English section. Toward the end of this section will be found lists of words under the word prefix. These prefixed words can be readily defined from the type of prefix and the root meaning itself. Thus, omissions are usually words built directly upon a specific word or root. Of course, the root word will always be defined in its proper place. The basic idea is in selection of words to be defined: where help to locate a word is unnecessary, the word is omitted, especially for the following forms of Lakota words:

1- Reduplicated forms. *
2- Ability forms: -pica(śni).
3- Diminutive forms: -la.
4- Causative forms: -ya(ŋ), -kiya.
5- Noun forms: -pi.
6- Reflexive forms: -ici-, -ic'i- ; gl for k or y; kp for p.

7- Reciprocal forms: -kici- .
8- Prepositional insert forms: -ki- , -kici-
9- Possessive forms: -glo- , gliyo- , -gla-
10- Contracted forms:

Ending	Omitted Contraction
-ata	-al
-eca, -ca	-el, -l
-ga, -ȟca	-ȟ
-ja	-ś
-ka	-g
-pa	-b
-tu	-l
-uta	-ul
-yaŋ	-ye
-za	-s

11- Adverbial forms:

-haŋ	-kel	-pa	-ata	-yaŋkel
-ka	-l	-kiya	-tu	-yela
-kab	-la	-śniyaŋ	-wapa	-taŋ
-ke	-na	-s'e	-ya(ŋ)	-taŋhaŋ
-ki (-ci)	-otaŋ	-ta	-yakel	

* Reduplicated forms:

Sample form	Reduplicated form
-nakeca	-nagnakeca
-nica	-nignica
-lega	-leglega
-leja	-leśleja
-ceca	-cekceca
-lila	-liglila
-luta	-lugluta
-zica	-zigsica

Confer prefix, suffix.

A LAKOTA GRAMMAR SUMMARY

based upon

Buechel's Grammar of Lakota

by

George Paul Casey, SJ

CONTENTS

The Parts of Speech in Lakota

NOUNS

Gender: Only real gender is used, not grammatical. A few specific forms do exist, but these are identified where "bloka" or "wiŋyela" are added to the generic noun for the male or female.

Number: There are singular, dual and plural. The plural is indicated by the suffix "pi" for animate nouns (men and animals) and is not indicated for inanimate nouns, except by means of a quantitative adjective or adverb. For the dual, cf. verbs.

Case : There are no strict case forms.

PRONOUNS

With the exception of the relative pronoun and the neuter "it", all English pronouns have a Lakota equivalent. Although Lakota has separate personal pronoun forms, it is the inseparate forms, both objective and subjective types, which are most important because they must be used by way of incorporation with verbs, nouns, adjectives, and these pronouns vary with each verb according to conjugation. Cf. verbs.

ADJECTIVES

Descriptive adjectives usually follow their nouns and pronouns; limiting adjectives usually precede them.
Plurality of adjectives often need not be expressed; when expressed, the suffix "pi" is used, or through a complex process the differentiating syllable of the adjective is reduplicated.
There are separate and inseparate possessive adjectives, the inseparate being the more important and incorporated with their objects. Different forms of these are used depending upon the class of things to which the possessed object belongs.

For comparison, Lakota does not use "-er" as in "wiser", but rather "sam", "more", as in "more wise", "sam ksapa".
For the superlative, "-est" is not used, but rather "iyotaŋ", "most", or some other like adverb, as in "most wise", "iyotaŋ ksapa".

ADVERBS

Adverbs usually precede the word they modify. Their use in Lakota is complicated by their large variety, their euphonic variations, and their lack of English equivalents except by way of circumlocution.

VERBS

Cf. syntax and paradigms.

PREPOSITIONS

The preposition usually follows its object; but often it is incorporated with the object personal pronoun, or is in other cases used without the object being expressed but with a verb following it. Cf. list.

CONJUNCTIONS Cf. syntax.

PARTICLES and INTERJECTIONS Cf. respective lists.

Subject and Predicate

AGREEMENT in NUMBER

1- Animate subjects:

singular subj. takes singl. predicate:	An owl is hooting.	Hiⁿháⁿ waⁿ hotóⁿ.
	The baby is crying.	Hokśíćala kiⁿ céye.
collective subj. takes plural predicate:	Your people are very numerous.	Nitá oyáte kiⁿ líla ótapi.
indefinite pron. may be plural in meaning:	None cried.	Tuwéni céyapi śni.
or singular:	No one cried.	Tuwéni céye śni.
compound subj. takes plural predicate:	The boy and girl cry.	Hokśíćala kiⁿ na wićíⁿcala kiⁿ céyapi.
compound subj. equally important and joined by "kici" or "ob" take plural pred:	Peter and Paul did not come.	Peter na Paul kicí hípi śni.
but with unequal subjs., singl. pred.:	Peter and the baby did not come.	Peter hokśicala kiⁿ kici hi śni.
plural subj. takes plural pred., but one sign of the plural is needed:	The children are crying.	Wakáⁿheja kiⁿ ceyapi.

2- Inanimate subjects:

plurality expressed with some adj. or adv., not by suffix "pi":	Many trees grow there.	Caⁿ óta el icáge.

AGREEMENT in PERSON

with two or more personal pron. subjs., pred. is plural in prefered order: 1st, 2nd, 3rd:	The boy and I will go.	Miś hokśila kiⁿ kici uⁿyáⁿpi kte.
with a plural pron. in the partitive genitive, preceded by a numeral or pron., the verb must agree with the plural pron. in person:	Three of us will go home.	Uⁿkíyepi kiⁿ yámni uⁿglápi kte.
* Except: with the use of "tukte waⁿji", "which one, any one", the "of" phrase is omitted in Lakota, or the inseparable personal pron. is used:	Which one of you will go home?	Nitúkte waⁿjí yagní kta he?
* Except: the "of" phrase may always be omitted when the meaning is clear:	Three of us will go home.	Yamni uⁿglápi kte.

The Linking Verb "to be"

General rule: if the predicate identifies the subj., "e", "to be", (plural, "epi") will be used for all 3rd person subjs.:	This man is the boss. This is my child. Who is this?	Wicáśa kiŋ le itáŋcaŋ kiŋ he e. Le miciŋca kiŋ e. Le túwe hwo?
1st and 2nd person subjs., "e" is in the pron.:	I am the boss.	Itáŋcaŋ kiŋ he míye.
But if the predicate describes the subj., no verb is used, the linking idea being expressed either by position of the noun and predicate for all 3rd person subjs.:	This man is good. This one is good. This one will be boss. What is this?	Le wicáśa kiŋ waśté. Le waśte. Le itáŋcaŋ kte. Le taku he?
or by the use of "kiŋ heca", "is such":	This man is boss. This one is boss.	Wicaśa kiŋ le itaŋcaŋ kiŋ héca. Le itaŋcaŋ kiŋ héca.
and with 1st and 2nd person subjs., the pron. may be incorporated with the predicate:	You are pitiful. I am sad.	Óŋniśike. Caŋtémaśice.
or incorporated with the "kiŋ heca":	I am a good boy.	Hokśíla waśté kiŋ hemáca.
Special cases: when "it" is the subject: of an impersonal verb, translate only pred.:	It is cold.	Osní yelo.
grammatically i.e., Lakota uses a substantive:	It is good to cry.	Céyapi kiŋ he waśté.
really meaning "the person, the thing":	It is a man. It is Peter. It is I.	Wicáśa kiŋ héca. Peter e. Míye yelo.
when "has" indicates a present state of being, a verb with "uŋ", "to be" is used:	He has come home.	Wána aglí uŋ.

Note: Most other English semi-copulative verbs have no Lakota equivalents; hence the thought must be rephrased.

The Simple Sentence

Direct OBJECTS		
simple:	God made the earth.	Wakántanka maká kin káge.
a double obj. is required after such verbs as "to teach, to ask etc.":	I will give you a horse.	Śúnkawakan cic'ú kte.
	I will teach you Lakota.	Lakóta iápi kin onspéciciyin kte.
or these verbs are used in their absoluteform:	I taught him.	Waónspewakiye.
a double obj. is required when an obj. represents a part of a man:	I shake your hand.	Napé ciyúze.
and when an animate obj. is had, "wica" is used:	I have children.	Wakánheja wicábluha.
a complement obj. is required for some verbs:	They made John chairman.	John itáncan kágapi.
Indirect OBJECTS		
are indicated by "ki" or "kici"; the more important of the two objects goes first:	I will give the money to John.	Mázaska kin le John wak'u kte.
	I will give John the money.	John mázaska kin le wak'u kte.
MODIFIERS		
adjective: (usually follows its noun)	John is a good man.	John wicáśa waśté kin héca.
noun or pronoun: (used descriptively they follow the noun; limiting, they precede)	This land is mine.	Le makóce mitáwa kin he e.
	The pine tree is very tall.	Wazí can kin líla hánska.
adverb: (usually precede the word modified)	She is really sick.	Lila kúja.
phrases: (as seen in English)		
infinitive: becomes a noun clausal substantive in most cases, esp. if used as a noun:	It is good for us to be here.	Lel unkúnpi kin he waśté.
adjectival: is recast keeping the adj. meaning	He is a man of great wisdom.	Wicáśa wan lila ksápa kin héca.
adverbial: used prepositionally, they can usually be kept so:	Man does not live by bread alone.	Agúyapi kin ecéla on wicáśa kin nipi śni.
infinitive of purpose: is used with a verb of locomotion, but it may be recast into an adverbial clausal substantive. Cf.	I came to see my child.	Micíнca kin wangláka wahi.

Complex Sentences: NOUN Clauses

Noun Clausal Substantives

Indirect Statements: introduced by "that", "kiŋ he"; the word order is: noun clause--kiŋ he--main clause:	I believe that he is a good man.	Wicáśa waśté kiŋ héca kiŋ he wicáwala.
*Except: in positive declarative sentences, esp. after verbs like "to know, to realize, to see etc.", the "kiŋ he" becomes "ca":	I know that man is a sinner.	Wicaśa kiŋ he waȟtáni s'a ca slolwáye.
In Indirect Quotations: the "kiŋ" combines with "éya, eciŋ, epcá" to form new words, "kéya, kéciŋ, képca":	He says he wants to eat.	Wóta ciŋ kéye.
In Direct Quotations: "éya, ekĭya, eciŋ" all follow their quotation:	"Hello!" he said.	"Hau!" éye.
unless they are used with "hécel, lécel":	He spoke thus to him: "Who are you?"	Lécel ekíye, "Nitúwe hwo?"
"leyá, heyá, leciŋ, heciŋ", if they are used, precede the quotation, but the corresponding "eya, eciŋ" are usually repeated at the end:	They said, "What is this?" they said.	Heyápi, "Le taku hwo?" eyápi.
In Indirect Statements: the "kiŋ he" may often be omitted in conversation, esp. when the subordinate verb is in the future tense:	I believe you will give me the money.	Mázaska kiŋ mayák'u kte wicáwala.

Complex Sentences: ADJECTIVE Clauses

Adjectival Clausal Substantives

Note: Because Lakota lacks a relative pronoun, relative adjective clauses must be turned into adjectival clausal substantives. These are

Restrictive: with antecedent known to the speaker, use "kiŋ he": (singular use)	The man whom you wish to see went home.	Wicáśa waŋ waŋláka yacíŋ kiŋ he kiglé.
(plural use)	The men whom you wish to see went home.	Wicaśa k'éya waŋwícalaka yacíŋ kiŋ héna kiglápi. (note article change after antecedent)
Restrictive: with antecedent unknown to the speaker, use "héci, heci he, hécina":	Whoever said that did not tell the truth.	Túwa heyá heci wicáke śni.
Descriptive: use "ca, caŋ, cána, cánahe, cáŋhe":	He saw a man who was well dressed.	Wicáśa waŋ táŋyaŋ iglúze ca waŋyáŋke.
	He who has a good wife is really lucky.	Túwa tawícu kiŋ waśté caŋ he líla táŋyaŋ wókini.
Identifying: esp. as "it" introduces the antecedent, use "ca":	It is John whom he meant.	John e ca ke.
	It is food which we came to buy.	Wóyute ca opétoŋ uŋhípi.
	Who is it who hit you?	Túwe ca anípa he?
Additive or Explanatory: co-ordinate the clause with the rest of the sentence:	He gave me a book which I read.	Wówapi waŋ mak'ú na blawá.

Complex Sentences: Adverbial Clauses

Adverbial Substantive Clauses

Note: These clauses are introduced by relative adverbs; when definite, use "kiŋ"; when indefinite, use "ca, caŋ, cána". Such clauses are of

TIME: "tohánl...hehánl":	When the sun goes down then you will come home.	Tohánl wi mahél iyáye kiŋ hehánl yaúpi kte.
"tohánnyaŋ...hehánnyaŋ":	When he lived with his mother then he was good.	Tohánnyaŋ húŋku kiŋ kicíti kiŋ hehánnyaŋ waśté.
	When he wants (then) he speaks to his friends.	Tohánl ciŋ caŋ (hehánl) takólaku kiŋ wókiyake.
PLACE: "tuktél...hel":	Where they killed the man, there they buried him.	Wicáśa kiŋ he tuktél ktépi kiŋ hel ȟápi.
	Where they killed an enemy, there they buried him.	Tuktél tóka waŋ ktépi cána hel ȟápi.
"tohaŋyaŋ...hehaŋyaŋ":	He went as far as he could.	Tohánnyaŋ okíhi kiŋ hehánnyaŋ iyaye.
MANNER: "tókel...hécel" (ecél, iyécel):	You will do it as I did it.	Tókel ecámoŋ kiŋ he iyécel ecánoŋpi kte.
	Do it as he told you!	Tókel éya cána ecél ecóŋ po.

Note: Often in conversation one or other adverb may be omitted, just as we do in English.

Other Adverbial Expressions:

"time while", "k'el, el, icuŋhaŋ":	Talk to a boy while he is growing.	Hokśíla waŋ icáge k'el wókiyaka yo.
"time since", "etáŋhaŋ, eháŋtaŋhaŋ":	It is three days since they came.	Hípi kiŋ eháŋtaŋhaŋ yamni caŋ.
"time until", "itókab" with "śni", pres. time:	He did not die until he talked to me.	T'e śni itókab wómakiyaka.
"time before", "itokab" and fut. time:	I want to see you before I go.	Mni kte itókab waŋcíyaŋka wacíŋ.
"time after", "ohakab, iyohakab":	All eat after they wash their hands.	Napé glujájapi kiŋ iyóhakab iyúha wótapi kte.
or simply coordinate:	All wash their hands and after they will eat.	Iyúha napé glujájapi na iyóhakab wótapi kte.
"place whither", "tókiyab":	Whither I am going you cannot come after me.	Tókiyab ble kiŋ ciŋ he miyátab yaúpioyákihipi śni.
"place whence", "tókiyataŋhaŋ":	Nobody will come whence I came.	Tókiyataŋhaŋ wahí kiŋ tuwéni u kte śni.

Complex Sentences: ADVERBIAL Clauses (continued)

Note: These adverbial clausal substantives are introduced by non-coordinating conjuntions which in English are of themselves subordinating conjunctions; thus

"although, though", "eśá, eśáŋ, eśáś, śaś, yeśá, yeśáŋ, yeś, weśá, weśáŋ, weś; keś; kayéś":	Although they really shot at him he got away unscathed.	Líla kutépi eśá iníhaŋśni hiyáye.
	Although it is only a lamb, you don't even give it to me.	Tóhaŋni táȟcaśúŋkala ciŋcála kayéś mayák'u śni.
"if, provided, unless", "kiŋ, kiŋháŋ, kinaháŋ, eháŋtaŋś, eháŋtaŋhaŋś":	If you have much, give to the poor.	Nitáwoyuha kiŋ óta eháŋtaŋś, waȟpánica wicák'u wo.
"if" (implying doubt), "héci-haŋ, hécinahaŋ, héci":	If that is right, tell it straight.	Hécetu hécihaŋ owótaŋla oyáka yo.
"because, since", "ca, caŋke, heoŋ, hecel, kiŋ oŋ, iciŋ":	I fired the man because he does not obey me.	Wicáśa kiŋ he namáȟ'oŋ śni ca ablúśtaŋ.
ca, caŋke used postpositively:	I fired him; the man does not obey me, that is why (I fired him).	Ablúśtaŋ; wicaśa kiŋ he nama-ȟ'oŋ śni ca.
iciŋ used prepositively:	I fired him for the man does not obey me.	Abluśtaŋ; iciŋ wicaśa kiŋ he namaȟ'oŋ śni.
"so that, in order that", "ca":	They stole the money in order to buy meat.	Taló opétoŋ ca mázaska kiŋ he manóŋpi.
or use "hecel":	They stole the money in order to buy meat.	Mázaska kiŋ he manóŋpi; hécel taló opétoŋpi kte.
"in order that not, lest", "owékiś, owékinaś, owékinahaŋś":	Don't do that, lest they will kill you.	Hécoŋ śni ye; owékiś niktépi kte.
"so, as a result", "ca, hecel":	He is very sick so that he cannot walk.	Líla kúja ca máni okíhi śni.
"as...as", make a simple sent.:	His clothes are as white as snow.	Taháyapi kiŋ wa iyécel ska.
or coordinate:	You know that as well as I.	Héna táŋyaŋ slolwáye; na niś éya táŋyaŋ slolyáye.
"as if, as though", "s'e, s'elececa":	We go about as if lost sheep.	Táȟcaśúŋkala s'e núniyaŋ uŋkó-manipi.
"than, more than", "sam, isám":	I cannot find a man wiser than you.	Wicáśa waŋ nisám ksápa ca iyéwaya owákihi śni.

The Verb TENSES

Note: The dual form is the same as the 1st person plural without the "pi" termination and is used only when one person addresses another and includes himself in the action, being or condition:

	Father, let us go home.	Até, uŋgni′ kte.

INDEFINITE: has two aspects,

Present: actually true now:	It is cold.	Osni′ yeló.
generally true now:	He never eats meat.	Taló yúte śni.
Past: took place in past:	We saw him yesterday.	Htálehaŋ waŋúŋyaŋkapi.
was generally true:	The Lakotas usually ate much meat.	Lakóta kiŋ taló óta yútapi s'a.

Note: an adverb helps fix past, and even present, time.

FUTURE: the indefinite with "kta, kte";

whenever used in English:	I will not go home.	Wagni′ kte śni.
the "kta" not repeated:	He will eat and go to bed.	Wótiŋ na iyúŋkiŋ kte.
when the verb is understood:	It will be warm today.	Leháŋl maśté kte.
used elliptically:	Will you come? I will not.	Yaú kta he? Kte śni.
substitute for imperative:	Give this to me.	Le mayák'u kte.
infinitive of purpose:	I have much to tell you.	Táku óta ecíciyapi kta bluhá.
purpose clauses: word order, purpose cl.--kta oŋ--main verb:	They called for the boy that they might question him.	Hokśíla kiŋ he wiyúŋgapi kta oŋ kicópi.
*with an imperative, simply coordinate:	Turn him loose that he may go.	Kiyúśka yo; iyáyiŋ kte.
express "is or was to, going to, sure to etc." by "kta uŋ":	He who steals is sure to be in prison.	Túwa wamánoŋ kiŋ he kaśkápi kta uŋ.

PRESENT PERFECT: the indefinite with some form of yuśtáŋ, to complete, finish, together with a fixing adverb:

	Now I have finished eating.	Wána wol miglúśtaŋ.

PAST PERFECT:

use "k'uŋ, uŋ" with the verb:	I had told him long ago.	Eháŋni owákiyake k'uŋ.
indicate prior action by "naháŋci...śni haŋni′", "not yet...when, before":	The boy went to look for the horses before the sun had risen. or The sun had not yet risen when the boy went to look for the horses.	Naháŋci wi hinápe śni haŋni′ hokśila kiŋ śuŋkóle iyáye.

FUTURE PERFECT: is expressed by the indefinite.

TENSES (continued) and The Subjunctive and Imperative MOODS

Progessive Tense:

indefinite with verb suffix "haŋ, he":	They were walking home leisurely.	Asníkiya glaháŋpi.
infinitive with inflected "yaŋká, uŋ":	Iwas listening to it.	Naȟ'óŋ maŋké.
	I am waiting for it.	Apé waúŋ.

Emphatic Tense:

"do", use verb with "kiśtó, kśto":	Somebody is coming.	Ku kśto.
	I did do that.	Hécamoŋ kśto.
"do", imperative, or "be sure to", use "ecáś":	Be sure to come. (Do come.)	Ecáś u wo.

SUBJUNCTIVE: a mood of

Wish: "may, would that"; use "Toké...ni":	I wish I were dead.	Toké mat'á ni.
"Toké eśá...ni":	May God have mercy on me.	Toké eśá Wakáŋtaŋka oŋśímala ni.
" ...ni":	May God have mercy on me.	Wakaŋtaŋka oŋśimala ni.
Contrary to fact: subord. cl.--k'eś or yuŋś--main verb and tka:	If I had a stick, I would kill the snake.	Caŋ waŋ bluhá k'eś, siŋtéȟla kiŋ wakát'a tka.
but subord. cl. omitted:	I would buy it (i.e. if I had the money).	Opétoŋ tka (i.e. mázaska kiŋ bluhá).

Uncertainty: present or future, use the indicative, factual mood.

IMPERATIVE: skeme of terminal particles to sentence:

ADDRESSEE	CONDITIONS	ADDRESSER MALE	ADDRESSER FEMALE
Singular:	3rd person singular verb; if verb ends in a, aŋ, e, i, iŋ or is negative:	yo	ye
	otherwise:	wo	we
Plural:	3rd person singular positive:	po	pi
	3rd person plural if negative:	yo	ye

Command:

terminal particles(above):	Come!	U wo.
future tense (with itó):	Let us pray.	(Itó) wacéuŋkiyapi kte.
strongest form: verb in 2nd person with terminal "kiló, ciŋ" (initial "uŋgna" optional):	Do not come near me!	(Uŋgná) kiyéla yaú kiló!

Imperative MOOD, (continued)

Request:

"yetó" (masc., fem.) or "nitó"(fem.) to imply one's bidding be done at once, for a good reason, or for just a minute:	Listen for a minute!	Anágoptaŋpi yetó.
"itó" is optional:	Now listen for a minute, friend.	Kóla, itó anágoptaŋ yetó!
"na, yemá" (by women only):	Listen to me!	Anámagoptaŋ yemá!
"eśá"--indicative--"śni":	Give me that money! (What is the matter that you don't?)	Eśá mázaska kiŋ mayák'u śni!

Entreaty: "please".

singl.: 3rd pers. singl. and "ye":	Friend, help me!	Kóla, omákiyi ye!
plur. : 3rd pers. plur. and "ye":	Friends, help me!	Kóla, omákiyaŋpi ye!

Consent: "very well, all right, etc.".

future indicative:	You may go.	Yiŋ kte.
"ho" and the future (ca):	You may go.	Ho, ca yiŋ kte.
"ho" and the imperative(ca):	You may go.	Ho, ca ya yo.

orders given to others, use
ho and wo, po (masc. singl., pl.); ho and we, pi (fem. singl., pl.) and term. particle.
orders including the speaker in the action, use
ho and ye, piye or yo (masc. singl., pl.); ho and na, and pi na (fem. singl., pl.) only and the future indicative; thus

ADDRESSER	ADDRESSEE SINGULAR	ADDRESSEE PLURAL	
masculine	Hówo iyáya yo!	Hópo iyáya po!	All right, go!
feminine	Hówe iyaya ye!	Ho iyáye pi!	All right, go!
masculine	Hóye uŋyíŋ kte!	Hópiye (Hópo) uŋyáŋpi kta!	All right, let's go!
feminine	Ho na uŋyíŋ kte!	Hópi na uŋyáŋpi kta!	All right, let's go!

MODAL Auxiliary Verbs: the following verbs have equivalents in Lakota, but only in a limited sense:

should, ought: "it is fitting", "iyéceca":	I should not do that.	Hécamoŋ iyéceca śni.
should: "it is likely", "itéke":	He should be coming home now.	Wáŋna ku itéke.
would: "customarily do, be", "śna": . . .	John would be drunk. or John is usually drunk.	John itómni kiŋ héca śna.
can, could: "ability":	I can sing.	Walówaŋ owákihi.
"possibility"	This song cannot be sung.	Olówaŋ kiŋ he lowáŋpica śni.

The INFINITIVE, PARTICIPLE and GERUND

INFINITIVE: may be a		
noun substantive: becomes a clausal substantive:	Boys like to play.	Śkátapi kiŋ he hokśíla kiŋ iyókipipi.
adjectival modifier: becomes		
either an adjective:	He is a man to be trusted.	Wicáśa waciŋyepica kiŋ héca.
or an appositive clausal substantive:	He is a man to be trusted.	Wicáśa waŋ túwe ke éyaś waciŋyaŋ okíhi kiŋ héca.
adverbial complement: infin.	He asked him to come.	U śi.
adverb of purpose: with a verb of locomotion; infin.:	I shall go to fish.	Hokúwa mni kte.
INFINITIVE Clause: these depend on the main verb; order, subordinate clause--main verb		
to wish, want, "ciŋ":	I want you to be good.	Niwáśte kta wacíŋ.
to believe, etc., "kéciŋ":	I believe this man is good.	Le wicáśa kiŋ he waśté kecámi.
to declare one to, "kéya".		
to consider, think one (one's self) to be, "la, kága, yawá, and reflexive forms".		
to see, hear, "waŋyáŋka etc." with a noun object:	I saw a dog bite your boy.	Śúŋka waŋ hokśíla nitáwa kiŋ yaȟtáka waŋbláka.
subord. cl.--kiŋ or ca--main verb		
to know, "slolyá":	I know this man is good.	Wicáśa kiŋ le waśté ca slolwáye.
infinitive--main verb		
to command, ask, etc., "śi":	You told me to come.	U mayáśi.
*Note "ciŋ" with infinitive:	I want to wash myself.	Miglújaja wacíŋ.
*Note double objects for		
waŋyáŋka, naȟ'óŋ (pron.):	I saw you coming.	Yaú waŋcíyaŋke.
apé (in all its subst. cls.):	I was waiting for you to arrive.	Yahí acípe maŋké.
PARTICIPLE and GERUND:		
subjective participial compl.:	He lay sleeping.	Iśtíŋma ȟpáye.
use the infinitive:	Taking all his possessions he went away.	Tawóyuha oyás'iŋ gluhá iyáye.
	He took it without saying a thing.	Táku eyé śni icú.
or recast in sense:	This looks bewildering to me.	Le awábleze śni.
objective compl.: subst. cl.:	I heard them singing.	Lowáŋpi nawáȟ'oŋ.
other participles and all gerunds: use the appropriate clausal substantives:	Having been blind, I now see.	Iśtámagoŋge, k'éyaś wána watóŋwe.
	I love going to school.	Wabláwa kiŋ he waśtewalake.

Common ADVERB List

ecána	soon	héktakiya	backward
ehá̄ŋni	long ago	héciya, hétkiya	in that direction
lecála	a little while ago	kákiya, kátkiya	toward yonder place
lecáś	just a minute ago	kútakiya	downward
nakéś	at last.	léciya, létkiya	toward this place
tokáta	later on	tóketkiya	toward some place
uŋgnáhela	suddenly	waŋkátkiya	upward
wáŋcak	at once	hógna	along that way
watóhaŋl	some time in future	lógna	along this way
ijéhaŋ	often	hehá̄ŋyaŋ	that far
óhiŋni	always	kahá̄ŋyaŋ	that far
téhaŋ	for a long time	lehá̄ŋyaŋ	this far
wáŋcala	once	eciŋśniyaŋ	thoughtlessly
wána	now	iwáśtela	slowly
hel, hétu, héci, héciya	there	oȟ'áŋkoya	quickly
kal, kákiya	yonder	śicáya	badly
kul, kúta	below	táŋyaŋ	well
lel, létu, léci, léciya	here	witkótkoya	foolishly
mahétuya	within	ecél	so, thus
taŋkál	outside	ecéȟci	exactly so
timá	inside	hécel, héceya	in that manner
téhaŋ	far	iyécel	in that manner
téhaŋtu	far	iyéceȟci	in exactly the same manner
tokáŋl	elsewhere	kákel	thus, so
tokáŋyaŋ	elsewhere	lécel, léceya	in this manner
tuktétu ke c'éyaś	in any place	hógna	in that way
tuktétu k'éyaś	in any place	lógna	in this way
waŋkál, waŋkáta	high up	tuktógna ke c'éyaś	in any manner whatever
hetáŋ	from there	áta, átaya	wholly, entirely
héciyataŋ	thence	icéwiŋś	unusually
kákiyataŋhaŋ	from yonder	iyótaŋ	most
kútaŋhaŋ	from below	kítaŋla	a little
letáŋ	from here	kitáŋyel	just a little
léciyataŋ	from here	líla	very
mahétaŋhaŋ	from within	hiyá	no
taŋkátaŋhaŋ	from without	śni	not
tehá̄ŋtaŋhaŋ	from afar	to, hau, haŋ, ohá̄ŋ	yes (men)
tokáŋltaŋhaŋ	from somewhere	haŋ, toś	yes (women)
tókiyataŋhaŋ	from some place	tákuwe	why
waŋkátaŋhaŋ	from on high	tóhaŋ	when
hecíyotaŋ	thereabout	tókel	now
kakíyotaŋ	somewhere yonder	tuktél	where
lecíyotaŋ	hereabout	tókiya	whither
tokíyotaŋ	somewhere	tókiyataŋhaŋ	whence
akókiya	beyond	séce, nacéce	perhaps

Personal ADJECTIVE List and RELATIONSHIPS

Separate Possessive ADJ.	Inseparate: property,	body parts,	incorporeal parts,	relationships
mitáwa	mita...	ma...	mi...	mi...
nitáwa	nita...	ni...	ni...	ni...
táwa	ta...			...ku
uŋkitawapi	uŋkita...pi	uŋk...pi	uŋk...pi	uŋki...pi
nitáwapi	nita...pi	ni...pi	ni...pi	ni...pi
táwapi	ta...pi	...pi	...pi	...kupi

<table>
<tr><th>RELATIONSHIP</th><th>A Male's</th><th>A Female's</th></tr>
<tr><td>father</td><td colspan="2">até</td></tr>
<tr><td>my father</td><td colspan="2">atéwaye kiŋ</td></tr>
<tr><td>thy father</td><td colspan="2">niyáte kiŋ</td></tr>
<tr><td>his, her father</td><td colspan="2">atkúku kiŋ</td></tr>
<tr><td>I have for father</td><td colspan="2">atéwaya</td></tr>
<tr><td>mother</td><td colspan="2">ína</td></tr>
<tr><td>my mother</td><td colspan="2">ináwaye kiŋ</td></tr>
<tr><td>thy</td><td colspan="2">nihúŋ kiŋ</td></tr>
<tr><td>his, her</td><td colspan="2">húŋku kiŋ</td></tr>
<tr><td>I have for</td><td colspan="2">ináwaya</td></tr>
<tr><td>grandfather</td><td colspan="2">tuŋkáśila</td></tr>
<tr><td>my</td><td colspan="2">mitúŋkaśila</td></tr>
<tr><td>thy</td><td colspan="2">nitúŋkaśila</td></tr>
<tr><td>his, her</td><td colspan="2">tuŋkáśitku kiŋ</td></tr>
<tr><td>I have for</td><td colspan="2">tuŋkáśilawaya</td></tr>
<tr><td>grandmother</td><td colspan="2">uŋcí</td></tr>
<tr><td>my</td><td colspan="2">uŋciwaye kiŋ</td></tr>
<tr><td>thy</td><td colspan="2">nikúŋśi kiŋ</td></tr>
<tr><td>his, her</td><td colspan="2">kuŋśítku kiŋ</td></tr>
<tr><td>I have for</td><td colspan="2">uŋcíwaya</td></tr>
<tr><td>grandchild</td><td colspan="2">takója</td></tr>
<tr><td>my</td><td colspan="2">mitákoja kiŋ</td></tr>
<tr><td>thy</td><td colspan="2">nitákoja kiŋ</td></tr>
<tr><td>his, her</td><td colspan="2">takójakpaku kiŋ</td></tr>
<tr><td>I have for</td><td colspan="2">takójawaya</td></tr>
</table>

<table>
<tr><th>RELATIONSHIP</th><th>A Male's</th><th>A Female's</th></tr>
<tr><td>older brother</td><td>cíye</td><td>tibló</td></tr>
<tr><td>my</td><td>ciyéwaye kiŋ</td><td>mitíblo kiŋ</td></tr>
<tr><td>thy</td><td>nicíye kiŋ</td><td>nitíblo kiŋ</td></tr>
<tr><td>his, her</td><td>ciyéku kiŋ</td><td>tiblóku kiŋ</td></tr>
<tr><td>I have for</td><td>ciyéwaya</td><td>tiblówaya</td></tr>
<tr><td>younger brother</td><td colspan="2">misúŋ</td></tr>
<tr><td>my</td><td colspan="2">misúŋkala kiŋ</td></tr>
<tr><td>thy</td><td colspan="2">nisúŋkala kiŋ</td></tr>
<tr><td>his, her</td><td colspan="2">suŋkáku kiŋ</td></tr>
<tr><td>I have for</td><td colspan="2">suŋkáwaya</td></tr>
<tr><td>older sister</td><td>taŋké</td><td>cuwé</td></tr>
<tr><td>my</td><td>mitáŋke kiŋ</td><td>cuwé kiŋ</td></tr>
<tr><td>thy</td><td>nitáŋke kiŋ</td><td>nicúwe kiŋ</td></tr>
<tr><td>his, her</td><td>taŋkéku kiŋ</td><td>cuwéku kiŋ</td></tr>
<tr><td>I have for</td><td>taŋkéwaya</td><td>cuŋwéwaya</td></tr>
<tr><td>younger sister</td><td>taŋkśí</td><td>taŋká</td></tr>
<tr><td>my</td><td>mitáŋkśi kiŋ</td><td>mitáŋka kiŋ</td></tr>
<tr><td>thy</td><td>nitáŋkśi kiŋ</td><td>nitáŋka kiŋ</td></tr>
<tr><td>his, her</td><td>taŋkśítku kiŋ</td><td>taŋkáku kiŋ</td></tr>
<tr><td>I have for</td><td>taŋkśíwaya</td><td>taŋkáwaya</td></tr>
</table>

(other family relationships may be found in Buechel's Grammar of Lakota)

Common PREPOSITIONS*

about	óksaŋ	aglágla	at edge of	kaglá	by, near
across	koákataŋ, ópta	akáŋl	on	kicí	with (one)
along	opáya	akótaŋhaŋ	other side	koákataŋ	beyond
among	égna, ópeya	égna	among	mahél	in, within
around	óksaŋ, ohómni	ékta	at, in	ob	with (many)
at	ékta	ektá	to	ógna	in
the edge of	aglágla	el	in, to, on	óhaŋ	through
beneath	oȟláteya	etáŋhaŋ	from	ohómni	around
between	okó	étkiya	towards	oȟláteya	under, beneath
beyond	akótaŋhaŋ, koákataŋ	iákaŋl	upon	okó	between
by, near	kaglá	ihákab	behind, after	óksaŋ	around, about
by means of	oŋ	iheciya	in that way from	oŋ	of, with, by
from	etáŋhaŋ	ihéktab	behind		means of, in ,
in	ektá, el, mahél,	ihúkul	under		on account of
	ógna, oŋ	ihútab	downstream from	opáya	along
near	aglagla, kagla	iȟéyata	in hills from	ópeya	with, together
of	oŋ	ikiyela	near to		with
on	akáŋl, el	ilazataŋhaŋ	back of	ópta	through, across,
on account of	oŋ	imáhel	within		over
on other side	akótaŋhaŋ, koákataŋ	isákib	beside, near to	-ata, -ta	at (insep. suff.)
over, across	ópta	isáŋpa	beyond	-etu, -tu	at (insep. suff.)
through	óhaŋ, ópta	itáhena	on this side of	-na	at
to	ektá, el	itáŋkal	on outside of	-kiya	toward
together with	ópeya	ítehaŋ	far from	-taŋ	from
towards	étkiya	itókab	before	-taŋhaŋ	from
under	oȟláteya	iwáŋkab	above	-wapa, -pa	beyond (and der.)
unto	el	iyóhakab	after	-íyotaŋ	in vicinity of
with	kicí, ob, oŋ, ópeya	iyécana	soon, thereafter	-íyotaŋhaŋ	about, in the
within	mahél				neighborhood of

*This list also includes some prepositional adverbs.

Inseparable "a": action is done on (not "a" for the 3rd pers. pl. of motion verbs).
Inseparable "o": place in or within which that action takes place.
Inseparable "é": (draws the accent) place at which (not "e" for 3rd pers. pl. of some verbs).
Inseparable "i": something is done with or happens with something; on account of, for, with reference to.

"i" prefixed to Nouns: after, following.
"i" prefixed to cardinal Numbers: makes them Ordinal.
"i" prefixed to Adverbs of place and time, and to some Prepositions: points out more clearly their relation to a preceding substantive.

INTERJECTIONS and INDEPENDENT ELEMENTS

a-a	Request to listen to, for.
apá	Surprise.
aś	Disapproval, friendly.
e	Joy to hear, see the pleasant.
ecé	Surprise, indignant.
ahó-hahó	Gratitude, joy for a gift.
epelá	Joy seeing much food.
háuŋ (m)	Pain, sorrow.
háye-háye	Delight at a gift.
hehé, hehehé	Regret at a misfortune.
héi (m)	Attract one's attention.
hépela-hépela	Joy, surprise seeing a friend.
hiná-hiná (f)	Regret at another's misfortune.
hinúŋ-hinúŋ(f)	Regret at own misfortune.
hókahe	Signal for action.
hokahé	Welcome to visitors.
huŋhé-huŋhé(f)	Regret.
huŋhuŋhé (m)	Regret.
ma (f)	Being taken by surprise.
oȟ, ȟoȟ (m)	Disgust.
tukí (f)	Wonder.
śi (f)	Attract attention, and many other meanings.
tulá (m)	Surprise, indgnant.
waŋ (m)	Surprise.
ya (f)	Fright, pretended.
yu (f)	Disapproval, prohibition.
yuŋ (f)	Pain, fatigue.

eceś (f)	Surprise, resentment at what another dares to say against the speaker.
iyúŋwiŋśkaś icíŋyuŋśkaś	Indignation at something said or done by another.
ma k'éye (f) waŋ k'éya (m)	Answer to a question or joke one considers foolish.
túwa kakéśa, túwa kakéśaś, túweȟca śkéka, ohúŋwela, All mean:	Strong indignation at a statement considered foolish.
waŋ ká waŋ waŋ lé waŋ (f) ma ká waŋ ma lé waŋ (f)	Surprise at suddenly seing something, thus: "Look at this (that)!"
... séce	... I think.
... nacéce	... I suppose.
... kcáma	... I thought (I was sure!)
Akśáka ...	It is too bad ...
Lotkúŋkeśni..	By the way...
Úŋś'keyapika	By the way...(returning to the subject).
nap'táhena	Something undone because it slipped one's mind.
Ho, (ca)...	Well, (then)...

éya... Well then... (to introduce one clause of a compound sentence when the other clause is coordinated with k'éyaś or tka).

ihó... Look, see, behold... (preceding a sentence to call attention to its subject).

itó... Come, come on, now then... (to arouse courage in self or another to do a certain thing; it precedes the sentence and takes the imperative or future verb).

íŋska (iŋ) ..., let me see, ... (can interrupt any sentence and indicates a pause to think).

Changeable VOWELS

Syllables with Changeable Vowels

gla	ȟma	kśa	pca	ska	ṫa	ca, pa, waŋ: (not in all words)
ga	ȟpa	ǩa	psa	śma	t'a	
haŋ	ȟta	k'a	pta	ṡpa	ya	bla, ha, la, kta, ṗa: (in inflections)
ȟca	kpa	ma	spa	tka	yaŋ	
kca	ksa	maŋ	śka	tkaŋ	za	ja: (in suffixes)

1. a, aŋ change to e : but sometimes the vowel may drop, esp. where there is an ellision and a change of consonants.

Endings of VERBS, ADJECTIVES, and ADVERBS are changeable.
Ending of SENTENCE is changeable.
Ending of COORDINATE CLAUSE is changeable; but not before ca, śka; and often not before caŋké.
Ending of DIRECT QUOTATION is changeable; but not at end of indirect questions.
Before PARENTHETICAL EXPRESSIONS there is a change; but not before śka.
Before certain words when they begin with the letters: e, ȟc, k, k', l, s, s', ś.

before: articles — some indefinite pronominal adjectives
prepositions — subordinate conjunctions

particles: adverbial, interrogative, imperative, declarative, subjunctive

Before: ya, kiya, ǩiya, laka, śi, kóŋza, kapíŋ, pica.

2. a, aŋ change to i or iŋ : before na
naiŋś
ye
future tense.

3. i of plural ending "pi" changes to e : in verbs before "lo".

Formation of VERBS

1. abs. - prep. vowel - ki - pron. - ki, kici - ka, pa, ya, yu - stem
   wa---------o--------ki---wicuŋ-------kici---ca---------------ksapi:
   waókiwicuŋkicicaksapi, We sever things in the middle for them.

2. abs. - prep. vowel - ki - na, wa, wo - pron. - ki, kici - stem
   wa---------o---------ki-------wa------wicuŋ-------kici---ksapi:
   waókiwawicuŋkiciksapi, We cut things through the middle with a knife for them.

3. abs. - pron. - ki, kici - ka, pa, ya, yu - prep. vowel - stem
   wa-----we-----ci-----------------ya------------o--------taŋiŋ:
   wawéciyaotaŋiŋ, I make things manifest for one.

4. abs. - na - prep. vowel - pron. - ki, kici - stem
   wa----na---------o---------wa----------------t'iŋza:
   wanáowat'iŋza, I press things in tight with my foot.

5. abs. - wa, wo - pron. - ki, kici - prep. vowel - stem
   wa--------wo----wa---------------------o---------ȟ'aŋko:
   wawówaoȟ'aŋko, I make lively by punching or shooting.

6. Verbs with the following initial syllables follow the rule of no. 2, above:
   ca- , ce- , co- , ǩo- , ǩa- , lo- , ma- , ƥa- , śu- , uŋ- ,

   as do their derivatives: ica- , ice- , waco- , cok'iŋ- , wako- , iko- , waka- , oma- ,
   wama- , etc.

Meaning of the Additives to Verbs:

-ka act of striking with, or of similar motion; motion of wind or water.
-pa act of pressing or weighing upon, pushing, sitting, lying upon.
wa- absolute (abs.) form of the verb (incapable of taking an object).
na- act of the feet; spontaneous action.
wa- action of a knife or saw.
wo- act done by shooting, poking, thrusting; blowing with mouth. (Note: this is not the contraction of "wa-o")
ya- action with the mouth, literally or figuratively.
yu- action with the hands; action in general.
ǩi- action performed in the middle.
-ki possessive form of the verb.
-k- , -kici- to or for someone.
a- , e- , i- , o- the inseparable prepositions.

Lakota VERBS of LOCOMOTION

ya	to be on the way to some place
i	to have gone to some place
u	to be coming to this place
hi	to arrive at this place
gla	to go to one's home
ǩi	to arrive at one's home
ku	to come to one's home here
gli	to arrive at one's home here

Suffix "huⁿni" indicates the arrival was not unexpected and is added to i, hi, ki, gli; iháⁿni, hiháⁿni, kiháⁿni, gliháⁿni.

Prefixes:

a-	accompanied by something not one's own.
glo-	accompanied by something one's own.
hiyo-	to go for something not one's own.
gliyo-	to go for something one's own.

Double Verbs: hiyúⁿka, To arrive at a place not one's own (the fact being mentioned there) and spend the night. Similarly other double verbs.

Special Double Verbs:

hiyú	to start to come
iyáya	to start to go
hiyáya	to pass by
glicu	to start to come home
kigla	to start to go home
gligla	to pass by on one's way home

Illustration: of the use of the eight verbs of locomotion. Let us suppose that A takes a journey to B's house and returns. Thus, the six steps of the journey:

A's viewpoint: mni kte, ble, wahi, wagla, waku, wagli
B's viewpoint: u kte, u, hi, gni kte, gla, ki
C's viewpoint(neighbor): yiⁿ kte, ya, i, gni kte, gla, ki

```
A   1 ———— 2 ———— 3   B
    6 ———— 5 ———— 4

           C
```

Uses of the Verb "TO BE"

yaŋká: temporary existence or accidental; in a certain place when an event occurs; with an animate subject:	Many men were there when he died.	Wicáśa óta yaŋkápi kiŋ hehaŋl t'e.
mere existence or presence in a certain place for an inanimate subject:	The money was there so I took it.	Mázaska kiŋ he yaŋká; caŋké icú.
to form the progressive:	I was listening to it.	Naȟ'óŋ maŋké.
uŋ: continued being in a place; animate subject only:	That we are here is good. He is mute.	Lel uŋkúŋpi kiŋ he waśté. Ié śni uŋ.
to form the progressive:	I am waiting for it.	Apé waúŋ.
oúŋyaŋ: remain as if it were one's home whereas it is not:	I stayed there six years.	Hel waníyetu śákpe owáuŋyaŋ.
ouŋyeya: make one's house in a place:	I lived there many years.	Hel waníyetu óta owáuŋyeya.
hiyeya: existence of inanimate things (singl. form, but pl. meaning):	He cut all the trees there were.	Caŋ hiyéya kiŋ kaśléśleca.
yuŋkáŋ (yuké), waníce (its opposite: something is or is not "on hand"):	There is meat on hand. There is no meat.	Taló yuké. Taló waníce.

Copulative form of "to be";

e, epi: for identification:	This man is the boss.	Le wicáśa kiŋ itáŋcaŋ kiŋ he le e.
for description: (understood)	This man is good.	Le wicáśa kiŋ waśté.

Some IRREGULAR Verbs and Particles

to carry away

ábla
ála
áya
uŋkáyapi
álapi
áyapi

ámni kte
áni kte
áyiŋ kte
uŋkáyapi kte
álapi kte
áyapi kte

to go away

iblábla
ilála
iyáya
uŋkíyayapi
ilálapi
iyáyapi

iblámni kte
iláni kte
iyáyiŋ kte
uŋkíyayapi kte
ilálapi kte
iyáyapi kte

to come forth

wahíyu
yahílu
hiyú
uŋhíyupi
yahílupi
hiyúpi

to eat

wawáta
wayáta
wóta
waúŋyutapi
wayátapi
wótapi

to eat something

wáta
yáta
yúta
uŋyútapi
yátapi
yútapi

to say something

epá
ehá
éya
éuŋkeyapi
ehápi
eyápi

to run

waímnaŋka
yaíŋaŋka
íŋyaŋka
uŋkíyaŋkapi
yaíŋyaŋkapi
íŋyaŋkapi

to go home

waglá
yaglá
gla
uŋglápi
yaglápi
glápi

wagní kte
yagní kte
gni kte
uŋglápi kte
yaglápi kte
glápi kte

to use something

muŋ
nuŋ
uŋ
uŋkúŋpi
núŋpi
úŋpi

to be

waúŋ
yaúŋ
uŋ
uŋk'úŋpi
yaúŋpi
úŋpi

to do something

ecámoŋ
ecánoŋ
ecóŋ
ecúŋkoŋpi
ecánoŋpi
ecóŋpi

to be

maŋká
naŋká
yaŋká
uŋyáŋkapi
naŋkápi
yaŋkápi

to recline

muŋká
nuŋká
yuŋká
uŋyúŋkapi
nuŋkápi
yuŋkápi

to think

ecámi
ecáni
eciŋ
uŋkéciŋpi
ecánipi
ecíŋpi

Interrogative Particles:

men: hwo, he, so
women: huwé, he so

Declarative Particles:

men: yelo (after e, i, iŋ an unchangeable a, aŋ)
lo (after changeable a, aŋ)
welo (after o, oŋ, u, uŋ)
women: we (after o, oŋ, u, uŋ)
ye (after i, iŋ)
yele (after unchangeable a, aŋ)

Note: no declarative particle is used after e or changeable a, aŋ, by women only.

VERB English	1st Class pron. prefix "to strike"	1st Class pron. insert "to receive"	2nd Class pron. prefix "to praise"	2nd Class pron. insert "to leave alone"
I strike	wakáśtaka	iwácu	blatáƞ	ablúśtaƞ
I strike thee	cicáśtaka	icícu	ciyátaƞ	acíyuśtaƞ
I strike him	wakáśtaka	iwácu	blatáƞ	ablúśtaƞ
I strike you	cicáśtakapi	icícupi	ciyátaƞpi	acíyuśtaƞpi
I strike them	wicáwakaśtaka	iwícawacu	wicáblataƞ	awícabluśtaƞ
thou strikest	yakáśtaka	iyácu	latáƞ	alúśtaƞ
thou strikest me	mayákaśtaka	imáyacu	mayálataƞ	amáyaluśtaƞ
thou strikest him	yakáśtaka	iyácu	latáƞ	alúśtaƞ
thou strikest us	uƞyákaśtakapi	uƞkíyacupi	uƞyálataƞpi	uƞkáyaluśtaƞpi
thou strikest them	wicáyakaśtaka	iwícayacu	wicálataƞ	awícaluśtaƞ
he strikes	kaśtáka *	icú *	yatáƞ *	ayúśtaƞ *
he strikes me	makáśtaka	imácu	mayátaƞ	amáyuśtaƞ
he strikes thee	nicáśtaka	inícu	niyátaƞ	aníyuśtaƞ
he strikes him	kaśtáka	icú	yatáƞ	ayúśtaƞ
he strikes us	uƞkáśtakapi	uƞkícupi	uƞyátaƞpi	uƞkáyuśtaƞpi
he strikes you	nicáśtakapi	inícupi	niyátaƞpi	aníyuśtaƞpi
he strikes them	wicákaśtaka	iwícacu	wicáyataƞ	awícayuśtaƞ
we strike	uƞkáśtakapi	uƞkícupi	uƞyátaƞpi	uƞkáyuśtaƞpi
we strike thee	uƞnikáśtakapi	uƞkínicupi	uƞníyataƞpi	uƞkániyuśtaƞpi
we strike him	uƞkáśtakapi	uƞkícupi	uƞyátaƞpi	uƞkáyuśtaƞpi
we strike you	uƞnicáśtakapi	uƞkínicupi	uƞníyataƞpi	uƞkániyuśtaƞpi
we strike them	wicúƞkaśtakapi	iwícuƞcupi	wicúƞyataƞpi	awícuƞyuśtaƞpi
you strike	yakáśtakapi	iyácupi	latáƞpi	alúśtaƞpi
you strike me	mayákaśtakapi	imáyacupi	mayálataƞpi	amáyaluśtaƞpi
you strike him	yakáśtakapi	iyácupi	latáƞpi	alúśtaƞpi
you strike us	uƞyákaśtakapi	uƞkíyacupi	uƞyálataƞpi	uƞkáyaluśtaƞpi
you strike them	wicáyakaśtakapi	iwícayacupi	wicálataƞpi	awícaluśtaƞpi
they strike	kaśtákapi	icúpi	yatáƞpi	ayúśtaƞpi
they strike me	makáśtakapi	imácupi	mayátaƞpi	amáyuśtaƞpi
they strike thee	nicáśtakapi	inícupi	niyátaƞpi	aníyuśtaƞpi
they strike him	kaśtákapi	icúpi	yatáƞpi	ayúśtaƞpi
they strike us	uƞkáśtakapi	uƞkícupi	uƞyátaƞpi	uƞkáyuśtaƞpi
they strike you	nicáśtakapi	inícupi	niyátaƞpi	aníyuśtaƞpi
they strike them	wicákaśtakapi	iwícacupi	wicáyataƞpi	awícayuśtaƞpi

* <u>This form is also the form of the infinitive.</u>

3rd Class VERBS and Reflexive forms	
I am suffering,	makákije
	nicákije
you...	kakíje
	uⁿkákijapi
	nicákijapi
	kakíjapi
I am tired,	wamátuka
you...	wanítuka
	watúka
	waúⁿtukapi
	wanítukapi
	watúkapi
I deceive myself,	mic'ígnayaⁿ
	nic'ígnayaⁿ
you...	ic'ígnayaⁿ
	uⁿkic'ignayaⁿpi
	nic'ígnayaⁿpi
	ic'ígnayaⁿpi
I said that to myself,	hemíc'iye
	heníc'iye
you...	heíc'iye
	heúⁿkic'iyapi
	heníc'iyapi
	heíc'iyapi
I appoint myself,	migláḣniga
	nigláḣniga
you...	igláḣniga
	uⁿkíglaḣnigapi
	nigláḣnigapi
	igláḣnigapi
I rouse myself,	mikpágica
	nikpágica
you...	ikpágica
	uⁿkikpagicapi
	nikpágicapi
	ikpágicapi

1st Class with "ki" ("kici") English	1st Class "ki" long form prefixed "to show to"	1st Class "ki" long form inserted "to do to one"	1st Class "ki" short form prefixed "to give back to"
I. to (for) thee	cicípazo	ocíciḣ'aⁿ	cícu
I....him	wakípazo	owákiḣ'aⁿ	wécu
I....you	cicipazopi	ocíciḣ'aⁿpi	cícupi
I....them	wicáwakipazo	owícawakiḣ'aⁿ	wicáwecu
thou....me	mayákipazo	omáyakiḣ'aⁿ	miyécu
thou....him	yakípazo	oyákiḣ'aⁿ	yécu
thou....us	uⁿyákipazopi	uⁿkóyakiḣ'aⁿpi	uⁿyécupi
thou....them	wicáyakipazo	owícayakiḣ'aⁿ	wicáyecu
he....me	makípazo	omákiḣ'aⁿ	mícu
he....thee	nicípazo	oníciḣ'aⁿ	nícu
he....him *	kipázo *	okíḣ'aⁿ *	kicú *
he....us	uⁿkipazopi	uⁿkókiḣ'aⁿpi	uⁿkícupi
he....you	nicípazopi	oníciḣ'aⁿpi	nícupi
he....them	wicákipazo	owícakiḣ'aⁿ	wicákicu
we....thee	uⁿnícipazopi	uⁿkóniciḣ'aⁿpi	uⁿnícupi
we....him	uⁿkípazopi	uⁿkókiḣ'aⁿpi	uⁿkícupi
we....you	uⁿnícipazopi	uⁿkóniciḣ'aⁿpi	uⁿnícupi
we....them	wicúⁿkipazopi	owícuⁿkiḣ'aⁿpi	wicúⁿkicupi
you....me	mayákipazopi	omáyakiḣ'aⁿpi	miyécupi
you....him	yakípazopi	oyákiḣ'aⁿpi	yécupi
you....us	uⁿyákipazopi	uⁿkóyakiḣ'aⁿpi	uⁿyécupi
you....them	wicáyakipazopi	owícayakiḣ'aⁿpi	wicáyecupi
they....me	makípazopi	omákiḣ'aⁿpi	mícupi
they....thee	nicípazopi	oníciḣ'aⁿpi	nícupi
they....him	kipázopi	okíḣ'aⁿpi	kicúpi
they....us	uⁿkípazopi	uⁿkókiḣ'aⁿpi	uⁿkícupi
they....you	nicípazopi	oníciḣ'aⁿpi	nícupi
they....them	wicákipazopi	owícakiḣ'aⁿpi	wicákicupi

1st Class: Short form "ki"

1) we (wa-ki), ye, ni, mi, ci carry the accent, except the mi in miye.

2) is used always before c and c'; usually before gl, gn, kc, ks, kś and kt; sometimes before h, s, and t.

1st Class Verbs: the reciprocal plural form only with "kici"; the reflexive form pronoun is "ic'i", but a "ka" prefix becomes "igla" and a "pa" prefix becomes "ikpa"; and the latter inflect as a third class verb. But the possessive form takes "ki" prefixed or inserted, and a "ka" prefix becomes "gla", the "pa" prefix "kpa"; inflection follows the first class.

1st Class "ki" short form inserted "to invite to"	1st Class "kici" prefixed "to be for"	1st Class "kici" inserted "to seek for"	1st Class "ki" and "kici" inserted "to pray for"	English
icíco	cícica	ocícile	wacécičiciya	I....thee
iwéco	wécica	owécile	wacéweciciya	I....him
icícopi	cícicapi	ocícilepi	wacécičiciyapi	I....you
iwícaweco	wicáwecica	owícawecile	wacéwicaweciciya	I....them
imíyeco	miyécica	omíyecile	wacémiyeciciya	thou....me
iyéco	yécica	oyécile	wacéyeciciya	thou....him
uŋkíyecopi	uŋyécicapi	uŋkóyecilepi	wacéuŋyeciciyapi	thou....us
iwícayeco	wicáyecica	owícayecile	wacéwicayeciciya	thou....them
imíco	mícica	omícile	wacémiciciya	he....me
iníco	nícica	onícile	wacéniciciya	he....thee
ikíco *	kicíca *	okícile *	wacékiciciya *	he....him
uŋkíkicopi	uŋkícicapi	uŋkókicilepi	wacéuŋkiciciyapi	he....us
inícopi	nícicapi	onícilepi	wacéniciciyapi	he....you
iwícakico	wicákicica	owícakicile	wacéwicakiciciya	he....them
uŋkínicopi	uŋnícicapi	uŋkónicilepi	wacéuŋniciciyapi	we....thee
uŋkíkicopi	uŋkícicapi	uŋkókicilepi	wacéuŋkiciciyapi	we....him
uŋkínicopi	uŋnícicapi	uŋkónicilepi	wacéuŋniciciyapi	we...you
iwícuŋkicopi	wicúŋkicicapi	owícuŋkicilepi	wacéwicuŋkiciciyapi	we....them
imíyecopi	miyécicapi	omíyecilepi	wacémiyeciciyapi	you....me
iyécopi	yécicapi	oyécilepi	wacéyeciciyapi	you....him
uŋkíyecopi	uŋyécicapi	uŋkóyecilepi	wacéuŋyeciciyapi	you....us
iwícayecopi	wicáyecicapi	owícayecilepi	wacéwicayeciciyapi	you....them
imícopi	mícicapi	omícilepi	wacémiciciyapi	they....me
inícopi	nícicapi	onícilepi	wacéniciciyapi	they....thee
ikícopi	kicícapi	okícilepi	wacékiciciyapi	they....him
uŋkíkicopi	uŋkícicapi	uŋkókicilepi	wacéuŋkiciciyapi	they....us
inícopi	nícicapi	onícilepi	wacéniciciyapi	they....you
iwícakicopi	wicákicicapi	owícakicilepi	wacéwicakiciciyapi	they....them

2nd Class Verbs: the reciprocal plural form is used with "kici"; the reflexive form is had by changing the "y" of the prefix to "gl", and then inflect as a third class verb. But the possessive form is similarly formed by changing the "y" of the prefix to "gl"; however, the verb is then inflected as a first class verb.

2nd Class VERBS "ki" prefixed "to open to"	2nd Class "ki" inserted "to tell to"	2nd Class "kici" prefixed "to count for"	2nd Class "kici" inserted "to think for"	English
cicíyugaŋ	ocíciyaka	cíciyawa	icíciyukcaŋ	I....thee
wakíyugaŋ	owákiyaka	wéciyawa	iwéciyukcaŋ	I....him
cicíyugaŋpi	ocíciyakapi	cíciyawapi	icíciyukcaŋpi	I....you
wicáwakiyugaŋ	owícawakiyaka	wicáweciyawa	iwícaweciyukcaŋ	I....them
mayákilugaŋ	omáyakilaka	miyécilawa	imíyecilukcaŋ	thou....me
yakilugaŋ	oyákilaka	yécilawa	iyécilukcaŋ	thou....him
uŋyákilugaŋpi	uŋkóyakilakapi	uŋyécilawapi	uŋkíyecilukcaŋpi	thou....us
wicáyakilugaŋ	owícayakilaka	wicáyecilawa	iwícayecilukcaŋ	thou....them
makíyugaŋ	omákiyaka	míciyawa	imíciyukcaŋ	he....me
nicíyugaŋ	onícíyaka	níciyawa	iníciyukcaŋ	he....thee
kiyúgaŋ *	okíyaka *	kíciyawa *	ikíciyukcaŋ *	he....him
uŋkíyugaŋpi	uŋkókiyakapi	uŋkíciyawapi	uŋkíciciyukcaŋpi	he....us
nicíyugaŋpi	oníciyakapi	níciyawapi	iníciyukcaŋpi	he....you
wicákiyugaŋ	owícakiyaka	wicákiciyawa	iwícakiciyukcaŋ	he....them
uŋníciyugaŋpi	uŋkóniciyakapi	uŋníciyawapi	uŋkíniciyukcaŋpi	we....thee
uŋkíyugaŋpi	uŋkókiyakapi	uŋkíciyawapi	uŋkíciciyukcaŋpi	we....him
uŋníciyugaŋpi	uŋkóniciyakapi	uŋníciyawapi	uŋkíniciyukcaŋpi	we....you
wicúŋkiyugaŋpi	owícuŋkiyakapi	wicúŋkiciyawapi	iwícuŋkiciyukcaŋpi	we....them
mayákilugaŋpi	omáyakilakapi	miyécilawapi	imíyecilukcaŋpi	you...me
yakílugaŋpi	oyákilakapi	yécilawapi	iyécilukcaŋpi	you...him
uŋyákilugaŋpi	uŋkóyakilakapi	uŋyécilawapi	uŋkíyecilukcaŋpi	you...us
wicáyakilugaŋpi	owícayakilakapi	wicáyecilawapi	iwícayecilukcaŋpi	you...them
makíyugaŋpi	omákiyakapi	míciyawapi	imíciyukcaŋpi	they....me
nicíyugaŋpi	oníciyakapi	níciyawapi	iníciyukcaŋpi	they....thee
kiyúgaŋpi	okíyakapi	kíciyawapi	ikíciyukcaŋpi	they....him
uŋkíyugaŋpi	uŋkókiyakapi	uŋkíciyawapi	uŋkíkiciyukcaŋpi	they....us
nicíyugaŋpi	oníciyakapi	níciyawapi	iníciyukcaŋpi	they....you
wicákiyugaŋpi	owícakiyakapi	wicákiciyawapi	iwícakiciyukcaŋpi	they....them

---

WORD SOURCES

A. Arrowside, Frank.
An. Antilope, Mrs. H.

B. Bergen, Wm.
Ba. Bordeaux, Alex.
Bc. Bordeaux, Charles.
BD. BearDog, Ed.
Bd. BigHead.
BE. Black Elk, Nick.
Be. Black Elk, Paul.
BF. BigFace.
Bf. Bordeaux, Felix.
BH. BraveHawk.
Bh. BlueHorse.
B.H. Bible History, Bue.
BIW. BearInTheWoods.
BL. BrokenLeg, Sam.
Bl. BullRing, Cleve W.
BM. BullMan, Ben.
BMj. BullMan, John.
BN. BullNation, Al.
Bn. Brown, Wm.
Bo. Boas, Franz.
BR. Sacred Pipe, Brown.
Br. Bryde, J. F.
BS. BoneShirt, T. and J.
Bs. BlackSpottedHorse, J.
Bm. Bordeaux, Wm.
BT. BigTurkey.
Bt. BlueThunder.
Bw. Brown, Wm.

CD. CrossDog, Wm.
CG. CrowGoodVoice.
CH. ChargingHawk.
Ch. Cottier, Henry.
Cl. Clifford, E.
CO. Colombe, John.
Co. ClownHorse.
CR. CrazyHorse, Mrs.

D. Deloria, Ella. (pg.)
Dakota Texts.
DE. DogEarCamp.
De. Desersa, M.
Du. Dubray, John.

EB. EagleBird, Wm.
ED. EagleDeer.
Ed. EagleDog.
EE. EagleElk, Jesse.
EF. EagleFeather, R.
EM. EagleMan.
ER. EagleRoad.
ES. EagleStar, Owen.
Es. ElkSky.
ET. EagleThunder.
Et. EagleTail.

F. Flood, Wm.
FB. FastBull.
FD. Densmore, Frances.
Teton Sioux Music.
FE. FoolishElk.
FH. FoolHead.
Fi. Fish.
FN. ForgetNothing, M.
FP. FillsPipe.
FR. FourHorns, Frank.
Fr. Frightened, Jos.
FW. FastWhirlwind.

GA. GoesAmong, A.
GB. GrayBuffalo, Mrs.
Gb. GoodBear, Jos.
Gr. Green, Charles.
Gramm. Buechel, Rev. E.
Lakota Grammar.
GS. GoodShield, Fred.
GT. GoodThunder.
GV. GoodVoice, Moses.
Gv. GoodVoice, Jesse.
GW. GoodWill, Moses.
H. Howard, James.
HC. HornCloud, Jos.
HH. HighHorse.
Hh. HuntsHorse.
HL. HorseLooking.
HM. HawkMan, Leo.
Hm. HolyMan.
Ho. Hoġaŋ.
HP. HighPipe.

IB. IronBull.
IS. IronShell, Peter.
Is. IronShell, Allan.

J. Janis, Wm.
Ja. Jackson, Jos.

K. Katola.
Ka. Kaśna, Mrs.
KS. KillsInSight, Chas.
KT. KnockOffTwo, Geo.

L. Little, Eugene.
La. Larvie, Tom.
LB. LittleBull, Tom.
LC. LittleCloud.
Lc. LoneCedar, Geo.
LE. LittleElk, Frank.
LH. LittleHawk.
Lh. LittleHorse.
LHB. LeftHandBull, Silas.
(also, SLB)
Lhb. LeftHandBull, P.
LM. LittleMoccasin.
LO. LameOmaha.

LP. LaPointe, Jacob.
LT. LittleThunder, Robt.
LTf. LittleThunder, Frank.
LWOW. Buechel, Rev. E.
Prayer Book.

M. Metcalf, Wm.
Me. Menard, George.
MF. MoccasinFace.
MG. MakesGood.
Mh. Makalȟpaya.
Mi. Mills, W.
MN. Moran, Narcisse.
MO. Mousseau, Louis.
MS. Buechel et Al.
Mss. Stories.
Mt. Buechel.
St. Matthew's Gospel.
MW. MakeNoiseInTheWoods.

NO. NoisyOwl.
NP. NightPipe, Alfred

OE. OldEagle, James.
OF. OwnsFire.
OH. OneHorn.
OS. OneStar, Michael.

P. Perrig, S.J., Rev. E.
Lakota Dictionary.
Pa. Pacer, Martin.
PB. PrettyBird.
Pb. (manuscript lost)
PD. PoorDog.
PLB. LeftHandBull, Peter.
PO. Pine, Oliver.

R. Riggs, Rev. S. R.
Lakota Dictionary.
RA. RunsAbove, Louis.
Ra. Randall, Wm.
Rac. Randall, Charles.
RB. RunningBear, Louis.
Rb. RedBird, Mrs.
RC. RedCloud.
RE. RedEyes.
RF. RedFeather.
Rf. RedFish, Wm.
RH. RunningHorse, Chas.
Rh. RunningHawk.
Rl. RingBull.
RO. Rooks, Charles.
RT. RingThunder, Sam.
RTj. RedTomahawk, John.
RTt. RedTomahawk, Tom.
RV. RunCloseToVillage, Mrs.

S. Shield, Tom, Norris, Sam.
SB. ShortBull.

WORD SOURCES (contin.)

Sb. StandingBull, Jake.
Sbj. StandingBull, Mrs.J.
SC. SpottedCalf, Wm.
SH. StrangerHorse.
SE. SoreEyes.
SI. Star, Ivan.
Si. Simpson, B.
SLB. cf. LHB.
Sp. Stampede, Mrs. Noe.
ST. SpottedTail.
St. Star, Pat.
SW. Schweigman, A.
Sw. Swift.
ŚG. Śuŋgleśka.

T. Trudell, Antoine.
TB. TwoBird.
TH. ThunderHawk.
Ti. Titus.
TT. TwoTeeth.

UW. UnderWater.

W. Walker, Alvina.
Wa. Walking, Mrs.
WC. Whissler, Clark.
Indians of Plains.
WE. WalkingEagle, Geo.
WF. WhiteFeather.
WH. WhiteHorse, Laban.
Wh. White, Frank.
WI. Williamson, Rev. J.
Dakota Dictionary.
Wi. WhiteHat, Emily.
WJR. Walker, J. R.
Oglala Sundance.
WL. WhiteLance, Jesse.
Wo. Wounded.
WR. WhiteRabbit.
WW. WhirlwindSoldier.
Ww. Whitewash.
Wwc. WhiteWolf, Charles.

YH. YellowHair.
Yh. YellowHawk, Ed.
YW. YellowWolf.

#(no.) Buechel et Al.

ABBREVIATIONS

a.	active.
abbrev.	abbreviation.
abs.	absolute.
adj.	adjective, adjectival.
adv.	adverb, adverbial.
altern.	alternate, alternative.
art.	article.
aux.	auxilliary.
cl.	clause.
col.	collective, collection.
coll.	" "
colloq.	colloquial.
comp.	compound, compounded.
conj.	conjunction.
coord.	coordinate, coordination.
dat.	dative.
defect.	defective.
def.	definite.
dem.	demonstrative.
deriv.	derivative.
dim.	diminutive.
e.g.	for instance (exempla gratia).
emph.	emphatic, emphasis.
encl.	enclitic.
esp.	especially.
exclam.	exclamation, exclamatory.
explic.	explicative.
fig.	figuratively, figure.
fut.	future.
imp.	imperative.
imper.	imperfect.
impers.	impersonal.
indef.	indefinite.
insep.	inseparable.
interj.	an interjection.
intj.	" " .
interrog.	interrogative, interrogation.
irreg.	irregular.
lit.	literally.
n.	noun.
neg.	negative.
no.	number.
nom.	nominative.
num.	number.
obj.	objective.
obs.	obsolete.
obs.	obscure.
opt.	optative.
p.	proper.
prop.	" .
part.	participle, participial.
particle.	(sic).
perhaps.	some doubt involved.
pers.	person.
ph.	phrase.
pres.	present.
pl.	plural.
pos.	possessive.
prefix.	(sic).
prep.	preposition, prepositional.
pron.	pronoun.
recip.	reciprocal.
red.	reduplicated.
ref.	reference, refering.
refl.	reflexive.
rel.	relative.
rhet.	rhetorical.
sing.	singular.
subj.	subjective.
suff.	suffix.
superl.	superlative.
syll.	syllable.
syn.	synonym.
t.	transitive.
v.	verb, verbal.
cont.	contraction.
a - a.	The dash (-) with a space before and after: the proximate word entry preceding is here mentioned.
(?)	There is doubt concerning or lack of definition, the word's function or meaning; see Appendix A.
#	Reference to Buechel's botonical lists.

LAKOTA-ENGLISH DICTIONARY

ă, exclam. Used on hearing a voice or noise so as to draw others' attention. A, anagoptaⁿ po.

ă, n. The arm-pit; the space between the forelegs of animals. Aoȟlate yumahel icu, She took it and hid it under her arm beneath her blanket. D.59.

a, prep. prefix insep.
1) Affixed to verbs and adjectives, it usually means "on" or "upon". Amani, To walk on. Cf. below.
2) In some cases, it gives a causative meaning to the word; thus, u, To come, and au, To bring; ya, To go, and aya, To take.
3) It forms a collective plural in the case of some verbs of motion. Au, They come. Aya, They go. Ahi, They have arrived.
4) Affixed to nouns, it sometimes makes adverbs of them; thus, wanica, None, and awanil or awanilya, In a destroying manner.
5) It makes nouns of some verbs, as wapta, To cut off from, and awapte, A cutting on; caⁿ awapte, A cutting board.

a'bebeya, adv. red. (abeya). Scattered, as a flock separately, singly; spreading out, scattering, as a herd of buffalo when chased. Cf. kaiyabebeya.
a'bekiya, adv. Scattered, separately.
a'beya, adv. Separately, scattering. - iyayapi or - akiyagle, Scattering, they went away. D.72.

ablag'yela, adv. Quietly, peacefully. Tohaⁿni - uⁿpi śni, as is said when a married couple do not get along well with each other. Bl.
ablak' hiⁿgla, v. To turn calm suddenly. B.H.117.11.
abla'ḱela, n. A calm. - ca wicaho ȟtani ca tokiya eyaś naȟ'oⁿpi kte. Bl. -- adj. Calm, still, without wind. - hiⁿgle, It suddenly became calm. D.21.

a'blaskabtoⁿyaⁿ, adv. Aside of another, flat or level. - uⁿȟpayapelo, They lie aside of one another.

abla'sḱaya, adv. Level, without ridges.
abla'ya, adj. Level on.

able'cahaⁿ, part. Scattered, fallen off, as from a pile of rock etc. Also, perhaps, oblecahaⁿ.

a'blelya oyu'spa, adv. Holding many things, e.g. flowers or hair, in the hand so that the upper ends hang down on all sides evenly. - haⁿ, i.e. as a bunch of plants. When the things held are kept straight, they say: ptayela haⁿ. Cf. oblelya.

ables', v.n. (ableza). To be clear. - iyaya, aya, To become clear. - amayaⁿ, I become clear, visible. Oyate kiⁿ taⁿyaⁿ - nayajiⁿpi kte.
ables'ya, v.a. To make clear, visible. Ableswaya. -- adv. Clearly. Also, ablésyaḱel.

able'za, v.a. Look into, notice, perceive. Awableza. -- v.n. To see clearly, be sober; to pay attention. Amableza.

abli'heca, v.n. (bliheca). To be industrious in regard to. Amabliheca.
abli'helic'iya, v. refl. To make one's self industrious about anything. Ablihelmic'iya.
abli'helya, v.a. To cause to be industrious about anything. -- adv. Industriously; stirringly.

ablo', n. The shoulder, the scapula. Hehaⁿ - anuⁿkatahaⁿ wicaȟpi num owawa.
ablo'hu, n. The shoulder bone or blade, the scapula.
ablo'iyoḱiju, n. The part between the shoulders. Also, abloiyokitahena.

ablo'ketu, v. imper. To come summer, to have lived until summer. Wana uⁿk'abloketupelo, We now have lived to summertime. Bl.

ablu'ḱehahaka, v. To pass over a thing very quickly and hence half and half, i.e. badly, as arrows. Bl.

aca'ġa, v.n. (caga). To freeze in, on,

or upon; become ice upon. Amacaga.

aca'glegle, adj. Scattered, with things far apart or motion this way and that. - wakagege, I made stitches far apart. Bl.
aca'glegleyakel, adv. (caⁿglegle, perhaps). Poorly written, with a letter placed here and there because of e.g. a shaking of the wagon. Also, okagligle. - wakagelo. Bl. LHB.

aca'ȟsnasna, v.n. (acage-snasna). To rattle, as icicles formed on anything.
aca'ȟsu, v. To form ice on something in little drops, as on trees, grass etc. Oⁿśtiⁿmapihiⁿ acaȟmasu, Little ice drops formed on my eyelids. Peji -. Bl.
aca'ȟsusu, v. red. (acaȟsu). Oⁿśtiⁿmahiⁿpi - imayayelo. Bl.
aca'ȟślaya, adj. (acaga-ślaya). All icy or covered with ice, as trees when rain is frozen on them.

aca'je iǵlata, v. refl. To give a name to one's self. B. LHB.

aca'mni, v.n. (camni). To sprout on.

acaⁿ'caⁿ, v.n. (caⁿcaⁿ). To shake on account of. Amacaⁿcaⁿ.

acaⁿ'iglaśka yaⁿká, v. refl. (acaⁿkaśka). To be fortified. B.H.62.9.
acaⁿ'kaśka, v.a. (caⁿ-kaśka). To bind wood on; to inclose on, fence in. Acaⁿwakaśka.
acaⁿ'kaśkaya, v.a. (caⁿ-kaśkaya). Make a fence, to enclose e.g. a fort; to bind wood together on. Acaⁿkaśkawaya.

acaⁿ'kśiⁿ, v.a. To step over, pass over or jump over. Also, acákśiⁿ. Acaⁿwakśiⁿ. Woacaⁿkśiⁿ, the Pasch. R. Bl.
acaⁿ'kśiⁿya, v.a. To cause to pass over. Acaⁿkśiⁿwaya.
acaⁿ'kśiⁿyaⁿ, adv. Passing over.

acaⁿ'kuȟiya, v. To go by a certain place on one's way somewhere. Hihaⁿni kiⁿ acaⁿkuwakiyiⁿ kte lo. WE. Cf. acaⁿkuya.
acaⁿ'ȟuya, v.a. (caⁿku). To make a road on, to pass through on. Acaⁿkuwaya. -- adv. Lying on e.g. a road, passing through. B.H.112.16;200.4.

acaⁿ'niyaⁿ, v.a. (caⁿniyaⁿ). To be angry for. Acaⁿmaniyaⁿ.

acaⁿ'nuⁿp̣a, v.a. (caⁿnuⁿpa). To smoke on or after, as after eating. Acaⁿnuⁿmuⁿpa.

acaⁿ'ṫeśica, v.a. (caⁿte-śica). To be sad on account of.
acaⁿ'ṫeśilya, adv. Sorrowfully for, sadly for. Also, acáⁿṫeśilyaȟel.

acaⁿ'ze, v.a. To be angry at. Amacaⁿze.
acaⁿ'zeȟa, v.n. To be or get mad or angry at. Amacaⁿzeka, He is angry with me; awacaⁿzeka, I am angry at him. Akicicaⁿzekapi, They are angry at each other. Acaⁿwicazekapi or awicacaⁿzekapi.

aca'pa, v.a. (capa). To stab on, stick in; to take stitches in or on. Acawapa.

aceb'ya, v.a. (acepa). To make fat for a certain purpose. Acebwaya.
aceb'yakel, adv. In a state of fattening for. - gle.

ace'jiya, v.a. To stick out the tongue to mock. Acejimayalapelo, You stuck out your tongue at me. Bl.

ace'p̣a, v.a. (cepa). To be fat for, be getting fat; to be in good order.

ace'sli, v.a. (cesli). To excrete on something. Acewasli. -- n. Something to urinate on; a diaper.

ace'ti, v.a. To make a fire on or at. Acewati.

ace'ya, v.a. To bemoan, bewail, cry out, cry for, mourn, weep for. Awaceya. Uⁿkaceyapi. -- acéyapi, part. Crying for, cried for.

aci'caȟlo, v.a. To growl about, complain of. Also, aśícaȟlo, which seems more correct. R. Bl.

aco'ȟata, (?). - imaⁿkeca, as a man would say who wants more than what he gets. Bc.

aco'pa, v.a. (copa). To wade into the water for anything. Acowapa. Witka acope uⁿyaⁿpi kte, Let us go for the eggs, i.e. found in the bulrushes. Bl.

acos'ya, adv. Warmly.
aco'za, v.n. (coza). To be warm on, be comfortable.

acu´, v.n. imper. (cu). To dew on, to bedew. -- n. and prep. With dew upon.

acuŋ´kaśk̇a, v.a. To fortify, surround with a fence or wall or palisade etc. Acuŋwakaśka. Acuŋkaśkapi. -- acúŋkáśk̇e, n. A fort, fortress, stronghold. Also, acoŋkaśke.

acu´wita, v.a. (cuwita). To be cold upon. Amacuwita.

acu´ya, v.a. To cause dew upon; to lay out something overnight to have it bedewed. Acuwaya. Syn.- katatabya. Bl.

a´ecela, adv. Just that, excluding or not including other things. Ihupa aecela iwacu, I took only the stem. - yaŋka, To be destitute of everything, even of necessities. Bc. Also, áecelakel, Being without, not having with one. B.H.115.17.

ae´celiyeic'iya, v. refl. To shut up one's self, as in a room. B.H.192.15.

ae´cetu, v.n. To fit to do something. Iśta aemacetu śni yelo, My eyes are not right, i.e. I cannot see well, as when they water. Owakita aemacetu śni yelo. Bl. LHB.

ae´gnaka, v.a. To add to. Bl.

ae´ṫulak̇eci, adv. In a little while. - wahi kte.

a´eṫulak̇e el, adv. ph. After a little while; rather at that time, very soon. Na - wiŋyaŋ k'uŋ hena iś eya ahihuŋni. B.H.137.14;183.2;259.5;304.5.

ae´yokas'iŋ, v. To peep in at. Aeyowakas'iŋ. Aeyouŋkas'iŋpi. Yuŋkaŋ paha k'oŋ el ehuŋni na aeyokas'iŋpi el lila pte otapi. B.H.112.11.

a´ġaŋ iḣpáya, v.n. To fall or jump into water with a splash. Áġiŋḣpaya yo.

aġi´, v.n. (gi). To be covered with rust, to have a rusty or brown stain; to be mildewed.

agla´, v.a. To be carrying or taking home. Awagla. Uŋkaglapi. Bl. Pte pa waŋjini ena iḣpeya śni oyas'iŋ - po. -- v. coll. pl. (gla). They go home. Tona glinapapi kiŋ hecena - ca miś eya wakiyagla na tiyata wagli.

agla´gla, adv. Along side of, in front of. - iŋyaŋka, To run in front of one. - inajiŋpi, They stand in front of one. Ecel - pazo au na nawajiŋ el ahihuŋni.

agla´ġeġe, v.a. pos. (akagege). To sew one's own upon.

agla´haŋ, v.n. To slip or slide out e.g. a tent-pole when a number are dragged along; to be dropping e.g. water continuously from a roof. Mni - . IS. -- part. perhaps. (agla). Carrying home. -- v. coll. pl. They keep on going home, one after another, as after a meeting.

agla´ḣṗa, v. pos. (akaḣpa). To throw e.g. a garment over one's own, to cover one's own. Awaglaḣpa.

agla´ḣṗek̇itoŋ, v. pos. (akaḣpetoŋ). To clothe or cover one's own. Aglaḣpewakitoŋ.

agla´ḣṗetoŋ, v. To clothe one's own. Aglaḣpewatoŋ.

agla´ḣpeya, v. (akaḣpeya). Aglaḣpewaya.

agla´ksa, v.a. pos. (akaksa). To cut off one's own upon. Awaglaksa.

agla´kśiś, v.n. To fall on top of one another; to be crossed, as do the legs. YH. To fall or lie down upon, as does a dog. Cf. aglaskica.

agla´kśuŋyaŋ yuŋka, v. To lie on one's belly. Bl.

agla´la, v.a. (akala). To scatter one's own upon. Awaglala.

agla´mna, v.a. pos. (akamna). To gather one's own, accumulate for a purpose. Awaglamna.

agla´paŋ, v.a. pos. (akapaŋ). To beat out or thresh one's own upon. Awaglapaŋ.

agla´ṗeṗeya, v. Cf. caḣ'aglapepeya, mniaglapepeya. Aglapepewaya. Bl.

agla´ṗoṫa, v.a. pos. (akapota). To beat in pieces one's own upon. -- v.n. perhaps. To float upon.

agla´psiŋṫa, v.a. pos. (akapsiŋta). To strike or whip one's own.

agla´psoŋ, v.a. pos. (akapsoŋ). To

spill one's own upon.

agla'pśuŋ, v.a. pos. (kapśuŋ). To put one's own out of joint on. Awaglapśuŋ.
agla'pśuŋyaŋ, adv. Bottom upwards, prone, upside down. - eḣpeya, iyeya, To turn bottom-side up.

agla'pṫa, v.a. (glapta). To cease to fall on or to rain. Amaglapta. -- v.a. To dip or ladle out from one's own kettle. Awaglapta. Cf. oglapta.

agla'ptus, adv. cont. Prone. - iḣpaya, To fall flat on the ground. Syn.- aglapśuŋyaŋ.

agla'sḱica, v.a. (akaskica). To press down on one's own, to lie on one's own. Awaglaskica. D.216.
agla'sḱiŋ, part. (aglaskica). On the face. Bl. - iḣpeya, To throw down on the face. - iḣpaya, To fall down on face.

agla'śkica, v. pos. (akaśkica, ayaśkica). To spit out on something of one's own. Awaglaśkica.

agla'śla, v.a. pos. (akaśla). To cut one's own in addition to. Bl.

agla'śna, v.a. pos. (ayaśna). To make a mistake in speaking. Awaglaśna.

agla'śṗa, v.a. pos. (akaśpa). To break a piece off one's own upon.

agla'śtaŋ, v. pos. (akaśtaŋ, ayaśtaŋ). To throw or spill e.g. water on one's own; to cease speaking or eating.

agla'ṫa, v.a. To chorus to, answer or respond to in music.

agla'ta, v. pos. (akata). To hoe one's own, e.g. one's corn. Awaglata.

agla'tkaŋ, v. pos. (ayatkaŋ). To drink one's own with or upon. Awablatkaŋ.

agla't'iŋza, v. To establish something for certain. Awaglat'iŋza. Ayaglat'iŋza he? Are you sure? Bl.

agle', v.a. To place or make stand on something, as a pitcher on a tray. - éwagle, 1st. pers. sing.; also, awagle; uŋkaglepi. Also, 3rd pers. pl. of agla, They go home. He - manipelo. B.H.171.10.

agle'haŋ, n. A frame; groundworks, a foundation. D.222.

agle'hiyeya, part. Placed one after another.

agle'ḱiya, v.a. To cause to take home. Aglewakiya.

agle'ṗa, v.a. (glepa). To vomit upon. Awaglepa.

agle'śḱa, n. A lizard or alligator. Bl. Also, agléśḱala.

agle'yela, n. An edge. - ihuŋni. Bl. LHB.

agle'yus, v. cont. (agleyuza). To hold against. - kute, To shoot, holding the gun against the object or very near it.
agle'yuza, v.a. To hold against, hold near to; to come near to. Aglebluza.

agli', v.a. To arrive at home, bring home. Awagli, uŋkaglipi. -- v. coll. pl. (gli). They all came back. About February 7th or 8th, the Indians say: Maga agli kte lo. BT.
agli'ceti, v. To come home and start a fire.

agli'haŋ, v. To fall on. Peta waŋ awicaglihiŋ na. B.H.65.10.
agli'he, v. (agliha n). To descend upon; to strike or hit by falling on. Maḣpiya waŋ akaḣpeya - .
agli'heya, v.a. To shine on. Wi kiŋ Jonas nata kiŋ - , The sun shone on Jonas' head. B.H.61.10;195.16;240.14.

agli'huŋni, v.a. To take something straight back home. Awaglihuŋni. -- v. coll. pl. They all arrived, coming straight back. Na waŋna uŋma kiŋ aglihuŋni. Awicaglihuŋnipi. Ecana - kte lo. Bl.

agli'ḣpaya, v.n. To fall on, hitting the ground, falling from above. Awagliḣpaya. Syn.- ahiŋḣpaya.

agli'ḣpeya, v.a. To leave something on one's way home, e.g. a horse that is played out. Agliḣpewaya.

agli'iyape, v. (agli-iyape). To wait for their coming home, to lie in wait by the way. Agliiyewape.

agli´naṗa, v. To bring out one's own. Na waŋna waŋjigjila tima iyayapi na - na taku yuja - . Yuŋkaŋ pte optaye kiŋ etaŋ aglinapapi. B.H.223.6.

agli´napiŋ, v. coll. pl. They camehome and stand there, as a herd of horses do coming from the pasture.
agli´psica, v. coll. pl. They come home and alight.
agli´ti, v. coll. pl. They come home and stay, i.e. camp. Tokśa, ptayetu kiŋ lel gliyatipi kte.

agli´ṫoḣiciksu, v. To bring along for somebody coming home. Kola aglitomiciksu wo. Bl.

agli´waŋyaŋka, v. coll. pl. They came back home to see their own.

agli´wota, v.n. To stop for one's meal on the way home. Agliwawota. Na waŋna aŋpo el ake akiya na wicokaŋhiyaya a-agliwotapi.

agli´yacu, v.a. To be on one's way home bringing something, as a missionary might a runaway boy. Awaġliyacu. -- v. coll. pl. They are on their way home. Also, agliyaku. D.251. B.H.48.1.

agli´yagla, v.a. To pass by with something to any place, as a policeman who passes by with a prisoner. -- v. coll. pl. They all pass by in sight, going home, taniŋyaŋ na glakiŋyaŋ. Waŋna uŋkisakib agliyagla eśa inila - . Waŋna oyas'iŋ lel witayela ku po, eya. Hecel el witayela - ca waś'ake owapa. Bl.
agli´yaglahaŋ, v. coll. pl. They continue to pass by, going home, as a column of soldiers does. Bl.

agli´yahaŋ, v. coll. pl. They came up a hill and stopped in sight on their way home. When ref. is made to one man only, we say: gliyahaŋ.

agli´yaku, v.a. (agli-aku). To be coming home with something. Awagliyaku. Hokśila - . Also, agli´yacu. -- v. coll. pl. They are coming home together. Lel iŋkpata wakpala uŋhe iyoḣloke kiŋ isam - , i.e. the enemies, ca hecena uŋgliyacupi, i.e. spies.

agli´yaoŋṗa, v. To come and place on. Agliwaoŋpa. Iŋyaŋ blaskaska ca el a-gliwicaoŋpapi. Cf. aoŋpa.

agli´yohi, v. coll. pl. (gliyohi). They reach home on returning. Bl.

agli´yoḣpaya, v. coll. pl. They came down from a hill. Na waŋna zuya k'uŋ - na wicoti el ukiya. MS.566. Bl.

agli´yotḣa, v. coll. pl. They stopped somewhere on their way home. In ref. to one only, we say: gliyotaka.

agli´yuġo, v.n. To arrive at home tired out. Agliblugo. RF.

agli´yuḣpa, v.a. To come home and lay down one's baggage, i.e. unload. A-wagliyuḣpa, I come home; agliblulpa, I unload. IS.

agli´yuḣaŋ, v. coll. pl. To come home and remain. Le wakpala cik'ala kiŋ opaya ukiya tka agliyukiŋ kte śni s'elececa yelo.

agli´yuŋḣa, v. To come home and sleep. -- v. coll. pl. They all camped on the way home. Gliyuŋka, ref. to one only. Na hetaŋ ukiya na wakpala waŋ wagacaŋ oju ca el - . Na wana ukiya na śakowiŋ agliyuŋkiŋ na aglihuŋni. Wakiŋyaŋ iġlag ukiye c'oŋ agliyuŋkelo. Bl.

aglo´gla, v. To carry home. Awaglogla. Bl.

aglu´blu, v. pos. (yablu). To plow one's own upon. Awaglublu.

aglu´ġaṫa, v. pos. (yugata). To open out e.g. one's hand on anything. Awa-glugata.

aglu´ha, v. pos. (ayuha). To have or take one's own on account of; to provide for some occasion, keep one's own for a certain occasion or purpose. Awagluha.

aglu´hete, v. pos. (ayuhete). To wait upon one's own; the sole object of one's thoughts, n.

aglu´homni, v. coll. pl. They all turn around to see. In ref. to one only, igluhomni. Bl.

aglu´ḣica, v. pos. (ayuḣica). To waken one's own upon. Awagluḣica.

aglu´ḣaḣa, (?). Bl.

aglu'kaŋ, v.a. To leave unmolested. Awaglukaŋ.

aglu'ǩawa, v. pos. (yukawa). To open up one's own.

aglu'kcaŋ, v. pos. (yukcaŋ). To understand one's own upon or in relation to. Awaglukcaŋ.

aglu'maŋ, v. pos. (yumaŋ). To grind one's own upon. Awaglumaŋ.

aglu'soťa, v. pos. (yusota). To use one's own up on. Awaglusota.

aglu'sťo, v. pos. (yusto). To smooth one's own down on, as one's hair. Awaglusto.

aglu'suťa, v. pos. (yusuta). To make hard one's own upon. Awaglusuta.

aglu'śǩica, v. pos. (yuśkica). To press out one's own upon.

aglu'śluśluta, v. Cf. yuśluta, oglikiya. Kaŋ iwapsake waŋ imicik'ege śni ca awagluślutiŋ kte lo. Bl.

aglu'śna, v. pos. (yuśna). To make a mistake over.

aglu'śťaŋ, v. pos. (ayuśtaŋ). To leave off something pertaining to one's self. Awagluśtaŋ.

aglu'śte, v.n. To be lame in. Siamagluśte, To sprain e.g. one's foot. Bl.
aglu'śteśte, v. red. (agluśte). To be numb or lame. Amagluśteśte. Bl.

aglu'ťa, v. pos. (yuta). To eat one's own with something upon something; to look at one's own. Awicaglutayelo. B.H.53.2;197.11.

aglu'ťiťaŋ, v. pos. (yutitaŋ). To stretch one's own upon; to pull down.

aglu'weğa, v. pos. (yuwega). To bend or break upon.

aglu'wi, v. pos. (yuwi). To wrap one's own around, as one's leggings on one's legs. Awagluwi.

aglu'za, v. pos. (yuza). To hold one's own to.

agna', adv. and perhaps prep. At once. Yuŋkaŋ lila kpeyela iyeya na - wouŋka na psuŋpsuŋkiya agliyuŋka. - mni k'uŋ waŋkal hiyu. D.217-8,269. -- agnágna, adv. red.

agna'haŋ, v.n. (gnahaŋ). To fall on, as fruit in anything.
agna'ǩa, v.a. To place on anything, apply externally e.g. medicine, poultice etc. Awagnaka, uŋkagnakapi.

agna'la, adv. Only with; with so many only.

a'gnawotapi, n. A table, anything to eat on, as a box etc.

agni', 3rd pers. sing. of agla. It is so changed before "na" following.

ağu', v.n. (gu). To burn on anything, burn on account of or by reason of anything. We agu s'e, All bloody. -- ağúğu, v.n. red. of agu. -- ağúğuya, v.a. (aguya). To cause to burn on. Also, ağúya. Aguwaya.

ağu'yap̌i, n. Bread; wheat.
- blu, Flour.
- blu ináze, A flour sifter.
- gmigmela, Biscuits.
- ha, Bran, chaff.
- hu, Straw, i.e. of wheat.
- icapa, A flail.
- ikácoco, A bread raiser.
- ipábla, A bread roller.
- iśpáŋye, A baking pan.
- okáğe, A bakery.
- óśpaŋyaŋ, A baker oven.
- owaślece, A slice of bread. Also, - wakaápi waŋji.
- sáka, Crackers; hard bread.
- skúya, Pastry; sweet crackers. Also, - skuyela.
- skuyéla gmigméla yuȟlókab, Doughnuts.
- su, A grain of wheat, seed wheat.
- śpaŋ, Baked bread.
- śpaŋ ha, Bread crust.
- tacáğu, A loaf of bread, which is light and spongy like to lungs.
- zíp̌ela, Pancakes. Also, - zibzíp̌ela.

ağu'yap̌i su oka'la, v. To sow wheat.

aha'hayela, adv. Not firmly, movably. Cf. hahayela.

ahahě', interj. An exlam. of thanks to one for a gift, something like: Three cheers for! Thus: (Name) ahahe, (repeat) ahahe. BT.

aha'kab, adv. After.

ahaⁿ', v.n. (haⁿ). To stand on, rest on. Awahaⁿ. Cf. aⁿbhaⁿkeya. -- v. imp. or interj. Look out! Be careful! as is said when something is losing its balance and will drop, as a lamp on the edge of a table. - hiⁿȟpayiⁿ kta! WE. R. -- Aháⁿ, n. p. A man in days of old who went out on some nice day in March, and he was not prepared for cold weather. So he froze to death when a blizzard suddenly came upon him. So, when a blizzard comes in the month of March, people say: Ahaⁿ taaⁿpetu welo. George Rogers uses the word as a warning for somebody to stop annoying one of the family, and he pronounces it: haháⁿ. D.197.

ahaⁿ'haⁿ, v. red. (ahaⁿ). To stand on. Pajola waz'áhaⁿhaⁿ, A hill beset with many pines. Bl.

ahaⁿ'hepiic'iya, v. refl. To wait until night overtakes one. B.H.77.4.

ahaⁿ'keya, adv. Immediately then, following. Hócoka kiⁿ - . Also, immediately behind. D.246.

ahaⁿ'keyela, adv. Previously, just before.

ahaⁿ'ḱiktapi, n. A wake, a watching at the body of a deceased person. Bl.

ahaⁿ'najiⁿ kuwa, v. To bother one constantly. Bl.

ahaⁿ'zi, v.n. imper. To be shady, over-shadowed. Amahaⁿzi.

ahaⁿ'ziya, v.a. To over-shadow, to cause shade upon, make dark upon, to screen from the sun. Ahaⁿziwaya. Wanagi ahaⁿziwayaⁿpelo, i.e. I am happy. BT.

ahe'ceca, v.n. To be rather better; to recover a little. Amahececa, uⁿkahececapi. -- ahécecake, adj. Rather better. Amahececake. Bl.

ahe'cel, adv. cont. of ahececa.

ahe'celya, adv. Pretty well, middling.

ahe'cetuka, adj. perhaps. Small, while something else is large. Bl.

ahe'heyela, adv. Not firmly. - yaⁿka.

ahe'ḱiya, v.n. (ahaⁿ-kiya). To cause to stand on; to step on, perhaps. - po, Step on that, i.e. to crush a bug. Bl.

ahe'yuⁿ, v.a. (heyúⁿ). To tie up a bundle on. Ahemuⁿ, ahenuⁿ.

ahi', v.a. To arrive at a place, bringing something. Awahi. -- v. coll. pl. They have come. Waⁿbli waⁿ hiyomahi na wicoti ekta amaki k'oⁿ na ake amahi k'oⁿ.

ahi'glaȟtaka, v.a. To grind one's teeth or with one's teeth.

ahi'gle, v.a. To bring and place, to set. Ahiwagle. Waⁿna woyute kiⁿ aupi na lel ahiglepo. Hoipate kiⁿ opuze kiⁿ ekta ahi yuslohu ahigle. - kte, To bet. B.H.275.17;302.8.

ahi'gnaka, v.a. To come and put down, to bring. Hecel wana cokab ahignakapi. Na iⁿyaⁿ tob - . D.98.

ahi'huⁿni, v. coll. pl. They arrive. Na waⁿna glihuⁿnipi icuⁿhaⁿ iś eya wamakaśkaⁿ ocaje oyas'iⁿ ahihuⁿni na waⁿna ataya okawiⁿg au. Ecel aglagla pazo au na nawajiⁿ el - . Waⁿna akicita - kte lo.

ahi'icu, v. To have come and taken. Taⁿcaⁿ kiⁿ ahiicupi. B.H.99.4;269.17.

ahi'ju, v.a. (ahi-ju). To bring and pile up. Also, ahitokśu. Ahiwaju. Bl.

ahi'kicigle, v.n. To bet for one. Ahiwecigle, ahiuⁿkiciglepi.

ahi'kte, v.n. To kill in battle. Bl.

ahi'k'u, v. To bring and give. Huⁿku kiⁿ haⁿpa eya - . MS.563.

ahi'mniciya, v. (ahi-mniciya). To assemble to, keep coming in one after another.

ahi'napa, v.n. To come out on, as do many sores. -- v. coll. pl. They come in sight. Cf. ahinape. -- v.a. To have one come out. Pilate ake Jesus taⁿkal ahinapiⁿ. B.H.264.19. -- ahínape, v. coll. pl. They come out on. Cf. ahinapa.

ahiⁿ'haⁿ, v.n. (hiⁿhaⁿ). To rain upon, fall, as rain does on things. Amahiⁿhaⁿ. Ahiⁿhe, It rains, is raining.

ahiŋ'heḱiya, v.a. To cause to fall on, as does rain. Ahiŋhewakiya. Also, ahiŋ́heya. Ahiŋhewaya.

ahiŋ'ḣpaya, v.n. (hiŋḣpaya). To fall on anything. Amahiŋḣpaya, uŋkahiŋḣpayapi. Yuŋkaŋ keya kiŋ wicaśa waŋ nata kiŋ akaŋ - . -- ahiŋ́ḣpayaic'iya, v.a. To make fall on one's self. Bl. LHB.
ahiŋ'ḣpayeya, v.a. To cause to fall on. Amahiŋḣpayeya.

ahi'oyuspa, v.a. To have come and captured. B.H.256.24.

ahi'ṗani, v. (ahi-pani). To shove with the elbow, to push or crowd against. Ahiwapani.

ahi'tebya, v. To come and devour. B.H. 200.4.
ahi'ti, v. To come and pitch one's tent. Ahiwati, ahiuŋtipi. -- v. coll. pl. They come and pitch their tents.

ahi'tokśu, v.a. Cf. ahiju.

ahi'ṫoŋwaŋ, v.a. To look towards one, to look upon, look to, regard. Ahiwatoŋwaŋ. Kul - yaŋka. Kuta ahiwatoŋwaŋ. Kul ahitoŋwiŋ ye.
ahi'ṫoŋwekiya, v.a. To cause to look towards. Ahitoŋwewakiya.
ahi'ṫoŋweya, v.a. To cause to look to. Ahitoŋwewaya.

ahi'uŋṗa, v. To bring and place. Ahiwauŋpa. -- v.a. To have come and lain down. B.H.99.5;120.7;187.8.

ahi'wicoti, n. An on-coming crowd. Israel oyate - kiŋ waŋyaŋkapi. B.H.69.2; 131.17.

ahi'wiṫaya, v. 3rd pers. pl. They have come together. B.H.64.21.

ahi'wiyoṗeya, v.a. To have arrived someplace and sold something. B.H.31.2
ahi'wota, v. To arrive and press against. B.H.71.12.

ahi'yagle, v.a. To bring home and place on. Also, v.n. -- v. coll. pl. They come and go on towards home. -- ahi'yagleya, part. Coming and going. Bl.

ahi'yahaŋ, v.n. To come and alight on, as a flock of birds on a field. -- v. coll. pl. They came up, i.e. on the other side of, a hill and stood in sight. In ref. to one only, we say: hiyáhaŋ. Waŋna akicita kiŋ ahiyahaŋ na waŋcak nataŋ ahiyu. Bl.

ahi'yaŋka, v.n. To come, i.e. many, and stay around. K'ośe ahiyaŋkelo.Bl.

ahi'yaya, v.a. To take and carry around, to hand around e.g. the pipe; to sing a tune. Awahiyaya, ayahilale, uŋkahiyayapi. -- v. coll. pl. They passed by. R. Olowaŋ num - . Olowaŋ waŋ ayahilala kiŋhaŋ. T'eblize śni wawiyaḣpaḣpaya ayahilale. Taŋcaŋ kiŋ el nape - śni yo. B.H.42.21;90.1.

ahi'yoḣpaya, v. coll. pl. They came down a hill. Hehaŋl uŋgna paha waŋ etaŋ wicáśa ota - na au na ahi. Yuŋkaŋ lila wicotapi na ahiwicoti.

ahi'yoḱakiŋ, v. To come and peep in and draw back the head. Ahiyowakakiŋ.
ahi'yoḱas'iŋ, v. To look in at a window or door, to peep in. Ahiyowakas'iŋ, ahiyouŋkas'iŋpi. In ref. to one only, iblokas'iŋ. Heciyataŋhaŋ - yaŋke, He sat looking from there. D.39. B.H.112.12. D.244. -- ahiýoḱas'iŋs'iŋ, v. red. (ahiyokas'iŋ). To appear and disappear; to peep and peep again.

ahi'yu, v.a. To be coming and bringing. Ahibu. Na he, i.e. cricket, lila i etaŋ we ahiyu. B.H.67.38;76.33. D.247. -- v. coll. pl. They are on their way home, as reported by somebody. Bl. Nataŋ - na kinil awicaupi. Lena tohaŋl okicize waŋji el uŋpi na kuwa awicahiyupi eśa napapi kte śni yelo. D.103.

ahi'yukaŋ, v. To come and make room, to come and shake off. Ahiblukaŋ.
ahi'yuŋḱa, v.n. (ahi-yuŋka). To come and sleep, i.e. collectively. -- v.a. perhaps. To bring and lie down.

ahi'yuslohaŋ, v.n. To come dragging along. -- adv. perhaps. Moving out. LHB. Hoipate kiŋ opuze kiŋ ekta - ahigle. B.H.301.27.

ahi'yuśtaŋ, v. (ahi-yuśtaŋ). To come and finish; to come to the end, as the last word in a talk. Ahibluśtaŋ. Ho, lecala ahiuŋyuśtaŋpi, i.e. we are now at the end of our fast, for we have plenty of meat. Bl.

ahi'yuweġe, v. coll. pl. They cross;

they came and broke it.

aho'coḱa, adv. (hocoka). In the midst.
aho'cokaya, adv. Around, surrounding. - uŋyaŋpi. -- v.a. To surround. Ahocokawaya.

aho'ḱipa, v. pos. (ahopa). To value as one's own, to respect one's own, as one's husband; to take care of. Ahowakipa.

aho'kśiwiŋkṫe, v. To get angry at e.g. a child, to act like a child towards one. Ahokśiwawiŋkte.

aho'pa, v.a. To take care of, to keep e.g. a regulation or commandment. Ahowapa, ahouŋpapi. Taŋyaŋ - yo. Ahokicipapi.
aho'peḱiya, v.a. To cause to respect or keep. Ahopewakiya.
aho'peya, v.a. To cause to observe. -- part. Respecting, honoring, observing. -- adv. Obediently.

aho'ṫaŋ, v.a. To make a noise around one. Ahowataŋ. -- ahóṫaŋka, n. One who makes noise around.

aho'toŋ, v.a. (hotoŋ). To cry out for, as a bird for food. -- ahótoŋtoŋ, v. red. To cry out for, bawl for anything.

aho'yasotkaya, v.n. To make expressions of anger. YH. Okiwaś'ag niśicelo ahoyasotkamayayelo, I am speechless to express my anger. Bl.

aho'yekiciyapi, n. A scolding of each other, a quarrelling with others; mutual recriminations. Cf. ahoyeya.
aho'yeya, v.n. To quarrel. Ahoyewaya, ahoyeuŋyaŋpi. Ahoyekiciyapi, They quarrelled with each other.

ahu'tkaŋyaŋ, adv. Branching, having many prongs or roots.

aḣab'ya, v. (ḣabya). To scare e.g. game. Aḣabwaya.

aḣaŋ'ḣaŋ, interj. An exclam. of some disgust, as in finding one's hands affected by touching poison ivy. - yelo. Bl.

aḣco', n. The upper part of the arm. Cf. isto.

aḣe'yuŋka, v.n. (ḣeyuŋka). To be frost on anything. Caŋáḣeyuŋke, There is frost on the trees, as at times during the winter.

aḣi'cahaŋ, v. (ḣicahaŋ). To stumble and fall on. Aḣicahe koŋze, He pretended to stumble and fall on. D.114. Also, aǧícahaŋ.

aḣlo', v.n. (ḣlo). To growl over or about a thing, as a dog does over a bone.

aḣmuŋ', v.a. To drown one in noise, be noisy about one. Lila amayaḣmuŋ. Inila yaŋki ye, amayahmuŋkelo, i.e. a person not wishing to get angry. Bl.

aḣni'yaŋ, v.a. To be angry, to take hold of angrily. Bl. -- aḣníyaŋyaŋ, v. red. (aḣniyaŋ). To be angry at, take hold of in anger. Awaḣniyaŋyaŋ, amaḣniyaŋyaŋ. Amayahniyaŋyaŋ hwo? Note: this word does not indicate the fondling or the handling e.g. of a baby lovingly. Bl.

aḣṫa'ni, v. (ḣtani). To labor for one, to work on anything; to sin, break a law. Awaḣtani.

aḣṫa'ṫa, adj. Languid, feeble. -- aḣṫáteca, adj. Weak, feeble.
aḣṫa'teśniyaŋ, adv. Without stopping or rest, continually in respect to something. Bl.

aḣwa'ic'iya, v. refl. To make one's self sleepy. Bl. Aḣwaic'iye s'e maŋkelo. -- aḣwáic'iyela, adv. Quietly. - yaŋka po, Be quiet. Bl.
aḣwa'ya, adv. Mildly. -- aḣwáyela, adv. Mildly, patiently, easily, gently. Cf. iwaśtela.

aḣ'a', v.n. To make noise, as does rain or hail when it strikes a window. Aḣ'ayelo. Cf. ḣ'ayéla.

aḣ'aŋ'ḣ'aŋ, v.a. To do a thing carelessly, not having one's mind on it. Awaḣ'aŋḣ'aŋ. -- aḣ'áŋḣ'aŋka, adj. Careless, negligent.

aḣ'a'yetoŋ, (?).

aḣ'e'ca, n. Things of minor importance, in opposition to important matters. - kiŋ oblakiŋ kte śni. BD.

aḣ'e'ḣ'eya, adv. Raggedly. - yaŋkelo,

She is in rags. S.

aH'iⁿ'H'iⁿciya, v.a. To make one's way carefully. AH'iⁿH'iⁿciyelaHci mawani yelo, Indeed I walked carefully!, e.g. among cactus or sharp rocks. Bl.

aH'iⁿl'H'iⁿlciyelakel, adv. Slowly and painfully. - mani, He walked, perhaps even groaning, as a person suffering from rheumatism. Bl.

aH'o'kaka, adj. Skillful, adept. Itowapi kaga aH'okekelo, He is skillful in taking pictures. Bl.

ai', v.a. To carry or take to a place. Awai, uⁿkaipi. -- v. coll. pl. (i). They reached a place. Waⁿna hocokata ai. Na waⁿna ake zuya ai na el opa.

ai'a, v.a. To talk or speak of or about; to consult in regard to; to speak evil of, to slander. Aiwaya, aiyaya, aiwicuⁿyaⁿpi. Oyate kiⁿ ake ainiyaⁿpi kte lo. Tuwa ca aie hwo? B.H. 316.16. -- aiápi, n. A consultation; a slander.

ai'cab, cont. of aicapa.

ai'caǧa, v. (icaga). To grow on or in; to yield, produce, accrue. Taku maka - , hena mitawa yelo. -- aícaǧe, n. Interest, as of money. B.H.268.22.

ai'caH, v. (aicaga). To produce. -- aícaHya, v.a. To cause to grow on, cause to produce. AicaHwaya.

ai'camna, v.n. (icamna). To storm upon, blow furiously on.

ai'capa, v.a. (ikapa). To open the mouth against any one. Also, aícapa.

ai'capa, v.a. (icapa). To stab one thing through or on another. Aicawapa.

ai'captaⁿptaⁿ, v.n. To roll over and over on anything. Amicaptaⁿptaⁿ.

ai'cazo, v.a. (icazo). To have drawn for a time upon, to take credit on account of. Aiwakazo.

ai'cikinica, v. To dispute among themselves. Yuⁿkaⁿ Juda wicaśa kiⁿ aicikinicapi na heyapi. B.H.227.21.

ai'cimani, v.n. (icimani). To journey upon, take a journey for some purpose. Aicimawani.

ai'citakigna, adv. On the other, folded on, double. Bl. Cf. aitagnaka.

ai'ciyoptepteya, adv. Crosswise, as four things at the four quarters about a point of reference. - yaⁿkapi, They stood crosswise. Bl.

ai'coǧa, v.n. (icoga). To gather on, to drift on anything.

ai'coza, v.n. (icoza). To be warm on or with. Aimacoza.

ai'c'ibleza, v. To understand, realize concerning one's self; to notice on one's behalf, on one's self. B. Akisni - . Mani kiⁿ aic'ibleze śni na ihaⁿble s'elececa. B.H.250.34;322.3. Cf. igluptaⁿyaⁿ. D.215,12.

ai'c'icaǧa, v.a. To make on one's self e.g. the Sign of the Cross. Caⁿic'ipawega - po. Amic'icaga, uⁿkaic'icagapi.

ai'c'ikita, v. refl. (akita). To seek one's self, to regard one's own interests. Amic'icita.

ai'c'ikiya, v. refl. (akiya). To be diligent, to make effort, bestir one's self. Amic'ikiya. -- adj. Diligent. - wauⁿ.

ai'c'iktaśni, v. To neglect one's self. -- v. (aktaśni). To despise, to heed not; to reject, slight. Cf. akta.

ai'e, Same as aia.

ai'ekiya, v.a. To cause to talk about, in either a good or bad sense; to consult with.

ai'glagcaⁿkúya, v. (?). Bl.

ai'glagya, v. refl. (iglaka). To move camp. Bl. LHB.

ai'glaHpa, v. refl. (akaHpa). To cover one's self. AmiglaHpa. -- aíglaHpeya, v.a. To cast about one. AiglaHpewaya. Taku aiglaHpeyapi, Clothes.

ai'glaka, v. To break camp. Bl. LHB.

ai'glala, v. refl. (aglala). To cast or throw upon one's self. - waśtemna, Perfume powder.

ai'glaptaⁿyaⁿ, v. To get something unexpectedly, what one has been wishing for. Bl.

ai'glap'o, v. refl. (akap'o). To get dusty, as by moving about. Makablu nisipi kiŋ el aniglap'opi kiŋ hena glatata po. B.H.222.17.

ai'glaśťaŋ, v. refl. (akaśtaŋ). To pour out or spill on one's self. Amiglaśtaŋ.

ai'glaťaŋ, v. refl. (yataŋ). To praise one's self for some quality or capacity. Amiglataŋ.

ai'gluha, v. refl. (yuha). To have or retain for one's own use, to provide for one's self; to be a citizen.

ai'gluhomni, v. refl. To turn on, to throw one's self at, as in battle. B.H.101.23.

ai'gluȟleca, v. refl. To tear one's own. -- ai'gluȟleȟleca, v. red. (aigluȟleca). To tear one's own to pieces. Aigluȟleȟlel, cont. B.H.34.37.

ai'gluȟpa, v. refl. (yuȟpa). To cause to fall on one's self, as the limb of a tree; to bring on one's self. Amigluȟpa. Wóťahi amigluȟpe. D.247.

ai'gluksa, v. refl. (yuksa). To break off, as a limb of a tree on one's self.

ai'glupoťa, v. refl. (glupota). To tear or rend e.g. one's own garment on one's self.

ai'gluptaŋyaŋ, v. refl. (igluptaŋyaŋ). To turn over on, roll over on. Amigluptaŋyaŋ, uŋkaigluptaŋyaŋpi. Caŋke el mahel (cega) iyuŋka na - . Cf. ayuptaŋyaŋ.

ai'glusota, v. refl. To use up one's own; to go all away, as ducks migrating.

ai'gluśica, v. refl. (yuśica). To get one's self into difficulty with. Amigluśica.

ai'gluśkehaŋ, v. refl. (yuśkehaŋ). To get busy on one's self, to bestir one's self, as a horse is supposed to do when a certain place must be reached. Bl.

ai'gluśla, v. refl. (yuśla). To cut e.g. grass and cover one's self with it. Peji amigluśla.

ai'gluťaŋ, v. refl. To pull the trigger of a gun on one's self; to besmear one's self with one's own emission.

ai'gluza, v. refl. (gluza). To dress or prepare one's self for an occasion. Amigluza.

ai'haŋ, v. coll. pl. They go and stand on anything.

ai'haŋbla, v.n. (ihaŋbla). To dream about. Aiwahaŋbla. Tataŋka pizi waŋ ota catka ca oŋ (tataŋka waŋ) aiyahaŋblelo.

ai'ȟat'a, v. To laugh, giggle at. Aiȟauŋt'api, They laugh at us.

ai'ȟpaya, v.n. (ihpaya). To fall on, as leaves do on anything.

ai'ȟpeya, v.a. To throw or place on; to bequeath, communicate, endow, dispose by will; to leave, entrust with one. Aiȟpewaya; aiȟpemaya, I inherit. Hokśila kiŋ miye aiȟpemaya yo. B.H. 42.16. -- ai'ȟpeyapi, n. An inheritance, a legacy.

ai'ic'ila, v. refl. To act as though one had brought in. B.H.310.7.

ai'ǩapa, v.a. (ikapa). To open the mouth upon; to scold. Aiwakapa.

ai'kcapťa, v. To talk much to, to reprove, scold.

ai'ǩia, v. pos. (aia). To talk about something that concerns one's self; to consider or talk against. Aiwakia.

ai'ǩoyag, cont. (aikoyaka). Sticking to. -- ai'ǩoyagya, v.a. To cause to stick to, link to or on. Aikoyagwaya.

ai'ǩoyaǩa, v.n. To stick to or on; to cleave to, be fastened to.

ai'kpablaya, v. refl. (pablaya, an old word). To make a fool of one's self by talking or acting foolishly. Also, aikpajuju. RF. Amikpablaya. Pablaya lends the fig.: to make one's self be a laughing stock, be helpless with one's back on the ground. Taku epe ciŋ eceȟci ecanoŋ śni kiŋ, anikpablayelo, taktokamo^n ta^{n}i^n śni yelo. BT. Ka ti^{n}skoya anikpablaye, lit., you have spread yourself flat, i.e. You are making a complete fool of yourself. D.72,75, note 1.

ai'kṗaġa^n, v. refl. (paga^n). To part with one's self for any purpose. Amikpaga^n. -- aikṗaġa^{n}ya^n, part. Parting with one's self for.

ai'kṗajuju, v. refl. (pajuju). To make a fool of one's self. Also, aikpablaya. Bl.

ai'kṗaṫa^n, v. refl. (pata^n). To reserve for one's self, i.e. for any duty or purpose. Amikpata^n. -- ai'kṗaṫa^{n}ya^n, part. Reserving one's self for.

ai'kpoġa^n, v. refl. (apoga^n). To blow on one's self, as with the mouth using water, medicine, etc. Na toha^{n}l okicize ecano^{n}pi ca (pejuta ki^n le) aikpoga^n po.

ai'kśi^{n}k̇iya, v.a. To make faces at. Aikśi^{n}wakiya.

ai'le, v.n. (ile). To burn or blaze on.
ai'leśaśa, adv. In the red flame. - yuza, To hold in the red flame. -- aileśaśaya, v.a. To put in or hold in the red flame to scorch. Aileśaśawaya.
ai'leya, v.a. To cause to burn on or around, to set fire to. Ailewaya. -- part. Setting fire to. Na wa^{n}ha cega wa^n lila ta^{n}ka ca ogna wizila k'o^n itiyopa el aileyapi.

ai'mniciya, v. coll. To gather together for a purpose.

ai'napa, v.a. (inapa). To come in sight of or upon. Ainawapa.

ai'natagya, adv. Beyond a hill. - naji^n. Bc.

ai'niha^n, v.n. To be afraid on account of. Aimaniha^n. -- aiḣiha^{n}ya^n, adv. Excitedly, fearfully.

a'inila, adv. Stilly or silently for, as in making the approach to game. - osni, Cold without wind.

ai^n'k̇icato^n, v.a. To put on an overcoat, shawl etc., or anything warm, around one, e.g. a child. Ai^{n}wecato^n.

ai^n'k̇ito^n, v. To wear an overcoat or shawl over one's clothes. Ai^{n}weto^n. Bl.

ai^n'ya^{n}k̇a, v. (i^{n}ya^{n}ka). To run on e.g. a floor, to run for, run to get. Awaima^{n}ka, ayaina^{n}ka, u^{n}kai^{n}ya^{n}kapi. Cf. i^{n}ya^{n}ka.

ai'ṗiyak̇a, v.a. To tie around one's self, to gird. Miniḣuhe ska wa^n aipiyake.

ai'ṗoġa^n, v.a. (ipoga^n). To blow upon. Aiwapoga^n.

ai'si^{n}ya^n, adv. Out of sight, behind something else. - iyaya. - iyotakapi, They sat down out of sight. Also, akota^{n}ha^n. R. D.39,71. Bl.

ai'śṫacelya, v.a. To catch a side glance or glimpse of anything. Aiśtacelwaye s'elececa, It seemed I noticed a signal. Bl.

ai'śtaecelya, v.a. To see, understand. Miyeś aiśtaecelwaye śni, I do not understand. Bl.
ai'śtagnag, cont. (aiśtagnaka). To gaze at. - kuwa, He placed his eyes on something, kept looking at it. -- aiśtagnagya, adv. Looking at intently. - kuwa, To watch closely. Bl. -- aiśtagnagyakel, adv. Intently looking at.
ai'śṫagnak̇a, v.a. (iśta-gnaka). To place the eyes upon, look at intently. Aiśtawagnaka.
ai'śṫagnak̇eśni, v. To neglect, not look after, as after one's child. Bl.

ai'śti^{n}ma, v.n. (iśti^{n}ma). To sleep on. Amiśti^{n}ma.

a'iṫaglaḣwe, adv. With the wind. - u^{n}ya^{n}pi. Also, áitaglaḣwek̇iya. - u^{n}glapi, We have the wind from the rear. - bla. Also, áitaglaḣweya. Bl.

ai'tagnagya, adv. Placing something on top of another. - k'i^n, To carry something on top of another. Bl.
ai'tagnaka, v.a. To place one on top of another, as in carrying. Aitawagnaka. R. Bl.

ai'ta^{n}ca^n, n. The ruler over. Taku ainita^{n}ca^n heci hena nici. B.H.94.21.

ai'teyuśi^{n}kiya, v.a. To knit the brows,

to cut faces at. Aiteyuśiŋwakiya.

ai'ťǩob, adv. Around. - u, To go around as around a horse to walk to it from the front so as to catch it. Bl.
ai'tǩoǩib, adv. Towards. - iŋyaŋka. Bl.
ai'tǩu, adv. Spoon-like, as in describing the lower lip of a baby crying.

ai'ťoheǩiciyapi, v. pl. They answer each other sharply. Bl.
ai'ťoheya, v. (ite-oheya). To turn one's face on, to look at; to answer accusations or hard words; to give one back. Aitohewaya. Bc. - yo. Cf. iteyeśni yaŋka, itohekiya, itoheya, To start for some place. D.101. Tohaŋl tuwa aitohewaya caŋśna tokel waciŋ ecel wakuwa yelo, When it becomes necessary for me to turn my face on some one, I can do with him as I please. Tuwa aitohewaya caŋ waȟmuŋgelo, I believe anybody that I look at. D.103.

ai'tokab, adv. Before, in time.

ai'toŋśni, v. To tell lies on. Aiwatoŋśni.

ai'waŋcayapi, v. 3rd pers. pl. They all talk bad about each other. Bl.

ai'yaciŋyaŋ, adv. Prudently, circumspectly. - ecoŋ. Syn.- owahecelya, kaiwaŋyaŋgya. Bl.

ai'yagle, v.n. To lead to, reach to, as a road; to lead to, as a result of conduct.
ai'yagleya, v.a. To lead to; merit, to deserve, bring upon one. Aiyaglewaya. Aiyagleic'iya. -- adv. Leading to, even to; until.

ai'yaȟṗaya, v.a. To fall upon. Aiyaȟṗawaya.
ai'yaȟpeya, v.a. To throw on or over, as a rope in catching a horse; to communicate to one e.g. a disease; to infect. Aiyaȟpewaya.

ai'yaǩab, cont. of aiyakapa.
ai'yaǩaṗa, v. To exceed, surpass. Obs.
ai'yaǩapťeya, adv. Uphill, ascending. Yuŋkaŋ tuwa ocaŋku waŋ ognaya ca ecel ihekab bla na - ya ca ecel bla na paha waŋ el iyahaŋ ca miś eya el iyawahaŋ. Paha waŋ taŋka - bla na iyawahaŋ. Cf. iyakapteya. R.

ai'yaǩaśǩa, v.a. To tie one thing on another. Aiyawakaśka. Iŋyaŋ oŋ wokpaŋpi waŋji tahu aiyakaśkapi. Cf. D.55. B.H.215.11. -- aíyaǩaśǩeya, part. Tying onto something else.

ai'yape, v.a. (iyape). To lie in wait for. Aiyawape.

ai'yaṗemni, v.a. (iyapemni). To wrap around, wrap up with. Aiyawapemni.

ai'yasaǩa, v.n. To stiffen or become hard on, as raw hide. Aiyamasaka.

ai'yecelya, adv. In much the same manner, in a way a little less to one than another. Iyohila tokel ośkiŋciyapi kte kiŋ - owicak'u.

ai'yohaŋsya, adv. In the shade. - ȟpaye. -- v.a. To over-shadow. Maȟpiya waŋ aiyohaŋswicaye. Nagi kiŋ aiyohaŋswicaye.

ai'yoȟpeya, adv. Down hill. -- n. A declivity. Na paha k'oŋ he - wicoti etkiya bla. Na uŋgnahela - tuwa kici ble ehaŋl weksuye. - mani. Also applied to a man older than 50 years. - iyaye. IS. D.9,67.

ai'yojaŋjaŋ, v.i. To shine on. -- aíyojaŋjaŋic'iya, v. refl. (aiyojaŋjaŋya). To have lighted one, be illuminated by. -- aíyojaŋjaŋya, v.a. To throw light on, illumine, as by a lighted match. Bl.

a'iyokipi, adj. Pleasant, agreeable.
a'iyokipiya, adv. Agreeably.

ai'yokpaza, v.n. To be darkened, confused. Aŋpahaŋ wi kiŋ aiyokpaziŋ kte.

ai'yopteca, adv. Less than.
ai'yopťel, adv. Towards, in the direction of; less. R. Also, aíyopťeťu, aíyopťeťuya. R.
ai'yopteya, v. To match with what one contributes. YH. Takuŋl aiyoptemayaye ciŋ hignaciyiŋ kte, as would a girl say to her lover, that he should buy her, give her something, so he does not throw her away. Bl. -- adv. In a straight line or direction. - iyayapi, They went directly, one place to another. Kaiciopteya kipazo, i.e. right opposite on a line with.

a'iyotaŋ, adv. More than, greater than, beyond. Aiyotaŋȟci. -- aíyotaŋic'ila,

v. refl. To push one's self ahead of others. Bl.

ai'yuḣeya, adv. Extremely, wonderfully. - waśte, Extremely good. - luzahaŋ. Bl.

ai'yuḣtata, v. To let loose on, give rope to e.g. a horse seemingly strangled. Bl.

ai'yukcaŋ, v.a. To think over something or think of something; to think much of one.

ai'zit̄a, v.n. (izita). To smoke or burn e.g. incense for some purpose.

a'jaya, adv. Plainly, - owicakiyake.

aji'ji, v. To whisper about a person or thing. Awajiji. Ojiji is used by men.
ajo', v. Cf. ajojo.
ajo'jo, v. To whistle about, to call by whistling, as a dog. Awajojo. -- ajójok̇iya, v.a. To cause to whistle for. Ajojowakiya.

ajuŋ'tka, n. The kidneys.

aju'toŋ, v. To add a little lie to one's narrative. Ajuwatoŋ. Bl.

ak̇ab', prep. Over, upon, beyond. - iyeya, To throw beyond. - iyaya, To overflow; to be pressed for work that is not done yet. Waŋna cega - iyaya. - iyayeśni makuwapi ca ecamoŋ śni, No end was there to bother, so I could not do it, i.e. what you wanted. Bc.
ak̇ab'haŋ, adj. or adv. Standing on the outside, as one does on the outside of a nest of tubs or kettles.

ak̇a'bla, v.a. (kabla). To cut into thin slices or strips, to slice in addition to. Awakabla.

a'kablablaġa, v. red. of akablaga. Heḣaŋl uŋgna waŋbli ca yaŋka na - .
a'kablaġa, v.n. To spread out over, as one's wings; to open e.g. the armpits or underparts of the wings for. D.81.
a'k̇ablaḣ, cont. of akablaga. - iyeya, To spread over, as a bird its wings.
a'k̇ablaja, v.a. To straddle, spread the legs apart. Awakablaja.
a'k̇ablas, cont. of akablaza. - iyeya.
a'k̇ablaś, cont. (akablaja). To be astride. - inajiŋ, To stand astride of.
a'k̇ablaya, v.n. To spread out over e.g. with one's wings. El ewatoŋwaŋ ehaŋl waŋbli waŋ akokiya - na itaŋnuŋk wicaḣpi.

ak̇a'blaza, v.n. To tear open on, as a bag on a horse.

ak̇a'bleca, v.a. (kableca). To break e.g. an instrument by striking it on something; to break one thing lying on another by striking. Awakableca.
ak̇a'blel, cont. To break to pieces on. - iyeya, eḣpeya.
ak̇a'blu, v.a. (kablu). To break up fine upon. Awakablu. Amayakablu welo, You raised dust settling on me; hence the meaning: to strike dust and make settle on someone. Bl. Cf. akapsica. -- v.n. To go up in dust. Wipa kiŋ paogmus egle yo, tusu ipataŋ toŋ wo, maka etaŋ kaspiŋ na wiluzignag toŋ wo, hecel akablu kta śni yelo. Bl.

aka'ecoŋ s'e, adv. Over-much, excessively. - ecoŋ. Syn.- aokaga. FH.
aka'ġa, v.a. To make on anything, to add; to tell a lie about, speak evil of; to exaggerate. Awakaga. He wicoḣ'aŋ kiŋ el akage śni ecoŋ po.

a'k̇aġal, adv. Stretching out to. R. - ḣpaya, He reached, stretching out and spreading his arms, as a little child towards its mother. Bl.
a'k̇aġalk̇iya, adj. Spread out or stretched out, as the hand or arm. BD. Cf. kagalkiya.
a'k̇aġaltkiya, adv. Stretched out, as the arms. - uŋ.

ak̇a'ġaṗi, n. Something made in addition; falsehood, exaggeration.

ak̇a'ġeġe, v.a. (kagege). To sew on or to, to patch on something else. Awakagege.

ak̇a'ḣaṗa, v. (kaḣapa). To drive or whip on. Awakaḣapa.
ak̇a'ḣaya, v.a. To spread news, exaggerate it all the while. Bl.
ak̇a'ḣla, v.a. To rattle, make sound by striking at or on account of. Awakaḣla. Na ḣlaḣla kiŋ awicakaḣlapi na caŋcega kiŋ kabupi na śiyotaŋka kiŋ yajopi na awicas'api.

aka'ḣpa, v.a. To cover, throw on or over, to cover up, conceal. Awakaḣpa. Amakaḣpa yo. Yuŋkaŋ el śina kpaŋyaŋpi waŋ el - egnaka na lowaŋ. - iḣpeya, To throw a robe over.

ak̇a´ḣp̣e, n. A bed cover, spread, a quilt; a covering, a shroud, veil. Ca^{n}pagmiya - , A wagon cover. Ite - , A veil. Hiyete - , A cloak, mantle.
aka´ḣpek̇ici´ciya, v. To cover up for one or to pass by a matter; to forgive. Akaḣpewecíciya.
aka´ḣpek̇icito^n, v.a. To cover for one. Akaḣpewecito^n. -- ak̇áḣṗek̇ito^n, v.pos. (akaḣpeto^n). To cover one's own. Akaḣpeweto^n.
ak̇a´ḣṗeto^n, v.a. To cover, throw on e.g. a covering; to cover up, conceal e.g. one's real opinion when used with ia. - iwaye. Awakaḣpeto^n. -- part. Covered, concealed. -- ak̇áḣṗeto^{n}to^n, v. red. - ia, To speak covertly, to deceive.
ak̇a´ḣpeya, adv. Covering. Maḣpiya wa^n śapa ca - he. - agliha. B.H.56.16;61.10. Cf. D.224.
ak̇a´ḣpiḣpeya, v.a. To throw over, cover over, as a blanket over a trunk etc. Bl.

ak̇a´ḣṫa^n, v.n. To soak into and come through on the other side, as grease through a skin. B.H.108.16. Also, to boil over on, flow over. Watage ota yelo waslipa po; u^{n}niha^n akaḣta^n yelo. BT. -- ak̇áḣṫa^{n}ya^n, v.a. To cause to cook in; to cut and make rough on. Akaḣta^{n}waya.

ak̇a´ḣwogya, v.a. To let fly over one. Peśnija akaḣwogmayayelo, You let the sparks (in smoking) fly over me. Bl.

aka´jipa, v.a. To shave with a knife or drawing knife upon. Awakajipa.

ak̇a´ka^n, v.a. (kaka^n). To beat, to strike off on anything, e.g. cherries off a bush onto a shawl spread out below. Awakaka^n, u^{n}kakaka^{n}pi. Also, to hew on anything. R. Cf. okak̇a^n.

ak̇a´kṗa^n, v.a. (kakpa^n). To pound fine on anything, to pound in addition to what is already done. Awakakpa^n.
ak̇a´kṗi, v.a. To crack on, as a nut on anything. Awakakpi.
ak̇a´ksa, v.a. (kaksa). To cut off on something, cut off from, cut off in addition to. Awakaksa.

ak̇a´kśa, v.a. To coil up on, as a rope. Awakakśa. -- akákśa^n, v.a. To go around to prevent one or to see him. Awakakśa^n, amakakśa^n. Bl. -- adv. Around, not in a straight course, as in going in a round-about way to catch a horse. Na wa^{n}na - nata^n u^{n}ya^{n}pi. Also, akákśa^{n}ya^n.
ak̇a´kśija, v.a. To bend into or round, as a piece of iron. Awakakśija.
ak̇a´kśiś, cont. of akakśija. - iyeya.
ak̇a´kṫa^n, v.a. To bend onto, bend around. Awakakta^n.

ak̇a´k̇uk̇a, v.a. To pound to pieces on. Awakakuka.

ak̇a´la, v.a. To pour out on, as grain, not liquids. Awakala. - hiyuya, To take one by surprise; apable hiyuya. Bl. -- ak̇álala, v. red. (akala). To pour out on anything. - iyeya.

ak̇al´ya, v.a. (kalya). To cause to heat upon. Akalwaya. R. Bl.

ak̇a´mna, v.a. (kamna). To acquire in addition to; to tear open on, as at a seam. Awákamna.

a´k̇amni iyaya, v.n. To separate with a splash e.g. snow with stepping on it when water is underneath.

ak̇a^n´, prep. On, upon. Used with a noun and without. Maka - . Maka ki^n le nitawapi kte lo ca - ota inicagapi kte lo. Cf. aka^{n}l.

ak̇a^n´, v.n. To become old on or with. Amaka^n.

ak̇a^n´ha^{n}pa, n. Overshoes.

aka^n´ iye´ic'iya, v. refl. To jump on e.g. a horse in mounting it.

ak̇a^{n}l´, prep. On, upon. Also, aka^n. Maka - . Yu^{n}ka^n i^{n}ya^n ta^{n}ka wa^n gliḣpa keye. Ca^{n}ke - inaji^n. - ogle, An overcoat. - ogle zizipila, A duster.

ak̇a^{n}l´ wau^n´ya^{n}pi, n. An altar. Aka^{n}l wau^{n}yeyapi, aka^{n}l wau^{n}yeyi^n kte: meaning the same. Aka^{n}l wawágluwaka^{n}pi, A sort of altar. B.H.11.10;58.5;108.1. Pb.33.

ak̇a^n´mná, v.n. To smell like something burning. Perhaps from kata-omna, yet the "k" is "k̇". R. Me.

ak̇a^n´ṫu, adv. Above. Paha - . -- n. The top one. -- adj. Living; in authority; common. Wicaśa - , Living men, men in authority, a common man. B.H.294.6.

akaⁿ'ṫuic'iya, v. To make much of one's self. Bl. Syn.- iglutaⁿiⁿ.

akaⁿ'ṫuya, adv. Above, high up; on the outside, without. Also, akáⁿṫuyakel. Wicaśa - . B.H.70.4.

akaⁿ'ṫuyela, adv. Outside, on the surface; almost on the top; above, high up. Bl.

akaⁿ' wapáblapi, n. An ironing board.

akaⁿ' waúⁿyaⁿpi, n. An altar. B.H.110.6

akaⁿ'yaⁿka, v. To ride a horse. Akaⁿmaⁿka, akaⁿuⁿyaⁿkapi. Nupiⁿ hiⁿkceka sapa akaⁿwicayaⁿkapi. -- akáⁿyaⁿkapi, n. A seat.

akaⁿ'yuⁿka, v. To lie on something. Akaⁿmuⁿka.

aka'pa, v. To beat or thresh off on, to pound. Awakapa.

a'kapa, adj. Larger somewhat, implying a comparison.

aka'paṫaⁿhaⁿ, adv. On the outside, exteriorly; from above; from another side or place.

a'kaṗeca, adv. Having something to spare. Bl.

aka'ṗeya, adv. Having to spare, as a coat; greater or higher; more than. Tipi kiⁿ le - wiyopeyapi, This house sold for more.

aka'ṗolṗol, cont. of akapolpota.

aka'ṗolṗoṫa, v. red. (akapota). To beat to pieces in many places on.

aka'ṗoṫa, v.a. (kapota). To beat to pieces on anything. Awakapota.

aka'psica, v.a. To make jump etc. on by striking, as by splashing water on one. Amayakapsicelo. Haⁿta yo anicapsiciⁿ kte. Bl. Cf. akablu.

aka'pṫa, v.a. (kapta). To cut off on, as part of a stick. Awakapta.

aka'pṫecela, v.a. To make shorter, to cut off a piece from a stick. Awakaptecela.

aka'saⁿpa, adv. Opposite, across, on the other side, as of a river. Note: The word is possibly obs.

aka'saⁿpaṫaⁿhaⁿ, adv. On the other side; from beyond, from the other side. R. Mini akasaⁿpataⁿhaⁿ: hutasaⁿpata. This is a Santee word; the Tetons say: ḱoákaṫaⁿhaⁿ.

aka'ska, v.n. To be greedy. Awakaska. Use obs. -- adj. Greedy, voracious.

aka'skica, v.n. To be pressing down, to press down.

aka'sni, v.a. (kasni). To extinguish on, as fire. Awakasni.

aka'sṫag, cont. of akastaka. - eȟpeya.

aka'sṫagya, adv. Sticking on or in.

aka'sṫagyakel, adv. Clinging to, sticking on.

aka'staka, v.a. To throw or daub on e.g. plaster, to bespatter. Awakastaka, uⁿkakastakapi. Ístiⁿma akastaka, To drop asleep (an express. not often used). Tiákastaka, To daub a house. IS.

aka'sṫo, v.a. (kasto). To smooth down on, as the hair on the head. Awakasto, uⁿkakastopi.

akā's'o, v. (kaso). To chop off a piece from. Awakas'o.

aka'śka, v.a. (kaśka). To bind upon. Awakaśka.

aka'śla, v.a. (kaśla). To cut or mow down upon, as grass upon a hay field. Awakaśla.

aǩa'śp̣a, v.a. (a and kaśpa). Cut or break off on. Awakaśpa. Na caᶯ eya śeca ca aletka kiᶯ hena akaśpapi. Maka kiᶯ taᶯiᶯ śniyaᶯ owaᶯjila yaᶯka śkelo (many buffalos) ca ikaᶯyela euᶯtipi na akaśpa icu wanauᶯsapi ktelo. Bl. -- v.n. Be provoked beyond endurance. Amákaśpa. -- aǩáśp̣eya, v.n. Remain longer than one can well endure, be provoked. Amakaśpeya. -- v.a. Provoke. Akaśpewaya.

aǩa'śp̣u, v.a. (a and kaśpu). Cut off a piece by striking, cut off on. Awakaśpu.

aǩa'śtaǩa, v.a. (a and kaśtaka). Beat one on another. Awákaśtaka.

aǩa'śṫaᶯ, v.a. (a and kaśtaᶯ). Pour out on, spill on, as water to baptize. Awakaśtaᶯ. Uᶯkakaśtaᶯpi.

aka'ṫa, v.n. (a and kata). Be hot on. Awakata.

aǩa'ta, v.a. Draw a bow, bend as a bow. Awákata. Na itazipa k'oᶯ ecel icu na wahiᶯkpe ecel akata na waᶯna ena waᶯkatakiya iyeya. Also, to hoe, dig about with a hoe, hill up, as corn, cover with dirt, cultivate. Awákata. Uᶯkákatapi. Wagmeza akata, Hoe corn. Peji akata (i.e. a hole) ca otaᶯiᶯ śni.

aǩa'ṫahaᶯ, adv. Above, overhead, on top, on the surface. Akaᶯtaᶯhaᶯ. R.

a'katanhaᶯ, adv. On the outside. Hiᶯ akataᶯhaᶯ, Hair of the robe outside. Note: The accent is on the first syllable, probably because of the hiᶯ.

aǩa'teya, v.a. Cause to hoe. Akatewaya.

a'ǩaṫiᶯ, v.a. Straighten on, as the arms. Measure with the arms stretched out on. Awakatiᶯ. -- ákatiᶯpi, n. The measure from fingertip to fingertip. SB. An ell, the length or distance of the fingers when the arms are stretched out. -- áǩaṫiᶯṫiᶯ, v. (red. of akatiᶯ). - mani, Walk, moving the arms sideways as in giving signs. Pejuta waᶯ aikpogaᶯ na akatiᶯtiᶯ. -- aǩáṫiᶯyaᶯ, v.a. Straighten slowly one way something that is crooked.

aǩa't'iᶯs, cont. (of akat'iᶯza).

aǩa't'iᶯza, v.a. (a and kat'iᶯza). Press anything down tight, as a weight over. -- aǩat'iᶯsya, v.a. Press down on anything by means of weights. Akát'iᶯswaya.

aǩa'uᶯg, cont. (of akauᶯka). - eȟpeya.

aǩa'uᶯǩa, v.a. (a and kauᶯka). Cut down, as a tree, on anything, make fall by cutting. Awákauᶯka.

aǩa'uᶯyaᶯ, adv. Lying across, as a body on a horse.

aǩa'weġa, v.a. (a and kawega). Break or fracture by striking on anything. Awákawega. -- aǩáweȟ, cont. (of akawega). - eȟpeya.

aǩa'wiᶯġa, v.n. Go round and round, as an eagle makes gyrations. R. Bl. -- aǩáwiᶯȟ, cont. (of akawiᶯga). Round and Round.

aǩa'wiᶯja, v.a. Bend down on, as grass on anything. Awákawiᶯja. -- akáwiᶯś, cont. (of akawiᶯja). - iyeya. - hiᶯȟpaya, Fall, as a tree, against a bank (not on the ground). Bl.

aǩa'zamni, v.a. (a and kazamni). Open upon one, throw open, as one's blanket. Awakazamni. - eȟpeya, Set open. - haᶯ, Stand open. -- akázamniyaᶯ, part. Opened on.

akce'ya, v.a. Cook or roast (ribs) partly and they dry. Awákceya.

aǩe', adv. Again, repeated, a second time. Cf. sam, which is more used in counting money. Ake, when used with numbers, is soft. Thus: aǩe záptaᶯ.

ake'napciyuᶯǩa, Nineteen.
ake'noᶯp̣a, Twelve. -- akénom, cont.
ake'nuᶯpa, Twelve.
ake'śaglogaᶯ, Eighteen.
ake'śaǩowiᶯ, Seventeen.
ake'śakp̣e, Sixteen.
ake'ṫop̣a, Fourteen. -- akétob, cont.
ake'waᶯji, Eleven. Also akéwaᶯjila.
ake'yamni, Thirteen.
ake'zapṫaᶯ, Fifteen.

ake' ececa, v.n. Recur.

ake'iyenakeca, adv. As much again.

aǩeś', adv. Again.

aŘe´śnaśna, adv. Again and again. B.H. 88.9.

aŘe´ya, v.a. Place on, make a roof on, place on the roof, make one roof on another. Akewaya.

aŘi´, v.a. Arrive at home carrying something. Awaki. Uⁿkakipi. -- v. coll. pl. They reach home. Hokśila kiⁿ he mni el aki Řiye.

aŘi´bleza, v. Think about. OȞ'aⁿ ekta akibleze, He thought about the treatment he had given (David). B.H.90.14; 108.22;240.16.

aŘi´caga, v.a. Make on, add to. Be unreasonable, go too far. Awecaga. -- aŘícaǧeca, v.a. Over-reach, cheat, want more than is right, be unreasonable. Awécageca. -- aŘícaȟ, cont. (of akicaga). -- aŘícaȟya, adv. Unreasonably.

aŘi´caśŘa, v.a. (of kaśka). Bind to or on, bind together. Akiwakaśka. Caⁿke akicaśkapi s'e iⁿyaⁿke, Cross-legged, have knock-knees. -- aŘícaśkaśka, v. red. of akicaśka). Baste on, sew on, as in basting. Akiwakaśkaśka.

aŘi´ceṗa, v.n. Become fleshy for or again. Amákicepa.

aŘi´ceti, v.n. Arrive at home and start a fire (when one's home is somewhere else).

aŘi´ceya, v. pos. (of aceya). Cry for one's own, mourn for, weep over one's own, as a dead relative. Awakiceya. Uⁿkakiceyapi.

aŘi´cicata, v. (of akata). Hoe for one, hoe for. Awecicata. Amicicata.

aŘi´ciciŧa, v. (of akita). Hunt a thing for another. Awécicita. -- aŘícikcita, v. pos. (of akita). Hunt one's own. R. Awecikcita. Bl.

aŘi´ciŘipapi, v. pl. (of akipa). They meet each other.

aŘi´cikśija, v. Retain anything not one's own for one, as a mother retains things in the name of her child. Bl.

aŘi´cikta, v. (of akta). Receive or accept from another, have respect unto. Awécikta.

aŘi´ciktaśni, v. (of aktaśni). Refuse, reject when offered by one. Awéciktaśni.

aŘi´ciktoⁿja, v.a. Forgive.

aŘi´cinica, v.a. (of anica). Withhold from, retain for. Awecinica. Woaȟtani awicakinicapi kta.

aŘi´cipa, v. (of apa). Strike for one. Awecipa. Uⁿkakicipapi.

aŘi´ciṗa, n. A flat tableland that lies higher than a creek. Wakpala iwaⁿkab akicipa k'el etipi ktelo. Bl.

aŘi´cipaṗi, v. pl. (of aŘipa). They meet each other.

aŘi´ciṗe, v. (of ape). Wait for one, hope for. Awecipe. Uⁿkakicipepi.

aŘi´ciŧa, v. (of akita). Hunt for another. Awecita.

aŘi´cita, n. A head warrior, one next to a chief, a warrior soldier, a policeman. Amakicita.

- awaⁿyaⁿg najiⁿ, Sentinel, sentry, guard.
- ehaⁿna ayuśtaⁿpi iyuⁿwiⁿ, Pension.
- hayapi, Regimentals, uniforms, military dress.
- ikceka, Private soldier.
- itaⁿcaⁿ, Captain, colonel, commander, lieutenant, officer.
- itaⁿcaⁿ Ȟaⁿtkahu zi (ska) yuha, Corporal, sergeant.
- itaⁿcaⁿ okihe, An adjutant.
- itaⁿcaⁿ taⁿka, General.
- itaⁿcaⁿ taokiye (or tawahośi), An orderly.
- iyeciⁿka opa, A volunteer.
- kicipasipi, Maneuver.
- omanipi, Parade.
- optaye, Company, corps.
- optaye itaⁿcaⁿ, Captain, commanding officer.
- optaye itaⁿcaⁿ taokiye, Lieutenant.
- optaye taⁿka, Brigade, division.
- optaye taⁿka itaⁿcaⁿ. Brigadier.
- ośpaye taⁿka, An army.
- ośpaye taⁿka opa, A regular.
- ota, Troops.
- owe, A troop, detachment, regiment.

akicitapi Ȟca, n. Rank and file.
- tamaza wakaⁿ, Muzzle loader. Or ikce okśupi, Bl.
- teca, A recruit.

- tipi, Barracks, fort, garrison, soldiers' quarters.
- tipi acuŋkaśkapi, Fortress, fortified camp.
- toŋweya omanipi, A patrol.

śuŋk'akaŋyaŋkapi akicita, n. Cavalry.

-- akicita kicipasi, v. Drill.

-- akicitakte, v. (akicita and kte). Punish officially, for the violation of law. Akícitawakte.

-- akicita najiŋ, v.n. Stand as a warrior soldier, stand on guard. A-nawajiŋ.

-- akicita nataŋtaŋ kaoŋspe, v. Drill.

aḱi'citoŋwaŋ, v. (of atoŋwaŋ). Look at for one, have the oversight for one. Awecitoŋwaŋ. Amicitoŋwaŋ.

aḱi'ciyukyuťa, v. (red. of akiciyuta). Look at one another. B.H.253.11.

aḱi'ciyul, cont. (of akiciyuta). adv. Face to face, looking at each other.

a'kiciyuptapi owoglake, n. Dialogue.

aḱi'ciyuťa, adv. Face to face.

a'kicizuya, v. Make war on one another. B.H.245.9.

aḱi'coŋs, v. (of akicoŋza). Keep one in suspense, avoid granting a thing with excuses. - iapi. - iwaye. - aya (abla).

aḱi'coŋza, v. Make resolutions without carrying them out. Bl. Aḱicoŋzahaŋ may perhaps be used as an adv.

aḱi'c'uŋc'uŋ, v. Do a thing repeatedly, glory in. Awéc'uŋc'uŋ. -- akíc'uŋc'uŋḱa, v. Do a thing repeatedly, overdo, be importunate, act or play recklessly, defiantly, contrary to orders. (Not akicic'uŋc'uŋka). Awéc'uŋc'uŋka.

aḱi'c'uya, adv. Much. - mak'u, Give me much.

aḱi'glagkicitoŋ, v. Patch for one. Akiglagwecitoŋ. R. Bl. -- akíglagkitoŋ, v. pos. (of akiglagtoŋ). Patch one's own. Akiglagwetoŋ. R. Bl.

aḱi'glagťoŋ, v. Put on a patch, patch, sew on a hole. -- part. Patched, having a patch on. Akiglagwatoŋ. R. Bl. -- aḱíglagya, v.a. Patch, put on a patch, use for a patch. Akiglagwaya.

aḱi'glaḱe, n. A sole of a shoe or moccasin (sewed on). Used only in connection with haŋpa. Haŋpákiglake, Sole of a moccasin.

aḱi'glasḱica, v. Press down one's own by sitting on it, as by sitting on one's overcoat, sit on one's own, as resting on one's heels. Cf. akiglaskiŋ. -- adj. Face downwards, prone. R. Lie on one's own, v.

aḱi'glasḱi(ŋ), cont. (of akiglaskica). Si kiŋ saŋni - yaŋka, Rest (sit) on one foot (placed below one) while the other is only bent. Si kiŋ nupiŋ - yaŋka, Rest on both feet while the knees are bent. Siyete saŋni - yaŋka, Rest (sit) on the heel of one foot while the other leg (knee) is only bent. RF.

aḱi'glaskil, cont. (of akiglaskica). - eȟpeic'iya. Throw one's self on one's face. -- aḱíglasḱilya, adv. Lying on the face, prone.

aki'glaśke, (?). Niyeś sipa - yauŋ welo. Bl. Buechel's translation is written with a hasty hand: A ruse (?) would say refusing to marry a woman.

aḱi'gle, adv. Again, more than once, once again. Times, used with numerals, e.g. nuŋpa akigle, Twice. Akigle means literally, set one on top of another. Added to any number, it means, so many times in succession. Cf. D.97. -- v. pos. (of agle). Place or make stand something on one's own, as the Indians took pith, put it in the hand or on the lower arm and lit it. To stand this was bravery. I have seen such marks. They call it, Pelákigle. Pelawakigle. -- akiglegle, adv. (red. of akigle). Many times. -- akígleya, adv. Repeatedly.

aḱi'gleglepa, v.n. Vomit on one's reaching home. Akiwagleglepa.

aḱi'gna, v. Sit, as a hen on eggs, have care for, as for off-spring. (Said of birds). - iyayelo. Bl.

aḱi'gna, adv. Through and through. Cf. glakiŋyaŋ. Śuŋgila kiŋ akigna o śke. - cawapiŋ kte lo. - caic'ipe.

aḱi'gnag, cont. (of akignaka).

aǩi'gnagya, adv. Placed on.

aǩi'gnaǩa, v. pos. (agnaka). To place one's own on. Awégnaka, ayegnaka.

aǩi'heca, adv. Close together. Bl.

aǩi'hececa, v.n. To become so, on reaching home, i.e. to get sick or well on one's arrival home. Akihemaceca.

a'ǩihenakeca, adv. Equally many, much. Also, ákilecelya. Akilecelya kicic'u po, as said when a sum of money is distributed and each one receives as much as the other. Bl.

aǩi'ȟoka, n. One who is skillful. -- akiȟoǩa, adj. Skillful, skilled in.

aǩi'ȟ'aŋ, v.n. To be without food, be hungry, starve. Amakiȟ'aŋ, uŋkakiȟ'aŋpi. Le wahiŋkpe kiŋ, tohaŋl amiciȟ'aŋpi ca oyate kiŋ witaya śna lapi na yeyayapi ktelo. -- aǩiȟ'aŋpi, n. A starving, famine. -- aǩiȟ'aŋt'a, v. To starve to death, die of hunger. Akiȟ'aŋmat'a. -- aǩiȟ'aŋt'eya, v.a. To cause to die of hunger. Akiȟ'aŋt'ewaya. -- aǩiȟ'aŋyaŋ, v.a. To cause to starve. Akiȟ'aŋic'iya, One's self to fast. -- adv. In a way fasting.

aǩi'ic'iya, v. refl. To prefer one's self. Acimic'iya. WW.

a'ǩijal, cont. of akijata. -- áǩijalya, v.n. To fork, as a stream. -- adv. In a manner forked. - woeye. Bl.

a'ǩijata, adj. Forked, as a stream.

aǩi'ǩaśka, v. To tie two things together. Same as akicaska. B.H.11.15.

aǩi'ǩiglaśka, v. To tie together, as one's torn moccasins; to tie up one's horse. Akiweglaśka. Bl.

aǩi'ǩiśniya, adv. All, entirely. Taku - oyas'iŋ ociciyakelo. Bl.

aǩi'kśija, v. pos. (akśija). To bend down e.g. the hand on; to retain anything. Awekśija.

aǩi'kťa, v. pos. (akta). To give heed to. Awákikta.

aǩi'kťoŋja, v.a. To forget, not remember. Awektoŋja, uŋkakiktoŋjapi, acikťoŋja, amiktoŋja. -- aǩíkťoŋś, cont. (akiktoŋja). -- aǩikťoŋśya, v.a. To make forget. -- adv. In a manner forgetful.

aǩil', cont. (akita). To seek for. - iyaya, He is gone to hunt something. Cuwiŋtku kiŋ tokel kte kta heciŋhaŋ he - ece-uŋ śke, i.e. she was on constant look-out for a good way to do away with her. D.167.

a'ǩilececa, adj. Equal to, of equal size. Tipi kiŋ oyasiŋ - . -- áǩilecel, adv. Like to, equal to. -- áǩilecelya, adv. Equally. Same as iyececa. Ikce wicaśa kiŋhaŋ waśicuŋ kiŋ nupiŋ - oniwaŋjilapi kta okihiśni yelo tohaŋyaŋ inicagapi hehaŋyaŋ. Wicaśa itaŋcaŋ uŋpi kiŋ tolute ece koyakapi.

a'ǩilehaŋ, adv. Just as far. -- áǩilehaŋhaŋkeca, adj. red. of akilehaŋkeca. -- áǩilehaŋhaŋyaŋ, adv. red. of akilehaŋyaŋ. -- áǩilehaŋkeca, adj. Of equal height, length etc. Kici akilemahaŋkeca, I am as tall as he. A man wants to buy posts and says: Iyuha - . Akiŋskokeca, Of the same size, as a team of horses. Nupiŋ akiŋskokeca opewatoŋ waciŋ, i.e. both are to be the same size. Here are always two or more things compared. -- áǩilehaŋwáŋkatuya, adj. Of the same height or length, as a man wants to have when he buys posts. Iyuha - . -- áǩilehaŋyaŋ, adv. Alike far, equally far.

a'ǩilenagnakeca, adj. red. of akilenakeca. -- áǩilenakeca, adj. Alike many, of equal number. Akileuŋnakecapi. Cf. iyenakeca.

a'ǩilenana, adj. Alike few.

aǩi'meya, adv. Around.

aǩi'mnamnaic'iya, v.n. To collect everyone his own little supply. - uŋpahipi na uŋkic'uŋpelo, Let us all everyone collect his own little supply, e.g. of sugar, coffee, etc., put it together and use it. Hena - bluha, These I have in a collection. Bl. Cf. akimanyaŋ.

aǩi'mnayaŋ, v.a. To collect one thing to another. Akimnawaya. Bl. Aŋpetu kiŋ le el tipi kiŋ le ekta miwoyuha lila ota akimnawaya yelo.

aki'mnimniciya, n. Each one's little bit that he brought. - okiciyapi, Many are giving only each a little bit. Bl.

aki'najiⁿ, v. Return and stand. Wakinajiⁿ. Na waⁿna leci wakpala waⁿ opaya ata akinajiⁿ el ake lecel eya... . Hecel el witayela agliyagla ca miś ake owapa na najiⁿpi k'oⁿ okśaⁿ akinajiⁿ. B.H.59.7.

aki'napa, v. Take out and home. Lena akinapa po. B.H.179.11.

aki'nataⁿ, v. pos. (of anataⁿ). Rush for one's own. Reach or arrive at the goal. Akinawataⁿ. Perhaps this second meaning is said by akinataⁿ.

aki'nica, v.a. (of anica). Hold for one.

aki'nica, v.a. Dispute about something, claiming it as one's own. Awakinica. Uⁿkakinicapi. Wiakinicapi, as male animals do in fighting one another.Bl.

aki'nihaⁿhaⁿ, (?). But this word seems to mean to make mistakes in speaking. Bl. While yat'iⁿsyakel ia seems to mean to speak plainly.

aki'nil, cont. (of akinica).
aki'nil, cont. (of akinica). - kignaka, Reserve something, placing it somewhere with the idea of getting it afterwards, cache.

aki'nilkiya, v. Cause to debate. Akinilwakiya. -- akinilya, v.a. Cause to dispute or debate about. Akinilwaya. -- adv. Disputatiously.

akiⁿ'glotaka, v. pos. (akaⁿ and iglotaka). This word in B.H.79.17 means, Saddle one's own, as one's ass. Cf. also B.H.68.6. Hiⁿś'a gleśka k'uⁿ he akiⁿglotaki na ya. MS.p.563.

a'kiⁿskokeca, adj. Of the same size, of equal size, as two horses, two logs etc. Nupiⁿ akiⁿskokeca opewatoⁿ waciⁿ. Two or more things are compared. Kici akiⁿmaskokeca, I am the same size as he. -- akiⁿskoya, adv. Of equal size.

akiⁿ'yaⁿ, v.a. (a and kiⁿyaⁿ). Fly over or on. Lena suta k'eś akiⁿye sekse uⁿkiyayapi kte, If the road were smooth, we'd go flying over it.

akiⁿ'yeic'iya, v. Push or thrust one's self upon or in upon. Cf. akaⁿ and iyeic'iya. Scili kiⁿ lila makuwapi. Tawa kiⁿ akiⁿyemic'iye lo.

aki'oⁿ, v.a. (of aoⁿ). Place on, as wood on one's own fire, place on for. Awakioⁿ. Yuⁿkaⁿ oyate kiⁿ caⁿ ota, eyaś tusu ece akioⁿpi. -- akioⁿpa, v. Return and place down. Akiwaoⁿpa.

aki'pa, v. pos. (of apa). Strike one's own.
aki'pa, v. Meet, as anyone travelling, come against, come upon one, happen to, befall one. Awakipa. Uⁿkakipapi. Woteĥi akipapi. Siⁿkpe ĥel amakipa ĥce lo. Wana ca na tahena iktomi waⁿ akipa.

aki'pab, adv. Divided, partaken of equally. - egnaka, Divided, separate. - iyeya, Divide.

aki'paja, v.a. Fold on, double over.

a'kipaptapi, v. pl. They break up and go in different directions. Bl. Wana auⁿkipaptapi kte lo.

aki'paś, v. cont. (of akipaja). Double over. - iyeya.

aki'paya, v.a. Cause to befall one.

aki'pe, v.a. Wait for one, wait for, expect, hope for. Awakipe. Uⁿkakipepi.

a'kipsoⁿwaheya, adv. (of papsoⁿ). Spreading out into a line. - kuśeya iyayapi, Spreading out, they go on (to intercept the buffalo, etc.). Bl. Connotation is that of a whole crowd moving down to one place in a body.LC.

aki'psapsa, adv. Close together, standing thick, as grain or grass, jammed together, as men or animals. Full of, as a lake of fish. R. Also said of many children in a family. Bl. -- akipsapsaya, adv. Thickly, close together. -- akipsaya, adv. Close together.

aki'ptaⁿ, v.n. Do together (many). Uⁿkakiptaⁿpi. -- adv. Together, joining forces. - uⁿyaⁿpi. - ecoⁿpi.

aki'sni, v. pos. (of asni). Get well, recover from sickness, recover from anger. Amakisni. Anikisni. Uⁿkakisnipi. Also said of the weather.

aǩi'sniya. v.a. Cause one to get well, cure. Akisniwaya. -- akísniya^n, adv. Getting well. Cf. asniya. B.H.184.23.

aǩi'sniyepicaśni, adj. Incurable. B.H. 114.22.

aǩi'śogya, adv. Thick, close together. LC.

aǩi'śoǩa, adj. (of śoka). Thick on, as leaves on covering the ground thickly. Peji ki^n akiśoke (kahihiyela) yu^{n}ke, an expression for Thick grass. Bl.

aki'ś'a, v.n. Shout, cheer. D.44. Akíś'api ki^n kowakipelo. D.103. Wa^{n}na akiś'api na utapi. Hecel u^{n}kiś wa^{n}na awicu^{n}ś'api na u^{n}kutapi.

aǩi'ś'ag, cont. (of akiś'aka).

aǩi'ś'agya, adv. Growing thickly, as wheat.

aǩi'ś'aǩa, adj. Thick, as wheat growing in the field. Applies also to weeds.

aǩi'ś'aś'a, v. red.(of akiś'a). Applaud. Wa^{n}na peha^n ki^n glinapi^n na akiś'aś'a.

aǩi'ťa, v.a. Seek for, hunt for, as something lost, make efforts to get. Awakita. U^{n}kakitapi. Acicita.

aǩi'ťaǩuniśni, v.n. (of atakuniśni). Become nothing, as in losing everything. Amakitakuniśni.

aǩi'ta^{n}i^{n}śniśni, adj. or adv. Appearing now and then again. - hi^{n}gla, Become invisible every now and then, as horses walking in hilly country at a distance. Bl.

aǩi'ťapi, n. An effort, a research.

aǩi'ti, v.n. Stop somewhere for the night on one's way. Akiwati. Cf. ahiti. Na glapi na akitipi na hiha^{n}na el wa^{n}na ake glapi.

aǩi'to, v. pos. (of ato). Tattoo, make blue marks on the body. Aweto. Ayeto. U^{n}kakitopi. Note: Whoever tattoos himself will be well off in the other world. The old woman who stands on the road in the spirit world will let him pass on to God. Whoever does not do it will be killed by the woman. This was an old belief.

aǩi'to^{n}wa^n, v.a. Look for something lost. Awákito^{n}wa^n. Akicito^{n}wa^n. Look for somebody or something lost.

aǩi'topi, n. Marks made by tattooing. -- part. Marked, tattooed.

aǩi't'a, v.n. Die after getting home, as a warrior wounded who is carried home. Akímat'a.

aǩi't'eya, adv. Crowded together, as books on a shelf. Same as akiśoka.

aǩi'wa^{n}yaka, v. Go and see one's own, as in the issue wagons at Pine Ridge. Akiwa^{n}blaka. Ewa^{n}yaka, They went to see something as a show.

aǩi'ya, v.n. Practice, give the mind to, consider. Awakiya. Na wa^{n}na heo^n wicaśa ita^{n}ca^{n}pi oyate el u^{n}pi k'u^n akiyapi na oyate ki^n nicitokab yaota^{n}i^{n}pi. Tokel eco^{n}pi waśteka heci^{n}ha^n he akiyapi, They conferred about what might be the best thing to do for him. D.218. -- v.a. Try one. Cf. akia, another possible spelling. Akimayapi, I am up for trial.

aǩi'yagla, v.a. (aki and awagla). Carry or take home. Awakiyagla. -- v. Go home. -- v. coll. pl. They all went of go home straightway. Bl. Akiyagla śke, They all left. D.92. Na u^{n}ma pte ki^n akiyagla. Yu^{n}ka^n śahiyela ki^n wahi^{n}wakpa etkiya iglaka akiyagla. K'oyéla akiyagla, See the clouds (storm) passed by. D.72.

aǩi'yataǩa, v. Be locked, as a horse's legs, etc. Ca^{n}ke akiȟa^n t'i^n kta ca cehupa ki^n akiyataka ca ś'i^{n}ś'i^{n}ya wota śke (the Wolf). Ca^{n}kpe akiyatake s'e mani, Cross-legged, have knock-knees. -- aǩiyataǩeca, adv. Touching, as hi^{n}yete akiyatakeca, Shoulders shrugged up, or hu - , Knock-kneed. Ca^{n}kpe - i^{n}ya^{n}ka, Run with knees touching one another, cross-legged, have knock-knees. Bl.

a'ǩiyeha^n, adv. Cf. opatko^{n}s. WE.

aǩi'yela, adv. Near.

aǩi'yotaka, v. Mount a horse. LHB. Iye kakeś glakca śni, najate ki^n pahi^n o^{n}z'aǩiyotake s'e. Bl.

akí'yucaŋpi, v. pl. Shake anything when several things hit together.

akí'yuǧo, v.n. Arrive somewhere tired out. Akiblugo. (A new word) RF.

akí'yuha, v.a. (of yuha). Have on, hold on, lift up. - aglapi, Carrying him (on their shoulders or so) they take him home. B.H.71.10;197.7. -- akí-yuhapi, v. pl. They bear, carry, when several do it together. Wicaša 60 seca (caŋ wakaŋ) akiyuhapi.

akí'yuȟpa, v. (aki and yuȟpa). Carry home and throw down. Akibluȟpa.

akí'yuŋka, v. coll. pl. They stop for the night somewhere on their way. Waŋna wakpa cik'ala kiŋ opaya akicita kiŋ akiyuŋka.

akí'yuskica, v. Tie fasten together, attach one to another. Akíbluskica.

akí'yutitaŋpi, v. pl. Pull different ways.

akí'yuweǧa, n. A crossing, a ford. Cf. kiyuwega. Paŋkeska wakpala kiŋ lila mni hiyaya. Caŋke tokaŋni akiyuwege šni.

akí'yuza, v. pl. They hold or take hold of one all around, seize. Akimayuzapi na...oiȟpemaya po. B.H.117.8,10. -- akiyuzapi, v. pl. They (two or more involved) hold or seize anything. R. Yuŋkaŋ wiŋyaŋ nuŋp el hipi...eyaš akiyuzapi na eyayapi.

akó', exclam. Welcome! (An old word). Same as caŋnako and waštaŋmi. Bl. -- adv. Beyond, on the other side of. Winuȟcala šica, ako gla yo. Ako ecoŋ wo.

ako'ecoŋ, v. imperat. only (?). Get away. Ya! Toskala akoecoŋ.

ako'itoheya, adv. Towards, with the face the other way, turned with the face from. R. - napelo, Bl.

akó'jal, adv. (cont. of akojata). Straddling. - najiŋ, Stand over a thing as a log, having it between the legs, or as in riding. Also akájal. Cf. D,37. Note: akojata is not used. -- akójalya, adv. Astride.

a'kókab, adv. Across, straight across, by a near way. - ya, Make a short cut. WE. -- ákokabya, v. Go across, go by a near way. -- adv. By a near way, across. -- ákokabyela, adv. Same as akokabya. Bl.

akó'kiya, adv. Beyond, from one, away from one, the other way. He ska ako-kiya. He e ca akokiya glahaŋ ške. D.220.

akó'taŋhaŋ, adv. Beyond, refering to place and time and things. From beyond. R. Hihaŋna akotaŋhaŋ iŋ, Day after tomorrow. Htalehaŋ akotaŋhaŋ, Day be-fore yesterday.

akó'wapa, adv. Further on, beyond a certain object mentioned. D.218. - najiŋ ye, Stand farther off from (the speaker). D.1. -- akówapataŋhaŋ, adv. From beyond.

akó'za, v.a. Make a motion at, attempt to strike. Awakoza. Na waŋna huŋka eya yaŋkapi k'oŋ hena awicakozapi.

akpa'bleca, v.a. (a and kpableca). Break in pieces one's own on something. R. Bl.

akpa'ǧaŋ, v.a. pos. (of pagaŋ). Give away one's own for some purpose. Awá-kpagaŋ. -- akpáǧaŋyaŋ, adv. Giving away for.

akpa'ha, v.n. Be without help. Aícikpa-ha maŋkelo, Nobody lends me a helping hand. BT.

akpa'hi, v.a. (a and kpahi). Gather up one's own on something. R. Bl.

akpaŋ'yaŋ, v.a. Tan over again, when it has not been done well, or tan hurriedly and carelessly. Akpaŋwaya.Bl.

akpa'spa, v. Suffer patiently, endure until it has passed off. Awakpaspa. Awakpaspiŋ ktelo, as a tired man would say, who makes for the place of his destination inspite of being tired.Bl. -- akpáspeca, n. One who suffers pa-tiently until his anger goes off, without saying a word. -- akpáspeya, adv. Patiently. Out of Sight. R. Also it has this meaning, - iyeya, Rub hard pressing.

akpas'ya, v.a. Cause darkness on,

darken. Akpaswaya. -- adv. Benightedly.

akp̆a'ťan, v. pos. (of patan). Reserve one's own for a purpose. Awakpatan. -- akpátanyan, adv. Reserving for a purpose.

akp̆a'za, v.n. (a and kpaza). Come night on one, be benighted. Amakpaza.

akp̆a'zo, v. pos. (of pazo). Point at one's own. Awákpazo.

akśa', adv. More, in addition to. Cf. akśáka.

akśa'ǩa, adv. Same as akśa. - onmaspe śni. - econ owakihi śni, It is a pity (too bad) to be unable to do more (again) for one reason or another. Akśaka miyecu śni ye, (Perhaps this use refers to kśaka in some way). Akśaka hel kuśeya winyan wan wicaśa śni ca un. D.109.

akśan'kśan, adv. To and fro, across and back.

akśi'ja, v.a. Take or retain something claimed by another. Awákśija.

akśiś', cont. (of akśija). - yuha. B.H.45.20.

akśu', v.a. Pile up on, load on. Awákśu. Paha ska kin hel akanl emaonpipi na iȟ'e amakśu po. Na wanna inyan lila ota akanl akśupi. -- n. A load. -- akśúǩiya, v.a. Cause to pile up on. Ajukiya is Riggs' spelling.

a'kťa, adv. Again, over again. Same as aké. -- prep. Of, about, concerning.

akťa', v.a. Have respect for, regard, keep in mind, give heed to. Receive. Awákata. From this are formed: akikta, akicikta, ihakta, wakta, etc.

akťa'kťa, adv. (red. of akta). Again and again, repeatedly. Gradually, little by little. -- akťákťaya, adv. Repeatedly.

akťa'śni, v. (of akta). Reject, despise. Awaktaśni. -- adv. Not well. - econ, Do a thing badly. -- akťáśniyan, adv. Unwillingly, against one's will. Cf. ektaśniyan. - ipaweȟ etonwe śni ye.

akťon', adv. More than. Wikcemna akton bluha, I have more than ten.

akťon'ja, adj. Forgetful. Amáktonja. -- v. Forget. -- akťónktonja, adj. (red. of aktonja). -- akťónkťonś, cont. (of aktonktonja). Also spelled aktunktuns. -- aktonś, cont. (of aktonja).

aktonś'ya, v.a. Make forget. Taku wan epin kte c'on aktónśmaya yelo. Bl. -- aktónktonśya, adv. (red. of aktonśya).

akton'yan, adv. Forgetfully. WE.

aǩu', v.a. Bring, come bringing home. Awaku. -- v. coll. pl. They are coming home. R. Na iktomni wan hel un ca he ayakupi kte lo.

aǩu'ǩa, v.n. Become old or rotten on one, as clothing. Amákuka.

aǩu'ta ku'wa, v. Be after a thing again and again, as when inquiring repeatedly if a thing has been done. Bc. WE. Riggs has this word.

ak'a', v. Dig on. Maka ak'a. Also, beat one in a game, i.e. throwing farther than the other. Amak'a. Ak'e lo. Note: I suppose this meaning is had, that in jumping and throwing, one deserves a mark in the ground (digging).

ak'in', n. Something to pack on. - ipatapi, A hide mounted with bead ornamentation and used as a saddle. - ska, A beaded saddle blanket. - kśupi. Tatanka okise śunak'in.

ak'o', Cf. ók'o.

ak'o'ǩa, v. Talk to one incessantly. Amayak'okelo. Bl.

a'laťa, adv. (abbrev. of alataya). All over. Owinji kin alata. Canku kin alata. Anpetu - . -- álaťaya, adv. Same as alata. Anpetu - ceya ke. Anpetu kin - heconhe. Pa kin - slowicakiciciye. B.H.79.1;203.5. D.85.

a'lehanyank, adv. Away from himself. - niwicaye, Others he saved, (himself he cannot save). B.H.266.7.

a'lehanyang, Cf. ilehanyang. - egnaka. Bl.

ale'ja, v.a. Urinate on something, as dogs do. Awaleja. -- n. A diaper.

ale'leya, v.a. Hold a green stick into the fire so that it gets parched. Alelewaya. Bl.

ale'śab, adj. Frost-bitten. Burnt or colored on the outside. - iniyaya hwo? Are your hands black and blue with the cold? Bl. -- alésabya, v.a. Roast but little and eat it although it is still raw. Bl.

ale'tka, n. Branch or limb of a tree. Caⁿ-áletka. D.34.

ali', v.a. Climb up. Cf. oskapa. Ascend as a hill. Awali. Also, step on. Thus, si amáli, He stepped on my foot. Si acíli. Na waⁿna owiciⁿhaⁿ paha kiⁿ uⁿkalipi. Caⁿke caⁿkiⁿ ali.

ali'agla, v.a. Climb a hill and disappear on the other side. Aliwagla.

ali'ḱiya, v.a. Cause to climb. Aliwakiya.

ali'li, v. (red. of ali). Awálili. Caⁿ kiⁿ alili iⁿyaⁿka na glicu. Mni kiⁿ alili iⁿyaⁿke. D.57. M.S.569. -- alíliya, adv. (red. of aliya). Na oyaya aliliya maka saⁿ oⁿ yuglakśikśaⁿ owapi. -- aliliyaḱel, adv. In a climbing manner.

ali'ya, adv. Climbing. -- v.n. Go climbing. Aliwaya. -- n. (?). A hike or climb. Aliya kiⁿ ogna owahececakelo ca ogna uⁿyaⁿpi ktelo. LB. - oḱit'eya, said of a road leading upward on a narrow ridge. RT. -- alíyakel, adv. In a climbing manner.

alo', v.n. Scorched, burnt, cooked. Iḣaⁿhaⁿ la keśa, alo śni, he asks for meat in vain, it is not thoroughly cooked yet. Bl. Śpaⁿ yeśa alo śni (or anapi' śni), drawing back one's hand as though something were hot. Cf. anapiⁿ.

alo'kiksohaⁿ, v. pos. (of aloksohaⁿ).

alo'ksohaⁿ, v.a. Put under the arm, as a book. Alowaksohaⁿ. Also, carry in the arms, as a child, or tucked under the arm as one might a garment. Alokso is not known. D.49. -- n. Armpit.

alos', cont. (of aloza).-- alósabya, v.a. Let something get black while roasting it. R. Bl. -- alóshiⁿgle, v.n. Feel a scorched sensation suddenly, be frightened suddenly, or suddenly angry. Aloshiⁿglemayakiye lo. Same as: Yuś'iⁿyaye mayayelo. BT. Cf. kagal hiⁿgle. D.47. -- alósloseca , v.n. Experience a burning sensation. Become angry. Alosloswayeca.

alo'sloza, v.n. (red. of aloza). Be scorched, but not cooked, as something held in the flame.

alos'ya, v.a. Scorch, as meat held in the flame. Have one's feelings touched by any circumstances, be made angry.

alo'waⁿ, v.a. Sing in praise of anyone, sing for, as for the death of an enemy. Awálowaⁿ. Uⁿkálowaⁿpi.

alo'wiṫaya, adv. (?). Bl.

alo'za, v.n. Be scorched, but not cooked.

alu'slus, cont. (of alusluza). Have the feeling all over one's body, teeth etc., caused by a grating sound. - hiⁿgla. - mahiⁿgla. Same as aloslos.

ama', interj. Of surprise and incredulity at something said, as one taps the arm of the speaker. Same as apá.Bl.

ama'ġaju, v. (a and magaju). Rain on. Amamagaju. Uⁿkamagajupi. -- amágajuḱiya, v.a. Cause to rain on. Amagajukiya. -- amágajuya, v.a. Cause to rain on. Amagajuwaya.

ama'ḣpiya, v.imper. Cloud over. -- adj. Cloudy, clouded over.

ama'ḣposaⁿṫagleya, adv. Silhouetted. - najiⁿ, Stand on top of a hill visible and inspite of the darkness one is set off against the sky. Bc. ED. M.

ama'ḱini, v. Walk on one's own. Toḱétu kec'eyaś oteḣi kta ca caⁿ waⁿ yaⁿke c'oⁿ hel amauⁿkinipi ktelo, Go back to the woods where we were because fierce weather is coming. Bl.

ama'ni, v. (a and mani). Walk on. Amáwani.

ama'śte, v.n. (a and maśte). Be warm on.

Amámaśte.

ama'śteic'iya ya^{n}ka , v. Sit to sun and warm one's self.

ama'śťenaptapta, n. The glimmering of vapor in the sun heat, the burning appearance in the prairie on a hot day, or on a stove. Bl.

ama'śťet'a, v.n. Have a sun-stroke. Amaśtemat'a.

ama'śťeya, adv. Exposed to the heat, in the sun. -- amáśteyaḱel, adv. Hotly.

ami'c'iciya, 1st pers. singl. of aic'iciya, which is perhaps from aya. R. Note: A man says this when he remains sitting and thinks while somebody calls him. Bl. Hence, Musing, or being distracted.

amna'ic'iya, v. refl. (of mnaya^n). Gather for himself, be selfish. Amnámic'iya.

amna^n'ya^n, v.a. (a and mna^{n}ya^n). Collect gather together to, add to. Amnáwaya.

amni', v. (a and mni). Spread out to dry on anything. Awamni. U^{n}kamnipi.

amni'ciyapi, v. pl. (a and mniciyapi). They assemble to on account of. Amniu^{n}kiciyapi.

amni'mni, v.a. Sprinkle on anything, sprinkle with water, etc. Awámnimni. U^{n}kamnimnipi. Acimnimni. -- amnímniya, v.a. Sprinkle on. We ki^n tiyopa ta^{n}kata^{n}ha^n amnimniyapi kte. B.H.52. 11.

amni'ťa^n, v.n. (a and mnita^{n}ka). Flow on or over. -- amníta^{n}ya, v.a. Cause to flow over, water a field. Amnita^{n}waya. Hence, Irrigate. -- amníta^{n}ya^n, adv. In an over-flowing manner.

amo^n'mo^{n}la, n. A childish word for a doll.

ana'blaġa, v.n. (a and nablaga). Open or spread out on.

ana'blas, cont. (of anablaza). - iyeya, Make burst by kicking.

ana'blaza, v.a. (a and nablaza). Tear open with the foot, burst open on. Anawablaza. -- anábleca, v.n. Spread out on, as grain when poured on anything. -- anáblel, cont. (of anableca). - eȟpeya, Scatter by pouring down.

ana'blu, v.a. Kick dust or dirt on. Anáwablu.

ana'bu, v.a. Make a noise on with the feet, stamp. Anáwabu. -- anábubu, v. (red. of anabu).

ana'ġibya, v.a. Clamp, hold fast, pin, as the spring of a trap does a mouse. Ito, nape ki^n anagibyapi; ca^{n}ke ikikcu śni. D.27. -- anáġipa, v. Be held fast, clamped, pinned, as by the spring of a trap, etc. Nape ki^n ena anagipa śke. Ikto nape ki^n glutita^n keś sutaya anagipa ke. D.22,27.

ana'glegleyakel, adv. (red. of anagleyakel). Slowly, step by step, limping. - mawani. The motion is as that of one suffering from rheumatism. Bl. -- anágleyakel, adv. Limping. - mani, He had a limp, as old people, not setting feet down firmly. Bl.

ana'gloḱa, v.a. Knock and injure on, sprain. Iśḱahu anawagloka. I sprained my ankle.

ana'gluśte, v.n. Be lame in the leg, limp. Break down, as one's leg does sometimes when they buckle. R. Bl. - iyaya. -- anágluśteśte, v. (red. of anagluśte). Bl.

ana'ġopťa^n, v.a. Listen to, hearken to, obey. Anáwagopta^n. Anáu^{n}gopta^{n}pi. -- anágopta^{n}ya, v.a. Cause to listen to. Anágopta^{n}waya.

ana'gwag, cont. (of anagwaka). - naji^n, Be complaining, criticizing. Bl.

ana'gwaka, v.a. (of nagwaka). Murmur against. B.H.55.2.

ana'ha, v.a. Kick a ball. Used in an Indian game. The ball is large and hangs on a string. Anáwaha. - iyeyapelo. Bl.

ana'haha, adv. Slowly, carefully. As, - mani, which refers to one; whereas nahaha is used in reference to more than one. F. -- v.n. Walk or run noiselessly after one. Anáwahaha. BD.

ana'huśteśteyakel, adv. Limpingly. - mani, Walk limpingly, as a horse. Cf. anápoksaŋyaŋkel. Bl.

ana'ȟa, adj. Rough, roughened up.

ana'ȟlaṫa, v. Hold on carefully, as a man to a horse. Anawaȟlata. Riggs gives the meaning, Crawl up carefully on anything.

ana'ȟloȟlo, v.n. Bubble up, as in boiling. Perhaps also, anagloglo.

ana'ȟloḱa, v.a. (a and naȟloka). Wear a hole in, as in a moccasin, on something. Anáwaȟloka.

ana'ȟma, v.a. Hide, conceal. Anáwaȟma. -- anáȟmaŋpi, n. A concealing, concealment. B.H.302.7. -- anáȟmeya, adv. Secretly, slyly, covertly. -- anáȟmeyahaŋ, adv. Secretly.

ana'ȟṗa, v.a. (a and naȟpa). Kick down on anything. Anáwaȟpa.

ana'ȟṫaḱa, v.a. (a and naȟtaka). Kick one on anything else. Anawaȟtaka.

ana'ic'ipsoŋ, v. refl. (of anapsoŋ). Spill on one's self by kicking, as by kicking over a bucket of water. Anámic'ipsoŋ.

ana'jiṗa, v. Pinch with the feet. Anáwajipa.

ana'ḱicigopṫaŋ, v. (of anagoptaŋ). Hearken to for one, listen, give ear, give heed to for one. Anáwecigoptaŋ. -- pl. They give ear to each other. Anáuŋkicigoptaŋpi. -- anáḱicigoptaŋyaŋ, adv. Listening to each other.

ana'kicikśiŋ, v. Come to one's aid. B.H.140.13. Cf. anakikśiŋ.

ana'ḱicipṫapi, v. pl. (recipr. of anapta). They stop or hinder each other. Anauŋkiciptapi.

ana'ḱicisoŋ, v. (?). Bl.

ana'ḱiciṫaŋ ecoŋpi, n. Game played by boys imitating the zuya yapi (war).Bl.

ana'ḱigopṫaŋ, v. pos. (of anagoptaŋ). Listen to, obey, as one's father. Anáwaḱigoptaŋ.

ana'ḱiȟma, v.a. and pos. Hide, conceal, refuse to tell, deny, affirm that it is not so. Anawakiȟma. -- anákiȟmaŋpi, n. Denial, a concealing. -- part. Concealed.

ana'ḱiȟmeya, v.a. Cause to conceal. Anákiȟmewaya. -- adv. Covertly, secretly. -- anáḱiȟmeyahaŋ, adv. Stealthily, privately.

ana'ḱikśiŋ, v.a. Stand over and defend one, interpose for one when in danger, expose one's self for another, work for one to let him rest. Anáwekśiŋ. Anácicikśiŋ. D.223. B.H.155.25.

ana'ḱipa, v. Flee from. Bl. SLB

ana'ḱipta, v. (?). Bl.

ana'kṗa, v. Fly away from, as sparks that fly away from a wood fire. Pelánamakpelo. Bl.

ana'ksa, v. (a and naksa). Break off a thing on something else with the foot. Anáwaksa.

ana'kśija, v. (a and nakśija). Bend down on with the foot, as grass on the prairie. Anáwakśija. -- anákśiś, cont. (of anakśija). - iyeya.

ana'kṫaŋ, v. (a and naktaŋ). Bend on or over with the foot.

ana'k'eza, v. Make smooth with the foot by treading on. Cf. onak'eza, which is more correct. R.

ana'mna, v.a. (a and namna). Rip on anything with the foot. Anáwamna. Haŋpa iŋyaŋ anamna, He ripped his moccasin on a stone.

ana'mni, v.n. Give way under the foot, as snow when there is water under it. - iyeya.

anaŋ'sa, v.a. (a and naŋsa). Hunt or go after, as buffalo. Anaŋwasa.

ana'pa, v.a. (a and napa). Run to for refuge. Anawapa.

ana'pca, v. (a and napca). Swallow on or after something else. Anáwapca.

ana'ṗiŋ, v.n. Be tasty. Śpaŋ yeśa anapiŋ śni iyecel yaglicu (omayani) welo.

This is said when somebody passes by in a hurry. BT. Špaⁿ yeśa anapiⁿ śni nace, inayaȟni. Bullring mentions both these phrases. Note: The meaning of the word is not quite clear. Buechel gives the meaning , Refuse to meat turned in a frying pan while frying.

ana'poksaⁿyaⁿkel, adv. In a limping manner. - mani, He walks in a limping manner, as a horse, the head going up and down. Bl. Cf. anáhuśteśteyakel.

ana'popa, v.n. (a and napopa). Burst on anything. Anámapopa.

ana'pota, v.a. (a and napota). Wear out on, as one moccasin on anything. Anáwapota.

ana'psaka, v.a. (a and napsaka). Break a string with the foot on anything. Anáwapsaka.

ana'psaⁿ, v.a. (a and napsuⁿ). Kick over and spill on anything. Anáwapsaⁿ, anámapsaⁿ, anáuⁿpsaⁿpi; or anáwapsuⁿ, etc. -- v.n. Boil over on anything.

ana'pśa, v.a. Break into a laugh after it had been suppressed. The word seems to be used only figuratively. BD. Riggs gives, Bubble up, as foul water when it is disturbed, for which use here anápśapśa. -- anápśapśa, v.n. (red. of anapśa). Boil up, come up, as bubbles on the water.

ana'pśuⁿ, v.a. (a and napśuⁿ). Dislocate, put out of joint on anything. Anawapśuⁿ.

ana'pta, v.a. Stop, hinder, forbid. Anáwapta. Anáuⁿptapi. -- v.n. Cease, stop. -kuwa, He cornered one. D.96. - aya, He surrounded them, as one drives them on. D.261. -- anáptapi, part. Stopped, ceased. Oⁿ - , That which produces a stoppage; the name given to paregoric.

ana'ptel, adv. Less, less than. -- anáptelya, adv. In a less manner. -- anáptelyakel, adv. Less, in a lessened manner.

ana'ptetoⁿ, v.a. Prohibit, lay a hindrance, lay an embargo. Anaptewatoⁿ. -- n. A prohibition, obstruction, hindrance.

ana'ptuja, v.a. (a and naptuja). Crack or split with the foot on anything. Anáwaptuja.

ana'p'iⁿ, adj. or adv. Stiff, frostbitten. - imayayelo, My hands are stiff from the cold. Bl.

ana'p'o, v.n. Come all over one, as ashes or steam, be fog on one. Anámap'o.

ana'sa, v.n. (of nasá). Rise up on, as a hog's bristles on his back, bristle up.

ana'slata, v.a. (a and naslata). Creep up to carefully, as a hunter to game. Anáwaslata. D.259. -- anáslatapi, n. A creeping up to game.

ana'śloka, v. Kick off, as one's moccasins. Anáwaśloka.

ana'ta, v. Bury with the foot, scrape dirt in with the foot. Anáwata.

ana'takiⁿyece, adv. (?). Tókiⁿśkiⁿś - . Bl.

ana'taⁿ, v.a. (a and nataⁿ). Flee to one, rush on any person or thing. Anáwataⁿ. -- anátaⁿpi, n. Attack, assault, the offensive in war.

ana'tapśija, v.n. Bubble up, come up, as bubbles on water.

ana'tipa, v.n. Crisp, shrivel, be burned.

ana'titaⁿ, v. (a and natitaⁿ). Push on with the foot, pull back on account of. Anáwatitaⁿ.

ana'tokelyakel, adv. Using the feet in an unusual manner. - mani, Walk in an unusual manner, as one who has sores. Bl. Mani maptahaⁿhaⁿ heoⁿ - mawani.

ana'tuka, v.a. (a and natuka). Wear off with the foot, as the hair from a buffalo-skin moccasin. Anáwatuka.

ana't'a, v.a. (a and nat'a). Kill with the foot on something. Anáwat'a.

ana't'iⁿs, cont. (of anat'iⁿza).

ana't'iⁿsya, adv. Firmly trodden.

ana'tʼiⁿza, v.a. (a and natʼiⁿza). Tramp down hard and tight. R. Also used for dancing, e.g. anauⁿtʼiⁿzapi kte.

ana'uⁿg, cont. (of anauⁿka). (Use is doubtful.) Anáuⁿgya owakihi yelo, as when one is looking for stock on foot or on horseback. -- anáuⁿgkiya, v.a. Cause to gallop on. Use is doubtful.

ana'uⁿka, v.a. (a and nauⁿka). Kick down on anything. Anáwauⁿka. -- v.n. Gallop, as a horse, on anything. Bl.

ana'wab, adv. Over against, beyond.

ana'wega, v. (a and nawega). Break on anything with the foot, but not to break off. Anáwawega. -- anáweh, cont. (of anawega). - iyeya.

ana'wiⁿja, v.a. (a and nawiⁿja). Bend down on with the foot. Anáwawiⁿja.

ana'wiⁿlwiⁿta, v. (red. of anawiⁿta).

ana'wiⁿś, v. (cont. of anawiⁿja). - iyeya.

ana'wiⁿta, v. (a and nawiⁿta). Scrape the foot on. Anáwawiⁿta.

ana'wiⁿyaⁿ, adv. Concealing by circumlocution. Steal up secretly by taking a round-about way. R. Bl.

ana'zica, v. Stretch something that is too short with the foot, i.e. holding it in the hands and bracing the foot against it, as a belt. Bl.

ani', v.n. (a and ni). Live on or for. Awáni.

ani'ca, v.a. Withhold, keep back from, retain something claimed by another, lay claim to. Forbid. Oppose. Awánica. From this word are formed akinica, and akicinica, Detain one. D.217.

anil', v. (cont. of anica).

ani'ni, n. Anything that collects on, as soot, thick scum, etc. - s'e hiyeya, said of soot that hangs loosely.

ani'ya, v.a. (a and niya). Breathe on. Awániya. Uⁿkániyaⁿpi.

anoⁿ'gopṫaⁿ, v.a. Obey, give ear to.

anoⁿh'keci'ya, v.a. Lend an ear to, listen to. - maⁿka.

anoⁿ'waⁿ, v.a. (a and noⁿwaⁿ). Swim for, swim on. Awánoⁿwaⁿ.

anuⁿg', adv. (of anuⁿka). On both sides. - opé, Sharp on both sides, two-edged. Anuⁿka, obs.

anuⁿg'kisoⁿ, n. Husband. An old word in the mouth of his wife. - waⁿ kici wauⁿ kiⁿ he, My husband. WR.

anuⁿg'pa uⁿ, v. Agree to. -- anúⁿg'ite uⁿ, v. Oppose each other. Bl.

anuⁿ'gwakicaśka, n. Saddle bags. Literally, something bound on both sides.

anuⁿ'g'ite, Cf. anuⁿgpa uⁿ.

anuⁿ'kasaⁿ, n. The bald eagle, or the white-headed eagle.

anuⁿ'kataⁿ, adv. On both sides, from both sides. Nap'anuⁿkataⁿ, With both hands. Nape saⁿnila, With one hand. Nap'- taku ojula icu na el (on the blanket) ognaka. Yuⁿkaⁿ cahli na okala. Na ake nape saⁿnila taku icu na ake el okala. Yuⁿkaⁿ mazakaⁿ wahiⁿsa. Itokeśaⁿ towicaya na pahte el kutakiya icazo na tapoⁿ kiⁿ anoⁿkataⁿ ecel na iku el oyas'iⁿ hecel owicawa. -- anúⁿkataⁿhaⁿ, adv. On both sides, from both sides, backward and forward. Na hehaⁿ ablo - wicahpi num owawa. B.H. 156.14.

Anuⁿk' Ite', n. A double face, a fabulous creature. D.245.

anuⁿ'kiyaⁿ, n. Cross-breed of any living thing. An eagle. Situpi kiⁿ ataya skaska, while their tail tips only are black. Bl.

anuⁿ'kpestola, n. Pick axe.

anuⁿ'wabya, adv. Off to one side

aⁿbce'ya, v. Cry in the day-time. Bl.

aⁿbhaⁿ'keya wi or ahaⁿ', n. The old name for half of March and April (about 6 weeks). The season when the weather changes frequently, half pleasant and half stormy (aⁿpetu-haⁿkeya). Bl. - ca wa kiⁿ tke s'e hiⁿhélo. Bl. Someone has said this is the name for the month of February.

a^{n}bśi'ceca, n. An unpleasant, rainy day. - yelo. Bl.

a^{n}bwa'śte, n. A pleasant day. - ca Ȟláȟla ki^n teha^n hóta^{n}i^n ktelo. Bl.

a^{n}ṗ', cont. (of á^{n}pa). Also a^{n}b in contraction. E.g. a^{n}b'icamna, A stormy day; and a^{n}bśiceca, A bad day. Bl.

a^n'ṗa, n. Daylight. Wa^{n}na - . Wa^{n}na - aya. -- á^{n}ṗaha^n, adv. In daylight. - el ipi kte. Hiha^{n}na ki^n - u^{n}gni kte lo. - wi ki^n aiyokpazi^n kte.

a^n'ṗaḱableza, n. Day-breaking, daybreak.

a^n'ṗaohoṫo^{n}la, n. Domestic fowls, so called from their crowing in the morning. Use in Holy Scripture.

a^n'ṗawi, n. The sun.

a^{n}pe'coḱa^{n}ya, n. Mid-day, noon. R. Bl.

a^{n}ṗe'ha^n, adv. Today, today as past, the past part. - cogi^n s'a wa^n owakaȟloke. D.113.

a^{n}ṗe'tacagu, n. Large grasshopper. Cf. aṗétacágu. Bl.

a^{n}ṗe'ṫu, n. Day. A word constructed from a^{n}pa and etu.

a^{n}pe'ṫuha^{n}ḱeyela, adv. Before noon. Bl.

a^{n}pe'ṫula, n. (dim. of a^{n}petu).

a^{n}ṗe'ṫutahena, adv. Before the day is done.

a^{n}ṗe'ṫuwaka^n, n. Sacred day, Sunday.

a^{n}ṗe'tuwi, n. The sun.

a^n'ṗo, n. (a^{n}pa and o). The dawn of morning. A^{n}pȯ is used for a Morning star. -- v.n. Dawn, as the coming of the morning. Nahaȟci - śni ha^{n}ni. B.H.186.1. -- á^{n}po kableze, n. Daylight. - ki^n leha^{n}l. B.H.134.13.

a^{n}ṗo'sḱa^{n}l, adv. (a^{n}pa and oska^{n}l). By day. B.H.127.19. -- a^{n}ṗósḱa^{n}ṫu, adv. By day, in the daytime. -- a^{n}ṗósḱa^{n}ṫuya, adv. By day. -- a^{n}ṗósḱa^{n}ṫuyaḱel, adv. By day, in the daytime.

a^{n}ṗo' wica'ȟpi, n. The morning star. Perhaps Jupiter. - su^{n}ḱáku, Brother morning star. Same as iȟúḱu kigle.

a^{n}pta'niya, n. Breath of day, the very first glimmerings of morn, vapors raised by the sun.

ao'cikpakpani, adj. (red. of aocikpani).

ao'cikṗani, adj. Not equal in length. -- aócikpanini, adj. (red. of aocikpani). Some longer and some shorter. -- aócikṗaniya, adv. Not equal in length.

ao'ci^n, v. (of oci^n). Desire some of a thing.

ao'cipṫel, adv. Not equal to, lacking. -- aóciptelya, adv. Not equal to. Lacking. -- aociptetu, adv. Unequal. Different.

ao'ǧi, adj. Blurred, as the eye. Wi kúwab ya ca na iśta ki^n lemaceca yelo; aogi amayelo. BT. A^{n}petu - yelo, A dreary day. Wi ki^n - s'elececa. Iśta aomagi^n. Bl.

ao'ǧi^{n}to^n, v. Make indistinct, hide. B.H.238.22.

ao'ǧi^{n}ya^n, adv. In a blurred manner. - wáwakiṫelo, I cannot distinguish very well. Bl. -- aóǧi^{n}ya^{n}kel, adv. In a blurry manner. - mu^n kte lo. Bl.

ao'glaḱa, v.a. (a and oglaka). Tell in regard to or in addition to. Aówaglaka, I am appealing. B.H.256.20.

ao'glaḱi^n, v.a. Peep around at one's own. Aówaglaki^n.

ao'glakśa^n, (?).

ao'glaṫa^n, v. pos. (of aokata^n). Lock up, nail up one's own, as one's house when leaving. B.

ao'gluta, v.n. Close up, fill up, as a hole or wound. Heal over. Aómagluta. -- aógluteya, v.a. Close up, cause to heal over. Press around, surround, overwhelm, close up on, as a war party. Aógluteways. -- part. Surrounding. -- adv. Throngingly. Le oya^{n}ke eta^{n}ha^n waśicu^n aogluteniya^{n}pi tka cik'ayela śicaya yelo. Yu^{n}ka^n tima iyaya; ca^{n}ke oyate ki^n aogluteyapi. D.215, 220,261,5.

ao´gmigma, v.n. Roll on. -- aógmigmeýa, v. a. Cause to roll on anything. Aógmigmewaya. -- aógmiyaŋyaŋ, adv. Round on anything.

ao´gnak̇a, v.a. (a and ognaka). Place upon, as a cover. Aowagnaka.

ao´haŋktoŋyaŋ, adv. and v. Be around, encircle, sit around, as a warm stove in cold weather. BD.

ao´haŋzi, v.n. (a and ohaŋzi). Shade, overshadow, be shade on. -- adv. In the shade, shade upon. -- aóhaŋziya, v.a. Cause shade upon, overshadow. Aóhaŋziwaya. -- adv. Shadowy, in the shade.

ao´hiyu, v.n. (a and ohiyu). Come out upon. Leak upon.

ao´homni, adv. Around, surrounding. - oglicu, Travel down around, as on a curved road. - hiyu, He step around (the bushes). D.270. RT. -- v.n. Go around so as to avoid something, avoid. Aowahomni. Natehaŋyaŋ ca na aohomnipi ca na he nakuŋ slolyapi. Note: This word has a meaning of waciŋ. D.117,189. -- aóhomnipi, v. The circuit. -- aóhomniya, v. Go around. Aóhomnibla.

ao´ḣ'aŋhaŋhaŋ, adv. Very skillfully. -- aoḣ'aŋhaŋhaŋkel, adv. Very skillfully.

ao´jaŋjaŋ, v.n. (a and ojaŋjaŋ). Be light on anything. Aómajaŋjaŋ. -- aójaŋjaŋya, v.a. Cause to be light upon, light. Aójaŋjaŋwaya. Tipi kiŋ aojaŋjaŋyapi, They lighted the tipi. B.H. 54.6. D.273. -- aójaŋjaŋyaŋ, adv. In an illuminated manner. - wacipi, A dance held in the evening near a big fire by those who intended to go on the war-path. Bl.

ao´k̇aġa, v.a. Add to, as in building, make something in addition to, do more than what one ought to do, exaggerate. Aówakaga. Lena (olowaŋ etc.) aokagapi śni yo. Ecéś eháś aoyakage lo. Bl. -- v.n. Drift down stream. Aómakaga. -- aók̇aġeca, v.a. Add to, do or say more than is fitting, be unreasonable. Aówakageca. -- n. One who is unreasonable in his demands, an importunate person.

ao´k̇ahi, v.n. Hang over, as the hair over the face. Bl. -- aók̇ahiya, adv. Through hanging hair. - wak̇ita, He looks out through the hair hanging over his face. Same as, kaózaŋ s'e wakita. Bl.

ao´k̇aḣ, cont. (of aokaga). - oyaka.

ao´k̇aḣniġa, v.a. (a and okaḣniga). Understand about, in consequence of. Aówakaḣniga.

ao´k̇aḣwog, cont. (of aokaḣwoka). Drifting or floating on. - iyaya.

ao´k̇aḣwok̇a, v.n. Drift on, float down stream.

ao´k̇aḣya, adv. Extravagantly, as in talking. -- aók̇aḣyak̇el, adv. Exaggeratedly.

ao´k̇ak̇i, v.a. Peep into, as through a key-hole or window, looking closely at something. Awáokaki. Bl. Aówakakiŋ. R. -- aókakiŋyaŋ, adv. Peeping into.

ao´k̇akśaŋyaŋ, adv. Around about, by a round-about way.

ao´k̇amna, v. Avoid, go around, sneak around stealthily, as in hunting game. Aówakamna. Cf. okamna and ayukśaŋyaŋ. Also, to avoid honoring a man, as one might do, not noticing a man when one might do so.

ao´k̇apol, cont. (of aokapota). Afloat, floating in a stream. - iyaya. -- aók̇apolya, v.a. Cause to float. Aókapolwaya. -- aók̇aṗoṫa, v.n. Float on, as a buoy, rise to the top, as anything in water.

ao´k̇asṫo, v.a. (a and okasto). Smooth down upon. Aówakasto.

ao´k̇aṫa, v.n. Be warm on. Aómakata.

ao´k̇ata, v.a. Cover with earth. Aówakata.

ao´k̇aṫaŋ, v.a. (a and okataŋ). Nail one thing on another. Aówakataŋ. Aóuŋkataŋpi. B.H.265

ao´k̇aṫica, v.a. Draw or scrape snow on anything. Aówakatica.

ao´k̇at'iŋs, cont. (of aokat'iŋza).

-- aóƙat'iⁿsya, adv. Pressed in or on tight. -- aóƙat'iⁿza, v.a. (a and o-kat'iⁿza). Press or pound in tight, as in packing flour. Hammer on tight, as a hoop. Aówakat'iⁿza.

ao'ƙawiⁿǧa, v.a. Encircle. Aówakawiⁿga. Na he oyate uⁿkihakab ai k'oⁿ hena a-nataⁿpi na aokawiⁿgapi. Na ecel tona kujapi hena ewicayuⁿkapi ca na aowica-kawiⁿgapi. Na waⁿna lila wicakutepi na icuⁿhaⁿ aowicakawiⁿgapi na ohaⁿketa egnagna iyayapi. B.H.72.7. D.269.

ao'ƙicaga, v.a. Deal falsely. Aómiye-cagapelo, (Although I treat you well,) you doñ't mind me. Bl. -- aókicagapi, n. Falsehood.

ao'ƙicaǧeca, n. Same as aókageca, and perhaps also aákicageca.

ao'ƙicip̄agi, v. (of opagi). Fill a pipe for one in addition to. Aówecipagi.

ao'ƙignaƙa, v.a. (a and okignaka). Put some in in addition to, help one to food a second time. Aówegnaka.

ao'ƙiȟp̄a, v.a. (a and okihpa). Rest or lie by for. Aówakiȟpa.

ao'ƙime, v.a. Encircle, go around, clasp, encircle with the arms. Aówa-kime. -- aóƙimeya, v.a. Cause to en-circle, go around. -- adv. Encircling.

ao'ƙiya, v. (a and okiya). Get together and plan on, make up something. Aówa-kiya. Aóuⁿkiyapi.

ao'kiye, n. Buggy topand cover. Cf. awokeya.

ao'kp̄aǧi, v. pos. (of aopagi). Fill one's pipe again. Aówakpagi.

a'okp̄ani, v.n. Be wanting, not suffi-cient. Heoⁿ owayawa kiⁿ tokata wakaⁿ-yeja kiⁿ aokpanipi kta iblukcaⁿ. Ta-kúku aomakpani yelo, I am short of various things. This is an old saying. HH. -- aókp̄aniyaⁿ, adv. Insufficiently, less than.

ao'kp̄as, cont. (of aokpaza). -- aókpa-sya, v.a. Darken, make dark upon. Aó-kpaswaya. -- adv. Obscurely, darkened.

ao'kp̄aza, v.n. Be dark on any place or thing. Aómakpaza.

ao'kp̄azaⁿ, v.a. Push into,as an arrow into a quiver or a feather into one's hair. Aówakpazaⁿ.

ao'kpazaⁿƙitoⁿ, v.n. Have a sheath or case upon, be sheathed or pushed in.

ao'k'o, v.n. (a and ok'o). Be a fuss made about. -- aók'oya, v.a. Buzz about, make a noise or fuss about. Aók'owaya.

ao'le, v. (a and ole). Seek for some-thing in addition to. Aowale.

ao'mna, v.a. (a and omna). Smell upon, smell in consequence of. Aówamna.

ao'naƙitaƙa, v. pos. (of aonataka). Fasten, as a door, on one. Aónawa-kitaka.

ao'napa, v.a. (a and onapa). Flee to, take refuge at. Aónawapa.

ao'nasloƙa, v.a. Run away from, leave or desert, as a friend in danger. Aónawasloka.

ao'natag, cont. (of aonataka). - iyeya. Aonaic'itag yaⁿkapi, as the Apostles did for fear of the Jews.

ao'nataka, v.a. Fasten on one, lock up. Tiyopa - , Fasten the door on one, shut one in. Aónawataka. Mazaska - , A safe.

ao'nat'iⁿs, cont. (of aonat'iⁿza). - iyeya. -- aónat'iⁿza, v.a. Press down tight in, as a box or barrel. Aónawat'iⁿza.

aoⁿ', v.a. Lay or place on, as wood on the fire. Awáoⁿ. Uⁿkáoⁿpi.

aoⁿ'p̄a, v. Place wood on the fire. R. Smoke in addition to, on, or after. This is conversational. BD. Thus, acaⁿmuⁿpa, or aompa, I smoke.

aoⁿ'śiya, adv. More poorly, in a worse condition. -- aóⁿśiyaƙel, adv. Still worse, worse and worse.

ao'pa, v. (a and opa). Follow with. Aówapa.

ao'p̄aǧi, v. (a and opagi). Fill the pipe again, fill the pipe after eat-ing. Aówapagi.

ao'ṗaṫica, v. Stick or push in or under or on, as a quilt under the tick. Cf. opatica.

ao'ṗazaⁿ, n. Eagle feathers, or anything the Indians, Mr. or Mrs., used to stick in their hair (head). Cf. opázaⁿ. Mitáaópazaⁿ. Cf. aókpazaⁿ, which may be the same word.

ao'ṗemni, v.a. (a and opemni). Roll up in. Aówapemni.

ao'peya, v.a. Add to, cause to follow with. -- adv. With, together with, included. D.37.

ao'ṗoġaⁿ, v.a. (a and opogaⁿ). Blow on. Aówapogaⁿ.

ao'pṫeca, adj. Less, little. -- aópṫel, adv. Less than.

ao'ptelya, v.a. Diminish. Aóptelwaya. -- adv. Less. -- aópṫelyaḱel, adv. Less, less than. -- aóptelyela, adv. Less, diminished.

ao'pṫeṫu, adv. Less in size. -- aópṫeṫuya, adv. Less, in a less manner.

ao'śla, n. Bare spot, as a place where the grass has been worn away by walking.

ao'śma, v. Heap up in on. Amákiośma yo, Give me much, as food, heap it up.

ao'ś'agya, adv. Tired out with difficulty. - wahi. RH. B.H.234.6.

ao'ṫalas'e, adv. More. - mak'u ye, Give me more.

a'oṫaⁿḱci, adv.(?). Chiefly. Cf. iyótaⁿḱci. - taku awaciⁿpi iyececa.

ao'taⁿiⁿ, adv.(?). Approaching dusk. - lake cel uⁿkihuⁿnipi ktelo, We shall arrive when it is getting dark. Bl. Taⁿyaⁿ wakita yo, aotaⁿiⁿ śni waⁿji yaⁿkelo. This is said when somebody is hiding somewhere.

ao'ṫehaⁿ, v.n. Be far. -- aóṫehaⁿṫu, v.n. Be a long time, be too late. Aómatehaⁿtu.

ao'tognaka, v.n. Dare, be foolhardy, risk one's life, take one's chances at.

ao't'iⁿs, cont. (of aot'iⁿza). -- aót'iⁿsya, v.a. Crowd or press about, beset. Aót'iⁿsmayaⁿ. -- adv. Crowding, besetting..

ao't'iⁿza, v.n. (a and ot'iⁿza). Be tight on, as a garment, be tight in, as anything inside another. Aómat'iⁿza

ao't'ognaḱa, v.n. Be foolhardy, dare, risk one's life. Aót'owagnaka.

ao'uⁿyaⁿ, v. (a and ouⁿyaⁿ). Be or abide on. Akaⁿ ouⁿyaⁿ.

ao'wehaⁿhaⁿ, v. (red. of aowehaⁿ). Jest, make sport. It seems this word is not used. Aówewahaⁿhaⁿ. Aóweuⁿhaⁿhaⁿpi. -- aówehaⁿhaⁿyaⁿ, adv. Jestingly, in sport.

ao wiṅśḱiya, v.a. Make a bed on for, e.g. to put a blanket down for a child to play on.

ao'yaḣe, v.n. Dry up on, soak in, evaporate on. Casmu ca mini oyasiⁿ - iyaye. Bl. - ayaⁿpa, All the water disappeared over-night. Bl.

ao'yaḱa, v. Add something while relating. Aóblaka. Ate tokel woniciyakapi kiⁿ aoyakapi ca heoⁿ lila caⁿteuⁿśicape. B.H.283.11.

ao'yutkuġa, v.a. Shut out.

ao'zeze, v.n. Dangle. -- aózezeya, adv. Danglingly.

ao'zica, v.a. Reach out after. Aówazica.

ao'zigzica, v.a. Stretch up after anything. Aówazigzica. -- aózigzil, cont. (of aozigzica). - najiⁿ, Stand stretching up. - wicapahi s'e ṫoki ai. This is said when people from here and there went to some meeting etc., picked out here and there, picking, as it were, on tip-toes. Bl.

ao'ziya, v.a. Cause to rest. Aoziwaya.

aṗa', interj. Same as amá. Bl.

apa', v.a. Strike or smite a thing in any way. Awápa. Amápa. Uⁿkápapi. Yuⁿkaⁿ tokeya ie kiⁿ mila waⁿ cuwi el apa na etaⁿ we hiyu.

aṗa' ayuśtaⁿ, v.a. Leave off, stop,

leave unfinished, quit. Apa owotaⁿla ic'ila, To pretend to be honest, recommending something bad as good. GV. FP.

aṗa'blasḱa, v.a. (a and pablaska). To make flat on anything. Awapablaska.

aṗa'blaya, v.a. (a and pablaya). To make level on anything; fig. to fatigue one, play one out, overcome, as a man by talking, a horse by riding. Awápablaya. Acipablayiⁿ kte lo, Well, I'll do it for you; it is all right with me. Ho wana niśtiⁿma ca acipablayelo. Wowapi kaḣ waśi k'oⁿ haⁿkeya awapablayelo. Bl.

aṗa'blaza, v.a. (a and pablaza). Burst open on, tear open on.

aṗa'bleca, v.a. (a and pableca). Break or crush on anything. Awápableca. -- n. A hill in front of and joining a higher hill and so forming a ridge. Paha waⁿkatuya k'el tahena - waⁿ yaⁿke uⁿ hel.... Bl. -- n., adj. Raised ground, a little hill, raised. - el najiⁿ. Bc.

apa'ble hiyúya, v. To surprise one, take one by surprise. Same as aḱála hiyuya. Bl.

aṗa'blu, v.a. To crush to powder on anything. Awápablu. -- v.n. To belch; to bubble up, as air from the water. Amápablu. Keya mni mahe iyaya, yuⁿkaⁿ - . -- aṗáblublu, v. red. (apablu). To bubble up with many bubbles.

aṗa'caⁿcaⁿ, v.a. (a and pacaⁿcaⁿ). To push or make tremble on anything, make one tremble by pushing. Awápacaⁿcaⁿ.

aṗa'coza, v.a. (a and pacoza). Rub and make warm on anything. Awapacoza.

aṗa'ġa, v.n. To beset with prickles. Amápagelo. Nape - , The hand is beset with prickles, having touched a cactus or anything like it. Bl.

aṗa'ġaya, v.a. To cause to be beset with prickles, as by throwing devil's grass or cactus etc. on one. Apágawaya. Bl.

aṗa'ġaⁿ, v.a. (a and pagaⁿ). To share or give away for a purpose. Awapagaⁿ.

aṗa'gliḣpaya, v.n. To fall on one wounded. Apawagliḣpaya, Na uⁿgna nitakuye waⁿji nikiyela - eśa el eyatoⁿwe kilo.

aṗa'gluśte, v.n. To be lame. R. Bl. Note: the word comes from huśte.

aṗa'gluśteśte, v. red. (apagluśte). Bl.

aṗa'gmigma, v.a. (a and pagmigma). To roll over on. Awapagmigma.

aṗa'gmiyaⁿyaⁿ, v.a. (a and pagmiyaⁿyaⁿ). To make round, as a ball, on anything. Awapagmiyaⁿyaⁿ.

aṗa'gmoⁿ, v.a. (a and pagmoⁿ). To twist or roll on anything. Awapagmoⁿ.

aṗa'gna, v.a. To shell e.g. corn. Awapagna.

aṗa'ġo, v.a. (a and pago). To carve or engrave on anything. Awapago.

aṗa'ġuḱa, v.a. (a and paguka). To sprain by rubbing on anything. Awapaguka.

apa'ha, v.a. (a and paha). To raise on or over, as the hand to strike one. Awapaha. Tohaⁿl uⁿci nazuⁿspe kiⁿ he taku - caⁿśna tokel niwaciⁿpicaśni yelo, Whenever my grandmother raised that axe over anything, there is no use trying to live. Caⁿ amapaha yeśaⁿ icuki yelo, He lifted a stick (to hit me), but he took it down again. D.103. B.H.66.9. Bl.

aṗa'ha he, (?). When a man in a meeting moved about unnecessarily much, they would tell him: Owaⁿjila yaⁿka yo; oⁿze saⁿ - s'e śkiⁿnic'iyelo. Thus, to make one's self busy over. BT.

aṗa'halaḱa, n. A low hill. -- adv. Hill-like. Same as apahalake. Na miś lel - waⁿ el huⁿḣ najiⁿpi ca el wakinawajiⁿ. R.

aṗa'haya, adv. Convexly.

aṗa'hi, v.a. (a and pahi). To pick up or gather on anything. Awápahi.

aṗa'hiⁿṫa, v.a. (a and pahiⁿta). To crush on anything. Awapahiⁿta.

aṗa'homni, v.a. (a and pahomni). To push on or shove around on anything. Awapahomni.

aṗa'huⁿhuⁿza, v.a. (a and pahuⁿhuⁿza).

Shake on anything. Awápahuŋhuŋza.

apa'ḣaḳayayapi, (?).

aṗa'ḣatḳa, adj. Against the grain, rough. -- apáḣatkaya, adv. Roughly, against the grain.

aṗa'ḣlagaŋ, v.a. (a and paḣlagaŋ). Make large on anything. Awápaḣlagaŋ.

aṗa'ḣlaltoŋ, v.a. (apaḣlata and toŋ). Bind or embroider with ribbon. Apáḣlalwatoŋ.

aṗa'ḣlaṫa, v.a. Embroider. -- apáḣlate, n. Ribbon, ferret, binding. Cf. śina apaḣlate. R.

aṗa'ḣleca, v.a. (a and paḣleca). Tear or rend on anything, rend by shoving with the hand, as the coat on one's back. Awápaḣleca.

aṗa'ḣloka, v.a. (a and paḣloka). Pierce or make a hole in, on anything. Awápaḣloka.

aṗa'ḣpa, v.a. (a and paḣpa). Throw down on. Awápaḣpa. Uŋkápaḣpapi.

aṗa'ḣpu, v.a. (a and paḣpu). Pick off on. Awápaḣpu.

apa'ḣṫa, v.a. (a and paḣta). Bind or tie on anything. Apáwaḣta. Apáuŋḣtapi. - yuha, Tie a knot, as in one's handikerchief in order to remember something. -yuha wagli yelo. LO.

aṗa'jaja, v.a. (a and pajaja). Wash by rubbing on anything. Awápajaja.

apa'jeje, adv. At the edge, or brim, as of a high bank, edge of a bench. Bl. - najiŋ (naiŋś iyotaka) yelo. BT. Kośkalaka k'uŋ maya-apajeje śuŋkkaśka yuha yekapiŋḣca ḣpayahaŋ śke. D.225. -- apájejeya, adv. Loosely, not securely, likely to fall, as a lamp placed on the edge of a table.

aṗa'jipa, v.a. Pinch by pressure on, as sitting on. Awápajipa.

aṗa'jola, n. Just a little raise on the ground. B.H.189.14.

aṗa'juju, v.a. (a and pajuju). Rub out on anything. Awápajuju.

aṗa'ḳiŋṫa, v.a. (a and pakiŋta). Wipe or rub off on anything. Awápakiŋta.

aṗa'ḳiŋyaŋ, adv. Leaning over as an old man does in walking, or as a tree to one side. - mani. Same as atakiŋya. Bl.

aṗa'ḳiza, v.a. (a and pakiza). Make a noise by filing or rubbing on.

aṗa'ko, v.n. (of pako). Bend over, become crooked.

aṗa'kṗaŋ, v.a. (a and pakpaŋ). Crush or make fine on. Awápakpaŋ.

aṗa'kṗi, v.a. (a and pakpi). Crack on, as a louse on anything.

aṗa'ksa, v.a. (a and paksa). Break off on. Awápaksa.

aṗa'ksoŋlya, v.a. Have the last word in a quarrel, win out by talking. Same as kipá. Bl.

aṗa'ksoŋtḳiciyapi, n. Quarrelling. Same as ahóyekiciyapi.

aṗa'kśija, v.a. (a and pakśija). Bend or double up on anything. Awápakśija.

aṗa'ḳuḳa, v.a. (a and pakuka). Rub to pieces on anything. Awápakuka.

aṗa'k'eġa, v.a. Rub smooth, as a tool on something else, using the hand. Awápak'ega. Cf. pak'ega. Cl. gives apabaga the same meaning.

aṗa'k'eza, v.a. (a and pak'eza). Make smooth by scraping on. Awápak'eza.

aṗa'k'oza, v.a. (a and pak'oza). Rub and make smooth on. Awápak'oza.

aṗa'laṗa, v. Make smooth, plane. Awápalapa.

a'pamagle, adv. Down-hill, descending. -- ápamagleya, adv. Down-hill, in a descending manner. Paha waŋ el śuŋkakaŋya waŋ ápamagleya u.

aṗa'maŋ, v.a. (a and pamaŋ). File, rub or polish on. Awápamaŋ. -- apáme, v. Same as apamaŋ. -- n. A file or rasp.

aṗa'mni, v.a. (a and pamni). Divide out on. Awápamni.

apa'pa, n.(?) (red. of apa).

aṗa'poṗa, v.a. (a and papopa). Make pop or burst on anything. Awápapopa.

aṗa'psak̇a, v.a. (a and papsaka). Break in two, as a cord, on anything. Awápapsaka.

aṗa'pson, v.a. (a and papson). Spill on anything, as water. Awápapson. We apápsonpi s'e, They were all bloody.

aṗa'pśun, v.a. (a and papśun). Put out of joint on anything, as the arm. Awápapśun.

aṗa'pṫan, v.a. (a and paptan). Roll over on anything. Awápaptan. -- apápṫanpṫan, v. (red. of apaptan). Roll over and over on anything.

aṗa'pṫuja, v.a. (a and paptuja). Make crack or split on anything. Awápaptuja.

aṗa'ṗuza, v.a. (a and papuza). Wipe dry on anything. Awápapuza.

aṗa'si, v.a. (a and pasi). Follow after, follow on, in order to deliver. Awápasi.

aṗa'sisa, v.a. (a and pasisa). Stitch on, patch, stick in or through, as a pin. Awápasisa.

aṗa'sk̇iṫa, v. (?). Bl.

aṗa'sleca, v.a. (a and pasleca). Split by rubbing on anything. Awápasleca.

aṗa'slohan, v.a. (a and paslohan). Shove or push along on anything. Awápaslohan.

aṗa'snon, v.a. (a and pasnon). Roast on or over anything. Awápasnon.

aṗa'sṫo, v.a. (a and pasto). Make smooth or brush down on anything. Awápasto.

aṗa'suṫa, v.a. (a and pasuta). Make hard or stiff by kneading on anything. Awápasuta.

aṗa'śica, v.a. (a and paśica). Soil or injure by rubbing on anything. Awápaśica.

aṗa'śiṗa, v.a. (a and paśipa). Break off close on anything, put out of joint on. Awápaśipa.

aṗa'śli, v.a. Squeeze out on. -- v.n. Ooze out. -- apáśliya, adv. In an oozing manner.

aṗa'ślok̇a, v.a. (a and paśloka). Pull or shove off on, as one's coat. Awápaśloka.

aṗa'śluṫa, v.a. Smear on. B.H.221.10.

aṗa'śṗa, v.a. (a and paśpa). Break off a piece on anything. Awápaśpa.

aṗa'śṗu, v.a. (a and paśpu). Pull off on anything, pick off or rub off, as one sticking on another.

aṗa'śuja, v.a. (a and paśuja). Mash or crush on anything. Awápaśuja.

aṗa'śwog, v. (cont. of apaśwoka). - iyeya.

aṗa'śwok̇a, v.n. (a and paśwoka). Come up on or over, as water, overflow.

apa'ṫa, v.a. (a and pata). Cut up on, as meat on a block, operate on. Awápata. Amápatapi.

aṗa'ta, v.a. Cut out and sew on, as in patching torn pants.

aṗa'ṫan, v.a. (a and patan). Reserve or take care of for a purpose. Awápatan. Also, Push against. The same as apátitan.

aṗa'ṫeṗa, v.a. Wear off short, as a pencil on paper.

aṗa'ṫica, v.a. (a and patica). Scrape off from, as snow from the ground. Awápatica.

apa'ṫiṫan, v.a. (a and patitan). Push or brace against. Awápatitan.

a'ṗatonyela, adv. Singling out one thing from others, as one horse from a herd. - wakuwa. Cf. áecela. Bc.

aṗa'ṫuja, v.a. (a and patuja). Stoop down on or over. Awápatuja. The word seems to convey the same meaning as akpaspa. Figuratively, Stooping down with the view of being more able to carry something. - po, Stoop down and you can do it, or Don't give up. WE.

Toketu k'eyaś awapaspiŋ ktelo, or awapatujiŋ ktelo, I will do it even if it be hard. Bl.

ap̄a'ťuś, v. (cont. of apatuja). - yaŋka, He is in a stooping position. -- apátuśya, adv. Stoopingly.

ap̄a'tuza, v. Stand stooping down on. Same as apatuś inajiŋ. Bl.

ap̄a't'a, v.a. (a and pat'a). Kill by pressing on anything. Awápat'a. -- ap̄át'at'a, v.n. Become numb, as by freezing on.

ap̄a't'iŋza, v.a. (a and pat'iŋza). Press tight on, make stiff on, as in making the thumb mark. Awápat'iŋza. - mazaska.

ap̄a't'o, v.n. Obstruct, oppose, prevent progress. Amáp̄at'o. -- ap̄át'oya, v.a. Obstruct, stop, hinder. Apát'owaya. -- adv. In an obstructing manner.

ap̄a'uŋǩa, v.a. (a and pauŋka). Push down on anything. Awápauŋka.

ap̄a'waǧa, v.a. Pulverize with the hands by rubbing and scatter over. Awápawaga. -- apáwaȟwaga, v. (red. of apawaga).

ap̄a'weǧa, v.a. (a and pawega). Break partly, as a stick, on anything. Awápawega. -- ap̄áweȟ, v. (cont. of apawega). - iyeya.

ap̄a'wiŋǧa, v.n. Go around in circles on or over. -- ap̄áwiŋȟ, v. (cont. of apawiŋga). - iyaya.

ap̄a'wiŋja, v.a. (a and pawiŋja). Bend or press down, as grass on anything. Awápawiŋja. -- apáwiŋś, v. (cont. of apawiŋja). - iyeya.

ap̄a'wiŋťa, v.a. (a and pawiŋta). Rub on. Awápawiŋta. Uŋkcela heca waksiŋ na oŋ apawiŋta.

a'p̄aye, n. Seasoning, anything like meat or grease boiled with corn. Cf. wapaya. -- áp̄ayeya, v.a. Use a thing for seasoning. Ápayewaya.

ap̄a'za, v. Stick up in a row, as bushes to sleep under. Hi kiŋ taku - sni, He has not got teeth anymore, i.e. he is now old. Bl.

ap̄a'zo, v.a. (a and pazo). Show or point to on anything, point at. Awápazo. Nape amapazo, He pointed his finger at me. Ecaŋnoŋ śni ehaŋtaŋś nap'acipazo kte lo.

ap̄a'zuŋťa, v.a. (a and pazuŋta). Stitch or sew up in sewing on anything. Awápazuŋta.

ap̄e', n. A leaf of a tree, leaves, a blade of common grass. A fin of a fish (thus, hoape). It is said also to mean Wing; thus, Ȟupáhu, as of grass-hoppers. Cf. apeśa, etc.

ape', v.a. Wait for, hope for. Awápe. Uŋkápepi. U ape, He waited for one to come. Ye ape, He waited for one to go, or He desires one to go along. Lel paha waŋ yaŋka ca el ye awicape ca kici el iyahaŋpi.

ap̄e'haŋ, v. (a and pehaŋ). Fold on anything. Awápehaŋ.

ape'ǩiya, v.a. Cause to wait for. Apéwakiya.

ap̄e'la tap̄i'ślecala iye'ceca, n. Prairie spurge, euphorbia petaloides eaplon. The name refers to the shape of the leaves. Bl.

ap̄e' śa, n. A grass-hopper whose inner wings are red. Bl.

ap̄e' taca'ǧu, n. A grass-hopper whose inner wings are black. Bl.

ape'ya, adv. Waiting for, hoping for.

ap̄e'yohaŋ, n. The mane of a horse.

ap̄e' zi, n. A grass-hopper whose inner wings are yellow. Bl.

ap̄i'c'iya, Cf. apiic'iya. -- v. refl.

ap̄i'ic'iya, v. refl. (of apiya). This word is used in reference to a society selecting new officers.

a'p̄ija, v.n. Be wrinkled on anything. Ámapija.

ap̄i'ǩiya, v. Get ready one's own, fix, make well. Pelijaŋjaŋye kiŋ apikiya. B.H.247.9.

a'p̄iś, v. (cont. of apija). -- áp̄iśṗija, v. (red. of apija). Be wrinkled on. -- áṗiśya, adv. In a wrinkled manner.

aṗi'ya, v.a. Mend on, apply medicine on, revive. Form a society. Poke a fire. The probable meaning as applied to society is to elect new officers. Awápiya. Cf. apiic'iya, apeic'iya. Paha sapa ki^n le Waka^{n}ta^{n}ka toha^n maka ki^n piye śni heha^{n}ya^n waġluha kte lo. ST.

aṗo', v.n. (a and po). Swell on. Amápo.

aṗo'ġa^n, v.a. (a and poga^n). Blow on, as water, medicine, etc. Awápoga^n. El pejuta apoga^n. Awícapoga^n.

apo'ȟpoga^n, v. (red. of apoga^n). Blow on medicine etc. repeatedly or in different places. D.257.

aṗo'mnamna, v.a. (a and pomnamna). Shake or wag the head about. Apówamnamna.

aṗo^n'ṗo^{n}yela, adv. Like soft and rotten wood. Used in a transferred sense. Woyuha ki^{n}ha^n he toha^n ci^n ki^{n}ha^n he maka - yuha ni kte laka, as they say to a fellow who will not loan out things. Bl.

apo'ṗa, v.n. Burst on, break open. -- apópaha^n, adv. or part. Bursting open.

apo'ṗta^{n}ṗta^n, v.a. (a and popta^{n}pta^n). Shake the head about, dissent from. Apówapta^{n}pta^n. Cf. apomnamna.

apo'śi^n, v. Make faces at. Apówaśi^n. Apomayaśi^n so, toke? Bl. -- apóśi^{n}śi^n, v.a. Make faces at, wrinkle the nose. Apówaśi^{n}śi^n. D.37,41 note 5.

aṗo'ṫaha^n, part.(?). Torn up on, used up on etc., as a coat on somebody. Le amapotahelo. Bl.

apsi'ca, v.a. Jump over anything, jump on. Awápsica. Wakpala apsica. -- apsil, v. (cont. of apsica).

apśa', v.a. (a and pśa). Sneeze on anything. Awápśa

apśa'pśa, adj. Thick, close together, as grass etc. R. Bl. -- apśápśaya, adj. Thickly set, in a close state. Bl.

a'ṗta^n, v.n. Roll over, as one shot. Amápta^n. Enaś - keye. -- ápta^{n}pta^n, v.n. (a and pta^{n}pta^n). Roll about on. Amápta^{n}pta^n. -- aptá^{n}ya^n, v.n. Roll over on, fall over. Amápta^{n}ya^n. R. Bl. Ha^n, mat'a eyi^n na - ke. D.13. -- aptá^{n}yetu, v. The season of fall comes on, have reached fall. Wana u^{n}k'á-pta^{n}yetupelo, We now have lived to the fall-time. Bl.

apṫu'jaha^n, part. Cracked or split on.

a'ṗus, v. (cont. of apuza).

aṗu'sk̇ebya, adv. In a filtering manner. Use is doubtful. -- apúskeṗa, v.n. (a and puskepa). Filter out on. Also in doubtful use.

aṗu'sk̇ica, v.a. Press down tight upon. Awápuskica. -- apúskil, v. (cont. of apuskica.

aṗu'sṗa, v.a. (a and puspa). Stick on, make stick on, scab. Awápuspa. -- apúspaṗi, n. Mucilage, solder. -- apúspeya, adv. In a sticking manner.

aṗu'sṗuza, v. (red. of apuza).

aṗu'stag, v. Crouch. - aya, Sneak, crouching up to, as to game. Cf. asloha^n, Crawl up on one's belly. Bl. -- apústagya, adv. Crouching. Bl.

aṗu'sya, v.a. (a and pusya). Cause to dry on. Apúswaya. -- adv. In the manner of drying on.

aṗu'tag, v. (cont. of aputaka). -- apútagya, v.a. Cause to touch. -- adv. In the manner of touching.

aṗu'taka, v.a. (a and putaka). Touch, lay on, as the hand etc. Awáputaka. Na peslete el awicaputaka. Nape awicaputakapi. B.H.285.11.

aṗu't'i^{n}s, v. (cont. of aput'i^{n}za). -- apút'i^{n}st'i^{n}s, v. (cont. red.). -- apút'i^{n}st'i^{n}sya, adv. Firmly, pressed upon. -- apút'i^{n}st'i^{n}za, v. (red. of aput'i^{n}za). -- apút'i^{n}sya, adv. Firmly.

aṗu't'i^{n}za, v.a. Press down upon, as is done in making the thumb mark. Awáput'i^{n}za.

aṗu'za, v.n. (a and puza). Dry on, become dry on one, as clothes. Amápuza.

a'p'eyela, adj. Very shallow. Said of water, such that one can walk through it without getting wet feet. Mini kiŋhaŋ - yuŋkelo. Bl.

ap'o', v.n. (a and p'o). There is fog on a thing.

asa'ḱa, v.n. (a and saka). Become dry or hard upon. Amásaka. B.H.112.4.

asaŋ', v.n. (a and saŋ). Become whitish or grayish.

asaŋ'ṗi, n. (aze and haŋpi). Milk of any kind.

- gwugwú, n. Thick milk.
- ináze, n. Milk separator. Some there are who say - inázeya.
- iyátke, n. Cf. napóštaŋ. So called because the top was used as a nipple. EM.
- niní, n. Thick milk, cream.
- pejúta, n. Cf. same meaning under itopa sapa tapejuta. Cf. also śuŋgleśka.
- skumnázi, Cf. asuŋpskunazi.
- súťa, n. Hard milk, i.e. cheese.
- s'amna, n. Cheese.
- wasná, n. Cheese.
- wasną icáge, n. A churn.
- wiglí, n. Butter, cream. Also - wasna.

asa'ṗa, v.n. (a and sapa). Become black on.

asas'ya, adv. (of asaza). Slowly, gently, stilly. -- asásyela, adv. Gently, slowly.

asa'za, adj. Gently. The word is used mostly with the negative. - śni, Inconstant, unchaste.

ascu', v. Look at others, apparently wishing to marry them. Awáscu. Amáscu. He says, Amayascu hwo? She says, Ya, he takuwe aciscu kacaś? Same as as'iŋ, perhaps. Bl.

asiŋ'ȟte, adj. Very desirable. Mniśa asiŋȟte. Cf. as'iŋ.

aska', v.n. (a and ska). Become white on.

askaŋ', v.n. (a and skaŋ). Melt on or thaw on, disappear from, as snow.

a'skaŋ, n. (aze and kaŋ). Cords and veins of the breast.

askaŋ' s'e, adv. Melting away as it were. Hehe, wana oyate uŋkotapi k'oŋ - uŋkayapelo. Bl.

aske'ṗa, v.n. (a and skepa). Leak out on.

asla', v.n. (a and sla). Be greasy on anything. -- asláya, v.a. (a and slaya). Make greasy, to grease. Asláwaya. -- adv. Greasily.

asli'ṗa, v.a. (a and slipa). Lick off, lick from, as a dog does.

aslo'haŋ, v.n. (a and slohaŋ). Crawl along on anything. Awáslohaŋ. -- aslóhaŋkel, adv. Slowly. Ed.

aslo'lya, v.a. (a and slolya). Know about, be wise about, know all about. Aslólwaya.

asna'sna, v. (a and snasna). Ring or rattle on.

asni', v.n. Recover or get well from sickness, recover from anger. Amásni. Anísni. Uŋkásnipi.

asni'ḱiya, v.n. Take a long rest, take a vacation. -- asníya, v. Cure, make well. Cf. ozíkiya, Take a brief rest. -- akísniya, v.a. Heal, cause to get well. Note that Riggs gives asnikiya the active meaning. -- asníḱiyeḱiya, v.a. Cause to get well. Asníkiwakiya. B.H.188.17. -- asníḱiyeya, v.a. Make well. B.H.188.20. -- asníṗica, adj. Curable. -- asnísniḱiya, v.i. (of asnikiya). Take a rest, rest often. - uŋyaŋpi kte lo. - hoyeyi na akeśna ceyahe, Resting ever so often, he called out, and again he wept; or, He lay shouting for help again and again. D.28.

asni'ya, v.a. Cause something to get well, cure, as a wound. Asníwaya. Cf. akisniya, which refers to persons, while asniya seems to refer to the thing to be cured.

asni'yaḱel, adv. In the way of recovering.

asni'yepicaśni, adj. Incurable.

asoŋ', v.a. (a and soŋ). Plait or braid on anything. Awásoŋ.

aso'so, v.a. (a and soso). Cut into strings on any place. Awásoso.

asṗaŋ', v.n. (a and spaŋ). Become soft or melt on, as snow on anything.

asṗa'ya, v.n. (a and spaya). Become wet on, suck in water, as in drowning. Amáspaya.

aspa'yeic'iya, v. refl. (of aspaya). - s'e uŋkupi, We are coming slowly, as though we were tired and pushing. Bl.

a'sṗeya, v.a. Cause to sink down, as an anchor in water. Bury up. Weigh. Áspewaya.

a'sṫaŋ, v.n. Be purple on, become purple.

a'sṫoya, v.a. (a and stoya). Smooth down upon.

asuŋ'kṫa, n. The kidney. - wayazaŋ, I have kidney trouble.

asuŋp'sk̇umnazi, n. Sour cream or sour milk. See the asaŋpi entry.

asu'ṫa, v.n. (a and suta). Become hard or strong upon. Amásuta.

asu'toŋ, v.n. (a and sutoŋ). Become ripe on or upon, as seed. R. Bl.

as'iŋ', v.n. Covet, secretly long for, hang about a place, look at something or somebody eating, wishing to get something too. Awás'iŋ. They say teasingly, Amáyas'iŋ he? Bl. -- as'íŋs'iŋ, v. (red. of as'iŋ). -- as'íŋyaŋ, adv. Desiringly. - ayuta. B.H.149.16.

aśa', v.n. Become reddish.

aśab', v. (cont. of aśapa).

aśab'ya, v.a. Defile, make dirty, tarnish, profane. Aśábwaya. -- adv. Dirtily, in a defiled manner.

aśa'k̇agle, adv. Holding loosely. - yuha, Hold something loosely so it might not drop. LH. -- aśák̇agleya, adv. Loosely(?). - okuwa, which is said when a man does something very difficult, hence with great pains, as when one fixes a piece of machinery in a car. J. -- aśák̇agleyela, adv. In a manner touching here and there. - peji to yajuŋpelo, They cropped the first green blades of grass here and there. Bl. - okihi, or - ecoŋ, He can or does with difficulty. Same as íśpaha yuzapi s'e. WE.

aśa'ṗa, v.n. (a and śapa). Become black or dirty on anything. Amáśapa.

aśe'ca, v.n. (a and śeca). Become dry or seasoned on anything.

aśi'ca, v.n. (a and śica). Become bad or unpleasant on or for.

aśi'cahowaya, v.a. Cry out on account of. Awáśicahowaya.

aśi'caya, adv. Badly, unpleasantly. -- aśicayak̇el, adv. Unpleasantly.

aśi'ḣtiŋ, v.n. Be poorly on account of, be defective.

aśil'woyak̇a, v. Speak evil of. LHB. B.H.164.6.

aśil'ya, adv. Badly, sadly. -- aśílyak̇el, adv. Badly, unpleasantly

aśiŋ'ḣte, adj. Worthless, no good, of poor quality, less good. B.H.84.13, 178.19. Woyuha - . Mniśa - . -- aśíŋḣteyak̇el, adv. (of aśiŋḣte). B.

aśka'hayela, adv. For a little while. Same as aśkatuyela. Also optelyela. Bl.

a'śk̇aŋs'e, adv. Later than expected, rather late. The word is opposed to taniś, Sooner than expected. - hi. Áśkaŋśni s'e, In no time at all, it seemed. D.27. Cf. taniś: taŋniś.

aśk̇aŋ'śk̇aŋ, v.n. (a and śkaŋśkaŋ). Move about on anything. -- aśkáŋśkaŋyaŋ, adv. Moving about on.

a'śkaŋyela, adv. Soon, quickly. - uŋkihuŋnipi, or uŋciupelo. - wahiyelo, I came in a hurry to leave soon again. The contrary is: Kat'eye taŋkáḣci wahiyelo, He came to stay for good. BT. Buechel questions the meaning of the word given by some to be, For a little while, not considering, in a hurry.

aśk̇a'ṫa, v.n. (a and śkata). Play on any place. Awáśkata.

aśk̇a'ṫula, adv. Lately, not long since. Same as lecala. Ba. -- aśkátuya, adv. Not long ago. -- aśkátuyela, adv. Lately, but a short time ago, near. - hwo? Is it near? Bl. Same as kaŋyela. Taku - hośi makaglipi. LH pronounces the word áśkatuyela.

aśk̇e', n. Tuft or bunch of hair which some Dakotas wear on the side of their heads. R. Lakota aśke gluwipi. RF. Gluwi means to wrap up one's own, as with a string.

aśk̇e'haŋ, v.n. (a and śkehaŋ). Do a thing carelessly, half and half. Amáyaśkehelo, You don't seem to care for (what I say). Bl.

aśkiŋ'yaŋk̇apila, adv. In a short time, from a short distance. Same as ecana. Ho wana letaŋ okaŋyela ca - onaślog uŋkihuŋnipi ktelo. Bl. - waglicu welo, I came back in a hurry from a little distance.

aśki'yaŋkel, adv. A short distance. B.

aśk̇i'yuwi, n. A strip of leather, hide or cloth wrapped around a bunch of hair, such as old Indian men used to wear on both sides of the head. BD. Aśke yuwipi, The bunch of hair tied up. R.

aśk̇ob'ya, adv. Crookedly, in an arched manner. -- aśk̇óṗa, v.n. (a and śkopa). Be crooked on or arched.

aśla', v.n. (a and śla). Be bare on anything. Use is doubtful. -- áślalyeta, adv. Bare, openly. Bc. -- áślaślayela, adv. (?). -- aśláya, adv. Openly, plainly.

a'ślayela, adv. Openly, plainly. - ociciyakiŋ kte, I will tell you plainly. - slolyayiŋ kte. - kajuja, Pay cash. Wi - hiyayelo. Bl. Ecaśni s'e caŋku kiŋ - yaŋkelo, implying there is no snow on the ground. Bl. B.H.229.3.

aślo', v.n. (a and ślo). Fuse or melt, as metals, grease etc., on anything. Slang: to be drunk. -- aślóya, v.a. Cause to melt on, solder. Aślówaya.

aślul'ya, v.a. (a and ślulya). Make slip on. -- aślúśluṫa, v.n. (a and śluśluta). Be slippery on.

aśma', v.n. (a and śma). Be deep, as water, on any place. Aśmélaka, Somewhat deeper. D.223.

aśme'ya, adv. Deeply, in a deep manner.

aśni'ja, v.n. (a and śnija). Be wilted or withered on or for.

aśni'yaŋyaŋ, v.n. Crawl or creep on, as a bug on one. -- adv. Creeping along, in a crawling manner.

aśo'k̇a, v.n. (a and śoka). Be thick, as a board, on anything.

aśo'ṫa, v.n. (a and śota). Be smoky on or at.

aśṗa'haŋ, part. Worn off, as the nap of cloth, threadbare, worn out. Bl.

aśṗaŋ', v.n. (a and śpaŋ), Be cooked or burnt on or by anything.

aśṫul'ya, v.a. Cause to thaw on. Aśtúlwaya.

aśṫu'ṫa, v.n. (a and śtuta). Thaw on anything.

aśuŋ'kt'eya, v.a. Kill one for misdemeanor. Tuwa naḣmala wanasa ca na lila akicita ktepi, aśuŋkt'eyapi naiŋś ecoŋpi śni ca na ti ayupotapi.

aśuŋ'śiyak̇el, adv. But little at all. Kitaŋyeḣci - waŋblakelo, I could not see it but with difficulty and little at all, as when wearing a poor set of glasses etc. Bl. -- aśúŋśiye, n. A little bit only. - lake waŋblakelo, I recognized but little. Bl. -- aśúŋśiyece, n. Only a little. Kitaŋyela - laka, He sees but little. Bl.

aśu'ta, v.a. (a and śuta). Miss, fail of. Aśúwata.

aśwu', v.n. (a and śwu). Drop, as water on anything. -- aśwúya, v.a. Cause to drop on, as water. Aśwúwaya.

aś'a', v.a. Shout at. Awáś'a. Akíś'a, Shout, cheer. Awákiś'a. Waŋna pehaŋ kiŋ hinapiŋ na akiś'aś'a. Na kici tiwegna wahiya kiŋ ayaś'api kta. Oyate kiŋ Ikto aś'api. D.112.

aś'ag', cont. of aś'aka.

aś'ag'ya, adv. In a coated manner. - yaƞka.

aś'a'k̇a, v.n. To be coated or furred, as the tongue in sickness; to be dirty, as a gun that needs cleaning out.
aś'a'kece, v. (?). Awaś'akece.

a'ṫa, prep. suff. To, at, on. Suffixed to nouns ending in "a","ata" becomes "ta" alone. In other cases, "y" is introduced for euphony; thus, tiyata. -- adv. Same as átaya.

atab'ya, v.n. To go one after another, to follow in Indian file. Also, atabaya. -- adv. Single filed manner. - atábuƞyaƞpi.

a'ṫabyela, adj. Thin, as a slice of bread.

ata'ḣnak̇ipca, v. To swallow one's saliva, as in desiring something. Atáḣnawakipce lo. Bl. Note: the word is used when a person desires very much to eat an appetizing thing and begins already to swallow because of a watering mouth. Bl. Cf. tage, napca.

aṫa'ja, v.n. (a-taja). To be rough or in waves on one. Amátaja. Amátajelo.

a'taja, v.n. To be filled to the brim. Ámatajelo, as is said when a man went the limit in eating. Bl.

ata'k̇iƞyaƞ, adv. Leaning on, not perpendicular, slanting. Wi - yaƞka, The sun is declining, as a tree leaning to one side. Bl. Cf. apakiƞyaƞ.

ata'kṗe, v.a. (a-takpe). To make an attack on. Atawakpe.

aṫa'k̇uniśni, v.n. To come to naught, become enfeebled, be ruined, become extinct; to wither away. Amatakuniśni. - amayaƞ. D.259,262. LHB.
aṫa'k̇uniśniṗica, adj. Perishable.
aṫa'k̇uniśniyaƞ, v.a. To bring to naught, to annul. Atakuniśniwaye.

aṫaƞ', v.a. To care for, have respect for. Awátaƞ. Ataƞpiśni,They pay no attention . B.H.241.2.

a'taƞiƞ, v.n. To appear on, be manifest. Ámataƞiƞ. Na waƞna - ayapi. Ataƞiƞśni aya na - iyaya. Hecel - śni iyaya.
a'taƞiƞiƞ, v. red. of ataƞiƞ.
a'ṫaƞiƞśniyaƞ, adv. In a lost manner. Ámataƞiƞśniyaƞ. Yuƞkaƞ iwaƞkam taku - haƞ ca waƞblaka. - kiƞyaƞ iyaya.

a'ṫaƞiƞya, v.a. To make appear, manifest. Ataƞiƞwaya. Le lehaƞl ataƞiƞwayiƞ kte śni. Ituƞka saƞ mato wakaƞ ataƞiƞyiƞ kta. Na kośkalaka nuƞp wakaƞ ataƞiƞyapi.

a'ṫaƞiƞyaƞ, adv. Appearing, manifestly, visibly. Si kiƞ ecela - najiƞpi.

ataƞ'k̇a, v.n. (a-taƞka). To be large on, in addition to, to be large.
ataƞ'kala, v.n. dim. of ataƞka.
ataƞ'kaya, adv. Widely, extensively.

ataƞ'oƞm, cont. of ataƞoƞpa. - iyaya, To have gone past perpendicular.
ataƞ'oƞmya, adv. In a leaning manner.

ataƞ'oƞṗa, v.n. To lean, as the sun does in the afternoon; to lean over, as a rider on a horse.

aṫaƞ' s'e, adv. Silently, stilly. - yuƞka.
aṫaƞ's'ela yaƞká, v. To be motionless, to take a long rest. Bl.
aṫaƞ's'iƞ, adv. At a standstill. - uƞ. - gluha, To keep things even with if one does not need or use them. Wi kiƞ - haƞ. Wicaḣpi - haƞ. B.H.25.24;73.8; 105.43;169.19. Note: ataƞs'e is the more correct form.
aṫaƞ's'iƞs'iƞ, adv. red. of ataƞs'iƞ. Same as owaƞjila yaƞka. - yaƞkapi, They were idle. B.H.52.4.

ataƞ'toƞśni, v. To have nothing of one's own, be not able to save. WE.

ataƞ'toƞyaƞ, v.a. To make one save so that he accumulates property. WE. Cf. taƞtoƞyaƞ.

ata'pa, v.n. (a-tapa). To follow after on anything. Awatapa.

aṫa'sak̇a, v.n. (a-tasaka). To become stiff or hard on, as clothes. Amatasaka.

ata'śośa, v.a. To spit on anything. Atawaśośe. Atacisośa.

ata'śośapina nabla'ǧa, n. Large-flowered yellow flax. Linum rigidum of the flax family. Same as canȟlogaŋ nablaga. The word refers to the capsule. #179. Bl.

aṫa'śṫaja, v.n. (red. of ataja). Be rough or in waves on one, as water.

ata'tapeśni, (?). - kuwa, He gave one no rest, i.e. he bothered one unceasingly. Bl.

ata'ṫeyaŋpa, v.a. (a and tateyaŋpa). Blow upon anything, as the wind does. The wind here seems to be a gentle wind. R. Bl.

a'taṫoheya, adv. On the windward side.

a'ṫaya, adv. Wholly, altogether, all, everything, universally. Alone, separately. -- áṫayaḱel, adv. All of it. Oyate kiŋ - ahiŋniciye. B.H.295.11. -- átayaḱinil, adv. Pretty near all. Na oyate kiŋ - au na ecel caŋ el aglagla inajiŋpi. -- átayaś, adv. The emphatic form of ataya. B.H.305.19.

a'ṫaya, v.a. To meet, as a person. Átawaya. Iktomi kákena ya na iya waŋ - .

aṫa'ya, v.n. Go directly, straight towards something. Atáwaya.

a'ṫayela, adv. Directly, without a medium, personally. Yuŋkaŋ śuŋka najiŋpi - uŋkihuŋnipi. - agliyagla. Toka waŋ koyakipapi ca atayela wakte yelo. Niyatayela, Right opposite you. - el ya ke, She walked straight to the camp. D.269. B.H.238.3.

a'ṫayeya, v. Meet. Átayewaya. Na ob atayekiciyapi, Thus they met together. B.H.121.4, 156.1, 155.23.

aṫe', n. Father, my father. Niyate, Your father. -- atéku, n. His father. Bl. claims that this form is used, but atkuku more so. Cf. inaku. -- atéya, v.a. Have for a father, sustain the relation of a child to a man. Atéwaya. Among the Dakotas one's father's brothers are also called até.

aṫe'btepaheyakel, adv. Worn out like, tattered, threadbare, worn short. Śina waŋ - iŋ k'oŋ, as is said when a person used to wear a worn out blanket. Cf. tepa. Bl.

aṫeb'ya, v.a. (a and tebya). Cut up or devour on. Atébwaya.

aṫe'ca, v.n. (a and teca). Become new on. - lake ciŋ, The younger people. B.H.283.6.

aṫe'ṗahaŋ, part. Worn off short on.

aṫi', v.n. (a and ti). Build a house or put up a tent at or on, pitch a tent or encamp at for a certain purpose.

aṫi'gnagya, adv. Nearby. R. Implied is the having of a man staying nearby. Bl.

aṫi'ole, v.a. Sponge on others. Atíowale. B.H.137.3.

atḱu'ḱu, n. His or her father.

ato', v.n. (a and to). Become blue or green on, to tattoo. Cf. akito. Amáto.

ato'kaŋ, adv. In or to another place.

ato'ḱeca, v.n. Become different.

aṫo'kśu, v.a. (a and tokśu). Carry or draw anything on, pile up at or on, as a horse's pack. Atówakśu.

aṫoŋ'waŋ, v.a. (a and toŋwaŋ). Look to or at. Awátoŋwaŋ. Uŋkátoŋwaŋpi. Ate, nata catkayataŋ wiŋawizi waŋ imakoyakiŋ kte lo, ca le - wo. Tuweȟci napata yuziŋ kta - . B.H.295.3. -- atóŋwaŋyaŋ, v.a. Cause to look at. Make a village at or on a place, probably because by making a village people are caused to look to or at a place. Atóŋwaŋuŋyaŋpi.

at'a'ȟya, v.a. Make dry, roughen, as a floor once wet and becoming rough through drying. Hence, Make not slippery. Cf. śluślute śni. Bl.

at'a't'aka, (?). Uŋgnahaȟci amáyat'at'ake s'elececa, implying to handle one lovingly. Bl.

at'e'ca, adj. Luke-warm, as water.
at'iŋs', Cf. at'iŋza.
at'iŋs'ya, adv. Tightly, in a squeezing manner. -- át'iŋsyaḱel, adv. (?). In a forced manner. - wahi, I came according to my promise, i.e. on definite terms. SLB.

at'in'za, v.n. (a and t'inza). Press on, be tight on. Amát'inza. -- at'ins, v. (cont. of at'inza).

at'o'za, v.n. (a and t'oza). Become blunt or dull on.

at'ung'ya, v.a. Suspect one, have an inkling of. At'úngwaya. Cf. t'ungya. Same as kenunyan. Tanakotanhan takunl at'ungyaye heci omakiyaka yo. BT.

au', v.a. Carry or bring anything towards. -- v. coll. pl. They come. R. Nape au yo, Shake hands. The word is also used in a figurative sense. Lakota ehanna tokel icagapi kin wicaȟcala ehanna owecinhan oyak aupi. Hecel ogna oyate au. Lena nitunkaśila yuha oyate kaȟ aupelo. Kośkalaka wan wonicupi psa ca hetan yin kta keye lo, eya au. Hecel wicowoyake aupi na ecel lehanl slolwaya. Yunkan anpetu wan el wicaśa wan eyapaha au na lecel eya. Yunkan oyate kin wicakico au. Wowapi kin pazo au. Le wicoȟ'an kin oyate kin econ aupi.

au', v.n. (a and u ?). Come out on, ooze out or run, as sap. Mini au.

aun', v.a. (a and un). Put wood on the fire. Awáun. -- v.n. Be on. Awáun. -- aúnyan, v.n. Be on or over. - iyaya, Pass over a hill, a fence etc. - kute, Shoot on the wing, or as the bird flies over. -- aúnyeya, v.a. Put on. Aúnyewaya. Hinyete - , Put on the shoulder, as a patch etc. or a sack. To wear as something about the shoulders. Same as awinyeya (a and in). -- v.n. (a and un). Approach from the windward side, i.e. come with the wind. Aúnyewaya. B.H.62.15, 265.3.

aun'yeyapi, n. Sand-berries, ground-berries, which if approached from the windward side are said to be bitter. But if from the opposite direction, sweet. -- aúnyeyapi hu, n. Western sand cherry, ground-cherry. Cf. taȟpiyogin, R. Prunus bessayi bailey, rose family; or icimagnuni. BT. #14.

awa', v.n. (a and wa). Snow upon, be snow on anything. Amáwa. Cf. Awáhinhe.

awa'bla, v.a. (a and wabla). Cut in strips on. Awáwabla.

awa'blaya, v.a. (a and wablaya). Smooth over by cutting with a knife, shave off lumps on. Awáwablaya.

awa'blaza, v.a. Cut or rip open. Awáwablaza.

awa'bleca, v.a. Break by cutting on anything, as something brittle. Cut up in pieces on. Awáwableca. -- awáblel, v. (cont. of awableca). - iyeya.

awa'ci, v.a. (a and waci). Dance on anything, or in honor of. Awáwaci. Topa can awacicipi kte.

awa'cin, v.a. (a and wacin). Think on or of, meditate upon, trust, believe in. Awácanmi. Awácanni. Awáuncinpi of unkáwacinpi. -- awácinȟel, adv. Thinking upon. -- awácinpi, n. A thinking upon, trusting in, faith.

awa'cinya, v.a. Influence someone. Awácinwaya. -- awácinyan, v. Influence another's thinking. Awácinwaye. -- adv. Thinking upon. -- awácinyaȟel, adv. In the manner of thinking on.

awa'gla, v.a. Shave off with a knife, as the fat from the guts. Awáwagla. -- awáglagla, v. (red. of awagla).

awa'hinhe, v.n. (awa and hinhe). Snow upon. -- awáhinheya, v.a. Cause to snow upon. Awáhinhewaya. -- adv.(?). Snowing upon.

awa'ȟpani, v.n. Be poor on account of. -- awáȟpanica, v.n. (a and waȟpanica). Become poor on account of or by means of. Amáwaȟpanica. -- awáȟpaniya, v.a. Make poor by means of. Awáȟpaniwaya. -- awáȟpaniyan, adv. Poorly off.

awa'ȟtani, v.a. Transgress a usage or law, sin on, fail to perform a vow. Awáwaȟtani. Awámic'iȟtani.

awa'ȟwayela, adv. Mildly, gently.

awa'ic'icin, v. (refl. of awacin). Think much of one's own self, as sickly people are liable to do. Awámic'icin. - s'e mankahelo. Bl.

awa'ic'iȟtani, v. (refl. of awaȟtani). Be guilty of a sin. Awáȟtani, Transgress a law, thereby one becomes guilty and hurts himself, which is awaic'iȟtani. Woaȟtani akipa, He meets a punishment. Cf. waic'iȟtani. R.

awa'jal, v. (cont. of awajata). - ośtaⁿ Sit astride, be placed on astride.

awa'jaťa, v.a. (a and wajata). Make a split on. Awáwajata.

awa'ǩa, v.a. (a and waka). Cut or split the feather from a quill. Awáwaka.

awa'kaⁿ, v.n. (a and wakaⁿ). Be sacred or incomprehensible on some account. -- awákaⁿǩa, v.n. Same as awakaⁿ. -- n. A supernatural being. -- awákaⁿyaⁿ, adv. Mysteriously, supernaturally.

awa'ǩaseya, part. (?). Withstanding the snow. - uⁿglapi ktelo, We shall have the snowstorm against us on our way home. Bl.

awa'ǩeya, v.a. Make a booth, spread over, as tree branches, make a shade, make an awning over. Awákewaya. -- awákeyap̌i, n. A booth.

awa'keza, v.a. (a and wakeza). Cut off smoothly as a feather for an arrow. Awáwakeza.

awa'ǩiciⁿ, v.a. pos. (of awaciⁿ).

awa'kpaⁿ, v.a. (a and wakpaⁿ). Cut fine on, make fine on, as in cutting tobacco. Awáwakpaⁿ.

awa'ksa, v.a. (a and waksa). Cut off, as a stick, on anything, with a knife. Awáwaksa. -- awáksaksa, v. (red. of awaksa).

awa'kśija, v.a. (a and wakśija). Shut upon, as a pocket-knife. Awáwakśija. -- awákśiś, v. (cont. of awakśija). - iyeya, It doubled or shut up, as a knife on anything.

awa'k'eza, v.a. Cut off smooth. Awáwak'eza. Also to split the feather end of a quill, cut off on, as the ribs of an animal.

awa'manoⁿ, v. (of amanoⁿ). Steal. Awámawicanoⁿpi, He stole from them. B.H. 80.20.

awa'mna, v.a. (a and wamna). Rip on, as with a knife. Awáwamna.

awa'nap̌iśkaⁿyaⁿ, v.a. Play with, as babies do with dolls etc. Awánamayapiśkaⁿyelo. Bl.

awa'nica, v.n. (a and wanica). Be or become nothing for some reason. Awámanica.

awa'nic'iglaka, v.a. Care for one's health. SLB. Perhaps the same as awaniglaka. B.H.194.18.

awa'nil, v. (cont. of awanica). The word is used adverbially. In a destroying manner. - iyeya.

awa'niyeťu, v.imper. (a and waniyetu). Come winter on one. Amáwaniyetu. Śuⁿkawakaⁿ kiⁿ tawocola awaniyetupi oa ota t'api. BT. Wana uⁿk'áwaniyetupelo. Bl.

awaⁿ'glag, v. (cont. of awaⁿglaka).

awaⁿ'glaǩa, v. pos. (of awaⁿyaⁿka). Oversee or take care of one's own. Awáⁿwaglaka.

awaⁿ'ic'iglaka, v. Beware, be on one's guard, look to one's self.

awaⁿ'ǩal, adv. Above, overhead.

awaⁿ'ǩiciyaⁿǩa, v. (of awaⁿyaⁿka). Watch or oversee for one. Awáⁿweciyaⁿka.

awaⁿ'yaⁿg, v. (cont. of awaⁿyaⁿka). - wauⁿ. - kuwa, He followed one with his eyes, watched closely, kept watch on. WE.

awaⁿ'yaⁿgǩiya, v.a. Cause to attend to or oversee. Awáⁿyaⁿgwakiya.

awaⁿ'yaⁿǩa, v.a. (a and waⁿyaⁿka). Look upon, see to, have the oversight of. Awáⁿblaka.

awa'p̌ol, v. (cont. of awapota).

awa'p̌oťa, v.a. (a and wapota). Cut in pieces on, destroy on anything by cutting with a knife. Awáwapota.

awa'psaǩa, v.a. (a and wapsaka). Cut off on, as a cord or string, with a knife. Awáwapsaka.

awa'psuⁿ, v.a. (a and wapsuⁿ). Unjoint with a knife on anything. Awáwapsuⁿ.

awa'p̌ťa, v.a. (a and wapta). Cut off from, as a piece, cut on, as clothes on a board. Awáwapta. -- awápte, n.

A cutting off from. Caŋ awapte, A cutting board.

awa'sḱica, v.a. (a and waskica). Press out on, as with a knife by cutting. Awáwaskica.

awa'sḱiṫa, v.a. (a and waskita). Press upon with a knife. Awáwaskita.

awa'sḱu, v.a. (a and wasku). Pare on, as an apple. Awáwasku.

awa'sleca, v.a. (a and wasleca). Split on. Awáwasleca.

awa'smiŋ, v.a. (a and wasmiŋ). Cut or shave off close, as meat from bones. Awáwasmiŋ.

awa'suic'iya, v. Make one's self do something, make a vow, take a pledge to be good, or refrain from certain things. Awásumic'iya. Tuwa teḣilapi ca na t'a ca nagi yuhapi na lila yuwakaŋpi na awasuic'iyapi.

awa'śaḱa, adj. Cheap, easily purchased. -- awáśakala, adj. Cheap, as goods.

awa'śiṗa, v.a. (a and waśipa). Cut off or prune upon anything. Awáwaśipa.

awa'śḱica, v.a. (a and waśkica). Press out upon, as by cutting with a knife. Awáwaśkica.

awa'śḱu, v.a. (a and waśku). Cut off upon, as corn from a cob. Awáwaśku.

awa'śla, v.a. (a and waśla). Make bare on, shave off with a knife on, cut as grass, in addition to what is already done. Awáwaśla.

awa'śloḱa, v.a. (a and waśloka). Cut a hole in or on anything. Awáwaśloka.

awa'śma, adj. Deep, as of piles or hills of snow, leaves, etc. Bl.

awa'śo, or awa'so, v.a. (a and waso). Cut off a string from, cut a string on anything. Awáwaso. -- awáśośo, or awásoso, v. (red. of awaso). Cut strings from, cut into strings on. Awáwasoso.

awa'śṗa, v.a. (a and waśpa). Cut off on, as a piece of a stick. Awáwaśpa.

awa'śṗaŋyaŋ, v.a. Make a feast on account of a person or event. He awaśpaŋyaŋpi kte. GA.

awa'śṗu, v.a. (a and waśpu). Cut up on, cut in pieces. Awáwaśpu. -- awáśpuśpu, v. (red. of awaśpu).

awa'śṫe, v.n. (a and waśte). Be good on or for, become better than. Amáwaśte. -- awáśteḱa, v.n. Be good for, befit. -- awáśteya, adv. Well, better than. -- awáśteyaḱel, adv. Better, in a better manner. - amayaŋ, I am becoming better.

awa'taŋiŋśni, adj. Dark, obscure, as in the dusk of the evening. - áyelo, It is getting dark. BT.

awa't'eca, adv. Cf. wawat'eca.

awa'wapṫe, n. A cutting board.

awa'yaṗiḱa, v.n. (a and wayapika). Be eloquent about anything, be more eloquent than someone. Awáblapika.

awa'yuṗiḱa, v.n. (a and wayupika). Be skillful about, be more skillful than. Awáblupika. -- awáyuṗiya, adv. Skillfully, well.

awe', v.n. (a and we). Become lean, as cattle do in the spring of the year. Bleed on.

awe'ṫu, v.n. (a and wetu). Become spring on one. Amáwetu. Toḱécala awematu welo. BT. Wana uŋkawetupelo, We have reached springtime. Bl.

awi'caka, v.n. Be true on, tell the truth. Awícawaka. -- áwicaḱehaŋ, adv. Truly of a truth. -- áwicakeya, adv. Truly. Waŋna (nazoŋspe) iwacu na waŋna - awapa. This word is used perhaps in regard to one person. -- áwicaḱeyahaŋ, adv. Of a truth. -- áwicaḱeyakel, adv. In earnest. B.H.80.23.

awi'caś'a, n. (of a aś'a). Shouting.

awi'cayasṗuya, n. The itch, itching.

awiŋ'yeya, v.a. Same as auŋyeya, (a and iŋ). B.H.265.3. -- adv. (a and wiŋyeya). Ready for anything. Cf. Wiŋyeya. Hiŋyetawiŋyeya yo, Carry it on the shoulder, as a gun. -- awiŋyeyapi hu, Cf. auⁿyeyapi.

awi'yakṗa, v.n. (a and wiyakpa). Glisten on anything.

awi'yaya, v. imp. Not to return before night, stay away over-night. The word corresponds perhaps to ayaⁿpa. BT.

awi'yukcaⁿ, v. Form an opinion on. Awíblukcaⁿ. Sicaya awimayalukcaⁿpi. B.H. 161.3.

awo'blaza, v.a. Tear open by shooting on anything. Awówablaza.

awo'bleca, v.a. Break in pieces by shooting or punching it. Awówableca. -- awóblel, v. (cont. of awobleca). - iyeya.

awo'blu, v.n. Fill up quickly, as a good well does. Awómablu. Riggs gives To blow up on, as by the wind, bubble up on as water. The word is used when a multitude gathers around one. Awómablu. -- awóblublu, v. (red. of awoblu).

awo'caⁿgle, v. Whirl and tumble, ricochet, as an arrow. - iyeya. The word is used of an arrow when it strikes its goal and then whirls around summersault-like. Bl.

awo'glaḱa, Cf. aoglaka. Awóciglake. Awómayaglake śni.

awo'ḣleca, v.a. (a and woḣleca). Split by shooting or punching on anything. Awówaḣleca.

awo'ḣloḱa, v.a. (a and woḣloka). Punch a hole in one thing on something else. Awówaḣloka.

awo'ḣṗa, v.a. (a and woḣpa). Make fall on by shooting. Awówaḣpa.

awo'juju, v.a. (a and wojuju). Break all up on, destroy upon. Awówajuju.

awo'ḱeya, n. A sort of roof. B.H.91.18. Tiyobleca kiⁿ wazi - tipelo, Have fine trees set up around the tent as a shelter. LB. -- awókeya sápa, n. A buggy.

awo'kṗaⁿ, v.a. (a and wokpaⁿ). Pound fine on. Awówakpaⁿ.

awo'ksa, v.a. Break off by shooting on or by punching on. Awówaksa.

awo'ḱuḱa, v.a. (a and wokuka). Shoot or punch to pieces on. Awówakuka.

awo'k'eġa, v.a. (a and wok'ega). Miss fire on, as in trying to shoot, snap a gun on. Awówak'ega. Same as awoto and awoskapa. -- awók'eḣ, v. (cont. of awok'ega). - iyeya. Cf. also awosna.

awo'paⁿ, v.a. (a wopaⁿ). Pound fine on, as corn. Awówapaⁿ.

awo'ṗoṫa, v.a. (a and wopota). Shoot to pieces on anything. Awówapota.

awo'psaḱa, v.a. (a and wopsaka). Break off, as a cord, by shooting on. **Awó**wapsaka.

awo'pṫa, v.a. (a and wopta). Punch off a piece, by striking on anything with the end of a stick. Awówapta.

awo'pṫuja, v.a. (a and woptuja). Split or crack, as an arrow by shooting against anything, or as a stick in punching. Awówaptuja. -- awópṫuś, v. (cont. of awoptuja).

awo'sḱaṗa, v.a. Miss fire on because the hammer does not strike the cap right. Awówaskapa. Same as awoto and awok'ega. Also cf. awosna.

awo'sleca, v.a. (a and wosleca). Split by shooting upon. Awówasleca.

awo'sna, v.a. (a and wosna). Miss fire on, as of a gun. Awówasna. Awówaśna.

awo'soksolya, adv. (?). - uⁿglihuⁿnipelo, Covered with snow. **Bl.**

awo'soṫa, v.a. (a and wosota). Use all up by shooting upon. Awówasota.

awo'śla, v.a. (a and wośla). Make bare on by punching. Awówaśla.

awo'śleca, v.a. (a and wośleca). Split off on, as a piece by shooting or punching. Awówaśleca.

awo'śloḱa, v.a. (a and wośloka). Shoot off on, empty the contents of a gun on anything by shooting at it. Awówaśloka.

awo'śluślul, (?). Awośluślul iyayapi, as is said when soft, heavy snow sticks to a person and gets between the clothes. M.

awo'śpa, v.a. (a and wośpa). Shoot a piece off on. Awówaśpa.

awo'śpu, v.a. (a and wośpu). Knock off upon, as anything stuck on, by punching or shooting. Awówaśpu.

awo'ștaka, v.n. Rebound, as an arrow on something hard not going in. Bl.

awo'takuniśni, v.a. (a and wotakuniśni). Destroy by shooting or punching on anything. Awówatakuniśni.

awo'to, v.a. Miss fire on. Awówato. Miss, because the gun hammer does not strike the cap right. Bl. Same as awoskapa and awok'ega.

awo't'a, v.a. (a and wot'a). Kill on by punching. Awówat'a.

awo'waśi econ', v. Work on something. Awowaśi ecamon. B.H.115.7,183.7,209.7.

awo'wega, v.a. (a and wowega). Break on, as by shooting or punching. Awówawega.

a'ya, v.a. Take or carry anything along. Abla. Ala. Amni kte. Ani kte. -- v. coll. pl. (of ya). They go together. It also seems to mean, to lead or rule. Itancan kage k'on he itancan na oyate awicaya. Le taku ca ala hwo? -- v.n. Become, be, be in or on. The form amáyan is doubtful. Maśte aya, It is getting warm. Wanna wicahcala na hunkeśni aya. Tohanl oiyokpaz aya ca na wicaśa lila waś'aka. Wana anpa aya. Lila waśma aya. Wanna atanin ayapi. Wanna hunkeśni amaye. Na wanna oglala kin hunh waziyata aya na ake Helazatan aya.

aya'blaska, v.a. (a and yablaska). Make flat with the mouth on anything.

aya'blaya, v.a. (a and yablaya). Make level with the teeth.

aya'blaza, v.a. (a and yablaza). Tear open with the teeth.

aya'bleca, v.a. (a and yableca). Crush on anything with the teeth.

aya'blu, v.a. (a and yablu). Chew fine on.

aya'bu, v.a. (a and yabu). Growl about. Abláblu.

aya'ceya, v.a. (a and yaceya). Make cry by talking to. Abláceya.

aya'gnayan, v.a. (a and yagnayan). Deceive with the mouth, tell a falsehood about. Ablágnayan.

aya'gopa, v.a. (a and yagopa). Suck up on. Ablágopa.

aya'gwa, v.a. Chew, as it were on something soft, with the front teeth. Ablágwa. -- ayágwagwa, v. (red. of ayagwa). Bl.

aya'hinta, v.a. (a and yahinta). Brush off with the mouth. Abláhinta.

aya'hepa, v.a. (a and yahepa). Drink up on. Abláhepa.

aya'hlaya, v.a. (a and yahlaya). Bite or peel off with the teeth on anything. Abláhlaya.

aya'hleca, v.a. (a and yahleca). Tear with the teeth on. Abláhleca.

aya'hloka, v.a. (a and yahloka). Bite a hole in on anything. Abláhloka.

aya'hpa, v.a. (a and yahpa). Throw down with the mouth on anything. Abláhpa.

aya'hpu, v.a. (a and yahpu). Bite off on, one thing on another. Abláhpu.

aya'htaka, v.a. (a and yahtaka). Bite one thing on another.

ayah'u, v.a. (a and yah'u). Peel off on. Ablah'u.

a'yaic'iya, v.n. Have a habit of doing something. Cannunpa - , He has the habit of smoking.

aya'jipa, v.a. Pinch upon with the teeth. Ablájipa.

aya'kca, v.a. (a and yakca). Untie with the teeth on anything. Ablákca.

aya'koka, v.a. (a and yakoka). Clatter

or gnash the teeth on or for anything. Ablákoka,

aya'kṗa, v.a. (a and yakpa). Bite out on. Ablákpa.

aya'kṗaŋ, v.a. (a and yakpaŋ). Chew fine on. Ablákpaŋ.

aya'kṗi, v.a. (a and yakpi). Crack with the teeth on anything.

aya'ksa, v.a. (a and yaksa). Bite off on. Abláksa.

aya'kśaŋ, v.a. (a and yakśaŋ). Bend with the mouth on. Ablákśaŋ.

aya'kśija, v.a. (a and yakśija). Double up with the teeth on anything. Ablákśija. -- ayákśiś, v. (cont. of ayakśija).

aya'kṫaŋ, v.a. (a and yaktaŋ). Bend with the mouth on. Abláktaŋ.

aya'ḱuka, v.a. (a and yakuka). Bite or tear in pieces with the teeth on anything. Ablákuka.

aya'k'eġa, v.a. (a and yak'ega). Gnaw on anything.

aya'k'eza, v.a. (a and yak'eza). Make smooth with the teeth on anything.

aya'k'oġa, v.a. (a and yak'oga). Bite or gnaw off on.

aya'k'oza, v.a. (a and yak'oza). Bite off smooth, as a horse eating grass.

aya'mna, v.a. (a and yamna). Gain on or for, by speaking.

ayaŋ'bic'iya, v. refl. (of ayaŋpa). Wake all night (purposely). Palani kiŋ tipi k'el ayaŋbmic'iye na wi waŋkab u kiŋ hehaŋ śuŋkawakaŋ ota wicawaki yelo. BT.

ayaŋ'ḱa, v.n. (a and yaŋka). Be on or for, be in such a condition.

ayaŋ'pa, v.n. Come light on, come morning, i.e. spend a sleepless night and be found sleepless by the dawn. Amáyaŋpa. Uŋkáyaŋpapi. Awaŋyaŋka ayaŋpi, Spend a sleepless night watching, as a sick person. Ístiŋme śni amayaŋpa. Ena ḣpaya, Sleep all night. Yuŋkaŋ ake iśnala - śke. Haŋhepi wocekiye wecaga el amayaŋpa, I stayed up all night praying for him. Cf. awiyaya.

aya'ogwu, v. Do something indistinctly, as speaking or singing. Abláogwu. Bl. -- ayáogwugwu, v. (red. of ayaogwu).

aya'onihaŋ, v.a. (a and yaonihaŋ). Praise on or for.

aya'otaŋiŋ, v.a. (a and yaotaŋiŋ). Make manifest on or for. Abláotaŋiŋ.

aya'pehaŋ, v.a. (a and yapehaŋ). Fold up with the mouth on anything. Ablápehaŋ.

aya'pemni, v.a. (a and yapemni). Twist with the mouth. on anything.

aya'ṗoṫa, v.a. (a and yapota). Bite in pieces on anything. Ablápota.

aya'psaḱa, v.a. (a and yapsaka). Bite off, as a string, on anything. Ablápsaka. - icu, He stopped talking, avoided quarrelling.

aya'psoŋ, v.a. (a and yapsoŋ). Spill with the mouth on anything. Ablápsoŋ.

aya'pśuŋ, v.a. (a and yapśuŋ). Pull out by the roots with the mouth on anything. Ablápśuŋ. -- ayápśuŋpśuŋyaŋ, adv. (red. of ayapśuŋ). Ituśeś mapagaŋka hi - mayuta yaŋke, as an old man would say when much food is given to him. BS.

aya'pṫaŋyaŋ, v.a. (a and yaptaŋyaŋ). Turn over on anything with the mouth.

aya'pṫuja, v.a. (a and yaptuja). Crack or split with the mouth on anything.

aya'sḱab, v. (cont. of ayaskapa). -- ayásḱabtoŋ, v.a. Make stick on, as a stamp on a letter, seal. Patch, as clothes. B.H.209.8. -- ayáskabtoŋpi, n. The lining, as in a coat. -- ayáskabya, v.a. Make stick on, seal.

aya'sḱaṗa, v.n. Stick to or on, adhere to.

aya'sḱu, v.a. (a and yasku). Pull off on with the teeth.

aya'sleca, v.a. (a and yasleca). Split

with the teeth on anything.

aya'smiꞃ, v.a. (a and yasmiꞃ). Pick off with the teeth on, make bare with the teeth on.

aya'sna, v.a. (a and yasna). Make ring, as a little bell, with the mouth on or over anything.

aya'soṫa, v.a. (a and yasota). Eat all up on. Ablásota.

aye'sṗaya, v.a. (a and yaspaya). Wet with the mouth on anything.

aya'sṫaꞃḱa, v.a. (a and yastaꞃka). Moisten on anything with the mouth.

aya'sṫo, v.a. (a and yasto). Lick smooth on.

aya'su, v.a. (a and yasu). Condemn on, condemn for or on account of. Ablásu.

aya'suṫa, v.a. (a and yasuta). Make firm or establish with the mouth by speaking. Ablásuta.

aya'swa, v.a. (a and yaswa). Pick to pieces with the teeth on anything. R. Bl.

aya'śaṗa, v.a. (a and yaśapa). Blacken or defile with the mouth.

aya'śkaheyela, v. Speak of as near. -- ayáśkaṫuyela, v. Speak of as near. Both words are doubtful.

aya'śḱica, v.a. (a and yaśkica). Press with the mouth upon, as in chewing tobacco. Abláśkica.

aya'śkoṗa, v.a. (a and yaśkopa). Make crooked or twisted by biting on.

aya'śluṫa, v.a. (a and yaśluta). Have the teeth slip on anything.

aya'śna, v.a. (a and yaśna). Miss with the mouth, let fall on from the mouth. Abláśna.

aya'śṗa, v.a. (a and yaśpa). Bite a piece off on anything. Abláśpa.

aya'śṗu, v.a. (a and yaśpu). Bite off on, as one thing that adheres to another.

aya'śṫaꞃ, v.a. (a and yaśtaꞃ). Cease from speaking or eating. Abláśtaꞃ. Na lecel eya, lowaꞃpi ayaśtaꞃpi hehaꞃl... . Oyate kiꞃ waꞃna wicaceya - . Waꞃna miś wol ablaśtaꞃ. Wota - .

aya'śuja, v.a. (a and yaśuja). Bite or mash up on with the teeth.

aya'ṫaḱuniśni, v.a. (a and yatakuniśni). Destroy with the mouth on anything.

aya'ṫaꞃ, v.a. (a and yataꞃ). Praise for. Ablátaꞃ.

aya'taꞃiꞃ, v.a. (a and yataꞃiꞃ). Make manifest upon or for, by speaking. Ablátaꞃiꞃ.

aya'ṫiṫaꞃ, v.a. (a and yatitaꞃ). Pull with the teeth on anything.

aya'tḱaꞃ, v.a. (a and yatkaꞃ). Drink, as water, on or after eating. Ablátkaꞃ. -- ayátḱaꞃyaꞃ, adv. Drinking on or after. B.H.109.12,15.

aya'togya, v. (of yatokeca). Conceal, change in telling. Ayátogwaye and ablátogye are used.

aya'uꞃḱa, v.a. (a and yauꞃka). Throw down with the mouth on anything.

aya'waja, v. Bite off on. Abláwaja.

aya'waśṫe, v.a. (a and yawaśte). Bless upon. Abláwaśte.

aya'weġa, v.a. (a and yawega). Fracture by biting on. Okiwaś'ag niśicelo, ahoyasotkamayayelo, cehupa aciyaweḣwegiꞃ kta yuꞃś, aciyawega ye, as is said to one who does not take advice. Bl. -- ayáweḣwega, v. (red. of ayawega. Cf. the above statement. Bl.

aya'zamni, v.a. (a and yazamni). Open or uncover with the mouth or by speaking.

aya'zaꞃ, v.n. (a and yazaꞃ). Be sick on. Amáyazaꞃ.

aya'zoḱa, v.a. (a and yazoka). Suck out on.

aya'zuꞃṫa, v.a. (a and yazuꞃta). Connect or weave together, as in talking.

a'yeǩiya, v.a. Make one take along. B.

a'yeya, v.a. Make one take along. Áyewaya.

a'yoka, (?). Tuwa ayoka kiŋ, iyopemiyaŋpi kte. Bl.

a'yoǩas'iŋ, v.a. Look into, peep into. Áyowakas'iŋ. Áokas'iŋ may also exist. -- áyokas'iŋyaŋ, adv. Peeping in upon.

a'yokoka, (?).Tuwa - yakaśigla iyececa yelo, an expression said in fun. Bl.

ayu'blasǩa, v.a. (a and yublaska). Make flat on.

ayu'blaya, v.a. (a and yublaya). Spread out on, unroll on.

ayu'blaza, v.a. (a and yublaza). Burst open on, make an incision on.

ayu'bleca, v.a. (a and yubleca). Break or crush on. Ablúbleca.

ayu'blu, v.a. (a and yublu). Plow on, pulverize, make mellow on. Ablúblu.

ayu'bu, v.a. (a and yubu). Make a drumming noise on anything.

ayu'caŋ, v.a. (a and yucaŋ). Sift or shake on or over. Ablúcaŋ. -- ayúcaŋcaŋ, v.a. (a and yucaŋ). Cause to shake or tremble.

ayu'čeǩa, v.a. (a and yuceka). Make stagger on any place.

ayu'ceya, v.a. (a and yuceya). Make cry on.

ayu'co, adv. Well, excellently. - kaga. -- ayúcoya, adv. Well. - ecoŋ. -- ayúcoyakel, adv. Well, finished. - ecoŋ.

ayu'coza, v.a. (a and yucoza). Make warm on any place.

ayu'ecet̄u, v.a. (a and yuecetu). Fulfil or accomplish on.

ayu'eciya, v.a. (a and yueciya). Turn wrong side out on anything. Ablúeciya.

ayu'ǧa, v.a. (a and yuga). To husk on, as corn. Ablúga.

ayu'ǧal, v. (cont. of ayugata). - inajiŋ, He stood with arms up-lifted. Śina waŋ yuha hinapa na yublaya egnake na ake haŋblaglaka na el - inajiŋ na uŋgnaȟila śina el epazo.

ayu'ǧalǧata, v. (red. of ayugata). Hold out, as the hand, on anything, the palms downward. Yuŋkaŋ le waŋbli ca - pe el ca piya waŋblakiŋ kta.

ayu'ǧaŋ, v.a. (a and yugaŋ). Open, as the door on anything.

ayu'ǧap̄a, v.a. (a and yugapa). Strip or pull off on, as the skin of an animal.

ayu'ǧat̄a, v.a. (a and yugata). Open out, as the hand, on anything, to lift one's hands over as in blessing, lift the hands towards heaven. Ablúgata. Wicaśa waŋ ataya ska igluza ca miwaŋkab hinajiŋ na amayugata.

ayu'ǧiic'iya, v. (refl. of ayugiŋ). Make one's self slumber, take a nap. Bl.

ayu'ǧiŋ, v.n. Slumber. Ablúgiŋ.

ayu'gla, v.a. (a and yugla). Uncoil or untwist.

ayu'gmigma, v.a. (a and yugmigma). Make round on.

ayu'gmuza, v.n. Shut the eyes on, as when something gets in. Ablúgmuza. Riggs gives v.a. Shut upon, as the hand upon anything. Nuŋge kiŋ ayugmuze. D.268.

ayu'gna, v.a. (a and yugna). Shell, as corn. To shake off on, as fruit.

ayu'gnayaŋ, v.a. (a and yugnayaŋ). Miss in trying to catch hold of.

ayu'ǧo, v.a. (a and yugo). Make marks on.

ayu'ǧuǩa, v.a. (a and yuguka). Sprain on, draw out, as one's sword from the scabbard.

ayu'gweza, v.a. (a and yugweza). Make rough on. R. Bl.

ayu'ha, v.a. (a and yuha). Have or possess on, hold or lift on, have for. Ablúha.

ayu'hel, adv. (of ayuhete). Waiting for. Constantly. - maŋke, I am waiting for them. - makuwapi. They are after me constantly. Bl. Hituŋkala waŋ wote c'uŋ el - kuwa, The boy kept edging around to where the mouse was gnawing. Lila wojapi kiŋ le ayuhel kuwa, He was very curious about the food and often stayed around. D.96,121.

ayu'heṫe, v.a. Think of and be after one thing. Ablúhete. Alúhete. Bl. Mazaśala waŋji wagluśna inaniptecapelo, cicupi amayaluhetepi eś kolakiciyapi waśte kiŋ hecela aluhetepi.

ayu'hiŋhaŋ, v. (of yuhiŋhaŋ). Rake or harrow over. Ablúhiŋhaŋ.

ayu'hiŋṫa, v.a. (a and yuhiŋta). Sweep or rake off on.

ayu'hoho, v.a. (a and yuhoho). Shake on, as anything loose.

ayu'homni, v.a. (a and yuhomni). Turn around on, as in bringing a gun round and pointing it at one. Ablúhomni.

ayu'huŋhuŋza, v.a. (a and yuhuŋhuŋza). Shake on or over, as a tree.

ayu'ȟa, v.n. Become attached to, stick to.

ayu'ȟab, adv. Crawling, creeping on or towards. - iyaya.

ayu'ȟeṗa, v.n. (a and yuȟepa). Absorb on.

ayu'ȟeyaṫa, v.a. (a and yuheyata). Push back on, push on one side.

ayu'ȟica, v.a. (a and yuȟica). Waken on upon. Ablúȟica.

ayu'ȟla, v.a. (a and yuȟla). Ring or rattle over.

ayu'ȟlaǧaŋ, v.a. (a and yuȟlagaŋ). Make large upon. Leave, forsake. -- ayúȟlagaŋśni, v. Not leave or forsake, to be with constantly.

ayu'ȟlaṫa, v.a. (a and yuȟlata). Scratch on.

ayu'ȟleca, v.a. (a and yuȟleca). Rend or tear on one, as a garment. Ablúȟleca.

ayu'ȟloḱa, v.a. (a and yuhloka). Make a hole on, open on. Ablúȟloka.

ayu'ȟmiŋ, v.a. (a and yuȟmiŋ). Sling or throw on one side, as a stone, on anything. Do crookedly, as in writing. -- ayúȟmiŋyaŋ, adv. Crookedly.

ayu'ȟmuŋ, v.a. (a and yuȟmuŋ). Make a buzz on, talk incessantly to one while he is still. Bl.

ayu'ȟṗa, v.a. (a and yuȟpa). Throw down on. Shut, as a window. Ablúȟpa.

ayu'ȟṗu, v.a. (a and yuȟpu). Make crumble on.

ayu'ȟṫaṫa, v.a. Loosen the lines on horses, so as to let them run. Ablúȟtata. Awícabluȟtata. The word may also be ayúoktata.

ayu'ȟuǧa, v.a. (a and yuȟuga). Break a hole in, upon anything.

ayu'ȟuŋta, v.a. (a and yuȟuŋta). Make soft on by rubbing.

ayu'ȟ'olȟ'ota, v. A vulgar word meaning to get on another's back, as steer calves do. Bl.

ayu'ȟ'u, v.a. (a and yuȟ'u). Peel off on,as bark.

ayu'jaja, v.a. (a and yujaja). Wash on.

ayu'jiṗa, v.a. (a and yujipa). Pinch upon with the hand. Ablújipa.

ayu'juju, v.a. (a and yujuju). Destroy or take to pieces.

ayu'juŋ, v.a. (a and yuju). Pull out by the roots on anything.

ayu'kaŋ, v.a. Go around, give place to. Cf. kiyukaŋ. -- ayúkaŋyaŋ, adv. Going around.

ayu'ḱaṫiŋ, v.a. (a and yukatiŋ). Straighten out on with the hand.

ayu'ḱawa, v.a. (a and yukawa). Cause to open on.

ayu'kca, v. (a and yukca). Unite on, disentangle on.

ayu'kcaŋ, v. Cf. yukcaŋ.

ayu'k̇iⁿca, v.a. Scrape off on, as in cleaning a fish. Ablúkiⁿca.

ayu'k̇iṗab, adv. Separately, divided.

ayu'k̇iṗat̄uja, v.a. Cause to stoop or bow down on. -- ayúkipat̄uśya, v.a. Make bow down. Ayúkipatuśwaya.

ayu'kṗaⁿ, v.a. (a and yukpaⁿ). Grind or make fine on. Ablúkpaⁿ.

ayu'ksa, v.a. (a and yuksa). Break off on, as limbs or sticks with one's hand. Ablúksa.

ayu'kśa, v.a. (a and yukśa). Bend, fold or double up on.

ayu'kśaⁿyaⁿ, adv. or v. Go around, out of the way. Bl. and MS,561.

ayu'kśija, v.a. (a and yukśija). Bend or double up on. Pull, as a trigger of a gun, on one. Ablúkśija.

ayu'kt̄aⁿ, v.a. (a and yuktaⁿ). Bend around on.

ayu'k̇uk̇a, v.a. (a and yukuka). Make rotten on.

ayu'kyuta, v. (red. of ayuta). Look at. Akiciyukyutapi, They looked at one another.

ayu'k'eġa, v.a. (a and yuk'ega). Scratch or scrape the hands on anything. Ablúk'ega. Cf. yak'ega.

ayu'k'eza, v.a. (a and yuk'eza). Make hard and smooth on, shave off close, as a mule's mane.

ayu'k'oġa, v.a. (a and yuk'oga). Scratch up, make rough.

ayu'k'oza, v.a. (a and yuk'oza). Make hard and smooth on.

ayul', v. (cont. of ayuta). - kuwa, and - yaⁿka, both have the meaning to continue to look at, to stare.

ayu'maⁿ, v.a. (a and yumaⁿ). Grind or file off on, sharpen by grinding.

ayu'mniġa, v.n. (of yumniga). Shrink on, settle on, as snow. Lehaⁿl waayumniyelo, Snow is now settled and hard, as on a road after traffic. Bl.

-- ayúmnih̄, v. (cont. of ayumniga). Waayumnih̄ iyaye, The snow is settling. Bl.

ayu'mnimni, v.a. Sprinkle on. B.H.58,6.

ayu'mnimnija, v.n. Ruffle, curl. -- n. A ruffle.

ayu'najiⁿ, v.a. (a and yunajiⁿ). Cause to stand on.

ayuⁿg', v. (cont. of ayuⁿka).

ayuⁿ'gya, v. Cause to lie on or for. Ayuⁿgwaya. -- v.n. Go and spend the night at. P.

ayuⁿ'k̇a, v.n. (a and yuⁿka). Be or lie on, lie in wait or spend the night out for, as for the purpose of killing deer.

ayu'oh̄t̄alya, adv. In a loose manner.

ayu'oh̄t̄at̄a, v. Loosen, as a noose.

ayu'ṗehaⁿ, v.a. (a and yupehaⁿ). Fold up on.

ayu'ṗemni, v.a. (a and yupemni). Twist or turn to one side on.

ayu'pot̄a, v.a. (a and yupota). Wear out on, tear to pieces or destroy on. Ablúpota. Ti ayupotapi.

ayu'psak̇a, v.a. (a and yupsaka). Break or pull in two on anything, as a string.

ayu'psoⁿ, v.a. (a and yupsoⁿ). Pour out or spill on, as water.

ayu'pśuⁿ, v.a. (a and yupśuⁿ). Pull out by the roots or extract, as teeth, on anything.

ayu'pt̄a, v.a. (a and yupta). Cut off on or pare, as a garment. Ablúpta. -- ayúpta, v.a. Answer, speak in return or opposition, give or grant a thing when asked. Ablúpta. Uⁿkáyuptapi. Acíyupta. Amáyalupta. Amálupta.

ayu'pt̄aⁿpt̄aⁿ, v.a. (a and yuptaⁿ). Turn or roll back and forth. -- ayúptaⁿyaⁿ, v.a. (a and yuptaⁿ). Turn or roll over on. Ablúptaⁿyaⁿ.

ayu'pt̄uja, v. Drop, as an arrow

in front of one's self by a slip of the hand while trying to shoot. Bl.

ayu'sk̇eṗa, v.a. (a and yuskepa). Make evaporate on or from.

ayu'sk̇ica, v.a. (a and yuskica). Press down tight on.

ayu'sk̇iṫa, v.a. (a and yuskita). Bind or bandage on. -- ayúskiskita, v. (red. of ayuskita). Tie or bandage on. D.220.

ayu'sk̇u, v.a. (a and yusku). Peel or pare off on.

ayu'sleca, v.a. (a and yusleca). Split on.

ayu'slohaŋ, v.a. (a and yuslohaŋ). Drag or draw along on. Ablúslohaŋ. Figuratively: tempt on, by holding out alluring things. Caḣ'áyuslohaŋ watokśupi (1826).

ayu'slohelaka, v. Pull off something on, as a bark on a tree, a skin over an animal. Bl.

ayu'sluta, v.a. (a and yusluta). Pull out on.

ayu'smak̇a, v.a. (a and yusmaka). Indent on.

ayu'smiŋ, v.a. (a and yusmiŋ). Make bare. Ablúsmiŋ.

ayu'sna, v. (a and yusna). Ring on or over, as a bell.

ayu'soṫa, v.a. (a and yusota). Use up on, expend on, spend money on.

ayu'sṫo, v.a. (a and yusto). Smooth down on, make smooth, as hair on the head.

ayu'suṫa, v.a. (a and yusuta). Make firm on.

ayu'swa, v. Dig under and make come down on, as sand.

ayu'swu, v.a. (a and yuswu). Make a rattling noise on or over.

ayu'śaṗa, v.a. (a and yuśapa). Blacken or defile on anything.

ayu'śica, v.a. (a and yuśica). Spoil or make bad on. Ablúśica.

ayu'śk̇ica, v.a. (a and yuśkica). Press out on.

ayu'śkoṗa, v.a. (a and yuśkopa). Make twist or warp on anything.

ayu'śla, v.a. (a and yuśla). Shave off on; cut, as grass, so to cover one with. Ablúśla. Amígluśla, I cut on or for myself.

ayu'ślok̇a, v.a. (a and yuśloka). Pull out on.

ayu'śluśluṫa, v. (red. of ayuśluta). Make smooth on, or perhaps sharpen. - yo. GA.

ayu'śluṫa, v.a. (a and yuśluta). Draw or slip out on anything.

ayu'śna, v.a. (a and yuśna). Drop or let fall on.

ayu'śpa, v.a. (a and yuśpa). Break off a piece on.

ayu'śṗi, v.a. (a and yuśpi). Pick, as fruit on a place.

ayu'śṗu, v.a. (a and yuśpu). Pick or pull off on. - amayaŋ welo, as they would say if one asked them for a little of the same thing again and again. Bl.

ayu'śṫaŋ, v.a. Stop or cease from, let go, let alone. Ablúśṫaŋ. Amayuśṫaŋ yo.

ayu'śṫaŋk̇iya, v.a. Put a check on, make and end of, put a stop to.

ayu'śuja, v.a. Sliver up on by twisting. -- ayúśuśuja, v. (red. of ayuśuja).

ayu'ś'e, v.a. Make drop on, as medicine. Ablúś'e. -- v.n. Fall in drops on. R. -- ayúś'eś'e, v. (red. of ayuś'e). B.H.199.2. -- ayuś'eya, adv. In a dripping manner.

ayu'ṫa, v. (of yuṫa). Eat, eat upon or in addition to. -- v.a. Look at, look steadily at. Ablúta. Itaŋcaŋ kiŋ - wicauŋ wo. Tuŋkaśila, amayuta yo. -- ayuta, v.a. Cover with earth, i.e. akata.

ayu'ťaǩuniśni, v.a. (a and yutakuniśni). Destroy or bring to naught on. Sam - amayaupelo, You make me "broke". Bl.

ayu'taŋ, v. (a and yutaŋ). Touch, put the hand upon. Ablútaŋ.

ayu'taŋiŋ, v.a. (a and yutaŋiŋ). Make manifest upon.

ayu'ťeb, v. (cont. of ayutepa). - amayaŋ welo, as they would say if one asked for a portion of the same thing (as food) again and again. Bl.

ayu'ťeca, v.a. (a and yuteca). Renew on.

ayu'ťepa, v.a. (a and yutepa). Wear off on.

ayu'ťica, v.a. (a and yutica). Scrape or paw on.

ayu'ťiṗa, v.a. (a and yutipa). Make cramp or draw up on.

ayu'ťiťaŋ, v.a. (a and yutitaŋ). Pull on. Ablútitaŋ.

ayu'togyakel, adv. Changing on. B.H.68.

ayu'tokaŋ, v.a. Shove away, put aside a little.

ayu't'iŋs, v. (cont. of ayut'iŋza). - hiŋgla, He pulled them suddenly tight together. B.H.78.4.

ayu't'iŋza, v.a. Squeeze.

ayu'uŋǩa, v.a. Make fall on. Ablúuŋka.

ayu'wakaŋ, v.a. (a and yuwakaŋ). Consecrate or make sacred for. Ablúwakaŋ.

ayu'waŋǩal, v.a. (a and yuwaŋkal). Exalt, make high for.

ayu'waśťe, v.a. (a and yuwaśte). Make good on or for.

ayu'waza, v.a. Scratch off with the fingernail on something. Abluwaza. Bl.

ayu'weġa, v.a. (a and yuwega). Break down on or fracture.

ayu'wi, v.a. (a and yuwi). Wrap on. Haŋpiśka sutaya - yo, uŋnihaŋ kiȟ'aŋ hi yelo. BT.

ayu'wicaka, v.a. (a and yuwicaka). Assure one, asseverate.

ayu'wignuni, v.a. (a and yuwignuni). Cause to perish, destroy on. - mayakuwa, You distract, bewilder, disturb, mix me up in my work. Bl.

ayu'wiŋja, v.a. (a and yuwiŋja). Bend down on.

ayu'wiŋťa, v.a. (a and yuwiŋta). Overlay, as wood with gold. Mazaskazi ayuwiŋtapi. B.H.60.23.

ayu'zamni, v.a. (a and yuzamni). Open on, set open on, as a door; unroll on.

ayu'ze, v.a. (a and yuze). Dip or skim out on.

ayu'zica, v.a. (a and yuzica). Draw or stretch on.

azaŋ'gzaŋka, v. Whine, as babies do. Bl.

a'ze, v.n. Get aground, stick fast, as a boat. Riggs gives azi.

aze', n. Breast of a female, the udder of a cow, etc.

aze'iŋkṗa, n. The nipple of the breast.

a'zeǩiya, v.a. Run aground, cause to stick. Ázewakiya. Riggs: azikiya.

aze'piŋkpa, n. (aze, pa and iŋkpa). The nipple of the breast, the teat or dug of a cow, etc.

aze'wicahiŋśma, n. A certain black caterpillar found in woods. Bl.

a'zeya, v.a. (aze and ya). Cause to get aground, run aground, as a boat. Ázewaya. Paohaha yo, - uŋ welo, Push the whole thing in, some is visible. Bl. Riggs: aziya. -- ázeze, v. (red. of aze). - uŋyaŋpi, We often get aground as we go. Note: this word is used also of dead fish etc.

azi'ic'iya, v. refl. Same as oziic'iya. Both words may be correct.

azi'lic'iya, v. refl. Apply smoke to one's self, smoke one's self. D.197.

azil'ǩiya, v.a. Burn incense, make a

good smell by burning, as cedar leaves in certain religious rites when one is sick. Aziĺwakiya.

azil´ťoŋ, v.a. To make a pleasant smell by burning leaves, to incense. Azilwatoŋ. Na waŋna hehaŋl tatiye topa kiŋ iyuha wazilyapi na azilmatoŋpi kta.

azil´ya, v.a. To incense or smoke smoething, as meat. Azilwaya. Na ciŋca k'oŋ - .

aziŋ´, v.a. To suck, as a child or the young of animals. Awaziŋ.

aziŋ´ǩiya, v.a. To give suck, to nurse as a mother her child. Aziŋwakiya.

azi´ťa, v.a. To smoke upon, to burn e.g. incense.

azi´ya, v.a. (a-ziya). To make yellow on anything.

azu´ya, v.a. (a-zuya). To make war on someone, to go to war against a people. Also perhaps, azúyeya. Azuwaya.

B

bla, v. 1st pers. singl. (ya). I go. -- prefix. Verbs commencing with "ya" change "ya" to "bla" to form the 1st pers. singl, and to "la" for the 2nd. Cf. kabla.

blabla'ťa, n. An upland plain. Bl.

bla'ȟa, adj. Broad at one end, tapering. Also, bláġa.

blasǩa', adj. Flat, as a board. Also, bláska. -- blaskáska, adj. red.
blasǩa'ya, adv. Flatly, on the flat side.

bla'ya, adj. Level, plain. - hiŋgla, He feels good. Waśpaŋka ognake k'oŋ taŋyaŋ iyojuwakiyelo ca - mahiŋgle lo, I filled that grub box well brimful, so I feel good. Bl.

bla'ye, n. A plain.
bla'yela, adj. Levelly, plain.
bla'yeya, adv. Evenly.

bla'ye zitka'tacaŋ hu stóla, n. Hairy prairie clover. Petalostemum villosum. The pulse family. Also, casmu huȟolȟota, waptaya huȟolȟota. The roots make a good purge; whereas the leaves and blossoms are eaten for an inside swelling of the throat. BT. Bc. #136.

blaza'haŋ, part. Ripped open of itself, torn open.

ble, n. A lake.

bleble'ca, adj. red. of bleca.
bleble'cahaŋ, part. red. of blecahaŋ.

blebles'ya, v. red. (blesya). To amuse one. Bleblesic'iya, He amuses, regales himself.

bleca', adv. Getting poorer and poorer, as from sickness. Mableca.

bleca'haŋ, part. Broken of itself.

ble'ġa, n. The American white pelican, a large whitish water-bird with white spots. Bl. FR.

blei'yoka, n. Little pools alongside a creek filled with weeds. Also, miniyuśpala. Bl.

blei'yośkokpa, n.(?). A buffalo wallow or hole where the water gathers after a rain. Bl.

bleǩi'yuťe, n. (ble and kiyute). An isthmus, a strait or channel in a lake.

ble'la, n. A little lake, a pond.

bleo'kaȟmi, n. A bog or beech.

bleo'śǩokp̄a, n. A lake basin.

bles', adj. (cont. of bleza).

blesya', v.a. Make clear, cause to recover from stupidity. Bleswáya. -- adv. Clearly. -- blesyáǩel, adv. Clearly.

bleya'ťa, adv. At the lake.

ble'za, but more probably blo'za, n. A loon, the great Northern Diver. BS.

ble'za, adj. Clear, clear-sighted. Iśta - , Sober. Mabléza. Wicableza s'e yalòwaⁿ k'oⁿ aluśtaⁿ, You stopped your cheering and singing. Bl. -- blézela, adj. Clear, as water.

ble'zesni, adj. Desperate, reckless. - s'e śkaⁿ, He acted excitedly. Bl.

ble'zic'iya, v. Recruit, restore one's health.

blihe'ca, v.n. Be lively or active, industrious. Mablíheca. Niblíheca. Uⁿblíhecapi. Le oⁿ lila niblihecapi kta ca eya, i.e. noⁿwaⁿpi. -- adj. Active, brisk, etc.

blihe'ic'iya, v. reflex. Take exercise, practise, exert one's self.

blihel'heca, v. (red. of bliheca).

blihel'ya, adv. In a lively manner.

blihe'ya, v.a. Make active, industrious. Blihéwaya. -- blihéic'iya, or blihíc'iya, v. Make one's self active, get busy. Blihémic'iya. Kola - yo. -- adv. Actively, industriously.

blo', n. A ridge or range of hills. Yuⁿkaⁿ blo inamni pte hotoⁿpi. Note: I have heard them use the word with reference to the Black Hills. -- n. An esculent root eaten by the Dakotas, in appearance and taste like the sweet potato ; potatoes. The opirs tuberosa.

bloa'ǩaťaⁿ, v. Cultivate potatoes, by making hills around plants.

bloa'liya, adv. Along the ridge.

bloblo'sǩa, n. The trachea tube.

blogyaⁿ'ka, v.n. Remain at home when others go out to hunt. Blogmáⁿka. Blogúⁿyaⁿkapi. Bl. R.

blo'hu, n. Potato-tops. Edible.

bloi'p̄ataⁿ, n. A potato masher.

bloǩa', n. The male of animals.

bloǩa'saǩ, n. A belch.

bloǩa'sǩa, v.i. and t. Hiccup, hiccough. Blowákaska. D.70. Blowakaska lo talo watiⁿ kte lo, as a man would say who got the hiccups.

bloǩe'coǩaⁿyaⁿ, n. Mid-summer.

bloǩe'haⁿ, n. Last summer.
bloǩe'ťu, n. Summer, next summer, this summer.

blo'ǩit'a, v. Be very tired or weary, as by walking, carrying a load. Bl. Blómakit'e. Makalȟpaya, He fell on the ground from weariness. R. -- bloǩit'eya, v.a. Make tired or weary, tire out, fatigue. Blokít'ewaya. R. Bl.

blopa'hi agu'yapi, n. potato-picking bread.

bloťa'huⁿǩa, n. A chief, the leader of a war party. Tuwa wazuya itaⁿcaⁿ ca he - . Miyeś le - wakte kte.

blowaⁿ'jila, n. A divide, a single upland plain between streams, top of a ridge. Also blowáⁿjia.

blo'za, n. The pelican. A big gray-black water bird with a long bill. The Indians used to make medicine bags of the lower jaw with its sack. Bl.

blu', adj. Powdered, pulverized, fine. Aguyapi - , Flour. Maka - Dust.

blublu´, adj. red. (blu). Mellow and dry, as apples or turnips. -- v. 1st pers. singl. of yublu.

bluye´la, adv. In a powdered, pulverized condition. - kaga.

bu, v.n. To make a noise, as of a drum that is beaten. Ptegleśka kiŋ ho bubi. Pte ota yelo eyapi; na waŋna buwicahiŋgla ca miś kakel inawape, ehaŋl ekta ewatoŋwaŋ. Oyate k'oŋ he lila bu anataŋpi.
bubu´, v. red. of bu. -- adj. Noisy. - s'e, as is said of one who has a large head etc. and everything large; hence, as a chunky fellow. Bubuke s'e.
bubu´ya, adv. red. (buya). Noisily, with a noise. - mani.

buya´, adv. Noisily, in the manner of one lowing. - mani, He walked noisily. - apa, It hit with a thud. D.217.
buya´ǩel, adv. In a noisy manner.
buye´ȟci, adv. (buya-ȟci). With a loud noise.

buyel´, adv. Noisily. - iŋyaŋka.

buye´la, adv. Same as buya.

ca, n. A step, the distance one steps. - niha^{n}ska. -- particle. At the end of a statement, it infers a wish: Won't you? Wagni kte, tokśa ya^{n}ka ca. Under other circumstances, if we omit ca, the statement becomes a command; thus: Takoja, uwa ye, u^{n}gni kte, leciya u^{n}tipi ca, eya. -- def. art. It is employed to indicate a descriptive relative clause. Yu^{n}ka^n wikośkalaka wa^n lila wi^{n}ya^n waśte ca ya^{n}ya^{n}ke. Yu^{n}ka^n winawizi wa^n catkayata^{n}ha^n ikoyaka ca wa^{n}ya^{n}ke. Yu^{n}ka^n itazipa wa^n lila ha^{n}ska ca yuha naji^n na wahi^{n}kpe wa^n lila ha^{n}ska ca naku^n iyagna. Lila kaȟmi wa^n waśte ca el etipi. Tuwa okihi ki^{n}ha^n he śu^{n}kawaka^n ca wicak'u kte. Yu^{n}ka^n taku k'eya cikcik'ala ca el okala. Wamakaśka^n hutopa ca cic'upelo. -- conj. Therefore. At the beginning of a sentence it is placed. Ota^{n}i^n hecel slolwaya ca ta^{n}ya^n oblaka. A^{n}pa ca wicoca^{n}lwa^{n}ka yelo; na ha^{n}hepi ca otuyaci^n utapelo. Ate u maśi ca wa^n na lena ociciyakapi kta ca wahi ca ta^{n}ya^n naȟ'o^n po. Hehé, le a^{n}petu ki^n lowaci^n ca ina weksuye lo. -- adv. conj. Because, that is why. At the end of a sentence it is put. Also, it can be interpreted: when. Niś eya ecamo^n ca, i.e. I did it because you also did. You are more than busy niśnala ca, i.e. because you are alone. Siiyotiyewakiye tuweni makagege śni ca, Because nobody mends my moccasins. Ho, ca eyaś wakokipe wicu^{n}kicapi kte lo. Ita^{n}ca^n mitawa eyayapi na tuktel eu^{n}papi ta^{n}i^n śni ca hece. B.H.271.7;282.7.

cae´gle, v.n. (ca-egle). To step, take a step. Caéwagle.
cae´glepi, n. A step, steps. - wa^{n}ji, One step measure, a yard.

ca´ġa, n. Ice. -- v.n. To freeze, become ice. - s'e, Icy.
ca´ġaṫa, adv. At, on the ice.
ca´ġaṫakiya, adv. Iceward, out on the ice.

ca´glawa, v. To count steps of one's own. - maunipi, We proceed slowly. Bl.

ca´glegle iyu´tapi s'e máni, express. To make big steps as though one were taking a measure of something.

cagle´pi, n. Cf. caegle. - ake zaptaŋ, 15 paces. D.99.

ca´ġoti, n. Ice house.

caġu´, n. The lungs. Lights.

caġu´ġukaca, n. A fool. Also witko oȟ'aŋ s'a. Bc.

caġu´ka, n. A fool.

ċahal´, idiom. I don't know. Perhaps the same as tokcel. It is used by both men and women.

ca haŋ´skaska ma´ni. A verbal expression meaning to take long steps in walking. Bl.

cahe´ce, conj. Because. P. Cf. ca hece.

caȟ´, n. (cont. of caga). - kul, Under the ice. - iyaya, The ice is gone. - hiyaya, Floating ice.

caȟa´gleyela, adv. Standing on ice, seen from afar.

caȟka´ȟloka, v. Make a hole into the ice by striking, as for watering horses.

caȟka´t'a, v. Be stunned or killed by a fall on ice, or by a piece of ice falling on one. Caȟmákat'a.

caȟka´zo, v. Slide in one's moccasins on ice. Caȟwákazo. Bl.

caȟli´, n. Charcoal, coal. Gunpowder.
- iyúȟpe, A large coal shovel.
- óp'iye, A powder magazine.
- ojúha, A powder-flask, powder-horn.
- sniyáŋpi, n. (?). RH.
- tipi, A powder house.
- tokśu, A coal bucket.

caȟna´juju, v. The word is used of the ice when the river breaks up in the spring.

caȟo´ťa, n. Ashes.

caȟsu´, n. Bare or smooth ice. Su refers to little ice drops.

caȟswu´la, n. Thin ice, ice not yet frozen solidly. Bl. Ch.

caȟu´wayazaŋ, or hoȟpa´wayazaŋ, n. Tuberculosis of the lungs, which did not exist in the early days.

caȟ'a´glapepeya, v. Make a flat stone skip or bound over the ice, as boys do. Bl. Caȟ'áglapepewaya.

caȟ'a´li, v. Walk on ice. Caȟ'awali.

caȟ'i´ċazo, n. Skates. - kic'uŋ, wec'uŋ, Skate or slide on the ice.

caȟ'ku´wa,v. Draw blocks of ice by means of a stick. Bl.

ca´ȟ'otila, n. The name for Eskimo.

caȟ'o´waŋcaya, adv. Ice all over. Maka owaŋcaya - . Makoce ataya - . Bl.

caȟ'o´wata, adv. Transparent, as newly formed ice.

caȟ'paŋ´paŋla, v. The ice is soft. Bl. - uŋkiyutapi kte.

caȟ'su´ta, v. The ice is thick. Bl.

cai´a, v. (ceya and ia). Talk crying. Cawáia. The word is perhaps not used alone. - iyaye, v. Talk crying and not while walking. - iblable.

cai´c'ipa, v. (refl. of capa). Used figuratively, to eat one's self full. Bl. Hehehe, camic'ipeȟcelo.

cai´glat'e, v. Sob, as they do before crying. This word is used for the old word cowaiglazaŋyaŋ. WL. Camíglat'e. Caúŋglat'api.

caje´, n. A name. Micáje, My name.

caje´glal, v. (cont. of cajeglata). Calling one's self. - hipi. B.H.245.5

caje´glaťa, v. (pos. of cajeyata). Call one's own by name. Cajéwaglata.

caje´iglaťa, v. refl. Speak one's own name. Cajémiglata.

caje´kaġa, v. Name, make a name for. Cajéwakaga. Na itazipa na wahiŋkpe hena ecel - .

caje´kiyaťa, v. Mention or speak of anything to one. Cajéwakiyata. B.H. 168.24.

caje'yal, v. (cont. of cajeyata). Calling by name. - wicakicopi.

caje'yata, v.a. Name, call by name, speak the name of a person or thing, mention by name. Cajéblata.

caju'nokapoja, n. Pneumonia.

caka', n. The palate, roof of the mouth, gills. Micáka.

caka'la, n. A liar. Nicákala, You are a liar.

caka'po, n. Piarrhoea of the teeth.

ca'kazigzitkiya, v.n. Make large strides. - iⁿyaⁿka, He drags his legs while running, as a tired horse. SLB. Bl.

caki'cipa, v. (of capa). Pierce for another, as a boil. Cawécipa.

caki'pa, v. (pos. of capa). Pierce one's own, as one's boil, open it with a pin. Cawákipa.

caki'pataⁿ, n. A riding bridle bit.

caki'yuhlate, n. (caka and yuhlata). A fish hook.

caksi', n. A wolf. Also yak'é, an old word. HM.

cak'i'glaska, v. Eat up quickly the little one has, just get a taste of it. Cak'iwaglaska. Bl. - iyeya. Cf. ićáska. -- n. Salts.

calo'kimna, adv. (cana and okimna). Between the knees. A vulgar word. R. Bl.

calo'tahena, adv. (cana and otahena). Between the knees. R. Bl.

camni', n. A sprout, germ or bud. - uya, To sprout. Also spelled caⁿmni, perhaps.

ca'na, adv. When, at such a time as. But the word always starts the sentence which may begin with tuwa, tohaⁿ, tuktel etc. or any word. The "na" of cana may be left out, or hehaⁿl added. Na haⁿhepi, cana hehaⁿl inajiⁿ yapi. Cf. Gramm. #148.1b.

cana', n. The groin, inside the thigh, the gland in the groin.

caⁿ, n. A tree, trees, wood. - stáⁿka, Wet wood.

caⁿ, cáⁿna, or cána, adv. conjs. They follow tohaⁿl, etc. and the dependent part of the sentence. When the word referring to indefinite time, "whenever", it has the coordinate meaning "then". Cf. above under cána. B.H. 60.9,23;61a.7;256.10.

caⁿ, n. A night or day. The numeral adjective always precedes it. Letaⁿ topa caⁿ uⁿgni kte.

caⁿa'gnakapi, n. A bier. - kiⁿ euⁿpapi. D.13.

caⁿa'kaⁿsmiyaⁿ, v. Prune trees.

caⁿa'kaⁿyaⁿkapi, n. A chair, bench, pew, anything to sit on.

caⁿa'kit'a, adv. Much brush, many trees.

caⁿa'lipi, n. Stairs, a ladder.

caⁿa'pakaⁿ, n. A crooked branch, one that grows downwards. (?). Bullring says caⁿápakiⁿyaⁿ.

caⁿa'pakiⁿyaⁿ, n. The branch of a tree that hangs downward, as children use for swinging.

caⁿbla'ska, n. A board, boards. - zibzipela, Shingles.

caⁿcaⁿ', v.n. Shake, tremble. Macáⁿcaⁿ. Lila macaⁿcaⁿ. -- caⁿcáⁿkiya, v.a. Make tremble or shake. Caⁿcáⁿwakiya. -- caⁿcáⁿpi, n. The ague, trembling. -- caⁿcáⁿs'e, adv. Hastily, quickly. - śkaⁿ. - iyaya. -- caⁿcáⁿya, v.a. Make tremble or shake, as by telling bad news. Caⁿcáⁿwaya. -- caⁿcáⁿyaⁿ, adv. Tremblingly.

caⁿ'ceġa, n. A drum. - ha, A drum head, a drum hide. - icábu, A drum stick.

caⁿciⁿ'śka, n. A wooden spoon.

caⁿgla'kiⁿyaⁿ, n. A neckyoke.

caⁿgle'gle, n. The scattering of trees. Wakpala - uⁿ hel. R.

caŋgle'glek̇a, n. Trees that stand here and there.

caŋgle'pi, n. Cord-wood, fire wood. - iyutapi waŋji, A cord of wood.

caŋgle'śk̇a, n. A hoop, a wheel. -- adj. Round, wheel-like. Tahuka - . - k̇uṫe, Play at shooting through a hoop while it is rolling.

caŋġu'ġu, n. A fire brand.

caŋ'ġuġu'ya gleśk̇a', n. The towhee or chewink. Its call, kijó, kijó, kijó and a smack with the lips. FR.

caŋ'ġuġu'ya śa, n. The wood thrush. - s'e iwaśicuŋlaḣ, as they say of a very talkative person. - s'e ia caŋ oegle wanil lila ie lo, as when a person talked unduly long. Bl.

caŋha', n. Bark.

caŋhaŋ'kayaŋkapi, n. A chair.

caŋ'haŋṗa, n. Shoes. - iśkahu haŋska, Boots.

caŋhaŋ'ṗi, n. Sugar, i.e. tree-sap. - blu, Powdered sugar.

caŋhaŋ'pokaġe, n. A shoemaker shop.

caŋha'ṗaślotaŋhaŋ, v. Take the inner bark of trees, e.g. maple, off with spoons to eat it. This was done in the spring when the sap was rising. Bl.

caŋha'saŋ, n. The sugar maple; also the white birch.

caŋha'śa, n. Cinnamon-bark.

caŋha'ślotaŋhe or caŋha'ślotaŋhaŋ, v.n. Peel off, as bark does from some trees. SLB. Caŋhaślotaŋtaŋheśni k'el caŋśaśa kaksa uŋyiŋ ktelo. Bl.

caŋha'yuślotaŋhaŋ, v. Take the inner bark of cotton trees which was used for horse feed, as good as oats they say. Bl.

caŋhe'yala, n. The wren. - iśnala itaŋcaŋ, a title given because of its loud voice.

caŋhu'ṫa, n. A stump. - iyukse, A stump puller.

caŋ'hute, n. Name of one of the 4 marks used on the hoop of the Paiŋyaŋkapi.

caŋhu'tkaŋ, n. The root of a tree. - sapa, Nigger head. The roots of a weed which are very tough, making roads over-rough and plowing a hard job.

caŋ'huya'pi, n. Crutches, stilts.

caŋḣa'ḣak̇e, n. A vertebra, a buffalo's hump. -- caŋḣáḣak̇eṫoŋ, v.n. Be humped having a hump.

caŋḣa'k̇a, n. (caŋ and ḣaka). Brush, a bush.

caŋḣcaŋ'ġa, v.n. Crunch or make a noise in chewing anything hard, as corn. Blacáŋġa. -- adj. Gristly, cartilaginous.

caŋḣiŋ'yaŋ, v.a. Be attached to one wishing always to be with him as fast friends, a loving couple. Caŋḣiŋwaya. He caŋḣiŋmaye śni, He has no use for me. BD.

caŋḣlo'ġaŋ, n. Hollow stalks, weeds. A weed is waptáye.

- ape pepe, n. A herb resembling forget-me-nots; any white-flowered species of oreocarya and related plants. Oreocarya perennis. Borage family. Bl. #290.
- ha śluśluta, n. White-flowered beard-tongue. Peatstemon albidus. Figwort family. Bl. #167.
- hu caŋ swula uŋ he tuktektel yuke, n. Prairie pink. Cf. maka caŋśiŋ hu. Bl. #142. BT.
- huḣla, or simply húḣla, n. Evening primrose, night willow. Herb oenothera biennis. Evening primrose family. WE. Its seeds are aromatic. BT. #134.
- hu pteptecela, n. Low erigeron, daisy. Erigeron pumilus. Composite family. Bl. #169.
- hu saŋsáŋ, n. Prairie evening primrose, white-stemmed evening primrose. Oenothera pallida. Evening primrose family. Bl. #190.
- hutkaŋ haŋska, n. Lance-leaved psoralea, tumble weed. Psoralea lanceolata. Pulse family. Bl. #211.
- hutkaŋ sabsapa, also śuŋktawote, n. A species of the buckwheat family.

Erigeron flavum. It is found in the Bad Lands. Bl. #109.

- hu waŋjila, n. Same as the hituŋkala nakpala, The mouse-ear-everlasting. Antennaria apricate grane. Composite family. Also, the hairy rock cress. Arabis hirsuta. Mustard family. Also, the wing-angled loose-strife. Lythrum alatum. The loose-strife family. Bl. #177,158, 286.

- Ḣlaḣla, n. Sharp-leaved beard-tongue. Peatstemon acuminatus. Figwort family. RT. #157.

- iŋkpa gmigmela, n. Lamb's quarters, pig weed. Chenopodium paganum. The goosefoot family. BT. #37. Note: the name belongs rather to the amaranth family.

- iśtawiyaowicaḣpaya, n. Froelichia. Froelichia floridanus. The amaranth family. Bl. #103.

- kcaŋkcaŋla, n. The western Venus' looking glass. Specularia leptocarpa. Bluebell family. Bl. #248.

- maḣ'áwaŋglakela, n. Prairie lily, showy mentzelia. Mentzelia decapetala. The blossom opens at night. Bl. #212.

- maka ayublaya, n. Same as the talagnake, The stiff or hard-leaved golden-rod. BT. #25.

- makatola, n. Purple fritillaria. Fritillaria atropurpurea. Lily family. Also, pejuta wahiŋheya ipiye. It is pulverized and made into a salve and rubbed on scrophulous swellings. Bl. #12.

- nablaga, n. Same as ataśóśapicana nablaga, The large-flowered yellow flax. Also, the low lupine. Lupinus pusillus. Pulse family. Bl. #179,213. Cf. ataśóśapina nablaga.

- ókihetoŋ, n. The hairy umbrella-wort. Oxybaphus hirsutus. Also, sweet hallionia. Four-o'clock family. K. #202. Cf. huokiha haŋskaska.

- oŋzipakiŋte, n. Ragweed. Bl. #21. Cf. caŋḣlogaŋ waśtemna.

- ówicak'o, n. Winged pigweed. Cycloloma atriplici folium. Goosefoot family. Bl. #42.

- pa, n. The western wall-flower, yellow phlox. Erýsimum asperrimum. The mustard family. Also, hu ḣolḣota; so named because of its bitter taste after chewing leaves or root; also, waḣcázi śícamna, because it has a disagreeable odor when the flowers wither away. Bl. HH. LB. #150.

- paŋpaŋla, n. Spiderwort, widow's or Job's tears. Tradescantia reflexa. Spiderwort family. Also, haŋp'inatapi. The blue flowers were used to paint moccasins and provided a blue, jelly-like paint. Bl. #197.

- paŋśpaŋjela, n. The great ragweed, horseweed, bitterweed. Ambrosia trifida. Cf. yamnumnuga iyececa.

- pepela, n. Dense-flowered aster, white wreath aster. Aster hebecladus. Composite family. Bl. #135.

- sotka, n. Prairie ragwort, Senecio platteasis. Composite family. Bl. #299.

- suta, n. Slender dalea; Riddell's senecio. Senecio Riddellii. Composite family. KS. Bl. #90,219. Cf. heḣak'tapejuta.

- śkiśkita, n. Cut-leaved nightshore. Solanum triflorum. Nightshore family. The berries are used for a stomach-ache. BT. #44.

- wabluśka hu, n. Tumble mustard; its leaves are fringed, leg-like. Sisymbrium altissimum. Bl. #65.

- waḣcazi paŋśpaŋjela, n. Tufted loose-strife. Nauburgia thyrsiflora. The primrose family. #173.

- wakalyapi, n. Golden coreopsis, the garden tickseed. Coreopsis tinctoria. Composite family. It is used for drinking tea that is very good. BS. Bl. #170.

- wapośtaŋ, n. Geyer's spurge. Euphosbia geyeri. Spurge family. Same as payá pejuta. It is so called because it was used as a protection for the head. Bl. BT. #24.

- wapośtaŋ kagapi, n. Pursh's plantain. Plantago Purshii. Plantain family. K. #200. Cf. - wapośtaŋ.

- waśtemna, n. Ragweed, Roman wormwood, hogweed, wild pansy. Ambrosia alatior. Composite family. Also, poipiye, As a tea from the leaves it is applied to swellings. Also, caŋḣlogaŋ oŋzipakiŋte, uŋma iŋkpa gmigmela. Also, Canadian wormwood. Artemisis Canadensis. Composite family. BT. Bl. #21. It has a pleasant odor. A tea is made from the root and is good for one who cannot urinate or whose bowels do not move or for a woman who is finding it difficult to give birth to her child. Le. The

roots when pulverized make a perfume. Pulverized roots they put on the face of a sleeping man so he will not wake up at night and thus people can steal his horses. BT. Bl. #47.
- waśtemna iyececa, n. Canada fleabane. Erigeron Canadensis. Composite family. Bl. #174.
- wicagnaśke, n. So-called because the basal leaves look somewhat like those of the gooseberry bush. A species of the Crowfoot family. Ranunculus cardiophyllus. HH. #260.

caŋḣlo'ġu, n. Weeds, pigweeds, any large weed.

caŋḣlo'ḣsnasnala, n. Cf. waḣpe t'oga. BT. #267.

caŋḣloḣ' su'ta, n. (?).

caŋḣloḣ' śluślu'ta, n. (?).

caŋḣo'tḱa, n. A kind of small bush. - hu. -- adj. Frosty, covered with frost. Note: The kind of bush referred to grows on the Platte River and was used for arrows. Bl.

caŋḣpaŋ', n. The American loot, mud hen, pied billed grebe.. Zintkala kiŋ ble kel uŋpi, pasu skaskapi. When a woman has been slandering and then goes away, they say of her: Eyiŋ na - ca miniali iŋyaŋke s'e ke gle. Bl. -- caŋḣpaŋ ṗezi, adj. Green. B. Also - pizi.

caŋ'ḣṗi, n. A war club, a tomahawk.

caŋḣu'naptaŋ, n. A group or bunch of bushes, as plum or buffalo berry bushes. The side of a hill covered with trees. R.

caŋ ica'ḣpe hu, n. The tall nettle with stinging hairs. The roots are used for a tea taken for pains in the stomach. Urtica gracilis. BT. #148.

caŋi'cajipe, n. A drawing knife, a plane.

caŋi'cakaŋ, n. (caŋ and kakaŋ). An adze or any instrument used in hewing wood or adzing.

caŋi'caślece, n. (caŋ and kaśleca). Something to split wood with, a wedge.

caŋi'ciṗaweġe, n. A cross. B.H.263.1. - aic'icaga po. Also used is caŋicipawega.

caŋi'coġa, n. Drift-wood.

caŋi'c'ik'oŋṗa, n. Two boards connected and serving for a cradle. Little babies were carried that way. Bl.

caŋi'naslelye, n. A saw-mill.

caŋ'iŋkpa, n. The ends of branches, the buds.

caŋ'iŋkpaṫa, adv. At the top of the tree. Bl.

caŋi'ṗajiṗa, n. A plane.

caŋi'ṗaḱize, n. (caŋ and pakiza). A violin, a piano.

caŋi'ṗame, n. (caŋ and pamaŋ). A wood-rasp.

caŋi'ṗapṫaŋye, n. A lever.

caŋi'sḱuye, n. A sweet-smelling shrub; the honeysuckle sweet wood. The connotation of it as a grocery is doubtful. Canwiskuye. R.

caŋi'taziṗa, n. Perhaps the aspen.

caŋi'ṫokśu, n. A mechanism replacing the wagon box, as a rack of a sort, for hauling wood.

caŋi'wakse, n. A saw, a hand or cross-cut saw.

caŋi'yawi ci'kala, n. Cf. its name under zuzeca tawote ptapta ikoyaka. Bl. #140.

caŋi'yuhomni cisci'la, n. A gimlet. Same as caŋiyumni.

caŋi'yuḣloḱe, n. An auger, a gimlet, a drill.

caŋi'yuḣuġe, v. Tie a rope to the top of a dry tree, and thus pull it down. Bl.

caŋi'yujiṗe, n. A drawing knife.

caŋi'yukize, or caŋyu'ḱizaṗi, n. An organ.

cani'yume, n. A rasp.

cani'yumni, n. An auger for boring holes.

cani'yuslohan, n. A sled. Bl. -- can-íyuslohe, n. A wood sled.

cani'yuṫaṗi, n. A cord of wood.

cani'yuwi or cani'yuwiwi, n. Curly wood, a vine. - cik'ala, for whose name cf. zuzeca tawote ptapta ikoyaka. - iyececa, The virginia creeper, the woodbine, the false grape, the American ivy or the five-leaved ivy. Quinque folia psedera. The vine family. The roots are bad. Hutkan kin peta s'elececa. Bl. #198. -- skaska naḣca, The western virginia bower. Clematis ligusticifolia. The crowfoot family. At times in the past when they had a head-ache, they made a tea of roots. A wash can be made with the roots. Horses eat the leaves. The word is otherwise given cuniyuwi ówicak'o, or ówicak'o hu. WE, Bc, Bw, BT.

canja'ṫa, n. A forked stick.

canḱa', n. A fire-steel.

canḱa'ġa, n. A log, any large piece of wood on the ground. - wan akan iyotaka.

canḱa'ġica, n. Touchwood, spunk or punk, i.e. soft, half-rotten wood. HM. Bl.

canḱa'ġiḣaḣa, (?). - wakagin kte, I shall whittle the stick so as it will have shaving curls intermittently. Bl.

canḱa'hohu, n. The spine.

canḱa'hoton, v. Make wood ring by striking, to play the harp and such like. - wayapika. B.H.85.20. -- canḱáhotonla, n. A zither.

canḱa'hu, n. (canka and hu). The spine, the backbone, the vertebrae.

canḱa'ḣonṗa, v.a. (cankaga and onpa). Lay or place logs to walk on, to bridge. Cankáḣwaonpa. -- cankáḣ'onṗaṗi, n. A log laid across, a bridge. - wan yunke lo.

canḱa'ḣpaḣpa, n. Shingles.

canḱa'ḣ'u, v. Peel the bark off a tree. Bl.

can'kaiciyo'pteya, (?). Crossed wood.

canḱa'ile, v. Make wood blaze by rubbing. -- cankáilepi, n. A match.

canḱa'ḱiza, v.n. Swing and creak, as trees in the wind.

canḱa'iyaṗi, n. A tea made of a certain bark.

can'kanka'pi, n. A chair.

can kap'o'jela, n. A tree. The word means light wood.

can'ḱaskusku, v. Hew a log. Cánwakaskusku.

canḱa'sluṫe, n. The spinal marrow.

canḱa'śḱa, v. (can and kaśka). Bind wood together, inclose with wood, fence in. Canwákaśka. - yanka. -- cankáśkapi, n. A fence, a fortification.

canḱa'śkokpaṗi, n. (can and kaśkopa). Wood hewed out, a trough. B.H.46.9.

canḱa'ṫaptaṗa, v. Hew logs, cut with a knife so that the chips fly off. Canwákataptapa. Bl.

canḱa'zontapi, canḱa'zuntapi, n. (can and kazonta or kazunta). Thin sticks or reeds woven together so they can be rolled up and used for bed curtains. But it is more probable they were used for bed matting. Bl.

canḱe', canḱeś', adv. or adv. conj. And so, and then, hence, therefore. The word is placed at the beginning of the sentence. -- adv. Same as ca when it is placed at the end of a sentence. That is why. B.H.83.2;136.10.

canḱe'laka, adv. conj. Therefore.

canḱi'caton, v. Play the harp for one. B.H.85.22.

cankin'ciṗagmiyan, n. A wagon without its box.

canko'gnake, n. A case for a fire-steel.

Cf. caŋka, ognake.

caŋk̇o'haŋ, n. The parts along the backbone.
caŋk̇o'haŋśiŋ, n. The fat along the back and sides.
caŋk̇o'opa, n. The back, as of man, in the very middle.

caŋk̇o'ye, n. A row, as of corn etc. Also, caŋkuye. R.
caŋko'yetoŋ, v. To be in rows or furrows. Also, caŋkuyetoŋ. R.
caŋko'yetoŋtoŋ, v. To make rows or furrows, as does a plough.
caŋko'yetoŋtoŋyaŋ, adv. In rows or furrows.

caŋk̇o'za, v. To swing a stick to hit. Caŋwákoza. Pajoke s'e caŋkoze, He whips with the left hand. Bl.

caŋkṗe', n. The knees, or the tibia bone. - hu, The knee bone.
caŋkpe'śka, adv. On the knees. - makagle najiŋ, He knelt down. Note: caŋkpe, Knee; śka, (?); maka, Earth; aglé, Set on; hence, To kneel. Variants are: caśkémakagle, caśkékamagle, caśkékpamakagle. Cf. D.99, note 5.

caŋksa', n. A policeman's club. - yuha, A policeman. - kiŋ le icu wo. Hehaŋ wicak̇pi hiŋk̇paya - waŋ icu.

caŋksi'ksizeca, adj. Saucy, morose.

caŋku', n. A road, way, path. - iyutapi, A mile. - icage, A road scraper.
caŋk̇u'jiṗa, n. The name of the stick or sticks (two) that are placed under the bedding on both sides (lengthwise) so as to prevent the bedding from spreading out too far, on the ground or floor.

caŋk̇u'naptaŋ, n. A slanting road, as one along a hill where one side is lower than the other. Bl. B.

caŋk̇u'te, v.n. To shoot at a target.

caŋk̇u'ya, v. To make for a road, have for a road. Caŋkuwaya. D.77.

caŋk'iŋ'ya, v. To go to get firewood. D.66.
caŋla'kisni, v.n. To recover from anger or sorrow. Also, caŋlásni. Caŋlamasni. B.H.88.26.

caŋla'sniyaŋ, v.a. To cause to recover from sorrow. Caŋlasniwaya.

caŋla'wakṗaŋ, n. (caŋli, awakpaŋ). A board on which to cut up and mix tobacco. Also, caŋli awakpaŋ, caŋliawakpaŋ.

caŋle', v.a. To gather firewood. Caŋwále. D.12.

caŋli', n. Tobacco. - ai, ahi, or yuśka, To make peace. Bl. Note: in making peace, tobacco was brought in a blanket wrapped up. When it was accepted and opened (yuśka), the proposition was accepted. Bl.
caŋli' awákpaŋ, n. Cf. caŋlawakpaŋ.
caŋli'caspek̇itoŋ, v. To satisfy one's self, as by eating. Bl.
caŋli'caspek̇iya, v. Cf. caŋlicaspeya. Caŋlicaspewakiya. Bl.
caŋli'casṗeya, v.a. To satisfy the desires of the heart, whether good or bad. Caŋlicaspewaya.

caŋli'ehánṫaŋ káǵaṗi héca, n. A ready-made cigarette.
caŋli'icahiye, n. A root grown in the Rocky Mountains, which when mixed with tobacco makes it aromatic, and no snakes will stay where they scent it; when medicated with tobacco and inhaled, it is good for bronchitis; and when boiled and rubbed on a sore face it relieves.

caŋli' iyóṗemni, n. A cigarette.

caŋli'mna, v. To be pleased with, be satisfied with, judge one satisfactory or up to standard. Taku ecamoŋ kiŋ oyasiŋ caŋlimayamna śni yelo, as a man would say to his dissatisfied wife. Caŋlicimna śni, I am not satisfied with you. LHB. Bl.

caŋli' oṗémnipi héca, n. A cigarette made when needed.
caŋli' yatápi, n. Chewing tobacco.
caŋli'yugmuŋ, v. To twist tobacco, to make cigars.
caŋli'yugmuŋpi, n. Cigars.
caŋli'yugmúŋpi úŋpapi, n. A cigar.
caŋli'yukṗaŋpi, n. A fine smoking tobacco.

caŋlni'yaŋ, v.n. To be angry, i.e. at women. Caŋlmaniyaŋ.

caŋlo'ǵu, n. Cigar ashes, dregs, remnants of tobacco. Cf. ogu. WL.

caŋlo'ġuha, n. (caŋli, yuha). A tobacco pouch.

caŋ'lowaŋk̇iya, v. (caŋ, lowaŋkiya). To play on an instrument, as on the violin.
caŋ'lowaŋkiyapi, n. A musical box; an organ.

caŋlwa'ḣteśni, adj. Looking forbidding or morose, displeased, as with somebody's visit. WE.

caŋlwaŋ'ka, v.n. To be a coward. Caŋlwaŋmaka. Caŋlwaŋuŋkapi.
caŋlwaŋ'kaic'iya, v. refl. To be afraid of everything, to fear for one's self, as in believing one's self sick. WE.
caŋlwaŋ'kala, adv. Cowardly.
caŋlwaŋ'kaŋ, adj. or n. (caŋte, waŋkaŋ). A coward, a weak-hearted man. Tuwa - ca lena el etoŋwaŋ ca naślute lo.
caŋlwaŋ'kapi, n. Cowardice.

caŋlwa'śte, v.n. To be happy, contented.
caŋlwa'śteya, v.a. To cheer one up, to make feel good. Same as caŋtopeya. Caŋlwaśtewaya. B. -- adv. Of good heart. - uŋ. B.H.88.24.

caŋlyu'ha, v.n. To be good-natured. Caŋbluha.
caŋlyu'hahaka, n. One who is good-natured, kind-hearted habitually. WE.
caŋlyu'hahapi, n. Good-heartedness, kindness. WE.
caŋlyu'haka, n. One who performed an act of kindness. WE.
caŋlyu'haya, v.a. To make one kind-hearted or good-hearted. Caŋlyúhamayayapelo. WE.

caŋl'a'snik̇iya, v.n. To recover from sorrow etc. - omanipi. B.

caŋl'o'ṗe, adj. perhaps. Grateful for a favor done, glad. Caŋl'omape. B.
caŋl'o'peya, adv. Gladly. Taku iyuśkiŋyaŋ ecoŋpi he kapi. -- v.a. To oblige one, to be good to one, to cheer one up. HC.

caŋmi'ḣce, v. 1st pers. singl. (awacaŋmi, ḣce). I want it very badly. BS. Obs.
caŋmi'lokataŋpi, n. A weapon used for striking by the Lakotas in war, consisting of a wooden handle with two or three knife blades fixed in it towards one end along the center

caŋ'nahaŋ, adv. conj. When, at such a time as. Wetu - maga agli.

caŋna'ḣmela k'el, n. perhaps. A place north of the Waśuŋ Wakpa where a bunch of trees is so located that one does not notice them until he is close by. Bl.
caŋna'k̇o, interj. Welcome. Same as akó and wastaŋmi. Bl. Obs.

caŋna'kṗa, n. A mushroom growing on trees.
caŋna'ksa, n. A war club.
caŋna'kseyuha, n. One who carries a club, a policeman.
caŋna'poṗa wi, n. The month of February, the moon when trees crack by reason of the cold. RH.
caŋna'slelya, v.a. To saw logs. Caŋnaslelwaya.

caŋni'yaŋ, v.n. To be angry at women, a word used of men only. Caŋmaniyaŋ, caŋuŋniyaŋpi.
caŋni'yek̇iciyapi, v. They are angry with one another, husband and wife.
caŋni'yekiya, v.a. To make a man angry with his wife. Caŋmiyewakiya.
caŋni'yeya, v.a. To be angry at or offended by a woman, as is said of men only. Caŋniyewaya.

caŋno'pa, n. (caŋna, opa, perhaps). (?). The crotch between the legs. (?).

caŋnum'k̇iya, v.a. To cause to smoke.

caŋnuŋ'ġa hu ptepṫécela, n. Solidago, goldenrod. Composite family. Bl.
caŋnuŋ'ġe, n. A bunch, a lump on a tree, i.e. a certain type of mushroom. Cf. nuŋge.

caŋnuŋ'pa, n. A pipe.
caŋ'nuŋpa, v.n. To smoke tobacco (caŋli uŋpa). Caŋnuŋmúŋpa, caŋnúŋnuŋpa, caŋnúŋk'uŋpapi.
Caŋnúŋpa hahiŋ iyapehaŋpi, A pipe with porcupine quill work wrapped about the stem, such as is used in the huŋkalowaŋpi etc.
Caŋnúŋpa iglaye, A wire pipe-stem cleaner. BD. Cf. glaya.
Caŋnúŋpa ṗahú, The bowl of a pipe.
Caŋnúŋpa siŋte, A pipe stem.

caⁿnuⁿp' aślo'ye wakśi'ca, n. A tin plate, an old word for maza wakśica. Cf. aśloya.

caⁿnuⁿ'pa wosláta, n. The original Indian pipe, consisting of a straight hollow deer bone. GA.

caⁿnuⁿ'p'ȟaka, n. Same as the huⁿkata caⁿnuⁿpa used in the huⁿka lowaⁿpi. It is not a real pipe. Bl.

caⁿo'gnaka, n. A box. Caⁿwognaka, Coffin.

caⁿo'haⁿzi, n. A bowery or the shade of trees, perhaps. Ake - el iyotaka. Ohaⁿziglepi, A bowery.

caⁿo'ȟloġeca, n. A hollow tree.

caⁿo'ȟloka, n. Same as caⁿoȟloġeca.

caⁿo'iali, n. A ladder. Also, oíale.

caⁿo'kajiṗe, n. Shavings.

caⁿo'kaśpu, n. Chips. B.H.116.6.

caⁿo'kṗaⁿ, n. Chips. Also, caⁿokpaⁿla.

caⁿo'nakṗaⁿ, n. Sawdust.

caⁿ'oniglat'a, n. Taku keśa waśakala kapi. Obs.

caⁿo'ṗajiṗe, n. Shavings.

caⁿo'ṗamna, n. Sprouts growing up around a stump.

caⁿ'oṗaṫiⁿyaⁿpi s'e, express. Tired of walking. - wamatuka welo.

caⁿo'ṗiye, n. A storage trunk.

caⁿo'ptuȟa, n. Small wood, i.e. chips, kindling wood. This is perhaps from ópte, i.e. what is left over. Yupta has the meaning: to cut out or off.

caⁿ'ot'oza, n. (caⁿ-t'oza). A round stick.

caⁿ'owaⁿcaya, n. Wood all over, i.e. a forest.

caⁿ'owoju, n. An orchard. - waśte, The Paradise.

caⁿpa', n. Choke-cherries.

caⁿṗa'gmiya ipátaⁿ, n. A spoke.

caⁿṗa'gmiyaⁿpi, n. A wagon. - caⁿkáhu, The underboard, as of a wagon, connecting front and hind wheels.
- cik'ala, A buggy without a top.
- hugáġeca, A wagon without the box, just the gear and wheels.
- hugmiyaⁿ, A wagon wheel. - hu nuⁿpa, A two-wheeled cart, a dray.
- ihupa, A wagon pole.
- ipahuⁿhuⁿze, A wagon spring.
- oaye, A train.
- śkokpa, A wagon box.

caⁿṗa'gmiya táⁿka, n. A lumber wagon.

caⁿṗa'gmiyuṫitaⁿ, n. A single or double tree; a whipple tree.

caⁿpa'hu, n. A choke-cherry bush. - caⁿ, The choke-cherry tree. Prunus Virginiana. The rose family. It was used in the making of arrows. Bl.#160.

caⁿ'ṗajipa, v. To shave or plane wood.

caⁿpa'jiṗe, n. A carpenter.

caⁿpa'kakaⁿ, n. The pigeon cherry.

caⁿpa'kaśki, n. Cherries that are mashed and dried, a favorite dish of the Dakota.

caⁿpa'kiza, v.n. To play on the violin.

caⁿpa'kizapi, n. A piano.

caⁿpa'ksa, n. (caⁿpa-ksa). A stump.

caⁿpa'sapa wi, n. The moon when the choke-cherries are black; July.

caⁿṗa'slaṫa, v. To set posts. - iyok'e, A posthole digger.

caⁿṗa'slaṫe, n. A post or stake.

caⁿpa'su oⁿ kicíopi, n. A mischievous pastime. They would eat a handfull of cherries and then sling one kernel after the other by means of a springy little stick, and so striking the bare skin of others. They hold the kernel to that part of the stick that is drawn backward. Bl.

caⁿpa'ṫa, n. A round bunch of bushes or trees. Also, caⁿwita, cuⁿśoke. Dense woods. WE. Cf. páta. Obs.

caⁿṗa'za najiⁿ, n. A tree. Bl. Obs.

caⁿ peju'ṫa cik'ala, n. A medicine.(?)

ca^{n}p̄e'p̄e, n. Brambles. B.H.263.10.

ca^{n}p̄e'tip̄iye. See winuȟcala taca^{n}petipiye, and taca^{n}pilipiye, n. A stick old women used to poke coals back into the fire.

ca^n'p̄iśko, n. The American red start, a little bird living in the woods. Bl.

ca^{n}psis' u^n, v. To be sad because neglected. U^{n}gnahaȟciś - onayaji^{n}ke.Bl.

ca^{n}pśu^n'ka, n. A block; large trees.

ca^{n}pta'yaha^n, n. The bush.

ca^{n}sa'kala, n. A switch, a twig, a rod. Oyasi^n - wicak'u.

ca^{n}sa'pa, n. (?) A tree.

ca^{n}sa'ta, n. A horizontal stick on which they hang up meat to dry. Cf. satglaki^{n}ya^n.

ca^{n}ska', n. A mulberry tree.

ca^{n}ski'skeya, v. To grow up in thickets and undergrowth. SLB. Ca^{n}skiskemayayelo, I am all confused, which can also be said, ca^{n}teokic'u^{n}mayayelo, or ca^{n}teokihiśnimayayelo. WR.

ca^{n}smna', adj. Unpleasant to the taste as the flesh of wolves, otters etc. R. Bl.

ca^{n}su', n. Hickory nuts, hickory-wood.

ca^{n}su'hu, n. The hickory tree, the walnut of New England.

ca^{n}swo'ju, n. A growth of trees in a bottom. Comp. of ca^{n}swu and oju). Bl.

ca^{n}śa'bśapa oju, n. A group of trees standing against a bank (maya). Bl.

ca^{n}śa'śa, n. The bark which the Dakotas mix with their tobacco for smoking. Dogwood, red osier dogwood. Cornus stolonifera. It grows along running water, as the Little White River (Ȟepeji). The dogwood family. #162. -- ca^{n}śaśaȟcaka, n. A species of dogwood, the bark of which is considered the best for smoking. -- ca^{n}śáśa ipúsye, n. The name for dipper, besides wicakiyuhapi. Also, ca^{n}śaśa ípusye, The constellation, perhaps Triangulum, named for its likeness to a willow stripped of its bark. WF.

ca^{n}śi'huṫa, (?). Ito iapi - wa^{n}ji epi^n kte lo, Let me too say a few words--speaking briefly. (An old saying) St. Śiyo s'e pa - laka ca ya^{n}ki^n na, which is said of a person with a little nose. Bl.

ca^{n}śil', adj. (cont. of ca^{n}teśica). Maśti^{n}cala ki^n - kigla.

ca^{n}śi'lya, v.a. To make sad. Ca^{n}śilwaya. -- adv. sadly, sorrowfully. -- ca^{n}śilyakel, adv. Sorrowfully.

ca^{n}śi^n', n. (ca^n and śi^n). The gum or resin that oozes from trees, pitch plaster, the pitch pine tree from which the gum oozes.

ca^{n}śi^n'kaȟp̄u, n. A small species of bird.

ca^{n}śi^n'śila, n. A plant from which gum oozes when it is broken off; perhaps a species of camomile.

ca^n'śiyo, n. The prairie sharp-tailed grouse. The same as śiyó cík'ala, The bob white. FR.

ca^{n}śka', n. A large hawk with a white breast, a snake eater. There are three kinds: - ġi, - sap̄ela, - wa^{n}blila, A hawk or kite, something like an eagle, an everglade kite. FR. Bl. The ca^{n}śka is the rough-legged hawk, the biggest species known in South Dakota. - hoyázela, The American Osprey hawk, a fish hawk, marsh hawk, a fish eater. - sápila, perhaps the same as - sapela. - śapela, The dark chicken hawk. - ú^{n}pigi, The red-tailed hawk. U^{n}pi is as upi, as in niupi. - u^{n}pígila, The yellow-tailed hawk.

ca^{n}śko'kpa, n. A wagon box.

ca^{n}śpu'śpula, n. Chips. (ca^n and yuśpu).

ca^{n}śu'śka, n. The box elder tree. Negundo interior (Britt). Acer negundo L. The maple family. Cf. taśuśka (crawling up and looking for sweet sap) . #123.

ca^{n}ta'gle, v.a. (ca^{n}te and agle). To desire, wish for, set the heart upon,

esp. to set the heart on for evil, determine evil against one. Caŋtáwagle.
caŋta'glepi, n. A determining of evil against.
caŋta'gleya, v.a. To cause to set the heart against. Caŋtaglewaya.

caŋ'taḣca, n. The Virginia white-tail deer. Also, siŋte haŋska.

caŋta'kseya, v. To cause a big tree to fall by setting fire to it at the root. Bl.

caŋte', n. The heart. Micaŋte.

caŋte'elai, v. To take to heart, be displeased. Caŋteelawai.

caŋte'elyuza, v. To have or hold in the heart, to esteem. Caŋteelbluza.

caŋṫe'hahala, adj. Quick-tempered. Caŋtemahahala. -- caŋṫéhahayela, adj. Irascible.

caŋte'huŋkeśniyaŋ, adv. Discouraged. B.H.6.4.

caŋte' húṫa, n. The aorta of the heart. Also, caŋṫéhuṫe. Bl.

caŋte'ḣniyaŋyaŋ, v.n. To be disturbed or distressed, as when one's foot hurts. Caŋtemaḣniyaŋyaŋ.

caŋte'ihála yaŋká, v. express. To be irascible.

caŋte'iyapa, v.n. To be flurried or excited, to have the heart heat unnaturally.
caŋte'iyapaṗi, n. Heart-heating, excitement.
caŋte'iyapaya, adv. Excitedly.

caŋte'ǩaptaŋyaŋ, adj. To be changeable in one's views. Caŋtemakaptaŋyaŋ. Bl.

caŋte'ǩazaŋ, v.n. To be distressed, as when one is thirsty while eating, or when one has swallowed too much smoke or something heady. Caŋtemakazaŋ.

caŋte'kiciciyapi, n. The loving each other.

caŋte'kic'uŋyaŋ, adv. (?). B.H.87.3.

caŋṫe'ǩiya, v.a. To love, to have an interest in or affection for, which prompts one to benevolent acts. Caŋtéwakiya.
caŋte'ǩiyapi, n. Love, benevolence; the one loved.

caŋte'ǩiyuza, v.a. To hold in the heart for good or ill; to have an opinion of whether good or bad. Caŋtewakiyuza. Ciŋcapi kiŋhe waŋji ke s'e caŋtekiyuze He loved it like one of his own children. B.H.93.12.

caŋte'mniskaŋojula, adj. Very sad on account of suffering. Bl.

caŋṫe'oġiŋ, n. The pericardium, the membranus bag protecting the heart.

caŋte'okic'unica, v.n. To be offended or angry at. Caŋteowec'unica. -- caŋtéokic'unil, cont. of caŋteokic'unica.
caŋte'okic'unilya, v.a. To offend, make angry by opposition. Caŋteokic'unilwaya.
caŋte'oǩic'uŋya, v. To do with heart, in a stirring manner. Caŋteokic'uŋmayayelo; or, caŋteokihiśnimayayelo; or, caŋskiskemayayelo. WE.

caŋte'okihiśniya, v. To have heart failure. SLB. Cf. caŋteokic'uŋya. WE.

caŋte'oŋśiǩa, adj. Low-spirited. Caŋteoŋmaśika.

caŋte'oyusya, adv. With the whole heart.

caŋte'oyuze, n. Inclination, intention. Nicaŋteoyuze kiŋ ognayaŋ makagi ye. Pb.32.

caŋte'ptaŋyaŋ, v.n. To be angry, be in a passion. -- adj. Angry.
caŋṫe'ptaŋyeya, v.a. To make angry, to provoke. Caŋteptaŋyewaya.

caŋte'suṫa, v.n. To be firm of heart, be brave. Caŋtemasuta. - kic'uŋ. Bl. -- adj. Brave.
caŋte'śica, v.n. To be sad, sorrowful. Caŋtemaśica. - ǩiyuza, To be grieved by somebody's enmity. - makiyuza. Bl.
caŋte'śicaya, adv. Sadly, sorrowfully.

caŋte'śilic'iya, v. refl. (caŋteśilya). To repent. Pb.40.

ca^{n}te´śilya, v.a. To make sad, sadden. ca^{n}teśilwaya. -- adv. Sorrowfully. -- ca^{n}téśilyakel, adv. Sadly.

ca^{n}te't'i^{n}s kic'u^n, v. To take courage. Bl. -- ca^{n}tét'i^{n}st'i^{n}za, adj. (red. of ca^{n}tet'i^{n}za). Bl. -- ca^{n}tét'i^{n}sya, v.a. To strengthen the heart, to encourage. Ca^{n}tet'i^{n}swaya. -- adv. Courageously.

ca^{n}te´t'i^{n}za, v.n. To be firm of heart, courageous. Ca^{n}temat'i^{n}za. - wacipi, A dance. - wapaha, seems to be a proper name, Lance of the Strong Heart.

ca^{n}te´wahi^{n}ya^n śi´ca, adj. Irascible. Bl.

ca^{n}te´waka^{n}heja, v.n. To be child-like, weak-hearted.

ca^{n}te´wānica, v.n. To be heartless, unprincipled, mean, wicked. Ca^{n}temanica.

cā^{n}te´waśte, v.n. Be glad, cheerful, joyful. Ca^{n}temawaśte. Ca^{n}tewaśtepo eya. -- ca^{n}téwaśteya, adv. Joyfully, cheerfully. -- v.a. To make glad, gladden. Ca^{n}tewaśtewaya. Pb.45.

ca^{n}te´yaśica, v.a. To make sad by talking, to dishearten. Ca^{n}teblaśica.

ca^{n}te´yaśniśnija, v.n. To have a tickling in the throat. Have a spell of coughing. Ca^{n}temayaśniśnija. B.

ca^{n}te´yat'i^{n}s, v. (cont. of ca^{n}teyat'i^{n}za).

ca^{n}te´yat'i^{n}za, v.a. To cheer up by words, to comfort, strengthen. Ca^{n}teblat'i^{n}za.

ca^{n}te´yawaśte, v.a. To make happy by words. Ca^{n}téblawaśte.

ca^{n}te´yaza^n, v.n. To be heart-sick, have heart trouble, to be very hungry. A heart disease.

ca^{n}te´yuka^n, v.n. To have a heart, be benevolent. Ca^{n}témayuka^n.

ca^{n}te´yukeya, adj. Reasonable.

ca^{n}te´yuślog, v. To have a change of mind towards a more necessary good. SLB. - iwekcu. BT.

ca^{n}te´yuza, v.n. To think, form an opinion. Ca^{n}tebluza. Pb.22. Tokel - he? What is your opinion?

ca^{n}ti´caśpeya, v.n. To satisfy the desires of the heart, whether good or bad, to gratify one's desires. Ca^{n}ticaspewaya.

ca^{n}ti´ha^{n}gya, v.a. To cause a heartache. Ca^{n}tiha^{n}gwaya. Also ca^{n}teiha^{n}gya. Bl. -- ca^{n}tíha^{n}g'ic'iya, v. (refl. of ca^{n}tiha^{n}gya). To give up, not being able to accomplish it. Bl.

ca^{n}ti´ha^{n}ke, adj. Worrying, sad, downcast, as when many children are sick in the family. Ca^{n}timiha^{n}ke. Bl.

ca^{n}ti´heya, v.a. To set the heart upon, to desire very much, covet, yearn for, long for. Ca^{n}tihewaya. B.H.92.5. Wicaśa ki^n iyuha (wikośkalaka ki^n) ca^{n}tiheyapi na yuzapi kta ci^{n}pi. D.46. -- adj. eager. -- ca^{n}tíheye, n. Self-control. Want or desire.

ca^{n}ti^n´yu^n, adv. Voluntarily.

ca^{n}ti´pa^n, n. (?) A sort of bird. Zi^{n}tkala ki^n ble kel u^{n}pi pasu skaska.

ca^{n}ti´yagle, v.n. To be angry, meditate evil. Ca^{n}tiyamagle. -- ca^{n}tíyaglepi, n. Malice, anger. -- ca^{n}tíyagleya, v.a. To be angry at, to make angry. Ca^{n}tiyaglewaya. -- adv. Angrily.

ca^{n}ti´yapa, v.n. Same as ca^{n}teiyapa. -- ca^{n}tíyapapi, n. Same as ca^{n}teiyapapi. -- ca^{n}tíyapaya, adv. Same as ca^{n}teiyapaya.

ca^{n}ti´yap'ic'iya, v. To feel sacred at one who has done something unintentionally. Bl.

ca^{n}ti´yokipiya, adj. Hearty. -- adv. Heartily.

ca^{n}ti´yokiśice, v.a. To be dissatisfied or outraged at something else. Ca^{n}tiyowakiśice. Ha^{n}kiya ca^{n}tiyomayakiśice. BD.

ca^{n}ti´yozikiya, v.n. To get over one's anger, sorrow, etc. Bl.

ca^{n}tka´ġiya, v.a. To let one wait and thus take his time. Ca^{n}tkagimayaye, which is rendered also: okā^{n}śnimayaye, or oúnc'o^{n}nilmayaye, or ohā^{n}naji^n mayakuwa. Bl. WE.

caŋtḱi'ya, v.a. To love one, make him one's heart. Caŋlwakiya. Caŋlmakiya.

caŋtḱu', n. The chest. Wakiŋyela s'e - kiŋ niśko naŋkiŋ na. - naiŋś Wahacaŋka Sapa, i.e. John Big Crow's grandfather, perhaps, invited many people to attend the wailing for his son who had been killed, and he heard the saying: Iŋs'e - ecela wicaśa ota ciŋ yelo; niconalapi eyaś bliheic'iya po. Bl.

caŋtḱu'ip̄asise, n. A breast pin, a badge.

caŋtḱu' sápela, n. A little bird with a black breast, a tail waŋblupi s'elececa, back black, i.e. ȟota, and head like that of the iśtanica taŋka. Bl.

caŋt̄o'ġiŋ, Same as caŋteogiŋ.

caŋt̄o'gnagya, v.a. To cause to place in the heart. Caŋtognawaya. -- adv. In a loving manner.

caŋt̄o'gnaḱa, v.a. (caŋte, ognaka). To place in the affections, to love. Caŋtowagnaka.
caŋto'gnakapi, n. Love.

caŋto'juha, n. A tobacco bag.

caŋt̄o'ḱignaka, v. pos. (caŋtognaka). To place in one's heart. Caŋtowakignaka.

caŋt̄o'kpani, v.a. (caŋte, okpani). To long for. Caŋtowakpani.
caŋto'kpanipi, n. A longing for.
caŋto'kpaniyaŋ, v.a. To cause to long for. Caŋtokpaniwaya. Wahaŋpi kiŋ caŋtowakpani yelo. Lehaŋyaŋ wahi kiŋ locaŋteowakpani yelo. -- adv. Longing for. Bl.

caŋt̄o'p̄eya, v.a. To cheer up. Same as caŋlopeya. Caŋtopewaya.

caŋuŋ'kcemna, n. Ill scented sumac; skunkbush. Also, caŋuŋkcemna caŋ or hu. Rhus coriaria variety, trilobata. The gray cashew family. The leaves are mingled with tobacco and smoked. Bl. #61.

caŋ'waciḱiyapi, n. A top.

caŋ'waȟpa táŋka, n. The bronzed grackle. He says: Mat'i ni, or: Cuȟli, i.e. tuwa końka ehaŋtaŋś. Bl. GA. FR.

caŋwa'kaŋ, n. A flag pole.

caŋwa'ksa, v. To saw wood. Caŋwawaksa.

caŋwa'kśica, n. A wooden dish or plate.

caŋ'wak'iŋ, n. A saddle. - hu, The saddle bow. - pasú, A saddle horn.

caŋwa'p̄e, n. Leaves; small branches. - ġi wi, September, the moon in which the leaves turn brown. - ḱasná wi, October, the moon when the wind shakes off the leaves. - wakaŋ. - woȟeśma, Thick leaves or foliage. Cf. caŋiyuwi iyececa.

caŋwa'pto wi, n. May, the moon in which the leaves are green.

caŋwa'sleca, v.a. To saw lengthwise.
caŋwa'slecapi, n. Wood sawed lengthwise, a plank, boards; sawing, the making of boards.
caŋwa'slesleca, v.a. To saw boards, to saw lengthwise of the wood often.

caŋwa't̄a, n. A log canoe, a skiff.
caŋwi'cajipe, n. A drawing knife.
caŋwi'cipaġa, n. A cross.

caŋwi'lut̄e, n. Logwood, containing red dye stuff.

caŋ'wiŋja, n. A floor.

caŋwi'p̄asnoŋ, n. A spit or stick to take hold of and roast meat on.

caŋwi't̄a, n. A little grove or island of trees. Cf. caŋpata.

caŋwi'yowa, n. (caŋ, wiyowa). A pencil. Mazawiyowa, A pen.
caŋwi'yut̄e, n. A wood measure, a cord stick.

caŋwi'yuwi, n. Curled wood, a vine.
caŋwi'yuze, n. A sharp stick to take meat out etc. from a kettle.

caŋwo'gnaḱa, n. A coffin. Note: caŋógnaka, A box.
caŋwo'jupi, n. A park, a tree nursery; an orchard.

canwo'slohan, n. A sled. Also, canwoslohe.

canwo'winǧe, n. Matted flooring. - kaga, The banner (wápaha) used in the ȟoka okólakiciye, i.e. a stick with the otter skin wrapped around it. - mak'upi, as is said when a person gets a certain job or office, as of collecting money for a certain purpose. Bl. Cf. wówinǧe.

canya'ȟ'u, n. Same as wagacan, Cottonwood. It is so called because in the olden times the Indian horses would feed on the bark.

canyang', cont. of canyanka. - yanka. - waecamon, i.e. worked inspite of sickness. WE.

canyan'ka, v.n. To be heart-sick, to groan. Canblaka, canunyakapi. Na hehanl wicaśa wan lila - ca el ahipi. Wicaśa wan toki - śke', A man groaned somewhere. D.224. B.H.230.1.

canyu'kizapi, n. An organ.

canyu'kťan, n. Bent wood. Canpagmiyanpi - , A wagon bow.

canyu'wacikizapi, n. A top.

canyu'wacipi, n. A top, the kind that one spins with two fingers.

canyu'wipi káǧapi, n. Two pieces of wood tied together which served as a boat for bows, guns etc. while they were swimming across a river. Bl.

canze', v.n. To become incensed or angry. Macanze perhaps, or canmaze. Hehan wicaȟpi hinȟpaya lila - . Pb.25.

canze'ka, adj. Angry. Canmazeka.

canze'ya, v.a. To make angry. Canzewaya. -- adv. Angrily.

canzi', n. Yellow wood, sumac; upland sumac, smooth sumac; scarlet sumac. The cashew family. Rhus glabra. The Indians did smoke the leaves turned red. #16.

cao'kit'a, v.n. To sob. Also, caokit'at'a. B.H.229.23. Note: ceyaokit'at'a is probably the original word.

cao'kit'at'aya, adv. red. (caokit'aya). In a sobbing manner.

ca on, B.H.83.2. Cf. each of these particles.

ca'p̄a, n. The beaver. - s'e nakpa cikcik'a, as is said of a big man with small ears. Bl.

capa', v.a. To stab or pierce, to thrust into, as with a knife. Cawapa.

capa'pa, v. red. (capa). To thrust into, as a knife into flesh, in different places. Cawapapa. Na iyaȟpaya na - kte na pahá icu.

capce'yakton, n. A beaver dam. - ota yelo. Bl.

capce'yazala, n. A plant growing along creeks with berries like gooseberries and sticky juice; the wild black currant. Ribes Americanum of the middle United States. Saxifraga family. RT. #164. Cf. capa, yaze.

cap̄un'ka, n. The mosquito. - s'e, Mosquito-like. - s'e śkatapi.

cap̄un'kwokeya, n. A mosquito net.

cap̄un'k'icuwa, n. A mosquito bar.

cap̄'i'gmunke, n. A trap for catching beaver.

cap̄'ťi'gnaka, n. A hole where beaver gather their provisions; a beaver dam. Bl.

cap̄'ni'ǧe, n. A beaver stomach. Bl.

cap̄'o'k'e, v. To dig out beavers, after the dam waters have been let off. Bl.

cap̄'o'naskiskita, n. A pastime for little children. Bl.

cap̄'sin'te, n. A beaver tail. Bl.

cap̄'sto', n. A fat, big beaver.

cap̄'wi'caȟca, n. An old beaver.

caska, suff. Appended to numerals, making them adverbs meaning: Together. Nunpincaska glipi, Both returned together. Ata iyuhacaska glipi, They all returned together.

caske', adj. Taking things not intended for one but for another. Camaske or macáske. - wicaśa. Wicaśa kiⁿ - s'a. WE. -- casǩé, v. To take by mistake, as in supposing a thing was intended for him, when it was meant for another. Cawáske. -- casǩéya, v. To cause one to take by mistake, as in handing somebody something, while another, thinking it was meant for him, reaches out for it. Caskewaya. Caskemayaye lo, You overlook me while distributing things. Bl.

casmu´, n. Sand. - ikácoco, A trowel. - húholhóta; for the English cf. blaye zitkatacaⁿ hu stola. -- casmúska, n. Sand. -- casmúsmu, adj. (red. of casmu). Sandy, much sand.

caś´, adv. Then. Hecegle - iye keye ca wana nauⁿȟ'oⁿpi, Just as well stop here, he said, so therefore.... B.H. 75.1 (same as tka). 101.1, 105.25, 110. 20, 174.17, 175.4 (ca is emphasized), 208.4, 211.24, 264.22.

caśki´toⁿ, v. (pos. of caśtoⁿ). To give a name to one's own. Caświkitoⁿ. D.106.

caśtoⁿ´, v. Make a name for one's self. Caśwátoⁿ. -- caśtóⁿpi, part. Named.

caś'a´ya, v. To praise one's bravery. Caś'áwaya. Perhaps also cas'aya. Bl.

caś'taⁿ´iⁿyaⁿ, adv. Having a great name. Bl. - skaⁿ, cf. B.H.87.2.

ca´ťa, n. Hard ashes, cinders. Bl.

ca´ťanaślogya, v. To hill corn with ashes. Catanaślogwaya. Bl.

catǩa´, n. The left hand. Micatka. -- adj. Left-handed. Camatka. -- catkáyataⁿ, adv. At the left side. Ate, nata - winawizi waⁿ imakoyakiⁿ kte lo. -- catkáyataⁿhaⁿ, adv. At the left hand of. - woglaka, wokilaka, To tell lies. Uⁿma hiⁿzi kiⁿ le - iyayiⁿ kte lo. Yuⁿkaⁿ nape - wase k'uⁿ he bluha.

catǩu´, n. The back part of a tent or house, the part opposite the door, the place of honor. - apáȟloka, n. An ornament fastened on the catku, the rear wall of the tent. -- catkúl, adv. At the back of a house or tent. -- catkúťa, adv. At the back of the tent, opposite the entrance which is the place of honor. - yaⁿka. -- catkúťaⁿhaⁿ, adv At the back part of a tent.

cau´kp̂ep̂ajo, n. The patella bone.

ce, interrog. particle, used at the end of a sentence to which one expects an immediate affirmative answer. The voice is raised in pronouncing it. Wóeye kiⁿ le yuhapi ce? They use this word, don't they? Lila woyute oteȟike ce, Food's scarce, isn't it? The word is also seemingly equivalent to "Say", in attracting somebody's attention. Ho, takoja wiⁿyaⁿ kiⁿ he uⁿyak'upi kta ce, eya śke. It means also: Is it not so? Or, Is it not right? Deloria (97) has ice, which seems to be au ce: Hituⁿkala he takula ca yatela so? Haⁿke wak'ula ye, miś eya watela kte. Ice, ice, etc. Won't you; won't you? Riggs uses ci. Katowotaⁿla kuye. Lehaⁿ waⁿciglak iblotaka ce, said when the man returned from looking for buffalo.

ce , n. The penis. Macé, nicé.

cea´ktoⁿ, v. To make a bridge. Ceawaktoⁿ. -- ceáktoⁿpi, n. A bridge.

cebce´p̂a, adj. (red. of cepa). Fat.

cebǩi´ya, v.a. (pos. of cebya). To fatten one's own. Cebwakiya.

ceblo´hu, n. The collar bone. The clavicle bone.

cebya´, v.a. To make fat, fatten. Cebwaya. -- adv. Fatly, liberally. -- cebyáp̂i, part. Fattened, fatted. --cebyéla, adj. Fat. Wicaśa - .

ceca´, n. The thigh.

ceca´hohu, n. The femur bone.

ceca´owagle, n. The femur bone, the hip-joint. -- cecáoakle, n. Pelvis.

ceco´wagle, n. (abbrev. of cecaowagle). The femur bone, the hip-joint.

ce e´yaś, Cf. kec'eyaś.

ce´ǧa, n. A kettle, pot, pail, bucket. -- cégaska, n. A white tin kettle.

cegnag´, cont. of cegnaka.

cegna´ǩe, n. A breech-cloth, a piece of cloth worn about the loins by Dakota men. Loin cloth. -- cegnáǩeǩitoⁿ,

cegna'ǩeǩitoŋ, v. To put on and wear a breechcloth. Cegnakewatoŋ.
cegna'kitoŋ, v. To put on or wear a breechcloth.

ceǧu'ǧu, adj. Burned black. BD.
ceǧu'ǧuya, v.a. To fry meat; to burn something black. Ceguguwaya. Waśiŋ - , To fry out fat. BD.

ceg'ya, adv. (ceka). Stumblingly.

ceg'i'yokaśke, Cf. ceȟ'iyokaśke.

cehiŋ'ka, n. An old man. Same as wicaȟcala. Bl. Obs.

cehiŋ'ka tapté, n. A large buffalo cow. Bl.

cehu'pa, n. The under jaw, the lower jaw. - glagla, The name of a bird, deriv. from its chattering in the evening so that people say that the weather will be cold. - naślel kinica, or - namaślel kinica, as is said when the jaws being tired refuse to move.
cehu'paglagla, v.n. To chatter, as do the teeth on account of the cold. Cehupawaglagla.
cehu'pa oágle, n. The place where the the jaw connects. Bl. Cf. paglá.

ceȟ, cont. of cega. - sapa, A black kettle. - ska, A white kettle.
ceȟci'scila, n. A small kettle or bucket.
ceȟka'ȟloka, n. A bucket or kettle with a hole on either side in which a wire is fastened perhaps. Bl.
ceȟhu'hataŋ, n. A kettle having legs.
ceȟi'kaŋ, n. A kettle-bail.
ceȟi'yokaśke, n. The stick or thing on which the kettle is hung. Same as sáta. Bl.
ceȟna'gila, n. dim. (ceȟnagi). Soot, perhaps. - s'e ahiyaye, He passes by all dressed in black. Bl.
ceȟni'getoŋ, n. A kettle that bulges in the middle. Bl.
ceȟpśuŋ'ka, n. A pail, small at the top and large at the bottom.
ceȟp'o', n. The steam from a kettle.
ceȟska', n. A tin can.
ceȟtaŋ'kiŋkiŋyaŋ, n. A large kettle. B.H.55.3.
ceȟwo'hota, n. A low wide kettle.
ceȟwo'yute, n. Clay cakes, etc. as little girls make. - skatapi.
ceȟ'i'ha, n. The lid or cover for a kettle or bucket.
ceȟ'i'hupa háŋska, n. A frying pan, a long-handled kettle.
ceȟ'i'hupatoŋ, n. A kettle or bucket with a bail.
ceȟ'na'ga, n. Soot, dead coals; whatever is black. Also, ceȟ'nagi, ceȟnagi.
ceȟ'o'ǩiyetoŋ, n. A kettle, such as a tea kettle.

ceȟṗi', n. Flesh. Micéȟpi.

ceja'ka, adj. Pigeon-toed, as when one walks such that there is much space between the legs. Cemajaka, macejaka. Bl.

ceji', n. The tongue. Miceji.
ceji'hute, n. The back part of the tongue.
ceji' iŋkpa, n. The point of the tongue.
ceji'jalya, adv. Deceitfully.
ceji'niyaŋ, n. A coated tongue, as from a fever. -- v.n. To have a sore tongue, as babies do. Cejimaniyaŋ.

cejiŋ', Cf. ce, jiŋ.

ce'ǩa, v.n. To stagger. Maceka.
ce'kceg, cont. of cekceka.
cekceg'ya, adv. Staggeringly, reeling. - mani.
cekce'ka, v.n. To stagger, reel.

ceǩi'cati, v. (ceti). To make a fire for me perhaps. Cewécati.
ceǩi'citi, v. (ceti). To make a fire for one. Cewéciti.

ce'ǩiciya, v. (cekiya). To pray or supplicate for another. Céweciya, I for another; céyeciya, You for another; céuŋkiciyapi, We for others; cémiyeciya, You for me. "God" seems to be the object of this word. Cf. wacekiya, cekiya.

ceǩi'ṗa, (?). Nape yuptaŋptaŋ cewec'i-peȟcelo, peta kiŋ oile ecetu śni ca.
ceǩi'papi, n. (?). Icimani - waŋji ceoŋpa yo, Roast a piece of pápa for the lonely traveller. Bl.
ceǩi'tipi, n. A feast of which virgins and men who have known women are said to partake.
ce'ǩiya, v. (ceya). To pray to, beseech. Cewákiya, cecíciya. Ceuŋniciyapi, We beseech you.
ceǩi'yaya, v. red. or adv. of cekiya. - wokiyake. B.H.227.6.
cekṗa, n. The navel. Cekpapi, A twin.

Macekpa. Hau cekpa, same as Hau kola. - agnake, The afterbirth. IS.

cekṗa'ta, adv. (of cekpa). - oŋ slolya, to have known before birth.

cekṗi'yuskiṫe, n. A child's swaddling-band.

cel, adv. About, nearly. Wikcemna cel, About ten. It is from ecel, meaning Or so. Na tahasopi k'oŋ hena oŋ wihuta opaḣlake el cel ikaŋyaŋ na caŋ pteptecela oŋ ecel okataŋ. -- particle, used at end of a sentence. Presumably, it must be. B.H.26.17; 64.13;99.16.

celi', n. A seed-like grass with long joints. -- celíhu, n. The seed stalk.

ceoŋp', (cont. of ceoŋṗa). -- ceóŋṗa, v.a. To roast as meat. Cewáoŋpa.

ce'ṗa, adj. Fat, fleshy. Macepa, nicepa, uŋcepapi.

ce'ṗela ṫaŋ'ka, n. The black-billed cuckoo. FR described it thus (1940): Bigger than a wood thrush, lives in the woods, brown shouldered, long tail, whitish breast and belly, black bill, nests close to the ground, four greenish eggs. It returns in May and leaves in September, sings in the morning, at noon and in the evening, and not at night. Its song is a short note at first, then many. It is called icóka sápa, which cf. When I showed FR Reed's bird book, he said that what we call the black-billed cuckoo looked like what he calls cepela taŋka. The yellow-billed cuckoo is also called cepela taŋka, but that variety is not called icoka sapa. FR.

cesli', n. The dung. -- v.n. To dung. Cewasli.

ceśi'kśice, n. The fat covering the paunch. Bl.

ceśka', n. The part of the breast near the collar bone.

ceśka'saŋsaŋ kśu'ṗi, n. A woman's beaded dress.

ceśki'kaŋ, n. (ceśka and ikaŋ). A button.

ceśki'kaŋ iyecece, n. Geyer's yellow monkey flower, mimulus geyeri Torr. The leaves float on water. Bl. #183.

ceśki'pazize, n. A breast pin.

ceśki'yuṫaŋ or ceśka'iyutaŋ, n. The suspenders, and also the martingale, i.e. a harness strap connecting the head-gear with the belly-band.

ceśko'ḣloke, n. The hollow place in the throat by the collar bone.

ceślo'ślo, v.n. To have diarrhoea. -- ceślóślo pejuta, n. Cf. peji swula cik'ala for the English name. Bl. #89.

ceṫaŋ', n. A hawk. - glegléga, The sharp-skinned hawk. The red-shouldered hawk. - śala, The sparrow hawk. - taŋka, The big hawk. The Indians knew of three kinds of hawk: cetaŋ taŋka; cetaŋ śala, The chickenhawk; and cetaŋ wataṗela, The shrike. Cetaŋ taŋka s'e tuweni takuwaye śni. Bl. -- cetaŋ wató̦ṗela, The loggerhead shrike. - s'e cik'ala tka pasu taŋka, said of a little man with big head and nose. Bl. -- cetaŋ wataṗela zi, The evening grossbeak, They call it that way because the bird goes much after other birds, but it is not a shrike. The bird lives on seeds and berries. BS.

ceṫe', n. The bottom of a vessel. -- cetéiyaskabyela, adv. Sticking to the bottom of a vessel, as a remnant of soap. Same as ceteyela. Bl. -- cetéḱaŋyela, adv. Little in, as water in a pail. Same as ceteyela. Bl. -- cetésapa, n. The suet. -- cetéṫa, adv. At the bottom of a vessel, or a river. Minicéteta. -- cetéṫala, adv. Having a little in, as a vessel. -- cetéyela, adv. Having a little in. Cf. cete.

ceṫi', v.a. To build a fire, make a fire. Cewáti.

cetu', adv. Then; so much; just so.

ceṫuŋ'te, n. The thigh bone.

ceṫuŋ'ṫośtaŋ, n. The neck or head of the femur, the articulation of the femur.

cet'uŋ'gla, v.a. To doubt, disbelieve. Cet'úŋwagla, cet'uŋuŋglapi, cet'uŋcigla.

-- cet'úⁿglaya, v.a. To cause to doubt. Cet'úⁿglawaya.

ce'ya, v.a. To cry, weep. - iglaƫa, To cry very hard, hysterically. Wacéya. B.H.46.2.

ceya'ƙa, n. Mint, the generic name of mints; wild mint, mentha canadensis. The mint family. Bl. #216. Note: ceyaka also means a dam in Santee, which explains the name ceyaktoⁿpi, Bridge.

ceya'ktoⁿ, ceya'ktoⁿpi, Cf. ceaktoⁿ, ceaktoⁿpi.

ce'yanaƙa, v.n. To twitch under the eyes or about the mouth. Céyamanaka.

ce'yaokit'a, v. To sob as children do. F. Cf. caókit'a.

ceya'ya, v. red. (ceya). - iyayapi. B.H.44.5. Cf. ceya.

ceyo'he, n. The abdomen. Bl.

ci, pers. pron. I-thee. Also the form ki, but ci after e or i ; same as the cont. v. insert wa-ni.

cica', adj. Rough; frizzled, curled up.

ċi'ċiye, n. A fabulous being. Indian women used to scare children with it when putting them to sleep. Takoja, iśtiⁿma ye; - waⁿ u kte na eniyayiⁿ kte. Cf. ħ'eya, mmla. PD.

ċikċi'k'ala, adj. red. (cik'ala). Very small. Pl. form, cikcik'apila.
ċikċi'k'aya, adv. (?). Śloślol s'e hu - huoƙihe taⁿkiⁿkiⁿyaⁿ kaca, as we say when a person has thin legs and thick knees. Bl.
ċikċi'scila, adj. red. (ciscila). Pl. form, cikciscipila. Lena - yeś t'api śni yelo.

ċi'k'ala, adj. Little, very small. Pl. form, cik'apila.
ċi'k'alakel, adv. A little. - icaske iyeuⁿyiⁿ kte, Let us smoke the pipe a little, or eating, smoking etc. a little. Bl.
ċi'k'ala śkátapi, n. A toy for girls.
ci'k'aya, adv. Small. Ite - . Bl.
ci'k'ayela, adv. Small, pent up in a small place.

cilo', part. Same as kiló; it is used after a 2nd pers. or imp. Note: it is der. from śni-lo-e.

ciⁿ, v.a. To desire, want. Waciⁿ.
-- def. art. The. It is used in the place of kiⁿ when the verb or adjective preceding has changed a or aⁿ into e . It is also used demonstratively, thus: Ciⁿ niyeś ehe kiⁿ, That is what you say. Ake ciⁿ talo kiⁿ iyuha ayakśijiⁿ kte, I suppose you will be claiming all the meat again. D.115.

ciⁿca', n. A child, the young or animals. Miciⁿca, niciⁿca. - íyanica, Inability to give birth to the child. Bl.

ciⁿca'ƙaġa, v. To beget a child. Ciⁿcawakaga.
ciⁿca'ƙiciƫoⁿ, v. To bear a child to or for one. Ciⁿcawecitoⁿ.

Ciⁿ'cakize, n. p. The Apaches. R. Bl.

ciⁿca'la n. Same as ciⁿca, but more in use for young of animals.

ciⁿca'ƫoⁿ, v.a. To have or give birth to a child. Ciⁿcawatoⁿ.

ciⁿca'ya, v. To have for a child, adopt as a child. Ciⁿcawaya.

ciⁿ'coġa, n. Bunches, as of dry grass, wood etc. left along a creek after a flood, driftwood. Also, caⁿicoga. R. Note: der. from caⁿ-icoga.

ciⁿco'ṗamna, n. A bunch of children together with their parents. Cf. canopamna.

ciⁿhaⁿ', conj. If, when. Same as kiⁿhaⁿ.

ciⁿhiⁿ'tƙu, n. His or her step-child. Bl.

ciⁿ'ħƫiⁿ, adj. Crooked. Note: this is an old word meaning śkopa.

ciⁿ'ƙa, adv., suff. to personal pron. Voluntarily. Miye - , niye - . -- v.a. To want, desire. Wacíⁿka.

ciⁿƙi'ya, v.a. To cause to desire.

persuade, advise. Ciŋwakiya.

ciŋ'kp̌a, n. (can-iŋkpa). Buds, a twig, the top of a tree, the end of a stick.

ciŋkś, n. My child! as is said by men to their children.

ciŋkśi', n. A son; a man's brother's son, or a woman's sister's son. Miciŋca hokśila, wiciŋcala. Niciŋca hokśila, etc. Miciŋkśi t'e śni itokab el u wo.
ciŋkśi'tǩu, n. His or her son.
ciŋkśi'ya, v.a. To have for a son, to be a father to one. Ciŋkśiwaya.

ciŋ'ktakta, v. (ceyiŋktakta perhaps). To cry sobbingly. Waciŋktakta perhaps.

ciŋpi'ca, adj. Desirable.

ciŋśǩa', n. A spoon. - cik'ala, Tea spoon; - ťuǩíla, A shell-shaped spoon or a very small spoon made of buffalo horn. - siŋte yukaŋ, The Big Dipper. Cf. wicaǩiyuhapi.

ciŋśka'yapi, n. A mountain sheep.

ciŋśni'yaŋǩel, adv. Detestingly. Wowaȟtani - nitawoope kiŋ ecel eciŋ kte. Pb.44.

ciŋťok', adv. (ciŋtoka). Certainly. -- interj. To be sure, expressing assent.

ciŋťo'ka, Cf. ciŋtok.

ciŋ'wakse, n. A saw.

ciŋya', v.a. To cause to desire, persuade. Ciŋwaya.

ciŋ'yaŋkel, adv. Desiringly. - yaŋka. Tohaŋl mini kiŋ śkaŋśkaŋ caŋ el iyayapi kte ciŋyaŋkel yaŋkapi. B.H.188.2; 192.13.

ċi'sċila, adj. Small.

ċi'sċiyela, 1) adj. Small, little; narrow, pent up, as a passage-way. - waciŋyayaŋpi. - tokeca. 2) adv. A little, for a little while. R.

ciya'nuŋ, n. A small tahuka caŋgleśka. Obs.

ciye', n. A man's older brother; my older brother. Niciye, Your elder brother. Note: male cousins from the father's side older than one's self are also called ciyé.
ciye'ǩu, n. His elder brother.
ciye'ya, v.a. To have for an elder brother. Ciyewaya.

ci'yotaŋka, n. A flute. Also, cotaŋka, śiyotaŋka. R. RT. Bc. Bl. B.H. 18.56.

ċo ċo, exclam. Of joy on seeing a friend unexpectedly. BS.

ċo, n. The kernel, core; the meat of grain; seed. - aya, To ripen. -- v.n. To ripen.

ċoċo', adj. Soft, as mud. Opposed to t'iŋza and suta. - hiŋgla kaluza.
coco'la, adj. Soft.
coco'ya, adv. Made or left soft. - śpaŋ, Not well cooked.

cogco'nala, adj. red. (conala). Very few, very little.

co'ǧeca, adj. Slovenly, with one's clothes not well put on. Macogeca.

ċoǧiŋ', n. The pith, as of wood; the core of anything, as of an apple. Wicagnaśka hu hena - taŋka. D.12.

coȟwaŋ'jica, n. The smaller kind of willow. - śaśa, The low, thin willow. - taŋka, The large willow.

coi'c'icoŋ, v. (cokoŋ). To determine evil against one's self; to be resolute. Also, icoic'ioŋ. R.

coǩa', adj. Empty, without anything. Śuŋkawakaŋ - wagli mazaska etc. Yuŋkaŋ lila wicaakiȟ'aŋ na le oyate omani ipi eśa - agli. Waye wai tka - wagli yelo, i.e. hunter for many but returned without any.

coǩa', n. A low bottom, a place where there are lakes or marshes.

ċo'ǩa, n. The Joker in playing cards; a joker, one who makes jokes.

ċo'kab, adv. In the midst, central. Mni cokab iȟpeyapi. D.79. Note: coǩáb úŋwiŋ, To be fighting in the middle while the hostile parties stand on both sides. Bl.

coka'ka, adj. (red. of coká).

coka'kala, adv. (red. of cokala).

cokal', adv. (cont. of cokata). In the midst. He itancan kaga na he - inajin. Itancan - ti. Yunkan ungnahela taji nump - hiyapi.

coka'la, adj. Naked, bare. Tanmácokala, I am without clothes. Simácokala, I am without shoes. Sícokala. Also means empty. Cf. R., kokala; also cf. P.

cokan', n. The middle. Na lena okicize kin - lecel oh'anye ci wanyakapi heon lila cajeyatapi. Peta kin - inajin. Blaye - kinapipi. Wicaśa wan ikányela yanka; canke hu kin - kaksa ihpeya.

cokan'gnagya, adv. Placed in the middle half. Same as okiseya. - ya. B.H.54.14. Miś - tima wai.

cokan'hiyuc'iya, Same as cokanhiyuic'iya, v. refl. To thrust one's self into, to come uninvited.

cokanl', n. or adv. The middle, or in the midst. - iśnala omani na enana inajin. - wawagli kte lo, similar to: isto tasicoska nupin taajuntka ognake kin nupin tanitahu kin tatahpa kin. Bl.

cokan'yan, n. (?). The middle. -- adv. In the middle. Yunkan hucan - hehanyan ataya we oha. Yunka blaye kin - taku wan śayela u. Itancan kin - najin. -- cokányangnaka, v.a. To place across the middle, place in the middle.

coka'pa, adv. In the midst, in the center.

coka'ta, 1) n. The middle. 2) adv. In the middle, in the midst. Wicaśa wan wakan - inajin. -- cokátakiya, adv. Towards the middle. -- cokátawapa, adv. Out in the middle, as of a stream.

cokco'nala, adv. (red. of conala).

co'kehanl, (perhaps co kin ehanl). Same as étukehanl. Bl.

cokon', v.a. To purpose evil against, desire to take the life of one. Cowákon.

coku', n. The inside of the cuticle, the underside of the skin, the thickness or stripe of the skin; the under part of the chin.

coku'kiton, v. To take on new flesh. Cokuweton. B.H.44.14.

ćok'in', v.a. To roast on spits over coals. Cowák'in. Cok'inpi, Roasting.

co'la, adj. Destitute, without, not having. Śina cola.

comni'glazanzan, v. (red. of comniglazan). To sob. Comniwaglazanzan. They now use caiglate. To sob as theydo before crying out loud. Comniglazi is not used. Bl. This is an old word.

ćo'nala, adv. A few.

co'nalaka, Same as conala śni, that is, ota. Cf. ka.

ćoni'ca, n. Flesh, meat of any kind; the meat or kernel of grain.

con'tehi, n. Thick woods.

conwi'yuġoġe, n. Brush breaker.

copa', v.a. To wade, go in the water. Cowapa. Mini cowapa.

cope'kiya, v.a. To cause to wade. Copewakiya.

cos, (cont. of coza).

cosco'za, adj. (red. of coza).

cosi'c'iya, v. (refl. of cosya). To warm one's self. Cosmic'iya.

cosya', 1) v.a. To cause to warm; to put out to dry, as cooked victuals; to dry and smoke, as meat. Coswaya. Taśupe cosyapi wanji ciscila hci ceonpa na hikśila kin k'u. 2) adv. Warmly. - igluze omani yo. Bl. -- cosyákel, adv. In a warm state.

cos'i'gluza, v. (refl. or pos. Coza and igluza). To dress up warmly one's self or one's own (?). Bl.

cowa'iglazan, v.n. To shiver as from cold or as when ready to cry. GB.

co'za, adj. Warm, comfortable; used

both in regard to persons and things, as clothing, houses etc. Macoza.

cu, 1) interj. Used following the sound of a gun-shot. Bl. 2) n. Dew. - śma, Heavy dew. R.

cuci'c'iŋ, v.a. To keep something with one's self, as a medicine in a bottle. Wácucic'iŋ. Cf. cutic'iŋ. Note: RF. knows only cutic'iŋ and claims that cucic'iŋ is a Yankton word.

cuglu'ƙaŋ, v. pos. (yukaŋ, To shake off a dew). To shake off, as a tree shaking (from the wind) off snow, ice etc., or dew (cu). Also, caŋglukaŋ. Iŋśe - . Note: the word is used when in spring ice forms on the branches of trees and drops; or when a cold spell comes in after warm weather in a change of weather.R.

cuhaŋ'zi, v. imper. singl. (cu, Dew; haŋzi, Shady, fig. to thaw). It is a day wrapped in a heavy wet fog. - yelo, as the old Indians said when the grass was full of dew and the sky cloudy, thus indicating it would be a warm day. RF. Obs.

cuȟci', adv. By one's self. It is used with the personal pronouns miye, niye etc., and sometimes with the numeral, but it is never used alone. Niye - ecoŋ wo, Do it yourself.

cuȟli', Same as Mat'i ni, tuwa kośka ehaŋtaŋś, the song of the caŋwaȟpa taŋka. GA.

cui'yohe, n. Moccasins made of old hides that have served as tents. Wizihaŋpa waŋji - micagege yo, One that does not turn hard from moisture. Wimiȟca - waŋji micaȟ yuha yo. Bl.

cuma'ȟpiya, v. It is cloudy.

cu'mni, n. Dew-drops.
cumni' ś'e, n. Dew standing in drops, dew-drops. Cf. aś'e.
cumni'ś'eś'e, n. Dew-drops all over anything.
cu'niyaŋt'a, n. A faint. Cf. sniyaŋt'a.
cuŋ'ȟaƙa, n. A brush or bush so dense that one cannot pass through. Also, caŋȟaka. R.

cuŋ'ȟloġeca, n. Dry wood that is rotten within.

cuŋi'yutapi, n. A yard measure.

cuŋi'yuwi ówicak'o, Cf. ówicak'ola hu. WE. #125.

cuŋ'ƙaśƙe, n. A fence, an inclosure; a fort.
- iyokataŋ, Staples.
- iyut'iŋze, Wire stretcher.

cuŋkś, n. My daughter, in addressing her. Men and women use it for girls.
cuŋkśi', n. A daughter; a man's brother's daughter, a niece; a woman's sister's daughter. Micúŋkśi.

cuŋkśi'la, adj. Toy. - wahiŋkpe, Toy bows and arrows.

cuŋkśi'tku, n. His or her daughter perhaps. Cuŋwitku is most often used.

cuŋkśi'ya, v.a. To have for a daughter. Cuŋkśiwaya.

cuŋ'k'iŋ, n. A back-load of wood, i.e. as mush as a woman can carry on her back.

cuŋ'k'iŋƫa, n. Any place where they go for wood.

cuŋ'peśka, cuŋ'peśka, n. Glue. Also, peśka. Note: the Lakotas generally obtain it by boiling buffalo heads and the residue they used in fastening on the points of their arrows. Cf. R.

cuŋ'śoke, n. Dense woods. " - kiŋ hel wauŋ kte waciŋ yelo", uŋkcekiȟa eya. D.260.

cuŋ'taŋka, n. (caŋ, taŋka). High wood; groves of timber. Cf. cuŋśoke.

cuŋ'waŋca, n. A forest.

cuŋwiŋ'ziye oyúze, n. A certain place where the Indians picked from pine trees a certain yellow resin or so, which they boiled and used for dyeing yellow. Bl.

cuŋwi'sƙuye, n. A species of plant, perhaps the honey-suckle. Also, caŋwiskuye. R. Cf. mániskuya.
cuŋwi'sƙuye hu, Cf. miniskuya, R.

cuŋwi'tku, n. His or her daughter.

cuŋwi'yape jiji', n. A tree of a sort.

ċuŋwi'yaṗehe, n. Grapes. Also, cuŋwiyapehela. - iyuśtaka, Purple. A. - iyuwi, Grape vines. Vitus vulpina. The wild grape. #124. - ojupi, A vineyard.

cuŋwi'yawa, n. A counting stick, as used in games such as - ksasu kutepi, haŋpapecoŋpi.

cuŋ'woḣeśma, n. Dense woods, forest.

cuŋ'yapehe (?) n. Raisins.

cuṗe', n. Marrow.

cusni', adj. Cool, as are dewy mornings and evenings.

cuṫi'c'iŋ, v. To carry at the side, as a powder-horn strapped over the shoulder and coming down under the arm. Note: This may be a doubtful translation. The word comes from ikute or icute and k'iŋ. RF. does not know the word cucic'iŋ. Ptehecutic'iŋ, A powder-horn. Cf. wacutic'iŋ.

cuṫi'k̇ic'iŋ, v. pos. of cutic'iŋ.

ċuwa'culuza, n. A scare crow; a spirit pest, originally. The word is said to be a Pawnee express. Cf. FD.81.

cuwe', n. A woman's older sister.

cuwe'ku, n. Her older sister.

cuwe'ya, v.a. To have for an older sister.

cuwi', n. The back, as the Oglalas say. - mayazaŋ, My back aches. - nuŋga, A hunchback. - okiniya, To gasp, breathe as one dying. - ozilkiya; cuwi ozilkiya wakiyaŋka; - kitoŋ; - wetoŋ kte: all these are funny expressions for taking a smoke.

cuwi'gnagya, v.a. To use for a gown. Cuwignagwaya.

cuwi'gnak̇a, n. A white woman's gown. - wiyakṗakṗa, A silk dress.

cuwi'nuŋġe, n. A camel.

cuwi' ogle, n. Bedding. - gliyomni kte, To go for my bedding. Bl.

cuwi'okini (?) v.n. To sigh. Cuwiowakini. Cf. comniglazaŋyaŋ. -- cuwi'okiniya, v.n. To gasp, breathe as one dying, to groan, to breathe deeply. Cuwiomakiniza. Cuwipuskica mat'e kinica yelo. D.l. Bl. B.H.119.29;137.25. D.229.

cuwi'ṗaha, n. The prominent part of the side below the arms.

cuwi'ṗusk̇ica, v.n. To be oppressed with sorrow, not anger. Cuwimapuskica. -- cuwi'pusk̇icat'ekinica, v. To be dying with pent-up sorrow; neither to rage nor to be in rage. Cuwipuskicamat'ekinica.

cuwi'ṫa, adj. Cold, feeling cold. Used only of living things. Macuwita, uŋcuwitapi.

cuwi'ṫagla, v. To be trembling with cold. Cuwitawagla. Bl.

cuwi'yuksa, adj. Cut off at the waist. Ogle - , A vest; hence, not - ogle.

cuwi'yuskiṫe, n. A vest; a corset, perhaps.

cuya', v.a. To cause dew, Cuwaya.

c'a, v. (k'a). To dig. Cf. kic'a.
c'el, cont. altern. form of k'el.
c'e'yaś, conj. Even if, although. The same as k'eyaś.

c'oŋ, Cf. k'oŋ which is changed to c'oŋ after an "a" turned into "e". Gramm.249 etc. Yuŋkaŋ waŋna emakiye c'oŋ weksuye. Hecel miś tokel emakiye k'oŋ ecel owakiyaka. Heḣaŋl kośkalaka eya waoŋspewicakiye c'oŋ hena tacaŋ kiŋ icupi na tima eoŋpapi. Caŋke kolaye c'oŋ ihuŋni na nupiŋ wicao.

c'oŋhaŋ', adv. When, ref. to the past. Same as k'oŋhaŋ.

e, v. irreg. To be. He e, That is. Epi, There are, there is. Ref. to something or person mentioned before. Pte śaŋ e ca okile hwo? Is it a white cow you look for? Na waŋna ti iglukśaŋ e enajiŋ na lila wicotapi. Lakota num wicakaḣnigapi, uŋma wahukeza waśte e na uŋma taśuŋke luzehaŋ e. Yuŋkaŋ he ate e ca kośkalaka lila owaŋyaŋk waśte. Yuŋkaŋ tipi kiŋ éśni. Waŋna kośkalaka kiŋ e na taŋkśitku kiŋ e na kuŋśitkula waŋ henakeca iglaka yapi keye. Tuwa e makagapi so? For whom do the people take me? B.H.67.7;11.1;167.5.

e, prefix. 1) Affixed to verbs and commonly signifies "to" or "at" and is equivalent to ekta; thus, eeḣpiya, To throw away at a place. It makes a location "from" of the verb and denotes that the action is done at a place; thus, ewaksa, To saw off at. There are two other location prefixes, "a" and "o". 2) Of some verbs commencing with "i", it makes a coll. pl. form; as inajiŋ, He stands, enajiŋ, They stand.

e, adv. On the other hand, instead. He e pila po. B.H.51.19;75.23;123.4.

eca', adv. Purposely. Hogaŋ taŋka waŋ eca yeye. B.H.117.12;266.4.

eca'...laka, It is ... there is. SLB. B.H.224.2;260.25.

eca', adv. Anyhow, it's too bad, ref. to something done in the past; really, truly. Cf. ehás. - wica waŋ akihaŋ t'iŋ lo. - okihi śni yelo. B.H.195.3; 266.4.

eča'ča, adv. perhaps. For diversion, in fun. - lowaŋ. Also, iḣaŋhaŋ, owehaŋhaŋ eya; at all, by all means; so, entirely; really, undoubtedly. - tokaḣ'aŋ, She was really lost. D.26,268. Before a verb it means to do thoroughly what the verb indicates; - iśtiŋma, He was deep in slumber, there is no doubting he was asleep. - ...hiyu. D.272,215.

eca'ecoŋk̇a, v.n. To follow e.g. a business; to pretend; to do as one likes, to do persistently against advice; to be self-willed. Ecaecamoŋka.

eca'haŋk̇eya, adv. Immediately, right after; at that time; continuously, completely. Also, ecahaŋkeyela. Bl.

eca'hecoŋk̇a, v. To feign, pretend; not to do, to do inspite of. Ecahecamoŋka.

eca'ḣ'e, adv. Indeed, truly, express. of impatience. Used only by women.

eca'ḣ'ek̇e, adv. or interj. Indeed! An express. of impatience. Also, ecaḣe. R.

eča'icijenaya, v. (?). Ecaicijenawaye. Bl.

eca'iciśniyaŋ, adv. Wrongly, entirely wrong. R. Bl.

eca'ic'ioŋ (?), v. refl. To determine evil against one's self. Ecamic'ioŋ. Also, icoic'ioŋ. R.

eca'k̇aleś, adv. At any rate. Not the same as ecákce. - cic'u kte śni, I want more for it, as for a horse, than what you offer. SB.

eca'kcana, adv. Soon, ref. to more than one event. Bl.

eca'kel, adv. Purposely, but at the beginning of. Wo mak'u ciŋ śni - ; - wo mak'u ciŋ śni. - yahi?

eca'k̇eleś, Same as ecakaleś.

eca'k̇icioŋ, v.a. (ecoŋ). To do for one, perhaps. B.H.74.2;250.8. Tokeśke caŋ śeca ecakicioŋpi kta hwo? B.H.265.18.

eca'k̇icoŋ, v. (ecoŋ). To do to one. Ecawecoŋ, ecayecoŋ, ecauŋkicoŋpi; ecacicoŋ, ecamiyecoŋ. Na śuŋk luzehaŋ num wicawaciŋ yelo, eya. Na wauŋ ecel ecakicoŋpi. Na taku ciŋpi kiŋ ecawicayecoŋ kta kehe k'oŋ. Oyate tokel ecawicuŋkicoŋpi kta hwo?

eca'k̇ioŋ, v. (ecoŋ). To do against. Ecawakoŋ, ecamakioŋ. Taku ecacicioŋ welaka? B.H.68.18;112.6;236.7;237.11.

eca'mna, adj. Having smell or taste, fragrant, savory. B.H.190.5.

eca'na, adv. Soon. - agliḣuŋni kte lo.

ecaŋ'k̇iŋ, v.a. To think so of, form an opinion of one. Ecaŋwakiŋ, ecaŋmayakiŋ. Heceś ipilapika ecaŋkiŋpi. D.202. Tuweni lena wayakapi ecawicakiŋ kte.

śni. D.252.

ecan̄l', adv. Just then, at that instant when suddenly.... This adverb is often preceded by a verb in the future tense. ...kte, tka ecan̄l... But perhaps Ȟcehan̄l is used here. Pb.68. B.H.69.4;299.9. D.5.

ecan̄l'eha, adv. But instead. B.H.99.

ecan̄'leś, adv. Instead, in place of that; in subordinate sentence, All the more. Na wan̄na kéya óṅśi íyahan̄ (i.e. on the blanket), tka - in̄yan̄ kin̄ ko opemnipi. B.H.212.7;245;255;290 311;41.

eca'owan̄caya, adv. All over. Bl.

eca'oyan̄keya, adv. Same as ośpeśpaya. Bl.

eca'oyasin̄, adv. All, emphatically. Same as ośpaśpaya and ecaoyan̄keya. Bl.

ecaś', express., Indeed, certainly, to be sure, to dispel doubt. Ecaś wau kte (you can depend on that). Na - topa can̄ kin̄ ake Ȟ'oká un̄hena el u wicaśi. B.H.41.22;79.5.

eca'śni, neg. (of ecaś). - s'e can̄ku kin̄ áślayela yun̄ke lo, i.e. no snow on the road. Bl.

eca'un̄, v. To be all alone by one's self. Bl. Miś lena tokel ecawicaun̄ kin̄ slolwaye śni. B.H.10.7. Cham tawicoicage kin̄ iyuha kinil apica makoce el ecaun̄pi.

eca'yauȟeca, 1) v.n. To remain in one place. Ecamauȟeca. 2) n. Something permanent, a fixture.

eća'... yélaka, Cf. ecá. B.H.90.7;113.19;172.5;177.18 (Is it possible?);180.9;184.8;191.25;210.17;229.26;239.12; 256.20;264.12. It is ... therefore. SLB.

eca'yuȟ'i, 1) n. Something that is all covered with buboes, as a toad. 2) adj. Rough, uneven on the surface.

ece', adv. Only. Same as ecela. Yun̄kan̄ huȟ'aka ece Ȟpaye. Wi num ece tokan̄l waun̄. Ístogmus ece wayacipi kta. Wa ece skan̄yan̄pi na yatkan̄pi.

ěcě', interj. Of disappointment at a refusal (friendly).

ece'ca, 1) v.n. To be so, be affected with, as with a cold or disease, to be like. Emaceca, un̄kececapi. Taku haye cin̄ owasin̄ taha ececa. Yun̄kan̄ wicaśa wan̄ ataya huhu ececa ca na Ȟayelo Ȟpaya. 2) adv. Thus, so.

ece'caȟe, adv. Just so, even so, that alone.

ece'ceca, adv.(?) (red. of ececa). Bl.

e'ċe cola yuha, v. To keep a horse free for work, spare it. Ece cola bluha kta. Bl.

ece'e, (?). Omaka wan̄ji ecee econ̄pi.

ece'glala, adv. Only that. Bl.

ece'Ȟci, adv. Just so, exactly (as one expected).

ece'kce or ecel'kce, advs. In the proper place or way, in place. Wan̄na ecelkce kiglapi, Each went his own way home. Wowapi ecekce égnaka ya, Put the books in their proper place. B.H.25; 35.10,13;284.23.

ece'kcel, adv. (red. of ecel). In this manner or way; so and so, thus and thus. B.H.25.15. -- ecékcelya, adv. Thus and thus.

ecel', adv. Thus, so (as it must be), as it was. Tiyopa ecel icu, So shut the door. Tiyopa ecel iyeya.

ē'cela, (?).

ece'la, adv. Only, alone.

ece'laȞcin̄, adv. Just so much, that alone.

e'celaȟel, perhaps adv. Itself alone, without help.

ecel'ya, v. (of ecel and iyeya; ecel, so as it must be). Tiyopa ecelya yo, Shut the door.

eceś', interj. Of unwillingness. Eceś ṫuwá le. Used by women only.

e'ceṫi, v. To build a fire to or at.

Écewati, éceuŋtipi.

ece'tk̇iya, adv. Towards (?). Bl.

ece'ṫu, 1) v.n. To be accomplished or fulfilled. Eyá letáŋ nuŋpa caŋ - kiŋ uŋyaŋpi kte lo. Tokata lena - kte lo. 2) adv. So, thus; just, right; about so many or so much. Yamni - , About three. B.H.112.1;117.25.

ece'ṫuk̇iya, v.a. To make so, to accomplish or fulfill. Ecetuwakiya.

ece'ṫuśni, adj. Null, void.
ece'ṫuśniya, v.a. To make a breach, of peace, contract etc.; to rescind.

ece'ṫuya, 1) v.a. To fulfill, accomplish, bring about. Ecetuwaya. 2) adv. About. St. Francis Mission etaŋ west etkiya three miles - ti.

ece'wakta, v. To attend to, to pursue such a course; to be accustomed to. Ecéwawakta.
ece'wakṫaya, adv. Attending to.

ece'yanuniya, v.a. To lead astray.

e'ciaiẏopteya, adv. Directly by, in the direction of. Bl.

e'cicaskaya, (?). Oyate kiŋ witaya ecicaskaya okimniciye kta keyapelo. Bl.

eciŋ', v.n. To think, suppose. Ecaŋmi, ecaŋni, uŋkiciŋpi. Na le tuwe hwo? ecaŋnipi nacece lo. B.H.47.6. Note: the thought is expressed before the word eciŋ.

eciŋ'ic'iciya, v.a. To bring one's self to do something.

eciŋ'k̇a, v. Same as eciŋ. To think, to hesitate or waver in one's opinions. Ecaŋmika.

eciŋ'śni, adj. Thoughtless, foolish, vain.
eciŋ'śniya, adv. Thoughtlessly, foolishly; wrong. - ecamoŋ.

eċiŋ'yaŋ, (?). Kitaŋ - pawósla iheya yaŋké, as is said when a sick person is about ready to die. LB.

e'cipa, v.n. (akipa). To meet together, as two ends of anything or as two armies in battle. Ecipapi. D.215.

e'ciṗeya, v.a. To cause to meet together, as two ends of anything. Écipewaya.

e'ciptaŋ, adv. (akiptaŋ). Together. - ecoŋkaŋpi kte lo.

e'ciśkaŋyaŋk̇el, adv. Together. Bl.

e'ciṫapa, adj. Agreeing with each other, fitted to; all of the same length.

eci'ya, v.a. (eya). To say to one. Ewakiya, uŋkekiyapi. Emakiya, eniciya. Emayakiya. Uŋkekiciyapi, We say to each other. Niś tokel eniciya hwo? Wowicake śni ca ayuśtaŋ yo, emakiya. Note: the "c" changes back into "k" after the "a" of the pronoun. It seems this word is introduced from Santee and should be: ekiya.

eci'yapataŋhaŋ, adv. Towards. Ḣtayetu - . B.H.17.11. SLB.

eci'yapi, v. 3rd pers. pl. or part. (eciya). Called, named. Same as ekiyapi.

eci'yaṫaŋ, adv. From, thence, hence. Na yamni caŋ ehaŋl aŋpa - tokicela ayaŋpa. Yuŋkaŋ taku waŋ skayela maḣpiya - u.

eci'yaṫaŋhaŋ, adv. From, of; on account of; concerning; hence. Tiyopa - .

eci'yawapa s'e, Same as akowapa.

e'ciyupta, v. (ayupta). To answer one another.

eco'k̇oŋ, v.a. (cokoŋ). To determine evil against one for any cause. Ecowakoŋ.

ecoŋ', v.a. To do, to work. Ecamoŋ or ecamuŋ, ecanoŋ or ecanuŋ, ecuŋk̇oŋpi or ecuŋkuŋpi. Omniciye - , To hold a meeting.

ecoŋ'k̇aṗiŋ, v. To be tired of doing, not to want to do. Ecoŋwakapiŋ. Cf. kapiŋ.

ecoŋ'k̇iya, v.a. To cause to do anything.

ecoŋ'ṗica, v. It can be done, is possible. - śni, It cannot be done. Pica

when joined to verbs denotes possibility.
econ'picaḣa, v. It is possible; it is impossible, perhaps. R. Mi.

econ'ṗicaśniśniyan, adv. red. (econpicaśniyan). Impossible. B.H.116.9.

econ'śi, v.a. To advise, exact.
econ'śipi, n. Orders.

econ'wacinśni, v. To be unwilling to do.

e'cuḣci, adv. At least. Also, ecuḣciś. Ota aun wo: ite - naot'insya unyankapi kte lo. Lel hanhepi wanji - amayanpa na hehanl mni kte, I shall spend at least one night here, then I will go. Bl. D.228.
e'cuḣcikel, Same as écela eśa.

ee', v. It is, that is. Hee, lee, etc. which includes the substantive verb. Hecel wanna kośkalaka num wicakaḣnigapi: unma "Mato topa" ee, na unma "Cetan akicita" ee. Na wana osniśni tka ee lila icamna na lila waśme.
ee...ee...ee, coord. conj. Rather... instead. B.H.184.22.

e'eś, adv. Indeed; that it is.

e'eḣiya, 1) v.a. To substitute for, to put for another; to regard as being something. 2) adv. Instead of. Ate, waku śni kinhan miye - wicaśa kin le wanji u kta.

e'ġeju, v. 3rd pers. pl. They assembled. B.H.132.8.

e'glaḣu, v. pos. (eyaka). To take up again, take back again, to take up one's own. Éwaglaku, éunglakupi. Bl.

e'gle, v.a. To place, set or make stand in a place. Éwagle, éunglepi.

e'gleġa, v. To overtake. Éwaglega.

e'glukśan, v. To return or turn around. Same as ékawinġe. Isam ewaglukśan yelo, I went around at a greater distance looking for something. Bl.

e'gluza, v. pos. (eyuẓa). To overtake and take one's own. Éwagluza.

e'gna, prep. With, in amongst, through, in the midst of. Wicegna, Amongst them. Oyate - . Ehanl pte otapi k'on ataya mak'o po na - taninśniyan iyayapi.

e'gnag, v. cont. of egnaka. - aya, To take and lay away.

e'gnagna, prep. red. (egna). With, in, amongst, through, in the midst of. Na ohanketa - iyayapi. Hena oyate - icaḣwicaye. B.H.104.23.

e'gnaḣa, v.a. To lay down or place, to lay away. Éwagnaka, eungnakapi or unkegnakapi. Éyagnake c'el isakib - yo. Bl.

e'gnalaḣci, adv. Amongst.

e'ha, adv. Instead, on the contrary. B.H.68.9;69.4;175.4. D.131, note 3; 204,23.

eha'hatun, n. Chapped lips.

eha'ḣaleś, express. Just for that, in that case. Also, eháeś. Nonge nakpayemayelo - . - ecamon kte. R. D.130, note 4. Bl. SB. Note: wicalaśni ḣeś.

eha'ḣe, 1) n. The last one. 2) adv. Yet, yet to come, a last time. - wanjila, One more. Heon - nape ciyuzapi.
eha'ḣeḣe, (?). - niun wele, as a woman says to a dog when it is to be killed. Bl.
eha'ḣela, 1) n. The last. Emahakela. Miś emahakela kta keya. Śunkakan yanka ośpaye wanji - manipelo. 2) adv. Yet, yet a little while.
eha'ḣelaḣecinhan, adv. Soon.

e'han, v. n. coll. pl. (ihan). They stand in or at. Hihanna oyate kin taku kapi na kawita - ca miś el owapa.

ehan', adv. Then, at that time; then, at that place; to, thus far. - na he - winyunga. Note: this ref. to past time.

ehan'ḣec'un, adv. Really, indeed. Same as ehank'un. - , Wakantanka Cinca kin he le e yelo. Wana - micunkśi héceya cinśni. GV. B.H.268.12. D.157. Cf. ehanon, which seems related to the word. Canke -

Lakota-wiŋyaŋ kiŋ slolyapi, It was plain she was a Lakota woman. D.270,2.

ehaŋ'k'ehaŋ, adv. Long ago. Same as ehaŋni, haŋbléblekel, or K̇iléleK̇el. B.H.190.22. Formerly. R. - homakśila waŋna wimacaḣcala.

ehaŋ'k'uŋ, adv. Indeed. This word is used when one is informed or convinced of something which he has doubted or disbelieved, or has been ignorant of. Same as lotkuŋkeśni, I see it now. WE. Takoja, - ecakel wasna kiŋ mawayakinoŋ ca wana slolwaye. D.

ehaŋl', adv. Then, at that time, ref. to past time alone. B.H.112.2. - wikoś kalaka k'uŋ t'a.

ehaŋ'na, adv. Long ago. Also, eháŋni.
ehaŋ'nitaŋhaŋ, adv. From along time ago.

ehaŋ'ṫaŋ, adv. Already, ever since. He - yasupi kiŋ heca yelo, He is already judged. B.H.180.20;191.8;233.9. Also, from the outset. D.141,154. Note: ehaŋṫaŋ plus a verb means that the first thing was already being done. - yuhapi, They had it already, before something else happened. D.258,261,56.

ehaŋ'ṫaŋhaŋ, adv. From, from that time or place. Hipi kiŋ - yamni caŋ, It is three days since they came. B.H.270.6.

ehaŋ'ṫaŋhaŋś, conj. If. B.H.98.23.
ehaŋ'ṫaŋś, conj. If. Tuwa tiwahe waste kiŋ he nakuŋ ciŋca tewicaḣila - le wicoḣaŋ kiŋ ecoŋ kte lo. Also, a doubtful meaning: Ehaŋtaŋś taogligle e yelo. B.H.293.20.

ehaŋ'tu, adv. At that time. Hehaŋ kośkalaka cik'ala na nahaḣci tawicutoŋ śni - . Ecel wagmeza k'oŋ egnakapi le wetu - . -- eháŋtuḣci, adv. Just at that time. -- eháŋṫuke, adv. Just then, then; indeed.

ehaŋ'ṫulaḣci, adv. Just there (?). Bl.

ehaŋ'uŋ, adv. Truly (?). This implies one had doubted something before, and it corresponds perhaps to the word ehaŋk'uŋ. Misuŋ, - toka śni. B.H.46. 3;104;102.9.

ehaŋ'yaŋ, adv. So far, as far as, up to a certain mark, as in filling a bottle. Hu - lila ataŋiŋ śni, i.e. the legs were not visible. Cf. Hehaŋyaŋ.

ehaś', adv. Surely, truly, certainly, indeed, unusually, undoubtedly. Ho heci - kiŋśitku kici tila k'uŋ wicaśa itaŋcaŋ tuŋkaŋyaŋ. Ito - taŋyaŋ wowak'u kte śni yeśaŋ, eya. Na - kaleḣlege s'e śaic'iye. The word implies that it was too much, more than one can accept. Cf. D.17, note 1.

e'huŋni, v. coll. pl. (ihuŋni). Na waŋna Susunipi kiŋ ikiyela - .

e'huweḣwéġaŋhaŋ, (?). Toki le tuwa inahniyela wawaśi ca iyaye c'oŋ toḱé ehuwehwegahe laka, toki iyaye taŋiŋ śni ye, as is said when a man, sent somewhere, stayed away longer than he ought to have. Bl.

e'ḣa, v.a. (ḣa). To take to and bury at a place, to bury there. E'waḣa. B.H.103.1;283.12.

e'ic'ila, v. refl. To take one's self for a certain thing. Wakaŋtaŋka - . B.H.3.11.
e'ic'iya, (?). v.a. To say to one's self or within one's self. The word is put at the end of a quotation. B.H.22.18.
e'ic'icaġa, v. To claim to be. Wakaŋtaŋka Ciŋca eic'icagelo. B.H.264.9.

e'iglaḱu, v. To help one's self to something when nobody gives it to us; to carry one's own back, as wood, when nobody helps. Bl.

e'iglujaja, v. refl. To wash one's self right there. B.H.221.11.

e'iḣpeic'iyaya, v.a. (?). Ońamniyeta eiḣpeic'imayayapelo, You let me stand alone when I had caught up with you, and then went back. Bl.

e'iḣpekiya, v.a. To take to and leave at, to throw away at. Eiḣpewakiya.

e'iḣpeya, v.a. To take and leave at, to throw away at. Mapehiŋ he tehaŋl paha waŋ ekta eiḣpeyapi kta.

ei'yaṗat'o, v.n. To strike against one.

Eiyamapat'o.

e'ƙaǧa, v.a. To make a thing at a place. 'Waĥpela' mato kagiⁿ kta ca tipi waⁿ ekagapi kte lo.

e'kaĥtaƙa, v.a. To barely touch there. Si kiⁿ mini kiⁿ ekaĥtakapi. B.H.71.11; 116.14.

e'kawiⁿǧa, v. Same as églukśaⁿ. Éwakawiⁿga. Isam ewakawiⁿyelo, I went around at a farther distance (looking for something). Bl. Ataⁿiⁿśniyaⁿ kiⁿyaⁿ iyaya na ekawiⁿgiⁿ na ake glihuⁿni. Kiⁿyaⁿ iyaye na - . MS.573.

e'ke e'yaś, Cf. kec'éyaś.

ē'ƙeśni, (?). Hiⁿhaⁿna - s'e hiⁿgni kta, It will be fine tomorrow. Bl. Uⁿkihuⁿnipi kiⁿ eke śni s'e hiⁿgni kte lo, There will be joy when we arrive. BT.

ē'ke s'e, Eke s'e waⁿji au wo, Bring one on that is even better. IS.

eƙi'cetu, v.n. pos. (of ecetu). To recover, become as before. Emákicetu. -- ekíceťuya, v.a. To cause to recover, make right again; to restore, raise up from the dead. Ekicetuwaya.

eƙi'cicetu, v.n. To become as before to or for one. Emicicetu, enicicetu, euⁿkicicetupi.

e'ƙiciglaku, v. To help one another loading up, as wood on the back. Bl.

e'ƙicigle, v. (of egle). To place for one. Éwecigle, éuⁿkiciglepi.

e'ƙicigluza, v. (of egluza). To take one's own from another; to retaliate. Éwecigluza.

e'ƙicignaƙa, v. (of egnaka). To lay away for one, put away and keep for one. Éwecignaka, émicignaka.

e'ƙicioⁿṗa, v. (of eoⁿpa). To place or set as a trap for anything; to lay away or place something for another. Ėwecioⁿpa.

e'ƙicipa, v. (of akipa). To meet and attack as two hostile bands. Bl.

e'ƙiciṗazo, v. (of pazo). To point to for one. Éwecipazo.

eƙi'ciya, v. Used only in the dual and plural: ekiciyapi, They said to each other. Uⁿkekiciya, We two say to each other.

e'ƙiciyaƙu, v. To help one load wood on his or her back. Bl.

e'ƙico, v.a. (of kico). To call through. B.H.46.7.

e'ƙigle, v. pos. (of egle). To place or lay away one's own. Éwegle, éuⁿkiglepi. Cuⁿśoke ekta śuⁿk ekiglepi.

e'kegleǧa, v. To overtake one. Éweglega, éuⁿkiglegapi, éwicuⁿkiglegapi. B.H.54.2;115.12. MS.563.

e'ƙignaka, v. pos. (of egnaka). To lay away one's own. Éwegnaka, éuⁿkignakapi. Yuⁿkaⁿ wak'iⁿ k'oⁿ ena paĥpa - na akaⁿl iyotaka.

e'ƙihuⁿni, (?). Hena éwakihuⁿni iyececa kiⁿ, hehaⁿl ake wowaśi ecoⁿkoⁿ ktelo. Bl.

e'kiṗazo, v. (of epazo). To show to one, point to for one. Éwakipazo.

e'ƙiťaⁿ, adv. Anyhow. Yuⁿ! tokinahaⁿś taku otaka ca - wamaśipi kte ĥciⁿ. Scepaⁿśi, - wawaⁿyaⁿk uⁿyiⁿ kte (they were warned not to do so).

eƙi'ya, v. To say to (to have said to).

e'ƙiza, v.a. (of kiza). To fight them there. B.H.73.10;91.12.

e'kśu, v.a. To pile up, lay up in a pile. Éwakśu. -- ékśupi, part. Piled up.

ekťa', prep. At, to. Wicoti ekta i na oyaka. Paha waⁿ ekta i.

ekťa'ƙiya, adv. To, towards.

ekťa'kťa, prep. red. (of ekta).

ekta' mai'ĥce, An old word in the 3rd person, He gives me just what I want. Ekta mayáiĥce, You are giving me just what I want. BT.

ekťa'na, adv. There behind, after. B.H. 171.9. Tuweni pa (buffalo here) kiⁿ - iȟpeyapi kte śni yelo. Ptepa waⁿ - iȟpeyayapi keye to eye lo, eya. Yuⁿkaⁿ (śiyo kiⁿ) caⁿ kiⁿ - otka keyapi. 98. Wicaśa k'eya wanase ipi na - waceuⁿpahaⁿpi. D.273.

ekta'śniśniyaⁿ, adv. (of ektaśniyaⁿ). Taku - waecoⁿpi kiⁿ etc.... B.H.80.18.

ekťa'śniyaⁿ, adv. Not according to. - ewatoⁿwaⁿ inaniptecapelo.

ekťa'wapa, adv. Close by something and facing it. Taśuⁿke luzahaⁿ - inajiⁿ na leya. Wicoȟaⁿ...hena tokata - ewagnake lo (set aside for the future). -- ekťáwapáya. Cf. D.135, éktawapaya.

ekte', v.a. (of e and kte). Hecena toka waⁿ ȟpaye k'oⁿ he ekte. To kill.

e'kťoⁿja, v.a. To forget something. Éwaktoⁿja, éciktoⁿja. -- éktoⁿjes'a, adj. Light-headed, forgetful.

e'ǩuwa, v.a. To follow right then, at once. B.H.54.1;110.18;115.12.

ek'e'yaś. Cf. kec'éyaś.

el, prep. In, at, to. This preposition following a verb has the meaning of the Latin "cum temporale". Bluśtaⁿ el owasiⁿ hecetu keyapi. Wauⁿcipi el ake emaceca. Pte kiⁿ kiyela au el waⁿna waⁿji kute. Kiyela u el hokśila k'oⁿ waⁿyakapi. Le waniyetu omake napciyuⁿka el hecel ecamoⁿ, I did this when I was nineteen....

elna'jiⁿ, v.n. To stand at a place. Elnauⁿjiⁿpi. -- elnájiⁿya, v.a. To cause to stand at; to bring to a stand as one following a deer when he overtakes it. Elnájiⁿwaya.

e'mniciya, v. coll. pl. They came together. Same as mnie'iyapi. Ecana lila tipi waⁿ taⁿka ca el - . B.H.206.6;257 5. Also, seemingly, To me meet there. B.H.293.15.

e'na, adv. Right here. Ena inajiⁿ, Stand right here. Ho ca ena uⁿ na ni waciⁿ yo. Ena naⁿkapi kiⁿ, niye ko henanipila kte lo. Wautaⁿyeyela tawicu kicila otowota ena uⁿpi.

ena'gnala, adv. Now and then, sometimes.

e'naȟci, adv. (of ena and ȟci). Same as kiyela. Tiyopa enaȟci iyotakapi.

e'najiⁿ, 1) v.n. To stand at a place. Eńawajiⁿ. 2) v.n. coll. pl. (of inajiⁿ). They stand. Cf. "e".

ena'ǩiya, v.a. To finish, quit, cease from. Enáwakiya. Na waⁿna le okicize kiⁿ enakiyapi.

ena'na, adv. Here and there; sometimes. Same as enagnala (?). Cokaⁿl iśnala omani na enana inajiⁿ na waⁿka na canumpa waⁿ okipagipi. Yuⁿkaⁿ enana leyapi: Lila zitkala otapelo, eyapi.

ena'naǩiya, adv. Here and there. - iyayapi. - mini olepi. B.H.54.4;171.15.

ena'naťaⁿhaⁿ, adv. From here and there. Na waⁿna okśaⁿtaⁿhaⁿ - heyoka k'oⁿ au.

e'napa, v. coll. pl. (of inapa). They come in sight.

e'okiyaka, v.a. To go there and tell. B.H.293.18.

e'oⁿpa, v.a. To place, lay (carefully). Éwaoⁿpa, éuⁿk'oⁿpapi. Le hihaⁿna kiⁿ mat'iⁿ kta ca tuktel paha waⁿji el taⁿyaⁿ emaoⁿpa po.

e'oyaka, v.a. (of oyaka). To tell there as a messanger. B.H.46.6.

e'paȟpa, v.a. To take to and lay down at. Éwapaȟpa.

e'pani, v.a. To crowd or shove, push with the elbows one's way through a crowd. Éwapani.

e'pataⁿ, v. To touch with the hand. Éwapataⁿ.

e'pazo, v.a. To point at, point to. Éwapazo. Na tuweni waepazo kiⁿ oⁿ epazo śni, napahuⁿka kiⁿ he oⁿ ecoⁿpi. Uⁿgnahela śina el epazo. Na itzapa k'oⁿ tatiye topa ku oyasiⁿ epazo.

epca', v. 1st pers. singl. I think. Epcéȟce. This is the only person ased. -- epcápca, v. 1st pers. (red. of epca). I thought so all the time, but didnot say so. Epcápcaȟce. Bl.

epce'ča, v. I think so. R.

epce'ce, v. red. perhaps, of epce. 1st pers. singl. - el epiη kte, I will say what come to my mind, while I think of it. - ecamoη kte, i.e. tokśa slolwayiη kte. Bc. Mh.

eś, particle, (iηś). Is it; if, supposing that something else cannot be done. Eś lecel ecamoη kiη waśte kta. Misuη, lecel yauηke ciη eś takuȟci koyakipe sece lo. Eś tok, misuη, tokaś, How about it, brother. Nakuη nimayayiη na ecel eś miciηkśi waηweglake. Hecel eś ciηka nake inila yaηka śke'. Lila tehaη glipi śni, caηke ecel eś ewicaktoηjapi, Very long they did not return; so at last indeed they forgot them. D.9,3,26. B.H.126.18.

eśa', adv. perhaps. At the beginning of a sentence and followed by śni, it conveys a wish. I wonder if. Eśa mayak'u śni 150 dollars cic'u kte, I wonder if you will sell the horse; I'll pay 150 dollars. Ito eśa waηbli gleśka mahiηgni na kiηyaη ble śni. Eśa uηkcekiȟa mahiηgle śni. D.144, 226. B.H.122.14;181.23;288.11. -- At the end of a sentence, it means: Although. Waśiglapi tuwa ciηca t'iη, naiηś tawicu eśa. Uηkisakib agliyagla eśa inila agliyagla. -- After a noun or verb, it means: Also; some, any, perhaps. Caη wiyopewagni kte naiηś peji eśa, iηś śuηka-wakaη eśa. Na hehaηtaη waηna waniyetu ota itahena eśa, lehaηyaη nahaȟci yuhapi. Naniȟ'oηpi śni eśa ceya howaya po. Lila kutepi eśa inihaη śni hiyaya. Hecel uηglipi na lila el ewacaηmi wawate eśa iηś imuηka ko. -- particle. After pronouns, it makes them universal. Taku eśa. Tohaη mat'e eśa hehaηl tokeca waηji (wahiηkpe) yuha kta. Tuweni wicaśa eśa el yiη kte śni. B.H. 185.6;227.9;274.4;275.20.

eśaη', Same as eśa. Lila eśaη, Also. B.H.274.24.

eśaś', conj. Eśa emph. Wowaȟtani oη kakiśuηyayapi kte iyececa eśaś, oηśiuηlapi ye. Pb.18. -- interj. Indeed.

e'śeś, particle. It indicates finality and a mark of contrast in judgment or fact; thus: Taku waηji ecoη śapi eyaś wicela śni ca eśeś ecamoη kte śni, eyiη kte, i.e. I do not have to. Eśeś mni kte śni, i.e. he lashes out when first he wanted to go along, whereas he did not for any indifferent reason. When one looks for another with whom he wanted to go some place, and when getting there he is told that his boy already went away; then he says: Eśeś tóka śni, O it is all right. A priest tells John to persuade Joe to give up drinking; John tries hard but has no success; John tells the priest about Joe: Eśeś okihipica śni. Clark thinks of going to Rosebud; then his brother Robert comes to his place in a car and says nothing about where he is going; Clark thinks Robert might go to Rosebud and hence says: Robert, Rosebud ekta mni kta waciη tka. Then Robert says: Eśeś heciya le ble lo, ca uηyiη kte. If Robert did not intend to go then he could not use eśeś. Here eśeś means perhaps: I have to, I have to go anyhow, so you can come along. I told him to have his wife join the Yatke Śni; so he goes home and tells her, but she says she could not do so. Then Amos comes back to me to tell me so, saying: Eśeś wicala śni. Amos tells me that he and his wife will go to Winner tomorrow. I say that I too want to go then and that they should take me along. He promises. Then in the morning he comes to me saying: Eśeś uηyaηpi kte śni. They changed their minds. Wowapi cic'u tka, eśeś ecamoη śni. Ho ca eśeś ena awape kte. B.H.89.7;118.3; 287.14.

e'ṫakṗa, v.a. To attack a certain person mentioned. Éwatakpe or étawakpe. Na waηji najiηyaηpi ca etakpiη na iyaȟpaya. Cf. takpé, To come upon and attack.

eṫaη', adv. 1) abbrev. of etaηhaη, From; on account of, concerning. Na etaη tima hiyu. I etaη. 2) Some, somewhat. Caηblaska etaη uηkicupi. Caη etaη makau po.

eṫaη'haη, prop. From; on account of, concerning. Maka gi oyuze el wicoti na etaηhaη zuyayapi. Oglala, S. D., emataηhaη uηketaηhaηpi. B.H.50.2; 273.1.

X. etaṅhaṅ na Y. hetaṅhaṅ, From X. to Y.

eṫaṅ'haṅhaṅ, prep. red. From different places, kinds, etc. Na ake woyute - icu na tatiye topa ecel epazo. B.H.50.2.

eṫaṅ'haṅś ṫoḱa, express. What difference does it make. Etaṅhaṅś he toka śni, It makes no difference. Bl.

eṫaṅ'na háṅṗa, n. Moccasins with no sole sewed on. Also, etáṅnajiṅ háṅpa, perhaps, as the Oglalas may say. Bl.

eṫaṅś', etáṅ emph. B.H.19.13;259.22.

eṫaṅ'śṫokaḱa, adv. express. What difference does it make.

eṫaṅ'ṫaṅ, Same as etaṅhaṅ.

e'taṗa, v. (tapa). To follow after. Étawapa. Bl.

e'teiyokiseyazaṅ, n. Neurology (a new word).

e'ṫi, v.a. To encamp at, pitch a tent at. Éwati, éuṅtipi. Hehaṅl ake wakpala waṅ lila taṅka ca el ihuṅnipi el etipi.

e'ṫiḱaġa, v. To camp at a certain place. B.H.5.5.

e'ṫikel, adv. Travelling and camping at nights, slowly. - uṅyaṅhaṅpi kte lo, i.e. to the Congress across the country. KS.

e'ṫiyóyaṅka, v. To live in a tent. Toke ti śni yeśaṅ etiyoyaṅkahe so? as a woman would say seeing a man live in a very small tent. Bl.

e'tḱiya, adv. Towards, to,with. Wakaṅtaṅka - taku okihipica śni wanice lo. Ca - iblabla. B.H.161.7.

e'tokiciksu, v. To haul for another. Étoweciksu. Bl.

e'toṅwaṅ, v.a. To look to or towards. Éwatoṅwaṅ, euṅtoṅwaṅpi. Ematoṅwaṅ. El - .

e'ṫu, adv. To, at, in there. Cuwi - , In the back. Makoce waṅ tokeya el wai k'uṅ he etu śni. B.H.196.19.

e'ṫuḱehaṅl, adv. (etu, kiṅ, ehaṅl). At the proper time. Same as cókehaṅl - wowapi wagnuni, Just when I should have the book, I lost it. Bl.

e'ṫulaḣci, adv. Just to, at, in.

e'ṫulaḱe, adv. After a while. - kiṅ. Cf. (?).

e'uṅ, v. To go and dwell or be; to dwell at. Éwauṅ.

e'uṅkekiyapi, (?). B.H.35.5. Cf. ekekiya.

e'wacekiya, v. To pray there. B.H.255 18.

e'waciṅ, v.a. To think of or concerning; to turn one's affections to. Ewacaṅmi, ewauṅciṅpi. Hecel uṅglipi na lila el ewacaṅmi wawate eśa iṅś imuṅka ko.

e'waciṅḱa, v.a. To think of, to turn the affections to. Ewacaṅmika, ewacaṅnika, ewauṅciṅkapi. Eya wacipi kiṅ el owapa eśa el ewacaṅmike śni.

e'waṅyaṅka, v. To look there. B.H.271.

e'wehiyu, v. To hemorrhage (a new word

e'wicoṫi, v. pl. coll. They camp together. Iṅyaṅ to oyuze el - . B.H. 71.8.

e'witaya, v. To assemble there; 3rd pers. pl. They assembled. B.H.107.6, 7;257.10.

e'woyaka, v. (woyaka). To tell there.

e'ya, v. To say anything. Epá, ehá, uṅkéyapi. -- adv. 1) Commencing a sentence: Well, as is said in English colloq. Eya, taṅyaṅ uṅkuṅpelo. 2) Also, too. Miś eya, I also. 3) Some. Na wakapapi eya mak'u. Cf. k'eya. B.H.83.3. -- conj. Although, anyhow. Eya...k'eyaś. Eya lila wamatuka k'eyaś el mni kta ("eya" must here be used). Lila wamatuka, k'eyaś eya el mni kte. Eya wacipi kiṅ el, owapa eśa el ewacaṅmike śni. Note: the form, eya...eśa, is perhaps used also. Eya ayupta, You will answer him thus. B.H.174.17. LHB.

e'yacaśtoŋ, v. To give a name to. Cf. caśtoŋ.

e'ya cekiya, v. To have said praying. B.H.78.3;80.9.

e'ya ceya, v. Answering he wept. B.H. 96.7.

e'yahaŋ, v. coll. pl. (iyáhaŋ). They go up a hill and stand on. Cf. iyáhaŋ.

e'yahe, v. Same as eyahaŋ. R. Note: this ref. to what is past; eyahaŋ, to what is present.

eya' hiŋgla, v. To commence or burst out saying.

e'ya hoyekiya, v. Saying he yelled out to him. B.H.122.25. LHB.

e'ya hoyeye, v. To say with a loud voice. B.H.90.9.

e'ya icekiye, v. Saying he besought him. B.H.63.15. LHB.

e'ya iwahoya, v. Saying he asked of me. B.H.94.11. LHB.

e'ya iwaktaya, v. Saying he was expecting. B.H.207.6. LHB.

eya'ke, adv. express. You don't say. Lila icamna lah - . Note: it is used by women on hearing an unexpected bit of news or something that everybody knows and then ironically the word is used.

e'ya kico, v. Saying he called him. B.H.81.6. LHB.

eya'kipaŋ, v. Saying he yelled at him. B.H.81.9. LHB.

e'yakpaha, v. pos. To herald out one's own. B.H.192.6.

e'yaku, v.a. To take up, take away. Éblaku, élaku, éuŋyakupi. Caŋ ota - wo. Bl.

eya'la s'e, adv. Seemingly all, apparently nothing but. Uŋpśija (mud) - wagli yelo, i.e. all bespattered with mud, apparently covered with mud. Wipatapi - , i.e. the man was so laden with such (porcupine quills) work that he seemed to be solid embroidery. Note: the same form is used for other things besides porcupine quill work. Also, we might speak of a camp thus: wakablapi - , i.e. the man is such a good provider that you cannot see his home for the racks of jerked beef drying around it. Bl. Cf. D.51, note 2.

eya' lecel, express. Do it if you can, but you cannot. A by-word used among friends as an answer to a big boast and expressing doubt. When the speaker adds it himself he shows that he does not wish to be taken seriously.

e'ya lowaŋ, v. Saying he sang. B.H. 88.4. LHB.

e'ya okiwa, v. To write saying. B.H. 111.21. LHB.

e'yapaha, 1) v. To herald, proclaim aloud; to stand out and make a speech. Eyawapaha, éyauŋpahapi. 2) n. A crier, a herald. Note: perhaps this should be iéyapaha (ie, apaha).

e'yapahaha, v. red. of ieyapaha. B.H. 117.23.

eya'pi ecéhce, eya' u ecéhce, express. Nothing but talk; nothing to it. GV.

e'yaś, adv. But then, familiarly. Hecel hoopta ble - wicemani kiŋ ataya kowakipapi. Otiwata wicaśa uŋ waŋji lel hi, - lila śicamna ca tima ye śni gle śipelo. Na - hehaŋyaŋ wana oyate kiŋ iye etkiya kicicupi kta oŋ iglu-homnipi. B.H.94.10.

e'ya śna, adv. Every now and then, every time. B.H.70;115;133;137;139; 159;166;191;209;307;192.

e'yaśtaŋ, v. coll. pl. (yaśtaŋ). They finish speaking or eating. Ake lowaŋpi na eyaśtaŋpi ehaŋl wicaśa k'oŋ he cokab inajiŋ na lecel eya. Olowaŋ kiŋ le - el waŋna ceyapi.

e'yaśtoka, express. I don't care; it makes no difference.

e'yaś tuká, adv. As you should recall. - uŋkicaŋte kiŋ uŋkoile s'elececa. B.H.273.14.

e'yawa, v. To take for. Also, e yawa. Jesus Messiah kiŋ eyawapi. B.H.269.3.

eya'wela s'e, adj. All bloody. - s'e ku.

e'yaya, 1) v.a. To take or have taken with one. Eblable, élale, éuŋyayapi. Takoja, iśtiŋma ye; ciciye waŋ u kta na éniyayiŋ kte, as a woman would say when putting children to sleep. PD. 2) v. coll. pl. (iyaya). They have gone. Same as iyáyapi. B.H.134.16; 137.9.

eya'ya, v. red. (eya). To say often, to repeat. Eṗáṗa, uŋkeyayapi. Tohaŋyaŋ oyakihipi ȟupahu ȟoza po eyáyiŋ. D.13.

eya'yalaka, v. red. To lie. Epapalaka.

eye'celeś, (?). A by-word: He said that a long time ago. WE.

eye' le, express. He said so, as is said when doubting a statement made by men. Eyá ke is used by women. Ke ... keyapi'.

eye'picaśni, adj. Absurd.

e'yeśaŋ, express. That is he. He Ikpi Huŋhuŋla - iyekiyapi śni keye. Note: deriv. from iye-eśa, or ee-eśa, perhaps.

eye'ya, v.a. To make say, to say something. Ituśeka taku waŋji eyemayayiŋ kte ȟciŋ tka aciyuptiŋ kte śni. Bl.

e'yoȟakiŋ, v.a. To look round into, as in at a door partly open; to look out of. Eýowakakiŋ.

e'yoȟas'iŋ, v.a. To peep in, as in through a key-hole, to look in by stealth. Eyowakas'iŋ, éyouŋkas'iŋpi. Ohloka waŋ lila ciscila etaŋ eyokas'iŋpi. Cuŋwiŋtku ti kiŋ el - , She looked (peeped) into her daughter's tipi. D.19.

e'yotaka, v. coll. pl. (iyotaka). Wol eyotake. B.H.124.3.

e'yuǧica, v.n. To wake up right there, to go to and wake up. B.H.117.3;134.15;203.9.

e'yuȟpa, v.a. To take and lay down at, to take off one's pack and rest it. Ebluȟpa. Ípaȟe éyuȟpapi (sic, ipaǧe), i.e. to rest somewhere before the place assigned for dinner. Bl.

e'yuŋȟa, v.a. To go and sleep at. Emuŋka, enuŋka. Iyayapi na wicoti kiŋ ikiyela eyuŋka. B.H.55.11. -- v. coll. pl. of iyuŋka.

e'yutaŋ, v.a. To go near and touch. Uŋgna emayalutaŋ kilo. B.H.256.23; 272.3.

e'yuweǧe, v. coll. pl. of iyuwega. Same as iyuwegapi. B.H.71.16.

e'yuza, v.a. To go and take at, seize and hold at or on the way, to hold to or at. Ebluza.

G

ġaġa'ya, adv. On the surface. - śpaŋ, To fry a piece of meat on its flat side or surface, as a slice of bacon.

ġalġa'ta, adv. Forked, pronged; open, as a piece of cloth.

ġaŋ, adj. (?). As is said of hair standing up or sideways, mussed up. Pehiŋ nigaŋ, Your hair is mussed up. Cf. ġaŋic'iya, wicagaŋgaŋ.

ġaŋġaŋ', adj. Open, as thin cloth.

ġaŋġaŋ'ic'ya, Same as gaŋic'iya.

ġaŋġaŋ'la, adj. Full of holes, as threadbare cloth appears to be etc. Magaŋgaŋla, i.e. I feel cold because of this clothing. Wana magaŋgaŋla ca iḣaŋhaŋ icaluza keś kaġaŋ mahiya welo. Bl.

ġaŋġaŋ'śni, adv. Crowded together, as men, animals, many wagons etc. - ahiyelo. WE. Cf. R.
ġaŋġaŋ'śniyaŋ, adv. Crowded together, there being no room between. B.H.51. 19;118.6.

ġaŋġaŋ'yela, adv. Clearing, as thick clouds grow thinner. Wana maḣpiya - u welo, i.e. clearing up. Bl. Cf. R. -- adj. Very sharp and thin, as the blade or bit of an axe.

ġaŋi'c'iya, v. refl. (gaŋ). To make one's own hair stand upright. Equivalently: pehiŋ pawosla iyeya.

ǧaᶯ´ka, adj. Bushy, as is said of hair. Nata - . Pehiᶯ magaᶯka.

ǧaᶯ´ s'e, adv. With the hair standing on end, not combed and waving in the wind. - manipi. Le tuktel yugmiᶯ ikikicapi laka; - he ye. Bl.

ǧaᶯye´la, adv. With the hair standing up not combed. Same as gaᶯ s'e.

ǧe´bniyaᶯ, v. (gepa, niyaᶯ). To breathe in a choking manner, as when the throat is swollen. Same as gemniyaᶯ.

ǧeǧe´ic'iyela, adv. To walk up and down in a room, or so in excitement. Bl. R. Cf. gegeya. - uᶯ.

ǧe´ǧeya, adv. Swinging, dangling. Same as zézeya. Tipi waᶯ el si nupiᶯ paȟtapi na pa - otkeyapi. Peta pa kiᶯ kutakiya - oktaᶯpi. B.H.305.28. -- v.i. To swing e.g. one's arms, as a drunken person. Also, gegéya, perhaps. Note: refl. gegeic'iya. Cf. R.

ǧe´mniyaᶯ, v. Same as gebniyaᶯ.

ǧe´p̣a, v.n. To gasp for breath, making a noise with the throat. Wagepa.

ǧi, adj. Brown, dark-gray, rusty-looking. Maka gi.

gica´haᶯ, v. n. To slip, misstep, stumble and fall, in the present time. Magicahaᶯ. In the past time: gicáhe, magicahe.

gica´he, v.n. To slip, stumble, in the past time. In the present: gicáhaᶯ.

gica´heya, v.a. To cause to slip and fall. Gicáhewaya.

ǧiǧi´, adj. red. (gi). Brown, rusty. -- n. Rust. Wana peji - aye lo. Bl.

ǧiǧi´ya, adv. red. (giya). Brown. Maȟpiya - kaȟwoka. Tohaᶯl maȟpiya - kaȟwoȟwok ahiyaye ciᶯ hehaᶯta kta śke'. Wana peji kiᶯ - aya. BT. D.92.

giᶯ´c̣a, v.n. To snivel; to grunt; to sob. Wagiᶯca.

giᶯ´cela, adj. Aching, convalescing. - ni k'uᶯ, as is said when a man is recovering from illness. LB.

ǧiᶯgiᶯ´ca, n. Ear wax; dross; quicksilver of looking-glasses; certain webs, etc. Also, ǧaǧéca. Noᶯge - omajula yelo, My ear is full of wax. Bl. Cf. R.

ǧiᶯlǧiᶯ´ca, v. red. (giᶯca). To make a noise like one choking.

ǧiᶯl´ǧiᶯcala, n. The Wilson snipe, so called on account of the noise it makes. Bl.

ǧitḳa´, adj. Grayish.

ǧitḳa´tḳa, adj. red. (gitka). Reddish, brownish or yellowish.

ǧiya´, adv. (?). Appearing brown. Mato ciᶯcála-hakáktala waᶯ giyéȟci yaᶯkela i.e. in his very brown coat. - śpaᶯ. D.116. -- v.a. To make brown; to roast, as corn or coffee.

gla, A syllable used to make the possessive form of verbs commencing with "ka" and "ya"; thus, for kaksa, glaksa, while the pronouns are prefixed.

gla, v. To go home. Wagla. Tiyatakiya wagla. -- v.a. To detest something repulsive. Waglá. B. Cf. wóglaya.

glabla´ya, v. pos. of kablaya.

glabla´za, v. pos. of kablaza and yablaza.

glable´ca, v. pos. (kableca, yableca). To break in pieces one's own by striking e.g. something brittle; to bite in pieces. Waglableca.

glablel´, cont. of glableca. - iyeya.

glablu´, v. pos. of kablu and yablu.

glace´ya, v. pos. of kaceya and yaceya.

glaco´za, v. pos. of kacoza.

glaǧa´p̣a, v. To tear or bruise a piece off.

glaǧe´ǧe, v. pos. (kagege). To sew one's own. Waglagege.

glagle´gleǧa, v. (?). Iktomi huhá glagleǧlegelo, they said when a fellow told lies. WE.

glagna'yaŋ, v. pos. of yagnayaŋ.

glaġo', v. pos. of kago.

glahaŋ', v.n. To ravel, to untwist, as twisted string.

glahe', adv. Unrolled of itself.

glahe'ya, adv. Continuously straight forward, without interruption. - ia, To speak continuously.
glahe'yapi s'e, adv. Same as kaniyeyapi s'e. - omani hihuŋni, i.e. doing what one wanted without stopping for anything else, thus without difficulties. Cf. glaheya.

glahiŋ'ṫa, v. pos. of kahiŋta. B.H. 174.9.

glaho'ho, v. pos. of yahoho or kahoho.

glaho'mni, v. pos. of yahomni or kahomni.

glaho'toŋ, v. pos. of kahotoŋ.

glahuŋ'huŋza, v. pos. of kahuŋhuŋza.

glaȟa', v. pos. (kaȟa). To curl, to knot one's own. Bl.

glaȟa'ṗa, v. pos. of kaȟapa.

glaȟeb', cont. of glaȟepa.

glaȟe'ṗa, v. pos. (yahepa). To drink up one's own. Waglaȟepa.

glaȟi'ca, v. pos. of yaȟica.

glaȟla'ȟlaya, v. red. of glaȟlaya. Bl.

glaȟla'ya, v. pos. (yaȟlaya). To bite obliquely, to bite off e.g. the skin of anything; to tell a lie. Waglaȟlaya. Bl.

glaȟle'ca, v. pos. (kaȟleca, yaȟleca). To break open one's own by smiting, kaȟleca; to tear open one's own by biting, yaȟleca. Waglaȟleca.

glaȟlel', cont. of glaȟleca. - iyeya, To break or smash open one's own suddenly.

glaȟlo'ka, v. pos. of kaȟloka and yaȟloka. Waglaȟloke śni ca paŋpaŋla waŋji mak'u wo, I can't chew it, so .... Bl.

glaȟni'ġa, v. pos. (kaȟniga). To choose one's own. Waglaȟniga.

glaȟṗa', v. pos. of kaȟpa.

glaȟṗu', v. pos. (yaȟpu). To pull or tear off with the teeth something of one's own that adheres to something else. Waglaȟpu. -- glaȟṗúȟṗu, v. red. of glaȟpu.

glaȟṫag', cont. of glaȟtaka. - iyeya.
glaȟṫa'ka, v. pos. (yaȟtaka). To bite one's own. Waglaȟtaka.

glaȟu'ġa, v. pos. of kaȟuga and yaȟuga. Cf. glaȟuȟuga.
gla'ȟuȟ, cont. of glaȟuga.
glaȟu'ȟuġa, v. pos. (kaȟuȟuga, yaȟuȟuga). To smash or break in one's own, as the skull of one's child, or as one's kettle by pounding; to break up one's own with the teeth, as bones which belong to one's self.

glaȟ'u', v. To peel with the mouth e.g. a turnip with the teeth. Bl.

glai'leġa, v. (?). Bl.

glaja', adj. or v.n. To be sick or diseased. Distinguished from wayazaŋka, as that means: an attack of sickness, this indicates a state of confinement. Maglaja.
glaja'ja, v. pos. of kajaja.

glaja'ta, v. pos. (yajalata). To bite and make forked. Bl.

glajib', cont. (glajipa). - yuta, To eat very slowly, to nibble off. - iyeya.

glaji'ṗa, v.a. pos. (kajipa). To shave one's own stick; to bite off or nibble one's own food. Waglajipa. Cf. yajipa.

glajo', v. pos. (yajo). To blow on one's own instrument. Waglájo.

glaju'ju, v.a. pos. (kajuju). To blot out or erase one's own; to pay one's debts. Wagláj uju.

glajuŋ'ke, v.n., adj. (glaja-uŋ). To be a confirmed invalid. Glaśmúŋke.

glakaŋ', v. pos. (kakaŋ). To hew one's own.

glaka'wa, v. pos. of yakawa.

glakca', v. pos. (kakca). To comb one's own. Waglakca.

glake', adj. Standing apart, alone, separated, as large trees without underbrush do; large-toothed, as a coarse comb. Cf. caŋglegle; caŋglaka, Ob.
glake'keyela, adv. (glakeyela). Not close together, but separated as men coming in a crowd and not close packed. Bl. - yaŋkapi, au, aye.
glake'ya, adv. Separately, at a distance from each other.
glake'yela, adv. Here and there, as shocks of grain in a field. Bl. BT.

glakiŋ'ca, v. pos. of kakiŋca.

glakiŋ'kiŋyaŋ, adv. (glakiŋyaŋ). In a zigzag line. Itaŋcaŋ k'oŋ he - el u na kaħol hiyuc'iya. Na ena - najiŋ ca lila kutepi. B.H.12.3.

glakiŋ'yaŋ, adv. Transverse, not crosswise, which is called kaicioptaya; but as one man standing and another passes by, not crosswise (-+-), but transversely (-┬-). Thus, a man - inajiŋ to the people when he has them at his right or left side. At right angles. Cf. D.199,112.

glaki'skiza, v. pos. red. of yakiza. Cf. higlakiskiza.

glakpaŋ', v. pos. (kakpa). To wink. Iśta waglakpaŋ, I wink my eyes.

glakpi', v. pos. of kakpi and yakpi.

gla'ksa', v. pos. (kaksa and yaksa). To cut, bite off one's own, as on'es own wood. Waglaksa. B.H.191.12.
glaksa'ksa, v. red. (glaksa). To cut or bite one's own in many pieces. Waglaksaksa.

glakśi'ja, v. pos. of yakśija.

glaku'ka, v. pos. of yakuka.

glak'e'za, v. pos. of yak'eza.

glak'o'ġa, v. pos. yak'oga.

glala', v. pos. (kala). To scatter one's own. Waglála.

glamna', v. pos. (kamna and yamna). To acquire or collect property; to acquire by talking. Waglámna.

glao'ksa, v. pos. of kaóksa.

glao'nihaŋ, v. pos. (yaonihaŋ). To praise one's own. Waglaonihaŋ.

glao'ta, v. pos. (yaóta). To count one's own many.

glao'taŋiŋ, v. pos. (yaotaŋiŋ). To manifest or declare one's own. Waglaotaŋiŋ. Hecel kéya ozuye tawa kiŋ ohitika keya - .

glapa', v. pos. (yapá). To take hold of one's own with the mouth. Waglapa.

glapaŋ', v. pos. (kapaŋ). To beat or thresh out one's own, as one's own corn. Waglapaŋ.

glapa'pa, v. red. of glapa. Śake - nawajiŋ.

glape'haŋ, v. pos. (yapehaŋ). To fold up one's own with the mouth. Waglapehaŋ.

glape'mni, v. (?). Bl.

glapol', cont. of glapota. - iyeya.

glapo'pa, v. pos. of yapópa.

glapo'ta, v. pos. (kapota and yapota). To beat one's own to pieces; to bite to pieces, destroy one's own by biting. Waglapota.

glapsag', cont. of glapsaka. - iyeya.

glapsa'ka, v. pos. (kapsaka and yapsaka). To cut off one's own by striking (kapsaka), as a branch of one's tree; to bite off one's own, as one's string. Waglapsaka.

glapsaŋ'psaŋ, v. pos. (kapsáŋpsaŋ).

To move to and fro one's own. Nape -. Cf. siᵑtóᵑpsaᵑpsaᵑ.

glapsiᵑ'psiᵑta, v. pos. (kapsiᵑpsiᵑta). To whip one's own child. Waglápsiᵑpsiᵑta.

glapsiᵑ'ta, v. pos. of kapsiᵑta.

glapsuᵑ', v. pos. (kapsuᵑ, yapsuᵑ). To spill one's own by striking or to spill with the mouth. Waglapsuᵑ.

glapśuᵑ', v. pos. (kapśuᵑ, yapśuᵑ). To knock out one's own by the roots, as a tooth; to knock out of joint, as one's leg; to bite out or knock out one's own, as a horse does in shedding his teeth. Waglapśuᵑ.

glapta', v. pos. (kapta). To lade out one's own. Bl. Note: yapta may perhaps be the basic word for this.

glaptaᵑ'yaᵑ, v. pos. of kaptaᵑyaᵑ.

glapte'cela, v. pos. of kaptecela and yaptecela.

glaptu'ja, v. pos. of kaptuja.
glaptuś', v. cont. of glaptuja. - iyeya.

glaptu'za, v. pos. of kaptuza. Bl.

glapu'za, v. pos. of yapuza. Bl.

glaskab', v. cont. of glaskapa.
glaska'pa, v. pos. (kaskapa). To clap, make strikes together. Nape - , To clap one's hands. Waglaskapa.

glaske'pa, v. pos. of kaskepa.

glaski'ca, v. pos. (kaskica, yaskica). To press one's own with the mouth. Wagláskica.

glasku', v. pos. (yasku). To bite or peel off one's own. Waglasku.

glasle'ca, v. pos. of kasleca.

glaslo'haᵑ, v. pos. of kaslohaᵑ, yaslohaᵑ.

glasni', v. pos. (kasni, yasni). To extinguish or cool. Peta uᵑglasnipelo, as they would say if the fire went out while they were talking. WH.

glasol', v. cont. of glasota. - iyeya.

glaso'ta, v. pos. (kasota, yasota). To eat up one's own, to use up words or language, i.e. to finish speaking; to cut all off, as one's own timber. Waglasota.

glasto', v. pos. of kasto.

glasu', v. pos. (yasu). To judge or condemn one's own; to perfect, to finish perhaps. Waglasu. R.

glasu'ta, v. pos. (yasuta). To confirm one's own words.

glas'i'c'iya, v. To be very lazy. Bl.

glaś, v. cont. (glaja). To be sick, be in a sick condition.
glaśuᵑ'ka, v. perhaps. and n. One who is often sick. MF.

glaśa'pa, v. pos. of yaśapa.

glaśi'ca, v. pos. (yaśica). To speak evil of one's own.

glaśka', v. refl. (kaśka). To bind one's own. Waglaśka. Śuᵑkuᵑglaśkapi ekta uᵑkipi.

glaśke'pa, v. pos. of yaśkepa. Bl.

glaśki'ca, v. pos. (yaśkica). To press one's own with the mouth, as in chewing tobacco. Waglaśkica.

glaśki'pa, v. pos. of yaśkipa.

glaśko'pa, v. pos. of kaśkopa, yaśkopa.

glaśla', v. pos. (kaśla, yaśla). To mow one's own meadow, to graze off one's own grass; to shave e.g. one's own beard. Waglaśla.

glaślo'ka, v. pos. of kaśloka. B.H. 191.9.

glaślu'ta, v. pos. of kaśluta.

glaśna', v. pos. (kaśna, yaśna). To blunder in speaking; to miss in taking one's food into the mouth; to miss in attempting to strike one's own; to talk incorrectly. Waglaśna.
glaśna'śna, v. red. of glaśna.
glaśna'śnayaᵑ, adv. Blunderingly,

as in talking, incorrectly.

glaśpa´, v. pos. (kaśpa, yaśpa). To knock or bite off a piece from one's own. Waglaśpa.

glaśpu´, v. pos. of kaśpu and yaśpu.

glaśta´ka, v. pos. (kaśtaka). To strike or smite one's own. Waglaśtaka.

glaśtaŋ´, v. pos. (kaśtaŋ, yaśtaŋ). To pour out one's own, to spill with the mouth, as one's coffee; to finish eating or speaking. Waglaśtaŋ.

glaśya´, adv. perhaps. Afflicted. - uŋpi ota akisniwicaye, i.e. he healed any sort of sickness. - makuja, I suffer a sickness that persists.

glata´, v. pos. (yata). To taste one's own, to chew over again, as a cow her cud. Waglata.

glataŋ´, v. pos. (yataŋ). To praise one's own. Waglataŋ.

glataŋ´ka, v. pos. of yataŋka.

glataŋ´yaŋ, v. pos. perhaps, of yataŋyaŋ. Bl.

glata´ta, v. pos. (katata). To knock and shake off one's own blanket; to take in the mouth and shake, as a dog does to something. Waglatata. B.H. 206.14. Cf. yata.

glata´ta, v. red. of glata. Waglatata. Pejuta kiŋ ikikca na - .

glateb´, v. cont. of glatepa. - iyeya. - aya.

glate´haŋ, v. pos. of yatehaŋ.

glate´pa, v. pos. (yatepa). To wear off one's teeth short. Waglatepa. Hi´glatepa.

glati´taŋ, v. pos. of yatitaŋ.

glatkaŋ´, v. pos. (yatkaŋ). To drink one's own. Waglatkaŋ.

glato´ie, v. To curse. Also, glatóie. Takuwe śuŋka owaŋke kiŋ le itaŋcaŋ wicaśayatapi mitawa kiŋ - hwo? B.H. 95.7. Cf. śigla tóie.

glato´kaŋ, v. pos. (yatokaŋ). To put one's own in another place with the mouth; to speak of one's own as in another place. Waglatokaŋ.

glato´keca, v. pos. (yatokeca). To speak of one's own as different. Waglatokeca.

glato´nana, v. pos. (yatonana). To count one's own few. Cf. glaota.

glato´to, v. pos. (katoto). To knock at one's own door. Waglatoto.

glat'a´, v. pos. (kat'a, yat'a). To kill one's own by striking; to bite one's own to death. Waglat'a.

glat'iŋs´, v. cont. of glat'iŋza. - iyeya.

glat'iŋ´za, v. pos. (kat'iŋza, yat'iŋza). To make one's own tight by driving; to press one's own tight with the teeth. Waglát'iŋza.

glauŋ´ka, v. pos. (kauŋka). To fell one's own. B.H.225.11.

gla´wa, v. pos. (yawa). To read one's own, to count one's own; to value one's own. Waglawa.

glawa´ci, v. pos. (kawaci). To make spin, as a top by striking. Bl.

glawa´kaŋ, v. pos. (yawakaŋ). To call one's own sacred. Waglawakaŋ.

glawaŋ´kal, v. pos. of yawaŋkal.

glawa´śte, v. pos. (yawaśte). To bless one's own.

glawa´ś'aka, v. pos. of yawaś'aka.

glawe´ga, v. pos. (kawega, yawega). To break or fracture by striking, as one's own axe handle; to break partly off with the teeth. Waglawega.

glaweh´, v. cont. of glawega.

glawe´hwega, v. red. of glawega.

glawi´caka, v. pos. of yawicaka.

glawi´yakpa, v. pos. of yawiyakpa.

glaya´, v.a. To push something through

a small hole, as made by a wire down a pipe stem. Glawaya. Caŋnuŋpa iglaye, A wire pipe stem cleaner. BD.

glayuŋg', cont. of glayuŋka. - iyeya.
glayuŋ'ka, v. pos. (kayuŋka). To cut down or fell one's own trees. Wagláyuŋka.

glaza'mni, v. pos. (kazámni). To open one's own. Waglázamni.

glaza'pa, v. pos. (kazápa). To cut off the fat with the skin, in skinning one's own. Waglázapa.

glaze', v. pos. (kaze). To lade out one's own, as one's food. Waglaze.

glazo'ka, v. pos. (yazoka). To suck one's own, as a child its own finger. Waglázoka.

glazuŋ'ta, v. pos. (yazuŋta). To connect one's words, to speak correctly; to praise or speak well of one's own. Waglázuŋta.

gle, v. To go home. Cf. gla.

gle, v.a. To put or place, make stand as is usually applied to things that stand on end, e.g. barrels etc.; to have by one. Mini wagle, I have water. Yuŋkaŋ winuŋhcala waŋ wiyohpeya glekeye (to go), wohaŋ gle (to set). Ho, uŋci, iblabla kiŋ le micicat'iŋ na ohaŋ migle yo. Note: this may be considered as the v.t. form of haŋ.

gleb, cont. of glepa. - hiyuyu, To vomit.

glebki'ya, v.a. To cause to vomit. Glebwákiya.

gle'ga, adj. Spotted, figured as calico.

glegle', adj. Scattered, here and there. Caŋglegle.

glegle'ga, adj. red. (glega). Spotted, speckled; brownish. R.
glegle'hya, adv. Made spotted. Bl.

glegle'ka, adj. Scattered, separated, one here and one there. Caŋglegleka.

glegle'za, adj. Striped, streaked.

glegle'zela, adj. dim. (glezela). Striped, streaked.

gleh'o'haŋ, v. To wear a stripe on. I kiŋ gleh'ówahaŋ waciŋ yelo. BT.

gleki'ya, v.a. To cause to go home, to send. Glewákiya.

gle'pa, v.a. To vomit, puke. Waglépa. Iglepa, To vomit up what one has eaten. Iwáglepa.

glesye'la, (?). Nige kiŋhaŋ tanásula ognake s'e - naŋke, i.e. one warming himself, his nigé. Bl.

gleśi', v.a. To send home, to order to go home. Glewáśi.

gleśka', adj. Speckled, spotted.
gleśka'śka, adj. red. (gleśka). Spotted, figured as calico.

gletoŋ', v.a. To correct a mistake, to make right. Glewátoŋ. Glemicitoŋ. WE.

gletoŋ', v.a. To repair, mend. Same as apiya. Glewátoŋ. WE.

gle'za, adj. Striped; in ridges or rows; fig. acting foolishly. He gleze yelo, He makes a fool of himself. WE.
gle'zela, adj. Striped. Igmu - .

gleze'zeka, adj. or n. Making a fool of one's self; a fool. Same as oileleka. WE.

gli, v. pos. (hi). To arrive at home. Wagli.

glia'pe, v.a. To await one's coming home. Gliáwape.

glicu', 1) v. To start to come home. Wagliyacu. Yuŋkaŋ ate inapa na ake tima glicu, i.e. he left the tent and came in again. 2) v. To get down from or away, as from a wagon.

glicu'ya, v.a. To cause to start home, to cause to camp. Glicúwaya. Leciya topa caŋ hehaŋyaŋ śna yujajape na hehaŋl oyate egna śna glicuwicayape.

gligla', v.n. To pass by something or

somebody, glakinyan, going home. Wanna wi gli'gle lo, as the Indians say about January 15th in ref. to the sun moving back to the east. Wana ȟeyáta gligla po, Now walk along back. D.92.

gligle'kiya, (?). Cannunpa kin - iyatanpi.

gligle'yakel, (?). - omani, To go here and there. - waun welo, as is said in watering trees here and there in a grove. Bw.

gligni', v. Come or go along towards one's house. Nitakuye tona tewicayaȟilapi heci hena owewicakiceya po, eya okawinȟ - .

glihan', v.n. To fall or come down and be standing, as an arrow. Inyan wan - ȟpaya. Wahinkpe kin tanwankatuya ya na wanna makata - . - gliȟpaya.

glihe'ya, adj. or adv. Steep. Mayá - , A steep bank. Maya - he lo. B.H.68. 11;228.7.

glihun'ni, v. pos. (hihunni). To reach home coming straight. Waglihunni.

gliȟpa', v. To fall down (once). Wagliȟpa. Yunkan inyan tanka wan - keye. Gliȟpaya, To fall again.

gliȟpa'ya, v. pos. (hinhpaya). To fall or lie down on coming home; to fall again; to fall down and lie, as a person or thing that drops. Wagliȟpaya. Apá - , To fall wounded. Ta - . B.H.283.5. D.199,247.

gliȟpe'ya, v.a. To throw someone down, as in wrestling. Gliȟpéwaya. Yunkan iś wicaśa wan ena winyan num hecel gliȟpewicaya.

glina'jin, v. pos. (hinajin). To return and stand. Waglinajin or waglinawajin. Ecel wagliyacu na tankal waglinawajin. Nawajin k'on el waglinawajin.

glina'pa, v. pos. (hinapa). To come in sight coming home; to come out of. Waglinapa and waglinawapá.

glinun'wan, v. To arrive at home swimming. Bl.

gli owa'yawa, n. A day school.

glipsi'ca, v. pos. (hipsica). To alight at home, jump down again. Waglipsica.

glipsil, cont. of glipsica.

gli'śni owáyawa, n. A boarding school.

glitan'inka, v. To arrive suddenly at home, i.e. where the speaker is. Toké tohinni tokiyatanhan yaglitaninke so? Bl.

gliu', v. (?). To be coming home.

gliya'cu, v. To be on one's way home with something, speaking of one. Wagliyacu, yagliyacu, also perhaps, glicu. Agliyacu, in speaking of many. Gla po, hecel wanna miś wagliyacu na wagli. Ecel wagliyacu (from a tent) na tankal waglinawajin. Hecel miglahomni na wagliyacu.

gli'yagla, v. (yagli-yagla, perhaps). To go from and return. Cf. yagla, To go over there.

gliya'gli, v. (?). To have gone and come back. Wagliyagli. Na wanna wagliyagli na wowiyuśkinka. Note: J. BearShield says there is no such word. Moreover, i in wagliyagli is perhaps a cont. of "na", wagla-na-yagli.

gliya'han, v.n. To appear on top of a hill in sight on one's way home. Wagliyahan. Agliyahan, in ref. to many. Ecel paha wan el wahiyoȟpaye k'on he ake aiyakapteya waku na el wagliyahan.

gliya'ȟpaya, v. pos. (iyaȟpaya). To come home and fall down upon one. Wagliyeȟpaya.

gliya'ku, v. pos. To return or start to come home. "He ókiksa" he kin hogna yagliyakupi kte lo. D.246. Note: only the 1st and 2nd persons are used: wagliyaku, yagliyaku, ungliyakupi; and the 3rd person is glicu.

gliyan'ka, v. (gli-oyanka). To go and be at home. Śunka wawíyeke (śunȟpab wowiyanka) s'e gliyankin kte lo. Bl.

gliyo', v. pos. of hiyo. Cf. hiyo.

gliyo'hi, v. pos. (hiyohi). To arrive somewhere <u>for</u> one's own, as parents for the school children. Gliyowahi. Wicagliyowahi. Cf. gliyoi.

gliyo'ḣpaya, v. To have come down from. Wagliyoḣpaya. When they are many: agliyoḣpaya. Na wanna wicaśa zaptanpi k'on hena gliyoḣpayapi (from a hill). Na oyate najinpi etkiya kupi na ikiyela glinajinpi.

gliyo'i, v. To go somewhere for one's own, as parents for their school children. Gliyowai. Wicagliyowai.

gliyo'kpeca, v. To have come back home from somewhere. Tokiyatanhan yagliyokpeca hwo? Bl. Cf. kiyokpeca.

gliyo'tak̇a, v. pos. (hiyotaka). Sit down on one's way home. Wagliyotaka. Unkipi na wazi iyohanzi wan el ungliyotakapi. Wanna glinapapi na oyasin tankal gliyotakapi.

gliyo'u, v. pos. (hiyou). To come to take one's own home. Hokśila gliyowau kte lo. Heon cigliyowaupi ca nunpa can asniwakinyin na unglapi kte lo. RC.

gliyo'ya, v. pos. (hiyoya). To go and get one's own. Ogle gliyoyapi kte śni. Hokśila mitawa kin hena wicagliyomni kta. ST. B.H.245.23. D.219.

gliyun'k̇a, v. pos. (hiyunka). To come asleep, to camp on the way home. Waglimunka, ungliyunkapi. Psunpsunkiya - .

gliyu'weġa, v. pos. (hiyuwega). To cross a stream by fording in coming home. Wagliyuwega. B.H.204.1.

glo, prefix. It forms the pos. of some verbs.

glo, v. To grunt, make a noise, as hogs and buffalo calves do. Lila pte hotonpi na glopi.

gloa'ya, v. pos. To carry one's own towards a place. Waglóaya. Tipi kin he wanna ungloayapi. B.H.47.

gloe'yaya, v. pos. To take or have taken one's own with one going some place, as in taking one's child. Wagloeyaya, ungloeyayapi. B.H.270.12.

glogla', v. pos. To carry one's own home. Waglogla. Waglogni kte. Nupin waglogni kte. D.120.

glogle'ska, n. The gullet, esophagus. Same as glogloska.

glogli', v. pos. To arrive at home with one's own. Waglogli.

glogli'yacu, v.a. To get something back, as after having loaned it out. B.H.61.6. MS.489. LHB.

gloglo', v. red. (glo). To grunt, as do hogs and buffalo calves, or as grouse. Also, glóglo. - u. D.84.

gloglo'lowan, v. To sing with a hoarse voice. Bl.

gloglo'sk̇a, n. The windpipe, i.e. the throat.

glohi', v. pos. To bring one's own to a place. Waglohi.

glohi'naṗa, v. pos. To lead one's own out. B.H.223.7.

gloi', v. pos. To take or have taken one's own to a place. Wagloi. Pb.37.

glo'in, v. pos. (in). Cf. glówin.

glok̇i', v. pos. To arrive with one's own, as children, at home. Wagloki. Note: the word is used of others.

glok̇i'yagla, v. pos. To have taken away one's own and be on the way home. Waglokiyagla.

glok̇u', v. pos. To be on the way home bringing (home) one's own, as children. Wanna - , as said when you see him coming with his children.

gloni'ca, v. pos. (anica). To refuse to give up what one claims, to forbid the use of one's own. Waglonica. Tiglonica, To forbid one's house. Tiyopa - , To hold the door, as the old saying goes. Bl.

glonil', cont. of glonica.

glonil'k̇iya, v.a. To cause to hold as one's own. Same as glonilya. Glonilwakiya.

glou', v. pos. To come bringing one's

own, as children to school; to bring something over, as a horse one wants to sell. Waglou. Same as au.

glo'wiŋ, v. pos. To put around one his own, as a blanket. Waglówiŋ. Na waŋna wicaśa waŋ śina hiŋ iakataŋ - . Cf. iŋ.

glu, prefix pos. Verbs commencing with "yu" form the pos., i.e. to or for one's own, by converting y to gl; these pos. forms have the pronouns prefixed.

glua'kipab, v. pos. (yuakipab). To divide or separate one's own. - ewagnaka, I make a division of my own.

glua'optetu, v. pos. (yuaoptetu). To make one's own less. Waglúaoptetu.

glubla'ya, v. pos. (yublaya). To spread out one's own, as one's blanket. Waglublaya. D.268.

glubla'za, v. pos. of yublaza.

gluble'ca, v. pos. (yubleca). To open out, take in pieces one's own. Waglúbleca.
glublel', v. cont. of glubleca.

glublu', v. pos. (yublu). To plow or make mellow one's own field. Waglublu.

glucaŋ', v. pos. (yucaŋ). To shake or sift one's own. Waglucaŋ.
glucaŋ'caŋ, v. pos. red. of yucaŋcaŋ.

glucaŋ'tat'a yaŋká, v. To have to wait long for a thing and so become impatient. Bc.

gluce'ġa, v. To dive with the head foremost. Uŋglúcegapi. Same as uŋglukśepi.

gluce'ka, v. pos. (yuceka). To try to pull out one's own. Na kuŋśitku tawala (horse) glucekahaŋ keye, i.e. it got mired.

gluce'ya, v. pos. of yuceya.

gluċo', v. pos. (yuco). To perfect, finish one's own, to arrange one's own. Waglúco.
gluċo'ċo, v. red. (gluco, yucoco). To make soft one's own. Waglúcoco.

gluco'kaka, v. pos. (yucokaka). To empty one's own barrel. Waglucokaka.

gluco'za, v. pos. of yucoza.

glue'cetu, v. pos. (yuecetu). To make one's own right, to take back what one has said. Wagluecetu.

glue'ciya, v. pos. (yueciya). To turn one's own the other side out, as one's own bag. Waglueciya.

gluġa', v. pos. (yuga). To pull off, as the husk of one's own corn. Wagluga.

gluġaŋ', v. pos. (yugaŋ). To open out one's own, as one's blanket or one's door. Waglúgaŋ.

gluġal', v. cont. of gluġáta. Nape - najiŋ, To stand with one's hands extended in an attitude of supplication.

gluġa'ta, v. pos. (yugata). To spread out one's own, as one's hands in prayer. Waglugata.

gluġe', v. pos. (yuge). To pick or gather up scraps from one's floor. Waglugé. R. Bl.
gluġe'ġe, v. red. (gluge). To gather up one's own by handfuls. Waglugege. R. Bl.

glugla', v. pos. (yugla). To untwist, uncoil, unroll, loosen one's own, as one's hair. Pehiŋ - . D.107.

gluglu'ka, adj. Saucy, disrespectful to superiors.

glugmi', v. pos. of yugmi.
glugmi'gma, v. pos. of yugmigma.

glugmuŋ', v. pos. (yugmuŋ). To twist one's own. Waglugmuŋ.
glugmuŋ'gmuŋ, v. red. of glugmuŋ. Pehiŋ - , i.e. curled her hair. Bl.

glugna', v. pos. of yugná.

glugnu'ni, v. pos. of yugnúni.

gluġo', v. pos. (yugo). To make marks or creases in one's own.

gluġu'ka, v. pos. (yuguka). To draw one's knife from one's pocket. Mila waŋ gluguke na wiŋyeya najiŋ. D.246.

glugwa', v. pos. of yugwa. Bl.

glugwe'ze, adv. (?). Swift. Same as glušniyaⁿyaȟce. Glugwezeȟce. - katka mani. Bl.

gluha', v. pos. (yuha). To have or possess one's own. Waglúha.
gluha'ha, v. red. (gluha). To embrace one's own. - ceyapi, They wailed over her. D.270. B.H.39.17;89.10.

gluha'ǩiya, v.a. To put one in possession of his own; to make one keep his own. Gluhawakiya. Mitoni kiⁿ le gluhamakiyi ye. Pb.41.

gluhiⁿ'ťa, v. pos. of yuhiⁿta.

gluho'ho, v. pos. (yuhoho). To shake one's own, as one's teeth. Waglúhoho.

gluho'mni, v. pos. (yuhomni). To turn one's own around. Wagluhomni. Nakpa kiⁿ saⁿni wagluhomni kte lo.

gluhuⁿ'huⁿs, cont. of gluhúⁿhuⁿza.
gluhuⁿ'huⁿza, v. pos. (yuhuⁿhuⁿza). To shake one's own, as one's tree. Waglúhuⁿhuⁿza.

gluȟeb', cont. of gluȟepa. - iyeya.
gluȟe'p̣a, v. pos. (yuȟepa). To dry up, to soak up and wipe out, as water from one's own canoe. Waglúȟepa.

gluȟe'yapa, v. pos. (yuȟeyapa). To remove or take away one's own. Wagluȟeyapa.

gluȟe'yapaya, v. refl. perhaps. To get away from. Wicaša šica wicagluȟeyapaya po. B.H.64.22;117.23;212.6;224.5.

gluȟi'ca, v. pos. (yuȟica). To wake up one's own. Waglúȟica.

gluȟla', v. pos. (yuȟla). To ring one's own bell. Waglúȟla.

gluȟla'ǧaⁿ, v. pos. (yuȟlagaⁿ). To loosen a little, as one's belt; to leave, as a wife her husband. Waglúȟlagaⁿ. - šni, To be constant, not to leave one's own.

gluȟla'ya, v. pos. (yuȟlaya). To peel off the skin of one's own, as one's potato. Waglúȟlaya.

gluȟle'ca, v. pos. (yuȟleca). To tear one's own, as one's coat. Waglúȟleca.
gluȟle'ȟleca, v. red. of gluȟleca.
gluȟlel', cont. of gluȟleca.

gluȟlog', cont. of gluȟloka.

gluȟlo'ȟloka, v. red. of gluȟloka.

gluȟlo'ka, v. pos. (yuhloka). To make a hole in one's own by boring. Waglúȟloka.

gluȟpa', v. pos. (yuȟpa). To take down one's own, as something hung up. Wagluȟpa. Na wiⁿyaⁿ kiⁿ he taku waⁿ k'iⁿ k'oⁿ he - .
gluȟp̣a'ȟp̣a, v. red. of gluȟpa.

gluȟp̣aⁿ'ȟp̣aⁿ, v. pos. To make soft one's own, as one's moccasins by putting them in water. Waglúȟpaⁿȟpaⁿ.

gluȟp̣u), v. pos. (yuȟpu). To pull off one's own, as one's seal or anything sticking fast. Waglúȟpu.
gluȟp̣u'ȟp̣u, v. red. of gluȟpu.

gluȟ'e'ȟ'e, v. pos. (yuȟ'eȟ'e). To do one's job only partly.

gluȟ'u', v. pos. (yuȟ'u). To pull off one's own, as bark with one's hands. Waglúȟ'u.

glui'yupse, v. pos. To take hold of one's own. Nakpa - po, Listen attentively. MF. Cf. iiglukse.

gluja', v. pos. (yuja). To stir one's own; to take one's own e.g. mush etc. Waglúje. Cf. gluze.

glujag'jaǩa, v. red. of glujaka.

gluja'ja, v. pos. (yujaja). To wash one's own. Waglújaja.

gluja'ǩa, v. pos. (yujaka). To pull open one's own, as one's eyes. Waglújaka.

glujib', cont. of glujipa.

glujiⁿ'ca, v. pos. (yujiⁿca). To pull or blow one's own nose. Waglújiⁿca. Caⁿke paȟli glujiⁿciⁿ kta.

gluji'p̣a, v. pos. (yujipa). To pinch one's own. Waglujipa.

gluju'ju, v. pos. (yujuju). To pull down or destroy one's own. Waglujuju.

glujuⁿ', v. pos. (yujuⁿ). To pull up one's own out by the roots, as one's tree. Waglujuⁿ. Hiⁿ wAⁿ - na k'u. MS.572.

glukaⁿ', v. pos. (yukaⁿ). To shake off one's own fruit. Waglukaⁿ.

gluka'ṗa, v. pos. of yukapa.

gluk̄a't̄iⁿ, v. pos. of yukatiⁿ.

gluk̄a'wa, v. pos. (yukawa). To open one's own, as one's mouth when one makes an effort with the hands. I waglukawa. Cf. icapa.

glukca', v. pos. (yukca). To untie one's own, to undo or unbraid, as a woman her hair. Waglukca.

glukcaⁿ', v. pos. To form an opinion of what concerns one's self, form an opinion of one's self. Waglukcaⁿ.

gluk̄iⁿ'ca, v. pos. (yukiⁿca). To scrape off e.g. dirt from one's own clothes by hand. Waglúkiⁿca.

gluk̄i'nuⁿkaⁿ, v. pos. (yukinuⁿkaⁿ). To divide one's own; to distract self.

glukiⁿ'yaⁿ, v. (?). Bl.

gluk̄i'ṗaja, v. pos. of yukipaja. Bl.

gluko'k̄a, v. pos. of yukoka.

glukṗaⁿ', v. pos. (yukpaⁿ). To grind one's own corn etc. Waglukpaⁿ.

gluksa', v. pos. (yuksa). To break off one's own, as a stick with the hands. Wagluksa.

gluksa'ksa, v. red. of gluksa; v. pos. of yuksaksa.

glukśa', v. pos. of yukśa.

glukśaⁿ', v. pos. of yukśaⁿ.

glukśe', (?). They call diving with the head foremost: glukśepi. Uⁿglukśepi, uⁿglucegapi cf. Bl.

glukśi'ja, v. pos. of yukśija.

gluk̄taⁿ', v. pos. (yuktaⁿ). To bend one's own. Wagluktaⁿ.

gluk̄u'ka, v. pos. (yukuka). To wear out or make old one's own. Waglukuka.

gluk'e'ǧa, v. pos. (yuk'ega). To scratch one's own. Wagluk'ega.

gluk'e'sk'eza, v. red. (gluk'eza). To shave off one's own close, as the hai[r] of one's head, one's dog. Wagluk'esk'eza.

gluk'e'za, v. pos. (yuk'eza). To shave or rub smooth one's own, as one's arrows. Wagluk'eza.

gluk'o'ǧa, v. pos. of yuk'oga.

gluk'o'za, v. pos. of yuk'oza.

glul, v. cont. of gluta. - wauⁿ, I am eating my food.

glumaⁿ', v. pos. (yumaⁿ). To grind and make sharp one's own, as one's axe or knife. Waglumaⁿ. Uⁿglumaⁿpi. D.195.

glumna', v. pos. (yumna). To rip one's own. Waglumna.

gluna'jiⁿ, v. pos. (yunajiⁿ). To make one's own stand up. Waglunajiⁿ.

gluna's'a, (?). Bl.

gluo'bleca, v. pos. (yuobleca). To scatter out one's own. Wagluobleca.

gluo'blel, v. cont. of gluobleca.

gluo'ȟlaǧaⁿ, v. pos. (yuoȟlagaⁿ). To loosen one's own a little, as one's girdle.

gluo'ȟlaȟ, cont. of gluoȟlagaⁿ. - icu, To loosen a little or untie a knot.

gluo'k̄iwaⁿjila, v. pos. (yuokiwaⁿjila) To place all one's own together, make one of them.

gluo'k̄iyut̄a, v. pos. (yuokiyuta). To close up one's own e.g. wound etc. Cf. R., okite, To heal up, as a wound Na oo kiⁿ - .

gluo'nihaⁿ, v. pos. (yuonihaⁿ). To honor one's own. Wagluonihaⁿ.

gluo't̄a, v. pos. (yuota). To multiply one's own. Wagluota.

gluo'taⁿiⁿ, v. pos. (yuotaⁿiⁿ). To

manifest one's own e.g. a law. Waglu-otaŋiŋ.

gluo'tk̇oŋza, v. pos. (yuotkoŋza). To make equal one's own; to do like. Wagluotkoŋza. Wana yagluotkoŋza hwo? Did you get your work done? Bl.

gluo'waŋcaya, v. pos. (yuowaŋcaya). To cause to spread all over, to make one's own go all over. Wagluowaŋcaya.

gluṗe', v. pos. of yupe.

gluṗe'haŋ, v. pos. of yupehaŋ.

gluṗe'mni, v. pos. of yupemni.

gluṗol', v. cont. of glupota.
gluṗol'ṗoṫa, v. red. of glupota.

glupo'ṗa, v. pos. of yupopa.

gluṗo'ṫa, v. pos. (yupota). To wear out one's own. Waglupota.

glupsag', cont. of glupsaka.
glupsa'k̇a, v. pos. (yupsaka). To break one's own with the hands, as a string or cord. Waglupsaka.
glupsa'psaka, v. red. of glupsaka.

glupsi'ca, v. pos. (yupsica). To make one's own jump, as one's horse; to pull up with a hook and line one's own fish. Waglupsica.
glupsil', v. cont. of glupsica.
glupsi'psica, v. red. of glupsica.

glupsuŋ'psuŋ, v. pos. (yupsuŋpsuŋ). To move back and forth one's own, as a cow her tail.

glupśuŋ', v. pos. (yupśuŋ). To pull out or extract one's own, as one's teeth. Waglupśuŋ.

glupṫa', v. pos. (yupta). To cut out one's own, as one's clothes.

glupṫaŋ', v. Cf. gluptaŋyaŋ.

glupṫaŋ'yaŋ, v. pos. (yuptaŋyaŋ). To turn over one's own. Wagluptaŋyaŋ.

glupṫe'cela, v. pos. (yuptecela). To shorten one's own. Wagluptecela.

glupṫu'ja, v. pos. (yuptuja). To crack or split anything of one's own by boring etc. Wagluptuja.
gluptu'ptuja, v. red. of gluptuja.
gluptuś', v. cont. of gluptuja.

gluptu'za, v. (?). Bl.

glus, cont. of gluza. - najiŋ, To stand holding one's own.

glusk̇a', v. pos. of yuska.

glusk̇a'ḣciŋ, v. To smoke, in ref. to clouds of smoke. Waglúskaḣciŋ kte lo. Uŋglúskapiḣciŋ kta lo. Bl.

glusk̇e'ṗa, v. pos. (yuskepa). To absorb one's own; to cause one's own to leak out or evaporate. Wagluskepa.

glusk̇i'ca, v. pos. of yuskica.

glusk̇il', v. cont. of gluskita.

glusk̇i'sk̇iṫa, v. red. (gluskita). To wrap or tie up one's own, as a Dakota woman does her baby. Wagluskiskita.
glusk̇i'ṫa, v. pos. (yuskita). To wrap or tie up one's own. Wagluskita.

glusk̇u', v. pos. (yusku). To cut close one's own, as the hair of one's child; to pare off, as the skin of one's own potato or apple. Waglusku.
glusk̇u'sk̇u, v. red. of glusku.

glusle'ca, v. pos. of yusleca.

gluslo'haŋ, v. pos. of yuslohaŋ.

glusluʼṫa, v. pos. (yusluta). To pull out, to draw out from under one's own. Waglusluta. Wiwakaŋ - .

glusna', v. pos. of yusna.

glusni', v. pos. of yusni.

glusol', v. cont. of glusota. - iyeya.
glusol'soṫa, v. red. of glusota.

gluso'ṫa, v. pos. (yusota). To use all one's own up. Waglusota.

glusṫo', v. pos. (yusto). To smooth down e.g. one's hair. Pa - , To smooth one's own hair.
glusṫo'sṫo, v. red. of glusto.

glusu'ksuṫa, v. red. of glusuta.

glusu'ťa, v. pos. (yusuta). To make firm or establish one's own. Waglusuta.

gluśab', v. cont. of gluśapa.
gluśa'bśap̣a, v. red. of gluśapa.

gluśi'ca, v. pos. (yuśica). To make bad or injure one's own. Wagluśica.

gluśi'ȟtiη, v. pos. (yuśiȟtiη). To weaken, enfeeble one's own, as one's horse; to wear out, spoil, make bad or injure one's own. Wagluśiȟtiη.

gluśi'kśica, v. red. of gluśica.

gluśǩa', v. pos. (yuśka). To untie or let go one's own. Wagluśka. D.65.

gluśǩaη'śǩaη, v. pos. (yuśkaηśkaη). To make one's own move about. Wagluśkaηśkaη.

gluśke'p̣a, v. pos. of yuśkepa. Bl.

gluśǩi', v. pos. (yuśki). To pucker, gather, plait one's own. Wagluśki.

gluśǩi'ca, v. pos. (yuśkica). To press with one's hands; to milk e.g. a cow.
gluśǩil', v. cont. of gluśkica.
gluśǩi'śǩica, v. red. of gluśkica.

gluśǩo'p̣a, v. pos. of yuśkopa.

gluśla', v. pos. of yuśla.

gluślog', cont. of gluśloka. - iyeya.
gluślo'ǩa, v. pos. (yuśloka). To pull off, as one's clothes; to pull out. Wagluśloka.
gluślo'śloka, v. red. of gluśloka.

gluślu'ťa, v. pos. of yuśluta.

gluśna', v. pos. (yuśna). To miss in regard to one's own. Wagluśna.
gluśna'śna, v. red. of gluśna.

gluśni'yaηyaη, v. To get away in a hurry, swiftly. Same as glugweğeȟce, kátka mani. Wagluśniyaηyaȟce. Bl.

gluśp̣a', v. pos. of yuśpa.

gluśp̣i', v. pos. of yuśpi.

gluśp̣u'. v. pos. of yuśpu.

gluśp̣u'ya, v. pos. (yuśpuya). To scratch one's own flesh. Wagluśpuya.
gluśpu'śpuya, v. red. of gluśpuya.

gluśťaη', v. pos. (yuśtaη). To finish one's own, to come to a conclusion. Wagluśtaη. Waηna haηbloglaka na - .
gluśťaη'śťaη, v. red. of gluśtaη.

gluśte', adj. Numb, as one's foot when it is asleep. Si wagluśte. Nape wagluśte.

gluś'a'ǩa, v. pos. (yuś'aka). To be burdened with one's own. Wagluś'aka.

glu'ťa, v. pos. (yuta). To eat one's own as food. Waglúta.

gluťaη', v. pos. (yutaη). To praise one's own; to touch one's own. Waglutaη.

glutaη'iη, v. pos. (yutaηiη). To make manifest one's own. Waglutaηiη.

glutaη'ǩa, v. pos. (yutaηka). To make large, enlarge one's own. Waglutaηka.

gluta'ta, v. pos. (yutata). To shake one's own, as one's clothes.

gluťe'ca, v. pos. (yuteca). To make new one's own. Wagluteca.

gluťe'haη, v. pos. (yutehaη). To make a long time; to put off, to defer. Waglutehaη.

gluťe'p̣a, v. pos. (yutepa). To make blunt, to wear off one's own. Waglutepa.

gluťi'ca, v. pos. (yutica). To scrape off e.g. the snow from one's own place. Waglutica.

gluťiη'ťo, v. To take all that has been staked in a game. Same as igluk'o. Waglutiηto. Bl.

gluťi'ťaη, v. pos. (yutitaη). To pull at one's own. Waglutitaη.

gluto'kaη, v. pos. (yutokaη). To remove one's own to another place. Waglutokaη.

gluto'ḱeca, v. pos. (yutokeca). To make one's own different. Waglutokeca.

glut'a', v. pos. (yut'a). To kill one's own by hanging, choking, etc. Waglut'a.

glut'iṅ'za, v. pos. of yut'iṅza.

gluwa'ci, v. pos. (yuwaci). To make spin, as a top with the hand. Bl.

gluwa'ḣṗanica, v. pos. of yuwaḣpanica.

gluwa'ḣwala, v. pos. of yuwaḣwala.

gluwa'kaṅ, v. pos. (yuwakaṅ). To make one's own sacred. Waglúwakaṅ.

gluwaṅ'ḱa, gluwaṅ'ḱal, v. pos. (yuwaṅkal). To lift or raise up one's own. Wagluwaṅkal. Iśta - . B.H.183. 2;230.7.

gluwa'śṫe, v. pos. (yuwaśte). To make good one's own. Wagluwaśte.

gluwa'ś'aḱa, v. pos. (yuwaś'aka). To make strong one's own. Waglúwaś'aka.

gluwa'za, v. pos. of yuwaza.

gluwe', v. pos. of yuwe. Bl.

gluwe'ġa, v. pos. (yuwega). To break or fracture one's own. Waglúwega.
gluweḣ', v. cont. of gluwega.
gluwe'ḣweġa, v. red. of gluwega.

gluwi', v. pos. (yuwi). To wrap up one's own, as with a string or thong. Lakota aśké gluwipi. Wagluwi.

gluwi'caka, v. pos. (yuwicaka). To make true or prove one's own. Wagluwicaka.

gluwiṅ'ġa, v. pos. yuwiṅga. Bl.

gluwiṅ'ja, v. pos. (yuwiṅja). To bend down one's own grass etc. Wagluwiṅja.
gluwiṅś', v. cont. of gluwiṅja.
gluwiṅ'świṅja, v. red. of gluwiṅja.

gluwiṅ'ṫa, v. pos. (yuwiṅta). To stretch out the hand to, implore, worship; to stroke one's own. Wagluwiṅta.

gluwiṅ'yeya, v. pos. of yuwiṅyeya and wiṅyeya, Ready.

gluwi'ṫaṅ, v. pos. (yuwitaṅ). To make proud or glorify one's own. Wagluwitaṅ.

gluwi'ṫaya, v. pos. (yuwitaya). Together with one's own. Cf. witaya.

gluwi'yakṗa, v. pos. of yuwiyakpa and wiyakpa.

gluwo'slata, v. pos. (yuwoslata). To place upright something of one's own. Wagluwoslata.

glu'za, v. pos. (yuza). To take or hold one's own; to take back again. Waglúza.

gluza'mni, v. pos. of yuzamni.

gluze', v. pos. (yuze). To dip or lade out e.g. victuals from one's own kettle. Wagluze.

gluzo'ḱa, v. pos. of yuzoka.

gmigma', v.n. To go round like a wheel.
gmigme'la, adj. Round, as a wheel. Aguyapi - , Biscuits. Aguyapi skuyela, - yuḣlokab, Doughnuts.
gmigme'ya, adv. Round and round, going round. Taku waṅ - skayéla yaṅka, i.e. something white and spherical. D.193.

gmigmi'yaṅ, adj. perhaps. Round, like a ball.
gmigmi'yaṅyaṅ, adj. red. of gmigmiyaṅ.

gmi'ḱa, adj. Light and small, as is said of men and animals. Magmika. - caṅke luzahaṅ.

gmi s'e, adv. (yugmi). In the manner of clearing off, raking off grass from a field. - úṅyaṅ émayaye, As though they had been cleared off, (the game I was after) got away from me. Syn.- hiṅte s'e.

gmiyaṅ', adj. Round, as a wheel.
gmiyaṅ'yaṅ, adj. red. of gmiyaṅ.
gmiyaṅ'yaṅla, n. Any little round things.

gmuṅ, adj. Twisted. Cf. kagmuṅ, yugmuṅ.

gmuṅk' waciṅ, v.a. To think of trapping one. B.H.241.23.

gmuŋ'ka, v.a. To set a trap, to trap anything, to catch in a trap. Wagmúŋka. Magmuŋkapi kiŋ ehaŋni omáyuspapi tka, as they say when they go to the same house repeatedly. B.H.258.8.

gmuŋ'smna, adj. Smelling like fish.

gmuŋ'za, adj. Slimy, fish-like, smelling strong, like spoiled meat.

gmus, cont. of gmuza.

gmus'ya, adv. Shut up.

gmuya'pi s'e, adv. Many things together, bunched up, crowded together, as children, horses, etc. Waglula kiŋ - etaŋhaŋ ahinape. Bl. B.H.155.14.

gmu'za, adj. Shut, as the mouth or hand, etc. Cf. ogmuza.

gnagna'lowaŋ, v. To sing a grunting song.

gna'haŋ, part. Fallen off of itself, as fruit.

gna'ka, v.a. To lay or place, lay away or lay up, as the dead. Wagnáka. Haŋpśikśica waŋjiȟci yagnaka hwo? Haven't you an old pair of shoes for me? Bl.

gnaŋgnaŋ' s'e, adv. In an intermittent manner, as in laughing, Ha-ha-ha; making a wavering tune with the voice as in singing. - olowaŋ. SLB.

gnaśka', n. The common frog. - hotoŋpi.
gnaśka'caŋli, gnaśka'caŋlila, n. A small kind of frog with a loud voice, the tree frog. Bl.
gnaśka' wakáŋ, n. A frog with a bray like a donkey; the bull frog, perhaps. Also, śúŋśuŋla iyececa. Bl.

gnaśkiŋ'yaŋ, v.n. To be wild, crazy, frantic. Śuŋgnaśkiŋyaŋ, A mad dog.
gnaśkiŋ'yaŋyaŋ, v.n. red. (gnaśkiŋyaŋ). To be oppressed, overcome, frantic. Magnaśkiŋyaŋyaŋ. Huŋȟ tokecapi na gnaśkiŋyaŋyaŋpi na t'a iȟpayapi.

gnawa'haŋ, part. Same as gnahaŋ.

gna'yaŋ, v.a. To deceive, cheat. Wagnayaŋ. Gnáye akú wo, Win him over by good treatment even if you don't feel like it. Bl.

gni, v. 3rd pers. singl. and used in the future tense of gla. Go to one's own home, to go home. Wagni kte, I will go home. Note: the future of gla is properly gni kte. Cf. mni.

gnugnu'śka, n. The grasshopper. - sapa The black grasshopper or out-door cricket.

gnu'ni, v.n. To wander, be lost, lose. Wagnúni. Note: this is the cont. of kinuni, perhaps.

ġobġo'bniya, v.n. To breathe hard.

ġobi'śtiŋma, v. To snore in sleep. Gobmiśtiŋma. WE.

ġob'ya, adv. In a snoring manner.

ġoġo' s'e, adv. Leaving a mark with one's foot. - mani, To walk dragging one's feet over the ground and leaving marks. Pahiŋ s'e uŋzica (?) - mani, as is said of old people who cannot lift their feet in walking. Bl.

ġoŋ'ġa, adj. The eyes gently closed. - maŋka. - uŋ, To be proud, not noticiing others as though one were blind.

ġo'p̄a, ȟo'p̄a, adj. Attractive, beautiful, handsome. Wiġópa, A pretty woman.
ġo'pa, v.n. To snore. Wagopa. D.272,33.
ġo'p̄eca, ȟo'p̄eca, adj. Beautiful, well-formed

ġu, v.n. To burn, singe, scorch, be burnt. Maġú, niġu, uŋġupi.

ġuġe'ca, n. The soft, spongy part of bones in which there is oil. Same as ġuyéca. Compare kaġeġe, kayeġe.

ġugnag'ya, ȟugnaȟ'ya, v.a. To burn down, destroy by fire. P.

ġuġu', v. red. (gu). To be burnt in

ġuġu'haŋ, adj. (?). He natá - , He is foolish, crazy. ED.
ġuġu' kaślá, (?). Lila waśigla na - na ceyahaŋ.

ġuġu'la, adj. Curled or ruffled as hair or fur. Same as yumníŋnija.

ġuġu'ya, v. red. (ġuyé). To cause to be burnt in different places, to burn in different places; to have more than one burn on a brand. Gugúwaya. Pséȟtiŋ waŋ guguyi na caŋksa waŋ kage. D.115.

ġuhe'heya, (?). red. of ġuheya. Wakpala óiŋkpa kiŋ - yuŋkelo, i.e. starting points of many canyons near together. Bl.

ġuhe'ya, (?). Caŋku kiŋ ǩitála - yuŋke lo, i.e. many roads on the prairie.Bl.

ġuȟ'ciŋ'cayela, (?). - uŋyaŋpi, i.e. coming from very far. Bl.

ġui'c'iya, v. refl. (guya). To burn one's self, as on a hot stove. Same as śpaŋíc'iya.

ġumna', adj. (ġu-omna). Smelling burnt. Onáġumna, It smells like a prairie fire.

guŋ'ga, adj. Proud; with eyes closed, not minding others, haughty. Same as ġoŋġa. - yaŋkahe, He was sitting haughtily. D.73.
ġuŋ'ġaġa, adj. red. of ġuŋġa.
ġuŋ'ġaġaya, adv. Proudly.

ġuśi'ca, adj. Burnt, and hence worthless.

ġuya', v.a. To burn, cause to burn. Guwaya.

ġuye'ca, n. The soft and spongy part of bones which holds oil. Compare kaġeġe and kayeġe.

gwa'haŋ, part. Bad, over-ripe, as fruit; turning soft and bad, as meat. Bl.

gwe'gwes, adj. (gwegwéza). Striped, used in ref. to the ribs. - hiŋgla, as is said of very lean men or animals that still move about. Tucuhu - hiŋgla yauŋ welo. Bl. Cf. R., ȟbeȟbeza.

gwegwe'za, adj. red. of gweza. Bl.
gwegwe'zela, adj. dim. of gwegweza. Bl.

gwe'za, adj. Lean, thin, ragged. Bl.

gwe'zela, adj. dim. of gweza.

gwu, adj. Curdled. Asaŋpi - .
gwugwu', adj. red. of gwu. Asaŋpi - .

gwu'la, adj. (?). Maka akaŋl taku - , taku kpaŋla hena oyasiŋ owakiyake. Bl.

ha, n. The skin or hide of animal or man; the bark of trees.

haa'ȟ'eȟ'e, adj. To have ragged clothes on. Haámaȟ'eȟ'e.
haa'ȟ'eȟ'eya, adv. In torn clothes. Bl. Syn.- haákaŋhaŋheyela.

haa'igluȟleȟleca, v. refl. To tear up one's clothing. B.H.38.4.

haa'ḱab, adv. On the outside, on the surface, said in ref. to the skin.
haa'ḱabyela, adv. On the surface, shallow, close under the skin, as ópi in opposition to śogyéla ópi, A serious wound. - eya, i.e. they do not mean what they say.

haa'kaŋhaŋheyela, adv. In torn clothes. Bl. Cf. haáȟ'eȟ'eya.
haa'ḱaŋhehéyela uŋ, v. red. To have on torn clothes.

haa'ḱaṗa, adv. On the outside.
haa'ḱaṗaṫa, adv. Externally.
haa'ḱaṗaṫaŋhaŋ, adv. On the outer surface.

haa'ḱaṫaṫa, v. To give one the last one has, turning the box upside down and shaking it over someone's hands. Haawakatata. Haacicatata. Bl.

haa'ḱuka, v. To have worn out clothes on. Hehé, haámakuke lo. GA.

haċi', n. A very young man, a grown-up boy. Also, haċila. Hamáci. Ataya hamaci yelo. Hacila kiŋ kopi kayeś opapi. B.H.117.21.

haċib', interj. An order to keep still or silent, esp. used in games. Naȟmapi kapi. BT. Cf. iyóhōb.

haċi'la, n. Children. B.H.117.21.

hacō'cola, adj. Naked, as said of men. Hamácocola. -- hacóla, adj. Naked, without clothes. Hacópila. Pl.

ha'eċe, ha eċe', adj. or adv. Empty. - hinajiŋ. Bl. B.H.106.6.

haha'ḱe, (?). Oŋs'mahahake s'elececa, as said when anxious to go somewhere. Bl.
haha'la, adv. Loose, easily moved, as a lamp on the edge of a table. Same as hahayela. Maháhala. Le aŋpetu kiŋ mahahala yelo. Taku iyuha eciŋ wakinica yelo. - s'e iŋyaŋka, Moving lively, as a good horse.

hahaŋ', Cf. aháŋ.

haha'yela, adj. Loose, not tight. - okoyake, as is said of fence wire that is held tight by staples, or as a box standing on a table and liable to drop.

haho' haho', express. Of joy on receiving something. - pilamaya.

haȟuŋ'ṫa, n. Thread, twine, cord. - iyáṗehaŋpi, Spool-thread.

hai'gluȟleȟlel, cont. of haigluȟleȟleca. - ceye. B.H.90.25.

hai'leyapi s'e, adv. Like one whose clothes are burnt near fire; bringing close to the fire, being not afraid of fire. - yaŋke lo, i.e. to sit. LB.

hai'ṗajaja, n. Soap.

haiyē', interj. Of joy at hearing good news, as when buffalo are near. "Pilapi" he kapi. RB. HH. Note: "ai" is pronounced as a diphthong in the word.

hai'yoṫiyeḱiya, v. To suffer in consequence of poor clothing. Haiyotiyewakiya.
haḱab', adv. Afterwards, in the meantime. - lena iglaka enajiŋ. D.261.

ha'kakśa, (?). Wojuha k'oŋ - waglagli yelo, I brought that full sack back empty. Pagé - iȟpeyayelo, i.e. gave your horse nothing to eat all day.Bl.

haḱa'ḱṫa, adj. Last, the last; the youngest child, boy or girl. Hamákakta, mahákakta; uŋhákaktapi. Uŋma wica he tokapa na uŋma wiŋyaŋ ca he - . Hokśiȟamakákta yelo. BT.
haḱa'ṫa, n. A man's or a woman's older or younger sister; a woman's brothers. Mahákata, My sister. Mihakata śuŋkawakaŋ owicawakile yelo. Bl. D.227, note 2. -- haḱáṫaḱu, n. Her relatives. D.229, note 5.

ha'ḱaṫaṫa, v. To give everything away. Wana háwakatata yelo. Bl.

haƙa'ťaya, v.a. To have for an older or younger sister. Hakatawaya. Both men and women use the word. Bl.

haƙe', n. The youngest child, boy or girl. Also, haƙéla, haƙáƙťa.

haƙi'kťa, v.n. To look behind, look back, turn around to look. Hawekta, hayekta, hauṅkiktapi. D.56. -- haƙí-ktakta, v. red. (hakikta). To look back often. - iṅyaṅkahaṅpi. D.66,67.

haƙi'toṅ, v. To have clothes on, to be dressed. Hawetoṅ. D.36.

haƙi'ya, v.a. To clothe one, give one clothes. Hawakiya.

ha'la, n. A flea, fleas. - śaśa, A red flea. Cf. psicala.

ha'lablaska, n. A bedbug. Bl.

halha'te, n. A magpie, so called because of its call. WE.

ha'mna, adj. Smelling of skin, not smelling well, as meat does at times.

ha'naȟpu, v. Cf. hanaȟpuȟpu.
ha'naȟpuȟpu, v. To appear ready to peel or drop off, as the rough bark of a tree or the skin e.g. of a snake.

ha'nasku, v. Cf. hanaskusku.
ha'naskusku, v.n. To crack and peel off as the skin of potatoes do by boiling.
ha'naskuya, v.a. To cause to crack and peel off. Hanaskuwaya.

haṅ, he, suff. These are affixed to verbs, although they may be the verb's part. form. They indicate the action is performed repeatedly or for awhile. Wiṅyaṅ waṅ céyahaṅ, keye. Wiṅyaṅ waṅ Ȟeyata céyahe kiṅ le, inayaye lo. Na waṅna oyate kiṅ kiblecahaṅpi. Note: It seems to be a rule that verbs ending in "haṅ" change to "he" when it concerns past time. Thus, aȟícahaṅ, He stumbles and falls on one; aȟícahe, He stumbled and fell on one.
haṅ, hiṅ, he, suff. Affixed to verbs, these are the same as śke, They say, It is reported. Waṅna mícicaṅ, hokśicala, owáuṅpiṅkte lo, eyahe. Hecena iyaya śke; yahiṅ na paha waṅ el asnikiya yaṅka śke. Eke blaye waṅ opta ya śke. Yahaṅ, yuṅkaṅ may also be the participial form.

haṅ, adv. Yes, of affirmation.

haṅ, n. cont. (haṅyetu). Night. Haṅicamna, A stormy night.

haṅ, v.n. To stand upright, as of things; to remain. Said of grass, arrows that strike the ground and stand; also, of cattle etc. that remain or stay in a certain locality. Hel haṅpiśke. Tataṅka optaye nuṅpa helo. BT.

haṅ, Same perhaps as haṅni and itokab. Mat'eśni haṅ, Before I die. B.H.39.7.

haṅble', v.n. To fast and dream or attain vision; a religious prayer ceremonial. Haṅwable. One is said to be ihaṅble.

haṅble'ble, adv. perhaps. Long ago. Same as haṅbleblekel and kilelekel. - taƙ'eye. -- haṅbléblekel, adv. Long ago. Also, ehaṅƙehaṅ, ƙileleƙel.

haṅble'ceya, v.n. To cry in the prayer of vision seeking. Haṅblewaceya.

haṅblo'glagia, v. To tell dreams and visions. Haṅbloglagiwaye.
haṅblo'glagyakel, adv. Prophetically. - leya oyake. B.H.69.8.
haṅblo'glaka, v.a. (haṅble-oglaka). To tell of one's own intercourse with the spirits, relate visions; to speak unintelligently; to pray. Haṅblowaglaka. Caṅ kapestopi top yuha najiṅ na - .

haṅco'kaṅ, n. Midnight. Wana - nacece.
haṅco'kaṅyaṅ, n. perhaps. Midnight. Na - enakiyapi. Ake lowaṅpi na - e ehaṅl hehaṅyela ecoṅpi. B.H.52.2.

Haṅge'okute, n. The Santee clan of the Sisseton Reservation.

haṅgla'wakel, (?). - uṅ. Bl.

haṅgnaġ'ya, adv. (?). - Ȟpaya, To lie down to sleep so that one is ready to get up early. Also, wiṅyeya Ȟpaya.

haṅhe'p̌i, n. Night. - cokaṅyaṅ, Midnight. - petijaṅjaṅ, A lantern. Note: Petijaṅjaṅ yuha omanipi. -- haṅhép̌i waśicuṅ, n. The Power of the night, its spirit or mystery. - Ȟmuṅgapelo, said when someone becomes sick very suddenly. Also, wiwíla ȟmuŋgapelo. -- haŋhéṗi wi, n. The moon.

haŋi'glaka, v. To travel by night. Bl.

haŋ'iśtiŋma, (?). Haŋiśtiŋme śni śkaŋ.

haŋi'yaciŋke śni, adv. (?). - wahiyelo, I came way late in the night. Bl.

haŋi'yaŋṗa, n. A moonlit night. Also, haŋwiyaŋpa. LB.

haŋka', n. A man's sister-in-law, i.e. his wife's sister or his brother's wife. Perhaps my sister-in-law. Nihaŋka, Your sister-in-law.
haŋka'ku, n. His sister-in-law.

haŋka'śi, n. A man's female cousin, i.e. his mother's brother's daughter, but not his father's brother's daughter. My female cousin. Nihaŋkaśi, Your female cousin.
haŋka'śitku, n. His female cousin.
haŋka'śiya, v. To have for a female cousin, i.e. for a man to have.

haŋka'toŋ, v.a. To have for a sister-in-law. Haŋkawatoŋ.
haŋka'ya, v.a. To have for a sister-in-law, as a man his wife's sister and his brother's wife. Haŋkawaya.

haŋk̇e', n. Half, a part of.
haŋk̇e'k̇e, n. red. (haŋke). Half and half. - wicak'u.

haŋk̇e'ya, adv. At. last, i.e. conveying the idea of having made good progress; having reached the middle, pretty much, little by little. Tapśkate ca - wayupika, i.e. learned how to play. B.H.54.5;64.12;82.1;91.13;170.6;207.7. Haŋhepi - etkiya napapi, i.e. through the night. - wicota ohimniciye. Pte waŋ kacegcegyi na - t'a gliȟpaye. - kiblecahaŋpi. D.52. -- n. A near relative, a blood relation. Note: the word is not used in the pl., as it refers to only one.. Hemahaŋkeya, He is a relative to me. EM. He nihaŋkeya, He is related to you. One may not say: Haŋkewaya. -- v.a. To halve, to have reached the middle. Haŋkewaya. -- haŋkeyaś, adv. Haŋkeya, emph. B.H. 29.5.

haŋki'gnaka, v. To delay, defer to the next morning, leave alone for the night. Takuku cipasi kta (last night) tka onikaŋ śni ca haŋcicignaka ca lehaŋl nitakuni śni. BT.
haŋk̇i'kṫa, v.n. To rise very early in the morning, to wake while it is yet night. Haŋwekta, haŋuŋkiktapi.

haŋko'kiṗa, 1) v.a. perhaps. To fear the night, be afraid at night. Haŋkowakipa. 2) adv. Cowardly, fearing the night. Haŋkokipeśni, Not afraid at night.

haŋkpaŋ', n. A shoe string.
haŋkpaŋ'oȟloka, n. The shoe string holes of a shoe.

haŋl iyáyapi s'e, (?).

haŋlo'waŋpi, n. A night song. Cf. wióweśte lowaŋpi.
haŋma'ni, v. To walk in the night; to be in the dark about anything, not to understand. Haŋmawani.
haŋma'nipike s'e, adv. (?). - wauŋ kiŋ, I know absolutely nothing about it.GA.

haŋmśi'celaȟcake, It is a very windy night. (?).
haŋmwi'tka, n. (haŋpa-witko). Fool moccasins, and not showing any pattern in the beadwork. WE.

haŋna'ṗa, v. To escape at night. EE.

haŋna'taŋtaŋ u, v. To come in the night feeling one's way with the feet.
haŋna'taŋtaŋkel, adv. Feeling one's way with the feet through the night.Bl.

haŋni', Same as itokab. El yapi śni - . B.H.61.6;17.6;177.23;186.1;204.6; 220.1;226.17;254.13.

haŋo'iyokipi, n. perhaps. A pleasant night. - yelo. Bl.

haŋo'luṫa, n. A warm night.

haŋo'mani, v. To walk at night. Haŋomani omaspe śni.

haŋo'pta, adv. Through the night. - iglaka. B.H.83.13.

haŋo'tk̇aŋ, n. A dark, sultry night, perhaps stormy. Also, haŋóluluta. Bl.

haŋ'ṗa, n. Moccasins.

haŋ'ṗaiṫak̇e, n. Cf. haŋpitake.

haŋpa'k̇iglak̇e, n. The sole of a shoe or moccasin; one of the badge-like decorations worn on the chest in the Sundance. Also, wakiglaka, haŋp'akiglake.

haŋ'pa kśúpi, n. Beaded moccasins.

haŋ'pa kutépi, n. A pastime for young men. Bl.

haŋ'ṗapecoŋṗi, n. (haŋpa-ape-ecoŋpi). A game in which a ball is hid in one of four moccasins or mittens and sought for by the opposite side; a hand game, in which is sung: Haŋpa hiyu wo; waŋna waktepi kte. R. MS.

haŋṗi', n. Broth, soup; gravy; juice. Caŋ-śuśka - , The sap of boxelders. Caŋpa - yatkaŋpi. Winuḣca, papala waŋ cik'ala yégnake c'oŋ - kaga yo, haŋp'uŋglatkaŋpi kte lo. Bl. Cf. wahaŋpi.

haŋṗi'kcek̇a, n. Moccasins.

haŋṗi'natopi, n. Same as caŋḣlogaŋ ḣlaḣla. Its blossoms are used to make blue paint for moccasins. Bl. #157, 197.

haŋṗi' ok̇áśkeya, (?). Bl.

haŋ'pisabye, n. Shoe blacking, polish.

haŋṗi'śka, n. (haŋpa-iśka). The upper part of a moccasin that covers the ankle; the upper part of a shoe or boot. - sutaya ayuwi yo, uŋnihaŋ kiḣ'aŋ hi yelo. BT.

haŋṗi'śk̇atoŋ, v. To sew an upper part to a moccasin, i.e. to make it like a rubber shoe for women. Haŋpiśkawatoŋ. Bl.

haŋṗi'ṫak̇e, n. The face or upper part of a moccasin; the tongue of a shoe, or what serves as such.

haŋpo'haŋ, v. To put on or wear moccasins. Haŋpowahaŋ.

haŋpo'hek̇iciciya, v.a. To put moccasins on one. Haŋpoheweciciya.

haŋpo'hek̇iya, v.a. To cause to put on moccasins. Haŋpohewakiya.

haŋ'poḣya, adv. (?). - wanuŋwe ḣce lo, as a man would say of himself who ran away moving arms and feet in excitement, as though to swim, nuŋwaŋ. GA.

haŋṗo'k̇ihaŋ, v. pos. (haŋpohaŋ). To put on or wear one's own moccasins; to wear one's shoes. Haŋpowakihaŋ. Kenátaŋtaŋ kte s'e haŋpokihe lo, as is said when a person's shoes are too wide.

haŋṗo'naśloke, n. Slippers. P.

haŋṗo'śṗu hokśícala, n. A doll.

haŋpsi'cu, n. A piece of tanned hide cut to size for a moccasin.

haŋpśi'śica, (?). - ca owakihi yelo.BT.

haŋptaŋ'ni, n. An old shoe or moccasin. - waŋjiḣci mak'u wo. Bl.

haŋp'ce'yaka, n. Moccasins with porcupine quill work. Bl.

haŋp'hiŋ'śma, n. Moccasins made of buffalo fur with the hair inside.

haŋp'i'ṗata, n. Moccasins covered with porcupine quill work.

haŋp'o'naśloke, n. Slippers.

haŋp'ṫi'ṫiŋyaŋka, (?). - waŋji micaga yo, Make me good shoes. Bl.

haŋ'sk̇a, adj. Long, tall, of time and distance. Waniyetu, caŋke haŋhepi kiŋ lila haŋske.

haŋ'skaska, adj. red. of haŋska. Pehiŋ - .

haŋ'sk̇eya, adv. Far, extending, long. Nupiŋ wáciŋhiŋ ikaŋ - itowe el iyaglaśkapi. - eya, To dwell on a topic, to speak long about something. Uŋma na uŋma kiŋ - .

haŋ'śni, neg. No! Not yes. Same as hiya.

haŋ'ṫa, v. imp. only. Get away, begone. - yo.

haŋ'tahena, adv. Before night. Iyúpaga po, tokśa - walaślapi kte lo, as said in addressing horses. - talo yutapi kte lo. BT. B.H.55.7.

haŋ'ṫaŋhaŋś, adv. If, in case that.

haⁿte'haⁿ, adv. Late in the night. Waⁿna kitaⁿla - ehaⁿl waⁿna toⁿweya k'oⁿ henayos kupi. Nahaȟci taku ota oblakiⁿ kta tka wana - yelo. Bl.

haⁿte' pepé iyéceca, n. Illinois Mimosa, curly-podded legume. Acuan illinoiensis.

haⁿtȟaⁿ', n. The fruit of a water plant called wihúta hu, Cat tail. When it is thoroughly ripe it is wooly. This material is used by mothers to make a sort of quilt, placed over sheeting and used for babies because it does not allow water to penetrate. Typha catifolia. #231.

haⁿ'tuk'e, adv. Indeed, for once.

haⁿ't'eya, adv. Wearily, as the moving of a sick person.

haⁿwa'cip̄i, n. The Night Dance, the name of a Dakota dance.

haⁿwa'hehaⁿtu, n. perhaps. A fixed time of the night at which something usually takes place etc. Wana - . Bl.

haⁿwa'kaⁿ, adj. perhaps. Mysterious, as a strange thing going on in the night. Haⁿhepi - s'elececa. Bl.

haⁿ'wakaⁿ, n. The aurora. P.

haⁿwa'tohaⁿlśna, adv. Anytime in the night, again and again in the night. Na waⁿna uⁿgnahaⁿśna - wacipi na ecel aⁿpa.

haⁿwa'tohaⁿtu, adv. Sometime during the night. - k'eyaś wau kte lo. Bl.

haⁿwi'yaⁿp̄a, n. Moonlight. Haⁿhepi waⁿ el - oiyokipi.

haⁿya'ġu, n. A robe dried out of doors in winter by freezing.

haⁿya'ġug, (?). Nape kiⁿ - imayayelo, My hands are stiff from cold. Bl.

haⁿyaⁿ'ȟeci, n. Tomorrow. Derived from haⁿyaⁿke kiⁿhaⁿ, or haⁿyaⁿkecihaⁿ, haⁿyaⁿkeciⁿhaⁿ, ref. to hihaⁿna ki(ⁿ). Haⁿhepi na hiⁿhaⁿna he kapi.

haⁿyaⁿ'ȟeciⁿhaⁿ, Same as haⁿyaⁿkeci.

haⁿyaⁿ'ȟeȟeciⁿ, n. red. (haⁿyaⁿkeci). Tomorrow, over night. Also, haⁿyáke-(ke)ci. B.H.194.5.

haⁿye', cont. of haⁿyetu.

haⁿye'cokaⁿ, n. Midnight.

haⁿye'tu, n. Night.

haⁿye'tula, n. dim. of haⁿyetu.

haⁿye'ťuwi, n. The moon.

haⁿye'wi, n. The moon. - yahilale ki, as addressed in prayer. RF.

haⁿyuⁿ'ȟa, v.n. To remain overnight, as something killed and left until morning; perhaps also in ref. to one staying overnight. Haⁿmúⁿke.

hao̅'k'u, v. To give, loan one's clothes to, or perhaps any clothes. Haowak'u.

hao'yasaȟa, adj. Skin dried to the bone, very lean.

ha'oyuȟ'u, n. A year's growth in a tree, i.e. with respect to its width of a ring. - ota yelo. Bl.

ha'paȟlaya, v. To throw off the skin, as do snakes.

hap̄a'śloka, v. To pull off skin, to chafe. Hawapaśloka.

hasaⁿ'ni, (?).

hasťaⁿ', adj. Dark-complexioned. Hamastaⁿ.

haś, interj. Of impatience, pride, discontentment. P.

hatoⁿ', v.n. To have chapped skin, as on the hands. Hamatoⁿ.

hau, interj. Of greeting or approbation. Hello! Yes! Fine! Good! Gramm. 121.

hauⁿ, interj. Of severe pain; used by men. Gramm.127.

haya', v.a. To have for clothing. Hawaya. Taku haye ciⁿ owasiⁿ taha ececa. Hena taȟca śuⁿkala tahaya koyagya el nihipelo. B.H.195.2.

haya'ȟe, n. Clothes.

haya'p̄i, n. Clothes, wearing apparel of any kind.

haya'p̄iyotke, n. A suit hanger.

ha'yuȟp̄u, v.n. To be scabbed. Hawágluȟpu. -- háyuȟp̄uȟp̄u, v. red.

ha'yuza, v.a. To skin, take off the skin of anything. Habluza.

ha'za, n. The whortleberry, huckleberry.

he, suff. Cf. ha^n.

he, 1) pron. dem. That. Hena, Those. 2) adv. There. Also, hel. It corresponds to le, lel. Na wa^{n}na iglakapi na ake wakpala wa^n el etipi na he ake wicoȟ'a^n wa^n eco^n. Hena hinaji^n na taku ehi^n kta heci eya yo. Tuweni he śni, or Tuweni okapte śni, All are there. Bl.

he, interrog. particle. Wicáyala he?

hē, interj. Look here!

he, n. A horn, the horns of animals; a louse. He ca^n aliǩiyeȟce lo. Cf. heyopuza.

hea'śketo^n s'e, adv. With the hair braids standing out, sideways. Bl.

heča', n. The buzzard, the turkey vulture. Wana - wa^n gli yelo; wana osni wanice, i.e. its arrival meant the end of cold weather. - wa^n ku welo, as they say when a scout returns seemingly with good news. Bl. Cf. skipipila.

he'ca, pron. and adj. Such, such like; belonging to such a clan, or such a description. Hemáca, heú^{n}capi. Taȟca śu^{n}kala yuha ki^n heca.

he'cac'u^{n}ś, adv. Nevertheless. B.H. 244.3.

he'caeśa, adv. Although it is such, not withstanding.

he'cakicio^n, v. To do that for one. Hecayecio^n iyececa. B.H.196.10;250.7.

he'caǩico^n, v.a. (heco^n). To do thus to one. Hecaweco^n.

he'caǩio^n, v. (heco^n). To do that, i.e. the same thing, to them. B.H.92.14.

heca^n'ǩi^n, v.a. To think so of one, form such an opinion of one. Hecá^{n}waki^n. Hecá^{n}cici^n.

hecaśka', adv. Still, nevertheless. Same as heecaśka.

heča' yu^{n}kápi, n. A place where buzzards (heca) are nesting and shed many feathers. Bl.

he'ce, adv. Thus, so, in this way; hence, therefore. Same as hecel. Tuweni wau^{n}śipi śni ca - . B.H.47.4; 67.9;199.14;235.6;283.4;290.5;271.7.

he'ceca, 1) adj. Like, such as, like that. Hemaceca. 2) adv. So, always so. Same as iyececa. Toha^n ki^n lena - kta heci. Na iśtogmus wowaci ki^n wacipi ki^n hena pte śake icicaśla nau^{n}kapi ki^n - . Tohi^{n}ni taku - wa^{n}yakapi śni. B.H.245.2.

he'ceca ca^{n}kéś, adv. Therefore, since that is the case, since that is the way it is. B.H.26.2.

he'ceca eśá, adv. Notwithstanding. Same as héceca eyáś. B.H.51.11.

he'cecaǩa, n. Such a one; a mean fellow.

he'ceca ki^n, adv. If so. B.H.69.9; 111.7;117.8;190.6.

he'ceca k'éyaś, adv. Nevertheless. B.H.52.1.

he'cegla, adv. Thus, so; only, only so far; that is all; only so little. Also, héceglala. Heo^n - eye, eya. - śka eca^{n}no^n śni, i.e. it was only so little trouble and you could not do it. Ta^{n}ya^n ecamo^{n}pi śni ki^n - kta. Yu^{n}ka^n - waci^n weksuye.

he'ceha^n, adv. Really. - wowicake nai^{n}ś wowicake śni heci, Is it really so or not?

he'ceȟci, adv. Just so, only so; altogether.

he'cekce, adv. red. (hece). In this manner, so thus. Ca o^n - iyaha^{n}bla. - iapi nawaȟ'o^n. - omawani. -eco^{n}pi, i.e. to one inquiring if he came for something special. Talo nai^{n}ś - yutapi. B.H.34;45.13;49.17;55.6;80.19; 136.19. Pb.28.

he'cekceca, adj. Of such a sort. Taku -, Something on that line or order. B.H.34.4.

he'cekcecaǩa, adj. Always such; bearing this character.

he'cekcekel, adv. red. of hecekcel or hecekce-kel perhaps. Mazaskazi na ca^{n}śi^n na pejuta waśtemna - kahipi. B.H.169.22.

he'cekcel, adv. red. (hecel). In this manner, so, thus; just as.

he´cekceťu, adv. red. (hecetu). So, in this manner.
he´cekceťuya, adv. After this manner.

he´cel, adv. Thus, so, in this way; hence, therefore. Taku - oŋ Susanna aiapi slolyapi śni. B.H.138.5.

hece´la, adv. That alone, only that. D.269.

hecē´laǩiya, adv. Only that way, that way alone, that alone.

hece´laya, v.a. To regard that alone. Hecelawaya.

he´celkiya, adv. That way. P.

he´celya, adv. So, thus, in that manner

he´cena, adv. Thus, conveying the idea that something keeps on happening; consequently; finally. Hecel aŋpetu topa apepi eśá, - t'a. Ho - tiyata kiya iŋyaŋke na tawicu kiŋ owicakiyake. Ekta nahaȟci lila wicotapi ca - waglicu. Hecel waŋna tipi iyohila kpamnipi, tka ecel ataya iyowicahi, i.e. coffee and sugar, na - yusotapi śni. Ho, misuŋ, waŋna wagni kte eya na - gla ca waŋyaŋk maŋka. - ecoŋ, To stick to work. - ya, i.e. right along. P.

hece´nicala, n. A yearling colt. R. Bl.

he´ceś, Same as héce, emph.

he´cetǩiya, adv. In that direction. - iglaka gle na otiwota kiŋ el akiti.

he´ceťu, adv. As, so, thus; that is the way; right, well. Hecetuȟca, Just so. Lena hecetuȟca slolwaya.
he´ceťuǩe, adv. As is common, as is usual.

he´cetula, v.a. To approve. B.H.175.5.
hece´ťulaǩa, v.n. To have an opinion, to think. Same as wicala, secelaka.
he´cetulakapi, n. Approval.

he´ceťuwaŋjica, adj. Always the same. - el uŋ, Always in the same place. Ho le - letaŋ yuha ya po, which ref. to a religious rite. - yaŋkapi.

he´ceťuya, 1) v.a. To make so, cause to be so or right. Hécetuwaya. 2) adv. So, thus, in showing one how.

he´ceya, adv. Really, certainly. Ho, wakokipe śni, - wani ye, Now, have yo fear of me; I am really alive. B.H.101.1;108.11;118,3;293.19,22. D.229,269,104.

he´ci, adv. In or at that place, there or away from the speaker. Also, it implies perhaps that I would like to know. Itokab tohaŋȟci le iyecel owaȟ'aŋ heci? I, did I ever .... Ca tuktogna oniglakiŋ kta heci? Ca tokeśke waoŋspeic'iciya heci? Tokeśke iyohipi kta heci? It is also paired as follows: tokel...heci; taku...heci; tohaŋ...heci. B.H.68.23;174.19;184.4; 208.9;78.2;252.16;112.6;245.2.

he´cina, (?). (heci-na). Makataŋhaŋ wicaśa waŋ wicoȟ'aŋ waŋ awahiyaya tka hena oŋ oŋśimala yo, tuwa waŋkataŋhaŋ initaŋcaŋ hecina.

he´cinahaŋ, adv. If, if it is so.

heciŋ´, v. (he-ciŋ). To think this, to think that, with the thought expressed following. Hecaŋmi, hecaŋni, heuŋkeciŋpi. B.H.47.5;199.3.

he´ciŋśǩayapi, n. The mountain sheep, so called because its horns are used for spoons (ciŋśká).

he´ciya, adv. At that place, there.

heci´ya, v. (heya). To say that to one. Note: I believe this is introduced from Santee through the Bible, whereas it should be hekiya. Hewakiya. Hemakiya, He said that to me. Heciciya, I say to you. Hekiciyapi, They say to each other.

he´ciyapaťaŋhaŋ, adv. Towards that time or place, on the side next to.

he´ciyaťaŋ, adv. From that place, thence. -- héciyaťaŋhaŋ, adv. From that place, therefore.

heci´yotaŋ, adv. In that direction.
heci´yotaŋhaŋ, adv. In that direction.

he´coŋ, v. To do that. Hécamoŋ, hécuŋkoŋpi. This takes up the action of the preceding sentence and continues it. Nazoŋspe caŋnuŋpa waŋ oŋ huhu kiŋ kaweȟweȟ apa śke lo. Hecoŋ na wicoti ekta i na oyaka.

he'e, v. That is it, it is he. Note: this, along with lée, includes the substantive and demonstrative pronoun.

he eca', adv. (?). Tuwa wiwicayuŋge ci he zuya itaŋcaŋ kiŋ he wowaśi tawa kiŋ - hecoŋ. "He eca u welo", eya, Now he is coming, he said. Yuŋkaŋ uŋma ciŋca k'oŋ he eca leya ... .

he eca' éyaś, adv. Nevertheless. B.H. 155.18.

he'ecaśka, adv. Still, nevertheless. Note: this may be der. of hee-ca-śka.

he'ehaŋ, adv. At that time, in ref. to the past.

he'ekiya, 1) adv. In the place of. 2) v.a. To call or count that to be the person or thing; to substitute, put one in place of another. Héewakiya.

heha'ha, v. red. 2nd pers. of héya.

heha'halake, v. 2nd pers. (heyayalaka). You lie, deceive.

he'haŋ, adv. At that time, then. Also, hehaŋ, perhaps.

hehaŋ'haŋkeca, adv. red. (hehaŋkeca). So long, each so long.

hehaŋ'haŋyaŋ, adv. red. of hehaŋyaŋ. B.H.153.9;208.10.

hehaŋ'hca, adv. Then and not until then.
hehaŋ'keca, adv. So long.

hehaŋl', adv. At or to that place; then. -- hehaŋleś, adv. emph. of hehaŋl. B.H.49.7;26.24.

he'haŋni, adv. (ehaŋni). Then. Ciŋcala - , When it was young, at the time of its youth. Kiyela yapi kiŋ - itkob hinapi, He came to meet them as they approached. D.152. B.H.93.10;122.14.

hehaŋ'pi, n. Night, last night. -- adv. Last night. P.
hehaŋ'pi wi, n. The moon.

hehaŋ'taŋ, adv. From that time; therefore. Oyate oyasiŋ le lecetu na - waniyetu opawiŋge śni makoce le waŋblaka. Na - waŋna waniyetu ota itahena eśa, lehaŋyaŋ nahahci (wahiŋkpe kiŋ) yuhapi. He toŋpi - huśte. - slolya wauŋ. D.100. B.H.31;86.22;145.7;156.3;199.21;280.2;272.14. -- hehaŋtaŋhaŋ, adv. From that time, therefore.

hehaŋ'tu, adv. At that time, then. Wana wicoh'aŋ tokaheya ecoŋ kte ci - . Waŋna wi hinapa - keya. Waŋna wicokaŋ saŋpa - waŋna hocokam tip waŋ el kagapi. Hokśiyuha kte kiŋ - . MS.526. B.H.165.14;246.3.
hehaŋ'tula, adv. Then. R. Bl.
hehaŋ'tulahci, adv. Just then.

hehaŋ'yaŋ, adv. So far, in ref. to places; so long, in ref. to time; from that time. At that time, then. Letaŋhaŋ tohiŋni iyopewaye śni ye, tohaŋyaŋ uŋni - . Yuŋkaŋ hucaŋ cokaŋyaŋ - ataya we apa. He waŋkatuya waŋca - ihuŋni. Eyaś - aŋpa caŋke. B.H.47.2;73.24;84.20;189.1;226.8;200.21;202.22;233.8;253.16;255.22;256.28;32.6;79.7.
hehaŋ'yakel, adv. Same as hehaŋyaŋ.
hehaŋ'yaŋyaŋ, adv. red. of hehaŋyaŋ.
hehaŋ'yela, adv. So far, only so far. Henihaŋyelapi. - woglake. - oihaŋke. Ho le wicowoyake kiŋ - oyakapelo. Lecel eya: - ye. - ecaŋnoŋpi kte lo. Ake lowaŋpi na haŋcokaya e ehaŋl - ecoŋpi.

hehe', interj. Alas! - mat'a nuŋseca, Alas, it seems as if I should die.
hehehe', interj. Alas! - waśicuŋ ota el mahipelo, tka ota óŋtoŋniyaŋpi śni.

hehe'la, 1) v. dim. (heha). You said so. Note: this is used in speaking to a child. 2) interj. You say so! A by-word.

hehu'te, n. Something, e.g. a string, ribbon, or band, to hold the aśke together, a tuft or bunch of hair that Lakota men used to wear on the side of their heads.

hehu'tela, n. An old bull buffalo whose horns are worn off and damaged badly. Bl.

heha'ka, n. The male elk, so-called from its branching horns. - iktomi, An elk with flat, broad horns, the prongs being short, a moose perhaps. Note: der. from he-haka.

heȟa'ka he, n. The tall gaura; the small-flowered gaura. Gaura parviflora. Bl. #40,119. Cf. wókaȟtaŋ blaskaska.

heȟa'ka tápejúta, n. The slender dalea. Dalea enlandra. Pulse family. The horsemint, wild bergawort. Menthaefolia graham. Mint family. The Indian distinguishes between the latter and waȟpe waśtemna; one grows in the open and the other, in thickets. Also, monarda menthaefolia graham; it is used for bad cuts with much blood issuing. The leaves are chewed and put under a bandage. This will stop the flow of blood. A tea of leaves, strained and kept in a soft cloth placed over sore eyes over-night benefits them. The tea is also effective against whooping cough or other coughing, according to CrazyHawk. The tea from the leaves is also good for people who faint. BT. FD.178,270-271.

heȟa'ǩatawoṫe, n. Elk food. Same as heȟakatapejuta, perhaps.

heȟa'ka wakṗá, n. The Yellowstone River, i.e. the Elk River.

heȟak' iktómi, n. A moose.

heȟa'ktaṗejúṫa, n. Elk medicine, a kind of mint.

heȟlo'ġeca, adj. Hollow-horned.
he'ȟloġeca iyéceca, n. A buffalo cow with long horns, which is an exception. Bl.

hei'ċakaŋ, n. A fine comb, a louse comb.

hei'c'iya, v. To say that to one's self, as at the beginning of a quotation.

hei'ǩaŋ, n. A string tieing the end of the hair. Mazaśa - . - iyaglaśka.

he'i ... ú yeṫo, v. To call to one, i.e. to men; to stop one.

hejaŋ'jaŋ, n. An unhatched louse, a nit, a body louse; so called because it is translucent.

heǩa'za, n. A yearling deer, i.e. with horns with one prong. Cf. táhejata.

heǩi'cinaǩeca, v.n. To be all used up to or for one, to have no more. Hemicinakeca.

heǩi'ya, v. To say this to.

he'kṫa, 1) n. That behind, what is passed or last, as applied to time and space. - weṫu, Last spring. 2) adv. Behind, back. - u, He come behind. - gla, He goes back home. - wagluha waciŋ śni, I do not want to have it back.
he'ktab, adv. Behind, after. Mihéktab.

he'kṫaǩiya, adv. Backward, whence one came. Hecel ake - ble k'oŋ he ogna waku. -- héktaktakiya, adv. red.
he'kṫapataŋ, adv. (?). Si - wikaŋ k'oŋ iyakaśka; caŋke iyutitaŋ.
he'ktapataŋhaŋ, adv. From behind, in the rear. - iyotaka, To get up behind, as behind a rider or driver. B.H.203.4

he'kṫaṫaŋhaŋ, adv. Behind.

he'kṫawapa, adv. Behind, after; backward.

he'kṫawapaṫaŋhaŋ, adv. From behind.

he'kṫawapaya, adv. Same as hektawapa.

hel, adv. In that place, there.

he'na, adv. Same as hel. - ouŋyeya yo

he'na, pron. pl. (he). Those.
he'na épi, ph. The pl. of hee. Tona kośkalaka taŋsna uŋpi kiŋ - kta keya. Waŋyaka po! Lena nitakuyepi ehaŋna icagapi k'oŋ hena epi ca ekta lapi kta lo.

hena'gnaǩeca, adv. red. (henakeca). So many of each.

hena'ǩe, (?).

hena'ǩeca, adv. So many; enough, sufficient; finished, all gone. Waniyetu 67 henamakeca. Tawicu kiŋ e na ciŋca hokśila num - ob Egypt etkiya iyayapi. B.H.48.26.

hena'ǩeȟci, adv. All these, so great

a quantity.

he'naḱel, adj. Only so many, only so much. P. Bl.

hena'ḱiya, adv. In so many ways.

hena'la, adv. Only so many or so much; none, all gone. Henamala, Mine all gone, I have none. Henákicila, All was gone for him, i.e. used up. D.27.
hena'laḱiya, adv. Only in so many ways or places.
hena'lapila, adv. pl. of henala.

hena'na, pron. red. of hena. - oyakapi. B.H.62.20.

henaŋ'gnaḱeca, adv. red. (henakeca). So many each.

henaŋ'gnaŋg, cont. (henaŋgnakeca). Each one so many.

hena'pila, adv. pl. of henala. Ena naŋkapi kiŋ niye ko - kte lo. Ho, henalapi icuŋhaŋ lecel wicaśa waŋ eya. Note: henalapi is also used.

hena'yos, heni'yos, pron. These two.

hena'yoza, Same as henayos.

he'nayuza, pron. Those two. Bl.

hena'yuzaḱiya, adv. Those two, these two times. Bl.

heni'yos, heni'yoza, Same as henayos.

heni'yoza, Same as hiniyos.
heni'yozaḱiya, adv. Those two, those two times.

he'oŋ, adv. For that, on that account, therefore.

he'oŋetaŋhaŋ, adv. Therefore.

heṗa', v. To fight. Hewapa, heyapa. Kici heyapa inicipi śni yelo. B.H. 86.21.

hepca', v. 1st pers. singl. I think that, I thought that. This is the only form used. Cf. epca, kepca.
hepca'pca, v. red. (hepca). I think that. Bl.

hepce'keśni, hepce'śni uŋ, v. Although I thought I would not. - ecamoŋ kte, i.e. still I'll do it. Hepceśni uŋ ecamoŋ kte, Although I had not intended to do it, I'll do it. WE.

heṗela', interj. Of surprise when hearing or seeing something foolish said or done by others. Also, héṗela. Same as huŋhuŋhé. - , śicaya ehelo. - , ecanoŋ yelo. Cf. śku.

heṗiŋ', v. 1st pers. singl. Same as hepa.

heṗi'ya, n. The side or flank of a hill. Ataya - el onakijiŋpi. Na waŋna paha waŋ - ca el iŋyaŋ blaskaska ca el agliwicauŋpapi. Oŋ cuwi-hepiya wahuŋ, He slashed an openning in the bull's side with it. Paha-hepiya e-wauŋpe. D.33,218.

heṗi'yela, adj. or n. On the grade of a hill. Hepiyelaḣci caŋku. Bl.

heṗo'la, n. A buffalo bull horn. Bl.

hesla'tḱala, n. A young male elk.

heś, interj. Why! Well! It may be. Eya heś taŋcaŋ zaniyaŋ taŋyaŋ wauŋ welo. Heś hécoŋ ehaŋtaŋś taŋyaŋ kte śni. Heś nila yeś waḣteyalaśni k'oŋ, Why! he is the one you rejected when he wanted you. D.204. B.H.48.7;131.5; 184.12;188.21;193.18;229.11.

heś'e'lake uŋ, express. That was you again (guessing).

heṫaŋ', adv. cont. (hetaŋhaŋ). From that place, from that time; therefore, on that account. Mato tipila ki - ilalapi kte lo. Itowe k'el mapehiŋ kiŋ - conala ate mayuha kta.

heṫaŋ'haŋ, adv. From that place or time; therefore, on that account. Iyaye k'oŋ - aŋpetu ake nuŋpa.

heṫaŋ'haŋś ṫoḱaḱa, ṫo'ḱa, express. What difference is it?

hetḱa'la, n. The ground squirrel, a kind of squirrel living in the woods or rocky places (iǧuǧa el), as in the Black Hills. Same as taśnaheca iyececa ǧiǧi. Bl.

he'ƫkiya, adv. Towards that place. Waŋna tipi k'oŋ - ukiye.

hetoŋ', adj. Horned. P.

hetoŋ' cik'ala, n. An antilope.

hetoŋ'toŋ, (?). Waŋ - mic'ila, said by a man who suddenly got what he always wanted and so feels greatly encouraged; or, wahácaŋka taŋka wak'iŋ s'elececa. Bl. Bm.

he'ƫu, adv. At that place, there.
he'ƫula, adv. There, then.

he'ƫulaḣci, adv. Just at that place or time. D.217.

he'ya, n. A louse, lice, head louse.

heya', v. (he-eya). To say that or this. Heƥá, hehá, heúŋƙeyapi. Heyeśni ciśi k'a, eya. - ayupta, That is what he answered. - hoyeya, To say with a loud voice. - iyuŋga, That is the way he asked. - owa, To write the following. - paŋ, To let out a cry. Heyapi śniś eyapika, i.e. to be indignant at a lie told. - wacekiya, To say the following prayer. B.H.81.7;199.10;59.5;76.5;99.19;108.2;207.4;236.7;111.17;236.4;80.6.

heya'ya, v. red. (heya). To say much, keep saying. Hepápa, hehāha, uŋkéyayapi. B.H.293.20.

heya'yalaƙa, v. red. (heya). To tell lies. Hepápalaka, hehāhalaka, heuŋyayapilaka, heyayalakapi or heyayapilaka. WE. Cf. eyaya.

heye'ceśni, (?). Heyapikeśni. Heyapikeśni k'oŋ. Bl.

heye'ƙiya, v.a. To cause to say that. Heyéwakiya.

heyō'ka, n. A clown. According to R. this is the name of a Dakota god called by some the anti-natural god. He is represented as a little old man with a cocked hat on his head, a bow and arrows in his hands and a quiver on his back. In winter he goes naked, and in the summer he wraps his buffalo robe around himself. Osni, yuŋkaŋ tiyoceyati śni naƙé maśte, yuŋkaŋ ceyati śni ehaŋ oŋ le heyonika yelo, as is said to one when he once had a fire while they called it warm weather.

heyo'ka oti', n. The house or place where a heyoka does his wakaŋ work.

heyo'ka tapeju'ta, n. Red false mallow, prairie mallow, malvastrum coccineum. A gray moss root. Magicians chewed their roots and rubbed their hands with it and so could dip them into the hottest water without being scalded. Sam Terry denied that it has the qualities just described. The roots chewed and laid on sores have a healing effect. NO. Bl. #168. Cf. FD. 167-8.

heyo'kicile, v. (heyole). To rid one of lice. D.109.

heyo'ƥaśƥu, n. A pin. Note: hiyopaśpu is more proper, but it is pronounced heyopaśpu.

heyo'ƥuza, adj. Lousy, full of lice or nits. -- v. To be lousy. Heyómapuza. D.109.

heyo'taƙe iƥa'śƥu, n. A tooth pick. Note: hiyotake is the word but is said heyotake.

heyu'ḣa, n. Name of all animals with branching horns. Also, heyúġa.

heyu'kƫaŋ, adj. Bent-horned. -- n. An animal with bent horns. Wicaśa kiŋ nakuŋ iteha kitoŋ na - waŋjigji ca na makikceka iic'iyúŋ.

heyuŋ', v.a. To tie up, wrap up a pack, pack up. Hemuŋ, henuŋ, heuŋyuŋpi. Taku henuŋ kiŋ suksutaya paḣta yo, napeceśni uŋkomani kte lo.
heyuŋ'ƥi, n. A wrapping up; what is wrapped around, as paper etc.

hi, n. A tooth, teeth; the bit or edge of an axe; the point of anything. Wicahi, Human teeth. Mahi.

hi, v.n. To arrive at. Wahi. El mahi, He came to me.

hia'ƙigle, v. To set the teeth firmly, as a dying person does. Waŋna t'iŋ kte ca - . - woglake s'elececa, He spoke through his teeth. EM.

hia'ƥe, v. To await one's coming. Hiawa pe.

hia'yaⁿṗa, v. (hi-ayaⁿpa). To come morning on, as in morning arriving.

hibu', v.n. To come or arrive. Wahibu. Obs.

hi'glaǩisǩis, cont. (higlakiskiza). To grate the teeth. - wauⁿ.
hi'glaǩisǩiza, v. To grate the teeth. Hiwaglakiskiza. Bl.
hi'glaǩiza, v. To grit or grind the teeth, as a cow or a man in his sleep; to crunch. Higlawakiza.
hi'glaǩoǩog, cont. of higlakokoka. - wauⁿ.
hi'glaǩoǩoǩa, v. To gnash the teeth. Hiwaglakokoka. Also perhaps, to shatter the teeth.

higna', n. A husband. Mihigna, nihigna, hignáka.
higna'ku, n. Her husband. - wóǩic'u, Meat above the knees of buffalos.HH.Bl.
higna'toⁿ, v.n. To have a husband, to be married. Hignawatoⁿ.
higna'ya, v. To have for a husband. Hignawaya.

hihe'ya, 1) v.n. (hi-iheya). To come and enter, as does a bullet or arrow. 2) v. coll. pl. They collect together, assemble in one place.

hihi', adj. Soft, as fur or down.
hihi'la, adj. Mellow, as ground or mud or sand. Caⁿku kiⁿ lila - , the wheels going in deep; hence, soft.
hihi' s'e, adj. Nappy, furry.

hihuⁿ'ni, v. To arrive at any place. Wahihuⁿni. Akicita najiⁿpi k'oⁿ el - na waⁿji paiyotak iȟpeya.

hi'ȟ'a, v. To gnash or show the teeth. Máyaśleca ciⁿca hakakta s'e makú - kaca, as is said of very lean people. Bl. -- hiȟ'aȟ'a, v. red. - iⁿyaⁿka.
hi'ȟ'akiya, v.n. To show one's teeth, to grin. Hiȟ'awakiya.
hi'ȟ'ayela, adj. Thin, poor, emaciated. - awayelo. Makú - yauⁿ welo. Bl. -- adv. Showing one's teeth, as a person does that has been sick in bed for a long time and is emaciated. - ȟpaya. Yuⁿkaⁿ wicaśa waⁿ ataya huhu ececa ca na - ȟpaya ca waⁿyaⁿkapi śke lo.

hii'ṗajaja, n. A tooth brush.
hii'paśpu, v. To pick the teeth. Hiiwapaśpu.
hii'śta, n. The eyetooth. GV.
hii'yat'iⁿze, n. Cloves.

hi'maza, n. A gold tooth.

himni'ciya, v. coll. pl. To come, assemble, to keep coming.

hinā', interj. Of surprise; used by women. -- hináhiná, interj. red.

hina'jiⁿ, n. The jaws of an arrow which hold the point. Bl. Also, hinája, hiwájatapi. R. Bl. -- v.n. To come and stand, to appear before. Wahinajiⁿ and perhaps wahinawajiⁿ. Hinauⁿjiⁿpi. Lehaⁿl wicaśa waⁿ u na - . Pb.27.

hina'pa, v.n. To come in sight; to come out of, come up, as something planted. Also, in ref. to the sun. Wahinàpa and wahinawapa.
hina'ṗeya, v.a. To cause to come in sight. Hinapewaya.

hinū', interj. Of gladness and surprise, as when one meets a friend, but used by women only. - , onapuza ca haⁿpi cola wówahele. BT. Also, That is funny, How funny! D.115. -- hinúhinú, interj. red. of hinu.

hi'num úya, n. A two-year old colt. Also, hinúmbuye.

hiⁿ, interj. Of disappointment over failure after a strained effort; used by men and women. Also, Whoops! I did not mean it, as when one accidentally offends another. The word is always said with a great expulsion of breath. D.100, note 1.

hiⁿ, n. Hair, fur, down. - naosakiya, To bristle up.

hiⁿa'ǩaⁿhaⁿhaⁿ, adv. or adj. Shedding one's hair, as do horses in spring. Also, hiⁿǩáⁿhaⁿhaⁿ.
hiⁿa'ṗaǩe, v. To have winter hair. Śuⁿkawakaⁿ kiⁿ nahaȟci - . Bl.

hiⁿgla', v.n. aux. This indicates a sudden action or movement, To become, to commence etc. suddenly. Mahiⁿgla. Otuyaciⁿ peta śaśa hiⁿglapi, utapi. Yuⁿkaⁿ taku eye, eyaś hi ece skaska hiⁿgle kiⁿ ecela waⁿyaⁿke.

Yuŋkaŋ (wahiŋkpe) iyoyaŋp - na taŋ waŋkatuya ya na waŋna makata glihaŋ. Pte ota yelo, eyapi; na waŋna buwica - ca miś kakel inawape; ehaŋl ekta ewatoŋwaŋ. Ataŋiŋ śni - . Mat'a - , toka kta he? Supposing I would die suddenly, what would you do? Iciyuta yuŋkaŋ śkaŋ nihiŋgle na kagal nihiŋgla.

ablak - , To die down, as the wind.
ataŋiŋśni - , To disappear.
buwica - , To charge upon.
ikópa - , To be wary, leary of one.
iyokiśica - , To fall into saddness. Also, iyokiśil - .
iyoyaŋp - , To brighten, to light.
kagal - , To jump; to jerk. Kagal nihiŋgla, You jumped in surprise.
kuja - , To get sick.
mat'a - , I am just about dead.
peta śaśa hiŋglapi, Flashes; sparks.
skaska - , To whiten, turn white.
śkaŋ nihiŋgla, You jumped in surprise.
toŋwaŋ - , To open one's eyes.
wakokipa - , To become afraid.

hiŋgnu', v.a. To singe off, as the down off a duck etc. Hiŋwágnu.
hiŋgnu'ṗi, part. Singed off. - s'e mahiŋgle lo, I am shocked. BT.

hiŋhaŋ', n. An owl.
- cik'ala, A small species of owl.
- ġi, The short-eared owl. Bl. Cf. National Geographic Magazine, Feb. 1935, p. 217, Owls of North America.
- hetoŋla, The horned owl.
- kap'ipila, The long-eared owl. It is a little owl.
- makȟótila, The burrowing owl; a little owl living in burrows with prairie dogs. Hiŋhaŋ makotila ciŋcala nataha s'e, as is said when hair stands up, unkempt. Hiŋhaŋ makotila ca ȟiŋyé s'e ȟ'aŋhiyeȟci upelo, as is said when people arrive very slowly. Bl.
- saŋ, The gray owl.
- sapa, The black owl.
- ska, The white or snowy owl; it has black spots on the belly. Its deep trumpet voice is heard late in the fall and even later on. It breeds in the winter on the prairie, coming down from the north. Bl.
- śa, The great horned owl.
- taŋka, The large great horned owl. There are five kinds of owls whose song goes: who-who-who--- . Spies were used to imitate this sound to indicate the enemy is near.

hiŋhaŋ', v.n. To fall, as rain or snow; hence, to rain, snow. Na waŋna waniyetu aŋpetu waŋ el wa - .

hiŋhaŋ'hotoŋ, v.n. To hoot as an owl. Na waŋna yapi el ośpaye etaŋ waŋji - ca na inajiŋpi.
hiŋhaŋ'ȟaġa, 1) n. An owl. 2) v. To hoot or shout as an owl, as young men do after dark; to act like an owl.
hiŋhaŋ' kap'ipila, n. Cf. hiŋhaŋ.

hiŋhaŋ'ke, n. or adv. (?). This end, the end this way. Bl.

hiŋhaŋ' makȟótila, n. Cf. hiŋhaŋ.

hiŋ'haŋna, n. This morning. Ho waŋna - el oyate kiŋ witaya aya na oimniciye.
hiŋ'haŋnaȟci, adv. (?). Very early in the morning.
hiŋ'haŋna ȟiŋ or ȟinhán, n. Tomorrow. - le ogna u kta. Tohaŋ kiŋhaŋ yaglapi kta he? Caŋke - eya. Note: ȟiŋ here is pronounced gi.
hiŋ'haŋni, n. Same as hiŋhaŋna. - kiŋ wiŋyaŋ oyasiŋ wayacipi kte lo.

Hiŋhaŋ'śuŋwaṗa, n. The Sicaŋgu or the Brule nation, who wear a little owl feather on the head.

hiŋhaŋ' tahánṗe, n. An appendix to a buffalo's heart; same as pśitola hu, so-called because of the shape of the leaves, broad-leaved, arrow-head, rilled, sagittaria latifolia, of the water plantain family. BT. # 126. Bl.

hiŋhe', v.n. To rain. Cf. hiŋhaŋ.
hiŋhe'ȟiya, v.a. To cause to fall, as rain or snow.

hiŋhe'ya, v.a. To cause to rain etc. Hiŋhéwaya.

hiŋȟpa'ya, v.n. To fall, fall down. Mahiŋȟpaya, uŋhiŋȟpayapi.

hiŋȟpe'ya, v.a. To throw down or away what one has in the hand. Hiŋȟpewaya. v.n. To be thrown down, be lying down. Wa oȟolya - , as said when snow lies in spots here and there. Bc.

hiŋ'ȟpiȟpila, n. A buffalo or horse in spring when they have shed their winter hair. Bl.

hi^{n}ȟte′ n. Thick fur, hair or nap.
hi^{n}ȟte′ya, adj. Furry, rough, the fur side out.

hi^{n}i′kceka, n. A dark bay horse. Also, hi^n íkceka.

hi^n′jijila, 1) adj. Downy, as young birds are. 2) n. Thin hair, as that on one's hands and arms.

hi^n′ǩaciceyela, adv. With the hair uncombed, matted. - naji^n. Bl.

hi^n′kceka, Same as hi^n ikceka.

hi^{n}ṗi′la, n. Short hair or fur, as that on robes taken in summer; robes with short hair. Peji - , A certain short grass growing in mat-like patches of light green. Bl. D.21.

hi^{n}l′ȟi^{n}cala, n. A gray water bird, so called on account of the noise they make. Bl.

hi^n′nasaǩiya, v.n. perhaps. To have the hair standing up, as does an angry dog ready to attack. Bl.

hi^{n}o′śkuśku, v. perhaps. To shed old hair, as horses do in spring. Wana śu^{n}kawakan hi^{n}ośkuśkupelo. Bl.

hi^n′pahi^n, n. A mouse colored horse. Miś - (i.e. horses) ki^n hena wicabluha kte lo.

hi^{n}ṗa′ȟla, n. A bunch of old thrown buffalo hair, which was held sacred and used as wotawe etc. Na tata^{n}ka - wa^n ku na pegnagkiya.

hi^{n}sǩa′, adj. Shed off, as is said of animals that have a new coat of hair; literally, hair white. Hi^{n}skála. Mato Hi^{n}skala, The name of Ribman of the village of Wounded Knee, S. D.

hi^{n}sǩe′, n. The long upper or canine teeth of animals.

hi^{n}ske′kagya, (?). - iyeya. - iyemayelo, He says the same thing I did without having heard me. Bl.

hi^n′sǩo, adv. So big, so large.

hi^n′sǩoǩeca, adv. So large, so great.

hi^n′sǩola, adv. So small.

hi^n′sǩosǩokeca, adv. red. of hi^{n}skokeca.

hi^n′sǩosǩoya, adv. red. of hi^{n}skoya.

hi^n′sǩota^{n}ka, adv. So great.

hi^n′sǩoya, adv. So far around, thus far.
hi^n′sǩoyela, adv. That big.

hi^{n}sta^n′, n. A chestnut-colored horse.

hi^{n}śa′, n. A sorrel horse.
hi^{n}śa′śa, n. red. of hi^{n}śa.

hi^n′ṫa, n. The bass, linden or lime wood. - ca^n, Bass-wood or lilia. also called paṫa. GW

hi^n′te s'e, v.t. (yuhi^{n}ta). To rake e.g. a field or garden etc. - naślog éyaye, As though they had been raked away, they (the game) got away. Cf. gmi s'e. Bl.

hi^{n}tka′, n. The nit or unhatched louse. Also, hi^{n}tkala.

hi^{n}tǩa^n′, n. The common cat-tail or typha.
hi^{n}tǩa^n′hu, n. The cat-tail stalk.

hi^{n}tō′, n. A gray horse.

hi^n′tokeca, 1) n. The color of something. 2) adj. Colored. P.

hi^{n}ya′jice, n. Fur, down; swan's down.

hi^{n}ya′ko^n, n. Stockings; the adversative for hu^{n}yako^n.

hi^n′ya^{n}ka, v. (hi^n, i.e. ha^n-ya^{n}ka). To wait, hold on. Used in the imp. only, when terminal "a" is used or terminal "i". Hi^{n}ya^{n}ka yo. Ito hi^{n}ya^{n}ka yo. Ito hi^{n}ya^{n}ki yelo. B.H. 43.17.

hi^n′ya^{n}kaġa, n. An owl. When the wild pigeons wail, the children say: - hoto^n welo, There is a ghost.

hi^{n}ya^n′kaȟ wacíyapi, n. A pastime for boys. Bl.

hiŋyaŋ'sela, adv. Wickely, badly. R.

hiŋyaŋs'gla, v. To be afraid on seeing something terrible. Hiŋyaŋswagla. R. Bl. D.47, note 2.

hiŋyaŋs'ya, 1) v.a. To provoke. Hiŋyaŋswaya. 2) adv. Sternly, crossly.

hiŋyaŋ'za, v.n. To be stern, cross. Mahiŋyaŋza. Tawaciŋ - , To be of surly disposition. -- hiŋyáŋzeca, adj. Stern, cross; sulky. Wicaśa - . -- hiŋyáŋzeƙe, adj. Stern; morose. Also, híŋyaŋzeke. -- hiŋyáŋziyela, adv. (hiŋyaŋza). Badly, wickedly.

hiŋye'ťaoŋṗa, v.a. To lay on the shoulder. Hiŋyetawaoŋpa.

hiŋye'ťe, n. The shoulder, the whole shoulder.

hiŋye'ťeawiŋyaŋ, v. To lay on the shoulder. Hiŋyeteawiŋwaya. Bl.

hiŋye'ťewak'iŋ, n. A shoulder insignia of a military general's rank. WHL.

hiŋ'zi, adj. Buckskin or cream colored. -- n. A buckskin horse.
hiŋ'ziśa, n. An orange colored horse.

hi'onaħ'ayela, adv. Showing the teeth, as a dying person or a skull, the lips removed. - ħpaya.

hi'paśku, v. To pick the teeth. P.

hipsi'ca, v. To jump down, as from a horse. Wahipsica.

hi'psoŋpsoŋla, adj. perhaps. Teeth on edge. Himapsoŋpsoŋla.

hisťo'la, n. An arrow; an arrow-head without barbs. Kesťóŋ, To have barbs.

hita'kaŋyuwi, v. (hi-takaŋ-yuwi). To bind an arrow-head on the shaft.

hiťi'gla, v.a. To loathe, dislike e.g. food. Hitiwagla.
hiťi'glaya, v.a. To cause to loathe or dislike. Hitiglawaya.

hi'ťobuye, n. A four-year old calf.

hituŋ'kala, n. A mouse, mice.

hituŋ'kala nakṗala, n. Mouse ear, pussy-toes, ladies' tobacco, white plantain; so called because of the shape of the leaves. It is a medicine. Also, the dwarf everlasting, the plantain-leaved everlasting. Antennaria aprica grave. The composite family. Bl. #158.

hituŋ'kala sápa, n. The field mouse. Paŋgi gnakapi. Also, a mole.

hituŋ'kala tawóyute, Cf. tokala tapejuta hu bloka. Bl. #249.
hituŋ'kala tuŋkce, n. The fall anemone long-fruited anemone, the summer anemone, thimble weed, so called for its leaves. Anemone cylindrica. The crowfoot family. B. #79.

hituŋ'ƙasaŋ, n. The large weasel, white in the winter, yellow in the summer. Bl. The gopher, wahiŋheya.

Hituŋ'ƙasaŋ Wicáśa, n. p. A tribe of western Indians. Bl.

hituŋ'k'naħábyapi, n. A pastime for boys. Bl.

hiťuŋ'ktaŋka, n. A rat. - s'e nakpa taŋktaŋka kaca, as is said of little men with long ears. Bl.

hiu'ya, v. To grow teeth, as a baby does. Hiuwaya.

hiwa'jaťapi, n. The jaws of an arrow that hold the head. Bl. Syn.- hinajiŋ.

hiya', adv. No, of negation.

hiya'gle, v.n. To reach to, as a road; to come upon one, also as a temptation. Mahíyagle, uŋḣiyaglepi. Also, It happens to one. Suŋkawakaŋ k'iŋnapapi mahiyagle. B.H.7.22;35.4;42.1;303.10.
hiya'gleya, 1) v.a. To cause to reach to; to bring upon one. Hiyaglewaya. 2) adv. Reaching to, leading to.

hiya'haŋ, v.n. To appear on top of a hill, so becoming visible; said in ref. to one. Wahiyahaŋ, uŋhiyauŋhaŋpi. When there are many we say: ahiyahaŋ. Use also, wahiyawahaŋ, yahiyayahaŋ.

hiya'ħpeya, v. perhaps. To throw over to one. Bl.

hiya'k̇apṫa, v.n. To come over, as a stream or hill. Wahiyawakapta.

hiya'k̇igle, Cf. hiakigle.
hiya'k̇iglegle, v. To chatter, as from cold or chill.

hi'yaŋka, v. (hi-yaŋka). To stay where one has arrived, to wait a minute. Also perhaps, hiŋyaŋka. The word is used only in the imperative mood; but note: Tate waŋ oyupemnipi s'e hiyaŋke lo. Bl. D.56, note 2. Cf. tíyaŋka yo.

hiya'nuŋ, adj. Puny, small and not able to grow. Mahiyanuŋ. Cf. k̇oyánuŋ.

hi'yatagle, v. (iyatagle). To have gone beyond, exceeded. Ekta toŋwéya ya po uŋgna - uŋyaŋpi kte lo. Bl.

hiya'ya, v.n. To come and pass along, to go by, go past. Wahiblabla, yahilala. Waŋna kiŋyela - po. Oyasiŋ hocokata - po. Haŋyewi, yahilale ki, as addressed in prayer. Paŋkeska wakpala kiŋ lila mini - . Amáya waciŋ śni yahilale lo, You pass by not thinking of taking me along. Bl.

hiya'ye, n. Semen. Also, ihíyaye. R.

hi'yazaŋ, v.n. To have a tooth-ache. Himayazaŋ.
hi'yazaŋpi, n. A tooth-ache.

hiye'ya, v.n. To become, to cause to be. Najiŋ - . Hiyeye ciŋ, Those who are, i.e. all. Waptaye najiŋ hiyeye kiŋ. Taku hiyeye ciŋ, All things. Oyate hiyeye ciŋ, All people. Uŋhiyeyapi, We are. Paha hiyeye kiŋ na wakpala yuŋke kiŋ hena yuptoka kiŋ ośkinic'iye, i.e. hunting buffalo. Wilwitaya eglepi, i.e. the grain, ca wana enanala na zazecayela hiyéye lo. Hel enana úta lila ota hiyeye, There lay about, i.e. were, many acorns. R. Bl. D.77. Gramm.319-320. Cf. iyeya.

hiyo', v. To come for something. The word is used with verbs as i, hi, iyaya etc. Woyute - mni kte. Waŋbli waŋ hiyomahi na wicoti ekta amaki. Śuŋkawakaŋ eya wicahiyo mni kte.

hiyo'au, v. pl. 3rd pers. (hiyo-au). They are coming for. B.H.18.3.

hiyo'hi, v. To come, arrive for. Hiyówahi.

hiyo'hik̇iya, v.a. To cause to come for. Hiyóhiwakiya.

hiyo'hiya, v.a. To cause to come for. Hiyohiwaya.

hiyo'ḣṗaya, v.n. To have come down from a hill, to be down, as said of a road. Wahiyoḣpaya. Gliyoḣpaya, as is said when one is coming down. Ecel paha waŋ el wahiyoḣpaye k'oŋ he ake aiyakapteya waku.

hiyo'ḣpeya, v.a. To come and let down. B.H.187.7.

hiyo'ṗatak̇e, n. A pin; a tooth-pick.

hi'yoṫak̇a, v.n. (hi-iyotaka). To sit down or stop on one's way someplace. Wahiyotaka. Manderson hel wahiyotaka. Hokśila, hel - yo.

hiyo't'iŋza, v. To come and crowd together. Iyuha hiyot'iŋze lo. Bl.

hiyo'u, v. To come for.
hiyo'ya, v.a. To bring or fetch. P.

hiyo'yatak̇e, n. (hi-oyatake). Anything sticking between the teeth, as meat etc. Hiyomayatake, A piece of meat got stuck between my teeth. Hiyomayatake ciŋ wakpaśpu kte lo, i.e. will pick it out. Bl.

hiyu', v.n. To come from out of, as a child being born; to come, come toward. Wahibu, yahilu. Tima - po. Tima - na tima hiyotaka. Taŋkal - . Caŋke waŋbli k'oŋ he waŋtaŋyeyela ti kiŋ iwaŋkab - . Hacocola wahibu ca ake hamacocola kte lo. Tokeśke tima yahilu hwo? B.H.43.12;241.15.

hiyu'k̇iciciya, v.a. To hand to one his own. Hiyuweciciya.

hiyu'k̇iya, v.a. To cause to come to somebody; to send or hand to, as a letter. Hiyuwakiya.

hiyuŋ'ka, v.n. To arrive somewhere and stop for the night. Wahimuŋka. B.

hi'yuskablu, n. Dentifrice. P.

hiyu'weġa, v.n. To cross a river or any water. Hiblúwega. Caŋke wata nuŋp oweciŋhaŋ hiyuwegapi keye.

hiyu'ya, v.a. To cause to come to, to send or hand to; to vomit. Hiyúwaya.

ho, prefix to adverbs. It makes them refer to a circle of camps. Cf. adverbs that follow.

ho, 1) adv. or interj. Of affirmation. Yes, all right. Ho, ca. 2) v.n. imp. only perhaps. Come on, come now. Wahó, uŋhópi. Ho wo. Ho po, etc. Aiyopteya yapi na ake hopi ca na iś eyą ecel hopi, na nauŋk nakicił'oŋpi. Śuŋkmanitu hopi. He wicaśa akaŋtu ho śni. B.H.63.16;294.6. Bl. 3) n. The voice either of man or animal.

hoa'glagla, adv. Along the tents of a camp circle, inside or outside. Hócokatuŋyaŋ - , i.ę. inside; holázataŋhaŋ - iyayapi, i.e. outside.

hoa'iciyopteya, adv. Through the middle of the tent.

hoa'ƙab hiyúya, v.a. To make one change in what he has said. Ablezin na eyá yo; miyeś le taku hecetu ca ociciyake lo; tka inihaŋśni hoakab hiyumayayiŋ kte ƙciŋ yelo. Bl.

hoa'ƙicipa, v. To talk for one, put in a good word for one. Hoawecipa. Hoacicipa. WE. B.H.88.25;237.9.

ho'aƙicipapi, n. A salutation. P.

hoa'nuŋk, adv. On two sides of the camp inside the circle, as when two men walk around from opposite directions, hoanuŋk hiyáyapi, and so are opposite and on both sides, i.e. diagonally opposite within the circle. Letaŋhaŋ - ataya najiŋyeyapi na ecel tipi he el anuŋk ihuŋniya po.

ho'apa śiŋ, n. Hard fat on the taníga. Bl.

hoa'pe, n. (hogaŋ-ape). Fish fins.

hoa'peśa, n. The red-fin, a species of fish; the short-headed red horse. Also, hoápeśaśa.

hobla'ska, n. The gizzard shad, perhaps.

ho'bu, n. A rough, unpleasant voice. Homabu.

ho'buƙiya, v.n. To speak with a gruff and unpleasant voice. Hobuwakiya.

hoca'ƙa, n. (hogaŋ-caka). Fish gills.

hoca'tkayataŋhaŋ, adv. At the left end of the open circle (camp). - tipi.

hoce'śpu, n. Fish scales. Cf. ceśpu.

hoce'te, n. The direct road to a drove of buffalo, in opposition to a round about way taken by some hunters as all set upon them for the hunt. Honuŋ piŋyaŋ uŋyaŋpi kte lo; akigle uŋyaŋpi kte lo. Bl.

ho'coƙa, n. A court-yard, an area surrounded by tents or houses. Na lila - otaŋkaya na iśtogmus wauŋcipi. D. 246.

ho'cokab, ho'cokam, adv. In the middle of the camp circle of tents. Tipi waśte waŋ - haŋ ca el akiyuha akignakapi.

ho'cokata, 1) n. The center place, a vacant spot within a circle of tents. 2) adv. In the center of a camp circle. - hiyaya po.

ho'cokatakiye, adv. Towards the middle of the camp. - bla, I went towards the center.

ho'coƙataŋhaŋ, adv. From the center or the midst of the camp. Wicaśa yamni - kupi ca el bla.

ho'cokatoŋyaŋ, adv. In a circle. - tipi, i.e. in a round village. - hoagla gla omani, He walked along the front of the tents, within the circle.

ho'cokatoŋtoŋyaŋ, adv. red. In their respective tribal circles. Wicoti waŋ yaŋke - . D.2.

hoco'śpu, n. A wart, scab; scales of a fish. Also, hocośpi, perhaps.

ho'ǧahaŋ, n. A rough, loud voice. Hómagahaŋ.

hoǧaŋ', n. Fish, the generic name. - mazognaka, A can of fish, as of sardines.

hoǧaŋ'mna, adj. (hogaŋ-omna). Smelling of fish, fishy.

hoǧaŋ'saŋla, n. Little fish, minnows. Same as hogaŋscila.

hoǧaŋ'scila, n. Little fish, minnows.

Same as hogaŋsaŋla.

hoǧaŋ'taŋka, n. A big fish, the name given to the whale.

ho'ǧaťa, n. A rough voice. Homagata.

ho'ǧita, adj. Hoarse, as a person's voice when he has taken cold. Hómagita.

ho'glaǧita, v. pos. (hoyagita). To make one's self hoarse by speaking. Howaglagita.

hogle'gleǧa, n. The grass pike; the rainbow fish. Bl. SLB.

ho'gluwaŋkal, adv. With a high voice. - lowaŋ. B.H.54.2.

ho'gna, adv. That way or direction, in that manner. Cf. logna. Niye tokel yaciŋ - kte. He ókiksa he kiŋ - yagliyakupi kte lo. Also, hógnakel. B.H. 255.10.

Ho'he, n. prop. An Assiniboin Indian.

ho'hetamáȟpiya, n. The northern lights. - ake taŋiŋ. Cf. maȟpiya taŋiŋ. Bl.

ho'hetapte, n. A buffalo cow apparently very thin and lean, but found with much fat when killed; a very lean cow. Bl.

hohi', v. imp. only. Take it. It is used only when a man hands the burning pipe to someone else. Cf. na.

hoho'la, adj. Loose, able to be shaken or moved. Hi mahohola, My teeth are loose.

hoho'ṗicaśni, adj. Immovable.
hoho'ṗicaśniyaŋ, adv. Immovably.

hoho'śni, adj. Silent. - yaŋka. Obs.

ho'hoťe, n. A swing; a hammock; a seesaw; a swing, as a grape vine hanging from a tree. - kic'uŋpi; si oŋ naȟtakapi. Also, hóhoťela.
ho'hotela akiciyapi, n. A sham fight between two groups of boys in which they use only their legs. Bl.
ho'hoťela kic'úŋ, v.n. To swing, to swing round. - wic'uŋ.
ho'hoťela kaśká, v. To make a swing. - kaśke uŋyiŋ kte. Caŋapakiŋyaŋ wanice k'eyaś caŋsakib uŋkaśkiŋ kte. Bl.

hohu', n. A bone. - s'e tasáke, as is said of something hard. Also, huhú. B. D.14. Hohúmila. D.33.

hohub', exclam. Of disappointment, as a light being extinguished. WE.

hohu'caŋȟpi, n. A club with a sharp horn attached to one end to kill animals with.

hohu'icaślece, n. A primitive axe with which the Indians split bones to get the marrow. Bl.

hohu'icaťe, n. A primitive hammer to crack bones with to get the marrow. Bl.

hohu'kazuŋta oŋ ósloȟaŋ kic'óŋpi, n. A sled made of buffalo bones.

hohu'mila, n. A bone knife. D.33.

hohu'saŋ s'e, adv. White-yellowish like bones. Also perhaps, adj. Maȟpiya kiŋ - u welo. Bl.

hohu'śuŋkakaŋ, n. The astroyolus bone. Part of the foot near the hoof. Also, hohu śuŋkawakaŋ. Bl. SLB.

hohu'wasmiŋpi, n. A soup made of the back bones; a hash. Bl.

hohu'yazaŋpi, n. Rheumatism.

hohu'yuȟmuŋpi, n. A toy for boys.

hoȟ, interj. Of displeasure at hearing something one does not like. Hoȟ, niyeś ecanoŋ śni, i.e. you do it yourself. D.196. LB. This is a man's word denoting objection or rejection of an idea that has been suggested.

ho'ȟaṗa, n. A rough voice. Homaȟapa. Cf. ȟapa.

ho'ȟeceś, interj. Of disbelief.

hoȟna'ǧicala hotóŋpi, n. A certain noise made by women with the tongue and used in a certain dance.

ho'ȟniyaŋyaŋ, v.n. To talk in a crying voice and excited manner, as is done from bashfulness. Hówaȟniyaŋyaŋ.

hoḣp̣a', v.n. To cough. Howahpa. - iglá t'a, or - miglat'a, To cough convulsively.
hoḣp̣a'ḣ'aṅ háṅska, n. Whooping cough.
hoḣp̣a'kujapi, n. Consumption.
hoḣp̣a'pi, n. Cough, the having a cold; consumption.

hoḣp̣i', n. A nest.
hoḣp̣i'ya, v.a. To have a nest; to make a nest of. Hoḣpiwaya.

hoḣwa', n. The calamus. The leaves are eaten, as well as the stalks, by the Dakota. It is a kind of water grass. The roots are called śuṅkcé. The word designates the leaves esp.

Hoḣwo'ju Wicáśa, n. A clan of the Sioux living on the Standing Rock reservation. The Huṅkpapáya.

hoḣya'zela, (?).

hoi'cuwa, n. (hogaṅ-kuwa). A fish hook or a fishing apparatus.

ho'iglaġita, v. pos. (hoiyagita). To make one's self hoarse by speaking. Same as hóglagita.

hoi'haṅke, n. Either end of the camp circle, i.e. at the entrance to the camp circle.

hoi'kceyaḳel, adv. Having not been educated or instructed; on the spur of the moment. - oyaka. - lowaṅ. Bl.

ho'iṅkp̣ala, adv. perhaps. Being barely audible because very distant. Hlaḣla kiṅ - hotaṅiṅ. LB.

hoi'p̣aṭe, n. (p̣ata). A fishing net. - yuze. BD. Cf. p̣ata.

hoi'śleyaṭaṅhaṅ, adv. At the right end of an open camp circle. - tipi.

hoi'śta, n. A match.

hoi'ṭokaġaṭaṅhaṅ, adv. perhaps. At the south side of the camp. Na waṅna - kigla.

hoi'wotka, n. A carp; the hog sucker. - s'e i cik'a kaca, i.e. for this fish has a small mouth and does not take to the bait easily; hence, fig. the word is applied to a person with a small mouth and who talks little. - s'e taṅcaṅ waśte, as they say of a well shaped horse. Bl.

hoiyo'ḣpaya, v.n. To become hoarse, by the wind blowing on one and thus affecting the voice. Hoiyómaḣpaya.

hoi'yoḳise, n. Half of a company, half of a camp.

ho'iyupsice, n. A fish hook.

ho'jahaṅ, adv. Roughly, hoarsely. - ia, To speak roughly, hoarsely.

hojilā', interj. How beautiful! Simply splendid!

hoḳa', n. The eel.

hoḳa', n. The thick-billed guillemot, Brunnich's murre.

hoka' ca haṅyé kiṅyé s'e, adj. Bewildered, hesitating, irresolute. - uṅkuṅpi. L.

hoka'ġapi, n. A flute, perhaps.

hoḳa'ġica, n. The snipe, a small kind of heron or the genus scolopax; the green-blue heron; the dim. of hokagica, hoḳáġicala. R. FR.

ho'ḳaġiṭa, v. To make the voice hoarse by speaking or singing. Hówakagita.

hŏḳahe', interj. Welcome! When a visitor has been bid to come in after rapping, by the invitation "Hau", on entering, the host says: - , hel iyotaka If he fails to say this, the visitor is displeased.

hokaḣ'glepi, (?). Said of those who come first for a big meeting and put up their tents. Bl.

hoka'ḣica, n. The stork.
hoka'manip̣ila, n. A place on the Niobrara River where there used to be a large colony of nested cranes. Bl.

ho'ḳapsaṅpsaṅ ia, v. To whine.

hoka'pta, v. To fill up. Howákaptelicelo, I fill myself up with food. Bl.

hoka'to, n. The blue heron.

hoke'luta, n. The full moon in the morning.

hoke'mila, n. Same as hokemi, hokewiⁿ.

hoke'wiⁿ, hoke'mi, n. The "man in the moon", thought of as a woman by the old Sioux, with a lot of clothes on. - ca najiⁿ yelo. - waⁿna wóze yelo (makal-hpaya), i.e. at full moon, she is stirring the kettle. Similarly, wiaceic'iti, i.e. she is making the fire (ceti). Also, hokéwiⁿ. BT.

hoke'wiⁿ s'e, adv. Like the woman, i.e. looking bulky, having on a lot of clothes. Makalhpaya. BT.

hoki'taⁿyaⁿkel, adv. Noisily. - nataⁿpi. B.H.134.14.

hoki'toⁿ, (?). Howétoⁿ. HM.

hokiyo'hloka wakpála, n. Pass Creek, on the eastern part of the Pine Ridge Reservation.

hoki'iyokpaza, (?). - iyécehci wauⁿ welo, I am unable to grasp anything. - cokáⁿ wauⁿ, I am bewildered. Bl. BT. Cf. hokómi.

hokśi', n. A child. - wablenica ca oⁿśiwicayalapi kte lo.

hokśi'cala, n. A baby. - kagapi, A doll. - toyuⁿke, A cradle.

hokśi'caⁿtkiyapi, n. The beloved son, one universally esteemed.

hokśi'cekpa, n. The Pasch flower; a certain species of round mushrooms without stems, supposedly looking like a baby's navel in the healing process because of the color and form reminding one of the baby's umbilical cord and navel; a gosling, a wild blue flower that appears first in the spring; the twin flower, pulsatilla. The buttercup or crowfoot family. The state flower of South Dakota. Also, - wanahca. Wana ptehiⁿcala wicatoⁿpi kte lo; wana - hinapelo, as is said in the springtime. IS. Bl. BT. # 149.

hokśi'ciwiⁿkte, adj. Childish, not man-like. Miye hokśicimawiⁿkte śni. Hokśiciwiⁿktepi śni po, Act like men. He hokśiciwiⁿkte s'a. WE.

hokśi' hakákta, n. The youngest child. Also, hakéla.

hokśi'hiyukiya, v.a. To cause an abortion. Note: not hokśihiyuyekiya.

hokśi'hiyuya, v. To have an abortion.

hokśi'ikpignaka, v.n. To be with child, be pregnant. Hokśiikpiwagnaka.

hokśi'ka, adj. Yet a boy, under-age. Homakśika.

hokśi'kaġa, v.a. To beget a child. Hokśiwakaga.

hokśi'keśni, adj. Of age, not a boy.

hokśi'kiksuya, v. To be laboring, as before childbirth. Hokśiyeksuya. B.H. 160.12;161.5.

hokśi'ksuya, v.n. To travail, be in childbirth, be in travail, to be in labor. Hokśiweksuya, hokśiyeksuya. D.122. B.H.164.10,15;245.24.

hokśi'k'iⁿ, v.a. To carry or pack a child on the back. Hokśiwak'iⁿ.

hokśi'la, n. A boy. Homakśila, hokśipila, houⁿkśipila.

hokśi'lala, n. dim. of hokśila.

hokśi'la wicáhca, n. A lazy young fellow, as if he were an old man.

hokśi'lic'iya, v. To act in a childish manner. WE.

hokśi'niġeśla, n. An inexperienced young man who tries to teach older people. - waⁿ taku emakiyelo. Bl.

hokśi'niġeślala, n. The last child in a family. Syn.- hakákta, hakéla.

hokśiⁿ'wiⁿkta, v. To be angry and act like a child, be pettish. Hokśiⁿmawiⁿkta.

hokśiⁿ'witkola, v. To be childish, silly.

hokśi'ouⁿpapi, n. An infant boy or

girl. Same as hokśiu^{n}papi. B.H.166. 20,10;169.15,19;170.4.

hokśi'paslohe, n. A go-cart.

hokśi'śniya^n ca^{n}nú^{n}pa, v. To let the smoke pass through the nose while smoking. BT.

hokśi'tokapa wóiyowaja, n. The first birthright. Also, wotokapa woiyowaja.

hokśi'u^{n}ke, (?). - śni eśá heco^n iyececa śni.

hokśi'u^{n}papi, n. An infant boy or girl. Same as hokśiou^{n}papi. B.H.166.10,20; 170.2.

hokśi'wi^{n}la, n. A virgin according to the flesh, one who has not had a husband. Bl.

hokśi'yuha, v. To give birth to a child. Hokśibluha. Piśko s'e - wośikśice ke. - kte, To conceive. LP.

hok̇u^n'ṗe śni, adv. (ho-ku-u^{n}pe). Babbling on. Lit., not laying down the voice. - wahoya, To instruct or talk to without interruption. - eya, To speak of something again and again. Same as yapsake śni. LC.

hoku'ta, adv. Down stairs.

hok̇u'wa, v. To fish, take or catch fish in any way. Howakuwa.

hola'zata, adv. Outside a circle, beyond the camp circle. D.251. -- holázata^{n}ha^n, adv. Outside the camp circle, at the rear of each tent. - hoaglagla hiyayapi, They walked around the camp outside.

ho'mna, adj. With the odor of fish, fishy, smelling like fish.
ho'mnaya^n, v. To gather or collect fish for a feast. Homnawaya.

hona'ġila, n. Tad-poles.
hona'witk̇ala, Tadpoles.

honu^n'ṗi^{n}ya^n.ya, v. To go around, surround going in a circle. On surrounding a buffalo herd they say: Honu^{n}pi^{n}ya^n u^{n}ya^{n}pi kte lo; akigle u^{n}ya^{n}pi kte lo. Bl. Also, honu^{n}pi^{n}ya, To surround in a half circle, as after having made an approach to a herd. Hi^{n}ha^{n}na ki^n honu^{n}pi^{n}wayi^n na wiḣpewayi^n kte. Bl. Cf. hocete.

ho^{n}ho^n', v.n. Cf. hu^{n}hu^n.

ho^{n}ho^n'zahela, Cf. hu^{n}hu^{n}zahela.

hoo'kawi^{n}ḣ, adv. Around the camp inside, as a man walking around making announcements from one end of the circle to the other. - ieyapahapi. - hiyaya. D.211,225.

ho'okihiṗicaśni, v. To be unable to get a chance to speak. Bl.

hoo'kśa^n, adv. perhaps. Around the circle outside.

hoo'pta, adv. Across the camp circle; through the camp, i.e. the circle of tents. - iyaya. Hecel - ble.

hoo'yaza s'e, adj. Crowded together like canned fish. NP.

hoṗa'śku, n. Fish-scales.

hoṗa'ta^n, v. To spear fish. Howapata^n.

hopa'ta^{n}k̇ala, n. A kind of fish like the perch. R. Bl.

hopa'waṫa, n. A fish. Bl.

hoṗe'ṗe, n. A fish, the stone roller. Bl.

hope'śka s'e, adj. With a comparison implied, as said of a knife with a long blade but short handle, or said of a fat man. Same as gmigmela s'e.Bl.

ho'ṗisk̇iya, v.a. To make the voice squeak, to speak with a squeaking voice.

ho'ṗiza, n. A small squeaking voice. Homapiza.

ho'po, v. imp. Cf. hówo, hóye. B.H. 62.7;148.26.

hosam', adv. On the other side of, beyond the camp. - éwato^{n}wa^n. Kákika - tiowa wa^n he ki^n heci ya ye. Also, hosá^{n}patáha^n.

hosa'mna, adj. Smelling of fish, fishy. Cf. hómna.

hosaŋ', n. Carp. Bl. SLB.

hosaŋ'nicaya, adv. On one side. - inajiŋ. B.H.64.15.
hosaŋ'paṫahaŋ, adv. Same as hosam.
hosaŋ'paṫa ya, v. To go visiting, i.e. away from the circle of tents. - mni kte lo. Bl. B.H.86.2.

hose'wimna, adj. Smelling like fish.

hośi', v. To tell news, take word. R. Note: It is used with other verbs.

hośi' ai', v. To go there with a message. B.H.56.9.

hośi'gla, v. To go home carrying word. Hośiwagla. P.

hośi'gli, v. To arrive at home with news. Hośiwagli. P.

hośi'glicu, v. To be on the way home with news. Hośiwaglicu.

hośi'glihuŋni, v. To reach home with a message. Hośiwaglihuŋni. B.H.43.6.

hośi'hi, v. To arrive somewhere with word. Hośiwahi. R.

hośi'i, v. To have gone to or to have been at to carry word. Hośiwai. R.

hośi'iyaya, v. To have gone to carry word.

hośi'kagla, v. To carry home word to one. Hośiwakagla.

hośi'kagli, v. To arrive at home with word to one. Hośiwakagli. Taku áśkatuyela hośimakaglipi. Miśnala wakpapta s'a hośicicagli. Bl. B.H.42.27.

hośi'kahi, v. To arrive somewhere with word to one. Hośiwakahi. Taku waŋ waśte waŋlakiŋ kte lo ca hośicicahi yelo. Cf. B.H.43.3.

hośi'kai, v. To go in somewhere bringing word to one. Hośiwakai. B. B.H. 262.20.

hośi'kaki, v. To have taken word home to one. Hośiwakaki.

hośi'kaku, v. To bring a message home to one. Hośimakaku po. B.H.169.15.

hośi'kau, v. To come to...with a message. B.H.272.8.

hośi'kaya, v. To take word to one. Hośiwakaya.

hośi'ki, v. To have reached home with a message. Hośiwaki. R.

hośi'ku, v. To be coming home with a message. Same as hośiú. Hośiwaku. R.

ho'śiśipa, express. Used in song by children playing. They would pinch others' hands, i.e. taking the skin between thumb and index finger and pulling upward. This was not supposed to hurt. FD.493. Śála.

hośi'u, v. To be coming with a message. Hośiwau.

hośi'ya, v. To go to take a message. Hośibla. R.

ho'śnaśna kic'uŋ', v. To hop on one leg, as children do for a pastime. - kakicipa ecoŋkoŋpi kta. Bl.

ho'śpeyela, adv. Loudly. - paŋ, To call with a loud voice. Bl.

hośti', interj. Oh, alas! expressing strong disappointment and regret.

hoś'ag'ya, adv. With a loud voice. B.H.3.10.

ho'taŋiŋ, v.n. To have one's voice heard. Homátaŋiŋ, perhaps. Waŋna maya k'el ikiyela inajiŋpi hotaŋiŋpi. B.H. 105.11.

ho'taŋka, n. A loud or great voice. Caŋke - lecel eya....
ho'taŋkakiya, adv. With a great or loud voice.

ho'taŋkaya, adv. With a loud voice. Lecel - eya....

Ho'taŋke, n. prop. The Winnebago Indian.

ho'taŋkiŋkiŋyaŋ, adv. - heya paŋ. B.H. 209.6.

hoṫoŋ', v. To cry out, put forth the voice as some animals do, as buffalo;

to crow; to thunder. Howatoⁿ. Wakiⁿyaⁿ - . Na waⁿna okśaⁿ - okawiⁿjapi (the buffalo). Note: it seems the word is not applied to birds.

hotoⁿ'kel, adv. Groaning. Also, hotoⁿk'el. Iś ena patuś hotoⁿk'el śkaⁿ. Iśnala tima iyayiⁿ na el - śkaⁿhiⁿ na uⁿgna glinapa.

hotoⁿ'ƙiya, v.a. To cause to bawl or cry out. Hotoⁿwakiya.

hotoⁿ'toⁿ, v. red. (hotoⁿ). Wahótoⁿtoⁿ. Lila - kiⁿyaⁿ.

hot'e'ca, n. Dead fish, such as are found in the spring.

houⁿ'ma, n. One of the sides of a surround on the buffalo hunt.

ho'uya, v.a. To send the voice to, cry out to one, to accost, shout. Hóuwaya. Na waⁿna aⁿpo ehaⁿl taśuⁿke luzahaⁿ lecel - . Ate, ahitoⁿwaⁿ yo, hóuciciye ca nayaȟ'oⁿ kta kihe k'uⁿ. D.244, 263.

ho'waƙaⁿ, v.n. To wail. Hómawakaⁿ. Pa izitapi; caⁿke - na óhaⁿketa t'a.

ho'wapaśiⁿ, n. The fat around the paunch. Same as taniga waśiⁿ. HH. BL.

howa'sapa, n. (hogaⁿ-owasiⁿ-sapa). The catfish. Also, hohasapa, perhaps the more correct. The black bass. SLB. Cf. huha, wojuha.

howa'śteya, (?). - waciⁿksapa yo.

howa'ya, v.n. To cry out, to groan. Howáwaya and wahowabla, yahowala. Ceya - , To clamor noisily, be noisy. Na nanih'oⁿpi śni eśa, ceya - po. R. D.196. B.H.27.22;262.26.

ho'we, adv. All right, meaning consent to. It is used by women; but Teton women may perhaps us hóna instead of hówe. Cf. hówo; D.9, note 4.

howi'wacipi, n. The Ghost Dance, perhaps, of 1891; a children's dance in which they say: Howi. Cf. howiwicaśa

howi'wicaśa, n. The Indians of the village of White Clay on the edge of the Pine Ridge Reservation, Oglalas; so called because they indulged in the Ghost Dance of 1891, in which they sang the word "howi", a word chosen because in the Ghost Dance the participants danced in a circle with hands joined just as in children's play (dance) they join hands and sing: Howi. LO. B. SLB.

howi'wotka, n. A rack for drying fish.

ho'wo, v. imp. All right! It carries the idea of consent or permission and is used by men. When addressing many they say: Hópo. Women say Hówe. B.H. 48.2;148.10. Cf. hóye.

howo'kśaⁿ, hoo'kśaⁿ, adv. Around the camp of tents, outside the camp; walking around outside, as is done by a spy.

hoya', v. To use the voice of another; to have another sing in one's stead. Howaya. Hociya.

hoya'zela ciƙ'ala, n. The belted kingfisher. It seems to be very ohitika and its cone is often used as wotawe. The heyóka kágapi used it as a wotawe, tying it on a spear. The kingfisher's fighting qualities, thus considered wayupika, were often so associated with the use of wotawe. Bl.

hoya'zela táⁿka, n. (?).

ho'ye, v. imp. All right, very well; meaning willingness in obeying an order or wish. It is used by men; in addressing many, we say Hópo. Also, hói. D.9, note 4. B.H.275.4.

ho'yeƙiya, v. (ho-yekiya). To cry to, to call to, pray to, address. Hoyewakiya. B.H.66.6;90.6.

ho'yeya, v.a. To cause the voice to go to, to call, cry out. Hóyewaya. Waⁿkalkiya yugal najiⁿ na - . Ena naⁿkapi kiⁿ niye ko henanipila kte lo, eya - .

ho'yeyeƙiya, v. red. (hoyekiya). To cry aloud to. B.H.107.20.

hu, exclam. A sound that is coyote-like and is made by boys when they bring beef home. Húhu, huhu, huhu, etc. The first hu is high, the second is lower in pitch. This they call wáglaś'api.

hu, n. The leg of man or animal. Mihu, nihu, wicahu. Hu mayukaŋ, The stock or stem of anything, as of a plant. Fig. the wheel of a wagon.

hua'kiś'aka, adj. Strong in one's legs, not easily tired. Bl.

hublo', n. The shin bone; the lower part of the leg.

hublo'yuŋke, n. The front muscle of the lower part of a man's leg. Cf. hucogiŋ. GV.

hucaŋ', n. The stem; the stock of a gun; the shaft of an arrow. Waŋna wahiŋkpe makata glihaŋ. Yuŋkaŋ - cokaŋyaŋ hehaŋyaŋ ataya we oha. Na - kiŋ lila paśluślutapi. B.H.62.13.

hu'ciŋśka, n. Green milkweed. Acerates vividi flora. Is is so called because of the shape of its leaves. Pulverized roots when swallowed help children with diarrhoea. Tea of the whole plant is good for mothers who have no milk. L. PLB. #258.

huco'ġiŋ, n. The calf of the leg, i.e. the muscle. - namatipa. Bl. Cf. hubloyuŋke.

hugla'ġo, v. pos. To make cuts on one's own arms and legs, as in mourning. Bl.

hugmi'ya ayút'iŋzela, n. An iron ring; the rim of a wheel.

hugmi'yaŋ, n. A wagon wheel.

hugmi'ya pepéla, n. A circular saw.

huha', n. The limbs of the body, as the legs and arms; the legs of a kettle. Śina - , The hide of the feet left on a robe. Śina - iyowakpataŋ kta, i.e. all around the shawl. WE.

huha'toŋ, v.n. To have legs or limbs. Huhawatoŋ.

huha'ṫop̣a, n. A quadruped, particularly the wolf; a particular kind of quadruped. Wahútopa is the generic name. R.

huha'ya, v.a. To have for muscles, to use for legs. Huhawaya.

hu'hohu, n. The leg bones.

huḣa'ka, adj. Lean, poor, nothing but bones; said fig. of an empty hay rack. - ece u welo. Bl.

hu'ḣla, n. Cf. caŋḣlogaŋ huḣla. WE. #134.

hu'ḣniyeya, v.a. To hurry one up, to make one lively, excited. Huḣniyeciye śni tka ociciyaka, i.e. you need not be in a great hurry about; I just tell you (what I want). BT. Cf. ḣniyeye s'e, wahuḣniye s'e.

hu'ḣ'a, adj. Lean, bony. Same as tamaheca. Bl.

hu'ḣ'a s'e, adv. A kind of lean look appearing; lean-like, bony. Bl.

hu'icignuniyaŋ, (?). - yuŋkapi, as is said of two friends who went on the warpath and being killed lie together. Bl.

hui'nak'eḣye, n. A wagon brake. - ecel icu, To put on the wagon brake. Cf. inák'eḣya.
hui'naṫaḣye, n. A wagon brake. Also, huinaṫ'age, perhaps. Bl.
hui'nat'aḣtoŋ, v. To put the (wagon) brake on. Bl.

hui'paḣte, n. Hobbles.

hui'yaḳaske, n. A piece of buffalo hide tied around the ankles, as is done in the Sundance.

hui'yaṫa, adj. Bony, as very lean men or animals. Ḣoka bloka s'e maku - heca, as said of persons with lean chests.Bl.

hui'yuŋ, adv. (hu-iyuŋ). On foot. - bla, I go on foot.
hui'yuŋḳel, adv. On foot, walking.

hui'yut'iŋze, n. Leggings.

huḳa', n. The skin.

huka'gmiya, n. A wagon wheel.

huḳa'ġopi, n. The making of cuts into one's arms and legs, as the Indians did in olden days when some near relative died. Bl.

huka'icicawiŋyaŋ yaŋká, v. To cross one's legs while sitting. Bl. -- huká-icic'uya, adv. With legs crossed.
hu'ƙaweǵapi, n. A fracture of the limbs. Bl.

hu'ƙiťaŋla, adv. Overloaded. - kuwelo, He returns overloaded. Bl.

hukpaŋ'ƙos iŋyaŋka, v. To run throwing the legs lively. Syn.- hniyaŋyaŋ, śniyaŋyaŋ. Bl.

huƙul', adv. Under, beneath.

huku'ta, adv. Below, under, at the lowest place. - lila icamna.

huƙu'ťakiya, adv. Deep downward.

huƙu'ťaŋhaŋ, adv. (?). Okiŋyaŋke ocaŋku ȟe - ewicoti.

huƙu'ya, adv. Below, at the lowest places.

hula'zata, n. The hind wheels.

huna'ṗobya, v. To have a blow-out in e.g. a tire. Hunapobwaya.

huna'pta, v. To have injured one's self and so to become lame. Hunawapte. R. Bl.
huna'śte, v. To sprain one's leg. Hunawaśte. R. Bl.

huna'ťiṗa, v.n. To have a cramp in the leg.

huni'śni, adv.(?). - lecel maŋkahelo, i.e. to be sitting motionless. Bl.

hu'noŋpa, n. (hu-nuŋpa). A biped; Man, in the sacred language.

huŋ, n. Mother, which is not used alone. Nihuŋ, Your mother; huŋku, His or her mother; ina, My mother.

huŋ'caje, n. A garter, for stockings. Also perhaps, huŋcaje s'e.

huŋhe', interj. Of astonishment or regret. Gramm.127.

huŋhuŋ', v.n. To shake, tremble, as a tree in the wind. WE.

huŋhuŋhe', interj. Alas! Of regret.

huŋhuŋs', cont. of huŋhuŋza.

huŋhuŋs'ya, 1) v.a. To cause to shake, to shake. Huŋhuŋswaya. 2) adv. In a shaking manner.

huŋhuŋ'za, adj. Shaking, trembling. Mahuŋhuŋza. WE.
huŋhuŋ'zahaŋ, part. Shaken, shaking.
huŋhuŋzahela, adv. Trembling, shaking, as on hearing bad news; also used fig.
huŋhuŋ'zayela, adj. Nervous. Mahuŋhuŋzayela s'elececa, as is said when one is anxious to get away on a trip. Bl.

huŋȟ, n. Some, a part of.
huŋȟ'huŋȟ, n. red. (huŋh). B.H.62.11.
huŋ'ȟlala, adv. Only a part.

huŋka', n. An ancestor.

huŋ'ka, (?). Húŋkehca kaca. Bl.

huŋƙa'ƙaŋ, v. To tell stories, yarns. Huŋwakakaŋ, huŋuŋkakaŋpi.
huŋka'ƙaŋpi, n. Stories, fables.

huŋƙa'ƙe, n. An ancestor; one's father, mother, brothers and sisters, hence immediate relatives. Mihuŋkake. Bl. Pb.35.
huŋƙa'ƙeya, v.a. To have for an ancestor. Huŋkakewaya.

huŋka'lowaŋpi, n. A rite or ceremony of the Dakotas, The Making of Relatives. BR.101.

huŋka'tacaŋ, n. The pipe rack, consisting of two upright sticks, each having a crotch at the top and another lying over them. Over against this rack the pipe rested.

huŋka'tacaŋnuŋpa, n. A wand used in the huŋkalowaŋpi and not a real pipe. Also called the caŋnuŋp'ȟaka.

huŋƙa'tacaŋnuŋp ťiowapi, n. A tipi with four pictures on the huŋkatacaŋnuŋpa painted on the surface outside. Bl.
huŋka'tawagmuha, n. A certain kind of rattle used in the huŋkalowaŋpi.

huŋƙa'ya, v.a. To consider and honor as a huŋka. Huŋkawaya.

huⁿk̇a'yapi, n. One who is called huⁿka.

huⁿ'k̇eśni, 1) adj. Slow, not fast in walking or working; sickly. Mahuⁿkeśni. 2) v.n. To be slow, sickly and lean, unable to do anything. Wahuⁿkeśni.
huⁿ'keśniya, v.a. To render powerless. Húⁿkeśniwaya.

huⁿ'kpa, n. The entrance to a camp when made in a circle or hollow square, with the entrance being made toward the west always. Huⁿkpa kaḣya tipi.

Huⁿ'kṗapa, n. prop. A clan or division of the Teton Sioux. Also called the Húⁿkṗapaya.

Huⁿ'kpaṫi, n. prop. The Lower Yanktonais, a clan of the Yanktonais Sioux. Also called the Húⁿkpaṫila.

huⁿ'ku, n. His or her mother.
huⁿ'k̇uya, v.a. To call mother, have for a mother. Húⁿkuwaya.

huⁿ'pe, n. The stick used in digging Indian wild turnips.

huⁿ'pe ok̇íjaṫa, n. A stick with a crotch in one end and used for bracing tent-poles inside; two of them are used to support a horizontal bar on which meat is hung to dry and are called saṫglak̇iⁿyaⁿ.

huⁿsk̇a', n. Leggings.
huⁿsk̇a'ya, v.a. To have for leggings, to make leggings of. Huⁿskawaya.

huⁿsk̇i'caḣe, n. Garters. R. Bl.

huⁿśe', adv. Surely, there is no doubt about it I feel now; undoubtedly, most evidently. D.227,23,56,120. B.H.26.22; 181.18;101.1.

huⁿ'tka, n. A large water-fowl, the cormorant, the double-crested cormorant. Kaⁿgi iyececa. Hena lila wakaⁿpi. Mni mahel witka yuhapi. RF. If an arrow hits them, they dive and return without it and so repeat their calls as if nothing ever happened. - s'e icewiⁿ nuⁿplala wicayuha, as is said of people who have only two children. Bl.

huⁿya'k̇oⁿ, n. Stockings. - iyáskabya. iyaskabwaye, iyaskabuⁿyaⁿpi, i.e. to darn stockings.

huo'kaḣmi, n. The hollow behind the knee.

huo'k̇ihe, n. A joint. Pehaⁿ s'e - miskosko, said when a man's joints are thick while his limbs are rather thin. - nito, You are still young, your joints (knees) are still limber. Bl.

huo'k̇ihe haⁿskáska, n. The narrow-leaved umbrella wort. Allinia linearis. The four-o'clock family. A tea made with the roots is used when there is difficulty in urinating. Bl. #215.

huṗa', n. One of the poles used for a horse travois; tent-poles tied together to pack on; a travois. Also, hupa waⁿjila, hupa waⁿjikśila. Suⁿóⁿk'uⁿpa, The dog travois. D.229, note 4. R. Bl. BS.

huṗa'gluza, v. To raise one's pipe while praying, as the Sioux did. - yo, Smoke! Note: hupa, ihupa, The pipe's stem; gluza, To hold. RF. Bl.

huṗa'heyuⁿṗi, n. A travois, tent-poles tied together to pack on. Cf. tuśúheyuⁿpi.

huṗa'k̇iyuza, v. To lift a pipe towards heaven while praying, as the Sioux did. Hupawakiyuza. RF.

huṗa'waheyuⁿ k'iⁿpi, n. The original vehicle used by the Indians when there were no wagons; a travois, having on it frequently an initiyuktaⁿ mounted upon a śuⁿktacaⁿgleśka. Also, hupaheuⁿ k'iⁿpi. HH. Cf. waheyuⁿ.
huṗa'waⁿjila, n. A pony-drag. Cf. hupawaheyuⁿ, waheyuⁿ.

hu'ṗaza, (?). (hu-paza). - makagle yaⁿka, To sit on the ground with knees bent up and feet drawn towards the body. - makagle ḣpaya, To lie flat on the back on the ground with the feet drawn towards the body, knees bent and sticking up. The idea behind " - makagle inajiⁿ" seems to be that the bent knees turned upward look like sticks set up, not expecting anyone in a deadly rest.

Perhaps the syllable "pa" is pahá, hill. Bl. Note: 1) pazá, v.a. To stick up bushes, as the Dakotas do to sleep under when on a journey. Wapaza. R. 2) pazá, n. A holy name for wood. Caŋpáza najiŋ, To pray. Hupaza makagle inajiŋ, To pray. RF.

hu'þazagle, v. To sit with the knees bent up. Húpazawagle.
hu'þazagleya, adv. On the back with the knees sticking up. - yuŋka, so to lie.

hu þe'þe, n. The hairy stickweed, lappula redowskii occidentalis; also, the sensitive brier, schrankia unicinata, the wild pulse family. Bl. #60,270.

huþe'stola, huþe'stostola, þesto'stola, n. Bayonet grass, bear grass, Spanish bayonet, soap weed, yucca glauca. The lily family. The roots are used for a tea and when mixed the roots of the uŋkcela blaska mothers are helped when they cannot bring forth a child. But there is danger that this root also makes the hokśiyuhapi śni pejuta since it seems to cut off the foetus, as has been observed by some and not by others. Pulverized, the roots of the hu pestostola can be mixed with tepid water and given to people who have a belly-ache. The root is also used for the making of soap. It also assumes a lila wakaŋ use, e.g. in the catching of a wild horse. The Indians would burn the root and let its fumes reach the animal and then they would catch and halter it easily. A tea made of the roots is used as a vermin killer by soaking the hair with it, and it also makes the hair grow. BD. BT. WE. Bl. #141. The stomach remedy was effective Oct. 28, 1917. The yucca plant.

huþe'yozaŋ, n. The outer seam e.g. on a legging. Huŋska hupeyozaŋ or hupeyohaŋ

hupu' caŋsa'kala, n. The bank swallow, a small but very swift bird living in holes on banks. Bl.
hupu' waŋblil̄a, n. Swallow-tailed kite.

husaŋ'gmi, adj. Very lean.
husaŋ'gmiyela, adj. Very thin. Same as wal̄panica. - amaye lo, I am getting thin, poor. Bl.

husaŋ'ni, n. One of a pair, an odd one, as one leg. Cf. saŋni.

husli', n. The lower part of the leg just above the ankle; the ankle. Tahusliyeyapi s'e uŋkupelo, as is said when driving a team fast. EB.

hu'st̄ag, cont. of hustaka.
hu'st̄agya, v.a. To enfeeble. Hustagwaya
hu'st̄ak̄a, v.n. To be faint, weak, weary or feeble in the legs. Humastaka.
huśte', adj. Lame. Humaśte.
huśte'k̄el, adv. Lamely. - mani.
huśte'śteyakel, adv. Limping. - mani.
huśt̄e'ya, 1) v.a. To make lame. Huśtéwaya. 2) adv. Limpingly.
huśte'yak̄el, adv. Lamely.

hu't̄ab, adv. cont. (hutapa). Downstream below.
hu't̄abk̄iya, adv. Downstream, towards.
hu't̄abya, adv. Downstream, opposed to iŋkpatak̄iya. Also, hút̄abyak̄el. R. Bl.

hu't̄anacut̄e, n. A rib of an ox or cow cut short, polished smooth and ornamented then thrown (game) on the ice or snow. -- v.n. To play with the - R. Also, hutínacute. Bl.
hut̄a'nak̄ut̄e, v.n. To play with the hutanacute. Cf. hutanacute. R.

hut̄a'saŋpat̄a, adv. On the other side of a creek or lake. Same as mini kiŋ koákataŋ, ak̄ásaŋpat̄ahaŋ. Cf. hutátahenat̄aŋhaŋ. FB.

hut̄a't̄a, adv. At the water by the shore.
hut̄a'tahenat̄aŋhaŋ, adv. On this side of a creek or lake. Same as mini kiŋ itahena, óhut̄atahenat̄aŋhaŋ. Cf. hut̄asaŋpat̄a.

hu't̄awabk̄iya, adv. (?).

hu't̄awapa, adv. At the water, by the shore.

hu't̄e, 1) n. The root of a tree or plant. Caŋhúte, A stump with sprouts, the bottom of a tree. Na waŋna el - kiŋ euŋgnakapi (caŋwakaŋ). 2) adj. Worn dull, as an axe.

hut̄e'iyul̄pa, adv. All, everything. Eceś, - cic'u yaciŋ yelo. Bl. B.H.157. 11.

hu't̄ela, n. A pistol.

huťi'paksa, v.a. To break off. B.H.62.14.

huťi'ṗak'oȟ, (?). (hutipak'oga). All, leaving nothing. B.H.39.3.

huťi'ṗak'oyela, adv. All, everything, nothing excluded. Hena - omáyakilakiŋ kte. HC. BS.

huťi'ṗaśpu, (?). - iyeya, To drive a-away or back, as enemies in battle.Bl.

huťi'yagleya, adv. From top to bottom. - kaȟ'u; - śeca, as a tree. Bl.

hutkaŋ', n. A root; fig. blood relationship. Caŋ - .

huto'kapataŋ, (?). The front wheels.

huťo'ṗa, adj. With or having four legs. Wamakaśkaŋ - ca cic'upelo. -- n. A four-legged. Cf. hunuŋpa.

huwa'ḱiś'aḱa, adj. Enduring, not easily tired.
huwa'ḱiś'ake, v. n. To be good on one's legs, have strong legs. Śuŋḱála s'e - .

huwa'ksa, v. To amputate, perform an amputation.

huwa'k'iṗe, n. The smaller bones in the lower leg and fore arm. Caŋkpe -, The fibula. Iśpa - .

huwi'cayuťipa, n. A little piece of meat that is found between the muscles below the knees of a buffalo. HH.

hu'woġa, adj. Having the knees bent while holding the legs in the air from a sitting position. - yaŋka. Bl.

huya', v. To have for a staff or leg. Cf. caŋhuyapi.
huya'kel, adv. Using as a leg, as a person using a horse to ride instead of walking. Le - omani yo. Caŋhuyapi, Crutches. -- huyáťa, adv. As the leg.

huye', hoiye', (?). - , hoapeśa waŋ mini ceteta ape kahihiya nuŋke, le u ciciye, so the Indians would say when throwing out the line to catch fish. Also, huyá, He, misuŋ, huya; Misuŋ, Hey, say younger brother, come here, my younger brother.

hu'yukśa, adv. Drawing towards one's body with one's feet, as one does with his feet when in pain. - yaŋka, - maŋke. RF. FR.

huyu'ťiṗa, v. To have cramps in the calf of the leg. Hehé, humáyutipe lo. Bl.

huza'zeca, n. The spokes of a wheel.Bl.

hwe', huwe', adv. The interrogative used by women as hwo is used by men.

hwo, adv. Of interrogation used by men.

ȟ, abbrev. of ȟce. Thus: ḱéyeȟ for kéyeȟce, He says that.

ȟa, v.a. To bury e.g. a dead person.

ȟab, cont. of ȟaṗa. - hiŋgla, - iyaya, To start up, as something sacred.

ȟabȟáb'ya, adv. red. (ȟápa). With a rustling noise. - iyaya, i.e. walking over dry leaves. Mini k'oŋ - ṗúzelo, That pond is entirely dry. Note: this word is a red. of ȟabya.

ȟabȟa'pa, v. red. (ȟapa).
ȟabȟa'ṗela, n. The name given to silk cloth of any kind. Note: the word is probably suggested by the rustling noise made in handling cloth.

ȟabya', v.a. To frighten or scare away anything, e.g. wild animals. Ȟabwáya.

Ȟaȟa'toŋwaŋ, n. p. The Chippewa or Ojibwa Indians, the names given them by the Dakotas, as those who make their villages at the falls. It is believed the name came from Sault Ste. Marie, and not the falls of the Mississippi.

ȟaȟa'ya, (?). Tipi kiŋ iwaŋkab taku ȟmuŋ s'elececa na tipi kiŋ - taku akalala hiyu na lila hececa.
ȟa'ḱa, adj. Branching, having many prongs, as some deer horns. Heȟáka, Elk.
ȟaka', n. A shooting instrument in a game. -- adj. Ruffled, not smooth, made rough, as a feather.

ȟaka'ḱuťe, v. To play or shoot the ȟaka.

Haka'ya, adv. Branched. - śkaⁿ, To do various things at the same time. BE.

Haⁿ, n. A scab. - hiⁿhpaya, The scab has fallen off.

Haⁿa'gnakela s'e, adv. Carefully, softly, as when touching a soft sore spot; gently. - kúwa, To handle people carefully. Bl.

Haⁿa'paha, v.n. To have a thick scab on a wound. Haⁿámapaha. Bl.

Haⁿhaⁿ', adj. red. Scabby. R. -- Haⁿháⁿpi, n. Sores. -- Haⁿháⁿyaⁿ, 1) v.a. To cause to be scabby. B.H.43.22. 2) adv. Like a scab. - hpaya. B.H.227.6.

Haⁿi't'a, v. To be covered with a rash, eruptions. Haⁿimat'a. Bl.

Haⁿi'yagnaka s'e, (?). - okuwa, To handle one very carefully. WE.

Haⁿte', n. The cedar, the western cedar juniperus scopulorum. HC. found that when its leaves are powdered and boiled make a fluid that, while absolutely harmless to man, will drive away potatoe bugs wherever it is poured. He saved his potatoe vines with this broth, on September 28, 1919. - caⁿhloġaⁿ, The common yarrow, milfoil, achillia millefolium. Composite family. - iyececa, Cf. peji swula cik'ala. - pepe iyececa, Illinois mimose, curley-podded legume, acuan illinoensis. Pulse family. # 192, 89, 244. Bl. -- Haⁿtéśa, n. The red cedar. Also, Haⁿtéśala.

Haⁿtkaⁿ'hu, n. The upper arm bone.

Haⁿtkaⁿ'hula, n. One who means to be a leader everywhere. Bl.

Haⁿtkaⁿ'huⁿzi, n. A military rank arm stripe. WHL.

Haⁿtkuⁿ'za, n. An ornament arm band, an armlet; bands for holding up the shirt-sleeves. Also Haⁿtkáⁿoyuze.

Ha'pa, v.n. To make a rustling noise, as in leaves or bushes; to rustle.

Hapa', adj. Rough, as the wind or the voice. Hoháṗa.

Hca, adv. Very. Le miye hca ca tokśa oyate el uⁿki kte, eya keya. Lena hecetu hca slolwaya. Wicaśa waⁿ śicahca. -- Hcahcá, adv. red. (Hca). Very. Le miye - slolwaya na el owapa.

Hca, 1) n. A flower blossom. Cf. wahca. 2) v.n. To blossom, bloom. - aya, To bloom.

Hca'ka, adv. suff. Very. Same as hca. Tólahcaka, Very blue. Waśtehcaka, Very good. Wazihcaka, The beautiful Black Hills spruce. Maśtuśtelahcake lo.

Hcaka'sa, adv. suff. Same as hcaka. Tokśa he na ecamoⁿ kte kiⁿ le taku - eyiⁿ. MS.95.

Hca'ya, v.n. To blossom. -- adv. Blossoming.

Hce, adv. Very. Yuⁿkaⁿ namah'oⁿpi kiⁿ icaⁿtemawaśte hce. Na macaje hce "Cik'ala Wicakte" emakiyapi.

Hcehaⁿl', adv. Just then. - śuⁿkmanitu waⁿ...toki-hiyaye. D.22. -- Hcehá ⁿl ...na, adv. correlative. No sooner... when. Hcehaⁿl wiⁿyaⁿ waⁿna ihuⁿni na hecenaś tokápa kiⁿ pakáksa. Note: Hepe hce, ehaⁿl hi, No sooner did I say that when he arrived.

Hci, adv. Very. It is post-positive. Hihaⁿnahci. Ecanahci. Iśnalahci. Ciscilahci.

Hci, 1) adj. Broken out in gaps. Cf. kahci. 2) n. A gap, as in the edge of an axe; a gash, cut scar. -- Hcihci', adj. red. (Hci). Gapped, notched, nicked, cut. Upi - , The fringed border of a garment. Pute - (rabbit lips) kuwi ye. Pute hcihcila. Bl. D.71,113. -- Hcihcíya, adv. (Hcihci). Tataⁿka s'e nakpa - yaⁿkiⁿ na, they say of a man whose ear lobes are pretty well torn, gapped. Wahiⁿheya s'e lohé - .Bl

Hciⁿ, suff. Same as hca, and is used with the future tense. Ktepi kte - .

Hciwa'haⁿ, part. Broken out in gaps, gapped.

Hco, adj. Slovenly, slatternly. Cf. nahcohco. -- Hcóka, adj. Slovenly. Hcóya, adv. In a slovenly manner. -- Hcóyakel, adv. Slovenly.

He, n. A high hill or ridge of hills; a mountain.

Ḣea'i, v.a. To have brought somewhere for burial. B.H.283.13.

Ḣe'blo, n. A hill top, a ridge.
Ḣe'bloḱa, n. Same as ḣeblo.

Ḣehe'ṗiya, adv. Part way up the hill.

Ḣehu'ḱul, n. The bottom or foot of a hill.

Ḣeiŋ'kṗa, n. The brink or brow of a hill, the end of a hill.

Ḣei'pa, n. The brow of a hill; esp. the head or commencement of the cotea des prairies.

Ḣekpaŋ'kpaŋla, n. Hilly land, i.e. all low hills. Same as pahá kutkúciyela. Bl.

Ḣeḱu', n. The foot of a hill back from a river. - uŋyaŋpi, We go at the foot of the hill.

Ḣel, adv. (Ḣe-el). Ashore, when the water retreats. Siŋkpe - amáḱiṗa ḣce. lo. BT.

Ḣema'ḱosḱaŋl, adv. In a desert place, an uninhabited place, a wilderness. Also, ḣemáḱosḱaŋṫu. - etaŋ oyate waŋ iglaka aya. - kiŋ he itahena na caḣli wakpa oiŋkpa kiŋ ogna uŋkiyayapi. - yapi. B.H.49.22.

Ḣema'ḱośikśica, n. Badlands. Bl.

Ḣema'ni, v. To walk on dry land.

Ḣe'mayacaŋ, n. A wooded hill.

Ḣena'ġi, n. The shadow of a hill. Pahá ohaŋzizi yukelo. Bl.

Ḣena'ke, n. A declivity, a slope. P.
Ḣena'ptaŋ, n. A declivity. P.

Ḣeo'ḣlaṫe, n. The foot or bottom of a big hill.

Ḣeo'śki, n. Rough lands. -- adj. Hilly, rugged, uneven, as country cut with many canyons. P. Bl. R. B.H.89.1.
Ḣeo'śkiśki, adj. red. (heośki). Hilly. P. Bl.

Ḣeśka', n. p. The Big Horn Mountains; the Rocky Mountains. D.225.

Ḣe'ta, adv. On or to the mountains, in the mountains.

Ḣe'ṫaḱiya, adv. Towards the hills. B.H.154.6.

Ḣetko'za, v. To give things away often, as though one were rich, when in reality one is poor.

Ḣeuŋ'napṫaŋ, n. A hillside.

Ḣewa'kṫokṫa, n. p. An Arickaree Indian.

Ḣeyab', adv. Away, elsewhere. - iya yo, Go or get away. - ecoŋ, Get away. - iḣpeic'iya, To shy, as a horse. Na iŋyaŋ kiŋ nakuŋ iyuha - yaŋka. D.204, 221. Note: this is a cont. of ḣeyápa.

Ḣeya'pa, adv. Away from, as standing away from a hot stove, etc. - inajiŋ. - yaŋka yo. -- v.n. To go away a little distance. Ḣeyáwapa. -- ḣeyápaya, adv. Away a little distance.

Ḣeya'ṫa, adv. On or to the ridge, bluff, plateau etc. as in contrast with lower places, esp. of the river bottoms etc. Cf. ḣéta.

Ḣeya'ṫaŋhaŋ, adv. On top of a hill. Na waŋna uŋkiyayapi na miś - wauŋ.

Ḣeyuŋ'ka, n. Frost, hoarfrost. Cf. aḣéyuŋka.

Ḣla, v.n. To rattle. Siŋteḣla, A rattle snake.

Ḣlaġaŋ', adj. Loose.

Ḣlahaŋ', adv. Loose, torn dangling.

Ḣlaḣla', n. A rattle; a herald, crier. - waŋji igni po. Bl. -- v. red. (ḣla). To rattle. Waḣláḣla.

Ḣla'ḣla húŋcaje, n. Garters with bells attached to them.

Ḣla'ḣla iyógnaka, (?). A little bird with a loud voice. Also, - s'e. W.

Ḣla'ḣla ṫáŋka, n. Bells.

Ḣlaḣla'ya, adv. Rattling, loosely.

Ḣlaḣla'yel, adv. Not securely. -- Ḣlaḣláyela, adv. Loosely, insecurely.

Ȟlaȟya', adv. To a distance; removing.
Ȟlaȟye'ca, v.n. To remove or go off to a distance.
Ȟlaȟye'śni, adv. Without leaving out or forgetting, even one single thing; every single thing included. Bl.

Ȟlaiŋ'śni, adj. Capable, skilful. Maȟlaiŋśni. Wicaśa - heca. BD.

Ȟlaye'la, adv. Ringing, tinkling, as little bells do while walking. Same as sna s'e. Bl.

Ȟlete', n. A very careless, irresponsible fellow who cares for nothing nor for anybody, and thus ruins every thing. Maȟléte. Wo.

Ȟli, 1) v.n. To break out in sores, be sore, raw. Maȟlí. 2) n. A running sore, a raw place.
Ȟliȟli', adj. red. (Ȟli). Broken out in sores; miring in mud.
Ȟliȟli'la, adj. Miry, muddy. Maka - oŋ iic'iyuŋ.

Ȟlo, v.n. To growl, as a dog. Waȟló.

Ȟloġe'ca, adj. Poor, thin, as a sick man; hollow, as a tree. - uŋ. - amáye lo. R. Bl.

Ȟlohaŋ', adj. Slovenly, not well put on, as clothes.
Ȟlohaŋ'haŋ, adj. (hlohaŋ). Untidy, slovenly dressed or put on. Taku ecaŋnoŋ kiŋ, śuŋkpala waŋji - kiŋ he iyeniceca yelo, as said when a man takes it too easy while working. Bl.
Ȟlohe'ca, adj. Slovenly.
Ȟlohe'ya, adv. In a slovenly manner.

Ȟloȟlo', v. red. of Ȟlo.
Ȟloȟlo'ǩa, adj. Full of holes.
Ȟloȟlo'ǩahaŋ, part. Full of holes. Ȟloȟloka icage, A crocket hoop.
Ȟlo'ǩa, adj. Hollow. -- n. A hollow. -- part. Hollowed.
Ȟlo'kece, n. A hollow object.

Ȟloǩi'ya, v.a. To make growl. Ȟlowákiya.
Ȟloya', 1) v.a. To make growl. 2) adv. Growling.

Ȟlu'ṫe, adj. Long-necked, as is said of man and beast.

Ȟlu'ṫe s'e, adv. perhaps. Of a sort long-necked.

Ȟmiŋ, adj. Crooked, misshapen. Siha - , A crooked foot.
Ȟmiŋȟmiŋ', adj. red. (Ȟmiŋ). Misshapen. caŋȟpáŋ s'e si - kacá, i.e. feetturned outward. Bl.
Ȟmiŋȟmiŋ'yaŋ, adv. red. (Ȟmiŋyaŋ). Crookedly.
Ȟmiŋ'yaŋ, adv. Crookedly, as in walking; sideways, fowl, sliced. Also, Ȟmiŋyaŋ śkaŋ. Tapa - u.

Ȟmuŋ, v.n. To buzz, hum, as the stones of a mill or the flapping of a bird's wings; to whistle, as a bullet. - hiŋgla, To make a buzzing noise suddenly.

Ȟmuŋ'ġa, v.a. To cause sickness; to cause kindly enchantment, to bewitch. Waȟmuŋga. Kiciȟmuŋgapi, i.e. bewitching each other. Tuwa aitohewaya caŋ waȟmuŋge lo. B.H.70.6. D.103.

Ȟmuŋȟmuŋ', v. red. (Ȟmuŋ). To buzz.

Ȟmuŋ's'e, Ȟmuŋ's'ekse, Ȟmuŋsece'ca, adv. In a buzzing way, as people speaking or praying together; altogether in a chorus. - cekiyapi, lowaŋpi. Na yamni t'api k'oŋ hena titakuye kiŋ Ȟmuŋs'ekse wicaceye. -- n. Noise.

Ȟmuŋya', v.a. To cause to hum, make buzz. Ȟmuŋwáya.
Ȟmuŋ'yaŋ, adv. Whizzing, buzzing. Mini kiŋ - he lo. Bl.
Ȟmuŋyĕ'la, Ȟmuŋ'yela, adv. Same as Ȟmuŋyáŋ. Mini kiŋ - hiyáye.

Ȟna, v.n. To snort, grunt, as does a person in anger. Waȟná.

Ȟnahaŋ', adj. Slovenly, not tidy, hanging, as a horse's lip. R. Bl.
Ȟnahe'ya, adv. Loosely, slovenly. R. Bl.
Ȟna'ȟna, v. red. (Ȟna). To grunt; to give forth the sound of a bear. Lila - uŋ, i.e. groaning (hauŋ) as one who is dying. D.219. Note: waȟnáȟna.

Ȟni'yaŋ, v.n. To be troubled, to have a stomach-ache. R. Note: this seems to be Wiciyela. -- Ȟniyáŋyaŋ, adj. red. (Ȟniyaŋ). Afraid, quaking for fear. Maȟníyaŋyaŋ. Pute - , To have the lips quiver, as from cold etc. Lehaŋl minagi kiŋ maȟniyaŋyaŋ. B.H.244.2.

Afraid, quaking for fear.

Hni'yeye s'e, adv. In haste, affrightedly.

Hoka', n. The badger.

Holho'ta, adv. red. of Hota.

Holwan'ca, adj. All in gray. - yelo, said when all are dressed in gray suits Thus also, Holyápi s'e ahi. Bl.

Holya', adv. Grayish, in a grayish or mixed manner, as is said of putting paint on the face. Mato s'e sicúha Holyahci, as said when a man has torn soles. Holyápi s'e ahi, All come dressed in gray. Bl. R.

Holye'la, adj. perhaps. Grayish. Yunkan winyan k'on u kin iwankab - han, mahpiya ekta iyagleyahan wanyakapi.

Ho'ta, adj. Gray, brown.

Hpahan', part. Thrown down, fallen down of itself.

Hpa'ka, adj. Very slow. BS.

Hpan, adj. To be becoming softened, as corn in water.

Hpanki'yan, v. pos. (Hpanyan). To soften one's own. Ito cante Hpanwakiyin kte lo, as a hungry man says. Máyaśleca ca tahuka Hpankiye s'e, as said when one hides some food someplace so as to eat it alone. Bl.

Hpanyan', v.a. To soak, steep in water. Hpanwáya.

Hpawa'han, part. Thrown off, down. R.Bl.

Hpa'ya, v.n. To lie down, recline. Kul - , He lies down. T'a - , He is dead. Canku kin kal - , The road lies over there. Wahpáya.

Hpa'yeya, v.a. To cause to lie down; to kill, as in battle.

Hpe'caka, adj. Faint, exhausted. Mahpecaka.

Hpe'la, adj. Weak. - hingla, To be discouraged, diverted from; to turn suddenly being reminded of something sad. - hingléḱiya, To make one sad suddenly. Bl. Note: the word is not used alone.

Hpeyun'ka, v.n. To stay with the young, hover over, as a hen does over her brood, to brood over, as is said of a young man when his first child is born. Bl.

Hpi, (?). Ihá Hpi, Hanging lips.

Hpihpi s'e, (?). Ref. to hair or hat bending under wind pressure. - inyanka, To run with hair flying in the wind. Wapośtan micihpi.

Hpi'ka, adj. Shaggy, bushy, as hair.

Hpo, (?).

Hpuhpu', adj. perhaps. red. (Hpu, Obs.). Crumbled off.

Hpuhpu'ya, adv. red. (hpuya). Crumbling away. Oyute kin yuogmuza ye, keya s'e oyute kin - , said when a woman's dress is torn near the hip-bone. Bl.

Hpuwa'han, part. Crumbled off, come apart, as things formerly stuck together.

Hpuya', adv. Crumbling off.

Htacu'śni, n. The cool of the evening.

Htahe'piyela, adv. Before night, before retiring perhaps. Bl.

Htai'yokpaza, v.n. To grow dark. B.H. 54.1.

Htaki'yaka, adv. Towards evening.

Htaki'yakel, adv. Towards evening.

Hta'lehan, n. Yesterday. - akotanhan, The day before yesterday.

Htama'kiyokpaza, v. To grow dusk. The same as awatanin śni, is Htamákiyokpazelo. Bl.

Htani', (?). - okile, To look for slowly, carefully; or: śkanśkan śni okile. Ablákela ca wicaho - ca tokiya eyaś nah'onpi kte. Bl. Note: Htaniśni may more properly be the word. Cf.

Htani'śni, adj. Motionless, without moving much. Same as śkanśkanśni. - inyanka, najin. WE. Cf. Htani.

Htao'janjan, n. A dimming.

Htao'sni, adj. Cold in the evening.

htaośni ayelo. Bl.

Ḣtao'taⁿiⁿśni, n. Dusk. Wana - aye. B.H.208.21.

Ḣtao'mani, v. To walk about at night. Maka waⁿ iye t'iⁿ kta yeś - yelo. Ed. BN.

Ḣta'ṫa, adj. Languid, weak. Maḣtata.
Ḣta'ṫeca, adj. Weak, beeble. Maḣtateca.

Ḣta'ye, adv. In the evening, last evening. Aⁿpetu waⁿ el - ehaⁿl.

Ḣta'yeṫamna, adv. perhaps. At dusk. Kaⁿgi s'e - iyuⁿka, i.e. to go to bed early. Bl.

Ḣta'yeṫu, n. The evening.

Ḣuġa'haⁿ, part. Broken in, dented.

Ḣuġe'ca, n. Cf. ġuġeca.

Ḣugna'ġa, v.n. To burn up, be consumed. Also perhaps, ġugnaġa.
Ḣugnaḣ'ya, v.a. To cause to burn up, to consume. Also, perhaps, ġugnaḣya. Ḣugnaḣwaya.
Ḣugna'ya, v.a. To burn down, destroy by fire. Also perhaps, ġugnaya. P.

Ḣuha', n. The scraping or shavings of hides taken off in making them thin enough for robes and eaten by the Dakotas. Cf. taḣuha.

Ḣuḣciⁿ'cayela, adv. Very high, very far away; too high, too far away so as to be seen well; to be shot etc. as a bird on top of a house or game passing by. - hiyaye lo. Thus, oicuśilya yaⁿke. Bl.

Ḣuḣu'ġahe s'e, adv. With a thundering noise. Caⁿ kiⁿ - yuⁿkahe. Wakiⁿyaⁿ hotoⁿ s'e. MG.

Ḣuḣ'ciⁿ'cayela, adv. At a great distance, very high up. - iyaye. - hiyaye. Lehaⁿl - uⁿkomanipi. Bl. Cf. Ḣuḣciⁿcayela.

Ḣuⁿwiⁿ', Ḣuiⁿ', v.n. To stink, become putrid, as does meat. Cf. Ḣwiⁿ.
Ḣuⁿwiⁿ'mna, adj. Stinking, smelling putrid. Mato - .
Ḣuⁿwiⁿ'ya, v.a. To cause to smell badly, make putrid. Ḣuⁿwiⁿwaya.

Ḣuṗa'hokoza, v.n. (hupahu-okoza). To flap or move the wings, to flutter.

Ḣuṗa'hu, n. The wing of a fowl.
Ḣuṗa'kiglake, n. A bat. Also, Ḣupakiglaḳela, The bird or part of a bird used as a wotawe.

Ḣuṗiⁿ'yuⁿ, adv. By the arms, without instruments, by main strength.
Ḣuṗiⁿ'yuⁿḳel, adv. By main strength, not minding the things that are in the way, as bad weather etc. - wauⁿ welo.

Ḣuṗu' caⁿsákala, n. (Ḣupahu perhaps). A little very swift bird living in holes on banks, the cliff swallow; the bank swallow, which lives not in round holes but in long narrow niches. Bl.

Ḣuṗu' waⁿblíla, n. The snow bunting. It stays sumer and winter; it has white feathers, but black wing feathers. Iśtanica taⁿka híⁿskokeca. Bl.

Ḣuwa'ṗaḣṗe, n. The meat left sticking to a hide.

Ḣuya', n. An aged eagle; a common eagle.

Ḣwa, adj. Sleepy, drowsy. Maḣwá, uⁿḣwapi.
Ḣwa'ḳa, adj. Sleepy; mild, gentle. Maḣwáka.
Ḣwa'ya, 1) v.a. To make sleepy. Ḣwawáya. 2) adv. Mildly, gently.
Ḣwa'yela, adv. Slowly, softly, gently.

Ḣwiⁿ, v.n. To stink, become putrid, as a dead body. Cf. Ḣuⁿwiⁿ.
Ḣwiⁿ'mna, adj. Smelling putrid.

Ḣ'a, v.n. To smell bad, as meat, bones cheese etc. when it has set for a few days. Waⁿna - yelo, they say of bones used for medicinal purposes when they are prepared just right, i.e. stinking. Wo. Cf. oḣ'amna, oḣ'aya. Note: the word seems akin to "grayish".
Ḣ'akṗa', adj. Not straight or level, a little curved or ruffled.
Ḣ'amna', adj. Smelling like stale meat; tainted. Same as oz'ámna.

Ḣ'aⁿ, v.n. To do, to work, act. Waḣ'aⁿ. Tókeśke yaḣ'aⁿ hwo? Na lila tokel ḣ'aⁿpi kiⁿ slolya.

H'aⁿ'haⁿska, v.n. To be long-winded, to be not soon tired.
H'aⁿ'haⁿska hoȟpápi, n. Whooping cough.

H'aⁿhi', v.n. To be slow at work, to advance slowly or leisurely. Waȟ'áⁿhi and maȟ'áⁿhi.
H'aⁿhi'ka, n. One who is slow at work, one who is incapable. H'aⁿwáhika.
H'aⁿhi'kiya, adv. Slowly, carefully, as in finishing a piece of work.
H'aⁿhi'la, adj. Very slow. Maȟ'áⁿhila. Cf. la.
H'aⁿhi'ya, adv. Slowly, with difficulty. Yuⁿkaⁿ hiⁿhaⁿ waⁿ kuciyela - kiⁿyaⁿ iyaya.

H'aⁿ'H'aⁿka, n. One who creates disorder or mischief wherever he goes, as do certain children, so that the people know at once the mischief maker. BH.

H'aⁿli'ta, v.n. To be active, make progress in work. - wauⁿ.

H'aⁿṗi'ca, v. That can be done. Tokel - śni, It cannot be done.

H'aⁿyaⁿ', v.n. To fail, decline, sink away, as in sickness; to be near death or very tired. H'aⁿwaya.
H'aⁿye'ca, v.n. To fail, decline; to sink away, as in approaching death. H'aⁿwáyeca.

H'aye'la, adv. Making a noise as hail, rain, or sand does non a roof or wall. - akála, He throws (shoots) all over the wall. Tipi - he lo, i.e. sand is battering the house.

H'eȟ'e', adj. Dangling, ragged. Haȟ'e-ȟ'e, Ragged clothes. Haáȟ'eȟ'e, To have ragged clothes on.
H'eȟ'e'ya, adv. (?). Śiyo śuⁿka s'e i-mniśtaⁿ - yaⁿkelaȟ. Bl.
H'eȟ'e'yela, adv. Ragged, torn, dangling, as clothes. -yaⁿka. Bl.

H'eya', n. A fabulous being Indian women use when putting restless children to sleep. Owaⁿjila ȟpaya; - waⁿ u we. Obs. Cf. ci'ciye, mmla.

H'o, v.n. To stand up on, as hair. Itowe - t'a. Cf. aȟ'o.

H'oka', 1) v. To sing with the drum. 2) n. A singer. Waⁿna waȟ'óka.

H'uⁿ'hikiya, 1) v.a. To finish, perfect. 2) adv. In a finished way, perfectly. - ecamoⁿ, I did it by way of finishing.
H'uⁿ'hiya, v.a. To finish, to perfect.
H'uⁿ'hiyela, adv. Exhausted, played out. - waglihuⁿni. BT.
H'uⁿ'hiyeśni, v. Not to have as much. H'úⁿhiwayeśni, or iyenakeca bluha śni. Note: originally H'uⁿ may have been H'aⁿ.

H'uⁿ'kṗani, v.n. To play out, be unable to reach or do, be unable to accomplish; to be in an unfinished state. - wauⁿ. H'uⁿwakpani śni.
H'uⁿ'kṗanikiya, v.a. To leave in an unfinished state, to fail to accomplish. H'úⁿkpaniwakiya.
H'uⁿ'kṗaniyaⁿ, v.a. To cause to fail to accomplish, to fail in finishing. H'úⁿkpaniwaya.

H'uⁿ't'a, v.n. To give out at work, be laid up by work, be exhausted. H'úⁿmat'a.
H'uⁿ't'eya, v.a. To cause to give out or exhaust one's strength; to oppress one with work. Kaiwaⁿyaⁿk oci'cuwa kte lo, owékinaś H'uⁿt'eciyiⁿ kte lo, i.e. lest I kill you by overworking you. Bl. Note: the word is perhaps from h'aⁿ-oⁿ-t'eya.

H'uⁿ'yaⁿ, v.a. To tire one. Maȟ'úⁿyaⁿpi. Obs. perhaps.

H'uⁿ'yela, adv. (?). Koġiⁿġiⁿ naⁿkahelo; - wahiyelo. BT.

H'uⁿwi'śtaⁿ śni, adj. Never quitting, incessant, persistent; all the time. Tuwa - caⁿku kiⁿ taⁿyaⁿ kaȟ au welo, Somebody has fixed a road in every bad place as he went on. Bl.

I

i, prefix. 1) Prefixed to verbs and adjectives, meaning "to, for, of, on, about, by means of, on account of, or in consequence of. 2) Prefixed to active verbs, it sometimes forms of them nouns of instrument; thus, kajipa, To shave: icajipa, A drawing knife. 3) Prefixed to the cardinal numbers, it forms of them ordinals; thus, nuŋpa, inuŋpa. 4) Prefixed to adverbs, it gives them the force of prepositions; thus, tehaŋ, Far: itehaŋ, Far from. 5) Prefixed to nouns, they signify time, meaning the next or succeeding one; thus, wetu, Spring: iwetu, The succeeding spring. Iblóketu, iptáŋyetu, íwaniyetu. Paha Sapa iwoglakapi (not "on the Black Hills"). Oyate kiŋ tokel taŋyaŋ uŋpi kte ciŋ he iwaŋyaŋke. Note: the meaning "on" is used less often than we would expect.

i, v.n. To have gone to, to have been at. Wai, uŋkipi. Mitakuyepi, waśicuta wai na Tuŋkaśila oti etaŋhaŋ waśicuŋ śakowiŋ el mahipi. R.

i, n. The mouth. Mii', nii', wicái.

ia', v.n. Same as iyá. To speak. Iwáya, iyáya, uŋkiapi. Taŋiŋyaŋ ia okihi śni. B.H.278.9.
ia'haŋ, part. Speaking.

ia'k̇aŋl, prep. (i-akaŋ). Upon, on top of. B.H.57.18.
ia'kaŋkaŋl, prep. red. (iakaŋl). On top of more than one thing. B.H.50.4.
ia'k̇aṫaŋhaŋ, adv. (akaŋ). On top of; upon, outside. Śina hiŋ - glowiŋ. B.H.60.21.

ia'k̇e, adv. Again, so many more. Note: the word is not used alone.
ia'k̇ehenak̇eca, adj. So many more than ten.
ia'k̇ek̇anak̇eca, adj. That number more than ten.
ia'k̇el, adv. Talking. Wicegna - yapi, They went talking among them.
ia'k̇elenak̇eca, adj. So many more than ten.
ia'k̇elenala, adj. Only so many more than ten.
ia'k̇enapciyuŋka, num. adj. The nineteenth.
ia'k̇enuŋṗa, num. adj. The twelfth.
ia'k̇eśaglogaŋ, num. adj. The eighteenth.
ia'k̇eśakowiŋ, num. adj. The seventeenth.
ia'k̇eśakṗe, num. adj. The sixteenth.
ia'k̇eṫopa, num. adj. The fourteenth.
ia'k̇ewaŋjila, num. adj. The eleventh.
ia'k̇eyamni, num. adj. The thirteenth.
ia'k̇ezapṫaŋ, num. adj. The fifteenth.

i'ak̇icuni, v. To desist from, grow tired and leave off. Cf. iyakicuni.

ia'k̇ic'uya, adj. Much. Cf. iyakic'uya.

i'ak̇ihehaŋk̇eca, adv. Alike in length.
i'ak̇iheha ŋyaŋ, adv. Alike in distance.
i'ak̇ihenak̇eca, adv. Of equal number with.
i'ak̇ilececa, adv. Alike, equal to, of one kind. Cf. iyakilececa.
i'ak̇ilecel, adv. Like to, equal to.
i'ak̇ilehaŋhaŋk̇eca, adv. red. (iakilehaŋkeca). Equal in size to.
i'ak̇ilehaŋhaŋyaŋ, adv. red. of iakilehaŋyaŋ.
i'ak̇ilehaŋk̇eca, adv. Equal in length to. Kici iakilemahaŋkeca, I am as tall as he.
i'ak̇ilehaŋyaŋ, adv. Alike in distance, as far as.
i'ak̇ilenak̇eca, adv. As many as.

i'ak̇ipapa, v. (i-apa). To strike on the mouth often, as young men do in shouting. Íawakipapa.

ia'ksape, adj. Wise in talking. B.H. 85.25.

ia'napta, v.a. To detain, prevent beforehand from proceeding. Cf. iyanapta.

i'aŋṗeṫu, n. The same or next day. - haŋkeyela, During that day. B.H.177.1. - yamni, Within the next three days. B.H.179.16.

ia'ouŋc'unica, v. To stutter, stammer. Iaouŋmac'unica. Bl.
ia'ṗi, n. A talk, one's speech or language. - kicága, To report one as saying things which he did not. - micagapelo; epe śni yelo. - otahena. WE.

ia'sni, v. To grow cold in or with reference to.

i'aś'a, v. To halloo, make a loud inarticulate noise. Iawaś'a, iauŋś'api.

i'aṫayela, pron. adv. That alone; personally, individually. Cf. iyatayela.

ia'uŋca, v.a. To imitate somebody's way of speaking. Note: uŋca alone is not used by the Oglala.

i'awaŋyaŋk, v. (iawaŋyaŋka). To keep one's eyes on. - kuwa. B.H.77.6.
i'awaŋyaŋka, v.a. To guard. B.H.133.23.

ia'wayáp̂ika, v. To speak nicely. Wiŋyaŋ ca witkowiŋ akisnis'e - , as when loose women speak nicely to others.Bl.

ia'wicaka, v.n. To speak the truth. Iawicawaka.

ia'wicak̂ehaŋ, adv. Truly, in truth.

ia'woglaka, v. To speak a language. B.H.278.4.

ible'za, v.n. To be enlightened about, to understand, as a person does gradually while waking up. Imableza. Bl.

ibli'helya, v.a. To stir up, excite. Iblihelwaya. B.H.128.15.

icab', cont. of icapa. - icu, To stick in and take out.
ica'bheya, adv. Right through, as a pain going through the chest. Also, icábeya, Pricked, injured in feelings. R. Note: the word is rarely used.

iča'blask̂a, v.n. (i-kablaska). To be flattened, as a bullet that is shot into wood.

iča'bu, n. (i-kabu). A drum stick.

iča'čaŋ, n. A sieve. Same as wičacaŋ.

i'čačaŋ, v.n. To trot, as a horse. Íwakacaŋ, I make it trot.

ica'ġa, v.n. (kaga). To spring up, grow, as grass, a child etc.; to become, as a man. Imacaga. Iŋyaŋ - , To turn into stone. D.222.

iča'ġe, n. (i-kaga). Something to make a thing with, an instrument, tool. -- v. (kage). To skim off. - icu, To take up in a bucket e.g. water; to take off or skim. - iwacu.

iča'ġejuya, 1) v. To come up with and go along with a company. Icagejuwicawaya. 2) adv. Together with, in company.

iča'ġeya, adv. Together. Oyate - tipi, The people were camped together.

iča'ġi, v.n. (i-kagi). To be hindered by, opposed by an obstacle. Imákagi. Taku - heci oyakiŋ kta, If there is an impediment, let him say so. Takuni imakagi śni omawani. Bl.

ica'ġiśniyaŋ, adv. Without obstacles. Takuni - omawani. Bl.

i'caġiya, i'caġeya, v.a. To bother, annoy one. Ícageciye. Ícagemayaye.Bl.

iča'gla, prep. (i-kagla). By the side of, near to. - ómakihaŋpo, Follow me closely. Bl.
iča'glala, prep. By the side of. Bl.

iča'glaya, adv. By the side of. Paha waŋ otoŋwahe kiŋ - haŋ. B.H.184.25.

iča'ġo, n. (i-kago). A mark or line drawn. -- v.a. (kago). To make a mark, draw a line, sketch. Iwákaġo, uŋkicagopi. Le iyákago kiŋ he itimahetaŋhaŋ opimic'iye lo. Caŋ waŋ oŋ ...maka kiŋ yumimeya - ...yo. D.34-5.
ica'ġoġo, v. (kago, perhaps). To make marks, perhaps, with. Pahiŋ ca mani s'e oŋze - la s'e, as is said of a woman who drags her too long robe or dress over the ground, comparing her to a porcupine that drags its tail over the ground. Bl.

iča'ġopi, n. A line. P.

iča'ġoya, 1) v.a. To cause marks, to cause to mark. Icaġowaya. -- 2) adv. Marking, in the way of marking.

iča'hi, 1) v.a. (i-kahi). To mix, stir up together. Iwákahi, uŋkicahipi. 2) v.n. To mix, mingle. Pte kiŋ ataya iwicuŋkahipelo, We bunched the cattle all up. Bl. -- ičáhihi, v. red. (icahi). To mingle, mix together.

iča'hihiya, adv. Mixed up with, together with.

iča'hik̂itoŋ, v. pos. To mix together one's own. Caŋlówakpaŋ hiyúmiciya yo;

caŋli ica'hiwetoŋ kte lo. GA.

iċa'hiŋṫe, n. (i-kahiŋta). A broom.

iċa'hitoŋ, v.a. To mix together e.g. tobacco. Icahiwatoŋ, icahiuŋtoŋpi.

iċa'hiya, v.a. To mix together, adulterate. Icahiwaya. Taspícahiye, Lemon extract.

iċa'homni, n. (i-kahomni). Something that is turned or turns, a wheel.

icaȟ', cont. of icaga. - aya, It keeps growing. Wana olute kiŋ - ayapelo, i.e. bones now growing fleshy, as during the spring. Bl.

ica'ȟabȟapela, v.n. To rustle, as the grass in a gentle wind.

iċa'ȟaṗe, n. (i-kahapa). Something to drive with, a whip.

iċa'ȟci, v.n. (kaȟci). To come off by wearing out, as a chain.
iċa'ȟciya, v.a. To make come off by wearing out. Icaȟciwaya.

icaȟ'ḱiya, v.a. To cause to grow, to rear, raise e.g. a child or a domestic animal. Icaȟwakiya.

icaȟ'ḱoḱela, adj. Cf. oicaȟ.

iċa'ȟli, v. To step into mud. Iwákaȟli. Iyákaȟli kilo. Bl.

ica'ȟmuŋ, v.a. To make buzz with. Iwakaȟmuŋ. Iŋyaŋ - , A sling. B.H.87.7.

ica'ȟniȟ, cont. of i-kaȟniga. - icu, To select, pick out.

iċa'ȟolȟoṫa, n. red. (icaȟota). Drops of rain, flakes of snow; so called because they fall like ashes. Cf. icaȟota.

iċa'ȟoṫa, n. (caȟota, perhaps). Drops of rain, flakes of snow, so called because they fall like ashes.

ica'ȟpe hu, n. The narrow-leaved purple cone flower, niggerhead. Braunerìa angustifolia. Composite family. It grows on the prairie. Otherwise it is called óŋglakcapi, or snake-root, which grows in the creeks, whereas the icaȟpe hu grows more on hills. As a medicine, it is chewed for tooth ache or for belly ache, or when one is thirsty or over-perspiring, as well as for swellings, for which last they chew the root and apply it to the swell. Makáblaye - . HM. PLB.

iċa'ȟṫag, cont. of icaȟtaka.

iċa'ȟṫagya, adv. Touching, as a cupboard does a wall or as a man leaning against the wall etc.; relating to, concerning. - haŋ. - inajiŋ. B.H. 111.2. -- v.a. To cause to touch. Icaȟtagwaya.
iċa'ȟṫagyaḱel, adv. Relating to.

iċa'ȟtaḱa, v.n. To come in contact in passing somebody, or as objects touch each other in a game, this being decided by the position, paiŋyaŋkapi; to touch e.g. poison ivy. Imakaȟtaka.

icaȟ'ya, 1) v.a. To cause to grow, to raise, rear, train up a child. Icaȟwaya. 2) adv. Conformed to, made like.

iċa'ijena, v. To mix up. Iwakaijena. Bl.

ica'ja, v.a. To think there is much or many; to do a thing much, as to give away much; to take more than is proper. Iwacaja.

iċa'jaja, v.a. To wash by shaking e.g. a bottle. Iwákajaja. Nasoŋspe oŋ icajajapelo. Bl.

ica'japi, n. Very much.

ica'je, adv. (caje). In the name of.

ica'jeḱa, v.n. To be named for or on account of.

ica'jeyal, adv. cont. (icajeyata). In the name of.

ica'jeyaṫa, adv. In the name of, in speaking the name of.

ica'jeyaṫapi, n. A candidate.

i'cajuju, n. The fare, the pay. P. Bl.

iċa'ḱaŋ, n. (i-kakaŋ). An adze. -- v.a. (kakaŋ). To strike and cut a piece out of. Iwakakaŋ, uŋkicakaŋpi.

iča'kija, v.n. To be in want of, lacking, suffering for. Imákakija, inicakija, uᵑkicakijapi. Na tuktel taku wanice naiᵑś taku icakijapi ca niwícaya omani keyapi'. Mini icakijapi. B.H.66.19. R.

iča'kije, n. (i-kakija). Affliction.

iča'kijeśniyaᵑ, adv. Not in want of, plentifully.

iča'kiś, cont. of icakija. - uᵑ, To be suffering for.

iča'kiśya, 1) v.a. To cause to suffer for, to afflict. Icakiśwaya. 2) adv. In a suffering manner; scantily.

iča'koᵑta, v.a. To cut a groove in, as one branch resting on another will do when swayed by the wind. WE. Cf. kakoᵑta.

iča'kpaᵑ, (?). Bl.

ica'kśa, v. (kakśa). To gather in a roll, as a blanket about the neck. Paícakśa iyeya, To gather or roll together about the neck. Paicakśa imáyaye.

ica'k'oǧe, n. A scraper.

ica'k'os, cont. of icak'oza. - iyaya.

ica'k'oza, v.n. To be made bare by, as by the wind.

i'čalu, n. (i-kalu). A fan, a wing to fan one's self with.

ica'luza, v. (kaluza). To flow over, flow with. Iwaśtegla tate - ca maka woblu welo. Wicayajipa tacaᵑhaᵑpi icaluza, i.e. flowing with milk and honey. B.H.47.14.

iča'ma, adj. Rough, as cloth or the beard; pricking, as do iron filings. -- v.n. To hurt or prick, as anything in the eye or elsewhere. Taku iśta imákama.

iča'mama, v. red. (icama). To prick.

iča'meča, v.n. To be pricked or have one's feelings injured by some little thing.

iča'meya, adv. Pricked, injured in feelings. - wauᵑ, My feelings are hurt. Cf. icapa.

iča'mna, v.n. To blow, bluster, storm, drive, as wind or snow; to be torn by anything and lose the contents, as a bag of corn carried along. Lila - . Cf. kamna, To rip.

i'čanah'o, (?). - welo, i.e. and carried away by the wind. Bl.

icaᵑ', adv. Whilst, in the meantime, just then.

icaᵑ'caᵑ, v.n. (i-caᵑcaᵑ). To tremble for, shake on account of. Imácaᵑcaᵑ.

icaᵑl', adv. But, just then. Yamni t'api k'oᵑ hena titakuye kiᵑ Hmuᵑsekse wicaceye eśa miś - lila wibluśkiᵑ niwagli kiᵑ heoᵑ. Htayetu el wakpala waᵑ el glihuᵑni na - oiyokpaza. MS.561. Cf. ecaᵑl.

icaᵑ'liyuha, (?). Taku icaᵑliniyuha yelaka, winiś'oś'okelo, i.e. in a good mood, hence ready to do. Bl.

icaᵑl'kaśpeya, v. To cheer up one's self, make one's self feel better by giving away etc. after the death of a dear one. Same as caᵑtiyozikiya. Icaᵑlkaspewaya. Bl.

icaᵑl'śica, (?). Takuni icaᵑlśice uᵑ wo. Lc.

icaᵑl'waśte, v.n. To be glad for. Icáᵑlmawaśte.
icaᵑl'waśteya, adv. Gladly for.

icaᵑ'l'iyu'hakel, adv. Same as caᵑtewaśte. - wauᵑ welo. St.

icaᵑ'śica, v.n. To be sad for, as when someone died. Icaᵑmaśica. B.H.302.24.

icaᵑ'śicapi, n. Tribulation.

icaᵑ'śil, cont. of icaᵑśica.
icaᵑ'śilya, 1) v.a. To make sad, grieve or disappoint one by means of something. Icaᵑśilwaya. 2) adv. Sadly, distressingly.

icaᵑ'tagle, v.a. To determine evil against one for some cause. Icaᵑtawagle.

ican'te, adv. In or at the heart.
icáŋtekic'uŋ, v.n. To encourage one's self by reason of. Icaŋtewec'uŋ. CH. Syn.- iśpákic'uŋ.
icáŋtekic'uŋyaŋ, adv. Encouragingly.
i'caŋtenica, v.n. To have no heart for, to be controlled by habit, so that will-power is gone. I'caŋtemanica.
icáŋteśica, v.n. To be sad on account of. Icaŋtemaśica. Ehaŋl wikośkalaka k'uŋ t'a; caŋke kośkalaka k'uŋ lila icaŋteśica.
icáŋteśicaya, adv. Sadly on account of.
i'caŋteśilya, v.a. To render happy by, make feel bad. Also, icáŋteśilya. I'caŋteśilwaya. R.
icáŋtet'iŋs, cont. of icaŋtet'iŋza. - kic'uŋ wo. B.H.46.4;122.7.
icáŋtet'iŋsya, 1) v.a. To encourage one by reason of. Icaŋtet'iŋswaya. 2) adv. Encouragingly.
icáŋtet'iŋza, v.n. To be encouraged or sustained by. Icaŋtemat'iŋza.
icáŋtewaśte, v.n. To be glad on account of. Icaŋtemawaśte. Yuŋkaŋ namah'oŋpi kiŋ icaŋtemawaśtehce.
icáŋtewaśteya, adv. Gladly on account of.

icaŋ'tognaka, v.a. To place in the heart with ref. to something; to purpose to give to one. Icaŋtowagnaka.

icaŋ'tokpani, v. To long for in ref. to. Icaŋtowakpani.

i'caŋyaŋ, adv. Leaning against e.g. a chair half reclined and leaning against the wall, or as a man so leaning. Tii'caŋyaŋ yaŋke, To lean against the house. B.H.173.18.

iċa'pa, v. To open the mouth; to open. Iwákapa, and perhaps iwácapa. - glukawa, To open the mouth without effort.

ica'pa, v. (i-capa). To stick into, to take a stitch; to stab with, to stick in e.g. a thorn or a stick. Icawapa. Caŋ icamapa. Na uŋma pestola k'oŋ he el icapiŋ na oŋ yumni. Waśiŋ - waciŋ yelo. GA.

iċa'paŋ, n. (kapaŋ). A thresher, a threshing machine; something to pound with. -- v.a. To pound to pieces. Iwakapaŋ. Bl.

ica'pcab, (?). Peji to mini - helo, i.e. drops of water on grass as it comes out of the ground. Bl.

ica'pe, n. (i-capa). Something that sticks in, a spear, a splinter; a stitch.

ica'pepeya, i'capepeya, (?). Maswiyokataŋ - yuwaŋkal iyeyapi. B.H.265.23.

i'capeya, adv. More than that. - waciŋ yelo. Bl.

ica'poġaŋ, n. (?). - waŋ hi, A snow storm started. Bl.

iċa'psake, n. (i-kapsaka). Something used in cutting off strings. Pahiŋ - , A porcupine quill cutter, a small knife.

iċa'psiŋte, n. (i-kapsiŋta). Something to whip with, a whip. - wiŋświŋśahela, A flexible whip, a buggy whip.

ica'pśiŋpśiŋcala ikpi' ska, n. The tree swallow. Upi'jata is practically synonymous.
ica'pśiŋpśiŋcala ikpi' śa, n. The barn swallow.

iċa'pśuŋ, n. (i-kapśuŋ). Anything to pry out or pull up by the roots with.

iċa'pta, v.n. (i-kapta). To break out, as the hold of meat in carrying it.

i'ċapta icu', v. To dip, to ladle out. Bl.

iċa'ptaŋptaŋ kic'úŋ, v.n. (kaptaŋptaŋ, To roll over much, roll about). To roll, as a horse does after a long drive. (Śuŋgleśka kiŋ) kul iyuŋki na - . D.257,99.

iċa'p'ośya, (?). Wapahlaya na - s'e iblabla. Bl.

iċa'p'taŋktaŋka, adv. With wide-open mouth. Le tohaŋ ceya ca - ceye. Bl.

iċa'saŋ, v.a. (i-kasaŋ). To whiten, make fade by touching or striking. Iwákasaŋ.

iċa'ska, (?). - iyeya. Icask'iyewayiŋ kte. Cik'alakel - iyéuŋyiŋ kte, Let us smoke, eat etc. a little in a hurry. Also, cak'iglaska. - iyewayiṅ kte lo.

ica'sḱica, v.n. To be pressed down. Imakaskica.
iċa'sḱice, n. (i-kaskica). A press.

ica'slece, n. (i-kasleca). Something to split with, a wedge.

ica'slohe, n. A marble, marbles; a stick made to slide along on snow or ice; the game of billiards. - ecoṅpi, To play billiards.

i'ċastaṅka, v. To moisten the mouth, as is done when people have little water. - uṅyaṅpi kte. Bl.

iċa'śe, n. (i-kaśe). Something rubbing against or fitted against; a hindrance.
iċa'śeya, v.a. To make a hindrance of, to hinder by means of. Icaśewaya.

iċā'śḱe, n. (i-kaśka). Something to tie or bind around with, a girdle, a sash; a prize. -- v. To play for, run a race for etc.
iċa'śkeya, v.a. To tie one with. B.H. 229.25.

iċa'śkice, n. (i-kaśkica). Something to pound with, a beetle.

iċa'śḱiṫa, v.a. To cut a little gash in, to cut notches. R. Bl.

ica'śla, n. (i-kaśla). Something to mow with. Peji - , A scythe. Putiṅ -, A razor.

iċa'śleca, n. (i-kaśleca). Something to split with, a wedge.

ica'śloka, adj. perhaps. Knocked out. Imákaśloke, colloq. I am all in, I am played out.
iċa'śloḱe, n. (i-kaśloke). (?). Caṅnuṅpa - , A thin stick used to press down the tobacco in a burning pipe, a poker.

ica'śośa, v. To mix by shaking together. Iwákaśośa.

iċa'śṗe, n. (i-kaśpa). An instrument for cutting out pieces. Mazicaśpe, A cold chisel.

iċa'śṗu, v.n. (i-kaśpu). To break off, come off as by over-heavy weight. -- n. Something to knock off with. R.

i'caśṫaṅ, adv. perhaps. Close up to one, as in running close up to one. - maṅka, I am close up to him. - mahiyaṅka, He ran close up to me. Hehaṅl wicaśa waṅ uṅgnahela - mahiyaṅkiṅ na lecel omakiyaka. Cf. icaśtiṅyaṅka.

i'caśtiṅyaṅka, v. To catch up with another running after him. Icaśtiṅmaṅka. Icaśtiṅyaṅke na oyuspa na tuweceeyaś iyugnayaṅ ca na he icaśtaṅ iṅyaṅkiṅ.

ica'ś'aḱa, v.n. (kaś'aka). Not to penetrate, as an axe that is dull.

ica'ta, v. (?). - iheya, To crowd together.

iċa'taṅtaṅ, (?). - ėhuṅni yo, Rub or spread it, i.e. glue, all over. Iwakataṅtaṅ. Bl.

ica'tḱayaṫaṅ, adv. To the left hand of. Micátkayataṅ.
ica'tḱayaṫaṅhaṅ, adv. To the left of. Micatkayataṅhaṅ. B.H.249.6.
ica'tkutaṅhaṅ, adv. To or at the back part of the tent from one.

i'cat'a, adv. Very. Śuṅkawakaṅ - taṅka, A very big horse.

iċa't'e, n. Anything to club to death with. Bl.

iċa'zo, 1) v.a. (kazo). To draw a mark or line, to take credit, to owe, be in debt. Iwakazo, uṅkicazopi. 2) n. A mark, a line drawn.

iċa'zoḱiya, v.a. To cause to mark; to cause to take things on credit, give credit to. Icazowakiya.

iċa'zopi, n. Credits.

iċa'zozo, v. red. of icazo.

ice', interrog. particle. Cf. cē.

iceb'ya, v.a. To fatten, make fat by means of. Icebwaya.

ice'ḱiya, v.a. (cekiya). To pray

to one for something. Icewakiya, icecíciya. Le miye (Wakantanka Cinca) ca tokśa taku icemayakiyapi ca na nawaȟ'on kte lo.

ice'ṗa, adj. (cepa). Fat on or by, fat by reason of. Imácepa.

icē'ṫe, n. The rim or lip of a kettle.

ice'ṫi, v. (ceti). To make a fire to or at. Icewati. - na mayujuju ye, Make a fire and undo my wrappings. D.228.

ice'win, adv. Grandly. Wicaśa wan kangi tanka s'e - pasu tanka keye, as is said of a man with a big nose. Huntka s'e - nunplala wicayuha, as said of people with only two children. Bl.
ice'winlakes'e, adv. perhaps. - iśtakte nuns'e amayuta yankelaȟ. Bl.
ice'winś, adv. Very much, implying wonder. - mayak'u. - ṫak'ṫoḱonka. - conamak'u we. - wokokipeka nacece, My, how awfully fearful he must be. Bl. D.153.

ici', prefix. Affixed to cardinal numbers making them ordinals. Icíyamni. -- To verbs, signifying "together". Koyáka, To put on; íćikoyaka, To fasten together. Iciwanyanka, To compare. -- To prepositions and adverbs, conveying the idea of space or time intervening between objects. Íćikiyela, Near to each other. Íćitehan, Far apart.

i'cicagmun, v.a. (kagmun). To tangle up. Íćiwakagmun.
i'cicahi, v.n. To mingle together, mix.
i'cicahiya, 1) v.a. To mix together, mingle, stir up. Íćicahiwaya. Wicaśa na winyan ko - mimeya enajin. Also, icíćahiya. D.262. 2) adv. Mingled. 7.
i'cicahiyakel, adv. Altogether. B.H.278.
i'cicahiyapi, part. Mixed together.

i'cicaȟabȟaṗa, v.n. To rustle, as the grass in a gentle wind. Also, icaȟabȟapela.

i'cicaskaya, v.a. To mix. Taśośe k'un he maka - . B.H.221.9.

i'cicasni, v. To make cool, as hot coffee by pouring it to and fro from one cup to another. Bl.

i'ciċaśka, v. To bind together.
i'ciċaśkeya, adv. Tied together, united. - eyapi, They say it all together.

i'cicaśla, adv. Making each other bare by striking. Pte na tahca ko naunkapi na śake - naunkapi.

i'cicaślaślayela, adv. Perhaps with a rattling noise. Makacega kin - kableblecapi. B.H.76.4.

i'cicaśnaśna, v. Perhaps to strike one another and make ring, as cymbals. Maza icicaśnaśnapi. B.H.92.3. -- n. Cymbals.

i'cicaśośa, v. To mix to cool off, a a liquid by pouring it to and fro from one cup to another. P. Bl.

i'cicawin, adv. Back again by the same way. - gla. Anunk - , Back and forth, perhaps. -- íćicawinwin, adv. red. of icicawin. -- íćicawinyan, adv. Back by the same way. - inyanka, To meet running in opposite directions. Bl.

i'cic'uya, adv. Passing by each other when coming from opposite directions. - iyayapi. Lenayos (lenaos) kakika paha wan lila tehanl yanke kin heci anunk - iyayapi kte lo.

i'ciglapśunpśunyan, adv. Piled on top of each other. Bl.

i'cigleglega, adj. Scattering, few. R.
i'ciglegleȟ, cont. of icigleglega. Wanji ska, i.e. porcupine quills, wanji sapa, wanji zi, inś toto iyoyaza owecinhan iyeyapi ca he - oyazapi ecin api. Used when the same colors occur again and again in the same order.

i'cigleśka, adj. Speckled, as corn of different colors.
i'cigleśkaśka, adj. red. of icigleśka.

ici'gni, v.a. To beat or maltreat, as a man his wife. Iwákigni, iunkignipi. A possible use: Na tanyan ecanonpi śni kin heceglala kta na niye inicignipte kte lo.

i'cignuni, v. To be mixed up, so as not to be distinguished. -- íćignuniya, v.a. To cause not to be distinguished. Íćignuniwaya.
i'cignuniyan, adv. Mingled, mixed up; during that time. B.H.56.17;201.6.

i'cihakṫaya, adv. (ihakta). Following each other.

i'cihehaŋhaŋyaŋ, adv. red. of icihehaŋyaŋ.
i'cihehaŋyaŋ, adv. Thus far apart.

i'ciȟloka, (?). - yuha, i.e. in ref. to dominos etc. Bl.

ici'ȟmiŋyaŋ, adv. Crookedly; incorrectly, confusedly. - naȟ'oŋ, To hear incorrectly. - wakaga, I made it wrong, differing from the other that is right.

i'ciiyoṗeya, v.a. (iyopeya). To barter, exchange one thing for another. Iciiyopewaya.
i'ciiyoṗeyapi, n. Barter, an exchange. Iciiyopekiciyapi, A market.

i'ciiyopta, adv. In a range, in the same direction.
i'ciiyopteya, adv. In that direction; across, through.

i'cijehaŋ, adv. Mingled, mixed up.Bl.R.
ici'jena, adv. Mingled, mixed up.

i'cikaŋkaŋyela, adv. red. of icikaŋyela.
i'cikaŋyela, adv. Near together.

i'cikikiyela, adv. red. of icikiyela.
i'cik̇iyela, adv. Close or near to each other.

i'cik̇oyag, cont. of icikoyaka. - iyeya.
i'cik̇oyagya, 1) v.a. To fasten one to another. Icikoyagwaya. -- adv. Linked, joined. Isto - manipi, They walk with arms linked.
i'cik̇oyak̇a, 1) v.n. To be fastened one to another. 2) adj. United.

i'cikpukpeya, adv. Scattered, mixed up. Cf. kpukpeya.

iči'kte, v. To kill one's self, commit suicide. BD. Cf. ic'ikte.

i'cilowaŋ, v. To wail alone (to one's self), as at the death of a relative.
i'cilowaŋpi, n. A death song.

ici'ma, adv. Ever; again. Haŋicima, hehaŋ, The night before.

i'cimani, 1) v.n. To travel, to go on a journey without one's family; to visit or go on an extended trip to another tribe or band. Iciwamani, icimauŋnipi. D.116, note 2. 2) n. A traveler.
i'cimani tipi, n. An hotel. Bl.
i'cimani cek̇iṗapi, n. The soft meat under the shoulders of buffalo. HH.Bl.
i'cimanipi, n. Traveling, visiting.

i'cimna, (?). - śni, He has no confidence in himself. B.H.74.21.

i'cinakśiŋ, v. coll. pl. (anakikśiŋ). To stand up for each other, to shield each other; to help each other. Also, écinakśiŋ. R. Used only with the pl. ending, either on itself or a verb following. (Cf. appendix).

ici'napciyuŋk̇a, adj. The ninth. Note: this form is not much used.
ici'nuŋpa, adj. The second; a second time, again, adv. Icinuŋpani śni, Not a second time. Icinuŋpani ihaŋgwicawayiŋ kte śni. B.H.9.2;181.20.

iciŋ', 1) conj. Namely, for you know. Mni kiŋ hel ihpeyapi ehaŋtaŋś niiyayiŋ kte ciŋ he (kéya kiŋ) slolkiya; - kéya kiŋ mini mahel uŋpi. 2) v. To desire one thing for another; to desire more of, in addition, as in asking more money for an object, thus for another. Okise iwakiciŋ kte. Iwásiŋ, iúŋciŋpi. - eyaś. B.H.157.20.

iciŋ'ca, n. A child, i.e. in ref. to. Toke niciŋcapi kiŋ iciŋcapi kiŋ na wicoicage iciyamni na itopa hehaŋyaŋ waŋwicayaglakapi ni. B.H.125.13.

iciŋ'iŋ, v. (kiŋiŋ). To throw at, strike with. Iwákiŋiŋ.

i'ciŋkciŋ, adv. Angrily, roughly, as one in speaking.

iciŋ'ya, v.a. To cause to desire. Iciŋwaya.

iciŋ'yuŋśkaś, interj. Of reproof. For heaven's sake! Wakaŋtaŋka ohoyalapi śni kiŋ. B.H.55.20. Cf. iyuwiŋśkaś.

ici'oŋb, adv. Off to one side, off from, out at one side of. Tipi kiŋ - bla, I went off on one side of the house. - ya, To swerve. P. -- ici'oŋbya, adv. perhaps. Out of the way. Same as icioŋb. - ȟpaya, as a strip of wood nailed under, serving to brace.

i'cipa, (?). Hecel iyawicapepi na ob icipapi na ob ecoⁿpi.
i'ciṗahaha, adv. Piled up, men and things. - egnakapi.
i'cipahahaya, adv. On top of one another. B.H.71.12;302.8.
i'ciṗaja, adv. perhaps. Dove-tailed together at the ends; inserted, laminated, fitted.
i'ciṗasisa, v.a. (pasisa). To stick to one another; to sew together, sew across. Iciwapasisa wicao śke, i.e. he pierced them all with one shot. D.113.
i'ciṗasiseya, adv. Pinned into one another, put close to one another. - yapi waⁿyaⁿke. B.H.22.6.

i'ciṗaś, cont. (icipaja). Back by the same way that one had left on. - glicu, glipi. D.227.
i'ciṗaśṗaś, adv. Backwards and forward; doubled on.

i'cipatkuh̄, (?). - yaⁿkapi, They sat close together. Also, okowanilya, icipat'iⁿs. Bl.

i'cipat'iⁿs, (?). Cf. icipatkuh̄. Bl.

i'ciṗawah̄wah̄, adv. perhaps. Crossing in all directions etc., as wood piled disorderly, or as hair tangled up. Caⁿ śeca ota yelo, - h̄payelo. Bl.
i'ciṗaweġa, v.n. (pawega). To cross, or to lie across.
i'ciṗaweh̄, cont. (icipawega). Crosswise. - okataⁿ, To nail on crosswise, to crucify.
i'ciṗaweh̄weġa, v. red. of icipawega.
i'ciṗaweh̄ya, adv. Crosswise, across.

i'ciṗiyela, adv. Sufficiently for one's self. - owiⁿja gluha wahi yelo, I came bringing just enough bedding for myself. - yaⁿka, To have barely room enough to sit on. Okáblayakel yaⁿka (the opposite), To have plenty of room to sit on. Bl.

ici'saⁿb, (?). - wómayakilahe, You interrupt me all the while. Bl.

ici'saⁿnica, (?). Wi - ye k'oⁿ ceti yelo, tate kte lo. BT.
ici'saⁿnicab, (?). More than one half, as having made over one half of one's way. Bl.

i'ciskuya, adj. (skuya). Alike, sour or sweet. Kici - , Alike sweet with.

ici'śagloġaⁿ, adj. The eighth.

ici'śah̄owiⁿ, adj. The seventh.

ici'śakṗe, adj. The sixth.

i'ciśleca, adv. or v. To be or stand so close together that one shot will kill more than one. - uⁿ, najiⁿ.
i'ciślecaya, adv. Mixedly close together. - wicoti, i.e. tents being close together and mixed up apparently, but a few in a line. Game may at times stand this way, where more than one can be shot with one bullet. - yaⁿkapi, or kaot'iⁿs yaⁿkapi, Packed close together, as people in a room. To many they say: iciyaiyopteya; or: - au; or: - aya. Obs. Syn.- icit'eyela.

i'ciśniyaⁿ, adv. Away off, not near anything. Also, wiciśniyaⁿ. Bl. R.
i'citakignag, adv. On top of each other while carried by somebody. Bl.
i'citakignagna, adv. red. - au welo, They are coming one bunch after another. Bl. Syn.- icikaⁿkaⁿyela.

i'citaⁿiⁿśni, v.n. (taⁿiⁿ). It is not manifest, i.e. which is the one between two or more.

i'citehaⁿ, adv. (tehaⁿ). Far apart. Also, i'citehaⁿhaⁿ, red.
i'citehaⁿyaⁿ, adv. Far apart from each other. Hecel nupiⁿ lila - iyayapi.

i'citḱoḱib, adv. Meeting face to face, i.e. opposite each other.
i'citḱoḱiṗaṗi, v. pl. (itkokipa). They met face to face.

i'citohaⁿ, adv. How long from? Also, i'citohaⁿhaⁿ, red. and i'citohaⁿhaⁿyaⁿ.
i'citohaⁿyaⁿ, adv. How far apart?

i'citokeca, adj. Different from each other.
i'citona, (?).

ici'toṗa, adj. The fourth.

i'cit'eya, adv. Very close together, crowding each other badly. -- i'cit'eyela, adv. Crowded together. Cf. iciślicaya.

i'ciwaŋyaŋka, v.a. (waŋyaŋka). To look at things together, compare. Iciwaŋblaka. Iciwaŋuŋyaŋkapi. B.H.136.20.
i'ciwaŋyaŋkapi, n. Comparison.

ici'waśte, v.n. To be good with. Taku -, With what is it good? Also, to be good for.

ici'wikcemna, adj. The tenth.

i'ciwotopi, v. 3rd pers. pl. (woto). Pe'iciwotopi, They run with their heads together, as rams do. Bl.

ici'ya, v.a. To take sides with, assist in a dispute or controversy, assist as an advocate. Iwákiya, uŋkikiyapi, imakiya.

i'ciyaciŋ, v. (iyaciŋ). To liken several things to each other, think equal. Íciblaciŋ. -- íciyaciŋyaŋ, adv. Likening to one another.

i'ciyaglaskiskiya, adv. red. In layers of flat or straight things, one upon another and horizontally; piled on top of each other. Bl. Cf. óciyuśtaŋśtaŋ, ócibcib.

i'ciyaglaskiya, adv. One above another, pressing on each other, as is said of flat or straight things; on on top of another. Bl. B.H.239.2;244.4. Cf. agláskica, óciyuśtaŋśtaŋ.

i'ciyaglaśka, v. pos. To unite together or tie one to another of one's own. Iciyawaglaśka. Nape iciyaglaśke oyuspa.

i'ciyagle, v.n. To reach one to another
i'ciyaglegle, v. red.
i'ciyaglegleya, adv. red.
i'ciyagleya, 1) adv. Reaching one to another. 2) v.a. To cause one to reach to another, cause to meet. Iciyaglewaya.

i'ciyahlah, (?). Nape - iyeya, To fold the hands for prayer, i.e. crossing the fingers. Bl. Cf. iciyaskabya.

i'ciyahlal, adv. (yahlata). Nape - okiciyuspewicakiya au na lecel eya, He folded their hands, as we do in prayer, but one man folding with another's. Nape - ogluspa, To fold one's hands. SI.

i'ciyahpaya, v.a. To catch from one another, to communicate to others, e.g. an infectious disease.

i'ciyaiglaśkapi, v. pl. To unite one to another, tie each other together, as man and wife.

i'ciyaiyopteya, adv. Cf. íciślecaya.

i'ciyakaśka, v.a. To tie or unite things mutually. Íciyawakaśka.

i'ciyakigle, adv. One by one, one after another. -- íciyakiglegle, adv. red.

ici'yamni, adj. The third, the third time. Na ake - ai na ake iyena wicaopi na agli.

i'ciyapa, v.n. To bump into somebody. Íciyamapa. Tate - yelo. Toké uŋśipi śni ca iciyawicawapa ni, as a woman would say, out of jealousy, in regard to two big men that she married. Bl. Cf. iyóto, iyápa.
i'ciyapapi, n. A collision.

i'ciyapuspa, v.a. (iyapuspa). To stick two or more things together. Iciyawapuspa.

i'ciyaskab, cont. of iciyaskapa. Stick to each other.
i'ciyaskabya, 1) v.a. To cause to adhere or stick to each other. Íciyaskabwaya. 2) adv. Adhering to each other. Nape - ogluspa, To place the hands together with palms together, as in going to Holy Communion. Bl.
i'ciyaskapa, v.n. (iyaskapa). To adhere or stick one to another.

i'ciyasyaza, adv. red. of iciyaza.

i'ciyawa, v.a. (yawa). To count up together. Íciblawa.

i'ciyaza, adv. red. (iyaza). In rows, in a range, from one to another, as in passing a thing around. Lena wicoicage - aupi.
i'ciyazaza, adv. red. One after the other, from one to the other. P.

i'ciyehaŋyaŋ, adv. Equally long. Bl.

i'ciyokihe, adj. Adjoining. - uŋ, To join, be adjoining. -- íciyokiheya, 1) v.a. To connect things, as two ropes, so as to make it longer. Iciyokihewaya. 2) adv. Over again and again, repeatedly, one after another.

i'ciyotatkoⁿs, cont. (iciyotatkoⁿza). Opposite to each other.

i'ciyotatkoⁿza, adv. (iyotatkoⁿza). Opposite to each other; equal to, even with.

i'ciyugmuⁿ, v.a. To twist together, as two threads. Íciblugmuⁿ. Wapepe iciyugmuⁿpi teślagkiyapi. Pb.38.
i'ciyugmuⁿyaⁿ, adv. Twisted. Caⁿpepe - yuktaⁿpi. B.H.263.10.

i'ciyumnahe's'e, adv. In various directions. - wicomani yelo, i.e. many people travelling in all directions. Bl.

i'ciyuⁿġa, v.a. To cross-question, examine by cross-questioning. Ícimuⁿga, íċinuⁿga, uⁿkíciyuⁿgapi.
i'ciyuⁿgapi, n. An examination.

i'ciyuota, v.a. (yuota). To multiply together. Ícibluota.

i'ciyuwi, v. To get entangled, entangle one's self. P.

ici'zaptaⁿ, adj. The fifth.

i'coġa, v.n. To lodge on, drift and lodge on, as a log of wood. B.H.8.4.

ico'kab, adv. Before. Micókab, uⁿkicokab. Wicicokab. Tipi kiⁿ - énajiⁿ. Na el caⁿ waⁿ glakiⁿyaⁿ otka na - wazilyapi. B.H.273.3.
ico'kabya, adv. Before; between. Waⁿji uⁿyaⁿkapi kiⁿ - iyotakiⁿ na taku hoyeya ....
ico'kaⁿyaⁿ, adv. In the middle, between. B.H.54.5.
ico'kapa, adv. (cokapa). Same as icokab.
ico'kapataⁿhaⁿ, adv. Before, in the midst; inside of.

ico'ka sápa, n. A bird whose mouth is black inside, whose tail is long; it lives in the woods and leaves in the fall; it is big as the caⁿwaḣpa taⁿka. Cf. hiⁿkcekapila, cépela taⁿka. Bl.

ico'kata, adv. In the middle of. Ahimniciya kiⁿ - . B.H.83.24.

ico̅l'ya, v. To make a base of operations. Tuktel icolyaya hwo? Where do you stay, make your home? Bl.

ico'ma, v.a. To draw up around the shoulders e.g. one's blanket; to wear a blanket held tightly around the body, the arms holding the edges in front of the body. Also, icómi. Śina iwácoma. Kośkalaka kiⁿ tilazata pamahel - najiⁿ. D.47.

ico'pa, v. (copa). To wade in, as in one's moccasins. Icówapa.

icos', cont. of icoza.

icos'ya, v.a. To make warm with. Icoswaya.

ico'za, v.n. (coza). To be warm by means of e.g. clothing. Imacoza.

ico'mi, v.a. Same as icoma, some using one form, others the other. Wiⁿyaⁿ waⁿ śina pamahel icomiⁿ (a form of icoma) na olowaⁿ waⁿ yawaⁿkal éyaye. D.261. R.

icu', v.a. To take, take up anything; accept, receive. Iwácu.

icu'cu, v. (?). Iyácucu lakelo, blihic'iya yo, as is said encouragingly to one who is on the point of winning a race. Also said is: Yakalulakelo, iyótaⁿla icu wo. Miye iwácucu kaca; eya śna wau welo, I am still active and so come now and then. Bl.

icu'ḣca, adv. The very one, the only one. Waⁿjila - au yo, Bring it even if but one. Note: this is not the same as icuḣciⁿ.

icu'kiya, v.a. To cause to receive; to hold one's self back in self control. Icuwakiya.

icuⁿ'haⁿ, adv. Whilst, during the time, in the meantime. Waⁿna aⁿpetu num mani kiⁿ - wicaśa waⁿ el hi. Yuⁿkaⁿ - taku owicakiyake ci he kiksuya. Na hecel nupiⁿ kawiⁿgapi na kiglapi le - oyate kiⁿ okiḣpayapi kte keyapi. Na ena lila tehaⁿ maⁿka - , taⁿke ena ate tokena yaⁿkapi. Note: it is used also without a noun.
icuⁿ'haⁿḣaḣci, adv. Just at that time.

icuⁿ'kśila, n. A little bow, such as

small boys use.

icuŋ'oŋb, adv. cont. (icuŋoŋpa). Out at one side of. Same as iciŏŋb. Tipi kiŋ - bla, I went off on one side of the house.

icuŋ'oŋpa, adv. Off to one side, off from, out of the way. Micuŋoŋpa, Off from me.
icuŋ'oŋpatanhaŋ, adv. Out of the way, off to one side.

icuŋś', cont. of icuŋza, which is obs. and der. from kuŋza.
icuŋs'ya, v. To be dilatory, not to do much, to have no mind to work; to work only for the pay. Icuŋswaya.
icuŋs'yakel, adv. Not heartily, pretending.
icuŋs'yeca, n. One who is not faithful or one who does not do his duty well. Also, perhaps, ecóŋsyeca. Perhaps it is der. from koŋza. R. Bl.

icu'pica, adj. Available. P.

icu'te, n. (kute). Something to shoot with, as the arrows one uses in a game. - wahiŋkpe, The name for the sticks used in the game called "painyaŋkapi". R.

icu'tu, n. A round stone to grind corn etc. on.

icu'wa, n. (kuwa). Something with which to hunt or catch anything. Hoícuwa, a fish-hook.

ic'i', pron. refl. It usually signifies that the action of the verb returns upon the actor, and sometimes indicates the action is done for one's self. Ic'icaga, To make one's self.

ic'i'blebleca, v. refl. red. To shake one's self, as a horse does. Kul iyuŋkiŋ na ȟnaȟna na icaptaŋptaŋ kic'uŋ na inajiŋ na - na eciyataŋhaŋ maka ǧi wobluya.

ic'i'caǧa, v. refl. (kaga). To make one's self; to make for one's self. Mic'icaga.

ic'i caŋ, v. refl. To cry over one's own self. Mic'icaŋ. BD. Cf. kicaŋ.

ic'i'caŋyaŋ, adv. Standing or planted firmly, as a post, a hay stack, a person. - najiŋ. Wopate waŋ lécegla - hiyeye ciŋ eya śke'.

ic'i'caśka, v. refl. (kaśka). To bind or tie one's self, to deliver up one's self to authorities. Mic'icaśka.

ic'i'coŋs, v. cont. (ic'icoŋza). - opa, To follow on one's own decision; to make a profession of religion.
ic'i'coŋskiya, v.a. To cause one to determine for himself.
ic'i'coŋza, v. refl. (koŋza). To determine for one's self, make up one's mind, to vow. Mic'ioŋza. Ekta yiŋ kta - . Eya aŋpetu kiŋ lehaŋl mic'icoŋza ca wana wahi yelo, i.e. came as I had promised. Bl.

ic'i'c'uya, adv. (k'u, To give). Giving one's self up; devotedly. - ecoŋ, He acts devotedly.

ici'glalu, v. refl. To fan one's self.

ic'i'gle, v. refl. (gla). To lay up for one's self. Mic'igle. Taku ic'iglepi, Furniture perhaps.
ic'i'gleka, n. One who has much, one who is always accumulating; a thrifty person.

ic'i'gnaka, v. refl. (gnaka). To place or locate one's self; to lay up for one's self. Mic'ignaka. Taku ic'ignakapi, Furnishings perhaps.

ic'i'gnayaŋ, v. refl. (gnayaŋ). To deceive one's self. Mic'ignayaŋ.

ic'i'ȟ'aŋ, v. refl. To extricate one's self, help one's self. B.H.76.14.

ic'i'ksapa, v. To save for one's self, to have gained experience, to be wise. Lenáke mic'iksapelo, This little nest I keep for tomorrow. Hecel oyate woyute ic'iksapapi. Bl.

ic'i'ksuya, v. refl. (kiksuya). To remember one's self, come to one's self. Mic'iksuya.

ic'i'kte, v. refl. (kte). To kill for one's self. BD. Note: icikte, To commit suicide.

ic'i'la, v. refl. (la). To say of or consider one's self. Waśte - , To consider one's self good.

ic'i'mnikel, (?). - muŋkelo, I lie all stretched out. LC.

ic'iŋ', n. A harness. -- ic'íŋikaŋ, n. Harness lines. -- ic'íŋpasu, n. The hame. -- ic'íŋyuḣlate, n. A snap.

ie', v. Same as ia.

i'ecana, Cf. iyecana.

ie'glaśna, v. pos. (ieyaśna). To blunder in speaking, speak falsely of one's own, as in telling one's dreams or visions; to stammer. Iéwaglaśna.
ie'glaśnaśna, v.n. To stammer, stutter.
ie'glaśna s'a, n. A blunderer.

ie'k̇aṗiŋ, v.n. To be tired of speaking, be unwilling to speak. Cf. kapiŋ.

ie'k̇iya, v.a. To cause to speak, make a speaker of; to have for interpreter. Iéwakiya.

ie'ksaṗa, v.n. To be wise in one's speech, be eloquent. Iémaksapa.

ie'laya, v. To put everything in the mouth, as do babies. - abla. Bl.

i'elgle, v. To reproach, blame. Íelwagle.

ie'sk̇a, 1) n. One who speaks well, an interpreter. Iyémaska, iyéniska. 2) v.n. To be fluent, to speak a language intelligibly. Iemaska.
ie'sk̇ak̇iya, v.a. To have for interpreter, cause to interpret from one language to another. Ieskawakiya.

ie'slota, adj. (?). One who tells the truth, perhaps. Bl.

ie'śni, v. Not to be able to speak, to be dumb.

ie'wicak̇a, v.n. To tell the truth. Iewicawaka. P.
ie'wicakeya, adv. Truly.

ie'yaṗaha, 1) v. To proclaim, publish. Iéyawapaha. 2) n. A public crier, a herald. The incorrect form is éyapaha.

ie'yaśna, v. To talk as one pleases, to talk falsely. Ieblaśna.
ie'yaśnaśna, v. red.

igla', prefix. It makes the reflexive form of verbs beginning with "ka" and "ya"; e.g. iglablaska, iwaglablaska. Bl.

igla'ciŋ, v. pos. (iyaciŋ). To liken one's own or one's self to. Iwaglaciŋ. Imiglaciŋ.

iglag', cont. of iglaka. - uŋyaŋpi.

igla'gleġleġa (?), v. refl. To make a fool of one's self.

igla'gnaśkiŋyaŋ, Cf. iyágnaśkiŋyaŋ.

igla'ġoġo, v. refl. (kagogo). To cut one's self in many places. B.H.108.10.

iglag'yak̇e, adv. (?). - hi, To come with all one's belongings, as on a trip. WE. Cf. iglaka.
iglag'yakel, adv. (?).

igla'hoġita, v.n. To become hoarse from speaking. Cf. yahogita.

igla'homni, v. refl. (yahomni). To turn one's self around. Miglahomni. Na waŋna tiyatakiya - na tipi ekiya glapi. Na waŋna - na tima kigla.

igla'ḣniġa, v. To choose for one's self; to choose one's self, perhaps. B.H.220.10.

igla'jata, v. refl. (yajata). To contradict one's self. Miglajata.

igla'jica, v. refl. (yajica). To speak of one's self as rich.
igla'jicak̇a, n. One who counts himself rich.

igla'k̇a, v.n. To move, to travel about with a family, pitching one's tent at short stages; to go camping. Iwaglaka, uŋkiglakapi.

igla'kata, v. refl. (kakata). To make one's self warm by moving the arms rhythmically. Bl.

igla'ksa, v. refl. (kaksa, yaksa). To cut off or bite off one's own. Miglaksa.

igla'lu, v. refl. (kalu). To fan one's self. Miglalu. Also, ic'iglalu.

igla'mna, v. refl. (kamna, yamna). To turn one's self around; to gain for one's self, get back one's own. Also, iglúhomni. Miglamna, uⁿkiglamnapi. Miś ena miglamna.

igla'ocoza, v. refl. (kaocoza). To make one's self warm by moving the arms rhythically. Bl.

igla'onihaⁿ, v. refl. (yaonihaⁿ). To praise one's self. Migláonihaⁿ.

igla'oⁿspe, v. refl. (kaoⁿspe). (?). Hena oⁿ (śuⁿkawakaⁿ) iglaoⁿspepi na hena oⁿ oyate icagapi kta.

igla'oⁿśika, v. refl. (yaoⁿśika). To speak of one's self as miserable. B.H. 74.16.

igla'otaⁿiⁿ, v. refl. (yaotaⁿiⁿ). To manifest one's self, proclaim one's self. Miglaotaⁿiⁿ.

igla'sto, v.a. (?). Iwaglasto. Imáglasto tka, I almost got left out, it almost did not reach me, i.e. in a distribution. Bl.

igla'su, v. refl. (yasu). To judge one's self; to see one's own wrongdoing and promise to do better. IS.

igla'śica, v. refl. To speak evil, to blame one's self.

igla'śka, v. refl. (kaśka). To bind one's self; to deliver one's self up to be punished. Miglaśka.

igla'śna, v. refl. (yaśna). To miss biting one's self, as a dog does in trying to bite his own tail.
igla'śnaśna, v. red. of iglaśna.

igla'śpa, v. refl. (yaśpa, kaśpa). To bite one's self loose, break loose. Mígláśpa. B.H.203.6.
igla'śpaśpa, v. red. of iglaśpa.

igla'śtaⁿ, v. refl. (yaśtaⁿ). To finish speaking or eating one's own food. Miglaśtaⁿ. Le yaglapi na taⁿyaⁿ wol miglaśtaⁿpi hehaⁿl.

igla'tamaheca, v. refl. To become leaning by speaking esp. by talking or slandering. Suⁿka tamaheca s'e iwaśicuⁿpi c'oⁿ iglatamaheca. Bl.

igla'taⁿ, v. refl. (yataⁿ). To praise one's self; to brag, boast. Miglataⁿ.
igla'taⁿ, v. pos. (iyataⁿ). To light one's own e.g. a pipe. Iwáglataⁿ. Ilege mak'u wo; iwaglataⁿ kte, Let me have your (burning) cigaret; I want to light mine.

igla'tata, v. refl. (katata). To shake dust off one's self.

igla'tokaⁿ, v. refl. (yatokaⁿ). To clear one's self, to prove an alibi. Miglatokaⁿ.

igla't'a, v. To have convulsions. Miglat'a. Hohpáiglat'a, To cough convulsively. -- v. refl. (kat'a perhaps). (?). Caⁿ oⁿ - omani, i.e. to walk slowly without paying attention to anything. Bl.
igla't'e, v. refl. (yat'a perhaps). To give in, to grant. Miglat'e. WE.

igla'wa, v. refl. (yawa). To count one's self, to esteem one's self. Waśte - , To consider one's self good. Miglawa. Wakaⁿ iglawapi. Iyaglawa. B.H.111.5. Cf. waśteic'ila.

igla'yekiya, v. To push into, as a straw to clear out a pipe stem.

igla'yeya, n. A pipe stem cleaner.

igla'zo, v. pos. (icazo). To mark one's self; to make marks on one's own e.g. blanket. Iwaglazo.

igla'zuⁿta, v. refl. To praise one's self. Miglazuⁿta.

i'gle, v. To use abusive language, to murmur. Iwagle. Moses el iglepi. Wicaśa el iglepi. B.H.54.6;235.13.

igleb', cont. of iglépa. D.33.

igleb'kiya, v.a. To cause one to vomit up what he has eaten. Iglebwakiya.

igle'glehya, adv. (?). - śkaⁿ, To be busy with many things at the same time.
igle'glehyakel, adv. (?). - taku ecoⁿ, To perform fickly. - pahi, To pick up

good and worthless things. Bl.

igle'glep̄a, v. red. (iglepa). To vomit or throw up what one has eaten . Iwagleglepa.

igle'p̄a, v.n. To vomit, throw up on account of. Iwáglepa.

igli', n. The soft fat of animals, grease, oil.

iglo'aya, v. To pay attention to one's self. Bl. -- v. refl. (aya). To advance one's self, get along well. B.H.130.10.

iglo'eyaya, v. (?). Bl.

iglo'hi, v. refl. (hi). To bring one's self to a place, as a deer that might come to be shot. Miglohi.

iglo'i, v. refl. (i). To take one's self to, take one's own to. Migloi.

iglo'k̄u, v. refl. (ku). To bring one's self towards home. Migloku.

iglo'nica, v. refl. To forbid one's self, to balk, refuse to go, as also men may do. Iwaglonica.

iglo'u, v. refl. (u). To bring one's self towards a place; fig. to induce one, as by studying etc. to bring one's self into the Church or into doing something. Bl.

iglo'ya, v. refl. (ya). To take one's self to a place, to take to one's self. Migloya.

iglu', prefix. Affixed to verbs in "yu", making them the refl. form.

iglu'bleza, v. refl. (ibleza). To make one's self see or think clearly.

iglu'caŋze, v. refl. (yucaŋze). To hurt one's self and so get angry; to fail to accomplish something and so get angry. Bl.

iglu'ceya, v. refl. (yuceya). To do something and so have tears come to one's eyes. Bl.

iglu'coscoza, v. refl. To warm one's self at a stove. Same as okaliciya. Bl.

iglu'ecetu, v. refl. (yuecetu). To make one's self right; to reform, repent. Migluecetu.

iglu'ek̄icetu, v. refl. To make one's self right, as before; to raise one's self from the dead, as Christ did. Migluekicetu.

iglu'ğuka, v. refl. perhaps. To make a fool of one's self, exposing one's self. WE.

iglu'ha, v. refl. (yuha). To possess one's self, be free; to restrain one's self, act well; to be able to carry one's own goods etc. Miglúha.
iglu'haya, v.a. To cause one to be free. Iyeciŋka igluhaye. Pb.20.

iglu'hi, v. refl. (yuhi, perhaps). To busy or arouse one's self. Uŋkigluhipi kte lo, Let us get busy, arouse ourselves. Bl.

iglu'hik̄a, v. refl. (yuhika). To quit a job to do something that wants attention immediately. Bl.

iglu'hiŋhaŋ, v. refl. (yuhiŋhaŋ). To lose one's patience, one's temper on account of being teased and when one wants peace. Migluhiŋhaŋ. Igluhiŋhe wakapiŋ, i.e. too angry to.
iglu'hiŋheya, v.a. To get one excited and make one lose his patience. Igluhiŋhewaya. Bl.

iglu'homni, v. refl. (yuhomni). To turn one's self around. Migluhomni.
iglu'homniya, v.a. To cause one to turn himself around; to be converted.

iglu'huk̄uciyela, v. refl. To lower one's self. B.H.168.3.
iglu'huk̄ul, v. cont. of igluhukuya. - iyeic'iya, To put one's self down.
iglu'hukulya, v. refl. of yuhukulya.
iglu'huk̄uya, v. refl. (yuhukuya). To lower one's self, be humble. Miglu-hukuya.

iglu'ȟci, v. pos. (iyuȟci). To tear or break out one's own button hole or eye of a needle. Hehé iwágluȟci yelo. GA.

iglu'ȟica, v. refl. (yuȟica). To waken one's self up. Miglúȟica.
iglu'ȟil, cont. - uŋ wo, Keep your eyes open, watch out, keep awake. BT.

iglu'ȟlaȟlata, v. red. To scratch one's self much or many times. D.40.

iglu'ȟlata, v. refl. (yuȟlata). To scratch one's self; to pinch one's self. Miglúȟlata.

iglu'ȟloka, v. refl. (yuȟloka). To open or unbosom one's self, to open for one's self. Miglúȟloka.

iglu'ȟniġa, v. refl. (yuȟniga). To dress up. Miglúȟniga.

iglu'ȟopa, v. refl. (yuȟopa). To make one's self look pretty. B.H.112.9.

iglu'ȟtaniḱapiŋ, v. refl. (yuȟtani and kapiŋ). To be unable to move one's self, as when sick in bed, or when one is very lazy. Iglúȟtaniwakapiŋ. WE. Bl. Cf. igluśkaŋśkaŋ kapiŋ.

iglu'iṗaweȟtu, v. refl. To leave the straight road. B.H.119.20.

iglu'jaja, v. refl. (yujaja). To wash one's self. Miglújaja.

iglu'juju, v. refl. (yujuju). To take to pieces one's own, as one's own bundle. Miglújuju.

iglu'ḱawa, v. pos. (i and glukawa). To open one's mouth. Iwaglukawa.

iglu'kcaŋ, v. refl. (yukcaŋ). To have an opinion of one's self, to understand one's self; to examine one's self; to make up one's opinion. Miglukcaŋ.

iglu'ksa, v. refl. (yuksa). To break one's own. Migluksa. Yuŋkaŋ pa - .

i'gluksaŋ, adv. Around, round about anything. Migluksaŋ. Na waŋna ti igluksaŋ e enajiŋ.
i'gluksaŋtaŋhaŋ, adv. Around from all sides. Also, igluksaŋyaŋ, Round about.

iglu'ḱuya, v. refl. To humble one's self. Cf. igluhukuya.

iglu'k'eġa, v. refl. (yuk'ega). To scratch one's self, to itch self. Bl.

iglu'k'o, v. To take it all, as to take all in a game that has been staked. Same as glutiŋto. Bl.

iglu'najiŋ, v. refl. (yunajiŋ). To rise by one's self. Pb.15.

iglu'nuŋpa, v. refl. (yunuŋpa). To make two of one's self; to have two pursuits on hand at the same time. Miglunuŋpa.

iglu'ocoscoza, v. refl. (yuocoscoza). To make one's self warm by putting on much clothing. Bl.

iglu'oḱinihaŋ, v. pos. To make one's own honorable.

iglu'onihaŋ, v. refl. (yuonihaŋ). To honor one's self. Migluonihaŋ.

iglu'oŋśika, v. refl. (yuoŋśika). To humble one's self. B.H.215.7;232.14.

iglu'oṫa, v. refl. (yuota). To multiply one's self, to do many things at the same time; to multiply. Migluota. Pb.44. B.H.45.3.

iglu'otaŋiŋ, v. refl. (yuotaŋiŋ). To manifest one's self. Migluotaŋiŋ.

iglu'otkoŋza, v. refl. (yuotkoŋza). To have become equal to others; to have become ready with everything like others, as in having things ready for a trip while others are waiting etc. Bl.

iglu'owotaŋla, v. refl. (yuowotaŋla). To straighten one's self up, to stand straight; make one's self upright or righteous. Miglúowotaŋla.

iglu'psica, v. refl. (yupsica). To prance or jump about, as does a frisky horse. Miglúpsica.

iglu'ptaŋ, v. refl. To roll over. P.
iglu'ptaŋptaŋ, v. red. Icapśiŋpśiŋcala waŋ - iyaye. MS.570.
iglu'ptaŋyaŋ, v. refl. (yuptaŋyaŋ). To turn around; fig. to change one's mind. B. D.35.

iglus', cont. of igluza.

iglu'soṫa, v. refl. (yusota). To use one's self up, to finish speaking, perhaps; to use up one's own. Miglusota.

iglu'suṫa, v. refl. (yusuta). To make one's self firm, establish one's one's self. Miglúsuta.

iglu'suyakel, adv. In the state of being ready. - yaŋka, To be ready, be on the spot. - maŋkelo. Bl. Cf. yusú egle.

iglu'śaṗa, v. refl. (yuśapa). To blacken, to defile one's self. Migluśapa.

iglu'śica, v. refl. (yuśica). To make one's self bad, get one's self into difficulty. Migluśica.

iglu'śiḣtiŋ, v. refl. (yuśiḣtiŋ). To enfeeble one's self, injure one's self in any way. Migluśiḣtiŋ.

iglu'śka, v. refl. To untie, to loose one's self. Migluśka. D.220.

iglu'śkaŋśkaŋḱaṗi(ŋ), v. refl. (yuśkaŋ-śkaŋ-kapi). To be unable to move one's self, as a sick person in bed. Same as igluḣtanikapi. Igluśkaŋśkaŋwakapi. WE.

iglu'śloḱa, v. refl. (yuśloka). To put off one's own, to divest one's self of e.g. one's garments. Migluśloka.

iglu'śṗa, v. refl. (yuśpa). To tear off one's self, as pieces of skin, scab, etc.; to tear one's self loose. B.H. 25.5.

iglu'śṫaŋ, v. refl. (yuśtaŋ). To finish or complete the things pertaining to one's self. Migluśtaŋ. Wakaŋtaŋka el wocekiye eyiŋ kta na he - kiŋhaŋ, hehaŋl.... Lol'iḣ'aŋ nigluśtaŋ kiŋhaŋ caŋ k'iŋ uŋyiŋ kte. Bl.

iglu'ś'aḱa, v. refl. (yuś'aka). To be pregnant, be overburdened with one's self. Iglumaś'aka.

iglu'ś'iŋś'iŋ, v. refl. (yuś'iŋś'iŋ). To tickle one's self repeatedly. D.40.

iglu'ta, v. pos. (iyuta). To measure one's self, measure or try one's own. Imigluta.

iglu'ṫakuniśni, v. refl. (yutakuniśni). To destroy one's self. Miglútakuniśni.

iglu'taŋ, v. refl. (yutaŋ). To paint one's self; to put on fine clothes or dress. Miglutaŋ, uŋkiglutaŋpi. Hecel waŋna oyate k'oŋ iglutaŋpi, i.e. for the Sundance. Yupi piya iglutaŋpi. B.H.108.1.

iglu'taŋiŋ, v. refl. (yutaŋiŋ). To manifest one's self. Miglutaŋiŋ. Togyé - , To simulate.

iglu'taŋḱa, v. refl. (yutaŋka). To make one's self great. Miglutaŋka.

iglu'taŋtaŋ, v. refl. (yutaŋ). To touch as with one's dirty hands; to touch often.

iglu'tata, v. pos. red. (igluta, iyuta, yuta). 1) To measure one's self, to try e.g. a coat etc. 2) To try, attempt repeatedly. Kiŋyaŋ - yaŋka.

iglu'ṫeca, v. refl. (yuteca). To make one's self new. Migluteca.

iglu'ṫemni, v. To perspire. Miglutamni.

iglu'ṫiṫaŋ, v. refl. (yutitaŋ). To struggle to tear one's self away. D. 163;206.

iglu'tokaŋ, v. refl. (yutokaŋ). To remove one's self to another place. Miglutokaŋ. Bl.

iglu'toḱeca, v. refl. (yutokeca). To make one's self different, to disguise one's self. Miglutokeca.

iglu't'a, v. refl. (yut'a). To kill one's self. - wikaŋ oŋ, by hanging.

iglu'waḣṗanica, n. One who throws away everything he has, a squanderer, a spendthrift. Also, iglúwaḣpanicala.

iglu'waŋḱaṫuya, v. refl. To raise one's self, be proud. Migluwaŋkatuya.

iglu'waśṫe, v. refl. (yuwaśte). To make one's self good, make reparation for a wrong done.

iglu'waś'aka, v. refl. (yuwaś'aka). To strengthen one's self. Migluwaś'aka.

iglu'waza, v. refl. (yuwaza). To rub one's self, as on account of a little itching. Bl.

iglu'wi, v. refl. (yuwi). To wrap or tie on one's own, as one's leggings. Migluwi.

iglu'wiŋyeya, v. refl. (yuwiŋyeya). To make one's self ready, to get ready. Miglúwiŋyeya. Cf. kenuŋic'iya.

iglu'wiṫaya, v. refl. (yuwitaya). To concentrate. P.

iglū'za, v. refl. (yuza). To dress up, put on a dress; paint one's self. Migluza. Wicaśa waŋ ataya ska - . Takuwe migluze k'oŋ iyecel ecaŋnoŋ hwo? Also, to refuse to give up one's own, to defend one's self. IS. WE. Note: the word is used instead of aigluza.

i'gluzeze, v. refl. To hold up one's self by, to cling to. Imigluzeze. Iŋyaŋ kiŋ le he Wakaŋtaŋka tawa lakaś tohiŋni wakaŋśica yujujupi okihi śni ca ikce wicaśa he - icagapi. MS.658.
i'gluzezeya, adv. Clinging to.

iglu'zica, v. refl. (yuzica). To stretch one's self, to stand on tiptoe. Migluzica. Uŋgna tataŋka waŋ inajiŋ na - .

igmu', n. A cat. Note: this is an abbrev. of igmuśuŋkala, its original name. Bl.
igmu'gleśka, n. The spotted wild cat, the genet.
igmu'gleza, igmu'glezela, n. The bobcat; the tiger.
igmu'ħota, n. The gray wild cat, lynx.
igmu'śuŋka, n. The domestic cat. Bl.
igmu'taŋka, n. A lion; fig. an Indian inspector.
igmu'watogla, n. A mountain lion; a wild cat.

igmuŋ'ke, n. A snare, a trap; poison to trap with.

igna'gnayaŋ, v. red. (ignayaŋ). To sport with; deceive by. Iwagnagnayaŋ.

i'gnagnaye s'e, adv. (?). - aupelo, They are coming in(for the meeting) slowly, i.e. one after another. Bl.

igna'śkiŋyaŋ, v.n. To be possessed with, be demonized; to be crazy for or by reason of. Imagnaśkiŋyaŋ.

igni', v.a. To hunt, seek for, follow after e.g. game; to call names. Iwagni, uŋkignipi. Caŋ - yo. Śuŋkmanitu imagni, He called me a wolf. Na oyate kiŋ kośkalaka top iwicagnipi.

igni'gla, v.a. To go home for. Iwagnigla.

igni'ya, v.a. To go for, take a journey for, to procure.

ignu', v.a. To blame with, charge with. Iwagnu. Eya ignupi, To utter slander. B.H.113.11.

iġu'ġa, n. Rock, a rocky place perhaps. Hetkala - el ti. - otila, i.e. the name of a bird. Cf. D.262.

iġu'ġaoṫila, n. A bird that lives in the clefts of rock. Thus, iguga oti, To live in the clefts. Igugala ecel uŋ, na holhotala na caŋheya hiŋskokeca, i.e. a very small bird with white stripes. Bl.

iha', n. The lower lip; the lid or cover of anything.

iha'ħpi, n. Hanging lips.

iha'islaye, n. (iha-islaye). Grease for the lips, a lip ointment.

iha'ƙab, adv. After, i.e. in place; behind. Mihakab, uŋkihakab. Cihakab wauŋ. - yapi. Mihakab u po.
iha'ƙabya, v.a. To follow.
iha'ƙaṗa, adv. After, behind.
iha'ƙapaṫaŋhaŋ, adv. From behind.

iha'ƙicikta, v.a. (ihakta). To accept of, take of one. Ihawecikta.

iha'ƙikta, v. pos. (ihakta). To have regard for one's own. Iháwekta, and ihawakikta perhaps.

iha'kta, v.a. To see to, be intent upon; to watch over, guard; to have regard for, love; to obey, follow; to wait for one. Iháwakta. Ihamakta yo, Wait for me! said when one walks faster than the other. Bl.
iha'ktakta, v. red.

iha'kṫaṗila, n. A pet.

iha'ktaya, 1) v.a. To cause to have regard for. Ihaktawaya. 2) adv. Having regard for.

iha'mnapi s'e, adv. Much...(?). Waśpaŋka - ahimayakigle kiŋ le ibluśkiŋ. Bl. BT.

ihaŋ', v.n. To stand in or at, to remain. Iwáhaŋ, iuŋhaŋpi. Na ehake hakela ecela - keye. Yuŋkaŋ itaŋcaŋ k'oŋ hena witayela ihaŋpi na lecel eyapi. Wana niśnala inihaŋ, You are the only one left.

ihaŋ'bla, v. To dream, to have visions. Iwahaŋbla, uŋkihaŋblapi. Taku iyahaŋbla hwo? Tataŋka waŋ iwahaŋblelo. Yuwipi wasicuŋ ca iwicawahaŋbla.

ihaŋ'ceti, n. Shavings laid ready in the evening to start the fire with in the morning, i.e. caŋ lecel kajipapi uŋ haŋhepi ehaŋ uŋcetipi. - oŋ ipogaŋpi. Bl. B.

ihaŋg', cont. of ihaŋke.

ihaŋ'gǩiya, v.a. pos. To destroy one's own, to destroy for one. Ihaŋgwakiya.
ihaŋg'ya, v. (ihaŋke). To destroy, to bring to an end. Ihaŋgwaya. Cf. ihaŋkeya.
i'haŋ iyu'pta, (?). - wau welo. Bl.
ihaŋ'ǩe, 1) v.n. To end, come to an end. Imahaŋke. 2) n. The end, termination; the border, boundary. He - ca el s'a-hiyela okitipi. He ska akokiya - kiŋ el lecel womayakiyaka. Ti - el uŋglapi.

ihaŋ'keťa, adv. At the end, at the last.

ihaŋ'keya, adv. At the end, at the last or lowest part. Pte kiŋ tukte - cepe kiŋ iyuha awicuŋglipelo ca nakeś taŋtaŋ wayatiŋ kte lo.

Ihaŋ'ktoŋwaŋ, n. prop. (ihaŋke-toŋwaŋ). The Yanktons, name of one of the divisions of the Dakota people.

i'hatoŋ, v. To have chapped lips. Íhamatoŋ. Ihamatoŋ ca islawakiyiŋ ktelo. Bl.

ihe', v. (?). Cf. tikta. Iwáhe. Wayátiktil ihe, To nag, find fault with others when there is no reason for it. LB.

i'hecegla, adv. At once. B.H.108.23; 117.10. -- ihéceglala, adv. Right at that minute. Yuŋkaŋ - toŋwe.

i'heciya, adv. In that way from.
i'heciyaťaŋ, adv. In that direction from.
i'heciyaťaŋhaŋ, adv. On that side of.

iheci'yoťaŋ, adv. In that direction from. R.

i'hehaŋhaŋyaŋ, adv. red. of ihehaŋyaŋ.
i'hehaŋyaŋ, adv. So far from.

ihe'kiya, v. pos. To have remaining. Ihéwakiya. Hehe kola, iktomila s'e léceglala ihewakiye lo. Bl. Note: it implies one has but little left. Cf. D.56.

ihe'ǩtab, prep. Behind, after one. Mihektab. -- ihéktabya, íhektabya, iheǩťapa, adv. Behind. Mihektapa, Behind me. -- ihéktapaťa, adv. At the back, behind. -- iheǩťapaťaŋhaŋ, adv. From behind.

ihe'ya, v. To go or pass through; to discharge from the bowels; to shoot, hit. Mini ecela - . Wakaŋgli makata iheyapi. Waŋwicayaŋk - ke, i.e. saw them at once. Kaotaŋ - . Cuŋkaśka kiŋ óhiye waŋjila iheyapi, They had only one fence row left. D.92;58;271;28.

ihiŋ'haŋna, n. The day following, the next morning. Aŋpetu wakaŋ - , Monday. Na waŋna - el wiyoȟpataŋhaŋ wicaśa waŋ hihuŋni.

i'hiťi, adj. Insisting on one's own opinion. Taku owakiyaka naȟ'oŋ śni piyeleś - yelo, He does not listen to what I say. Caŋheyala s'e inihiti yelo. Bl.

iho', v. Behold, listen, be it so, see then. The imp. only is used. Iho le icinuŋpa wicoȟaŋ ecoŋ eśa lila śogya ecoŋ yawapi. Iho, miciŋkśi, lena aokagapi śni yo. Leci kuwo eya. Hecel ekta mni na el wai; yuŋkaŋ "Iho taku tokel slolyaye kiŋ olakiŋ kte lo", eya. Iho, misuŋ, waŋna yagni kta. Note: iho-wo and iho-po are doubtful derivatives of the word. Ito seems to infer arousing one to do something, the speaker including himself.

iho'eceś, adv. Just as well, might as well. - hecel ecuŋkoŋpi kte. Cf. itoeceś, itoceś.

iho'hucaťe, n. A big stone hammer to break up bones in order to get the marrow. Ihonicata, The small stone hammer used to pound cherries etc. with. Bl.

iho´nicata, n. A stone **hammer** to pound meat and cherries with. Ihóhucate, A large hammer used to break bones for retrieving marrow. Ohúⁿnicata, A club. Note: ihúnicata is incorrect. D.16.

iho´yeya, v.a. To utter with reference to, to pronounce. Uⁿgna...woyaśica ihoyeyaya kilo. B.H.67.16.

ihu´, v. An obscene by-word relating to copulation. Oⁿze ihu, To commit sodomy. Note: hu seems to be used alone.

i´hubloya, v. To strike on the lower part of the legs as punishment. Ihublowaya. Ihublociyiⁿ kta. Hecanoⁿ śni kiⁿhaⁿ, ihublociyiⁿ kte lo. IS.

ihu´ku kigle, n. Same as itkob u, or áⁿpo wicáhpi suⁿkáku. WE.

ihu´kukuya, adv. red. of ihukuya.

ihu´kul, adv. Under, beneath. Oyuⁿke - . - iyeya, To put underneath.

ihu´kuya, adv. Under, beneath anything, down below. Mihukuya.

ihuⁿ´ni, v.n. To reach, get across; to finish, to come to the end of. Iwáhuⁿni. Aⁿpetu 60 niopeyapi wauⁿ kte lo. Na he - kiⁿ ate ekta wagni kte lo. Hel uⁿkihuⁿnipi.
ihuⁿ´nikiya, v.a. To cause to reach.
ihuⁿ´nikiya, v.a. To go through with, finish, complete, as the reading of a book. Ihuⁿniwakiya. Waawaⁿyaⁿke k'uⁿ he ihuⁿnikiye. B.H.160.9.
ihuⁿ´niyaⁿ, adv. Clear through, entirely. Wicokaⁿhiyaye ci - taku talo ke eyaś yatapi kte śni. -- v.a. To cause to reach. Ihuⁿniwayaⁿ. Letaⁿhaⁿ hoanuⁿk ataya najiⁿyeyapi na ecel tipi he el anuⁿk ihuⁿniyaⁿ po. Waⁿna tipi kiⁿ ti ce kiⁿ hehaⁿyaⁿ - waśma kiⁿ.

ihu´pa, n. The bail or handle of anything; a stem, shaft, thill etc.; a wagon tongue, an axe-handle. - iyuhomni, A crank. P.
ihu´pakicitoⁿ, v.a. To put in a handle etc. for one. Ihupawecitoⁿ.
ihu´pakitoⁿ, v. pos. To bail or handle one's own. Ihupawetoⁿ.
ihu´patoⁿ, v. To have a handle, to be handled; to put a handle or bail to anything. Ihupawatoⁿ.

ihu´tab, adv. Down stream of, below.

ihu´tawab, prep. (?). The prefix i suggests the prep. Below (local), at the end of, as of the month. Waśiⁿ wakpa iyohloke el kitaⁿla - he ewicoti.

iha´, v. (i-ha). To laugh, laugh at, make fun of. Iwaha. Imaha.
iha´ha, v. red. (iha). To laugh at, make fun of, ridicule. Iwáhaha. - ia, To commit rape. - kuwa, To treat one like a boy, imitate him. Bl. BD.
iha´hake, n. One who is always jesting, a fool.
iha´haya, v.a. To cause to jest or laugh at. Ihahawaya. -- adv. Laughingly, jestingly. Pb.24.

iha´hpiya, iha´hpiya, adv. With hanging lips. Bl.

iha´ke, v. To laugh, jest. Iwahake.

iha´kiya, v.a. To cause to laugh. Ihawakiya.

i´haⁿhaⁿ, adv. Jestingly, in fun, not in earnest; for awhile. - el wauⁿ kte. - śuⁿkawakaⁿ bluha kte. - kiⁿ iⁿyaⁿkapi (without a prize), i.e. temporarily. - caje, A nickname. D.260.

iha´t'a, v.n. To laugh hard. Iwahat'a.
iha´t'at'a, v.n. To laugh immoderately. Ihamat'at'a.

iha´ya, v.a. To cause to laugh, be the occasion of laughter. Iháwaya.

i´hca, v.n. (i-hca). To be sure to have gone to, to be sure to be there. Ihciⁿ kte. Waíhciⁿ kta.

ihci´wahaⁿ, part. Broken out in gaps, gapped; torn, as a button-hole.

ihe´yab, adv. (?). Wicaśa kiⁿ le ayuśtaⁿ na - iyaya yo. B.H.203.8.

ihe´yata, adj. or prep. (heyata). Back from, behind. Miheyata. Tipi kiⁿ - , Back of the house.
ihe´yataⁿhaⁿ, adv. From behind.
ihe´yatataⁿhaⁿ, adv. From behind.
ihe´yatiyeya, v.a. (iheyata-iyeya). To thrust. P.

i´hli, n. or adj. A sore mouth. Ímahli.
ihli´, v.n. To have a sore or break-

ing out in consequence of. Imáhli.

i'hnahan, v.n. To have the under lip hanging down. Imáhnahan.

ihni'yanyan, v.n. To be troubled with, excited about. Imahniyanyan.

I'hoka, n. p. The name of a class or band of Tetons; the name of a dance, perhaps. - okolakiciye, The Badger Society, a military organization.

ihpa'ya, v.n. To fall, fall down; to become sick. Iwahpaya, iyahpaya, unkihpayapi. T'a ihpayapi.

ihpe'kiciciyapi, n. Throwing each other away, a divorce.
ihpe'kiciya, v. To throw away for or to.
ihpe'kiya, v.a. pos. (ehpeya). To throw away, forsake, leave one's own. Ihpewakiya. Note: ehpeya, however, does not exist.
ihpe'ya, v.a. To throw down, throw away; to leave, forsake. Ihpéwaya. Kaksa - okicaslel.

ihta'hepi, n. Before night, before the day is out.

i'htalihan, adv. (?).
i'htalihanhan, adv. (?).
i'htayetu, n. The next evening, the evening following the time mentioned.

ihu'haotíla, n. A sparrow. Cf. iguga otila.

ihun'win, 1) v.n. To smell of, to stink. 2) n. A bad smell, stink.

i'hwahwa s'e, adv. Slowly, in a drowsy manner, gradually. - igluwinyeya. L. Bl.

ih'an', v.n. (h'an). To do, work; do in ref. to; to be busy with something. Iwáh'an. Canpa - , i.e. picking, pounding, etc. cherries. Bl.

ih'e', n. A rock; gravel. Same as inyan. - tipi, A concrete building. Paha ska kin hel emaonpapi na - amakśu po.

ih'e'h'e canhlógan, n. The silky or low Townsendia, or perhaps more correctly the Townsendia ex scapa. Townsendia grandiflora. Composite family. Bl. #285.

ih'e' maká ceyáka, n. The long-flowered penny royal. Hedeoma longiflora. Mint family. It is used in wahanpi, soup, the leaves being stirred into it. Bl. #269.

ih'e' swū'la, n. Little stones, as found on ant hills or at the bottom of a river; gravel, fine rocks.

i'ic'icel, cont. (iic'icita). - un, To watch one's self well so as not to do anything wrong. Bl.

ii'c'igni, v. refl. (igni). To hunt e.g. game for one's self. Imic'igni. BD.

ii'c'ihaha, v. refl. (iha). To make one's self a laughing-stock, as is said of one who commits adultery. Imic'ihaha.

ii'c'ikcu, v. refl. (icu). To help one's self, take what one is to have. Imic'ikcu.

ii'c'iyun, v. refl. (iyún, iun). To rub on one's self e.g. medicine.D.257.

ii'gluge, v. To act absurdly, to blunder. Imigluge, inigluge. - yelo. Bl. Syn.- aikpablaya.

ii'glukse, v. refl. To break or cut off one's own for a purpose. "A" eyapi na nakpa - po, "Attention". MF. Cf. gluiyupse.
ii'kcu, v. To take or obtain what one expects. Ptan, he taku kin húnkeśni ca yuptanyan - canna ake luzahan hecel on tunkaśila ptan eyacajewicaśton. BT.

i'ikiya, v. To ask back what one has given.

ii'kpakinte, n. A napkin, anything to wipe one's mouth with. Bl.
ii'kpustan, v. pos. of ipustan.

i'ikputaka, v. pos. To kiss one's own, as one's relatives. Also, íiputaka, perhaps. Iiwakputaka.

i'inkpata, adv. At the point of anything.

i'iputaka, v. To touch mouths, to kiss. Iiwáputaka. Hehanl hiyu na iiputake na leya ... .

i'iślayataŋhaŋ, ii'ślayataŋhaŋ, adv. To the right side of. B.H.159.11;249.5;260.6.

i'itkob, adv. Cf. iitkopataŋhaŋ.
i'itḱopataŋhaŋ, adv. Returning the compliment, as in saying to another what is fitting to be said to him alone. R. Bl.

i'iyuwi, n. Something to tie around the mouth. Śuŋg - , A halter.

ijaŋ'jaŋ, 1) v.n. To give light, as a candle. 2) n. A light. -- ijáŋjaŋya, v.a. To light e.g. a candle; to cause to give light. Ijaŋjaŋwaya. -- ijáŋjaŋyaŋ, adv. Giving light for.

i'jata, adj. Forked-mouth, double tongued.

i'jehaŋ, adv. Among, into the midst. - iyaya, He went among them. Note: ijéhaŋ, cf.

ije'haŋ, adv. Often, frequently, repeatedly, right along. Śuŋkawakaŋ - bluha kte lo (a prayer). R.
ije'haŋyaŋ, adv. Often.
ije'haŋyaŋkel, adv. Frequently.

ije'na, adv. Mixed up, e.g. different kinds together.

iji'ca, v.n. To be rich in goods; thus in distinction from waśéca and iwáśeca, To be rich in provisions.
ijil'ya, 1) v.a. To cause to be rich. Ijilwaya. 2) adv. Richly.

iji'mna, v.n. To smell like something burning, as fat or bones or cloth.

i'jog, cont. of ijoka.
i'joḱa, v.n. To have the lips pushed out. -- íjoḱiya, v. To push out the mouth at, to twist the mouth; to whistle. Ijowakiya. Cf. jo.

iḱa'bluya, adv. Crushing fine. -- v. To crush to dust. - iyukpaŋ. B.H.240.14.
iḱa'caŋ, v.a. To sift or shake as in sifting. Iwakacaŋ.

i'kacaŋ, 1) v.n. To trot, as a horse does. 2) v.a. To adjust something carried on the back, as a baby, by jerking it upward. Iwakacaŋ.
i'kacaŋcaŋ, v.n. (?) (kacaŋcaŋ). To trot towards, as a horse does perhaps. - waŋna el u na tipi tiyopa aiyopteya waȟpe waŋ paslatapi ca haŋ.

iḱa'ġi, Cf. icagi.

i'ḱahaŋ, adv. So far from.
i'ḱahaŋyaŋ, adv. So far from.

iḱa'ḱeiŋ, (?). To lean on something bending (also applied to trees). WE. Cf. ikaki.

i'ḱaḱi, adv. On that side of.
i'ḱaḱiya, adv. On that side of.
i'ḱaḱiyataŋhaŋ, adv. In that way from, on that side.
iḱaḱi'yotaŋ, adv. In that direction from.

iḱa'mna, v. To rip by striking. Ogle - . Iwákamna.

ikaŋ', n. A cord, string, rope; the bail of anything. Also, wíkaŋ.
ikaŋ'cola, n. A bow-like spear used by members of the tokala okolakiciye. The same as the tokala tawahukeza, which is perhaps the tokala tawokoŋze.
ikaŋ'cola mas'a'ṗapi, n. A radio, a wireless. Also, mazacola winaȟ'oŋ, tatuye oŋ winaȟ'oŋ. - waŋ yuha s'elececa, as one would say to a woman who gossips much about other people.

ikaŋ'ḱicitoŋ, v.a. To put or tie a string or strap on for one to carry by. Ikaŋwecitoŋ. -- ikáŋḱitoŋ, v. pos. (ikaŋtoŋ). To tie a string on one's own pack to carry it by. Ikaŋwetoŋ. -- ikáŋtoŋ, v.a. To put a string or strap on a bag etc. to carry it by. Ikáŋwatoŋ. Na haŋpośpu hoksicala waŋ anok ikaŋtoŋpi ca yuhapi. -- ikáŋtoŋtoŋ, v. red. D.211.

iḱaŋ'yaŋ, v.a. To have for a string or handle. Ikáŋwayaŋ.

ikaŋ'ye, adv. Towards the center, as towards the fire.

iḱaŋ'yela, adv. Near to. Note: the better form seems to be ikíyela.

ikaŋ'yetaŋ, adv., n. The front; in front of. Mikaŋyetaŋ, In front of me.--

ikáŋyetaŋhaŋ, adv. On the river or lake side of an object; in front of. Mikaŋyetaŋhaŋ.

i'kaṗa, v.a. (i-kapa). To open the mouth on, talk loud to. Íwakapa. Ímakapa.
i'kaṗaka, n. One who scolds, perhaps; a talkative person.
i'kaṗas'a, n. One who scolds, a scold.

ika'ṗeya, adv. Beyond, more than.

ika'pta, adv. Through. - hiŋhpaya, To fall through.

i'kaskab, cont. of ikaskapa.
i'kaskabya, adv. Smiting on the mouth.
i'kaskaṗa, v.a. To slap on the mouth. Íwakaskapa.

ika'sli, v. To have one's self, a finger or so, bruised by something, as a door. Imákasli.

i'kato, v.n. To gallop, as does a horse.

i'kawawa, v.n. red. To move the lips, open the mouth often. Bl. Cf. íśpaśpa.

ikcaŋ', v. To want to do a thing but with you first trying it. Imákcaŋ.Bl.

ikca'pta, v. pos. (icapta). To be angry and talk badly. Mikcápta, uŋkíkcaptapi.

ikce', 1) adj. Common, wild, in a state of nature. Haŋpikceka, Moccasins. - wicaśa, An Indian person. 2) adv. For nothing, freely, in the common way. - mac'u, i.e. gave it for nothing. - heya. B.H.230.9.
ikce'ka, adj. Common.
ikce'kce, adv. red. of ikce.
ikce'kceka, adj. red. of ikceka. Pb.24
ikce'kceya, adv. red. of ikceya.
ikce' okśúpi, n. A muzzle loader (shot gun). Also, akicita tamazawakaŋ. Bl.
ikce' wicáśa, n. Common men, wild men; Indians, not white men.
Ikce'woaie owe opa, n. p. A Democrat.P
ikce'woaiepi, n. Democracy. P.
ikce'ya, adv. In a common manner, commonly, ordinarily; freely, wildly, naturally. Lehaŋl - waŋwicalakapi kte lo, i.e. they see spirits without being wakaŋ. - u wanice, He does not come without a special reason. WE.
ikce'yakel, adv. Ordinarily.
ikci'a, v. (ikce-ia). To speak frankly truthfully. - niwánicelo, You are a liar. BT.

iki'bleza, v. (i-kibleza). Cf. kibleza
iki'caga, v.n. (icaga). To become, to grow to be. Imakicaga.
iki'cazo, v.a. (icazo). To take credit of one. Iwecazo. Imicazo.
iki'cicaga, v.n. (icaga). To grow for one. Imicicaga.
iki'cicu, v. (icu). To take or get for one. Iwecicu. Imicicu.
iki'cigni, v. (igni). To hunt something as deer etc. for one. Iwécigni.
iki'cihaŋ, v. (haŋ). To remain for one. Imicihaŋ.
iki'cihahapi, v. recip. They laugh at each other.
iki'ciksaṗa, v. (iksapa). To be wise for one, instruct one in the right way. Iweciksapa.
iki'cilowaŋ, v. (ilowaŋ). To sing to one, to praise one for another. Iwecilowaŋ.

i'kiciŋ, v.a. To desire something for what one has given or will give. Iweciŋ. Iwakiciŋ. Bl.

iki'ciyukcaŋ, v. (iyukcaŋ). To judge of or from another opinion about anything for another. Iweciyukcaŋ. Imiciyukcaŋ. Iciciyukcaŋ.

iki'ciyuŋ, v. (yuŋ). To rub on for. Iweciuŋ or iweciyuŋ. B.H.199.2.

iki'ciyuśkiŋ, v. To congratulate. P.

iki'ciyuśtaŋ, v. (iyuśtaŋ). To take care of e.g. a sick person. Iweciyuśtaŋ.

iki'co, v.a. To invite to, as to eat corn or meat. Iweco. Imico.

iki'gni, v. pos. To hunt one's own.

iki'ha, v. pos. (iha). To laugh at one's own. Iwakiha.
iki'haha, v. red. (ikiha). To make fun of one's own.

iki'h'aŋ, v. (?). Iwakih'aŋ. To, ka cik'ala imákih'aŋ yo, said when a sick person wants something and one gives it to him. Bl.

iki'jica, Cf. ijica. Tuŋkaśila mazaska iśnala - kte. BT.

ik̄i'kcu, v. pos. (icu). To take back what one has given, to take one's own. Iwekcu. Hece wicaśa kiŋ maza wakaŋ - na ekta - .

ik̄i'k̄iyela, adv. red. (ikiyela). Near to many things, as houses; ikiyéla, Near to one thing.

ik̄i'ksab, v. cont. of ikiksapa.
ik̄i'ksabya, 1) v.a. To cause one to be wise in ref. to his own. Ikiksabwaya. 2) adv. Wisely, cautiously.
ik̄i'ksap̄a, v.n. To be wise for one's own, to consult. Iwákiksapa.

ik̄i'k'o, v. To be excited by tumult. Waná hiŋhaŋna caŋke taku ħmuŋ s'e ikik'opi, It was morning and the camp was in an uproar. Taku ikik'opi, There was an uproar about something. B.H. 239.4;263.3. D.269,78.
ik̄i'k'ok'o, v. red. (ikik'o). To create a disturbance, in ref. to many. B.H.250.7.

ik̄i'nica, v.a. To grab, try to get something, as a bunch of dogs a cat, or boys candy. Na el Pehiŋ Haŋska, i.e. Custer, nataŋ hi na ecel iwicakinicapi. Na waŋna heyoka uŋmapi k'oŋ cega k'oŋ ikinicapi.
ik̄i'nil, v. cont. (ikinica). To try to get, where persons are crowded together grabbing for or trying to get; to kill, each trying to kill. - awicaupi.

ik̄iŋ't̄a, v.n. Same as ipiŋta. Imákiŋta. Bl.
ik̄iŋ't̄eśni, adj. Dull, as a knife, axe etc. that cannot be used. Kaŋ iẃapsake waŋ imicikiŋteśni, i.e. my knife is dull. BD. Bl.

ik̄iŋ'yela, adv. Nigh to, ref. to time and place. Tipi waŋ ena haŋ ca - śuŋkawakaŋ kiŋ hu pawicaħtiŋ na tipi k'oŋ tima i.

iki'p̄acica, Cf. kipacica. Waŋ, owekiŋś hiŋ imayakipaciciŋ kte lo.

ik̄i'p̄ajiŋ, v.a. (kipajiŋ). To quarrel with one for or on account of anything. Iwakipajiŋ. B.
ik̄i'p̄ajiŋyaŋ, adv. Opposing. Tawaciŋ - , Denying one's self. B.H.214.12;70.8.

ik̄i'p̄aŋ, v.a. (kipaŋ). To call to one for something. Iwakipaŋ.

ik̄i'p̄atitaŋ, v.a. To push one sideways as in running a race and trying to beat one. Iwakipatitaŋ. Imakipatitaŋ. WE.
ik̄i'p̄emni, v. To wrestle with and take away from. Imakipemni. Bl.

ik̄i'p̄i, v. (kipi). To need for one's self. - śni, To be unworthy. Imakipi śni, I am not worthy. - śni iwaŋglake. Mazaska ota - . Uŋkikipipi kte. B.H. 55.15;111.5;175.3;202;226.16;295.15. Pb.31.
ik̄i'ya, v. To assist, to side with, take sides with. Same as iciya, perhaps, which cf. Jesus el imayakiyiŋ kta iceciciye. B.H.46.12;297.1. Pb.10.

ik̄iye'la, adv. Cf. ikikiyela.

ik̄i'yuŋ, v. pos. (iuŋ). To rub on one's self. Iwakiuŋ or iwakiyuŋ. Uŋkikiyuŋpi. Nape maka - .
ik̄i'yuŋyuŋ, v. red. To rub on one's self, in ref. to many. Na wana pejuta iśta noŋge ko ikiyuŋyuŋpi.

ik̄i'yut̄a, v.a. To measure out to, perhaps. Makoce kiŋ yuśpaśpaya iwicakiyuta. B.H.73.13.
ik̄i'yuwi, v.a. To bridle, to put a rope in the mouth of one's horse. Obs.
ik̄o'ak̄at̄aŋhaŋ, adv. Across the river from. B.H.203.3.
ik̄o'glamnaya, v.a. To get ahead of somebody and put one's self in the way; to get before, as a horse by making short cuts or a round-about way. Ikoglamnawaya. Also, ikoglamnayaŋ iyaya. Bl.

ikō'k̄ab, adv. Before, out in front in both time and place. Tka he - Taśuŋke Luzahaŋ tokeya waŋ eyapi.

iko'k̄top̄awiŋġe, adj. The one thousandth.

iko'pa, v.a. To be afraid of, fear e.g. some event. Ikowapa. B.H.136.16. Pb.45.
iko'p̄egla, v.n. To be in the state of fear on account of. Ikopewagla.
iko'pek̄iya, v.a. To cause to

be afraid of or for. Ikopewakiya.

iko'yag, cont. of ikoyaka. - iyeya.
iko'yagya, 1) v.a. To fasten to, as a horse to a cart; to join one thing to another; to clothe, put on. Ikoyagwaya. 2) adv. Fastened to. - haŋ, Standing fastened to.
iko'yagyakel, adv. Fastened to. B.H. 76.7.
iǩo'yaǩa, v.n. To adhere to, stick to, to be fastened to. Ikomayaka, ikouŋyakapi. Na talo tukteni ikoyake śni. Ate, nata catkayataŋ winawizi waŋ imakoyakiŋ kte lo. Na heoŋ ceȟpi ekta waconica taŋka inikoyaka.

iǩo'ze, v. To shake, move with the hand. Iwákoze. Na le caŋ eya wiyaka iyakaśkapi kiŋ hena icu na "lena huŋka - yelo" eya.

ikṗa'ǧaŋ, v. refl. (pagaŋ). To spare one's self, yield up one's self. Mikpagaŋ.

ikṗa'ǧe, n. The notch in the end of an arrow by which the string is pulled backwards. - ecela taŋiŋyaŋ wao welo, i.e. shot the arrow so deep that only the notch is visible. Bl.

ikṗa'ǧica, v. refl. (pagica). To wake up. Ikpagica po. Bl.

ikpa'hi, v. refl. pos. (pahi). To pick up for one's self. Nuŋpa caŋ kipiya ikpahipi. B.H.55.17.

ikṗa'huŋhuŋza, v. refl. pos. of pahuŋhuŋza.

ikṗa'ȟloǩa, v. refl. (paȟloka). To pierce through, make a hole for one's self, as the muskrat does. Mikpáȟloka. Hecena kéya śina kiŋ etaŋhaŋ ikpaȟloke na mini mahel wíyuśkiŋśkiŋ.

ikṗa'ȟṗa, v. refl. (paȟpa). To throw one's self off, as from a horse. Mikpaȟpa.

ikpa'ǩiŋťa, v. refl. (pakiŋta). To wipe, rub one's own. Mikpakiŋta. Na peji ȟota oŋ ikpakiŋtapi. Cf. kpakiŋta.

ikpa'kiśkija, v. refl. (pakiśkija). To make sore by rubbing perhaps. Iśta kiŋ - na lila ic'icuwa. B.H.119.15.

ikṗa'kṗi, v.n. To pick a hole, break a hole, as a young chicken in its shell; to hatch out one's own; used in ref. to chickens. R.

ikpa'k'eǧa, v. To rub one's self against something to stop from itching. Mikpak'ega. Cf. ikpáwaza, said of animals; and igluwaza.
ikpa'k'eȟk'eǧa, v. red. of ikpak'ega.Bl.

ikṗa'pťaŋ, v. refl. To turn one's self over, to roll over. Mikpaptaŋ. D.216.
ikpa'pťaŋpťaŋ, v. red. (ikpaptaŋ). To turn one's self over, roll over, as when not sleeping well; to toss. Bl.
i'kpapťaŋyela, adv. In the manner of rolling over. - ȟci wahihuŋni yelo.BT.

ikpa'śloka, v. refl. (paśloka). To slip out of, as out of a too big suit; to take off. B.H.87.5.

ikṗa'taka, v. pos. To lean on one's own, to brace one's own.

ikṗa'ťaŋ, v. refl. (pataŋ). To be careful of one's self. Mikpataŋ.
ikṗa'ťaŋyaŋ, adv. Taking care of one's self, carefully.

ikṗa'tiťaŋ, v. refl. (patitaŋ). To push along, as a boat with a pole, to steer a boat.

ikpa'waza, v. refl. To rub one's self against something, as cattle do on a tree. (Sapa gleśka kiŋ) mniyatki na hehaŋl caŋ waŋ el inajiŋ na ikpawazahe. D.257.

ikṗa'zo, v. pos. To show one's self. Mikpazo.

ikṗi', n. The belly, abdomen.
ikṗi'gnag, cont. of ikpignaka. - iyeya.
ikṗi'gnagya, adv. Placed in around the belly.
ikṗi'gnaka, v.a. To place in or put around the body, as a blanket when tied around one. Ikpiwagnaka. Inawaye ciŋ ikpimagnake wi 7 k'el matoŋ welo. BT.
ikṗi'paťaŋhaŋ, adv. In around the body.
ikṗi'sǩayayuŋka, v. To lie with the belly turned up, as a dog does.
ikṗi'yonapa, v. To take shelter in; to flee toward. Ikpiyonaciṗelo, wawatiŋ kte lo, as a man would say coming in and wanting to eat. Bl.

ikṗu'kṗa, adv. Mixed up, as people of different nations dwelling together, or as different kinds of corn growing together in the same field.
ikṗu'kṗeya, adv. Same as ikpukpa.

i'ksab, v. cont. of iksapa.
i'ksabya, v.a. (iksapa). To make anything to do anything. Íksabwaya.

iksab'ya, 1) v.a. (ksapa). To make wise for or concerning. Iksábwaya. 2) adv. Wisely.
iksa'ṗa, v.n. To be wise about anything. Iwáksapa.

i'ksaṗa, v.n. To be much engaged about something, to be unfortunate, not to obtain; to be burdened with e.g. other people's troubles. B.H.129.22. Note: ímaksapa.

i'kśiŋƙiya, v.a. To make faces at. Also, perhaps ikśiŋƙiya. Íkśiŋwakiya. Ikśiŋmakiya.

ikṫa'hela, adv. Moderately, carefully, gently. Bl.

ikṫe', v. (kte). To kill with anything. Iwákte.
ikṫe'ƙa, n. Something to kill with, as a gun. - manica, I have nothing to kill with.

ikṫo'mi, n. A spider; a fabulous creature like the fox in English folk lore. - s'e ciŋca ota laḣcak, as is said of little people who have many children. - tawókaśke, A spider web. Cf. Uŋktomi. Note: wókaśke, A place of imprisonment. But children may be heard to say: Iktomi tahókaśke; but that is wrong. Bl.

iku', n. The chin.
iƙu'hu, n. The chin.

iƙu'ja, v.n. To be sick or indisposed on account of. Imákuja.

iƙu'ka, v.n. To be decayed by reason of, worn out by; to be boiled to pieces together with.
iƙu'ƙeya, adv. Rotten or boiled to pieces with. - śpaŋ, It is cooked all to pieces.

i'ƙusaŋ, n. A mink, a small kind of mink with a light-colored jaw. Mustela vison lacustris. Also, íƙusaŋla.

iƙu'śe, (?). Woecoŋ kiŋ le - najiŋ.
iƙu'śic'iya, v. refl. To prevent one's self.
iƙu'śetoŋ, v.a. To block the way with something. Iŋyaŋ taŋka waŋ ikuśetoŋpi na kiglapi. B.H.269.12.

iƙu'śeya, adv. In the way of. B.H. 114.3;230.2.

iku'ta, (?). Noŋpegnakapi - ewicoti.

iƙu'ṫe, 1) n. Ammunition, something to shoot with, a gun. Icute, however, is the better form. 2) v.a. To direct something against another. Wicoḣ'aŋ śica imayakutepi, i.e. bad work directed against one. B.H.88.13;41.13.

i'ƙuteka, v. To throw hints. B.H.99.

i'ƙutƙuteƙa, v.n. To make trial, to endeavor beforehand to know how one can succeed, for instance, in asking for anything. Iwakutkuteka.

ik'e'ġe śni, adj. Dull, as a knife which cannot be used to scrape with. Kaŋ íwapsake waŋ imicik'ege śni, or imicik'iŋte śni. Bl.

ik'o', v. To get worried. Ik'opi kta, i.e. the same as ilitapi kta. Bl.

ilag', v. cont. of ilaka.
ilag'ya, v.a. To cause to serve, have for a servant; to make use of. Ilagwaya. B.H.251.13.

ila'ƙa, v.a. To have for a servant, to control, govern, rule over. Iwalaka.

ila'zaṫa, adv. Back from, behind something. Milazata, By my side, perhaps. Wicaśa waŋ nilazata najiŋ he k'oŋ he tuwe he? Ce - najiŋ.
ila'zaṫaŋ, adv. From the side of, perhaps
ila'zaṫaŋhaŋ, adv. In the rear of, behind, from the side of perhaps. Paha zizipela el - hel wicoti na etaŋ zuya aya.

ile', 1) v.n. To burn, to blaze. 2) n. A blaze.

i'leciya, adv. On this side of.
i'leciyaṫaŋ, adv. On this side of.
i'leciyatanhaŋ, adv. From this side of, in this way from.
i'leciyotaŋ, adv. In this direction from.

ile´ǧa, v.n. To shine, glitter, as do stars. Wicaȟpi waŋ lila ilege ciŋ he waśtewalaka. MS.1.

i´leǧa, v.n. To speak evil about somebody, to spoil one's reputation. Same as yatakuniśni. Iḿalega; wayatakuniśni. BD.

ile´ǧe, n. A burning thing, a light. - mak'u wo; iwaglataŋ kte, Let me have your burning (cigaret); I want to light mine.

i´lehaŋ, adv. So far off.
i´lehaŋhaŋ, adv. red. of ilehaŋ.
i´lehaŋyaŋ, adv. So far off. Ilehaŋyaŋg egnaka. Ilehaŋyaŋg ic'icuwa yo. Bl. Cf. alehaŋyaŋg.

ileȟ´, cont. of ilega.
ile´ȟleǧa, v. red. (ilega). To shine, sparkle, twinkle, as the stars. Hehaŋ wicaȟpi iyuha lila - waśteśte. MS.1.
ileȟ´ya, 1) adv. In a shining manner. 2) v.a. To cause to shine. - caŋnuŋpapi, - úŋpapi, A cigar. Bl.

ile´nilyakel, (?). - wanasapi, i.e. hunting the few remaining buffalo. Bl.

ile´ya, v.a. To burn, cause to burn, to set fire to. Ilewaya.

ili´ṫa, v. (?). Ilitapi kte lo, i.e. the same as: Ik'ópi kte lo. Bl.

ili´ṫaka, v.n. To be animated for, be brave for or on account of. Ilimataka.

ilo´ciŋ, v. To be hungry on account of. B.H.111.11.

ilo´waŋ, v.a. (lowaŋ). To sing to or for, to sing the praises of, to praise one. Iwalowaŋ.

ima´cuka, express. colloq. That gets me, i.e. implying one has a liking for a person or thing. Same as maktéka. Inicuka.

ima´ǧaǧa, v.n. (magaga, perhaps). To be amused with, cheered by. Imamagaga.
ima´ǧaǧaic'iya, v. To recreate self.

ima´ǧajuya, v.a. To cause to rain by means of something. B.H.157.7.

i´mahel, adv. Within.

ima´helwapa, adv. Towards the inside, inwards.
ima´heṫa, adv. Within. - mayázaŋ.
ima´heṫaŋhaŋ, adv. From within.
ima´heṫu, adv. Within.
ima´heṫuya, adv. Inwards, within.
ima´heṫuyaḱel, adv. In the inside of, within.

ima´ȟ'aḱaṫe, n. A cultivator. WL.

ima´ni, v.a. (mani). To walk to or for a thing. Imawani, imauŋnipi.
i´mani, v. To go home. Iḿawani. Miś eya imawani kte lo, I too shall go home. Imauŋnila kte lo. Bl. WH.

ima´s'oyuspe, n. Pincers, tongs.
ima´ziyapa, n. A hammer.

i´mna, v.n. To be satisfied, to have sufficient of. Iḿamna, iúŋmnapi. Tawaoŋspe kiŋ woitoŋpeyapi na imnapi. B.H.171.19. Cf. woimna.
i´mnahaŋ, adv. Satisfied, to satisfaction, enough, sufficiently.
i´mnahaŋhaŋ, adv. Sufficiently, very much, awfully. - iȟaȟa.

imna´haŋhaŋ, n. Part of the guts of animals, perhaps the fourth or smallest manyple of animals.

i´mnahaŋyaŋ, adv. Sufficiently.
i´mnahaŋyaŋkel, adv. Very much, a great deal, sufficiently. - ecoŋ.
i´mnaic'iya, v. refl. (imnayaŋ). To fill self with food, to satisfy one's self with. D.28.

imna´yaŋ, v.a. (mnayaŋ). To gather together by means of. Imnawaya.

i´mnayaŋ, 1) v.a. To fill, satisfy. Iḿnawaya. 2) adv. Filled, satisfied. - wotapi. B.H.208.15.

imni´cahu, n. Same as omnica hu. Strophostyles pauciflora. Bl. #292.

imni´ciya, v.n. To make an assembly for some purpose. Imnimiciya.

imni´coyapa, (?). Haŋp'ceyaka waŋ imnicoyapelo. Bl.
imni´ja, (?). Ehaś - s'e cepelo, as is said of an unusually fat man or animal Bl.
imni´śtaŋ, n. Water running from the mouth. - au, To drivel, slaver. - mau, The water is running from my

mouth. Śiyó śuᶯka s'e - ȟ'eȟ'eya yaᶯkelaȟ. Bl.

imni'ťaᶯ, v.n. To spread out. -- n. A flood. - kiᶯ u. B.H.71.18;195.16.
imni'ťaᶯyaᶯ, v.a. To flood. Imnitaᶯwaya. B.H.7.12.

ina', n. Mother, my mother.

ina'blablaza, v. red. (inablaza). To burst open because of something. B.H. 112.17.

ina'blaska, v.n. To tramply under foot. Inάwablaska. Aᶯpetu topa kiᶯhaᶯ caᶯku kiᶯ - iȟpeyapi kte lo, i.e. the sand will be trampled hard and flat. Bl.

inab'ya, adv. Taking refuge in, sheltered by. Tipi - wauᶯ. Cf. inapa.

ina'ġihaha, v.n. To feel scared hearing something. RF.

i'nagnaka, v. (i-nagnaka). To have the lips twitch. Ímanagnakelo. Bl.

ina'hahaya, adv. Loosely, as wood corded badly.

ina'ȟci, v.a. To pierce and have the hold break out of anything, to have the hold break out, as of a stirrup. Inάwaȟci.

ina'ȟco, Cf. naȟco.

ina'ȟloǩa, v.a. To wear a hole with the foot by means of something, as in one's moccasins or stockings. Inawaȟloka. Haᶯpa iᶯyaᶯ inawaȟloka, I have worn a hole in my moccasins on a stone.

ina'ȟma, v.a. To hide, keep secret, conceal. Also, v.n. Inawaȟma. Cf. D.56.

i'naȟma, v.a. To seduce, to commit fornication or adultery with one. I'nawaȟme. - s'e (secretly) mila waᶯ oglikiyi na yuha tima iyaye. D.272. Cf. wiinaȟma.
i'naȟmaᶯpi, n. Seduction.
ina'ȟmayakel, adv. Secretly, unknown to others. B.H.105.14.
ina'ȟmeǩiciciyapi, n. The game of hide and seek. Inaȟmekiciciya ecoᶯpi. Bl. Note: inaȟmekiciyapi is incorrect.

ina'ȟmeǩiya, v.a. To hide from, conceal from one. Inaȟmewakiya.
ina'ȟmeya, adv. Secretly, slily, covertly.
ina'ȟmeyahaᶯ, adv. In secret, secretly.

ina'ȟni, 1) v.n. To be in haste, in a hurry. Inawaȟni. 2) adv. Quickly, in haste. - ecoᶯpi.
ina'ȟnikel, adv. In a hurry. B.H.253.16.
ina'ȟniǩiya, v.a. To cause to make haste, to hasten one. Inaȟniwakiya.
ina'ȟniṗi, n. A hastening, haste, hurry.
ina'ȟniya, v.a. To hasten one, make hurry. Inaȟniwaya.
ina'ȟniyaᶯ, adv. In haste, hastily.
ina'ȟniyela, adv. Same as inaȟniyaᶯ.

ina'ȟṗe, n. (naȟpa). That which is stepped on and sets off a trap, the pan of a trap.
ina'ȟṗela, n. dim. of inaȟpe.
ina'ȟuġa, v. To mash by stepping on. Same as naȟúġa. Inawaȟuga. Cf. inakuka. -- inάȟuȟuġa, v.a. To mash up or crash by trampling on. Inawaȟuȟuga.

ina'ȟ'uȟ'u, v. To scatter with the feet what has been piled up. - ahiyu élale. Bl.

ina'jabjapa, v. red. of inajapa. Bl.
ina'jabya, (?). Bl.
ina'jabjabyela, adv. (?). Waníśiṗeś śicála tanuᶯka śni k'oᶯ, nakeś sipa kiᶯ - yaglilotake. Bl.

i'najalyeya, v. To keep the mouth open. Bl.

ina'japa, v. To wear out the tip of one's shoes. Bl.
ina'jiᶯ, v.n. To rise up to one's feet, to step to. Inawajiᶯ. Miwaᶯkab hinajiᶯ na amayugata. Yuᶯkaᶯ isakib inawajiᶯ. -- inάjiᶯǩiya, v.a. To cause to stand up, to raise up.

i'nakiȟma, v. pos. (inaȟma). To entice away one's own. Inawakiȟma.

ina'ǩikśiᶯ, v. To take shelter in or behind, to make a shelter of, as of a tree. Inawakikśiᶯ.
ina'ǩiᶯlya, v.a. (?). Wóloťa kiᶯ inakiᶯlmaya upelo, i.e. want to borrow from me, but I will not do it. Bl.
ina'ǩiᶯťa, v. To be able in no way to finish a job. Inawakiᶯta. Haᶯkeya inakiᶯtelo. Bl.

ina'ƙiṗa, v. pos. (inapa). To take refuge in one's own; to trust in something that sustains some relation to myself. Inawakipa.

ina'ƙiwizi, v. pos. (inawizi). To be envious of one's own relations, to be jealous of one's own. Inawakiwizi.

ina'ku, n. His mother. Also, huŋku. BL. Cf. ateku.

ina'kuka, v. (nakuka). To crush or destroy with the foot. Inawakuka.

ina'k'eȟya, v. To make a scraping noise as a wagon brake. Huínak'eȟye.

ina'k'esya, adv. Near by, along side of.

ina'mni, adv. Beyond, over, as over the hill from. Yuŋkaŋ blo - pte hotoŋpi.

i'naŋgnaŋg, cont. of inaŋgnaŋka.

i'naŋgnaŋka, v. To move the lips, as in reading to one's self. Ímanaŋgnaŋka.

ina'pa, v.n. To come out, to get things; to live through e.g. a winter; thus, to take refuge in, to take shelter in or from a storm, or any evil; to trust in. Inawapa, inauŋpapi. R.

ina'paŋ, (?). Aŋpetu yamni kiŋhaŋ caŋku kiŋ ataya - iȟpeyapi kte lo, i.e. the snow will be packed and hard after three days. Bl.

i'napcapca iyéya, v. To suppress one's anger, to swallow one's anger, not answering. Tuwa taku waŋji eniciye c'eyaś - yo; hececa kiŋ nicaŋte kiŋ suta kte lo. - owamani yelo. Bl.

ina'pciyuŋ(g)yuŋƙa, adj. red. (napciyuŋka). Every ninth one.
i'napci(ŋ)yuŋƙa, adj. The ninth.

i'naṗeya, 1) v.a. To cause to come in sight or come out of, cause to appear on the other side; to shoot through; to cause to live through, as through a winter; to cause to trust in. Inápewaya. 2) adv. Appearing; trusting in; coming in sight. Also, inápeya. R.

ina'ṗiśkaŋ, v.a. To waste things foolishly.Ináwapiśkaŋ.
ina'ṗiśƙaŋyaŋ, v. To do little things, to pass away time, to kill time. Inawapiśkaŋyaŋ.
ina'ṗiśƙaŋyaŋpi, n. Toys, playthings.

ina'ṗoṫa, v.a. (napota). To wear out e.g. one's moccasins by some means. Ináwapota.

ina'psaƙa, v.a. (napsaka). To break off e.g. a string with the foot, by some means or other. Inawapsaka.

ina'pśa, v.n. To make a noise, as one walking with water in his moccasins. Inawapśa. -- inápśapśa, v. red. of inapśa. Ináwapśapśa.

ina'ṗṫa, v.a. To wear out a thing, e.g. a shoe. Inawapta.

ina'pṫeca, v.n. To be prevented by. Inapṫecaśni, Not to be prevented by anything. Inamápteca śni. Maza śala waŋji wagluśna inaniptecapelo, cicupi amáyalúhetepi eś kolakiciyapi waśte kiŋ heuŋcapi kta.

i'nap'ibiyeya, v.a. To drop the lower lip, as when on the point of crying, i.e. to contract the muscles below the mouth, as is specially noticed in children. Ínap'ibiyemaye, ínap'ibiyeuŋyapi.

i'nap'ip'iyeya, v.a. To make one start crying, i.e. to drop the lower lip (nap'iŋ) before crying, as is noticed in babies. Inap'ip'iyemayelo. Bl.

i'nasaƙa, (?). Ínamasaka. Iśta caŋ inamasaka, i.e. when a splinter flew in one's eye. Bl.

ina'sli, v.a. To crush with the feet. Ináwasli.

ina'śloƙa, v. To pass on beyond; to wear through, wear out something, as shoes; to get one's self away, escape, as from danger; to slip off, as a cover from something. Ináwaśloka.

ina'take, n. (i-nataka). A fastener, i.e. a bolt, lock, bar; a fence; a fort etc.

i'naťaŋ, v.a. To press upon with the foot. Siíŋataŋ, Something on which the foot presses, thus, stirrups.

inā'ťibya, v. To roast humidly, as meat on coals; to make curl up.

ina't'aǧe, n. The brake of a wagon. Cf. huinak'eȟye.
ina't'aȟya, 1) v.a. To use the brake on a wagon. Cf. inak'eȟya. 2) adv. In a sliding, careful way. - ya, To walk carefully on slippery ground so as not to fall, walking in a sliding way.

ina'wizi, v. To be jealous, to be envious of. Inawawizi.
ina'wizipi, n. Jealousy, envy.
ina'wiziya, 1) v.a. To cause to be jealous. Inawiziwaya. 2) adj. Enviable. P.

ina'ya, v.a. To call mother, have for a mother. Ináwaya.

ini', v.n. To take a vapor bath, to steam one's self; to take a sweat. Iwani, iyani, uŋkinipi. To make this bath wakaŋ, one would wash and steam himself four times by pouring water over hot stones and accompanying this with singing etc. This is done ceremonially after killing an enemy or a royal eagle. R.

ini'haŋ, v.n. To be scared, frightened or amazed, be astonished. Imanihaŋ, uŋkinihaŋpi.
ini'haŋpi, n. Amazement. Cf. wowinihaŋ.
ini'haŋšni, adv. Fearlessly, persistently. Lila kutepi eśa - hiyaya.
ini'haŋšniyaŋ, adv. Persistently. B.H. 213.6.
ini'haŋya, v.a. To frighten, scare, amaze, astonish one. Inihaŋwaya. Optelyela inihaŋmayaŋpelo. Bl.
ini'haŋyaŋ, adv. In amazement.

ini'hiŋciya, v. To be alarmed on seeing etc. something because of something else. Heya naȟ'oŋpi k'uŋ hecena - hiŋglapi. B.H.67.5;172.4;128.1. Bl.
ini'hiŋciyešniyaŋ, adv. Fearlessly. B.H.302.18.

ini'ǩaǧa, v.n. To make "ini", to take a vapor bath, or an initi, iniopa. Inikagapi wókeya, A sweatlodge.

ini'la, adj. Still, silent. - maŋka.Bl. - agliyagla. Inila uŋ, A gentle snake.
ini'laya, v.a. To cause to be silent, make still. Inilawaya.

ini'opa, v.n. To take a vapor bath with others.
ini'p̄i, n. A steaming, sweating.

ini'ti, 1) n. A sweat-house. 2) v.n. To take a vapor bath; to make a little house and sweat in it. Iniwati.

ini'ťiyukťaŋ, 1) n. The little booth fastened on two poles and drawn by horses or dogs, in which babies are transported. 2) v. To bend willows over for a booth. Initibluktaŋ. Bl.

ini'woǩeya, n. A sweat house.

ini'ya, v.a. (niya). To breathe from. Iwaniya.

i'niyaŋ pejúta, i'niyaŋpi, n. Annual erigeron; erigeron annuum. The buckwheat family. It is so called because it is used for children with sore mouths (i); a tea is made from the whole plant; also it is used as a tea for those who cannot urinate well. Oŋ wahiŋyuŋtoŋpi. BT.
i'niyaŋpi, n. Cf. iniyaŋ pejuta. Also, an Indian child's sickness, i.e. soreness of the mouth. Bl.

inum', cont. of inuŋpa.
inu'mnum, cont. of inumnuŋpa.
inu'mnuŋpa, adv. Every second one.

inuŋ'pa, adj. The second.

i'nuŋpa, n. (i-nuŋpa). Two mouths. Mazakaŋ - , A two-barrelled gun.

inuŋ'waŋ, v. To swim. Bl.

iŋ, adv. of negation. Same as hiyá. Obs. BT. -- v.a. To wear around the shoulders e.g. a blanket. Waíŋ, yaiŋ, uŋk'iŋpi. Śina hiŋ akatahaŋ iŋ. BD.
iŋ, iŋ'šǩa, interj. Expression of hesitancy when not finding the right word at once. Let me see.

iŋǩi'ya, v.a. To cause to wear e.g. a shawl. Iŋwakiya.

iŋ'kp̄a, n. The end of anything, the

small end, the head or source, as of a stream. Yuŋkaŋ caŋ - kiŋ iwaŋkam gla na ecel ataŋiŋśni iyaya.
iŋ'kpat̆a, adv. At the end, at the head or source; upstream, above.
iŋ'kpat̆ahaŋ, adv. From the end, from the head of, as of a stream.
iŋ'kpat̆aƙiya, adv. Upstream, towards the head of a stream, as opposed to hútabya, Downstream.
iŋ'kpat̆ala s'e, adv. Near the head or top of something. Oŋjiŋjiŋtka wakpala he el okijata el - ewicoti.

iŋ'ska, interj. Of hesitancy: Let me see; Wait a minute. Also, iŋska iŋ. B.H.47.2.

iŋ'sƙoƙeca, adv. So large. Na tacaŋ kiŋ śuŋkawakaŋ tacaŋ -.
iŋ'sƙoƙiníca, v.n. To be doubtful which is the largest. Also, híŋskokinica (hiŋsko-akinica).

iŋś, conj. Same as naiŋś. Hecel uŋglipi na lila el ewacaŋmi wawate eśa - imuŋka ko. - waŋyaŋka yo. B.H.90.8. Note: ko usually ends the sentence.

iŋ'śe, adv. perhaps. Just, only; implying excuse or explanation. - eca ca ecamoŋ, I did it only for fun. -le śuŋgmanitu tawote ca wauŋ welo. Wanikaŋ śni tka - hetataŋka pizi waŋ ota latkaŋ ca oŋ aiyahaŋble lo. Kola, niśnala gla po, ena waŋ kte, eya śke'. Yuŋkaŋ oyasiŋ "Hiya, lena - waniyetu el icagapi ca osni kiŋ okihipelo" eyapi'. - he toka śni śka hepelo. Le - oyate wowicawak'a kta ca lecamoŋ, i.e. an excuse. Also, of course, evidently. Mini kiŋ hel iȟpeyapi ehaŋtaŋś niyayiŋ kte ciŋ he (keya kiŋ) slolkiya; iciŋ kéya kiŋ mini mahel uŋpi, tka - wicagnayaŋ. Eya takuni ota epiŋ kte śni tka - takuku iciyuŋgiŋ kte lo. B.H.88.13;306. D.71,77;20, note 1. Gram.201.

iŋ'śeśekel, Same as úŋśkeyapika, lotkuŋkeśni. - he wóyak maśipi k'uŋ, I was supposed to say that, but I had forgotten all about it.
iŋ'śeśelakeś, 1) n. An instance. 2) adv. For instance. P.
iŋ'śeyapika, Same as uŋśkeyapika. MN.

iŋś he'cel, iŋś he'ce, express. It is all the same to me. That is all right I do not care, so the saying goes.

iŋś to'ka, iŋś tok', express. Or else? Used at the end of a questioning attitude. Ho, eca, ina-iyokihe kiŋ he - . D.9. B.H.198.2.

iŋ'ś'uŋmakeci, Cf. uŋś'uŋmakeci.

iŋ'yaŋ, n. A stone, stones. - cega, A stone jar. - icaȟmuŋ, A sling.

iŋ'yaŋg, cont. of iŋyaŋka. - ble kta, I will go on a run. - śkaŋ.

iŋ'yaŋha, n. A sea-shell.

iŋ'yaŋȟe, n. A rocky hill.

iŋ'yaŋƙa, v.n. To run. Waimnaŋka, yainaŋka, uŋkiŋyaŋkapi. Pte cepa waŋji cepa kici wimnaŋkiŋ kta. Note: this may be the same word as: i-yaŋka, ya-i-naŋka, wa-i-mnaŋka.

iŋ'yaŋ kapémni, n. A stone war-club.
iŋ'yaŋ maká, n. Cement.
iŋ'yaŋ óŋyeyapi, n. A sling to throw little stones with.
iŋ'yaŋ sápa, n. A slate.
iŋ'yaŋ śa ók'e, iŋ'yaŋ śók'e, n. A place at Black Pipe where is found red earth to paint with. Bl.
Iŋ'yaŋ Woslál Haŋ, n. p. The Standing Rock agency. D.222-223.

io'ape, n. An hour. - yamni hehaŋl, Three hours after this. B.H.283.6.

i'oblula, n. A sheltered place where the wind does not blow.

io'glamniyaŋ, adv. Following around the curves, as of a stream.

i'ogmus, v. cont. (iogmuza). - maŋka, I keep my mouth shut. - yatapi. - yuza To gag. - gluza, To clamp one's palm over one's mouth. D.268,2,6.
i'ogmusya, v.a. To cause to shut the mouth.

i'ogmuza, 1) n. A closed mouth. 2) v.n. To have the mouth shut, to lay the hand on the mouth. Íowagmuza.

io'gnag, v. cont. of iognaka. -- íogna-

gkiya, v.a. To put into the mouth of another, to give to eat, cause to eat. Iognagwakiya. B.H.144.3.
io'gnagya, v.a. To cause to put into the mouth, give food to. Iognagwaya.

io'gnaka, v.a. (i-ognaka). To put into the mouth e.g. food. Iowagnaka.

i'ohitika, adj. To be brave in words, pugnacious.

i'ojugjuya, v. red. Wata kiŋ nupiŋ iojugjuyapi. B.H.186.12. Cf. iojuya.

i'ojula, adj. (ojula). Full to the brim.
i'ojulaya, v. To make full, to fill. Aŋpetu tahena pustag mahiŋgniiojulawayelo, i.e. will do much work today. Bl. -- i'ojuya, v.a. To fill to the brim. Iojuwaya. B.H.71.18.

io'kapaza, v.n. To be pungent in the mouth, as pepper. Also, iokáza. Iowakapaza. BD.

iō'katan, v.a. To nail one thing on another; to nail and hold an axe on the other side to buttress. Also, i'okataŋ. Iowakataŋ. BD.

iō'kawiŋh, adv. Following around the circle.

io'kogna, adv. In the midst, between. B.H.7.11.

io'kpakpas, adv. Moving the lips. - yaŋka.

i'omaka, n. The year next to, the next year. B.H.78.5;112.1.

ioŋ'śila, v. (oŋśila). To have mercy or compassion on one in ref. to something; to grant, bestow. Ioŋśiwala.
ioŋ'śilaya, adv. Having compassion on one in ref. to something.

i'oŋwiyúta, v. To make a motion with the mouth, to gesture to one with the mouth. Ioŋwibluta.

io'pawiŋge, adj. The one hundredth.

iŏ'stan, n. (ośtaŋ). A cork, stopper for a vial etc.
io'śtaŋpi, n. Same as iośtaŋ.

io'wa, n. (owa). Something to write or paint with; a pen or pencil.

i'owoic'iśloka, v. To dig out in a hurry some turnips e.g. Iowomic'iślokiŋkta ca hecamoŋ we. Bl.

i'oyaśkaŋ, v.a. To get one to talk. Ioblaśkaŋ. Ioblaśkaŋ na oŋ lila woglake. PO.

io'yuspe, n. A handle. B.H.60.11.

ipa', Cf. talipa.

ipa', n. The top of anything, the high end hill of a ridge; a cape, a promentory etc. are said to be he ipa. - k'el akaŋl iyotakayo; hecoŋ na taŋyaŋ wákitayo. Bl.

i'paceka, v.a. To push and make stumble. Iwápaceka. Bl.

ipa'cica, v.t. (?). Pehiŋ kiŋ ipácicapi s'e, as is said when a man's hair is disheveled and pressed down. Bl.

i'paga, (?). Hiŋhaŋna kiŋ waŋcag - mauŋhipi ktelo, i.e. go on a buffalo hunt. Also, ipahe, perhaps. - eyuhpapi, To rest someplace before reaching the place assigned for dinner. Bl.

ipa'gaŋ, v. (pagaŋ). To push aside, as a tent door, for the purpose of looking out.

ipa'gloka, v. To be dislocated, as a joint, by anything.

ipa'gmuŋg icu', v. cont. (ipagmuŋka). To dip up e.g. water with a vessel. Cega kiŋ mni kiŋ ekta ipagmuŋg ojula icu waciŋ, i.e. tried to dip out a pailful of water. D.223.

ipa'gmuŋka, v.n. To be capable of being dipped up with a bucket.

ipa'go, n. (i-pago). Something to carve or engrave with, a carving implement.

ipa'goya, adv. Passing by, exceeding in length or size; exceeding in speed, as when one horse outruns another.

ipa'ha, v. (?). - iyeya, To raise up e.g. a curtain, to hoist up. Wipa kiŋ

- égle. D.196-7.

iṗa'hiŋ, 1) v.n. To lean the head against, to have for a pillow. Iwapahiŋ. 2) n. A pillow.
iṗa'hiŋk̇itoŋ, v. To rest; to make a resting place out of.
iṗa'hiŋya, v.n. To have for, use for a pillow. Ipahiŋwaya.

iṗa'hotoŋpi, n. A pop-gun, as the Indians used to make them.

iṗa'ȟlala, adv. In a row, facing one way, lined up like soldiers in rank formation. Also, ipaȟlalya, ipaȟlaȟlalya. - najiŋpi. - au, They came on lined up. Catku el - ewicagnaka. Óṡpaṡpaye ecel - au. - k'iŋ caŋglákiŋyaŋ, A four-horse evener. D.77.

iṗa'ȟlok̇a, v.a. To make a hole in, to punch through.

ipa'ȟna, adv. (?). - o, To shoot an arrow through something so the point is visible on the other side (not said of bullets). Caŋke apaha najiŋ na - o, He stood aiming at it and then sent his arrow piercing it. - iheya. Sb. D.193. Note: R. gives ipaȟdaŋ. Cf. D.117.
ipa'ȟnaheya, adv. Right through. Same as ipázeya. - yazaŋ. Cf. D.112, ipaȟna o, To pierce.

iṗa'ȟo, v. To brush up, as hair from the forehead, to brush into a curl. Iwapaȟo.

ipa'ȟṫe, n. (i-pahta). Something to tie up with, a string.

i'paȟṫe, n. A bridle. Note: i-paȟta.

iṗa'jiŋ, v.n. To be prevented by something from proceeding; to come to a stand, not to be able to go on. Imapajiŋ.

i'ṗajiŋ, v. To resist difficulties, to overcome difficulties, to go on bravely, not to fear dying. Iwapajiŋ.

iṗa'jiŋyaŋ, adv. Prevented by, in opposition, opposing.

iṗa'jiṗa, v.a. (pajipa). To stick in, to prick with. Iwapajipa.
iṗa'jiṗe, n. Something that pricks, a pricker.

iṗa'juŋṫa, v.a. To give when it is not wanted, to force upon one. Iwápajuŋta.

iṗa'k̇a, v.n. To draw back, as meat from ribs when cooked, or as husks of corn when ripe. Iwápaka. - yuha, To hold together like a bunch of feathers, grass, etc., i.e. a handful. Bl.

iṗa'k̇iŋja, v. To rub, as one's eyes with the hands. Iwapakiŋja.

iṗa'k̇iŋṫa, v.a. To wipe off. Iwápakiŋta
iṗa'k̇iŋṫe, n. (i-pakiŋta). Something to wipe with, a towel.

iṗa'k̇oṫe, n. A probe.

iṗa'kśaŋ, n. A bend in a river etc. D.249.

iṗa'la, n. Something corresponding to sausage. Same as ipá. Nata kiŋ - s'e wau welo (or wauŋ welo), as is said when a man has lost his hair above the forehead. Bl. Note: cf. talipa (talo-ipa).

iṗa'maŋ, v.a. (pamaŋ). To rub, rub on, as in filing. Iwapame.
iṗa'me, n. Something to rub with or to file with. Caŋ - , A file. Waŋ - , A stone with which to rub arrows.

iṗaŋ'hoyeya, adv. Screamingly, above the natural voice. Note: der. perhaps from paŋ-hoyeya.

iṗa'psak̇e, n. A small knife for cutting porcupine quills.

iṗa'pṫaŋ, v. To turn over. - eȟpeic'iya, To turn one's self over. Bl.

iṗa'ṗuza, n. Something to wipe dry with, a towel.

iṗa'saŋ, v.a. To put on white paint with the end of a stick, make white dots, to rub on and whiten with. Iwapasaŋ.

iṗas'haŋ, n. Anything that comes through and holds; a trip, or trigger, a small iron that comes over and holds a set trap; a needle.

iṗa'sisa, v.a. To stick in, as a needle

or pin; to fasten, as with a wiping screw. Iwápasisa.
iṗa'sise, n. (i-pasisa). A pin.

ipa'sli, v.a. To crush by pressing against something. Iwápasli. Si kiŋ maya - . B.H.68.12.
i'ṗasliya, 1) v.a. To press one against the wall. Iwapasliya. 2) adv. Pressing against something. Tiipasliya yaza yo, Hold him against the wall. Bl.

iṗa'sminyaŋ, n. The ram rod for a gun. Mazawakaŋ - . BD.

iṗa'sotka, adj. Conspicuous, extending up, as a tall tree or steeple; one thing larger or taller than others, as the protruding ends of the logs in a log cabin. Bl.
iṗa'sotkaya, adv. Conspicuously. Tipi - , A high house, a tower. Bl.

iṗa'sṗa, v.a. To drive in, as tent pins. Iwapaspa. R. Bl.

iṗa'spaya, v.n. To become wet, as by sitting on moist ground. Bl.

iṗa'swayazaŋ, n. Pleurisy.

iṗa'śkica, v. (paśkica). To rub, as clothes on a wash board. Iwapaśkica.

iṗa'ślog, cont. of ipaśloka. - iyeya.
iṗa'śloka, v.a. To draw off over the head e.g. a shirt; to live through, as through a winter or a sickness.

iṗa'śpeyuŋk, (?). - iŋyaŋka, To run close together and jolt one another, as in a narrow path. Bl.

iṗa'ta, v. To embroider; to work quill work, work with quills of the porcupine. Iwapata. Haŋpa waŋ lila yupiyela iye he - , i.e. embroider with porcupine quills. Haŋpa k'el glakiŋkiŋyaŋ ipatapi. D.226-7.

iṗa'tag, cont. of ipataka.
iṗa'tagtoŋ, v.a. (ipatake-toŋ). To brace out or stretch, as in drying hides and skins. Ipatagwatoŋ. Cana kiŋ caŋ ipatagtoŋpi s'e iŋyaŋke, To run with feet far apart. Bl.
iṗa'tagya, v.a. To cause to brace out or up; to sustain, reinforce. Ipatagwaya.
iṗa'taka, v.a. To stretch out by means of cross-sticks; to have for a staff or support, be dependent upon. Iwapataka.
iṗa'take, n. (i-patake). A prop or brace, a stick to stretch a skin on. Siŋkpe ha - , A stick to stretch a muskrat skin on.

iṗa'taŋ, n. A prop or brace. Tuśu - toŋ wo; wakiŋyaŋ ukiye eyaś lila tate kte lo. Bl.

iṗa'taŋ, v.a. To mash up one thing on another. Iwápataŋ.

iṗa'taŋgle, v.a. To brace.

iṗa'taṗi, n. Embroidery, ornamental work.

iṗa'tkuġa, adv. Abreast, in a row, in a phalanx. R. Bl.
iṗa'tkuhya, adv. In a row, abreast. R. Bl.

iṗa't'iŋza, 1) v.a. To make firm by means of. Iwapat'iŋza. 2) n. (i-pat'iŋza). Anything that makes firm, sustenance, nourishment.

iṗa'waġa, v. To rub, scrub or scour e.g. a floor. Iwapawaga. Pehiŋ kiŋ ipawagapi s'e hpayelo, With uncombed or matted hair.... Bl.

iṗa'weġa, v.n. To bend across, to intersect, come into or cross, as one road does another. Perhaps obs.
iṗa'weh, cont. of ipawega. - ecoŋ, To do something incorrectly.
iṗa'wehwehya, adv. red. of ipawehya.

iṗa'wehya, 1) v.a. To cause to intersect. Ipawehwaya. 2) adv. Crossing, instersecting; aside, out of the way; incorrectly.

iṗa'wiŋta, v.a. To rub on with. Iwapawiŋta.

iṗa'zeya, iṗa'seya, adv. Right through, as a pain runs right through the chest. - mayazaŋ. RF. Rh. Pershaps obs. Cf. ipásisa.

iṗa'zica, adv. Bulged out, as a tent when one leans against it.

ip̂a'zilya, adv. Convex, as opposed to skokpa. - haŋ. Tipi - , A high house, tower. Bl. Bt.

ip̂e'sleťaŋhaŋ, adv. (?). Taŋcaŋ kiŋ ȟpaya tka k'uŋ hel - iyotakiŋ na .... B.H.271.4.
ip̂e'slete, (?). - tka k'uŋ hel, When his head had been lying. B.H.109.10.

i'pi, adj. Full, satisfied as from eating. Ímapi. Mazaska - nit'e. Íwicapi. BT. B.H.55.8. Cf. wíp̂i.

ip̂i'ğa, 1) v.n. (piga). To boil e.g. water; to foam. 2) n. The foam of boiling water.

ip̂i'glag, cont. of ipiglaka.
ip̂i'glagǩitoŋ, v.a. To put on one's girdle, gird one's self. Ipiglagwetoŋ.
ip̂i'glagtoŋ, v.a. To put on a girdle, to be girded. Ipiglagwatoŋ.
ip̂i'glaǩa, v. pos. (ipiyaka). To put on one's own girdle. Ipiwaglaka.
ip̂i'glaǩe, n. A girdle.

ip̂iȟ', cont. of ipiga.

i'p̂iic'iya, v. refl. (ipiya). To fill one's self with. Mini ipiic'iyapi. B.H.55.25.

ip̂i'la, v.a. To deny to, refuse to give, withhold from, as too good for one. Ipíwala. Pel'ipimayala ca nacicipiŋ ktelo, i.e. your room is cold. Bl. D.202, note 3; 53, note 2.

ip̂i'laye, n. Something that gladdens.

ip̂iŋ'ťa, v.n. To be defective in some part, be too short or too little, be not as usual. Imapiŋta. R. Bl.

i'p̂iya, v.a. To make full, to fill. Ípiwaya.

ip̂i'yag, cont. of ipiyaka.
ip̂i'yagǩicitoŋ, v.a. To put on a girdle for one, to gird one. Ipiyagwecitoŋ.
ip̂i'yagǩitoŋ, v.a. pos. To put on one's girdle, to be girded. Ipiyagwetoŋ.
ip̂i'yagtoŋ, v.n. To gird, put on a girdle; to be girded, perhaps. Ipiyagwatoŋ.

ip̂i'yaǩa, v.a. To gird one's self, to put on a girdle. Ipiblaka. Ipiyakasapa íkuje, A strap buckle. Ipiyakasapa iyúȟloke, A harness punch. Ipiyakasapa uŋzoǧe, Cowboy riding pants (uŋzoge hiŋśma).
ip̂i'yaǩe, n. A girdle, sash, belt. Ipiyake kśúpi.

ip̂i'ye, n. Something to repair with.

ip̂o', n. A swelling.
ip̂o'ǧaŋ, v.n. To breathe out, exhale. Iwapogaŋ. - yo, i.e. to make fire blaze by blowing at it. Bl.
ip̂oȟ', cont. of ipogaŋ. - iyeya, To blow on, blow in, blow away.
ip̂oȟ'ya, 1) v.a. To cause to breathe out, exhale. Ipoȟwaya. 2) adv. Blowing, perhaps.

ipsi'ca, v.n. To jump down from, to jump, jump over. Iwapsica, uŋkipsicapi. Cokaŋ inajiŋ na uŋgnahela jiŋlhiŋgni na tokaŋl - .
ipsil', cont. of ipsica.
ipsi'psica, v. red. (ipsica). To hop, as a grasshopper.
ipsi'psil, red. of ipsil. - iyaye. B.H.280.10.

ipśiŋ'cala, (?). Ité - kaca, as they say of a man with a small and wrinkled face. Bl.
ipu'ȟniyaŋ, adj. Anxious, eager, in a hurry to do something, as horses, i.e. yapi ciŋpi.

ip̂u'skep̂a, n. A strainer. P. Bl.

i'p̂usǩica, v.n. To be close to, to touch, press on. Ímapuskica. - wicaśa ota hipi. Bl. -- íp̂usǩil, cont.
i'p̂usǩicela, adv. Pressed close together. - iyotaŋkapi, They sit close together.
i'p̂usǩilya, 1) v.a. To cause to press on. Ipuskilwaya. 2) adv. Pressed together. Also, íp̂usǩisǩil. - iyeya, To shove close together.
i'p̂usli, v.n. To be close to, to press upon, to touch anything. Imapusli.
i'p̂usliya, 1) v.a. To cause to press on. Ipusliwaya. 2) adv. Touching. Makipusliya, On the ground.

ip̂u'sp̂a, v.a. To stick, paste, glue on. Iwapuspa. -- ip̂úsp̂e, n. Anything that sticks to, as a seal, a wafer. - s'e yaŋkelo, He holds his peace.

iṗu'sṫag, v. cont. of ipustaka. Makipustag iḣpeic'iya, To throw one's self on the ground.

iṗu'sṫaka, v.n. To be flat; wanting, defective. Imapustaka.

iṗu'sṫaŋ, adv. (?). - yuza, To clap up against, as a coal of fire. Bl.

iṗus'ye, n. Something to dry on or with, a dryer. Same as wiṗusye.

ipu'ś'iŋ, n. The outside of a bend or curve, as in a river. Bl.

iṗu'tag, cont. of iputaka.
iṗu'taḱa, v.a. To touch, kiss. Iwápu-taka.

i'ṗuza, v.n. To have the mouth dry, to be thirsty. Ímapuza.
i'ṗuzapi, n. Thirst.
i'ṗuzat'a, v.n. To die or be dying of thirst, to be very thirsty, to suffer from thirst. Íṗuzamat'a.

ip'ō', n. (p'o). Steam.

ip'o'za, v. Cf. ip'ozeca.
ip'o'zeca, v.n. To be out of humor about anything. Imap'ozeca.

isab'ye, n. Blacking.

isa'ḱib, adv. On the side of, along side of. Caŋku - iyotaka. Mísakib, At my side. Uŋkísakib akiyagle, They passed by on the side of us.
isa'ḱibya, adv. On the side of, beside. B.H.36.19.

i'sam, adv. (isaŋpa). Beyond that place or time. Hecel - iblabla. Yuŋkaŋ - (beyond the woods) lila wicoti na lila iyokipi.
isam'tu, adv. More than. Same as isaŋbtu, isaŋpatu. Wicataŋcaŋ kiŋ he wokoyake kiŋ - śni hwo? B.H.193.23.
isam'ya, adv. Further on, on the other side of, beyond. Also, isamyá. - hehaŋl. Misamya waś'agya uŋpi. Bt.
isam'yeś, adv. More than before, all the more. B.H.261.11;263.2.

Isaŋ'aṫi, n. prop. The Santee Indian, so called because they used to stay long at the place where they got the material for their stone knives, hence isaŋ-ati, i-saŋ (knife). WE.

i'saŋb, adv. (isaŋpa). More than. B.H. 67.19.
i'saŋbtu, adv. More than. Same as isamtu, isaŋpatu. B.H.252.18;193.23.
i'saŋbya, Cf. samya. Misaŋbya waś'agya uŋpi. Taku kiŋ oyas'iŋ - caŋteciciye. B.H.78.
isaŋ'pa, adv. Beyond that place or time; more than. Taŋyaŋ ecaŋnoŋpi kiŋ ake - ecaŋnoŋpi kte lo. Inisaŋpapi. Isáŋpapi, Those beyond, far away.
i'saŋpaṫaŋhaŋ, adv. From beyond that, beyond. Yuŋkaŋ - makoce waŋ lila caŋwape to na makoce kiŋ togéla yuŋká.
i'saŋṗaya, adv. More than. Niyepi kiŋ hena wicinisaŋpayapi śni hwo? B.H. 193.26;194.6.

isaŋ'yaŋ, v.a. To communicate the whiting e.g. from one's robe to another by rubbing against. Isaŋwaya.

Isaŋ'yaṫi, n. prop. Same as Isaŋati.

isa'ṗa, v.n. To be blackened by anything. Imasapa.

isi', (?). (i-si). - wagluha kte, I am going to go. Na - el ite makipastoya gliḣpic'yi na wopila eye. Pb. 235.

isi'ṫuṫece, (?). - śni u, To come well prepared, having made all preparations. LC. Cf. iśitutece śni.

isi'yaṫaŋhaŋ, adv. Near the feet of. Taŋcaŋ kiŋ ḣpaya tka k'uŋ hel iyotake ca. B.H.271.4.

i'sḱuya, adj. The mouth watering for. Ímaskuya.
i'sḱuyagla, v.n. To have one's mouth water for anything, as for different kinds of food. Ískuyawagla.
i'sḱuyeya, v.a. To make one's mouth water for; to salt, thus to sweeten (skuyewaya), perhaps.
isla'ye, n. Ointment, salve. - ojuha, An oil bag.
islol'ya, v.a. To know by means of. Islolwaya. D.246.
isṗaŋ'sṗaŋheca, n. Ironwood, hornbeam. Of the ostrya virginica, the birch family, perhaps. Its flowers look like hops, the leaves like those of the elm tree. It was used for bows and its blossoms for painting the face; hence the saying: Śa wóilag

ota yelo. Also, American hop hornbeam, iron wood, lever wood; itúhu caŋ, caŋ maza, uspaŋspaŋheca. R. BT. Bl. HM. # 19.

isti'koyagya, v.a. perhaps. To hold with the arms. B.H.77.24.
isti'hohiya, v. To reach with the arm. -- adv. Within arm's reach.

isto', n. The arm of a person; the lower part of the arm, perhaps.
isto'glukatiŋ, v. pos. To stretch out one's arm. Istowaglukatiŋ.
isto'gluksaŋ, v. pos. To bend one's arm.
isto'iyohiya, 1) v. To reach with the arm. Istoiyohiwaya. 2) adv. Within arm's reach.
isto'katiŋkiya, v.a. To cause to stretch out the arm. Istokatiŋwakiya.
isto'paksaŋ, n. The bend of the arm.
isto'paksija, v. To bend the arm. Istowapaksija.
isto'staka, adj. Tired in one's arms. B.H.56.2.

isto'śniśkiye, v. To squint with one or two eyes. Cf. iśtokśiŋkiye.

isto'yeya, v. To stretch out one's hand or arm. Same as napeyeya. Bl.

isto'yukaŋ, v. To have arms. Istómayúkaŋ.

isto'yukśija, v. To bend up the arm. Istóbluksija.

iswu', n. Small stones.
iswu'la, n. dim. (iswu). Gravel.

iś, pron. He, she, it. Iś iye, He himself.

iśa'gloġaŋ, adj. The eighth.
iśa'glogloġaŋ, adj. red. Every eighth one.

iśa'kowiŋ, adj. The seventh.
iśa'kowiŋwiŋ, adj. red. Every seventh one.

iśa'kpe, adj. The sixth. -- n. A six-shooter, a pistol.
iśa'kpekpe, adj. Every sixth one.

iśa'mna s'e, adv. perhaps. Reddish. Na hocokam oyate kiŋ - oimniciye, The whole crowd seemed to be red.

iśi', v. To pay wages. Iwaśi. -- n. perhaps. Wages.

iśi'ca, v.n. To be hurt, harmed, injured. Imáśica. Bl. D.59. Cf. iwicawaśte.

iśi'cawaciŋ, v.n. To be greedy, covetous, desiring more.

iśi'cola, adv. Without remuneration. Cf. wiśi.

iśi'gla, v. (śigla). To be angry about. Iśilwagla, perhaps.

iśi'htiŋ, v.n. To be feeble from, be injured by, enfeebled. Imaśihtiŋ.

I'śikciŋ, adv. Angrily, crossly. Also, iśiŋhciŋ, iśikciŋ, but not iŋśiŋkciŋ. - kuwa, To treat somebody mean. C. P. GV. Note: it is der. perhaps from i-śica-ciŋ.

iśi'kiciŋ, v. To want pay. Iśiweciŋ.

iśi'kigla, v.n. To be angry on account of; to be sad about, affected by or for. Imaśikigla.
iśi'kiglaya, v.a. To make angry by, to make angry and torment, to afflict for. Iśikiglawaya.

iśil' áya, v. To be bad on account of. B.H.155.15.

iśiŋ'htiŋ, v. (?). Bl.
iśiŋ'kihtiŋ, v. (?). Iśiŋwehtiŋ. Bl.

i'śiŋl, adv. Quickly. - kah wacaŋmi tka owakihi śni.

iśi'tutece śni, adv. Being equipped with everything before starting on a journey etc. Syn.- wapikiyece śni.LC.

iśka'hu, n. The ankle bones. Caŋhaŋpa - haŋska, Boots.
iśka'hutoŋ, v.a. To put tops on moccasins. Iśkahuwatoŋ.
iśka'kaŋ, n. The large tendon extending from the heel up the leg; the large tendon in the back of the neck, perhaps.

iśkaŋ', v. cont. (iśkata). Petiśkaŋ, To come near the fire, draw up to the fire, to warm one's self. Petimaśkaⁿ.

iśkaⁿ'ƙap̄iⁿ, v. To be lazy by reason of. Imáśkaⁿkapiⁿ.

i'śkaⁿśkaⁿ aƙi'ƭa, express. To look at with a hungry mouth, as children do when others eat. Iśkaⁿśkaⁿ amáyakita ye, tuktehaⁿ akiȟ'aⁿ t'emayayiⁿ kte, as a woman would say to grandchildren.

i'śkaⁿyaⁿ, v.a. To get one to talk by teasing etc. Iśkaⁿwaya. Bl.

iśƙa'ƭa, v.a. To play to or for anything. Iwáśkata.

iśki'śkeyece, (?). Bl.

iśƙō'ġiⁿ, n. The long hair on an ankle of a horse; a bare spot on part of the forelegs above the knees, its odor being ugly. R. Bl. Note: there is some question of iśka-ogiⁿgiⁿ, To nod, being the word's der.

iśla'yapaƭaⁿhaⁿ, adv. From the right side. BD.

iśla'yaƭaⁿ, Same as iślayataⁿhaⁿ.

iśla'yaƭaⁿhaⁿ, adv. At the right hand of. Na uⁿma hiⁿśa kiⁿ le - iyayiⁿ kte lo.

i'śloye, n. Something to hold or melt metal with; a pair of tongs or a ladle. Maza su - . Bl.

iśna'la, pron. Alone; he or she alone. Miśnala, niśnala, uⁿkiśnapila. Hokśila - yuhapi kiⁿ hemaca. B.H.123.8.

iśna'śnala, pron. red. (iśnala). Each one by himself. D.157.

iśna'ƭi, v.n. To have the menses; lit. to dwell alone or in a separate house. -- n. Menstruation, the menses. - waⁿjini kiyela (or nikiyela) u kte śni. -- iśnáƭip̄i, n. Dwelling alone; the menses.

iśna'woglaka, v. To talk to one's self. Miśnáwowáglaka.

iśni'ƙaleś, adv. Within a little, nearly, pretty near.

i'śokśoƙap̄ila, n. Thick lips.

iśo'ƭa, n. Smoke; cloud. Maka (skunk) kiⁿ ohiⁿni - waⁿ el kakiśyapi.

iśp̄a', n. The elbow. - taiⁿśpa akipa, To meet with disaster. - ha yuzapi s'e owakihi yelo (ohiwayelo), i.e. fig. carrying a thing through although they may even catch a hold of the skin of one's elbow, which is held up for protection. Bl. GA.

iśp̄a'hu, n. The bones of the lower part of the arm, the radius and ulna.

iśp̄a' ƙi'c'uⁿ, v. To use one's elbows, perhaps. Iśpa kic'uⁿpi caⁿna (cana) okihipelo. GA.

iśp̄a' ƙi'c'uⁿyaⁿ, adv. (?). - maka hewayelo. Bl.

iśp̄a'kic'uⁿ, v.n. To take courage; to get busy. Same as bliheic'iya. CH.

iśpaⁿ'śpaⁿeca, n. Cf. iśpaⁿspaⁿheca. HP.

i'śpaśpa, v.n. To move the lips, as some persons do when reading to themselves. Same as íkawawa. - maⁿka. R. Bl.

iśp̄a'zihiⁿ, (?). Of a buffalo. Bl.

i'śpuƙitoⁿ, v. To eat little, because there is little on hand. Iśpuwakitoⁿ. Bl.

iśƭa', n. The eye, eyes. Miiśta, uⁿkiśtapi. Le maiśta oⁿ waⁿblaka.

iśƭa'akaȟpe, n. The eye-blinds of horses.

iśƭa'bles, cont. of iśtableza.

iśƭa'blesya, v.a. To make clear-sighted. Iśtableswaya.

iśƭa'bleza, v.n. To be clear-sighted. Iśtamableza.

iśƭa'glakp̄a, v. pos. (iśtakakpa). To put out one's own eye. Iśtawaglakpa.

iśƭa'ġoⁿġa, v.n. To be blind, not to be able to see well. Iśtamagoⁿga.

iśƭa'ġoⁿgapi, n. Blindness.

iśƭa'ġoⁿgaya, adv. In a blind state. - toⁿpi. B.H.221.21. -- v.a. To make blind, to blind. Iśtagoⁿgawaya.

iśƭa'ġoⁿġe, n. A blind person.

iśƭa'ha, n. The eyelid.

iśƭa'ȟca, (?). Śiyo iśtaȟcapi, as they say when it is very foggy in the spring or winter. Tuwa yatoⁿwaⁿpi kiⁿhaⁿ, iśtaniȟcapi kte lo. D.21.

iśƭa'ȟe, n. The ridge above the eyebrows. -- iśṫáḣehiŋ, n. The eye brow. -- iśṫáḣe hiŋśmáśma, express. Used in playing cards when one does not deposite money because he has nothing. Bl. -- iśṫáḣeṗi, n. The eye brows. Note: this form is doubtfully used. Cf. iśtaḣe. -- iśṫáḣeṗihiŋ, n. The eye lashes. R. Bl. -- iśṫáḣe yuślá, n. A tool, pincers, to pull out hairs, as those of the eye brows, beard etc.

iśṫa'ḣmiŋ, adj. Cross-eyed.

iśṫa'iyohiya, adv. As far as the eye can reach.

iśṫa'iyośnija, 1) v.n. To have the eyes blinded or dazzled by the light. 2) v.a. To dazzle, perhaps.
iśṫa'iyośniśya, v.a. To dazzle the eyes, as bright light does.

iśṫa'iyotapa, v. To look in the direction someone else is looking. Iśtáiyotawapa, I look in the direction that someone else is looking. Iśtáiyotamapa, He is looking in the direction that I am looking. Note: used as the infinitive of otapa.
iśṫa' jotókte, (?). Iśta jotomakte yelo. Bl.

iśṫa'kakṗa, v.a. To strike and put out an eye. Iśtawakakpa.

iśṫa'k̇akṗaŋ, v. To wink the eye. Iśtawakakpaŋ. Note: iśtawakakpaŋ, red. is doubtfully used.
iśṫa'k̇akpáŋpi s'e, adv. Winking the eyes quickly, as done in excitement etc. Ehaŋni - śkiŋmic'iye; yuŋkaŋ lehaŋl owakihi śni yelo. Bl.

iśṫa'kṗa, v.n. To be blind, having the eye put out. Iśtamakpa. -- iśṫákṗeya, v.a. To make blind. Iśtakpewaya.

iśṫa'kśiŋ, v. To be squint-eyed or cross-eyed. Iśtamakśiŋ.
iśṫa'kśiŋk̇a, n. A squint-eyed person.
iśṫa'kśiŋkśiŋ, v.n. red. of iśtakśiŋ.

iśṫa' kte nuŋ s'e, adv. express. With piercing eyes staring at one. - ayuta. Bl.

iśṫa'maza, n. Eye-glasses.

iśṫa'mniġaġa, adv. In tears, with tearful eyes running. Note: there may be a variant spelling.
iśṫa'mnihaŋpi, n. Tears. Also, iśṫámniyaŋpi, the more correct form.
iśṫa'mnioślo, adv. With water standing in the eyes. Also perhaps, iśṫámniojula.
iśṫa'mniyaŋ, adv. Running at the eyes, being blear-eyed. Note: iśtámaniyaŋ is doubtfully a variant. - kowakipe. Bl. Pb.47.

iśṫa'nagléśk̇iya, v. To look sternly at one with eyes widely open. Same as iśtanatogkiya.

iśṫa'nagnaŋk̇a, v.n. To have the eye twitch repeatedly. Iśtamanagnaŋka.
iśṫa'nak̇a, v.n. To have the eye twitch just once. Iśtamanaka. Cf. iśtanagnaŋka.
iśṫa'natógk̇iya, v. To look sternly at one, changing the eyes, as it were.
iśṫa'natogyeya, (?). Wicaśayatapi kiŋ - nacaŋcaŋ. B.H.140.6.

iśṫa'nica táŋka, n. The horned lark; the snowbird, one of the first to be with us in the spring, and it stays here all winter, being seen along the roads; its call: Opteptecela, opteptecela. Also, maśtékola.

iśṫa'niyaŋ, v. To have sore eyes. Iśtamaniyaŋ. Iśtawicaniyaŋpi wi, The month of March. Note: iniyaŋ, To have a sore mouth inside.
iśṫa'niyaŋpi, n. Soreness of the eyes, a disease the Sioux are subject to in the spring. Bl.

iśṫa'oḣcá, express. Used of the snow that forms ice in the eyes.
iśṫa' otóya, v.a. To give one a blue eye. Iśta otowaya.
iśṫa'saŋk̇iya, (?). - kici uŋpi, To regard with jealousy. Bl.
iśṫa'su, n. The eye-ball. Bl.

iśṫa'tólas'e ayúta, v. To look at angrily. He takuwe iśtatolas'e amayaluta hwo?

iśṫa'waíyojaŋjaŋ, (?). Iśtawaiyomajaŋjaŋ yelo. Bl.
iśṫa'wakáśke, n. An eye disease, the right corner of the right eye and the left corner of the left eye becoming red. KT.

iśṫa'wicaniyaŋ, n. An epidemic of sore eyes. - wi, March, the sore eyes moon.

iśṫa'wicayazaŋ wi, n. March, the month in which sore eyes prevail.

iśṫa' wi'yoḣpayiŋ kte waŋ, express. Used when a spy made signs as of buffalo being near while he was standing on a hill. Bl.

iśṫa'yeya, v. To look into the distance Iśtayewaya. Yuŋkaŋ tohaŋyaŋ iśtayeyapi hehaŋyaŋ pte kiŋ au. Bl.

iśṫe'ca, v.n. To be ashamed, be bashful. Imaśteca. -- iśṫél, cont.
iśṫe'lic'iyeya, v.a. To baffle, make bewildered. Iśtelic'iyewaya. Bl.
iśṫe'lk̇iya, v.n. To make one ashamed; to disappoint one. Iśtelwakiya.
iśtel'ya, v.a. To make ashamed, to dishonor. Iśtelwaya, iśtelmayaya.

iśṫi'haŋke, n. The outer corner of the eyes. Bl.

iśṫiŋ'ma, v.n. To sleep, be asleep. Miśtiŋma.

iśṫi'yagna, adv. (?). - kuwa, To watch closely. B.H.303.3.

iśṫi'yojaŋjaŋya, v.a. To dazzle one. Same as iśtáiyojaŋjaŋya. Iśtiyojaŋjaŋmayayelo, as a man would say if somebody came all dressed up; or, iśtaiyówalmayayelo. Bl.

iśṫi'yośnija, v.n. To have the eyes blinded or dazzled by the light. Also iśtaiośnija. Iśtiomaśnija. -- iśṫíyośniśya, v.a. To dazzle one. B.H.155.26

iśṫi'yotapa, v.n. To look towards when somebody points. Iśtiyotawicapiŋ. B.H. 244.3.

iśṫi'yowalya, v.a. To dazzle one. Iśtiyowalmayayelo, as they said to a person who was dressed up very richly; or, iśtiyojaŋjaŋmayayelo. Bl.

iśṫo'ġiŋ, n. The eyelids, perhaps. Note: iśṫóḣehiŋ may be the word.
iśṫo'ġiŋk̇iya, adv. Eyes partly closed.

iśṫo'gmus, cont. of iśtogmuza. - waci.
iśṫo'gmusya, 1) v.a. To cause to shut the eyes. Iśtomuswaya. 2) adv. Having the eyes shut.
iśṫo'gmuza, 1) v.n. To shut the eyes. Iśtówagmuza. 2) adj. Blind-folded, with the eyes shut.
iśṫo'gna, adv. In the eyes. Na ḣliḣlila oŋ - śna ap'api keye.
iśṫo'gnake, n. The socket or orbit of the eye. Bl.
iśṫo'ḣli, adj. Blear-eyed, having sore eyes.
iśṫo'juha, n. Any cover for the eyes.

iśṫo'k̇icicaśtakapi, n. A mischievous pastime in which they chew the fruit of rosebushes, gather all the kernels in the hand and fling them into other peoples' faces. Bl.
iśṫo'kśiŋ, v.n. To close one eye and look with the other. Iśtowakśiŋ. Bl.
iśṫo'kśiŋk̇iya, v.a. To look at with one eye closed. Iśtokśiŋwakiya. R. Bl.

i'śuŋmakeci, Cf. uŋś'uŋmakeci.

iśu'ta, v.n. To fail of accomplishing, be unable to do a thing; to miss in shooting at. Iśuwata.
iśu'ṫeya, v.a. To cause to fail of. Iśutewaya.

iś'a'k̇e huŋ'keśni, adj. Feeble, said of old men. Bl.

iś'o'ś'o, adj. Scampering, not easily restrained; hasty, quick. Imaś'oś'o. Cf. wiś'oś'o.
iś'o'ś'ok̇a, n. One who obeys cheerfully, who is quick. - na walitake. Cf. wiś'oś'oka.
iś'o'ś'oya, adv. Quickly, hastily, cheerfully, eagerly. - śkaŋpi. Ikto iś'oś'oyeḣci eya ke, Ikto began eagerly. D.103.

i'tab, adv. Soon after; quickly. D. 272.56,74.

iṫa'glaḣwe, adv. With the wind, the wind in the back. Yuŋkaŋ itaglaḣwetaŋhaŋ śuŋka-wakaŋ ota au. Note: íśtaglaḣwe, n. form. Paha - uŋyaŋpi, We go to the leeward of the hill. R.
iṫa'glaḣwek̇iya, adv. With the wind.
iṫa'glaḣweṫaŋhaŋ, adv. From the direction whence blows the wind. He ti kiŋ iśtaglaḣwetaŋhaŋ yau kte. Note: the word may be a cont. of iśtaglaḣwe.

Na tohaŋl - iyayapi ca waśtemna, i.e. that woman. -- iťáglaȟweya, adv. With the wind.

iťa'gna, adv. (?). - kuwa, To watch closely. Ww.

ita'gnagya, adv. Placed one on top of another. R. Bl.
ita'gnaka, v.a. To place one on top of another. Itawagnaka.

ita'hena, adv. On this side of, i.e. in time or place.
ita'henaťaŋhaŋ, i'tahenaťaŋhaŋ, adv. On this side of.

iťa'ƙaha, n. The instep. Siíťakaha, The top of the foot, the instep.

iťa'ƙaȟpe, n. Cf. itéakaȟpe.

iťa'ƙe, n. The upper part of a haŋpa, in opposition to the sole. Bl.

iťa'ƙignag, adv. With something on top of something else.

itam'ye, v. To die. Toki itamwaye kiŋ, itamyaye kiŋ, itamye kiŋ, When I, you, he dies, as men say. Women say: iwátamye, iyatamye, itamye.

itaŋ', adv. (taŋ). On the side. - anuŋk, On both sides. Mitaŋtaŋhaŋ, At my side. Mitaŋkiyela, Near me, etc. -- n. Same as wikaŋ. Ceji - kiŋ yuśkapi. Mark 7:35. HH.
itaŋ'anuŋk, adv. On both sides. D.57.
itaŋ'anuŋkaťaŋhaŋ, adv. On both sides.

i'ťaŋ, v.n. To be proud.

itaŋ'caŋ, n. A ruler, lord, master. Imataŋcaŋ.
itaŋ'caŋƙa, n. The chief one, lord or master.
itaŋ'caŋƙiya, adv. In a lordly manner, with authority.
itaŋ'caŋƙiya, v.a. To have for or acknowledge as master, to make lord or chief. Itaŋcaŋwakiya.
itaŋ'caŋya, v.a. To have for a chief or master. Itaŋcaŋwaya.
itaŋ'caŋyaŋ, adv. With authority, chief-like. - ecoŋ, To preside. Yuŋkaŋ Śuŋkmanitu Ohitika eciyapi waŋ - ecoŋ kta keyapi' (wacipi). Ito taku waŋ - oblakiŋ kte ciŋ he le e. BT.
itaŋ'caŋyaŋkel, adv. In the manner of a chief, which one is not. Cf. kel.

itaŋ'gluzaza, (?). Itaŋmagluzaza. Itaŋwicagluzaza s'e. Bl.
itaŋ'gluzazaya, (?). Itaŋgluzazamayaye, You scare me, perhaps; you make me shine. Bl. Cf. taŋgluzaza.
itaŋ'ic'iya, v. refl. To improve one's self, e.g. one's health by eating, or one's property by working. WE.
itaŋ'igluksaŋ, adv. Round about one.

itaŋ'iślayataŋhaŋ, adv. At the right side of somebody. B.H.286.3.
itaŋ'ƙal, adv. Without, outside of. Tiyopa eciyataŋhaŋ - hinajiŋpi.
itaŋ'ƙaťa, adv. Outside of. Otoŋwahe kiŋ - . B.H.229.18.
itaŋ'ƙaťaŋhaŋ, adv. From without.Pb.47.

itaŋ'ƙiyela, adv. Near to one. Mitaŋkiyela.

itaŋ'nuŋk, adv. (iťaŋanuŋk). On both sides. Tiyopa kiŋ etaŋhaŋ itokagatakiya - enajiŋ. Cf. itaŋ.
iťaŋ'nuŋkwak'iŋƙiyapi, n. A load carried by a horse on both sides without using tent-poles. Cf. tuśuheyuŋpi.

itaŋ'okśaŋ, adv. Around about, on all sides. Also, itáokśaŋ. - eic'itoŋwaŋ, He looked about himself.

i'ťaŋpi, n. Pride, vainglory.

itaŋ'sak t'a, (?). (taŋ-saka). B.H. 280.13.

i'ťaŋťaŋ, v. red. (itaŋ). To be vain, proud of, to glory in. Imátaŋtaŋ, uŋkitaŋtaŋpi.
i'ťaŋťaŋpi, n. Pride, glorying, arrogance.
i'ťaŋyaŋ, v.n. To be proud by reason of. Itaŋwaya.

iťaŋ'yaŋ, (?). Well on account of. Iśtiŋme kiŋ, - kte lo. B.H.229.1.

itaŋ'yaŋ, v. To be well off by reason of working etc., perhaps. WE.

i'ťaŋyeśni, v.n. To receive no benefits from, to be of no use. Ímataŋyeśni.

ita'okśaŋ, adv. Round about, on all sides, all around something, as a fence around property; on all sides. Tipi kiŋ itawokśaŋ caŋwape topakiya eglepi. Hecel wicitawokśaŋ uŋyaŋpi na okiwaŋjila uŋkutapi. Cf. R.:

itanokśan. Na hetanhan paha sapa - tiwahepi kin omaniyan unpi. D.215.

ita'śośa, v. To spit out.

ita'ťowab, adv. To the windward side of, on this side of.
ita'ťowal, adv. Same as itatowab.
ita'ťowapa, adv. On this side of, to the windward side of. Also, itáťowapaťanhan.
iťa'ťowaťa, adv. In the direction whence the wind blows, against the wind; to the windward of. Cf. tatowata.

ita'wacin, (?). Hunhunhe mazaska - śice lo. BT.

i'ťawank̇agle, adv. Up hill, ascending.
i'ťawank̇agleya, adv. Ascending, up a very steep hill.

iťa'ziṗa, n. A bow to shoot with. Mitazipa. - ikan, A bow string. - ṗeconpi, A game, a boys' pastime. Also, - ṗecónpi. Bl.

iťe', n. The face. Miite.

iťe'ak̇aḣpe, n. A cover for the face, a veil.

iťe'anung, adv. On both sides of the face. Also, iťéanunkatanhan.

iťe' aśníyanpi, n. Squirrel-tail grass, fox tail. Hordeum jubatum. The grass family. Bl. #186.

ite' awíćaśniyan hu, n. Witch grass. Panicum capillare. The grass family. BT. #43.

iťe'cinhin, n. The hair over the forehead; the forelock.

iťe' (e)yéśni, adj. perhaps. Not paying attention to others, i.e. out of pride or anger. - yanka. GA.

iťe'ha, n. A mask, as the medicine man used; a halter. Yunkan giic'iya ca - wan un he sinte lulyapi kaga.

i'ťehan, adv. (teha). Far from.
i'ťehanhan, adv. red. of itehan.
i'ťehanhanyan, adv. red. of itehanyan.
i'ťehanlake, adv. After a while. - ci; - ki. T'in na - wicaśa wakan el kihi. Glayo, - wau kte. Na - k'el eciyatan kupi.
i'ťehanťanhan, adv. Far away from.
i'ťehanyan, adv. Far away from.

iťe'hohu, n. The cheek bones.

iťe'iyaskabya, v. To put a stamp on.
iťe'iyaskabye, n. A postage stamp. Cf. wiciteiyaskabye.

iťe'k̇a, adv. or v. impers. Time for, due, timely; likely indeed. Wanna hi - , Now he ought to come. Wana capa ota itekalo, There ought to be many beavers here. Lit., on the face of it, evidently; it appears. B.H.36.15. D.251.

iťe'lazatanhan, adv. Behind the back.
iťe'naśinśinkiya, v. To cut faces. P.

iťe'owa, v. To draw, sketch. P.
iťe'owapi, n. A photograph, snapshot.

iťe'oyuze, n. A look, the cast of countenance, appearance, complexion. - waśte, A pleasant face.

iťe'ṗak̇inťe, n. A towel. Cf. epakinte.

iťe'śa hinglé, v. To blush. Bl.
iťe'śinkiya, v. To frown, to grin. Iteśinwakiya.
iťe'śinśin, n. A wrinkled face. Itemaśinśin.

ite'śnioṗa, (?). The face is frozen. IS.

iťe'śniśniyan, adv. red. of iteśniyan.

iťe'śniyan, adv. Truthfully. - epe. B.H.87.3;259.9.

iťe'ťanhan, v. or adv. To be queer, as is said when a man who is considered good does something wrong. Bl. Sb.

i'ťeťanhan, adv. In front, face on towards a person or animal. - ya, To place one's self in front, as in approaching a horse lest one be kicked by being at its side. Bl.

iťe' watógla, n. A horse that is very sensitive on the head, and hence dodges the bridle on being caught. Bl.

iťe'we s'e hiŋgle, v. To blush. Bl. Also, iteśa hiŋgle.
iťe'ya, adv. Almost, apparently. D.67.
iťe'yakel, adv. Likely, it stands to reason; apparently. D.99. B.H.31.7; 121.4.

iťe'yukoǩiya, v. To frown, scowl, look severe. Also, iťéyukoǩiya.

iťe'yukśilkiya, v. To cut faces. P.
iťe'yukśiŋkiya, v. To make faces at.
iťe'yuśiŋǩiya, v.a. To draw up the face at one, to frown. Iteyuśiŋwakiya. Also iťéyuśiŋǩiya.

iťe'yuśiŋśiŋ, adj. With face wrinkled.
iťe'yuśiŋśiŋkiya, v. To cut faces. P.

iťe'zi, (?). Taku - mayazaŋ, as is said when one is not satisfied with something. Bl.

iťi'caǧa, v. To set up a tent for a certain purpose. Itiwakaga. Hocokam tipi waŋji iticicagepi kiŋ, el wau na oyate kiŋ wowicawakiyakiŋ kte lo. Tipi waŋ taŋka iticagapi k'uŋ el agla na el aki. Tipi waŋji cokab iticagapi. MS.566. D.230.

iti'cicaśke, n. The three first and main tent poles, which are usually tied together.

iťi'gnila, n. The pocket gopher; a little animal piling up provisions for the winter. FH. Bl.

iťi'pakiŋte, n. A towel.

iťi'sabye, n. (iteisabye). (?). Bl.

iťi'yohila, adj. Each one. Bl. B.H.64.7.
i'ťiyoṗa, adv. Near the door. Na waŋna tipi kiŋ - el caŋ waŋ paslatapi. Kici ku na tipi k'oŋ - el kinajiŋpi.

itǩa', n. A blossom, the capsule; an egg; the seed of anything; the testicles.
itǩa'sǩa, n. The white of an egg.
itǩa'zica, n. The yolk of an egg.

itǩob', adv. Again, back again, in return, in reply. - ahi, They returned. - wicaye, He went forward to meet them. D.230.
Itǩob' U, n. p. The star Arcturus, of the first magnitude, which is alpha Bootes and one of the brightest stars, rising in the northwest during the spring. It is so called because it comes to meet the returning birds from the southeast and south. Also, because below it they return and pass by, it is called Ihuku Kigle. When the Itkob U stands in the mid heavens they say it is summer. BT.

i'tǩoǩib, cont. (itkokipa). Meeting; in the presence of, before. Mitkokib.
i'tǩoǩipa, v.a. To meet, come together from opposite directions. Itkowakipa. Itkokib u. - na kaśka yuzi na agla. Ciŋca itkokib u. Tuweni waziya itkokipiŋ kta okihi śni. MS.566.

itǩoŋ', v.n. To burn, blaze, as fire.

i'tǩoŋs', cont. of itkoŋza. Eye kiŋ - , At the same time. B.H.259.4.
i'tǩoŋskiya, Cf. itkoŋsya.
itǩoŋs'ya, adv. Even with. Also, iťkoŋs ya. -- íťkoŋsya, v.a. To make even, To have accomplished one's task. Toǩ'aŋ kiŋ he itkoskiye. B.H.73.16.

itǩoŋ'yahaŋ, part. Burning, alive, as coals.
itǩoŋ'yaŋ, v.a. To make burn or blaze. Itkóŋwaya.

i'tǩoŋza, adv. Even with.
i'tǩoŋzela, adv. Even with, coming up to the mark, not more and not less, as the fluid of a quart measure is even with the mark denoting the qt. measure.

ito', v.n. To become blue by means of.

iťo', adv. Come; well. - le haŋhepi kiŋ ake ewicuŋkizapi na taśuŋkepi kiŋ oyasiŋ wicuŋkipi ktelo. - wagni kte, eya śke; yuŋkaŋ uŋma k'oŋ he iś eya: Ito wagni kte, eya śke. - ceye, wicoti ekta uŋyiŋ kta.

iťo'btob, adj. cont. of itobtopa.

iťo'bťoṗa, adj. red. (itopa). Every fourth one.

ito'ceś, interj. (ito-eceś). Of disappointment at not being welcome etc., thereupon giving away. Also, itóeceś. Itoceś Ǩaǩi mni kte. Cf. ihoeceś.

iťo'el, Cf. toel.
iťoe'yaś, Cf. toeyaś.

i'ťoglaza, n. A head ornament, tied on top of the head and connected at the other end with the hair braid. Ww.

iťo'gna, adv. In the face. - ayap'api kte. -- iťógnagna, adv. red.
iťo'gnagya, adj. Looking like a lord, with the appearance of a lord. B.H. 256.9;263.9.
iťo'gnake, n. The face, countenance, visage, appearance; presence. Mitognake.
Iťo'gna Opi, n. prop. Name of the father of Miwaka^n Yuha, Sword. RF.

i'ťoha^n, adv. How far from? How long from? Mahel naji^n yo; ta^{n}ya^n wa^{n}ya^{n}ka yo; - iyewayi^n kte; ta^{n}ya^n awa^{n}ya^{n}ka yo. Bl. Also, red. íťoha^{n}ha^n.
i'ťoha^{n}ya^n, adv. A little ways off. Na - ahinaji^n. - naji^n. B.H.46.4;259.8.

iťo'heheya, v. red. (itoheya). In different directions. - iyayapi. B.H. 241.2.
iťo'heǩiya, v. To go on home. Itohewakiyi^n kta. L. Bl. Syn.- wagni kte.
iťo'heya, v.a. To go on to any place. Na Jordan wakpala itaokśa^n makoce ki^n ataya - . Takuni etkiya itohewayi^n kte lo. Hektakiya - , To go backwards. Bl. L. LWOW.180.

itō' hi^{n}ya^{n}ka yo, imp. express. Wait a a little! B.H.93.21.
ito'hiya^{n}ki yetó, imp. express. Hold on! B.H.20.26.

i'ťohomni, v.n. perhaps. To turn round, end round. Itohomni wec'ú^n.

iťo'ic'íkowa, v. To have one's picture taken. Also, perhaps, iťóic'íkuwa.
iťo'juha t'a ca, express. A saying, used when a man is plain spoken. Itojuha nit'a ca^{n}ke iyeyaglaśna sece. Bl.

i'ťoǩa, (?). Nothing the matter with. Eta^{n}ś he iu^{n}tokapi eśa yelaka? What is that to us? B.H.259.22;277.5.

iťo'ǩab, adv. Before, in ref. to time and place. Mitokab. Na - hinaji^n. Before (Latin ante) his death. The word always follows śni and its verb: T'e śni - , Before his death; kigle śni - , Before he went. This is contrary to our expectations: Le wicaśa ki^n hi^{n}ha^{n}na wicoha^n hiyaye śni ecel kigni kte. Ti wegna ye śni - iglutokeca, owa^{n}ya^{n}g śica ic'icaga. Also, iťóǩabťu, iťóǩabťuya. -- iťóǩabya, adv. Before, up to that time. Nitokabya, mitokabya. B.H.32.1;98.21;75.1.

iťo'ǩaġa, 1) n. The south. 2) adv. Southward. -- iťóǩaġaťa, n. The south, at the south, adv. --iťóǩaġaťaǩiya, adv. Towards the south. Tiyopa ki^n eta^{n}ha^n - itanu^{n}k enaji^n. -- iťóǩaġaťa^{n}ha^n, adv. To the south of, on the south side of, from the south. -- iťóǩaȟ, cont. (itokaga). Southward. - bla, I am going south. - iyaya, an euphemistic phrase for "To have died"; lit. "To have gone south". A soul was supposed to travel to spirit land via the Milky Way, from north to south. Its fate was determined where the Milky Way divides into two branches in the south. Sb. - iťóǩaȟǩiya, adv. Towards the south, southwards.
iťo'ǩaȟwapa, adv. Towards the south.

ito'ǩamna, adv. Before that, up to that time. Also, itokabya. Bl. B.H.96.8; 97.2;138.5;303.7.

i'toka^{n}l, adv. In another place away from; opposed to sakib. Also, itóka^{n}l. - iyaya, To go somewhere else away from. B.H.293.25.

ito'ǩapa, v.a. To be before one in birth, be older than. Mitokapa, He is older than I.
ito'ǩapaťa^{n}ha^n, adv. Before, from before; from the presence of. Mitokapata^{n}ha^n.

i'ťoǩaśni, v. It makes no difference, does not concern, influence. Imatokaśni. Iu^{n}tokapiśni. Na ena glaki^{n}ki^{n}ya^n naji^n ca lila kutepi eśa - . Taȟca śu^{n}kala ki^n el iwicatokeśni. B.H.220. 7;223.23.
i'ťoǩaśniya^n, adv. In vain, without reason. P. Bl. -- íťoǩawacı^{n}śni, (?). Unconcerned in something. B.H.28.3.

ito'ǩeca, v.n. (tokeca). To be altered, changed; to be affected by in any way. Imatokeca. Perhaps better, ítokeca.
ito'ǩecaśni, v. perhaps. Eta^{n}ha^n - , It is none of his business, or perhaps, It makes one no difference or no dif-

ference to him. Also, ítokeca śni. Imatokecaśni. B.H.305.19.

ito'kehaŋ, adv. At the first, formerly.

i'ťoǩi, adv. Where from? Which way from? Cf. toki.

iťo'ǩicile, (?). (ite-ole-kici). Itomiyecile yelo, You are aiming at my face, i.e. striking. Bl.

i'ťoǩiya, adv. Which way from?
i'ťoǩiyapa, adv. Which way from?
i'ťoǩiyapaťaŋhaŋ, adv. Same as itokiya.
i'ťoǩiyaťaŋhaŋ, adv. In what direction from?

i'ťoǩiyopeya, v.n. To trade, exchange. B.H.19.13.

iťo'kśaŋ, adv. (ite-okśaŋ). Around the face, as in painting a circle. - tokiyapi.

i'toktog, adv. Alternately. P.
i'toktogye, adv. In different ways. B.H.77.13.
i'toktoǩaŋl, adv. Alternately. Bl.
i'toktoǩeca, adj. Alternately. - ecoŋpi.

ito'k'ehaŋ, adv. Formerly, of old.

ito'k'eyaś, adv. Let me see, wait a little. R. Cf. toéyaś.

iťō'la kiŋ héhaŋ, iťō'la k'oŋ héhaŋ, adv. Long ago. Same as lila ehaŋni. Obs. Cf. itokab.

iťo'leś, (?). - heya śke c'uŋ, as is said when somebody makes a bad remark Bl. Cf. itóla.

iťo'mni, adj. Drunk, dizzy from drinking. Imátomni. Cf. itomnimni.
iťo'mniic'iya, v.n. To carouse, revel, get drunk. P.
iťo'mnimni, adj. Dizzy, i.e. from sickness. Imátomnimni. Cf. itomni.
iťo'mnipi, n. A turning around, as of the head; drunkenness.
iťo'mnis'a, n. A drunkard.
iťo'mniya, v.a. To make dizzy or drunk Itómniwaya.

i'ťona, adv. Of how many? Which number?
i'ťonaǩa, adv. Of how many?
i'ťonaǩeca, adv. Of what number?

itoŋ', v.n. To tell the truth. Note: the word is not used alone; rather, e.g. itoŋśni.
itoŋ'ic'ipa, v. perhaps. To be astonished at one's self; to praise one's self to.
itoŋ'ǩipa, v. pos. (itoŋpa). To wonder at one's self or one's own, to praise one's self.
itoŋ'ǩip̣eya, adv. Astonished at one's self, praising one's self.
itoŋ'pa, v.a. To be surprised, astonished, to wonder; to praise one. Itóŋwapa. Le hecetu na oyate kiŋ waŋyaŋkapi na lila itoŋpapi. Le takuwe itoŋyapapi hwo? B.H.280.14.
itoŋ'p̣eya, adv. perhaps. Surprisingly, wonderfully, astonishingly, praiseworthily.
itoŋ'p̣eyahaŋ, adv. Same as itoŋpeya.
itoŋ'piśni, n. Untruth, lies.
itoŋ'śni, v.n. To tell an untruth. Iwatoŋśni. Akśakaȟci he - k'oŋ. Bl.
itoŋ'śniśni, v. red. of itoŋśni.
itoŋ'śniyaŋ, adv. Falsely.
itoŋ'waŋ, v.n. (toŋwaŋ). To look or see with, as with one's eyes. Iwátoŋ waŋ.

iťo'oicacu, n. A camera.

iťo'p̣a, adj. The fourth. Imátopa.

iťo'pťa sápa, n. (ite-opta-sapa). The black-footed ferret, so called for a black stripe across its face. Its home is with prairie dogs and is very difficult to kill. Hence, it is said to be wakaŋ; and whoever kills one will soon die himself. BD.
iťo'pťa sápa tapeju'ťa, n. Snow on the mountain, showy milkweed or spurge, white marginal spurge, a milkweed with blossoms half white and half green. Euphorbia marginata, the spurge family. It grows in gumbo and near prairie dog homes. Also, asaŋpi pejuta. A tea from it is used by mothers without milk. Also, crushed leaves in warm water makes a liniment for swellings. SG. BT. Bl. # 214.
ito'to, v.n. red. (ito). To be made blue by.

iťo'wap̣i, n. A picture. Cf. iteowapi. - naśǩáŋśǩaŋyaŋpi, Moving pictures.
iťo'wapognake, n. A little metal frame in which photos are held.
iťo'wapojuha, n. A picture frame.
i'ťowe, i'ťoe, n. The forelock. Bl. - k'el mapehiŋ kiŋ hetaŋ conala ate

mayuha kta. Nupiᵑ waciᵑhiᵑ ikaᵑ haᵑskeya - el iyaglaśkapi; note that R. gives itoye, Face, appearance.

i'ṫoye, i'ṫoe, n. The forelock; the face, appearance. Also, íṫoyehiᵑ. Cf. ituhu, Forehead. R.

i'ṫoyeḱitoᵑ, i'ṫoeḱitoᵑ, v. pos. To wear braids of hair or ornaments in front. Itoyewetoᵑ. R. Bl.

i'ṫoyetoᵑ, i'ṫoetoᵑ, v.n. To have braids or ornaments dangling about one's face. Itoyewatoᵑ. R. Bl.

i'ṫoyewoblu, v.n. To have hair stand up, as from the wind blowing. Also, itoewoblu. Psáloka hecoᵑpi.

i'ṫoyeyuḣ'o, v.n. To have hair stand up on the head. Itoyemayuḣ'o.

iṫo'yuha t'éḱiya, (?). Bl.

iṫu', adv. Wildly, without being planted or tamed. - icaga, It has grown up of itself, for nothing. R. Bl.

itu'hu, n. The forehead, the frontal.

iṫu'hu, n. The black oak. - caᵑ, Black oak wood. Same as ispaᵑspaᵑheca. Bl. # 19.

iṫu'ḣci, adv. For nothing, gratuitously, without cause. Same as otuḣci.

iṫu'ḱaleś, adv. Truly, indeed.

iṫu'maḱoskaᵑ, adv. In vain, to no purpose.

ituᵑ'gtaᵑḱa, n. A rat.

ituᵑ'ḱab, adv. (ite-uᵑkapa). On the back, reclining backward. As opposed to aglapśuᵑyaᵑ. Na tataᵑka ha waᵑ owiᵑjapi ca el - iyuᵑka na hecina t'a. - naicabyeya iśtiᵑme. WL. Bl. D.104.

iṫuᵑ'ḱabṫu, adv. On the back.

iṫuᵑ'ḱabyela, adv. On the back. - gliḣpaya, i.e. throws himself on the back on his return. - ḣpaya. D.272.

ituᵑ'ḱala, n. A mouse.

ituᵑ'ḱasaᵑ, n. The weasel. Also, ituᵑkasaᵑla.

ituᵑ'psicala, n. The field mouse. Also ituᵑpsipsicala.

iṫu'psápsa s'e, adv. Disorderly. Same as psápse s'e. - uᵑ, To be disorderly in one's looks, i.e. with ragged clothes, dishevelled hair etc. Bl.

iṫu'śeḱa, adv. By all means, nevertheless; by repetition, perseverence in doing it over and over again. - owakihi kte lo. R. GA. Bl. - taku waᵑji eyemayahiᵑ kte ḣciᵑ, tka aciyuptiᵑ kte śni yelo. Ituśaka is incorrect.Bl.

itu'śeś, adv. Indeed. - iśica mawaciᵑka pcelyela mayuta taᵑke.

iṫu'ṫu, adv. red. of itu.

iṫu'ṫuya, adv. red. of ituya. R. Bl.

iṫu' uᵑ, v. To be in a wild state. R.

iṫu'ya, adv. For nothing, without a cause, gratuitously. R. Bl.

iṫu'yaḱel, adv. Without cause, gratuitously. R. Bl.

it'a', v. (?). Bl.

it'e'ca, adj. Slightly warm, lukewarm, tepid, as is said of fluids only.

it'el'ya, v.a. To make slightly warm or tepid, e.g. water.

it'e'nihaᵑ, (?). - śni.Taku - ecóᵑśnimayáyapelo, You give me no time to do my work. - woteśni, To eat but little because one is bothered. Bl.

it'e'waciᵑ, v. To intend to die on account of. Same as oᵑ t'ewáciᵑ. Tokeś'uᵑlaka wayatkaᵑpi kiᵑ - . Bl.

it'iᵑś', v. cont. of it'iᵑza.

it'iᵑs'ya, v.a. To make firm by means of. It'iᵑswaya.

it'iᵑ'za, v.n. To be firm by reason of.

it'iᵑ'ze, n. (i-t'iᵑza). A strengthener, a tightener, as an elastic garter.

it'uᵑ'gḱiya, v. To suspect concerning one's self.

it'uᵑg'ya, v. To suspect.

it'uᵑ'ḱeca, v.n. Unwilling to do; to be suspected of. Imat'uᵑkeca. BD.

i'waciᵑ, v. To think of going to. Iwacaᵑmi.

iwa'ciᵑgnuniyaᵑ, adv. (?). Bl.

iwa'ciᵑjata, v.n. To be undecided about anything. Iwaciᵑmajata.

iwa´ciŋko, v.n. To be impatient about, be out of humor on account of. Iwaciŋmako.

iwa´ciŋtokaŋkaŋgnagnaya, adv. (?). Ca hecel kohaŋ - omawani yelo. Bl.

iwa´ciŋtoŋ, v. To be intelligent by reason of. Iwaciŋwatoŋ.

iwa´ciŋyaŋ, 1) v.a. To trust in for or in reference to. Iwaciŋwaya, iwaciŋciya. Le aŋpetu kiŋ el taku waŋ iwaciŋciyelo; so, what he wants follows. Pb.34. 2) adv. Trustingly.
iwa´ciŋyeȟci, (?). Pb.41.

iwa´glamna, n. An extra or fresh horse. The Indians would have another horse along in case the one they were riding played out, or a horse were needed for an escape or the carrying of meat home. Na ecel iwaglamna yuha najiŋpi kiŋ el aglihuŋni.

iwa´hoḱiciyapi, v. pl. (iwahoya). They promise to each other. Olowaŋ kiŋ he uŋkahiyayapi kta kéya-iwahouŋkiciyapi k'uŋ, We agreed (promised) to sing that song. D.224.

iwa´hoḱoŋḱiya, v.a. To instruct in regard to, to counsel or advise concerning. Iwahokoŋwakiya.
iwa´hoḱoŋḱiyapi, n. Instruction, counsel.

iwa´hoya, v.a. To send word to concerning anything; to promise; to grant, permit; to warn, let know. Yúsyus iwahociyiŋ kte. Iwahowaya. Hecel waŋna oyuspa. Yuŋkaŋ iyokipi. Hecel waŋna iwahoyiŋ na "Hihaŋna kiŋ aŋpahaŋ uŋyiŋ kte lo" eya. Niyate taku tona iwahomaye. D.11,13,236. B.H.112.7.

iwa´hukeza, n. (?). Akicita num - yuhapi. - yamni yuha. B.H.95.26.

i´waȟtelaśni, v.a. To dislike on account of something, to dislike something in one, to disesteem, think lightly of for some reason, to be disgusted with one on account of. Iwaȟtelwalaśni. D.33,268.

iwa´ȟwayela, adv. (?). Haŋkeya - glapelo, The storm clouds passed by without much noise. Bl.

iwa´ȟ'aŋic'ila, v. refl. To be proud of. Iwáȟ'aŋmic'ila.

iwa´ic'iniyaŋ, v. refl. (iwakiniya). To be dissatisfied with one's self.

i´wakaŋ, 1) adj. Talkative, tattling, gabbling. 2) n. A babbler.
i´wakaŋyaŋ, adv. In a babbling manner.

iwa´kaŋyaŋ, adv. Supernaturally.

iwa´kaŋyeja, (?). Taku keśa imawakaŋyeja yelo, I am satisfied with any amount be it ever so little. Bl.

iwa´ḱici, v.n. To dance for one, in praise of one; to dance the Scalp Dance. Iwawakici. R.
iwa´ḱiciȟci, v. (iwaȟci). To tear off and take for one; to make fringes. Iwakiciȟcipi kte. Iwamiciȟci. Na waŋna - mila oŋ. Note: paȟci´, To cut or break out notches by cutting. R.
Iwa´ḱiciwacipi, n. p. The Scalp Dance.

iwa´ḱicoŋza, v.a. (koŋza). To influence one, command one in regard to. Iwawecoŋza.
iwa´ḱicoŋze, n. A commandment, decree.

iwa´ḱiniya, v.a. To get out of humor with; neglect, contemn. Iwawakiniya.

iwa´kťa, 1) v.n. To be on one's guard, be on the look-out, to guard. Iwawakta. B.H.160.10;174.9. 2) n. A mark, sign; a pledge.
iwa´kťaya, 1) v.a. To have a look-out for, put on one's guard; to forewarn, admonish. Iwaktawaya. 2) adv. Guardedly. B.H.55.14;157.22.

iwa´ktegla, v.n. To go home in triumph having taken scalps. Iwaktewagla.
iwa´kťegli, v.n. To come home in triumph bringing scalps. Iwaktewagli.
iwa´kteḱiyagla, (?). Waniyetu amakeśakowiŋ el Scili kiŋ iwaktemakiyaglapelo. BT.

iwa´ḱuwa, v.a. To provoke one, make one angry.

iwa´litake, adj. Active. Same as iyuśkiŋyaŋ śkaŋ. Iwalitakelo. Bl.

iwa´nağiyeya, v.a. To trouble one in regard to, to disturb one with.

iwa'niṫi, v.n. To go and spend the winter at for some purpose. Iwaniwati.

i'waniyeṫu, n. The succeeding winter, the next winter.

iwaŋ'glag, cont. of iwaŋglaka.

iwaŋ'glaka, v. pos. (iwaŋyaŋka). To look to, have regard for one's own. Iwaŋwaglaka. Ikipiśni iwaŋglake, He deemed himself unworthy. B.H.175.3.

iwaŋ'ic'iglaka, v. refl. To look at one's self; to guard one's self. Iwaŋmic'iglaka.

iwaŋ'iglag, cont. of iwaŋiglaka.

iwaŋ'iglaka, v. To look at one's self in a glass; to watch over, guard one's self; to set a guard. Iwáŋmiglaka.

iwaŋ'jica, (?). Waciŋ - śni, Getting angry easily. Bl.

iwaŋ'k̇ab, adv. Above something. Miwaŋkab. Na tipi kiŋ - ikiyela hinajiŋ, i.e. a cloud. Na wa kiŋ - iyeya, i.e. on top of a house.
iwaŋ'k̇abic'iya, v. refl. To exalt one's self. B.H.161.2.
iwaŋ'k̇abtu, adv. Above, up. Woilake uŋ kiŋ he itaŋcaŋye kiŋ he - śni. Also, iwáŋk̇abṫuya, iwáŋk̇abṫuyakel, iwáŋk̇al.
iwaŋ'k̇apa, adv. Above, up above one. Also, iwáŋk̇apaṫa.
iwaŋ'k̇apaṫaŋhaŋ, adv. From above one. Also, iwáŋk̇aṫahaŋ. Huŋḣ wakpala kiŋ opaya ya po; na huŋḣ - ya po.

iwaŋ'k̇iciyaŋk̇a, v. To look to, watch over for one. Iwaŋweciyaŋka.
iwaŋ'k̇iciyaŋk̇api, v. pl. They look to, watch over one another. Iwaŋuŋkiciyaŋkapi.

iwaŋ'yaŋg, cont. of iwaŋyaŋka.
iwaŋ'yaŋgya, adv. perhaps. Watching out, being careful. - conala etaŋ caŋtewaśteya wicak'u wo. B.H.120.15. Bl.
iwaŋ'yaŋgyeḣci, adv. Examining very carefully, keeping one's eyes open. - omani. Syn.- kicuŋniyaŋkel.

iwaŋ'yaŋk, cont. of iwaŋyaŋka. B.H. 153.18.

iwaŋ'yaŋk̇a, v.a. To look to or at; to survey, examine, spy at, watch at: to judge. Iwaŋblaka. Hetaŋhaŋ hihaŋna ca na tuktogna oti iwaśte kiŋ he ogna kaḣnigapi naiŋś iwaŋyaŋkapi na tokiyataŋhaŋ oge waśte kiŋ he ogna na oyate tonakecapi kiŋ hena taŋyaŋ iyukcaŋpi. B.H.89.12;45.5;194.13.
iwaŋ'yaŋk̇api, n. Spies; surveyors.
iwaŋ'yaŋk̇e, n. Something by which to see, the sight of a gun, a telescope or field glass. Maziwaŋke cf.

iwa'ṗe, v. To make sharp by. Iwawape. Iwapeśni, To make dull on.

iwa'ṗetog, cont. of iwapetokeca.
iwa'ṗetogtoŋ, v.a. To mark or brand with. Iwapetogwatoŋ.

iwa'ṗetokeca, n. A mark, a sign.

i'wapsaka, v. To cut off with, as with a knife or some other thing. Kaŋ iwapsake waŋ imicikiŋte śni, i.e. my knife is dull, pe śni.

iwa'saza, v.n. To take hard, get sick over. Iwamasaza.

iwa'śeca, v.n. To be rich, esp. in provisions. Iwamaśeca.

iwa'śi, v.a. To employ for a certain purpose. B.H.7.18;85.20;227.7.

i'waśicuŋ, v.n. To be talkative; to talk badly. Ímawaśicuŋ.

iwa'śṫe, v.n. (waśte). To be better by means of, be benefited by. Imawaśte. Hetaŋhaŋ hihaŋna ca na tuktogna oti - kiŋ he ogna kaḣnigapi.
iwa'śṫegla, adv. Same as iwaśtela.
iwa'śṫeglala, adv. red. of iwaśtegla.
iwa'śṫeka, v.n. To be none the better for.
iwa'śṫela, adv. Slowly, moderately, carefully. Hehaŋl - ie śi.
iwa'śṫeya, adv. Better.
iwa'śṫeyak̇el, adv. A little better.

iwa'ś'ag, cont. of iwaś'aka.
iwa'ś'agya, v.a. To strengthen by means of. Iwaś'agwaya.
iwa'ś'ak̇a, 1) v.n. To be strong by reason of or for. Ceḣpi' - . Iwamaś'aka. 2) n. Strength, the source of strength. - śni, To be weak, be unable to recover. Ceḣpi imáwaś'ake śni.

i'waṫohaᶯl, adv. perhaps. Sometime, one day in ref. to something. - uᶯgna wicacokam waśicuᶯ waᶯ hinajiᶯ na atayaś waᶯjini uᶯkayutapi śni. B.H.8.3; 32.1;74.18;259.8.
i'waṫohaᶯtu, adv. Sometime. B.H.31.6; 90.17.

iwa'ṫoḱiya, v.n. To be much concerned by. Waeyapi kiᶯ oᶯ lila iwatokiyapi śke'. D.225.
iwa'ṫoḱiyaśṇi, v.n. To be none of one's business. Iwamatokiyaśni.
i'waṫoḱiyaṫaᶯhaᶯ, adv. Out of concern. BT.

iwa'ṫoṗeḱiya, n. An oar or paddle, anything to row a boat with.

iwa'ṫuka, v.n. To be tired or or on account of anything.

i'waṫukte, (?). John tipi kiᶯ he - el ti yelo. BT.

iwa'wiḱuwa, v.a. To do something to make one angry, to provoke one. Iwawiwakuwa.

iwa'yazaᶯ, v.n. To be sick in consequence of. Iwámayazaᶯ.

iwa'yuṗiḱa, v.n. To be skillful, handy on account of or in doing. Iwáblupika.
iwa'yuṗiya, adv. Handily, nicely, well. - spaᶯyaᶯ. B.H.20.19;77.11.

iwa'ziyapa, adv. To the north of.
iwa'ziyapaṫaᶯhaᶯ, adv. To the north of.
iwa'ziyata, adv. At the north of.
iwa'ziyataᶯhaᶯ, adv. Northward of.

iwe', v.n. To bleed by reason of. Imawe.

iwe'ceya, v.a. To have regard for, do. as one commands. Iwecewaya.

i'wehiyu, v. To bleed from the mouth. Iwemahiyu.
i'wehiyupi, n. A bleeding from the mouth, a sickness among the Sioux.Bl.
i'wehiyuya, v. To raise blood, spit blood. Iwehiyuwaya.

iwe'śleka, v.n. To do something worthy of honor; to wear or have as evidence of bravery. Iwewaśleka. The custom was to wear a split feather as a sign of having been wounded by the enemy. R. Bl.

iwe'yośaya, adv. perhaps. With a blood mouth. Na taḣca na pte ko - kacegceg omanipi. Note: der., i-we-ośaya.

iwi'cableza, n. Enlightenment.
iwi'cacaġa, n. A generation. - śakowiᶯ hehaᶯyaᶯ ocic'u ktelo. Bl. MS.514.
iwi'cagnayaᶯ, n. (gnayaᶯ). Deception.
iwi'cahupi, n. (hu). Sodomy. Note: thi is now a vulgar word, and byword.
iwi'cakcaśla, n. A clipper.

i'wicamna, adj. (imna). Satisfying, furnishing much nourishment.

iwi'caṗo, n. (po). A swelling, an inflation on account of.

i'wicapuza, n. (puza). Thirst.

iwi'caśṫeca, n. (iśteca). Shame, bashfulness.
iwi'cawaśṫe, adj. Nourishing, nutritious, as food; being good for them, as certain things might be. P. Bl.
iwi'cayuṫaᶯ, adj. Lovely, tempting. P. Bl.

iwi'kcemna, adj. The tenth.
iwi'kcemnamna, adj. red. Every tenth one; tithes.

iwiᶯ'kṫe, v.n. To glory in, be proud of. Imawiᶯkte, uᶯkiwiᶯktepi.
iwiᶯ'kṫekṫe, v. red. of iwiᶯkte.
iwiᶯ'kṫepi, n. A glorying in.
iwiᶯ'kṫeya, v.a. To cause to glory in. Iwiᶯktewaya. -- adv. Glorying, proudl

iwi'śṫaᶯ, v.a. To treat well, as a sick person. Iwawiśtaᶯ.

iwi'tko, v.n. (witko). To be drunk on. Imawitko. Taku - , Something that intoxicates, liquor.
iwi'tkotkoka, v.n. To become foolish by means of.
iwi'tkoya, v.a. To make drunk with. Iwitkowaya.

i'wiyohiyaᶯpaṫa, adv. At the east of.
i'wiyohiyaᶯpaṫaᶯhaᶯ, adv. To the east of.

iwi'zilye, n. Frankincense, weed etc. P

iwo'blasḱayela, adv. Made flat, flattened by force of. Yuᶯkaᶯ maza su num iwoblaskayela mahel uⁿ.

iwo'blu, v.n. To be blowy, snowy; to bluster; to drift, blow up e.g. snow or dust; a blizzard, n. - taⁿka.D.249.
iwo'blublu, v. red.

iwo'cajeyalya, v. To sing one's praises on account of. B.H.88.2. -- adv. In praise of one. - woglaka. Bl.

iwo'c'u, n. A churn. Cf. woc'u.

i'wog̈ag̈a, n. A rifle. Le kośkalaka kiⁿ wahiⁿkpe na - waⁿ hecel yuha ȟpeya śka. - s'e haiẏotiyekiya, To have clothes on with many holes, as though many bullets went through them. Bl.

iwo'glaǩa, v. pos. (woyaka). To speak in ref. to one's own. Iwowaglaka.

iwo'hiⁿyaⁿsyakel, adv. (?). - wakiⁿyaⁿ ukiye, An awful thunderstorm is coming. Bl.

iwo'ȟtaǩa, v.n. To hit or strike against, bump. Iwomahtaka. D.28. -- v.a. Iwowaȟtaka. Same as iwóto.
iwo'ȟtaǩe, n. A billiard stick or cue; the hammer of a gun.

iwo'ic'iťo, v. (iwoto). To run one's self against. Bl. Cf. iikpustaⁿ.

iwo'ju, n. A seed drill. Wagmeza - . - su. B.H.200.3.

i'wokoǩiṗeǩe, n. One with a sharp tongue. Bl.

i'wokpaⁿ, (?). Bl.

i'wona s'a, (?). - iyeyapi s'e uⁿkiyayapelo, i.e. going fast, as in an automobile over high and low places. Also perhaps, iẃowaⁿka. - iyaye s'e hiyu.Bl.
i'wonas'iyaya, v. To pass over a target and high into the air, as an arrow.Bl.

iwo'paⁿ, 1) v. To shoot to pieces. 2) n. A pestle. Cf. wopaⁿ.

i'wopsil, (?). Same perhaps as iwowaⁿka. - wao. Bl.

iwo'sla, (?). Nakpa - ikikcu, To prick up one's ears; similarly, Nakpa yuwaⁿkal ikikcu. Bl.

iwo'sli, n. A squirt; a syringe; a squirt gun, which is made by Dakota boys out of the common elder or boxwood.

iwo'slohaⁿ, v. To blow along lengthwise. - iyeya.
iwo'slohaⁿhaⁿ, v. red. To fly over the ground, as snow in a blizzard. Waiwoslohaⁿhaⁿ, Snow drifting. Bl.

i'woś̄o, n. Pouting lips.
i'woś̄oǩa, adj. Pouting with the mouth pushed up. R. Bl.
i'woś̄oǩiya, v.n. To push out the lips; to pout. Iwośowakiya.

iwo'ś'aǩa, v. (woś'aka). To hit with little force, to indent. Iwowaś'aka. Waciⁿ - , To be discouraged. Hecel waciⁿ iwomaś'akiⁿ kte śni. Pb.42.

iwo'ťaniⁿśniyaⁿ, adv. Visible only very close by. - haⁿ na kaska iyaya.

iwō'ťo, v.n. To hit or strike against, butt against. Also, iyóťo. Iwomato. Iwoic'ito.

i'wowaⁿka o, v. To hit something after first striking another thing, as an arrow the ground first. Iwowaⁿka wao. Iwowaⁿka iyeyapi s'e uⁿkiyayapelo, as in going fast in an automobile through a draw to a higher point. Bl.

iwo'yaǩa, v.a. To relate, tell of; to speak in ref. to. Iwoblaka.

iya', v.n. To speak. Also, iá. Iwáya, iyáya, uⁿkiyapi. Note: iáa, v.n. red. where the "y" is dropped. D.105,note 1.

I'ya, n. prop. A fabulous creature.

iyab', cont. (iyapa). Striking against. Tiyopa - iblabla, I struck against the door.

iya'blagyela, adv. Calmly. Aⁿpetu waⁿ okatakiⁿ wanica ca - helo. Bl.

i'yableza, v.a. Watch, with ref. to something. Miniyatkaⁿpi kiⁿ iyawicableza yo. B.H.75.14.

iyab'ya, adv. Singly, separately scattered, as in hunting. - uⁿyaⁿpi, We go separately. Also, butting or striking against.

i'yabya, adv. Scattering around, dispersedly. - najiŋpi. - uŋkolepi, Scattering ourselves around we hunted.

iya'cica, adj. Rough, ruffled up, as is said of hair or feathers.

iya'ciŋ, v.a. To liken to, compare with. Iblácin. -- iyáciŋȟel, adv. By way of comparison. -- iyáciŋpi, n. A likeness, resemblance. -- iyáciŋyaŋ, adv. Like to, in like manner, equal to; parabolically, metaphorically. -- iyáciŋyaŋȟel, adv. Somewhat like.

iya'ġegnag, n. A cluster-like group, as of grapes. Also, iyáge. R. - yaŋka, P. Bl. -- iyágeya, adv. In clusters, in bunches. Bl.

iya'ġi, v. To be rusty, perhaps. Bl.

iya'glapśiŋyaŋ, v.a. To turn over upon anything.

i'yaglapśiŋyaŋ, adv. (aglapśiŋyaŋ). Bottom upwards.

iya'glasȟi, cont. of iyaglaskica. - mayaŋka, It is pressing on me.
iya'glasȟica, v.n. (aglaskica). To lie on, press on; to cover. Iyamaglaskica.
iya'glaskilya, v.a. To cause to press upon. Iyaglaskilwaya.

iya'glaśȟa, v. pos. (iyakaśka). To tie one's own to. Iyáwaglaśka. Nupiŋ wáciŋhiŋ ikaŋ haaskeya itowe el iyaglaśkapi. Yuóŋjiŋcayela iyaglaśka, To tuck up one's robe or dress. Bl.

iya'glaśna, v.n. To make a mistake, to blunder in speaking. Same as iéglaśna. Iyawaglaśna.

iya'gle, v.n. To go or come to; to reach to, extend or lead to, as does a road; to meet, come upon one. Cf. iyagleya.

iya'glegleġa, v. To tell lies. Iyamaglegleġa. Bl.

iya'gleic'iya, v.n. To get one's self into trouble or difficulties that one cannot overcome, as does a thief; to be in for trouble, to meet obstructions on one's way. Same as iyokaic'iya.

iya'gletoŋ, v.a. To have on or over. - ecoŋ, He does it on something else, as to knit on.
iya'gletoŋyaŋ, adv. Over, having something under. - kaksa, To cut one stick off on another.

iya'gleya, 1) v.a. To cause to reach to, to lead or bring one to, as a man into trouble. Pte otapi el ai na maya waŋ el iyaglewicayapi. Yuŋkaŋ wiŋyaŋ k'oŋ u kiŋ iwaŋkab Ȟolyela haŋ, maȟpiya ekta - haŋ waŋyakapi. Iyaglewaya, iyaglemaya. 2) adv. Leading somewhere, as does a road; reaching to, even to; on top of something, as a house on its foundation. Caŋku kiŋ le Manderson (otoŋwahe) - ihuŋni. Htayetu - hecoŋhaŋpi. - haŋ. Petijaŋjaŋ - egle yo, i.e. put it on; or, Petijaŋjaŋ agle egle yo. Le woeye kiŋ lehaŋ - , This (old) word is in use until the present day. Le aŋpetu kiŋ - Until this day. B.H.108.10;259.29. EM. Cf. B.H.113.7;274.13;108.3.

iya'gluȟa, v. pos. (iyayuȟa). To follow after one's own, as a colt its mother. Iyawagluȟa and iyabluȟa.

iya'glupta, v. refl. To slip away, break loose, escape, as an animal one had tried to kill. Iyamaglupta, iyaniglupta. Bl.

iya'gluza, v. (?). Hecélaȟci wana iyawagluzelo, Now I gave everything away. Bl.

iya'gna, prep. After, behind, following; with, together with. Same as iyáyustog. Yuŋkaŋ itazipa waŋ lila haŋska ca yuha najiŋ na wahiŋkpe waŋ lila haŋska ca nakuŋ - . Waŋna yamni caŋ miyagna uŋpi (Mark 8.1). Maȟpiya śapa iagna u kiŋ. St. B.H.258.7.
iya'gnagna, prep. red.
iya'gnaȟel, adv. In the manner of following.

iya'gnaśkiŋyaŋ, v. To say foolish things in anger. Iyamagnaśkiŋyaŋ. Bl.

iya'gtoŋ, v. (iyake). To put a feather on an arrow. Iyagwatoŋ.

iya'ġuya, v. To burn, as a little mush in a kettle after the water is evaporated. Also perhaps, iyáġu.

iyaġ'ya, Cf. iyáke. Waŋbli Ȟupahu.

wiyaka ca iyagyapi (arrows, i.e.).

i'yagyaťayela, adv. red. (iyatayela). Individually, personally, self alone. B.H.60.4.

iya'haŋ, v.a. To go up a hill and stand, in ref. to one man; where there are many, we say éyahaŋ. Iyawahaŋ, uŋkiyahaŋpi. Na waŋna paha k'oŋ el iyahaŋpi. Paha kiŋ kal iyawahe. Bl. BT. -- part. Speaking.

i'yahaŋ, v.a. To put the foot on, step on anything. Íyawahaŋ. Na waŋnaś śina waŋ, iŋyaŋ eya ko el ahipi na waŋna kéya oŋśi - .

i'yaȟagyela, adv. Too little left, too short. Same as iyapat'oyela. - tókaŋl iyawakaśke śni, i.e. the two ends of the string were too short to tie them together. Tuwa iyaȟagyelaȟci omiglaptelo, i.e. left me very little. Bl.

iya'ȟpaȟpaya, v.n. To scramble. Also, iyákiciȟpayapi, They scramble. P. Bl.

iya'ȟpaya, v.n. To fall upon, grab, seize. Iyawaȟpaya, iyauŋȟpayapi. Na kici iyakiciȟpayapi. Huŋku kiŋ ceya iyayiŋ na (hokśila tawa) iyakiȟpaya kéye. R.

iya'ȟpeȟiciciya, v.a. To put or throw on for one e.g. a load on a horse.

iya'ȟpeȟiya, v.a. To put on or throw over e.g. the back of a horse. Hō---- waŋna - yo, as an old man called out before moving on.

iya'ȟpeȟiya, v.a. To give or hand to one e.g. the pipe; to put on or throw over, as in loading a horse; to touch the ground with and then hold up to heaven, as is done before smoking the pipe.

iya'ȟpeya, v.a. To throw over or on, throw out, as a rope on a horse's head or as a fishline. Iyáȟpewaya. Wakaŋtaŋka - , To make God favorable by prayers (a saying used by the Indians of old). Caŋnuŋpa - po, Smoke! RF. Bl.

iya'ic'ikpehaŋ, v. refl. (iyapehaŋ). To wrap one's self around, as does a snake. Zuzeca waŋ hiyu na Paul nape el - . B.H.304.2.

iya'ic'ipa, v. To knock against, as one's head against a wall. Wanuŋ - yelo. P. Bl.

iya'iglaśka, v. refl. (iyakaśka). To tie one's self, to give one's self up to be bound. Iyámiglaśka.

i'yaȟa, n. A glutton, one who eats too much.

i'yaȟab, adv. (i and akab). In addition, more than what is due, than what one needs, to spare. Taku oyasiŋ - yuha. - ecoŋ, To overdo. - iyeya, To surpass. B.H.149.22. P.

i'yakabtu, adv. Surpassingly. Same as iyakab. R. Bl.

i'yaȟaȟpe, n. (akahpa). A cover or lid for the mouth of anything. B.H. 60.20. -- íyaȟaȟpeya, adv. Serving as a cover. - haŋ. B.H.23.6.

iya'kaŋwiŋlake s'e, adv. (?). - tak'eye, He says so, but I doubt it. Bl.

i'yakapa, v.n. To be larger than, to surpass. Íyamakapa.

iya'ȟapaťaŋhaŋ, adv. Afterwards; behind.

i'yaȟapaťaŋhaŋ, adv. Over or on top.

i'yakap̣eic'iya, v. refl. To go beyond one's self, to be intemperate.

i'yakap̣ep̣eya, adv. red. of iyakapeya. B.H.178.9.

i'yaȟap̣eya, 1) v.a. To pass, go beyond, overcome; to persuade, succeed in persuading. Iyakapewaya. 2) adv. More than surpassing.

iya'ȟapťa, v.a. To climb, as a hill, to reach the top; to pass over or beyond. Iyawakapta, iyauŋkaptapi, uŋkiyakaptapi.

iya'ȟapťeya, 1) v. To cause to pass up or over. Iyakaptewaya. 2) adv. Beyond, going over; going up-hill.

iya'ȟasaŋni, n. One side or half of something. -- iyáȟasaŋnila, n. One side only.

iya'ȟaśȟa, v.a. (kaśka). To tie one thing to or on another. Iyawakaśka. Na le caŋ eya wiyaka iyakaśkapi kiŋ hena icu.

iya'ǩaťiŋ, v. (akatiŋ). To measure by means of e.g. a yard-stick. Iyáwakatiŋ.

i'yaǩawiŋ, v.n. (akawiŋ). To exceed, go beyond bounds, overflow, as a river does its banks.

iya'ǩe, n. The feather end of a quill, the feather on an arrow.

iya'ǩicaśka, (?). - ówaheȟce, as a man says to another who is very lazy and does not want to be disturbed and thus wants to help him along. - óciciheȟcelo, i.e. follow you closely. - ómakihaŋ yo, Follow close behind me. Bl.

iya'ǩiciȟpaya, v. To bounce on each other. Bl.

iya'ǩiciyuha, v. To be attached to, as one horse to another. Iyaweciyuha. R. Bl. -- iyáǩiciyuȟa, v.n. To be attached to, follow those one loves. Iyábluȟa.

i'yaǩicuŋni, v.n. To become tired and leave off, to give up. Íyawecuŋni. D.59. Na wana iyawicakicuŋnipi na awicayuśtaŋpi. MS.565.
i'yaǩicuŋniya, v.a. To cause to leave off or cease from. Íyakicuŋniwaya.
i'yaǩicuŋniyaŋ, adv. Leaving off.

iya'ǩic'u, 1) v.n. To be much, to increase. 2) adv. Much more than one needs.

iya'ǩic'uŋc'uŋka, n. One who does more than is usual; one who keeps on begging.

iya'ǩic'uya, adv. Much, a good deal, plentifully, in abundance. - bluha, I have a great deal. Cf. akic'uya. -- v.a. To have more than one needs. Iyákic'uwaya.

iya'ǩigle, adv. Times. Zaptaŋ - . B.H. 37.7. Pb.36. -- v.n. To surpass, overlap, reach beyond the time, as old corn lasting until the new comes. -- adv. Like to, as. Wetu - maśte, It is as warm as spring. -- iyáǩiglegle, adv. Over and over again, repeatedly.

i'yaǩigleǧa, v. To go on and overtake R. Bl. -- íyaǩigleȟ, cont. R. Bl. --

iyáǩigleya, 1) v.a. To cause to reach round to; to make surpass. Iyakiglewaya. 2) adv. Surpassing. Nuŋpa - Śakowiŋ - . B.H.112.8;217.2.

iya'ǩigna, adv. In layers, one on another.

iya'kiȟpaya, v. pos. (iyahpaya). To grab, seize one's own, as one's gun. D.248;266.

iya'ǩiju, adv. perhaps.(ju). Together, united; put, placed, laid up together. Hocokab tipi - ihaȟpeya, To join 2 to 4 tents into one big one for meeting purposes. Na el akicita wóhaŋpi na oceti śakowiŋ el iwoglakapi. Hihaŋna kiŋ hocokab tipi - iyaȟpeyapi kta śke lo.
iya'ǩijuya, adv. Together. - okala. - omaka 102 ni uŋ na t'e. Bl. B.H.128.11.

i'yaǩilececa, adv. Like, alike.
i'yaǩilecel, adv. Alike. Iyákilecel is a doubtful form. B. B.H.191.20,21; 235.10.

i'yaǩilehaŋkeca, adv. Of the same length with.
i'yaǩilehaŋyaŋ, adv. Of equal distance.
i'yaǩilenakeca, adv. Of equal number.

i'yaǩilenala, adv. As few as.

iya'kili, v.a. To climb up on one's own, perhaps. B.H.8.5.

i'yaǩiniskoǩeca, adv. Of the same size.

i'yakipapa, v. Cf. iakipapa.

iya'ǩiṗe, v.a. To wait for, hope for; to befall, happen to. Iyawakipe. - maŋkelo (or: ape maŋkelo). Iháwakta na ena maŋkelo. Iyamakipe yo, Wait for me, Look for me. Bl. D.202,219.
iya'ǩiṗeya, adv. Waiting for.

i'yaǩiś'a, v. To shout at one's own.
i'yaǩiś'aś'a, v. red. B.H.72.14. Cf. iyaś'a.

iya'ǩiťa, v.a. To urge on, as slow horses; to chase away e.g. dogs. Iyawicakita yo, i.e. the horses; hurry them up if you want to get home. RTj.

i'yaǩiťa, v.a. (akita). To have an eye to, keep watch on, lest one commit some depredation; to hunt for charges against one. Iyawakita.

iya'k̇itaŋiŋ, (?). -lake uŋki kiŋhaŋ, waśte yelo, Better to go in daylight. Aŋpetu - śni yelo, i.e. foggy. Bl.

i'yako, adv. Beyond anything. Cf. ako.
i'yakotaŋhaŋ, adv. Beyond, from beyond.

iya'ksaṗa, v.a. To make wise by talking.

iya'kṫaśni, v.a. (aktaśni). To disregard. Iyáwaktaśni, íyauŋkiciktapi śni. Note: iyakta is not used. Bl.

iya'k'iŋtoŋ, v. To sew, glue, lay something on, e.g. a piece of leather. Bl.

iya'k'oza, n. A horse that has big knuckles, i.e. swollen. Same as wohé, iyanuŋga, which cf. - waŋ yuhapi. Kul Wicaśa - waŋ yuhapi. Bl.

iya'li, v.a. (ali). To climb up on. Iyawali.

iya'mni, adj. The third.
iya'mnila, adj. Only the third one.
iya'mnimni, adj. red. Every third one.

iya'mnimni, ia'mnimni, v. (amnimni). To sprinkle, as water on anything. Iyawamnimni.

iya'najica, v. To run with what one has taken, as a run-away horse with a wagon, or a man with a horse. Iyánawajica. Taśuŋke kiŋ zaptaŋ iyanawajice lo. BT.

iya'napṫa, v.a. (anapta). To detain, to go before and prevent from proceeding. Iyanawapta. - k̇uṫé, To obstruct, step in the way, and shoot. Bl.

iya'nica, i'yanica, v.n. (aníca). To be prevented, detained or hindered by; remain fast, be unable to go on. Iyamanica, iyauŋnicapi. Magaju kiŋ he iyamanica. D.22.

iya'nuŋġa, v.n. To become hard, callous or unfeeling, as a scarred place. Iyamanuŋga. Same as iyak'oza. Note: this is said of the knuckles of a horse when they are swollen.
iya'nuŋḣ, cont. - iyeya.
iya'nuŋḣya, v.a. To cause to become callous. Iyánuŋḣwaya.

iya'oṗemni, v.a. To cover, enclose, shroud. Iyaowapemni. P. Bl.

iya'pa, v.a. (apa). To beat or strike against; to beat, as the heart; to strike or knock against, as with the foot. Iyamapa, iyauŋpapi. Iyaic'ipa. Lila caŋte - waŋyaŋk yaŋkahaŋ. Lila caŋte iyamapa. Iyawapa. Tokśa, iyacicipe kte.

i'yapa, n. A snow storm. - waŋ hi yelo. GA. B.H.69.12.

i'yaṗaháyela, adv. Brimful, much of anything, as is said of dry things as grain that heaps on top. Also, íyaṗaśniśyela. Bl. Cf. íyujibyela.

iya'pakel, adv. Unexpectedly, all of a sudden. - waŋblake lo. Bl.

iya'papa, v. red. of iyapa. Icapśiŋpśiŋcala ic'icage na mni - kiŋyaŋ ya. MS.573.

i'yaṗaśniśyela, adj. Brimful. Same as íyapahayela. P. Bl.

i'yaṗaśtag, cont. of iyapaśtaka.
i'yaṗaśtagya, v.a. To creep up and fall upon before one is aware, to take by surprise. Iyapaśtagwaya. R.Bl.
i'yaṗaśtaka, v.n. To be taken by surprise. Íyamapaśtaka. R. Bl.

i'yaṗṫaŋ, (?). - glus kat'iyewayelo, I shot it from nearby. Bl.

i'yaṗat'o, i'yaṗat'ola, v.n. To butt against, be struck by; to press on, be cramped by e.g. a short moccasin. Íyamapat'o. Haŋpa iyamapat'ola. Si iyamapat'o ca si mapani ye, said when the shoes are too short. Bl.
i'yaṗat'oya, v.a. To run against; to hinder, prevent. Íyapat'owaya.
i'yaṗat'oyak̇el, adv. In the manner of pressing against; pressed together, cramped together, close together, as in sitting close together or as books stand close together on a shelf. Also, íyaṗat'oyela. - uŋyaŋkapi.

iya'paya, v.a. To run against, be thrown against, as in an automobile. Iyapawaya. Bl.

-- iyápayaȟel, adv. Encountering, as stormy weather. - waŋuŋkiciyaŋkapi ca takuni taŋyaŋ uŋkoglakapi śni yelo, i.e. we met in cold weather, so talked briefly and accomplished nothing. Bl.

i'yaṗe, adv. Near, close. Míyape, Near me. Níyape, Near you. Taŋká miyape yaŋka. -- v.a. (ape). To wait for, lie in wait for, lie in ambush. Íyawape. Tokśa iyácicipe kte.

iya'ṗehaŋ, v.a. (pehaŋ). To fold up with, to wind on, as the thread on a spool, to wrap around. Iyawapehaŋ. Haȟuŋta iyapehaŋpi, Spool-thread. Caŋnuŋpa pahiŋ iyapehaŋpi, A pipe whose stem is covered with porcupine quill-work wrapped around. Taśupa caŋ iyawapehaŋ na cewaoŋpiŋ kte lo. Bl.
iya'ṗehaŋyaŋ, adv. Folding up.

iya'ṗeȟel, adv. (?). - kuwa, To watch in order to catch, waiting for a chance to catch. B.H.230.11.

i'yaṗela, adv. Near, close at hand.

iya'ṗemni, v.a. (aopemni). To wrap around, wind up in. Iyawapemni.
iya'ṗemniyaŋ, adv. Wrapped up in.

iya'ṗeya, 1) v.a. (iyape). To cause to lie in wait for. Iyapewaya. 2) adv. Lying in wait for.

iya'ṗusṗa, 1) v.a. To glue, stick on with glue or paste. Iyawapuspa. 2) v.n. To stick to, as wet clothes; to be glued, as sore eyes. Iyamapuspa.
iya'ṗusṗeya, 1) v.a. To cause to glue on. Iyapuspewaya. 2) adv. In a glued or sticking manner.

iya'p'op'oya, adv. Misty. - hiyaya ca osni yelo, as is said when it is foggy and cold, as also: Maȟpiya ġiġiya kaȟwog hiyayelo. Bl.

iya'p'osp'os, (?). - ahiyayelo, as said when it is very cloudy and then clear again. Bl.

i'yap'oyela, adv. Misty. B.H.56.16.

iya'sag, cont. of iyasaka.

iya'saȟa, v.n. To be dried hard on, as skin or garments on one. Iyamasaka.

iya'sȟab, cont. of iyaskapa.
iya'sȟabya, 1) v.a. perhaps. To make stick to, as a postage stamp. Cf. iyaskapa. 2) adv. Sticking to.
iya'sȟabye, n. Glue. WE.

iya'sȟaṗa, v.n. (askapa). To stick to, stick on, adhere to. Iyámaskapa. B.H. 135.24. Iŋyaŋ kiŋ ena - , i.e. stuck to the rock. D.73.

iya'sȟi, cont. of iyaskica.

iya'sȟica, v.a. To press or suck one thing on another, as corn on the cob. Iblaskica.
iya'sȟilya, adv. Pressing, sucking on.

iya'sȟisȟa, v.n. To be smoothed down, as the hair on an animal by swimming in the water. Iyamaskiska.

iya'sni, v.n. (asni). To become still, as a noise ceasing; to recover from, as from anger or sickness; to die down, as a fire with only coals left. D.197. Iyámasni.
iya'sniya, v.a. To give to one unexpectedly; to make quiet. Iyasniwaya.

iya'su, v.a. (yasu). To judge of, judge on account of, condemn for. Iblasu.

i'yas'e, n. (iya). A glutton.

iya'śka, (?). Yuŋkaŋ hokśila kiŋ he - hokśila ic'icaga ke.

i'yaślalya, v.a. To prove one to be a liar; to catch one in a suspected action. Iyaślalwaya. D.279.

i'yaślata, v. To be found guilty of a lie. Iyamaślata. El ayakage ciŋhaŋ tokata Tuŋkaśila ekta wai kiŋ iyaniślatiŋ kta ca taŋyaŋ ecoŋ wo, as was said to a government representative.ST.

i'yaślaya, adv. Plainly, clearly.

iya'śoṫa, (?). - s'e omawani, i.e. the breath is steam because it is cold. Bl.

i'yaś'a, v. (aś'a). To shout at, shout against. Iyawaś'a.
i'yaś'ayapi, n. The war-whoop. P. Bl.

i'yaś'ápi, n. An acclamation. Bl.

iya'ṫa, v.a. To say that one intends to give something to a person that is absent. Iblata. Iyatahe c'on wan k'uwelo. Bl. Cf. R.

iya'ta, v. To chew something with something else. Taṗi' ca waśinlo iyatapi s'e, as is said when through disputing much confusion is created. Bl.

iya'tab, adv. After; soon, soon again. Miyatab u wo, Follow me. - ya. B.H. 177.14;205.1;234.3. D.73.
i'yatabyela, adv. Soon after.

i'yatagle, 1) adj. To go beyond, surpass, to go beyond ordinary bounds, be excessive. Iyamatagle. 2) adv. Full, running over. Le anpetu kin iyamatagle ca heon ośkinc'iye maśicelo, ca ito le hanhepi kin ake ewicunkiyapi kte lo. Ungna taku iyanitagle kin ikan lupsake cin oteḣi wan slolyayin kta.

i'yaṫagle, v., adj. To be speechless from surprise. Iyamatagle, iyanitagle.

i'yatagleic'iya, v.n. To surfeit, to be immoderate. - śni, Be moderate, temperate. P.
i'yatagleya, 1) v.a. To go beyond, surpass, to do more than is right or exact, do too much; to cause to go beyond; to be intemperate. Iyataglewaya. 2) adv. Too much.

iya'ṫan, v.a. To light e.g. a pipe. Iblatan. Na cannunpa unhe wanna iyatanpi na unpwicakiyapi. Ilatan hwo? Hau, iwaglatan. Na gliglekiya iyatanpi. BT.
iya'tan, v.a. To touch with the mouth. Iblatan.

iya'taninlaḣe, n. The while it is yet daylight. - c'el ecamon ktelo. Bl.

iya'ṫasag, cont. of iyatasaka.
iya'ṫasagya, adv. Stiffly.
iya'ṫasaḣa, v.n. (tasaka). To become hard or stiff on one, as skin that has been wet and dried stiff or frozen on. Iyamatasaka.

i'yaṫayéla, adv. pron. Personally, individually; it alone. Also, íatayela. - śunkawakan kipi, It alone cost one horse.

iya'unṗa, v.a. (aunpa). To lay on, place on; to accuse of, blame with. Iyawaunpa. Lena taku iyaniunpapi kin takuni alupta śni he?
iya'unṗaṗi, n. An accusation.
iya'unṗeṗicaśni, adj. Blameless. Le weyapi kin iyaunpemapicaśni yelo. B.H.263.4.
iya'unṗeṗicaśniyan, adv. Blamelessly.
iya'unṗeya, adv. In a blaming or accusing way.

iya'wa, v.a. (yawa). To count by or according to, count together; to figure with, settle. Iblawa. B.H.33.2; 217.4.

iya'wanyangkiciya, v. (?). Wakantanka toogligle waśte wan iawanyangkiciyin kte kin he wicawala yelo. B.H.122.19.

iya'ya, v.n. To have gone; to be more than, to go over, be more than enough, be a surplus. Wicokan sam - . Na tona (i.e. sugar and coffee) iyaye k'on hena kala iyeya, tka ayuta naunjinpi kin hecena takuni śni. Unkiyayapi.

iya'yahan, part. (iyaya, of iya or ia). Talking, chatting. Pb.24.

iya'yeḣiya, v. To pretend to go away, to act as though one was going away. Iyáyewakiya. Bl.

iya'yeya, v.a. To cause to go or have gone, to send; to turn away, rout. Iyayewaya. Na śunkawakan kin unyan iyayewicunyapi kte. Wiyatke kin le miyopteya iyayeyi ye. Pb.41.

iya'yuḣ, cont. (iyayuḣa). To go closely behind another. - un. - iyaya. - ocimani yacin. Mitaoyate kin nahaḣci waziyata pte - unpi ca tohanl agli kinhan iwanweglakin kta. OH.
iya'yuḣe, v. To have an attachment for, be a follower of; Latin, cara. Iyabluḣe, iyáciyuḣe. Iyáciyuḣa yacin. Iyamayaluḣepi śni. B.H.101.15;107.10.
iya'yuḣḣiya, (?). Wicaḣpi kin...na yapi. B.H.169.18.
iya'yuḣya, adv. Following. B.H.112.3.

iya'yukśan, prep. Around. Otonwahe - . B.H.72.12.

iya'yus, cont. of iyayuza. - yuza, To

hold anything close to another.

iya'yuscola, adj. Unarmed. BD.

iya'yusťak, cont. (iyayustaka). With, together with. Wowapi nuŋpa - yuha, He holds two books together (in his hand). B.H.115.24;287.7.
iya'yusťaǩa, v. (?). Iyayustag heyuŋ, To tie one thing on another. Iyayustag hemuŋ.

iya'yuwi, v. To grow warped, become curled or twisted. Iyamayuwi, iyaniyuwi. Leceya nape kiŋ caŋ iyamayuwi kte lo, i.e. the hands stiff. Nape caŋ iyaniyuwi ȟca hwo? Bl.

iya'yuza, 1) v.a. (yuza). To hold to or at. Iyabluza. 2) n. A holder, as a cloth to hold a hot iron with.

iya'za, adv. One after another, as going from one home to another. Tipi - omani. Tiíyaza. Wópate kiŋ - wol omani hi. Hecel wicaȟpi hiŋȟpaya oyate - omani na taku ecoŋpica śni ecoŋ keyapi. Cf. oyaza.

iya'zaŋ, v.n. (yazaŋ). To be sick on account of or by means of; to be affected by sympathy with cr for. Imayazaŋ.

iya'zi, v. To be convalescent. Tóhaŋ watuka iyanizi keci hehaŋl..., When you have recovered. Bl.

iya'zil, cont. of iyazita.
iya'zilya, v.a. To burn e.g. sweet leaves, to burn incense. Iyazilwaya.
iya'zita, v.n. To burn e.g. cedar leaves, to smoke and make a pleasant odor.

i'ye, pron. pers. He, she, it. Iyepi, They.

i'yecana, adv. Soon after, near to, soon. - yahi, You came soon after. - wau kta.

iye'ceca, 1) v.n. To be like to; it is fitting, proper. Iyemaceca. Hecamuŋ kta - . 2) adv. Like, like as, like that, such as, the same as.
iye'cecaśniyaŋ, adv. Unlike, such as not. Itazipa...na yuwegapi - suta ca ecoŋpi. Syn.- iyécecaya.
iye'ceȟci, adv. Just like. Hoǩiiyokpaza - wauŋ welo, I cannot grasp anything. He (zitkala) - hehaŋl śinasapa wicablumihaŋ yelo. BT.
iye'cekceca, adv. red. of iyececa. Huŋhuŋhé, le uŋci si - yelo, How her feet resemble grandmother's! D.55.
iye'cekcelya, adv. red. of iyecelya. B.H.63.11.
iye'cel, prep. Like; in like manner. - ecoŋ, To conform to, to be consistent; to imitate. Le t'iŋkte - oȟ'aŋ yelo. B.H.1.20;258.12.
iye'celya, adv. Like; a little less, not much. - śica ayapi. B.H.9.3.
iye'ceťu, 1) v.n. To be so, become so, to be as was expected; to come to pass or take place. B.H.174.22. 2) adv. So, thus; right.
iye'ceťuya, adv. So.
iye'ceťuyaǩel, adv. In this manner.

iye'ciŋǩa, adv. Of one's self, of one's own accord, without advice. Miyeciŋka. - iglúha, To be a citizen.
iye'ciŋkala, Same as iyeciŋka. Miyeciŋkala, uŋkiyeciŋkalapi. - hena iyaġnipi kta.
iye'ciŋǩiŋyaŋka, n. An automobile.

i'yeeś, pron. emph. He, she, it.

iye'ha, adv. (eha). Instead, rather he (she). Yuŋkaŋ haŋkaku kiŋ - nagiyeya śke'. Bl. Note: The word indicates something like: It is you who does it, as is said when one is accused of doing what the speaker is doing.LP.

iye'haŋ, adv. At the time appointed. Waŋna iyemicihaŋ, My time is on, i.e. for being on duty.
iye'haŋhaŋkeca, adv. red. of iyehaŋkeca
iye'haŋhaŋťu, adv. red. (iyehaŋtu). At the times referred to; at referred to places, perhaps.
iye'haŋhaŋyaŋ, adv. red. of iyehaŋyaŋ.
iye'haŋkeca, adv. Being of the same length, as two things compared. Same as iyehaŋyaŋ.
iye'haŋl, adv. At the time, just then. Same as wahehaŋl. B.H.22.2;53.3;61.17. Note: the word refers to past as well as future time.

iyehaŋtu, adv. At the time; now, it being the time now. Na waŋna aŋpetu waŋ el kipi kte ci - wicokaŋyaŋ to eyaś

asnikiyapi. - kiᵑhaᵑ ake wau kta. Na wotapi kte k'uᵑ he wana - . Na waᵑna - k'oᵑ hehaᵑ ukiya, i.e. at the appointed time, when it was time.
iye'haᵑt̄ula, adv. Just at the time.
iye'haᵑt̄ulahci, adv. Exactly at the time. R. Bl.
iye'haᵑtuśni, adv. Not time yet.
iye'haᵑtuya, adv. At the time. B.H.148.14.
iye'haᵑwapa, adv. Towards the time.

iye'haᵑyaᵑ, adv. To be even, of the same size, length, height etc. Same as iyehaᵑkeca; also, perhaps used as adj. - śni, It does not come up to the mark, one being smaller than the other. - ciᵑ, as is said when in buying a hat one wants the same size he had before. Tuweni - uᵑ śni. Tuweni - śni haᵑskiᵑ. Tuweni iyenihaᵑyaᵑ kte śni. Takuni niyehaᵑyaᵑ taᵑka śni. B.H.43.16;86.4;98.18;100.22;191.12;194.4. Note: the word is used in comparing or measuring two things and seems always to call for an adj., at least in the mind.

iye'ic'iya, v. refl. (iyeya). To find one's self; to put or thrust one's self. Ogna - , To push, crowd one's self in.

iye'jak̄ak̄eś, adv. Unable, failing by a little, as in what one is accustomed.

iye'k̄aeś, pron. Even he. Also, iyék̄aleś

iye'k̄ap̄iᵑ, Cf. iekapiᵑ.

iye'k̄icihaᵑt̄u, v.n. To be suitable for one, be fitting or belonging to one; to be the time or opportunity for one. Iyémicihaᵑtu, iyeuᵑkicihaᵑtu. B.H.172.3

iye'k̄iya, v.a. pos. (iyeya). To find one's own, to recognize; to put or push one's own in. Ate, iyemayakiyiᵑ kta. Wímakaᵑ nitawa ojúha el - yo.

iye'k̄t̄aśni, adv. Incorrectly, not according to rule.

iye'na, pron. As many (as), so many. Tipi tonakeca kiᵑ yawapi na lena (coffee and sugar) - wicak'upi kte lo. Na ake iciyamni ai na ake - wicaopi na agli. Oyate peji - , A nation as many as the blades of grass. Na - ca mini yatkaᵑpi śni naiᵑś wotapi śni... waᵑna enakiyapi. B.H.111.5.
iye'nak̄a, adv. So many as.
iye'nakeca, adj., pron. As many, as much. Iyemanakeca, iyeuᵑnakecapi. Ake ecoᵑpi na ake - (buffalos) naceca wicaopi. B.H.58.2;93.19;247.7.
iye'naᵑgnakeca, adv. red. of iyenakeca.

iye'nayaᵑ, v.n. To give up, to be tired of. Iyenawaya. - uᵑpi. P. BD. Bl. B.H. 118.12.

iye'piśni, v. They did not seem to be the same people anymore. - s'e kuᵑśitku kici kas'ala yaᵑkapi keye.

iye'ska, Same as ieska.

iyeś', pron. Same as íyeeś and carries the notion: It is better. Itaᵑcaᵑ kiᵑ itokab wawahtani kte śni ca - waśte ye. B.H.138.1,2.
i'yeśkalaka, pron. He himself, even he. Same as iyeśtuka laka. Also, íyek'e, (Yanktoᵑ). Cf. D.71. R.

iye'śnica, interj. You don't say so! It cannot be.

iye'śt̄uka, (?). Uᵑkíyeśtuka he waᵑbli yeś kte yeśaᵑ, i.e. was fooled inspite of his smartness. - oyuspe, He caught it while everyone else had missed it. Yuᵑkaᵑ - wakaᵑ; caᵑke..., i.e. had supernatural powers. - laka. Bl. D.158, 119. B.H.88.3.

iye'ya, v. aux. It is appended to verbs commencing with ka, na, pa, wa, wo, ya, yu, and to some adverbs and generally emphasizes and expresses quickness or suddenness of action. Iyewaya, iyeuᵑyaᵑpi. -- v.a. To find, to put, place, thrust into, shove at. Iyewaya. Na wa kiᵑ iwaᵑkal (on the house) iyeya. Taku waᵑ iyewayelo ca iwacu welo. -- iyéyaya, v.a. emph. of iyeya. P.

iyo', prep. in comp. (i-o and euphonic y). To, in, into.
iyo'blaye, n. (oblaye). A plain extending from, as from a hill.

iyo'blula, 1) adv. Sheltered. 2) n. A sheltered place. Same as ioblula.

iyo'cokaya, adv. (i-ocokaya). In the midst of; all put into the mouth;

all swallowed up in.

iyo'cosyakel, adv. (?). - owahelo. Bl. Syn.- iyowiŋhahayakel,

iyo'coza, v.a. To be warm in, as in a coat. He imacoza.

iyo'glagla, adv. Rattling. - s'e iyaya. To make a noise, as of a bullet put into the muzzle of a gun; to go down with a rattling noise.

iyo'glamna, adv. Circuitously, round all the crooks and turns.
iyo'glamnayaŋ, adv. Circuitously, particularly. - woglaka.
iyo'glamniyaŋ, adv. Round about.

iyo'gli, n. A razor strap, a steel hone perhaps. -- iyógliya, v.a. To rub back and forth, as in whetting or strapping a razor. Iyogliwaya.

iyo'gluś't'eya, (?). Iyogluś't'ewaya. Iyogluś't'emayayelo, as a man who wants to live in peace would say to another who is always after him; meaning: You make me sick with you talking. Bl.

iyo'gluze, n. Wearing apparel. Bl.

i'yogmus, Cf. iogmus, iogmusya, iogmuza.

iyo'gnag, Cf. iognag. - iyeya. Bl.
iyo'gnagkiya, Cf. iognagkiya.
iyo'gnagya, Cf. iognagya.
iyo'gnaka, v.a. To put into the mouth, as food. Iyowagnaka. Cf. iognaka.

i'yohaḣab, adv. After, in time, subsequent to.

i'yohaḣabtoŋ, v. To close or seal, as a full box or letter after it is finished. Bl.
i'yohaḣabtu, adv. Afterwards.
i'yohaḣabṫuyaḣel, adv. A little after.
i'yohaḣabṫuya, adv. Afterwards.

iyo'haŋ, v.a. (ohaŋ). To boil one thing with another. Iyowahe.

iyo'haŋzi, n. (ohaŋzi). A shady place, a bower. Wazi - waŋ el uŋgliyotakapi.

i'yohe, n. Something wrapped around the fee; socks, stockings.

iyo'hi, adj. Each, every one.

iyo'hi, v.a. To reach, get to arrive at a place; to be sufficient for, reach to one, as in a division of articles; to be large enough for, as a garment. Iyowahi, iyomahi, iyouŋhipi. Hecel tipi opawiŋge sam iyaye yawapi na hena waksica ogna pamnipi na ecel ataya iyowicahi. Hecel tipi iyohila k̇pamnipi (i.e. coffee and sugar), tka ecel ataya iyowicahi na hecena yasotipi śni.
iyo'hik̇iya, v.a. To cause to reach or arrive at; to give to each one, make go around, as in dividing articles. Iyohiwakiya.

iyo'hila, adj. Each one.

iyo'hiśni, v. Not to reach to.
iyo'hiśniyaŋ, v.a. To cause to not reach to.

iyo'hiya, v.a. To cause to reach a place; to extend the hand to; to make reach to all. Iyohiwaya.

iyo'hōb, interj. When playing hide-and-seek all hide themselves, one would say Iyohob! and thus start the one seeking. BT. Bl. Ob. Cf. hacib.

iyŏ'ḣa, n. The lower part of the face, the side of the face; the lower jaw of animals; the gills of fish. Bléga s'e - ziyela. - caŋnuŋpa, The common short-stemmed pipe. Bl.

iyo'ḣahiŋ, n. Whiskers.

iyo'ḣaḣa, n. Water-falls. Mini íyoḣaḣa.

iyo'ḣlaṫe, adv. Underneath. - inajiŋ.
iyo'ḣlaṫeya, adv. (oḣlaṫeya). Underneath. B.H.109.5;95.22.

iyo'ḣlogya, adv. By, through, by means of. Niye - wicoicage oyasiŋ wicayawaśtepi ktelo. Ieska waŋ - wokiyake, To speak through an interpreter. Wicaśa śica - yuakagal oyakataŋpi. B.H. 10.10;35.5;136.3;279.22.

iyo'ḣloke, n. The mouth of a river or of two rivers that form into one. Wakpala kiŋ le - el iyawicuŋpepi kta. Cf. okijata.

iyo'ȟpaya, v.n. To go down from a hill, away from the speaker. Iyowaȟpaya.

iyo'ȟṗek̇iya, v.a. Same as iyoȟpeya.
iyo'ȟṗeya, v.a. To throw or cast into; to cook, throwing meat into the kettle. Iyoȟpewaya.

i'yoic'iktek̇a, v. refl. (iyokteka). To reprove one's self, to repent, Syn.- iyopeic'iya.

iyo'ja, (?). Tasiha taŋka waŋ iyojahe s'e ye uŋyaŋpelo, said while following retreating enemies. Caŋpagmiyaŋpi iyojahe s'e, when the rattling of a wagon is heard from a distance. Bl.

iyo'jaŋjaŋ, n. (ojaŋjaŋ). Light. B.H. 244.14. -- v.n. To shine, shine into, to give light to. Iyonijaŋjaŋpi el mani po. B.H.244.15. -- iyójaŋjaŋyaŋ, 1) v.n. To shine, to shine into, to give light. 2) adv. Shining, giving light. -- iyójaŋjaŋye, n. Light. Maka kiŋ - kiŋ he miye yelo. B.H.221.8.

i'yojuk̇iya, v. pos. (iyojuya). To make one's own brimful. Waśpaŋka ognake k'oŋ taŋyaŋ iyojuwakiyelo. Bl.
i'yojuya, v.a. To make brimful. Bl.

i'yok̇aġa, adv. (okaga). South of.
i'yok̇aġaṫaŋhaŋ, adv. South of.
i'yok̇aȟ, cont. of iyokaga.
i'yok̇aȟk̇iya, adv. South of.
i'yok̇aȟwapa, adj. In a southerly direction.

iyo'kaȟmiŋ, n. A point of land.

iyo'kaic'iya, v. To get one's self into trouble. Syn.- iyáleic'iya.

i'yok̇ak̇iśya, v. To give a sharp answer after one has kept silent for a while. Iyokakiświaya. Bl.

iyō'k̇al, adv. cont. (iyokata). To warm. - śpaŋyaŋ, To toast or roast by holding to the fire. - aya, To hold near fire and make warm. Bl.

iyo'k̇ala, 1) v.n. (okala). To empty or pour into, as grain. Iyowakala. 2) n. Something into which anything is poured, and so to measure with; a measure.

iyo'k̇alic'iya, v. To get one's self into trouble by too much talking, and thus to be caught as a liar; to become an unwilling creditor, as when on gives away something good but receives a thing less valuable. Iyokalmic'iye lo.

iyo'k̇aluza, 1) n. Air in motion, a breeze. 2) adj. Airy, cool.

iyō'k̇alya, 1) v.a. To warm, make hot in; fig., to make hot, excited; to heat with e.g. a stove a room. Iyokalwaya. 2) adv. perhaps. By the heat.

iyo'k̇aniyaŋ, v.n. To be jarred or shaken by a striking. Iyomakaniyaŋ.

iyo'kaŋ, (?). Tipi - el caŋ wicayakaku kte lo. Bl.

iyo'k̇apa, v. (kapa). To surpass. Iyowakapa.

iyo'k̇apas, cont. of iyokapaza.
iyo'k̇apasya, v.a. To exert an evil influence upon, as on a sick person by one's presence; to make worse. Iyokapaswaya.
iyo'k̇apasyeca, v.a. Same as iyokapasya.

i'yok̇apataŋhaŋ, adv. Behind, after; younger than. Miyokapataŋhaŋ.

iyo'k̇apaza, v.n. To be pungent, make smart, as does pepper or mustard seed in the mouth. Iyomakapaza.

iyo'k̇apṫe, n. (kapte). Something to dip with, a dipper, ladle. Cf. okapta.

iyo'k̇askica, v. (?). Paȟli iyomakaskicelo, when the nose clogs. Bl.

i'yok̇aśeyela, adv. Closely, close to, as in holding a horse's halter close to the mouth. - kaśka yuze. - okataŋ, To drive a nail up to the head.

iyo'k̇aśk̇e, n. (kaśka). Something that connects or is used to bind with.

i'yok̇aśtaŋ pestóla, n. A funnel. Bl.

iyo'k̇aṫa, v.n. (okata). To be warm in, warm by reason of; to be hot inside, as from liquor.

iyo'k̇aṫaŋ, v.a. (okataŋ). To drive in,

as a nail on something. Iyowakata^n.

iyo'ḱatḱuġe, n. (katkuga). A nail, a screw; a nut of a screw.

iyo'ḱawi^{n}ġa, v. To turn round and round
iyo'ḱawi^{n}ḣ. Cf. iokawi^{n}ḣ.

iyo'ḱi, v.a. To permit, encourage. Note: The word is not used except with śni, or in a negative way.

iyo'ḱicasleca, v.a. (kasleca). To split in two in the middle. Iyokiwakasleca.

iyo'ḱicaśḱa, v.a. (kaśka). To tie together, as two strings. Iyokiwakaśka.
iyo'ḱicaśḱeya, adv. Tied together, connected or following each other, as the seasons without any intervening time.

iyo'ḱicaśṗa, v.a. (kaśpa). To divide in the middle. Iyokiwakaśpa.

iyo'ḱignag, cont. of okignaka. - hi^{n}gla, At the same instant, as is said of guns fired off simultaneously.

iyo'ḱignaḱa, v.a. (akignaka). To put or place in together, to put in one's own mouth. Iyowakignaka.

iyo'ḱihe, n. A joint.

i'yoḱihe, 1) v.n. To be next to, be second. Iyowakihe. 2) adj. Second, next to. Cf. D.3, note 2.
i'yoḱiheya, adv. Lengthened out, added to; next to, following, succeeding.
iyo'ḱiheya, v. To continue something commenced by others (?). Iyokihewaya.

iyo'ḱihi, v.a. (okihi). To be able for; to come upon, come up with. Iyowakihi.
iyo'ḱihiya, 1) v.a. To make able for. Iyokihiwaya. 2) adv. Ably.

iyo'ḱiniha^n, adj. (okiniha^n). Honored for.
iyo'ḱiniha^{n}ya^n, adv. Honorably.

iyō'ḱiṗi, 1) v.a. To please, be pleasing to others. Iyowakipi. 2) v.n. To be pleased with, like. Iyomakipi, iyou^{n}kipipi; iyonimakipi, I am pleased with you, You are pleasing to me. Pb.35
iyo'ḱiṗiśniya, v.a. To cause one to feel displeased.
iyo'ḱiṗiśniya^{n}kel, adv. Unpleasantly. - naji^{n}pi, They felt awkward standing. B.H.277.17.

iyo'ḱiṗiya, 1) v.a. To please, cause to be pleased. Iyokipiwaya. 2) adv. Delightfully, pleasantly.

iyo'ḱise, n. (okise). The half of anything cut in two. Maka - tata^{n}ka ota nawaḣ'o^n. Tawoyuha ki^n wicak'u. BT.
iyo'ḱiseya, adv. (iyokise). Half. Maka - tata^{n}ka ota nawaḣ'o^n. Ito, taku u^{n}kaglipi ki^n he - u^{n}k'upi kte. Bl. B.H. 125.5;127.4.

iyo'ḱiśica, v.n. To be sad, sorry, grieved. Iyomakiśica, iyoniciśica, iyou^{n}kiśicapi.
iyo'ḱiśicapi, n. Sadness, sorrow.
iyo'ḱiśicaya, 1) v.a. To make sad, to sadden. 2) adv. Sadly.
iyo'ḱiśil, cont. of iyokiśica. - hi^{n}gla. B.H.234.4.
iyo'ḱiśilya, 1) v.a. To sadden, grieve, displease, disappoint. Iyokiśilwaya. 2) adv. In a manner producing sadness, sadly. - naji^n. D.14.

iyo'ḱiśni, v.a. To forbid, prevent, hinder; to advise vigorously against something. Iyowakiśni, iyou^{n}kipiśni, iyomakiśni. R. D.116. Cf. iyoki.

iyo'ḱita^{n}i^n, n. (ota^{n}i^n). Manifestation.
iyo'ḱita^{n}i^{n}ya^n, adv. Manifestly.

i'yoḱiwi^n, v. To motion, point somewhere with one's mouth. Íyowakiwi^n, íyomakiwi^n. Bl. -- íyoḱiwi^{n}wi^n, v. refl. of iyokiwi^n. Iyowakiwi^{n}wi^n. Bl.

i'yoḱiyusleca, v.n. (yusleca). To split in two, be divided in customs.
i'yoḱiyuslel, cont. (iyokiyusleca). To be divided in customs.

iyō'ḱo, n. Space, as between heaven and earth. Maka ki^n na maḣpiya - el wau^n. Hel - ogna iyotaka yo. D.58.
iyō'ḱogna, adv. (iyoko-ogna). Between places, between one place and another. Cf. iókogna.

i'yoḱoṗeya, adv. Opposite to, beyond, in sight.

iyo'kṗani, v.n. To lack, be wanting; to be less than, not enough; to fail, not to reach in time, not to accomplish. Iyomakpani. -- iyókṗaniya, v.a. To cause to lack etc. Iyokpaniwaya. --

iyókp̄aniyaⁿ, adv. Lacking, failing of. Wiciyokpaniyaⁿ yauⁿ śni. B.H.169.10. Cf. iokpaniyaⁿ.

iyō'kp̄ata, v.a. To sew on, to put a patch on. Iyowakpata. Śina huhá iyowakpatiⁿ kta.

i'yōkteƙa, v.a. To scold, reprove, speak sharply to. Iýowakteka. D.268 and 16. -- iyoktekteka, v. red. To scold often. Iýowaktekteka.

iyo'mnaya, v.a. To put much in the mouth, as corn, cherries, etc. Iyomnawaya. Bl.

iyo'naniyaⁿ, v.n. To be jarred or shaken by foot. Iyonawaniyaⁿ.

iyo'napa, v. To take shelter in. Egypt makoce kiⁿ - yo. B.H.170.3.

iyo'nataƙe, n. A bar, anything to bar with or to close up with.

i'yonataⁿ, (?). - mayakuwayelo, you always push me, give me time and I'll do it. Bl.

iyo'niyaⁿ, (?). Hlaƙla kiⁿ - hotaⁿiⁿ, dimly hearable because very distant. LB.

iyo'p̄asƙica, v.a. To press in, ram in, as in loading a gun.

i'yop̄aśťag, cont. of iyopaśtaka. - wauⁿ, I am exciting. -- iyopaśťagya, adv. Encouragingly.

i'yop̄aśtaƙa, v.a. To excite, incite, encourage, actuate, urge. Iýowapaśtaka. D.221.

iyo'p̄ata, v.a. To patch, sew a piece on. Iyówapata. Hakéla pehiⁿ śikśicela k'eyaś huhá k'el ecuƙiciⁿ iyowapatiⁿ kte. D.87.

i'yop̄aťaⁿ, v.a. To push abruptly one, to make one go on (i.e. without constant pressure). Iýowapataⁿ.

i'yop̄azaⁿ, v.a. (of opazaⁿ). To put into the mouth. Iyowapazaⁿ. -- iyóp̄azaⁿ, n. Something to bind or hold in, as a ferrule (a bushing); the brass ring that holds in the ramrod of a gun; the ramrod itself; the bore of a gun. R. Bl.

iyō'p̄eic'i'ya, v. refl. (of iyopeya). To blame one's self, reprove one's self, to repent. Iyópemic'iya. -- iyóp̄eic'iyapi, n. A blaming one's self, repentance, contrition.

iyo'p̄eƙiya, v.a. To reprove, chide, scold, punish. Iyópewakiya.

iyo'pemni, n. A cigaret.

iyō'p̄eya, v.a. To reprove, correct, punish. Iyopewaya. -- iyóp̄eya, v.a. To make one tree lodge on another. Iyopewaya. Bl. Cf. R., iyepeya.

iyo'p̄eya, v. To exchange, sell. Mazaska iyopeyaye kiⁿ hena yagluha oyakihi tka. B.H.283.1. -- n. The price paid; exchange.

iyo'psica, v.n. To hop, jump down. Iyowapsica. Waⁿmayaⁿka po, miś iyowapsiciⁿ ktelo. Bl. Mni kiⁿ ekta iyopsicapi. D.29. -- iyópsilkaƙicipa ecóⁿpi, n. A pastime for boys. Bl.

iyo'pśa s'e, (?). Said when the report of a gun is hardly hearable. Bl.

iyo'pśapśa, v.n. To boil up in bubbles.

iyo'pśaya, perhaps adv. Said when the report of a gun is hardly audible. Bl.

iyo'pťa, v. To pass through. Tokśa iyouⁿptiⁿ ktelo, i.e. will leave now. Bl. B.H.293.10. - iyaya, To pass through, pass on. - iyeya, To purge. -- iyóptaiyeyapi, n. A purge, cathartic.

iyo'pťe, (?). Miyopte śni ehaⁿtaⁿś, Except through me. B.H.254.22. -- iyópteya, adv. Through, straight through, passing on. - ya. Miyopteya iyayeyi ye. B.H.255.9. Hecel emakiya kiⁿ hehaⁿl waⁿna - iblabla. Hehaⁿl ake - icimani ya. B.H.54.9. Wiyatke kiⁿ le miyopteya iyayeyi ye. Pb.41. -- v.n. To have acquired some skill, made some progress. Iyoptewaya.

iyo'ptiyeya, v.a. To cause to pass through. Contraction of iyopta iyeya.

iyo'p̄uƙli, n. A cork wadding for a gun. -- iyóp̄uƙliya, v.a. To use for gun wadding.

iyo'p̄uskice, n. A ramrod.

iyo'sniyaŋ, (?). Tate waŋ - uye lo; wasu hiŋhiŋ kte laka. Bl. -- iyósniyaya, v.a. To cool. Iyosniyawicaye. Tate waŋ iyosniyawicaye. B.H.139.23.

iyo'staŋ, n. (of oštaŋ). Something pushed into the mouth of anything, a vial cork, a stopper.

iyo'śala s'e, adv. All in red. - ahiyaye, They pass by all dressed more or less in red. Bl.

iyo'śnija, v.n. To be blinded by the sun or snow. Iyómaśnija. Iśta kiŋ wi iyośnije, The sunlight blinded her eyes, (or is it, The reflection of the sun in her eyes blinded the mother so she could not see well.) D.222.

iyo'śtaŋpi, n. A cork, a stopper.

i'yotag, cont. of iyotaka. - hiyeya. -- iyótagkiya, v.a. To cause to sit down. Iyotagwakiya.

iyo'tahe'na, adv. Between, forgotten. Same as naptahena. Iapi - epiŋ kte, I speak of something that, as you remember, we talked about before. Cf. lotkuŋkeśni. WE. - owaŋjigjila yaŋka yo, said to a fellow who always bums around, Stay at home. RF. This is an old word.

iyo'tahepi, adv. Between one place and another. -- iyótahepiya, adv. On the way, this side of the place of destination. B.H.39.14.

i'yotaka, v.n. To sit, sit down, rest, camp perhaps. Be sitting. Wayawa - iblotaka. Na waŋna wizipaŋ paha kiŋ ohlate wakpala el iyotakapi. -- iyótakehaŋ, part. Sitting.

iyō'taŋ, 1) adv. Most, very. - waśte. 2) adj. Great, greater, greatest, chief. Used in comparing one thing with another. Imayotaŋ. -- iyótaŋhci, adv. Chiefly, most of all.

iyo'taniŋ, v. To shine on account of. Mahpiya kiŋ lila - . B.H.166.4.

iyo'taŋla, 1) v.a. (?). Woyuha kiŋ iyotaŋyala. Pb.26. 2) perhaps adv. Same as taŋyaŋ. This is an old word. - oyah'aŋ yelo. - omayakihaŋ yelo. RF. Sagye kiŋ le e ca yaciŋ heci, icu na - icu wo. BT.

iyo'taŋlaka, v.a. To esteem most, value most highly. Iyotaŋwalaka.

iyo'taŋyaŋ, adv. Greatly.

iyo'tatkoŋs, cont. (of iyotatkoŋza). Opposite to, over against. -- iyótatkoŋsya, adv. Even with, opposite to. -- iyótatkoŋza, adv. (of otatkoŋza). Opposite to, over against, even with.

i'yotitaŋla, (?). Ogle iyomatitaŋla yelo, too small, too tight for me.Bl.

iyo'tiyekiya, v.n. To have troubles, to suffer, find it hard. - yauŋpi, or Iyotiyeyakiyapi. Miye ekta - mayahipi. Haiyotiyekiya, haiyotiyewakiye, To suffer from poor clothing. Siiyotiyekiya, To suffer from one's feet. --iyótiyeic'iciya, v. refl. (of iyotiyekiya), spelling of refl. doubtful. To bring trouble, sufferings on one's self. WE.

iyō'to, v.n. To bump against. Tiyopa iyówato. Cf. iċiyapa.

iyo't'ognag, cont. of iyot'ognaka. - bla, I go at the risk of my life. -- iyót'ognaka, v.n. To hazard life, risk one's life, go into danger.

i'yot'iŋst'iŋs, (?). Wana peji to kiŋ - yaślapi iyececa yelo, they shined themselves with grass. Bl.

iyo'wa, n. Writing materials.

iyo'waja, perhaps adv. (of owaja). Near to, equal to, relating to, concerned in, having a right to. Iyomawaja. Iyouŋwajapi. Also, iyowaja. D.260. -- iyowajaka, adv. Used with the meaning of iyowajaśni. -- iyówajaśni, adv. Not near to, not equal to, having nothing to do with. -- iyówajaśniniyaŋ, adv. Not near to.

iyo'walya, (?). Cf. D.124. Also, cf. wal'iyowalya.

iyo'waŋg, cont. of iyowaŋke. -- iyowaŋgya, perhaps v.a. To have one as imitator, set an example for, be imitated. Iyowaŋgwaya, I am his example, He does as I do. Iyowaŋgmaya, He is my example, i.e. I do as he does. BD. Cf. owaŋgya. Bl.

iyo'waŋke, n. An example set for.

iyo'waś, cont. of iyowaja. - waun śni, I am not near to. - yuha. B.H.19.13.

iyō'wata, perhaps v. or adj. Meaning perhaps, To reflect. This is said of a sunrise on a cold winter morning when a long ray of bright light goes straight up. The Indians say it means cold weather. Wi kiⁿ - , or simply, Iyówata. Miyoglasiⁿ oⁿ iyowatwayiⁿ kte, they say when they give signals with a looking glass. Tipi waⁿ - , would be said when in the distance a house is visible on account of a fire throwing its light on it. -- iyówatya, v.a. To make visible by throwing light on. Cf. iyowata.

iyo'wicajaⁿjaⁿ s'e, adv. Same as kale-hleǵápi s'e koyaka. - koyaka, To dress very attractively. Bl.

iyo'wiⁿhahayakel, adv. Same as iyoco-syakel. - owahelo. Bl.

iyo'wiⁿhala, adv. In jest, jestingly. -- iýowiⁿhala, v.a. To fulfil some-body's wishes. Iyowiⁿhacila. Bl. -- iyówiⁿhayela, adv. In jest, jestingly. Bl.

iyo'wiⁿic'iya, v. refl. (of iyowiⁿyaⁿ). To declare one's willingness. D.221.

iyo'wiⁿkiya, v.a. To permit, allow. Iyowiⁿwakiya. Iyowiⁿuⁿkiyapi. Iyówiⁿ-mákiya yo.

iyo'wiⁿyaⁿ, v.a. To bear, consent, en-dure, permit, accept, to be sufficient for. Iyowiⁿwaya. Ate hecel iyowiⁿye śni. Caⁿke uⁿmapi uⁿhena iyowiⁿyaⁿpi. Hecel wiⁿyaⁿ kiⁿ - . -- iyówiⁿyeśni, adv. Without leave, contrary to orders insufficiant, inoperative as medicine.

iyo'wiwila s'e, (?).

iyo'wotaⁿiⁿ, n. A place from which one can see to a great distance, as a hill. Perhaps used as adj. too. Wana maka - śni hiⁿgla. MS.563. -- v. per-haps imp. Said when in winter it is rather foggy and one cannot see well. Bl. P'o waⁿ iyowotaⁿiⁿ śni, A heavy fog filled the land. D.208. -- iyó-wotaⁿiⁿśniyaⁿ, adv. Invisibly. Hecena mahpiya eciyataⁿ ośota s'e hiyu na - najiⁿ. Iyowotaⁿiⁿ śni may also be an adj., as above: Maka ... hiⁿgla. -- iyówotaⁿiⁿśniyela, adv. Śóta - kuwapi śka opi śni gli yelo.

iyo'ya, v.n. To gape, yawn. Iyowaya. BD. used iyówawa. Cf. icápa.

iyo'yag, cont. of iyoyaka.

iyo'yagwagwa, v. To chew in a way, i.e. with the front teeth, what cannot be chewed as something soft, in order to taste it. Bl.

iyo'yagya, v.a. To hurt one's feelings. Iyoyagwaya. Bl. Also, to displease, offend, to make sick.

iyo'yaka, v.n. To be offended, dis-pleased; to be made sick. Iyomayaka.

iyo'yakeca, v.n. To be sorrowful, dis-tressed. Iyomayakeca.

iyo'yalal, adv. (of iyoya). In a sleeping manner perhaps. - ecoⁿkoⁿpi.

iyo'yam, cont. of iyoyaⁿpa. -- iyó-yamya, 1) v.a. To shine on, illumin-ate, enlighten. Iyoyamwaya. 2) adv. Illuminated, in an illuminated manner. This is of iyoyaⁿbya.

iyo'yaⁿbya, v.a. (?). Of iyoyaⁿpaya. Pb.29. -- iyóyaⁿbyela, adv. Being in the light. B.H.113.4. Na waⁿna lila - cetipi.

iyo'yaⁿpa, 1) v.n. To shine, give light. 2) n. Light. Yuⁿkaⁿ (?) iyoyap hiⁿgla na taⁿwaⁿkatuya ya na waⁿna maka ta glihaⁿ. Taku waⁿ ite kiⁿ ataya iyo-yam mahiⁿgle na toyela iyaya. Waⁿna ake iyoyam mahiⁿgle. Hehaⁿl uⁿgnahela ite kiⁿ iyoyam mahiⁿgla na ecel waⁿna lila mat'iⁿ kta seca. Yuⁿkaⁿ ataya iyoyam hiⁿgla na ataⁿiⁿ śni. Waⁿka-taⁿhaⁿ toyela - ca, i.e. water is blue. -- iyóyaⁿpaya, v.a. To enlight-en, shine on. Iyoyaⁿpawaya.

iyo'yas'iⁿ, adv. With, on. Pa he - , A head with the horns on. One could not say: Pa wapośtaⁿ - . Śuⁿkwiⁿ-yela ciⁿcala - . B.H.238.4. -- iyó-yas'iⁿyaⁿ, adv. With, on. This may perhaps not be used by the Tetons. They use iyoyas'iⁿ. D. spells the word iyówas'iⁿyaⁿ. D.28 and 98.

iyo'yaya, v.a. To make yawn.

iyo'yaza, v. To string as beads, or

to put a string through a needle.

iyo'zi, n. (of ozi). Rest, repose. -- iyóziǩiya, v.a. To cause to rest. Iyoziwakiya. -- iyóziya, adv. At rest. -- iyóziziya, adv. red. Leisurely.

iyu'blaȟ, (?). Tipi - iyeya, To open the whole front part of the tent, to raise the walls of a tent. Yuŋkaŋ waŋna tipi kiŋ - iyeyapi. Waŋna tipi - iyeyapi waŋ eglepi.

iyu'caŋ, 1) v.a. To riddle, sift. P. Iblucaŋ. Bl. 2) v.n. To be short of things. Caŋli imayucaŋ, I am short on tobacco. Loliyucaŋkelo, He has little to eat. Bl. Woyute iyucaŋpi śni. B.H.106.8.

iyu'caŋteśica, v.a. To make feel bad on account of, in consequence of.

iyu'caŋyaŋkel, adv. A little, very little of, as food. - yuha. - yaŋke. Bl. Peji - najiŋpi kte śni nacecelo, i.e. meaning the horses. Bl.

iyu'ecetu, v.a. To perfect, make right by means of. Ibluecetu.

iyu'ġeya, adj. All, the whole.

iyu'gmigma, n. (of yugmigma). Something that turns a thing, a turner, as a water-wheel.

iyu'gnayaŋ, v.n. (of yugnayaŋ). To be deceived, as in the prospect of receiving something. Imayugnayaŋ. Iyugnayenic'iyelo. MS.488. Woyute eciyataŋhaŋ - ayapi, i.e. getting out of grub. B.H.55.10.

iyu'ġuka, v. (?). Ibluguka. Cekpa ibluguka ca hece, a man says when a friend always wants him back. Bl.

iyu'ha, adj. All. - kaska, All in all. P. -- iyúhaha, adj. red. of iyuha. B.H.50.3.

iyu'hahaya, adv. red. of iyuhaya.

iyu'haya, adv. Loosely, slovenly.

iyu'hiŋhe, n. A harrow.

iyu'hiŋta, n. The intestines. This is perhaps iyuhota. - kiŋ ataya waŋkatakiya mau, i.e. the feeling to vomit.

iyu'hiŋte, n. (of yuhiŋta). Anything to rake with, as makiyuhiŋte.

iyu'homni, n. (of yuhomini). Something to turn with, as a door knob.

iyu'hota, n. Intestines, all the inside organs of an animal.

iyu'ȟci, v.a. To break out, make it break, as the eye of a needle; to tear a button-hole. Iblaȟci. Uŋkiyuȟcipi. Nakpa - . Bl.

iyu'ȟepe, n. (of yuȟepa). An absorber, a sponge. P. Bl.

iyu'ȟlaȟlaya, (?). Wokoyake kiŋ coku kiŋ ekta iyaskapa keś - kiyuślokapi.

iyu'ȟlata, v.a. (of yuȟlata). To catch hold of with, as with a hook; to scratch with. Ibluȟlata. -- iyúȟlate, n. (of i and yuȟlata). Something to catch with, something to scratch with.

iyu'ȟleȟlel, adv. Being scratched. - icu, Tearing up while taking it. Bl. Oŋjiŋjiŋtka oju waŋ el iyayapi na - iyayapi.

iyu'ȟloke, n. (of yuȟloka). Something to open with or make a hole with. Tiyopa - , A door opener, a key.

i'yuȟmiŋ, v.n. To be distorted. Ibluȟmiŋ, the word being difficult to say well, however. Wanagi - , the people say when a person's face, half of it, as it happens among the Indians, is distorted. Wanagi imayuȟmiŋ.

iyu'ȟmuŋ, n. (of yuȟmuŋ). A sling.

iyu'ȟpa, v. To be all, completed, indicating: That's it, or That's all. B.H.95.23. -- adj. All, the whole. Same as iyuha. Bl. Tóke léceya caŋte - niwanica hwo? Bl. -- iyúȟpala, adj. Same as iyuȟpa.

iyu'ȟpe, n. (of yuȟpa). Something to pull down with.

iyu'ȟ'eyayapi, n. A certain part of the meat on the shoulder blades of buffalos. HH. Bl. Same as tisto conica.

iyu'ijena, v. To mix. Ibluijena. Cf. iyukpukpa. Bl.

iyu'jaja, 1) v.a. (of yujaja). To wash with, to be washed with; to wring out, BD. 2) n. Something to wash with, as a wash-tub, wash-board, etc.

i'yujibyela, adv. Brimful, as of fluids. Bl. Cf. Iyapahayela.

iyu'jiṗa, n. The upper end of the forehead where the hair begins. - el o. MS.77. -- iyújiṗe, n. (i and yujipa). The front lock of a man's hair; also, something to pinch or lay hold with, as maziyujipe, Tongs. Little girls often had the hair fixed together in this sort of fastener. - pakiḣte ciŋ etulaḣci kute. D.88. -- perhaps v. To pinch with an instrument or pull out hairs.

iyu'k̇akija, v.a. To cause to suffer by. B.H.266.4. -- iyúk̇akiśya, perhaps adv. Causing pain. - ecakicoŋpi. B.H.167.11.

iyu'kcaŋ, v.a. (of yukcaŋ). To understand, have an opinion or understanding of, to think, guess; to judge. Iblukcaŋ. Uŋkiyukcaŋpi. Iciyukcaŋ, imayalukcaŋ. -- iyúkcaŋk̇e, n. One who forms an opinion. -- iyúkcaŋk̇el, adv. Guessing. - aya, To go on guessing. -- iyúkcaŋyaŋ, 1) v.n. To cause to understand. Iyukcaŋwaya. 2) adv. Thinking, having an understanding of.

iyu'k̇iŋ, v.a. To wrench, pry. Iblukiŋ. -- iyúk̇iŋk̇iŋ, v. red. To pull to and fro as a fence post in order to loosen it. Bl. Iblukiŋkiŋ. -- iyúk̇iŋyaŋ, adv. Prying. - icu. The word implies prying with a lever. Bl. Cf. iyupseya icu.

iyu'k̇iṗab, adv. Divided. The word is not much used.

iyu'koltkeyela, adv. (?). - otke lo, to hang on something without touching the ground as a piece of wood or a bag on a fence. Bl.

iyu'kṗaŋ, 1) v.a. (of yukpaŋ). To rub up fine, as with the fingers; perhaps to pulverize by means of. Ikabluya - . B.H.240.14. 2) n. Something to make fine with, a mill.

iyu'k̇ṗukṗa, v.a. (of yukpukpa). To break up fine and mingle together. Also, to mix as tobacco and caŋśáśa. Same as iyuijena. Iblukpukpa. Bl.

iyu'ksa, v.a. (of yuksa). To break off with, cut off with. Ibluksa. -- iyúkse, n. Something to break or cut off with. Snuffers.

iyu'kśaŋ, v.n. To go off, curve off, as a road.

iyu'k'eġe, n. (of yuk'ega). Something to scratch with, as a piece of wood. R. Bl.

iyu'k'eze, n. (of yuk'eza). A scraper.

iyu'k'o, v. (?). Ibluk'o. Hi - welo. Bl.

iyul', cont. (of iyuta). To eat with, as one thing with another. -- iyúlk̇itoŋ, n. Something to eat with, i.e. a sauce. -- iyúltoŋ, n. Something to eat with other things, sauce, condiment.

iyu'maŋ, n. (of yumaŋ). Cf. iyume.

iyu'me, n. Something to rub with. Hence maziyume, A file.

iyu'mni, n. (of yumni). Something that turns around. Tate - , A whirlwind. Caŋiyumni, An auger.

i'yuŋ, v.a. To rub on, apply, as ointment or soap, etc. Iwayuŋ. Uŋkiyuŋpi. Na maka ḣliḣlila oŋ iic'iyuŋ. Le wicaśa tuwa ayiŋ kta ciŋ he pejuta iwayuŋ kta. Sla wakaŋ imáyuŋpi. Pb.45.

iyuŋg', cont. (of iyuŋka). To lie out as for deer.

iyuŋ'ġa, v.a. To inquire of one, ask one a question. Imuŋga. Inuŋga. Iciyuŋga. Uŋkiyanuŋgapi, You ask us. B.H.281.10. -- iyúŋġapi, n. Inquiry. -- iyúŋḣ, cont. of iyuŋga.

iyuŋ'k̇a, v.n. To lie down, go to bed. Imúŋka. Inúŋka. Uŋkiyuŋkapi. Wakpala waŋ el iyuŋkiŋ kta iyukcaŋ.

iyuŋ'kala, adv. Personally. Iye - he. B.H.14.10;53.1;88.10;102.5;300.16. Atkuku kiŋ iye - taŋkal hinajiŋ.D.203.

i'yuŋk̇el, adv. (?). Hu - , On foot.

iyuŋ'pi, n. Unction, anointment. This should perhaps better be wiúŋpi. B.

iyuŋ'toŋ, v.a. To put grease or brains

on a skin in order to dress it. Iyuŋwatoŋ.

iyuŋ'wiŋ, n. Remuneration, something to pay with. - yukaŋ, There is pay.
iyuŋ'wiŋtoŋ, v. To have the means of paying, have something to give for. Iyuŋwiŋwatoŋ. -- iyúŋwiŋyaŋ, v.a. To have or use as pay. Iyuŋwiŋwaya.

iyu'paġa, v.a. To gather up in the hand e.g. the mouth of a bag for tying; to seize, lay hold of, arrest e.g. a desperate fellow. The word seems obs.; iyupaḣ is rather used. Iyupaḣ icu. - po! as said in goading horses to hurry. - po, tokśa haŋtahena walaślapi kte lo, i.e. the horses. BT.

iyū'paḣ, cont. (iyupaga). Together, in a bunch with none missing. - nauŋk au, They come together on the gallop. This may correspond to kinil. - yuza, To clasp tight, as the mouth of a bag. - okala. R. Bl. B.H.39.2.
iyu'ṗaḣya, adv. Grouping, into bunches. - okala. Bl.

iyu'paŋ, v.a. To break or rub up, as in the hand. Iblupaŋ.

iyu'ṗiza, adj. Wrinkled.

iyu'psepseya, adv. red. of iyupseya.

iyu'pseya, adv. Crookedly, zigzag. - icu, To lift with a stick, as by pushing something under the stick, i.e. to operate with a rod and fulcrum. Bl. Cf. iyukiŋyaŋ.
iyu'pseyakel, adv. Crookedly perhaps. - taku tokanoŋ. Bl. Cf. iyupsiya, a word not entered since it seems to be commonly in the form of iyupseya.

iyu'pśaya, adv. Mixed up; all together as good and bad.

iyu'pṫa, v. To take up with a spade, to dig and take up, as in spading. - icu, iwacu.

I'yupṫala, n. prop. A society like the Omaha Dance Society.

iyu'ṗuza, v.a. (yupuza). To make dry with. Iblupuza. -- iyúṗuze, n. Something to make dry with, a towel.

iyu'saḣe, n. A gad, a whip.

iyu'sk̇aṗa, v.a. To crack a whip and strike something or somebody.

iyu'k̇iṫe, n. A bandage. Cf. yuskita.

iyu'slohaŋ, v. To drag something. - eyaya, i.e. to drag or take along with all that is lying on it, as a blanket and things lying on it. Bl.
iyu'slohe, n. (yusloha). Something to drag along.
iyu'slohetoŋ, v. To drag something along. Iyuslohewatoŋ.
iyu'slohetoŋyaŋ, adv. Draggingly. - aya. Also, iyusloheya. Bl.

iyu'sna iyéya, v. To pull out, as pins from a tent. Na waŋna tipi k'oŋ he wiceśka - iyeyapi, na waŋna ḣ'oká etaŋhaŋ hinapapi.

iyu'sol, cont. of iyusota. - eyaya, All passed by.
iyu'soṫa, v.a. (yusota). To use all up with, to use up for. Iblusota.

iyu'sotka, v. To clear up. - iyaya. Note: the only use of this word is in ref. to clouds of a thunderstorm or clouds of smoke disappearing. LP.

iyu'sṫo, v. To smooth down, as the hair. Iblusto. Peślete el awicaputakiya na etaŋhaŋ anuŋk kutakiya si ekta iyagleya - ewicayaya.

iyu's'eya, adv. Barely, - migluśtaŋ, I barely finished. - otaŋiŋ, It is hardly visible. Cf. iyuzeya.

iyu's'o, v. (?). When a man rides through water and gets wet inspite of lifting his legs. Cf. yus'o. Bl.

iyu's'oya, adv. In an exhausted condition; reluctantly, with difficulty. - iyowiŋkiye. - ihuŋni. B.H.109.4.
iyu's'oyaḣci, adv. With difficulty.
iyu's'oyakel, adv. Just a little, hardly. Kitaŋyel - iyewayelo, That is all I could find. - kini. LB.B.H. 38.12.

iyu'śica, v. (yuśica). To injure by means of, make bad with. Igluśica.
iyu'śice, n. Something that makes bad or injures.

iyu'śiŋktiŋyaŋ, adv. (?). - najiŋ, To stand leaning one way. Bl.

iyu´śḱa, n. (yuśka). Something by means of which to untie a bundle.

iyu´śḱi, cont. of iyuśkica.
iyu´śḱica, v.a. To press on and cut accidentally, as with a knife; to wring out of, as out of water. Ibluśkica.
iyu´śḱice, n. (yuśkica). A press.

iyu´śḱi^{n}, v.n. To rejoice, be glad, to rejoice in. Ibluśki^{n}.
iyu´śḱi^{n}ḱiya, v.a. To cause to rejoice. Iyuśki^{n}wakiya.
iyu´śḱi^{n}śḱi^{n}, v. red. of iyuśki^{n}.
iyu´śḱi^{n}śḱi^{n}ya^{n}, adv. red. of iyuśki^{n}ya^{n}.
iyu´śḱi^{n}ya^{n}, 1) v.a. To make glad, to gladden, rejoice. Iyuśki^{n}waya. 2) adv. Gladly, rejoicingly.

iyu´śla, n. (yuśla). Shears, scissors. Mitaiyuśla. D.59.

iyu´ślok, cont. (?). Śina ki^{n} ecela - kipi.
iyu´śloḱa, n. (yuśloka). Something to pull out with, as a cork screw.
iyu´śloḱe, n. A key.

iyu´śluśluta, n. (yuśluśluta). Something to make smooth with, a rubber, a polisher.

iyu´śna, n. (yuśna). One that has lost its mate, an odd one.

iyu´śṗa, v.a. (yuśpa). To pick off from, as a scab. Ibluśpa.

i´yuśpeśni, adj. Silent, not opening one's mouth. - ma^{n}kelo. Cf. iśpaśpa.

iyu´śṗeyeya, adv. (?). - eco^{n}, To do somebody's work that he neglected, i.e. work besides one's own. WE.

iyu´śṗu, v.a. (yuśpu). To pick off from as corn from the strings. Ibluśpu.

iyu´śtaḱa, (?). Cu^{n}wiyapehe iyuśtakapi s'e, that suggests the color purple.

iyu´śṫa^{n}, v.a. (yuśta^{n}). To finish inside, to finish for. Ibluśta^{n}.

iyu´ś'i^{n}yaya, v. To be surprised at or with regard to. Also, iyuś'i^{n}yaya. B.H.163.1;181.9;252.1. MS.157.
iyu´ś'i^{n}yeya, v.n. To be frightened. Imayuś'i^{n}yeya. B.H.289.5.

iyu´ṫa, v. (yuta). To eat with, as one thing with another. Iwáta, iyáta may be perhaps the 1st and 2nd pers. forms.

iyu´ta, v.a. To measure, weigh; to try or attempt. Ibluta, Iciyuta, yu^{n}ka^{n} nihi^{n}gla na kagal hi^{n}gla, I tried you, i.e. to get something, etc. BT. -- v.a. (uta). To taste.

iyu´ṫa^{n}, 1) v. To tempt; to be tempted or tried. Imayuta^{n}. 2) n. The trigger of a gun. Tuśu - to^{n} wo; waki^{n}ya^{n} u^{n}kiye eyaś lila tate kte lo. Bl. Cf. ipata^{n}.

iyū´ta^{n}, v.a. To put in grease and mix up, to mix up e.g. grease and cherries to make pemmican; to mingle. Ibluta^{n}.

iyū´ta^{n}ta^{n}, v.a. (yutá^{n}). To touch, to feel in several places. Ibluta^{n}ta^{n}.

iyu´ṫa^{n}ya^{n}, adv. Stretched out, as was Christ's body on the cross. - otké. Cf. iyutita^{n}ya^{n}. -- v.a. To tempt, to try or prove. Iyuta^{n}waya. -- adv. Tempting, trying.

iyu´ṫapi, n. A measure. Wojiyutapi, An acre; makiyutapi, A mile; tekuiyutapi, A pound.

iyu´ṫeḱiya, v.a. To cause to measure; to adjust, arrange; to appoint. Iyutewakiya.

iyu´ṫepa, v.n. (yutepa). To be worn out by anything.

iyu´ṫeṗicaśni, adj. Unmeasurable, immense, fathomless. P.

iyu´ṫeya, 1) v.a. To adjust. Iyutewaya. 2) adv. By measure.

iyu´ṫiṫa^{n}, n. A tug; a double-tree. -- v.a. (yutita^{n}). To pull by. Iblutita^{n}. -- v.n. To be stretched or pulled by.
iyu´ṫiṫa^{n}ya^{n}, adv. Stretched by.

iyu´tḱuġe, n. Something to fasten or lock with, a key.

iyu´to^{n}, v.a. To grease a hide, as

when it is to be tanned. Iblutoŋ. Bl.

iyu'tutkayakel, adv. Partly and imperfectly. - ecoŋ, To do a job imperfectly. LP.

iyu'waŋǩa, adv. Up. Wicaśa num wicakico na wihuta yujuŋpi na - eglepi.

iyu'waśte, 1) v. (yuwaśte). To make good, benefit by means of. Ibluwaśte. 2) n. Something that benefits.

iyu'weğa, v.a. To pass through, to cross or ford e.g. a stream. Ibluwega.
iyu'weȟ, cont. (iyuwega). - iyaye, To ford a stream. B.H.95.1.
iyu'weȟya, adv. Crossing, fording.

iyu'wi, 1) v.n. To curl, twist, as a vine or curled wood. 2) n. Anything twisted or tied, a vine.

iyu'wicola, adj. Not bandaged or dressed, as a sore. -- n. (iyuwi). Anything twisted.

iyu'wiŋ, Cf. iyuŋwiŋ.

iyu'wiŋśkalake s'e, (?). Bl.

iyu'wiŋśkaś, adv. emph. or interj. For heaven's sake! i.e. with a reproving tone. - taku waŋ okihi waciŋpi he kapi, i.e. and for a long time. Also, iyúwiŋśka. Syn.- iciŋyuŋśkaś.

iyu'wiya, adv. Tangled, in a snarl, as hair or thread.

iyu'za, v.a. (yuza). To hold on or to, to put the hand on and hold. Ibluza. Nape - . B.H.42.20.
iyu'ze, n. (yuza). Something to hold with, a holder; something to take out food with, a ladle.

iyu'zigzil, cont. of iyuzigzica. Oyaya kiŋ yuakagal - okataŋpi. B.H.265.22. Cf. yuzigzica.

iyu'ziya, adv. Partly in sight, as is said of anything seen over a hill.
iyu'ziziya, adv. In sight.

iza'ptaŋ, adj. The fifth.
iza'ptaŋptaŋ, adj. red. Every fifth one.

ize'zeya, adv. Dangling. Taku - ikoyake. Bl.

izi'gziťa, v. red. (izita). Izilwaya, izigzilwaya. Ehaŋl izigzita na uŋgna yuile. Note: the cont. form seems to be used in the conjugation of the word. Cf. izita.

izil', cont. of izita.
izil'toŋ, v.a. To make a smoke; to smoke anything. Izilwatoŋ.
izil'ya, v.a. To cause to smoke e.g. a deer skin; to incense. Izilwaya. Na waŋna wizilya eya icu na - . Taku waśtemna waśteȟce kiŋ izilyapi. B.H. 61.2.

izi'ťa, v.n. To smoke, as a prairie fire or a firebrand, or fat held over a fire. -- v.a. perhaps. To smoke something, holding it in smoke. Pa gegeya otkeyapi na oȟlate cetipi na pa izitapi. Wakeya waŋ lila taŋka ca etaŋhaŋ śota izitahe. D.47.

izo', n. An upland plain that is a peninsula. R. Bl.

izu'yapi, n. What the Dakotas carry with them in going to war, i.e. the Palladium of the expedition, this sometimes being a pipe, sometimes the skin of an animal.

izu'za, n. A large, rough whetstone for the grinding of axes etc. Míoglè is that used for knives.

* * * *

J

ja, Cf. yuja.

jag, cont. of jata.

jagja'lya, adv. red. (of jalya). Forkedly, doubly. - waŋyaŋka, to see one thing multiplied by a defect of the eyes, as in old age. - wakita, to see things doubly from bad eyes. Bl. -- jagjályakel, adv. Same as jagjalya.Bl.

jagja'ťa, adj. red. (of jata). Forked, rough.

jahaŋ', adj. Rough, harsh, making a loud noise, as an animal. Ho - . --- jaháŋhaŋ, adj. Rough, unpleasant, grating. Hojahaŋhaŋ.

jahe's'e, adv. Noisily, unpleasantly. - apa, To strike and make a loud noise - ia, To speak hoarsely. Bl. -- jahéya, adv. Roughly, harshly, not melodiously, as the voice. - ia.

jaja', Cf. yujaja.

jaja'haŋ, (?). Uŋkcela heca waksiŋ na oŋ (the painted hide) apawiŋta ca he tohiŋni jajahe śni. MS.482.

ja'jaya, adj. Clearly, plainly. Jájayeḣci, Very plainly. B.H.137.6. Pb.23. -- jájayela, adv. Clearly, distinctly. - waŋyaŋka.

ja'ka, adj. Rolling or straining, as the eyes.

jal, cont. of jata. -- jalyá, adv. Forkedly. - wiyukcaŋ, To be of two minds, to be undecided.

jaŋjaŋ', n. A vial, a bottle, a glass of any kind; window glass. - okáśleca or - okableca, Pieces of broken glasses or bottles. - wakśica, A drinking glass.

jaŋjaŋ'la, perhaps adj. Clear, transparent, as glass beads. Psita - . -- jaŋjáŋyela, adv. Clearly, distinctly. - waŋyaŋka.

jā'ťa, adj. Forked, as a stick, stream.

ji, adj. Thin and bristly, as the hair on the hands and arms, also like a young duck. Iśpá ji. Héji.

jia'lepa, n. Same as tajíagnuŋpa. The meadow lark. BE. Wo.

ji'ca, adj. Rich. Majica. Jiciḣicagelo, they say to a man who watches everywhere that nothing be wasted or spoiled. BT. -- jicáka, adj. Rich. Majicaka.

jiji', v. To whisper. Wajiji. -- jijíloway, v. To sing in a low, whispering, drawling manner. Jijiwalowaŋ.

jiji'ya, adv. red. (of jiya). Standing up, as the hair on one's hands.

jiji'yahaŋ, adv. Whispering.

ji'la, adj. Thin and bristly, as hair.

jilya', v.a. To make rich. Jilwaya. -- jilyéca, v.a. To make rich. Jilwayeca.

jiŋ, v.n. To stand erect, stiffen up. Majiŋ. Said of the penis of man.

jiŋ'ca, v.n. To blow out from the nose, to blow the nose, snuff up. Also to hiss, perhaps. Wajiŋca. - yo!

jiŋ'lhiŋgla, v. (jiŋca and hiŋgla). To whistle, pushing out air suddenly. Jinlmahiŋgla. Cokaŋ inajiŋ na uŋgnaḣela jiŋlhiŋgni na tokaŋl ipsica.SI.

ji'ṗa, Cf. kajipa. -- jiṗáhaŋ, part. Cf. jipáheca. -- jiṗáheca, part. Becoming smooth or hollowed out of itself.

ji'ya, adv. Thin and standing up, as hair; thin scattered, and sparkling in the sunbeams.

jiya'haŋ, perhaps adv. Whispering, soft, with a subdued voice. - lowaŋ. - cekiya. -- jiyáhaŋlowaŋ, v. To sing in a low, whispering, drawling manner, as while practising. Same as Ḣwayela lowaŋ.

jiye'la, adv. Thinly, sparsely, as the hair on the hands.

jō, v. To whistle, as a man does. Wajó. -- johōtoŋ, v. To whistle, as the birds. -- johótoŋla, n. The bob white, whose call is like whistling to somebody (jo). Same as pakóśkala. Is.

jō'jo, v. red. (of jo). To whistle for a while, to whistle for. Wajojo. -- jojólowaŋ, v. To whistle a tune. Jojowalowaŋ.

jojo'yagtoŋ, v. To make a loop, noose, or lasso. -- adv. In a noose. R. - icu, To make it into a noose. Bl. -- jojóyake, n. A noose or slip-knot.

jolo'waŋ, v. To whistle a tune. Wajolowaŋ. -- jolówaŋwaŋ, v. (?). - naŋke lo. Bl.

joto'kte, (?). Ísta jotomakte yelo, wipápiya po, i.e. the smoke makes me blind. Bl.

ju , v. To root; to put, place, lay up. Waju. Cf. aju and oju.

ju'ju, Cf. kajuju.

juju'wahaŋ, part. Broken, fallen to pieces, as a house; become loose.

juŋ , Cf. yujuŋ.

jutoŋ', v. To fill one's self with food. Juwatoŋ welo. Bl.

k , prefix. It makes the possessive form of verbs commencing with "p". E.g. pagaŋ, kpagaŋ, To part with one's own.

ka , 1) interrog. part. 2) Same as the article kiŋ. Tokel ciŋ ka lecel uŋ wica śi. B.H.133.14. Iŋś toka tokeca waŋji uŋkapepi kte ka? B.H.198.3;242.2. Tokaŋtaŋhaŋ oniciyakapi ka? Ito, tuwa icu ka, Let us see who gets it. B.H.266.4. Ito, Elias u na eglaku ka yaŋke. B.H.268.4. Caŋkel hecel omani ka ..., While he .... B.H.318. Tohaŋl iyokipi ka caŋ kakiswicayahe. B.H.87. Cuŋkś, tohaŋ yaciŋ ka lel uŋ wo, Daughter, stay here as long as you like. D.60. Waciŋ ka yuŋkaŋś ehaŋnihci cacipapakta tka ye lo. D.71. Toki yaciŋ ka ya ye. D.98.

ka , prefix. To a class of verbs whose action is performed by striking, as with the hand, or with an ax, club or other instrument; or by the action of the wind or water. The pronouns of the verb are prefixed.

ka , suffix. To verbs and nouns. In most cases it does not seem materially to alter the signification. R. Yet, it seems that "ka" emphasizes a word, that a thing is done well or is a very good thing, or done by all. It a noun of verbs. Na waŋna wagliyagli na wowiyuśkiŋka na toeyaś tohaŋl wicaakihaŋ kiŋ ake wo nic'upi kta keyapelo, eya. -- ka , adv. suffix. The equivalent of śni, Not; and it is sometimes used ironically, as waśte, Good, waśteka, Not good. B.H.179.18; 222.4. Otaka, otaśni, conala; conalaka, conalaśni, ota tase heca ka (It is not that.), are all indicative of the negative. The word otaŋiŋka, To appear, be manifest, R. says is sometimes used in the sense of otaŋiŋśni, as, Taku otaŋiŋka, or Takuwaŋ otaŋiŋ śni, There is no news. Also cf. R., oŋspeka. Taku isaŋp kokipepicaka? What further fear should I have than that? D.103. -- ka , suffix. Meaning "Almost". T'aka, He almost died. Hiŋhpaya ka, He almost fell down. However this may be the same as "tka". -- ka, adv. Same as laka. Rather, pretty much. Wicaśa taŋktaŋka ka uŋpi. B.H. 111.16. Juda oyate kiŋ waptaŋyaŋpi ka. B.H.143. Le kagiśniśni oh'aŋke lah. Bl.

ka , v.a. To mean, signify; take for, consider; to ask for, demand. Waka. Cica. He wake, That is what I mean. Oyate taku kapi, The people in question. Ic'ice ki(ŋ), He means himself. Śuŋka mayaki yelaka? B.H.87.9. -- v.t. To mean.

ka , adv. There, yonder. Tohaŋl iyokipi ka caŋ kakiświcaye. B.H.76.14.

ka , demonstr. pron. There, that yonder. The plural: kaná. It is used when the thing spoken of is not quite close, when we use le. Gramm.23. Kacáŋ, That tree there. Katipi. Ka tipi waŋ taŋka he kiŋ he uŋtipi ca el uŋgni kte lo. Ito, ka cik'ala imakih'aŋ yo, Let me have some of that.

kaa'beya, adv. Scattered, as horses. - iyaya.

kaa'blel iye'ya, v. To scatter by striking. Kaáblel yeyá, To scatter as one's hair by loosening one's braids. Yuŋkaŋ witaŋśna uŋ k'oŋ nupiŋ kaablel yeyapi.

kaa'glapśiŋ, adv. Bottom side up, turned over. - ihpeya. -- kaaglapśiŋyaŋ, adv. Same.

kaa'iyohpeya, adv. Down hill, down a steep descent.

kaa'kokiya, adv. In another direction, another way. Waŋbli waŋ - kiŋyaŋ iyaya. Also, cf. MS.574.

kaa'opťel, v. cont. of kaaopteca, which is not known. - ecoŋ, To do less than. BD.

kaa'opťeťu, v. To lessen. - ecoŋ, To do less, or make it less. -- kaáopťeťuya, adv. In the way of diminishing. -- kaáopťeťuyakel, adv. Diminishingly.

kaa'pamagle, adv. Sloping down hill, gently sloping. -- kaápamagleya, adv. Down-hill, sloping.

kaa'takiŋyaŋ, adv. Leaning.

kaa'takuniśni, v.a. To destroy by striking.

kaa'ya, v.a. (of aya). To be taking to

one. Wakáaya. Unkaayapi. R.

ƙaa'yasƙab, adv. Clinging to or touching. - inajin, To lean on, cling to, standing touching one. Bl.

ƙabla', v.a. To cut meat thin for drying as the Indian women do. To slice up. Wakábla. -- ƙabláblapi, n. Preparing meat for drying by slicing thin. Slices. Cf. wakablapi. P.

ƙabla'ǧa, v. To spread out, as a bird does its wings. -- ƙabláȟ, cont. of kablaga. - iyeya. -- ƙablája, v.a. To spread open, as the legs, to straddle. Wakáblaja. Kablaje s'e iyunka, i.e. indicating, perhaps, tiredness. Bl.

ƙabla'pi, n. Something cut up in slices or thin pieces, as meat for drying.

ƙablas', cont. of kablaza. - iyeya.

ƙabla'sƙa, v.a. To flatten by beating, to make flat by striking, as a leaden bullet, or as done with an axe. To hew. Wakablaska.

ƙabla'sƙiya, v.a. To cause to rip or burst open. Kablaswakiya.

ƙablaś', cont. (of kablaja). Spread apart. - inajin, To stand astride of anything. -- ƙabláśya, v.a. To cause to straddle. Kablaśwaya.

ƙabla'ya, v.a. To make level by beating, e.g. a holy place. Wakablaya. -- v.n. To open, as the eyes of a young dog for its first sight. LB.

ƙabla'za, v.a. To make rip open or burst by striking or throwing down, to burst something open, as a ball by striking. Wakáblaza.

ƙable'bleca, v.a. red. (of kableca). To break to pieces. Wakablebleca. -- ƙabléblel, cont. of kablebleca.

ƙable'blesic'iya, v. refl. To rest one's mind by walking around after hard work. MG. Kableblesmic'iyin kte. Cf. kazilic'iya.

ƙable'ca, v.a. To break something brittle by striking, e.g. glass. Wakableca. -- ƙablél, cont. (of kableca). To throw down and break to pieces. - iyeya; - iȟpeya. Peji kinhan - (same as alili) najinpi ktelo, said of horses when there is much hay to eat. Bl. - kingni kte. B.H.240.13. -- ƙablelƙiya, v.a. To cause to break. Kablelwakiya. -- ƙablélya, v.a. To cause to break to pieces.

ƙa'blelya, adv. Scattered, loosened. Pehin - śkatapi, They play with their hair loosend

ƙables', cont. of kableza.

ƙables'glepi s'e, adv. (?). - un. Anpetu - , A clear day without any mist. Tohunhunniyan k'eyaś - unpi śni, i.e. always standing together. Bl.

ƙables'ya, v.a. To cause to be clear, to clear off, as the wind does fog. -- ƙabléza, v.n. To become clear, clear off, as fog clears away. Anpó - . Ecel anpa na kableze el kośkalaka k'on inapin na leya .... MS.153. -- ƙabléześni, 1) v. To be still foggy or dark, i.e. before the day dawns. Nahaȟci - . 2) v.a. To strike and make frantic. Wakableześni.

ƙablo'blo, v. red. (of kabló). To hit hard many times, hence perhaps to cause swellings by striking. Bl. D. 196. B.H.68.16.

ƙablu', v.a. To pound fine, pulverize, to strike, as ground etc. Wakablu. Na makoce kin oyate kin ataya kaȟminpi na kablupi. -- ƙablúblu, v. red. -- ƙablúƙiya, v.a. To cause to make fine. Kabluwakiya. -- ƙablúpi, n. Something fine, as powdered sugar. -- ƙablúya, v.a. To cause to make fine.

ƙabu', v.a. To beat, as on a drum. Cancega kin kabupi. -- ƙabúbu, v. red. (of kabu). To beat often. Wakabubu.

ƙabu'buya, adv. red. (of kabuya). Knocking.

ƙabu'ya, adv. Striking, knocking.

ƙaca', 1) neg. suff. Not. Okihi kaca, He cannot do it. 2) Same as hececa, which is he iyececa, and often used that way. B.H.62.13.

ƙacan', v.a. To shake, clear by shaking, to sift. Wakacan. -- v.n. To shiver. Oblula wanice ca uᵑkácaᵑpi kte lo. Wakacaᵑhelo, would be said while one moved his body and drew his clothing tighter for feeling cold. Bl.

ḱacaᵑ'caᵑ, v.n. To trot, as a horse. -- v.a. red. (of kacaᵑ). To clean by shaking, as in sifting; to shake. Wakácaᵑcaᵑ. -- ḱacáᵑcaᵑyaᵑ, adv. Shaking. -- ḱacáᵑcaᵑyela, adv. Shaking, shivering with cold.

kacaᵑ'glegleya, (?). Húᵑpe kacaᵑglegleyapi s'e iᵑyaᵑkelo, when a man runs making big strides. Legs, huᵑpe. Bl.

ḱacaᵑ'gle iye'ya, v. To throw something round, as a hoop, and thus make it go on.

ḱacaᵑ'he, v. To shake with the cold. Wakacaᵑhe.

ḱacaᵑl', (?).

ḱacaᵑ'lab iye'ya, v. To cheer one up. Same as kacaᵑlwaśte iyeya. Bl. -- ḱacáᵑlwaśte iyéya, v. To cheer one up. Bl.

kacaś', interrog. Of doubt or hesitation, meaning: What then? What of it? Tase, le ciciyuha - , haᵑke cicu ka. Grammar.361(3). Waśtekaca, It is not good. R.

ḱace'ǵu uᵑ, n. proper. A Congregationalist, the short-coated one. Sw.

kaceg'ya, adv. Staggering, in a staggering manner. - mani. -- ḱacék, cont. (of kaceka). - iyeya, To make stagger by striking. -- ḱacéḱa, v.a. To strike and make stagger. Wakáceka. -- ḱacékcegya, adv. red. of kacegya. -- ḱacēkcēk, cont. red. (of kaceka). Staggering. - najiᵑ. - ya. D.199. -- ḱacékceka, v.t. and v.i. red. (of kaceka). To stagger. Makácekceka. Tate waś'akelo oᵑ makacekcekelo. Bl. Mahuᵑkeśni ca makacekceke. D.114.

ḱacel', Same as taᵑiᵑśni. Tokel...ekta mni kte - . B.H.147.7;222.7. Tuwa - , Some one or other, someone who.

ḱace'slisli, v. (?). - s'e mani, i.e. weak-kneed. Bl.

ḱace'ya, v.a. (of ceya). To make cry by striking. Wakaceya.

ḱaci'ca, v.a. (?). An old word used thus: Taha - , To smoothen a hide, i.e. by rubbing with a piece of iron to get it dry, giving the hide the finishing touch. RF. Bl. Wakácica.

ḱaci'k'ala, v.a. (of cik'ala). To make small by chopping off. Wakacik'ala. -- ḱacík'ayela, v.a. (of cik'ayela). To make small by striking. -- ḱací'scila, v.a. To make small by cutting.

ḱaco'co, v.a. To mix up, as eggs, to beat up. Wakácoco.

ḱaco'za, v.a. To make warm by striking. R.

ḱa'e, pron. That is he.

ḱae'cetu, v.a. To make right or accomplish by striking. Wakaecetu.

ḱae'haᵑ, adv. Before that event takes place. The word is something like kohaᵑ. - migluwiᵑyeya kte. Bl. Wiᵑyaᵑ kiᵑ t'iᵑ kte kiᵑ heoᵑ - caᵑwognaka ikignipi kte. M.

ḱae'ktawapaya, perhaps adv. Far. - laka ca kohaᵑ miye wapami kte ḣcelo, i.e. moves away slowly. Bl.

ḱaeś', pron. That one. R. Waᵑjila - el uᵑpi śni, Not one was in. Hee - hi śni, That one did not come, i.e. the one expected did not come or appear.

kae'tulake el, (?). B.H.11.2. - peji owayaśla kiᵑ wanil aye.

ḱae'yaya, v.t. (of eyaya). To have taken something belonging to another, to have carried away. Wakáeblabla.Bl. R. gives: keyaya. Uᵑkcekiḣa waᵑ wososo kaeyaye c'oᵑ iyatap ye. D.73.

ḱa'ǵa, v.a. To make, form, to cause to be, be the cause or author of; to execute. Wakaga. -- ḱaǵe' yuzá, v. Meaning perhaps, to take hold of me. Bl.

ḱaǵab', cont. (of kagapa). To make spread out or open by cutting. - iyeya. -- ḱaǵábya, adv. Gaping open, as a wound.

kaǵal' hiᵑgle', v.n. To be disappointed suddenly in one's expectations, to throw up one's hands, i.e. with the

idea of falling over on one's hands, perhaps. Kagal mahi^{n}gle. Kagal hi^{n}gle-mayakiyelo. BT. B.H.38.4. Cf. alóshi^{n}gle.
K̇aġal'ġata, adv. red. of kagata.
K̇aġal'k̇iya, adv. Spread out, stretched out, as the hand or arm. Cf. ákagalkiya.

K̇aġa^n', v.n. To open, make an opening in, to come through, as the wind does through one's clothing; to open by itself or by the wind. Tate ki^n - mahiyu. Wana maga^{n}ga^{n}la ca iḣa^{n}ha^n icaluza keś, - mahiyuwelo. Bl. R. PD.
K̇aġa^n'ġa^{n}ya^n, adv. red. of kaga^{n}ya^n.
K̇aġa^n'ya^n, adv. Open, spread out.

K̇aġa'ṗa, v.a. To cut, spread open by cutting, to spread open. Wakagapa.

K̇aġa'ṫa, adv. Spread out, as the hands or fingers.
K̇aġa'tkiya, adv. Same as kagalkiya.

K̇aġe', v.a. To skim off e.g. cream milk. Asa^{n}pi - . Wakáge.

K̇aġe'ġe, v.a. To sew. Wakagege. -- v. red. perhaps (kaġe). - icu, To take out repeatedly, i.e. by handfuls; to take out a handful, k̇aġé icú. Note: the word is not used alone.

K̇aġi', v. To stop one's progress, to be in one's way, as a river; not to be able to proceed; to hold in esteem to respect. Wakagi. Makagi.

K̇aġi'ca, v.a. To wake up by striking. Also, kaḣíca. Wakágica. D.26.

K̇aġi^{n}l'ġi^{n}ca, v.a. To strike and make spit fumes, as it were. Same as kaji^{n}kji^{n}ca. Bl.

K̇aġi'śni, adv. Without obstruction. - iyeya, To pass on without obstruction.
K̇aġi'śniśni, adv. red. Not hindered, not influenced by any number of people present, doing as one pleases; without fear or regard for anything. - oḣ'a^n. U^{n}ḣcegila s'e - wala yelo. WE. Cf. wito^{n}peśni. -- K̇aġíśniśniya^n, adv. Same as kagiśniśni. - woglaka. B.H.282.3.
K̇aġi'ya, v.a. To hinder, obstruct, make go slow, to bother. Kagiwaya, kagiu^{n}ya^{n}pi. Kagimayaya. Nihu^{n}keśni ni ca kagimayayi^n kta ca ni kte śni yelo, eya (ref. to going to war). -- adv. Hindering.

K̇agla', adv. By the side of, nearby. Kaglálaka hwo? Is it near? -- v.a. (agla). To take home to one. Wakagla. He - yo. -- v.n. To unfold, to stretch out at full length, unçoil, as a snake or rope. Wika^n - . Supe ki^n - hi^{n}hpaye. D.247.
K̇agla'gla, adv. red. (kagla). Alongside of.
K̇agla'k̇i^{n}ya^n, adv. Sticking, perhaps sideways, from the side. Tate - u^{n}glapi ktelo, We will have the wind from the side. Cf. glaki^{n}ya^n.
K̇agla'la, adv. red. of kagla. - hiyaya yo.
K̇agla'ya, adv. By the side of.

K̇agle'ġa, v.a. (glega). To mark across or make stripes or figures, to make rough. Wakaglega.
K̇agle'ġleġa, v. red. (kaglega). To make stripes across by cutting.
K̇agle'gleza, v. red. of kagleza.

K̇agle'ṗa, v.a. To make one vomit by striking on the back, as one in whose throat something got stuck. -- v.n. To vomit on account of dizziness caused by rapid circular motions. Makaglepa.

K̇agle'za, v.a. (gleza). To mark across or around by cutting; to make in stripes or figures. Wakagleza. R.
K̇agle'zela, v.a. To stripe, make striped.

K̇agli', v.a. (agli). To bring home to one (the "k" indicates). Wakagli. Wa^{n}na waśi^n wa^n yapa - śke'.

K̇aglog', cont. of kagloka. - iyeya.
K̇aglo'glo, v. red. (ka-glo, To grunt). To hit hard in anger, to make howl. Bl.
K̇aglo'gloka, v.a. red. (kagloka). To shake e.g. in the way an old wagon box does, or a wagon.
K̇aglo'k̇a, v.a. To put out of joint by striking. Wakagloka. -- v.n. perhaps. To make a misstep, thus feeling pain but without a dislocation (kapśu^n). Tahuka - .

K̇agmi', v.a. To cut all down, to clear

away, as timber, grass. R. Wakágmi. Also, To hoe.

kagmi'gma, v.a. To make round by striking or rolling. Wakagmigma. -- v.n. perhaps. To roll along. Tapa kiŋ le waŋkayewaya kiŋ hehaŋ kuta - iyaye ci, kuwapi kte lo.

ḱagmi'pi s'e, adv. (?). - yaŋkapi, They have nothing whatsoever left, are entirely poor. Same as: keye cola yaŋkapi. Bl.

ḱagmi'yaŋyaŋ, v.a. To make roll by striking, as a ball. Wakagmiyaŋyaŋ.

ḱagmuŋ', v. To spin or twist with the extended hand. Wakagmuŋ.

ḱagna', v.a. To shake off by striking, as corn, striking the kernels off, or as fruit from a tree. Wakagna.

ḱagna'yaŋ, v.a. (of gnayaŋ). To miss partly while striking, e.g. in splitting wood and striking off a little piece. Wakagnayaŋ.

ḱaġo', v.a. To draw a line, i.e. on land, as a Reservation line. Also, To mark, make marks, cuts or gashes, to vaccinate. Wakago. -- ḱaġóġo, v.a. To make marks, to gash.

ḱaġo'p̂a, v.a. To strike one asleep, to wake partly up and make snore. Wakagopa. Seems derived from ka and ġopa.

ḱaġug', cont. of kaguka. - iyeya.

kagwa', v. To bruise one, to strike and skin. - iyeya. - iyemayayelo. Bl.

kagwe'za, v.a. To make rough by striking. Wakagweza. Bl.

ḱagwu', v. To make curdle, thick, by striking or moving. Wakagwu.

kagye'la, adv. Rattling, like an old wagon etc.

ḱahaŋ', adv. To this, thus far. Word is used when one is pointing at the same time, as in saying: He emptied the bottle so far. - niś toka hwo? B.H. 119.18. Cf. lehaŋ, ehaŋ, hehaŋ, iyehaŋ. -- ḱaháŋhaŋ, adv. red. of kahaŋ. -- ḱaháŋhaŋḱeca, adv. red. of kahaŋkeca. -- ḱaháŋhaŋyaŋ, adv. red. of kahaŋyaŋ. -- ḱaháŋḱeca, perhaps adv. To this, thus far, so long. -- ḱaháŋl, adv. To this, at this, thus far. -- ḱaháŋt̄u, adv. To that, so far, so long. - kiŋhaŋ. Bl. -- ḱaháŋt̄uk'e, adv. Now then. Also, kahaŋtuk'el. R. Bl. - katkaŋhaŋyaŋ wiyukcaŋpo. Bl. -- ḱaháŋt̄uya, adv. So far. -- ḱaháŋyaŋ, adv. Thus far. - inajiŋ yo. -- ḱaháŋyaŋka, adv. Some distance off, as in counting relationship. -- ḱaháŋyela, adv. Only so far, only so long. P. Bl.

ḱaha'yeya, v. To go away, leave. Hihaŋna kiŋ kaháyewayiŋ kte. Bc. Bl. R. gives: kaha iyeya. Wana - po, said when they prepared to go and are now ready, being said by the leader or so of the group. Rb.

ḱahe'ktaḱiya, (?). - kacekcekapi, They staggered backward. B.H.256.11.

ḱahe'piya, adv. and perhaps n. On the side of. Caŋku kiŋ he - ȟpaya, That road goes along the hill, i.e. on it. Yuŋkaŋ - waŋ el taku waŋ ȟpaya. MS. 160.

kahi', v.a. (of ahi). To bring to oné, to arrive bringing something to one. Wakahi. Le cik'ala cicicahi ye. Pte kiŋ ataya iwicuŋkaȟpelo, i.e. we bunched them up. Bl. -- v.a. To stir, to rummage. Wakahi. -- ḱahíhiya, adv. Moving, as a fish's fins in water, or as feathers in the wind. Huyé (or Hoiyé), hoapeśa waŋ miniceteta ape - nuŋke, le uciciye, the Indians said when throwing out the line to catch fish. -- ḱahíhiyela, Same as akiśoka. Peji kiŋ - yuŋke, i.e. much grass.Bl.

ḱahiŋ'ȟpeya, v.a. To run over something. To make fall over or down, to overthrow. Na wasabglepi kiŋ he - glicupi. Hece na - iyaya na kte. MS.521.

ḱahiŋl', cont. (of kahiŋta). To brush or sweep off or out. - iyeya. - eȟpeya.

ḱahiŋ't̄a, v.a. To sweep or brush up, as a floor. Wakahiŋta. Owaŋ -.

ḱahiŋt̄u ska, (?). - iyaya. The word is used when the wind clears a place, sweeping it clear. Bl.

kahi'yaya, v. (?). Olowaŋ -, To sing a hymn, a song. B.H.54.2. Hogluwaŋkal olowaŋ - . U na waŋjila eśa, i.e. olowaŋ waŋ, at least one, uŋkicahiyayapi ye. D.20.

k̇aho'ho, v.a. To loosen something by striking, as a fence post; to strike and knock loose, as a torch or stick set in the ground. Wakahoho. Wihuta iyuha - po, i.e. announced before breaking up camp. -- k̇ahóhola, v. Same as kahoho.

k̇aho'mni, v.a. To make something turn around by striking, as a top; to turn around, as a wheel by striking; to spin, as a top. Wakáhomni. -- k̇ahómnimni, v. red. of kahomni. B.H.87.17.

k̇aho'toŋ, v.a. To make animals cry, not dogs however, by striking, e.g. pigs. Wakáhotoŋ. To make howl out by striking. -- k̇ahótoŋtoŋ, v. red. of kahotoŋ. Bl.

k̇aho'wa, v. To make dogs howl by striking them.

k̇ahu'k̇ul, adv. Down. - iyeya, To put down by striking. -- k̇ahúk̇ulwapa, adv.

k̇ahuŋ', v.a. To make a mark by striking with an ax. Wakáhuŋ.

k̇ahuŋ'huŋs, cont. of kahuŋhuŋza. - iyeya. -- k̇ahúŋhuŋsya, adv. Shaking. - haŋ, It stands shaking.

k̇ahuŋ'huŋza, 1) v.a. To shake, make shake by striking, as a tree, or as the wind does trees. Wakáhuŋhuŋza. 2) v.n. To be shaken as on a wagon, rocking chair etc. Mak̇áhuŋhuŋza. -- k̇ahúŋkuŋza, v.a. To pretend to strike with an ax.

k̇ahu'ṫe, v.a. To wear to a stump by striking, as an ax. Wakahute. -- k̇ahúṫela, perhaps part. Worn to a stump.

k̇aḣ , cont. of kaga. - áya, To continue making.

k̇aḣa', 1) v.a. To curl, to knot; to make rough or to notch by striking. Wakaḣa. 2) n. A curl, a knot.

k̇aḣab, cont. (of kaḣapa). To drive along, as cattle or horses. - aya. -- k̇aḣábḣapa, v. red. (of kaḣapa). To beat against and make a rustling noise as the wind blowing against grass.

k̇aḣa'ḣa, v.n. red. (of kaḣa). To curl up, as a flame, to sparkle or send up sparks.

k̇aḣa'ṗa, v.a. To drive along, as a team or bunch of cattle; to whip, drive by whipping. Wakaḣapa.

k̇aḣci', v.a. To gap, to break a gap in something, as in the edge of an ax. Wakaḣci. -- k̇aḣcíḣci, v. red. To break out gaps from the edge of an ax. Wakaḣciḣci. -- k̇aḣciýa, v.a. To cause to break a gap in an ax. Kaḣciwaya.

k̇aḣeb', cont. of haḣepa. - iḣpeya, To empty by lading out. The word is used only of liquids.

k̇aḣe'ṗa, v.a. To bail out, throw out, as water with the hand or a cup etc. until it is all gone. Wakaḣepa.

k̇aḣe'yaṫa, adv. (of ḣeyata). Back, on one side. - iyeya, To shove or throw back or to one side.

k̇aḣk̇a'ġa, v. To cough, belch, pretending to cough up something that got into the person by magic. Note the sound "kaḣ". Yuŋkaŋ heceglala uŋma k'oŋ - . Na ake uŋma k'oŋ he - na iś ake uŋma k'oŋ ecoŋ.

k̇aḣk̇i'ya, v.a. To cause to make. Kaḣwakiya. Na caŋli wapaḣta kiŋ hena kaḣkiyapi.

k̇aḣla', v.a. To make sound by striking, to ring, as a bell. Wakaḣla.

k̇aḣla'ġaŋ, v.n. To lengthen out, become long, extend. - yeya, To give away what has been given one. -- Kaḣlaḣ, cont. of kaḣlagaŋ. - aya, It lengthens out.

k̇aḣla'ḣla, v. red. (of kaḣla). Perhaps to rattle. Wakaḣlaḣla.

k̇aḣla'ḣlaġaŋ, v. red. of kaḣlagaŋ. -- k̇aḣlaḣlaḣ, cont. of kaḣlaḣlagaŋ. -- k̇aḣlaḣlaḣya, adv. Lengthening out. - aya, To become long or lengthen out, as the days.

k̇aḣla'ṫa, v.a. To catch something with a sharp hook, as with a fish hook or a hawk preying on an animal.

kahla'te, adv. Below something. - owá-k'a.
kahla'teya, adv. Below, undermining perhaps. - wak'á.

kahla'ya, v.a. To cause one to ring or sound. Kahlawaya. -- v.n. To fall off, as a sticking plaster; to come off, as paint or paste or scales. D.248.

ka'hlayela, adv. (?). - iyuha oⁿspeciciyelo, i.e. I have taught you all. Bl.

kahle'ca, v.a. To tear open by striking to split open, to fracture. Wakahleca.
kahle'hleca, v. red. To break in e.g. the skull, to fracture. Wakahlehleca.
kahlel', cont. of kahleca. - iyeya.
kahlel'ya, v.a. To cause to fracture. Kahlelwaya.

kahli', v.n. To mire, stick in the mud. Wakahli. D.77. -- kahlihli, v. red.
kahli'ya, v.a. To cause to mire. Kahliwaya.

kahlo'geca, (?). Huⁿhé - yeyéle, as a woman would say when a man asks for food continually. Owipi wotehi. - yewáyehcelo, as said by one who eats without end. Waⁿ lila wawata śka - yewayelo, i.e. still hungry inspite of having eaten much. Bl.

kahlo'gostaⁿpi, n. A vest, a garment made without sleeves.

kahlog'ya, v.a. To cause to make a hole in. Kahlogwaya. Also, to break into, as a burglar into a house. Pahte kiⁿ kahlogmayehcelo, i.e. the cold has made a hole into my forehead, it is very cold! P. Bl. -- adv. perhaps. Pahte kiⁿ - wicatasakelo. Bl.

kahlo'hloka, v. red. of kahloka. B.H. 274.19.
kahlok', cont. (kahloka). To knock a hole in. - iyeya. - ya, To go on without minding anything. Uⁿkigluśtaⁿpi na - uⁿkigni ktelo, When done with our work we will go home at once. Kahlóhlok iyaye ole, He looked for it in all directions.
kahlo'ka, v.a. To break a hole in anything, to make a hole by striking, as with an ax or club into ice.

kahlu'hlul, adv. (?). - hiyu, as leaves coming out in abundance and therefore hanging down. - hiuic'iya, To stand up and talk too often. - ihpeic'iyapi. WE. Cf. kah-yuhlata, kahlu-hla-ta.

kahmi', n. An inside corner, a bend in a river, a bay, a point of land etc. R.

kahmiⁿ', v.a. To bend by striking. Wakahmiⁿ.

kahmuⁿ', v.a. To make buzz, to whirl and cause to make noise. -- v.n. Caⁿ lila - tate ca. Wakahmuⁿ.
kahmuⁿ'hmuⁿ, v. red. of kahmuⁿ.
kahmuⁿ'hmuⁿyaⁿ, adv. Buzzing.
kahmuⁿ'yaⁿ, adv. Whirring, buzzing.

kahni'ga, v.a. To choose, select, elect, appoint. Wakahniga. Kośkalaka nump wicakahniga po.
kahnih', cont. of kahniga. - icu, To take one's choice.
kahnih'kiya, v.a. To cause to choose. Kahnihwakiya.
kahni'hniga, v. red. of kahniga.
kahni'hnih, cont. of kahnihniga.
kahni'hpica, adj. Eligible.
kahnih'ya, adv. Choosing.

kaho'ta, v.n. To make gray by striking. Wakahota.

kahpa', v.a. To knock down anything hanging up, to make something fall. Wakahpa. - iyeya yo! as is said before breaking up camp.
kahpa'hpa, v. red. To strike and make pieces fly off, as from wood or ice. Wakahpahpa.
kahpe'kiya, v.a. To cause to knock down. Kahpewakiya.

kahpu', v.a. To knock off something sticking, as pine gum; to scale off. Wakahpu. -- kahpúhpu, v. red.
kahpu'ya, adv. Scaling, falling off.

kahśi', v.a. To get a thing done; to order something.

kahta'keke, (?). Wakahtakeke, i.e. my words do not please him, though I said nothing bad. Bl.

kahtaⁿ', v.n. To soak up, to soak in, as does grease in wood. R. Bl.

kahtaⁿ'ka, v. To be attached to, have an affection for, as one animal has for another. R. Bl.

kaḣtaŋ´yaŋ, v.a. To cause to spread, as one does grease. R. Bl.

kaḣṫa´ṫa, v. To enfeeble, make unwell by striking. Wakaḣtata.

kaḣṫu´ṫeśni, adv. Not well made.

kaḣu´ġa, 1) v.a. To break up or break in e.g. the skull by striking; to crack something by striking. 2) v.n. To be deformed by being dropped or knocked about. Cega - .
kaḣuḣ´, cont. To crack something by striking. - iyewaya. Yuŋkaŋ wicaśa waŋ icu na keya - apiŋ kte keciŋ.
kaḣuḣ´ḱiya, v.a. To cause to break or knock in. Kaḣuḣwakiya.
kaḣu´ḣuġa, v. red. (kahuga). To smash e.g. eggs, a head, anything brittle.
kaḣuḣ´ya, adv. Breaking or staving in.

kaḣuŋ´ta, v. To wear out gradually and soften, as a church-bell rope. Also, kaḣuŋte. A.

kaḣwa´, v.a. (ḣwa). To make sleepy by striking or shaking, as in a wagon. Caŋpagmiyaŋ makaḣwa.

kaḣwog´, cont. of kaḣwoka. - iyaya, It has drifted off, carried along by wind or tide; blown off. - iyeya, To blow away.
kaḣwog´ya, v.a. To cause to drift; to wave, as a flag. Kaḣwagwaya.
kaḣwo´ḣwog, cont. of kaḣwoḣwoka. Tohaŋl maḣpiya gigiya - ahiyaye ciŋ hehaŋtu kta śke, i.e. when brown clouds drift in the wind. D.92.
kaḣwo´ḣwoḱa, v. red. of kaḣwoka.
kaḣwo´ka, v.n. To be carried away by wind; to float like the clouds, or wave as a flag. Tate ca wowapi kaḣwokelo. Óḱaḣ u, He comes floating down river. BT.

kaḣya´, 1) n. (kaga). Make, a kind, a sort. 2) adv. Made like, like, in the form of. Iktomi tawogmuŋke - , Made like a spider web. Wakiyela - , In the form of a dove. Lakol - wicoḣ'aŋ, A sort of Lakota work. Waḣ'eca - hiŋhelo.
kaḣya´kel, adv. In appearance. Tuwa tokeca - , Looking like someone else, disguised, with the form of another; with meaning unknown. B.H.272.3.

kaḣya´payalakes'e, (?). Wana lowaŋ kta ca - omniciye. MS.159.

kaḣ'a´kṗa, v.a. To hollow out, as in whittling or notching; make a hollow place by cutting with an ax. Wakaḣ'akpa. Bl.

kaḣ'aŋ´hiya, adv. (h'aŋhiya). A little slower, slowly, as in walking, reading, speaking etc.

kaḣ'e´, v.t. (?). Ptepa kah'epi s'e oyaka, i.e. to tell something with all its details. Bw.

kaḣ'ol´, v. aux. (kah'ota, obs.). - iyeya, To throw away e.g. a ball. - hiyuc'iye (of uya, To have thrown down), He gets off a horse, or down from a wagon. - yeic'iya. Bl.

kaḣ'u´, v.a. To peel off by striking, to skin, as a potato thrown on a hard surface.
kaḣ'u´ḣu, v. red. To make rough by breaking the bark or skin in many places. Wakaḣ'uḣu.

kai´, v.a. (ai). To go in, bringing something to one; to take to one. Wakai, uŋkaipi.

kai´caŋyaŋ, adv. Leaning against. Same as icaŋyaŋ. - egle, To lean against. - najiŋ, To lean against something.

kai´cic'uya, adv. Crossing each other, crookedly. Hukaicic'uya yaŋka, To cross one's legs while sitting. RF.

kai´ciopteya, adv. Crosswise, as two roads intersecting. - iyaya. - ikázo, To make or mark with a cross. Also, kai´c'iopteya. D.4. Cf. glakiŋyaŋ.

kai´cisaŋnica, (?). - ahiyayelo, ecel egnaka yo, i.e. the wind etc. have blown it half off (the tablecloth), so put it back.

kai´ciyaṗehaŋ, adv. (apehaŋ, To fold on anything). Tangled up. Si - yaŋka, To sit with one foot lying on the other. Hu - yaŋka, To sit, on the ground, with the legs crossed, i.e. in Indian fashion, before one. Hu - najiŋ, To stand with feet lying on one another. RF. -- kai´ciyaṗeheya, adv.

(?). Hu - ħpaya, Lie with legs crossed. Bl.

ķai'coġa, v.n. To come off, slide away as wood in water; to gather in bunches as old hay, twigs etc. Bl. -- ķaićoħ. v. contr.

ķai'ġejuya, adv. Crowding in.

kai'gluwiⁿyaⁿ, (?). - hiyayelo. Bl.

kai'hakteya, (?). - s'e magaju, It rains just a few drops. Bl.

ķai'ħeju, v.n. To be sore from riding. - katuta. Bl. -- ķaíħejujuya, adv. red of kaiħejuya. - uⁿpelo. Almost the same as kaiħeya, the the difference is uncertain. Bl. -- ķaíħejuya.

ķai'ħeya, adv. (?). - aya, ahinajiⁿ, i.e. coming together in groups or bunches. Said of people and also of things as driftwood. Bl.

ķai'jena, v.a. To confuse, mix up as the wind does. Tate - . Bl.

ķai'le, v. (of ile). To make blaze by fanning or as the wind does. -- ķaíleħleġa, v.a. To strike, as a fire, and cause to send sparks. -- ķaílele, v. red. of kaile. Bl.

kai'naħni, v. To hurry up in working, be busier. - yo. Bl. -- ķaińaħnila,v. To hurry up, run, in the manner of old people. Wakainaħnila. Bl. -- kaińaħniyaⁿ, adv. or v. perhaps.

ķaiⁿ'yaⁿg iye'ya, v. To throw and make run, as a rabbit etc. - iyaya. Bl. -- ķaíⁿyaⁿkelaka, v. To run like old people, taking short steps and not advancing fast. Wakáiⁿyaⁿkelaka. Bl.

ķai'ṗatkuħya, adv. In a line fronting.

ķai'ṗazilya, adv. High. - lakese haⁿ, He stands higher than the others. Bl.

ķai'psilyalakes'e, adv. (?). - iⁿyaⁿka, To be a little ahead of others in running. So is also the middle finger ahead of the others. Bl.

ķai'ṗusťagya, adv. Crowding, pressing against.

ķai'śťaminihaⁿpi hiyu'ya, v. Perhaps to bring tears into one's eyes, as the wind does. -- ķaíśťaminioju iyéya, v. Same.

ķai'śuta, v. To stumble, i.e. once; to make a misstep. The word is used with another verb. - iyaya. Cf. kaiśutata. - iyaya, i.e. when speaking of a wagon, when it jolts going transversely over ruts etc. - iblabla, as on hard snow. Same as kaíśloślog iyaya. Bl. -- ķaíśutata, v. To stumble and labor until one gets on one's feet again. - iyaya. It is used with other verbs.

ķai'ťeb, adv. Diagonally, not straight. -- ķaíťebya, adv. Crosswise, slanting diagonally, slanting. - kaksa.

kai'ťececaśni, (?), (of ka, ite, and ececa śni). - iyemayayelo, which is said in fun: You make me angry. Bl.

kai'tehaⁿlake, adv. A little farther off (place); a little later (time). Na ake - ehaⁿl ake u.

ķai'ťeṗa, v.a. To cut diagonally. Wakaitepa.

kai'ťeyeśni iye'ya, v. Perhaps, to make one suddenly serious by a hurting remark. Bl.

ķai'tķob, adv. Back again. - gliħpaya, To fall back again, rebound.

ķai'tķobya, adv. Opposite, but a little to one side, not looking quite straight at one. -- ķaítķoķib, adv. With the face towards one, meeting. -- ķaítķoķibya, adv. Facing one. -- ķaítķoķipaťaⁿhaⁿ, adv. Opposite to, fronting one.

ķai'toķab, adv. Before, in advance of, as of a travelling party. - gli, To come home before the rest. - ya, To go before, prepare or break the way. -- ķaítoķabya, Same as kaitokab.

ķai'tokaⁿl, adv. Out to one side. - iyeya, To shove aside.

ķai'ťokṗas, cont. of kaitokpaza. - iyeya.

ķai'ťokṗaza, v.a. To bring darkness over for a little while by smiting, to stun by striking. Wakaitokpaza.

ƙai'ťomni, v.n. To be dizzy, having been struck on the head or been turning swiftly around on or in, as on a merry-go-round. Makáitomni.

kai'tuŋkab, adv. Same as kaituŋkabya. - glilipaye, He lost his balance and fell backward. D.74,note3. Cf. ituŋkab, Flat on the back, lying looking upward. -- ƙaíťuŋƙabya, adv. Reclining one's body, as when riding horseback. Bl.

kai'waŋyaŋgya, adv. Prudently, circumspectly, carefully, as in carrying a load without dropping things. - ecoŋ, To do a thing in such wise. Same as owahecelya, kaiyaciŋyaŋ, aiyaciŋyaŋ. - magaju, i.e. it rains by a few drops. Bl.

kai'waŋyaŋk, v. (of kaiwaŋyaŋka). To watch one. - ocicuwa ktelo, owekinaś ȟ'uŋt'eciyiŋ ktelo. Bl. Kaiwaŋyaŋka seems not to be used or to exist.

ƙai'yab, (?). - iyeya, To make bound off, as an arrow, after striking obliquely. Bl. Śuŋkmanitu - ihaŋ, i.e. to meet a wolf, he coming from the opposite direction; this happens to be EM.'s Indian name. Oyate waŋ taŋka wicoti ca - ihaŋ, Without any warning, he came upon a great camp of human beings. D.207-8.

ƙai'yabebeya or ƙai'yap̄ep̄eya, adv. red. In all directions. B.H.304.4. -- ƙaiýabeyekiya or ƙaiýap̄eyekiya, adv. Scattered. - iyayekiyapi, They are running in all directions, as horses that are chased.

kai'yaciŋyaŋ, adv. Carefully. - ecoŋ, He does it carefully, as carrying a load without dropping anything. Bl. Same as kaiwaŋyaŋgya.

ƙai'yakap̄eya, adv. Exceeding, a little more than. R. Bl. -- ƙaiýakap̄eyala s'e, adv. A little ahead. - iŋyaŋka, To be a little ahead of others in running.

ƙai'yaƙapťeya, adv. Uphill.

kai'yaƙic'ula s'e, (?). - mak'u śni, icewiŋś conala mak'u we, i.e. expected much, but received little. Bl. - yahipi kiŋ icaŋlmawaśte. Bl.

ƙai'yaƙic'uya, adv. A little more.

ƙai'yap̄ehaŋ, v. To get entangled, swung around. B.H.95.23.

kai'yocatka, (?).

ƙai'yoȟpeya, (?). Bl.

kai'yokpaniyaŋ, adv. Unevenly. Note a similar use: Oćihiśniśniyaŋ ecoŋpi he kapi. Bl.

ƙai'yoťag, v. cont. (of kaiyotaka). To be seated. - gliȟpaya, To fall down in attempting to be seated. -- ƙaiýotagtag, cont. red. of kaiyotag. - gliȟpaya, To bump up and down as when seated in a wagon on a bad road. Bl.

ƙai'yoťaƙa, v. To be seated. - gliȟpaya, To fall down when being seated.

ƙai'yowas, cont. (of kaiyowaza). To cause an echo by striking. - iyeya.

ƙai'yowaza, v.a. To make echo by striking with the hand, make resound. Wakaiyowaza.

kai'yoyagya, (?). Kawaŋkaka iyaya ca iyoȟa kiŋ - iyeye. Similar to: Tapoŋ naśkaŋ s'e iŋyuŋke. Bl.

ƙai'yuzeya, adv. A little way off; not a long way off. - icu, To take by reaching, to reach for. - hinajiŋ. B.H.231.3,11;232.10. - enajiŋ.D.4. -- ƙaiýuzeyakel, adv. Same. -- ƙaiýuzeyataŋhaŋ, adv. From a distance. - o, To hit, although one is very far away. - yeśaŋ, apelo. This word may be the same as kaiyusyataŋhaŋ. Cf. kaiyuzeya.

ƙaja', v.a. To split a little, to make gape. Wakaja. Also, to hit and split. - wao. Same as kaślel. Bl.

ƙaja'bjap̄a, v. red. of kajapa. Bl. Makájabjapelo, I am very tired from riding.

ƙaja'haŋ, v.a. (of jahaŋ). To make open out by striking, to press open. Wakajahaŋ. -- ƙajáhaŋhaŋ, v. red.

ƙaja'ja, v.a. To wash away, as a bridge by a flood; to wash away by pulling back and forth. Wakajaja. - iyaya.

ƙaja'ƙa, v.a. To squeeze open, as a

wound; to strain or knock open. Wakájaka.

ǩajal', cont. of kajata. - iyeya. -- ǩajálya, adv. (?). Tiśkakaŋ - yaŋk, as is said when with a lean person the two muscles on the neck are protruding and there is a hollow between the two. Bl.

ǩajaŋ'jaŋ, v.n. (of jaŋjaŋ). To become light, as clouds after rain clear; to dawn. B.H.186.2. ---ǩajáŋjaŋǩa, v.n. Same as kajaŋjaŋ. -- ǩajáŋjaŋyaŋ, adv. Dawning. - u, It is dawning.

ǩaja'p̂a, v.a. To strike and make dull, as an ax or knife by hitting it on something hard, so that the thin part of it turns around. Bl.

ǩaja'ťa, v.a. To make forked by cutting with an ax. Wakájata.

ǩajib', cont. (of kajipa). To shave off quickly or by a stroke. - iyeya.

ǩajib'jip̂a, v. red. of kajipa.

kaji'nica śni, (?). Takuni - keś, i.e. to take the whole thing instead of only a part of it (Doubtful interpretation). TH.

kajiŋ'kjiŋca, v. Same as kagiŋlgiŋca.

ǩaji'p̂a, v.a. To shave with a knife or drawing-knife, to plane. Wakajipa.

ǩajo', v.n. To purge, have diarrhoea; to whistle, as the wind does. Wakájo. Tate - . Nóŋge tate makajo ca taŋyaŋ nawaȟ'oŋ śni. Bl. - iyeya.

kajo'joyeya, v. red. (of kajo and yeya). To throw, as a piece of wood, with a whizzing sound. Also refers to diarrhoea. Bl.

kaju', v. (?). Tiŋpsiŋla wana hukáju, as is said in August when the stems of the wild turnip are dry and break off. A. Sb.

ǩaju'ju, v.a. To knock off; to blot out, efface; to pay off, as one's debts.

ǩajuŋ', v.a. To knock out somebody's tooth by hitting with a ball, or striking; to pull up, as birds do corn; or to come out or moult, as the quills of geese. R.

ǩajuŋ'he s'e, (?). - inajiŋ, To get mired, perhaps. Bl.

ka'ǩa, adj. Stiff, rattling, as a stiff hide when beaten; sounding dull, as a bell sometimes does. Iyeś - wowaśi ecoŋ, as one would say to another to incite him to work pointing at another (iyeś) who does work hard. BE.

ǩaǩa', n. A baby's word for grandfather.

ǩaǩab', (?). - iyeye, To push away perhaps. - iȟpeya. Bl. Same as kaha iyeya, and kahiŋȟpeya. Si - iyeya, To trip one by holding the foot in his way while he is moving. LT.

ka'kag, cont. (of perhaps kakaka). To sound, rattle, like an old kettle when shaken with stones in it. - hiŋgla. -- kakágya, adv. Rattling, as an old kettle when shaken; rattling, as an empty wagon. -- kakágyaǩel, adv. Rattling.

ǩaka'ǩa, v.a. To make a dull noise by beating an old kettle or a stiff hide. Wakakaka.

ǩakaŋ', v.a. To hew, as a log; to adze; to knock off, as fruit from a tree. Wakákaŋ.

ǩaǩaŋ', v. To make marks, notches into something hard. Wakákaŋ. -- ǩaǩáŋǩaŋ, v. To cut notches in or knobs on.

ǩaka'p̂a, v.a. To strike a ball that is thrown and send it back. Wakakapa. Cf. pakapa.

ǩaǩa'ťiŋ, v.a. To straighten out by striking, as round or coiled wire, or a horse shoe. Wakakatiŋ.

ǩaǩa'wa, v.a. To make open by striking, i.e. to strike something off and thus open it partly e.g. a tin can. Wakakawa.

ǩakca', v.a. To comb, as hair; to disentangle. Wakakca.

ǩa'ǩeca, adv. In this manner, thus.

ka'ǩeca, adj. Stiff, making a noise

when felt or handled, as parchment. Cf. kaǩa.

ǩa'ǩel, adv. So, thus; in some direction somewhere. - ecoⁿ wo, Do it in this manner. Na - kawiⁿȟ iyayapi. - ecamoⁿ we, That way I do, i.e. That's the trick I work. - na - . D.21,114.
ǩa'ǩelya, adv. Thus, so.
ǩa'ǩena, adv. Somewhere, in some direction. Iktomi - ya na Iya waⁿ ataya.

ǩaǩe'stoⁿ, v.a. To make barbed, as an arrow. Kakeswatoⁿ. R. Bl.
ǩaǩe'stoⁿyaⁿ, adv. With barbs. Bl.

ǩaǩeś', adv. indef. Any. Tukte uⁿma - , What one, no matter which. Tuktektetu - , Anywhere. Iye - glakca śni ȟajute kiⁿ pahiⁿ oⁿz'ákiyotake s'e. Bl. B.H. 108.10. -- ǩaǩéśǩeś, adv. red. of kakeś. Taku - , Anything. SW. B.H.60.3.

ǩa'ǩeťu, adv. In this way, so, thus. Also, ǩáǩeťuya.

ǩa'ǩi, adv. There, yonder. - mni kte. - ka, Yonder. - ka caⁿcega waⁿ hotaⁿiⁿ kiⁿ hel niyate ti yelo, Yonder, where the drum is singing, is your father's house. D.208. Cf. leci, heci.

ǩaǩi', v.a. (aki). To have taken home or somewhere else to one. Wakaki, uⁿkakipi. Miye talo kiⁿ he wakaki. D.244

kaǩi'cipapi, (?). (kapa). Kignuⁿ - , A swimming game, an underwater race.

ǩaǩi'ciṗehaⁿ, v. (?). Mini - .B.H.71.12

ǩaǩi'ja, 1) v.n. To suffer, be afflicted. Makakija, nicakija. 2) adj. Suffering, afflicted.

ǩa'kiǩa, adv. Over there. Same as kakiya. Also, kaki ka. Hehaⁿl lenayos - paha waⁿ lila tehaⁿ yaⁿke kiⁿ heci anuⁿk anuⁿk icicuya iyayapi kte lo. Nitaⁿke niyate ob - tipi waⁿ he kiⁿ he tipelo.

ǩaǩi'nuⁿk, adv. Each one his own way. - iyayapi. B.H.89.10.
ǩaǩi'nuⁿkaⁿ, adv. Apart. - iyeya, To force apart, to separate. Tate hiyu na caⁿ k'uⁿ hena - iyeye. D.22.
ǩaǩi'nuⁿǩaⁿǩiya, adv. Cf. kinuⁿkaⁿkiya. Mini kiⁿ - iyaye. B.H.112.4;113.9.

ǩaǩiⁿ'ca, v.a. To scrape e.g. hair from a hide. Wakakiⁿca.
ǩaǩiⁿl', cont. of kakiⁿca. - iyeya, To scrape off. -- ǩaǩíⁿlkiⁿca, v. red of kakiⁿca. Bl.

kaǩi'pa, v. (kapa). To surpass, excel one, get through successfully. Kawakipa. Oiyoȟpaye kiⁿ śica ca kawakipe ciⁿhaⁿ iyowakita kte lo. Bl.

ǩaǩi'ṗaś, adv. Wrinkled, loose fitting
ǩaǩi'ṗaśṗaś, adv. red.

ǩaǩis', cont. of kakiza, - iyeya.
ǩaǩi'sǩiza, v. red.

ǩaǩiś', cont. of kakija.
ǩaǩi'śic'iya, v. To make one's self suffer.
ǩaǩiś'ya, 1) v.a. To inflict or make suffering; to punish. Kakiśwaya. 2) adv. Afflicted, suffering.
ǩaǩiś'yaǩel, adv. In pain. - wauⁿ.

ǩa'ǩiya, adv. Yonder, there.
ǩa'ǩiyaťaⁿhaⁿ, adv. From yonder place; in this wise, in this way, by this means.
ǩaǩi'yotaⁿ, adv. In that direction.
ǩaǩi'yotaⁿlahci, adv. Just that way, just in that direction.

ǩaǩi'za, v. To make creak by rubbing, as two trees do that rub against each other, or as door hinges that are not well oiled. Tiyopa - , The door is creaking. Caⁿ numb icicameya haⁿ caⁿke tate hiyu caⁿ icicakiⁿzahaⁿ śke, i.e. two trees rubbed together making a loud squeaking noise. Caⁿ numb tate caⁿ iyena icicakiⁿzahaⁿ. D.21,26.

ǩaǩmiⁿ', v.a. To clear off e.g. weeds from a field. Wakakmiⁿ. Na makoce kiⁿ oyate kiⁿ ataya kakmiⁿpi na kablupi.

ǩakog', cont. of kakoka. - hiⁿgla.
ǩakog'ya, adv. Rattling.
ǩakog'yaǩel, adv. Rattling.

ǩako'ǩa, v.a. To produce a dull sound by striking, but not by drumming. Wakakoka. Kabu, To drum.
ǩako'koǩa, v. red. of kakoka.

ǩaǩoⁿ'ťa, v.a. To cut in ridges; to wear thin a rope, a strap etc. by striking. BD. Wakakoⁿta. -- ǩaǩóⁿtkoⁿťa, v.a. red. (of kakoⁿta). To hollow out in grooves or ridges. Wakakoⁿtkoⁿta.

ķakp̣a´, v.a. To strike and make a hole in, cut a vein. Wakakpa. Tezi - . BT. Iśta kiⁿ nupiⁿ kakpapi, They put out his both eyes. D.220. - iyeya, To shoot through, as an arrow or bullet.

ķakp̣aⁿ´, v.a. To beat fine, mash up; to wink, as the eye. Wakakpaⁿ. Cf. iśtakakpaⁿ.

ķakp̣i´, v.a. To crack or break, as a nut. Wakákpi. -- kakpiýeya, v.a. To pierce through. Pte - . Bl.

ķaksa´, v.a. To separate by striking with an axe, to split; to cut off with an axe or by striking. Pa - . Wakaksa. -- ķaksáksa, v. red. (of kaksa). To cut off often, to cut up, as wood for fire. Wakaksaksa. Wana maȟpiya - ca kaskiyayiⁿ kte lo. WE. Caⁿkáksaksapi, To cut off one piece after another, as pieces from a stick. Bl.

kaksi´ȟpeya, v.a. (of kaksa and iȟpeya) To strike and sever. B.H.133.26.

ķakśa´, abbrev. (of kakeśa). 1) v.a. To coil, roll up, as a rope, wikaⁿ; to wind, as yarn; to fold up. Wakakśa. 2) adv. Coiled up. Pagé hákakśa omawani yelo, i.e. indicating to be hungry. Bl. Tuwa - , as a man says to another when doubting his truthfulness LB. -- ķakśakśa, adv. red. (of kakśa). Coiled up, in coils, rolled round. -- ķakśala, adv. Coiled up.

ķakśaⁿ´, v.a. To bend, bend up. Wakakśaⁿ. -- ķakśaⁿkśaⁿ, adv. Crookedly, in a zigzag manner. - iⁿyaⁿka. Also spelled: ķakśáⁿkśiⁿ. Bl.

kakśi´ja, v.a. To bend up, double up by striking e.g. a leg opposite the knee, thus getting him on his knees; to shut up, as a pocket knife. Wakakśija. -- kakśiǩśa, The word is doubtful. Leceya makakśikśelo, i.e. tired. Bl. -- ķakśiǩśija, v. red. of kakśija. To be tired from riding, though this is a very doubtful meaning. Bl. -- ķakśiś, cont. (of kakśija). To double up. - iyeya. -- ķakśiśya, v.a. To cause to shut up. ķakśiśwaya.

ķakťaⁿ´, v.a. To bend by striking, to make something curved, as a horse shoe. Wakaktaⁿ. -- ķakťaⁿkťaⁿ, v. red. of kaktaⁿ. -- ķakťaⁿyaⁿ, adv. Bending.

ķaǩu´, v.a. (of aku). To start to bring home. R. Waⁿji makaku yo. Tipi iyokaⁿ el caⁿ wicayakaku kte lo. Bl.

ķaǩu´ka, v.a. To wear out by friction, striking etc. Wakákuka. R. gives v.a.

ķaǩuⁿťa, Cf. kakoⁿta. -- ķaǩúⁿtǩuⁿťa, Cf. kakoⁿtkoⁿta.

ķaǩye´la, adv. With a noise, perhaps of something dropping. Taku - wakśica el ohiⁿȟpaya.

ķak'e´ǧa, v.a. To make a grating noise. Wakak'ega.

ķak'es´, cont. (of kak'eza). To blow off and leave bare and hard, as when the wind blows the snow from the ground. - iyeya.

ķak'e´za, v.n. To leave hard and bare, as wind does the ground.

ķak'ō´ǧa, v.a. To scrape off with a knife or stick, as dirt from shoes, clothes, paint from the wall etc. Wakak'oga. -- ķak'oȟ, cont. of kak'oga. Tiⁿpsila - ỵutapi, Scraping turnips they eat them.

ķak'os´, cont. of kak'oza. - iyeya.

ķak'o´za, v.a. To make the ground bare and thus harden it, to make hard, to leave hard and bare as the wind does the ground, or by sweeping etc. Wakak'oza. Cf. ot'oza.

ķal, adv. cont. (perhaps of kakiya). - ewicoti. Paha kiⁿ kal iyawahe. BT.

ķal, cont. of kata. Kal aya, It is getting hot.

ķala´, v.a. To scatter, as grain, and once not applied to liquids. Wakála.

ķalab´, cont. perhaps of kalapa. - iyekiya, To salute with the hand. - iyeuⁿkiciyapi kta. WE.

ķala´la, v. red. (of kala). To scatter, sow, throw, broadcast, soidoing repeatedly. Wakalala. - iyeya. Sipa kiŋ - s'e yaŋka, i.e. when the toe end of moccasins is all torn. Taku inayaḣni ca - s'e yainaŋke, i.e. to put clothes on carelessly. Bl.

K̇ala´ṗa, v.a. To rub smooth and level. Note: kalab iyekiya, a more used form of the word. Bl.

K̇ale´bleṗa, v. red. (of kalepa). To notch by cutting. Wakaleblepa. R. Bl.

K̇ale´cala, adv. Soon, pretty soon. -- K̇alecalakes'e, adv. (?). Ww.

K̇ale´ġa, v.a. To fan, perhaps; to make shine by striking. Ḣupáha oŋ peta kalegahiŋ na ena t'a śke. MS.71.

kale´haŋyaŋk, (?). Away. - iyeya. B.H. 249.4.

K̇ale´ḣleġa, v. red. of kalega. -- K̇aléḣlegapi s'e, perhaps adv. - hiŋgla, To sparkle suddenly as it were, as a piece of metal that is being polished. Bl. - koyaka, To dress very attractively. Bl. Same as iyówicajaŋjaŋ s'e koyaka.

K̇aleḣ´ya, v.a. To make shine by striking, as a fire.

K̇ale´ktehaŋ, adv. Stumbling, tottering. K̇aléktehaŋhaŋ, adv. red. of kalektehaŋ. -- K̇aléktehaŋhaŋyaŋ, adv. Stumblingly. -- K̇aléktehaŋyaŋ, 1) v.a. To cause to stumble along. Kalektehaŋwaya. 2) adv. Stumbling.

K̇ale´ṗa, v.a. To cut a notch in. Wakalepa. R. Bl.

kalkal´ya, adv. Bitingly, in anger. - eya. SH.

K̇alob´, cont. (of kalopa). To mire. - iyaya. -- K̇alóbk̇iya, v.a. To cause to mire. Kalobwakiya. -- K̇alóblob, red (of kalob). Miring, wading, as a horse in mud. - iyaya. -- K̇alóbloṗa, v. red. of kalopa. -- K̇alóbya, v.a. To cause to mire. Kalobwaya.

K̇alō´ciŋ, v.n. To be hungry from being shaken up, as from having ridden on a wagon or on horseback. Makálociŋ.

K̇alo´ṗa, v.a. To strike something soft that does not give way, but at most shows a hole. Pi - . -- v.n. To mire, stick in the mud. Wakalopa. Cf. kaḣli. -- K̇aloṗe s'e, v. To give a love tap. - apa, To strike one without hurting him.

K̇alu´, v.a. To blow or brush away a little with the hand. Wakalu. Also, to fan. -- K̇alúlak̇a or K̇alú lák̇a, perhaps n. The fastest runner, men or horses. Yakalu lakelo, iyotaŋla icu wo, i.e. you alone win, all others were far behind.Bl. -- K̇alúlu, v. red. (of kalu). To be fanning. Wakálulu. Miglalu, I fan myself. Lowaŋ na icabu waŋ oŋ el (śina kpaŋyaŋpi waŋ) - iyeya.

K̇alus´, cont. of kaluza. -- K̇alúsya, 1) v.a. To cause to flow. Kaluswaya. 2) adv. Flowing, swiftly. -- K̇alúsyalak̇es'e, adv. Fast, but as it were and not in reality. - uŋgni ktelo. The word is used by old people and children. Bl.

K̇alu´za, v.n. To flow rapidly, as water; to be filled with. Toŋ - . We - . B.H.43.22;49.18.

K̇alya´, v.a. (of kataya). To heat, as rocks. Wakálya. Na iŋyaŋ k'oŋ hena - . -- K̇al'ić'iya, v. To warm one's self.

K̇a´makal iye´ya, v.a. To strike down. Bl.

K̇ama´k̇atak̇iya or K̇ama´k̇atka, (?). - uwate k'uŋ. Tate waŋ - iḣpemayelo. Bl.

K̇amas´ya, adv. As hard as iron. Caŋku kiŋ - yuŋka ca śluślutelo, i.e. hard as iron and slippery. Bl.

K̇ama´to, v.a. To provoke one and encounter resistance on his part. Wakámato. Cicámato. Bl.

K̇ame´yakel, adv. Squatting down, meaning to remain somewhere. Miméya is of doubtful use. Ka - maŋke. EB.

K̇ami´ma, v.a. To make something flat and round by striking with an ax, as a wheel might be formed. Wakamima.

K̇amna´, v.a. To get, obtain, earn. Wakamna. -- perhaps v.n. To rip, as a seam, come open. BE. Also, to rip by striking, as a ball is ripped when struck often; to rip,as a coat. --

k̇amnák̇iya, v.a. To cause to get or obtain. Kamnawakiya. -- k̇amnáyaŋ, v.a. To cause to get or obtain. Kamnawaya.

kamni'mni, v. red. (of namni, v.n.). To hang loosely, dangle; to swing, as a blanket in the wind. -- kamniȟnila, n. Earrings, such as always dangle, and are made of a triangular shape. R. Cf. owiŋ. Wapaha - el kśupi. MS.153.

kaną', pron. dem. pl. (of ka). Those yonder. Grammar,23. D.38.

k̇ana'k̇e, adv. So many, so much, all these. -- k̇anak̇eca, adv. Same. -- k̇anák̇eȟci, adv. So many. -- k̇anák̇iya, adv. All these, so many, in so many ways.

k̇ani'ca, v.a. (of ka and nica). To cut off clean, as meat from bones. R. Bl. Same as akaśpu. -- k̇ani', v.a. Same.Bl.

k̇aŋ, adj. Aged, worn out with age. Mak̇áŋ. Uŋkaŋpi. Waŋna - , i.e. in opposition to former youthful strength.

kaŋ, abbrev. (of kaŋta). The word is used in simile. There are red plums among the black ones that seem to be bad, but in reality they a re ripe and good. The meaning is something like: another kind. Bl. also says it indicates doing a thing poorly, as writing, since one does not know how. Kaŋġiġi yuśpiśpi s'e. Bl.

k̇aŋ, n. A vein, artery; a sinew, tendon; the nerve; a cord, string. - masuksuta. Taȟca - . Pte - . Kaŋ wamaś'akelo. -- kaŋák̇alaya, adv. (?). - yaŋka, To be very lean, i.e. when the veins are very visible and thick. Pehaŋ s'e napsu kiŋ - . Bl.

kaŋġi', n. A crow. -- kaŋġi' cehúpa ska, n. A crow. Cf. kaŋgi taŋka.

k̇aŋġi'ha migna'ka, n. A feather disk resembling the uŋȟcela kagapi, called a bustle by H. Crow feathers, hence kaŋgiha, were used for it. A feather ornament fastened on the back and dangling down. Worn in the Omaha Dance. Note: the upper flower-like part is called uŋȟcela kagapi. Bl.

kaŋġi' oyuŋ'ke, n. A certain place known to the Indians where many crows are nesting. Bl.

kaŋġi'tame, n. Black shale; a certain black soil; a black smooth stone found along White River. MS.356.

kaŋġi' t̄aŋ'k̇a, n. The large crow, the raven. To the Indians there were three kinds of crow: 1) kaŋgi taŋka, 2) uŋciśicala, and 3) kaŋgi cehupa ska. She cries out in the morning: Wakalya, wakalya, and also: Kaȟ, kaȟ.... Bl. They were taught to speak.

Kaŋġi' Wica'śa, n. The Crow Indian.

kaŋhaŋ', adv. Dangling and falling off or out; tattered, old; falling, as ripe fruit etc. Hiŋ - , i.e. when the horses lose their hair in spring. -- kaŋháŋhaŋ, adj. Tattered, ragged; dangling. Iktomi ehakeȟciŋ - s'e iyaya śke. MS.104. Cf. Haakaŋhaŋhaŋ, referring to the clothes of old people. Hiŋakaŋhaŋhaŋ, when speaking of horses as they shed their hair.

kaŋhe', v.n. To shell out, as ripe corn.

kaŋhe'ca, adj. Ragged, tattered, as one's clothes. Makáŋheca.

kaŋhe'heyela, adv. Ragged, perhaps. Wicota kawél - , uwelo, i.e. when many come in a hurry having old clothes on. Bl.

k̇aŋ'hi, v.n. To live to be old, reach old age. Káŋwahi.

kaŋ'ȟtal, (?). (of kaŋ and ȟtata). - imacu, I feel lazy. Bl.

kaŋi'cakp̄e, n. (of kaŋ and kakpa). A lancet.

k̇aŋ'ihuŋ'ni, v.n. Same as kaŋhi. Káŋiwahuŋni.

kaŋi'naśkaśkaŋ, n. A medical battery.

k̇aŋi't'a, v. To die of old age. Kaŋimat'e.

k̇aŋi'wapsak̇e, n. Something, e.g. a knife, to cut off a sinew or string etc. Cf. wapsáka. - waŋ imicikiŋte śni, or imicik'eye śni, My knife is dull, i.e. not sharp. Bl.

k̇aŋi'yeyapi s'e, adv. (?). - ya, or - u, To go or come cheerfully without meeting with any difficulties. Bl. - oyaka, To tell something well, with all its details and to the end. BE.

kaⁿka'kp̣a, v.a. To cut a vein, to bleed one. Kaⁿwakakpa.

kaⁿke'ca, n. A water bird with a thin long bill. Bl. The pileated woodpecker, or woodcock. R. gives The large red-headed woodpecker, but Bl. denies this. The latter says it is as tall as a crane with a bill about 1 decimeter long, but along the Missouri River about 3 inches and yellow. Hena wakaⁿ. The head was used as an ornament on the huⁿkatacanuⁿpa. Bl. Note in D.72 the photograph. At Saⁿtee the kaⁿké is said not to be a water bird. But it lives in the woods, a woodpecker the size of a wild pigeon, with a black body, a red stripe on the head and a black, heavy, sharp bill about one and a half inches long. T. D.71 and other places.

kaⁿki'cakp̣a, v.a. To strike a vein for one, bleed one. Kaⁿwecakpa. Kaⁿcicakpa. Kaⁿmicakpa.

kaⁿna', n. Blisters, that may appear on waist or ankles of men and horses. - witka hiyu welo. Bl.

kaⁿna'ceġa, n. (?). - itazipa, a bow whose shape reminds one of ceġa.

kaⁿ'naṫip̣a or kaⁿna'ṫip̣a, v.n. To draw up, to cramp, as the nerves or muscles.

kaⁿsu', n. Plum stones; playing-cards; any ticket. -- kaⁿsúkuṫe, v.a. To shoot plum stones; to play cards. Kaⁿsuwakute. -- kaⁿsúkuṫep̣i, n. Playing cards. -- kaⁿsú ziⁿtkalą, n. Perhaps the American redstart. Śkeluta iyececa. Some call the redstart: ġuġuya śku. Also, caⁿpiśko.

kaⁿ'śniśnilak, (?). - ataya, To meet one unexpectedly whom one wanted to see. IS.

kaⁿ'ṫa, n. A plum, plums. -- káⁿṫahu caⁿ, n. The plum tree or bushes. Prunus Americana. #112. -- káⁿṫa sapa, n. Prunes. -- káⁿṫaśa wi, n. The moon when the plums are red, i.e. August. -- kaⁿṫúhu, n. Plum bushes. Same as kaⁿtahu.

kaⁿye', adv. Inwards, towards the center, as of a house.

kaⁿyē'ja, n. A child. Bl.

kaⁿye'la, adv. Near. Waⁿna pte otapi ca kaⁿyela yapi.

kaⁿye'ṫa, adv. or n. Before, in front of.

kaⁿye'ṫaⁿhaⁿ, adv. On the inside of.

kaⁿye'wapa, adv. Within, towards the center.

kao'blaġaheya, adv. perhaps. Scattered out from a central place. Said of a line of men, as soldiers, moving farther apart, lengthening the line, and thus being less likely to be hit. Icitehaⁿyaⁿ yapi he kapi. Same as naóblel aye s'e. Bl. -- kaóblelya, adv. Scattered away from each other, leaving a free center. - waci. Bl.

kao'blotoⁿ, v.a. To make edged, cornered by striking. To form a corner. Bl.

kao'cikp̣ani, v.a. To make uneven, unequal, of different sizes, by striking. Wakáocikpani. -- kaócikp̣aniyaⁿ, adv. Unequally.

kao'ciⁿśica, v.a. To strike and make mean. Bl.

kao'cipteca, adv. Not equal. R. Bl. -- kaóciptel, adv. Unequal, one large and one small; diminishing or increasing in size. R. Bl. -- kaóciptelya, adv. Unequally. R. Bl. -- kaóciptetu, adv. Unequal in size etc. R. Bl.

kao'gmigma, v. To make roll into something by striking. To make roll over and over by striking. R.

kao'gna iye'ic'iya, v. refl. To copulate, have intercourse. Bl. Same as kaokajaya iyeic'iya.

kao'heye, (?).

kao'ḣlagaⁿ, v.n. To get loosened, as bolts on a wagon, or as belts on any machine. Cf. kaḣlagaⁿ. -- kaóḣlagyela, adv. Loosely, loose like a coat that is too big. - nuⁿ, i.e. wearing a coat that is too big. A.

ƙao'ȟlaȟyalaka, v. perhaps imp. Not near to and not very far from, as a place. Nahaȟci - . Kitaⁿla - ca yuinaȟni po, i.e. it is pretty far yet, so you better hurry up. Bl.

kao'ȟlakala, adj. Loose, as a wire on a car which was once tight, or as one on a tree in which it once was imbed but now is loose.

ƙao'ȟmiⁿ, v.a. To cause to move obliquely, as a man on horseback does with a running cow, going against her; to throw obliquely. R. Wakáoȟmiⁿ. -- ƙaóȟmiⁿyaⁿ, adv. Obliquely, moving sideways like a horse that is struck on one side. - iyaya, To throw obliquely. Bl.

ƙao'ȟp̄a, v.a. To break through, smash, to knock in, break through by striking, e.g. somebody's skull. Wakáoȟpa. Nata kaoȟpe. D.103. -- ƙaóȟp̄eƙiya, v.a. To cause to knock a hole in. Kaoȟpewakiya. -- ƙaóȟp̄eya, 1) v.a. To cause to strike through. 2) adv. In the manner of striking through.

ƙao'ȟya, adv. Leaning, sloping, twisting. - egnaka.

ƙao'ȟ'aⁿko, v.a. (of oȟ'aⁿko). To strike and make go or work fast. Wakaoȟ'aⁿko. -- ƙaóȟ'aⁿkoya, adv. With greater hurry. - śkaⁿ yo. Bl. B.H. 148.10.

kao'iyokipi, v. To be in good spirit. B.H.92.4.

ƙao'ƙajaya iye'ic'iya, v. refl. To have sexual intercourse, to copulate. Bl. Same as kaógna iyéic'iya. -- ƙaóƙajayata ektá iyéic'iya, v. To get into the fork of a river so that one must retreat. Bl.

ƙao'ƙic'uya, adv. Deluge like, said of water spreading all over. - iyaya. B.H.54.15.

ƙao'koƙab, adv. Around, across, before. - ya, Go around, to hedge up the way, as in chasing buffalo.

ƙao'ksa, v.n. To fall off or over, to crumble down, as a bank, fall in, cave in. -- v.a. To cut a hole into or through, as in ice. Wakaoksa. Bl. Cf. ptuȟ'á. Also see B.H.43.9;72.15. --

ƙaókseya, v.a. To cause to break in, fall in, as a bank. Kaoksewaya.

ƙao'ktaⁿ, v.a. To bend and pound in. Wakaoktaⁿ. -- ƙaóktaⁿyaⁿ, 1) v.a. To cause to bend in. Kaoktaⁿwaya. 2) adv. Bending into.

kao'lusic'iya, v. refl. To cool off by fanning one's self. - yaⁿka. The spelling is doubtful.

ƙao'mnimni, n. perhaps. A whirling around. - iyecel caⁿteluze lo; - iyecel wilukcaⁿ yelo: words used of one who makes all sorts of statements, i.e. he lies. BT.

ƙaō'na, v.a. To drive or hammar on, as an iron ring on a stick by striking. Wakáona.

ƙaoⁿ'sp̄e, v. (of oⁿspe). To train, teach, as a horse; to break. Wakaoⁿspe. -- ƙaóⁿsp̄eśni, adj. Untrained, untaught.

ƙaoⁿ'ze woslal, adv. Heels up. - iyeya, iȟpeya.

ƙao'p'o, v. To raise dust, as in sweeping.

ƙao'p'ośya, v. To cause a stove to smoke by openning a room door etc.Bl.

ƙao'smaƙa, v.a. To make an indentation by striking. R. Also, to make a hole, through-like, into the ground. Osmaka is a gulch.

ƙao'sni, (?). -- kaósniic'iya, v. refl. (perhaps of kaosniya). To cool down, refresh one's self in the open air; to cool off by fanning one's self. Also used is kaolusic'iya. -- kaósnisni, v. red. of kaosni.

ƙao'sp̄a, v.a. To strike and bruise in. Wakaospa.

ƙao'sp̄eya, v. To weigh down. -- ƙaósp̄eyetoⁿ, v. To weigh anything.

ƙao'swa, v. (?). - hiⁿȟpaya, To fall off, as from a bank into a river.

kao'ślok iya'ya, v. To make a misstep and almost fall but then go on. Yuⁿkaⁿ - imayaye s'e hiⁿgla.

k̇ao'ślośl̇og, Same as kaiśuta iyaya.

kaō'śpa, v. To fall. - hiŋhpaya, To fall off, as from a bank into a river. This may be incorrect, since the word seems to be confused with kaóswa.

k̇ao'ṫa la'k̇e s'e, adv. A few more. B.H. 67.18;120.14.

k̇ao'ṫaŋ, v.a. To pound tight into, as a board that stands out between others back among which it is knocked. Wakaotaŋ. Bl. D.58. Cf. kaona.

k̇ao'taŋiŋ, v.a. (of otaŋiŋ). To make manifest or apparent. Wakáotaŋiŋ.

k̇ao'ṫehehaŋ, (?). Nahaḣci - lakelo. Cf. kaoḣlaḣyalaka. Bl.

kao'tkuǧa, v.n. perhaps. To close and be locked of itself, as a door with a night-latch. BD. -- k̇aotk̇uḣ, cont. (of kaotkuga). To go and get on the other side, as a door way; to go through and be on the other side of a door when slammed behind. Bl. R. gives katkuḣ.

k̇ao't'iŋs, cont. of kaot'iŋza. - iyeya. - yaŋkapi, They are crowded together, as in a room packed full. Bl.

k̇ao't'iŋza, v.a. (of ot'iŋza). To drive or pound tight into a hole, as a fence post, or a screw into a hole that was there; to pound in tight something that is loose, as a loose nail in a wall. Wakaot'iŋza.

kao'waŋya, (?). Saŋb kaowaŋye s'e, i.e. the story grows while it is told to others. Bl.

k̇ao'wiŋḣ iya'ya, v. To walk in a circle. Hihaŋna el waŋna wanase aya na paha waŋ eya (perhaps) he ehaŋl - iyaya na 'pte otayelo', eyapi.

kao'wotaŋ, v.a. To straighten out beads or notches, as in wire, by striking. Wakaowotaŋ. Bl.

k̇ao'wotaŋiŋ, v.n. To clear away, as a storm or anything that obstructs vision. Also, to clear off, become so that things can be seen at a distance.

k̇ao'wotaŋla, v.a. (of owotaŋla). To straighten, make straight by striking in any way. Wakaowotaŋla.

kao'yaḣe, v. To empty a vessel. Wakaoyaḣe. Bl.

k̇ao'yuṫaŋyaŋ, n. perhaps. A cut made into a tree with an axe and leaves it then later. B.

k̇ao'zaŋ s'e, Cf. aokahiya wakita. - wakita. Bl.

k̇ao'zeze, v.n. To swing, dangle, as by the wind. Cf. paozeze. -- k̇aózezeya, adv. Swinging, dangling. - yaŋka.

k̇apa', v.a. To beat or thresh off, as corn; to pound up, as meat. Wakápa.

kapa', v.a. To pass by in running, to beat in a race; to excel, surpass in anything; to go beyond, transgress. Kawápa. Kauŋpapi. D.107.

k̇apaŋ', v.a. To beat or thresh off, as corn,or to beat meat. Hence, pápa. Wakapaŋ. -- k̇apáŋpaŋ, v.a. To beat soft, make mellow. Wakapaŋpaŋ. -- k̇apáŋyaŋ, (?). (of kapaŋ). - yaŋka, or iyotaka, yo, Make a soft seat for yourself to sit on, i.e. by beating and smoothing hides etc. Bl.

k̇aṗe', v.a. To chisel. Iŋyaŋ kapepi. B.H.100.7.

k̇aṗe', v.a. (of pe). To sharpen by pounding, as a scythe. Wakape. Wakape.

kaṗe', v.a. Same as kapa, To excel. Ki iŋyaŋkapi na Joe kape, i.e. Joe came in first.

k̇aṗe'mni, v.a. (of pemni). To make crooked or awry by striking. Wakápemni. Taḣca topapi eyaś - k'iŋ. MS.75. k̇aṗémnimni, v. red. of kapemni. B.H. 203.6. -- k̇aṗémnimniyaŋ, adv. Dangling. - otkeic'iyapi, i.e. giant strides. Bl. -- k̇aṗémniyaŋ, adv. Crookedly, dangling, swinging, as scissors tied by a string. Uŋgna - micignake ci. Bl.

k̇aṗe'ṗe or kaṗe'ṗe, v. red. of k̇ape and of kape.

k̇aṗe'sṫo, v.a. (of pesto). To make sharp-pointed with an ax. Wakápesto. Na caŋ kapestopi top yuha najiŋ. -- k̇aṗestopi, n. An arrow all of wood, the head end make sharp and thin to kill birds or other little animals. Bl.

kaṗe'ya, 1) v.a. (of kapa). To go or pass beyond, do more; to cause to surpass. Kapewaya. 2) adv. Beyond, further, greater than, surpassing.

ḱaṗiŋ', v.n. To be indisposed or unwilling to do a thing; to be tired. Wakapiŋ. Mani - . Ecoŋ - . Ie - . Ape - , To be tired of waiting. D.81.

ḱaṗiŋ'ja, v.a. To shorten a horse's tail. Wakapiŋja.

ḱaṗis', cont. of kapiza.

kaṗi'yehaŋ, adv. perhaps. A certain length of time, as implied in: A long time ago I saw you and have seen you again; you were well and still are. Gb.

ḱaṗi'za, v.a. To make squeak or squeal by striking. Wakápiza.

ḱaṗo', v.n. To swell, as one's flesh. Makápo.

ḱapob', cont. (of kapopa). To burst with a noise. - iyaya. - iyeya, To cause to burst.

ḱaṗo'ġaŋ, 1) v.n. To puff out and become tied; to swell like a sail for the wind. 2) v.a. To puff up as a bladder. -- ḱaṗóh, cont. of kapogaŋ. - iyeya. -- ḱaṗóhya, 1) v.a. To make swell out, as anything filled with air. Kapohwaya. 2) adv. Rising, swelling out. Mini - hiyotake, i.e. a blister.

ḱaṗol'ṗoṫa, v. red. of kapota.

ḱaṗoŋ'ya, v. To remove the last rough places from a hide with the wahiŋtka. Kapoŋwaya. Bl.

ḱapo'ṗa, v.a. To make a popping noise by striking, i.e. smashing, and making burst; to strike and make burst with a noise. Wakapopa. -- ḱapóṗaṗi hu, n. The closed or blind gentian. Also the bottle gentian. Gentiana Andrewsii. Gentian family. Also called wahca waśte. Bc. Bl.

ḱaṗo'ṫa, v.a. To tear by striking, as clothes hung out and torn by the wind. Also v.n. Wakapota.

ḱapo'ya, v.a. To brush, as one's coat. Kapowaya.

ḱapsag', cont. (of kapsaka). To break violently. - iyeya or ihpeya. - hiŋhpaya. -- ḱapsagya, 1) v.a. To cause to break. Kapsagwaya. 2) adv. Broken, as a string.

ḱapsa'ḱe, v.a. To cut something limbed in two by striking, like string or wire etc.; to break, as a string. -- v.n. To be cut in two. Wikaŋ kiŋ kapsakahe. D.66. Kapsag hiŋhpaya.

ḱapsaŋ'psaŋ, v.n. To dangle, swing back and forth; to sway to and fro, as a limb in water. -- v.t. perhaps. Cf. sicapsaŋ.

ḱapsa'psaḱa, v. red. of kapsaka.

ḱapsi'ca, v.a. To make jump by striking, as in playing shinney. Tabkápsicapi. Wakapsica. -- ḱapsil, cont. - iyeya. Also used as a contration of kapsiŋta, perhaps. R.

ḱapsiŋ'psiŋṫa, v.a. To whip, scourge. Same as yupsiŋpsiŋta; correct by whipping. Pb.38. Wakapsiŋpsiŋta.

ḱapsiŋ'ṫa, v.a. To whip, flog; to correct, as a child by whipping. Wakapsiŋta. -- ḱapsíŋtapis'e, adv. Whipped, as it were. Léceya, kola - śkiŋmic'iye lo. BT.

ḱapsi'psica, v. red. (of kapsica). To make jump much by striking. Wakapsipsica. -- ḱapsípsil, cont. To throw out and make skip about, as in fishing. - iyeya. D.217.

ḱapsoŋ', v.a. To spill something by striking. Wakapsoŋ. -- ḱapsóŋpsoŋ, v. red.

ḱapśuŋ, v.a. To break something by striking, as a ball hitting a tooth. To knock out, as a tooth; to dislocate, as a joint, by striking. Wakapśuŋ.

ḱapśuŋ'ḱa, v.a. To make round or knoblike. Wakapśuŋka.

ḱapśuŋ'pśuŋ, v. red. of kapśuŋ. -- ḱapśúŋyaŋ, v.a. To cause to knock out of place. Kapśuŋwaya.

ka̦pta', v.a. To lade or bail out, as water from a boat. Wakapta. - iyaye, To break, burst under a heavy weight, as a sack when the contents are too heavy.

ka̦ptaⁿ'ptaⁿ, v.a. To turn over and over. Wakaptaⁿptaⁿ.

ka̦ptaⁿ'yaⁿ, 1) v.a. To cause to fall over; to turn over, upset, as a canoe. Wakaptaⁿyaⁿ. 2) adv. Turning over. -- ka̦ptáⁿyeya, v.a. To cause to fall over, to overturn. Kaptaⁿyewaya.

ka̦pta'pta, v.n. To fall to pieces, as something rotten.

ka̦ptu'ġa, v.a. To break off a piece by striking. Wakaptuga. BD.

ka̦ptu'ħ'a, v.a. To scrape off, whittle off, as for kindling. Bl. -- ka̦ptú-ħ'aħ'a, v.a. To scrape off little things, as fibers from a hide. Bl.

ka̦ptu'ja, v.a. To cause a board or so to come over by striking it on one end. Wakaptuja. BD. Also, to split or crack by striking, but not to split open. R. -- ka̦ptúptuja, v. red. Cf. kaptuja for possible meanings. -- ka̦ptúptuś, cont. of kaptuptuja. - iyeya. -- ka̦ptúś, cont. of kaptuja. - iyeya. -- ka̦ptúśkiya, v.a. To cause to make crack. Kaptúśwakiya.

kaptu'za, v. (?). Bl.

ka̦pu'za, 1) v.a. To make something dry by shaking it in the wind. Wakápuza. 2) v.n. To become dry by being shaken by the wind, as wash. BT. used this word also for voting "dry" for the state of South Dakota.

ka̦p'i', v. Perhaps the same as kaħwoka, To float or wave, as in the wind. Tate ca wowapi kap'iyelo. BT. -- ka̦p'í-p'i, v.n. perhaps red. (of kap'i). To wink, blink, as when something gets into the eye or dazzles one. Iśta wiyoħpemayiⁿ kte seca ca - wawakita yelo.

ka̦p'o', v.a. To raise dust, as in sweeping. Wakap'o.

ka̦p'o'ja, adj. Light, not heavy. Also, kap'ójela. -- ka̦p'óśic'iya, v. To balance one's self. -- ka̦p'oś kic'uⁿ, v. To walk lightly and carefully, as when passing on or over ice, in order not to break through. Bl. -- ka̦p'ó-śp'oja, adj. red. (of kap'oja). Light. Kap'ośp'oje s'e mani, or Henala s'e mani. Bl. -- ka̦p'óśp'ojela, adv. red. of kap'ojela. - s'e mani, To walk lightly, without any noise. Bl. -- ka̦p'óśyela, adv. (?). Taku oyasiⁿ - yaciⁿ. Bl. Kap'ojela, The name of the father of Taśuⁿke Witko, Crazyhorse. RF.

ka̦sa', v.a. To bury in the snow, cover over with snow. Wakasa.

ka̦sab'sabyela, adv. red. (of kasabyela). Heavily. - hiⁿħpaye, She dropped to the ground repeatedly from weakness. D.270.

ka̦sab'yela, adv. Heavily. - hiⁿħpaya, To fall heavily, as from weakness. Cf. kasabsabyela.

ka̦sag', cont. of kasaka. - iyeya.

ka̦sa'ka, v.a. To switch, whip. Wakasaka. -- ka̦sa'ksaka, v. red. (of kasaka). To whip, to hit one. Wakasaksaka.

ka̦saⁿ', 1) v.n. To turn white, as paint does from rain. 2) v.a. To whiten by scraping. Wakasaⁿ. -- ka̦sáⁿsaⁿ, v. red. (of kasaⁿ). To scrape and whiten. Wakasaⁿsaⁿ.

ka̦se'p̣a, v.n. To wash off, as the rain does paint. R. B.

ka̦ska', v.a. To bleach by striking or dragging. Wakaska. -- v.n. To become clear, to clear off, as clouds, smoke etc. Maħpiya kiⁿ - iyaya. Na wicaśa waⁿ najiⁿ k'oⁿ el owotaⁿiⁿśni na - iyaya na hecena oyate kiⁿ waⁿyaⁿk najiⁿpi na ecel ataⁿiⁿ. -- (?). Numbkaska, Two together. Cf. ićicaska. WE.

ka̦skab', cont. (of kaskapa). To strike off with the hand. - iyeya.

ka̦ska'p̣a, v.a. To strike, as with the hand; slap; to strike hands together. Nape glaskapa, To strike one's hands together. Wakaskapa. The word is <u>not</u> ka<u>ś</u>kapa.

ka̦ska'ya, v. To make clear up. Ośota ca kaskawaye.

ka̦skeb', cont. of kaskepa. - iyeya.

ḱasḱeb'ḱiya, v.a. To cause to bail out e.g. water from a canoe. Kaskebwakiya.
ḱasḱeb'ya, v.a. To bail or empty out.

ḱasḱe'p̄a, v.a. (skepa). To empty something, as a bucket, gradually by drinking from it; to bail out, empty e.g. a pond etc. Wakaskepa.

ḱasḱi'ca, v.n. perhaps. To settle down, as does a haystack. -- v.a. To press, press down on by striking, this latter meaning being the more correct. R.

ḱaski'glag, (?). - wicoti, i.e. camping together without order. Bl.

ḱasḱil', cont. of kaskica. - yuza, To clasp in the arms.
ḱasḱil'ya, v.a. To cause to settle down or to press down. Kaskilwaya.

ḱasḱi'sḱa, (?).
ḱasḱi'sḱasḱa, v. (?). Bl.
ḱasḱi'sḱasḱakel, (?). - kagege, To work out a pattern, map-like, as in beadwork etc. - wakagege k'oŋ wana kitaŋyaŋkel wagluśtaŋ. Bl.

ḱasḱi't̄a, v. To press, clasp.

ḱasḱu', v.a. To peel off e.g. bark with an ax. Wakasku. BD.
ḱasḱuḣ'ya, adv. Cutting off squarely.

ḱasḱ'i'yaya, v.n. (kaska-iyaya). To clear up, as the weather. P. Bl.

ḱasla'la, adv. Slowly and carefully, not having expression. - mani ya. - woglaka. Same as kat'éyakel. Bl. Cf. slata.

ḱasle'ca, v.a. To split e.g. wood with an ax. Wakasleca.
ḱaslel', cont. of kasleca. - iyeya.
ḱaslel'ya, v.a. To cause to split. Kaslelwaya.
ḱasle'slel, cont. of kaslesleca.

ḱasli', v.a. To strike and force something out, as water from a bladder or rubber ball, or grease from the same. Wakasli. - ḱut̄é, To shoot at something many times. BD. -- ḱasliýa, v.a. To cause one to press out. Kasliwaya.

ḱaslo'haŋ, v.a. and v.n. To make something or somebody slide by striking. - iyeya. - yeya or yemaya, i.e. to slide, as a wagon does on a slanting and slippery road. Kaslohelo. - glihpaye, Sliding, he fell. BT. D.84.
ḱaslo'haŋhaŋ, v. red. of kaslohaŋ. - iḣpaya, To fall again and again, like a drunken man perhaps.

ḱasma'ḱa, v.a. To indent or make concave by striking; to make a track, as does a wagon. Wakasmaka.

ḱasmiŋ', v.a. To strike off something by means of an axe. Wakasmiŋ.
ḱasmiŋ'yaŋ, v. To make bare, as in striking off.
ḱasmiŋ'yaŋyaŋ, v. red. of kasmiŋyaŋ.

ḱasna', v.a. To make ring or sound by striking e.g. a piece of iron or a kettle. Wakasna.
ḱasna'sna, v. red. (kasna). To make ring; to trim or cut off e.g. the limbs from a tree and so leave it bare. Wakasnasna.

ḱasni', v.a. (sni). To put out, extinguish by beating a fire; to cool food by shaking it or pouring it from one vessel into another. Wakasni. Bl.
ḱasni'sni, v. red.

ḱasol', cont. (kasota). To use up by striking; to get or clear out of the way what is waste. - iyeya, eḣpeya. - iyayelo, kaska iyayelo, i.e. clouds clearing away.

ḱaso't̄a, v.a. To use up by striking, as by felling trees and thus getting farm land; or by killing off cattle and by having men fall in battle to use up. Wakasota. Cf. R. -- v.n. To clear off, as the sky. Kasol iyayelo.

ḱasp̄a'ya, v.a. (spaya). To wet, moisten, as in sprinkling the floor before sweeping. Wakaspaya.

ḱasp̄e'ya, v.a. To weigh, esp. something heavy. Kaspewaya.
ḱasp̄e'yela, adv. Rather heavy. - ku welo, i.e. carrying too heavy a burden, and sweating he returns. Bl. Cf. kaspeya.

ḱast̄ag', cont. (kastaka). To throw on. - ihpeya, To throw and make stick e.g. mud.

ḱast̄a'ḱa, v.a. To throw on, as mud; to

dump something, not liquid, e.g. mud or grain, from a basin. Wakastaka.

k̇aṫaŋ'ka, v.a. To moisten by pounding. Wakastaŋka.

k̇asṫo', v.a. To smooth down, to stroke, as the hair with the hand. Wakasto. Hena - wicuŋyuhapi, i.e. perhaps to value highly. -- k̇asṫósṫo, v. red. (of kasto). To stroke, make smooth. Wakastosto. -- k̇asṫoya, adv. Smoothly.

k̇asu'ksuta, v. red. of kasuta.

k̇asu'ṫa, v. (of suta). To pound and make hard or tough, as pounding a hide; to make boys tough by striking. Wakasuta.

k̇aswa', v.a. To make lint; to curry. Wakaswa. -- k̇aswáka, v. (?). May be related to kaza, or kazazeca. Bl. -- k̇aswáswa, v. red. of kaswa.

kaswu', v.a. To cut into small strips, cut into dangles, make fringes. Wakaswu. -- k̇aswúk̇iya, v.a. To cause to cut into strips. Kaswuwakiya. -- k̇aswúpi, n. Dangles, fringe. - s'e, (adverbial) Fringed as it were; said of old torn clothes. Bl. -- k̇aswúswu, v. red. (of kaswu). To cut into strips and let hang. Wakaswuswu.

k̇as'a', 1) v.a. To strike and make hiss as a snake. Wakas'a. Kas'a haŋpi. 2) v.n. To sail or glide in the air, as birds. BD. R. Bl. -- k̇as'ak̇iya, v. To warm one's self. Nape - , To warm one's hands, holding hands spread out over a stove like wings (kas'a). Nape kas'awakiyelo. Bl.

k̇as'a'la, adv. Proud, putting on airs. Seems to be from okás'a, To soar. Wicaśa - inajiŋ. Wicaśa - yaŋka. -- k̇as'álakel, adv. Unconcerned. - yaŋka, To be unconcerned in anything around one. Bl.

kas'iŋ's'iŋ, v. perhaps. To dangle, as phlegm from the mouth of a sick person who is not strong enough to spit it all out. Imniśtaŋ - . Cf. s'iŋs'iŋya. BD. -- k̇as'íŋs'iŋyaŋ, adv. red. of kas'iŋyaŋ. - ikoyake. Bl. -- k̇as'íŋyaŋ, adv. Dangling, like phlegm from the mouth of a cow etc. Bl.

k̇aś, Same perhaps as k̇a, but this emphasizes. - iyuŋga yo. -- pron. perhaps indef. Latin cumque. (perhaps the same as k'eyaś). Tuweni - heca wanice. Tuweni - hecoŋ kiŋ he śni, Nobody could ever (I don't care who) do it; i.e. I am the very one.

k̇aśe', v.n. To strike against, stumble. Sipa - . Makaśe. Cf. ptehu kaśe, the name of a plant, elephant's trunk. This is the old form. Some call it ptehu kaśeiŋ.

k̇aśe'ca, v.a. To make dead or dry by striking, to deaden by cutting around, as around a tree. Wakáśeca. -- k̇aśélk̇iya, v.a. To cause to deaden. Kaśelwakiya.

k̇aśe'ya, 1) v.a. To obstruct, fend off. Kaśewaya. 2) adv. Hitting against.

k̇aśib', cont. of kaśipa. - iyeya. -- k̇aśíbyela, adv. Bent. - mani, To walk bent under a burden.

k̇aśi'ca, v.a. (of śica). To spoil by striking, as spoiling a table with an axe. Wakaśica. -- k̇aśíc̄ahowaya, v.a. To cause to cry out by striking, e.g. a dog. Wakaśicahowaya. D.196. -- k̇aśíkśil, (?). - wakaŋpi sece.BT.

k̇aśi'ṗa, v.a. perhaps. To knock or cut off close, as branches from a tree, legs from a chair or pot, or rivets from a knife. Wakaśipa. -- v.n. To be bent under the weight of something, as a hay rack

k̇aśk̇a', v.a. To tie, bind; imprison. Wakaśka. - yuha, To lead. D.227. - gle, To picket, as horses. D.258. - gluza. MS.352. - yus kte ayepi. B.H.130.6. - yus ayiŋ kte. B.H.148.8. Zaptaŋ-kaśka wiciŋcala k'uŋ ole yapi. D.157. -- k̇aśk̇áhaŋ, part. Tied, bound.

k̇aśkaŋ'śkaŋ, v.n. To be shaking, being shaken up, as when sitting on a heavy wagon, i.e. bumping or hitting. Makáśkaŋśkaŋ. Same as kahuŋhuŋza. Cf. also naśkaŋśkaŋ.

k̇aśk̇a'ṗa, v. To make a noise, as by striking water. Wakaśkapa. Cf. paśkapa.

k̇aśka'ṗiya, v.a. To cause one to be bound, to have one arrested. Kaśkapiwaya. B.H.217.15. -- k̇aśk̇aśka, v.

red. of kaśka. B.H.284.19.

ƙaśkeb', cont. (of kaśkepa). To strike out, to press out by striking, as water from anything.

ƙaśƙe'haŋ, v.a. (of śkehaŋ). To make skip about by striking. Wakáśkehaŋ.

ƙaśƙe'ṗa, v.a. To strike and press out, as water. Wakaśkepa.

kaśke'ya, v.a. To have one arrested. Kaśkewicaye. B.H.286.4.

ƙaśƙi', v.a. To pound, grind, e.g. cherries. Wakaśki. Caŋpákaśkipi.

ƙaśƙi'ca, v.a. To press by striking; to pound or to batter out e.g. clothes. Wakaśkica. -- ƙaśƙil, cont. of kaśkica. - iyeya. -- ƙaśƙiśƙa, v.a. To make rough by striking, as with an ax or stick. Wakáśkiśka.

ƙaśki'śkiṫa, v.a. To mark in equal lengths for cutting. Bl.

ƙaśƙob', cont. of kaśkopa.

ƙaśƙo'ƙṗa, v.a. To hollow out, make concave, cut out as a trough. Cf. kaosmaka. Wakaśkokpa. -- ƙaśƙóƙṗaƙṗa, v. red.

ƙaśƙo'ṗa, v.a. To make crooked or twisted by striking, but not to curve (cf. kaktaŋ). Wakaśkopa.

ƙaśku', v.a. To scrape off, as scales from a fish, corn from a cob. Bl.

ƙaśla', v.a. To cut off, make bare; to shave, to mow. Wakaśla. -- ƙaśláśla, v. red. of kaśla. -- ƙaślaya, v.a. To cause to make bare. Kaślawaya.

ƙaśle'ca, v.a. To split, as wood by striking with an ax. Wakaśleca. Makaśleca. -- ƙaślel, cont. of kaśleca. - wao. Bl. Same as kajá wao. -- ƙaślésleca, v.a. red. (of kaśleca). To split up fine, e.g. wood. Wakaśleśleca. Na tipi kiŋ icokab caŋ kaśleślecapi ota pahayela eglepi.

ƙaślog', cont. of kaśloka. - iyeya.

ƙaślo'ƙa, v.a. To knock off or out, as the helve from an axe or a nail from its hole; to fall out, as an arrow that has been shot into an animal; to clean out, as a pipe. B.H.116.3.

ƙaślul', cont. (of kaśluta). To cause to glance off. - iyeya. - iyaya, To glance off, as an ax.

ƙaślu'śluṫa, v. red. (of kaśluta). To polish; to smooth by striking, to planish. Wakaśluśluta.

ƙaślu'ṫa, v.a. To strike and make glance off. Wakaśluta.

kaśme'yalake s'e, adv. Many sitting, perhaps, together. - naŋkapi. Bl.

ƙaśna', v.a. To miss in attempting to strike, as e.g. a ball. Wakáśna. -- ƙaśnáśna, v. red.

ƙaśni'ja, v.a. (of śnija). To make wither by striking e.g. weeds. Wakaśnija.

kaśni'yaŋyaŋ, (?). Minikaśniyaŋyaŋ, i.e. shallow water passing over rocks. -- kaśníyaŋyaŋla, (?). Mini kiŋ - yuŋkelo, i.e. it rippled. Bl.

ƙaśo'śa, v.a. To stir up and make turbid, as water with a stick or rock etc. Wakaśośa.

ƙaśṗa', v.a. To separate, cut loose from; to strike off a piece, perhaps. Wakaśpa.

ƙaśṗa'ṗi, n. Name for a dime. -- ƙaṗáṗila, dim. of kaśpapi.

ƙaśṗe'ṗicaśni, adj. Not capable of being separated. -- ƙaśpeṗilṗicaśni, (?). Le tuwa - , oie ƙitoŋ k'oŋ, as is said when a man disappears suddenly having said he would stay. Bl.

ƙaśṗe'ya, v.a. To cause to separate or break off. Kaśpewaya.

ƙaśṗi', v.a. To knock off e.g. mulberries by striking the bush or tree under which a sheet has been spread, thus picking, śpi. Wakaśpi.

ƙaśṗu', v.a. To knock off something by striking. Wakaśpu. -- ƙaśṗúśṗu, v. red. Wakaśpuśpu. The word implies knocking or striking off one piece after another from a log until it is used up. Bl. Caŋkáśpuśpupi.

k̇aśtag´, cont. of kaśtaka. - yeya, To throw e.g. a hutanacute.

k̇aśṫa´k̇a, v.a. To strike, beat, whip. Wakaśtaka.

k̇aśṫaŋ´, v.a. To pour out, said of liquids only. Wakaśtaŋ. Cf. papsuŋ, To spill.

k̇aśta´śtag, cont. red. of kaśtaka. - ogliya, To hone in the manner of striking. Bl.

k̇aśtu´śta, v.n. To be tired from riding. Makaśtuśta. Bl.

k̇aśu´ja, v.a. To bruise, batter; to mash, crush by striking. Pa - , To make the nose bleed. Wakaśuja.
k̇aśuś´, v. cont. (kaśuja). To bruise or mash down. - iyeya.
k̇aśu´śuja, v.a. red. of kaśuja.
k̇aśu´śuś, cont. (kaśuśuja). To break or mash down. - iyeya.
k̇aśu´śuśya, adv. Battered, bruised.
k̇aśuś´ya, 1) v.a. To cause to batter or bruise. Kaśuśwaya. 2) adv. Bruisedly, batteredly.

k̇aśwu´, n. Urine. - mahiyu welo. Bl.

k̇aś'ag´, cont. of kaś'aka.
k̇aś'ag´ya, v.a. To cause to strike feebly. Kaś'agwaya.
k̇aś'a´k̇a, v.a. To strike with too little force to penetrate. Wakáś'aka.

k̇aś'iŋ´, v.n. To bend backwards, to be bent toward the inside (concave), like the back of a sway-back horse, or a pug nose. Makaś'iŋ. Nicaś'iŋ. Mila - . - aya.
k̇aś'iŋ´yaŋ, adv. Bent backwards.

k̇ata´, v.a. To assemble together. Wakata. - iheya. - iheuŋpi. Hohu wakatiŋ kte. Bl.

k̇a´ṫa, adj. Warm, hot, as applied to persons and things. Makáta.

kata´ġa, v. (tage). To make foam, as the running water does.
kataḣ´, cont. (kataga). To make to foam, e.g. by beating eggs.

k̇ata´ja, v. (taja). To make waves, as the wind does.

k̇ata´kiŋkiŋ, v. red. (katakiŋ). (?). Katakiŋkiŋḣci wagli yelo, i.e. staggering to right and left as though one were hit. - la s'e mawani yelo. Bl.
k̇ata´k̇iŋyaŋ, adv. (takiŋyaŋ). Leaning. - haŋ, To stand leaning.

k̇ata´k̇oha, v.a. To hold in one's arms e.g. a baby. Wakatakoha. Also, katáku yuhá, katákoyuha. D.247, note 1. B.H.129.16;227.9.

k̇ata´k̇iŋ, v.a. (takiŋ). To strike and cause to lean. Wakatakiŋ.

k̇aṫa´k̇uni śni, v.a. To beat to pieces, destroy, as by striking with an axe. Wakátakuni śni.

k̇ataŋ´, v.a. To pound on e.g. beef before it is fried, to make beef steak or a piece of hide. Wakataŋ. Cf. wákape.
k̇ataŋ´blablas, adv. perhaps. (?). - gliḣpeic'iya, To throw one's self on both sides on the back, as a horse does to stop itching. Bl. Cf. ikpaptaŋptaŋ iḣpeic'iya. Note: the word cannot be used in ref. to man.

k̇ataŋ´iŋ, v.a. (taŋiŋ). To make apparent; to clear off e.g. anything covered up. Wakataŋiŋ.

k̇ataŋ´k̇a, v.a. (taŋka). To beat out large, to enlarge by striking. Wakataŋka. -- k̇atáŋk̇aya, v.a. To make something larger that has been finished before. Wakataŋkaya.

k̇ataŋ´oŋb, cont. (kataŋoŋpa). Leaning at an angle about 45 degrees.
k̇ataŋ´oŋbya, adv. Leaning.
k̇ataŋ´oŋṗa, v. (kataŋ-oŋpa). To lean.

k̇ataŋ´taŋ, v. red. of kataŋ.

k̇ata´ṗa, v. To shake and make dry, as the wind does clothes; to dry by shaking.

k̇ata´pśija, v.a. To cause to rise, as bubbles in water by throwing something in. Wakatapśija.
k̇ata´pśiś, cont. of katapśija. - iyeya.

k̇aṫa´ptaṗa, v.a. To hew e.g. rocks. Caŋ - , To hew off thin pieces of wood from a dry log, as for kindling. Bl.

Caⁿkátaptapapi. Bl. Iⁿyaⁿ - . B.H. 100.7.

kaťa'ťa, v.a. To shake off e.g. dust from a blanket; perhaps to brush off with the hand or with a brush. Wakatata. R.

kata'ta, v.a. To make blunt by striking e.g. a tent pin at the upper end, the head where it is to be struck. Wakatata.

kata'tabya, v. Bl. Cf. katatapa.
kaťa'ťap̄a, v. red. of katapa.

kaťeb', cont. of katepa. - iyeya. - aya, To wear out from being used.

kaťe'haⁿ, adv. (tehaⁿ). Far, at a distance. -- kaťéhaⁿyaⁿ, adv. At some distance, a little distance off.

kaťe'p̄a, v.n. To wear out by itself through striking against something. -- v.a. To cut to a stump, to cut tapering. Wakatepa.

kaťi'ca, v.a. To stir or perhaps to mix up. Wakatica.

kaťi'ca, v.n. To be obstructed, as the nostrils.

kaťi'kťica, v. red. (katica). To thicken by stirring.

kaťiⁿ', adj. Straight, straightened out, as the arm. Makatiⁿ.
kaťiⁿ'ǩiya, v.a. To stretch out, make straight. Isto - .
kaťiⁿ'ťiⁿyeya, adv. Continuously. Śuⁿkaⁿ s'e - omani, i.e. to walk apparently aimlessly here and there, as old horses do although there be plenty of grass. Also, katiⁿtimyeya.
kaťiⁿ'yaⁿ, adv. Straight; directly; continuously, without stop; immediately, off-hand. Wi k'oⁿ - yaⁿkelo; maśte kte lo. - ecoⁿ śni, To dally. P. R. Bl. Mh.
kaťiⁿ'yeya, adv. Directly; continuously, without stop; straightened out. - el hi. - owotaⁿla ku wo. Iśtiⁿma owakihi śni. BD. -- v.a. To straighten out. Br.

katǩa', v.n. To choke or be choked, as in eating; to stick in the throat. Makátka.

ka'tka, adv. Briskly. Also, glugwezeȟce, gluśniyaⁿyaȟce. - mani. Bl.

katǩaⁿ'haⁿyaⁿ, adv. Slowly, soundly. Kahaⁿtuk'e - wiyukcaⁿ po, Now then, think well. Bl. Syn.- kat'iⁿsya.
katǩaⁿ'heya, adv. Slowly and soundly. - wiyukcaⁿ, To think slowly and soundly, a good trait. Tka-heya suggests a ref. to taking one's time, as in thinking and in opposition to yuptaⁿpila s'e wiyukcaⁿ. - śkaⁿ. Bl.

katǩe', Same as katká.
katǩe'ye, v. a. To cause to choke. Katkewaya.

ka'tkiya, adv. That way, over yonder (pointing) somewhere. Hokśila - iyaya. Letkiya, This way. Cf. kal, kakiya, kiya.

ka'tǩiya, v. pos. To heat one's own. Cuwi - yuⁿka, i.e. warming one's back. Also, kalkiya. Bl.

katku', adj. Rather short of something, having very little, e.g. of sugar, coffee etc. R. Bl.

katǩu'ġa, v.a. To strike off square pieces. Wakatkuga. BD.

katǩuⁿs', cont. of katkuⁿza.
katǩuⁿ'tǩuⁿta, v. Cf. kakuⁿtkuⁿta.

katǩuⁿ'za, v.a. To cut off square. Wakatkuⁿza. Caⁿ - s'e maȟpiya waⁿ taⁿiⁿ yelo, i.e. when long clouds rise evenly, in a front, on the horizon. Bl.

katku'tǩuġa, v. red. of katkuga.

katku'yakel, adv. Rather little, few of something; rather short. Bl.

kato', v.a. To strike and not make an indentation; to rap, make a sound. Wakato. -- kaťóhaⁿ, v. (kato-haⁿ). To stand and tap, as does a woodpecker on a tree.

kaťo'nauⁿg, cont. of katonauⁿka. - iyaya. - hiyaya. Na uⁿgna tahenakiya hiyu na lecegla - hiyaya ca akiś'api. - omawani ye, i.e. I roam, galloping.
kaťo'nauⁿgkiya, v.a. To make gallop slowly. Katonauⁿgwakiya.

kaťo'nauⁿka, v.n. To gallop slowly,

as a horse might.

ƙaƭo'ƭo, v. red. (kata). To knock or beat on e.g. a door. Wakatoto.

ƙaƭo'wotaŋla, (?). - kuyé. Lehaŋ waŋciglak iblotaka ce, as is said when the man return who looked for buffalo. BT.

ƙaƭo'yeyapi s'e, adv. Alone. - omawani, i.e. I went alone. Wicahcala kiŋ takośku kici - yaŋkapi, ihuŋnipi, as is said when one or two are left alone by others. Bl.

ƙaƭu'ƙa, v.a. To knock off e.g. fur; to destroy by smiting. Wakatuka.

kaƭuŋp', (?). Waśma iyecel uŋpśiś - omawani, i.e. walking through gumbo. Cf. tuŋtúŋpa.

ƙatu'ta, v.n. To be sore from riding etc. Makatuta. Bl. Syn.- kaiħeju.

ƙatu'tka, v.a. To break in small pieces or to pound up fine. Wakatutka. R. Bl.

ƙat'a', v.a. To kill or stun by striking. Wakat'a. - iyeya, To kill by shooting. - eħpeya, To knock over dead. Tuwa śigla ca kat'api. Thus, fig.: Śni makat'elo. -- v.n. To die by hitting an object. B.H.302.24.

ƙat'a'ǧa, v.a. To shake and make dry, as the wind does a wet cloth. Wana maka kiŋ - , The ground is becoming dry now, i.e. as in the spring. Maśte tate, hecel maka kiŋ kat'agiŋ ktelo. Bl.

kat'a'pt'apa, v. To signify by a certain gesture of the head that expresses contempt, dislike, hatred etc. It consists in opening one's closed fist and moving it toward the object disliked and thus making the fingers outstretched; or in snapping one's finger in the sign of contempt. Also, okat'apt'ap. D.37,88. RTj.

kat'a't'a, v. red. of kat'a. Kat'at'api s'e u welo, as is said of a man who comes e.g. on horseback very slowly and seemingly exhausted. RTj. A.

kat'e'la, (?). - tacaŋcega icabu, A long drumstick used by women. Bl.

ƙat'e'yaƙel, adv. Slowly, leisurely. - hi, To come slowly. - ya, To go without being in a hurry, slowly. Bl. Syn.- kaslalaya.

ƙat'e'yetaŋka, adv. Sitting still for a long time in a lazy manner, conveying the idea of being at leisure, not watching out, not being intent on anything; to sit in the Lakota fashion for men, with legs crossed almost under the buttox. - yaŋka, To sit flat on the ground, with the legs outstretched and the knees bent partly out. - nasuŋyaŋ yaŋka, To sit flat on the ground with legs out-stretched and both touching each other. - mani, To walk about leisurely. - najiŋ, To stand unaware of anything, i.e. watoglaśni najiŋ. - u, i.e. iwaśtegla u. Kat'eyetaŋkaħci wahi, I came to stay awhile, I came very slowly. - wowaśi ecoŋ, i.e. ħaŋhiyeħci wowaśi ecoŋ. Bl. Obs.

ƙat'i'ic'iya, v. refl. To shoot one's self. Bl.

kat'iŋħ'ya, adv. Grunting. - glihpaya, To grunt while suddenly falling down.

ƙat'iŋs', cont. of kat'iŋza.

ƙat'iŋs'ya, 1) v.a. To cause to be solid or at rest. 2) adv. Same as katkaŋhaŋyaŋ. - wiyukcaŋ.

ƙat'iŋs'yakel, adv. Pounded tight. - maŋke, I am sitting here for good. EB.

ƙat'iŋ'za, v.a. (t'iŋza). To pound tight, make tight or firm. Wakat'iŋza.

ƙat'i'yeya, v.a. To kill by shooting. Kat'iyewaya.

ƙat'o'za, v.a. To dull or make blunt by striking. Wakat'oza.

ƙat'uŋ'ƙeca, v.a. To suspect one. Wakat'uŋkeca. R. Bl.

ƙat'uŋ'ƭuŋƙeca, v. red. Bl.

ƙau', v.a. (au). To be bringing something to. Wakau. Caŋ etaŋ makaú po. Caŋnuŋpa waŋ cicicaupi ca yanipi kte lo. Wigli waśtemna k'oŋ hena micaupi nito. Micaupi, i.e. "mi" because it is her perfume. B.H.137.16.

ƙauŋg', cont. of kauŋka. - iħpeya.

kauŋħ'ye, (?). Same perhaps as kawiŋħye. The number 100 is represented in this manner: Nape nupiŋ ƙaská - . HH.

ƙauŋ'ƙa, v.a. To cut down, fell e.g. trees; to strike down e.g. persons; to blow down, as the wind does trees. Wakauŋka. -- ƙaúŋƙaƙa, v.n. To be jolted or bounced up and down, as in a wagon. - yemaya. -- ƙaúŋƙiya, adv. Leaning over, as a half felled tree. Caŋ kiŋ he - haŋ, The tree leans over. Also, kauŋgƙiya.

kau'ta, v.a. To make a gun go off, by striking it. -- v.n. To go off, accidentally by itself. Kaúte.

ƙawa', v. To open, as a flower. Bl.

ƙawa'ci, v.a. (of ka and waci). To cause to dance, by striking; to spin by whipping, as a boy does his top. Wakawaci.

ƙawa'ciŋksab, (?). - iyeya.

ƙawa'haŋ, part. Opened.

ƙawa'ja, v.a. To work at a difficult thing, keep at a thing though hardly able to do it. Wakawaja.

ƙawaŋ'ƙab, adv. Upward. Wi - u kiŋ lehaŋl. B.H.118.4.

kawaŋ'kaka, v.n. To be jolted or bounced up and down as in a wagon. Kawaŋkaka imayaye, I was bounced. Same as kauŋkaka. BD. - iyaya ca iyoȟa kiŋ kaiyoyagya iyeye. Bl.

ƙawaŋ'ƙal, adv. Upwards. - iyeya, To knock upwards. Na yaśtaŋ el ȟolyela he ake - iyaya. Na śna - kiglahaŋpi. MS.106. -- ƙawáŋƙalwaƥa, adv. A little up.

kawa'swas, red. (of kawas, of kawaza). Caȟota kiŋ - iyeye, He, the wolf, brushed the ashes off. D.22.

ƙawaś', cont. of kawaja. - yaŋka, He keeps at it.

ƙawa'śte, v.a. To make well, by striking or cutting with an ax, or by whittling, sewing etc. Bl.

ƙawa'ś'aƙa, v.n. (of waś'aka). To be made strong by packing or carrying loads. Makawaś'aka.

ƙawa'tuƙa, v.n. To be tired from long riding on a wagon or on horseback, by reason of shaking (ka). Śuŋkakaŋ yaŋkapi makáwatuka. Caŋpagmiyaŋpi makawatuka.

ƙawa'za, v.a. To throw up e.g. ground with a stick. R. Bl.

ƙawe'ǧa, v.a. To break by striking, but not to break entirely off. -- ƙawéȟ, cont. of kawega. - iyeya. -- ƙawéȟweǧa, v. red. of kawega. -- ƙawéȟweȟ, cont. (of kaweȟwega). To fracture or break in several places. - iyeya. - apa. -- ƙawéȟya, 1) v.a. To cause to break. Kaweȟwaya. 2) adv. Breaking.

ƙawel', Same perhaps as kawitaya. Wicota - kaŋheheyela uwelo. Tula, le tuwe kiŋ witka welaka cu - haŋp' ceyaka waŋ ohaŋ hiyayele. Bl.

ƙawe'we, v.a. To strike and make bleed, make bleed. Wakawewe. Bl.

ƙawi'gnuni, v.a. To destroy by striking, to break in pieces. Wakawignuni. R. Bl.

ƙawil'wiƭa, (?).

ƙawiŋ'ǧa, v.n. To turn in one's course, i.e. go back. Wakawiŋga. - iyaya, He went turning. Kola, - yo, heci yai kiŋ, niktepi kta. Hecel nupiŋ kawiŋgapi na kiglapi. -- ƙawíŋȟ, cont. of kawiŋga. - iyaya, To turn short. - uśi, To call one back. P.

ƙawiŋ'ja, v.a. To beat down, mat down by striking e.g. grass etc. Wakawiŋja. -- ƙawíŋś, cont. of kawiŋja. - iyeya. - iȟpeya.

ƙawiŋ'świŋja, v. red. of kawiŋja. -- ƙawíŋświŋś, cont. of kawiŋświŋja.-- ƙawíŋświŋśya, adv. Matted down.

ƙawiŋś'ya, 1) v.a. To cause to mat down. Kawiŋśwaya. 2) adv. Beaten down, fallen down.

ƙawi'ƭa, adv. Together. - upo. - awicakuwa. Bl. Petaga kiŋ - egle. MS.568. -- ƙawíƭaya, adv. (of witaya). Together. - agli el caje oglaka. - awicayapi, Rounded them into a small area. D.211.

kaye'ǧe, Same perhaps as kaǧeǧe. Kayege refers to the present; kagege, to the past, where someone else is doing it. It is heard repeatedly among the Sicaⁿgu.

ƙayeś', adv. It emphasizes a pronoun or other word. Miye - , I myself. Niye - , You yourself. Iś iye - eye kiⁿ. Kawiⁿga yo, miye - tehaⁿyaⁿ ca owakihi śni. Miye - waśicuⁿ kiⁿ ehaⁿni maktepelo. Heci Wakiⁿyaⁿ Oyate kiⁿ el - maktepi śni yelo, eya. MS.155. Niyeś sipa - akiglaśke śni yauⁿ welo. Bl. -- pron. That one, even such. Uⁿgna tuwa tasi cogiⁿ - iħpeyayapi kilo. Bl. New B.H. 54;111;126;187;196;206;208;210;245;303.

ƙaye'ya, v. To wave e.g. a blanket. Kayewaya. Śina waⁿ kayeyelo, He waves a blanket, i.e. as a sign indicating the number of buffaloes one sees. Bl.

ƙayō'la wacipi, n. A dance. Also called isaⁿbati wacipi. Bl.

ƙayo'yo s'e, adv. With fleshy parts shaking. - mani, To walk like very fleshy men or animals. Bl. R.

ƙayuⁿś', (?). B.H.115.4.

ƙaza', v.a. To pick to pieces e.g. the takaⁿ or sinew, tearing off one string after another and twisting it for use in sewing. Wakaza. -- n. A job. - ota, Many jobs. MO.

ƙaza'mni, 1) v.a. To uncover or open out, as anything covered. Wakazamni. Also, to push away, i.e. with the hands, e.g. bed clothes. Pámahe yauⁿ kiⁿ ite - . 2) v.n. To open e.g. a door from a draft. -- ƙazámnimni, v. red. (of kazamni, v.n.). To open and close continually, as a door does in the wind. Tiyopa yuokiyuta yo, - iyayelo, taⁿyaⁿ iyakaśka yo. Bl. -- ƙazámnimniyela, (?). - tipi k'oⁿ, as is said of a tent flapping, not tied up, in the wind.

ƙazaⁿ', 1) v.a. To hurt, to make feel pain by striking; to render motionless. Wakazaⁿ. Hiⁿyete kazaⁿpi, Bruised shoulders. B.H.265.3. 2) v.n. To fill up, have the sense of fullness. Bl. R. gives kazi'. Yuⁿkaⁿ pi kazaⁿpi ca na oniyaⁿ śice k'oⁿ iyemaceca amahi. Lociⁿ wawatiⁿ na caⁿte makazaⁿ yelo. Caⁿte - , or caⁿte makazaⁿ, To have heart burn.

ƙazaⁿ'ṗeya, v.a. To smoothen a stick and make it sharp at one end. Bl.

ƙazaⁿ'yaⁿ, adv. Parting, separating e.g. grass in passing through it. This seems to be derived from kazá.

ƙaza'za, v.a. To cut into fine strips and let hang; to slash. Wakazaza. D.36. -- ƙazázapi, n. The ermine, so-called because the skin is cut up into strips to wear on the head. -- ƙazázeca, v. Same as kaswaka. Bl.

ƙaze', v.a. To lade or dip out with a spoon or ladle. Wakaze. Mícaze ye, Lade out for me, i.e. serve me some. Wakśica taⁿka waⁿ ojula - , i.e. she served a big dish full. D.54.

ƙa'zela, adj. Shallow, not very deep, as water when a man can walk through without swimming. Bl.

kaze' wie's'e, adv. Limping. - u, To come limping like a horse. - iyaya. SC.

ƙazil'ic'iya, v. refl. (of kazilya). To stretch one's self out; to lie down and rest leisurely, as after hard work or meals. Kazilmic'iyiⁿ kte. Cf. kablebles ic'iya. MG.

ƙazil'ya, v. To stretch out, straighten.

ƙazoⁿ'ta, v.a. To weave e.g. cloth; to twist in e.g. in making baskets or snow shoes or bed folders (mats). Also, kazuⁿta. Cf. caⁿkazuⁿta.

kazu'ksugyela, adv. Wet through, sopping wet, i.e. from rain or perspiration. - omawani yelo. Bl.

ƙazuⁿ'ta, Same as kazoⁿta.

kca, adj. Loose, disentangled, straight. -- kcaháⁿ, part. Coming loose, untying of itself. -- kcakcá, adj. red. of kca. Napsuhu - kacá, as is said when a person has long fingers. Bl.

kca'ma, defective v. I thought. B.H. 230.5;232.2;278.9.

kcaⁿ, Cf. yukcaⁿ. It is not used alone.

kcaŋ'ka, n. One who fails in doing what he said he would. R. Bl.

kcaŋkcaŋ'la, adj. Tall and very movable as men or trees may be; unsteady, as is said of a man's mind, tawaciŋ. Bl.

kcaŋpte'pte, adv. Seemingly occupied with one's thoughts. - Ȟca maŋkelo, i.e. thinking deeply in silence. - Ȟca amayaluta, You look at me as though you wanted to say something. Bl.
kcaŋpte'ptekel, adv. Burdened with the knowledge of something. -ku welo, He returns with a message. BE. Also, caŋpteptekel.

kcawa'haŋ, part. Having come untied.

kce'ḱiya, v. To hold or hang over. Nape - yauŋ welo, i.e. holding the spread-out hands over the stove to warm them, i.e. nape kaś'akiya yauŋ welo.
kceya', v. To cook by hanging over the fire; the side or ribs of an animal, n. Wakceyapi.

kco, abbrev. for kicó.

ḱe, abbrev. of ka, itself an abbrev. of laka. He iaŋpetu tonakeca ke el. Ke ci(ŋ), or ḱéci, an abbrev. perhaps of lake ciŋ (kiŋ or ci) and idiom denoting: Pretty much, nonetheless. Hecel uŋhe keci, While he was there for awhile. Taku mazaska zi keci oŋ lila wiyakpayela he. Hecoŋhaŋpi keci, While they were doing that. Misuŋ, lecelyauŋ ke ciŋ eś takuȟci koyakipe sece lo. D.3, note 3. B.H.133.18;101.3;89.5;67.6;226.5.

ḱe, n. A turtle. Kenatantaŋ kte s'e haŋpokihe lo, as is said when shoes are too wide. Note: the word is used commonly in connection with other words.

Ḱeca', n. A long-haired dog. Also, Ḱecála.

Ḱecaŋ'ȟ'a, n. A species of turtle. Bl.

ḱe'caŋḱiŋ, v.a. To think of as such, to regard as. Kécaŋwakiŋ.

ḱeci', Cf. ḱe. Also, ḱéci.

ḱe'ciŋ, v. To think that. Kécaŋmi, kécaŋni. Kéuŋkeciŋpi or kúŋkeciŋpi. Wakaŋ - śni yo, Do not think that you are wakaŋ. Kéwicakiŋpi. B.H.129.23; 137.6;272.13. B.
ḱe'ciya, v.a. To say to one that it is so and so. Kéwakiya, kéuŋkiyapi. Note: the word is introduced from Santee through the Bible; hence, the word should be kékiya.
ḱe'coŋ, v. To do that. Taŋyaŋ - ic'ilaca, He thinks he has done that well.

ke c'e'yaś, ke e'yaś, k'e'yaś, ce e'yaś, e k'e'yaś, e ke e'yaś, particles. They follow pronouns and make them universal. Tuwé - , Anybody. Taku wato ke c'eyaś. B.H.202.22.

ke eśa', Cf. keśa.

kee'yaś, adv. Although, all the same. Hakela pehiŋ śikśice - śina huhá iyowakpatiŋ kta. -- particle. Same as ke éyaś. Cf. ke c'eyaś.

Ḱegle'zela, n. A spotted or striped turtle living on land; the sand turtle perhaps. Cf. patkáśa.

ḱe'ha, v. 2nd pers. sing. of keya.

Ḱe'ha, n. (keya-ha). A tortoise shell.

Ḱehu'ḱu, n. An arrowhead diamond shaped. Bl. Cf. kestoŋ, wismahiŋ ikceka.

Ḱeȟ'aŋ'la, n. A species of small turtle. GA.

Ḱeiŋ'yaŋhaŋ, part. Roof-like, sloping.

ḱeḱi'ya, v. To say that. Kewakiya. B.H.70.11;111.20;153.26;196.8;208.21; 217.7;293.19.

kel, adv. suff. In a way, as it were, in a manner of speaking. Itaŋcaŋyaŋ, i.e. doing something like a chief which one is; itaŋcaŋyaŋkel, i.e. like a chief (which one is not), as it were. Htaleh aŋkel, Yesterday, as it were. D.222,278. Cf. wiŋhahayakel.

Ḱenuŋ'ic'iya, v. To get ready. Kenuŋic'iya yo. Kenuŋmic'iya. Syn.- igluwiŋyeya.

Ḱenuŋ'nuŋja, n. The soft-shell turtle.

Ḱenuŋ'yaŋ, v. To know partly, suspect.

Kenúⁿwaya. Same as at'uⁿgya.

ke'pa, v. 1st pers. sing. of keya.

ke'pa, n. (keya and pa). A tortoise's head.

ke'pca, v. 1st pers. sing. I thought that.

keston', v.n. (keze and toⁿ). To be barbed, have a barb, as a fish hook or arrow. -- n. A barbed arrow-head. -- kestóⁿśni, n. An arrow-head not barbed.

kes'a'mna, n. A species of turtle. The stink turtle. Ra. Bl.

ke s'e, Same as lake s'e. Iⁿyaⁿkapi - wowaśi ecoⁿ. Le kagiśniśni oh'aⁿ ke lah. Bl. B.H.58.7;181.9;236.23. Ikaⁿyela - hinajiⁿ. Taka lila iyoyake s'e yaⁿkahaⁿ ke. D.8,note 6.

keś, conj. But, although. Toka kiⁿ nicasotapi kte - iyuhaha wicawakte yelo. Wiⁿyaⁿ waⁿji yuha - ihpeyahaⁿke. MS.92. R. gives: conj. Although. It is always used in reference to past time. Tohaⁿl wanasapi kta - kaⁿgi ska waⁿ pte kiⁿ owicakiyaka ca lila napapi.

keśa', particles, perhaps adv., following pronouns to make them universal. Tuwe keśá, Whoever. Taku - , Anything. Aⁿpetu tukte - . Miye - el ciyiⁿ kta iyececa śni. Nakuⁿ - . B.H.196.12; 228.6.

keśko'kpa, n. A species of turtle. Bl.

kewa'pa, n. The water lily; a water plant with round large leaves that lie flat in the water. Bl.

kewo'yuspa s'e, adv. perhaps, and used figuratively. (?). - leniceca yelo, as is said of one who is strong and does things although they are hard to do; for, it seems to be hard to drag a turtle out of the mud. BT.

ke'ya, v. To say that. Képa. Kéha. Uⁿkeyapi. Letaⁿ waniyetu topa kiⁿ oyate waⁿ ahi kta keyelo, eya. Note: Kéya, kéciⁿ, kecaⁿkiⁿ are from eya, eciⁿ, ecaⁿkiⁿ. Those of the latter class indicate that the subject of the preceding verb is identical with the person who says or thinks, which those of the former class do not.

ke'ya, v.a. To make a roof of. Kewaya. Na hel caⁿha keyapi. -- n. The large tortoise; a roof. Keya s'e upihcihci, as is said of women when their dresses, i.e. the lower border is all fringed. Oyute kiⁿ yuogmuza ye, - s'e oyate kiⁿ hpuhpuya.

Kéya, To say that:
Keya cajeyata. B.H.64.1.
Keya iwahoya. B.H.81.4;205.5.
Keya okiyaka. B.H.62.23;94.1;188.23; 256.14.

ke'ye cola, adv. (?). - yaⁿkapi or iyayapi, They are entirely destitute, having nothing. Bl. Also, keye cocola. Same as kagmipi s'e yaⁿkapi.

keze', n. The barb of a fish hook, the sharp point of anything. - śice, An arrow whose head hooks are also hooked, and thus cannot be pulled out or backward. St.

ki., prefix. Affixed perhaps to some verbs, which indicates that the action is performed through the middle. Thus: kiwaksa, To cut in two in the middle. It does not, however, draw the accent.

ki, v.a. To take from one by force, to rob. Waki. Taśuⁿkepi kiⁿ oyasiⁿ wicuⁿkipi kte lo. Na taku luhapi kiⁿ hena oyasiⁿ ko nicipi ciⁿpi kta. -- v.n. To arrive at one's home or where one lives. This is used when the person speaking is away from the home spoken of. Waki. Uⁿkipi. R.

ki, prep. in comp. To; of. It is prefixed to or incorporated into verbs and always takes the accent of the verb. Kícaga, To write a letter to. When prefixed to verbs of motion commencing with a vowel, the "i" is dropped; thus, kau. In some instance it has the meaning of kici, For. Wicakiyuajaja. B.H.273.7;273.14. -- pron. pos. in comp. One's own. Thus, okile, To seek one's own. This ki does not draw the accent. -- abbrev. of kiⁿ or kiló, which cf. Uⁿgna waciⁿniwaś'akala ki. B.H.68.18. MS.350.

kia'guyapi, v. To turn into bread. B.H.175.15.

Ƙia'ṗe, v.n. To wait until one reaches home. Kiawape.

Ƙible'ca, v.n. (of bleca). To break up e.g. a gathering of people. Kiblecahaⁿ seems to be the word always used. Na waⁿna oyate kiⁿ kiblecahaⁿpi.

Ƙible'za, adj. Convalescent. -- v.n. To recover from a drunken fit; to get sober. Wakibleza.

Ƙi'ća, v. pos. (of ka). To mean one's own or demand one's own. Wakica or wéca. Yéca. Uⁿkićapi. Nahaƞci weca śni. Taku waⁿji mitawa ca weca, k'eyaś mic'upi śni iyecel wauⁿ welo. Bl. Cf. B.H.36.3;179.19

Ƙića', prep. in comp. For. Thus: opetoⁿ, To buy; opekicatoⁿ, To buy for.

Ƙi'cableca, v. (of kableca). To break for one by striking e.g. brittle ware. Wecableca.

Ƙića'ǧa, v.n. (of caga). To become ice again.

Ƙi'caǧa, v.a. (of kaga). To make to or for one. Wowapi - , To write a letter to. Woope - , To make a law for. Tuⁿkaśitku kiⁿ wahiⁿkpe - na wakute oⁿspekiya. Wecaga. Micaga. Cicaga.

Ƙi'ćagla, v. (of kagla). To fall out or unroll for one. Micagla.

Ƙi'caǧo, v. (of kago). To make a mark for one; to vaccinate.

Ƙi'cahi, v. (of kahi). To rummage for one. Wecahi.

Ƙica'ƞpa, v.a. To knock off for one, remit to one e.g. his debts. B.H.217.11.

Ƙica'kca, v. (of kakca). To comb or curry one's own. Wecakca.

Ƙi'caƙiⁿca, v. (of kakiⁿca). To scrape e.g. fish, for one. Wecakiⁿca.

Ƙi'cakṗa, v. (of kakpa). To strike into for one. Kaⁿ - , To cut a vein for one, to bleed one.

Ƙica'ksa, v.a. To cut in two in the middle with an axe, or by striking; to break e.g. a law, to disobey. Kiwákaksa.

Ƙi'caksa, v. (of kaksa). To cut in two for one, as a stick with an ax. Wécaksa

Ƙi'caƙuka, v. (of kakuka). To pound to pieces or destroy for one e.g. clothing. Wecakuka.

Ƙi'ćala, v.a. (of kala). To spill e.g. grain for another. Wecala.

Ƙi'camna, v. (of kamna). To earn for one. Wecamna.

Ƙi'camna, v. (?). Wamniomni - yelo, i.e. a hurricane. Bl. Wicaśa ota -

Ƙica'mnayaⁿ, adv. (?). - ahiyaye, To pass by in large numbers. Bl.

Ƙicaⁿ', v. To call on the dead, when wailing for them, as in crying: Miciⁿkśi, miciⁿkśi. Wecaⁿ. Uⁿkicaⁿpi.

Ƙicaⁿ'ic'iya or Ƙiciⁿ'ciya, v. refl. To get ready, make one's self ready e.g. for a walk. Kicaⁿmic'iya. -- Ƙicáⁿƙiya, v. pos. To arrange, get ready one's own; pack up. Owiⁿja kiⁿ - . B.H.290.8.

Ƙićaⁿ'yaⁿ, v.a. To work, till, cultivate e.g. the ground; to tend, care for. Talo - , To dress out beef etc., i.e. cut into pieces. Kicaⁿwaya. D. 199 and 271.

Ƙi'capsag, cont. of kicapsaka. - iyeya.

Ƙica'psaka, v.a. To cut in two e.g. a string at the middle. Kiwakapsaka.

Ƙi'capsaka, v. (of kapsaka). To cut in two e.g. a string for one. Wecapsaka.

Ƙi'capsuⁿ, v. (of kapsuⁿ). To knock over and spill out e.g. water for one. Wécapsuⁿ. -- Ƙićapśuⁿ, v. (of kapśuⁿ). To strike or knock off e.g. a horse for me. Wecapśuⁿ.

Ƙi'casleca, v. (of kasleca). To split in two for me something soft or light. Wécasleca.

Ƙi'casto, v.a. To smooth the hair for one. Wecasto. Bl.

Ki'caśla, v. (of kaśla). To make bare for one, to cut low; to shave. B.H. 76.6.

Ki'caśleca, v. (of kaśleca). To split in two for one something hard, to cut with effort. Wécaśleca.

Kica'śpa, v.a. To cut into the middle e.g. of an apple. Kiwákaśpa.

Ki'caśpa, v. (of kaśpa). To divide for one. Wécaśpa.

Ki'cawega, v. (of kawega). To partly break or fracture for one. Wecawega.

Ki'cawignuni, v. (of kawignuni). To destroy for one e.g. a toy. Wecawignuni. R. Bl.

Kici', prep. With, together with. Hehaⁿ wicaĥpi hiⁿĥpaya takolaku kiⁿ - iś eya yapi.

Ki'ci, prep. in comp. For. The syllable ki always keeps the accent of the verb it is connected with. Kići mauⁿ, He is with me.

Kici', prep. and perhaps pron. in comp. To each other. It makes the reciprocal form of verbs. Ecakicicoⁿpi, They do to each other. Waśtekicilapi, They love each other.

Kici'atakiciya, v. To meet face to face, to meet squarely. Kiciataweciya.

Kici'ca, v.n. or v.t. To be with, together with, following with, on the same side with; to have for a companion. Wécica, I am with him. He makicica, perhaps He is with me. He uⁿkicicapi, He is with us. Uⁿkicicapi uⁿ. B.H.164.16. Na wica waⁿ wecica k'oⁿ he icu, nazoⁿspe) na iś eya ake kahuⁿkoⁿza. Kicića ota, i.e. of the same age with. Toke Itaⁿcaⁿ taogligle wakaⁿ kiⁿ yecicapi ni. B.H.125.6;197.5. Mi5 cica yauⁿ. B.H.227.11.

Ki'cicableca, v. (of kableca). To break up for one e.g. dishes by striking. Wecicableca.

Ki'cicacaⁿ, v. (of kacaⁿ). To sift for one. Wécicacaⁿ.

Ki'cicaga, v. (of kaga). To make anything for another. Wecicaga. Uⁿkicicagapi. Note: kićaga, To write a letter to one; kićicaga, To write a letter for another, i.e. other than the one to whom it is written.

Ki'cicagege, v. (of kagege). To sew anything for one. Wecicagege.

Ki'cicagla, v. (of agla). To take to one's home for him. Wecicagla.

Ki'cicagli, v. (of agli). To bring to one's home for him. Wécicagli.

Ki'cicahi, v. (of ahi). To bring to a place for one. Wecicahi.

Ki'cicahiⁿta, v. (of kahiⁿta). To sweep for one. Wecicahiⁿta.

Ki'cicaĥniga, v. (of kaĥniga). To choose or select for one. Wécicaĥniga.

Ki'cicaĥuga, v. (of kaĥuga). To fracture for one, break in e.g. the skull or a barrel-head, for one. Wécicaĥuga. -- Kićicaĥuĥuga, v. red.

Ki'cicai, v. (of ai). To take to a place for one. Wecicai.

kici'caic'iya, v. refl. To take sides with. B.H.3.12;89.4.

Ki'cicajuju, v. (of kajuju). To pay for anything for another; to erase for one; to forgive one. Wecicajuju. Uⁿkicicajujupi.

Ki'cicakaⁿ, v. (of kakaⁿ). To hew for one. Wécicakaⁿ.

Ki'cicakca, v. (of kakca). To comb e.g. hair for one. Wecicakca.

Ki'cicaki, v. (of aki). To have taken to one's home for him. Wecicaki.

Ki'cicakiⁿca, v. (of kakiⁿca). To scrape for one. Wecicakiⁿca.

Kici'cakiya, v.a. To join one's own to. Pb.43.

Ki'cicaksa, v. (of kaksa). To cut off e.g. a stick for one. Wecicaksa. -- Kićicaksaksa, v. red. To cut up e.g. firewood for another.

Ki'cicaku, v. (of aku). To be bringing

something home for one. Wecicaku.

ki'cicakuka, v. (kakuka). To pound to pieces for one. Wécicakuka.

ki'cicala, v. (kala). To pour out or or spill for one. Wécicala.

ki'cicasleca, v. (kasleca). To split e.g. something light for one. Wécicasleca. -- ki'cicaslesleca, v. red.

ki'cicasni, v.a. To put out, extinguish e.g. a prairie fire for another. Wécicasni. Bl.

ki'cicaśka, v. (kaśka). To tie or bind for one. Wécicaśka.

ki'cicaśla, v. (kaśla). To cut or make bare for one, as in mowing. Wécicaśla.

ki'cicaśleca, v. (kaśleca). To split e.g. a log or something heavy for one. Wécicaśleca. -- ki'cicaśleśleca, v. red.

ki'cicaśpa, v. (kaśpa). To deliver from, to relieve or free from one; to separate for one. Wécicaśpa.

ki'cicaśtaka, v. (kaśtaka). To smite for one. Wécicaśtaka.

ki'cicaśtaⁿ , v. (kaśtaⁿ). To pour out or spill for one, in ref. to liquids. Wécicaśtaⁿ.

ki'cicau, v. (kau). To bring for one. Wécicau, mi'cicau.

ki'cicaweġa, v. (kawega). To break or partly break for one. Wécicawega.

kici'cawota, n. One of the same age. Kicicamawota, I am of the same age as he, of one age with him. Cf. kicica.

ki'cicaya, v. (kaya). To take or carry to a place for one. Wécicabla perhaps.

kici'caya, v. To be with another. Also, ki'cicaya. Ni'cicaya maktepi kte. Miyécicaya yauⁿ kte. Nicicaya uⁿyaⁿkapi. - uⁿpi. B.H.254.11;267.16;292.6;306.12.

ki'cicazuⁿta, v. (kazuⁿta). To weave for one. Wécicazuⁿta.

ki'ciceya, v.a. To bewail. P.

ki'ciciⁿ, v. (ciⁿ). To desire or ask for for another. Wéciciⁿ, mi'ciciⁿ.

kici'copi, v. recip. (kico). To call each other. Uⁿkicicopi. Kicico wotapi, A feast in which a general invitation is given. Na waⁿna haⁿhepi el - na el aya ca miś ake el owapa.

kici'co wótapi, n. A public feast.

ki'cicute, v. (kute). To shoot anything for another. Wécicute.

kici'cutepi, v. recip. To shoot each other, as in the wakaⁿ wacipi. Uⁿkicicutepi.

ki'cic'iⁿ, v. (k'iⁿ). To carry or pack for one. Wécic'iⁿ.

ki'cigle, v. (gle). To place or set for one. Wecigle.

ki'ciglohi, v. (glohi). To bring one's own to him, to return his own. Wéciglohi. R. Bl.

ki'cigloi, v. (gloi). To have taken one's own to him. Wécigloi. R. Bl.

kici'glonica, v. To refuse to give up for one, as a mother prevents a child giving away its own. Bl.

ki'cigloya, v. (gloya). To take one's own to him. Wécigloya. R. Bl.

ki'cignaka, v. (gnaka). To lay away or lay up for one. Wecignaka.

ki'cihaⁿ, v. (haⁿ). To be or remain for one. Micihaⁿ.

ki'cihiyohi, v. To go and fetch for one.

ki'ciȟa, v. (ȟa). To bury for one. Wéciȟa.

kici'ȟapi, v. 3rd pers. pl. They laugh or smile at each other. Bl.

kici'ȟmuⁿġapi, v. recip. (ȟmuⁿga). To bewitch each other. Uⁿkiciȟmuⁿgapi.

ki'ciȟ'aⁿyaⁿ, v. (ȟ'aⁿyaⁿ). To fail or become worse for one, as one's sick child. Mi'ciȟ'aⁿyaⁿ.

kici'ic'iya, cont. (kicaⁿic'iya). To make one's self ready. Cf. kiciⁿciya.

ki'ci'kpamni, v. (pamni). To divide among themselves. Suⁿk kicikpamnipi na mazawaka ko tona na mazasu ko. Also, ki'cikpamni.
kici'kpamnipi, v. recip. To divide among themselves. Uⁿkicikpamnipi.

ki'ciksuya, v. (kiksuya). To recollect for one. Wéciksuya. Also, kicíksuya.

kici'kśaⁿ, v. To wrestle with; to make love, have love-play. Also, ki'cikśaⁿ. Uⁿki'cikśaⁿ(pi).

kici'ktepi, 1) v. recip. To kill each other. Uⁿkiciktepi. 2) n. Murder.

ki'cikuja, v. (kuja). To be sick for one, as one's child.

kici'la, adv. With, only with. - ti.

kiciⁿ', v. (ciⁿ). To desire one's own, desire for one or of one. Taku mayakiciⁿ na hecanoⁿ hwo?

kiciⁿ'ciya, v. refl. To get ready, make ready one's self, as for a walk. Also, kicaⁿic'iya perhaps. B.H.165.8;170.6. Cf. igluwiⁿyeya.

kiciⁿ'iⁿ, v. pos. (kiⁿiⁿ). To throw e.g. stones at one's own. Wéciⁿiⁿ, uⁿkiciⁿiⁿpi.

ki'cipa, v.a. To assist one e.g. with something to carry on a game in gambling; to reserve, espouse e.g. a girl with the intention of marrying her; to keep for one. Wécipa. Cícipa.

ki'cipableca, v. (pableca). To break for one. Wécipableca.

kici'paesya uⁿpi, v. They are against each other as husband and wife. Bl.

ki'cipagaⁿ, v. (pagaⁿ). To part with for one. Wécipagaⁿ.
kici'pagaⁿpi, v. recip. To part with each other, as a man his wife. Uⁿkicipagaⁿpi.

ki'cipagmuⁿ, v. (pagmuⁿ). To twist e.g. a string for one. Wécipagmuⁿ.

ki'cipago, v. (pago). To carve for one. Wécipago.

ki'cipahi, v. (pahi). To pick or gather up for one. Wécipahi. Micipahi.

ki'cipajaja, v. (pajaja). To wash out e.g. a gun for one. Wecipajaja.

kici'pajiⁿpi, v. recip. (kipajiⁿ). They oppose each other. Uⁿkicipajiⁿpi.

ki'cipajuju, v. (pajuju). To erase for one. Wecipajuju.

ki'cipakca, v.(pakca). To comb out straight for one. Wecipakca.

ki'cipakiⁿta, v. (pakiⁿta). To wipe for one. Wecipakiⁿta.

ki'cipame, v. (pamaⁿ). To file for one. Wecipame.

ki'cipaⁿ, v. (paⁿ). To call to one for another. Wecipaⁿ.

ki'cipapsoⁿ, v. (papsoⁿ). To spill or pour out e.g. water for one. Wecipapsoⁿ.

kici'pasi, v.n. To drill, excercise as soldiers do. P.

ki'cipasnuⁿ, v. (pasnuⁿ). To roast e.g. meat for one. Wecipasnuⁿ.

ki'cipasuta, v. (pasuta). To knead or make stiff e.g. bread for one. Wecipasuta.

ki'cipata, v. (pata). To cut up or carve for one. Wecipata.

ki'cipataⁿ, v. (pataⁿ). To take care of for one. Wecipataⁿ.

ki'cipazo, v. (pazo). To point to for one. Wecipazo.

ki'cipehaⁿ, v. (pehaⁿ). To fold up for one. Wecipehaⁿ.

ki'cipemni, v.n. (pemni). To become crooked or twisted for one. Micipemni.

kicis', cont. of kiciza. - waciⁿpi, They want to fight.

ki'cisoⁿ, v. (soⁿ). To braid for one. Wecisoⁿ.

ki'cisuta, v.n. (suta). To become hard of firm for one. Micisuta.

k̇i'ciśica, v.n. (of śica). To become bad to or for one. Miciśica.

k̇ici'śkata, n. A playmate.

k̇ici'śnala, pron. Alone with any one or any thing.

k̇i'citehaŋyaŋlake s'e, adv. A little apart, not far from each other. Yuŋkaŋ tipi nuŋp - haŋ.

k̇i'citoŋ, v. (of toŋ). To bear or have a child to or for one. Wecitoŋ. Micitoŋ.

k̇i'cit'a, v. To die for. B.H.153.16.

k̇i'ciwaśṫe, v.n. (of waśte). To be good or become good for one. Miciwaśte.

k̇i'ciya, v. To go in place of another, go for another. Weciya. Miciya, He goes in place of me. Niciya, He goes in place of you.

k̇i'ciyaḣeṗa, v. (of yaḣepa). To drink up for one. Weciyaḣepa.

k̇i'ciyaḣleca, v. (of yaḣleca). To tear in pieces with the mouth for one. Weciyaḣleca. -- k̇i'ciyaḣleḣleca, v. red.

k̇i'ciyaḣṫak̇a, v. (of yaḣtaka). To bite for one. Weciyaḣtaka.

k̇i'ciyamna, v. (of yamna). To acquire for one by talking. Weciyamna.

k̇i'ciyaŋka, v.n. (of yaŋka). To be or exist for one. Miciyaŋka.

k̇i'ciyaonihaŋ, v. (of yaonihaŋ). To praise for one. Weciyaonihaŋ.

k̇i'ciyaotaŋiŋ, v. (of yaotaŋiŋ). To make manifest for one. Wéciyaotaŋiŋ.

k̇i'ciyapa, v. (of yapa). To suck for one, as in conjuring, the affected part of a sick person. Weciyapa.

k̇i'ciyaṗoṫa, v. (of yapota). To tear up with the mouth for one. Weciyapota.

k̇i'ciyapsak̇a, v. (of yapsaka). To bite off e.g. a string for one. Weciyapsaka.

k̇i'ciyasu, v. (of yasu). To judge or condemn for one. Weciyasu. -- k̇ici'yasuṗi, v. recip. (of yasu). To judge or condemn each other. Uŋkiciyasupi.

k̇i'ciyaśṗa, v. (of yaśpa). To bite off a piece for one. Weciyaśpa.

k̇i'ciyaṫaŋ, v. (of yataŋ). To praise for one. Weciyataŋ.

k̇i'ciyataŋiŋ, v. (of yataŋiŋ). To make manifest or declare for one. Weciyataŋiŋ.

k̇i'ciyawa, v. (of yawa). To count for one, to account to one. Weciyawa.

k̇i'ciyublaya, v. (of yublaya). To spread out for one. Weciyublaya.

k̇i'ciyublu, v. (of yublu). To plow or break up for one. Wéciyublu.

k̇i'ciyucaŋ, v. (of yucaŋ). To shake for one. Weciyucaŋ.

k̇i'ciyuġa, v. (of yuga). To husk e.g. corn for one. Weciyuga. Not of yugaŋ as R. has.

k̇i'ciyugaṫa, v. (of yugata). To open out e.g. the hand for one. Weciyugata.

k̇i'ciyugmuŋ, v. (of yugmuŋ). To twist for one. Weciyugmuŋ.

k̇i'ciyuha, v. (of yuha). To have or keep for one. Weciyuha. Uŋkiciyuhapi.

k̇i'ciyuhaŋska, v.a. To lengthen out for one. Taaŋpetu kiŋ yeciluhaŋskiŋ kte. Pb.40.

k̇i'ciyuhomni, v. (of yuhomni). To turn around for one. Weciyuhomni.

k̇i'ciyuhuŋhuŋza, v. (of yuhuŋhuŋza). To shake for one. Weciyuhuŋhuŋza.

k̇i'ciyuḣleca, v. (of yuhleca). To tear for one. Wéciyuḣleca.

k̇i'ciyuḣlok̇a, v. (of yuḣloka). To open or make a hole for one. Weciyuḣloka.

k̇i'ciyuja, v. (of yuja). To make mush for one. Weciyuja.

k̇i'ciyujaja, v. (of yujaja). To wash for one. Wéciyujaja.

Ki'ciyujuju, v. (of yujuju). To tear down or tear to pieces for one. Weciyujuju.

Ki'ciyujuŋ, v. (of yujuŋ). To pull out by the roots for one. Weciyujuŋ.

Ki'ciyukṗaŋ, v. (of yukpaŋ). To grind e.g. grain for one. Weciyukpaŋ.

Ki'ciyuksa, v. (of yuksa). To break off for one. Weciyuksa.

Ki'ciyukśaŋ, v. (of yukśaŋ). To bend for one. Weciyukśaŋ.

Ki'ciyumaŋ, v. (of yumaŋ). To grind e.g. an ax for one. Weciyumaŋ.

Ki'ciyuota, v. (of yuota). To multiply for one. Weciyuota. Pb.44.

Ki'ciyuowotaŋla, v. (of yuowotaŋla). To straighten for one. Weciyuowotaŋla.

Ki'ciyuṗoṫa, v. (of yupota). To wear out or destroy for one. Weciyupota.

Ki'ciyupsaka, v. (of yupsaka). To break e.g. a cord for another. Weciyupsaka.

Ki'ciyupśuŋ, v. (of yupśuŋ). To pull out or extract e.g. a tooth for one. Weciyupśuŋ.

Ki'ciyusapa, v. (of yusapa). To blacken for one. Wéciyusapa.

Ki'ciyusk̇isk̇iṫa, v. red. of kiciyuskita.

Ki'ciyusk̇iṫa, v. (of yuskita). To bind up or wrap up for one. Weciyuskita.

Ki'ciyusoṫa, v. (of yusota). To use up for one. Weciyusota.

Ki'ciyusṫo, v. (of yusto). To make smooth for one. Weciyusto.

Ki'ciyusuṫa, v. (of yusuta). To make firm for one; to insure. Weciyusuta.

Ki'ciyuśaṗa, v. (of yuśapa). To defile for one. Weciyuśapa.

Ki'ciyuśica, v. (of yuśica). To make bad or spoil for one. Weciyuśica.

Ki'ciyuśiŋḣtiŋ, v. (of yuśiŋḣtiŋ). To enfeeble for one, to injure for one. Weciyuśiŋḣtiŋ.

Ki'ciyuśk̇a, v. (of yuśka). To loosen for one. Weciyuśka.

Ki'ciyuślok̇a, v. (of yuśloka). To pull off e.g. the clothes for one. Weciyuśloka.

Ki'ciyuśna, v. (of yuśna). To make a mistake for one. Weciyuśna.

Ki'ciyuśpi, v. (of yuśpi). To gather or pick off e.g. berries for one. Weciyuśpi.

Ki'ciyuśṫaŋ, v. (of yuśtaŋ). To finish or perfect for one. Weciyuśtaŋ.

Kici'yuṫa, v. To eat with one. Kiciwata. -- Ki'ciyuṫa, v. (of yuta). To eat anything for one. Weciyuta.

Ki'ciyuṫakuniśni, v. (of yutakuniśni). To destroy for another. Weciyutakuniśni.

Ki'ciyutaŋ, v. (of yutaŋ). To touch for one. Weciyutaŋ.

Ki'ciyutaŋiŋ, v. (of yutaŋiŋ). To manifest for one. Weciyutaŋiŋ.

Ki'ciyutaŋk̇a, v. (of yutaŋka). To enlarge for another. Weciyutaŋka.

Ki'ciyuṫeca, v. (of yuteca). To make new for one. Weciyuteca.

Ki'ciyuṫehaŋ, v. (of yutehaŋ). To make a delay for one, prolong, put off for one. Weciyutehaŋ. T'iŋ kte kiŋ he yeciluteháŋ. Pb.41.

Ki'ciyutokaŋ, v. (of yutokaŋ). To put in another place or remove for one. Weciyutokaŋ.

Ki'ciyutok̇eca, v. (of yutokeca). To make different for one. Weciyutokeca.

Ki'ciyuwaśṫe, v. (of yuwaśte). To make good for one. Weciyuwaśte.

Ki'ciyuwaś'ak̇a, v. (of yuwaś'aka). To make strong for one. Weciyuwaś'aka.

Ki'ciyuweġa, v. (of yuwega). To partly break for one, as a stick. Weciyuwega.

ki'ciyuza, v. (of yuza). To hold for one. Weciyuza.

ki'ciyuzamni, v. (of yuzamni). To open out or uncover for one. Weciyuzamni.

kici'yuzapi, v. recip. To take each other, as man and wife. Wakan - , Marriage.

kici'za, v. (of kiza). To fight. Kici - , To fight, quarrel with one. Kici weciza. Hanhepi ataya kici kicizelo. -- kici'zapi, n. A fight.

kico', v.a. To call, invite e.g. to a feast. Weco. Mico.

kicon'za, Cf. kicunza.

kico'śniyan, adv. With being not invited, uninvited. Micośniyan. B.H.147.7.

kico'za, v. To wave at someone. Nape wicakicozapi. B.H.186.11.

kicu', v. (k'u). To restore to one, give to one what belongs to him. Wécu. Yécu. Unkícupi. Mícu. Nícu. Cícu. According to analogy this should be kic'u, but it is not. Na wanna tawicu cinca ko wicakicu ca ob oyate el gli.

kicun'ni, v. To leave off, abstain from what one was about to do; to give over, be discouraged; to excuse, not press any further. Wecúnni. -- kicúnniyan, adv. Carelessly, not heartily. -- kicúnniyankel, adv. Circumspectly, looking about carefully. - omani, To go on carefully watching the road. Same as iwányangyekci. Bl.

kicun'skehan, adv. Half full, as a vessel.

kicun'za, v. To determine in regard to. Wecúnza.

kicu'wa, 1) n. A friend. Same as kola. Hau kicuwa. 2) v.pos. (of kuwa). To follow up, pursue, as in trying to give medicine to one's child. Wecúwa.

kic'a', v. pos. (of k'a). To dig one's own; to dig for one. Wec'á.

kic'in', v. pos. (of k'in). To carry or pack one's own, e.g. one's child or one's things. Wec'in. Unkic'inpi. Kic'in refers to carrying on one's back; whereas, k'in refers to carrying on one's shoulder, perhaps. BS.

kic'un', v.a. To put on or wear e.g. clothes, hat etc. Wéc'un. Yéc'un. Unkíc'unpi. Na wase kic'unpi kin hena kpakintapi na glapi kte lo. When used with certain verbs, the word shows that the action is done to themselves. Thus: itohomni - , oslohan - , hośnaśna - , hohotela - , icaptanptan - . -- kic'únkiciciya, v.a. To put on for one, help one to put on e.g. clothes. Kic'unweciciya. -- kic'unkiya, v.a. To cause to put on. Kic'unwakiya. -- kic'unskehanyan, adv. Having little in, as perhaps in a vend. The same perhaps as ceteyela. Bl. -- kic'unya, v.a. To cause to put on. Kic'unwaya. -- kic'unyan, perhaps adv. In a clothed manner, perhaps. Tancan - . B.H. 69.11.

kigla', v.n. To have gone home. Note: In all the persons, except the third, "ya" is inserted, as if from the word kiyagla. Wakiyagla. Yakiyagla. Unkiyaglapi. -- kiglé, Same as kigla. Perhaps also v. (of gle). To place for, make ready for one; to place or lay up one's own. Wegle. -- kiglékiya. v. To start home at once. Kiglewakiya. Cf. ukiya.

kiglē'ga, v.a. To overtake one. Weglega. Na wanji - ca na oyuspa. Icizaptan can el wicakiglega. MS.353. D.56.

kigle' s'a, n. A truant.

kigle'ya, v.a. To send off home. Kiglewaya.

kigli', v. (?). Tokeya - . MW.

kiglu'śpa, v. pos. To break in two one's own. Kiwagluśpa.

kigma', v.n. To look like, resemble. Wegma or wakigma. -- kigmáic'iya, v. To imitate.

kigna', v.a. To caress, soothe; to fondle e.g. a child. Wegná. Yegná. He - yo!

kignag', cont. of kignaka. - wahi, I came to lay away. -- kignágna, v. red. of kigna. -- kignágya, v.a. To cause to lay up one's own. Kignagwaya.

ḱigna'ḱa, v.a. (of gnaka). To lay up for , keep for one; to lay up one's own; to put off, to adjourn. Wegnaka. Yegnaka.

ḱigna'śkiⁿyaⁿ, v. To turn crazy. B.H. 204.10.

ḱigna'yaⁿ, v.a. To caress; to fondle. Perhaps, wakignayaⁿ.

ḱigni', v.n. irreg. He will go home. Wagni kte, I will go home. Yagni kte, You will go home. Gla, He goes home. Grammar,78.

ḱignug', cont. (of kignuka). To dive. - iyaya, To go under water, dive. Mni kiⁿ el kignuⁿk iblamni na cawapapa. D.70. Kignuⁿk ekta iyaye. D.74. There is some doubt about kignuⁿka. -- ḱi-gnúgḱiya, v.a. To cause to dive. Ki-gnugwakiya.

ḱignu'ḱa, v. To dive. Wegnuka.

ḱignuⁿ', (?). - kacicipapi, A swimming race under water, i.e. one would swim and then another, trying to swim the farthest. Bl.

ḱihaⁿ', (?). Tukte kawita uⁿḱíhaⁿpi kte lo, i.e. perhaps the same as uⁿ-kiwitayapi kte. Bl.

ḱihe', (?). - laka yo, Get busy now, stick to it. IS.

ḱihi', v.n. To be fledged, as young birds; to become large enough; to provide for one's self. Cf. uⁿcihi. -- ḱihíya, v.a. To raise, as a child; train up to manhood. Kihiwaya. Cf. uⁿ-cihiya.

ḱiho'waya, v. (of howaya). To talk loud to. B.H.115.6.

ḱihuⁿ'ni, v.n. To get through, reach home or the goal etc. Wakihuⁿni. Uⁿ-kihuⁿni.

ḱiȟlo', v. pos. (of ȟlo). To growl over one's own e.g. a bone, as is said of dogs. Makiȟlo.

ḱiȟpa'ya, v. (?). MW.

ḱiȟ'aⁿ', n. Stormy weather, a storm. Haⁿpiśka sutaya ayuwi yo, uⁿnihaⁿ - hi yelo. BT. - waⁿ hi yelo. Bl. Also, perhaps, ḱiȟ'aⁿ. Tokel - kte k'uⁿ he ikopa keye. B.H.136.16.

ḱiȟ'aⁿ'ḱa, (?). Caⁿ wákiȟ'aⁿkelo, I split wood. Bl.

ḱiȟ'aⁿ'yaⁿ, v. (of h'aⁿyaⁿ). To be likely to die to or for one e.g. one's child. Makiȟ'aⁿyaⁿ. R. Bl.

ḱii'glaksa, v. refl. (of kicaksa). To injure one's self. Kimiglaksa. Kini-glaksa.

ḱii'gluśpa, v. refl. To free one's self; to wrestle. This is used, perhaps, only in the plural. R. Caⁿke naȟmakel kiigluśpiⁿ kta waciⁿyuze. B.H.164.7.

ḱiiⁿ'yaⁿḱa, v.n. (of iⁿyaⁿka). To run with one for something, to race. - waⁿ kuwelo. BT. Kiiⁿyaⁿkapi, They run races. Kiiⁿyaⁿk ape. D.2;107. -- ḱiíⁿyaⁿḱapi, n. A running, a race.

ḱiiⁿ'yeya, v.a. To shoot or make fly an arrow. Kiiⁿyewaya. -- ḱiíⁿyeyapi, n. A bow shot.

ḱija'nicaśni, (?). - yuha yo, Try and get it even if it is impossible. Ba.

ḱijo', v.a. (of jo). To whistle for, call by whistling. Wakijo. Le kijo-pica śni, as is said of a man with whom one has to be careful; for, not able to stand a joke etc., he hits back. Bl. -- ḱijójo, v. red. (of ki-jo). To whistle for, to call one's own e.g. one's dog by whistling. Wa-kijojo.

ḱikcaⁿ'pta, v.a. To console, comfort one; to take sides with, desire to help one. Doubtfully, wekcaⁿpta. Wicákikcaⁿpte, A comforter, the Holy Spirit. Cikcaⁿptapi kte. Pb.40;45.

ḱiḱi'gla, v.n. To go home and leave one e.g. one's dog or horse. Maki-kigla.

ḱiḱi'ḱa, adj. or n. All covered with scrophulous sores. Bl.

ḱiḱi'yaḱel, adv. (?). - uⁿ, a figure of speech used when a married couple or other people do not getalong with each other very well; i.e. tokiⁿś caⁿtewaśtepi śni. Bl. Cf. oiglukiki.

kikpa'mni, v.a. (of kpamni). To divide or distribute one's own to.

kiksa'pa, v.n. (of ksapa). To become wise; to consult. Wakiksapa.

kiksu'ya, v.a. To remember; to be conscious. Weksuya. Miksuya. Ciksuya. -- kiksúyekiya, v.a. To cause to remember. Kiksuyewakiya. -- kiksúyeśni, v.n. To be conscious in no way, be unconscious; to be numb. Nape weksuyeśni, My hand is numb. -- kiksúyeya, v.a. To cause to remember. Kiksuyewaya.

kikśaⁿ', v.a. To wrestle, perhaps. Wakikśaⁿ. Also, to violate, commit rape on; to take without leave. Wakikśaⁿ.R. -- kikśaⁿpi, n. Rape.

kikta', v.n. To awake from sleep, be awaken. Wekta. - hiyaya. - iyotaka ke, He sat bold upright, having been lying on his back. D.105. -- kiktáhaⁿ, part. Awake, keeping awake. - uⁿ. -- kiktá iyotaka, v. To sit up, i.e. from a lying position. B.H.109.10. -- kiktáya, adv. Awake. - wauⁿ.

kikte', v.a. (of kte). To kill one's own; to kill for one. Wekte.

kiku'ja, v. pos. (of kuja). To be sick for one, to have one sick e.g. a child Makikuja.

kiku'te, v. (of kute). To shoot anything for another, such as ducks. Wakikute.

kila', 1) v. (of la). To ask or beg of one. Wakila. 2) v. pos. (of la). To think, esteem. Waśtekila. The word is not used alone.

kilē'le, adv. Long ago. Same as kilelekel and haⁿbleblekel. - tak eyé. Also, just as it happens. R. -- kiléleKel, adv. Long ago. Same as ehaⁿni, haⁿbleblekel, ehaⁿkehaⁿ.

kilo', particle. Meaning "śni yo", and seemingly following the 2nd pers. or imperative. Indicates: Beware of, or Do not. Eyatoⁿwe kilo, Pay no attention to it. El le - , Do not go there. Women drop the "lo". Nita akicita kiⁿ uⁿgna wicyagnaya kilo. Aktoⁿś mayaye cilo, Don't let me forget it. B.H. 176.4;57.22;47.7;89.14.

kilo'waⁿ, v. (of lowaⁿ). To sing to, as to a child. Wakilowaⁿ. B.H.128.4.

kilya'kel, adv. (?). - ecoⁿ, To do something slowly but surely. Bl.

kima'ka, v. To turn into soil, as anything rotting in the ground.

kimi'mila, n. The butterfly. --

- gleglega, The speckled butterfly.
- sapa, The black butterfly.
- ska, The white butterfly. Also, the little moths that fly around at night and go for every light they notice. Hence the saying: Kimimila ska s'e takuni kokipapi śni; i.e. ska s'e takuni kokipapi śni, To be as fearless as a white moth.
- śa, The red butterfly.
- to, The blue, purple or green butterfly.
- zi, The yellow butterfly. Bl. --

kimímila tawanahca, n. The large-flowered beard tongue. The figwort family. Penstemon grandiflorus. Nutt. Also, the bind weed, hedge bindweed; the morning glory. The morning glory family. Convolvulus sepinus. L. BT. Bl. # 2 and 203.

kimna'haⁿ, v.n. To fall off; to rip off for one. Makimnahaⁿ.

kimni', v. (of mni). To spread out one's own to dry in the sun. Wemni. Yemni.

kinahaⁿ', conj. If, when. Cf. kiⁿhaⁿ.

kina'jiⁿ, v. To reach home and stand; to stand again in one's place; recover one's position. Wakinawajiⁿ. Na miś lel apahalaka waⁿ el huⁿh najiⁿpi ca el wakinawajiⁿ. Na blaye cokaⁿ kinajiⁿpi.

kina'ksa, v. pos. (of naksa). To hurt one's foot by stepping on e.g. glass. Also, pronounced kináksa, v.a. To break in two with the foot, to break in the middle. Kinawaksa. Kinauⁿksapi.

kina'pa, v. To come or go forth out of; to have passed through in going home. Wakinapa. B.H.217.11;185.10.

kina'psaka, v. (of napsaka). To break in two in the middle with the foot, as a string. Kinawapsaka.

k̇inaś', interj. Then, well then. Perhaps an abbrev. of kiŋnahaŋś. - huŋḣ mak'u we, i.e. expecting to get it. - takuwe ecaŋnoŋ hwo? - he mayak'u śni, i.e. then give. Note: The word is sometimes contracted to kiŋś, and always begins a sentence which offers a suggestion, Well, in that case etc. Kinaś inatokapa kiŋ kici le śni. D.9, note 1.

k̇ina'śṗa, v. (of naśpa). To break off about half with the foot. Kinawaśpa.

k̇ini', v.n. (of ni). To live again, to return to life from the dead; to revive, recover from fainting. Wakini. Uŋkinipi. - aŋpetu, Easter Day.

Kini' Aŋpetu, n. prop. Easter, Resurrection Day.

k̇ini'ca, v.n. To strive, try to; to be anxious to. Wakinica. Ecoŋ wakinica. Na lila ake ekta, i.e. to the spirit land, ye wakinica.

k̇ini'haŋ, v.a. To honor, respect, reverence; have confidence in. Wakinihaŋ. -- k̇iniḣaŋpi, part. Honored, respected. -- k̇iniḣaŋśniyaŋ, adv. Dishonorably. -- k̇inihaŋyaŋ, adv. Honorably, respectfully.

k̇ini'k̇iya, v.a. To cause to live again. Kiniwakiya.

k̇inil' or k̇iŋnil', adv. Almost all, but with a few missing. Iyaye - maŋka, i.e. trying to. Oyasiŋ - inajiŋpi, All except a few stood up. Haŋke taŋiŋ - oye iyaye lo, as is said of a fresh wagon trail. BT. Temnit'e - kupi, i.e. almost overcome by perspiration. D.40.

k̇ini'ya, v.a. To raise to life.

k̇inuŋ'k̇aŋ, adv. Separately, between two; divided, each having a part. - wicak'u, i.e. two things. Hehaŋ - , i.e. two women, wicayuzapi. -- k̇inúŋkaŋk̇iya, adv. Separately. Caŋ k'uŋ hena - iyaya, The two trees sprang apart, i.e. separated as the wind blew. D.27. -- k̇inúŋkaŋyaŋ, adv. Separately.

k̇inuŋ'kiciyapi, v. To tell each other. RH.

k̇inuŋ'waŋ, v.n. (of nuŋwaŋ). To swim home, swim back again. Wakinuŋwaŋ. Also, to return swimming. Bl.

k̇iŋ, def. art. The. Also, ki. Note: When "a" or "aŋ" changed to "e" precedes, "ki" becomes "ci". Tuwa ohiye ci toka hwo? -- conj. cont. If, when. Ina iyeyakiye śni kiŋ, niktepi kta. Hence, at the beginning, also, at the first part of the sentence, kiŋ seems to have the meaning of the Latin cum temporale, i.e. when. Oyate icagapi kiŋ, tuweni t'e śni uŋpi. At the end of the sentence or independent clause, it gives the idea: It is a sure thing. Ninive otoŋwahe kiŋ ihaŋgyapi kte kiŋ. Therefore, in a sense, it functions as the terminal "yelo" or "epe kiŋ". B.H.117.20. Miyeś taŋtaŋ waceye kiŋ. MS.67. -- adj. or perhaps v. (?). When the Śahiyela tiŋpsila grow spongy, i.e. puff out and turn bad in June, the old Indians said: Waŋna kiŋ yelo. Now they say of them: Waŋna popópi. -- particle ending a rhetorical question. Also, ki. Tokayelaka hecaŋnoŋ kiŋ? Takuwe miniwicayakaśtaŋ kiŋ? Grammar,362. B.H.174.23. -- adv. clause substantivalized. Kiŋ accompanies various adverbs, thus:

kiŋ hecel. B.H.85.21;98.11.
kiŋ hehaŋl. B.H.15.11;94.11.
kiŋ hehaŋyaŋ. B.H.52.14.
kiŋ lehaŋl. B.H.55.1;71.11;76.1;81.4; 86.12;118.4;122.23;124.3;14.11.
Grammar, 247ss.

k̇iŋ'ca,, adj. Scraping. The word is **not used alone.** Cf. yukiŋca..

k̇inca'haŋ, part. Bare, fallen off, as hair from a dead animal, or as scales.

kiŋhaŋ', conj. If when. After "a" and "aŋ" changed into "e" the word becomes ciŋhaŋ.

k̇iŋiŋ', v.t. To throw at, to assail with something thrown. Iŋyaŋ oŋ - , To pelt with stones, to stone. Wakiŋiŋ. Makiŋiŋ. Niciŋiŋ. Wahukeza waŋ oŋ - . When considered v.i., we say <u>ma</u>kiŋiŋ. D.58 and 63, note 1.

kiŋ'ja, v.i. To whine, as babies do when they want something. LT.

k̇iŋ'sk̇ok̇eca, adv. So large. -- k̇iŋskosk̇ok̇eca, adv. red.

kiŋ'skoskoya, adv. red. of kiŋskoya.

kiŋ'skoya, adv. Thus far around.

kiŋśka', n. A horn spoon.

kiŋśye'la, adv. Whizzing, as a bullet, a bird, a fast horse. - ya. Cf. śliyela. Bl.

kiŋyaŋ', v.n. To fly, as birds do. - iyaya, It went away flying. -- kiŋyáŋpi. Those that fly, birds.

kiŋye', v. Same as kiŋyaŋ. Taku kiŋye ciŋ, i.e. birds.

kiŋye'kiyapi, n. A kite; an air ship. P. Bl.

kioŋ'pa, v. pos. (of oŋpa). To lay or place on one's own.

kipa', v. pos. (of pa). To blame one's self or one's own; to suffer in consequence of one's own course. Wakipa. Toś kipahci, i.e. suffers for his own foolishness. Also, to murmur, kick because somebody does not help one. BT. To silence one by talking and having the last word. Same as apaksoŋlya. Bl.

kipa'ble, v. (?). The word is used in speaking of horses when they stop running and stand still. Bl. Same as kipámna.

kipa'cica, v. pos. To wear out or off by knocking or rubbing against, as the hair of a quiver that bumps against one while walking.

kipa'hci, v. (of kipa, perhaps). Cf. kipá. Toś - , as is said when something hard happened to a man through his own fault because he did not listen. Toś is about the same as ito. Ba. SB. Bl.

kipa'jiŋ, v.a. (of pajiŋ). To stand up against, oppose. Wakipajiŋ. -- kipájiŋpicaśni, adj. Irresistible. P. Bl. -- kipájiŋyaŋ, adv. Opposing.

kipa'kiŋta, v.a. (of pakiŋta). To cleanse away for one, wipe off. Wakipakiŋta.

kipa'kiya, v.a. To cause to blame one's self. Kipawakiya.

kipa'mna, (?). Kipamnapi, as is said of wild horses or buffalo when they scatter after the hunting and wounding has begun. Bl. The word is related or the same as kipáble, i.e. implying coming to a stand-still.

kipa'na, v. To make a little room for one by pressing closer to the others. - po. Lel cicipana, tahena le ku wo. Wakipana. Bl.

kipaŋ', v. (of paŋ), To call to one. Wakipaŋ. Fr. Henry wicohaŋ waśte oŋ Greenwood ekta makipaŋ kiŋ he lila iyomakipi.

kipa's'a, n. One who is lazy, gets along with difficulty and blames himself much.

kipa's'iyaya, v. To evade, elude, turn sideways, avoid. Bl. Same as taŋhmiŋkiya iyaya. B.H.68.12.

kipa'ta, v. pos. (of pata). To join together e.g. skins in making one's own tent.

kipa'ta, v. pos. (of pata). To cut up one's own e.g. meat. Kpata may be the correct word.

kipa'taŋ, v. (of pataŋ). To keep for one; to mash up as food. Wakipataŋ.

kipa'titaŋ, v. (of patitaŋ). To push with all one's might. Wakipatitaŋ.

kipa'yehca, v.n. To rise up again, recover itself, as grass bent down. R. Bl.

kipa'zo, v. (of pazo). To point to for one, to show to one. Wakipazo. Makipazo.

kipca', v. (?). Lowaciŋ ca oŋ tahna wakipcahe lo. Bl.

kipe'haŋ, v.a. To roll up, perhaps; to fold one's own. Taśina kiŋ kipehe. B.H.112.4.

kipi', v.n. To hold, contain; to carry as a vessel, to cart etc.; to be large enough for, as a coat; to be sufficient for. Makipi.

kipi'ya, 1) v.a. To cause to fit. Kipiwaye. 2) adv. Fittingly, properly;

enough for. - kaga, To adapt, adjust to. - ecamoⁿ. Nuⁿpa caⁿ - , Enough, i.e. of it, for two days. Tkeiyutapi waⁿji - . B.H.55.17;237.4.

kipi'za, v. To smack one's lips or produce a sound at somebody, as a babies. Wakipiza. Bl.

kipsa'kaheśni, part. perhaps, Uninterrupted, continuous. - au welo. Bl.

kipsi'ca, v. To jump down from, alight from, as from a horse. Wakipsica.

kis, cont. of kiza.

kisag'ye, v.n. To turn into a cane, rod. B.H.48.14.

kisaⁿ', v.n. (of saⁿ). To become whitish for one. Makisaⁿ.

kisa'pa, 1) v.n. (of sapa). To become black, or bare again as does the ground by the disappearance of snow. 2) n. Bare ground. Also, kisápa.

kisiⁿ'c'iya, Cf. piic'iya.

kisiⁿ'kpe, v. (?). Wakisiⁿkpe. Wakisiⁿkpe na mak'u welo, i.e. to have received something one wanted very badly. Makisiⁿkpe na uⁿgnayelo. Bl.

kisiⁿ'te, v. (?). Wakisiⁿte. Wakisiⁿte cik'a na mak'u welo, i.e. when a person gets what he wanted very badly. The word may really be kisiⁿkpe. Bl.

kiska', v.n. To bleach. Fig., To recover common sense. Bl. Cf. kiwaśte.

kiski'za, v. red. (of kiza). To grate or gnash e.g. the teeth; to squeak, as shoes.

kisli'pa, v. (of slipa). To lick up one's own again, as dog does his vomit. Weslipa.

kisna'haⁿ, v.n. To break and fall off, as beads from a strand, for one. Makisnahaⁿ.

kisni'kiya, v.a. To cure one. Kisniwakiya. Bl.

kiso', v. pos. (of so). To cut a string from a hide, to cut up one's own.

kisoⁿ', v. pos. (of soⁿ). To braid one's own. Wesoⁿ. Wakisoⁿ also.

kiso'ta, v.n. (of sota). To be used up for one. Makisota. Nicisota.

kispa'ya, v. (of spaya). To be or become wet for one. Makispaya.

kisye'la, adv. With a grating sound. - mani, i.e. to make a grating noise in walking through snow in cold weather. Bl.

kis'iⁿ's'iⁿ, (?). Wakis'iⁿs'iⁿ. Cf. kas'iⁿs'iⁿ and s'iⁿs'iⁿya. Bl.

kiśi'ca, v.a. To check, oppose, put a stop to; to forbid, command to stop; to drive or kick out e.g. a dog from a house; to cast away; to be mean to; to order back. Taⁿkakula kiⁿ - he c'uⁿ, Who had been so mean to her younger sister. D.120.

kiśkaⁿ', v.a. (of śkaⁿ). To do to, act towards one. Wakiśkaⁿ.

kiśka'ta, v.a. (of śkata). To play to or with, to play for. Wakiśkata. -- kiśkáta, v. perhaps pl. To wrestle with others in fun, playfully, as also do horses sometimes. Bl.

kiśle'ya, v. To hold and feel, to force; to commit rape. Kiśléyaya. Bl. Also v.a. To annoy, vex, continue to press or urge one; to make ashamed, to offend, dishonor. R.

kiśpa'haⁿ, v. To break up and go. Wakiśpahaⁿ. Na hihaⁿna el oyate kiśpahaⁿpi ca wazitakiya aya. Also, kiśpáhaⁿ.

kiśto', adv. Cf. kśto.

kita'la, adv. Close together, as one hole near the other. Caⁿku kiⁿ - guheya yuⁿkelo, i.e. many roads together. Bl.

kitaⁿ', v.n. To stick to e.g. an opinion, continue to assert, to insist upon and not yield. Wakitaⁿ. Nihiⁿciye kiⁿ oⁿ sam lila kitaⁿpi, i.e. that the turtle be thrown into the water. Kéyaś lila kitaⁿpi, They insisted. D.20;117. B.H.49.21.

ki'taⁿ , adv. Scarcely, hardly. -- ki'taⁿeciⁿyaⁿ, adv. Slightly, just able. -- kitaⁿhci, adv. At last. - miglustaⁿ, At last I am through, or perhaps too: Scarcely am I through. R. D.262;100. Mi.

ki̇taṅ'iṅ, v. (of taṅiṅ). To appear or be visible for. Makitaṅiṅ. -- ki̇táṅiṅśni, v.n. To be lost for one. Makitaṅiṅśni. D.268-9.

ki̇ṫaṅ'kognagyelaḣci, (?). - uṅpi, as is said of a couple that is not affectionate to each other and think of getting a divorce. Bl. - oyaśtaṅ yelo.

ki'ṫaṅla, adv. A little, very little, in a slight degree. - tokeca, A little different. - oiyokpaza. Na waṅna wicokaṅyaṅ kitaṅla saṅpa hehaṅl waṅna eyapaha oṅhe ake u. Na hocoka kiṅ - isam uṅkiyaglapi. Wata kiṅ - pacokab iyeye. B.H.66.9;186.5.

ki̇ṫaṅ'ṗawoslaheyelakel, adv. (?). - maṅke c'oṅ nawajiṅ yelo. Bl.

ki'ṫaṅ s'e, adv. With difficulty.

ki̇ṫaṅ'yaṅ, adv. Continuously; insisting upon. -- ki̇ṫáṅyaṅḱel, adv. With the greatest difficulty; contrary to all expectation, perhaps. - ecamoṅ, I did it, i.e. although I thought I was unable, e.g. as lifting a heavy weight which one thought one could not lift. Same as yus'óyakel. -- ki̇ṫáṅyeḣci, adv. With difficulty; not thoroughly. R. Mini el iyayapi na minit'api, tka - glinapapi. -- ki̇ṫáṅyel, adv. With difficulty. - mikpanajiṅkelo. Bl. - otaṅiṅ, It is hardly, just a little, visible. WE. -- ki̇ṫáṅyelakeleś, (?). - emáca.

ḱita'ta, adv. Near together; frequently, in close succession. -- ki̇tátala, adv. (of kitata). Near together, close in succession. Same as icikaṅyela. - yutapi wakaṅ iwacu kte.

ki̇ṫi'yus'eya, adv. Barely. - taṅiṅyaṅ, Barely visible. - bluśtaṅ, I hardly finished it. Also, kitiýuzeya. Br.

ḱitoṅ'waya, (?). Tehaṅ - lo. Bl.

ki̇ṫoṅ'yaṅ, adv. perhaps. In an increasing manner, growing. Ceḣpi - ,i.e. my flesh growing. B.H.44.15.

ki̇t'a', v.n. (of t'a). To die or be dead for one, as one's child. Makit'a.

ḱiuṅ', (?). Tehaṅ - na, i.e. went far away. Bl.

ki̇uṅ'uṅ laḱe, v. To act foolishly, unreasonably, when no one else does.Bc. Wakiuṅuṅlake. Wiṅyaṅ nuṅb ataya cagu-iyuḣpa wanicapelo. Lena tuktel kiuṅuṅpilake lo, i.e., freely translated, where did they grow up anyway? The word, as we might say, means: they must live some life! "Ki", is a dative; uṅ, To be, to exist, and is reduplicated; pi, they; la, refers to one who is open to mild ridicule.

ki̇uṅ'yaṅ, v. To lose for one, lose what belongs to another. Wakiuṅyaṅ.

ki̇wa'kaṅheja, v.n. To desire to be with; to be on good terms with; to be intimate with. Wakiwakaṅheja.

ki̇wa'kaṅyeś, adv. Carefully. - au wo. - uṅkomanipelo. - eyakas'iṅ yo. - oyakilehaṅ ca he cicu welo. - woyakile s'elececa. Bl. The word is used in referring to babies, wakaṅheja.

ḱiwa'ksa, v.a. To cut in two in the middle e.g. a stick. Kiwawaksa.

ki̇wa'nice, v. To turn to nothing, vanish. Lit., there is nothing there whatsoever. Bl.

ḱiwaṅ'jica, (?). Taku - śni slolye, He understands everything thoroughly. Bl.

ḱiwa'psaḱa, v.a. To cut a cord or string in two in the middle. Kiwawapsaka.

ḱiwa'sleca, v.a. To slit or saw in the middle something soft. Kiwawasleca. -- ḱiwáśleca, v.a. To saw in the middle something hard. Perhaps this word is not used.

ḱiwa'śṗa, v.a. To cut in two in the middle, as an apple. Kiwawaśpa.

ki̇wa'śte, v.n. To become good, convert, return to God; to be on good terms again. P. Cf. kiská. Makiwaśte. Bl. B.H.54.9. -- ki̇waśteśte, adj. red. of kiwaśte refering to many. -- ki̇wáśteśteka, (?).

ḱiwa'ś'agpica śni, adj. One who acts

wrong inspite of all good advice. Bl.

Ǩiwa'ś'aka, adj. Strong, having strong muscles. Bl.

Ǩiwi'ťaya, 1) v.n. To assemble. Uŋkiwitayapi kte. Bl. Ptaŋyetu kiŋhaŋ lel ake kiwitayapi kte, They will meet here again in fall. D.225. 2) adv. (of witaya). Together, assembled together, i.e. of their own accord, spontaneously. B.H.61a.4.

Ǩiwi'tkotkoka, v. To be or become foolish. B.H.104.18.

Ǩiwi'wila, v. To turn into a spring. B.H.181.21.

Ǩiwo'ksa, v.a. To shoot in two in the middle. Kiwowaksa.

Ǩiwo'psaǩa, v.a. To shoot off in the middle e.g. a cord.

Ǩiwo'śpa, v.a. To shoot e.g. an apple in two. Kiwówaśpa.

Ǩi'ya, 1) v. aux. To cause, to make to be. Ecoŋkiya. It is always affixed to the verb etc.; whereas the pronoun is inserted before the "kiya". 2) Ǩíya, v. aux. poss. (of ya). -- adv. Towards. Tokatakiya. Ektakiya. 3) adv. Separately, in different ways or in different places. Oyate nuŋpakiya wicoti. Na el taniga k'oŋ he topakiya paȟloka.

Ǩi'yagla, v. To have gone home. The word is not used but in the 1st and 2nd pers. Wakiyagla. Yakiyagla. Cf. kigla. Uŋkiyaglapi. Hecel waglinawapa na tona glinapapi kiŋ hecena agla ca miś eya wakiyagla na tiyata wagli. Lecel totaŋkaya eya: Uŋkiyaglapi kte lo. Cf. D.219, uŋkiyagni kte.

Ǩiya'glapťa, v. pos. (of kiyakapta). To have passed over e.g. a hill in going home. Wakiyaglapta.

Ǩiya'haŋ, v.n. To climb a hill etc. and stand; to stand on top. Wakiyahaŋ. Yuŋkaŋ paha el kiyahaŋpi.

Ǩiya'he, v. (of kiyahaŋ). Same as kiyahaŋ. A North Dakota Indian in the 1870's had the name Waŋbli Kiyahe. His English name was Climbing Eagle. Yuŋkaŋ paha waŋ etaŋ u k'oŋ - śni ecel ataŋiŋ śni iyaya.

Ǩiya'ǩapťa, v.n. To have passed over e.g. a hill in going home. Wakiyakapta.

Ǩi'yaǩiju, v.n. To unite. Also, Ǩíyokiju. R. -- Ǩíyaǩijuya, 1) v.a. To put together, cause to unite. Kiyakijuwaya. R. 2) adv. Together, unitedly.

Kiya'ksa, n. prop. (Ǩiyáksa). A band of Dakotas, so called, it is said, from the inter-marrying of relatives among them.

Ǩiya'ksa, v. (of yaksa). To bite in two in the middle. Kiblaksa.

Ǩiya'mna, v. (of yamna). To acquire for another by talking. Wakiyamna.

Ǩiya'pa, v. (of yapa). To suck for, take in the mouth and suck, as the Dakota conjurers did. Wakiyapa. A k'uŋ el - . D.59. -- Ǩiyápapi, n. Drawing with the mouth.

Ǩiya'taŋiŋ, v.a. (of yataŋiŋ). To make manifest to or for. Wakiyataŋiŋ.

Ǩiye', adv. (?). - au wo. BT.

Ǩiye'la, adv. Near, near to. Refers to time and place. Cf. ikiyela. Tokśa nikiyelapi wauŋ kte lo.

Ǩiyo'kpeca, v. To have come back to one's home that is away. Tokiyab kiyokpeci na u kapiŋ yelo, i.e. does not care to come back. Cf. gliyokpeca. Wakiyokpeca.

Ǩiyo'naǩijiŋ, v. To arrive and take refuge in with others. Waŋna napapi na paha waŋ el kiyonakijiŋpi.

Ǩiyo'ťaǩa, v.n. (of ki and iyotaka). To arrive and remain at home. This is used by the person who arrives, or by another person, when away from the place. Wakiblotaka. Yakilotaka.

Ǩiyu'ajaja, v.a. To explain to one. B. -- Ǩiyúajajaya, v.a. To explain to one. Wowapi wakaŋ kiŋ - . B.H.288.7; 301.3.

Ǩiyu'gal, cont. (of kiyugata). To lift one's arms. - wacekiya. B.H.55.28.

ǩiyu'ǧaⁿ, v.a. (of yugaⁿ). To open for one, as a door. Wakiyugaⁿ. -- ǩiyúǧaťa, v.a. (of yugata). To open e.g. the hand, to stretch out the hand to; to implore, as in worship. Wakiyugata. Also, to hold out one's arms towards somebody, as a baby towards its mother. Bl.

ǩiyu'ha, v. (of yuha). To have or keep for one. Wakiyuha. Wowaciⁿye kiyuhapi kiⁿ he Jesus iyokipi. Wakaⁿtaⁿka wowaciⁿye - , i.e. he trusts in God. B.H. 187.8;266.6.

ǩiyu'ȟa, v.a. To copulate as animals do.

kiyu'inaȟni, v.t. To hurry things for one. Makiyuinaȟni yo. Wanagi el mahipelo. Cf. D.244.

ǩiyu'jaja, v. (of yujaja). To wash for another. Wakiyujaja.

ǩiyu'juju, v.a. To repeal.

ǩiyu'kaⁿ, v.a. To make room for e.g. in a room; to be for one. Wakiyukaⁿ. Makiyukaⁿ. Ciciyukaⁿ. Catku el makiyukaⁿpi. Makiyukaⁿ yo, hel waku welo, Get out of the way for me, I am coming yonder. Bl. D.71. B.H.224.17. -- ǩiyúkaⁿyaⁿ, (?). Taťúye - uⁿyaⁿpi kta, i.e. to drop dust so as to know which way the wind blows, in order to get to the leeward of the buffaloes. -- ǩiyúǩo, v. To make room for one between others by moving closely together. Ciciyuko. Bl. This is perhaps kiyuoko. Cf. oko.

ǩiyu'ksa, 1) v. (of yuksa). To break or cut in the middle. Kibluksa. Šuⁿka waⁿ cokaⁿ - na śpaⁿśni yuta. 2) v.a. To break in two for one. But this is pronounced ǩiyúksa, and kibluksa is doubtful as the 1st pers.

ǩiyu'kseya, adv. perhaps. Separately. - egle. Cf. kiyuśpeya. Fr.

ǩiyuⁿ'ǩa, v.n. To go home and lie down, go and sleep at home. Wakimuⁿka. Psuⁿpsuⁿkiya - . B.H.81.8.

ǩiyu'śe, v.a. To hate one, do evil to one. Wakibluśe. Lila - , She maltreated her. D.270.

ǩiyu'śǩa, v.a. (of yuśka). To loose, untie, unharness; to release from prison or confinement. Wakiyuśka and wakibluśka.

ǩiyu'śpa, v.a. and v.n. (of yuśpa). To break into pieces, divide e.g. bread; to deliver or free, as from a trap or evil of any kind. Kibluśpa and wakibluśpa. Letaⁿhaⁿ oyate kiⁿ nuⁿpakiya - iyayapi kte. D.225. -- ǩiyúśṗapi, n. A dividing, delivering. -- ǩiyúśṗaśṗa, v. red. of kiyuśpa. B.H.208.13. -- ǩiyúśṗeya, adv. Separately. Cf. ǩiyúkseya. - egle. Fr.

ǩiyu'ťe, n. A strait or channel, an isthmus.

ǩiyu'tokaⁿ, v.a. To remove for one. Wośica mitawa kiⁿ oyas'iⁿ miyetaⁿhaⁿ mayakilutokaⁿ kte. Pb.30.

ǩiyu'weǧa, v. To break something belonging to another, to break to. Wakiyuwega.

ǩiyu'weǧa, v. (of iyuwega). To cross e.g. a stream in going home. Wakibluwega. Na ake mini el kiyuwegapi na oyate kiⁿ napapi etkiya agla na etipi.

ǩiyu'za, v.a. (of yuza). To hold to one. Wakiyuza. Waciⁿ ipaweȟ mayakiluzelo, i.e. you don't mind me. Bl.

ǩiyu'zamni, v.a. (of yuzamni). To open to or for one, to uncover for one. Wakiyuzamni.

ǩi'za, v.n. To creak, to grate.

ǩi'za, v.a. To fight, quarrel with. Waǩiza.

ǩizo'mi, v. To covet. Wakizomi. Wakizomi na mak'u welo, as is said when a man gets where he wanted. Makizomi na magnayelo. Bl. Cf. kisiⁿte. Woyuha taku k'eyaś etkiya yakizomi kilo. B.H.57.26.

ǩizu'zeca, v.n. To turn into a snake. B.H.48.12.

ǩo, conj. And, too, also. It is placed after the word it belongs to. Miye - kte, Me too. Waⁿna caⁿpa na kaⁿta - yutapi. Na iȟ'e waⁿ lila zizipela ca ko wicaku po. -- v. To desire strongly, to be anxious for. It follows another verb, as in oȟ'áⁿǩo, oȟ'aⁿwaǩo, To be anxious to do a thing, to be quick about it. Waciŋḱo. Ptehiḱo, ptehiwako, i.e. to perform ceremonies to attract the buffalo. Note, maśteḱola, another name for iśtanica taŋka, The horned lark, which cf. Gliwaḱó, I am anxious to see him return. Wi. Wagleksuŋ bloka osniḱo s'e huholyéla. Same as: osni kte ciŋ. Bl. Hacila kiŋ ḱópi kayeś ópapi. B.H. 117.21.

Ḱoa'ḱaṫaŋ, adv. Over the river, across the river. Also, hutasaŋpata. -- Ḱoáḱaṫaŋhaŋ, adv. From beyond the river.

Ḱog, cont. (of koka). To make a sound, to rattle. - hiŋgla.

koġiŋ'ġiŋ, (?). Tipi kiŋ iyaza caŋnuŋp' - omani. - naŋkahelo ḣ'uŋyela wahiyelo. BT. -- koġiŋġiŋkel, adv. (?). - yaŋka, To be slow, to stay away long. Bl. -- koġiŋġiŋlag, (?). - naŋka nahina taku yakáhe? FB.

Ḱogla'mna, adv. Around, over. -- Ḱoglámnayaŋ, v.a. To surround, restrain, cut off retreat. Koglamnawaya.

Ḱogli', adj. Clear, translucent. -- Ḱoglígli, adj. red. of kogli. The flint corn is so called from its translucency.

Ḱo'gna, adv. On that side. Also, kaogna.

kogna'gyela, adv. (?). Kitáŋ - ile, It burns just a little. Bl.

Ḱohaŋ', adv. Now, quickly; meanwhile, before something else is done. - iyaya, tokśa wau kte. Kola, - gla yo, lena mau kiŋ na tokśa ehakela waku kte lo. Wica kiŋ - paha waŋ el eyokasiŋ. - mak'u wo. -- Ḱoháŋḱe śni, (?). - iyaye kiyelo. Bl.

Ḱohaŋś', adv. Since that, so that.

Ḱoḣtiŋ'laḣ, Same as lecála. WE.

koi'yayuḣḱiya, (?). Also perhaps, kaiyayuḣḱiya. - iyaya, as is said of a road that leads to and into another at a small angle. Bl.

Ḱoja'gjal, adv. Apart. - mani, To walk with the legs apart. Jata, Fork-like.

koḱa'. n. A keg, barrel. - maza, A water tank.

ko'ḱa, n. The sound created by knocking.

Ḱoḱab', adv. Before one, in the way of. - inajiŋ, To stand in the way of one, so as to hold him. Same as kuśeya najiŋ. -- Ḱoḱábya, v. To go before one, ahead of one. Also, perhaps adv.

Ḱoḱa'la, n. dim. (of koká). A small keg.

Ḱoka'mna, (?). Palani - hi s'e lila owewakaŋkaŋ, as is said when a person tells lies. La.

Ḱoḱa'ojuha, n. An empty barrel.

ko'ḱela, 1) v. To make a noise, to rattle e.g. dishes. Caŋcaŋ s'e śkaŋ yo: wiohiyaye - yelo, i.e. the sun will set soon. Bl. Tawaciŋ kokelapi śni yo. B.H.194.7. 2) adv. Quickly, rapidly.

koḱi'caśpa, v. To dig two holes into one; to shoot twice in the same place. Cf. kokiyuḣci. Kowecaśpa is doubtful. R.

ko'ḱiciyas'iŋ, adv. Uniting, coming together and flowing on, as two streams in one; stuck or fastened together, as dogs after copulating; also used of potatoes in a bunch. R. Bl.

Ḱoḱi'jaŋjaŋ, v.n. To become thinner and lighter here and there, as clouds or the prairie. Bl. Same as kokiwotaŋiŋ.

Ḱo'ḱiju, v.n. To come together. -- koḱíjuya, 1) v.n. To cause to unite together. Cf. okijuya. 2) adv. Unitedly, together. Also, koḱíjuya.

Ḱoḱi'pa, v.a. To fear, be afraid. Kowakipa. Kouŋkipapi. Komakipa. -- Ḱoḱípaṗi, part. Feared. Hence, wokokipe. -- Ḱoḱíṗeḱiya, v.a. To cause to fear. Kokipewakiya. -- koḱíṗeśniyaŋ, v.a. To render fearless. Kokipeśniwaya. Pb.45. Takuni kokipeśniniyiŋ kta ciŋ. -- Ḱoḱíṗeya, 1) v.a. To cause to fear, make afraid of. Kokipewaya. 2) adv. Timidly. -- Ḱoḱíṗeyahaŋ, adv. Fearing, fearful, afraid.

koki'ptaŋ, (?). Tawat'elwaye śni tka yelo; tka Lakota kiŋ komayakiptaŋpi ca heoŋ blelo. MS.532.

kok̇i'woḣci, v. (?). Kokiwowaḣci. Bl.

kok̇i'wotaŋiŋ, v.n. To become thinner and lighter, as clouds, or a prairie etc.; to be transparent, as a mosquito net. Bl.

k̇ok̇i'yuḣci, v. To unite two holes that are close together into one, by tearing the separating material. Kokibluḣci. Cf. kokicaśpa.

ko'ko, red. (of ko). Also. It is used when refering to more than one thing. B.H.39.12.

k̇ok̇o'gya, adv. (of kokoka). Rattling.

kok̇o'juha, n. (of koka and ojuha). An empty barrel. Same as kokaojuha.

k̇ok̇o'ka, v.n. To rattle e.g. a stiff skin.

k̇ok̇o'yaḣaŋla, n. A chicken, fowls. So called, perhaps, on account of their quick picking up. The rooster sings: Mato kawiŋge. Bl. Cf. kóka. Also, k̇ok̇óyaḣ'aŋla. Bl. - otí, A chicken coup.

koko'yela, adv. Hurrying, hastening a little, in quick succession.

k̇okṫa', adj. One thousand. - śica, A billion. LT. Also, k̇okṫáśica, A million. According to Rac., the word indicates everything beyond a million, wóiyawa.

k̇o'kṫa, adv. Also, besides. -- k̇ókṫaya, adv. Besides.

k̇okṫo'ṗawiŋġe, adj. A thousand. -- k̇októṗawiŋġeġe, adj. red. B.H.57.8.

k̇o'la, n. A friend, the particular friend of a Lakota man. Mitakola. Nitakola. Takolaku. -- k̇olák̇iciyapi, n. Friendship. -- k̇oláya, v.a. To have for a particular friend. Kolawaya.

kome'ya, v.a. To destroy. Komewaya. B.H.51.10;72.20;244.5.

komi', v.n. To melt, perhaps. Wa kiŋ - kta. Bl.

k̇ona'tk̇e, adv. High. Ciŋcala - s'e micitoŋpi, A pretty tall colt was born to me. Oŋzoge - s'e uŋ elo, The pants are drawn up high. -- konátkeya or konátkeyela, adv. High, as a high tree with a bushy crown and a thin trunk, i.e. caŋ - hiyeya. - waókśupi, i.e. a high wagon. Ḣlaḣla - otke, A big heavy bell on a thin stand. - omani, i.e. a big heavy man with very thin legs.

k̇oŋ, v. To desire, to covet. Wakoŋ. -- k̇óŋla, v. dim. To desire. P. It is used by children or women. Wakoŋla. Owaś'ag koŋla taogliḣpaye lo. B.H.195.21.

k̇oŋs, cont. of koŋza. Nah'oŋ śni - hiyaye, Pretending not to hear, he went along. D.20. -- k̇oŋsyá, adv. Pretending. Also, k̇oŋsyákel.

k̇oŋ'za, v. To pretend. Wakoŋza. Kahúŋ - , To pretend to strike. Witko - , To pretend to be ignorant. Iyopteya ye - , He pretends to go on. B.H.273.8. -- v.a. To wish evil to one. Wakoŋze. Mayakoŋze. Wicakoŋzapi. B. B.H.148.28.

k̇o'ṗegla, v.n. To be afraid, be in fear. Kopewagla.

k̇o'ṗeya, 1) v.a. To make afraid. Kopewaya. 2) adv. Insecurely.

k̇os, cont. of koza. - hiyaya. Hupahu - iyuta. MS.145.

k̇osaŋ', adv. Onward, farther on than was intended. - iyaya, i.e. travelling a little farther than was expected because the sun was still up high. Na he ozuye kiŋ huŋḣ hetaŋ namni agli na huŋḣ - éyaya. - éyaya, He kept on following the calling. Note: R. gives ákosaŋ, adv. Whilst, in the meantime.

k̇oska', n. Gonorrhoea.

k̇ō'sk̇os, v. cont. (of koskoza). To swing. Haŋpośpu hokśicala k'oŋ waŋna - najiŋpi.

k̇ō'sk̇oza, v. red. (of koza). To wave, beckon; to swing. Na mila el - śke lo.

k̇osya', v.a. To cause to wave or make a signal. Koswaya.

ḱośḱa', v. To be affected with venereal disease. Komáśka.

kośka'la, n. A youth, young man. Same as kośkalaka. R. Bl.

ḱośḱa'laḱa, n. A young man. Komaśkalaka. The word is not kośká. -- kośkáśkalaka, n. A boy turning, growing into manhood and acting like a man. - mani. Bl. -- kośkáuⁿcihikaca, (?). The word is used teasingly of a girl that did not seem to care to marry. Bl.

ḱo'ya, conj. And, too, also. Na waⁿna oyate kiⁿ tipi kiⁿ ojuṗila na taⁿkal - . Wakaⁿheja śuⁿka - yuaḣwayela miyeciluziⁿ kta. Bl.

ḱoyag', cont. of koyaka. - wauⁿ, I am wearing. - uⁿ, i.e. hitched. P. -- ḱoyágḱiya, v.a. To cause to put on or wear. Koyagwakiya.

ḱoyag'ya, 1) v.a. To cause to put on; to attach to. Koyagwaya. 2) part. Clothed. Hena taḣca śuⁿkala tahaya - el hihipelo. B.H.195.2.

ḱoya'ḣ'aⁿ, v.n. To be quick in doing a thing, to hasten, hurry. Koyawaḣ'aⁿ. Koyámakiḣ'aⁿ yo, nituwa heci? Koyámakiḣ'aⁿ yo. D.90. -- koyáḣ'aⁿna, adv. Quickly, immediately. R. Bl. -- koyáḣ'aⁿyela, adv. Quickly. Same as inaḣni.

ḱoya'ḱa, v.a. To put on or wear e.g. clothes. Koblaka. Kouⁿyakapi. -- ḱoyákapi, part. Clothed. Taku - , Clothing.

ḱoya'kiḣ'aⁿ, v. To be quick in doing perhaps one's own. Taku ecanoⁿ kta heci - yo. B.H.253.15. Koyamakiḣ'aⁿ yo, nituwa ka heci?

ḱoya'nuⁿ, adj. Of quick growth; precocious. Makoyanuⁿ. Cf. hiyánuⁿ.

ḱoyaⁿ', adv. Quickly. - upi yo. Bh. -- koyáⁿla, adv. Quickly. R. Bl.

koye'la, adv. Promptly, quickly.

ḱo'za, v.a. To shake, to wave e.g. a signal; to swing. Hupahu - . Śina - . Nape kícoza, To wave the hand at.

kpa, pos. prefix. Verbs that take "pa" as a prefix, make the possessive form by adding "k". Thus: pagaⁿ, kpagaⁿ.

kpa, 1) v.n. To swell, as rice does in cooking. 2) adj. Durable, lasting, not soon eaten up, as some kinds of food e.g. rice. 3) adj. Punched out. Noⁿge kpa, deaf; iśta kpa, blind.

kpabla', v. pos. of pabla. Bl.

kpabla'za, v. pos. of pablaza. Bl.

kpable'ca, v. pos. (of pableca). To break in pieces one's own by pressure. Wakpableca.

kpaǧaⁿ', v. pos. (of pagaⁿ). To spare or part with one's own; to leave or separate from one's own. Wakpagaⁿ.

kpagmuⁿ', v. pos. (of pagmuⁿ). To twist one's own. Wakpagmuⁿ.

kpaha'haṗiḱa, n. One who is put forward in company. Makpahahapika.

kpahi', v. pos. (of pahi). To gather or pick up one's own. Wakpahi. Uⁿkpahipi.

kpaḣle'ca, v. pos. (of paḣleca). To make a hole in one's own, to lance. Wakpáḣleca.

kpaḣṗa', v. pos. (of paḣpa). To lay down or put off one's own load. Wakpaḣpa. B.H.38.2.

kpaja'ja, v. pos. (of pajaja). To wash out one's own e.g. a gun. Wakpajaja.

kpaju'ju, v. pos. (of pajuju). To rub out one's own. Wakpajuju.

kpaḱiⁿ'ta, v. pos. (of pakiⁿta). To wipe one's own. Wakpakiⁿta. Uⁿkpakiⁿtapi. Cf. ikpakiⁿta. Na wasé kic'uⁿpi kiⁿ hena kpakiⁿtapi na glapi kte lo.

kpakpas', cont. (of kpakaza, of kpaza). adj. red. Dark. Ite - mahiⁿgle lo, i.e. to have a spell of dizziness. GA.

kpakṗi', v. pos. (of pakpi). To crack or break one's own, as a chicken breaking its shell.

kpakśi'ja, v. pos. (of pakśija). To double up one's own. Wakpakśija.

kpaku'ka, v. pos. (of pakuka). To wear out one's own by rubbing. Wakpakuka.

kpamaŋ', v. pos. (of pamaŋ). To file, to polish one's own. Wakpamaŋ. Hekpamahaŋ. D.91.

kpamni', v.a. To divide, distribute. Wakpamni. Hecel waŋna tipi iyohila kpamnipi. R. gives v. pos. (of pamni). To divide out one's own. -- kpamnipi, n. A distribution.

kpana'jiŋka, v. refl. (of panajiŋ). To get up from the ground on one's limbs, as do old people. Kitaŋyel mikpanajiŋkelo. Bl.

kpaŋ, adj. Fine, as flour.

kpaŋkpaŋ'la, adj. red. (of kpaŋla). Fine, soft. Makoce - k'el, Prairie with little elevations all over. Bl.

kpaŋ'la, adj. Fine, soft. Taku - ota ca yawapica śni, as was stated by Bl. when referring to the fact the Lakota has countless fine little words.

kpaŋyaŋ', v.a. To tan, to dress e.g. a skin. Kpaŋwáya. Taha kpaŋyaŋpi kiŋ ohomni waso. Lila taŋyaŋ - yuśtaŋ. Yuŋkaŋ śina kpaŋyaŋpi waŋ el akaȟpa egnaka. WI. refers to the word as from kpaŋ, Fine, soft; but this is doubtful.

kpaoŋ'jiŋjiŋtka yaŋka, v. To be in a stooping position out of sorrow, i.e. hiding one's face, as it were. Cf. k kpaśiŋśiŋ. Bl.

kpao'wotaŋka, v. pos. (of paowotaŋka). To make one's self right, i.e. get thihgs one needs badly and receives e.g. clothing, weapons etc. Kitaŋyel mikpaowotaŋkelo. Bl.

kpapsoŋ', v. pos. (of papsoŋ). To spill over one's own e.g. blood. Wakpapsoŋ. Pb.32.

kpapta', v. To leave one's company, escape; to leave before company breaks up; to free one's self and go away, as from jail, while the others remain. Wakpapta. Tokel kpaptiŋ kte ciŋ iyukcaŋ. Miśnala wakpąpta ca hośicicagli. Minit'e śni - . B.H.42.27;304.4. - iyaya, To go through breaking things, as cattle through a fence; to free one's self and go away. Hecel uŋkpaptapelo. Bl.

kpapu'za, v. pos. (of papuza). To make one's own dry by wiping. Wakpapuza.

kpasmiŋ'yaŋyaŋ, v. To load a gun, hammering in the load with the rod. Bl.

kpasnoŋ', v. pos. (of pasnoŋ). To roast one's own meat. Wakpasnoŋ.

kpasu'ta, v. pos. (of pasuta). To make hard by kneading one's own bread. Wakpasuta.

kpaśiŋ'śiŋ yaŋka, v. To be in a sitting and stooping position, as the Indians do when in sorrow; to be silent out of sorrow. - maŋka. Pa. Bl. Cf. kpaóŋjiŋjiŋtka. Śiŋśiŋ refers to wrinkles. Cf. also uŋjiŋcala, i.e. with a round and short tail.

kpaśpu', v. pos. (of paśpu). To loosen one's own. Hiyomayatake ciŋ wakpaśpu ktelo, i.e. will remove that piece of meat that got stuck between the teeth. Bl.

kpa'ta, v. pos. (of pata). To cut up or carve one's own meat. Wakpata.

kpataŋ', v. pos. (of pataŋ). To take care of one's own, to save one's own; to think much of, so as to spare or not use up; to save, as money. Wakpataŋ. Niȟ'kpataŋ, i.e. to eat little, little knowing that something better is coming. Bl. B.H.214.13. Pb.26.

kpataŋ'taŋkel, adv. Sparingly, using little by little, slowly. Woeye ciscila bluha ca - oblakelo. Bl. Kpataŋtaŋ may be used, perhaps.

kpat'a', v. pos. To kill one's own by pressure. B.H.99.4 -- kpat'át'a, v.n. To be numb or asleep. Siha wakpat'at'a.

kpawa'ś'aka, v. pos. pawaś'aka. (?).

kpawi'yakpa, v. pos. of pawiyakpa. Sicaŋ kiŋ - , To polish one's thigh. D.1.

kpa'za, adj. Dark. Also, kpasa.

kpazaŋ', v. pos. (of pazaŋ). To part or separate one's own. Wakpazaŋ.

kpazi'gzica, v. pos. (of pazigzica). To stretch one's own. Wakpazigzica. Hel ota wohaⁿpi ca nige - yo. Bl.

kpazo', v. pos. (of pazo). To show one's own. Ceji - . Hayapi kpazopi. B.H.153.18;290.16.

kpe, Same as kpa, adj.

kpehaⁿ', v. pos. (of pehaⁿ). To fold up one's own. Wakpehaⁿ.

kpe'ya, adv. Sounding. - apa, To strike anything and make a sound.

kpeyē'la, adv. perhaps. Resounding, with a loud sound, report, as a gun shot off. Na lila - iyeya.

kpi, syll. Suggests the act of breaking open. Cf. pakpi.

kpukṗa', adj. Boiled up, mixed up, not clear; full of dirt, as is said of water slightly turbid, or of soup which contains floating particles. -- kpukṗéya, adv. Mixed up, all kinds together.

kpusṗa', v. pos. (of puspa). To glue or seal one's own. Wakpuspa.

kputa'ka, v. pos. (of putaka). To touch one's own.

ksa, adj. Separated. It is used with prefixes ya etc.

ksab', cont. of ksapa.

ksabya', 1) v.a. To make wise. Ksabwaya. 2) adv. Wisely, prudently. - wauⁿ. -- ksabyáhaⁿ, adv. Wisely. -- ksabyákel, adv. Wisely. B.H.45.7.

ksa'haⁿ, part. Broken in two of itself.

ksaksa'ṗa, adj. red. of ksapa.

ksa'ṗa, adj. Wise, prudent. Waksapa.

ksawa'haⁿ, part. Broken into.

ksi'zeca, adj. Cross, grum, stern. It is used now more than and instead of wóhiⁿyaⁿze. It is said also of wild animals. Maksízeca.

ksi'zeke, adj. To be good on, i.e. boastingly. Maksizeke, I am a good one.

ksize'oie, n. A laughable word, a word that causes laughter. Also, ksizéoíe.

ksizi'c'ila, n. or adj. A bully. Ksizmíc'ila.

ksuⁿkaḣ', v. To deceive, fool. - kuwa. EE.

ksu'yeya, v.a. To hurt, injure, inflict pain on. Ksúyewaya.

kśa, adj. Bent, rolled. Cf. yukśa. -- kśáka, adj. Bent up, as an aged person, decrepit. Makśaka. -- kśála, adj. Bent.

kśaⁿ, adj. Crooked. Kśa and kśaⁿ are probably the same root. R. -- kśaⁿkśáⁿ, red. of kśaⁿ.

kśaⁿ'kśaⁿ, v.n. To wriggle, as a fish.

kśaⁿkśaⁿ'yaⁿ, adv. Crookedly.

kśaⁿyaⁿ', 1) v.a. To make crooked, to crook, bend. Kśaⁿwaya. 2) adv. Crookedly.

kśi'ja, adj. Bent, doubled up. Cf. yukśija. -- kśijáhaⁿ, part. Bent up, doubled up.

kśikśa', adj. Numb, stiff with cold.

kśikśaⁿ', adj. Crooked.

kśikśe', adj. Makśíkśe, Makśikśe s'elececa, I am tired. Bl. Cf. kśikśa.

kśikśe'ca, adj. Numb. Nape makśikśeca.

kśikśe'ya, v.t. To make tired, tire out. Owekinaś kśikśeciyiⁿ kte lo, Perhaps I'll make you tired. Bl.

kśiś, cont. of kśija. Kśiśic'ilaka, To regard one's self as bent up.

kśto or kśt, suff. It is affixed to verbs, emphasizing a fact about which others have a doubt or know nothing of. Thus: ecamoⁿ kśto, kepékśt. It has the force of an emphatic assertion, implying that the thing which is asserted has been doubted. Nakuⁿ lece śna waceye kśto, eyiⁿ na, Kuwa, kuwa, eye. Cf. kiśto.

kśu, v.a. To bead things e.g. a saddle blanket, moccasins etc. Ak'iⁿ kśupi, hanpa kśupi etc. Wakśú. Na ilazatanhan can eya śayapi ca wiyaka kśupi. Hena (i.e. wiyaka) wapaha na wahukeza ko el kśupi kte lo. MS.153.

kśunka'ḣyakel, adv. In a deceiving manner. Same as zomiyankel. KS.

kta, particle. Indicates futurity: to be on the point of something when.... Hecel waglinawapin kta, yunkan eyapaha unhe leya.... Lepin kte ḣcin ehanl. Kta, yunkan, ehanl, tka ecanl: but just then. -- Indicates also intention: to do something intended, expressed by the future. Yunkan anpetu wan el wicaśa unpin omani iyayapi kta.

kta, v. To wait for, to neglect doing and expecting another to do. Wakta. -- ktáḱa, v. To wait, expect another to act. Waktaka. Seemingly only the 1st pers. is used.

ktan, adj. Crooked, curved. Cf. yuktan. -- kt̔ankt̔án, adj. Crooked, as a tree. Same as śkośkópa. -- ktanktánḱiya, v.a. To bend, to make somebody bend himself. Ktanktanwakiya. Cuwi ktanktankiyin na taku kakyela wakśica el ohinḣpaya. -- ktanktánḱiya, adv. Crookedly, indirectly. -- ktanktányan, adv. Crookedly. Also, ktanyán.

kte, v.a. To kill anything; to overcome one in a game. Wakte. Cf. makteka. When two Indians were fighting, the one would say: Mato wakte ḣce; the other, badly beaten, replied: Mato makte ḣce.

kte, v. Same as kta.

kteḱi'ya, v.a. To cause to kill. Ktewákiya.

kte'la, v.a. To overcome, be victorious over, to win, beat. Waktela.

ku, v.n. To be coming home or back, to come towards home. R. Waku. Unkupi. Unci, he ku wo. Ate, waku śni kinhan, miye cekiya wicaśa kin le wanji u kta. Leci ku wo.

ḱu, (?). - k'el tanyan śni, Something is wrong in the lower parts, as in a wagon. Bl.

ḱu, suff. pron. His, hers, etc.

ḱu'ciyela, adv. Low down, low of stature, short. Yunkan hinhan wan - ḣ'anhiya kinyan iyaya. Wi - ḣcehanl. D. 209 and 227.

ḱu'ja, adj. Sick. Makuja.

ḱuka', adj. Rotten, tender, worn out, as clothes; spoiled, as meat. Hehé haámakuke lo.

ḱuḱe'ya, 1) v.a. To make rotten; to wear out. Kukewaya. 2) adv. Rotten, spoiled, decayed, fallen to pieces. - śpan, To be cooked too much.

ḱuḱu'śe, n. A hog, hogs, pork. - śin, Fat pork, pickled pork. - wigli, hog's lard.

ḱul, adv. Below, under, beneath, down. - ḣpaya. -- ḱulḱúciyela, perhaps adv. red. of kuciyela. Paha - yukelo. Maḣpiya - kaḣwóg au welo. Bl. -- ḱúlḱul, adv. red. (of kul). Below, under, beneath, down. - ḣpayapi. -- ḱúltḱiya, adv. Downwards.

Kul'wicaśa, n. prop. The Lower Brule. - iyak'oza wan yuhapi.

kun, v. To covet. Cf. kon.

ḱun, n. Mother-in-law. Nikún, Your mother-in-law. Kúnku, His or her mother-in-law. -- ḱúnkśitku, n. Cf. kunśi. -- ḱúnku, n. His or her mother-in-law.

ḱun'śi, n. Grandmother. Nikunśi, Your grandmother. Kunśitku, His or her grandmother. Cf. unci.

kun'tkunta, adj. Grooved.

ḱunya', v.a. To have for a mother-in-law. Kunwaya.

kun'za, Cf. konza.

ḱuse', v.n. To leak, as a vessel. R. Bl.

ḱuse'ton, v.a. To bar, stop. Kusewaton. - najin. B.H.155.4.

ḱuś, cont. (of kuja). Inactive, feeble. - amayan, I am growing feeble.

ḱuśe'ya, 1) v.a. To put in the way of, to stop something e.g. a ball. Kuśe-waya. B.H.78.12. 2) adv. In the way of. - uⁿ, inajiⁿ, egnaka. Kuśéciya, I am in your way.

kuśi'paton, v. (?). Caⁿ kuśipawatoⁿ kte lo. Bl.

kuśle'ca, n. The kingfisher. Another word for hoyazela. From this the name Kuśleca Wakpa comes. Bl. R. -- Kuślé-ca Wakpa, n. prop. The Loup fork of the Platte River of Nebraska.

kuś'i't'a, v. (of kuja and it'a). To die or be dying of laziness, to be very lazy. Kuś'imat'a.

kuś'koⁿ'za, v. To pretend to be sick. Bl.

ku'ta, adv. Low down. - gla yo. MS.356. Lel paha waⁿ yaⁿka...yuⁿkaⁿ - lila ta-taⁿka na pte otapi. Oyate - uⁿpi el lila cajeyatapi. - ahiwatoⁿwaⁿ. MS.355. -- Kútagleya, adv. Downward. Pa - i-hpeya, To throw one down head foremost. Bl. -- Kútakiya, adv. Downward. Ito-kśaⁿ towicaya na pahte el - icazo na tapoⁿ kiⁿ anoⁿkataⁿ ecel ecoⁿ na iku el oyasiⁿ hecel owicawa. -- Kútaⁿhaⁿ, adv. Under, as one under the other while wrestling; from below. Ikce wi-caśa kiⁿ lila - ehakela at nicagapi heoⁿ.

kute', v.a. To shoot anything with a gun or arrow. Wakúte.

ku'tkiya, adv. Downwards.

ku'wa, v.a. To follow after, chase, hunt; to treat or act towards one evil or good; to pursue, prosecute e.g. a piece of work. Wakuwa.

ku'wa, v. imp. Come here. - yo, po. The word is used in the imperative only. Kúwi ye. D.71, note 2.

ku'wab, adv. Downward. Wi - ya ca na iśta kiⁿ lemaceca yelo; aogi amayelo. BT. Kuwapa as an expanded source of the word is doubtful.

kuwa'ciⁿ, v. To think of coming home.

ku'wapica, adj. Manageable. P.

ku'ya, adv. Below, beneath, under, un-derneath; down. Pb.27. -- Kúyataⁿhaⁿ, adv. From below.

k'a, v.a. To dig e.g. the ground. Wa-k'a. Ic'ic'a, To dig for one's self. Kicic'a, To dig for another. Wecic'a. Maka ekta ciscila wak'elo. B.H.108.17. Maka k'e k'oⁿ.

k'a'najiⁿ, v.n. To refuse to do some-thing. The idea is, one would suppose, taken from a boy who while being pull-ed digs his feet in the ground for support.

k'e, v.a. To dig. Same as k'a.

k'e'ga, v. To grate, scrape. Wak'ega.

k'eh, cont. of k'ega. -- k'ehk'éga, v.n. red. (of k'ega). To have a rat-tling in the throat, as anthing chok-ed to death. Wak'ehk'ega. -- k'ehk'éh, cont. of k'ehk'ega. -- k'ehk'éhya, adv. In a scraping manner etc.

k'el, cont. (of kiⁿ and el). There. Waⁿna ob toka iyayapi k'el glipi. Na yuśtaⁿ k'el lecel eya. Htayetu k'el eyapaha waⁿ u. Na kośkalaka kiⁿ hpaye k'el okśaⁿ enajiⁿ. Also, c'el.

k'e'leś, cont. of he é k'eś. Hé e - , as is said when recognizing something that one lost. Bl.

k'es, cont. of k'eza.

k'esk'e'za, adj. red. (of k'eza). Smooth, trodden down.

k'eś, adv. If. Hecoⁿ k'eś wakasaksa-kiⁿ kte. Also, even, as for me. P. B.H.68.20;229.8. Ablezapi k'eś kolá-kiciyapi waśte kiⁿ heuⁿcapi tka yelo. MS.649. He é k'eś, as is said when recognizing something lost. Bl. Cf. k'éleś.

k'e'ya, pron. adj. Some, that kind. Caⁿpá - etaⁿ hiⁿhpaya. Yuⁿkaⁿ tokeya paⁿgi - wicakipazo. Na iⁿyaⁿ - śakpe agli. Yuⁿkaⁿ taku - cikcik'ala ca el (caⁿwakśica) okala.

k'e'yaś, cont. Although, but. Cf. ke-c'eyaś. Keya kiⁿ nuⁿwaⁿ niuⁿ, - oya-te kiⁿ iś t'a keyapi. B.H.253.11.

k'e'za, adj. Hard, smooth, trodden down.

k'e'ze, adj. Short but hardy. Wicaśa - . Also, k'eza, which cf. R.

k'iⁿ, v.a. To carry, bear, carry on the back. Wak'iⁿ. Kic'iⁿ, To carry one's own. Śuⁿkawakaⁿ waⁿji wawateca ca tohaⁿl aya ca na k'iⁿ mawani kte lo. B.H.113.4. BS. indicates that k'iⁿ means to carry on one's shoulders, whereas kic'iⁿ, to carry on one's back. But this may be doubtful. -- k'iⁿkiya, v.a. To cause to carry. K'iⁿwakiya. B.H.102.6.

k'iⁿ'napa, v. (of k'iⁿ and nape). To run away with, as a horse with a wagon.

k'o, n. The noise created by making hum, buzz, by bustling, talking together etc. Na waⁿna k'o hiⁿgla.

k'o'ǧa, v.n. To rattle, make a rattling noise. -- k'oȟ, cont. of k'oga. - iyeya. -- k'oȟk'óǧa. v. red. of k'oga. -- k'oȟk'óȟ, cont. of k'oȟk'oga. -- k'oȟk'óȟya, 1) v. To cause to rattle, to make a rattling noise. k'oȟk'oȟwaya. 2) adv. Rattling.

k'oⁿ, cont. art. Same as c'oⁿ and k'uⁿ. Cf. k'uⁿ.

k'osyē'la, adv. Smoothly. - yuⁿka, i.e. smooth as a floor.

k'ō's'e, adv. Apparently, all gone; perhaps noisily. - éyaye c'oⁿ miyeś ehakela ble c'oⁿ taȟca waⁿ kaⁿyela uⁿ k'oⁿ wao welo.

k'oyē'la, adv. All, everything. - éwicayaya, They, i.e. the cattle, every one of them disappeared, not one can be seen. Cf. hutipak'oyela. - glasota, i.e. he says the last word, or eats up one's last. Caⁿli kiⁿ - henala, i.e. not a bit left. - akiyagle, i.e. all the thunderstorm clouds passed by. Bl.

k'u, v.a. To give anything to one. Wak'u. Kicu, To give one his own. -- k'ukiya, v. To cause to give. K'uwakiya.

k'uⁿ, def. art., or dem. pron. That, referring to the past, to something done or said before, to some person or thing mentioned in a previous sentence. When the word immediately preceding changes "a" or "aⁿ" to "e", c'oⁿ is used. K'uⁿ he. K'uⁿ hena. K'uⁿ hehaⁿ. Ehaⁿl wikośkalaka k'oⁿ t'a. Niye el taku ecoⁿ mayaśi k'oⁿ hena waⁿna wagluśtaⁿ. Tokel yaciⁿ k'oⁿ ecel ecamoⁿ. SI. Huⁿhuⁿhe, miciⁿkśi oⁿśiwakila k'oⁿ. Ake tokel ecoⁿ k'oⁿ ecel ecoⁿ. Taku ciⁿpi kiⁿ ecawicayecoⁿ kta kehe k'oⁿ. Ate, ahitoⁿwaⁿ yo, hóuciciye ca nayaȟ'oⁿ kta kehe k'oⁿ. Tokel waⁿbli waⁿ amai k'oⁿ na tokel icimani wai k'oⁿ he ecel owaglaka. Taku waⁿ taⁿke mak'u k'oⁿ he nape ogna bluha. Nitakola k'oⁿ miye. Note: Following a verb, the word seems to make it past time; I did it, or I have....Thus: Lecaś ecamoⁿ k'oⁿ, i.e. someone asks a person a second time to do a thing which he already had done. Heś nila yeś waȟteyalaśni k'uⁿ, Why, he is the one you rejected when he wanted you. D.204. Ehaⁿni owakiyake k'oⁿ, I thought I told him long ago. BD. Monday k'oⁿ hehaⁿ waⁿciyaⁿkiⁿ kta waciⁿ, I wanted to see you last Monday. Hehehe, he mitawa śni, owalote k'uⁿ, eye. B.H.116.4. Hinúⁿ, ótaś k'iⁿ s'a k'uⁿ, How funny, he used to carry more than that. D.115. Also note: While k'uⁿ generally stands as the past form of the definite article, at times it furnishes the "whereas" in a compound sentence; thus, Whereas you commanded me to take nothing, I took an owl. Cf. k'oⁿ.

k'uⁿhaⁿ', adv. When. This always refers to past time. It becomes c'oⁿhaⁿ after "e" which has taken the place of "a" or "aⁿ".

k'uⁿ he'haⁿ, adv. When. Uⁿkipi - . Nahaȟci honikśila - . Wicat'a haⁿhepi el wicayaȟa - . Niteca - , When you were young. B.H.35.4;271.1;121.6; 127.20;276.6. -- k'uⁿ hehányaⁿ, adv. coord. conj. So long. Thus: Na tohaⁿyaⁿ yugal uⁿ - Amalekites kiⁿ napewicayapi. B.H.56.1;96.2;156.1;124.10; 129.20. -- k'uⁿ hetáⁿ, adv. conj. From e.g. a place. Yuⁿkaⁿ Wakaⁿtaⁿka maȟpiya śape - ho taⁿiⁿ na heye. B.H. 56.19.

k'u'śi, v. To comand to give. K'uwaśi.

k'uwa'ciⁿ, v. To be disposed to give. K'uwácaⁿmi.

*

la, v.a. To ask, demand. Walá. Kila, To ask for one. -- v.a. To form an opinion of, whether good or bad; to think of or esteem in any manner; to take for. Wala. The word is used esp. with waśte and śica. Wakaŋtaŋka la. B.H.267.10.

la, 1) suff. It seems to make a word a superlative, Very. Śicela, Very bad. Kolapila, uŋgna nayapapi kilo. Cepela, Very fat. Ḣ'aŋhila, Very slow. 2) dim. suff. It terminates pronouns, adjectives, verbs and adverbs. When suffixed to numeral adjectives, demonstrative pronouns and adverbs, it signifies "Only"; thus: waŋjila, Only one; henala, Only these.

labya', adv. Very much so, intensely, as working or giving something very good. Labyelo. - waecoŋ.

laḣ, abbrev. of laḣca, perhaps; suff. (?). Waciŋlaḣ. Huŋhe, lote waśicuŋlaḣ. Bl.

laḣcaka, suff. particle. Very. Tataŋka ota ópilaḣcakelo. BT. Noŋge caŋ oyaglukse laka he wapaŋhe laḣcake c'oŋ. Bl. The Santee, in order to express the superlative to a verb, adds "ḣca", Very. But, the Teton inserts the "la" and "ka", so that we have added to the verb laḣcaka. D.57, note 1.

lak̇a', v.a. To have an opinion of. Waláka. Waśte walaka, I think well of him. Hecetulaka.

lak̇a, adv. enclitic. Much, rather. Also lake. Wicaśa taŋka laka, i.e. rather old, oldish. Kakiśyaye laka, i.e. rather much. Heya hotaŋiŋ laka. B.H.69. 12;104.22;106.15;256.10;120.13;227.10.

lak̇a or laka, encl. suff. Implies a question: Why don't you? Waŋkál étoŋwelake, He looked up, i.e. without the others knowing it to infer "Try". Waŋkal etoŋwelaka, Look up, why don't you. Tokiya egnaka laka, Where did you ever place it anyhow? Cf. yelaka. Noŋge caŋ oyagluksa laka he wapaŋhelaḣcake c'oŋ. Omawani kta, kohaŋ śkaŋlaka yo. Tate waŋ iyosniyaŋ uye lo wasu hiŋhiŋ kte laka. Bl. Yugnayelaka, He must have missed him, or evidently missed him. D.84. Takowe miye heci wai ktelaka, How in the world could I go do such a thing? D.279. Cf. D.101. Ie laka yo. B.H.211.7;212.9;261.14. Icimani k'uŋ el ilaka caŋ ayaśtaŋ iyeyi na heya ke, The instant the traveler reached him he stopped shouting and said to him. Cf. note 2. Laka is an enclitic which, added to any active verb, means: The instant he did so and so. It is always followed by caŋ, Then.

lak̇aś', adv. Indeed, truly, of course.

lak̇e, adv. encl. (of laka). Rather. It follows an adjective. Wicaśa taŋkiŋkiŋyaŋ lake eya. B.H.83.3. - ci, or - ciŋ, Pretty much, rather. B.H. 67.7;134.18. Ateca lake ciŋ, The younger people. B.H.283.6. - s'e, Apparently pretty much. Kaipazilya - s'e haŋ, i.e. is a little higher than the others. Kaipsilyalakes'e iŋyaŋka, i.e. running a little ahead of the others. Bl. Hotaŋka - s'e. Kaoḣ'aŋkoya lake s'e. B.H.108.5;148. 18. -- lak̇el, adv. encl. (of laka). It forms an adverb of manner. Cf. tokel okihilakel. Grammar,187.

Lak̇ōl', adj. prop. Lakota. - ia, To speak Lakota. - iẃaya. -- Lak̇ólk̇iciyapi, n. A Lakota confederacy.

lak̇ol'ya, v.a. To be friendly with, to have for a friend. Lakolwaya.

Lak̇o'ṫa, n. prop. The Dakota.

la'ṗa, adj. Smooth, level. -- láṗela, adj. Level, as a floor; smooth, as a face without wrinkles. Ite wicalapela k'el éceka yelo. Bl.

laṫa'k̇uwaciŋ, v. To make much of a little thing, exaggerate, in jesting. Syn.- lawicoḣ'aŋwaciŋ. WE.

lawico'ḣ'aŋwaciŋ, v. To make much of a little thing, to exaggerate in jesting. Lawicóḣ'aŋwacami. WE. Syn.- latakuwaciŋ.

laza'ṫa, adv. By the side of, behind. -- lazáṫak̇iya, adv. Backward. - mani. B.H.9.14. -- lazáṫaŋhaŋ, adv. Back, behind. Cokaŋ huŋḣ t'a ḣpayapi na nakuŋ - huŋḣ ḣpayapi. Oglala kiŋ huŋḣ waziyata aya na ake ḣelazataŋhaŋ aya.

le, pron. This. It may be placed before the noun or after the article. Le wicaśa kiŋ, or Wicaśa kiŋ le. --

adv. Here; now. Le na ti po. Yuⁿkaⁿ mini el noⁿwaⁿ na, le wanoⁿwe lo, eya na le iyuha ecoⁿ po. Le kiⁿyela uⁿyaⁿpi kte lo, hiyupo, eya. Oyate waⁿ le wicoti kiⁿ lena nitawa kta. Ate le u kta keya, eya. Le yaglapi na taⁿyaⁿ wol' niglaśtaⁿpi hehaⁿl....

lē, particle. It is used by women, when men say "lo". Hinu, onapuza ca haⁿpi cola wówahe le. BT.

le'ca, pron. Such as this. B.H.171.17.

leca'kcala, adj. New, as a new suit. Hayapi - .

le'caǩicioⁿ, v.a. (?). Caⁿ teca kiⁿ el lecakicioⁿpi kiⁿ, tokeśke caⁿ śeca ecakicioⁿpi kta hwo? B.H.265.17.

le'caǩicoⁿ, v.a. To do thus to. Lecawecoⁿ. Lecauⁿkicoⁿpi. Perhaps the same as lecakicioⁿ.

le'caǩioⁿ, v.a. To do this to. Lécawakioⁿ.

leca'la, adv. Lately, a little while ago; soon, perháps.

lecaś', adv. Just a little while ago. - lel hi na iyaye.

le'ce, Same as lécel. Nakuⁿ - śna waceye kśto, eyiⁿ na, Kuwa, kuwa eya.

le'ceca, adv. Like this, such as. Lececapi. Lemaceca. He kiⁿ heca waⁿ el wicowoyake waⁿ - . Íśtiⁿmapi na oikpaȟicapi kiⁿ - sehiⁿgle. B.H.39.4.

le'cegla, adv. Close, as standing close to. Wópate waⁿ - icicaⁿyaⁿ hiyeye kiⁿ, eye śke. -- léceglala, adv. Only this close; this is all. Na uⁿgna tahenakiya hiyu na - kaťōnauⁿk hiyaya ca akiś'api. Yuⁿkaⁿ itagleȟwetaⁿhaⁿ śuⁿka wakaⁿ ota au na - ahinajiⁿ na najiⁿpi. MS.148. Wana - ca wagluśtaⁿ kte.D.56.

le'cekceca, adv. red. (of lececa). Such as these.

le'cekcel, adv. red. of lecel. -- lécekcelya, adv. red. of lecelya.

le'cel, adv. Thus, after this manner. -- lecéla, adv. This alone. -- lécelya, adv. So, thus.

lece'tkiya, adv. This way, pointing out the whole road. The word is different from letkiya. Oyate kiⁿ - igláka eyaya ca etkiya uⁿgni kte lo. MS.54.

le'ceťu, adv. Thus, so, right; this is right. Oyate oyasiⁿ le - na hehaⁿtaⁿ waniyetu opawiⁿge śni makoce le waⁿblaka. -- léceťuǩel, adv. In this manner.

le'ceya, adv. This is so, right now, really, certainly. D.8 and 32. - , kola, kapsiⁿtapi s'e śkiⁿmic'iye lo. BT. - caⁿte matakuni śni yelo. Bl. Toke - caⁿte iyuȟpa niwanica hwo? Bl.

le'ci, adv. Here, in this place. Na waⁿna - wakpala waⁿ opaya ata akinajiⁿ el ake lecel eya.

leciⁿ', v. To think that. Hecel el iyotaka na - : Le wicaśa kiⁿ takuwe isto saⁿni wanica hwo? eciⁿ. MS.143.

le'ciya, adv. Here, about here. -- léciyaťaⁿ, adv. From this. -- léciyaťaⁿhaⁿ, adv. From this place, on this side.

leci'yotaⁿ, adv. In this direction. -- lecíyotaⁿhaⁿ, adv. In this direction, this way.

le'coⁿ, v.a. To do this, act in this way. Lécamoⁿ. Le iⁿśe oyate wowicawak'u kta ca - . - s'e, In this manner; like doing this; hence, thus. Topa akigle oblake ciⁿ - s'e ecoⁿpi, Just as I have described it, this was done four times. D.199 and 106. MS.163.

le'e, v. This is it. This, and also hee and ee, contain the substantive verb.

le'ǧa, adj. Glittering. Bl.

lehaⁿ', adv. Now, thus far; at this place. -- léhaⁿhaⁿ, adv. red. of lehaⁿ. Śuⁿksi kośka s'e śaké - , i.e. when nails are unusually long. Bl. -- leháⁿhaⁿǩeca, adv. red. of lehaⁿkeca. -- leháⁿhaⁿla, adv. red. of lehaⁿla. -- leháⁿhaⁿyaⁿ, adv. red. of lehaⁿyaⁿ. -- leháⁿkalkaťaⁿhaⁿ, adv. (?). Oyate - ahipi, i.e. people from other countries, foreigners. B.H.34.3. -- leháⁿkaťa, (?). Cf.

wicaśa - , A foreigner. B.H.27. -- lehaŋḱeca, adv. So long, so high, so short. -- leháŋl, adv. Same as lehaŋ. -- leháŋleś, adv. Nowadays. - héceca, It is like that nowadays. Sbj. -- leháŋtaŋhaŋ, adv. From this.

lehaŋ'ṫu, adv. To this, thus far; now. B.H.15.23. -- leháŋṫuḱel, adv. Just so far, in this way; just now. -- leháŋṫuya, adv. To this extent, on this wise. -- leháŋṫuyaḱel, adv. Just now, on this wise. -- leháŋyaŋ, adv. So far, in space; so long, in time. Na hehaŋtaŋ waŋna waniyetu ota itahena eśa - nahaḣci yuhapi, i.e. wawakaŋ. B.H.102.15. -- leháŋyaŋk, adv. Away, somewhere else, apart. - iyaya. Oyate - uŋpi kiŋ, Other people, people living in other places. - egnaka. B.H. 83.6;123.2;201.14 and 24;271.14. -- leháŋyela, adv. Thus far, just now.

lehiŋ'cita, adv. So often, again and again, more than expected. - iyuŋgahe. Cf. kitatala. B.H.77.12. - iyuŋk yapi, They travelled often lying down. D.2. Perhaps from lehaŋic'ita.

lehiŋ'yagleya, adv. Until this day. B.H.280.8. Perhaps from lehaŋ and iyagleya.

leḣle'ġa, adj. perhaps. red. of lega.

lei'c'iya, v. (of leyá). To say this to one's self, as at the beginning of a quotation. B.H.22.18.

le'ja, 1) v.a. To urinate. Waleja. 2) adj. (?). Leś waciŋtaŋka, i.e. one who does not have to urinate often. Bl. -- léjapi śni, n. Inability to urinate, a sickness known to the Sioux. Bl.

leki'ya, v. To say this to one. Cf. ekiya and hekiya. B.H.16.19;169.9;178.2.

lekśi', n. Mother's brother; uncle, my uncle. One's father's brother is called até. Nilékśi. -- lekśiṫku, n. His or her uncle. -- lekśiya, v.a. To have for an uncle. Lekśiwaya.

lel, adv. Here, in this place.

le'na, pron. pl. (of le). These.

lena'gnaḱeca, adv. red. of lenakeca.

lena'ḱe, Cf. lenakeca. - mic'iksapelo, That much I save for tomorrow.Bl.

lena'ḱeca, adv. So many, so much. Lemánakeca. Leuŋnakecapi. Pb.28.

lena'ḱeḣciŋ, adv. All these. Also, lenakeḣci.

lena'la, adv. Only so many, so few.

lena'na, pron. red. of lena. B.H.62.10.

lena'os, adv. These two, both these. -- leniṫos, adv. Both these. Also, leniyos.

le'ogna, adv. Around here. Also, lógna. Hihaŋna kiŋ le ogna u kta ca kokipe śni oyuspa po.

lepca', v. 1st pers. sing. (of le and epca). I thought this. Note: No other form is used.

leśle'ja, v.n. red. (of leja). To urinate often.

leṫaŋ', adv. From this place, from this time; after, the Latin post. Ca - waŋna tuktogna iyonicipipi kiŋ ogna iyaya po. - waniyetu topa kiŋ oyate waŋ ahi kta keye lo. - topa caŋ kiŋhaŋ hehaŋl.... Syn.- letaŋhaŋ. -- leṫáŋhaŋ, adv. From this place or this time. Lemátaŋhaŋ.

le'tka, (?). Maletka, I am "broke".Bl.

le'tkiya, adv. This way, pointing towards one's self. - u wo.

le'ṫu, adv. Here, at this place or time. Literally, now. -- léṫuḣca, adv. Just here.

leya', v. To say this. Leṗá. Lehá. Leúŋḱeyapi. - hoyekiya. B.H.212.8. - hoyeya. B.H.86.7;215.5. - óstegla. B.H.95.4. - owa. B.H.175.16. - oyaka. B.H.69.8. - ṗaŋ. - omani. B.H.172.5. - wacekiya. B.H.100.20.

li'glila, adv. Very. An emphasized form. - lúzahaŋ, húŋkeśni, ohitika, iyuŋka, iŋyaŋka, wowaśi ecoŋ. Bl.

li'la, adv. Very. - kaḣmi waŋ waśte.

li'laḣ, adv. Exceedingly. Also, lílaḣci.

li'laǩa, adj. Being good on something, i.e. skillful e.g. in running etc. Malílaka.

li'lakel, adv. Very much. B.H.66.4.

lili'ťa, n. A children's word for white man. Bl. - uⁿyaⁿpi kte; whereas another would say to the children: Go to town.

liťa'śkaⁿ, v. To get busy. Litawaśkaⁿ. Bl.

lo, n. Food. Soft, tender, moist stuff e.g. fresh meat, or soft hide. Tahálo saka kaksapi waciⁿ śni, lo ca waciⁿ yelo.

lo, particle. It is used at the end of a sentence or phrase, for the sake of emphasis or euphony. Men say lo, or yelo; women, ye. Na le tuwa hwo? ecaⁿnipi nacece lo.

lobya', adv. Cf. lolobya. - śpaⁿ.

lociⁿ', v. To want food, be hungry. Lowaciⁿ. Loúⁿciⁿpi. -- lociⁿpi, n. Appetite. -- lociⁿya, v.a. To cause to feel hungry e.g. by speaking of good food.

lo'gna, adv. This way or in this manner. Cf. hógna. - yakagege kta.

loǧu'ťe, n. The hollow of the flank of man or beast.

loȟe', n. The parts of the cheeks and throat which are loose and not fastened to the bones. Gills. B.H.122.26.

loi'gni, v. To hunt food. Also, loligni. Loiwagni. Mini yuśpala loiwagni yelo, Perspiring I am looking for food. Bl.

lolȟwa'ǩa, adj. Unable to eat much. Lolwaȟwaka. Bl. The word is used when a man wants to eat more than what he got. Syn.- lolwazaze. Bl.

loli'cupi, n. Issueing food, rations.

loli'gni, v. To look for food. B.H.181.5.

loli'ȟ'aⁿ, v. To prepare food, to cook. Loliwaȟ'aⁿ. Haⁿpa cicagapi naiⁿś lolicicíȟ'aⁿpi kta ca wau we.

lolo', adj. red. (of lo). Soft, damp, fresh.

lolob'ya, 1) v.a. To boil soft e.g. meat, corn etc, to cook until tender. Bl. Lolobwaya. D.12. 2) adv. perhaps. Tenderly, very tender. It is said of meat well cooked. - śpaⁿ, Cooked tender. -- lolōbyapi, n. Meat, beans etc. cooked so that they are very soft, overboiled. Lhb. -- lolóbyela, adj. Soft, very soft.

lolo'p̣a, adj. Soft. Among the Teton, the word does not seem to have the meaning of "miry".. -- lolóp̣ela, adj. Too soft, flabby. Used of over-ripe fruit.

lolwa'nagi, (?). - yewaye c'uⁿ taⁿyaⁿ wíyewaye lo, i.e. has his full. Bl.

lolwa'zaze, (?). It is said when a man wants to eat more than what he got. Bl. Syn.- lolȟwaka.

lol'i'jicayakel, adv. Having many provisions. - uⁿ welo. Bl.

lol'i'yucaⁿ, v. To have hardly anything to eat. Bl. Also perhaps, lol'iyucaⁿka.

lol'o'petoⁿ, v. To buy grub. B.H.208.2.

lol'ō'p̣iye, n. A leather bag to keep meat etc. in.

lop̣a', adj. Soft; doubtfully, miry.

loťe', n. The throat. - ayáskabyapi, A neck-band, wanap'iⁿ.

loťe'ogmus yuza, v. To throttle.

loťe' ona'ȟnaȟna, v. To have a rattling in the throat. Lote onámaȟnaȟna. Also, lotónaȟnaȟnaȟna. WE.

loťe' p̣o'pi, n. A sickness of the throat, swelling which the Sioux knew. Bl.

loťe' waśicuⁿ, n. One who desires to eat very much, very often. Bl.

lotǩu', n. The throat of man and animals; the part immediately under the jaw.

loťkuⁿ'ǩeśni, adv. perhaps. It corresponds to the English "Oh" when, while talking one forgets something and it comes to mind: Oh! I wanted to tell you.... - wociciyakiᶯ kte. Also, just "Oh!"

loťo'gmus yuza, v.a. To seize by the throat, to throttle. P. Bl. Cf. lote ogmus yuza.

lowaᶯ', v.n. To sing. Walówaᶯ. -- lowáᶯp̄i, n. Hymns; singing. -- lowáᶯwaᶯ, v. red. of lowaᶯ. B.H.140.1.

lowi'ťaya, adv. All fresh, raw, as meat. - icu, yuha iyoȟpeya yo. Bl.

loya', adj. Moist, not dry; fresh, as meat. -- loyáǩe, adj. Fresh, not dried. - uᶯ. -- loyáǩel, adv. In a moist condition.

luglu'ta, adj. red. of luta. Bl.

lul, adv. (of luta). Red. -- lulúťa, adj. red. (of luta). Red. It is used in speaking of leaves turning color. -- lulyá, v.a. To color or paint red or scarlet e.g. porcupine quills. Lulwaya. Siᶯte lulyapi, The red-tail deer. SI.

lu'p̄i, adj. perhaps. Dangling. Bl. Cf. yulúpi śni, and walúpi śni. Syn.- woyá.

lus, adv. Swiftly. - ya, To go fast. -- lusǩíya, v.a. To cause to be swift. -- luslúzahaᶯ, v. red. of luzahaᶯ. -- lusmáni, v. To walk fast. Lusmawani. BT. Lusmani po, Walk fast; in opposition to Mani glapo, Walk slowly. Bl. -- lusyá, v. To make swift. Luswaya.

lu'ťa, adj. Red, scarlet.

lu'zahaᶯ, v.n. To be swift, fast running. Malúzahaᶯ. Nilúzahaᶯ.

*

mă, interj. For calling attention: Look here! Attention! It is used by women. D.78, note 2.

ma, pron. obj. Me. It is also used with a class of neuter and adjective verbs, when it is translated by the nominative I; and with some nouns it is used as the possessive, My, mine.

maca', n. Another name for śuⁿkmanitu.

maǧa', n. A goose, geese. The word may also be, perhaps, maȟ'á.

ma'ǧa, n. A cultivated spot or field.

maǧa'ǧaic'iya, v.n. To be amused, amuse one's self. -- maǧáǧak̇iya, v.a. To amuse, comfort one. Magagawakiya. -- maǧáǧaya, v.a. To amuse, divert one. Magagawaya. Thus: magagaic'iya.

ma'ǧahu, n. Cornstalks.

maǧa'ju, 1) n. Rain. 2) v.n. To rain. -- maǧájuk̇iya, v.a. To cause to rain. Magajuwakiya. -- maǧájumini, n. Rain-water. -- maǧájuya, v.a. To cause to rain, cause rain. Magajuwaya.

maǧa'k̇iciyapi, n. A pastime in which boys taking a swim will dive and grab somebody's leg and say: Maga niciⁿca tonakeca hwo? The aggressor will push the other under so many times. The game is announced by saying: Maǧá úⁿyaⁿpó. Then all dive and try to grab somebody.

maǧa'ksica, n. A duck, ducks, i.e. the general name. They say: Magá, magá, magá. Bl. - agli wi, The moon when the ducks come back, April.

maǧa'ska, n. The swan. Also, maǧáska taⁿka. - s'e ahiyaye, To pass by dressed in white.

maǧa'śapa, n. The common wild goose, the Canadian goose. Also, maǧáśapa taⁿka, The black swan. A woman teasing her brother-in-law would say while she goes: Eyiⁿ nahaⁿ magaśapa ca mániye s'e kagle (i.e. with a waddling gait). Bl.

maǧa'śekśecala, n. The brant. R. A big white water bird with bill about 3 in. long like that of a crane, and tall as it with legs 2 dm. long. - s'e ho waśte, as they would say of a fellow with a good voice. Bl.

maǧa'śniyaⁿla, n. The red-headed duck. Also the name for other ducks. Maǧá-śniyaⁿyaⁿla ȟupahu skaska, The red-headed duck. The word is applied to other ducks as well. - ikceka, The black duck. - iśtóȟlate ska, The blue winged teal. - nawáṫe to, The green winged teal. - pa to, The bald-pate duck. Magaśniyaⁿyaⁿla ȟota, The gadwall duck, a wild duck about the size of the mallard.

maǧa'ṫa, adv. At or in the field.

maǧa'taⁿk̇a, n. A goose. The swan. R.

maǧa'taⁿka u, n. Swellings on the back or elsewhere with matter therein. EM. Bl.

maǧa' taśuⁿpe, n. A swift, round and black waterbug. A long-legged bug that walks on the water. Bl.

Maǧa' Wakpa, n. prop. The Laramie River.

maǧa' wapa'ha, n. (?). - iwekcu ktelo; and now I shall go begging from house to house: tiiyaza tiole ayiⁿ kte.Bl. Cf. wapaha.

ma'ǧa yuśla', v. To weed a field.

maǧi'cahiⁿṫe, n. A rake, a harrow.

maǧi'camna, n. A hoe, hoes. Also perhaps, maǧ'i'camna.

maǧi'yublu, n. A plow.

maǧi'yuhiⁿṫe, n. A rake, harrow.

mahe', prep. Within, in, into. Maka - iyemayelo.

mahel', prep. Within, in, into. Same as mahé. Caⁿ - . Tipi kiⁿ - haⁿ, i.e. in the snow pile. -- mahélhel, prep. red. (of mahehe). - iyaya, To go up and down behind something, so that the head disappears and appears again, as children do. Syn.- yusnisnis. WE. The word is fundamentally from mahel. B.H.36.5.

mahel'hetuya, adv. red. of mahetuya.Bl.

mahe´logle, n. An undershirt.

mahe´luŋzóġe, n. Drawers, undershorts.

mahe´lwapa, adv. Inward, towards the interior.

mahe´ṫaḱiya, adv. Towards the inside, inwards. Na ake waŋji o, tataŋka, ca na he hiŋ kiŋ - ihpeyapi. Hecel waŋna ouŋ waśteicíyapi.

mahe´ṫaŋhaŋ, adv. On the inside, as is something lying a ways under or among other things. Timahetaŋhaŋ, In the house. Minimáhetaŋhaŋ, In the water.
mahe´ṫaṫaŋhaŋ, adv. From inside, from within.

mahe´ṫu, adv. Within, inward; deep.
mahe´ṫuya, adv. Deep in. Yuŋkaŋ - o. Hecel taku oŋ (an arrow) opi kiŋ, lila - iyayiŋ kta. MS.481.
mahe´ṫuyalake s'e hiyáya, v. To go into, e.g. a crowded room, and pass through all to find a place. Bl.

maḣ, cont. of máġa and maġá.

maḣa´ḱata, v. To hoe e.g. corn. Manawakata.

maḣciŋ´ca, n. The young of geese and ducks.

maḣgla´gmi, v. To clear off e.g. weeds from a field; to cultivate, to hoe. Maḣwaglagmi.

maḣi´cahiŋṫe, n. A rake or harrow.

maḣi´yublu, n. A plow.

maḣi´yuhiŋhe, n. A harrow, a drag.

maḣi´yuhiŋṫe, n. A rake, a harrow.

maḣḱa´śla, v. To hoe a field.

maḣḱi´caŋyaŋ, v. To work or till a field.

maḣṗi´ḣpiya, n. red. (maḣpiya). Scattering clouds.

maḣṗi´ohaŋzi, n. A shadow caused by a cloud. - ahi.

maḣṗi´ya, n. The clouds, the sky, the heavens; Heaven.
- ayáskapa, n. An isolated cloud. Maḣpiya ayaskapa wanice, Not one cloud is visible. Bl.
- śáṗa, Black clouds.
- śóka, Thick clouds.
- śpuśpu, Long broken clouds.
- tacéjiksica, Little white clouds scattered over a part of the sky. To the Indians, this looks like the thin layer of fat covering the paunch.
- taŋiŋ, The northern lights, the aurora borealis. When this sort of event took place, the Indians would paint their faces, sit up all night and burn leaves as incense.
- to, The blue sky.
- tola, The clear sky, blue sky.

Maḣṗi´ya To, n. p. The Arapahoe Indians.

maḣṗi´yohaŋzizi, n. perhaps. The passage of clouds, at intervals obstructing the sunlight. Bl.

maḣta´ni, n. An old field.

maḣ'a´waŋglaḱe, n. A cicada or harvest fly; the seventeen-year locust. So called because it is doing nothing but singing all day and apparently watching the fields. Also, maḣ'áwaŋglakela. BT.

maḣ'o´wiŋje, n. A corn husk tick. Wi.

maḣ'wa´ṗajiŋ, v. To have the ducks against one's self, i.e. unable to kill any while others kill aplenty. Maḣ'wamapajiŋ yelo. Bl. Cf. maga, wapajiŋ.

maḣ'yu´śla, v. To make a field bare, i.e. to pull weeds. Maḣ'bluśla.

maka´, n. The skunk or polecat. Also, maŋká. - ciŋcala, A young skunk.

maḱa´, n. Ground, earth, the earth. - namaḣ'oŋ, as they would say touching the ground in taking an oath. If one should then tell a lie, he was sure to stumble with his horse. - naniḣ'oŋ he? Ómaka, A season, winter or summer; a half-year season. Omaka tahena Scili kiŋ ake śuŋkawakaŋ wicawakiyelo. Cf. wakiŋyaŋ.
Maḱá aḣ́śniśni s'e mani, To walk lightly and without noise. Bl. BT.
Maḱáblu, Dust.
Maḱácaḣli, Coal.

Makácanákpa, A flower, the lady's slipper. It is eaten. BE.
Makácanśinhu, The prairie pink, a rush-like lygodesmia. Lygodesmia Juncea. Composite family. It can be chewed. A tea made of the whole plant is supposed to stop the diarrhoea of children. WE. # 143. BT. Cf. canhlogan hu can swula. A leafless plant.
Makáceġa, An earthen vessel or pot.
Maká ceyaka, Lance-leaved sage. Salvia lanceolata. Of the mint family. #159.
Maká ceyaka iyececa, Lemon mint. Monarda citriodora. #289. This was new to the State herbarium.
Makágle, adv. End on the ground. Same as makegle. R. Canpeśka - inajin.
Maká gleśka, The little spotted skunk; the civet cat.

maka'gleya, v.n. To fall down, as a long stick, endwise. Canpeśka - inajin To kneel.

maka'gna, adv. (of maká and ogna). Same as tehan. - tehan yahi śni, i.e. you let us wait for you very long. Inyankehanla ilale c'un - yaun welo, Although you went away running, you were there very long. Bl. - lakes'e, Very slowly, late. Bl. Kiktayo, kiktayo, - lakes'e tehan nunkelo, i.e. as is said when a person sleeps too long. Bl.

maka'heya, v.a. To finally accomplish what one has long desired. Iśpá kic'unyan makahewayelo, i.e. I killed him. Bl.

maka'hlihlila, n. Mud. Also, makahlihli.

maka'ik'e, n. A pick axe.

maka'iyuhloke, n. An auger to dig post holes. R. Bl.

maka'iyu'ksaksa, n. A cultivator.

maka' iyupte, n. A breaking plow. R.Bl.

maka'iyuta, v. To measure land, to survey. -- makáiyutapi, n. A measuring-chain, surveyor's chain; an acre of ground, perhaps.

maka' kiciinpi, n. The mud and willow game. Bl.

maka'k'ak'a s'e, adv. Pawing. - najin, i.e. shuffling with the feet, as it were, pawing the ground. Bl.

makal', adv. On the ground. - hpaya.

maka'mani, n. and v. A pedestrian, one who travels on foot. Makamawani.

maka'mani in'yanka, v. To ride a bicycle.

maka'nongeya, v. To know it already, as if having the earth as an ear. Makanongewaya. Ehanni nawahon welo; maka kin nongewayehcelo, as an old saying goes. EM.

maka'oi'yute, n. A piece of surveyed land, an allotment, i.e. a quarter, half, full section etc. The size of it is defined by adding śokela etc. Tamáka oiyute, His allotment. Cf. makaowaśpe.

maka' ok'e, n. A dug-out, pit. Also, makók'e. -- maká ook'e, n. An old cistern. B.H.27.20.

maka'opaśpe, n. A measured tract of land.

maka'ośpe, n. An acre. WI. Bl.

maka'owan'ke, n. The bobolink. A little bird, so called because it has two white stripes over the back, from head to tail, like a skunk; otherwise the bird is black, and lives near water among bulrushes. Bl. Also, makaowankela and manká zintkala which cf.

maka'owaśpe, n. A piece of measured, surveyed land, defining the size by adding śokela, okise etc. Cf. makaoiyute. Also, makowaśpe or makopaśpe.

maka'pa, n. A skunk's head.

maka' pte, n. Buffalos made of clay to play with as a pastime. Bl.

maka'san, n. Whitish or yellowish clay.

maka'sanpa, n. Next year, next season.

maka'sitomni, n. The whole world. -- makasitómniyan, adv. All the world over.

maka'suhula, n. Sandy soil.

maka'śpaŋ, n. A brick. Bl. -- makáśpaŋyáŋpi, n. A brick.

maka' śuŋkawakaŋ, n. Horses made of clay to play with.

maka'ta, adv. At the ground, on the ground; on the floor. Na waŋna wahiŋkpe kiŋ - glihaŋ. -- makátakiya, adv. Towards the earth. - amayuta yo, i.e. as the Indians prayed to God.

maka'tanasula, n. A kind of soil with whitish streaks, a clay perhaps, that boys used for making clay horses. Bl.

maka'teca iyu'blu, n. A breaking plow. EB.

maka' tipi, n. A cellar, a sod house.

maka'to, n. Blue earth. Hence, Mankato, a city in Minnesota.

maka'tomnica, n. The trailing wild bean. Strophostyles helvolva. Also, omnica, and Lakota omnica. #111.

maka' to'oyuze, n. A place this side of the Powder River where the Indians got blue earth to paint with. Bl.

maka'wakśica, n. Earthen plates or dishes.

maka' wana'kajata, adv. Long ago. -- maká wanákajataŋhaŋ, adv. Long ago. -- maká wanákaś, adv. Long ago. Bl.

maka'wase, n. Red earth used as paint. -- makáwase śa, Red earth, used by the Dakotas as a paint instead of vermillion.

maka'yublu, v. To plow.

maka'zi, n. Brimstone, sulphur.

maka' ziŋtkála, n. Same as maŋka owaŋke. FR.

make'glakiŋyaŋ, adv. Across the earth. Only this form is used, although one would expect the form, makáglakiŋyaŋ. - omani, To come from afar, from far away. Sb.

maki'cima, n. A two-year-old horse. Also, a young horse only a few years old, in opposition to one that is old (kaŋ).

maki'cinoŋ, v. (of manoŋ). To steal anything for another. Mawecinoŋ.

maki'glata, v. To take much leave. Tuwa - iyahe tokel iyayelo, as is said if a man came on foot and wanted to stay a few days, but then suddenly disappears. Bl.

maki'gleya, adv. Endwise; downwards, perhaps. Pa - , With the head downward.

maki'gluksaŋ, adv. To go around the world, to go very far. - omawaniyelo. Makókawiŋh is much the same. - owakawiŋge. Bl.

maki'haŋke, n. The end of the world. BT. Bl.

maki'inaskilye, n. A roller.

maki'kablaska gli'hpeya, v.a. To beat flat to the ground. B.H.239.1.

maki'kacoco, n. A machine for mixing mortar, cement.

maki'kaśpe, n. A pick axe.

maki'kceka, n. The land, as opposed to water; soil, as opposed to clay or gravel; the layer of good soil, as opposed to sand etc. below the humus. Loam. P. - ic'iuŋ. -- makíkceya, adv. On land.

maki'naksaksa, n. A harrow.

maki'napte, n. A spade. -- makínaśpe, n. A spade.

maki'noŋ, v. (of manoŋ). To steal, take back secretly what one has given. Mawákinoŋ.

maki'pabluya, adv. Raising dust e.g. by falling. - ihpeic'iya, To throw one's self into the dust. B.H.64.10.

maki'pahlala, (?). - wakiŋyaŋ ukiye lo, i.e. storm clouds all along the horizon and coming towards one. Bl.

maki'papte, n. A shovel. Spade. R.

maki'pasise, n. (of maku). A breast pin.

maki'pastoya, adv. (?). - ihpeic'iya.

B.H.215.7.

maǩi'ṗusǩica, v.n. (of maka and ipuskica). To press on the ground, lie flat on the ground. -- maǩíṗusǩil, cont. of makipuskica. - iȟpeic'iya, To throw one's self on the ground. -- maǩíṗusli, adv. With the face on the ground, prone. -- maǩíṗusliya, adv. Bowed down to the ground.

maǩi'saŋpa, n. The next season.

maǩi'waŋyaŋke, n. A compass; a surveyor.

maǩi'woȟliya, adv. perhaps. Sticking tight in the ground. Tawahukeza kiŋ oŋ akigna - cawapiŋ kte lo. B.H.89.13.

maǩi'yagle, (?). - yuziŋ na akaŋ iȟpeic'iya, i.e. hold it, i.e. the sword, against the ground and throw himself on it. B.H.90.22. -- maǩíyagleya, adv. To the ground, to the earth. Ozaŋ kiŋ - okinaȟlece. B.H.268.7.

maǩi'yaǩasaŋni, n. A side or part of a country.

maǩi'yapa, v. perhaps a. To hit the ground, as in falling. Makiyawapa. Ite makiyamapa. B.H.59.2.

maǩi'yap'oya, adv. perhaps. Raising much dust. - upi, i.e. they raise much dust as they are coming. Bl.

maǩi'yeya, (?). Wicaśa - yuŋka, i.e. sick and foresaken. Bl. Cf. makóǩaȟciyela.

maǩi'yoǩiṗi, v.n. To be acclimated, to like it in a certain country. Bl. -- maǩíyoǩiṗiya, v.a. To acclimate. WI. Bl.

maǩi'yublu, n. A plow. - iwoju, A lister. EB.

maǩi'yuhiŋhe, n. A cultivator.

maǩi'yuhiŋte, n. A harrow.

maǩi'yuȟloǩe, n. An auger to dig post holes.

maǩi'yupťe, n. A breaking plow; the wheel or cutter of a breaker.

maǩi'yuťaŋ, n. (of maku and iyutaŋ). A cinch, a saddle girth.

maǩi'yut'iŋze, n. A surcingle, girth.

maǩo'blaye, n. A plain.

mako'cajeyate, n. The direction on a letter.

maǩo'ce, n. A country, a place.
- átaŋiŋ, A mirage.
- iwaŋyaŋkapi, Surveyors.
- oihaŋke, A globe.
- oṗaśpe taŋka, A country. P. Bl.
- owapi, A map, maps.

mako'gmigma, n. A globe. P.

maǩo'ȟloǩa, n. A hole in the ground, a cave. - waŋ el mahel iyaya.

mako'icago, n. A boundary line of land. B.H.39.18.

mako'ǩaȟciyela, (?). - ȟpaya, i.e. nobody looks after him. Bl.

mako'ǩawiŋȟ, adv. Around the world. WE. Syn.- makigluksaŋ.

maǩo'ǩocaŋku, n. A road with fences on each side. BT. Bl.

mako'k'api, n. A bulwark, an intrenchment. P.

maǩō'k'e, n. A dug-out, a pit. B.H. 108.25.

mako'mnica hu, n. James' cristatella; the earth bean. Cristatella jamesii. The caper family. D.97. Bl. #57. -- makómnica hu ȟoȟóta, n. The silky sophora. Sophora sericea. The pulse family. #301.

maǩoŋ'caǧe, n. A season, the seasons.

maǩo'ṗaśpe, n. (of maka and opaśpe). A section of land.

mako'p'oya, (?). - upi, i.e. raise much dust while coming. Bl.

maǩo'sǩaŋ, 1) adv. For naught, in vain. 2) n. A place where no one dwells.

maǩo'sǩaŋl, adv. In the wilderness; doubtfully, for naught or in vain. Yuŋkaŋ hihaŋha el wicaśa k'oŋ iśnala - auŋyaŋpi śke. Waŋna lila tehaŋ iśnala - uŋpi keye. B.H.180.15. -- mak̇ósk̇aŋṫu, adv. and n. Desert-like, away from trees or dwellings. -- mak̇ósk̇aŋṫuya, adv. Away from any dwelling. -- mak̇ósk̇aŋṫuyak̇el, adv. In a desert place.

mak̇o'smak̇a, n. (of maka and osmaka). Any low place, a ditch.

mak̇o'śica, n. Bad land, desert.

mak̇o'śice peji Ḣota, n. The long-leaved mugwort. Artemisia longifolia. The composite family. It is found in the Bad Lands. Bl. #144.

mak̇ō'śla, n. Bare ground. D.205.

mak̇o'tahe'na, adv. Far from any dwelling. Bl.

mak̇o'wak̇ic'iṗa, n. A place or little hollowing, a light hollow or depression in the prairie.

mak̇o'waŋca, n. All the earth. -- mak̇ówaŋcaya, adv. All over the earth.

mak̇o'wapi, n. A map of a country; maps.

mak̇o'waśṗe, Cf. makaowaśpe.

makṫe'k̇a, explic. That kills me, i.e. overcomes me. Lit.: ma-kte-ka, as a person or thing. It is used by one loving irresistibly a person or catching a fancy for something. Nikteka. Syn.- imácuka.

mak̇u', n. The breast.

mak̇u'ak̇aḣpe, n. A bib, a napkin.

mak̇u'hu, n. The breast-bone. The sternum.

mak̇u'ipatitaŋ, n. A breast strap, going between the forelegs.

mak̇u'nusnuŋja, n. The lower extremity of the breast-bone.

mak̇u'ṗiŋkṗa, n. The end of the breast, the part just above the navel.

ma k'e'ya, interj. Rediculous! It is used by women in answer to a remark considered foolish or rediculous. B.H.43.25;111.13. Cf. waŋ k'eya.

mak'e'yak̇e s'e, adv. Apparently unwillingly. - ayuśtaŋpi.

ma'ma, n. A woman's breast.

ma'ni, v.n. To walk. Mawáni.

mani'ca, v.n. 1st pers. (of nica). I have none.

ma'nihaŋ, part. Walking.

ma'nik̇el, adv. Walking.

ma'nik̇iya, v.a. To cause to walk. Mániwakiya.

manil', adv. Abroad, away from the house; into the wilderness. - ya. - tehaŋl eiḣpeya wicaśi. B.H.50.25.

ma'nióṗawak̇iŋyela, n. The spotted sandpiper.

mani'ṫak̇iya, adv. Disappearing from camp. - iyaya. Kośkalaka k'oŋ he (wanagi) Ḣeyab iyaya na - gla, i.e. to disappear from the camp without giving a reason why, for doing something wrong apparently. Bl. MS.166. Hece - tacejikśica k'u wo. MS.55.

mani'ṫuk̇ala, (?). Children playing run around in one line zigzag holding a shawl up behind, making it look like a tail and sing: Manitukala sinte onamaśloke. Bl.

ma'niyaŋ, adv. Walking. Maka gi oyuze el wicoti na etaŋhaŋ zuyayapi maka - . Hecel nupiŋ - uŋpi. Cokata - wauŋ. -- mániye s'e, (?). A woman teasing her brother-in-law would say, when he goes: Eyiŋ nahaŋ maga śapa ca - kagle. Bl.

manoŋ', v.a. To steal anything. Mawánoŋ. Mauŋnoŋpi. -- manóŋpi, n. Stealing, theft.

maŋ, interj. Look here! Also, ma! -- maŋ, le maŋ, exclam. One of surprise when seeing something used by women. Cf. waŋ, le waŋ, used by men. Bl.

maŋka', v.n. 1st pers. sing. of yaŋka.

maŋka' ziŋtkala, Cf. makaowaŋke. FR.

ma'ṗiḣ'a, n. A toad. Syn.- witápiḣa,

matapiȟ'a.

masce'ga, n. Cf. maza cega.

masi'caśpe, n. A chisel.

masi'waⁿyaⁿke, n. A telescope; field glass; a microscope.

masƙa'p̄e or maskáp̄a, n. (of maza and kapa). A blacksmith. B.H.302.9. Cf. mazkápe. Note: there is question of the p̄ .

masƙiⁿ'sƙa, n. Cf. mazakiⁿska.

mas'a'hi, v. To arrive with freight, as iron goods were often with what they hauled to the agencies. IS. Mas'áwahi.

mas'a'papi,caⁿ, n. A telephone post.Bl.

mas'caⁿ'wapaika, n. A check strap.

mas'caⁿ'yapa, n. A bridle. - ikceka, A riding bridle. -- mas'cáⁿyapa ikú swu, A bridle bit, with dangling ornaments. LB.

mas'i'cicaȟaȟa, n. Iron made in links, a chain. Also, perhaps, mas'íćicaǧaǧa, hence from maza ici kagaga.

mas'i'gmuⁿke, n. A trap. Cf. cap'igmuⁿke, from capá.

mas'i'ƙuśe, n. A buckle. P. Bl.

mas'i'yume, n. A file.

mas'p̄e'p̄e, n. Barbed wire.

mas'wa'kśica, n. Tin plates.

mas'wi'cayeǧe, n. A sewing machine. Note: the "y" instead of ǧ.

mas'wi'coⁿpi, n. A frying pan.

mas'wi'yogli, n. A steel to sharpen knives on.

mas'wi'yokataⁿ, n. A nail.

mas'wō'gnaƙa, n. Canned food.

maśe', n. A man's brother-in-law. It is used if they are on very good terms. Sbj. Cf. waśé, a woman's sister-in-law. Syn.- taⁿháⁿ. -- maśéya, v.a. To have for a maśe, brother-in-law. Syn.- taⁿháⁿya.

ma'śke, n. A friend. It is used by women as men say kóla. -- maśkéya, v.a. To have, i.e. for a woman, for a female friend. Maśkéwaya.

mā'śleca or maya'śleca, n. A coyote.

maśťe', adj. Warm, hot, as applied to weather.

maśťe'aglihaⁿ, v.n. To get a sun-stroke. Maśteamaglihaⁿ.

maśte'caⁿhaⁿp̄a, n. Slippers; warm-weather shoes.

maśte'ƙo, n. A little grayish bird. Its call as it rises is: oosh-oosh-oosh. BE. Cf. maśtekola.

maśte'ƙola, n. The iśtanica taⁿka, the horned lark. The name is derived from maśteko, To desire warm weather. The Indians called it that because there would be good weather (warm) whenever it went straight up into the air singing: Maśte ko. Bs. Cf. ptehiko, oȟ'aⁿko, osniko. Cf. the Handbook of Birds of the Western U. S., by Florence Merriman Bailey, p.247.

maśťe'napťapťa, n. Hot waving air, as on a hot day over a field, or over a stove.

maśťe'osni, n. Clear and cold; cold and bright.

maśťe'śťe, adj. red. of maśte.

maśťe't'a, v.n. To be killed by heat.

maśťe' wapośtaⁿ, n. A summer bonnet.

maśťe'ya, adv. In a warm state, warmly. -- maśťéyaƙel, adv. Warmly, hotly.

maśťiⁿ'ca, n. The rabbit. -- maśtiⁿcala, A rabbit.

Maśtiⁿ'cala Wicaśa, n. prop. The Cree Indians. Also, Maśtiⁿcala ha śina iⁿ. Bl.

maśtiⁿ'ca pute', n. A bush bearing red edible berries, the buffalo berry. -- maśtíⁿca puté caⁿ, The buffalo berry, the rabbit berry. Argentea oleaster family. Bl. #223. -- maśťiⁿca puté hu caⁿ, n. The buffalo berry bush.

maśťiⁿ'sap̄a, n. The common rabbit, the cotton-tail rabbit. Also, maśtiⁿsapela. -- maśťiⁿska, n. The hare or jackrabbit. The prairie rabbit. Bl.

maťa'p̄iħa, n. The toad. D. spells the word: matápeħ'a. D.47.

maťe'ťe, n. (of tete). The side or rim, the edge of anything e.g. creek, table etc.

mato', n. The gray or polar bear. - s'e sicuha ħolyeħci, as is said when the soles of one's shoes are worn out.Bl.

Mató ciⁿcála, A bear's cub.
Mató ħoťa, The grizzly bear.
Mató kiciyapi, A game played by boys. The boy acting the bear hides in the bushes while the hunters are outside holding switches. He goes for them, iyaħpaya, tickling them while they hit him with their switches. Mato miniśośe kiⁿ hehaⁿyaⁿ uⁿkuwapi, as was said. Bl.
Mató taspáⁿ, n. The round-leaved hawthorn. Crataegus chrysocarpa. It is seen in the Bad Lands. RO. #256.
Mató tatíⁿpsila, n. The large bracted psoralea. Psoralea cuspidata. The pulse family. Bl. says it has the same qualities as the auⁿyeyapi. It is also a medicine. Bl. #217.
Mató ťip̄ila, n. A constellation of eight stars, as they say, standing in a circle. The gemini, Castor and Pollux,are prominent among them. BT. denies this name. Mh.

maťu'gna, n. The crayfish. Also, matuśka, Crawfish. - s'e ti śikśica, as they say of one who has a poor house. - ok'e uⁿyiⁿ kte, for their claws were boiled and treated with grease, whereupon they turned red and were used for ornaments. - kiⁿhaⁿ mini awakaśtaⁿ ktelo, i.e. thirsty. Bl.

maya', n. A steep place, a bank e.g. of a river.

ma'yaca, n. A name for śuⁿkmanitu.

maya'gliheya, n. A steep bank. Yuⁿkaⁿ mni kiⁿ okigluslece na itamuⁿk - s'e yuⁿke, na ocokaⁿyaⁿ ocaⁿku kaħya pusyela he. - kiⁿ ataya iⁿyaⁿ. D.29.

mayal', (?). Ozuye taⁿka k'uⁿ - yewicaye. MS.563.

ma'yaśle, n. A small species of wolf, the jackal.

maya'śleca, n. A coyote. OE. Also, máyaśleca. WL. Máyaślecala s'e ite sok'iⁿyaⁿ, as they said of a man with a small face. Bl.

ma'za, n. Metal of any kind.

- agléħaⁿ, An anvil. Also, - aglehe.
- aglíheya, To print. - aglihewaya.Bl.
mázablaska, A flat iron.
mázacaħ'íćazo, Skates.
mázacaⁿku, A train, a railroad.
máza cáⁿku p̄etíjaⁿjaⁿ, A conductor's lantern.
mázacaⁿku tipi, A railroad car. RH.
mázaceġa, An iron pot, a kettle.
mázaceśkikaⁿ, Metal buttons.
máza cola wiħaħ'oⁿ, A radio. Also, ikaⁿcola mas'áp̄api, or ťatúye oⁿ wíħaħ'oⁿ.
máza eglé, To set a trap; to put up a store. Bl.
mázaħlaħla, A bell.
mázaiciyokihe, A chain.
mázaiyokaťaⁿ, Nails.
mázaiyokatkuġe, A nut, iron nuts for bolts.
mázakaġa, A worker in metal, a blacksmith. Cf. maz'kape.
mázakaⁿ, A gun, rifle. Tona - luhapi oyasiⁿ u po.
mázakaⁿ i, The muzzle of a gun, the barrel of a gun. P.
mázakaⁿ i núⁿpa, A double-barreled gun.
mázakaⁿ íyopazaⁿ, The tubes or ferrules which hold in the ramrod; the ramrod.
mázakaⁿ iyópuħli, Gun-wadding.
mázakaⁿnawaťe, The plate of a gunlock; the lock of a gun. P.
mázakaⁿnoġe, A gun lock, esp. the pan, the nipple.
mázakaⁿpahu, The breech of a gun.
mázakaⁿ śup̄úťe, The butt of a gun.
mázakaⁿ úta, To shoot, fire off a gun.
mázakiⁿskа, An iron spoon, spoon.
mázalowaⁿkiyap̄i, A talking machine.
mázamna, Smelling of iron. - s'e woyaka, as is said when someone speaks of his serious troubles and difficulties that are hard to listen to, as when using harsh words. BE.

mázanapsiohli, Finger-rings.
mázaoceti, An iron fire-place, a stove
mazápa, To telephone. Mazawapa.
mázapepe, Barbwire.
mázapośla, A tack with a big round head, something like a thumbtack.
mázapsonpsonla, Wire.
mázasapa, Black metal, iron.
mázasiiiahtake, A spur.
mázaska, Money, white metal; silver; a dollar.
mázaska aónatake, A safe.
mázaska el ahígle, To bet. Bl.
mázaska igní, To raise money. P.
mázaska kamná, To raise money. P.
mázaska kpánla, Currency, change.
mázaska ógnake, A pocket book, a money bag. Mazáskaognake, A safe.
mázaska omnáye, The treasury.
mázaska wanáp'in, A silver medal.
mázaska wanjíla, One dollar.
mázaskazi, Gold, yellow silver.
mázasu, A bullet, bullets; shots, cartridges.
mázasu íśloya, Something to melt lead in.
mázasu íyokaśtan, Bullet molds.
máza sutá, Steel.
mázaśa, Copper, red metal.
mázaśala, A penny. The penny which a person receives who is appointed to collect money for the fourth of July celebration.
mázaśkanśkan, A clock, a watch.
mázaśkanśkan íkan, A watch chain and fob.
mázaśkanśkan tanka, A clock.
- śkópa, A hook.
mázaśloyapi, Pewter. So called because it is used for running on the bowls of Dakota pipes.
mázaśunkákanyanka, A bicycle.
mázawakan, A gun, rifle.
mázawakan śupúte, The butt of a gun.
mázawakan úta, To shoot a gun, fire off a gun.
mázawakśica, Tin or iron pans.
mázawiyowa, A pen. Can wiyowa, A pencil.
mázawiyúhomni, A jack-screw. Bl.
mázawiyute, A carpenter's square.
- wiyuwanka aya, A jack-screw. Bl.
mázawoyuspa, Pincers, tongs. Bl.
mázayajopi, Brass instruments; a brass band.
mázazazéca, Screen wire.
mázazi, Copper, yellow metal.

ma'zcanyapa, Cf. mas'canyapa.

ma'zicukeya, n. A chain.

mazi'wanke, n. abbrev. An opera glass or telescope.

mazi'wanyanke, n. A telescope. Also, maziwanke. Na - yeyapi.

mazi'yapa, n. A hammer.

mazi'yuhomni, n. A wrench. Also, a screw driver; a drill to make holes with.

mazi'yuhloke, n. A can opener. -- maziyúhloke, n. A drill to make holes into iron.

mazi'yukce, n. A trimmer's snip.

mazi'yuwi, n. Bridle bits.

mazkin'ska, n. An iron spoon.

mazo'piye, n. A store. - wicaśa, A trader, a merchant.

mazo'yuspe, n. A pliers.

ma'z'icakse, n. A chisel.

maz'i'gmunke, Cf. mas'igmunke.

maz'i'pame, n. A file.

maz'i'yokatan, n. A nail.

maz'ka'pe, n. (of maza and kapa). Cf. maskápe.

maz'o'ceti, n. A stove.

mi, pron. pos. in comp. My or mine; me; for me or to me. Thus: mikte, He kills for me. Cf. ni.

mica', pron. and prep. in comp. (of kica). For me. Opemicaton, He buys for me.

mica', n. The hip-bone. According to TT., this does not refer to the lean meat on the side of the animal near the rump, as R. translates it. BD. says we use instead tamíca and tamícahu.

mi'caga, v. (of kicaga). To make to or for one.

mica'hu, n. The bone near the hip-bone. R. Bl.

mi'caki, n. The bone near the hipbone. Also, micáhu. R.

mi'caksica, n. A small wolf. Cf. mi'yaca, mi'yaśleca.

mi'capeca, n. Porcupine grass; needle, spear or devil's grass, a grass armed with a long sharp beard. Stipa spartea. The grass family. WE. RH. - ota kiŋhaŋ, waniyetu waśme kte. #178.

mi'capeca oŋ kici'opi, n. A mischievous pastime in which boys would take a bunch of devil's grass (micapeca) and, to hurt those without coats on, throw it on them. Bl. Syn.- wicapeca.

mi'ci, pron. with prep. (kici). For me, i.e. not with me. Mici uŋ, In my stead or for me; kici mauŋ, With me. Witaŋśna uŋ num omak'u po; hena caŋnuŋpa miciyuhapi kte lo.

mici'caya, Cf. kicicaya. Pb.45.

mic'i', pron. refl. Myself. Mic'ikte, I kill myself, i.e. for myself. Mic'icaga, I make for myself, or I make myself. Cf. nic'i', ic'i'.

mignag', cont. of mignaka. - wauŋ.

migna'ka, v.a. To put in under the girdle e.g. a knife or hatchet; to wear around the loins. Miwagnaka. Hohumila waŋ - ; caŋke ikikcu. Uŋgna kapemniyaŋ micignake ci, i.e. boasting. D.33. Bl. Note: the word seems to be used usually with mila, or in ref. to mila.

mi'gnaka, v. (kignaka). He lays up for me.

mi'la, n. A big knife. Hohu - , A modern but old knife. Tablo - , A modern knife.

mi'lahaŋska, n. A long knife; an American.

mi'la kaś'iŋ, n. A sickle.

mi'lapaksa, n. Round-pointed knives; table knives; a case knife.

mi'laya, v.a. To have or use for a knife. Milawaya.

mi'liyuma, n. A grind stone.

mima', adj. Round, circular. Also, mimé.

mime'la, adj. Round, as a disc, but not as a ball, which is gmigméla.

mime'la wáȟcazi, n. The stiff or hard-leaved goldenrod. Solidago rigida. BT. #25. Cf. tal'agnake, caŋȟlogaŋ maka ayublaya, waȟpe ape blaskaska.

mime'ya, adv. In a circle. - najiŋpi.

mime'yela, adv. Round. - yuktaŋ. Bl. MS.349.

mi'na, n. A knife. Note: the word is used by the Tetons also. Cf. mila.

mini', Same as mni.

mini'mahel zuzeca, n. A water snake. Bl.

minio'huṫa aglágla waȟcazi, n. The stickseed, beggar's tick, beggar's lice; the stickseed sunflower, sticktight; pitchforks; bur marigold. Bidens glaucescens. The composite family. BT. #68.

minio'pakiŋyéla, n. A bird.

minio'pawakiŋyela, n. The spotted sand piper. Bl.

minisaŋ'tuhu, n. Schweintz cyperus. Cyperus Schweinitzii. The sedge family. LB. #247.

mini'wicagnaśka caŋ, n. (?).

miŋ'ska, n. A piece of tin to scrape hides with. BD. Note: there may be another name for this.

mi'oglas'iŋ, n. A mirror.

mi'ogle, n. A whet-stone. Note: deriv. mila and egle, To place, or ogle.

mio'juha, n. A knife-sheath.

mi'ska, n. Same as tahi'ŋcacice.

miś, pron. I. Miś miye.

miśna'ka, pron. I alone. - kes'e, As if I alone. Bl.

miśna'la, pron. I alone.

miśna'lakes'e, adv. and pron. As if I alone.

miśna'sanica, adv. On my side.

mita', pron. prefix. My, mine.

mi'tahe, n. A tomahawk-like weapon, consisting of a wooden handle and a number of knives sticking out to one side at the other end. Syn.- caṇmilokataṇpi.

mita'wa, pron. My, mine. Cf. tawa and nitawa. Nimitawa ktelo, You will be mine. Unitawapi kte. But these are doubful: Manitawa kte, I will be yours. and, Niuṇkitawapi kte.

mi'wakaṇ, n. A sword. - iyuze, The hilt of a sword. P.

Miwa'taṇni, n. prop. The Mandans.

mi'woṡtaḱe, n. (of mi and woṡtaka). A blunt-pointed arrow, i.e. one all of wood with the head thicker than the shaft, used to kill birds. Bl.

mi'yaca, n. The prairie wolf. Cf. micaksica.

mi'yaṗahe, n. Anything to cover the loins with, such as our Lord on the Cross had. - kitoṇ. -- miýaṗeheḱiya, v.a. To use as a cover for the loins. Ṡina - , To use a robe for a cover.

mi'yaṡleca, n. A small kind of wolf; the coyote. Cf. micaksica.

mi'ye, pron. I, me.

miye'ciṇ, Cf. miyeciṇka.

miye'ciṇḱa, pron. I myself. Syn.- miyecuḣci.

miye'cuḣci, pron. emph. I myself. Cf. miyeciṇka.

miyē'k'e, pron. emph. Even I, such a one as I. R. Bl.

miyē'k'eṡ, pron. emph. superl. I myself. R. Bl.

miyeṡ', pron. emph. I.

mi'yoglas'iṇ, n. A mirror, looking-glass; round mirrors fastened to a sash called ptaṇhá wanap'i', i.e. of otterskin. - hiyuya, To give a signal with mirror reflections. Bl.

mi'yogli or mi'ogle, n. A whet-stone.

Mi'yoglioyuze, n. prop. The Whet-stone Agency.

mi'yoḱaṡ'iṇ, n. The small of the back. Syn.- miyopawega.

mi'yokṡijaṗi, n. A pocket knife. - ope, The blade of a pocket knife. Also, miyukṡija.

mi'yoṗaweġa, n. The small of the back. Syn.- miyokaṡ'iṇ. Specifically, that part of the spinal column that is bent. Bl.

mi'yuġiṇġiṇ, (?). Agleṡka s'e - hiṇgla mani, i.e. as in walking, the skin wrinkles as a lizzard's. It is used with reference to old people.Bl.

miyu'ṫaṗaṗi mila, n. A kitchen knife, the upper point of which is missing. Bl.

M'mla, n. prop. A fabulous being Indian women used when putting restless children to sleep. Inila Ḣpaya; Mmla waṇ úwe. This is an old word whose meaning is lost. Syn.- ciciye, Ḣ'eyá. PD.

mna, v.n. To swell. Ṡupe mnala yelo. Cf. yumna.

mnahaṇ', 1) n. A rip. 2) part. Ripped of itself. -- mnaháṇhaṇ, red. of mnahaṇ.

mnaḣca'ḣca, n. The prairie lily. The word is perhaps not used.

mnai'c'iya, v. To gather for one's self. B.H.193.25.

mnaḱi'ya, v.a. To take up a collection for one; to gather one's own. Waḣpaye mnakiyapi. B.H.260.20.

mnayaṇ', v.a. To gather together, collect. Mnawaya. Mnauṇyaṇpi. -- mnayáṇpi, n. A collecting, collection. -- mnayéḱiya, v.a. To cause to collect. Mnayewakiya.

mni, Cf. yumni.

mni, n. Water. -- v.a. To lay up to dry, spread out in the sun to dry. Wamni'. -- v. 1st pers. sing. of ya. - kta, I will go. Ni kta, You shall go. The following are derivatives of mni, Water:

mniagláṗeṗeya, v. To make a flat stone skip on the water. Bl.

Also, mniáglapepeya. Mniáglapepewaya.
mniáḣaśṫaŋ, v. To baptize, pour water on. Br. WI.
mniáli, (?). Caŋhpaŋ - iŋyaŋke, i.e. moving over the water, using the wings. Bl.
mniápaḣta, 1) v. To carry water in a skin. 2) n. A skin bottle for water.
mniáp'eyela, n. Very shallow water. Bl.
mnicágla, adv. By the water.
mnicáḣmuŋ, n. The noise made by a stream flowing over a rocky bed. Cf. mnikahmuŋ. RTj.
mnicáluza, n. Rapid water.
mnicáśkilyela, adv. All wet, soaked, in the manner of pressing out water. - uŋkomanipi. Bl. Syn.- mniḣ'eḣ'eyela.
mnicáśniyaŋyaŋla, adj. or n. Rippling water. Mni kiŋ kaśniyaŋyaŋla yuŋkelo.
mnicátomni, n. A windmill.
mnićiya, v. To assemble e.g. a feast; to make a feast or call an assembly. Mnimiciya. Mniniciya. Mniuŋciyapi or mniuŋkiciyapi. Taku oŋ mniciyapi ca oŋ inaḣni oyate kiŋ witaya awicayau kte lo. Note: this word seems to be rather derived from, mni, I go.
mničóčo, adv. Slushy.
mnic'á, v. To dig for water. Bl. B.H. 49.20.
mnic'ápi, n. (of mni and k'a). A well of water, a spring; a little hole made where the water gathers more plentifully. Syn.- wiwiła. Also, minic'api.
mniǵa, Cf. yumniga. Not deriv. of mni water.
mnihiṗi s'e, (?).
mnihiẏaya, n. A flood of water.
mniḣáḣa, (?). Ísta - maŋke, i.e. water is running from my eyes. Bl.
mniḣúha, n. Linen or cotton cloth, calico; paper. Not deriv. of mni, water.
mniḣúha caŋnuŋpa, n. A cigarette.
mniḣúha ipatiŋ, n. Starch.
mniḣúha iyówa, n. A pen, pencil.
mniḣúha kakaŋḣa, n. Writing paper. Also, newspaper.
mniḣúha mazaska, n. Paper money.
mniḣúha mazaskaiċu, n. A bank check.
mniḣúha ogle, n. A shirt.
mniḣúha óhaŋzi, n. An awning, a shade.
mniḣúha opemni caŋnúŋpa, n. A cigaret.
mniḣúha ośṗúla, n. Pieces e.g. of calico etc. P. Bl.
mniḣúha owápi śni, n. A blank, blanks.
mniḣúha oyúḣlece, n. A rag. R. Bl. P.
mniḣúha paŋpáŋla, n. Silk.
mniḣúhaska, n. White cotton or muslin; white paper, writing paper.
mniḣúhaska śoka, n. Bed-ticking.
mniḣúhaska zibzipela, n. Fine muslin.
mniḣúha tóḣca, n. Blue cloth, as distinguished from green.
mniḣúha wanap'iŋ, n. A neckerchief.
mniḣúha wápaḣlate, n. Crape.
mniḣúha wiẏuma, n. Sand paper. P.
mniḣ'eḣ'eyela, adv. With the water dripping from one. - uŋkomanipelo. Bl. Syn.- mnicaśkilyela.
mniḣ'ić'iya, v. refl. To pay close attention to a certain thing. - yaŋka, To be silent and thinking, i.e. while others talk; i.e. so to sit, drawn up in a stooping position. Bl. - omani. But, cf. wákicokic'uŋ. Perhaps mniḣya is not used. Cf. yumniga.
mniićapsiŋpsiŋ, n. perhaps. The slashing rain. - hiŋhelo. Bl.
mniiẃosli, n. A water spout.
mniiẏatke, n. A drinking vessel, a dipper to drink with.
mniiẏokaśtaŋ, n. A pitcher.
mniiyósnisniyapi s'e, adv. In the manner of shrinking back from cold water. - taku tokoŋ, To work at a thing in intervals, hesitatingly, not knowing much about it. Lehaŋyaŋ wauŋ kiŋhaŋ mniyósnisniyapi s'e wauŋ. Bl. - ḣpaya. Doubtfully, mniyosnisniyaŋpi s'e.
mniiẏuḣepe, n. A sponge. B.H. 268.2.
mniiyúḣlogyápi, n. A flume.
mniiyúsli, n. A water faucet. Mniiẏusli, A squirt.
mniḣáataja, n. (of mni and taja). Waves.
mniḣáḣmuŋ, n. The roaring of waves.
mniḣákiciṗehaŋ, n. Rolling waves. B.H. 71.12; 203.6; 209.4.
mniḣákiṗehaŋ, Cf. mnikakicipehaŋ, which seems the better form.
mniḣáŋoju, of mni, kaŋyela and ojupi. Cf. mnikooju.
mniḣáośkokpa, n. A canyon made by floods.
mni kaṗóḣya hiyótaḣe, n. A blister.
mnikiẏupta, v. To make a ditch.
mnikiẏuptapi, n. A ditch.
Mniḣówoju, n. prop. The name of a band of the Teton Sioux.
mnil, adv. In the water.
mnil't'a, v.n. To drown, be drowned. Mnilwát'a.
mnil't'eya, v.a. To drown, cause to drown. Mnilt'ewaya.
mnináṗas hiyuye, n. A blister. P. Also, mninakáṗoḣ hiyuye.
mninátake, n. A dam. Also, mninatákapi.
mniógnake, n. A water pitcher. Also,

a large water tank or reservoir.
mnióhuta, n. The shore, the edge of a river. Hecel wakaŋ k'oŋ - el inajiŋ na haŋbloglaka.
mnióȟpaya, v.a. To rinse.
mníoícu, n. A made well. Syn.- omniowe.
mnióȟablaya, n. Water spread out, inundation.
mnióśkokpa, n. A gutter. Also, mniwóśkokpa. Bl.
mniót'a, v.n. To die in the water. Mniomat'a.
mnióť'eya, v.a. To cause to die in the water. Mniot'ewaya. Mnit'éic'iya, To drown one's self. D.45.
mniówamniyomni, n. An eddy.
mniówaŋca, n. The ocean, all over water.
mniówe, n. A well or spring of water. Also, a fountain of water. - aȟiȟicapi k'el, i.e. a certain spring somewhere near the Platte River. Bl.
mnipásli, n. A pump.
mnip̆átajapi, n. A water faucet opening by pressure from a pump-jack; a pump, perhaps. Syn.- mniyutajapi.
mnípataje, n. A pump. Syn.- mnipasli.
mnip̆éji, n. Slough grass.
mnip̆íǧa, n. Beer, ale; Seltzer or soda water. Bl.
mnísap̆a, n. Ink.
mnísap̆a ip̆ap̆uze, n. An ink blotter.
mnisáp̆a wicázo, n. A penholder.
mniskáŋmni, n. Water obtained by melting snow. - ota kta lo, as is said when much snow is expected to thaw.
mniskŭya, n. Salt. This word is pronounced slowly so as to make meaning differences clear. Hence, mnĭskŭyă, Vinegar; mnĭskŭyă, Lemonade, and also mniiskuya.
mniskúya ógnake, n. A salt shaker.
mniskúya oyúze, n. Salt lake.
mniskúyetoŋ, v.a. To salt. B.H.123.4.
mnisōl iyáya, v. To have gone never to return, as a man who went far away, or as horses lost, etc. Toké tokiyab mnisol ilaleȟce c'oŋ tohiŋni yagli so? BE.
mniśá, n. Red water, i.e. wine, cider or ale.
mníśośe, n. Turbid water. Mniśośe, n. prop. The Missouri River.
mniś'ēś'e, v.n. To sprinkle, fall in drops, as rain.
mnitácaŋku, n. A ditch, channel.
mniťáǧa, n. Foam, froth, spittle.
mnitáŋ, 1) v.n. To overflow, be flooded. 2) n. A flood. R. gives mnitáŋ; but, that the word is from mnitaŋka is highly doubtful.
mniťáŋya, v.a. To cause to flood. Mnitaŋwaya.
mnitáťe, n. Waves, as caused by the wind. Bl.
mnít'a, v.n. To drown. Mnímat'a.
mnit'éya, v.a. To drown.
mníwakaŋ, n. Whiskey.
mniwakáŋ ska, n. Alcohol.
mníwamnúȟ'a, n. Snails, periwinkles, which are used as ornaments. Tuŋslá ognake. R. Bl.
mniwáŋca, n. The sea, the ocean.
mniwáŋca okáȟmiŋ, n. A bay, a gulf.
mniwáŋcawaťa, n. A ship.
mniwáŋjila papsuŋ, v. It rains unceasingly. B.H.8.2.
mniwáśtemna, n. Perfume.
mniwátaǧe, n. Foam, perhaps. Syn.- mniwaticoga. Bl.
mniwáťicoǧa, n. The scum on stagnant water; water-moss.
mniwíťoye, n. A certain blue water dye.
Mni Woblú, n. prop. Fall River.
mniwóȟaȟa, n. A water falls. P.
mníwosli, n. A syringe.
mníwosli i, n. A nozzle.
mniwót'a, v.n. To be drenched, soaked with water. Mniwomat'a. Bl.
mniwŏzaŋ, 1) n. Fine, drizzling rain; a mist. 2) v.n. To drizzle. Cf. R. bozáŋ.
mníyapataŋhaŋ, adv. Next to the river, by the river, by the water.
mniyóȟcaya, adv. perhaps. (?). Ísta - waceyakiye, i.e. with eyes full of tears. B.H.127.18.
mniyóȟp̆aŋyaŋ, v. To soak in water.
mniyósniya, v. (?). Mniyósnisnikiciyapi ktelo. Hiya, mni kiŋhaŋ áp'eyela yuŋkelo, i.e. the water is very shallow. Bl.
mniyówaŋca, Cf. mniowaŋca.
mniyówe, Cf. mniowe.
mniyóweglepi, n. A well of water.
mniyúpiza, v. To drink noisely. Mniblúpiza. Bl.
mníyuśpála, n. A puddle, a waterhole. - loiwagni yelo, i.e. looking for food causes one to perspire. Bl.
mniyúśpaśpayela, n. or adv. perhaps. Little water pools. Magaju akisni; yuŋkaŋ - ota. Wakpa - opaya omawani yelo. BD.
mniyúśp̆aye or mniyúśp̆ayela, n. A pool. Note: temniyuśpala, Perspiring much. B.H.50.1.
mniyútaja, v. To pump.
mniyútajapi, n. A faucet; a pump jack. Perhaps also, a pump. Cf. mnipatajapi

and taja.
mnizí, n. Bile, which is accumulated in the stomach. Also, perhaps, beer, whiskey.
mnizícinca, n. (mnizi and ciŋ). A drunkard. Mh.

mnuǵa, v. To crunch, as a horse does in eating corn.

mnuȟ, cont. of mnuga. -- mnuȟmnúǵa, v. red. of mnuga. Cf. yamnúmnuga. -- mnuȟyéla, adv. In a crunching way.

mnu'mnus, v. To creak. - hiŋgla, To creak suddenly, as a piece of wood when one breaks it in two. LC.

*

na, prefix. It is affixed to verbs, indicating that the action is done with the foot; but less commonly it is also used to express the effects of frost, heat etc., as well as to suggest rapid motions e.g. of machines or spontaneous motions. Cf. náka, napca.

na, v. imp. Take it. Thus: Mak'u na. Wakalya na. It is added to verbs and used with anything offerred. However, Hohi', Take it. refers only to a burning pipe offerred. RF. In being added to verbs, it is employed the same as "ye", except that it is used by everybody. R. RF.

na, conj. And, moreover, also. People often say it twice in succession, one seemingly belonging to the first half of the sentence, the other to the second. Woligluśtaⁿpi na, na lecel eya. Waⁿna caⁿ wakaⁿ el egle na na waⁿkal kiya yugal najiⁿ. Also, To, that, the Latin "ut". This is expressed in two coordinated but not subordinated sentences. Thus: Okiyaka yo na ecoⁿ kte, Tell him <u>to</u> do it. Wicaśa num wicakico na wihuta yujuⁿpi.

naa'blaya, v. To make level by trampling on. Naawablaya.

naa'glapśuⁿ, v. (of aglapśuⁿ). To kick over. - eħpeya. Naawaglapśuⁿ. -- naáglapśuⁿyaⁿ, v. (of aglapśuⁿyaⁿ). To kick anything over. - iyeya.

naa'ƙaħliyeya, (?). Ceji - , i.e. to let one's tongue hang out, as dogs do in hot weather.

naa'ƙakciya, Cf. naakaś'iⁿyaⁿ. Bl.

naa'ƙamni, v. To cause to burst or spread out, as one's moccasins. R.Bl. -- naákamnitoⁿ s'e, adv. Burst open. - yaⁿka, as is said when the moccasins or leggings burst open. Bl.

naa'ƙaś'iⁿ, v. To bend backwards, as the written "t". - iyaya. R. Bl. -- naáƙaś'iⁿyaⁿ, adv. perhaps. Bending backwards. Bl. Syn.- naákakciya.

naa'kawiⁿś, Cf. naakaś'iⁿyaⁿ. - iyeya. Bl.

naa'ƙiyatagtáke s'e, (?). When a woman has slandered someone and goes home, the others say: Ya, heyiⁿ nahaⁿ ka - (has "x" shaped legs) gle. Bl.

naa'okpani, v.n. To lack. Tawowicala kiⁿ - śni. B.H.42.2.

naa'taⁿiⁿśni a'ya, v. To obliterate tracks with the foot. Bl.

nabkaⁿ', n. (of nape and kaⁿ). The sinews of the wrist.

nabla'blaǧa, v. red. of nablaga. -- nablábIaħ, cont. of.

nabla'ǧa, v.n. To swell out, burst open, as corn in boiling. -- nabláħ, cont. of nablaga. - iyaya. -- nabláħya, v. (of nablaga). To cause to burst open, as corn. Nabláħwaya. Wagmeza nabláħyapi, Popcorn.

nablas', cont. of nablaza. - iyeya.

nabla'ska, v.a. To flatten with the foot. Nawáblaska.

nabla'ya, 1) v.a. To make level or smooth with the foot. Nawablaya. 2) v.n. To become level, spread out.

nabla'za, 1) v.a. To kick open, make burst by kicking e.g. a football. Nawablaza. 2) v.n. To burst, as a kettle by freezing; to burst open, as hominy by boiling.

nable'bleca, v. red. of nableca.

nable'blel, cont. of nablebleca. - kaoksa. B.H.72.15.

nable'ca, 1) v.a. To break e.g. glass by kicking or stepping on. Nawableca. 2) v.n. To blossom, unfold, as waħca, flowers; crack open as seeds do.

nablel', cont. of nableca. - iyeya. -- nablélya, v.a. To cause to break with the foot. Nablelwaya.

nablu', v.a. To pulverize with the foot. Nawablu. 2) v.n. To become dry and fine, as sugar stirred up. -- nablúblu, v. red. of nablu. -- nablúya, v.n. To be plain or manifest as tracks not long since made.

nabu', v.a. To drum with the foot, beat on the ground, stamp. Maka - . Nawabu. -- nabúbu, v. red. To make a noise by stamping. Nawabubu.

naċa´, n. A chief. Note: In former times there were only naca, naca okolakiciye. The itaŋcaŋ was introduced by the white man. RF.

naċaŋ´ċaŋ, 1) v.n. (of caŋcaŋ). To shiver, tremble. Namácaŋcaŋ. TT. pronounces the word nacáŋcaŋ. 2) v.a. To make shake with the foot. R. -- nacáŋcaŋyeya, v.n. or adv. perhaps. To tremble. Nacaŋcaŋyemaya. - heye. B.H. 289.2.

nacaŋ´ḱutoŋ, v. To make a track or path somewhere e.g. by going or riding repeatedly. Nacaŋkuwatoŋ.

nacaŋ´teśilya, adv. (?). - wipi, i.e. having eaten all one can take and being sorry for not being able to eat more. Bl.

nacaŋ´ze, v.a. To make angry by kicking or tapping with one's foot. Nawácaŋze.

naca´pcab, cont. of nacapcapa. - ya, To go on a trot. -- nacápcabya, v.a. To cause to trot. Nacapcabwaya.

naca´pcaṗa, v.n. To trot, as a horse.

nace´ca, adv. Perhaps, probably, it may be. It is placed after the word it belongs to. B.H.184.12. D.249. Na le tuwe hwo? ecaŋnipi nacece lo. Ake ecoŋpi na ake iyenakeca - wicaopi.

naceg´, cont. of naceka. -- nacégcég, cont. of nacegceka. -- nacégceka, v. of naceka. -- nacégyeya, v. To make stagger by kicking. Same as naceg iyeya. Nacegyewaya.

naċe´ḱa, v.a. To make stagger by kicking, as in trying to kick down a fence post that will not yield. Nawaceka.

nace´ya, v.a. (of na and ceya). To make cry by kicking. Nawaceya.

naci´k'a, Same as nacik'ala.

naci´k'ala, v. (of cik'ala). To make small by trampling. Nawacik'ala.

naci´scila, v.a. (of ciscila). To make less by trampling on. Nawáciscila.

nacō´ċo, v. To make soft with the feet e.g. the mud. Nawacoco ca ȟliȟlila. Cf. coco.

naġa´, v.n. To gape open, as a wound. Yamnipi k'oŋ maya el yapi na - s'e hiŋgla. Yuŋkaŋ mahel iyayapi.

naġab´, cont. of nagapa. - iyeya.

naġa´ġá, v. red. (of naga). To spatter or fly out, as grease on the fire. -- naġáġaya, adv. Partly molten, as is said of grease. Also, adj., naġáġayela.

nagal´, cont. of nagata. - iyeya. -- naġálġata, v. red. of nagata.

naġaŋ´, v.n. To gape open, as a wound. R. gives naġá. Na lila tehaŋ tiyopa s'e maya kiŋ nagahaŋ. B.H.293.11. -- naġáŋġaŋ, v. red. B.H.299.25.

naġa´ṗa, v.a. To strip off the skin of anything with the foot, as a horse might do to a man by kicking. Nawagapa.

naġa´ṫa, v.n. To stretch out the foot. Nawagata.

naġi´, n. The soul, spirit; the shadow of anything, as of a man (wicánagi) or of a house (tinági). Minagi. Uŋnagipi. - iyaya, He has gone to the spirit world. Opta hiyaye ka, - kiŋ aiyohaŋswicaye kiŋ oŋ akisnipi kte. B.H.283.4.

naġi´ aktoŋś´ya, v.a. To surprise e.g. game by stealing close by. Bl.

naġi´ca, v.a. To wake one up with the foot, or by making a noise with the feet. Nawagica.

nagi´haha, adj. Scared, nervous on hearing something. WE.

nagi´iya´ya, v.n. To yield up one's spirit, to die.

nagi´ksabic'ila, v. refl. To think one cannot be taken by surprise. Bl. -- nagiksabya, adv. Observantly. - omani, To walk with open eyes, watching everything. Bl. - oṗic'iya.

nagi´ksaṗa, adj. (?). The word is used to indicate when one made a good guess and is now glad over it. MF.

nagil', cont. of nagica. - iyeya.

naǧi' nii'c'iya, v. To save one's soul. Nagi nimic'iya.

nagi'toŋ, v. To be haunted; lit. to produce ghosts. He - , The place is haunted. SH.

naǧi'yeya, v.a. To trouble, vex, bother one. Nagiyewaya.

nagi'yuwaśte, adj. Salutary. P.

nagla', v.n. To uncoil of itself. Maza wikaŋ - . -- adj. perhaps. Loose, not tied tight; untied.

nagla'gla, adj. Moving, i.e. as the ribs of a buffalo. -- nagláglaǩe s'e, adv. perhaps. Standing out, i.e. as the ribs of a poor animal; lean, very poor, as is said of animals whose ribs stand out.

nagla'ǩe, v.n. To stand out, as the ribs of a poor animal when lean, very poor. Namáglake. -- nagláǩeya, adv. Sticking out, as the ribs of an animal. -- naglákeyeya, (?). Tucúhu - wí́mapi yelo, i.e. to be overloaded with food, so that the ribs are stretched far apart. Cf. naiŋyaŋyeya, nawizipaŋyeya. Bl.

nagla'ǩiŋyaŋ, adv. Set crosswise or turned out, as the foot. Si - iyeya, To turn the foot out.

nagla'pśuŋyaŋ, v. To turn bottom up with the foot.

nagla'pťus, cont. of naglaptuza. - iyaya.

nagla'pťuza, v.n. To fly back, as a bow that is bent or a tree that is pulled and let go.

nagle'gles, cont. of naglegleza. - aya, To become striped, staring. D.275.

nagle'gleza, v.n. To be checkered or marked.

naglō'ǩa, v.a. To knock and injure, as the joint of one's leg. R. Nawagloka. Caŋkpe - . Nagloke s'e, With injured limbs, as it were. Nagloke s'e waku.

nagmi'gma, v.a. To make round with the foot. Nawágmigma.

nagmi'yaŋyaŋ, v.a. To make roll with the foot, as a football. Nawagmiyaŋyaŋ.

nagmu'gmuŋ, v. red. (of nagmuŋ). To curl or crisp e.g. bark or burned leather. R. Note: this is v.a.

nagmuŋ', v.n. To twist of itself, curl or crisp, as bark or burnt leather. -- nagmúŋyaŋ, adv. Curled.

nagna', v.a. To knock off with the foot, as fruit. Nawagna.

nagna'ka, Cf. nagnaŋka.

nagnaŋ'ǩa, v. red. (of naka, or perhaps naŋka). To twitch, as the muscles of the eyes, mouth etc. cause the flesh. When they had presentiments that somebody was coming, they said: Nóŋȟmapaŋ yelo, sicuha managnaŋkelo, icimani ahi kte lo. Cf. naŋka, naka. Managnaŋka. Note: The word also seems to be used for the beating of the heart.

nagna'yaŋ, v.a. To stumble, to miss step; to miss in trying to kick; to miss something partly, i.e. not meeting it right, with the foot, as in kicking a ball partly and so giving it a wrong direction. Nawágnayaŋ.

naǧo'ǧo, v. To make scratches, as on the floor by walking, with the shoes etc.

naǧo'ya, v.a. To scratch out, erase with the foot, e.g. something written in the sand. Nagówaya.

naǧu'ǩa, v.a. To sprain, as one's ankle.

nagwag', cont. of nagwaka. - iyeya. Si - iyeya makaȟliȟlila nakiŋtapi. -- nagwágwaka, v. red. of nagwaka.

nagwa'ka, v.n. To kick out the foot; to struggle; fig. to criticize etc. Nawágwaka. R. gives nabaka.

naha'ha, adv. Slowly, carefully; putting down the feet carefully, stealthily, walking on the toes, tiptoeing. - waimnakelo. Bl.

naha'hci, adv. Still, yet. Le winyan kin - niun keyapi. Nahahci...śni, Not yet. -- naháhcike, adv. Not really yet, a little time left.

naha' iyeya, v. To kick out of the way. R. Nahéyab iyeya, Bl. says is the same.

nahan', conj. And, then, also, besides. Hokśila kin kici canpagmiyanpi kin el iyotaka - lila luziyayapi.

naheb'yela, adv. (?). - mankelo. - iyotaka, To sit on one's haunches. Bl. - yanka, To be sitting with one knee bent and the other almost touching the ground and resting on this lower leg. RF.

nahinl', cont. (of nahinta). To scrape off with the foot. - iyeya. Wa k'ecel - owalekte, wanjihci ektonjapi naceca ca wapahi ktelo. Bl.

nahin'ta, v.a. To scrape or wipe off with the foot. Nawáhinta.

naho'ho, v.a. To shake or make loose with the foot. Nawáhoho.

naho'mni, v.a. To turn round with the foot, as in the operation of a bicycle. Nawahomni.

nahō'ton, 1) v.a. To make howl e.g. a dog by kicking. Nawahoton. 2) v.n. To sound by machinery e.g. by any form of talk-reproducing machine.

nahun'huns, cont. of nahunhunza. - iyeye.

nahun'hunza, v.a. To shake or rock with the foot. Nawahunhunza. Makoce kin si on nahunhunza.

naha', v.n. To become rough, as one's hands when chapped by the wind, or as roads when thawing after the winter. Also perhaps, to stand up on end, as grains of corn when boiling. Namáha. Maka kin - . A.

nahab', cont. (of nahapa). To scare or drive away by stamping. -- nahábhapa, v. red. of nahapa.

naha'pa, v.a. To scare away by stamping. Nawahapa.

nahci', v.a. To tear off a piece by stepping, to break out a piece with the foot. Nawahci.

nahco', v.n. To loosen or untie, as do one's shoestrings or stockings. Also, nahcóhco. Nahcohco omani, i.e. walking about with stockings down and open shoes. Hinyakon nahcohco. -- nahcóka, v.n. To come loose, as one's leggings. -- nahcóya, adv. Loose, untied, as the strings that hold up one's leggings.

nahe'yab, v. perhaps. To kick out of the way. Syn.- naha iyeya. Bl.

nahe'yata, v.a. To kick off to one side. Nawaheyata.

nahla', v.n. To ring, as a telephone bell. R. gives v.a. To rattle with the foot. Nawahla.

nahla'ġan, v.n. To open, spread out, be enlarged.

nahla'hla, v. red. of nahla.

nahla'hlal, cont. of nahlahlata. - un, To be scratching. D.98.

nahlal', v. cont. of nahlata. -- nahlálmnimni, n. A spring to which it is hard to go because of steep banks.-- nahlál mniówe, n. (?). -- nahlál unkúnza, v. To pretend holding back. D.79. Bl.

nahla'ta, v.a. To scratch with the toes. Nawáhlata.

nahla'ya, v.n. To peel off of itself, to fall off, as a scab. B.H.126.15.

nahle'ca, v.a. To rend or tear open with the foot. Nawahleca.

nahle'cela s'e, adv. perhaps. Almost bursting. It is said of very fleshy men or animals. - un. Bl.

nahle'hleca, v. red. of nahleca.

nahlel', cont. of nahleca.

nahli' v.n. To step into mud. Nawáhli. -- nahlíhli, v.n. To trample in mud. Nawáhlihli.

nahlog, cont. of nahloka. - iyeya.

naȟlo'ȟloka, v. red. of naȟloka. -- naȟlóȟloke s'e, (?). -mani, To walk lightly, without noise. Bl.

naȟlo'k̇a, v.a. To make a hole with the foot; to wear a hole in the foot by walking. Nawaȟloka.

naȟma', v.a. To hide, conceal. Also perhaps, adv. Nawáȟma. Naciȟma. - iyaya, glapi, glipi, icupi. -- naȟmáȟmala, adv. red. of naȟmala. -- naȟmákel, adv. Secretly. B.H.164.7;229.17. -- naȟmála, adv. Secretly, slyly, covertly. Also, naȟmálakel. B.H.35.9.

naȟme', v. Cf. naȟma. -- naȟméyahaŋ, adv. Secretly.

naȟmi'ȟa, v. To laugh slyly. Naȟmíwaȟa.

naȟmiŋ', v.a. To turn outward or make turn out e.g. one's heels. Nawáȟmiŋ. Siyéte - .

naȟni'yeyela or naȟníyela, (?). Naȟniyeyelaȟci omani, To walk and run by turns. Bl.

naȟol', cont. of naȟota. Oyé - iyaya, He makes tracks as he goes.

naȟo'ta, v. Cf. naȟol.

naȟṗa', 1) v.a. To throw down with the foot, to kick to make fall. Nawaȟpa. 2) v.n. (?). -- naȟṗáȟṗa, v. red. (of naȟpa). To have the stockings hanging down and hindering one's gait; to be slovenly, untidy. - s'e. Bl. - s'e omani, as is said when an old man walks slowly like a heavy horse with its long-haired knuckles. Also, napśápśaśe omani. Bl. -- naȟpáȟpaka, n. One who is slovenly, untidy. He naȟpaȟpake c'uŋ, That one, she is untidy. D.9. Cf. yuȟpáȟpa s'e.

naȟṗaŋ'yaŋ, v. To moisten with the foot. Nawaȟpaŋyaŋ.

naȟṗe'ya, v.a. To cause to make fall with the foot, as kicking a box on which someone is sitting. Naȟpewaya.

naȟpi'ȟpi s'e, adv. perhaps. Slouchy. Is said of little heavy horses with long hair at the ankles. Bl. -- naȟpíȟpiya, (?). Slouchy, with things hanging down. Bl.

naȟṗu', v.a. To knock off with the foot anything sticking. Nawáȟpu. -- v.n. To fall off of itself. -- naȟṗúȟṗu, v. red. (of naȟpu). To fall off, as anything that has been stuck.

naȟtag', cont. of nahtaka. - iyeya. -- naȟtágya, v.a. To typewrite. Naȟtagwaya. LB.

naȟta'ȟtaka, v. red. of naȟtaka. Maka naȟtaȟtakapi. D.67.

naȟṫa'ka, v.a. To kick anything. Nawaȟtaka.

naȟu'ġa, v.a. To crack e.g. a nut with the foot or by knocking. Nawaȟuga.

Naȟu'ya Hoȟpi' Wakpala, n. prop. A creek south of the Niobrara. Bl.

naȟwa', v.a. To put to sleep by rocking with the foot. Nawaȟwa.

naȟ'aŋ'hiya, adv. Slowly.

naȟ'e'ȟ'eyakel, adv. In a bitten-off manner, not evenly, looking ragged and torn. - nakseya, i.e. he cut the grass unevenly leaving some here and there. Similarly, onák̇ik̇iyakel nakseya. Bl.

naȟ'oŋ', v.a. To hear anything; to listen to; to attend to; to obey. Nawaȟ'oŋ. -- naȟ'oŋk̇iya, v.a. To cause to hear, to relate, make hear. Naȟ'óŋwakiya. -- naȟ'óŋyaŋ, v.a. To cause to hear. Naȟ'oŋwaya.

nai'cabya, adv. With the mouth wide open. Hogaŋ waŋ taŋka - anataŋ. B.H. 122.24. Also, naícabyeya. D.104.

nai'coġa, v.n. To come loose, to slip down e.g. one's leggings. Cf. naȟcoka.

nai'coȟ, cont. (of naicoga). To cause to come untied and slip down e.g. one's leggings. - iyeya. Thus, to loosen one's belt, drop one's pants; to kick one's quilt to the feet, as children do etc. Taŋyaŋ ecel iyuŋka - aya u we. Bl.

nai'c'iȟma, v. refl. (of nahma). To hide one's self. Namic'iȟma.

nai'c'iȟmiŋyaŋ, v.n. To get out of gear, out of place, as a wheel etc.

as is said of any vehicle (na), machinery etc.

nai'c'ijin, v. To defend one's self, speak for one's self, instead of having a lawyer or the like. Cf. nakicijin.

nai'c'ik'ega, v. refl. To scratch one's self. Bl.

nai'c'iocoza, v. To make one's self warm by running. Bl.

nai'c'iśnaśna, v. refl. (of naśnaśna). To scratch one's self with the foot, perhaps. Cf. naśna. Bl. MW. Syn.- naic'iwaza.

nai'c'iśpa, v.n. To get away from danger or trouble.

nai'c'iwaza, v. refl. (of nawaza). To scratch one's self with the foot, as dogs do. Bl.

nai'kpiska, v. Lit., as animals often have a white belly, ikpi ska. - eḣpeya, To kick over, as a dog, on its back.

nai'leġa, v. To make shine, perhaps, by kicking, poking e.g. the fire with one's feet. Nawailega. Bl. Also, nalega.

nai'leḣ, cont. of nailega. -- naíleḣya, v. To make shine or sparkle with the foot. R. Bl.

nainl', (?). Wagugeca kaga ca nainlpica śni. Bl.

nainś', conj. Or.

nain'yanyeya, (?). Nige - wipi, To be filled up with food, i.e. the stomach is the stone, inyan. Bl. Cf. nawizipanyeya, and naglakeyeya.

nai'ṗaweḣ, cont. (of naipawega). To kick something out of one's way, keep away with the foot.

nai'ṫunḱab, v. To go over backwards, as a horse when its head is pulled back. - yanká. - eḣpeya, To kick over backwards, as a cow may one when being milked. - iyeya, Turn over backwards.

nai'yojaheyakel, adv. Rattling by itself, as the loose spokes of an old wheel. - naunkelo. Syn.- kakag hingle. Bl.

nai'yowas, cont. of naiyowaza. - iyeya.

nai'yowaza, v.a. To cause an echo by stamping. Nawaiyowaza.

nai'yoyaḣe, v.n. To evaporate by itself.

naja', v.a. To crush by trampling on e.g. rice. R. Bl. Nawaja.

naja'ja, v.a. To wash out with the feet, trample out. Nawajaja. R. gives To wash out by boiling, which is a bit doubtful.

naja'ḱayela, adv. Lying open. - han, as is said of a wound when the margin is swollen and showing a deep cut. Bl.

najal', cont. (of najata). To spread or gape open, as a wound. - iyeya. -- najályakel, adv. Open as a wound. P.

najan'janyelayeye, (?). The word is used of a boil etc. that is ripe and shining. Bl.

naja'ta, v.a. To make forked by kicking, to split. Nawájata.

najib', cont. of najipa. - iyeya.

naji'ca, v.n. To run away, to flee, retreat. R. Bl.

najil', cont. of najica. - iyaya.

na'jin, v.n. To stand. Owanjila - , To stand still. Note: inájin, To rise up. Inawajin.

najin'ca, v.n. To run away, flee or retreat. Nawájinca.

na'jinhan, part. Standing. - najin, To rise up and stand.

na'jin hiya'ya, v. To stand up, go get up. Also, perhaps, inajin hiyaya. Canke iheceglala najin hiyayapi. B.H. 170.2;273.15.

na'jinḱiya, v.a. To cause to stand,

to raise up, lift up. Najiⁿwakiya.

na'jiⁿyaⁿ, v.a. To cause to stand, to stop; to corner, to hold at bay; perhaps, to cause to fight. Nájiⁿwaya. Na waⁿji najiⁿyaⁿpi ca etakpiⁿ na iyaȟpaya. B.H.73.1. D.71, note 3.

na'jiⁿyeyapi, v. pl. They stand in a row, i.e. ipahlalya inajiⁿpi, from one thing to another. Letaⁿhaⁿ hoanuⁿk ataya - na ecel tipi he el anuⁿk ihuⁿniya po.

naji'pa, v.a. To prick or pinch with the toes; to punch or touch with the foot. Nawajipa.

naju', n. The back part of the head.

naju'ju, 1) v.a. To kick to pieces. Nawajuju. 2) v.n. To come to pieces of itself.

naju'ƙaosnisni s'e, (?). - iⁿyaⁿka, as is said of a man who has but little hair left and this is waving in the wind while he runs. Bl.

najuⁿ', v. To pull out, or kick, something with the foot.

naju'ťe, n. The back of the head, the occipital bone, the base of the skull. - el apapa. -- najúťośkókpa, n. The hollow of the neck behind.

naƙa', v.n. To twitch, as the eye or flesh at times does involuntarily; also, the ringing of the ear, the latter being taken as a sign that something happened. Ísta manáke. Noge manake. Sicuha manake.

nakab', cont.(of nakapa). To kick out of the way. - iyeya.

naka'ƙa, v.a. To make rattle with the foot, as stiff hides might be. Nawakaka.

nakaⁿ', v.a. To thresh out e.g. corn etc. with the feet by treading. Nawakaⁿ.

naka'p̄a, v.a. To kick e.g. a ball. Nawakapa. Tapa nakapapi, A game played by girls.

na'ƙap̄as, (?). Mini - hiyuya, as is said of drops of water that appear when one has scalded one's self. - hiyumayelo. Bl.

naƙa'p̄o, v.n. To swell, as a dead body, dough etc. or wood after a rain, as in a door that cannot be closed. -- naƙáp̄oǧa, v.n. To rise, swell up, as bread or any swelling of the body. -- náƙap̄oȟ, (?). Mini - hiyuya, as is said of the drops of water that appear in the place where one scalded one's self. Bl. - hiyumayelo. Syn.- náƙap̄as.

naƙa'ś'iⁿ, v. To bend backwards. Nakaś'iⁿc'iya. D.215. - yeya, as is said of the man riding and bending back while pulling back the head of the horse.

naƙa'ťiⁿ, 1) v.a. To straighten with the foot; to straighten the foot. Nawakatiⁿ. 2) v.n. To become straight of itself.

naƙa'wa, v.i. To spring open; also, to shrink, as a door and so does not stay closed. -- v.t. To kick open. Nawákawa.

nakca', v. To be smooth of itself. Pehiⁿ namákca.

naƙe', adv. The emphatic form perhaps of nakeś. Osni, yuⁿkaⁿ tiyoceyati śni; naké maśte, yuⁿkaⁿ ceyati ehaⁿ oⁿ le heyónika yelo. GA. Nake iśta apiyiⁿ kte ȟciⁿ eyaś wicala śni keye. MS.96.

naƙe'ȟca, adv. At last, as one wanted. Bl.

naƙe'nula, adv. A short time, a little while. - wani, I have lived but a little while. This word seems to refer rather to a sudden death inflicted by an enemy; thus it is a saying: - ni wauⁿ welo. GA. - waniyelo, i.e. an excuse for leading a merry life, with the attitude: Be merry while you live. Ba.

nakeś', adv. At last; just now. Also, naké. - tiwahe waⁿ tokata uⁿkicu kte lo. Hihaⁿna - wahi kte. Pte kiⁿ tukte ihaⁿkeya cepe kiⁿ iyuha awicuⁿglepelo ca - taⁿtaⁿ wayatiⁿ kte lo. MS.95. B.H.58.

naki'blaya, v. pos. (of nablaya). To trample one's own level. Nawakiblaya.

nak̇i'bleca, v. pos. (of nableca). To break one's own by treading on it. Nawakibleca.

naki'ca, v.a. To scrape with the foot, to paw as a horse, scraping towards one's self. Note: this is not natica.

naki'capca, v. pos. (of napca). To swallow down one's own e.g. spittle, or blood from a bleeding tooth.

nak̇i'ciblaya, v. (of nablaya). To make level by trampling on for one. Naweciblaya.

nak̇i'cibleca, v. (of nableca). To break e.g. a plate for one with the foot; also, to break for one by freezing etc. Namicibleca.

nak̇i'cibu, v. (of nabu). To drum with the foot for one. Nawecibu.

nak̇i'cigmuŋ, v. (of nagmuŋ). To twist for one, to become twisted on. Namicigmuŋ.

nak̇i'cihuŋhuŋza, v. (of nahuŋhuŋza). To shake for one. Nawecihuŋhuŋza. -- nak̇i'cihuŋhuŋzapi, n. See-sawing.

nak̇i'ciḣma, v. (of naḣma). To conceal for one. Naweciḣma.

nak̇i'ciḣṫaka, v. (of naḣtaka). To kick for one. Naweciḣtaka.

nak̇i'ciḣ'oŋ, v. (of naḣ'oŋ). To hear for one. Naweciḣ'oŋ. Nakiciḣ'oŋpi, They hear each other.

nak̇i'cija, v. (of naja or nakija). To tread out for one; to hull for one e.g. rice by treading. Nawecija. R.Bl.

nak̇i'cijiŋ, v.a. To stand for one, represent somebody as a delegate; to defend. Thus, deriv. of na-kici-jiŋ. Nawecijiŋ. Tuŋkaśila oyate kiŋ nacicijiŋ kte. Namic'ijiŋ, I defend myself. Nanic'ijiŋ, You defend yourself. Naic'ijiŋ, He defends himself. Namicijiŋ, He defends me. Nanicijiŋ, He defends you. Oyate kiŋ lila nacicijiŋpelo. -- nak̇icijiŋka, v. To stand up for one, stand by one. Nawecijiŋka.

nak̇i'ciksa, v. (of naksa). To break off with the foot for one. Naweciksa.

nak̇i'cikśiŋ, v. (of nakikśiŋ). To stand up for one in danger, to stand by one. Nawecikśiŋ. R. Bl.

nak̇i'cik̇uk̇a, v. (of nakuka). To wear out with the foot for one. Nawecikuka.

nak̇i'cipa, v. (of napa). To flee from any person or thing. Nawécipa. Ḣcehánl pte kiŋ taku nakicipapi iteya iyayapi. D.257 and 99.

nak̇i'cipaŋ, v. (of napaŋ). To trample of tread out e.g. grain for one. Nawecipaŋ.

nak̇i'ciṗoṫa, v. (of napota). To wear out e.g. moccasins for one. Nawecipota.

nak̇i'cipsak̇a, v. (of napsaka). To break e.g. a cord with the foot for one. Nawecipsaka.

nak̇i'cisuṫa, v. (of nasuta). To tread hard for one. Nawecisuta.

nak̇i'ciśpa, v. (of naśpa). To release one from trouble, as a lawyer his client. BD. Naweciśpa.

nak̇i'ciśpu, v. (of naśpu). To kick off for one anything sticking. Naweciśpu.

nak̇i'citak̇a, v. (of nataka). To fasten or lock for one. Nawecitaka.

nak̇i'ciweġa, v. (of nawega). To break e.g. an ax-handle for one by treading on it. Naweciwega.

nak̇i'ciwizipi, v. recip. (of nawizi). They are jealous of each other. Nauŋkiciwizipi.

nak̇i'cuŋniniyaŋkel, adv. red. of nakicuŋniyaŋkel. Syn.- nat'oŋt'oŋgyaŋkel. Bl. -- nak̇i'cuŋniyaŋkel, adv. Same as nat'oŋgyakel or nat'uŋgyakel. Bl.

nak̇i'gmuŋ, v. (of nagmuŋ). To become twisted of itself for one. Namakigmuŋ.

nak̇i'ḣma, v.a. pos. (of naḣma). To hide or conceal one's own. Nawakiḣma.

nak̇i'ḣtaḣṫak̇a, v. pos. (of naḣtaḣtaka). To kick one's own e.g. horse. Naweḣtaḣtaka.

naǩi'ȟ'oŋ, v. pos. (of naȟ'oŋ). To hear one's own e.g. what one has said or is reported to have said. Nawakiȟ'oŋ.

naǩi'ja, v. pos. (of naja). To tread out one's own e.g. rice. R. Bl.

naǩi'ksa, v. pos. (of naksa). To break one's own with the foot. Naweksa or nawakiksa.

naǩi'kśiŋ, v.a. To defend one's self. R. Cf. anakikśiŋ. Nawekśiŋ. Nauŋkikśiŋ pi. Yupin nakikśiŋ, To work hard and hurriedly in order to finish a job in a certain time, to be anxious to finish a job. Bl.

naǩiŋ'ca, v.a. To scrape off e.g. hair with the foot. Nawakiŋca.

naǩiŋl', cont. (of both nakiŋca and nakiŋta). To scrape off with the foot. - iyeya. -- naǩiŋlǩiŋl, v. cont. of nakiŋl. - ȟpayelo, He slipped with feet backwards and fell. Bl. This can also be said: nak'elk'eȟ ȟpayelo.

naǩiŋ'ťa, v.a. To brush or wipe one's feet on something; to brush off with the foot. R. Nawakiŋta. Caŋke si nagwag iyeya makaȟliȟlila nakiŋtapi.

naǩiŋ'ťǩilya, adj. Tender, as meat.

naǩi'pa, v. pos. (of napa). To flee or retreat towards home; to turn back for fear. Nawákipa.

naǩi'pca, v. pos. (of napca). To swallow down one's own e.g. spittle. Nawakipca.

naǩi'psaǩa, v. pos. (of napsaka). To break with the foot one's own string. Nawakipsaka.

naǩi'psoŋ, v. pos. (of napsoŋ). To spill over one's own with the foot. Nawakipsoŋ.

naǩi'p̌usǩica, v.a. To press close together with the feet. Nawakipuskica.

naǩi'śloka, v. pos. (of naśloka). To extricate one's self from; to kick off one's own moccasins.

naǩi'śna, v. pos. (of naśna). To miss one's footing, to slip; to miss while trying, being in a hurry; to put on one's shoes; to mind one's own. Nawakiśna. Hehe, huŋkahe nawicakiśna, i.e. he does not care for or look after his nearest relatives. Bl.

naǩi'taǩa, v. pos. (of nataka). To fence, fasten, bolt or bar one's own. Nawakitaka.

naǩi'weǧa, v. pos. (of nawega). To break or splinter one's own with the feet, or somebody else's stick with one's feet. Nawakiwega.

naǩi'wizi, v.a. (of nawizi). To be envious of, jealous of. Nawakiwizi. Namakiwizi.

naǩi'za, v. To make one's shoes or so creak. Caŋhaŋpa nakizapi.

nakog', cont. of nakoka. - iyeya.

nako'ǩa, v.a. To knock with the foot and thus producing a noise. Nawakoka. -- nakókoǩa, v. red. of nakoka.

naǩoŋ'ťa, v.a. To wear out partly with the foot e.g. a rope, strap etc., i.e. make it thinner. BD.

nakp̌a', n. The external ear of animals and men. Also, nakpala, Large ears. - saŋni waglahomni kte lo. -- nakp̌á-huťe, n. The root of the ear, where it is grown to the head. Bl.

nakp̌a'kp̌a, v.n. To crackle, pop, as wood burning.

nakp̌aŋ', v.a. To grind with the feet by treading. Nawakpaŋ.

nakp̌a' oǩo'gna, ph. Between the ears.

nakp̌a'stogya, adv. Moving the ears to and fro, as a horse does.

nakp̌a' wica'ȟci, n. A pointed piece of fat attached to a buffalo's heart. Bl.

nakp̌a' yuwo'slal iki'kca, v. To prick up the ears e.g. of a horse at anything.

nakpe'yeya, (?). Noŋȟ'nakpeyemaye.Bl.

nakp̌i', v.a. To crack with the foot, as boys do with the eyes of butchered cattle. Nawákpi. To crack nuts: naȟu-ga. -- nakṗíkṗi, v. red. (nakpi). To make successive sounds, as a gun sometimes does in hanging fire.

nakṗi'ślayaṫaŋhaŋ, n. (nakpa-iślayataŋhaŋ). The right ear. B.H.256.18.

nakpo'ṫa, v. pos. (napota). To wear out one's own moccasins etc. Nawakpota. R. Bl.

nakpu'kpa, v.n. To mix together, as in boiling e.g. a stew. P.

nakṗu'taḱe, n. An ear wrapper, a scarf. Note: deriv. possibly from nakpa and pútaka.

naksa', v.a. To break off e.g. a stick in two with the foot. Nawaksa.
naksa'ksa, v. red. of naksa.
naksa'ya, v. To cause to break with the foot. Naksawaya.

nakse'ya, v.a. To cut e.g. hay. Naksewaya.

nakśa', 1) v.a. To coil or to roll up with the foot e.g. a rope. Wikaŋ nawakśa. 2) v.n. To coil, roll up, as anything burnt. Also, nakśála.

nakśaŋ', v.a. To bend with the foot e.g. a stick by two hands and bent with the foot. Nawakśaŋ.
nakśaŋ'kśaŋ, v. red. of nakśaŋ.

nakśe'capi, n. (nakśa). A sickness of the Sioux consisting in cramps, the limbs being contracted and leading to death. Bl.

nakśi'ja, 1) v.a. To double up anything with the foot, to bend up the leg. 2) v.n. To double up on, as the stockings do in hanging down. Huŋyakoŋ nawakśikśija.

nakśi'kśija, v. red. (nakśija). To double up, e.g. with the foot.

nakśiś', cont. (nakśija). To bend up e.g. one's legs. - iyeya.

naktaŋ', v.a. To bend with the foot by stepping on and giving permanent bend to. Nawaktaŋ.
naktaŋ'ktaŋ, v. red. of naktaŋ.
naktaŋ'yaŋ, v.a. To cause to bend with the foot. Naktaŋwaya.

naḱu'ḱa, v.a. To wear out with the feet. Nawakuka.

naḱuŋ', conj. And, also. Na often precedes it, thus: Wicaśa waŋ kaga na nakuŋ wiŋyaŋ waŋ kaga.
naḱuŋś', emph. nakuŋ.

nak'e'ġa, v.a. To scratch, using the spurs upon a horse. Nawák'ega.

nak'eḣ', cont. of nak'ega.
nak'eḣ'k'eġa, v. red. of nak'ega.
nak'eḣ'k'eḣ, red. of nak'eḣ. - Ḣpayelo, He slipped out with the feet backward, not finding a hold and falling. - uŋ. Bl. D.98. Syn.- naśluślul, nakiŋlkiŋl.

na'la, adv. Alone, only. Note: the word is used with the pronouns miś, niś, iś, and uŋkiś.

nale'ġa, v.a. To make shine or sparkle, as in pushing up or kicking the fire with the foot. Nawalega. -- v.n. To sparkle, scintillate. R. Bl.

naleḣ', cont. of nalega. - iyeya. Bl.
nale'ḣleġa, v. red. (nalega). To kick or punch up the fire with the foot. Nawaleḣlega. Also, naíleḣleġa.
naleḣ'ya, v.a. To make sparkle e.g. burning wood by kicking. R. Bl.

nalo'loṗa, v.a. To trample and make limber. Nawalolopa. Bl.

namna', 1) v.a. To rip, e.g. the seam of a coat. Nawamna. 2) v.n. To rip of itself. -- namnámna, v. red. of namna.
namna'yaŋ, v.a. To cause to rip e.g. one's moccasins. Namnawaya.

namni', v.n. To turn back when going on a journey. Nawamni. Na he ozuye kiŋ huŋḣ hetaŋ namni agli na huŋḣ kosaŋ eyaya, i.e. coming back before one reaches the destined place. Note: it is used with verbs. - gli, wagli.

namni'ġa, v.n. To shrink, draw up, as cloth by washing.
namniḣ', cont. of namniga. - iyeya.
namniḣ'ḱiya, v. To shrink, to full up.
namniḣ'ya, v.a. To cause to shrink. Namniḣwaya.

namni'mni, v. red. (namni). To swing,

e.g. one's blanket.

namnu'mnuza, v. red. (of namnuza). To crackle, as green wood in fire or as a prairie fire. R. Bl. Syn.- pelnakpakpa.

namnus', cont. of namnuza. - iyaya. R. Bl.

namnu'za, v.a. To make creak or sound, as when one walks on newly formed ice. Nawamnuza. R. Bl.

na'na, conj. red. (of na). The word is used by women in handing anything, or telling people when others offer them something. It means: Take it; here it is.

nani', v.a. To touch or jog with the foot, to rouse up. Nawani. -- naníni, v. To jog with the foot, to wake up. Nawanini.

nani'yaⁿ, (?). Sore feet. Onaȟlokiⁿ kte laka - ca caⁿku ipaweȟ ecé iⁿyaⁿka ciⁿ yelo. Bl. Si - , The feet pain one. Si nawaniya.

naⁿka', 2nd pers. sing. (of yaⁿka). To be. -- v.n. To twitch, as the eye lid. Same as naka. Cf. also nagnaⁿka. Iśta manaⁿke lo, mitakuye ake waⁿji t'e.GA.

nao'blel, (?). - aye s'e, or kaóblagaheya, as is said of a line of men, e.g. soldiers, when they move farther apart, thus lengthening the line and being less likely to be hit. Bl.

nao'glapśuⁿ, v. To kick anything over. - iȟpeya, To kick anything over bottom up. R. Bl. -- naóglapśuⁿyaⁿ, adv. Kicking over. - iyeya, To kick over. R. Bl.

nao'gluta, v.a. To close up or cover with the foot. Nawáogluta.

nao'gmigma, v.a. To roll anything with the foot, down hill. - iyeya. Nawaogmigma. Also, naogmigmeya. D.217.

nao'gmus, cont. of naogmuza. - iyaya. Iśta - amaya. Bl.

nao'gmuza, 1) v.n. To close up of itself; to close or shut up, as a flower does. 2) v.a. To close up or cover with the foot. Naowagmuza.

nao'ȟmiⁿ, v.n. To glance off sideways. - iyaya.

nao'ȟpa, v.n. To press or sink down into e.g. mud or water; to break through ice. Nawaoȟpa.

nao'ȟpeya, v.a. To cause to sink down into, to make break through. Naoȟpewaya.

nao'ȟ'aⁿk̇o, v.a. To quicken one's movements by kicking him. Naowaȟ'aⁿko.

nao'k̇iyut̔a, v. To close up or heal e.g. a crack or a wound. Namaokiyuta. B.H.65.8.

nao'ko, v.n. To open, split. B.H.157.8.

nao'k̇otoⁿtoⁿyaⁿ, adv. red. of naokotoⁿyaⁿ. B.H.65.6.

nao'k̇otoⁿyaⁿ, adv. Making a crack, split. Maka kiⁿ - nasleslece. B.H. 65.4.

nao'kpani, v.a. To miss, be short of; to have lost. Naowakpani. Ehaka taku waⁿjila naoyakpani. B.H.234.1;254.4; 298.11.

nao'ksa, v. To break through, as when walking on ice or crusted snow. Naowaksa. -- naóksaksala s'e, adv. Trippling along. - hiyaya, To pass by trippling, as people with short legs. Bl.

naō'kśija, v.a. To bend double, to double up in with the feet, as in bed sheets. Naowakśija.

nao'kt̔aⁿ, v.a. To bend into with the foot. Naowaktaⁿ. -- naókt̔aⁿyaⁿ, adv. Bent in.

nao'mnumnus, cont. (of naomnumnuza and naomnuza). To make creak or sound, as when one walks on newly formed ice or on potatoes. - mani.

nao'mnuza, v.a. To make creak or sound as when one walks on newly formed ice or in a pile of potatoes. The use of this word is doubtful.

na oⁿ, Cf. oⁿ. B.H.79.10.

naoⁿ'ziwosla, v. To kick bottom upwards. - iyeya. - iyeic'iya, To turn a somersault.

nao'ṗemni, v. perhaps a. To prevent from moving, as in walking and getting entangled, twisted, wrapped around, as a rag lying in a rut that gets around a wheel, or a too long overcoat that flaps around the limbs and makes walking difficult. Miniḣuha (rag) hugmiyaŋ - . - s'e u, as is said of a man coming, his too long overcoat flapping around the legs; thus, in a way hindered in one's walking by something entangling e.g. the lower ends of a too long overcoat. Cf. naopemni.

nao'ṗijela, adv. Loose fitting.

nao'po, v.n. To warp; to draw together, as a flower; to shut up.

nao'siŋ, v.a. To make into a hard knot by kicking, as a horse its traces, or by using the foot. R. Bl.

nao'siŋyaŋ, adv. In the manner of a hard knot. - iyeya, To make a knot hard by using the foot, as in closing a loop. R. Bl.

nao'swa, v. (?). Nawaoswa. Bl.

nao'śli, v.n. To press up around, as when one sits down in soft mud. -- naóśliya, adv. Puffed up around. - po, Swelled up full.

nao't'iŋs, cont. of naot'iŋza. - iyeya. - ayapelo. -- naót'iŋsya, 1) v.a. To cause to press down tight in, as a horse's foot. Naot'iŋswaya. 2) adv. Ota auŋ wo, ite ecuḣci naot'iŋsya uŋyakapi kte lo. Bl.

nao't'iŋza, 1) v.a. To press in tight with the foot e.g. the ground around a fence post. 2) v.n. To become fat, as horses in the pasture. Syn.- cepa'ya.

nao'waŋcaya, v. To spread out. - aya, To spread out e.g. a heap of sand with the feet. Bl.

nao'wiŋġa, v. To turn in the toes. Naówiŋḣ mani. -- naówiŋġes'e, adv. - mani, To walk with the feet turned in. Cf. ḣmiŋḣmíŋ, as in: Si ḣmiŋḣmiŋ mani, To walk with the toes turned out, perhaps. R.

napa', v. perhaps n. To run away, to flee e.g. from a fight. Nawapa. Pel'ipimayala ca nacicipiŋ ktelo, i.e. it is cold in your room, so I am leaving you. Bl.

naṗa'gle, v.a. (of nape and agle). To place the hand on, rest it on. Napawagle. Nata - iśtima, To sleep resting the head on one's hand. -- naṗáglepi, n. (of nape). The distance from the end of the thumb to the end of the middle finger when stretched out; a span. Bl.

napa'huŋka, n. The thumb. Tuweni waépazo kiŋ oŋ epazo śni, - kiŋ he oŋ ecoŋpi.

naṗa'ḣpaġa, v.n. To snap or crackle, as corn parching. Bl.

naṗa'ḣpaḣ, cont. of napaḣpaga. - iyeya. Bl. -- naṗáḣpaḣya, v.a. To parch e.g. corn. Napaḣpaḣwaya. Bl.

naṗa'ḳaha, n. A piece of leather stretched over the left hand while shooting with arrows so as to protect it against friction. But R. gives this to be, the back of the hand; whereas for the latter we say napitakaha.

naṗa'ḳaza, n. The five fingers of a hand, or claws of a foot. Capa s'e - ksaksa kaca, as is said when a man's fingers are half cut off. Peháŋ s'e - haŋskaska kaca. Bl.

naṗa'ko, v.n. To bend up of itself. -- naṗákoya, adv. Rounded up. - po, Swelled up.

napaŋ', v.a. To trample fine, to tread out e.g. grain. Nawapaŋ. -- napáŋpaŋ, v. red. of napaŋ.

napa'pa, (?). Waecakca nuŋkiŋ na - umayaye, so a father would say to his child or wife, if they did wrong. - taku ecoŋ mayayapelo, i.e. you bother me unceasingly. Bl.

naṗa'ṗazo, v. To shake the finger at one, as in scolding. Napamayapazo yelo. Bl.

naṗa'ṫa, adv. By the hand. - yuza, To hold by the hand. - yus aya. Tuweḣci - yuziŋ kta atoŋwe. B.H.289.6;295.2.

napa'tuja, v.a. (of patuja). To kick and make bend. Napatuś iyeya.

napca', v.a. To swallow e.g. food. Nawapca. -- napcápca, v. red. (of napca). To put in one piece into the mouth after another. -- napcéya, v.a. To cause to swallow. Napcewaya.

napcin'yungyunka, adj. red. (of napcinyunka). Nine and nine, nine on both sides, by nines.

napcin'yunka, num. adj. Nine.

napco', n. The lean meat near the back bone, the longissimus dorsi; the tenderloin. Cf. tanapco.

napco'ka, n. (of nape and cokaya). The palm of the hand. Waowe śica (bear) s'e - kin yuh'iyela yankin na, as is said when a person's hands were scratched badly. Bl.

napco'kanyan, n. The middle-finger.

nape', v. Cf. napá.

nape', n. The hand. Manape on wakaga.

nape'apaha, v. To raise the hand to, to strike anything. Napéawápaha.

nape'ceśni, adv. Slowly, perhaps; not being afraid or bashful etc. - u, iśtima, kul hpaya. - waun, as they used to say, whereas we now say: Cantewaśteya waun. RF. Taku henun kin suksutaya pahtayo; - unkomanipi kte, i.e. slowly.

nape'glaskapa, v.n. To clap the hands, to applaud.

nape'glujaja, v. To wash one's own hands.

nape'i'cicaśka, v. To tie somebody's hands together. Napéi'ciwakaśka.

nape'ikpa'hin, v. (of nape and ikpahin). To lie with the head on the hand. Napeiwakpahin.

nape'kicoza, v. (of napekoza). To wave the hands to, beckon to with the hand, to gesticulate.

nape'koza, v. To beckon with the hand, wave the hand.

nape'kśikśa, v. To have the hands numb or stiff with cold. Napemakśikśa.

nape'mni, v.n. (of pemni). To twist of itself.

nape' ogle cekutepi, n. A game played by one man throwing a pronged stick as far as he can to make it stand upright, and others who try to win by having their's fall the nearest to his.

nape'oicu, n. Handwriting. Also, napóicu. - tokeca, A different handwriting. NP.

nape' oi'lekiyapi, n. The clasping-leaved dogbane. Apocynum canbinum, hyperici folium. The dogbane family. Indian hemp. It is so called because they used to place the wooly seeds on their hands and light them. While they burn up very rapidly, it does not hurt. Nape oilekiyapi hu tanka un heca yelo: hanta po, i.e. snakes often hide under them. BT. #105.

nape'ojula, n. A handful.

nape' onwogláka, v. To use the sign language. Cf. wíyuta.

nape'ośtan, Cf. napośtan.

nape'picaśni, adj. Inevitable.

nape'pinkpa, n. The tip of a finger.

nape'wicáśpan, n. A thin layer of meat adhering to the small ribs on the inside. Bl.

nape'ya, v.a. To cause to flee, to drive or scare off or away. Napewaya.

nape'yahan, adv. Carefully, watching out. Takunl icu wacin po na - śkan po.

nape'yekiya, v. To stretch out the hand to. -- napéyeya, v. To stretch out one's hand. Syn.- istoyeya. Bl.

nape'yupśunka, 1) n. The fist. 2) v.n. To clench the fist. Bl.

nape'yuza, v. To shake hands.

napi'caśka, v. (of nape and kaśka). To tie to the hands of one. Ptehe wan

- ca ki. MS.574. -- napícaśkeya, adv. Tied to the hand, i.e. always with one and following one about. - uⁿ, To accompany constantly.

napi'kceyakel, adv. By hand. - icahya. B.H.93.11.

napiⁿ', adj. Satisfying, tasty; strong, rich, oily, as some kinds of food are. Ptehiⁿcala pi - , which saying is supposed to be one of the meadow lark's sayings.

napiⁿ'kpa, n. (of nape and iⁿkpa). Gloves. - ot'óza, Mittens. -- napiⁿkpayuġaġa, n. Gloves. R. Bl.

napiⁿ'yuⁿ, adv. With the hands or arms alone, without weapons.

napi'śkaⁿ, v.n. To put the hand to for evil, lay hands on, to move the hand about on; to touch with evil design. -- napíśkaⁿkiya, v.a. To cause to move the hands on, caress. Napiśkaⁿwakiya.

napi'śkaⁿyaⁿ, v.a. To hurt or destroy anything, to kill, esp. what is not one's own. Napiśkaⁿwaya. Tokśa tuwa ciⁿ kiⁿ, napiśkaⁿmayiⁿ kte. Bl.

napi'ślayataⁿhaⁿ, adv. At the right hand. B.H.284.8.

napi'śtaⁿ or napi'śtaⁿka, n. One who is always active, one who accomplishes much. -- napíśtaⁿyaⁿ, v. To be active and accomplishing things. Napiśtaⁿwaya. -- napíśtaⁿkiya, v.a. To keep one busy and accomplishing things. Napiśtaⁿwakiya.

napi'takaha, n. The back of the hand. Cf. napakaha. Nape okazoⁿte kiⁿ - kiⁿ nupiⁿ iciyagleya iyakaśkapi. MS.340. Cf. siitakaha.

napi'yagleya, v. To lay hands on. Napiyaglemayayapi śni, You did not lay hands on me. B.H.256.25.

napi'yaya, cont. of nape and iyaya.

napi'yayus, adv. perhaps. Held in the hands. - yuha, To hold tight in one's hands. B.H.48.10.

napi'yeya, v. To have a hand in something. Deriv. of nape and iyeya. SLB. B.H.122.26.

napi'yuⁿ, Cf. napiⁿyuⁿ.

napi'yuskiya, v.a. To cause to capture one. B.H.255.24;271.2. Pb.199 gives the sense: He shall be delivered to the gentiles, i.e. they shall cause the gentiles to have power over him.

napi'yusya, v.a. To deliver into somebody's power, hand over, to make hold. B.H.72.5. -- adv. Controlling. - śkaⁿ, To control by guiding others.

napi'yuza, v.a. To lay hands on, capture. Napibluza. Napiwicayuzapi. Bl. Note: napiyeya uⁿyuzapi. B.H.163.9.

napi'yuzeca, v. To take things into one's own hands, to do it one's self. Napibluzeca.

napi'za, v.n. To make a creaking noise, as when one steps on a mouse and it creaks or squeaks; to creak, make a creaking noise.

napkaⁿ', n. (of nape and kaⁿ). The sinews or tendons of the wrist.

napka'wiⁿte s'e, (?). - śkaⁿ, i.e. acting as though one were wiping or fanning something away, which meaning to steal. Bl.

napki'coza, v.a. To wave the hand to. Napwecoza. Also, napekicoza.

napko'za, v. To wave the hand. Napwakoza.

napo', v.n. To swell, as soaked corn.

napob', cont. (of napopa). To burst with a noise. - hiⁿgla. - iyeya, To cause to burst and make a noise. -- napóbyapi, n. Fire crackers.

napō'ġa, v.n. To swell, raise, as corn soaked or dough; to ferment. Note: this is not used in ref. to a swelling hand. Napogapi, A swelling. - kuja, One who has that disease. Aguyapi - śni. HM.

napo'glecekutepi, n. A game (?). Bl.

napo'gmus, cont. of napogmuza. Yuⁿkaⁿ - icu na kul ihpeya.

napo'gmuza, v.a. To close the hand on.

Napowagmuza. Napogmus oyuspa. Napomayagmuzapi. B.H.137.27.

naṗo'gna, n. What is in the hand, a handful. Caŋhaŋpiska - mak'u. -- naṗógnaka, v.a. To put into the hand. Napowagnaka.

naṗoḣ', cont. of napoga. - iyeya. -- naṗóḣya, v.a. To cause to ferment, to leaven, make light. Napoḣwaya. -- naṗóḣyapi, n. Leaven.

naṗo'k̇aśk̇e, n. Cuffs, a bracelet. Syn.- napoktaŋ. - kśupi, Beaded cuffs. Formerly, metal bands, i.e. napoktaŋ, were used.

naṗo'k̇azuŋte, n. The fingers.

naṗo'kṫaŋ, n. A bracelet, an armband.

naṗol', cont. of napota. - iyeya.

naṗol'pota, v. red. (of napota). To wear out with the feet.repeatedly.

naṗoŋ'yaŋ, v. To crush, to grind with the feet. Bl.

napo'ṗa, 1) v.n. To burst, as a boiler, a gun, corn (popcorn). 2) v.a. To burst something.

naṗo'ṗawaǧa, v.a. To rub in the hands. Napowapawaga.

napo'poṗela, n. A motor-cycle.

napo'śiŋ. v.n. To shrivle up while drying. Bl.

naṗo'śṫaŋ, n. A thimble. Also, the prairie coneflower, the long-headed coneflower. Lepachys columnaris. The composite family. Also called asaŋpi iyatke. WE. EM. It is so called because of the shape of the fruit. BT. gave it to horses when they could not urinate. WE. said that a tea of it is good against belly-ache. RV. said a tea of the tops is good for head-ache. WE. #66. Also, napéośtaŋ.

naṗo'ṫa, v.a. To wear out with the feet e.g. one's shoes. Nawapota.

napo'waya, v. To fringe, perhaps. Nawapowaya. Syn.- naswáya.

naṗo'yublaya, (?). Letaŋhaŋ napoyublayapi s'e yuŋka ca napeceśni waimnakiŋ ktelo, i.e. the road is now level. Bl.

naṗo'yujaja, n. A wash basin.

napsag', cont. of napsaka. - iyeya.

napsa'ka, v.a. To break e.g. a cord with the foot, to break something in two with the foot. Nawapsaka.

napsaŋ'ni, n. (of nape and saŋni). The hand on one side, one hand of a person.

napsa'psaka, v. red. (of napsaka). To break in different places e.g. a string. B.H.77.1. -- napsápsakela s'e, (?). - mani, To go trippling. Bl. The napsaka suggests the tearing of a cord with the foot. Bl.

napsi'ca, v.n. To skip, hop, jump around. Nawapsica.

napsil', cont. of napsica. - iyaya. -- napsílya, v.a. To make jump, make dance.

napsi'psica, v. red.(of napsica). To dance about. Also, to spatter out e.g. hot grease when water is dropped into it. Nawapsipsica.

napsi'psil, cont. of napsipsica. - iyaya. -- napsípsilya, v.a. To make skip or dance about. Napsipsilwaya.

napsi'yoḣli, n. A finger-ring, a ring. Also, perhaps, napsiyoḣle.

napsi'yoḣli kutepi, n. A game in which one person holds a stick carrying six rings and tosses them into the air to catch thereafter as many as possible on the same stick. Bl.

napska'śni, adj. Of unclean hands; a sinner.

napsoŋ', Cf. napsuŋ.

napsu', n. A finger. Minapsu. Napsúhu, A finger bone. B.H.274.20.

napsu'haŋska, n. The middle-finger.

napsu'hu okō', n. The spaces between the fingers.

napsu'kaza, n. The five fingers. P. Bl. Cf. napsuokiha, the knuckles of the fingers. Bl.

napsuⁿ', v.a. To kick over and spill. Nawápsuⁿ.

napsu'okaza, n. The fingers.

napsu'okihe, n. The knuckles of the fingers. Bl.

napśa', v. Cf. napśapśa. The word is doubtfully used. -- napśápśa, v. red. of napśa. It refers to something hindering one's walking. - s'e omani, as is said when an old man walks slowly; similarly, nahpahpa s'e omani. Bl. -- napśápśa s'e, adv. With difficulty, slowly. Waśicuⁿ tawa s'e - hiyayelo, as is said when a person walks with difficulty on account of too long clothing, pants or stockings hanging down, like Arabian horses with their hairy feet. Bl.

napśi'ja, v. (?). Bl.

napśuⁿ', 1) v.n. To break by kicking, to dislocate the foot or leg. 2) v.a. To put out of joint e.g. a foot or leg. Nawapśuⁿ.

napśuⁿ'ka, n. Any round growth on one, a lump or swelling. Cf. pśuⁿka.

napta', v.a. To throw over ground, as is done in using a spade. Also, to wear off. Nawapta. Makinapte, A spade.

napta'hena, adv. (?). - ecamoⁿ śni, I did not do it because I forgot all about it. RF. This is an old word. Cf. lotkuⁿkeśni.

naptaⁿ'yaⁿ, v.a. To upset by kicking e.g. a coal bucket; to kick over. Nawaptaⁿyaⁿ. -- naptáⁿyaⁿkel, adv. In the manner of turning over.

napte'ca, adv. Less. Cf. aopteca.

naptel', cont. of napteca. Cf. aoptel. -- naptélya, adv. Less. Cf. aoptelya. -- naptélyela, adv. Less, diminished. Cf. aoptelyela.

napte'tuka, adj. A few. Wicaśa - . BS.

naptu'ga, 1) v.a. To break off with the foot a piece. Nawaptuga. 2) v.n. To break off of itself, as a piece of ice. BD.

naptu'ja, v.n. To crack, split of itself, or by the action of heat or cold. -- naptúptuja, v. red.

naptuś', cont. of naptuja. - iyaya.

nap'a'kaśpeya, v. To let slip or drop from the hands because it is too heavy, or hot etc. Nap'ámakaśpeya.

nap'a'nuⁿk yuza, v. To take hold of something with both hands. Nap'anuⁿk haⁿ, Both his hands are sore.

nap'iⁿ', v.a. To wear around the neck e.g. beads etc. Nupiⁿ śiyotaⁿka nap'iⁿpi. -- nap'íⁿkiya, v.a. To cause to wear on the neck. Nap'iⁿwakiya. -- nap'iⁿpi, n. A yoke. Caⁿ - , An ox-yoke.

nap'i'takaha, n. The back of the hand. Cf. napitakaha.

nap'kuwa ś'aka, v.n. To grasp firmly. Nap'kuwa maś'aka.

nap'o', v.n. To raise dust with the feet, as horses do walking etc. Nawap'o.

nap'o'mna, v.a. To cause to smell by stepping on. Nawap'omna.

nasa', 1) v.a. To hunt buffalo, to surround and kill, as they do in the buffalo hunt. Nawasa. Also, nasé. 2) v.n. To stand erect, as hogs' bristles. Lecetaⁿhaⁿ taku ahinapa, tka nasa s'e ahinapelo: iglakapi śni yelo: śuⁿkakaⁿyaⁿkapi s'elececa yelo. Bl.

nasa'tiⁿ, v. To stretch out, as an animal when dying; to become straight. -- nasátiⁿtiⁿ, v. red. (of nasatiⁿ). To be straight. - iyaya, To go straight as e.g. a hutanacute.

nasa'ya, adv. Prickly, knobby, sharp. - haⁿ. Bl.

naseb', cont. (of nasepa). To go scraping along, cleaning off, brushing off. R. Bl.

naska', v.n. To bleach, get white.

naskeb', cont. of naskepa.

naske'p̣a, v. (of skepa). To leak out, be empty. B.H.106.7.

naski'ca, 1) v.a. To press down with the feet, as a man walking on a hay wagon to get it down. 2) v.n. perhaps. To go down or become less of itself; to settle.

naskil', cont. of naskica. - iyaya, To abate or go down, as a swelling.

nasla', v.a. To grease with the foot. Nawasla.

naslal', cont. (of naslata). Without noise, stilly. - ya, bla, i.e. to walk or crawl up without noise. -- naslaslal, cont. of naslâslata. - omani, ya. D.272.

nasla'slata, v. red. of naslata.

nasla'ṫa, v.a. To go softly up to anything, to crawl up to. Nawaslata.

nasle'ca, 1) v.a. To crack or split. 2) v.n. To crack of split of itself, as a board or the earth in winter. Maka kiⁿ - . Bl. D.67.

naslel', cont. of nasleca. - iyaya. -- naslelya, v.a. To cause to split or crack. Naslelwaya. Caⁿ - , To saw boards on the saw mill.

nasle'sleca, v. red. of nasleca.

nasli', v.a. To crush with the foot e.g. a bug etc. Nawasli. -- v.n. perhaps. To hiss, as wet wood in the fire. -- naslísli, v. red. of nasli. -- naslíya, adv. Oozing out, as sap from a tree.

naslo'haⁿ, v.a. To make slide by kicking e.g. a dog.

naslū'ṫa, v.a. To kick out with the feet, as from one's bed. Nawasluta. -- v.i. To slip out, as a foreign object from an ulcer. D.60.

nasmiⁿ'yaⁿ, v.a. To scrape off with the foot. Nawasmiⁿyaⁿ. -- nasmiⁿyaⁿyaⁿ, v. red. (of nasmiⁿyaⁿ). To scrape or wear off with the feet and leave bare. Nawasmiⁿyaⁿyaⁿ.

nasna', 1) v.a. To make a rattling noise with the feet, as with the spurs. Nawasna. 2) v.n. perhaps. To fall off of itself, as rice when the tying breaks. -- nasnásna, v. red. of nasna. - mani, To make a tinkling as one walks.

nasni', v.a. To put out a fire with the foot. Nawasni.

nasoⁿ', Cf. nasuⁿ. For nazuⁿspe, nasoⁿspe; nasoⁿsoⁿ, nasuⁿsuⁿ; nasoⁿyaⁿ, nasuⁿyaⁿ.

nasoⁿ'spe, n. An ax. Cf. nazuⁿspe.

naso'ṫa, v.a. To use up; to destroy with the feet. Nawasota.

nasp̣a', v.n. To get wet. Yuⁿkaⁿ haⁿpa kiⁿ naspapi. -- nasp̣áya, v.a. To wet the feet, shoes; to wet with the feet. Nawaspaya. Si namicispaya ca ito k'eyaś pusmic'iyiⁿ ktelo.

nasṫaⁿ'ka, v.a. To moisten with the feet. Nawastaⁿka.

nasu', n. The upper part of the head; the brain. -- nasúhu, n. The skull, the cranium. Syn.- natahu.

nasu'kaza, n. The knuckle.

nasu'la, n. dim. (of nasu). The brain, the cerebrum. For this we do not use nasú. Nasu kaosnisni s'e, as is said when a person has got little hair left and standing in all directions. Bl.

nasuⁿ'p̣akce, n. A comb. Note: this is from nasu and pakca. - swula, A fine comb.

nasuⁿ'suⁿ, v. red. (of nasuⁿ). To struggle. Nawasuⁿsuⁿ.

nasuⁿ'yaⁿ, adv. (of nasuⁿ). With the feet and legs stretched out. Kat'eyetaⁿka - yaⁿka, To sit on the ground with both legs stretched out. - ḣpaya. RF.

nasu'suza, v. red. (of nasuza). To snap, as ice forming.

nasu'śtiⁿca s'e, (?). The word is used for a person who has very little hair left, thin and looking ragged. Bl.

nasu'ṫa, v.a. To trample hard.

nasu'za, v.n. To splinter or fly off, as a piece of a bone; to snap, as water freezing.

naswa', v.n. (?). The word is used to denote what is done when one steps e.g. on a silk dress and it stretches partly, i.e. the thread tears one way.

naswa'ka, v. To fall off, as feathers.

naswa'ya, v. To fringe. Nawaswaya. Bl. Cf. napowaya.

nas'a', v.n. To simmer, make a slight noise, as water before boiling. It is said also of a fast horse. Bl.

nas'iŋ'yela, (?). Ituŋkab - yuŋka, i.e. to lie on the back.

nas'ō's'o, v.n. To shuffle, to scrape the feet along as in dancing, to draw the feet over the floor as Indians do to show their anger. Nawas'os'o. - mani. Bl.

naś, conj. emph. (of na). And. B.H.19. 7;123.5. B.H.(book): 92,99,108,124, 133,135,136,145.

naśa', v.n. (of na and śa). To become red, to blush. Ite naśa hiŋgla, His face colored up.

naśab', cont. of naśapa. - iyeya. -- naśábya, v.a. To cause to soil with the feet. Naśabwaya.

naśā'ḱayela, adv. Fresh, not closed up as yet, as a wound. Oo kiŋ - haŋ na we hiyu.

naśa'k'oḣayeya, (?). - ayugal wauŋ welo, peta kiŋ, i.e. spread out hands over the stove. Bl.

naśa'pa, v.a. To soil, blacken, defile with the feet.

naśe'ca, v.a. To make wither by trampling on e.g. grass. Nawaśeca.

naśel'ya, v.a. To cause to trample on and make wither. Naśelwaya.

naśib', cont. of naśipa. - iyaya. -- naśibśib, v. red. of naśib. - iyeya. - mani, as one does when the shoe laces are loose.

naśi'ca, v.a. To defile, spoil with the feet. Nawaśica.

naśi'cahowaya, v.a. To make howl by kicking e.g. a dog, and not a human being. Nawaśicahowaya.

naśiŋ'śiŋ, v.n. To contract and wrinkle as warm glue does when cooling off etc., or a wet cloth when drying. -aya. Bl. - iyaya, as is said of something that has been stretched and cut in two, and then the two pieces crinkle, i.e. shorten.

naśi'pa, v.a. To bend e.g. a stick by stepping on. Nawaśipa.

naśka', 1) v.a. To untie with the foot. Nawaśka. 2) v.n. To come untied of itself.

naśkab'ya, v.a. It seems to mean to make a spinning top run on another top. Naśkabwaya.

naśka'haŋ, part. Untied, loose, as a knot. R. Bl.

naśkaŋ', (?). Tapoŋ - s'e iŋyaŋke, i.e. the cheeks go up and down from the jolting of the wagon. Bl.

naśkaŋ'śkaŋ, 1) v.a. To shake or move about with the foot. Nawaśkaŋśkaŋ. 2) v.n. To move rapidly, as by machinery. Itowapi - , Moving pictures. Also, to be shaking, trembling, as on an automobile when the engine starts. Note: The difference between this word and kaśkaŋśkaŋ which means a shaking from slow bumping or hitting or striking is that naśkaŋśkaŋ is a rapid motion. For the same reason, moving pictures are called itowapi naśkaŋśkaŋ.

naśka'ṗa, v. (?). The word is used of two tops which while spinning run against each other. Bl.

naśka'wahaŋ, part. Untied, loose, as a knot. R. Bl.

naśki'ca, v.a. To press with the foot, press out by trampling on. Nawaśkica.

naśkil', cont. (of naśkica). To press out with the foot e.g. the intestines after butchering. - iyeya.

naśki'śka, v.a. To make rough e.g. the ground by trampling on it. Nawaśkiśka. Caⁿku naśkiśkapi ca caⁿpagmiyaⁿpi t'iⁿzani mani śni yelo. Bl.

naśko'kpa, v.a. To indent, make a hollow place with the foot. Nawaśkokpa.

naśko'pa, 1) v.a. To twist with the foot. Nawaśkopa. 2) v.n. To twist or become crooked of itself. -- naśkóśkopa, v. red.

naśla', v.a. To make bare with the feet. Nawaśla. -- naśláya, v.n. To come off, as the hull from corn when boiled. -- naśláye, (?). - niktepi, They bother you always. Śehaⁿśtuka tuweni - nikte śni hwo? For once, at last, they leave you unbothered, don't they? Bl.

naśle', (?). Cehupa namaśle kinica, as one says chewing suddenly into something very sour. Bl.

naśle'ca, v.a. and perhaps n. To split something heavy or big with the foot and with effort.

naślel', cont. of naśleca. - iyaya. -- naślélya, v.a. To cause to split. Naślelwaya.

naśle'śleca, v. red. of naśleca.

naśli', v.n. To swell and form sores; to ooze out, as sap from trees or juice from meat roasting. Namaśli.

naślog', v. cont. (of naśloka). To run or flee away suddenly, as horses do at times. - glicú, To start off home suddenly. Kos hiyuya na - iyaya.

naślo'ka, 1) v.a. To kick off e.g. one's shoes. Nawaśloka. 2) v.n. To come off, escape, fly out, as the cork of a bottle.

naślul', cont. (of naśluta). To slip without falling. - Hpayelo. Bl. -- naślúlya, v.a. To cause to slip. Naślulwaya. -- naślúślul, cont. (of naśluśluta). To slip repeatedly as horses do on ice.

naślu'śluta, 1) v.n. To slip often. 2) v.a. To make smooth with the feet. Nawaśluśluta.

naślu'ta, v.n. To slip, slide, slip down. Nawaśluta. Perhaps also v.a.

naśna', 1) v.n. To slip, miss one's footing. 2) v.a. To miss something in kicking. Nawaśna. Caⁿku nauⁿśnapi, tka taⁿyaⁿ uⁿkupelo, i.e. inspite of missing one's road when coming home. Bl. -- adv. again and again, always. - apapi. There is some doubt about the use of śna, adv. compounded this way. Cf. śna. -- naśnáśna, v. red.

naśni'ja, 1) v.a. To trample on and kill e.g. the grass. Nawaśnija. 2) v.n. To be withered, as after a frost.

naśo'ka, v.n. To thicken, swell, as a piece of wood in water; to get a thick skin on one's feet from walking. Namaśoka.

naśo'śa, v.a. To make turbid or dirty e.g. water with the feet. Nawaśośa.

naśpa', v.a. To break off anything with the foot. Nawaśpa. -- naśpáśpa, v. red. (of naśpa). To break off many things with the foot.

naśpe'ya, v.a. To cause to break off with the foot e.g. by pushing somebody. Naśpewaya.

naśpi', v.a. To break off e.g. fruit with the foot. Nawaśpi.

naśpu', v.a. To break off with the foot something sticking, e.g. pumpkins; to knock off something with the foot. Nawaśpu. -- naśpúśpu, v. red. (of naśpu). 1) v.a. To break off pieces, break in pieces with the foot e.g. tallow. Nawaśpuśpu. 2) v.n. To come to pieces, as in boiling.

naśta'śta s'e, adv. As though tired out or exhausted. - mani, To walk as though one's legs were weak. WE.

naśu'ja, v.a. To bruise or crush with the foot. Nawaśuja.

Naśuⁿ'hape, n. prop. A Flathead Indian. Also, Natableca. SB.

naśuś', cont. of naśuja. - iyeya.

naśu´śka, (?). Tezi naśuśkayeya wiṁaṗe nat'iⁿsya he kapi.

naśu´śuja, v. red. (of naśuja). To bruise or mash by trampling on. Nawaśuśuja. -- naśúśuś, cont. B.H.112.16.

naṫa´, n. The head of man. Cf. pa.

nata´, v. To kick up, perhaps to kick out of the way. - ole, as they say to a child that kicks its cover to the feet where it is heaped up. - aya.Bl. - iyeya.

naṫa´ akaḣpe, n. A hat. It is an old word. WR.

Nata´ bleca´, n. prop. A Flathead Indian. -- n. A square head.

naṫa´coḱuḣpuḣpu, n. The dandruff. P.Bl.

natag´ haⁿ, cont. (of nataka). To stand fastened, as a closed up fence. - iyeya, To fasten, as in a hurry perhaps.

naṫa´ġuġu, n. A curly head, e.g. a Negro. Bl.

naṫa´ha, n. The skin of the head. Bl.

naṫa´hu, n. The skull, the cranium.

naṫa´ḣpuḣpu, n. Dandruff.

nata´ḣtoⁿyaⁿ, v.a. To beat e.g. eggs. Nataḣtoⁿwaya. P. Bl.

nata´ḱa, v.a. To bolt, bar e.g. a door; to close up, fence e.g. a field; to stop a leak. Nawataka.

nata´ḱuniśni, 1) v.a. To destroy with the foot. Nawatakuniśni. 2) v.i. To turn into nothing by itself, vanish by itself, evaporate.

naṫa´naśuⁿṗakce, n. A side comb, an ornament.

nataⁿ´, v.a. To touch with the foot, feel with the foot. Nawataⁿ. Haⁿ nataⁿtaⁿ.

naṫaⁿ´, v.a. To make an attack, go after and rush upon e.g. the enemy. Nawataⁿ. Hecel - aglinajiⁿ.

nataⁿ´ka, v.n. To enlarge, become larger, as a shoe.

nataⁿ´oⁿb, adv. Leaning, inclined. -- natáⁿoⁿbya, adv. Leaning. - haⁿ, It stands leaning.

naṫaⁿ´ṫaⁿ, v. red. (of naṫaⁿ). To rush upon, perhaps repeatedly, or in great numbers. - hiyupi.

nataⁿ´taⁿ, v.a. red. (of nataⁿ). To feel one's way with the feet. Nawataⁿtaⁿ. Haⁿ - . Kenataⁿtaⁿ kte s'e haⁿpokihe lo. Bl. -- natáⁿtaⁿkel, adv. (of nataⁿtaⁿ). Thus feeling one's way with the feet. - iwaśtegla yahe. D.223.

naṫa´śla, adj. Bald-headed.

naṫa´ṫa, v.a. To shake off e.g. dust from one's feet or blanket. Bl.

nata´ta, v.a. To heap up with the feet, as is done when boys wrestle and pile up ground with the feet; or as children kick down their bed clothing and heap it up at the feet. Also, perhaps, naṫaṫa.

naṫa´ yazaⁿpi, n. A head-ache, a sickness the Sioux were subject to.

naṫeb´, cont. of natepa. - iyeya. -- naṫébya, v.a. To cause to wear off e.g. one's horse's hoof. Natebwaya.

naṫe´mni, v. To sweat from excitement. B.H.255.19. - yeye. Also, to perspire from heat, warm weather. Namatemni.

naṫe´ṗa, 1) v.a. To wear off with the foot e.g. one's shoes; to wear short, as a hoof or shoe. Nawatepa. 2) adj. Worn off, worn out, as a shoe.

naṫib´, cont. of (natipa). To draw up as a person dying; to draw up, as a hide in dying. -- naṫíbṫiṗa, v.n. red. (of natipa). To have the cramps. Namatibtipa. -- naṫíbya, v.a. To cause to draw up. Natibwaya.

naṫi´ca, v.a. To scrape with the foot, i.e. away from one, but not pawing like a horse nor like a child kicking off the bed clothes.

naṫi´kṫica, v.n. To thicken by boiling; to trample, make thick by tramping.

natil', cont. of natica. - iyeya.

natiŋ', v. To be in convulsions. - ȟpaya, To lie in convulsions, as a dying person or an animal. Bl.
natiŋ'tiŋ, v. red. of natiŋ. Bl.

naŧi'ṗa, v.n. To draw up, as does leather when put on the fire; to crisp; to cramp, contract the muscles. He lecel eya ayaśtaŋ kiŋ icuŋhaŋ skayela (maȟpiya) he k'oŋ natipe s'e, waŋkatakiya kigla.

naŧi'ṗasise, n. Hair pins.

naŧi'ŧaŋ, v.a. To pull backwards or forwards by bracing the feet, as a horse in pulling, as a person in using the brake on a wagon or in stretching something. Nawatitaŋ.

nati'yuskite, n. (nata-iyuskite). A wreath or crown. Wateślaleke and nakputake are misnomers.

natku'ǧa, 1) v.a. To break square off with the foot. 2) v.n. To break square off of itself, to break by itself, as a mirror or window pane. BD.

natog'yeya, (?). Iśta - yauŋ welo, i.e. you look terrified. Bl.

naŧo'ǩiiŋyaŋke, n. (nata-okiiŋyaŋka). The sutures of the skull. EF.

naŧo'ŧo, v.a. To knock at something, e.g. a door with the foot; to make a noise by knocking with the foot. Nawatoto.

naŧu'ȟŧuȟ, v.a. (tuga). To lift or pull and so becoming hunched over; to make horses pull hard. - yeya. Bl.

natu'ja, v.i. To have the itch. Namatuja. LT.

naŧu'ǩa, v.a. To stamp off and destroy e.g. fur. Nawatuka.

naŧu'ta, v.n. To smart, as one's feet by travelling much. Si namatuta.

naŧu'tka, v.a. To knock pieces off with the foot. Nawatutka.

nat'a', v.a. To kill by kicking. Nawat'a.

nat'e'ǩinica, v. (nat'a-kinica). To annoy, vex; to worry, to beg to death.

nat'e'ya, v. To kill by running e.g. a wagon.

nat'iŋ'ȟyeya, v.a. To cause to grunt, as with a medicine given to a woman in the throes of childbirth. FB.

nat'iŋs', cont. of nat'iŋza. - iyeya.
nat'iŋ'za, v.a. To press hard with the foot. Nawat'iŋza.

nat'o'ṗe s'e, adv. In a tottering manner, when e.g. one walks a great distance and then is ready to drop. - omani.

nat'uŋg'yakel, adv. Hesitatingly, carefully as though afraid. St. Obs. Syn.- kokipeya.

nat'uŋ'ka, v.n. To refuse to go, hesitate, hold back, as a man not liking an order or such. Nawat'uŋka.
nat'uŋ'kiya, v.a. To make afraid, make hesitate. Nat'uŋwakiya.
nat'uŋ't'uŋgyakel, adv. red. of nat'uŋgyakel.

nauŋg', cont. (nauŋka). To gallop, as a horse does. - iyaya.
nauŋg'ǩiya, v.a. To cause to gallop.
nauŋ'ka, v.n. To gallop, as a horse does. Nawauŋka. Nauŋka, or nauŋg, u, He came galloping. Pte na taȟca ko nauŋkapi na śake icicaśla nauŋkapi. Also perhaps, to kick and make fall.

nawa'kaŋkaŋla, adv. Carefully, quietly. - mani, To walk carefully. Bl.

nawa'nica, 1) v.a. To trample to nothing, destroy by trampling on. Nawawanica. 2) v.i. To turn into nothing by itself, disappear, evaporate.
nawa'nil, cont. (nawanica). To walk or run off sickness or fatigue; to destroy or annihilate.

nawaŋ'ǩal, v. To rise upward. - hiyu, To spring upon, as on the boards of a floor. - iyeya, To blow up, as with powder. Etaŋhaŋ (cega) wicanape waŋ - hiyu śke, From it a human hand rose to the surface. D.54.

nawa´ťe, n. The temples. Nawate anuⁿk mayazaⁿ.

nawa´za, v.a. To scratch with the foot; to move the foot to and fro, as in crushing a bug or in putting out a fire; to scratch with the foot, as chickens do. Nawawaza. Naic'iwaza, To scratch one's self with the foot, as do horses or dogs.

nawe´ġa, v.a. To break by kicking, to break with the foot. Nawawega. Śuⁿka-wakaⁿ namaȟtaka na namawega.

naweȟ´, cont. of nawega. - iyeya.
naweȟ´ķiya, v.a. To cause to break with the foot. Also, naweȟya. Naweȟwaya.

nawi´cakśeca, n. The cramps, an old-time sickness that led to death, convulsions. Bl. LT. Obs. Syn.- nawicatipa, nakśecapi.

nawi´caśli, n. The measles, a rash.

nawi´caťipa, n. Cramping, cramps.

nawi´ciťe, n. The flesh or muscles on the upper arm near the shoulder. - el mayazaⁿ. Bc.

nawi´gnuni, v.a. To destroy with the foot. Nawawignuni. R. Bl.

nawi´lwiťe s'e, (?). - mani, To drag one's feet over the ground as though one gathered snow together. Bl.

nawiⁿ´ceśni, adj. Immovable, by the feet perhaps, as a rock set firmly in the ground.

nawiⁿ´ja, v.a. To trample down e.g. grass; to mat down; to bend something by stepping on it, e.g. a fence wire. Nawawiⁿja.

nawiⁿl´ iyeya, v.a. To scratch one with one's foot; touch one, as when attracting another's attention. Bl.

nawiⁿś´, cont. of nawiⁿja. - iyeya.
nawiⁿ´śķiya, v.a. To make one bend down with the foot, as a fence wire. Also, nawiⁿśya.
nawiⁿ´świⁿja, v. red. (nawiⁿja). To make crooked or bent by stepping on repeatedly; to cause to trample down.

nawiⁿ´ťa, v. (?). P.

nawi´zi, v. To be jealous, envious. Nawawizi.
nawi´zipaⁿyeya, (?). Nige - wipi, To be filled up with food, as a full bag. Bl. Cf. naiⁿyaⁿyeya, naglakeyeya.
nawi´zis'a, n. A jealous person.

nawo´holyeya, (?). Ila kiⁿ - matásakelo, i.e. the mouth is tube-like, with lips protruding and stiff from the cold. - po, To swell into the shape of a tube.

nawo´saķiya, v.n. To bristle up, stand erect, as hair. Hiⁿ - .

nawo´sla iyeya, v. To cause something to stand upward by stepping on, as on a pile of wood.

naye´ic'iya, v. refl. To make one's self perspire, as in a sweat lodge. Note: the word is quite doubtful.

naza´mni, v. To open by kicking away, as children kick away the bed clothes. - s'e. Bl.

nazaⁿ´, v. To hurt; to stun by kicking. Nawazaⁿ.

naze´ya, v. To filter. Nazewaya. P. Bl.

nazi´ca, adj. Over-stretched, as a machine belt that becomes too wide. -- v. perhaps a. To stretch e.g. a rope by means of the knees or feet. Bl.

nazi´gzil, (?). Yuⁿkaⁿ taku - iwahaⁿ waku. MS.356.

nazoⁿ´spe, n. An axe. - ihupa, An axe handle. - opetaⁿka, A broad-ax.

ni, pron. in comp. Thee, thou; thy, thine; your, yours. Cf. ma, mi.

ni, suff. It converts a word into the contrary (śni); thus: Waⁿjini, haⁿkeni, tukteni. Eyaś tostos haⁿkeni wate śni ka, eye. Icinuⁿpani. B.H.282.8.

ni, v.n. To live. Wani.

ni, particle. Cf. toke...ni, nuⁿwe. B.H.84.4;245.20. As a particle it is put after the verb expressing a wish.

nica', v. (of ka). He means you.

ni'ca, v.n. To be destitute of, have none of. Manica. Ninica. Uⁿnicapi. -- ni'caole, v. To look for poor people. Nicaowale.

ni'ci, pron. and prep. For you. Note: this does not mean "with you", although BD. holds it means both for and with you. Cf. nicica.

nici'ca, prep. and pron. With you. Tokśa - wauⁿ kte lo. B.H.48.2. Itaⁿcaⁿ kiⁿ - yauⁿ, The Lord is with you. B.H. 74.14. -- nicicaya, (?). - wauⁿ. Pb.6.

nic'i, refl. pers. pron. of 2nd pers. Yourself.

niġe', n. The paunch, the stomach.

niġe' saⁿla, n. An antelope. Bl. Also, the prairie antelope or the gazelle. Syn.- tatokala.

niġe'taⁿka au'pi, n. A sickness of the Sioux; the swelling of the abdomen with the arms and legs lean. Bl.

niġe' taⁿkiⁿ'yaⁿ, n. A by-name for chiefs. - wacipi kte lo, i.e. each one having a hatchet. BT.

nihaⁿ', adj. Afraid. Manihaⁿ. -- niháⁿyaⁿ, v.a. To scare. Nihaⁿwaya. R. Bl.

nihiⁿ'ciya, v.n. To be frightened, scared, to cry or scream as in fright; to hurry. Nihiⁿmiciya. Nihiⁿuⁿkiciyapi. -- nihi'ⁿciyakel, adv. In fright.

niḣka'zilk̇iya, v. (of nige and kazilya). To fast, i.e. stretch one's stomach. Niḣkazilwakiyiⁿ kte. Bl.

niḣ'kpa'ṫaⁿ, v. To eat little, knowing that something better is coming. Bl.

niḣ'ṫo'kayeyaśni, v. To fill one's self. Niḣ'tokayewayaśni. Bl.

nii'c'iya, v. To make one's self live, save one's self, to escape, have a narrow escape. Pb.35.

nik̇a', (?). Wicanike c'oⁿ hehaⁿ lena ocaⁿku, i.e. in olden times there were roads. BT.

nik̇i'ya, v.a. To prevent, stop. Niwakiya. Niciciya. WE. Syn.- anaptaⁿ.

nik̇i'ya, v.a. (of ni). To cause to live. Niwakiya. Pb.42.

nil, cont. of nica.

nini', adj. Coagulated, curdled, as is said of thick sour milk; quivering. Asaⁿpi nini. -- n. perhaps. Jelly.

niⁿ, interj. May it be, would that it were. Toke bluha niⁿ, I wish I had it. Cf. toke...ni.

nise'hu, n. The hip-bone; os ilium. -- niséhu aglé, n. Something soft to put under one's back while resting. BMj. Bedding. - glihomni kte. Bl.

ni'sk̇o, adv. So large. -- ni'sk̇ok̇eca, adv. So large, so great. -- ni'sk̇ola, adv. Small, only so large; very little, very small (with the idea of derision or contempt). R. Ptehiⁿcala waⁿ - toⁿpelo. He--owaⁿjila eśa ektana nake śni, niskole, takuwe yau ca? Here it is used as a name of contempt. Wicaśa nimaskola. Taḣca ciⁿcala s'e tahu kiⁿ - kagle. Bl. -- ni'skosko, adv. red. of nisko. Maśtiⁿcala iśta - . Bl. Iyotaⁿ honiskosko paⁿpaⁿpi. B.H.108.9. -- ni'sk̇osk̇ok̇eca, adv. red. of niskokeca. -- ni'sk̇osk̇ola, adv. red. of niskola. -- ni'sk̇otaⁿk̇a, adv. So large. -- ni'sk̇oya, adv. So far around. -- ni'sk̇oyela, adv. Only so far around.

niś, pron. You. - niye, You yourself. Cf. iś, miś, uⁿkiś.

niśna'la, pron. pers. You alone, sing. and pl. Niśnapila, You alone. Cf. iśnala, miśnala, uⁿkiśnala.

niśṫu'śṫe, n. The rump, the heavy part near the tail. The lower part of the back. Syn.- nite.

nita', pron. in comp. Your, yours, sing. and pl. Cf. ta, mita, uⁿkita.

nita'wa, pron. Your, yours. Cf. tawa, mitawa, uⁿkitawa.

niṫe', n. The lower part of the back, the rump.

niṫe'hep̣i, n. A woman's skirt, a petticoat. - okíjata, A pair of pants. This is an old word. WR.

nito´, imp. form. This is a woman's imp. form, whereas a man says: yeto. B.H.137.16.

nito´śki, n. A woman's underskirt. Bl. Also, nitośke. R.

ni´uᵑ, v. To be living. Níwauᵑ.

niya´, v.n. To breathe. Waniya. - śni, He does not breathe. -- niyáśniśni, adv. All out of breath. D.272.

niya´ke, adj. Alive. Maniyake. - yuza, To take alive. -- niyákel, adv. Alive, in a living manner. B.H.99.19;114.21.

niyaᵑ´, 1) v.a. (of ni). To cause to live, make live, revive, e.g. a sick person. Niwaya. Also, to let live, miss or fail of killing e.g. game or an enemy. 2) v.n. perhaps. To breathe, take breath, inhale. Cf. niyá. Niya kiᵑ śota s'e hemaceca yelo. Bl.

niya´śniśni, adv. All out of breath. Cf. niya.

niya´śni t'eya, v.a. To choke to death. Niyaśni t'eyapi kte epceȟce. BT. Niyaśniśni kihuᵑni, He arrived at home breathless. D.120.

niya´śota s'e, adv. As though smoke were coming from the nostrils, as it seems with horses in the cold weather. Śuᵑkawakaᵑ kiᵑ - iᵑyaᵑkelo. Bl.

niya´ya, v. red. (of niya). To blow out one's breath vigorously. D.208.

ni´ye, pron. You. Niyepi, You pl. Cf. iye, miye, uᵑkiye.

niye´, v. To cause to live. Cf. niyaᵑ.

ni´ye, v. imp. Take it. The word is used by men.

ni´yecuȟciᵑ, pron. <u>You</u> at any rate. -- niyeȟaleś, pron. Even you. Cf. iyekaleś. Also, niyekeś. P.

ni´yeś, pron. emph. You. Cf. iyeś.

noᵑ´ga, Cf. nuᵑga.

noᵑ´ge, n. The ear, the sense of hearing. -- nóᵑgekpa, adj. Deaf, hard of hearing. Nóᵑgemakpa. -- nóᵑgekpeya, v.a. To make deaf. Nóᵑgekpewaya. -- noᵑgéogmus gluza, v. To hold one's ears tight so as not to hear. B.H. 286.3.

noᵑ´geoȟloka, n. The orifice of the ear.

noᵑ´ge yuza, v. To obey, listen to, heed. El - śni. B.H.35.4.

noᵑ´goptaᵑ, v. (of noᵑge and ptaᵑ). To turn the ear towards, to listen, attend to. Noᵑgowaptaᵑ. Tipi el opa lowaᵑ wicaśi na " - ecoᵑ po" eya. Hokśila kiᵑ iśtiᵑma; caᵑke el - . MS.97. -- nóᵑgoptaᵑptaᵑ, v. red. (of noᵑgoptaᵑ). To listen. - najiᵑ, To stand listening. D.19.

noᵑȟcaᵑ´, adj. Deaf. Manáᵑȟcaᵑ. -- noᵑȟcáᵑ śihuta, v. To pretend not to hear. Noᵑȟcaᵑmaśihuta. Bl. -- noᵑȟcáᵑśihutayela, adv. Pretending to be deaf or not to hear, because one does not care to hear. Bl. - yaᵑka.

noᵑȟka´tiya, v. To awaken one by a sudden noise; to talk very loud, so one does not hear well. Miśtiᵑma tka noᵑȟkátimayáyelo. BT. Bl. -- noᵑȟkátiyece, v.a. To hear suddenly. Capuᵑka noᵑȟkatimayece lo, i.e. hear suddenly the buzzing of a mosquito. Bl. Note: this is not noᵑhkat'iyece.

noᵑ´ȟkeciya, v. To bend one's head sideways, trying to hear.

noᵑ´ȟpaᵑ, n. (of noᵑge and paᵑ). The ringing of the ears. R. Nóᵑȟmapaᵑ, My ears are ringing. Bl.

noᵑȟpe´kic'uᵑ, (?). - yaᵑkahe c'uᵑ taku waᵑ onóᵑȟ s'ake. Bl. -- noᵑȟpékic'uᵑśniyaᵑ, (?). Bl.

noᵑ´ȟsuhute, n. The base of the ear. Also, nóksuhute.

noᵑȟ´ s'aka, v. To be listening, although one does not seem to. Nóᵑȟmas'akelo. Same as nagoptaᵑ eyapi. St. This is an old word.

noᵑȟwa´coka, n. (of noᵑge and wacoka). The cavities on the outer ear. Bl.

noᵑȟwa´zaza, (?). Noᵑȟwámazaza tka

noŋȟkatimayayelo, as a man says when asked why he is silent while the other people talk much. Bl.

noŋȟwica'ȟloke s'e, (?). - ociciyakiŋ kte, I'll explain it to you, that is.

noŋ'ȟ'opaya, adv. (of noŋge and opaya). (?). - yazaŋ, To have an ear-ache.

noŋwaŋ', v.n. To swim. Also, nuŋwaŋ. Wanoŋwaŋ. Yuŋkaŋ mini el - na "Le wanoŋwaŋ welo", eya; "na le iyuha ecoŋ po". - niuŋ.

num, cont. (of nuŋpa). Two. -- númkaskaska, adv. By twos. - ye wicaśi. B.H.218.13. -- númlala, adj. Two alone, only two. -- númnum, adj. Two and two,

nu'mnuŋṗa, adj. red. (of nuŋpa). By twos.

nu'mnuza, adj. Creaking or sounding, as a house does when shaken by the wind. Tipi haŋhepi ataya - he.

nu'ni, v. To wander, to miss the road and wander about, get lost; to be mistaken about a thing. Wanuni. Hece caŋku yanuni kte śni. -- núniniyaŋ, adv. red. of nuniyaŋ. -- núniya, v.a. To cause to wander. Nuniwaya. -- núniyaŋ, adv. Wandering, lost. - mani. To blunder one's way.

nuŋ or nuŋwe, fut. particle. It is used in place of kta. P. Bl.

nuŋ, v. 2nd pers. sing. (of uŋ). To use.

nuŋ'blala, adj. Only two.

nuŋ'ġa, adj. Enlarged, grown-out and hardened. It is used in speaking of a place that grows after being sprained or so, e.g. the back etc. Thus: cuwi - , A hunch back; iśkahu - , An enlarged ankle; tacaŋ nuŋȟnúga, A lumpy body. Nuŋȟnuga, With many lumps. Manúŋga.

nuŋȟcaŋ', v. To be deaf, hard of hearing. Nuŋȟmacaŋ.

nuŋȟnuŋ'ġa, adj. red. (of nuŋga). Swollen up.

nuŋ'ȟ's'a, v. To hear well. Nuŋȟmas'a, I hear well. WE.

nuŋ'ka, v. 2nd pers. sing. of yuŋka.

nuŋ'pa, num. adj. Two; twice. -- núŋṗaḱiya, adv. Twice; in two ways.

nuŋ'ṗoweciŋhaŋ, Cf. oweciŋhaŋ. B.H. 293.9.

nuŋs'e', adv. Almost, nearly. Cf. ka, suff. T'e - ake kini. Sa - , Almost red. Waniyetu nuŋs'iyohakab. MS.164. Tohaŋl kte - nicuwapi kiŋ. MS.571. -- nuŋs'eléceca, adv. Almost, pretty near. Tipi kiŋ tiyo nawapa - yelo.

nuŋśnuŋ'jahela, adj. Flexible, perhaps, as bones of a child; tender, like fresh young leaves. Also, nuŋśnúŋja. Caŋiŋkpa kiŋ - .

nuŋwaŋ', Cf. noŋwaŋ.

nuŋwe', v.n. and explic. Let it be so, expressive of desire; may it be so, Amen. Wakaŋheja otuyubleza; maka iyokiseya tataŋka ota nawaȟ'oŋ ca wakaŋheja wagluhika - . Bl.

nuṗiŋ', adj. Both. -- nupiŋcaska, adv. Both together.

nuṗiŋ'ṫu, adv. Alike, equal, as two things.

nuṗiŋ'yaŋ, (?). - zaniyaŋ okanuŋkihuŋnipi kte. B.H.124.25.

*

o , prefix. It forms nouns of verbs; thus: kaśpá, okáśpe.

o , prep. prefix. 1) cont. (of ogna). In, into. Prefixed to verbs, it makes the locative form in "o"; thus: okáśtaŋ, To pour into. 2) cont. (of oŋ). For. It is prefixed to verbs to indicate purpose, for the purpose of; thus: okuwa waśte, It is good for following, i.e. easily followed.

o , v.a. To shoot, to hit when shooting. Wao. Uŋk'opi.

oa'ble, adv. In a pile, as in placing pieces of beef in a pile. This is an old word. - éoŋpa. Also, oáblel.

oa'gle, n. The end of the stem that is inserted into the bowl of a pipe; a place of holding or resting something. R. Bl. -- oáglehaŋ s'e, adv. As a foundation. B.H.120.3.

oa'he, Cf. owahe.

oa'hececa, adj. Better, pretty well, as is said of one sick. Aliya kiŋ ogna - kilo ca ogna uŋyaŋpi ktelo, i.e. going along ridges is better, when the snow is not drifted. LB.

oa'hiyaye, n. (of ahiyaya). A going or taking sound; a tune, the air of a tune.

oa'ie, n. (of aia). Slander.

oa'ƙaȟpe, n. A cover e.g. for a bed etc. Bl. P.

oa'ƙaŋƙaŋ, n. A seat. - haŋska, A bench. -- oáƙaŋƙe, n. Anything used for a seat; a wagon seat. This is a cont. of oáƙaŋyaŋƙe.

oa'ƙate, n. The drawing of a bow. - waśte, A bow easy to draw. - śica, A bow hard to draw. Bl.

oa'ƙiȟ'aŋ, n. (of akiȟ'aŋ). Starving.

oa'ƙinica, n. (of akinica). A dispute, perhaps.

oa'kiyecoƙaŋ, adv. In the middle, before others. Na ob ecoŋpi el - ecoŋ na ake tawa kiŋ opi, i.e. he was fighting in the middle, between the two conflicting parties.

oa'ƙiyela, adv. (of akiyela). Near, not far.

oa'kśu, n. A load; an armful.

o'aletka omni'ciye, n. Cf. aletka.

oa'li, n. A step, as on a buggy or in a flight of stairs.

oaŋ'petu caŋ, adv. Daily. Also, oaŋpetu ka caŋ. - wacekiyapi kta. LP. Oaŋpetu iyohi, ohiŋhaŋna oyasiŋ. Oaŋpetu ka caŋ na hiŋhaŋnaȟci kikta na. B.H.60.23;185.3;42.6;29.2. Bl.

oa'p̄e, n. (of apa). Strokes, stripes, beatings; the striking of a clock; an hour.

oa'śica, adj. (of aśica). Unpleasant, disagreeable, as the country, the weather etc. Also, in the sense that something does not stand well on something else. Bl.

oa'śilya, adv. Not standing well on, not up to standard. - helo, It does not stand well. Bl. Also, perhaps, oáśilyakel, i.e. when something does not mix well or appear appealing, not presentable or pleasant.

oa'śkayela, adv. Near, short. Bl.

oa'u, n. Access to. Bl.

oa'waŋyaŋke śi'ce, adj. perhaps. Hard to watch. Bl. Syn.- oyuha śice.

oa'ye, n. (of aya). Continuation; progressing thing. Iapi - etaŋ uŋkagiŋ kte, i.e. we will continue finding words when I come again. Taku ota tiwahe - na oigluha.

oa'yuśtaŋ, n. (of ayuśtaŋ). A stop, cessation from.

ob, prep. (of opa). With, together with (more than one being ref. to). Kici is used when speaking of one. Na ob taŋyaŋ upi, na ob taŋyaŋ uŋpi.

obe', n. A division, class, sort.

o'bic'iya, v. refl. Same as opeic'iya. Caŋkeś - wol iyotake. To join, conform self to. B.H.3.13;46.5;65:10;

78.8;273.10.

obla'ska, n. (of blaska). The flat side of anything. -- obláskaya, adv. On the flat side, flat.

obla'ya, adj. (of blaya). Level. -- obláye, n. A level place, a plain; a valley. -- obláyela, adv. Level. Also perhaps, adj. -- obláyeya, adv. Evenly.

oble'ca, 1) adj. Cornered, edged, as a board or a house (tent). Hence, tiyobleca, A square (cornered) tent. 2) n. The edge e.g. of a board or a blanket; the edge or bit of an ax etc.

oble'cahaŋ, part. Broken into fragments, as the bones of a dead animal; scattered, as a people. B.H.254.8. -- óblecaheya, adv. Scattered. - aya.

oble'caya, adv. On the side, with the sharp part up, not on the flat surface.

o'blel, cont. of obleca. -- óblelya, adv. Scattered. - naŋkapelo, i.e. you are not ready yet, although we will go now. Bl. -- óblelyakel, adv. In a scattered condition.

obles', cont. of obleza. -- oblésya, adv. Clearly, brightly; soberly.

oble'toŋ, adj. Square-edged. Cf. oblotoŋ.

oble'za, v.n. (of bleza). To be clear, sober. Omableza.

oblō'toŋ, 1) n. A corner of anything, an angle. 2) adj. Cornered, having corners. Caŋna - , Any piece of wood with corners, e.g. 2" x 2" etc.; but not a board, which is caŋ blaska. -- oblótoŋtoŋ, adj. red. (of oblotoŋ). Having many corners, angular.

oblo to'pa soŋ, v. To braid, weave together four strings. Bl. -- oblo yámnila soŋ, v. To braid, weave together three strings. Bl.

o'blula, n. or adj. Rain or wind-proof, as of the roof or walls of a house. Tipi - . EM. Also, calm, sheltered, protected. Waŋna - . Le - , This is a sheltered place. - wanice ca uŋkácaŋpi kte lo.

obśi'ś'ic'iya, v. To have much but not giving anything away. Bl. Ecaca - naŋkelo. BT.

o'btu, prep. With (referring to more than one). B.H.41.7.

oca'ǧa, v.n. (of caga). Freeze or become ice in.

oca'ȟsu, v. (?). Wakpala oguhaŋ oyasiŋ - ca oomani śice. Bl.

oca'je, n. Kind, sort, species; name. Na wamakaśkaŋ - oyasiŋ ahiyaya. Na taku woyute - oyasiŋ etaŋhaŋ icu.

ocaŋ'koze, n. The swinging of a stick, towards an object that is distrusted to keep it away. Na oonakijiŋ el ihuŋni na - k'oŋ hecena iyawicaȟpayapi na wicakasotapi. Na Wana ekta ikiyela yapi; ehaŋl owicakiyapi; ehaŋl Taśuŋke Witko ekta tokeya okaȟ'ol iyeic'iyiŋ na ocaŋkoza. MS.527.

ocaŋ'ku, n. A road, street, way. -- ocáŋku s'e, adv. (?). -- ocáŋkutoŋyaŋ, adv. Forming a road, perhaps. B.H.112.5. -- ocáŋkuya, perhaps adv. or n. A path, in the manner of a road. B.H.54.14;112.15. Ocaŋkuyapi k'aŋ ogna iȟpeyapi.

ocaŋ'naslece, n. A sawmill. P.

ocaŋ'naṫuȟci, adv. In the middle of something. Bl. - uŋ welo. Bl. St. Syn.- cokata kapi.

ocaŋpa'jipe, n. A carpenter shop.

ocaŋ'ṫeśilya, adv. Sadly. -- ocáŋteśilyakel, adv. In a saddened condition. - kigle. B.H.89.9;234.4.

ocaŋ'yuȟize, n. A place or a house where there is an organ.

ocaŋ'ze, v.n. To anger easily. Macáŋze. Uŋcáŋzepi. -- ocáŋzewakaŋ, adj. Hot-headed, ill-tempered. P. Bl. -- ocáŋzeyakel, adv. In an angry manner. - heya.... B.H.5.19. -- ocáŋzeze hiŋgla, v. To become suddenly angry. Bl.

oca'ṗe, n. A wound. B.H.130.10;274.21.

oca'śtaŋiŋ, v. To be famous. B.H.91.7.

oca'śtoŋ, v. To make a name for one's

self, by doing something great. Ocaśmatoⁿ. BT. Bl. -- ocáśtoⁿka, v. To make a name for one's self in doing something great. Na wana lila - . MS.154.

oce'oⁿ, part. Cooked. - waśte, Something that is cooked easily. - śica. Bl.

oce'sli, v. (of cesli). To defecate in. - tipi, A privy.

oce'ti, n. (of ceti). A fire-place, a chimney. Maza - , A stove. - ipásotka, A coal stove, i.e. one that is high in the shape of a frustum,, tapering to the top, in contrast to a wood stove. EB. - sam iya, A stove pipe. - śol iyeya, A chimney, i.e. the flue. - wóslahaⁿ, A stove pipe.

o'cib, adv. One after another. Na ohaⁿketa - ota ayapi na śuⁿkawakaⁿ kiⁿ heepi slolyapi. -- ócibcib, adv. red. With many things piled on one another, i.e. many flat and straight things.

o'ciblaǧaheya, adv. Abreast, in a row. P. Bl. Cf. ociblagaⁿ, óweciⁿhaⁿ.

o'ciblaǧaⁿ, adv. Abreast, in a row.P.Bl.

o'cihiśniśni, v.n. Not to be unanimous in judgment. Wwc. - uⁿhipi: uⁿptayapila śni. Bl. As for a meeting together, see ociwaśte, ociśica. -- ócihiśniśniyaⁿ, adv. Being strung out in a file, unequally spaced, as horses coming in to the finish line; unequal in size, as the children of a family. - ecoⁿ. Bl. Wwc.

o'cikaⁿ, adv. Having room, roomy.

oci'kcik'aya, red. of ocik'aya. Cf. cik'aya. B.H.194.26.

o'cikpakṗani, adj. red. (of ocikpani). Some longer and some shorter, referring to many. Note: more used perhaps is ocikpanini. -- ócikpakpaniyaⁿ, adv. perhaps. B.H.92.13.

o'cikṗani, adj. Not equal in length, i.e. one taller than the other, as the pipes of an organ, or boys lined up according to size. Syn.- aócikpani. -- ócikṗanini, adj. red. (of ocikpani). Some longer and some shorter.

oci'k'ala, adj. (of cik'ala). Small within. Ti - , A small room. -- oci'k'ayela, adj. (of cik'ayela). Small inside, of small dimensions. Pb.31. Hehé, - ca teḣi iblotaka, i.e. sitting tight between others. Bl.

ociⁿ', v.a. To desire, beg, ask for. Owáciⁿ. Uⁿkóciⁿpi. Mitakoja wakablapi waⁿji ociⁿ u maśi ye. Itaⁿcaⁿ kiⁿ he ociⁿ yelo. B.H.238.6.

o'ciⁿḣiⁿyaⁿpi, v. recip. (of oḣiⁿyaⁿ). They are offended at each other, they feel themselves slighted.

ociⁿ'ḳiwakaⁿ, v. perhaps n. To be unwilling to help one out; to speak so as to bring harm to another. Óciⁿwaḳiwakaⁿ. Bl. Wwc. Ociⁿmayáḳiwakaⁿ yelo, i.e. you do not want to help out, give me one. Ociⁿmic'iwakaⁿ.

ociⁿ'śica, v.n. To be cross, bad-tempered, ill-disposed. Ociⁿmaśica. -- ociⁿ'śicaya, adv. Evilly disposed.

ociⁿ'śilya, adv. Cf. ociⁿśicaya. He kici - wauⁿ. A.

ociⁿ'wakaⁿ, adj. Unwilling to help out; forgetful. Ociⁿmawakaⁿ. Ecakel ociⁿniwakaⁿ yelo, i.e. on purpose you do not want to help me out. Bl.

ociⁿ'waśteya, adv. Well disposed. He kici - wauⁿ. A.

o'ciⁿyaⁿ or o'ciyaⁿ, v. To threaten. Ociniyaⁿpi kiⁿ hena wacewicakiciciya po. B.H.191.17.

o'cipteca, adj. Shorter than. R. Bl.

o'ciptel, adv. Not equal to, lacking. R. Bl. -- ócipteptel, adv. red. of ociptel. Bl. - ecoⁿ. -- óciptetu, adv. Unequal in length, or otherwise. R. Bl.

oci'scila, adv. Little, for a little while. -- oci'sciyela, adv. (of cisciyela). For a little while.

o'ciśica, adj. Being on bad terms with, not getting along with. Fi.

o'citkoⁿs, cont. of ocitkoⁿza. Wicaśa - waciⁿpi, Men think alike.

o'citǩoŋza, adj. Equal, alike, of the same size or length. Caŋ - , Trees of the same height.

o'cit'iŋza, v.n. To be crowded together. R. Bl.

o'ciwaśte, adj. Making up with, being on good terms with. Kici - yo. B.H. 88.27. BD. Cf. ociśica. Note: perhaps both ociwaśte and ociśica are ociŋ waśte and ociŋ śica. -- óciwaśteya, adv. On good terms with. Ake kici - wauŋ welo, I am again on good terms with him. Bl. B.H.157.13.

o'ciyuśṫaŋ, v. (of oyuśṫaŋ). To be one in another, as kettles or cups; to be doubled up, as a blanket. -- óciyuśtaŋśtaŋ, v. red. (of ociyuśṫaŋ). To be placed one inside of another, as kettles, cups, etc. - egnag ayapi. Bl.

oco'ǩab, adv. (of cokab). In the midst.

oco'kaka, v.n. (of coka). To be empty, not full e.g. of persons in a house; there is room.

oco'ǩaŋya, adv. (of cokaŋya). In the middle. Ti - , In the middle of the house. Tipi - , The tent in the middle of the other tents. D.4. B.H.54.11.

ocos', cont. (of ocoza). Warm. - maŋka, I am in a warm place. -- ocósya, adv. In a warm condition. - igluza, To put warm cloths on, dress warmly. ES.

oco'za, 1) adj. Warm, as a house that keeps warm because well-built. Macuwita ca yukśala muŋke; hecel omacoze. Bl. 2) n. Warmth, heat.

ocu', v.n. (of cu). To become damp in; to have drops of water inside.

ocuŋ'wanice, n. A free place with timber on both sides. Bl. Syn.- otiŋtoska.

ocu'ya, v.a. To dampen with dew. - egnaka, To spread out, as a hide, to have dew fall on it. Bl.

oe'ceca, v.n. Slow in coming to boiling, as when at last something is boiling in. Bl.

oe'čiye, Cf. oekiya. Taku - śice: owahokoŋkiye śice, oyaksab śice, wanagoptaŋ śice. Bl.

oe'coŋ, n. (of ecoŋ). Doing, work. - waśte, Good to do, easy to do.

oe'coŋȟca uŋ, v. To do frequently at some place; to go often for a special purpose, as to go frequently to a bawdy-house. R. Bl.

oe'coŋla ecoŋ, v. To do things excitedly before others, in the center. Na waŋna oyate kiŋ ȟaka uŋpi na hocokata oecoŋla ecoŋpi.

oe'coŋśilya, v.a. To cause one to do his work badly by bothering him too much. Taku oecoŋśiluŋyayapelo. Bl.

oe'gle, 1) v.a. (of egle). To set or place in. Oewagle. 2) n. (of egle). A setting down; a saying, a verse, a sentence. Ca - nisuksuta k'el blihic'iya yo.

oe'gnaka, n. (of egnaka). A placing down; a stop. R. Bl.

oe'haǩe, n. perhaps. (of ehake). The last. Na waŋna - kiŋ uŋkisakib ukiye ehaŋl ake uŋgnahela ouwicuŋtapi. Aŋpetu - kiŋ. B.H.44.14;178.19;229.12. Pb.34-5.

oe'ǩiye, v.n. or n. To convince one of something, persuade one of. Taku - śica, i.e. one hard to advise. Wwc.

oe'ṫi, n. (of eti). An encampment ahead. - ataya coco welo. - śicelo. Hececa k'eyaś aliya ekta hinajiŋ yo, tokeś opicakelo. Bl.

oe'ye, n. (of eya). A saying, a verse, sentence. Tuktuŋma le - waśte hwo? Yamni akigle - . B.H.187.13. Pb.37.

o'ġejuya, 1) v. To take hold, as of one's clothes. 2) adv. Together with; among. - yuza.

o'ġeya, adv. Just as it is, whole, altogether, the whole thing. - icu, i.e. to take it as it is. Wicaśa k'uŋ he taoyuŋke - hiyoȟpeyapi. B.H.187.7.

oġi', n. Rust. -- v. To rust. B.H. 193.12. -- oġi', adj. perhaps. Brown. Iśta omagi. BT.

o'ġiŋ, n. Clothes covering, a sheath.

o'ǧiᶯǧiᶯ, v.n. To nod, be nodding, as in one's sleep. - yaᶯka.

o'ǧiᶯkicitoᶯ, v. To clothe for one. Ogewecitoᶯ. -- óǧiᶯkitoᶯ, v. pos. (of ogiᶯtoᶯ). To put clothes on one's own. Oǧewetoᶯ.

o'ǧiᶯtoᶯ, v.a. To put on a cover or a wrapping on something. Oǵewatoᶯ. Ogeic'itoᶯ, To clothe one's self. Hena oᶯ ogenic'itoᶯpi.

oǧi'ya, v. (of gi). To paint yellow.

oglag', cont. of oglaka. He - wahi, I came to tell that.

ogla'ȟniǧa, v. pos. (of okaȟniga). To understand one's own affairs. Owaglaȟniga. -- ogláȟniȟ, cont. - maᶯka.

ogla'ka, v. pos. (of oyaka). To tell of one's own. Owaglaka. Uᶯkoglakapi. Caje - .

ogla'ǩiᶯyaᶯ, n. and perhaps adv. (of glakiᶯyaᶯ). Width, breadth. - ópta. B.H.60.10.

ogla'la, v. pos. of okala.

Ogla'la, n. prop. The name of one of the clans of the Teton Sioux. Omaglala. Cf. okala, To scatter; hence, oglala, To scatter one's own.

ogla'pśuᶯ, v. pos. (of glapśuᶯ). To break or twist or loosen one's own. Owaglapśuᶯ. The word refers to the action of one when he pulls off the bowl of his pipe and holds the stem in his mouth. Bl.

ogla'pta, v. pos. (of oyapta and okapta). To leave some of one's own. Owaglapta. Ha ecela omiglapte, i.e. you gave away everything but the skin. Bl.

ogla'ya, v. To thrust into, as a stick into a tube. -- ogláyeya, v. To shove into.

ogle', v.a. (of gle). To set or place in. Owagle.

o'gle, n. A shirt, a coat. - wakaᶯ, A ghost shirt. - áȟco wanice, A vest. Bl.

oglece'ǩuťe, v. To play the game oglecekutepi which consists in shooting arrows so as to come near as possible to where the first arrow sticks in the ground. Ogleceuᶯkutepi kte. Bl. -- oglecéǩuťepi, n. 1) Two bright stars standing opposite each other, one in the east and the other in the west. 2) The shooting off of arrows to see whose will stick closest to the first. Also, a gambling game with bow and arrow, by trying to strike the bowstring with one's arrow. Mh.

o'gle ci'yuksa, n. A vest.

o'gle haᶯska, n. An old word for "wife" in the mouth of her husband. - waᶯ kici wauᶯ kiᶯ he, i.e. my wife. WR.

o'gle hiᶯśma, n. A fur coat.

o'gle iyo'tkeye, n. A clothes peg. Bl.

o'gle ǩauᶯ'jica, n. A short coat, as opposed to a Prince Albert.

o'gle papo'a, n. A clothes brush.

o'gle ťahu', n. The collar of a coat.

o'gle u'pi haᶯska, n. A Prince Albert coat.

ogle'za, adj. (of gleza). Striped in, in ridges or rows in, streaked. Ite onigleza, You have streaks in your face, i.e. dirty face.

o'gle zigzi'ca, n. A sweater.

ogli'cu, v. To get down into. Wata kiᶯ etaᶯhaᶯ mini - . B.H.209.4. Also, to go down, as from a table or high ground. Aohomni - , To travel downhill on a curved road. Wwc. RTj.

ogli'gla, v.n. (of gligla). To go on a journey, travel from place to place. Owagligla.

ogli'gle, 1) part. Going from place to place. - ya. 2) n. The messangers and guardsmen appointed for a meeting. - wakaᶯ, An angel. -- oglíǵleǩiya, v.a. To cause to go from place to place. Ogliglewakiya.

ogli'gle waǩaᶯ, n. An angel.

ogli'gleya, 1) v.a. To send hither and thither. Ógliglewaya. 2) adv. Going from one place to another. - waun. -- ogligleyapi, n. Those sent, messangers, apostles.

ogli'han, v.n. To fall in anything endwise. -- oglíheya, v.a. To cause to fall in endwise. Oglihewaya. -- oglí-heyakel, adv. Causing to fall in endwise.

ogli'ȟpaye, (?). Owaś'ag konla taogli-ȟpaye lo, i.e. its fall was terrible. B.H.195.21.

ogli'kiya, v. To sharpen. Kan iwapsake wan imicikinte śni ca ogliwakiyin kte lo. Cf. miogle, agluśluśluta. Bl.

o'glimniciye, v. col. pl. They assemble in. Na wanna oglimniciye el saśicun k'on agla opawinge.

o'gliwiṫaya, n. A place to which all roads lead or to which people return. Wwc. Lel ogliwitayelo, as is said of many roads joining in one leading to some place. Bl.

ogli'ya, v.a. To hone e.g. a knife. O-gliwaya. Kaśtaśtag - . Cf. miogle, altern. spelling: miogli.

o'gliyotke, n. A screw eye.

ogli'you, v. (of gliyou). Wana awicapa po, wanna - waśteyelo, i.e. now we are in sight of home, or any place one is called to. Bl. BT. gives oglíhiyou.

oglu', n. Luck, fortune. - śica, Bad luck; - waśte, Good luck. P. Bl.

oglu'homnimni, v. To turn something to and fro constantly. Owagluhomnimni. Yunkan wanji nakpa sanni - .

oglu'ksa, v. refl. To stop abruptly in one's speech. Omigluksa. Nonge can o-yaglukse laka he wapanhe laȟcake c'on. Nonge can oyagluksa laka, taku onici-yakapi kinhan anayagoptan śni yelo.Bl.

oglu'maza, v. pos. (of oyumaza). To hit one's own mark. Owaglumaza.

o'glunǧe, v. pos. (of oyunge). To put on, wear one's own. Owaglunge. Also, ogluge. R.

oglu'sota, v.n. To go off, leave; be all gone, as ducks in the fall of the year.

oglu'spa, v. pos. (of oyuspa). To catch, take a hold of one's own. O-wagluspa. Unkogluspapi. Nonge ogmus - , To close one's ears with the hands.

o'gluṫa, v.n. To be closed up, as a wound. -- ógluṫeya, v.a. To close up. Oglutewaya.

oglu'ze, v. pos. (of oyuze). To dip out from into one's own dish. Owa-gluze.

ogmun'heca, v. To gurgle, as a bad egg. Syn.- oȟlaganla, okaċoċo, oka-ċo.

o'gmus, cont. of ogmuza. I - waun, My mouth is shut. Nonge - ogluspa, To stop one's ears. -- ógmusya, v. perhaps n. To shut, cause to shut. O-gmuswaya.

o'gmuza, v.n. To be shut or closed. Iśta - .

ogna', prep. In, in the direction of (place); in the way of, in one's speech. Nape - taku yuha. Tokel on-nispepi k'on - onspewicakiya po. I-tancan kin he tokel iyukcan na oni-ciyakapi ca - unpo. Na u k'on - gla ca oyate wanyankapi. - nuns'e, A-bout that way. Tipi - . Tokel econ wicaśi k'un - econpi. Woope - . B.H. 45.13;124.15;136.18;118.4;137.26; 154.1;242.2. Also, ógna. R.

ognag', cont. of ognaka. - waśi, I told him to put it in.

ogna'gna, prep. red. of ogna. Ungna toka śka yaiteśla ciyuzin na - acipe cin. Bl. Iye iapi kin - wowicakiya-kapi. B.H.278.7.

ogna'gnaka, v. red. of ognaka. -- o-gnágnaḱapi, n. Something in which things are put or laid away; a chest.

ogna'ka, v.a. To place in. Owagnaka. Unkógnakapi. Na ake hunȟ el - na ota śpanyan. -- ognáḱapi, n. A placing in, a deposite. -- ógnaḱe, n. A place to keep things in. Wakśica - , A cup-board. Minióngnake, A water pitcher; a water tank. Miniskuya - , A salt shaker.

ogna'la, adv. (?). Napognala, Only a handful.

ogna'yaⁿ, adv. Accordingly. Tokel wicaśayatapi kiⁿ ecoⁿ niśi kiⁿ - oyate kiⁿ awaⁿwicalakiⁿ kta.

ogna'yeȟci, adv. Closely, nearly, about. Taku oyasiⁿ - owicakiyake. P. Bl.

ogna'ye-waśte, adj. Easy to fool. D.71.

oǧu', 1) v.n. (of gu). To burn in, as in a kettle. Ite kiⁿ ogu s'e, as is said when the face has not been washed. Bl. 2) n. Scraps, dregs, e.g. coffee grounds, but not the sediment of dirty water.

oǧu'ǧuye, n. A brand, a mark burnt in.

oǧu'haⁿ, n. (?). Wakpala - oyasiⁿ ocaȟsu ca oomani śice, i.e. roads through valleys are icy.

oǧuⁿ'ǧa, v.n. To doze, be drowsy, to be half asleep or awake; to slumber. Omaguⁿga. Yuⁿkaⁿ omaguⁿga na wacipi el cokam muⁿka ena wekta na lila caⁿtemaśica.

oǧu'ya, v.a. To cause to burn in, as meat. Ogúwaya.

oǧu'ye, n. A brand, as on cattle.

ogu'ye, n. A handful. - waⁿji mak'u ye, Give me a handful.

ogwa'haⁿ, part. Fallen to pieces in a hole.

ogwu', v.n. To curdle, to become rather cheesy, as milk. Cf. gwu. -- ogwúgwu, adj. Curdled in e.g. a jar.

o'ha, v.n. To stick to, to adhere to, as do feathers or paint. Omaha. Yuⁿkaⁿ hucaⁿ cokaⁿyaⁿ hehaⁿyaⁿ ataya we oha. Si kiⁿ makaȟliȟlila ohapi. Iyakicoska ówahehcelo, as a man says trying to help another who is being lazy. Bl.

o'haƙab, adv. Afterwards, after. Na le - Ȟliȟlila wakpala el tate ahi. Hecel le hecoⁿpi na - waⁿna waciⁿksapapi. Pb.45. -- óhaƙabya, adv. After.

o'haƙapataⁿhaⁿ, adv. Afterwards. Also perhaps, ohákapataⁿhaⁿ. R. B.H.37.9.

oha'mna, adj. Smelling of skin.

ŏhaⁿ', interj. Oh, yes.

ohaⁿ', v.a. 1) To boil e.g. meat. Owahaⁿ. 2) To put on e.g. socks, to wear. Owahaⁿ. Uⁿkohaⁿpi. Na waⁿna he haⁿpa - omani i.

o'haⁿ, v. To try, attempt; to apply one's self; to study. Ówahe. R. Bl. -- n. A straight place in a river between two bends. R. Bl.

o'haⁿ, prep. Among, within e.g. the woods, in water, fire. Wa - iyaye. Caⁿ ogu - iyaye. Wicota - iyaye. Wicohaⁿ opa. - wicauⁿpi. B.H.55.11;90.4;116.7;118.1;226.1.

o'haⁿgle, v. Cf. ohaⁿgleya.

o'haⁿglela, adv. Through all, through the middle. Syn.- óhaⁿgleyela.

o'haⁿglegleya, adv. red. of ohaⁿgleya. B.H.51.9.

o'haⁿgleya, 1) v.a. To keep near one, follow about, as a colt its mother. Ohaⁿglewaya. 2) adv. Right through, walking through a city e.g. B.H.33.14;265.4. -- óhaⁿgleyela, adv. In the middle, through the middle.

o'haⁿhaⁿ, prep. red. (of óhaⁿ). Within, among, through. Peta kiⁿ okśaⁿ psilya na ecel peta k'uⁿ - iyayapi.

ohaⁿ'hepi, n. perhaps. A given night. - el, On a certain night. B.H.30.8.

o'haⁿketa, adv. At length, at the end; finally, after a while. Lila waⁿyakapi na oyuspapi na lila kuwapi na waⁿna - oyate el uⁿ.

ohaⁿ'pi, part. Boiled.

ohaⁿ'ska, n. (of haⁿska). Length. -- oháⁿskeya, adv. In length. B.H.7.8; 60.10. - epiⁿ kte.

o'haⁿzi, n. Shade, a defense from the heat, shadow. Caⁿwegna - el iśtiⁿma. -- óhaⁿziglepi, n. A bower made of branches. Something set up for a shade e.g. the branches of trees; an arbor; a porch. -- óhaⁿzizi, n. red. perhaps. Shadow. Kenági paha - yukelo, he kapi. Bl.

ohe´, n. A place, a niche; a bed; the old or former place. Mitóhe, nitohe. K'iŋ - , The collar mark. B.H.110.14; 238.9. -- ohé ećé, adv. Without, empty. Caŋke - wahukeza kiŋ gliȟpaye, i.e. it did not hit anything. Caŋke śuŋśuŋla kiŋ - iyaye. - hinajiŋ, wahinawajiŋ, To come to a place and find it deserted. Bl. B.H.88.9;95.24.

ohe´gle, n. A good place for camping, resting etc. Same as oheglepi. WE. Bl.

ohe´glepi, n. A bed-stead, a bed.

ohe´yuŋ, n. A wrapper. -- v.a. To wrap up in. Ohemuŋ, ohenuŋ.

o´hi, v.a. To be able to reach to, tall enough to reach up to, long enough to reach down to. Ówahi, ómahi. Also, to reach to one, be large enough for. Ohipicaśni, as very deep snow, where one cannot get through.

ohi´ic'iya, v. refl. To gain for one's self. Waoŋśila ohiic'iyapi kte. B.H. 189.6.

ohi´ic'iya wicóȟaŋ, n. A pension.

ohi´ḱiya, v. pos. (ohiya). To win back one's own; to give something to another of what one has won, to win for another. Ohiwakiya.

o´himniciye, v. coll. pl. They come together for a meeting. Ake lel ohinimniciyepi kte lo.

o´hinaṗe, n. (hinape). A place of egress.

ohiŋ´haŋna, n. The morning, during the forenoon. - iyohila, Every morning. Also, ohiŋhaŋni. - kiŋ iyohila taŋkal hinajiŋ. - oyasiŋ wowaśi ecoŋ. Bl. D.113. B.H.86.6;105.15.

ohiŋ´ȟpaya, v.n. (hiŋȟpaya). To fall into; to fall from; to forsake. Omáhiŋȟpaya. Yuŋkaŋ gnugnuśka waŋ i etaŋ nape el - . Na taku kakyela wakśica el - .

o´hiŋni, adv. Always. Na hetaŋ - caŋ mahel ecé tipi. -- óhiŋniḱiya, v.a. To cease from, to finish. Ohiŋniwakiya. Also, óhiŋniḱiya.

o´hiŋniyaŋ, adv. Always, all along, all through. Żiŋtkala maka - uŋpi kiŋ iyuha awicagli. B.H.69.13.

ohiŋ´yaŋsyela, adv. In bad humor. - omawani śka wiŋkcekce naŋka yelo. - tak'takamna welo. BT.

ohiŋ´yaŋzeca, v.n. To be stern, cross. Owahiŋyaŋzeca. Wicaśa waŋ ciŋca wahokoŋkiye śni laka wamanoŋ ohiŋyaŋzekelaȟcak. Also, ohiŋyaŋzeke. Bl.

ohiŋ´yaŋzeka, adj. Cranky. Wiŋyaŋ waŋ tokiyataŋhaŋ - hi yelo. Bl.

o´hiṗica śni, v. It cannot be reached, because it is too high. Bl.

ohi´ṫika, v.n. To be furious, terrible, brave. Omahitika.

ohi´ṫila, v.a. To consider brave, furious. Ohitiwala. -- ohiṫilaḱa, n. A brave person. Bl. -- ohiṫi waciŋ, v. To mean to be brave. Bl. -- ohiṫiya, adv. Furiously, terribly. Tona - oȟ'aŋyaŋpi kiŋ hena ecel ewicaglepi. MS.521.

o´hiwitaya, v. coll. pl. perhaps. They assemble. Bl. Syn.- óhimnic'iye.

ohi´ya, v.a. To win, acquire; to get the better of one in any way, as in a game. Ohiwaya. Waŋna tipi he ohiyayelo. Ecel okicize kiŋ ohiyapi. B.H. 56.4.

o´hiya, v.a. To cause to reach. Ohiwaya. -- adv. Reaching to, hanging over, as hair.

ohi´yaye, n. A setting, arrival, term, conclusion. Caŋcaŋ s'e śkaŋ yo; wi - kokela yelo, Hurry up with your work; the sun will set soon. Bl.

o´hiye, n. One length of anything, a line, as in a book. - yamni, when speaking of fence wires. - num zi, - yamni zi, i.e. the police or soldier arm stripes. Ikaŋ kiŋ tablokaŋ ca - num pagmuŋpi. Cuŋkaśke - tob cuŋkaśkapi. MS.481. D.92.

ohi´yeḱiya, v.a. To cause to win. Ohiyewakiya.

ohi´yeya, v.a. Same as ohiyekiya. Ohiyewaya.

o´hiye zaptaŋ, n. A 10' x 12' tent; ohiye topa, An 8' x 10' tent.

ohi'you, (?). - waśte, as is said when one comes near the place of his destination, a place not his own. Bl. Cf. ogliyou.

ohi'yu, v. (of hiyu). To come through, as water through a roof; to leak, to come into, come through on; to pass through, as through a crack. - śica, A bad place to pass through.

oho'ȟpa, v.a. (of hoȟpa). To cough and spit into. Ohowaȟpa.

o'hoƙa, n. One who is respected, while in reality he should be punished.

oho'ƙila, v. pos. (of ohola). To honor one's own.

oho'la, v.a. To respect, honor, worship. Ohowala. Ohouⁿlapi. Also, ohólaƙa. Ohowalaka.

oho'mni, adv. Around, round about. He ki - lapi kte; but they also say: ohomni yo, i.e. Go around that, since the road is bad or there is a carcas lying on it. GA. Omáhomni po, Go around me, avoid me. Bl.

oho'mniƙuwa, v. To hint at; to go round about in regard to. Ohomnimakuwa.

oho'mniyaⁿ, adv. Around, round about; evasive.

oho'wakáⁿyaⁿƙel, adv. (?). - iⁿyaⁿ oⁿ iglaśpaśpa ouⁿye. B.H.203.6.

ohuⁿ'ƙaƙaⁿ, n. A story, myth, fable.

o'huⁿƙeśni, v.n. To be weak, not strong. B.H.249.17. -- ohúⁿƙeśniya, v.a. To cause one to be weak. B.H.74.6. -- ohuⁿkeśniyaⁿ, adv. Poorly. - kuwa. B.H. 93.1.

ohuⁿ'wela, interj. It expresses doubt. B.H.26.16. Bl.

o'huƭa, n. The place where the water meets the feet, the edge or shore. Also, óhute. B.H.45.21. D.37. -- óhuƭapa, adv. At the edge or shore. -- óhuƭaƭa, adv. At the shore. -- óhuƭatahenaƭaⁿhaⁿ, adv. On this side of the shore or water. Syn.- mini kiⁿ itahena, hutátahenataⁿhaⁿ. FB.

ohu'ƭe, n. (of hute). The root, the bottom. -- ohúƭeƭanajiⁿ, adv. In the very beginning. Wh.

ohu'tkaⁿ, n. The beginning of things. B.H.1.1.

oȟ, interj. It expresses disbelief. B.H.44.1.

oȟa'ƙa, v.n. To be stuffed with food, surfeited; to be injured or made sick with food. Omáȟaka. -- adj. Forked, as a stream. -- n. The forks of a stream. -- oȟáƙayaƙel, adv. In many ways. B.H.70.9.

oȟa'ƥe, (?). - taⁿiⁿśniyaⁿ yaⁿkelo, as is said when a man sitting between others is overlooked. Omniciye tipi el tuweni - eśa uⁿ śni. Bl. Tuweni - uⁿ śni, i.e. one finds nobody at home. NP. Haⁿhepi - taⁿiⁿśni wakiyagle, i.e. went home in the evening without anybody knowing it. Bl.

oȟa'ya, v.a. To fill up e.g. a hole with brush wood. P. Bl.

oȟci', v. To dangle or hang perhaps. Bl. -- oȟciȟci, adv. Hanging, dangling. -- oȟciȟciƙes'e, adv. Not having washed one's self and dressed carelessly and raggedly. Bl. -- oȟcíȟciya, v. To make dangle.

oȟiⁿ'yaⁿ, v. To pout, be out of humor about, to be dissatisfied with one's portion or treatment; to slight; to refuse. Owaȟiⁿyaⁿ. Uⁿkoȟiⁿyaⁿpi. Śuⁿśuⁿla ca wak'iⁿ oȟiⁿye s'e, as is said when a man does not care to do even a little job, because mules are slow with a light load, but fast with a heavy one. Bl.

oȟla'ǧaⁿ, adj. Not fitting, loose; as is said of a small thing in a large place. -- oȟláǧaⁿla, adj. or adv. Loosely, not fitting, loose, as a small bolt in a large hole; too small e.g. for a form, frame etc. Also, said of the gurgling of a bad egg, etc. Bl. -- oȟláǧaⁿyela, adv. Loosely. - muⁿ welo, The coat is too large for me. BL.

oȟla'ȟlayela, adv. Loosely, as knitting; not stretched, as a cord.

oȟlaȟ'yela, adv. Loosely, as in too big clothes. B.H.87.4.

oȟla'iŋ, (?). - manice, or - wanil waśkaŋ, I am always busy. Bl.

oȟla'ťe, adv. Under, beneath. Maya - caŋku iyaya, The road goes under the hill or bank. Waŋna wizipaŋ paha kiŋ - wakpala el iyotakapi. Pa gegéya otkeyapi na - cetipi. -- oȟláťeťaŋhaŋ, adv. From beneath. -- oȟláťeya, adv. Beneath, under. Uŋkiś huŋȟ le maya kiŋ - uŋyaŋpi ktelo. Caŋ kiŋ le - uŋyaŋkapi kte. Bl.

oȟli', adj. Filthy in or within, as unwashed dishes. Omáȟli. Iśtoȟli, with ref. to eyes. Bl.

oȟli's'e, adv. Crowded about, as people around a tent to see a dance. Na isam wiŋyaŋ waŋ ena wicaśa waŋ kici yaŋkahaŋpi ca - hiŋglewicakiyapi. Yuŋkaŋ tipi waŋ el - haŋ ca tima iyaya. Ehaŋl - makuwapi.

oȟli'ya, adv. In a filthy manner. Wakśika kiŋ - haŋ, The dishes remain unwashed. Bl.

oȟlo'geca, adj. perhaps. Covered with. We - , All bloody.

oȟlo'ȟloka, n. red. of oȟloka. Nakeś wa k'oŋ - yelo, i.e. a dry spot visible here and there. Bl.

oȟlo'ka, n. A hole.

o'ȟmiȟmiŋyaŋ, adj. Crooked. Also, óȟmiŋyaŋ.

oȟmuŋ'yece, (?). Oȟmuŋyayece lo, as is said when a person passes by with paying attention to one. Bl. Cf. waóȟmuŋyece, A talkative person.

oȟol'ya, adv. Grayish. Wa - hiŋȟpeya, i.e. when it snows the snow remains only here and there. Bc.

oȟō'p̣a, adj. Looking well in e.g. a suit, attractive. Cf. ȟopa, ǧopa. Hayapi kiŋ omáȟopa.

oȟpa', v.n. To drop. Pa - hiŋgni. B.H. 268.6.

oȟpaŋ', v.n. To be wet or moist in. -- oȟp̣áŋkiya, v.n. To dabble, splash gently. -- oȟp̣áŋkiya, v.a. To dip into, sop or soak in; to wet or soak, e.g. so as to take off the hair. Oȟpaŋwakiya. -- oȟpáŋyaŋ, v.a. To soak e.g. wash in water. Oȟpáŋwayaŋ.

oȟpa'ye tipi, n. Dormitory quarters.

oȟpu'ȟpuya, adv. (?). - aya, as is said when a wound is healed and the skin is coming off. Peeling off, perhaps.

o'ȟťaȟťa, adj. Loose, not stretched tight, as a slackened bow-string. -- óȟťaȟťayela, adv. Loosely, not stretched.

oȟta'ni, v. perhaps. Laboring. Ziŋtkala - śni kas'a kiŋyaŋpi. Bl.

oȟta'teya, (?). MS.142.

o'ȟtayeťu, n. (of ȟtayetu). The evening. - iyohila, Every evening. B.H. 86.6;105.15.

o'ȟya, adv. Obliquely, from corner to corner; sloping, as the characters in writing.

oȟ'a', adj. Gray; black and white specks on a black ground.

o'ȟ'abyela, adv. Not quite full, almost full. Bl.

oȟ'a'ka, adj. Gray, black appearing through the white; all colors intermingled.

oȟ'a'mna, v.n. To smell moldy, to stink. Cf. ȟ'a. Bl. Syn.- oniyemna.

oȟ'aŋ', 1) v. To do, to work. Owaȟ'aŋ. Tokel - kiŋ hena slolwaya. 2) n. Work, action; custom, artifices. Mioh'aŋ oyasiŋ cic'u kte. MS354. - witoŋpe śni oyaȟ'aŋ he? Teȟiya omiciȟ'aŋ yelo, as one would say if his companion had plenty without letting him share. Uŋk'oȟ'aŋpi, We are in for it. B.H.38.7. Śikśica oyaȟ'aŋ ca hece. Le t'iŋ kte iyecel oȟ'aŋ yelo. B.H.68.19;258.12.

o'ȟ'aŋ, v.n. To be slow, perhaps. To be long in doing. Ómaȟ'aŋ. - ekta akibleza, i.e. thought of the treatment he had given David. B.H.90.14.

oȟ'aŋ'eciŋśniyaŋ, adj. Impolite. P.

oȟ'aŋ'glawa, v. pos. perhaps. To call

something one's own work; to say to have worked, when in reality it does not amount to much. Taku ecanon kin - ecanon we, so a woman would say to her husband who thought he did much work. - tak'tokanon.

oh'an'hanhan, v.n. To do odd things, to play pranks, cut capers; to do badly. Oh'anwahanhan. Na ungna - s'e wahinkpe wan ekta egle, And suddenly, as if in fun, he set an arrow in place. D.26. - sicápsanpsan nankelo. Bl. Also, oh'ánhanhanka.

oh'an'hi, v.n. To be slow in. Wicalapi kte kin el onih'anhipi. B.H.273.4. -- oh'ánhiya, v.a. To cause to be slow.

oh'an'kihanhan, v. To play pranks upon one; to do badly to. Oh'anwakihanhan.

oh'an'ko, 1) v.n. To be quick in doing anything, handy. Omah'anko. Onih'anko. Unkoh'ankopi. 2) n. A minute, 60 seconds. Walehantu ca śunkawakan hunkeśni oh'ankopelo, i.e. spring. Bl. -- oh'ánkoya, adv. Quickly. -- oh'ánkoyakel, adv. Rather quickly. B.H.170. 6. -- oh'ánkoyela, adv. Quickly, suddenly.

oh'an'optelic'iya, Cf. oh'óptelic'iya.

oh'an'pi, v.n. (of oh'an and pi). To be generous, liberal. Oh'ánmapi. -- oh'ánpiya, adv. Generously, liberally.

oh'an' sinkpekpe, v. To be muskrat-like, to be fearless in one's doings. BT.

oh'an'slata, v.n. (of oh'an and slata). To be slow in one's movements; to work slowly and deliberately. Oh'anmaslata.

oh'an'śica, v.n. To be ill-behaved, be stingy; to be of a mean or cross disposition. Oh'anmaśica. -- oh'ánśicaya, adv. Badly. -- oh'ánśilya, 1) v.a. To make stingy, make bad. Oh'anśilwaya. 2) adv. Badly, wickedly.

oh'an'śunkeca, v.a. perhaps. To give up hope, be hopelessly lost, as one who will die; to act disastrously. Also v.n. Owah'anśunkeca. Wanji unyan el oyapapi kin oyah'anśunkecapi kte lo. Bc. ED. D.58, note 2.

oh'an'tehan, v.n. (of oh'an and tehan). To be long in doing a thing. Oh'anmatehan.

oh'an'tokeca, adj. To be queer in one's way. BD.

oh'an'wakankanyan, (?). Kukuśe s'e - wakita, i.e. to see everything, boys have clear eyes. Bl.

oh'an' waśicun, n. One who can make all sorts of things like a white man. EB.

o'h'anwaśte, 1) n. Order, courtesy. 2) adj. Well-behaved, good, generous, good-humored, open-hearted; orderly. -- oh'ánwaśte, v.n. To behave well, be good, be generous. Oh'ánmawaśte.

oh'an'wiha, adj. Funny, cute. Hokśila - .

oh'an'yan, v.n. To do work, to act. Owáh'anya. Oyah'anya. Unkoh'anyanpi. Tona ohitiya oh'anyanpi kin hena ecel ewicaglepi. MS.521. Also, óh'anyan, To do, habitually work, be active. Owáh'anbla. Unkoh'anyanpi. Also ówah'anyan. Tona wakan oh'anyayanpi k'on oyasin hocokata hiyaya po. Note: although BD says óh'anyan is not used, still we have oh'anyayanpi.

oh'an'ye, n. The doings of a person. - ci wanyakapi, heon lila cajeyatapi.

oh'an'yeya, v.a. To cause to do. Oh'anyewaya.

oh'a'ya, adv. In a grayish or mixed manner, as is said of putting paint on the face. Cf. h'a.

oh'e'h'e, (?). Śunka aze oh'eh'es'e wahanpi waśtelake, i.e. when someone likes broth very much.

o'h'eya, v.n. To have but little in.

oh'i'tonkipa, v. To do something against orders and have bad luck, but not showing it. Also, oh'ánitonkipa.

oh'o'kpaya, (?). Wanagi s'e iśta - , as said when the eyes are sunk in deep. Bl.

oh'o'ptelic'iya, v. To slacken and give up one's work. Also, oh'ánoptelic'iya. Oh'optelmic'iya. Oh'optelmic'iyeśni na pilamic'iyelo, I am glad I did not give up. Bl.

oi'ali, n. Stairs in a house.

oi'caġa, v.n. (of icaga). To grow in anything; to grow up. Oimacaga.

oi'caġe, n. (of oicaga). A growing; a generation, not wicoicage; creation; interest taken on money lent. A. B.H. 62.12. Cuⁿwiyapehe -.

oi'cahitoⁿ, v.a. (of icahi). To mingle, mix together in, as tobacco and bark, in anything. Oicahiwatoⁿ. -- oi'cahiye, n. (of icahiye). A mixture, a mixing.

oi'caħ, cont. (of oicaga). - kokela, Of quick growth. - tehaⁿ, Of slow growth. -- oi'caħwaⁿkala, adj. Growing easily. -- oi'caħya, v.a. To yield, produce; to make grow; to cause to produce. Oicaħwaya. B.H.157.8.

oi'cazo, n. (of icazo). A marking, credits, taking things on credit, giving things on credit.

oi'cimani, n. (of icimani). Travelling; a company of travelers, many, while icimani has ref. to one. Iyotiyeyakiyapi heoⁿ - kiⁿ le cic'upi. - waśte yuhapi kte kiⁿ he Wakaⁿtaⁿka icekiye. B.H.36.7.

oi'cipa, Cf. oic'ipa.

o'icoġa, (?).

oi'cu, n. A place where one finds or receives things, as when one goes for e.g. gravel, rocks etc.; a quarry or pit. Oicu śica. - śilyá, Hard to get or to reach. - śilyá yaⁿkelo. -- oi'cuwaśte, adj. (of icu). Good to take, acceptable.

oi'c'iglaka, v. (of oiglaka). To say to one's self concerning one's self. Also, oi'ciglaka. Woic'icoⁿze- , To make a vow. B.H.22.18.

o'ic'igmigmela, adv. or adj. With one's self rolled up. - muⁿkelo, i.e. to lie with knees drawn towards the body. LC. Syn.- óic'ipśuⁿpśuⁿkel.

oi'c'ihi, v. refl. (of okihi). To be able for one's self; to be rich; to get for one's self, be selfish. Omic'ihi; to be able to accomplish things; to profit. R.

oi'c'iħ'aⁿ, (?). Wóteħi omic'iħ'aⁿ.Bl.

oi'c'ikp̄ani, v. refl. (of okikpani). Not to be able to take care of one's self or family, to be poor. Omic'ikpani.

oi'c'imani, n. A trip. P.

oi'c'ipa, v. (?). Caⁿku oic'ipe, Side roads going into a main road. Bl. Also, oi'cipa.

o'ic'ipśuⁿpśuⁿkel, adv. Curled up. - muⁿkelo, i.e. to lie with knees drawn towards the body. LC. Same as óic'igmigmeyela muⁿkelo.

oi'c'iwa, v. refl. (of owa). To write one's self. Caje - , To sign one's own name.

o'ic'iya, v. refl. (of okiya). To help one's self. B.H.290.6.

oi'c'onica, v. To control one's self, not giving in to one's temper. Omic'onica. Ouⁿkic'onicapi.

oi'e, n. (of ia). A word; a saying or speech. Wicaśa waⁿ oie owotaⁿla ehaⁿtaⁿś he eca kaħnigapi. Oie yuspica śni. Bl.

oi'eħicatoⁿ, v.n. To use language. Oiewecatoⁿ.

oi'eħic'uⁿ, v.n. To command, enforce obedience. Oiewec'uⁿ.

oi'eħitoⁿ, v.n. To use language, words. Oiewetoⁿ. Waśagyela oieyetoⁿpi kiⁿ mitaakicita ob wamayalakapi kte lo. ST.

oi'e p̄ep̄eka, (?). Oie pepekelaħcak, i.e. taku eye ciⁿ oyasiⁿ caⁿzéka ecé ca heoⁿ heyapelo. Bl.

oi'e tatúyeyeke, adj. Changing one's views often. Oie matatuyeyeke. Also, tatúyeke. Bl.

oi'e waśi'cuⁿ, n. (?). -- oi'e waśi'kśicuⁿ, n. red. (of oie waśicuⁿ). (?). Oie niwaśikśicuⁿ welo. BT.

oi'eya, v.n. To use words, to speak. Oiewaya. Wóiȟa oieyaye lo. Also, oíeye. Itaŋcaŋ tuwa kaca he oieye nawaȟ'oŋ. B.H.49.4.

oi'glagya, adv. Travelling in. B.H.63. 20;165.7.

oi'glak, cont. of oiglaka. - uŋpi, They are moving. Na oyate kiŋ - uŋpi. Wi yamni - uŋpi. B.H.56.1.

oi'glaǩa, 1) v. To move, be moving, as a family or camp travelling. BD. says this sense is not used. 2) v. refl. (of oyaka). To make one's self known, tell one's own name; to confess. Omiglaka. B.H.127.10;174.19;221.14.

oi'glake, n. (of igláka). An expedition, journey, excursion. Wana maśteśte, - kte taniga waŋji pusya yuha yo. Bl.

oi'glapta, v. To take all that is left when things are distributed. Omiglapta. Bl. Also perhaps, to pour out for one's self. D.66.

oi'glonica, (?). B.H.165.7.

oi'gloye, n. Making progress; getting along. Onigloye ekta tokeca? or: Oigloye nitawa tokeca he? How are you getting along? BD.

oi'glubleca, v. refl. To scatter, as a crowd of people do. B.H.10.2.

oi'gluha, v. pos. To have one's self, to be well off. Omigluha. Wicaśa ksapapi lena wawiyaksapapi ca oyate kiŋ ogna - yapi. MS.483.

oi'gluǩiǩi, v. To be dissatisfied etc. and finally speak against those who seem to be against us. Oiglukikipiśni, as is said of a man so people would get along with each other well. Bl. Cf. kikiyakel. Omiglukiki. -- oíglu-ǩiǩiya, v.a. To cause to quarrel with each other by backbiting etc. Bl.

oi'gluśica, v. refl. To spoil one's own reputation. Omigluśica.

oi'gluśǩaŋ, v.n. To have a relapse, become sick again.

oi'gluze, n. (of igluza). What one puts on, clothing.

oi'haŋke, n. (of ihaŋka). The end of time, space etc.; the end of a story. B.H.170.13. -- oihaŋkeya, v.a. To make an end of, destroy.

oi'heya, v.a. (of iheya). To shoot into. Oihewaya. -- oíheye, n. The place where the shot is sent. R.

oi'heye tipi, n. (of iheya). A toilet.

o'ihuŋni, 1) v.a. (of ihuŋni). To land in or at. Oiwahuŋni. 2) n. A landing. Tipi kiŋ - waśte, i.e. easy to reach. D.251.

oi'ȟaȟa, v.a. To ridicule, laugh at, scorn. B.H.77.22. -- oiȟaȟaya, adv. In a mocking manner. - ia. B.H.57.11; 108.5. -- oiȟaȟayakel, adv. Mockingly. B.H.111.13;263.8.

oi'ȟpeȟpeya, v. red. (of oiȟpeya). O-iȟpeȟpeyapi s'e wicoti, as said when a few tents are scattered over a valley. Bl. Syn.- yawawapilas'e.

oi'ȟpeya, v.a. To throw into. Oiȟpewaya. Na mini śma ciŋ el (keya kiŋ) oiȟpeyapi.

oi'kcapta, v. pos. perhaps. To talk angrily to one's self. B.H.44.8.

oi'kpaġica, (?). Hecel - na lila wiyuśkiŋ. MS.152.

oi'kṗahúŋzapi, n. A rocking chair.

oi'kpaȟica, v.n. To wake up. Omikpaȟica. Uŋkoikpaȟicapi.

oi'kpaptaŋśilya, adv. (?). - mayakuwapelo, i.e. you are hard after me, a few, with your talk. Bl. - ic'iya. Bl. -- oikpaptaŋwaśteya, adv. (?). - epelo, To say truthfully, as is said when somebody doubts a statement. Bl.

oi'kpasya, adv. In darkness. - haŋ, To be in darkness. B.H.1.2.

oi'kpat'a, 1) v.n. (of ikpi). To be still-born, die within on account of pressure from outside. 2) n. An abortion, as of a child. Omíkpat'a, as the mother says when it happens to her child. 3) v. refl. To have an abortion accidentally, by pressure as while digging with the huŋpe. Oni-kpat'iⁿ ktelo.

oi'kwa, v. pos. (of owa). To write one's own, paint or draw one's own e.g. name or picture. Caje, ite -.. Ite omikwa. Omikwa, omic'ikwa, I write my name. Caje - yo, Write your name. Uⁿkoikwapi. -- oikwaya, v.a. To cause one to write his name. Oikwawaya.

oi'le, 1) v.n. (of ile). To blaze in, burn within. Peta kiⁿ - ecetu śni.Bl. B.H.273.14. 2) n. A flame.

oi'leleka, n. A good-for-nothing, a fool. Perhaps, oiṁaleleka. Omáileleka. WE. Note: oi'lelepi, which refers to more than one.

oi'leya, v.a. To set on fire. B.H.241.6.

o'imniciye, v. col. pl. They go, i.e. for a meeting. Oyate kiⁿ ataya hocokata wicakico au na hecel waⁿna - .

oi'naḣme, n. A hiding place. P. Cf. ináḣmekiciciyapi, The playing of hide and seek.

oi'najiⁿ, n. (of inajiⁿ). A standing place, a starting place.

oi'najiⁿta, n. The place of standing, a goal. It is a name applied to the town of Valentine, Nebraska.

oi'naṗe, n. A place of coming out.

oi'nikaġa, (?). MS.344, 349. - tipi.

o'iⁿkṗa, n. The end of anything. Hemakoskaⁿtu kiⁿ he itahena na caḣli wakpa - kiⁿ ogna uⁿkiyayapi. Wakpala - kiⁿ ġuhéheya yuⁿkelo. Bl. -- óiⁿkpata, adv. In the very beginning e.g. of ancestry etc. - oyate toká icagapi hehaⁿl. Bl.

o'iⁿyaⁿka, v.i. To run about in. D.35.

oiⁿ'yaⁿke, n. A race track.

oi'ṗakśaⁿ, n. A bend, crook, angle.

oi'ṗaktaⁿ, n. A bend in a stream.

oi'ṗasilya, adv. Cf. ipasilya.

oi'ṗeya, n. A shelter from the wind which faces the sun east or west. Tipi - el maⁿka. BD. Also, a sheltered place, a warm place out of the wind. R. - k'el ololuta helo. - eciyataⁿhaⁿ puza oh'aⁿko welo. Bl. Syn.- oblula.

oi'ṗiyaḱe, n. (of ipiyaka). The place around which the girdle is put, the waist.

oi'ṗutaḱe, n. (of iputaka). A kiss.

oi'puza, v.n. To thirst after. B.H. 189.4.

oi'sa, n. The outer corner e.g. of a house. - yamni, A triangle, as the Indians call it.

oi'śtaglewaⁿjila, n. A steady gaze, a fixed look.

oi'śtiⁿme, n. (of iśtiⁿma). A bed-room. Ikpaptaⁿptaⁿ ihpeic'iyelo, - śica ca, i.e. in sleep. Bl.

oi'taⁿcaⁿ, n. The head man. Na oyate el - uⁿpi kiⁿ. Ti el - kiⁿ he, i.e. the head servant. B.H.97.21;204.6. -- oítaⁿcaⁿyaⁿ, adv. At the head. - uⁿpi. - waawaⁿyaⁿka. B.H.100.8,11.

oi'ṫomni, v. To be dizzy, as from looking downward from a high place. Bl.

oi'wawaⁿyaⁿgwaci, n. Any place where there has been held a Sundance. RTj.

o'iwiṫaya, v. To assemble. - yelo, They came together. Bl. Syn.- kiwitaya, ókimniciye.

oi'yaciⁿyaⁿ, adv. In the same manner as somebody else, after the same pattern etc. - ecoⁿkoⁿpi kte kaga, i.e. as a pattern of bead-work. Bl. WE.

oi'yagle, n. A road leading to. B.H. 194.24.

oi'yahaⁿ, v.n. (of iyahaⁿ). To alight down in. R. Bl.

o'iyahe, n. A reaching the top.

oi'yaḣṗeya, v. To hold up the pipe to, as the Dakotas do to the Great Spirit before smoking.

oi'yaḣpeye, n. What can be thrown over the back of a horse. - waⁿjila,

One load.

o'iyakapeya, adj. Steep, as a road; going upward. Canku - , i.e. where the road leads up it is steep.

oi'yakaśka, v.a. To tie into. Oiyawakaśka. -- oiyakaśke, n. A tying into, a knot.

oi'yanica, v.n. To be prevented in. Oiyamanica. D.51.

oi'yanil, cont. of oiyanica. -- oiyanilya, v.a. To prevent, be the cause of prevention, to clog.

o'iyapa, (?). Also, oiyapa.

oi'yaye, n. A getting through e.g. over a bad road or through deep snow. Bf. - wanice, It is impossible to get through. Also note: oiyanica , He cannot get through, for one reason or another, snow, quarantine etc.; and oiyamanica, I cannot get through. Inikagapi tima - kin. MS.351. - śilya nawicatakapi. B.H.118.7.

oi'yayeśilya, v. To prevent one from leaving, as by speaking to him although he is anxious to go. Oiyayeśilmayayelo, oúnc'unnilmayayelo. Bl.

oi'yekiye, n. (of iyekiya). Recognition. - śicapi. D.224. - waśteya, Easily recognized, easy to find out. - waśteya wiyaskabtonpi. B.H.269.22.

oi'yeye, n. A wound, a hole made by a shot.

oi'yoblula, n. A shelter, such as brush, a hill etc.

oi'yobluya, adj. or n. A calm. Also, oiyobluyela.

oi'yognag, cont. of oiyognaka. - tonala, A few mouthfuls.

oi'yognaka, n. (of iyognaka). A mouthful, very little.

o'iyohanzi, n. A wagon umbrella.

oi'yohpaya, v. To fall into. Oiyóhpabla. Also, óiyohpaya, adj. Steep, i.e. downward. Canku - .

o'iyohpaye, n. A ford, or crossing. P. Bl. Cf. óiyuwege.

oi'yohpayeya, v. To make fall, perhaps, into; to go into. Taku epe cin, nonge oiyohpayeyayeśni yelo. BT.

oi'yohpeya, v.a. To throw or cast into, to go into e.g. a river at a ford. Oiyohpewaya.

oi'yokipi, 1) v.n. To be pleased with. Oiyomakipi. 2) adj. Pleasant, agreeable. This is not said of persons, but of places and of the weather. Wanna lila maśte, lila - . Hanwiyanpi - A pleasant moon-light. 3) n. Attraction. P. - t'a nuns'e, as is said when the crowd has a very jolly time. - tajontka, A buffalo kidney is good to eat (an old saying). GT. -- oiyokipiya, adv. Pleasantly, agreeably. - oyate ounkijupi.

oi'yokiśica, adj. Disagreeable, as the weather; unhappy, feeling badly. Oiyomakiśica. - ahi, It storms. Hecel wanna wakanheja wanjigji wola ceyapi na lila - .

oi'yokiśilya, (?). Tipi kin - he, This room, house, is in great disorder. Bl. - yaceya yelo, How sad to see you weeping. D.122. -- oiyokiśilyela, adv. Disagreeably etc.

oi'yokpas, cont. (of oiyokpaza). To turn dark. - hingla. B.H.52.2. -- oiyokpasya, 1) v.a. To make dark. 2) adv. Darkly, in darkness. - han, He stands in darkness. B.H.54.7.

oi'yokpaza, n. Darkness. Tohanl oiyokpaz aya ca na wicaśa lila waś'aka.

oi'yokśica, adj. Ill-matched. P.

oi'yopa, v.n. To be affected, have a swelling etc. in consequence of a sore etc. in another place of the body. Oiyomapa. Cf. sniyopa. WE.

oi'yopeye, n. (of iyopeya). A scolding.

oi'yotake, n. (of iyotaka). A seat, a sitting place.

oi'yotiyekiya, v. (?). Oiyotiyewakiya. B.H.104.20.

oi'yuktan, n. (of yuktan). A bend.

oi'yusƙilya, adv. Oppressed in, as from smoke in a room. - maŋkelo. BT.

oi'yuskite, n. (of iyuskita). A place where a band goes around e.g. around the arm or wrist.

o'iyuspe, n. The handle, i.e. that part of a handle which is grasped, like the wooden part of a bucket handle.

oi'yuƫe, n. Dimension, rate. - ciscila, An inch. P. - waŋji, One section; - okise, A half-section; - śokela, A quarter section. - caŋku, A section road.

oi'yuweġe, n. A ford, crossing, a place of crossing a stream.

o'izilya, v. (?). Itóizilwayiŋ kte lo.

oi'ziƫa, v.n. To smoke, as a stove.

ojaŋ'jaŋ, n. Light, a light. -- v. perhaps. Tohaŋl oiyokpaz aya ca na wicaśa lila waś'aka, na - ca na huŋkeśni. Na tuktel - ca na natakapi. MS.351.

ojaŋ'jaŋglepi, n. A window, windows. - akáȟpe, A shutter, curtain, shade. P. Bl.

oja'te, n. (of jata). A fork, the forks of a road or stream.

oji', v.a. To whisper about. Owaji. Owicawaji. Okicijipi.

oji'ċaka, (?). - ca wawicak'u we. Bl.

oji'ji, v. red. (of oji). To whisper about, whisper to. Owajiji. -- oji'jiya, adv. In a whispering manner, secretly. -- oji'jiyahaŋ, adv. Whispering.

o'jilaka, n. perhaps. The young ones, of both men and animals. - ko óimnic'iye, All the children too were in the meeting.

oju', v.a. To plant or put in the ground, one by one as in planting corn. Owaju. -- n. A growth, field etc. e.g. of weeds etc. Hehaŋl uŋkcela oju waŋ el awicai. Na oŋjiŋjiŋtka oju waŋ el awicai. Wagacaŋ oju.

oju'gjula, adj. red. of ojula.

oju'ha, n. A sheath or case for anything, an empty bag. Wíwakaŋ nitawa - el iyekiya yo.

oju'ju, v.n. To fall to pieces in any place. -- ojújuwahaŋ, part. Fallen to pieces in, as an old wagon or a house.

oju'ƙiciton, v. (of ojutoŋ). To fill a bag for one. Ojuweciton.

oju'ƙitoŋ, v. pos. (of ojutoŋ). To fill up one's own bags etc. Ojuwakitoŋ.

oju'la, adj. Full, filled. Onijula. Omájula. -- ojúlaya, v.a. To fill full. Ojulawaya.

oju'miniyatke, n. A tank. Also perhaps, ośuŋminiyatke. Cf. śuŋminiyatka.

oju'pi, 1) part. Filled, planted. 2) n. Something to plant or sow, seed.

oju'toŋ, v.a. To fill up into sacks etc. Ojuwatoŋ. -- ojútoŋpi, n. Filled bags.

oju'ya, v.a. To cause to fill or plant. Ojuwaya. Woptuȟ'a ojumayayelo, You got the scraps all over me. Bl. Pb.34. -- adj. Same as ojula. Apamagleya u na isam lila ośota - haŋ (perhaps also ojuyahaŋ).

oƙa'bla, n. (of kabla). A piece cut off broad and flat, as meat cut for drying; a slice.

o'ƙabla, adj or adv. Spread out on or perhaps over; enlarging, as the foot of a stand. - aya, i.e. as spilled water. Cf. óƙaśƙe.

oƙa'blaya, adv. (of kablaya). Peacefully, without obstruction; expanded; plain, level; freely, as in discoursing; having good luck. - mayuhapelo. - muŋkiŋ ktelo, i.e. will have the whole room for myself. Tuweni nagiyewicaye śni ca - uŋpi. D.109. - wicaśa, A free man. - igluśtaŋ kte, He will finish easily, without trouble. -- oƙáblayakel, adv. In a conveniently open place. - yaŋka, To be or sit in a comfortably large place, as opposed to íċipiyela. Bl. - uŋyaŋkapelo, We get along with one another.

oka'blaye, n. A level place, a plain. Also perhaps, okáblaya.

oka'blebleca, v. red. of okableca. B.H. 303.14.

oka'bleca, v.a. (of kableca). To break to pieces in anything. Owakableca. -- okáblecahan, part. Broken in. -- oká-blece, n. A breaking in. -- okáblel, cont. (of okableca). To break or crush to pieces in. - iyeya.

oka'blu, v.n. To blow into, as the wind does. -- okábluya, 1) v. To cause a draft in the room, by opening the door. Okabluwaya. Tiyopa yugan s'a ye, - tka. Bl.

oka'cagla, v. perhaps. To be too large for one, as a coat, a shoe etc. Hanpa omákacagla. Bl. -- okácaglayela, adv. When e.g. one's coat is too large for one. - un, mun, ohlágan yela mun welo. Bl.

oka'co, v.n. To make a noise in, as a bad egg, gurgling. Bl. -- okácoco, v. red. of (kaco). To make a noise in, gurgle, as a bad egg. Bl. -- okácoya, adv. Producing a gurgling sound. Pagé - omawani, i.e. with an empty stomach. Also perhaps, okác'oya, Making a noise in, as fluid in a partly filled bag when shaken. Iwanyank wawatin na page - wagni kte, i.e. to go home with almost an empty stomach, like a horse when it has drunk only water.Bl.

oka'c'oya, Cf. okacoya.

oka'ga, 1) v.a. To copy, to make a model; to add to. This sense seems not to be used. 2) n. Same as okage. Maka - eciyatanhan. Pb.195. -- okágapi, n. A copy, model, image. The word is doubtfully used.

oka'gaya, v.a. To stick into, as something sharp, as arrows. The word is also applied to sharp words. Also perhaps, okáhaya.

o'kage, v. To float. B.H.8.6;116.8.

oka'ge, n. (of kaga). Creation; things made in the same manner, kinds, as a bundle or bundles of arrows made alike. Wicaśa - , A class of people. Maka - . B.H.245.27.

oka'gege, n. (of kagege). A place where anything is sewed, a seam. Wakeya - owoblu, as is said when in a blizzard the fine snow is blown into the tent through the seam. M.

oka'glala, adv. By the side of. -- okaglayela, adv. Near to, close by. R. Bl.

oka'glogloka, v. red. To rattle, as a car. Br.

oka'hi, 1) v.n. To hang over, as grass over the road, or hair over the forehead. 2) n. Hair bangs. -- okáhika, n. One who wears hair bangs. P.

oka'hinhan, (?). Wa okahinhe, ca oye kin tanyan ablespica śni, It snowed on the track so it cannot be clearly seen. Bl.

oka'hiya, 1) v.a. To cause to hang over, comb the hair over the face. Okahiwaya. 2) adv. Hanging over.

okah', cont. of okaga. - waśte, Of good form.

o'kah, adv. Floating. - u, To come floating. - ya, To float down, as a song. Mihakab - u wo. D.32.

o'kahhiyaya, v. To float by.

oka'hleca, v.a. (of kahleca). To tear a hole in, tear in pieces, to fracture. Owakahleca. -- okáhlece, n. A rend, a fracture. -- okáhlel, cont. of okahleca. - iyeya.

oka'hlog, cont. of okahloka. - iyeya.

oka'hlohloka, v. red. of okahloka. Mahpiya ahi k'on mahpiya tola okahlohloke. Bl.

oka'hloka, v.a. To make its way through, as water through cloth, to come through. Omakahloka. Cogin śa oyakahloke ehantanś, i.e. when you strike a tree with red pith. D.12. -- okáhloke, n. (of kahloka). A hole, a gash, made by striking. B.H.274.20.

oka'hmin, n. A corner, as made by houses; a bay.

oka'hniga, v.a. To understand, comprehend. Owákaȟniga. Uⁿkokaȟnigapi.

oǩa'ȟniȟ, cont. of okahniga. - waśte, Easy to understand; - śica, Hard to understand, abstruse. -- oǩáȟniȟǩiya, v.a. To cause to understand. Okaȟniȟwakiya. -- oǩáȟniȟpica śni, adj. Incomprehensible. - woglakelo. P. -- oǩáȟniȟya, v.a. To make to comprehend, to explain to one. Okaȟniȟwaya.

oǩa'ȟo, v.n. To sail, soar, glide in the air, as hawks etc. do. Bl. Syn.- okás'a.

oǩa'ȟp̂a, v.a. (of kaȟpa). To make fall into by striking. Owákaȟpa.

oǩa'ȟp̂u, v.a. (of kaȟpu). To knock or brush off into. Owakaȟpu.

oǩa'ȟťaⁿ, v.n. (of kaȟtaⁿ). To soak in, become soaked e.g. from water, grease etc. -- oǩáȟťaⁿyaⁿ, v.a. To dip in, sop up, sponge, to soak in, absorb. Okaȟtaⁿwaya. Okaȟtaⁿuⁿyaⁿpi. -- oǩáȟtaⁿye, n. A sponge.

oǩa'ȟtogtogye, red. of okaȟtogye.

oǩa'ȟtogye, adv. Made in a different manner. Tuwa...uⁿgna wakuwapi el wahiⁿkpe waⁿjila oⁿ pte num wicao na wahiⁿkpe kiⁿ - kagapi. MS.482.

oǩa'ȟwaⁿjila, n. The same form. BD.

oǩa'ȟwoǩa, v.n. To float in the air; to travel around much, as is said of a man who travels much. Owákaȟwoka.HC.

okaȟ'ya, (?). Śuⁿkwiⁿyela waⁿ cincókaȟya, i.e. more than one colt which one wished. Bl.

o'ǩaȟya, 1) v.a. To cause to float down stream. 2) adv. Floating. - u.

oǩa'ȟ'ol iyeya, v. To throw away into. Na śna noge - iyewicaya. -- oǩáȟ'ol iyéya ecoⁿpi, n. A game played on ice. Bl.

oǩa'jaya, adv. Between, in the forks of.

oka'ǩab, cont. of okakapa. To hit into, as a ball into a room. Mniyokakab iyemayayiⁿ kte lo, You will knock me into the water. D.33.

oǩa'kaⁿ, v.a. (of ǩakaⁿ). To shake into, as buffalo berries into a pail.

oǩa'ǩaⁿ, 1) v.a. (of ǩaǩaⁿ). To hew in anything. Owákakaⁿ. 2) v.n. To be broken to pieces, as a wagon during a runaway.

oǩa'kap̂a, v.a. To hit into, as a ball into a room. Owakakapa.

oǩa'ǩiⁿ, v.n. To peep in. Owakakiⁿ. Cf. aokakiⁿ. Taku oyasiⁿ - inajiⁿ slolye, i.e. knows everything. Bl.

oǩa'ǩiśya, adv. Abusively.

oǩa'ǩosǩoza, v. red. (of okakoza). To dangle. D.273.

oǩa'ǩoza, v.n. To dangle. P. Bl.

oǩa'kp̂aⁿ, v.n. To be broken up in. - yaⁿke nawaȟ'oⁿ welo, I did not hear (understand) it very well. Bl. -- oǩákp̂aⁿyaⁿkel, adv. Broken up in; dimly. - waⁿyaⁿka, To see it unclearly, just a little bit of it. - naȟ'oⁿ. - wayakita hwo? Bl. WE. Syn.- ciscila otaⁿiⁿ, kitaⁿyel otaⁿiⁿ.

oǩa'ksa, v.a. (of kaksa). To cut down a tree or root that is in the way. Owakaksa. Okakse śica, Difficult or hard to cut. D.66. -- oǩákse, n. Pieces cut out, cuttings; a notch cut in. -- oǩákseya, adv. (?).

oǩa'kśaⁿ, adv. Around about, by a roundabout way. EE. Also, oǩákśaⁿyaⁿ. - iblabla. Cf. akakśaⁿ, aokakśaⁿyaⁿ.

oǩa'kśe, n. (of kakśa). A roll of ribbon or cloth, a skein of thread.

oǩa'la, v.a. To scatter in or on e.g. to sow grain; pour out into; sow, plant. Owakala. Uⁿkokalapi. Yuⁿkaⁿ taku k'eya cikcik'ala ca el - i.e. caⁿwakśica el.

oǩa'laiheya, v. To load a gun in haste without a wad. Okalaihewaya.

oǩa'lala, v. red. of okala.

oǩa'lic'iya, v. refl. To warm up, warm one's self in. B.H.258.6. Bl.

okal'tǩiya, adv. Towards a warm place.

Cuwi - ȟpaya, To lie with one's back to the fire.

oǩa'lus, cont. of okaluza. -- oǩálusya, adv. Airy.

oǩa'luza, 1) n. Air in motion, a draught of wind. Lila okalus hiyu. 2) v.n. To blow through or into, blow on one. Omakaluza. 3) adj. Airy. - śni, Close, as a room. P.

oǩal'ya, v.a. To make hot in.

oǩa'ma, v. To hit the center, as in shooting. Owákama. Bl.

oǩa'mna, v. To avoid, to go around, go out of the way. R. Bl. Syn.- ayukśaŋyaŋ, aokamna. -- n. (of kamna). Earnings, wages, pay. - waśte, Good pay. -- oǩámnayaŋ, adv. Going round, avoiding, taking care, picking one's steps, as in walking. - mani. R. Bl.

oǩa'mnimni, v. To whirl around, as snow or sand around houses. Okamnimniyelo. Bl.

okaŋ', v.n. There is room, room for; it is not crowded; to be at the disposal of others. Ómakaŋ.

oǩaŋ', n. (of kaŋ). Old age; one's youth when spoken of by old men. - kiŋ ektab. - ihuŋni. B.H.97.8;124.25. -- oǩáŋǩe, adv. At old age; at the last, at the end. - ektab waśte, Good in the end.

okaŋ'śniyaŋ, adv. Having no time. - uŋ. B.H.200.23. - mayukuwapelo. Bl. Blaye kiŋ ataya - pte hiot'iŋza śke, They found the prairies crowded with buffalos. D.204. WE.

oǩaŋ'ťehaŋ, v.n. (of kaŋ and tehaŋ). To be long becoming old, bear old-age well, retain a youthful appearance; being old, one looks young. Also, oǩáŋťeȟiǩe.

okaŋ'yaŋ, adv. Roomy. B.H.225.3.

okaŋ'yela, adv. Near. Wana letaŋ - , i.e. the house. Bl. Also, nearby. B.H.69.10.

oǩa'pa, v.n. To be spoiled by standing in a vessel. R. Bl. Also, to bite, as do pepper, onions, tobacco etc. Ceji owicakapa. A.

oǩa'paŋ, v. (of kapaŋ). To pound in. Owakapaŋ.

oǩa'paza, v. To make smart, as pepper does the mouth. Omákapa.

oǩa'p̄o, v. To make swell by striking.

o'ǩap̄ol, cont. of okapota. - iyaya. - hinápa, To come up from the bottom of a creek or lake, as fish, or a piece of wood thrown in and coming up again, to float in water. BD. Me. says, floating on the water; thus, Caŋ waŋ - u welo. -- óǩap̄olya, v.a. To cause to float on. Okapolwaya.

o'ǩap̄oťa, v.n. To be borne upon, float on water.

oǩa'p̄ota, v.n. To be torn by shaking, as a pocket by keys carried in it.

oka'psica, v. (?). Hecel mini kiŋ ota - . B.H.203.7.

oǩa'pťa, v.a. To dip out into, lade out; to take out one's wages gradually. Owakapta. Na waŋna mini - na glicu kte ehaŋl. Wacowak'iŋla k'uŋ écuȟciś omiyecapta ceś, At least I hope you have left for me what is cooking in the ashes. Zuzeca k'uŋ hecela okaptapi, The snake alone was remaining. D.22 and 59. -- v.n. perhaps. To be left. Tuweni - śni, i.e. all are here. Miśnala omakapta ca hośi cicahi yelo. Wicaśa wakaŋ kiŋ miśnala okaptapi lel wauŋ welo. B.H.43.3;107.12. -- oǩápťapi, n. What is left, leavings; remnants. -- oǩápťe, v. To lade out into.

oǩa'saǩeciyataŋ, n. The right horse, the one whipped. - k'iŋkiya yo. P.Bl.

oǩa'sǩe, n. A bunch or lump of things sticking together as candy, sugar etc. Caŋhaŋpi - , caŋhaŋpokaske. Wowapi - , Any book with many leaves. -- oǩáskeska, n. red. of okaske. -- okáskeskeya, adv. red. of okaskeya.

oǩa'skeśilya, adv. perhaps. Gathered together. - op̄iic'iya, as is said when men and animals are mixed up in a bunch. Bl.

oka'skeya, adv. Sticking together in

a lump, as candy. Bl.

oǩa'slaťa, v.n. To stick in,as a splinter.

oǩa'sleca, v.a. (of kasleca). To split within,anything that can be split easily, without effort. Owakasleca.

oǩa'slohaƞ, 1) v.a. (of kaslohaƞ). To make slide in. 2) v.n. To make a trail by being dragged along in.

oǩa'slohe, n. A mark of anything dragged along, a trace, a trail.

oǩa'sloslo, v.a. To bruise, mash or crush in or into. Owakasloslo.

oǩa'sluťa, v. To hit the center, as in shooting and knocking out a piece perhaps. Bl. Cf. okama, okat'iƞza.

oǩa'sni, v. (?). Omakasni yelo, as is said when the wind comes in through the sleeves etc.

oǩa'sōl, cont. of okasota.

oǩa'soťa, v. To use up, destroy. Owakasota.

oǩa'sp̄eya, v. To make sink into, to immerse.

oǩa'sťag, cont. (of okastaka). To throw on or in e.g. mud. - iyeya, iȟpeya.

oǩa'sťaka, v.a. (of kastaka). To throw on or in, make stick on, as in daubing a house. Owakastaka.

oǩa'sťo, adv. (of kasto). Making or leaving a trail in the grass, as that made by another. - ya. Note: R. makes the word a n.

oǩa'su, n. A fringe, perhaps. Cf. okaswu.

oǩa'swu, n. (of kaswu). Fringe. Śina kaswupi, A shawl with fringe.

oǩa's'a, v.n. To sail or soar, glide in the air, as birds do.

oǩa's'ayakel, adv. Proudly. - ayuta. B.H.232.1.

oǩa's'iƞ, v. To look into.

oǩa'śǩa, v.a. (of kaśka). To tie into, as a scalp into a hoop; to fasten up, as green hide to dry. Owakaśka.

oǩa'śǩaƞ, v.n. To be injured internally, as a woman during pregnancy. Omakaśkaƞ. Note: oiglaśkaƞ, To hurt one's self inwardly.

oǩa'śǩaƞtoƞ, v.a. To bring forth before its time. Okaśkaƞwatoƞ. -- oǩáśkaƞtoƞpi, n. A abortion.

o'ǩaśǩe, 1) adj. Large at one end and small at the other. 2) n. The large end of a thing. R. Taśnaheca bloka s'e pa - , as is said of a man with a big nose. Bl.

oǩa'śǩe, n. (of kaśka). A place where one ties up things, as horses, ships. -- oǩáśǩe najiƞ, v. To stand tied, or bound to, as a horse to a post.

oǩa'śǩi, v.n. To be mashed in,or become jelly, as berries carried in a vessel; to pound or mash in. -- oǩáśice, v.n. To be mashed in, made jelly of. Wojuha zizipela ca caƞpa iyuha okaśkicelo. Bl.

oǩa'śleca, v.a. (of kaśleca). To split within anything that requires effort. Owakaśleca.

oǩa'śna, v.a. (of kaśna). To miss, to pass over e.g. a day.

oǩa'śp̄a, v.a. (of kaśpa). To strike a piece off in; to expectorate in perhaps. Owakaśpa.-- oǩáśp̄e, n. A piece struck off. Also, the word for those people living in one district.

oǩa'śpetoƞtoƞyaƞ, adv. red.(of okaśpetoƞyaƞ). By or in groups. B.H. 208.9. OS. Bl.

oǩa'śťaǩa, v.a. (of kaśtaka). To smite one in a place, as in a house. Owakaśtaka. --oǩáśtaǩe, n. A smiting, punishment. Kikta hiyayiƞ na loliȟ'aƞ oƞspic'iya yo; lecanoƞ kiƞ tuktel hignayatoƞ kiƞ - Ȟca yauƞ kte lo; he wicawake lo. GA.

oǩa'śťaƞ, v.a. (of kaśtaƞ). To pour into, fill into, as is said of liquids. Owakaśtaƞ.

oǩa'śuśuje, n. Bruises. B.H.130.10.

o'ǩaś'agya, adv. Prevented, hindered, as by having too much clothing on. - un. R. Bl.

oǩa'ta, v. (of kata). To fill up e.g. holes, to cover up in. - aya, as is said when things heap up by sweeping together. - kuwa, To stop, prevent. Bl.

oǩa'ťa, 1) v.n. To be warm inside. Ti-ókata, A warm house. 2) n. Heat.

oǩa'taǩin, v. (of katakin perhaps).(?). Anpetu wan - wanica ca iyablagyela helo, i.e. a calm day. Bl.

oǩa'ťan, v.a. To drive in e.g. a nail or pin; to nail, make fast with nails. Owakatan. Na can pteptecela on ecel - . Ptehan kin he lila yat'ins okatanpi. MS.482.

oǩa't'a, v.a. To kill by striking in, to beat to death in, e.g. a cat in a sack, or young animals in their mother's womb. Also, okat'e.

oǩa't'ins, cont. of okat'inza. - iyeya.

oǩa't'inza, v.a. To pound in tight, make tight, fill up. Owakat'inza. Also To hit the center in shooting. Bl.

oǩa'waton, v. To be alright, recovered. -- oǩáwatonyan, adv. Without hindrance or obstruction, as also applied to the weather.

oǩa'winġa, v.n. (of kawinġa). To go round and round at a distance. Owa-kawinġa. Na wanna okśan hoton okawinġapi. Lila wanbli ota okawinġapi wan-yanka. MS.148.

oǩa'winȟ, cont. of okawinġa. - ya, To go round and round, as the sun does. - au. Wamakaśkan ocaje oyasin ahihun-ni na wanna ataya - au na oyate kin okśan au na wicakat'api. -- oǩáwin-ȟela, n. A merry-go-round. -- oǩáwin-ȟya, adv. Round and round.

oǩa'yege, n. Seams. - wanice. B.H.266, 2.

oǩa'za, n. (of kazá). The articular bones of the arms and feet. Takan - , A thread of takan (sinew).

oǩa'zap̌a, v. To cut up and spread nicely, to cut the meat e.g. of deer along the spinal column into long strips. Owakazapa. Bl. Syn.- taká-ȟloka.

oǩa'ze, v.a. (of kaze). To dip out in-to. Owakaze.

o'ǩazeze, v.n. To swing, as something suspended from a cord. -- óǩazezeya, adv. Swinging, dangling.

oǩa'zonťe, n. (?). Napokazonte, The fingers. Nape - kin napitakaha kin nupin iciyagleya iyakaśkapi. MS.340. Siokazonte, The toes.

oǩi', prefix. It is affixed to verbs, signifying: through the middle. The prefix is composed of two prep. par-ticles, ogna and ki.

oǩi'bliheca, v.n. (of bliheca). To be smart in doing anything. Owakibliheca.

o'ǩiblotonton, adj. (of obloton). Having many corners, angular.

oǩi'cablaza, v.a. (of kablaza). To cut or rip open in the middle, e.g. anything soft, as a melon. Okiwaka-blaza.

oǩi'cableca, v.a. (of kableca). To break in two in the middle e.g. a plate or wood etc. by striking. Oki-wakableca.

oǩi'caȟa, v. To pull a knot very tight. Bl. Also, to tie one thing to an-other, tie a knot. Oǩiwaǩaȟa. -- o-ǩícaȟaȟapi, adj. Knotty, full of knots.

oǩi'caȟniġa, v.a. (of okaȟniga). To understand, to comprehend. Oǩiwaǩa-ȟniga.

oǩi'caksa, v.a. (of kaksa). To cut in two in the middle, as a stick with an ax. Okiwakaksa.

oǩi'canye, n. (of kicanyan). Work; tillage, cultivation. - ota, Compli-cated, as a piece of mechanism.

oǩi'capta, v.a. (of okapta). (?). He-cel Chanaan makoce kin he Abraham o-kicaptapi. B.H.11.15.

oǩi'captuǧa, v.a. To split in two in the middle, as with a chisel. Okiwakaptuga.

oǩi'casleca, v.a. To split something light, with little effort, in two, in the middle. Okiwakasleca. Note: where sleca and śleca are used, the former is used to indicate splitting when no effort is needed. -- oǩi'caslel, cont. (of okicasleca). To split in two in the middle. - iyeya. - iȟpeya. - uŋkaglipi kte. Bl.

oǩi'caśǩa, v.a. To tie into, to knot, tie knots in. Okiwakaśka.

oǩi'caśleca, v.a. To split in the middle, as a log. Okiwakaśleca. Note: śleca refers to hard splitting, sleca to easy splitting of. -- oǩi'čaślel, cont. - iyeya.

oǩi'čaśpa, v. (of kaśpa). Tosmite in two in the middle. Okiwakaśpa.

oǩi'čaśtaŋ, v.a. (of okaśtaŋ). To pour one's own into, to pour into for one. Owecaśtaŋ.

oǩi'cičaśtaŋ, v. (of okaśtaŋ). To pour into for one, as into a vial etc. Owecicaśtaŋ.

oǩi'ciciŋ, v. (of ociŋ). To desire of one for another. Owecicaŋ.

oki'ciciya, v. (of oǩiya). To talk together, as in courting. Okiciciyapi.

oǩi'cico, n. (of kico). Inviting each other, as to feasting.

oǩi'cicuwapi, v. (of okuwa). They follow or run after each other, as children do in a game.

oǩi'cignaǩa, v.a. (of ognaka). To put or place in for one. Owecignaka.

oǩi'cihaŋ, v. (of ohaŋ). To boil anything for another. Owécihaŋ.

oǩi'ciiŋ cokaŋ', n. No man's land. Also, owáǩihe cokáŋ. Co.

oǩi'ciji, v. To whisper to one another. -- oǩi'cijiji, v. red. B.H.210.17. -- oǩi'cijipi, n. Whispering. -- oǩi'cijiya, adv. Whisperingly.

oǩi'ciju, v.a. (of oju). To fill for another, plant for another. Oweciju.

oǩi'cile, v. (of ole). To seek anything for another. Owecile.

oǩi'cilota, v. (of olota). To borrow of one for another. Owecilota.

oǩi'ciŋ, v. (of ociŋ). To ask or desire of one, beg something of one. Owakiciŋ. Uŋkokiciŋpi. El yiŋ na wakablapi waŋji omakiciŋ yo.

oǩi'cipa, v. (of opa). To follow for anything; obey e.g. commands. Owecipa.

o'kiciśtaŋ, v.t. (of ośtaŋ). To put in e.g. a cork for another. Hiŋhaŋ iśta k'eya el okiciśtaŋpi, They put in a pair of owl's eyes in the place of the ruined ones. D.220.

oǩi'ciwa, v. (of owa). To write for one. Oweciwa.

oǩi'ciwaśakala, adj. Easily purchased for one. Bl.

oǩi'ciwaśte, adj. (of waśte). Good together, as two things eaten together; advantageous.

o'ǩiciya, v. (of óǩiya). To help another. Note: to help each other, perhaps óǩiciciya. Okiciciyapi.

oǩi'ciyak aupi, n. Tradition. B.H. 305.11.

oǩi'ciyapta, v. (of oyapta). To leave e.g. a part of one's food for one.

oǩi'ciyusiŋpi, v. recip. (of oyusiŋ). To fall out with one another, quarrel.

oǩi'ciyustaŋ, v. (of oyustaŋ). To put one into another for one, as one kettle into another. Oweciyuśtaŋ.

oǩi'ciyas'iŋ, v.n. To unite, to come together and flow, as two streams; to cling to each other, as several potatoes hanging together; to be fastened together, as two dogs in copulation. -- adv. perhaps. Cf. kokiciyas'iŋ.

o'ǩiciyuśtaŋśtaŋ, adv. Placing one in with the other. Oye - uŋyaŋpi ktelo, i.e. will follow in each other's footsteps. Oyé óciyuśtaŋśtaŋ ciu ktelo, I will follow your footsteps. Bl.

oki'ciyuze, n. (of yuza). Taking each other, as in marriage. - waŋ uŋkagapi, We shall have a marriage. - waśte waŋ kagapi. D.232.

oki'ciyuze wakaŋ', n. Matrimony.

oki'cize, n. (of kiciza). War, fighting a battle.

oki'c'u, (?). Yu-iye kayeś iyoha saŋni - śni wote, i.e. chews only on one side. Bl.

oki'c'unica, v.n. To be made angry, to be offended. Caŋte owec'unica. -- okí-c'unilya, v.a. To provoke to anger, to offend. Okic'unilwaya.

oki'glaha, v. pos. (of okicaha). To tie perhaps one's own together tight, e.g. one's string. Bl.

oki'glahniga, v. refl. To know or understand what pertains to one's self. Oweglahniga.

oki'glusleca, v. refl. To split in the middle. B.H.54.9. -- okíglusleIya, adv. Split in the middle. B.H.54.15.

o'kignagtoŋtoŋ, adv. In layers, having many layers. R. Bl. Also, okígnagtoŋtoŋyaŋ, - ahiyaye, To pass by in smaller groups. Bl.

oki'gnaka, v. pos. (of ognaka). To place one's own in. Owegnaka. Na cahli k'oŋ na wahiŋśa k'oŋ hena ecel owegnaka na lila wakaŋwala.

oki'gnuŋka, v.n. (of kignuŋka or kignuka). To dive or put one's head under the water in a vessel or bath.

oki'haŋ, 1) v. pos. (of ohaŋ). To put on, wear one's own e.g. moccasins. Kenataŋtaŋ kte s'e haŋpokihe lo, as is said when shoes are too wide. 2) v. pos. (of ohaŋ). To boil for one. Owakihe.

o'kihaŋ, v.a. To follow or be after one in travelling; to follow in years, be younger than. Owakihaŋ. Waniyetu yamni omayakihaŋ. Icagla omakihaŋpo. Bl. Also, okihe, cf.

o'kihe, 1) v.a. To follow or be after one, as in travelling; to follow in years, be younger than. Ówakihe. Waniyetu waŋjila ocicihe, I am one year younger than you. 2) adj. Next to, following, second. 3) n. A joint, as of a finger. -- ókiyeya, adv. Secondly, after.

oki'hi, v.a. To be able, able to accomplish. Owakihi. Uŋkokihipi. Also, to overcome, win over etc. Tehaŋ omakihi śni. Na wasu nakuŋ - śni, Hail cannot destroy it. -- okíhiic'iya, v. Cf. okihiya. Taku waśte yaciŋ kiŋ he okihinic'iyiŋ kte na wicakeya ceya yo. MS.350. -- okíhika, v.n. To be able. -- okíhikiya, v.a. To make able for. Okihiwakiya. -- okíhila, v. dim. of okihi, and used by children.

oki'hipica, adj. Possible, that can be done. - śni, Impossible.

oki'hiśniya, v.a. To thwart, disable. Okihiśniwaya. -- okíhiśniyaŋ, adv. Oic'iya - kuś hpaye. B.H.290.6.

oki'hiya, 1) v.a. To render able, cause to be able for. Okihiwaya. 2) adv. According to ability.

oki'hpaya, v.n. To rest, remain in the same place, not to remove. Owakihpaya. Uŋkokihpayapi. Le icuŋhaŋ oyate kiŋ okihpayapi kta keyapi. Caŋ ota eyaku wo, okihpayapi kte lo. Bl. B.H.122.21;171.12. -- okíhpayekiya, v.a. To cause to lie by or rest. Okihpayewakiya.

oki'hyaŋ, (?). Bl.

oki'h'aŋ, v. (of oh'aŋ). To do to one. Owakih'aŋ. Iyotaŋla omayakih'aŋ yelo. Tehiya onicih'aŋ ca uŋyak'upi kte lo, i.e. the wolf said. When one's companion would not let one share of his plenty, one would say: Tehiya omayakih'aŋ yelo. Taŋyaŋ - kiŋ atkuku kiŋ okiyake. Śica ocicih'aŋ śni. Wicaśa owotaŋla kiŋ he tuktognani - śni ye. B.H.126.23;235.16;262.19.

oki'h'aŋ śuŋkē'ca, v.a. To do badly to, treat like a dog; to destroy what one has depended on, e.g. food; not to give food to. Owakih'aŋ śuŋkeca. Uŋkokih'aŋ śuŋkecapi. Kicuŋniyaŋ wilukcaŋ kiŋhaŋ oyate kiŋ owicakih'aŋ śuŋkeca kte lo.

oki'h'anyan, v. (of oh'anyan). To do to, act towards. Owakih'anyan.

oki'jata, n. The dividing of two rivers with one river dividing in two; a fork - el. Also, okijate. -- adj. Forked. Hehan can - tob waksa agli.

oki'jeya, adv. Together. Ataya - . B.H.9.20.

o'kiju, v.n. To be united; to meet, as two parties. Blokecokanyan ehanl oyate yamni - . Oiyokipiya oyate ounkijupi.

oki'ju, v. (of oju). To sow or plant one's own, to plant for one; to fill up, e.g. a bag.

o'kijuya, 1) v.a. To cause to unite. Okijuwaya. 2) adv. Unitedly, together.

oki'kaha, v. To tie a knot. Okiwakaha.

oki'kahniga, v. To understand one's own perhaps. Na tokel eonpi kin okiwakahnige śni ca eya wacipi kin el owapa eśa el ewacanmike śni.

oki'kaśleca, v.a. To split in the middle. B.H.99.22.

oki'kcanpte, (?). Cf. kcanptepte. - niśicelo, as is said when two are disputing and another is butting in; they say to him. Bl.

oki'kiyakel, adv. Covered with scrophulous sores. - un. Also, it is said of a meeting: - inyanka.

oki'kpani, v.a. To be unable for a thing, be impotent. Owakikpani. -- okikpaniya, v.a. To render unable. Okikpaniwaya. -- okikpaniyan, adv. Not being able, incompetently. - waun.

oki'ksab, cont. of okiksapa. -- oki'ksabya, 1) v.a. To cause to experience or know. Okiksabwaya. Okiksabic'iya, To make one's self wise. 2) adv. Wisely.

oki'ksahe, n. An abyss.

oki'ksapa, v.n. (of ksapa). To be wise in respect to, to have gained wisdom by experience. Owakiksapa.

oki'ksuye, 1) v.a. (of kiksuya). To remember. - waśte, It is easily remembered. 2) n. Remembrance.

oki'kśu, v. pos. To fill one's own; to put into one's own, e.g. into one's pocket.

oki'le, v. pos. (of ole). To seek for one's own. Owakile.

oki'litaton, (?). - śkan, To work in excitement. Cf. owilita. Bl. Kangi wicaśa to yo najinwicayapi na - . MS.526. Cf. owolutaton.

oki'lota, v. (of olota). To borrow anything of one. Owakilota, unkokilotapi, omakilota. Ocicilota.

o'kime, 1) n. A seam, a joint. 2) v.n. To join, meet; go round, circle, encircle. -- ókimeya, 1) v.a. To cause to go round, encircle, enclose. Okimewaya. 2) adv. Encircling.

o'kimniciye, (?). Oyate kin witaya ecicaskaya - kta keyapelo. Syn.- kiwitaya, óiwitaya.

oki'nablaga, v.n. (of nablaga). To burst open, as corn in boiling.

oki'nablaza, v.n. (of nablaza). To burst open, as corn in boiling. Same as okinablaga.

oki'nableca, v.a. To break in two, e.g. a plate, etc. by trampling on it. Okinawableca. -- okinablel, cont. - iyeya.

o'kinahan, adv. Perhaps. The word occurs at the beginning of a clause.

oki'nahleca, v.n. To tear in the middle. B.H.268.7.

oki'naksa, v.a. (of naksa). To break anything in two in the middle with the foot. Okinawaksa.

oki'nasleca, v.n. (of nasleca). To split or burst open lengthwise, beso done very easily.

oki'naśpa, v.a. (of naśpa). To divide in the middle, break off. Okinawaśpa.

oki'ni, v.a. To share, receive a part in a division; to obtain a share in any way, where there is a small amount.

Owakini, uᶯkokinipi. Kal ótkeya yo (the táblo, at the door) hecel ptejiᶯcala ake uᶯkokinipi kte lo; this is a superstitious old saying. Bl. Tabló waᶯ ecela ai śke. Heceglaȟci - ca. D.119. Also, oǩini.

ō'ǩini, adv. Perhaps, possibly. The word is used at the beginning of a clause.

oǩi'nica, (?). Bl.

oǩi'nihaᶯ, 1) v.a. To single out for praise. Owakinihaᶯ. 2) adv. (of kinihaᶯ). Honorably, honorable.

oǩi'niǩiya, v.a. To give a share of, cause to partake. Okiniwakiya. Pb.30.

oǩi'niyaᶯ, v.n. (of niya). The word is used with cuwi, cuwi' - , To gasp, breathe as one dying, to breathe deeply, to heave a deep sigh. Ehaᶯl cuwi owakiniyaᶯ keyapi. D.88 and 90.

oǩiᶯ' oᶯ śica, Cf. okiuᶯ śica. The expression is used of man or horse that refuses to obey. Bl.

oǩiᶯ'yaᶯ, 1) v.n. (of kiᶯyaᶯ). To fly in, to fly about overhead. 2) adj. in comp. with waśte. Docile, gentle. Zitkala iyuha okiᶯyaᶯpi na okawiᶯȟ au na kiyela okiᶯyaᶯpi. Icuᶯhaᶯ piśko k'eya okiᶯyaᶯhaᶯpi. D.73.

oǩiᶯ'yaᶯka, v. (perhaps of oki and iᶯyaᶯka). (?). Okiᶯyaᶯke oᶯspic'iciya yo. GA.

oǩi'pa, v. pos. (of opa). To follow or obey one's own; to follow e.g. the habits or trade of one's father. Owakipa. Le hiyu ca oye - gle lo, He went home on the same road he came on. Bl.

oki'paǧi, v. To fill the pipe for. D.249.

oǩi'p̄ata, v.a. (of pata). To join one to the other; to patch on. Okiwapata. -- oǩip̄atap̄i, n. Patchwork.

oǩi'p̄e, v. Same as okipa.

oǩi'p̄eča, v.n. To do as one has been accustomed to do. Owakipeca.

oǩi'p̄eǩiya, v.a. To cause to follow one's own. Okipewakiya.

oǩi'p̄emni, v. pos. (of opemni). To wrap around one's own. Owakipemni.

oǩi'p̄eya, 1) v.a. To cause to follow one's own. Okipewaya. 2) adv. Following. - wauᶯ.

oǩi'p̄i, v. (of kipi). To be large enough for; to hold, admit, receive. Omakipi, onicipi, uᶯkokipipi. Pa kiᶯ lila taᶯka caᶯke - śni. D.28.

oǩi'sabya, adv. Blackish. Maka - yuᶯkelo, as is said when there is but little snow in winter. Bl.

oǩi'sap̄a, v.n. (of kisapa). To become bare, black, as a spot of ground while the snow remains around.

oǩi'se, n. A part; the half of anything. -- oǩi'sela, n. dim. of okise. Maza śa - muᶯ. B.H.243.6. -- oǩi'seya, adv. Half. Taśuᶯkepi kiᶯ - wicuᶯktepi. Also, oǩi'seyela.

oǩi'soťa, v.n. (of sota). To be used up, all gone.

o'ǩisoťa, v. col. (of yusota). They are all gone. Cf. ósota. B.H.71.16.

oǩi'sťaǩa, v.n. To be enfeebled by, or on account of.

oǩis'yakel, adv. Is used to or is only fighting. - uᶯ. Owicakisyakel is doubtfully used. B.H.86.22.

oǩi's'as'a, (?). Iśtiᶯma uᶯkokis'as'a. Bl.

oǩi'śilia, v. (?). Bl.

o'kiśtaᶯ, v. pos. perhaps. (of ośtaᶯ). To put in place of, to put in one's own. Yuᶯkaᶯ isto k'oᶯ ecel ikikcu na ecel - na ku. MS.147.

okiś'yakel, adv. (?). - naᶯke lo, ot'iᶯȟyakel naᶯke lo, as is said by a visitor whò is received in silence as though he were not welcome. Bl.

oǩi'taᶯiᶯ, 1) v.n. To appear, be conspicuous, as a hill. 2) n. Manifestation, perspicuity. - waśte. -- oǩi'taᶯiᶯyaᶯ, adv. Manifestly, gloriously. - uᶯpi, i.e. became famous. D.258.

oki'ti, v.n. To live in some place, have a residence. He ihaⁿke ca el Śahiyela okitipi.

oki't'a, v.n. To be tired, fatigued or worn out by; to be made sick by. Wamatuka yelo, takuiyuha owakit'e lo, as a man would say when he did not care for anything any more.

oki't'eya, v.a. To obstruct in, prevent. Caⁿku - , as is said of a narrow road. - uⁿyaⁿkapi, i.e. crowded together because room is small. Bl. RTt. Also, to tire out, bother unceasingly. B.H.58.6;137.25;238.24. -- adv. Silent from exhaustion. - maⁿke lo. BT. -- okit'eyakel, adv. Obstructing, preventing. Cf. patagya. Syn.- patagyakel. -- okit'eyela, adv. Too large, bulky; tired out. R. Bl.

oki'uⁿ śica, adj. Hard to handle, as a lively horse or a child on account of its tossing. Bl.

oki'wa, v. (of owa). To write for one. Owakiwa.

oki'wablaza, v.a. (of wablaza). To rip open in the middle. Okiwawablaza.

oki'wableca, v.a. (of wableca). To break through the middle e.g. of a plate by cutting on it. Okiwawableca.

oki'waksa, v.a. (of waksa). To cut with a knife through the middle. Okiwakaksa.

o'kiwaⁿjila, adv. Continually, always; uniform, alike. - naȟmala kigla. Hecel wicitawokśaⁿ uⁿyaⁿpi na - uⁿkutapi.

oki'waptuġa, v.a. To cut in two with a knife in the middle, as pemmican, anything crusted or half frozen.

oki'wasleca, v.a. (of wasleca). To slit, rip down something soft e.g. an apple in the middle with a knife or saw. Okiwawasleca. Cf. oki. Na ake tataⁿka waⁿ o na oⁿ ha kiⁿ - . -- okiwaslel, cont. of okiwasleca.

oki'waśleca, v.a. (of waśleca). To slit or rip down e.g. a log or board in the middle with a saw. Okiwawaśleca.

oki'waśpa, v.a. (of waśpa). To cut into halves, in two in the middle e.g. an apple with a knife. Okiwawaśpa.

oki'waśpu, v.a. (of waśpu). To halve e.g. a potato with a knife. Okiwawaśpu.

oki'waś'ag śica, adj. Describing one who cannot be advised or does not listen to advice. Bl.

oki'wiⁿja, (?). Na wana, Lel yaⁿka ye, eyiⁿ na pteha okise waⁿ - . MS.143.

o'kiwitaya, adv. perhaps. Gathering about something.

oki'wośleca, v.a. To split by shooting. Okiwawośleca.

oki'wotahena, adv. By mere chance. - waⁿkiciyaⁿkapi. Bl. -- okiwotahena, adv. Between two places, things or persons. - ti, To live alone away from the crowd. - iblotake. - egnaka. Bl.

oki'ya, v.a. To talk with; to court, as a man courts a woman; to make peace with. Owakiya. D.51 and 269.

o'kiya, v.a. To help, assist one in anything. O'wakiya.

oki'yag, cont. of okiyaka. He - wahi.

oki'yaka, v.a. (of oyaka). To tell anything to one. Owakiyaka, uⁿkokiyakapi; and also, owakiblaka, oyakilaka.

oki'yapta, v. (of oyapta). To leave, e.g. food, for one. Owakiyapta.

oki'yasiⁿ, v.n. To stick together, as potatoes growing on the same root.

oki'yaskapa, v.n. To stick on, stick together, cleave to; to fall in and become flat, as an animal that is poor.

o'kiyekiya, v.a. To make one help. B.H.265.9.

oki'yuslel, cont. (of okiyusleca). To divide. Woyuha...okimakiyuslel śi yo. Talo kiⁿ hena - icupo, eya ke. B.H. 224.2. MS.96.

o'ḱiyuṫa, v.n. To heal up e.g. a wound; to grow over, as bark cut on a tree.

oḱi'zi, v.n. To heal up, recover from a hurt or wound. Omakizi. -- oḱi'ziḱiya, v.a. To cause to heal up. Okiziwakiya. -- oḱi'ziya, v.a. To cause to heal, make well; cause to take a rest. Okiziwaya.

oḱō', 1) n. A crack, hole, aperture, as in a house; a space. 2) adv. Between. Oko waŋjica, One week. Oko oyate ob mayani kte, as the chief is told when he is inaugurated. Okoya ayuśtaŋ, To leave a space free. Caŋ kiŋ he oko kiŋ ogna iblable. Le Sept. 25-30 oko el St. Francis Mission ekta wai kte lo. Yuŋkaŋ makoce kiŋ owaŋcaya waśicuŋpi na Lakota kiŋ oko oyasiŋ ceya uŋpi. MS.355. Cf. sióko, napsúhu-.

oḱō'gna, adv. Between.

oko'gnagnaka, v. To put between others, e.g. a child between a number of persons so that it cannot fall etc. Bl.

oḱo'ḱiṗe, n. Danger, fear. -- oḱóḱiṗeya, adv. In fear.

oḱo'laḱiciye, n. A league, fellowship; society, a community or society.

oḱo'laya, v. To have for a friend. Ake hokśila waŋ - .

oḱoŋ', n. Desire.

oḱoŋ'ze, n. A rule, a law.

oko'ṗe, n. (of kope). Fear.

o'ḱoṗeya, adv. Seen through a hole, as one seen through an opening in the bushes. - waŋblaka. - owojuŋ waŋ taŋiŋyaŋ he lo, A garden (field) is just a little visible between the hills. BT.

oḱo'śniyaŋ, adv. There being no space. - haŋ. B.H.130.9.

oḱō'toŋ, v. There is a crack, there is a hole. -- oḱótoŋyaŋ, n. An opening or communication; expanse, space, the expanse of the heavens, the firmament. R. -- adv. perhaps. With free spaces. Okotoŋyaŋ ayuśtaŋ, To leave a space free, as in putting boards on a wall and leaving a space for windows.

oḱo'wanilya, adv. With no room between. - yaŋkapi, i.e. sit close together; also, íċipat'iŋs yaŋkapi. Bl. Also, in the obverse sense, all over. B.H. 50.4.

oḱō'ya, adv. Between. - ayuśtaŋ, To leave a space free between rows.

okṗa'ǵi, v. pos. (of opagi). To fill one's own pipe with one's own tobacco. Owakpagi.

o'kṗani, v.n. To be lacking; less than, i.e. to what one already has, as money etc.

o'kpaŋkpaŋ, (?). Śuŋkhiŋśa wicaȟcala s'e ite saŋ - . Bl.

okpaŋ'la, adj. Crumbled, as coal, bread etc. Aguyapi - . Bl. B.H.213. 7.

o'kṗas, cont. of okpaza. - icu, To become dark.

okpa'spa, v. (?). Owakpaspa. Waciŋ - , as is said of a man when he keeps silent inspite of his anger. Bl.

o'kṗasya, 1) v.a. To darken, make dark. Okpaswaya. 2) adv. Darkly, in the dark. Wanagi s'e iśtokpasya, as is said when the eyes' sockets were very deep. Śuŋkite pśuŋka s'e poge kiŋ - , as is said when a man's nose points upwards. Bl.

o'kṗaza, 1) v.n. To be dark. 2) n. perhaps. Darkness, night.

okpa'zaŋ, (?).

o'kṗe, v. To meet and assist in carrying a load or in taking part of one's load. - ya. Taŋke, ciye okpewica ni kte lo, teȟiya kupi ca iya yo. MS.74. - śni heyáhe, he kept on saying that without helping. D.71.

okpi'kpi, (?). Maka ciŋcala s'e iśta cikcik'aya iśta - kaca, i.e. very small eyes. Bl.

okṗu'kṗa, adj. Full of dirt, not clear, as water, soup etc. -- okṗúkṗe, n.

okṗu'kṗe, n. (of kpukpa). Dregs, lees.

o'ksa, v.n. To break off e.g. a stick in a hole. -- oksáhaⁿ, part. Broken off in, fallen in e.g. in a corn-hole. -- oksáhe, part. Same as oksahaⁿ.

oksa'ṗe wo'ṫeḣi, ph. Stupid, hard to teach. Bl. Syn.- tehaⁿ ksape śni.

o'kse, n. Anything broken off short.

ō'kśaⁿ, prep. and adv. Around, round about. - kiⁿyaⁿ, To hover. Na waⁿna haⁿhepi el ataya tipi kiⁿ - enajiⁿ. -- ókśaⁿiṗata, v. To put edging around quill-work. -- ókśaⁿkśaⁿ, adv. red. of okśaⁿ. Wekta na - ewatoⁿwaⁿ na lila caⁿtemaśica. - wakita. Iśnala pahata - etoⁿwaⁿ, i.e. viewing the country round about. B.H.234.5. D.120. MS.162. -- ókśaⁿṫaⁿ, adv. From all around, from all directions. Tohaⁿl letaⁿhaⁿ ble ci hehaⁿl - awicaupi kte lo. Also, ókśaⁿtaⁿhaⁿ. Waⁿna okśaⁿtaⁿhaⁿ el au.

okśu', v. pos. (of oju). To load e.g. one's gun; to load a wagon. Owekśu. Caḣli ecel okśupi kiⁿ iyecel uwata na takuni śni. Hohu - wo, Pile up the bones, i.e. in a kettle. Kola, omicikśu wo; omani mni ktelo. Bl.

okte', n. perhaps. A killing, in regard to killing. Ziⁿtkala owe oyasiⁿ kiⁿyaⁿpi na okte śicapi. MS.479.

oḱu'ja, v.n. (of kuja). To be sick on account of. Omakuja. -- oḱúje, n. Sickness; doubtfully, laziness. R. - tipi, A sick room.

okuⁿ', adj. in comp. - oⁿ waśte, Gentle or mild. ER.

oḱu'ṫe, n. (of kute). A shooting, a shot.

oḱu'wa, v.a. (of kuwa). To chase, run after. Owakuwa. Taku - , She worked with something. D.272.

ok'a', v.a. (of k'a). To dig into, dig through, out, up. Owák'a, uⁿkók'api. Śuⁿkmanitu waⁿ hi na omak'iⁿ na imacu welo. Itaokśaⁿ maka kiⁿ ok'iⁿ na. -- ok'ápi, n. A digging into. -- ok'é, n. A digging; a mine.

ok'iⁿ', 1) v. (of k'iⁿ). To carry in. Owak'iⁿ. 2) n. (also of k'iⁿ). A pack, load, something to carry or pack in e.g. in a blanket or a sack. - waⁿji kage. D.66.

ok'i'ṗe, n. Something staked, the prize.

o'k'o, v. To stick to or on, as feathers or down or flour dust; to gather around for something to eat. Owak'o, ómak'o. Eceś lila ómak'opi kelaḣ, They crowd me fearfully for. Bl.

ok'o', n. A noise, hum, buzz, bustle; a disturbance. - hiⁿgla. Lila wakiⁿyaⁿ ukiye na lila wasu ko hihaⁿha wakaⁿgli makata iheyapi na lila - na ecel aⁿpa el akisni. Ok'o uⁿkagiⁿ ktelo. Icuⁿuⁿpa, icúⁿoⁿpa, - kta waciⁿ śni. Bl. BM. -- ok'ŏḱa, n. (of ok'o and ka). Noise, disturbance, tumult. Na waⁿna lila - . Syn.- ok'ós'e. Also perhaps v. To cause disturbance. Hohaⁿpataⁿhaⁿ taku ok'oke; yuⁿkaⁿ el gli. MS.164.

ok'o's'e, n. Disturbance, tumult.

ok'o'ya, v.n. To make a noise or bustle. Ok'owaya. Na wana oyate k'uⁿ oimniciye na lila - śkaⁿpi. MS.577. -- adv. perhaps. Noisely. - yaⁿka. Na cokata lila wicotapi na taku - śkaⁿpi. B.H.205.5. MS.342. R. Also, ok'ŏyakel, Na waⁿna ok'oyakel śkaⁿpi.

ok'u', 1) v.a. To lend anything to one. Owak'u. 2) v.a. (of k'u). To give to, e.g. food; to give a portion to. Caⁿke śuⁿk ok'upi na lila wicota ko ekta waⁿyaⁿk ahi. Also, to share with. D.97, note 3.

olab'ya, v.a. To cheer up, make glad by giving; to give much. Olabwaya. Olabciya. LHB. Bl. -- adv. Very much. P. Also, olábyaḱel, Exceedingly, very much; gratifyingly.

ola'kol, cont. of olakota. - kaga, To make a treaty, make peace among, make friends with. P.

ola'ḱolḱi'ciyapi, n. Friendship, peace. Wakaⁿpi - , The communion of Saints.

ola'kolwicaye śni, adj. Not caring for relatives, without natural affection.

ola'kolya, v. To have for a friend. -- adv. perhaps. As friends. - uⁿpi kte kiⁿ oihaⁿke wanicin kte. B.H.129.8

ola'koť, cont. of olakota. Olakotkaga. Also, olakol.

ola'ǩoťa, n. Friendship, alliance, fraternity.

o'lanuⁿs'e, (?). Bl.

ole', v.a. To seek for, hunt for anything. Owale, uⁿkolepi.

ole'ja, 1) v. (of leja). To urinate in anything. Owaleja. 2) n. The bladder perhaps; a chamber-pot.

olol', cont. of olota.

olo'lobya, v.a. To over-boil something in. Ololobwaya.

olo'ťa, v.a. To borrow anything. Owálota.

o'loťa, adj. red. (of ota). Much of various kinds. Lila - . Hecel top zuya ipi kiⁿ iyuha - waoⁿtoⁿyaⁿpi.

olo'ťapi.uⁿ, n. A hireling; anything borrowed from others. Bl. P.

olo'waⁿ, n. A song, hymn, a tune.

olu'luťa, 1) n. Heat. 2) adj. Warm, hot, as a room or the weather; sultry. P.

olu'ťe, n. The large muscle or flesh on the thigh, legs. Wana - kiⁿ icaȟ ayapelo, i.e. get fat from grass in the spring. Bl.

olu'zahaⁿ, n. (of luzahaⁿ). Swiftness.

Oma'ha, n. prop. An Omaha Indian.

o'maka, n. A year; a season. - opta tawoecoⁿ wowapi, An historical book, a record. B.H.147.25.

oma'ni, 1) v. (of mani). To walk in or according to, as in a road; to travel. Omawani, omauⁿnipi, uⁿkomanipi. 2) n. A walk. -- omániyaⁿ, v. To go on a walk. Omawaniyaⁿ. Waⁿna ake omaniyaⁿpi kta. -- omániyaⁿkel, adv. Walking. - wauⁿ.

oma'sǩaṗe, n. A blacksmith shop; a blacksmith. P.

oma's'ǩaġe, n. A blacksmith shop.

oma'śte, 1) n. Heat, warmth; the sunshine; where the sun shines. 2) v.n. (of maśte). To be hot in.

oma'wahitoⁿ, n. The two fathers of husband and wife call each other by this title; and the mothers as well. Omawahitoⁿ mitawa, nitawa. The word may be derived from uⁿmawatoⁿ. Also, omáwahetoⁿ. This is a term of direct address, used regardless of sex between the parents, aunts, uncles, and grandparents of a person, when speaking either of or to that person's spouse's parents, uncles, aunts and grandparents. D.199, note 1. -- omáwahitoⁿkiciya, v. refl. To have each other for omawahitoⁿ. -- omáwahitoⁿya, v.a. To have for a omawahitoⁿ. Omawahitoⁿwaya. Cf. omawahitoⁿ. Also, omáwahetoⁿya.

oma'zape, n. A graphophone.

o'mazape, n. A telephone apparatus.

omi'meyela, adv. Encircling.

omini'owe, n. A made well. Syn.- mini oicu.

o'mna, 1) v.a. To smell something, such as whiskey, burnt herbs etc. Ówamna, ouⁿmnapi. 2) n. A smell. Ciⁿca k'oⁿ azilya. Yuⁿkaⁿ - na akisni.

o'mnaǩiya, v. To give a smoke to. Omnamakiyi ye, Give me a smoke.

omna'yaⁿ, v. (of mnayaⁿ). To gather into. Omnawaya. Wicawe waⁿjila el omnauⁿyaⁿpelo.

omni'ca, n. Beans. Also, maǩátomnica, Lakota omnica. The trailing wild bean. Strophostyles helvola; also falcata comosa. Pulse family. Waȟpe wakaⁿ heca ota yelo. As a medicine, you pulverize the leaves and put them on swellings together with any salve; lila waśte. BT. #111. -- omníca gmigmí, n. Peas. Also, omnica gmigmela. -- omnicahu, n. The legumen, strophostyles pauciflora. Bl. #292. -- omníca taⁿkiⁿyaⁿ, n. Large beans.

omni'ciye, n. (of mniciya). An assembly. - ecoⁿ, To hold a meeting.

omni'mni, v. To sprinkle into.

omni'yatke, n. A place to drink water. Pb.31.

o'mniyela, adv. perhaps. (?). - wayatapelo, as they say when some ate sitting with others and without sharing with them. Ena - ayuhel wicakuwi, as horses do in a small place. BT. GA.

ona', n. A fire, a prairie fire. Cf. onikuseya, oninatake.

ona'blu, v. To raise dust by walking through sand. Onawablu.

ona'cu, (?). Haⁿpa kiⁿ onawacu welo, My moccasins are frosty inside. Bl.

ona'glo, v.n. To rattle in the throat. -- onágloglo, v. red. To rattle in the throat, have a rattling in the throat, as one about to die. The word is also applied to things boiling and rattling in the kettle. D.272.

ona'ǧu, n. A place where a prairie fire burned everything. Ataya - pte kiⁿ au welo, i.e. so full of buffalos that the prairie looks black.

ona'ǧumna, v. perhaps. (of ona and gumna). To smell like a prairie fire.

ona'gwu, v.i. To curdle in, as milk in a pot.

ona'ȟlaṫe, n. (of naȟlata). A scratch.

ona'ȟleca, v.a. To tear a hole in a hole. Onawaȟleca. -- onáȟlece, n. (of naȟleca). A rent, a tear.

ona'ȟloḱa, v.a. To make a hole either in the ground with the foot, or in the foot by walking. Onawaȟloka.

ona'ȟna, n. The death rattle of a dying person. Also perhaps, onaglo.

ona'ȟṫaḱa, v. (of naȟtaka). To kick in. Onawaȟtaka. -- onáȟṫaḱe, n. A wound made by kicking.

ona'ȟ'oⁿ, 1) v. (of naȟ'oⁿ). To hear what is reported, to hear of or concerning. Onawaȟ'oⁿ. 2) n. Hearing. - waśte, It is good hearing. -- onáȟ'oⁿḱiya, v.a. To cause to hear of, to communicate to concerning. Onaȟ'oⁿwakiya. -- onáȟ'oⁿpi, n. Hearing. -- onáȟ'oⁿya, v.a. To cause to hear, to communicate to, to announce. Onaȟ'oⁿwaya.

ona'jaja, v.n. (of najaja). To cleanse or wash out e.g. clothes by boiling.

ona'jiⁿ, v. (of najiⁿ). To stand in, to take refuge in or at. Onawajiⁿ. P'osyakel - k'oⁿ. Bl.

ona'juju, v.n. (?). It is applied to a wagon when its wheels are broken. BT.

o'naḱab, cont. (of onakapa). To kick into. - iyeya. Si oⁿ caⁿ kiⁿ peta ekta - iyeya śkaⁿ.

ona'kaⁿ, 1) v.a. To strike and knock off into, to tread off in. Onawakaⁿ. 2) v.n. To be kicked to pieces, as the teeth of one's mouth. Hi ataya onamakaⁿ.

ona'ḱicitaⁿpi, v. recip. (of onataⁿ). To kick each other, as boys in play. Onauⁿkicitaⁿpi.

ona'ḱijiⁿ, v.i. To take shelter or refuge in or behind, as behind a tree in a battle. Onawakijiⁿ. Hecena ataya hepiya el onakijiⁿpi.Cf.onakikśiⁿ.

ona'ḱiḱiyakel, adv. Unevenly. - naksey, To cut grass unevenly, leaving some here and there. Syn.- naȟ'éȟ'eyakel. Bl.

ona'ḱikśiⁿ, v.a. (of nakkśiⁿ). To take shelter or refuge in or behind, as behind a tree in battle. Onawekśiⁿ.

ona'ḱiśośe, v. To stir up water with the foot, so that others cannot use it. Fig., to spoil somebody's chance to buy things that someone else wants etc.; to spoil things for another that he wanted to do. Onamayaḱiśośe lo. Bl.

ona'kṗa, v.n. (of nakpa). To burst within something.

ona'kṗaⁿ, n. A mill. Aguyapi - , A

flour mill. -- v. perhaps. (of na and kpaŋ). To make fine in, as by machinery.

ona'ksa, v.a. (of naksa). To break into or through, as in walking on ice. Onawaksa. Siyete ośoke k'el uŋkcela onawaksa. Bl. -- onákse, n. A breaking in.

ona'kśaŋ, n. (of nakśaŋ). A bend, a crook.

ona'kťaŋ, 1) v.n. To bend into of itself. Cf. naktaŋ, naoktaŋ. 2) n. A bend.

ona'k'eġa, (?). Ite pśuŋka waŋ onamak'ega helo, as is said when desiring a smoke. BT.

ona'k'esk'eza, v. red. of onak'eza.

ona'k'eza, v.a. To make smooth by stamping on. Onawak'eza.

ona'k'os, cont. of onak'oza. -- onák'osk'oza, v. red.

ona'k'oza, v.n. To trample on and make hard. Onawak'oza.

o'namnimni, v. To be on one's way. -icu, To be on the way to some place repeatedly but go back again. Bl. -- onamniyeta, adv. (?). - éiȟpeic'iyaya, To go on in a crowd somewhere, but return when someone else has caught up. - eiȟpeic'imayayapelo. Bl.

ona'ṗa, v.a. (of napa). To flee to, take refuge in. Onawapa.

ona'pce, n. A bite; the act of swallowing; the esophagus, perhaps. Pusyá śpaŋyayapi ca - omaśicelo. P. GA. -- onápceśilya, (?).

ona'ṗe, n. A place of refuge, where enemies cannot harm one.

ona'ṗe, n. or adv. In hand. Miye kayeś - el able śni wak'u welo, i.e. gave him something new, something never handled. Bl.

ona'piga, v.n. To foam, froth; to spoil as spoiling meat.

ona'ṗoȟya, v.n. To swell out, puff up. -- onáṗoȟye, n. Leaven.

ona'ṗoṗa, v.n. (of napopa). To burst within something.

ona'ṗuza, (?). Hinu, - ca haŋpi cola wowahete, as a woman would say when all the soup had evaporated. BT.

ona'se, n. The buffalo chase.

ona'slata, (?). Caŋku onaslatapi, They advance slowly, i.e. as slow horses. Bl.

ona'sto, v. To tramp down, make bare with the feet in. Ṗeji - eȟpeya. Hopo, waŋna waȟpe, wokiya ekta owaŋka - lapi kte lo. Tokel owaŋka onastopi he oŋspewicakiya.

ona's'amna, (?). Bl.

ona's'eya, v.n. To begin to boil, simmer in, as water in a pot. Bl.

ona'śkaŋ, v.n. To become sick again, to relapse. Onawakśaŋ.

ona'ślaśla, v. red. (of onaśla). To bare or make bare with the feet. Onawaślaśla. Na hiŋ ko onaślaślapi.

o'naślog, cont. of onaśloka. - iyaya. Wauŋ letaŋ okaŋyela ca aśkiŋyaŋkapila - uŋkihuŋnipi kte lo. Bl.

o'naśloka, v.n. (of naśloka). To leave behind, run off and leave. Oňawaśloka.

ona'śloka, v.a. To pull off in, as shoes in the mud. Onáwaśloka. Wicaśa waŋ nata kiŋ ataya - ca iśta kiŋ akaȟpeya hiyu, A man with his entire scalp peeled off so that it hung in front of his eyes. D.224.

ona'ś'o, v.n. To pace, as a horse. -- onáś'ola, n. A pacing horse. -- onáś'oś'o, v. red. of onaś'o.

o'natag, cont. of onataka. - iyeya.

o'nataka, v.a. (of nataka). To fasten, bar, bolt, lock e.g. a door; to fasten e.g. a fence; to fasten or lock up in. Oňawataka.

ona'take, n. A cage, a pen.

ona'taŋ, v.a. To kick, to crush upon; fig., harsh words to be used. Onawataⁿ. Onacitaⁿ. Also, onátaⁿyaⁿ. D.215.

ona'ť'iⁿs, cont. of onat'iⁿza. - iyeya.

ona'ť'iⁿza, v.a. (of nat'iⁿza). To make firm by treading on. Onawat'iⁿza.

ona'ť'os, cont. of onat'oza. -- onát'ost'oza, v. red.

ona'ť'oza, v. To make smooth by stamping on.

ona'ya, v. To start a prairie fire. Onawaya. Bl.

ona'zoⁿ, (?). Tatamni - . Bl.

oni', n. Life. - mitawa kiⁿ wakpagaⁿ yelo. B.H.254.2.

oni'ǩuśeya, n. perhaps. A fire guard. The word seem to be of ona and ikuśeya. Cf. oninatake.

oni'natake, n. A fire guard. Also, onáinatake.

oni'sǩoǩeca, adj. So large.

oni'ya, v. (of niya). To breathe into, to breathe out of. Owaniya. - śica, To have bad breath. -- oniyaⁿ, n. Breath. - haⁿska.

oni'yaśni t'e, v. To choke to death. WE.

oni'ye, n. Breath. Pb.34. -- oníyemna, v. To have a foul breath; to smell bad. Bl.

oni'yetoⁿ, v.n. To be affected by some internal hurt or disease; to have the lungs affected, as in pulminary consumption. Oniyewatoⁿ.

onoⁿȟ'hoyeya, v. To hear with one's own ears. Onóⁿȟhoyewaya. Miś eya onóⁿȟhoyewayelo. Bl.

onu'ni, v.n. (of nuni). To wander in. owanuni. -- onúniśniyaⁿ, adv. (?). Taku oyasiⁿ - waéhelo, as they say to a joker. Bl. -- onúniya, v.a. To cause to wander in a place. Onuniwaya. -- onúniyaⁿ, adv. Wanderingly, lost. -- onúniyata, adv. Wandering. R. Bl.

onuⁿ'we, n. A bath tub.

oⁿ, prep. For, on account of; of, by means of, with, i.e. when used with cause or instrument. Maza oⁿ kagapi, i.e. made of iron. Si oⁿ caⁿ kiⁿ peta ekta onakab iyeya. Maka ȟliȟlila oⁿ iic'iyuⁿ. Nazoⁿspe caⁿnuⁿpa waⁿ oⁿ huhu kiⁿ kaweȟweh apa śke lo. Tona iśta oⁿ waⁿlakapi kiⁿ hena kokipa po. Hena oⁿ oⁿnitoⁿpi kta. Taku mitawa oⁿ owicakiyapi kta. Taku tona cic'upi owasiⁿ oⁿ miksuya po. Note: when the word is used alone, it means "with". Na taha kpaⁿyaⁿpi kiⁿ ohomni waso na oⁿ tuśu kiⁿ hena paȟta. Tataⁿka pizi waⁿ ota latkaⁿ ca oⁿ aiyahaⁿble lo. -- prep. cont. When the word is put at the end of a sentence, it gives what has just been said to be the reason. That's why. It may also occur within the sentence. B.H. 96.8 and 11.

oⁿ'aziⁿpi, n. A nipple. Cf. aziⁿ.

oⁿ'cablu oju, n. A pile of snow or rubbish carried together by the wind; perhaps the place where snow etc. are so piled. Bl.

oⁿci', Cf. these words under uⁿ- .
oⁿ'cihi,
oⁿ'cihiya,
oⁿci'śi,
oⁿci'śicala, etc.

oⁿ'c'ikṗani, v.n. To be poor, not able to sustain one's self. Oⁿmic'ikpani, and perhaps oⁿmac'ikpani. -- óⁿc'ikṗaniyaⁿ, adv. In a destitute condition. - wauⁿ.

oⁿ'c'uⁿnica, v.n. To be delayed, be prevented; to wait until the thing cannot be done. Oⁿmac'uⁿnica. -- óⁿc'uⁿnilya, v.a. To stop, keep from doing, prevent, hinder. Oⁿc'uⁿnilwaya.

oⁿ'eciyataⁿhaⁿ, adv. By means of; on account of.

oⁿ'eṫaⁿhaⁿ, adv. Therefore, for that cause.

oⁿ'glakcapi, Cf. icaȟpe hu which is the same. The plant grows in the hills and is used as a tooth-ache medicine.

oⁿ'gloġe, n. A shirt.

oⁿ'gluȟpe, n. (?). - maota, i.e. much

work, no time. MO. Also, óŋgloḣpe.

oŋ'gluze, (?). - maota kaca, I have a lot of things to tend to. Bc.

oŋ'gnawiċaśke, n. A bed. This is an old word for oyuŋke. HM.

oŋ'gnaye, (?). - k̇aḣk̇aḣ ahitipelo, i.e. arrived ahead of the others. Bl.

oŋ huŋk̇a'lowaŋpi iye'ceca, n. Same as zuzeca tapejuta. It is so called because the plant resembles somewhat the huŋkatacanuŋpa. The leaves are opposite, their position reminding one of the strains of horse hair attached to the huŋkatacaŋnuŋpa at intervals. Bl. #5.

oŋ'iglujajapi, n. A wash basin.

oŋjiŋ'jiŋtka, n. The rose, roses, rosebuds. - hu, Rose bushes. - mazognaka, Canned tomatoes.

Oŋjiŋjiŋ'tka Wakpa, n. prop. The Rosebud River.

oŋ'k̇iciśkatapi, v. recip. (of oŋśkata). To jest, joke or banter each other, as persons within a certain degree of affinity are at liberty to do among the Dakotas. R.

oŋ'kiśkata, v.a. (of oŋśkata). To talk as one pleases with, boast, brag; joke with one. Oŋwakiśkata. This privilege is allowed only between brothers-in-law and sisters-in-law. This an old word. R.

oŋ'naṗe watog'ya, (?). - maza wakaŋ, maza ska bluha kte, i.e. for emergency's sake, to be prepared for anything. Bl.

oŋ'napṫaŋ, adj. Sideling. Heóŋnaptaŋ, A side-hill.

oŋ'ṗa, v.a. To place or lay any long object in a reclining attitude. Waoŋpa. Wayaka kiŋ tima paḣta oŋpapi. Also, úŋṗa.

oŋspe', v.n. To know how to do a thing. Oŋmaspe, uŋkoŋspepi. Oŋmaspe waŋji glaḣniga po. Also, oŋspék̇a, which is sometimes used in the sense of oŋspeśni, Not to know how. -- oŋspék̇iya, v.a. To cause to know how, to teach. Oŋspewakiya, oŋspemakiya. Oŋspeciciya. Oŋspeic'iciya, To learn.

oŋs'co'kalaka, n. One who loafs on horseback a great deal and thus has lean horses. - caŋke, as they say of a loafer's lean horse. Bl.

oŋs'ha'ha, adj. Sitting restlessly, wishing to get away. Uŋgnahela oŋsmahaha yelo, All at once I have a desire to travel. BT. Bl.

oŋ'śi, adj. Poor, miserable. Oŋmaśi, oŋuŋśipi. Na waŋna kéya - íyahaŋ. -- óŋśic'iya, v. refl. To make one's self miserable, pretend to be in misery. Oŋśimic'iya. Hecena keya ceya iyaya na lila oŋśiic'iya. Also, óŋśiic'iya.

oŋ'śiḣ'aŋ, v.n. (of oŋśi and ḣ'aŋ). To be humble, to act humbly. Oŋśiwaḣ'aŋ. -- óŋśiḣ'aŋka, v.n. To be humble, to try to excite compassion; to fawn. Oŋśiwaḣ'aŋka. -- óŋśiḣ'aŋpi, n. Humility.

oŋ'śiic'icaḣya, adv. Humbling one's self deeply. - pasto. Cf. B.H.43.11.

oŋ'śik̇a, adj. Poor destitute, miserable. Oŋmaśika, oŋuŋśipika.

oŋ'śikiḣ'aŋ, v.a. (of oŋśiḣ'aŋ). To humble one's self to another, act humble towards. Oŋśiwakiḣ'aŋ.

oŋ'śikila, v. pos. (of oŋśila). To have mercy on one's own. Oŋśiwakila. Ate...oyate kiŋ oŋśiwicakila ye. Pb. 35. Also, óŋśik̇ilaka.

oŋ'śila, 1) v.a. To have mercy on, to pity. Oŋśiwala, oŋśimala. 2) interj. Poor thing! It is used by women to infants. Kola, oŋśiuŋlapo. -- óŋśilak̇a, v.a. To have mercy, to pity. Oŋśiwalaka.

oŋ'śiśiya, adv. red. (of oŋśiya). Dolefully, pitifully. - ceyaya. B.H. 35.3;117.20.

oŋ'śiya, adv. and perhaps adj. Poorly, miserably. - imacage lo. Tuwa - waŋyakapi kiŋ oŋśila wicaśi. Miciŋkśi - , miye ekta iyotiyekiya mayahipi. Hokśicala - ḣpaya ciŋ waŋyaŋka. -- oŋśiyaca, adj. Miserable. Oŋśimayaca. Also, oŋśiyeca. P. -- óŋśiyakel, adv.

Pitifully. - yanka, To sit pitifully. D.55.

on'śkata, v.n. To talk as one pleases, brag, jest, as brothers and sisters-in-law are privileged to do among the Dakotas. Onwaśkata.

onśpa', n. A piece of anything. - oniwaja, It concerns you partly, you are concerned in it. BT. -- onśpála, n. dim. A little piece.

on'śtinma kpat'a, v. To kill one's own by lying on in one's sleep. B.H.99.4.

on'śtinma nihin'ciya, v. To feel scared in one's sleep. B.H.31.10.

on'śtinmapihin, n. The eye-lashes. The word explains itself: on iśtinmapi hin. BD. Onśtinmapihinpi acaȟsusu imayayelo. Bl.

on'śtinmat'a, v. To die in one's sleep. D.33. Also, to be very sound asleep. B. -- ónśtinmat'aya, v.a. To cause one to sleep very soundly. B.H.2.15.

on'śunk'nasapi hu, n. Same as zuzeca tawote, Wolf berry. #10.

on'śunk'oyu'spapi, n. Same as tatawabluśka ta canȟlogan. It is used by chewing and rubbing on the hands. #8.

on tan'tanhan, prep. and adv. For the sake of. Wakantanka caje kin - . B.H. 49.2;117.9.

on'ton, v.n. To be injured. Onmaton, onuntonpi. Hena on onnitonpi kta. -- óntonic'iya, v. refl. To injure one's self. -- óntonśniyan, adv. Without being hurt. Daniel igmu tanka egna - yankahe. B.H.145.2. -- óntonyan, v.a. To hurt, wound, injure. Ontonwaya. Ota ontonniyanpi śni. Óntonic'iya. Óntonmic'iya.

on't'ewácin, v. Intend to die on account of. Tokeś'unlaka wazatkanpi kin -. Bl. Syn.- it'éwacin.

on'wahin'yuntonpi, n. Annual erigonum. So called because it was mixed, its blossoms, with nasula tapi', tapiśleca, and rubbed into the hides of animals to bleach them. Hecel skayela kpanyanpi. Bl. Cf. iniyan pejuta. WC.61. Bl. #54.

on we'ojutonpi, n. Same as taśoka.Bl.

onwe'ya, n. Provisions. Le - tehan bluha ktelo, i.e. papa etc.

Onwe'ya Wakan, n. Viaticum. Pb.44.

onwi'yutapi, n. (of on and iyuta). Something to weigh or measure with; a standard measuring tool.

on'wohanpi océti, n. A cooking range.

onze', n. The rump, anus.

onze'hu, v. To copulate.

onze'kte, v. To give birth to another child, while still nursing one.

onze'okaśtanpi, n. An injection.

onze'pija, v. To be the oldest of two infants, one of which was born before the other was weaned. Bl.

on'zeslohan, v.n. (?). WE.

onze'ś'aś'ákiya, v. To yelp, as wolves and coyotes do. Bl.

onze'yugmuza, v.a. To shut up or hold shut the anus.

onzi'natan, n. The tail strap.

onzi'wosla, onzi'woslal, adv. Head over heels. - najin, yanka, To turn a summer-sault, stand with the heels up; to be in a flurry, not know what one is about. - najin, To stand with the heels up.

onzo'ġe, n. (of onze and oge). Pants. - pteca, Knickerbocker pants. - to, Overalls.

ŏo', n. A wound, a place where one is shot.

oo'gnake, n. A holder. Petijanjan ska - , A candle stick.

oo'he, n. (of ohan). A boiling, enough to boil at once. - waśte, Something that is cooked easily, or fig., that fits or wears well, as shoes or clothes. Bl.

Oo'henunpa, n. prop. A clan of the Teton Sioux, the Two Kettles. Tatáȟpa kiŋ le Oohenuŋpa he awagli ktelo.

oo'hiye, n. (of ohiya). Victory.

oo'ju, v. (of oju). To plant in. Oowaju.

oo'k̇aȟniȟteȟike, adj. Obscure. P. Bl.

oo'k̇aȟniȟ waśte, adj. Easily understood, obvious. Ookaȟniȟ niwaśte. Bl. B.H.259.10.

oo'k̇aśtaŋ, v.a. Cf. okaśtaŋ.

oo'kihi, (?). - śica. Hecel le wicoȟ'aŋ kiŋ - śica. MS.489.

oo'kiye, n. (of ókiya). An assistant; a servant.

oo'kśu, n. A load.

oo'k'e, n. Cf. maka ook'e.

oo'mani, n. A walking on; a sidewalk. Wakpala oguhaŋ oyasiŋ ocaȟśu ca - śice. Bl. - teȟike. D.200.

ooŋ'ṗa, v. (of oŋpa). To put or place in. Owaoŋpa. Ouŋk'oŋpapi.

ooŋ'śila, n. or adj. Hard to please, perhaps. - niśicelo. BT. D.33.

oo'petoŋ, n. (of opetoŋ). A fare. Tiyopa - , A toll gate.

oo'taŋiŋ, v.n. (of otaŋiŋ). To be manifest through.

oo'wa, n. (of owa). A letter, character, as the letters of the alphabet; a figure or mark of any kind. Śina - śa naiŋś to naiŋś gi...kaȟpapi. D. 113.

oo'waptaya, n. (oowa and ptaya). The alphabet.

oo'yake, n. (of oyaka). The act of telling a story; a relation, narrative.

oo'yuȟpa, n. A place of resting or throwing down burdens. Also, oéyuȟpa. R. Bl.

oo'yuspe, n. The handle of anything. Itazipa...- waśteya ecoŋpi. MS.481.

ō'ṗa, v.a. To go with, follow; be present at, take part in. Ówapa, óuŋpapi. Oyate kiŋ lila oimniciye ca el owapa. Miye kiŋ el omapa śni. B.H.301.7.

opa', (?). Syn.- el uŋ. Yuŋkaŋ wakpala waŋ opá caŋku ca opaya aya ewicuŋkiglegapi.

oṗa'gi, v.a. To fill or cram a pipe with tobacco. Owápagi, uŋkopagipi. Caŋnuŋpa waŋ opagipi na wicitokab eoŋpapi. Omáyakipági śni, toka? as they would say when on visiting the pipe was not offerred. -- n. A pipeful of tobacco.

oṗa'ha, v. To push over a bank. Owapaha. Also, mayá opáha. R.

opa'hi, v. (of pahi). To gather or pick up into. Owapahi.

oṗa'ȟci, n. A ravine, a hollow; the hollow among the hills where creeks head; a gully with or without water.

oṗa'ȟleca, v. (of paȟleca). To tear in. Owapaȟleca. -- oṗáȟlece, n. A rent.

oṗa'ȟloka, v. (of paȟloka). To pierce in; to wear holes in, as a sick man's bones do when they come through the flesh. Owapaȟloka. -- oṗáȟloke, n. A hole. Ceśikaŋ - , A button hole. Na taha k'oŋ hena oŋ wihuta - el cel ikaŋyaŋ na caŋ pteptecela oŋ ecel okataŋ.

opa'ȟta, v. (of paȟta). To tie or bind in. Opawaȟta. Śina waŋji taŋka opaȟtapi kte, i.e. a turtle. -- oṗáȟtaȟta, v. red. of opaȟta. B.H.35.13; 201.15. -- opáȟte, n. A package, a bundle; a bale of blankets; a bunch of beads.

oṗa'k̇iŋslasla, (?). Iśta kiŋ - iyewakiyelo, i.e. to rub the eyes because a lot of dust got in. Bl.

oṗa'mna, 1) v.n. To rip e.g. a seam. 2) n. A rip or rend.

opa'nakseye, n. A gibbet. B.H.147.22.

oṗaŋ'ga, v.n. To be bulky; to hinder or impede one, as cumbersome clothes do. Omapaŋga.

opaŋ'ǧeca, v.n. To be hindered by bulky articles, to be bulky. Omápaŋgeca. -- opáŋǧece, adj. perhaps. Having on too much clothing. Omapaŋgece. Bl.

opaŋ'ȟya, 1) v.a. To hinder, impede. Opaŋȟwaya. 2) adv. Bulky, not compressed. -- opáŋȟyaȟel, adv. Bulkily. -- opáŋȟyela, adv. Not well arranged, bulkily.

opa'pa, adv. perhaps. red. (of opa). Many along in, as head of cattle grazing along a creek.

opa'paya, adv. perhaps. red. of opaya. Caŋku - ewicaglepi. B.H.283.3.

opa'pinslasla iyeya, (?). Ista kiŋ - , To rub impurities out of the eyes.Bl.

opa'poŋ, n. The border or edge of anything; the stripe of a blanket, the edge of a book, the stripes or points that are put into white blankets to show their size. Caŋke (wikaŋ) ihaŋke oŋ wiŋyaŋ taśina - el iyakaśka.MS.353.

opa'psoŋ, v. (of papsoŋ). To pour out into, spill into. Owapapsoŋ. Also, opapsuŋ.

opa'ptaŋ, v. (of paptaŋ). To turn over. - iyeya. -- opáptaŋptaŋ, v.n. To roll over and over in anything. -- opáptaŋyaŋ, v.a. To roll anything on or into. Owapaptaŋyaŋ.

opa'puŋ, Cf. opapoŋ.

opa'puŋtaŋhaŋ, adv. From under the bottom of a tent.

opa'seb, cont. of opasepa. - gnaka, To lay away with care.

opa'sepa, v.a. To keep with care. Owapasepa.

opa'si, v. (of pasi). To follow after in, as in a road. Owapasi.

opa'ska, v.t. To press down and flatten e.g. dough in a bread pan. Aguyapi - . But for a bread pan, cf. wópaska. Syn.- yut'iŋza.

opa'skaŋ, v. To melt by lying on. Uŋkopaskaŋpi etiktelo, i.e. will camp here at the snow. Bl.

opa'slata, v. To stick in, as a sliver or splinter. Caŋ ómapaslata, I ran a splinter into e.g. my hand.

opa'sleca, v.a. To split, slice, cut e.g. wasna in something. MS.143. -- opáslesleca, v. red. of opasleca. Na wasna waŋ icu na caŋ wakśica waŋ el - na k'u. MS.143.

opa'spa, v. To push under in the water, press down into the water. Owapaspa. -- opáspaspa, v. red. Bl.

o'paśniya, v.a. To except, exempt, exclude. Opaśniwaya.

opa'śuśuja, v. To mash up in.

opa'śwoka, v. To push in e.g. a stick and splash.

opa'taŋ, v.a. To push into, to mash up in. Owapataŋ. -- opátaŋtaŋ, v. red.

opa'tica, v.a. To stick or push in or under, as a handspike. Owápatica. -- opátil, cont. (of opatica). To push under, as a crow-bar.

o'patkoŋs, cont. of opatkoŋza. WE. Cf. ákiyehaŋ. -- ópatkoŋsyela, adv. In line, fronting one way, facing one way.

opa't'a, v.a. To kill by pressure in, as a cat in a sack, or young animals in their mother's womb.

opa'waǧa, v.a. (of pawaga). To roll over anything in the hands, to rub in the hands. Owápawaga.

opa'wiŋǧe, adj. One hundred. -- opáwiŋǧeǧe, adv. By hundreds. Also, opawiŋȟwiŋge.

opa'wiwi, adv. Tangled together, in a mass; many, e.g. a great many maggots, or a great many people. -- opáwiwis'e, adv. Shaking, as a mass of anything.

opa'wiya, adv. Many together, as a herd.

opa'ya, adv. Along in. Caŋku - , Along in the way. Na waŋna wakpa cik'ala kiŋ - akicita kiŋ akiyuŋka. Wakpala kiŋ - ya po. -- opáyaya, adv. red.

of opaya. B.H.135.17.

oṗa'yeya, (?).

oṗa'zaⁿ, v.a. To push into or under, as into a sheath or belt; to push under and over, to interlace, as in making baskets. Owapazaⁿ. -- oṗázaⁿyaⁿ, adv. Running under. -- oṗázaⁿzaⁿ, v. red. (of opazaⁿ). To weave into. Owapazaⁿzaⁿ. B.H.55.11.

oṗa'zo, n. A protuberance.

oṗa'zoⁿta, v.a. To wrap around, wind up in, as a dead body in a winding sheet or a spool with thread. Owapazoⁿta.

opceb'yela, adv. For a short time. - ob ye. - wowicala yuhapi. B.H.14.2; 200.21;244.14.

ope', n. The edge, the sharp part of anything; a plow share, a blade, as of a knife. Miyokśijapi - . Nazoⁿspe - . B.H.116.3.

oṗe'haⁿ, v. (of pehaⁿ). To fold up in. Owapehaⁿ. -- oṗéhe, n. (of pehaⁿ). A fold; a bolt of cloth.

o'ṗeic'iya, v. refl. To side with, to follow. B.H.3.9. Óbic'iya, abbrev.

oṗe'ji ƙaśla k'el, n. perhaps. A certain place somewhere near the Platte River where one Indian saw hay cut for the first time. Bl.

oṗe'ƙicatoⁿ, v. (of opetoⁿ). To buy for one with one's own money. Opewecatoⁿ, opeuⁿkicatoⁿpi. -- oṗéƙicitoⁿ, v. (of opetoⁿ). To buy in place of another. Opewecitoⁿ.

oṗe'ƙitoⁿ, v. pos. (of opetoⁿ). To buy or purchase one's own, to redeem. Opewakitoⁿ, opeuⁿkitoⁿpi. -- oṗéƙitoⁿpi, part. Redeemed, redeeming. -- oṗéƙitoⁿyaⁿ, v.a. To cause to redeem. Opekitoⁿwaya.

oṗe'mni, v.a. To wrap around, as a garment. Owapemni, uⁿkopemnipi, Also, to be wrapped in. -- oṗémniyaⁿ, adv. Wrapped around. - uⁿ.

oṗe'sto, n. A point.

oṗe'toⁿ, v.a. To buy, purchase; hire. Opéwatoⁿ, opeuⁿtoⁿpi.

o'peya, 1) adv. With together. Aⁿpetu 60 niopeyapi wauⁿ kte lo. Wakaⁿtaⁿka niopeya uⁿ ni. B.H.124.12. Wiⁿyaⁿ wicopeya. 2) v.a. To cause to go with. Opewaya.

o'ṗeya uⁿ, n. An adherent, one belonging to a gang. Bl.

oṗi', v. perhaps. To be pleased. - śni, Displeased. Takuku - śni oⁿ t'iⁿ kta awaciⁿ, i.e. not contented. B.H.86. 14;109.5.

o'ṗi, n. or part. Wounded, one wounded, a wound. B.H.112.3.

oṗi'caƙa, (?). Ataya coco welo, i.e. soft ground after the melting of snow; oeti śicelo; hececa k'eyaś aliya ekta hinajiⁿ yo, tokeś opicakelo, i.e. perhaps it is not so bad after all. Bl.

oṗi'c'iye, n. and v. perhaps. A good place for resting; a camping place. Syn.- ohegle. WE. As v. refl., To act. Tawaciⁿhiⁿyaⁿsyakel - . Cf. opiic'iya.

oṗi'ic'iya, v. refl. To form an opinion and act for one's self, to get ready; to conduct one's self. D.2 and 35. Ptaⁿśkiśka iyecel opinic'iyelo, śkiⁿnic'iyelo.

oṗi'jeca, adj. Wrinkled, as an old person.

oṗi'ƙila, v.n. To be satisfied with e.g. food. Opiwakila. - uⁿkomanipi; śikigla uⁿkomanipi, i.e. we are making headway, we get on pretty well. Bl. Also, opikilaƙa.

opiś'yela, (?). - uⁿ.

opi'ya, (?). Perhaps to tie or be alike. BD.

oṗi'ye, 1) n. A place where things are put away and kept, a box. 2) v.n. (of piya). To mend or make well. - śica, Bad to doctor or make well.

o'ṗo, v.n. To be warped, be shrunken.

oṗo', v.n. To be swelled. Omápo.

oṗo'ǧaⁿ, v.a. To blow in upon, to

blow out from. Owápogaⁿ. -- oṗóḣ, cont. (of opogaⁿ). To blow away, blow from the mouth. - iyeya.

o'popo, v. red. (of ópa). To be warped, be shrunken. Capa s'e śake - kaca, as is said when a person has long fingernails. Bl.

oṗo'ṗoya, adv. red. perhaps. (?). B.H. 130.10.

o'psuⁿpsuⁿ, v.a. To draw back and forth in the water, to rinse.

o'pśuⁿpśuⁿyela, (?). - ic'ignaka po, i.e. be ready, for we will go soon.Bl.

opśuⁿ'wahe, (?). Bl. Also, opsuⁿwahe.

o'pṫa, adv. Through, across (locally). Yuⁿkaⁿ blaye waⁿ - ya śke. - ya. B.H. 54.3;283.4. -- ópṫapṫa, adv. red. (of opta). Through and through. Bl.

opṫa'ye, 1) n. A herd of animals. 2) adv. perhaps. In a bunch. - yaⁿkapi, They sit together in a bunch. Pte - kiⁿ etaⁿ aglinapapi.

o'pṫe, n. (of yupta). What is left, leavings.

opteb'yela, adv. A little while. - el wauⁿ kta. Also, a little distance. Letaⁿhaⁿ na owakpamni - , It is a little ways from here to Pine Ridge. - taⁿkal aye wicaśi. B.H.284.13.

opṫe'ca, adv. Less.

o'pṫeheca, adv. Almost empty, as is said of vessels.

opṫe'kte, n. A slaughter house.

opṫe'lic'iya, v. refl. To cease from, as from anger or strife, become gentle. Optelmic'iya. Cf. aópteca.

o'ptelyela, adv. For a little while; fora short time. - ocic'u welo, I loan it to you for a short time. - tatóheya uⁿglapi ktelo, i.e. for a little while against the wind. Bl. The same as optébyela.

optu'ḣaḣala, n. Crumbs, leavings. Winuḣcala, pápa - eśa igni yo; wanagi el mahipelo. Bl. Cf. ópte.

oṗu'ġi, v.a. To push into, as hay into moccasins; to stuff, fill, as with hay. Owapugi. -- oṗúġipi, n. A stuffing.

oṗu'ġitoⁿ, v.a. To put in stuffing, as in moccasins. Also, to mount, as a bird for display. Opugiwatoⁿ. -- oṗúġitoⁿyaⁿ, adv. In a stuffed manner.

oṗu'ḣli, v.a. To stuff anything into, as an old coat into a broken window. -- oṗúḣliyahaⁿ, adj. Stopped up, clogged. Cf. iyopuḣli. B.H.129.19.

oṗu'ḣtiⁿyaⁿkel, adv. Angrily. - ia, iwaya, i.e. to talk angrily. Bl.

oṗu'skebya, adv. Filtered. Bl.

oṗu'sḱica, v.a. To press down in. Owapuskica. -- oṗúsḱil, cont.

oṗus'ya, adv. Teeming with, infested with e.g. vermin in something. Teḣmuⁿga - yaⁿkapi. RA.

opu'ś'iⁿ, n. A curve, as of the outer side opposite the string of a bow. Cf. ipúś'iⁿ. Bl.

oṗu'taḱa, v. (of putaka). To touch in. Owaputaka. Oyate el tuwa wayazaⁿ kiⁿ le oputakiⁿ kta, eya.

oṗu'tḱaⁿ, v.a. To dip into, lay or put in e.g. the fingers; to sop, as with bread. Owaputkaⁿ. Ninape kiⁿ uyiⁿ na micuwi kiⁿ el - yo.

oṗu'za, v.n. To be covered with e.g. vermin etc., being dry as it were. Oko wanilya opuzapi. B.H.50.4. Cf. heyopuza. -- oṗúze, n. The dry edge of a river or sea. - kiⁿ el inajiⁿ, i.e. stepped on the shore. B.H.175.8;275.17.

op'o', n. Fog, steam; a cloud of dust. Pte otapi k'oⁿ ataya mak'op'o na egna taniⁿśniya iyayapi. Na el op'o waⁿ iwaⁿkab haⁿ waⁿyakapi.

op'o'sa, adj. Clear and cold, with particles of snow in the air. -- op'ósya, adv. Clear and cold.

op'ŏ'ya, adv. In a cloud, as of dust, mak'op'oya, snow, wa op'oya, etc. Yuⁿkaⁿ taku waⁿ, heya, mak'op'oya naunk u. Yunkan wa - inyankin na glinajin. Kiyela kupi ecel ataya okśan mak'op'oya han na wanna glihunnipi. Na lila tehan maka - han ecel wiyaya tka. Yunkan etanhan wanna maka - han.

op'o'za, adj. Same as op'osa.

osan'ƙayakel, adv. Void of game, such as deer etc. - yunkelo, as is said of a creek.

osan'sanƙe s'e, (?). The word is used in ref. to one whose hair and beard are white. Bl.

osin'kpekpeyakel, adv. (?). - taku ecannon welo. Bl. Perhaps syn.- iyupseyakel.

osin'sin, v.n. To leave a mark, as tears drying on one. Omásinsin.

o'sƙab, cont. of oskapa. -- óskabya, adv. Sticking to, adhering.

osƙa'ƙa, adj. Bare, as a tree whose leaves are fallen off; open, as a country without thickets.

o'sƙapa, v.a. To climb up e.g. a tree, a pole. Also perhaps, to stick in, adhere to. Owaskapa. B.H.223.2. -- óskapi, n. Ornamental work, such as is put on pipe stems. R. Pehin on wikan wan iyapehanpi, he - eciyapi. Waké - , Ornaments attached to the walls of a tent. - s'e woyaka, To give a nice, clear talk. BE.

o'sƙica, adj. (of yuskica). Tight, drawn around, as a garment. -- óskicela, adj. Tight, well fitting.

oski'ske, n. A draw. - wan el unglicupi, We got into a hollow, i.e. in the ground or land. Bl.

o'sƙisƙita, v. red. of oskita.

o'sƙita, v. To bind up in, as a child.

osku'mna, Same as oskumna. Cf. skumna.

osƙū'ya, adj. Sour, e.g. as milk. Skuya, Sweet.

osla', v. (of sla). Greased in anything.

oslo'han, 1) v.n. To slide, slip, slide down to the ground. Ómáslohan. - kic'un, To slide on a board or sled or one's feet. - wec'un. 2) n. A drawing or sliding in. D.247.

oslol'ya, v.a. To know of. Oslolwaya. Canku - . Wakantanka oslolyapi śni, Pagans. Takuni oslolye śni, i.e. of what had happened. B.H.121.8;283.7.

oslol'yapiśniyankel, adv. Unnoticed, not recognized. B.H.212.7.

oslol'ye, n. Knowledge.

o'smaka, n. A ditch, hollow, gulch, ravine, valley. B.H.172.6.

osmi'smiƙa, adj. Bare, without leaves, as a tree.

osna'ze, n. A scar. Also, osnázeca.

osni', 1) n. Cold weather; winter; year. - tanka wan hi. 2) adj. Cold in. Ti - , Cold in the house. Note: frozen (as fingers), frost-bitten, śpan. -- osniƙa, osniƙe, adj. Cold.

osni'ƙo, n. The screech owl. Perhaps from osni and ƙo, to desire. Syn.- paglá, popótka. Is.

osni'sni, red. (of osni). Very cold.

osni'tawanáp'in, n. A tippet, scarf, necktie.

oso', v. To cut open e.g. the skin of an animal in preparing to skin it. Owáso.

oson', v.a. (of son). To plait or braid e.g. hair. -- n. A braid of hair. Winyan wan - k'el oyuspe, hecena mina icu na - nupin owaksa. MS. 560.

ō'soƙa, v. col. (of yusota). They are all gone, used up, killed. Wanna - . Cf. sota. B.H.71.14.

ospan'spanheca, adj. (?). This refers to a swelling in which dents are left when one presses it. Ómáspanspanheca.

ospa'ya, v. (of spaya). To become damp in. -- ospáye, n. Moisture.

o'speya, v.a. To sink, make sink.

o'sťag, cont. of óstaka. -- ósťagya, v.a. To make stick on. Ostagwaya.

osťa'ǩa, v. (staka). To be feeble on account of, to be debilitated.

o'sťaǩa, v.n. To stick on or in e.g. dirt on a plow or mud in a house; to stick on, as does flesh. Omastaka.

osu'ǩa^{n}lyuza, v. To take one's choice, to take the best. Osuka^{n}lbluza. R.Bl.

osu'ťa, (?). Ha^{n}keke waksapi na - ece yúzapi s'e, as is said when a man, although little himself, has fleshy arms and legs. The is also applied to a horse with short legs. Also, osúťe. Bl.

osu'ťaya, adv. For good. Ho lena - yuha yo na ekto^{n}je śni yo.

osu'to^{n}ya^{n}, adv. Fig., fairly well. - eco^{n}.

o'swaha^{n}, part. perhaps. Caving in, as sand, coal etc., when some is taken from below. Na paha okise maya oswahe ki^{n} heca wa^{n}ya^{n}ka. MS.563.

o'swaswaya, part. Sinking in, as feet in soft snow or soil. Also perhaps, óswaya. Bl.

os'a'mna, adj. Sour smelling, smelling like stale meat, tainted. Si - , Feet that stink. Syn.- Ȟ'amna.

o's'ica, n. Misfortune, bad luck, which suggests a sudden craning, throwing a person on his back. Hecel yau^{n} ki^{n}, - ayakipa kte lo, i.e. to meet with bad luck for not listening to good advice. - akipe ki^{n} naké miyeksuyi^{n} kte, as an old lady once said. BE. Syn.- woteȟi, taku śice. BT.

os'i'c'iya, Same as oziic'iya, in all probability. U^{n}gnaheląȟci a^{n}petu wa^{n}ji - yau^{n} welo. BT.

ośa'pa, v.n. To be dirty in e.g. one's face. Ístihuku maka u^{n}kośapapelo, i.e. dust gathered below the eyes. Bl.

ośi'ca, adj. Bad with, as one kind of food with another, not agreeing, as sweet and sour. Wabluśka mayuta yelo, - kta secelo, as they would say when on account of a head-ache or knee-ache or rheumatism they felt that a storm was coming.

ośi'camna, (?). Bl.

ośi'ceca, adj. and n. Stormy, a storm. Wi u k'o^{n} cetiyelo ca - kte lo. - ahiyelo. Bl.

ośi'cecaǩe, adj. Unpleasant, as rainy weather, not pleasing, as certain country.

ośi'cecakiksuya, v. To know by one's feelings when bad weather is coming.

ośi'gla, adj. Excitable, irritable.

o'śikśicela, n. and adj. perhaps. Worthless things. - ece mayak'u welo waśteśte ki^{n} yakpahi na. Bl.

ośi'kśiloȟ'a^{n}ka, v.n. To act badly, wickedly. Also, ośílȟ'a^{n}ka. Ośilwaȟ'a^{n}ka.

ośil'ya, adv. In disorder. Tipi ki^{n} - he lo, This room, house, shows great disorder. Bl. Cf. D.125.

ośil'ye oȟ'á^{n}, v.n. To act badly. Ośilye owáȟ'a^{n}.

o'śiṗa, n. Clusters. B.H.62.14.

ośi'tǩigla, v.n. (śitkigla). To be angry with.

ośi'tǩiglaya, v.a. To make angry, cause to suffer. Ośitkiglawaya.

ō'śǩa^{n}, n. Motion, movement. Tka migluśke k'o^{n} heha^{n} - ewato^{n}we.

o'śǩa^{n}śilya, v.a. To impede one's progress, prevent from moving freely.

ośǩa'ťa, v. (śkata). To play in. Owaśkata.

ośǩa'ťe, n. Play, diversion. - tipi, A playroom.

ośǩi', n. Poor land, with hills and canyons. Wazi - . Oblaye - .

ośǩi'iyaza ocá^{n}ku, n. A road from hill to hill as hidden after a heavy snowstorm. FB.

ośǩi^{n}'c'iye, n. An occupation. Le a^{n}petu ki^{n} iyamatagle ca heo^{n} - maśicelo.

ośǩi^{n}'ic'iya, v.n. To busy one's self about, be busy. Ośki^{n}mic'iya. Tokel wicaśa ośkiⁿc'iyapi he slolye waciⁿpi.

oślí'śla, adj. (śkiśka). Abrupt, rough in word; intricate.
ośki'śkelya, adv. Confusedly.
ośki'śkeyà, v.a. To make complicated or confused, create difficulties, to perplex. Óśkiśkewaya. -- adv. Crookedly; with difficulty. Also perhaps, óśkiśkiya.

ośki'śki, n. Broken land, bad country, i.e. with hills and canyons.
ośki'śkiic'iya, v. refl. To get confused, as in disputing. Bl.

ośkō'kpa, n. A concavity, a hollow place. Tawicu k'oⁿ lel - mahel kiglapi, i.e. hokśila kici.

ośku'mna, adj. Sour, spoiled, as food. Also, oskumna.

ośla', n. perhaps. An open place. Makośla yuⁿke el, i.e. bare, grassless ground. Bl. Cf. ślayá. Syn.- otiⁿtoska.

óslo'kahaⁿ, part. Coming off, peeling off, as a scab. Also, oślókahe, in ref. to past time.
óslo'ślokahaⁿ, part red. of oślokahaⁿ.

ośme', n. Depth.

o'śnapi, n. Crumbs, scraps. R. Bl.

ośni'yaⁿyaⁿ, v.n. To move about, as worms in the stomach.

ośog'ya, adv. (śogya). Thickly.

ośo'ka, adj. (śoka). Thick. -- n. Thickness. Also, ośoke.

ośo'śe, (?). Bl.

ośō'ta, adj. (śota). Smoky, filled with smoke, as a tent. -- n. Smoke. Hecena makpiya eciyataⁿhaⁿ - s'e hiyu na iyowotaⁿiⁿ śni. - mat'iⁿ kte, misuⁿ, eya śke. - yelo, wipipaha egle po.
ośo'tamna, n. The smell of smoke. Na tatiye kiⁿ caⁿli śota naiⁿś - eśa hena slolye waciⁿpi.
ośō'ta ogna iyáya, n. A chimney. B.H. 51.3.
ośo'ta t'a, v. To suffocate from smoke. D.196.
ośō'taya, adv. Smoky. Yuⁿkaⁿ oyate waⁿ wicoti ca lila wicomani na - wicoti. -- v.a. To make smoke. Ośotawaya.

ośō'tiyaye, n. A chimney. Cf. ośota ogna iyaye.

ośpa'śpaye, adv. red. (ośpaye). By groups. - ecel ipaklaklalya au.

ośpa'ye, n. A drove, a herd consisting of different kinds of animals; a company separated from the main body. Śuⁿkakaⁿyaⁿka - waⁿji ehakela manipelo.
ośpa'yetoⁿtoⁿyaⁿ, adv. In groups. Bl.

ośpe', n. A verse; a breaking off, a piece or part of a section of land. In ref. to Sacred Scripture: oégle. Cf. yuśpa.

o'śtaⁿ, 1) v.a. To put on, to put in, as a cork, a handle into an ax, etc. Ogle, wapośtaⁿ, haⁿpa - . 2) v.n. To be on e.g. a hoop, or in e.g. as a stopper; to be in agreement with; to be in place of. 3) prep. perhaps. In place of, on, at. 4) adv. perhaps. On, at. Mazaśkaⁿśkaⁿ waⁿjila - , At one o'clock sharp. Tuⁿkaśila taaⁿpetu he - matoⁿpi, I was born on Washington's birthday. Wismahi ca el, i.e. arrow, ośtaⁿpi. Toośtaⁿ maⁿkelo, I am in a rented house. Bl. MS.481.

ośtaⁿ'haⁿ, part. Being in or on. -- n. A running watery sore. -- v.n. To ooze out e.g. water from a sore.

ośtaⁿ'iyótaka, v.n. To take one's place e.g. as a temporary superior.

ośtaⁿ najiⁿ, v.n. Same as ośtaⁿiyotaka.

ośte', adj. Deformed. Omáśte.

ośte'gla, v.a. (ośte-gla). To mock, call names, revile, abuse, insult, defy. Óśtewagla. Wakaⁿtaⁿka - , To blaspheme.
ośte'glapi, n. Contempt, opprobrious language.

ośtē'ka, adj. Ugly, deformed, crippled. Omáśteka. Syn.- taⁿśica.

ośte'kaya, v.a. To unmold, spoil e.g. a good horse. -- ośtékekiya, v.a. To

Cripple, deform.

oś'te'keśni, adj. Inviolate, immaculate.

ośte'la, adj. Deformed.

oś'te'ś'teya, adv. (of ośteya). Imperfectly, clumsily. - wicakuwapi, They teased them disagreeably. D.45. -- ośtéśteyakel, adv. red. of ośtéyakel.

oś'te'ya, adv. Imperfectly, clumsily; by chance, accidentally. -- oś'téyakel, adv. Deformedly.

ośti', interj. Oh, alas! It expresses strong disappointment and regret, and it would seem to be taken good-naturedly. It indicates sudden and unlooked for disappointment. Also, huśti'. D.28, note 2.

ośtul'ya, adv. Soft, not frozen. - yaⁿka, To remain soft, as meat buried in the snow. Bl.

ośuⁿg' iȟpéya, v.a. To maltreat.

ośuⁿ'gśuⁿgye, adv. red. (of ośuⁿgye). Very much, violently. - iȟpeya, To destroy things.

ośuⁿg'ye, adv. Too much, more than one can take care of; very much, violently. - wo mak'u, He gave me more food than I could eat. - iȟpeya, To destroy things, spoil them, i.e. breaking windows, tearing up things etc. Lila anuⁿk - iȟpekiciyapi. MS.521. Hihaⁿna kiⁿ honuⁿpiⁿyaⁿwayiⁿ na wiȟpewayiⁿ kte, i.e. kill many buffalos. Wasna na papa ko - kiⁿ, i.e. carried pemmican and dried meat in great abundance. D.201. -- ośúⁿgyela, adv. Violently, very. Slang: lots. Also, wośuⁿgya. R. Talo - yuȟpa. D.271. Bl.

ośuⁿ'kayaⁿkel, adv. In a miserable condition. - ȟpaya. This is an old word. Bl.

ośuⁿ'kecalaka, n. A very little thing; a very sick person.

ośuⁿ'kowote, n. A manger.

ośuⁿ'koyuspe, n. A corral.

ośuⁿ'k'ogleśica, adj. perhaps. There being no room for large crowds.

oś'a'ka, v.n. To become hard, as gravy in a kettle.

oś'e', n. A drop e.g. of water. -- v.n. To drop into. -- oś'éś'e, v.n. red. of oś'e. -- oś'éya, v.a. To make drop in, as water.

o'ta, adj. Much, many. Uⁿkotapi. Wicota, A great company. Iśta mini maota. Waniyetu maota. He ota śuⁿkmanoⁿ. MS.487.

otab', v. (of otapa). To follow after one, as in a road. - glau. Oyé - : taku oye - omani, i.e. to follow the track, as of game. -- otábtab, red. of otab. -- otábya, v. To trail, follow tracks.

ota'caⁿ, n. The principal part of anything, something very good, very prominent. Also perhaps, otaⁿcaⁿ. -- otácaⁿke, n. Something very good, very nice; the greatest, as giving something very nice. Also perhaps, otaⁿcaⁿke.

o'tahela, adv. perhaps. Many or much piled up.

o'tahena, adv. On this side, as in meeting one suddenly on this side of the place where one was looking for him. - iapi, as is said when coming back to something that was talked about but not settled. Bl.

ota'hepi, adv. Between places. -- otáhepiyela, adv. By the way, between places.

o'taja, n. One of the four marks seen on the hoop used in the game paiⁿyaⁿkapi.

o'taka, adj. Many, much. R. Also, the same as óta śni. Cf. ka. Mi.

o'takiya, adv. In many places, times, ways; often. Otoⁿwahe - wahokoⁿwakiyiⁿ kte, i.e. in many cities in different directions. B.H.186.4.

ota'kuye, n. Brotherhood, relationship, relations, kinsfolk, kinship. Palani - . D.220. -- otákuyeya, v. Form a relationship. Hel Raguel eciyapi waⁿ nitośpaye kiⁿ otakuyewicaya ca uⁿ welo. B.H.123.3.

otaᶯ'caᶯ, n. (of taᶯcaᶯ). The chief, the greatest. Cf. itaᶯcaᶯ. -- otáᶯcaᶯke, n. The greatest in members, as the greatest herd, the largest war-party. -- otáᶯcaᶯkeya, adv. In the greatest numbers.

otaᶯ'glakiᶯyaᶯ, n. Breadth. Syn.- oglakiᶯyaᶯ.

o'taᶯiᶯ, v.n. (of taᶯiᶯ). To be manifest, visible. Taᶯkaya onitaᶯiᶯ kte lo. - hecel slolwaya ca taᶯyaᶯ oblaka. Si ecela otaᶯiᶯpi. Peji iᶯkpa ecel - yelo, i.e. deep snow. -- ótaᶯiᶯka, v.n. To appear, be manifest. Note: this is used sometimes in the sense of otaᶯiᶯ śni. -- ótaᶯiᶯśniyaᶯ, adv. Not manifestly. Na lowaᶯ wacipi kiᶯ - haᶯ na toksa taᶯiᶯśni. -- ótaᶯiᶯyaᶯ, adv. Manifestly, openly. Waᶯna - kupi.

otaᶯ'ka, 1) n. (of taᶯka). Greatness, largeness. 2) adj. Large, broad.

otaᶯ'kala, v.a. To have in the greatest estimation. Otaᶯkawala. -- ótaᶯkalaka, v.a. To esteem most highly. Otaᶯkawalaka. -- otáᶯkaᶯ, adv. Singl- one out. Syn.- apatoᶯyela. WE.

otaᶯ'kaya, adj. Largely, extensively; spacious. Kaħmi waᶯ lila - ca el etipi. R. -- adv. Largely, extensively. Oyate ota hocoka - wicoti śke lo. Waᶯna lila hocoka - oimniciye. Hocoka kiᶯ lila - na cokata lila wicotapi. Wakpa waᶯ - na śma ca el iyoħloke. D.198 and 37. -- otáᶯkayaka, n. Greatness.

otaᶯ'kiᶯkiᶯyaᶯ, adv. In a big circle. Oyate iglak omanipi na waᶯna hocoka - wicoti.

otaᶯ'ktaᶯkaya, adv. red. of otaᶯkaya. D.225.

otaᶯ'la, 1) v.n. To be proud, vain. Omataᶯla. 2) v.a. To treasure, consider valuable, as one's clothes etc.

otaᶯ'toᶯ, adj. Abundant. Bl. -- otáᶯtoᶯka, adj. Large, prodigious. -- otáᶯtoᶯyaᶯ, adv. Very lively, zealously, excitedly, as playing, fighting etc. - ecoᶯpi. -- otáᶯtoᶯyaᶯkel, adv. Exaggeratedly. - ia, To speak in a dissatisfied way.

otaᶯ'yaᶯ, v.n. perhaps. To be well, feel no pain. Omataᶯyaᶯ. Minit'eyapi kiᶯ he - kte tka, i.e. it were better for him .... B.H.215.12.

ota'pa, v. (of tapa). To follow after one, e.g. on a road; fig., to imitate, follow after e.g. Christ. Oye - . Otawapa, otauᶯpapi and uᶯkotapapi. Uᶯkonitapapi, uᶯkotanipapi. Woeye kiᶯ otapiᶯ kte hciᶯ. Otamayapapi. B.H. 107.3;103.4;58.4;199.7;234.5;234.2. -- otápeya, adv. Following. B.H.63.2; 66.15;301.9.

o'tapi s'e, adv. perhaps. In large numbers. - ahiyaye, To pass by in large numbers.

o'tasagya, (?). MS.483.

ota'śośa, v. To spit in. Otáwaśośa. -- otáśośe, n. A spittoon.

ota'te, n. A clime, climate.

o'tatkoᶯza, adj. Equal to, parallel.

ota'waᶯjila, n. Two alike, a pair of one kind.

ota'wat'elśica, adj. Unendurable, unbearable. Otáwat'elniśicelo. Bl. -- otáwat'elśilya, adv. Exceedingly bad.

ota'wat'elya, v. To be willing, be willing to do. Otawat'elwaya.

ota'wat'eśica, adj. Great, fearful, numberless.

oteb'ya, v. To gnaw on or into, as a mouse does on cheese, or a wolf to a carcass. Mahel - .

ote'haᶯ, adv. Far, a long distance. -- otéhaᶯya, v.a. To hinder, cause to be long about a thing, to let one wait long for a thing. Otehaᶯwaya. Taku ecamoᶯ tka otehaᶯmayayelo. Bl. -- ótehaᶯyalaka, adv. perhaps. It will be a little while (ref. to the future). Hótaᶯiᶯpi tka ka ótehaᶯyalake oᶯ oyate kiᶯ taᶯyaᶯ naħ'oᶯpi śni. Syn.- tehaᶯ.

ote'ħi, n. Misery, difficulty; a thicket of bushes or brush one cannot pass through without difficulty. -- otéħika, adv. Very hard to endure, trying, difficult; expensive. Taku - hiyagle. B.H.42.1.

oťi', 1) v.n. To dwell in. Owati, uŋkotipi. 2) n. A house, dwelling. Tuŋkaśila oti, The White House. -- oťíķiya, v. To make camp. Lel otiwakiyeȟcelo. Bl.

oťiŋ'ťoska, n. An open place in the woods. R. Bl. Syn.- ocúŋwanice. -- oťíŋťoskaskaya, adv. With open places in the woods here and there. Bl.

oťi'woťa, n. An old encampment. -- oťíwoťaŋl, adv. At the old camping ground. MS.67. Also, otiwotata.

oťi'yohi, adj. Each one, every one. Also, otoiyohi. Śuŋkawakaŋ śaglogaŋ wicaśa itaŋcaŋpi hena iyuha - wicawak'u welo. BT.

otķa', v.n. To hang from, be suspended from anything, e.g. from a tree. Wikaŋkaŋ num el - . Also, otke, cf.

otķab'ya, v.a. To make stick on, to daub. Otkabwaya.

otkaŋ', v. To storm, perhaps. Wana - hwo? Haŋótkaŋ ktelo. Bl.

oťka'p̄a, v.n. To clog.

otķe', v.n. To hang from, to be hung up, as a coat. -- ótķeya, v.a. To hang up, suspend anything; to advertise. Ótkewaya. -- otķéyahaŋ, part. Hanging up. -- otķéyapiya, v.a. To have one hung. Eca le yuakagal otkeniyaŋpiwayiŋ naiŋś ciyuśka wowaś'ake bluha kiŋ slolyaye śni yelaka? B.H. 264.12.

otķe'yuťe, n. A weight.

otķiŋ', v.n. To become damp in.

o'tķoŋs, cont. of otkoŋza. - yuksa, To break off even. Wicaśa waŋ tawicu kici tawaciŋ kiŋ - wakiksapelo, i.e. are of one mind on everything. Bl. -- ótķoŋsela, adv. Evenly. Also, ótķoŋsyela. - wana henámala, i.e. have nothing anymore. Bl.

o'tķoŋza, adj. Even, equal, parallel.

oto'gmuŋ, (?). Tipi kiŋ - śni he, This room looks very disorderly. Bl.

oťo'haŋyaŋ, adv. For a short time or distance. - oholaya kuwa. B.H.206.2. D.67. --oťóhaŋyaŋkel, adv. For some time. - lel maŋkiŋ ktelo. Bl.

oťo'iyohi, adj. Each one, every one. Na taku waśpaŋka ecoŋpi kiŋhaŋ hena - etaŋhaŋ icupi. -- oťóiyohihi, adj. red. perhaps. Some of each, perhaps. Oyate - ahi yelo, Some of each tribe arrived. BD. -- oťóiyohila, adj. perhaps. Same as otoiyohi. B.H.195.5.

oto'ķahe, n. The beginning, that which goes first. - kiŋ le uŋȟpayapi kiŋ isam akiyagle kiŋ hehaŋl ouwicuŋtapi kte lo, eya. - le waku welo. Wagli - ku welo. -- otóķaheta, adj. At the head. BD.

oto'ķaheya, 1) n. The first, the beginning. 2) adv. At the beginning. - oyaŋke, The first place. B.H.242.9.

oto'ķaťa, adv. Before, foremost.

oťo'ķeťu, (?). Owicatoketu taŋiŋśni, as is said when somebody did not do well and others did not care to hear about it. WE.

oťo'kiyotaŋ, n. perhaps. A way. B. Syn.- ocaŋku. B.H.254.20.

oto'kśu, 1) v. (of tokśu). To haul or transport in e.g. a cart. Otowakśu, otouŋkśupi. 2) n. Hauling, transporting. - waśte, It is good hauling.

otoŋ', v.a. To put on and wear e.g. leggings or pantaloons. Owátoŋ. Huŋskowetoŋ kta, I shall put my pants, i.e. Lakota pants, on. Wizi waŋ kazazapi ca otoŋ. D.36.

otoŋ'wahe, n. A cluster of houses, a village, a town, a city; the city of Washington. -- otóŋwaheťu, prep. n. At or to the city of Washington. - yiŋ kte, He will go to Washington.

oťoŋ'waŋ, v. (of toŋwaŋ). To look into. Owatoŋwaŋ, uŋkotoŋwaŋpi.

otoŋ'we, n. Sight, eye-sight. B.H. 236.9.

otoŋ'yaŋ, adv. (of toŋyaŋ). Suppurating.

o'ťop̄i ķa, (?). A word used by boys.

Otopi ka nuŋke.

oťo'sa, adj. Blunt, round; not cut up. - śpaŋ, Cooked whole. Cap'stó s'e ite kiŋ - kaca, i.e. when the face is big. Bl. -- oťósya, adj. Blunt, round.

oťo'ťaŋhaŋ, prep. perhaps. From every kind, as taking some away from each kind. BD. Also, oťóťaŋhaŋhaŋ. Na oyate - Omaha tipi el zuya ai. MS.520.

oťo'ťola, adj. perhaps. Clear of brush, long grass etc.; thinly, as grass. Also, totola. Syn.- owaŋke waśte, zazecala. ET. Bl.

oťo'yasiŋ, adv. (of otoiyohi and oyasiŋ). Every single one, all. BD.

oťo'za, adj. Blunt, round, round and long as a stick; not split. Caŋ - , A round stick.

oťu'ȟci,. adv. In vain, for nothing; gratis. Also, ituȟci. - peji opetoŋpi, i.e. they bought it for your horses but you did not come.

oťu'ȟ'aŋ, v. To give away, make a present. Otuwaȟ'aŋ. -- oťúȟ'aŋpi, n. The giving away things.

oťu'kiȟ'aŋ, v.a. (of otuȟ'aŋ). To make a present of to, to give to one. Otúwakiȟ'aŋ.

oťu'makoskaŋl, adv. Without cause.

oťu'tȟa, n. Small articles, trinkets; crumbs, a little to eat. Also, tutká. Takuŋl onitutka ka hwo? i.e. at least a little to eat. Hiya, takuni omatutka śni ye. Bl. -- oťútkala, (?). - eśa tuweni el uŋ śni yelo, i.e. nobody is in. Bl.

oťu'ťuyaciŋ, adv. red. of otuyaciŋ.Bl.

oťu'woťa, n. An old deserted camping place. Bl. Also, otiwota. Waŋtaŋyeyela tawicu kicila - ena uŋpi. MS.100.

oťu'ya, adv. In vain, groundlessly, for nothing. - iyaya. -- oťúyaciŋ, adv. At random; in vain, for nought. Haŋhepi ca - utapelo. Also, otuyaciŋyaŋ. Wakaŋtaŋka - waciŋyaŋpi kte śni. B.H.120.19.

oťu'yauŋ, v. To be in a wild state.

oťu'yubleza, v. To wake up, arouse perhaps by shaking (yuhi). Wakaŋyeja - ; maka iyokiseya tataŋka ota nawaȟ'oŋ ca wakayeja wagluhika nuŋwe, as an old man would call out before going on a buffalo hunt. Bl.

ot'a', v.n. (of t'a). To die in any place; to have the stomach overloaded, to die of a surfeit; to be sick from eating or drinking too much. Omat'a. - ȟpaya. B.H.133.19;133.20.

ot'e', v. perhaps n. To die, by dying. - teȟi, Hard to die, tenacious of life. Wi s'e ot'eyuha uŋ ke, i.e. when a person faints often. Bl. - ikicihuŋni, About to die. B.H.40.2.

ot'e' ikicihuŋni, v. About to die, to be near death. B.H.255.19.

ot'e' iyagleya, adv. perhaps. Unto death. Minagi kiŋ ot'iyagleya iyokiśice. Also, ot'íyagleya. B.H.255.7.

ot'e' kpaǧaŋ, v. To give up one's life. B.H.223.19.

ot'i'kicihuŋni, Cf. ot'eikicihuŋni. B.H.255.19.

ot'iŋ', v. perhaps a. To drink much, greedily. Owat'iŋ.

ot'iŋȟ'yakel, adv. (?). - naŋke lo, okiśyakel naŋke lo, as is said by a visitor who is received silently by the person he came to see, as though he were not welcome. Bl.

ot'iŋs', cont. (of ot'iŋza). To choke. - yaŋka. Iyuhiŋta kiŋ ataya i etkiya na - amau. - ahiyotake. Maku - ape. D.111,248,58.

ot'iŋśt'iŋza, red. of ot'iŋza.

ot'iŋs'ya, adv. Tightly, firmly. Also, ot'iŋsyaȟel.

ot'iŋ't'iŋ, v. red. of ot'iŋ.

ot'iŋ'za, v.n. To be tight or fast in e.g. clothes that are too small, and food that sticks in the throat; to be too small for so many, as a church might be. Omat'iŋza.

ot'i'yagleya, Cf. ot'e iyagleya. B.H. 255.7.

ot'o'gnag, cont. of ot'ognaka. - lowaⁿpi, A death song, i.e. one in which a person cares nothing whether he lives or dies. Ja. -- ot'ógnagya, adv. At the risk of life.

ot'o'gnaka, v.n. To risk life, be foolhardy; to be willing to die. Ot'owagnaka. -- ot'ógnakel, adv. Although unwilling. B.H.147.11.

ot'o'ja, Same as ot'oza.

ot'o'za, adj. Hard, as a mud floor of a house or as a road. Also, ot'oja. Wa ca caⁿku - kiⁿhaⁿ paslohaⁿpi uⁿk'oⁿpi kte. Bl.

ot'uⁿ'yaⁿkel, adv. Contrary to one's liking. - ecamoⁿ.

ouⁿ', v.n. (of uⁿ). To be, to be in. Owauⁿ. -- n. (of uⁿ, To use). A load of a gun; a dose of medicine; what is used at once; ammunition. -- n. (of uⁿ, To be). A condition, state; place, room; one's ways. Nitaouⁿ kiⁿ ogna manipi śni. Hecel waⁿna ouⁿ waśteiciyapi. B.H.7.6;83.5;175.1. Cf. B.H. 175.1.

ouⁿ'caġe, n. Likeness; form, kind; growth. Ouⁿmacage. Lehaⁿl - tokel imacage ciⁿ ociciyakiⁿktelo. BT. Uⁿkouⁿcagepi kiⁿ iyecel uⁿkagapi kte. B.H.1.20.

ouⁿ'c'oⁿnilya, v. To hold one back by speaking to him, as he is anxious to leave. WE. Also, perhaps, uⁿc'oⁿnilya. R. Ihacikta na ouⁿc'oⁿnilmayayelo. Syn.- caⁿkagiya, oiyayeśilya. Bl.

ouⁿ' leca'la, n. The New Deal. Also, oúⁿteca.

ouⁿ'p̄a, v.a. To lay in and bind up e.g. an infant on a board. Owauⁿpa. Waⁿ ouⁿpapi s'e ocaⁿku, A road as straight as an arrow. BT. Waⁿna micicau, hokśicala, owauⁿpiⁿ kte. -- oúⁿpapi, n. One bound in, an infant. Hokśioúⁿpapi.

ouⁿ'śila, (?). Ka wicaśa - waśte, as they say of a man who is always ready to help. Bl.

ouⁿ'ṫeca, n. The New Deal. Also, ouⁿ lecála.

ouⁿ'yaⁿ, v.n. To be or stay habitually, perhaps, in a certain district; to live somewhere; to live. B.H.9.18; 39.4;86.12;173.1;203.6. Owáuⁿyaⁿ. Bl.

ouⁿ'ye, n. Nature, one's being; home. Toke eśa nitouⁿye kiⁿ he nuⁿpa iyakigleya bluha ni. Iye taouⁿye ogna yapi. Jerusalem el ouⁿye kiⁿ. B.H. 112.8;200.22;278.6. -- oúⁿyek̇iya, v.a. To cause to dwell in; to cause to rule over. Ouⁿyewakiya. -- oúⁿyeya, v.a. To cause to dwell in, give power to. Ouⁿyewaya. Also, to make a place one's home. Tuktel ouⁿyeye kiⁿ okiyakapi. Makata - . Jerusalem el ouⁿyeye kiⁿ. Hena - yo. B.H.62.21; 89.5;101.1;169.5;170.4. Pb.31.

ou'ṫa, v.a. To shoot, as with a gun, not a bow. Ouwata. Haⁿhepi kiⁿ ouwicuⁿtapi kte lo. Wakaⁿgli kiⁿ outapi. Tipi kiⁿ outa. MS.564. B.H.56.15.

ou'ye, n. (of uya). The coming, the springing up, as of the grass; a quarter of the heavens; tateouye topa, The four quarters of the wind.

owa', v.a. To paint, write, sketch; figure. Owawa. Waⁿna glinapapi na oic'iwapi. Wokpaⁿ owa wayupikapi. MS.482.

owa'cek̇iya, v. (of wacekiya). To pray in. - owayawa, A denominational school. -- owácekiye, n. A church building; the Church. B.H.306.17,18; 213.11.

owa'ci, n. A dance hall.

owa'ciⁿksab, cont. of owaciⁿksapa. -- owáciⁿksabya, adv. Intelligently.

owa'ciⁿksap̄a, adj. (of waciⁿksapa). Intelligent, wise, understanding. Owaciⁿmaksapa.

owa'ġo, v.a. To score. Owawago.

owa'he, n. (of ohaⁿ, v.n.). Something to stand on.

owa'hecelya, adv. Prudently, far-seeingly, circumspectly. - ecoⁿ. Syn.- aiyaciⁿyaⁿ, kaiwaⁿyaⁿgya. - kaga, To know something about what one could not do for a long time. Bl. Also, owáhecelyakel. Kitaŋyel - bluśtaŋ yelo, i.e. to improve something a little. Bl.

owa'hegle, n. A platform.

owa'heglepi, n. A foundation. Bl. Also, owáhegle.

owa'hinaƀe, n. (of ahinapa). The springing up of vegetables, water, etc. -- owáhinaƀeya, v.a. To cause to spring up. Owahinapewaya.

owa'hoƙoŋƙiye, n. A pulpit. - śica, One hard to advise. Bl.

owa'huŋ, n. A gash. Bl.

owa'ḣabya, 1) v. (of oyasiŋ and ḣabya). To scare all away. Owaḣabwaya. 2) n. One who scares away.

owa'ḣlaġaŋ, v. To enlarge, as by cutting a hole with a knife.

owa'ḣlaye, n. (of waḣlaya). Parings, as of an apple. Also perhaps, something to peel off in.

owa'ḣloƙa, v.a. To cut a hole in when shaving, as in making a dish. Owawaḣloka. -- owáḣloke, n. (of waḣloka).

o'waḣƀanica, adj. (of waḣpanica). Poor. Omawaḣpanica.

owa'ḣƀaniya, v.a. To make poor. Owaḣpaniwaya. -- owáḣƀaniyaŋ, adv. Poorly, miserably.

owa'ḣwayakel, adv. B. (?).

owa' icu, v. To make a memorandum of something. To note, take note of.

owa'iḣƀeye, n. A dumping place, a dump.

owa'izilye, n. A vessel to put in incense, a censer. B.H.64.14.

owa'ja, v.n. To be concerned in. Omawaja, oniwaja. Cf. iyowaja.

owa'ƙaḣla, n. A belfry, a steeple, a bell-tower.

owa'ƙihe coƙaŋ', n. No man's land. Co.

o'waƙiṫa, (?). Owakitapi s'e lemaceca, as old people say when they cannot see well anymore. Bl.

owa'ƙiya, v.a. (of okiya). To speak to or with; to speak harshly to, to reprimand; to offend. Owawakiya. Owaciciye.

owa'ƙiya, v.a. (of owa). To cause to write. Owawakiya.

owa'ƙoŋze, n. (of koŋza). Determination.

owa'kƀamni, n. An Indian agency, a place of distribution.

owa'ksa, v.a. To cut within. Ceji kiŋ owaksa icupi. B.H.153.8. Mina icu na osoŋ nupiŋ owakse. MS.560. -- owákse, n. A cut. Bl.

owa'kta, v.a. To look out for, wait for one. Owawakta. Owacikta. Miśna owamaktapelo, i.e. they want me alone for work. Bl. -- owáktayakel, adv. Looking out for. - wauŋ, I am looking out for. Bl.

owa'manoŋ, 1) v. (of manoŋ). To steal in or from any place. Owamawanoŋ. 2) n. A thief.

owa'mniomni, n. An eddy, whirl-pool; a cyclone. It is said one finds fish wherever there is a whirl-pool.

owa'naḣ'oŋ, (?). Minitáte ca - śice. Bl.

owa'nasapi, n. A place of chasing buffalo.

owa'nase, n. (of nasa). A place of chasing buffalo, the buffalo chase. Na le ohakab ḣliḣlila wakpala el tate ahi na owanaseta akicita...nataŋ ahi.... -- owánaseṫa, adv. (of owanase). At or on the buffalo hunting place. Owanase wakpala iyoḣloke, The slaughterhouse canyon.

owa'nataŋye, n. A grinding mill. BD.

o'waniyeṫu, n. Winter.

o'waŋca, adv. All over, everywhere; all together. Also, ówaŋcaya. Yuŋkaŋ lila makoce kiŋ owaŋcaya pte ojula. Maka owaŋcaya caḣ'ówaŋcaya, i.e. ice everywhere. Bl.

owaŋg', Cf. owaŋka. Also, owáŋ.

owaŋg'kiciya, v. To infect one another. Wicokuje śikśica oŋ owaŋgkiciyapi kte. B.H.245.10.

owaŋg'ya, v.a. perhaps. To resemble, imitate; take lessons from; to follow the example of. Owaŋgwaya. Also, to be similar to one another, as sick like another. Owaŋgkiciyapi. B.H.63. 12.

owaŋ'g'ic'iya, v. To be in the habit of. -- adj. Habitual. P.

owaŋ'ji, adv. At rest, at leisure. - yaŋka, To be at rest. -- owáŋjigjila, adv. red. of owaŋjila. Iyótahéna - yaŋka yo. -- owáŋjila, adv. At rest, disengaged, unemployed. - yaŋka, To be unemployed.

ō'waŋjila, adj. Alike, the same. - i-gluzapi. Ateyapi na Ciŋhiŋtku na Wo-niya Wakaŋ ki ówaŋjilapi. Kici we o-uŋwaŋjilapi. B.H.28.4.

owaŋ'ka, n. A place to lie on, a floor; a place for pitching a tent, the ground. Also, owaŋg, owaŋ. Owaŋ kahiŋ-ta, To sweep the floor. Hopo, waŋna waȟpe wokeya ekta owaŋka onasto lapi kte lo. Cokata owaŋka yakagiŋ kta. MS.349. Owaŋk, abbrev.

owaŋ'kaicahiŋte, n. Something to sweep with, a broom.

owaŋ'ke, n. perhaps. (perhaps of owaŋ-yaŋke). Likeness, size perhaps. Iya taŋka - , Like unto a big Iya. Oma-waŋke. Śuŋka - . Wicat'e owaŋkepi, i.e. look like corpses. B.H.95.6;231. 6.

owaŋ'kiyuhiŋte, n. A rake.

owaŋk' kaga, v. To prepare a place. B.H.92.9.

owaŋ'k'icahiŋte, n. A broom.

owaŋ'k'ipakiŋte, n. A mop, floor-cloth.

owaŋ'yag, cont. of owaŋyaŋka. - waśte, Good-looking, beautiful. - śica, ugly.

owaŋ'yaŋka, v.a. (of waŋyaŋka). To look upon. Owaŋblaka. -- owáŋyaŋke, n. A sight, a show, a vision; appearance, looks. B.H.32.5. -- owáŋyaŋke-śniyaŋ, adv. Invisibly. - wiŋyaŋ waŋ wowakaŋ lapi. B.H.302.11.

owaŋ'yeye, n. A place to look out at, a porthole, a loophole. -- owáŋyeye-toŋ, v. To have port-holes, as for shooting. R. Bl.

owa'paȟlokehaŋ, (?). Iśpa ha - owakihi yelo, i.e. although they bruise the skin of my elbow, held up for protection, I will carry it out. GA.

owa'pate, n. (?).

owa'pi, part. Figured, written.

owa'pśuŋ, v.a. To disjoint. B.H.153. 10.

owa'sabglepi, (?). Tipi - , Something used for a tower, a tower, a high monument. B.H.9.4.

owa'sku, 1) v. To pare in anything. Owawasku. 2) n. (of wasku). A paring.

owa'slece, n. (of wasleca). A split, splitting. -- owáslel, cont. of owa-sleca. - waśte, Good to split.

owa'smiŋ, n. (of wasmiŋ). Something to shave off into.

owaś', cont. of owaja. - wauŋ śni, I am not affected by, not concerned in.

owa'śakala, adj. Cheap, easily purchased.

owa'śkaŋyela, adv. Not far, near. - tipi. Bl.

owa'śpaŋye, n. An oven.

owa'śpe, n. (of waśpa). A piece cut off.

owa'śte, adj. Pleasant, wholesome, as weather etc. Ȟtayetu - ca etaŋhaŋ a-glihuŋni. B.H.156.9. -- owáśteca, adj. Cf. owaśtecaka. -- owáśtecaka, adj. Pleasant, as a place, weather etc. Aŋpetu waŋ lila - . Oblaye - , A pleasant open plain. D.216.

o'waśtekal, adv. Picking, choosing. - icu, To take the pick of. Syn.- otaŋkaŋ, apatoŋyela. WE.

owaś'ya, v.a. (of owaja). To bring near to, cause to be near. Okiyapi keś, wikośkalaka kiŋ, owaśyapi śni, Although they courted her, they did not succeed. D.51. Note: The word is commonly used with the negative; as, owaśwaye śni. Owaśwayeśni yelo, i.e. did not accomplish it because of unfavorable weather. Bl.

o'waś'ag, cont. of owaś'aka. Na - koŋla taogliḣpaye lo, i.e. its fall was terrible. B.H.195.21.

owa'ś'ak̇a, v.n. (of waś'aka). To be strong for the accomplishment of anything. Owamaś'aka. Taku kiŋ oyasiŋ oki'ciwaś'akapi. B.H.218.15.

owa'taŋk̇aya, v.a. To cut larger, as a hole. P. Bl. Syn.- oyutaŋkaya, yutaŋkaya.

owa'ṫohaŋṫu k̇a waŋ, n. ph. (?). - el wokcaŋ wicaśa ciŋca kośkalapi eya ... ipi. B.H.116.1.

owa'ṫohaŋyaŋ, adv. For a short time. Also, owáṫohaŋyaŋkel. - yewicaśipi. B.H.290.1;132.1;205.16. - śni, But a little time afterwards, a short time after. B.H.132.11. Also, owátohaŋyela. Woyute waŋ - takuni kte śni kiŋ he. B.H.209.5;205.16.

owa'uŋyaŋ, 1) v. perhaps. To sacrifice in any place. 2) n. A place of sacrifice, an altar.

owa'uye, n. (of uya). The growing, springing up of things.

owa'wopte, n. (of wopta). The place from which a tiŋpsila or turnip has been dug.

owa'yakpaŋ, n. (of yakpa). What is chewed fine, as the muskrat's food. R. Bl.

owa'yaśla, n. A pasture. Peji - kiŋ wanil aye. B.H.11.2;223.14.

o'wayáwa, n. A school, a school room.

owa'yujaja, n. A Laundry; a bath tub; anything to wash in.

owa'yukṗaŋ, n. (of yukpaŋ). What is ground up fine.

owa'yuśna, 1) v. (of yuśna). To sacrifice in any place. Owáblusna. 2) n. A place of sacrifice, an altar. Syn.- owauŋyaŋ.

owe', n. A class, division, order, kind. Ziŋtkala owe ota, Many kinds of birds. Owe toktokeca, A different kind.

owe'ceya, v.n. To cry over one, as in praying for one. Jerusalem cuŋwiŋtkupi, owemaceyapi śni yo. B.H.265.12.

o'weciŋhaŋ, adv. In succession, in Indian file, i.e. one behind the other. Lakota ehaŋna tokel icagapi kiŋ wicaḣcala ehaŋna - oyak aupi. - wicakico. D.248. -- óweciŋhaŋhaŋ, adv. red. of oweciŋhaŋ. - yaŋkapi. -- óweciŋhaŋyaŋ, adv. In Indian file.

owe'coŋkel, (?).

o'wehaŋhaŋ, v.n. To jest, make fun. Owewahaŋhaŋ. -- ówehaŋhaŋka, n. A jester. -- ówehaŋhaŋkel, adv. In jest. - ecoŋ, To mean no harm. -- ówehaŋhaŋkeśniyaŋ, adv. In earnest, not fooling. -- ówehaŋhaŋyaŋ, adv. Jestingly.

owe'haŋk̇eṫa, adv. At the end.

owe'heca, n. An arrow thrown for a mark for others to shoot at.

o'weḣca, (?). Ya-óweḣca makihaŋhaŋ ye, as a woman says refusing an offer of marriage. Bl.

owe'k̇iceya, v.n. To cry over the loss of one's own, as when someone died. Owewakiceya. Cf. oweceya. Nitakuyepi tona tewicayaḣilapi heci hena owicakiceyapi po, i.e. ghost dance. B.H.41.4;91.1;170.13. D.28.

owe'k̇inahaŋś, adv. Lest. - waḣtanipi. P. B.H.42.8.

owe'k̇inaś, adv. Perhaps. B.H.45.8. -- owék̇iś, adv. Perhaps, it may be, lest. Hecoŋśni ye - anip'api naiŋś niktepi kte. MS.51. B.H.58.3.

owe'k̇iwakaŋ, v. (of owewakaŋ). To lie about one. Owewakiwakaŋ. Pb.23.

owe'naṗe, n. A place of shelter, as

against rain etc. R. Bl.

owe'śleke, n. A war- prize, such as a feather; a decoration. Cf. iweśleke.

owe'śťe, v.n. To use a by-word, a well-known phrase, as: Iciŋ niyeś ehe kiŋ, etc. Owewaśte. -- owéśťeka, n. A by-word. -- owéśťepi, n. By-words, cant phrases. -- owéśťeya, adv. In the manner of a by-word. - ia.

owe'śuŋkeca, v.n. To be unable to do a thing. Owewaśuŋkeca. R. Bl.

owe'wakaŋ, v.n. To lie, tell an untruth. Owemawakaŋ. Also, owéwakaŋkaŋ. Owemawakaŋkaŋ, oweniwakaŋkaŋ, oweuŋwakaŋkaŋpi.

owi'caȟe, n. A graveyard.

owi'caȟkóȟela, adj. Precocious, as a child who walks early; also said of plants etc. that grow early or quickly.

owi'caȟtehaŋ, adj. Of slow growth or development, as applied to all living things. R. Bl. Owicaȟmatehaŋ.

owi'cakaśke, n. A jail.

owi'cakuja, n. An unhealthy locality or house.

o'wicak'ola hu, n. Western virgin's bower, traveller's joy, the old man's beard. Clematis ligustici folia. The crowfoot family. BT. #125.

owi'cawapi, n. A list, as of names.

owi'haŋke, Cf. oihaŋke. -- owíhaŋkeśniyaŋ, adv. Endlessly, eternally. -- owihaŋkeťa, adv. At the end. Tokśa - ate ijehaŋ oniciyapi kta. -- owíhaŋkewanica, adj. Endless. -- owíhaŋkewanil, adv. Always, ever; interminably. -- owíhaŋkeya, v.a. To bring to an end, destroy. Owihaŋkewaya.

o'wihe s'e, adv. In a large number. - ahiyaye, They pass by in large numbers. Bl.

owi'ȟ'aŋ, n. (?).

owi'keśni, v.n. To be strong, not to fail, as the strength of a person; to accumulate without being used, as property. Omawikeśni. -- adv. Staying together, not scattering, as cattle; not scattered, not spent. - najiŋpi. MG. Bl.

owi'lita, (?). - śkaŋ, To work in good spirits. Bl.

owiŋ', v.n. To wear e.g. an ornament. To wear e.g. rings in the ears, as an ornament. Owawiŋ, ouŋwiŋpi. -- n. An earring or ornament.

o'wiŋġa, adj. perhaps. Crooked, as a road.

o'wiŋġe, n. A curl, as of hair.

o'wiŋȟya, adv. Curved, curled. Pehiŋ - waglakca. - wakaga, i.e. trying to bend something straight and getting it curved.

owiŋ'ja, 1) n. Something spread to light down or sit on; a bed, a floor. Caŋ - , A wooden floor. 2) v.a. To make a bed of, use for a bed. Owawiŋja, uŋkowiŋjapi. Na tataŋka ha waŋ owiŋjapi ca el ituŋkam iyuŋka na hecena t'a. Peji ȟota owiŋjapi.

owiŋ'ja akaȟpe, n. A bed quilt.

owiŋ'ja popópa, n. A quilt.

owiŋ'kiya, v. To cause to wear jewels.

owiŋ'la, n. Ear-jewels.

owiŋ'pi, n. Earrings, jewels.

owiŋś', cont. of owiŋja. -- owíŋśkiya, v.a. To make a bed of, strew or spread down for a bed. Owiŋśwakiya. -- owiŋśtoŋ, v.a. To make a bed of. Owiŋśwatoŋ, owiŋśuŋtoŋpi. Śina hiŋśma tonakel nakuŋ opemnipi hena kuya - . D.229.

owiŋś'ya, v.a. To make a bed of. Owiŋśwaya.

o'wiŋśya, adv. Bent downward, as a tree.

owi'ṗi, (?). - woteȟi, as is said when a person does not stop eating. Bl.

owi'tko, v.n. (of witko). To be drunk with. Omawitko. -- owíťkoťko, adj. Foolish. -- owíťkoťkoya, adv. Foolishly. -- ówitkoya, adv. Acting foolishly from choice, playing the fool. -- owítkoyakel, adv. Foolishly.

owi'wila, (?). - s'e uŋ, as is said of a very fleshy man or animal. Bl. -- owíwiyela, adv. In a swampy place. Psaowoju - haŋ. B.H.31.5.

owi'yuśkiŋyaŋ, adv. With joy. Wakaŋtaŋka oholaya - wotapi. B.H.125.16.

owo'blu, v.i. To blow in, as fine snow does through cracks etc. Wokeya okagege - , i.e. snow comes in, blows in through the seams of a tent. M.

owo'glake, n. A place of council; a parlor; a council, consultation. Na waŋna otoŋwahetaŋhaŋ agli, i.e. the delegates, na - na Maȟpiya Luta lecel woglake. - tipi, A council house, chamber.

owo'he, n. A place where a feast is to be; a kitchen. Bl. - uŋkaȟnigapi kta. Ed.

owo'hitika, adj. (of ohitika). Brave on or in something. Owomahitika.

owo'ȟeśma, adj. Thick in, as in weeds within a garden or corn field etc. Cf. woȟeśma.

owo'ȟloke, n. (of woȟloka). A hole made by punching.

owo'iciślok, abbrev. of owośloka. Waŋjila eśa i - waciŋ śni, i.e. he too should get one. Bl.

owo'ju awacekiyapi, n. The name for the procession held on one of the Rogation Days.

owo'ju waśte, adj. Fertile. P. Bl.

owo'kśaŋ, n. A curve. P.

owō'lu, v.n. To blow in, as the wind does through a hole causing a draft. Lila - . Note: this word may be owóblu. - hiyu welo. Bl.

owo'lutatoŋ, 1) v.n. To make a noise or bustle. Owowalutatoŋ. 2) n. Noise, bustle, clamor. -- owólutatoŋyaŋ, adv. Clamorously. - yaŋka. B.H.205.3.

owo'pota, v.a. (of wopota). To shoot to pieces in anything. Owowapota.

owo'pte, n. The place from which a turnip is dug. This word is rarely used. Cf. owawopte.

owo'skica, v.a. (of woskica). To punch or ram hard in a hole. Owowaskica. -- owóskil, cont. of owoskica. - iyeya.

owo'slal, adv. Straight up. - hiyaye. B.H.53.2.

owo'slata, n. Height, perpendicularity.

owo'śloka, v.t. To throw, sling, fling into. Cf. wośloka. Tiŋpsila wotapi kiŋ waŋjila eśa i owomic'iślokiŋ kte. Waŋjila eśa i owouŋkiciślokapi kte, as women would say going to dig turnips. Bl.

owo'śpe, n. (of wośpa). A piece shot or punched into.

owo'ta, (?). - aya, as is said when snow or sand etc. is drifting to a certain place and heaping up. Bl.

owo'taŋ, v. (of wotaŋ). To ram or pound hard in a hole. Owowataŋ.

owo'taŋiŋ, 1) adj. Clear, manifest. - śni, Foggy, hazy, smoky. 2) n. Clearness, appearance. - śni, Haziness. Na wicaśa waŋ najiŋ k'oŋ el owotaŋiŋśni. -- owótaŋiŋka, adj. Same as owotaŋiŋ. -- owótaŋiŋyaŋ, adv. Clearly. Taku owotaŋiŋśniyaŋ haŋ. MS.570.

owo'taŋla, adj. Straight, not crooked; right, just, upright. Owomataŋla, owouŋtaŋlapi. -- owótaŋlakel, adv. Justly. B.H.241.22. -- owótaŋlaśniyaŋ, adv. Unjustly. Pb.26. -- owótaŋtaŋla, adj. red. of owotaŋla. MS.351.

owo'te, n. (of yuta). A place to eat in. Tuktel - otiyaye so? B.H.251.11. - tipi, A dining room; a hotel. -- owóteya, v.a. To use for a dining room. B.H.251.12.

owo't'iŋza, v. (of wot'iŋza). To pound in hard and tight. Owowat'iŋza.

owo'uŋka, adj. Lying, knocked down or killed in, as in a house, valley etc.

Cf. tikauŋka.

owo'wicak'u, n. An issue station.

owo'zaka, v. To rush, be in a hurry.

oya', 1) v.n. and v.a. To stick to; to come off one, as white-wash; to stain, sully. Omaya. 2) n. The arms, legs, the limbs.

oyā', adj. Mouldy, perhaps; spoiled, as meat may be. Talo oya yuta.

o'ya, (?). - huŋkeśni.

oya'ġi, v.a. To impede, as high grass does in walking; to scratch; to affect as choke-cherries do the throat. Oblagi. Omayagi.

oya'ġiya, v.a. To cause to impede, as by sending one into the brush; to pierce right through. Oyagiwaya. B.

oya'ġiyela, adv. Impeded by. - capa, To stab right through. B.

oya'gloglo, v.n. To rattle, as water in a pipe. MG. Cf. onagloglo. R.

oya'gṗicaśni, adj. Unspeakable, beyond expression. P.

oya'gwa, v. To chew on and thus spoil. Oblagwa. Bl.

oya'ȟe, v.n. To dry up, evaporate e.g. water; to fall or diminish e.g. water in a stream or in a vessel when a little is taken out, or in a pond. Minióyaȟe yelo, as in a pond. Casmu ca mini oyasiŋ aóyaȟe iyaye. Bl. B.H. 108.26.

oya'ȟekoȟela, adj. Boiling away fast, as is said of a pot or kettle. Cf. kokela.

oya'ȟeya, v.a. To cause to boil away or evaporate. Oyaȟewaya.

oya'ȟloȟlog, cont. of oyaȟloȟloka. - eya, To talk like a baby, or like one who does not know what he is talking about. - ia. R.

oya'ȟloȟloka, v. To begin to speak, as does a very young child. Oblaȟloȟloka.

oya'ȟloḱa, v.a. To bite a hole in anything, to make a mark with the teeth, to bite in.

oya'ȟloḱe, n. A hole bitten in.

oya'ȟ'u, n. A stump or stub. Caŋli - muŋpa yelo, i.e. smoke a cigar stump. Bl.

oya'ḱa, v.a. To relate anything, to report, tell e.g. a story to somebody or a person his name. Oblaka, uŋkoyakapi. Ociyakiŋ kte, I will report you. Omayaka, He told on me.

oya'ḱe tipi, A parlor.

oya'ksa, v.a. (yaksa). To bite anything off in. Oblaksa.

oya'ksab śica, adj. One hard to teach because he pays no attention. Bl.

oya'ksaksa, v. red. of oyaksa.

oya'ksaksayakel, adv. Biting off in.

oya'kse, n. A biting off.

oya'k'oġa, v. To bite or gnaw off in.

oya'k'oza, v. To bite off short, as do horses.

oya'ma, v. To guess, as when one holds something hidden and lets others figure what it is; to gnaw in or on. Oblama, olama. Heca sece; hiya, olame śni. Bl.

oyaŋ'ka, v.n. To be, be in a place. Tioyaŋkapi kiŋ nahuŋhuŋs hiŋgle. B.H. 278.2;282.3.

oyaŋ'ḱe, n. A place of residence; a seat; a room. B.H.293.10.

oya'ṗe, v. To put or take in the mouth e.g. a pipe. Blaṗé, lapé, oyápapi. -- n. (yapa). The small end of a pipe-stem which is taken in the mouth.

oya'pṫa, v.a. To leave, have over and above what one eats. Oblapta, ouŋyaptapi. B.H.112.18. -- oyápṫapi, n. Remnants, crumbs, i.e. of a meal.

oyas', abbrev. of oyasiŋ.

oya'saḱa, adj. Dried hard on or in, withered.

oya'siŋ, Same as oyas'iŋ.

oya'ska, v.a. To clean off, i.e. by

passing through the mouth. Oblaska.

oya'smiⁿyaⁿ, adv. Being gnawed at, as by wolves. Iⁿśe le śuⁿkmanitu - muⁿkiⁿ kta ca wauⁿ welo. MS.486.

oya's'iⁿ, adj. All, everyone.

oya'śica, v.a. (of yaśica). To speak ill of, give bad impressions of, give a bad character to. Oblaśica.

oya'śkiśka, v. (of yaśkiśka). To speak unintelligibly. Oblaśkiśka.

oya'śpaśpa, v. red. (of oyaśpa). To tear off with the mouth from, as birds do with meat etc. B.H.31.6.

oya'ś'iⁿś'iⁿ, v.n. To itch, to feel as if something wanted to be rubbed, itched. Omayaś'iⁿś'iⁿ. Poge omayaś'iⁿś'iⁿ hecel oⁿ wapśahelo. Bl.

oya'tag, cont. of oyataka. -- oyátagya, v.a. To cause to stick or drag heavy, as a sled on bare ground. Oyatagwaya.

oya'taka, v.n. To stick or drag heavily. Lociⁿ wawata tka hiyomayatake, i.e. referring to tough meat. Bl.

oya'taⁿ, v.a. To bite or press on with the teeth. Oblataⁿ.

oya'taⁿiⁿ, v.n. To show, manifest, testify. Oblataⁿiⁿ.

oya'taⁿtaⁿ, v. red. of oyataⁿ.

oya'taⁿyaⁿ, (?). Bl.

oya'te, n. A people, nation, tribe, band.

Oya'tenúⁿpa, n. prop. The Omahas. They are said to have camped in two concentric circles. R. Bl.

oya'teya, adv. As a people. - uⁿpi. B.H.118.8.

Oya'teyámni, n. prop. The name given to the Ponkas. Cf. Oyatenuⁿpa. R. Bl.

oya'tkaⁿ, v.a. (of yatkaⁿ). To drink in anything. Oblatkaⁿ.

oya'tkaⁿkaⁿ, 1) v. red. (of oyatkaⁿ). To drink repeatedly. 2) v. To come to a head, as a sore.

oya'tkapa, v.n. (of otkapa). To stick on or in anything.

oya'tke, n. Drink; a draught or drink of anything.

oya'toto, v. To eat off clean, as a horse does the grass.

oya't'a, v.a. (of yat'a). To bite to death in.

oya't'aǧe, adj. (of yat'aga, which is not used perhaps). Rough, roughened, as a screw so it does not work etc., or a tongue by medicine.

oya't'e, n. A biting to death.

oya'wa, v.a. (of yawa). To count; to read, to read or count in; to go to school. Oblawa, ouⁿyawapi. - tipi, A school house.

oya'ya, v. red. (of oya). To be musty, moldy.

oya'ya, n. The limbs of the body of e.g. a horse, arms and feet; a string, a bunch, a skein, as of beads. Yuⁿkaⁿ taku waⁿ - topa ca u na cokam hinajiⁿ. - kiⁿ yuakagal iyuzigzil okataⁿpi. B.H.265.22. - topa.

oya'yamna, v. (of oya). To smell moldy.

oya'yatopa, adj. Four-footed; on all four. Also, huhá topa. Bl.

oya'za, 1) v.a. To string e.g. beads. This is used of the past time only. Oblaza. Pśito oyazapi, Strings of beads. 2) n. (of yaza, which is not used). Things strung on together, as a string of beads. Cf. iyaza. -- oyázahaⁿ, v. To continue to string beads. Oblazahaⁿ.

oya'zaⁿ, v.n. To be sick for, sick in consequence of. Omayazaⁿ. -- oyázaⁿic'iya, v. refl. of oyazaⁿ. Taku oⁿ oyazaⁿmic'iye. Bl.

oya'zaza, v. red. of oyaza.

oye', n. A track of something; footsteps, foot-prints; marks left by anything. Maoye. Yuⁿkaⁿ ake pte ca oye akiyagla śke. Ate, tohaⁿl yau kiⁿ oye kiⁿ taⁿyaⁿ omale yo. -- oyéhaⁿ, v. To leave tracks. Waⁿ lel oyemahelo,

Here are my tracks. Bl. Hecel el ipi na el oyehanpi na hetanhan wana glicupi. MS.157.

oyo'pta, (?). Oyomapta. Kaṫinyeya oyoptin kta, i.e. will go straight. Bl.

oyu'blaya, v.a. To spread out in. Na-p'oyublayapi s'e yunkelo, i.e. land as level as one's hand. Bl.

oyu'blaye, n. A page in a book.

oyu'bleca, v.a. (of yubleca). To divide out, scatter; break to pieces within something. Oblubleca. -- oyúblece, n. A breaking in. -- oyúblel, cont. of oyubleca. - iyeya. - egnaka, To open out. - iḣpeya, To cause disorder, confusion, as in a room. Cf. oyuglaglaya iḣpeya. Bl.

oyu'blu tanka, n. perhaps. A field, perhaps large, to plow.

oyu'cokaka, v. To take all out of, as the load of a gun. Cf. wayucokaka.

oyu'cokaḱa, v. To produce a noise, as by squeezing somebody's arm and making the bones jar.

oyu'glaglaya, v. To tangle. - iḣpeya, To tangle up, confuse e.g. ropes etc. Cf. oyublel iḣpeya. Bl.

oyu'ha, v. (of yuha). Used in connection with waśte, etc. - waśte, Good to have. - śice, Hard to watch, look after, handle, manage etc. This is said of persons and things. Bl. Same as oáwanyanke with śice.

oyu'hi, v. To scatter about, to spread e.g. hay for horses to eat. -- oyúhihi, v. red. of oyuhi. - iḣpeyayo.

oyu'hinhan, v. To scatter about. The same as oyuhi. Obluhinhan.

oyu'ḣlaġan śni, v.n. To stay, remain in the same place.

oyu'ḣlaṫa, v.a. (of yuḣlata). To scratch in. Obluḣlata. -- oyúḣlaṫe, n. A scratch.

oyu'ḣleca, v.a. (of yuḣleca). To tear in, as in an old hole. Obluḣleca. -- oyúḣlece, n. A rent.

oyu'ḣloka, v.a. (of yuḣloka). To bore or make a hole in, to make holes in, e.g. as hard snow does in horses' legs. Obluḣloka. -- oyúḣloke, n. An opening.

oyu'ḣpa, v.a. (of yuḣpa). To put or pull down in. Obluḣpa, oúnyuḣpapi. -- oyúḣṗe, n. A throwing down.

oyu'ḣ'eḣ'eyakel, adv. (?). - e ayuśtan, To quit one's work, i.e. that one has done only in places, here and there, and not well.

oyu'ḣ'i, n. (of yuḣ'i). A pimple, a rough place, pimples.

oyu'juju, v.a. To pull asunder e.g. a package of letters. P.

oyu'junkjunta, v. red. (of oyujunta). To thrust into, as the hand into a pail, repeatedly. Oblujunkjunta. Canke a oyujunkjuntapi, They thrust their hands between the legs of the turtle, i.e. to tickle her.

oyu'junṫa, v. To thrust into, as the hand into a pail. Oblujunta. Na cega wan pihya he k'on ekta - na śunka pa k'on icu. Also, to lay in. Na maku el ocape k'un he oblujunte śni kin. B.H.274.21.

oyu'kaḱa, v. n. perhaps. To rattle in, as a little pebble in a rattle. -- v.a. To rattle in a place.

oyu'ḱiḱiḱe, v.a. (?). Bl.

oyu'kṗukṗa, v. a. perhaps. To crumble in, to crumble and scatter about in.

oyu'ksa, v.a. (of yuksa). To break off e.g. a stick in a hole. Obluksa. -- oyúkse, n. A piece broken off. Aguyapi - , A broken off piece of bread. B.H.253.14.

oyu'kśa, (?). - imunkelo. Bl.

oyu'kśan, n. A link. P. Bl.

oyu'kṫan, 1) v.a. (of yuktan). To bend anything into something else. Obluktan. 2) n. A bend, a crook. -- oyúkṫanyan, adv. Bent into.

oyu'ḱunṫa, v. To pick in e.g. the nose

or ears.

oyul', cont. of oyuta. - waśte, Good to eat.

oyu'ma, v. To confirm. Oyumapi s'e oyake lo, i.e. he says the same thing another said, he confirms. Oyume lo. Bl. Syn.- oyuślata.

oyu'maza, v.t. To make a hit, as in hitting a target in the center, or to hit something in the intended place. Oblumaza.

oyu'mni, v. To rove, wander about, roam aimlessly. Oblumni. Oblumni kte lo, I'll walk around, i.e. here or there. Miś miye tokel wacinˀ ecel oblumni. Maka tanˀka oblumni, i.e. went very far. Bl. D.100. -- oyúmnimni, adv. Round and round.

oyunˀg', cont. of oyunˀka.

oyunˀ'ka, v. To lie down in. Omunˀka. -- oyúnˀke, n. A bed, a place to lie down. - hu, A bed-stead.

o'yunˀke hugmi'ya, n. A bed caster.

oyunˀ'k'akanˀyanˀkapi, n. A lounge.

oyu'pemni, v. To whirl. Tate wanˀ oyupemnipi s'e hinˀyanˀkelo, i.e. a whirlwind. Bl.

oyu'ponˀwaya, v. To scatter and thus waste e.g. sugar. Oblupoˀwaya. Bl.

oyu'pota, v.a. To tear to pieces in, as a cat sticking her paw into a hole and grabbing a mouse, or an eagle grabbing a rabbit. Cf. yupota. -- oyúpote, n. A torn place, a rent.

oyu'psonˀpsonˀ, v. To spill orsprinkle e.g. water on a floor.

oyu'pta, v.a. To cut out in or of, as clothes. Oblupta. -- oyúptaptapi, n. Scraps, remnants such as cloth. -- oyúpte, n. Pieces left in cutting out a garment; scraps, remnants.

oyu'ptuh'ayakel, adv. In small quantities. - egnaka, i.e. tobacco. Bl. Cf. oyututkayakel.

oyu'sinˀka, v. To hate. Oblusinˀka, unˀkoyusinˀkapi.

oyu'sinˀyanˀ, adv. Out of humor with.

oyu'skiskita, v. red. (of yuskita). To wrap up in, as a babe in its blankets, to bind tightly in. Obluskiskita, unˀkoyuskiskitapi. Yunˀkanˀ ataya omayuskiskitapi ca wekta kta k'oⁿ owakihi śni. Ptehinˀśma wanˀ ataya oyuskiskitapi. D.245.

oyu'skita, v.a. (of yuskita). To wrap up in, as a babe in its blankets. Obluskita.

oyu'slohanˀ, v.a. To make slide in. -- v.n. perhaps. Cf. okislohanˀ.

oyu'slohe, n. A mark of anything dragged along, a trace, a trail. Cf. okaslohe.

oyu'sni, (?). - ewegnakinˀ kte, i.e. so to cool off a pipe.

oyu'spa, v.a. To hold, to catch, to take hold of. Obluspa. Napóyuspa.

oyu'spaya, v.a. (of yuspaya). To make wet with the hands in anything. Oblúspaya.

oyu'spekiya, v.a. To cause to lay hold of one. Oyuspewakiya.

oyus'ya, adv. Laying hold of.

oyu's'o, (?).- unˀ, i.e. to be deep in water and swimming, as one does not touching the bottom. Bl.

oyu'śica, v. To fall out with one, get into a quarrel with one. Obluśica. Obluśica na lila howayelo. P. Bl. Also, to do wrong in respect of. Omayuśica, unˀkoyuśicapi. -- oyúśice, n. That which injures.

oyu'śkanˀ, v. To relapse, to become restless. Omigluśkanˀ.

oyu'śkeya, adv. Lively in movement, on the alert. - unˀ, econˀ. - he lo.

oyu'śkica, v.a. To press out, as juice from grapes. B.H.30.20.

oyu'ślata, v. To make something smooth, as a wall being plastered; fig., to confirm what another said. Obluśluta.

oyu'śna, 1) v.a. (of yuśna). To let

drop or fall into, to waste. Obluśna, uŋkoyuśnapi. D.37-8. -- n. Something dropped. BD. -- oyúśnaśna, n. Many things dropped, as crumbs, scraps etc.

oyu'śťaŋ, v.a. (of yuśtaŋ). To finish within, as a house; to put one into another, as buckets, or as a cork into a bottle. Obluśtaŋ.

oyu'ś'e, v.a. To make drop in, e.g. into a glass when pouring medicine. Obluś'e.

oyu'taŋ, v.a. To touch, feel. Oblutaŋ, uŋkoyutaŋpi. Tohaŋyaŋ, i.e. wagmeza, śeca śni kiŋ, hehaŋyaŋ tuweni - kte śni.

oyu'taŋȟaya, Cf. yutaŋkaya, owataŋkaya.

oyu'taŋtaŋ, v. red. (of oyutaŋ). To feel. Oblutaŋtaŋ.

oyu'taŋ waŋka'la, n. A two-barrelled muzzle-loader, a powder loader. Bl.

oyu'ťe, n. Eating, food.

oyu'ťe, n. The parts just above the hips, the sides. Na tataŋka kiŋ - el - wicaśi. - kiŋ yuogmuza ye, keya s'e oyute kiŋ ȟpuȟpuya, as said when the dress is torn on the side near the hip. Bl. - el apiŋ na yuǧiciŋ na.... B.H.293.4.

oyu'ťepa, (?). Cecá kiŋ izuza oyutepe s'e, as is said when a man or horse is very lean. Sicáŋ kiŋhaŋ izuza oyutepe s'e, as is said when the hips are as lean as a whetstone. Bl.

oyu'tȟoŋza, v.a. To make equal, break off and make equal with something else. Oblutkoŋza. -- oyútȟoŋze, n. Something that makes equal.

oyu'tȟuǧa, v.a. To fasten e.g. a horse in a stall, to lock e.g. a door. Oblutkuga, uŋkoyutkugapi. B.H.77.6. -- oyútȟuǧahaŋ, part. Fastened, locked.

oyu'ťutkayakel, adv. In small quantities. - egnaka, To put in in small quantities, bits. Bl. Cf. oyuptuȟ'ayakel.

oyu't'a, v.a. (of yut'a). To kill in. Oblut'a.

oyu't'iŋza, v.a. (of yut'iŋza). To make firm in. Oblut'iŋza. -- oyút'iŋze, n. A strengthener.

oyu'wi, adj. Vine-like.

oyu'zaŋ, v.a. To spread out, as a curtain.

oyu'ze, v.a. (of yuze). To take or dip out food into. Obluze. -- n. A catching, a taking; a place where one finds or takes many. Mini skuya - . Maka gi - el wicoti. Iŋyaŋ to - el ewicoti. Miogli - el. Cf. yuza.

o'za, adj. Both. Lenioza, heniyoza.

o'zaŋ, n. A curtain. Ozaŋpi, Bed-curtains. B.H.268.7.

ozaŋ'niyaŋkel, adv. (?). - piuŋkiyiŋ kta na uŋkiśtiŋma ktelo. Bl.

ozaŋ'yela, adv. (?). Ikpáȟ'ozáŋyela iŋyaŋgya, i.e. to shoot an arrow so deep into an animal that only the end notch is visible. Bl.

o'ze, v. (of yuza). To catch. Oze waśte, Good to catch, to takę, get.

oze'zeya, adv. Swinging.

o'zi, v.n. To rest. Omazi, uŋkozipi.

o'zica, v.n. To stretch out arm and body to reach or get something. Owazica.

ozi'ic'iya, v.n. To refresh one's self, to rest. Ozimic'iya. Note: the idea of stretching one's self (zi) seems to be underlying.

ozi'ȟiya, v.n. To rest, take a brief rest, stretch. Oziwakiya. Asnikiya, To take a long rest.

ozil'ya, v.a. To make a smoke, to fumigate. Ozilwaya.

o'ziwanil, adv. Continually, without rest.

ozi'ya, v. (of ozi). To rest, take a rest. Oziic'iya, To rest one's self. Ozimic'iya.

ozu'ye, n. (of zuya). War; a war-party; an army.

*

ṗa, prefix. Affixed to verbs, denoting that the action is done by pushing or drawing, rubbing or pressing with the hands or arms. The pronouns are prefixed.

pa, 1) n. The head of man or animal; the principal part of anything. Pte pa. Mato pa. 2) The nose. Pa we hiyu. 3) The beak or bill of birds.

ṗa, v.a. To push, urge perhaps; complain, murmur. Mayapa śni kiᶯhaᶯ, waśte yelo, kola. BT.

pa, v.n. To fall, as snow. P.

pa, v.a. To bark. This is not used as a root word. Cf. pápa.

pa, adj. Bitter. Pejuta pa.

ṗaa'glapśuᶯ, adv. Turning bottom upward. - iȟpeya, To turn bottom upward by pushing etc. -- ṗaáglapśuᶯyaᶯ, adv. Bottom upwards, overturned by pushing. - iyeya, To turn bottom upwards.

ṗaa'los, v. To make one start up suddenly, as by stinging. - iyeya. Bl.

ṗabla'ska, v.a. (of blaska). To press out flat, to flatten. Wapablaska.

pa'blaska, n. The broad bill of a duck.

ṗabla'ya, v.a. (of blaya). To spread out, e.g. dough; to make level; to iron e.g. clothes, to make smooth. Wapablaya.

ṗabla'za, v.a. To burst open, tear open e.g. a bag by sitting on it. Wapablaza.

ṗable'bleca, v. red. of pableca.

ṗable'ca, v.a. To break or crush e.g. brittle ware, glass etc. by pressing, pushing or sitting on. Wapableca. -- pablel, cont. (of pableca). To break something brittle suddenly, quickly. - iyeya.

ṗablel'ya, v.a. To cause to break something brittle. Pablelwaya.

pablu', v.a. To crush, to pulverize by pushing, as hogs do running their snoots through the ground; to flatten. Wapablu. Bl. -- ṗablúka, v. (?).

ṗabu', v.a. To drum on with the fingers. Wapabu. -- ṗabúbu, v. red. of pabu. -- ṗabúya, v.a. To cause to make a drumming noise with the hand. Pabuwaya.

ṗacaᶯ'caᶯ, v.a. To push and make tremble e.g. one's arm by hard pushing. Wapacaᶯcaᶯ.

pacaᶯ'gleya hiyúya, v. To roll toward one e.g. a hoop, tahuka caᶯgleśka. Also, kacaᶯgleya. D.198-199.

ṗacaᶯ'naᶯl, adv. Shoved off. - iyeya, To shove out e.g. a boat from the shore. - aya, To push ahead.

pa'caᶯśihuṫa, n. The English sparrow, short, thick billed.

ṗaceg', cont. (of paceka). To push aside and make stagger. - iyeya. -- ṗacégceg, cont. of pacegceka.

ṗace'gceka, v. red. (of paceka). To make stagger. Wapacegceka. -- ṗacégyeya, v.a. To make one stagger suddenly by pushing. Bl.

ṗace'ka, v.a. To push and make stagger. Wapaceka.

pacē'ṫe, n. The nostrils.

paci'ca, v.a. To mix up e.g. the hair by rubbing. Cf. ipacica.

ṗaci'k'ala, v.a. (of cik'ala). To make small by rubbing. Wapacik'ala. -- ṗacík'ayela, v.a. Same as pacik'ala.Bl.

ṗaci'scila, v. (of ciscila). To make small by rubbing or pressing. Wapaciscila. Also, ṗacísciyela. Bl.

ṗaċo'ċo, v.a. (of coco). To rub soft e.g. mortar, paint etc.

ṗaco'kab, (?). To push into the middle. - iyeya. B.H.186.5.

ṗaċo'kaka, v.a. To empty, push or drawn out entirely. Wapácokaka.

paco'la, adv. Without a head.

ṗaco'za, v.a. (of coza). To make warm by rubbing. Wapacoza.

ƥae', v.a. To inflict punishment in order to prevent future lapses. Wapáe. Ww.

ƥae'ceca, v.a. To make something go the way it ought to by pushing etc., as aflashlight. Wapaececa.

ƥae'cetu, v.a. (of ecetu). To adjust as it was or should be, push into the right place e.g. a dislocated joint. Wapaecetu.

ƥaes'ya, adv. Being against. - uᶯ, To be against. Bl.

ƥaē'za, v.a. To be against, work against. Wapaeza. Bl.

ƥae'ze, v.a. To rival, seek to supplant

ƥaǧab', cont. of pagapa. - iyeya.

ƥaǧaᶯ', v.a. To be able to spare, i.e. for the giving away. To part with, give away, spare. Wapagaᶯ. Also, to open by pushing, to open up e.g. land of the Reservation. -- ƥaǧáᶯǧaᶯ, v. red. of pagaᶯ.

ƥaǧaᶯ'ya, 1) v.a. To cause to give away. 2) v. To cause to open. Pagaᶯwaya. -- ƥaǧáᶯyahaᶯ, part. Habitually inclined to part with things. - uᶯ. Bl. -- ƥaǧáᶯyaᶯ, adv. 1) Parting with. 2) Opening.

ƥaǧa'ƥa, v.a. To push off with the hand e.g. the skin of ananimal. Wapagapa. Also, to get skinned, wounded while pushing or thrusting.

ƥaǧe', n. The diaphragm, abdomen, belly. - hákakšа omawani yelo, i.e. walk around with an empty stomach.Bl.

ƥaǧe'ya, v.a. To make flee, run away. Pagewaya. -- adv. (?). Anuᶯkataᶯhaᶯ upi na - najiᶯpi; caᶯke hehaᶯl wana tokicikpapi, i.e. stood ready to charge and then they began to fight. D.267. - akinajiᶯ.

ƥagiᶯ'ǧe śni, adv. perhaps. Going without stopping. - iyaya, To go without stopping in any place. WL. MS.105.

ƥagiᶯ'giᶯ, v.a. To make wrinkles e.g. on cloth by rubbing in one direction. Bl.

ƥagla', n. A very small owl whose call is first to be heard in spring: Pagla waᶯ hotoᶯ welo. It is said to be the same as the cehúpaglagla, not the screech-owl. They claim it is a very tame bird and very small. WF. It seems to live in tree holes and hence hardly ever seen. This is also an old name for any kind of woodpecker, but doubtfully screech-owl. - waᶯ caᶯ śtuta iyutelo; wana wetu welo. HH. Wc. says nobody knows what kind of bird it is, or perhaps animal. But its call in the evening is a sign of spring. RF. indicates it to be abird. It is a little owl with ears, the same as the cehupaglagla and the uᶯgnagicala, the screech-owl. WF. It is also the same as the popotka and the osniko. Is. The bird is so named for its snapping of the bill, snapping mandibles, and its wavering call, and it goes by the names also of: cehupaglagla, uᶯgnagicala, popotka. Properly, the saw-whet.

pa'glaȟuǧa, v. (?). Páwaglaȟuǧa. Bl.

ƥagla'ǩiᶯyaᶯ, adv. Pushing or crowding to one side.

pagla'ptus iyeya, v. To tip over. Apajeje iblotaka ca paglaptus iyewayelo, i.e. was sitting at one end of the bend and so tipped over. Bl. Syn.- paoᶯze wosla iyeya.

ƥagle'ǧa, v.a. To mark off e.g. names on a list.

ƥagle'za, v.a. (of gleza). To make spotted or ringed by rubbing. Wapagleza.

ƥaglo'glo, v. (?). Bl.

ƥaglo'ǩa, v.a. To dislocate, put or push out of joint. Wapagloka.

ƥagmi'ca, v.a. (?). Wapagmica. Bl.

ƥagmi'gma, v.a. To make round e.g. like a ball with the hands; to roll e.g. a barrel with the hand, pushing against it. Wapagmigma.

ƥagmi'yaᶯ, v.a. To roll with the hand e.g. a barrel, to roll by pushing against. Wapagmiyaᶯ. Wa pagmiyaᶯpi, Rolling snow. Also, ƥagmíyaᶯyaᶯ. Wapagmiyaᶯyaᶯ

ṗagmuŋ´, v.a. (of gmuŋ), To twist with the hand, to roll up something with the hand. Wapagmuŋ. Tablokaŋ ca ohiye num pagmuŋpi. MS.481. -- ṗagmúŋpi, n. A skein of yarn, yarn; anything rolled up, as a hide, blanket etc.

ṗagna´, v.a. To shake off e.g. fruit with the hand; to shell off e.g. corn with the hands by rubbing; to make fall off by rubbing, as by rubbing two ears of corn together to remove the kernels.

pa´gnagya, adv. Doing something with one's head set, not losing sight of it, not giving up, going straight for it. WE.

pa´gnaka, v. To have resolved upon something, set one's head towards a thing. Takomni etkiya pawagnakelo, I am resolved to go there. Bl.

ṗagna´śkiŋyaŋ, v.a. (of gnaśkiŋyaŋ). To make furious by pushing about. Wapagnaśkiŋyaŋ.

ṗagna´yaŋ, v.a. (of gnayaŋ). To miss something partly trying to rest on something and thus fall down e.g. from a chair. To miss in pushing. R. Wapagnayaŋ.

ṗago´, v.a. To carve, engrave; to mark e.g. by a line for a race, to pace ground. Wapago. -- ṗagógo, v.a. red. (of pago). To mark, scribble, as a baby does with a lead pencil. Wapagogo. -- ṗagóḱiya, v.a. To cause to carve or engrave. Pagowakiya.

paġoŋ´ṫa, n. The mallard duck; the loon; the common tame duck, and other ducks.
- nawate ska, The hooded merganser.
- pa to, The shoveller.
- pa sapa, The pin-tail and the lesser scaup duck.
- iśta śa, The wood duck, said to be wakaŋ selececa, on account of its head feathers.

There is a saying when a woman is always with her husband: Pagoŋta s'e wiyuḣlagaŋ śni; for, the mallard duck is monogamous in its wild state, but becomes polygamous in captivity.

pago´ṗaṫića, v. (page and opatica). To put in under the girdle e.g. a knife. -- paġóṗaṫil, cont. - iyeya.

paġo´ptaŋ, adv. perhaps. (of page). Around the waist. - yuza, To hold a person about the waist.

ṗaġo´ya, v.a. To cause to mark; to make carve etc. Pagowaya.

ṗaġug´, cont. of paguka. - iyeya.

ṗaġu´ka, v.a. To sprain by rubbing etc., to rub down, as in dressing skins. Wapaguka.

paġuŋ´ṫa, Cf. pagoŋta.

ṗagwes´, cont. of pagweza. - paḣpa, To remove the meat from a hide scraping with the wahiŋtka in the same parallel direction; this is done when the hide is to be used for a tipi. Cf. gwegwes.

ṗagwe´za, v.a. To make somewhat rough by rubbing. Wapagweza.

ṗaha´, n. A mound, a hill.

ṗaha´, 1) v.a. To raise to strike, be ready to strike. - najiŋpi. 2) v.a. To push onward, push aside; to oppose, reject. - iḣpeya, iyeya. Mapaha ye, Push me, as on a swing. Cf. patokaŋ iyeya. Bl.

pa´ha, n. The hair of the head, the scalp. - icu, He took a scalp. Waŋna kośkalaka waŋ - zizi ca śina hiŋ akataŋiŋ ca hinajiŋ na lecel eya....

ṗaha´ha, v. red. of ṗahá. Uŋgna toka śka - iḣpeciye ci. Bl.

paha´hayela, adv. red. (of pahayela). In great numbers, abundantly. - tebwicaye. D.106.

ṗahaŋ´skeya, v.a. To make bigger by rubbing or rolling e.g. a cake. Bl.

ṗaha´ohaŋzi, n. Dusk. Bl. Cf. maḣpiohaŋzi.

ṗaha´ṗajola, n. A prominent or conspicuous hill.

ṗaha´ta, adv. At or on the hill. - mni kte, I shall go on the hill. - iyotakapi.

ṗaha´ya, adj. Piled up, projecting, prominent. -- ṗaháyela adv. In a pile, abundantly. - egle. Caŋ kaśle-ślecapi ota - eglepi.

ṗahi', v.a. To pick up, gather up, to collect e.g. words. Wapáhi

ṗahi'higla, (?). - toki ipi, i.e. went alone there, nobody else. Bl.

ṗahi'hilag, (?). - óhimic'iye, i.e. for once I am first. Bl.

ṗahi'ḣaḣa, v.a. To strike one in the face, so that his face (hi) looks twisted and crooked. Bl.

pahiŋ', n. The porcupine; the quills of the porcupine.

ṗahiŋl', cont. (of pahiŋta). To brush or wipe off quickly and completely. Bl. - iyeya.

pahiŋ' nasuŋ'ṗakce, n. The tail of a porcupine, which is used as a comb.

pahiŋ'pabla, n. A tool to flatten porcupine quills with when ornamenting.

pa'hiŋsk̇ayela, adv. (?). Hena - omayakilaka waciŋ, i.e. tell one all you know about it. Wociŋ yahi ca cic'u; yuŋkaŋ - cic'u yaciŋ yelo. Caŋli kiŋ - uŋglasotapi, i.e. used up the last bit. - akiyagle, i.e. all the storm clouds passed by. Bl. HC. Yh.

ṗahiŋ'ṫa, v.a. To rub, brush or wipe off. Wapahiŋta.

ṗaho'ho, v.a. To shake or move, make loose by pushing e.g. a tooth, a fence post. Wapahoho. -- ṗahóhośniyaŋ, adv. Immovably.

ṗaho'mni, v.a. To push anything round. Wapahomni. Caŋtepi kiŋ ake wicayapahomni kiŋ akiblezapi kte. B.H.108.22.

ṗaho'toŋ, v.a. (of hotoŋ). To cause to make a noise, as iron by filing, or an animal by stabbing. Wapahotoŋ.

pahu', n. The large part or head of anything, as the caŋnuŋpa pahu, the bone of the pipe; blo pahu, the root of a Dakota potato; tiŋpsiŋla pahu, the upper part of the tiŋpsiŋla; wagmeza pahu, the butt-end of a corn cob.

pa'hu, n. The skull-bone.

ṗahu'k̇ul, adv. With head down. - iyeya, To bow somebody's head, to push one's head down, to push or shove down.

ṗahuŋ'huŋs, cont. of pahuŋhuŋza. - iyeya. -- ṗahúŋhuŋsya, v.a. To cause to shake with the hand. Pahuŋhuŋswaya.

ṗahuŋ'huŋza, v.a. (of huŋhuŋza). To shake, make shake by pushing, as a tree. Wapahuŋhuŋza.

pahu'ṫe, n. The place where the head and neck meet; the ridge of the nose at the base between the eyes. R.

pa'huṫe, n. The upper hard part of the nose. Bl.

pahu'zi, n. An old-time pistol, on account of the yellow handle.

ṗaḣa', v.a. To make rough by rubbing. Wapaḣa. -- ṗaḣáḣa, v.n. To be rough, as ice sometimes is.

ṗaḣci', v.a. To tear out a piece, pick out a piece. Wapaḣci. -- ṗaḣciḣci, v. red.

ṗaḣe'yab, cont. (of paḣeyapa). To push aside quickly. - iyeya.

ṗaḣe'yapa, v. To shove aside. Wapaḣeyapa. -- ṗaḣéyaṫa, v. To push aside. - iyeya, To push back or out to one side.

paḣgla'jiŋca, v. To snivel, perhaps. Paḣwaglajiŋca. Bl.

ṗaḣiŋ' hiyu'kiya, v. To excell one, do better than another. Also, paḣiŋ iyek̇iya. Paḣiŋ hiyumakiyelo, as a man, to whom one had talked and then yet another very urgently, would say. Bl.

ṗaḣla'gaŋ, v.a. To enlarge, to cause to lengthen out. Wapaḣlagaŋ.

paḣla'jiŋca, v. To sniff or snuff the nose.

ṗaḣla'ṫa, v.a. To scratch or scrape along. Wapaḣlata.

paȟla'ṫe, n. The internal parts of the nose, the nasal fossae, the root of the nose; the holes in the skull communicating with the nostrils.

ṗaȟla'ya, 1) v.a. To rub or roll off something sticking, as a piece of wet paper; to peel off, pull off e.g. the skin of a potato. 2) v.n. To peel off of itself.

ṗaȟle'ca, v.a. To tear to pieces, pull to pieces; to tear something by pushing or leaning against it. Wapaȟleca. -- ṗaȟléȟleca, v. red. of paȟleca. -- ṗaȟlel, cont. (of paȟleca). - iyeya, i.e. as a wild horse running into a tent.

ṗaȟli', v.a. To stick in the ground e.g. a stake or stick. Wapaȟli.

paȟli', n. The excretion of the nasal fossae.

ṗaȟli'ȟli, v. red. of ṗaȟli.

paȟli' i'yoḱaskica, v. (?). This is used in speaking of the discharge from the nose that is very adhesive so that one cannot get it out. Paȟli iyomakaskica.

paȟli'ṗakiⁿte, n. A handkerchief.

ṗaȟli'ya, v.a. To cause to push into the ground. Paȟliwaya.

ṗaȟlog', cont. of paȟloka. - iyeya, where the action is indicated to be performed quickly.

ṗaȟlo'ȟloka, v. red. (of paȟloka). To make many holes.

ṗaȟlo'ḱa, v.a. To make a hole in, pierce, run through, bore; break through e.g. ice; pierce e.g. the ears by pushing or pressure. Wapaȟloka. Num caⁿte paȟlokapi kta. Na maka el paȟlokiⁿ na el mahel egnaka.

ṗaȟni'ȟṗilṗicaśni, (?). - wawapahi, i.e. picked up all sorts of things, good and worthless ones. Bl.

ṗaȟṗa', v.a. To throw, as a horse its rider; to take down e.g. something hanging up; to lay down or put off e.g. one's load; to scrape off e.g. the flesh sticking to a hide. Wapaȟpa.

ṗaȟṗe'ya, v.a. To cause to throw down. Paȟpewaya.

ṗaȟṗu', v.a. To break or pick off in small pieces, as with a chisel. Wapaȟpu. -- ṗaȟṗúȟṗu, v. red. of paȟpu. -- ṗaȟṗúya, v.a. To cause to pick off. Paȟpuwaya.

paȟṫa', v.a. To tie up. Pawáȟta. Hu páȟta, To hobble a horse. Na oⁿ, straps, tasu kiⁿ hena - . Si nupiⁿ paȟtapi. Iyujipa pakiȟte ciⁿ etulaȟci kute. D.88. -- paȟṫáȟṫa, v.a. To tie and make into bundles. Wapaȟtaȟta. -- paȟṫápi, n. A bundle, a pack.

paȟte', n. The forehead; the space on the brow, directly above the bridge of the nose. D. Itokśaⁿ towicaya na - el kutakiya icazo na tapoⁿ kiⁿ anoⁿkataⁿ ecel ecoⁿ. -- paȟṫéyukóḱiya, v. To frown. Perhaps, paȟteblukokiya. Also, paȟṫeyukoḱiya.

ṗaȟu'ġa, v.a. To break or push a hole in e.g. a kettle; to crack by pushing e.g. an egg. Wapaȟuga. -- ṗaȟúȟ, cont. (of paȟuga). - iyeya, To crack or crush quickly. -- ṗaȟúȟuġa, v. red. of paȟuga.

paȟwa'yaśkabya, (?). Lila iȟat'emayayapi na paȟwayaśkabmayayapelo. Bl.

paȟwa'yaśkapa, v.n. (?). Paȟwayamaśkapa, as is said when one laughs so heartily that the peritoneum contracts. Bl.

paȟyu'ṫibya, v. To cause one to laugh very heartily. Paȟyutibwaya. Lila iȟat'emayayapi na paȟyutibmayayapelo. Bc. Also, paȟwáyaśkabmayayapelo.

ṗai'ċaksa, (?). - éyaye. Bl.

pai'cisaⁿnica. (?). - iyeya. Bl.

ṗai'kpiska, adv. With belly up. - iȟpeya, To throw over on the back, belly up as a dog; thus, pa-ikpi-ska.

ṗai'le, (?). - iheya yo, oteȟike, i.e. when it is cold. Bl.

ṗai'leġa, v. To make a fire shine or sparkle by poking. Wapailega. Bl.

ṗai'lepi, n. A flashlight.

pain̄l'pica, (?). Can̄te kin̄ - śni, i.e. cannot make an impression on him, persuade him. Bl.

pain̄'yan̄ka, v.a. (of in̄yan̄ka). To shoot or throw a stick through a hoop when rolling; to push through with the hand. Perhaps, wapain̄yan̄ka.

pain̄'yan̄kapi, n. The hoop-game; an Indian game played by two or any number of twos. Each one has two sticks connected by a strap. a hoop with four marks is rolled on; when it stops and tips sideways, each player throws his pair of sticks under it. The position of the sticks with respect to the marks decides the game. - un̄, To play the hoop-game. D.2.

pai'puskica, v.a. (of ipuskica). To press down on with the hand. Wapaipuskica. -- paípuskil, cont. of paipuskica. - iyeya.

pai'tkon̄s, cont. of paitkon̄za.

pai'tkon̄za, v.a. To make even by pressing; to strike off level, as a measure of grain. Wapaitkon̄za.

pai'waśtela, adv. (of iwaśtela). Slowly. - iyeya, To shove along slowly. -- paíwaśteya, adv. Slowly, gently.

pai'yapat'o, v.n. (of iyapat'o). To be pushed by. - ihemic'iye. - iyeya, To push e.g. a door to make it catch and be fully closed. Bl.

pai'yotag, adv. Down. - ihpeya, To make sit down, to set one down. - egnaka. Akicita najin̄pi k'on̄ el hihun̄ni na wan̄ji - ihpeya.

pai'yowaza, v.a. To make echo by striking with the hand. Wapaiyowaza.

pai'yuwiya, adv. Tangling. - ihpeya, To tangle up, mix up etc. by rolling on, as buffalo do while rolling in weeds. Bl.

paja', adv. Through. - capá, To stab through.

paja'ja, v.a. To wash e.g. a floor, to mop. Wapajaja.

pajal', cont. of pajata. - iyeya. -- pajáljata, v. red. of pajata.

paja'ta, v.a. To make forked by punching or thrusting something into. Wapajata.

paje'je, paje'jeya, v.n. To be in danger. - najin̄, To stand or be at the edge of something and so be in danger of following. A.

pajib', cont. (of pajipa). - iyeya, To sting quickly or suddenly. - kuwa, To be after one for something. Bl. -- pajíbjipa, v. red. of pajipa.

pajin̄', v. To prevent. R. Bl.

pajin̄'ca, v.a. To make croak by shaking up. Wapajin̄ca. Bl.

pajin̄'gjin̄ca, v. red. of pajin̄ca. Bl.

paji'pa, v.a. To prick with a pin, to press against and make penetrate; to sting. Wapajipa.

pajo', n. (?). Sun̄śun̄la s'e ituhu - kaca, as is said of a man whose forehead is very convex, bill-like. Bl. -- pajójo, (?). Śún̄śun̄la ikpi san̄ s'e iśtahe - kaca, as is said of a man with heavy eyebrows. Bl.

pajo'ke s'e, (?). - can̄koze, i.e. he whips with the left hand. Bl.

pajo'la, n. A high knoll or hill, peak. -- adj. perhaps. A hill. Paha pajola, A prominent, conspicuous hill. -- pajóya, adv. Hill-like; swelled-up, as pimples. - kaga, i.e. as a road in the middle so that the water may flow off.

paju'ju, v.a. To rub out, cross out, erase. Wase kic'un̄pi k'on̄ hena peji hota on̄ wicakicipajuju. Also, to get out of joint by pressure, as a box loosening where the nails hold the corners. Wapajuju.

pajun̄', v.a. To push down and pry up e.g. roots; to pull up, as ducks do grass roots under and in water. Wapajun̄.

pajun̄'ta, v.a. To touch, as a bunch of hair the eyes. Iśta mapajun̄ta. Bl.

paka', 1) v.a. To split or cut a slit in for an arrowhead. 2) v. with iyeya, To push down or break down e.g.

ribs of an animal.

ṗakab', cont. of pakapa. - iyeya. To throw or toss e.g. a ball; to run against one. - iyeciyiŋ kte lo, so the bull calf has said.

paḱa'huŋghuŋg, v. red. of pakahuŋka. -iyeya, To nod, as horses do constantly when chasing away flies. Syn.- pamaglegle iyaya. Bl.

paḱa'huŋḱa, v.a. To bow or nod the head to one, as in assenting. Pawakahuŋka. Cf. pómnamna.

pa'ḱaic'ícuya, n. The American red cross-bill. Also, - haŋpi, and paká-ic'icuyela. They are said to breed in mid-winter. FH.

paḱa'ksa, v.a. To strike off a man's head. Pawakaksa.

ṗa'ḱaŋ, v.n. To prevent. Mini - , To be prevented by water, as in making a journey.

ṗakaŋ', v.a. To rub off dirt, rub clean e.g. a dirty window. Wapakaŋ.Bl.

ṗaḱaŋ'yaŋ, adv. Along, alongside. - ya, To go alongside e.g. a lake, or as a horse along a fence trying to get away. Mini kiŋ śina ca - blelo. Bl. Syn.- aglagla.

ṗaka'ṗa, v.a. To toss; to strike a ball that is thrown and send it back; to strike or stab before falling; to push away. Wapakapa. Cf. kakapa.

paḱa's'iŋ, v.t. or v.n. To be with one's head raised, to raise one's head. Pawakas'iŋ. Yuŋkaŋ ake - na waŋcala eyi na ake t'a, i.e. he raised his head. D.13,28.

ṗaḱa'tiŋ, v.a. (katiŋ). To straighten out e.g. the arm when bent at the elbow. Wapakatiŋ.

ṗaḱa'wa, v.a. To make a split, split.

ṗakca', v.a. To comb, disentangle, untie. Wapakca.

paki'cahuŋka, v. (pakahuŋka). To bow or nod the head to one. Pawecahuŋka.

ṗaki'gni, (?). Hupakignipi, i.e. they tie up the tent poles, i.e. the two long ones, to the vehicle. BT.

ṗaḱi'gnuŋg, cont. of pakignuŋka. - iyeya.

ṗaḱi'gnuŋḱa, v. To push under water, make dive. Wapakignuŋka.

paḱi'ȟṫa, v. pos. (paȟta). To tie up or bind together one's own, to pack up. Pawakiȟta. Iyujipa pakiȟte ciŋ etulaȟci kute. D.88.

ṗaḱiŋ', v.n. To stand leaning, stooping. - iyaya, To walk stooping down. Cf. takiŋ iyaya, pakiŋyaŋ. Bl.

ṗaḱiŋl', cont. (pakiŋta). To wipe. - iyeya, To wipe off all quickly.

ṗaḱiŋ'ṫa, v.a. To wipe e.g. dishes, to rub off, cleanse; to clean e.g. a gun barrel by rubbing up and down. Peji ȟota oŋ wicapakiŋta.

ṗaḱiŋ'yaŋ, v.n. To walk stooping. -- adv. With the upper part of the body leaning forward, as one who has a back-ache. - mani. Bl.

ṗaḱi'ṗaś, v. To strike and make bend, i.e. where one was hit. Bl.

ṗaḱi'ṗuskica, v.n. To be pressed tight together. -- ṗaḱiṗuskil, cont. of pakipuskica. - iyeya, To press together. - egnaka, To lay on for the purpose of pressing down.

ṗaḱi'ṗuskiṫa, v.n. To be pressed together.

ṗaḱis', cont. of pakiza.

ṗaḱi'śḱiza, v. red. of pakiza.

paḱi'ya, adv. Leading. Iŋyaŋ waŋ tiihaŋke el - he lo. B.H.240.10.

paḱi'yaḱel, adv. Same perhaps as pakiya. - yaŋka. B.H.281.14.

ṗaḱi'za, v.a. To make creak by rubbing. Wapakiza.

ṗaḱo', v.a. Cf. pakol.

ṗaḱo', adj. Crooked, bent around.

ṗaḱol', v.a. cont. of pakota. - iyeya.

ṗaḱo'natke, v.a. To press together and make bulky. Bl.

ṗakoŋ´ťa, v.a. To wear partly out e.g. a rope, a strap etc. by pressure, rubbing etc. BD.

ṗaǩo´śkala, n. Some bird like the hiŋhaŋ kap'ipila, but not an owl; the whippoorwill, living in the woods. Also, the johótoŋla, and perhaps the bobwhite. Is. Bl. - s'e i kiŋ nisko, as they say of a man having a big mouth. Bl.

ṗaǩo´ťa, v.a. To dig or take out marrow from a bone, to probe. Wapakota.

ṗaǩo´za, v.a. To push back and forth, to swing. Wapakoza.

ṗakṗa´, v.a. To pierce, gouge out e.g. an eye. Wapakpa.

ṗakṗaŋ´, v.a. To crush, make fine by pressing. Wapakpaŋ. -- ṗakṗáŋkṗaŋ, v. red.

ṗakṗi´, v.a. To crack open, mash e.g. a louse or flea. Wapakpi. -- ṗakṗikṗi, v. To prick holes in e.g. bread before baking; to dot all over.

ṗaksa´, v.a. To break something with the hand by pushing or pressure; sitting e.g. on a board and breaking it. Wapaksa. -- ṗaksáksa, v. red. of paksa.

paksa´ s'e, adv. (?). - najiŋ, To stop walking, as when tired or because it is very warm. Syn.- wotoka s'e. Bl.

ṗakśa´, 1) v. To fold e.g. a blanket. 2) adj. Bent down, like an old person.

ṗakśaŋ´, v.a. To bend, make bend by pushing. Wapakśaŋ. -- ṗakśáŋkśaŋ, v. red.

ṗakśa´yela, adv. In a bent condition.

ṗakśi´ja, 1) v.a. To double up anything, e.g. folding chairs, beds to put them away. 2) v.n. To sit down, in the fashion of old people. Wapakśija. Uŋpakśijiŋ kte lo. Bl. To eyaś uŋpakśijapi kte lo, Let us sit down and rest. Bl.

ṗakśi´kśaŋ, adj. Crooked, zigzag.

ṗakśi´kśija, v. red. of pakśija. -- ṗakśiś, cont. of pakśija. - iyeya.

ṗakťaŋ´, v.a. To bend around with the hand. Wapaktaŋ. -- ṗakťáŋkťaŋ, v. red. of paktaŋ. -- ṗakťáŋyaŋ, 1) v.a. To cause to bend. 2) adv. Bent around.

pa´ǩuciyela, adv. Head down. - yuza, To hold the head down. R. Bl.

ṗaǩu´ǩa, v.a. To wear out by handling, as the knees of one's pants by rubbing them often with the hand. Wapakuka.

paǩu´ťagleya, adv. With head down. - iȟpeya, To throw one down head foremost. Bl.

ṗak'e´ǧa, v.a. To scrape with the hand and with glass. Wapak'ega. -- ṗak'éȟ, cont. of pak'ega. - iyeya. -- ṗak'ék'eǧa, v. red. of pak'ega. Note: not pak'eȟk'ega. R.

ṗak'es´, cont. of pak'eza. - iyeya. -- ṗak'ésk'eza, v. red. of pak'eza.

ṗak'e´za, v.a. To make a noise by rubbing, as in filing. Wapak'eza. Also, to scrape, make smooth by scraping.

ṗak'os´, cont. of pak'oza. - iyeya. -- ṗak'ósk'oza, v. red. of pak'oza.

ṗak'o´za, v.a. To rub and make smooth and hard. Wapak'oza.

ṗal, v. cont. (of páta). To cut up e.g. meat. Pal iyuta, He tries to cut up. Pal yuśtaŋ. D.199.

pa´la, n. dim. A little nose. "Poor" little nose, yaoŋśiyakel eyapi. Pala kiŋ haŋke kiŋ kaksapi s'e, as is said when the nose is very short. Bl.

Pala´ni, n. prop. The Pawnee Indians. -- n. A liar, as the Pawnee were known to be liars. Mapálani kéyeȟ, He claims that I am a liar. Mh.

Pala´ni taziŋtkala, n. A bird living in prairie dog holes, but not an owl. It is thin billed, the bill about an inch long; ȟolȟotapi and looks somewhat like a śloślola. Bl.

ṗala´ṗa, v.a. To smooth off e.g. a rough road. B.

ṗale´ǧa, v.a. (?).

pale'haᶯyaᶯk, (?). - yuza. B.H.297.13.

ṗale'ȟleġa, v.a. To poke the fire. -- ṗaléȟya, v.a. To make shine by.

ṗalōb', cont. of palopa. - iyeya, egle. D.121. -- ṗalóblōb, v. red. of palob. - iyeya.

ṗalō'ṗa, v.a. (of lopa). To push into the mud, bemire. Wapalopa.

pama'gle, adv. Head bowed down. - yaᶯka, To bow one's head. - inajiᶯ. -- pamáglegle, adv. red. of pamagle. - iyaya, To nod constantly, as horses do in summer chasing away flies. Syn.- pakáhuᶯghuᶯg iyeya. Bl. -- pamáglela, adv. Head bowed down; prone. Also, pamágleyela.

pa'mahe, pa'mahel, adv. The head covered as by a shawl. - inajiᶯ. Pamahe yauᶯ kiᶯ, ite kazamni; hece wicaśa iyecel wowiyukcaᶯ taᶯktaᶯka luha kte.

ṗama'hehe, v. To push under water repeatedly. - iyeya. Bl.

ṗama'hel, adv. (?). - iyeya, To push in.

ṗamaᶯ', v.a. To file. Wapamaᶯ. Lila peya pamaᶯpi. MS.481. -- adj. perhaps. Filed.

ṗame', v.a. To file. The same as pamaᶯ. Wapame.

pami', v.n. To move away slowly. Kaéktawapaya laka ca (it is far) kohaᶯ miye wapami kteȟcelo.

ṗami'ma, v.a. To make round, i.e. flat and round like a coin, by filing. Wapamima.

pa'mima, adj. (of pa and mima). Round and pointed.

ṗamna', v.a. To rip e.g. one's coat-sleeve. Wapamna. -- ṗamnámna, v. red. of pamna perhaps.

ṗamni', v.a. To divide, distribute. Wapamni. Wagmeza kiᶯ he wakśica ogna pamnipi. Note: kpamni seems to be used most usually. BD.

pamni's'e u, v. To have a cold, a catarrh, i.e. water running from the nose. Pamnis'e mau, makaluza. Pamnis'e hiyu. Pamnis'e kaluza. Bl.

pamnu'mnuġa, n. The gristle or cartilage in the end of the nose; the end of the nose.

ṗanag', v. To start. - iyeya, To make start suddenly, as by pinching or stinging. Bl.

pa'nakseya, v.a. To hang somebody. Pánaksewaya.

ṗani', v.a. To push or jog one with the elbow; to touch one secretly as a sign to come along. Wapani. Bl. -- ṗaniȟi, v.a. To push or jog with the elbow or hand; to wake out of sleep by jogging. Wapanini.

ṗanuᶯ'ġa, v.a. To sprain e.g. the arm or hand. Wapanuᶯga.

paᶯ, n. An Indian woman's work-bag. D.229.

paᶯ, v.n. To yell, call, halloo. Wapáᶯ.

ṗaᶯ'ġa, adj. Drunk. Note: this seems to be, however, slang.

ṗaᶯ'ġece, adj. Bulky, puffed out; many e.g. people. Mapaᶯgece. R. Bl.

paᶯgi', n. The artichoke. Helianthus tuberosus. - hu, The artichoke stalk, which is edible. D.97. P.
- haᶯska, The parsnip.
- pepe, śaśa, The raddish, beet.
- zizi, The carrot.

Paᶯgi' Taᶯkiᶯ'kiᶯyaᶯ iyóȟloke k'el, n. ph. A little creek going into the Powder River near its mouth. Bl. Perhaps the Mizpah Creek.

ṗaᶯȟṗaᶯ'ȟya, adv. Breaking out. - hinape, yaᶯke, Eruption, breaking out. WE. Also, ṗaᶯȟyákel. Bl.

ṗaᶯ'ja, adj. Puffed up, soft, bunchy. -- páᶯjela, adj. Puffed out, bulky

paᶯke'śka, n. Crockery, China-ware; celluloid; large shells. - hokśicala, A doll.

Paᶯke'ska Wakpa, n. prop. The Platte River.

pannun'pala, n. The showy milkweed. Asclepias speciosa. The milkweed family. It is a medicine, being eaten. Syn.- waȟcaȟca. #76.

ṗanṗan', v. red. (of pan). To yell, make a noise, shout, as Dakota young do. Wapanpan. D.244.

panpan'la, adj. Soft, as a deer skin; tender, like meat. Also, panpányela. Hayapi - .

panśa', n. A suitcase.

panśpan'ja, adj. Soft, bunchy. -- panśpanjela, adj. Soft, as furs, cotton, wool; bulky, puffed up, like bread.

panś'ya, adv. Bulky, bunchy.

pan'wak'in, n. A sort of saddle consisting of a piece of leather and two stirrups only. Bl. Bs.

ṗan'wiyopeyapi, n. An auction sale.EB.

panwo'ṫuka, n. An Indian woman's bag, in which she keeps her sewing apparatus; a work-bag.

ṗan'yan, adv. Crying out. -- ṗanyánhan, adv. Crying out, yelling. - eya.

ṗao'blelya, v.a. To spread by rubbing. Bl.

pao'gla, v. (?). - iyeya. Bl. -- ṗaóglaya, adv. Singly, one by one, in a row far apart. - yankapi.

ṗao'gluta, v.a. (of ogluta). To close up or over e.g. a hole by rubbing. Wapaogluta. -- ṗaógluṫeya, v.a. To cause to close up by rubbing. Paoglutewaya.

ṗao'gmus, cont. of paogmuza. Wipá kin - egle yo. Bl.

ṗao'gmuza, v.a. To shut or close with the hand, as a door. Wapaogmuza. Wanna wipa tiyapa ko paogmuzapi.

ṗao'ha, v.a. To push one into, e.g. into a creek or a hole. Wapaoha. Mini paoha. -- ṗaóhaha, v. red. (of paoha). To turn around e.g. meat in a frying pan. Wapaohaha. - yo, ázeya un welo, i.e. push the whole thing and everything on it in. Bl.

ṗao'ȟmin, v. To jump sideways, to shy from, as some horses do when an automobile passes by. Bl.

ṗao'ȟṗa, v.a. To stick through with something. - iyewaya. Yunkan maka kin - iyeya na kutakiya huȟpaya, i.e. hunpe on.

ṗao'ḱaǧa, adv. Exceedingly, extravagantly. Hokśicala wan waśte - . B.H. 46.1.

ṗao'kanśniyan, v. or adv. perhaps. To crowd out. B.H.200.6.

pao'ḱihe, n. (pa and okihe). The bridge or ridge of the nose, bone and cartilage.

ṗaō'ḱiju, v. To put together e.g. playing cards. Cf. ókiju.

ṗao'ḱiyasḱaṗa, v.n. To be bent in, jammed in.

ṗao'ḱogna iyeic'iya, v. To squeeze one's self into a row of men. Bl.

ṗao'ḱoton, v. To make a split, in order to insert something. - o. Bl. Syn.- pakawa.

ṗao'ksa, v.a. To make cave in e.g. a ditch etc, so as to fill the cavity and level the ground. Wapaoksa.

ṗaō'na, v.a. perhaps. To push on e.g. a ring on a stick; to shove on. Wapaona. Bl.

ṗaon'ze wosla iyéya, v. ph. To tip over. Apajeje iblotaka ca paonze wosla iyewayelo. Bl. Syn.- paglaptus iyeya.

ṗao'po, v.n. To warp; to push and make a hollow place. Cf. naopo.

ṗao'ṗusḱica, v.a. To press down into. -- ṗaóṗusḱil, cont. of paopuskica.

ṗao'sḱica, v.a. To cram. Wapaoskica.

ṗao'sṗa, v.a. To push under, as in water. Wapaospa.

ṗao'ślog, cont. (of paośloka). To break through. - iyeya, To break through suddenly, as through ice, or get into deep water suddenly;

to break through e.g. ground that is undermined.

ṗaō'śloḱa, v.a. To make go in by pressure, as a stick into the ground, or a nail into a hollow wall where, unexpectedly, it suddenly goes in. Wapaośloka.

ṗao'tḱoⁿs, cont. of paotkoⁿza.

ṗao'tḱoⁿza, v.a. To press in full, make even full; to strike off level, as in measuring grain. Wapaotkoⁿza.

ṗao'tḱuǧa, v.a. To push and thereby lock e.g. a door with a night latch.

ṗao't'iⁿs, cont. (of paot'iⁿza). To press tight e.g. a half-closed door. - iyeya, iyotaka. Hena papa na waśiⁿ icicahi - ognakapi. MS.483.

pao't'iⁿza, v.a. To press in hard and tight with the hand. Wapaot'iⁿza.

pao'waⁿcaya, v. To disperse by. Bl.

ṗao'wotaⁿ, v.a. To make straight, make stand upright. Wapaowotaⁿ. - hiyuic'iya, To make one's self sit up, having been on one's back. Bl. Also, ṗaówotaⁿla.

ṗao'zeze, v.n. To swing, dangle, hang, as berries. Cf. kaozeze. -- ṗaózezeya, adv. Swinging, dangling. Cf. kaozezeya.

papa', v. To bark, as dogs do. Śuⁿka mapapa, i.e. barked at me. Suⁿka waⁿ ska ca u na papa. MS.573. SI.

ṗa'ṗa, n. Dried meat. - saka. Cf. wakablapi. Winuȟcala, pápala waⁿ cik'ala yegnake c'oⁿ haⁿpi kaga yo; haⁿp'miglatkaⁿpi ktelo. Bl.

ṗaṗa'ǧa, v.n. To pop e.g. corn in parching, or meat. R. Bl.

ṗapaȟ'ya, v.a. To parch e.g. corn, meat etc. R. Bl. -- ṗaṗáȟyapi, n. (of papaga). Dried intestines, that were filled with fat and then roasted like sausage. Bl. Syn.- talipa, taśupa caⁿ iyapehaⁿpi. Bl.

pa'pala, adj. red. (of pa). Bitter, biting, as pepper.

pa'piⁿkpa, n. The point of the nose.

ṗaṗi'sṗiza, v. red. of papiza. Bl.

ṗaṗi'za, v.a. To make creak by pressure or by sitting on. Wapapiza. Bl.

ṗapob', cont. (of papopa). To burst. - iyeya, To make burst.

ṗapo'ṗa, v.a. To make burst or pop squeezing or pressing. Wapapopa.

ṗaṗo'ṫa, v.a. (?). Wapepeka oⁿ pa kiⁿ uⁿpapotapi. Pb.27.

ṗapo'waya, v.a. (of powaya, which is not used). To rub or brush up e.g. fur or nap on a hat or blanket. Wapapowaya.

ṗapsag', cont. (of papsaka). To break in two. - iyeya, To break a rope or wire in two, and the like, by one's quick and sudden pressure. -- ṗaṗságya, v.a. To cause to break e.g. a cord, wire etc. by pressure. Papsagwaya. Also perhaps, v.n. To break away as a horse from a rope, to break loose or through.

ṗapsa'ka, v.a. To break or tear in two by pressure or by sitting e.g. in a swing. Wapapsaka. Hokśila hohotela - .

ṗapsi'psica, v. red. (of papsica). To push and make fly as chips. Bl. Papsica is not used, it seems. Cf. psica.

papsuⁿ', v.a. To spill. Wapapsuⁿ. Cf. kpapsoⁿ.

ṗapsuⁿ'psuⁿla, v. To rub and make smooth and round, as an arrow shaft. Wapapsuⁿpsuⁿla.

ṗapśuⁿ', v.a. To put out of joint or dislocate e.g. one's arm; to sprain one's own. Wapapśuⁿ. Kpapśuⁿ, wakpapśuⁿ. Nape kiⁿ, i.e. of the waziya, - iȟpeya.

ṗapśuⁿ'ḱa, v.a. To make blunt e.g. a pointed stick, needle etc. Wapapśuⁿka. Cf. pśuⁿka.

ṗapśuⁿ'pśuⁿ, v. red. of papśuⁿ. Tokel owanaseta nape - kiⁿ oⁿ kokipe.

ṗapta', adv. Through. Tipi kiⁿ - uⁿki-yaglapi. Waŋna caŋ kiŋ - iblabla.

ṗaṗtaŋ', v.a. To turn over. Wapaptaŋ. -- ṗaptáŋptaŋ, v.n. red. (of paptaŋ). To wallow about, roll over, to writhe. Wapaptaŋptaŋ. -- ṗaptáŋptaŋyaŋ, adv. Wallowing about, rolling. D.220. -- ṗaptáŋyaŋ, 1) v.a. (of paptaŋ). To cause to turn over, upset or turn over by pushing. Wapaptaŋyaŋ. Paptaŋyepica śni. 2) adv. Rolling about.

pa'ptehiŋcala, n. A buffalo cow with a head similar to that of a calf. Bl.

ṗaptu'ġa, v.a. To break off a piece by pressure. Wapaptuga. BD.

ṗapṫu'ja, v.a. To split, to crack by working with the hands. Wapaptuja. -- ṗaptúptuja, v. red. of paptuja.

ṗapṫus', perhaps cont. of paptuza. - iyuŋka. -- adv. In a stooping position. R.

ṗapṫuś', cont. paptuja. - iyeya. -- ṗapṫuśya, v.a. To cause to crack or split. Paptuśwaya.

ṗaptu'za, v.n. perhaps. To stoop, bend over.

ṗaṗus', cont. of papuza. - iyeya.

ṗaṗu'za, v.a. (of puza). To rub dry, wipe dry. Wapapuza.

ṗap'ō'ḣ'a, v.a. To make the hair stand straight up with the hand. Wapap'oḣ'a.

ṗaseb', cont. of pasepa. - iyeya. R.Bl. -- ṗasébsepa, v. red. of pasepa. Bl.

ṗase'ṗa, v.a. To rub off e.g. whitewash. Wapasepa. R. Bl.

ṗasi', v.a. To inquire about something secretly; to escort somebody, as a prisoner to jail; to march one on. - agla. D.105 and 270. Wapasi.

ṗasi'sa, v.a. To pin together; to stick in, as a needle or pin. Wapasisa.

ṗasi'yakel, adv. Watching, following up. B.H.258.6. Lh.

pa'ska, adj. White-headed.

ṗasḱa', v.a. To bleach; to rub and make white. Wapaska.

ṗasḱe'ṗa, v.a. To rub off or move away water or any fluid with the hand, as from a table. Perhaps also, paśkepa. R.

ṗasḱi'ca, v.a. To press down on with the hand; Slang: to swipe, i.e. steal. -- ṗasḱiĺ, cont. of paskica - iyeya.

pa'sla, adj. Bald-headed.

ṗaslal', cont. of paslata. Na caŋ eya okijata ca - he k'oŋ hena icu.

ṗa'slalyēla, adv. Steadily. - ecoŋ, To work slowly but steadily. Bl.

ṗasla'ṫa, v.a. To set up a pole in the ground, to drive in as a stake. Wapaslata.

ṗa'slayela, adv. Slowly. - uŋ, To keep quiet and do nothing, take it easy. - ḣci omawani. Bl. Perhaps also, the same as paslalyela.

ṗasle'ca, v.a. To split e.g. a hide, sack etc. with a knife. Wapasleca. -- ṗasléĺ, cont. of pasleca. - iyeya. -- ṗaslésleca, v. red.

ṗasli', v.a. To squeeze out by pressure. Wapasli.

ṗaslo'haŋ, v.a. To push or shove along e.g. a sled. -- ṗaslóhaŋhaŋ, v. red. of paslohaŋ. -- ṗaslóhaŋpi, n. A long stick with a large head which the Dakotas make slide on the snow and ice.

ṗaslu'ka, n. Masturbation, onanism.

ṗaslul', cont. of pasluta. -- ṗaslúsluta, red. of pasluta.

ṗaslu'ṫa, v. To push out of, as dirt from a pipe stem. Wapasluta.

ṗasmag', cont. of pasmaka. - iyeya.

ṗasma'ka, v.a. To make a hollow in by pushing, to indent. Wapasmaka.

ṗasmiŋ'yaŋ, v. Cf. pasmiŋyaŋyaŋ. -- ṗasmiŋyaŋyaŋ, v.a. To rub or scrape off, make smooth or clean. Wapasmiŋyaŋyaŋ.

ṗasna´, v.a. To make rattle or ring by pushing e.g. a door-bell. Wapasna.

ṗasni´, v.a. To extinguish a firebrand or a light, by sitting on it or pushing it into the ashes. Wapasni.

ṗasnoŋ´, v.a. To roast e.g. meat on a spit or stick. Wapasnoŋ.

ṗasnuŋ´, Cf. pasnoŋ.

ṗaso´ta, v.a. To use up by rubbing with the hand, as soap. Haipajaja wapasota.

ṗasṗa´ya, v.a. To make wet, to sponge; in a vulgar sense, as also tawiŋtoŋ, to have sexual intercourse. Wapaspaya.

ṗasṫaŋ´k̇a, v.a. To moisten; in a vulgar sense, as tawiŋtoŋ, to have coitus. Syn.- paspaya.

ṗasṫaŋ´k̇iya, v.a. To cause to take off the hair, as in dressing a skin. Pastaŋwakiya.

ṗasṫo´, v.a. To smooth, brush down e.g. the hair. Wapasto. Cf. kasto.

ṗasṫo´ iḣpáya, v.n. To fall on one's hands and knees, or on one's face. - iwáḣpaya. - iyuŋka. Makata pasto iḣpeic'iye. B.H.43.11;133.9. Bl.

ṗasṫo´sṫo, v. red. of pasto. - iḣpeic'iyapi, i.e. get on their knees with heads on the ground. - iwaḣpaye. Bl. B.H.109.1.

ṗasṫo´ya, v.a. To cause to brush down. Pastowaya. -- adv. Brushing down.

pasu´, n. The human nose; the beak or bill of birds.

pasu´blaska, n. A broad-billed duck.

ṗasu´ṫa, v.a. (suta). To make stiff and hard by kneading, as dough. Wapasuta.

ṗaswu´ v. To push into, bury, as in a barrel of corn; to cut into strings. - iyeya, To make rattle, as corn by pushing into it. Taha - , To make fringes on a skin.

ṗaswu´ic'igle, v. To squeeze one's self in, to be important, obtrusive. Paswumic'igle. Bl.

ṗaswu´pi, n. Fringe, fringes.

ṗaswu´swu, v. red. of paswu.

ṗaswu´ya, v.a. To rattle by pushing. -- adv. Rattling.

ṗaśa´, v.a. (śa). To make red by rubbing. Wapaśa.

ṗaśib´, cont. of paśipa. - iyeya.

ṗaśi´bśib, red. of paśib.

ṗaśi´bśiṗa, v. red. of paśipa.

ṗaśi´ca, v.a. (śica). To spoil with the hands or by rubbing; to soil, injure. Wapaśica.

ṗaśi´cahowaya, v.a. (śicahowaya). To make cry out by pushing with the hand; to push or punch and make cry out. Wapaśicahowaya.

ṗaśi´ḣtiŋ, v. To make badly, to do a thing incorrectly.

ṗaśi´ṗa, v.a. To bend something giving it another form. Wapaśipa.

ṗaśka´, v.a. To loosen by pressure, as in untieing a knot. Bl.

ṗaśkaŋ´gle, v. To take as a sign, perhaps. Bl. Note: wiṗaśkaŋglepi seems only to be used.

ṗaśk̇a´ṗa, v. To make a noise with one's hands in water. Wapaśkapa. Cf. kaśkapa.

ṗaśkeb´, cont. of paśkepa. - iyeya. Bl.

ṗaśke´haŋ, v. To push or toss away. - iyeya, To push sideways with the head, toss away. - kuwa. Syn.- pakab iyeya.

ṗaśk̇ē´ṗa, Same as paskepa.

ṗaśk̇i´ca, v.a. To press out with the hand, not by twisting but pressing. Note: yuśkica, To wring. Wapaśkica.

ṗaśk̇i´śk̇a, v.a. To disarrange by rubbing. Wapaśkiśka.

ṗaśk̇i´ṫa, v.a. To press, squeeze out by pressing. Wapaśkita.

ṗaśkō´kṗa, v.a. To make a cavity or ditch by pressure with the hands, or by sitting. Wapakokpa.

ṗaśku´, v.a. To shell corn, by pressing a stick between the rows of kernels and thus prying them off. Bl.

ṗaśla´, v.a. (śla). To make bare, rub off e.g. hair. Wapaśla.

paśla´, adj. Bald-headed. Note: this is used only of animals such as turkeys.

ṗaśla´ya, v.a. To cause to make bare. Paślawaya.

pa´ślayela, (?). - s'e wóyaka yo, i.e. tell the full truth. La. Syn.- hepáśpupi s'e.

ṗaśle´ca, v.a. To split something hard or heavy by pressure. Wapaśleca.
ṗaślel´, cont. of paśleca. - iyeya.
ṗaśle´śleca, v. red. of paśleca.

ṗaślo´k̇a, v.a. To push or shove off e.g. one's coat sleeve. Wapośloka.

ṗaślu´śluta, v. To keep popping up. Na hucaŋ kiŋ lila paśluślutapi. MS.481.

ṗaślu´ta, v. To loom up. - hinapa, To loom up before one suddenly, as when passing through a draw unseen and thence coming up and into sight. WE.

ṗaśna´, v.a. To miss while thrusting or pushing. Wapaśna.

paśni´ja, v. (?). Bl.

ṗaśṗa´, v. To cut or break a piece off with a knife pressing hard.
ṗaśṗa´śṗa, v. red. of paśpa.

ṗaśṗe´k̇iya, v.a. To cause to break off, to cause to come out, perhaps as does a stain. Paśpewakiya.

ṗaśpe´śni, adj. Indelible. Bl.

ṗaśṗe´ya, v.a. To cause to come out, as a stain etc. Paśpewaya.

ṗaśṗu´, v.a. To break off, as a bulb or excrescence; to loosen and make fall off by pushing; to wash out, as a stain. Hepáśpupi s'e woyaka yo, Tell all about it. (He, Lice, and -) Wapaśpu.
ṗaśṗu´śṗu, v.a. red. (paśpu). To break off or cut in pieces e.g. a cake. Wapaśpuśpu.

ṗaśṫaŋ´, v.a. To soak and take the hair off, as from a hide. Wapaśtaŋ.

ṗaśtu´ta, v. To rub perhaps, as the feet with snow. ED.

ṗaśu´ja, v.a. To crush with the hand; to break or mash by punching.
ṗaśuś´, cont. of paśuja. - iyeya.

ṗaśu´śuja, v. red. (paśuja). To mash up, break in pieces e.g. bones. Wapaśuśuja.

ṗaśwo´ka, v.n. To come over, overflow.

ṗaś'a´k̇a, v.a. To push of strike with too little force to penetrate, to dent. Wapaś'aka.

ṗata´, adv. Together, crowded. - iheya, They crowd together. -- v.a. To cut out and sew up, as in making a tent. Wapata.

pa´ṫa, v.a. To cut up e.g. meat. Wapáta. Nupiŋ wicao, pte, na wicapata. -- n. A grove of timber. R. MG. Bl. Syn.- hiŋta. Cf. caŋpata.

ṗatag´, cont. (pataka). To come to a stop after running, as horses do; to stop short. - inajiŋ. D.19,77,271.
ṗata´gtag, cont. red. of patag. - iŋyaŋka. Bl.
ṗatag´ya, v.a. To prevent, scare. Patagmayayelo, okit'emayayelo. Bl. -- v.n. To stop short. -- adv. Haltingly. Also, nat'uŋgyakel. SI. Syn.- kokipeya.
ṗatag´yakel, adv. Bringing to a stop. Bl. Syn.- okit'eyakel.
ṗata´k̇a, v. To dodge about, run here and there; to come to a stand, as a horse does. - inajiŋ. Patake śni keś katiŋyeya iyaya po. R. Bl.
ṗata´ktaka, v. To stop. Taŋyaŋ uŋkomanipi; yuŋkaŋ kal ecela uŋpataktakapi, i.e. stopped. Bl.

ṗaṫaŋ´, v.a. To esteem highly; to take care of, to save. Wapataŋ. Miniśa waśtek̇ce kiŋ lehaŋ yapataŋ yelo. B.H. 178.20; - najiŋ, To resist. - mauŋpi s'elececa, They seem to be against me, seem to push me away. - iyeya, To save things.

ṗataŋ´, v.a. To mash up e.g. potatoes. Wapataŋ. Also, to feel for by pushing with anything other than the hand. Wapataⁿ. -- ṗaṫáⁿhaⁿ, part. Pushing against.

ṗataⁿ'iⁿ, v.a. To rub and make appear. Wapataⁿiⁿ. -- ṗatáⁿiⁿśni, v.n. To rub off, to obliterate. Wapataⁿiⁿśni.

ṗataⁿ'ka, v.a. To push out, make larger by pushing. Wapataⁿka. Also, pataⁿkal iyeya. Pataⁿkal hiyuya. B.H.52.15;130.9.

ṗaṫaⁿ'ṫaⁿ, v. red. of paṫaⁿ. Pataⁿtaⁿpi s'e mayani hwo? i.e. you walk as though they were pushing you on. Bl.

ṗataⁿ'taⁿ, v. red.(of pataⁿ). To push into, as a stick into the sand in hunting for tortoise eggs, feeling around with the stick. Kepataⁿtaⁿ. -- ṗatáⁿtaⁿyaⁿ, adv. Pushing for e.g. turtle eggs in the sand. - kuwa.

ṗa'ṫaⁿwaⁿjila, adv. Directly, in one path, with one purpose, unchangeable.

ṗaṫaⁿ'yaⁿ, adj. Reserving, keeping.

ṗataⁿ'yaⁿ, adv. Pushing against.

pa'ṫapi, n. A cutting up of meat.

ṗaṫe'ca, v.a. To make new, rub up and make new again, to furbish. Wapateca.

ṗaṫe'ṗa, v.a. To wear off by rubbing, to wear out by pressure, as the spring on a wagon. Wapatepa.

ṗaṫi', cont. of patica. - iyeya.

ṗaṫi'ca, v.a. To work up, by pressing on e.g. dough when sticky and soft; to shove, to push. Wapatica. -- paṫíl, cont. of patica. Paṫimahel - iyeya, To shove into the house. -- ṗaṫima iyeya, hiyuya, v. To push in, as a person into a room. To thrust, force into. FE. D.44.

ṗatiⁿ', adj. Stiff, as a new ribbon; firm, not springing or yielding; stiff with the cold. Mapatiⁿ. Cf. katiⁿ, satiⁿ. -- ṗatíⁿyaⁿ, v.a. To cause to become stiff. Patiⁿwaya.

pati'ṫaⁿ, v.a. To push against, to push e.g. a wheelbarrow. Wapatitaⁿ. -- ṗatíṫaⁿyaⁿ, adv. Pushing against.

patḱa'śa, n. A small species of turtle that lives in the water. Cf. keglezela. Also, patḱáśala.

ṗatḱu'ǧa, v.a. To break in square pieces by pushing or punching. BD. Wapatkuga. -- ṗatḱúḣ, cont. of patkuga. - iyeya. -- ṗatḱútḱuǧa, v. red.

ṗato'ḱaheya, v.a. To push to the front. B.H.93.2.

ṗato'kaⁿl iyeya, v. To push aside. Also, paṫókaⁿl iyeya. Patókaⁿl iyéwaya. Cf. pahá iyeya.

ṗaṫoⁿ'waⁿwaⁿ, (?). - iyeya. Iśta kiⁿ - iyewakiyelo, i.e. to rub one's eyes in order to see better. Bl. - iyeyiⁿ na taⁿyaⁿ ables waciⁿ yo. Bc.

patu'ja, v.n. To bend over, lean forward, stoop down to get something. Wapatuja. -- paṫuś, cont. of patuja. - inajiⁿ, To stand bent over forward. - hotoⁿkel śkaⁿ. -- ṗaṫúśṫuś, v. red. - iyaya, Pass on by stooping. Bl. -- paṫúśya, v.a. To cause to bend forward or stoop, to make bow down. Patuśwaya.

ṗat'a', v.a. To kill by pressure, as by lying on. Wapat'a. -- ṗat'át'a, v.n. To be numb; to be asleep, as a limb.

pat'ē'ca, v.a. To make soft by pressing e.g. fruit. Wapat'eca.

ṗat'i'ḣpeya, Cf. pat'a and iḣpeya.

ṗat'iⁿs', cont. of pat'iⁿza. - iyeya. -- ṗat'iⁿst'iⁿza, v. red. of pat'iⁿza.

ṗat'iⁿ'za, v.a. To make stiff by kneading, as in mixing up bread, to press down tight. Wapat'iⁿza.

ṗauⁿ'ka, v.a. To push and make fall down. Wapauⁿka. Colloq., to eat one out of grub (push down), one who gives a feast. CG.

ṗawa'ǧa, v.a. To roll or twist in the hand. Wapawaga.

pa'waksa, v.a. To behead. Pawawaksa.

pa'wak'iⁿ, n. A saddle, pack-saddle.

ṗawaⁿ'ƙal, adv. Upward. - iyeya, To shove up, raise. - yuza, To hold up high. Pb.17. B.H.244.10.

ṗawa'za, v.a. To rub and push, as one cow does to another. Also, to annoy or vex by pushing. R. Wapawaza. Cf. ikpawaza.

pa'we, v. To bleed at the nose.

ṗawe'ǧa, v.a. To break with the hand, but not entirely off, or by pushing, falling, sitting etc. Wapawega. Hehé kola lociⁿ wapáwegeȟcelo, i.e. when wanting food very badly. Bl.

pa' we hiyu, v. To bleed at the nose. Also, pawéhiyu. Pawemahiyu.

ṗaweȟ', cont. of pawega. - iyeya, To break with the hand, as a stick suddenly or quickly. -- ṗawéȟweǧa, v. red. of pawega. -- ṗawéȟya, v.a. To cause to break by pushing against. Paweȟwaya.

pa'weƙaluzapi, n. A violent bleeding of the nose, a sickness among the Indians of old. Bl.

ṗawe'we, v.a. To make bleed. Wapawewe. Mikpawewe, I made myself bleed.

ṗawi', (?). Cf. wáṗawi.

ṗawi'cegna, (?). - hiyuya. BT.

ṗawi'gnuni, v.a. (?). Wapawignuni. R. Bl.

ṗawi'ƙa, v.n. To be still strong, have some vitality left, as is said of a person that will die. Wapawika. Nahaȟci - . Cf. owik'e śni. -- adv. Many. BD.

ṗawiⁿȟ'ya, adv. Turning out of a straight direction.

ṗawiⁿ'ja, v.a. To bend or press down e.g. grain by one's weight, as in sitting on a branch, or a knife while cutting with it. Wapawiⁿja. -- ṗawíⁿś, cont. of pawiⁿja. - iyeya. -- ṗawíⁿświⁿja, v. red. (of pawiⁿja). To bend down, to make shake.

pawiⁿ'ta, v.a. To rub. Wapawiⁿta.

ṗawi's'e, adv. Crowded together, as cattle or sheep etc. Also, moving, as maggots. R. Bl. - iⁿyaⁿka. Note: this word seems to carry the idea of crawling over each other, as a moving mass.

ṗawi'ṫaya, v.a. (of witaya). To gather with the hand, as in gathering crumbs. Wapawitaya.

ṗa'witayela, adv. Sticking the heads together, as when crowding around a messenger to hear the news. Taku kápelaka: wozá hiⁿglapelo; wána el yucik'ayela el ahiyayelo; wana - el ahiyayelo. Bl.

ṗawi'wi, adv. red. (of pawi). In crowds. R. Bl. -- ṗawíwis'e, adv. (of pawis'e). Crowded together and moving en masse. Also, shaking. R. Bl. -- ṗawíya, adv. Teeming with e.g. flies on something. RA.

ṗawi'yaƙel, adv. Still strong, as is said of a person that will die. - ȟpaya. BD.

ṗawi'yakṗa, v.a. (of wiyakpa). To make shine, to polish, to brighten by rubbing. Wapáwiyakpa.

ṗawo'slaheyelakel, adv. Cf. pawoslata. Kitaⁿ - maⁿke c'oⁿ nawajiⁿ yelo. Bl.

ṗawo'slal, cont. of pawoslata. - iyeya, To push up e.g. a tent to make it stand. - egle. B.H.163.5. Also, with egle, To put something up such as a pole. Wowapi - iyeya, To hoist the flag. Natahe kpaⁿyaⁿpi kiⁿ ohomni waso na oⁿ tuśu kiⁿ hena paȟta na - eglepi. Na waⁿna caⁿ wákaⁿ kiⁿ - euⁿglepi. B.H.163.5. To set up straight.

ṗawo'slata, v. To push up straight.

paya' ṗejúṫa, n. Cf. caⁿhlogaⁿ wapośtaⁿ. BT. #24.

paya'ṫa, adv. In or at the head.

pa'yayala, Cf. yayála. Bl.

ṗaza', v.a. To stick up bushes, as the Dakotas did to sleep under; to put up, e.g. sticks, in a row closely together, as a fence. Wapaza. - egle. Cf. hupaza.

pa'za, adj. Bitter, as gall.

ṗazaṅ', v.a. To part or separate e.g. the hair. Wapazaṅ. Also, to hurt or kill by striking.

pazaṅ', adv. With the head concealed, as a hen in the bushes, i.e. with the head invisible. - ḣpaya. - egle, To conceal e.g. a stick in deep grass. Bl. Also, pasáṅ, perhaps.

ṗazaṅ'yaṅ, adv. Dividing, parting. Taté - , i.e. tatoheya, uṅglipi ktelo, i.e. go against the wind, parting the wind.

pazaṅ'yaṅ, adv. Under the brush, but without the idea of concealment. - iyuṅka, To sleep under the brush. Perhaps also, ṗazaṅyaṅ.

pa'zeca, adj. Bitter; fig., bitter, as in one's remarks. Bl.

pa'zeze, adv. Swinging, nodding. - maṅka. Also, letting the head drop, as in sleep. Also, pázezela, pázezeya, pázezeyela. - íśtiṅma.

ṗazi', v.a. To push into, as a stick into the sand in hunting for turtle eggs. Wapazi. R. Bl.

ṗazi'ca, v.a. To roll out or stretch with the hand, to stretch by pressing against. Wapazica. -- ṗazígzica, v. red.

ṗazo', v.a. To show, present anything in view. Wapazo. - yeṫó, Let me see. -- ṗazóḱiya, v. To cause to show. Pazowakiya.

ṗazuṅl', cont. of pazuṅta.

ṗazuṅ'ṫa, v.a. To sew or run up at the sides some distance from the edge e.g. of leggings, to lace. Wapazuṅta. D.228.

pazu'ya, v. To crack e.g. a bone, to break. Hu mapazuye, I cracked my bone. Ka. Cf. zuya.

pce'cela, adj. Short.

pcelye'la, adv. Awhile, for a short time, briefly.

pcepce'cela, adj. red. of pcecela.

pcepcel'yela, adv. red. of pcelyela.

ṗe, n. The top of the head. Pe awicaputaka na oyasiṅ asnipi.

ṗe, adj. Sharp, as edged tools; pointed.

ṗe, particle. The precating pl. imp. termination of verbs, used by women, while men say: po. Ecoṅ pe, Do ye do it.

ṗe, adv. The modal pl. ending, the old form for "pi", and used by women only.

ṗea'glaṫaṫa, v. To use all up, to exhaust one's supply by giving to others. Peawaglatata.

ṗea'gnagkiya, v.a. (?). Aṅpetu waṅji towaṅjica ca peagnagwicakiyiṅ ktelo, i.e. an all blue day is to shine on them. LP.

ṗeco'ḱaṅ, n. The scalp lock the Indians used to let grow on the back of the head, a round tuft.

Peco'ḱaṅ Haṅ'ska, n. prop. A Chinaman, i.e. the big scalp lock.

ṗeco'ḱaṅyaṅ, n. The scalp lock. - Haṅska, A Chinaman. -- ṗécoḱaṅyaṅkisoṅpi, n. The scalp lock.

pe'gnagḱiya, v.a. (of pegnaka). To cause to wear in the hair or on the head. Na tataṅka hiṅ paḣpa waṅ k'oṅ na - .

pe'gnaḱa, v. To wear in the hair or on the head e.g. a wotawe, a bunch of buffalo hair etc. D.36. -- ṗégnaḱapi, n. Ornaments worn in the hair or on the head, e.g. feathers etc.

ṗehaṅ', n. A crane. - s'e napakaza haṅskaska kaca, i.e. long fingers. Bl. -- peháṅska, The heron. -- peháṅ śa, The little blue heron. -- peháṅ ṫo, The great blue heron.

ṗehaṅ', v.a. To fold up anything. Wapehaṅ. - egnaka, To fold up and lay away.

ṗehaṅ'ġila, n. The gray or sand-bill crane.

ṗehaṅ'haṅ, v. red. (of pehaṅ). To fold up much or all. - egnake, To fold up all and lay away.

ṗehaṅ'saṅ, n. The large white crane.

pehiṅ', n. The hair of the head. Mapehiṅ.

ṗehiṅ'cicila, n. The killdeer, a plover.

ṗehiṅ'icasṫo, n. A hair brush.

ṗehiṅ'islaye, n. Hair oil.

ṗehiṅ' iyo'stola, n. A hair net.

ṗehiṅ' papo'a, n. A hair brush.

ṗehiṅ'ṗasise, n. Hair pins.

ṗehiṅ'ṫuṫa, adj. Dishevelled, unkempt. Pehiṅmatuta. Bl.

ṗeḣni'ġa, adj. Red hot. -- v.n. To be red hot. -- n. That which is heated to a red heat. Compare peśnija.

ṗeḣniḣ', cont. of peḣniga. -- ṗeḣniḣniġa, v. red. of peḣniga. -- ṗeḣniḣya, v.a. To make red hot. Peḣniḣwaya.

ṗeji', n. Grass, herbs, hay.
- blaskaska, Blue grass, perhaps.
- icape, pejiċape, A pitch fork.
- icaśla, pejiċaśla, A scythe.
- icaśla opé, pejiċaśla opé, A mowing sickle.
- háṅskaska psi iyececa, Hungarian or awnless brome grass. Bromus inermis. The grass family. BT. #41.
- hiṅkṗila, Moss; a short grass growing in light-green, mat-like patches.

pejiḣcaka, Slender wheat grass. Agropyron occidentalis. The grass family. Also called salt grass. When it is abundant and tall, it was said that the coming snow would reach to its head and horses etc. would eat just that. Bl. #185.
- ḣóta, Dark leaved mugwort. The composite family; a herb of whitish or grayishappearance: wild sage. Artemisia ludoviciana. #77.
- ḣota aṗé blaskaska, Prairie mugwort, the western or cudweed mugwort; white sage, artemisia gnaphalodes, sagebrush, wormwood, artemisia natroninsia. Composite family. BT. Bl. #63,146.
- ḣota ṗeṗé, A grass. (?).
- ḣota skúya, (?). A medicine.
- ḣota swúla, Silvery wormwood. Artemisia filifolia. Composite family. A medicine. Bl. #287.
- ḣota śicamna, Rabbit brush, the rayless goldenrod. Chrysothamnus graveolens. Bl. #188.
- ḣota taṅka, Big sage brush. A medicine.
- ḣota totó, Blue sage brush. A medicine.
- ḣota waśtemna, Pasture sage brush, wormwood sage. Artemisia frigida. The composite family. Bl. #64.
- icaśla (of kaśla). A scythe.
- inakse, A mowing machine.
- iṅkpa, Oats. Also, wayahota.
- ipaḣte, A baler; a bundle.
- ité oṅ aśniýakiyapi, Cf. ite aśniyaṅpi. Also, pejijiji. #186.
- iṫokśu, A hay rack.
- iwiċakoyaka, Dark-green bulrush. Scirpus atrovirens. Sedge family. Buffalo grass. Buchloe dactyloides. The grass family. Also, sipáwicaśe. There are two specimens, one male and the other female. EM. #69,182.
- iyuhiṅte, A hay rake.
- iyúwaṅka aya, v. To unload a wagon into a barn.

pejiǰiji, Cf. peji ite oṅ aśniyakiyapi (tickle). #186.

pejiḱaśla, v. To cut hay or grass, to mow. Pejiwakaśla.
- miċapeca, Cf. micapeca.

pejiṅakse, A mowing machine. Cf. peji inakse.
- oakśu, A wisp of hay; what hay one can hold in his arms or on a fork. P. Bl.
- ojupi, A lawn. P.
- okaśla, A place to cut hay, a meadow, hay ground.
- ókihe totó, A grass growing along rivers.
- okiǰaṫa, Grama grass, mesquite grass. Bouteloua oligostachya. The grass family. Most specimens of these plants have two spikes. But for the sake of sport, the Indians would hunt for those with three; spikes one and three are gray. YW. #224.
- onakseyapi, Hay land.
- owiṅja, A tick.

pejiṗaha, A hay stack.

pejiṗata aye, A hay stacker.
- psuṅpsúṅla, Heavy sedge. Carex gravida. The sedge family. Bl. #184.

pejiptaptahaṅ, adv. In stacks.

- skuya, Barnyard grass, cockspur grass, water grass. Echinochloa crus-galli. The grass family. Bl. #230.
- suksúta, Alkali grass, salt or marsh spike grass. Distichlis spicata. The plant cannot be eaten. Bl. #175.
- swula, Same as waŋyeca swula. BT.
- swula cik'ala, The low milkweed. Asclepias pumila. The Milkweed family. Also called ceśloślo pejuta, or ȟaŋte iyececa. They make tea of it for children who have diarrhoea. Bl. BT. #89.

pejíśaśa, A grass that cattle do not eat.
- śaśa iŋkpa jiji, Indian grass. Sorghastrum nutans. The grass family. Bl. #243.
- śaśa óǩihe taŋǩíŋkiŋyaŋ, Blue stem, forked beard grass. Andropogon furcatus. The grass family. Bl. #240.
- śaśa swula, Beard grass, little blue stem, broom beard grass. Andropogon scoparius. The grass family. Bl. #242.
- śicamna, June grass, spear grass, Kentucky blue grass. Poa prattensis. Bl. #293.
- takáŋ, Sand dropseed, rush grass. Sporobolus cryptandrus. The gray grass family. It is so called because the sheath is as tough as takaŋ. Bl. #85.
- takáŋ kaza, The three-awned bemch grass, wire grass. Aristida purpurea. The grass family. Lhb. #201.

pejítokśu, A hay rack. Cf. peji itokśu.
- uŋkcékcela, Sand burs.
- uŋkcéla, The sandbur. R. Small burr-grass. Cenchrus carolinianus. The grass family. #23.
- wabluśka, An insect, the walking stick. WE.
- wacáŋǧa, Sweet grass.
- wakaŋ, Scribner's panic grass. Panicum scribnerianum. Horses die eating it. WE. Bw. BH. #98.
- woǩéya oti kiŋ, Same as susuni.

pejíyuhiŋta, v. To rake hay.
- yuskíta kutepi, A pastime for boys.
- zizi, Gutierrezia, broomweed. Gutierrezia Sarothrae. The composite family. The Indians make a tea of the whole plant, boiling it, for coughing and colds. WE. BT. #59.

pejo'gnake, n. A hay loft.

peju'ta, n. Medicine. Lit., grass-roots.
- gmigmela, Round medicine, pills.
- ha sapa, Cf. pejuta waȟ'e śa. Bl. #165.
- hu ókihe toŋtoŋ, A medicine used for sore joints. (?).
- ȟáka, A medicine. (?).
- icu śi, v. To prescribe a medicine.
- jaŋjaŋ s'ele, Alum.
- niǧe taŋka, The bush morning glory. Ipomoea leptophylla. The morning glory family. BS. heard from his grand-mother that in olden days when there were no matches they used to start fire in the roots, wrap them up and hang them outside. The fire would keep seven months (petaga). As a medicine, the root is used. The kernel of the large root is eaten raw. Bl. Old CD. scraped some off the big root to eat when he had stomach trouble. HM. #18.
- sapa, Coffee.
- sapsápa, The narrow-leaved puccoon. Lithospermum angustifolium. The borage family. A medicine. Bh. #155.
- ska hu, A plant like astragalus recemosus or canadensis; locoweed, milk vetch or tragacanth. Ho. calls it pejuta zi, the root being so colored. The roots were BT.'s big medicine for pains of the chest and back; the roots are pulverized and chewed. It can be used with another herb against spitting blood. A tea of the roots is taken for coughing. Ho. BT.
- skuya, The slender milkweed. Astragalus parviflorus. The pulse family. The roots are medicinal. Mothers chew the roots when they have no milk.
- swula, Same as waŋyeca swula. Bw.
- tiŋpsila, A medicine. (?).
- totó, A medicine. (?).
- wahiŋheya iṗiye, Same as caŋȟlogaŋ maka tola. Bl. #12.
- waȟ'e śa, The hairy puccoon, hairy gromwell, red-root. Lithospermum gmelini. The borage family. Also, pejuta ha sapa, for a black skin covers the red root. They make a powder of the roots and let people take it when they are wounded in the chest. A girl who had been shot through the chest was treated with this powder as a medicine and recovered inspite of a doctor's prediction of death. L.
- wicaśa, A medicine man, a physician.

peju'taya, v.a. To use as a medicine.

B.H.123.3.

ṗel, n. cont. (of peta). Fire.

ṗela'ƙigle, v. To place pith on one's arm, light it and let it burn until up thereon. To stand it was bravery. Pelawakigle. Cf. akigle.

ṗeli'cagla, adv. Near the fire, by the fire.

ṗeli'cu, n. A little coal shovel.

ṗeli'jaŋjaŋ, n. A torch, lamp. - ihupa, A candle stick. P. - iŋkpa, A lamp chimney. -- ṗelíjaŋjaŋ ska, n. A candle. -- ṗelíjaŋjaŋ wigli, n. Lamp oil, kerosene. -- ṗelíjaŋjaŋpi, n. A torch. B.H.75.22.

ṗeli'jaŋjaŋye, n. A lamp. B.H.247.1.

ṗeli'kceya, adv. Over fire. - ceoŋpa, To roast over fire. B.H.53.1.

ṗeli'leyapi, n. Something to light a fire with; kindlings.

ṗeli'mna śni, (?). Not afraid of fire. LB.

ṗeli'ṗoġaŋ, n. Bellows.

ṗeli'śƙaŋ, v.n. To draw near the fire, warm one's self. Pelimaśkaŋ.

peli'yaglaśyahaŋ, (?). Peliyaglaśyahelo, i.e. The fire is glimmering under the ashes. Bl.

ṗelkaŋ'ye, adv. Near the fire. Also, ṗelƙáŋyela.

ṗelko'kipa, v. To be afraid of fire. Kimimila ska s'e pelkokipe śni yelo. Bl.

ṗelmna', 1) v.n. To smell of fire. 2) adj. Smelling of fire, smelling burnt. Pelmnaśni naŋkahaŋpelo, i.e. when there is no heat in the house. Bl. -- ṗelmnámnaya, v. red. (of pelmnaya). To roast beef, turning it around all the time.

ṗelmna'ya, v. To make smell of fire. Pelmnayaŋpo, hecel waśte yelo, i.e. start a fire. Bl.

ṗelna'kpakpa, v.n. (of peta and nakpakpa). To crackle, as fire. Bl. Syn.- namnumnuza.

ṗelwi'yuśkiŋ, (?). The word is used of fire when in it the sparks are flying from little explosions. - yelo. Bl.

ṗel'i'yucaŋyaŋkel, (?). - naŋka hwo? Bl.

ṗel'ƙi'toŋkel, (?). - naŋka hwo? i.e. stay near fire? Bl.

ṗe'maƙiwoṫo, v. perhaps. The head to strike the ground. - gliḣpeya. B.H. 184.25. -- ṗémaƙiwoṫoya, adv. The head striking the ground. B.H.112.14.

ṗemni', 1) adj. Warped, twisted, crooked. 2) v.n. To warp, twist, to become crooked, become entangled. -- ṗemnímni, v. red. of pemni. -- ṗemníyaŋ, adv. Crookedly, perversely, twisting.

peo'wiwila, n. The soft spot in the top of an infant's cranium.

peō'zaŋ, n. The line where the hair of the head is divided, parted.

ṗeṗe', adj. red. (of pe). Prickly, jagged. Maza - , Barbed wire. Uŋkcela - . -- ṗeṗéya, adv. Prickly, sharp or rough, as a frozen road. - hiyeya.

pesle'te, n. The top of the head. Na - el awicaputaka. - owíŋġe, The crown of the head. R. Bl. - owamniomni.

pesle'teśa, n. The red comb of a cock chicken.

ṗe'sṫo, adj. Sharp-pointed; a grayhound, n. -- ṗésṫola, adj. Sharp-pointed; the diamond in cards, n. -- ṗesṫósṫola, adj. red. of pestola. -- ṗestóstoya, adv. red. of pestoya. D.67.

ṗe'sṫoya, adv. In a sharp-pointed manner. -- adj. perhaps. Pointed. Tokala s'e ite cik'aya, ite - , cehupa cik'eik'a kaca, i.e. when a man has a very small face. Bl. -- ṗéstoyela, adv. In a sharp-pointed manner. Yuŋkaŋ iŋyaŋ waŋ icu zizipela ca na he - kaga.

ṗe'śa, n. The headgear used in the Omaha dance.

Pe'śa, n. prop. The Kwapas.

peśa', n. The comb of the domestic rooster or hen, the fleshy crest or caruncle on the head of a domestic cock or hen. Also, a headgear used in a certain dance and is made of porcupine skin, the Omahas being the first to use it. FR. Cf. pesleteśa.

ƥe'śa, n. The jack in playing cards.

ƥeśka', n. The air-bladder of a fish. It is sometimes used for making glue, and hence the name, coⁿpeśka.

pe'śni, adj. Dull, as a knife.

ƥeśni'ja, n. Sparks of fire. Peta ca kaħwoka caⁿna - . - akáħwagmayayelo, i.e. while smoking. Bl.

ƥeť, cont. of peta. Thus, in petijaⁿjaⁿ.

ƥe'ťa, n. Fire.

ƥeťa'ǧa, n. Burning coals. - kiciiⁿpi, A pastime practiced by boys to test one's bravery, throwing burning pieces of wood at each other. Bl.

ƥeťa'gaiceoⁿpa, v. To broil on the coals. Petagaicewaoⁿpa.

ƥeťa'kigle, Cf. pelakigle.

ƥeťaⁿl', adv. On the fire. - iħpeya, To throw on or in the fire. B.H.195.9.

pe'ta yuha'la, n. The walking fire, night fire, will o'the wisp, ignis fatuus. This is well known to the Indians who see all sorts of colors. It is sometimes near the ground, but also high up. They know that it may come from rotten wood, but do not know it originates in swampy places, esp. along the upper White River.

ƥeťi'jaⁿjaⁿ, n. A lamp.
- agleħaⁿ, A candle stick. Bl.
- ǧeǧéya, A lantern. Bl.
- iħupa, A candle stick. R. Bl.
- iyókaśtaⁿ, A funnel to pour oil into a lamp. Bl.
- iyukse, A candle snuffer. R. Bl.
- jaⁿjáⁿ wosláħaⁿ, A lamp chimney.
- ośtáⁿ, A candle stick. Bl.
- ska, A candle.
- ska oognake, A candle stick.B.H.60. 25.

peťi'jaⁿjaⁿye, A lamp, perhaps. B.H. 300.4.
- yuha omanipi, A lantern.

ƥeťi'leyapi, n. Kindling.

ƥeťi'leye, n. Kindling. Wazizi - , Pine wood kindling. LB. - wiⁿyeya gnakapi caⁿke yuile icupi; but D. says this would be better pelileye. D.279.

ƥeťi'śkaⁿ, v.n. To draw near the fire, warm one's self. Petimaśkaⁿ.

ƥeťka'gla, adv. (of peta and kagla). Near the fire, by the fire.

ƥeťka'ile s'e, adv. In the manner of fanning a fire. - yainaⁿkelo, You run with swinging arms.

ƥeťki'yela, adv. Near the fire.

ƥeťō'kalic'iya, v. refl. To warm one's self on a fire. -- ƥeťókalya, v.a. To warm up the fire. Petokalwaya.

ƥeťo'wayake, n. Any big piece of wood laid in the stove to keep up the fire over night. Caⁿ taⁿka ileya ayaⁿpa kta iyececa; sni okihi śni. Also, petowoyake.

ƥeťu'sƥe, n. A firebrand.

ƥeťu'sťe, n. A firebrand to start another fire with. Caⁿ haⁿke Huħnage śni yaⁿke kiⁿ - eciyapi. R.

ƥe'wiwila, n. The soft spot in the cranium of infants. Note: peówiwila is more often used.

pe'ya, adj. or adv. Sharp, as edged tools. Wahiⁿkpe k'oⁿ he yumaⁿ. Hecel lila - kaga na nakuⁿ pestola. - pamaⁿpi. MS.481.

ƥeyo'haⁿ, n. The line running over the middle of the head from the forehead, the parting of the hair. Also, ƥeyóhaⁿla.

peyo'zaⁿ, n. The place which is left on the head by separating the hair, a part.

ƥezi', n. The king in playing cards.

pi, n. The liver. Mapí. Wicápi. Tapi, The liver of animals. Cf. pica, abbrev.

pi, suff. The common pl. termination of verbs, nouns, pronouns, adjectives and sometimes adverbs and prepositions. It often becomes "pe" before yelo, when the "ye" is lost; e.g. hecoⁿpe lo for hecoⁿpi yelo.

pica', adj. Good. Taku - yuha śni icíkte. Bl.

pi'ca, v. aux. It has the force of "caⁿ" and conveys the idea of power or possibility. Ecoⁿpica, That can be done. Na taku ecoⁿpicaśni ecoⁿ keyapi. Opte iyayepica śni waⁿ el kuśeya najiⁿ. Wakaⁿtaⁿka tawoope ateuⁿyaⁿpi etaⁿhaⁿ uⁿkicupi kiⁿ hena kicaksauⁿpicapi śni. Mapica śni. B.H.68.14;153.6. Paiⁿlpica. Opta iyayepica śni waⁿ el kuśeya najiⁿ. Kisakauⁿpicapi śni. Woope kiⁿ kisaksauⁿpicapi śni. Taku slolyepica śni k'uⁿ. Iyauⁿpemapica śni. B.H.139.12,16. Pi, abbrev. of pica. Eḣpeye pi, Able to hit. RA.

pica'ka, v. aux. It sometimes has the force of pica, and sometimes with that of pica śni. The "ka" may in some cases be interrogative. -- adj. A little good, a little better than some other.

pica'lake, adj. More perfect than some other. - ciⁿ he icu yo, i.e. take the best one.

pica'śni, v. It cannot be, it is impossible.

pica'ya, adv. Well.

pi'ġa, v.n. To boil, i.e. foaming, bubbling, as heated water etc. Na waⁿna iⁿyaⁿ k'eya kate k'oⁿ caⁿ okijata oⁿ icu na el ognaka na oyasiⁿ el ognaka na lila piga.

pi'ġes'e, adv. Bubbling with a noise, as a swimmer but with a bubbling noise, with bubbles rising. Cf. piga.

piḣya', adv. Boiling. - haⁿ, To stand boiling. Also, ipiḣya. R. Na cega waⁿ piḣyáhe k'oⁿ ekta oyujuⁿta.

pii'c'iya, v. refl. (of piya). To prepare one's self, get ready. Pimic'iya. Syn.- kisíⁿc'iya. Bl.

piki'cila, v. To be glad or thankful with or for another, to take part with one in his thankfulness. Piwecila.

piki'ciya, v. To make one well. Bl.

piki'la, v.n. To be thankful, glad. Piwakila.

piki'ya, v.t. To mend, repair, reset, rearrange one's own. D.22. Piwakiya.

piki'ya, piki'ya, v. To get one's bed ready. Sa. Waⁿna piyakiyiⁿ na inuⁿkiⁿ kte, i.e. now you make ready to go to sleep, don't you? Bl. Also, to doctor, treat; to conjure, as the Dakotas do to doctor. Piwakiya. D.59,226. ES.

pila', v.n. To rejoice, be glad, thankful. Piwala, piyala, piuⁿlapi. Pb.29. -- piláic'iya, v. refl. To make one's self thankful. -- pilákiya, v.a. To make glad, make thankful. Pilawakiya. -- piláya, 1) v.a. To make glad. Pilawaya. Pilamaya. 2) adv. Gladly. -- pilíc'iya, v. refl. To make one's self thankful.

pilya', (?). Pilyapelo, i.e. they ate up all the grass. Bl.

piⁿ'ja, adj. Destitute of hair.

piⁿ'kpa, n. The top, as of a tower etc. B.H.9.4.

piⁿ'ksihu, n. Same as saⁿtuhu taⁿka, i.e. in water. Bl.

piⁿśpiⁿ'jela, adj. Thin, scattering, as hair or grass.

piⁿ'zece, adj. perhaps. Becoming small, little, dwindling down, as snow, a crowd. Wa kiⁿ - ciⁿhu. Wana - lo. Bl. Cf. yupiⁿpiⁿtapi s'e.

pipi'ya, adv. red. (of piya). Well, anew; again and again, thoroughly. - kipaⁿpi, Again and again they called to him. - iyuⁿka, Again and again he settled down, i.e. in a lying position. D.20,52,81.

pi'saⁿsaⁿ oḣ'aⁿ'ke, (?). This is used when a man gets an idea of doing something and starts at once doing it without thinking it over before. One is said to have had a pisaŋ and died of it. Sb.

ṗiṡṗi'za, n. The prairie dog; the ground squirrel.

ṗi'ṡṗiza, v. red. (of piza). To squeal as a ground squirrel when caught, to make a noise with the lips, as in whistling for a dog.

ṗiṡṗi'za tawo'te, n. Fetid marigold, false dog-fennel. Dyssodia papposa. The composite family. One of BT.'s medicines: he pulverizes the leaves and gives them to people when they find breathing difficult. BT. #34.

ṗi'śko, n. The night hawk. Also, piś. Piśko waśiŋ aglipi hehaŋl. The piśko returns last of all the birds. At that time the grass is in good condition and the buffalo are fat. So piśko brings on the fat. Piśko s'e hokśi yuha wóśikśice ke, as is said of a woman who loses her children through carelessness. Piśko is said to lay her eggs any place, having no nest. LP. Piśko ca wanigle s'e uŋglahaŋpi, as is said when we cannot get on fast going home. The night hawks do a lot of flying around in the fall while other birds go south directly (wanigla). RA.

ṗiśle'ca, n. The spleen.

ṗiśṗi'ja, adj. red. (of pija). Wrinkled. Mapiśpija. - hiyeya, To shrivel. -- ṗiśṗi'jela, adj. Wrinkled or shrivelled, as one's hands from being in water; withered. Mapiśpijela. -- ṗi'śṗiś, cont. of piśpija. - hiŋgla, To become wrinkled. Bl.

ṗiya', v.a. (of pi, good). To make anew, mend up, repair. Piwaya. To conjure the sick.

ṗi'ya, adv. Well anew; again. - kaga, To mend, make anew. Tokata - inicagapi ktelo. MS.355. D.22.

ṗiya' iyotake, v. To move away in a sitting position. WE.

ṗi'ya iyukcaŋ, v. To take another view of; to change one's mind.

ṗiye', Same as piyá.

ṗiye'leś, adv. Notwithstanding; heedlessly. It is used of one who does not listen to what is said to him. But the word is not used. Bl. WE.

ṗiye'ṗica, adj. Reparable. Piyepicaśni, That cannot be repaired.

ṗi'za, v.n. To creak, as a shoe. Cf. kiza.

ṗizi', n. The gall. Mapizi. Iŋśe he tataŋka pizi waŋ ota latkaŋ ca oŋ aiyahaŋble lo.

ṗizo', n. Same as heyoka. - waŋ u welo. Bl.

ṗō, v.n. To swell, puff out. Mapó.

ṗo, suff. The pl. termination of verbs in the imp. mood. It is probably formed from "pi" and "wo".

pōb, cont. of popa. - iyaya, and - hiŋgla, To burst out, snap suddenly. -- pobyá, adv. Snapping, popping with a sudden noise, as when hitting a table with one's knuckles. - awaṗelo.

ṗō'ġaŋ, 1) v.a. To blow, as with the mouth. Wapógaŋ. 2) v.n. To spread out, as a bladder when blown. Le pejuta waŋ tatuye topa oyasiŋ wapogaŋ kta. - na yatkaŋ yo, i.e. when things are hot. Bl.

po'ġe, n. The nose. Perhaps <u>ma</u>poge. - glujiŋca, To blow the nose.

Po'ġe Hlo'ka, n. prop. The Nez Percé Indians. Also, n. The nostrils.

pogiŋ'jo, v. To sniff, as when breathing causes a whistling sound in the nose. Bl.

ṗogo', n. Same as wicaśa itaŋcaŋ, wakicoŋza. It is apparently an old word. Pogo uŋyaŋkapelo, as they might say to a new-comer. GS. Lc. A.

po'ha, 1) adj. Having a lot of hair and all unkempt; standing up and moving, as long hair. Pehiŋ mapóha. 2) v.a. To make the hair stand up by running the fingers through it. Wapóha.

po'hahas'e, adv. Shaking, as a buffalo

shaking his head. R. -- póhas'e, adv. Having an abundance of hair,on the head, that stands out disorderly.

po'ȟcante, n. The wings of the human nose. Bl.

poȟwo'mnankel, adv. Cf. pójanjan. Bl.

ṗoi'ṗiye, n. The name for any medicine good for swellings. Cf. śunkcankahupiye. WE. BT. RT. #21,115,158. Cf. hitunkala nakpala.

po'janjan, v. To snuff up, as an animal does the wind; to snuff, sniff, scent, as a dog does. Cf. póśin.

po'ḱimnamna, v.a. (of pomnamna). To shake the head at one. Powakimnamna,

po'ksan, v. To shake the head to the right and left. Wapoksan. - s'e, Shaking the head to the right and left.

ṗol, cont. of pota.

ṗolṗo'ṫa, adj. red. (of pota). Worn out. -- ṗolṗóṫanhan, part. red. (of potahan). Full of holes, torn, ragged, as a worn-out garment.

po'mnamna, v. To shake the head, as in refusing or denying a thing. Wapomnamna. Cf. pakáhunka. -- pómnamnaḱiya, v. To shake or wag the head at. Pomnamnawakiya. Also, pomnamnaḱiya, To cause to wag the head.

po'nunuje, n. The lower part of the nose. Bl.

ṗonṗon', adj. Rotten, as wood; soft. Also, ṗonṗónla.

poo'waśte, n. Cf. waȟpe pa. BT. #228.

pō'ṗa, v.n. To burst.

ṗoṗo', v.n. red. (of ṗo). To swell, puff out. Also perhaps, popó

popo'ṗa, adj. Full of pith. -- n. Cotton. Owinja - . -- popóṗes'e, adv. As is said of nap on a blanket or fine fur on a robe.

ṗoṗo'tḱa, n. A screech-owl, hinhan. Its call: Hohí', hohí'. Also, popotkala. Same as paglá, osniko, ungnagicala.

ṗoṗo'tḱaḱiya, v.t. To silence one by one's argument or saying, for the popotka is said not to move when shot. Is.

ṗo'ptan, v. To turn one's head, in one direction perhaps. Hinhán makotila s'e - waśicun, as is said of a person who is rubber-necked,i.e. turning the head all round like a burrowing owl. Bl.

po'pṫanpṫan, v.n. To shake the head, signify dissent. Powaptanptan. Cf. pomnamna. -- póptanptanḱiya, v. To shake the head at. Poptanptanwakiya. -- pópṫanpṫanḱiya, v.a. To cause to wag the head. Poptanptanwakiya.

ṗō'sḱi, cont. (of poskica). By the neck. Also, poskil, obsc. "l". Na poski omayuspa. Poski mayuza. -- pósḱica, v. To clasp around the neck.

pō'skil, Cf. poski. -- pósḱil iyakaśka, v.a. To tie around the neck, as a halter perhaps. -- pósḱil kte, v. To kill by choking. Poskilwakte. -- pósḱil yut'a, v. To put to death by hanging. Poskil mayalut'e kinica yelo. Bl. -- pósḱil yúza, v. To clasp about the neck, to put the arms around the neck of one, to embrace, to hold in one's arms. Poskil bluza. D.222.

ṗō'sḱisḱi, red. (of poski). Holding, squeezing by the neck. - mayuza.

po'śin, v.n. To sniff, snuff up the nose; make a face at. Pówaśin. -- póśinśin, v. red. (of pośin). To make faces at. Pówaśinśin.

ṗośla', adj. Rounded off at one end. Maza - . Nata - . WE.

po'ślicoma, adj. or v. perhaps. To have the head covered e.g. with a blanket. Pośliwacoma. Bl. BD.

po'śliśli, v. To have one's face always covered, i.e. out of bashfulness. - un. -- pośliśliḱa, n. One who keeps his face covered with his blanket. Also, póśliślis'a.

ṗo'śṫan, 1) v. To wear e.g. a hat or head covering. Powaśtan. 2) n. A hood, a child's cloak with a hood. - ipatapi, A hood-like ornamented, quill-work, piece of leather in which little babies are tied up. A bonnet-like baby cradle.

p̄ó'ṫa, adj. Worn out, spoiled, as shoes etc. Also, potáhaⁿ, part. Haⁿpa potahe lo. Potahewayelo.

powa'ya, 1) n. Nap, fur. 2) adj. Having nap, rough, made rough, fur-trimmed. P. Coming off, as dry paint. 3) v.a. To brush e.g. a coat. Uⁿkcela heca waksiⁿ na oⁿ apawiⁿta, i.e. the painted hide, ca he tohiⁿni jajahe śni naiⁿś powayeśni. MS.482. -- powáyela, adj. Having nap.

po'wiwila, Same as peowiwila.

psā, n. A kind of rush or water grass.

psa ciⁿ'ca, n. Pithy grass or rush. Also, psa swula, psa pópoṗela. It is edible. WE. Bw. Bc.

psa'ka, adj. Broken. Cf. yupsaka. -- psákahaⁿ, part. Broken, as a string; broken-hearted. R. Also, psakáhaⁿ. Note: In ref. to past time, psákahe. -- psaḱáheca, (?). Tuweni psakahece-śni niuⁿpi k'oⁿ hehaⁿ lena ocaⁿku, i.e. these were roads in past days. BT.

Psa'loka, n. prop. A Crow Indian.

psaⁿpsaⁿ'ka, adj. Easily changing one's views. - caⁿke. Cf. siⁿtoⁿpsaⁿpsaⁿ. -- n. A fool. GV.

psa o'blotoⁿ, n. An edible plant. (?). Also, oblotoⁿtoⁿ. L.

psa o'ju, n. A growth of rush. B.H.45. 21. Also, psaóju, psáoju.

psa'owiⁿja, n. Rush mats.

psa'oyuⁿke, n. Rush mats. P.

psapsa'kahaⁿ, part. red. of psakahaⁿ.

psa' swula, n. Cf. psa ciⁿca.

psawa'cipi, n. The Crow Indian dance.

psa'wapośtaⁿ, n. A straw hat. Also, psápośtaⁿ.

psawo'gnake, n. A basket.

pse, n. A water bird, i.e. a very restless bird that never remains sitting or standing for any length of time in the same place. BT. Hence, the saying: Pse kiⁿyaⁿpi eśa ekta opa iyececa yelo, which saying is applied to people that never stay at home long, but go to every gathering there is anywhere. EM.

pse'ḣte, pse'ḣtiⁿ, n. The ash. Colloq., a pipe, since pipe stems are made of ash wood. - icu wo, okihe kaḣya uⁿyaⁿkapi kte lo. WE.

pse'ḣtiⁿ caⁿ, n. The green ash. Fraxinus lanceolata. The olive family. Also, pseḣte. The wood is used for bows. #120. MS.481.

psi'ca, adj. Jumping. Cf. yupsica, ipsica.

psi'cala, n. A flea.

psil, cont. of psica. - iyaya, To jump or hop away. -- psilyá, adv. Jumping.

psiⁿ, n. Rice, wild rice. - ská, White rice, barley.

psiⁿ uⁿ'wohaⁿpi, n. A double boiler, since it is used to cook rice.

psipsi'ca, v. red. (of psica). To jump much, to skip.

psipsi'cala, n. The grasshopper.

psi'psicala, n. The jumping mouse.

psipsi'cala sapa, n. The jumping mouse or the field cricket.

psi'psil, cont. of psipsica. - ya, iⁿyaⁿkapi. - itkobwicaye. D.120.

psohaⁿ'p̄a, n. Indian snow shoes.

psoⁿpsoⁿ'ḱiya, adv. With the face down. - gliyuⁿka, i.e. he lay face downward. Also, psoⁿpsóⁿkiya.

psoⁿpsoⁿ'la, adj. Supple, lithe, bendable, as is said of a willow stick or a wire that can be moved in all directions. Also, psoⁿpsoⁿyela.

psuⁿpsuⁿkiya, Cf. psoⁿpsoⁿkiya. -- psuⁿpsuⁿla, Cf. psoⁿpsoⁿla. Also cf. psoⁿpsoⁿyela for psuⁿpsuⁿyela.

pśa, v.n. To sneeze, as from a cold. Wapśa. Poge omayaś'iⁿś'iⁿ hecel oⁿ wapśahelo. Bl. Cf. apśa. -- pśapśá, v. red. perhaps. -- pśapśá s'e, adv. Appearing disorderly. - uⁿ, To look disorderly, i.e. in ragged clothes and dishevelled hair. - glepa. Cf. itúpśapśa s'e uⁿ. -- pśayá, v.a. To cause to sneeze. Pśawaya.

pśica', n. A swallow; the flying squirrel. Also, pśiⁿcá, icapśiⁿpśiⁿcala. - kiⁿyékiyeȟcelo, as they say of him who is riding fast. R. BT.

pśiⁿ, n. Leeks, onions.

pśiⁿca', n. A swallow. - kiⁿyé s'e, as is said when a crowd disbands suddenly, like a bunch of swallows. LC. Cf. pśica.

pśiⁿ hublo'ka, n. An onion or onion-like plant poisonous to man.
pśiⁿ śica'mna, n. The wild onion. Allium reticulatum. The lily family. It is edible. #265.
pśiⁿ taⁿ'ka, n. The mariposa lily. Calochortus nuttallii. The lily family. Bl. #300.

pśitō', n. Beads.

pśito'la hu, n. The broad-leaved arrow head. Sagittaria latifolia. So called because of the roots that are edible and eaten as a medicine. WE. Bl. #126. Syn.- hiⁿhaⁿtahaⁿpė.
pśito'lahu iyéceca, n. The black bindweed (leaves). Polygonum convolvulus. Bl. #296.

pśito' suhúla, n. Very small beads.
pśito'śuhúla, n. Intermediate beads.

pśu'ǩe, (?). Pa ca - kaca yaⁿkiⁿ na, as is said of one with a short, crooked nose. Bl.

pśuⁿ, adj. Shed, fallen off, as horns; drawn out. Cf. yupśuⁿ, kapśuⁿ.
pśuⁿhaⁿ', part. Fallen off, dislocated.
pśuⁿǩa', adj. Round, short and thick. Paha - . -- n. perhaps. A bulge, a knot, as on a tree; a pill.
pśuⁿka'ka, n. Tiny round things, pills.
pśuⁿǩa'la, n. Any tiny round thing.
pśuⁿǩa'ya, adv. In a bunch, in a heap, as an animal curled up. - yaⁿka.

pśuⁿǩa'yaǩel, adv. In a bunch, drawn up together.
pśuⁿǩa'yela, adv. In a bunch, as rags and not animate things.

pśuⁿpśuⁿ'wahaⁿ, part. red. of pśuⁿpśuⁿwahe and pśuⁿwahaⁿ. Same as śibśipahaⁿ. -- pśuⁿpśuⁿwahela, adj. perhaps. (pśuⁿpśuⁿwahaⁿ). Note: the word is used in ref. to little things.
pśuⁿwa'haⁿ, part. Dropped out, fallen off. Awicakehaⁿ mapśuⁿwahelo, i.e. I am sore broke. Bl.

pta, Cf. yupta.

ptahaⁿ', part. Cut off, cut out.
ptahaⁿ'haⁿ, part. red. of ptahaⁿ. Mini maptahaⁿhaⁿ, heoⁿ anatokelyakel mawani, i.e. water running down from sores, so I walk in a lame manner. - yelo, i.e. his clothes all are ragged and torn everywhere. Bl.

ptaⁿ, n. The otter. In the sacred dialect it is called hepaⁿ. - s'e taⁿ lehaⁿ hu pteptecela kaca, as is said when a person has a heavy body but short legs. R. Bl. Cf. yuptaⁿ.
ptaⁿha', n. The otter skin.

pťaⁿpťaⁿ', adj. Unsteady, rocking, as a canoe. -- pťaⁿpťáⁿla, adj. Unsteady in mind; not defined as tottering.

ptaⁿśǩi'śǩa, adj. perhaps. (ptaⁿ-śkiśka). Up and down and right and left, as is the way of a mole. - iyecel omani yelo; miś eya owale yelo. - iyecel opinic'iyelo, śkinic'iyelo. BT.Bl.

ptaⁿ'tacaⁿǩu, n. An otter's trail; the trail of small animals in general.

Ptaⁿ'uⁿpi Wakpála, n. p. A little creek going into the Tongue River at its mouth; Pumpkin Creek. Bl.

ptaⁿyaⁿ', adv. Flurried, excited, as is said of animals.

ptaⁿyē'tu, n. Autumn, fall. Also, ptaⁿyela. - kiⁿ, kiⁿhaⁿ.

pťa'pťaya, adv. red. (ptaya). Together, collectively. - uⁿkomani; - eglepi, To shock e.g. grain. Wilwitaya eglepi is much the same.

pta'ya, adv. Together, collectively. - uⁿyaⁿpi kta. Hokśila - najiⁿpelo.BT. Also, ptáyela.

pte, n. The female buffalo.

ptea'saⁿp̂i, n. Cow's milk. -- pteásaⁿpinini, n. Thick, curdled milk. -- pteásaⁿpiwasna, n. Butter. Also, pteásaⁿpiwigli.

pteblo'ka, n. A steer.

ptece', n. Buffalo dung. - pahi uⁿyiⁿ kte. Bl. MW.

ptē'cela, adj. Short. Maptecela.

pte'ġa, n. The dense grass around a lake. Cf. ptegaglonica.

pte'ġagloniča, n. The ziⁿtka ślila, ziⁿtka tanagila. A little gray bird living on the prairie in swampy places and able to alight on weeds. Its call: (smacking) tch, tch, tch---s s s s (hissing). Bl. Note: ptega (a marsh. R.) is not used alone.

ptegle'śka, n. Tame cattle.

Ptegle'śka caⁿli', n. Bull Durham tobacco.

pteġo'p̂eca, n. The marsh hawk; a kind of hawk, so called because it frequents marshes. Its nité, rump, is white, its feet yellow. Bl. R. - śa. - ska. Bl.

pteġu'ya, v.a. To brand cattle.

pteha'hiⁿśma, n. A buffalo robe, a buffalo skin with thick hair.

pteha'śla, n. A buffalo hide from which the hair has been removed. Cf. teȟpi.

ptehe'ciⁿśka, n. A spoon made of a cow horn.

ptehe'cutic'iⁿ, n. A powder horn (of a cow) carried at the side.

ptehe'śťe, n. A thin, short stick with a short horn fastened to one end and used by men in a game for throwing and sliding over ice.

ptehe' wapa'ha, n. A horned headdress.

pte'hiko, v. To perform ceremonies in order to locate buffalo. Ptehiwako. "Kipazo ptehiko." from a winter-count for 1871-72. RB.

ptehiⁿ'cala, n. A calf.

ptehiⁿ'cicila, n. The killdeer, the American ring plover. Its call: Tiblō, tibló, tiblo; or: Tiblo wewe, tiblo wewe. The Lakota answers: How. FR. Note: this is a doubtful comp. of ptehiⁿca and ic'ila.

ptehiⁿ'p̂aȟp̂a, n. Tags of buffalo hair; old matted hair shed and fallen from buffalo. D.36.

ptehiⁿ'śma, n. A thick or long-haired buffalo.

ptehiⁿ'śmaha, n. A buffalo robe.

ptehi'yap̂a, (?). La.

ptei'caȟape, n. A blacksnake whip.

ptei'ciyuȟa uⁿma, n. The blossoms (iⁿkpa zizi) of this plant boiled with pispiza tawote make a good tea for the spitting of blood. Name, (?). Ti.

ptei'śta, n. A buffalo's eye. Bl.

ptejiⁿ'cala, n. A new-born buffalo calf. Kal otkeya yo, i.e. the táblo, at the door, hecel - ake uⁿkokinipi ktelo, which is an old superstitious saying. Bl.

pte'kiciyapi, n. A pastime for boys. Bl.

ptelye'la, adv. For a short time. Hehaⁿl ehake - wauⁿcipi na enauⁿkiyapi. This seems not to be used by the Titoⁿwaⁿ.

ptema'ǩicima, n. A heifer.

ptema'ǩokawaze, n. A buffalo wallow. WF.

ptemna'yaⁿpi, n. Gathering cattle, a round-up.

ptena'kpa, n. A buffalo's ear. Bl.

ptenuⁿ'weǩiyapi, n. A dipping of cattle.

pteo'k̇icaśka, n. Work-oxen; perhaps a span of oxen. Bl. Also, pteákicaśka.

pteo'najiŋ, n. A cow barn.

pteo'ptaye, n. (of pte and optaye). A herd of buffalo.

pteo'waci, n. A buffalo wallow. Cf. D.207, note 4. Syn.- ptemakokawaze.

ptepa' k̇aḣ'épi s'e, adv. With great care. - ecoŋ, oyake, To do, say etc. something very carefully. Bl.

pte pa'pala, n. Fig., the main news, what is new. Br.

ptepte'cela, adj. red. (of ptecela). Short, ref. to more than one thing. Note: all duplication suggests plurality.

ptesaŋ', n. A white buffalo cow, a rarity whose hide is used in religious ceremonies.

pteta'mak̇a, n. A lean cow.

ptetaŋ', n. The meat perhaps of the middle of the back of a buffalo. Bl.

pteta'wanap'iŋ, n. An ox-yoke.

pteta'woṫe, n. The ground plum. Astragalus caryocarpus. The pulse family. It is a prairie plant that bears juicy berries. Lit., buffalo's food. As a medicine it is good for horses. L. RT. #154.

ptewa'k'iŋ, n. Work-oxen. - akikaśka. B.H.110.15. R. Bl. Syn.- pteók̇icaśka. - íċicaśkapi, A span of work-oxen. B.H.42.11.

ptewa'niyaŋpi, n. Tame cattle.

ptewa'togla, n. A wild cow.

ptewiŋ'kte, n. A fat and dry buffalo cow. Bl.

ptewiŋ'yela, n. A cow.

ptewo'yak̇e, n. The large grasshopper without wings. It would seem they tell of buffalo. R. It is an insect found along sand, roads; it is brown and the upper legs are very wide, and is really not a grasshopper. Also, the fifth bone in the tasiha uŋpi.

pteya'ḣota, n. Wild rye, nodding white rye. Elymus canadensis. The grass family. BT. #86.

pteya'ḣpa, n. The cowbird. Bl. Syn.- waḣpa ḣota.

ptiŋ'haŋ, n. Last autumn. (?). HM. -- ptíŋhaŋna, (?). - hecoŋpelo. BT.

ptuḣ'a', v.n. To crumble down. Cf. kaoksa. -- ptuḣ'áḣ'a, v. red. of ptuḣ'a. -- ptuḣ'áḣ'ayakel, adv. In small crumbs etc. Aŋpetu waŋ takuśniśni - pahi uŋkomani yelo. Bl.

ptu'ja, adj. Split, cracked. Cf. yuptuja. -- ptujáhaŋ, part. Cracked of itself.

ṗu, v. 1st pers. singl. I am coming. An old word meaning waú. Cf. śku.

ṗucaŋ'caŋ iyaya, v. To pass under, stooping. Bl.

ṗu'ġa, v.n. To snort, as a horse does when frightened.

ṗulki'ċiŋkel, adv. (?). - uŋ, To let one's lips hang down because one is displeased with something. Bl.

ṗuŋṗuŋ', v.n. To decay, **to rot**, said of wood etc. **not animal matter.** -- adj. Rotten, as wood. Cf. poŋpoŋ. Also, ṗuŋṗúŋla.

ṗu'sa, Same as puza.

ṗusk̇eb', cont. of puskepa. - okaśtaŋ.

ṗusk̇e'ṗa, v.a. To pour all out, to empty. Wapuskepa. R.

ṗusk̇i'ya, v.a. To dry or cause to dry, as wet clothes. Puswakiya.

pusṗa', v.a. To stick on, glue; to seal. Wapuspa. Yuŋkaŋ taŋkśitku coŋpeśka waŋ oŋ iśta - , keye; caŋke iśtagoŋga keye. MS.94. -- ṗusṗék̇iya, v.a. To cause to glue on or seal. Puspewakiya. -- ṗusṗéya, v.a. To cause to seal or glue.

ṗusṗu'za, adj. red. of puza.

ṗusṫag', cont. of pustaka. - iyuŋka,

To squat down. - eȟpeic'iya, To get down so as to hide, bow down, squat down. -- ṗusṫáǧṫuk̇el, adv. Squatting down.

ṗusṫa'k̇a, v.n. To squat down. Wapustaka. Pustake s'e emauⁿpi kte. Bl. Cf. patuja. -- ṗusṫákel, adv. Into a squat position. - iȟpeya, To make one squat down, to put down. Bl.

ṗusta'stak, v. To stoop. - iyaya, To pass below something, stooping. Bl.

ṗusya', 1) v.a. To dry, cause to dry. Puswaya. 2) adv. In a drying manner. - henamala, i.e. have nothing anymore. Bl. -- ṗusyák̇el, adv. In a drying manner. -- ṗusyáśpaⁿ, adj. Cooked dry. -- ṗusyáśpaⁿyaⁿ, v. To cook dry, cook too long. -- ṗusyéla, adv. Dry. - haⁿ. B.H.54.10;112.5. -- ṗusyéya, v. (?). Wanagoptaⁿpi c'oⁿ caka na pusyemayelo, i.e. listening with open mouth; it is also used fig. Bl.

ṗuśk̇i', adv. In a bunch, as rags and not cattle. Cf. pśuⁿkayela.

ṗuśk̇i'ca, v.a. To press or rub out with the hand. Wapuśkica.

ṗuśk̇il', cont. of puśkica. - yaⁿka. -- ṗuśk̇ilya, adv. Pressed, squeezed.

ṗuś'iⁿ'ś'iⁿ, Cf. opúś'iⁿ, ipuś'iⁿ. Bl.

ṗutag', cont. of putaka. - iȟpaya, To fall down with the hands on the ground.

ṗuta'k̇a, v.a. To touch, as with the hand when one falls. Waputaka.

ṗuṫaⁿ'la.s'e, adv. Short, small and thick, as a man, horse, wagon etc. Bl.

ṗuṫaⁿ'yela, adv. (?). Itoceś - mic'ignakiⁿ kte, Alright, I shall hold my tongue. Bl.

ṗuṫe', 1) n. The upper lip. Ihá, the lower lip. 2) n. The nose and mouth of animals, e.g. horses.

ṗuṫe'ȟniyaⁿyaⁿ, v.n. To have the lips quiver with cold or in anger. Putemaȟniyaⁿyaⁿ.

ṗuṫe'ok̇icu, n. The elephant.

ṗuṫiⁿ'hiⁿ, n. The beard, especially what grows on the upper lip; the mustache. Also, ṗuṫíⁿhiⁿ. - icáśla, A razor. - ipájaja, A shaving brush.

ṗuṫo'kicu, n. (of pute and wokicu). An elephant. Also, putéokicu.

ṗut'iⁿ'ǧela, (?). Wakiⁿyela maku kaca, - s'e yaⁿkiⁿ na, as is said of a proud, short and fleshy person. Bl.

ṗu'za, adj. Dry, as wood. This is not pusa.

ṗuzal', cont. of puzata. - iyayeya, To run one ashore; fig. meaning only, to show that one has told a falsehood.

ṗu'zala, n. A cat. This is a word old women use.

ṗuzaⁿl', Same as puzal. - yeya, To prove that one is a liar. - yeciyiⁿ kte. - ni kte lo. BT.

ṗuza'ṫa, adv. Lit. on dry land; fig., caught in a lie. - glicu, To reach shore. Bl.

ṗu'zela, adj. Shallow, as a stream of water; nearly dry.

p'e, n. The elm tree. -- p'écaⁿ, n. The white elm. Ulmus Americanus. The elm family. #127. - ṫuⁿṫúⁿpa, The slippery elm. Bl. -- p'eik̇ceka, n. The common elm.

p'o, 1) n. Fog, mist. 2) adj. Foggy, misty. P'o yelo, so they say and thus indicate that it will be warm; whereas the old Indian said: Cuhaⁿzi yelo. Cf. cuhaⁿzi. P'o wakitapi s'elececa, as they used to say when they could not see well, for fog it seems. Bl. -- p'óp'o, adj. red.

p'osya'kel, adv. Out of humor, displeased. - uⁿk'uⁿ wiⁿhahakelo, i.e. after we did not like it in the beginning, we are in good spirits now. Bl.

p'o'wak̇iṫa, (?). Ísta kiⁿ p'owakitapi s'elemaceca yelo, i.e. do not see well, blurred, foggy. P'owakitapi s'e wauⁿ, My vision is blurred. Bl.

p'oye'la, adj. Steaming. Na Waⁿna

P'OZECA
cega kiŋ el u na waŋna - haŋ.

p'o'zeca, v.n. To be out of humor. Ma-p'ozeca.

sab, cont. of sapa.

sabsa'pa, adv. red. of sapa. -- sabsapya, adv. perhaps. red. (of sapya, sabya). Black, dark.

sabya', 1) v.a. To blacken, as shoes. Sabwaya. 2) adv. Darkly, blackly. -- sabyáhaⁿ, adv. perhaps. Dark, blackish, as water seen at a distance. -- sabyakel, adv. Blackish; in sight, far off. Also, sabyéla, Yuⁿkaⁿ i etaⁿ taku waⁿ sabyela nape el ohiⁿȟpaya.

sagsa'ƙa, adj. red. (of saka). Raw, uncooked; hard, dried. This ref. to many things.

sagya', v.a. (of saka). To make hard, stiff. Sagwaya. Syn.- yusáka.

sagye', n. A cane, a staff. -- sagyéƙitoⁿ, v. To use a staff in walking, as an old person. Sagyéwetoⁿ. Also, sagyétoⁿ. Sagyéwatoⁿ. -- sagyéya, v.a. To use anything for a staff. Sagyéwaya.

sak, cont. of saka.

sa'ƙa, adj. Hard, stiff, dried, as an old hide. Páṗa sáƙa.

saƙa'la, adj. Green, limber. Caⁿ - , A switch.

saƙib', adv. Together. Cf. isákib. Nupiⁿ - , Two side by side. Caⁿsákib uⁿkaśkiⁿ kte. Heciyataⁿhaⁿ le wau ca - uⁿgni kte lo, I just came from there now; so we two shall go home together. D.102. Bl. -- saƙíbṫu, adv. Two together. -- saƙíbṫuƙel, adv. Both together

sam, adv. cont. (of saⁿpa). More, beyond, more than. Sam iyaya, To go beyond, surpass. Sam iyeya, To make go over or beyond. Sam taku ota slolyayapi kte lo. Sam kiyela ya po. Sam tahenakiya u. Tuwa yuha kiⁿ sam toketu kiⁿ slolyiⁿ kta. Note: Sam is used more than aké in counting money. Sam iyaye, More than. Tipi opawiⁿge sam iyaye yawapi. -- samsám, adv. red. of sam. -- samsáⁿpa, adv. red. of saⁿpa. -- samyé s'e, adv. More, as it were; increasingly. - iyotaⁿ śica ayapi.

saⁿ, adj. Gray, whitish, or yellowish. Pehiⁿ saⁿ. Maka saⁿ.

saⁿ a'ya, v. To fade.

saⁿb, cont. of saⁿpa. - ecoⁿ. B.H. 287.14.

saⁿni', adj. Of one side, on one side. Nakpa kiⁿ - wagluhomni kte lo. Na nape - pejuta waⁿji ca yuha. -- saⁿníca, adv. On one side, sideways. Wapośtaⁿ - kic'uⁿ. -- saⁿníla, adv. Of only one side. Na ake nape - taku icu na ake el okala.

saⁿo'kpukpa, adj. Gray, black and white mixed, as hair.

saⁿ'opapa, adj. Gray hairs here and there on one's head; turning gray. Syn.- saⁿókpukpa.

saⁿ'pa, adv. More, more than, over, beyond. Lena - taku tona oⁿnispepi kta waciⁿ. Waⁿna wicokaⁿyaⁿ - ehaⁿl uⁿgna waⁿna u. -- sáⁿpataⁿhaⁿ, adv. From beyond. -- sáⁿpsaⁿpa, adv. red.

saⁿsaⁿ', adj. red. (of saⁿ). Whitish. P. B.H.35.19. -- saⁿsáⁿopapa, adj. red. of saⁿopapa.

saⁿṫu'hu, n. A species of red grass with a hard round stalk and strong blade. Note: this is not pejiśaśa. -- saⁿṫúhu ȟcaka, n. Sand grass, long-leaved reed grass. Calamovilva longifolia. The grass family. It is used for pipe cleaning. Chief Crazy Horse wore the top of this plant as a wotawe on the head instead of a feather. Bl. BT. #145. -- saⁿṫúhu óƙihetoⁿ, n. Cf. peji śaśa okihe taⁿkiⁿkiⁿyaⁿ. WE. #240. -- saⁿṫúhu taⁿka, n. Tall marsh grass. Spartina cynosuroides. The grass family. #281.

saⁿyaⁿ', 1) v.a. To whiten, whitewash. Saⁿwaya. 2) adv. Whitish. Aⁿpo - hinapa, The dawn appears brightly.

saⁿye'la, adj. Grayish. Makoce - .

sa'ṗa, adj. Black. Masápa.

sa'ṗa taⁿ'ka, n. The spade in playing cards.

Sa'pa Wicaśa, n. prop. A Ute Indian.

sa'pa yuğa'ğa, n. The club in playing

cards.

sā'ṫa, n. A forked stick. Syn.- húŋṗe oḱijata.

saṫgla'kiŋyaŋ, n. The horizontal stick resting on two others with forked ends, a stick to dry meat on. Also, caŋsáta. Cf. huŋpe okijata. Note: The "t" is made liquid in sounding it. R. SE. -- v. perhaps. To hang out, as in drying something.

saṫiŋ', adj. Stretched out straight, as in death. -- saṫíŋs'e, adj. Stretched out, as it were; tall. Haŋska he kapi. Bl. -- saṫíŋṫiŋ, adj. red. of satiŋ. -- saṫíŋyela, adv. Stretched out, as one dead. - Ḣpaya.

saṫi'yaḣaśḱe, n. That which ties up on the sáta.

satka'ksa, v. To cut poles which are used in the tent to hang things on. Satkakse uŋyaŋpi kte. Bl.

sazu', n. The cross-sticks of the Ḣaká, an Indian game. This is an old name. Also, tucuhu.

sċe'paŋ, n. A woman's sister-in-law. -- sċépaŋku, n. Her sister-in-law. Also, ścépaŋku. D.269. -- sċépaŋśi, n. A woman's female cousin; my female cousin; perhaps her husband's brother's wife. Nisċepaŋśi. -- sċépaŋśitku, n. Her female cousin; her husbands's brother's wife. -- sċépaŋśiya, v.a. (for a woman). To have for a female cousin; to have for a husband's brother's wife. Scépaŋśiwaya. -- sċépaŋya, v.a. (for a woman). To have for a sister-in-law. Scépaŋwaya.

Sċi'li, n. prop. The Pawnee Indians, perhaps. They have almost the same language. Grinnell, in "The Story of the Indians", calls them the "Skidi". p.127,128,132.

scu, v. To make one's self important, as by dressing up; to attract attention. Na tokel okihi scu. MS.104. Cf. wawáscuscuke.

se'ċa, adv. As though, seemingly; I thought so. Na Lakota akicita seca ehakela nakuŋ manipelo. Uŋgnayeḣci uŋkiyepi na niyepi koya ikipi kte śni seca ca, eyaś heca wiyopeye kiŋ ekta yapi na.... B.H.247.13. Also, séce. Sece k'uŋ. B.H.69.4;93.15;175.4.

se'celaka, v.n. To have an opinion, think. Sécewalaka. Ho le hecel slolwaya na lila wakaŋyaŋ ecoŋpi secewalaka. Syn.- wicala, hecetulaka.

sē'hiŋgla, adv. So happening. Waŋlaka sehiŋgle ciŋhaŋ, If you happen to see him. R. Iśtiŋmapi na oikpaḣicapi kiŋ lececa sehiŋgle, i.e. as though he woke up from a deep sleep. B.H.39.5. Wanuŋ eśa tokel omayaluspe sehiŋgle ciŋhaŋ yatuŋwiŋ kte, If by accident you <u>somehow</u> happen to catch me, you will see. Tiwegna glicu caŋke k'o - śke. D.35.49.

se'kse, adv. Same as s'elececa, as it were. Yublapi - hiŋḣpaye, as is said when snow falls here and there in large flakes. Yunap'iyeyapi - iŋyaŋkelo, as is said of a horse running off in a curve. Tiŋpsila kiŋ itka nahca ca wagacaŋ - hiyeyelo. Wagmu apapi - apa, i.e. to strike one so that it sounds. Lena suta k'eś akiŋye - uŋkiyayapi tka yelo, i.e. if the road were hard we would go over it flying. Bl.

sē'ksel, adv. Like.

sĕ'mni, n. A loafer, bum; an unmarried young man. Syn.- sinté, kośkalaka. Bl. Cl.

sewi'mna, adj. Rancid, as fat that stood long. -- sewíye, adj. Spoiled, rancid, as rotting meat etc.

si, n. The foot.

sia'kśa, adj. Pigeon-toed, in opposition to siháḣmiŋ. Siamakśa. Bl. -- siákśakśa, adj. red.

sicaŋ', n. The outer side of the thigh. - kaŋ namatipelo. Bl. D.1.

Sicaŋ'ġu, n. prop. The Brule Indians, the Rosebud Indians. Lit., burned thighs. Sicaŋmagu.

sicaŋ'oṗiye, n. (of sicaŋ and opiye). A side pocket, as in one's pants or coat; any pocket.

sica'psaŋ, v. To shake the foot. Siwakapsaŋ. Cf. kapsaŋpsaŋ. -- sicápsaŋpsaŋ, v. red. (sicapsaŋ). To move one's feet right and left, like a dog wagging its tail. Oh'aŋhaŋhaŋ - naŋkahelo. Bl.

sico'cola, adj. red. of sicola.
sico'kakala, adj. red. of sicokala.
sico'kala, adj. Bare-footed. Sicomakala.
sicō'la, adj. Bare-footed.
sicu'ha, n. The sole of a shoe, or foot. -- sicúhatoŋ, v. To sole, put a sole on a moccasin. Bl.

sicuŋ', n. That in a man or thing which is spirit or spirit-like and guards him from birth against evil spirits. Thereafter he may derive other sicuŋpi through the toŋ of other beings, esp. animals. The shaman's sicuŋ, his implements etc., used to be kept in his wakaŋ-bag (wasicuŋ), just as the medicines etc. were the sicuŋpi of the pejuta wicaśa. Such sicuŋpi can be lent to others. Other and evil sicuŋpi are derived through bad and similar means. WJR.158-9.

si'glapsaŋpsaŋ, v. To swing the feet. Also, siglápsaŋpsaŋ. Siwaglapsaŋpsaŋ. Cf. kapsaŋpsaŋ, sicapsaŋ.

si'gluha, v.n. To escape, get out of the way, i.e. having a bad conscience. Síwagluha.

siha', n. The sole of the foot, the skin of the feet; the feet of horn-footed animals (horses etc.); a hoof.
siha'ħmiŋ, adj. The toes pointed sideways, as in walking; in opposition to siákśakśa. Sihámaħmiŋ. Bl.

Siha' Sápa, n. prop. The Blackfeet Sioux.

sihu', n. The bones of the foot, the toes.
sihu'kaŋ, n. Same as sihutkaŋ. Syn.- iśkákaŋ.
sihu'tkaŋ, n. The place on the leg just above the heel, i.e. the muscle or tendon of the heel; the foot ligament. Also, sihukaŋ. D.92. Bc.
siħa'p̄e, n. The hollow of the foot. Also, sióħap̄e.

sii'c'iyapa, v. To strike the feet together in walking. Also, siíc'iyapapa, v. red.

sii'nat̄aŋ, n. Stirrups. - akáħpe, A covered stirrup. Cf. ínataŋ.
sii't̄aħaha, n. The top of the foot, the instep. Also, siitaka.

si ito'ħab égle, v. ph. To make one fall over one's foot while wrestling with him. Bl.
si'iyot̄iyeħiya, v. To have pains in one's feet for lack of good shoes. Siiyotiyewakiye, tuweni makagege śni ca. GA. Bl.

siiyu'te, n. A foot measure.

si ħakab' iyeya, v. ph. To make one fall by holding the foot in his way while he is running. Bl.

siko'śkapi, n. A sickness of horses, swollen hoofs. Bl.
siksa', adj. Club-footed.
si nani'yaŋ, v. The feet hurt. Si nawaniya. Also, sínaníyaŋ. Bl.

siŋkp̄e', n. The muskrat. Also, wasiŋkpe. P. -- siŋkp̄éicuwa, n. Spears, traps, axes etc. used in killing muskrats. -- siŋkp̄éla, n. The muskrat.
siŋkp̄e'oŋzemna, n. Musk. Bl.
siŋkp̄e'tawot̄e, n. Calamus, sweet-flag, the acorus calamus. Used as medicine for cramps of the arms and legs. The roots are pulverized, mixed with gun powder and given as a drink in water.
siŋkp̄e'yakel, adv. In the manner of a muskrat. - lila wota, wipiic'iya.

siŋsiŋ', adj. Besmeared, slimed, as with fish; dried on, glued or glazed over.

siŋt̄e', n. The tail of an animal; fig. a young man, kośkalaka, or the bait accompanying a purchase, i.e. a sale's bonus. He siŋte yelo, He is no baby any longer.
siŋt̄ē'haŋska, n. The Virginia white-tailed deer; fig., a young buck, a rowdy. Syn.- caŋtaħca.
siŋte'ħla, n. A rattle snake.

Siŋte'ħla Wicáśa, n. prop. The Snakes; the Comanches.

siŋt̄e'lulyapi, n. The red-tailed deer. IS. St.

siŋt̄e'sap̄ela, n. The mule-deer; the black-tailed deer.

siŋte'waksápi, n. The bob-tail deer. P.

siŋtē'wiŋyaŋ, n. An unmarried young woman. Cf. sinte, kośkalaka. Bl.

siŋtoŋ'psaŋpsaŋ, v. To wag the tail. Also, siŋtúpsaŋpsaŋ, also red. of siŋtupsaŋ. Cf. psaŋpsaŋka, kapsaŋpsaŋ. B.H.126.11. P. Bl.

sio'cokaŋ, n. The middle toe.

sio'ȟape, n. The hollow of the foot. Also, siȟape.

sio'kaza, n. The toes. Cf. siokazuŋte. Bl.

sio'kazuŋte, n. The toes, all taken together, or taken singly perhaps. - waŋji. Note: siōko, The spaces between the toes.

sio'kiciyaȟlalyapi, n. A pastime for children.

siō'ko, n. The spaces 'twixt the toes.

sio'śtuŋkala, n. The soft claws of a buffalo calf. Bl.

sipa', n. The front part of the foot a man steps on; the toes, the end of the big toe. -- sipáhuŋka, n. The big toe.

sipa'gnagya, (?). - éyayelo. This is said of tracks. BT.

si'paha iyeya, v. To kick away sideways. Bl.

sipa'iyókihe, n. The second toe.

sipa'ksize, n. The lower part of the leg of animals.

sipa'wakaśe , v.n. To stumble. Sipawamakaśe. P. Sipawamakaśe hena maȟica yelo. Bl.

sipa'wicakaśe, n. Buffalo grass. Also, peji iwicakoyake. Buchloe dactyloides. The grass family. #182.

sipa'wicayaksa, n. A certain black beetle that snaps. When people have pain in the tips of the toes, they use this word to denote it, assuming that this beetle has bitten them. EM.

sipiŋ'kpa, n. (sipa and iŋkpa). The toes. -- sipíŋkpakpala, adv. On the toes. - mani, To walk on tiptoes. Bl. Syn.- naslaslal. - mani.

sisaŋ'ni, n. One foot, the foot on one side.

Sisi'toŋwaŋ, n. prop. The Sisitonwans, a band of the Dakota.

siśa'śte, n. The little toe. - iyókihe, The fourth toe.

si'śtaȟe, n. The two little bones, claws, on the feet of cows and horses.

sito'mni, adv. All over, throughout. Waŋna maka - eyapaha. Maka - wakiŋyaŋ agli. MS.101. -- sitómniyaŋ, adv. All over.

situ'pi, n. A bird's tail feathers. Cf. siŋtupsaŋ, situpsaŋ.

situ'pi aȟ'áyetoŋpi, n. The lark sparrow. The tips of the tail feathers are white, otherwise it is gray, and hence the name. Its breast is whitish and head gleglega. These white tips appear like white feathers glued to the tips of the eagle feathers used in war bonnets etc. Hence, aȟ'ayetoŋ. -- sitúpi waŋblila, n. The magnolia warbler. Bl.

situ'psaŋ, siŋtóŋpsaŋ, v. To wag the tail. - iyeya, To switch the tail. D.33. -- sitúpsaŋpsaŋ, v.n. To wag the tail, as a dog's or bird's. Cf. kapsaŋpsaŋ.

si't'at'a, adj. Asleep, numb, as the foot.

siya'payakel, adv. (?). - iyotiyekiye, i.e. to suffer from wet feet perhaps. Bl.

siye', adv. perhaps. As a warning, to a person not to do a certain thing because one is sure he cannot do it. Hiya, oyakihi śni siye. LE. -- siyé epé, v. To tell the truth, as is said when one is asked about one's statement. Siye epiŋ kte, i.e. I'll tell the truth. Siye epe lo.

siye'mila, (?). - , wakiŋyaŋ maktepi,

maka niye śni śka. Sb.

siye'te, n. The heel. - mayazaŋ. -- siyéťe iýahe, n. The ball and heel of the foot. The word iyahe alone does not seem to be used. -- siyéťe ośkóke, n. The thick skin of the heel. - k'el uŋkcela onawaksa tka oteȟike. Bl.

siyo'kaja, Cf. siokaza.

Siyo'ko, n. prop. A mythical wicked man, whose name is used to scare children. Siyoko u!

siyō'ǩo, Cf. sioko.

siyo'naťica, v. (?). Siyonawatica. Bl. -- siyónaťiktica, v. red. Bl.

si'yuha, v. To go to die. Hena taŋyaŋ wakagiŋ kte ȟciŋ yelo, uŋgna uŋyaŋ siwicabluha hehaŋtaŋś iye hena slolyapi kte, i.e. if I should die. Bl.

ska, adj. White, clear. -- skāǩa, adj. Doubtfully white or gray, as a house seen from a distance. Ti - . -- skála, adj. dim. (of ska). White.

ska'niyaǩa, (?). Túweȟca - , i.e. that is a lie. Bl.

skaŋ, v.n. To dissolve, melt, as snow and not as butter, metal etc. Cf. ślo. -- skaŋyáŋ, v.a. To melt. Skaŋwaya. Mini yatkaŋpi śni, wa ece skaŋyaŋpi na yatkaŋpi.

skaŋye'ca, adj. Blue. - s'e, Bluish. Bl. Pejiȟcaka - s'e yuŋke, i.e. very blue or green. Bl.

skaska', adj. red. of ska. - hiŋgla hiyaya, To turn away one's eyes in passing so as not to notice one, i.e. the white of his eyes. Bl. -- skaskála, adj. red. of skala.

skaya', v.a. To whiten. Skawaya.

ska'ya, adv. White.

skaya'kel, adv. Purely, undefiled. -- adv. perhaps. White, whitish; purely. R. Yuŋkaŋ taku waŋ - maȟpiya eciyataŋ u na yuzukapi s'e haŋ.

skebya', v.a. To draw all out, as a fluid; to exhaust. Skebwaya.

sǩē'ǩa, interj. An expression of doubt, used when a man makes a statement who told lies before. MG. Tóŋweȟca - .

ske'ṗa, v.n. To leak out slowly, escape, pass away by evaporation, as do fluids. -- skeskéṗa, v. red.

ski'ca, Cf. kaskica.

skica'haŋ, part. Pressed down, close.

skiska', n. The wood duck. Cf. pagoŋta.

sǩisǩi'ca, red. of skica.

sǩisǩi'cahaŋ, part. All pressed together.

skiski'ťa, red. (of skita). To be marked, as a log by worms having eaten away under the bark. Cf. yuskiskita.

ski'ťa, adj. Tied, bound, fastened, as a child on a board. Cf. yuskita.

skoko'gli, (?). Taku - , i.e. I do not believe it.

sǩowe', adv. perhaps. Wrong. This is an old word. Taku - ecanoŋ he? BT.

sku, adj. Broken out a little. Cf. wasku.

skumna', adj. Sourish; smelling badly or sour, as the scalp when dirty. Bl.

sǩusǩu', red. (of sku). Shaved off. Pa - .

skusǩu'ya, adj. red. of skuya.

sku'ya, adj. Sweet. Oskúya, Sour.

skuyē'la, adj. Delicious. P.

sku'yeya, v.a. To make sweet. Skuyewaya

sla, n. Grease, oil, ointment, salve. Sla wakaŋ. -- slaǩíya, v.a. pos. (of slaya). To grease, anoint one's own. Slawakiya. -- slaǩíyapi, n. Ointment; grease for greasing. -- sláojuha, n. An oil-bag. Also, islaye ojuha.

slasla'ťa, adj. red. of slata. Oie - .

sla'ťa, adj. Slow, feeble. Toȟ'aŋ - , Slow at his work. Oie - , Slow of speech. Also, sláťeca. Maslateca.

slaya', v. To grease, anoint. Slawaya.

sle'ca, Cf. kasleca.

sleca'han, part. Split of itself.

sli, adj. Tapering. -- v.n. To ooze, as gum from a tree. P.

slib, cont. of slipa. - iyeya. -- slibkiya, v.a. To cause to lick. Slibwakiya. Also, slibyá.

sli'hingla, v. To fire a shot. Sliwahingla. -- slihingle, 1) adv. With the loud report of a gun. Cf. hingla. 2) n. The report of a gun. Lena (a medicine man's powder and shots) on taku wakute kin lila - śni, iwaśtela iyaya na taku wakute kin wancag wicawao.

sli'pa, v.a. To lick, lick up anything. Waslipa.

slisli', adj. red. of sli. Bl.

sli'slipa, v. red. of slipa.

slisli'ya, adv. red. of sliya. - apa, To strike with a switching sound. Ungna toka śka yupatuś icicu na - acipe ci. Bl.

sliya', adv. Hissing, the sort made by a rapidly moving switch. Canke śiyo k'un iyuha - wacipi, i.e. as the prairie chickens dance with a booming caused by beating the wings against the air.

slohan', v.n. To crawl. Waslohan. - ku. - omani, as is said of horses. BT. -- slohánhan, v. red. (of slohan). To crawl along, as in getting near ducks. Waslohanhan. Slohanhanhca wagliyelo, as is said of one who drags his feet when he is very tired. -- slohans'e, adv. Same as slohes'e.

slohē's'e, adv. Slowly, as if crawling along.

sloli'c'iya, v. refl. To know one's self; to feel. P.

slolki'ciya, v. To know one another. - unkicagapelo. Bl.

slolki'ya, v. pos. (of slolya). To know one's own. Slolwakiya. Tokeśke wahan kin slolwakiye śni. -- slolkíyeya, v.a. To cause one to know something that pertains to himself; to alarm, to put on one's guard.

slolya', v.a. To know, have knowledge of anything or person. Slolwaya. Slolwicakiciyapi, i.e. to know it of them. B.H.282.6.

slolye'ic'iya, v. To make one's self known. -- slolyékiya, v.a. To cause to know. Slolyewakiya. -- slolyéśni konza, v. To disown, disavow. - wakonza. B.H.253.19;254.13. -- slolyéwacin, v.a. To inquire; fig., to beat the bush. P. -- slolyéya, v.a. To cause to know. Slolyewaya. Pb.28.

sloslo'la, adj. Turning soft, as meat, e.g. bacon, and other foodstuffs such as ice cream when it begins to melt. BS. A.

slo'ta, adj. (?). Iéslota, One who tells the truth, perhaps. Iémaslota. Bl. Cf. slolya.

smag, cont. of smaka. -- smagsmágya, adv. red. of smagya.

smagya', adv. Indented, concave. Also, smagyákel.

sma'ka, 1) adj. Hollow, concave. 2) n. A hollow, a sunken place.

smi, adj. Cf. smismi.

smin, Cf. wasmin. -- smínyan, Cf. sminyanyan.

sminyan'yan, adj. Clean, nothing extraneous or sticking to, bare, smooth as a worn blanket.

smismi', adj. Clear of limbs, as a tree; stripped. Cf. smiyan. -- smismíyan, adv. Destitute, deprived of everything.

smi'yan, Same as sminyan.

sna, v.n. To ring, sound. Wahácank sna, Ringing shield. Cf. kasna. -- snahán, part. Ringing, rustling, as leaves falling in autumn. -- snahánhan, red. (of snahan). Falling off, rustling.

snan'za, sna'za, sna's'a, 1) v.n. To

draw up, as burnt skin; to be scarred. 2) n. A scar. R.

snasna', red. (sna). To ring, rattle.
snasna'la, adj. Bare, as a tree when its leaves have all fallen off.
sna' s'e, adv. Tinkling, ringing. Bl. Syn.- Ȟlayela.
snaye'la iyáya, v. To ring, sound as iron etc. do when struck. - iyeya. Snayéla, adv.

sna'za, Cf. snaŋza. -- snazé, n. P.

sni, adj. Cold, as the weather or as ice; gone out, as peta sni, i.e. fire. -- n. Cold. Sni mákat'elo. Talo sni, Cold meat (after cooking). Petijaŋjaŋ sni, The lantern went out.
snica't'a, v. To feel sleepy from heat or cold. Snimakat'a. Ȟtayetu sniuŋkat'api ca lila uŋkiśtiŋmapi. BT.
snisni', adj. red. of sni. Haŋ - , Cold nights.
sniya', v.a. To cool. Miceji kiŋ sniyiŋ kte lo. B.H.228.3.
sniya'hoṫa, v.n. To take cold, draw in the cold by breathing. Sniblahota.
sniyaŋ', v. To become cold, as the weather. - uya.
sniyaŋ' kat'a, v. To knock somebody senseless.
sniyaŋ' t'a, v. To faint.

sniyo'pa, (?). WE. Cf. oiyopa.

so, v.a. To cut into strings. Wasó. Na taha sópi k'oŋ hena oŋ wihuta opaȞloke el cel okataŋ.
so, particle interrog. Same as hwo and he, except that so implies one is expecting an affirmative answer, but he one is leaving the answer to the addressee. Hokśila kiŋ le waniyetu tona ilukcaŋ so? Kola, tohaŋl wanasapi kte so? F.

sokso'ṫa, adj. red. of sota. Iśta - , Blurred, bad eyes.
sol, cont. of sota. - iyeya, aya, To disappear, die gradually. B.H.51.1.
solḱi'ya, v.a. (sota). To use up or expend or destroy for one. Solwakiya. Cf. kasota, yusota.
solya', v.a. To have used up e.g. one's wood supply. Solwaya. Bl.

soŋ, v.a. To plait or braid e.g. the hair, or thin cords into a rope. Wasóŋ. Wikaŋ sóŋpi, A lasso to catch horses with. Śupe wasoŋ kte, i.e. will call him to order.
soŋ'pi, n. Braids, strings of corn.

so'so, v.a. To cut into strings, as a hide. Wasóso. Tahalo k'oŋ he haŋke - .
so'soṗi, n. A strip or string cut from hide.

so'ṫa, adj. perhaps. Used up, gone; hazy. Iyuha sotapi, All are dead. Cf. kasota, yusota, solkiya.

sotka', adj. As one tall thin tree standing among smaller ones.

sṗaŋ, v. To thaw, perhaps. Aŋpetu waŋ spaŋ s'e waśte he yelo, i.e. a quiet pleasant day in winter. Bl.
sṗaŋ'la, v.n. To become soft, melt, as snow. Wa - . -- sṗáŋlaya, v.a. To cause to thaw, as snow. Spaŋlawaya.

spaspa'ya, red. of spaya.
spa'ya, v.n. To be wet, as in one's clothes. Maspaya.
spa'yeya, v.a. To wet, cause to wet or moisten. Spayewaya.

stag, cont. of staka.
stagya', v.a. To make feeble. Stagwaya. -- adv. Feebly, languidly.
stagya'kel, adv. Feebly. Also, stagyéla.
sta'ḱa, adj. Feeble, weary, not able to walk, sick and lying down from exhaustion. Mastaka. Caŋkahu mastaka. Cuwistaka. Hupahu staka. MS.145. Uŋgnahaȟci le aŋpetu kiŋhaŋ iśta mastaka s'elececa. Bl.

staŋ, adj. Moist, wet. Cf. pastaŋ. Also, purple, grape-colored, dark. Śa staŋ, Dark-red. Ha - , Dark complexioned.
staŋka', adj. Moist. Caŋ - .
staŋ'ḱa, adj. Purple

stasta'la, adj. Pliable. - s'elececa, as is said of a bow when it bends well, or of a gun when the hammer works well (oiled etc.). Itazipa kiŋ - s'e (or lolopela s'e) awakate lo.Bl.

sto, adj. Smooth, lying smooth, as hair. Cap'sto s'e nakpa cikcik'a, as is said of a man who has little ears. Bl. Cf. kasto.

sto'la, adj. Small and neat. Mastola.

stosto´, adj. red. (sto). Smooth, lying flat.

stoya´, v.a. To make smooth, smooth down e.g. hair. Stowaya.
stoya´kel, adv. Smoothly. Also, stoyéla.

stu, adj. Proud. Mastú. Uⁿstúpi.

stu´ic'ila, v. refl. To think much of one's self, be proud. Stumic'ila.

stusta´, adj. Tired, weary, unable to move. Mastusta. Caⁿkahu mastusta.
stuste´ya, adv. Wearily, tired out, in an exhausted condition. - waglihuⁿni. -- v.a. perhaps. To weaken. P.

su, n. The seed of anything; a bullet, maza su. Wasu, Hail.

sukpaⁿ´la, n. A shot gun; shot. R.

suksu´ta, adj. red. of suta.
suksu´taya, adv. red. of sutaya. Bl.

suⁿ, n. cont. of suⁿka. Misúⁿ, My younger brother, which is used in addressing him by men and women. -- v. To braid. Cf. soⁿ.

suⁿ´ka, n. A man or woman's younger brother; certain cousins are likewise so called. Misuⁿka, My younger brother.
suⁿka´kiciyapi, n. Brethren, those related as brothers. Suⁿkauⁿkiciyapi.
suⁿka´ku, n. His or her younger brother.
suⁿka´ya, v.a. To have for a younger brother. Suⁿkawaya.

suo´juha, n. A pod.

supe´stola, n. A muskmelon. Same as suzizila.

susu´, n. The testicles.
susu´ icu, v. To castrate. Bl.

Su´suni, n. prop. The Shoshone Indians. Also, Peji´ Wokéya Oti´ kiⁿ.

suśa´śala, n. A 22-caliber rifle.

suta´, adj. Hard, not yielding to the touch; capable of endurance, strong. Masuta. -- sutáka, adj. Tough, hardy. -- sutáya, adv. Firmly, hard. -- sutáyakel, adv. Firmly.

suto´, n. A metal cartridge filled. Na mazasu waⁿ - ikoyaka.

sutoⁿ´, v.n. To ripen, have seed; to be ripe, fit for use, as corn.

suzi´zila, n. Muskmelon. Syn.- supestola.

swa, Cf. yuswa.
swahaⁿ´, part. Ravelled.
swaka´, adj. Ragged, as an old flag, fringed. -- swaswáka, adj. red.

swu´la, adj. Small, fine, as beads etc.
swu´swula, adj. red. of swula.
swuwa´ya, adj. Soft and fine, as snow in warm weather. Wa kiⁿ - ca taⁿyaⁿ oomani waśteyelo. Bl.

s'a, v.n. To hiss, as a serpent or angry people do. Was'a. Also, to splash, as does water.

s'a, aux. suff. To verbs, signifying frequency of action. Wai s'a. It also gives to verbs the force of nouns of agent. Wamanoⁿ s'a, A thief.

s'amna´, adj. Smelling sour, stinking.

s'e, adv. Like, as though. Syn.- s'elececa, It seems as if, it appears so. Hecel he hiⁿhaⁿ s'e waciⁿpi oⁿ hecoⁿpi. Na makoce waⁿ peji to ca akaⁿl maglihe s'ececa na mani iblabla. Also, s'ecéca, s'elé. But s'ececa may be Yankton. B.H.149.8;150.19.
s'ele´ceca, adv. As if, it seems so. Uⁿyaⁿpi kiⁿ slolyapi - . Atkuku toki iyayapi s'e s'elemaceca, as is said at the departure of one who was like a father. Bl.

s'ē´wacaⁿmi, v. 1st pers. sing. (s'ewaciⁿ). I think it is so. This form is used when one is speaking of something that is not distinctly recollected.
s'ē´waciⁿ, v. To think it to be so. Caⁿke tibloku kiⁿ he ciⁿca - na ceya iyayiⁿ na icu keye. MS.96.

s'iⁿ, adv. Craning one's neck, or stretching one's throat or so, as is done when choking or swallowing with difficulty. S'iⁿ napca. Ahiyokas'iⁿ. Cf. s'iⁿs'iⁿ, eyokas'iⁿ. - s'e iⁿyaⁿka, i.e. as a horse, throwing up its head while running. Thus also, Yukós'iηpi s'e iηyaηka. Bl. -- s'íηs'iη, adv. red. Also perhaps, s'íηs'iηya, s'íηs'iηyaη. Caηke akiȟaη t'iη kta ca cehupa kiη akiyataka ca - iyaya wota śke. - iyaya wanapca. Bl. Tókiyataη taákiȟ'aη wahi yelaká s'iηs'iηyaη wanawapce lo. Bl. Cf. kas'iηs'iη, kis'iηs'iη.

ś, A letter that seems to be added to words for dem. emph. Hence, it is like to ȟci. Waηcakeś, At once. Hecenaś. Eȟaś. Miyeś. Waηnaś.

śa, adj. Red. We śa, Crimson. P.

śa' ayaskapa, n. A patent in fee, perhaps because of the red seal attached. HH.

śab a'ya ku'ja, v. ph. To have consumption, i.e. of the bones.

śabśab'ya, adv. red. of śabya. Maȟpiya - kaȟwokelo. Bl.

śabya', 1) v.a. (of śapa). To soil, to defile. Śabwaya. 2) adv. Dirtily.

śagi', adj. Auburn, sandy. P.

Śagla'śa, n. prop. An Englishman.

śaglō'ġaη, num. adj. Eight. -- śaglóġaηla, adv. Only eight. -- śaglóglo-ġaη, adv. By eights.

śa' hiηgla, v.n. To glow. P. Ite - . Bl.

Śahi'ya, n. prop. A tribe of western Indians, not the Śahiyela. Bl.

Śahi'yela, n. prop. The Cheyenne Indians.

śahi'yela tatiη'psiηla, n. The white-flowered parsley. Cogswellia orientalis. The parsley family. The roots are eaten. #263. - huzizi, The yellow-flowered parsley. Cogswellia montana. The parsley family. Also, waȟcazi iyawicaskapa, so called because the plant is sticky when perhaps young. Bc. #262.

śai'c'iya, v. refl. (of śaya). To paint one's self red; to dress well. P. B.H.112.9.

śake', n. The nails of the fingers and toes; the claws of birds and beasts; the hoofs of animals.

śake'haηska, n. The grizzly bear.

śake'hute s'e hiηgla, v. To become very angry, i.e. like a bear. Bl.

śake' ta'ṗa, n. A sickness known to the Indians, consisting in the swelling of the finger tips. Bl.

śaki'ya, v.a. To paint red one's own, or for one; to redden, as the Dakota do scalps. Śawakiya; to make glad by gifts. Nupiη giic'iyapi na itokśaη śakiyapi.

śako'wiη, num. adj. Seven. -- śakówiηla, adv. Only seven. -- śakówiηwiη, adv. By seven.

śa'kpe, num. adj. Six. -- śákṗekṗe, adv. By sixes. Also, śakpékṗe.

śaktoη' s'e, (?). Bl.

śak'o'yazaη, v.n. To have pains under the finger nails because of cold weather.

śa'mna, adj. Dark brown. Bl.

śaη, n. The vagina.

śaη, adv. Same as eśaη, put at the end of the sentence. Uηśila waη leciś maηke śaη, He who was kind to your grandfather sits over here. D. 116.

śaηke', n. A step-mother; a father's other wife. R. Bl. -- śaηkeya, v.a. To have for a śaηke. Śaηkewaya.

śaη'ku, n. An old form for huηku. Mh.

śa'ṗa, adj. Dirty, defiled; blackened. Maśapa. Nape maśapa. Also, śáṗe. Maśape.

śape'stola, n. The diamond in cards.

śapśa'ṗa, adj. red. of śapa. -- śapśáṗe, adj. red. of śape.

śaṗ'a'yapi, n. A sickness of Indians. They refuse any food after they have tasted. Consumption. Bl. EM.

śaś, Same as eśaś, eśa. B.H.28.4.

śaśa', adj. red. of śa.

śaśa'ya, 1) v.a. To dye or paint red. Śaśawaya. 2) adv. Redly.

śaśte', n. The little finger

śaśte'iyókihe, n. The third finger, the ring finger, i.e. that next to the little finger.

Śawa'la, n. prop. The Shawnees. R. Tóka ca kapi.

śaya', 1) v.a. To paint red; to give clothes to somebody, to clothe one. 2) adv. Redly.

śaye'la, adv. Reddest. Maśtiṅcapute - ota.

śe, interj. Hist! Used by men. Cf. śi.

śe'ca, adj. Dry, dead, as wood; rotten.

śehaṅ', (?). He, kola kola tatuye topakiya nataṅ hiyuye - tamuṅka śni ye. MS.101. RT.

śehaṅ'leś, adv. How much more; how much less. B.H.101.2;194.6. Niciye epi kayeś iyeyapi śni k'uṅ, - le hanikakta kiṅ taku oyakihi kte laka, Even your elder brothers have not found her; then how much less will you who are the youngest have any luck?

śehaṅś', adv. A word denoting impatience. R. Micopi ca el wai na lila wicotapi tka - wana slolwaya. MS.341. Na nakuṅ suṅkakupi kiṅ heciya - tehilapi heci henana oṅ Benjamin lila apatoṅyela kuwa. B.H.43.3.

śehaṅ'śka, adv. At any rate. R. Bl. Also, śeháṅśkalaka. R. Bl.

śehaṅ'śtuka, adv. Well, but; this time sure, at last. Aṅbwaśte ca - hlahla kiṅ tehaṅ hotaṅiṅ ktelo. Bl. R. - ecamoṅ kta, This time I will not forget to do it, i.e. as I did before inspite of my resolutions. - okata heci waśteyelo, as a man says coming into and finding the room warm for once. FB. - tuweni naślaye ni kte śni hwo? i.e. at last not one is after you? Bl. - akipa ca, Finally he was really punished. SHB. B.H.68.14.

śeskśe'ca, adj. red. of śeca.

śelya', 1) v.a. To make dry, to lay up to season, make wither. Śelwáya. 2) adv. Seasoning, withered. -- śelyákel, adv. In dry condition. - yaṅka. B.H.65.20.

śē'na, adj. Having used up, spent, sold etc. everything, and hence having nothing. Maśéna. Mazaska maśena. Also, jena. Cf. yuijena etc.

śeya'ka, n. A tea drunk by Indians as westerners drink theirs. It is made of a water plant, perhaps peppermint, but the non-medicinal mint, ceyáka.

śi, interj. Hist! Hark! Heh! It is used by women to call attention privately.

śi, v.a. To command, bid. This word is always preceded by another verb. Ecoṅ śi. Waśí.

śibśi'paha ṅ, part. red. of śipahaṅ. Syn.- psúṅpsuṅwahaṅ.

śi'ca, śi'ce, adj. Bad, ugly, wicked. Maśíca.

śica'howa, v.n. To cry out. Śicahowawa. -- śicáhowaya, v.n. To moan, scream. Śicahowabla. Śicahowala. Śicahowauṅyaṅpi. Na ataya akicita k'oṅ śicahowayapi na Lakota ko.

śi'cakicilapi, v. recip. Hating each other. Also, śilkícilapi.

śi'cakila, v. pos. (of śicela). To hate one's own. Śicawakila. Also, śilkíla.

śi'cakiya, v.a. To think low of. Śicawakiye. P. Also, śilkíya.

śica'mna, adj. Bad smelling. Niśicamna ca gni na yaki kiṅ ikpakiṅtiṅ na u wo.

śica'waciṅ, 1) v.n. To be frightened, to hurry overmuch; to scream out. B.H.112.9. 2) adv. Frantically. - wau. D.194 and 4.

śica'ya, adv. Badly, not well. - kuwa, To treat meanly. Also, śicáyakel.

śicē'ca, n. A child, little children.

This is doubtfully used by the Tetons. R. Bl.

śi'cela, v.a. To esteem as bad, to hate. Śíc̣ewala. Cf. waȟtela śni, śillá.

śi'celaȟ, adj. dim. (of śica). Funny, cute, as applied to babies etc. for an endearing name.

śi'celaka, v. To think bad, to hate. Śíc̣ewalaka.

śici'a, v.n. To talk angrily. Śiciwaya.

śi'cit'e, adj. (of śica and it'a). Very bad; worthless; lit., dead of badness.

śico'ķiya, v.a. (of śica and okiya). To speak evil to one's spouse. Bl.

śicun', Same as sicun.

śic'e', n. A woman's brother-in-law and mine, i.e. her husband's brother and her sister's husband. Niśic'e. -- śic'eku, n. Her brother-in-law, i.e. husband's brother and sister's husband. -- śic'éśi, n. A woman's male cousin, and my male cousin. Niśíc'eśi. -- śic'éśitku, n. Her male cousin. -- śic'éśiya, v.a. To have for a male cousin. Śic'éśiwaya. -- śic'éya, v.a. (for a woman). To have for a brother-in-law, i.e. husband's brother and sister's husband. Śic'ewaya.

śigla', v.n. To be or become angry, take offense at. Śilwagla, śiunglapi. Tuwa śigla ca kat'api. Śiyagla. Bl. Note: that "l" is introduced before the pronouns. R. -- śiglápi, n. Anger, wrath. -- śigláya, v.a. To make angry, provoke. Śiglawaya.

śiȟṫin', adj. Bad, poorly made, imperfect. -- śiȟṫínyan, adv. Poorly made, imperfectly.

śika, interj. Pitiful one! This word has no accent and can stand or be omitted without affecting the sense of the sentence. It is something of an aside by the person telling the story to stir pity in the hearers for a character in the tale. - onśiyeȟci omaśte wan el anpetu ataya ȟpayela ke, i.e. the helpless animal sought out a sunny spot and lay there all day. Tima lekśitkula k'un wayaka s'e tisanpatanhan pa icu śni yanka, There sat his uncle, like a pitiable captive, on the opposite side of the tipi, never once raising his head. Note: this last example illustrates the omission of śika from its place immediately after k'un. D.123, 110.

śiķi'gla, v. To be satisfied with. - unkomanipelo, We are making good headway. Bl. Syn.- opikila.

śikśi'ca, adj. red. of śica. -- śikśíc̣aya, adv. Badly. - mani. Ota - econ. B.H.199.6.

śikśil', cont. (of śikśica). Badly. - ia, To talk badly. - iwaya. -- śikśíloȟ'an, v. To act badly, to do wickedly. -- śikśíloȟ'anka, n. One who does badly. -- śikśílya, adv. (of śilya). Badly.

śila'ptanyeya, v.a. To cause to have bad luck, to curse. B.H.67.9.

śila'wacin, v. To think bad of, have bad desires for. B.H.191.7.

śil ecón ape', v. To solicit. Also, Wicoh'an śica econ ape. B.H.29.

śilgla', v. To detest, not wishing to see it. Śilwagla. This may more properly be śigla. -- śilglá tóie, v. To curse. Śilwicagla toie, He cursed them. Śilwagla mitoie. B.H.113.12. Cf. glatóie.

śilȟ'an', v.n. To behave badly. Śilwaȟ'an. -- śilȟ'ánka, n. One who acts badly. Bl. -- śilȟ'ányan, adv. Behaving badly.

śilki'cilapi, Cf. śicakicilapi.

śilķi'la, Cf. śicakila.

śilķi'ya, Cf. śicakiya.

śilla', v. To esteem bad. Śilwála.

śilo'ȟ'an, v. To do wrong. Śilowaȟ'an. - ape. B.H.94.3;137.20.

śilo'iepi, n. Bad talk. B.H.103.7.

śilwa'econ, v. To act badly, commit wrong deeds. - śni yunś tohanni unnicahipi śni tka yelo. B.H.260.16.

śilwa'kipa, v. To have bad luck. B.H. 44.3.

śilwa'nakih'oⁿ, v. (?). Śilwanakiȟ'oⁿpi s'e inila maⁿkehelo, i.e. I am silent. Bl.

śilwi'yauⁿpa, v. B.H.164.6.

śilwi'yukcaⁿ, v.abs. To plan evil. Śilwiblukcaⁿ. D.258.

śilwo'ȟaȟniȟya, v.a. To scandalize e.g. little ones, to teach evil to little ones. B.H.215.10.

śilwo'yaka, v. To talk bad about others.

śilya', v.a. To spoil. Śilwaya. Syn.- yuśica. -- adv. Badly.
śilya'ȟel, adv. Badly.

śilye'ȟci, (?). - Ȟlogeca it'eyela, as is said when a man is very lean. Bl.

śilye'la, adv. Sadly; badly. - t'a ȟpaye. D.273.

śil'a'nagoptaⁿ, v. To hear stories about others and spread them.

śina', n. A blanket, shawl, robe.
śiná apaȟlate, Ribbon, ferret.
śiná apaȟlate zibzipela, Silk ribbon.
śiná caⁿkohaⁿ, The center beaded back part of a shawl, a blanket beaded across the middle. R.
Śinágleglega, n. prop. The Navajos.
śináhiⁿśma, A buffalo robe.
śináȟota, The common white blanket.
śináikceka, A buffalo robe.
śináipatapi, A robe ornamented with quill-work.
śinájaⁿjaⁿ, A red blanket.
śiná ȟasúpi, A fringed shawl.
śiná okásu, The fringe of a shawl.
śináokipata, A quilt made of pieces.
śináopapuⁿ ciscila, A blanket with a small border, save list cloth.
śináopapuⁿ ȟota, Gray list cloth.
śináopapuⁿ ska, White list and stroud.
śináopehe, A bale of blankets.
śinásaⁿ, A blanket.
śináśa, A red blanket.
śináto, Blue skirt cloth; a blue or green blanket.
śináto zibzipela, Blue broad cloth.
śinázibzipela, Broad cloth.
śinóȟasu, Cf. śina okásu.

śiⁿ, n. The fat part of animals, esp. fat meat; the sappy part of wood, thus: caⁿśiⁿ.

śiⁿkciⁿ'yaⁿ, adv. Cranky. - uⁿ, To be angry always and cranky. Bl. Note: Wawohilhitikiⁿ kte ȟciⁿ ca hecel kapi.

śiⁿkpaⁿ'ȟahu, n. Food roots; the name of an edible root that grows in low lands. Also, śiⁿkpáⁿka. D.97.

śiⁿśiⁿ', adj. Wrinkled.

śiⁿta'to cegnáke, n. A loin cloth made of blue or black cloth.

śipa', Cf. kaśipa, yuśipa.
śipa'haⁿ, part. Broken off close, as the limbs of a tree, the teeth of a comb. Also, śipawahaⁿ, pśuⁿwahaⁿ.

śiśo'ka, n. The robin. R. FR.

śi'yagla, n. A duck.

śiya'ȟa, n. The American eared grebe; the teal duck; a boil. D.130.

śiya'ka, n. A boil. - upi, i.e. a little hard swelling containing hard matter. EM.

śiya'taȟala, n. The American dipper, the water ouzel, a small black bird that lives near water. Bl.
śiya'taȟaⁿla, n. A small bird that frequents rice lakes. R. Bl.

śiyo', n. The grouse, the prairie hen. The male heralds forth the morning: Wi̇jo bū .... The female answers: Mabú, mabū .... - s'e pa caⁿśihuta laka ca yaⁿkiⁿ na, as is said of a person with a little nose. Male prairie chickens inflate their neck sacs as sounding boards and send their "oom-boom-boom" often two miles across the prairie. Śiyó wacipi.

śiyo' cik'ala, n. The quail, the bob-white. Also, can śiyo. FR.

śiyo' iśtóȟcapi wi, n. prop. The month of March.

śiyo'ka, n. A bird. (?).

śiyo'śuⁿȟa, n. A bird dog.

śiyo'taŋka, n. A large śiyo. - yajo.

śiyō'to, n. The muscle in the front side of the upper part of a man's leg. In times past, men always died when that muscle was hurt badly. Gv.

śiyo' wacipi, n. The drumming performed by the grouse in spring during the mating season.

śiyū'ťakaȟpe, n. (śiyute and akaȟpe). An apron.

śiyū'ťe, n. The front part of the legs, the lap. - akaȟpe, An apron.

śka, conj. But, and yet. Nikuja śka taŋkal ilala, You are sick and yet you want outside. Iŋśe he tokaśni śka hepelo. B.H.181.10.

śǩa, Cf. śke.

śkabyē'la, adv. With a noise such as made by a rock etc. thrown in. Thus: śkáb hiŋglá.

śkal, cont. of śkata. - iya.

śkalǩi'ya, v.a. To cause to play. Śkalwakiya.

śka'lwayup̄ika, adj. Skillful at games.

śkaŋ, v.n. To do, to act, to move about. Waśkáŋ. - hiŋgla. D.217.
śkáŋhiŋgleǩiya, v. To make one start up. Bl.
śkaŋǩáp̄iŋ, adj. Lazy, unwilling to move about.
śkaŋǩáp̄iŋp̄i, n. Laziness.
śkaŋǩiya, v.a. To cause to move about. Śkaŋwakiya.
śkaŋśkáŋ, v. red. (of śkaŋ). To stir, move about, change place. Waśkaŋśkaŋ. Maza śkaŋśkaŋ.
śkaŋśkáŋ oǩíle, v. To make it comfortable for one's self, to rest. Bl.
śkaŋśkáŋ waśicuŋ, n. A restless person. Same as woslotoŋ śni, wanaptoŋka. Bl.
śkaŋśkáŋyaŋ, 1) v.a. To cause to move about. Śkaŋśkaŋwaya. 2) adv. Moving, in motion. Also, śkaŋyáŋ.

śka'ťa, v.n. To play. Waśkáte.

śke, v.n. impers. It is said, they say, it is reported. Hecel wicakte śke. Cf. D.1, note 1.

śkeca', n. An animal similar to an otter. R. Bl. - ha, The pelt of a little black animal used in ornamenting ladies' winter coats. Bl.

śke'haŋ, adj. Wild, prancing, as a horse; ambitious. -- śkeháŋhaŋ, adj. (of śkehaŋ). Jumping around, frolicsome.

śke'he, Same as śkehaŋ. -- śkehéca, n. An animal that is wild or unsteady. -- śkéheśni, adj. Gentle. -- śkehéya, v.a. To make wild, make prance about. Śkehewaya. -- śkéheya, adv. Ambitiously.

śke'lo, Same as śke.

śǩelu'ťa, n. An oriole; perhaps an auduban. It is often used as a wapegnaka. -- śǩelúťa taŋka, n. The Baltimore oriole. Śǩelúťa cik'ala, The orchard oriole. FR. Śkeluta s'e ahiyaye, To pass by dressed more or less in yellow with a little black and white. Bl.

śkica', Cf. yuśkica.

śkica'haŋ, part. Squeezing, pressed.

śkiŋ'c'iya, v. To move one's self. Śkíŋmic'iya. Hehaŋl wicat'e k'uŋ - . Also, śkiŋciya. R.

śki'p̄ip̄i, śki'p̄ip̄ila, n. The chickadee. The Lakota say it has a sevencleft tongue. It begins to split in October; the seventh split occurs in April when it heals up again. Then it asks of the buzzard (heca) returned: Gli hwō? Upon the Indians answering: Gli yelo, the bird is satisfied and remains silent for a long time. When the buzzard is back, there will be no cold weather anymore, it is said. Also, śkíbibila, wiyáwala, ǧuǧuya śkula. BS. D.88.

śkiśka', adj. Rough, not smooth and level, as a road.

śkiśke'ya, 1) v.a. To make rough. Śkiśkewaya. 2) adv. Roughly.

śkiśki'ťa, adj. Rough, not smooth and level.

śkiśki'ťa hu, n. Cf. caŋȟloǧaŋ śkiśkita. Bl. #236.

śkob, cont. of śkopa. - iyaya.

śkobya', 1) v.a. To make crooked. Śkobwaya. 2) adv. Crookedly.

śkoġiŋ'ġiŋlak yaŋka, v. To sit idle. An old word. BD.

śkokpa', adj. Hollowed out, concave, as a shell.

śkō'pa, adj. Crooked, warped, concave. Pa śkopa, A crooked nose.

śko'pela, n. A banana. Also, zizi' śkopela.

śkośko'pa, adj. red. (of śkopa). Crooked, warped, concave; curled, as hair. RF.

śku, v.n. To be wholly or partially roasted, i.e. red from the heat; to be covered with red spots, as one who lies too close to the fire in cold weather. Maśkú. Ikpi niśku. R. HC.

śku, Same as "yau". An old word. A man would say on seeing and recognizing another: Hepela niyeyo, tokiyataŋ śku hwo? Our visitor would then answer: Heciyataŋ pu welo. Pu is equivalent to waú. Bd.

Śku'tani, n. prop. The Kootenai.

śla, adj. Bald, bare.

śla e'gna, ślae'gna, adv. Openly, exposed, in full view, uncovered; without a house, defenseless. - haŋ, Unsheltered, standing out. Cf. ślaégnag.

ślae'gnag, adv. In a barren place, where nothing grows (śla). Caŋ - haŋ, A tree stands in a bare country, i.e. nothing else is growing.

ślaśla', adj. red. of śla. Bare in different places, as a pasture or doze, a place of fallen timber.

ślaya', 1) v.a. To make bare. Ślawaya. 2) adv. Nakedly, without covering. Maka - yuŋke kiŋ, Bare, grassless ground. Now they say: makóśla, (of maka and ośla). Makośla yuŋke el.

śle'ca, Cf. kaśleca.

śli, 1) adv. Hissing, fizzing, as two persons whispering to each other. 2) v.n. To ooze out, as gum. Nawicaśli. -- śliyéla, adv. perhaps. Making the noise of rain. Also, śliyélahaŋ. Magaju kiŋ śliyelahaŋ. Also, Whizzing, as a bullet in the air. Kóŋśyéla ya, i.e. the whizzing of a bullet. But this seems to be no word, rather a comp. of koŋs and śliyéla. Also, śliyela. R.

ślo, v.n. To melt, as butter, grease, metal, ice. Mini ślo ayelo, i.e. the snow is melting. Bl. -- v. To lisp. IS.

ślo'ka, Cf. kaśloka.

śloka'haŋ, part. Out of place, as an ax-head off the handle, or an eye out of its socket.

ślośló', 1) v. red. (of ślo). To melt. 2) adj. Soft, melted, as fat.

ślośló'kahaŋ, part. perhaps. Falling off. Śake kiŋ - . B.H.231.5.

ślo'ślola, n. The upland plover. Its rolling sound and its nocturnal flights (migrating) to and from the pampas of South America is a forelorn sound. - ca ikpakpi s'e, as they say when a man has greased his hair, like a bird fresh from the shell. - s'e hu cikcik'aya hu okihe taŋkiŋkiŋyaŋ kaca, as is said of a person who has thin legs but thick knees. Bl. IS.

śloślō'la, n. Slush; the soft fat parts in an animal perhaps. R.

śloya', v.a. (of ślo). To make melt, as butter, grease. Ślowaya. Waśiŋ śloyapi, Fried bacon. -- śloyágnaka, v.a. To place near the fire to soften or melt. Cf. tasagyagnaka. Bl. -- śloyápi, n. That which is melted.

ślu'ślu'ta, adj. Slippery, as a road; smooth, as ice, a horn etc. He - . Also, fig., Penniless, "broke", having spent everything. Waŋna maśluśluta. Bl. Noŋge niśluśluta, i.e. you do not listen to me. BT.

ślu'ta, adj. Cf. yuśluta, naśluta.

śma, adj. Deep, as water or snow; dense, as foliage; thickly set, as hair. -- śmaśmá, adj. red.

śme, Same as śma. -- śméya, adv. Deeply, densely. Wa śmeya hiⁿhpeya ca, i.e. deep snow. B.H.8.2. -- śmeyáťa, adv. In the deep.

śmi, adj. Bare. -- śmiśmí, adj. red. of śmi. -- śmiśmíka, adj. perhaps. Hairless. Nasu - . Bl. Bald.

śna, Cf. yuśna.

śna, adv. Again and again, continually, ref. to something that so occurs. Śna apápi. Le oⁿ śna wocekiye yakagapi kta. Caⁿ śna yaⁿka, Always there, here, now. MS.73. R. B.H.61.6;178.19; 265.5;257.14. Also, sometime, sometimes. Aⁿpetu śna. B.H.257.14. Le wahiⁿkpe kiⁿ, tohaⁿl amiciȟaⁿpi ca oyate kiⁿ witaya śna lapi na yeyayapi kte lo. Kośkalaka k'oⁿ he omani i na śna taȟca na pte na heȟaka hecel śna wagli ca tawicu k'oⁿ wakabla. Wauⁿyaⁿpi el śna ihpeyapi. Hena wi waⁿji caⁿ okaśpe waⁿji el śna omniciye ecoⁿpi. Na śna uⁿkcepi na śna kawaⁿkal kiglahaⁿpi. MS.143,158,344,106.

śna'śnayela, adv. At times, a little. Wa - hiⁿhpayelo, i.e. a little snow. LB.

śni, adv. The particle of negation. Not. It follows verbs, nouns, pronouns and as well adjectives, adverbs etc. Cf. D.9, note 2. Gramm.352,289.

śni'ja, adj. Withered, dead, dried up, as leaves by the sun; blurred, indistinct. Iśtómaśnija.

śni' ṗuťe' ya, v. To play a game in which players throw the bow. Bl.

śniś, adv. Śni emph. I śniś gli yelo, i śni kayeś gli yelo, as is said when one returns after nobody knew of his whereabouts. Bl. Note: I śnis may more properly be iśniś.

śni'śni, red. of śni. The word ref. to some repetition. Maka ali - s'e mani, i.e. to walk lightly, inaudibly. Bl.

śniśni'ja, adj. of śnija.

śniśya', 1) v.a. To make wither or dry up. Śniśwaya. B.H.200.6. 2) adv. Withered. Also, fig., To shrink; to disappoint one. Śniśmaya, He (or she) disappointed me, i.e. by not coming or giving praise. WW.

śniyaⁿ, śniyaⁿkel, suff. Affixed to verbs and nouns, making them negative adverbs. Na iye el uⁿśniyaⁿ taku wokage keśa wokage śni. LWOW.183. Wowicakeśniyaⁿ waayataⁿiⁿ kta eya awicakitapi. MS.279.

śniyaⁿ'yaⁿ, adv. Very rapidly, ref. to the motion of e.g. the wings etc. Cf. hukpáⁿȟos iⁿyaⁿka. Syn.- ȟniyaⁿyaⁿ. - kiⁿyaⁿ, iⁿyaⁿka. -- śniyáⁿyaⁿla, n. The rapid moving of wings. Bl. Cf. kaśniyaⁿyaⁿla.

śni'yeca, (?). Wa śniyeca, as when snow melts on touching the ground.Bl.

śnuⁿśnuⁿ'jela, adj. Pliant. Syn.- kcaⁿkcaⁿla, wiⁿświⁿjahela. Bl.

śog, cont. of śoka. -- śogśógya, adv. red. of śogya.

śogya', adv. (of śoka). Strongly, firmly; thickly; seriously, badly; greatly, much; piled, as clothes heaped on each other etc. - awaciⁿ, sutaya awaciⁿ. - kaga. - opi, i.e. seriously wounded. Iho le icinuⁿpa wicoȟaⁿ ecoⁿ eśa lila - ecoⁿ yawapi. Also, śogyéȟ

śoho'toⁿla, n. The black-billed cuckoo.

śō'ka, adj. Thick, as applied to solids such as cloth, board wood; dense, as woods. Na caⁿ - etkiya ya.

śo'ȟela, n. A quarter of a dollar; a quarter section of land. Cf. śoka.

śokśō'ka, adj. red. of śoka. Caⁿ kaśleślecapi ota pahayela eglepi na caⁿha - ko na lila ota ileyapi.

śok'iⁿ', (?). Taȟca ciⁿcala s'e ite kiⁿ - laka ca yaⁿkiⁿ na, as is said of a man with a little face. -- śok'iⁿyaⁿ, (?). Mayaślecala s'e ite - , as is said of a man with a strikingly small face. Bl.

śol, cont. of śota.

śola'nini, n. Soot,smut.

śola'śaṗa, v.n. To become dirty from smoke.

śolki'ya, v. To make smoke. Pute mayukaŋ ca śolwakiyiŋ kte, as an Indian may say when he is ready to smoke a pipe.

śolya', v. To make smoky.

śoŋ'śoŋ ikpisaŋ, śoŋ'śoŋ ikpiska, n. A donkey. Also, śóŋśoŋkpisaŋ, abbrev.

śoŋ'śoŋla, 1) adj. Long-eared, hanging down, as the ears of many dogs do. 2) n. A mule.

śośa', adj. Turbid, muddy, as water.

śośe', adj. Same as śośa. -- śośéya, 1) v.a. To make turbid or muddy, to stir up. Śośewaya. 2) adv. Turbidly.

śo'ṫa, 1) n. Smoke. 2) v.n. To smoke, as does fire.

śo'ṫa sam iyáye, n. ph. A chimney, one built on the roof.

śo'ṫiyowotaŋiŋśniyaŋ, adv. Invisible from smoke, surrounded by smoke. - maŋkelo, I am sitting in the smoke. Bl. Syn.- śótiyuskilya.

śo'ṫiyuskilya, adv. Enveloped by smoke. - naŋkahaŋpelo, as is said when people sit in a smoky room. Bl. Cf. śotiyowotaŋiŋśniyaŋ.

śotk̇a'zi, 1) n. Soot. 2) adj. Smoked black, sooty.

śoṫō'ju, adj. Smoky, full of smoke; hazy, as the atmosphere. R. Tak waŋyaŋgpica śni ohiŋniyaŋ śotoju. Bl. -- śoṫójuya, v. To make smoky, to fill with smoke. Śotojuwaya.

śpa, Cf. yuśpa.

śpahaŋ', part. Broken off. -- śpaháŋhaŋ, red. (of śpahaŋ). Broken off, crumbling away. Wayakayaḣ'u śpahaŋhaŋpi. B.H.114.21;184.21.

śpaŋ, adj. Cooked; burnt or frozen, as parts of the body by heat or cold. Talo - . Noge maśpaŋ. -- v.n. perhaps. To be cooked, burnt or frozen. Na tehaŋ hecel - el icu na ake huŋḣ el ognaka na ota śpaŋyaŋ. Caŋke waŋji icu (a hot dog's head) tka nape - . Maka śpaŋpi, A brick. Yupiyela wana wapasnoŋ k'uŋ - , There was some meat on spits just about done. D.22.

śpaŋi'c'iya, v. refl. (of śpaŋyaŋ). To get burned or frozen. Cf. ġuíc'iya.

śṗaŋk̇a'ġapi, n. Green corn dried.

śpaŋk̇i'ciciya, v.a. To cook for one. Śpaŋweciciya.

śpaŋk̇i'ya, v.a. pos. To cook one's own food, to cook for another. Śpaŋwakiya.

śpaŋ'la s'e ia', v. To speak excitedly, angrily. - ielo. Bl.

śpaŋ'śni, adj. Raw, not cooked. - yutapi, What is eaten raw, i.e. melons, cucumbers.

śpaŋśni'yuṫapi iyéceca, n. The buffalo burr, sand-burr. Solanum rostratum. The nightshade family. Bl. #222.

śpaŋyaŋ', v.a. To cook e.g. food. Śpaŋwaya.

śpe, Cf. śpa.

śpi, Cf. yuśpi.

śpu, Cf. yuśpu.

śṗu'k̇eśni, adj. A very lively character. Hokśila-hakaktala waŋ - , yuŋkaŋ he e, i.e. wide awake. D.14. WE. Syn.- bliheca.

śpu'la, adj. perhaps. dim. Little things torn from something; nicknacks, trifles. Taku - . Bl. Taku - kiŋ oyas'iŋ teḣila, kpagaŋ śni, i.e. to be attached to all sorts of little things such as nicknacks. Bc. -- śpuśpúla, adj. red. (of śpula). Taku - keci, All sorts of little things. Bc.

śpuwa'haŋ, part. Fallen off of itself, as anything that adhered, e.g. a telephone wire.

śtag, cont. of śtaka. -- śtagyá, 1) v.a. To mash up; to make preserves. Śtagwaya. 2) adv. Mushy, as said of soft ice..

śta'ka, adj. Soft, as ice. Cf. kaśtaka.

śtan, Cf. kaśtan, yuśtan.

śtaśta', adj. Weak, brittle. -- śťaśťáka, adj. red. of śtaka. -- śtaśtála, adj. Brittle. -- śtaśtáyela, adj. Soft, tender, as skin may be.

śtei'c'ila, v. refl. To think much of one's self.

śtela', v. To rate high, admire. Śtewala. Śtelapi, n. Admiration. -- śteláka, v. To rate high. Śtewalaka.

śtulya', v.a. To thaw out, as anything frozen. Śtulwaya.

śťunka', adj. Unripe, as fruit. -- śtunkála, adj. Soft, mellow; not ripe, as corn in the milk.

śtuśťa', adj. Soft, as the flesh of animals when hard chased, wanting flavor.

śtuśte' la, adj. Same perhaps as śtuśta. Also, Tired out, in ref. to man. Maśtuśte la ȟcakelo. Bl. BT. -- śtuśťéya, v.a. To chase so as to make weary and render the meat flavorless. Śtuśtewaya.

śtu'ťa, 1) adj. Thawed, warmed. Nape maśtuta. Pagla wan ca śtuta iyutelo. 2) v.n. To be thawed, warmed. Wana unśtutapelo. HH.

śun, n. The large feathers of birds' wings.

śung, cont. of śunka.

śunga'k'in, n. A saddle blanket.

śungblo'ka, n. The male of a horse or dog.

śunghu'la, n. A short-legged horse, a pony; a small horse, a shetland pony.

śunǧi'la, n. The fox.

śungle'śka, n. A spotted horse.

śungma'ǩicima, n. A young horse.

śungma'nitu, n. A wolf.

śungnan'kpoǧi, n. A brown-eared horse.

śungni'ni, n. A wild horse. Bl.

śungnu'ni s'e yanka, v. To be silent and sad, as though one had lost one's horses. WE.

śungwin'yela, n. A mare.

śung'i'cakce, n. A horse curry.
śung'i'capsinte, n. A horse whip.
śung'i'caśke, n. A picket-pin, anything to fasten a horse with.
śung'i'kan, n. A strap to tie a horse.
śung'i'kte, n. Poison; lit., that by means of which a wolf is killed.
śung'i'naȟtake, n. A spur.
śung'i'najipa, n. A spur.
śung'i'paȟte, n. A bridle.
śung'o'najin, n. A stable, horse barn.
śung'o'naś'o, n. A pacing horse.

śunȟpa'la, n. A puppy, little dog.

śun'ǩa, n. A dog.

śun'kace, n. A bulbous esculent root that grows in swamps. R. The root of the calamus plant, whose leaves are called hoȟwá. Also, śunkcé.

śun'ka ce'mila, n. A knife with a crescent like blade which is used in butchering. The cutting edge is along the outer side. Bl.

śunkaho', v. To howl like a dog.

śunka'ȟlowanpi, n. A parade with singing made by those who were on the point of going on the warpath. Bl.

śunka'in, n. A horse blanket. - ȟloȟlóka, A fly cover. Also, śunkak'in, śungak'in.

śun'ka iťe' pśunǩa, n. A bull dog.

śunka'kanyanka, n. A rider, man on horseback. -- v. To ride horseback. Śunkakanmanka. - ośpaye wanji ehakela manipelo.

śunkan'yan, adv. (?). Talo wan - iyayelo, as they say when they failed to catch a rabbit etc. for food. BT. Lecala taku wan oyé iyaya, tka - oye iyayelo, i.e. it seems to be a fresh track. Bl. -- śunkányankel, adv. (?). - igluza, To have poor clothing on that does not protect; also, zanzanyela igluza. Bl. - mak'u, He gave me only a little. Tulá śunkanya yaun welo, mato wayakita yelo, i.e. meeting one who did not notice one's coming and was afraid. Le pahiⁿ s'e - mani tka taⁿktaⁿkaya omani yelo. Bl.

śuⁿka'śtaka, v.a. To abuse a horse by striking. B.H.68.10.

śuⁿ'ḱawakaⁿ, n. A horse.

śuⁿ'ḱawakaⁿ tapejúta, n. Silvery groundsel. Senecio canus. The composite family. Bl. #94.

śuⁿ'kawakaⁿ' tawanap'iⁿ, n. A horse collar.

śuⁿ'ka wicaśa, n. A monkey.

śuⁿkcaⁿ'kahuiṗiye, n. Western false gromwell. Onosmodium occidentale. The borage family. The roots and seeds are used for horses as a tea and for rubbing in. It is also used for swellings on men. BS. #115.

śuⁿkce', n. The root of the calamus plant; the leaves are called hoḣwá. Cf. śúⁿkace.

śuⁿkce'cahuśte, n. A horse that is lame in the hip. Bl.

śuⁿkciⁿ'ca, n. A young coyote.

śuⁿkciⁿ'cala, n. A colt.

śuⁿkciⁿ'ca oti, n. A wolf's den.

śuⁿkhiⁿ'śa, n. A sorrel horse. Same as hiⁿśa. - wicaḣcala s'e ite saⁿ okpaⁿkpaⁿ. Bl. - gleśka, A spotted sorrel horse. MS.561.

śuⁿkhu'la, n. A horse with short legs. - s'e huwakiś'ake, as is said of a man with short legs who is good at running. Bl. A short-legged pony. Cf. śuⁿghula.

śuⁿkhu'śtiṗiye, n. Wooly white hymenopappus. Hymenopappus tenuifolius. The composite family. From the plant are made tea and salve to treat horses' hoofs. Bl. #268.

śuⁿki'cakca, n. A horse curry.
śuⁿki'capowa, n. A horse brush.
śuⁿki'capsiⁿte, n. A horse whip.
śuⁿki'ċaśke, n. A picket-pin, a stick, pin, to tie horses to.

śuⁿḱi'coco, v. To call one's dogs. Bl.

śuⁿki'gmuⁿḱe, n. Poison; anything to use in trapping wolves.

śuⁿki'ṫepesṫo, n. A grayhound.

śuⁿkko'yakya, v. To rope a horse. Śuⁿkkoyakwaya.

śuⁿkle'ja hu, n. Racemose milk vetch. Astragalus racemosus. The pulse family. Bl. #39.

śuⁿḱlu'zahaⁿ, n. A race horse.

śuⁿkma'niśniḱiya, (?). Walking in the manner of a played out horse. Bl.

śuⁿkma'niṫu, n. A coyote.

śuⁿkma'niṫuho, v.n. To howl like a wolf. Śuⁿkmaniṫuwaho.

śuⁿkma'niṫu táⁿka, n. A wolf.

śuⁿknoⁿ'ġekpa s'e, adv. (?). Huⁿhé, wokiyakapi kiⁿ el ewaciⁿ śni - , as is said when a person does not listen. Bl. Roboam - wokiyakapi k'uⁿ el ewaciⁿ śni. B.H.103.10.

śuⁿknu'ni, n. A wild horse.
śuⁿ'koⁿpa, Same as śuⁿoⁿk'oⁿpa.
śuⁿko'waśakala, n. The Canadian milk vetch, Canadian rattleweed. Astragalus Canadensis. The pulse family. The seeds are an eating delight to horses. BT. #118.

śuⁿko'wote, n. A nosebag.

śuⁿksi'kośka, n. A horse with a swollen foot. Bl.

śuⁿksi'maza, n. A horse shoe.

śuⁿkśa'kiyuksa, n. A hoof trimmer.

śuⁿkśaⁿ', n. An old worn-out horse. Śuⁿkśáⁿḣca yeś peji k'iⁿ yelo; as an old horse may be used on occasion for hauling hay, so also a lazy man works once in a while, or works for once. Bl.

śuⁿkta'caⁿgleśka, n. The basket-like hoop laid over the two poles of the śúⁿkoⁿpa in which loads and children are packed.

śuⁿkta'haⁿpa, n. Real horse-shoes made of leather to protect the hoofs, as old-time Indians employed.

śuŋkta'hu waś'áka, n. A horse with a very strong neck, so that it cannot be guided easily. Bl.

śuŋkta'maḳa, n. A lean horse or dog. Cf. támaka.

śuŋkta'pejuta, n. Stemless loco-weed, crazy-weed; Colorado loco vetch. Oxytropis lamberti. The pulse family. Horses eat it and even dig out the roots. L. #4. Cf. FD.257.

śuŋkta'wanap'iŋ, n. A horse collar.

śuŋkta'wote, n. Same as śuŋktapejuta. One of the three kinds of zitkatacaŋ: false indigo, bastard indigo, and river-locust. Amorpha practicosa. The pulse family. Also, branched eriogonum. Eriogonum multiceps. The buckwheat family. BT. WE. Bl. #4,130,288.

śuŋk'i'śtakpa s'e, adv. Walking or going about in the manner of a blind horse, fearlessly when it should fear; wandering, as certain women do. - omani. Bl.

śuŋk'i'yoṗeya, v.a. (?). Śuŋk'iyopewaya. Wahaŋpi śuŋk'iyopewayelo, as a man says when he has no teeth anymore and eats not meat but soup only. Bl.

śuŋk'lō'ṫe, adj. perhaps. Slow because one is tired, seemingly not able to take care of one's self. Tuwa úŋciḣiśni he kapi. Śuŋk'málote.

śuŋk'na'sapi, n. A pastime for boys shooting arrows through a waleġa in which worms get water. Bl.

śuŋk'nu'nikiciyapi, n. A pastime for boys. Bl.

śuŋ'k'ohaŋpi, n. A wakaŋ wicoḣ'aŋ instituted by marriageable women to get a husband; a feast of boiled dog.

śuŋk'o'iyaḳilsuṫa s'e, adv. In the manner of a horse that slackens again and again inspite of all urging and whipping. - kagiśniśni nagwaka, as is said of a man who continues to criticize inspite of all explanations. Bl.

śuŋk'o'ḳaḣ, (?). - waŋjica nuŋb wicayuha, He has two horses perfectly alike. Bl.

śuŋk'o'ḳaḣwog, (?). - uŋ ca śicelo, as is said of a horse that changes its owners very often. Bl.

śuŋk'o'kasak'suta, n. A horse that does not react to urging or whipping. Bl.

śuŋk'o'naś'ake, n. An old, worn-out horse. Bl.

śuŋk'o'naś'ola, n. A pacing horse. Cf. śuŋg'onaś'o.

śuŋ'k'oŋjica, (?). - s'e yusniza s'a ye, i.e. breaks wind often. Bl.

śuŋ'luta, n. The red-shafted flicker, the wood-pecker. The under-side of its wings and tail is red. They sing when good weather is coming. RF.

śuŋmni'yaṫa áya, v. To water the horses.

śuŋoŋ'k'oŋpa, n. (śuŋka-oŋ-k'iŋpi). A pony drag, the original vehicle of the Dakotas when there were no wagons. It consisted of two poles, one pair of ends being fastened together and placed on the back of the pony (or dog) with a strap around the breast, the other pair of ends dragging over the ground. The baggage rested on the śuŋgtacaŋgleśka which is tied across the poles behind the horse's tail. A dog drag. Also, śuŋúŋk'oŋpa. Cf. hupa waheyuŋpi.

śuŋpa', v.n. To moult, shed, as birds do their feathers; to be in moulting.
śuŋṗa'ḣliḣli, v. To have the feathers partly grown, as geese.
śuŋṗe'la, adj. perhaps. Moulting. Bs.

śuŋ'śuŋ ikpisaŋ, n. A donkey. Also, śúŋśuŋ ikpiska, śúŋśuŋkṗisaŋ.

śuŋ'śuŋla, n. A mule. - ikpi saŋ iśtaḣe pajojo kaca, as is said of one with heavy eye-brows. Bl.

śuŋto'to, v.n. To have the feathers partly grown.

śuŋuŋ'k'oŋṗa, n. A dog or pony travois. Also, perhaps, śuŋkuŋk'oŋpa. BS.

śuŋzi'ca, n. The northern flicker, a wood-pecker. It is colored brown, and it says: Aŋpētu waśtē, aŋpétu waśté. FR. Huŋhé, śuŋzica s'e śaké haŋskaskalaḣ, as is said when a person has very long fingernails. Bl.

śuṗe', n. Guts, intestines.

śuṗe'ośica, 1) adj. Hard to digest; disagreeing with one. 2) n. Anything hard to digest.

śuptaŋ'ka, n. (of śupe and taŋka). The large intestines.

śuṗu'ṫe, n. The pit of the stomach, i.e. below the navel. Also, A gun stock.

śuśka', adj. Slow, tardy; good for nothing, worthless. Maśuśka. -- śuśkáka, n. A worthless fellow.

śu'śuś hiŋgla, (?). Bl.

śuta', v. To miss, fail of, to be unable to obtain; to miss, as in shooting. Śuwate. Ehaŋl waŋji kiyela śumata.

śu'taḱaḣpe, n. An apron. Cf. śiyute akahpe, abbrev.

śuṫe'ya, v.a. To cause to fail or miss. Śutéwaya.

śwē'ḱa, adj. Having used up everything, "broke". Waŋna maśweka. Bl.

śwōśwō'ke s'e, adv. Extraordinarily fleshy, as a man or his nose, lips etc. Bl. Syn.- waśóśo s'e, kayóyo s'e.

śwu, v.n. To drop, as water or any other liquid. R. Bl. Cf. s'e. -- śwuśwú, v. red. of śwu. Cf. s'es'é.

ś'a, v.n. To shout. Waś'á.

ś'agi'c'iya, v. refl. To sustain one's self, have command over one's self, to be resolute.

ś'agś'a'ḱa, adj. red. (of ś'aka). Strong. Bl.

ś'agya', v. Cf. ś'agic'iya. -- ś'agyakel, adv. Steadily. Tate waŋ - u. B.H.278.3.

ś'a'ḱa, adj. Strong. Maś'aka. Cf. waś'aka, yuś'aka. Nap'kuwa - , To grasp firmly. Bl. Miwaŋkab - , i.e. stronger than I. B.H.174.7. -- ś'áḱeca, adj. Mighty, powerful; hard to deal with, severe, austere. Bc. R. Maś'akece. Uŋś'akapi. Cf. waś'aka.

ś'ā's'e, n. Noise caused by a large gathering of men etc. Cf. s'a, part. Note: s'as'ehe yaŋkapi. B.H.179.5.

ś'e, v.n. To drop, as water. -- ś'éś'e, v. red. (of ś'e). To drop, trickle, as water. Miniś'éś'e, To sprinkle, fall in drops, as rain. -- ś'eyá, v.a. To make fall or drop, as in drops. Ś'ewáya. -- ś'eyápi, n. Drops.

*

ta, prefix. Affixed to such nouns as signify the various members of the body, limiting them to the corresponding parts in ruminating animals; thus: ceji, The tongue; tacéji, A buffalo tongue. Hence, "ta" may properly be considered as the generic term for all ruminating animals, since it enters into comp. of the names of most of them, as tataŋka, taȟca.

ta, adj. One of; a pair. Tawaŋjila, A pair. Tanuŋpa, Two pairs.

ta, pron. in comp. His, hers, its; theirs, i.e. with "pi" at the end of the noun.

t̄a, prep. in comp. At, to, on. It is affixed to nouns as a suff., giving them the force of adverbs, thus: makata; ata, yata, cf.

taa'juŋtka, n. A buffalo's kidneys. Bl. -- taájuŋtk'ognake, n. (?). Bl.

taa'kiȟ'aŋ, (?). (of taŋ and akiȟ'aŋ). Being very hungry perhaps. - wahiyelo, i.e. come being very hungry. Bl.

tab, cont. of tapa.
tabi'cakap̄e, n. A ball club, a bat.
tabi'capsice, n. A ball club, shinny stick.
tabi'yeya, v. To throw a ball.
tabi'yukape, n. A catching glove.
tabk̄a'kab, cont. of tabkakapa. - iyeya, To play ball by striking and knocking. -- tabk̄ákabkab, red. of tabkakab. - iyeya.
tabk̄a'psica, v. To play ball by taking up the ball in the club and throwing it. Tabwakapsica.
tabk̄a'psicapi, n. The game of shinny. Cf. kapsica.

tablas', Cf. taŋblas.
table'cakiya, Cf. taŋblecakiya.

ta'blo, n. The shoulder of cattle and horses. -- t̄áblohu, n. The shoulder-blade of animals. Na waŋna tablo waŋ ake iŋyaŋ oŋ kaśleca na yumaŋ.

t̄ablo'k̄a, n. The male of the common deer, a buck.

ta'blokaŋ, n. The sinew of the shoulder-blade.

tabu'bu, n. Something very large, but unknown and talked of by the old people; a monster. - kaga, i.e. to have a boy stand with back bent and other children pile robes on him, and so he would become something big. Bl. -- tabúbu s'e, adv. Tabúbu-like. This ref. to something round and big that no one ever saw. Bt.

tab waŋka'yeyapi, n. A religious ceremony of the Dakotas, the Throwing of The Ball. Also, Tapa Waŋkáyap. The giving of gifts seemed to be in favor of orphans. BR.127.

taca'ǧu, n. Lungs of man and animal.

taca'k̄a, n. The roof of the buffalo's mouth. Bl.

tacaŋ', n. The body.

tacaŋ'ȟaȟaka wapa'ha, n. (?).

tacaŋ'ȟaȟake, n. The first bones of the buffalo's spinal column. Bl.

t̄acaŋ'ȟp̄i, n. His war club.

tacaŋ'kahu, n. The middle part of the spinal column. Bl.

t̄acaŋ'k̄asluṫa, n. The white nerve running over the back of animals and going to the brain.

t̄acaŋ'k̄ohaŋhaŋke, (?). Oie -, as is said of a man who talks nicely, does not use harsh words.

tacaŋ'koye, n. perhaps. Extra thick layers of fat covering a buffalo. St.

tacaŋ'kp̄e o'gnak̄e, n. The meat above the knees of cattle. Also, tacaŋkpognake.

t̄acaŋ'ksa, n. His club.

t̄acaŋ'p̄aȟmiyaŋ, adv. With the body bent to right or left, crooked.

t̄acaŋ'ṫa, n. 1) The heart of the buffalo, the ox etc. 2) The heart in playing cards. -- tacáŋṫamnumnuǧa, n. Fleshing hanging on a buffalo's heart. Bl. -- tacáŋṫa iŋkpa, (?). Bl. -- tacáŋṫa oǧiŋ, n. The membranous bag that surrounds and protects the buffalo's heart, the pericardium. It was used as a glove in mixing greasy foodstuffs. BD. Also, tacáⁿtogiⁿ. MS.483. -- tacáⁿťasu, (?). -- tacáⁿťopazaⁿ, n. A piece of fat attached to a buffalo's heart. Bl.

ťace'ji, n. The tongue of ruminating animals.
tace'ji iⁿkpa, n. The point of a buffalo tongue. Bl.
tace'ji oka'slute, (?). Bl.
tace'ji ozi, Cf. ozi. Bl.
tace'ji su, (?). Bl.

tace'sli, n. The dung of ruminating animals, esp. the buffalo.

ťace'śikśice, tacéjikśica, tacéjigjica, n. The thin layer of fat that covers the paunch, the lumps of white fat that surround the paunch. - waⁿji na waśiⁿ waⁿji kici uⁿyak'upi kte lo. Mahpiya - , as they say of the heavens covered with balls and patches of white clouds. WE.

tace'śka ha śuⁿk'a'k'iⁿ, n. A part of the buffalo hide used as a saddle blanket, the ceśka, i.e. the part near the collar bone. Taceśka-ha is also used fig., one who sticks to his job, does not give up; thus: tacéśkamaha, I do not give up. Es. Bl. Tacéśkamaha keyapelo, he, as is said of one who is very brave in battle. Bl.

tace'toⁿte ośtaⁿ, n. The place where the legs join the body. Bl.

taciⁿ'cala, n. The young of deer, a fawn.

tacu'pala s'e, adv. As one easily losing his self-control, having no opinion of himself. - uⁿ, To lose one's self control easily, to be a health scrupler. Bl. Cf. tacupe.

tacu'pe, n. Marrow. Hence I say: Ehaⁿni tacupala s'elemaceca, I used to be weak. Bl.

ta'ǧa, n. An issuance. Minitaga, Froth or foam. -- taǧé, n. Froth, foam, spittle, scum.

taǧi'ca, n. A lean buffalo. Bl.

taglo'gloska, n. The wind-pipe in animals.

taǧu'ha, n. A scabby singed or old bull. GA.

taha', n. A deer-skin.
taha'iyokataⁿ, v. (iyokataⁿ). To stretch out e.g. a hide with pins. Tahaiyowakataⁿ.
taha'kalala, n. (kalala, cf.). A woman's buckskin dress, usually ornamented with fringes etc.
taha'kpaⁿyaⁿ, v. To tan a hide, i.e. rub it on a pole until it is soft and pliable. Tahakpaⁿwaya.
taha'lo, n. A hide. - saka kakśapi, A stiff rolled-up hide.
taha'opahloke, n. The slits cut in a hide by which it is stretched.
taha'pe, n. A tanned hide.
taha'pe napiⁿkpa, n. Mittens made of buffalo fur with the hair outside. Bl.
taha'pe wapośtaⁿ, n. A cap made of buffalo fur with the hair outside.Bl.
ťaha'saka, n. Dried skin, parchment; a skin with the hair taken off but not yet dressed.
ťaha'sopi, n. Leather strings.
taha'yuśtaśta, v. To soak a hide, e.g. for one night, after it has been treated with gall, brain and marrow. Tahabluśtaśta.

tahe'capśuⁿwi, n. The moon in which the deer shed their horns, i.e. December. R. Bl.

tahe'gle, n. A stick with a buffalo or deer horn fastened to it at one end and used in the paslohaⁿpi game. Also, when the horn is fixed perpendicularly, it is used as a weapon. Cf. tahezeze.

ta'hejata, n. A two-year old deer, i.e. one with two prongs, one fork on either horn. Bl. Cf. hekaza. Also perhaps, the male elk or deer. Bl.

ťahe'na, adv. On this side, in ref. to time and place. Aⁿpetu - , Before the evening. Aⁿpetu - waⁿblakiⁿ kta hwo? -- tahénakiya, adv. Towards one, this way. Le waśicuⁿ kiⁿ - waktepi kta ca le ohomni uⁿyaⁿpi. Na uⁿgna - hiyu. Tehaⁿl ye śni ecel wicaśa waⁿ lila haⁿska ca - u, i.e. towards him. D.102. -- tahénaťaⁿhaⁿ, adv. From this side.

tahe'pi, adv. By the way, on the road, between one place and another. Iglag tahepi wanaunsapi ktelo. Bl.

tahe'piya, adv. On the side of. On the side of a wall. B.H.7.10. Wicaśa śunkawakan - otka, i.e. he hangs on the side of the horse. Na paha kin - ȟpayapi.

tahe'zeze, n. (ta-he-zeze). A stick with a horn fastened to it perpendicularly at one end and used originally to kill smaller animals; in some cases the horn was fixed to swing at the end of the stick.

tahin', n. Buffalo or deer's hair.
tahin'cacice, n. An instrument made from tin to scrape hair off skins.
tahin'paǧuke, n. The knee-bone used as a pemmican stone and as a tool to scrape hair from hides, and thus the name. Also, pteȟcaka hinyete. Cf. paguka.
tahin' pakince, n. An instrument for scraping hides. Also, taȟca tahin pakince.

tahin'śpa, n. An awl, a needle make from the upper part of an elkhorn. - cik'ala, A needle. - cik'ala ipásisapi, A pin cushion. Also, tahinśpa ipásise.

Tahin' Wicaśa, n. prop. Another name for the Cheyenne Indians living down south. Maśte maka el unpi, itokaga.

tahin'yete, n. (of hinyete). The shoulder of animals. - ośtan, The place where the arms join the shoulder. Bl.

taho'gmi, n. The hoop on which a scalp or hide is stretched. - kaȟyá, The figure (four curves forming a four-sided figure with the concave sides outward) painted on that part of a robe which covers the back. - kagapi hanpa, A moccasin with a hoop-like design on the upper side. Bl.

taho'kaśke, n. The cross bars inside a tent on which a skin is fastened to dry. -- tahókatan, v. To stretch out a hide on pickets for tanning. Tahowakatan. Bl.

tahu', n. The back of the neck.
tahu'akaȟpe, n. A cape for the neck.
tahu'ceȟkiya, v. To shrug the shoulders, draw up the shoulders. Syn.- tahúślikiya.
tahu'hute, n. The nape of the neck, the prominent articulation of the neck behind.
tahu'icosya, n. A scarf or comforter.
tahu'iyutitan, n. The check strap.
tahu'jipa kicun, v. To somersault on the neck.

tahu'ka, n. The hide of a buffalo, a green hide. - cangleśka, A hoop with leather straps drawn over it, thus making it like a sieve; as such it is used in the game tahuka cangleśka. D.198. - wacipi, Jumping rope, as children do. - wata kagapi, A hoop with a hide stretched over it and serving as a boat for things to be placed on while swimming across a river; a bullhide boat. Bl.

tahun'sapa wikan, n. A rope made of hair from the horse's mane.

tahun'ska, n. Leggings made of deer skin. Also, a shirt-collar.

tahu'sliyeya, v. To speed, gallop loudly. Tahusliyeyapi s'e unkupelo, i.e. we sped in coming like gallopping horses. EB.

tahu'ślikiya, v. perhaps. To draw up or shrug the shoulders. Cf. tahúceȟkiya.

tahu'wanap'in, n. A horse collar.

ta'ȟca, n. The common deer. - taló, Mutton.
taȟca ito'pta sapa, n. A deer with a black streak across the face. Such specimens were considered wakan. Bl.
ta'ȟca nakpa'la, n. Same as hitunkala nakpala. Bh. #158.
ta'ȟca śin ślo u kte, ph. Expressed when the weather is to be very warm.
ta'ȟca śúnkala, n. A sheep.

taȟgla'hota, v. To swallow the wrong way. Taȟwaglahota. WE. -- taȟgláśkape, v. To have one's saliva go the wrong way and feel choked. Taȟwaglaśkape. WE.

taȟna', (?). Lowacin ca on - wakipcahe lo. Bl.

taȟpa', n. The lower part of the neck and breast of animals; the part between the shoulders of a man; the muscle across the abdomen.

taȟpi'yoǧiŋ, n. A muscle below the tataȟpa which is thrown away. Bl.

taȟtoŋ', v. (of tage). To have scum.

taȟu'ha, n. The scrapings of hides or skins, which are used when food is scarce.

taȟu'wap̄aȟp̄a, n. The thin layer of flesh that sticks to a hide, near the ribs on both sides.

t̄a'ja, 1) n. Waves. 2) adj. Rough, as water agitated.

taji', n. A red (śaśa) buffalo calf; usually they are black when young. Yuŋkaŋ pte saŋ waŋ taji waŋ kici iśtiŋmapi el gli.

ta'joŋtk̄a, n. The kidneys in animals.

taju'śka, n. The ant, ants. Cf. taśuśka.

ta'k̄a, v.a. To roast off the hull, as of rice; to roast e.g. coffee. Wataka.

tak̄a'ȟloka, v. To cut the meat of deer along the spinal column so as to get long slices, to cut up and spread nicely. Tawakaȟloka. Syn.- okazapa, and possibly onakazapa which seems not to exist. Bl.

takaŋ', n. The sinew taken from the back of the deer, buffalo or cow which is used for thread. - ok̄áza, A string or thread of takaŋ. Cf. kazá.

takaŋ'gi, (?). - toki hilu we? yau we? as they say to a fellow who would not go with the bunch but would want his own ways and left, but finally came back to them. Also: - taku yaka hwo? Bl.

takaŋ'hecala hu, n. The black raspberry, black cap, scotch cap thimble berry bush. Rubus occidentalis. The rose family. #129. Takaŋhecala, raspberries. Takaŋhecahu, The raspberry bush But also, takáŋhecala, The American wood strawberry. Fragaria Americana. The rose family. It is so called because of its string(kaŋ)-like runners. Waȟpe skuya yutapi. Ba. #261. Also, takaŋyecala.

takaŋ'itazipe, n. A bow the back of which is overlaid with sinews.

takaŋ'yecala, n. Raspberries. Cf. takáŋhecala.

tak̄i'kpe, v. pos. perhaps. (of takipa). Cf. takipa. - uŋglapi ktelo. Bl.

tak̄iŋ', v.n. To lean sideways. - iyaya. Pakiŋ iyaya, To lean forward.

tak̄iŋ'tazipa, n. (of takaŋ and itazipa). A kind of bow to whose one side sinews are glued. Cf. takaŋitazipa.

takiŋ'wapsake, n. A knife to cut off the takaŋ when one is through with sewing.

tak̄iŋ'yaŋ, adv. Leaning, not perpendicular.

tak̄i'pa, v. (of tapa). To follow one and take one's own from him, i.e. what he has stolen. Tawakipa. Bl.

tak̄i'yuȟa, n. Any bull of cattle, deer, etc. -- tak̄íyuȟa wi, n. The month when deer copulate, November.

tako'ja, n. A grandchild. Mitákoja or mitákoś. -- tak̄ójakpa, n. His or her grandchild. Also, tak̄ójakpak̄u. Winuȟcala waŋ - waŋ kici ti. -- takójaya, v.a. To have for a grandchild.

t̄ak̄o'lak̄iciyapi, n. Particular friends. -- tak̄ólak̄u, n. His particular friend. -- tak̄ólaya, v.a. To have one for a particular friend. Takolawaya.

t̄ak̄o'mni, adv. Nevertheless, still; always, ever, at any time; (with śni following) at no time. - el owapa kte lo, Although I advised not to do so. MS.103. B.H.42.19.

takoś', n. A son or daughter-in-law. Mitákoś, nitákoś. -- takóśku, n. His or her son or daughter-in-law. -- takóśya, v.a. To have for a son or daughter-in-law. Takoświya.

takp̄e', v.a. To come upon, attack. Tawakpe. - ya, To go to attack. -- takp̄éya, adv. Attacking.

t̄a'k̄u, 1) n. Something. 2) pron. interrog. What? 3) n. That ref. to a relative. Cf. takuye. Taku hutopapi.

B.H.291.15.

ťa'ǩuca, pron. interrog. What?

ťa'ǩueya, pron. Something. Yuŋkaŋ - ceuŋpahaŋ.

taku' ic'iȟ'aŋ, Cf. taku iȟ'aŋ. Bl.

ťaǩu' iȟ'aŋ, v. in comp. ph. - yahi hwo? What have you come to do? R. Bl.

ťa'ǩu ǩe c'e'yaś, pron. indef. Anything or whatever. Also:
táku ke eśá.
táku ke éyaś.
táku keśá.
táku k'éyaś. Tawoyuha taku k'eyaś etkiya yakizomi kilo. B.H.57.26.

ťaǩu'kiciyapi, n. Relatives, relationship.

ťa'ǩukiya, v.a. pos. To value one's own. B.H.153.19.

ťaǩu'ǩu, n. red. (of taku). Small articles, trinkets, one thing or another. Misuŋ eś - koyakipe secelo. - kouŋkipapi kiŋ hena uŋkoglakapi kte. D.103. -- ťaǩúǩuǩel, adv. Of everything, all sorts of things. - itaŋcaŋ kiŋ kaaye wicaśi. - el onaȟ'oŋ, i.e. heard all sorts of things about him. B.H.36.4; 261.18.

ťa'kula, pron. interrog. What? Note: He takula hwo? R. Bl.

ťaǩu'mna, v.n. To have taste or smell. - śni, To be without smell, taste or aroma.

ťa'ǩuni, n. Nothing. It is generally followed by śni. - ota epiŋ kte śni. Lena ecamoŋ kiŋ - śica slolyayiŋ kte śni. MS.481. -- ťáǩunikel, adv. In no way. - toka śni, Nothing happened. B.H.117.24. - akipa śni, i.e. an uneventful journey. D.269. -- ťáǩuniśni, 1) n. Nothing. 2) v.n. To come to nothing, fail, perish. Matákuniśni. -- ťáǩuniśniyaŋ, adv. Gone to nothing, perishing.

ťaǩuŋl', n. Something, anything. - yulpica eśa yaglepi hwo? B.H.274.4. Na waŋna oŋ (a bow) - kute iyuta. Taŋyaŋ ecoŋ po na takuŋl icu waciŋ po na napeyahaŋ śkaŋ po. Hecena iśtogmus wawaci kiŋ - slolwaye tka iblukcaŋ. - aiyoptemayaye ci hignaciyiŋ kte. - onitutka k'u hwo? i.e. something little to eat. Bl. - cic'u kta iyececa yalaka hwo? B.H.147.16;

ťa'ǩu oŋ, n. The why, the reason why. - kiŋ he. B.H.81.23.

ťa'ǩuśaśa, n. Any red thing.

ťa'ǩu śaśála, n. Swamp smart weed. Polygonum emersum. The buckwheat family. Bl. #303. Also, the foxglove, which is edible. - ececa uŋma iŋkpa śaśa uŋ he, The smart weed, lady's thumb, pink knot weed, the joint weed. Polygonum pennsylvanicum. BT. #226. - hu iyececa, The tall dock, the peach-leaved dock. Rumex altissimus. This is Bullring's medicine, an effective remedy for stomach cramps, diarrhea or hemorrhage. Bl. #229. -- ťáǩu śaśála hu swúla, n. Lady's thumb, heart weed. Polygonum persicaria. The buckwheat family. DE. Bl. #304. -- ťáǩu śaśála hu wiŋyela, n. The dock-leaved or pale knotweed. Polygonum lapatifolium. The buckwheat family. Bl. #302.

ťaǩuśa'śala, n. Jelly..

ťa'ǩuśkaŋśkaŋ, n. A power working, moving things secretly; oneof the powers in the wakaŋ wicoȟaŋ. That which causes everything to move. WJR.154.

ťa'ǩuśni, n. Nothing. -- ťáǩuśniśni, n. Small articles, trifles.

ťa'ǩuwe, pron. interrog. Why, What for?. Kola, - migluze k'oŋ iyecel ecaŋnoŋ hwo? Also, tákowe. Bl. - ca, Why. B.H.30.10.

ťaǩu'ya, v.a. To have one for a relation. Takuwaya. -- ťaǩúye, n. A relative. Mitákuye, uŋkitakuyepi.

ťa'k'eya, v. To say something. Yuŋkaŋ glakiŋyaŋ inajiŋ na - . Yuŋkaŋ .... Ták'epa, ták'uŋkeyapi. -- ťák'eyaya, v. red.

ťa'k'ole, v. To look for something. - yahi he? What have you come for?

tale'ja, n. Urine.

tali'oakse, n. A butcher saw.

tali'ṗa, n. (of talo and ipá). Something corresponding to sausage. Long slices of beef are cut and put into gut casings; they are tied and cooked that way. - eciyapi wakagiṅ ktelo.Bl.

ťalo', n. Fresh meat. - waṅji, A piece of meat. -- ťaló iyukpaṅ, n. A meat chopper. -- ťalóyukp̌aṅpi, n. Cut meat, as sold in stores.

tal'a'gnaka iyececa, n. The western iron weed. Veronia fasciculata. The composite family. Bl. #147. -- tal'á-gnake, n. The stiff or hard-leaved goldenrod. Solidago rigida. The composite family. The leaves are laid under meat. Also, caṅȟlogaṅ or maka ayublaya, waȟpe ape blaskaska, mimela waȟcazi. Bl. #25.

ťama'heca, adj. Poor, lean, not fat. Matamaheca.

tama'hel, adv. In the body, within. -- tamáhelheca, adj. red. of tamaheca. -- tamáhelya, adv. Poorly, not in a fat state.

ta'maka, adj. Poor, lean. Ptetamaka, A lean cow.

tama'koyuṅka, n. A deer that, contrary to habit, used to stay in the same place and hence became fat. Bl. The word is applied to a deer that leaves an impression in the ground where it has been lying for a long time. - s'e leniceca yelo, as is said of a man who sleeps unduly long. Bl.

tama'ǩuhu, n. The breast-bone of animals.

tama'śkeku, n. Her female friend.

tami'ca, n. The short sharp bone ends found in the single parts of the spinal column. Bl. Also, the lean meat on the side of an animal near the rump, the small of the back; the lean meat of the thigh.

tami'cahohu, n. The bone near the hip-bone.

ťamna', (?).

tamna'tkaṅ, n. The meat on the front side below the knee of the buffalo; the corresponding part in other animals is called tasićoǧiṅ. Bl.

ťamni', n. The womb; the afterbirth or sack which envelopes the foetus.

tamni'oȟpi caṅ, n. A fig tree. B.H. 177.23;225.15. -- tamníoȟp̌i hu, n. The clammy ground-cherry. Physalis heterophylla. The nightshade family. It grows about a foot high with green berries that turn yellow, looking like little bags filled with yellow grease when frozen. Give three to five, one after the other, to one who has no appetite. Children eat them. The may also be the word used for fig. BT. #131.

tana'ǧila, n. A hummingbird. Zitka - s'e iniwaśicuṅ welo, You are as talkative as a little bird, as is said of a little person. Bl.

tana'jica, v. To flee. Bl. -- taná-jilhi, v. To come fleeing. Tanajilwahi. Bl.

tana'pco, n. The lean meat near the back bone; the longissimus dorsi of an animal. Cf. napco.

tana'pkaṅ, n. The fleshy part on the leg below the knee of an animal; the cords in the leg of animals. Also, tasicogiṅ. Also, tanakpaṅ. R.

tana'sula, n. The brain of animals.

tana'wiciťe, n. The little bulbous piece of meat on the foreleg.

ťani'ǧa, n. The paunch of a buffalo, or cow.

tani'ǧa miniyaye, n. A paunch for carrying water, made of the buffalo paunch.

tani'ǧa śiṅ, n. The fat covering the paunch. Bl.

tani'ȟyusku, v. To empty the paunch of a buffalo.

tani'ȟ'ohiṅ'śma, n. The curved half of the paunch proper (- ośkokpa). It is used for various purposes. Bl. -- taniȟ'ośkókpa, n. The curved half of the paunch proper. Also,-hiṅśma. Bl. -- taniȟ'ośla, n. One half of the paunch proper which is smooth inside while the other half is called tani-ȟ'ohiṅśma or taniȟ'ośkokpa. Bl.

ťani'ǩa, adj. Old. Cf. taṅnika.

tani'śtuśta, n. The meat in the quarters of an animal. Bl. Cf. niśtuśte.

tani'ťahu, n. The backbone of the buffalo. Na - ko aku wacinpo. Bl.

tani'tkoȟloke, n. The meat inside the thigh bones of a buffalo. Bl.

tani'ya, n. His or her breath or life. Cf. woniya.

tanum', Cf. tanuⁿb. -- tanúmnum, adj. num. red. In two sets. Wokoyake - , Two sets of suits. B.H.115.15.

tanuⁿb', adj. num. His or her two. Also, tanum. Ogle - , His two coats. B.H.206.4.

tanuⁿ'ȟ'śiⁿ, n. The fat behind the ears. HC. Also, tanúⁿȟ'suhute. HC.

taⁿ, adj. cont. (of taⁿka). Very. It is prefixed usually to other adj., thus: taⁿwaⁿkatuya, Very high. Wahiⁿkpe kiⁿ taⁿwaⁿkatuya ya. Taⁿ naké uⁿhipelo, At last we are here, i.e. we ought to have come sooner. Cf. taⁿtáⁿ.

taⁿ, cont. of taⁿcaⁿ. Táⁿhaⁿska.

taⁿ, n. A side of the beef, including the bones. Taⁿ waⁿjila, One side or half the animal cut down the middle of the backbone.

taⁿ, Cf. yutaⁿ.

ťaⁿ, prep. or adv. suff. It is used in word, esp. adv., formations. Thus: heciyataⁿ.

taⁿaǩo'ťaⁿhaⁿ, adv. Beyond a person or animal, i.e. something with a body.

taⁿa'ťayela, adv. Towards a person. Cf. taⁿiyatayela.

taⁿblas', cont. (of taⁿblaza, which is apparently not used). On the side. - yuⁿka, To lie on the side, as animals do. Same as taⁿblecakiya.

taⁿble'caǩiya, adv. On the side. Also, táⁿblecakiya. - yuⁿka, To lie on the side. Caⁿkahu mastake ca - muⁿke. - hiyu, To come walking sideways, i.e. with the side towards something.

taⁿcaⁿ, n. The body. Mitaⁿcaⁿ, uⁿtaⁿcaⁿpi. Also, tacáⁿ. -- taⁿcáⁿ oyúze, The exterior, the looks of a person. B.H.85.5. Cf. iteoyuze. -- taⁿcáⁿtoⁿ, v. To have a body; to be ripe, full-grown.

taⁿca'tkayataⁿhaⁿ, adv. At the left side of the body. - iyayiⁿ na ake el iyeya (shot) na ake wouⁿka. B.H.265.24.

taⁿco'cola, adj. red. of taⁿcola. -- taⁿcókala, adj. Naked, without clothing. Taⁿcomakala.

taⁿco'la, adj. Nearly naked, poorly clad, naked. Cf. hacócola.

taⁿgla'ǩiⁿyaⁿ, adv. Crosswise, across something else.

taⁿglu'sasaseca, v. To be frightened, as at a ghost or at anything; to be made sick by seeing anything. Taⁿmaglusasaseca. -- taⁿglúsasaya, adv. In a state of fright.

taⁿglu'zaza, v. (?). Taⁿwićagluzaza s'e oyaȟ'aⁿ ye. Bl.

ťaⁿhaⁿ', prep. From. Note: it is usually suff., thus: heciyataⁿhaⁿ.

taⁿhaⁿ', n. A man's brother-in-law, a wife's brother, and a man's sister's husband; my brother-in-law. Nitáⁿhaⁿ, Your brother-in-law. -- taⁿháⁿǩiciyapi, n. Brothers-in-law. -- taⁿháⁿku, n. His brother-in-law.

taⁿhaⁿ'śi, n. A man's male cousin; my male cousin. Nitáⁿhaⁿśi. Note: this does not include a father's brother's sons who are brothers. -- taⁿháⁿśitku, n. His male cousin. Cf. taⁿhaⁿśi. -- taⁿháⁿśiya, v.a. To have for a male cousin. Taⁿhaⁿśiwaya. Cf. taⁿhaⁿśi.

taⁿhaⁿ'ya, v.a. (for a man). To have for a brother-in-law.

taⁿȟmiⁿ'ǩiya, adv. Bending one's body away, as a horse does when passing something it fears. - iyaya. Bl. Syn.- ǩiṗáś iyaya.

taⁿi'catkayataⁿhaⁿ, adv. At the left side of somebody. Cf. taⁿcatkayataⁿhaⁿ.

ƭaƞiƞ', v.n. To appear, be manifest, be visible. Mataƞiƞ, uƞtaƞiƞpi. Tokel ecamoƞ kta - śni. -- taƞíƞiƞ, v.n. red. (of taƞiƞ). To appear occasionally, as one passing under a hill, or as the suņ through clouds; to flicker. P. -- taƞiƞiƞyaƞ, adv. red. (of taƞiƞyaƞ). Appearing occasionally. - iyaya.

ƭaƞiƞ'śni, v.n. To be lost, to have disappeared. Mataƞiƞśni. -- taƞíƞśniyaƞ, adv. Out of sight, lost. Ataya mak'op'o na egna - iyaya.

ƭaƞiƞ'yaƞ, adv. Manifestly, openly, without concealment.

ƭaƞ'iƞyuƞla, adv. perhaps. Being deprived of what is necessary for life, or for a certain kind of work. - éyotakiƞ kte, as is said of a meeting when the books are missing. TB.

taƞ'ipa, n. The meat along the spinal column of a buffalo. Bl.

ƭaƞi'ślayaƭaƞhaƞ, adv. At the right side of a person. B.H.265.23. -- ƭaƞíśleyaƭaƞ, adv. At the right side of somebody (taƞ). Naślog hiyu na - iyayiƞ na el iyeya (shot).

taƞi'yatayela, adv. Individually; directly, in person. - glajuju, To pay each one for himself. Cf. taƞátayela.

taƞi'yohila, pron. indef. Each one, every one.

taƞi'yupse, v. To turn one's body to the side in order to see something. Bl. -- taƞíyupseya uƞ, v. To be turned sideways and look. Bl.

taƞi'yut'iƞze, n. A corset.

taƞ'ka, adj. Large, great in any way. Mataƞka.

taƞka', n. A woman's younger sister; mitáƞ, My younger sister. Nitáƞ. Mitaƞ, toké wicaȟpi waƞ lila ilege ciƞ he waśtewalaka. -- taƞƙákiciyapi, n. They who are sisters.

taƞ'ƙaƙiya, adv. Largely. Ho - , With a loud voice.

taƞka'ku, n. Her younger sister.

taƞƙal', adv. Out of doors, without. - iyaya, To go out. - iyeya, To turn out, put out of doors. - iya, To go to the toilet.

taƞ'ƙala, v. To consider great.

taƞƙa'ƭa, adv. Out of doors. Cf. taƞƙal. -- taƞƙáƭahaƞ, adv. Outside or from the outside. Na oyate kiƞ el - waƞyaƞk najiƞpi.

taƞka'ya, v.a. To have for a younger sister (for women).

taƞ'kaya, adv. Greatly, to a great extent. - onitaƞiƞ kte lo. B.H.194.24.

taƞke', n. A man's older sister. Mitáƞke, nitaƞke. -- taƞkéku, n. His older sister. -- taƞkéya, v.a. To have for an older sister. Taƞkewaya.

taƞƙiƞ'ƙiƞyaƞ, adj. red. pl. (of taƞka and taƞkiƞyaƞ). Very large, very important, as men in authority. B.H. 67.7.

taƞƙiƞ'yaƞ, adj. Very great, large. -- taƞkiƞyaƞyaƞ, adj. red.

taƞkśi', n. A man's younger sister. Mitáƞkśi, nitaƞkśi. -- taƞkśitku, n. His younger sister. -- taƞkśíya, v.a. To have for a younger sister.

taƞktaƞ'ka, adj. red. (of taƞka). Very great. -- taƞktáƞƙaya, adv. red. (of taƞkaya). Largely. Maka taƞktaƞƙaya omani ye. Bl. B.H.62.14.

taƞku', n. abbrev. (of taƞkéku). His older sister. Also, táƞku. Mh. Note: this is an old form.

ƭaƞla', v.a. To love, honor, respect; to be patient. Taƞwala. Also, ƭaƞláƙa.

taƞ'mahel, adv. In the body, within. -- táƞmaheltaƞhaƞ, adv. From within the body.

taƞna'ƙeƙiya, adv. On the side; with the head on one side. - yuƞka. -- taƞnáƙeya, adv. On the side; with the head turned to one side, as a drowsy person. Also, taƞnáƙiciya, adv. -- taƞnáƙiƞc'iya, v. refl. or adv. (taƞnakaƞ-ic'iya). To bow one's body away, as a timid horse does while passing by something it is afraid of. Taŋnákiociya is very doubtful. Bl. Syn.- taŋḣmiŋkiya.

taŋ'napa, v. To be scared, as by a sudden motion, and flee; to jerk involuntarily; to move sideways, as when one is frightened. Bl. -- táŋnapapa, v. red. (of taŋnapa). -- adv. Bending one's body to the right or left while passing through something lest one touch something or tear one's clothes. - ya. Bl. - uŋ, To be timid or hesitating (for fear) while going to some place. Bl. -- táŋnapek̇iya, v. To bend one's body sideways so as to avoid being hit. Bl.

ṫaŋni', 1) adj. Old, worn out. 2) adv. Of old; before; already. - kta s'e (not: - kte śni s'e) oyaka, To tell something hurriedly, i.e. lest it become old. Bl.

taŋ'nicala, n. Tiny flies that pester horses etc. during the hot weather. Also, táŋnicela, Small insects; gnats.

taŋni'k̇a, adj. Old, worn out, ancient.

taŋni' kta s'e, adv. ph. In great haste, sooner than expected; before others. - oyaka, ecoŋ, tebya. - womakiyakelo. Bl. B.H.273.16.

taŋni'la, 1) adj. Old, ahead of others, before others. 2) adv. Long ago. Syn.- ehaŋni. Yuŋkaŋ śuŋka najiŋpi atayela uŋkihuŋnipi na - Taśuŋke Luzahaŋ el uŋ. Yuŋkaŋ giic'iya waŋ - t'a ḣpaya. Yuŋkaŋ - slolya na leya, i.e. she knew it before I told her.

taŋni'ni, adj. red. (of taŋni). Worn out.

taŋniś', adv. emph. Already, i.e. sooner than expected. - hi. - luśtaŋ so? Hiŋḣota akaŋyaŋka waŋ ena kinajiŋ tka - Caŋtku Waŋkatuya kte. MS.530. Later than expected, aśkaŋs'e. Bc.

taŋni'śpaŋ, n. Red earth used for painting one's self. Bl. Cf. wase acetipi.

taŋo'haŋglegleya, adv. Parting the body in two. - yusleslel kte. B.H. 76.12.

taŋo'k̇ik̇aśleca, v.a. To split in two in the middle. B.H.99.16. -- taŋók̇isese, n. The halves of the body or any body. B.H.99.16.

taŋo'kśaŋ, adv. Around about, surrounding. Uŋkitaŋokśaŋpi, Around us. Lit., around the body. D.74.

taŋoŋb', cont. (of taŋ and oŋpa). Leaning to one side. -- taŋóŋbya, v. To walk with the body leaning to one side. Taŋoŋbiblabla. -- taŋóŋbyaŋka, v. To sit with the body leaning to one side. Taŋóŋbmaŋka.

taŋṗa', n. A little basket in the cuŋwiyawa kaŋsu kutepi game played by women.

taŋsag', cont. (of taŋsaka, which is not used). To frighten. - t'a, To die of great fright, to faint. -- taŋságt'eya, v.a. To frighten very much. Taŋsagt'ewaya.

taŋ'saŋni, n. One side of the body. - awagli kte lo. Bl. Note: the word is said: tasáŋni. -- taŋsáŋni t'a, v. To be paralyzed on one side.

taŋsi'ṫomni, n. The whole body. -- taŋsíṫomniyaŋ, adv. All over the body.

taŋsmi'yaŋyaŋ, adv. Alone, deprived of everything. -- taŋsmíyaŋyaŋka, n. One who is alone, without relatives.

taŋśi'ca, adj. Ugly, deformed. Taŋmáśica.

taŋśiŋ', n. The fat on the ribs.

ṫaŋśna', adj. Alone, single, unmarried. Wicátaŋśna, An unmarried man. Witáŋśna, An unmarried woman, a virgin. -- taŋśnála, adj. Alone, without one's family.

ṫaŋṫaŋ', adv. Very good, very well, very nicely. - wayatiŋ kte lo. MS. 95. - ceye. Cf. taŋ.

taŋ'ṫaŋhaŋ, adv. For the sake of one. Nitaŋtaŋhaŋ ecamoŋ, I did it for your sake. Le nitaŋtaŋhaŋ iyopemayaŋpi. David - oŋ. He oŋ - . Mitaŋtaŋhaŋ, uŋkitaŋtaŋhaŋpi.

taŋ'taŋiŋśniyaŋ, adv. In a way unnoticed. - ecoŋ, To do things unnoticed. Bl.

taṉtaṉ'yaṉ, adv. red. of taṉyaṉ. -- taṉtáṉyaṉkel, adv. red. of taṉyaṉkel.

taṉtoṉ'śni, v.n. To be unsubstantial, as some kinds of food, e.g. wojapi; or as a thrown off calf that may be only a month or two old, i.e. still formless. Bc. BT. -- taṉtóṉśniyaṉ, 1) v.a. To spoil meat etc., as by negligence while cooking. Bl. Taṉtoṉśniwaya. 2) adv. Unsubstantially, destitute. -- taṉtóṉya, v. To let e.g. vegetables or other eatables spoil because one has too much. Bl. -- taṉtóṉyaṉkel, adv. Excessively, intemperately. - oȟaṉ, ohitiya oȟaṉ.

taṉ't'at'a, adj. Paralyzed. B.H.187.1, 4.

taṉwa'śte, adj. Of fine form, handsome. Taṉmawaśte.

taṉyam', adv. In behalf of one. - ia, To take one's part, speak for one, as when a few are disputing. R. Bc. He - iwaye.

taṉ'yaṉ, adv. Well. - uṉ, ecoṉ, slolya. Also, táṉyaṉkel. - iyaye. B.H.99.6. D.81.

taṉya'takiya, adv. Towards one. - hiyu.

taṉye'ȟci, adv. Very well, exceedingly well.

taṉye'kel, adv. Whole, without injury.

taṉyē'la, adv. Well. - waṉblake. - Ȟugnaȟye. B.H.108.23.

taṉye'ni, adv. Not well. - iśtiṉme śni. B.H.111.11.

taṉ'yutkaṉ'la, taṉ'yutkaṉ'lak, adj. Much of something as food. - oṉweya yuha uṉyaṉpi, i.e. go with much grub. Caṉli kiṉ - yuha. Bl.

taṉza'ni, adj. Healthy, in health, sound, not injured in body. Taṉmázani. -- taṉzánike, adv. Well, in good health. -- taṉzániyake, adv. Without injuring, as killing an animal without injuring its hide. - kat'a. -- taṉza'niyaṉ, adv. Whole, not wounded.

tao', v.a. To wound by shooting, wound but not kill. Tawáo. B.H.112.3.

tao'kaśka, Cf. iktomi taokaśke.

tao'kiye, n. His disciple or assistant. Mitaokiye. -- taókiyeya, v. To have for one's servant or helper.

tao'pi, 1) n. A wound. 2) part. Wounded, a wounded person. Na hel - k'oṉ he waṉji akignaka iyeyapi ca he t'a ca ena ȟapi. Note: taniyopi, They wound. Pb.36.

tao'uṉye, n. His dwelling.

tao'yate, n. His people. Mitaoyate.

ta'pa, n. A ball. Śaké nitapa kte, as mothers would tell their children when they point at a rainbow; i.e. their fingertips would be as round as a ball, which was to say they should not do it. Bl.

tapa', v.a. To follow after one who has gone; to follow e.g. game; to pursue e.g. an enemy. Tawapa. Na tawicapa. MS.352.

tapa'ga, n. The diaphragm of man and animal.

tapa'kśiṉ, n. The fat that sticks to the kidneys. R. Bl.

ta'pa naka'papi, n. A game for girls.

tapa'pa, v. To hit a ball.

tape'te, n. The back, the upper part of the back. Also, tapéto, tapétu. BD.

tape'tognagya, adv. Placed on the back.

tape'tognaka, v. To put or place on the back. LB.

tape'tokatkiya, adv. (tapeto-kata-kiya). With the back against the fire.

tape'to ska, (?). Bt.

tape'tota, adv. On the back. Also, tapetuta.

tape'totaṉhaṉ, adv. On the back. R. Bl.

tape'tu, n. The back, the upper part of the back. Waṉbli waṉ - el owawa (on the ghost shirt). Cf. tapete.

tape'ya, v.a. To go after, follow, i.e. in order to catch. Tawapeya.

tapi', n. The liver of animals.

tapi'śleca, n. The spleen of animals.

taṗi'yeya, v. To throw a ball.

taṗi'zi, n. Gall.

tapo', n. The duodenum; one of the stomachs of ruminating animals; the crop of fowls.

tapoŋ', n. The cheek. -- tapóŋhu, n. The cheek-bone.

taṗo'ṗoska, n. Anything nicely round. R. Bl.

tapsi'psiza, v. red. of tapsiza. -- tapsiś, cont. of tapsiza. - hiŋgla, To bubble up, as water when anything is thrown in, or spontaneously.

tapsi'za, v. To bubble up, come up, as bubbles on water. Also, tapśi'ja, anátapśija.

tapuŋ', Cf. tapoŋ.

taṗ'i'cakape, n. A bat.

taṗ'i'capsice, n. A shinny stick, a baseball bat. Also, tap'i'capsiṫe. Wakiŋ hotoŋpi śni k'el - kaksa uŋyiŋ kte. Bl. Cf. icapsiŋte.

taṗ'i'yukape, n. A catching glove for baseball.

ṫasag'ya, 1) v.a. To cause to harden. 2) adv. In a hardened state. - gnaka, To lay away to harden.

ṫasa'ḱa, adj. Stiff, hard; frozen, hardened by cooling, whether at a temperature above or below the freezing point; hard, as tallow; cold, as napé matásaka.

tasaŋ'ni t'a, v. To be paralyzed on one side. Note: this should be taŋsáŋni.

ṫase', interj. Of course not! An expression of contradiction or discredit, followed by ka, ḱaḱeca, or kacaś. Tasé, le ciciyuha kacaś, huŋke cic'u ka eye. Tase wanagi waŋ ceḣpi na hohu ikoyake ka. B.H.274.1.

tasi'coġiŋ, n. The fleshy part on the leg below the knee of an animal on the rear side. Meat on the front side corresponding is called tamnatkaŋ. Tasicogiŋ itself is a piece of meat in the lower leg of ruminants and is full of sinew and a most undesirable part of the meat. Hence, fig., something better than nothing. D.116. Bl.

tasi'coska, n. The white meat on the thigh bone perhaps of the buffalo.Bl.

tasi'ha uŋpi, n. A string of five deer bones, a few beaded loops, and a pin to catch them on while swinging the bones. A game played mostly by women.

ṫasiŋ'ta, n. (of siŋte). The tail of a buffalo. D.37.

ṫasi'tupahu, n. The lump of fat above the tail of a fat buffalo. Bl.

ta'skakṗa, n. The wood tick.

taspaŋ', n. The red haw; apples.

taspaŋ'haŋpi, n. Cider.

taspaŋ' hiŋśma', n. Peaches.
taspaŋ' hu, n. The hawthorn. R. The common hawthorn, white thorn, scarlet-fruited thorn, red haw, thorn apple, mayflowers. Crataegus sheridana. The berries are mixed with other medicines and thus taken. Bl. #218. Note: this is of the rose family.
taspaŋ'hu caŋ, n. The hawthorn; an apple tree.
taspaŋ' oŋ'wohaŋpi, n. A sauce pan, i.e. in which to boil sweets.
taspaŋ' ope'mnipi, n. A pie.
taspaŋ' pesto'stola, n. A pear. HL.
taspaŋ' puzyapi, n. Dried apples.
taspaŋ'sloslola, n. The dwarf red haw. R. Bl.

ṫaspi'cahiye, n. Lemon extract. Also, taspiŋcahiye. Cf. icáhiye.

tasp'o'pemnipi, n. Apple pie. P. BD.

tasu'su, n. The narrow-leaved American vetch. Vicia linearis. The pulse family. It is so called because of its little beans. B. #156. -- tasúsu caŋḣlóġaŋ, n. Long-leaved milk vetch. Astragalus longifolius. The pulse family. Bl. #252.

tasu'ṫaṗahu, (?). Also, tasúṫuṗahu.Bl.

taśi'śake, n. The nails or hoofs of animals. The Dakotas used them for rattles. R. Bl.

taśi'yagnuⁿpa, n. The meadow lark. This is its elaborate lingo:
Şcepáⁿ, mícakca.
Śic'é, mícakce.
He túwa, tí hwo?
Kiktápo, wáⁿna aⁿpa yelo.
Ptehíⁿcala, pí napiⁿ.
Kóla, ptehíⁿcala waciⁿ yelo.
Kóla, wakiⁿyaⁿ ukíyelo, tiyo napa po.
Kóla, kiyáksi kiglág aú welo. (Oglala)
Héci cíye t'elo.
Míye imátaⁿcaⁿ yelo.
Ítoye cik'a tiblo.
Wówaglakiⁿ kte lo.
Two meadow larks meet; the one says: Taśiyagnuⁿpa, nitakoja waⁿ gli yelo, iwakici yo. Whereupon, the other dances and sings: Hahé, hihohó, or, Híye, ahéye hi. Bl. Tajiyagnuⁿpa is a doubtful spelling.

taśi'yaka, n. The pylorus or lower orifice of the stomach of ruminating animals; the large intestines. - imnáhaⁿhaⁿ. Bl.

taśna'heca, n. The striped ground-squirrel. -- taśnáheca siⁿté, n. The name for millet.

taśo'ka, n. The fourth cavity of a ruminant's stomach called seed or rennet (abomasus). Also, oⁿ wéojutoⁿpi. Bl.

taśo'śa, v. To spit.

taśpu', n. The stem, as of a pumpkin. Uⁿkcela - , The cactus berry. Hehaⁿ uⁿkcela - wicakipazo. Also, a knob, a door-knob.

taśuⁿ'śiⁿ, n. The fat on both sides of the neck of a buffalo. Bl.

taśū'pa, n. Intestines, guts; a hose. Also, śupé. - waśiⁿ. - caⁿiyawapehaⁿ na cewaoⁿpiⁿ ktelo. The word "hose" is applied to the word by transfer, for a garden e.g. or gasoline etc. hose, because they convey fluids from one place to another. Bl. D.197. - caⁿ iyapehaⁿpi, Dried intestines (casings) which are filled with fat and roasted; sausage, papahyapi, talipa. -- taśúp'kśaⁿkśaⁿ, n. The intestines. Bl. -- taśúp'okáhmi, (?). Bl. --

taśup'owotaⁿla, n. The colon. Bl.
taśu'śka, n. A common ant.
taśu'śka kiⁿyaⁿ, n. The flying ant. Cf. tajuśka. Bl.
taśu'śka sapa, n. The black ant. Bl.
taśu'śka śaśa, n. The red ant. These ants are mashed and mixed with other medicines for people to drink when they are shot. Bl.

tata', adj. Dull, blunt, bruised up, as the point of a stick etc. R. Bl.

tata'hu, n. The back of the neck of cattle; the neckbone of animals.

tata'hpa, n. The breast of animals.Bl. - payápa, (?). Bl.

tata'mni, n. That which surrounds the foetus, the womb of animals. Cega waⁿ ile ca - ota kte lo: an old superstitious saying. - onazoⁿ. Bl.

tataⁿ'ka, n. The male buffalo. - hé-śluśluta, A buffalo bull with exceptionally smooth horns. Bl. - wiⁿkte, A buffalo whose testicles are exceptionally small. Bl.

tata'pa, adj. Almost dry, as wash, meat etc. hanging in the wind. -- tatápeśni, adj. Still quite wet, as wash, meat.

tata'po, n. The third stomach of ruminating animals, the omasum or manyplies or psalterium. Cf. tapo, the fourth stomach, the duodenum.

tata'psiⁿ, n. (?). Bl.

tata'wabluśka, n. The horsefly. - hota, The gray horsefly. Bl. - sapa, The black horsefly. Bl. -- tatáwabluśka tacáⁿhlogaⁿ, n. Scarlet gaura, wild honey-suckle. Gaura coccinea. The evening primrose family. Also, óⁿśuⁿkoyuśpapi. B.T. #8.

tate', n. Wind, i.e. air in motion.

ta'te, n. Hunting, chasing. - ai, ahi. Na le ohakab tate ahi. Manil tatetipi, They lived alone while he was deer-hunting. Also, táte. D.271.

tate'iyumni, n. A whirlwind. R. Bl.
tate' kahwógyapi, n. A toy for little boys.
tate' kajo', v.n. To storm and make

things creak.

tat́e'k̇as'a, v. To whistle, as the wind.

tat́e'ouye, n. A quarter of the heavens. - topa, The four quarters of the universe.

Tat́e'tacaⁿku, n. A tributary to the Platte River. Bl.

ta't́eya, v. To hunt. Also, tát́e aya, To go on a hunt with a large party. Cf. t́át́e.

tat́e'yaⁿp̣a, 1) n. A blast of wind. 2) v. The wind blows; to blow as the wind. - hi, A heavy wind set in. - kte. Bl. Cf. B.H.43.8.

tat́iⁿ'gleska, n. Intestinal worms.

tat́i'p̣ogaⁿ, n. perhaps. A wind storm. B.H.195.16.

tat́i'wok̇itahena, adv. (?). Ito he hecel ecoⁿpi śni kiⁿhaⁿ, oyate - iyotiyekiya uⁿ tka yeśaⁿ. Bl.

tati'ye, Cf. tatuye.

tatk̇a'śa, n. A species of turtle. Also, patkaśa.

tat́o'hek̇iya, adv. Against the wind or current, up-stream. Also, tat́óheya. - uⁿglapi kte lo. - yapi. Bl. B.H. 208.22.

tato'k̇a, n. The big horned antelope.

tato'k̇ahe ciⁿśka, n. A spoon or dipper made of the horn of a mountain sheep.

tato'k̇ala, n. The gazelle or prairie antelope. Syn.- nigesaⁿla.

tato'na, n. A pair. Also, tona. Rh. SI. Haⁿpa - yaciⁿ, i.e. how many pairs do you want? Na waⁿna oyate - oimniciye k'oⁿ he etaⁿhaⁿhaⁿ na waⁿna waci au.

tat́o'wab, cont. (of tatowapa). Up stream or against the wind. - uⁿyaⁿpi. -- tat́ówal, adv. cont. (of tatowata). On the windward side of anything. Mitátowal iyaya, He went to the side where the wind hits me.

tat́o'wapa, adv. Up Stream, up the river, against the wind. -- tat́ówapat́aⁿhaⁿ, adv. From above, i.e. perhaps from up stream, from the wind. -- t́at́ówat́a, adv. With the wind against one. Tateowataⁿhaⁿ is also used. Komakipapi na mitátowata ece ahiyaya, i.e. the wind came from my direction. Cf. itatowata.

tā't́u, n. A root used as a liniment when boiled. It can also be taken as a tea or chewed to check the spitting of blood. Bl. BD.

tat́u'cuhu, n. The ribs of cattle, cutlets. - wapáha.

tatuⁿ'kce, n. Manure. - ptaya glepi, A dung hill. B.H.43.23. - taⁿkálhiyúya, To clean a stable out.

tat́u'ye, n. (of tateouye). A quarter of the heavens, as north, east, etc. - topa, The four quarters, always honored in religious ceremonies by directing the sacred pipe etc. in these directions. Also, tatiýe. Le pejuta waⁿ - oyasiⁿ wapogaⁿ kta.

t́at́u'yekt́aśniyaⁿ, adv. With the wind coming sideways, right or left, as in walking.

t́at́u'ye oⁿ winaḣ'oⁿ, n. A radio. Syn.- mazacola winaḣ'oⁿ, ikaⁿcola mas'ápapi.

tat'e'ca, n. (of ta and t'eca). The carcass of a ruminant. Bl. B.H.246. 11.

tat'e'caⁿnuġa, n. A weed called the snakeroot. Also, tat'écaⁿ nuⁿga hu, The dotted button snake-root, blazing star. Liatris punctata. The composite family. It is said that once there was found in the intestines of a deer all the contents (excrement) hardened into balls like the bulbous roots of this plant, and hence its name. The roots are pulverized and taken when one does not have an appetite. BT. HM. #17. -- tat'écaⁿ nuⁿġa huiyececa, n. The large button snakeroot, the blue blazing star, rattlesnake master, devil's bite. Ligulistylis. The composite family. Syn.- wazimniⁿkpa iyececa. Bl. #102.

tauⁿ'kaśni, v. To be unwilling to do. Tamuⁿkaśni, tanuⁿkaśni. He---kola, kola, tatuye topakiya nataⁿ hiyu ye śehaⁿ tamuⁿkaśni ye. MS.101. Lecoⁿpi tamuŋkaśni. Bl. RT. LP. Syn.- tawat'elyeśni.

ṫa'wa, pron. adj. His, hers, its. Mitawa, nitawa.

ṫawa'ciŋ, n. The mind, will, understanding; disposition, purpose; thought. Mitawaciŋ.
tawa'ciŋ hahála, adj. Fickle. P. Bl.
tawa'ciŋhaŋska, adj. Patient, long-suffering. -- tawáciŋhaŋskeya, adv. Patiently.
tawa'ciŋhiŋyaŋsyakel, adv. Melancholically.
ṫawa'ciŋhiŋyaŋza, adj. Morose.
tawa'ciŋkic'uŋ, v.n. To be resolute, obstinate, have a mind of one's own. Tawaciŋwec'uŋ. -- tawáciŋkic'uŋyaŋ, adv. Resolutely.
tawa'ciŋ k̇iksúya, v. To assume reason, become reasonable again. Bl.
tawa'ciŋk̇itoŋyaŋ, adv. Holding great promise. B.H.123.17.
tawa'ciŋ páŋpaŋla, adj. Weak minded, credulous, easy to fool. Bl.
tawa'ciŋsuṫa, adj. Firm, resolute, not easily influenced. -- tawáciŋsuṫaya, adv. Resolutely.
tawa'ciŋśica, adj. Of a bad disposition. Tawaciŋmaśica.
ṫawa'ciŋśilwoṫe, v.n. To eat greedily not wishing to share with others. Tawaciŋśilwawate.
tawa'ciŋ tok̇eca, adj. Whimsical. -- n. A whim. P.
tawa'ciŋ t'at'áka, adj. Stupid. Waéktaŋjaśni he kapi. Bl. P.
tawa'ciŋwaŋkala, adj. Fickle, easily influenced.
tawa'ciŋ waśák̇ala, adj. Venal, easily seduced or fooled. Syn.- kat'iŋsya wiyukcaŋśni, tawaciŋ paŋpaŋla. Bl.
tawa'ciŋwaśte, adj. Of a good disposition. Tawaciŋmawaśte.

tawa'ġaŋ, n. A step-son or step-daughter; any step relation. -- tawáġaŋk̇u, n. His step-son. - wiŋyaŋ, His step-daughter. WE. -- tawáġaŋya, v.a. To have for a step-son or -daughter.

ta'waic'iya, v. refl. To own one's self; to be free. -- táwaic'iyapi, n. Freedom, liberty.

tawaŋ'ji, n. One of anything, a pair. Tanúŋpa, Two pairs. Tayámni, Three pairs.

tawa'pśuŋk̇ak̇aŋ, n. The glands on both sides of the throat or neck. They are so called because they break out on the surface looking like gopher hills which suggest another name, wahiŋheya opi.

ṫa'waśe, n. A woman's female friend. Mitáwaśe, derived from tawaśe or perhaps waśe. -- ṫáwaśetku, n. Her friend, a female's friend. Mitáwaśe, My friend (said by women). Tawaśetku kiŋ okiyapi. Na waŋna uŋkitawaśetku kiŋ lila ahiyu. Note: this seems to be of waśe. -- táwaśeya, v. To have for a female friend.

ṫawa't'elk̇iya, v.a. To be willing to have such a thing happen to one. Tawat'elwakiya. -- ṫawát'elya, v.a. To be willing for anything, desirous to do or suffer. Tawat'elwaya.

ṫa'waya, v.a. To possess anything, have for one's own. Tawawaya. Pb.34. -- táwek̇iya, v.a. To cause to own. B.H.111.22.

ta'welaha, n. A heavy kind of summertime robe with pug hair and used as a summer robe. R. Bl.

ṫawi'cu, n. His wife. Mitawicu, nitawicu. -- tawi'cutoŋ, v. To have a wife, be married. Tawicuwatoŋ.

tawi'napce, n. The gullet of animals.

tawiŋ', n. A wife. Note: this is used only with the pron., thus: mitawiŋ, nitawiŋ. -- tawiŋtoŋ, v.a. To have sexual intercourse with a woman. Tawiŋwatoŋ. Also, ṫawiŋya. Tawiŋwaya. tawiŋmaya.

ṫawi'yela, n. The female of the common deer, a doe or hind.

ṫawo'ecoŋ, n. His work, business, doing.

tawo'gmuŋk̇e kaĥya', cl. He made it like a spider web, as is said e.g. of a tahuka caŋgleśka or a pattern, say in beadwork.

tawo'hiyaye wica'wote, n. The Paschal Lamb. Also wicawotapi. - uŋniciyawiŋyeyapi. B.H.251.4,6,12,14,16. -- tawóhiyaye wótapi, n. The eating of the Paschal Lamb. B.H.251.20.

tawo'k̇oŋze, n. His influence or purpose. Note: this is used for the Spirit of God; Nitawokoŋze. R.

tawō'sa, n. A lump of fat found on both sides of a cow's neck below. It was ordinarily boiled for use.

tawo'śitku, n. His or her helper, one that sides with him or her. Bl.

tawo'waśi, n. A helper or servant. - kiŋ inaḣni caŋpagmiya ikoyagyapi. -- ṫawówaśiya, v.a. To have for a helper.

tawo'yute, n. His food.

tawo'ze, n. The fat found behind the ears of buffalo and cattle. Bl.

Taya'mni, n. prop. A constellation of stars composed of the stars of Orion and the Pleiades of Taurus. There are seven stars in it: - pa, The Pleiades of Taurus; - caŋkahu, The belt or studded girdle of Orion. - tucuhu, The two flanking stars, Betelgeuse and Rigel; - siŋte, The last of the other large stars of Orion lying off from the tip of Orion's sword. Bl. BT.

ta'za, n. The inner, fleshy part of a cow's udder, which is a good dish.

ṫebk̇i'ciciya, v. To eat up for one. -- ṫebk̇i'ciya, v. (of tebya). To eat up provisions of any kind for another. Tebweciya. -- ṫebk̇i'ciyapi, v. They eat each other up. -- ṫebk̇i'ya, v. pos. To eat up one's own. -- v.a. To eat up another's or for another. Tebwakiya.

ṫebṫe'ṗa, adj. red. of tepa.

ṫebya', v.a. To eat all up, to devour. Tebwaya.

ṫe'ca, adj. New, young. Niteca k'uŋ hehaŋ, When you were young. B.H.276.6.

ṫe'caya, 1) v.a. To make new, renew. 2) adv. Newly. Also, ṫécayak̇el.

ṫe'haŋ, adv. Far, long, in ref. to time and place. - wote śni. -- téhaŋhaŋ, adv. red. of tehaŋ. Hecel lila - yanipi kta. -- téhaŋl, adv. Far, long. Lila - yapi. -- téhaŋ lake, téhaŋlake ci, adv. After a little while. - uwo, Come after a little while. -- téhaŋtaŋ, adv. From afar. Also, ṫéhaŋtaŋhaŋ. - teḣiya uŋkupelo. -- ṫéhaŋṫu, adv. Far off, to or at a great distance. Also, ṫéhaŋṫuya, ṫéhaŋṫuyak̇el.

ṫe'haŋwaŋk̇al, adv. High up. -- ṫeháŋwaŋk̇aŋṫu, adv. Very high. Also, ṫeháŋwaŋk̇aṫuya. -- ṫeháŋwaŋk̇aṫuyak̇el, adv. Loftily, high up.

te'haŋyaŋ, adv. Far away. Hena yamni - yapi. Na tokeya śuŋkakaŋyaŋka - manipelo. Na taku okiyaka, tka - ; heoŋ nawaḣ'oŋ śni.

ṫeḣi', adj. Difficult, hard to be done. Hard to be endured. -- ṫeḣíḣik̇a, adj. of teḣika. -- ṫeḣíḣiya, adv. red. of teḣiya.

ṫeḣi'k̇a, adj. Hard to do or hear, difficult; dear, costly, valuable; hard to get along with; unreasonable. Mateḣika.

ṫeḣi'k̇ek̇ila, v. pos. (of tehikela). To value one's own. Teḣikewakila. Also, ṫeḣík̇ek̇ilak̇a.

ṫeḣi'k̇ela, v.a. To think hard or difficult; to value very much. Teḣikewala. Also, ṫeḣík̇elak̇a.

ṫeḣi'la, v.a. To love, value very highly; to be unwilling to part with. Tewaḣila.

ṫeḣi'slolyek̇iya, v. To punish, to cause to suffer.

ṫeḣi'ya, adv. Hardly, with difficulty, badly. - ecoŋ, To do with difficulty, to do badly. - owaḣ'aŋ yelo, omakiḣ'aŋ yelo, waku welo. Bl. Also, ṫeḣíyak̇el.

ṫeḣi'yak̇uwa, v.a. To follow after for evil, to treat badly, to persecute.

ṫeḣmi'soha, n. A tanned hide. Bl. Syn.- teḣpiceha.

teḣmi'sopi, n. A leather strap. WR.

teḣmuŋ'ġa, n. The horsefly, flies. Cf. tatawabluśka.

ṫeḣṗi', n. A skin with the hair taken off worn as a blanket. Syn.- ptehaśla. -- ṫeḣṗíceha, n. A tanned hide. Bl. Syn.- teḣmisoha. -- ṫeḣpí haŋpa, n.

Moccasins with the rough surface of the skin outside.

ṫeḣṗi'wiḱan, n. A strap cut out of a dry hide.

ṫeḱi'ciḣila, v. To value, hold precious for one, as a mother values her child or does in the name of her child things for it. Bl.

ṫemni', v.n. To sweat, to pant, give out. Temamni, teunmnipi. -- ṫemni't'a, v.n. To sweat very profusely, to die of sweating. Temnimat'a. Śunka temnit'api ktelo, as is said when predicting a warm day. -- ṫemni't'eyela, adv. Perspiring profusely. - wowaśi econ. B.H.235.15. -- ṫemni'yan, adv. Sweating. Ite - wayatapi ktelo. Bl. BT.

ṫe'ṗa, adj. Root form, worn off, as in katepa. -- ṫeṗáhan, part. Worn off.

ṫeślag', cont. of teślaka. -- ṫeślágḱiton, v. To put on or wear a crown or fillet on the head; to put on or wear a Lakota hat, which has no roof but only a rim. -- ṫeślágḱiya, v.a. To make one wear on the head as a wreath etc. Pb.38. -- ṫeślágton, v. To put on or wear a fillet around the head. Teślagwaton.

ṫeśla'ḱa, v. To wear, as a crown or fillet, around the head. Tewaślaka. Ha kin le hanke tewaślakin kte. D.23.

ṫewa'pa, n. An esculent root growing in the water, which the Dakotas take, boil and eat. R. Bl.

tewi'camni, n. (of temni). Sweating.

ṫe'ya, n. One who has more than one wife. -- ṫéyaḱiciyapi, n. Those who stand in the relation of "teya" to each other. -- ṫéyaḱu, n. Her teya. -- ṫéyaya, v.a. To have one for a teya. Teyawaya.

ṫezi', n. The stomach. - natiptípa, Stomach cramps.

ṫi, 1) v.n. To live, dwell, abide. Wati'. 2) n. A house. Cf. tipi.
ṫia'kastaḱa, v. To daub a house. IS.
ṫia'ḱaśluṫa, n. A trowel. P. Bl.
ṫia'nunḱatanhan, adv. In both sides of the house.
ṫia'ṗiya, v. To repair a house.

ṫia'wanyanka, v. To stand guard about a house; to stay at home and watch the house.

ṫiblo', n. A woman's elder brother; my elder brother (used by women). Nitiblo. -- tiblóku, n. Her elder brother. -- tiblóya, v.a. To have for an elder brother. Tiblowaya.

ṫi'ca, Cf. patica. To scrape off.

ṫica'ǧa, v. To put up a tent; t o build a house. Tiwakaga.

ṫica'han, part. Scraped off, falling off of itself.

ṫi'canica, n. The long-billed curlew. It has a long and thin bill and says: Mniśwū, mniśwū...(a trembling sound). The ticanica tanka sings: Optepteptecela, opteptepteceIa. - s'e pasu kin lehanḣci, as is said of a man with a long nose. FR. Bl. LT. IS.

ṫi'canicahu, n. A plant growing on the prairie, similar to the wild turnip, but not hairy like it. Its tough stems when green were made into a sort of basket to carry meat in home. It is also used as a medicine. -- ṫi'canicahu ḣloḣota, n. The silver-leaf psoralea. The psoralea argophylla. The pulse family. It is fed to horses when they are tired, i.e. the root.. BT. #3. -- ṫi'canicahu tanka, n. A large bushy plant very common on the prairie. The few-flowered psoralea. Psoralea tenuiflora. The pulse family. A tea is made from the root as a remedy for headache. A smudge made from the plant is specially good against mosquitoes. Bl. #13. Lhb. -- ṫi'canicahu tinpsila, n. Digitate psoralea, wild alfalfa. Psoralea digitata. The pulse family. Bl. #187.

ṫican'kahu, n. The long cross beam of a roof against which both sides rest. Cf. cankahu, the spine or backbone.

ṫica'tkayatahan, adv. At the left side of a tent, to the left of the catku. -- n. the left side of the tent. -- ṫica'tḱu, n. The part of the tent or house opposite the door, the place of honor. -- ṫicátḱuṫa, adv. Opposite the door.

ṫice', n. The top of a tent or house,

the hole where the smoke goes out, the roof, the ceiling. -- ťicéiⁿkpa, n. The top of a tent, the ridge of a house. Also, ťicéśka. -- ťicéśkaoȟloka, n. The hole at the top of the tent by which the smoke escapes. -- ťicóȟloka hukútahaⁿ, n. The part just below the tent hole, in the front and above the wicéśka. -- ťicóȟloke, n. The hole at the top of a tent by which smoke escapes. -- ťicópa, n. The center hole of a tent.

ťigi'yapi, n. A tipi painted brown.

ťigle', v. To have a family, be married; to make a home. Tiwagle, tiuⁿglepi.

ťigli'yoya, v. To come and camp at the place of hunting and butchering buffalo. Toketu keś yukpaⁿhaⁿ po, ota yaopi kiⁿ na tigliyouⁿyaⁿpi ktelo. Bl.

ťiglo'nica, v. To forbid one's house, to prevent others from coming in. Tiwaglonica.

ťiglu'ȟlaǧaⁿ śni, v. To always stay at home.

ťiglu'juju, v. pos. (of yujuju). To fold up one's tent. B.H.12.4.

ťihu'ȟa, n. The poles of a tent left standing, the skeleton of a tent or of a log house. R. Bl. -- ťihúȟaka, n. The skeleton of a tent or an unfinished log house. R. Bl.

ťi'ȟaha, n. The second of the stomach cavities, the reticulum. Also, tiȟamnamna. Bl. Cf. R. under iȟaha.

ťi'ȟamnamna, n. The second of the stomach cavities in ruminants, the honeycomb or reticulum, next in size to the taniga. - waⁿ ena tacupe waⁿ hecel mak'u ca iwacu na wawata.

tii'caskapi, n. A trowel.

tii'haⁿke, n. A house nearly completed. Also perhaps, the corner of a house. B.H.240.10;281.13.

ťii'ȟeyapaya, adv. Out on the prairie.

ťii'kceyakel, adv. In tents. - ti, To live in tents. B.H.6.6.

ťii'ṗaslaťe, n. A brace to support a roof with, a pillar. Also, tipaslate. B.

tii'ṗasotka, n. A tower. B.H.239.3.

ťii'saⁿye, n. Paint.

tii'ślayatahaⁿ, n. The right side of a tent, the right of the catku.

tii'yaza, adv. From house to house. - tiole ayiⁿ kte. Bl.

tii'yokaȟmi, n. A corner of a room. - k'el, tiúⁿgnaǧa k'el. Bl.

ťii'yuṗaȟ, adv. perhaps. "Bag and baggage", "of the whole bunch." B.H.39.2.

ťiǩa'iťeṗa, n. perhaps. A pent house; a shed or little house with a roof only on one side and built onto another; a lean-to. Cf. kaitebya, kaitepa.

ťiǩa'uⁿǩa, n. perhaps. A tent or house knocked down by the wind. Cf. kauⁿka, owauⁿka.

ťiǩi'cii, v. (?). Tiwecii and timicii. Bl.

ťikte', v.a. To murder. Tiwakte. D.249.

ťikťi'ca, adj. Thick, as hair; stiff, as mush; sticky. Also, ťikťica. R. BD.

ťil, cont. (of ti el). In the house. Til hiyu.

ťi'la, v. (of ti). To dwell. Kici tila, To take sides with. Watila.

ťile'haⁿg, abbrev. of tilehaⁿyaⁿg. - iyayelo, He went visiting. LB. -- ťiléhaⁿyaⁿg ya, v. To go visiting. Tilehaⁿyaⁿg yeśni wauⁿ. FE. Bl.

ťima'hel, ťima'he, adv. Inside the house, within. - iyayapi, i.

ťima'heťakiya, adv. Towards the interior.

ťima'heťaⁿhaⁿ, adv. From within.

ťima'heťu, adv. Within.

ťima'ma iyaya, v. To go in to more than one thing. B.H.50.3.

ťiⁿ'gleśka, n. A fawn. -- ťiⁿ'gleśkala,

n. The young of deer, so called because they are spotted. Also, ťakiᶯ́gleśkala. Niǧé kiᶯhaᶯ - s'e leniceca yelo, as they said of the old Indian men whose abdomens became spotted from exposure when they did not wear European style clothes. Bl.

ťiᶯ'psila, n. The wild turnip. The turnip, prairie apple, pomme blanche. Psoralea esculenta. The pulse family. - kiᶯ wicapaȟli s'e hinapelo. - kiᶯ itká naȟcá yelo ca wagacaᶯ sekse hiyeyelo. Bl. #205. -- ťiᶯ'psila pejuta, n. The narrow-leaved milkweed. Acerates angustifolia. The milkweed family. The root is given to children when they have no appetite. CH. #257.

ťiᶯ'psiᶯla itka'ȟca wi, n. The moon when the seedpods of the Indian turnip mature, June.

ťiᶯ'psiᶯla skaska, n. The white turnip.
ťiᶯ'psiᶯla śaśa, n. The raddish, beet.
ťiᶯ'psiᶯla zizi, n. The carrot.

ťiᶯ'sko, adv. interrog. How large? R.
ťiᶯ'sǩoǩeca, adv. interrog. How big? How large? Cf. hiᶯskokeca.
ťiᶯ'sǩosǩoǩeca, adv. red. of tiᶯskokeca.
ťiᶯ'sǩosǩoya, adv. red. of tiᶯskoya.
ťiᶯ'sǩoya, adv. interrog. How far around, how extensively? Ka - anikpablaye, i.e. you certainly spread your ignorance over a great area. D.72,75.
ťiᶯ'śkola, adv. Of what size, how small? Cf. hiᶯśkola. Note: tiᶯsko is used more as a rhet. interrog.

ťinťiᶯ'yaᶯ, adj. perhaps. Lean, beginning to dry up. Tahu kiᶯ - . Bl. Cf. t'iᶯt'iᶯ. Syn.- tamaheca.
tiᶯ'yaᶯka, Same as tohiᶯyaᶯka.
ťio'ǩitahena, n. The space in between farms and ranches. Br.

ťio'ǩo, n. A house yard.
tio'kśaᶯ, adv. Around the house, inside or outside. - wawakita.
tio'kśu, v.a. To carry into the house. Tiowakśu. Na woyute tokel hoǩśicala kiᶯ yutiᶯ kte ciᶯ - .
ťio'kťe, v. To kill in the house, to commit homicide, in distinction from killing in war.
ťio'le, v. To hunt a house for lodging or for a meal. - mni kta.
ťio'nablu, v. To raise dust with the feet in the house. Tionawablu.
ťio'naǩipa, v. To flee to the house.
tio'napa, v. To flee to, take refuge in the house. Tionawapa. Ikce wicaśa tipi kiᶯ tionawapa nuᶯs'elececa yelo.
ťio'sni, adj. Cold in the house.
ťio'śpaye, n. A band; a clan; a party under one chief.
tio'wa, n. A painted tipi or tent, i.e. red etc. Cf. e.g. tiśayapi, witiowapi etc.
tio'waᶯjila, adj. perhaps. Living with others. - ti, To live in one house with others. Living in one house. B.H.99.2.
ťio'yaᶯǩapi, n. A room. Bl.

ťi'p̌a, Cf. yutipa.

ťi'p̌ahiᶯ, n. (of ipahiᶯ). His pillow.

ťi'paǩel, n. The meat behind the head over the spinal column of buffalo. HH. Bl.

ťip̌a'slaťe, n. A pillar of a house. B.H.77.23. Tiip̌aslate, A brace.

ťi'p̌i, n. A tent, house, dwelling. - wakaᶯ, A church.
ťi'p̌i ipa'sotkaya, n. A church tower, as it seems to suggest a wahúkeza when ornamented, thin and tapering to about six or seven feet in height.
ťi'p̌i iyo'ǩiheya, ťi'p̌iyóǩiheya, n. A council tent, contructed by joining a number of tents and capable of seating about 500 people at once. D.3, 225,246; 3 note 3.
ti'pila, n. A little house. Mato - kiᶯ hetaᶯ ilalapi kte lo.
ťi'pi wakaᶯ', n. A sacred house, church.
ťi'piyokihe, n. Cf. tipi iyokihe.

ťisam', adv. Beyond the tent or house, on the other side of the house. Cf. hosam.
tisaᶯ'patahaᶯ, n. The side wall of a tent (inside).
tisa'pa, n. The top of a buggy.

ťi'sto conica, n. A certain part of the meat on the shoulder blades of a buffalo. HH. Bl. Syn.- iyuȟ'eyayapi.

tiśa'yapi, n. A tipi painted red.

ťi'śǩakaᶯ, n. (of iśkakaᶯ). The large sinew or muscle in the neck. - kajalya yaᶯka, as when the two muscles are very prominent with lean persons and form a cavity between them. Bl.

ṫi'śṫaśiŋ, n. The fat found behind the eyes at the temples of buffalo and cattle. Bl.

ṫiṫa'heṗiya, n. The middle part of a tent between the wipá and the wihuta śa. - kaḣol yeya. D.247. -- ṫitáhepiya, adv. On the wall. B.H.140.5.

ṫi'ṫak̇uye, n. The immediate relatives. D.230.

ṫiṫaŋ', v. To pull to or in a certain direction. Caŋte kiŋ nahaḣci wakaŋ wicoh'aŋ etkiyaŋ - yelo. BT. Isam yatitaŋ kte śni, i.e. to bother one (for something). - śni s'e mani, i.e. does not seem to pull. Bl.

ṫi'taŋ waya'wa, v. To attend a day school.

ṫiṫa'zipe, n. (of itazipa). His bow.

ṫito'kaŋl, adv. As a guest. - uŋ, i, hi. P.

Ti'toŋwaŋ, n. prop. (tiŋta, not used, and toŋwaŋ). The Tetons, those bands of the Dakotas living on and beyond the Missouri River west. They probably represent the majority of the whole Sioux nation. Their language differs from the dialects of the other bands in their use of "l" for "d". R.

ṫi'ṫuṫuk̇a, (?). - wiḣmapi yelo, as is said when coming from other houses where one got one's fill. Bl.

ṫiuŋ'gnaġa, n. The corner of a room. - k'el. Bl. Syn.- tiŋyokaḣmi.

tiuŋ'ma k'el ya, v. To go visiting. - mni kte lo. Bl.

ṫiuŋ'napṫaŋyaŋ, n. (of uŋnaptaŋ). The sides of a house, sides of the roof.

ṫiwa'he, n. A household, including persons as well as things. Uŋtiwahepi.

ṫi' wakṗala el, ṫi'pi wakṗala el, ph. A house or houses standing on a creek.

tiwaŋ'kata, adv. Upstairs.

ṫi'wicakṫe, 1) n. A murderer. 2) v.a. To commit murder. Tiwicawakte. Na waŋjini - heca kte śni. -- ṫiwicaktepi, n. Murder.

ṫiwo'haŋ, adv. Between, among the tents. B.H.89.9. Cf. egna. - omanipi. -- ṫiwóhaŋhaŋ, adv. red. of tiwohaŋ. Waŋna ihiŋhana yuŋkaŋ tataŋka kiŋ - ahiyu. D.209.

ṫiwo'k̇itahena, adv. Away from houses. Also, tiyokitahena. -- n. The wilderness. - onáṗeya uŋ, To be a fugitive. B.H.6.3;173.1. - ouŋye.

ṫiwō'slaṫa, n. A miner's tent, i.e. without side walls and roof-like.

ṫiya'kiḣpeca, (?). This applied to a young man who is attached to a relative and wants to marry her. HH. Cf. ómniyela.

ṫi'yaŋk̇a yo, interj. Wait! Hold on! interrupting one in his speech or action etc. Note: the word seems to be from: ito hiyaŋka, hi and yaŋká, and not from ṫo and iŋyaŋka.

ṫiya'ṗa kte, v.a. To massacre. B. - wicaktepi, A massacre. Bl. B.

ṫiya'ṫa, adv. At the house, at home.
ṫiya'ṫak̇iya, adv. Toward the house, home. - iŋyaŋke.
ṫiya'ṫana, adv. At home. B.H.34.8;115.5.

ṫiye'ṗa, n. The door of a tent, consisting of a piece of leather. - caŋyúktaŋ, The two flaps with which the upper part of a tent can be closed or opened. Cf. wipipaha. - hukútahaŋ, The part of a tent below the door and corresponding to a door sill. -- ṫiyéṗaṫa, adv. At the door.

ṫiye'yak̇e, (?). - wicayuś'iŋyeya, i.e. surprising them in their winter quarters. Bl.

tiyo', adv. Same as timá.

ṫiyob', cont. of tiyopa.
tiyo'bcok̇atoŋ, v. Bl. (?).
tiyo'bleca, n. A square tent, with corners (obleca), not a Dakota tent.

tiyo'bleze śni s'e śkaŋ, v. ph. To move about excitedly in the house without accomplishing anything. Bl.

ṫiyob'ya, v.a. To have or use for a door. Tiyobwaya.

ṫiyo'gnaka, n. The household.

tiyo'gnaśkiŋyaŋ s'e śkaŋ, v. ph. To move about excitedly in the house without accomplishing anything. Bl.

ṫiyo'haŋk̇ok̇iṗa, v. To be hungry, i.e. a fig. express. for: to be afraid of the ghosts in the night. Also, ṫióhaŋk̇ok̇iṗa. Tiyohaŋkowakipelo, - . WH. Cf. wanagi el mahipelo. Note: this may be said in day-time too; and it is also said of one who comes first for a big meeting but remains alone for a long time and so uses up his provisions.

ṫiyo'he, n. A household; a place where a house once stood, a deserted house. Cf. tiwahe.

ṫiyo'hiyukśa, (?). - naŋkahe. Bl.

ṫi'yoḣa, n. The cheek of a buffalo. Lel ṫiyoḣaś wicoti. Bl.

ṫiyo'ḣeyuŋk̇a, n. (ti, ḣeyuŋka). Frost settling on the inside wall of houses or tents. Caŋ ota aŋpo - au welo. BT.

ṫiyo'ḣeuŋk̇a wi, n. February, the moon when there is frost inside the house. Caŋ ota aŋpo - au welo. BT.

ṫiyo'ḣwaic'iya, v. To rest. Bl.

ṫiyo'kalya, v. To warm up a room. Tiyokalwaya. Tiyokalya; hececa kiŋ mabliheca kte lo. Bl.

ṫiyo'k̇aśkapi s'e śkaŋ, v. ph. To move away from somebody, disliking him, as far as one can in a room, thus acting like a timid horse etc. that is tied but tries to get away when someone comes near. Bl.

ṫiyo'k̇awiŋḣ, v. cont. (ti, okawiŋga). To go around in a circle in the house. - omani.

ṫiyo'k̇itahena, adv. Between houses. Also, tiokitahena, tiwokitahena. -- n. Spaces between farms or ranches. Br.

ṫiyo'k̇iṫi, n. One who lives in his own tipi. - Waŋ, as is said of one who, owning a tipi, is buried in it, i.e. resting on a scaffold; one who had no tipi was placed on the scaffold without a tent around it. D.227. Cf. MS.487.

ṫiyō'k̇o, adv. Between houses. Cf. tioko.

ṫiyo'k̇uṫa, adv. Downstairs.

ṫiyo'lolya, v. To go and rent a house. Bl.

ṫiyo'mnak̇iya, v.a. To gather one's own in the bin, to store up. B.H.174.10.

ṫiyo'ṗa, n. A door, the place of entrance.
- gmigma, A door knob.
- gmigmela, A door knob.
- iyokatkuġe, A nail, nails, screws such as are used in connection with a door.
- oyúṫkoġi, A door lock, a padlock.

ṫiyo'ṗaṫa, adv. At the door.

ṫiyo'ṗa wíśimnaye, n. A publican, a toll collector. B.H.232.1.

ṫiyo'ṗeyapi, n. The camping around a herd of buffalo. This was done in days of old when this animal was gentle, it is said. Bl.

ṫiyo'p'ik̇uśé, n. The bolt of a door on the inside. Note: ikuśeya, In the way of.

ṫiyo'p'inatake, n. A door lock.

ṫiyo'p'iṗátak̇e, n. A stick to hold the door of a tent tight from within. Bl.

tiyo'ślola, adj. With a kind of rolling sound in the house. Wabluśka - , A cricket.

ṫiyo'śṗaye, n. A band, a division of a tribe, a community. Also, tióśpaye.

ṫiyo'ṫahena, adv. Away from any house. Also, tiwótahena. - owaŋjigjila yaŋka yo, i.e. stay at home, and in this sense iyotahena seems to be used. RF.

ṫiyo'tateśni, n. A close, warm room. P. Bl.

ṫiyo'ṫi, v. To set up a soldiers' lodge. Tiyouŋtipi.

ṫiyo'ṫipi, n. A soldiers' lodge, set up for the purpose of making laws generally to regulate the buffalo chase and to provide for their being carried into effect.

ṫiyo'ṫoŋwaŋ, v. (ti, otoŋwaŋ). To look into a house.

tiyo'ṫ'ebleze śni s'e śkaŋ, v. ph. To move about excitedly in the house without accomplishing anything. Bl.

tiyo'woslata, n. A wall in a house. P.

ṫiyu'kaŋ, v. (of yukaŋ). To leave the house, as is said when the women and children leave the tent for the men to feast in. Cf. kiyukaŋ.

tiyu'ktaŋ ḣpáya, v.n. To sleep in a tiyuktaŋ wakeyapi. -- tiyúktaŋ wakéyapi, n. A round lodge like a sweat-lodge. When an Indian had no tent while travelling, he would take any sticks, bend and slip them in the ground and cover them with hides. Cf. wakéya, kéya.

tka, 1) conj. cont. (of tuka). But. Mini el iyayapi na minit'api, tka kitaŋyeḣci glinapapi. B.H.174.15;182.3. Note: The Wiciyela for the conj. use tuká. 2) particle. The sign of the subjunctive.

tka, v.a. To scrape the hair off a hide. Watká. -- adj. Heavy.

tkab'ya, adv. Stiffly.

tka kiŋ, Cf. tka k'uŋ. B.H.204.15.
tka k'uŋ, Cf. tka, particle. Tawa tka k'uŋ. Jesus oyusiŋka tka k'uŋ. B.H. 109.10;114.4;115.23;119.1,6;140.4;157.19;289.27;271.3;278.9;289.27.

tka'ṗa, adj. Adhesive, clammy, as rice when there is hardly any water in it.

tkaś, emph. tka. Yuś'iŋyemaya tkaś.

tke, adj. Heavy. Same as tka. -- tkeiyúṫa, v.a. To take up and feel the weight, to weigh anything. Tkeibluta, or perhaps tkeiyuwata. -- tketké, adj. red. of tke. -- tkeúta, v.a. To weigh anything. Tkeuwata. -- tḱéya, adv. Heavily. - k'iŋ, To carry heavily. -- tkéyawak'iŋḱiya, v. To load heavily, to overload.

tkoŋsḱi'ya, v. To finish a job, be done. Wana tkoŋswakiyelo.

tkoŋsya', adv. Evenly. Also, tkoŋsyéla.

tkoŋ'za, adj. Even, square with; just, exactly. -- tkóŋzela, adj. Even, in numbers, as twenty, thirty, etc.

tku'ġa, Cf. katkuga.
tkuġa'haŋ, part. Broken off.
tkutku'ġa, red. of tkuga.
tkutku'ġahaŋ, part. Broken off in several places.

ṫo, n. The noise made by a blow. Cf. katoto.

to, Same as ito.

ṫo, ṫo'i, ṫoś (used by women), adv. The affirmative: Yes.

to, adj. Blue, green.

to, pron. adj. It is used in some cases for "ta" when the noun begins with "wo"; thus, wocaŋniye, tocaŋniye.

ṫob, cont. (of topa). Four. Tob kiŋ, The four winds; the messanger of all the world powers. WJR.153.
ṫo'blala, adv. Only four.
ṫobṫōb', adv. red. (of tob). By fours, four and four. -- n. Four by four, four times four. Tobtob kiŋ, The four general world powers related, multiplied by four other relations, thus to the product of sixteen relations: Wikaŋ-Haŋwikaŋ; Taku Śkaŋśkaŋ-Tatekaŋ; Tob kiŋ-Yumnikaŋ; Makakaŋ-Woḣpe; Iŋyaŋkaŋ-Wakiŋyaŋ; Tataŋkakaŋ-Hunuŋpakaŋ; Wanagi-Waniya; Nagila-Waśicuŋpi. WJR.153-4.

to'caŋniye, n. (of wocaŋniye). His wrath against his wife.

ṫo'el', conj. But before, but first. It indicates that time is taken before doing something important; to do something else first, but the speaker is impatient with the delay, does not approve of it. Using tóéyaś, which cf., would show that the speaker approves of the delay. Talo k'uŋ ataya tebmakiyapelo eyiŋ na lociŋ caŋke toel woyute owekiceya śke. Waciŋhiŋ k'uŋ he ataya ikoyaka caŋke ena toel gluśpuhiŋ na wana wicaśa sapa k'uŋ he glihuŋni kta haŋl. D.109;28, note 1.

ṫo'e'yaś, conj. Same as tóél. Also, ṫók'éyaś, iṫók'éyaś, iṫóéyaś. Cf. toel. Iŋśe le ociciyapi kta tka toeyaś wauŋśiyalapi heciŋhaŋ he slolwayiŋ kta waciŋ ye. D.67. Hecel toeyaś okuwa śni ca ayuśtaŋ. Na waŋna aŋpetu waŋ el kipi kte ci iyehaŋtu wicokaŋyaŋ toeyaś asnikiyapi. Hehaŋl waŋna wauŋcipi na toeyaś huŋḣ ececapi ehaŋl asṅikiyapi. Lecel eya: itoeyaś hena najiŋ po. Uŋgnahela leya: itoeyaś asnikiya po, eya. MS.156. Yuŋkaŋ: toeyaś ena najiŋ po, eya. Na waŋna oyate k̇iŋ kiblecahaŋpi na toeyaś wol akiyagla, i.e. as they were told to do. Oya te kiŋ lel amapepi kte lo; toeyaś paha ekta mni na wicokaŋ hiyaye kiŋ wagli kta.

to'ġaŋgaŋ ok̇i'waslecapi, n. A very fat cow. HH. Bl.

togmoŋ'śni, adv. Topsy-turvy, disorderly. Bl.

to'gmuŋ s'e, adv. (?). - uŋ, as is said of a man who has poor property and troubles with relatives. - yauŋ welo. Bl.

togto'ka, (?). Caŋ kiŋ - aoŋpo, tiyoḣeyuŋka au welo, i.e. put more wood on. Bl.

ṫogye', adv. In a different manner, differently, a little different, in a different set of many ways, as one word is a little different from another. Oglala ciscila - eyapi. Heoŋ ecaŋna - iwaŋblakiŋ kte lo na ecel ecamoŋ kte lo ca oyaka yo. - kaga, To make different.

tog'i'a, v. To talk a strange language. Tog'iwaya.

ṫo'haŋ, adv. indef. Sometime; when, at what time, at what place? Ake - waŋciyaŋkiŋ kte. -- adv. interrog. When? - kiŋhaŋ. - hecetu kta? - gnaśka hiŋhaŋ uyapi kiŋ, hehaŋ hecetu kta he? Bs.
tohaŋ....ca na, Whenever....then. - iglakapi ca na eyapaha waŋji el uŋ.
tohán...hehán, As long as. - yani eśa hehán, As long as you live. B.H. 80.8.
tohaŋ...hehaŋ (subordinated), Until. Na toŋweya k'oŋ hena ena najiŋpi kte lo - uŋkupi śni hehaŋ, eya. Na hel tohaŋyaŋ glipi śni (the delegates). hehaŋ hel wicoti (the people).
ṫohánhaŋ, adv. red. of tohaŋ. At what time? At what times, places? How far?

ṫohaŋ'haŋk̇eca, interrog. red. of tohaŋkeca.

ṫohaŋ'haŋyaŋ, adv. red. of tohaŋyaŋ.

ṫohaŋ'huŋniyaŋ, adv. As long as. Also, tohuŋhuŋniyaŋ. Bo.

ṫo'haŋḣci, adv. indef. Some other time in the future perhaps. - wouŋglakiŋ kte.

ṫohaŋ'k̇eca, adv. How long? This usually ref. to space. Cf. lehaŋkeca, hehaŋkeca.

ṫohaŋl', adv. conj. and interrog. When, when? Also, tohán. Na - waŋna akisnipi lila wiyuśkiŋpi. - oiyokpaz aya ca na wicaśa lila waś'aka. Kola, - wanasapi kte so?
tohaŋl....ca na,
tohaŋl....caŋ, B.H.80.19.
tohaŋl....eśa, B.H.120.5;61.6.
tohaŋl....kiŋ hehaŋl, B.H.94.11.

ṫo'haŋni, adv. Never. B.H.48.8;68.24; 98.17;138.5;222.10. Pb.29.
ṫo'haŋśna, adv. Sometime.

ṫohaŋ'taŋ, adv. or noun. For all the past time. - kiŋ iyotiyewakiye, All my life I have had a hard lot. D.269.

ṫohaŋ'ṫu, adv. interrog. When? - kiŋ takpé-ayiŋ kta śka hwo. D.91.

ṫohaŋ'ṫuk̇a waŋ, adv. At a certain time. Wana - lila tiyata gla ciŋ, A certain time whe wanted to go home. Itohaŋtuka yuŋkaŋ leya śke. D.60,91.

ṫohaŋ'ṫu ke c'eyaś, adv. Whenever, at any time. Also, ṫohánṫu k̇eś, R. Bl. tohaŋtu k̇eśá, tohaŋtu k'e éyaś.

ṫohaŋ'yaŋ, adv. As long as, as far as; interrog., for how long? - oyakihipi ḣupahu koza po. Letaŋhaŋ tohiŋni iyopemaye śni ye, - uŋni hehaŋyaŋ. - iśtayeyapi hehaŋyaŋ pte au. B.H.55.15; 249.18;256.20. - ye śni ḣci, He had not gone far yet. B.H.121.3. - śni haŋni, In no time. B.H.256.20. - yapi; yuŋkaŋ, i.e. for some time, a while. D.157.
tohaŋyaŋ....hehaŋyaŋ, B.H.61.11. Na - maḣpiya kiŋ he owaŋjila hecel haŋ ca hehaŋyaŋ oyate kiŋ owaŋjila tipi; na tohaŋl maḣpiya kiŋ ḣeyab iyaya caŋ na iś eya iglakapi.
tohaŋyaŋ....iyehaŋyaŋ. B.H.55.15;98. 17;100.22;267.11.

ṫohaŋ'yaŋkel, adv. How far, to where. ṫohaŋ'yaŋ śni haŋni, (?). B.H.256.20.

to'he, n. His place, his camp; his office or position. B.H.218.3.

ṫo'hiŋgla, v.n. To resound. Cf. ṫo.

ṫo'hiŋni, adv. It is used usually in coord. with śni: - ....śni. Never.

to'hiŋyaŋką, v. imp. Hold on. Wait a minute. This is used by a speaker who does not wish to be interrupted. Same as toeyaś. - po, wicaśa waŋji t'iŋ kta keś ehake ḣotaŋiŋ na t'e lo. MS.101. Cf. ṫiŋyaŋka yo, interj.

ṫohuŋ'hiŋniyaŋ, Cf. tohuŋhuŋniyaŋ. B.H.12.1.

ṫohuŋ'huŋniyaŋ kiŋ, adv. Always, forever. He wicaśa kiŋ - cajeyatapi kte. Bl. B.H.152.21;12.1.

to'ḣca, adj. Blue, as distinguished from green.

to'ḣ'aŋ, n. His acts. Cf. oḣ'aŋ. Wicaśa iyecel toyaḣ'aŋ. B.H.134.22.

ṫo'i, Cf. ṫo.

ṫoi'a, v. To knock, criticize. Toiwaya.

to'ie, n. His word.

ṫoi'ehaŋpi, Cf. toies'a, B.H.66.3.

ṫoi'es'a, n. A crank, a knocker, critic. This is used for one person; for more than one, toiehaŋpi. Cf. to, n. A noise made by a blow.

to'iyok̇itaŋiŋ, n. His manifestation.

tojaŋ', n. A niece; my niece, when the person is addressed. Mitojaŋ, nitojaŋ. Note: this form is used by women. Cf. toŋjaŋ. -- tojáŋk̇u, n. Her niece. -- tojáŋya, v.a. To have for a niece (a woman). Tojaŋwaya.

toje'la, adj. Short. Du. Syn.- ptecela.

ṫo'k̇a, n. An enemy, one of a hostile nation.

to'ka, adv. interrog. Why? How is it? What is up? - hwo? What is the matter? D.224. Ina, - ca ate iḣpeya uŋgni kte he? Tuwa ohiye ci - hwo? Tuŋkaśila, - ca he yaglumaŋ hwo? Taku - hwo? What is up, what is the news? Taku - kiŋ nah'oŋpi, i.e. what is the matter. B.H.278.6;45.23;81.7. Tomáka, There is nothing the matter with me. Sp. Cf. tokeca; tomakeca śni, nothing the matter, not sick.

tok̇a', adv. At the first. Tuwa - hi na wawaŋyaŋka cana iśta ḣca yelo. Na hehaŋl waŋna ob - iyayapi k'el glipi.

tok̇ab', cont. of tokapa. - ya, To go before.

ṫo'kaca, adv. (toka, why; and ca, and). interrog. Why, wherefore? Cf. toka.

tok̇a'he, 1) n. The first, the beginning. B.H.30.15. 2) v. To be first, to go before. B.H.215.3. -- tok̇áhekiya, v. To go ahead of others. B.H. 126.5. -- tok̇áhek̇iya, v.a. To cause to go before. Tokahewakiya. -- tok̇áheya, 1) adv. At the first, before, in the beginning, primo. - oyate tona lel yauŋpi kiŋ hihaŋna kiŋ wocic'upi kte lo. 2) n. The first.

to'k̇ahu, n. The thistle. Carduus lanceolatus. R. -- tókahu wahiŋkpe oŋ ziyápi, n. The Pricly poppy. Argemone intermedia. The poppy family. The name indicates with it they dye arrows. K. #294.

tok̇a'ḣci, adv. At the first, the very first.

tok̇a'ḣtayetu, n. The first of the night. R. Bl.

ṫo'kaḣ'aŋ, v.n. To lose, to suffer loss. Also perhaps, adj. What has become of it? and I say: Tokaḣ'aŋ, It is gone, i.e. I do not know how it happened. Tokamaḣ'aŋ. Ogle na huŋska, na śina ko el uŋ na tacaŋ kiŋ tokaḣaŋ. Na ake uŋgnahela - na ake pte pa śeca k'oŋ eca yaŋka. Yuŋkaŋ tokaḣaŋpi na wikośkalaka k'oŋ el uŋpi. Hecel oyate iśtapi kiŋ etaŋhaŋ tokaḣaŋ. Yuŋkaŋ - ca,el etoŋwaŋ po, epa. Yuŋkaŋ - na miśnala ena nawajiŋ.

tō'k̇aiápi, n. A foreign language; an enemy's language.

ṫok̇a'ic'ignaka, v. To make note of,

write down for one's self e.g. a word. Tokamic'ignake śni; tokanic'ignake śni. Tokič'ignake, abbrev. Bl.

toka'kala i^{n}ya^{n}ka, v. To run like a horse with body bent, as when the head is pulled back and sideways. Bl.

toǩa' kata', v. To throw a bow on the ice, but then strike the ice at once because one does not know how to do it, i.e. the trick in throwing. Bl.

ťo'ǩaǩa ye śni, v. Not to be able to go any place, having no horses etc. Bl. Also, ťóǩani ye śni.

to'ǩaǩiciyapi, n. Enemies.

toka'ǩiciyut'api, n. A game played by boys. Bl.

ťo'kaǩico^n, v. (of toko^n). To do to or for one.

ťo'kaǩiȟ'a^n, v. To suffer injury or loss; to lose something. Tokamakiȟ'a^n. B.H.77.17;53.14.

toǩa' ǩi^n heha^n'na, adv. ph. At the first, formerly. - pejuta k'upi ki^{n}ha^n akisni kta iyeca tka yelo, If they had given him medicine in the beginning of the sickness, he would have got well. Bl.

ťo'ka kte, cl. Something may happen, it ought be something. Owekiś - sece.

toǩa'k'eha^n, adv. At the first. Also, toǩák'u^{n}héha^n.

ťo'ǩa la, v. Not to be influenced by. Toka wala. B.H.241.27.

toka'la, n. A small gray fox, and very fast.

toǩa'laȟci, adv. For the very first time.

toka'la taṗejúta hu bloka, n. White prairie clover. Petalostemum candidum. The pulse family. Bl. #249. -- tokála taṗejúta hu wi^{n}yela, n. The violet or purple prairie clover. Petalostemum purpureum. The pulse family. It is used as a medicine. The root is chewed as a gum. Bl. L. #176.

toka'la waci'pi, n. The fox dance.

ťo'kamo^n, v. 1st pers. singl. of toko^n.

ťo'kani, adv. In no way, having no means or way. It is usually followed by a verb with śni. Mni ki^n el - hiyu śni ki^n heo^n. D.132: no way of crossing the river. - ble śni, i.e. no way of going, no horses, no wagon, no nothing. Hecel toeyaś - okuwa śni ca ayuśta^n. Ca^{n}ke - akiyuwege śni, i.e. the fall Pa^{n}keska Wakpa. Ca heo^n - tak'epe śni yelo. - tak'epe śni ki^n o^n lila ca^{n}temaśice. D.278: I would not say anything, and that is why I am very unhappy. - glicu śni, i.e. had no way of coming out. D.28. Cf. D.32.

ťo'kano^n, v. 2nd pers. singl. of toko^n.

toka^n', toǩa^{n}l', 1) adv. In another place, elsewhere; another way. Leta^{n}ha^n nihu^n kici - u^{n}ya^{n}pi kte lo. 2) n. Another, as another person. - tawa. Wa^{n}na ake iglakapi na - yapi. Ho heha^{n}l - iblabla na wi num ece - wau^n. B.H.5.5. -- toká^{n}lka^{n}l, adv. red. R. Bl. -- toká^{n}lťa^{n}ha^n, adv. From another source, place or person. Jerusalem el - yahi yelaka? B.H.272.7; 223.2;232.3;260.24. -- toká^n ośta^n, Cf. tokóśta^n. -- toká^{n}ya^n, adv. Having ref. to another place. R. Bl.

toǩa'pa, n. The first, first born, eldest. Tokamapa, tou^{n}kapapi. D.1.

toǩa'paťa^{n}ha^n, adv. Ahead, before.

toǩa'ṗaya, adv. Leading. - śka^n, To lead. B.H.61.24.

toǩaś', adv. Perhaps, maybe. - kigle sece. Also, possibly. - éciciya owakihi kte séce, It is just possible that I can help you. B.H.174.15;182.21;222.3;242.2. D.270.

ťo'ka śka, cl. There is something said. U^{n}gna - pahaha iȟpeciye ci.

ťō'ǩaśni, adv. cl. It does not matter. Lila wanasapi na lila wawicaśeca na - u^{n}pi. MS.348. -- ťóǩaśniǩiya, v.a. To make light of. P. Tokaśniwakiya. -- ťóǩaśniya^n, adv. Without any trouble. - wawa^{n}ya^{n}ke, He saw without any trouble. D.220. Also, with no resistance, more or less willingly but reluctantly. Takuni - u^{n}pi, i.e. are all right with one another. - niwicayuzapi, i.e. took them alive without much resistance on their part. B.H. 135.7;80.3. SLB.

toka'ta, 1) adv. In the future, in future, yet to come. - aⁿpetu wakaⁿ. 2) n. The future.

toka'tahaⁿ caⁿblaska, n. A dash board.

toka'takiya, adv. In the future. Pb.27.
toka'tayab, adv. or adj. perhaps. Ahead, future. Bl.

toka' uⁿ śni, Cf. toka. Wiśi ca wacaⁿmi na wok'iⁿ toka wauⁿ śni yelo, i.e. got more than he expected and can hardly take care of it. Bl.

to'kaya, v.a. To have for an enemy. Tokawaya. B.H.201.4.

to'kayelaka, to'kayelakaś, adv. interrog. For what reason, what for, why? Sometimes kiⁿ is added to the word. Cf. yelakaś. - hecaⁿnoⁿ kiⁿ? Why did you do that? implying, you should not have done it. Ito, le wouⁿptiⁿ kta; - heyapi kiⁿ? eya, i.e. they were told not to dig turnips. Iho, oh'aⁿ emacetu śni eśa ; takoja, taku wotehi ota tka - nituⁿkaśila lehaⁿ amahi yelo. MS.477. D.198.

tō'kčel, tō'kicel, adv. or interj. Somewhere, I don't know where; perhaps, expressing doubt or ignorance, as in answer to a question of the whereabouts of something, i.e. of place only. P.

to'kciⁿciⁿyaⁿ, adv. As pleases; anyhow. Also, tokeciⁿciⁿyaⁿ, tokciⁿkiⁿyaⁿ. R.

To'kciⁿka Wota, n. prop. The Cheyenne Indians living on the Tongue River Reservation.

to'kciⁿkciⁿka, (?). - waipeyelah, i.e. throws everything away into any place etc. Bl.

toke', interj. Listen! i.e. on hearing a noise unexpectedly.

to'ke, opt. particle. I suppose, of course. Toke, ota icazo, eyaś kicipajuju k'uⁿ he e cel. B.H.199.15;221.12. Also perhaps, tóki.
toké eśá....ni, I wish I .... B.H.84.4;112.7;122.10,14.
toké....laká, Would that ...., implying a wish. B.H.55.4.
toke....ni, Oh that, I wish. This infers a wish, that something may be. Toke he bluha ni, I wish I had it. Toke mat'a ni, I wish I was dead. Toke Itaⁿcaⁿ taogligle wakaⁿ kiⁿ yecicapi ni. B.H.125.6;157.8.
toke....so? B.H.264.4. Really. Toke yagli so? Did you really come back? as I was afraid you would not. Toke, ti śni yeśaⁿ etiyoyaⁿkahe so? Bl. Mitaⁿ, toke wicahpi waⁿ lila ilege ciⁿ he waśtewalaka, i.e. really I suppose. MS.1.

to'keca, adj. Different, another. Wicaśa - , Another man. Matókeca. R.

to'keca, adj. Unwell, sick. Tómakeca, tonikeca, touⁿkecapi. Tokecaśni, To be well. Cf. tokecela.

tokē'caca, adv. Unconcernedly. - omani. Also, toké ecaca, Without specific purpose, at random. - omanihaⁿ. D.19. Bl. Syn.- wiⁿkcekceya.

to'kecae, adv. Why? Bl. R.
to'kecakacel, adv. For no reason. R.Bl.

toke'cakel, adv. In case of need. - owiⁿja luha, Have you got an extra blanket, one to spare? S. Syn.- wanuⁿtokayakel.

to'kecaśni, adj. Well, recovered; there is nothing the matter. Hecel waⁿna kuje k'oⁿ tipi k'oⁿ etaⁿ - aglinapa na tiyatakiya glapi. Cf. tokecela.

toke'cela, adv. Slowly, gradually; weakly, from weakness. - hpaye. Ake mini el iyayapi kta, tka - aglagla inajiⁿpi. - glihuⁿni. Aⁿpa eciyataⁿ - ayaⁿpa. - hóyekiya, To call out softly to one. - manila, Barely walking. D.67,219.

to'keciⁿ, adv. Anyhow. As one pleases. Also, tókeciⁿciⁿ. - wauⁿ, i.e. I do as I please. -- tókeciⁿciⁿyaⁿ, adv. As pleases. Also, tokeciⁿyaⁿ. - uⁿ. MS.485.

toke' ecaca, Cf. tokecaca. D.19.

to'kehci, adv. Howsoever.

ťoǩe'ǩekel, adv. (of ťoǩé). With ripe concernedness. - tókiyataŋhaŋ yaku welo, as is said when one returns hurriedly as though something had happened or he was bringing a message. - nayajiŋpi s'elececa, You seem to stand there listening and talking about something. Bl.

ťō'ǩel, adv. and interrog. How, in what way, why? ; somewhere, to some place; as. Tokel oŋ wibluśkiŋ kta hwo? B.H.225.8;122.4. Tokel okihi, As hard (loud, strong etc.) as one can. - ȟ'aŋ. B.H.45.7;58.14;225.8;252.5. tokel....ca na ecel, As....so. Tokel eya ca na ecel ecoŋ po. tokel ȟ'aŋp̌ica śni, Nothing can be done about it. Gramm.191. B.H.152.17. - iyaya, To disappear. D.221.

to'ǩelǩelťu, adv. In whatever way.
ťo'ǩelǩelťuya, adv. In what way soever. R. Bl.
to'ǩelǩiyaťaŋhaŋ, adv. On what side, from where, from what direction. B.H. 118.9.

ťō'ǩel oki'hika, cl. (okihi and laka). Cf. tókel. B.H.125.3;139.19;95.22;119.10;140.1. Tokel okihilakel, By all means, in every way, with all might. B.H.105.3.

ťo'ǩena yaŋka, v. To remain while others move, to stay partly the way they were. Na ena lila tehaŋ maŋka icuŋhaŋ taŋke ena ate kici tokena yaŋkapi k'oŋ hecetuwaŋjica yaŋkapi.

ťo'ǩeni, interj. cl. Waŋ - wowaȟtani el nitoŋpi tka waohola śni waoŋspeuŋyakiyapi wacaniyelo. B.H.222.13. Tokeniś nawicaȟ'oŋ śni iyecel iye kapi śni s'e hiyaya ke, i.e. he paid no attention, as if they did not mean him. D.29.

ťo'ǩeś, adv. As. Cf. tokel. Tokeś he niye s'e wacaŋmi, I thought that was you. R. Bl.

ťo'ǩeśa, adv. After a little while, at any rate. This is an adv. of assent to word or action. Cf. tokśa.

ťo'ǩeśǩe, adv. How, how in the world? in whatsoever way. Takoja, - yaȟ'aŋ hwo? What have you been doing. He kigna yo! - naka he? eya. - yaȟ'aŋ na hecel naŋka hwo? - waȟ'aŋ kiŋ slolwayeśni. - yahilu hwo? B.H.241.15;60.6;80.22;184.11;211.7. - ecoŋ ciśi k'uŋ hecehci ecoŋ wo. D.200. -- ťóǩeśǩeśǩe, adv. red. (of tokeśke). How in various ways. - wauŋyeyapi naiŋś... hena okiyake. B.H.60.6;80.22. -- ťóǩeśǩe uŋpi s'e ománi, v. To travel over very bad roads or on no roads at all, as in hilly country. Syn.- teȟiȟiya omani, ptaŋśkika s'e omani.

ťo'ǩetǩel, adv. red. of tokel. R. Bl.
ťo'ǩetǩiya, adv. In whatever way. Bl. - mni kta hwo? B.H.28.3;298.4.

ťo'ǩeťu, adv. How is it? As it is. - kiŋ ecel oblakiŋ kta. - he? How is it, what is the matter? Toniketu? How is it with you, how are you? - taŋiŋ śni. - kakeś, As it happens.

to'ǩĕťu kec'eyaś, adv. However, in whichever way. Toketuke c'eyaś, No matter what happens. D.12.

ťo'ǩeťu ǩeś, adv. perhaps. No matter what, all the same. Le yaciŋ niś yaciŋ śni, śice nacece; hiya, - mak'u wo. Bl.
ťo'ǩeťuya kakéś, adv. In whatever way; at random perhaps.

to'kewaciŋśni uŋ, v. To pretend to be unaware of something, as when somebody come who has wronged one long ago, and acts as if nothing ever happened. Tokewaciŋśni wauŋ, wowaglaka. Yuŋkaŋ isam lila wicoti na lila oiyokipi ca el tokewaciŋśni bla.

ťo'ǩeya....ca hehaŋl', adv. coord. conj. Before, Latin antequam. Tokeya wicoȟaŋ waŋji, num, yamni ecoŋpi, ca hehaŋl tawicutoŋpi.

toke'ya, adj. or n. The first, in opposition to others following.

ťŏǩĬ', interj. Of admiration for something beautiful and a word used by women.

ťo'ǩi, adv. Where, somewhere. Waŋna toki iblabla taŋiŋ śni. B.H.232.2. Also perhaps, tóke. Toki wi wikcemna ecetu.

toki'čic'oŋ, v. (of tokic'oŋ). To take vengeance on for one. Towecic'oŋ, touŋkicic'oŋpi.

toƙi'cikśu, v. (of tokśu). To transport for one. Towecikśu.

to'ƙiconze, n. (of wokiconze). His law or determination.

toƙi'c'un, v.a. To revenge, take revenge on. Towec'un. - wacinhanpi, i.e. thought of taking revenge. B.H.135.9.

tō'ƙi e'iƕpeya, v. To misplace something. P. -- tóƙi iƕpéƙiya, v.a. To lose one's own, misplace one's own. Toki iƕpewakiya. R. -- toƙí iƕpeya, v. To lose, misplace, drop. Bl.

to'ƙi iyaye s'a, n. One who is gone much; a tramp. - tanin śni. D.81.

to'ƙinahanś, adv. Same as tokinaś. Ya! - taku otaka ca ekitan wamaśipi kte ƕcin.

to'ƙinaś, interj. Maybe. - yacin śni s'elececa. - he niye s'e wacanmi. Syn.- seca, tokaś.

toƙin'....ni, Same as toké....ni. Konpi s'e eyapi.

to'ƙinś, adv. Well, implying that one was mistaken in one's assumptions. - he niye s'e wacanmi, I thought that was you. - waśicun wakan kin hi kte sece, i.e. yunkan hi śni. - le wapośtan s'elececa; yunkan heca śni. Rf. - el mahi. B.H.115.3.

toƙinś', adv. Carelessly, wrong. - ecannon, yakage. Tóhinni - wote śni, Never did he eat carelessly. D.120-1.

toƙin'śeśeś', adv. Luckily enough, almost too good to be true. - oyakihi keci (kecin), as is said when encouraging one, knowing that he can do it. - iyowinyan ce. D.160, note 3.

toƙin'śƙinś, (?). - anátakinyece. Bl.

toƙinś'yaƙel, adv. Carelessly, without care.

toki'ya, v.a. To paint blue. Towakiya. Itokśan tokiyapi.

to'ƙiya, adv. interrog. Where, in what place. Also, where did he go? Cf. toki. -- tóƙiyab, adv. (of tokiyapa). Where, in what direction? - tuwa can katoto hwo? - omani ye śi. Yunkan - cancega naƕ'on ke. MS.97. - inaƕma yo. B.H.88.23. -- tóƙiyala, v. Where are you going? This does not mean just "where". R. -- tóƙiyani, adv. Nowhere, to no place. - ya. - yin kte śni, i.e. will go nowhere. Bl. B.H.52.3. D.133. Cf. tokani. -- tóƙiyapa, adv. Where. -- tóƙiyatan, adv. Whence, from what place? - hi? Na tuwepi nunpapi kin - śunkahopi ca na aiyopteya yapin na ake hopi. Wicaśa wan hi - . Wan! hokśila wan - waohola śni yaƕ yelo. -- tóƙiyatanhan, adv. Whence, from what place? from some place. Yunkan wicaśa wan kośkalaka wan kici - glipi. Tonikiyatanhan hwo? B.H.264.10. Cf. leciyatanhan etc. -- tóƙiyawapa, adv. Where, in what place.

tokiyo'ṗeƙiciyapi, n. Barter, exchange.
tokiyo'ṗekiya, v.a. To barter, exchange one thing for another with one. Tokiyopewakiya. Tokiyopeciciya, I exchange with you. Cf. iyopekiya.
toƙiyo'ṗeya, v.a. (toki and iyopeya). To barter, exchange one thing for another. Tokiyopewaya.

toƙi'yotan, adv. Somewhere, in some direction, towards somewhere; at once. Yunkan hakela - iyaya keye. D. 220,244,79. Cf. leciyotan, heciyotan, kakiyotan. Also, toƙíyotanhan.

to'ƙon, v.a. To do; to misplace, thus being unable to find. Tókamon, tókanon, tókunk'onpi. Inyan k'on he tokanon hwo? Mazaska wikcemna tókanonpelo. Tokamayanon oyakihi śni tka. PD. B.H.264.14. Anpetu kin lena el taku tokonpi kin hena slolyaye śni yelaka? B.H.272.7.

toƙon'ṗica, adj. Useful, good for something.

toko'śtan, v.n. To sprain, dislocate one's own. Cankpe tokomaśtan, i.e. when knees do not work well. Cecá tokomaśtan. Cf. tokan ośtan. -- tokóyuśtan, v.a. To displace, dislocate, put one in the place of another. Tokobluśtan. R. Bl.

to'ksaṗe, n. (of woksape). His wisdom. Nitoksape.

tō'kśa, adv. Presently, by and by, before long; yes. Le miye ƕca ca - oyate el unki kte eya keya. - ohinni awaŋciyakapi kte lo.

tokśu', v.a. To transport, carry, draw; to go back and bring. Towakśu, touŋkśupi. Hecel towicakśupi, i.e. they picked up the wounded.

toktōg', adj. Another. Waŋji -, By turns. Waŋji toktog asaŋpi yuslipi, They milk by turns, i.e. every morning another boy. Uŋma -, By turns, in ref. to two persons. Also, itógto, adv. Alternately. R. -- toktógye, adv. red. (of togye). In different ways. B.H.277.5;278.4. -- toktógyek̇el, adv. In different ways.

ṫokṫo'k̇eca, adj. red. (of tokeca). Different. D.250.

ṫo'kṫu, adv. How is it? Haŋska naiŋś ptecela, - ? Tuwa le yuha kiŋ sam - kiŋ slolyiŋ kta. Tokata - kte ciŋ ob gluśtaŋpi kte lo. Cf. toketu. - ke c'éyaś, However, in whichever way.

ṫo'k̇yab, Cf. tokiyab.

ṫok'e'yaś, Cf. toéyaś.

tō'laḣcak̇a, adj. Very blue. Cf. ḣcáka.

ṫo'las'e, adj. (of to and s'e). Cf. iśta tolas'e ayuta.

tolu'ṫe, adj. Purple. Tahayapi kiŋ - ece koyakapi. B.H.91.23;263.9.

to'mawahitoŋ, to'mawahetoŋ, n. His omawahitoŋ, cf. Perhaps the word is derived from uŋma-he-toŋ.

ṫō'na, adv. How many, which? Taku - oŋnispepi kta waciŋ. Ake lel wicoḣaŋ tona ecoŋ kta ca ake u wo. -- ṫónacaŋ, adv. How many days? -- ṫónagna, adv. How many? Also, ṫónagnag, ṫónagnak̇eca (of tonakeca). -- ṫónagnala, adv. red. of tonala, perhaps the same as tonana.

ṫo'nakeca, adj. Some, a few. Also, interrog. how many, how much? Pejuta waŋ icu na tonakecapi oyasiŋ wicak'u. Waŋna hokśila kiŋ waniyetu - na waŋna mani luzahaŋ. Oniye tonamakeca heci hena oyas'iŋ cic'u. Pb.34. Cf. lenakeca etc. -- ṫónakec'eyaś, adv. How many soever. -- ṫónakel, adj. A few, some, a few times; several, a fair number. Na el wicaśa - yaŋkapi. - ewicuŋktepi. Na ikiyela maya ca - ob wauŋ. MS.535. - owicakaptapi. B.H.135.9. Hiŋśma - owiŋśtoŋ. D.229. -- ṫónak̇iya, adv. How many, how many times? in how many ways. Hecel oyasiŋ - wapatapi kiŋ ptepa olepi eśa taŋcaŋ ecoŋpi.

ṫo'nana, adv. A few, how few. Lena waŋwicayakapo; - wicaopi kiŋ waŋyaŋka po.

ṫo'naŋgnaŋg, cont. Cf. tonagnag.

tō'ni, n. His life.

toŋ, 1) v.a. To have, to give birth to; to possess, acquire. Ciŋca toŋ. Watóŋ. Oŋzoge wetoŋ kte; ogle wetoŋ kte. 2) n. An endowed spiritual or quasi spiritual power or quality that makes a person or thing wakaŋ. Thus, the wicaśa wakaŋ is one who has the power to make wakaŋ other things. WJR.152. Also, matter, pus.

toŋ'haŋ, v.a. To be afraid of. Toŋwahaŋ. This is an old word. R. Bl. Also, tóŋheca.

toŋḣli'ḣli, v. To lossen the phlegm in the throat by coughing. Bl.

toŋi'k̇aśṗa, v. To expectorate, spit. Toŋiwakaśpa.

toŋjaŋ', n. A man's niece. A woman's niece is tojaŋ. Toŋjaŋku, toŋjaŋya, cf. tuŋjaŋ, tuŋjaŋku, tuŋjaŋya.

toŋka'śṗa, v. To spit out phlegm. Toŋwakaśpa. Bl.

ṫoŋ'kce, n. Excrement.

ṫoŋ'la, adj. Weak. Ehaŋni - s'elemáceca, tacúpala s'elemaceca, I used to be weak. Bl. -- tóŋla s'e uŋ, v. To be idle on account of not feeling well, to be too much afraid for one's health. Bl. Toŋlas'e wauŋ welo. BT.

toŋo'gnagagya, adv. Matter on sores here and there. - ḣaŋpi. B.H.231.4.

toŋśka', n. A nephew, my nephew. Women say tośka. Mitoŋśka. Also, tuŋśka. -- toŋśkáku, n. His nephew. -- toŋśk̇áya, v.a. To have for a nephew.

toŋ'toŋ, v. red. of toŋ. -- n. That

which has physical properties. Hence, toŋtoŋśni, That which is without physical properties. -- tóŋtoŋyaŋ, adj. Visible from its properties; hence, toŋtoŋśniyaŋ, Invisible because of properties. WJR.153.

toŋt'e', n. His death. B.H.229.2. Cf. wicoŋt'e.

toŋwaŋ', n. Any kind of arrows. Mitoŋwaŋ. R. Bl. - śikśica, tka mak'u welo, i.e. gave he poor arrows. - waśteśte, Good arrows. Bl.

ṫoŋwaŋ', v.n. To look, see. Watoŋwaŋ, uŋtoŋwaŋpi. Hecel pamagle iblotake na iśtogmus iblotake na waŋna watoŋwaŋ. Iśtogmus ece wayacipi na yatoŋwaŋpi kte śni. -- ṫoŋwáŋhaŋ, part. Looking, seeing.

toŋwaŋ'yeca, v.n. To dwell at a place, to live there. Toŋwaŋwayeca. Bl.

ṫoŋ'wel, adv. (tohaŋ el). Once upon a time. Tóŋwĕl(ĕ) wéṫu ká wăŋ, Long ago in springtime. - ptaŋyétu ká waŋ, Long ago in fall. - waniyetu ka waŋ. Cosya igluze omani yo; tuwa - śuŋkmanitu cuwita kacaś. - wetuka wicaḣcala, as is said of a young man or boy who acts or talks like an old man or who grew very fast. Bl. Also, tuŋwel, ehaŋni. Note: this is doubtfully derived from ṫoŋwáŋ.

ṫoŋ'weni, adv. When? Huŋhuŋhé, - yahi hwo? When did you come? (I knew nothing about it. Bc. Bl. Note: this is perhaps derived from tóhuŋweni, which is not used. -- ṫóŋweni....śni, adv. Never. Nilekśi tuŋweniḣciŋś hi śni. D.154,81. Cf. toŋwel. Note: LP. says toŋweni is the deriv. of toŋwel-ni.

ṫoŋwe'ya, 1) n. A spy, a guide. 2) v.n. To go to see, to go as a spy. Perhaps toŋwebla. Toŋweuŋyaŋpi. 3) v.a. To cause one to see, give sight to. Toŋwewaya.

toŋyaŋ', v.n. To suppurate.

to'ope, n. His law. Mitoope.

ṫo'ṗa, num. adj. Four. Also, tob. Wicaśa uŋtopapi. -- ṫópaḱiya, adv. In four ways, four times.

to ṗe'stola, n. The hoary or mullein-leaved vervain. Verbena stricta. The vervain family. BT. #27.

ṫo'ṗṫoṗa, adj. red. (of topa). By fours; four and four. Cf. tóbtob.

tosaŋ', adj. Light blue. -- tosáŋya, v.a. To make light blue. B.H.60.14.

tosa'ṗa, adj. Grape-colored.

ṫosḱa'la, n. The downy and hairy woodpecker. On the head it has a red spot. Ya! - akoecoŋ. FR.

ṫoś, adv. Yes, yea; an affirmative expression used by women only. Cf. ṫo and haŋ.

tośa', adj. Purple. B.

tośe', adj. Dull, blunt. -- tośéyaḱel, adv. Bluntly.

ṫośka', n. A nephew, my nephew. Mitośka, nitośka. This form is used by women only, while men say toŋśká or tuŋśka. Mitośka yuha maŋkiŋ kta. -- tośḱáḱu, n. Her nephew. -- tośḱáya, v.a. To have for a tośka. Tośḱáwaya.

to'śkiŋciye, n. (of śkiŋciye). His or its work, his field, his occupation, as is said on seeing trees felled in a creed and concluding that beavers are at work there. Bl.

ṫōśṫōś', adv. red. (of toś). Yes, yea. Eyaś - haŋkeni wate śni eye.

ṫoṫiŋ'yaŋka, interj. Wait a little. - yo. Cf. ito.

toto', adj. red. of to. -- totóla, n. Blue beads, green beads.

ṫoṫō'la, adj. Bare. Also, otótola. ET. Cf. yutoto.

tōtō'ṗa, adj. All wet, as moccasins from rain or snow. Matótopa. Ma k'eya, nitotopiŋ kte, i.e. you will be wet from dew or fog. Bl.

toto'ṗela, (?). Hokśi - iyeniceca yelo, You act like a child, are childish. Bl.

toto'ya, adv. red. of toya. MS.340.

to'wakaŋ, n. His wakaŋ or spirit. Cf.

wowakaŋ.

towaŋ'jica, adj. All blue. Aŋpetu waŋji - ca ṗeágnagwicakiyiŋ kte lo, A clear blue day (sky) is to shine on them. LP. -- towáŋjila, n. The blue sky, all blue.

to'waoŋjila, n. (of wowaoŋśila). His mercy. Nitowaoŋśila.

to'waśťe, n. (of wowaśte). His goodness. Nitowaśte.

tō'waś'aǩe, n. (of wowaś'ake). His power or strength. Nitowaś'ake.

ťo'weni, adv. Never. Also, tóŋweni.... śni. Kośkalaka kayeś - taku emakiye śni yelo. Bl.

to'wicaǩe, n. (of wowicake). His truth. Nitowicake. Na - ca taŋiŋśni, i.e. although he might have spoken the truth.

to'wiŋje, n. (of owiŋja). His bed. Mitowiŋje.

toya', v.a. To dye or paint blue or green. Towaya. -- tóya, adv. In a blue or green manner. -- toyákel, adv. In a blue or green form. -- toyéla, adj. Bluish, greenish.

tozi', adj. Light green. -- ťózitka, adj. Greenish. Syn.- caŋȟpáŋ pizí.

ťucu'hu, n. A rib, the ribs.

ťucu'śťe, n. The side below the ribs, the flank.

ťū'ǧa, 1) adj. Hunch-backed, as a man or a camel. Matúga. 2) n. A hump or hunch.

ťuȟma'ǧa, Same as tuȟmuŋga. - ȟota, A gray bee or wasp. Bl.

ťuȟmuŋ'ǧa, n. Bees, wasps, hornets.
ťuȟmuŋ'ǧa caŋhaŋ'pi, n. Honey. B.
ťuȟmuŋ'ǧa taŋka, n. The bumble-bee.
ťuȟmuŋ'ǧa tuŋkce, n. Honey.
ťuȟmuŋ'ǧa wigli, n. Wax.

ťuǩa', conj. But. This seems to be used only in combinations, thus: Eyaś tuka uŋkicaŋṭe kiŋ uŋkoile s'elececa. B.H.273.14. Śehaŋś tuka. Miyeśtuka, Even though nobody else acts, I will. D.71, note 4.

ťu'ǩa, Cf. katuka.

ťuǩa'haŋ, part. Scabby, i.e. having lost one's hair, as a dog, horse etc. Also, spoiled, destroyed (said of fur). R.

ťuka'ǩa, part. Tired. Miyeś - , wanagi el mahipelo. BT.

ťuǩaś', adv. But. R. Bl.

ťuǩi', interj. Is that so? This is used by women. D.115. Tuki yaȟi so?

ťuǩi', n. A clam.
ťuǩi'ha, n. A shell, without the animal.
ťuǩi' pśitō, n. A pearl.
ťuǩi'winuŋkala, n. A large shell. Bl. Also, a small round clam shell. Bl.

ťukťe', pron. interrog. Which? Uŋma tukte, Which of the two? - ehaŋ, When? - e, Which is it? Ho, niciŋca kiŋ - ehe ci ikikcu wo. - oyate ca enitaŋhaŋ hwo? Wicaśa nitukte waŋjipi. B.H.121.26;224.9.

ťukťe' e k'e'yaś, ťukťe' eke e'yaś, pron. indef. Anybody. Tukte....ke c'eyaś, Whichever. Tukte aŋpetu k'eyaś, Whichever day. B.H.52.10.

ťukťe'haŋ, (?). Iśkaŋśkaŋ amayakita ye, - akiȟ'aŋ t'emayayiŋ kte, as a woman would say to grandchildren who want to eat along. Bl.

ťukťe' ihāŋkeya, (?). - caŋ otehike kiŋ oŋ kage, i.e. the best of wood. B.H.60.9.

ťukťe'kťe, pron. red. of tukte. -- tukťe'kťel, adv. red. (of tuktel). Sometimes, once in a while, now and then; in some places.

ťukťe'kťeťaŋhaŋ, (?). MS.343.

ťukťe'kťeťu, adv. red. of tuktetu. - ǩaǩéś, Anywheres. B.H.108.10. - ke s'e, It is hard to choose, every one is good. Also: oyasiŋ waśte s'elececa. Na waŋna lila oiyokipi kośkalaka k'oŋ tuktektetu ke s'e waŋna enajiŋ na waŋna lowaŋpi.

ťukťel', adv. Where? in what place?

somewhere. Ake - iśtiŋma. Waŋna tipi he ohiyayelo. ca - kagapi yaciŋ hwo? Le hihaŋna kiŋ mat'iŋ kta ca - paha waŋji el taŋyaŋ emaoŋpa po. -- ťukťél ....hel, adv. coord. Where....there. Tuktel wicaȟapi kiŋ,hel woyute eśa egnakapi.

ťukťe'na, (?). - Israel oyatepi tka k'uŋ otaŋiŋpi śni. B.H.119.1.

ťukťe'ni, adv. Nowhere. This is used with the negative śni. Huhu ece ca na tukteni talo ikoyake śni yelo.

ťukťe'ognagna, red. of tukteogna. B.H. 88.25. Cf. tuktogna.

ťukťe'ťaŋhaŋ, adv. From what place?
ťukťe'ťu, adv. At what place? - Ȟapi taŋiŋ śni. -- ťukťéťu ǩaǩeśǩeś, adv. At most any place. Wakaŋtaŋka wauŋyekiyapi. B.H.60.3. Cf. kakeśkeś. -- ťukťéťu k'éyaś, ťukťéťu ke c'éyaś, adv. In any place, everywhere, wherever. Also, tuktetu ǩaǩéś. - iyomakepi. B.H.50.3;154.2.

ťukťo'gna, ťukťéogna, adv. Where? in what direction, which way? - uŋyiŋ kte he? Letaŋ waŋna tuktogna iyonicipipi kiŋ ogna iyaya po. - oti iwaśte kiŋ he ogna kaȟnigapi. - ktepi kta taŋiŋ śni. B.H.45.6,12;46.2;266.13. -- ťukťógnagna, adv. red. of tuktogna. B.H.88.25. -- ťukťógna ke c'éyaś, adv. However, in which ever way. B.H.137. 25;266.3. -- ťukťógnakel, adv. In no way. - iwayapiya gnaye iyuŋȟ śipi. - waayupte śni. B.H.77.11;261.21. -- ťukťógnani, adv. (tukte-ogna-ni). In no way. - napa okihi śni. B.H.72.3; 262.18;292.7.

ťuktu'ǩahaŋ, adj. Spoiled, as furs when the hair is off. R. Bl.

ťukťuŋ'ma, adv. Either one of two. B.H. 199.14;187.13.

ťula', interj. For shame! An exclam. of surprise or protest.

ťum, n. The whistling or whizzing sound made by a flying bullet.

ťuŋjaŋ', n. A man's niece. A man's brother's children and a woman's sister's children are considered as children and are not tuŋśki or tuŋjaŋ. Mituŋjaŋ, nituŋjaŋ. -- ťuŋjáŋku, n. His niece. -- ťuŋjáŋya, v.a. To have for a niece (a man). Tuŋjaŋwaya.

ťuŋǩaŋ', n. A father-in-law. Mitúŋkaŋ, nituŋkaŋ. Also, in the sacred language, a sacred stone supposed to have great power and used in the oinikage tipi. This stone is also called the yuwipi waśicuŋ. HM. FD.204. -- ťuŋǩáŋǩu, n. His or her father-in-law. -- ťuŋǩáŋśi, n. My father-in-law. Nituŋkaŋ, Your father-in-law. -- ťuŋǩáŋśiya, v.a. To have for a father-in-law. Tuŋkaŋ waśicuŋ, n. Cf. waśicuŋ. -- ťuŋǩáŋyaŋ, v.a. To have for a father-in-law. Tuŋkáŋwayaŋ.

ťuŋǩa'śila, n. A grandfather, my grandfather. Nituŋkaśila. -- Ťúŋǩáśila, n. prop. The president of the United States; the Supreme Being, the Godhead. -- Ťúŋǩáśila Oti, n. prop. The White House, the president's house. -- ťuŋǩáśilaya, v.a. To have for a grandfather. Tuŋkaśilwaya. -- ťuŋǩáśitku, n. His or her grandfather.

ťuŋ'kce, n. Excrement, faeces; breaking wind.

ťuŋsla', n. The snail, the leech.

ťuŋśka', n. A nephew. Mituŋśka, nituŋśka. Taŋkeku ciŋca hokśila. -- ťuŋśkáku, n. His nephew. -- ťuŋśkáya, v.a. To have for a nephew. Tuŋśkawaya.

ťuŋťuŋ'pa, adj. Slippery, ropy, slimy. Thus, p'e - , The slippery elm. R.Bl.

ťuŋ'weȟca, This is used usually with śǩéka. An expression of disbelief, doubt, when a man makes a statement who is known to be a liar. MG. - śkeka, lila oniwakaŋkaŋ ye. B.H.99.10.

ťuŋ'wel, Cf. toŋwel. -- ťúŋwelwel, adv. red. Bl.

tuŋwi'cu, n. His or her aunt, on the father's side. -- tuŋwícuya, v.a. To have for one's aunt. Tuŋwicuwaya.

ťuŋwiŋ', n. An aunt, my aunt, on the father's side; an uncle's wife. Nituŋwiŋ, Thy aunt. Note: a mother's sisters are called ína. -- ťuŋwíŋya, v.a. To have for an aunt, on the father's side. Tuŋwiŋwaya.

tusla' wa'yaskape s'e, adv. Sticking in the manner of a leech. Tusla wayaskape s'e kuwa, To be intent upon speaking to a person and hence come again and again, while the other knows nothing about this and does not ask either. Bl.

ťuswe'ca, n. A dragon fly. Bl.
ťuswe'ca śa, n. The red dragon fly. Bl.
ťuswe'ca taŋka gleglééa, n. The large speckled dragon fly. Bl.
ťuswe'ca taŋka zizi, n. The large yellow dragon fly. Bl.
ťuswe'ca to, n. The blue dragon fly.

ťuśu', n. A tent pole, tent poles, a lodge pole.
ťuśu'heyuŋpi, n. A travois, tent-poles tied together to pack things on. Cf. hupáheyuŋpi.
ťuśu' iŋkpa, n. The upper (visible) ends of tent-poles. Also, ticé iŋkpa.
ťuśu' ipa'ťaŋtoŋ, v. To brace the inner wall of a tent lest it shake too much during a storm. Bl.
ťuśu' iyu'ťaŋtoŋ, v. To put a rope around the tent-poles above and fasten it inside to the ground so as to hold it tightly together while a heavy wind blows. Bl.

ťuta', adj. Smarting, chapped by the wind. Ite matuta.

ťutka', n. Small articles, trinkets; but not insects. -- ťutkála, n. dim. of tutka. -- ťutkátka, n. Small, trifling articles or trinkets. -- ťutkátkayakel, adv. In bits, small quantities. - wawakamna, Make money in small quantities at a time. Bl. Syn.- yuȟ'eȟ'eyakel, ptuȟ'aȟ'ayakel, tutkáyakel.

ťu'wa, pron. rel. Who. Tuwa ohiye ci toka hwo?
túwa....ca na he (or ca he), Who (whom)....he (him); if one....he. Tuwa naȟmala wanasa ca na akicita ktepi (rel. useage).
túwa....eśa, Anyone or someone. Tuwa icimani eśa. B.H.57.17.
ťu'wa e kága, v. To take for, mistake for. B.H.221.16.

ťu'wa ka keśá, interj. It is impossible, never heard of. Also, tuwe kakśa and tuwekakeśa, tuwakakśa and tuwa akákeśa. R. D.160. B.H.179.18. Absurd! Preposterous! Also, ťúwa ka keśaś.

B.H.29.10;179.26.

ťu'wa tawa, pron. Whose?

ťuwa'ťulúza, (?). Bl.

ťuwe', pron. interrog. Who? which? (rarely). - ca, Who? B.H.148.20.
ťuwe' ce e'yaś,
ťuwe' ȟci k'éyaś,
ťuwe' ke c'e'yaś,
ťuwe' ke e'yaś, prons. Anybody, everybody, all, whoever. - slolyapi na miś slolwaya. Wicaśa - . B.H.236.11.

ťu'weȟca, pron. Who indeed? - śkéka, i.e. doubting. - śkeka lila oweniwakaŋkaŋ. B.H.99.10.

ťu'wekaleś, pron. Whoever. R.
ťuwe' keśa', pron. Whoever. B.H.190.23;261.7.
ťuwe'la, pron. Who. He - hwo? - waŋwicayaŋke śni. R. Bl.

ťuwe'ni, pron. Nobody. - uŋ śni. Ciŋkśi, nitaŋkśila manil - uŋ śni ekta kici ti na awaŋyaŋka yo. Tehaŋl - uŋ śni waŋ ekta etipi keye.

ťuwe'śka, interj. Who is this? - hwo? Bl.

t'a, v.n. To die, faint away, lose consciousness temporarily. Mat'a.

t'a'ǧa, adj. Rough, as a floor on account of sand strewn over it; bitter or astringent, as oak bark.

t'a'ǧela hu, n. Same as wahpe taga. BT. #267.

t'a'hiyuya, v.n. To be still-born.

t'aȟt'a'ǧa, adj. red. (of t'aga). Rough, not smooth. Ocaŋku - kiŋ hena yualapapi kte. B.H.172.8.

t'a'nuŋs'e, adv. About dead.

t'at'a', adj. Numb, asleep, as a limb. Hu mat'at'a. -- t'at'áka, adj. Numb, palsied. Mat'at'aka.

t'e, v.n. To die. Same as t'a.

t'eble'ze śni, v. To be frantic, wild. Hokśila k'uŋ - na ceye. D.98. - wawiyahpahpaya ayahilala, i.e. to wrestle for fun. Bl.

t'eca', adj. Lying dead. Pte - , A dead cow.

t'e'ca, adj. Warm, lukewarm, tepid, as water.
t'e'caya, adv. In a dead state, still a little warm. Also, t'écayaƙel. Note: the word is used of fluids, as coffee.

t'egna'śkiŋyaŋ s'e, (?). - ole, To look for one high and low in great excitement. Bl.

t'eho'waya, v.n. To cry out badly, to scream for fear, as is said of men and animals. Wat'éhowabla.
t'eho'wayeya, v.a. To cause to cry out badly. T'ehowayewaya.

t'ei'cakiś, adv. In a dying state. Also t'eícaƙiśya.

t'eƙi'nica, v.n. To contend with death; to be doubtful whether one dies or lives. T'emakinica. Hecel yaŋkahe c'oŋ he ceya lila iyokiśica oŋ - śke', As he sat there, he felt as though he must die of grief. D.225.

t'eƙi'ya, v.a. To cause to die. T'ewakiya.

t'eƙoŋ', v. To wish to be dead. T'ewakoŋ.
t'eƙoŋ'za, v. To wish one dead, to curse.

t'e'la nuwé, n. A small kind of lizard found on the hills; the sand lizard. Also, t'éla nuwéla. S. Bl.

t'eśni'yaŋkel, adv. Not dying. Elias - waŋkatakiya eyayapi. B.H.113.5.

t'eya', v.a. To cause to die. T'ewaya. Ota t'ewiceyaya.

t'eya'su, v. To condemn to die (a new word).
t'eya'suƥi, part. Condemned to die.

t'iŋ, v.n. To die. Same as t'a. It is used when followed by "kta", the sign of the future.

t'iŋ'ǧa, v.n. To snivel, to grunt; to labor, as a woman in childbirth. Wat'iŋga.

t'iŋs'ya, 1) v.a. To make firm. T'iŋswaya. T'iŋsic'iya, To restrain one's self, to brace up. 2) adv. Firmly, without fear.
t'iŋsya'ƙel, adv. Firmly, bravely.

t'iŋt'iŋ', adj. perhaps. Beginning to be dry. Same as púza aya. Tauŋkce nuŋb waŋblaka; yuŋkaŋ uŋma puza na - yelo. Bl.

t'iŋ'za, adj. Hard, stiff, as mud; firm, brave. Wowaśi - , A hard worker. Caŋte - , Brave heart.

t'iŋza'ni, adv. Stilly, smoothly, calmly. Caŋku naśkiśkapi ca caŋpagmiyaŋpi - mani śni yelo, i.e. rough roads and unpleasant riding. - najiŋ okihi śni, i.e. was not able to stand calmly still. Bl.

t'o'ja, adj. Dull, pointless.

t'ośya, adv. (t'oja). Bluntly. - kaga.

t'uŋgya', v.a. To suspect, have a suspicion of a thing. T'uŋgwaya.
t'uŋgya'kel, adv. Unwillingly. - ecoŋ.
t'uŋgye'śni, adv. perhaps. Not unwillingly. B.H.5.16.

t'uŋ'ka, v. Cf. t'uŋkeca. Mat'úŋka. Sp.
t'uŋ'ƙeca, v.n. To be suspicious, to be suspected. Mat'uŋkeca.
t'uŋƙi'ya, v. To suspect concerning one's self.

u, v.n. To come, be coming. Wau, uⁿkupi. R.

u'c'ita au, 1) n. The name for the morning parade held on July 4th. Also, uc'ita nataupi, uc'ita au iⁿyaⁿkapi. Fr. 2) v. (of uic'ita, utá). To march or celebrate the 4th of July. Uc'ita uⁿkaupi kte lo. Bl. Hiⁿhaⁿna el wana uc'ita ayiⁿ kta ca toka ktepi hena oḣ'api k'uⁿ ecel ewicaglepi. MS.565. Na wana uc'ta ahiyaya. MS.565.

uk̇a', n. The skin, hide, esp. the skin of a living animal. R. Bl. The skin without hair, in opposition to ha, which is a hairy hide. Bl.

uk̇i'ya, v. col. pl. They are on their way home, i.e. where the speaker is; this is said of many, whereas ku is said of one. Wana agli yelo, They have arrived at home, i.e. where the speaker is. Wakiⁿyaⁿ ukiye lo. Na waⁿna iyehaⁿtu k'oⁿ hehaⁿ ukiya na waⁿna ake zaptaⁿ ca el owakpamni el agli. Note: wana glapelo, They are on their way to their home, i.e. the speaker being absent. Wana tiyata kipelo, They have arrived at their house, i.e. the speaker absent. LB. Wagli ukiyelo, i.e. successful in the chase, they were returning. D.3.

uk̇i'ya, v.a. To cause to come. Uwakiya. R. -- uk̇íya, v.n. col. pl. They are coming. Also v.n. Wakiⁿyaⁿ ukiye lo, Thunder is coming.

umaⁿ', adj. The one, the other. Cf. uⁿma.

uⁿ, 1) v.n. To be. Waúⁿ, yaúⁿ, uⁿk'uⁿpi. 2) v.a. To use anything, have for use. Muⁿ, nuⁿ, uⁿk'uⁿpi. Also, to play. Ḣaka uⁿpi, i.e. play Ḣaka. Nupiⁿ tataⁿka wapaha uⁿpi. 3) pron. in comp. We, us. 4) v.a. To wear. Note thatthis is the same as iⁿ; sapuⁿ, skauⁿ.

uⁿ, uⁿ'pi, particle perhaps. Same as oⁿ. It has perhaps the Latin meaning of ens, being. Uⁿ seems to take the place of the article kiⁿ, or perhaps it is the same as k'uⁿ (k'oⁿ). Caⁿke kaⁿgi uⁿ lila oⁿśic'iya. Na pte uⁿpi kiⁿ el egna iyaya. Hehaⁿ wicaśa hiⁿśma uⁿ hiyu. B.H.190.20;85.7;14.11; 15.16.

uⁿ'azipi, n. A nipple for sucking. Also, oⁿaziⁿpi.

uⁿ'ca, v.a. To mock, imitate, ridicule one. Úⁿwaca, úⁿuⁿcapi.

uⁿ'cabloju, n. (of uⁿcablu and oju). Deep snow, drifts, as along fences. This is an old word. Bl.

uⁿci', n. A grandmother, my grandmother. Nikuⁿśi. Cf. kuⁿśi. A woman calls her mother-in-law uⁿci. -- Uⁿcí, n. prop. Earth, Mother Earth, a term so applied by the Sioux in former times as a subject of concern in their prayers.

uⁿ'cihi, v.n. To have attained one's growth; to be able to take care of one's self. Uⁿmacihi, uⁿuⁿcihipi. -- úⁿcihiya, v.a. To cause to sustain one's self; to raise, train up to manhood. Uⁿcihiwaya.

uⁿci'la, n. dim. of uⁿci.

uⁿci'śi, n. A mother-in-law, my mother-in-law. Uⁿciśi nitawa.

uⁿci'śicala, n. The crow, crows. The corvus Americanus. Also, the little crow, and so perhaps what R. calls uⁿgnaġicala, a bird like a small owl. - s'e ho śica tka lowaⁿ, as they say of a fellow who has a bad voice. Bl. Note: kangi is the raven.

uⁿci'śila, n. dim. of uⁿciśi.

uⁿci'śiya, v.a. To have for a mother-in-law. Uⁿciśiwaya.

uⁿci'ya, v.a. To have for a grandmother. Uⁿciwaya.

uⁿ'c'oⁿnica, v.n. To give up, yield, not try to escape; to be prevented, penned up; to be stage-struck, to be frozen on the spot. Uⁿmac'oⁿnica. Uⁿc'uⁿnica hiⁿgla, i.e. the words stuck in her throat and she could not utter them. D.271, note 1; 244.

uⁿ'c'oⁿnil, v.n. cont. of uⁿc'oⁿnica.

uⁿ'c'oⁿnilya, 1) v.a. To obstruct, prevent; disarm. Uⁿc'oⁿnilwaya. Hecoⁿ kiⁿ oⁿ - , i.e. she disarmed him. D.271. 2) adv. Prevented.

uⁿ'c'uⁿnica, Cf. uⁿc'oⁿnica, and also for uⁿc'uⁿnil, uⁿc'uⁿnilya.

uⁿgna´, interj. Perhaps, I do not know but that. Na - , nitakuye waⁿji nikiyela apa gliȟpaya eśa, el eyatoⁿwe kiló. Kolapila, - nayapapi kilo na wipe kiⁿ kiksuya po. Na waⁿna wicokaⁿyaⁿ saⁿpa ehaⁿl - waⁿna u. - ṫóka śka pahaha iȟpeciye ci. - kapemniyaⁿ micignake ciⁿ. Bl. B.H.81.1.

uⁿgna´ǧaṫa, adv. At or in the uⁿgnaga, in the corner behind the door.

uⁿgna´ǧe, n. The places on both sides of the tent door inside; the corner of a room, and as such is an okaȟmiⁿ behind the door; the place fenced off on each side of the door of a lodge. R. LO.

uⁿgna´ǧicala, n. A screech owl, a bird like a small owl. It wails in the night, sitting in the tree. Women imitate it in a certain dance. Also, it is called the popotka, and the pagla. - hotoⁿpi, as the women do, "lilililili" in the dance. Cf. hoȟnáǧicala hotoⁿpi.

uⁿgna´haȟci, adv. Possibly, it may be so. - le aⁿpetu kiⁿhaⁿ iśta mastaka s'elececa. Bl.

uⁿgna´haⁿla, adv. Suddenly, immediately.

uⁿgna´haⁿś, uⁿgna´haⁿśna, adv. Every now and then, at certain times. Caⁿte paȟlokapi kiⁿ henayos - yutitaⁿpi, as is done in the Sundance.

uⁿgna´hela, uⁿgna´helake, adv. All at once, suddenly. Yuⁿkaⁿ - wekta. Yuⁿkaⁿ - taji nuⁿp cokab hiyupi. -- uⁿgnáhelaya, v.a. To surprise one. Uⁿgnahelawaya. B.H.76.6.

uⁿ´gnaȟ'icaśke, n. A tripod of three sticks to which is fastened the caⁿkázoⁿta, over which robes were spread to sleep on. GA. Bl.

uⁿ´gnak̇aȟ ecóⁿ, uⁿ´gnayek̇aȟ, (?). Makoce ataya caȟ'owaⁿcaya; yuⁿkaⁿ uⁿgnayekaȟ skaⁿ ayelo. Hena wana uⁿgnayekaȟ ablezapi, They understand things now. Bl.

uⁿgnaś´, interj. emph. Perhaps. Same as uⁿgna. - ecaⁿna nit'api kte lo.

uⁿgna´yeȟciś, interj. emph. Perhaps, possibly. B.H.34.27;117.4.

uⁿ´gnayek̇aȟk̇ah, Cf. uⁿgnakaȟ ecoⁿ. - peji uya ayelo. Bl.

uⁿhe´, uⁿhe´na, pron. dem. That. Cf. k'uⁿ he, k'uⁿ hena. Na eyapaha uⁿhe taⁿkal hinapiⁿ na lecel eya. Ehaⁿl eyapaha k'uⁿ he eyapaha au na lecel eya. Uⁿkoniciyakapi uⁿ he le aⁿpetu kiⁿ e yelo. MS.71. B.H.55.14;136.22. Wakaⁿtaⁿka aguyapi eya iwaktaniyaⁿpi uⁿhe lena e yelo. Yuⁿkaⁿ Juda hokśila eya topapi k'uⁿ hena ceb ayapi na taⁿyaⁿ uⁿpi na uⁿmapi uⁿhena hececapi śni.

uⁿȟce´ǧila, n. Probably the mastodon, or other large animals whose petrified remains are found in the Dakota territory. - s'e kagiśniśni wala yelo. -- uⁿȟcéǧilahu, n. The bones of the uⁿȟcegila. They were used for the making of medicines.

uⁿȟce´la, n. The mescal bean.
uⁿȟce´la blaska, n. The flat cactus.
uⁿȟce´la k̇a´ǧapi, n. The feather disk attached to the back of a dancer, so called because the central part appears like a cactus.
uⁿȟce´la pte, n. A toy for boys.
uⁿȟce´la taⁿka, n. The tall cactus.
uⁿȟce´la taśṗu´, n. The cactus berry.
uⁿȟce´la yu´ta ṫawo´ȟtate, n. The paraphernalia used in the peyote service of the Native American Church. LTf.

uⁿ´iglujajapi, n. A wash basin.

uⁿjiⁿ´cala, n. A fledgling bird before the tail has grown, any bird with a short tail. - iblotakelo, as a man says when in sitting down he almost tips over in a forward direction. Bl.

uⁿjiⁿ´jiⁿtk̇a, n. A tomatoe.
uⁿjiⁿ´jiⁿtk̇a hu, n. A rosebush.
uⁿjiⁿ´jiⁿtk̇ahu caⁿ, n. The wild rose bush. #29.

uⁿkcaⁿś´, adv. Same as tokśa.

uⁿ´kce, v.n. To defecate with sound, to break wind. Uⁿwakce, úⁿuⁿkcepi. - hiⁿgla. D.73. -- n. A breaking wind. R. -- úⁿkcekce, v. red. of uⁿkce. Uⁿwakcekce. BT.

uⁿkce'k̇iħa, n. The magpie. Its call: Halháta, halhata, hal, hal, hal. - s'e waśiⁿ waśtelake. Bl. RF. Rl.

uⁿkce'la, n. The cactus. Cf. uⁿħcela. - taśpu, The cactus berry. - blaska, The flat cactus. - kagapi, An ornament of feathers and looking like a blossom which is attached to the seat of a man in the Omaha dance. Bl. - taⁿka, The tall cactus. The roots of the uⁿkcela blaska in being boiled make a tea good for people who cannot urinate. Cf. hu pestostola, or pestola. Lakota maka sapa na wase ocaje oyasiⁿ oⁿ owa na yuśtaⁿ ca nahaħci spaye ci el piya yuspaya na - heca waksiⁿ na oⁿ apawiⁿta ca he tohiⁿni jajahe śni naiⁿś powaye śni. MS.482.

uⁿkce'la ṗeṗe', n. Bur-grass, sand-bur. Cenchrus carolinianus. The grass family. BT. #23.

uⁿkce'pagmigma, n. The tumble bug. Also, uⁿkcépagmiyaⁿyaⁿ.

uⁿki'....pi, pron. in comp. We, us.
uⁿkiś', pron. We, ourselves. Cf. iś, miś, niś. - huⁿħ le maya kiⁿ oħlateya uⁿyaⁿpi kte lo. -- uⁿkiśnala, pron. dual. We two alone. Uⁿkiśnapila, pl.

uⁿk̇i'ta, pron. pos. in comp. with "pi" to terminate the word. Ours. -- uⁿk̇itawa, pron. dual. Ours, i.e. yours and mine. Uⁿkitawapi, pl.

uⁿk̇i'ya, v.a. (of uⁿ and kiya). To cause one to use or wear, as a coat; to help him on with something, as with a coat. Uⁿmíciciya yo, Help me putting it on. Pb.31.

uⁿki'ye, pron. We two, us. Uⁿkiyepi, pl. Cf. iye, miye, niye.

uⁿkṫo'mi, n. The spider; a fabulous creature like the fox in western folklore. Cf. iktomi. -- uⁿkṫómi tao'k̇aśke, n. A spider's web.

uⁿk'uⁿ'pi, v. pl. We are.

uⁿ'la, v. dim. To use.

uⁿma', adj. The one, the other. - tukte, Which of the two.

uⁿma'ciyaṫaⁿ, adv. (of uⁿma eciyataⁿ). From the other side, on the contrary.

uⁿma' ece'tk̇iya, adv. On the contrary.
uⁿma' eciyaṫaⁿhaⁿ, adv. From the other side, on the contrary. Cf. uⁿmaciyataⁿ.

uⁿma'gma, adj. One or the other, either of two. Le - icupo, Take any one of the two you wish.

uⁿma'la, adj. with śni. Neither.
uⁿma'ni, adj. None of two, neither. - waśte śni, Both are bad. Bl. - uⁿyuha kte śni. B.H.99.21. Heceś - o śni. D.111.

uⁿma' ṫo'kṫok, adv. By turns, one after another. - ecoⁿpi. B.H.92.12;252.14. - iśta waⁿkal yekiyapi. D.33. -- úⁿmaṫokṫok, adv. Two by two in turns, only two by turns. - ecoⁿpi.

uⁿ'nahaⁿ, adv. At last, soon, shortly. Cf. uⁿnihaⁿ.

uⁿ'naptaⁿ, adj. perhaps. Sideling, inclined toward one side. Same as heṗiya. -- úⁿnapṫaⁿyaⁿ, adv. Slanting.

uⁿ'nihaⁿ, adv. At last, soon, shortly. Same as uⁿnahaⁿ. - śakómayazaⁿ yelo. BT. Wana - ataya tebye sece c'uⁿ. D. 96,194,74.

uⁿ'ṗa, v.a. To place. Also, oⁿpa. Wauⁿpa.

uⁿ'ṗa, v.n. To smoke e.g. tobacco. Muⁿpa, nuⁿpa, uⁿkuⁿpapi. Caⁿnuⁿpa kiⁿ le nuⁿpapi kta.

uⁿpaⁿ', n. The female elk.
uⁿpaⁿ'ha, n. Elk skin.
uⁿpaⁿ'hiⁿsk̇e, n. Elk teeth.
uⁿpaⁿ' tawoṫe, n. The smaller red-root. Ceanothus ovatus. The buckthorn family. The leaves are used for drinking tea. The eastern variety, ceanothus americanus, was used by American troops during the Revolution. BT. #52.

uⁿ'ṗi, v. pl. (of uⁿ). They are.

uⁿpśi'ja, n. Mud. - s'e, as is said of a large herd of buffalo. - eyala s'e wagli yelo, i.e. all bespattered with mud. Bl. This word applies to thin mud, while ħliħlila ref. to light mud. Be. -- uⁿpśiśya, adv. Muddy.

uⁿsiⁿ', n. The small end of a porcupine quill; the large quills in the porcupine's tail.

uŋ'śtiŋmaṗihiŋ, n. Cf. oŋśtiŋmapihiŋ.

uŋśṫo', suff. Affixed to verbs, meaning that a thing has already been said or done. Heṗé - , hehé - .

uŋ'ś'ḱeyaṗiḱa, uŋ'śḱeyaṗiḱa, adv. But coming back to our subject, as is said when forgetting all about the subject or point of one's conversation. LP. Syn.- iŋśeyapika, iŋśkeyapika. Waŋ, - he woyak maśi, ewektoŋje. BT. Cf. lotkuŋkeśni, toŋwel. SI. This is an old word.

uŋ'ś'uŋmaḱeci, interj. Oh yes; just because. One man explains something to another who in turn tries to explain the same thing to a third person but asks questions continually because he did not understand in the first. Then the first man says to the second: Uŋś'uŋmakeci kiyuieska ye, i.e. speak bluntly for another. - eya ca heoŋ hecoŋ. - woglakahapi na awektoŋje, Just because they were talking I forgot all about it. MN. Also perhaps, iŋś'uŋmakeci, iśuŋmakeci. Lit., iś-uŋma-ka-ciŋ, i.e. as for one, the other one of two, in a manner of speaking, the. It then means something like this: Then he, the other one of a pair. In other words, this second person that comes up for consideration is instantly labelled as being exactly as stupid, silly, ridiculous, as the other just mentioned. -- úŋś'uŋmakec'uŋ, interj. Same as uŋś'uŋmakeci, but ref. to something mentioned before. MN.

uŋwe'ya, n. Provisions for a journey.

uŋ'wohaŋpi océti, n. A cooking range.

uŋ'yaŋ, v.a. To lose. Waúŋbla, yauŋla, uŋk'uŋyaŋpi. Wauŋmni kta. Taku waŋ úŋyaŋpi k'oŋ he ole. B.H.237.3. To drop out of sight. - kigle. - kiglapi. - imayayapi. Hena - uŋkinapapi kte śni. Hopo, waŋjini - napapi śni po; - inawicapin. Hena (i.e. iŋyaŋ gmigmela) - okicize el yapi kte śni. - iwicayayapi. B.H.166.15;239.14;80.14. MS.353,351. - kigla, To forsake. P.

uṗi', n. The lower border of a garment. Situpi, The tail of a bird.
uṗi'gleġa, n. A Balmoral skirt.

upi'jaṫa, n. The generic name for the swallow, by reason of their forked tail. The forked-tail swallow. Its nest is made in banks of streams. Same as the icapśiŋpśiŋcala. The upijata taŋka is black, others white, a large bird with a bill two inches long. Hena iś eya zuzeca yutapi.

uśi', v.a. (of u and śi). To command to come, send. Uwaśi.

uta', v.a. To try, as a gun by firing it; to fire off. Tokśa, aŋpa ca wicocaŋlwaŋka yelo, na haŋhepi ca otuyaciŋ utapelo, eya. To give one much more food than he can eat, he utapelo. Bl.

u'ṫa, n. The hazelnut; acorns. R. D.77.
u'ṫahu, n. An oak tree. Also, iṫúhu.
u'ṫahu caŋ, n. The burr oak, the scrub oak, the mossy cup oak. Quercus macrocarpa. The beech family. #114. Oak wood.
u'ṫahu caŋḣlo'ġaŋ, n. The flour-of-an-hour, the venice mallow, the modesty. So named from its shape of leaf. The hibiscus trionum. The mallow family. Bl. #307.

u'wa, v. imp. Come! This is used by women. Men say: Uwa yo. Takoja, uwa ye, uŋgni kte. But Jairus said: Uwi na ninape kiŋ aputaki ye. B.H.204.24. Misuŋ uwi ye, Iktomi said. D.117.

uya', 1) v.a. To cause to go, to send, to start. B.H.86.6. 2) v.n. To come; to become. Sniyaŋ uya, It is becoming cold. Also, to grow, spring up, as grain. Tokiyataŋhaŋ uya hwo? i.e. where does the wind come from? Bc. Tate waŋ waś'agya uye lo. Bl.

uye'ḱiya, v.a. To cause to grow or spring up. Uyewakiya.

uye'ya, v.a. To cause to come. Uyewaya.

* *

wa, prefix. When it is used with verbs it usually puts them into the absolute or intransitive sense, i.e. the verb is changed into an adjective neuter, or passive verb; thus, óⁿśila, To have mercy upon, becomes waóⁿśila, Merciful. In some cases it forms of them nouns denoting the agent or actor. Indeed, the absolute forms may all be so used, as in Wanikiye, The Savior. When it is prefixed to nouns, it makes their meaning more general. Moreover, it indicates in some action words that the action is done by a sawing motion, as with a knife or saw.

wa, pron. in comp. I.

wa, n. Snow.

waa'bles, cont. of waableza. - hiⁿgla. B.H.293.13. -- waáblesya, v. To make one observe. Aware, adv.

waa'bleza, v. To be observing, to be clear-sighted, have the use of one's senses. Waawableza.

waa'caⁿkśiⁿ, v. (of acaⁿkśiⁿ). To step over e.g. kettles and dishes standing on the floor. Bl. Waacaⁿwakśiⁿ.

waa'caⁿze, v. (of ocaⁿze). To be angry at others, ill-tempered. Bl. -- waácaⁿzeḱa, v.n. To be ill-tempered. -- waacaⁿzeya, adv. In a surly manner.

waa'gla, v. (of agla). To take home. Waawagla.

waa'glaheya, v. Same as waahiⁿḣpaya. Bl.

waa'gleca, v. To take home. Waawagleca. R. Bl. Cf. waagla.

waa'gli, v. (of agli). To bring home. Also, wágli.

waa'gliheya, v. (of agliheya). To come down and smite, as lighting. B.H.129.24.

waa'gna glepi, n. Any table. B.H.60.22.

waa'haⁿnajiⁿ, v. To come to stand. - kuwa, To come again and again trying to speak to one but finding him busy. Bl.

waa'hiⁿḣpaya, v. To be fallen on something. Bl.

waa'hoṭaⁿka, n. One who bawls out, one who vociferates. Waahowataⁿka.

waa'hotoⁿ, n. Something that makes a noise, as thunder etc.

waa'hoyeya, v. (of hoyeya). To reprove, scold. Note: the 1st pers. singl. is not used.

waa'ia, v. (of aia). To talk about, to slander; to try a case in court. Waaiwaye, waaiuⁿyaⁿpi. -- waáiapi, n. A talking against, slander; consultation; a trial in court.

waa'ies'a, n. A slanderer.

waa'jaja, v.a. To take off clean, as meat from bones. Waawajaja. Bl. GA.

wā'ka, n. A prisoner of war.

waa'ḱaġa, v. (of akaga). To add to, to make a lie on. Waawakaga. -- waáḱaġapi, n. A making on; a blasphemy perhaps.

waa'ḱaḣpa, v. (of akaḣpa). To cover. Waawakaḣpa. -- waáḱaḣṗe, n. A covering. Cf. woakaḣpe. -- waáḱaḣṗetoⁿpi, n. A cover, lid, as of a basket. B.H. 46.1.

waa'kaⁿl, (?). - yaⁿka. Bl.

wa'aḱata, v. To cover with snow.

waa'ḱi, v. (of aki). To have taken home, which is away from the speaker. Waawaki. B.H.36.12.

waa'ḱicaġa, v. To play jokes on; make sport of.

waa'ḱiciyataⁿiⁿ, n. (of kiciyataⁿiⁿ). Manifestation.

waa'ḱikṫoⁿja, v. (of akiktoⁿja). To forget. Waawektoⁿja. -- waáḱikṫoⁿjapi, n. Forgetfulness.

waa'ḱil, cont. of waakita.

waa'ḱinica, v. (of akinica). To dispute. Waawakinica. -- n. One who disputes. -- waáḱinicapi, n. A dispute over something.

waa'ḱinil, cont. of waakinica. - uŋpi, They are disputing. -- waáḱinilya, adv. In the way of disputing.

waa'ḱit̄a, v. (akita). To hunt, seek. Waawakita.

waa'ḱiyecetu, (?). Waákiyeuŋcetupi.

waa'kśija, v. of akśija.

waa'ḱu, v. To bring home. Bl.

waa'naǧopt̄aŋ, v. (anagoptaŋ). To listen to, obey. Waanawagoptaŋ.
waa'naǧopt̄aŋyaŋ, adv. Obediently. - wauŋ.

waa'naic'ipta, v. refl. To stop, forbid one's self. Waanamic'ipta.

waa'naḱiciǧopt̄aŋ, n. A listener, an audience.

waa'naḱikśiŋ, v. (anakikśiŋ). To expose one's self for others, to take the place of one in danger. Waanawekśiŋ.
waa'naḱikśiŋyaŋ, adv. Exposing self for others.

waa'napta, v. abs. (anapta). To stop, forbid people. Waanawapta.

waa'naśap̄a, v. (anaśapa). To defile or soil by trampling upon. Waanawaśapa.

waa'naśloka, n. Something that flies out or refuses to stay in, as a cork etc.

waa'nat̄aŋ, v. (anataŋ). To rush on, make an attack. Waanawataŋ.

waa'nica, v. (anica). To refuse to give up. Waawanica.

wa'aoḱiyapi, n. A mutual plan. Bl.

waa'pa, v. (apa). To strike. Waawapa.

waa'pe, v. (ape). To wait, be in waiting. Waawape. - yaŋkahaŋpi. D.194,219, 251.

waa'sḱab, cont. of waaskapa.

waa'sḱabya, v. (askabya). To cause to stick on, make adhere. Waaskabwaya.
waa'sḱabyapi, n. Sticking plaster.

waa'sḱap̄a, v. (askapa). To stick on.
waa'sḱap̄e, n. Something that sticks, a sticking plaster.

waa'sniyaŋ, v. (asniyaŋ). To heal, make well. Waasniwaya. -- n. A healer, a healing. B.H.184.13.

waa's'iŋ, v. (as'iŋ). To covet, desire what is another's; to stay where others are eating expecting to share. Waawas'iŋ. Note: this ref. is to food only, perhaps.

waa'śap̄a, v. (aśapa). To be defiled. Waamaśapa.
waa'śap̄e, n. Dirt, as on soiled hands, grease etc.; a blotter, perhaps.

waa'ślaya, v. (aślaya). To skin an animal. Waawaślaya.

waa'śluśluta, v. To be smooth and slippery from dirt, as a boy's sleeves sometimes become. Bl.

waa'ś'aka, v.n. To be loaded with or coated, as the tongue in sickness. Cf. waś'aka.

waa'ś'akece, n. A noisy person. Bl. Syn.- waóḣmuŋyece.

waa'ś'api, n. Applause by acclamation. Bl.

waa't̄aya, v. (ataya). To be lucky, fortunate. Waatawaya. Bl.
waa't̄ayes'a, n. A fortunate one, as a good hunter.

waa't̄oŋwaŋ, v. (atoŋwaŋ). To be observing. Waawatoŋwaŋ.

waa't̄oŋwe, n. An observer.

waa'uŋyeya, v. To scare away, as game by one's coming. Bl.

waa'waciŋ, v. (awaciŋ). To think about, consider, be thoughtful. Waawacaŋmi. When persons did not intend to stay, having their thoughts somewhere else, they would say: Waawacaŋmi śni yelo. BT. -- n. An interest. -- adj. Devout, sincere. P.

waa'wacinyan, v.a. To cause to think or consider. Waawacinwaya. -- n. One who makes others think.

waa'wanglag, cont. of waawanglaka.

waa'wanglaka, cont.(of awanglaka). To watch over one's own. Waawanwaglaka. -- waáwanglake, n. One who watches over, a shepherd etc.

waa'wanyangkiyapi, n. One who is employed to observe; a steward.

waa'wanyank, cont. of waawanyanka. - unpi. B.H.270.7.

waa'wanyanka, v. (of awanyanka). To oversee, watch over etc. Waawanblaka. -- waáwanyanke, n. A watchman. B.H. 293.10.

waa'ya, v. (of aya). To take or bear to. Waabla.

waa'yaśkaheyela, v. (of ayaśkaheyela). To speak of as near. Waablaśkaheyela. Bl. Also, waáyaśkatuyela.

waa'yaśtan, v. (of ayaśtan). To complete with the mouth, as eating or speaking.

waa'yata, v. (of ayata). To guess, predict, foretell. Waablata.

waa'yatanin, 1) v. (of ayatanin). To proclaim, make manifest, bear witness, testify. Waablatanin. 2) n. A witness. B.H.216.4;257.19. -- waáyataninyan, adv. Testifying.

waa'yate, n. A prophet. Cf. ayata.

waa'yupta, v. (of ayupta). To answer. Waablupta.

waa'yuptanyan, v. (of ayuptanyan). To turn back on one, redound on one's self or one's relatives.

waa'yupte, n. One who answers.

waa'yus'o, v. (of ayus'o). To wade after.

waa'yuta, v. To look at. Waabluta, waaunyutapi.

waa'zilton, v. (of azilton). To burn incense to or for. Waazilwaton. B.H. 159.9.

wabla', v.a. To cut in slices, as bread. Wawabla. -- wablábla, v. red.

wabla'blaza, v. red. of wablaza.

wablas', cont. of wablaza. - iyeya, To rip open. - iyewaya. -- wablásblaza, v. red. of wablaza.

wabla'ska, v.a. (of blaska). To make dull or flat on the edge, as a knife by shaving. Wawablaska.

wabla'ya, v.a. (of blaya). To make flat with a knife, to have off lumps etc. Wawablaya.

wabla'za, v.a. (of blaza). To rip open lengthwise, as in butchering an animal, cutting open a watermelon, a boil etc.

wable'bleca, v. red. of wableca.

wable'ca, v.a. To break, as brittle ware, with a knife. Wawableca.

wablel', cont. of wableca. - iyeya.

wable'nica, n. An orphan, one without relatives. Wamablenica.

wa'bles, cont. of wableza. - kic'un, To try and understand. Bl. Yunkan - hinglapi, Their eyes were then opened. B.H.273.11. -- wablésya, v. To see, be seeing, i.e. with the eyes. Wableswaya. Iśtagunge kin wablesyapi. LWOW.177. Tanyan - śke, i.e. he was seeing well. D.35. Wh. -- wablésyehci, adj. Sharp-sighted, clear-sighted. - blihel hingle. B.H.39.5;69.7. Also, wablesyehca.

wa'bleza, 1) v.n. To see clearly, to understand. Wawableza. 2) n. An inspector.

wa'bloska, n. The lark bunting. Calamospiza melanocorys. The white-winged black bird. When taking to flight it sings: Ska, ska, ska; to, to, to; śa, śa, śa; zi, zi, zi; hol, hol, hol. And while alighting: Wil, wil, wil. Bl. R.

wa'blośa, n. The red-winged black bird. Its songs are: Tōke, mat'ā nī. Nakun miyē. Miś eyā. Cap'cehlī. Cf. wapagica. Bl. RF.

wablu'śka, n. A bug, an insect.
wablu'śka hiŋśma iyececa, n. The blue lettuce, the large-flowered blue lettuce. It is cut-leaved and reminds one of a beetle or other hairy insect. Lactuca pulchella. The composite family. Bl. #254.
wablu'śka huha ota peji, n. Crab grass. It reminds one of the insect called the "walking stick". Schedonuardus paniculatus. The grass family. Also, peji wabluśka iyececa. Bl. #282.
wablu'śka tiyoślo, n. A cricket. Also, wabluśka tiyoślola.

waca'jeḣiyaṫa, v.a. To mention the names of deceased relatives to one and beg for their sakes. Wacajewakimblata. Wakaŋtaŋka ni uŋ kiŋ oŋ wacajeciciyate, By the living God tell us your family line. Mt.26.63. -- wacájeyaṫa, v. (of cajeyata). To ask for or beg in the name of the dead; to make a parliamentary motion. Wacajeblata. -- wacájeyaṫapi, n. A petition. -- wacájeyal, cont. of wacajeyata.

wacaŋ'ġa, n. A species of sweet-smelling grass used in religious ceremonies.

wacaŋ'ḣiŋyaŋ, v. abs. (caŋḣiŋyaŋ). To be attached, devoted to others. Atayeś wacaŋḣiŋye śni uŋ, He has no use for his relatives at all, i.e. always avoiding them. LB.

wacaŋ'kśu, v. To dry things on a stick. Wacaŋwakśu.

wacaŋl'ḣiya, v. Same as wacaŋtkiya. Pb.36.

wacaŋ'mi, v. defect. I thought.

wacaŋ'śilya, v. To make sad.

wacaŋ'ṫeiyo'ḣiśica, adj. Sad. B.H.85.18
wacaŋ'ṫeśica, adj. (of caŋteśica). Unhappy. Wacaŋtemaśica.
wacaŋ'ṫeśilya, v.a. To make sad. Wacaŋteśilwaya.
wacaŋ'tiyoḣiśica, adj. Displeased, vexed, provoked, as when many bother one. WE. Cf. wacáŋteiyóḣiśica.
wacaŋ'tkiya, v. (of caŋtekiya). To be gracious, kind, benevolent, generous in giving love. Wacaŋlwakiya, wacaŋluŋkiyapi. -- wacáŋtḣiyapi, n. Benevolence.
wacaŋ'ṫognaḣa, 1) v. (of caŋtognaka). To be generous, affectionate. Also, wacaŋteognaka. Wacaŋtowagnaka. 2) adj. Generous, affectionate. -- wacáŋṫognaḣapi, n. Generosity, affection.
wacaŋ'ṫokṗani, v. (of caŋtokpani). To desire much, long for; to be impatient. Wacaŋtowakpani.
wacaŋ'zeya, v. (of caŋzeya). To make angry. Wacaŋzewaya. Pb.26. -- wacáŋzezeka, n. One easily made angry, susceptible, easily irritated.

waca'pe, v. To stab. Wacawape.

waca'ítoŋ, 1) v. (of caśtoŋ). To name, give a name. Wawacaśtoŋ. 2) n. A namer, one who names.

wace'ic'iciya, v. refl. To pray within one's self; to pray in one's behalf perhaps. B.H.232.5.
wace'ḣiciciya, v. To pray for one.
wace'ḣiya, v. (of cekiya). To pray. Wacewakiya.

wace'oŋpa, Cf. waceuŋṗa.

wace't'uŋgla, v. (of cet'uŋgla). To doubt, disbelieve. Wacet'uŋwagla. -- n. One who always doubts. -- wacét'uŋglapi, n. Unbelief, doubting. -- wacét'uŋglaya, adv. Doubtingly.

wace'uŋṗa, 1) v.a. (of ceuŋpa). To roast e.g. meat. Wacewauŋpa. 2) n. One who roasts anything.

Wace'uŋṗa, n. prop. The Yankton and Sicaŋġu clans of the Sioux. Wamáceuŋpa.

wace'ya, v.a. (of ceya). To make cry by cutting. Wawaceya.

waci', v.n. To dance. Wawaci.

waci'k'ala, v.a. (of cik'ala). To shave small. Wawacik'ala.

waci'k'ayela, n. A little. - aya yo. Bl.

waciŋ', v. 1st pers. sing. of ciŋ.

waciŋ', v.n. To think, purpose, try to; to be anxious to, to aim at. Wacaŋmi, wacaŋni, wauŋciŋpi. Ni - yo, Wish to live! Mazawakaŋ kiŋ icu - po. Icúwaciŋ, To try to get it. Ohiye -

To try to win. Yus-iŋyaŋkmawaciŋ yo, Try to get a hold of me. D.35,34,28. Note: this word requires another verb in the infinitive mood to precede it.
waciŋ'bleza, v.n. To be clear-headed; to be smart, quick to comprehend.
waciŋ'cik'ayela, adj. Fickle-minded. Waciŋmacik'ayela. Also, waciŋcisciyela. Waciŋmacisciyela.
waciŋ'ektayuza, v.n. To be kind, forebearing, long-suffering. Waciŋektabluza.
waciŋ'gnugnuni, adj. red. (of waciŋgnuni). Wandering in mind, bewildered, oblivious. Waciŋmagnugnuni.
waciŋ'gnuni, v.n. To be wandering or bewildered. Hehaŋl waciŋgnunipi kte lo. -- adj. Bewildered. -- waciŋgnuniya, v.a. To bewilder, distract, puzzle. Waciŋgnuniwaya. P. -- waciŋgnuniyaŋ, adv. Confusedly. Bl.
waciŋ'hahela, adj. Easily excited or alarmed. Also, waciŋhahála. Waciŋmahahela, waciŋmaháhala. Cf. tawaciŋhahála. BD.

wa'ciŋhiŋ, n. The head-dress of a Dakota man; anything standing up on the head, e.g. feathers. etc. Down or soft feathers. P. Bl.
wa'ciŋhiŋ sapsapa, n. Black plumes, ostrich feathers.
wa'ciŋhiŋya, v.a. To use for a plume. Waciŋhiŋwaya.

waciŋ'hiŋyaŋza, adj. Cruel, morose. Waciŋmahiŋyaŋza.

waciŋ'huŋkeśni, adj. Impatient, irascible. Waciŋmahuŋkeśni. -- waciŋhuŋkeśniya, v.a. To irritate, provoke. B.H. 45.12.

waciŋ'ic'iyapi, n. Self-reliance. P. Bl.

waciŋ' iha'la, adj. Easily excited to anger. Cekpa s'e waciŋihala. yaŋke. Bl.
waciŋ'iwoś'ag, cont. of waciŋiwoś'aka.
waciŋ'iwoś'agya, v. To discourage.
waciŋ'iwoś'ak , cont. of waciŋ iwoś'aka. - hiŋgla. B.H.62.24;209.5.
waciŋ'iwoś'aka, v.n. To be discouraged, to be out of heart. Waciŋiwowaś'aka. Cf. iwoś'aka.
waciŋ'iyok̇iṗi, v.n. To be contented, satisfied with. Waciŋiyomakipi. -- waciŋiyok̇iṗiya, adv. Contentedly.
waciŋ'iyok̇iśica, v.n. To be displeased with; to be sad on account of, to regret. Waciŋiyomakiśica.
waciŋ'iyok̇iśilya, adv. Displeased with.
waciŋ'jaṫa, adj. Forked mind, i.e. undecided, hesitating. Waciŋmajata.
waciŋ'k̇a, v. Same as waciŋ.
waciŋ'kiciyapi, n. Confidence. Bl.
waciŋ'k̇iciyuzapi, v. recip. Having regard for each other. Cf. waciŋkiyuza.
waciŋ'kiksuya, v. To remember all things well. Waciŋweksuya. Yuŋkaŋ heceglala waciŋweksuye.
waciŋ'k̇iya, v. pos. (of waciŋyaŋ). To trust in, as in anything laid up for one's own use; to trust to or have confidence in e.g. a friend. Waciŋwakiya.
waciŋ'k̇iyuza, v.a. To think of, hold in the mind, either for good or for evil. Waciŋwakiyuza.
waciŋ'ko, adj. (waciŋ and ko). Ill-natured, pouting. Waciŋwako, waciŋuŋkopi. -- waciŋkok̇ela, adj. dim. of waciŋko. -- waciŋkoṗi, n. Passionateness. -- waciŋkoya, adv. Passionately; crossly.
waciŋ'ksab, cont. of waciŋksapa. Taŋyaŋ - kic'uŋ wo. Bl.
waciŋ'ksabic'iya, v. refl. of waciŋksabya. Pb.33.
waciŋ'ksabya, adv. Wisely, discreetly. D.215, note 1.
waciŋ'ksaṗa, adj. Intelligent, wise, conscious, with presence of mind. Waciŋmaksapa, waciŋuŋksapapi. Na miś icuŋhaŋ waciŋmaksapa na wacipi kiŋ asnikiya yaŋkapi. -- v.n. perhaps. To be aware. - yo.
waciŋ'nuŋṗa, adj. Hesitating, undecided as to doing or not doing. Waciŋmanuŋpa. -- waciŋnuŋṗaśniyaŋ, adv. Honestly, truthfully. - iyuha taŋyaŋ ociciya ktelo. Bl.
waciŋ'oaye, n. Inclination. - manica, i.e. I am discouraged.
waciŋ'oyuze, n. (of waciŋyuza). Thought or one's thinking.
waciŋ'śica, adj. Bad dispositioned.
waciŋ'taŋgya, adv. Patiently. B.H.201. 1;227.2.
waciŋ'taŋka, adj. Patient, magnanimous, long-suffering, enduring long. Waciŋmataŋka. Na waciŋnitaŋka kiŋ heoŋ wicaśayatapi ka oyapa kte lo. -- waciŋtaŋk kic'uŋ, v. To have patience. BD.
waciŋ'ṫeḣi, v. To take interest in nothing. -- adj. perhaps. Indifferent. Bl.
waciŋ'toŋ, v. To have understanding, have a mind of one's own, be wise. Waciŋwatoŋ.
waciŋ'toŋgnagya, v.a. To comfort, us-

ually by giving to the afflicted; to cause to have a different view. Waciŋtoŋgnagwaya.

waciŋ´toŋgnake, n. (waciŋ-toŋ-gnaka). A comforter. Also, wakicaŋpte.

waciŋ´toŋśni, v.n. To be foolish. Waciŋwatoŋśni.

waciŋ´t'a, v.n. To be forgetful. Waciŋmat'a. Also, waciŋt'at'a. Waciŋmat'at'a. -- waciŋt'at'ake, n. One who is weak-minded and forgetful.

waciŋ´waśakala, (?) Uŋgna waciŋniwaśakala ki, i.e. beware of. MS.350.

waciŋ´wiḱic'uŋ´śni, v.n. To be indifferent about.

waciŋ´yaŋ, 1) v.a. To trust in, depend upon, to need one; to believe in. Waciŋwaya. Waciŋciya. Waciŋmaya. 2) adj. Confiding. -- waciŋ´yaŋpi, n. Trust, confidence, faith; trustiness.

waciŋ´yeh̆ci, adv. Very confidently. Pb.35.

waciŋ´yeḱiya, v.a. To cause to trust in. Waciŋyewakiya. -- waciŋyeṗica, n. Something that can be trusted in, depended upon, faithful, reliable. P. B.H.220.9.

waciŋ´yeya, v. To purpose, set the mind to; to cause to trust in. Waciŋyewaya śni, I am discouraged, lose hope in. D.221.

waciŋ´yeyeśni, v. To object to, to lose hope in. Waciŋyeyapiśni. Bl. B.H.66.3.

waciŋ´yusya, v.a. To cause one to have a certain opinion. Tokel Jesus el waciŋluze kiŋ iyecel ohiŋniyaŋ Jesus el waciŋyusmayiye. Pb.10.

waciŋ´yuza, v. To have an opinion; to be inclined. Waciŋbluza. Hel waciŋbluza wauŋ, That is my mind. Nah̆makel kiigluśpiŋ kta waciŋyuze. B.H.164.7. -- waciŋ´yuze, n. The intention. P. Tokata hecel ecoŋ kte iyukcaŋ. Bl.

waci´ṗi, n. (of waci). Dancing, a dance.

waci´scila, v.a. (ciscila). To make small by cutting. Wawaciscila.

wacō´ḱa, n. Level land, a bottom with hills on both sides, low land near a river or lake without timber. - el iyotaŋ waśmelo. R. Bl.

waco´ḱoŋ, v. (of cokoŋ). To desire to take life. Wacowakoŋ. -- wacóḱoŋpi, n. A desire of taking life.

wać̌o´k'iŋ, v. abs. (of cok'iŋ). To roast something on coals. Wacouŋk'iŋpi ktelo, i.e. wasting potatoes etc. in fire. D. spells the word: cok'iŋ. D.22. Wicówak'iŋ.

waco´nica, n. (of conica). Venison, wild meat of any kind, fresh or dry. -- waconicaka, n. Wild meat dried.

wacōs´ya, v. To cause to warm, to put out to dry, as cooked victuals; to dry and smoke, as meat. Wacoswaya. -- wacósyaṗi, n. Smoked pork; a paunch half-boiled and hung out to dry.

wa´cuṫic'iŋ, n. Anything carried diagonally over the chest from the left shoulder to the right hip. - wakaŋ, A certain wotawe. BT. Cf. cuṫic'iŋ.

wae´cakca, (?). - nuŋkiŋ na napapa umayaye, so a man would say to a child or wife when they did foolish things. Bl.

wae´caḱioŋ, v. To treat. Waecawakioŋ. B.H.63.11.

wae´coŋ, 1) v. (of ecoŋ). To do things or make preparations, as for a feast. Waecamoŋ. B.H.64.3;88.25;90.14;57.20; 305.9. 2) n. An actor. Teh̆iya waecamoŋ, I have done a tragic deed. D. 249.

wae´coŋcoŋka, n. (of waecoŋ). A jack of all trades, one who does all sorts of things. Waecamuŋmuŋka. WE.

wae´coŋh̆ca ic'ila, v. To make much of one's own little actions, to brag, exaggerate. Hecoŋ na - . Bl.

wae´coŋḱiya, v. To tax one's strength. P. Bl.

wae´kiciŋciŋke, n. One who wants a thing very badly and asks for it often. ED.

wae´ḱignaka, v. To lay something away. Wanagi - , To put something, i.e. some of one's food, away for souls before eating. It is a sort of grace before meals. BT.

wae´ḱiya, v. To speak to one. Waewakiya. Bl. B.H.47.7;157.9;184.16;186.3.

wae´ktaŋjaśni, adj. Unpliable, lacking docility, not educable.

wae´kṫaśniyaŋ, adv. Improperly, falsely. - iyeya. Bl. Syn.- waipaweh.

wae'lhiyayake, n. (?). - takuni oⁿspe śni tka, i.e. wants to help work but knows nothing about it. Bl.

wae'lhoyeya, v. (?). Bluskaka, yuⁿkaⁿ waelhoyeyiⁿ kte hciⁿ, i.e. gave him a new suit, but was ungrateful. Bl.

wae'pazo, n. The index or fore-finger. Tuweni - kiⁿ oⁿ epazo śni, napahuⁿka kiⁿ he oⁿ ecoⁿpi. - kiⁿ oⁿ wojapi kiⁿ cokayelahci palob egle na yazoka ke. D.121. Also, a pointed piece of meat on the shoulder blades of buffalo. Bl. HH.

wae'ya, v. (of eya). To speak. Waepa. Taku oyasiⁿ onuniśniyaⁿ waehelo, as they would say to a habitual joker. Tokel waeya kiⁿhaⁿ oblakiⁿ kta waciⁿ. Niciye Aaron waeyiⁿ kta okihi. B.H. 48.24;55.6;68.27;139.14;166.12;242.4; 199.7.

wae'yaku, v. (of eyaku). To take, carry away by force. Waeblaku, waeuⁿyakupi.

wae'yece, (?). Wicaśa waⁿ - śni uⁿ k'uⁿ heye lo, i.e. he is telling the truth. BE. Cf. waiece.

wa'ġa caⁿ, n. The western cotton-wood. Populus sargentii. The willow family. Also, caⁿyah'u. #193.

waġal'ġata, v. red. (of wagata). To make marks, each cut or sawed in anything. Wawagalgata.

waġa'pa, v.a. (of gapa). To take off e.g. the skin of an animal with a knife; to skin, to open with a knife. Wawagapa.

waġa'ta, v.a. (of gata). To make marks, to mark or cut with a knife; to carve or hack. Wawagata.

wagla', v.a. To take off, as tallow from entrails, with a knife; to shave off with a knife; fig., to sicken one. Wawagla. F. D.202. -- waglágla, v. red. of wagla.

wagla'glaka, v. To criticize food, to find nothing good enough. Wawaglaglaka. -- wagláglake, n. One who is dissatisfied with the food offerred, does not find it tasty enough. Hence, one who is finicky, very particular, exacting, easily excited. B.

wagla'mni, v. To go after what one has left. Cf. glamni.

wagla'ślośl o, v. To whistle, i.e. one note: ti-ti-ti.... To play a tune is yajó. Wawaglośloślo. Yuⁿkaⁿ el u na śiyotaⁿka waglaśloślo.

wa'glaś'api, n. The shout that is made by the children when meat etc. is brought into camp. They meet the men returning; and when the women hear them shout, they say: Waⁿna - ; and they get busy starting a fire. BT. Uká hu. Cf. hu.

waglé, 1) n. A storehouse, storage, provisions. SLB. Hituⁿktaⁿka - , The provisions of rats carried together. Bl. 2) v. (of gle). B.H.107.21.

wagle'kśuⁿ, n. The wild turkey. - s'e nape pepé kaca, as is said when pieces of skin hung on one's hands. Bl.

wa'gle wo'śnapi, n. An altar.

wagle'za, n. The garden snake, or garter snake. D.273.

wagli', v. 1st pers. sing. of gli.

wa'gli, v. (of agli). To bring home game, meat etc. Wáwagli, wáuⁿglipi. Pte naiⁿś wamakaśkaⁿ hecekce wawicaglipi. MS.557. -- n. perhaps. Hunted game. Wágli otokahe kuwelo. BT.

wagli'gla, v. (of gligla). To travel, to go about from place to place. - wauⁿ.

wagli'gleca, n. One who is always travelling. R. Bl.

wa'gligli, v. red. (of wágli). To arrive at home with meat. Taku wágliglipi. Bl. D.273. Cf. wagliku. -- wágliku, v. To bring home meat. Wágliwaku. Wicaśa waⁿ - ca wahaⁿpi uⁿyatkaⁿpi kte, as they say when a man brings meat home. Bl.

wagli'nawapa, v. 1st pers. sing. of glinapa with a double inseparable pron. Hecel waglinawapiⁿ kta, yuⁿkaⁿ eyapaha uⁿ he leya. Cf. wahinapa.

wa'gliukiya, (?).

wa'gliyoya, v. To go after one's own. Also, perhaps, wagliyoya. -- wágliyoyapi, n. A pastime for children. Bl. It was played in olden times in imitation of camp life with a boy as chief. They needed provisions, so the chief let a certain number of the children bite into a stick and those had to go home and get from their parents whatever these wanted to give. Thus, is created an imitation of wágliku. Bl.

waglu'ha, v. (of gluha). To have one's own, to keep. Wawágluha. -- waglúhahaka, adj. Saving, frugal, parsimonious. Wawágluhahake lo miye tka pilamic'iye lo. BT.

waglu'hahakeći, n. A parsimonious person.

waglu'hahakteca, adj. Going to become a parsimonious person, giving promise of so becoming.

waglu'hika, v. To hush, keep silent by threats etc. Also perhaps adj. Maka iyokiseya tataⁿka ota nawah'oⁿ ca wakaⁿyeja - nuⁿwe. Bl. BT. Cf. for other meanings wayuhi, wayuhika.

wa'gluhe, v.n. To live with one's wife relatives, to be a hanger-on. Wawagluhe.

Wa'gluhe, n. prop. The Loafer band of the Oglalas.

waglu'htata, v. To offer one's own. Wawagluhtata.

waglu'la, n. Maggots, worms; tapeworm.

waglu'śna, v. To drop one's own.

wa'glutapi, n. A table. - akáhpe, A table cloth.

waglu'za, v. To take back what one has given. Wawágluza.

wagme'za, n. Corn.

wagme'zahu, n. Corn stalks.

wagme'za icákse, n. A corn sickle.

wagme'za nabláġa, n. Popcorn. Also, wagmeza nablahyapi.

wagmu', n. Gourds, pumpkins, squash etc.

wagmu' blu, n. A squash.

wagmu'ha, n. A rattle, as used in the wapiyapi.

wagmu'hu, n. Pumpkin vines.

wagmuⁿg', cont. of wagmuⁿka. - bla, I am going trapping.

wagmuⁿ'ka, v. (of gmuⁿka). To trap, hunt with traps. Wawagmuⁿka. Also the 1st pers. sing. of gmuⁿka. -- wagmúⁿkapi, n. Trapping.

wagmu'śkopa, n. The Japanese pumpkin.

wagmu'śpaⁿśni yutapi, n. Water melon.

wagna', v.a. (of wa-gna). To cut off e.g. corn from the dried ear which is called waśtuⁿkala; to make fall off by cutting, as fruit from a tree. Wawágna.

wa'gnag, cont. of wagnaka. - cola.

wa'gnagtoⁿ, n. Something put with another thing. - k'u, To give, e.g. a blanket, with a gun; or to furnish e.g. a pad on a horse's sore back.

wagna'ka, v. 1st pers. sing. of gnaka.

wa'gnaka, v. (of agnaka). To place on, put on e.g. poultices on sores etc. Wawagnaka. Cf. wakicignaka.

wagna'śkiⁿyaⁿ, v.a. (of gnaśkiⁿyaⁿ). To make crazy or frantic by cutting or stabbing. Wawagnaśkiⁿyaⁿ. -- n. A lunatic. P.

wa'gna wo'ṗetoⁿpi, n. A counter in a store.

wa'gna wośnapi, n. An altar of sacrifice.

wa'gnawotapi, n. A table to eat on.

wagna'yaⁿ, 1) v.a. (of gnayaⁿ). To miss in attempting to strike with a knife. Wawagnayaⁿ. 2) v. To deceive. 3) v. 1st pers. sing. of gnayaⁿ.

wagna'ye, n. An imposter. P.

wa'gnayutapi, n. A table.

wagnu'ka, n. The red-headed woodpecker. FR. Also, wagnuka ṗe śa. D.38.

waġo', v.a. To make marks or gashes in the flesh; to mark, carve or engrave with a knife in wood. Wawago. -- waġókiya, v.a. To cause to carve. Wagowakiya. -- waġópi, n. One of the four marks seen on the hoop used in the paiⁿyaⁿkapi game.

wağu'ğeca, n. Hardened, crusted snow. Waśpaⁿla ca wakaśloyakel maunipelo; - kiⁿhaⁿ teȟiya uⁿkupi tka yelo. Bl. Cf. waiśnaheca, Soft snow.

wağu'ğuya, v.a. To cause to burn, scorch. Waguguwaya. -- wağúya, v.a. To scorch. Waguwaya.

wagwe'za, v.a. (of gweza). To carve, make rough with a knife. Wawagweza.

waha', n. Hides, in opposition to anything else. Bl.

waha'caⁿka, n. A shield.
waha'caⁿka kic'iⁿ', n. A snail, one who carries his shield on his back. Also perhaps a kind of lizzard. Bl.
waha'caⁿka waⁿ ska(saⁿ) k'iⁿ, v. ph. To be generous, liberal, benevolent. This is a phrase used in winter; in summer is used: wahacaⁿka waⁿ śayapi k'iⁿ. R. Bl. BT.

wahaⁿg'ya, v. To destroy. Wahaⁿgwaya. D.216. -- wahángyeca, n. One who destroys everything.

wahaⁿ'pi, n. Broth, soup of any kind. Wicaśa waⁿ wagliku ca - uⁿyatkaⁿpi kte. Bl.

waha'ṗaȟpa, v. To flesh a robe or skin while the hide is still fresh. Wahawapaȟpa. Cf. wahatka, wahiⁿtka. R. Bl.
waha'śla, n. A tanned hide.
waha'tka, v.a. To scrape a dry hide, taking off any meat there may yet be on it. Wahawatka. Bl. Cf. wahiⁿtka. Hóhe uⁿ wiⁿyaⁿ - ca tiyopa el kat'iwaye lo. BT.

wahe'cekcetu, adv. perhaps, red. (of wahecetu). About. Wiyute nuⁿpa naiⁿś yamni - ca he. B.H.178.12.
wahe'cel, adv. About that time. SLB. Omaka yamni - . B.H.225.1.
wahe'cetu, wahe'cetuya, adv. About. Opawiⁿge - . B.H.82.6. Syn.- sece.

wahe'haⁿ, adv. Betimes, in good time.
wahe'haⁿl, adv. About at that time, i.e. past and future. Na wana lila lowaⁿpi - tice ekta śiyotaⁿka k'oⁿ he yajopi. MS.340. Haⁿcokaⁿyaⁿ - . B.H. 247.7;17.12;77.7;137.8. Syn.- iyéhaⁿl.

wahe'ķic'uⁿ, v. pos. To pack up or tie one's own. Wahewec'uⁿ. Cf. waheyuⁿ.
wahe'yuⁿ, v. (of heyuⁿ). To pack up in bundles. Wahémuⁿ, wahenuⁿ. -- wahéyuⁿpi, n. Packing up. Śuⁿkawakaⁿ waⁿ hupa waheuⁿpi waⁿ k'iⁿķiyapi na ekta hipi.

wahi'bu, v. 1st pers. sing. of hibu.

wahi'nawapa, v. 1st pers. sing. of hinapa with a double pron. Cf. waglinawapa.

wahiⁿ', n. Hairs.

wahiⁿ', n. (of waⁿ and hi). A flint, flints.
wahiⁿ'cola, n. An arrow when the head (wismahiⁿ) came off. Bl.

wa'hiⁿhe, v. (of hiⁿhaⁿ). It snows. Wáhiⁿhiⁿ kta, It will snow.

wahiⁿ'heya, n. The pocket gopher.
wahiⁿ'heya ipi'ye, n. Roots. Same as waȟcaȟca hu bloka. Bl. #250.
wahiⁿ'heya opi, n. Swollen and opened glands, a frequent occurrence among Indians; hence the name because they appear as gopher hills.
wahiⁿ'heyaṗablu, n. Gopher-hills.

wahiⁿ'kṗe, n. An arrow, arrows.
wahiⁿ'kṗe hina'jiⁿ, n. The jaws of an arrow which hold the point (wismahiⁿ). Bl.
wahiⁿ'kṗe kiⁿiⁿyeyapi, n. A bow-shot.

wahiⁿ'ṗaȟpa, n. A fleshing-knife or chisel used in preparing green hides for drying.
wahiⁿ'paspa, n. Tent pins. Same as wihiⁿpaspa.

wahiⁿ'sķe, n. The long-grained or southern corn, so called because the grains resemble the canine teeth of animals.

wahiⁿ'śa, n. Gun caps.

wahiⁿ'śma, n. Furs. B.H.60.13.

wahiⁿ'tka, n. An instrument used in scraping hides, i.e. a bit of steel fixed to an elk-horn handle and used as a hoe on the flesh side, making the hide the same thickness.

wahiŋ'yajice, n. Down, fur, such as is used by the Dakotas in their sacred ceremonies.
wahiŋ'yuŋtoŋ, v. (of iŋyuŋtoŋ). To rub tanasula (brains), marrow and gall on hides to prepare them for tanning. Bl.

wahi'śnaheca, n. Soft new snow. Waíśnaheca is used in speaking of snow that will fall tomorrow. Pa.

wahi'yo, v. abs. of hiyo.
wahi'yohi, v. To come for or after but without mentioning what. Also, wahiyowahi. Wawahiyohi, wauŋhiyohipi. BD.
wahi'yoi, v. To have gone after. Wahiyowai.
wahi'yu, v. 1st pers. sing. of hiyu.

waho'coȟa, n. An inner courtyard. P. Cf. hocoka.

waho'gnugnu, (?).

waho'ȟṗi, n. (of hohpi). Nests. But note: ziŋtkala hoȟpí.

waho'kiya, v.a. To send word to. Wahowakiya. Mato waglamna wahokiye lo, The bear sends for extra help. D.115.

waho'ȟoŋkiya, v.a. To instruct, counsel, advise one. Wahokoŋwakiya. -- wahóȟoŋkiyapi, n. Instructions, counsel, advice; counselled, adj.

waho'śi, v. (of hośi). To carry word, to bring or carry news; to be an apostle. - waŋ...David okiyak śipi. B.H. 96.1;189.2. Note: this word is always used with i, hi, ya, etc.
waho'śi gli, v. To bring home news. SLB. B.H.62.18.
waho'śi hi, v. To arrive somewhere with a message. B.H.43.7. Also, wahośi kahi. B.H.262.18.
waho'śiyaṗi, n. One sent with a message, an apostle. Also, wahóśiye wakáŋ. Pb.42.
waho'ya, v.a. To send for one; to send word to one, to promise something to one; to order something by mail. R. Wahowaya. Leciya wacipi kta śki na wahomayaŋpi ca le inaȟni omawani, i.e. sent for me. D.20. -- wahóyapi, n. Sending word to.

wahu'aṗa, n. Corn, an ear of corn.

wahu'aťaya, v.n. To find one's self all at once unable to proceed, to be unable to escape for fright or some other cause. Wahuatawaya. -- wahúaťayeya, v.a. To frighten or in some way make unable to escape. Wahuatayewaya.

wahu'ȟniye s'e śkaŋ, v. To work hurriedly. Cf. huȟniyeya, inaȟni. Bl.

wahu'ḱeza, n. A spear.

wahu'nuŋpa, n. A biped, an appelation for man. R. Bl.

wahuŋ', v.a. To cut across, i.e. in one's flesh or in meat of any kind; to slash or gash or cut the flesh, as the Dakotas are accustomed to do in behalf of the dead. Wawáhuŋ. Waic'ihuŋ, To cut or gash one's self. D.33.

wahuŋ'cala, (?). - s'e waínakiȟniȟnike; wána kákena iyayelo, as is said when one of a crowd is in a great hurry and goes on while the others are rather slow in getting ready. ED.

wahuŋ'huŋ, v.a. red. (of wahuŋ). To make loose by cutting, to cut off e.g. ropes in different places. Inaȟni wiciŋ kiŋ wohohopi. Also, wahoŋhoŋ.

wahu'ťaktáyakel, adv. At the end, lastly. - mni kte, i.e. when all others have gone. Bl.

wahū'ťe, n. A stump of anything, stumps. Caŋhute, The stump of a tree. The word implies stumps in opposition to anything else.

wahu'ťoṗa, n. Quadrupeds, the generic term for quadrupeds;in the sacred dialect, the dog or wolf. R.

wahu'waṗa, n. An ear of corn, corn unshelled. - agóŋ, Cornsilk. Bl.

wahu'waťaya, v. To move one's arms as in running, so as to cause that impression for the enemy, instead of fleeing. MW. Bl. Cf. wahuataya. -- wahúwaťayeya, v.a. Cf. wahuatayeya.

waȟa', v. (of ȟa). To bury many things or in many places. Also, 1st pers. sing. of ȟa. Wawáȟa.

waȟab'ya, v. (of ȟabya). To frighten

or scare away, as game by one's coming. Wahabwaya. Bl.

waha'pi, n. A burying; something buried.

wahca', n. The generic name for flowers. - nableca, To unfold or blossom.
wahca'hca, n. Flowers, blossoms. Also, the showy milkweed. Asclepias speciosa. The milkweed family. The blossoms boiled and mixed with flour make a very good dish. Bl. Eating flowers is not a modern idea. North American Indians used the floral bud clusters of the milkweed to thicken soups and stews, and cut up the full-blown flowers for a sort of preserve. BT. #76. Same as paⁿnuⁿpala.
wahca'hca hu bloka, n. Swamp milkweed. Asclepias incarnata. The milkweed family. Bh. #250.
wahca' pepe'la, n. The Joe Pye weed, trumpet weed, purple thoroughwort, gravel or kidney root, the tall or purple boneset. Eupatorium purpureum, variety maculatum. The composite family. BT. #117.
wahca' waśte, n. The closed or blind gentian, the bottle gentian or barrel gentian, Cloistered Heart. Gentiana andrewsii. The gentian family. BT. #133.
wahca'ziblu, n. The rock goldenrod. Solidago canadensis. The composite family. BT. #28.
wahca'zi cik'ala, n. The yellow prairie mallow, tooth-leaved primrose. Oenothera serrulata. The evening primrose family. BT. #7.
wahca'zi kaⁿ'ta mna uⁿma hu táⁿka, n. The golden parosela. Parosela aurea. The pulse family. BT. #275.
wahca'zi suta, n. Same as peji hota waśtemna. BT. #64.
wahca'zi śicamna, n. Same as caⁿhlogaⁿ pa. LB. #150.
wahca'zi taⁿka, n. The sunflower. This has medicinal use. Cf. caⁿhlogaⁿ wahcazi paⁿśpaⁿjela.
wahca'zi waśte, n. White prairie aster. Aster commutatus. The composite family. - ota yelo, hiyu po. Hu paksa ayapi Lakota waśtelakapi. BT. #137.
wahca'zi waśtemna, n. The cut-leaved sideranthus. Sideranthus spinulosus. The composite family. Also, caⁿhlogaⁿ pepela. BT. #100.
wahca'zizi, n. Yellow flowers; the sunflower.

wahci', v.a. (of hci). To cut or break out notches by cutting. Wawahci.

wahciⁿ'ca, n. The small, thin poplar tree. - oju. Bl.

wahe'yata iyeya, v. To push back; one who pushes others back, n.

wahla', v.a. (of hla). To make rattle with a knife. Wawahla.

wahla'gaⁿ, v.a. (of hlagaⁿ). To enlarge e.g. a hole by cutting around. Wawahlagaⁿ.

wahla'hla, v.a. (of hlahla). To make rattle by cutting. Wawahlahla.

wahla'ya, v.a. To pare off; to circumcise. Ha - , To peel. Wawahlaya.

wahle'ca, v.a. To cut or break in pieces with a knife, rend in cutting. Wawáhleca. -- wahléhleca, v. red. of wahleca. -- wahlél, cont. of wahleca. - iyeya.

wahlog', cont. of wahloka. - iyeya.

wahlo'hloka, n. Lace.

wahlō'ka, v.a. (of hloka). To cut a hole in anything with a knife. Wawahloka.

wahna', v. To groan. Bl. -- wahnáhna, v. red. Bl.

wahna'hnaheca, n. The wild cucumber. The mock apple. Echinocystis lobata. The gourd family. CR. #225.

wahpa', v.a. To cut off anything and let it fall. Wawahpa.

wa'hpa hóta, n. The cow bird. Also, pteyáhpa. It is accustomed to sitting on cattle and horses. R. Bl. FR.

wahpa'ka, n. perhaps. One who being sickly has not put his clothes on well. Hehe, he wana wahpakelo. Bl.

wahpa'nica, adj. Poor, destitute, having nothing. Mawahpanica, uⁿwahpanicapi.
wahpa'nikiya, v. pos. To make self poor. Ite wahpaniwakiye, i.e. to make my face look sorrowful, so as to attract sympathy.

waȟpa'nila, v.a. To consider poor. Waȟpaniwala.
waȟpa'niya, v.a. To make poor, cause to be poor. Waȟpaniwaya.
waȟpa'niyaᵑ, adv. Poorly, in a destitute way. - hakitoᵑ. B.H.133.8.
waȟpa'niyaᵑkel, adv. In a destitute way. - wahi.

waȟpaᵑ'yaᵑ, v. To soak anything; to soak and take the hair off. R. Waȟpaᵑwaya.

wa'ȟpa taᵑka, n. The common black bird.

waȟpa'ye, n. Anything one has of movable goods, baggage; the paying for a living somewhere; hence, taxes. - mnakiyapi. B.H.260.20. - glajuju, To pay tax. -- waȟpáyeca, n. Baggage.

waȟpe', 1) n. Leaf, leaves. 2) n. Tea.
- aȟkikaśkapi, Common hop. Humulus lupulus. BT. #74. Syn.- winakapo.
- aṗé blaskaska, Same as tal'ágnake. Bl. #25. Syn.- mimela waȟcazi. BT.
- blaskaska, Winter-greens.
- caᵑli, A leaf used for tobacco, a small vine that runs on the ground as the winter-green, the leaf of which serves as a tobacco.
- caᵑsakala, Same as wapepeka. BT. #33.
- ceyaka, Virginia mountain mint. Pycnanthemum virginianum. The mint family. A tea made from it is used for coughing. BT. #121. Also, waȟpe icikoyagyaka.
- ȟcaȟca, Texas croton, skunk weed. Croton texensis. This is the female plant; the male has no blossoms. Tea of the leaves is good for stomach pains. Bl. BT. #208.
- ȟla, The clammyweed. Polanisia trachysperma. The caper family. Bl. #309.
- ȟ'eȟ'e, Pink cleome, common bee plant, stinking clover. Cleome serrulata. The caper family. BT. #20.
- icikoyagyaka, Same as waȟpe ceyaka. BT. #121.
- iᵑkpa jiji, Strong-scented lettuce. Lactuca virosa. The composite family. WE. #110.
- iᵑkpa ṗeṗé, Same as wókaȟtaᵑ blaskaska. BT. #119.
Waȟpékute, n. prop. The Leaf-shooters, a band of Dakotas among the Nebraska Santee.
- maká ayublaya, Prostrate ameranth. Ameranthus blitoides. BT. #36. Also, the small-flowered verbena. Verbena bipimatifida. The vervain family. BT. #274.
- pa, The false boneset. Kuhnia eupatorioides. The composite family. WE. #228.
- peji, Alfalfa.
- ṗeṗé, The Douglas phlox. Phlox Douglasii andicola. The phlox family. Bl. #266.
- ṗeṗéla, Knotgrass, doorweed, goosegrass, dooryard weed. Polygonum aviculare. The buckwheat family. BT. #35.
- poṗa, A species of willow.
- poṗa caᵑ, The large species of willow. L.
- skuya, Veined dock. Rumex venosus. The buckwheat family. The leaves are sour. Tea of the roots is given to women when an afterbirth does not come in time. L. Also, lady's sorrel, upright yellow wood sorrel. Oxalis stricta. The woodsorrel family. Bl. BS. #235.
- swula, Yellow melilot, sweet clover, millet; the balsum flower, king's clover, king's crown. Melilotus officinalis. The pulse family. Bl. #279.
- śica, The burweed marsh elder. Iva xantifolia. The composite family. Waȟpe śica ota yelo; uᵑgna el lapi kilo. The seeds cause irritation on the bare skin. BT.
- śluśluta, Entire-leaved groundsel. Senecio perplexus. The composite family. HH. #151.
- tiᵑpsila, The whorled milkweed. Asclepias verticillata. The milkweed. Mothers use it when they have no milk. SG. #220.
- to, The prairie violet. Viola pedatifida. The violet family. HH. #152.
Waȟpétoᵑwaᵑ, n. prop. A band of Dakotas on the Lake Traverse Reservation.
- t'aga, Alum root, rough heuchera. Heuchera hispida. The saxifrage family. It has tuberous roots used for making a medicinal tea for diorrhoea. When powdered and thrown into the water it makes it red. This powder is also used on sores. Also, caᵑhloȟ snasnala, t'agela hu. BT. Bs. #267.
- wacaᵑġa hu bloka, Cleavers, goose grass, cleaver-wort. It is not sweet-scented. Galium aparine.

The madder family. Bl. #305. Cf. waḣpe wacaŋga hu wiŋyela.
- wacáŋġa hu wiŋyela, Sweet-scented bedstraw. Galium trifolium. The madder family. Cf. the non-scented, hu bloka. L. #172.
- waśtemna, Wild bergamont, horsemint. Menthalfolia monarda. The mint family. It is noted for its fragrance and is similar to heḣaka tapejuta. The leaves are often chewed while singing and dancing. FD.178,270. Bl., #209.
- wizilya, The sandbar willow. Salix fluviatilis. BT. #104. Also, coḣwáŋ jica.
- wok̇eya, A bower.
- yataṗi, Fragrant giant hyssop. Agastache foeniculum. The mint family. It has the aroma of anise and hence is called also lophantus anisatus. As a tea for drinking, it is very good. BS. #206. This herb grows in the canyons about Pine Ridge, S.D. and serves as a substitute for tea.
- yatápi iyececa, The tumble weed. Amaranthus graecizans. The amaranth family BT. #32. Also, the western figwort. Scrophularia occidentalis. Bl. #199. Also, the false dragon head, obedient plant, lion's heart. Physostegia virginiana. Bl. #237. Also, lopseed. Phryma leptostachya. Bl. #138.
- yazokapi, Downy painted cup. Castilleja sessiliflora. The figwort family. The honey can be sucked from its blossoms. Bl. #264.

waḣṗe'yuṫaṗi, n. Cabbage.

waḣṗo'k̇ijate, n. The few-flowered psoralea. Psoralea tenuiflora. The pulse family. BT. #13.

waḣṗu', v.a. To cut off in small pieces. Wawaḣpu. -- waḣṗúḣṗu, v. red.

waḣṫa'ni, v. (of aḣtani). To transgress a law, to sin. Wawáḣtani.
waḣṫa'nic'iya, v. refl. To make one's self commit sin. Pb.13.
waḣṫa'nis'a, n. A transgressor, a sinner.
waḣṫa'niya, v.a. To cause to transgress or sin. Waḣtaniwaya.

waḣṫē'k̇a, adj. No good for the purpose designated, as a bad cigar.
waḣṫe'kaca, adj. Bad.
waḣṫē'k̇eśni, adj. Skilful, good in something. Wamáḣtekeśni. Wowaśi ecoŋ - . Iapi ecoŋ - .
waḣṫe'laśni, v.a. To dislike, abominate. Waḣtewalaśni.
waḣṫe'śni, adj. Bad, worthless, wicked. Mawáḣteśni. - kiŋ! The worthless one. - śicapi kiŋ uŋci míktepi, i.e. worthless bad ones. - śicapi kiŋ. - śica. D.16,57,56,105.
waḣṫe'śniit'a, interj. A curse word meaning: You are practically dead for today I will kill you. When ref. is made to more than one, they say waḣteśniit'api. Waḣteśniit'api kiŋ aŋpetu tahena iyuha wicawakte kte śaŋ, eya keye. Also, sick and tired of. Waḣteśni imát'e, mni kta tka, I am sorry I missed my good luck or chance, i.e. because I was absent when things were distributed.
waḣṫe'śni t'a, n. perhaps. One who gets away with misdeeds. Waḣteśni t'e kiŋ magnaye yelo, The rascal deceived me!

waḣtiŋ'kiya, v. pos. (of waḣtiŋyaŋ). To be fond of one's own. Waḣtiŋwakiya.
waḣtiŋ'yaŋ, v.a. To care for, be fond of, love, as in expressing love of any members of the family. Waḣtiŋkiciyapi, as is said of a married couple. Waḣtiŋmaye kacá, He does not care for me. Waḣtiŋciye śni! which is akin to cursing.

waḣu'gnaḣya wauŋyaŋpi, n. A holocaust. B.H.61.8.
waḣu'ḣnaḣya, v. To burn up as rubbish. Waḣuḣnaḣwaya.

waḣuŋ'wiŋye, v. (ḣuŋwiŋye). To smell, stink, as meat does in the hot weather.

waḣu'ṗak̇oza, n. Wing-flappers, i.e. fowls, domestic fowls. MS.477.

wa'ḣwa, adj. Mild, gentle. R. Bl.
wa'ḣwaka, adj. Mild. Mawaḣwaka. Bl.
wa'ḣwak̇eca, adj. Gentle.
wa'ḣwak̇iya, adv. Gently, noiselessly. - tima hiyu welo. Bl.
wa'ḣwak̇iyak̇el, adv. Gently, in ref. to one's own. Ho - ake hewicakiye. - iyopewicaye. B.H.38.6;80.23. Also, waḣwak̇iyela, perhaps adj. B.H.238.9.
wa'ḣwala, adj. Gentle, mild. Mawaḣwala. Oḣ'aŋ - .
wa'ḣwaya, adv. Mildly, gently, peacefully. David wicaśa kiŋ - uŋpi kiŋ

heca. B.H.96.1;198.12. Also, wáhwayakel, wáhwayela.

wah'aⁿ'hiya, adv. (of h'aⁿhiya). Slowly, as in cutting perhaps.
wah'aⁿ'h'aⁿic'ila, v. refl. To be self-sufficient, self-important. Wah'aⁿh'aⁿmic'ila. EM. Cf. wah'aⁿic'iya.
wah'aⁿ'h'aⁿic'iya, v. red. of wah'aⁿic'iya. Bl.
wah'aⁿ'ic'ila, v. refl. (of wah'aⁿla). To think highly of one's self, to be proud. Wah'aⁿmic'ila.
wah'aⁿ'ic'ilapi, n. Pride.
wah'aⁿ'ic'iya, v. To pretend to do much work, while very little is done. Bl.
wah'aⁿ'ka, v. To find it hard to work; to do difficult things well. Wawah'aⁿka. R. Bl. Haⁿwáⁿji amayaⁿpa caⁿna wawah'aⁿke lo.

wah'aⁿ'ksica, n. The marten. WH.

wah'aⁿ'la, v.a. To esteem, think highly of one. Wah'aⁿwala.

wah'e'ca, n. Round white hail, like to shot.

wah'u', v.a. To cut the hull or rind off, to peel e.g. an orange with a knife by scraping. Wawah'u. -- wah'úh'u, v. red. of wah'u. Wawáh'uh'u.

wah'uⁿ't'eya, v. (h'uⁿ and t'eya). To tire one out.

wai'caǧa, v. (of icaga). To grow, produce, as a field or plants. Yuⁿkaⁿ wagmeza kiⁿ lila - . Tamaka el lila waicage. B.H.225.2.
wai'cahya, v. abs. (of icahya). To produce, raise things, as horses, children etc.; to create. Waicahwaya. D.257.
wai'cahyapi, n. That which is produced or raised.
Wai'cahye, n. prop. The Creator.

wai'caskaⁿ, v. To melt snow. Bl.

wai'cihaha, n. A jester, an insolent fellow; one who does evil to others and laughs at the mischief he has done. -- wai'cihahapi, n. Insolence.

wa'iciksuksu, v. To cover one's self with all sorts of ornaments; pahayela wakoyake. Wamiciksuksu. Bl.

wai'cisniyaⁿ, v. To run the knife out of the right course in cutting. - iyeya. Also, wawicisniyaⁿ. R.

wai'ciya, v. (of iciya). To assist, take one's part. R. Bl.

wai'cu, v. (of icu). To take. waiwacu. Kagisnisni waiculah, Helps himself unceremoniously. Bl. B.H.236.12.
wai'cucuka, n. A pilferer.
wai'cucukteca, v. To be going to be a pilferer.
wai'cucukte hciⁿ, v. To covet. P.

wai'c'igluhtata, v. To offer a sacrifice for one's self, e.g. parts of one's flesh, as was a custom.
wai'c'iglusna, v. refl. (of wayusna). To sacrifice one's self, to let one's self fall. Wamic'iglusna.
wai'c'ihoⁿ, v. refl. (of wahoⁿ). To cut or gash one's self. Wamic'ihoⁿ.

wa'ic'ihtani, v. refl. (of wahtani). To sin against one's self. Wamic'ihtani. Cf. awaic'ihtani.

wai'ecesni, v. To tell lies. Waiwayecesni. WE. Tuwe ca hosi gli hwo? Aksaka he - k'oⁿ, Oh, that is an old liar. Bl.

wai'elgle, n. (of ielgle). One who casts up to another, an accuser. -- v. To accuse. P.

wai'glamna, v. (of iglamna). To make a living for one's self. B.H.171.1.

wai'gluhtata, v. To offer one's self in sacrifice as did Christ.
wai'glusna, v. refl. (of wayusna). To sacrifice one's self. Wamiglusna.

wai'glustaⁿ, v. refl. (of yustaⁿ). To finish what pertains to one's self. Wamiglustaⁿ. B.H.268.5.

wai'hakta, v. To make one wait and follow. WE. -- adj. Fond.

wai'hpeya, v. (of aihpeya). To throw away; to give to others; to sacrifice, give to the spirits, gods. Waihpewaya.

wai'kalelepake, (?). Waikalelepakelahcake, as is said if a man acts as if he knows everything and bosses everywhere. Bl.

wai'kceya, adv. perhaps. (of ikceya). Instead of something else. - k'u, To give something else instead of the article asked for. - mnayaŋ, To have received, i.e. at a collection tour, all sorts of things, as calico etc., instead of money, which was asked for.

wai'kicu, v. To take from others; to remove, take from others by magic, as medicine men pretended to do. Waiwakicu.

wai'kikcu, v. (of ikikcu). To take one's own. B.H.245.22.

wai'leya, v. (of ileya). To burn, set fire. Wailewaya.

wai'nakiȟni, v. To be always in a hurry about one's self. B.H.75.17. -- waínakiȟniȟnike, (?). Wahuŋcala s'e - ; wana kakena iyayelo, as is said when one of a crowd is in a great hurry and goes on while the others are slow in departing. ED.

wai'ṗaṫe, n. A snow plow. An. Gr.

wai'ṗaweȟ iyeya, Same as waektaśniyaŋ. Bl.

wai'ṗila, n. (of ipila). One who forbids or refuses to part with what he has.

wai'śkahu, n. Knuckles. - nuŋġa, Swollen knuckles of a horse. - nuŋġa waŋ yuha yelo. Bl.

wai'śnaheca, n. Soft new snow. For a difference cf. wahiśnaheca, wagugeca.

wai'śteca, adj. Bashful. -- waíśṫelya, v.a. To put to shame. Waiśtelwaya.

wai'ṫebya, adv. Cut shorter on one side. Cf. watepa.

wai'yakaṗeya, v. (of iyakapeya). To give one no chance to speak while one is talking angrily. Bl.

wai'yaṗat'oya, v. To obstruct, bear down on. Waiyapat'owaya. Bl.

wai'yaṗe, v. (of iyape). To lie in wait. -- waíyaṗeṗi, n. An ambush.

wai'yatagle, v. To have exceeding much e.g. work and hence cannot do it. Waiyamatagle. -- waíyatagleic'iya, v. refl. To overdo, overtax one's self; to fail, having overtaxed one's strength. -- waíyatagleya, v. To urge on over-much. Waiyataglewaya.

wai'yekiya, v. To find one's own. Waiyewakiya.

wai'yeya, v. (of iyeya). To find. Waiyewaya.

wai'yeyeca, n. One who finds much.

wai'yojaŋjaŋ, v. (of iyojaŋjaŋ). To dazzle, blind. Iśta waiyomajaŋjaŋ yelo, Light dazzles me, as when one has sore eyes. Bl.

wai'yuŋġa, v. To inquire. B.H.96.2.

waja'gjaṫa, v. red. of wajata.

Waja'je, n. prop. A clan among the Oglalas and Sicaŋgu. GA.

wajal', cont. of wajata. -- wajáljaṫa, v. red. of wajata. -- wajálya, v.a. To cause to cut forked, make forked. Wajalwaya.

waja'ṫa, v.a. (of jata). To make forked by sawing or cutting, as one end of an arrow notched for the string; to cut into a fork. Wawajata.

waju', v. 1st pers. sing. of ju.

waju'ju, v.a. (of juju). To quarter, to cut up e.g. beef; to cut in pieces, cut up e.g. an animal. Wawajuju. B.H. 107.15. GA.

waka', v.a. To cut or strip, as the feather from a quill; to cut off e.g. the ribs of an animal; to split a quill in the middle. Wawaka.

waka'ajaja, v. To lay bare, to uncover, as by sweeping. Also, wakáaślaya.

waka'bla, v. (of kabla). To slice. Wawakabla. Also, 1st pers. sing. of kabla. D.271.

waka'blapi, n. Meat cut up for drying, dried meat, hence the same as ṗáṗa.

waka'blaya, v. (of kablaya). To cut in thin slices, as meat for drying; to make level, spread out; 1st pers. sing. of kablaya. Wawakablaya.

waka'blaza, v. (of kablaza). To rip open; 1st pers. sing. of kablaza. Wawakablaza.

waka'bleca, v. (of kableca). To dash to pieces; 1st pers. sing. of kableca. Wawakableca.

waka'blu, v. (of kablu). To pulverize; 1st pers. sing. of kablu. Wawakablu.

waka'bu, v. To drum. P.

waka'ga, v. (of kaga). To make; 1st pers. sing. of kaga. Wawakaga. -- wakágapi, n. An image, picture, idol; something made. Wicaśa - , A scarecrow; the Pawnee being: cuwá culúza. Cuwa culuza waⁿ apapi kiⁿ hehaⁿ. BL.

waka'gege, v. (of kagege). To sew; 1st pers. sing. of kagege. Wawakagege.

waka'gi, 1) v. (of kagi). To hinder or prevent by one's presence, as to keep one from speaking or from doing something to be feared; to be revered; 1st pers. sing. of kagi. Wawakagi. 2) n. One who restrains by his presence. -- wakágiya, 1) v.a. To hinder, obstruct, keep others from going fast. Wakagiwaya. 2) adv. Slowly, preventing, detaining.

waka'gmigma, v. (of kagmigma). To make round; 1st pers. sing. of kagmigma. Wawakagmigma. -- wakágmiyaⁿyaⁿ, v. (of kagmiyaⁿyaⁿ). To roll; 1st pers. sing. of kagmiyaⁿyaⁿ. Wawakagmiyaⁿyaⁿ.

waka'gmuⁿ, v. (of kagmuⁿ). To spin, twist; 1st pers. sing. of kagmuⁿ. Wawakagmuⁿ. -- wakágmuⁿpi, n. Spinning.

waka'haⁿ, part. Split, as the feather end of a quill.

waka'haⁿl, adv. Sometime in the future. Bl.

waka'hi, v. (of kahi). To rummage through, as children do trunks etc.; 1st pers. sing. of kahi. Wawakahi. Also, to bring. Wamakahi, He brings to me. -- wakáhika, n. One who rummages.

waka'hiⁿhpeya, v. To knock down and run over one or something, as a horse over-running a child. Wakahiⁿhpewaya.

waka'hiⁿta, v. (of kahiⁿta). To sweep; 1st pers. sing. of kahiⁿta. Wawakahiⁿta, wauⁿkahiⁿtapi.

waka'hoho, v. (kahoho). To shake, make loose; 1st pers. sing. of kahoho. Wawakahoho.

waka'homni, v. (of kahomni). To make turn round; 1st pers. sing. of kahomni. Wawakahomni.

waka'huⁿ, v. (kahuⁿ). To make marks, cuts, by striking with an axe or knife. Wawakahuⁿ.

waka'huⁿhuⁿza, v. (kahuⁿhuⁿza). To shake by striking; 1st pers. sing. of kahuⁿhuⁿza. Wawakahuⁿhuⁿza.

waka'hapa, v. (kahapa). To drive along; 1st pers. sing. of kahapa. Wawakahapa.

waka'hepa, v. (kahepa). To bail out; 1st pers. sing. of kahepa. Wawakahepa.

waka'hica, v. (kahica). To waken up by striking; 1st pers. sing. of kahica. Wawakahica.

waka'hla, v. (kahla). To rattle, to rummage; 1st pers. sing. of kahla. Wawakahla.

waka'hlaka, n. One who pilfers much.

waka'hleca, v. (kahleca). To break open, to fracture; 1st pers. sing. of kahleca.

waka'hlihli, v. To become mired. - wau welo, i.e. to wade through deep mud. Bl. Cf. kahlihli.

waka'hliya, v. (kahliya). To make mire. Wakáhliwaya.

waka'hloka, v. (kahloka). To make a hole in; 1st pers. sing. of kahloka. Wawakahloka.

waka'hniga, v. (kahniga). To choose; 1st pers. sing. of kahniga. Wawakahniga.

waka'hpa, v. (kahpa). To throw down; 1st pers. sing. of kahpa. Wawakahpa.

wa'kahpa, v. (akahpa). To cover. Wáwakahpa.

waka'hpu, v. (kahpu). To tear down; to strike and make fall down; to strike and loosen from its fastenings; 1st pers. sing. of kahpu. Wawakahpu.

wak̇a'ḣṫak̇a, v.n. To be easily hurt, touchy, nervous. Wamakaḣṫaka.
wak̇a'ḣṫak̇eca, n. One who is made sick by a little matter, one who is nervous. Wamakaḣtakeca.
wak̇a'ḣṫak̇ek̇e, n. On who is nervous, fretful, dissatisfied with everything; a grumbler. Bl.

wak̇a'ḣuġa, v. (kaḣuga). To break e.g. the skull, kettles etc.; 1st pers. sing. of kaḣuga. Wawakaḣuga.

wak̇a'ḣuŋṫa, v. (kaḣuŋta). To make rough, as birds do tearing open husks of corn.

wa'k̇aḣ'o, v.n. To linger about something, as buzzards do about a carcass.

wak̇a'ḣ'u, v. (kaḣ'u). To peel off e.g. bark; 1st pers. sing. of kaḣ'u. Wawakaḣ'u.

wak̇a'ile, v. (kaile). To make blaze. Wawakaile.

wak̇a'jaja, v. (kajaja). To wash by drawing back and forth in the water; to see well; 1st pers. sing. of kajaja. Wawakajaja.

wak̇a'jiṗa, v. (kajipa). To shave. Wawakajipa.

wak̇a'juju, v. (kajuju). To pay off; to erase; to forgive; 1st pers. sing. of kajuju. Wawakajuju.
wak̇a'jujukiya, v. To tax, impose a tax. P.

wak̇a'juŋ, v. (kajuŋ). To tear up by the roots.

wak̇a'kab iḣpéya, v. To push out of the way. Bl. Cf. kakab iḣpeya.

wak̇a'kaŋ, v. (kakaŋ). To hew; to beat or strike off e.g. berries or grain, to hammer on, strike, as in shaping a stone; 1st pers. sing. of kakaŋ. Wawakakaŋ. - uŋyaŋpi kte. Bl. B.H. 201.14.

wak̇a'kca, v. (kakca). To comb, to disentangle; 1st pers. sing. of kakca. Wawakakca.

wak̇a'k̇iŋca, v. (kakiŋca). To scrape; 1st pers. sing. of kakiŋca. Wawakakiŋca.

wak̇a'kiśya, v. (kakiśya). To cause to suffer, give trouble. Wakakiśwaya. D.268.

wak̇a'kok̇a, v. (kakoka). To make rattle; 1st pers. sing. of kakoka. Wawakakoka.

wak̇a'kṗaŋ, v. (kakpaŋ). To pound fine; 1st pers. sing. of kakpaŋ. Wawakakpaŋ.

wak̇a'k̇sa, v. (kaksa). To cut off with an axe; 1st pers. sing. of kaksa.

wak̇a'kśa, v. (kakśa). To roll up. Wawakakśa.

wak̇a'kśaŋ, v. (kakśaŋ). To bend; 1st pers. sing. of kakśaŋ. Wawakakśaŋ. Also, wák̇akśaŋ. Bl.

wak̇a'kśija, v. (kakśija). To double up. Wawakakśija.

wak̇a'kṫaŋ, v. (kaktaŋ). To make bend; 1st pers. sing. of kaktaŋ. Wawakaktaŋ.

wak̇a'kuka, v. (kakuka). To pound to pieces, destroy; 1st pers. sing. of kakuka. Wawakakuka.

wak̇al'ya, v. To boil. Wakalwaya. -- wak̇ályaṗi, n. (kalya). Anything boiled; generally used for coffee.

wak̇a'mna, v. (kamna). To collect, gather; to earn, to make money, to earn or merit; 1st pers. sing. of kamna. Wawakamna. Pb.30.
wak̇a'mnak̇a, n. One who collects.
wak̇a'mnaŋpi, n. Collecting, earning.

wak̇aŋ', adj. Sacred, consecrated; special; incomprehensible; possessing or capable of giving toŋ, i.e. an endowed spiritual quality which is received or transmittable to beings making for what is specially good or bad. WJR.152-3. Mawakaŋ, or perhaps wamakaŋ. Taku iyahaŋbla ca wanikaŋ keha he? eya. Miś eya heoŋ mawakaŋ yelo. MS.244.
wakaŋ'ecoŋ, v. To do tricks of jugglery. Wakaŋecamoŋ.
wakaŋ'ecoŋṗila, n. Magic, tricks of jugglery.

wak̇aŋ'gli, n. The lightning. - makata iheyapi. MS.258.

wakaŋ'heja, n. (kaŋheja). A child, children. Also, wakaŋyeja. -- adj.

Poor, distressed, feeble. Waníkaŋheja śni. Note: the adj. does not seem to be used in Teton. Bl.

wakaŋ' h'aŋ, v. To court, as by playing a flute etc. Bl.

wakaŋ' ia, v. To foretell. Wakaŋ iwae. B.H.67.4;145.2. Cf. wakiŋya.

wakaŋ'ic'icoŋza, v. To profess e.g. faith. P.

wakaŋ'ic'ila, v. refl. (wakaŋla). To esteem one's self holy or wakaŋ, to be proud. Wakaŋmic'ila.
wakaŋ'ic'ilapi, n. Pride.

wakaŋ'ka, n. (kaŋ). An old woman. Wamakaŋka.

wakaŋ'ka, adj. Doubtfully mysterious, i.e. it is doubtful if certain person or thing is wakaŋ. Wamakaŋka.
wakaŋ'kaǧa, v. To make wakaŋ, perform acts of worship according to ideas of the Dakotas. Wakaŋwakaga.

wakaŋ'kala, n. dim. Same as wakaŋka.

wakaŋ' kaŋ'pi, n. (?).

wakaŋ'kaŋyaŋ, adv. red. (wakaŋyaŋ). - mioh'aŋ, The miracles I wrought. B.H.63.17;114.22.

Wakaŋ'kiciyuzapi, n. The sacrament of Matrimony.

wakaŋ'kila, v. pos. (wakaŋla). To regard one's own as sacred. Wakaŋwakila.
wakaŋ'la, v.a. To reckon as holy or sacred; to worship. Wakaŋwala. Na cahli k'oŋ na wahiŋśa k'oŋ hena ecel owegnaka na lila wakaŋwala. Also, wakáŋlaka.
wakaŋ'la s'e uŋ, v. To be a health scrupulant. Bl.

Wakaŋ'śica, n. prop. Satan, the devil, the Bad Spirit.

Wakaŋ'taŋka, n. prop. God, the Creator of all things, the great Spirit; also, all wakaŋ beings because they are all as one. WJR.152.

wakaŋ' wacipi, n. The sacred dance.
wakaŋ'wohaŋ, v. To make a sacred feast. Wakaŋwowahe. -- wakáŋwohaŋpi, n. A sacred feast.

wakaŋ'yaŋ, adv. Sacredly, holily, mysteriously. Wiŋyaŋ kiŋ le otuyaciŋ u śni yelo, - u welo. Also, wakáŋyaŋkel. - wóha naŋké, as is said to one who travels with much luggage. Bw. - wóecoŋ, To do wonderful deeds, wonderful deeds done. B.H.290.9,20.

wakaŋ'ya wówaŋyaŋke, n. A sacred vision. B.H.291.13.

wakaŋ'yeja, n. Same as wakaŋheja. - otuyubleza, He woke the children. Cf. kaŋyeja.

wakaŋ'yelak, wakaŋ'yelakel, adv. With great difficulty, only by overcoming almost insurmountable obstacles. - icu.

wakaŋ'yuza, v. To take a wife after the manner of Christians. Wakabluza.

waka'ohpa, v. (kaohpa). To break through; 1st pers. sing. of kaohpa. Wawakaohpa.

waka'pa, v. (kapá). To excel, exceed, surpass; win a race. Wakawapa.

waka'pa, v. (kapá). To pound off; 1st pers. sing. of kapa. Wawakapa.

waka'paŋ, v. (kapaŋ). To pound off e.g. corn; 1st pers. sing. of kapaŋ. Wawakapaŋ.
waka'paŋpaŋ, v. (kapaŋpaŋ). To pound soft; 1st pers. sing. of kapaŋpaŋ. Wawakapaŋpaŋ.

waka'papi, n. Mashed-up meat mixed with marrow, pemmican.

waka'pcecela, v. Same as wakaptecela.

wa'kape, n. A piece of leather on which to mash beef, cherries etc. Na - waŋ ogna wakapapi ojula ahimigle.

waka'pemni, v. (kapemni). To twist, to swing e.g. a lasso; 1st pers. sing. of kapemni. P.

waka'pesto, v. (kapesto). To sharpen; 1st pers. sing. of kapesto. Wawakapesto.

waka'peya, v. To excel, cause to excel. Wakapewaya.

waƙa'poƥa, v. (kapopa). To make burst; 1st pers. sing. of kapopa.

waƙa'popo, v. To make a noise in deep snow by walking and compressing the snow. Also, wa kapopo. - wau welo. Bl.

waƙa'ƥoƭa, v. (kapota). To pound to pieces; 1st pers. sing. of kapota. Wawakapota.

waƙa'psaƙa, v. (kapsaka). To break in two, as a string; 1st pers. sing. of kapsaka.

waƙa'psica, v. (kapsica). To make hop; 1st pers. sing. of kapsica. Wawakapsica.

waƙa'psiⁿpsiⁿƭa, v. (kapsiⁿpsiⁿta). To whip; 1st pers. sing. of kapsiⁿpsiⁿta. Wawakapsiⁿpsiⁿta.

waƙa'psoⁿ, v. (kapsoⁿ). To spill; 1st pers. sing. of kapsoⁿ. Wawakapsoⁿ.

waƙa'pśuⁿ, v. (kapśuⁿ). To dislocate; 1st pers. sing. of kapśuⁿ. Wawakapśuⁿ.

waƙa'pƭa, v. (kapta). To dip out; 1st pers. sing. of kapta. Wawakapta. Wana - po, as they say when ready to eat. LO.

waƙa'pƭecela, v. (kaptecela). To cut off shorter; 1st pers. sing. of kaptecela. Wawakaptecela.

waƙa'ƥus'ƙiya, v. To hang up to dry. Wakapuswakiya. Bl.

waƙa'sa, v. (kasa). To bury in the snow. Wawakasa.

waƙa'se, n. (kasaⁿ). A thing growing old and white. Bl.

waƙa'sƙa, v. 1st pers. sing. of kaska. To whiten.

wa'ƙaska, v. (akaska). To eat greedily, eat long. Wawakaska. Toki etoⁿwe śni wauⁿkaskapi. R. Bl.

waƙa'sƙeƥa, v. (kaskepa). To bail out.

waƙa'sƙica, v. (kaskica). To press or pound tight. Wawakaskica.

waƙa'sleca, v. (kasleca). To split without effort; 1st pers. sing. of kasleca.

waƙa'sli, v. (kasli). To strike and make fly out, to make spirt out by striking, as matter from a sore. Wawakasli.

waƙa'slohaⁿ, v.n. To drive along, as the wind does a boat.

waƙa'smaƙa, v. (kasmaka). To indent by pounding. Wawakasmaka.

waƙa'smiⁿyaⁿyaⁿ, v. To make bare, as the wind does the ground by driving off the snow.

waƙa'sna, v. (kasna). To make ring; to shake off, as the wind does leaves from a tree; 1st pers. sing. of kasna.

waƙa'sni, v. (kasni). To extinguish; 1st pers. sing. of kasni. Wawakasni.

waƙa'soƭa, v. (kasota). To use up, expend, make an end to; 1st pers. sing. of kasota. Wawakasota.

waƙa'soteka, n. A spendthrift. B.H. 226.1.

waƙa'sƭo, v. (kasto). To smooth down.

waƙa'swu, v. (kaswu). To cut in strips. Wamakaswu. -- waƙáswuƥi, n. Dangles.

waƙa'śaƥa, v. To make black or dirty by smiting. Wawakaśapa.

waƙa'śeca, v. (kaśeca). To deaden; 1st pers. sing. of kaśeca.

waƙa'śeya, v. (kaśeya). To obstruct. Wakaśewaya.

waƙa'śicahowaya, v. (kaśicahowaya). To cause to cry out by smiting. Wawakaśicahowaya.

waƙa'śiƥa, v. (kaśipa). To break off, as limbs from a tree; 1st pers. sing. of kaśipa. Wawakaśipa.

waƙa'śƙa, v. (kaśka). To bind; 1st pers. sing. of kaśka. Wawakaśka.

waƙa'śƙica, v. (kaśkica). To press, pound; 1st pers. sing. of kaśkica. Wawakaśkica.

waƙa'śkokƥa, v. (kaśkokpa). To hollow out e.g. a trough; 1st pers. sing. of kaśkokpa. Wawakaśkokpa.

waǩa'śkop̌a, v. (kaśkopa). To cut crookedly; 1st pers. sing. of kaśkopa. Wawakaśkopa.

waka'śleca, v. (kaśleca). To split with a knife or axe by striking and making real effort; 1st pers. sing. of kaśleca. Wawakaśleca.

waǩa'śloǩa, v. (kaśloka). To knock off e.g. the head from an axe handle. Wawakaśloka.

waǩa'śloyakel, adv. In a manner causing melting. Waspaŋla ca - mauŋnipelo. Bl.

waǩa'śluťa, v. (kaśluta). To make glance, as an axe; 1st pers. sing. of kaśluta. Wawakaśluta.

waǩa'śna, v. (kaśna). To miss in striking; 1st pers. sing. of kaśna. Wawakaśna.

wa'ǩaśoťa, adj. (wa and śota). Blackened with smoke.
wa'ǩaśoťeśni, adj. Clean, not defiled, pure; virgin, n. Also, wotiyemnaśni. ED.
wa'ǩaśoteśniyaŋ, adv. Purely, undefiled. R. Bl.

waǩa'śp̌a, v. (kaśpa). To cut off a piece; to expectorate; 1st pers. sing. of kaśpa. Wawakaśpa.

waǩa'śťaǩa, v. (kaśtaka). To smite; 1st pers. sing. of kaśtaka. Wawakaśtaka.

waǩa'śťaŋ, v. (kaśtaŋ). To pour out; 1st pers. sing. of kaśtaŋ. Wawakaśtaŋ.

waǩa'śuja, v. (kaśuja). To crush by striking; 1st pers. sing. of kaśuja. Wawakaśuja.

waǩa'ś'aka, v. (kaś'aka). To strike with too little force to penetrate; 1st pers. sing. of kaś'aka. Wawakas'aka.

waǩa'taŋni, v. (kataŋni). To wear out by striking; 1st pers. sing. of kataŋni.

waǩa'ťaťa, v. (katata). To shake e.g. a bed; 1st pers. sing. of katata. Wawakatata.

waǩa'ťepa, v. (tepa). To cut to a stump; 1st pers. sing. of katepa. Wawakatepa.

waǩa'ťica, v. (katica). To scrape off; to mix up e.g. mortar. R.

waǩa'ťiŋ, v. (katiŋ). To straighten with a knife, cut straight. Wawakatiŋ.

waǩa'tǩa, v. (katka). To choke. Wamakatka.

waǩa'tǩuǧa, v. (katkuga). To cut up short.
waǩa'tǩuŋza, v. (katkuŋza). To cut off square. Wawakatkuŋza.

waǩa'ťoťo, v. (katoto). To knock e.g. on a door; doubtfully, to clear land for plowing; 1st pers. sing. of katoto.

waǩa'ťuǩa, v. (katuka). To spoil by striking e.g. furs. Wawakatuka.
waǩa'ťutǩa, v. (katutka). To break into small pieces. Wawakatutka.
waǩa't'a, v. (kat'a). To kill by striking. Wawakat'a.
waǩa't'iŋza, v. (kat'iŋza). To pound in tight. Wawakat'iŋza.
waǩa't'ozapi, n. A stone hammer. Syn.- ihonicata. WR.
waǩa'uŋǩa, v. (kauŋka). To chop down e.g. timber, to blow down as the wind does trees; 1st pers. sing. of kauŋka. Wawakauŋka.
waǩa'weǧa, v. (kawega). To break or fracture. Wawakawega.
waǩa'wignuni, v. (kawignuni). To destroy. Wawakawignuni. R. Bl.
waǩa'wiŋja, v. (kawiŋja). To bend down by striking. Wawakawiŋja.
waǩa'zaŋ, v. (kazaŋ). To strike and make sick. Wawakazaŋ.

waǩa'ze, v. (kaze). To lade or dip out e.g. food from a kettle. Wawakaze.

waǩa'zoŋťa, v. (kazoŋta). To weave; 1st pers. sing. of kazoŋta. Also, wakasoŋta (soŋ). Wawakazoŋta.

wakcaŋ'yaŋ, v. To observe and report. - waku welo. R. Bl. -- wakcáŋyeya, v.a. To cause to go and spy out. Wakcaŋyewaya. R. Bl.

wakce'ya, v.a. To hang over the fire

to roast. Wakcewaya. -- wakcéyapi, n. The ribs of an animal, the roasting piece, because the ribs are generally so prepared. Cf. kceya.

wake'ya, 1) v.a. To have for a tent. Wakewaya. 2) n. A round Lakota skin tent. D.246.
wake'yaska, n. A canvas tent.
wake'yaton, v.a. To make a tent of, form a wakeya. B.H.61.3.

wakĕ'za, v. (?). Wawákeza. Bl.

waki', v. (ki). 1st pers. sing. of ki, To arrive; to rob. Wawaki.

waki'bleca, v. pos. (wableca). To break one's own, i.e. by attempting to cut with a knife. Wawakibleca.

waki'caġa lowánpi, n. (?).

waki'camna, v. (kamna). To make money for one. Wawicakicamna. B.H.299.16.

waki'cepa, (?). - mini wohlecelo, as is said when just a few drops of rain do fall. Bl. Hehlokeca tanka wakinaśleca - , as is said of fat buffalo. Bl.

waki'ciblaza, v. (wakiciksa). To cut open or cut lengthwise for one. Waweciblaza.

waki'cigluhtata, v. To offer something of one's own as a sacrifice for another, as God gave his Son for the world.

waki'cignaka, v. (gnaka). To lay away for one. Wawecignaka.
wa'kicignaka, v. (agnaka). To lay on for one, apply a poultice to one. Wawecignaka.

waki'ciġo, v. (wago). To cut or carve for one. Wawecigo.

waki'cihon, v. (wahon). To cut or gash for one. Wawecihon. -- waki'cihonhon, v. red.

waki'cih'u, v. (wah'u). To cut the rind or hull off for another. Wawecih'u.

waki'cikpan, v. (wakpan). To cut off fine e.g. tobacco for one. Wawecikpan.

waki'ciksa, v. (waksa). To cut off for one. Waweciksa. -- waki'ciksaksa, v. red. of wakiciksa. Wawéciksaksa.

waki'cipa, (?). Wamicipa. BT.

waki'cipta, v. (wapta). To cut off or trim for one. Wawecipta.

waki'cisku, v. (wasku). To peel or pare for one. Wawecisku.

waki'cisleca, v.a. (wasleca). To split with a knife or rip with a saw for one. Wawecisleca.

waki'ciśla, v. (waśla). To cut or shave off with a knife for one. Waweciśla.

waki'ciśloka, v. (waśloka). To cut out, cut a hole for one; to take out a piece for. Waweciśloka.

waki'ciśpa, v. (waśpá). To cut off a piece for one. Waweciśpa. -- wákiciśpaśpa, v. red. Taku oyasin - kte hcin, i.e. he makes big deeds of all his little actions. Bl.

waki'ciśpu, v. (waśpu). To cut off something that was stuck on, for another. Waweciśpu.

waki'ciunyan, v. To offer sacrifice for one.

wa'kicokic'un, adv. Carefully. - aya yo. Bl.

waki'conza, waki'conze, n. One who determines or decides, a leader of a travelling band of Indians, i.e. older men used to go in formation ahead of the others; a magistrate. Also, wakicunza. Na wicahcala top - wicabluha na ob wati kin hena tehan nipi kta. D.225,262. -- v.a. To purpose, determine for one; to resolve to do to or for one. Waweconza. -- waki'conze, n. A delegate.

wa'kicoya, adv. Just a little, slightly. - wanblakelo. - wao, I wounded it slightly. Bl.
wa'kicoyakel, adv. Well finished, well done. - kagelo. Bl.

waki'cuwa, waki'cuwaya, v. (kicuwa). To follow up. - yahi hwo? i.e. did you come for lease etc., and money? BT.

waki'c'uⁿpi, n. What is taken and used by all, common property; a gift or alms perhaps. Bl.

waki'glaka, n. Dressed skin, leather, such as is used to make and mend moccasins.

waki'gle, n. What one has laid up; a store, stores.

waki'gluhtata, v. To sacrifice one's own.

wa'kigna, n. Newly born animals. Wana wetu ca - ota ktelo. Bl.

waki'gnag, cont. of wakignaka. - wahi.

waki'gnaka, v. (kignaka). To store away one's own. Wawegnaka. -- waki'gnakapi, n. What is laid up, as money etc.

waki'go, v. pos. (wago). To cut or carve one's own; to engrave. Wawakigo.

waki'hiyece, n. perhaps. (kihiya). One who raises up children. Wakihiyecelah, as is said of a man who brought up many children. Bl.

waki'hoⁿ, v. pos. (wahoⁿ). To cut or gash one's own. Wawakihoⁿ. -- waki'hoⁿhoⁿ, v. red. of wakihoⁿ. Wawakihoⁿhoⁿ. Also, wakihuⁿhuⁿ, To make slight cuts or indentations in the surface of anything one's own. Wawakihuⁿhuⁿ. Itazipa ikaⁿ kiⁿ - , To cut nicks in one's bowstring. D.111. Cf. wahuⁿhuⁿ.

wa'kihtani, v. (wahtani). To sin against. Cf. awahtani.

waki'h'aⁿke, n. perhaps. One who does all sorts of hair work. Bc.

waki'janignica śni, (?). This is said when one wants to have everything. Bl.

waki'kcaⁿpta, 1) v.a. To comfort, console. Wawekcaⁿpta. 2) adj. Compassionate. -- wakikcaⁿpte, n. A comforter.

waki'ksa, v. pos. (waksa). To cut off one's own with a knife or saw. Wawakiksa, and waweksa. -- wakiksaksa, v. red. of wakiksa.

waki'ksapa, (?). Wicaśa waⁿ tawicu kici tawaciⁿ kiⁿ otkuⁿs wakiskapelo, as is said when a couple is of one mind. Bl.

waki'ksuya, v. (kiksuya). To remember or recall; to hold communion with, receive communications from supernatural beings; to call to remembrance a dead friend; to see signs of enemies, to be frightened by signs. D.2. -- wakiksuyapi, n. Remembering the past; having dreams or visions.

waki'kśu, v. (?). Wawakikśu. Bl.

waki'kśukśu, v. To hang many ornaments on one's own as children do. Bl.

wa'kiktoⁿja, v. (akiktoⁿja). To forget. Wáwektoⁿja.

wa'kil, cont. of wakita. Taⁿyaⁿ - ble c'oⁿ iśtagmus makilowahce lo. BT. Waⁿkatakiya - śi. B.H.13.10.

waki'la, v. (kila). To ask or beg of one. Wawakila. Pb.36. B.H.120.11.

wakil'kitaⁿ, v. red. (wakitaⁿ). To do things wrong and defend them anyhow. Wawakilkitaⁿ. -- wakilkitaⁿyaⁿ, adv. red. Obstinately, perseveringly.

waki'naśleca, (?). Héhlokeca taⁿka - wakicepa, as is said of fat buffalo. Bl.

wa'kinica, v. (akinica). To dispute, argue. Wáwakinica. Wácikinica. Wacikinil wahiyelo. Bl. B.H.285.13. -- wákinicapi, n. A disputation, contest.

waki'nihaⁿ, v. 1st. pers. sing. of kinihaⁿ.

wa'kinil, cont. of wakinica. - wauⁿ. - wahiyelo, I came to dispute with you.

waki'niya, v.n. To be touchy, get out of humor. Wawakiniya.

wakiⁿ'iⁿ, v. (kiⁿiⁿ). To throw at, to stone; 1st pers. sing. of kiⁿiⁿ. Wawakiⁿiⁿ.

wakiⁿ'ya, v. cont. (wakaⁿ ia). To say something that comes true, foretell.

Wakinwaya. He wakinya śke; but in Santee, He waayata śke.

wakin'yan, n. (kinyan). The thunder, the cause and source of thunder and lightning, supposed by the Dakotas to be a great bird; one of the 16 wakan beings Wakantanka, that associated with the west and which is never a carrier to our prayers, but rather is defied by them; hence, the wakan being usually counter-posed to Inyan, as Wi is to Han; thus, the winged Wakantanka. Cf. Wakantanka. Na ecel lila wakinyan agli. - namah'on, which is used for an oath; and it is believed that whoever would say this and lie anyhow was sure to die or be killed by lightning. Cf. maka namah'on. -- v. To fly, as does a bird. WJR.152-6.
- ha, The sharp-shinned hawk. Cetan iyececa.
- hotón, The thunder; lit., the thunder uttered its voice.
- hotón s'e, adv. With a thunder-like noise, thunderingly. Can kin - hoton s'e yunkahe. MG.

wakin'yanla pahli'hu, n. Water-plantain. Alisma plantago-aquatica. Bl. #298.

wakin'yan ona'yanpi, n. A prairie fire started by lightning.

wakin'yanpi, n. (kinyan). Those that fly, birds. R. Bl.
wakin'yanpi, n. The coming true of something foretold by a medicine man. BD. Cf. wakinya.

wakin'yan tonwan'pi, n. Sheet lightning, summer lightning. Hence, heat lightning. Lit., the thunderbird's look. Cf. wakinyan. -- wakinyan tónwanpi petijajan, n. A flashlight. Wakinyan tónwanpi, An electrical apparatus where sparks are seen, as an X-ray machine. Also, electric lights.

wakin'yela, n. The mourning dove. Its song: M...., m..... When she sounds this wail, children say: Hinyankaġa hoton welo, i.e. there is a ghost there. - s'e hupteptecela kaca, as is said of a person having a heavy body but short legs. - s'e cantku kin nisko nankin na, i.e. a broad chest. Bl.

waki'pa, v. (?). Bl.

wa'kipa, v. (akipa). To befall, happen, to have an accident. B.H.35.1; 58.5.

waki'pajin, v. (kipajin). To oppose; 1st pers. sing. of kipajin. Wawakipajin, waunkipajinpi.

wa'kipapi, n. An accident, casualty.
wa'kipaya, v.a. To cause one to have bad luck. B.H.106.4.

waki'pi, n. Robbery; spoiling.

waki'pika, adj. Roomy, as anything that can contain much. Bl.

waki'pśapśa, adv. Thick, close together. R. Bl.

waki'pta, v. pos. (wapta). To pare, cut off or trim one's own. Wawakipta.

waki'puskica, v. (kipuskica). To clap together and make fit or adhere by shaving. Wawakipuskica. -- wakipuskil, cont. of wakipuskica. - iyeya.

wakis', cont. of wakiza. - iyeya.

waki'scu, (?). Also, wakisca. He miye wawescu, i.e. this will be mine, let <u>me</u> shoot this bird, i.e. glonica. Bl.

waki'skiza, v. red. of wakiza.

waki'sku, v. pos. (wasku). To pare one's own, e.g. an apple or potato. Wawakisku.
waki'skusku, v. pos. (waskusku). To slice off one's own. Wawapasnon k'on waweskusku ktelo. Bl.

waki'sleca, v. pos. (wasleca). To split or rip e.g. a board or stick with a knife or saw. Wawakisleca. -- wakislesleca, v. red.

waki'śkita, v. pos. (waśkita). To cut across on one's own. Wawákiskita.
waki'śla, v. (waśla). To cut off and make bare, as in cutting one's own grass, with a knife. Wawakiśla. -- wakiślaśla, v. red.
waki'śpa, v. pos. (waśpa). To cut off a piece from one's own. Wawakiśpa. -- wakiśpaśpa, v. red.
waki'śpu, v. pos. (waśpu). To cut up one's own in pieces, as potatoes for planting. Wawakiśpu. -- wakiśpuśpu,

v. red. of wakiśpu.

waǩi'ś'ag, cont. of wakiś'aka.
waǩi'ś'agya, v.a. To make endure. Wakiś'agwaya.
waǩi'ś'aka, adj. Capable of endurance, strong to endure hardship or suffering; not easily exhausted or overcome, indefatigable. Wamakiś'aka, waniciś'aka.
waǩi'ś'ake, n. Strength.

wa'ǩita, v. (akita, which seems not to be used). To look out, watch. Wáwakita, wáuŋkitapi. Ipá k'el akaŋl iyotaka yo; hecoŋ na taŋyaŋ - yo. Bl. Pb.47.

waǩi'ṫaŋ, v. (kitaŋ). To insist upon; to persist in doing; 1st pers. sing. of kitaŋ. Wawakitaŋ. -- waǩiṫaŋǩa, n. One who insists upon.

waǩi'toŋtoŋǩa, v.n. To be frugal, economical. Wawakitoŋtoŋka. Le hokśila wakitoŋtoŋke lo. Cf. wagluhahaka. Also, one who is frugal etc., who saves everything, one who tries to save and have things, n.

waǩi'uŋyaŋ, v. To sacrifice or make an offering to one, to sacrifice one's own. Wawakiuŋyaŋ, waciciuŋya, waniciuŋya. Waic'iuŋye. Wawakiuŋmni kte. Wakaŋtaŋka cekiyapi na wakiuŋyaŋpi. Bl. Pb.12,43. Cf. wauŋyaŋ.

wa'ǩiya, v. To talk about, discuss; try e.g. a case in court. Wáwakiya.
wa'ǩiyapi, n. A trial.
wa'ǩiyaṫipi, n. A courthouse; a council house.

waǩi'yazaŋ, v. pos. (wayazaŋ). To become sick for one, as one's child. Wamakiyazaŋ, waniciyazaŋ.

waǩi'yela, Cf. wakiŋyela.

wa'ǩiye wica'śa, n. A lawyer.

waǩi'yuśe, v. (kiyuśe). To oppose, to hate. Wawakiyuśe.

waǩi'yuśǩa, v. (kiyuśka). To loosen, release; 1st pers. sing. of kiyuśka. Wawakiyuśka and wawakibluśka.

waǩi'yuśna, v.a. To drop for one, as bread for a dog; to sacrifice to, offer to in sacrifice. R. Wawákiyuśna.

waǩi'yuwanice, (?). Wakiyuwanicelaȟ, as is said perhaps of one who had nothing yet received much from others. Bl.

waǩi'yuza, v. (kiyuza). To gesture holding to or towards one, to hold up the pipe towards heaven etc., as the Dakotas did before smoking. Wawakiyuza.

waǩi'za, v.a. (kiza). To make a scraping, squeaking noise with a knife or saw. Wawakiza.

wako', n. A horse whose tail has been cut short. Also, waúŋjiŋca. Bl.

wako'gla, n. A gully, gulch, a ravine made by water.

waǩo'ǩiṗa, v. (kokipa). To be afraid, fearful. Wakowakipa.
waǩo'ǩiṗeǩicaǧa, v. To make afraid, frighten into a measure. Wakokipewecaga. B.H.128.4;174.2;223.3;282.7. -- waǩóǩiṗewicaǩicaȟ wawícaǩi, n. A hold-up man, a robber. B.H.223.3.
waǩo'ǩiṗeya, adv. Timidly. B.H.209.4.

waǩoŋ', v. (koŋ). To desire; 1st pers. sing. of koŋ.
waǩoŋ'la, v. To covet.

waǩoŋ'niyaŋ, v. To have done much, performed much. Wakoŋniwaya. Bl.
waǩoŋ'niyeya, v. To destroy everything. Bl.

waǩoŋ' s'e, (?). Wakoŋpi s'e naŋkapi, i.e. you are in good spirits. BT.

wakoŋ'ṫa, v.a. (koŋta). To dig out with a knife, to hollow or groove. Also, to wear out partly with a knife a rope, strap etc., i.e. making it weaker. Wawakoŋta. -- wakóŋtkoŋṫa, v. red. (wakoŋta). To make in grooves or ridges. Wawakoŋtkoŋta.

waǩoŋ'za, v. (koŋza). To influence, to determine, to decree; 1st pers. sing. of koŋza. Wawakoŋza. -- waǩóŋze. n. Influence.

waǩo'yagkicatoŋ, v. To clothe. B.H. 194.6.
waǩo'yagya, v. (koyagya). To put on, to clothe; to cause to put on. Wakoyagwaya.

wak̔o'yak̔a, v. (koyaka). To put on clothes. Wakoblaka, wakouŋyakapi.
wako'yak̔eca, n. One who puts on clothes one who dresses up. Wakomayakeca.

wakp̄a', n. A stream of water, a river. -- v.a. To cut off, cut from; to cut out or cut into. Wawakpa.

wakp̄a'la, n. A small stream, a creek.

wakp̄a'mni, v. (kpamni). To serve out one's own, to distribute; 1st pers. sing. of kpamni. Wawakpamni. Na hehaŋl yul wicaśi. Caŋke oyate kiŋ wakpamnipi na catewaśteya wotapi. -- wakp̄ámnipi, n. A distribution.

wakp̄aŋ, v.a. (kpaŋ). To cut up fine with a knife, e.g. tobacco. Wawakpaŋ. -- wakp̄áŋkp̄aŋ, v. red.

Wakp̄a' Śice, n. prop. The city of Pierre, S. D., named from the western tributary to the Missouri there.

wakpa'ťaŋk̔a, n. (kpataŋ). One who is economical.

wakp̄i', v.a. To cut open e.g. a nut with a knife; to crack with a knife. Wawakpi. -- wakp̄íkpi, v. red.

wakp̄i'cagla, adv. By the side of a stream. -- wakp̄ikp̄i, v. red. of wakpi.
wakp̄o'gna, adv. On the stream.
wakp̄o'pťa, adv. Across the stream.

wakp̄u'kp̄a, n. Dirt, dust, motes of dust. -- wakp̄úkp̄eca, n. Anything scattered about, dust.

waksa', v.a. (ksa). To cut off e.g. a stick with a knife or saw; to separate anything by cutting crosswise. Wawaksa. -- waksáksa, v. red. (waksa). To cut off in several places, cut in pieces with a knife or saw. Wawaksaksa. Na waŋna talo k'oŋ he haŋke - . Waŋsák - , To cut sticks for arrows. D.40.

wakśi', n. abbrev. (wakśica). A dish, pan, bowl, plate. - egle, yujaja, taŋka. B.H.207.10.

wakśi'ca, n. A dish, a bowl, a pan, a plate.
- blaska, A plate.
- ognake, A cupboard.
- op̄iye, A cupboard.

wakśi'ja, v.a. (kśija). To shut up e.g. a knife blade when in the act of cutting. Wawakśija.

wakśi'op̄iye, n. A cupboard. R. Bl.
waksi'skokp̄a, n. Soup plates, saucers.

wakśiś', cont. of wakśija. - iyeya.

wakśi'ťap̄ela, n. A flat plate.
wakśi'yatabla, n. A plate.

wa'kśu, v. (akśu). To pile on, load on, lay on. Wáwakśu. Bl.

wakśu', v. To make beadwork, do beading. Wawakśu. -- wakśúpi, n. Beadwork.

wakťa', 1) v. abs. To look out for, watch for, be on one's guard. Wawakta. 2) n. A sign, a mark. Zuya itaŋcaŋ kiŋ lila waktapi. Waktaśnil̔ca haŋl ite kiŋ cal̔li onapobyapi śke. D.219.
wakťa'k̔el, adv. On the look out for, guardedly, expecting it. D.12.

wakťaŋ', v.a. (ktaŋ). To make crooked by shaving. Wawaktaŋ. -- wakťáŋkťaŋ, v. red.

wakťa'ya, 1) v.a. To put on one's guard, to warn. Waktawaya, waktauŋyaŋpi. 2) adv. On one's guard, warily, prudently. -- wakťáyak̔el, adv. On the look out. - wauŋ. Bl.

wakťe', v. (kte). To kill, to have killed or scalped; to triumph. Wawakte. - hi, To come in triumph. - agli, They come home in triumph. - gli, They come home in triumph. - gla, ku, ki, etc. Wakte agli ca ite sabkiyapelo. D.9. B.H.88.16. Also, 1st pers. sing. of kte.
wakťe'agli, v. 3rd pers. pl. They return having killed enemies. Bl.
wakťe'ka, n. One who kills much.

wakťo'glag, cont. of waktoglaka.
wakťo'glagk̔iya, v.a. To cause to tell how many scalps one has taken. Waktoglagwakiya.
wakťo'glak̔a, v. pos. (wakte-oglaka). To tell over one's own war-like exploits, tell how many scalps one has helped to take. Waktowaglaka.
wakťo'k̔iciyak̔a, v. (wakte-okiciyaka). To tell to one the war-like deeds of another for him. Waktoweciyaka.
wakťo'kiyaka, v. (wakte-okiyaka). To

tell one of war-like exploits. Waktowakiyaka.
waktoʹyaka, v. (wakte-oyaka). To tell what one has done in killing enemies. Waktoblaka.

wakuʹkiye, v. (wakte-ukiye). To come in triumph. -- n. A triumph celebration. Yuŋkaŋ - el oyate kiŋ David tawicoh'aŋ kiŋ nah'oŋpi. B.H.88.1.

wakuʹni, (?). Maka ohiŋniyaŋ lila - yelo. MS.649. Cf. wakoŋniyaŋ.

wakuŋʹza, Cf. wakoŋza.

wakuʹte, v. abs. (kute). To shoot, to be shooting; 1st pers. sing. of kute. Wawakute. Miyeśtuka wawakute kte. - oŋspekiya. D.71.
wakuʹtepi, n. A shooting.

wakuʹwa, v. (kuwa). To hunt, hunt for furs; 1st pers. sing. of kuwa. Wawakuwa. Na waŋna - na lila cepa waŋ o keya. Also, a manager. P.
wakuʹwapi, n. Hunting e.g. furs.

wak'aʹ, v. (k'a). To dig; 1st pers. sing. of k'a. Wawak'a.

wak'eʹġa, v. To butcher. Kohaŋ - yo, Hurry up to butcher. Also, to choke or strangle. Bl.

wak'esʹya, part. Cutting off. - aya, To strip off clean e.g. meat from bones. - abla.

wak'eʹza, v. (k'eza). To smooth over by shaving. Wawak'eza.

wak'iŋʹ, v. (k'iŋ). To pack, carry on one's back; 1st pers. sing. of k'iŋ. Wawak'iŋ. B.H.298.4. -- n. A pack, a burden; luggage, baggage. Yuŋkaŋ - k'oŋ ena pahpa ekignaka na akaŋl iyotaka. - yuha yaŋkapi. D.251.
wak'iŋʹkiya, v.a. To cause to pack or carry, i.e. on the back, as a horse.
wak'iŋʹk'iŋla s'e, n. Something like a pack, i.e. a square or cube.
wak'iŋʹlas'e, n. Same as wak'iŋk'iŋla s'e.
wak'iŋʹpi, n. A burden, a pack.

wak'uʹ, v. (k'u). To give; 1st pers. sing. of k'u. Wawak'u. Wakaŋtaŋka wawicak'u kiŋ he mazaska oŋ opetoŋpica kecani. B.H.287.6.

wal, cont. of wata. A boat.

walaʹ, v. (la). To ask, beg. Wawala. B.H.98.14. Cf. wakila.
walaʹkel, adv. Begging. - yaŋkahe. B.H.236.2.

walaʹkotaśni, adj. Not caring, having no regard for one's own people, as Indians for Indians. Walamakotaśni. Ite - , in ref. to an angry face. Cf. olakolwicayeśni.

walaʹla, v. red. of wala.
walaʹlaka, n. A beggar. Wawalalaka.

walceʹte, n. The bottom or keel of a boat.

waleʹġa, n. The bladder.
waleʹġa miniyaye, n. A bladder to carry water in. Bl.

waleʹhaŋ, adv. By this time. Also, walehaŋl. B.H.37.9.
waleʹhaŋtu, adv. At this time. Waŋyaŋg omani po; - ca śuŋkawakaŋ huŋkeśni oh'aŋkapelo. Bl.

waleʹlepa, v. red. (walepa). To cut rounded notches e.g. on a feather. Bl. Cf. waśkiśkita.

walheʹktab, cont. (walhektapa). At the stern.
walheʹktapa, n. The stern of a boat.
walheʹktapataŋhaŋ, n. The stern of a boat; at the stern, adv.

waliʹta, adj. Brave. Wamalita.
waliʹtagya, adv. Bravely. - kipajiŋ.
waliʹtake, adj. Brave, active and courageous. Also, iyuśkiŋyaŋ śkaŋ. Wamalitake. Walitakelo. Bl.
waliʹtaya, adv. Actively, bravely together with others. - śkaŋ. Syn.- waś'agya. Note: this is said to be a Sissiton word.

waloʹgnaka, n. (?).
waloʹh'egnaka, n. A cow bladder, used in times past like the paper bags of today. Bl.
walōʹlobya, v.a. To boil until tender, to over-boil and thereby turn things into mush or meat, beans etc. Walolobwaya. D.54.
walōʹlopela, n. Slush, half-molten snow.

walo'ogna, n. A bag to keep dried meat in.

walō'ṗela, n. Meat, beans etc. overboiled and mush-like. Lhb. Cf. walolopela.

walo'ṫeṫeke, n. (loté). One who is hungry often, is fond of food. Wamaloteteke. Bl. Inaȟni uŋglapi k'uŋ - . Wamaloteteke caś slolyaye c'uŋ (caś: ca emph.). D.12.

wa'lowaŋ, v. abs. Cf. olowaŋ.
wa'lowaŋpi, n. The huŋkalowaŋpi. Bl. BD. A rite by which we establish a relationship on earth, which is a reflection of that real relationship which always exists between man and Wakaŋtaŋka; one of the seven Sioux religious rites. BR.101.

walpa', n. The bow of a boat.
walsiŋ'ṫe, n. A steering oar, the helm, the rudder of a boat.
walsiŋ'ṫe yuhomni, 1) v. To pilot or steer a boat of any kind. 2) n. A helmsman.
waltu'cuhu, n. The ribs of a boat.

walul'ya, v. (lulya). To dye red or scarlet. Walulwaya.
walul'ye, n. A dyer of scarlet.

walu'ṗi śni, n. Something that is still whole, intact, where nothing has been cut off as yet, as fresh ham etc. Walupi śni waŋji ikikcu wo. Bl. Cf. yulupi śni.

wal'i'caśke, n. An anchor. - eȟpeya, To cast anchor.
wal'i'caśpe, n. A tool for hollowing out a canoe.
wal'i'ṫoṗe, n. An oar, a paddle.

wal'i'yaciŋ, v.a. To adopt a child in place of one that died, because it has the same looks and features; an old custom among the Indian peoples. Such children will receive goods but not real estate. Wal'iblaciŋ. D.269.

wal'i'yoṗeya, v.a. To accuse one of doing what another has done. Wal'iyopewaya.

wal'i'yowalya, v. To let someone else do what one was supposed to do; to excuse one's self. Wal'iyowalwaya.

wal'o'ihuni, n. A boat landing. Also, wal'óinajiŋ.

wama' el i, (?). Wama el ipi s'e, as is said of a flock of birds in confusion and making a great noise. Bl.

wama'heṫuyaḱel, adv. By one's self. - ecoŋ, oyaka, To do or say something great without advice from anybody.

wama'ka maniśni, adv. Suddenly and without being noticed, not having one's footsteps heard. - hi. - tehaŋ yahi so? - tak eya, He said something that was not expected, and hence ceases doubts. Bc. OS.

wama'ḱaśḱaŋ, n. The generic word for the animal kingdom; all things that move (śkaŋ) upon the earth (maka); creeping things.
wama'ḱaśḱaŋ s'e, adv. Brutally, like wild animals.

wama'ka ṫehaŋṫulaḱe s'e, adv. From afar. - yahi. BS.

wama'ḱinoŋ, v. (makinoŋ). To steal from one. Wamawakinoŋ.

wama'ḱognaka, n. The contents of the world, the whole of creation; Creation. R. Bl.

wama'nika, n. (?). Wicaśa - , i.e. a man who visits or sees people much, but not to pass the time, but for business of any kind; one who does not loaf. UW. - oyamani hwo? You came alone? - agli yelo. Bl.

wama'noŋ, v. (manoŋ). To steal. Wamawanoŋ, wamauŋnoŋpi.
wama'noŋpi, n. Stealing, theft.
wama'noŋs'a, n. A thief.

wama'yal, adv. (wamayata). Toward a bank (mayá). - i s'e yaŋkapi, as is said when a meeting is full of much talking by many present at once, and ref. is made to a bank where there come echoes.

wa'mini, n. Snow-water.

wamna', v.a. To rip e.g. a seam with a knife. Wawamna.

wamna'ic'ila, v. refl. (wamnala). To be proud, to think much of one's own abilities. Wamnamic'ila. -- wamná-ic'ilapi, n. Pride.

wamna'la, v.a. To honor, respect, fear; to consider brave or energetic; to think little of one. Bl.

wamna'mna, v. red. of wamna.

wamna'yaᶯ, 1) v. (mnayaᶯ). To gather, collect. Wamnawaya, wamnauᶯyaᶯpi. 2) n. A collector. -- wamnáyaᶯpi, n. A gathering; a collection. -- wamnáye-kiya, v. To take up a collection for.

wamni', v. (mni). To dry by spreading out e.g. shelled corn; 1st pers. sing. of mni. Wawamni.

wamni'akaśtaᶯ, 1) n. One who baptizes. John Baptist, - . B.H.172.1. 2) v. To baptize. Wamniawakaśtaᶯ. B.H.176.8

wa'mnimni, v. (amnimni). To sprinkle; one who sprinkles, n. Wáwamnimni.

wamni'omni, n. A whirlwind, a hurricane; a whirlpool; a small worm or puppa, a caccoon. Bl. D.218.

wamni'pi, n. (wamni). Fruit etc. spread out thinly.

wamni'ťu, n. A whale. Also, a hippopotamus.

wamnu'ȟ'a, n. A small shell called a cowry and used for an ornament on dresses. - cuwignaka. -- wamnúȟ'ala, n. dim. of wamnuȟ'a.

wamuᶯ'lmuᶯťa, adj. red. (wamuᶯta). Cf. wamuᶯta. Si kiᶯ - , as is said when the nails are off a birds foot. Bl.

wamuᶯ'ťa, adj. Short a nd rounded off when it should be long, as a horse's tail. Śuᶯkawakaᶯ waᶯ siᶯte - . WE. -- n. An ear of corn well filled and flat at the end. R.

wana', adv. Now, already. Also, waᶯná.

wana'blaska, v. (nablaska). To flatten with the foot. Wanawablaska.
wana'blaya, v. (nablaya). To spread out with the feet. Wanawablaya.
wana'blaza, v. (nablaza). To burst open.
wana'bleca, v. (nableca). To break in pieces with the foot. Wanawableca.

wa'nabu, v. (anabu). To make a drumming noise with the foot on the ground drum the foot on the ground. Wanawabu. -- wánabubu, v. red.

wana'caᶯcaᶯ, v. (nacaᶯcaᶯ). To shake with the foot. Wanawacaᶯcaᶯ.
wana'cekceka, v. (nacekceka). To make stagger by kicking. Wanawacekceka.
wana'ceya, v. (naceya). To kick and make cry. Wanawaceya. -- wanáceyes'a, n. One who kicks and makes cry.

wana'ġi, n. (nagi). The soul when separated from the body; a ghost, the spirits of the departed; a shadow. - okaśke, Purgatory.
wana'ġi ktepi, n. A disease consisting in the distortion of the face to one side; a stroke.
wana'ġitacaᶯku, n. The Milky Way.
wana'ġitaȟimimila, n. A miller or moth. Bl.
wana'ġitamaȟoce, n. The world of spirits.
wana'ġitaśośa, n. A ghost spittle, a kind of exudative found around some plants; cuckoo-spittle; heavy dew.
wana'ġi tiᶯpsila, n. The prairie larkspur. Delphinium virescens. The crowfoot family. Bl. #180.
wana'ġitipi, n. The house of spirits, the abode of the dead; Hades.
wana'ġiya, v.n. To go to the spirit land.
wana'ġiyaťa, adv. In the land of spirits. - i, To go to the spirit land, an expression used at the time of the Ghost Dance.

wana'ġiyeya, v. (nagiyeya). To annoy, trouble, vex. Wanagiyewaya.

wana'gmuᶯ, v. (nagmuᶯ). To curl or twist.

wana'gna, v. To kick off e.g. fruit from a bush. Wanawagna.

wa'nagnaᶯka, Cf. wanagnuᶯka.

wana'gnayaᶯ, v. To slip, slide; to deceive. -- wanágnaye, n. A slipping, a deception.

wana'gnuᶯka, wana'gnaᶯke, (?). - śni s'e tak eyé, i.e. he does not tell the truth. RF.

wa'nagoptaᶯ, (?). Wánagoptaᶯpi c'oᶯ caká na ṗúsyemáyelo. Bl.

wana'goptaŋ śica, n. One hard to advise, a heedless person. Bl.

wana'ğuka, v. (naguka). To sprain. Wanawağuka.

wana'gwagiyeya, v. (nagwaka). To kick awaya, kick out the foot.
wana'gwaka, v. (nagwaka). To kick out the foot.

wana'hiŋl, cont. (nahiŋta). - iyeya, To scrape away with the foot. Bl.
wana'hiŋta, v. (nahiŋta). To scrape off with the foot. Wanawahiŋta.

wana'hoho, v. (nahoho). To make loose with the foot. Wanawahoho.
wana'homni, v. (nahomni). To turn round with the foot. Wanawahomni.
wana'hotoŋ, v. (nahotoŋ). To cause to make a noise by kicking. Wanawahotoŋ.
wana'huŋhuŋza, v. (nahuŋhuŋza). To shake with the foot. Wanawahuŋhuŋza.
wana'ȟapa, v. (naȟapa). To scare away by walking; one who frightens game, n. Wanawaȟapa.

wana'ȟca, n. Flowers, esp. cultivated flowers. -- wanáȟca totó, n. Same as caŋȟlogaŋ ȟlaȟla. BN. #157.

wana'ȟci, v. (nahci). To break out a piece with the foot; to break out a piece e.g. from a horse's hoof.

wana'ȟeyaṫa, v. (naȟeyata). To kick out of the way. - iyeya. R. Bl.
wana'ȟica, v. (naȟica). To waken up with the foot. Wanawaȟica.
wana'ȟla, v. (naȟla). To rattle with the foot. Wanawaȟla.
wana'ȟlata, v. (naȟlata). To scratch with the foot; one who scratches with the foot, as a cat. Wanawaȟlata.
wana'ȟleca, v. (naȟleca). To tear with the foot; one who tears, n. Wanawaȟleca.
wana'ȟloka, v. (naȟloka). To wear holes in the feet by means of something. Wanawaȟloka.

wana'ȟma, v. (naȟma). To conceal. Wanawaȟma, or wawanaȟma.
wa'naȟma, v. (anaȟma). To conceal; to deny a charge. Wawánaȟma, or possibly wánawaȟma.

wana'ȟṗa, v. (naȟpa). To knock or shake down, as one may do by walking on an upper floor. Wanawaȟpa.

wa'naȟpa, v. To kick or cast about snow with the feet, as buffalo and horses do.

wana'ȟṗu, v. (naȟpu). To kick off pieces.
wana'ȟtagya, v. (naȟtaka). To typewrite. Wanaȟtagwaya.
wana'ȟṫaḱa, v. (naȟtaka). To be in the habit of kicking. Wanawaȟtaka.

wana'ȟ'oŋ, 1) v. (nah'oŋ). To hear, hearken, obey. Wanawaȟ'oŋ. Cf. anagoptaŋ. 2) adj. Hearkening, obedient.
wana'ȟ'oŋpi, n. The act of listening, hearkening.
wana'ȟ'oŋśni, v. To be disobedient. Wanawaȟ'oŋśni.
wana'ȟ'oŋśniyaŋ, adv. Heedlessly.

wana'ic'iȟma, n. One who conceals himself, a hypocrite.

wana'iyeya, v. To kick down with the foot, to kick aside. Also, wanahaiyeya.

wana'jaja, v. (najaja). To wash by boiling, as clothing. -- wanájajaya, v.a. To cause to wash out or come clean by boiling. Wanajajawaya.

wana'jica, n. A run-away; a truant. P. Bl.

wana'jiṗa, v. (najipa). To pinch or scratch with the toes. Wanawajipa.
wana'juju, v. (najuju). To kick down, kick to pieces; one who kicks to pieces, n. Wanawajuju.
wana'kaḱa, v. (nakaka). To make rattle with the foot e.g. icicles, stiff hides etc. Wanawakaka. -- wanákakaḱa, v. red.

wana'kaŋyaŋ, v. (nakaŋ). To thresh e.g. wheat.

wana'ḱatiŋ, v. (nakatiŋ). To stretch out with the foot. Wanawakatiŋ.

wa'nakiȟma, v. (anakiȟma). To conceal. Wánawakiȟma.
wa'naḱiȟmaŋpi, n. Hypocrites.

wa'naḱikśiŋ, v. (anakikśiŋ). To interpose and defend one by taking his place in danger. Wánawekśiŋ, wanamikśiŋ.

wana'koḱa, v. (nakoka). To rattle with

the foot. Wanawakoka.
wana'ksa, v. (naksa). To break off with the foot. Wanawaksa. -- wanáksaksa, v. red.

wana'kseya, v. To mow grass, harvest grain. B.H.201.14. -- wanákseye, n. One who cuts grain. B.H.201.14.

wana'kśija, v. (nakśija). To double up with the foot. Wanawakśija.
wana'kťaŋ, v. (naktaŋ). To bend with the foot. Wanawaktaŋ.
wana'kuka, v. (nakuka). To wear out with the feet. Wanawakuka.
wana'kukeca, n. One who wears out moccasins badly.
wana'mna, v. (namna). To rip with the foot, as moccasins. Wanawamna.
wana'mnaka, n. One who rips his moccasins much.
wana'oȟƥa, v. (naoȟpa). To break into with the feet. Wanawaoȟpa.
wana'oksa, v. (naoksa). To break through, as through ice in killing muskrats. Wanawaoksa.
wana'okťaŋ, v. (naoktaŋ). To bend into with the foot. Wanawaoktaŋ.
wana'ot'iŋza, v. (naot'iŋza). To tread in tight. Wanawaot'iŋza.

wana'pa, v. (napa). To flee. Wanawapa.

wana'paŋ, v. (napaŋ). To crush out with the feet, tread out. Wanawapaŋ. R. Bl. -- wanápaŋpaŋ, v. (napaŋpaŋ). To make soft by treading. Wanawapaŋpaŋ.

wana'pca, v. (napca). To swallow. Also perhaps, the general word for eating. Wanawapca. - iyeya. Oyaŋke waŋji wakaȟnigiŋ na hel wakaŋheja taŋyaŋ iśtiŋmapi na taŋyaŋ wanapcapi kte lo, the saying of Sitting Bull. - yuha kte, Will have something to live on. MS.540.

wana'ƥe icage yuha, v. To have power over all, to be feared by all. Also, wanáƥicageyuza. R. BD.

wana'ƥeya, v. To drive off, cause to flee; one who makes flee, n. Wanapewaya.

wana'ƥiċaġe, n. (?). - yuha, as is said of an angry person who bosses everybody while the rest remain quiet. LC. Syn.- wauŋkec'ila.

wana'ƥiśkaŋyaŋ, v. To play with, as children do with toys; to exhibit, perform, as in a circus.

wana'ƥiśťaŋyaŋ, v. (napiśtaŋyaŋ). To destroy or injure everything.

wana'pobya, 1) v. To cause to burst. Wanapobwaya. 2) n. Fire-crackers.

wana'ƥognaka, v. To put or hold in the hands.

wana'ƥoȟya, v. (napoȟya). To leaven, cause to rise. Wanapoȟwaya. -- wanáƥoȟyapi, n. A balloon.

wana'poƥa, v. (napopa). To burst.

wana'ƥoťa, v. (napota). To wear out with the feet. Wanawapota.
wana'ƥoťeca, n. One who wears out with the feet. Wanawapoteca.
wana'psaka, v. (napsaka). To break e.g. a string with the foot. Wanawapsaka.
wana'psoŋ, v. (napsoŋ). To spill by kicking, to kick over. Wanawapsoŋ.

wana'ptoŋka, n. A restless person. Syn.- wosloton śni, śkaŋśkaŋ waśicuŋ. Rl.

wana'pťuja, v. (naptuja). To split or crack.

wana'p'iŋ, n. A medal; a necklace of beads; and handkerchief; anything worn around the neck, a comforter etc.
- blaska, A necklace of beads interwoven.
- kicatoŋ, v.a. To put on as a wanap'iŋ; to cause to wear a necklace etc. Wanap'iŋwecatoŋ.

wana'p'iŋya, v.a. To have or use for a wanap'iŋ. Wanap'iŋwaya.

wana'sa, v. (nasa). To hunt by surrounding and shooting e.g. buffalo; to chase buffalo. Wanawasa, wanauŋsapi. Tohaŋl pte ota ca wanasapi. Maka kiŋ taŋiŋśniyaŋ owaŋjila yuŋka śkelo (fall of buffalos) ca ikaŋyela euŋtipi na akaśpa icu wanauŋsapi kte lo. Bl.
wana'sapi, n. The buffalo chase.
wana'seya, v. To go on a buffalo hunt; to make a surround.

wa'naslata, v. (anaslata). To crawl up to. Wánawaslata.

wana'sleca, v. (nasleca). To split light things.

wana'sna, v. (nasna). To make ring with the feet. Wanawasna.

wana'sni, v. (nasni). To trample out e.g. fire.

wanaś', adv. emph. of waná.

wana'śapa, v. (naśapa). To defile with the feet. Wanawaśapa.
wana'śeca, v. (naśeca). To trample and make dry, as grass. Wanawaśeca.
wana'śica, v. (naśica). To injure with the feet. Wanawaśica.
wana'śipa, v. (naśipa). To break off with the feet. Wanawaśipa.
wana'śkica, v. (naśkica). To press with the foot; one who presses with the foot, n. Wanawaśkica.

wana'śkiśkilya, v. To ruffle, as a dress.

wana'śla, v. (naśla). To make bare with the feet.

wana'śleca, v. (naśleca). To split heavy things and with effort.

wana'ślogya, v. To hull corn, i.e. with ashes as the old Indians did; to make hominy. Wanaślogwaya. Wagmeza cahota oᶯ wanaślogyapi. Cf. catanaślogya.

wana'śloka, v. (naśloka). To pull off e.g. pantaloons. Wanawaśloka.

wana'śnija, v. (naśnija). To trample down e.g. grass and make wither. Wanawaśnija.

wana'śośa, v. (naśośa). To foul e.g. water with the feet. Wanawaśośa.
wana'śpa, v. (naśpa). To break off with the feet. Wanawaśpa.
wana'śpu, v. (naśpu). To break off, as in trampling on pumpkins. Wanawaśpu.
wana'śuja, v. (naśuja). To bruise with the feet. Wanawaśuja.

wana'taka, v. (nataka). To fasten up. Wanawataka.

wa'nataᶯ, v. (anataᶯ). To run upon, to attack. Wánawataᶯ.

wana'tepa, v. (natepa). To wear off short with the foot. Wanawatepa.
wana'tica, v. (natica). To scrape away e.g. snow; to paw, as does a horse. Wanawatica.

wana'tipa, v. (natipa). To cramp.

wana'titaᶯ, v. (natitaᶯ). To pull or push against. Wanawatitaᶯ.

wana'tuka, v. (natuka). To stamp to pieces e.g. furs; one who destroys by stamping, n. Wanawatuka.

wana't'a, v. (nat'a). To kick to death. Wanawat'a.

wana'uᶯgya, v. To scare away e.g. game by one's coming near. Bl.

wana'uᶯka, v. (nauᶯka). To kick and make fall down; to start off on the gallop, as a herd of buffalo.

wana'wega, v. (nawega). To break with the foot. Wanawawega.
wana'wiᶯja, v. (nawiᶯja). To bend down with the foot e.g. grass. Wanawawiᶯja.

wani', v.a. To shake in cutting, as jelly; to cut off e.g. the fastenings of a skin stretched out; to rip. Wawani.

wani'ca, adj. (nica). None, without any. Manica, ninica, uᶯnicapi.

wani'cokaᶯ wi, n. The mid-winter moon, December. -- wanícokaᶯyaᶯ, n. The mid-winter.

wani'gla, v. To go home on account of the winter, go south as do birds. Piśko ca - s'e uᶯglahaᶯpi, as is said when one's horses or cattle cannot make head-way, being too slow. The night larks do much travelling, but it stays in the same place while other birds go on fast. The same is true when they begin to leave for the south. RA.

wani'gnica, adj. red. of wanica.

wani'haᶯ, n. Last winter. Last summer, blokéhaᶯ.

wani'heyuᶯka, n. Winter frost, when

winter-time begins. - iwahuⁿni. Cf. ȟeyúⁿka, aȟéyuⁿka.

wani'ƙiya, 1) v. (nikiya). To save, to cause to live. Waniwakiya. Pb.45. 2) n. One who makes live; a savior. Wanikiye, The Savior.

wa'nik'ala, n. A very little. R. Wana - ihelo, i.e. very little left. Bl.

wanil', cont. of wanica. Owihaⁿke -, Endless. - aya, To die out, become extinct.

wani'ni, v. red. of wani.

wani'ṫi, v. To spend the winter, to winter. -- waniṫipi, n. A winter encampment.
wani'uⁿ, v. To winter, spend the winter.

wani'yaⁿ, v. (niyaⁿ). To cause to live. Waniwaya.
wani'yaⁿpi, n. Domestic animals. Also, waniyaⁿṗiṗi.

wani'yeṫu, n. Winter; a year. -- wani'yeṫu wi, The winter moon, November.
wani'yeṫu oƙiśaṗa, n. An open winter, i.e. little snow here and there. Bl.

wanoⁿ'ȟkaṫiyece, v. (noⁿȟkatiyece). To hear the buzzing of things, suddenly catch sound of. Bl.

wanu'ȟci, adv. All of a sudden. Uⁿgnahela kapi. BT. Cf. Waⁿna.

wanuⁿ', adv. By chance, accidentally. Also perhaps, wanuⁿ kta śni. - ecoⁿ, To do by accident, as killing, not purposely. Wanúⁿ kta śni epe, I did not mean it.
wanuⁿ'ȟci, adv. By accident. R. Bl.
wanuⁿ'ƙeca, v. To escape. An old word. - gle lo. BT.
wanuⁿ'ƙel, adv. Accidentally.
wanuⁿ'kta śni, adv. Not purposely. - epe, I did not mean it.
wanuⁿ'ṫokaheya, adv. Prudently. An old word. Waktaye eyapi. - lena hepa.

wanuⁿ'ṫokakayaƙel, adv. red. of wanuⁿtokayakel, having ref. to more than one thing. Ten dollars - bluśpuśpu, i.e. to use it for any emergency in any way not known as yet; or, as in taking more blankets along than one needs, thinking that one might need them. - wauⁿ, i.e. I am waiting, looking for one, watching for one. Bl.
wanuⁿ'ṫoƙayaƙel, adv. For any emergency. Akaⁿ ogle waⁿ - yuha mni kte lo, as in the summertime one takes a heavy overcoat along. Bc.

wanuⁿ'waa'ṫayela, v. To strike it well by chance. Bl.

wanuⁿ'wakipa, v. To have bad luck or a bad accident. Bl.
wanuⁿ'woakipa, n. An accident.

waⁿ, interj. An introductory expletive. Why! Look! See! Waⁿ! hokśila waⁿ tokiyataⁿ waohola śni yahi yelo. B.H.123.5. Hoȟ, waⁿ, kola, nikuⁿśi ...waȟtemalaśni. Waⁿ! kakiya ka Ikto wak'iⁿ na hiyaye. D.97,20,78. Cf. Gramm.266-7.

waⁿ ka waⁿ, exclam. Of surprise when seeing something at a distance.
waⁿ le waⁿ, exclam. Of surprise when seeing something nearby. It is used by men. Bl. Cf. maⁿ, le maⁿ, which is that used by women.

waⁿ, n. cont. (waⁿhiⁿkpe or wahiⁿkpe). An arrow. Waⁿju, A quiver. Na śuⁿkawakaⁿ tawa waⁿ-yamniyaⁿpi naiⁿś waⁿ-nuⁿpayaⁿpi. Waⁿ oⁿ o. Waⁿ oⁿ t'eya. Waⁿtaⁿyeya.

waⁿ, art. indef. A, an. This applies to the modification of its own substantive word, or even the whole sentence. Nic'iya yo waⁿ, Save yourself, why don't you? Niuⁿyaⁿpi ye waⁿ. Teȟislolyiⁿ kta waⁿ ikicihuⁿni, i.e. a time of suffering. Mnilatke ciⁿhaⁿ mayaluśnakte lo waⁿ. Ma, zuya hila seca waⁿ, It is possible he has really come to war. Kola, waⁿ, taⁿka s'e mak'u ye waⁿ, Friend, give me a larger portion. D.97,78,33. B.H.98.14;182.21; 183.7;248.21;266.4;267.4;294.4. Cf. Gramm.328-9.

waⁿa'payapi, n. An arrow that hits and sticks in the wound. A.

waⁿbli', n. The royal war eagle. - gleśka. The Indians knew of four kinds of eagles: waⁿbli gleśka, anuⁿkiyaⁿ, anuⁿkasaⁿ, and the common eagle ȟuyá.
waⁿbli'gleśka, n. The spotted eagle. Also, n. prop. The epitome of powers

of the north. - s'e iśta blezelo, as is said of a man with sharp eyes. Bl.

waᶯbli'tahe'ya, n. The American goldfinch.

waᶯblu'p̂i, n. (waᶯbli-upi). Eagle-tail feathers.

waᶯ'ċa, num. adj. or adv. Once.
waᶯ'caeś, adv. At once.
waᶯ'cag, adv. At once. - wicakuwapi.
waᶯ'cagcala, adv. (waᶯcala). A few times; now and then once, once a piece. R. Bl.
waᶯ'cagna, adv. At once, immediately. B.H.147.5. D.105.
waᶯ'caȟci, adv. Just once, for once, at least once. - he bluha kte, as a man would say as he grabbed for something whereas others received plenty and he got nothing. Ho (iṫo) - Ikto wawapilaya śke. D.5.
waᶯ'cakcala, adv. Once a piece, seldom, a few times. P.
waᶯ'cakeś, adv. At once. Hokśila kiᶯ he ayaupi śni ehaᶯtaᶯś, - yaupi kte śni. B.H.36.5.
waᶯ'cala, adv. Only once.
waᶯ'caleśa, adv. (waᶯcala-eśa). At least once. - ecamoᶯ kta.
waᶯ'cayeś, Same as waᶯcaeś.

waᶯ'ċi, adj. One, used in counting.

waᶯgla'ka, v. pos. (waᶯyaᶯka). To see one's own. Waᶯwaglaka.

waᶯ'glegleġa, n. The bull snake.

waᶯhi', n. (waᶯ-hi). A flint, flints, so called perhaps from the fact that arrow-heads were formerly made from flint stone. R.

waᶯhiᶯ'kpe, Cf. wahiᶯkpe.

waᶯhi' ośtaᶯpi, n. The kind of gun once distributed at the wakpamni taᶯka with which no caps as yet were used but only powder. Bl.

waᶯi'glaka, v. refl. (waᶯyaᶯka). To look at one's self. Waᶯmiglaka, waᶯuᶯkiglakapi.

waᶯi'pame, n. A tool, i.e. two rocks each with a groove to match the other and by which arrows were made round and smooth by drawing the tool to and fro.

waᶯ'iyaȟpeya, v.a. To shoot arrows.
waᶯi'yuġola, n. (waᶯyugo). An instrument for the making of crooked lines on arrows.
waᶯ'iyuk̇eze, n. An instrument for making arrows.

waᶯji', num. adj. One.
waᶯji'ca, 1) adj. One. 2) adv. In one way. Hecetu - , In the same state, without change.
waᶯji'gji, adj. red. (waᶯji). One a piece, each one one; some. Taȟca - ataya k'iᶯpi. B.H.115.15;235.11.
waᶯji'gjila, adj. red. (waᶯjila). One by one, singly; one a piece. Oyasiᶯ - tima yaupi kte lo ca tohaᶯl cicopi ca u po.
waᶯji'la, num. adj. One. Wawáᶯjila. Waᶯjipila, They are one.
waᶯji'laȟel, adv. In one manner. Also, waᶯji, adj. B.H.32.3.
waᶯji'laȟiya, adv. In one way.

waᶯji'lak'iᶯ, n. A body cart with two wheels.

waᶯji'ni, pron. None. Hopo, - uᶯyaᶯ napapi śni po.

waᶯji'ṫokṫok, adv. One after the other, by turns. - ecoᶯpi. B.H.159.7.

waᶯ'ju, n. A quiver. - puṫe, The lower end of a quiver where it is sewed together, giving the appearance of lips. Bl.

waᶯk̇ab', adv. (waᶯkapa). Above. Miwaᶯkab. Na wi - u kiᶯ hehaᶯ śuᶯkawakaᶯ ota wicawaki yelo. BT. Wicaśa waᶯ ataya ska igluza ca miwaᶯkab hinajiᶯ. MS.645,355.

waᶯka'ġa, v.a. To make arrows. Waᶯwakaga. -- waᶯkáȟ, v. abbrev. of waᶯkaga. - wicaśipi. - wayupika, Skillful in making arrows. Bl.

waᶯk̇al', adv. Above, up high. - otkeyapi. Le lowaᶯpi kiᶯ oyasiᶯ - etoᶯwaᶯ po.

waᶯka'la, adj. Weak, tender, soft; brittle, easily broken or torn. Mawaᶯkala.

waᶯk̇al'k̇aṫuya, adv. High. Cuᶯkaśke - haᶯ. B.H.72.2.

waᶯk̇al'ṫipi, n. An upper room, upstairs.

waŋȟal'tȟiya, adv. Upwards; uphill. P. - yugal najiŋ na hoyeya.

waŋȟa'p̄a, A word not used. Cf. waŋkab.
waŋȟa'paya, adv. High up, in a high position. Tuwa ehakela ȟci eyaś - uŋ kte. BT. Taakicita itaŋcaŋ waŋkapayehce kiŋ kico. B.H.92.27.
waŋȟa'ṫahaŋ, adv. From above.
waŋȟa'ṫaȟiya, adv. High upwards. - kigla. Na waŋna wahiŋkpe kiŋ - iyeya.
waŋȟa'ṫaṫaŋhaŋ, adv. From above. Miyeś waŋkatataŋhaŋ wahi yelo.
waŋȟa'ṫȟiya, adv. Upward.

waŋȟa'ṫu, adv. Up above, high up.
waŋȟa'ṫuya, adv. High up. Wahiŋkpe kiŋ taŋwaŋkatuya ya. Also, waŋȟáṫuyaȟel.

waŋȟa'yeic'iya, v. refl. of waŋkayeya. Bl.
waŋȟa'yekiciya ecoŋpi, n. A pastime for children. Bl.

waŋ'kayela, adv. Loose, free to turn.

waŋȟa'yeya, v. To throw something high up, e.g. a ball. Waŋkayewaya. Wicaśa kiŋ keya icu na tice etkiya - .

waŋȟi'ciyaŋȟapi, 1) v. recip. (waŋyaŋka). To see each other. 2) n. A visit.

waŋ'ȟip̄aksa, n. A lizzard that can separate off its tail, a four-legged creature. Bl.
waŋ'ȟipaksela, n. A small lizzard. BH.

waŋk'e'ya, interj. It is used when one sees something done in the wrong way; or when one says things but does not do them. TT. BT. It means something like: But the fact is; it is ridiculous. - , miyeȟca ca pte kiŋ hena wicawao welo, Why, the fact is that it is I who shoot all the game. D.114. B.H.108.5;188.15;279.7. The word is a men's word.

waŋli'la, interj. Of surprise at the great quantity or quality of things. TT.

waŋ'lwaŋcala, adv. red. of waŋcala. - oie waśteśte, For once he spoke right. Bl.
waŋlwaŋ'lwaŋcaśniyaŋ, adv. Many different articles but all of one kind, as differently shaped pipes. - yuké.

waŋna', adv. Now, already.

waŋnuŋ'p̄aya, v. To hit something e.g. game with two arrows. Waŋnuŋpawaye.
waŋo'ṫaya, v. To hit one with arrows in many places. Bl.

waŋ' ouŋpapis'e ocáŋku, n. A road as straight as an arrow. BT.

waŋsa'ȟa, n. Arrows before they are ready to be used, i.e. dry sticks cut to size etc. Waŋsák-waksaksa hiyaye. D.40. Wakiŋyaŋ hotoŋpi śni k'el waŋsak'kaksa uŋyaŋpi ktelo. Bl.

waŋtaŋ'yeya, v. To be skillfu in shooting. Waŋtaŋyewaya. -- waŋṫáŋyeyela, n. One who shoots (arrows) well. B.H. 19.5. Cf. MS.97.

waŋ'to, n. The blue racer snake.

waŋwaŋ'ca śni, adj. Uneven as to size, or to kind, character etc. The word is used in ref. to many, a crowd. WE.

waŋwaŋ'yaŋȟa, n. A spectator. Wiŋyaŋ waŋwaŋyaŋkapi kiŋ śicahowaya eyaya. Na ake - k'oŋ kiyela au na waŋyaŋk inajiŋpi.

waŋyaŋg', cont. of waŋyaŋka. - he, To come to see.
waŋyaŋg'ȟiya, v.a. To cause to see anything. Waŋyaŋgwakiya.
waŋyaŋ'gpica, adj. Visible.
waŋyaŋg'ya, v.a. To cause to see or perceive. Waŋyaŋgwaya.
waŋyaŋ'ȟa, v.a. To see, perceive anything. Waŋblaka.

waŋye'ca, n. Rushes; the fire fly, the lightning bug.
waŋye'cahu taŋka, n. (waŋ-iyececa). The scouring rush, pipe stem. Equisetum hyemale. The horsetail family. Horses get fat on it. Bl. BT. #122.
waŋye'ca swula, n. Horsetail, scouring rush. Equisetum variegatum. The horsetail family. L.

waŋye'ya, v.a. To shoot arrows, to shoot in the sacred dance. Waŋyewaya. Compare waŋtaŋyeya.

waŋyu'ǧo, v.a. (waŋ-yugo). To make the crooked marks or furrows on arrows, which are considered essential to a good arrow. Waŋblugo.

waŋyu'ǧuka, v. To draw an arrow out of the quiver.

waŋ'yukpaŋhaŋ, v. To shoot arrows one after another. Waŋblukpaŋhaŋ.

waŋyu'za, v. To be able to handle bow and arrow, as is said of a boy. Wana waŋyuze, He can now handle bow and arrow. TT.

wao', v. (o). To hit in shooting; 1st pers. sing. of o. Wawao.

wao'hola, v. (ohola). To honor, worship. Wawaohola. Hokśila waŋ tókiyataŋ waohola śni yahi yelo. B.H.63.10.
wao'holaśniyaŋ, adv. Irreverently. B.H.80.21.

wao'ȟmuŋyece, n. A very talkative person, one who makes much noise wherever he is. Bl.

wao'ka, n. A marksman; a good hunter. Wawaoka. Waópika, pl. D.64.

wao'kaȟniǧa, v. To be intelligent, to be skillful in finding game. Waowakaȟniǧa. Waokaȟnigelo, wigni wayupikelo. Bl. Wicaśa ksapa na waokaȟnigeȟce. B.H.32.7.

wao'kaȟwaŋjica, n. or adj. One "make", one style; all made in the same manner, as arrows. Bl.

wao'kala, v. of okala. B.H.248.17.

wao'kicaȟniǧa, v. To have understanding, be wise. Waokiwakaȟniǧa. B.H. 121.2. Bl.

wao'kihi, v. (okihi). To be able, to have ability. Waowakihi. Bl.
wao'kihika, n. One who is able. Waowakihika.
wao'kihiya, 1) v.a. To make able. Waokihiwaya. 2) adv. Ably, powerfully.

wao'kiya, v. (o-kiya). To let one do the shooting etc. while hunting. Bl.

wa'okiya, v. To command. R. Bl.

wao'k'u, v. (ok'u). To lend. Waowak'u.

wao'mani, (?).

waoŋ'spe, v. (oŋspe). To know how. Waoŋmaspe. Wicaśa - , A learned man. B.H.172.1.
waoŋ'speic'iya, n. A scholar. P.
waoŋ'spekiya, v. (oŋspekiya). To teach. Waoŋspewakiya.
waoŋ'spekiye, n. A teacher. B.H.177.5.
waoŋ'spewicakiye, n. An apostle, disciple. B.H.177.1.

waoŋ'śila, adj. Merciful, gracious. Waoŋśiwala.

waoŋ'toŋkiya, v. pos. To ruin, spoil one's own. Bl.
waoŋ'toŋyaŋ, v.a. To spoil, miss. Waoŋtoŋwaya. Bl. Also, to injure.

waoŋ'ze, n. A nickname for a bear. Bl.

wao'po, v.a. To push in with a knife, make a hole in. Wawaopo.

wao'p'o, n. Light snow flying in the sunlight.

wao'śtegla, v. (ośtegla). To speak evil of, call bad names; to revile, to slander. Waośtewagla.

wao'ta, n. Much of anything. - luha yelo, You have a lot of things. Also, plentiful. B.H.32.25.

wao'tape s'e, adv. (otapa). Following a certain plan unintentionally. B.H. 157.20.

wao'weśica, n. A generic name for the bear. - s'e napcoka kiŋ yuȟ'iyela yaŋkiŋ na, as they say when a person has many scratches on his hands. Bl.

wao'yataŋ, v. To talk bad secretly about somebody, to spoil one's reputation; to bite unawares, as a dog or animals do. Waoblataŋ. Cf. wayatawaciŋhiŋyaŋza.

wao'ye, n. Tracks. - ótalaȟcake. Bl.

wao'zeze, v.a. To cut nearly off with a knife and let swing. Wawaozeze.
wao'zezeya, v.a. To cause to cut in strips or dangles. Waozezewaya.

wapa', n. (pa). The head of anything, as a dog's used as a head-dress for dancing; the source for locomotion, as the engine or locomotive of a train; anything that is placed at the lead position. SLB. -- adv. Towards, upwards. This is usually suffixed to the word it develops. Tokatawapa, Forward, toward the future. Ektawapa inajiⁿ, To stand farther on.

waṗa'aglapśuⁿyaⁿ, v. (paaglapśuⁿyaⁿ). To turn bottom upwards. - iyeya.

waṗa'bla, v. To spread out, make level; to iron e.g. clothes. Wawapabla. Also, wapablaya.

waṗa'blaska, v. (pablaska). To make flat; 1st pers. sing. of pablaska. Wawapablaska.

waṗa'blaya, v. (pablaya). To make smooth; to iron, as clothes; 1st pers. sing. of pablaya. Wawapablaya.

waṗa'blaza, v. To make burst by pressing; 1st pers. sing. of pablaza. Wawapablaza.

waṗa'bleca, v. (pableca). To crush to pieces; 1st pers. sing. of pableca. Wawapableca.

waṗa'blu, v. (pablu). To pulverize; 1st pers. sing. of pablu. Wawapablu.

waṗa'bu, v. (pabu). To beat, drum; 1st pers. sing. of pabu. Wawapabu.

waṗa'caⁿcaⁿ, v. (pacaⁿcaⁿ). To make shake; 1st pers. sing. of pacaⁿcaⁿ.

waṗa'caⁿnal iyeya, v. To shove toward the middle or center. R. Bl.

waṗa'ceḱa, v. Cf. wapacekceka.

waṗa'cekceḱa, v. (pacekceka). To push and make stagger; 1st pers. sing. of pacekceka.

waṗa'eze, n. A person who does not like everybody; a rival, jealous person. Also, wapayezaha. R.

waṗa'ġaⁿ, v. (pagaⁿ). To part with; to open; 1st pers. sing. of pagaⁿ. Wawapagaⁿ.

waṗa'ġaṗa, v. (pagapa). To push off e.g. the skin of an animal; 1st pers. sing. of pagapa. Wawapagapa.

waṗa'ġeya, v. (pagaⁿ, perhaps). To scare away a crowd of men or animals. Wapagewaya. -- waṗáġeyeca, (?).

wa'paġica, n. The yellow-headed blackbird. - s'e oie caⁿtet'inst'iⁿzelo, as is said when a man speaks angrily. Bl. FR. Cf. wabloska.

waṗa'gmigma, v. (pagmigma). To make round; 1st pers. sing. of pagmigma. Wawapagmigma.

waṗa'gmiⁿyaⁿyaⁿ, v. (pagmiⁿyaⁿyaⁿ). To roll; 1st pers. sing. of pagmiⁿyaⁿyaⁿ. Wawapagmiⁿyaⁿyaⁿ.

waṗa'gmuⁿ, v. (pagmuⁿ). To twist; 1st pers. sing. of pagmuⁿ. Wawapagmuⁿ.

waṗa'gmuⁿḱe, n. One who twists; a spinner.

waṗa'gmuⁿpi, n. Twisted thread, yarn.

waṗa'gnaśḱiⁿyaⁿ, v. To make crazy; 1st pers. sing. of pagnaśkiⁿyaⁿ. Wawapagnaśkiⁿyaⁿ.

waṗa'gnayaⁿ, v. (pagnayaⁿ). To miss, as in attempting to stab; 1st pers. sing. of pagnayaⁿ.

waṗa'ġo, v. (pago). To carve; one who carves or engraves; 1st pers. sing. of pago. Wawapago. -- waṗáġoya, v.a. To cause to carve.

waṗa'gweza, v. (pagweza). To make rough. Wawapagweza.

wapa'ha, n. A headdress of feathers. Nupiⁿ tataⁿka - uⁿpi.

wa'ṗaha, n. The shaft or pole on which are tied feathers of various colors and used in the Dakota dances; a standard, banner, flag.

wapa'ha hetóⁿpi, n. A horned headdress.

wapa'ha héyuġa, n. A branch-horned headdress.

waṗa'ha iyeya, v. (paha-iyeya). To push down. R. Bl.

wapa'ha iyúslohetoⁿ, n. A warbonnet with one tail that falls in a train.

wa'ṗaha kamni'mnila ṗeji, n. So called because of the sharp, upper end (wapaha) of the grass blades. Tall grama grass. Bouteloua curtipendula. The grass family. Also called anthers vermillion or cinnamon red. Bl. #221.

wapa'ha mimá, n. A round warbonnet without a tail. Bl. Also, wapaha miméla.

wapa'ha oḱi'jata, n. A warbonnet with

two tails.

wa'ṗaha payu'ktaⁿ, n. A sort of spear looking almost like a bishop's staff and used by the Wiciⁿska and Ḣoka Okolakiciye, military societies among the Oglala Sioux. FD.313.

wapa'ha yuslohe, n. The lower part of a warbonnet, its trailer.

waṗa'hi, v. (pahi). To gather or pick up; 1st pers. sing. of pahi. Wawapahi.

waṗa'hiⁿl, cont. of wapahiⁿta. Suⁿkawakaⁿ - wota yelo, i.e. to scratch snow away and eat grass. LB.

waṗa'hipi, n. A gathering or picking up.

waṗa'hoho, v. (pahoho). To shake or make loose.

waṗa'homni, v. (pahomni). To turn around; 1st pers. sing. of pahomni. Wapahomni.

waṗa'hotoⁿ, v. (pahotoⁿ). To make cry out; 1st pers. sing. of pahotoⁿ. Wawapahotoⁿ.

waṗa'huⁿhuⁿza, v. (pahuⁿhuⁿza). To shake with the hand, shake by pushing against; 1st pers. sing. of pahuⁿhuⁿza. Wawapahuⁿhuⁿza.

waṗa'ḣatḱa, v. To rub against the grain; 1st pers. sing. of paḣatka.

waṗa'ḣci, v. (paḣci). To tear out pieces; 1st pers. sing. of paḣci.

waṗa'ḣeya, waṗa'ġeya, v. Cf. wapaḣewaya. Bl.

waṗa'ḣlaġaⁿ, v. (paḣlagaⁿ). To enlarge; 1st pers. sing. of paḣlagaⁿ.

wa'ṗaḣlaltoⁿ, v. To work with ribbon; to embroider. Wapaḣlalwatoⁿ.

wa'ṗaḣlaṫa, v. (apaḣlata). To embroider.

waṗa'ḣlatapi, n. The burying of meat in snow. Hecel talo kiⁿ ośtulya yaⁿkiⁿ kte, tasakiⁿ kte śni yelo. Bl.

wa'ṗaḣlaṫe, n. A ribbon, ribbons.

waṗa'ḣleca, v. (paḣleca). To tear, rend; 1st pers. sing. of paḣleca. Wawapaḣleca.

waṗa'ḣli, v. (paḣli). To push into the ground or mud.

wapa'ḣloḱa, v. (paḣloka). To make holes, to pierce; 1st pers. sing. of paḣloka. Wawapaḣloka.

waṗa'ḣmiⁿ, v. (paḣmiⁿ). To make crooked.

waṗa'ḣṗa, v. (paḣpa). To throw down; 1st pers. sing. of paḣpa. Wawapaḣpa.

waṗa'ḣṗu, v. (paḣpu). To pick off; 1st pers. sing. of paḣpu. Wawapaḣpu.

wapa'ḣṫa, v. (paḣta). To tie in bundles; 1st pers. sing. of paḣta. Wawapaḣta.

wa'ṗaḣṫa, n. A bundle, a pack. Caⁿli - etaⁿ kagapi.

waṗa'ḣuga, v. (paḣuga). To break holes in; 1st pers. sing. of paḣuga. Wawapaḣuga.

waṗa'ḣwuḣwu, v. (?). - waimnaⁿkelo, i.e. to run through snow and fall over on one's hands. Bl. Note: paḣwuhwu seems more proper, but that itself does not seem to exist.

waṗa'jaja, v.(pajaja). To wash; 1st pers. sing. of pajaja. Wawapajaja.

waṗa'jiⁿ, v.n. To be prevented, not to be able to accomplish. Wamapajiⁿ.

waṗa'jipa, v. (pajipa). To pinch; 1st pers. sing. of pajipa. Wawapajipa.

waṗa'juju, v. (pajuju). To erase; to demolish; 1st pers. sing. of pajuju. Wawapajuju.

waṗa'juⁿ, v. (pajuⁿ). To dig up with the bill, as ducks do under water.

waṗa'ḱaṫiⁿ, v. (pakatiⁿ). To straighten out.

waṗa'ḱawa, v. (pakawa). To open out.

waṗa'kca, v. (pakca). To comb; 1st pers. sing. of pakca.

waṗa'ḱiⁿta, v. (pakiⁿta). To wipe; 1st pers. sing. of pakiⁿta. Wawapakiⁿta.

waṗa'ḱiza, v. (pakiza). To make creak; 1st pers. sing. of pakiza.

waṗa'ḱo, v. (pako). To push away from each other to make room for somebody. Wawapako. Bl.

wapa'ko, v.a. (pako). To cut or saw crooked. Wawapako.

waṗa'ḱoṫa, v. To probe or dig out; 1st pers. sing. of pakota.

waṗa'kṗa, v. (pakpa). To pierce; 1st pers. sing. of pakpa. Wawapakpa.

waṗa'kṗi, v. To pick open e.g. eggs; 1st pers. sing. of pakpi. Wawapakpi.

waṗa'ksa, v. (paksa). To break off with the hand; 1st pers. sing. of paksa. Wawapaksa.

waṗa'kśija, v. (pakśija). To make double up; 1st pers. sing. of pakśija. Wawapakśija.

waṗa'kṫaⁿ, v. (paktaⁿ). To crook, make crooked; 1st pers. sing. of paktaⁿ. Wawapaktaⁿ.

waṗa'k'eġa, v. (pak'ega). To scratch; 1st pers. sing. of pak'ega. Wawapak'ega.

waṗa'k'eza, v. (pak'eza). To make hard and smooth; 1st pers. sing. of pak'eza. Wawapak'eza.

waṗa'maⁿ, v. (pamaⁿ). To file; 1st pers. sing. of pamaⁿ. Wawapamaⁿ.

wapa'mima, v. (pamima). To make round; 1st pers. sing. of pámima. Wawapamima.

waṗa'nini, v. 1st pers. sing. of panini.

waṗaⁿ'geyeca, (?). Cf. páⁿgece.

waṗa'ogluta, v. (paogluta). To close up; 1st pers. sing. of paogluta. -iyeya.

waṗa'oksa, v. (paoksa). To push or break through; 1st pers. sing. of paoksa. Wawapaoksa.

waṗa'osṗa, v. (paospa). To push under e.g. water; 1st pers. sing. of paospa. Wawapaospa.

waṗa'ot'iⁿza, v. (paot'iⁿza). To press in tight; 1st pers. sing. of paot'iⁿza. Wawapaot'iⁿza.

waṗa'owotaⁿ, v. (paowotaⁿ). To make straight. Wawapaowotaⁿ. -- waṗáowotaⁿla, v. (paowotaⁿla). To make straight; 1st pers. sing. of paowotaⁿla. Wawapaowotáⁿla.

wapa'pa, v. red. (wapa). To bark, as does a dog. Śuⁿka - ota kte lo.

waṗa'ṗaḣya, v. (papaḣya). To parch e.g. corn, fat etc. Wapapaḣwaya. R. Bl.

waṗa'poṗa, v. To burst open, as corn; 1st pers. sing. of papopa.

waṗa'psaḱa, v. (papsaka). To break e.g. cords; 1st pers. sing. of papsaka.

waṗa'psoⁿ, v. (papsoⁿ). To spill e.g. water; 1st pers. sing. of papsoⁿ. Wawapapsoⁿ.

waṗa'pṫuja, v. To take out a piece, as with a chisel; to split or crack; 1st pers. sing. of paptuja. BD. R.

waṗa'ṗuza, v. (papuza). To make dry by wiping; 1st pers. sing. of papuza. Wawapapuza.

waṗa'sḱa, v. To make white by rubbing; 1st pers. sing. of paska. Wawapaska.

waṗa'slata, v. To set up, e.g. a pole in the ground; 1st pers. sing. of paslata. Wawapaslata.

waṗa'sleca, v. (pasleca). To split; 1st pers. sing. of pasleca. Wawapasleca.

waṗa'smaka, v. To indent; 1st pers. sing. of pasmaka. Wawapasmaka.

waṗa'smiⁿyaⁿyaⁿ, v. To make bare and clean; 1st pers. sing. of pasmiⁿyaⁿyaⁿ.

waṗa'snoⁿ, v. (pasnoⁿ). To roast e.g. meat; 1st pers. sing. of pasnoⁿ. Wawapasnoⁿ. D.22.

waṗa'sṫaⁿka, v. (pastaⁿka). To moisten. Wawapastaⁿka.

waṗa'śaṗa, v. (paśapa). To defile. Wawapaśapa.

waṗa'śiṗa, v. (paśipa). To break off close e.g. the limbs of a tree; 1st pers. sing. of paśiṗa. Wawapaśipa.

waṗa'śḱica, v. (paśkica). To press, squeeze. Wawapaśkica.

waṗa'śkiśka, v. (paśkiśka). To make rough.

waṗa'śkokṗa, v. (paśkokpa). To make hollow, to cut or dig out.

waṗa'śkoṗa, v. (paśkopa). To make twist or become warped. Cf. śkopa.

waṗa'śleca, v. (paśleca). To split with an effort; 1st pers. sing. of paśleca. Wawapaśleca.

waṗa'śna, v. (paśna). To miss. Wawapaśna.

waṗa'śṗa, v. (paśpa). To push away; to break off; to wash out e.g. stains; 1st pers. sing. of paśpa; that which is capable of being washed out, n. Wawapaśpa.

waṗa'śṗu, v. (paśpu). To break off. Wawapaśpu.

waṗa'śuja, v. (paśuja). To crush; 1st pers. sing. of paśuja. Wawapaśuja.

waṗa'ś'aka, v. (paś'aka). To push or stab with too little force; 1st pers. sing. of paś'aka. Wawapaś'aka.

wapa'ṫa, v. (pata). To cut up, as a butcher does an animal; 1st pers. sing of pata. Wawapata. Hecel miś num wicawao na wawapata.

waṗa'ṫaⁿ, v. (ṗataⁿ). To be saving of; 1st pers. sing. of pataⁿ. Wawapataⁿ.

waṗa'taⁿ, v. (ṗataⁿ). To push; to mash; 1st pers. sing. of pataⁿ. Wawapataⁿ.

waṗa'ṫaⁿḱa, n. One who is saving. Same as wakpataⁿka.

wapa'ṫaṗi, n. Meat cut up; the act of cutting up meat.

waṗa'ṫica, v. (patica). To work up by pressing on e.g. dough when sticky and soft; to shove, push; 1st pers. sing. of patica. Wawapatica.

waṗa'toⁿyaⁿ, v. To put to flight, to make flee. Wapatoⁿwaya. Bl. -- waṗátoⁿyece, n. One who puts all to flight. Bl.

waṗa't'iḣpeya, v.(pat'iḣpeya). To push out of the way. Bl.

wapa't'iⁿza, v. To press hard e.g. dried wash; 1st pers. sing. of pat'iⁿza. Wawapat'iⁿza.

waṗa'waġa, v. (pawaga). To roll, twist; 1st pers. sing. of pawaga.

waṗa'weġa, v. To break or fracture; 1st pers. sing. of pawega. Wawapawega.

waṗa'wi, wa'ṗawi, v. To gather about something, as buzzards do a carcass. Tuḣmuḣ - s'e nicuwapelo, i.e. many wasps buzzing about one. Bl. -- waṗáwiya, adv. Yet moving about. KE.

waṗa'wignuni, v. (pawignuni). To destroy; 1st pers. sing. of pawignuni. Wawapawignuni. R. Bl.

wapa'wiⁿja, v. (pawiⁿja). To bend down e.g. grass; 1st pers. sing. of pawiⁿja.

wa'ṗawiⁿta, v. (apawiⁿta). To rub on, to plaster; what is put on, as in plastering, n. Wawapawiⁿta.

wapa'yalake s'e, (?). Na wana ka ekta - kupi. MS.150.

wa'ṗaye, n. Grease; meat; seasoning of any kind.

wa'ṗayeya, v.a. To use for seasoning. Wapayewaya.

waṗa'zaⁿ, v. To separate, part e.g. hair; 1st pers. sing. of pazaⁿ. Wawapazaⁿ.

waṗa'zo, v. (pazo). To show; 1st pers. sing. of pazo. Wawapazo. -- waṗázopi, n. A show, an exhibition.

wape', v. (pe). To sharpen with a knife. Wawape.

wa'pe, n. Leaves, obsol. Caⁿwapa, Foliage.

wape´gnaka, n. (?).

waṗe´haŋ, v. To fold; 1st pers. sing. of pehaŋ. Wawapehaŋ.

waṗe´mni, v.a. (pemni). To make crooked or twisted by shaving. Wawapemni. -- waṗemniyaŋ, part. Shaved twisting.

waṗe´ṗe, n. The Russian thistle, Russian tumbleweed. Also, waṗéṗeka, waȟpe caŋsakala. Salsola tenuifolia. The goosefoot family. BT. #33.

wape´peǩa, n. Thorns, prickles, briers.

waṗe´sťo, v.a. (pesto). To shave to a point. Wawapesto.

wa´ṗetogtogya, adv. Marvelously, miraculously.
wa´ṗetogtoǩeca, n. Signs, marks; miracles, wonders.
wa´ṗetogtoŋ, v.a. To mark anything, have a sign. Wápetogwatoŋ. B.H.6.10.
wa´ṗetogtoŋpi, n. Marks, signs.
wa´ṗetogtoŋyaŋ, adv. Signed, marked. He - ayaskabtoŋ, i.e. has signed. B.H. 209.8.
wa´ṗetogya, adv. Marvellously.
wa´ṗetogyakel, adv. Distinctively, peculiarly. SLB. Toktogna - yapazo, i.e. sure sign. B.H.209.12.
wa´ṗetoǩeca, n. A sign, mark; a bound or limit; a miracle.

wā´ṗi, adj. lucky, fortunate. Wámapi.
wā´ṗiǩa, adj. Fortunate. Wawapika. B.H. 27.29. Bl.
wa´ṗiǩe, n. One who is fortunate.

waṗi´ǩiya, v. To put up and lay away things well, to rearrange. Wapiwakiya. Wapikiye-koŋs taku okuwa, She pretended to put the room in order and worked with something. D.272.

waṗi´ǩiyece śni, adv. Having prepared one's self well, provided one's self with everything before starting on a journey etc. LC. Syn.- iśitutece śni.

wāṗi´la, v.n. To be thankful. Wawapila.
waṗi´lapi, n. Gratitude. Pb.33.
waṗi´lapiśni, n. Ingratitude.
waṗi´laśni, v.n. To be unthankful, ungrateful. Wawapilaśni.

wā´ṗiśni, adj. Unfortunate.

waṗi´ya, v. To conjure the sick; to powwow in the Indian way. Wapiwaya.

wa´ṗiya, 1) v.a. To make fortunate. Wapiwaya. D.260. 2) adv. Fortunately.

waṗi´yapi, n. Conjuring.
waṗi´yeȟci, adv. Sound and well. - waki ehaŋtaŋś. B.H.22.19.
waṗi´yeǩiya, v.a. To cause one to apply Indian medicine. Pb.24.

wapo´bleca, n. Cf. wapáha.

waṗol´, cont. of wapota. - iyeya, To rip or destroy with a knife.
waṗol´ṗoťa, v. red. (wapota). To cut to pieces. Wawapolpota.

wapo´śťaŋ, n. A hat, a bonnet. - gmigma, gmigmela, A cap. - gmigmela hiŋśma, A fur cap.
waṗo´śťiyu´t'iŋze, n. A hat band.

waṗo´ťa, v.a. To destroy by cutting; to cut to pieces, as in cutting up a tent; to make holes while cutting, as in taking off the hide of an animal. Wawapota.

wapsag´, cont. of wapsaka. - iyeya, To cut off suddenly with a knife e.g. a string. Yamni śuŋk wápsak iwacu welo. RC. D.92.

wapsa´ǩa, v.a. To cut off, e.g. string or cord with a knife; to saw or cut something in two with a saw or knife. Wawapsaka. -- wapsápsaǩa, v. red.
wapsi´ca, v. To make chips fly.
wapsi´psica, v. red. (wapsica). To cut and make the chips fly off. Bl.

wapśuŋ´, v.a. (pśuŋ). To cut round a joint, to joint with a knife, to cut or saw asunder, as when two bones are tightly joined. Wawapśuŋ. -- wapśúŋpśuŋ, v. red.

wapťa´, v.a. To cut off a piece, trim off the edge of anything; to cut out e.g. a garment; to cut through. Wawapta. - iyeya, To trim off with a stroke.

wa´pťaŋyaŋ, adj. or v. Lucky. Caŋke Juda oyate kiŋ wáptaŋyaŋpi ka woyuha olota yuha glipi. B.H.134.17.

wapťa´pťa, v. red. of wapta.

wapťa´yahujiji, n. The snake root. It

and all its forms are medicines.
wapťa'yaȟla, n. A form of snake root.
wapťa'ya ȟota, n. Snake root.

wapta'ye, n. A weed.

wapťe'cela, v.a. (ptecela). To cut short, to cut too short. Wawaptecela.

waptu'ǧa, v.a. To cut or saw off a piece. Wawaptuga. BD.
waptuȟ', cont. of waptuga. - iyeya. Bl.
waptu'ptuǧa, v. red. of waptuga. Bl.

wa'puskeṗa, v. To empty; 1st pers. sing. of puskepa.

wa'ṗusṗa, v. (puspa). To glue, to seal; 1st pers. sing. of puspa. Wáwapuspa.

wa'ṗusťaka, v. (pustaka). To stoop down; 1st pers. sing. of pustaka. Wáwapustaka. Bl.

waṗus'ya, v. (pusya). To dry e.g. clothes. Wawapusya.

wa'ṗutaka, v. (aputaka). To touch with the hand, press upon. Wawaputaka.

wasab'gle, v. To set up signs, to set up a stick in the ground to point the way one is going; to place for a landmark, to place something black for a sign. Wasabwagle. R. Bl. Cf. R., caⁿpakiⁿ. -- wasábglepi, n. (sapa-gle). The mark or boundary, a stake etc., as is used in playing ball. Inaȟni - waⁿji kagapi na ilazatаⁿhaⁿ enajiⁿ. -- wasábgleya, adv. In the manner of a sign.

wasab'ya, v. (sabya). To blacken. Wasabwaya.

wasaⁿ'yaⁿ, v. (saⁿyaⁿ). To whiten. Wasaⁿwaya.

wasas', cont. of wasaza.
wasa'sḱiya, v. To care for tenderly. Wasaswakiya, wasasmakiya, wasasciye. Hauⁿ, hauⁿ, wasaswakiye c'oⁿ, as they wail at a child dead.
wasas'yela, adv. Mildly, gently.
wasa's'ic'iya, v. refl. To take more care of one's self than is right. Bl.
wasa'za, adj. Well guarded and protected from evil and hardships. Wamasaza.

wasa'zeca, n. One who is easily made sick; one who is getting well.

wase', n. Red earth, vermillion. - kic'uⁿpi kiⁿ hena kpakiⁿtapi na glapi kte lo.
wase' acetipi, n. Flat pieces of clay burned in fire and used for painting one's self. It is first pulverized. Bl. Cf. taⁿniśpaⁿ.
wase'kic'uⁿ, v. To paint red, to put on vermillion.
wase'yaⁿka, v.n. To have a spot on one's face. Wasemayaⁿka. -- n. A pimple.

wasiⁿ'kpe, P. Cf. siⁿkpe.

waska'ska, n. White things. Bl.
waska'ya, v. To whitewash. Also, wasaⁿyaⁿ.

wasḱi'ca, v.a. To press out with a knife. Wawaskica.
wasḱil', cont. of waskica and waskita.
wasḱi'ťa, v.a. To press upon with a knife. Wawaskita.

wasḱu', v.a. To pare or shave off, as the skin of a potato or apple and as flesh from a hide. Wawasku. Blo wásku, To peel potatoes.
wasḱu'sḱu, v. red. of wasku.

wasku'yeca, n. Fruit of all kinds.

wasla'ya, v. (slaya). To oil, to grease. Waslawaya.

wasle'ca, v.a. To saw, to slit or rip up by sawing; to split something with a knife. Wawasleca.
waslel', cont. of wasleca. - iyeya, To split with a knife or saw.
wasle'sleca, v. red. (wasleca). To saw up, as a log into boards; to cut into small strips. Wawaslesleca.
wasle'slel, cont. of waslesleca.

wasli', v.a. To press out with a knife or by cutting. Wawasli.
wasli'ṗa, v. (slipa). To lick with the tongue; 1st pers. sing. of slipa. Waslipa. Watage ota yelo, - po; uⁿnihaⁿ akaȟtaⁿ yelo. BT.
wasli'sli, v. red. of wasli.

wa'slohaⁿ, v. To crawl. Wáwaslohaⁿ. Bl.
waslol'ya, v. (slolya). To know. Waslolwaya. Huⁿȟ t'api na waslolwayapi. B.H.171.12.

waslol'yapi, n. Knowledge.
waslol'yapiśni, n. Ignorance. P.
waslol'ye, n. One who knows.
waslol'yewaciŋ, v. To be eager to learn. Waslolyewacaŋmi.
waslol'yeya, v. To cause to know. Waslolyewaya.

wasma'ka, v.a. (smaka). To indent or make a hollow place by cutting with a knife. Wawasmaka.

wasmiŋ', v.a. To cut or shave off clean, as meat from a bone. Wawasmiŋ. Hohu wasmiŋpi, A soup made of the back-bones. P. -- wasmíŋsmiŋ, v. red. (wasmiŋ). To pare or trim the meat off clean from the bones. Wawasmiŋsmiŋ. -- wasmíŋyaŋ, part. Cutting off very smoothly.

wasna', n. Lard, grease, tallow; a mixture of pounded beef and marrow and kept in a powdered state. Wagmeza - , A mixture of corn and marrow. Caŋpa - , A mixture of cherries and marrow. R.

wasna'snaheca, n. The kingbird. Also, - ikpi ska, - ikpi zi. Hokśicala, hokśicala, hokśicala eyapi. - ciŋcala s'e ipaȟlala uŋyaŋkapelo, i.e. sit close together in a row.

wasna'ťasa'ka, n. Tallow, hardened grease.

waso', v. To cut a strip or string, as from a hide. Wawaso. Na taha kpaŋyaŋpi kiŋ ohomni waso na oŋ tuśu kiŋ hena paȟta na pawosla eglepi.

wasoŋ', v. (soŋ). To braid in strings, as corn or hair; 1st pers. sing. of soŋ. Wawasoŋ.

waso'so, v. red. To cut into strips or strings. Wawasoso.

waspaŋ'la, n. Melting snow, slush. - ca wakaśloyakel maunipi yelo. Bl. -- adv. Slushy. R.

wa'spayeic'iya, v. refl. To make one's self wet, to perspire. Wáspayemic'iyelo, as they say after eating plenty. Bl.

wasťaŋ'mi, interj. Welcome! An old word. Bl. Syn.- ako, caŋnako.

wastu'steya, v. To weary one. Wastustewaya. Cf. waśtuśteya.

wasu', n. Hail.
wasu'hiŋhaŋ, v. To hail.

wasu'hula, n. Iroquois used for necklaces. R.

wasu'kiya, v.a. To decree, make a decree; to judge, condemn. To hold sacred. Wasuwakiya. Na akicita kiŋ hena oyate wasuwicakiyapi na omani śni wasuyapi. Ate hecel wasuuŋkiyapelo.

wasu'la, n. abbrev. (wasuhula). - cuwignaka. - wabluśka.

wasu'snaka, n. The narrow side of a feather, the narrow barbs on one side of the shaft or quill which are used on the notch end of arrows. - hena iyagya yo, hecena kiŋ oȟ'aŋko ktelo. Bl.

wasu'ťoŋ, v. (sutoŋ). To get ripe, ripen, as does grain or fruit.
wasu'toŋpi, n. The harvest.
wasu'toŋ wi, n. The harvest moon, August.
wasu'toŋyaŋ, v. To bring forth fruit. B.H.240.12.

wasu'ya, v. To make a law; to judge, condemn. Wasuwaya.

was'o'juha, n. A bag to keep the wasé in.

waśag'kiciya, v.a. To render weak for one. B.H.75.6.

waśag' la, v. To consider one not very intelligent. Waśagwala, waśagcila, waśagmayala. Bl.

waśag'ya, v.a. To beat one easily. Waśagwaya. B. Cf. waśakala, waś'aka.
waśag'yela, adv. Easily, cheaply. Śuŋkawakaŋ - wak'u, i.e. for a little money. - oieyetoŋpi kiŋ mitaakicita ob wamayalakapi kte lo. ST.

waśa'kala, adj. Cheap, easy. Śuŋka waśakalapi, i.e. easy to get.
waśa'kayela, adv. Easily, cheaply. WE.
waśa'kśakala, adj. red. of waśakala.

waśa'śte, n. Cf. śaśte. - wapáha.

waśe', n. A woman's female friend, corresponding to kóla; a woman's sister-in-law, thus a word used if persons are not on very good terms. Cf. maśe, A brother-in-law. Sb.

waśe'ca, adj. Rich, esp. in provisions. Wamaśeca. D.116.
waśe'caya, adv. Richly, i.e. esp. in provisions. Lila talo ota yuhapi na - tipi.

waśe'kiciya, v. To have each other for special friends. Used by women only.

waśe'p̣a, adj. Unclean. BT.

waśe'ya, v. To have for a friend, as is said of women only. Waśewaya.

waśi', v.a. To employ. Wawaśi. Yuŋ! tokinahaŋś taku otaka ca wamaśipi kte ȟciŋ. Le wiŋyaŋ kiŋ tuktel waśipi ca hel wokajuju k'upi. Wamaśipi śni yelo, as once said a medicine man. Wawaśi. MS.482.

waśib', cont. of waśipa. - iyeya.
waśi'bśipa, v. red. of waśipa.

waśi'ca, v.a. (śica). To spoil by cutting. Wawaśica.
waśi'cahowaya, v.a. (śicahowaya). To cause to cry out by cutting; to cry out badly, to moan, groan. Wawaśicahowaya.
waśi'celaka, v. (śicelaka). To dislike; one who dislikes, n. Waśicewalaka.

waśi'cuŋ, n. The white man, as used esp. disparagingly; any person or thing that is wakaŋ, as tuŋkaŋ - , yuwipi -, etc. The white man seemed to be wakaŋ so they called this new comer among Indians, coming from across the ocean, mni - ; while others met in the central United States, pusyata - . Buechel speculates that the word may be wa-śica-uŋ, One (wa) wearing (uŋ) bad or short (to the Indian eye) clothes, as is said: sapuŋ, skauŋ. Also, a person or thing having or characterized by special powers resident in the universe and looked upon as a container or carrier of toŋ, i.e. that by which the person or thing is wakaŋ; also, any object into which has been put toŋ by a person such as a wicaśa wakaŋ for his ceremonials and carried about by him in a bag, not the medicine bag. Waśicuŋpi. WJR.153.
waśi'cuŋ ciŋca, n. A mixed blood.
waśi'cuŋ hokśila, n. A white man's boy.
waśi'cuŋ wak̂áŋ, n. The white man's doctor.
waśi'cuŋ wiciŋcala, n. A white man's girl.
waśi'cuta, prep. n. At or to a white man's town. - wai na waśicuŋ śakowiŋ el mahipelo. Otoŋwaheta yiŋ kte, i.e. he will go to Washington, D. C.

waśi'gla, v. To mourn for the dead; to paint one's self black, as in mourning. Waśiwagla. B.H.71.1. -- n. Mourning habiliments. Miciŋca oŋ waśiqagla.
waśi'glagla, v. red. (waśigla). To get angry often.
waśi'glaka, n. One who gets angry at everyting. Also, waśiglake.
waśi'glaya, adv. Mourning.

waśi'ȟtiŋ, v.a. (śiȟtiŋ). To enfeeble by cutting; to do poorly with knife or saw. Wawaśiȟtiŋ.

waśi'kśica, v. red. of waśica.

waśil'ȟ'aŋ, v. (śilȟ'aŋ). To act wickedly. Waśilwaȟ'aŋ. R. Bl.

waśil'kigla, v. To be angry.

waśil'kiglaya, v. (śilkiglaya). To distress or make angry; one who makes angry, n.

waśil'kte, n. Pulmonary consumption, a lingering disease; failing in health, to be covered with scrophula. R. Bl.

waśiŋ', n. Fat not dried out, fat meat; pork. - cosyapi, Smoked ham or bacon, plain bacon. - śloyapi, Fried bacon.

waśiŋ'keȟa, n. (ikceka). Tallow.

waśiŋ'lo, n. A fresh and juicy piece of waśiŋ. Bl.

Waśiŋ' Wakpa, n. prop. The South Platte River.

waśi'p̣a, v.a. To cut off e.g. a branch from a tree, to prune; to cut off e.g. a pin with a knife. Wawaśipa.

waś iye'ya, v.a. To find one to be weaker than one's self. B.H.25.1.

waśi'yuta, n. (waśicuta). A place where white people live. - mni kte. - wai. This was the first name for an Agency, and perhaps a first attempt for Washington.

waśkaŋ'śkaŋyaŋ, v. (śkaŋ). To cause to move; one who causes to move or live. Waśkaŋśkaŋwaya.

wa'śke, (?). Wayaśkehelo, as is said when there is much on hand but only little is brought; thus, in cutting what tobacco I brought, I dropped some, and then the remark is made. Bl.

waśk̇i'ca, v.a. To squeeze by cutting; to press out e.g. water from a cloth with a knife; to scrape out. Wawaśkica.

waśk̇il', cont. of waśkica and waśkita.

waski'śkica, v. red. of waśkica.

waśki'śkiṫa, v. red. (waśkita). To cut much, gash; to make an edge toothed, as a feather. R. Wawaśkiśkita. Bl. Cf. walelepa.

waśk̇i'ṫa, v. To make notches, to cut across, gash. R. Wawaśkita.

waśk̇u', v.a. To cut off e.g. corn from the cob. Wawaśku. -- waśk̇úśku, v. red.

waśla', v.a. (śla). To make bare by cutting with a knife; to shave or scrape off e.g. hair from the hide. Wawaśla. -- waśláśla, v. red.

waślog', cont. of waśloka. - iyeya.

waślo'k̇a, v.a. (śloka). To cut a hole in, to cut out a piece, cut out e.g. an eye; to cut loose something that is fast in etc. Wawaśloka. -- waślóśloka, v. red.

waślo'ślotkiya, waślo'ślotkiyece, Cf. wasloslotkiya and wasloslotkiyece.

waślo'ya, v. To melt, smelt e.g. metal. Waślowaya.

waśni'ja, adj. Withered. Cf. śnija.
waśniś'ya, v. To cause to wither; one who causes to wither. Waśniśwaya.

waśoŋ', n. Cf. waśuŋ.

waśo'śe, n. A daring warrior. An old word.

waśō'śo s'e, Same as śwośwoke s'e, kaẏoyo s'e.

waśṗa', v.a. (śpa). To cut off a piece, cut up, to scalp. Wawaśpa. - iyeya. - yusota, - kte. MS.100,102.

waśpaŋ'k̇a, n. Cooked food. Na hehaŋl taku - ecoŋpi kiŋhaŋ hena otoiyohi etaŋhaŋ icupi. B.H.31.19. - ognake, A case for dried meat, a grub box. - ognake k'oŋ taŋyaŋ iyojuwakiyelo, i.e. the stomach. Waśpaŋk'ognake kiŋ matasake, i.e. stomach. Bl.

waśpaŋ'kiya, v. (?). B.H.31.11.

waśpaŋ'śni, adj. Raw, not cooked.
waśpaŋ'yaŋ, v. (śpaŋyaŋ). To cook, as food; to make a feast. Waśpaŋwaya.

waśṗa'śṗa, v. red. (waśpa). To cut into many pieces e.g. meat. Wawaśpaśpa. Caŋke taŋcaŋ kiŋ - ayapi. MS.101.

waśṗi', v.a. To cut off e.g. fruit from a tree. Wawaśpi. -- waśpíśpi, v. red.

waśṗu', v.a. To cut up, cut into pieces; to rip e.g. a seam, to rip up, cut as in ripping; to cut off a piece. Wawaśpu. -- waśṗúśṗu, v. red. (waśpu). To cut up into small pieces. Wawaśpuśpu.

waśṫe', adj. Good, pretty. Mawaśte.
waśṫe'ca, adj. Cf. waśtecaka.
waśṫe'cak̇a, adj. Good, well-disposed.
waśṫe'k̇ca, adj. Very good.
waśṫe'ic'ila, v. refl. (waśtela). To love one's self, to be selfish, to be proud. Wastemic'ila.
waśṫe'k̇a, adj. Good-hearted; good, little good, doubtfully good. Cf. ka, suff.; like to wakaŋka, Doubtfully mysterious. Cf. D.194 note 1, Sort of good. BD. Waśtekelo, He is a fine (ironically) fellow.

waśte'k̇icilapi, v. recip. Loving each other.
waśte'k̇ila, v. pos. (waśtela). To love one's own. Waśtewakila. Also, waśtékilaka. Waśtewakilaka.

waśťe'la, v.a. To esteem good, to love. Waśtewala. Waśteic'ila.
waśťe'laƙa, v.a. To love. Waśtewalaka.
waśťe'lakapi, n. Love; one who is loved.

waśťe'mna, adj. (omna). Sweet smelling, odoriferous. -- waśťémnaya, v.a. To perfume; to embalm. Waśtemnawaya

waśťe'śťe, adj. red. of waśte.
waśťe'śťeya, adv. red. of waśteya.
waśťe'ya, 1) v.a. To make good. Waśtewaya. Hecel waŋna oŋ waśteiciyapi. 2) adv. Well, in a good manner. Ooyuspe - ecoŋpi. Also, waśťéyaƙel. MS. 487.

waśtul'ya, v. (śtulya). To thaw, cause to thaw things that are frozen. Waśtulwaya.

waśtuŋkala, n. Corn on ears boiled and dried, a favorite Indian provision.

waśtu'śteya, v. (śtuśteya). To weary out. Waśtuśtewaya.

waśuŋ', n. The den or hole of small animals, of snakes and bugs; any hole in the ground. BD.

waśuŋ'kajuŋ, v. To moult or shed feathers. Bl. Cf. waśuŋkaśloka.

waśuŋ'kaśloka, v. To moult or shed feathers. Also, waśuŋkajuŋ. Bl.

waśu'ta, v. To shoot and miss. Waśute śni, Never Misses a Shot, a family name.

waś'ag', cont. of waś'aka. - hiŋgla, To become strong.

waś'a'gic'iya, v.n. To strengthen one's self.

waś'a'ƙa, adj. Strong. Wamaś'aka.

wa'ťa, n. A boat. -- v. (yuta). To eat. Wawata, wayata, wota, wauŋtapi. Also, 1st pers. sing. of yuta. Talo watiŋ kte lo.

wata'ǧe, n. Froth, foam, as in a boiling kettle. - ota yelo, waslipa po; úŋnihaŋ akaȟtaŋ yelo. BT.

waťa'kp̌e, v. (takpe). To attack or to attempt to seize. Watawakpe.

waťa'ƙuniśni, v.a. (takuniśni). To cut to pieces, destroy by cutting. Wawatakuniśni.

waťa'ƙuyapi, n. Relatives. B.H.171.12.

wata'mahelheca, adj. Lean. Bl.

wataŋ', n. Bait, as used in fishing. To bait a hook, ikoyagya. Hoye, hoapeśa waŋ miniceteta ape kahihiya nuŋke, - śaśala yeciciye.

wataŋ'caŋ, n. Appearance of material things. - iwaŋyaŋkapi śni yo, i.e. judge not. B.H.194.13. - iwaŋyaŋke, thus: waoholaśni.

wataŋ'iŋśni, adj. Lost.

wataŋ'ƙa, v.a. (taŋka). To cut large. Wawataŋka.

wataŋ'ka, n. One who is great or rich.
wataŋ'kaic'ila, v. refl. To esteem one's self highly, to be proud.
wataŋ'kaic'ilapi, n. Pride, haughtiness.

wataŋ'kala, v.a. To esteem great. Wataŋkawala.

waťaŋ'ƙaŋl, (?). - oye uŋ welo, It is a fresh track, i.e. after snowing. - uŋȟpayapi kte lo, i.e. will scrape snow away and camp here for the night. Bl.

waťaŋ'kic'ila, (?).
waťaŋ'ni, n. Old things. Hena - .

wa'taŋtoŋśni, v. To be poor, destitute in consequences of sickness etc.; to have lost everything. Wámataŋtoŋśni.
wa'taŋtoŋśniyaŋ, adv. Having lost everything, become poor. Bl.

wataŋ'ya, v.a. To use a thing for bait. Wataŋwaya.

wata'pa, v. (tapa). To pursue. Watawapa.

wa'ťap̌eťa, n. A steamboat.

wata'tabƙiya, v. To hang up, to dry. Watatabwakiya. Bl. Syn.- wakápuskiya.

wa'tawat'elya, v. (tawat'elya). To be willing to do or suffer. Watawat'elwaya.

wa'ťe, v. abs. (yuta). To eat something Wawáte, waúntapi. Wota, 3rd pers. sing. of wáte and yuta.

waťeb', cont. of watepa. - iyeya.
waťeb'ķiciciya, v. (tebya). To eat up for one. Watebweciciya.
waťeb'ķiya, v. pos. (watebya). To eat up one's own; to eat up for one. Watebwakiya.
waťeb'ya, v. (tebya). To eat all up, to devour; one who eats up, as does a wolf, n. Watebwaya.

waťe'ca, n. A part of one's food, esp. which one takes home from a feast.

wa'ťeca, n. Snow lately fallen.

waťe'ћiķa, adj. Difficult, hard, as a man in his dealings; dear, as goods etc. R. Bl.

waťe'ћila, 1) v. (teћila). To withhold what one has; not to give away; to be stingy. Watewaћila. 2) n. A miser. -- waťéћilapi, n. Parsimony.

waťe'þa, 1) v.a. To shorten by cutting off at the end with a knife, to cut short. Wawatepa. 2) v. (tepa). To wear off short, be worn out.

waťe'ślagķicaton, v.a. To crown one. Pb.38.
waťe'ślagķiton, v. (teślagkiton). To wear a fillet or garland around the head. Wateślagweton.
waťe'ślagkiya, v. To make wear a crown.
waťe'ślagton, v. (teślagton). To have or wear a garland or civic crown. Wateślagwaton.

waťe'ślaķe, n. A fillet, a wreath, a civic crown, anything wrapped around the head.

waťe'zi, (?). Ituhu - ka ca yankin na, as they say when a man has a prominent, balding forehead. Bl.

watķa', v. (tka). To scrape, as one does to hides. Wawatka.

wato', n. Grass, green grass, weeds.

waťob', cont. of watopa. - bla.

wato'gcin, v. To desire another kind of food. Watogwacin. BT.

wato'gla, adj. Wild, untrained, skittish. Wamatogla. Cf. watoka.

watog'ya, v.a. To spoil, ruin. Watogwaya. Bl. Also, to take vengeance, retaliate, to kill. D.268,271. Cf. toka. -- watógyapi, n. Reprisal.

waťo'hanhanl, adv. red. (watohanl). Sometime. - śna oћ'an waśtepi śni. B.H.128.2.

waťo'hanl, adv. Sometime. - śna. B.H. 128.2;81.1.

wato'hantu ka wan, (?). B.H.12.6.

Waťo'ћťaťa, n. prop. The Oto tribe, a western tribe. R. Bl.

waťo'ihuni, n. A landing place.

wato'ķa, n. Vegetation. B.H.51.19.

wato'kankan, adv. Evasively. - woglaka, To talk of something else when others talk to us, to dodge. Bl.

wato'ķapa, n. (tokapa). The first born; the birthright. Watomakapa. R. Bl.

waťo'keca, n. (tokeca). A different kind of food from what one has been accustomed to, fruits, vegetables; a contrast. P. Le maka akanl - nakun ca tanyan yaunpi kta.

waťo'ķelķeťuya, adv. In certain amounts. B.H.79.6.

waťo'ķeťuka, adv. Being pretty good-sized. B.H.171.2.

wato'kicon, 1) v. abs. (tokicon). To take vengeance. 2) n. An avenger.
wato'kiconpi, n. The reprisal made, retaliation. P.

waťo'kikśu, v. To haul one's own things.

waťo'ķiya, (?). BT.

wato'ķiyopeya, v. (tokiyopeya). To trade. B.H.179.11.

waťo'kśu, v. (tokśu). To carry, transport. Watowakśu, watounkśupi.
wato'kśupi, n. Transportation.

waton'ķa, n. One who is rich.

watoⁿ'śni, v. To own nothing, be poor. Wawatoⁿśni. WE.

waťo'pa, v. To paddle a canoe. Watowapa.

Waťo'paȟlaťe, n. prop. A tribe of northern Indians. Also, Waťópala, who live on the other side of Ȟeska. Bl.

waťo'paṗi, n. Rowing, paddling.

waťo'ṗeǩiya, v.a. To make paddle or row. Watopewakiya.

waťo'ṗeya, adv. By boat. - gle wicaśi. B.H.208.20;294.8. Cf. opeya. Also, waťóṗeyakel. - iyaya. B.H.303.10.

wato'toǩa, n. red. of watoka. Taku - ojupi kiⁿ heca ecela yutapi. B.H.136.14.

wato'toya, adv. Grass-like, green.

wato'ya, adv. Greenly.

waťu'cuhu, n. (tucuhu). Ribs.

waťu'ǩa, adj. Faint, weary, exhausted. Wamátuka. -- v.a. To cut off e.g. hair or fur; to destroy e.g. furs by cutting. Wawatuka.

waťu'kaya, v. To make tired, to weary.

waťu'kte, pron. of tukte. BT.

waťu'śekśeca, n. Dust, dirt, sweepings, manure.

waťu'śetka, n. Old, withered weeds. OS.

waťu'tǩa, v.a. (tutka). To cut up into crumbs, to cut into bits or scraps, to whittle. R. Wawatutka. -- n. Little things, e.g. scraps, shavings, crumbs and bits etc. -- waťútǩala, n. Very small things. -- waťútǩatǩa, n. Trifles; trinkets. R.

wat'a', v.a. (t'a). To kill with a knife. Wawat'a.

wat'uⁿg'ya, v. (t'uⁿgya). To suspect, have an indistinct knowledge of.

wauⁿ', v. (uⁿ, To be). To be well-off; 1st pers. sing. of uⁿ. Wawauⁿ.

wauⁿ'ca, 1) v. (uⁿca). To mock, imitate one. Wauⁿwaca. 2) n. A mocker. Also, waúⁿcala.

wauⁿ'jiⁿca, n. A horse whose tail is cut short. Also, wakó, n. Bl.

wauⁿ'ka, v.a. To fell by sawing e.g. a tree. Bl.

wauⁿ'ǩeic'ila, v. refl. To be proud, think one is all "it". Also, wauⁿkaic'ila. B.H.3.5;151.2;101.2;232.13. D.49.

wauⁿ'ǩe śni, (?). - tka heye lo, i.e. he is lying. BE.

wauⁿ'ǩic'ila, v. To think much of one's self, be proud. Cf. wauⁿkeic'ila.

wauⁿ'uⁿǩa, n. One who wanders about, a vagabond, a tramp.

wauⁿ'yaⁿ, v.a. To offer sacrifice, e.g. in the form of money etc. ; to lose. Wauⁿwaya, and perhaps wawauⁿya. B.H. 5.6;61.4;108.23. Taku wauⁿyepica. Cf. wakiuⁿyaⁿ.

wauⁿ'yaⁿṗi, n. Sacrifices, things offered. Oyate kiⁿ tipi iyohila wauⁿyaⁿpi au po. Caⁿ waⁿ paslatapi na el - kiⁿ eglepi. Hel - ecoⁿpi. MS.351. The word seems to imply the offering of something promised before, somehung up and not edible. Cf. wayuȟtatapi.

wauⁿ'yaⁿṗi iťáⁿcaⁿ, n. A high priest. B.H.146.6.

wauⁿ'ye, n. The act of offering. B.H. 8.1.

wauⁿ'ye iťáⁿcaⁿ, n. A priest of the Old Testament. - taⁿka, A high priest. B.H.97.11;259.19;262.16.

wauⁿ'yekiya, v. To make offerings to. Wauⁿyewicakiciciyapi. B.H.11.20;39.9; 49.23;156.6.

wauⁿ'yeya, v. To offer sacrifices. - itaⁿcaⁿ, A priest. B.H.60.6;61.1; 260.26.

wau'ta, v. To give to eat. Wautapi, They give away much food. Waumatapi, They give me much to eat. Bl.

wawa'bla, v. (wabla). To cut in slices. Wawawabla.

wawa'blablaza, v. red. of wawablaza.

wawa'blaza, v. (wablaza). To rip open or up. Wawawablaza.

wawa'bleca, v. (wableca). To cut up, break to pieces with a knife. Wawawableca.

wawa'caⁿlilike, n. One who is always smoking. Bl.

wawa'ġap̄a, v. (wagapa). To skin animals, be in the habit of taking off skins. Wawawagapa.

wawa'gla, v. (wagla). To make uncoil by cutting. Wawawagla.

wawa'gna, v. (wagna). To cut off, as in shelling corn with a knife; to make fall by cutting. Wawawagna.

wawa'gnayaṉ, v. (wagnayaṉ). To miss in trying to cut. Wawawagnayaṉ.

wawa'ġo, v. (wago). To carve, engrave. Wawawago.

wawa'gweza, v. (wagweza). To make rough; to haggle. Wawawagweza.

wawa'ha, n. The generic name for furs or peltries.

wawa'heye śni, adv. Pretending. - omani, To move about as though one knew the country, although one is a stranger. BE.

wawa'hiyaṉsk̄alak̄a, adj. Morose, cross.
wawa'hiyaṉsyakel, adv. Roughly, crossly.
wawa'hiyaṉzeca, n. A morose person.

wawa'hokoṉkiya, v. (wahokoṉkiya). To exhort, advise. B.H.173.1;252.1.

wawa'hoya, v. abs. To order things.
wawa'hoyap̄i, n. Things ordered by mail.

wawa'huṉ, v. (wahuṉ). To cut, gash. Wawawahuṉ.
wawa'huṉhuṉ, v. red. (wawahuṉ). To cut e.g. a piece of meat nearly off in many places. - wak'u, I gave it to him to cut in many pieces.

wawa'hutela, v. (wahutela). To wear off to a stump, as a knife. Wawawahutela.

wawa'ȟlaġaṉ, v. (wahlagaṉ). To make large, to cut so that a thing becomes larger. Wawawaȟlagaṉ.

wawa'ȟlaya, v. (waȟlaya). To pare, to cut off the rind or skin. Wawawaȟlaya.
wawa'ȟlayela, n. Parings.

wawa'ȟleca, v. (waȟleca). To tear in attempting to cut. Wawawaȟleca.

wawa'ȟloka, v. (waȟloka). To cut holes. Wawawaȟloka. Cf. wawaśloka.

wawa'ȟobȟop̄ece, n. One who is proud of his wearing apparel, while he does not look good otherwise. Bl.

wawa'ȟp̄aniyaṉ, v. (waȟp̄aniyaṉ). To make poor. Wawaȟpaniwaya.

wawa'ȟ'u, v. (waȟ'u). To peel, pare. Wawawaȟ'u.

wawa'juju, v. of wajuju. - niśipi.

wawa'k̄aṉ, n. The sacred arrow, the wahiṉkpe wakaṉ that the Cheyenne Indians are supposed to have received.

wawa'kaṉkaṉ, n. or v. One who does wonderful things. Wawakaṉkaṉpi keci. B.H.67.6.

wawa'kaṉkaṉka, adj. Acting in a mysterious manner, soothsaying. Wawamakaṉkaṉka. Wicaśa wawakaṉkaṉpika. B.H. 49.11.

wawa'kiciśpaśpake, (?). The word is used in ref. to one who has given away much, distributed and given more in addition. Bl.

wawa'k̄ip̄ajiṉ, v.n. To rebel against, oppose; to be a rebel. Wawawakipajiṉ.
wawa'k̄ip̄ajiṉpi, n. Opposition, rebellion.
wawa'k̄ip̄ajiṉyaṉ, adv. Rebelliously.

wawa'k̄oṉt̄a, v. (wakoṉta). To cut or notch. Wawawakoṉta. -- wawák̄oṉtk̄oṉt̄a, v. red.

wawa'kp̄aṉ, v. (wakpaṉ). To cut up fine. Wawawakpaṉ.
wawa'kpaṉśni, adj. (kpaṉ). Fine, active, stirring, as a man; nervous, quick stepping, as a horse; fleet, as a dog. Wawamakpaṉśni. Note: this word is used in the neg. form only.

wawa'ksa, v. (waksa). To cut off. Wawawaksa.

wawa'kt̄ak̄a, v. (wakta). To look for. Wawaktakeśni uṉhipelo, Our coming was a surprise to them. Bl.

wawa'ktaṉ, v. (waktaṉ). To cut so as to make crooked. Wawawaktaṉ.

wawa'ktayapi, n. Something expected, as a child. SLB.

wawa'k'eza, v. (wak'eza). To make smooth by cutting. Wawawak'eza.
wawa'k'eze, n. A board on which to trim feathers or to shave wood.

wawa'k'oŋśni, adj. Active. Syn.- śpukeśni, bliheca. WE.

wawa'mna, v. (wamna). To rip with a knife. Wawawamna.

wawa'mnala, 1) v. (wamnala). To respect one, honor, have a high opinion of. 2) n. One who respects. Wawamnawala.
wawa'mnalaśni, n. One who respects nothing.

wawa'nice, v. or n. To be nothing; a dearth. Wawaniciŋ ktelo. B.H.32.26.
wawa'niceca, v. There is nothing or very little.

wa'waŋk̇e, n. (waawaŋyaŋke). A watchman.
wawaŋ'yaŋk, cont. of wawaŋyaŋka. - mni kta. B.H.269.21.
wawaŋ'yaŋk̇a, v. (waŋyaŋka). To look in, see. Wawaŋblaka. Tuwa toka hi na - ca na iśta ḣca yelo, i.e. sore eyes.
wawaŋ'yaŋk̇e, n. A looker-on, spectator.
wa'waŋyaŋk̇e, n. A policeman, an overseer.

wawa'ṗesṫo, v. (wapesto). To shave to a point. Wawawapesto.

wawa'ṗilak̇iya, 1) v. (pilakiya). To make glad. Wawapilawakiya. 2) n. One who makes glad.

wawa'ṗilaya, v. abs. To give cause for gratitude; to do a favor. D.5.

wawa'ṗoṫa, v. (wapota). To destroy by cutting. Wawawapota.

wawa'psaka, v. (wapsaka). To cut off e.g. a cord. Wawawapsaka.

wawa'pta, v. (wapta). To cut out, pare around. Wawawapta.

wawa'pṫecela, v. (waptecela). To cut off short. Wawawaptecela.

wawa'ptuḣ'a, v. (waptuḣ'a). To scrape off crumbs, as from a medicine root. Bl.

wawa'sċusċuk̇e, n. One who dresses well in order to be noticed by the women folk. Bl.

wawa'sk̇u, v. (wasku). To pare e.g. potatoes. Wawawasku.

wawa'smiŋ, v. (wasmiŋ). To make bare with a knife. Wawawasmiŋ.

wa'was'iŋ, (?). Bl.

wawa'śagya, v. To spoil, render worthless. B.H.34.18.

wawa'śicuŋke, n. One who imitates or tries to be like a white man.
wawa'śicuŋyaŋ, adv. (waśicuŋ). Like a white man.
wawa'śikśicuŋke, n. One who imitates or tries to be like a white man.

wawa'śilkigla, 1) v.n. To be angry, vexed. 2) n. One who is angry.
wawa'śilkiglaya, v. (śilkiglaya). To make angry. Wawaśilkiglawaya.

wawa'śk̇iṫa, v. (waśkita). To cut, gash. Wawawaśkita.

wawa'śla, v. (waśla). To shave off. Wawawaśla.

wawa'śloka, v. (waśloka). To cut out of. Wawawaśloka.

wawa'śṗa, v. (waśpa). To cut off pieces. Wawawaśpa.

wawa'śṗu, v. (waśpu). To cut in pieces. Wawawaśpu. -- wawáśṗuśṗu, v. red. (wawaśpu). To cut up in pieces e.g. tallow. Wawawaśpuśpu.

wawa'ṫak̇uniśni, v. (watakuniśni). To destroy.

wawa'ṫeṗa, v. (watepa). To wear off to a stump; to cut off short. R.

wawa't'a, v. (wat'a). To kill with a knife.

wawa't'eca, adv. Gentle, mild. Śuŋkawakaŋ waŋji - k'iŋ mamani kte lo.
wawa't'ecaka, n. One who is kind, as a gentle horse.

wawa'yuśna, 1) v. (wayuśna). To sacrifice. Wawabluśna. 2) n. One who sacrifices; a priest.

wawe'čeya, v. abs. (weceya). To have confidence in people. Wawecewaya.
wawe'čeyeśni, v. To distrust. Wawecewayeśni. Bl.
wawe'čeyeśniśni oȟe kitóᶯ, v. To slander and spoil one's good name. Bl.

wawi'caȟya, v. (icaȟya). To cause to grow, to form; to create.
wawi'caȟye, n. A maker, a former; the Creator.

wawi'cak'u, v. To donate, make a donation. Wawicawak'u. P.
wawi'cak'upi, n. A gift. Bl.

wawi'cekiya, v. To solicit help, support. Wawicewakiya.

wawi'ciȟaȟa, n. One who commits adultery; one who sins against others and makes light of it.
wawi'ciȟaȟapi, n. A laughing stock; adultery. B.H.233.14.

wawi'ciya, n. (iciya). An advocate, one who helps (supposing two are fighting) and assists one against the other. Also, waniciye.

wawi'gni, v. To search for something, to hunt. Wawiwagni.

wawi'haᶯgya, v. (ihaᶯgya). To destroy. Wawihaᶯgwaya. B.H.14.12;50.17.
wawi'haᶯgye, n. A destroyer.

wawi'ȟa, v. (iȟa). To laugh at. Wawiwaȟa. -- wawiȟaȟa, v. red.

wawi'ȟaka, n. One who makes sport, a jester.

wawi'ȟapi, n. Jesting, making sport.

wawi'ȟat'eya, v. Not to understand one's business, to do it wrong; to make others laugh at one's ignorance. Bl.

wawi'ȟaya, 1) v.a. To cause to laugh at. Wawiȟawaya. 2) adv. Wittily.

wawi'ȟpeya, v. To give away. Wawiȟpewaya.

wawi'ȟ'aᶯka, n. One who is always doing something, a hustler.

wawi'koyaka, n. Same as wokaȟtaᶯ blaskaska. Bl. #119.

wawi'maǧaǧayeca, n. One who cheers up others by his talk. Bl.

wawi'mnaśniyaᶯ, adv. Haughtily, considering others weaklings. B.H.86.13.

wawi'naȟni, v. (inaȟni). To be in haste.
wawi'naȟniyaᶯ, v. To hasten, cause to hurry. Wawinaȟniwaya. Wawinaȟniwaya tka wablaȟlokeśni, I tried to get them busy, but I made no impression on them. Bl.

wawi'nakiȟni, v. To be in haste, to do beforehand. Wawinawakiȟni.
wawi'nakiȟnika, n. One who is in haste.

wawi'nihaᶯ, adj. (inihaᶯ). Fearful, afraid; inspiring fear, excited. - maᶯka. -- wawinihaᶯyaᶯ, v. To make afraid. Wawinihaᶯwaya.

wawi'piic'ila, v. refl. (wawipila). To think more of one's self than of anyone else.

wawi'pila, v. (ipila). Not to give, to refuse. Same as waipila. Iyeś waᶯuśila na taku yuha kiᶯ tohiᶯni - śni na tuwa oᶯśika ca taku yuha kiᶯ oᶯ okiya keya okiyaka. D.214, 53 note 2.

wawi'śtaᶯyeca, n. One who can cheer up others by his funny talking. Bl.

wawi'śteca, adj. Modest, ashamed. Cf. wiśteca, the better form.
wawi'śtelya, 1) v. To make ashamed. Wawiśtelwaya. 2) adv. Ashamedly, bashfully.

wawi'tkoya, v.(witkoya). To make drunk. Wawitkowaya.

wawi'toᶯpa, v. (itoᶯpa). To praise. Wawitoᶯwapa.
wawi'toᶯpapi, n. Praising.
wawi'toᶯpapiśni, n. Not praising.

wawi'wahoya, v. To issue orders. B.H. 231.1. -- wawiwahoye, n. One who gives orders.

wawi'waktaya, v. To cause one to expect or wait for something, as for a call. B.H.157.12;242.2. SLB.

wawi'yaciᶯ, v. (iyaciᶯ). To liken to, to use parables. Wawiblaciᶯ.
wawi'yaciᶯyaᶯ, adv. Figuratively.

wawi'yaȟpaȟpaya, v. red., perhaps from wawiyaȟpaya. (?). T'ebleze śni - ayahilale, i.e. to wrestle for fun. Bl.

wawi'yaȟtagia, v. To find fault. Wawiyaȟtagiwaya, perhaps. -- wawi'yaȟtaka, v. (yaȟtaka). To find fault.

wawi'yakaṗeic'iya, v. refl. (wawiyakapeya). To exceed one's self, to be intemperate.

wawi'yakaṗeya, v. To exceed, go beyond.

wawi'yaksapa, v. (iyaksapa, perhaps). To say wise words. Wawiblaksapa. WH. Wicaśa ksapapi lena wawiyaksapapi ca oyate kiȠ ogna oigluhayapi. MS.483. Na tokel okihi scu na taku eyaś wawiyaksapiȠ na taȠyaȠ kiȠye wicaśi. MS. 104.

wawi'yaṗe, 1) v. (iyape). To lie in wait. Same as waiyape. Wawiyawape. 2) n. An ambush. -- wawi'yaṗeṗi, Same as waiyapepi.

wawi'yayuȟ, cont. (wawiyayuȟa). Following, as a colt its mother.
wawi'yayuȟa, v. (iyayuȟa). To follow, be attached to. B.H.290.10. -- n. One who follows.
wawi'yayuȟya, adv. Following.

wawi'yeke s'e, (?). ŚuȠka wawiyeke s'e gliyaȠkiȠ kte lo, as was said of Father Westropp, a missionary of the Pine Ridge in the first quarter of the 20th century. ŚuȠkpala...wowiyuśkiȠ. Bl.

wawi'yeḱiya, v. (iyekiya). To recognize something. Wawiyewakiya.

wawi'yeya, v. (iyeya). To find. Wawiyewaya. -- wawi'yeyeca, n. One that finds much, as does a good dog.

wawi'yohi, v. (iyohi). To reach to, extend to, to be sufficient for. Wawiyowahi. -- wawi'yohiya, 1) v.a. To cause to reach to. Wawiyohiwaya. 2) adv. Reaching to.

wawi'yoḱiṗi, v. (iyokipi). To be pleased with. Wawiyomakipi. -- wawi'yoḱiṗiya, adv. Joyfully, gladly, pleasantly. -- wawi'yoḱiṗiye, n. One liked by others at first sight. B.H.85.14.

wawi'yoḱiśica, v. (iyokiśica). To be sad. Wawiyomakiśica. -- wawi'yoḱiśil, cont. (wawiyokiśica). Sad. - wauȠ. -- wawi'yoḱiśilya, 1) v. (iyokiśilya). To make sad. Wawiyokiśilwaya. 2) adv. Sadly, sorrowfully. Wawiyokiśilwaya iyecel wahi yelo. Bl. BT.

wawi'yoḱiśni, v. To forbid. B.H.111.8; 260.20.

wawi'yoṗaśṫaḱa, v. (iyopaśtaka). To encourage, urge on.

wawi'yoṗeḱiya, v. (iyopekiya). To sell; to reprove. Wawiyopewakiya.
wawi'yoṗeya, v. (iyopeya). To reprove. Wawiyopewaya.

wawi'yowiȠyaȠ, part. Accomodating. Bl.

wawi'yuḱaḱija, v. (yukakija). To make suffer. Wawiblukakija.

wawi'yukcaȠ, v. (iyukcaȠ). To judge, to examine. WawiblukcaȠ. -- wawi'yukcaȠka, n. One who examines and judges.

wawi'yuȠġa, v. (iyuȠga). To inquire, ask questions. WawimuȠga, wawiuȠyugapi. B.H.236.3.
wawi'yuȠġapi, n. An inquiry.
wawi'yuȠġe s'a, adj. Inquisitive. P.
wawi'yuȠȟ, cont. of wawiyuȠga. - bla.
wawi'yuȠȟṫuḱel, adv. In an inquiring manner. - omani. R. Bl.
wawi'yuȠȟya, adv. Inquiringly.

wawi'yuṗiya, adv. Well, expertly.

wawi'yuta, v. (iyuta). To measure. B.H.194.14.

wawi'yuṫaȠ, n. What solicits as to temptation. SLB. - awakipa kiȠ, Jesus oȠśimala ye. Pb.34.
wawi'yuṫaȠyaȠ, v. (iyutaȠyaȠ). To tempt. WawiyutaȠwaya.
wawi'yuṫaȠye, n. One who tempts, a tempter. - oyas'iȠ kowakipiȠ kte. Pb. 27.

wawo'blaya, v. (woblaya). To make spread out by shooting or punching. Wawowablaya.

wawo'blaza, v. (woblaza). To tear open by shooting etc. Wawowablaza.

wawo'bleca, v. (wobleca). To break in pieces by shooting or punching. Wawowableca.

wawo'blu, v. (woblu). To pound fine, to pulverize. Wawowablu.

wa'woblu, v. The snow flies. Iwaśtegla tate yeśaŋ, wáwoblu welo. Bl.

wawo'ceḱa, v. To make stagger by shooting. Wawoceg iyeya.

wawo'c'o, v. (woc'o). To churn. Wawowac'o.

wawo'gna, v. (wogna). To knock off e.g. fruit by shooting. Wawowagna.

wawo'gnaśk̇iŋyaŋ, v. (wognaśkiŋyaŋ). To make crazy by pounding, punching or shooting. Wawowagnaśkiŋyaŋ.

wawo'gnayaŋ, v. (wognayaŋ). To miss in shooting. Wawowagnayaŋ.

wawo'haiyeya, v. (wohaiyeya). To make tumble over by shooting.

wawo'hilhitika, adj. perhaps. (?). Wawohilhitikiŋ kte ḣciŋ. Siŋkpela s'e úŋśika tka wawohilhitikece, as is said when an old woman inspite of her helplessness takes care of her husband and household. Bl.

wawo'hiŋṫa, v. (wohiŋta). To sweep all off by shooting. Wawowahiŋta.

wawo'hoho, v. (wohoho). To make loose by shooting. Wawowahoho.

wawo'huŋhuŋza, v. (wohuŋhuŋza). To make shake by shooting. Wawowahuŋhuŋza.

wawo'ḣci, v. (woḣci). To shoot or punch out pieces. Wawowaḣci.

wawo'ḣiŋyaŋ, v. (oḣiŋyaŋ). To be dissatisfied with. Wawowaḣiŋyaŋ.

wawo'ḣloka, v. (woḣloka). To shoot or punch holes. Wawowaḣloka.

wawo'ḣmiŋ, v. (woḣmiŋ). To make crooked by shooting. Wawowaḣmiŋ.

wawo'ḣṗa, v. (woḣpa). To shoot on the wing.

wawo'ḣtaka, v. To knock with the end of anything. Bl.

wawo'jaja, v. (wojaja). To wash out by punching. Wawowajaja.

wawo'ji, v. (ojiji). To tell secretly. Wawowaji. -- wawójiji, v. To whisper; a whisperer, n. Wawowajiji.

wawo'kaḣṫaŋyaŋ, v. (okaḣtaŋyaŋ). To have much influence over. Oyate...wawokaḣtaŋwaye.

wawo'ḱicaḣniġa, adj. Of quick understanding.

wawo'k̇ihi, v. (okihi). To be able. Wawowakihi.

wawo'k̇ihik̇a, n. One who is able.
wawo'k̇ihiya, v. To make able. Wawokihiwaya.

wawo'k̇iya, v. (okiya). To help; to be with, to accompany. Wawowakiya. Takomni wawowicakiyapi waŋ yuk̇e. -- wawók̇iye, n. One who helps, a helper; Help.

wawo'kpani, v. (okpani). To be unsuccessful, unlucky. Bl.

wawo'kṗaŋ, v. (wokpaŋ). To pound fine. Wawowakpaŋ.

wawo'ksa, v. (woksa). To break off by shooting or punching. Wawowaksa.

wawo'kṫaŋ, v. (wo-ktaŋ). To bend by shooting or pounding. Wawowaktaŋ.

wawo'kuka, v. (wokuka). To destroy by pounding or shooting. Wawowakuka.

wawo'ḱuwa, v. (okuwa). To follow constantly, to chase. Wawokuwa.

wawo'k'oya, n. Excitement, tumult. - taŋka. B.H.303.3. -- v.n. To be clamorous, noisy, to make noise. Cf. owolutatoŋ.

wawo'k'oyece, n. (?). As is said when a crowd of people disperses in all directions, as when suddenly noticing a snake among them. Bl.

wawol'wicayeśni,uŋ, v. (?). - yauŋ. Bl.

wawo'paŋ , v. (wopaŋ). To pound fine, as hominy. Wawowapaŋ. -- wawópaŋpaŋ, v. (wopaŋpaŋ). To make soft by pounding.

wawo'paŋpi, n. Cornmeal,or anything pounded fine.

wawo'p̄emni, v. (wopemni). To twist by shooting etc. Wawowapemni.

wawo'p̄ot̄a, v. (wopota). To shoot or pound to pieces. Wawowapota.

wawo'psaka, v. (wopsaka). To shoot off, as strings. Wawowapsaka.

wawo'pt̄a, v. To cut out e.g. turnips. Wawowapta. Hence, to dig up by striking with a stick endwise, as in digging tiⁿpsiⁿla. D.243.

wawo'pteca, (?). - śni, Active, energetic; none being greater. Pb.21

wawo'slat̄a, n. Hollow bones used for ornaments. A kind of long bead and large in the middle; worn by the Dakota. R. - wanap'iⁿ, An ornamental breast cover made of hollow bones.

wawo'sleca, v. (wosleca). To split by shooting. Wawowasleca.

wawo'sni, v. (wosni). To blow out, extinguish. Wawowasni.

wawo'sot̄a, v. (wosota). To exterminate by shooting. Wawowasota.

wawo'śkiśkeyece, n. One who butts in and causes confusion when others are disputing about something. Bl.

wawo'śla, v. (wośla). To shoot off bare. Wawowaśla.

wawo'śloǩa, v. (wośloka). To shoot or punch out, as an eye. Wawowaśloka.

wawo'śna, v. (wośna). To miss in shooting. Wawowaśna.

wawo'śp̄a, v. (wośpa). To shoot off a piece. Wawowaśpa.

wawo'śt̄egla, 1) v. (ośtegla). To call bad names. 2) n. One who speaks evil of. Wawośtewagla.

wawo'śuja, v. (wośuja). To shoot to splinters.

wawo'ś'aǩa, v. (woś'aka). To shoot or punch with too little force to penetrate. Wawowaś'aka.

wawo't̄a ihaⁿ, n. A snow drift. Also, wawota iheya.

wawo't̄akuniśni, v. (wotakuniśni). To shoot to pieces or destroy. Wawowatakuniśni.

wawo't̄ica, (?). Bl.

wawo't̄iyekiya, v. To plead for. Oyate kiⁿ wawotiyewicakiyapi kta on. B.H. 49.9.

wawo't'a, v. (wot'a). To kill by punching. Wawowat'a.

wawo't'iⁿza, v. (wot'iⁿza). To pound tight. Wawowat'iⁿza.

wawo'weǧa, v. (wowega). To break or fracture by shooting or punching. Wawowaweǧa.

wawo'yaǩa, 1) v. (oyaka). To relate. Wawoblaka. 2) n. One who relates, a narrator.

wawo'yusiⁿ, v. To hate, to be out of humor with. -- wawóyusiⁿǩe, n. One who hates.

wawo'yusp̄a, 1) v. (oyuspa). To seize, to arrest as a prisoner. Wawobluspa. 2) n. A policeman. -- wawóyusp̄api, n. The making of arrests.

waya'aglapśuⁿyaⁿ, v. (yaaglapśuⁿyaⁿ). To root over, as a hog does anything. - iyeya.

waya'aślaya, adv. (yaaślaya). Explaining, unfolding.

waya'ataⁿiⁿ, 1) v. (yaataⁿiⁿ). To make manifest, proclaim. Wablaataⁿiⁿ. 2) n. A prophet. B.H.197.11.

waya'blaska, v. (yablaska). To make flat with the mouth. Wablablaska.

waya'blaskaska, v. (yablaskaska). To talk about unimportant things per longum et latum, to make much of a little thing, to add details; to thrash out.

waya'blaya, v. (yablaya). To make level with the mouth. Wablablaya.

waya'blaza, v. (yablaza). To bite or tear open with the teeth. Wablablaza.

waya'bleca, v. (yableca). To break, crush or tear to pieces with the teeth. Wablableca.

waya'bleza, v. (yableza). To cheer up by speaking. Wablableza.

waya'blu, v. (yablu). To chew fine. Wablablu. -- wayáblublu, v. red.

waya'caŋcaŋ, v. (yacaŋcaŋ). To make shake with the mouth. Wablacaŋcaŋ.

waya'caŋze, v. (yacaŋze). To have the habit of making people angry by talking. Wablacaŋze.

waya'caskeskeke, v. To eat slowly. Wablacaskeskeke. Bl.

waya'caśkeśkeke, v. To eat a small ration of food slowly so as to make it last longer. Wablacaśkeśkeke. Bl.

waya'cekceka, v. (yacekceka). To make stagger by biting etc. Wablacekceka.

waya'ceya, v. (yaceya). To make cry by scolding etc. Wablaceya.

waya'cik'ala, v. (yacik'ala). To speak of as small, to underrate. Wablacik'ala.

waya'ciscila, v. (yaciscila). To underrate. Wablaciscila.

waya'coco, v. (yacoco). To make soft by biting, to chew. Wablacoco.

waya'ċoċoka, n. One who always gives his own opinion. R. Bl.

waya'coza, v. (yacoza). To make warm by biting etc. Wablacoza.

waya'c'o, v. To smack the lips while eating. Śuŋkwíċaḣcala s'e walac'o.Bl.

waya'ececa, v. (yaececa). To persuade, talk into. IS. WE.

waya'ecetu, v. (yaecetu). To accomplish or bring to pass by speaking. Wablaecetu.

waya'ġa, v. (yaga). To bite off, as husks. -- wayáġaṗa, v. (yagapa). To bite off the skin or husk. -- n. One who bites, as a horse.

waya'ġica, v. (yagica). To waken up, cause one to awaken by speaking to him. Wablaġica.

waya'gla, v. (yagla). To draw out or uncoil, as a dog does when eating the fat from entrails.

waya'glakiŋyaŋ, v. (yaglakiŋyaŋ). To set at variance, to make mischief between others. Wablaglakiŋyaŋ. - na heyahelo. Bl.

waya'gloka, v. (yagloka). To put out of joint with the teeth.

waya'gmigma, v. (yagmigma). To make round with the mouth. Wablagmigma.

waya'gmiyaŋ, v. (yagmiyaŋ). To make roll with the mouth. Also, wayágmiyáŋyaŋ. Wablagmiyaŋyaŋ.

waya'gnaśkiŋyaŋ, v. To make crazy by talking to. Wablagnaśkiŋyaŋ.

waya'gnayaŋ, v. To miss with the mouth, to deceive, to tell a falsehood. Wablagnayaŋ.

waya'hahake, n. One who causes to waver by biting. -- wayáhahayela, v. To make waver or to render unstable by biting. Wablahahayela.

waya'ha iyeya, v. To throw down by biting, as one horse does another.

waya'hiŋṫa, v. (yahiŋta). To brush away with the mouth. Wablahiŋta. -- n. One who names every point of his speech, and thus brushes it away.

waya'hoho, v. (yahoho). To make loose by biting. Wablahoho.

waya'homni, v. (yahomni). To turn one around by talking, persuade one to change his opinions. Wablahomni.

waya'hoṫa, n. Wild rice, oats.

waya'hoṫa blaska, n. The name for spelts.

waya'hoṫa hiŋśmáśma, n. Barley. P.

waya'hoṫoŋ, v. (yahotoŋ). To make cry out by biting. Wablahotoŋ.

waya'huŋhuŋza, v. (yahuŋhuŋza). To shake with the mouth. Wablahuŋhuŋza.

waya'ḣaṗa, v. (yaḣapa). To scare up by talking, as game. Wablaḣapa.

waya'ḣci, v. (yaḣci). To bite out a piece. Wablaḣci.

waya'hepa, v. (yahepa). To drink all up. Wablahepa.

waya'heyata, v. (yaheyata). To get (others) away by talking. Wablaheyata. R. Bl.

waya'hla, v. (yahla). To rattle with the mouth.

waya'hlata, v. (yahlata). To scratch with the teeth.

waya'hleca, v. (yahleca). To tear with the teeth. Wablahleca.

waya'hloka, v. (yahloka). To bite a hole in. Wablahloka. Also, to make an impression by talking, to persuade. Wawinahniwaya tka wablahloke śni. Bl.

waya'hpa, v. (yahpa). To throw down with the mouth. Wablahpa.

waya'hpu, v. (yahpu). To bite off anything that had been glued on. Wablahpu.

waya'htagia, v. To find fault.

waya'htaka, v. (yahtaka). To bite; to abuse by speaking evil of; one that bites, as a dog, n. Wablahtaka.

waya'huğa, v. (yahuga). To crush with the teeth. Wablahuga.

waya'hugnağa, v. (yahugnaga). To slander and thus spoil other people's good name. Bl.

waya'hwa, v. (yahwa). To make sleepy by talking to. Wablahwa.

waya'h'aŋhihike, v. (yah'aŋhike). To eat slowly. Bl. Wablah'aŋhihike.
waya'h'aŋhike, v. To eat very slowly.

waya'h'u, v. (yah'u). To peel off with the teeth. Wablah'u.

waya'iha, 1) v. (yaiha). To make laugh by talking. 2) n. One who jests and makes others laugh.

waya'iiyowaja, v. To speak of as pertaining to.

waya'ijena, v. (yaijena). To make trouble between others by talking. Wablaijena. - na heyahelo. Bl.

waya'inahni, v. To hasten, make hurry by talking. Wablainahni. -- wayáinahniya, v. To hasten one by speaking to him.

waya'inila, v. (yainila). To put to silence by speaking. Wablainila. -- wayáinilya, adv. Putting to silence. - ia.

waya'iśteca, v. To make ashamed by talking to.

waya'iyoya, v. (yaiyoya). To make yawn by talking.

waya'jaja, v. (yajaja). To wash or clean with the mouth, as a wolf or dog does by licking bones.

waya'jata, v. (yajata). To seduce, making others give up their good views. Wablajata. WE.

waya'jipa, v. (yajipa). To bite, as mosquitos do.

waya'jo, v. (yajo). To blow an instrument. Wablajo.
waya'jopi, n. A horn, a cornet, etc. B.H.75.22.

waya'juju, 1) v. (yajuju). To demolish with the mouth, as an argument by counter argument; to tear to pieces, as a dog does anything with its mouth. 2) n. One who demolishes with his mouth. Wablajuju.

waya'ka, n. A captive taken in war, a prisoner. - oyuspapi.

waya'kaka, v. (yakaka). To champ, as does a horse.

waya'kapa, v. (yakapa). To catch in the mouth. Wablakapa.

waya'katiŋ, v. To straighten with the mouth.

waya'kawa, v. (yakawa). To open with the mouth.

waya'kayah'u wico'kuje, n. Leprosy, something like eczema, white. - śpahaŋhaŋpi. B.H.114.20;129.23;184.21.

waya'kiza, v. To grit or grind the teeth, as does a cow.

waya'kokoka, v. To make the teeth rattle. Wablakokoka.

waya'ḱoⁿtḱoⁿta, v. To indent or notch with the teeth. Wablakoⁿtkoⁿta.

waya'kp̄aⁿ, v. (yakpaⁿ). To masticate. Wablakpaⁿ.

waya'kpi, v. (yakpi). To crack with the teeth, as a louse. Wablakpi.

waya'ksa, v. (yaksa). To bite off. Wablaksa. -- wayáksaksa, v. red.

waya'ksapa, v. (yaksapa). To make wise by instruction, to teach. Wablaksapa.

waya'kśaⁿ, v. (yakśaⁿ). To bend with the mouth. Bl.

waya'kśija, v. (yakśija). To double up with the teeth. Wablakśija.

waya'kťaⁿ, v. (yaktaⁿ). To bend with the teeth. Wablaktaⁿ. -- wayákťaⁿyaⁿ, adv. Bending with the teeth.

waya'kuka, v. (yakuka). To bite to pieces. Wablakuka.

waya'k'eǧa, v. (yak'ega). To gnaw with a grating noise. Wablak'ega.

waya'k'eza, v. (yak'eza). To bite smooth with a grating noise. Wablak'eza.

waya'k'oǧa, v. (yak'oga). To gnaw. Wablak'oga.

waya'mima, v. (yamima). To make round in the mouth. Wablamima.

waya'mna, v. (yamna). 1) To rip with the teeth. 2) To gain by talking. Wablamna.

waya'mnuǧa, v. (yamnuga). To grind, as in eating parched corn. Wablamnuga. -- wayámnumnuǧa, v. red. (wayamnuga). To gnaw, as a dog does a bone.

waya'ohiⁿyaⁿze, v. (yaohiⁿyaⁿze). To persuade one to give up by representing the thing as bad. Bl.

waya'oȟ'aⁿko, v. (yaoȟ'aⁿko). To make quick by speaking to. Wablaoȟ'aⁿko.

waya'ojigjica, (?). Tajiyagnuⁿpa s'e - as is said when a man desires meat. Bl.

waya'okp̄aniyaⁿ, v. To speak of as unequal, to make unequal.

waya'oksa, v. (yaoksa). To bite through Wablaoksa.

waya'okťaⁿ, v. (yaoktaⁿ). To bend into with the teeth. Wablaoktaⁿ.

waya'ol'otake, v. To eat slowly so as to make a small ration last long. Bl.

waya'onihaⁿ, v. (yaonihaⁿ). To praise, to honor. Wablaonihaⁿ. -- wayáonihaⁿyaⁿ, adv. Práising.

waya'opťelya, v. To make less with the mouth.

waya'oťaⁿ, v. To exhort. P.

waya'otaⁿiⁿ, 1) v. (yaotaⁿiⁿ). To make manifest. 2) n. One who makes manifest.

waya'p̄a, v. (yapa). To hold in the mouth. Wablapa. 2) n. Something edible taken home. NP.

waya'p̄emni, v. (yapemni). To twist with the teeth. Wablapemni.

waya'p̄esťo, v. (yapesto). To bite to a point. Wablapesto.

waya'p̄i, v. Cf. wayapika.

waya'p̄ika, v.n. To be fluent, to speak a language well, to be eloquent. Wablapika.

waya'p̄iⁿsp̄iⁿzece, v. To eat very slowly because the ration is very small. Bl. Wablapiⁿspiⁿzece.

waya'p̄iya, adv. Fluently.

waya'pizapi, n. A mouth organ.

waya'pop̄a, v. (yapopa). To make burst by biting. Wablapopa.

waya'p̄oťa, 1) v. (yapota). To tear to pieces with the mouth, to rend, be ravenous. 2) n. One who tears in pieces with the teeth, as does a dog. Wablapota.

waya'psaka, v. (yapsaka). To bite off e.g. cords. Wablapsaka.

waya'psica, v. (yapsica). To make hop by biting. Wablapsica.

waya'psoŋ, v. (yapsoŋ). To spill with the mouth. Wablapsoŋ. Also, wayapsuŋ.

waya'pśuŋ, v. (yapśuŋ). To shed, as a horse his teeth.

waya'ptaŋyaŋ, v. (yaptaŋyaŋ). To turn over with the mouth, roll over. Wablaptaŋyaŋ.

waya'ptecela, v. (yaptecela). To bite off short.

waya'ptuja, v. (yaptuja). To split e.g. a tooth. Wablaptuja.

waya'skapa, v. To smack one's lips; to kiss. Ho wáyaskapa, as is said of the noise made by fish when they come to the surface of the water, or as in kissing. Cf. wayaśkapa.

waya'sk̄ep̄a, v. (yaskepa). To drink all out.

waya'sk̄ica, v. (yaskica). To press on with the mouth. Wablaskica.
waya'skita, v. To press on with the mouth, make tight. Wablaskita.

waya'sku, v. (yasku). To peel off with the teeth, bite off the skin or rind. Wablasku. -- wayáskusku, v. red. (yasku). To bite off the rind or hull. Wablaskusku.

waya'sleca, v. (yasleca). To split with the teeth.

waya'slohaŋ, v. (yaslohaŋ). To drag along with the mouth, as a wolf or other animal does his prey.

waya'sluta, v. To pull out with the teeth, as does a dog.

waya'smaka, v. (yasmaka). To bite and make indentations.

waya'smiŋ, v. (yasmiŋ). To gnaw off, as dogs do. -- wayásmiŋyaŋyaŋ, v. To be eaten off smooth.

waya'sna, v. (yasna). To make ring with the mouth; to ravel. Wablasna.

waya'sni, v. To make go out by talking, talk until the fire goes out.

waya'sota, v. (yasota). To eat all up e.g. food; to use up e.g. words. Wablasota.
waya'soteca, n. One who eats up much.

waya'spaya, v. (yaspaya). To wet with the mouth. Wablaspaya.

waya'st̄aŋka, v. (yastanka). To moisten with the mouth.

waya'st̄o, v. (yasto). To lick down, as one cow does the hair of another.

waya'su, 1) v. (yasu). To judge, condemn. Wablasu. 2) n. A judge.

waya'sut̄a, v. (yasuta). To make firm with the mouth, to establish or decree. Wablasuta.

waya'suya, adv. In the manner of judging.

waya'swaka, v. (yaswaka). To make fringed but trying to bite a piece off a tough piece of meat, i.e. not getting off much. Wablaswaka. Bl.

wayas'yazaŋka, adj. (?). WE.

waya'śap̄a, v. (yaśapa). To soil with the mouth.

waya'śica, v. (yaśica). To speak evil of, to curse. Wablaśica.

waya'śigla, v. (yaśigla). To make angry by talking to.

waya'śiȟt̄iŋ, v. (yaśiȟtiŋ). To enfeeble by biting, or perhaps talking to; to spoil or make bad with the mouth; to talk badly about, to find fault with. -- wayáśiȟt̄iŋȟa, n. One who always finds fault.

waya'śipa, v. (yaśipa). To bite off close.

waya'śka, v. (yaśka). To untie with the mouth.

waya'śkaŋśkaŋ, v. (yaśkaŋśkaŋ). To cause to move with the mouth.

waya'śkapa, v. To make the noise of lapping water. Ho wáyaśkapa, as is said of the noise made by splashing wato, grass. Cf. wayaskapa.

waya'śkica, v. (yaśkica). To chew and press with the mouth, as in chewing tobacco.

waya'śkiśka, v. (yaśkiśka). To bite and make rough; to get into difficulty by talking; to misrepresent. Wablaśkiśka.

waya'śkokpa, v. (yaśkokpa). To gnaw out a hollow place. Wablaśkokpa.

waya'śkoṗa, v. (yaśkopa). To make warp or twist with the mouth.

waya'śla, v. (yaśla). To graze, browse, make bare as cattle do by grazing. Iyupaga po, tokśa haŋtahena wayaślapi kte lo. BT. Cf. B.H.42.25. Note: this word is used in the present time of their doing it now.

waya'ślaḱiya, v.a. To herd. B.H.85.11.

waya'śloka, v. (yaśloka). To bite out.

waya'śna, v. (yaśna). To miss or let fall from the mouth; to make mistakes in talking, to stammer. Wablaśna.

waya'śpa, v. (yaśpa). To bit off pieces. Wablaśpa.

waya'śpi, v. (yaśpi). To pick off fruit as do birds.

waya'śpu, v. (yaśpu). To pick off with the mouth something that has been stuck on.

waya'śuja, v. (yaśuja). To crush with the mouth.

waya'ta, v. (wota). To chew. Wablata.
waya'ťa, v. 2nd pers. sing. of wota.

waya'ťakuniśni, v. (yatakuniśni). To destroy with the mouth. Wablatakuniśni.

waya'ťaŋ, v. (yataŋ). To praise. Bl.

waya'taŋiŋ, v. (yataŋiŋ). To make manifest. Wablataŋiŋ.

waya'taŋḱa, v. (yataŋka). To speak of as large. Wablataŋka.

waya'tata, v. To chew.

waya'tawaciŋ'hiŋyaŋ'za, v.n. To have the habit of taking others for morose persons.

waya'ťehaŋ, v. To speak of as far.
waya'ťehaŋhaŋ, v. To speak slowly. Wablatehaŋhaŋ.

waya'ťeȟika, v. (yateȟika). To speak of as difficult.

waya'ťekoŋza, v. (wayata-koŋza). To chew the cud, as do cows; lit. to pretend to chew.

waya'ťeṗa, v. (yatepa). To wear off the teeth. Wablatepa.

waya'tiktil ihe', v. To find fault with others when there is no reason for it, to nag. LB. Wayatiktil iwáha.

waya'ťiťaŋ, v. (yatitaŋ). To pull with the teeth. Wablatitaŋ.

waya'tḱaŋ, v. (yatkaŋ). To drink. Wablatkaŋ.
waya'tḱe, v. (yatke). To drink. Wablatke. -- wayáťḱeḱiya, v.a. To cause to drink; to give medicine to. Wayatkewakiya.

waya'tkoŋza, v. (yatkoŋza). To make equal. Wablatkoŋza.

waya'togtogya, v. (yatogtogya). To lie while narrating something. Perhaps also, wayatogtog ia.

waya'tokaŋ, v. (yatokaŋ). To speak of as in another place. Wablatokaŋ.

waya'toḱeca, v. (yatokeca). To alter, change, speak of as different. Wablatokeca.

waya'ťuḱa, v. (yatuka). To nibble off e.g. hair etc. Wablatuka.

waya'tuta, v. To make smart by biting. Wablatuta.

waya't'a, v. (yat'a). To bite to death. Wablat'a.

waya't'iŋza, v. (yat'iŋza). To make firm with the mouth; to establish, declare.

waya'uⁿka, v. (yauⁿka). To bite and make fall, as a beaver does trees. R. Bl. Wablauⁿka.

waya'wa, v. (yawa). To read, count; to go to school. Wablawa.
waya'wahiⁿyaⁿza, Cf. wayuwahiⁿyaⁿza.
waya'waja, v. (yawaja). To bite or gnaw at, as dogs do.

waya'wakaⁿ, v. To speak of as sacred. Wablawakaⁿ.

waya'wapi, n. Reading; numeration, arithmetic.

waya'waśakala, v. To speak of as easy or cheap. Wablawaśakala.

waya'waśte, v. (yawaśte). To bless. Wablawaśte.

waya'waś'aka, v. To call strong. Wablawaś'aka.

waya'waza, v. (yawaza). To bite, as dogs do in playing with one another.

waya'weğa, v. (yawega). To break partly off with the mouth. Wablawega.

waya'wicaka, v. To call true. Wablawicaka.

waya'wicaśaśni, v. To speak of as wicked. Wablawicaśaśni.

waya'wignuni, v. (yawignuni). To confuse by butting in and saying hard words. Wablawignuni. R. Bl.

waya'wiⁿja, v. To bend down with the mouth. Wablawiⁿja.

waya'wiyakpa, v. of yawiyakpa.

waya'zamni, v. (yazamni). To uncover with the mouth.

waya'zaⁿ, v. (yazaⁿ). To feel unwell, to have pains. Wamayazaⁿ. Cf. yazáⁿ.
waya'zaⁿgla, v. To feel pain. Wayazaⁿwagla.
waya'zaⁿka, 1) v. (yazaⁿ). To be sick. Wamayazaⁿka. 2) n. One who does not feel right.

waya'ze, v. (yaze). To take out food with the mouth, as does a dog.

waya'zica, v. To stretch anything with the mouth. Wablazica.

waya'zoka, v. (yazoka). To suck e.g. sugar or candy. Wablazoka.

waya'zoⁿta, v. (yazoⁿta). To praise an undeserving person.

waye', v.a. To hunt for edibles, for game. - omani, i, ya, iyaya, mni kte. Wayeya coka ukiye s'elececa. - wai tka coka wagli yelo. Also, to look for money gotten at the agency. - coka kau welo, as is said when a man returns without having found anything. LT. Bl. Ja. Waye i na wana ȟtayetu haⁿl watuka gli. D.232.

wayu'ablaya, v. (yuablaya). To make level.

wayu'aglapśuⁿyaⁿ iyeya, v. To turn bottom up.

wayu'akiȟ'aⁿ, v. (yuakiȟ'aⁿ). To make starve. Cf. akiȟ'aⁿ.

wayu'akipab, adv. Separately. Cf. yuakipab, akipab.

wayu'apako, v. (yuapako). To make crooked. Cf. apako.

wayu'aśkayela, v. (yuaśkayela). To make near. R. Bl. Cf. aśkatuyela.

wayu'aślaya, v. (yuaślaya). To make manifest; to uncover. Wabluaślaya. Cf. aślaya.

wayu'aślayapi, n. Interpretation. B.H. 30.13. Cf. aślaya.

wayu'azi, v. (yuazi). To run aground, as a boat. Cf. áze.

wayu'blaska, v. (yublaska). To make flat. Cf. blaska.

wayu'blaya, v. (yublaya). To spread out, make level. Wablublaya.

wayu'blaza, v. (yu-blaza). To rip open. Cf. blazahaⁿ.

wayu'bleca, v. (yu-bleca). To crush, break in pieces. Wablubleca. Cf. blecahaⁿ.

wayu'blu, v. (yu-blu). To make mellow; to plough. Wablublu.

wayu'bu, v. (yu-bu). To make a drumming noise. -- wayúbubu, v. red.

wayu'ca^n, v. (yu-ca^n). To sift. Wabluca^n. -- wayúca^{n}ca^n, v. red. (wa-yuca^n). To shake, sift.

wayu'ceǩa, v. Cf. wayucekceka.
wayu'cekceka, v. (yu-cekceka). To make stagger. Wablucekceka.

wayu'ceya, v. (yu-ceya). To make cry.

wayu'cik'ala, (yu-cik'ala). To make small, to compress. Wablucik'ala.
wayu'ciscila, v. To make small.

wayu'co, adv. (ayuco). Well, neatly. -- wayúcoco, adv. red.

wayu'cokaka, v. (yu-coka). To take out or empty e.g. the load from a gun. Wablucokaka.

wayu'coya, adv. Well. Cf. ayucoya.

wayu'coza, v. (yucoza). To make warm by kindling a fire. Wablucoza. Cf. coza.

wayu'ecelya, v. (yuecelya). To make a thing as it ought to be. Wabluecelya. Bl.

wayu'eceṫu, v. (yu-ecetu). To make right, fulfil, accomplish. Wabluecetu.

wayu'eciya, v. (ayueciya). To turn wrong side out. Wablueciya.

wayu'ektaśniya^n, v. (yu-ektaśniya^n). To act wrong. Wabluektaśniya^n. B.H. 82.6.

wayu'ġa, v. (yuga). To open out or pull off, as in husking corn; to husk corn. Wabluga.
wayu'ġa^n, v. (yuga^n). To open. Wabluga^n.

wayu'ġapa, v. (yugapa). To take off the skin, as from an animal; to flay. Wablugapa.

wayu'ġata, v. (yugata). To spread out e.g. the hands. Wablugata.

wayu'gla, v. (yugla). To untwist, uncoil. Wablugla.

wayu'gloka, v. To dislocate. Wablugloka.

wayu'gmigma, v. (yugmigma). To make round. Wablugmigma. Also perhaps, to roll. Bl.

wayu'gmiya^{n}ya^n, v. (yugmiya^{n}ya^n). To make roll. Wablugmiya^{n}ya^n.

wayu'gmu^n, v. (yugmu^n). To twist. Wablugmu^n.

wayu'gna, v. (yugna). To shake off e.g. fruit.

wayu'gnaśǩi^{n}ya^n, v. (yugnaśki^{n}ya^n). To make crazy. Wablugnaśki^{n}ya^n.

wayu'gnaya^n, v. To miss; to deceive.

wayu'ġo, v. (yugo). To make crooked marks. Wablugo.

wayu'ġuǩa, v. (yuguka). To stretch, strain; to sprain. Wabluguka.

wayu'gweza, v. (yugweza). To make rough.

wayu'ha, v. (yuha). To have things, possess things, have or own properly. Wabluha. Pb.26. D.106. - iyeya.
wayu'hahaka, n. (yuha). One who possesses much. Wabluhahaka.
wayu'hahayela, v. (yuhahayela). To make unsteady. Wabluhahayela.

wayu'hi, v. (yuhi). To drive off e.g. game; to arouse, startle etc. Wabluhi. Mato Wayuhi, The name of Bear Shirt's old father.
wayu'hiǩa, adj. Disturbing, troublesome.

wayu'hi^{n}l, cont. of wayuhi^{n}ta. Śu^{n}kawaka^n - wotapelo, i.e. it scratched snow away and ate grass. LB.

wayu'hi^{n}ta, v. (yuhi^{n}ta). To sweep off. Wabluhi^{n}ta.

wayu'hoho, v. (yuhoho). To catch and hold loosely, as something too large to grasp. Wabluhoho.

wayu'homni, v. (yuhomni). To turn round on.

wayu'hoto^n, v. To cause to make noise.

wayu'hu^{n}hu^{n}za, v. (yuhu^{n}hu^{n}za). To

shake. Wabluhu^{n}hu^{n}za.

wayu'ȟatka, v. (yuȟatka). To make rough.

wayu'ȟepa, v. (yuȟepa). To drain off; to absorb.

wayu'ȟeyata, v. (yuȟeyata). To shove aside, push back.

wayu'ȟica, v. (yuȟica). To waken one up, cause to awaken. Wabluȟica.

wayu'ȟiyaya, v. (yuȟiyaya). To be awkward, to bungle. Wabluȟiyaya.
wayu'ȟiyayaka, n. A bungler.

wayu'ȟla, v. (yuȟla). To make rattle.

wayu'ȟlağa^n, v. (yuȟlaga^n). To make larger, to enlarge.

wayu'ȟlata, v. (yuȟlata). To scratch, to dig under.

wayu'ȟleca, v. (yuȟleca). To tear. Wabluȟleca.

wayu'ȟloǩa, v. (yuȟloka). To make a hole, to open. Wabluȟloka.

wayu'ȟmi, v. (yuȟmi). To make crooked.

wayu'ȟmi^n, v. (yuȟmi^n). To throw off sideways.

wayu'ȟmu^n, v. (yuȟmu^n). To buzz or make buzz.

wayu'ȟpa, v. (yuȟpa). To lay down, throw down.

wayu'ȟpu, v. (yuȟpu). To pick off pieces.

wayu'ȟťaťa, v. (ȟtata). To offer sacrifices; to kill in sacrifice. Wabluȟtata. Note: this word is used generally of animate objects, whereas wau^{n}ya^n is used of inanimate ones. -- wayúȟťaťapi, n. Sacrifices, animals or things offered in sacrifice, esp. to avoid some evil, but also to express one's community with departed spirits. Thus, pieces from one's meal are offered to a wanagi before one sets to eating, by dropping them on the ground so that animals and birds may pick them up. Cf. wau^{n}ya^{n}pi.

wayu'ȟuğa, v. (yuȟuga). To break holes in. Wabluȟuga.

wayu'ȟu^{n}ťa, v. (yuȟu^{n}ta). To make soft or pliant e.g. a skin by rubbing. Wabluȟu^{n}ta.

wayu'ȟu^{n}wi^n, v. (yuȟu^{n}wi^n). To cause to putrify. R. Bl.

wayu'ȟ'a^{n}hi, v. To make slow, to retard.

wayu'ȟ'a^{n}hica, v. To play out a horse by not knowing how to handle it.

wayu'ȟ'a^{n}hihike, n. One who is slow in his actions. Ww.

wayu'ȟ'iyayaka, (?). Wabluȟ'iyayaka.

wayu'ȟ'u, v. (yuȟ'u). To peel. Wabluȟ'u.

wayu'icicahi, v. (yuicicahi). To mingle.

wayu'ieska, v. To translate; an interpreter, n. -- wayúieskapi, n. An interpretation. B.H.30.13.

wayu'ile, v. (yuile). To make blaze.

wayu'inaȟni, v. (yuinaȟni). To cause to hasten. Wabluinaȟni.

wayu'i^{n}ya^{n}ka, v. To get ahead of others by hurrying. Wablui^{n}ya^{n}ke. IS.

wayu'iśteca, v. (yuiśteca). To make ashamed.

wayu'iyowaza, v. (yuiyowaza). To cause an echo.

wayu'ja, v. (yuja). To stir up; to make mush or hasty pudding. Wabluja.

wayu'jaja, v. (yujaja). To wash e.g. clothes; to do a washing. Wablujaja.

wayu'jaǩa, v. (yujaka). To pull open. Wablujaka.

wayu'ji^{n}ca, v. (yuji^{n}ca). To pull or blow e.g. the nose. Wabluji^{n}ca.

wayu'jipa, 1) v. (yujipa). To pinch. 2) n. One who pinches. Wablujipa.

wayu'juju, v. (yujuju). To tear down, to demolish. Wablujuju.

wayu´ju^n, v. (yuju^n). To pull out by the roots. Wabluju^n.

wayu´k̇ak̇ija, v. (yukakija). To make suffer.

wayu´ka^n, v. (yuka^n). To shake off e.g. dew.

wayu´kaṗa, v. (yukapa). To catch in the hand e.g. a ball. Wablukapa.

wayu´k̇aṫi^n, v. (yukati^n). To straighten out.

wayu´k̇awa, v. (yukawa). To open out, push back. Wablukawa.

wayu´kca, v. (yukca). To unbraid, untie. Wablukca.

wayu´kca^n, v. (yukca^n). To examine, investigate. Wablukca^n.

wayu´k̇eċa, v.n. (yuka^n). There is some.

wayu´k̇i^{n}ca, v. (yuki^{n}ca). To scrape.

wayu´k̇iṗaja, v. (yukipaja). To double or fold up.
wayu´k̇iṗeha^n, v. (yukipeha^n). To fold up.

wayu´k̇iza, v. (yukiza). To make creak. Wablukiza.

wayu´kok̇a, v. (yukoka). To rattle, giving a dull sound. Also, wayúkokok̇a.

wayu´kṗa^n, v. (yukpa^n). To make fine, to pulverize, grind e.g. grain. Wablukpa^n.

wayu´ksa, v. (yuksa). To break off, cut grain. Wabluksa. B.H.79.2. -- wayúksaksa, v. red.

wayu´ksapa, 1) v. (yuksapa). To make wise. 2) n. One who makes wise, an instructor.

wayu´kse, v.a. To break off e.g. ears of corn, to harvest e.g. corn. B.H. 183.6.

wayu´kśa, v. (yukśa). To roll up.
wayu´kśala, v. (yukśala). To bend up.

wayu´kśa^n, v. (yukśa^n). To bend.

wayu´kśija, v. (yukśija). To double up.

wayu´kṫa^n, v. (yukta^n). To bend. Wablukta^n.

wayu´kuka, v. (yukuka). To spoil, wear out.

wayu´k'eġa, v. (yuk'ega). To scratch with a grating noise.
wayu´k'eza, v. (yuk'eza). To make smooth with a grating noise.
wayu´k'oġa, v. (yuk'oga). To scratch, make rough with a grating noise.
wayu´k'oza, v. (yuk'oza). To make smooth by scraping away.

wayu´mahel iyeya, v. To put or push into.

wayu´ma^n, v. (yuma^n). To whet, file, grind e.g. edged tools. Wablume.

wayu´mima, v. (yumima). To make round by grinding. Wablumima.

wayu´mna, v. (yumna). To rip.

wa´yumni, v. (ayumni). To turn round on.

wayu´mniġa, v. (yumniga). To make shrink or draw up.

wayu´naji^n, v. (yunaji^n). To cause to stand up. Wablunaji^n.

wayu´na^{n}k̇eya, v. (yuna^{n}keya). To turn on one side.

wayu´niyaśni, v. (yuniyaśni). To suffocate, to strangle. Wabluniyaśni.

wa´yu^{n}ka, v. To watch and stay with the buffalo kills. Wau^{n}yu^{n}kapi kte lo, as some men said when they wanted to stay with the buffalos killed, while others went off to call the people. Bl.

wayu´obleca, v. (yuobleca). To scatter abroad, to disperse. Wabluobleca.

wayu´ocikṗani, v. (yuocikpani). To make unequal.

wayu´oci^{n}śica, v. (yuoci^{n}śica). To make cross.

wayu´oḣmi^n, v. (yuohmi^n). To miss, to throw on one side of the mark.

wayu´oḣṗa, v. (yuoḣpa). To break

through into.

wayu'oh'aⁿko, v. (yuoh'aⁿko). To make hasten. Wabluoh'aⁿko.

wayu'okahwoka, v. (yuokahwoka). To cause to float in the air.

wayu'okinihaⁿ, v. (yuokinihaⁿ). To make honorable.

wayu'okiwaⁿjila, v. (yuokiwaⁿjila). To make into one, to unite.

wayu'onihaⁿ, v. (yuonihaⁿ). To honor; to be respectful. Wabluonihaⁿ. -- wayúonihaⁿyaⁿ, adv. Respectfully.

wayu'opeśa śni, (?). - nahahci ni wauⁿ, i.e. to insist on having something although one does not understand it so well. BT.

wayu'optel, cont. of wayuopteca.

wayu'optetu, v. Same as wayuptecela. Bl.

wayu'oseya, v. (yuoseya). To tie in a fast knot.

wayu'ota, v. (yuota). To multiply. Wabluota.

wayu'otaⁿiⁿ, v. (yuotaⁿiⁿ). To make manifest. Wabluotaⁿiⁿ.

wayu'otkoⁿza, v. (yuotkoⁿza). To make equal.

wayu'ot'iⁿza, v. (yuot'iⁿza). To make tight in. Wabluot'iⁿza.

wayu'owotaⁿ, v. (yuowotaⁿ). To straighten, to make upright. Wabluowotaⁿ. Also, wayúowotaⁿla.

wayu'paⁿġa, v. (yupaⁿga). Same as wayuota. Bl.

wayu'paⁿpaⁿ, v. (yupaⁿpaⁿ). To make soft. Wablupaⁿpaⁿ. Also, wayúpaⁿpaⁿla.

wayu'patuja, v. (yupatuja). To bend down.

wayu'pcecela, v. (yupcecela). To shorten. Cf. wayuoptecela.

wayu'pehaⁿ, v. (yupeha). To fold up.

wayu'pi, v.n. To be skillful, ingenious. Wablupi.

wayu'pika, v.n. To be expert, skillful. Wablupika.

wayu'piya, adv. Skillfully, expertly, well. Oh'aⁿ - tak tokoⁿ. Bl. Also, wayúpiyahaⁿ, wayúpiyakel.

wayu'popa, v. (yupopa). To cause to burst.

wayu'pota, v. (yupota). To wear out, cut up. Wablupota.

wayu'poteca, n. One who wears out or uses up much.

wayu'powaya, v. (yupowaya). To brush up e.g. fur.

wayu'psaka, v. (yupsaka). To break e.g. cords. Wablupsaka.

wayu'psica, v. (yupsica). To make jump. Wablupsica.

wayu'psoⁿ, v. (yupsoⁿ). To spill out. Wablupsoⁿ.

wayu'pśuⁿ, v. (yupśuⁿ). To pull out by the roots, to dislocate. Wablupśuⁿ.

wayu'pta, v. (yupta). To cut out e.g. clothes. Wablupta.

wayu'ptaⁿyaⁿ, v. (yuptaⁿyaⁿ). To turn over. Wabluptaⁿyaⁿ.

wayu'ptayela, v. (yuptayela). To put together, collect. Wabluptayela. Bl.

wayu'ptecela, Cf. wayupcecela.

wayu'ptuha, v. (yuptuha). To pick to pieces.

wayu'ptuja, v. (yuptuja). To crack, to split.

wayu'saⁿ, v. (yusaⁿ). To whiten, to whitewash.

wayu'sapa, v. (yusapa). To blacken.

wayu'sepa, v. (yusepa). To rub off e.g. dirt or paint. Wablusepa. R. Bl.

wayu'ska, v. (yuska). To whiten, make white; to clear one who has been charged with a crime, to acquit. Wabluska. -- wayúskapi, n. One who has been cleared from charges laid against him.

wayu'sk̄eṗa, v. (yuskepa). To draw all out, to exhaust.

wayu'sk̄ica, v. (yuskica). To press; to be neat and tidy; to surpass all others; one who is feared by or restrains others. Wabluskica.

wayu'skit̄a, v. To bind, press. Same as wayuskica.

wayu'sku, v. (yusku). To shear off close, pare, shave off. Wablusku. -- wayúskusku, v. red.

wayu'slaslata, v. red. To do a thing slowly, deliberately.
wayu'slat̄a, v. To do a thing slowly.

wayu'sleca, v. (yusleca). To split. Wablusleca.

wayu'slohaⁿ, v. (yuslohaⁿ). To draw along. Wablislohaⁿ.

wayu'sluta, v. (yusluta). To pull out. Wablusluta .

wayu'smaka, v. (yusmaka). To hollow out; to indent.

wayu'smiⁿ, v. (yusmiⁿ). To pick off, make bare.

wayu'sna, v. (yusna). To ring, to rustle, as leaves falling; to ravel out. Wablusna.

wayu'sni, v. (yusni). To make cold, to extinguish.

wayu'sota, v. (yusota). To spend, use up, consume. Wablusota.

wayu'sto, v. (yusto). To smooth down. Wablusto.
wayu'stoka, n. One who makes smooth.

wayu'su, v. (yusu). To get things ready. Wablusu.

wayu'suta, v. (yusuta). To make strong, to establish. Wablusuta.

wayu'swa, v. (yuswa). To pick to pieces

wayu'swu, v. (yuswu). To make a noise, as in handling shelled corn.

wayu's'o, v. (yus'o). To cut off a strip at the edge e.g. of paper.

wayu'śa, v. (yuśa). To make red.

wayu'śapa, v. (yuśapa). To soil. Wabluśapa.

wayu'śeca, v. To make dry up or wither.

wayu'śica, v. (yuśica). To make bad, to spoil. Wabluśica.

wayu'śiȟtiⁿ, v. (yuśiȟtiⁿ). To make bad; to injure in any way.

wayu'śikśica, n. One who does nothing well, spoils things because he does not know how. Also, wayúśikśiceca. Cf. wayuśica.

wayu'śipa, v. (yuśipa). To break off close.

wayu'śka, v. (yuśka). To untie.

wayu'śkaⁿśkaⁿ, v. (yuśkaⁿśkaⁿ). To cause to move or stir about. Wabluśkaⁿśkaⁿ.

wayu'śkehaⁿ, v. (yuśkehaⁿ). To make wild or unsteady, to cause to prance.

wayu'śk̄i, v. (yuśki). To plait. Wabluśki.

wayu'śk̄iśk̄a, v. (yuśkiśka). To make rough; to make difficult or confused; to make mischief. Wabluśkiśka.

wayu'śkokpa, v. (yuśkokpa). To hollow out.

wayu'śkopa, v. (yuśkopa). To make twisting.

wayu'śla, v. (yuśla). To make bare, cut off. Wabluśla.

wayu'śleca, v. (yuśleca). To split with an effort.

wayu'śloka, v. (yuśloka). To pull out.

wayu'śluśluṫa, v. (yuśluśluta). To make slippery.

wayu'śna, 1) v. (yuśna). To drop, let slip, make a mistake. Wabluśna. 2) v.a. To sacrifice, offer sacrifice. -- wayúśnapi, n. A sacrificing, a sacrifice.

wayu'śnaśni, adj. Accurate. Bl.

wayu'śośa, v. (yuśośa). To make turbid.

wayu'śṗa, v. (yuśpa). To break off pieces. Wabluśpa.

wayu'śpi, v. (yuśpi). To pick off as berries. Wabluśpi. Cf. wośpi.

wayu'śpu, v. (yuśpu). To pick off anything stuck on. Wabluśpu.

wayu'śtaŋ, v. (yuśtaŋ). To finish. Wabluśtaŋ. -- wayúśtaŋka, n. One who finishes.

wayu'śuja, v. (yuśuja). To crush.

wayu'ś'agya, v.a. To overload e.g. an animal. Wayuś'agwaya.
wayu'ś'aka, v. (yuś'aka). To be overloaded. Wabluś'aka.

wayu'ś'iŋś'iŋ, v. (yuś'iŋś'iŋ). To tickle. Wabluś'iŋś'iŋ.

wayu'ś'iŋyeya, v. (yuś'iŋyeya). To frighten. Wayuś'iŋyewaya. D.215.

wayu'ťa, v. (yuta). To eat up; one who eats all up. Wawata. Cf. wota. R. Bl.

wayu'taŋ, v. (yutaŋ). To touch.
wayu'taŋcola, v. (yutaŋcola). To make naked.

wayu'taŋiŋ, v. (yutaŋiŋ). To make manifest, to expose. Wablutaŋiŋ.

wayu'taŋka, v. (yutaŋka). To make large.

wayu'taŋni, v. (yutaŋni). To make old, wear out. Wablutaŋni.
wayu'taŋniḱa, n. One who wears out

wayu'taŋtaŋ, v. red. (yutaŋtaŋ). To feel all over.
wayu'taŋyaŋ, v. (yutaŋyaŋ). To make things well. Bl.

wayu'ťeca, v. (yuteca). To make new, to renew. Wabluteca.

wayu'ťehaŋ, v. (yutehaŋ). To make long, to be slow.

wayu'ťehaŋhaŋka, v. To be always long in doing a thing. Wablutehaŋhaŋka.

wayu'ťeḣika, v. (yuteḣika). To make difficult. Wabluteḣika.

wayu'ťeṗa, v. (yutepa). To wear off.

wayu'ťica, v. (yutica). To scrape away, as a horse does snow by pawing.

wayu'ťiṗa, v. (yutipa). To cramp, draw up.

wayu'ťiťaŋ, v. (yutitaŋ). To pull.

wayu'tḱoŋza, v. (yutkoŋza). To make even. Wablutkoŋza.

wayu'tkuğa, v. (yutkuga). To break off. R. Bl.

wayu'tokaŋ, v. (yutokaŋ). To put in another place, to remove. Wablutokaŋ.

wayu'toḱeca, v. (yutokeca). To make different, to alter. Wablutokeca.

wayu'tuta, v. (yututa). To make smart by rubbing. Wablututa.

wayu'ťutḱa, v. (yututka). To break into small pieces.

wayu't'a, v. (yut'a). To kill, choke to death. Wablut'a.

wayu't'iŋza, v. (yut'iŋza). To make firm. Wablut'iŋza.

wayu'uŋka, v. (yuuŋka). To throw down.

wayu'waciŋtoŋ, v. (yuwaciŋtoŋ). To make intelligent. R. Bl.

wayu'wahiŋyaŋza, v. To make morose or ill disposed. Also, wayawahiŋyaŋza. Cf. wayatawaciŋhiŋyaŋza, yatawaciŋhiŋyaŋza; waciŋhiŋyaŋza. R.

wayu'waḣa, v. To conciliate. B.H.129.7.

wayu'waḣṗanica, v. (yuwaḣpanica). To make poor. Wabluwaḣpanica.

wayu'waḣwala, v. (yuwaḣwala). To make gentle or mild. Wabluwaḣwala.

wayu'wakaŋ, v. (yuwakaŋ). To make sacred, to consecrate. Wabluwakaŋ. B.H. 66.17.

wayu´waŋk̇al icu, v. To lift up.
wayu´waŋk̇al iyeya, v. To raise or pry up.

wayu´waśak̇ala, v. (yuwaśakala). To make cheap or easy. Wabluwaśakala.

wayu´waśte, v. (yuwaśte). To make good, improve. Wabluwaśte.

wayu´waś'ak̇a, v. (yuwaś'aka). To make strong, to invigorate. Wabluwaś'aka.
wayu´waś'akeśni, v. To make weak. Wabluwaś'akeśni.

wayu´waza, v. Cf. yuwaza. Bl.

wayu´weġa, v. (yuwega). To break partly off. Wabluwega.

wayu´wi, v. (yuwi). To wrap around.

wayu´wicaka, v. (yuwicaka). To make true.

wayu´wicaśaśni, v. (yuwicaśaśni). To make bad, debase, corrupt. Wabluwicaśaśni.

wayu´wignuni, v. (yuwignuni). To make wander. R. Bl.

wayu´wiŋja, v. (yuwiŋja). To bend down.

wayu´wiŋṫa, v. (yuwiŋta). To stroke. Wabluwiŋta.

wayu´wiŋyeya, v. (yuwiŋyeya). To make ready. Wabluwiŋyeya. Cf. wayusu.

wayu´wiṫaŋṫaŋ, v. To make proud by giving good things. R. Bl.

wayu´wiṫaya, v. (yuwitaya). To gather together, to collect. Wabluwitaya.

wayu´witko, v. (yuwitko). To make naughty.
wayu´witkotkoka, v. To make foolish.

wayu´wiyakpa, v. Cf. yuwiyakpa.

wayu´woslaṫa, v. (yuwoslata). To set upright.

wayu´za, v. (yuza). To take; to take the clothes of those who come home in triumph. R. Bl.

wayu´zamni, v. (yuzamni). To uncover. Wabluzamni.

wayu´zaŋ, v. (yuzaŋ). To part or separate e.g. the hair on the head.

wayu´ze, v. (yuze). To lade or dip out from a kettle. Wabluze.

wayu´zica, v. (yuzica). To stretch. Wabluzica.

wayu´zoŋṫa, v. (yuzoŋta). To make honest, better men. Wabluzoŋta. R. Bl.

wazab´, cont. of wazapa. - iyeya.
waza´bzaṗa, v. red. of wazapa.

wa´zaŋzaŋ, n. A fine snow mist. - u welo, as is said when a few snowflakes very little drop here and there. Cf. mniwozaŋ, A drizzle.

waza´ṗa, v.a. To skin, cut off; to cut e.g. meat for drying. Wawazapa.

waza´za, 1) v.a. To cut into fringes. Ogle, huŋska wawazaza. 2) v.n. To be fringed, dangle. Cf. kazaza. 3) adv. In dangles. -- wazázaṗi, n. Fringe, dangles.

wazi´, n. A pine tree, pines.
wazi´caŋ, n. The western pine. Pinus scopulosum, ponderosa. The common pine tree.
wazi´ḣcaka, n. The Black Hills spruce.

wazil´ya, v.n. and perhaps a. To burn as does incense. Cf. zilya. Wazilwaya. Hehaŋl tatiye topa kiŋ iyuha wazilyapi. Hecel - na azilwicaya. B.H. 64.17.

wazi´mna, n. Same as wazimniŋkpa.

wazi´mniŋkpa, n. (wazimna-iŋkpa). The tall meadow-rue. Thalictrum polygamum, cornuti. The crowfoot family. Bl. #194. The seeds have a pleasing odor and are given to horses to make them lively. And when the seeds are chewed and rubbed on the hands, they serve as a pleasant lotion. WE. Bc. Bn. BH.
wazi´mniŋkpa iyececa, n. The large button snake root, the blue blazing star, the rattle snake master, devil's bite. Liatris ligulistylis. Same as tat'ecaŋnuŋga hu iyececa. Also, the maple-leaved goosefoot. Chenopedium hybridum. Bl. #153.

wazi´ṗiŋkṗa, n. Pine cones.

wazi′ s'e, adv. Pine-like, very tall. R. Bl.

wazi′ śiyo, n. The spruce grouse.

wazi′śk̇eca, n. The strawberry. Fragaria Americana. Also, wazíśk̇ecala.

wazi′ṫak̇iya, adv. Towards the north. Ihiha^{n}na el oyate kiśpaha^{n}pi ca - aya.

wazi′wica′gnaśk̇a, n. Pine berries.

Wazi′ya, n. prop. The name for, and personification of, the power or powers, the nature characteristics of the north, e.g. Tate, the winds; Waśicu^{n}pi, bearers of powers that esp. make it possible to walk in a sacred way. The word used for Santa Claus.

wazi′ya ce′k̇aga, n. A pastime enjoyed by Indian children of old. They would dip a branch into water and then place it upright in very cold weather. It would freeze, and then they would suck it as it were a piece of stick candy. Bl.

wazi′yapa, adv. At the north, to the north.
wazi′yapaṫa^{n}ha^n, adv. Northwards; from the north.
wazi′yaṫa, n. The north, at the pines.
wazi′yaṫak̇iya, adv. Towards the north.
wazi′yaṫa^{n}ha^n, adv. At the north, from the north. Also, wazíyaṫaṫa^{n}ha^n.

Wazi′yaṫa Wicaśa, n. prop. A branch or group of the Assiniboins.

wazi′zi, n. Pieces of pine. - pet'ileye, Pine kindling wood. LB.

wazi′zi^{n}tkala, n. The pine siskin, the pine finch.

waz'o′ju, n. (wazi-oju). A place where many pine trees grow, as in canyons.

we, 1) n. Blood. 2) adj. Bloody. 3) v.n. To bleed.

we, pron. insep. It is compounded of "wa" and "ki". Cf. Gramm.45.

we, particle. Sign of the imp. sing. used by women. Mihakab u we. Iwacu we na cicu we. Israel el woita^{n}ca^n ta^{n}ka yau^n we. B.H.111.13. Cf. ye.

we′ceya, v.a. To be on good terms with one's relatives, have regard for them. Wécewaya. Also, to have confidence in a person or thing, trust, believe in the ability of one or of a thing. Héco^n kta keye, eyaś wecewaye śni, He said he would do it, but I do not believe he will, i.e. I do not believe he can or will do it. Wécekiciyapi, They trust one another.
we′ceyeṗica, adj. Trustworthy, reliable, as is said of persons and things. Wéceyemapica.
we′ceyeśni, v.a. To disregard, to slight; to have a grudge against a relative, not looking at him or her; to have no confidence in, to doubt about the ability of somebody or an animal doing something, as in distrusting a poor horse making a long trip, etc. Wécewayeśni. Syn.- wóimna śni. B. B.H.115.4.

we co′lakel, adv. Unbloody. B.H.61.5.
we′ eya′la s'e, adv. All bloody. - gli ye. Bl.

we′ġa, adj. Broken. Cf. yuwega, etc.
weġa′ha^n, part. Broken, but not entirely off. Isto mawégaha^n. Mawégahe yelo, I am really "broke".

we′gna, prep. Among. Paha ca^n - ya^{n}ka, Hill in the Woods, i.e. the name of a hill in the White River valley some 10 miles north of Oglala, S. D.

we′ha^n, n. Last spring. - hécamo^n welo.

wei′c'iya, v. refl. To bleed one's self.

wei′glak, v. cont. (iglaka). To travel camping along the way. Wanáka - ayi^n ktelo.

we′k̇alu′zapi, n. An unnatural flow of blood, a sickness of women; hemorrhage. Bl. Syn.- we nápoṗaṗi.

wek̇i′ciya, v.a. To bleed each other.

we′laka, adv. Same as yelaka. Le wicaśa taku - . B.H.203.13;68.18;161.8.

we′la s'e, adv. All bloody. - śka^{n}pi, i.e. all bloody from cutting themselves.

wena′poṗaṗi, n. An hemorrhage typical of women. Bl. Cf. wékaluzapi.

we'ośṗaŋ, v.n. To dry up, cease to flow as does blood in a critical point of afterbirth. Wémaośpaŋ.

we'oṫa, n. A blood clot. Wéyota is the Santee form of the word. WW. D.113.

weś, Same as yeś, yeśa, yeśaŋ; weśa, weśaŋ. B.H.123.6.

weśle'k̇api, n. The wearing of honors, esp. feathers, signs of honorable wounds. R. Bl.

we'ṫu, n. The spring of the year. Iwétu, Next spring, the following spring.

wĕ'-wĕ'-wĕ', interj. It is used by women in calling dogs.

wewe', adj. Bloody.

We' Wicaśa, n.p. A Blood Indian, a Sioux of the north.

weya', v.a. To shed blood, make bleed; hence, to put to death. Wewaya. B.H. 263.6.

weyo'ḣlogelya, adv. All bloody. - gli ye. Bl.

we'yota, n. A clot of blood. Cf. weota.

we' yuk̇e'ya, adv. Bloody. B.H.61.3.

wi, prefix. Some verbs commencing with "i" make the abs. form by prefixing "w" instead of "wa"; thus, iyúkcaŋ, wíyukcaŋ.

wi, n. The sun, the moon; a month; a personification of the most immense power in creation, for it determines all seasons. FD.86. WJR.153. Aŋpetu wi, The sun. Haŋhepi wi, The moon. Wi hinapa, The sun rises. Wi mahel iyaya, The sun has set.

wi, cont. of wiŋyaŋ. Thus, wiinahma.

wi'ace'ic'iṫi, n. (wi-aceti). Sundogs; there are sundogs, v. A ring around the moon; there is a ring around the moon, v. MG. Also, wíacic'iṫi. It is said the sun does this because it will be cold or stormy. Fr.

wi'ahinapa, v. To have the sun rise on one.

wi'ataŋoŋmya, adv. When the sun is leaning; in the afternoon.

wica, prefix. It is affixed to verbs to make it pl., and it is used when one is speaking of a unit, a certain crowd of people, or all people in general. Lila wiciśtiŋmelo, as is said of a family, or visitors, or members of a meeting, etc. Iśtiŋmapi ref. to individuals singly and not belonging together.

wica', n. A male of the human species, a man. Wimáca.

wica', pron. in comp. With verbs, this represents the 3rd pers. pl. obj., them. Thus, wicawakte, I killed them. But, when it is used with neuter verbs and adj., it generally forms what may be regarded as abstract nouns. Thus, caŋcaŋ, To shake; wicacaŋcaŋ, The ague.

wica', adj. Male, pertaining to sex; human. This adj. is prefixed to nouns that have ref. to man. When the noun begins with a vowel, the "a" of wicá is dropped. Thus, iśta, An eye; wiciśta, The human eye.

wiċa', n. The raccoon. Also, wicíteglek̇a. R. Bl. Cf. D.36.

wica'akiḣ'aŋ, n. Starving, famine. Oyate wicoti na lila - na aŋpetu waŋ el wanasapi. Waniyetu zaptaŋ - kte. B.H.39.5.

wica'atk̇uk̇u, n. A father, their father.

wica'bapi, n. Blame. Also, wicaṗapi.

wi'ċablece, n. (kableca). An instrument to break in pieces with, e.g. a sledge.

wi'cabwoṫaṗi, n. A table fork.
wi'cabyuṫapi, n. A meat fork.

wica'caje, n. Names, names of persons. - wowapi, A catalogue, list of names.

wi'ċacaŋ, n. (kacaŋ). A sieve. Also, wíyucaŋ.

wica'caŋcaŋ, n. The ague.

wi'ċacaŋpi, n. A measure.

wica'caŋṫe, n. The human heart.

wica'caȠt̄eoyuze, n. The thought of the heart.

wica'ce, n. The human penis.
wica'ceḣp̄i, n. Human flesh.
wica'ceji, n. The human tongue.
wica'cep̄a, n. Human fatness, obesity.

wica'cep̄ahala, n. A certain high but not wide mountain. Bl.

wica'cesli, n. The excrement of the raccoon; human excrement.

wica'ceya, n. Weeping, crying. Also, wicáceye. Oyate kiȠ waȠna - ayaśtaȠ.

wi'ċacice, n. An instrument used in brushing up the fur of skins.

wica'ciȠca, n. Children, posterity, offspring.

wica'ċok̄oȠ, n. (cokoȠ). Threatening, intending evil.

wica'cuwit̄a, n. The sense of cold experienced by human beings, the feeling of coldness.

wica'ġaȠġaȠ, adj. Not crowded; a sprinkling of people, n. Br.

wi'ċaġe, n. (kaga). An instrument to make something with.

wi'ċaġeġe, n. Anything to sew with, thread or lace. Mas'wicayege, a sewing machine.

wica'glat̄a, n. The women who follow the men in singing at the war dance or other like dances. Cf. aglata.

wica'gnak̄ap̄i, n. Dead bodies laid on top of the ground or scaffolds; the scaffold on which a dead person is placed. YuȠkaȠ - waȠ tima otka.

wica'gnaśk̄a, n. The goose berry.
wica'gnaśk̄ahu, n. The goose berry bush; the golden, the buffalo, the flowering currant. Ribes longiflorum. The saxifrage family. It was used for the making of arrows. Wicaśa waȠji na yamni na tob oyate el wahiȠkpe kaga wayupikapi ca hena waȠkaḣ wicaśipi, wiśiyukeya. - hena cogiȠ taȠka heoȠ. MS.481. Bl. OF. Bh. #163.
wica'gnaśk̄a taȠka, n. The large goose berry.

wica'gnaye, n. (gnayaȠ). A person who deceives; deception. - s'a, Treacherous, wily; a trickster, n.

wi'ċago, n. (kago). An instrument to mark with.

wi'ċaġuk̄e, n. Same as wicacice.

wica'hi, n. Human teeth.

wi'ċahi, n. Something to mix with, e.g. a mush-stick.

wica'hi kage, n. A dentist.

wi'ċahiȠt̄e, n. (kahiȠta). A broom, a rake.

wi'ċahiya, v. (icahiya). To mingle. Wicahiwaya.

wi'ċahiyut̄api, n. Seasoning, spices, sauce etc. Also, wicáhiyayutapi. P.
wi'ċahiyut̄api toto', n. A salad. P.
wi'ċahiyut̄api zi, n. Mustard. P.

wica'ho, n. The human voice. - waȠ nawaḣ'oȠ.
wica'hohu, n. Human bones.

wica'ho kaḣwo'gyapi, v. To radio broadcast.

wica'hooyúsp̄a, n. A voice or sound record; a sound recorder. Also, wicaho oyuspe.

wica'huha, n. The limbs of the body.
wica'huhu, n. A human skeleton.

wica'huȠk̄ak̄e, n. Ancestors.

wica'huȠk̄u, n. A mother, mothers

wica'ḣaȠḣaȠ, n. The small fox.

wica'ḣapi, n. (ḣa). Bodies interred, graves, tombs.
wica'ḣapi ognake, n. A coffin. Also, caȠwógnaka.

wica'ḣca, n. An old man; a father-in-law.
wica'ḣcala, n. An old man of any kind.

wi'caḣep̄a, n. (kaḣepa). A ladle. R. Bl.

wi'caḣlece, n. (kaḣleca). Something to tear or bruise with.

wi'čaȟloke, n. (kaȟloka). Something to make holes with, e.g. a gimlet.
wica'ȟmuŋga, 1) v. To shoot or send by magic something, e.g. a knife, nail or bullet, into one as some Dakota wizards pretend to do; also, to remove such things by magic, i.e. wokabiyeya. 2) n. One who practices such shooting, a magician. Also, wicáȟmuŋǧes'a.

wi'čaȟpe, n. An instrument to throw down with. Cf. kaȟpa.

wica'ȟpi, n. A star.
wica'ȟpi hiŋȟpa'ya, n. The falling of the stars, applied to the year 1833.
wica'ȟpi siŋtéton, n. A comet.
wica'ȟpi śa, n. A planet. BT.

wi'čaȟpu, n. (kaȟpu). An instrument to pick off with.

wi'čaȟuǧe, n. (kaȟuga). Something to break in with.

wica'ȟuŋwiŋ, n. (ȟuŋwiŋ). Putrifaction.

wica'ȟwa, n. (ȟwa). Drowsiness.

wica'i, n. The human mouth.
wica'iha, n. The human lips.

wica'jipa, n. A wasp. - mayajipa.

wi'čajiṗe, n. (kajipa). Something to smooth or shave with, a plane.

wica'ka, v. (ka). To mean; he means them.

wiča'ka, v.n. To speak truth, to be true. Wicawaka.

wica'kahiyaya, v. (kahiyaya). To carry round to them, to sing to them.

wica'kahuŋ'huŋzapi, n. A cradle.

wica'kaȟaṗa, n. (kaȟapa). A driver, one who drives.

wica'kaŋl, adv. (wica-akaŋl). Behind them. - wauŋ welo. Bl. Syn.- wicilazate.

wica'kapiȟca, adj. Dead sure, absolutely certain. P.

wi'čakca, n. (kakca). A curry comb.

wiča'kela, v.a. (wicaka-la). To esteem true, to believe. Wicakewala. Wicakeic'ila, To believe one's self true, continue to affirm. Yuŋkaŋ wicaśa kiŋ Jesus eye kiŋ - na ekta gla.
wiča'kelakiya, v.a. To convince. P.

wica'keya, adv. In truth. Taku waśte yaciŋ kiŋ he okihinic'iyiŋ kta na - ceya yo. MS.350.

wica'kicaśla, n. A barber.

wica'kicičajujupi, n. Forgiveness.

wica'kicila, v. To comply. -- adj. Positive. P.

wica'kicilowaŋ, v. (lowaŋ). To wail or sing for, as for those who have gone on the warpath etc.

wica'kicopi, n. (kico). Calling, invitation.

wica'kiȟ'aŋ, v. (kiȟ'aŋ). Same perhaps as wicaakiȟ'aŋ. B.H.106.2.

wi'čakije, n. (icakija). Distress, suffering.
wi'čakijeśniyaŋ, adv. Lacking nothing. D.64.

wica'kikcaŋpte, n. (kikcaŋpta). A comforter. The Holy Spirit, n. prop.

wica'kini, n. Resurrection. B.H.229.12.

wi'čakiŋce, n. (kakiŋca). Something to scrape with.

wica'kipi, n. Robbery.

wi'čakiśya, v. To cause to suffer. Wicakiśwaya. -- adv. perhaps. - uŋkuŋpi, i.e. in our necessities.

wica'kiyapa, v. Cf. kiyapa.

Wica'kiyuhapi, n. prop. The constellation of the Big Dipper or the Great Bear. Bl. Ciŋśkásiŋteyukaŋ is also another name. IS. Cf. ki, v.

wi'čakoke, n. (kakoka). A rattle; a rattler.

wi'čakṗe, n. A lancet.

wica'ksaṗa, n. Wisdom. Cf. wicoksape.

wi'čakse, n. (kaksa). An instrument

to cut off with.

wica'ktepi, n. Killing.
wica'ktes'a, n. One who kills.

wica'k'upi, n. Giving.

wiča'la, v.a. To believe, put confidence in; to agree to. Wicawala.
wiča'laȟa, v.a. To believe. Wicawalaka.

wica'lapela, (?). Ite - k'el écela yelo, as they say encouragingly to a warparty. Bl.

wiča'lapi, n. Belief, believing, faith.
wiča'lapica, adj. Worthy of belief.
wiča'laya, v.a. To cause one to believe, to persuade. Wicalawaya. Wicake s'elececa yelo, wicalamaye lo, epa.

wica'leja, n. Human urine.

wi'calu, n. A fan.

wica'luzahe, n. (luzahaᵑ). Swiftness.

wica'nakśecapi, n. (nakśeca). The cholera.

wica'naᵑka, n. Tremor. Cf. na(ᵑ)ka.

wica'nape, n. The human hand. B.H. 140.6.
wica'nasu, n. The human brain. Also, wicanasula.
wica'nataśloka, n. A dry human skull.

wica'ni, v.n. They live. -- n. Life, prosperity. It is used of many; wiconi is used of one.

wica'nite, n. The loins.
wica'noġe, n. Human ears.

wica'oȟ'aᵑko, n. (oh'aᵑko). Dexterity.

wica'paha, n. The human scalp.
wica'pahu, n. The human skull.
wica'paȟli, n. The excretion of the human nose. Tiᵑpsila kiᵑ - s'e hinapelo. Bl.

wica'paptapta iyaye ole', v. (?).

wi'cape, n. (capa). A fork, a table fork; a piercer.

wi'capeca, n. (capa). A kind of grass armed with a long sharp beard. Same as micapeca.

wica'pehiᵑkaġapi, n. False hair, a wig.

wi'capela, n. dim. of wicape.

wica'pi, n. The human liver.

wica'po, n. A swelling.

wica'poġe, n. The human nose.

wi'čapote, n. (kapota). An instrument to rend with.

wi'čapsice, n. (kapsica). Anything to make jump with.

wi'čapsiᵑte, n. A whip.

wi'časkice, n. (kaskica). A press.

wi'časlece, n. (kasleca). Something to split with, a wedge.

wica'sote, n. A general dying, the decease of many. Bl.

wi'často, n. (kasto). Anything to smooth with, a brush.

wica'śa, n. Man, a man, mankind. Wimacaśa.
- akaᵑtu, One of human kind, a mortal, distinguished from the dead and spirits.
- ha, A term for a lazy man. Iyotiyewakiye, wicaśa há waᵑ kici wauᵑ ca, as a woman would say of her lazy husband. GA.
- iglawa, One who counts himself a man; a chief.
- ikte, Poison.

wicáśake, Human nails of the toes or fingers.
- lehaᵑkata, A foreigner. B.H.27.30.
- śiᵑ, The meat on the breast of buffalo. HH. Bl.
- śni, adj. Mean, wicked, prankish. Wimácaśaśni. Also, to be tricky, deceptive, crooked in dealings; mischievous, as a child; waggish, as a man or woman. D.25. SLB.

wicáśaśniyaᵑ, adv. Wickedly.
- taᵑka, A middle-aged man. Yuᵑkaᵑ wicaśa taᵑka kiᵑ he wicaȟpi waᵑ lila ilege ciᵑ hée. MS.1.
- wakaᵑ, A priest; formerly the Indian shaman.

wicaśayataᵑpi, A king. Cf. yataᵑ. Also, wicaśayatápi, A ruler or chief, a king. -- wicaśayátapiya, v.a. To have for a king. B.H.263.

9;264.24. -- wicaśayatat̄apika, Same as wicaśayatapi.
Wicáśa Yut̄a, A tribe of western Indians who are said to have been cannibals; the Utes. Bl.

wi'ćaśke, n. Something to tie with, bonds.

wi'ćaśḱice, n. A press.

wi'ćaśkiƞ, n. A hammer to pound cherries with. W.

wi'ćaśla, n. (kaśla). A scythe.

wica'śni, v. To tell a falsehood. Wicamicaśni, wicanicaśni. WE. Wicaśni s'e gnayaƞ, In a childish manner. Bl.

wica't̄akuniśni, n. Destruction.

wica't̄aƞcaƞ, n. The human body. Pb.35.

wica'taƞkaǧapi, n. A tent with certain figures representing ribs and hearts, seemingly, painted somewhat horizontally around on the outer surface of the tipi.

wica'taƞkala, n. The gull; a bird that is white, breast blackish, legs short, bill short and not broad like that of pigeons; it lives near lakes, and it flies always over the water. Bl. Also, wiƞyaƞ taziƞtkala.

wica'taƞśna, n. A single man. - s'e tawak'iƞ taƞka, as is said when a man has much baggage.

wića'tawi, n. The raccoon moon, February. R. Bl.

wi'catkuḣye, n. The nut of a hub.

wica'toka, n. A male captive.

wica'toḱeca, n. Differences; things different. -- wicátoḱtoḱeca, n. red.

wica't̄ut̄e, n. Roughness, as of the hands, but not chapping, which is: wicayuḣ'i.

wica't'a, n. The dead.

wi'ćat'e, n. An instrument to kill with

wi'ćat'iƞze, n. Something to make tight with; a screw or nail.

wi'ćaweǧe, n. Something to break with.

wica'wiwazica, n. A widower.

wica'woḣa, n. A son-in-law, my son-in-law. - nitawa. Also, a man who lives with his relatives, lit. a buried man, or one who being attracted to a family stays on with them. Cf. D.14, note 4.

wica'woḣa tata'ḣca, n. A small-sized nige saƞla, antilope. Bl.

wica'woḣaya, v.a. To take or have for a son-in-law. Wicawoḣawaya.

wica'wot̄a, n. A feast or banquet. - taƞka kte. - kagapi. B.H.77.21;178.17.

wica'ya, adv. Manly.

wica'yajip̄a, n. A bee, bees. - tacaƞhaƞpi, Honey. B.H.173.4. - hiƞśma, A fuzzy bee, larger than a honey bee. Bl. - zi, The yellow bee. Bl.

wica'yasupi, n. Condemnation; pronouncing sentence.

wica'yat̄aƞpi, n. Praise, compliments.

wica'yazaƞ, n. A being sick, a sickness.

wica'yuhe, n. A master.

wica'yuḣ'i, n. Chapping, as of the hands. Cf. wicatute.

wica'yusḱap̄i, n. Purgatory. Also, peta cik'ala.

wica'yuś'iƞ'yaƞyaƞ s'e, (?). - wawakipa, i.e. I saw something suddenly that I never saw before.

wica'yuwaḣp̄anica, n. Making poor.

wica'yuwiƞtapi, n. Honoring, as the Dakotas do at feasts, calling the host by some signifying relationship or title of friendship, or the gesture of stroking in or before the face in token of respect or friendly greeting and saying: Haiýe, haiye.

wi'ćazo, n. A pen or pencil.
wi'cekiya, Same as wicekiye.
wi'ceḱiye, n. Something to pray with; to solicit help with e.g. a printed prayer, v. Also, to solicit signa-

tures on a petition paper; to apply for help. Wicewakiya.

wice'śka, n. The hole or opening in the top of a tent. R. The two overlapping ends of a tent between the upper part (wipá), the large flaps, and the entrance and held together with pins. Also, the pins that hold these two ends together. RF. SI. Na waⁿna tipi k'oⁿ he - iyusna iyeyapi, i.e. pull out the pins. Yuⁿkaⁿ leya - kiⁿ ogna kute kte sece c'uⁿ. D.111. - iṗásise, The pins which hold the wiceśka of a tent together, the overlapping ends above the entrance. Also, wicéśkipasise, Tent pins; a badge. R. - oȟlóke, The pin-holes for the holding of the wiceśka together.

wi'ceṫi, n. Same as wiaceic'iti.

wi'ceuⁿṗe, n. A frying pan. B.H.153.7.

wici'bleza, n. Clearness, pleasantness.

wici'ċaśke, n. Strips of blanket or ornamented strips of anything, worn over the shoulders and trailing on the ground, as a wicicaśke wapaha, A headdress so ornamented.

wici'napciyuⁿka, adj. num. The ninth.
wici'nuⁿpa, adj. num. The second.

wiciⁿ', v. To desire women, hunt after women. Wiwaciⁿ.

wiciⁿ'ca, n. A girl.
wiciⁿ'cala, n. A little girl. Wimáciⁿcala.

wiciⁿ'pi, n. The desiring women.

Wi'ciⁿska Oko'lakiciye, n. prop. The White-Marked Society, a military society among the Oglala Sioux. Also, Wiciska. FD.313. Wiciⁿska-waci ahiyaye, They went by, doing the Wiciⁿska dance, the Pack-strap-white-dancing.

wiciⁿ'śkaⁿ, v. To be flirting or courting while busy at some kind of work.

wici'śagloġaⁿ, adj. num. The eighth.
wici'śaḱowiⁿ, adj. num. The seventh.
wici'śakpe, adj. num. The sixth.

wici'śnala, adj. None with one, alone.

wici'śṗa, n. The fore-arm, the distance from the elbow to the end of the middle finger, a cubit.

wici'śṫa, n. The human eye.

wici'śṫiⁿme, n. Sleep; they are asleep.

wici'ṫe, n. The human face, the countenance.

wici'ṫegleġa, n. The raccoon.

wici'ṫeiyaskabye, n. A postage stamp.

wici'ṫe owapi, n. The picture of a face; a photograph.

wici'ṫiyekiyapi s'e, adv. (wica-ite-iyekiyapi). As though they recognized one another after a long time. - waⁿblakelo, as is said when greeting one another very heartily, as though one did not meet for a long time. BF.

wici'toḱapa, n. The eldest born.

wici'ṫoṗa, adj. num. The fourth.

wici'ṫowa, v.a. To photograph. Wicitowawa. Wicitowapi, A pictured postcard.

wici'wikcemna, adj. num. The tenth.
wici'yamni, adj. num. The third.

Wici'yela, n. prop. The Yankton Indian, as applied by the Tetons to the Yanktons and Yanktonais. R.

wici'yoḱiṗi, n. Excellence, beauty, pleasantness.

wici'yuⁿka, n. Bed-time.

wici'zaptaⁿ, adj. num. The fifth.

wico'ahoṗe, n. (ahopa). Law, custom; ceremony.

wico'aie, n. (aia). Slander.

wico'ayuśtaⁿ, n. (ayuśtaⁿ). Leaving off.

wico'bliheca, n. (bliheca). Activity.

wico'cajeyate, n. (cajeyata). Traditions.

wico'caⁿlwaḱaⁿ, n. A coward. Tokśa, aⁿpa ca - yelo, na haⁿhepi ca otuyaciⁿ utapelo.

wico'caⁿniye, n. (caⁿniyaⁿ). Anger, malice of husband towards wife.

wico'caⁿtagle, n. (caⁿtagle). Evil intention, malice.

wico'caⁿte, n. The human heart.

wico'caⁿte'iyutaⁿye, n. Temptation.
wico'caⁿteoyuze, n. Thought, purpose, disposition, wish.
wico'caⁿteśica, n. Sadness.
wico'caⁿtewaśte, n. Gladness.
wico'caⁿti'heye, n. Desire, covetousness.
wico'caⁿtiyagleya, n. What is desired.

wico'caⁿzeka, n. (caⁿzeka). Anger, malice.

wico'ecetu, n. (ecetu). Uprightness.

wico'ekicetuye, n. (ekicetuya). Restoration.

wico'gligle, n. Travelling.

wico'haⁿ, adv. (wica-ogna). Into the crowd. R.

wico'ḣtani, n. (ḣtani). Labor, work.

wico'ḣ'aⁿ, n. (oḣ'aⁿ). Work, custom, habit.
wico'ḣ'aⁿya, v.a. To have for a custom. B.H.262.11.

wico'ḣ'uⁿca, v. To ape, mimic. Wicoḣ'aⁿ úⁿwaca. BT.

wico'icaġe, n. (icaga). A generation.

wico'ie, n. (oie). A word, speech; a story, legend, etc.

wico'iglataⁿ, n. (iglataⁿ). Boasting.

wico'inaḣni, n. (inaḣni). Haste, hurrying.

wico'iśtiⁿme, n. (iśtiⁿma). Sleep.

wico'itoⁿpe, n. (itoⁿpa). Carefulness.

wico'iyokiśice, n. Sorrow.

wico'iyopeic'iye, n. Repentance.

wico'jice, n. (jica). Riches.

wico'jula, n. (ojula). Fullness; full of people.

wico'kaġi, n. (kagi). A hindrance.
wico'kaġiye, n. An obstruction.

wico'kakije, n. (kakija). Suffering.

wico'kaⁿ, n. Age. - uⁿkitawa k'uⁿ tasagye kiⁿ iyacu. B.H.122.13.

wi'cokaⁿ, n. (wi-cokaⁿ). Noon. Na waⁿna - kiyela hehaⁿl inajiⁿ na waⁿkal etoⁿwaⁿ najiⁿ na lowaⁿ. Na waⁿna - saⁿpa hehaⁿl eyapaha k'oⁿ he ake u.
wi'cokáⁿhiyaya, n. Afternoon. Also, wícokaⁿ sam iyáya. Le wicaśa kiⁿ hihaⁿna - śni ecel kigni kta.

wico'kaⁿhiyuic'iya, v. (wica-cokaⁿhiyuic'iya). To come unasked.

wi'cokaⁿyaⁿ, n. Noon. Na waⁿna - saⁿpa ehaⁿl uⁿgna waⁿna u. Na waⁿna - kitaⁿla saⁿpa hehaⁿl waⁿna eyapaha oⁿhe ake u.

wico'kaśke, n. A prison. P. Bl.

wico'kcota, red. of wicota. B.H.82.19.

wico'kicamna, (?). Le aⁿpetu kiⁿ - yelo. Bl.

wico'kiciyuwaśte, n. A blessing, peace.

wico'kicize, n. (kiciza). Fighting.

wico'kipajiⁿ, n. (kipajiⁿ). Opposition.

wico'koⁿze, n. Influence, law; a kingdom.

wico'ksape, n. (ksapa). Wisdom.

wico'kuje, n. (kuja). A sickness.

wico'mniciye, n. (mniciya). An assembly.

wico'nawizi, n. Jealousy. Bl.

wico'ni, n. (wica-oni). Life, of the present but esp. of that to come; a lifetime. - owihaⁿke wanica, Eternal life.

wico'nihiⁿciye, n. A general fear, turmoil, panic, as at the Flood. Bl.

Wico'niyaⁿpi, n. p. Salvation. - kte

kiŋ he Juda oyate kiŋ etaŋhaŋ kte lo. B.H.182.10.

wicoŋ'ťe, n. (wica-oŋ-t'a). Death. Hehaŋl - kiŋ hi kta.

wico'oŋśike, n. (oŋśika). Poverty.

wico'owewakaŋ, n. (owewakaŋ). A lie, a falsehood; deceit. Also, wicóowewakaŋkaŋ.

wico'owotaŋla, n. (owotaŋla). Righteousness.

wico'peya, prep. ph. (wica-opeya). Among them. Iktomi - , i.e. the piśko, iyaya śke. MS.105.

wico'suťa, n. (suta). Firmness, strength.

wico'śice, n. (śica). Evil.

wico'śiȟtiŋ , n. (śiȟtiŋ). Debility.

wico'śkaŋśkaŋ, n. (śkaŋśkaŋ). Moving, motion; government, rule, governance. R.

wico'śkate, n. (śkata). Play.

wico'śkiśke, n. (ośkiśke). Difficulty, distraction.

wico'śṗi, n. A wart. Also, wicóśṗe.

wico'ťa, n. Many persons, a multitude. Wiúŋcotapi.

wico'ťakuniśni, n. Destruction.

wico'ťakuye, n. (takuye). Relationship, brotherhood.

wico'tala s'e, adv. Rather many. - yahipi kiŋ icaŋlmawaśte. Bl.

wico'tapiśniyaŋkel, adv. Away from a crowd. B.H.251.1.

wico'tawaciŋ, n. Disposition.

wico'ťeca, n. (teca). Newness.

wico'ťi, n. A village, a camp; 3rd pers. pl. of oti. Na ȟtayetu hehaŋl - kiŋ kiyela glapi.

wico'ťoketu, adv. interrog. How is it? - taŋiŋ śni, How it is is not apparent.

wico'uŋ, n. A family, all that are related by blood; a place where men live; covenant. Also, wicotakuye. Bl. R.

wico'waciŋko, n. (waciŋko). Bad temper.

wico'waȟwala, n. Gentleness.

wico'waśťe, n. (waśte). Goodness.

wico'waś'aké, n. Human strength.

wico'we, n. (owe). Relationship between brothers, sisters and cousins; these and their aunts and uncles. Also, a generation, son-father-grandfather etc. R. Na waŋna aŋpa ca na hehaŋl - naiŋś owapate naiŋś śuŋkawakaŋ ceslipi naiŋś tokel wicaśa ośkiŋciyapi hena slolye waciŋpi. -- wicówepi, n. Same as wicowe.

wico'wicaśaśni, n. Villainy. B.H.31.1.

wico'woglaké, n. Relating stories, biography. - k'u, To let one make a speech.

wico'woyaké, n. (oyaka). A declaration, narration; doctrine; chapter.

wico'yuťakuniśni, n. That which causes destruction.

wico'zaŋni, n. Health. Pb.38.

wičuŋ'keśni, n. One who knows nothing or does not care to do anything, is incompetent to keep house. Lila taŋyaŋ loliyaȟ'aŋ śni yelo; - ca loliȟ'aŋ s'e, as they would say of a woman whose cooking was very poor, intimating that for this reason she had many husbands. Note: the word is applied only to women. GA.

wicuŋ'ksu, n. The pole on which meat is dried. Bm.

wi'cuŋs ia, v. To make a wrong statement unintentionally. Hehehé wicuŋs iwayelo. BT.

wi'cuŋśkayeśni, v. Not to pay attention. Wicuŋskawayeśni. Wicuŋskaye is not used. Syn.- el etoŋwaŋśni. EM.

wi'cuŋśni, Cf. wicuŋkeśni. The word

is applied to a woman who is incompetent, cannot cook or keep house etc. La.

wic'i'caĝe, n. A growth of men, a generation. Also, wic'óⁿcaĝe. SLB.

wi'c'iⁿ, n. (k'iⁿ). The strap which the Dakotas use in carrying meat. Inaȟni - kiⁿ wahuⁿhuⁿpi.

wie'yaku, v.a. To take away a woman. Wiéblaku.

wigla'ȟpa, v. pos. To strike or take down one's own tent. Wiwaglaȟpa.

wigla'śtaka, v. pos. To beat one's wife. Wiwaglaśtaka.

wi'glawa, v. (iglawa). To count one's self. Wiwaglawa. Also, to settle, figure. B.H.248.3.

wi'gli, n. (igli). Oil, grease.

wi'gligla, v. To travel to and fro away from one, as does the sun. Wíwagligla. WE.

wi'gli oⁿ káĝapi, n. Indian bread.

wi'gli zaze'cala, n. The drops of grease floating on a good soup, seemingly like floating eyes. Bl.

wi'gloceti, n. An oil stove.

wi'glukcaⁿ, v. (iglukcaⁿ). To understand one's own or one's self, to form an opinion; to judge one's self. Wiwaglukcaⁿ. Pb.23.

wi'gmuⁿke, n. The rainbow. Mas'ígmuⁿke, A trap or snare. According to the Indians, the rainbow is not the result of rain, but it stops further rain.

wi'gnagnaye, (?). - toⁿpi s'e amaupelo. Bl.

wi'gni, v. (igni). To look for provisions, to hunt e.g. deer, to provide. Wiwagni. Pb.24. He écuȟciś taⁿháⁿka na haⁿkaku wiwicakigni kte, i.e. he will provide for. D.12.

wi'gnu, v. (ignu). To murmur; to reproach; to be displeased with. Wiwagnu. -- wígnupi, n. A murmuring.

wi'ĝuye, n. An instrument to make brands with e.g. on cattle etc., a branding-iron.

wiha'kakta, n. The fifth child, if a daughter; so called probably from its usually being the last. In March the Indians would say: Iśtawicaniyaⁿpi wi taⁿiⁿ yelo; wihakakte iyuha wiyuśkiⁿ po; ake wigli luzapi kte lo. BT. Hoihákakta, the youngest of a man's wives.

wiha'kakta ce'papi, n. The month of April. The youngest wife had to crack bones; for, on the marrow they would get fat. Bl.

wi'haⁿblapi, n. A dreaming.
wi'haⁿble, v. Same as ihaⁿbla.
wi'haⁿbles'a, n. A dreamer.

wihi'gnatoⁿ, n. A married woman. Pb. 25.

wi'hinaṗa, n. The sun rising, the east.

wihiⁿ'ṗasṗa, n. Tent pins, picketpins. Same as wahiⁿpaspa. - kaksa. Bl.

wi'hiyala, (?). - tonakeca, What time is it? FN.

wihu'ta, n. The lower border of a tent. - iyuha kahohopo, as is announced before breaking up camp. BT.

wihu'ta hu, n. The broad-leaved cattail. Typha latifolia. The cat-tail family. A water plant three to four feet tall with thin broad leaves and one round stalk bearing fruit which is called haⁿtkáⁿ. Bl. #231.

wihu'ta hu iyececa, n. Eastern plantian, wayside plantain, healing blade. Plantago major. Bl. #181.

wihu'ta hu swula, n. The great bulrush. Scirpus validus. BT. #70.

wihu'ta inatake, n. Something used to fasten up around the bottom of a tent, e.g. grass.

wihu'ta śa, n. The lowest part of a tent, the border, which is usually painted red. -- wihúta śa oȟlóke, n. The holes made in the lowest part of a tent through which tent pins go.

wi'ḣmuᵑġe, n. Witch-medicine.

wi'ḣpaᵑyaᵑpi, n. Dry pápa.

wi'ḣp̣eya, v.a. To give away things. Wiḣpéwaya. Also, to give, as after a death in a family. Hihaᵑna kiᵑ honuᵑpiᵑyaᵑwayiᵑ na ośuᵑgye wiḣpewayiᵑ kte, i.e. intending to kill many buffalo. R. Bl. -- wiḣp̣eyapi, n. The practice of giving away property on the death of a member of the family; things laid out for giving away. - bluha kte. GA.

wiḣu'p̣a, n. The flaps of a tent. Cf. wipipaha.

wi'ḣ'aᵑ, v. (ih'aᵑ). To be busy with many things. Wiwaḣ'aᵑ. -- wiḣ'aᵑpi, n. Being busy about many things.

wii'ċaḣṫaḱeśni, adj. Not having known women.

wii'cigni, v. To scold or whip a woman. Wiiwecigni or wiiwakigni.

wi'ic'iglukcaᵑ, v. To make a vow, a resolution, a promise to do a certain thing. Wímic'iglukcaᵑ. Bl.

wii'c'igni, v. abs. (wigni). To provide for one's self e.g. good food etc.; to look out for things one's self. MS.557.

wi'iglukcaᵑ, v. To form one's opinion.

wii'ḣp̣eya, v.a. To throw away a woman, leave a wife. Wiiḣpewaya.

wii'naḣma, v. To conceal a woman, take her off; to commit fornication. Wiinawaḣma.

wii'yagluḣa, v. To be a constant companion of one's wife. Bl.

wii'yaḣpaya, v. To commit rape, to force a woman.

wii'yanajiᵑce, v. To run away holding a woman.

wii'yaoᵑp̣api, n. Charging with infidelity or with having had illicit intercourse.

wi'iyap̣aḣice, n. The fastenings of a tent at the top.

wii'yap̣e, v. To wait for a woman in order to talk to her, to court her.

wi'iyaya, v. The sun sets; sun-down, n.

wii'yayuḣ, adv. In the path of the sun, i.e. from east to west. - ya, To go with the sun. R. Bl.

wi'iyayuḣa, v. To leave home and take a wife at another village and live with her friends. Wiiyabluḣa.

wiiyu'ḣlate, n. A pipe wrench.

wiji'ca, 1) adj. (ijica). Rich. Wimajica. Lila wak'upi caᵑke wijica ke. D.270. 2) n. Riches. Wíjica, The rich. B. -- wíjicaya, v.a. To enrich. P.

wi'jimna, v.n. To smell like something burning, such as fat, bones etc.

wi'kalye, n. A tea or coffee pot.

wi'ḱaᵑ, n. A leather cord, a packing strap. - soᵑpi, A lasso, strands of thin cords twisted into thick cord. D.257.

wi'ḱaᵑgigike, n. One who is very anxious to acquire things as he has nothing. Wímakaᵑgigike. Bl.

wi'ḱaᵑḱaᵑ, n. A double rope. Na - num el otka, i.e. as in the Sundance.

wi'ḱawaᵑḱap'u, n. The hour of about 7:00 or 8:00 A.M. Cf. kawaᵑkalwapa.

wi'kaze, n. A gravy strainer.

wikce'mna, adj. num. Ten. - nuᵑpa, Twenty. - yamni, Thirty. Etc.
wikce'mnamna, adj. num. Ten by ten. P.

wi'ḱicaᵑyaᵑpi, n. A tool, tools.
wi'ḱicaye, n. Tools, implements. Also, wikicaᵑye. R.

wi'ḱiciyuᵑgapi, n. (iyuᵑga). Mutual inquiry, a questioning of one another.

wi'ḱic'uᵑ, adv. With a concern. Waciᵑ - śni, One who is indifferent.

wiḱi'kśaᵑ, v. To play with one's wife. To love-play. Wiwakikśaᵑ. BD.
wiḱi'kśaᵑpi, n. Playing with one's wife, love-play. BD.

wi'ǩinica, v. To pick up, grabbing what others drop. Wíwakinica. Akicita k'oŋ waŋna ti uŋyaŋ éyaya na lila wiuŋkinicapi.

wiǩi'śkata, v. (wi-kiśkata). Same as wikikśaŋ.

wiǩi'śleya, v.a. To offer insults to a woman. Wikiślewaya.
wiǩi'śleyapi, n. Rape.

wi'ǩiyuťa, v. To beckon to, talk by signs. Wiwakiyuta. Nape oŋ - . B.H. 160.6.

wi'kopa, v. (ikopa). To bear with, be afraid. Wikowapa.
wi'koṗeca, n. One who is afraid.
wi'koṗeśniyaŋ, adv. Without fear, securely.

wiko'śka, n. A venereal disease of women.

wiko'śǩalaǩa, n. A young woman.

wiko'śka tapejúta, n. The small western poison ivy. Rhus rydbergii, or taxicodendron rydbergii. The sumac family. When touched it causes irritations, hence the name. It is not a medicine plant. BT. #92. Cf. wikośka.

wi'kpi zi, n. The yellow-breasted chat which sings at night. FR.

wi'ksaṗa, v. (iksapa). To comprehend well, to have experience looking after a thing intelligently. Wiwaksapa. - iyaye ciŋ he waśte tka yelo. Bl.

wikte', v. To beat one's wife.

wi'ǩuciyela, n. That time towards sunset, late in the afternoon.

wi'ǩuwabya, n. That time about 3:00 in the afternoon.

wi'lecala, n. The crescent of the moon between New Moon and First Quarter.LB.

wi'lulye, n. Anything to color red with, cochineal.
wi'lute, n. Red, scarlet dye, i.e. a fluid to dye something e.g. porcupine quills scarlet.

wilu'zignagtoŋ, v. To make the tent tight around the lowest part, the border, by pins or by putting hay etc. all around. Osni kte lo, - wo, as they say when a storm is coming, thus to cover up the tipi at the bottom all around so the wind may not blow in. BT.

wilu'zignake, n. Insulation. Bl.

wi'lwiťa, adv. In groups, in bunches. Peji śaśa - haŋ. Bl.
wi'lwiťaya, adv. red. (witaya). In groups, assembled in different places. - eglepi, Shocked grain.

wi'mahel iyáye, n. The setting of the sun. Wimahel iyayetkiya etoŋwe.

wi'makaheya, n. That which enables one to earn or accomplish much.

wi maka'ťaŋhaŋ, n. The moon between Full Moon and Third Quarter. - u, i.e. it rises late and from the earth. LB.

wi mima', n. The Full Moon. LB.
wi mima'ǩaŋyela, n. The moon between First Quarter and Full Moon, i.e. when it is gibbous. LB.

wi'mna śni, v. To have no confidence, to doubt one's ability. B. Syn.- weceyeśni.

wi'naǧiyeya, (?).

wi'naȟtagye, n. A typewriter. LB.

wi'naȟ'oŋ, v. (naȟ'oŋ). To hear, to be able to hear. Winawaȟ'oŋ.

wi'najaja, n. A washing machine.

wi'nakaŋye, n. A threshing machine.

wi'naǩaṗo, n. Common hop. Humulus lupulus. The nettle family. It is used in making bread. Also called waȟpe aǩícaśkapi. Baking powder; hops, yeast. R. BT. Bl. #74.

wi'naǩiwizi, v. To be jealous or envious of. Winawakiwizi.

wi'napce, n. The esophagus. - mahel popi, Swollen tonsils.

wi'naṗiŋśkaye, n. A toy, toys, playthings. Also, wínaṗiśkaŋye.

wi'naṗoȟye, n. (napogaŋ). Leaven, yeast.

winap'i'la, n. (?). A bird. Also perhaps, wiňap'iŋla.

wi'nataȟe, n. (inataka). A fastening, a lock.

wina'wizi, n. The cockle burr or clot burr. - hu, i.e. the plant itself. Ate, nata catkayataŋ - waŋ imakoyakiŋ kte lo.

wi'nawizi, v. To be jealous or envious. Wiňawawizi. Cf. winakiwizi.

wina'wizi cik'ala, n. Wild liquorice (licorice), burr legume, buffalo burr. Glycyrrhiza lepidota. The pulse family. As a medicine, the root is used by BT. who mixes it with pejuta ska. This is his great medicine. The root is bitter when chewed and often used during the flu. BT. #78.

wina'wizi hu taŋka hca, n. The cockle burr or clot bur. Xanthium echinatum. The composite family. As medicine, it is used as śilyapi in ceremonies. MS. 356. BT. #108.

wi'nawizipi, n. Jealousy.
wi'nawizis'a, n. A jealous person; of a jealous disposition, adj.

wi'naze, n. A strainer, a filter. Cf. nazéya.

winu'ȟca, n. A man's mother-in-law. BD. - , cuiyohe waŋji micaȟ yuha yo. Bl.
winu'ȟcala, n. An old woman. Wimanuȟcala.
winu'ȟcala tacaŋ'ṗetiṗiye, n. (caŋ-peta-apiya). A poker, any piece of wood to poke a fire with. Caŋ tukte oŋ peta apiyapi he e lo. Also, winuȟcala tacaŋpelipiye. Caŋtetipiye is an incorrect word.

winuŋ'kala, (?). Bl.

wiŋ, adj. Female, of a woman or wife. This word is commonly suffixed to the name of women, much the same as Mrs. is prefixed to a woman's name.

wiŋ'ġa, v. Bending. This is a root word.

wiŋ'haha, adj. Jovial, good-natured.
wiŋ'hahaka, n. One who is pleased with trifles. P'osyakel uŋk'uŋ wiŋhahakélo.
wiŋ'hahakel, adv. In good spirits. - uŋ. Caŋtewaśte kapi. SI. Also, wihahayakel, wiŋhahayakel. D.278.
wiŋ'hahaya, adv. Easily pleased. - icu, To take trifles gladly.
wiŋ'hahayakel, adv. Apparently in good spirits, happily. Cf. wihahayakel, which seems to be Santee. Cf. kel, suff. D.278.

wiŋȟ, cont. of wiŋga.
wiŋȟya', adv. In a bent manner.

wiŋja', Cf. yuwiŋja.
wiŋja'haŋ, part. Bent down, as grass.

wiŋ'kcekce, adv. Unconcerned; not in a hurry, not concerned or minding anything. - mani. Iye amawicawani śni s'e - yaŋkahaŋpelo. BT. D.4. Takuni onah'oŋ - naŋkahelo. Bl. Also, wiŋkcekceya; to no purpose. R. Syn.- ťoȟécaca.

wiŋ'kte, n. A hermaphrodite.

wiŋś, cont. of wiŋja.
wiŋśķi'ya, v.a. To make bend, bend down.
wiŋświŋ'ja, adj. Flexible. Bl.
wiŋświŋ'jahela, adj. Limber, pliant, not stiff; tender. Maza wiŋświŋjahela. Also, wiŋśwíŋjela.

wiŋ'yaŋ, n. and adj. A woman. Wiŋmáyaŋ. The Queen in playing cards.

wiŋ'yaŋciŋ, v. To buy a wife.

wiŋ'yaŋ cokab ti wiŋ, n. A virgin. Bl. Syn.- witaŋśna uŋ.

wiŋ'yaŋ tapeji'ȟota, n. Same as peji ȟota swula. HM. #287.

wiŋ'yaŋ tawiyaka, n. Same as wiŋyaŋ tazitkala. BT.

wiŋ'yaŋ taziŋtkala, n. The gull. It is so called because women used its feathers for quill-work and on account of its belly. Also perhaps, the ptehiŋcicila. One species has red legs, the other green. It is a water bird with wings and back white, black wing tips, bill like that of śloślola, tail white, legs about 2 dm. long. Its call: Tibló wewé, tibló wewé. The male answers: Uhu, úhu. Bl. Rl. The American avocet.
wiŋ'yaŋ toŋwiyaka, n. Same as wiŋyaŋ

taziⁿtkala. BT.

Wiⁿ'yaⁿ Wakpala, n. prop. A creek south of the Niobrara River of northwestern Nebraska. Bl. The Loup River, perhaps.

wiⁿ'yaⁿyaṫapi, n. A queen.

wiⁿ'yela, n. A female animal.

wiⁿ'yeya, adv. Ready, prepared. - nakapi hwo? Waⁿna tipi waⁿ - eglepelo, i.e. for religious ceremonies. Hihaⁿna kiⁿ wocic'upi kte lo ca - uⁿ po.

wiⁿ'yuṗiⁿ, n. Paint, such as is used on walls etc. Also, wiyupi, wiyuⁿpi.

wiō'caⁿ, n. A dumb woman. Iéśni, A dumb man.

wio'cok̇aⁿyaⁿ wi, n. The middle moon, applied to January and to July. R. Bl.

wi'ohinaṗaṫaⁿhaⁿ, adv. From the east.

wio'k̇iciciya ecoⁿpi, n. An innocent pastime practicing courting between boys and girls.

wi'ok̇iseya, n. The Firt Quarter of the moon, approaching Half Moon.

wio'k̇iya, v. (okiya). To court or talk with a woman; to enjoy converse with a woman. Wiowakiya. -- wiók̇iyapi, n. Courting.

wio'ptasabyápi, n. A tent with a black ring painted all around, in the middle. Bl.

wi'ośaya, n. The aurora.

wio'ṫeȟika, n. The hard moon, January.

wi'otkeye, n. A hook or string etc. on which to hang up things. Bl.

wio'wa, n. A painted tent.

wio'weśte lowaⁿpi, n. Night songs, love songs. Also, wi oyeśte lowaⁿpi. IS.

wio'yuspa, v. To stop a woman and detain her in order to court. D.52, note 1.

wipa', n. A windflap, the upper part of a tent with the ventilating flaps.

It is painted red or black on a given kind of tent. D.4.

wi'ṗabla, n. A sadiron, flatiron; anything to flatten things with, or to smooth with. Also, wiṗablaye. Cf. pablaya.

wi'ṗaġuke, n. (paguka). A bone or iron used for scraping down skins in the process of dressing.

wi'paȟte, n. A string; anything used for tying.

wi'ṗajaja, n. (pajaja). Soap. Cf. ha ipajaja.

wi'ṗajiⁿ, v. To be prevented from succeeding in what one attempts to do by having lost a friend etc. Wimapajiⁿ.

wi'ṗajuju, n. A rubber eraser.

wi'ṗame, n. A file.

wiṗa'ṗiya, v. To open the flaps. - po; ośota yelo. Iśta joṫómakte yelo; - po. Bl.

wi'ṗaṗowaya, n. A clothes brush. P.

wiṗa'sabyápi, n. A tent whose upper and lower ends are painted black. Bl.

wi'ṗasise, n. A safety-pin.

wi'ṗaslohaⁿ, n. A wheel-barrow.

wi'ṗasnoⁿ, n. A stick to roast meat with. Bl.

wi'ṗaspe, n. Tent pins.

wiṗa'śayápi, n. A tent whose upper and lower ends are painted red. Bl.

wi'ṗaśk̇aⁿglepi, n. Fires made by a returning war party as a sign of their returning. Bl.

wi'ṗaśk̇ice, n. (paśkica). A press; a washboard. Also, wiṗaśk̇iṫe, wiṗaśkiśkite.

wi'ṗaṫa, v. (ipata). To ornament, work with porcupine quills. Wiwapata. -- wiṗaṫapi, n. Quill-work, embroidery. - eyalas'e. D.51, note 2.

wi'ṗatiŋ, n. Starch.

wi'ṗazukaŋ, n. A species of red berry that grows in small bunches and is good to eat; the service berry, sometimes called the June berry. Also, wipazokaŋ. Bl. It is used for making tahuka caŋgleśka because it does not break easily. Also, wipazuka waśte wi, The month of June. -- wiṗazuḱahu, n. A shrub used by Indians for making the tahuka caŋgleśka. The caŋpaha and the wicagnaśkahu are used for arrows. Bl.

wi'ṗazutkaŋ, n. Same as wipazuka. The June berry, service berry, May berry. Amelanchier canadensis. The rose family. The shad bush. RT. #161.

wi'ṗe, n. (pe). Sharp instruments; arms, weapons of any kind, fire-arms. Wiṗenica, Without weapons. Kolapila, uŋgna nayapapi kilo na wipe kiŋ kiksuya po. Na taŋyaŋ wipe yuha. MS.352.

wi'ṗeḱitoŋ, v. To equip one's self with gun, ammunition etc. Wipewetoŋ. Bl.

wi'ṗemnaśni, adv. Without being wounded; dead but not wounded, dead without apparent cause.

wi'ṗemnayaŋ, adv. Wounded, with a wound. - t'a, To die from an arrow or bullet shot. Bl. Tuwa - ḣpaya ca waśte yelo. MS.486.

wi'ṗeoḣloḱa, n. A wound from a spear.

wi'ṗeya, v. To sell a woman or girl in marriage, as once the Dakotas did.

wi'ṗi, v.n. (ipi). To be full of food, to be satisfied. Wímapi. Waŋna wimapi.

wiṗi'ṗa, n. Tent-flaps.

wiṗi'ṗaha, n. The two ventilating flaps on the top of a round tent. Oślota yelo; - egle yo. - ośtaŋpi, The pockets of the two tent flaps in which the two supporting poles fit.

wi'ṗiya, 1) v.a. To fill, cause to be filled or full. Wipiwaya. Wipiic'iya, To satisfy one's self with eating. 2) adv. Full.

wi'ṗusye, n. (puspa). Something to dry on or with, a dryer. Same as ipúsye.

wi'p'osyakel, adv. Morosely, cross. This is an old word. - uŋ. Tawaciŋ śica na inila uŋ. SI. Cf. p'osyakel. Syn.- hiŋyaŋzeke.

wi'sabye, n. Anything that gives a black hue. blacking.

wi'saŋye, n. Whiting.

wi'sḱuye, n. Anything that sweetens, or sours, other things.

wi'slolye, n. Something to know by. B.H.127.17. Also, a thermometer, a barometer etc.

wisma'hiŋ, n. An arrow-head. - íkceka, An arrow-head in exact form of a triangle, without a neck for tying. Cf. kestoŋ, kehuku. Bl.

wiśaŋ', n. The mons veneris, the vagina, inner and outer lips.

wi'śaślayela aye, v. n. The sun becomes clear and distinctly seen.

wi'śaye, n. Anything used in coloring red.

wi'śi, n. Hire, pay for work, remuneration. Wiśi nic'u kte lo.

wi'śikaḣya, adv. Instead, in lieu of wages. B.H.266.1.

wi'śimnaye, n. One who collects toll; a publican. B.H.173.23;191.23.

wi'śitoŋ olotapi, n. A hireling. B.H. 223.22.

wi'śitoŋyaŋ, adv. For wages. - olota. B.H.223.19.

wi'śi yuḱe'ya, adv. For payment. B.H. 100.3.

wi'śpaŋ, n. Iodine. OS.

wi'śṫeca, adj. Modest, bashful. Wimáśteca.

wi'śṫelḱiciyapi, n. The being ashamed of each other.

wi'śṫelḱiya, v.a. To be bashful or reserved, to be ashamed of, as a man is of some of his wife's relations, esp. the females; or a woman of her husband's relations, esp. the males. Wiśtelwakiya. -- wiśṫelkiyapi, n. The habit of being ashamed or reserved in the presence of one's spouse's relatives, esp. of the other sex.

wi'śtelya, v.a. To cause to be ashamed. Wiśtelwaya.

wi'śṫeśṫeca, adj. red. (wiśteca). Modest.

wi'śuṫe, v. To fail doing or miss. Also, wiśuta. Wiśuwate. Mazawakaŋ kiŋ le tohaŋtaŋ bluha kiŋ wiwognaye wanicelo. Yuŋkaŋ lehaŋtu kiŋ wiśuwatelo. Bl.

wiśwe'epi, interj. Almost, nearly; Oh! BD. Cf. wiświ eyepi.

wiświ' eye'p̄i ihe'ya, v. Whew! He just missed, i.e. in shooting. Wiświ eyepi okapta, Man! He is down almost to the last bit. Wiświ eyepi is idiomatic and indicates a very close accident or dangerous circumstance has been avoided. Wiświ', interj. D.141, notes 1 and 3. Bl.

wi'ś'oś'o, adj. Hasty, quick. Wímaś'oś'o. CG.
wi'ś'oś'oka, n. One who is lively; ready for work, wishing to work, adj. Wímaś'oś'oka. Taku icaŋliniyuha yelaka winiś'oś'okelo. Bl.

wi'ta, n. An island. -- v. To gather. Wiúŋtapi kte.

wi'take, n. A frying pan.

wi'takiŋyaŋyaŋka, n. The afternoon.

wi'takiya, adv. Together, en masse.

wi'taŋ, adj. Proud, elated. Wímataŋ.

witaŋ'śna uŋ, n. A maiden, one who is without a husband; one who lives alone and hence witaŋśna uŋ, which is also pl.

witaŋ'śnahu, n. The fig tree, a name given by Mr. Renville.

wi'taŋtaŋ, v. red. (witaŋ). Proud, vain. Wimataŋtaŋ. Pb.25,28.
wi'taŋtaŋka, n. One who is proud, as one may in having good clothes on.Bl.
wi'taŋtaŋpi, n. Vain-glory, pride.
wi'taŋtaŋya, v.a. To make proud.
wi'taŋtaŋyaŋ, adv. Glorying.

Wi'tap̄ahatu, n. prop. The Kiowas or Osages. R. M. Also, Witapaha.

wita'piĥa, n. A toad.

wita'wat'elya, v. To be willing. Cf. tawat'elya.

wi'taya, adv. Together, in company. - tipi. - wicakico. Oyate kiŋ - awicayau kte lo. Waŋna hihaŋna el oyate kiŋ - aya na oimniciye.

wi'tayaiheya, v. To assemble together. Witayaiheuŋyaŋpi.
wi'tayela, adv. Together, in company. Same as witaya. - ihaŋpi, au. Waŋna owasiŋ lel - ku po. Oyate kiŋ ataya - tipi. D.225. Wana pa - el ahiyaye lo, i.e. sticking the heads together to listen as they gather around a messanger. Bl.

wi'tiowapi, n. A tipi with the picture of the sun painted above the door. Bl.

wi'tka, n. An egg.
wi'tkatoŋ, v. To lay eggs, as fowl do.

wi'tkeyute, n. A scale; weights of measure; a pound. Also, witkeute.

witko', adj. Foolish. Wimatko.
witko'kaġa, n. The fool-maker; an imaginary being said to visit one in one's dreams.
witko'koŋza, v.n. To pretend to be foolish. Witkowakoŋza.
witko'p̄i, n. Foolishness.
witko'tko, adj. Foolish. Wimátkotko, wiuŋtkotkopi.
witko'tkōka, v.n. and n. To act foolishly. Wimátkotkoka. A fool, n. R.
witko'tkopi, n. Foolishness.
witko'tkoya, adv. Foolishly.
witko'wiŋ, n. A foolish woman, a harlot. Also, witkówiŋla.
witko'wiŋ waśtelaka, n. A lewd fellow.
witko'ya, 1) v.a. To make foolish. Witkowaya. 2) adv. Foolishly. - oĥ'aŋ.
witko'yahaŋ, adv. Foolishly, sillily. Also, witkóyakel. - oyaĥ'aŋ yelo. Bl.

wito'ka, n. A female captive.

wi'toŋp̄eśni, adv. Without fear or regard for anything, not honoring. Cf. itoŋpa.

wi'toye, n. Something that dyes blue or green; green or blue blanketing.

wit'e', n. The New Moon. LB.
wit'iŋ'kta kaŋyela, n. The moon between Third Quarter and New Moon. LB.

wi'wahoya, v. (iwahoya). To warn, order. Wiwahowaya. Wiwahoyapi uŋ ektoŋjiŋ na. Wiwahociyapi kiŋ hena ecanoŋpi śni. B.H.15.16;101.15. -- wíwahoye, n. An order. B.H.16.7.

wi'wakoŋza, v.a. To wail for those who have gone out on a war party. Wiwawakoŋza. Wiwicayawakoŋza.

wi'waŋkaṫuya, n. The hour about 9:00 A.M. - u, hiyu.

wi'waŋyaŋka, v. To observe, judge. B.H. 63.10;85.5;224.3.

Wiwaŋ'yaŋk Waci'pi, n. p. The Sundance, the Sioux national celebration.

wiwa'śte, n. Cf. wiwaśteka.

wiwa'śṫeka, n. A beautiful woman, a lady.

wiwa'yaka, n. A woman captive from another people.

wiwa'zica, n. A widow.

wi'wicagnupi, n. Accusation, blaming.

wi'wicajica, n. Riches.

wi'wicayuŋġapi, n. Questions.

wiwi'la, n. A water spring. Also, minic'ápi.
wiwi'la kapa'pa, n. A swamp, where the earth surface lies in water.
wiwi'la tapeji', n. Swamp grass. BT.
wiwi'yela, adj. Boggy, marshy from the presence of springs.

wi'wognaye, n. No missing of the aim. Mazawakaŋ kiŋ le tohaŋtaŋ bluha kiŋ - wanicelo; yuŋkaŋ lehaŋtu kiŋ wiśuwatelo. Bl.

wiwo'ha, n. A woman who lives with her husband's relatives. - , wakśu niśipi kiŋ tokeśke yaḣ'aŋ kte hwo? wawiḣayayiŋ kte lo. GA. Cf. wicawoḣa.

wi'wośṫake, n. A blunt arrow such as boys use to kill birds with. The shaft tapers large at the point end. R. Bl. Syn.- miwośtake.

wiwo'ṫikiya, v. To ask for a wife for another man. Cf. wotikiya.

wi'yaciŋ, v. (iyaciŋ). To liken to, compare to or with. Wiblaciŋ. B.H. 246.1.
wi'yaciŋiapi, n. Parables, similitudes.
wi'yaciŋpi, n. Likeness, resemblance, similitude.
wi'yaciŋyaŋ, adv. In the form of a similitude, parabolic.

wiya'gyata, (?). - inaḣme s'e eyatoŋwelo, i.e. you look secretly, as it were, at the sun. BT.

wi'yaḣloka, v. (?). Wiblaḣloka. Cehupa wiblaḣloke śni s'elececa, i.e. made no impression upon him apparently, although I told him repeatedly. Bl.

wi'yaka, n. A quill, a feather of the wing or tail of geese. Also, the two feathers fastened to the peśa and hence called Peśa Ogle.

wi'yakaḣpe, n. A cover. B.H.60.13.

wi'yakapaŋ, n. A flat bag for keeping tools or cherries etc. in. Tahasaka - . Cf. paŋ.

wi'yakaśke, n. A band to tie with.

wi'yako, v.n. To feel nausea, feel like vomiting on seeing or smelling something bad. Wiblako. Bl.

wi'yakojuha, n. (wiyaka-ojuha). The gullet, esophagus of ruminating animals and so called because it was used to fill with air and so to dry. Then feathers were kept in this sausage-like bag, as well as grease. Bl. BD.

wiya'kpa, 1) v.n. To shine, glisten, reflect. 2) adj. Bright, glistening. Pśito - , as do metal beads. Pśito jaŋjaŋla, Glass beads.
wiya'kpakpa, red. of wiyakpa.
wiya'kpakpayela, adv. red. of wiyakpayela. B.H.270.9. D.209.
wiya'kpapi, n. Brightness.
wiya'kṗaya, adv. Brightly.
wiya'kpayela, adv. Brightly, flashing. - ku, iyojaŋjaŋ. B.H.59.20;100.18.

wi'yaksapa, v. To make clear to, to tell intelligently to. Wiblaksapa. Bl.

wi'yanajiŋce, v. To hurry away with what one has received. Wiyanawajiŋce. GA.

wiyaŋ'keca, v.n. To remain at home and keep one's self busy with something. Bl.

wi'yapaḣica, n. The one pole in the middle of the rear wall of a tent. - hiŋḣpaya ehaŋtaŋś wakeya ataya hiŋḣpaye. Hence, one of the three main tent poles that stands at the rear and with it stands or falls the tent itself. Cf. wiiyapaḣice.

wi'yaṗe, v. (iyape). To lie in wait, as for game. Wíyawape. Haŋhepi el - iyaya śke. - kute ya. Bl.

wi'yaskabtoŋ, v.a. To seal. Iŋyaŋ taŋka k'uŋ he - . B.H.269.22.

wi'yaskabye, n. Mucilage; solder. R. Bl.

wi'yaśpapi, n. The Third Quarter of the moon. LB.

wiya'ta, adv. At the sun; at the moon. BS.

wi'yatagle, v. To have exceeding much. Wiyamatagle. -- wíyatagleya, adv. Having much, surpassingly.

wi'yataŋomya, n. Cf. wiataŋomya.

wiya'ṫaṗik̇a waci'ṗi, n. A dance performed by single young women only and two young men do the drumming and singing. Bl.

wi'yatke, n. A drinking cup.
wi'yatke agle'he, n. A saucer.

wi'yauŋṗa, v. (iyauŋpa). To charge with slander. Wiyawauŋpa, wiyauŋkuŋpapi. B.H.142.23. Also, wiyaoŋpa.
wi'yauŋṗapi, n. An accusation. Bl. Syn.- woiyauŋpa.
wi'yauŋṗeṗica śni, adj. Blameless. - uŋ, To be or walk blamelessly. B.H. 159.4.
wi'yauŋṗeṗicaśniyaŋ, adv. Without possibility of blame, perfectly. - uŋ. B.H.192.1.

wiya'wapi, n. A calendar; a month.

wi'yayuskiṫa, v. To bind around. Wiyabluskita. -- wíyayuskiṫe, n. A bandage.

wi'yeya, v. To dine well. Taŋyaŋ wiyewaye lo, I ate well. Bl. Lol'wanagi yewaye c'uŋ taŋyaŋ wiyewaye lo.

wi'yohaŋ, v. (iyohaŋ). To boil. Cega cik'ala (cegiscila) - popa, The tiny kettle burst into boiling. Cegiscila wiyohaŋpi popa. Bl.

wi'yohi, v. (iyohi). To reach to, to be sufficient for.

wiyo'hiyaŋṗa, n. The east; the sun rising.
wiyo'hiyaŋṗaṫa, 1) n. The east. - eciyataŋhaŋ, From the east. 2) adv. At the east, eastward.
wiyo'hiyaŋṗaṫahaŋ, adv. From the east.

wi'yoḣpaya, v. (iyoḣpaya). To come down from. Iśta wiyomaḣpaya, i.e. something got into my eyes. Bl.

wi'yoḣṗeya, v.a. (iyoḣpeya). To put or throw into, as meat into a kettle to boil. Wiyoḣpewaya. Yuŋkaŋ tima cega waŋ ogna wiyohpeyapi na lila kalyahaŋ na wicaśa ota tima yaŋkapi. MS.145.

wiyo'ḣṗeyaṫa, n. The west, where the sun sets, at the west.
wiyo'ḣṗeyaṫak̇iya, adv. Westward, towards the west. Yuŋkaŋ lila waŋkatuya - kiŋyaŋ gla.
wiyo'ḣṗeyaṫaŋhaŋ, adv. From the west.

wi'yojaŋjaŋ, v. (iyojaŋjaŋ). To shine.

wi'yokatkuǵye, n. A wood screw.

wi'yok̇ihe, n. A banner, a flag.

wi'yok̇ihehela, n. Wampum, like the wasuhula, but straight.

wi'yoṗek̇iya, v. (iyopekiya). To sell something or one's own. Wiyopewakiya. B.H.179.6.
wi'yoṗeya, v. (iyopeya). To sell, to trade. Wiyopewaye, wiyopeuŋyaŋpi.
wi'yoṗeye, n. A seller, a merchant; merchandise for trade.

wi'yotkeye, n. A hook or peg.

wi'yowa, n. Paint, something to mark or write with; ink. Maza - , A pen. Caŋwiyowa, A pencil.

wi'yucaŋ, n. A sieve. Also, wicacaŋ. Also, wíyucaŋcaŋ.

wi'yuhiŋte, n. A common rake.

wi'yuhomni, n. A wrench.

wiyu'ḣlaǵaŋ śni, v. To have one's wife with one all the time, wherever one goes. Paǵoŋta s'e - . Bl.

wi'yuȟloka, v. To get hold, to hold, with the view to opening. Wibluȟloka. Matasaka ca nape kiⁿ wibluhloke śni, i.e. cannot take a good hold of it, as one's hands are stiff. Toké, nape kiⁿ wiyuhloke śni so? as they say when somebody drops things. Bl. -- wíyuȟloke, n. An opener, a key. Cf. iyuȟloke.

wi'yuȟoⁿṫe, n. A rope made of sinew on which they make a hide pliant by pulling it over to and fro. Bl.

wi'yujaja, n. Something to wash in, as corn; a colander, a basket, a tub.

wi'yukcaⁿ, 1) v. (iyukcaⁿ). To understand, have an opinion. 2) n. One who forms an opinion. Wiblukcaⁿ, wiuⁿyukcaⁿpi. -- wíyukcaⁿṗi, n. Forming an opinion. -- wíyukcaⁿyaⁿ, adj. Judicious.

wi'yuḱeze, n. The instrument for making the zigzag or winding marks on arrows. R. Bl. Also, wíyuḱezeṗaha.

wi'yuḱiⁿce, n. Something to scrape with.

wi'yukpaⁿ, n. A mill to grind with, a coffee mill, etc.

wi'yukse, n. Anything to cut off with, such as a knife, a scissors etc. - luha he? a man asks when he wants to cut off a string. Bl.

wi'yuⁿ, v. (iyuⁿ). To anoint. Wíwayuⁿ. B.H.183.5.

wi'yuⁿġa, v. (iyuⁿga). To ask questions or inquire. Wimuⁿge, winuⁿge, wiuⁿyugapi; wimayanuⁿge. Ho le wimuⁿge k'oⁿ hecel amayupta. -- wíyuⁿġapi, n. Questions.
wi'yuⁿȟ, cont. of wiyuⁿga. - wahi.
wi'yuⁿȟya, v.a. To cause to inquire. Wiyuⁿȟwaya.

Wi'yuⁿpi Wakaⁿ, n. p. The Anointing for the Sick, a sacramental rite of the Catholic Church. Pb.44.

wi'yuskiṫe, n. A bandage; a press.

wi'yuslohaⁿ, n. A sled, a sleigh. Also, wíyuslohe.

wi'yuśḱice, n. A wringer; a press.

wi'yuśḱiⁿ, v. (iyuśkiⁿ). To rejoice, be glad. Wibluśkiⁿ.
wi'yuśḱiⁿḱiya, v.a. To cause to rejoice.
wi'yuśḱiⁿpi, n. Rejoicing.
wi'yuśkiⁿśkiⁿ, v. red. of wiyuśkiⁿ. Wibluśkiⁿśkiⁿ. Hecena keya śina kiⁿ etaⁿhaⁿ ikpaȟloke na mini mahel - .
wi'yuśḱiⁿyaⁿ, 1) v.a. To cause to rejoice. Wiyuśkiⁿwaya. 2) adv. Rejoicingly, gladly.

wi'yuśla, n. An instrument for shearing, a shears. Note: iyuśla only seems to be used.

wi'yuṫa, v. (yuta). To eat one thing with another. Wibluta.

wi'yuta, v. (iyuta). To measure, to weigh; to make signs, to talk by signs, to motion to. Wibluta. Wíyutab, They talk in signs. Waⁿyaⁿka yo, wíniciyutelo. Bl. B.H.295.8.
wi'yutapi, n. A measure.
wi'yuṫe, n. A measure, a measuring tape, a steel yard.

wi'yuwi, n. Something tied around, a bandage etc. Caⁿ wiyuwi, A vine.

wi'yuza, v. To hold or take things with one's left hand (catká). Wiyuzapi wakute ktelo. MS.483.

wizi', n. An old smoky tent, or part of one.
wizi'haⁿpa, n. Moccasins made of an old tent hide.
wizi'la, n. dim. An old smoky tent.

wi'zilya, v. To offer incense. Wizilwaya. -- wízilye, n. Incense, such as herbs, grasses etc. Na waⁿna wizilye eya icu na izilya.

wizi'paⁿ, n. The rawhide sack or satchel made by the western Sioux; the native trunk or carpet bag (round), made from untanned hide, but not a suitcase which is paⁿśá; a container in which to gather berries. SB. BS. - sapa, A satchel.

wi'ziye, n. Something to color yellow with; varnish.

wo, prefix. Affixed to verbs, signifies that the action is done by shooting, punching, pounding with the end of a stick, or by blowing. It is also used when the action of rain is expressed. The insep. pron. is placed after the prefix.

wo, n. Food. Cf. woyute. Śuŋkawakaŋ tawócola awaniyetupi ca ota t'api. BT.

wo, particle. Sign of the imp. sing. used by men, instead of yo the more common form. It is used when a "u" sound precedes, similarly as yelo and welo, when preceded by a "u" sound. Caŋksa kiŋ le icu wo. Itaŋcaŋ kiŋ ayuta wicauŋ wo. Le atoŋwaŋ wo. Ake u wo. Wicakico wo. But also: Ektoŋje śni wo.

wo'acaŋkśiŋ, n. (acáŋkśiŋ). A stepping over; the Passover. Yuŋkaŋ - , Juda oyate taaŋpetu wakaŋ waŋ he waŋna ikiyela ihaŋ.

wo'agla, n. A taking home.
wo'agli, n. A bringing home.

wo'ahoƀe, n. Reverence, a ceremony; a commandment, custom, law, rule, regulation. P.

wo'aȟtani, n. (aȟtani). A transgression, sin.

wo'ai, n. The act of taking to a place.

wo'aie, n. (aia). A talking about, slander.

wo'aiȟpeye, n. (aihpeya). Leaving to, a will, a testament; that which is left to one, a legacy. Also, responsibility for things entrusted to one. - kiŋ miye wak'iŋ kte. B.H.36.3.

wo'akaġe, n. A making on; blasphemy.

woa'kaġeġe, n. Things sewed on; lacework etc. sewed on ladies' dresses for decoration.

wo'akaȟƀe, n. (akaȟpe). A covering.

woa'ƙaŋhiyuya, v.a. To cause to rise to the top, as scum or froth, by shooting in, as in water. Woakaŋhiyuwaya.

wo'aƙeye, n. A curtain, a screen, something thrown up around like a tent. Cf. awakeyapi.

wo'akiktoŋje, n. (akiktoŋja). Forgetfulness.

wo'aƙinice, n. A competition; a dispute, a row. P. Bl. B.H.297.1.
wo'aƙinilya, v. To dispute. B.H.168.19.

wo'aƙipa, n. (akipa). An event, fortune; misfortune. - kiŋ le uŋhiyaglepi. B.H.35.4;81.5.

wo'akta, n. (akta). Regard. Note: this is always used with śni. Hence, wóaktaśni, Disregard.

wo'aktoŋje, n. Forgetfulness. Bl.

wo'anaġoptaŋ, n. (anagoptaŋ). Obedience. -- wóanagoptaŋyaŋ, adv. Obediently.

wo'anaȟma, n. Concealment; a secret. B.H.164.4. Also, wóanaȟme.

wo'anapte, n. (anapta). A stopping, restraint; something astringent.

wo'anice, n. Detention. P.

wo'aoƙiye, n. A promise. WE. Syn.- wóiwakta, wóiwahoye.

wo'aƀe, n. (ape). Waiting for, expectation; hope.

wo'asni, n. (asni). Recovery from sickness.
wo'asniƙiye, n. A lasting rest. Pb.18, 30.

wo'aśaƀe, n. (aśapa). Defilement.

woa'ślaya, v.a. (aślaya). To make bare or lay open, expose by shooting in. - iyeya.

wo'aƭakuniśni, n. (takuniśni). Destruction.

wo'awaciŋ, n. (awaciŋ). Thinking on, cares, thought; faith. B.H.156.9; 200.23.

wo'awaŋyaŋke, n. Care, protection. P.

wo'ayupte, n. (ayupte). An answer.

woblas', cont. of woblaza. - iyeya.

wobla'sƙa, v.a. (blaska). To flatten by shooting, as in shooting a bullet against a stone. Wowablaska.

wobla'ya, v.a. (blaya). To spread out by blowing or punching. Wowáblaya.

wobla'za, v.a. To tear open by shooting e.g. the bowls of an animal. Wowablaza.

woble'bleca, v. red. (wobleca). To batter.
wo'bleca, v.a. To break open e.g. a trunk. Also, to scatter things, as is done by a child in searching a trunk.
woble'ca, v.a. To break in pieces by striking with a pestle or by shooting; to shoot something to pieces, to shatter. Wowábleca. D.30.
wo'blece s'a, n. One who breaks open trunks and while searching scatters things.
woblel', cont. of wobleca. - iyeya.

wo'bliheca, n. Activity; industry.

woblu', 1) v.a. (blu). To pound up fine, crush. Wowáblu. 2) v.n. To blow in fine particles, drift, as does snow; to blow about, as dust; to boil up, as does water in a spring. Iwaśtegla tate icaluza ca maka - welo. Bl. Caȟota - iyeya. D.77.
wo'blu, v. (yublu). To pulverize; to plough. Wabúblu.

woblu'blu, v. red. of woblu.

woblu'ya, part. Blowing up, as the wind blows dust or snow. -- v. To blow, to spit on. Wobluwaya. Maka śa - i etaŋhaŋ.

wo'cajeyalya, v.a. To give expression to. Caŋte mahel wokiksuye yuhapi kiŋ hena lecel wocajeyalyapi. B.H.135.16. Wócajeyate, the words of a song. This is derived from the custom of naming a man, to sing his praises, in song; wocajeyalya is used for the words of the song of one's man's praises. D. 261, note 2.

wo'cajeyaṫe, n. The words of a song in praise of the name of another. D.261, note 2.

wocaŋ'caŋ, v.a. (caŋcaŋ). To make trouble by shooting. Wowacaŋcaŋ.

wo'caŋȟiŋyaŋ, v. To be very much attached to one. Cf. caŋȟiŋyaŋ. BD.

wo'caŋkśu, n. Meat hanging on a long stick to dry.

wo'caŋlwaŋka, n. Cowardice.

wo'caŋniye, n. (caŋniyaŋ). A man's anger against his wife.

wo'caŋśice, n. Sorrow.

wo'caŋṫagle, n. (caŋtagle). Evil intention against, malice; the object of evil purpose.

wo'caŋṫehahayela, n. Over-sensitiveness perhaps. P.

wo'caŋṫeiyapaya, adv. With a beating heart. - na teȟiya uŋkiŋyaŋpi. MS. 103.

wo'caŋṫeiyoḱiśice, n. Sadness. Iwaśicuŋ ca - . Bl.

wo'caŋṫeiyuṫaŋ, n. Temptation. B.H. 92.2.
wo'caŋṫeiyuṫaŋke, n. Something that tempts. Bl.
wo'caŋṫeiyuṫaŋye, n. Temptation.

wo'caŋṫeḱapṫaŋya, n. Irritation, the becoming upset; anger. - yuha. Bl.

wo'caŋṫeḱiye, n. Love. Cf. wocaŋtkiye.

wo'caŋṫeoyuze, n. Infatuation.

wo'caŋṫeśice, n. Sorrow, adversity. - wanice. Pb.47.

wo'caŋṫewaśte, n. Gladness.

wo'caŋṫiheye, n. Ardent desire.

wo'caŋṫiyuṫaŋ, n. Temptation. Cf. wocaŋteiyutaŋ.

wo'caŋtḱiye, n. Love, benevolence. Cf. wocaŋtekiye. Pb.36.

wo'caŋṫognaḱe, n. Compassion, pity. Pb.31.

wo'caŋṫokṗani, n. A longing for.

wo'caŋze, n. Anger.
wo'caŋzeḱa, n. Rage.

wo'cas'aya, n. That which is noteworthy, known, prominent. Makoce waŋ - ka ca, A prominent and well-known country. B.H.62.13.

wo´cas'ayakel, adv. Very famous. Iyotaⁿ - uⁿ. Solomon - cajeyatapi. B.H.88.17; 102.4.

woceg´, cont. of woceka. - iyeya.
woceg´ya, adv. Staggeringly.

woce´ka, v.a. To make stagger by shooting or punching. Wowáceka.
woce´kceka, v. red. of woceka.

wo´cekiye, n. (cekiya). Crying to; prayer.

wo´cet'uⁿgla, n. (cet'uⁿgla). Unbelief. - yuhaśniyaⁿ oholapi. B.H.169.20.

wo´ceye, n. (ceya). Crying. Cf. wicaceya.

wō´ciⁿ, v. (ociⁿ). To beg, ask for; to be begging. Wówaciⁿ. - yahi ca cic'u; yuⁿkaⁿ páhiⁿskayela cic'u yaciⁿ yelo. Bl.
wo´ciⁿla, n. A beggar. P.
wo´ciⁿpi, n. Begging, craving; hunger.

wo´cokoⁿ, n. (cokoⁿ). A threat, a curse.

woc'o´, v.a. To churn. Wowác'o.
woc'o´c'o, v. red. of woc'o.

wo´ecetu, n. (ecetu). Fulfillment; simplicity. P.

wō´ecoⁿ, n. Work, doing. - ota woitoⁿpeya ecoⁿpi. B.H.66.17;156.2;192.10.

wo´ecoⁿka, n. Work, that can be easily done, but is not done by many.

wo´ecoⁿla, v. To consider something hard work but it is not.
wo´ecoⁿlaka, n. A difficult work. BD.

wo´ecoⁿyaⁿ, v. To do; one who is always doing, n. Woecoⁿwaya.

wo´ekicetu, n. Renewal; resurrection.
wo´ekicetuye, n. Restoration.

wo´ektoⁿje, n. Forgetfulness.

wo´eye, n. A speech or saying. Yuⁿkaⁿ - kiⁿ le slolyapi śni. Cf. wóie, a word.

woġa´, adv. Spreading out, straddling, sprawling. - s'e najiⁿpi.

wo´ġa, v. To husk e.g. corn. Wabluga, wauⁿyuhapi. Cf. wayúga.

woġa´ġa, v.n. To shoot out in different directions, as rays of light or the branches of a tree. Also, yuġáġa. R.
woġa´ġaya, adv. Spreading, as a tree top when cut down, its brances shooting out from a center.

wo´ġapi, n. The act of husking corn.

woġa´ya, adv. Shooting out from a point. Also, yuġáya. R.

wo´ġi, n. (gi). Brownness.

wogla´, v.a. To shell off by shooting or punching. Wowágla.

wo´gla, n. Something that is detested. Woglapi, mihakab iyaya po, i.e. ye cursed, despised. B.H.249.21.

wo´glaglaka, v. red. (woglaka). To chat.

wo´glaka, v. (oglaka). To converse of one's affairs, to talk, counsel. Wówaglaka.
wo´glakapi, n. Telling one's own affairs. Woglakapi wakaⁿ, Penance, the sacramental confession.

wogla´kiⁿyaⁿ, v. (glakiⁿyaⁿ). To cause to glance, as a bullet.

wo´glawa, n. Something bitter or disagreeable. B.H.191.24.

wo´glaya, v. To consider something a detestable thing. Cf. gla. Tona woglawicayaye kiⁿ hena tehiya uⁿpi kta, i.e. whom you curse. Cham woglayapi uⁿ kte lo. B.H.4.16;6.1;9.16;67.11. -- wóglayapi, n. A detestable thing. - yauⁿ kte.

wo´gligleye, n. A pattern, design, as for bead-work. Also, wogligleyapi. IS.

woglo´glo, red. v. To grunt, as do pigs or buffalo. Bl. Also, woglóka. Bl.

wo´gmuⁿke, n. (gmuⁿke). A place where trapping is done. Iktomi tawogmuⁿke, A spider-web. BD.

wogna´, v.a. To shoot off, as fruit

from a tree. Wowágna.

wo'gna, prep. In. Cf. ogna.
wo'gnaka, v. (ognaka). To put or place in. Wowagnaka.
wo'gnakapi, n. A basket or receptacle.

wogna'śkiⁿyaⁿ, v.a. (gnaśkiⁿyaⁿ). To make crazy or furious, as an animal, by shooting it. Wowágnaśkiⁿyaⁿ.
wo'gnaśkiⁿye, n. Lunacy, madness. P.

wogna'yaⁿ, v.a. (gnayaⁿ). To miss partly in shooting or striking with end of a stick, i.e. not hitting e.g. an animal well so that it can get away. Wośná, To miss. Wowágnayaⁿ.

wo'gnaye, n. (gnayaⁿ). Deceit, delusion.

wo'ǧu, n. Scraps, as of tallow dried out.

wo'ha, n. abbrev. (woyuha). Property. Lecel - na Wakaⁿtaⁿka lila ohola kiⁿ oⁿ iś eya oyas'iⁿ oholapi. B.H.42.13.

woha', v. To shoot or punch over. - iyeya.
woha'hayela, v. To make totter by shooting or pushing.
woha'iḣpeya, v.a. To shoot or make fall and thus to punch over.

wo'hakakta, n. The youngest, the last.

wo'haⁿ, v. (ohaⁿ). To cook, boil; to make a feast. Wówahaⁿ, wóuⁿhaⁿpi.
wo'haⁿpi, n. A boiling, a feast. - kaga, To make a feast.

wohe', n. A horse with big knuckles. Syn.- iyák'oza. Bl. Cf. iyánuⁿga. Wohé eśaⁿ lila luzahaⁿ. Bl.

wo'he, v. Cf. wóhaⁿ.
wo'hela, n. A cook.
wo'hekiya, v.a. To cause to cook, to have for a cook. Wohewakiya.
wo'hekiyapi, n. A cook. Cf. wohela.

wo'heyuⁿ, n. (heyuⁿ). A package, a parcel, bundle, as of dried meat. - top yaⁿka ca waⁿji tokeya yajuju.

wohil', cont. (wohiⁿta). To sweep all off, as men in a battle-field; to blow away.

wohiⁿ'ḣpaya, v.a. To make fall by shooting or punching.

wohiⁿ'ta, v.a. To sweep off by shooting e.g. men in a battle field; to blow away. Wowahiⁿta.

wo'hiⁿyaⁿsya, adv. Sternly, crossly. Cf. hiⁿyaⁿsya.
wo'hiⁿyaⁿsyakel, adv. In a cross or stern manner; like quite unpleasant or stormy weather. - uⁿ, as is said of an ornery, fierce-looking bull. - magaju. Bl. Cf. ohiⁿyaⁿsyela.
wo'hiⁿyaⁿsyela, adv. Sternly. B.H.34.17.
wo'hiⁿyaⁿze, adj. Stern, cross, as could be said of a mean man or animal, e.g. a mean horse. - H'aⁿ, To act sternly. Note: this is less usually used; rather preferred, ksíze-ca.
wo'hiⁿyaⁿzeke, n. A stern man, one who is feared.

wo'hiti, adj. Furious, terrible.
wo'hitigla, n. (hitigla). Something loathed.
wo'hitigya, adv. Bravely. - uⁿ, He is brave. B.H.62.9.
wo'hitika, adj. (ohitika). Terrible, furious, violent; energetic. Wómahitika; wóhitipika, pl. Na okicize el wohítipiké ci hena wicaka.
wo'hitila, v.a. To regard as furious. Also, wóhitilaka.
wo'hitiya, adv. Furiously, violently; energetically.

wo'hiyaye, n. A passage, as of the sun going from east to west. -- Wóhiyaye, n. p. The Passover. B.H.61.2;171.8; 179.2.

woho'ho, v.a. To shake or lossen by shooting. Wowáhoho.

woho'ta, adj. Short and thick, chubby.

woho'taniⁿ, v.a. (hotaⁿiⁿ). To make cry out by punching. Wowahotaⁿiⁿ.
woho'toⁿ, v.a. (hotoⁿ). To make bawl by shooting or punching. Wowahotoⁿ.

wohuⁿ'huⁿs, cont. of wohuⁿhuⁿza. - iyeya.
wohuⁿ'huⁿsya, part. Shaken by shooting or punching.
wohuⁿ'huⁿza, v.a. (huⁿhuⁿza). To shake e.g. a tree by shooting it. Wowahuⁿhuⁿza.

wo'ha, n. (ha). A place to bury in, a place of deposite in the ground; a cellar, a pit; something buried. Miniwóha.

wo'haka, 1) n. (ohaka). Something eaten that does not agree with the stomach; poison; also, a job with much incidental work, oécoⁿ ota. R. Bl. WE. 2) v. To be poisoned, to feel bad after eating something. Wómahaka. R. Bl.

wohci', v.a. To break out a piece by punching, as from the end or edge of a chisel. Wowahci. -- wohcíhci, v. red.
wohci'hciya, adv. In dangles, dangling.
wohci'ya, adv. Same as wohcihciya.

wo'hešma, adj. Thick, as grass or under brush.

wo'heyaka, n. Presents for one having been cured. B.H.115.9.

wo'hiⁿyaⁿ, v. (ohiⁿyaⁿ). To be dissatisfied with, to take offense at. Wówahiⁿya. Hence, to pout. -- wóhiⁿyaⁿpi, n. Dissatisfaction, offence.

wohla', v.a. To make rattle by shooting. Wowáhla.

wohla'gaⁿ, v.a. (hlagaⁿ). To make loose by shooting. Wowahlagaⁿ.

wohla'hla, v. red. of wohla.

wohla'ya, v.a. To peel off by shooting, as the bark of a tree. Wowahlaya.

wohle'ca, v.a. To tear through by shooting or running into something, e.g. a wagon tongue into a tent. Wowahleca. Wakicepa mini wohlece lo, as is said when just a few drops of rain fall. Bl.
wohle'hleca, v. red. of wohleca.
wohlel', cont. of wohleca. - iyeya.

wohle'pe s'e, adv. Standing upright, as hair. Itoye kiⁿ - he c'oⁿ. Bl.

wo'hli k'el, adv. (?). - ahiyaya. Bl.

wohlog', cont. of wohloka. - iyeya.
wohlo'hloka, v. red. of wohloka.
wohlo'ka, v.a. (hloka). To shoot or punch a hole, by shooting to make a hole. Wowáhloka.

wohlo'kapi šni pejúta, n. Waxwork; climbing bitter-sweet. Celastrus scandens. The stafftree family. The red roots are chewed and smeared all over the body, as it was thought, so one would be impervious to wounding. BT. #46.

wohmiⁿ', v.a. (hmiⁿ). To make a gun crooked shooting. Wowahmiⁿ.
wohmiⁿ'yaⁿ, part. Crooked by shooting.

wohpa', v.a. To make fall by shooting, to shoot down, as a bird on the wing. Wowahpa. MS.100. -- wohpáhpa, v. red.

wo'hpani, n. Something perhaps to mix in e.g. paint.

wohtag', cont. of wohtaka.
wohta'ka, v.a. (htaka). To pound, punch or knock with the end of anything. Wowahtaka.

wohu'ga, v.a. To break in or break open by shooting or punching, to crack something by shooting or running against something like a rabbit's head by a shot. Wowáhuga.
wohuh', cont. of wohuga. - iyeya.
wohu'huga, v. red. of wohuga.

wō'h'aⁿ, n. Something that is hard to do, a hard proposition. Also, wóh'aⁿka.
wō'h'aⁿhi, v.n. To be slow, to be long doing something, taking much time at doing. Also, óh'aⁿ. Wómah'aⁿhi, wóuⁿh'aⁿhipi. R. Bl.
wo'h'aⁿka, n. A hard proposition.
wo'h'aⁿyaⁿkel, adv. With difficulties of all sorts. - caⁿli iyátaⁿ, It took quite a while to light his cigaret.

wo'h'iyaya, v. To do a thing poorly, badly. Wómah'iyaya.
wo'h'iya'yaka, v. To do one's work not well at all, yet pretending to be very busy and know all about it. Akšaka he woh'iyayaka. Bl.

woh'u', v.a. To peel off e.g. bark by shooting; to strike and scrape along. R.

wo'icage, n. (icaga). A growth, a generation.
wo'icahye, n. The produce. P.

wo'icaje, adj. Many, very many; many kinds, a great variety. Also, wóicajeka.

wo'icaŋśica, n. Sadness, a cause of sadness.

wo'icaśyela, adv. (caje). Wonderfully much. Blo - mak'u welo. BS.

wo'icazo, n. (icazo). Debt, credit.

wo'iciȟaȟaya, adv. In a mocking manner. - eya. B.H.57.10.

wo'icu, n. (icu). A receiving, acceptance; a reception.

wo'ic'icoŋze, n. (koŋza). A resolution, a binding one's self by an oath or resolution. - oic'iglaka, To make a vow. B.H.284.16.

wo'ic'igle, n. One who lays up for himself; substance.

wo'ie, n. A word. Wóeye, A saying. B. B.H.69.13;103.9.

wo'ielgle, n. A casting up, a charging with.

wo'iglaka, v. refl. (woglaka). To declare one's self, declare one's purpose, to vow. Wómiglaka. Na hihaŋna el tona caŋte pahloka woiglakapi heci hena waŋna hocokata ai.

wo'iglaťaŋ, n. (iglataŋ). Boasting.

wo'igluzeze, n. (igluzeze). A clinging to, a support, a hope. Tuŋkaśila tahokśila yauŋpi kiŋ niś eya he - sloľyayapi; iciŋ he uŋkokiyakapi kiŋ tóki. MS.648.

wo'ignu, n. Murmuring.

wo'ihakta, n. The regard.

wo'ihamnayaŋ, adv. Generously, richly. - kajuju. B.H.13.3.

wo'ihaŋble, n. A dream.

wo'ihaŋgye, n. Destruction. P.

wo'ihaŋke, n. A conclusion; end; loss. P. B.H.13.18.

wo'iȟa, n. (iȟa). Something laughable. - oieyaye lo.
wo'iȟaȟa, n. Raillery.

wo'iȟaka, v. To laugh at, to jest. - lo.
wo'iȟala, n. Something that causes laughter.
wo'iȟaya, adv. Laughably, ludicrously; oddly, funny, queer. Wośkatela waŋ oȟ'aŋ wowiȟaya ecuŋhaŋpi. Taku oȟ'aŋ wówiȟaya zuya hila ye. D.33,78.
wo'iȟayaȟel, adv. Ludicrously. Wóciŋ hi ca k'upi yeśaŋ - iyuha k'upi ciŋ. Bl.

wo'iȟoíe, n. A laughable word.

wo'iȟpekiciye, n. A divorce. B.H.232. 20.
wo'iȟpeye, n. (ihpeya). Putting or throwing away.

wo'ijajapi, n. A tub.

wo'ijaŋjaŋ, n. A light. B.H.168.14.

wo'ijica, n. Wealth, with reference to or in terms of. He - uŋglawa ye. B.H.122.16.

wo'ikazo, n. Cf. woicazo, Debts. B.

wo'ikiksape, n. (ikiksapa). Experience.

wo'ikope, n. (ikopa). Fear; anything frightful or discouraging. B.H.45.6.

woi'kpiska, v. To shoot or punch and knock over on its back. - eȟpéya.

wo'iksape, n. Something difficult.
wo'iksapeca, n. That which is difficult.

wo'ikuśe, n. Resistance, obstacles, an impediment.

wo'ilagic'iya, v. refl. To make one's self a servant, to serve. El -. B.H. 243.11;44.1.
wo'ilagya, v. To employ. P.
wo'ilake, n. A person or thing made to serve for a definite purpose, that one uses. Woimalake. Oŋśicilake kiŋ heoŋ kici woinilake kiŋ niś eya oŋśiyalakiŋ kta iyececa śni hwo? B.H.

woi'le, v.a. (ile). To blow and make blaze, as a fire. Wowáile.
woi'leya, v.a. To cause to make blaze by blowing. Woilewaya.

wo'imaġaġa, 1) v.n. (imagaga). To be cheerful or merry. Wóimamagaga. 2)

n. An amusement, entertainment, something cheering. - wośkate.

wo'imna, adj. Famous. WE. B.H.160.13.
wo'imnamna, adj. red. (woimna). Popular; capable, strong. Ituyaĥcin woimnamnapi na takuni okihipi śni. Bl.
wo'imnanka, adj. Powerful, strong, capable.
wo'imnayan, adv. Ably, capably. Bl. With satisfaction. Also perhaps n. Cf. ímnayan.

wo'inaĥme, n. (inaĥma). Concealment.

wo'inaĥni, n. (inaĥni). Haste.

wo'inaƙiwizi, n. (inakiwizi). Jealousy.

wo'inaṗe, n. (inape). A refuge, a retreat.
wo'inaṗeƙa, n. What is threatening ; harm. Takuni - ecacicion kte śni yelo. B.H.90.15.
wo'inaṗeya, v.a. To use for or have for a refuge. Pb.26.

wo'inapiśkanye, n. (?). Lena - ca cic'u welo. MS.356.

wo'inawizi, n. (inawizi). Jealousy, envy; the cause of envy.

wo'inihan, n. (inihan). Something frightful, fear.
wo'inihanyan, adv. Fearfully. D.215.

wo'iṗutaƙe, n. A kiss. B.H.256.6.

wo'iśtinma, n. (iśtinma). Sleep. Also, woiśtinme.

wo'iṫan, n. A thing of honor. Taku wanji - yalá hwo? - waśte kagelo, i.e. performed a good deed. Bl.

wo'iṫancan, n. Leadership. - wicak'upi. Also, authority, power; government. - tanka yaun we. Wicaśa - yuha kin hemaca. B.H.111.13;196.15.

woi'tkon, v.a. (itkon). To kindle or make burn by blowing. Wowaitkon.

wo'itonṗe, n. A surprise, a cause for wonder. Woimatonpe. Pb.31. Waś'aka -, A wonder of strength. Waś'aka woimatonpe. B.H.76.10;222.8.
wo'itonṗeṗeya, adv. red. of woitonpeya. B.H.135.2.
wo'itonṗeya, v. To be a surprise. Taoonspe kin woitonpeyapi na imnapi. B.H.171.19. -- adv. Wonderfully, surprisingly, abundantly. Wagmeza kin - yuke. Bl. B.H.178.1.

wo'it'inze, n. A supporter, a support. Maza kin takuni - śni, The iron (fence posts) was no support at all, i.e. the iron being soft. Bl.

wo'it'ungye, n. A suspicion. P.

wo'iwahoye, n. A promise. P. WE. B.H. 7.14. Syn.- wóiwakta, wóaoƙiye.

wo'iwakta, n. A promise. WE. B.H.13. 17. Syn.- woaokiye, woiwahoye.

wo'iwanyanƙe, n. A review, an example; a fair proposition. P. B.H.107.22; 252.15.

wo'iwapetogye, n. A signal, sign or mark. Taku - eśa on yau kte. B.H. 245.2.

wo'iyaksape, n. Useful and wise advice. - on woglak wicaśi kte. Bl. MS.482.

wo'iyaṗat'oye, n. A hindrance.

wo'iyaunpa, n. An accusation. Also, woiyaunpe. Bl. B.H.36.14;174.3.

wo'iyawa, n. A million. What is beyond this number is called kokta śica. Rac.

wo'iyecetu, n. Fulfillment, uprightness.

wo'iyoƙiṗi, n. Pleasure, satisfaction. P. Pb.40.

wo'iyoƙiśice, n. Sorrow, sadness. Pb. 40.

wo'iyopaśtake, n. Pressure. P.

wo'iyopeye, n. A scolding, punishment.

wo'iyoṫiyeƙiya, n. Suffering. B.H.120.6. Also, adversity. P. R. Bl.

wo'iyowaja, n. A share of, an inheritance; business. P. B.H.240.3;261.1.

woi'yowas, cont. (woiyowaza). To make an echo by shooting. - iyeya.
woi'yowaza, v.a. To make an echo by shooting. Wowáiyowaza.

wo'iyowiŋkiye, n. A permission.

wo'iyukcaŋ, n. Same as wowiyukcaŋ.

wo'iyuŋ, n. An anointing; anointment. B.H.83.22.

wo'iyuŋġe wo'wapi, n. A catechism.

wo'iyuśkiŋ, n. Gladness.
wo'iyuśkiŋya, v. To make something the occasion for much rejoicing. B.H.88.2.

wo'iyutaŋke, n. Something that tempts. Bl.

wō'ja, v. (yuja). To mash, to stir as a mush, to make mush. Wówaja, or wablúja.

woja'gjata, v. red. of wojata.

woja'ja, v.n. To wash, as rain does the road. Also, a wash-tub, n. P.
wo'jajapi, n. Washing.

wō'japi, n. Something mashed and stirred up; mush, a stew of any kind mixed. Caŋpa, kaŋta wojapi.

woja'ta, v.a. (jata). To make forked by punching, as is done to a turnip digger. Wowájata.

wo'jice, n. (jica). Riches.

wo'ju, 1) v. (oju). To sow, to plant. Wówaju, wóuŋjupi. 2) n. A sower.

wo'juha, n. An empty bag, a sack; a case.

wo'juhaglatata, v.a. To exhaust, use all up e.g. one's supply by giving to others. Wojuhawaglatata.

wo'juhala, n. A small bag.

wo'juiyu'tapi, n. An acre. - 40.

woju'ju, v.a. (juju). To break to pieces or destroy by shooting; to knock or punch to pieces; to break, as the rain does ice, or as a flood does a bridge. Wowájuju.

wo'juju, v. (yujuju). To take to pieces; to demolish; to unpack. Wowajuju or wablujuju.
wo'jujupi, n. A taking to pieces, dismantling.

wo'jupi, n. A sowing or planting a field or garden.
wo'jupi wi, n. The moon of planting, May.

wo'juti, n. A farm-house; a farmer.

wo'jutoŋ, 1) v. To fill up into bags or sacks. Wojuwatoŋ. 2) n. A filled sack. B.H.38.3.
wo'jutoŋpi, n. A bag or sack filled. Also, wojútoŋpi. Águyapi wojútoŋpi.

wo'juwicaśa, n. A farmer.

woka'biyeya, v.a. To remove what has been sent into another's body by magic. Wokabiyewaye. Cf. wicahmuŋga.
woka'bkab, v. To issue. Toŋ - hiyuya, To expectorate freely, spit out phlegm freely. Bl. Syn.- woślóślog.

wo'kaġe, n. (kaga). Anything made, creation; forms. Maka - kiŋ hetaŋhaŋ. B.H.165.14.
wo'kaġe tipi, n. A factory.

wo'kaġi, n. (kagi). A hindrance.
wo'kaġiye, n. One who obstructs.

wo'kahniġa, v. (okahniga). To understand. Wowakahniga.
wo'kahniġe, n. (kahniga). Choice. B.H. 107.9.

wo'kahtaŋ, n. Small grass burs which easily stick to one's clothing.
wo'kahtaŋ blaskaska, n. The showy tick trefoil, sticktights. Desmodium canadense. The pulse family. WE. #119.

wo'kakije, n. (kakija). Suffering, misery.
wo'kakiśye, n. The cause of suffering.

wo'kala, v. (kala). To scatter. Wowakala. B.H.248.21.

wo'kamna, n. Income, a salary, wages, livelihood.

wokaŋ', v.a. To punch or shoot off. Wowákaŋ.

wo'kapa, n. Something pungent. Taku eye' ciŋ oyasiŋ - ececa, All his words are cutting. Taku waŋji epe ciŋhaŋ hena - ca epe s'elececa. Bl.

wo'kapaŋ, n. Pounded meat; a meat-block.

wo'ǩapaza, n. Pungency, anything pungent, e.g. pepper.

wo'ǩap̌e, n. A hide on which to pound cherries, meat etc., the hide from the head of the buffalo; a rawhide container; a going beyond, a transgression, cf. kapa. R.

wo'kap̌e, n. One who catches a ball, a catcher.

wo'kase, n. (kasa). A deposit in the snow. R. Bl.

wo'ǩaslat̄e, v. (okaslata). To stick in, as a splinter into the finger. Womakaslate. R. Bl.

wo'ǩasote, n. The using up of a thing.

wo'ǩaswu, n. Fringes. Hena paŋ ipatapi na anuŋg - heca ipatapi. MS.483. IS.

wo'kaśeya, n. Something opposing, a hindrance.

woǩa'ťiŋ, v.a. (katiŋ). To make stretch or straighten out by punching. Wowákatiŋ.

wo'kcaŋ, n. A seer. Wokcaŋ wicaśa, A prophet. -- v. To see for one's self, with one's own eyes. - ya, To go and find out for one's self. - i. Note: this word is used with another word, generally speaking.

wo'kcaŋka, n. One who understands things.

woǩe'ya, n. An Indian dwelling made of straw, psa, grass, peji, etc. Some tribes lived in such houses. Waȟpe - , A certain lodge used in the Sundance. B.H.9.15.

woǩi'blebleca, v. red. of wokibleca.

woǩi'bleca, v. pos. (wobleca). To break one's own by pounding or shooting. Wowakibleca.

woǩi'blel, cont. of wokibleca. - iyeya.

wo'ǩicaȟniǧa, v. To detect, see through or understand e.g. the deception or untruthfulness of another. Cf. okicaȟniga.

woǩi'cibleca, v.a. (wobleca). To break for another, by shooting or punching. Wowécibleca.

woǩi'cic'o, v. (woc'o). To churn for one. Wowécic'o.

woǩi'ciȟloka, v. (woȟloka). To shoot or punch a hole for another. Wowecíȟloka.

woǩi'ciȟp̌a, v. (woȟpa). To shoot down something on the wing, or that is hanging up, for another. Wowecíȟpa.

wo'ǩiciju, n. (woju). To sow or plant for one. Wóweciju.

woǩi'cikp̌aŋ, v. (wokpaŋ). To pound for one. Wowecikpaŋ.

woǩi'ciksa, v. (woksa). To shoot or punch off e.g. a limb or an arm, from one. -- woǩiciksaksa, v. red.

wo'ǩiciŋ, n. An entreaty. P.

wo'kicipasi, n. A military evolution, a maneuver. P.

woǩi'cipťa, v. (wopta). To dig or pry up for one, as in digging a turnip. Wowécipta.

woǩi'cisni, v. (wosni). To blow out e.g. a candle for one; to blow and cool for another, as hot food. Wowecisni.

woǩi'cisoťa, v. (wosota). To kill off for one by shooting e.g. cattle. Wowecisota.

woǩi'ciśloǩa, v. (wośloka). To shoot off a gun for one. Woweciśloka.

woǩi'ciśna, v. (wośna). To miss in shooting for one. Woweciśna.

woǩi'ciśp̌a, v. (wośpa). To shoot off a piece for one, to shoot or kill for one and relieve from danger, as from a wild animal. Woweciśpa.

woǩi'ciweǧa, v. (wowega). To break, but not entirely off, for one by shooting or punching. Woweciwega.

wo'ǩicize, n. (kiciza). Fighting.

wo'ǩicoŋze, n. Law, government, dominion, authority; a kingdom. - yuha. B.H.173.8. Cf. kicoŋza, koŋza.

woǩi'hiŋta, v. pos. (wohiŋta). To make

clear a place, as is said of rain clouds that pass by with a few drops of rain falling only. Syn.- wokiśloka.

wo'kiȟye, v. To have missed something good by not being there and so being sorry for it, to regret. He wokiȟye. IS. Wowakiȟye.

wo'kija, v. (woja). To make hasty-pudding for one. Wowakija.

wo'kikaȟniġa, v. (okikaȟniga). To have understanding. B.H.273.3.

wo'kikcaⁿpte, n. (kikcaⁿpta). Comfort, consolation. Pb.44.

woki'ksa, v. pos. (woksa). To break in two one's own by shooting or punching. Wowakiksa. -- wokiksaksa, v. red.

wo'kiksuye, n. (kiksuya). Remembrance, commemoration. - aⁿpetu, An anniversary.

wo'kiksuyeya, v.a. To have for a remembrance, to remember by. B.H.237. 16;253.7.

wo'kikśaⁿ, n. Friendly teasing, such as between males and females.

wo'kikta, n. (kikta). Watching, waking.

woki'ktaⁿ, v. pos. (woktaⁿ). To crook one's own by shooting, as one's arrow. Wowakiktaⁿ.

wo'kilapi, n. The act of requesting.

wo'kimnaⁿka, adj. Liberal, large; good, wise; honored. R. Bl.

wō'kini, v. (okini). To get a share, be lucky in getting something. Wowakini. Lila taⁿyaⁿ wowakini yelo; śuⁿkawakaⁿ mak'u yelo.

wo'kinihaⁿ, n. Honor, respect; one's part. Wicaśa iyuha niyawaśtepi kte na - luha kte.

woki'nuⁿkaⁿ, v.a. (kinuⁿkaⁿ). To separate by shooting. - iyeya.

wokiⁿ'ca, v.a. To scrape or scratch in shooting; to make sting or smart by shooting. R.

wokiⁿl'kiⁿca, v. red. of wokiⁿca.

wokiⁿ'tkiⁿca, v. red. of wokiⁿca.

wo'kipajiⁿ, n. Opposition, rebellion.

woki'powaya, v. pos. of wopowaya.

woki'puskica, v.a. (kipuskica). To drive up close together by punching or shooting; to rain on. Wowakipuskica. -- wokipuskil, cont. (wokipuskica. - iyeya.

wo'kisapa, v. pos. (wosapa). To make one's self black by shooting; to rain on, as snow, and make the ground bare.

woki'śla, v. pos. (wośla). To injure or lay bare by shooting. Wowakiśla.

woki'ślaya, v.a. To make bare or expose by shooting. Wowakiślaya.

woki'śleca, v. pos. (wośleca). To split off a piece from one's own by shooting or punching. Wowakiśleca.

woki'śloka, v. pos. (wośloka). To shoot or punch a hole in one's own, shoot off one's own gun, to blow out and make clear, as a tube. Also, it is said of rain clouds that pass by with only a show of a few rain drops. Bl. Syn.- wokihiⁿta.

woki'śna, v. pos. (wośna). To miss in attempting to shoot one's own. Wowakiśna.

woki'śpa, v. pos. (wośpa). To shoot off a piece from one's own. Wowakiśpa.

wo'kitaⁿ, n. A little of anything. R. Waⁿciglakapi kte hciⁿ ca - hci wau na wahi yelo. Bl. Wokitaⁿhci, tehiya.

wo'kitaniⁿ, n. (okitaniⁿ). Manifestation, renown.

wo'kitaⁿiⁿyaⁿ, adv. Gloriously.

wo'kit'a, v. (okit'a). To be tired out. Wowakit'a and womakit'a. -- n. Weariness, exhaustion. - wanice. Bl.

wo'kiya, v. (okiya). To speak with, talk with, to make peace. Wowakiya. R. Bl.

wo'kiyag, cont. of wokiyaka. - wahi, I have come to announce to one.

wo'kiyaka, v. (okiyaka). To speak to, to tell to one, declare to. Wowakiyaka, and perhaps wowakiblaka. Lila taⁿyaⁿ womakiyakelo.

wo'kiyakakiya, v.a. To make speak to. Niye wouⁿkiyakapi ye...tka Wakaⁿtaⁿka wouⁿkiyakapikiye śni ye. B.H.58.2.

wō'ǩiye iyaya, v. To go to buy, trade at a store. - mni kte. Tehaⁿ wokiye wahi.

wo'ǩiyuȟe, n. (kiyuȟa). Copulation.

wo'ǩiyuśke, n. (kiyuśka). A setting free, deliverance.

wo'ǩizi, n. (okizi). The scar left after healing; a healing; salve. R.

woǩo'ǩa, v.a. To make rattle by shooting or punching. Wowakoka.

woko'kipapake śni, (?). - mani. Bl.

wo'ǩokiƥe, n. (kokipa). Fear, the cause of fear. Maka ȟliȟlila oⁿ iic'iuⁿ nata ko. Caⁿke lila puza ca wokokipe. B.H.120.5.

wo'koǩiƥeya, adv. Fearfully. - magaju. Bl. Syn.- wohiⁿyaⁿsyakel.

wo'ǩoⁿ, n. (koⁿ). Desire; something desirable.

wo'ǩoⁿǩa, n. Something desired.

wo'ǩoⁿze, n. (koⁿza). A decree, law; an influence.

wo'koyaǩe, n. (koyaka). Clothing.

wo'ǩoze, n. (koza). A swinging, a brandishing.

wokƥa', v.a. (kpa). To shoot out, punch out. Wowákpa. - iyeya.

wo'kƥamni, n. A pile, a share, a distribution.

wokƥaⁿ', v. pos. (wopaⁿ). To shoot to pieces. Wowakpaⁿ.

wo'kpaⁿ, v. (yukpaⁿ). To grind e.g. grain. Wablúkpaⁿ.

wokƥaⁿ'kƥaⁿ, v. red. of wokpáⁿ.

wokƥi', v.a. To crack with the thumb. Wowákpi.

woksa', v.a. (ksa). To break off by punching or shooting e.g. a stick, limb etc.; to break while running, as a team running against a tree and breaking the neck-yoke etc. Wowaksa.

wo'ksa, v. (yuksa). To pull e.g. corn. Wabluska, wauⁿyuksapi. Yuⁿkaⁿ wagmeza kiⁿ lila waicaga. Hecel oyate kiⁿ woksapi.

woksa'ksa, v. red. (woksa). To break off in many places by shooting. Wowaksaksa.

wo'ksaƥe, n. (ksapa). Wisdom.

wo'ksapi, n. Pulling corn, harvest; those engaged in harvesting, reapers.

wokśe'ca, v.a. To shoot and make keel over, to shoot and make double up. Wowákśeca.

wokśel', cont. of wokśeca. - iyeya.

wo'kśije, n. Something bent or folded up. - topa c'uⁿ: waⁿji eyé lo, as is said when somebody tells a big lie. Bl.

wokťaⁿ', v.a. (ktaⁿ). To bend or make bend by punching. Wowaktaⁿ.

wokťe', v.a. (kte). To kill by punching. Wowakte.

wo'kťe, n. (kte). A killing, slaughter, massacre.

wo'kuje, n. (kuja). Sickness, indisposition.

woǩu'ǩa, v.a. (kuka). To shoot or punch all to pieces.

wō'k'e, n. (k'a). A digging; a place dug to bury in; a pit. Ȟoká wok'e, A heap of soil before a badger's hole or the hole itself perhaps. Bl.

wok'e'ǵa, v.a. To snap, as a gun; to miss-fire, as in firing a gun; to scrape, as a gun missing fire. Wowak'ega. Mazawakaⁿ kiⁿ śice c'eyaś - śni uⁿ kiⁿ owaⁿjila yuha uⁿ wo. Bl.

wok'eȟ, cont. (wok'ega). To go off after a long time. - hiⁿgla. - iyaya, To hang fire, as with a gun.

wok'eȟya, part. Missing fire, as a gun.

wo'k'iⁿ, n. (k'iⁿ). A pack; a carrying. - mayut'e lo, as is said when the burden is very heavy. Bl.

wo'k'iⁿyut'eya, v.a. To overload.

wo'k'u, v. To give food to; to lend. Wówak'u.

wo'k'upi, n. A lending, giving to.

wol, cont. of wota. Le yaglapi na

taŋyaŋ wol niglaśtaŋpi, hehaŋl.... Wol eyatake. B.H.124.3.

wo'la, v. To beg food; begging, n. Wówala, wóuŋlapi. Hecel waŋna wakaŋheja waŋjigji wola ceyapi.

wo'laǩolǩiciyapi, n. Amity, cordiality, mutual esteem, friendship; peaceful mutual relations. B.H.189.7.
wo'laǩoťa, n. Peace, friendship. - kagapi.

wo'las'a, n. A beggar.

wo'le, v. (ole). To seek for. Wowale.

woli'gluśtaŋ, v. refl. To finish eating. B.H.37.6.
wolǩi'ya, v.a. (wota). To cause to eat, to feast. Wolwakiya.

wo'lol, cont. of wolota. - wahi, I have come to borrow.
wo'loťa, v. (olota). To borrow; to hire; borrowing, n. Wowalota. - kiŋ inaǩiŋlmayaupelo. Bl.
wo'loťapi, n. A borrowing.

wo'luťa, n. The round of a beef animal when dried. Cf. olute. - śapa. Bl.

wo'luzahe, n. Swiftness; one who is swift. Cf. wicoluzahe.

wol'wicayapi, n. A banquet, a feast. P.
wol'wol, cont. of wolwota. - wouŋglakapi kte. Me.
wol'woťa, v. To eat, be eating.

wolya', v.a. To make a feast. P. B.H. 93.15.

wo'mime, n. A circle. P.

wo'mna, v. (omna). To smell, perceive smell; an odor, n. Wowamna.
wo'mnaǩa, n. A person or animal that perceives easily a scent, as a bird, dog etc. Also, a bird dog. P.
wo'mnaśni, n. One who does not perceive smell.

wo'mnaye, n. (mnayaŋ). A collection.

wo'mniciye, n. An assembly. R. Bl.

wo'naǧiyeye, n. A bother.

wo'naȟ'oŋ, n. Information.

wo'naŋke, n. (naŋka, naka). A tremor, an omen.

wo'nap̌e, n. (napa). Flight, for fear of something. Bl.

wo'nase, n. (nasa). A hunting of buffalo. D.113.

wona'suŋsuŋ, v. To make struggle by shooting. - iyeya.

wo'nata, v. To get far ahead of others, leave far behind; fig., to be unsuccessful in everything while other are. Wónamatapelo. Bl. EM.

wo'nate, v. To beat, as in a race, to excel. Wónawate. Inaȟni śkaŋ yo: wonanitapi ktelo, i.e. the enemies will catch you if you stay behind, a fig. of speech. Bl. P.

wo'naťaŋ, n. A military maneuvre. P.

wo'nawizi, n. Jealousy. Hehaŋl oyate kiŋ - oŋ waŋjigji kuwapi. MS.525. B.H.37.1;65.11.

woni', v.a. (ni). To resuscitate by blowing. Wowani. - iyeya.

wo'nihiŋciye, n. (nihiŋciya). Fright. B.H.76.7. Pb.22.

woni'ya, v.a. (niya). To resuscitate by blowing. Wowaniya.

wo'niya, n. Spirit, life, breath.
Wo'niya Wakaŋ, n. p. The Holy Spirit.

wo'oglake, n. (oglaka). A declaring of one's own rights or intentions. Siŋte Gleśka - el opa. MS.525.

wo'ohitike, n. Courage, fury, bravery, hardihood.

wo'ohiye, n. (ohiya). Victory, conquest; merit, prize; an inning.

wo'ohola, n. (ohola). An honoring, respect. Pb.33.

woo'ȟpa, v.a. To break in e.g. the skull by shooting or punching. Wowaoȟpa.

woo'ȟ'aŋko, v.a. (oȟ'aŋko). To make lively by punching or shooting. Wowáoȟ'aŋko. Also, speed, n. Wóoȟ'aŋko.

wo'oḣ'aŋka, n. The speed of a thing.

wo'oiyokipi, n. Same as woiyokipi. B.H.155.9.

wo'ok̇aḣniġe, n. (okahniga). The understanding of things, comprehension.

wo'okihi, n. (okihi). Power, ability.

wo'ok̇itaŋiŋ, n. Manifestation.

wo'ok̇iye, n. (okiya). Help. Cf. wowaḣwa.

wo'oksa, v.n. To break off in, as the bank of a river. - iyeya.
woo'kse, n. A washout made in a bank by water flowing in the stream. Bl.

woo'kṫaŋ, v.a. To bend into by punching. Wowaoktaŋ.
woo'kṫaŋyaŋ, v.n. To become crooked, as an arrow, by being shot into anything. - iyeya.

wo'olota, n. Lease, rental.

wo'oŋṡpe, n. (oŋspe). A precept, lesson.
wo'oŋṡpekiye, n. (oŋspekiya). Teaching. Jerusalem otoŋwahe kiŋ - nitawapi kiŋ oŋ ojuwicayayapelo. B.H.284.3.

wo'oŋśila, n. Mercy. B.H.63.14.

wo'oṗe, n. (opa). Law, custom.

wo'ośkiśke, n. (śkiśka). Confusion, difficulty, complexity.

wo'otaŋiŋ, n. (otaŋiŋ). Manifestation; news.

woo't'iŋza, v.a. To press in tight, as with a pole the ground around a fence-post. Woówat'iŋza.
woo't'iŋza, v.n. To be tight. Caga - , The ice is firm.

wo'owoglake, n. An address, a speech, an oration.

wo'owotaŋla, n. (owotaŋla). Righteousness, uprightness.

wo'oyusiŋke, n. Hatred. B.H.97.4.

woo'zeze, v.a. To shoot almost off and let swing. Wowaozeze.
woo'zezeya, adv. Shot almost off and swinging. - egle.

wo'ozikiye, n. A brief rest. Asnikiyapi, A long rest.

wo'ṗaġi, n. The noise made by a drum stick, a percussion. R. Bl.
wo'ṗaġik̇iya, v. To make a rhythmic noise, as in drumming. Wahiŋkpe waŋ ena itazipa waŋ hecel yuha na waŋna itazipa el wopagikiyiŋ na lowaŋ.

wo'paḣta, n. A bundle, a bale. P.

wo'ṗajiŋ, v.n. (pajiŋ). To be prevented by, be made unsuccessful. Womapajiŋ.

wo'ṗak̇aŋ, v.n. (pakáŋ). To be honored. Womapakaŋ. R. Bl.

wo'ṗak̇iŋṫe, n. (pakiŋta). A wiping.

woṗa'k̇o, v.a. (pako). To knock crooked, by shooting or punching. Wowapako.

wo'ṗamnayaŋ, adv. Collected together.

wo'ṗani, (?). Bl.

wopaŋ', v.a. To pound fine, as corn in a mortar. Wowapaŋ.
wopaŋ'paŋ, v. red. of wopaŋ.
wopaŋ'paŋla, v.a. (paŋpaŋla). To pound soft with the end of a stick. Wowapaŋpaŋla.

wo'ṗask̇a, n. A bread pan, one for baking.
wo'ṗask̇a taŋka, n. A dish pan, one for mixing flour or for washing dishes.

wo'ṗasmi, n. (pa-smi). Spite, anger. R.

wo'ṗasnoŋ, n. (pasnoŋ). A roast, a roasting of meat.

wo'paṫa, n. (pata). A place for cutting up meat; the act of cutting up meat. A butcher shop, n.

wo'pataŋ, n. The saving of things.
wo'paṫe, n. The things thrown away in butchering when meat is plentiful, the head, intestines, backbone etc. The heap of such things. Ito - ekta śuŋkmanitu kuwa uŋyaŋpi ktelo. Bl.

wo'pat'iŋze, n. A pressure. P.

wop̆e'mni, v.a. (pemni). To turn aside or twist by blowing or shooting. Wowapemni.

wo'p̆emni, n. A rolling up; an accumulation.
wo'p̆emnik̆ağapi, n. Something made into a roll; a pie, pies.

wop̆e'mniyaŋ, part. Twisting or turning aside by blowing or shooting.

wop̆e'st̆o, v. (pesto). To shoot or punch to pieces, destroy by shooting. Wowapesto.

wo'p̆etoŋ, 1) v. (opetoŋ). To buy, to buy and sell, to trade. Wopewatoŋ. 2) n. A trader, a merchant.
wo'p̆etoŋ ikazopi, n. A bill, an account or debt. P.
wo'p̆etoŋpi, n. Commerce.

wo'p̆ik̆a, adj. Skillful in making anything. Cf. wayupika.

wo'p̆ila, n. (pila). Thanks; joy, gladness. - k'u, eciya, To give thanks.
wo'p̆ilak̆iye, n. Something that makes glad.
wo'p̆ilaye, n. That which makes glad; an advantage. P.

wop̆iŋ'sp̆iŋza, v. To inflict light wounds. Wowapiŋspiŋza. Wanotayapi, tka wopiŋspiŋzapelo. Bl.

wo'piŋta, part. Causing trouble to one. Cf. wośkiśka.

wo'p̆iye, n. (opiye). A case, box, bag; a medicine bag; any place in which things are kept. D.229.
wo'p̆iyeya, v.a. To have for wopiye. Wopiyewaya.

wop̆ol'p̆ot̆a, v. red. of wopota.
wop̆o't̆a, v.a. (pota). To shoot or punch to pieces, destroy by shooting; to make many holes by shooting. Wowapota.

wopo'waya, v.a. (powaya). To make soft by blowing up e.g. nap or fur; also, by striking with the fingers. Wowapowaya.

wopsag', cont. of wopsaka. - iyeya.
wopsa'k̆a, v.a. (psaka). To break off e.g. a cord by shooting or punching; to cut something in two by shooting. Wowapsaka.
wopsa'ksaka, v. red. of wopsaka.

wo'pśuŋ, v. To break something by dropping, or by falling.

wopta', v. To punch or dig with the end of anything, to dig e.g. turnips. Wowapta, woyapta, wouŋptapi. Tiŋpsila wopte yapi.

wo'pta, v. (yupta). To tear in two e.g. a blanket. R. Bl.

wopt̆aŋ'yaŋ, v.a. (ptaŋyaŋ). To make glance off, as in shooting; to make turn over by shooting e.g. a boat. Wowaptaŋyaŋ.

wopt̆a'pt̆a, v. red. of woptá.

wo'ptecaśni, adj. Not a little; immeasurable. R. Cf. opteca.

woptu'ǧa, v.a. To shoot off a piece. Wowaptuga. BD.

wō'pt̆uȟ'a, n. Remnants, leavings, scraps; rubbish, litter, as in a room. Caŋ - , Wood chips. - ojumayayelo, You got the scraps, i.e. splinters, little bits of things as stickseeds etc., all over me. Bl.

woptu'ptuǧa, v. red. of woptuga. Bl.

wopt̆u'za, v.a. To make a man fall on his knees by shooting. Wowaptuza.

wop̆u'sk̆ica, v.a. (puskica). To ram in tight. Wowápuskica.

wop̆u'sk̆il, cont. of wopuskica. - iyeya.

wo'putkaŋ, v. (oputkaŋ). To dip in. Aguyapi waŋ oŋ woputkaŋpi. B.H.253.13.

wosaŋ'kayakel, adv. Void of everything, desolate, as a country, with nothing there to be obtained, no game etc. R. Bl.

wo'sap̆a, n. (sapa). Blackness.

woska', v.a. To wash off, as rain does whitewash.

wo'ska, n. One who makes white; ornamental work.
wo'skaka, n. One who makes white or who works moccasins.

wosƙaŋ', v.n. To cause to melt and flow off, as rain does snow.

wosƙa'p̄a, v.a. To make a noise, as with a pop-gun or toy pistol; to miss fire, as when the cap explodes but does not ignite the charge. Wowaskapi. -- wosƙáp̄ap̄i, n. The pop of a toy gun.

wo'sƙapi, n. Quill-work, quill design.

wosƙi'ca, v.a. To press down tight by pounding. Wowaskica.
wosƙil', cont. of woskica. - iyeya.
wo'sƙilya, v.a. To crush. Also perhaps, wosƙilya. Woskilmayayelo. Bl.

wo'sƙuye, n. (skuya). Taste, savor.

wosla', adv. or adj. Upright, straight up. Yuŋkaŋ śina ikceka heca waŋ - yaŋke s'elececa waŋyaŋke. Tehaŋ - inawajiŋ owakihi śni, as says a man with back-aches.
wosla'haŋ, adv. Upright, up. P. MS.71.
woslal', adv. cont. (woslata). Upright, straight up. - najiŋ. Also, woslálhaŋ, woslásla. Iŋyaŋ - haŋ. Śota kiŋ - haŋ.
wo'slaslate, n. One slow and good e.g. at working. Ww. Syn.- wayuȟ'aŋhihike.
wo'slaslateke, (?). Cf. wosláta.
wosla'ťa, adv. On end, erect, perpendicularly. Also, woslát̄u.

wosle'ca, v.a. To split by shooting or punching. Wowasleca.
woslel', cont. of wosleca. - iyeya.
wosle'sleca, v. red. of wosleca.
wosli', v.a. To push down in, as in churning; to squirt. Wowasli.

woslo'haŋ eȟpéya, v. To make cattle e.g. slide shooting them.
wo'slohe, n. A drag, a sled.

wo'slolye, n. (slolya). Knowledge.

wo'slotoŋ śni, v. To be careless, always jumping at first impressions and not showing planned caution. Woslowatoŋ śni, woslotoŋpi śni. Rl. PD. Cf. wanaptoŋka, śkaŋśkaŋ waśicuŋ.

wosna', v.a. (sna). To make a bell ring, and thus try shooting at it; to make ring by shooting. Also, the noise of leaves falling when they are shot from trees. Wowasna.
wosna'sna, v. red. of wosna.

wosni', v.a. (sni). To blow out e.g. a candle; to cool by blowing. Wowasni. -- v.n. To put out, as rain does fire.
wosni'sni, v. red. of wosni.

wosol', cont. of wosota. - iyeya.
wosol'soťa, v. red. of wosota.

wo'soso, n. Meat cut in strips or strings. - haŋskaska kaga yo; wiuŋpipi ktelo. - k'uŋ yuha kiŋyaŋ iyaye. Bl. D.73. Cf. soso.

woso'ťa, v.a. (sota). To kill all off, use all up by shooting; to use up all one's shot; to shoot all the game, such as ducks. Su iyuha wowasota. Wowásota.

wośp̄a'ya, v.n. (spaya). To wet by raining on.
wo'śp̄aye, n. Wetness.
wosťaŋ'ƙa, v. (staŋka). To moisten by raining on.

wo'sukiye, n. Law, its fulfilment or completion perhaps.

wosu'ksuťa, v. red. of wosuta.
wosu'ťa, v. (suta). To make hard by punching or ramming; to make hard by raining on. Wowasuta, wouŋsutapi.

wo's'icu, v.a. To take by force.

wo'śa, n. (śa). Redness.

wo'śape, n. (śapa). Anything that defiles, filth.

wośib', cont. of wośipa. - iyeya.
wośi'bśip̄a, v. red. of wośipa.

wośi'ca, v.a. (śica). To injure or spoil by shooting or punching. Wowaśica. Also, to commit evil deeds.
wo'śica, v. To commit evil deeds. Wowaśica, wouŋśicapi. Tona wośicapi s'a kiŋ hena tanagi kiŋ tokakiyapi. B.H.127.16.

wośi'cahowaya, v.a. (śica-howaya). To make cry out by shooting or punching.

wo'śice, n. (śica). Evil, badness. The cause of disease. Pb.39.

wo'śigla, n. (śigla). Anger.

wo'śiȟtiŋ, n. (śiȟtiŋ). Feebleness, debility.

wo'śiĦ'aŋ, n. (śiĦ'aŋ). Wickedness.

wo'śikśiceke, n. (?).

wo'śil iyagle, v. To meet with bad luck, be cursed. Wośil iyamagle. B.H. 4.25.

wośi'p̣a, v.a. To shoot off e.g. a branch or anything projecting from another body. Wowaśipa.

wo'śitkigla, n. (śitkigla). Affliction, displeasure.
wo'śitkiglaya, v. To afflict, to make angry.

wo'śkaŋkap̣iŋ, n. Sloth, laziness. P.

wo'śk̇aṫe, n. (śkata). Play.

wo'śk̇ehaŋ, v. perhaps. Making totter and fall by shooting. Tokeya - , One who on the warpath kills the first enemy. Bl. Cf. paśkehaŋ.

wośk̇i', v.a. To pound e.g. corn not well dried. Wowaśki.
wośk̇i'ca, v.a. To squeeze out by ramming. Wowaśkica.

wo'sk̇ica, v. (yuskica). To press.

wośk̇il', cont. of wośkica. - iyeya.

wo'śkiŋciye, n. Action; occupation, work. Bl. B.H.57.13.

wo'śkiśka, part. Causing trouble to many. - Ħe óśki. Cf. wopiŋta.
wo'śkiśke, n. (ośkiśke). Trouble, confusion. Wośkiśki is an incorrect spelling; whereas, Ħeóśki is correct.

wo'śkopa, n. The curve of something.P.

wośla', v.a. (śla). To make bare by shooting, shoot off e.g. hair etc. Wowaśla.
wośla'śla, v. red. of wośla.

wośle'ca, v.a. To split off a little piece by shooting or punching. Wowaśleca.
wośleI, cont. of wośleca. - iyeya.
wośle'śleca, v. red. of wośleca.

wō'śleślecap̣i, n. Hominy.

wośloǵ, cont. of wośloka.

wośło'k̇a, v.a. To fire off a gun, shoot out a load; to blow out, clear out by blowing and through a tube. Wowaśloka.

wośło'śłog, cont. of wośłośloka. Toŋ - hiyuya, To expectorate, spit out phlegm freely. Bl. Syn.- wokabkab.

wośło'śłok̇a, v. red. of wośłoka.

woślul', cont. (wośluta). To make glance, as a bullet. - iyeya.
wośłū'ṫa, v.n. (śluta). To glance, as ą bullet.

wo'śme, n. Depth. P.

wośna', v.a. To miss in shooting, miss the mark. Wowaśna.

wo'śna, v. (yuśna). To sacrifice; to drop something in offering. Wowaśna. -- n. Something offered to God in sacrifice.
wo'śnak̇aǵa, n. One who offers sacrifice, a priest.
wo'śnak̇iya, v.a. To cause to sacrifice. Wośnawakiya.
wo'śnap̣ik̇aǵa, n. Same as wośnakaga.

wośna'śna, v. red. of wośná.
wośna'ya, v.a. (wośna). To cause to miss. Wośnawaya.

wośo'k̇a, adj. Puffed out, enlarged, ending in a knob.

wośō'śo s'e, adv. Extraordinarily thick or fleshy, as is said of a man or his nose or lips. Bl. Syn.- śwośwoke s'e.

wośp̣a', v.a. To punch or shoot off a piece, knock off a piece by shooting or punching. Wowaśpa.

wośp̣i', v.a. To shoot off e.g. fruit. Wowaśpi.
wo'śp̣i, v. (yuśpi). To pick e.g. berries. Wabluśpi, waluśpi, uŋwośpipi. - eyaya.
wośp̣i'p̣i kaǵapi, n. The distribution of Christmas presents from the tree.
wośp̣i'p̣i, v. red. of wośpi.

wośp̣u'śp̣u, v. red. (wośpu). To punch to pieces, as a cake of tallow. Wowaśpuśpu.

wośṫa'ḱa, Cf. śtáka. Bl.

wo'śṫaŋ, Cf. óśtaŋ. Wóśtaŋpi.

wośte', interj. Horrible!

wo'śṫepi, n. Trite phrases. Cf. oweśtepi.
wo'śtepi iyeya, v. To throw, as it were a bow onto ice. Bl.

wośu'ja, v.a. (śuja). To crush by punching; to crush or mash up, as a bullet does bones. Wowaśuja.
wośuś', cont. of wośuja. - iyeya.
wośu'śuja, v. red. of wośuja.

wo'ś'a, adj. Overloaded. - ku welo, He returns overloaded. Bl.

woś'ag', cont. of woś'aka.
woś'ag'ś'agya, part. red. of woś'agya.
woś'ag'ś'aka, v. red. of woś'aka.
woś'ag'ya, part. Shooting with too little force.

woś'a'ḱa, v.a. To shoot with too little force to penetrate; to make no impression with one's words. Wowaś'aka. He wowaś'ake lo, woyaś'ake lo, woś'ake lo. Bt.

wo'ś'akel, adv. Overloaded. - omawani. Bl.

wo'ś'iŋ, n. A bull frog. Bl.
wo'ś'iŋś'iŋḱiye, n. Something that invites interest or curiosity. - wógnake yagle yelo, You placed there an attractive box. BT. - k'el. Bl.
wo'ś'iŋyeye, n. A surprise, a scare.

wota', v. To press against. - iyeya, To blow off. B.H.71.12.

wō'ṫa, v. (yuta). To eat. Wawáṫa, waúŋṫapi. Waúŋyutapi. B.H.226.23.

wota'ḱa, v. To desist, give up, stop suddenly. B.H.10.4;107.9.

wo'takṗe, n. (takpe). An attack, an assault.

wota'ḱuniśni, v.a. (takuniśni). To destroy by punching or shooting; to shoot all to pieces; to carry off, as rain does snow. Wowátakuniśni.

wo'ṫaḱuye, n. Consanguinity. P.

wotaŋ', v.a. To pound, as in washing clothes.

wo'taŋ, v. (yutaŋ). To touch, to feel; anything that feels about for food, as the raccoon.

wo'taŋglusasayakel, adv. As if getting into everything. - magaju, It rains terribly. Bl. Syn.- wokokipeya, wohiŋyaŋsyakel.

wo'taŋiŋ, 1) v. (otaŋiŋ). To be apparent. 2) n. News.

Wo'taŋiŋ Waśte, n. p. The Gospel. P.

wo'taŋiŋ wowapi, n. A newspaper.

wo'taŋka, n. Largeness, anything large. Wotaŋkaȟci mak'u welo, But he gave me much! but meaning very little. Bl. Paŋgi siŋte kayeś - yelo, as a person said when he gave half of the little he had. Bl. Hena yuta yo; paŋgi siŋte yeś, - yelo, as is said when giving only a little food because there is not much on hand.

wotaŋ'ḱiya, v.a. To cause to pound. Wotaŋwakiya.

wo'taŋtoŋ, n. Abundance. Bl.

wo'ṫapi, n. Eating.

wota'ta, v.a. To make dull, as a pestle by pounding it in a mortar, or as an arrow by shooting.

wo'tawaciŋ, n. Desire, ambition. - waśte. Takuwe - kiŋ le nicaŋte mahel luha hwo? B.H.13.10;283.3.

wo'tawe, n. Armor, weapons consecrated by religious ceremonies; a charm relied upon in war.

woṫeb', cont. of wotepa. - iyeya. To wear off, as the point of an arrow.

wo'ṫeca, n. (teca). Newness.

wo'ṫeȟi, n. Something hard to be endured, difficulty, trouble. Lila aiapi ca - akipapi.
wo'ṫeȟiȟiya, adv. With great difficulty. B.H.94.2.
wo'ṫeȟiḱe, n. Difficulty, hardship.

wo'ťektegla, v.n. To be hungry. Wotektewagla. -- wóťekteglapi, n. Hunger.

wote'pa, v.a. (tepa). To wear off short, as an arrow by shooting. Wowatepa.

woťi'ca, v.n. To make spatter out e.g. mud by shooting. Wowatica.

wo'ťica, n. perhaps. (tica). Scraping or pawing, as a horse does snow. R.Bl.

wo'ťikiciciya, v. To petition for. B.H.212.11.
wo'ťiǩiya, v. To beg of one for another. Also, ikicituka. Wotiwakiya.

woťiƞ', v.n. To take a stiff position, become stiff, be stiff, as a dead person; to stand upright. -- adj. Stiff, standing up, as horses ears.
wo'ťiƞǩiya, adv. Stiffly. Tahu - . B.H. 285.21.
woťiƞ'ťiƞ, adj. red. (wotiƞ). Stiff, standing up.
woťiƞ'ťiƞyaƞ, adv. red. of wotiƞyaƞ.
woťiƞ'yaƞ, adv. Stiffly.

woťi'ťaƞ, v. To pull a load.

woťi'ťi, adv. Irresolutely; unsteadily. - mani, i.e. as a blind man. - ecoƞ, To do it hesitatingly. - inajiƞ, To stand undecided. - uƞ.
wo'ťiťikel, adv. Unsteadily, in a shaky manner. Iśtamagoƞga ca - wahi yelo.Bl.

wo'ťiye, v. To plead. - wauƞ. PD. Cf. iyotiyekiya.
wo'ťiyeǩiya, v. To plead with one for a favor, for deliverance from trouble. B.H.147.4.

wo'ťiyemnaśni, adj. Pure, clean, as a person or a house etc. B.H.8.16.

woťi'yeya, adv. Idle because of inability. - wauƞ welo. BT. Cf. wotiti.

wotǩu'ǧa, v.a. (tkuga). To shoot off square e.g. a stick, to shoot and break partly off; to strike and crack e.g. a plate. Wowatkuga.
wotǩuȟ', cont. of wotkuga.

woťo', v.n. To miss fire, as a gun because of faulty loading or a poor cartridge; to knock with the end of anything. Mazawakaƞ - yelo. - inawajiƞ, i.e. I found the door closed. Wouƞtopi kte, i.e. Let us dance

wo'togye, v.a. To do things in a different way. Bl.

woťo'ǩa, adj. Pounded off short, short. He wotoka.

woťo'kapa wóiyowaja; n. The first birthright. B.H.19.12.

woťo'ka s'e, adv. Immovably, like a post. Also, wotokasekse, paksá s'e. - inajiƞ, To stop walking and stand still, as in warm weather or when one is tired. Bl.

woťo'ǩeca, v.a. (tokeca). To alter and make different by punching or shooting.

wo'toǩic'oƞ, n. (tokic'oƞ). Revenge.

woťo'ťo, v. red. of woto.

woťu'ǩa, v.a. To spoil e.g. the fur of an animal by shooting. Wowatuka.
woťu'ǩaǩa, v. red. (wotuka). To spoil or hurt by shooting; to make smart by shooting. Wowatukaka.

woťu'tǩa, v.a. (tutka). To shoot or punch off pieces. Wowatutka.

wot'a', v.a. (t'a). To kill by punching or shooting; to strike so as to endanger life, to stun. Wowat'a. - iyeya. Woic'it'a, To stun one's self by shooting, to shoot and kill one's self. Mini - , To drown one out, to drench, as when the water leaks on one through the roof.

wo't'a, v. To be dead of food, to have eaten too much, to be surfeited. Womat'a.
wo't'e, n. Death caused by food.
wo't'eic'iya, v. To over-eat one's self, even to becoming sick.
wo't'eye, n. The cause of death.

wot'iƞs', cont. of wot'iƞza. - iyeya.
wot'iƞ'st'iƞza, v. red. of wot'iƞza.
wot'iƞs'ya, adv. Tightly.

wot'iƞ'za, v.a. (t'iƞza). To tighten make tight by punching; to blow up tight e.g. a bladder. Wowat'iŋza.

wot'o'ġa, (?).

wot'o'ja, v.a. To make short or blunt by shooting. Wowat'oja.
wot'oś', cont. of wot'oja.

wouŋ'k̇a, v.a. To make fall, as an animal when shot. Wowauŋka. Yuŋkaŋ lila kpeyela iyeya na ogna - na psuŋpsuŋkiya gliyuŋka.

wo'uŋyeya, v.a. To have for a victim. B.H.130.5.

wo'wa, v. (owa). To mark, to paint, to write. Wowawa, woyawa. Wiŋyaŋ waŋ - wayupike ci he. MS.482. B.H.198.17.

wo'waaiḣpeye, n. A written legacy.

wo'waci, n. (waci). A dance, dancing.

wo'waciŋ, n. Faith, confidence. Cisciyela wowaciŋ luhapi kiŋ. B.H.203.12.

wo'waciŋgnuni, n. Delirium. P.

wo'waciŋko, n. (waciŋko). Irascibility.

wo'waciŋtaŋka, n. Patience, perseverance.

wo'waciŋyaŋ, n. (waciŋyaŋ). Trusting in, reliance upon, faith.
wo'waciŋye, n. Something one needs badly, a necessity; same as wowaciŋyaŋ. - kiŋ ojumaye. Pb.34. D.259. - waśte, An interest, what is interesting.
wo'waciŋyeya, v. To depend on rely on. Wowaciŋyewaya. Itazipa na wahiŋkpe kiŋ hena wowaciŋyeyapi na oŋ woyute icupi. D.106.
wo'waciŋyuze, n. Emotion, inclination, propensity, tendency. P.

wo'wahecoŋ, n. Kindred, relationship; names expressing relationship. Also, wowahicoŋ. Mitáwowahecoŋ. Wiŋyaŋ kiŋ le iyuha wowahicuŋ uŋkiyuhapi, i.e. she is some relation us us all. Wowahicuŋ tonakeca kiŋ iyuha cajeyate. D.57,220.

wo'wahokoŋk̇iye, n. (wahokoŋkiya). Instruction, advice, counsel.

wo'waḣṗanica, n. (waḣpanica). Poverty.

wo'waḣṫani, n. Cf. woaḣtani.

wo'waḣtelaśni, n. (waḣtelaśni). Abhorrence, dislike.
wo'waḣtelaśniya, v.a. To dislike. B.H. 93.26;216.1.
wo'waḣtelaśniyaŋ, adv. Not pleased with.

wo'waḣwa, n. Peace. B.H.166.14.
wo'waḣwala, n. (waḣwala). Gentleness, meekness.

wo'wak̇aŋ, n. (wakaŋ). Something supernatural. Hecel - kiŋ le slolwaya. Wawákaŋ, The sacred arrow.

wo'wakiś'ake, n. Endurance. P.

wo'wak̇iṫaŋ, n. (wakitaŋ). Something that is contended for.
wo'wak̇iṫaŋye, n. That which causesobstinacy or determination, resolution.

wo'wak̇oŋze, n. (wakoŋze). Determination; law, rule, justice.

wo'wakṫa, n. (wakta). A mark, a sign; circumspection.
wo'wakṫaya, v. To make a mark or sign.

wo'wala, n. Petition. Pb.34.

wo'wamanoŋ, n. Theft.

wo'wanaḣ'oŋ, n. Obedience. - śni, Disobedience, insubordination. P.

wowa'nica, v.a. (wanica). To shoot or punch to nothing.
wo'wanice, n. The state of nothingness. B.H.1.1.

wo'wanik̇iye, n. (wanikiya). Salvation. Wakaŋtaŋka towanikiye kiŋ waŋyaŋkapi kte lo. B.H.172.9.

wowa'nil, cont. of wowanica. - iyeya, To shoot to pieces, destroy by shooting.

wo'waŋk̇e, n. A wonder to see, as in times past it was said when a woman had twins, or when a meadow lark was found in the stomach of a deer, or when even an old woman was found in the belly of a deer! Bl.

wo'waŋyaŋk̇e, n. A vision, a sight, a show. - yukeya, Publicly. B.H.300.14; 289.9.

wo'waoⁿspe, n. (waoⁿspe). Precept, instruction.
wo'waoⁿspekiye, n. Instruction.

wo'waoⁿśila, n. Mercy, pity, kindness. Le na - ca ecamuⁿpi na tehaⁿhaⁿ yanipi kta.

wo'wapetogtoⁿ, n. (wapetogtoⁿ). A mark or sign.
wo'wapetokeca, n. A sign, a wonder, a miracle.
wo'wapetoktokeca, n. red. (wowapetokeca). Signs. B.H.70.5.

wo'wapi, n. (owa). A picture, letter, book; the flag. - paósla iyeya, To hoist the flag.

- icage, Something used to paint or write with; a pen or pencil.
- ináhtagye, A typewriter.
- kaga, 1) v. To write, make a book. Wowapi wakaga. 2) n. A scribe, a clerk.
- naśkáⁿśkaⁿye, A moving picture projector.
- oh'áⁿko, A postcard.
- oíhpeya, v. To vote.
- okijate, A flag of truce.

Wo'wapi Wakaⁿ, n. p. The Holy Bible.

wo'wasukiye, n. A law, rule, regulation. - oholapi. - waⁿjila ahouⁿpapi kte. D.20,231.

wo'waśagya, v. To overcome easily. B.H. 123.14.

wo'waśi, 1) n. Work, labor. 2) n. A hired man. B.H.81.17;86.23.
wo'waśiya, v.a. To make work, have for a hired man. B.H.45.12.

wo'waśpe, n. (waśpa). A piece cut off.

wo'waśte, n. (waśte). Goodness. B.H. 123.3.
wo'waśtelake, n. Love, complacency.

wo'waśtemna, n. A pleasing odor. Pb.33.

wo'waś'agya, adv. Strongly.
wo'waś'ake, n. (waś'aka). Strength.

wo'watuka, n. Weariness. P.

wo'wauⁿye, n. The victim for a sacrifice, the gift that serves as a sacrifice. Wakiⁿyela waⁿ hece śna - aipi. Wakiⁿyela waⁿ hece śna - aipi. Wakiⁿyela nuⁿblala śna wowauⁿyiⁿ kta aipi. B.H.16.20;167.5,6;168.3. Pb.16.

wo'wauⁿyeic'iye, n. The offering of one's self, self immolation. Pb.34.

wo'wawokiye, n. (wawokiya). Help.

wo'wawoyuśtaⁿ, n. Finishing, perfection or completion.

wo'wayazaⁿ, n. (wayazaⁿ). Sickness, disease.

wo'wayupike, n. Adroitness, art, cleverness. P. D.205.

wowe'ga, v.a. To break, but not off by shooting; to break something by falling. Wowawega. Tahu - .
woweh', cont. of wowega. - iyeya.
wowe'hwega, v. red. of wowega.
woweh'ya, part. Broken by shooting, but not entirely off. - yaⁿka.

wo'wicagi, n. An impediment, obstacle, difficulty.

wo'wicagnaye, n. Deception. Cf. wognaye.

wo'wicahtake wanica, v.n. To be irritable, easily provoked; to be unwilling to be touched. Wowicahtake manice.

wo'wicake, n. (wicaka). Truth, reality, fact. - śni ca ayuśtaⁿ yo, i.e. there is no truth in it. -- adj. Genuine, serious. P.
wo'wicakeśniyaⁿ, adv. Falsely. - waayataⁿiⁿ, A false witness. B.H.257.19.
wo'wicakeya, adv. Truthfully. B.H.129.14.
wo'wicakeyataⁿhaⁿ, adv. Of a truth, truly.

Wo'wicakigna, n. p. The Holy Spirit, the Comforter. A comforter, n. B.H. 254.22;298,13.

wo'wicak'upi, n. Allowance, distribution, issue; offering. P.

wo'wicala, n. (wicala). Belief, faith.
wo'wicalaya, v.a. To cause to believe, to persuade. Wowicalawaya.

wo'wicaśaśni, n. Spite; mischief;

meanness. B.H.245.15.

wo´wignu, n. (ignu). Murmuring.

wo´wihaŋble, Cf. woihaŋble.

wo´wiḣa, n. (iḣa). Cf. woiha.
wo´wiḣaḣa, n. Laughing, making fun; adultery. Na lena kohaŋ taku - ece ecoŋpi. Wowiḣa oyaḣ'aŋ yelo, as is said when a man acts badly.
wo´wiḣaḣak̇iya, v. To laugh at one's own. Wowiḣaḣawakiya. R. Bl.
wo´wiḣaḣaya, adv. Shamefully. D.33.
wo´wiḣala, n. Fun; something laughable.
wo´wiḣaya, Cf. woiḣaya.
wo´wiḣayakel, Cf. woiḣayakel.
wo´wiḣ'oi´yeya, v. (wowiḣ'a-oiyeya). To say something evil about a person, thinking he or she is not present whereas he is and hears. Bl.

wo´wijica, n. Wealth. - yuhakiyiŋ kta. B.H.86.16.
wo´wijica waciŋ, n. Avarice, overly ambitious desire.
wo´wijice, n. (wijica). Riches.

wo´wilag, cont. of wowilaka.
wo´wilagya, v.a. To make a servant of, to have for a servant, to cause to serve. Wowilagwaya. Wamakaśkaŋ waŋ hutopa ca cic'upelo ca he wowilagyayapi kta.
wo´wilak̇e, n. A servant, a hired man.

wo´wimaġaġa, Cf. woimagaga.

wo´winaḣni, Cf. woinaḣni.

wo´winak̇iwizi, Cf. woinakiwizi.

wo´winaṗe, Cf. woinape.
wo´winaṗeya, Cf. woinapeya.

wo´winawizi, n. Jealousy. D.260. Cf. woinawizi.

wo´winihaŋ, Cf. woinihaŋ.
wo´winihaŋyaŋ, Cf. woinihaŋyaŋ.

wo´wiŋye, n. Little packets of tobacco offered as a sacrifice. - kaga. Bl. Cf. caŋwowiŋye. Caŋli wápaḣta sece.

wo´wiŋyeya, v.a. To use as an instrument. Wowiŋyewaya. R. Bl.
wo´wiŋyeyapi, n. Tools, instruments. R. Bl.

wo´wiśtece, n. (iśteca). Shame.

wo´wiśṫelya, v.a. To consider disgraced. B.H.101.19. -- adv. Disgracefully, shamefully.
wo´wiśtelye, n. The cause of shame.

wō´wiṫaŋ, n. (itaŋ). Honor, glory, pride.
wo´wiṫaŋyaŋ, 1) v.a. To glory in. Wowitaŋwaya. 2) adv. Honorably, gloriously.

wo´witoŋṗe, n. (itoŋpa). Something one thinks great or strong.

wo´wiyakpa, n. A reflexion; splendor. P. Bl. B.H.166.5.

wo´wiyukcaŋ, n. A thought.

wo´wiyuŋ kaġapi, n. A ceremony performed before a buffalo hunt. When many buffalo were seen, wowiyuŋ kagapi, i.e. they put down red blankets which were sacrifices for the Great Wonder, God. BT.

wo´wiyuśk̇iŋ, n. (iyuśkiŋ). Gladness, rejoicing. Wicaśa kiŋ lila - aŋpetu kiŋ he el ojula keyapi.
wo´wiyuśk̇iŋyaŋ, adv. Gladly, rejoicingly.

wo´wiyuṫaŋ, n. (iyutaŋ). Temptation. - oŋ iniyute. B.H.127.2. - oyas'iŋ kipaju. Pb.46.
wo´wiyuṫaŋpi, n. Probation.
wo´wiyuṫaŋye, n. Temptation.

wowo´t'iŋza, v.a. To ram down tight in.

woya´, adv. Ragged, dangling. Also, woya s'e, lúṗi.

wo´yag, cont. of woyaka. - wahi, I have come to tell.
wo´yagk̇iyapi, n. A witness; one made to testify.
wo´yagya, v.a. To talk about things everywhere. He makoce kiŋ hel woyagyapi. LWOW. 23. Pent.

wo´yak̇a, v. (oyaka). To tell, relate, declare; publish. Woblaka, wouŋyakapi. Yuŋkaŋ lecel woyakapi.
wo´yak̇aṗi, n. A declaration, a narration.
wo´yake, n. Indication; report. P. B.H.306.1.

wo´yaonihaŋ, n. A eulogy. P.

wo'yaptapi, n. (oyapta). Leavings, fragments of food.
wo'yapte, n. Cf. woyaptapi.

wo'yasu, n. (yasu). Judgment, condemnation.

wo'yaśica, n. A curse. Uⁿgna - ihoyewicayaya kilo, Beware of uttering a curse at them. B.H.67.16.

wo'yataⁿ, n. (yataⁿ). Praise. B.H.239.3.

wo'yatke, n. (yatkaⁿ). Drink.

wo'yat'aǧe, n. (yat'aga). Something astringent; acrimony.

wo'yawa, n. (yawa). A counting. - taⁿka, A million.

wo'yawaśte, n. (yawaśte). Blessing, praise. -- v. perhaps. To bless. B.H. 102.11.

wo'yawataⁿka, n. A great count. A million.

wo'yaya, n. A string of beads. Preferably, oyáya. BD.

wo'yazaⁿ, n. An ache; disease, infirmity. P. Pb.47.

wo'yuaślaye, n. (?). B.H.168.20. Things concealed, but now revealed.

wo'yuecetu, n. (yuecetu). A making right.

wo'yuha, n. (yuha). Property. Nitawoyuha kiⁿ uⁿciⁿpelo.
wo'yuha oicaǧe, n. One's income, revenue. P.
wo'yuhaya, v.a. To have for property, consider one's property or one's own, to own. Pb.22.

wo'yuȟtani, (?). Bl.

wo'yuȟuptoⁿyaⁿkel, adv. Bravely. Táⁿyutkaⁿlak, or tanyutkaⁿla, - omawani, i.e. walk around strong and bravely. Bl. Syn.- woś'akel.

wo'yukcaⁿ, n. (yukcaⁿ). Opinion, judgment.

wo'yuonihaⁿ, n. An honor; honor.

wo'yuptiⁿnaƀe, v. To come and explain or ask for help by explaining what one is charged with. Bl.

wo'yuska, n. Ornamental work, such as cutting strips into skins and winding them with quills.

wo'yusote, n. Expense.

wo'yusu, n. (yusu). A making right, finishing.

wo'yusuta, n. (yusuta). A making firm.

wo'yuśice, n. Harm, bad quality. P. Also, that which makes bad.

wo'yuśiȟtiⁿ, n. That which makes feeble; that which injures or makes bad.

wo'yuśke, n. Absolution. B.H.214.3.

wo'yuśkiśke, n. (yuśkiśka). That which causes difficulty.

wo'yuślayegnak, adv. Cf. ślaégnag. - najiⁿ.

wo'yuśna, n. (yuśna). A missing something, letting fall; the sacrificing of something.
wo'yuśnaśnaƀi, n. Things dropped and left. - pahi, To pick up etc. things that were dropped or lost. Bl.

wo'yuśtaⁿ, n. (yuśtaⁿ). A finishing, completion, perfection; putting one in another. Ňa hel woyajupi na niciⁿcapi hel wayawapi kte lo, tka cuwignaka sapa oⁿ ca Tuⁿkaśila wakila ca. "How" eyelo ca he - heca yelo," eya. RC.

wo'yuś'iⁿyaye, n. Terror. P.
wo'yuś'iⁿye, n. Astonishment, wondering. P.

wo'yutakuniśni, n. Ruin.

wo'yutaⁿiⁿ, n. Disclosure, evidence.

wo'yute, n. (yuta). Food, something to eat.

wo'yutehaⁿ, n. Duration. P.

wo'yuteya, v.a. To have or use as food. Woyutewaya.

wo'yutitaⁿ, n. Tension. P.

wo'yutkoŋze, n. (yutkoŋza). A making equal.

wo'yuwaśte, n. (yuwaśte). That which makes good.

woza', v. To start, respond. - hiŋgla. To start up all at once, as a company on hearing some startling intelligence from a messanger around whom all suddenly gather.

wozaŋ', 1) v.a. To hurt or feel pain by shooting, as with a pop-gun. Wowazaŋ. 2) v.n. To get hurt by running against something.

wo'zaŋ, n. A curtain. Miniwozaŋ, A slow rain, a mist.

wo'zaŋni, n. (zaŋni). Health.

wo'ze, n. (yuze). Taking out, lading out of a kettle. Le hihaŋna kiŋ - kta ca tona el oyapapi kte ci hena el ya po.
wo'zepi, part. Laded out.

wo'zi, n. Cf. zi.

wo'zuŋte, n. Honesty, doing things rightly. PD.

* * * *

Y

yā, interjection of exclamation expressing fear. It is used by women only; whereas a man would simply utter the "ȟnaȟna", a bear-like expression, so as to make himself brave. D.52, note 1. Ya! toskala akoecoŋ. B.H.46.3. Also, an exclamation of indignation.

ya, prefix. It is affixed to a large class of verbs and signifies that the action is done with the mouth by biting, talking etc. Thus, yaksa, To bite off. Affixed to adjectives, and sometimes to nouns, it makes of them verbs meaning to speak of as such, or to make so with the mouth; thus, yawaśte, To call good. Yawicaśa, To speak of as a man. In these cases, the different persons are formed as in ya, To go.

ya, pron. in comp. Thou, you.

ya, suff. The causative suffix, to cause, to make; to have for, to regard as. It is affixed to verbs, adjectives etc.; thus, ecoŋya, sabya. The insep. pron. is placed before. Also, ateya, To have for a father. -- ya, yakel, yaŋ, adv. suff. Terminations of advs. made from adjs.; also, adv. and part. terminations of verbs. Thus, śicaya, Badly. Yuktaŋyaŋ, Bending, crookedly.

ya, v.n. To go, to start, to proceed. Bla, la, uŋyaŋpi. The fut., mni kte, ni kte, yiŋ kte. Ake hocokata lapi kte lo.

yaa'jaja, v. To speak plainly and in detail. Bl.

yaa'los iyeya, v.a. To hurt the feelings of one. Bl. Syn.- yaiẏoyagiyeya.
yaa'losloza, v. (alolosloza). Fig., to singe. - s'e iyeya, To say something that makes another feel uncomfortable, to injure one's feelings.

yaa'opteca, v.a. (aopteca). To speak of as being small, to underrate. Blaaopteca.
yaa'opṫel, cont. of yaaopteca. - iyeya.
yaa'opṫelya, adv. In a depreciating manner.
yaa'opṫetu, v.a. (aoptetu). To speak of as less, to underrate. Blaaoptetu.
yaa'opṫeṫuya, adv. Underrating.

yaa'ṗako, v. (pako). To bend or twist with the mouth.

yaa'śḱala, v.a. (aśkala). To speak of as near. Blaáśkala.
yaa'śḱaśkala, v. red. of yaaśkala.
yaa'śḱaya, adv. Speaking of as near. WE. Syn.- yaaśkayela.
yaa'śḱayakel, adv. Same as yaaśkaya. Also, yaaśkayela.
yaa'śḱayela, adv. and v.a. To speak of as near. Blaaśkayela.

yaa'ślaya, v.a. To explain or talk about what somebody has said. Blaaślaya.

yaa'taŋiŋ, v.a. To prove. B.H.257.16.

yablas', cont. of yablaza. - iyeya.

yabla'sḱa, v.a. (blaská). To flatten with the mouth. Blablaska.

yabla'ya, v.a. (bláya). To make level with the teeth. Blablaya.

yabla'za, v.a. (blazá). To tear open with the teeth. Blablaza.

yable'bleca, v. red. (yableca). To shake up with the mouth, as a dog does something he caught.

yable'bleza, v. red. of yableza.

yable'ca, v.a. To break or crush with the teeth, to break e.g. a bottle or one's teeth with the mouth. Blableca.
yablel', cont. of yableca. - iyeya.

yables'ya, adv. Cheeringly. - ia, To speak cheeringly.

yable'za, v.a. (bleza). To make sober by talking to; to enlighten, cheer. Blableza.

yabli'heca, v.a. To make active by talking. Blabliheca.

yablu', v.a. To make fine by chewing.
yablu'blu, v. red. of yablu.

yabu', v.a. (bu). To make any loud but distinct sound or some disagreeable noise, as children do with horns etc.
yabu'bu, v. red. of yabu.
yabu'ya, adv. Hoarsely. - ia, To speak

with a hoarse voice.

yacaŋ'caŋ, v.a. (caŋcaŋ). To make shake with the mouth, as a dog does its prey.

yacaŋ'ǧa, v.n. To make a noise in chewing anything hard, e.g. corn. Blacaŋga. Cf. caŋkcaŋga.

yacaŋ'lecéca, v.a. To make one downcast by saying things. Blacaŋlececa. Bl.

yacaŋ'liyapa iyeya, v. To say something to hurt another's feelings.

yacaŋ'ťiyapa iyeya, v. Same as yacaŋliyapa.

yacaŋ'zeka, v.a. To make angry by talking to. Blacaŋzeka.

yaca'śkeśkeke, v. To eat up slowly. Cf. wayacaśkeśkeke.

yačeg' iyeya, v. To make stagger with the mouth. Bl.

yače'ka, v.a. Cf. yacekceka.

yače'kcek, cont. of yacekceka. - icu, Taking his breath he jerked Ikto towards him. D.l.

yače'kceka, v.a. To biteand make stagger. Blacekceka.

yace'ya, v.n. To cry for having been bitten. Blaceya. Also, to make cry by talking or biting. R.

yaci'k'ala, v.a. (cik'ala). To count small; to make small with the mouth; to under-value. Blacik'ala.

yaci'scila, v.a. (ciscila). To speak of as small, to count as little or few. Blaciscila.

yačo'čo, v.a. To chew up fine, to mash. Blacoco.

yaco'kaka, v.a. To empty by eating out the side, as do dogs a dead animal.

yaco'nala, v.a. To speak of as few.

yaco'za, v.a. To call warm, to make warm with the mouth. Blacoza.

yae'ceca, v.a. To talk somebody into something, to persuade. Blaececa. Also, to make one believe a thing to be so.

yae'cela, v.a. To speak of as right, to make right with the mouth. Blaecela.

yae'celya, adv. Rightly told. - oyaka, To tell a thing as it ought to be told.

yae'cetu, v.a. To tell a thing as it ought to be told, to correct a statement. Blaecetu.

yae'ceťuya, adv. Speaking correctly.

yaǧa', v.a. To peel off with the teeth; to husk with the mouth. Blaga.

yaǧab', cont. of yagapa. - iyeya.

yaǧa'ǧa, v. red. of yaga. - iyeya.

yaǧal'ǧaťa, v.a. To make forked with the mouth, to prevaricate. Blagalgata.

yaǧaŋ', v.a. To open with the mouth. Blagaŋ.

yaǧa'ṗa, v.a. To bite off e.g. the skin or bark from anything. Blagaṗa.

yaǧa'ta, v. Cf. yagalgata.

yaǧe', v.a. To drink up e.g. water from a spring. To gather with the mouth, as cattle do grass. Blage.

yaǧe'ǧe, v.a. To gather with the mouth, as cattle do grass.

yaǧi'ca, v.a. To waken one, arouse with the mouth or by talking. Blagica.

yaǧil', cont. of yagica. - iyeya.

yaǧī'ťa, v. To become hoarse. Hóyagita, To make the voice hoarse by speaking. Cf. hógita.

yagla', v.a. To bite off, as a dog does the fat from entrails with the mouth.

yagla'gla, v.a. To uncoil with the mouth, as a dog does entrails.

yagla'heya, adv. Explaining. - ia, To set in order; to lay open, explain.

yagla'kiŋyaŋ, v.a. (glakiŋyaŋ). To go across in one's speech, to contradict one's self, to tell what is false. Blaglakiŋyaŋ.

yagla'pis'e, adv. Fluently, plainly. - oyaka.

yaglo'ka, v.a. To put out of place by

means of the teeth. Blagloka.

yagmi', v.a. To clear off, to bite off, as a cow does grass.
yagmi'ca, v. To catch by the hair, using the mouth. Blagmica.

yagmi'gma, v.a. To make round with the mouth. Blagmigma.

yagmi'pi s'e, adv. Rounded off, as a bunch of grass or weeds whose tops have been bitten off.

yagmi'ya^{n}ya^n, v.a. To roll in the mouth and perhaps with the mouth. Blagmiya^{n}ya^n.

yagmu^n', v. To twist e.g. thread with the mouth and hand.

yagna', v.a. To drop something from the mouth while breaking it, as does a horse when eating a cob of corn; to shake off e.g. fruit with the mouth. R.

yagna'ya^n, v.a. To miss something partly with the mouth in attempting to catch; to tell a falsehood. Blagnaya^n. R.

yagnu'ni, v.a. (gnuni). To cause to wander in the wind by talking to , to confuse. Blagnuni.

yaġo', v.a. To make a mark with the teeth. Blago.

yaġōb', cont. (yagopa). To gobble. - iyeya. P. - yatka^n, To sip e.g. water or other liquid.
yaġo'ṗa, v.a. To draw in one's breath with a noise; to sip making noise, trying to get the remnants of a fluid; to suck, as did the old pejuta wicaśa. Blajopa. Also, to make feel proud by talking. Cf. yatita^n.

yaġu'ġugapi ca^n, n. The American nettle tree; the hackberry or sugar berry tree. Celtis occidentalis. The nettle family. Also, yamnumnugapi ca^n. WE. #227.

yaġu'ḱa, v.a. To strain e.g. one's neck by biting something. Blaguka.

yagwa', v.a. To shell with the mouth, to bite off. Blagwa. R. Bl.

yagwe'za, v.a. To bite and make rough. Blagweza.

yaha'hala, v.a. To shake or move with the mouth; to move one in his purpose by talking to, to persuade. Blahahala.
yaha'hayela, v.a. To move by talking to, to shake in one's purpose. Blahahayela.

yaha'iyeya, v.a. To throw down with the mouth, to turn aside with the mouth. R. Bl. Syn.- yaceg iyeya.

yaha^n', v.n. To prick or run into one, as a splinter, thorn etc. Mayáha^n. Yu^{n}ka^n wicaśa wa^{n}jila u^{n}kcela wa^n - keyapi.

yahi^{n}l', cont. (yahi^{n}ta). To eat all up. - iyeya.
yahi^n'ṫa, v.a. To brush away with the mouth, to eat all up. Blahi^{n}ta.

yaho'ġilya, adv. Hoarsely.
yaho'ġita, v.n. To become hoarse from singing.

yaho'ho, v.a. To shake or make loose with the mouth. Blahoho.
yaho'hoya, adv. Shaking with the mouth.

yahol'ya, v.a. (yahota). To cause to inhale and thus cough. Yaholwaya.

yaho'mni, v.a. To turn one round by arguments, to make one change his views, to be converted or convert someone else, for which the red women are well known. -- v.n. To believe anything at once and talk just as old women do.
yaho'mniṗicaśniya^n, adv. Unchangably. - ca^{n}zeka. B.H.89.7.

yahō'ṫa, v. To draw in with the breath, to inhale e.g. cold air, dust etc. Also, to draw in water into the wrong pipe and thus to cough, to smoke and thus cough, having inhaled. Blahota. -- yahóṫe, n. An inhalation.

yaho'to^n, v.a. (hoto^n). To bite and cry out. Blato^n.

yahu^n'hu^{n}s, cont. of yahu^{n}hu^{n}za. - iyeya.
yahu^n'hu^{n}za, v.a. To shake with the mouth; to shake one's resolution by talking to. Blahu^{n}hu^{n}za.

yaḣab', cont. of yaḣapa. - iyeya, To scare away e.g. game by talking.
yaḣa'p̄a, v. To frighten or scare up e.g. game by talking. Blaḣapa.

yaḣci', v.a. To tear out a little piece with the teeth. Blaḣci.
yaḣci'ḣci, v. red. of yaḣci.

yaḣeb', cont. (yaḣepa). - iyeya, To drink up at once.
yaḣeb'ḣepa, v. red. of yaḣepa.
yaḣe'pa, v.a. To drink up, to empty e.g. water etc. Blaḣepa. Yuŋkaŋ (tataŋka) opi ca he pizi kiŋ blaḣepa.

yaḣe'yal, cont. of yaḣeyata. - iyeya.
yaḣe'yat̄a, v. To put aside with the mouth or in speaking to reject. Blaḣeyata.

yaḣla', v.a. To make rattle with the mouth. Blaḣla.

yaḣla'ġaŋ, v.a. To enlarge with the mouth. Blaḣlagaŋ.

yaḣla'ḣla, v. red. of yaḣla.

yaḣlal', cont. of yaḣlata. - ia, To speak as one does who is starving to death.
yaḣla't̄a, v. To speak as one dying. Blaḣlata.

yaḣla'ya, v.a. To bite or peel off the skin or rind of anything with the teeth; to tell a lie. Blaḣlaya. R.Bl.

yaḣle'ca, v.a. To tear with the mouth something from something else, as a piece from a newspaper. Blaḣleca.
yaḣle'ḣleca, v. red. of yaḣleca.
yaḣlel', cont. of yaḣleca. - iyeya.

yaḣlog', cont. of yaḣloka. - iyeya.
yaḣlo'ḣloka, v. red. (yaḣloka). To bite and tear, as dogs do. Blaḣloḣloka.
yaḣlo'ḣa, v.a. To bite a hole in, to bite open, to gnaw. Blaḣloka. Papa blaḣloka owakihi śni. Hituŋkala kiŋ wak'iŋ hiyeye ciŋ mahel - . Syn.- yas'aka.

yaḣmiŋ', v.a. To crook or turn aside with the mouth; to distort. Blaḣmiŋ.
yaḣmiŋ'yaŋ, adv. Turning aside with the mouth. - egnaka.

yaḣmuŋ', v. To make a humming or rattling noise with the mouth. Yaḣmuŋs'e yatapi.
yaḣmuŋ'ḣmuŋḣela, v. red. To make a noise as in dissolving a piece of hard candy in one's mouth. Blaḣmuŋḣmuŋḣela. Also, yaḣmuŋḣmuŋḣla.

yaḣpa', v.a. To pull something with the mouth so as to make it come down, as a dog jumping at a piece of beef. To throw anything down with the mouth. R.
yaḣp̄a'ḣp̄a, v. red. of yaḣpa.

yaḣp̄aŋ', v.a. To moisten or soak in the mouth, to dissolve in the mouth e.g. pills. Blaḣp̄áŋ.
yaḣpaŋ'ḣpaŋ, v. red. (yaḣpaŋ). To make soft with the mouth e.g. a quill or sinew (thread). Blaḣpaŋḣpaŋ.

yaḣpe'ya, v.a. To cause to throw down with the mouth. Yaḣpewaya.

yaḣp̄u', v.a. To bite off in small pieces e.g. pine gum, to bite off something sticking on another. Blaḣpu.
yaḣp̄u'ḣp̄u, v. red. of yaḣpu. Blaḣpuḣpu.

yaḣtag', cont. of yaḣtaka. - iyeya.
yaḣtag'ḳiya, v.a. To cause to bite anything. Yaḣtagwakiya.
yaḣt̄ag'ya, 1) v.a. To cause to bite. Yaḣtagwaya. 2) adv. Biting.
yaḣt̄a'ḳa, v.a. To bite, to take a hold of with the mouth. Blaḣtaka. Also, capuŋka mayáḣtaka.

yaḣu'ġa, v.a. To bite into; to crush with the teeth, to chew; to crack something such as a nut with the mouth. Blaḣuga.
yaḣu'ġapi, n. Peanuts; nuts, because they are cracked with the teeth.

yaḣu'gnaġa, v.a. (ḣugnaga). To speak evil of, to destroy one's character, as if one were being consumed or as if one's character were burnt up. Blaḣugnaga.
yaḣuḣ', cont. of yaḣuga. - iyeya.
yaḣuḣ'ḳiya, v.a. To cause to crush or bite into. Yaḣuḣwakiya.
yaḣu'ḣuġa, v.a. red. (yaḣuga). To crack open. D.70.

yaḣuḣ'ya, v.a. To cause to crush with the teeth. Yaḣuḣwaya.

yaḣuŋl'ḣuŋṫa, v. red. of yaḣuŋta.
yaḣuŋ'ṫa, v.a. To draw through the mouth and make pliable, as sinews for sewing and bark for tying. Blaḣuŋta.

yaḣwa', v.a. To make sleepy by talking to. Blaḣwa.

yaḣwu', v.n. To make a noise, as in chewing snow or ice, to make a crunching noise.

yaḣ'a'kṗa, v.a. To bite and make rough. Blaḣ'akpa.

yaḣ'aŋ'hike, v. To eat quite slowly.

yaḣ'aŋ'hiya, adv. (ḣ'aŋhi). Making slow by talking to.

yaḣ'i'yaya, v. To be awkward with the mouth, as in speaking etc. Blaḣ'iyaya.

yaḣ'u', v.a. To peel off e.g. a rind or hull with the teeth, or a piece of skin with the mouth etc. Blaḣ'u.

yaī', interj. Indicating doubt and surprise when something funny has been stated. Girls alone seem to use it.

yai'gnuni, v.a. To confuse by interrupting etc. Bl.

yai'ḣa, v. (iḣa). To make laugh by talking to. Blaiḣa.

yai'jena, v. (ijena). To speak confusedly.

yai'kceya, v.a. (ikceya). To speak of as worth little. Blaikceya. WE. B.H. 291.20.

yaik̇i'yuta, v.a. To taste drinking. B.H.265.20.

yai'kpiska iḣpeya, v. (ikpi-ska-iḣpeya). To make turn over on the back, as a dog, by speaking to or biting.

yai'le, v.a. (ile). To make blaze by blowing with the mouth. Blaile.

yai'naḣni, v.a. (inaḣni). To make haste by speaking to. Blainaḣni.
yai'naḣniya, adv. Hastening by speaking to.

yai'nil, cont. of yainila. - iyeya, eḣpeya, To put to silence by argument.
yai'nila, v.a. (inila). To put to silence by speaking to. Blainila.

yaiŋ'ceśni, v. To be unable to eat up anything given, to leave over much. Blaiŋceśni. Bl. Syn.- yaowiśni.

yai'oyaya, v.a. (iyoya). To make yawn by speaking to. Also, yaiyowa. Blaiyoya.

yai'ṗaweḣ iyeya, v. To represent something different from what it is.

yai'śṫeca, v.a. (iśteca). To make ashamed by speaking to. Blaiśteca.
yai'śtelya, 1) v.a. Same as yaiśteca. 2) adv. Making ashamed by speaking to.

yai'tokaŋ, v.a. To put aside, reject. Blaitokaŋ.

yai'yowa, v.a. (iyowa, iyoya). To make yawn by speaking. Blaiyowa.

yai'yowaja, v.a. (iyowaja). To speak of as near, to speak to the point. Blaiyowaja.
yai'yowajaśni, v.a. To speak beside the point. Blaiyowajaśni.

yai'yowas, cont. of yaiyowaza. - iyeya.

yai'yowaś, cont. of yaiyowaja. - ie śni, He does not speak to the point.

yai'yowaza, 1) v.a. To make echo by speaking. Blaiyowaza. 2) n. An echo.

yai'yoyag iyeya, v. To make sad by speaking to. R. Bl. Syn.- yaalos.
yai'yoyak̇a, v.a. (iyoyaka). To make sad by speaking to.

yaja'ja, v.a. To lick or wash with the mouth, as does a cat.

yaja'ta, v.a. To seduce one, to persuade to give up one's good resolutions. WE.

yajib', cont. of yajipa. - iyeya.
yaji'bjiṗa, v. red. of yajipa.
yajib'yela, adv. Nibbling. - yaḣtaka, To chew up with the front teeth something very small. Bl.

yajiŋ'ca, v.a. To snuff up the nose. Caŋli - , To take snuff. Blajiŋca.

yaji´ṗa, v.a. To bite or pinch with the teeth, to bite as bugs or mosquitos, to sting as does a wasp. Blajipa.

yajo´, v.a. To blow on an instrument, to play on a fife or flute. Blajo. Śiyotaƞka yajo.
yajo̅´jo, v. red. of yajo. Blajojo.
yajo´ḱiya, v.a. To cause to blow on an instrument. Yajowakiya.

yajo´pi hu, n. The hemlock water parsnip, the water hemlock. Sium cicutaefolium. The parsley family. The stems are streaked with purple if it is hemlock. The roots are used for medicine to treat the stomach. The fleshy roots of the poison hemlock contain a deadly poison. The stems children use for whistles. BT. #128. Also, the poison hemlock. -- yajópi hu cik'ala, n. The small water hemlock. BT.

yajo´ya, v.a. To make one blow a fife or flute. Yajowaya.

yaju´ju, v.a. To tear down or tear to pieces with the mouth; to refute or demolish an argument. Blajuju.

yajuƞ´, v. To pull up by the roots with the mouth, as birds do corn. Blajuƞ. Aśakagleyela peji to yajuƞpelo, i.e. the horses cropped the first green shoots of grass.

yaḱa´, v.a. To split with the mouth, as the feather end of a quill. Blaka.

yakab´, cont. of yakapa. - iyeya.

yaḱa´ḱa, v.a. To champ, as does a horse his bit.

yaḱa´ḱija, v.a. (kakija). To make suffer by scolding or biting. Blakakija.

yaḱaƞ´yela, v. To speak of as near, i.e. not talking loud. M.

yaḱa´ṗa, v.a. To catch in the mouth anything that is tossed. Blakapa.

yaḱa´ṫiƞ, v.a. To straighten or bend out straight with the mouth. Blakatiƞ.
yaḱa´ṫiƞṫiƞ, v.a. To straighten by talking, to set right, criticize. Tokśa nihu yakatiƞtiƞpi kte, as is said when one says or does many things wrong. Tokśa niyásmiƞpi kte. Bl.

yaḱa´wa, v.a. To open or push back anything with the mouth. Blakawa.

yakča´, v.a. To untie with the mouth, to disentangle. Blakca.

yaḱel, suff. An adv. termination; as, yus'oyakel. Cf. ya, suff.

yaḱi´ṗaja, v.a. To double or fold up with the mouth so as to make the ends meet. Blakipaja.
yaḱi´ṗaś, cont. of yakipaja. - iyeya.
yaḱi´ṗehaƞ, v.a. (pehaƞ). To double or fold up with the mouth, so as to make the ends meet. Blakipehaƞ.
yaḱi´ṗusḱica, v.a. To press close together with the mouth. Blakipuskica.
yaḱi´ṗusḱilya, adv. Putting close together with the mouth.

yaḱis´, cont. of yakiza. - iyeya.
yaḱi´skiza, v. red. of yakiza.

yaḱi´yela, v. Same as yakaƞyela, except the former refs. also to nearness of time.
yaḱi´yelaḱel, adv. Near.

yaḱi´za, v.a. To make a grating or creaking noise with the teeth, to gnash. Blakiza.

yakog´, cont. of yakoka. - iyeya.
yako´ḱa, v.a. To rattle with the teeth, chatter, gnash. Blakoka.

yako´ḱela, v.a. (kokela). To make active by talking to. Blakokela.

yako̅´ḱipa, v.a. (kokipa). To make afraid by talking to. Blakokipa.

yako´kog, cont. of yakokoka.
yako´kogya, 1) v.a. To cause to make a chattering with the teeth. Yakokogwaya. 2) adv. Chattering.

yako´koḱa, v.a. (yakoka). To rattle the teeth, chatter, gnash. Blakokoka.

yaḱo´natke, adv. With high words. Cf. konatke. - makuwapi, They are after me with high words, as is said by one who does not get a chance to defend himself and his case because others always counter-attack with high-sounding words. Thus similarly: yawaƞkal makuwapi; kul k'u śni maktepi. Bl.

yaḱoƞ´ṫa, v.a. To wear out partly with

the mouth a rope, strap etc., i.e. making it thinner and less strong. BD. Also, yaku^{n}ta. BD.
yako′ṗegla, v.a. (kopegla). To make afraid by talking to. Blakopegla.

yakṗa′, v.a. To bite out, bite through. Blakpa. -- adj. Hard of hearing on account of noise. Noġe mayákpa.
yakpa′kṗa, v. red. of yakpa.

yakṗa^n′, v.a. To chew fine, to masticate. Blakpa^n.
yakṗa^n′kṗa^n, v. red. of yakpa^n.
yakṗa^n′ya^n, adv. Chewing fine.

yakṗi′, v.a. To crack with the teeth e.g. lice. Blakpi.
yakṗi′kṗi, v. red. of yakpi.

yakṗu′kṗa, v.a. To bite in small pieces, to crumble with the teeth. Blakpukpa.

yaksa′, v.a. To bite off e.g. a stick. Blaksa.
yaksa′ksa, v. red. (yaksa). To bite off often. Blaksaksa.
yaksa′ksayakel, adv. Biting off.

yaksa′ṗa, v.a. To make wise by talking to. Blaksapa.

yaksa′ya, 1) v.a. To cause to bite off. Yaksawaya. 2) adv. Biting off.

yakśa′, v.a. To bend up with the mouth. Blakśa.
yakśa′kśa, v. red. of yakśa.
yakśa′la, v.a. To bend up with the mouth. Blakśala.

yakśa^n′, v.a. To bend with the mouth. Blakśa^n.
yakśa^n′kśa^n, v. red. (yakśa^n). To bend or curl up. Blakśa^{n}kśa^n.

yakśi′ja, v.a. To double up with the teeth.
yakśi′kśija, v. red. of yakśija.
yakśiś′, cont. of yakśija. - iyeya.

yakta^n′, v.a. To bend with the mouth. Blakta^n.
yakṫa^n′kṫa^n, v. red. (yakta^n). To bend in several places with the mouth.
yakṫa^n′ya^n, 1) v.a. To cause to bend with the mouth. Yakta^{n}waya. 2) adv. Bending with the mouth.

yaku′ka, v.a. To destroy with the teeth, bite to pieces. Blakuke.

yaku^n′tku^{n}ṫa, v.a. To bite notches in. Blaku^{n}tku^{n}ta.

yak'e′, n. A wolf. Also, śu^{n}kmanitu.

yak'e′ġa, v.a. To make a grating noise with the teeth. Blak'ega.
yak'eḣ′, cont. of yak'ega. - iyeya.
yak'eḣ′k'eġa, v. red. of yak'ega.

yak'es′, cont. of yak'eza. - iyeya.
yak'e′sk'eza, v. red. of yak'eza.
yak'e′za, v.a. To make smooth with the teeth and making a grating noise. Blak'eza.

yak'ō′ġa, v.a. To bite or gnaw off e.g. something hard. Blak'oga. Hitu^{n}kala wa^n taku yak'oġaha^n ca naḣ'o^n. D.96.
yak'oḣ′, cont. of yak'oga. - iyeya.
yak'oḣ′k'oġa, v. red. of yak'oga.

yak'os′, cont. of yak'oza. - iyeya.
yak'o′sk'oza, v. red. of yak'oza.
yak'o′za, v.a. To make smooth with the mouth; to eat all off smooth, grass. Blak'oza.

yal, cont. of yata. Thus, cajeyata, cajeyal, In the name of.

yale′blepa, v.a. To bite notches in. Blaleblepa. R. Bl.

yale′cakcala, v.a. (lecakcala). To speak of as near perhaps. Blalecakcala. WE. Syn.- yaaśkaśkala.
yale′cala, v.a. (lecala). To speak of as near in time. Blalecala.

yale′ha^{n}ya^{n}g, v.a. (leha^{n}ya^{n}k). To speak of as away somewhere else. - iyeya. Bl.

yalus′ icu, v. To draw in the smoke of one's pipe through the mouth. Yalus iwacu.
yalus′ yatka^n′, v. To sip in. Bl.

yalu′zaha^n, v.a. To call swift. Blaluzaha^n. Naku^n le, i.e. a played-out horse, śu^{n}śu^{n}la ikpi ska k'eyaś - iyececa yelo. Bl.

yama′, v.a. To gnaw, to bite off e.g. a thread sticking out of a coat etc. Blama.

yama′he e′yaya, v.a. To snatch with the mouth, as a dog does. Yamahe iwacu, iyewaya. Tuwa mini hiyo i ca

wamnita waⁿ mini mahetaⁿhaⁿ yamahe ewicayaya keyapi. Ito, miś eya waniya na yamahe eciyayiⁿ kta eya. B.H.127.1.
yama'heliyeya, v.a. To push into the mouth. Yamaheliyewaya.

yame'ca, v.a. To gnaw, to chew. Blameca. - yo, Eat all you can (there is much on hand). Bl.

yami'ma, v.a. To make round e.g. a wheel with the mouth. Blamima.

yamna', 1) v.a. To rip with the mouth, as a dog or a horse might do to one's coat. Blamna. 2) v.a. To win over by talking, to acquire by talking or in any other way with the mouth; to gain. Bl. R.
yamna'ǩiya, v.a. To cause to gain by talking etc. To cause to rip. R. Yamnawakiya.
yamna'yaⁿ, v.a. To cause to rip, as a dog by making him go after somebody. Yamnawayaⁿ.

yamni', v. 2nd pers. sing. of mni.

ya'mni, adj. num. Three.

yamni'ǧa, v.a. To make shrink by biting, as some big bite of food through chewing. Blamniga. Syn.- yapiśitka.

ya'mniǩiya, adv. In three different ways or places. - wai, I went to three different places.
ya'mnila, adv. Only three.
ya'mnimni, adv. By threes. - manipi. Witka - icupi, Each received three eggs.

yamni'yeya, v.a. To turn or change the course or plan of one by speaking to or with. Yamniyewaya. Bl.

yamnu'mnuǧa, v.a. To crunch, crush, grind, champ, or make noise with the teeth, as in eating. Blamnumnuga.

yamnu'mnuǧa iyececa, n. The great ragweed, the horseweed, bitterweed etc. Ambrosia trifida. The composite family. Its seeds are medicinal. B. #48. Cf. caⁿȟlogaⁿ paⁿśpaⁿjela.

yamnu'mnuǧapi, n. The hackberry tree; so called because animals crunch its berries. Also, black pepper. - can, The hackberry tree. Also, yaǧúǧuǧapi caⁿ.

yana'jiⁿ, v.a. (najiⁿ). To cause to stand by speaking. Blanajiⁿ.

yanaⁿg', v.a. To make one jerk sideways etc. suddenly by biting, as a bee does a person, or as one horse another. Bl. - iyeya.

yaⁿ, 1) suff. A termination for adv. and part. 2) v. A causative suffix to verbs. Hence, also, suff.

yaⁿǩa', v.n. To be; to sit. Maⁿka, naⁿka, uⁿyaⁿkapi. El - , To be at home. D.96, note 3.

yao'cikp̄ani, v.a. (ocikpani). To make unequal with the mouth. Blaocikpani.

yao'cipteca, v.a. To count less, make less, under-estimate. Blaocipteca. R. Bl.
yao'ciptel, cont. of yaocipteca.
yao'ciptelya, adv. Speaking of as less or unequal.
yao'ciptetu, v.a. To count less. Blaociptetu.
yao'cipt̄et̄uya, adv. Speaking of as less, as unequal. Also, yaócipt̄et̄uyaǩel.

yao'glapśuⁿ, v. To turn over with the mouth. - iȟpéya.
yao'glapśuⁿyaⁿ, adv. (oglapśuⁿyaⁿ). Turning over with the mouth. - iyeya.

yao'gmus, adv. (ogmus). With the mouth shut. - s'e ia, To talk with the mouth full.

yao'gwu, v. To speak stiffly, mouthing one's words. Lila s'e eyi'ye, laogwu welo. To sip e.g. hot soup.

yao'ha, v.a. To make fall over with the mouth. Bl. Cf. yaceg iyeya, yaha iyeya.

yao'hiⁿyaⁿze, v. To persuade one to give up by representing the thing as bad. Blaohiⁿyaⁿze.

yao'ȟloka, v.a. To bite a hole in.

yao'ȟmiⁿ, v. To say anything sideways, to hint, insinuate. Blaoȟmiⁿ. - iyeya.

yao'ȟp̄a, v.a. To bite into. Blaoȟp̄a.

yao'ȟ'aⁿǩo, v.a. (oȟ'aⁿko). To hasten

one by speaking to. Blaoħ'a^{n}ko.

yaoʹƙiniha^n, v.a. (okiniha^n). To honor with the mouth, to praise. Blaokiniha^n. R. Bl.

yaōʹksa, v. To bite through. Blaoksa.
yaoʹksaksa, v. red. of yaoksa.

yaoʹkťa^n, v.a. To bend in with the mouth.
yaoʹkťa^{n}ya^n, adv. Bending with the mouth.

yaoʹl'otake, v. Cf. wayaol'otake.

yaōʹniha^n, v.a. To praise, honor. Blaoniha^n.
yaōʹniha^{n}ya^n, adv. Praising.

yao^{n}ʹśiyakel, adv. Speaking meekly. Pála (Little Nose) - eyapi. Bl.

yaoʹpo, v.a. To compress by biting.

yaoʹꝑo^n, v. To spread e.g. news by telling it; lit., to bite off and blow away, as flowers. Blaopo^n. R.Bl.
yaoʹꝑo^n iyeya, v. To spread something as news more and more and to exaggerate. Syn.- akaħaya. Bl.

yaoʹślog iyeya, v. To swallow something inadvertently that one should not, e.g. to swallow one's tooth pick.

yaōʹťa, v.a. To speak of as many, to multiply. Blaota.

yaōʹta^{n}i^n, v.a. (ota^{n}i^n). To make manifest, to proclaim. Blaota^{n}i^n.
yaoʹta^{n}i^{n}ya^n, adv. Declaring.

yaoʹťeħiƙa, v.a. (oteħika). To make difficult with the mouth, speak of as difficult. Blaoteħika. Nitu^{n}kaśila ki^n taku tob yaoteħikapi tka....

yaōʹt'i^{n}s, cont. of yaot'i^{n}za. - iyeya.
yaoʹt'i^{n}za, v.a. To get something as meat into a hollow tooth or between; to press in tight with the mouth. R. Talo blaot'i^{n}za.

yaoʹwi^{n}ġa, v.a. To bite or pull round with the teeth, as in making moccasins. Blaowi^{n}ga.
yaoʹwi^{n}ħ, cont. of yaowi^{n}ga. - iyeya.
yaoʹwi^{n}ħwi^{n}ġa, v. red. of yaowi^{n}ga.

yaoʹwiśni, v. To be unable to eat up everything given, to leave over much. Blaowiśni. Bl.

yapaʹ, v.a. To take in the mouth e.g. a pipe in smoking or in the wapiyapi; to hold in the mouth, as a dog does a bone. Blapa. Also, to bite. Waśi^n wa^n - kagli śke. Toeyaś blapi^n kta, as they say taking a few puffs on the pipe in a hurry. BlW.

yapa^{n}ʹpa^n, v.a. To make limber or pliable by biting, as in making moccasins. Blapa^{n}pa^n.
yapa^{n}ʹpa^{n}la, v.a. (pa^{n}pa^{n}la). To make soft with the mouth. Blapa^{n}pa^{n}la.

yapaʹpa, Cf. yapa. Bl.

yapceʹcela, v.a. To shorten with the mouth; to speak of as short.

yaꝑeʹ, v.a. (pe). To bite sharp. Yapeśni, To make dull e.g. the teeth by biting. Blapeśni.

yaꝑeʹha^n, v. (peha^n). To fold up with the teeth. Blapeha^n.
yaꝑeʹmni, v.a. (pemni). To twist, turn or make crooked with the mouth. Blapemni.
yaꝑeʹmniya^n, adv. Twisting with the teeth.

yaꝑeʹsťo, v.a. To make sharp-pointed with the teeth. Blapesto.

yaꝑiʹ, v.a. (pi). To declare good. Blapi.

yaʹꝑi, v. 3rd pers. pl. of ya. They go.

yaꝑi^{n}ʹja, v.a. (pi^{n}ja). To pull out long hairs from a skin with the teeth. Blapi^{n}ja.

yaꝑi^{n}ʹśꝑi^{n}zece, v. red. of yapi^{n}zece, not used. Cf. wayapi^{n}spi^{n}zece.

yaꝑisʹ, v. cont. (yapiza). To squeak with the mouth. - yatka^n, To drink slowly, sip, to drink in draughts; to drink carefully, as though something bad was floating on the fluid. Bl.

yaꝑiʹśitka, v.a. To reduce in size by chewing, as a big lump of food. - wota, To eat with repugnance, and therefore little. Bl.

yaṗi'za, v. (piza). To make squeak with the mouth. Blapiza.
yaṗi'zapi, n. A mouth organ.

yaṗi'zapi hu, n. Wild spikenard, false Solomon's seal. Smilacina racemosa. The lily family. So called because the Indians used to produce musical tones with its leaves. Also, zuzeca tawote hu iyececa. BT. SH. #1.

yapi'zapi iyececa, n. The sand lily, the little white lily, Mayflower. Lencocrinum montanum. The lily family. BT. #276. Also, the prairie false dandelion. Agoseris cuspidata. The composite family. Bl. #278.

yaṗo', v.a. To compress by biting. Blapo.

yapōb', cont. of yapopa. - iyeya, To make pop suddenly or quickly.

yaṗol'ṗol, v. cont. of yapolpota. B.H. 114.2.
yaṗol'ṗoṫa, v. red. of yapota.

yapō'ṗa, v.a. (popa). To make pop, as in blowing a leaf. Blapopa.

yaṗō'ṫa, v.a. (pota). To tear in pieces with the mouth. Blapota.

yapo'waya, v. (powaya). To blow up or make rough, as nap or fur. Blapowaya.

yapsag', cont. of yapsaka. - iyeya, To bite e.g. a thread suddenly in two, to bite suddenly and quickly.
yapsāg'ya, 1) v.a. To cause to bite in two. Yapsagwaya. 2) adv. Biting off e.g. cords.

yapsa'ḱa, v.a. (psaka). To tear a thing, e.g. a string, in two with the mouth. Blapsaka.
yapsa'ḱe śni eye, v. To speak of something again and again. LC. Syn.- hokuⁿpe śni eye.
yapsa'psaḱa, v. red. of yapsaka.

yapsi'ca, v.a. (psica). To cause to skip or jump by biting. Blapsica.
yapsil, cont. of yapsica. - iyeya.

yapsoⁿ', v.a. To turn over and spill with the mouth.
yapsoⁿ'psoⁿ, v. red. of yapsoⁿ.
yapsuⁿ', Same as yapsoⁿ.

yapśa', v.n. 2nd pers. sing. of pśa. You sneeze. Wapśá, I sneeze. Someone is said to sneeze when a lover mentions the name of his beloved. Tuwa cajemayate laka mayapśa yelo. Bl.

yapśuⁿ', v.a. To cast off or shed e.g. teeth; to pull and break with the mouth. Blapśuⁿ. BD. Cf. yupśuⁿ.

yapṫa', v.a. To bite off around. Blapta.

yaptaⁿ'yaⁿ, v.a. (ptaⁿyaⁿ). To turn over with the mouth. Blaptaⁿyaⁿ.

yapte'cela, v.a. (ptecela). To bite off short, to shorten with the mouth. Blaptecela.

yaptu'ǧa, v.a. To bite off a piece. Blaptuga. Hi waglaptuga. BD.
yaptuḣ', v. cont. of yaptuga. - nape el okignake, i.e. the mouse had bitten it off into his palm. D.97.

yapṫu'ja, v.a. (ptuja). To crack or split with the mouth. Blaptuja.
yapṫu'pṫuja, v. red. of yaptuja.
yaptuś', cont. of yaptuja. - iyeya.
yapṫuś'ya, v.a. To cause to crack with the mouth. Yaptuśwaya.

yaṗu'za, v. To dry with the mouth. Bl.

yap'o', v. (p'o). To make steam with the mouth, as in breathing in cold air. Blap'o.

yasaⁿ', v.a. To whiten with the mouth. Blasaⁿ.
yasaⁿ'ka, v. Cf. yasaⁿ.

yaska', v.a. To make clean with the mouth. Blaska.

yasḱaⁿ', v.a. To let dissolve in one's mouth. Blaskaⁿ.

yasḱa'ṗa, v.a. To make a noise as in kissing. Blaskapa.

yasḱeb', cont. of yaskepa. - iyeya.
yaske'ṗa, v.a. To drink up. Blaskepa.

yasḱi'ca, v.a. To press with the mouth, To suck or lick e.g. bones. Blaskica.
yasḱil', v. cont. of yaskica. - iyeya.

yaski'ska, v. (?).

yaŝki'sk̄iťa, v.a. To bite and make soft e.g. a hard string. Blaskiskita.

yask̄u', v.a. To bite off or peel off with the teeth, as the skin from an apple. Blasku.
yask̄u'sk̄u, v. red. of yasku.
yask̄u'ya, v. To act, by a certain noise, as though something was sweet, and so by chewing it induce children to take it. Blaskuya.

yasla', v.a. To grease with the mouth, as a dog does anything.

yasle'ca, v.a. To split with the teeth. Blasleca.
yaslel', cont. of yasleca. - iyeya, To split with one's teeth suddenly and quickly.
yasle'sleca, v. red. of yasleca.

yasli', v.a. To bite and press out, as grease from a bag. Blasli.

yasli'tk̄a, v.a. (slitka). To make knobbed or tapering with the teeth. Blaslitka.

yaslŏ'haŋ, v.a. (slohaŋ). To drag along with the mouth, as does a dog. Blaslohaŋ.
yaslo'haŋhaŋ, part. and v. red. of yaslohaŋ. - iŋyaŋka, He ran dragging something in his mouth. R.

yaslŭl', cont. of yasluta. - icu, To pull out with the teeth.
yaslū'ťa, v.a. To pull out with the mouth. Blasluta.

yasmiŋ', v.a. To bite off e.g. meat from a bone, to make bare with the mouth, to gnaw, to eat the meat off. Blasmiŋ. D.14. R.
yasmiŋ'kiya, v.a. To cause to eat off, make bare with the teeth. Yasmiŋwakiya.
yasmiŋ'smiŋ, v. red. of yasmiŋ.
yasmiŋ'yaŋ, v.a. To cause to make bare with the teeth. Yasmiŋwaya.
yasmiŋ'yaŋyaŋ, v.a. To make bare with the mouth; to eat off close and smooth.

yasna', v.a. To cause to ring with the mouth; to ravel with the teeth. Blasna.

yasni', v.a. (sni). To blow, cool by blowing. Blasni.

yasōl', cont. of yasota. - iyeya.
yasol'ya, adv. Eating up.
yasō'ťa, v.a. (sota). To use up with the mouth, to eat all up. Blasota.

yaspa'ya, v.a. (spaya). To wet with the mouth. Blaspaya.

yasťaŋ'k̄a, v.a. To moisten with the mouth. Blastaŋka.

yasťō', v.a. To lick smooth e.g. hair. Blasto.
yasťo'sťo, v. red. of yasto.

yasu', v.a. To make right by speaking; to judge, to decree. Blasu. Wayásu wicaśa. Na waŋna mini mahel ayapi kta yasupi.

yasu'ksuťa, v. red. of yasuta.

yasu'pi, n. Condemnation.
yasu'piśniyaŋ, adv. Without hearing. - kasaksaka. B.H.300.14;303.4.

yasu'ťa, v.a. (suta). To make firm with the mouth, to establish. Blasuta.

yasu'ya, adv. Judging, condemning.

yaswa', v.a. To pick in pieces with the teeth. Blaswa.
yaswa'ka, v.a. To make fringed by trying to bite of a piece from a tough piece of meat, and not getting much.
yaswa'swa, v. red. of yaswa.

yaswu', v. To take in small bead-like pieces with the mouth. - s'e yuta, To eat in little pieces or strings. Cf. swula.

yasya'zaŋ, v. red. (yazaŋ). To be lame or sick all over, as from hard labor. Mayasyazaŋ.

yas'a', v.a. (s'a). To make a ringing or roaring noise in speaking. Blas'a.

yas'a'ka, v. To be unable to bite or chew e.g. tough meat. Blas'aka. Bl.

yas'o's'o, v.n. To be stiff from the cold. Nakpa kiŋ mayas'os'ohcelo, My ears are stiff from the cold. Bl.

yaśab', cont. of yaśapa. - iyeya.
yaśa'ṗa, v.a. (śapa). To soil with the mouth. Blaśapa.

yaśib', cont. of yaśipa. - iyeya.
yaśi'bśiṗa, v. red. of yaśipa.

yaśi'ca, v.a. (śica). To make bad with the mouth, to speak evil of, curse. Blaśica.

yaśi'gla, v.a. To insult by talking. Blaśigla.

yaśi'ḣtiŋ, v.a. To make feeble by biting. Blaśiḣtiŋ.

yaśil', cont. of yaśica. - śi. B.H.69. 3.
yaśil'ṗicaśni, adj. Faultless, blameless. P.

yaśi'ṗa, v.a. To bite off close, as an animal does the branches or twigs of a tree. Blaśipa.

yaśka', v.n. To untie with the mouth. Blaśka.

yaśkaŋ'śkaŋ, v.a. To make move about by talking to. Blaśkaŋśkaŋ.

yaśke'ṗa, v. Cf. yaskepa. Bl.

yaśke'śkeke, v. (?).

yaśk̇i'ca, v.a. To press with the teeth or mouth. Blaśkica. Caŋli - , To chew tobacco.
yaśk̇il', cont. of yaśkica. Caŋli - uŋ.

yaśki'ṗa, v. To bite and make full up.

yaśki'śka, v.a. To make rough with the mouth; to disarrange by talking to, raise objections, to make difficulty. Blaśkiśka.

yaśkob', cont. of yaśkopa. - iyeya.
yaśko'kṗa, v.a. To bite out and make concave. Blaśkokpa.

yaśko'ṗa, v.a. To make crooked or twisting with the mouth. Blaśkopa.

yaśla', v.a. To bite or graze off, make bare, as cattle do a pasture. To have been grazed, cropped. Cf. wayaśla.
yaśla'śla, v. red. of yaśla.
yaśla'ya, adv. Grazing off.

yaśla'yegnag, Cf. yaaślayegnag.

yaślog', cont. of yaśloka. - iyeya.

yaślog'ya, adv. Pulling out with the teeth.

yaślo'ia, v. To speak with much saliva in the mouth; to make a whistling or hissing sound with the teeth in talking. Yaśloiwaya.

yaślō'k̇a, v.a. To pull out with the teeth e.g. a cork. Blaśloka.

yaślo' s'e, v. To whistle as the upland plover, not producing any sound, but as they do when they both go and come back again. CO.

yaślul', cont. yaśluta. - iyeya.
yaślu'śluṫa, v.a. To make slippery with the mouth. Blaśluśluta.
yaślu'ṫa, v.a. To let slip from the mouth; to have the teeth slip off from anything. Blaśluta.

yaśna', v.a. To miss while trying to catch with the mouth; to blunder in speaking. Blaśna.
yaśna'k̇iya, v.a. To cause to miss with the mouth. Yaśnawakiya.
yaśna'śna, v. red. (yaśna). To stammer, to falter.
yaśna'ya, v.a. To cause to miss with the mouth; to make stammer. Yaśnawaya.
yaśna'yaŋ, adv. Mistaking, blundering with the mouth.

yaśni'ja, v.a. To make wither by biting. Blaśnija.
yaśniś', cont. of yaśnija. - iyeya.
yaśni'śnija, v. red. of yaśnija. Caŋte mayaśniśnijelo heoŋ howaḣpahelo. Bl.

yaśo'śkoṗa, v. red. of yaśkopa.

yaśpa', v.a. To bite off a piece, to break off a piece with the mouth. Blaśpa.
yaśṗa'ṗi, part. Bitten off, as is said of the moon when it has commenced waning.
yaśpa'śpa, v. red. (yaśpa). To bite off a piece in different places. Blaśpaśpa.
yaśṗe'k̇iya, v.a. To cause to bite off a piece. Yaśpewakiya. Also, yaśṗeya.

yaśṗi', v.a. To pick off, as do birds berries.

yaśpu', v.a. To bite off anything

stuck on. Blaśpu.
yaśpu'śpu, v. red. (yaśpu). To bite in pieces e.g. candy, ice etc.
yaśpu'ya, v. To bite, as lice do; to make itch, to itch. Mayaśpuya. Iśta mayaśpuya. -- adj. Itching.
yaśpu'yaya, v. red. (yaśpuya). To itch. Iś eya waci kinica na sicuha kiⁿ ya-śpuyaye. D.43.

yaśťaⁿ', v. To finish speaking, to keep quiet. Blaśtaⁿ. Oyak - , To cease speaking.

yaśū'ja, v.a. To crush, as a dog does a bone; to mash up. Blaśuja.
yaśuś', cont. of yaśuja. - iyeya.

yaśu'śka, v.a. (śuśka, perhaps). To belittle, not appreciate a favor. Ma-yaśuśka, He did not appreciate what I did for him. BD. Note: this is an old word.

yaśu'śuja, v. red. of yaśuja.

yaś'a'ka, v.a. To make no impression with the mouth. Blaś'aka. Ia - .

yaś'iⁿ'ś'iⁿ, v. To strain in the peak of copulation. Blaś'iⁿś'iⁿ.

yata', v.a. To chew; to try by taste. Blata.

yā'ťa, 1) prep. in comp. At, by, to. Thus: Ĥeyáta. 2) v. 2nd pers. sing. of yuta. 3) v. To speak, utter. Thus: cajeyata, wicaśayatapi.

yata'ǩiⁿ, v.a. To make lean with the mouth, as a dog in trying to pull down a stick.
yata'ǩiⁿyaⁿ, adv. Making leaning with the mouth.

yaťa'ǩu, v.a. (taku). To make something of in relating, make up a story about. Blataku.
yaťa'ǩuǩa, v.a. To make something of nothing in narration; to overestimate. Blatakuka.
yaťa'ǩuniśni, v.a. To eat up, destroy with the mouth; to speak contemptuously of. Blatakuniśni.
yaťa'ǩuniśniyaⁿ, adv. Destroying with the mouth.
yaťa'ǩuśni, v.a. To speak of as being of no value, depreciate. Blatakuśni.
yaťa'ǩuya, adv. Speaking of as if it were something. - oyaka.

yaťaⁿ', v.a. To speak well of, praise. Blataⁿ.

yataⁿ', v.a. To touch with the mouth, to pull as in sucking. Blataⁿ.

yataⁿ'iⁿ, v.a. (taⁿiⁿ). To declare anything, make manifest. Blataⁿiⁿ. B.H.137.21.
yataⁿ'iⁿyaⁿ, adv. Manifestly.

yataⁿ'ǩa, v.a. To speak of as large or great. Blataⁿka. Pb.41.

yataⁿ'ni, v.a. To wear out or make old with the mouth. Blataⁿni.

yaťaⁿ'ťaⁿ, v. red. (yataⁿ). To praise. Blataⁿtaⁿ. Ake oyate kiⁿ wicaĥpi hiⁿ-ĥpaya yataⁿtaⁿpi.
yaťaⁿ'yaⁿ, adv. Praising.

yata'ta, v. red. (yata). To chew for a while. Blatata. Na pejuta waⁿ - najiⁿ. D.257.

yata'waciⁿhiⁿyaⁿza, v. To speak of one as a morose person, to make cross or surly by talking to. Blatawaciⁿhiⁿ-yaⁿza.

yaťeb', cont. of yatepa. - iyeya.

yate'haⁿ, v.a. (tehaⁿ). To speak long, to speak of as long or as far in the future. Blatehaⁿ.
yaťe'haⁿhaⁿ, v. red. of yatehaⁿ.

yaťe'p̣a, v.a. To waar off with one's teeth; to bite off short, wear off, as the teeth. Blatepa.

yaťi'ca, v.a. To scrape away with the mouth e.g. snow.

yaťi'ǩťiťaⁿ, v.t. To draw, breathing in repeatedly, to draw smoke as in smoking. Blatiktitaⁿ. D.103.

yaťil', cont. of yatica. - iyeya.

yaťi'mahelicu, v.a. To call one into the house where one is. Yatímaheli-wácu.

yaťi'ťaⁿ, v.a. To pull with the mouth, as a dog holding a bone under foot and pulling meat off. Blatitaⁿ.
yaťi'ťaⁿyaⁿ, 1) v.a. To cause to pull with the teeth. Yatitaⁿwaya. 2) adv. Pulling with the teeth.

yatk̇aŋ´, v.a. To drink. Blatkaŋ.
yatk̇aŋ´tk̇aŋ, v. red. of yatkaŋ. Wakalyapi - k'el na wolwol wouŋglakapi kte lo. Me.
yatk̇aŋ´yaŋ, adv. Drinking.

yatk̇a´ṗa, v.a. To eat e.g. something that is viscid or sticksin the mouth. Blatkapa.

yatk̇e´k̇iya, v.a. To cause to drink. Yatkewakiya.

yatk̇u´ġa, v.a. To bite or pull and break with the mouth. Blatkuga.

yatk̇uŋs´, cont. of yatkuŋza. - iyeya.

yatk̇uŋ´tk̇uŋṫa, v. Cf. yakuŋtkuŋta.

yatkuŋ´za, v.a. To bite off even. Blatkuŋza.

yatk̇u´tk̇uġa, v. red. of yatkuga.

yato´gtogya, v.a. To tell lies while narrating something. Also, yatogtog ia.
yatog´ye, adv. Telling differently. - oyaka, To relate a thing differently.

yato´kaŋ, v.a. To put in another place with the mouth, speak of as being in another place. Blatokaŋ.

yato´k̇eca, v.a. (tokeca). To alter with the mouth, to speak of as different. Blatokeca.

yaṫo´ṫo, v.a. To eat up, as a horse does grass. Blatoto. Pejuta waŋ - .

yaṫu´k̇a, v.a. To nibble off, spoil, as mice do furs.

yaṫu´tk̇a, v.a. To bite into little pieces. Blatutka.

yat'a´, v.a. To bite to death. Blat'a.

yat'a´ġa, v.a. To make rough by biting. Blat'aga.

yat'iŋs´, cont. of yat'iŋza. - oyaka, To relate firmly and with authority.
yat'iŋs´ya, adv. Firmly. Hena imanuŋga ca iyuha - ociciyakelo. Bl.
yat'iŋs´yakel, adv. Well and clearly. - ia, To speak well, correctly, pronouncing the words well. Bl.

yat'iŋ´za, v.a. To make firm with the mouth, to affirm. Blat'iŋza. Cf. wicaka.

yauŋ´ca, v. To ridicule with one's speech. Blauŋca. Bl.

yauŋg´, cont. of yauŋka. - iyeya.

yauŋ´k̇a, v.a. To throw down, pull down with the mouth e.g. trees as beavers do. Blauŋka.

yawa´, v.a. To say over, to read; to count; to consider. Blawa. Tipi tonakeca yawapo. Tipi opawiŋge sam iyaye yawapi. Le pejuta kiŋ lila wakaŋ yawapi.

yawa´ciŋhiŋyaŋza, Cf. wayuwahiŋyaŋza.

yawa´ciŋk̇o, v.a. To make angry by talking. Blawaciŋko.

yawa´ciŋtoŋ, v.a. To make intelligent, to instruct. Blawaciŋtoŋ.

yawa´ḣwaka, v.a. To make gentle, pacify by talking kindly to. Blawaḣwaka.
yawa´ḣwala, v.a. To make gentle by talking to, to soothe; to make one sleepy by talking. Blawaḣwala.

yawa´ja, v.a. To split fork-like with the mouth. Blawaja. To make a noise with the mouth. Also, yahotoŋ. WE.

yawa´kaŋ, v.a. To consider wakaŋ, or to consider supernatural. Blawakaŋ.

yawaŋ´k̇al, v. To raise or elevate the voice. - makuwapi, They are after me with high sounding arguments. Bl. Cf. yakonatke. - yeya, iyeya.

yawa´ṗicaśni, adj. Innumerable.
yawa´ṗicaśniśniyaŋ, adv. red. (yawapicaśniyaŋ). Numberless. B.H.50.2.
yawa´ṗicaśniyaŋ, adv. Numberless. Śiyo cik'ala kiŋ - maḣpiya kiŋ taŋiŋśniyaŋ kiŋyaŋ au. B.H.55.10.

yawas´, cont. of yawaza.

yawa´śak̇a, v. Same as yawaśakala.
yawa´śak̇ala, v.a. To count cheap or easy, to underrate. Blawaśakala.

yawa´śṫe, v.a. To declare good, bless.

Blawaśte.

yawa'ś'ag, cont. of yawaś'aka.
yawa'ś'agya, adv. In a strengthening manner.
yawa'ś'aka, v.a. To strengthen by talking to, to encourage. Blawaś'aka.
yawa'ś'akeśni, v.a. To make weak by talking to. Blawaś'akeśni. Śuⁿka kiciyawaś'akeśni s'e ake lehaⁿl wakinicahaⁿpelo, i.e. done quit quarrelling like fighting dogs. Bl.

yawa'wa, v. red. (yawa). To be easily counted, being distinctly separated. Yawawapila s'e uⁿpelo. Yawawapila s'e wicoti, i.e. when the tents of a camp are rather scattered. Syn.- oiȟpeȟpeya. Bl.

yawa'za, v.a. To bite or gnaw, as a horse does wood. To bite in play, as do horses or dogs.

yawa'zeca, v.a. To gnaw at; to annoy by begging. P. Bl.

yawe'ġa, v.a. To break e.g. a stick with the mouth but not entirely off. Blawega.
yaweȟ', cont. of yawega. - iyeya.
yaweȟ'ḱiya, v.a. To cause to break with the mouth. Yaweȟwakiya.
yawe'ȟweġa, v. red. of yawega.
yaweȟ'ya, v.a. To cause to break with the mouth. Yaweȟwaya.

yawi'ca, v.a. (wica). To call a man, to call brave. Blawica.

yawi'caka, v. (wicaka). To speak of as true; to affirm to be true. Blawicaka.
yawi'caḱeya s'e, adv. Deceptively; ironically. - oyaka, To tell a thing not as it is, to make a statement of which the very reverse is true.
yawi'caḱeyeȟci, adv. Making appear as true. - oyaka, To try to make a thing appear true by telling it as true.

yawi'caśa, v.a. (wicaśa). To call a man. Blawicaśa.
yawi'caśaśni, v.a. To make one mischievous by talking to; to call bad; to make bad by talking to, to corrupt. R. Blawicaśaśni.

yawi'gnuni, v.a. To destroy with the mouth, to talk bad. R. Bl.

yawi'nuȟcala, v. (winuȟcala). To call a woman, to speak to as a woman. Blawinuȟcala.

yawiⁿ'ja, v.a. (wiⁿja). To bend something with the teeth, as a fork in the mouth; to bend down with the teeth. R. Blawiⁿja.
yawiⁿś', cont. of yawiⁿja. - iyeya.
yawiⁿś'ḱiya, v.a. To cause to bend down with the mouth. Yawiⁿśwakiya.
yawiⁿ'świⁿja, v. red. of yawiⁿja.

yawiⁿ'yaⁿ, v.a. (wiⁿyaⁿ). To call a woman, to speak to as a woman. Blawiⁿyaⁿ.

yawi'ṫaya, v.a. (witaya). To collect together with the mouth. Blawitaya.

yawi'yakpa, v.a. To make shine with the mouth; to interpret. Blawiyakpa.

yawo'sla, v. (wosla). To set up with the mouth.

ya'ya, adv. Undecided, bewildered. - najiⁿ, To stand bewildered. WE.

yaya'la, adj. Limber, pliant, not stiff. Bl. Syn.- wiⁿświⁿja.

ya'yaya, adv. Same as yaya. - najiⁿ. Syn.- yuhelhel, wotiti. Sb. Also, Stubborn. Taku ociciyake ciⁿ namayaȟ'oⁿ śni na - inayajiⁿ yelo. Bl.

yaza'he s'e, adv. Bead-like. Bl. Syn.- owéciⁿhaⁿ. Bl.

yaza'mni, v.a. To open or uncover with the mouth; to lay bare or expose by argument. Blazamni.

yazaⁿ', v.n. To feel pain. Mayazaⁿ. Nata - , To have a head-ache. Cf. wayazaⁿ.
yazaⁿ'gla, v.n. To feel pain and be touchy about it, i.e. not wanting anybody to touch the suffering limb. Mayazaⁿgla, or perhaps yazaⁿwagla.
yazaⁿ'hiⁿgla, v.n. To become sick suddenly.
yazaⁿ'ya, v.a. To make one sick. Yazaⁿwaya.

yaze', v.a. To take out with the mouth from something, as food from a kettle the way a dog does, or a killed duck from a pond. Blaze.

yaze'ze, v.a. To make swing with the

mouth.

yazi´ca, v.a. To stretch anything with the teeth. Blazica.
yazil´, cont. of yazica. - iyeya.
yazil´ya, adv. (yazica). Slowly, drawing out. - lowaŋ, To sing slowly, drawing the notes. NP.

yazō´ka, v.a. To draw or sip a fluid to see what it tastes like. Syn.- yagopa, To suck the honey from a blossom; aziŋ, To suck, as a baby in nursing the breast.

yazo´kapi hu, n. The white-flowered gilia. Gilia longiflora. The phlox family. When fresh, the flowers appear a little purple. BT. #83.

yazoŋ´ta, v.a. To praise one who ought to be reproved.
yazuŋ´ta, Cf. yazonta.

ye, pron. 2nd pers. comp. of "ya" and "ki"; thus, yeksuya, of kiksuya for yakiksuya.

ye, particle. 1) It often follows at the close of a sentence to give emphasis to what is said. It is used by women as is yelo by men. Moreover, it seems that after an "u" sound the "y" is changed to "w". 2) A sign for a precatory form of the imp. sing., used by women and men, but chiefly women. Komakipe śni ye (a woman speaker). Ate, oyate kiŋ oŋśiwicakila ye (a man speaking). B.H.78.12.

yea´pe, v.a. To wait for one; to come along. Bl. Yeawape.

yeka´piŋ uŋ, v. To linger. P.

yeki´ya, v.a. To bet, to stake anything. Yewakiya. B.H.117.4.

yeki´ya, v.a. (ya). To cause to go, to send, to drive; to extend to e.g. one's hand. Icokab u; caŋke kute yekiyapi, na ake ataya ihuŋni.

yeki´yapi, n. A bet, gambling stake. P. Bl. Syn.- ahigle.

ye´la, suff. Affixed to adjectives and making them adverbs. Thus, sabyela, Blackish; toyela, Greenish; Holyela, Grayish. As adv. these tend to shift toward adj. again.

yélaka, ye´lakaś, adv. Indeed, truly; since, as, because. Tokeśke pte kiŋ cepapi śni - waśiŋ cola śna wawatelo ca awicakupo, eya ke. Toka - ecamoŋ kiŋ? Why did I do that? Hehe takoś, eya, wanikau - hehelo. Taku icaŋliniyuha - , wini ś'oś'okelo. Bl. MS. 144,94. Tokiyataŋ taakiH'aŋ wahi - s'iŋs'iŋyaŋ wanamapce lo. Bl. Niśnála tokeca niglawa - , Evidently you regard yourself as different, in a different class by yourself. D.53, note 3. B.H.142.10;185.6;204.2;235.19;259.22;272.7,8;276.11,14.

yele´, particle. It is used by women to indicate the real fact of the statement preceding. Men will use yelo. B.H.46.3.
yelo´, particle. Used by men to terminate a statement with emphasis, so as to stress fact. Hence, often a brief pause precedes the particle. After a plural termination "pi" the "ye" is often dropped and the "pi" becomes "pe". Hecel ecoŋpelo. Cf. ye.

yema´, particle. An imp. form of ye, used by women. T'a yemá. B.H.43.26.

yeś, conj. abbrev. of yeśa. But, although. Ziŋtkala waŋ iye wipe yuha śni yeś ciŋca awicakikśija. MS.479. Tipi ocoza bluha yeś waniyetu cokaŋyaŋ. Lena cikciscipila yeś t'api śni yelo. B.H.95.9.
yeśa´, yeśaŋ´, conj. Although. Also, eśá. Wociŋ hi ca k'upi yeśaŋ woiHayakel iyuha k'upi ciŋ. Bl. Ito ehaś taŋyaŋ wowak'u kte śni yeśaŋ, eya ke. B.H.66.9;194.15;30.1.
yeśaś´, conj. Though, although, even if. Tuwé waŋkatuic'iya (iglawaŋkatuya) yeśaś kul glicu kte. BT.

yeśi´, v.a. To command to go, to send. Yewaśi.

yeto´, particle. Same as yo. Ku - . Pazo - , to pazo, Let me see it for a second. Ito hiŋyaŋki - . B.H.20.26; 43.17.

yeya´, v.a. To cause to go, to send, to extend to. Yewaya, yeuŋyaŋpi. Na waŋna wawakaŋ kiŋ le yeyiŋ kta.

yeye´, v. To be, to continue, to last. Hecel wanase kiŋ paha kiŋ tohaŋ yeye kiŋ (as long as it lasts), hehaŋ ipaHlalya aya, na kakel enape kiŋ hecena ptaptaye wan opawinge wahecetu ca ataya kulkul ħpayapi. Na wakpala kin tohan yeye kin hehan aglagla wicoti na tipi kin oyasin akilececa na ośota śni.

yo, particle. The sign of the imp. sing., used by men. Cf. wo. Note: when there are two imperatives in one sentence (e.g. Go and see.), only the second one has the yo; whereas, the ending of the first is "in" instead of "a", supposing the verb does end in "a". Iyayin na nape nupin el oyuspa yo. Blihec'iyapi na tokel econ ciśipi kin iyecel econ po. Paha skan kin hel akanl emaonpipi na iħ'e omakśu po.

yu, exclam. A woman's protest or exclamation when scolding. Yu! tokinahanś taku otaka ca ekitan wamaśipi kte ħcin. Note: The woman's exclamation in prefacing a reprimand is in a rather high voice; but, the same is true of a declaration of disapproval.

yu, prefix. It expresses the idea of causation in some way not conveyed by ka, na, pa, wa, wo, ya. Thus, yunajin, To cause to stand or to lift up. Sometimes it conveys the idea of pulling. Affixed to adj., and sometimes to n. it forms verbs of them and means: to make or cause to be. Thus, yuwaśte, To make good.

yua'blaya, v.a. To make level on, to spread something, as a rug, on level ground. Bluablaya. B.H.172.7.

yua'glapśunyan iħpeya, v. To upset e.g. a kettle. Bl.

yua'ħwayela, v. To cause gently. Śunka yuinila miciyuza, śunka - miciyuza. Taku aśkatuyela hośimakaglipi.

yua'jaja, v.a. To explain, make clear e.g. a doctrine. Bluajaja. Hh.

yua'kaǧal, adv. With arms stretched out crosswise. - otkeya, To crucify. - okatan. MS.100. B.H.262.23. RT.

yua'kaħpa, v. (akahpa). To cover, conceal. - icu, To draw anything over one, as a blanket turned down.

yuā'ƙan, v. (akan). To cause to come up. - hiyuya, To cause to come up, as a fish on a line. - eħpeya, To cause to come up and be thrown out, as a fish.

yua'ƙanl icu, v. To pull up from on something, as from a hole. Ehaś ota (hogan) - awicaupi. B.H.27.21;186.1. Nape - icupica śni yelo, i.e. it's very cold. Bl.

yua'ƙazamni, v.a. (akazamni). To open out, uncover. Bluakazamni. - iyeya.

yua'ƙiħ'an, v.a. (akiħ'an). To cause to starve. Bluakiħ'an.

yua'ƙiṗab, adv. (akipab). Separately. - egnaka, To separate, divide.

yua'ƙiṗaja, v.a. (akipaja). To place across. Bluakipaja.

yua'ƙiṗaś, cont. (of yuakipaja). Crossing each other; in bows. - icu, To tie in a bow-knot.

yua'kowapa, adv. Further on, beyond. - egnakelo, He prolonged it. Cunkaśke - egnake, He moved the fence a little back.

yua'laṗa, v.a. To smooth off e.g. a rough road. Ocanku t'aħt'age kin hena yualapapi kte lo. B.H.172.8. Cf. paláPa.

yua'los, v. To scare. - iyeya. Bl.

yua'losloza s'e iyeya, v.a. To injure one's feelings in any way.

yua'okpani, v.a. To lessen, cut down. B.H.150.21.

yua'opteca, v.a. To make less. Bluaopteca. R. Bl.

yua'oṗtel, cont. of yuaopteca. - iyeya, To make less, as in making a price lower.

yua'oṗteťu, v.a. To make less, lessen. Bluaoptetu.

yua'oṗteťuya, adv. Lessening.

yua'ṗaƙo, v.a. To make crooked. Bluapako.

yua'ṗaƙoya, adv. Making crooked, twisting.

yua'sni, v. To quiet down, soothen e.g. a person excited or sad. Bluasni.

yua'sniyan, v.a. To console. B.H.229.6.

yua'śaṗa, v.a. (aśapa). To defile. Bluaśapa.

yua'śka s'e, adv. Near, nearby in a sense. - taᶯiᶯyaᶯ yuᶯkelo, It seems to be near, e.g. a hill; or even to afar off, tehaᶯtu. Bl.
yua'śkayela, v.a. To make near, to bring near. Bluaśkayela. R. Bl.

yua'ślaya, v.a. To uncover, expose; to expose what one should not tell, i.e. secrets etc. Bluaślaya.
yua'ślayela, adv. Explaining, clearly, plainly. - oyaka. B.H.60.7.

yua'taᶯiᶯ, v. To manifest. B.H.213.9.

yua'taś, v.a. To absorb. P.

yua'ṫaya, v.a. To make whole, complete; to cure. B.H.232.4.

yua'zi, v.a. (azi). To run aground, pull ashore e.g. a boat. Bluazi.

yubla'blaya egnaka, v. To lay out and spread e.g. a blanket. Bl.

yubla'ġa, v.a. To spread out e.g. an umbrella, or the toes, as of a duck. Oiyohaᶯzi - . Maga siha yublaga po! Use your brain, think! Bl.
yublaḣ, cont. of yublaga. Maga siha - maᶯkelo, i.e. I am thinking. Bl.

yubla'pisekse, adv. Openly, distinctly. - hiᶯhpaye, as is said when snow falls in heavy flakes here and there. Ehaᶯna - wawakita, I could see things well when time was. Bl.

yublas', cont. of yublaza. - egnaka, To open out, as in dressing a cow. - iyeya. D.247.

yubla'ska, v.a. To make flat. Blublaska.
yubla'ya, v.a. To open, spread out, unfold, make level. Blublaya. Na oyate najiᶯpi etkiya, i.e. śina kpaᶯyaᶯpi kiᶯ, - pazo. Śina waᶯ yuha hinapa na - egnaka.

yubla'za, v.a. To burst open. Blublaza.

yuble'bleca, v. red. of yubleca.
yuble'ca, v.a. To break to pieces or crush e.g. brittle ware by pressing with the hands. Blubleca, lubleca.
yublel', cont. of yubleca. - iyeya.

yublel'kiya, v.a. To cause to break to pieces. Yublelwakiya.

yublē'za, v.a. To make clear. Blubleza.

yubli'heca, v.a. To make active, lively. Blubliheca.

yublu', v.a. To make mellow; to pulverize, to plough. Blublu.
yublu'blu, v. red. of yublu. Blublúblu.
yublu'ḱiya, v.a. To cause to plough. Yubluwakiya.
yublu'ya, v.a. To cause to pulverize. Yubluwaya.

yubu', v.a. To make a drumming noise. Blubu.
yubu'bu, v. red. of yubu.
yubu'ya, adv. In a drumming manner.

yucab', cont. of yucapa.
yucab'cabḱiya, v. red. To cause to trot.
yucab'caṗa, v. red. of yucapa.
yucab'kiya, v.a. (yucapa). To cause to trot. Yucabwakiya.
yuca'bluzahaᶯ, 1) v. To trot rapidly. 2) adj. Fast trotting, as a horse.

yucaᶯ', v.a. To sift, shake in a sieve; fig., not to have, be without. Caᶯli mayucaᶯ, I have no tobacco. Blucaᶯ.
yucaᶯ'caᶯ, v.a. To make shake, in sifting. Blucaᶯcaᶯ.

yucaᶯ'lasni, v.a. (caᶯte-asni). To soothen, quiet down. Blucaᶯlasni. B.H.170.13;255.21.
yucaᶯ'lwaḣteśni, v.a. To make angry. Blucaᶯlwaḣteśni. Bl.

yucaᶯ'nal iyeya, v. To push into the middle of a room etc. R. Bl.

yucaᶯ'ṗis'e, adv. Shivering. - inajiᶯ.

yucaᶯ'ṫewaśṫe, v.a. To cheer up. B.H. 85.22.
yucaᶯ'ze, v. To cause to become angry. Bl. To make angry.
yucaᶯ'zeḱa, v.a. To make angry. Blucaᶯzeka.

yuca'ṗa, v. To trot, as a horse. Trotting, ikacaᶯcaᶯ.

yuceḣ, v. cont. To hold, as in holding a bucket. - nauᶯka, To gallop with the head (of the horse) drawn towards the breast.

yuće'ka, v.a. To pull in vain, i.e. what cannot be pulled out; to make stagger. R. Syn.- yutitaⁿ. Blucéka.
yuće'kćeka, v.a. To make stagger. Blucekceka.

yuce'ya, v.a. To make cry. Bluceya. Mayuceya.

yuci'k'ala, v.a. To make small, compress e.g. a coat that is too baggy. Blucik'ala.
yuci'k'ayela, adv. In a small space, pressed together, compactly. Wana el - el ahiyaye lo, i.e. a crowd. Bl.

yuciⁿ'kťakťa, v.a. To make one cry or sob by catching him, i.e. a runaway boy; meaning, He will if I catch him! Bluciⁿktakta. Perhaps lit., yu-ceyiⁿkta kta.

yuci'scila, v.a. To make small. Bluciscila.

yućō'ćo, v.a. To make soft as mortar, i.e. by pouring in water. Blucoco.

yuco'ka, v.a. To empty, make empty. Blucoka.

yuco'kab, adv. cont. (cokapa). Making centrally located. Ośota yelo, wipipaha egle yo iⁿś eśa tiyopa kiⁿ - icu wo. BT.

yuco'kaka, v. red. of yucoka.
yuco'kakaya, v. or adv. (yucokaka). To make empty by setting all in order. Tipi waⁿ taⁿka iticagi na timahel - egle, i.e. erected a large tipi and arranged things attractively inside. D.15.

yuco'kala, v.a. To keep free for work e.g. a horse and let it rest. P. Syn.- éćecola.

yucō'nala, v.a. To make few, to lessen in number or quantity. Bluconala. B.H. 45.17.

yuco'scoza, v. red. of yucoza.

yuco'ya, adv. Finished, well. R. Bl. Syn.- wakicoyakel. Wakicoyakel kagelo. Bl.

yuco'za, v.a. (coza). To make comfortably warm e.g. a room. Blucoza.

yue'ceca, v.a. To make something go or act the way it ought to, as one does in winding a train or cranking an automobile. Bluececa.
yue'celya, v. To make a thing as it ought to be. Bluecelya. 2) adv. Rightly, correctly. Also, yuécelyakel. Bl.

yuē'ceťu, v.a. (ecetu). To fulfill, to accomplish; to correct a wrong statement; thus, gluecetu. To straighten e.g. a house. Bluecetu.
yue'ceťuya, 1) v.a. To cause to fulfill. Yuecetuwaya. 2) adv. Fulfilling, making right.

yue'ciya, v.a. To turn wrong side out e.g. a garment or a bag. Blueciya.

yue'ktaśni, v. To do a thing in a wrong way. Also, yuéktaśniyaⁿ. Luektaśniyaⁿpi kiⁿ, wayaȟtanipi kta. Syn.- ipaweȟ ecoⁿ.

yuǧa', v.a. To husk e.g. corn. Bluga, lugá, uⁿyúgapi.

yuǧāb', cont. of yugapa. - iyeya.

yuǧa'ǧa, 1) v.n. To spread out, open out, display. 2) adv. Spread out, open.

yuǧal', v. cont. of yugata. - iyeya, To lift one's arms, to stretch out one's arms upwards. - najiⁿ, uⁿ. - yaⁿka nape nupiⁿ oⁿ. Na waⁿkalkiya yugal najiⁿ na hoyeya. - iwahoya. B.H.56.1;163.8;276.7.
yuǧal'ǧata, v. red. (yugata). To stretch out or raise the arms, as do babies etc.
yuǧal' ic'icoⁿza, v. To promise under oath. B.H.207.2.
yuǧal'kiya, v.a. To administer an oath, make one swear. P. Ho yugata yo.
yuǧal'ya, v. To speak out to, to worship.
yuǧal'yapi, n. Worshipping, worship.

yuǧaⁿ', v.a. To open e.g. a door. Blugaⁿ.

yuǧaⁿ'ǧaⁿla, v.a. To make open or flimsy.
yuǧaⁿ' iȟpeya, v.a. To fling open, uncover e.g. a sleeping person. P. Yuⁿkaⁿ tiyopa kiⁿ yugaⁿ iȟpeyapi. Syn.- yuzamni ihpeya, akazamni ihpeya.
yuǧaⁿ'yaⁿ, v.a. To cause to open. Yu-

gaŋwaya.

yuġa'p̄a, v.a. To strip or pull off e.g. the skin from an animal, to skin. - s'e mahiŋgle lo, fig. GA.

yuġa't̄a, v. To stretch out the hand and arm upwards, to swear. Blugata. Waŋkatuya - . B.H.52.2.

yuġe', 1) v.a. To take out with the hand. Bluge. 2) n. A part or portion; some. - icu wo. - uŋyuhapi kte lo. Yugehci omicapta po. Note: the word is probably not used.

yuġe'ġe, v.a. To gather up in the hand, to take up by handfuls. - icu. Bl.

yuġe'k̄icaġa, Cf. yugekicaħ.
yuġe'k̄icaħ, v. cont. (yugekicaga). To hold out tempting things. - au, To lead on by holding out tempting with e.g. oats for a horse, holding it before its face and making it come along. WE. Bl. Syn.- ayuslohaŋ au.

yuġe'la, n. A big quantity, much. Bl.

yuġi'ca, v.a. To arouse one, wake one up. Blugica.
yuġil', cont. of yugica. - iyeya.

yuġi'mnamna, v. To make brown a little. Bl.

yuġi'payela, adv. Closely, as when one wound is inflicted near to the first one. - opi.

yugla', v.a. To untwist, unroll, uncoil; to stretch. Blugla.
yugla'gla, v. red. (yugla). To stretch out, to unwind. - aya, To go one after another, to follow in Indian file. D.54.
yugla'k̄ek̄e, (?). Tucuhu - hiŋgla yauŋ welo, i.e. you are getting thin. Bl.

yugla'kiŋyaŋ, adv. Transversely, across or athwart. - icu, To pull or put something so that it is transverse to one.

yugla'k̄iya, v.a. To cause to uncoil or stretch out. Yuglawakiya.

yugla'kśiŋkśaŋ, adv. In a zigzag line. Makasaŋ oŋ - owa, To paint, i.e. write, a zigzag line with white earth. - kiŋye, To fly in a zigzag line.

yugla'kśiŋkśiŋ, adj. Zigzag, or in all kinds of ways, as children mark on the snow. B.H.172.7.
yugla'kśiŋkśiŋya, adv. In a zigzag line. - mani.

yugla'ya, v.a. To cause to uncoil. Yuglawaya.

yuglo'glo, v.a. To make grunt e.g. a buffalo calf by catching it. Bluglo-glo. Also perhaps, to hit hard in anger and make howl. Bl.

yuglo'ka, v.a. To sprain badly, dislocate. Blugloka.

yugmi', v.a. To clear off e.g. grass etc. from a field. Blugmi.

yugmi'ca, v.a. To catch by the hair of the head, to pull one's hair. Blugmica. Miciglugmica. Iciglugmica, To pull one's own hair.

yugmi'gma, v.a. To make into a ball e.g. a bunch of paper, but not a snow ball; to make round. Blugmigma.
yugmil', cont. of yugmica. - yuza, To take hold of the hair of the head.

yugmi'yaŋyaŋ, v.a. To make roll with the hand. Blugmiyaŋyaŋ.

yugmi'yus, (?). - yupocaŋcaŋ, To take one by the hair and pull him to and fro. Bl.

yugmuŋ', v.a. To twist e.g. string or tobacco. Caŋli yugmuŋpi, Cigars.
yugmuŋ'gmuŋ, v. red. of yugmuŋ.

yugna', v.a. To shake e.g. fruit from a tree; to make fall off, as corn in shelling it.

yugna'gnayaŋ, v. (yugnayaŋ). To take a loose hold of. Yugnagnayaŋ wakuwa.

yugna'śkiŋyaŋyaŋ, v. red. (yugnaśkiŋyaŋ). To cause to rave, be possessed. B.H.185.21.

yugna'yaŋ, v.a. To miss, as in trying to grasp something. Blugnayaŋ. D.84.

yugnu'ni, v.a. To cause to wander. Blugnuni.

yuġo', v.a. To make scratches. Blugo. -- v.n. To be tired, fatigued, as is said of man and animal. Blugo.

yuǧo'ǧo, v. red. (yugo). To make marks by scratching. Blugogo.

yuǧo'yakel, adv. In an exhausted condition.

yuǧu'ka, v.a. To draw from the pocket and open a knife; to stretch, strain; to pull out e.g. an arrow from the quiver. Bluguka. Mila - .

yugwa', v. (?). Bl.

yugwa'yaⁿ, v.a. To drop while holding. BD.

yugwe'za, v.a. To make rough. Blugweza.

yugwog'gwog, (?). - Ȟpaya, as is said of a person that is unable to swim but keeps himself above water by moving. Bl.

yuha', v.a. To have, own, possess; to have given birth to a child; to lift, be able to carry (with this meaning, the terminal "a" is not changed to "e"). Bluha śni, I am not able to carry it. -- part. Carrying with one; it is almost a prep. meaning "with". Śina waⁿ yuha hinapa na yublaya egnaka. Tahca ha waⁿ yuha najiⁿ.

yuha'ha, (?). Śuⁿkawakaⁿla k'oⁿ uⁿśilapica śni - yuzapi s'e nauⁿke, as is said when a played-out horse comes on trotting. Bl.

yuha'hala, v.a. To make not firm, to unsettle. Bluhahala.

yuha'hapika, (?). Uⁿgnahaȟci - lowaciⁿ yelo, as a hungry visitor would say who, being told that there is nothing in the house, thinks that they have still something hidden away. Bl.

yuha'hayela, v.a. To move, shake, make unstable. Bluhahayela.

yuha' iyeya, v. To find or receive something unexpectedly. Bl.

yuha'kiya, v.a. To make one have, to cause one to have.

yuhaⁿ'ska, v.a. To lengthen out, make longer, prolong. Bluhaⁿska.

yuha'pi, part. Owned, held. - ciⁿ, He wants to be hired.

yuha'śniyaⁿ, adv. perhaps. Without. Wocet'uⁿgla - oholapi. B.H.169.20.

yuha'ya, adv. In the manner of having; having. - uⁿ.

yuhel'hel, adv. Bewildered. Yáyaya, yuhelhel, wotiti najiⁿ, To stand still and bewildred. Sb. Not knowing what to do. - nawajiⁿ. But also, Bluhelhel wauⁿ.

yuhi', v.a. To drive off e.g. game; to arouse, startle. Bluhi.

yuhi'ka, v.a. To shake up, as in waking one up; to arouse. Bluhika. Mayaluhikelo. Uⁿma nahaȟci luhike śni hwo? Bl.

yuhiⁿ'haⁿ, v.a. To tease, to provoke one so as to get him angry. Bluhiⁿhaⁿ. Bl.

yuhiⁿl', cont. of yuhiⁿta. - iyeya.

yuhiⁿ'ta, v.a. To rake away, to rake a field, yard. Bluhiⁿta.

yuho'ho, v.a. To move, shake anything not firm. Bluhoho. Pb.34.

yuho'hola, v.a. To shake, as something not solid. Bluhohola.

yuho'hopicaśni, adj. Immovable.

yuho'hoya, 1) adv. Shaking. 2) v.a. To cause to shake.

yuho'mni, v.a. To turn around anything, to turn e.g. a grindstone. - taciyotaⁿka. Bluhomni.

yuho'mnimni, v. red. of yuhomni.

yuhoⁿ'hoⁿza, Cf. yuhuⁿhuⁿza.

yuho'taⁿke, v.a. To make one cry. Bluhotaⁿke. Bl. Syn.- yuceya.

yuho'tapi s'e, adv. Clearing away obstacles. - iyaye, He went on, as though there were no obstacles. R. Bl.

yuho'waya, v.a. To make whine etc., as dogs do. Bluhowaya. Ayuśtaⁿ na luhowayahe, Let the dog alone, you make it whine. Bl.

yuhu'kul iyéya, v. To cast down, to humble. - iyewaya.

yuhu'kuya, v.a. (hukuya). To humble, bring down. Bluhukuya.

yuhuⁿ'huⁿ, v.a. To move, shake something not firm. Bluhuⁿhuⁿ. Pa - na inajiⁿ.

yuhuⁿ'huⁿs, cont. of yuhuⁿhuⁿza. - uⁿ.
yuhuⁿ'huⁿsya, 1) v.a. To cause to shake and move. Yuhuⁿhuⁿswaya. 2) adv. Shaking, moving.
yuhuⁿ'huⁿza, v.a. To shake e.g. a tree with the hands. Bluhuⁿhuⁿza.

yuĦa', 1) v.n. To curl, branch out. 2) adj. Curled, frizzled. Nata - .
yuĦa'Ħa, 1) v. red. (yuĦa). To become curled or branched. 2) adj. Curly, having many branches or prongs. Haⁿp yúĦaĦa kśupi, A moccasin with a design on the upper side, i.e. lines going in all directions. Bl.
yuĦa'tka, v.a. To ruffle, e.g. the hair or feathers. BluĦatka.

yuĦeb', cont. of yuĦepa. - iyeya.
yuĦeb'Ħepa, v. red. of yuĦepa.
yuĦeb'ya, v.a. To imbue. P.

yuĦe'kicaĦ au, v. To coax one on, lure against one's will, in order to entrap by going ahead and showing a small number; to decoy. WE. Bl. Also, yuĦekicaĦ aya.

yuĦe'pa, v.a. To empty a vessel by lading out. BluĦepa.

yuĦe'yab, cont. of yuĦeyapa. - iyeya, To put aside. - icu. B.H.46.1.

yuĦe'yal, cont. of yuĦeyata. - iyeya, icu.

yuĦe'yapa, v.a. To put a little back, put aside. BluĦeyapa. Also, to get out of the way. -- v.n. To make room. - yo, Get away from here. R.
yuĦe'yapaya, v.a. To leave alone, get away from one. MayuĦeyapaya yo. B.H. 52.10. Tipi wakaⁿ kiⁿ yuĦeyapaye śni. B.H.168.23.

yuĦe'yata, v.a. To put back, reject. BluĦeyata.

yuĦla', v.a. To ring e.g. a bell, to rattle. BluĦla.

yuĦla'ġaⁿ, v.a. To enlarge; to separate from, leave. BluĦlagaⁿ. Ti gluĦlagaⁿ śni, To stay always at home. WiyúĦlagaⁿ śni, To be always in company with one's wife. Pagoⁿta s'e wiyuĦlagaⁿ śni. Bl.

yuĦla'Ħla, v. red. of yuĦla.

yuĦla'Ħlata, v. red. of yuĦlata.

yuĦla'Ħlaya, v. red. of yuĦlaya.

yuĦlal', cont. of yuĦlata. - iyeya.
yuĦla'ta, v.a. To scratch, as does a cat. BluĦlata.

yuĦla'ya, v.a. To pull off e.g. paper sticking to the wall; to peel off, take off e.g. sticking plaster. BluĦlaya.

yuĦle'ca, v.a. To tear in pieces with the hands. BluĦleca.
yuĦle'Ħleca, v. red. of yuĦleca.
yuĦlel', cont. of yuhleca. - iyeya. - icu, To receive a partial payment, as on a lease etc.
yuĦlel'kiya, v.a. To cause to rend. YuĦlelwakiya.
yuĦlel'ya, v.a. To cause to tear up. YuĦlelwaya.

yuĦli'Ħli, v.a. To make dirty, slimy, slippery. Bl.

yuĦlo', v.a. To make growl. BluĦlo.

yuĦlog', cont. of yuĦloka. - iyeya. YuĦlog haⁿ, To stand open.
yuĦlog'kiya, v.a. To cause to open. YuĦlogwakiya.

yuĦlo'hela s'e, adv. Seemingly burdened or unwell. - mani, To walk slowly as though one carried a heavy burden or were sick. Bl.

yuĦlo'Ħloka, v. red. (of yuĦloka). To make holes in. BluĦloĦloka.
yuĦlo'ka, v.a. To make a hole, using the hand. BluĦloka.

yuĦmiⁿ', v.a. To twist out of joint; to sling e.g. a stone sideways; to make go crooked. R. BluĦmiⁿ.
yuĦmiⁿ'Ħmiⁿ, v. red. of yuhmiⁿ. B.H. 294.17.
yuĦmiⁿ'yaⁿ, adv. Off sidewise, crookedly, as a ball might go; sliced, as in golf.

yuĦmuⁿ', v.a. To make whizz, as in throwing a stone from a sling. BluĦmuⁿ.
yuĦmuⁿ'Ħmuⁿ, v. red. of yuĦmuⁿ.
yuĦmuⁿ'yaⁿ, adv. Making whizz.

yuĦni'ġa, v.a. To dress one up nicely. BluĦniga. MigluĦniga, I am dressed up.

Cf. igluhniga.
yuhni'yan, (?). Pute yuhniyanpi s'e najin yankelo, i.e. with quivering lips as from fear. Bl.
yuhni'yanyan, v. red. of yuhniyan. Pute yuhniyanyanpi s'e nanke hwo? Bl.

yuhon'ta, v.a. To make soft e.g. flax in dressing it; to rub soft e.g. a skin by pulling the hands back alternately. Bluhonta. Also, yuhunta.

yuhpa', v.a. To pull something, so as to make it fall; to loosen the bow string after use; to throw down e.g. one's load, to shake off. Bluhpa.
yuhpa'hpa, v. red. of yuhpa. - s'e kinyan, To fly slowly, i.e. as a big bird, dragging something, as it were.

yuhpan', v.a. To soak and make soft e.g. a piece of leather. Bluhpan.
yuhpan'hpan, v. red. (yuhpan). To soak and make a little soft e.g. a piece of leather work. Bluhpanhpan.

yuhpe'ya, v.a. To cause to throw down, shake off. Yuhpewaya. Misun, (śiyo kin) miciyuhpeye. MS.98.
yuhpi'hpeya, v.a. To throw down.

yuhpu', v.a. To pick off a piece. Canśin - . Bluhpu.
yuhpu'hpu, v. red. of yuhpu. Bluhpuhpu.

yuhta'ka, v.a. (?). Ehaś maka kin yuhtakin kte s'e inyankelo, as is said of a horse that holds the head down while running. Bl.

yuhtan', v.a. To make rough. Cf. yuhtanyan.
yuhtan'yan, v.a. To make rough, to whet or do a rough edge. Bluhtanyan.

yuhtu'te śni icu, v. To take the whole leaving nothing. Yuhtute (have in use) śni k'u, To give the whole thing, such as a box of cigars, without keeping anything back. Et.

yuhu'ġa, v.a. To crack something, using the hand. Bluhuga.

yuhu'gnaġa, v.a. To cause to burn up. Bluhugnaga.

yuhuh', cont. of yuhuga. - iyeya.
yuhu'huġa, v. red. of yuhuga.
yuhunl'hunta, v. red. of yuhunta.
yuhun'ta, v.a. To make soft e.g. a piece of thread; to rub soft e.g. a skin. Bluhunta. Also, yuhonta.

yuhun'win, v.a. To make putrify e.g. flesh. Bluhunwin.

yuhwa', v.a. To make drowsy. Bluhwa.

yuh'a'kpa, v.a. To make curved e.g. an edge of a knife that has been long in use. Bluh'akpa.

yuh'an'hi, v.a. To make slow. Bluh'anhi.
yuh'an'hika, adj. Slow.

yuh'e'h'e, Cf. yuh'eh'eyakel.
yuh'e'h'eyakel, adv. In bits, in small quantities. - wawakamna, Making money in small quantities at a time. Syn.- tutkayakel. Bl.

yuh'i', v.n. To pimple, be pimpled or rough; be chapped, as hands; to be broken out full of pimples. Nape mayuh'i. Ite yuh'i.
yuh'i'h'i, v. red. (yuh'i). To be pimpled, rough.
yuh'i's'e, adj. Chapped-like.
yuh'i'ya, v. To be made rough. Nape kin yujaja kangi tanka nape s'e nape kin sabyela - , as is said when a person's hands are rough from dirt. Mato s'e siyete - . Bl.
yuh'i'yaya, v.a. To do badly, bungle. Bluh'iyaya.
yuh'i'yela, adv. or adj. Marked, pimpled, rough, as by scratches or gouging. Waowe śica (bear) s'e napcoka kin - yankin na, as when a person's hands are scratched. Bl. Cf. waoweśica, example.

yuh'u', v.a. To take off the hull or rind, to peel e.g. the bark with the hand; to pull off a little piece of skin. Bluh'u.

yui'capa, v.a. To open somebody's mouth, as a horse's. Bluicapa.

yui'ćićahi, v.a. To mix together, to mingle. Bluicicahi.
yui'ćićahiya, adv. Mingling. - iyeya.
yui'ćićawin, v.a. To make turn back on the same way. Bluicicawin.

yui'c'ic'uya, v.a. To cause to pass by over or alongside of each other, as the two ends of anything; to make overlap each other. Bluic'ic'uya.

yui'eska, v.a. To interpret, explain e.g. a piece of the Holy Scripture. Bluieska.
yui'ha, v.a. To make laugh. Bluiha.

yui'jena, v. To stir or mix together. Bluijena. Fig., to mix up things, confuse. Mayaluijena. Ciyuijena. BT.

yui'kpiska ihpeya, v. To turn anything over on its back, as a dog.

yui'le, v.a. To cause to blaze, to kindle a fire. Bluile. Ehanl izigzita na ungna yuile.
yui'lepi, n. A match to start fire.

yui'nahni, v.a. To hasten one, to make someone hurry. Bluinahni. Makiyuinahni yo; wanagi el mahipelo, as the Indians say when they are very hungry.
yui'nahnikiya, v.a. To cause one to hasten.
yui'nahniyan, adv. Hastening. - śkan. Bl. Also, yuinahniyela. Bl.

yui'nila, v.a. (inila). To make still, put to silence. Bluinila. - yuza, To caress and make still, as a mother does her child. Bl.
yui'nilya, adv. Putting to silence.

yuin'yanka, v.a. To make run. Bluinyanka.
yuin'yank'inyanka, v.n. To run dragging one along, making one run along. Yuinyankwaimnanke.

yui'pahtu, v.a. To reverse a thing, to undo a thing. Bluipahtu. B.H.20.11.

yui'śteca, v.a. To make one ashamed. Bluiśteca.

yui'śtogmus, cont. of yuiśtogmuza.
yui'śtogmuza, v.a. (iśtogmuza). To make one shut his eyes; to deceive. Bluiśtogmuza.

yui'tannunk, adv. On both sides. - iyakaśka, To tie a horse to both sides of one's team.

yui'teśla, Cf. teślaka. Ungna tóka śka - ciyuzin na ognagna acipe ci.Bl.

yui'tokan, v.a. To put out of the way; to remove from; to reject. Bluitokan.

yui'tomni, v.a. To turn around and around, thus making him dizzy. Bluitomni.

yui'yakipab, adv. Dividing, separating. Also, red. yuiyakipapab.

yui'yotag, cont. of yuiyotaka. - ehpeya, To push one down, make sit down, i.e. by force.

yui'yowajaśni, v. To place afar off.

yui'yowas, cont. of yuiyowaza.
yui'yowaś, cont. of yuiowaja. - iyeye śni. Cf. yuiyowajaśni.

yui'yowaza, v.a. To make resound, to make echo. Bluiyowaza.

yui'yoyag, v. To scare and get a person excited. Bl. - iyeya. Cf. oyaka.

yui'yupse icu, v. To close a tent door very tight from within. Bl.

yuja', v.a. To mash, make mush; to stir up e.g. mush. Bluja. Tahuha bluja kte pangi icahi. Wa kin yujapi s'e yunkelo, as is said of snow when thawing. Bl.

yujag', cont. of yujaka. - iyeya.

yuja'han, 1) v.a. To make a jarring noise. Blujahan. 2) adj. Sounding.
yuja'heya, adv. Sounding, harshly.

yuja'ja, v.a. To wash e.g. clothes. Blujaja.

yujā'ka, v.a. To pull open or strain open somebody's eyes. Blujaka.

yuja'pi, part. Mixed up, as mush.

yujib', cont. of yujipa. - iyeya.
yujib'jib, v. To pinch. - kuwa, To bother, treating roughly. SLB.
yujib'jipa, v. red. of yujipa.
yujib'yela, v. To pinch up with the fingers, as in pinching the skin. Blujibyela. -- adv. Pinching up with the fingers. - yuza.

yujin'ca, v.a. To pull or blow e.g. the nose. Blujinca.

yuji'pa, v.a. To pinch. Blujipa.

yujo', v.a. To whistle to. Blujo.
yujo'jo, v. red. of yujo. Blujojo.

yuju´ju, v.a. To tear down, destroy, deface; to pull in pieces, undo, open e.g. a bundle; to make void e.g. an agreement etc. Blujuju.

yuju^n´, v.a. To pull up with the roots something that is tight, pulling up straight. Bluju^n. Wicaśa num wicakico na wihuta yuju^{n}pi.

yuju^n´ṫa, v.a. To thrust into. Iśta - , To thrust something into the eye, to strike the eye.

yuk̇a´, v.a. To strip off e.g. the feather part of a quill. Bluka.

yuk̇ab´, cont. of yukapa. - iyeya, To jerk.

yuka´ġal, Same as yuakagal. - otkeyapi. MS.102.

yuka´kak̇a, v. (?). Otutkala eśa tuweni el u^n śni yelo; ca tiyopa blukakaki^n na wagliyacu welo. Bl.

yuk̇a´kija, v.a. To cause to suffer. Blukakija. Oyate eya wicalukakije na ota t'ewicayaya.

yuk̇a^n´, v.n. To be; there is. It lacks forms for the 1st and 2nd pers. sing. Pl.: u^{n}kanpi, luka^{n}pi, yuka^{n}pi. It is often used with a pl. meaning, as in: tahca yuka^n, hu mayuka^n. Pute mayuka^n ca śolwakiyi^n kte, as the Indian says when he fills a pipe. -- v.a. To give room. Kiyúka^n, To make room for one.

yuka^n´, v.a. To shake off e.g. dew. Bluka^n. Cf. cugluka^n.

yuk̇a^n´, v.a. (k̇a^n). To make old. Bluka^n

yuka^n´ka^n, v. red. of yuka^n.

yuka^n´nakśa ika^n´to^n, v. To keep a firm hold on something and not letting it go. - ḣcelo. Bl.

yukā´ṗa, v.a. To catch e.g. a ball in the hand. Blukapa. Tabyúkapa.

yuka´pojela, v.a. To lighten. P.

yuka´ṫa, v.a. (kata). To make warm by rubbing. Blukata.

yuk̇a´ṫi^n, v.a. To straighten out with the hand. Blukati^n.

yuk̇a´wa, v.a. To open e.g. a wound, a sore, or somebody's mouth; implying effort being made in so opening. Blukawa. B.

yuk̇a´wak̇iya, v.a. To cause to open e.g. a sore, wound etc. Yukawawakiya.

yukca´, v.a. To loose a knot, untie, unwrap; open what is tangled. Blukca.

yukca^n´, v.a. To comprehend anything, to understand; to know, guess; to have an opinion, judge. Blukca^n.

yúkca^n´ya^n, adv. Comprehending, guessing.

yuk̇e´, v.n. To be. Cf. yuka^n.

yuk̇e´ya, adv. Being, having, possessing. Peta - wau^n kte. Hena wa^{n}kaḣ wicaśipi wiśi - . MS.481.

yuk̇i´cahipi s'e, adv. (?). - wiyukca^n, To be unsteady in one's actions. - wiblukca^n yelo. BT.

yuk̇i´k̇ik̇e, v.a. To pull e.g. a tree at its top towards the ground. Bl.

yuk̇i´k̇ṫa, v. To cause to wake up. Blukikta. Isto el yuzi^n na yukikta.

yuk̇i´ni, v.a. To cause to live again, to make recover. Blukini. Na wa^{n}na yukinipi na wota okihi.

yuk̇i´nuk̇a^n, v.a. To divide between, as apples etc. between those present; to separate e.g. cattle. Blukinuka^n. - wicayus-waci^n, He planned to hold them apart, i.e. two trees. D.21,27. -- adv. Divided. Yukinuka^n egnaka, To place out separately.

yuk̇i´nuk̇a^{n}k̇iya, v.a. To part in two, separate. B.H.233.10. -- adv. Divided, separately. - u^{n}pi.

yuk̇i´nuk̇a^{n}ya^n, adv. Separately.

yuk̇i^n´, v.a. To give room to pass, to lean to one side. Bluki^n.

yuk̇i^n´ca, v.a. To scrape off with the hand or finger; to clean e.g. taniga by pulling it through two fingers. Bluki^{n}ca.

yuki^n´ja, v. (ki^{n}ja). To make whine. Tate wa^n yuki^{n}japi s'e u welo, i.e. howling. Bl.

yuk̇iŋ'k̇iŋ, adv. To and fro, from side to side.

yuk̇iŋl', cont. of yukiŋca. - icu.

yuk̇i'ṗaja, v.a. To bend anything around, to double over e.g. a piece of paper, a blanket, a string so as to make the ends meet; to hem, as in sewing. Blukipaja.
yuk̇i'ṗaś, cont. of yukipaja. - iyeya. - yuza, To double around and hold. - iyakaśka, To tie a knot with a loop. Bl. Syn.- yuśiŋyaŋ icu.
yuk̇i'ṗehaŋ, v.a. To fold, to lay in folds. Blukipehaŋ. - egnaka.

yuk̇i'ṗusk̇ica, v.a. To put close together, to press. Blukipuskica.
yuk̇i'ṗusk̇il, cont. of yukipuskica. - yuza, To hold one thing close to another.
yuk̇i'ṗusk̇ilya, adv. Pressed close to.

yuk̇is', cont. of yukiza. - iyeya.
yuk̇i'sk̇iza, v. red. of yukiza.

yuk̇i'yela, v.a. To make near. Blukiyela.

yuk̇i'yuṫeya, adv. Crisped or drawn up.

yuk̇i'za, v.a. To make creak. Blukiza. Caŋíyukize, A piano.

yuk̇ō', v.a. To make a hole larger with the hand. Bluko.

yukōg', cont. of yukoka. - iyeya.
yukō'k̇a, v.a. To ring or rattle, as an old kettle. Blukoka.

yuko'k̇ela, v.a. To make active, to stimulate. Blukokela.

yuko'k̇iya, v.a. To make wrinkle. Ite - , To frown or scowl.

yukō'kok̇a, v. red. of yukoka.

yuk̇oŋ'ṫa, v.a. To wear partly out by handling e.g. a strap or rope, i.e. to make it thinner. BD. Blukoŋta.

yuko's'iŋ, v. To throw high, crane one's neck. Yukos'iŋpi s'e iŋyaŋka, i.e. running with the head thrown high up, as a horse craning. Bl. Cf. s'iŋ s'e.

yuko'yaḣ'aŋ, v.a. To cause to be quick, to hasten. Blukoyaḣ'aŋ.

yukṗa', v.a. To ruin, crush, quench, stifle. Iśta - , To make blind. Blukpa.
yukṗa'kṗa, v.a. Cf. yukpa. P.

yukṗaŋ', v.a. To grind e.g. corn etc., to make fine, to pulverize. Blukpaŋ.
yukṗaŋ'kṗaŋ, v. red. of yukpaŋ. Blukpaŋkpaŋ.
yukṗaŋ'ṗi, n. Grinding.
yukṗaŋ'yaŋ, v.a. To cause to grind. Yukpaŋwaya.

yukṗi', v.a. To crack or burst e.g. a louse. Blukpi.
yukṗi'kṗi, v. red. of yukpi.

yukṗu'kṗa, v.a. To make fine, to crumble up and scatter about. Blukpukpa.

yuksa', v.a. To break off e.g. a stick with the hand. Cf. huyuksa.
yuksa'ksa, v. red. of yuksa. Bluksaksa.

yuksa'pa, v.a. (ksapa). To make wise. Bluksapa.

yuksa'ṗi, n. A breaking off; monthly payments, as on deposites etc.

yukse'kseya, v. red. of yukseya.
yukse'ya, 1) v.a. To cause to break off, as in trapping. Yuksewaya. 2) adv. Broken off, as if straight down; Cliff-like, as is a bluff shore where the water is deep and the bank appears broken off.

yukśa', v.a. To bend or double up, e.g. a blanket. Blukśa. Hu - śni uŋkiŋyaŋpelo. MS.104.
yukśa'kśala, adj. red. of yukśala. PD.
yukśa'la, adv. Bent up, crooked. - icu. Macuwita ca - muŋke; hecel omacoze. Bl. Wi k'oŋ - yaŋkelo, wioteḣi kte lo. BT.
yukśaŋ', v.a. To bend. Blukśaŋ.
yukśaŋ'kiya, v.a. To cause to bend. Yukśaŋwakiya.
yukśaŋ'kśaŋ, v. red. (yukśaŋ). To bend and make crooked. -- adv. In a crooked line, in a manner zigzag. - mani.
yukśaŋ'ya, adv. Curved. - iyaya, He went in a curved line.
yukśaŋ'yaŋ, v.a. To cause to bend. Yukśaŋwaya.
yukśaŋ'yeya, adv. Bent around, in a circle.

yukśa'yela, adv. Bent, with the knees drawn up, in a bent position. - Ḣpaya.

yukśi'ja, v.a. To double up e.g. a knife or one's arm, i.e. gluksija.
yukśi'kśija, v. red. of yukśija.
yukśiś', cont. of yukśija. - iyeya.
yukśiś'ya, v.a. To cause to double up. Yukśiśwaya.

yuktaⁿ', v. To bend with the hand. Bluktaⁿ. B.H.263.10.
yukťaⁿ'ḱiya, v.a. To cause to bend anything. Yuktaⁿwakiya. -- yukťáⁿḱiya, adv. Crookedly.
yukťaⁿ'kťaⁿ, 1) v. red. (yuktaⁿ). To bend, to crook. 2) adj. or adv. Zigzag, bent.
yukťaⁿ'kťaⁿḱiya, adv. red. of yuktaⁿkiya.
yukťaⁿ'kťaⁿyaⁿ, adv. red. of yuktaⁿyaⁿ.
yukťaⁿ'yaⁿ, adv. Crookedly.
yukťaⁿ'yeya, adv. Not in a straight line, crookedly.

yuku'ka, v.a. To pull to pieces; to make rotten, to destroy. Blukuka.

yukuⁿ'ta, Cf. yukoⁿta.

yuk'e'ġa, v.a. To scratch, as after itching. Cf. yuḣlata, how this differs.
yuk'eḣ', cont. of yuk'ega. - iyeya.
yuk'eḣ'k'eġa, v. red. of yuk'ega.
yuk'eḣ'ya, 1) v.a. To cause to scratch or scrape. Yuk'eḣwaya. 2) adv. Scratching, scraping.
yuk'e'k'eġa, v. red. of yuk'ega.

yuk'ěs', cont. of yuk'eza. - iyeya.
yuk'ě'sk'eza, v. red. (yuk'eza). To shave off close and smooth e.g. the hair of the head. Bluk'esk'eza.
yuk'e'za, v.a. To shear, clip off close e.g. the hair of the head. Bluk'eza. Also perhaps, to make hard and smooth.

yuk'ō'ġa, v.a. To scratch up, make rough with the nails. Bluk'oga.
yuk'ōḣ', cont. of yuk'oga. - iyeya.
yuk'oḣ'koġa, v. red. of yuk'oga.

yuk'ōs', cont. of yuk'oza. - iyeya.
yuk'ō'sk'oza, v. red. of yuk'oza.
yuk'ō'za, v.a. To make smooth and hard by taking off the grass or hair etc. Bluk'oza.

yul, cont. of yuta. - wicaśa. Na heḣaⁿl yul wicaśi, caⁿke oyate kiⁿ wakpamnipi na caⁿtewaśteya wotapi.

yulab', cont. of yulapa. - iyeya.
yula'blapa, v. red. of yulapa.

yula'kota, v. To do a thing in the way of a Lakota, to change things so that they suit a Lakota. PB.

yulā'ṗa, v.a. To make smooth. Blulapa.

yule'bleṗa, v.a. To make notches in, to make a jagged edge, as with a scissors. Bl. To produce a serrate margin, edge.

yule'na, (?). - s'e yaglihuⁿni yelo, as is said when a person returns from a long trip sooner than expected. Hm.

yule'śleja, v. red. (leja). To make urinate. Bl.

yulḱi'ya, v.a. (yuta). To feed, cause to eat. Yulwakiya.

yulo'loṗi, adj. Many. Also, ota. Heheheé, oyate - lel ohimniciye na oiyokipilaḣcake el waⁿweglaka, yuⁿkaⁿ caⁿtemaśice, as was said on seeing a place where big gatherings used to take place in times of old.

yulpi'ca, adj. Edible. Takuⁿl - eśa yaglepi hwo? B.H.274.4.

yulu'ṗi śni, n. Something that is yet whole, intact, not opened, as a fresh bag of tobacco untouched by hands. - Ḣca waⁿji ahigleyo. Bl. Cf. walupi śni.

yulu'zahaⁿ, v.a. (luzahaⁿ). To make swift. Bluluzahaⁿ.

yulya', v.a. To feed, cause to eat. Yulwaya.
yul'yul, adv. red. of yul. Hena tokeya - waku kte lo. D.54.

yuma'hel iyeya, v.a. To push one thing into something else, to insert, to hold in. Yumahel iyewaya. Yumahel icu, To draw back, to hide under one's clothes. D.39,114.

yumaⁿ', v.a. To sharpen by grinding, filing or whetting e.g. an axe. Blumaⁿ. Also, yumé.

yumī'ma, v.a. To make round e.g. a wheel. Blumima.
yumi'meya, adv. In a circle, circular. - yaŋke, iyotaka, po, Sit round in a circle. D.34.

yumna', v.a. To rip a seam with scissors, or by pulling. Blumna.
yumna'k̇iya, v.a. To cause to rip. Yumnawakiya.
yumna'mna, v. red. of yumna.

yumni', v.a. To turn round e.g. a crank. Blumni. Na uŋma pestola k'oŋ he el icapa na oŋ - .
yumni'ġa, v. To shrink, draw up.
yumni'ja, adj. Ruffled, as hair on a hide.
yumni'mni, v.n. and v.a. To turn round and round, to whirl.
yumni'mniġa, v. red. of yumniga.
yumni'mnija, 1) v.a. To curl. 2) adj. red. (yumnija). Curled, ruffled, as the hair on a hide.
yumni'mniś, cont. of yumnimnija. - iyeya.
yumni'mniśya, 1) v.a. To cause to curl. Yumnimniśwaya. 2) adv. Curly.
yumni'mniyaŋ, adv. Turning round and round. - otke, i.e. as a flag in the wind.

yumnu'mnuġa, v.a. To make a noise, as in handling corn. Blumnumnuga.

yuna'jiŋ, v.a. To cause to stand, to raise or lift up. Blunajiŋ. Pb.47.
yuna'jiŋk̇iya, v.a. To make stand. Na uŋma waŋna tokeya - . Nape el oyuspiŋ na - . B.H.290.19.

yuna'k̇e, v. Cf. yunakeya.
yuna'k̇eya, v.a. To turn anything partly, turn on one side. Blunakeya.

yunaŋ'k̇e, v. 2nd pers. sing. (yu-yaŋka). To cause you to be present; you become or come present. - nuŋs'e uŋkanipepi, i.e. waiting long thinking you would come soon, but you did not. Bl.

yuna'p'iyeya, v. (?). Yunap'iyeyapi sekse iŋyaŋkelo, as is said of a horse that runs off in a curve. Bl.

yuna's'a, v.a. To try hutanacute by making it hop in one's right hand above one's head, before slinging it, to see if it balances well. Bl. Cf. nas'a, as said of a horse.

yuna'ya, v. To pass something along. Yunawaya.
yuna'yek̇iya, v.a. To pass on, give to someone else. Bl.

yuni', v.a. To touch one, so as to call his attention to something. Bluni. Cf. pani.
yuni' kuwa, v. To bother, annoy by pulling or touching. Yuni Wakuwa. Bl.
yunī'ni, v. red. (yuni). To touch so as to arouse one, or call his attention to anything. Blunini.

yuni'yaśni, v.a. To put out of breath, to strangle. Bluniyaśni.

yunuŋ'ġa, v.a. To make a hard or callous place, by strain or otherwise. Blunuŋga.

yunuŋ'pa, v.a. To divide into two. B.H.60.15.

yuŋ, interj. An exclam. used by women when feeling pain. Oh! O dear me. R.

yuŋgyuŋ'ka, v. To rock or sway from side to side. P. Bl.
yuŋgyuŋ'k̇ahaŋ, v. To rock or sway from side to side, as a sailor does in walking. Mayuŋgyuŋkahe. Caŋke wikośkalaka yamnipi k'oŋ hiŋhaŋ kiŋ kuwa eyayapi na yuŋgyuŋkahaŋ Ḣpayapi na waŋji oyuspa. Na ecel yuŋgyuŋkahaŋpi.
yuŋgyuŋ'k̇e s'e mani, v. To walk as a sailor, to sway from side to side.

yuŋk̇a', v. To lie along. Muŋka, uŋyuŋkapi. Hecel miś wiyeya muŋka. Yuŋkaŋ isaŋpataŋhaŋ makoce waŋ lila caŋwape to na makoce kiŋ toyela yuŋka.
yuŋk̇a'haŋ, v.n. To lie down, fall down. Mayuŋkahe.
yuŋk̇a'he, adv. Lying prone, as a tree cut down, or as a whole fence.
yuŋk̇a'heya, 1) v.a. To throw down, cause to fall. Yuŋkahewaya. 2) adv. Obliquely, as the characters are placed in writing. - ówa.

yuŋ'k̇aŋ, conj. And, also, then.
yuŋ'k̇aŋś, conj. If. Also, yuŋkáŋś. Note: but by far more commonly used is k'eś.

yuŋk̇a'pi, n. A lying down, an encampment.

yuŋś, conj. If, provided. Hecoŋ śni - ,

If he had not done it. Śilwaecoŋ śni - , B.H.260.16. Okiwaś'ag niśicelo, ahoyasotkamayayelo, cehupa aciyaweȟwega kta - , aciyawega ye. i.e. when a person does not listen to advice. Note: Yuŋś is used when only the speaker knows or claims to know the fact indicated in the conditional cl.; whereas, k'eś is used when both the speaker and the person addressed are aware of it. Gramm.284.

yuo'bleca, v.a. To divide, disperse, break in pieces, scatter abroad, as does a people. Bluobleca. -- v.n. To be with the narrow or sharp part up. - yuza, To hold the sharp part up, as the edge of a board.
yuo'blecahaŋ, part. In a dispersed state, scattered.
yuō'blel, cont. of yuobleca. - iyaya, To go off, disperse. - iyeya, To cause to scatter abroad.

yuō'cikp̣ani, v.a. To make unequal. Bluocikpani.

yuō'ciŋśica, v.a. To make cross, angry. Bluociŋśica.

yuo'cipteca, v.a. To make one shorter than another; to make a difference, to diminish. Bluocipteca. R. Bl.
yuo'ciptel, cont. of yuocipteca. R. Bl.
yuo'ciptelya, adv. Diminishing by degrees. R. Bl.
yuo'ciptetu, v.a. To make of different size, to lessen. Bluociptetu. R. Bl.
yuo'ciptetuya, adv. Lessening. R. Bl.
yuo'ciptetuyakel, adv. Of different sizes. R. Bl.

yuō'citkuŋza, v.a. To make equal, even. Bluocitkuŋza.

yuo'coscoza, v. red. (yuocoza). To make one feel warm by, let him wear much clothing.
yuo'coza, v.a. To make one feel warm and comfortable, e.g. by rubbing his hands and putting good clothing on him. Bl. Bluocoza.

yuo'gla, adv. Lined in a row. - icupo, as is said to a group, to line up in a row. Bl. Cf. ociblagaheya.

yuo'glapśuŋ, v. To turn something over. - iȟpeya, To turn and throw over.
yuo'glapśuŋyaŋ, adv. Turning over.

yuō'gmus, cont. of yuogmuza. - icu, To close up e.g. a door; to button e.g. one's coat. - icu yo. Na ake tiyopa kiŋ - icupi.
yuo'gmuza, v. To wrap up in, to close up or button closed. Wakaŋheja wicayuogmuza yo, hiŋhaŋna iglakapi kte lo, as a herald said on the day before moving away. The word also ref. to the mending of children's moccasins. Oyute kiŋ - ye, Close up that hole (tear) in your side (dress). Bl.

yuo'gna icu, v. To open e.g. the barrel of a gun in order to put in a cartridge. Bl.

yuo'ha, v.a. To push one into e.g. a hole, or a water hole. Bluoha.

yuo'hoho, v.a. To shake something in a tight place, as a tree stump around which is made a hole but none is able to pull it out. WE. Bluohoho.

yuō'ȟaŋk̇oya, adv. Hastening.
yuo'ȟaŋśica, v.a. To make act badly. Bluoȟaŋśica.

yuō'ȟlaġaŋ, v.a. To loosen, make loose. To become loose, v.n. Also, to loosen e.g. a nut on a bolt. R.
yuo'ȟlaȟ, cont. of yuoȟlagaŋ. - icu, To make loose. Also, to become loose, v.n. R.

yuō'ȟp̣a, v.a. To break off through and into, to pull through and into. Bluoȟpa.

yuo'ȟp̣eya, v.a. To cause to break through. Yuoȟpewaya.

yuoȟ'ya, adv. Obliquely, as characters are placed in writing. - egnaka.

yuō'ȟ'aŋk̇o, v.a. To make hasten. Bluoȟ'aŋko.

yuo'k̇aȟwoka, v.a. To make wave in folds, as does a flag etc. Bluokaȟwoka.

yuo'k̇ap̣oṫa, v. To cause to be borne up, as in water. To float.

yuo'k̇inihaŋ, v.a. To make honorable.

yuō'k̇iwaŋjila, v.a. To make alike or similar. Bluokiwaŋjila.

yuo'ḱiyuta, v.a. (okiyuta). To close up, by drawing to together e.g. a wound for healing. Tiyopa kin - yo, kazamnimni iyayelo, tanyan iyakaśka yo, i.e. the tent door is flapping to and fro. Bl.

yuō'ḱo, v.a. To make a hole. Bluoko.

yuō'ksa, v.a. To break off into; to pull through into. Bluoksa. Cf. yuoḣpa.

yuo'kťan, v.a. To bend into. Bluoktan.

yuo'nihan, v.a. To honor, treat with attention. Bluonihan.
yuō'nihanyan, adv. Honoring, treating politely.

yuon'jincayela, adv. (?). - iyaglaśka, To tuck up one's robe or dress. Bl.

yuon'śi, adj. perhaps. Reducing to weakness, humble. Osni wan - unyuzapelo, A cold wave hit us mercilessly. Bl.
yuon'śika, v.a. To reduce to littleness, to humble. B.H.232.13.

yuo'ṗeja, v. (?). Ciyuopeja śni s'elececa. To, mayaluopeja śni yelo, I do not seem to disturb you. No, you do not come in. Bl.

yuo'po, v.a. To press out of shape, press in at the sides e.g. a kettle; to make warp. Bluopo.

yuo'pťeca, v.a. To make less. Bluopteca.
yuo'ptel, cont. of yuopteca.
yuo'pťelya, adv. Making less.
yuo'pťeťu, v.a. To make less. Bluoptetu.
yuo'pťeťuya, adv. Lessening.

yuo'sekse, n. Same as yuos'e.

yuō'seya, 1) v. To get into a hard knot. 2) adv. Tightly, in a hard knot. - iyakaśka. - iyaya, A knot to become real tight. Bl. Cf. yuśkepicaśni. - icu, To tie in a bow knot. - kagege, To tuck. P.

yuo'smag, cont. of yuosmaka. - iyeya.
yuo'smagsmaka, v. red. of yuosmaka.
yuo'smaka, v.a. To make a hollow place or indent. Bluosmaka.

yuo'spe icú s'e máni, v. To limp; to go with a catching gait.

yuo'swa, Cf. óswahan.

yuo's'e, n. One who shoots but does not hit, seemingly used ironically.

yuo'śin, v. To tie in a bow knot or loosely.
yuo'śinśin, v. red. of yuośin. Bl.
yuo'śinyan, adv. Loosely; tied in a bow knot.

yuō'ťa, v.a. To multiply. Bluota.

yuo'tan, v. To make straight e.g. a crooked road with many bends. Also, yuówotan.

yuō'tanin, v.a. To make appear, make manifest, to spread news. Bluotanin.
yuo'taninyan, adv. Making manifest; celebrating.

yuo'tanḱaya, v.a. To make larger e.g. a road by removing things.

yuo'ťapi, n. A multiplying; multiplication.

yuo'ťeḣiḱa, v.a. To make difficult, make hard to be endured. Bluoteḣika.

yuō'tḱonza, v.a. To make of equal length, to finish, to cut off evenly. Bluotkonza.

yuo'tḱuġa, v.a. To lock a door with a key or by hand. BD.

yuo't'ins, cont. of yuot'inza. - icu, To draw in tight. - iyeya.
yuo't'inst'inza, v. red. of yuot'inza.
yuo't'inza, v.a. To press in tight; to make firm in. Bluot'inza.

yuo'wancaya, v. To make or cause all over, everywhere. Bl. Cf. owancaya.

yuo'wanjila, v.a. To unite. Pb.35.

yuō'wecinhan, v. To place in a row, one behind the other. Bluowecinhan.

yuo'wiśni, v. To be unused; to accumulate without being drawn upon, as provisions. R. Bl.

yuo'wotan, v.a. To make straight; to make upright, justify. Bluowotan. -

icu, To set up straight what fell or was upset. Bl.
yuō'wotaⁿla, v.a. To make straight, to make right. Bluowotaⁿla.

yuō'yaȟe, v.a. To absorb, cause to absorb, as with a blotter. To empty a well by pumping. Bluoyaȟe. -- v.n. To evaporate, as water being gone.

yuo'yaṫaⁿyaⁿ, (?). Bl. Cf. oyataⁿyaⁿ.

yupa', v.a. To make bitter. Blupa.

yuṗa'ǧa, v.a. To grasp tightly. Blupaga.
yuṗaȟ', cont. of yupaga. - yuza, To hold tightly.

yuṗaⁿ'ǧa, v.a. To make somebody drunk; to tie up loosely, to make a large bundle. Blupaⁿga. R.
yuṗaⁿȟ', cont. of yupaⁿga. - iyeya.
yuṗaⁿȟ'ya, adv. Loosely, in a large bundle.

yuṗaⁿ'ja, v.a. To seize something soft, e.g. hair, wool. Blupaⁿja.

yupaⁿ'paⁿ, v.a. To make soft by rubbing. Blupaⁿpaⁿ. Maka - . Iⁿyaⁿ na caⁿ oⁿ yupaⁿpaⁿpi, i.e. ten hides.
yupaⁿ'paⁿla, v.a. To make soft e.g. leather. Blupaⁿpaⁿla.

yuṗaⁿś', cont. of yupaⁿja. - iyeya, oyuspa.

yuṗa'ṫuja, v.a. (patuja). To cause to stoop down, to get or bend down. Blupatuja.
yuṗa'ṫuś, cont. of yupatuja. - iyeya. Uⁿgna toka śka - icicu na slisliya acipe ci, i.e. watch out, I will hit you. Bl.

yupce'cela, v.a. To make short, to shorten. Blupcecela.
yupcel'yela, 1) v. To make short, to shorten. Blupcelyela. 2) adv. Shortening, fastening.

yupe', v.a. To make sharp. Blupe.

yuṗe'haⁿ, v.a. To fold up. Blupehaⁿ.
yuṗe'mni, v.a. (pemni). To twist, make warp, as a board. Blupemni. Wociciyaka; yuⁿkaⁿ - mazakiyelo. Bl.
yupe'mnimni, v. red. (yupemni). To warp, crook, twist. Blupemnimni.
yuṗe'mniyaⁿ, adv. Crookedly.

yuṗe'sṫo, v.a. To make pointed, as in shaping a hat. Blupesto.

yuṗi', v.a. To make good. Blupi.
yuṗi'ḱa, 1) v.a. To clothe one well, to make look well. Blupika. 2) n. One who dresses well, one who does things neatly.

yuṗin' naḱi'kśiⁿ, v. To work hard and hurriedly, in order to finish a job in a certain time. Bc. To be anxious to finish a job, by working hard. Cf. kapiⁿ, śkaⁿkapiⁿ. Bl.

yuṗiⁿ'ja, v.a. To pull out the coarse hair from a skin; to pull off the hair or fur. Blupiⁿja.

yuṗiⁿ'ṗiⁿṫapi s'e, adv. (?). - iⁿyaⁿka, as is said of little animals running. Bl.

yuṗiⁿś', cont. of yupiⁿja. - iyeya.
yuṗiⁿ'śpiⁿja, v. red. of yupiⁿja.

yuṗi'ṗiya, adv. red. (yupiya). Nicely. - iglutaⁿpi. B.H.108.1.
yuṗi'ṗiyeȟci, adv. red. of yupiyeȟci. B.H.227.5.

yuṗis', cont. of yupiza. - iyeya.
yuṗi'sṗiza, v. red. of yupiza.

yuṗi'ya, adv. Well, nicely, finely, beautifully. Pb.44.
yuṗi'yakel, adv. Same as yupiya. - igluza. Syn.- taⁿyeȟci.
yuṗi'yeȟci, adv. Very nicely, pleasantly. - aiyohaⁿsya ȟpaye. B.H.118.2. Pb.44.
yuṗi'yela, adv. of yupiya. - tap'ká-psicapi, They played ball beautifully. D.3.

yuṗi'za, v.a. To make creak. Blupiza.

yuṗō', v.a. To make swell, as by scratching. Blupo.

yupōb', cont. of yupopa. - iyeya, To cause to snap, burst.

yupo'caⁿcaⁿ, v. (?). Yugmiyus - , To take one by the hair and shake him to and fro. Bl.

yuṗŏl', cont. of yupota. - iyeya.
yuṗŏl'ṗoṫa, v. red. of yupota.

yupō'ṗa, v.a. To cause to snap or

burst. Blupopa.
yuṗo´ta, v.a. To tear to pieces, as does an eagle a rabbit with the bill and not by scratching. To wear out, to tear to pieces e.g. a garment, to use up. R. Maśtiŋcala hiŋ yupoteȟcelo, as they say of only a few snow flakes falling. Bl.

yupō´waya, v.a. To roughen up e.g. fur or nap. Blupowaya.

yupsa̱g´, cont. of yupsaka. - iyeya.
yupsa̱g´ya, 1) v.a. To cause to break e.g. a string. Yupsagwaya. 2) adv. Breaking, as a cord.
yupsa´ka, v.a. To break or pull in two e.g. a string. Blupsaka.

yupsaŋ´psaŋ, v.a. To wag e.g. the tail; to cause to move back and forth.

yupsa´psaḱa, v. red. of yupsaka.

yupsī´ca, v.a. To make jump, to toss. Blupsica.
yupsil´, cont. of yupsica. - iyeya.

yupsiŋ´psiŋta, v. To whip.

yupsi´psica, v. red. of yupsica.
yupsi´psil, cont. of yupsipsica. - iyeya. B.H.203.7.

yupsoŋ´, v.a. To turn over and spill e.g. water, to spill something by pulling. Blupsoŋ. Also, yupsúŋ.
yupsoŋ´la, v.a. To move something limber, as a willow or a piece of wire. Blupsoŋla. Cf. psoŋpsoŋla.
yupsoŋ´psoŋ, v.a. red. (yupsoŋ). To wag, cause to move back and forth, as in sprinkling a lawn. Cf. glupsuŋpsuŋ.
yupsoŋ´psoŋla, v.a. To make round, to take off the corners. Blupsoŋpsoŋla.
yupsuŋ´, Cf. yupsoŋ etc.

yupśuŋ´, v.a. To pull out sideways, to pull and break, i.e. not by the roots which is yujuŋ. Blupśuŋ.
yupśuŋ´ka, v.a. To double up in a round bunch. Nape glupśuŋka, To clench the fist. Blupśuŋka.
yupśuŋ´ḱaya, adv. Doubled up. Nape - gluza, He struck him in the face with closed fists. B.H.258.15.
yupśuŋ´pśuŋ, v. red. (yupśuŋ). To roll into a wad. Blupśuŋpśuŋ. - iȟpeya, To roll and throw away. D.2. B.H.271.14. To make round like a ball with the hands. Bl.

yupṫa´, v.a. To cut out e.g. a garment after a pattern; to cut off, as in making two shawls out of one big one. Blupta.

yupta´egnag, adv. All together, collectively. - naślog iyayapi. R. Bl.

yuptaŋ´pila s'e, adv. Quickly and in disorder, disorderly, as opposed to katkaŋheya. - wiyukcaŋ; katkaŋheya wiyukcaŋ. - pimic'iye lo; śkeheya pimic'iyelo. Pa - yaŋka, He sat turning his head from side to side, as it were. D.5. BT.
yuptaŋ´ptaŋ, v.a. To turn or roll back and forth with the hand, to rock. Bluptaŋptaŋ. - waŋyaŋka, i.e. a kernel of corn. Nape - cewec'ipeȟcelo, peta kiŋ oile ecetu śni ca. Bl. Makiyuptaŋptaŋ. Ciciyuptaŋptaŋ.
yupṫaŋ´pṫaŋyaŋ, v.a. To roll back and forth, to roll over and over. Bluptaŋptaŋyaŋ.
yupṫaŋ´yaŋ, v.a. To turn over by pulling. Yuptaŋyepicaśni. -- adv. Rolling over. Bluptaŋyaŋ.

yupta´pta, v. red. (yupta). To throw over or down in lumps, as in plowing hard ground. Bluptapta.

yupta´ya, adv. (ptaya). Together, collectively. - egnaka.
yupta´yela, v.a. perhaps. To put together, collect. Bl.

yupte´cela, v.a. To shorten. Bluptecela.
yuptel´yela, adv. Cf. yupcelyela.

yupṫi´napa, v. To take shelter, hide. Yuptinawapa. Yuptinamapa yo, Hide behind me. Bl.
yupṫi´naṗeyakel, adv. In hiding. - muŋ kte lo. Bl.

yupṫo´ḱakiŋ, v. To look around, look for. Yuptowakakiŋ. Cf. okakiŋ. Paha hiyeye kiŋ na wakpala yuŋke kiŋ hena - ośkinic'iye. Makoce lena - onicage tuktel iyayahin na tataŋka ośkiŋciye waŋlake heci pilamayakiye. BT. Taku sitomni - slowayelo, i.e. I know everything. Bl.

yuptu´ǧa, v.a. To pick to pieces. Bluptuga. Also perhaps, yuptuȟ'a.

yupṫu'ja, v.a. To make crack or split, e.g. a board by boring. Bluptuja.
yuptu'ptuja, v. red. of yuptuja.

yuptu'ptuta, v. To scatter in bits here and there, like heavy snowflakes. Bl.

yuptuś', cont. of yuptuja. - iyeya.
yuptu'śḱiya, v.a. To cause to split or crack. Perhaps, yuptuświwakiya, or yuptuświwaya.

yuṗu'ḣṗuġa, v. To hit hard in anger. Bl.

yuṗu'za, v. To make dry, to wipe dry.

yus, cont. of yuza. - najiŋ, To hold one standing. - aya, To lead. Pb.19, 29. Kaśka yus aya, To lead on a bridle or so. Yus iyeya, To throw away. D. 208.

yusa'ḱa, v.a. To whip, snapping. Kasaka, To whip somebody or something; to make a stiff hide soft by bending it to and fro.

yusa'ḱib, adv. Both together. - uŋpi, They both stay together. Also, yusaḱibṫu.

yusa'ksaka, v. To hit from a distance, as horses with a long whip.

yusaŋ', v.a. To make brownish or whitish, to make fade. Blusaŋ.

yusaŋ'pa, v.a. (saŋpa). To make more, cause to increase. Blusaŋpa.

yusa'ṗa, v.a. To blacken. Blusapa.

yuscu', v.a. To have captured some young man or woman's affection or attention and to be elated over it, esp. in ref. to future marriage. Bluscu, luscu. Mascu, I am captured. Cf. ascú.

yuseb', cont. of yusepa. - iyeya.

yus e'napa, v. To lead out of doors. Yus enawicape. B.H.283.8.

yuse'ṗa, v.a. To rub off e.g. paint, to deface; to wear off e.g. the skin from the hand. Blusepa.

yus' icu, v.a. To grasp and take along.

yusiŋ'c'iya yaŋka, v. To be apparently asleep, to say nothing. Haŋkeya - maŋkelo, To look hostile at one. Bl.

yus' iŋ'yaŋka, v.a. To run and catch. Sinte kiŋ - yo. B.H.48.13;217.12.

yusḱa', v.a. To whiten, cleanse, to gather with the fingers. Bluska.

yuska'ḱa, v.a. To equip one with new clothes. Bluskaka. Bl.

yusḱa'ḱiya, v.a. To cause e.g. linen to bleach. Yuskawakiya.

yuska'pa, v. To crack a whip, without striking. Icapsiŋte - .

yusḱa'ṗila s'e, adv. Neatly, clearly, as a job done.

yusḱa'ṗis'e, adv. Close together.

yusḱeb', cont. of yuskepa. - iyeya.
yusḱe'ṗa, v.a. To cause to escape, to drain off, to evaporate. Bluskepa.

yuski'ca, v.a. To press, make tight. Bluskica.
yuskil', cont. of yuskica and yuskita. - iyeya.
yuski'skil, cont. of yuskiskica and yuskiskita.
yusḱi'sḱiṫa, v. red. (of yuskita). To wrap around and round, as in fastening a child on a board. Bluskiskita.
yusḱi'ṫa, v. To bind or tie something hard with a string or so, as a bundle or package; to bind, bandage; to hoop e.g. a barrel. Bluskita.

yusḱi'ya, v.a. (yuza). To cause to marry. Yuswakiya.

yusḱu', v.a. To peel off the skin with the hand; to pare. Blusku. Caŋke kaŋgi na halhata kici waśiŋla kiŋ yuskupi na manil etokśupi keye. MS.96.
yusku'sḱu, v. red. of yusku.
yusḱu'ya, v.a. To make sweet or sour etc., to flavor. Bluskuya.

yusle'ca, v.a. To split with one's hands, to tear e.g. meat. Blusleca.
yuslel', cont. of yusleca. - iyeya.
yuslel'ḱiya, v.a. To cause to split. Yuslélwakiya.
yuslel'ya, v.a. To cause to split. Yuslelwaya.
yusle'sleca, v. red. of yusleca.
yusle'slel, cont. of yuslesleca. - kte.

B.H.76.12.

yusli', v.a. To squeeze out, as matter from a sore; to milk. Blusli.
yusli'tk̇a, v.a. To make taper; to make small by pinching. Bluslitka.

yuslo'haŋ, v.a. To pull a sled, to drag or draw along. - aya, To tow. Bluslohaŋ. - icu, To pull off on, as bark on a tree. Bl. Cf. ayuslohelaka.
yuslo'haŋhaŋ, v. red. of yuslohaŋ. Bluslohaŋhaŋ.
yuslo'haŋyaŋ, adv. Dragging along.
yuslo'hekiya, v.a. To cause to draw along. Yuslohewakiya.
yuslo'slo, v.a. To make soft by pressing with the hand, as an apple. Blusloslo.

yuslul', cont. of yusluta. - icu, iyeya.
yuslul' icu'ṗi, n. A drawer.
yuslul' ognake, n. A bureau, with drawers.
yuslu'ťa, v.a. To pull out, to draw out from under, as a splinter from under a fingernail, or a book from a shelf. Blusluta. Hecel oka hi na ḣeyata - śke. B.H.122.26.

yusmiŋ', v.a. To pull off, pick off what is not tight. Hiŋtkala - . Blusmiŋ.
yusmiŋ'yaŋyaŋ, v.a. To pick off e.g. meat from a bone. Blusmiŋyaŋyaŋ. Cf. R.

yusmi'smi, v. red. (yu-smi). To shave off short e.g. the hair. Blusmismi.

yusmi'smiŋ, v. red. of yusmiŋ. Blusmismiŋ.

yusna', v.a. To ring or tinkle, as with little bells. Blusna. To pull off anything being on a string, as beads, to ravel out e.g. a stocking. Same as yuswa.
yusna'sna, v. red. of yusna. Blusnasna.

yusni', v.a. To put out, extinguish e.g. a fire, to turn out a light, lamp; to make cold. Petijaŋjaŋ - . Blusni.
yusni'sni, v. red. of yusni. Blusnisni.
yusni'snis icu, Cf. yusnis'. Same as mahelhel, mahehe, iyaya. WE.
yusnis'', v. To become invisible. Yusnis' iyaya, iblabla, To be visible with one's head and then invisible, as children do hiding their head behind something by lowering themselves. If this is done repeatedly, we say: Yusnisnis' icu. WE.

yuso', v.a. To cut in strings or strips e.g. a hide. Bluso.

yusol', cont. of yusota. - iyeya.
yusol'kiya, v.a. To cause to use up. Yusolwakiya.
yusol'ya, v.a. To cause to use up. Yusolwaya.

yuso'so, v. red. of yuso. Blusoso.

yuso'ta, v.a. To use up, make an end of, expend. Blusota.

yuspa'ya, v.a. To make wet, to sponge. Bluspaya.

yusťaŋ'k̇a, v.a. To moisten. Blustaŋka.

yusťo', v.a. To smooth down e.g. the hair, to make smooth. Blusto.
yusťo'k̇iya, v.a. To cause to make smooth. Yustowakiya.
yusťo'sťo, v. red.(of yusto). To stroke. D.257.
yusťo'ya, v.a. To cause to make smooth. Yustowaya. -- adv. perhaps. Making smooth. Iyake kiŋ - taŋyaŋ ecoŋ wo. MS.481.

yusu', v.a. To make right; to make things ready. Also, yuecetu. Blusu. - egle, To put things ready, so as to have them one hand when needed. Syn.- yuwiŋyeya.

yu'sus, cont. of yusyuza. Same as yúsyus (yusyuza). - iwahoya etc., To instruct one impressively, i.e. taking hold of his arm repeatedly, to be sure to instruct. - iwahowicaya yo na taŋyeḣci ecoŋpi kte lo. EM. Bl.

yusu'ťa, v.a. To make firm. Blusuta.

yusu'ya, 1) v.a. To cause to make right. Yusuwaya. 2) adv. Ready. Taku oyasiŋ yusuya he. - egle. B.H.241.1; 251.7.

yuswa', v.a. To ravel out e.g. a stocking, to pick to pieces e.g. wool. Bluswa. Same as yusna.
yuswa'swa, v. red. of yuswa. Bluswaswa.
yuswa'ya, v. or adv. To pick to pieces.

yuswu´, v.a. To make a rattling noise, as in taking hold of shelled corn. Bluswu.
yuswu´pi s'e, adv. of yuswu. Léceya taku au tka - au welo, i.e. iglaka au śni, hekapi. - icagapelo, as is said when all the children of a family do grow up well. Bl.
yuswu´swu, v. red. of yuswu.

yus´yus, cont. of yusyuza. Also, yusus.

yus'o´, v.a. To cut off a strip at the edge of something. BD. -- v.n. To swim as a duck or muskrat; to come up for air, as a muskrat brings its head above water and so gulps air. - nunwan. Perhaps the idea of exhaustion is suggested from the apparent comp. yuza-o.
yus'o´ǩiya, v.a. To cause to swim ducklike, to make come to the surface. Yus'owakiya.
yus'ō´las'e, adv. In an exhausted manner, as one tired. - igluśtan.
yus'ō´s'e, adv. Almost, scarcely, hardly. - t'a, He almost died.
yus'o´s'o, v. red. of yus'o.
yus'o´ya, adv. perhaps. All tired out. Kitanyel - wawatelo, i.e. have eaten but little. Bl.
yus'o´yaȟel, adv. In an exhausted manner, all tired out; contrary to all expectation. - ecamon. - waglihunni yelo. BT. Same as kitanyankel.
yus'o´yeȟci, adv. Same as yus'oyakel. - wahi. Bl.

yuśa´, v.a. To make red by rubbing or touching. Bluśa.

yuśab´, cont. of yuśapa. - iyeya.
yuśab´ya, v.a. To cause to soil. Yuśabwaya.
yuśa´ṗa, v.a. To soil, blacken, to defile anything. Bluśapa.

yuśe´ca, v.a. To deaden; to make dry. Bluśeca.
yuśe´kśeca, v. red. of yuśeca.
yuśel´, cont. of yuśeca. - iyeya, To cause to wither.

yuśib´, cont. of yuśipa. - iyeya.
yuśi´bśiṗa, v. red. of yuśipa.

yuśi´ca, v.a. To make bad, to injure, spoil. Bluśica.

yuśī´gla, v.a. To make angry. Bluśigla.

yuśi´ȟtin, v.a. To enfeeble, to debase. Bluśiȟtin.
yuśi´ȟtinpi, n. Feebleness.
yuśi´ȟtinyan, adv. Feebly.

yuśil´ȟ'an, v.a. (śilȟ'an). To make act badly. Bluśilȟ'an.
yuśil´ȟ'anyan, adv. Causing to do badly.
yuśil´ya, adv. Treated badly. - ecanicompelo, They wronged you. Bl.

yuśi´na iȟpéya, v. To take away one's shawl. Yuśina tancocola iȟpeya, To take away shawl and render naked. Bl.

yuśin´, v.n. To wrinkle. Paȟte yuśinwakiya.
yuśin´kiya, v.a. To make wrinkle e.g. the forehead. Ite, paȟte - , To frown at. Yuśinwakiya.
yuśin´pi, n. Wrinkles.
yuśin´śin, v. red. (yuśin). To wrinkle.
yuśin´yan, adv. Wrinkled, folded. - iyakaśka, icu, To tie a knot in such a manner (with a loop) that it can be loosened by pulling; yukipaś iyakaśka. Bl.

yuśi´ṗa, v.a. To bend e.g. wire etc. Bluśipa.

yuśka´, v.a. To loosen, to untie. Bluśka.

yuśkan´śkan, v.a. To cause to move about, to shake up somebody or something. Bluśkanśkan.

yuśka´śka, v. red. of yuśka. B.H.38.2.

yuśǩe´han, v.a. To make wild. Bluśkehan. Bluśkehin kta.
yuśǩe´hanhan, v. red. (yuśkehan). To make prance about; to stir up e.g. people. Bluśkehanhan. B.H.261.13.

yuśke´pa, v.a. To wring out e.g. water from wet clothes. Bl.
yuśke´ya, adv. Free, loose. - napapi, unpi.

yuśǩi´, v.a. To plait. Bluśki.
yuśǩi´ca, v.a. To press, squeeze, wring e.g. clothes; to press out water by twisting, to wring e.g. a wash rag. Bluśkica.
yuśǩil´, cont. of yuśkica. - iyeya.
yuśǩī´ṗi, part. Plaited, gathered in folds.

yuśki'śka, v.a. To make rough, make notches. Bluśkiśka.
yuśki'śkeya, v.a. To cause to make difficult. Yuśkiśkewaya.
yuśki'śkica, v. red. of yuśkica.

yuśkōb', cont. of yuśkopa. - iyeya.
yuśkō'kpa, v.a. To hollow out e.g. a trough. Bluśkokpa. -- adj. or adv. perhaps. Śina - yuza yo, el ognakiŋ kte, i.e. to hold the blanket in such a way as to make a concavity for things to be poured in.
yuśkō'pa, v.a. To bend, to make crooked or twisting. Bluśkopa.
yuśko'śkopa, v. red. of yuśkopa.

yuśku', v.a. To shell off e.g. corn with the hand. Bluśku.
yuśku'śku, v. red. of yuśku.

yuśla', v.a. To make bare or bald; to cut off the hair, to shear e.g. sheep; to pull out weeds. Bluśla.
yuśla'kiya, v.a. To cause to pull, pluck or shear off. Yuślawakiya.
yuśla'śla, v. red. of yuśla. Pejí-hota - , i.e. pulling up quantities of sage brush. D.112.
yuśla'ya, v.a. To cause to make bare, bald etc. Yuślawaya.

yuśle'ca, v.a. To split with the hand. Bluśleca.

yuśli', v.a. To press or squeeze with the hand. Bluśli.
yuśli'ya, adv. Pressing. - iyakaśka, To squeeze up and tie tight.

yuślog', cont. of yuśloka. - iyeya.
yuślōg'ki, v.a. To snatch away. Yuślogwaki.
yuślog'ya, v.a. To cause to pull off or out. Yuślogwaya.
yuślō'ka, v.a. To pull off e.g. a garment; to pull out e.g. a cork. Bluśloka.
yuślo'śloka, v. red. of yuśloka.

yuślul', cont. of yuśluta. - iyeya.
yuślu'śluta, v. red.(of yuśluta). To make smooth or slippery; to let slip from one. Bluśluśluta.
yuślu'ta, v.a. To slip out, to let slip from one, as a fish. Bluśluta.

yuśma', v.a. To make deep e.g. by pouring water. Also, yuśmé. Bluśma.
yuśme'ya, adv. Deeply.

yuśna', v.a. To drop anything, to let slip; to miss while trying to catch. Bluśna.
yuśna'koŋza, v. To pretend to make a mistake. Yuśnawakoŋza.
yuśna'pi, n. A mistake.
yuśna'śna, v. red. (yuśna). To try to catch and fail often, to miss. Bluśnaśna.
yuśna'śni, adv. Accurately. Bl.
yuśna'śni ecoŋpi, n. Accuracy. Bl.

yuśni'ja, v.a. To cause to wither. Bluśnija.
yuśni'śnija, v. red. of yuśnija. Bluśniśnija.

yuśō'śa, v.a. To make muddy e.g. water. Bluśośa.

yuśpa', v.a. To break off, to divide. Bluśpa. Igluśpa, To free one's self from. Wicaśa kiŋ le - śni ca eniyayiŋ kte, This man is not honest, has no good intentions, so stay away from him. FP.
yuśpa'śpa, v. red. (yuśpa). To break into pieces e.g. bread; to scratch off pieces. Bluśpaśpa. - wiyopeya, To retail. Also, yuksaksa. Bl.
yuśpa'śpaya, adv. In parcels, pieces. Makoce kiŋ - iwicakiyute. B.H.73.13.

yuśpi', v.a. To pick or gather e.g. berries, to pull off, pick off e.g. cherries from a tree. Bluśpi.

yuśpi'ka, (?). Íogmus - waeye eyelo. Bl.

yuśpi'śpi, v. red. of yuśpi.

yuśpu', v.a. To pull off what is tight with the hand. Bluśpu.
yuśpu'la ota, n. Red root, green amoranth. Amoranthus retroflexus. BT. #22.

yuśpu'śpu, v. red. of yuśpu. Bluśpuśpu.
yuśpu'śpupi, n. Pieces broken off; change, coin money.

yuśtaŋ', v.a. To finish anything, to perfect; to settle e.g. a question in a meeting; to have decreed. Bluśtaŋ. Zitkala taŋka oyasiŋ kiiŋyaŋkapi kta gluśtaŋpi.

yuśta'śta, v. To soak a skin, hide,

as a preparation for dressing it; to moisten one's skin. Bluśtaśta. Tahayuśtaśta.

yuśtu'ta, v. To rub or soak the feet as with snow. Ed.

yuśu'ja, v.a. To crush e.g. bones; to break in slivers, e.g. by twisting a tough piece of wood. Bluśuja.

yuśuŋ'oŋṗa, n. The form or shape of a "V", like that made by the poles of a travois on the back of a dog, or that made by cranes traveling either way off and back from the wing tips of the leader. - kahya. MS.104. Yuśuŋuŋk'oŋpa kahya. BS.

yuśuś', cont. of yuśuja. - iyeya.
yuśu'śuja, v. red. of yuśuja.

yuś'ag', cont. of yuś'aka.
yuś'ag'ya, 1) v.a. To over-burden, overload. Yuś'agwaya. 2) v.n. To have much of a thing considered a burden. He tuwa śuŋḣpala yuś'agye, yuś'ag ble lo, i.e. then somebody has plenty of little dogs. Bl.
yuś'a'k̇a, v.n. To be heavily laden, have much as one can carry. Bluś'aka.

yuś'e', v.a. (ś'e). To cause to fall in drops, to make drip e.g. drops of medicine. Bluś'e. Cf. ś'eś'e.
yuś'e'ś'e, v. red. of yuś'e. Bluś'eś'e.

yuś'iŋ'ś'iŋ, v.a. To tickle, e.g. under the arm.

yuś'iŋ'yaya, v.n. To be afraid, be frightened, be surprised. Mayuś'iŋyaya. Wicayuś'iŋyaye s'e taku waŋblaka, nawaḣ'oŋ, I saw, heard, unexpectedly something very beautiful. BE. D.215.
yuś'iŋ'yeya, v.a. To frighten, scare. Yuś'iŋyewaya.

yū'ṫa, v.a. To eat anything. Wáta, yáta, uŋyútapi.

yuta'egle, v. To sweep together in a heap e.g. of hay, rubbish etc. GA. BT.

yuṫa'hena, v.a. To make nearer, to put towards. Blutahena. - icu, To draw it this way or towards himself.

yuta'k̇iŋ, v.a. To cause to lean. Blutakiŋ. Toki - śni lecel maŋkahelo, i.e. to be sitting motionless. Bl.
yuta'k̇iŋyaŋ, adv. Leaning.

yuṫa'k̇u, v.a. To make a thing to be something. B.H.70.4.
yuṫa'k̇uniśni, v.a. To destroy. Blutakuniśni.
yuṫa'k̇uniśniyaŋ, adv. Destroying.
yuṫa'k̇uśni, v.a. To bring to naught; to frustrate. Blutakuśni.

yutaŋ', v.a. To touch, to feel. Blutaŋ. Cf. yutitaŋ.

yuṫaŋ', v.a. To honor, glorify. Blutaŋ. Cf. yataŋ.

yuṫaŋ'cola, v.a. To make naked. Blutaŋcola.

yutaŋ'iŋ, v.a. To make manifest. Blutaŋiŋ.
yutaŋ'iŋyaŋ, adv. Manifestly, openly.

yutaŋ'k̇a, v.a. To make great or large, to enlarge. Blutaŋka.

yutaŋ'kal icu, v.a. To call one outside. Yutaŋkal iyeya, To take one outside.

yutaŋ'ka s'e, adv. Seemingly made big. Bc.
yutaŋ'k̇aya, v.a. To enlarge something, as by adding e.g. a picture made larger, or a house given an addition. Cf. yuotaŋkaya. -- adv. Largely, greatly. - kaga.

yutaŋ'ni, v.a. To make old, wear out. Blutaŋni.
yutaŋ'nik̇a, v.a. To wear out e.g. clothes, to make old. Blutaŋnika.

yutaŋ'om, adv. Leaning. - egle, To place leaning. BD. - haŋ, It is leaning.
yutaŋ'oŋpa, v.n. To lean. P.

yutaŋ'taŋ, v. red. of yutaŋ. Blutaŋtaŋ.
yutaŋ'taŋkel mani, v. To grope, as a blind person does. Bl.

yuṫaŋ'yaŋ, v.a. perhaps. To make good. -- adv. Praising.
yuṫaŋ'yaŋk̇el, adv. Really, in earnest, for good. - ecamoŋ kta.

Yu'ṫapi Wakaŋ, n. prop. Holy Communion.

yuťa'ťa, v.a. To shake off e.g. dust from a garment; to scrape or brush off with the hand. Blutata.

yuta'wacinhinyanza, v.a. To make cross. Blutawacinhinyanza.

yuťēb', cont. of yutepa. - iyeya.
yuťe'bťeṗa, v. red. of yutepa.

yuťe'ca, v.a. To make new, renew. Bluteca. Pb.35.

yuťe'han, v.a. To put off, prolong, to make slow, retard. Blutehan.
yuťe'han s'e, adv. Delaying. Bc.

yuťel'ya, v.a. To renew. LP.

yuťe'pa, v.a. To wear off short, as a bolt on a wagon. Blutepa. R.

yuťib' iyaya, v.n. To draw up, as does leather when it is near a fire. Bl.
yuťib'ya, adv. (yutipa). To be drawn up, as burned leather, or as a muscle cramp. - yanka.

yuťi'ca, v.a. To scrape away, e.g. to slide snow away with the hand; to paw, as does a horse. Blutica.
yuťil', cont. of yutica. - iyeya.

yuťi'mahel, adv. Into the house. - icu, To take into the house. Bl. B.H.249. 11.

yuťī'ṗa, v.a. To cramp e.g. the muscles to make crisp or draw up e.g. burned leather. Siyutipa-simayutipa, To have cramps in the feet, my feet. Teziyutipa, To have cramps in the stomach. Tahuyutipa, To have a cramp in the neck.

yuťi'ťan, v.a. To pull. Blutitan. Cf. yuzica, To stretch. - icu, To get by pulling, as in a tug-of-war, or as in treating a stubborn horse.
yuťi'ťanyan, v.a. To cause to pull at. Yutitanwaya.

yutkab' omani, v. To walk with difficulty, as through gumbo. Bl.

yutkan'la, adj. Plenty, plenteous; much, abundant. P. Bl. Syn.- yugela.

yutǩe'ya, adv. Deeply, as is said of a bluff shore where the water is deep.

yutǩons', cont. of yutkonza. - iyeya.
yutkon'za, v.a. To cut off even, as with shears. Blutkonza.

yutǩu'ǧa, v.a. To break off square. Blutkuga.
yutkuȟ', cont. of yutkuga. - iyeya.
yutkun'za, Cf. yutkonza.

yutku'tǩuǧa, v. red. (yutkuga). To break or divide in several pieces.

yutog'ye, v.a. To make different. - econ.

yuto'kan, v.a. To put in another place, remove; to reject. Blutokan.
yuto'kankan, v. red. of yutokan. - iyeya, To scatter abroad.
yuťō'ǩanl, adv. In another place. - iyeya, To remove, push away. - yuza, To lead away. - unkiciyuzapi ye. Pb. 18.
yuto'kanyan, adv. In another place, removed. - iyeya,

yutō'keca, v.a. To alter, revoke. Blutokeca.

yuťo'ťo, v.a. To clear off e.g. a field. Blutoto.

yuto'tobya, v.a. (yutotopa). To soak and make soft. Yutotobwaya.
yuto'toṗa, v.n. To become soft, as leather by soaking.

yuťug'ťuǩa, v. red. (yutuka). To pick to pieces e.g. furs.

yuťuȟ'yela, adv. Bent, doubled up, stooped, as an old man. - hiyaya, mani.

yuťu'ǩa, v.a. To pull or destroy e.g. furs; to spoil. Blutuka.

yuťun'ťunpa, v.a. To make slimy or slippery. R. Bl.

yuťu'ta, v.a. To make smart. Blututa.

yutu'tka, v.a. To break in small pieces. Blututka.
yutu'tkayakel, adv. In parts, pieces, in small amounts. - econ, eya, To do or say something only partly and imperfectly. LP.

yuťu'ťuǩa, v. red. of yutuka.

yut'a´, v.a. To choke to death. Blut'a.
yut'a´t'a, v. red.(of yut'a). To benumb. P.

yut'iⁿs´, cont. of yut'iⁿza. - iyeya.
yut'iⁿ´st'iⁿza, v. red. of yut'iⁿza.
yut'iⁿ´za, v.a. To draw tight, to tighten e.g. a saddle-girth. Kola, - yo, as a visitor would say who wanted to smoke the pipe.

yuuⁿg´, cont. of yuuⁿka. - iyeya.
yuuⁿ´ka, v.a. To make lie down, throw down; to demolish. Bluuⁿka. Ciyuuⁿke kiⁿ wakaⁿ kte lo, na mayaluuⁿke kiⁿ pilaniciyiⁿ kte lo, eya.

yuuⁿ´zi, v.a. To take one around the waist and pull backwards. Bluuⁿzi. Na waⁿna caⁿte paȟloke el caⁿ eya ikoyagya na - hekta pagopta yuziⁿ na icu na topa lila yutitaⁿ. Syn.- yutitaⁿ.

yuwa´ciⁿko, v.a. To make angry. Bluwaciⁿko.
yuwa´ciⁿksapa, v.a. To make wise. Bluwaciⁿksapa.
yuwa´ciⁿtaⁿka, v.a. To make magnanimous; to make stubborn. Bluwaciⁿtaⁿka.
yuwa´ciⁿtoⁿ, v.a. To make intelligent. Bluwaciⁿtoⁿ.

yuwa´ğa, v.a. To twist, roll, turn, as the hands in running. Bluwaga.

yuwa´ȟpanica, v.a. To make poor. Bluwaȟpanica.
yuwa´ȟwaka, v.a. To make mild or gentle. Bluwaȟwaka.
yuwa´ȟwala, v.a. To make gentle. Bluwaȟwala.

yuwa´kaⁿ, v.a. To make holy, consecrate or make special. Bluwakaⁿ.
yuwa´kaⁿyaⁿ, adv. Consecrating, keeping holy, piously. Lila - ecoⁿpi. B.H. 57.12;73.7.

yuwa´nica, v.a. To destroy, annihilate; to spend one's money. Taku wowaś'ake luhapi kiⁿ ko niyuwanicapi ciⁿpi.
yuwa´nil, cont. of yuwanica. - aya, To bring to naught.

yuwaⁿ´jila, v.a. To make into one, unite. B.H.233.9.

yuwaⁿ´kal, v. To cause to move upward. - icu, To lift or raise up. - iyeya. - aya, To raise, put on a high place, to honor. Nakpa - ikikcu, To prick up one's ears.

yuwaⁿ´kala, v.a. To make soft or tender. Bluwaⁿkala.

yuwaⁿ´kaṫu, v.a. To raise, exalt. B.H. 232.14.
yuwaⁿ´kaṫuya, 1) v.a. To raise e.g. a curtain, i.e. let it go up; to promote. 2) adv. Upwards, above.

yuwas´, cont. of yuwaza. - iyeya.
yuwas´ kte, v.a. To bother, annoy by pulling him here and there. Yuwas wakte.

yuwa´sla, v.a. To grease, by rubbing salve on one's hands. Bluwasla.

yuwa´sna, v.a. To make any food very tasty; wasná was always a very much sought-for dish. Bluwasna. He luwasna.

yuwa´swaza, v. red. of yuwaza.
yuwas´ya, adv. In a twisting manner; vexing.

yuwa´śakala, v.a. To make cheap or easy. Bluwaśakala.

yuwa´śte, v.a. To make good; to bless. Bluwaśte.

yuwa´ś'ag, cont. of yuwaś'aka. - iyeya.
yuwa´ś'agya, v.a. To cause to make strong. Yuwaś'agwaya.
yuwa´ś'aka, v.a. To make strong; to strengthen. Bluwaś'aka.
yuwa´ś'akeśni, v.a. To make weak, feeble. Bluwaś'akeśni.

yuwa´za, v.a. To twist or turn, as the handsdo in running; to vex, tease, annoy and continue to do so; to throw up dirt with the foot and let it down on the back as a bull does. Maka yuwaza. Cf. igluwaza.

yuwe´, v. To make bleed. Bl.

yuwe´ğa, v.a. To break e.g. a stick with the hands but not entirely off. Bluweğa.
yuweȟ´, cont. of yuwega. - iyeya.
yuwe´ȟweğa, v.a. To break something in different places; to hike out. Bluweȟwega.
yuwe´ȟweȟ, cont. of yuweȟwega. - iyeya.
yuweȟ´ya, v.a. To cause to break. Yuwe-

ȟwaya.

yuwi´, v.a. To wrap around, bind up; to bandage. Bluwi. R.

yuwi´caǩa, v.a. To make true, to prove or convince; to show that a cause is true, and to establish it. Bluwicaka. Tokśa, bluwicakiᵑ ktelo, In time, I will prove it.
yuwi´caǩeȟca, adv. Truthfully. - oyaka, To tell a thing not as it is, to make a thing appear true by telling it as true. Cf. yawicakeyeȟci.
yuwi´caǩeya, adv. perhaps. Telling a thing as true. B.H.70.4. Same as yuwicakeya s'e.

yuwi´caśa, v.a. To make manly.
yuwi´caśaśni, v.a. To make mean; to get excited. Bluwicaśaśni.

yuwi´coȟ'aᵑ, v.a. To turn a trifling affair into something big. EE.

yuwi´gnuni, v.a. To cause to perish, to destroy. Bluwignuni. R. Bl.
yuwi´gnuniya, v.a. To cause to destroy. Yuwignuniwaya. R. Bl.

yuwil´witaya, adv. Made to be grouped in different places. - ahiyaye, A big crowd together but then smaller parties and persons about nearby. Bc.

yuwi´nuȟcala, v.a. To make a woman of, to render effeminate. Bluwinuȟcala.

yuwiᵑ´ǧa, v.a. To turn around, turn back. Bluwiᵑga. Bl.
yuwiᵑȟ´, cont. of yuwiᵑga. - iyeya.
yuwiᵑ´ȟwiᵑǧa, v. red. of yuwiᵑga.
yuwiᵑȟ´ya, adv. Coming around. - glicu.

yuwiᵑ´ja, v.a. To bind down e.g. with a piece of wire; to make limber or pliant.
yuwiᵑś´, cont. of yuwiᵑja. - iyeya.
yuwiᵑ´świᵑja, v.a. To make limber. Bluwiᵑświᵑja.
yuwiᵑś´ya, v.a. To cause to bend down. Yuwiᵑświya.

yuwiᵑ´ťa, v.a. Ite - , To salute, as the Dakotas do when they desire peace etc., to wipe the face of another with the hands, not actually, but in gesture, a sign of friendly relations.

yuwiᵑ´yaᵑ, v.a. Same as yuwinuȟcala.
yuwiᵑ´yaᵑke s'e, adv. Being a bad woman. - uᵑ, One who is a bad woman, but who wishes to be thought good.

yuwiᵑ´yeya, v.a. To get ready, make ready, prepare. Bluwiᵑyeya.

yuwi´pi, n. Transparent stones, usually found on ant hills and used in the wakaᵑ wicoȟ'aᵑ called yuwipi, which consists in one being tied all round and being loosed by magic.
yuwi´pi waśi´cuᵑ, n. A sacred round hard stone that is supposed to have power in the hands of those who have dreamed. - iwicawahaᵑble. Same as tuᵑkaᵑ. Cf. waśicuᵑ.

yuwi´ťaᵑ, v.a. To honor, glorigy. Bluwitaᵑ.
yuwi´ťaᵑťaᵑ, v.a. To make proud by giving good things.

yuwi´ťaya, 1) v.a. To collect together or assemble e.g. horses. Bluwitaya. 2) adv. All together, assembled.

yuwi´tko, v.a. To make foolish. Bluwitko. B.H.102.16.
yuwi´tkotko, v.a. To make foolish. Bluwitkotko. Also, yuwitkotkoka.

yuwi´wihe s'e, adv. In large numbers. - ahiyaye, To pass by in crowds. Bl.

yuwi´yakp̣a, v.a. To make shine; fig., to interpret. Bluwiyakpa.

yuwo´hol, Same as yuwaᵑkal, iwosla. Nakpa kiᵑ - ikikcu, To prick up one's ears. Bl.

yuwo´otaᵑla, v.a. To adjust. P.

yuwō´slal, v. (woslal). To make upright. - egle, iyeya, icu, To set up on end. B.H.280.10. Pb.44.
yuwō´slaťa, v.a. To set upright e.g. a flag pole. Bluwoslata.

yū´za, v.a. To take hold of, catch; to take a wife. Bluza. Caᵑnuᵑpa ciciyuziᵑ kte, as an Indian would say to Wakaᵑtaᵑka, i.e. will hold the pipe for you, i.e. will pray. BT.

yuza´haᵑ, v.a. To make a noise, one made by tearing cloth. Bluzahaᵑ.

yu´za hi´yaᵑka, v.a. To grab running. Taśina el yuza hiyaᵑke. B.H.29.14.

yuza'mni, v.a. To uncover, to open by pulling something away, as in uncovering a bed by pulling away the blankets etc.; to find one by pulling away a screen or curtain; to spread out. Bluzamni. Tiyopa kiƞ - hiyeya.

yuza'mnihaƞ, adv. Standing open. - egle.

yuza'mnimni, v. red. of yuzamni.

yuza'mniyaƞ, adv. Open. Maȟpiya tatiyopa kiƞ - haƞ. B.H.286.2.

yuzaƞ', v.a. To part or separate e.g. tall grass, to push aside; to raise up e.g. a curtain. Bluzaƞ.

yuza'za, v. To pick to pieces e.g. sinew or a piece of cloth.

yuze', v.a. To dip, lade out e.g. food from a kettle; to skim. Bluze.

yuzi'ca, v.a. To stretch e.g. a skin or a rubber. Bluzica. Amagaju nahaƞ cu kiƞ(haƞ) yuzicapi s'e u ktelo, It will grow fast (as grain) when it rains and dews. Bl.

yuzi'gzica, v. red. (yuzica). To stretch, make pliable. Bluzigzica.

yuzil', cont. (of yuzica). Stretching. - icu, To stretch.

yuzoƞ'ta, v.a. To make honest; to make them better men. Bl.

yuzug', cont. of yuzuka. - icu.

yuzu'ka, v.a. To stretch out from one. Bluzuka.

yuzu'kapis'e, adv. Moving in a straight direction up or down, or in any other direction. Yuƞkaƞ taku waƞ skayela maȟpiya eciyataƞ u na - haƞ na tipi kiƞ iwaƞkal ikiyela hinajiƞ.

yuzu'zeca, v.a. To turn into a snake. B.H.49.2.

* * * *

Z

za, Cf. yuza.

zahaŋ', adj. Cf. zazahaŋ.

zamni', Cf. yuzamni.
zamni'mni s'e, adv. As though uncovering. Bl.
zamni'yahaŋ, part. Uncovered. Bl.
zamni'yaŋ, adv. Uncovered. - uŋ. Bl.

zaŋ'kel, adv. With a whimpering cry. - ie, To speak with a whining, crying voice, so as to call for pity.

zaŋni', adj. Well, not sick. Mazaŋni.
zaŋni'ǩa, adj. Healthy, sound, well. Mazaŋnika.
zaŋni'yaŋ, adv. Well, in good health. - wauŋ. Also, zaŋníyaŋǩel.

zaŋzaŋ'la, n. Gauze, mosquito net, etc. -- adv. Scattered, standing far apart. R.
zaŋzaŋ'yela, adv. Unprotecting, thinly covering. - igluza, To have very light clothing on, that does not protect. Same as śuŋkaŋyaŋkel. Bl.

za'pťaŋ, adj. num. Five.
za'pťaŋǩiya, adv. In five ways, in five places.
za'pťaŋla, adv. Only five.
za'pťaŋpťaŋ, adv. By fives, five apiece.

zaza'haŋ, adj. Ragged.

za'zeca, adj. Here and there, few, as trees standing about, or the few hairs on a person's head. Cf. huzazeca.
zaze'cala, adj. dim. (zazeca). Thinly, thinly strewn and the like. Peji kiŋ - yuŋkelo, i.e. thin. Bl. Syn.- ototola.
zaze'cayela, adv. Scattered, here and there as shocks of grain. - hiyeyelo. Bl. Syn.- glakeyela.

ze, adj. Disturbed. Cf. caŋze.
ze'ǩa, adj. Shaken, disturbed. Caŋzeka.
ze'ya, v. root. Cf. caŋzeya.

zeze', adv. perhaps. Hanging, dangling. - ikoyake, To hangs downward, dangling as a lap robe does on the sides. BT.
ze'zeya, adv. Swinging, dangling. - otka. - otkeic'iya.

zi, adj. Yellow.

zibzi'ṗela, adj. Thin, fine, as is silk or fine cloth.

zica', n. The reddish gray squirrel.

zi'ca, Cf. yuzica.

zica'ȟota, n. The common gray squirrel. R. Bl.

zigzi'ca, adj. Flimsy, not firm; elastic; a rubber hose, n. Ogle - , A sweater.

zilya', v.a. To smoke, fumigate. Zilwaya. Pejuta kiŋ he zilya ye.

ziŋl'yeic'iya, v. refl. To have spent everything. Ziŋlyemic'iya. Bl.

ziŋtka'caŋȟpaŋla, n. A small water bird with a large bill. R. Bl.

ziŋtka'la, n. The generic name for small birds. Also, zitkála.
- iṗátapi, Moss, mold. R. Bl.
- ógnake, A bird cage.
- sitúpi háŋska, A peacock. Bl.
- slila, A kind of bird. Same as the ptegaglonica, ziŋtka tanagila. Bl.
- wíṗatapi, The thin moss growing in figures on rocks, said to be ornaments made by bird. Bl.
- tacaŋ, The false or bastard indigo, the river locust. Amorpha practicosa. The pulse family. Mini aglagla uŋpi, growing near water. It seems to be a shrub and not a weed like the other kinds of ziŋtka tacaŋ. It is so called because birds alight on it in the prairie where there are no trees. They were used to make arrows from the stalks. Also, śuŋktawote.

ziŋtka'to, n. The blue bird.
ziŋtka'to gleglega, n. The blue jay.
ziŋtka'to ikpi'ska, n. The blue bird, a jay. Common in the Black Hills.
ziŋtka'zila, n. The warbling vireo.
ziŋtka'zila cik'ala, n. The yellow-billed fly catcher.

ziŋtki'scila, n. The tree sparrow.

ziṗaŋ', n. A youngster about ten years old or younger, boy or girl.

zi'ṗela, adj. Thin, fine. Aguyapi - , A pancake. Cf. zibzipela.

ziśa', adj. Reddish.

zi'ťa, v.n. To smoke. Cf. izita.

zitka'la, Cf. ziⁿtkala.
- tawote, n. Prairie bird'sfoot trefoil. Hosackia americana. The pulse family. BT. #93. Also, pepper grass. Lepidium apetalum. Bm. #280. It in the form of a tea is good for the kidneys.
- wiṗatapi, wakśupi, n. Two kinds of thin moss growing on rocks. A third kind is iⁿyaⁿ wakśupi. Bl.

zitka'tacaⁿ, n. Wild tea, lead plant, shoe strings. Amorpha canescens. The pulse family. Also, śuⁿktawote, blaye zitkatacaⁿ hu stola. HM.BT.#11. #130. #136.
- mini aglagla uⁿpi, Same as ziⁿtkala tacaⁿ. Bl. #130.

zitka'to cik'ala, n. The blue bird, a corn eater. In April the Indian would say: Waⁿna zitkato agli yelo, wiⁿyeya uⁿpo igluwiⁿyeya po. After his return there occur cold rains that kill many horses, because they have shed their winter hair. BT. Ziⁿtkato s'e ahiyaye, i.e. pass by dressed in blue. Bl.

zitka'to glegleġa, n. The blue jay. Also, zitkato taⁿka. FR. Note: iwaśikśicuⁿ.

zitka'zi cik'ala, n. The yellow-billed fly catcher.

zitka'zila, n. The warbling vireo.

ziya', 1) v.a. To dye or paint yellow. Ziwaya. 2) adj. Yellowish.
ziya'to, adj. Green.
ziye'la, adj. Yellowish. Bl.
zizi', adj. red. (zi). Yellow.

zizib'yela, adv. Thinly, finely. - opi, To inflict a slight, non-dangerous wound.
zizi'ṗela, adj. Fine, thin. Yuⁿkaⁿ iⁿyaⁿ waⁿ icu - ca na he pestoyela kaga.

zizi' śkoṗela, n. A banana. Also, śkoṗela.

zohe'la, adv. Very slowly, as in going. - bla.

zomi', adj. Trying to get things from others by pretending to be poor. Mazomi.
zomi'ǩa, n. One who tries to get things from others by pretending to be poor.
zomi'yaⁿǩel, adv. In a tricky manner. - icu, To get things in a sly way by pretending to be poor.

zoⁿlya'ǩel, adv. (zuⁿta). Right, honestly. - ecoⁿ wo, Do it right. Bt. B.H.155.17.

zoⁿ'ťa, adj. Honest, trustworthy. Waⁿ! nizóⁿte śni yelo, You do not act right. Bt. Cf. zuⁿta.
zoⁿ'ťaheca, n. An honest person. R.Bl.

zoⁿťa'heya, adv. In close succession; connectedly.

zuhaⁿ', adj. Striped. Also, zuháⁿhaⁿ, red.
zuhe'ya, adv. In a striped manner.

zuⁿlyá, adv. Well, correctly; joined. Also, zuⁿlyákel.

zuⁿmi'yaⁿkel, adv. Same as siⁿkpeyakel. - lila wota, wipiic'iya.

zuⁿ'ta, adj. Connected, braided, woven together.
zuⁿ'ťeśni, adj. Incorrect, disjoined, as language.

zuya', v.n. To go on a war party, to make war, to lead out a war party. Wazuya, uⁿzuyapi. - iyaya, kupi.

zuze'ca, n. A snake.
- blaska, A flat-looking snake. Bl.
- hoġaⁿ, n. An eel. Also, hoká.
- ǩiⁿyáⁿpi, n. A flying snake. Bl.
- luzahaⁿ, n. A fast-moving snake. Wáⁿto, The blue racer; waⁿglegleġa, The bull snake.

zuze'ca tapejuta, n. The slender beardtongue. Penstemon gracilis. The figwort family. The roots are used against snake-bite. BT. #5.

zuze'ca tawote, n. The wolf berry, buckbrush, buckbush. Symphoricarpos occidentalis. The honeysuckle family. Also, óⁿśuⁿk'nasapi hu, because they used to make arrows of the bush and shoot them at dogs in play. Bl. RT. #10.

zuze'ca tawóťe hu taⁿkíⁿyaⁿ heca, n. True Solomon's seal. Polygonatum com-

ZUZECA TAWOTE PTAPTA
mutatum. The lily family. BT. #132.

zuze'ca tawote ptápta ikóyaka, n. The carrion flower, Jacob's ladder. Smilax herbacea. The lily family. WE. #140.

zuze'ca tawote úŋma ap̄é totó he, n. The great lobelia, the blue cardinal flower. Lobelia syphilitica. The bell flower family. BT. #84.

a, an, def. art. Waŋ.

abandon, v.a. Aonasloka; Ḣ'uŋkpani: -kiya, (finishing); -yaŋ; oḣ'opteli-c'iya, - one's work. Cf. leave.

able, v. Oic'ikpani, v. refl. Not - to care for own. Okihi, v.a. (power): iy- ; oic'ihi, v. refl. Be - for self; waw- , Be - ; waw-ka, n. An - person; -ya, Make able. Pica, v. aux. Have power, ability: -ka; -śni, Cannot be, be impossible.

abominate, v.a. Waḣtelaśni.
abortion, n. Okaśkaŋtoŋpi. Okaśkaŋtoŋ, v.a. Abort. Oikpat'a, v.n. Be still-born, have an - ; n. Cf. pregnancy.

about, adv. (approximately). Cetu, cel: e-ya, wahe- .

above, adv. Akaŋtu; adj. Auŋyaŋ, v.n., Be - . Waŋka: -ta, adv. Up high; a-ta; i-ta; -pa; i-pa; i-btu.

abreast, adv. Ȯciblagaŋ.
abroad, adv. Manil (from home).
absolution, n. Woyuśke.
absorb, v.a. Yuataś. Ayuḣepa, v.n. - on.

abstain, (leave off). Kicuŋni, v. - from.
abundant, (prodigious). Otaŋtoŋ, adj.: -ka; w- , n. Abundance. Wiyatagle, v. Have super-ly: -ya, adv. -ly.

abuse, adv. Okakiśya, abusively.
abyss, n. Okiksahe (vastness).
accept, Cf. get. Oicuwaśte, adj. -able.
access, n. Oau (to).

accident, (bad luck). Cf. deformed, befall. Ośteya, adv. -ally, by chance. Wakipa: -pi, n.; -ya, v.a. Make have bad luck. Wanuŋ, adv. -ally: -ḣci, -kel; -woakipa, n.

acclimate, v.n. Makiyokipi, Be -ed.
accomodate, part. Wawiyowiŋyaŋ, -ting.
accompany, v. Wawokiya, Be -ing, of help.
accomplish, v.a. Makaheya. Oḣ'aŋye, n. -ments. Wakoŋniya, v. Have -ed much.

Wayaecetu, v. (speaking).
according, adv. Ektaśniya. Ognayaŋ, adv. -ly.
accumulate, n. Wopemni, -tion. Yuowi-śni, v. Be unused.

accurate, adv. Yuśnaśni, -ly: - ecoŋpi, n. Accuracy.
accuse, v. Ṡilwiyauŋpa (of evil). Wi-wicagnupi, n. An accusation.

acquire, (possess). Kiciyamna, v. (by talking for). Toŋ, v.a. Possess, give birth to.
acrimony, n. Woyat'age.
across, Cf. opposite.

act, (do, move). Ecoŋ, v. Do: l- , - this way; śilwa- , - badly, wrong. Oḣ'aŋ: t- , n. His acts; yu-śica, v.a. Make - badly. Opiic'iya, opic'iya, v. refl. - on one's own, conduct self. Ṡkaŋ, v.a.: ki- , v.a. - towards, do to.

active, (lively). Iś'oś'o, adj. Hasty; iwalitake, wawak'oŋśni, śpukeśni, bliheca. Yakokela, v.a. Make - (talk-ing). Blihe: -ya, v.a. Make - ; -ca, v.n. Be - ; -lya, adv. -ly. Ḣ'aŋlita, v.n. Progress in work.

actor, n. Waecoŋ.
add, (over-do). Egnaka: a-, v. - to; a-okignaka, v.a. Help - . **Kaga**: a- , v.a. - an untruth; akicaga, v.a. O-verdo; ao- , v.a., v.n. - more; aoka-geca, v.a. Aopeya, v.a. - with. Ao-yaka, v. (in talking).

address, n. Makocajeyate.
adhere, Skapa: aya- , v.n. - to; waa-skabya, v.a. Make - . Tkapa, adj. Ad-hesive.

adjacent, adv. Yugipayela, Closely.
adjourn, v.a. Kignaka.
adjust, (measure, set). Iyuteya, v. Paecetu, v.a. - rightly, set in place. Yuwootaŋla, v.a.

admire, (rate). Ṡtela, v. Rate high: -ka, v.; -pi, n. -ation.
admit, adv. Tokiŋś, - edly.

adopt, v.a. Wal'iyaciŋ (a child).
adorn, v. Ẇaicikśukśu (self).

adultery, Cf. intercourse.
advise, Cf. instruct. Ecoŋśi, v.a.: -pi, n. Advice. Owahokoŋkiyeśica, n. One hard to - ; wanagoptaŋśica. Woiyaksapa, n. Good advice.

affect, (badly). Oiyopa, v.n. Be -ed (with a sore). Oniyetoŋ, v.n. Be -ed by.
affection, adv. Olakolwicayeśni, Without natural - .

affirm, v.a. Yat'iŋza.
afraid, Cf. fear. Kope: -gla, v.n. Be - ; -ya, v.a., adv. Nihaŋ, adj.: -yaŋ, v.a. Frighten; wawi- , adj.; wawi-yaŋ, v. Make - . Nihiŋciya, v.n. Be - .

after, adv. Ektana, etulake. Hakab, adv.: i- ; ihakapa; iyo- ; o- . Itehaŋlake, iyakapataŋhaŋ. Iyatab, adv.: -yela. Letaŋ, adv. - this, afterwards (place, time). Ohaŋketa, adv. - a while.

again, (often). Ake, adv.: -ececa, v.n.; -iyenakeca, adv.; -ś, adv.; -śnaśna; akigle, adv.; i- . Icima; icinuŋpa; iciyokiheya, adv. - and - . Itkob; lehiŋcita, adv. - and - . Piya, adv.: pi- , adv. - and - .

against, adv. Kicipaesya, Being - each other.

age, (old, worn out). Kaŋ, adj. -ed (opposed to youthful). Kicicawota, n. One of same - . Wakase, n. Thing growing old and white.

agency, (reservation). Miyoglioyuze, Whet-stone Agency. Owakpamni, n. An Indian agency.

ago, Cf. late.
agree, (disagree). Ośica, adj. Incompatible (sour vs. sweet). Wicouŋ, n. Covenant.
aground, v. Aze, Run - . Cf. Yuazi, v.a. Run - .

ahead, (before). Kaipsilyalake s'e, adv. A little - . Kaiyakapeya, adv. A little more than. Taŋnila, adj. - of others, before others. Tokapataŋhaŋ, adv. Before.

aimless, adv. Oyumnimni, Round and round.

airplane, n. Kiŋyekiyapi, An air ship.
alarm, adj. Waciŋhahela, Easily -ed; waciŋhahala.
alert, (lively). Oyuśkeya, adv. On - .
alight, (jump down). Oiyahaŋ, v.n. - in.
align, Cf. flush.
alike, (equal). Cf. equal. Nupiŋtu, adv. Waŋjila: o- , adj. Identically - ; ota- , n. Two - , a pair.

all, adv. Ataya: -kinil, Near - . Cf. Akikiśniyaŋ, ecaoyasiŋ. Ecaoyaŋkeya, - by groups. Eyala (s'e). Hute: -iyuȟpa; hutipak'oȟ, hutipak'oyela. Iyuha. Kinil, adv. Almost - . K'os'e, adv. (those buzzing about); k'oyela. Ośpaśpaya, adv. - by groups. Oyasiŋ, oyas'iŋ, adj. Sitomniyaŋ, adv. - over; alata. Owaŋca, adv.: eca-ya. Eśeś, particle, - right; howe, adv.; howo, hoye.

allow, (permit). Iyokiśni, v. (encourage); iyowiŋkiya, v. Permit. Wowicak'upi, n. -ance, an issue.

ally, n. Wawiciya, waniciye.
almost, (nearly, scarcely). Nuŋs'e, adv.: -lececa. Ognayeȟci, yus'o s'e.

alone, v. Ecauŋ, Be - . Ece, adv.: Cf. Hece: -gla, adv.; -la. Iatayela, pron. adj. Icuȟca, adv. Iśna: -la, pron. or adj. (only); -ti, v.n. Live alone; kic-, v. Be - with; wic-la, adj. Nala, adv. in comp. with pron. Katoyeyapi s'e, adv. Taŋsmiyaŋyaŋ, adv. Deprived of all: -ka, n. One - . Taŋśnala, adj. Without one's family.

along, (by side of). Aglagla, adv. - side; ho- , adv. - side; pakaŋyaŋ. Opaya, adv. - in.

already, adv. Ehaŋtaŋ, Ever since. Taŋniś, Sooner than expected.

also, (besides). Ko, conj.:-kta, adv.; -ya. Eśa, eśaś, śaś (used after n. or v.).

altar, n. Wagle wośnapi, wagna wośnapi.
alter, v.a. Wotokeca.
alternate, adv. Itokto: -g; -gye; -kaŋl; -keca, adj.

although, (but). Eśa, eśaś, śaś (ending sentence). Keś, adv., conj. But; keeyaś, c'eyaś. Weś, weśa, weśaŋ; yeś, yeśa, yeśaŋ, yeśaś, conj.

always, (ever). adv. Ohiŋni, adv.: -yaŋ. Okiwaŋjila; tohuŋhuŋniyaŋ kiŋ, adv. Forever. Takomni, adv. At any time.

amateur, adj. Wayuśikśica.
amazement, Inihaŋ: -pi, n.; -yaŋ, adv. In - .
ambitious, Śke: -haŋ, adj.; -heya, adv. -ly.
among, adv. Egna: -laḣci; w- , prep. Ijehaŋ, adv. perhaps. Opeya, adv. Together with: wic- , prep. ph. - them.
amputate, Cf. cut.

amuse, v. Bleblesya. Magaga: i- , v.n.; -ya, v.a.

ancestor, Cf. family. Huŋka, n.: -ke, n.; -keya, v.a. Have as - ; -ya, v.a.; -yapi, n.; wica-ke, n. -s.

ancient, Cf. old. Taŋnika, adj.

and, (also, too). conj. Ko (follows the word joined). Na, naś, nahaŋ, nakuŋ(ś). Yuŋkaŋ, conj. Also, then; yuŋkaŋś, conj. Also; if; k'eś.

angel, n. Ogliglewakaŋ.

angle, n. Oipakśaŋ. Okiblotoŋtoŋ, adj. Many cornered.

angry, (wrath). Aḣniyaŋ, v.a.: -yaŋ. Aho: -kśiwiŋkte, v.; -yasotkaya, v.n. Akaśpa(e), v.n.: -ya, v.a. Caŋlniyaŋ, v.n. Caŋni: -yaŋ, v.n.; -yekiciyapi, v. Caŋte: -hahala, adj.; -okic'unica, v.n.; -okic'unilya, v.a.; -ptaŋyaŋ, v.n., adj.; -ptaŋyeya, v.a.; -wahiŋyaŋśica, adj. Caŋt: -iyagle, v.n.; -iyaglepi, n.; -iyagleya, v.a.; -iyaglewaya, adv. Caŋze, v.n.: -ka, adj.; -ya, v.a.; -waya, adv.; na- , v.a. Make - ; waya- , v. Have habit of making - (talking). Iciŋkciŋ, adv. Igluhiŋhaŋ, v. refl. Ikcapta, v. pos. Iśi: -gla, v.; -kciŋ, adv.; -kigla, v.n.; -kiglaya, v.a. Opuḣtiŋyaŋkel, adv. Angrily. Ośitkigla, v.n. Be - with. Śakehutę s'e hiŋgla, v. Become - as a bear. Śicia, v.n. Talk angrily. Śigla: -pi, n. Wrath; -ya, v.a. Provoke; wa-gla, v. Get - often; waglaka, n. An irritable person. Waśilkigla, v. Be - : -ya, v. Make - ; n. A person who makes angry.

animal, (and reptiles, rodents).
1. In general: wamakaśkaŋ, n.
2. Parts of: ta-, prefix.
bladder, waloḣ'egnaka.
brain, tanasula.
breast, tataḣpa.
colon, taśup'owotaŋla.
flank, tucuśte.
flesh, taḣuwapaḣpa (near knee); tanapkaŋ (below knee); tanawicite (foreleg).
gall, tapizi.
gullet, tawinapce, wiyakojuha.
intestines, taśupa.
kidney, tajoŋtka.
kidney fat, tapakśiŋ.
liver, tapi.
muscle, taḣpiyogiŋ.
neck, tatahu (back).
nerve, kaŋ; tacaŋkasluta (over back).
paunch, taniga.
rib, tucuhu, kceya, wakceyapi.
shoulder, tablo, tahiŋyete.
shoulder blade, tablohu.
shoulder sinew, tablokaŋ.
spleen, tapiśleca.
stomach, tapo. Cf.
tendons, kaŋ, tanapkaŋ (leg), tasicogiŋ.
tongue, taceji.
udder, taza (flesh).
wind-pipe, taglogloska.
womb, tatamni.
3. Names of animals:
antilope, hetoŋ cik'ala, nigesaŋla, tatoka (big-horned), tatokala (prairie), wicawoḣatataḣca.
badger, hoka.
bear, mato: -Ḣota, śakehaŋska, The grizzly, nicknamed waoŋze; waoweśica (in gen.).
beaver, capa, cap'.
bull, takiyuha (in gen.).
calf, ptehiŋcala, hitobuye.
cat, igmu.
cattle, ptegleśka, ptewaniyaŋpi.
cow, pte, hohetapte. Cf.
coyote, maśleca, mayaśleca, miyaśleca, śuŋkciŋca, śuŋkmanitu.
cub, matociŋcala.
deer, taḣca, hekaza. Cf.
doe, tawiyela (hiñd).
dog, śuŋka.
domestic animal, waniyaŋpi.
donkey, soŋsoŋ ikpisaŋ.
elephant, puteokicu, putokicu.
elk, hehaka, heslatkala, uŋpaŋ.
ferret, itopta sapa.
fox, śuŋgila, tokala, wicahaŋhaŋ (small).

frog, waś'iŋ (bull).
gazelle, nigesaŋla.
gopher, itignila, wahiŋheya (pocket).
grayhound, pesto.
ground squirrel, pispiza, taśnaheca.
heifer, ptemakicima.
horse, śuŋkawakaŋ. Cf.
jackal, mayaśle.
lion, igmu taŋka, igmuwatogla.
lizard, agleśka, t'elanuwe (sand), waŋkipaksa.
marten, waḣ'aŋksica.
mastodon, uŋḣcegila.
mink, ikusaŋ.
monkey, śuŋkawicaśa.
mouse, (h)ituŋkala, ituŋpsicala, psipsicala (jumping).
mule, soŋsoŋla.
muskrat, siŋkpe.
otter, ptaŋ, hepaŋ; śkeca.
pig, kukuśe.
porcupine, pahiŋ.
prairie dog, pispiza.
rabbit, maśtiŋca(la).
raccoon, wica, wiciteglega.
rat, ituŋgtaŋka, hituŋktaŋka.
sheep, ciŋśkayapi, heciŋśkayapi, taḣcaśuŋkala.
skunk, maka.
squirrel, hetkala, zica (red), zicaḣota (gray).
steer, ptebloka.
toad, mapiḣ'a, witapiḣa, witapiḣa.
weasel, (h)ituŋkasaŋ.
wolf, śuŋkmanitu taŋka, caksi, yak'e, huhatopa, maca, mayaca, mayaśle, micaksica.

annihilate, v.a. Nawanil. Cf. destroy.
annoy, (vex). Kiśleya, v. Continue to urge, make ashamed, to pet, rape. Nat'ekinica, v. Beg to death. Wanagiyeya, v. Trouble. Yawazeca, v.a. (beg). Yunikuwa, v. (pull, touch). Yuwas kte, v.a. (pull).

anoint, (unction). Iyuŋpi, wiuŋpi, n. An unction. Slaya, v. To grease.

another, Cf. different; turn. Tokaŋ(l), adv. In - place, way; n. - person: -taŋhaŋ, adv. From - source; -yaŋ, adv. - place (in fef. to). Toktog, adj.

answer, v.a. Aglata, aitoheya, ayupta; aitohikiciyapi, eciyupta. Iyokakiśya, v. (sharply).

anticipate, Cf. expect; hurry. Wawinakiḣni, v. Do in anticipation of.
anxious, adv. Tokekekel, Most -ly.

any, Cf. all, every. Kakeś, indef. adv. Kaś, keśa, indef. adj. (Latin cumque). Ke c'eyaś etc., (makes pron. universal). Taku ke c'eyaś, pron. -thing, whatever. Takuŋl, n. Anything, something. Tukte e k'eyaś, pron. Anybody. Tuktektetu, adv. Anywhere.

anyhow, adv. Eca: -kaleś. Ekitaŋ. Cf. please.

apart, (asunder). Iciteha ŋ, adv.: k-yaŋlake s'e, A little - . Icitohaŋ, adv. Kakinuŋk, adv. (own way). Kojagjal, adv. Oyujuju, v.a. Pull asunder. Zaŋzaŋla, adv. Standing far -, scattered.

apostle, Cf. news. Ogligleyapi, n. Wahośiya(e): -pi, n.; - wakaŋ, n.

apparent, Cf. appear. Kaotaŋiŋ, v.a. Make - .

appear, v.n. Taŋiŋ: a- , v.n. Be visible, manifest; aki-śniśni, adj., adv. -ing; -iŋ, v.n. - occasionally. Hinajiŋ, v.n. Hiyahaŋ, v.n. Napa: hi-, v.n.; e- , v. coll. pl.; gli-, v. pos. Come in sight going home.

appearance, (looks, countenance). Iteoyuze, n. Kaḣyakel, adv. In - . Taŋcaŋ: -oyuze, n. The exterior of a person; wa- , n. - of material things.

appetite, adv., adj. Lolḣwaka, Without - ; yaiŋceśni, yaowiśni.

applaud, n. Waaś'api, Applause.
apply, (put on). Gnaka: a- , v.a.; wakici- , v. - medicine to.

apportionment, (division). Akipab, adv. In allotments.
approve, v. Hecetula: -kapi, n. -al.
arithmetic, n. Wayawapi. Cf. read.

arm, Cf. weapon. Napoktaŋ, n. -band. Oakśu, n. -ful. Pagopatica, v. - self with; wipekitoŋ, v. - self.

around, Ahocokaya, adv. Aitkob, akimeya; aokime, v.a. Go round; aohaŋktoŋyaŋ, v., adv.; ayukaŋ, v.a.; iyo-glamna, adv.; hiⁿskoya, adv.; honuⁿpiⁿyaⁿ ya, v. Surround; kaokokab, v. Go - . Kśaⁿ: ayu-yaⁿ, v., adv. Go - , out of way; hoo- , howo- , iglu- , itaⁿiglu- , itaⁿo- , itao- ; iyayu- , prep.; oka- , adv.; o- , prep., adv.; o-taⁿ, adv.; oka-yaⁿ; taⁿo- , adv. Surrounding. Ohomni, adv. - about: a- , adv. Wiⁿga, wiⁿh: aka- , adv.; aoka- , v.a.; hooka- , adv.; yu- , v.a. Turn - , back; adv. Coming - .

arrest, Cf. tie. Kaśkapiya, v. Have -ed; kaśkeya.

arrive, Cf. come.

arrow, Kehuku, n. - head. Kestoⁿ, n. A barbed - head. Wahiⁿ: -cola, n. - with no head; -kpe, n.; -hinajiⁿ, n. Jaws of - ; -kiⁿiⁿyeyapi, n. Bow-shot. Waⁿ, n.: -ju, n. Quiver; toⁿ- , n. (of any sort); -apayapi, n. - stuck in a wound; -kaga, v.a. Make - ; -nuⁿpaya, v. Strike with two -s; -otaya, Strike with many -s; -saka, n. - in the making; -taⁿyeya, v. Be a good shot; -taⁿyeyela, n. One good at shooting - ; -yeya, v.a. Shoot -s; -yugo, v.a. Incise an - well; -yuguka, v. Draw an - ; -yukpaⁿhaⁿ, v. Let fly many -s; -yuze, v. Handle bow and - . Wismahiⁿ, n. - head. Wiwośtake, n. A blunt - ; miwośtake. Wawakaⁿ, n. p. The Sacred Arrow of the Cheyenne.

article, Kin, ki, ci, ka, The (def.). Waⁿ, A, an (indef.). Uⁿ, uⁿpi, The; kiⁿ, k'uⁿ, oⁿ, k'oⁿ (being).

as, adv. Tokel, tokeś, As...as one can. Toketu, adv. As it is. Sekse, adv. As it were; s'elececa. Iyena, pron. (so many): -ka, adv.; -keca, adj., pron.; -ⁿgnakeca, adv. red. Seca, adv. Seemingly; s'e, adv. Like, as though, as if; s'elececa.

ascending, adv. Aiyakapteya. Ali, v.a. Ascend: -agla, v.a. ; -kiya, -li; -liya, adv.; -ya, adv., v.n., n. Climbing. Itawaⁿkagle, adv.: -ya.

ashame, (having disobeyed). Oh'itoⁿkipa, v. Do without shame. Wiśtelya, v.a. Make -ed; wiśtelkiciyapi, n. -edness.

ashes, n. Cahota, caⁿlogu.

aside, (back). Kaheyata, adv. To one side. Kaitokaⁿl, v. Push - .

ask, (desire). Ciⁿ, v.a. - for: o- , v.a.; oki- , v. - of; waeki-ciⁿke, n. One anxious to get (askiṅg). La, v.a.: ki- , v. - of.

assemble, (come together). Aokiya, v. Egeju, v. They -ed. Hiheya, v. col. pl. Ignagnaya s'e, adv. Coming one at a time. Kata, v. Mniciya(e), v.: a-pi, v. pl.; e- , v. col. pl.; i- , v.n.; ogli- , v. col. pl. (meet); ohi- , v. col. pl.; oi- , v. col. pl. Go to a meeting; oki- , v.n.; o- , n. An assembly. Witaya: e- , v.; ki- , v.n.; ohi- , v. col. pl.; oi- , v.n.; -iheya, v.

asset, (substance). Woic'igle, n. One who saves; one's assets.

assist, (serve). Cf. help. Okiye: o- , n. An -ant, servant; ta- , n. His -ant, disciple. Okpe, v. Give an - .

assure, v.a. Ayuwicaka.

astonish, n. Woyus'iⁿye, -ment.

at, adv. Ecuhci(ś). Ekta(kta), prep. El, prep. Etulahci, adv. Yata, prep. in comp. (by, to)

attach, v. Ikoyaka, Adhere to; iyak'iⁿtoⁿ. Yuha: iyakici- , v.; iya- .

attack, v. Ekicipa. Nataⁿ: a- ; a-pi, n. Takpe, v.a. Assault: a- ; e- .

attempt, (try). Akoza, v.a. Iglutata, v. pos. Ohaⁿ, v. Study.

attend, (attentive). Ecewakta, v. Mnih'ic'iya, v. Give attention to. Oyaksab śica, adj. Inattentive. Titaⁿwaya, v. - school. Wicuⁿskayeśni, v. Pay no attention; el etoⁿwaⁿśni.

attract, Iwicayutaⁿ, adj. -ive. Oiyokipi, n. -ion.

auction, n. Paⁿwiyopeyapi, n. - sale.

audition, (listen, hear). Wanah'oⁿpi, n.

available, adj. Icupica.

avarice, Wikaⁿgligike, n. An avaricious person. Wowijica waciⁿ, n.

avenge, Cf. vengeance. Watokicoⁿ, v.; n. An -er.

avoid, (evade, elude). Kipaś'iyaya, v.

AWARE
Okamna, v.: a- . Taŋȟmiŋkiya iyaya, v. Ayukśaŋyaŋ, v.

aware, v. Tokewaciŋśni uŋ, Pretend to be un- of; waciŋksapa, v.n. Be - .
away, adv. Haŋyaŋk: ale- ; kale- ; le- , Somewherelse. Ȟeyapa, ȟeyab, ȟlaȟya, iciśniyaŋ, ihehaŋyaŋ.

awkward, Cf. bungle. Wayuȟiya, v. Be - . Yaȟ'iyaya, v. Be - (speaking etc.)

babble, n. Iwakaŋ: -yaŋ, adv. -ing. Oyaśkiśka, v.

back, (backward). Takiya: hek- , adv.; kahek- , adv. Backwards; laza- . Ituŋkab(tu), adv. Kaitkob, adv. Again. Tapete(o,u), n.: -gnagya, adv. Placed on the - ; -gnaka, v. Place on - ; katkiya, adv. With - against the fire; -ta, adv. On the - ; -taŋhaŋ.

bad, (ugly, wicked). Śica, adj.: kici- , v.n. Become - to for; oḣ'aŋya, adv. Badly, wickedly; -ya, adv. -ly, not well; -yakel. Ośikśiloḣ'aŋka, v.n. Act -ly; ośilye oḣ'aŋ, v.n. Śicit'e, adj. Very - . Śilya, adv. -ly.

badge, n. Ipasise: caŋtku- , Breast pin; wiceśk- , n.

baffle, v.a. Iśtelic'iyeya.
bag, n. Lol'opiya (meat). Ojuha, n.: was'- (wasé). Paŋ, n. Work - (woman's); -wotuka, Sewing - ; wiyaka- , Tool - (and cherries etc.). Waloogna, n. (meat). Wopiye, n. Medicine - .

baggage, n. Waḣpaye(ca).
bail, (empty). Kaḣepa, v.a. - out; kapta.
bait, n. Wataŋ, n.: -ya, v.a. Use for.
balance, v.a. Yunas'a, - a hutanacute.

bald, (bare). Śla, adj.: nata- , adj. (head).
ball, n. Tapa, tap', tab, n.: -pa, v. Hit a - ; -icakape, n. A bat; -icapsice, n. Shinny stick; -iyeya, v. Pitch a - ; -iyukape, n. Catching glove; -kakab iyeya, v. To bat - ; -kapsica, v. Bat out a - ; -icapsice, n. A - bat.

band, Cf. arm band. Haŋtkuŋza, n. Arm - . Oiyuskite, n. Place for a - to be fit. Wiyakaśke, n. (tying).
bandage, n. Iyukite. Wiyayuskita, v.; wiyayuskite, wiyuskite, n.

bank, (earthen). Cf. m oney. Maya, n.: -gliheya, n. (steep); wa-l, adv. Toward a - .
banquet, Cf. dine.

baptize, Cf. sacrament. Wamniakaśtaŋ, n. One that -es.
bar, n. Iyonatake.

barb, Pepe, adj. -ed, jagged, prickly, rough. Kestoŋ, v.n.: ka- , v.a. Keze, n. A sharp point.
barber, n. Wicakicaśla.

bare, Cokala, adj.: sima- , v. Hacola, adj. K(c)ak'oza, kak'os, v.a.: i- , v.n. K(c)ak'eza, v. Leave - . Kiŋcahaŋ, adj. Ska: o-ka, adj. - of, open; otiŋto- , n. An open place. Smiŋ: ayu- , v.a. Snaṣnala, adj. (tree); kasmiŋ, v.a. Śla, adj.: ao- , n.; a- , v.n.; a-lyeta, adv.; a-ya, adv.; awo- , v.a.; icica- , adv.; kica- , v. Make - ; na- , v.a.; ona- , v.a.; o- , n. An open placę; pa-ya, v.a.; wo- , v.a. (shoot). Śmi, adj.; totola, adj.: o- .

bark, v.a. Papa; wapapa.
barn, n. Pteonajiŋ, Cow - ; śuŋg'onajiŋ, Horse - , stable.
barrel, (keg). Koka, n.: -la; -ojuha, An empty - ; kokojuha.
barren, adv. Ślaegnag, In - country.

basin, n. Uŋiglujajapi, A wash - .
basket, n. Psawognake.
bat, v.a. Kapa: ka- , - a ball; pa- .
batter, v. Woblebleca.
bawl, v. Hotoŋ: -toŋ; -kel, adv.; -kiya, v.a. Make - . Howaya, v.n.
bay, n. Okaḣmiŋ.

be, (exist, well). Eca...laka, It is ...there is. Ece: -ca, v.n., adv.; -ḣci, adv.; -kcel, -l, -tu. Ee, v.: l- , This is; h- , That is. Hiyeya, v.n. Uŋ, v.n.: o- , v.n., n. Be, a condition or state, a place, room; one's ways, being; -k'uŋpi, v. We are; -pi, They are; wa- , v. Be well-off. Yaŋka, maŋka, naŋka, v.n.: a- ; kici- , - for; o- , - in. Yukaŋ(e), v.n.; There is some, wa-ca; -ya, Be, have.

bead, v.a. Kśu. Pśito, n.: -suhula, Very small - ; -śuhula, Medium - . Totola, n. Blue or green - . Oyaya, n. A string of beads; woyaya. Yazahe s'e, adv. Bead-like; oweciŋhaŋ.
beard, n. Putiŋhiŋ; mustache.

beat, (strike). Cf. thresh. Aka(agla)pota, v.a. - in pieces. Akapsica, v.a. (jump). Aka(agla)śpu, v.a. (cut off). Aokat'iŋza, v.a. (pack). Akawega, v.a. (break on). Blo: ihu-ya, v. - legs; ka-blo, v. Make swell. Eiyapat'o, v.n. - against. Icicaśnaśna, v. (sounding off). Icigni, v.a. Maltreat. Ikaskapa, v.a. Ka(gla)bleca, v. - to pieces. Kabu, v. (drum). Katakuniśni, v. To - to pieces. Koza: a- , v.a. Try to - ; caŋ- , v. Swing a stick to - . Kte, v.a. (a game); ktela. Makiblaska gliȟpeya, v. - flat. Nataȟtoŋyaŋ, v.a. (eggs). Pa: aka- , v. Thresh off on; akici- , v. - for; aki- , v. pos.; a- , v.a. Smite; a-pa, n. A blow; ekici- , v. Attack one another; iakipa, v. - the mouth (whoop); iya- , v.a. (heart) - against; ka- , v. - off; wo-gi, n. - of a drum; wo-gikiya, v.a. Make a rhythmic - . Paŋ: aka-(agla)- , v.a. Thresh; gla- , v. pos. Thresh own; ica- , v.a. - to pieces; ka- , v. - off. Śtaka: a'ka(agla)- , v.a. - one another; ka- , v.a.; wigla- , v. pos. - own wife.

beau, (dandy). Wawascuscuke, n.

beautiful, adj. Gopa, ȟopa, gopeca. Igluȟopa, v. refl. Make self - . Owaŋyaŋgwaśte, adj. (to eye).

because, Cf. indeed. Ca, caheca, conj. adv. Welaka, yelaka, adv.

beckon, (wave, signal). Koza, kos: koś- , v.a.; nape- ; -ya, v.a. Signal. Wikiyuta, v. - to.

become, v.n. Akihececa (arriving home). Aya; uya.

bed, n. Ohe, oheglepi, oyuŋke.
Bedding, Cuwiogle, maȟ'owiŋje (cornhusks), nisehuogle.
Bed-room, Oiśtiŋme.
Bed-stead, Oyuŋke hu; uŋgnaȟ'icaśke (tripod support for robes).
Caster, Oyuŋke hugmiya.
Tick, Peji owiŋja; towiŋja, His - .
Ticking, Mniȟuhaskaśoka.
Aowiŋskiya, v.a. Make - on for. Owiŋja, v.a. Use for a - : -akaȟpe, n. A quilt; -popopa, n. Quilt; owiŋśkiya, v.a. Make a - of. Wiciyuŋka, n. Bedtime.

befall, (accident). Wakipa, v. Have an accident.

before, Haŋni, adv. Ikokab, icokab (time, place); kokab, adv. In the way of. Iȟtahepi, n. - evening. Ikaŋyetaŋ, adv.: -haŋ, adv. From in front of. Ikoglamnaya, v.a. Go, get ahead of. Itetaŋhaŋ, adv. Face to face. Itoka: a-b, adv.; -btu, -ya, -mna, adv. -pa, v.n. Ahaŋkeyela, adv. Just - .

beg, (ask). La, wala, v.: -kel, adv. Begging; -laka, n. -gar. Wociŋ: -la, n. -gar; -pi, n. -ging, craving, hunger; wola s'a, n. -ging (food).

begin, Ohutetanajiŋ, adv. In the very -ning; ohutkaŋ, n. The beginning of things. Oiŋkpata, adv. In the -ning. Otokahe, n. The -ning, first; -ta, adj. At the head; -ya, n. The first; adj. At the -ning.

behalf, (part). Taŋyam, adv. In - of.

behave, v.n. Śilȟ'aŋ, - badly; śilȟ'aŋka, n. Behavior.

behead, v.a. Pakaksa, pawaksa.

behind (back). Hekta(pa,b), adv., n.: i- . Iheyata, adj., prep. Iyokapataŋhaŋ, adv. (age). Iyagna, prep. Lazata, adv.: i- , adv., n. Wicakaŋl, adv. - them; wicilazate.

belch, v.n. Apablu. Blokasak, n.

believe, (agree to). Wicala, v.a.: -ka, v.; -pi, n. Faith; -pica, adj. Worthy of belief; -ya, v.a. Make - .

belittle, v.a. Yatakuśni; yatakuya, adv. Belittling.

bell, (steeple). Ȟlaȟla taŋka, n.; owakaȟla, n. A belfry.

belly, n. Ikpi; paikpaska, adv. With the - up.

below, Cf. under. Kuya, adv.: -taŋhaŋ, From - .

bend, (crook, angle). Akata, v.a. Draw a bow. Huwoga, adj. Bent. Ȟmiŋ: ka- , v.a.; taŋ-kiya, adv. -ing body away. Kaś'iŋ, v. - concave: naa- , v. - backward; na- . Kpaŋ: apa- , v.a. Make fine. Kśa, adj. Decrepit: ayu- v.a. Fold, double up on; pa- , adj. Bent, aged; yu-yela, adv. (posture). Kśaŋ: ipa- , n. A fold; istoglu- , v. pos. - own arm; istopa- , n. - of the arm; kiciyu- , - for; na- , v.a. - by foot; oipa- , n. A crook, angle; oŋ- , n.; pa- , v.a. Make - . Kśija: aka- , v.a. - into, round; aki- ; ana- ; ayu- ; istopa- , - the arm; istoju- . Ktaŋ: aka- , v.a. - around, onto; ana- ; ayu- ; ka- , kao- , na- , nao- , oipa- , oiyu- , ona- , oyu- , pa- , woo- , yao- , yuo- . Ko: pa- , Bent around; na- , v.n. - up. Naakakciya, v. - backward. Napatuja, v.a. - (kick). Naśipa, v.a. (step on).

Pakipaś, v. (strike). Paokiyaskapa, v.n. Be bent in. Wega: aglu- , v. pos. - upon. Wiŋga, wiŋḣ, v. Be -ing; -ya, adv. In a bent manner. Wiŋja: ana- , v.a. - down on by foot; ayu- ; na- ; owiŋśya, adv.; pa- ; -haŋ, part. Bent down.

benefit, (make good). Iyuwaśte, v. - by.
benevolence, Cf. gracious.
beside, adv. Isakib.
besmirch, Oḣlogeca, adj. Covered with.

bet, v.a. Ahigle; ahikicigle, v.n. Yekiya, v.a. Stake something on: -pi, n. A stake.

better, adj. Ahececa: -ke; o- , (of the sick). Waśte: a- , v.n.; a-ya, adv. ; i- , v.n.; i-ya, adv.

between, adv. Oko: i-gna, -gna; -gnaka, v. Put - others. Tahepi: o- , adv. - places; iyo- ; iyo-ya, adv. On this side.

beverage, (alcoholic etc.). Mni, n. Water: -piga, Beer, ale, soda-water; -śa, Wine, cider, ale; -wakaŋ, Whiskey; -wakaŋska, Alcohol. Mniiskuya, mniskuya, Lemonade.

bewail, v.a. Kiciceya.
bewildered, (wandering, oblivious). Waciŋgnuni, adj.; yaya, adv. Undecided; yuhelhel, adv.
bewitch, (enchant, sicken). Ḣmuŋga, v.a.: kici- , v. - each other.

beyond, adv. Ainatagya. Akab, prep. Ako, adv.: -kiya, -taŋhaŋ, -wapa(taŋhaŋ). Hosam(ŋ), adv.: -patahaŋ. Isam (ŋ), adv.: -pa. Iya: -kapeya, v.a. Go - , overcome; -kapta, v.a., adv. Pass over and - ; -ko, adv.; -kotaŋhaŋ. Iyokopeya, adv. - in sight. Na: a-wab, adv.; i-mni.

Bible, n. p. Wowapi Wakaŋ.
bicycle, Makamani iŋyaŋka, v. Mazaśuŋkakaŋyaŋka, n.

bier, n. Caŋagnakapi.
big, Cf. large.
bill, (beak, debt). Pa, n.: -blaska, n. (duck's); -su, n. Beak. Wopetoŋ ikazopi, n. Debt.
bind, Cf. tie. Kita: o- , v. - up in (a child); s- , adj. Tied, fastened. Wipaḣte, n. - string etc. Yuwiŋja, v.a. - down.

bird, n. Anpaohotoŋla, Domestic - ; wakiŋyaŋpi, Winged creatures; ziŋtka(la), - in general; uŋjiŋcala, A fledgling.
bat, hupakiglake.
black-bird, wablośa (red-wing); waḣpataŋka; wapagica (yellow-head).
bluebird, ziŋtkato.
bobolink, makaowaŋke, maŋkaziŋtkala.
brant, magaśekśecala.
bunting, wabloska (lark).
buzzard, heca.
chat, wikpizi.
chickadee, śkipipi, wiyawala, guguya, śkula.
chicken, kokoyaḣaŋla.
comorant, huŋtka.
cowbird, pteyaḣpa, waḣpakaḣota.
crane, pehaŋ, pehaŋska (white).
cross-bill, pakaic'icuya (red).
crow, kaŋgi, uŋciśicala. Cf.
cuckoo, cepela taŋka, śohotoŋla.
curlew, ticanica.
dove, wakiŋyela (morning).
duck, magaksica, pagoŋta Cf., magaśniyaŋla (red-head), pasublaska (broad-bill), śiyagla, śiyaka (teal).
duckling, maḣciŋca.
eagle, anuŋkasaŋ, ḣuya, waŋbligleśka (spotted).
finch, waŋblitaheya (gold), waziziŋtkala (pine).
flicker, śuŋluta, śuŋzica.
flycatcher, ziŋtkazila cik'ala (yellow-bill).
gold-finch, waŋblitaheya.
goose, maga, maga sapa (wild).
grackle, bronze, caŋwaḣpa taŋka.
grouse, prairie, caŋśiyo, śiyo, waziśiyo (spruce).
gull, wicataŋkala, wiŋyaŋtaziŋtkala.
hawk, caŋśka (red-leg), cetaŋ, piśko (night), ptegopeca (marsh), wakiŋyaha (sharp-shinned).
heron, hokagica, hokato (blue), pehaŋska (white), pehaŋgila (sand-bill).
hummingbird, tanagila.
jay, ziŋtkatogleglega.
killdeer, pehiŋcicila, ptehiŋcicila.
kingbird, wasnasnaheca.
kingfisher, hoyazela cik'ala, hupucaŋsakala, kuśleca.
lark, iśtanica taŋka, maśtekola (horned).
loon, bles, bleza, bloza, blega.

BIRD (contin.)
magpie, halhate, uŋkcekiḣa.
meadowlark, jialepa, taśiyagnuŋpa. Cf.
mud hen, ziŋtkala caŋḣpaŋla.
oriole, śkeluta.
ousel, śiyatakala (water).
owl, hiŋhaŋ. Cf. Hiŋyaŋkaga (hoot), osniko (screech), pagla, popotka, uŋgnagicala (screech).
peacock, ziŋtkala situpi haŋska.
pelican, bleza.
plover, śloślola.
quail, śiyo cik'ala.
raven, kaŋgi taŋka.
red-start, caŋpiśko, kaŋsu ziŋtkala.
robin, śiśoka.
sand-piper, maniopawakiŋyela, miniopawakiŋyela.
saw-whet, pagla.
shrike, cetaŋ watapela.
snipe, giŋlgiŋcala, hokagica.
snow-bunting, hupuwaŋblila.
sparrow, iḣuḣaotila, pacaŋśihuta (English), situpi aḣ'ayetoŋpi (lark), ziŋtkalaslila (grasshopper), ziŋkiscila (tree).
stork, hokaḣica.
swallow, hupucaŋsakala (cliff), icapśiŋpśiŋcalaikpiska (tree), icapśiŋpśiŋcalaikpiśa (barn), psiŋca, upijata.
swan, magaska.
thrush, caŋguguyaśa.
towhee, caŋguguyagleśka.
turkey, wagleksuŋ (wild).
vireo, ziŋtkazila (warbling).
warbler, situpiwaŋblila.
whippoorwill, pakośkala.
woodcock, kaŋkeca.
woodduck, skiska.
woodpecker, toskala, wagnuka (redhead).
wren, caŋheyala.

Pa, pasu, n. Beak; pa, n. Head. Siŋte, n. Tail. Ape, n. Wing.
Hokamanipila, n. Nesting place (crane).

birth, Cf. pregnancy. Hokśiyuha, v. Give - to; hokśitokapa woiyowaja, n. First -right; wotokapa woiyowaja. Oŋzekte, v. Give - (when nursing); oŋzepija, v. Be unweaned at - of another. Toŋ, v.a. Give - to: -pi, n. T'ahiyuya, v.n. Be still-born.

bit, n. Wokitaŋ, A little - of anything. Yuḣ'eḣ'eyakel, adv. In -s.

bite, (use of mouth, teeth). v.a.
Aya:
-ḣlaya, Peel.
-ḣleca, Tear on.
-ḣloka, - a hole in.
-ḣpu, - off on.
-ḣtaka, - one on another.
-jipa, Pinch, -ing.
-kca, (untie).
-kpa, - out on.
-kpi, Crack.
-ksa, - off on.
-kśaŋ, Bend by mouth.
-kśija, Double up by mouth; -kśiś.
-ktaŋ, Bend.
-kuka, Tear in pieces.
-k'ega, Gnaw on.
-k'oga, Gnaw off on.
-k'oza, - off smooth.
-pemni, Twist by mouth.
-pota, - in pieces.
-psaka, - off.
-pśuŋ, Pull out by teeth.
-sleca, Split.
-smiŋ, Clean, strip off.
-śkica, Chew.
-śkopa, Twist by mouth.
-śpa, - off a piece on.
-śpu, - off (what sticks).
-śuja, Mash.
-titaŋ, Pull by mouth.
-waja, - off on.
-wega, Fracture.

Gla: (pos. form for ka- and ya-).
-jata, Fork.
-pa, Take hold of.
i-śna, Miss with the mouth.

kalkalya, adv. Bitingly (anger).
Kiciya:
-ḣtaka, - for.
-psaka, - off for.
-śpa, - off for.

Kiya: -ksa, - in two.
O:
-kapa, v.n. (spices, tobacco etc.).
-napce, n. A wound, bite.
-yaḣloka, v.a. - a hole in, mark.
-yaksa, v.a. - off.
-yak'oza, v. - short.
-yataŋ, v.a. - down on.

Pa: -pala, adj. -ing (pepper).
Waya: -smaka, v. (make marks).

Ya:
-gapa, Peel.
-gla, Strip off.

-gmipi s'e, adv. Bitten off.
-ȟtaka, Take hold by mouth.
-ȟuga, - into, chew, crack.
-kpukpa, - into small pieces.
-oȟpa, - into.
-owiⁿga, Pull about with the teeth.
-pa.
-pta, - off around.
-ptuga, - off a piece.
-śpa, - off a piece; -śpapi, part. Bitten off.
-śpu, - off; -śpuya, v. Make itch.
-tkuⁿza, - off even.

bitter, (fig.). Iwokokipeke, n. A sharp-tongued person. Pa, adj.: -za, adj.; -zeca, adj. (words). T'aga, adj. Astringent. Woglawa, n. A - thing.

black eye, v.a. Iśta otoya, Give one a - .
blacksmith, (smithy). Maskape, maz'kape, n. : o- , n. - shop; mazakaga, n.; omas'kage, n. - shop.

bladder, n. Peśka, Air - (fish); walege, n.
blade, n. Ope. Cf. edge.
blame, Ielgle, v.; ignu, v.a. Iyauⁿpa(e), v.a.: -pi, n.; -picaśni, adj.; -ya, adv. Kipa, v. - self, own: -kiya, v. Make - self. Wicapapi, n. Yaśilpicaśni, adj. -less.

blanket, (robe, shawl, quilt). Śina, n. Cf. Witoye, n. Blue, green -ing.
blasphemy, n. Woakage.
blaze, (fan, flame). Ile, v. Fire: ka- , v.a. Make - ; o- , v.n., n. Flame.

bleach, (clear). Oⁿwahiⁿyuⁿtoⁿpi, n. (for hides). Ska: ka- , v. Become clear; ki- , v.n.; na- , v.n.; pa- , v.a.

bleed, v. Kaⁿkakpa, kaⁿkicakpa. We: i- , v.n.; i-hiyu; i-hiyupi, n.; i-hiyuya, v.; i-yośaya, adv.; kawe- , v. Make - ; pa- , v.n.; pa-hiyu, v. - at the nose; pawe- , v.a. Make - .

bless, v.a. Ayawaśte; glawaśte, v. pos.
blind, Iśtaakaȟpe, n.; iśtakakpa, iśtaglakpa, v.a.; iśtakpa, v.n.; iśtakpeya, v.a. Iśtagoⁿga(e), v.n.: -pi, n.; -ya, adv.; iśtagoⁿge, n. Iyośnija, v.n. Be -ed; iśta- , v.n.
blink, v. Kap'i.

blister, n. Kaⁿna, mnikapoȟya hiyotake, mninapas hiyuye.
block, v.a. Ikuśetoⁿ. Wokapaⁿ, n. A meat - .

blood, Cf. bleed. We, n., adj., v.n.: - colakel, adv. Un-y; - eyala s'e, adv. All -y; a- , v.n. Bleed on; eyala s'e, adj. -y; -ic'iya, v. Bleed self; -kiciya, v. Bleed each other; -la s'e, adv.; -ośpaⁿ, v.n. Cease - flow (afterbirth); -ota, -yota, n. - clot; we- , adj. -y; -ya, v. Shed - ; -yoȟlogelya, adv. All -y; -yukeya, adj. -y.

blossom, (bloom). Itka, n. Kawa, v. Open, bloom. Nableca, v.n.

blow, v.a. Ataeyaⁿpa (wind). Blu: iwo- , v.i. - in; owo- v.n. Icamna, v.n. Jiⁿca, v. - the nose: yu- , v.a. Pull, - the nose. Jo: gla- , v. pos. - on own (instrument); ya- , v.a. - a musical instrument. Kak'es, v. - off. Lu: ka- , v. Brush away; owo- , v.n. - in. Pogaⁿ, v.a. (by mouth): aik- , v. refl.; ai- , v.a.; ao- , v.a.; a- , v.a.; apoȟ- , v.; o- , v.a. - in upon, out from. Slohaⁿ: iwo- , v. Wosni, v.a. - out, extinguish. Wośloka, v.a. - out, clear, empty.

blowout, v. Hunapobya, Have a - .
blunder, Cf. laugh, sport. Wawiȟat'eya, v. - in one's business. Yaśna, v.a. (speaking).
blunt, Katata, v.a. Make - . Papśuⁿka, v.a. Make - . Tata, adj. Dull, bruised. Tośe, adj. Dull: -yakel, adv. Wot'oja, v.a. Make - (shoot).

blur, Aogi(ⁿ), adj.: -toⁿ, v.; -yaⁿ, adv. Śnija, adj. -red, indistinct.
blush, v. Iteśahiⁿgle, itewe s'e hiⁿgle.

board, n. Wawak'eze, Work - (for cutting).
boast, (brag). Cf. jest. Oⁿkiśkata, v.a.

boat, n. Caⁿyuwipi kagapi, n. A float. Wata, wal, n.: caⁿ- , n.; mniwaⁿca- , A ship; -peta, n. Steam- ; -opeya, adv. By - ; -hektab, adv. At the stern; -siⁿteyuhomni, v. To pilot, a helmsman, n.; wal'oihuni, n. - landing; wal'oinajiⁿ. Wal: -hektapa, n. The stern; -cete, Keel, bottom; -pa, The bow; -siŋte, n. The helm, rudder; -tucuhu, n. Ribs; wal'icaśke, n. Anchor. Wal'icaśpe, n. Canoe router. Wal'itope, n. Oar, paddle.

body, n. Taŋcaŋ, tacaŋ, taŋ. Cf. bone.
abdomen, ceyohe, ikpi (belly), page, śupute (lower).
afterbirth, tamni.
ankle, iśkahu.
arm, a, aḣ'co (upper), isto (lower).
back, cuwi, cuwinuŋge, miyokaś'iŋ (small), miyopawega, tapete(o,u).
brain, nasu.
breast, ceśka (upper), maku.
bridge (nose), pahute, paokihe.
brow, iyujipa.
cheek, itehohu, tapoŋ.
chest, caŋtku, taḣpa (upper).
chin, iku.
diaphragm, tapaga.
ear, noŋge (hear). Cf.
elbow, iśpa.
esophagus, winapce.
eye, iśta.
finger, śaśte.
flesh, ceḣpi, nawicite (upper arm).
foot, si.
forehead, ituhu, paḣte (brow).
fossae, paḣlate (nasal).
gall, pizi.
gland (throat), tawapśuŋkahaŋ.
groin, cana, caŋnopa, logute.
gullet, glogleska.
hair, hiŋ.
hand, nape. Cf. (fingers).
head, pa, peslete (top), naju (back), najute, nata, natableca (square), natagugu (curly).
intestines, iyuhiŋta, iyuhota, śupe.
jaw, cehupa, iyoḣa.
joint, okihe.
kidney, ajuŋta, asuŋkta.
knee, huokaḣmi (back), caŋkpe.
knuckle, nasukaza.
lap, śiyute.
leg, hu.
limb, huha.
lips, iha, wiśaŋ (vagina).
liver, pi.
lungs, cagu, tacagu.
mouth, i.
nails, wicaśake.
navel, cekpa.
neck, tahu (back), najutośkokpa (back), pahute (nap), tiśkaŋkaŋ (muscle).
nerve, kaŋ.
nose, pa(la), pasu, poge. Cf.
nostrils, pacete.
palate, caka.
penis, ce.
rib, tucuhu.
rump, niśtuśte, nite, oŋze (anus).
scalp, nataha.
shoulder, ablo, hiŋyete.
side, cuwipaha (below arms), oyute (above hips).
skull, nasuhu, natahu, natokiiyaŋke (sutures).
soft-spot, peowiwila, pewiwila.
spine, tacaŋḣaḣake (first vertebrae), tacaŋkahu (middle).
spleen, piśleca.
stomach, nige (paunch), tezi.
temples, nawate.
tendon, kaŋ.
testes, itka, susu.
thigh, ceca, olute, sicaŋ (outer), śiyoto (front).
throat, ceśkoḣloke (lower), lote, lotku.
tongue, ceji. Cf.
tonsils, winapce.
vagina, śaŋ.
vein (artery), kaŋ.
waist, oipiyake.
wind-pipe, glogloska.
womb, tamni.
wrist, nabkaŋ, napkaŋ (sinews.

Aloksohaŋ, v.n. Carry under arm.
Caŋkpeska, adv. On knees.
Huhatoŋ, v.n. Have limbs; huhaya, v.a.
Ikpignaka, v.a. Put about belly. Cf.
Istoyukaŋ, v.n. Have arms.
Oŋzeyugmuza, v.a. Hold anus shut.
Tacaŋpaḣmiyaŋ, adv. With - bent.
Tamahel, adv. In the - ; taŋmahel.
Taŋakotaŋhaŋ, adv. With a - ; beyond flesh.
Taŋcaŋtoŋ, v. Have a - ; be full-grown.
Taŋohaŋglegleya, adv. Dividing the - in two; taŋokikaśleca.
Taŋokisese, n. Halves of the - .
Taŋsaŋni, n. A side of the - .
Taŋsitomni, n. The whole - ; taŋsitomniyaŋ, adv. All over the - .

boil, Cf. dry. Anaḣloḣlo, v.n. Bubble up. Magataŋka, n. Oececa, v.n. Be slow to - . Ohaŋ, v.a. (meat); ohaŋpi, part.; iyohaŋ, v.a.; okicihaŋ, v. - for; okihaŋ, v.; oohe, n. A -ing. Ololobya, v.a. Over- in. Onas'eya, v.n. Simmer in. Oyaḣeya, v.a. Make - away. Piga(e), v.n.: - s'e, adv. -ing with noise; piḣya, adv.; i- , v.n., n. Pśa: ana-pśa, v.n.; iyo-pśa, v. (in bubbles). Siyaka, n. Wakalya, v.a.

boisterous, (garrulous). Waohmuŋyece, n. A - person. Yas'a, v.a. Roar (in speaking).

bold, adj. Iohitika.
bolt, (fasten, lock). Nataka, v.a. Tiyop'i: -kuśe, n. A door - , lock; -natake, -patake.

bond, n. Inatake.
bone, n.
hohu, (in gen.).
gugeca, Marrow; guyeca, cupe.
wicahuhu, The human skeleton.
caŋkahu, Spine; caŋkohaŋ, caŋkahohu, caŋkaslute.
caukpepajo, Patella - .
ceblohu, Collar - .
cecahohu, Femur.
cecaoakle, Pelvis.
cehupaoagle, Jaw joint.
cetuŋte, Thigh.
cetuŋtośtaŋ, Femure head.
hohuśuŋkakaŋ, Astroyolus - .
hutanacute, Rib.
huwak'ipe, An outer extremity - .
iśpahu, - of the lower arm.
tamakuhu, Breast - .
mica, Hip - : -hu, -hi, -ki, ta-hohu, Part near hip - ; nisehu.
okaza, Arm, foot.
pahu, skull.
tatahu, Neck.
tamica, Spinal end.
tapoŋhu, Cheek - .

bonus, n. Siŋte (fig.), Sale's - .
book, n. Wowapi. Cf. picture, flag.
booth, Awakeya, v.a. Make a - : -pi, n.
bore, (drill). Ḣloka: oyu- , v.a.; pa- , v.a.

born, T'ahiyuya, v.n. Be still- . Wakigna, n. An animal new-born.
borrow, v. Olota, v.a.: -pi, n. Okicilota, v. - of for; okilota, v.

both, Nupiŋ, adj.: -caska, adv. - together. Oza, adj.; lenioza, heniyoza. Yusakib, adv. - together; -tu.

bother, v.a. Icagiya, icageya, iwaḣagiyeya. Kuwa: ahaŋnajiŋ - ; akuta - , Ok'o: a- , v.n. a-ya, v.a.

bottom, Cete, n. etc. - of a vessel. Coka, n. Kaaglapśiŋ, adv. - up. Kaoŋze woslal, adv. Heels up. Cf. dish.

bounce, v. Iyakiciḣpaya.
bow, (incline). Ayukipatuja(śya), v.a.
bowér, n. Waḣpewokeya.
box, n. Caŋognaka, caŋwognaka; wopiye.
brace, (out, up). Ipataka, ipatag, ikpataka, v.: -toŋ, v.a.; -ya, v.a.; ipatake, n. Ipataŋ, n.: -gle, v.a. Owaś'aka, v.n. Be -ed for. Oyut'iŋze, n.

brag, v. Waecoŋḣca ic'ila.
braid, Soŋ: a- , v.a.; kici- , - for; -pi, n. -s; ki- , v. - own.

brake, Inat'a(e): huinak'eḣye, n.; hu-ḣtoŋ, v.; -ge, n.; -ḣya, v.a., adv.; huinataḣye, n.

branch, adv. Ahutkaŋyaŋ. Aletka, n. Caŋapa: -kaŋ, n. A crooked - ; -kiŋyaŋ, n. A - growing down. Caŋiŋkpa, n. - ends: -ta, adv. At - top. Ḣaka, adj. -ing: -ya, adv. -ing. Yuḣa, v.n. - out, curl: -ḣa, v., adj. Many pronged; curly.

brand, n. Caŋgugu (by hot iron). Guye: ogu- , n. (burnt in); o- , n.; pte- , v.a. (cattle); wi- , n. -ing iron.
brave, Caŋtet'iŋza(s), v.n. Be - : -kic'uŋ, v.; -ya, v.a.; -waya, adv. Lita: i-ka, v.n.; wa- , adj.; wa-gya, adv. -ly; wa-ke, adj. Active, courageous; wa-ya, adv. Actively; waś'agya. Owohitika, adj. - on, in. T'iŋza, adj. Firm. Woyuḣuptoŋyaŋkel, adv. -ly. Woś'akel, adv.

bread, (wheat). Cf. aǧuyapi. Aguyapi, n.: blopahi- , n. Potato - ; ki- , v. Turn into - ; - wigli oŋ kagapi, n. Indian - . Cf. aǧuyapi pasteries.

break, v. (prefix-root).

Prefix	Root
a- (on,cause,col.).	blaza (rip).
ahi- (arrive).	*bleca (open).
ahiyu(glu)-	blu (fine).
aka(gla)- (hit).	hiŋta (clear off).
ana- (by foot).	*ḣci (tear out).
apa(kpa)- (hand).	ḣleca (open).
awa- (cut).	ḣloka(e)(g) (hole).
awo- (shoot).	ḣpa(e) (lie).
aya(gla)- (mouth).	ḣuga (pierce).
ayu(glu)- (hand).	juju (to pieces).
hutipa- (entire).	kaŋ(kpaŋ) (broken).
i- (to, on).	kpi (crack).
ica(ka)- (hit).	*ksa(e) (separate).
ina- (foot).	kuka (pound).
ipa(kpa)- (hand).	popa (burst).

BREAK (contin.)

Prefix	Root
iwakici- (for).	psaka(e)(g) (two).
iyu(glu)-	pśuŋ (fallen off).
ka(gla)- (strike).	pta (out).
kao- (through).	ptuga (crumble).
ki- (for).	sku (swell).
kica(ka)-	sleca (split).
kicica(ka)- (for).	sna (topple, rock).
kicipa-	śipa (close).
kiciyu(glu)-	śpa (divide).
kina-	śpu (pull off).
na- (with foot).	śuja (mash).
naki-	tkuga (square).
nakici-	*wega (fracture).
nao- (through).	
o- (on, into).	* The most common roots.
oka(gla)-	
okica(ka)-	
okiwa-	
ona-	
oyu(glu)-	
pa(kpa)- (crush).	
wa- (cut).	
wo- (shoot, punch).	
woo- (through).	
ya(gla)- (speak, mouth, bite).	
yu- (by hand).	
yuo-	

Note: To compose: yu-bleca, i.e. by hand to break what falls to pieces as glass etc. when it is struck with the hand: yubleca.

Some suffixes: -haŋ, -wahaŋ (in gaps). These form participles, thus: Oblecahaŋ, o-bleca-haŋ, i.e. into pieces broken.

Hukawegapi, n. Fractured limb.
Paŋḣyakel, adv. Breaking out, swelling.
Wopśuŋ, v. Break, letting fall.
Wowega, v.a. Break, in falling.
Yuoḣpeya, v.a. Make break through.
Yuśpa, v.a. Break in pieces.

breast, n. Askaŋ, Veins of - . Aze, n. Udder: -iŋkpa, Nipple; -piŋkpa, Teat; oŋaziŋpi, uŋazipi. Maku, The breast: -hu, - bone; -nusnuŋja; -piŋka, Pit of the stomach. Mama, n. (woman's).

breath, Niya, v.n. Breathe: a- , v.a.; gobgob- , v.n.; i- , v.a.; -śniśni, adv. Without - ; -ya, v. Breathe out vigorously; o- , v. Breathe into, out of; oniye, n.; oniyemna, v. Have foul - , smell bad. Niyaŋ: geb- , v.; gemniyaŋ, gepa; o- , n. Breath. Yus'o, v.n. Duck under water and then come up for - ; yus'okiya, v.a. Make surface.

breed, n. Anuŋkiyaŋ.
brick, n. Makaśpaŋ (blocks).
bridge, v. Ceaktoŋ, ceyaktoŋ: -pi, n.

bright, (intelligent, alert, shine). Waciŋbleza, v.n. Be - . Wiyakpapi, n. -ness. Cf. glisten.

bring, v.a. Aya(e), v.a., v. col. pl.: -kiya, v.a.; -ya, v.a. Eciŋic'iciya, v.a. - self to do. Eke s'e, adv. -ing something better. Gli: ka- , v.a. - home; kicica- , - home for; wa- , - home meat. Hi: a- , v.a.; a-gle, a-k'u, a-uŋpa, a-gnaka, a-yagle, a-yu; glo- ; -yoya; ka- ; kiciglo- . I: aigluḣpa, v. refl.; ka- . Ku: a- , v.a.; ka- . U: au, v.a., v. col. pl.; glou, kau.

brisk, Katka, adv. -ly.
bristle, adj. Ji, Bristly and thin: -jiya, Standing on end; -la, adj. Nasa, v.n.; a- ; nawosakiya, - up.
brittle, (weak). Śtaśta, adj.

broadcast, v. Wicaha kaḣwogyapi. (radio).
broil, v. Petagaiceoŋpa (on coals).
brood, v.n. Ḣpeyuŋka.
broom, n. Icahiŋta(e): owaŋka- , owaŋk'- , w- .
broth, n. Haŋpi, hohuwasmiŋpi.

brotherhood, (fellowship). Cf. relative, friend.
bruise, (batter). Cf. mash, crush. Ka: i-sli, v.; -gwa, -ośpa, -śuja, o-sloslo; o-śuśuje, n. Naśuja, v.a. (by foot). Wicaḣlece, n. That used to tear or - .

brush, v.a. Hiŋta: aya- , - off; pa- , Rub, wipe, comb off; ya- , - away (by mouth). Ipaho, v. - up. Okaḣpu, v.a. - off into. Po: ka-ya, pa-waya (coat), -waya. Pasto, v.a. - down, smoothen. Yutata, v.a. - off (by hand). Pazaŋyaŋ, adv. Under the brush. Cf. head.

brutal, Wamakaśkaŋ s'e, adv. -ly.
bubble, v. Anaḣloḣlo, v.n.; anapśapśa, apablublu. Tapsiza, v. - up; tapśi: ana-ja, v.n.; ka-ja.

buck, Cf. throw off. Paḣpa, v.a.
bud, n. Caŋiŋkpa.

buffalo, n. Tataŋka, ta. Pteoptaye, A - herd.
Kinds:
cehiŋka tapte, Large cow.
hehutela, Old bull.
heḣlogeca, Horned cow.

BUFFALO (contin.)
hiⁿȟpiȟpila, Animal that shed old hair (horse, buffalo, etc.).
pte, Cow.
ptejiⁿcala, Calf.
ptesaⁿ, White cow.
ptewiⁿkte, Fat dry cow.
tagica, Lean - .
taguha, Old scabby - .

Parts:
hiⁿhaⁿtahaⁿpe, Part of heart.
huwicayútipa, Leg meat.
iśkakaⁿ, Tendon.
nakpawicaȟci, Part of heart.
nige, Paunch.
ptece, Dung.
pteiśta, Eye.
ptenakpa, Ear.
ptetaⁿ, Cut of the back.
taajuⁿtka, Kidney.
tacaka, Mouth roof.
tacaⁿkoye, Fat layers.
tacaⁿta, Heart: -mnumnuga, Flesh about the heart; -ogiⁿ, Membrane; tacaⁿtopazaⁿ, Heart fat.
taceji iⁿkpa, Tongue tip.
taceśikśice, Paunch fat.
taceśka ha śuⁿk'ak'iⁿ, Saddle hide.
tacetoⁿte ośtaⁿ, Trunk of body.
tamnatkaⁿ, Leg meat.
taniga, Paunch: -śiⁿ, Fat; taniȟyusku, Empty - ; taniȟ'ohiⁿśma, Curved part of - ; taniȟ'ośkokpa; taniȟ'ośla, The smooth half of the - .
tanitahu, Backbone.
tanitkoȟloke, Thigh (inner) meat.
tanipa, Meat along the spine.
tasicoska, Thigh white meat.
tasiⁿta, Tail.
tasitupahu, Tail fat.
taśuⁿśiⁿ, Neck fat.
tipakel, Head (back) meat.
tistoconica, Shoulder meat; iyuȟ'eyayapi.
tiyoȟa, Cheek.
wicaśaśiⁿ, Breast.

Onase, n. - chase: owa- ; owa-ta, adv. At, on a - chase; owanasapi, n. A - run; wanasapi, n. - chase; wa-ya, v. Go on a - chase.

buggy, n. Aokiye, tisapa (top of).
bulge, (protuberance). Ipazica, adv. -ing. Opazo, n.
bulky, Cf. fluff, hinder, soft. Pakonatke, v.a. Make - (pack). Paⁿ: -gece, adj. Puffed out; -śya, adv. Bunchy.

bully, Ksizic'ila, n., adj.

bump, v.n. Iciyapa: -pi, n. Iyoto, v. (against).
bunch, Iyupaȟ, adv. In a - .
bundle, (bunch). Cf. heap. Paȟta: -ȟta, v.a. Tie up in -es; -pi, n. A pack; wapaȟta, n. Puśki, adv. In a - .

bungle, Cf. awkward. Wayuȟiya, v.: -yaka, n. -er; yuȟ'iyaya, v.a. Do badly.

burden, n. Itaⁿnuⁿkwak'iⁿkiyapi. Yuȟlohela s'e, adv. Seemingly -ed.
burgeon, Ouye, n. Burgeonning; owauye, n. Growing of.

burn, Cf. fire. Ogu, v.n. - in. Śpaⁿ, adj. Burnt (from heat or cold): adj.; v.n. Be burnt; -ic'iya, v. refl. Get burnt or frozen.

burst, Cf. break. Blaga: na- , v. - open; okina- . Blaza: ka- , Rip open; na- , v.a. (by foot); pa- ; ayu- , v.a.; inabla- . Hleca: na-la s'e, adv. -ing. Onakpa, v.n. - within. Naakamni, v. Make - open. Popa, v.n.: na- , v.a., v.n. Explode; ona- , v.n. - within; apa- , v.a. - on; pa- , Make - (squeezing). Kapta iyaye, v. Okinablaza, v.n. - open.

bury, v.a. Ha(e): e- , v.a.; kici-, - for; -ai, v.a. Bring for burial; wa-pi, n. Burial. Wakasa, v. - in snow.

bush, n. Caⁿ: -ȟaka, (in gen.); -ȟotka, (used for arrows); -ȟuⁿaptaⁿ, Group of -es; -icaȟpe hu, Nettle; -ptayahaⁿ, n. (in gen.). Cuⁿȟaka, n. A brush of -es. Gaⁿka, adj. -y. Hpika, adj. Shaggy. Paza, v.a. Make -es erect (for sleeping under).

business, Iwatokiyaśni, v.n. Be none of one's - . Tawoecoⁿ, n. His work, doing. Woiyowaja, n.
busy, Cf. work. H'aⁿ: o-yaⁿ, v.n. Be active; wi- , v. Be - with much; wipi, n. Occupation. Wiyaⁿkeca, v.n. - self at home. Kihe laka yo, Keep - , stick to it.

but, conj. K'eyaś, Although. Śka, Yet. Tka, tuka. Toel, toeyaś, But first, but before. Tuka(ś), conj. in comp. with eyaś, śehaⁿś, a pron. etc.; eyaś tuka, As you should recall.

butcher, v. Wak'ega.

butt, (push, rub). Pawaza, v.a. (annoy).

butter, Cf. milk.
button, n. Mazaceśkikaŋ (metal).
buy, (hire, purchase). Ope: -toŋ, v.; -kitoŋ, v. - own, redeem; -kicitoŋ, v. - in place of; -kicatoŋ, v. - for. Wokiye iyaya, v. Go to - , trade.

buzz, Ħmuŋ, v.n.: ayu-, v.a.; -s'e, adv.; -s'ekse, -sececa; -ya, v.a.; -yaŋ, -yela, adv.; ica- , v.a.; ka- , v.a. Make - . K'o, n. (busy people); -s'e, adv. With the - gone, apparently. Ś'as'e, n. (crowd of men).

by, (agent). In Lakota, agent exists only as the subject of action. (near). Cf. (means). Iyoħlogya, adv.; oŋ, prep.

cabinet, Cf. drawer. Yuslul ognake, n. A bureau.
cache, n. Wokase, - made in snow.
cactus, n. UŋȞcela, Mescal bean: -blaska, Flat cactus; -taŋka, Tall - ; -taśpu, - berry; uŋkcela.

cage, Cf. pen. Onatake, n. Ziŋtkala ognake, Bird - .
calculate, (figure). Owa, v.a.

calendar, n. Wiyawapi.

call, (cry out, slander). Kicaŋ, v. - to the dead. Kico, v.; ekico, v.a. Paŋ, v.n. - out, yell: iki- , v.a.; kici- , v. - for; ki- , - to; -yaŋ, adv. -ing out; -yaŋhaŋ, adv. Wawośtegla, v. - bad names; yatimahelicu, v.a. - into the house. Hei...uyeto, Hey, top there, wait!

callous, v. Iyanuŋga(Ȟ), v.n.: -ya, v.a.; yunuŋga, v.a. Make - . Iyak'oza, n.

calm, Ablaka(e)(g): -yela, adv. -ly; -hiŋgla, v.; -la, n., adj.; iy-yela, adv. Caŋtiyozikiya, v.n. Be - . Oiyobluya, n., adj.

camera, n. Itocicacu.

camp, (encamp). Gliyuŋka, v. pos. Hoiyokise, n. Aiglagya, v. Ohegle, n. A good place to - ; opic'iye, n. Ti: a- , v.n. Be en-ed; ahi- , v.; e- , v.a.; e-kaga, v.; e-kel, adv.; e-yoyaŋka, express.; ewico- , v. col. pl.; o- , v. Make - ; o-wota, otuwota, n. An old en-ment; o-wotaŋl, adv. At an old en-ment; -gliyoya, v. - at the hunting area; oe- , n. An en-ment ahead; -yopeyapi, n. A -ing about the herd.

can, Mas'wognaka, Canned food, n.
candid, Aślaya(e), adv.: -la, adv.
candidate, n. Icajeyatapi,
candle, n. Pelijaŋjaŋ ska: -ihupa, n. - stick; -iyukse, n. Snuffer; -ośtaŋ, n. - stick; -ska oognake, n. - stick. Petijaŋjaŋ ska, n. Pelijaŋjaŋ aglehaŋ, n. - stick.

cane, n. Sage: kisagye, v. Turn into a - ; sagye; sagyetoŋ, v. Use for a staff in walking; sagyeya, v.a.

canyon, (valley, draw, gulch). Mnikaośkokpa.
capable, Cf. unable. Okihi, v. Be - . Okipi, v. Be - to hold, admit, receive. Oweśuŋkeca, v.n. Incapable of. Mnaŋyaŋ, adv. Capably; woimnaŋka, adj. Strong; woimnaŋyaŋ, adv.

capture, (captive). Gmuŋka, v.a.; gmuŋk waciŋ, v.a. Ahioyuspa, v.a. Napiyuskiya, v.a. Make - ; napiyuza, v.a. Wicatoka, n. A male captive; witoka, A female captive; wiwayaka, n. A captive from another people.

carcass, n. Tat'eca (a ruminant).
care, (keep). Awaŋyaŋ(gla)ka, v. Look after; awaŋkiciyaŋka, v. Watch over. Cucic'iŋ, v.a. Gnaka(e): ekici-, v.; haŋa-la s'e, adv. -fully; haŋiyas'e, adv. -ing, holding -fully. Ahopa, v.a.; ahokipa, v. pos. Kśija: akici-, v.a.; a- , v.a. Nica: akici- , v.a. Ekicioŋpa, v. Pa(kpa)taŋ: i- , v. refl.; kici- , v. - for. Ataŋ, v.a.: -toŋyaŋ, v.a. Walakotaśni, adj. Not caring for own. Wasaza(s), adj. Well-guarded from hardship: -kiya, v. - for tenderly. Woawaciŋ, n. Cares. Ikiciyuśtaŋ, v.

careful, Ikpataŋyaŋ, adv.; iktahela; kaiwaŋyaŋgya (prudently); kaiyaciŋyaŋ, kaslala; kiwakaŋyeś (with babies); nawakaŋkaŋla; napeyahaŋ; ptepakaȞ'epi s'e, adv. With great care. Wakicokic'uŋ, adv. -ly.

careless, adj. AȞ'aŋȞ'aŋka; aȞ'aŋȞ'aŋ, v.a. Do -ly. Aśkehaŋ, v.n. Ȟlete, n. -ness. Tokiŋś, adv. -ly; tokiŋśyakel.

caress, v.a. Kigna. Cf. fondle.
carpenter, n. Caŋpajipe: o- , n. - shop.

carry, v.a. Agla(ya), gloaya, glogla. Ai, v.a., v. col. pl. Ahiyaya(gla), v.a. Akiyuhapi, v. pl.; akiyuȞpa, v. Au, v.a., v. col. pl. Awiŋyeyapi, v. pl. Cutic'iŋ, v.; cutikic'iŋ, v. pos. Hośikaya, v. K'iŋ, v.a. Pack: o- , v., n. Tokśu: a- , v.a. Transport, - off, away, pick up; etokicikśu, v. Wotakuniśni, v.a. - off (by rain).

cart, Cf. wagon. Waŋjilak'iŋ, n. Two-wheeled - .

cartilage, (gristle). Pamnumnuga, n. (of nose).
carve, v.a. Go: apa- , v.a.; ipa- , n.; kicipa- ; wagata, v.a. (by knife); wa- , wa-kiya, v.a.; wa-pi, n. Mark on a game hoop; wakici- , v. - for; waki- , v. pos. - own. Wagweza, v.a. Roughen with a knife.

castrate, v. Susu icu.
catch, (hold). Cf. hold. Icaśtiŋyaŋka, v. - up with. Iciyaȟpaya, v.a. Infect others. Kapa(e): wo- , n. A -er; ya- , v.a. - in mouth; yu- , v.a. - a ball. Oze, v. Take, get. Yagmica, v. - the hair (by mouth). Yuza(s), v.: oyuspa, v.a. Take hold of.

catechism, n. Woiyuŋge wowapi.
caterpillar, n. Azewicahiŋśma.

cause, v. aux. Kiya, Make be, do etc. Oŋ, prep. (means, reason, purpose): -eciyataŋhaŋ, adv. By means of, because of; -etaŋhaŋ, adv. For that reason. Otumakoskaŋl, adv. Without - .

caution, v.a. Aȟ'iŋȟ'iŋciya; aȟ'iŋlȟ'iŋlciyelakel, adv. Anahaha, adv.

cave, Cf. sink. Oswahaŋ, part. -ing in. Paoksa, v.a. Make - in.
cease, v. Yaśtaŋ (talking).

celebrations, (days, occasions). Jesus Toŋpi, Christmas. Kini Aŋpetu, Easter. Wiwaŋyaŋkwacipi, Sundance; oiwawaŋyaŋgwaci, Site of the Sundance. Woacaŋkśiŋ, Passover.

cellar, n. Maka tipi (sod house).
celluloic, (cellophane). Paŋkeska, n.
cement, n. Iŋyaŋ maka.
cemetery, n. Owicaȟe.
censer, n. Owaizilye.
center, n. Cogiŋ; cokab, adv.; hocokata, n., adv. Ikaŋye, adv.

ceremony, n. Wakaŋ wicoȟ'aŋ. Caŋnuŋpa Wakaŋ, The Sacred Pipe. Haŋbleceyapi, Vision Quest. Hokśicaŋkiyapi, Releasing the Soul. Huŋkapi, Making Relatives; huŋkalowaŋpi, walowaŋpi. Inipi, Purification Bath. Iśnata Awicalowaŋ, Maiden Advance to Womanhood. Tapa Waŋyaŋkap, Throw the Ball; tab waŋkayeyapi. Wiwaŋyaŋk Wacipi, Sundance. Ptehiko, v. Do a - for buffalo. Wahiŋyajice, n. Fur for a sacred - . Waŋyeya, v.a. Shoot arrows in a sacred dance. Wowiyuŋkagapi, n. - before a buffalo hunt.

certain, Ciŋtok(a), adv. -ly. Ecaś, ecaśni, eeś, ehaś, adv. Ehaŋkec'uŋ, ehaŋk'uŋ, adv. Haŋtuk'e, adv. Hecehaŋ, heceya, adv. Huŋśe, adv. Wicakapiȟca, adj. Absolutely - .

chair, (seat). Caŋakaŋyaŋkapi, n.; caŋhaŋkayaŋkapi, caŋkaŋkapi. Oikpahuŋzapi, n. A rocking - .
champ, v.a. Yakaka.

chance, Okiwotahena, adv. By mere - .
change (alter). Caŋtekaptaŋyaŋ, adj. Changeable in own views; caŋteyuślog, v. Hoakab hiyuya, v.a. Piya iyukcaŋ, v. - one's mind. Itokeca, v.n.; ayatogya, v.; ayutogyakel, adv. Yamniyeya, v.a. Alter course (by speaking to).

channel, (strait, isthmus). Kiyute, n.
chap, Tuta, adj. -ed. Yuȟ'i: - s'e, adj. -ed-like; wica- , n. -ping.

charm, (palladium). Izuyapi, n.; wiciyokipi, n. Excellence, beauty; wotawe, n. (for use in war).
chase, Cf. run, hunt, buffalo. Okuwa, v.a.; wawokuwa.

chatter, v. Hiyakigle. Yakoka, v.a. (the teeth).
cheap, (easily bought). Awaśaka, adj.: -la, o-la; waśagyela, adv. Easily.

check, (latch). Cf. latch, money. Iyopazaŋ, v. Paglega, v.a. - off (a list).
cheer, v.n. Akiś'a. Caŋlwaśteya, v.a.; caŋteyat'iŋza, caŋteyawaśte, caŋtopeya, icaŋlkaspeya; kacaŋlabiyeya, v. - up. Olabya, v.a. - up (by gifts). Wawimagagayeca, n. A cheery person; wawiśtaŋyeca. Yableza, v.a. Enlighten, make sober.

cheese, Cf. milk.
cherish, v.a. Pataŋ.
chew, v..a. Aya: -bleca, -blu, -gwa; oyagwa, v. - on and spoil. Iyata, v.; wayata; yata, v.a. (taste). Yas'aka, v. Be unchewable. Yaśkica, v.a.

chief, Cf. lord, government, military. Itaŋcaŋ, n. President, chairman. Naca, n. An able voice of the community. Nigetaŋkiŋyaŋ, n. Nickname for a - .

child, (little children). Ciŋca, n. Wakaŋheja, n.; wakaŋyeja. Zipaŋ, n. A youngster.

chimney, n. Ośota ogna iyaya, ośotiyaye, śota sam iyaye.

chisel, v. Kape. Cf. tool.
choke, (crane). Katka, v.; katke. Niya: -śnit'eya, v.a. - to death; o-śni t'e, v. - to death. S'iŋ, adv. Craning.

choose, (elect). Apiic'iya, v. refl. Ka(ca,gla)ȟniga, v.: i- , v.; kica- , - for. Osukaŋlyuza, v. Take one's choice. Owaśtekal, adv. -ing, picking.

chunky, adj. Pśuŋka. Wohota, adj. Chubby.

church, n. Owacekiya, The Church; the church building. Tipi wakaŋ, n. The church building, chapel. Tipi ipasotkaya, n. - tower.

churn, n. Iwoc'u. Woc'o, v.a.
cider, n. Taspaŋhaŋpi.
cinder, n. Cata. Catanaślogya, v. Hill corn with ashes.

circle, (encircle). Hocokatoŋyaŋ, adv. Kaowiŋȟ, adv. In a circle. Mime: -ya, adv. In a - ; okimeya, v.a. En- , enclose; adv. -ling; o-yela, adv. Enling; wo- , n.; yu-ya, adv. Circular, in a - .

circumcise, v.a. Waȟlaya.
circumspect, (careful). Kicuŋniyaŋkel, adv.; owahecelya, aiyaciŋyaŋ, kaiwaŋyaŋgya. Wowakta, n. -ion.
citizen, Aigluha, v. refl. Provide for self.

claim, v. Eic'icaga. Glogliyacu, v.a. Oȟ'aŋglawa, v. pos. - as own, lay - to.
clamor, Cf. noise.
clamp, v. Anagipa; anagibya, v.a.
clap, (applaud). Glaskapa, v. pos. Napeglaskapa, v.n.

clasp, v. Kaskita, - in the arms.
class, n. (sort, kind, division, species). Cf. name. Obe, n.; owe, ocaje, okage.

clatter, v.a. Ayakoka.
claw, v.a. Oyupota, - to pieces; oyupote, n. - mark. Siośtuŋkala, n. Buffalo calf - ; siśtaȟe, n. Little - on the foot of cow or horse.

clean, v. Iglatata, v. refl. Pakaŋ, v.a. (rub). Pasluta, v. (push out). Waajaja, v.a. Take off - .

clear, adj. Bleza(s): a- , v.n.; a-ya, v.a.; blezela, adj., Caȟ'owata, adv. Gaŋgaŋyela, adv., adj. Gmi: - s'e, v.t. - off, crop; yu- , v.a. Icagiśniyaŋ, adv. Iglatokaŋ, v. refl. Iyaślaya, adv. Iyusotka, adj. (weather). Jajaya, adv. Plainly. Jaŋjaŋla, adj. Transparent. Ka: -hmiŋ, v. - off (field); -owotaŋiŋ, v. - off (weather); owotaŋiŋ, adj.; -skaya, v.a. Make - up; ska, adj.; -sk'iyaya, - up; -sota, v. - up, use; -taŋiŋ, v. - off, make apparent. Kogli, adj. Translucent. Ototola, adj. - of brush; owaŋkewaśte, zazecela.

clearing, n. Ocuŋwanice (in woods), otiŋtoska.

clerk, n. Wowapikaga, A scribe.
clever, Wowayupike, n. -ness.
climb, v. Iyali, v.a.; iyakili. Kiyahaŋ, kiyahe, v.n. Oskapa, v.a. - up, shinny up.
cling, Cf. stick. Kaayaskab, okiyaskapa, v.n. -ing to, cleave to. Kiyuza, v. - to. Okiyasiŋ, v.n. - together.

clock, (watch, appurtenances). Mazaśkaŋśkaŋ, n. A watch: -ikaŋ, Fob; -taŋka, Clock.
clog, Cf. stick. Otkapa, v.n.

close, (near, together, shut). Aki: -pśaya, adv.; -ptaŋ, adv. Together, joined; -śoka, adj. Thick stand; -śogya, adv.; -t'eya, adv.; -ś'agya, adv.; -ś'aka, adj. Aogluta, v.n.; aogluteya, v.a., part., adv. ; aoyutkuka, v.a.; kaotkuȟ, - behind, shut. Naogluta, v. Shut up; ogluta, v.n.; paogluta, v.a. - up, over (rub). Gmuza: iśto- , v.n., adj.; pao- , v.a. Shut by hand. Yuiyupseicu, v. Shut tight (tent). Kita: -la, adv. - together; na-ka, v.a. pos. Shut in own. Ektawapa, adv. Goŋga, adj. Icaśtaŋ, adv. Ici: -pasiseya, -śleca, adv. Ipu: -skica, v.n.; -sli, v.n. Iyokaseyela, adv. Lecegla, adv.

cloth, (linen, etc.). Mniȟuha, Linen, cotton; paper: -ośpula, Pieces of - ;

-oyuȟlece, Rag; -paⁿpaⁿla, Silk; -ska, Muslin; white paper; -skazibzipela, Fine muslin; -toȟca, Blue - ; -wapaȟlate, Crape. Opehe, A bolt of -. Śinaópapuⁿ, List - , Cf. Śinazibzipela, Broad - , Cf. Śina apaȟlate, Ribbon.

clothe, Cf. cover. Ogiⁿtoⁿ, v.a. Wakoyagkicatoⁿ, v. Yupika, v.a. - well; n. One who dresses well.

clothing, n. Oigluze (in gen.).
bonnet, Maśtewapośtaⁿ.
coat, Ogle: -kauⁿjica, Short - ; -hiⁿśma, Fur - ; -tahu, - collar; mniȟuha - , Light - ; -upihaⁿska, Prince Albert - ; aiⁿkicatoⁿ, v. Wear a - .
drawers, Maheluⁿzoge (shorts).
gloves, Napiⁿkpa.
hat, Wapośtaⁿ.
loin cover, Miyapahe.
neckerchief, Mniȟuhawanap'iⁿ.
pants, Nite okijata, oⁿzoge.
scarf, Nakputake.
shawl, v. Aiⁿkitaⁿ, Wear a -.
shirt, Ogle.
skirt, Nitehepi.
stockings, Hiⁿyakoⁿ, huⁿyakoⁿ, iyohe.
sweater, Oglezigzica.
undershirt, Mahelogle, nitośki.
vest, Kaȟlogośtaⁿpi, ogleciyuksa.

brush, Ogle papoa.
peg, Ogle iyotkeye.

cloud, n. Maȟpiya, Heaven; sky. Cf.: ama- , v., adj. Cloud over; cu- , v. Maȟpihpiya, adj. Scattered - . Maȟpiohaⁿzi, n. - shadow. Op'oya, adv. In a - (of dust, snow).

clover, Cf. herbs. Blaye zitkatacaⁿ hu stola, n.

clown, n. Heyoka, On who flaunts by his antics the faults and unreasonableness of men. Pizo, n.

club, n. Caⁿȟpi, caⁿksa; hohucaⁿȟpa, icat'e.

clumsy, Cf. deformed.

cluster, Cf. bunch, pack. Iyagegnag, n.; iyageya, adv. Ośipa, n.

coal, n. Caȟli, Charcoal; makacaȟli.

coated, Aś'aka, v.n. Get - ; aś'agya, adv.

coffee, Cf. medicine. Pejuta sapa, n. Wakalyapi, n.

coffin, n. Wicaȟapi ognake, caⁿ wognaka.

cohabitate, Cf. intercourse. Wiinaȟma, v.

coil, v.a. Kakśa: a- , v.a. Wawagla, v. Make un- (cut).

cold, Cowaiglazaⁿ, v.n. Be - . Cuwita, adj.: a- , v.n.; -gla, v. Op'oza, adj. Cold and clear (frosty): op'osa. Pamni s'e u, v. Have a - . Sni: adj., n.; Ȟtao- , adj.; ia- , v.; o- , n. (weather, winter, year); adj.; o-ika, adj.; -yaȟota, v.n. Take - , breathe in - ; -yaⁿ, v. Become - (weather).

collapse, Cf. zigzag. Kakśaⁿ, v. (bend up).

collect, Cf. gather. Mna: waka- , v.; waka-ka, n. A -or; wa-yaⁿ, n. A -or; wopa-yaⁿ, adv. -ed together. Yuptaegnag, adv. -ively; yuptaya, adv. Together; yuptayela, v.a. To put together.

color, n., adj. Hiⁿtokeca (in gen.).

Black:
sapa, śapa, adj.
saⁿokpukpe, adj. Gray.
saⁿopapa, adj. Turning gray.
wisabye, n. -ing.
wosapa, n. -ness.
asapa, aśapa, ayaśapa, ayuśapa, isabye, isapa, v. -en.
kiciyusapa, v. -en for.
kisapa, v.n. Become - , bare (ground).
sabya, v.a. -en; adv. Darkly.
wakaśapa, v. Make - (strike).
wasabya, v. -en.

White:
saⁿ, Gray, whitish, yellowish; saⁿyela, adj.
ska, White, clear; skaya; skayakel, adv. In a clear manner.
śaⁿśaⁿ, adj. Whitish.
asaⁿ, aska, icasaⁿ, ipasaⁿ, isaⁿyaⁿ, v.a. Make - .
kasaⁿ, v. Turn - ; kasaⁿsaⁿ, v. Scrape - .
kisaⁿ, v. Become - for.
saⁿyaⁿ, v.a. -en; adv. Whitish.
waskaska, n. - things.
waskaya, v. To -wash.
wisaⁿye, n. Whiting.

Red:
luta, lul, adj. Scarlet.
śa, adj.
śayela, adv. Reddest.

ziśa, adj. Reddish.
takuśaśa, n. A - thing.
wiśaye, n. Red coloring.
wośa, n. Redness.
aśa, v. Be - .
naśa, v. Become - .
paśa, v. Rub - .

Yellow:
zi, zizi, ziya, ziyela, adj.
hohusaŋ s'e, adj. Light yellow.
aziya, v. Make - .
ogiya, v. Paint - .
ziya, v. Dye or paint - .

Blue, Green:
to, adj. Blue, green.
toto, adj. Green.
skaŋyeca, adj. Blue.
toḣca, adj. Blue.
tolaḣcaka, adj. Very blue.
tosaŋ, adj. Light blue.
towaŋjica, adj. All blue.
tozi, adj. Light green.
tozitka, adj. Greenish, caŋḣpaŋ pezi.
wato(to)ya, adv. Grass-like green.
ziyato, adj. Green.
witoye, n. Dye or paint of blue or green.
ato, ito, itoto, v.n. Be blue or green.
tokiya, toya, v. Dye or paint blue or green.

Miscellaneous:
astaŋ, v. Make purple.
kaḣota, v. Make gray.
hiŋzi, adj. Cream.
gi, Brown: wo- , n.; yu-cala, v. Make a little - .
ḣota, adj. Gray, brown: ḣolya, adj. Gray; oḣolya.
ogi, adj. Rust brown.
oḣ'a, adj. Black and white speckled; oḣ'aka, adj. Gray, all colors mingled.
staŋ, adj. Dark purple; staŋka, adj. Purple.
śagi, adj. Auburn, sandy.
śamna, adj. Dark brown.
tolute, adj. Purple.
tośa, adj. Purple.
tosapa, adj. Grape.
gleśka, adj. Spotted, striped.

comb, Kca: gla- , v. pos.; ka- , v.; kica- , v. - own; kicica- , - for; kicipa- , v. - out; nasuŋpa- , n.; pahiŋnasuŋpa- , n. - (of porcupine tail); pa- , v.a. Disentangle. Kaswa, v. Curry. Pesleteśa, n. Cock's - .

come, (arrive).
auŋ, v.n. - with the wind.
gli, v.n. Arrive home:
a-yoḣpaya, v. col. pl.
-cu, v.
-yoni, v. pos.
-yoḣpaya, v.
gloki, v. pos.
haŋnataŋtaŋ u, v.
ahi, v.n. Arrive at; v.a.:
-gnaka, v.a. -yahaŋ, v.n.
-icu, v. -yaŋka, v.n.
-mniciya, v. -yohpaya, v. col.
-napa, v.n. -yokakiŋ, v.
-oyuspa, v.a. -yu, v.a. (hiyu).
-tebya, v. -yukaŋ, v.
-ti, v. -yuŋka, v.n.
-witaya, v. -yuslohaŋ, v.n.
-wota, v. -yuśtaŋ, v.
-yagle, v.a., v.n. -yuwege, v.

hi, v.n. Arrive:
-bu, v.n. -yakapta, v.n.
-ayaŋpa, v. -yuŋka, v.n.
-heya, v.n.
-huŋni, v. iglo- , v. refl.
-mniciya, v. col.

hiyo, v. Come for:
-hi, v.
-hikiya, v.a.
-hiya, v.a.
-ḣpaya, v.n.
-ḣpeya, v.a.
-yo u, v.

hiyu, v.n. Come from out of:
ao- , v.n.
iglo- , v. refl.
-kiya, v.a.
-ya, v.a.
o- , v. (through).
wicoŋkaŋ-ic'iya, v. - unasked.

ho, v.n. imp. Come now: hośi:
-hi. -kai.
-i. -kau.
-kahi. -u.

i, v. Have gone to:
ainapa, v.a. iglagyake, adv.
igloi, v. refl. iglonica, v. refl.
icagejuya, v. iyagle, v. refl.

aki, prep. in comp. For:
-najiŋ, v. -yugo, v.n.
-nataŋ, v. pos.
kiyokpeca, v.a. Have - back.

okaḣloka, v.a. - through.
paśpeya, v.a. Make come out.

u, v.n. Be Coming:
ukiya, v. pl. They - home; v.a. Make come.
uyekiya, v.a. Make come.
uwa, uwiye, v. imp. Come! (women).
uwa yo, v. imp. Come! (men).
au, v.n. - out on; v. col. They - .

ya, suffix. Of cause.
oya, v.n., v.a. Come off, wash off.
igloya, v. refl.

comfort, Waciŋtoŋgnake, n. -er; waciŋtoŋgnagya, v.a. Wicakikcaŋpte, n. A -er. The Holy Spirit. Wowicakigna, n. -er.

comical, (funny, cute). Cf. laugh. Oȟ'aŋwiȟa, adj.
command, (enforce). Iwakicoŋza(e), v.a. n. Oiekic'uŋ, v.n. Enforce obedience. Ši, v.a. Bid one. Waokiya, v. Cf. imperatives.

commerce, (trading). Wopetoŋpi, n.
common, Hecetuke, adv. Ikce, adj., adv.: -ka, adj.; -ya(kel), adv. Kiska, v. Recover - sense. Wakic'uŋpi, - property.

compare, Cf. figure, parable. Wiyaciŋ, v. - to, with.
compassion, (pity). Ioŋšila, v. Have - on: -ya, adv. Wakikcaŋpta, adj. -ate. Wocaŋtognake, n. pity.

complain, v.a. Acicaȟlo, v.a. Anagwag, v.a.; anagwaka. Igle, v. Pa, v.a. Bark. Wayašihtiŋka, n. A -er.
complete, Akigna, adv. -ly. Iyuȟpa, v. Be al finished.

complex, Woošsiške, n. -ity.
complicate, (confuse, abrupt). Ošśkiška, adj. -ed; ośkiśkiic'iya, v. refl. Get confused.
compliment, n. Wicayataŋpi, Praise.

comply, v. Wicakicila.
comprehend, (know, opinion, guess). Yukcaŋ, v.a.
compress, v.a. Yaopo (bite), yapo.
concave, (hollow). Ośkokpa, n. Concavity. Šmaka, adj.

conceal, Cf. hide. Woinahme, n. -ment.
concern, Iwatokiya, v.n. Be -ed. Iyowaja, adv. -ed in; owaja, v.n. Be -ed in. Wikic'uŋ, adv. With a - ; waciŋ-śni, n. One unconcerned.

conciliate, v. Wayuwaȟa.
condemn, v.a. Yasu:a- , v.a.; glasu, v. pos.; wasuya, v. Judge; -pi, n. -ation.

condiment, (sauce). Iyul: -kitoŋ, -toŋ, n. Sauce. Mniskuya, n. Salt. Yamnumnugapi, v. Black pepper.
cone, n. Wazipiŋkpa, Pine - .

confer, Cf. council. Owoglake, n. A conference room, council chamber.
confess, v. refl. Oiglaka, Make self known.
confidence, Waciŋ: -kiciyapi, n.; -yeȟci, adv. Very confidently; -yekiya, v.a. Make have - ; -yepica, n. Source of - ; -yeya, v. Cause to take - ; wo- , n.

confirm, (corroborate). Oyuma, oyuślata, v.
confuse, Hoka ca haŋye kiŋye s'e, adj. -ed; hokiiyokpaza, adj. Come into darkness. Wośkiśka(e), part. Causing - ; n. Trouble bewilderment. Yaignuni, v.a. (interruptions).

conjure, (sucking etc.). Kiciyapa, v. Suck for (as if drawing off poison). Piya, v.a. Repair: wa- , v. - the sick, to powwow; wa-pi, n. -ing.

connect, v.a. Ayazuŋta. Iciyokihe, adj.: -ya, v.a.
consanguinity, Cf. relative. Wotakuye, n.
conscious, (remember). Kiksuya, Be - .

consecutive, Iyaza, adv. -ly.

consider, v.n. Akiya. Bleza: aki- , v.; iyu- , v. refl. Caŋteyuza, v.n. Eciŋ, v.n.; -ka, v.; h- , v. Epca, v.: -pca, v. red.; epceca, v.; h- , v. Ecaŋkiŋ, v.a.: h- , v.a. Hecetulaka, v.n. Heceyala, v.a. Ayu(glu)hete, v.a. Awi(i)yukcaŋ, v.a. Ic'ila, v. refl. Awaciŋ, v.a.: -kel, adv.; -pi, n. -ation; -ya, adv.; -yakel, adv.; awakiciŋ, v.a. pos.; ewaciŋ, v.a.: -ka, v.a.; iwaciŋ, v. Igluwitaya, v. refl. Yawa, v.a.

consistent, (congruous, connected). Cf. weave. Zoŋtaheya, adv. -ly.
console, (comfort). Kcaŋpta(e): ki- , v.a.; waki- , v.a. Comfort; wakikcaŋpte, n. Comforter. Yuasniyaŋ, v.a.

conspicuous, adj. Ipasotka: -ya, adv. Okitaŋiŋ, v.n. Be - .

consult, (wise). Kiksapa, v.n.
contain, (hold, carry). Kipi, v.n. Be sufficient for. Ognake, n. A -er for keeping things.

contemn, v.a. Iwakiniya, Get out of humor with. Kat'apt'apa, v.a. (gesturing).
contend, Wowakitaŋ, n. A point of contention, of a resolution set; wowakitaŋye.
content, v.n. Waciŋiyokipi, Be -ed.

continue, v. Yeye, To last.
continual, (unceasing, continuous). Aḣtateśniya, adv. Glaheya, adv. Ḣ'uŋwiśtaŋ śni, adj. Incessant. Katiŋtiŋyeya, adv. With no stop. Kipsakaheśni, adv. Oaye, n. Continuation. Oziwanil, adv. Without rest. Śna, adv.

contract, (shrink). Naśiŋśiŋ, v.n. Natipa, v.n. Draw up, curl, cramp.
contradict, Cf. oppose. Yaglakiŋyaŋ, v.a. - self.

contrary, (against). Ot'uŋyaŋkel, adv. - to liking. Uŋmaciyataŋ, adv. On the - , from the other side; uŋma ecetkiya, uŋma eciyataŋhaŋ. Yus'oyakel, adv. - to expectations.

control, v.a. Ilaka. Napiyusya, adv. -ling. Oic'onica, v. - self. S'agic'iya, v. refl. - self, be resolute. Tacupala s'e, adv. Easily losing self control.

convalesce, Kibleza, adj.
convenient, Wicakijeśniyaŋ, adv. Convenienced.
convert, (persuade, change). Yahomni, v.a. Turn one around by arguments.

convex, Ipazilya, adv.
convince, (persuade). Glahomni, v. pos. Oekiye, v.n.; n. Conviction. Wicakelakiya, v.a.
convulse, v.n. Natiŋ.

cook, v.n. Alo, aloza(s): alesabya, alosabya, v.a.; -ya, v.a. Kceya, v. Hang over: a- , v.a. Apasnoŋ, v.a. Śpaŋ, adj. -ed; v.n. Be -ed: a- , v.n. -yaŋ, v.a.; -kiciciya, v.a. - for; -kiya, v.a. - own. Loliḣ'aŋ, v. Oceoŋ, part. -ed. Wohaŋ(e), v.: -la, n. One who cooks; -kiya, v. Have for a - ; -kiyapi, n.

Utensils:
boiler (double), Psiŋuŋwohaŋpi.
colander, Wiyujaja.
knife (kitchen), Miyutapapi.
pan (bread), Wopaska; wopaska taŋka, A dish - ; mas'wicoŋpi, Frying - ; wiceuŋpe, witake.
pot (kettle), cega. Cf.
range (cook), Oŋ(oŋ)wohaŋpi oceti.
sieve, Icaŋcaŋ, wicacaŋ, wiyucaŋcaŋ.
strainer, Ipuskepa; wikase, Gravy - .

cool, Sni: cu- , adj; Ḣtacu- , n.; icica- , v.; iyo-yaya, v.; kao- , v. Refresh; -ya, v.a.; Wo-, v.a. (blow).

coordinate conj., adj.
tohaŋ (tohaŋl,tohaŋyaŋ)...ca na: Whenever...then.
tohaŋ...hehaŋ: As long as (until, as far as)...then; tohaŋhuŋniyaŋ, tohuŋhuŋniyaŋ.
tohiŋni...śni: Never...ever.
tokel...cana ecel: As...so.
tokeya...ca hehaŋl: Before...then.
tuktel...hel: Where...there.

Uŋma, umaŋ, adj. The one...the other.
Uŋmagma, adj. One or the other.

copy, (model). Okaga, v.a.: -pi, n. Model, image.
cord, Cf. string.
cordial, Wolakolkiciyapi, n. Amity, -ity.

corner, Cf. bend. Oblece, adj. -ed. Blotoŋ: kao- , v.a. Make a - ; o- , n., adj. Kaḣmi(ŋ), n. An inside - ; o- , n. (of houses). Najiŋyaŋ, v.a. Hold at bay. Oisa, n. The outer - . Uŋgnagata, adv. In the - behind the door; uŋgnage, n. -s within either side of the door.

corral, n. Ośuŋkoyuspe.
correct, v.a. Gletoŋ. Iyokteka, v. Reprove. Iyopeya, v. Punish, scold; iyopekiya. Paśiḣtiŋ, v. Do incorrectly. Yaecetu, v.a. - a statement. Zuŋlya, adv. -ly, joined.
corrupt, (make bad, injure). Iyuśica, v.a.

cotton, Cf. pith. Popopa.
cough, v.n. Have a spell of -ing. Hoḣpa, v.n.: - Ḣ'aŋ haŋska, n.; -pi, n.

Kaȟkaga, v. - up. Toŋȟliȟli, v. - up phlegm.

council, (consultation, conference). Cf. consult, confer. Owoglake, n. - chamber.

count, v. Glaota, glatonana (one's own). Yawa, v.a.: glawa, v. pos.; ici- , v.a.; kici- , - for; o- , v.a. - in; i- , v.a.

courage, Cf. terrible.
court, n. Wakiyatipi (house); okiya, v.a. Talk to; okiciciya, v. Talk together. Wakaŋȟ'aŋ, v. - a woman (by music); wiyapė, v. Wait for a woman; wiokiya, v. Talk flirtingly: -pi, n. Courting. Wioyuspa, v. Detain a woman.

cover, (clothe).
cegnake, n.: -kitoŋ, v.; cegnakitoŋ.
cekpiyuskite, n.
ceśka: -saŋsaŋ kśupi, n.; -ikaŋ, -ipazize, -iyutaŋ, n.
cuwi: -gnagya, v.a.; -gnaka, n.; -yuskite, n. Aiglagla, v. refl. Aigluśla, v. refl. Iglutaŋ, v. refl.: a- . Gluza(e): ai- , v. refl.; i- , v. refl.; iyo- , n. Wearing apparel.
ha: -kitoŋ, v.; -kiya, v.a.; -ya, v.a. -yake, n.; -yapi, n.
igluȟniga, v. refl.
iŋkiya, v.a.
iśtojuha, n.
ka(gla)ȟpa(e): a- , v. pos.; a-kitoŋ, ai- , v. refl.; a- , a-kitoŋ, a-toŋ, v.a.; a-ya, adv.; akaȟpikpeya, v.a.; a- , n.; itea- , n.; iya- , n.; wiya- , n.; iya-ya, adv.; oa- , n. (bed); wa- , v.
kasa, v.a. - with snow.
naataŋiŋśni aya, v. - tracks.
aognaka, v.a.
aokata, v.a.
iyaopemni, v.a.
poślicoma, v. Have head -ed; pośliśli, v. Have face -ed.
auŋyeya, v.a.
yuta: a- , v.a.; naogluta, v.a. (foot) ayuwiŋta, v.a. Overlay.

covet, v. Kizomi, koŋ(uŋ), waicucukteȟciŋ.
cow, (ruminant). Pte, n.: -gleśka, Tame cattle; -waniyaŋpi; -makicima, Heifer; -watogla, Wild - ; -wiŋyela, female - . Togaŋgaŋokiwaslecapi, n. A very fat - .

cowardice, Cf. fear.

crack, (deform).
ȟuga(ȟ): ka- , v. Break; na- , v.a.; pa- , v.a. (push on); ya- , v.a. Open, crush; yu- , v.a. (by hand).
kpa: pelna-kpa, v.n. red. Crackle.
kpi: ka- , v. Open, pierce; kpa- , v. - own (shell); na- , v. (by foot); pa- , v.a. Mash.
ptuja, adj. -ed: ka- , v.a.; na- , v.n.
sleca: na- , v.a., v.n.
wega: kiciyu- , v. Fracture.
zu: pa-ya, v. (bone).

cradle, n. Caŋic'ik'oŋpa, wicakahuŋhuŋzapi.
cram, v.a. Paoskica.
cramp, Tipa: ayu- , v.a.; huna- , v.n.; huyu- v.; kaŋna- , v.; yu- , v.a. (of muscles etc.), fold up, crisp.

crane, v. Yukos'iŋ, - the neck.
cranky, Śiŋkciŋyaŋ, adv. Toies'a, n. A crank, a critic.
crawl, v.n. Slohaŋ: a- . Śniyaŋyaŋ: a- , v.n., adv.; o- , v.n. - about within. Ayuȟab, adv.

crazy, Gnaśkiŋyaŋ: ki- , v.n. Turn - ; waya- , v. Talk one - . Cf. fool.

creak, Kiza: caŋka- , v.n.; ka- , v.a. Make - (rub); na- , v.a. (shoes); pa- , v.a. Make - (rub). Mnuza: na- , v.a.; nao- ; nu- , adj.; mnumnus, v. Piza, v.n.: na- , v.n.; pa- , v.a. Make - .

cream, Cf. milk.
create, Oicage, n. Creation; okage, n.; Waicaȟye, n. The Creator; wawicaȟya, v.; wawicaȟye, n. Maker, creator. Wamakognaka, n. Creation, the universe.

credit, Icazo: a- , v.a.; -pi, n.; ik- , v.a.; oicazo, n. Taking of things on - .
credulous, adj. Tawaciŋpaŋpaŋla, Weak-minded, naive.

creep, (move noiselessly). Naslata, v.a. - up to.
crest, Cf. comb. Peśa, n.
crinkle, v.n. Kakeca.
crippled, Cf. deformed. Ośteka, adj. Taŋśica, adj.

crisp, Yukiyuteya, adv. Drawn up.
criticize, v.n. Nagwaka (fig.). Toia, v. To knock. Waglaglaka, v. - food, be finicky. Yakatiŋtiŋ, v.a. Set

right (talking).
croak, v.a. Pajiᶯca, Make - (shake).
crooked, adj. Ciᶯȟtiᶯ. Glakiᶯkiᶯyaᶯ, adv. Ȟmi(ᶯ), adj.: ayu-yaᶯ, adv.; -yaᶯ, adv.; ici-yaᶯ, adv.; o-ȟmiᶯyaᶯ, adj.; wapa- , v. Make - ; wayu- , v. Kśaᶯ, adj.: kśi- , adj. Ktaᶯ, adj. Bent; owiᶯga, adj. Pemni: ka- , v.a. śkopa(b), adj.: a-ya, adv.; a- , v.n.; aya- , v.a.; -ya, v.a., adv. Wapako, v. Cut, saw - .

crop, v.a. yagmi.
cross, v. Akokabya. Caᶯwicipaga, n. Hiᶯyaᶯza(e), v.n. Be - : -ca, adj.; o-ca, v.n. Be stern, cranky; ksizeca, adj. Stern. Hukaicicawiᶯyaᶯ yaᶯka, v. Kaicic'uya, v. (legs). Kaiciopteya, adv. (intersecting). Ociᶯśica, v.n. Be bad-tempered: -ya, adv. Evily disposed. Wega(e): ahiyu- , v. col. pl.; akiyu- , n.; caᶯicipa- , n. The Cross, crucifix; hiyu- , v.n.; icipa- , v.n.; iyu- , v.a.; kiyu- v. (a stream).

cross-eyed, adj. Iśtaȟmiᶯ. Iśtakśiᶯ, v.
crosswise, adv. Glakiᶯyaᶯ: na- , Set - , turned outward; taᶯ- , Across. Kaiteb, adv. Diagonally. Aiciyoptepteya, adv. Icipawaȟwaȟ, icipaweȟ, icipaweȟya, adv.

crowd, Gaᶯgaᶯśni, adv.: -yaᶯ. Hooyaza s'e, adj. Icata, v. Kaigejuya, adv. -ing in. Kaipustagya, adv. -ing against. Oȟli s'e, adv. -ed about. Paglakiᶯyaᶯ, adv. -ing to one side. Pani: ahi- , v.; e- , v.a. Paokaᶯśniyaᶯ, v. - out. Pata, adv. -ed together. T'eya: aki- , adv.; ici- , adv. T'iᶯza(s): ao-ya, v.a., adv.; hiyo- , v.; oci- , v.n. Be -ed. Wicoha, adv. Into the - . Wicotapiśniyaᶯkel, adv. Ahiwicoti, n.

crown, (fillet). Teślagkitoᶯ, v. Put on a - .
crumble, Ȟpu: ayu- , v.a.; ȟpu- , adj. -wahaᶯ, part.; -ya, adv. Kaoksa(e), - down: -ya. Oyukpakpa, v. - in. Okpaᶯla, adj. -ed. Ptuȟ'a, v.n. - down. Śpahaᶯhaᶯ, part. -ing away.

crumbs, Cf. leavings. Otutka, n.
crunch, v.n. Caᶯȟcaᶯga; adj. Mnuga, v.; mnuȟ. Yacaᶯga, v.n. Yaȟwu, v.n. Make a -ing noise.

crush, Cf. grind. Kpableca, v. - own; pableca, v.a. (weight from above) . Pakpaᶯ, v.a. Woskilya, v.a. (pound). Nasli, v.a. (by foot). Onataᶯ, v.a. - upon (harsh words). Yaśuja, v.a. (by mouth). Yuśuja, v.a. Naja, v.a. (by foot).

crutch, n. Caᶯhuapi,
cry, (moan). Cf. pout, sob, shout. Ceya, v.n.: wa- , v.a.; na- , v.a. (kick); owe- , v.n. - over. Śicahowa, v.n. - out: -ya, v.n. Moan; kahotoᶯ, v. Make - out.

cube, Cf. pack. Wak'iᶯlas'e, n.
cubit, n. Wiciśpa.
cultivate, (till, work). Cf. hoe. Maȟglamni, v.a. Okicaᶯye, n. -tion.

cumbersome, Cf. hinder. Oᴅaᶯga(e), v.n. Be - ; -ca, v.n. Be encumbered.

cupboard, n. Wakśica ognake.
curdle, (thicken by beating). Kagwu, v.; ogwu; onagwu, v.i. - in. Nini, adj. -ed.

cure, (heal). Aki: -sniya, v.a.; -sniyepicaśni, adj. Aogluta(e), v.n.: -ya, v.a. Asni: -ya, v.; -kiya, v.a.; -kiyekiya, -kiyeya; -pica, adj.; -ya, v.a.; kisnikiya, v.a.

curious, Woś'iᶯś'iᶯkiye, n. A curiosity.
curl, v.n. Ayumnimnija. Glaȟa, v. pos. Gugula, adj. Iyuwi, v. Twist; n. A vine. Nagmugmuᶯ, v.a. Crisp; nagmuᶯ, v.n. Owiᶯge, n. (hair); owiᶯȟya, adv. -ed, curved. Śkośkopa, adj. -ed. Yuȟa, v.n. - and branch out: -ȟa, adj. Curly.

current, Tatohekiya, adv. Against the - ; tatoheya.
curse, v. Glatoie. Śilaptaᶯyeya, v.a.; śilgla toie. Wayaśica, v. Speak evil of. Wośiliyagle, v. Be -ed, meet bad luck.

curtain, n. Ozaᶯ, wozaᶯ.
curve, Cf. geometry. Apahaya, adv. Convexly. Opuś'iᶯ, n. Arc, arch, a convex line. Owokśaᶯ, n.; wośkopa.

custom, (law, ceremony). Cf. work, follow. Oȟ'aᶯ, n.: wic- , n. Habit; -ya, v. Have for a - . Ope: wicoahope, n. Ceremony; wo- , n.

cut, v.a. Cf. break, Note on composing.

Prefix	Root
a-	*bla(ya) (flat).
aiyu(glu)-	blaza (rip open).
aka(gla)- *	*bleca.
awa- *	gapa.
cuwiyu-	gmi (fell).
huka(gla)-	gna.
huwa-	go.
ica(ka,gla)- *	huŋ (slash).
itena-	*ḣci (notch).
iwa-	ḣleca (to pieces).
ka(gla)- *	ḣloka (hole, out).
kai-	ḣpa (fall).
kaoyu-	ḣpu (bits).
ki-	ḣtaŋ.
kica(ka)- *	kaŋ.
kicica(ka)-	keza.
kiwa- (in two).*	koŋta (fray).
na-	*kpa (out).
o-	kpaŋ (cut fine).
oka-	kpi (crack).
okica(ka)- *	*ksa (cut off).
okiwa-	k'eza.(off clean).
owa- *	ni (fasten).
oyu-	nica (clean).
pa-	pako (crooked).
ta- (deer).	pata (cut up).
wa- *	pota(l) (destroy).
waki-	psaka.
wakic-	psica (jump).
wao-	pśuŋ.
ya-	pta(e) (cut out).
yu-	ptecela. (small).
	ptuga.
	skica (press).
	skita.
	sku.
	skuḣya (square).
	smiŋ.
	so (string).
	swu (strips).
	s'o.
	śiŋśiŋ.
	śipa.
	śkica.
	śkita (across).
	śku.
	śla (shave).
	śloka.
	śo.
	śpa(e) (part).
	śpi (pluck).
	śpu (stick).
	takuniśni
	taŋ (body).
	taŋka (large).
	tepa(b) (food).
	uŋka(g).
	zapa.
	zeze (dangling).

Waiciśniyaŋ, v. Cut crooked.
Suffixes: -kiya, -yaŋ, -ya, -haŋ (part.).

cute, adj. dim. Śicelaḣ.

cutting board, n. Awawapte, caŋlawakpaŋ, caŋliawakpaŋ.

cyclone, Cf. eddy. Owaomniomni, n.

Dakota, (clans etc.). n. p. The more proper name for the Sioux, which is the short for Nadowessioux, from the Chippewa Nadowesiw, lit. little snake (enemy). Cf. nation.

dam, n. Capceyaktoⁿ, mninatake.
damage, Taⁿzaniyake, adv. Un-ed.
damp, (moist). Cf. wet, dew. Ocu, v.n. Become - in: -ya, v.a. Ospaya, v. Become - in; ospaye, n. -ness. Otkiⁿ, v.n. Become - in. Tatapa, adj. Almost dry; tatapeśni, adj. Still wet.

dance, (kinds, regalia). Waci, v.: -pi, n.; a- , v.a.; iwakici, v.n.; o- , n. - hall.
Kinds: -wacipi:
Haⁿ- , Night Dance.
Howi- , Ghost.Dance.
Iwakici- , Scalp Dance.
Kayola- , Isaⁿbati- , Santee Dance.
Omaha- , Omaha Dance.
Maśtiⁿca- , Rabbit Dance.
Psa- , Crow Dance.
Tokala- , Fox Dance.
Wakaⁿ- , Sacred dance.
Wiwaⁿyaⁿk- , Sundance. Cf. celebrations.
Wiyatapika- , Young Woman's Dance.

Regalia:
huiyakaske, Ankle ornament for the Sundance.
kaⁿgiha mignaka, Feather bustle.
peśa, Omaha Dance headgear.
ptehe wapaha, Horned headgear.
uⁿḣcelakagapi, Bustle fixed to the rear.
waciⁿhiⁿ, Headdress: - sapsapa, Black plumes; -ya, v.a. Use as a plume.
wapaha, Headdress.

dandruff, n. Natacokuḣpuḣpu, nataḣpuḣpu.
danger, Cf. fear. Okokipe, n. Fear; okokipeya, adv. In fear. Pajeje, v.n. Be in - .

dangle, Kapemnimniyaⁿ, adv. -ling. Lupi, adj.-ling. Okakoza, v.n.; okakoskoza, v.n. Woḣciya, adv. In -s. Zeze: i-ya, adv. -ing; ao- , v.n.; pao-ya, adv. -ing.

dare, v.n. Aotognaka, aot'ognaka.

dark, (confusion). Paza, kpaza: aiyo- , v.n.; ao- , v.n.; oiyo- , n. -ness; o- , v.n. Be - ; n. Night; kpas: a-ya, v.a.; ao- , v.n.; ao-ya, v.a., adv.; oi-ya, adv. In -ness; oiyo- , v. Turn - . Okisapa, v.n. Become - ; okisabya, adv. (in color). Taⁿiⁿ: ao- , adv.; awa-śni, adj.

date, Cf. time, day.
daub, Cf. stick. Otkabya, v.a. Make stick on. Tiakastaka, v. - a house.

dawn, n. Aⁿpo, aⁿpakableza, aⁿptaniya. Kajaⁿjaⁿ, v.n. Cf. day.
day, n. Aⁿpa, aⁿp(e), n.: -haⁿ, adv. In -light; -kableza, n. -break; -cokaⁿya, n. Noon; -haⁿ, adv. Today. Aⁿpetu, n.: -haⁿkeyela, adv. Before noon; -la, n. dim.; -tahena, adv. Before - is done; -wakaⁿ, n. Sunday; i- , n. The same or next - ; o- caⁿ, adv. Daily.Aⁿbśiceca, n. A bad - ; aⁿbwaśte, n. A good day. Aⁿpo, n., v.n. Dawn: -kableze, n. -light; -skaⁿl, -skaⁿtu(ya), adv. By - . Aⁿptaniya, n. First beak of light. Caⁿ, n. Date, day. Ihiⁿhaⁿna, n. Next day, morning.

daylight, Cf. day. Iyotaⁿiⁿlake, n.

dazzle, Iśti(ai)yośnija(ś), v.n., v.a.: -ya, v.a. Iśtiyowalya, v.a. Iyojaⁿjaⁿ: iśt- , v.a.; wa- , v. To blind.

deaf, adj. Noⁿḣcaⁿ; nuⁿḣcaⁿ, v.n.; noⁿḣcaⁿsihutayela, adv. Pretending not to hear.

debase, Cf. feeble. Yuśiḣtiⁿ, v.a.
debility, n. Wośiḣtiⁿ.
debt, n. Woikazo.
decay, Cf. rot.

deceive, Cf. lie. Gnayaⁿ(e): iyu- , v.n. Be -ed; wana- , v.a., n. Deception; wayu- , v. Cf. miss; wowica- , n. Cejijalya, adv. Deceitfully. Kśuⁿkaḣ, v.: -yakel, adv. In a manner deceiving.

decide, Cf. plan.
declare, (manifest). Yataⁿiⁿ, v.: kici- , - for. Woyakapi, n. A -ation.
decoration, n. Oweśleke, A war prize.
decoy, v. Yuḣekicaḣ au, Coax into a trap.

decree, (judge, condemn). Cf. influence. Wakoŋza, v. Determine. Wasukiya, v.a.
deep, (down, below, beneath). Hukutakiya, adv. (downward). Śma(e), adj.: a- , v.n.; a-ya, adv.; awaśma, adj.; o- , n. Depth; wo- , n. Yutkeya, adv. Deeply.

deer, n.
sintehaŋska, White-tailed - .
sintelulyapi, Red-tailed - .
sintesapela, Black-tailed, mule - .
sintewaksapi, Bob-tailed - .
tabloka, Buck.
taciŋcala, Fawn.
tahejata, Two-year old - .
taȟca, Common - .
taȟca itopasapa, Black-faced - .
tamakoyuŋka, Fatted deer.
tiŋgleśka, Fawn.

deface, v.a. Yusepa, Wear off.
defame, v.n. Ilega. Iglaoŋśika, v. refl. Śica: gla- , v. pos.; igla- , v. refl.; oya- , v.a.; aśilwoyaka, v.

defecate, Cf. excrete. Uŋkce, v.n. Break wind; n.
defect, (fault). Aśiȟtiŋ, v.n. Ipiŋta, v.n.
defend, v. refl. Naic'ijiŋ, - self (speaking). Nakikśiŋ, v. - self.

defile, v.a. Śapa(b): aya- ; iglu- ; kiciyu- , - for; -ya, v.a., adv. Dirtily; wapa- , v. Igluśica, v. refl.

deformed, (imperfectly, clumsy, accidental). Ośte, adj.: -la, adj.; -ya, adv.
degree, (of adj., adv.).
Dim., -la, suffix. Very, only.
Comparative, sam, isam, isaŋpa in comp. adv.
Superlative, -ȟca(e), suffix; iyotaŋ, lila.

delay, v.a. Caŋ-kagiya, caŋkagiya. Haŋkignaka, v. Oiyayeśilya, v. Oŋc'uŋnica, v.n. Be -ed; ouŋc'uŋnilya, v.a. Tehaŋ: oȟ'aŋ- , v.n. - in doing; kiciyu- , v. Make - for; o-ya, v.a. Cause - .

delegate, n. Wakicoŋze.
deliberate, v. Wayuslaslata, Do -ly.
delirium, n. Wowaciŋgnuni.
deliver, v.a. Kaśpa.
deluge, Cf. inundate.

demolish, (throw down). Yuuŋka, v.a. Make lie down.
demonstratives, (intensifiers). Cf. that, this. Kayeś, for pron.: Miye - , I myself. Uŋhe(na), for pron., That.

den, n. Śuŋkciŋca oti (wolf); waśuŋ, A hole.
dense, adj. Śma, Thick. Woȟeśma, adj.

dent, (indent). Smaka: kao- , v. Make a - ; ka- , v. - , make a track; pa- v.a. Indent. Paś'aka, v.a. (push, strike).
dentist, n. Wicahikage.
depart, v. Gluśniyaŋyaŋ.
depend, (trust, believe). Waciŋyaŋ, v.a. - upon, need one.

deposite, Cf. place. Ognakapi, n.
descend, Apamagle, adv.: -ya, adv. Glicu, v.: -ya, v.a.

design, (pattern). Wogligleye, n.; wogligleyapi.

desire, Asiŋȟte, adj. As'iŋ, v.n.: -yaŋ, adv. Caŋmiȟce, v. Caŋt: -agle, v.a.; -aglepi, n.; -iheya, v.a., adj.; caŋtiheye, n.; -okpani, v.a.; -okpanipi, n.; -okpaniyaŋ, v.a.; -okpaniwaya, adv.; i-okpani, v. Ciŋ, v.a.: ao- , v.; -ka, v.a.; -kiya, v.a.; -pica, adj.; -ya, v.a.; -yaŋkel, adv.; i- , v.; i-ya, v.a.; iki- , v.a.; ki- , v. - own; okici- , v. - of for; wi- , v. - women, hunt women; wi-pi, n. - for women. Ikcaŋ, v. Koŋ: -la, v.; o- , n. Waciŋ: Śila- , v. Have bad - for; wota- , n. Ambition.

desist, v. Wotaka, Stop suddenly.
desolate, adv. Wosaŋkayakel, Void.
despair, v. refl. Caŋtihaŋgiciya. O-ȟ'aŋśuŋkeca, v.a., v.n.

destitute, (poor). Keyecola, adj. Entirely - . Nica, v.n. Be - of: waȟpa-, adj. Poor, having nothing; waȟpanikiya, v. pos. Make self - ; waȟpanila, v.a. Consider poor; waȟpaniya, v.a.; waȟpaniyaŋ, adv. Wataŋtoŋśni, v. Be - of everything: -yaŋ, adv. Having lost all.

destroy, Cf. ruin, injure. Haŋgya: wa- , v.: wa-ca, n. One who -s; wawi- , v.; wawihaŋgye, n. Komey, v.a. Napi: -śkaŋyaŋ, v.a. - own; -śtaŋyaŋ, wa-śtaŋyaŋ, v. - everything. Okiȟ'aŋśuŋkeca, v.a. - one's necessities. Takuniśni: kaa- , v. (strike); kiciyu- , v. - for; na- , v.a. (by foot); wica- , n. Destruction; wo- , v.a. (shoot). Tuka: ka- , v. (knock off); wa- , v.a. - (cut). Wakoŋniyeya, v. - everything. Wignuni: ka- , v.a.; kica- , v. - for; wapa- , v. Wopesto, v. (shoot). Yakuka, v.a. Bite to pieces.

determine, Kicuŋza, v. - in regard to; owakoŋze, n. Determination.

detest, Ciŋśniyaŋkel, adv. -ingly. Gla, v.a.: wo-ya, v. Consider -able; wo-yapi, n. A -able thing; śi- , v.

detour, v. refl. Igluipaweḣtu.
devil, n. Wakaŋśica, Satan.
devour, v. Wayuta; n. One who -s.
dew, Cu: a- , v.n. imper., n., prep.; a-ya, v.a.; a-waya, v.a.; -mni, n.; -mni ś'e, n. - in drops; -ya, v.a. Katatabya, v.a. Wanagitaśośa, n. Heavy - . Cf. damp, wet.

desterity, n. Wicaoḣ'aŋko.
diarrhoea, Kajo, v. Have - .

die, (dead, deaden). Gleya, adv. Unto death: -kpagaŋ, v. Give one's life. Kiḣ'aŋyaŋ, v. Be likely to - for. Itamye, v. Kaśeca, v.a. Deaden. Siyuha, v. To go to - . T'a(e): akih'aŋ- , v.; aki- , v.n.; i-waciŋ, v.; kaŋi- , v. - of old age; ki- , v. - for; maśte- , v. - from heat; oŋiśtiŋma- , v. - in sleep; oŋwaciŋ, v. Intend to die for; i-waciŋ, v. Intend death for; t'a, v.n.; kici-, v. - for; o- , v.n. - in a place, - from gluttony; ot'e, v.n.: -ikicihuŋni, v. About to - ; -iya; temni- , v.n. (sweat); t'a, v.n. Faint away, lose consciousness; -nuŋs'e, adv. About dead; -ca, adj. Lying dead; -icakiś, adv. Dying; -kinica, v.n. Struggling for life; -kiya, v.a. Make - ; -ya, v.a.; toŋ- , n. His death; -koŋ, v. Wish to be dead; -koŋza, v. Want to be dead; -śniyaŋkel, adv. Not dying; -yasu, v. Condemn to - ; wica-, n. The dead; wicoŋ- , n. Death; wo- , v. - from eating; n. ; wo-ic'iya, v. Get sick eating. Yaḣlata, v. Speak as one who is dying.

different, Cf. another. Etaŋhaŋś toka, express.; etaŋśtokaka, adv.; hetaŋhaŋś tokaka, adv. Togye, adv. In a - manner: okaḣ- , adv. Made -ly; toktogye, adv. In - ways; tok-kel; wo- , v.a. Do in a - way; ya- , adv. Telling -ly. Tokeca, adj.: a-, v.n.; ici- , adj.; iglu- , v. refl.; kiciyu- , v. Make - from, for; wica- n. Difference.

difficulty, (hard). Kitaŋ s'e, adv. With - ; kitaŋyaŋkel, adv. With greatest difficulty. Napśapśa s'e, adv. With - . Iyus'oya, adv. Exhausted, reluctantly, hardly. Teḣi, adj. Difficult, hard to endure; -ka, adj. Hard to do or bear, costly, unreasonable; -kela, v.a. Think hard or - ; waya-ka, v. Speak of as difficult; wayu-ka, v. Make difficult; wo- , n.; wo-ḣiya, adv. With - ; wo-ke, n. Hardship. Wakaŋyelakel, adv. With great - . Woyuśkiśke, n. Source of a - .

diffident, Wimna śni, v. Be - ; weceyeśni, v.

dig, Ikpaḣloka, v. refl. K'a(e), c'a, v.a.: a- , v.; iyo- , n.; o-, v.a. - into, through, out, up; o-pi, n. -ging into; kic'a, v. - own for. Pakota, v.a. - out, probe. Iyupta, v. Spade up; owawapte, n. A dug hole of a turnip. Iwoic'iśloka, v. Ayuswa, v.

digest, Śupeośica, adj. Hard to - ; n. What is hard to - .
diligent, (attentive). Aic'ikita, v. refl.; aicikiya, v. refl., adj.; aic'iktaśni, v. (negative).

dim, Htaojaŋjaŋ, n.
diminish, Cf. less. Yuociptelya, adv. -ing be degrees.

dine, Owohe, n. A dining hall, room. Owote, n. Place to - : - tipi, n. Dining room, cafe, restraunt; -ya, v.a. Use for dining. Wiyeya, v. - well.

dip, (skim). Ka(ca)pta icu, v.; iyokapte, n. Dipper. Mniyatke, n. Dipper. Ipagmuŋka, v.n. Oputakaŋ, v.a. - into (with fingers). Ptenuŋwekiyapi, n. -ping of cattle. Woputkaŋ, v. - in. Ze: ayu- , v.a.; gla- , v. pos. - out own; oglu- , v. pos.; oka- , v. - out into.

direct, (directly, indirectly). Ataya, v.n.; atayela, adv. Eciaiyopteya, adv.; iciiyopta, iciiyopteya. Katiŋyaŋ, adv. -ly, immediately, off-hand. Ktaŋktaŋkiya, adv. In-ly. Pataŋwaŋjila, adv. -ly, without veering.

direction, (geographic).
Wiyoȟpeyata, n. The west.
Waziyata, n. The north.
Iwiyohiyaŋpata, n. The east.
Itokaga(ȟ), iyokaga, n. The south.

Wiyoȟpeyata, n. The west: -kiya, adv. Westward; -ŋhaŋ, adv. From the west. Waziya:i-pa, adv. Northward; wazitakiya, waziyatakiya; -pa, adv. At, to the north; -pataŋhaŋ, adv. Northwards, from the north; -taŋhaŋ, adv. At, from the north.
Wiohinapataŋhaŋ, adv. From the east; wiyohiyaŋpa, n. The east.

Kaakokiya, adv. In another - . Kakel, adv. In some - ; kakena. Kakiyotaŋ, adv. In that - .

dirt, (dirty). Anablu, v.a. Anini, n. Oȟli, adj. - within,in. Okpukpa, adj. Full of - , mirky. Apaśica, v.a. P'o: aigla- , v. refl.; kao- , ka- , v. Raise dust. Aś'aka, v.n. Get -y. Śapa(e), adj. -y, blackened; aśab, aśabya, v.a., adv.; a- , v.n.; o- , v.n. Be -y; waa- , n. (hands).

disable, (thwart). Okihiśniyaŋ, v.a.
disagree, (not unanimous, unpleasant). Cf. quarrel. Apoptaŋptaŋ, v.a. Ocihiśniśni, v.n. Not be unanimous. Oiyokiśica, adj. Disagreeable.

disappear, (lost). Kacel, particle. Indicates uncertainty. Manitakiya, adv. (from camp). Taŋiŋśni, v. Be lost, have -ed: -yaŋ, adv. Out of sight, lost.

disappoint, v. fig. Śniśya. Kagal hiŋgle, v. Be -ed.
disarm, v.a. fig. Uŋc'oŋnilya.
disband, (break up, go). Kibleca, v.n. Kiśpahaŋ, v.

discharge, v. Kauta, Fire a gun by accident.
disciple, (pupil, student). Waoŋspewicakiye, n. Also, an apostle.
disconsolate, Wipajiŋ, v.

discourage, v.n. Waciŋiwoś'aka, Be -ed.

discuss, Cf. try. Wakiya, v. Talk about.
disease, Cf. sickness.
disentangle, v. Ayukca.

dish, (tableware). Wakśi(ca), n. (in gen.).
cupboard, Ognake (opiye).
pitcher, Mniiyokaśtaŋ, mniognake.
plate, Yatabla, ognake tapela, wakśica blaska (flat), caŋwakśica (wooden), makawakśica (clay), mas'(za)-waǩśica(tin).
saucer, soup-plate, Ognake skokpa, wiyatke aglehe.
shaker, Mniskuya ognake.

Cete, n. Bottom of a vessel: -iyaskabyela, adv. Sticking to the bottom; -kaŋyela, adv. Little in the bottom; -sapa, n. Suet in the bottom; -ta, mniceteta, -yela, adv. Cf. bottom.

dishevel, v.a. Pacica, Mix up.
disjoin, Zuŋteśni, adj. -ed, incorrect language. Cf. weave.
disjoint, Cf. joint.
dislike, v.a. Hitigla: -ya. Iwaȟtelaśni, v.a. Waśicelaka, v.; n. One that -s.

dislocate, (joint). Cf. joint, sprain. Gloka: ipa- , v.; pa- , v.a. (joint); yu- , v.a. Sprain badly. Pśuŋ: ana- , v.a.; apa- , v.a.; ka- , v.; na- , v.n., v.a.; pa- , v.a. Put out of joint.

dismantle, (disassemble). Wojuju, v. Take to pieces: -pi, n. Disassembly.
disobey, (break a law). Kicaksa, v.a. - a law, lit. cut in two. Wanaȟ'oŋ, śni, v. Be disobedient.

disorder, (disarrange). Itupśapśa s'e, adv.Ośilya, adv. In - : Paśkiśka, v.a. (rub). Togmuŋśni, adv. Topsy-turvy. Yuptaŋpila s'e, adv. -ly. Katkaŋheya, adv. Orderly.

disown, (disavow). Slolyeśni koŋza, v.
disperse, v. Paowaŋcaya, - by. Yuobleca, v.a. Scatter, divide: -haŋ, part. -ed.

displace, v.a. Tokoyuśtaŋ.
displease, (feel bad). Caŋlwaȟteśni, adj.; caŋteelai, v.; caŋtiyokiśice, v.a. Be outraged at; iyucaŋteśica, v. Feel bad. Waciŋiyokiśica, v.n. Be -ed. Hiŋyaŋzeke, adj. Ip'ozeca, v.

dispose, (on terms with). Ociŋwaśteya,
adv. Well -ed; ociwaśte, adj.; ociŋ-
śicaya, adv. Evilly -ed; ociśica,
adj. Ill-disposed towards. Ohiŋyaŋs-
yela, adv. In bad humor. Waciŋ: ta-
śica, adj. Of a bad disposition; ta-
waśte, adj. Of a good disposition;
-śica, adj. Badly dispositioned. Wa-
śteca(ka), adj. -ed well.

dispute, (argument). Akinica, v.a. -
about; o- , n.; wa- , n. A disputant;
wa-pi, n.; w- , v.; w-pi, n. Contest.
disregard, v.a. Iyaktaśni.
disrespectful, adj. Glugluka.
dissatisfy, v. refl. Iwaic'iniyaŋ.

dissolve, (melt). Skaŋ, v.n. (snow).
distance, (distant, away). Itohaŋyaŋ,
adv. Kaiyuzeya, adv. A little - away.
distinct, Yublapisekse, adv. -ly, o-
penly.

distort, (deform). Cf. twist. Iyuȟmiŋ,
v.a.
distract, Wicośkiśke, n. -ion, difficulty.
distress, (suffer). Wicakije, n.

distribute, (divide). Pamni, v.a. Divide; kpamni: ki- , v.a. - own; -pi,
n. An issue, -tion; wa- , v. - own;
wa-pi, n. -tion. Owowicak'u, n. -tion
center.

district, (people of). Okaśpe, n.
disturb, Caŋte: -ȟniyaŋyaŋ, v.n. Be
-ed; -ihala yaŋka, v. express.; -iya-
pa, v.n.; -iyapaya, adv.; -iyapapi,
n. -ance; -kazaŋ, v.n. Ok'os'e, n.
A tumult. Ze, adj. -ed: -ka.

ditch, (trench, bulwark). Mako: -k'api,
n. An entrenchment; -smaka, n. Mni-
kiyupta, v. Make a - ; -pi, n.; mni-
tacaŋku, n. Channel.

dive, v.n. Glucega. Kignuŋka, v.: o- ,
v.n.; pa- , v. Make - .
divert, Cf. turn. Kawiŋga, v. - one's
course.
divest, v. refl. Igluśloka; igluśpa.

divide, v.a. Apamni; kicikpamni, v. To
- among selves. Kicaśpa, v. - for:
iyo- , v.; okinaśpa, v.a. Okiyuslel,
v.a. Yuiyakipab, adv. -ding. Yunuŋpa,
v.a. - in two.
divorce, n. Woiȟpekiciye.

dizzy, Cf. stun. Itomni: ka- , v.
Be struck - ; o- , v. Be - .

do, Cf. work. Caŋteokic'uŋya, v. -
with heart. Ecoŋ, v.a.: ecakicioŋ,
v.a. - for; ecakicoŋ, ecakioŋ, v.;
-kiya, v.a.; hecakicioŋ, hecakicoŋ,
hecakioŋ, v.; hecoŋ, lecoŋ, kecoŋ;
lecakicoŋ, v. - thus to; lecakioŋ, v.
- this to; tokakicoŋ, v. - to, for.
Gluȟ'eȟ'e, v. pos. - partly. H'aŋ,
v. Work at: -pica, v. Able to - ;
o- , v., n. Work; oki- , v. - to.
Akiptaŋ, v.n. - together.

docile, (gentle). Cf. fly. Okiŋyaŋ-
waśte, adj.
doctor, n. Pejuta wicaśa (Indian);
waśicuŋ wakaŋ (white man). Pikiya,
v. Treat, conjure.

dodge, Cf. stop. Pataka, v. - about.
dog, Cf. animal. Śuŋka, n.; śuŋgnaśkiŋyaŋ, n. A mad - ; śiyośuŋka, n.
Bird-dog; śuŋȟpala, n. Puppy; śuŋka-
itepśuŋka, n. Bull - ; śuŋkitepesto,
n. Grayhound; śuŋkicoco, v. Call one's
dog. Keca, n. Long-haired - .

doll, n. Amoŋmoŋla, haŋpośpu hokśicala.
domineer, Cf. power. Wanapicage, n.
Domination. Wauŋkec'ila, v. Be proud.

donate, v. Wawicak'u: -pi, n. Gift.
door, (entrance). Cf. house. Tiyopa,
n.: -gmigma, -gmigmela, n. - knob;
-iyokatkuga, n. - screws, nails;
-oyutkogi, n. - lock, padlock; -ta,
adv. At the - .

dormitory, n. Oȟpaye tipi.
double, (bend up). Cf. shut. Jagjalya,
adv. Doubly. Kipaja: ya- , v.a. - up,
ends meeting (by mouth); yu- , v.a.
- over; yukipaś. Kśija, v. - up: ka- ,
v. - up; kpa- , v. - up own; na- ,
v.a. - up (by foot), ends meet; v.n.;
nao- . Iglunuŋpa, v. refl.; inuŋpa,
n. - mouthed. Yupśuŋka, v.a. - up in
around, bunch: -ya, adv. -ed up. Ici-
paśpaś, adv.

doubt, v.a. Cet'uŋgla(ya).
down, Cf. deep, under. Iyoȟpeya, v.
Throw, cast into: ai- , adv., n.;
kaa- , adv. - hill. Kaȟ'ol, v. Throw,
get - . Kuta(l), adv.: kahu- , adv.
(put); kutkiya, adv.; kuwab, adv.
-ward. Makigleya, adv. -ward, endwise.

downcast, Yacaŋlececa, v.a. Make - (talking).

downstream, Hutab, adv.: -kiya, -ya, -yakel, i- , adv.
doze, (drowsy, slumber). Oguŋga, v.n. Yusiŋc'iya yaŋka, v. Seemingly asleep, say nothing.

draft, Okabluya, v.a. Cause a - ; o-kabluza, n. (wind); v.n. Blow some; adj. Drafty.
drag, v.a. Yuslohaŋ, - along (by mouth) pulling; i- , v. ; iyuslohe, n.

draw, (pull, sketch). Cf. hollow. Ipaka, v.n. - back. Ipaśloka, v.a. - off over, divest. Oakate, n. (of a bow). Oyuzaŋ, v.a. (curtain), spread out. Yalusicu, v. Take a - (pipe); yalusyatkaŋ, v. Take a draught of. Yataŋ, v.a. (suck); yatiktitaŋ, v.t. (smoking). Yuguka, v.a. - a knife, arrow. Yuslohaŋ, v.a. Pull, drag: -yaŋ, adv. Yusluta, v.a. Pull out. Iteowa, v. (sketch); oikwa, v. pos.; owa, v.a. Cf. write.

drawer, Cf. cabinet. Yuslul icupi, n.
dream, v.n. Haŋble(a,o), Fast for vision: ai- , v.n.; -ceya, v.n.; -gla-gla, v.; -glagyakel, adv.; -glaka, v.a.; i- , v.; wi-pi, n.; wi-s'a, n. A dreamer.

dregs, (scraps). Ogu, n. Okpukpe, n. The lees.

dress, Cf. cover, clothe. Waḣpaka, n. One poorly -ed. Wakoyakeca, n. A well -ed person. Wawaḣobḣopece, n. A prim -er. Yuḣniga, v.a. - up nicely. Yupika, n. A good -er. Ḣolwaŋca, adj. -ed in gray; iyośala s'e, -ed in red. Kicaŋyaŋ, v. (meat); okazapa, v.; kipata, kpata; pastaŋkiya, v.a. Dehair, - a skin.

drift, (carried away). Kaḣwoka, v. - off. Oŋcablu oju, n. Wawota ihaŋ, n. A snow - .
drink, Hepa: aya- , v.a.; gla- , v. pos.; kiciya- , v. - up for. Ot'iŋ, v.a. - much, greedily. Mniyupiza, v. - quietly. Yage, v.a. - up. Yatkaŋ(e) v.a.: a- , v.a.; glatkaŋ, v. pos.; omni- , n. -ing place; o- , v.a. - in; n.; wi- , n. -ing cup. Yaskepa, v.a. - up.

drive, v.a. Ipaspa, v.a. Naḣapa, v.a. - away (stamping). Okataŋ, v.a. - a nail. Wicakaḣapa, n. -er. Yuhi, v.a. - off (game).

drool, (drivel). Imniśtaŋ, n. Iskuya, adj.: -gla, v.n.; -ya, v.a. Kas'iŋ-s'iŋ, v. Drivel.

drop, v.n. Oḣpa. Ayuptuja, v. Yuśna: a- , v.a.; o- , n. Fall (waste); o-śna, n. Crumbs. Nap'akaśpeya, v.a. Let slip from the hands. Śwu, v.n. Precipitate: a- , v.n.; a-ya, v.a. Ś'e, v.n. (water); ayu- , v.a., v.n.; -ya, adv.; o- , n. (of water); v.n. - into; oyu- , v.a. Make - in; -ś'e, v. red. Trickle; -yapi, n. Drops of water.

drown, v.n. Mnilt'a; mnilt'eya, v.a. Mniot'a, v.n.; mniot'eya, v.a. Mni-t'a, v.n.; mnit'eya, v.a.

drum, n. Caŋcega. Icabu, n.; nakicibu, v. - for (by foot); pabu, v.a. - on, (by finger).

drunk, adj. Itomni: -ic'iya, v.n.; -mni, adj.; -pi, n.; -s'a, n.; -ya, v.a. Mniziciŋca, n. A -ard. Paŋga, adj. (slang). Witko: i- , v.n.; i-tkoka, v.n.; i-ya, v.a.; o- , v.n. Be - with; wa-ya, v. Make - .

dry, Akceya, v.a. Aśeca, v.n. At'a-ḣya, v.a. Ayuskepa, v.a. Blublu, adj.; nablu, v.n. Become - and fine. Gluḣepa, v. pos. Hemako: -skaŋl, adv.; -śikśica, n. Katapa, v. (shake). Kat'aga, v. Shake - . Mni, v.a. - in the sun. Oyaḣe, v.n. - up, evaporate, go - : aoyaḣe, v.n. Puza(s), adj.: apa- , v.; apus- , v.; -ya, v.n.; iyu- , v. Make - with; ka- , Make - ; wakapus'kiya; kpa- , v. - own; o- , v.n. Be - all over; opuze, n. - land; pa- , v.a. Rub - ; -kiya, v.a. Make - ; -yaśpaŋyaŋ, v. Cook - ; waka-kiya, v.; - aya, adj. Beginning to - ; wi-ye, n. Drier. Saka, adj. Dried stiff: a- , v.n.; oya- , adj, Dried hard on, in; withered. Satglakiŋyaŋ, v. Hang out to - . Śelya, v.a. Make - , wither; adv. Śnija, adj. Dried up. T'iŋt'iŋ, adj. Beginning to - . Wacaŋkśu, v. - on a stick; wicuŋksu, n. -ing pole (meat). Watatabkiya, v. Hang and - .

due, Cf. timely.

dull, Cf. blunt, stupid. Icaś'aka, v.n. Ikiŋta, v.n. Ik'ege śni, adj. Kajapa, v.a. Kat'oza, v. Make - . Peśni, adj. Wotata, v.a. Make - (by pounding).

dumb, Ieśni, n. One who is - (man). Wiocaŋ, n. One who is - (woman).
dump, n. Owaiȟpeye.

duration, n. Woyutehaŋ.
dusk, Cf. evening. Pahaohaŋzi, n.
dust, (dusty). Cf. dirt, dirty, fog. Katata, v. (shake). Makablu, n.; makipabluya, makiyap'oya, makop'oya, adv. Raising - . Nap'o, v. Raise - (feet). Onablu, v. Raise - (walking). Wakpukpeca, n.

dwell, (live in). Euŋ, v. Iśnati, v.n. - alone, have menses; iśnatipi, n. Oti, v.n. - in; n. -ing. Ouŋyaŋ, v.: a- , v.; ta- , n. His -ing. Toŋwaŋyeca, v.n. - at, live at.

dwindle, (lessen). Piŋzece, adj. -ling down.

dye, (stain). Mniwitoye, n. Blue - . Walute(l), n. - that is red: walulye, n. A dyer of scarlet; wilulye, n. Red - stuff.

each, (every). Iyohi: it-la, adj.; ot- , adj. - one; oto- , adj.; ot-hi, adj. Some of - ; taŋ-la, pron. - one, every one. Ototaŋhaŋ, prep. From, away from - kind; otoyasiŋ, adv. Every single one.

eager, adj. Ipuḣniyaŋ.

ear, Nakpa, n.: -hute, n. Root of - ; -okogna, adv. Between the -s; -stogya, adv. Moving the - ; -yuwoslal ikikca, v. Prick up the - ; nakpiślayataŋhaŋ, n. The right - . Noŋge, n.: -kpa, adj. Deaf; -kpeya, v.a.; -ogmusgluza, v. Hold one's -s; -oḣloka, n. - hole; noŋḣcaŋ, adj. Deaf; noŋḣkeciya, v. Bend one's - ; noŋḣpaŋ, n. Ringing -s; noŋḣsuhute, n. Base of - ; noŋḣwacoka, n. Outer ear. Śoŋśoŋla, adj. Long-ed, drooping -s.

earn, v.n. Iweśleka. Kamna, v.a. (get): kicamna, v. - for; wa- , v. Make money, - merit; wa-ŋpi, n. -ing.

earnest, Yutaŋyaŋkel, adv. In - , for good.

earth, (clay, soils, ground, land, country, world). Cf. land. Maka(k), n. Earth, ground: -glakiŋyaŋ, adv. Across the - ; -gle, adv. With end on the ground; -ta(l), adv. On the ground; -saŋ, n. Light-colored clay; -suhula, n. Sandy soil; -to, n. Blue earth; -tooyuze; -sitomni, n. Orb of the earth, the world; -tanasula, n. Moulding clay; -wase, n. Red earth (paint); -wase śa, n. Vermillion paint makikceka, n. Land, soil, loam; -ikceya, adv. On land; -ipusli, adv. On the ground; -iyagleya, adv. To the ground; -iyakasaŋni, n. Part of the country; -iyapa, v. Hit the ground; makoce, n. Country, place; makoce oihaŋke, n. A globe; makoḣloka, n. Cave; -okawiŋḣ , adv. Around the world; -ośica, n. Bad land, desert; -óśla, n. Bare ground; -owaŋca, n. All the - . Taŋniśpaŋ, n. Red - (paint). Cf. wase. Uŋci, n. p. Mother Earth.

easy, Paslayela, adv. Slowly, going - : - uŋ, v. Take it - . Waśakala, adj. Cheap. Cf.

eat, v.
ayaśtaŋ, aglaśtaŋ, v.a.
cak'iglaska, v. - up fast; wakaska.
caic'ipa, v.
glajipa(b), v.a.
iśpukitoŋ, v.
niḣkpataŋ, v. - little; niḣtokayeya-śni, v. Fill self.
teb: ahi-ya, v.a.; a-ya, v.a.; -kiciciyapi, v. - up for; -kiciya, v. - up provisions; -kiciyapi, v. They - each other; -kiya, v. - own; v.a. - up another's; -ya, v.a. Devour.
wate, v. abs.: -bya, v. - all up.
wota(l), v.: -igluśtaŋ, v. refl. Finish -ing; -kiya, v.a. Make - ; -wota, v. Be -ing.
yacaśkeśkeke, v. - up slowly.
yaowiśni, v. Be unable to - up all.
ayasota, v.a. - all up; glasota, v. pos. - own all up.
yatoto, v.a. - up (as grass).
yuta, v.a.: a- , v.; agluta, v. pos.; i- (l), v. - with; kici- , v. - with, for; wauta, v. Give to - ; wi- , v. - with.

echo, Iyowaza: ka- , na- , pa- , wo- , ya- , v.a. Make - ; n.
economical, adj. Wakpataŋka; n. An - person.
edible, adj. Yulpica.
eddy, (whirlpool, wind, cyclone). Owamniomni, n.

edge, (border, bottom). Agleyela, n. Apajeje, adv. Kaobloton, v. Make -ed. Matete, n. (creek etc.). Obleca, adj. -ed; n. ; obletoŋ, adj. Square-ed. Okśaŋipata, v. Put an - on. Ope(a), n. (blade): -poŋ, n. Border (cloth); -puŋtaŋhaŋ, adv. From under the bottom of the tent.

effort, n. Akitapi.
egg, n. Itka: -ska, -zica, w- , n.; w-toŋ, v. To lay eggs.
either, Tuktuŋma, adv. - of two.

elastic, Cf. flexible, pliable. Zigzica, adj.
elated, adj. Witaŋ, Proud.
elder (eldest). Wicitokapa, n. Eldest son born, or daughter.

elect, Cf. choose. Kaḣniga.
eloquent, (fluent). Wayapi: a-ka, v.n.; -ka, v.n. Be - ; -ya, adv. -ly.
elsewhere, adv. Atokaŋ.

emaciate, Okiyaskapa, v.n. Be -ed.
embrace, v. Poskilyuza, Hold in arms.
embroider, v. Ipata, v.: -pi, n. Wa-paĦlata(l), v.: -toŋ, v. Work with ribbon.

emergency, (urgency). Wanuŋtokayakel, adv. For any - .
emphasis, (to the fact of). -kśto, -kśt, suff. to v. Yelo, lo, le, ending a sentence.

employ, Owaŋjila, adv. Unemployed. Waśi, v.a. Woilake(g), n. -ee, a hireling; -ya, v.

empty, adj. Coka: si-la, adj.; glu-ka, v. pos. Haece, adj.; ohe ece, adv. Without; opteheca, adv. Almost - . KaoyaĦe, v.a.; yuĦepa, v.a. Lade out. Iyokala, v.n., n. (measure). Ħloka, adj. Kaskepa(b), v. - by drinking; puskepa, v.a. Awośloka, v.a.

enchant, Cf. bewitch.
encircle, Cf. around.
end, Cf. old. Hocatkayataŋhaŋ, hoisleyataŋhaŋ, adv. Haŋke: hiŋ- , n., adv. - this way; hoi- , n.; i- , v.n., n.; ihaŋg; i-ta, adv. At the - ; i-ya, adv.; kaki- , n. - of the world; owi-śniyaŋ, adv. Eternally; owi-ya, v.a. Bring to an - ; oi- , n.; oi-ya, v.a. Make an - of; owi- , n.; owe-ta, adv. At the - . Wahutaktayakel, adv. At the - , lastly. Iŋkpa, n. Point, tip: o- , n. - of anything.

endure, (strength). Akpaspa, v. Haiyotiyekiya, v. Icakisya, v.a., adv. Iyowiŋyaŋ, v. Consent to. Otawat'el-śica, adj. Unendurable. OteĦika, adv. Hard to - , trying, excessive. Waki-ś'aka, adj. Long-suffering: hu- , adj. -ing; wakiś'agya, v.a. Make - ; waki-ś'ake, n. Strength, -ance; wowakiś'a-ke, n.

enemy, Cf. foreign. Tokakiciyapi, n. pl.
energetic, (ready for work). Wiś'o-ś'oka, n. An - person.
enfeeble, Cf. weak. WaśiĦtiŋ, v.a. (cut).
enforce, v.n. Oiekic'uŋ, - obedience.

engage, v.n. Iksapa.
engrave, (mark, carve). Go: pa- , v.a. Mark with a line, scribble; wa- , v.a. Carve; waki- , v.
engulf, (press up around). Naosli, v.n. (in mud).
enlarge, Cf. large.
enlighten, Iwicableza, n. -mant.
enslave, v.a. Ilag.
entangle, Cf. ravel.
entertain, Woimagaga, n. -ment.
entice, (solicit, subvert). Cf. intercourse. InakiĦma, v. pos.

entrance, n. Huŋkpa.
envy, (jealousy). Nawizi, v. Be jealous: inakiwizi, v. pos.; i- , v.; i-pi, n.; - s'a, n.; i-ya, v.a., adj.

equal, (even, parallel, square with). Akile: -ceca, adj.; -cel, -celya, -haŋ, -haŋyaŋ, adv.; -haŋkeca, -haŋ-waŋketuya, adj.; -haŋyaŋ, adv.; -nagnakeca, -nakeca; -nana, adj. neg.; iy-haŋkeca, adv.; iy-haŋyaŋ, iy-nakeca, adv. Akiŋskokeca, adj.; akiŋ-skoya, adv.; iyakiniskokeca, adv. Of the same size. Ecitapa, adj. Iyehaŋ-keca, iyehaŋyaŋ, adv. Tkoŋza(e), adj. Even, exactly: oci- , adj. Alike (size, length); ota- , adj. - to, parallel; o- , adj. Even, parallel; oyu- , v.a. -ize; n. -izer; pai- , v.a. -ize; igluo- , v. refl.

equip, v.a. Yuskaka, - with new clothes.

erase, v.a. Nagoya (scratch). Juju: gla- , v.a. pos.; kicipa- , v. - for; pa- , v.a. Rub out, cross out; wipa- , n. A rubber eraser.

erect, v. Jiŋ, Be, stand - .
err, v. Wicuŋs ia.
erupt, PaŋĦpaŋĦya, adv. -ing.

escape, (flee, leak, dissipate). Haŋ-napa, v.; napa, v.n. Inaśloka, v. Iyaglupta, v. refl. Sigluha, v.n. Get out of the way (from bad conscience). Wahuataya, v.n. Unable to - . Yuskepa, v.a.

escort, v.a. Pasi, March one.
esteem, -kila, suff. Thus: waśtekila. Śilla, v. - bad. Taŋ: iyo-laka, v. - most highly; o-kala, v.a. - greatest, most highly (singling out). Wa-Ħ'aŋla, v.a.

estrange, (without affection). Kitaŋ-kognagyelaĦci, adj. -ed.

eulogy, n. Woyaonihaŋ.
evaporate, v.n. NaiyoyaĦe. Natakuni-śni, v.i. Nawanica, v.i.

evasive, Watokaŋkaŋ, adv. -ly.
even, Cf. equal. Itkoŋza(e), adv.: -ya, adv.; -ya, v.a.; -la, adv. Oblayeya, adv.

evening, Hta: -kiyaka, adv. -makiyokpaza, v.; -otaŋiŋśni, n.; -yetamna, adv.; -yetu, n.; o-yetu, n.; i-yetu, n.

event, Wakiŋyaŋpi, n. A foretold eventuality. Woakipa, n.

every, Cf. each, all, any. Owaŋca, adv. -where; o- . Tuktetukakeś, adv. -where. Tuwe ce eyaś, pron. -body, anybody.

evil, (do, plot). Ecaic'ioŋ, v. refl. Ecokoŋ, v.a. Hiŋyaŋsela, hiŋyaŋziyela, adv. Icaŋtagle, v.a. Koŋza, v. Wish to do - . Iśilaya, v.; śicokiya, v.a. Speak - to; wośica, v. Commit - ; wośice, n.

exact, Tkoŋza, adj. Just -ly.
exaggerate, Aokicageca, n. -tion. Otaŋtoŋyaŋkel, adv. Yatakuka, v.a. - the unimportant. Waciŋ: lataku- , v. (jest); lawicoȟ'aŋ- , v. ; yuwicoȟ'aŋ, v.a. - a trifle into a big thing.

exalt, (praise, honor). Cf. praise. Iwaŋkabic'iya, v. refl.
examine, v.a. Iciyuŋga. Iwaŋyaŋka, v.a. Look at; iwaŋyaŋgyeȟci, adv. Looking intently. Wawiyukcaŋ, v. - for judgment; wawiyukcaŋka, n. A judge.

example, (model, hero, ideal). Iyowaŋke, v. Set an - ; iyowaŋg; owaŋgya, v.a. Follow the - of; woiwaŋyaŋke, n.

exceed, Cf. more. Kaiyakapeya, adv. A little more, ahead. Olabyakel, adv. -ingly.

excel, Cf. surpass. Pahiŋhiyukiya, v. - one; pahiŋiyekiya. Wonata, v. Get far ahead of.

exchange, (barter). Iyopeya: ici- , v.a.; ici-pi, n.; tokiyopekiciyapi, n. Barter; tokiyopekiya, v.a. Barter; tok- , v.a.

excite, v.n. Ikik'o. Iyopaśtaka, v.a. Urge. Otaŋtoŋyaŋ, adv. Ptaŋyaŋ, adv. Flurried (animals). Caŋteiyapa, v.n. Be -ed: wo-ya, adv. With heart beating.

exclamations, Cf. interjection.

exclude, Aecela(kel), adv. Exclusively. Opaśniya, v.a.
excrete, (defecate). Aleja, v.a., n. Urine. Cesli, n., v.n.: a- , v.a.; acewasli, n.; o- , v. - in; o-tipi, n. Outhouse, toilet room; ta- , n. Dung. Kaśwu, n. Urine. Paȟli, n. Nose excretion. Toŋkce, n. Excrement; tuŋkce, n. Breaking wind; tatuŋkce, n. Manure.

excuse, (leave off, abstain). Kicuŋni, v.n. Be discouraged. Wal'iyowalya, v. - self, leave to others.
exercise, (drill). Kicipasi, v.n.
exhale, v.n. Ipogaŋ; ipoȟya, v.a., adv.
exhaust, Yus'olas'e, adv. In an -ed manner; yus'oya, adv. Tired all out; yus'oyakel, yus'oyeȟci.

exhibit, (display, perform). Wanapiśkaŋyaŋ, v.
exhort, (encourage). Wayaotaŋ, v.
exit, n. Ohinape, oinape.
expand, v.a. Akamna.

expect, Wawaktayapi, n. One -ed, a child.
expend, Woyusota, n. Expense.
experience, n. Woikiksape.
expert, Cf. ingenious. Wayupi: -ka, v.n. Be - ; -ya, adv. -ly; -yahaŋ, -yakel, adv.; wawiyupica, adv. -ly.

explain, v. Woyuptiŋnape, Come to - (ask for help). Yuajaja, v.a. Make clear: ki- , v.
expose, (in the open). Śla egna, adv. -ed. Yazamni, v.a. Open, uncover, by arguments.

expression, (by-word, nickname). Oweśte, v.n. Use pet -s: -ka, n. A pet - . Oyagpicaśni, adj. Beyond - , unspeakable.
extend, (hold out, extensive). Kcekiye, v. Hold, hang over. Otaŋkaya, adj. Extensive, large, spacious. Yekiya, v.a. - to (the hand). Yaya, v.a. - to.

extinct, Atakuniśni, v.n.
extinguish, Sni: aka- , v.a.; ka- , v.a.; kicica- , v.a.; na- , v.a. (fire); pa- , v.a. Snuff out.

extract, (exhaust). v.a. Skebya (fluid) Yaze, v.a.

extravagant, Aokaḣya, adv. -ly; paokaga, adv.

eye, n. Iśta: - su, n. - ball; iśtiha^{n}ke, n. Outer corners of the -s; iśtogna, adv. In the -s; iśtognake, n. Socket; iśtaha, Lid; o^{n}iśti^{n}mapihi^{n}, Lashes; iśtaḣe, Ridge: -hi^{n}, Brow; -pi, Brows; iśtaḣepihi^{n}, Lashes. Skaska, adj. White of the eyes. Iśtaiyohiya, adv. As far as the - can see.

eyeglasses, n. Iśtamaza.

fables, (story). Huⁿkakaⁿ, v.: o- , -pi, n.

fabulous, (beings). Ciciye, n. A ghost. Iya, n. The Eater. Mmla, The Giant. Iktomi, The Trickster. Siyoko, The Wicked One. Tabubu, The Monster. Waziya, Santa Claus.

face, (human). Apośiⁿ, v. Make -s at. Ikśiⁿkiya, v.a. Ite, n.: -anuⁿg, adv.; -śiⁿśiⁿ, n. A wrinkled - ; -yukśilkiya, v.; -yukśiⁿkiya, v.a.; -yuśiⁿkiya, v.a.; itogna, adv.; itognake, n. Countenance; itokśaⁿ, adv. Kaitkobya, adv. Facing, fronting. Opatkoⁿsyela, adv. -ing one way. Psoⁿpsoⁿkiya, adv. With - down.

fact, (emphasis). Yelo, yele, lo, le, particle concluding a sentence to give emphasis to the - stated.
factory, n. Wokage tipi.
fade, v. Saⁿ aya.

fail, v.n. Iśuta, v.n.; iśuteya, v.a. Iyatakuniśni, v.n. Kiciħ'aⁿyaⁿ, v. - for. Maħ'wapajiⁿ, v. - getting (in hunting).

faint, Cf. die. Cuniaⁿta, n. Ħpecaka, adj. Sniyaⁿ t'a, v.
faith, n. Awaciⁿpi, wowicala (belief); wowicalaya, v.a. Cause to believe.

fall,
aglakśiś, v.n.
aglapta, v.n.; kaptapta, v. - to pieces.
agli: -haⁿ(e), v.; -hpaya, v.n.
aħicahaⁿ, v.
aśwu, v.n.: -ya, v.a.
ayaśna, v.a.
gli: -haⁿ, v.n.; -ħpa, v.; -ħpaya.
gnahaⁿ, part.: a- , v.n.
hiⁿ: a-haⁿ, v.n.; a-ħpaya, v.n.; -haⁿ, v.n.; -heya, v.a.; -hpaya, v.n.
Ħpa: aiglu- , v. refl.; awo- , v.a.; ikpa- , v. refl.; ka- , v. Make - ; ka- , v.a. Fell; oka- , v.a. Fell; yu- , v.a. Fell (pull), loosen, drop.
Ħpaya: agaⁿ i- , v.n.; aglaptus i- , v.n.; aiya- , v.a.; ai- , v.n.; apagli- , v.n.; i- , v.n.; oiyo- , v. - into; pasto i- , v.n. - prostrate, on hands and knees.
Ħpeya: na- , v.a. Make - (foot); wohai- , v.a. Make - (shoot).

naħpu, v.a. - off (what is stuck).
jujuwahaⁿ, part. -en to pieces; oju-ju, v.n. - to pieces; ojujuwahaⁿ.
kaⁿhaⁿ, adj. -ing (hair, fruit etc.).
kaośpa, v.
kimnahaⁿ, v. - off.
makagleya, v. - down endwise.
naswaka, v. - off (feathers).
ogliħaⁿ, v.n. - in endwise.
ogwahaⁿ, part. -en to pieces.
pa, v.n. (snow).
si itokab egle, si kakab iyeya, v. Make trip over one's feet.
śloślokahaⁿ, part. -ing off, shedding.
śpuwahaⁿ, part. -en off.
uⁿka: ayu- , v.a.; pa- , v.a. Push to make - ; wana- , v. Fell; wo- , v.a. Fell.
yaoha, v.a. Make - over (by mouth).

falls, n. Iyoħaħa, mniwoħaħa, Water- .
false, Cf. lie. Wicaśni, v. Tell a -hood. Yatogtogya, v.a. Falsify.

family, (members, relatives). Tiwahe, n. Household. Takuye, n. A relative; ahaⁿ, v. Be related; haⁿkeya, n. A relative. Tigle, v. Make a home. Wicotakuye, n. Family residence.
aunt, Tuⁿwicu (his); tuⁿwiⁿ.
baby, Hokśicala.
brother, Ciye, hakata (man's); in-law, Maśe, śic'e (woman's), taⁿhaⁿ (man's).
child, Ciⁿca(la), iciⁿca, ciⁿhiⁿtku, ciⁿkś (son), hokśicaⁿtkiyapi, kaⁿyeja; in-law, Takoś.
children, Wakaⁿheja, hacila.
cousin (female), Scepaⁿśi (woman's), haⁿkaśi (man's); (male), śic'eśi (woman's), taⁿhaⁿś (man's).
daughter, Cuⁿwitku, cuⁿkś.
elder (brother), Tiblo (woman's), ciye (man's); (sister), cuwe (woman's) taⁿke (man's).
father, Ate, ateku, atkuku; in-law, Tuⁿkaⁿ.
girl, Wiciⁿca(la).
grandchild, Takoja.
grandfather, Tuⁿkaśila.
grandmother, Uⁿci, kuⁿśi.
in-law, Haⁿka; omawahitoⁿ, Title of paternal and maternal.
last child, Hakakta, wihakakta (female).
mother, Ina, huⁿku; in-law, Kuⁿ, uⁿciśi, winuħca (man's).
nephew, Toⁿśka (man's); tośka, (woman's)
niece, Tojaⁿ (woman's), toⁿjaⁿ (man's).

FAMILY (contin.)
older, Cf. elder.
sister, Cuwe, hakata (woman's); taŋkakiciyapi, Sisters; in-law, Scepaŋ (woman's), haŋka (man's). Cf. elder.
son, Ciŋca, ciŋkś; in-law, Wicawoħa.
step- mother, Śaŋke; child, Tawagaŋ.
uncle, Lekśi.
wife, Tawicu (his), tawiŋ, mitawiŋ.
younger (brother), Suŋka, suŋkaku, misuŋ; (sister), Taŋka (woman's), taŋkśi (man's).
youngest child, Hake.
grandfather (baby's language), Kaka.

famous, (well-known). Ocaśtaŋiŋ, v.n. Be - . Woimna, adj.
fan, v. Kalulu; ic'iglalu, v. refl.; iglalu; kaolusic'iya, v. - self.

far, (farther, from, off). Cf. interrogative. Ilehaŋ, itehaŋ, adv.; katehaŋ, adv. At a distance; kaitehaŋlake, A little farther (time, place); kahaŋ, Thus - . Kaektawapaya, adv.; kasaŋ, Farther on. Kaoħlayalaka, Not - from. Lehaŋtukel, Just so - , just now; lehaŋtuya, lehaŋyaŋ, lehaŋyela. Makotahena, adv. - from. Tehaŋ: o- , adv. (distance); -taŋ, From a- ; -taŋhaŋ; -tu, - off; to, at a great distance; -tuya, -tuyakel; -yaŋ, - away; wamaka-tulake s'e, adv. From a- .

fare, (toll). Icajuju, oopetoŋ, n.
farm, n. Wojuti, - house, -er; wojuwicaśa, n. -er.

fast, (swift, from food). Kaluluka, n. The -est; kalusyalakes'e, adv. Akih'aŋic'iya, v. refl., adv. Starve. Haŋble, v.n. Cf. dream. Niħkazilkiya, v.

fasten, (bar, lock). Cf. tie, latch, lock. Okaśka, v.a. - up, tie into, hide. Onataka, v.a. Oyutkuga, v.a. Tie, lock: -haŋ, part. -ed.

fat, Cf. meat, animal. Ceśikśice, n. (covering paunch); talipa, taśupa caŋ; papaħyapi, n. Containers for - . Tanuŋħ'śiŋ, n. - between ears. Taŋśiŋ, - on ribs; tawosa, - on lower neck; tawoze, n. - behind ears. Tiśtaśiŋ, - at the temples.

fatigue, v.n. Yugo, Be -ed: -yakel, adv. In an exhausted condition.
fatten, Cf. fat. Cepa(b), adj.: a-ya, v.a.; a-waya, adv.: a- , v.n.; -kiya, v.a.; -ya, v.a.; -waya, adv.; -yapi, part.; -yela, adj.; i-ya, v.a.; i- , adj. Hoapa śiŋ, n. Fat on the taniga; howapaśiŋ.

fault, Wawiyaħtaka, Find - ; wawiyaħtagia, wayaħtagia.

fear, v.n. Caŋlwaŋka: caŋlwaŋmaka, v. refl.; -la, adv.; -ŋ, n., adj.; caŋtewakaŋheja, v.n. Hiŋyaŋsgla, v. Inagihaha, v.n. Inihaŋ, v.n.: wo-yaŋ, adv. -fully; inihiŋciya, v. Kopa(e): haŋkokipa, v.a., adv.; i- , v.a.; i-gla, v.n.; i-kiya, v.a.; kokipa, v.a.; okokipeya, adv. In - ; o- , n.

fearless, (not bashful). Inihaŋśni, adv.; inihiŋciyeśniyaŋ. Napeceśni, adv. Unabashedly. Oħ'aŋsiŋkpekpe, v. Be - in doing. Śuŋk'iśtakpa s'e, adv. Going about -ly.

feast, v.a. Awaśpaŋyaŋ. Cekitipi, n. Kicico wotapi, n. Public - ; wicawota, n. Banquet; wǫlwicayapi; wolya, v.a. Make a - . Śuŋk'ohaŋpi, n. Dog feast. Wakaŋwohaŋ, v. Make a sacred - : -pi, n. A sacred - .

feather, n. Aopazaŋ. Iyake(a), n.; wiyaka, n. - quill; iyagtoŋ, v. Situpi, n. Tail - . Śuŋ, n. The large wing -s: -paħliħli, v. Have -s partly grown; -toto, v.n. Waŋblupi, n. Eagle-tail - . Wasusnaka, n. Narrow side of a - .

feeble, (weak). Kaħtata, v. Make - . Kuja, v.n. Be sick, weak. Staka: o- , v. Be - because of; oki- , v.n. Be en-ed by. Śiħtiŋ: ya- , v.a. Make - (bite); yu- , v.a. En- ; yu-pi, n. -ness; yu-yaŋ, adv. -ly. Ś'ake: i-huŋkeśni, adj.; yuwa-śni, v.a. Make - .

feed, v.a. Iognaka(g): -kiya, -ya, v.a. Yulkiya, yulya, v.a.
feel, v. Aluslus; yualosloza s'e iyeya, v.a. Injure one's -ings. Taŋ: ayu-, v. Touch; iyu-taŋ, oyu- , v.a.; pa- , v. - about for with; wo- , v. Touch; n. One that -s.

fell, Cf. cut. Uŋka: ka- , v.; wa- , v.a. - (saw).
female, n. Wiŋ (of woman, wife): -yela, n. (animals).

fence, v.a. Acaŋka(gla)śka(e): -ya, v.a.; - yaŋka, v. refl.; acuŋkaśka, v.a.; acoŋkaśke, n.; cuŋkaśke, n. Inatake, n.

ferment, (leaven). Napoȟya, v.a.: -pi, n. Leaven.
fertile, adj. Owojuwaśte.
fetch, (get). Kicihiyohi, v. Go and - for.

few, (some, several). Conala, adv.: cog- , adj.; -ka, adj. Many. Iyakilenala, adv. Naptetuka, adj. Tona: -nala, -gnala, -na, adv. How - , a few; -keca, adj. Some; -kel, adj. Several (times, number).

fickle, (false promises, whimsical). Kcaŋka, n. One who is - ; kcaŋkcaŋla, adj. Tawaciŋ: -hahala; -tokeca, adj. Whimsical; -waŋkala, adj.; waciŋcik'ayela, adj. -minded.

field, n. Maga, Cultivated - : -ta, adv. In the - ; maȟtani, n. Old - . Oju, n.: owoju, n. Garden, a planted - . Oyublu taŋka, n. (for plowing).

fight, (quarrel). Cf. quarrel. Kiza, v.a.; kiciza, v.; kicizapi, n.; okisyakel, adv. Used to -ing.
figure, Cf. count. Wawiyaciŋyaŋ, adv. Figuratively. Wiglawa, v. Settle, calculate.

file, (rasp). Ayumaŋ, v.a. Pamaŋ(e), v.a., adj. -ed; kpamaŋ, v. - own; kici- , v. - for. Oweciŋhaŋ, adv. In single file (succession).

fill, v.n. Awoblu. Hokapta, v. Oȟaya, v.a. - up. Ipi: -ic'iya, v. refl.; -ya, v.a. Ju: io-ya, v.a.; -toŋ, v. - self (eat); o-kicitoŋ, v. - a bag for; o-kitoŋ; o-la, adj. -ed; o-pi, n.; o-toŋ, v.a. - in sacks; o-tóŋpi, -ed bags; o-ya, v.a.; okici- , oki- , v. - up for; okikśu, v. pos. Pa(kpa)gi: aokici- , v. (pipe); ao- , v. pos. and v.; o- , v. pos. - own pipe. Okata, v. - up, cover over. Ataja, v.n.

filter, v.a. Caŋ: ayu- , ika- , iyu- (sift), v.a. Puskepa(b): a- , v.n.; a-ya, adv.; o-ya, adv. -ed. Nazeya, v.

filth, n. Wośape.
final, Ohaŋketa, adv.
find, v.a. Iyeya(e), Go and - : -ya, v.a.; wa-ca, n. One that -s much; waw- , v.; yuha - , v. Receive unexpectedly.

fine, (small, soft). Swula, adj. (as beads); swuwaya, adj. Soft and - .
finger, Cf. hand. Napsu, n. Napapazo, v. Shake the - at; waepaza, n. Index or forefinger. Śąk'oyazaŋ, v.n. Pain under the nails. Śaśte, n. Little - : -iyokihe, n. Middle - .

finish, Cf. settle. Co: glu- , v. pos.; yu-ya, adv. -ed; waki-yakel, adv. Well. Ȟ'uŋhikiya, v.a., adv.; Ȟ'uŋhiya, v.a.; Ȟ'uŋhiyela, adv. Ohiŋnikiya, v.a. Cease from. Staŋ: ahiyu- , v.; igla- , v. refl.; iyu- , v.a.; oyu- , v.a. - within; yu- , v.a. Perfect. Tkoŋskiya, v. - a job, be done. Yupiŋnakikśiŋ, v. Be hurried to - work.

fire, (burn).
auŋ, v.a.; aoŋ.
caŋtakse ya, v. Set - to root.
ceti, v.a.: a- , v.a.; acewati, v.a.; aki- , v.n.; cekikati, v.; cekiciti, v.; e- , v.; i- , v.; o- , n. -place; mazao- , n. Stove.
gu, v.n.: a- , v.n.; a-ya, v.a.; ce-gu, adj.; ce-guya, v.a.; -gnagya, v.a.; -mna, adj.; -śica, adj.; -ya, v.a.; iya-ya, v.
hiŋgnu, v.a.: -pi, part.
hugna: -ga(Ȟ), v.a.; -gaya, v.a.; -ya, v.a.
ile, v.n., n.: a- , v.n.; a-śaśa(ya), adv.; a-ya, v.a., part.; caŋka- , v.; ha-yapi s'e, adv.; -ya, v.a.; o-ya, v.a. Set on - .
itkoŋ, v.n.: -yahaŋ, part.; -yaŋ, v.a.
le: a-leya, v.a.; a-sab, v.a.
lo: a- , v.n.; a-kiksohaŋ, v. pos.; a-za(s), v.n.: -abya, v.a.; -hiŋgle, v.n.; -losyeca, v.n.; -loza, v.n.; -ya, v.a.
natipa(b): a- , v.n.; i-ya, v.
ona, n. Prairie - : -gu, n. Burnt prairie; -gumna, v. Smell of a - ; -ya, v. Start a - ; onikuśeya, n. Fire-guard; oninatake, -inatake.
oŋ, uŋ: a- , v.a.; ce-pa, v.a.
peta(l,t), n.: -akigle, v. - self; -icagla, adv. Near - ; -ikceya, adv. Over - ; -ileyapi, n. Kindlings; -imna śni, v. Be unafraid of - ; -iśkaŋ, v.a. Draw near - . Cf. warm. -ikaŋye, adv. Near - ; -kagla, adv.; -kiyela, adv. Near - ; -kokipa, v. Fear - ; -mna, v.n. Smell of - ; adj. -aga, n. Coals; -aŋl, adv. On - ; -yuhala, n. Walking - , night - ;

-kaile s'e, adv. Fanning the - . -owayake, n. Chunk of wood to bank a fire; -uspe, n. - brand; -uste, n. Aśpaŋ, v.n. Aiziya, v.n. Wakiŋyaŋ onayaŋpi, n. Prairie - started by lightning. Wipaśkaŋglepi, n. - for a triumph.

firesteel, n. Caŋka, caŋkognake.
firm, Ahahayela, aheheyela, adv. neg. Aiyasaka, v.n. Suta: apa- , v.a.; a- , v.n.; ayu- , v.a.; caŋte- , v.n., adj.; iglu- , v. refl.; o-ya, adv. Śogya, adv. -ly. T'iŋza(e,s): ana-ya, adv.; aput'iŋs-ya, adv. red.; ipa- , v.a., n.; i-ya, v.a.; i- , v.n., n.; ka- , v. Make - ; ona- , v. (by foot); oyu- , v.a. Make - in, brace; -ya, v.a.; adv. -ly, bravely.

first, Toka(e), adv. At the - : -ḣci, adv.; -he, n. The beginning; v. Be - ; -hekiya, v. Go ahead of others; -heya, adv. At the beginning, first; n. The - ; -ḣtayetu, adv. At the - of night; -k'ehaŋ, adv. At the - ; -k'uŋhehaŋ, adv.; -laḣci, adv. For the - time; -pa, n. -born, eldest; -ya, adj. n. The first.

fish, (marine life). Hogaŋ, n. (in gen.).
carp, Hoiwotka, hosaŋ.
catfish, Howasapa.
clam, Tuki.
crawfish, Matuśka.
crayfish, Matugna.
eel, Hoka, zuzecahogaŋ.
frog , Gnaśka. Cf.
leech, Tuŋśla.
minnow, Hogaŋsaŋla, hogaŋscila.
pike (grass), Hogleglega.
rainbow, Hogleglega.
red-fin, Hoapeśa.
shad, Holaska.
snail, Mniwamnuḣ'a, tuŋśla, wahacaŋkakic'iŋ.
stone-roller, Hopepe.
toad, Matapiḣa, matapeḣ'a.
turtle, Ke, keya. Cf.
whale, Hogaŋtaŋka, wamnitu.

fin, Hoape.
gill, Hocaka.
scale, Hoceśpu, hopaśku.

dead fish, Hot'eca, n.
fish, v. Hokuwa. Homnayaŋ, v. Collect - . Hopataŋ, v. Spear - .
fishy smell, Hogaŋmna, homna, hosamna, hosewimna, adj.

fish-hook, n. Cakiyuḣlate, hoicuwa, hoipate, hoiyupsice.

fit, (able, suited to, join). Aecetu, v.n. Be able. Kipiya, v. Make - ; adv. Wakipuskica, v. - closely, tightly together.

flabby, (shaking). Kayoyo s'e, adv. Lolopa, adj. Soft.

flag, n. Wiyokihe, Banner. Wowapi, n.: -okijata, n. Truce - .
flame, Kaḣaḣa, v. - up, lick. Oile, n.
flap, (beat). Cf. swing. Kaozeze, v. (by wind). Śniyaŋyaŋ, adv. -ping (wings); ḣniyaŋyaŋ.

flash, (spark). Pailepi, n. -light; wakiŋyaŋ toŋwaŋpi petijaŋjaŋ. Wakiŋyaŋ toŋwaŋpi, n. Spark.

flat, adj. Blaska: -ya, adv.; ica- , v.n.; iwo-yela, adv.; ka- , v.a.; na- , v.a. -ten; o- , n. The - side; o-ya, adv. On the - side; pa- , v.a. Wipablaye, n. -iron. Opaska, v.t. -ten. Ipustaka, v.n.

flatter, v.a. Yazoŋta.
flavor, v.a. Yuskuya (sweet, sour). Śtusta, adj. Lacking - ; śtuśteya, v.a. Make lose - .

flax, n. Ataśośapina nablaga.
flay, v. Wayugapa.
flee, v.a. Napa: anakipa, v.; a- , v.; ao- , v.a.; ikpiyo- , v.; nakipa, v. (homeward); napeya, v.a. Make - ; o- , v.a. Take refuge. Najica: iya- , v.; najiŋca, v.n.; nakicipa, v.n.; ta- , v.; tanajilhi, v. Come -ing. Naic'iśpa, v.n. (danger, trouble); pageya, v.a. Make - ; wapatoŋyece, n. Person that makes - . Cf. refuge.

flesh, Cf. body. Akicepa, v.n.; coku, n.; cokukitoŋ, v.; conica, n. Huwapaḣpe, n. Śwośwoke s'e, adv. Very -y; waśośo s'e, kayoyo s'e.

flex, v.a. Yupsoŋla.
flexible, (pliant, fresh, tender). Nuŋśnuŋjahela, adj.; nuŋśnuŋja. Psoŋpsoŋla, adj. Supple, lithe. Wiŋświŋje, adj.; wiŋświŋjahela, wiŋświŋjela.

flimsy, adj. Zigzica.
flinch, Cf. shy.
flirt, v.n. Wiciŋśkaŋ, Be -ing.

float, v. Okage(ȟ): ao-wog, ao-woka, v.n.; -woka, v.n. (in air); -ya, v.a. Make - ; adv. -ing. Aokapota(l), v.n.; aokapolya, v.a.; okapota, v.n.; aglapota, v.a. pos. - upon.

flood, (overflow). Mnitaŋ, v.n.: i-, v.n., n.; i-yaŋ, v.a.; -yaŋ, v.n.
floor, n. Caŋwiŋja, caŋwowiŋge. Owaŋka, owaŋg, owaŋk, n. (for rest, tent).

flour, n. Owayukpaŋ.
flow, (trickle). Amnitaŋ, v.n.: -ya, v.a.; -yaŋ, adv. Kaluza, v. - rapidly; kaluskaluza; icaluza, v.

flower, (weed). Waȟca, n. The genus. Wanaȟca, ȟca, n. Blossom; ȟcaya, v. Waptaye, n. Weed. Caŋȟlogaŋ, n. Hollow stalk. Cf. medicine, grass.

amaranth, Waȟpe maka ayublaya.
anemone, Hituŋkala tuŋkce.
aster (dense), Caŋȟlogaŋ pepela; waȟcazi waśtemna (prairie).
beard-tongue, Caŋȟlogaŋ: - haśluśluta, - ȟlaȟla; haŋpinatopi.
bedstraw, Waȟpewacaŋga huwiŋyela.
bee-plant, Waȟpe ȟ'eȟ'e.
beggar's lice, Miniohuta aglagla waȟcazi.
bindweed, Kimimila tawanaȟca, psitola hu iyececa.
bitter-sweet, Woȟlokapiśni pejuta.
blue cardinal flower, Zuzecatawote apetotohe.
boneset, Waȟpe pa.
buckwheat, Caŋȟlogaŋ hutkaŋ (species).
bullrush, Wihuta huswula.
burr, Śpaŋśniyutapi iyececa (sand).
burweed, Waȟpeśica.
calamus, Siŋkpetawote.
cat-tail, Haŋtkaŋ, hiŋtkaŋ, wihutahu.
clammyweed, Waȟpeȟla.
cleavers, Waȟpewacaŋga hubloka.
clover, Tokalatapejuta hubloka; waȟpeswula.
cockle-burr, Winawizi.
coneflower, Nap(e)ośtaŋ.
crowfoot, Caŋȟlogaŋ wicagnaśke (species).
cyperus, Minisaŋtula.
daisy, Hupteptecala.
dalea, Caŋȟlogaŋ suta.
dogbane, Napeoilekiyapi.
doorgrass, Waȟpe pepela.
downy painted cup, Waȟpeyazokapi.
erigeron, Oŋwahiŋyuŋ toŋpi.
flax (lupine), Caŋȟlogaŋ nablaga.
fleabane, Caŋȟlogaŋ waśtemna iyececa.

flower (contin.)
froelichia, Caŋȟlogaŋ iśtawiyowicaȟpaya.
gentian, Kapopapi, waȟcawaśte.
gilia, Yazokapiȟu.
goldenrod, Caŋȟlogaŋ makaayublaya, caŋnuŋgahu pteptecela, mimela waȟcazi, tal'agnake (stiff), waȟcaziblu (rock).
gromwell, Śuŋkcaŋka huipiye.
groundsel, Śuŋkawakaŋtapejuta, waȟpeśluśluta.
hawthorn, Matotaspaŋ.
honey-suckle, Tatawabluśka tacaŋȟlogaŋ, oŋśuŋkoyuśpapi.
hops, Waȟpeakikaśkapi.
iron-weed, Tal'agnaka iyececa.
ivy, Wikośkatapejuta (poison).
Jacob's ladder, Zuzecatawote ptaptaikoyaka.
knot-weed, Takuśaśala huwiŋyela.
lady's thumb, Takuśaśala huswula.
lark-spur, Wanagitiŋpsila.
lady's slipper, Makacanakpa.
lily, Caŋȟlogaŋ maȟ'awaŋglakela (prairie), kewapa (water), mnaȟcaȟca (prairie), pśiŋtaŋka (mariposa), yapizapi iyececa.
loco-weed, Śuŋktawote.
looking-glass, Caŋȟlogaŋ kcaŋkcaŋla.
loosestrife, Caŋȟlogaŋ wahcazi.
mallow, Utahu caŋȟlogaŋ, waȟcazi cik'ala.
milkweed, Panuŋpala, waȟcaȟca, tiŋpsila pejuta.
mimosa, Haŋtepepe iyececa.
mint (lemon), Makaceyaka iyececa.
monkey flower, Ceśkikaŋ iyececa.
mouse ear, Caŋȟlogaŋ huwaŋjila, hituŋkalanakpala, taȟcanakpala.
mugwort, Makośice pejiȟota.
mustard (tumble), Caŋȟlogaŋ wabluśkahu.
nettle, Caŋicaȟpe.
penny royal, Iȟ'e makaceyaka.
oreocarya, Caŋȟlogaŋ apepepe.
Pasch flower, Hokśicekpa.
pigweed, Caŋȟlogaŋ iŋkpagmigmela, owicak'o, caŋȟlogu.
plantain, Caŋȟlogaŋ wapośtaŋkagapi, wakiŋyaŋla paȟlihu, wihutahu iyececa.
prairie-pink, Caŋȟlogaŋ hucaŋswula, makacaŋśihu.
prickly poppy, Tokahuwahiŋkpeoŋziyapi.
primrose, Huȟla, husaŋsaŋ.
psoralea, Matotatiŋpsila, ticanicahu, waȟcazi kaŋtamna uŋmahutaŋka, waȟpokijate.
pyeweed, waȟca pepela.
ragweed, Caŋȟlogaŋ oŋzipakiŋte.

ragwort, Caⁿḣlogaⁿ sotka.
red-root, Uⁿpaⁿtawote, yuśpulaota.
rose, Oⁿjiⁿjiⁿtka(hu).
sage, Makaceyaka.
sideranthus, Waḣcazi waśtemna.
smartweed, Takuśaśala.
snake-root, Tat'ecaⁿnuga, wazimniⁿkpa iyececa, wazimniⁿkpa (button).
sophora, Makomica.
Solomon's seal, Yapizapihu, zuzecatawote hutaⁿkiⁿyaⁿ heca.
spiderwort, Caⁿḣlogaⁿ paⁿpaⁿla.
spurge, Caⁿḣlogaⁿ wapośtaⁿ, apelatapiślecala iyececa.
stickweed, Hupepe.
sunflower, Waḣcazi taⁿka, waḣcazizi.
thistle, Tokahu, waḣpepe(ka) (Russian)
townsendia, Iḣ'eḣ'e caⁿḣlogaⁿ.
tumble-weed, Hutkaⁿhaⁿska, waḣpeyatapi iyececa.
umbrellawort, Caⁿḣlogaⁿ okihetoⁿ.
vervain, Topestola.
vetch, Śuⁿklejahu (milk), śuⁿkowaśakala (Canadian), śuⁿktapejuta (loco), tasusu (American).
violet, Waḣpeto (prairie).
virgin's bower, Owicak'olahu.
wallflower, Caⁿḣlogaⁿ pa.
winter-greens, Waḣpeblaskaska.
wolfberry, Oⁿśuⁿk'nasapihu, zuzecatawote.

fluent, Yaglapi s'e, adv. -ly, plainly.
fluff, Cf. soft.
flush, (level, align). Kaotaⁿ, v.a. Make - . Paotkoⁿza, v.a. Make - with.

fly, (escape, scatter). Kiⁿyaⁿ, v.n.: o- , v.n. - in, about; o-waśte, adj. Docile; akiyaⁿ, v.a. Naśloka, v.n. - off, out: waa- , n. One persisting to fly off, out; akaḣwogya, v.a. Papsipsica, v. Make - (push).

foam, Cf. spit, issue. Ipiga, n. Kataga, v. Make - ; mniwataga, n.; mniwaticoga, n. Skum.

fog, (steam, dust). P'o, n. Mist; adj.: ana- , v.n.; a- , v.n.; o- , n.

fold, Aicitakigna, adv. Iciyaḣlal, adv. Apako, v.a. Kśa: ayu- , v.a.; pa- , v. (blanket). Kśija: apa- , v.a. Double up; pa- , v.a. - up. Akipaja(ś), v.a. Pehaⁿ, v.a. - up: aya- , v.a.; ayu- , v.a.; gla- , v. pos.; iya- , v.a.; iya-yaⁿ, adv.; kici- , v. - up for; kpehaⁿ, v. - up own; o- , v. - up in; opehe, n.

follow, v.n. Ecaecoⁿka. Ahaⁿkeya, adv. Immediately -ing; ohaⁿgleya, v.a. - about. Icihaktaya, adv. Ihakabya, v.a. Ioglamniyaⁿ, adv. Iokawiⁿḣ, adv. Iyayuḣya, adv.; iyagluḣa, v. pos. Kuwa: e- , v.a.; kicuwa, v. - up, after. Wawiyayuḣa, v. Tag along; n. One that tags along; wawiyayuḣya, adv. Okihaⁿ, v.a. Be after; okihe, v.a., adj. -ing, next. Opa, v.a.: -si, v. - after in; a- , v.; a-ya, v.a.; okicipa, v. - for, obey; okipa, v. pos. - ways of others, obey; okipeca, v.n. Do as accustomed to; okipekiya, v.a. Make - own; okipeya, v.a. Make - own; adv. -ing; -si, v. - after in. Pasi: a- , v.a.; -yakel, adv. -ing up. Tapa(b): a-ya, v.n.; a- , v.n.; o- , v. - after; fig., imitate; waotape s'e, adv. -ing unintentionally.

fond, (care for). Waḣtiⁿkiya, v. pos. - of own; wahtiⁿyaⁿ, v. Be - of. Waḣtiⁿciye śni! (cursing) You do not love me!

fondle, (hold). Katakoha, v. Hold in arms. Kignayaⁿ, v. Caress.
food, n. Lo (soft stuff); walopela, n. - overboiled (mushy). Wota(e), v.: -pi, wol, n.; heḣakatawote, n. (for elk); wo, n.; wola, v. Beg - . Wateca, n. Part of one's - taken home from a feast. Watogciⁿ, v. Desire other - . Yute, o- , n. Eating; tawo-, n. His - ; wo-ya, v.a. Have or use as - .

fool, Aikpajuju, v. refl. Aikpablaya, v. refl. Eceyanuniya, v.a. Eciⁿśni, adj. Glezezeka, adj. Guka: ca- , n.; iglu- , v. Heyoka, n. Iglagleglega, v. refl. Iḣaḣake, n.; iic'iḣaḣa, v. refl. Kiuⁿuⁿlake, v. Act - . Oileleka, n. Ot'ognaka, v.n. Be -hardy, rish life. Psaⁿpsaⁿka, n. A - . Caske(ya), v. Waciⁿtoⁿśni, v.n. Be -ish. Witko, adj. -ish: ki-tkoka, v. Be -ish; o-tko, adv. -ish; -kaga, n. - maker; -koⁿza, v.n. Pretend to be -ish; -pi, n. -ishness; -tkoka, n. A - ; v.n. Act -ishly; -tkopi, n. -ishness; -tkoya, adv. -ishly; -ya, v.a. Make a - of; adv.; -yahaⁿ, adv. Sillily.

foot, Kpaḣajiⁿka, v. Get to one's feet; anatitaⁿ, v.; anatokelyakel, adv.; anatuka, v.a.; anat'a, v.a. Si, n.: -akśa, adj. Pigeon-toed;

-haḣmiŋ, adj. Toes pointing out; -capsaŋ, v. Shake the - ; -glapsaŋpsaŋ; -cola, adj. Bare-footed; -cuha, n. Sole of the - or shoe; -ha, n. Sole, hoof; -hutkaŋ, n. - ligament; -hukaŋ; -ḣape, n. Hollow of the - ; -oḣape; -ic'iyapa, v. Strike feet together (walking); -itakaha, n. Instep; -iyotiyekiya, v. Pain one in the - ; -ksa, adj. Club-footed; -naniyaŋ, v. The - hurts; -pa, n. Front of - ; -saŋni, n. One in a set of feet; -yete, n. Heel; -yeteośkoke, n. Skin of the heel. Oyayatopa, adj. Four-footed, on all four; huhatopa, n. A quadruped. Huiyuŋ, adv.

for, -kica- , -kici- , prep. in comp.

forbid, (oppose, check, stop). Kiśica, v.a. Wawiyokiśni, v.

force, v.a. Kasli, - out, press out.

ford, n. Oiyoḣpaye. Gliyuwega, v. pos.; oiyuwege, n.

foreign, Cf. enemy. Toka, n. Enemy, hostile. Wicaśa lehaŋkata, n. -er.

foremost, Cf. begin. Otokata, adv.

forest, n. Caŋnahmela k'el; caŋowaŋcaya, cuŋwaŋca; caŋowoju, caŋwita; coŋteḣi, Thick - ; cuŋśoke, cuŋtaŋka, cuŋwiŋziye oyuze, cuŋwoheśma, n. Cf. timber.

foretell, Cf. predict. Wakaŋ iya, v.; wakiŋya.

forget, Ociŋwakaŋ, adj. Purposely -ful. Waciŋt'a, v.n. Be -ful. Ktoŋja: aki- , v.a.; a- , adj.; aktoŋ- , adj.; aktoŋśya, v.a.; aktoŋyaŋ, adv.; e- , v.a.; waki- , v.

forgive, v.a. Kicicajuju: wica-pi, n. -ness. Akiciktoŋja, v.a.

fork, Cf. silverware. Jata(l), adj.: aki- , adj.; oki- , n.; jag- , adj. Forked, rough; o- , n.; okajaya, adv. In the forks of; ka- v.; na- , v.a.; pa- , v.a. Make -ed; wa- , v.a.; wo- , v.a. (punch). Ohaka, adj. -ed, n. (stream): -yakel, adv. In many ways.

form, (likeness, kind, image). Ouŋcage, n. Likeness. Okaḣwaŋjila, n. One of the same form, style.

formerly, adv. Itokehaŋ, itok'ehaŋ, itola kiŋ (k'oŋ) hehaŋ.

forsake, (fall from). Ohiŋḣpaya, v.n. Ayuḣlagaŋ, v.a. Leave.

fortune, Cf. luck. Wapi, adj. Lucky; -ka, adj.; -ke, n. -ate person; -śni, adj. Un-ate; -ya, v.a. Make -ate; adv. -ately.

foundation, n. Oagle, owaheglepi.

fowls, Cf. birds. Aŋpaohotoŋla, n. Domestic - . Waḣupakoza, n.

fracture, Cf. break. Kawega, v.; kicawega, v. - for. Okaḣleca, v.a.

fragment, n. Owośpe, A piece shot, punched off.

frame, Agle, v.a.: -hiyeya, part.; -haŋ, n.

frantic, Śica waciŋ, v.n. Be frightened, hurrying, screaming; adv. -ally. T'ebleze śni, v. Be - , wild.

fray, Swaka, adj. -ed. Wakahuŋta, v. Make - , peeling off.

free, (extricate). Igluha(ya), v.a. Iśicola, adv.; ituḣci. Kiigluśpa, v. - self (wrestle). Kpapta, v. - self and leave. Nakiśloka, v. - self. Tawaic'iya, v. refl. Be - : -pi, n. -dom, liberty. Yuśkeya, adv. Loose.

freeze, Acaḣślaya, adj. Caga, n.: a- , v.n.; acaḣślaya, adj.; acaḣsu, v. Aḣeyuŋka, v.n.; anap'iŋ, adj., adv. Heyuŋka, n. Haŋyagu, n.

freight, Mas'ahi, v. Arrive with - .

frequent, v. Oecoŋḣca uŋ.

fresh, adj. Lolo (meat), loya.

friction, Cf. rub.

friend, Kola, n. (men): -kiciyapi, n. -ship; -ya, v. Have as a - ; o-ya, v.; ta-kiciyapi, n. Particular - ; ta-ku, n. His particular - . Lakota(l): -ya, v.a. Be -ly with; o-ya, v. Have as a - ; adv. As - ; o-kiciyapi, n. -ship, peace; o- , n. -ship, alliance, fraternity; wo- , n. -ship, peace. Tawaśe, n. Female - (woman's): -tku, n. Her - (female). Kicuwa, n.

frighten, Cf. scare. Nagihaha, adj. -ed. Oŋśtiŋmanihiŋciya, v. Be -ed in sleep. Owaḣabya, v. - all away; n. One who -s. Taŋglusasaya, adv. In fright; taŋglusasaseca, v. Be -ed, sick at seeing. Taŋsag, v.: -t'eya, v.a. - very much. Yuś'iŋyeya, v.a.

fringe, Napowaya, v.; naswaya, v. Okasu, okaswu, paswupi, n. Waozezeya, v.a. Cut in -s; wazaza, v. Cut -s; adv. In -s; wazazapi, n. Dangles.

frog, n. Gnaśka: -caᶯli(la), -wakaᶯ. Honagila; honawitkala, n.
frolic, Śkehaᶯhaᶯ, adj. -some.

from, Eciyataᶯ, adv.; eciyataᶯhaᶯ, heciyataᶯ; iheciya, adv.: -taᶯ, iheciyotaᶯ, adv. Ehaᶯtaᶯhaᶯ, adv.; etaᶯ, adv.; etaᶯhaᶯ, prep.: -haᶯ, prep.; etaᶯtaᶯ, prep. Ikahaᶯ(yaᶯ), adv. K'uᶯ hetaᶯ, conj. There. -taᶯ, -taᶯhaᶯ, prep. suff.

front, Cf. before. KaipatkuȟYa, -ing. Kaᶯyeta, adv. In - of.
frost, n. Waniȟeyuᶯka, First - .
froth, (foam). Onapiga, v.n.
frown, v. Iteśiᶯkiya, iteyukokiya, Grin. Paȟteyukokiya, v.

frugal, adj. Wagluhahaka, Saving, parsimonious. Wakitoᶯtoᶯka, v.n. Be - , economical.

fruit, (berries). Cf. vegetables.
apple, Taspaᶯ (haw), taspaᶯpuzapi (dried).
artichoke, Paᶯgi.
banana, Śkopela, ziziśkopela.
berry, Auᶯyeyapi, capceyazala, haza.
buffalo-berry, Maśtiᶯcapute.
cherry, Caᶯpa, caᶯp' , tamnioȟpihu (ground).
fig, Tamnioȟpi.
gooseberry, Wicagnaśka.
grape, Cuᶯwiyapehe, cuᶯyapehe.
lemon, Taspicahiye (extract).
muskmelon, Supestola, suzizila.
peach, Taspaᶯ hiᶯśma.
pear, Taspaᶯ pestostola.
pineberry, Waziwicagnaśka.
plum, Kaᶯta, kaᶯsu (stone), ptetawote (ground).
raspberry, Takaᶯhecala (black).
red-haw, Taspaᶯsloslola.
sandberry, Auᶯyeyapi.
serviceberry, Wipazukaᶯ (June berry), wipazokaᶯ, wipazutkaᶯ.
strawberry, Takaᶯyecala, waziśkeca.

Wasutoᶯyaᶯ, v. Bring forth fruit.

fulfill, (accomplish). Ecetu, v.n.: ayu- , v.a.; -kiya, v.a.; -ya, v.a.; wo- , n. -ment. Enakiya, v.a. Glaheyapi s'e, adv.
full, adj. Ojula: i- , adj.; ojuya; iyojukiya, v.; iyujibyela, v. (to brim. Ipi, adj.: w- , v.n. Be - , satisfied (with food). Iyapahayela, adv.; iyapaśniśyela, adj.; iyatagle, adv. Kazaᶯ, v. Feel - . Kicuᶯskehaᶯ, adj. Half- . oȟ'abyela, adv. Almost - . Yaśkipa, v. Bite and make - up.

fume, v.a. Kagiᶯlgiᶯca, Make - . Ozilya, v.a. Fumigate; zilya.
fun, Ecaca, adv. In - , as a diversion. Iȟaᶯhaᶯ, adv.

funnel, n. Iyokaśtaᶯ pestola.
fur, (nap). Cf. hair. Powaya, n.; adj. -trimmed; powayela, adj. Having nap. Wahiᶯśma, n.

furious, Cf. terrible. Pagnaśkiᶯyaᶯ, v.a. Make - (pushing about).
future, Tokata, adv. In - ; n. The - : -kiya, adv. In the - ; -yab, adj. Wakahaᶯl, adv. Sometime in - .

futurity, (intention). Kta, particle; nuᶯ, nuᶯwe.

gain, Cf. win. Ohiya, v.a. Acquire, win, get the better of. Yamna, v.a. - by talking; yamnakiya, v.a.

gallop, (speed). Cf. run. Nauŋka, v.n.: kato- , v. - slowly; wa- , v.a. Start off on a - . Tahusliyeya, v. Speed.
game, (hunted). Osaŋkayakel, adv. Void of - .

game, (pastime). (Boys'), haŋpakutepi; hiŋyaŋkaḣwaciyapi; hituŋk'naḣabyapi; iyopsilkakicipa ecoŋpi; pejiyuskita kutepi; petekiciyapi; tokakiciyut'api. (Girls'), tapanakapa; tasihauŋpi.

In general:
cuŋwiyawa kaŋsukutepi, Plum pit.
haŋpapecoŋpi, Hand guessing.
hutanacute, Cow bone.
kignuŋkacicipapi, Underwater race.
magakiciyapi, Water duck.
makakiciiŋpi, Mud and willow.
matokiciyapi, Tickling game.
micapeca oŋkiciopi, Mischievous game.
napeoglece kutepi, Stick throwing; napoglece kutepi.
napsiyoḣli kutepi, Stick and ring.
oglece kutepi, Arrow shooting.
okaḣ'oliyeya ecoŋpi, Ice game.
paiŋyaŋkapi, The hoop; otaja, n. Mark on one of the four hoops.
paslohaŋpi, The tahegle for sliding on snow or ice.
petagakiciiŋpi, Testing with coals.
ptewoyake, Bone girls use in the tasihauŋpi.
sazu, Cross-sticks of ḣaka, a game shooting instrument.
śnipute ya, v. Throw the bow.
śuŋk'nasapi, Shooting arrows through a walega.
śuŋk'nunikiciyapi, (?).
tabkapsicapi, Shinny.
taŋpa, Small basket used in the cuŋwiyawa kaŋsukutepi.
tokakata, v. Throw a bow on ice.
wiokiciciya ecoŋpi, Game to practice courting.
woohiye, An inning.
(Children's), inaḣmekiciciyapi, Hide-and-Seek; siokiciyaḣlalyapi, waŋkayekiciya ecoŋpi, waziyacekaga.

gap, Ḣci, adj., n.; -ḣci, adj.; -ḣciya, adv.; -wahaŋ, part.; ka- , v.a. Make a gap.

gape, (spread out, lie open). Kagapa, v. - open; naga, v.n. - open; nagaŋ. Najakayela, adv.; najata(l), v.a.

garbage, n. Woyatapi. Cf. leave.
garments, Cf. clothing.
garrulous, Cf. boisterous.
garter, n. Huŋcaje (s'e): ḣlaḣla - , n.; huŋskicaḣe, n.

gash, n. Owahuŋ. Wago, v.a. Mark the flesh. Waic'ihoŋ, v. refl. - self; wakihoŋ, v. pos. - own, cut nicks; wakicihoŋ, v. - for. Waśkita, v.

gasp, Cf. rattle. Okiniyaŋ, v.n. (with cuwi). Onaglo, v.n. Rattle in the throat; onaḣna, n. A dying breath.

gather, (collect). Caŋle, v.a. Coga: ai- , v.n.; kai- , v. Bunch. Gluge, v. pos.; ogejuya, v. - up one's clothes; yage, v.a. (by mouth). Mna: aki-mnaic'iya, v.a.; aki-ya, v.a.; a-ŋyaŋ, v.a.; gla- , v. pos.; i-yaŋ, v.a.; -ic'iya, v. -for self; -kiya, v. Take a collection, - own; -yaŋ, v.a.; -yekiya, v. Make - ; o-yaŋ, v. - into. Mniciya: ai- , v. col. pl. Cf. assemble. Pahi: ak- , v.a.; a- , v.a.; kici- , v. - for; kpaḣi, v. - own; o- , v. - into. Wita, v.: oki-ya, adv. -ing about; owikeśni, adv. -ed to gether, not spent; pa-ya, v.a. (by hand); pa-yela, adv. -ing heads together; wapawi, v. - about, swarm, flock about.

gauze, Cf. net. Zaŋzaŋla, n.
gaze, Oiśtaglewaŋjila, n. A steady -
gear, Naic'iḣmiŋyaŋ, v.n. Get out of - , out of place.

generation, n. Iwicacaga, oicage, wic'icage, wic'oŋcage, woicage.
generous, Caŋlyuha, v.n.; caŋteyukaŋ. Oḣ'aŋpi, v.n. Be - . Woihamnayaŋ, adv. -ly.

gentle, Cf. mild. Asaza(s), adj.: -ya, -yela, w-yela, adv. Gently, mildly. Iktahela, adv. Okuŋoŋwaśte, adj. Mild. Waḣwa, adj.: a-yela, adv.; wo-la, n. -ness. Paiwaśteya, adv. Wawat'eca(ka), adv., n.

geometry, (figures). Oisa, n. Angle: - yamni, Triangle. Opesto, Point. Ohiye, Line. Otatkoŋza, adj. Parallel. Owokśaŋ, opuś'iŋ (convex), Curve. Owoslata, Perpendicularity.

get, Aiglaptaⁿyaⁿ, v. (unexpectedly). Ayamna, v.a. Caⁿk'iⁿya, v. - firewood. Icu, v.: -kiya, v.a. (control); ikic- , v. Ikinica, v.a.; ikinil. Kicikta: a- , v.; akta, adv.; iha- , v.a. Oigloye, n. Progress, one's - ting along; oiyaye, n. Getting through (a bad road).

get ready, Cf. prepare.
ghost, n. Nagi, n.: -toⁿ, v. Make -s; wa- , n.
gibbet, n. Opanakseye.

gift, n. Wakic'uⁿpi. Wośpipikagapi, n. -giving at the Christmas tree.
gills, n. Iyoȟa, loȟe.
gimlet, Cf. drill.
girdle, (gird). Ipiya(gla)ka(e,g), v.a. -kitoⁿ, v.a.; -toⁿ, v.a.

give, (gift, present). Hetkoza, v. Yield to. Hiyukiciciya, v.a. Iglat'e, v. refl. - self away. Iyaȟpekiya, v.; wiȟpeya, v.a. - away things: -pi, n. Akpagaⁿ, v.a. pos.: -yaⁿ, adv.; pagaⁿya, v.a. Make - away. K'u, v.a.: hao- , v.; o- , v.a.; -śi, v. Command to - ; -waciⁿ, v. Be disposed to - ; wo- , v. - good food to, lend; w-pi, n. A lending, giving away to; wowica-pi, n. Issue, allowance. Akimnimniciya, v. - away, make a present: -pi, n. Give-away; anamni, v.n. Otuȟ'aⁿ, v. - away (a present): -pi, n. Give-away; otukiȟ'aⁿ, v.a. - to one (present). Ayukaⁿ, v.a. Yield to.

glad, Cf. thank. Waśte: caⁿteya- , v.a. -den; icaⁿl- , v.n. Be - ; icaⁿl-ya, adv. Wawapilakiya, v. Make - ; n. A good angel.

glance, (miss partly). Kagnayaⁿ, v. Kaiyab, v. - off. Kaśluta(l), v. - off; wośluta, v.n. Naoȟmiⁿ, v.n. v.n. - off. Woglakiⁿyaⁿ, v. Make -. Woptaⁿyaⁿ, v.a. Make - off, ricochet.

glass, (container). Jaⁿjaⁿ, n. Vial, bottle, pane, drinking - .
glaze, Siⁿsiⁿ, adj. -ed over.
glisten, (glitter, shine). Lega, adj. -ing. Wiyakpa, v.n.; adj. -ing: -pi, n. Brightness; -yela, adv. Flashing; a- , v.n.

glory, Iwiⁿkte, v.n.: -pi, n.; -ya, v.a., adv. Yutaⁿ, v.a. Glorify; o-kitaⁿiⁿyaⁿ, adv. Gloriously.

glow, v.n. Śa hiⁿgla.
glue, Cf. seal. Apuspapi, n. Mucilage; kpuspa, v. - own. Cuⁿpeśka, coⁿpeśka, n. Wiyaskabye, n. Mucilage.

glutton, n. Iyaka, iyas'e. Lotewaśicuⁿ, n.; waloteteke, n. Wot'a, v. Glut self.
gnash, Cf. grind. Yakiza, v.a.; kiskiza, v. red. Yak'ega, v.a.

gnaw, (nip). Otebya, v. - on, into, at. Yak'oga, v.a. - off: o- , v. Yasmiⁿ, v.a. - off, eat off: -kiya, v.a.; o-yaⁿ, adv. Being -ed at. Yak'eza, v.a. - smooth. Yama, v.a. - off; yameca, v.a. Chew. Yawaza, v.a. Nip one; yawazeca, v.a. - at; wayawaja, v. - at.

go, v. imp. Akoecoⁿ, Get away!; haⁿta. Gla(e), v. Go home: akiya- , v.; -kiya, v.a.; -śi, v.a.; gli-yakel, adv.; gliyagli(a), v.; gliyoi, v.; gliyoya, v. pos.; iya- , v.n.; ki- , v.; kiki- ; oglicu, v. -down in; ogligle, part. Going from place to place.
Hośi ai, v.; hośi iyaya, v.; hośiya.
Ȟlaȟyeca, v. Go off a distance.
I, v.n. Have gone to, been at: aihaⁿ, v. col. pl.; aitkob, adv.; akiwaⁿyaka, akiyagla, eokiyaka, iheya, iȟca, imani, itohekiya, itoheya, iyahaⁿ, v.; wahiyoi, v. - after; kigni, v. He will go home; makiglukśaⁿ, v. Go around the world, far.
Iyaya(e), v.n. Have gone: akil- , v.; -kiya, v.; -ya, v.a.; iyayuȟ, v.; iyoȟpaya, v. - down, away; kahayeya, v. - away; timama- , v. Go in to more.
Ya, bla, la, mni (fut.), v.n. Go to, start for, proceed: kici- , v. - in place of; aohomni, v.; onamnimni, v. Be on the way; waglamni, v. - for, after; yekiya, v.a. Make - .

goad, (quicken). Naoȟ'aⁿko, v.a. (kick).
goal, Cf. stand. Oinajiⁿta, n.
gobble, v. Yagob iyeya.
go-cart, n. Hokśipaslohe.

God, n. p. Wakaⁿtaⁿka: Tuⁿkaśila - , God-Head. Ateyapi, Ateuⁿyaⁿpi (our), The Father; Wakaⁿtaⁿka Ciⁿca, the Son; Woniyawakaⁿ, Wicakikcaⁿpte,

Tawokoⁿze, Wowicakigna, The Holy Spirit.

good, Ayuco, adv.: -ya, -yakel, Well done. Lilaka, adj. - at, on (skilled) Pica, adj.: -ka, adj. Little - , better. Waśte, adj.: a- , a-ka, v.n.; a-ya, a-yakel, adv.; ayu- , v.a.; caⁿl- , v.n.; caⁿl-ya, v.a.; ici- , v.n.; iglu- , v. refl.; kici- , v. Be - for; kiciyu- , v. Make - for; -Ȟca, adj. Very - ; ki- , v. Become - , convert to God; okici- , adj. - together; to- , n. His -ness; -ka, adj. -hearted, a little - ; -ya, v.a. Make - ; adv. Well; wo- , n. -ness. Yapi, v.a. Declare - . Yupi, v.a. Make - . Cf. wakaⁿka.

gopher-hills, n. Wahiⁿheyapablu.
gorge, Zuⁿmiyaⁿkel, adv. -ing self. Cf. muskrat.

Gospel, n. p. Wotaⁿiⁿ Waśte.

gossip, Cf. talk. Oiglukiki, v. Śil'anagoptaⁿ, v. Spread - . Yahomni, v.n.
gouge, (pierce). Pakpa, v.a. - out.

government, Wokicoⁿze, n. Governance; wicośkaⁿśkaⁿ. Itaⁿcaⁿ, n. Chairman, president, chief.
gracious, (benevolent). Wacaⁿtkiya, v. Be - , generous with one's love: -pi, n. Benevolence.

gradual, Cf. slow. Tokecela, adv. -ly (from weakness).

grain, (corn, wheat etc.). Cf. grass.
barley, Wayahota hiⁿśmaśma.
corn, Wagmeza: -nablaga, Popcorn; wahiⁿske, Southern - ; wahuapa, wahuwapa; wamuⁿta, An ear of - ; magahu, Stalks; waśtuⁿkala, Dried - .
millet, Taśnaheca siⁿte.
oats, Wayahota.
rice, Wayahota (wild).
rye, PteyaȞota.
spelt, Wayahotablaska.
wheat, Aguyapi su.

grasp, v.a. Napogmuza; nap'kuwaś'aka, v.n. - firmly. Yugnayaⁿ, v.a. - at.

grass, (hay, grain, rush, straw). Peji, wato, n. Psa, n. Pithy - . Cf. grain.
alfalfa, WaȞpepeji.
barley, Psiⁿska.
bayonet, Hupestola.
beard, Pejiśaśa swula.
blue, Pejiblaskaska.
blue-stem, Pejiśaśa okihetaⁿkiⁿkiⁿyaⁿ.
brome, Pejihaⁿskaskapsi iyececa.
buffalo, Sipawica(ka)śe.
bullrush, Pejiiwicakoyaka (buffalo).
calamus, HoȞwa (watergrass).
cockspur, Pejiskuya.
crab, Wabluśkahuota peji.
goldenrod, PejiȞota śicamna.
grama, Pejiokijata, wapahakamnimnila.
Indian, Pejiśaśa iⁿkpajiji.
June, Pejiśicamna.
lade-side, Ptega.
marsh, Pejisuksuta, saⁿtuhu, piⁿksihu.
milkweed, Pejiswula cik'ala.
moss, Pejihiⁿkpila, ziⁿtkala (w)ipatapi.
oats, Pejiiⁿkpa, wayahota.
panic, Pejiwakaⁿ.
porcupine, Micapeca, wicapeca.
rice, Psiⁿ.
river, Pejiokihetoto.
rush, Pejiswula; waⁿyecaswula (horsetail); pejitakaⁿ (grass); psaciⁿca (pithy); psaswula; waⁿyeca, wayecahutaⁿka (pipe stem).
sage, PejiȞota waśtemna (pasture).
salt, PejiȞcaka (wheat).
sand-bur, Uⁿkcelapepe.
sand, SaⁿtuhuȞcaka.
sedge, Pejipsuⁿpsuⁿla.
seed-grass, Celi.
slough, Mnipeji.
squirrel, Iteaśniyaⁿpi.
sticktights, WokaȞtaⁿ.
swamp, Wiwilatapeji.
sweet, Wacaⁿga.
water-grass, HoȞwa, psa (rush).
wire, Pejitakaⁿkaza.
witch, Iteawicaśniyaⁿhu.

Pejiyuhiⁿte, v. Rake hay; pejiptaptaha, adv. In stacks; pejipaha, n. Hay stack; pejioakśu, n. Whisp of hay; pejioju, Lawn; pejiokaśla, n. Hay land, meadow; pejionakseyapi, n. Hay land; pejognake, n. Hay loft.

grate, Cf. noise. Kiza(s), v.n.: -yela, adv. With a -ing sound. K'ega, v. Scrape: ka- , v. Make - .

grateful, adj. Caⁿl'ope: -ya, adv.; olabya, adv. Gratifyingly. Wapila, v.n. Be - : -pi, n. Gratitude; -piśni; -śni, v. Be Un- ; wa-ya, v. abs. Give cause for gratitude, do a favor.

gratuitous, Cf. free. Ituya, adv.: -kel, adv.

gravel, n. Iswula.
graze, (crop). Oyatoto, v.
grease, (lard, oil). Sla: a- , v.n.; a-ya, v.a., adv.; na- , v.a. (by foot); o- , Be -ed in; ihai-ye, n. Iyu(ŋ)toŋ, v.; iyutaŋ, v. Add - , lard. Igli, n. Oil; wigli, n.

great, (number, size, quantity). Cf. large. Iyutepicaśni, adj. Immense. Śogya, adv. -ly: śogyeḣ. Taŋka, adj.: o- , n. -ness; adj. Large, broad; i-yotaŋyaŋ, adv. -ly; otaŋcaŋ, n. The -est: -ke, n. -est in numbers; -keya, adv. In -est numbers; o-yaka, n. -ness; -kiya, adv. Largely; -la, v. Consider - ; -ya, adv. To a - extent; taŋkiŋyaŋ, adj. Very - , important; taŋk- , adj. Very - ; wa- , n. - and rich person; wa-la, v.a. Esteem - .

greed, Akaska, v.n., adj. Amnaŋyaŋ, v.a. Iśicawaciŋ, v.n.; tawaciŋśil-wote, v.n. Eat -ily.

greeting, n. Hoakicipapi.
grid, Cf. network.
grim, (serious). Kaiteyeśni, v. Make -.
grin, v. Iteśiŋkiya.

grind, Aḣiglaḣtaka, v.a. Ayak'ega, v.a. Higlakiskiza; higlakokoka, v. Ikabluya, adv. Inakuka, inasli, v. Kpaŋ: apa- , v.a.; ayu- , v.a.; kici-yu- , v. - for (corn); yu-pi, n. -ing; yu-yaŋ, v.a. Make - ; na- , v.a. - under foot. Napoŋyaŋ, v. (by foot). Owanataŋye, n. -ing mill. Yumaŋ: aglumaŋ, v. pos.; a- , v.a.; kici- , v. - for (axe). Cf. pulverize.

grip; v. Wiyuhloka, Take a - on. Yu-paga, v.a. - tightly.
groan, (cry out). Waśicahowaya, v.a.
groove, (plush, rout). Paśkokpa, v.a. Make a - , cavity (by hand, sitting). Koŋta: wa- , v.a. To rout; wakoŋt- , v. Make in ridges; kuŋtkuŋta, adj. -ed.

grope, v. Yutaŋtaŋkel mani.
ground, Cf. earth. Tokakayeśni, v. Be -ed; tokaniyeśni.

group, Cf. district, strike. Caŋnuŋ-ge, n. Bunch or lump on a tree. Ciŋ-coga, n.; ciŋcopamna, n. Kaiḣeya, adv. -ing, in bunches. Okaśpetoŋtoŋ-yaŋ, adv. By, in -s; ośpaśpaye, adv. Wilwita, adv. In -s.

grow, Haoyuḣ'u, n. Growth. Icaga(ḣ), v.n.: o- , v.n. - in, up; oicage, n.; -kiya, v.a.; -ya, v.a.; ikicicaga, v.n.; waw-ya, v. Make - , form; ik- , v.n. - to be. Koyanuŋ, adj. Of quick growth. Oju, n. A growth, field. U-ya(e), v.n. - up, spring up; -kiya, v.a. Make - up.

growl, Ayabu, v.a. Ḣlo, v.n.: -kiya, v.a.; -ya, v.a., adv.; ki- , v. - over.
gruff, (harsh, noisy, rough). Jahaŋ, adj. (voice); jahe s'e, adv. Harshly.

grumble, v. pos. Oikcapta. Wakaḣta-keke, n. A -er.
grunt, v. Glo. Ḣna, v.n. T'iŋga(ḣ), v.n. Snivel and - (in labor pains): ka-ya, adv.; na-yeya, v.a. Make - .

guage, Cf. meter, measure.
guard, Wakta: i- , v.n.; i-ya, v.a., adv.; -kel, adv. -edly, expecting; -ya, v.a. Put on - ; adv. On - .

guardian, n. Caŋnakseyuha. Iawaŋyaŋka, v.a.
guess, v. Oyama, Take a - . Yukcaŋyaŋ, adv. -ing.
guest, Titokaŋl, adv. As a - .

guillemot, n. Hoka (thick-billed), Murre.
guilt, Awaic'iḣtani, v.

gullible, adj. Ognaye waśte.
gully, (ravine). Wakogla, n.

gun, Cf. weapon. Hutela, n. Pistol. Mazakaŋ, mazawakaŋ, n. Rifle: -i, n. Muzzle; -inuŋpa, n. Double-barreled - ; -iyopazaŋ, Ferrules; -iyopuḣli, n. Wadding; -nawate, Lock; -noge, Pan; -pahu, Breech; -śupute, Butt; -uta, v. Fire a - . Waŋhiośtaŋpi, n. A flintlock. Caḣli, n. -powder.

gurgle, v. Ogmuŋheca. Okaco, oyagloglo, v.n.

H

habit, Ayaic'iya, v.n. Owaⁿgic'iya, v. Be in the - of; adj. -ual.

hail, n. Wasu: -hiⁿhaⁿ, v. Waȟ'eca, n. (shot-like).

hair, n. Aśke: he-toⁿ s'e, adv. Hiⁿ, n.: -ȟte, n.; -jijila, n.; -kaciceyela, adv.; -kpila, n.; -nasakiya, v.n.; -ośkuśku, v.; -paȟla, n.; -yajice, n.; iyoȟa- , n. Whiskers; iteciⁿ- , n. Hpiȟpi s'e, adv. Iśkogiⁿ, n. Itoye, itowe, itoe, n.; -woblu, v.n.; -yuȟ'o, v.n. Okahi, n. Bangs: -ka, n. One wearing bangs; -ya, v.a. Make bangs. Paha, n. (of head); paśtaⁿ, v.a. To de-hair (hide). Pehiⁿ, n. (of head). Piⁿjaⁿ, adj. -less. Ptehiⁿpaȟpa, n. Tags of buffalo - . Tukahaⁿ, part. Losing - , scabby; tuktukahaⁿ, adj. Spoiled (loss of hair). Wakiȟ'aⁿke, n. A worker in - .
<u>Grooming</u>:
aśkiyuwi, Hairband.
hehute, Hairband.
natipasise, Hairpin.
pehiⁿ: -icasto, Hairbrush.
-islaye, Hair-oil.
-iyostola, Hairnet.
-papoa, Hairbrush.
-pasise, Hairpin.

half, n. Haⁿke: -ya, v.a. Icisaⁿnicab; iyakasaⁿni, n. Iyokise, okise, n.; okiseya, adv. Okiwaśpa, okiwaśpu, v.a. Cut in - .

halt, Ogluksa, v. refl. Stop abruptly in one's speech. Patagya, adv. -ingly; nat'uⁿgyakel, kokipeya, adv.

hand, n. Nape(a): -gle, v.a. Put a - on; -glepi, n. A span; -kaha, n. -guard; -ta, adv. By - ; -(o)apaha, v. Raise the - ; -glujaja, v. Wash -s; nap(eic)icaśka, v. Tie -s; -ikpahiⁿ, v. Tie head on -s; -kicoza, v. Gesticulate; -koza, v. Beckon; -kśikśa, v. Have the - numb; nap(e)oicu, n. -writing; -ojula, napogna, n. -ful; -yekiya, v. Stretch out the - to (istoyeya); -yupśuⁿka, v.n. Clench the fist; -yuza, v. Shake -s; napikceyakel, adv. By - ; napiśkaⁿ, v.n. Put the - to evil; napiyagleya, v. Lay a - on; napiyayus, adv. Held in - ; napiyeya, v. Have a - in; napiyusya, v.a. - over, make hold; napiyuzeca, v. Take into own - ; napkicoza, v.a. Wave the - to; napkoza; napognaka, v. Put into - ; napsaⁿni, n. The - on one side; o- , n.; adv. In - . Pastoiȟpaya, v.n. Fall on -s and knees. Yuge, v.a. Take a -ful.
<u>Parts</u>:
napahuⁿka, Thumb.
napakazaⁿ, Fingers, claws.
napcoka, Palm.
napcokaⁿyaⁿ, Middle finger.
napepiⁿkpa, Finger tip.
napeyupśuⁿka, Fist; v.n. Clench fist.
napitakaha, Back of hand; nap'itakaha.
napokazuⁿte, Fingers.
napsu, Finger:
-hu oko, Spaces between the fingers.
-okaza, Fingers, claws.
-okiha, Knuckles.
oguye, Handful.
yuge, Handful.

handkerchief, n. Paȟlipakiⁿte.

handle, n. Ihupa: -kitoⁿ, v. pos.; -kicitoⁿ, v.a.; -toⁿ, v. Iyuhomni, n. Knob. Iyuze, n. Holder; oiyuspe, ooyuspe, n.

handsome, adj. Oȟopa, taⁿwaśte.

hang, (suspend). Kamnimni, v. - loosely (blanket). Kceya, v. - over and cook. Oȟci, v. Dangle: -ȟci, adv.; -ȟcikes'e, adv. Raggedly; -ȟciya, v.a. Okahi, v.n. - over: a- , v.n.; a-ya, adv.; -ya, v.a. Otka, v.n. - from; otke, v.n. Be hung up; otkeya, v.a. - up. Panakseya, v.a. - one. Paozeze, v.n. (berries); zeze, adv. -ing; zezeya, adv. Swinging. Cf. dangle.

hanger, (poles). Satkaksa, v. Cut - ; wiotkeye, n. (hook, cord). Wagluȟe, v.n. Be a hanger-on.

happen, Cf. become. Akipaya, v.a. Sehiⁿgla, adv. So -ing, - to. Toka kte, express. Something may - .

happy, (cheerful, without difficulties). Kaⁿiyeyapi s'e, adv. Happily.

harangue, v. Waiyakapeya.
hard, Cf. firm. Kamasya, adj. (iron). K'oza: ayu- , v.a.; ona- , v.n. Make - (by foot); ot'oza, adj. - packed; ot'oja, adj. Saka(g), adj.: a- , v.n.; -ya, v.a. Stiffen; yu- , v.a.; ta-ya, v.a. -en; adv. -ed; ta- , adj. Stiff, frozen; oś'aka, v.a. Get - .

Suta, adj.: aglu- , v. pos. Make - ; kici- , v. Become - for; na- , v.a. Trample - ; wo- , v. Make - . Wateȟika, adj. - in dealings, dear, treasured. Ayuk'eza, v.a. Make - (shave).

hardly, Cf. scarcely. Kitiyus'eya, adv. Barely.

hardware, (bolt, nail, screw, hinge, bell, etc.)
iyopazaŋ, Bushing, ferrule.
iyokatkuge, Bolt, nail, nut, screw: maza- , wiyokatkugye.
wicatkuye, Hub-nut.
mazaȟlaȟla, Bell. Cf.
maziciyokihe, Chain; mazicukeya.
mazapepe, Barbed wire; mas'pepe.
mazapośla, Tack.
mazapsoŋpsoŋla, Wire.
mazazazeca, Wire screen.
mas'iyume, File. Cf. tool.
ogliyotke, Screw-eye.
okataŋ: a- , v. Nail; mazaiy- , maz'iy- , i- .
was'wiyokataŋ, Nails.

hardy, Cf. sturdy.
harlot, n. Witkowiŋ(la).
harm, Cf. injure, hurt. Ociŋkiwakaŋ, v. Speak, bring - .

harvest, n. Wasutoŋpi, woksapi.
haste, Huȟniyeya, v.a. -en; ȟniyeye s'e, adv. With - . Taŋnikta s'e, adv. In great - . Wiś'oś'o, adj. Hasty. Yuoȟaŋkoya, adv. -ening.

hat, Cf. clothing. Wapośtaŋ, n.; wapośtiyut'iŋze, n. -band.
hatch, v.n. Ikpakpi.

hate, (ill-humor). Siŋka(e): oyu- , v.; oyusiŋyaŋ, adv. Out of humor with; wawoyasiŋ, v. Be out of humor; wawoya- , n. One that hates. Śica(e): -kila, v. - own; -kiya, v.a. Think low of; śilkiya, v.; -la, v.a. Esteem bad.

haughty, Wataŋkaic'ilapi, n. -iness. Wawimnaśniyaŋ, adv. -ily. Cf. wimna śni.
haul, (transport). Otokśu, v., n.; watokikśu, v. - own.

haunt, v.n. Nagitoŋ.

have, Cf. possess, keep, pregnancy, Yuha, v.a. Possess, give birth to, lift, having, carrying with one: ki- , v. - for, keep; -kiya, v.a. Make - ; -ya, adv. Having. Iyoyas'iŋ, adv. With, wearing, bearing.

hay, Cf. grass.

he, she, it, pron. Iye, iś, iyeś, iyeeś, iyekaeś, iyeśkalaka. Kae, That is he.

head, Cf. body. Pa, n. Generic name for the top end of something, the nose, beak. Pe, n. Top of the - ; peslete, n. Oitaŋcaŋ, n. - man: -yaŋ, adv. At the - . Oyatkaŋkaŋ, v. Come to a - .
Pa: -cola, adv. Without a - .
-gnagya, adv. -ed right for.
-hu, n. - of anything: -kul, adv. With - down; -te, n. Junction of - and neck.
-kas'iŋ, v.t., v.n. Have - raised.
-kuciyela, adv. - down; pakutagleya, adv.
-magle, adv. - bowed down.
-mahel, adv. With - covered.
-ska, adj. White -ed.
-sla, -śla, adj. Bald -ed.
-yata, adv. In, at the - .
-zaŋ, adv. With - concealed.
Po: -kimnamna, v.a. Shake - at.
-ksaŋ, v. Shake - right and left.
-mnamna, v. Shake - (denial): -kiya, v. Wag - at, make - wag.
-ptaŋptaŋ, v.n. Shake - (dissent).
-ślicoma, v. Have - covered.
taŋnakekiya, adv. With - to one side.

headdress, Cf. dance. Wapaha, n.: -hetoŋpi, n. Horned - ; -heyuga, n. Branched-horn - ; - iyuśloheton, n. Warbonnet (with one tail).

heal, v.n. Okiyuta, - up: na- , v. Close up (wound). Okizi, v.n.: -ya, v.a.
health, (sound, whole). Owicakuja, n. Un-y place. Taŋzani, adj. In - , sound: -ke, adv. In good - ; zaŋni, adj. Well, sound: taŋ-yaŋ, adv. Whole; wo- , n.; -ka, adj.; -yaŋ, adv. In good - .

heap, Pśuŋkaya, adv. In a - , bundle: -kel, adv. Drawn together.

hear, v.a. Anagoptaŋ: -ya, v.a.;

anakicigoptaŋ, anakigoptaŋ, v.; anoŋgoptaŋ, v.a.; anoŋḣkeciya, v.a.; noŋḣkatiyece, v.a. - suddenly; onoŋḣhoyeya, v. - with own ears; nuŋḣ's'a, v. - well. Gluiyupse, v. pos. Hoiŋkpala, adv.; hotaŋiŋ, v.n.; iho, v. Naḣ'oŋ, v.a.: nakiciḣ'oŋ, v. - for; nakiḣ'oŋ, v. pos.; o- , v. - a report, - of; n. A hearing; -ya, v.a. Announce to; wa-pi, n. -ing. Yakpa, adj. Hard of -ing. Yasupiśniyaŋ, adv. Without a -ing.

heart, n. Caŋte: -huta, n. Aorta; -kiciciyapi, n. Love of each other; -kiya, v.a. Have affection for; -kiyapi, n. Benevolent love; -kiyuza, v.a. Hold a given disposition; -ogiŋ, caŋtogiŋ, n. Pericardium; -okihiśniya, v. Have - failure; -oŋśika, adj. Low-spirited; -oyusya, adv. With the whole - ; -waśte, v.n. Be glad; -waśteya, adv. Cheerfully; v.a. Make glad; -yazaŋ, v.n. Be -sick; caŋtihaŋgya, v.a. Cause -ache; caŋtiyokipiya, adj., adv. Hearty; caŋtognagya, v.a. Place in the - ; caŋtognawaya, adv. In a loving manner; caŋyaŋka, v.n.; i- , adv. in comp. In, at the - ; icaŋtognaka, v.a. Purposely put in the heart.

heat, Cf. warm. Katkiya, v. - own; kalya, v. Olululuta, n., adj. Sultry. Omaśte, n., v.n. Be hot in.

heaven, Cf. sky. Maḣpiya, n. The -s, clouds.
Bodies and Phenomenon:
aŋpetu wi, aŋpawi, Sun.
aŋpowicaḣpi, Morning star.
haŋhepi wi, Moon.
hohetamaḣpiya, Norther lights.
maḣpiya, Clouds, heavens.
wi, Sun, moon.
wiyośaya, Aurora. Cf. star.

Constellations:
matotipila, The eight stars about Gemini.
tayamni, Orion and the Pleiades.
wanagitacaŋku, Milky Way.
wiaceic'iti, Sundogs.
wicakiyuhapi, Big Dipper.

heavy, (weight, fatigue). Kasabyela, -ily. Tka, adj.; tkeya, adv. -ily.
heed, Akikta, v. pos. Anakicigoptaŋ, v.; anakigoptaŋ, v. pos. Kiwaś'agpica śni, n. One who acts -lessly. Piyeleś, adv. -lessly, notwithstanding. Wanaḣ'oŋśniyaŋ, adv. -lessly.

height, Cf. high.
help, v. Anakicikśiŋ. Ekiciyaku, ekiciglaku, eiglaku, v. Icinakśiŋ, v. Stand up for others. Ic'iḣ'aŋ, v. refl. Extricate self. Iic'ikcu, v. refl. Ikiya, v.; iciya, v.a. Take sides with; oic'iya, v. refl. - self; okiciya, v. - another; okiya, v.a.; wawokiya, v. Accompany; wiceye, v. Apply for - . Ociŋkiwakaŋ, v. Be unwilling to - ; ociŋwakaŋ. Tawowaśi, n. A -er, servant.

hem, n. Upi.
herb, n. Blayezitkatacaŋ hustola, Clover. Ceyaka, hehakatapejuta, Mint. Hiiyat'iŋze, Cloves. Peji ḣota, Gray grass, wild sage. Cf. medicines, grass.

herd, (bunch, drove). Kaḣapa, v. Opawiya, adv. In a - ; optaye, n., adv. In a - . Ośpaye, n.: -toŋtoŋya, adv. In groups. Wayaślakiya, v.a.

here, adv. Ena: -nakiya, -nataŋhaŋ. Le, adv.: -ci, -ciyataŋ, -ciyataŋhaŋ; lel, -tu (place or time); -ogna, logna, adv. Around - .

hermaphrodite, n. Wiŋkte.
hesitate, Kokipeya, adv. -ingly. Nat'uŋgyakel, adv.; nat'uŋka, v.n. Wotiti, adv. -ingly, unsteady: -kel.

hew, v. Kakaŋ; kicicakaŋ, v. - for; okakaŋ, v.a. - in. Kataptapa, v. (rocks).
hiccough, (hiccup). Blokaska, v.i.

hide, (conceal, skin). Aisiŋyaŋ, adv. Out of sight. Naḣma, v.a. Conceal: oi- , n. Place to - ; nakiciḣma, v. - for; nakiḣma, v.a. pos.; a- , v.a.; a- , v.a.; a-ŋpi, n.; anaḣmeya, adv.: -haŋ, adv.; i- , v.a.; inaḣmekiya, v.a. Anakima(e), v.a.: -ŋpi, n.; -ya, v.a.; -waya, adv.; -yahaŋ, adv. Anawiŋyaŋ, adv. Aogiŋtoŋ, v. Inabya, adv. Inakikśiŋ, v. Inapa, v.n. Ioblula, n.; iyoblula, adv., n. Yuptinapeyakel, adv. In hiding.
(Skin) ptehaśla, n. Buffalo - . Taha, n. Deer-skin: -kalala, Buckskin dress; -lo, n. Hide; -opaḣloke, Slit holes for stretching - ; -pe, Tanned - ; -penapiŋkpa, Fur mittens; -pewa-

poštaⁿ, n. Fur cap; -saka, n. Dried skin, parchment; -sopi, Leather strings; tahiⁿ, Buffalo, deer hair; tahuka, Green buffalo hide; uka, Skin (living) without hair; ha, Skin with hair. Teȟpi, n. Skin used as a blanket; ptehaśla. Tahaiyokataⁿ, v. To stretch a -. Tahiⁿcacice, n. Tool to remove hair; tahiⁿpaguke, pteȟcaka hiⁿyete, tahiⁿpakiⁿce, taȟca tahiⁿpakiⁿce, n. Tahokaśke, n. Hide stretcher; tahokataⁿ, v. Stretch for tanning. Teȟmisoha, n. Tanned - ; teȟpiceha, wahaśla, n. Wahapaȟpa, v. Flesh a fresh - ; wahatka, v.a. Scrape a dry -. Tahakpaⁿyaⁿ, v. Tan - . Tahayuśtaśta, v. Soak a - . Wahiⁿyuton, v. Rub on gall, marrow etc.

high, adj., adv. Gliheya. Huȟciⁿcayela, adv. Kaipazilya, adv. Konatka, adv. Owoslata, n. Height. Pajola, adj. - in the center (of road). Waⁿka: tehaⁿ-tu, adv. - up, very - ; -lkatuya, adv.; -paya, adv. - up, in a - position; -takiya, adv. - upwards; -tu, adv. - up; -tuya, adv.

hill, Apa: -bleca, n., adj.; -halaka, -jola, akicipa, n. Hepiya, n. -side. He, n. Mountain: -blo(ka), -hukul, -iⁿkpa, -ipa, -kpaⁿkpaⁿla, -ku, -mayacaⁿ, -nagi, -ohlate, -uⁿnaptaⁿ, iⁿyaⁿ- , n.; -hepiya, -takiya, -yataⁿhaⁿ, adv. Paha, n. Mound, hill: -pajola, n. Prominent - ; -ta, adv. At, on the - .

hinder, Cf. prevent, stop. Kagi, v. Stop progress: -śni, adv. Without hindrance. Okaś'agya, adv. Prevented. Oⁿc'uⁿnilya, v.a. Opaⁿȟya, v.a., adv. Bulky; opaⁿȟyela, adv. Poorly arranged.

hint, (insinuate). Ikuteka, v. Ohomnikuwa, v. - at. Yaoȟmiⁿ, v. Insinuate.
hippopotamus, n. Wamnitu. Cf. animal.
hire, Cf. borrow. Olotapi uⁿ, n. A -ling. Yuhapi, part. -ed. Cf. own.

his, hers, its, pron. adj. prefix. Ta-, tawa- ; adj. Suffix, -ku.

hiss, (fizz). Nasli, v.n.; śli, adv. -ing. S'a, v.n.: ka- , v.a. Make - .

hit, Cf. beat. Iwoȟtaka, v.n., n. Iwowaⁿka o, v. Iyapat'o(la), v.n.: -ya, v.a.; -yakel, adv.; iyapaya, v.a.; iyab, v. Okakapa, v.a. - into. Okama, v. - center; okasluta, v. Oyumaza, v.t. Make a - (on target); oglumaza, v. pos. - own mark. Yusaksaka, v. - from a distance, while whipping.

hitch, n. Okaśke.
hoarse, Gita: ho- , adj.; hogla- , hoigla- , v. pos.; iglaho- , v.n.; ya- , v. Become - . Hoiyoȟpaya, v.n. Hojahaⁿ, adv.

hobbles, n. Huipaȟte.
hoe, Cf. tool. Akata(e), v.a.; aglata, v. pos.; -ya, v.a.; akicicata, v.; maȟakata, v.a.; maȟkaśla.

hold, v. Yuza(e), yus, za, v.: agle- , v.a.; a- , v. pos.; aki-(pi), v. pl.; igluzeze, v.refl.; igluzezeya, adv.; iyayus, iya- , v.a., n.; i- , v. - by hand; kici- , v. - for; nap'anuⁿk - , v. Take - ; o-pekiya, v.a. Make lay - of, catch; o-ya, adv. Laying - of. Akinica, v.a. Ayuha, v.a.; akiyuha, v.a. Anaȟlata, v. Ayugata(l), v.a. Oognake, n. A -er. Wayuhoho, v. - loosely, awkwardly. Yugnagnayaⁿ, v. Take a loose - of. Yukaⁿnaksa ikaⁿtoⁿ, v. Keep a firm - on.

hole, Hloka(g): ayu- , v.a.; glu- , v. pos.; Hlo- , adj.; Hlo-haⁿ, part.; ka-ya, v. Make a - ; kiciyu- , v. Open a - ; na- , v.a.; o- , n.; oka- , n. Cut, gash; ona- , v.a. Make a - by or in the foot; opa- , n.; owa- , v.a. Cut a - in; owo- , n.; oya- , n. - bitten in; wa- , v.a. Cut a - in; wa- , v.a. Ayuȟuga, v.a. Break a - in. Gaⁿgaⁿla, adj. Kakpa, v. Make a - , pluck out; kicakpa, v.; ikpakpi, v.n. Kaoksa, v. Cut a - . Kokicaśpa, v. Dig two -s into, shoot twice in some place. Oko, n. Aperture, space. Wopota, v.a. Make -s (shoot).

hollow, Cf. empty, valley. Jipa, v. - out, smooth. Kaȟ'akpa, v. Śkokpa, adj. -ed out: ka- , v. - out. Makowakic'ipa, n. (of land). Opaȟci, n. Gully. Ośkiske, n. Draw. Smaka, n. Sink: o- , n. Ditch, ravine, valley; wa- , v.a. Make a - ; wayu- , v. Papopo, v.n. Push up to make a - .

holocaust, n. Waȟugnaȟya waunyanpi.

home, (come, bring).
aglekiya, v.a. Make take - .
agli, v.a. Arrive at - : v. col. pl.;
-ceti, v. Arrive and start a fire.
-hunni, v.a. Take straight back - ; v. col. pl.
-ȟpeya, v.a. Leave on way - .
-iyape, v.
-napa, v.
-napin, v. col. pl.
-psica, v. col. pl.
-ti, v. col. pl.
-tokicikśu, v.
-wanyanka, v. col. pl.
-wota, v.n.
-yacu, v.a., col. pl.
-yagla, v. col. pl.
-yaglahan, v. col. pl.
-yahan, v. col. pl.
-yaku, v.a., col. pl.
-yacu, v.a.
-yohi, v. col. pl.
-yotaka, v. col. pl.
-yugo, v.n.
-yuȟpa, v.a.
-yukan, v. col. pl.
-yunka, v. col., v. col. pl.
aglogla, v.
aȟiyagle, v.a., v.n.
aki, v.a.; gli:
-gni, v. Go towards - .
-hunni, v. pos.
-nunwan, v.
-taninka, v. Arrive suddenly at - .
-u, v. Be coming - .
-yacu, v.
-yahan, v.n.
-yaȟpaya, v. pos.
-yaku, v. pos.
-yokpeca, v.
-yotaka, v. pos.
-you, v. pos.
glo- , v. pos.
glokiyagla, v. pos. Go - taking own.
akiceti, v.n.
aku , v.a. Come bringing - .
gloku, v. pos. Coming - with own.
hośi: -gla, v. Go - carrying news;
-gli, v.
-glicu, v.
-glihunni, v.
-kagla, v.
-kagli, v.
-kaki, v.
-kaku, v.
-ki, v.
-ku, v.
ignigla, v.a. Go - for.
tiglonica, v. Forbid entrance to - .
tigluȟlagansni, v. Stay always at - .

hoop, n. Tahogmi (for hides).
holy, adj. Wakan, Special, sacred: a- , v.n.; ayu- , v.a.; i-yan, adv.

hominy, n. Wośleślecapi. Cf. vegetables.
honest, Wacinnunpaśniyan, adv. -ly. Zonta, adj. Trustworthy: -heca, n. An - person; zonlyakel, adv. -ly; wozunte, n. -y, doing rightly.

honor, Cf. praise, respect. Ohola, v.a. Okinihan, adv. -ably: w- , n. One's share. Weślekapi, n. Wearing of -s. Wicayuwintapi, n. Giving of a title of - . Wopakan, v.n. Be -ed. Wowitan, n. Glory, pride: -yan, v.a. Glory in; adv. -ably. Yaonihan, v.a.: -yan, adv. Praising; yuonihan, v.a. Treat with attention, politeness.

hoof, Cf. nail.
hook, (catch hold). Cf. fish. Iyuȟlata, v.; kaȟlata, v. Kacangle iyeya, - a hoop. Wiyotkeye, n. A peg.

hoot, v.n. Hinhanhoton, hinhankaga.
hop, v. Hośnaśnakic'un. Napsica, v.n. Cf. jump, skip.
hope, v.a. Ape, - for.
horn, He, n.: -hlogeca, adj.; -pola, n.; -ton, adj.; -yuha, n.; -yuktan, adj.,n.

horse, n. Śunkawakan.
<u>Kinds</u>:
hecenicala, Yearling colt.
hinȟpiȟpila, Shedding - .
hinikceka, hinkceka, Dark bay - .
hinpahin, Mouse-colored - .
hinstan, Chestnut-colored - .
hinśa, hinśaśa, Sorrel - .
hinto, Gray - .
hinzi, Buckskin - : -śa, Orange - .
hinum uya, makicima, Two-year old - .
itewatogla, A - sensitive to its head.
iwaglamna, A spare - .
iyak'oza, Large-knuckled - .
okasakeciyatan, The whipping (right) horse.
onaś'ola, Pacing - ; śung'onaś'o.
śungbloka, Stud.
śunghula, Pony, shetland pony.
śungleśka, Spotted - .
śungmakicima, Young - .
śungnankpogi, Brown-eared -.
śungnini, Wild - .
śungwinyela, Mare.

šuŋkcecahuśte, - lame in the hip.
śuŋkciŋcala, Colt.
śuŋkhiŋśa, Sorrel - .
śuŋkhula, Short-legged - .
śuŋkluzahaŋ, Race horse.
śuŋknuni, Wild horse.
śuŋksikośka, Swollen-footed - .
śuŋkśaŋ, Old worn-out - .
śuŋktahuwaś'aka, Strong-necked - .
śuŋktamaka, Lean - .
śuŋk'okasak'suta, Stubborn - .
śuŋk'onaś'ake, Worn-out - .
śuŋk'onaś'ola, Pacing - .
wako, wauŋjiŋca, - with a cut tail.
wohe, iyak'oza, Large-knuckled - .

apeyohaŋ, Mane.
siŋte, Tail.

śuŋkmaniśnikiya, v. Walk as a played-out - ; śuŋkkoyakya, v. Rope a - ; śuŋkaśtaka, v.a. Abuse a - ; śuŋmniyata aya, v. Water a - .

<u>Harness</u>: ic'iŋ, ic'i
cakipataŋ, Bit.
ic'iŋikaŋ, Lines.
ic'iŋpasu, Hame.
ic'iŋyuḣlate, Snap.
ikiyuwi, Bridle.
ipaḣte, Bridle.
iteha, Halter.
iyutitaŋ, Tug, double-tree.
makiyutaŋ, Cinch.
makiyut'iŋze, Surcingle.
makuipatitaŋ, Breast strap.
mas'caŋwapaika, Check strap.
mas'caŋyapa, Bridle.
mas'ikuśe, Buckle.
mazasiinaḣtake, Spur.
mazcaŋyapa, Bridle.
maziyuwi, Bit.
nap'iŋpi, Yoke.
oŋzinataŋ, Tail strap.
pawak'iŋ, Brief saddle, pack saddle.
śuŋgak'iŋ, Saddle blanket; śuŋkaiŋ, śuŋkak'iŋ.
śuŋg'inaḣtake, Spur; śuŋg'inajipa.
śuŋg'ipaḣte, Bridle.
śuŋkawakaŋ tawanap'iŋ, Collar.
tahuiyutitaŋ, Check strap; ceśkiyutaŋ.
tahuwanap'iŋ, Collar.

śuŋg'icakce, wicakca, Curry.
śuŋg'icapsiŋte, Whip.
śuŋg'icaśke, Hitch.
śuŋg'ikaŋ, Hitching strap.
śuŋkicapowa, Curry brush.
śuŋksimaza, śuŋktahaŋpa, Shoe.
śuŋkśakiyuksa, Hoof trimmer.
śuŋkowote, Nosebag.

hot, Cf. angry, warm. Kata, adj.; kal. Maśte, adj. (weather). Peḣniga, adj. Red- ; n., v.n.

house, n. Tipi, ti, oti, Dwelling, house, room, tipi, tent. Tiwahe, tiyognaka, tiyohe, n. A household.
<u>Kinds</u>:
heyoka oti, Heyoka's place of works.
tikaitepa, Pent house, lean-to.
tikauŋka, Knocked down - .
tipila, Small - .
tiwakpela el, A - on a creek.
tiyohe, A deserted - .
tiyuktaŋwakeyapi, Improvised shelter.
wokeya, Straw - .

<u>Parts</u>:
ticatku, Place opposite the door.
tice(śka), Top vent, ridge of roof.
ticopa, Center tent pole.
tiihaŋke, Corner of a - .
tiiyokaḣmi, Corner of a room.
tioko, Yard about a - .
tioyaŋkapi, Room.
tipaslate, Pillar, brace.
tiuŋnaptaŋyaŋ, Sides of a - , roof.
tiyopa, Door, entrance, gate.
tiyowoslata, Wall.

<u>Related to</u>:
tianuŋkataŋhaŋ, adv. In both sides of a house.
tiapiya, v. Repair a - .
tiawaŋyaŋka, v. Watch a - .
ticaga, v. Build a - .
ticatkayatahaŋ, adv. At the left side of the - .
tiihaŋke, n. A - short of completion.
tiiyaza, adv. From - to - .
tiiyupaḣ, adv. With all one's belongings.
til, timahel, tima, tiyo, adv. In the house.
tiokśaŋ, adv. Around, in, out of - .
tiokśu, v.a. Carry into the - .
tiokte, v. Kill in the - , commit homicide.
tionablu, v. Raise dust in the - .
tionakipa, v. Flee to the - ; tionapa.
tiosni, adj. Cold in the - .
tisam, adv. Beyond the - .
tiwaŋkata, adv. Upstairs.
tiwokitahena, tiyotahena, adv. Away from homes.
tiyata, adv. At the house, home; tiyatana.

tiyatakiya, adv. Toward the - , home.
tiyobleze śni s'e śkan, v. Move about purposely with excitement; tiyognaśkinyan s'e śkan, tiyot'ebleze śni s'e śkan.
tiyobya, v. Use for a door.
tiyokawinȟ, v. Go around in a circle in a - .
tiyokuta, adv. Downstairs.
tiyololya, v. Rent a - .
tiyoślola, adj. With a rolling sound in a - .
tiyotonwan, v. Look into a - .
tiyukan, v. Leave the - .
yutimahel, adv. Into the - .

how, Cf. manner.
however, adv. Unś'keyapika (coming back to the subject; inśeyapika, inśkeyapika.

howl, v. Ho(glo): ka-glo, v. Make - ; ka-ton, ka-wa, na-ton (kick); naśicawaya,v.a.; paśica-waya, v.a.; śunka- , v. (a dog); śunkmanitu- , v. (wolf).

hull, v. Wanaślogya (corn).
humble, (little). Ku: igluhu-ciyela, v. refl.; igluhu-ya, iglu-ya; hu-l iyeya, hu-ya, v.a. Bring down. Onśiȟ'an, v.n. Be - : -ka, v.n. Excite compassion; -pi, n. Humility; onśikiȟ'an, v.a. - self before; yuonśi, adj. Reducing to weakness; yuonśika, v.a. To humble.

humor, Cf. displease, hate. P'osyakel, adv. Out of - ; p'ozeca, v.n. Be out of - .
hump, Cf. hunch. Canȟaȟake, n.: -ton, v.n. Tuga, n.

hunch, Natuȟtuȟ, v.a. (pull, lift); tuga, n.; adj. -backed.
hunger, (hungry). Locin, v.: i- ; ka- , (shake). Tiyohankokipa, v. fig. Be hungry. Wocinpi, n. Wotektegla, v.n. Be hungry: -pi, n.

hunt, (pursue, trap, surround, chase). Cf. military. Igni, v. Stalk (game): iic'- , v. refl.; ikic- , v.; ikigni, v. pos.; lo- , v. - food; lol- , v. Akita, v.a.: akicicita, akicita, akitonwan, v. Cf. Kuwa, v.a.: icuwa, n.; wa-pi, n. -ing. Mazaegle, v. Set a trap. Nasa, v.a. - buffalo, cf.; anansa, v.a. Tate, n. -ing, chasing: -ye, v.; -aya, v. Go on a - . Waye, v.a. - for food, supplies, money.

hurricane, (cyclone, tornado). Wamniomni, n.

hurry, v.n. Inaȟni: -kel, adv.; -kiya, v.a.; -pi, n.; -yan, adv.; -yela, adv.; ka- , v.; kiyu- , v. - for; wainakiȟni, v. Be always hurried; waw-(yan), v. Be in a - ; wawinakiȟni(ka), v.n. Iyakita, v.a. Koya(e): kaoȟ'an-, adv. With a great - ; ko-la, adv.; -ȟ'an, v. - doing; -kiȟ'an. Owozaka, v. Be in a - , rush.

hurt, Aglapśun, v.a. pos.; apapśun. Apaguka, v.a. Apaśica, v.a.; iśica, v.n. Hunapta, v. Icama, v.n.; icabheya, adv. Igluśiȟtin, v. refl. Enfeeble self. Iyoyagya, v. - one's feelings. Ksuyeya, v.a. Wakaȟtaka, v.n. Be easily - . Wozan, v.a. Feel pain; v.n. Get - . Yacanliyapa iyeya, v. - one's feelings; yacantiyapa iyeya.

husband, Cf. family. Anungkison, n. obs. Higna, n.: -ku; -ton; -ya.
hush, Cf. silent. Wagluhika, v. Keep silent (threat).

husk, Yuga: a- , v.a.; kici- , v. - for. Woga, v.: -pi, n. -ing.

hypocrit, n. Ohoka. Wakanic'ila, v. refl. Be -ical: -pi, n. Hypocrisy. Wanaic'iȟma, n. A - ; wanakiȟmanpi, n.

I

I, (we, my, our). Miye, miyeś, miś, pron. I, me; miyeciŋka, miyecuḣci, miyek'e(ś), pron. I myself, even I; miśnaka, miśnala(ka), pron. I alone. Wa, pron. in comp. (subject); we, pron. in comp. (wa-ki), I...to; ci, (wa-ni), I...you; ma, mi, pron. in comp. (object); mic'i, pron. refl. in comp. Mitawa, mita, pron. prefix. My, mine; ma, mi, pron. pos. My. Mica, mici, pron. in comp. For me. Uŋkiye(pi), uŋkiś, pron. We, us; uŋkiśna(pi)la, pron. We alone. Uŋ, uŋki-pi, pron. in comp. We, us. Uŋkita(wa)-pi, pron. adj. Our.

ice, n. Caga(Ḣ): -ta, -takiya, adv.; cagoti, n.; -agleyela, adv.; -kaḣloka, -kat'a, -kazo, -najuju; -su, n.; -swula, n.; -'owaŋcaya, adv.; -paŋpaŋla, The - is soft; caḣ'suta, The - is hard or thick; ki- , v. Become - again.

identify, v. refl. Eic'ila.
idle, Wotiyeya, adv. (inability).

if, Cf. when, although. Ehaŋtaŋś. Kiŋhaŋ, If when; ciŋhaŋ. K'eś, adv. Yuŋkaŋś, conj.; yuŋś, conj. Provided, if.

ignorance, n. Waslolyapiśni.
image, (picture, idol). Wakagapi, n.
imbue, v.a. Yuḣebya.
imitate, v.a. Iauŋca. Kigmaic'iya, v. Resemble. Otapa, v. fig.

immeasurable, adj. Woptecaśni.
immediate, (sudden). Agna, prep., adv. At one notice, at once. Ecahaŋkeya, adv. Ihecegla, adv. Uŋgnahaŋla, adv. -ly; uŋgnahela(ke), adv. All at once.

immolation, n. Wowauŋyeic'iye, n. Self - .
immovable, adj. Hohopicaśni: -yaŋ, adv. Igluḣtanikapiŋ, v. refl. Igluśkaŋśkaŋkapi, v. refl. Nawiŋceśni, adj. Wotoka s'e, adv. Immovably; wotokasekse, paksa s'e.

impatient, Waciŋ: i-ko, v.n.; -huŋkeśni, adj. Irascible; -ihala, adj. Easily excited.
impede, v.a. Oyagi, Hinder, scratch.

imperfect Iyututkayakel, adv. -ly. Śiḣtiŋ, adj. Poorly made.

imperitives:

	singular	plural	Beckon
Men:	yo (wo)	po	yeto, to
Women:	ye (we) yema	pe	nito

important, (principal, very good, nice). Otaŋcaŋ, n. - part; otacaŋ: -ke, n. The finest. Scu, v. Make self - .
impose, v.a. Ipajuŋta.
imposter, Cf. deceive. Wagnaye, n.

impoverish, Wicayuwaḣpanica, n. -ment.
impress, v. Wayaḣloka, Make an -ion talking. Ś'aka: wo- , v.a. Make no impression on; ya- , v.a. Make no -ion talking.

improper, Waektaśniyaŋ, adv. -ly; waepaweḣ.
improve, v. refl. Itaŋic'iya.

in, (into, within, front of). Iyo, prep. in comp. (i-o). In, into. El, prep. In (place). Mahel, mahe, prep. Within, in, into; imahel, adv. Within. Ogna, prep. In (direction, manner); wogna. Aglagla, adv. Along side, in front of.

incense, Zil: iwi-ye, n.; wi-ye, n.; iya-ya, v.a., iyazita, v.n.; wi-ya, v. Offer - .
incline, Waciŋoaye, n. Inclination.

income, n. Wokamna, Livelihood. Woyuhaoicage, n. Revenue.
incorrect, Cf. mistake. Iyektaśni.
incorrigible, Śuŋk'oiyakilsuta s'e, adv. -bly.

increase, v.n. Iyakic'u; adv. Kitoŋyaŋ, adv. In an -ing manner.
incurable, adj. Asniyepicaśni.
indecision, Iwaciŋjata, v.n.

indeed, Ituśeś, adv. Ecaḣ'eke, adv. Truly (used by women). Lakaś, adv.; welaka, yelaka, adv. Cf. because.

indelible, adj. Paśpeśni.
indent, Cf. dent. Naśkokpa, v.a.

indicative mood: Cf. subjunctive, futurity. Yelo, lo, particle for the stress of fact.

indifference, Itokaśni, v. Waciŋ: -teḣi, adj. Indifferent; -wikic'uŋśni, v.n. Be indifferent about.

indisposed, (tired). Cf. unwilling, tired.
indistinct, Ayaogwu, v.; ayogwugwu.
individual, Iyagyatayela, adv. red.; iyatayela, adv.: taŋ- , adv. -ly.

induce, v.a. Inapeya.
industrious, Blihe: a-ca, v.n.; a-lic'iya, v. refl.; a-lya, v.a.; -ya, v.a.; -ic'iya, v., adv.; -ca, v.n., adj.; -lheca, v. Aigluśkehaŋ, v. refl. Napiśtaŋ, n. One active who is busy and does much. Wimakaheya, n. Industry.

inept, Cf. skillful. Waḣteka(ca), adj.
infatuate, Wocaŋteoyuze, n. -tion.
infect, (infest). Opusya, adv. Infested with.
infidelity, n. Wiiyaoŋpapi, Charge of.

inflate, v.n. Pogaŋ.
influence, v.a. Awaciŋya(ŋ). Tokala, v. Be not -ed by. Wakoŋza, v. Determine, decree; wakoŋze, n. Wawokaḣtaŋyaŋ, v. Have great - over. (philosophy) Toŋ, n. The action of a thing by which knowledge of the thing comes to be, known, i.e. in itself and in its characteristics.

inform, v.a. Iwahoya.
ingenious, (expert). Skillful. Wayupi, v.n. Be - .
inhale, Cf. intake. Yaholya, v.a. Cough; yahote, n. An inhalation.

inherit, Woiyowaja, n. Share of an -ance.
injure, Cf. corrupt, feeble, hurt. Kiiglaksa, v. - self. Okaśkaŋ, v.n. Be -ed internally. Oŋtoŋ, v.n. Be -ed: -yaŋ, v.a. Oyuśice, n. Misunderstanding. Kiciyuśiŋḣtiŋ, v. - for. Wanapiśtaŋyaŋ, v. - everything.

ink, (mark, write). Wiyowa, n. Marking material.

inquire, (investigate). Pasi, v.a. - about secretly. Slolyewaciŋ, v.a. Wiyuŋga(ḣ,e): wa- , v.; wa- s'e, adj. Inquisitive; wa-ya, adv. In an -ing way; wikiciyuŋgapi, n. Mutual inquiry.

insect, (bug, butterfly). Wabluśka, n. (in general).

insect:
ant, Tajuśka, taśuśka. Cf.
bedbug, Halablaska.
bee, Tuḣmuŋga: - taŋka (bumble); - caŋhaŋpi, - tuŋkce, n. Honey.
beetle, Sipawicayaksa (black).
butterfly, Kimimila. Cf.
cicada, Maḣ'awaŋglaka.
cricket, Psipsicala, wabluśkatiyoślo.
flea, Hala, psicala.
fly, Taŋnicala, taŋnicela; tusweca, Dragon - .
gnat, Cf. fly.
grasshopper, Gnugnuśka, a(ŋ)petacagu, apeśa, apezi, psipsicala, ptewoyake (wingless).
horsefly, Tatawabluśka, teḣmuŋga.
lightning-bug, Waŋyeca.
locust, Cf. cicada.
louse, Heya.
maggot, Waglula.
mosquito, Capuŋka.
moth, miller, Wanagitakimimila.
spider, Iktomi, uŋktomi.
tapeworm, Cf. maggot.
tick, Taskakpa (wood).
tumblebug, Uŋkcepagmigma, uŋkcepagmiyaŋyaŋ.
walking-stick, Pejiwabluśka.
wasp, Wicajipa, wicayajipa. Cf. bee.
water-bug, Magataśuŋpe.
worm, Tatiŋgleska (intestinal). Cf. maggot.

insert, v.a. Yumahel iyeya, Hold in.
inside, Ayueciya, v.a. Make -out. Kaŋye: -taŋhaŋ, adv. On the - ; -wapa, adv. Within, towards the center. Mahe: -taŋhaŋ, adv. On the - ; -tu, adv. Deep within; -tuya.

insist, Ihiti, adj. -ing. Kitaŋyaŋ, adv.
insolent, Waiciḣaḣapi, n. Insolence.

inspector, n. Wableza.
instance, n. Iŋśeśelakeś; adv.
instead, adv. E, ecaŋleha, ecaŋleś, eekiya, eha, iyeha.

instep, n. Itakaha.

instruct, v.a. Wahokoŋkiya, Advise: -pi, i-pi, n. Advice. Ksapa: iya- , v.a.; wayu- , n. -or. Wowaoŋspe, n. -ion: -kiye, n. Yawaciŋtoŋ, v.a. Yusus, yusyuza, v. - earnestly.

instrument, n. Icage.

insufficient, (lack, need). Icakija, v.n. Ikipi, v. Okpani: a- , v.n.; a-yaŋ, adv.; iy- , v.; na- , v.n. To lack.

insult, (contempt). Aikśiŋkiya, v.a. Ośtegla, v.a. Revile: -pi, n. Scolding. Yaśigla, v.a. (in speech).
insure, (firm). Cf. firm. Kiciyusuta, - for.

intake, Cf. inhale. Yahota, v. Draw in air and water with the breath.

intelligent, Iwaciŋtoŋ, v. Waokaȟniga, v. Be - , skilful. Waśagla, v. Consider not - .
intemperate, Taŋtoŋyaŋkel, adv. Excessively. Wawiyakapeic'iya, v. Be - ; wawiyakapeya, v. To exceed.

intend, Caŋteoyuze, n. Intention. Waciŋ, v.n. Try, think, be anxious to: -yuze, n.; -yeya, v. Set one's mind to, purpose.
intense, Labya, adv. -ly.
intercede, v. Wotikiya, wotikiciciya.

intercourse, (sexual, adultery, copulation, fornication).
adulterer, Wawiciȟaȟa.
adultery, Wawiciȟaȟapi, wowicaȟaȟa.
climax, v. Yaś'iŋś'iŋ.
copulate, v. Kaogna iyeic'iya, kaokajaya, kiyuȟa (animal), oŋzehu (human) (Vulgar) Paspaya, pastaŋka, tawiŋtoŋ, tawiŋya.
deposite (seed), n. Oŋzeokaśtaŋpi.
masturbation, n. Pasluka.
onanism, n. Cf. masturbation.
sodomy, n. Iwicahupi.

interest, n. Waciŋ: waa- , n.; -teȟi, v. Take - in nothing.

interior, Cf. within. Timahetakiya, adv. Toward the - .

interjection, (exclamations, expressions).
(accusation) Okiŋoŋśica, disobeying. Tula, For shame! Yu (women), You are a bad one!
(affirmation) Hau, Good! To, toį, toś, Yes (women). Haŋ, ohaŋ, Yes. Śehaŋś, Most certainly! Śehaŋśtuka, Finally, to be sure! Tokaśka, There is something said. Uŋś'uŋmakeci, Oh yes! Oŋś'uŋmakec'uŋ, Oh yes! Waŋk'eya, Why, the fact is...!
(attention) Haho, Look at this! He, Look here! Ma, maŋ, Look! (women) Śe (men), śi (women) Hist! Ś' , same as śe. Toke, Listen! Waŋ, waŋ ka waŋ, Look, see!
(bidding) Nįye, Take it!
(contrary) Śehaŋśka, At any rate.
(denial) Eceś, No sir! Hiya, No. Hoȟ, Don't give me that. Tase...ka, Of course not!
(doubt) Ama, apa, Who can believe that? Hoȟeceś, Who will believe that! Iyeśnica, You don't say so! Ohuŋwela, oȟ, I have my doubts! Seca, May be. Skeka, I have my doubts about. Tokaś, tokinaś, tokinahaŋś, May be. Tuŋweȟca śkeka, There are doubts about this. Tuwakakeśa, tuwakakśa, Impossible! Uŋgna(ś,yeȟciś), Perhaps, possibly. Yai, Whee!
(fear) Ya, Geee...
(greeting) Caŋnako, Welcome! Co co, Hello, hello! Hau, Greetings!
(hope) Niŋ, May it be so!
(impatience) Haś, Nuts! Why! Well! Heś, Well! Hiŋ, Rats! Whoops! Iciŋyuŋśkaś, iyuwiŋśkaś, For heaven's sake! Waȟteśniit'a, I'm sick and tired of!
(joy) Haiye, A great day is here!
(narrow miss, escape) Wiśwepi, wiświ, Whew!
(pain) Yuŋ (women), Oh! dear me! Makteka, imacuka, That kills me!
(patience) Itok'eyaś, Wait a little! Tiyaŋkayo, tohiŋyaŋka, totiŋyaŋka, Wait a little!
(pity, compassion) Ece, Sorry! Hehehe, Alas, too bad! Huŋhuŋhe, Too bad, such is the case. Oŋśila, Poor thing! Śika, Pitiful one!
(praise) Ahahe, Three cheers for...
(question) Tuweśka, Who is this?
(readiness) Iyohob, Ready, here I come.
(rejection) Iŋś hecel, Who cares! Wośte, Horrible! Mak'eya, Rediculous!
(sadness) Itoceś, Oh my! Ośti, hośti, Alas, that's bad!
(silence) Hacib, Hush up!
(sounds, calls) Cu, gun report. Ś..., Leave! We-we-we, Come! (for dogs).
(thought) Iŋska iŋ, Let me see now.
(warning) Ahaŋ, Be careful, look out! Eyalecel, Try is you will; you know what I mean. Hinahina, Oh, oh! Hośti, That's bad! Hu, Hey, hey, hey! Siye, Watch out! Be on your guard!
(wonder) Hinuhinu, How grand! Hohub, What do you know! Hojila, Beautiful! Lotkuŋkeśni, Oh! Toki, How wonderful! (women) Tuki, Is that so! (women). Waŋlila, Tremendous.

intermittent, Gnaŋgnaŋ s'e, adv. In an - manner.

interpret, v. Wayuaslaya: -pi, n. -ation. Wayuieska, v. Translate: n. -er; -pi, n. -ation. Yawiyakpa, v.a.

interrogative:
Mood Particles:
(doubt) Kacaś, terminal.
(rhetorical) Kiŋ, terminal.
(expected affirmation) So, ce, terminal.
(expected information) Hwo, hwe, huwe, he, terminal to sentence.
(expected consent) Ka, terminal.

Pronouns:
Who? Tuwe, tuweca, tuwela, tuweḣca.
Which? Tona, tukte, uŋma tukte (of two).
What? Taku, takuca, takula.
Whose? Tuwatawa.

Adverbs:
How? Tokel, tokeśke, toketu, toktu, wicotoketu:
- extensively? Tiŋskoya. Cf. large.
- far? Itohaŋ (from), tohaŋhaŋ, tohaŋyaŋkel.
- large? Tiŋsko(keca), tiŋskola (dim)
- long? Tohaŋkeca (length).
- many? Itona, tona (quantity), tonakiya (times); tonagna(g), adv.; tonakeca, adj. (quantity). Of how many? Itonaka, itonakeca (number).
- much? Śehaŋleś (more, less).
When? Tohaŋ(l), tohaŋhaŋ, tohaŋtu, toŋweni.
Whence? Tokiyataŋ(haŋ), tuktetaŋhaŋ.
Where? Tohaŋhaŋ. Cf. Whither?
Whither? Tokiyab, tokiyawapa, tuktogna; tuktetu (place), tuktel (place).
Why? Takuwe, tokaca, tokayelaka(ś) kiŋ, tokecae, tokel. Cf. How?

interrupt, Wawośkiśkeyece, n. He who -s.
intersect, v.n. Ipawega(ḣ): -ya, v.a., adv.

intimate, (good terms). Kiwakaŋheja, v. Desire to be - .
introduce, Kpahahapika, n. He who is put forward.

inundate, (flood). Kaokic'uya, adv. Inundating.
investigate, (examine). Wayukcaŋ, v.
invisible, Cf. visible. Yusnis', v. Become - .

invite, (call, feast). Kico: i- , v.a.; -śniyaŋ, adv. Un-ed; okicico, n. The -ation of each other.

inwards, adv. Maheta(l): i-wapa, imahetuya, -wapa, -kiya. Kaŋye, adv. To center.

irascible, Wowaciŋko, n. Irascibility.
iron, Cf. metal. Mazasapa, n. Wapabla, v. Press clothes; akaŋ wapablapi, n. Ironing board.

irrespectful, Witoŋpeśni, adv. -ly.
irresponsible, Wicuŋkeśni, n. An - woman; wicuŋśni.

irritate, (excite). Ośigla, adj. Waciŋhuŋkeśniya, v.a. Wowicaḣtake wanica, v.n. Be irritable.

island, n. Wita.
isolate, (alone, apart). Cf. apart. Okiwotahena, adv. In an -ed place.
issue, n. Taga, Issuance, froth, spittle, scum. Wokabkab, v.; wośloślog. (philosophy) Toŋ.

itch, n, Awicayaspuya; yaśpuya, v. Make - ; adj. -ing.

J

jack (of all trades), n. Waecoⁿcoⁿka.

jam, (entangled). Naopemni, v. Entangle. Paokiyaskapa, v.n. -med in.
jar, v. Iyonaniyaⁿ.

jealous, Cf. envy. Nawizi: nakiciwizipi, v. pl. recip.; nakiwizi, v.a.
jelly, n. Takuśaśala.

jerk, v.a. Yanuⁿg, Make - sideways.
jest, (joke, banter). Oⁿśkata, v.n. Brag; oⁿkiciśkatapi, v. recip. Owehaⁿhaⁿ, v.n.: -ka, n.; a- , v. Iyowiⁿħala, adv. In - ; wayaiħa, n. A joker.

jewelry, (ornaments).
bracelet, cuff, Napokaśke, napoktaⁿ.
comb (side), Natanaśuⁿpakce.
ear ring (jewels), Owiⁿla, owiⁿpi, kimnimnila.
ring (finger), Napsiyoħli.
wear, make, v. Owiⁿkiya.

jingle, (tinkle). Nasna, v.a.,v.n.
join, Cf. sew. Kicicakiya, v. - own to. Zuⁿlya, adv. -ed.

joint, Okihe: hu- , n.; iyokihe, n. Kagloka, v. Put out of - . Wapśuⁿ, v.a. Cut a - : o- , v.a. Disjoint; apapśuⁿ, v.a.

jolt, (jostle). Kauⁿkaka, v.n.
journey, Cf. travel. Aicimani, v.n. Haⁿiglaka, v. - by night. Oiglake, n. Expedition.

jovial, adj. Wiⁿhaha, Good-natured: -ka, n. A - person; -kel, adv. In good spirits; -ya, adv. Easily pleased, happily.

joy, Cf. rejoice. Owiyuśkiⁿyaⁿ, adv.
judge, (condemn, right). Yasu, v.a.: i- , v.a.; kici- , v. - for; kici-pi, v. - each other; wo- , n. -ment, condemnation; iglasu, v. refl. Wiyukcaⁿyaⁿ, adj. Judicious; ikiciyukcaⁿ, v.

jump, (hop, skip). Agaⁿ iħpaya, v.n. - into water with a splash. Akaⁿ iyeic'iya, v. refl. Psica, adj. -ing: aka- , v.a.; a- , v.a.; gli- , v. pos.; hi- , v.; iglu- , v. refl.; i- , v.n.; ipsi- , v. red.; iyo- , v. Hop down; ka- , v. Make - ; ki- , v. - down, alight from; psi- , v. Skip.

junction, (roads). Ogliwitaya, n. A road - , con- of many roads.

just, (right). Iⁿśe, adv. Only. Owotaⁿla, adj. Right, upright; yuowotaⁿ, v.a. Make upright, -ify.

K

keep, (reserve). Cf. care. Kiciyuha, v. - for. Kignaka, v. - for, lay up for. Opasepa, v.a. - with care. Patanyan, adj. Reserving.

kettle, (pot). Cega(ḣ), n.: -ciscila, -kaḣloka, -huhatan, -ikan, -iyokaske, -nigeton, -pśunka, -p'o, -ska, -tankinkinyan, -wohota, n.; -'iha, n. A lid; -'hupa hanska, , Frying pan; -'ihupaton, n. Bucket with a handle; -'naga, n. Soot; -'okiyeton, n. Tea - . Kannacega, n. That which has a - shape. Mazacega, mascega, n. A metal - .

key, (opener). Iyuḣloke, iyuśloke, n. Iyutkuge, n. Lock or key.

kick, Ana: -ḣpa, v.a.; -ḣtaka,-ic'ipson, -ha, -psaka, -psan, -ptuja, -sloka, -ta. Na: -aglapśun, v. - over; -ha iyeya, v. - away; -ḣeyab, v. - away, to one side; -ḣeyata, -ipawega; -ḣpa, v. - down; -ḣtaka, v.a.; -ikpiska, v. - over on one's back; -jipa, v.a. Nudge with the foot; -juju, v.a. - to pieces; v.n. Come to pieces; -jun, v. Pull and - ; -kapa, v.a. (a ball); -kawa, v.a. - open; -kiciḣtaka, v. - for; -kiciśpu, v. - off for; -kiḣtaḣtaka, v. pos.; -oglapśun, v. - over; -onziwosla, v. - bottoms up; -sluta, v.a. - out; -śloka, v.a. - off; -ta, v. - up, away. Ona: -ḣtaka, v. - in; -ḣtake, n. Injury done by -ing; -kab, v. - into; -kan, v.a. - off in; v.n. Be -ed to pieces; -kicitanpi, v. recip. - each other. Sipaha iyeya, v. - away sideways. Wanaiyeya, v. - down, aside; wanahaiyeya.

kill, Kte, v.a.: ahi- ; aśunkt'eya, v.a. - for misdemeanor; ici- , i- ; kici-pi, v. pl. They - each other; ki- , v. - for, own; o- , n. A -ing; wa-ka, n. A -er. T'a, v. Die: akiḣ'ant'eya, v.a.; pa(kpa)- , apa- , v.a.; awo- , v.a.; caḣka- , v. (by a fall on ice); gla- , v. pos.; iglu- ; ka- , v. Stun; kat'iyeya, v. - self; na- , v.a. (kick); nat'eya, v.a. (running); oka- , v.a. (strike); onśtinma kpa- , v. - own (lying on); opa- , v.a. (press); oya- , v.a. (bite); oyu- v.a. - in; pa- , v.a. (press); wa- , v.a. (by knife); wo- , v.a. Stun. Wosota, v.a. - all off.

kin, Cf. relative. Otakuye, n. -folk.
kindle, Cf. fire. Petileyapi, n. Kindling; petileye, n.

king, n. Wicaśayatapi(ka). Wicokonze, n. -dom.
kink, Kaowotan, v. Straighten out a - .

kiss, v.a. Iputaka;iiputaka, v.; iikputaka, v. pos.; oiputake, n.
kitchen, n. Owohe.
knead, (stiffen). Kicipasuta, v. Make stiff for. Pat'inza, v.a. Stiffen by -ing.

knee, Cf. body. Makagleinajin, v.n. Kneel. Woptuza, v.a. Make fall to one's -s (shoot).

knife, n. Mila, n. A large - : -paksa, Round-pointed - ; -ya, v. Have, use a - ; hohu- ; śunkacemila, n. Crescent-bladed - . Icapsake, ipapsake; takinwapsake, Sinew - . Hopeśka s'e, adj. Cf. mila.

knob, n. Taśpu (door).

knock, (sound). Gla: -pśun, v. pos.; -śpa, -tata, -toto, -unka. Iyaic'ipa, v. Ka: -bu(bu)ya, v.; -kan, v. - off; -śipa(b), -śloka(g); -śpu, v. Chip away at; -toto; -tuka, v. - off; kicapśun, v. - off for; koka, n.; sniyankat'a, v. - cold, senseless. Na: -gloka, v.a. Injure; -gna, -ḣpu, v. - off; -koka, v.a. (foot); -toto; -tutka, v.a. - off pieces (foot); o-kan, v.a. - off into. To, n. A blow sounded with the fist etc. Wo: a-śpu, v.a.; o-unka, adj. -ed down, killed; -ha, v. - over (shoot); -ikpiska; -juju, v.a. - to pieces; -śpa, v.a. - off (shoot); -śpi, v. (pick); -tutka, v.a. - off pieces.

knot, Kaḣa, v. Curl; okicaḣa, v. - very tight; okicaḣaḣapi, adj. Knotty. Naosin, v.a. Oiyakaśke, n.; okicaśka, v.a. Pśunka, n. (of tree). Yuoseya, v. Get into a - ; adv. In a - .

know, v. Slolya: i- , v.a.; o- , v.a. - of; oslolye, n. -ledge; waslolye, n. One who -s; wa-pi, n. -ledge; waslolyeya, v.a. Make - . Makanongeya, v. - already. Onspe, v.n. Have knowhow, the savoir-faire: -kiya, v.a. To teach.

L

labor, (work). Aȟtani, v.; oȟtani, v., adv. -ing. Awowaśi ecoⁿ, v.

lace, Cf. sew. Pazuⁿta, v.a. - up. Waȟloȟloka, n.
lack, Cf. wanting. Okpani, v.n. Be -ing. Yucaⁿ, v.a. fig. Be -ing in. Cf. sift.

ladder, n. Caⁿoiali, oiale.

lade, (empty). Cf. utensil. Kaȟepa, v. - out. Okapta, v.a. - out into. Kaze, v. - out; oyuze, v.a. - out into.
laden, Cf. burden. Yuś'aka, v.n. Be heavily - .

lake, n. Ble: -la, -kiyute, -óśkokpa, n.; -yata, adv.

lame, adj. Huśte: -kel, adv.; -ya, v.a., adv.; agluśte, v.n.: an- , ap- , v.n.
lamp, Cf. lantern. Pelijaⁿjaⁿ, petijaⁿjaⁿ, n.: -iⁿkpa, - chimney; -wigli, - oil (kerosene); -ye, n.; -gegeya, n. Lantern; -iyokaśtaⁿ, n. - oil funnel; -pi, n. Torch; - jaⁿjaⁿ woslahaⁿ, n. - chimney; -yuha omanipi, n. Lantern.

land, (country, survey, division). Makaoiyute, n. Piece of surveyed - ; makaowaśpe, makaopaśpe, makowaśpe, makaopaśpe taⁿka, n. A country. Makaośpe, n. An acre of - ; wojuiyutapi. Makopaśpe, n. A section of - ; śokela, n. A quarter section of - . Makaowapi, n. Map; makowapi. Makogmigma, n. Globe. Makoicago, n. Boundary. Oihuⁿni, v.a. (a boat etc.); n. A -ing: wat- , n. -ing place. Okiciin cokaⁿ, n. No-man's - ; owakihe cokaⁿ. Óśki, n. Poor - (tumbling).

language, (tongue). Ie, iya, v., n.: oie, n. A word, speech; oiekicatoⁿ, v.n. Use - ; oiekitoⁿ; tog'ia, v. Talk a strange - ; tokaiapi, n. A foreign - . Oowa, n. Letter, character; oowaptaya, n. Alphabet. Zuⁿteśni, adj. Incorrect - . Ieska, English T.

lantern, n. Haⁿhepi petijaⁿjaⁿ; petijaⁿjaⁿ yuha omanipi.

large, Akapa, adv. -er some. Hlagaⁿ: apa- , v.a. Make - on; ayu- , v.a. Make - upon; owa- , v. En- (cut); pa- , v.a. En- , lengthen out; wa- , v.a. En- (cut). Taⁿka, adj.: a- , v.n. Be -er; a-la, v. dim. Very little -er; a-ya, adv. Extensively; iglu- , v. refl. Make self great; ka-, v. Beat - ; na- , v.; kiciyu- , v. En- for; owa-ya, v.a. Cut -er; oyuya, yu-ya; pa- , v.a. En- (push out); wo- , n. Anything - , -ness. Bubu, adj. Chunky. Hiⁿsko, adv. So big: -keca, adv. So - ; -taⁿka, adv. So great; -yela, adv. That big; iⁿskokeca, adv. So - ; iⁿskokinica, v.a. Be doubtful which is -est; kiⁿskokeca, adv. So - ; nisko, adv. So - ; oniskokeca, adj. So - . Nuⁿga, adj. En- . Okacagla, v. Be too - for. Okaśke, adj. Bauble, knob-like; wośoka, adj. - , knobby, en-ed. Pahaⁿskeya, v.a. En- (rub, roll). Yuko, v.a. En- (by hand).

last, (order, time, duration). Ehake, ehakela, n., adv.; oehake, n. The - . Hakakta, adj.; hekta, n. Haⁿkeya, adv. Kitaⁿȟci, adv. At - , soon; nake(ś,ȟca), uⁿnahaⁿ, uⁿnihaⁿ, adv. Kpa, adj. Durable, lasting.

latch, n. Ipashaⁿ.
late, adv. Áśkaⁿs'e, Rather - ; aśkatula, aśkatuya, aśkatuyela. Haⁿtehaⁿ, adv. Lecala(ś), adv. Awhile ago, -ly.

laugh, v.a. Amapśa. Iȟa, v.: a-t'a, v.; -ȟaya, v.a.,adv.; -ke, v.; -kiya, v.a.; -ⁿhaⁿ, adv.; -t'a(t'a), v.n.; -ya, v.a.; iciciȟaȟapi, v. recip.; ik- , v. pos.; kic-pi, v. pl. They - at each other; naȟm- , v. - slyly; waw- , v. - at; waw-t'eya, v. Ridicule; waw-ya, v.a. Make - at; adv. Wittily; wo-ka, v. - at, jest; wo-ya, adv. Ludicrously; woiȟoie, n. -able word; wow-ȟakiya, v. - at own; wow-la, n. Fun. Ksizeoie, n. -able word. Paȟyutibya, v. Make - heartily.

laundry, n. Owayujaja.

law, (rule). Cf. condemn. Okoⁿze, n.: wo- , n.; tokicoⁿze, n. His - . Cf. koⁿza. Toope, n. His - . Wasuya, v. Make a - .
lawyer, Cf. discuss, try. Wakiye wicaśa.

lay, Cf. place. Mignaka, v. - up for me. Kioⁿpa, v. - on own. Paȟpa, kpaȟpa, v.a. - down (a load).
layer, Iyakigna, okignagtoⁿtoⁿ, adv. In, with many -s.

lazy, Glas'ic'iya, v. Škaŋkapiŋ, adj. Unwilling to move: i- , v.; -pi, n. Laziness; kaŋḣtal, adv. Kipa s'e, n. A - person. Kuś'it'a, v. Die from laziness.

lead (reach). Aiyagle, v.n. - to; adv.: -ya, v.a. Akagal, adv. Glohinapa, v. pos.; yus enapa, v. - out of doors. Pakiya, adv. -ing. Tokapaya, adv. -ing: -śkaŋ, v.

leader, (ruler). Aitaŋcaŋ, n.; woitaŋcaŋ, n. -ship. Blotahuŋka, n. Haŋtkaŋhula, n.

leaf, n. Ape, wape, caŋwape; waḣpe.
leak, (escape). Ohiyu, v.: a- , v.n. Skepa, v.n. - out, evaporate: a- , v.n.; na- , v. - out, empty.

lean, (slope, thin). Kiŋyaŋ: apa- , adv. -ing over; ata- , adv. Slanting; kaata- , adv. -ing; kata- , v. Stand -ing. Takiŋ, v.n. - sideways, forward: kata-yaŋ, v. Stand leaning; ka- , v. Make - ; -yaŋ, adv. -ing. Taŋoŋpa(b), adv. -ing to one side; -ya, v. Walk -ing; -yaŋka, v. Sit -ing; a- , v.n. - over, incline; atanoŋmya, adv.; ka- , v.; kataŋoŋb, adv. -ing at a 45 deg. angle; na- , adv. Icaŋyaŋ, adv. -ing against: ka- , adv. Ikakeiŋ, v.n. - on. Ikpataka, v. pos. Brace self. Iyuśiŋktiŋyaŋ, adv. -ing one way. Kaoḣya, adv. Sloping, twisting. Yukiŋ, v.a. - to the side, give passage. Gweza, adj. Thin, ragged, poor. Huḣaka, adj.; huḣ'a, adj.; huḣ'as'e, adv. With a - look. Huiyata, adj. Bony; husaŋgmi, adj. Very - . Kaŋakalaya, adv. Very - . Tamaheca, adj. Thin; tamahelya, adv. Poorly; tamaka, adj. Poor; watamahelheca, adj. Tiŋtiŋyaŋ, adj. Beginning to dry up, grow thin.

learn, v. Slolyewaciŋ, Be eager to - .
leather, Cf. hide, Wakape, n. - for mashing on; wokape, n. Wakiglaka, n. Dressed skin.

leave, Cf. omit. Ayuśtaŋ, v. - alone. Yuhlagaŋ, v.a. Separate from: a- , v.a. Forsake. Haŋta, v. imp. Get away. Iglutitaŋ, v. refl. Iglutokaŋ, v. refl. Aglukaŋ, v.a. - alone. Kicuŋni, v. - off, excuse. Oyapta, v.a. Have left-overs; oglapta, v. pos. - some of own; okiciyapta, v. (food); okiyapta, v. Oglusota, v.n. Go off. Onaśloka, v.n. - behind. Opte, n. -ings; optuḣaḣala, n. Crumbs. Ośnapi, n. Scraps.

leaven, Cf. ferment. Onapoḣye, n.; winapoḣye, n.; winakapo, n. Hops; waḣpe akicaśkapi; baking powder, yeast.

left, (hand, side). Catka, n. - hand: camatka, adj.; -yataŋ, adv.; i-yataŋ, adv.; taŋ-yataŋhaŋ, adv. At the - side of the body; taŋi-yataŋhaŋ.

leg, n. Hu: -akiś'aka, adj.; -blo, -bloyuŋke, -cogiŋ, -hohu, -iyut'iŋze, -ŋska, n.; huŋskaya, v.a.; -saŋni, -sli, n.; -topa, adj., n.; -wakiś'ake, adj.; -ya, v.; -yakel, -yata, adv. Sipaksize, n. Lower - .

legacy, n. Wowaaiḣpeye, A written - .
leisure, (rest). Kat'eyakel, adv. -ly. Owaŋji(la), adv. At rest, unemployed.

lend, (give). Cf. give. Ok'u, v.a. - to.
length, (lengthen, extend). Cf. large. Haŋska: kiciyu-, v. -en out for; o- , n.; ohaŋskeya, adv. In - . Kaḣlagaŋ, v. -en.

less, Aiyopteca(l), aiyoptetu(l), adv.: - than; -ya, -yakel, adv. In a less manner. Aokpaniyaŋ, adv. Wanting in. Aopteca(l), aoptetu, adv.: -ya, v.a., adv.; -yakel, -yela; glu- , v. pos.; ka- , v. Lessen, diminish; napteca, naptelya, opteca, adv.; wayoptelya, v. Make - by mouth.

lesson, n. Wooŋspe. Owaŋgya, v.a. Take a - from.
lest, (so as not). Owekinahaŋś, adv.
letter, n. Wowapi, Written discourse.

level, adj. Blaska: a-btoŋyaŋ, adv.; a-ya, adv.; apa- , v.a.; aya- , v.a.; ayu- , v.a.; -ya, adv. Blaya(e), adj.: a- , adj.; apa- ; aya- , v.a.; ayu- , v.a.; -la, adj; -ya, adv.; gla- , v. pos.; ka- , v. Make - ; naa- , v. Make - (by foot); na- , v.n., v.a.; naki- , nakici- ; o- , adj.

lever, n. Caŋipaptaŋye. Iyupseya, adv. Crookedly (fulcrum operated).
lewd, Witkowiŋwaśtelaka, n. A - person.

liberal, Cf. generous. Wahacaⁿka waⁿ ska (saⁿ) k'iⁿ, v. fig. Be - (in winter); wahacaⁿka waⁿ śayapi k'iⁿ (in summer). Wokimnaⁿka, adj. Wise, honored.

lick, v.a. Slipa: a- , v.a.; ki- , v. - own. Ayaspaya, v.a. Ayastaⁿka, v.a. Ayasto, v.a. Oyaska, v.a. - clean. Yajaja, v.a. Wash (by mouth). Yaskica, v.a. (what is eaten).

lie, (falsehood). Itoⁿśni, v.: itoⁿpiśni, n.; -yaⁿ, adv.; a- , v. Ajutoⁿ, v. Akaga, v.a.: -pi, n.; aokicaga, v.a.; aokicagapi, n. Gnayaⁿ, v.a.: aya- , v.a.; ic'i- , v. refl.; igna- v. red.; iwica- , n. Cakala, n. A liar. Eyayalaka, v.; heyayalaka. Glagleglega, v.; iyagleglega, v. Glaȟlaya, v. pos. Ieyaśna, v. Ijata, adj. Iyaślata, v. Puzata, adv. fig. Caught in a - . Waieceśni, v. Tell lies. Iyaślalya, v.a. Owekiwakaⁿ, v. - about; owewakaⁿ, v.n. Palani, n.

lie, (recline). Yuⁿka: aglakśuⁿyaⁿ - , v. - on belly; ahi- , v.a.; akaⁿ- , v.; ayuⁿgya, v.; a- , v.a.; iyuⁿg, v. - hidden; i- , v. - down in bed; ki- , v.n. God home and - down; o- , v. - down in; -haⁿ, v.n. - along, down; -he, adv. Lying prone; -pi, n. Encampment; yuuⁿka, v.a. Make - down. Akauⁿyaⁿ, adv. Akiglaskil, v. Aokiȟpa, v.a. Haⁿgnagya, adv. Ȟpaya, v.n.; ȟpayeya, v.a. Ic'imnikel, adv. Kazilya, v. Stretch out. Makipuskica, v. - on the ground.

life, Cf. live. Oni, n.: t- , n. His - ; wic- , n.
lift, Cf. raise. Kiyugata, v. - arms in prayer.

light, (illumine, not heavy). Jaⁿjaⁿ: ao- , v.n.; ao-ya, v.a.; ao-yaⁿ, adv.; i- , v.n., n.; i-ya, v.a.; i-yaⁿ, adv.; iyo- , n., v. (shine). Gmika, adj. (small). Hohetamaȟpiya, n. Iyataⁿ, v.a. Iyoyaⁿpa, v. Give - ; iyoyam. Kap'oja, adj. Not heavy; kap'oś kic'uⁿ, v. Walk -ly; yukapojela, v.a. -en. Tokaśni, adv. Not mattering: -kiya, v.a. Make - of. Wakaⁿgli, n. Lightning; wakiⁿyaⁿ toⁿwaⁿpi petijaⁿjaⁿ, n. Electric - .

lightning, Cf. flash. Wakiⁿyaⁿ toⁿwaⁿpi, n.

like, adj.,adv. Hececa; hecetuwaⁿjica, adj.; lececa, adv. - this; lecekceca, adv. red. - these. Iaki: -hehaⁿkeca, -hehaⁿyaⁿ, -henakeca, -lececa, -lecel, -lehaⁿkeca, -lehaⁿyaⁿ, adv. Icaȟya, adv. Iyaki: -lececa, -lecel, adv. Yaciⁿ: ici- , v.; ici-yaⁿ, adv.; iglaciⁿ, v. pos.; i- , v.a.; i-kel, adv.; i-pi, n. -ness; i-yaⁿ, i-yaⁿkel, adv.; wi-pi, n. -ness, resemblance. Iyece: -ca, v.n.; -ȟci, -kceca, -kcelya, -lya, adv.; iyecel, prep. Owaⁿke, n. -ness. Seksel, adv.

limb, n. Oya, Extremity of the body: -ya, n. Bodily extremities, limbs.
limber, Nalolopa, v.a. Make - (by foot). Sakala, adj. Green.

limit, (boundary). Wapetokeca, n. Wasabglepi, n. Stake marker.
limp, adv. Anahuśteśteyakel; anagluśte, v.n. Be - . Anaglegleyakel, adv.; anagleyakel. Anapoksaⁿyaⁿkel, adv. Yuospe icu s'e mani, v. Kaze wie s'e, adv.

line, (a length). Ohiye, n. (of fence, print, etc.).
linger, v.n. Wakaȟ'o, - about, hover over. Yekapiⁿ uⁿ, v.

link, n. Oyukśaⁿ.
lip, n. Ehahatuⁿ, Chapped -s; iha, n.: -hpi, n.; -toⁿ, v.; -ȟpiya, adv. Iȟnahaⁿ, v.n. Ijoka, v.n.; ijokiya, v. Ikawawa, v.n. Iśokśokapila, n. Iśpaśpa, v.n. Pulkiciⁿkel, adv. With hanging -s (sad); pute, n. Upper - ; iha, n. Lower lip.

liquidate, (efface, knock off, pay off). Kajuju, v.
lisp, v. Ślo.
list, n. Owicawapi (names).
listen, (heed, obey). Noⁿgeyuza, v. Obey; noⁿgoptaⁿ, v. Attend to.

little, Cf. small. Iyucaⁿyaⁿkel, adv. - of. Kitaⁿla, adv. Very - . Ociscila, adv. (time); wacik'ayela, n.; wanik'ala, n. A very - . Oȟ'eya, v.n. Have little in. Ośuⁿkecalaka, n. A very - thing. Cf. sick. Wamnala, v. Think - of. Optebyela, adv. A - while, distance; optelyela, adv. For a short time. Snaśnayela, adv. - at times. Tehaⁿlake, adv. After a - while.

live, (lively). Cf. active. Ni, v.n.: a- , v.n.; ki- , v. - again; ki-kiya, v.a. Make - again; ki-ya, v. Raise to life; -ic'iya, v. Make self - ; -kiya, v.a.; -un, v.n. Be -ing; -yake, adj. Living, alive; -yakel, adv.; -yan, v.a. v.n. Inhale, breathe, live; wicani, v. pl. They - ; n. Lives; wiconi, n. One's life. Ti, v. Dwell: oki- , v.n. - in, have residence; -la, v. Dwell; -owanjila, adj. -ing with others; tipi, n. A dwelling place. Waiglamna, v. Make a -lihood for self. Śpukeśni, adj. Very lively; bliheca.

load, Kśu: a- , v.a.; o- , v. pos. - own; oo- , n.; wa- , v. - on, pile on. Iyopazan, v. Kpasminyanyan, v. (gun). Okalaiheya, v. (a gun). Oun, n. (of a gun). Tkeyawak'inkiya, v. - heavily, over- . Oyucokaka, v. Un- . Peji iyuwanka aya, v. Un- a wagon into a barn.

loaf, Ons'cokalaka, n. - on horseback. Wagluḣe, v.n. Be a hanger-on. Semni, n. A bum, an unmarried young man.

lock, Taka: akiya- , v.; aonaki- , v. pos.; aona- , v.a.; nakici- , v. Fasten. Aoglatan, v. pos. Otkuga: ka- , v. Close; pa- , v.a. (push); yu- , v.a. - a door.

long, (far). Hanska, adj.; hanskeya, adv. Hehan: -hankeca, adv.; -yan, -yela. Iciyehanyan, adv. Makagna, adv. Very - . Tehan, adv. (time, distance); far.

long ago, adv. Ehank'ehan; ehanni, ehanna, ehannitanhan; hanbleble(kel), kilele(kel). Maka wanakajata, adv. Tannila, adv.

long-winded, H'anhanska, v.n.

look, v.a. Ableza. Iśta: a-celya, v.; a-gnaka, v.a.; a-gnagyakel, adv.; -iyotapa, v.; -yeya, v.; iśtiyotapa, v.n.; iśtokśin, v.n. Okaki(n): aoglakin, v.a.; a- , v.a.; ey- , v.a.; okas'in, v. - into: aey- , v.; ay- , v.a.; eyokas'in, v.a. Hakikta, v.n. Nakiśna, v. pos. - after own. Nicaole, v. - for poor people; tak'ole, v. - for something. Ascu, v. Akita, v.a.: iśkanśkan - , ph. Tonwan, v.n. See, take a - : ahi- , v.a.; akici- , v.; aki- , v.a.; a- , v.a.; a-yan, v.a.; waatonwe, n. Observer; e- , v.; i- , v.n.; o- , v. - into. Wanyanka: a- , v.a.; e- , v.; ia- , v.; ici- , v.a.; o- , v.a. - upon; owanyanke, n. Looks, appearance; owanyeye, n. Place for a -out; iwanic'iglaka, v. refl.; waniglaka, v. refl. - at self. Iyowotanin, n. A -out: -śniyan, adv. Invisibly. Ayuta(l), agluta, v.a.: akiciyukyuta, v.; akiciyuta(l), adv.; ayukyuta, ayul, v.

loom, v. Paśluta, - up, pop up.
loop, (noose, lasso). Jojoyagton, v. Make a - .

loose, Apajejeya, adv. Aśakagle, adv. Glugla, v. pos. Hahala, adv.; hahayela, adj.; inahahaya, adv. Ḣlagan, adj.: glu- , v. pos.; Ḣlahan, Ḣlaḣlayel, adv.; kao- , v. Get - ; kaoḢlakala, adj. Loosened; o- , adj.; oḣlaḣyela, adv. Kahoho, v. Knock - : glahoho; hohola, adj.; nahoho, v.a. Shake - ; pahoho, v.a.; wohoho, v.a. Ḣtata: aiyu- , v.; ayu- , v.a.; ayuoḣtalya, adv.; ayuo- , v. Igluśka, v. refl.; kiciyuśka, v.; kiyuśka, v. Unharness; paśka, v.a. Iglaśpa, v. refl. Kableya, v. -en hair. Kca, adj. Straight, untangled. Kpaśpu, v. -en own. Nagla, adj. Naḣco, v.n. Become - . Naopijela, adv. - fitting. Wahunhun, v.a. Make - (slash). Wankayela, adv. (free to turn). Yuḣpa, v.a. -en (bowstring). Yupanḣya, adv.

loquacious, adj., n. Iwakan.
lord, n. Itancan: -ka, n.; -kiya, -yan, -yanḣkel, adv.; -kiya, -ya, v.a.; itognagya, adj. Cf. chief.

lose, (misplace, drop). Cf. disappear. Aikpagan, v. refl. Onuniyan, adv. Lost (wander); gnuni, v.n. Unyan, v.a.: ki- , v. - for. Tokaḣ'an, v.n. Suffer a loss; tokakiḣ'an, v. Suffer injury, loss; toki eiḣpeya, v. Misplace. Tokon, v.a. Misplace. Wataninśni, adj. Lost.

loud, Cf. noise.
lounge, n. Oyunk'akanyankapi.
louse, n. Heya, hejanjan, hintka; heyokicile, v.; heyopuza, adj.,v.

love, Cf. heart. Canḣinyan, v.a. Be attached to one as one's mate, a loving couple; cantkiya, v.a.; cantognaka, v.a.: -pi, n. Ic'ic'uya, adv. Kicikśan, wikikśan, wikiśkata, v.a. Make - , have love-play. Teḣila, v.a.

Value highly. Waśtela(ka), v.a.: -pi, n. Love of benevolence; the beloved. wowaśtelaka, n. Love of complacency.

low, (short). Kuciyela, adv. - down, short.

luck, (fortune). Oglu, n. Fortune. Śilwakipa, v. Have bad - . Tokiŋśeśeś, adv. -ily enough. Waataya, v. Be fortunate; waatayes'a, n. A lucky one. Wanuŋwaatayela, v. Strike it well; wanuŋwakipa, v. Have bad - , an accident. Waptaŋyaŋ, adj.,v. Be lucky.

luggage, Cf. baggage, bag. Paŋśa, n. Suitcase. Wizipaŋ, n. Satchel.

lump, n. Caŋnuŋge (on a tree). Okaske, n. (things stuck together).

lungs, n. Cagu; caȟuwayazaŋ, hoȟpawayazaŋ, n. Tuberculosis of the - .

magic, n. Wicaȟmuŋga, A magician. Wokabiyeya, v.a. Remove by magic. Cf. bewitch.

magistrate, (delegate, representative). Wakicoŋza, n.; wakicuŋze.

maiden, Cf. virgin. Witaŋśna uŋ, n.
make, v.a. Kaga(H): aic'icaga, v.a. - on self; akicaga, v.a.; e- , v.a.; ic'icaga, v. refl.; -kiya, v. Cause to - ; -tuteśni, adv. Poorly - ; -ya, n.,adv. A make, sort; wao-waŋjila, n.; kicaga, v. - for; kicicaga, v. - for; micaga, v. - for. Iksab, v.a.

male, n. Bloka. Wica, n., adj. (human).

man, n. Wicaśa, wica. Haci(la), n. A lad. Hokśinigeśla, n. A pretentious adolescent. Hokśila wicaȟca, n. A lazy boy. Hunuŋpa, n. The biped: wa- n. Man in the sacred language. Ikcewicaśa, n. Common man. Kośkala(ka), n. Young - ; fig. siŋte. Wicaȟca(la), n. An old - . Wicaśaakaŋtu, n. Living - ; wicaśaha, Lazy - ; wicaśaiglawa, n. Chief, one counting self as a - ; wicaśataŋka, Middle-aged - . Wicataŋśna, n. A single man. Wicaya, adv. Manly. Waśicuŋ, n. The white man: - ciŋca, Mixed-blood person; - hokśila, wiciŋcala, White man's boy, girl; wa-ke, n. Imitator of white men; wayaŋ, adv. Like a white man; wawaśikśicuŋke, n. An aper of white men. Cf. family.

manage, Cf. pursue. Kuwapica, adj. -able. Oyuha, v. in comp. with waśte.

manger, n. Ośuŋkowote.
manifest, (visible, clear, open). Cf. show. Nablaya, v.n. Become - , plain. Taŋiŋ: kiciyao- , v. Make - for; kiciyu- , v.; kiya- , v. - to, for; okiyaŋ, adv.; oo- , v.n. Be - through; o- , v.n. Be - ; toiyoki- , n. His -ation; waakiciya- , n. -ation; wayaa- , v. Make - , proclaim.

manner, (courteous, orderly, generous, cheerful; pattern, mode). Oȟ'aŋwaśte, n., adj. -ly; v.n. Oiyaciŋyaŋ, adv. In the same - . Toke: -ȟci, adv. Howsoever; -lkeltu, -śke, -tkiya, -tu ke c'eyaś, -tuya kakeś, tuktogna ke c'eyaś, adv. Toketu keś, adv. No matter what.

many, Cf. much. Ota, adj. Hena: -gnakeca, adv. So - of each; -keca, adv. Just - enough; -kel, adj. Only so - ; -kiya, adv. In so - ways; -la, -lapila, adv. Only so - , all gone; -ŋgnakeca, adv. So - each. Iakehenakeca, adj. So - more than ten; iakelenala, adj. Only so - more than ten. Icaja(e), v.a. Think there are - : wo- , adj. Very - , great variety. Kanake, adv. So - ; lenake, lenala. Pawika, adv. Tonakec'eyaś, adv. Howmanysoever. Yulolopi, adj.

marble, n. Icaslohe.

mark, Go: ayu- , v.a.; glu-, v. pos.; -go s'e, adv.; ica- , v.a.,n.; ica-pi, n.; ica-ya, v.a.,adv.; ka- , v.; pa- , v.a. - off ground; pa-ya, v.a. Make - , carve; ya- , v.a. - with the teeth. Icazo, v.a.,n.: -kiya, v.a.; iglazo, v. pos. Iwapetokeca,iwapetog, n.: -toŋ, v.a.; wapetokeca, n. Sign, miracle. Gle: ka-ga, v. - across; na-gleza, v.n. Be -ed, striped; wasab- , v. - one's way, - a boundary. Kahuŋ, v. (chip). Kaśkiśkita, v. - in equal lengths. Naȟota, v. Iwakta, n.; wowakta, n. Mark, sign: -ya, v. Make a sign.

marksman, Cf. arrow, shoot. Waoka, n.

marry, Cf. sacrament. Kiciyuzapi, v. recip., n.; okiciyuze, n. Marriage. Tawicutoŋ, v. Be married. Teya, n. A polygmaous man. Wipeya, v. Sell in marriage. Yuskiya, v.a. Make - .

mash, v.a. Śuja: apa- , v.a.; aya- , v.a.; opaśu- , v. - up in; pa- , v.a.; wo- , v.a. Pataŋ, v.a. - up: bloi- , n.; ki- , v.; o- , v.a. - up in; i- , v.a. Inaȟuga, v. Kakpaŋ, v. Beat; owayakpaŋ, n. - made by chewing. Okaśki, v.n. Be -ed in, made jelly of; wośki, v.a. Pound. Śtagya, v.a. - up; adv. Mushy. Woja, v. Make a mush: -pi, n. A stew; yuja, v.a. v

mask, n. Iteha.
massacre, v.a. Tiyapa kte; tiyapa wicaktepi.
master, n. Wicayuha.

masturbate, Pasluka, n. -tion, onanism.
mat, (beat down). Owiŋja, n.; kawiŋja, v. - down.

match, n. Hoiśta, yuilepi. Aiyopteya, v. - with what another contributes. Oiyokśica, adj. Ill-matched.

mate, Kaȟtanka, v. Be a - .
maturity, Uncihi, v.n. Have attained-.

meal, (pounded, ground). Wawopanpi, n. Cornmeal.
mean, (signify, cruel). Ka, v.a. Consider, ask for, signify; kica, v. pos.; nica, v. He means you. Kaocinśica, v. Make - ; oȟ'anśica, v.n. Be ill-behaved, cross.

means, (way). Tokani...śni, adv. With no - to.
meanwhile, adv. Kohan.

measure, (weight, length). Iyuta(e), v. Weigh, try: -pi, n. A - , an acre, a mile, a pound; -kiya, v.; -ya, adv. By - ; o- , n. A dimension, a rate: - ciscila, An inch; - wanji, A section; - okise, Half section; - canku, Section road; onwiyutapi, n. A standard for - ; canwiyute, n.; igluta, v. pos.; ikiyuta, v.a. Iyakatin, v.; akatinpi, n. Standard of - from finger-tip to finger-tip. Otkeyute, n. A weight; siiyute, n. Foot - ; witkeyute, n. Scale, weights, a pound; wiyutapi, n.; wiyute, n. -ing tape or rod. Wicacanpi, n.

meat, (cuts, kinds). Patapi, n. Butchering, dressing. Kabla, v. Cut for drying. Taloiyukpan, n. - chopper; taloyukpanpi, v. Cut - for sale.
Parts:
iyuȟ'eyayapi, Shoulder (buffalo).
napco, Tenderloin.
napewicaśpan, - under the small ribs.
tacankpe ognake, - above knees; tacankpognake.
tamica, Thigh.
tasicogin, - below knee, front side.
tanapco, - near spine.
taniśtuśta, Quarters of beef.
tan, A half beef.
tatucuhu, Cutlets.
woluta, A round of beef.
Kinds:
papa, papasaka, Dried - .
śin, Fat parts.
śloślola, Soft fat parts.
talo, Fresh - .
talipa, Sausage.
wakapapi, Pemmican.
wasna, Pounded beef and marrow etc.
waśinlo, Juicy fat parts.
wiȟpanyanpi, Dry papa.
wocankśu, - drying.
wokapan, Pounded - .

medal, (necklace). Mazaskawanap'in, Silver - .
mediate, Cf. friend.

medicine, n. Pejuta. Pśunka, n. Pill. Pejuta wicaśa, n. The Indian medicine man skilled in the use of herbal remedies. Waśicun wakan, The doctor of the white man. Pejutaya, v.a. Use - . Wapiyekiya, v.a. Make apply - .

Aches: icaȟpela, napośtan, onglakcapi, icaȟpehu, pejutahu okihetonton, waȟpataya ȟota, Snakeroot, coneflower.
Appetite: tinpsila pejuta, Milkweed.
Breath; pispizatawote, Fetid marigold.
Chest; pejutaskahu, Loco-weed.
Childbirth; canȟlogan waśtemna, yamnumnuga iyececa, Ragweed; hu(pestola), stola, Yucca, soapweed; waȟpeskuya, Dock (afterbirth).
Colds, coughs; hehakta pejuta, Mint; pejizizi, Broomweed; waȟpeceyaka, Mountain mint; waȟpeicikoyagyaka.
Cramps; takuśaśala hu iyececa, Tall dock. Cf. diarrhoea.
Diarrhoea: hucinśka, Green milkweed; pejiswula cik'ala, Low milkweed; takuśaśala hu iyececa, Tall dock.
Excretion: canȟlogan waśtemna, Ragweed.
Head: matotatinpsila, ticanica hutanka, Psoralea.
Hemorrhage: takuśaśala hu iyececa, Tall dock.
Horses: ptetawote, Ground plum; śunkhuśtipiye, Hymenopappus.
Kidneys: zitkala tawote, Bird's-root.
Lotion: pejiȟotaswula, tanka, toto, Sages, gray grass; wazimninkpa, Meadow-rue.
Milk (mothers'): hucinśka, Green milkweed; pejutaskuya, Tender milkweed; waȟpetinpsila, Milkweed.
Mouth: inyanpejuta (iniyanpi), onwahinyuntonpi, Erigeron.
Poison; pejiwakan, Panic grass; yajopi, Water hemlock.
Snake-bite: zuzecatapejuta, Beard-tongue.
Sores: pejutajanjan s'ele, Alum; waȟpet'aga, Alumroot; wiśpan, Iodine.
Stomach;(hu)pestola, stola, Yucca, soapweed; pejutanigetanka, Bush morning-glory; waȟpeȟcaȟca, Croton,

skunkweed; caŋȟlogaŋśkiśkita, Nightshore.
Swelling: caŋȟlogaŋ makatola, Purple fritillaria; hituŋkala nakpala, White plantain; omnica, Beans; poipiye, White plantain; śuŋkcaŋkahuipiye, False gromwell.
Wound: pejutawaȟ'e śa, Hairy puccoon.

meditate, v.a. Awaciŋ.
meet, v. Akipa; akicikipapi, v. pl.; akicipapi, v. pl.; ecipa, v.n.; ecipeya, v.a. Ataya, v.a.; atayeya, v. Icitkokipapi, v.; itkokib, v.a.; itkokipa, v.a. Kiciatakiciya, v. - face to face, squarely.

mellow, adj. Śtuŋka, Soft, not ripe.
melon, n. Wagmu, Gourd, pumpkin, squash, etc.: -blu, Squash; -hu, Pumpkin vine; -śkopa, Japanese pumpkin; -śpaŋśni yutapi, Watermelon.

melt, v.n. Askaŋ: - s'e, adv. Aspaŋ, v.n. Aśla, v.n. Aśloya, v.a.; ślo, v.n.: -ya, v.a. -yapi, n. Melted matter; wakaśloyakel, adv. In manner of -ing. Komi, v.n. Opaskaŋ, v. (from lying on); waicaskaŋ, v. - snow.

member, (adherent). Opeya uŋ, n.
memory, n. Wakiksuyapi, Memories, dreams, visions.
menses, n. Iśnatipi; iśnati, v.n. Have a menstrual flow.

merchant, (trader). Mazopiye wicaśa, n.; wiyopeye, wopetoŋ, n.
mercy, Oŋśila, v. Have - on, pity: -ka, v.a.; oŋśikila, v. pos.; oŋśiya, adv. Miserably, pitifully; wowa- , n. Towaoŋjila, n. His - .

messanger, n. Ogligle, ogligleyapi. Wahośiyapi, n.
mess, adj. Gaŋ, -ed: -gaŋic'iya, v.; -ic'iya, v. refl.; -s'e, adv.; -yela, adv.

metal, n. Maza: -mna, adj. Smelling of - ; -skazi, Gold; -suta, Steel; -śa, Copper; -śloyapi, Pewter; -zi, Copper.

meter, Cf. guage, measure. Wislolye, n.
middle, (midst). Coka: aho-, adv.; iyo-ya, adv. Cokaŋ, n.: -gnagya, -l, -yaŋ, i-yaŋ, o-ya,oakiyecokaŋ, adv. Cokapa, adv.; hocokab, hocokam, ocockab, adv. Cokata, n.,adv.: cokal, a- , -kiya, -wapa, i- , adv. Egna, prep. Amidst. Hoaiciyopteya, adv. Ocaŋnatuhci, adv. In the - . Yucaŋnal iyeya, v. Push into the - of.

midnight, n. Haŋcokaŋ, yaŋyecokaŋ.
migrate, v. Wanigla (southward).
mild, Aȟwaya, aȟwayela, adv.
military, (personnel, rank etc.). Cf. itaŋcaŋ.

milk, n. Asaŋpi: pte- , n. Cow's - ; pte-nini, n. Curdled - ; pte-wasna, n. Butter; pte-wigli.

mimic, (ridicule, mock). Uŋca, v.a.; wicoȟ'uŋca, v. Ape.
mind, (disposition, thought, understanding). Tawaciŋ, n.

mine, Cf. dig. Ok'e, n.
minor, (unimportant). Cf. unimportant.
miracle, Wakaŋyaŋ, adv. Miraculously, sacredly: - wicoȟ'aŋ, v. Perform -s. Wowapetokeca, n. Sign, wonder.

mirage, n. Makoceataŋiŋ.
mire, (stick). Kaȟli, v. Kajuŋhe s'e, v. Kalopa(b), v. Hit a soft spot; palopa, v.a. Be -ed in.

mirror, n. Mioglas'iŋ, miyoglas'iŋ.
mischief, Wayuśkiśka, v. Make - .
miser, Obśiś'ic'iya, v. Be -ly.
misery, (difficulty). Oteȟi, n.
misfortune, Cf. luck. Os'ica, n.
misplace, Cf. lose.

miss, (fail). Śuta, v. - hitting (target): a- , v.a. Śna: ayaśna, v.a.; ka- , v. - batting; oka- , v.a. - a day; pa- , v.a. - pushing, thrusting; wo- , v.a. - shooting; ya- , v.a. - with the mouth. Gnayaŋ: ayu- , v.a.; pa- , v.a. - one's hold, seat; wa- , v.a. - with a knife; wiwognaye, n. Shooting accuracy; wo- , v.a. - shooting, striking; ya- , v.a. - with the mouth. Iwonas'iyaya, v. Aokamna, v. Go around, avoid. Naokpani, v.a. Be short of. Wayuoȟmiŋ, v. - throwing.

missfire, v.a. Awok'ega, awoskapa, awosna; woto, v.n.: a- , v.a.
misstep, (stumble, twist foot). Kagloka, v. Kaoślok iyaya, v. Near fall.

mistake, Śna: agla- , v.a. pos.; aglu- , v. pos.; gla- , v. pos.; glaśna-yaŋ, adv.; kiciyu- , v. Make a - for; yu-koŋza, v. Pretend a - ; iyagla- , v.n.; ya- , v. Blunder in speaking; yu- , v.a. Let drop; yu-pi, n. A miss. Ecaiciśniyan, adv. Iigluge, v. Ipawehya, adv. Incorrectly. Tuwa e kaga, v. - for.

mistress, Wiiyayuha, v. Go to one's -.
misunderstanding, (falling out with). Oyuśica, v. Have a - with.

mix, v.a., v.n. Icahi: -hiya, adv.; -kiton, v. pos.; -ton, -ya, v.a.; ic-, v.n.; ic-ya, v.a., adv.; o-ton, v.a.; o- , n. Mixture; w- , n. -ing stick; w-ya, v. Mingle. Ijena, adv.: ica- , v.; icijehan, adv.; ic- , adv.; ka- , v. - up; iyu- , v. Icaśośa, v.: ic- . Icicaskaya, v.a. Icignuni, v.: -ya, v.a.; -yan, adv. Kpukpa(e): ici-ya, adv.; i- , adv. Varied; iyu- , adv. -ed fine; na- , v. - together. Iyupśaya, adv. -ed, good and bad. Kacoco, v. Beat together. Wohpani, n. Something to - in. Gluja, v. pos.

moccasins, n. Cuiyohe. Hanmwitka, n. Fool - . Hanpa, n.: -itake, hanpitake, -kiglake, -kśupi; tehpi- , n. - with rough side out; wizi- , n. - made from old tent hides. Hanp: -ikceka, -iśka(ton), -itake, n.; -ohan, -ohekiciciya, -ohekiya, -okihan, v.; -tanni, n. Hanp': -ceyaka, -hinśma, -ipata, n. Iśkahuton, v.a. Woska, n. A worker of moccasins.

mock, Cf. imitate. Wauncа(la), n. One that -s. Woicihahaya, adv. In a -ing manner.
moderate, Iktahela, adv.
modest, (bashful, ashamed). Wiśteca, adj.; wiśtelkiya, v.a. Be reserved.

moist, Cf. sponge, wet. Pastanka, v. -en; wostanka, v. -en (rain).
mold, v. Oyaya, Be moldy, musty: -mna, v. Smell -y.

money, (coins, keep, use).
Penny, mazaskaśala.
Dime, kaśpapi.
Quarter, śokela.
Dollar, mazaska.
Coins, change, yuśpuśpupi.
Currency, change, mazaskakpanla.
Paper - , mnihuha mazaska.
Bank check, mnihuha mazaskaiicu.
Pension, ohiic'iya wicohan.
Interest, oicage.
Safe, mazaska aonatake.
Pocketbook, mazaska ognake.
Treasury, mazaska omnaye.

Mazaska igni, v. Raise - ; mazaska kamna, v. Raise - . Mazaska el ahigle, v. Bet .

month, n. Wi, wiyawapi (calendar).
January, wiocokanyan wi, wiotehika wi.
February, cannapopa wi, tiyoheyunka wi, wicata wi.
March, iśtawicayazan wi, śiyo iśtohcapi wi.
April, wihakaktacepapi wi.
May, canwapto wi, wojupi wi.
June, tinpsinla itkahca wi, wipazukawaśte wi.
July, canpasapa wi, wiocokanyan wi.
August, wasuton wi.
September, canwapegi wi.
October, canwapekasna wi.
November, takiyuha wi, waniyetu wi.
December, tahecapśun wi, wanicokan wi.

moon, Cf. heaven. Hanhepi wi, hanwiyanpa, hanyewi, hanyetuwi, n. Hokeluta, hokemi, hokemila, hokewin, n.
Wilecala, n. Crescent moon.
Wimima, n. Full moon.
Wimakatanhan, n. Full third quarter.
Wiyaśpapi, n. Third quarter.
Wimimakanyela, n. First quarter full.
Wiokiseya, n. First quarter.
Wit'e, n. New moon.
Wiyata, adv. At the - , sun.

mop, n. Owank'ipakinte, Floor - . Pajaja, v.a.

more, Iyakapa(e): a- , v.; icapeya, adv.; ikapeya, adv.; iyakab, iyakabtu, adv.; -ic'iya, v. refl.; -ya, adv. Aiyotan, adv. Akta, akton, adv. Aotala s'e, adv.; kaotalake s'e, adv. A few more. Ipagoya, adv. Sanpa(b), adv. - than, over, beyond: i-samyeś, adv.; i- , i-tu, i-ya, adv. Iyakawin, v.n.; iyakic'unc'unka, n.; kaiyakic'uya, adv. A little - .

morning, adv. Anpetuhankeyela, Before noon. Hinhanna, hinhanni, n.: o- , n. Forenoon; -hci, adv.

morose, (melancholy). Cf. displease. Wacinhinyanza, adj. Cruel: ta- , adj. Wahinyanza: wayu- , v. Make one ill-disposed; wawahiyanskalaka, adj. Cross; wawahiyanzeca, n. A - person.

mortality, n. Wicasota.
mosquito, n. Capuŋka, capuŋkwokeya, capuŋk'icuwa.

motion, (free movement). Óśkaŋ, n.: -śilya, v.a. Prevent, impede - .

motorcycle, n. Nap̣opopela.
moult, Cf. shed. Śuŋpa, v.n.; śuŋpela, adj. -ing. Waśuŋkajuŋ, v.; waśuŋkaślo-ka.
mount, v. Akiyotaka.
mountain, Cf. hill. He, n.: -ta, adv. Wicacepahala, n. High wide - .
Hesapa, n. p. The Black Hills; Pahasa-pa.
Heska, n. p. The Big Horns, The Rocky Mountains.

mourn, v.a. Aceya; akiceya, v. pos.; owekiceya, v.n. - over. Waśigla, v. - for the dead; n. -ing garments etc.: -ya, adv. -ing.

mouth, n. I: icap'taŋkataŋka, adv. With - wide open; naicabya, adv.; ie-laya, v. Put things in the - ; iiyuwi, n. A halter for the - ; iniyaŋpi, n. Sickness of the - ; iyognaka, v.a. Put into the mouth: o- , n. -ful; iyoȟlo-ke, n. - of a river, delta. Oyape, v. Take in the - ; yaśloia, v. - words.

move, Ahiyuslohaŋ, adv. Iglaka, v.n.; aiglagya, v.; naglagla, adj. -ing. Akatiŋ mani, v.n. Skaŋ, v.n. - about: -kiya, v.a.; -śkaŋ, v.; -yaŋ, adv. In motion; aśkaŋ- , v.n.: -yaŋ, adv.; na-śkaŋ- , v.n. - rapidly; wa-śkaŋyaŋ, v. Make - ; n. One causing to live. Gla-psaŋpsaŋ, v. pos. Inaŋgnaŋka, v. - the lips (reading). Iokpakpas, adv. Ioŋwiyuta, v. Pahohośniyaŋ, adv. Im-movably. Pami, v.n. - away slowly. Piyaiyotake, v. - away (sit). Śkiŋc'i-ya, v. - self.

movie, n. Wowapiśkaŋśkaŋ; wowapina-śkaŋśkaŋye, n. Movie projector.

mow, Cf. cut. Kaśla, v.a.: peji- , v.

much, (too, so). Akaecoŋ s'e, adv. O-ver-much. Akeiyenakececa, adv.; hena-keȟci, adv.; lenake, lenakeca, adv. So - , many. Akic'uŋc'uŋka, v. Do repeatedly, over-much; akic'uya, adv.; iakic'uya, adj.; iyakic'uya, adv., v.a. Icajapi, n. Very - ; icakije-śniyaŋ, adv.; woicaśyela, adv. Won-derfully - . Ihamnapi s'e, adv. Iyatagle, adj., adv.: -ic'iya, v.n.; -ya, v.a., adv. Ka, laka, suff. Ra-ther - . Ota, adj. Much, many: ol- , adj. Of great variety; -ka, adj.; -hela, adv. Piled up. Ośuŋgye, adv. Too, very - . Taŋyutkaŋla, adj. - of something.

mud, n. Makaȟliȟli (thin). Uŋpśija, n. (light).

multiply, v.a. Yuota: ici- , v.a.; i-gluota, v. refl.; kici- , v. - for; -pi, n. A multiplication.

murder, v.a. Tikte; tiokte, v.a. Com-mit homicide; tiwicakte, n. A -er; v.a. Commit - .
murmur, (rebel). Kipa, v. pos.

mush, v. Yuja, Make - ; kiciyuja, v. Make - for.

music, (instruments).
Drum, caŋcega. Cf.
Flute, ciyotaŋka, hokagapi.
Harmonica, yapizapi, wayapizapi.
Harp, caŋkicatoŋ.
Horn (brass), wayajopi, mazayajopi.
Organ, caŋiyukize, caŋyukizapi; ocaŋ-yukize, An organ pit.
Piano, caŋipakize, caŋpakiza.
Violin, caŋipakize.

musk, Cf. perfume. Siŋkpeoŋzemna.

my, pron. adj. Cf. I.

mystery, Wakaŋka, adj. Doubtfully mysterious; wawakaŋkaŋka, adj. Of a mysterious activity.

N

nag, v. Wayatiktil ihe.
nails, (claw, hoof). Cf. claw. Śake, n. (fingers, toes, etc.): taśi- , n. Hoof.

naked, adj. Śla: -ya, adv. -ly. Taŋcola, taŋcokala, adj. Poorly clad.

name, n. Caje: a- iglata, v. refl.; -glal, v.; -glata, -iglata, -kaga, -kiyata, v.; i- , adv.; i-ka, v.n.; i-yata(l), adv.; o- , n.; wa-kiyata, v.a. - one's deceased relatives. Caś: -kitoŋ, v.; -toŋ, v.; -'taŋiŋyaŋ, adv. eya-toŋ, v.; o-toŋ, v. Make a - . Eciyapi, i.e. ekiyapi. Glawakaŋ, v. pos.

napkin, n. Iikpakiŋte. Makuakaḣpe, n. A bib.

nation, (clan, group, tribe). Oyate, n.: -ya, adv. As a - .
American, Milahaŋska.
Apache, Ciŋcakize.
Arapahoe, Maḣpiyato.
Arickaree, Hewaktokta.
Assiniboin, Hohe, Waziyata Wicaśa.
Blackfoot, Sihasapa.
Brule, Sicaŋgu, Hiŋhaŋśuŋwapa, Kul Wicaśa.
Cheyenne, Śihiyela, Śiyela, Śahiya, Tahiŋ Wicaśa, Tokciŋkawota.
Chinese, Picokaŋhaŋska.
Chippewa, Haḣatoŋwaŋ
Comanche, Cf. Snake.
Cree, Maśtiŋcala Wicaśa.
Crow, Kaŋgi Wicaśa, Psaloka.
Dakota, Dąkota Oyate; Kiyaksa (band).
English, Śaglaśa.
Eskimo, Caj'otila.
Flathead, Natableca, Naśuŋḣape.
Ghostdance Group, Howi Wicaśa (Oglala).
Huŋkpapa, Hoḣwoju, Huŋkpapa. Cf. Minniconju.
Kootenai, Śkutani.
Kwapa, Peśa.
Leaf-Shooter, Waḣpekute; Waḣpetoŋwaŋ.
Lakota, Titoŋwaŋ; Dakota.
Loafer, Wagluḣe (Oglala).
Mandan, Miwataŋni.
Minniconju, Miniowoju. Cf. Teton.
Nez Perce, Pogeḣloka.
Northern tribe, Watopaḣlate, Watopala, We Wicaśa (Blood).
Oglala, Titoŋwaŋ, Oglala; Wajaje.
Omaha, Oyatenuŋpa, Omaha.
Osage, Witapaha(tu), Kiowa.
Oto, Watoḣtata.
Pawnee, Palani, Scili.
Ponka, Oyateyamni.
Santee, Isaŋati.
Shawnee, Śawala.
Shoshone, Susuni, Pejiwokeya Oti kiŋ.
Sioux, Dakota Oyate.
Sisseton, Haŋgeokute, Sisitoŋwaŋ.
Snake, Siŋteḣla Wicaśa.
Tetoŋ, Titoŋwaŋ; (bands) Iḣoka, Oglala, Mnikowoju etc.
Two Kettle, Oohenuŋpa.
Ute, Sapa Wicaśa, Wicaśa Yuta.
Winnebago, Hotaŋke.
Yankton, Huŋkpati (Lower), Ihaŋktoŋwaŋ; Waceuŋpa, Wiciyela (Yanktonais).

nausea, Wiyako, v.n. Feel - .

near, adv. Kiyela, - to (time, place): a- , adv.; ici- , iciki- , iki- ; i-kiŋyela; itaŋ- ; oa- , adv. Atignagya, adv. Kagla, adv. Nearby: icagla, prep.; icaglaya, adv.; o-la, adv. By the side; o-yela, adv. Kaŋyela, adv.: ici- , i- , o- , owaś- , adv. Inak'esya, adv. Isiyataŋhaŋ, adv. Iyokal, adv. Iśnikaleś, adv. Itiyopa, adv. Iyape, adv.: -la, v.a. Kitata, adv. - together, in close succession. Owasya, v.a. Bring, cause to be - . Yaaskala, v. Speak of as - ; yaaskayela. Yuaśka s'e, adv. Nearby.

neat, adj. Stola, Small and - . Wayaco, adv. -ly. Yuskapila s'e, adv. -ly.

necessity, (need). Kpaowotaŋka, v. Get necessities for self. Napepicaśni, adj. Inevitable. Taŋiŋyuŋla, adv. Deprived of necessities (of life, work, etc.).

neck, Ḣlute, adj. Long: - s'e, adv. Poskica, v. Clasp about the - ; poskil, adv. By the - ; poskiski, adv. Squeezing by the - . Tahu, n. Back of the - : -hute, n. Nape of the - .

necklace, (kerchief, medal, etc.). Wanap'iŋ, n.: -blaska, n. (beads); -kicatoŋ, v.a. Wear as a - ; -ya, v. Have use of as a - .
need, Cf. necessity. Tokecakel, adv. In case of - .

neglect, v. Aiśtagnakeśni, v. Iwakiniya, v.a. (from contempt). Wiśute, v. - doing, miss.

neither, adj. Uŋmala...śni; uŋmani... śni, adj. - of two.

nervous, Wakaȟtakeca, n. A - person; wakaȟtakeke, n. A fretful person.
nest, n. Hecayuŋkapi; hoȟpi, n.: -ya, v.a.
net, Cf. apart. Zaŋzaŋla, n. Netting.

network, (grid). Tawogmuŋkekaȟya, cl. He made a web of it, a pattern.
neurology, n. Eteiyokiseyazaŋ.

never, adv. Tohaŋni, toŋweni...śni, toweni...śni.
nevertheless, (still, yet). Hecac'uŋś, hecaeśa, hecaśka, adv.; hececaeśa, hececa k'eyaś, he eca eyaś, he ecaśka, adv. Ituśeka, adv. Nahaȟci, adv. Yet, still. Takomni, adv.

new, adj. Teca, Young: a- , v.n.; ayu- , v.a.; iglu- , v. refl.; kiciyu- v. Make - for; pa- , v.a. Make - , furbish; wo- , n. -ness; -ya, v. Renew; adv. Newly. Lecakcala, adj.

news, n. Ptepapala, The main - . Wahośi, v. Bring - . Wotaŋiŋ, n.
newspaper, n. Mniȟuhakakaŋka, wotaŋiŋwowapi.

next, (continue, follow, second). Iyokihe, v., adj.; okihe.
nibble, v. Oyak'oza, v. Bit short; wayaol'otake, v. - on. Yaȟpu, v.a. (on what sticks). Yajipa, v.a. Yatuka, v.a. - off.

nice, Yupiya, adv. -ly, finely, pleasantly, with grace and skill.
nick, v.a. Woȟci (by tool).
nicknack, (trifle). Śpula, n., adj. Bits of.

night, Cf. dark. Akpaza, v.n. Ayuŋgya, v.n. Haŋ, n.: -yetu, -hepi; ohepi, n. A certain - ; -iyaŋpa, n.; haŋnataŋtaŋkel, adv.; -oiyokipi, n.; -oluta, n.; -opta, adv.; -otkaŋ, n.; -tahena, adv.; -tehaŋ, adv.; -wahetu, n.; -wakaŋ, adj.; -watohaŋlśna, adv.; -watohaŋtu; -yetu, n.; he-pi, n., adv. Ĥtahepiyela, adv.

no, adv. Hiya, iŋ; haŋśni, interj.
nobody, pron. Tuweni...śni.
nod, v.n. Ogiŋgiŋ (in sleep). Pakahuŋka, v.a. - to; pakicahuŋka, v. Bow to. Pazeze, adv. -ding, swinging.

noise, (bustle, clamor, disturbance, tumult). Aȟmuŋ, v.a.; waoȟmuŋyece, n. Aȟ'a, v.n. Make - ; Ȟ'ayela, adv. (of rain, hail). Bu, v.n.: ana- , v.a.; ayu- , v.a.; -ya, -yakel, -yeȟci, -yel, adv. Apakiza, v.a. Ayuswu, v.a. Giŋlgiŋca, v. Hoȟnagicala hotoŋpi, n. Peculiar sound of women's voices singing; hokitaŋyaŋkel, hośpeyela, adv.; waahotoŋ, n. - maker; wayuhotoŋ, v. Make - . Ĥuȟugahe s'e, adv. With thundering - . Inapśa, v.n. Kakyela, adv. With - . K'o, n. Bustling of people; o- , n.; o-ya, v.n., adv. Owolutatoŋ, v.n. Make a - ; n. Bustle, clamor; owolutatoŋyaŋ, adv. Oyucokaka, v. Make crunch (squeeze). Pak'eza, v.a. Make a rasp sound, filing. Waaś'akece, n. A noisy person.

none, Cf. destitute. Wanica, adj. Without anything, any. Waŋjini, pron.

nose, n. Pa: -cete, n. Nostril; -hute, n. Upper part of - ; -ȟlate, - fossae; -su, n. Bill, beak; -piŋkpa, n. Tip of the - . Poge, n.: poȟcaŋte, n. Wings of the - ; ponunuje, n. Lower - , snoot.

not, (negative). Kaca, neg. suff. Kilo, Same as śni yo. Śni, adv. particle of negation; śniś, neg. intensive.

notch, n. Ikpage. Kakaŋ, v.; okakse, n. Lepa: kaleb- , v.; ka- , v.; wale- , v. Cut round -es; yaleb- , v.a. Bite -es in; yuleb- , v.a. Make -es in.

note, (memorandum). Owaicu, v. Take - of. Tokaic'ignaka, v. Take - of.

nothing, (none). Nica, n.; wa- , adj., v.n. Have - , none; a- , v.n.; wawanice, v., n. Be - , a dearth : -ca, v. There is - , or little; wowanica, v.a. Reduce to - ; wowanice, n. State of -ness. Takuni...śni, n.; v.n. Come to - ; takuniśni, n. Eyapi eceȟce, ph. Nothing but talk.

nourish, Iwicamna, adj.; iwicawaśte, adj.
now, (already). Iyehaŋtu, adv. At the time. Lehaŋleś, adv. Nowadays; lehaŋtuyakel, adv. Just - . Uŋgnahaŋśna, adv. - and then, at certain times. Wana(ś), waŋna(ś), adv. Now (present).

nudge, v.a. Pani, panini.
null, adj. Ecetuśni: -ya, v.a.
numb, adj. Gluśte. Kśikśa, adj.; kśikśeca. T'at'a, adj.: kpa- , adj. Asleep; pa- , v.n. Be asleep (limb); si- ; -ka, adj. Palsied.

number, Kicamnayaŋ, otapi s'e, owihe s'e, pahayela, yuwiwihe s'e, adv. In large -s. Otawat'eśica, yawapicaśni, adj. -less.

Cardinal:

waŋji, waŋci, waŋ,	One.	1
nuŋpa (nuŋb, num),	Two.	2
yamni,	Three.	3
topa (tob),	Four.	4
zaptaŋ,	Five.	5
śakpe,	Six.	6
śakowiŋ,	Seven.	7
śaglogaŋ,	Eight.	8
napciyuŋka,	Nine.	9
wikcemna,	Ten.	10
ake waŋji,	Eleven.	11
ake nuŋpa,	Twelve.	12
ake yamni, etc.	Thirteen.	13 etc.
wikcemna nuŋpa	Twenty.	20
wikcemna nuŋpa ake waŋji,		21
wikcemna nuŋpa ake nuŋpa,		22
wikcemna nuŋpa ake yamni, etc.		23 etc.
wikcemna yamni ake waŋji, etc.		31 etc.
opawiŋge,	One hundred.	100
opawiŋge sam yamni,		103
opawiŋge sam ake yamni,		113
opawiŋge sam wikcemna yamni ake yamni, etc.		133 etc.
opawiŋge nuŋpa sam wikcemna yamni ake yamni,		233
opawiŋge yamni sam wikcemna yamni ake yamni, etc.		333 etc.
koktopawiŋge,	One thousand.	1000
opawiŋge wikcemna,		1000
opawiŋge wikcemna kiŋ yamni,		3000
opawiŋge wikcemna kiŋ wikcemna,		10000
opawiŋge wikcemna sam opawiŋge yamni sam wikcemna yamni ake yamni,		1333
opawiŋge wikcemna kiŋ wikcemna ake yamni sam opawiŋge yamni sam wikcemna yamni ake yamni,		13333
opawiŋge wikcemna kiŋ opawiŋge,		100000.
Kauŋȟye, kawiŋȟye, opawiŋge,		100.

By Groups:

numnuŋpa,	By twos.
napciŋyuŋgyuŋka,	By nines.
opawiŋgege,	By one hundreds.

Alternates:

inumnuŋpa,	Every second one.
iyamnimni,	Every third one.
itobtopa,	Every fourth one.
iwikcemnamna,	Every tenth one.

Limits:

nuŋblala,	Only two (-la suff.).
tanum,	His two.
tanumnum,	In two sets.
numkiya,	In two different ways, places.

Ordinals:

tokeya,	1st.
inuŋpa, (w)icinuŋpa,	2nd.
iyamni, (w)iciyamni,	3rd.
itopa, (w)icitopa, etc.	4th.
iwikcemna, iciwikcemna,	10th.
iwikcemna yamni, etc.	30th.
iyopawiŋge,	100th.
iake yamni,	13th.
wikcemna yamni iake yamni,	33rd.
opawiŋge sam iake yamni,	103rd.

nut, n. Yuȟugapi. Uta, n. Hazel- , acorn.

O

oar, Cf. paddle.
oath, Yugalkiya, v.a. Administer an -.

obey, v.a. Anagoptaŋ, anoŋgoptaŋ; anakigoptaŋ, v. pos.; waanagoptaŋyaŋ, adv. Obediently.

object, v. Waciŋyeyeśni, - to, lose hope in. Yaśkiśka, v.a. Raise -ions to.
oblique, Kaoḣmiŋ, v. Move -ly. Oḣya, adv. -ly, slanting: yu- , adv. -ly.

obscure, adj. Ookaḣniḣteḣike,
observe, (keep). Iwaŋyaŋka, v.a.: -pi, n.; owaŋyeye, n. Place to - . Wosukiye, n. Observance (of law).

obstacle, n. Wowicagi. Yuhotapi s'e, adv. Removing -es.
obstinate, (opiniated). Okiwaś'ag śica, adj. Waektaŋjaśni, adj. Wanting docility. Wakilkitaŋyaŋ, adv. -ly.

obstruct, (prevent). Uŋc'oŋnilya, v.a. Prevent, disarm; adv. Prevented. Woikuśe, n. Obstacles.
obtrusive, Cf. fringe. Paswuic'igle, v. Be - , important.

obvious, adj. Ookaḣniḣwaśte.
occupy, (occupation, job; busy). Kcaŋptepte, adv. (in thought). Ośkiŋc'iye, n. Occupation; ośkiŋic'iya, v.n. Busy self; wośkiŋciye, n. Occupation, work.

odd, Iyuśna, n. One with no mate.
odor, n. Wowaśtemna, A pleasing - .

offend, v.a. Iyoyaka, Displease, make sick of. Okic'unica, v.n. Be made angry. Śigla, v.n. Take offense at.

offer, v. Wagluḣtata, - own; wakicigluḣtata, v. - a price, a sacrifice for. Wauŋye, n. Act of -ing: -kiya, v. Make -s to. Wowicak'upi, n. -ing.

often, adv. Ijehaŋ: -yaŋ, -yaŋkel. Otakiya, adv. (place, time, manner).

oil, Cf. grease. Wiglizazecala, n. Floating droplets of - .
ointment, (oil, grease, salve). Sla, n.: i-ye, n.; -ojuha, n. Oil bag.

old, Akaŋ, v.n.; kaŋhi, v. Live to be - ; okaŋ, n. -age; okaŋke, adv. At -age, at the last; -tehaŋ, v.n. Bear -age well. Tanika, adj.; taŋni, adj. Worn-out; adv. Of - , already, before; wataŋni, n. - things.

omit, (let alone). Agluśtaŋ, v. pos.

on, (upon, at). A, prep. insep., prefix. Akaŋ(l), prep.: i- , prep.; i-akataŋhaŋ, adv. Ata, prep. suff. Auŋyaŋ, v.n. Be - , over. Iyagletoŋ, v.a.: -yaŋ, adv. Óstaŋ, prep. On, at; adv.: -haŋ, part. Being on, at.

once, Cf. waŋji. Toŋwel, adv. - upon a time. Ehaŋni, adv. Waŋca, adj., adv. num.: -eś, adv. At - ; -g, -gna, -yeś, -keś; -gcala, adv. - in awhile; -ḣci, adv. For, just, at least - ; -caleśa; -kcala, adv. Only - in awhile, seldom; -la, adv. Only - .

one, Cf. number. Waŋji, adj.: -ca, adj.; adv. In - way; -gji, adv. - a-piece, some; -gjila, adv. -by- , singly; -la, adj.; -pila, v. They are - ; -lakel, adv. In one manner; -lakiya, adv.; -toktok, adv. - after the other, in turns.

only, Cf. alone.
ooze, (supperate). Au, v.n. Sli, v.n.: na- , v.n.; na-ya, adv. Śli, v.n. - out: na- , v.n. Óstaŋhaŋ, v.n. - out. Otoŋyaŋ, adv.; toŋyaŋ, v.n.

open, Blaga: ama- , v.n.; iyublaḣ, v. (tent). Kablaya, v. (eyes): o- , adv. Free, level. Anablaza(s), v.a. Glubleca, v. pos. Gaŋ, gaŋgaŋ, adj.: ayu- , v.a.; glu- , v. pos.; ka- , v. Spread out; kiyu- , v. - for; pa-ya, v. Make - , part with; pa-yaŋ, adv. -ing, parting with; ya- , v.a. (by mouth); yu- , v.a. (door). Gata: aglu- , v. pos.; gal- , adv.; kiciyu- , v. - out (hand). Hloka: ayu- , v.a.; iglu- , v. refl.; oyuḣloke, n. An aperture; wiyuḣloke, n. An opener, key. Kajahaŋ, v. Press - ; kajaka, v. Squeeze - ; Glujaka, v. pos.; inajalyeya, v. Aikapa, v.a.; icapa, v. Kawa: aglu- , v. pos.; ayu- , v.a.; iglu- , v. pos.; ka- , v. Make - ; wapa- , v. - out. Kpi, adv. Breaking - . Naśakayela, adv. (wound). Yuogna icu, v. (gun). Naoko, v.n. Split. Anapopa, v.a. Taŋiŋyaŋ, adv. -ly, unconcealed. Iyuwicola, adj. (sore); n. Bandage. Zamni: aka- , v.a.;

aya- , v.a.; ayu- , v.a.; kiyu- , v. - to, for; gla- , v. pos.; na- , v. - by foot; yu-yaŋ, adv.

opinion, La, laka, v.a. Form, have an - of. Waciŋyuza, v. Have an - . Wayacocoka, n. One giving ever his own opinion. Kitaŋ, v.n. Be opiniated, obstinate.

opportune, Ecekce, ecelkce, express. Kehaŋl: co- , adv.; etu- , adv.

oppose, Cf. stop. Pajiŋ: kici-pi, They - each other; ki- , v. Stand up against. Paesya, adv. Against.

opposite, (across). Akasaŋpa, adv.: -taŋhaŋ, adv. Akokab, adv. Hoopta, adv. Icitkokib, adv. Iyotatkoŋs, adv. - to, against, even: ic- , adv.; iciyotatkoŋza.

oppress, Oiyuskilya, adv. -ed in.

optative mood, Cf. subjunctive. Toke, particle in comp., I suppose of course; toki. Toke eśa...ni, I wish I; toke...laka, I wish that; toke... ni, Oh that; tokiŋ...ni; toke...so? Did you really want...?

or, conj. Naiŋś.
order, (get done; arrangement). Kaȟśi, v. Place an -. Kaskiglag, v. Spread without - . Wawahoya, v. abs. - things: -pi, n. Things -ed (by mail); wiwahoye, n. An - .

ornament , Cf. jewelry. Ska: o-pi, n. -al work; wo- , n. -al work; woyu-, n. Owiŋ, v.n. Have - on - ; n. Pegnakapi, n. Hair - . Wakikśukśu, v. Hang -s on own. Wamuȟ'a, n. Cowry shell. Wasuhula, n. Necklace Iroquois; wasula. Wawoslata, n. Bone beads. Wicicaśke, n. Strips worn over shoulders and trailing.

orphan, n. Wablenica.
oscillate, (vibrate). Ogluhomnimni, v.a. (turn). Yupsoŋpsoŋ, v.a. (as in sprinkling).

other, adj. Uŋma, umaŋ, The one...the other: -ciyataŋ, adv. From the - side; -gma, adj. One or the - . Itokaŋl,adv.

out, Kajuŋ, v. Knock, pull, fall - .

outside, adv. Akapataŋhaŋ; akabhaŋ, adj. Akaŋtuya, akaŋtuyela, adv. Akataŋhaŋ, adv. Holazata, adv. Taŋkata(l), adv. Out-of-doors, without: i- , adv.; i-ŋhaŋ, adv.; -haŋ, adv. From the - .

outstanding, (singular). Sotka, adj.
oven, n. Owaśpaŋye, Baking - .
over, Cf. beyond. Iyakapataŋhaŋ, adv.
overflow, v.n. Paśwoka: a- , apaśwog.
overlap, v.a. Yuic'ic'uya, Make - .
overload, Hukitaŋla, adv. Wok'iŋyut'eya, v.a. Woś'a, adj. -ed.

overseer, n. Wawaŋyaŋke, Policeman.
overshadow, Cf. shade.
overtake, Glega: e- , eke- , iyaki- , ki- , iyakigleȟ, v.a.

overturn, (topple). Paaglapśuŋ, adv.

own, Cf. poor. Watoŋśni, v. - nothing. Yuhapi, part. -ed, held.

ox, n. Pteokicaśka, pteakicaśka, Workoxen; ptetawanap'iŋ, n. Ox-yoke; ptewak'iŋ, n. Work-oxen.

P

pace, v.n. Onaś'o.
pack, (bundle, carry, luggage, order). Kaot'iŋza, v. - tight; naot'iŋza, v. Kic'iŋ, v. - own; kicic'iŋ, v. Carry; wahekic'uŋ, v. pos. - own; wak'iŋ, n. Baggage: -pi, n. A pack. Oiyaȟpeye, n. Horse - . Opaȟte, n. -age, bundle, bunch, bale; pakiȟta, v. pos. Tie up own, - up. Owotaŋ, v. Ram in; wopuskica, v.a. Ram tight. Waheyuŋ, v. - in a bundle.

paddle, v. Watopa(e), - a canoe: -pi, n. Rowing; i-kiya, n.
page, n. Oyublaye (book).

pain, (hurt). Kazaŋ, v.a. Yazaŋ, v.n. Feel - : -gla, v.n. Be touchy.
paint, Cf. write. Owa, v.a. Tiisaŋye, n. Wi(ŋ)yu(ŋ)piŋ, n. Wall - .

pair, n. Otawaŋjila, - of a kind; ta, adj. One of, a pair of; tatona, n. A pair; tona, n.; tawaŋji, n. One, a pair; tanuŋpa, n. Two pairs.

pan, n. Taspaŋ oŋwohaŋpi, Sauce pan.
pander, v. Wiwotikiya.

paper, n. Mniȟuha: -owapi, Blanks; -ska, Writing - .

parable, n. Wiyaciŋiapi; wiyaciŋyaŋ, adv. In parables, parabolic; wawiyaciŋ, v. Use -es. Cf. figure.

parade, n. Śuŋkaȟlowaŋpi, War - . U-c'ita au, n. July 4th - .

paralyze, v. Taŋsaŋni t'a, Be -ed on one side of the body; taŋt'at'a, adj. -ed.

parch, v.a. Papaȟya (corn, meat etc.).
parent, Cf. family. Wakihiyece, n. One who raises children.

parlor, Cf. confer. Oyake tipi.

part, (separate). Cf. some, imperfect. Zaŋ: ka-yaŋ, adv. -ing; kpa- , v. - own; yu- , v.a. Separate; pa- , v.a. (hair); pa-yaŋ, adv. Dividing; peo- , n. - in the hair; peyo-, n. Pagaŋ: kici- , v. - with for; kici-pi, v. They - with each other; kpagaŋ, v. - with own; -yahaŋ, part. Ready to - with. Kpapta, v. Leave own, - with one's company. Okise, n. - of; oŋśpa, n. Opa, v.a. Take - in. Peyohaŋ(la), n. Line at the part.

particles, Cf. according to each purpose to which they are put.

particular, (squeemish). Wayuskica, n. A very - person.

Paschal Lamb, n. prop. Tawohiyayewicawote; Wicawotapi, n. prop.

pass, (over, by etc.). Abluhehahaka, v. - over quickly. Acaŋkśiŋ: -ya, v.a.; -yaŋ, adv.; acaŋkuya, acaŋkkukiya, v. Gligla, v.n.: wi- , v. Come and - by. Hiyaya, v.n. Icic'uya, adv.; Inaśloka, v. Inapiska, v. (time). Iyopta, v. - through; iyoptiyeya, v. - through. Kinapa, v. - through. Kiyaglapta, v. - over; kiyakapta, v. - over. Pucaŋcaŋ iyaya, v. - under (stooping). Yunaya, v. - along; yunayekiya.

passionate, Waciŋkopi, n. -ness; waciŋkoya, adv. -ly.
pasture, n. Owayaśla.

patch, Pata: iyo- , v.; oki- , v.a. - on; oki-pi, n. Patchwork.
patent, n. Śa ayaskapa, - in fee.

patience, Cf. endure. Waciŋ: ta-haŋska, adj. Long-suffering; ta-haŋskeya, adv. Patiently; -ektayuza, v.n. Be fore-bearing; -taŋka, adj. Patient; - taŋk kic'uŋ, v. Have - .

pattern, Cf. network.

paw, (throw up dirt). Kawaza, v.a.; yuwaza, v.a. - the ground. Makak'ak'a s'e, adv. Wotica n. -ing, scraping.

pay, Cf. wage. Iśi, v.; iśikiciŋ, v. Iyuŋwiŋtoŋ, v. (have to -). Kicicajuju, v. Pray - for for. Yuksapi, n. Monthly -ments.

peace, Cf. gentle. Wowaȟwa, n. Okiya, v.a. Make - ; court a woman. Ablagyela, adv. -fully.

peak, (top). Pajola, n. High hill; adj. Prominent; pajoya, adv. Humped, hill-like.

pedestrian, n. Makamani.

peel, v.a. Ayugapa; yaga, v.a. - off (with teeth). Ḣlaya: glu- , v. pos.; na- , v.n. - off; owaḣlaye, n. Parings; pa- , v.a., v.n. - off; wa- , v. Pare off, circumcise; wo- , v.a. - off (shoot); ya- , v.a. (with teeth) yu- , v.a. - off. Ḣ'u: ayu- , v.a.; caŋka- , v.; gla- , v.; ka- , v. - off; wa- , v.a.; wo- , v.a. - off; ya- , v.a. (by mouth); yu- , v.a. Sku: ayu- , v.a.; gla- , v. pos.; hana- , hana-ya, v.a.; ka- , v. - off; owa- , v. - in; n. Paring; wakici- , v. - for; wa- , v.a. Shave off; yu- , v.a. - off, pare. Caŋha(pa, yu)ślotaŋhaŋ(e), v.; oślokahaŋ, part. -ing off; oślokahe.

peep, v.n. Okakiŋ, - in.
pellet, Cf. bullet, hail, seed, shot. Su, n.; sukpaŋla, n. Shot.

pen, (pencil). Mazawiyowa, n. Pen; caŋwiyowa, n. Pencil. Wicazo, n. Pen or pencil. Onatake, n. Cage.

penetrate, v.a. Paośloka.
peninsula, (plain). Iźo, n.
penniless, adj. fig. Śluśluta.
people, Cf. nation. Oyate, n.
perfect, adj. Picalake, More - than. Wowawoyuśtaŋ, n. -ion, finishing, completion.

perform, v. Oecoŋla ecoŋ, - excitedly. Wanapiśkaŋyaŋ, v. Exhibit, play.
perfume, (cosmetics). Mniwaśtemna, n. Waśtemna, adj. Sweet-smelling: -ya, v.a.

perhaps, (possibly). Naceca, adv. Okinahaŋ, okini, adv. (begins clause). Owekinaś, owekiś, adv. Lest - . Tokaś, adv. Uŋgna, adv., interj.

perish, v.n. Atakuniśni: -pica, adj. Yuwignuni(ya), v.a. Make - , destroy.
persecute, (bedevil). Teḣiyakuwa, v.a. Bedevil.
perseverance, n. Wowaciŋtaŋka.
persist, v. Ipajiŋ.
persistent, Inihaŋśniyaŋ, adv.

person, Iyuŋkala, adv. -ally. Taŋatayela, adv. Towards a - ; taŋiyatayela, adv. Individually, in - .

perspicuity, (awareness). Okitaŋiŋ, n.
perspire, v. Iglutemni; natemni, v. Nayeic'iya, v.a. refl.

persuade, Cf. convince, believe. Wicalaya, v.a. Yahahala, v.a. (by talk); yahahayela, v.a. Shake in one's purpose. Yaohiŋyaŋze, v. - to give up.
perverse, (crooked, twisted). Pemniyaŋ, adv. -ly.

pestle, n. Iwopaŋ.
pet, n. Ihaktapila.
petition, n. Wacajeyatapi.

peyote, n. Uŋḣcela: - yuta tawoḣtate, n. Gear for a - cult ceremony.

phonograph, n. Omazape.
photograph, n. Iteowapi; itoic'ikowa, v.; wicitowa, v.a.

pick, Ikpahi, v. refl. pos.; pahi, v.a. - up, collect. Paḣci, v.a. Tear, - out. Ḣpu: apa- , v.a.; pa- , v.a. - off (in small pieces); yu- , v.a. - off a piece. Icaḣniḣ, v. cont. Oyukuŋta, v. - at, in. Yuptuga, v.a. - to pieces; yuptuḣ'a. Smiŋ: aya- , v.a.; yu- , v.a. - off; yu-yaŋyaŋ, v. Swa: ya-(ka), v.a. - to pieces (with teeth); yu-ya, v. - to pieces. Iyuśpa, v. - , pluck (corn, etc.). Śpi: ayu- ,v.a.; ka- , v. (knock off); kiciyu- , v. - for; wo- , v. (berries); ya- , v.a. - off (as birds do); yu- , v.a. Gather berries. Śpu: apa- , v.a.; ayu- , v.a.; iyu- , v.a. Pluck, - (corn). Kaza, v. - to pieces; yuzaza, v. - to pieces (sinew, cloth).

picket-pin, n. Wihiŋpaspa.
picture, Cf. photograph. Itowapi, n.; wowapi, n. Cf. book. Itowapognake, n. - frame; itowapojuha.

pie, n. Taspaŋ opemnipi, tasp'opemnipi, Apple - . Wopemni, n.
piece, (parcel, part). Cf. part. Óśpe, n.
pierce, Cf. stab. Okagaya, v.a. Paḣloka, v.a.: o- , v. - in; wa- , v. Make holes in. Paoḣpa, v.a. - through Waopa, v.a. Make a hole (knife).

pile, v.a. Ahiju, aośma, ekśu. Iciglapśuŋpśuŋyaŋ, icipahaha, iciyaglaskiskiya, adv. Pahaya, adj. -ed up, prominent.

pilfer, Waicucuka, n. -er; waicucukteca, v. Become a -er. Wakaḣlaka, n. -er.
pillow, Pahiŋ: i- , v.n., n.; i-ya,

v.n.; ti- , n.

pimple, (roughness). Yuḣ'i, v.n. Be -ed, rough, chapped: o- , n. Waseyaŋka, v.n. Have a spot on the face; n.

pin, n. Heyopaśpu, hiyopatake. Ipasisa(e), v.a., n.: mak- , n. Breast - ; w- , n. Safety - ; pasisa, v.a. Pin together. Wipaspe, n. Tent pins.

pinch, v.a. Jipa: ana- , v.; apa- , wapa- , ayu- , glu- , yu- , v.a. Waiciya, v. Pinch-hit, assist.

pine, Cf. tree. Wazi, n. - tree; wazizi, n. Pieces of - ; waz'oju, n. A - timber.

pipe, n. Caŋnuŋpa: - hahiŋiyapehaŋpi, n. Pipe with stem wrapped in quills; - woslata, n. Pipe made from a hollow straight deer bone. Opagi, n. A tobacco-filled pipe. Caŋnuŋp'Ḣaka, n. A wand, imitative of the pipe. Icaśloka, n. Poker for a pipe. Iglaye, n. Pipe cleaner. Oyape, n. Mouth-piece. Pahu, n. Bowl of a pipe. Siŋte, n. Pipe stem; oagle, n. Stem insert for the bowl; oskapi, n. Ornamental work for the stem. Opagi, v.a. Fill a - ; okipagi, v. Fill a - for. Oiyaḣpeya, v. Gesture with the pipe. Wakiyuza, v. Gesture with, hold up the pipe.

pit, (dug-out). Cf. quarry. Makaok'e, n.; makok'e. Oyuze, n. (sand, etc.).
pitcher, Cf. dish.
pith, Popopa, adj. -y, fluffy.

place, (set).
akeya, v.a.
aloksohaŋ, v.a.
caŋpaslata, v. Set posts.
eekiya, v.a.
ehaŋtulaḣci, adv.
gle, v.a.: a- , v.a.; a-hiyeya, part.; ahi- , v.a.; ahiya- , v.a., v.n.; e- , v.a.; ekici- , v.; ic'i- , v. refl.; ic'i-ka, n.; eki- , v. pos.
gnaka, v.a.: ahi- , v.a.; aitagnagya, adv.; aita- , v.a.; akignaŋya, adv.; aki- , v. pos.; ao- , v.a.; e- , v.a. ic'i- , v. refl.; eki- , v. pos.; o- , v.a. - in; oki- , v. pos.
iḣpeya: a- , v.a.; eyuḣpa, v.a.; iyaḣpekiciciya, v.a.; iyaḣpekiya, iyaḣpekiya, v.a.
iyomnaya, v. - much in the mouth.
ohe, n. A niche; otahepi, adv. Between places.
aoŋ, aoŋpa, auŋ, auŋpa, oŋpa, uŋpa, v.a.: agliyaoŋpa, v.; ahiuŋpa, akioŋ, eoŋpa, hiŋyetaoŋpa.
ośtaŋ, prep. In -of: -iyotake, v.n. Take one's place; -najiŋ, v.n. glastokaŋ, v. pos.
ślokahaŋ, part. Out of - .
tuktetu kakeśkeś, adv. At most any - ; tuktetu k'eyaś, adv. In any - .
awiŋyeya, v.a.; glowiŋ, v. pos.
yagloka, v.a. Put out of - (with teeth).

plain, Cf. manifest. Blaye, n.: mako- , n.; o- , n.; oka- , n. Blablata, n. Blowaŋjila, n.

plait, v.a. Yuśki: -pi, part. -ed, gathered in folds.

plan, v. Aokiya, Mutually - . Ic'icoŋza(s), v. refl. Iglukcaŋ, v. refl.
plane, n. Caŋicajipe, caŋipajipa; caŋiyujipe, n. Draw knife.
plant, v.a. Oju: -pi, part. -ed; -ya, v.a.; o- , v. - in; okiciju, v. - for; okiju, v. - for. Cf. flower, medicine, grass, tea, chew.

plaster, n. Waaskabyapi, Adhesive; waaskape.
plateau, n. Iyoblaye.
platform, Cf. stand. Owahe, n.; owahegle.

play, v.n. Śkata: a- , v.n.; i- , v.a.; ki- , v. - to, for; kici- , n. -mate; o- , v. - in; ośkate, n. Diversion; śkalkiya, v.a. Make - ; wanapiśkaŋyaŋ, v. - with toys: a- , v.a. Ecaca, adv. Uŋ, v.a. Kicikśaŋ, v. Make love, have love-play.

playing cards, n. Kaŋsu: -kute, v. Play cards.
coka, Joker.
pezi, King.
wiŋyaŋ, Queen.
peśa, Jack.
sapataŋka, Spades.
tacaŋta, Hearts.
pestola, śapestola, Diamonds.
sapayugaga, Clubs.

plead, v. Wotiye: -kiya, v. - with for.
pleasant, Iyokipi: a- , adj.; a-ya, adv.; o- , adj. Owaśte, adj. Wholesome. Wicibleza, n. -ness (weather).

please, (pleasant). Iyokipi, v.: o- , v.n. Be -ed with; waw- , v.; waw-ya, adv. Gladly; waw-ye, n. A pleasant appearing person; opi, v. Be -ed; pila, v. Be -ed. Cf. pleasure. Ooŋśila, n., adj. Hard to - . Tokciŋciŋyaŋ, adv. As -s, anyhow; tokeciŋciŋyaŋ, tokciŋkiŋyaŋ, tokeciŋ.

pleasure, Pila, v. Be pleased: i-ye, n.
pleat, Cf. ruffle.

pledge, n. Iwakta.
plenty, n. Waota; adj. Plentiful. Yutkaŋla, adj. Much, abundant; yugela.

pliable, (limber). Yuwiŋja, v.a. Make - ; wiŋświŋjahela, wiŋświŋja, adj. Śnuŋśnuŋjela, stastala, kcaŋkcaŋla, adj. Yayala, adj. Yahuŋta, v.a. Make - (by mouth). Yapaŋpaŋ, v.a. Make - .

plot, v.a. Cokoŋ. Śilwiyukcaŋ, v. - evil.
plow, Blu, adj. Pulverized: aglu- , v. pos.; ayu- , v.a.; glu- , v. pos.; kiciyu- , v. - for; makayu- , v.

plug, (stop). Nataka, v.a. (a leak).
plunge, v. Kaśkapa, Make noise of striking water; śkabyela, adv. With a - .

plural, -pi, suff. to v., n., pron., adj., adv., prep.

pocket, n. Sicaŋopiye.

point, Pazo, v. Present: akpazo, v. pos.; a- , v.a.; ekici- , v.; eki- , e- , v.a.; kici- , v. - to for; ki- , v. - to for. Iyokaȟmi ŋ, n. - of land. Iyokiwiŋ, v. Iiŋkpata, adv. Pesto, adj. Sharp-ed; o- , n.; -la, adj. -ya, adv., adj. T'oja, adj. -less, dull; tośya, adv. Yaiyowajaśni, v.a. Speak beside the - .

poison, n. Śuŋg'ikte, śuŋkigmuŋke, wicaśakte.
poke, v.a. Paleȟlega, - a fire.
pole, Cf. tipi. Caŋwakaŋ, n. Paslata, v.a. Set a - . Hupa, n.: -heyuŋpi, -waheyuŋk'iŋpi, -waŋjila, n.

police, Cf. seize. Caŋnakseyuha, n. Guardian. Wawoyuspa, n. -man.

polish, Śluśluta: iyu- , n. -er; ka- , v. Kpamaŋ, v. - own. Pawiyakpa, v.a.

pool, n. Ble: -iyoka, -iyute, -iyośkokpa, -la, -okaȟmi.

poor, (bad). Cf. destitute. Ataŋtoŋśni, v. Hpani(ca): awa- , v.n.; oic'i- , oŋic'i- , v.n. Be - ; owa- , adj.; owa-ya, v.a.; wa- , adj.; wowa- , n. Poverty. Cola, adj. Hlogeca, adj. Kagmipi s'e, adv. Entirely - . Woh'iyaya(ka), v. Do -ly, badly. Oŋśi, adj.: -ka, adj. Destitute. Letka, adj. "Broke".

pop, (noise, crackle, snap). Popa: ka- , v. Make - : kapol, v.; na- , v. Explode. Nakpakpa, v.n. Namnumnuza, v. red. Napaȟpaga, v.n. Parch (corn); papaga, v.n. (corn). Woskapa, v.a. Make -: -pi, n. A pop.

positive, Wicakicila, adv.
possess, v.a. Yuha: a- , v.a.; gluha, v. pos.: -kiya, v.a. Ignaśkiŋyaŋ, v.n. Tawaya, v.a.; tawekiya, v.a. Make - . Tiiyupaȟ, adv. All one's belongings.

possessives. Some are formed where:
Ka becomes gla.
Pa becomes kpa.
Ya becomes gla.
Glo and gliyo are inserted.
Ta is prefixed; to is formed of ta and wo.

possible, Pica: ecoŋ- , v.; ecoŋ-ka; ecoŋ-śniyaŋ, adv.; okihi- , adj. Possibly. Cf. perhaps.

post, n. Mas'apapi caŋ, Telephone - .
postage, n. Wiciteiyaskabye, - stamp.
postcard, n. Wowapi oȟ'aŋko.

pottery, (earthen). Makacega, n. Pot. Paŋkeska, n. Crockery, China-ware.

pound, Cf. beat. Kataŋ, v. (meat): iyo- , v.a. (nail, etc.); wotaŋ, v.a. (wash): -kiya, v.a. Make - . Kaona, v. - on. Kapa, v. (meat): kapaŋ, okapaŋ. Kaśki, v. Grind; kaśkica, v. - out. Kakuka, v. - to pieces; kicakuka, v. - to pieces for. Okat'iŋza, v.a. - in tight. Woȟtaka, v.a. - with.

pour, Śtaŋ: aigla- , v. refl.; aka- , v.a.; gla- , v. pos.; ka- , v. - out; oka- , v.a. - into; okica- , v.a. - own into for; okicica- , v. - for. Kala, v. - out: a-(la), v.a.; kicicala, v. - out for. Anableca(l), v.n.

Psoŋ: ayu- , v.a.; kicipa- , v. - for; opa- , v. - out into; opapsuŋ.

pout, Cf. dispose. Aitku, adv. Ayaceya, v.a. Inap'ibiyeya, inap'ip'iyeya, v.a. Iwośo, n.: -ka, adj.;ikiya, v. Ohiŋyaŋ, v. Waciŋko, adj. -ing.

powder, Blu, adj. Fine, as - : -yela, adv. Caȟli, n. Gun- .

power, (nature, being). Ouŋye, n.: -kiya, v.a. Cause to have - over, to rule; -ya, v.a. Give - to. Ś'ake(ca), adj. Mighty, -ful: towa- , n. His - , strength; wowa- , n. Strength. Takuśkaŋśkaŋ, n. (philosophy) - setting in motion. Sicuŋ(pi), n. Holder of - ; śicuŋ, wasicuŋ, waśicuŋ. Cf. tuŋkaŋ. Toŋ, n. An endowed or communicable spiritual quality, a manifestation of the presence of - . Wanape icage yuha, v. Have - over all; wanapicageyuza, n. Domination. Waŋbligleśka, n. p. Epitome of - of the north; Waziya, n. p. - proper to the north. Wookihi, n. Ability.

prairie, Tiiȟeyapaya, adv. Out on the - .

praise, Taŋ: aigla- , v. refl.; aya- , v.a.; gla- , v. pos.; igla- , v. refl. iitkopataŋhaŋ, adv. (iitkob); kiciya- , v. - for; ya- , v.a. Speak well of. Onihaŋ: aya- , v.a.; gla- , v. pos.; igla- , v. refl.; iglu- , v. refl.; iyokinihaŋ, adj.; kiciya- , v. - for; yu- , v. Treat with attention. Caś'aya, v. - one's bravery. Glazuŋta, v. pos.: i- , v. refl. Ikiciyuśkiŋ, v. Ilowaŋ, v.a. Iwocajeyalya, v. Wawitoŋpa, v.; -pi, n.

prance, v.a. Śkeheya, Make - about, Make wild.

prank, (caper). Oȟ'aŋhaŋhaŋ, v.n. Play a - . Waiciȟaȟa, n. -ster. Cf. insolent.

pray, v. Cekiya: -ya, v., adv.; ewa- , v.; eya - , v. ph.; i- , v.a.; cekiciya, v.; owa- , v. - in; waceic'iya, v. refl. - within self; wicekiye, n. -er card, a printed -er; wacekiya, v.; wocekiye, n. -er.

precede, (ahead, before). Kaitokab, adv. Ahead of.

precipitate, v. Wosloton śni, Be - , careless.

precocious, adj. Koyanuŋ, owicaȟkokela.

predict, v. Waayata, Foretell, guess.

prefer, v. Akiic'iya, v. refl.

prefix:
a , On.
e , They - .
i , To, for, on; about, on account of.
k , (to "p") Makes pos. of the v.
ka , Strike.
na , By foot, with speed or motion.
o , In, into; for purpose of; makes verbs into nouns.
oki , Through the middle.
pa , Push, pull, rub, press.
ta...(pi), His, hers, its, theirs.
wa , (to adj.) Makes into v.a.
(to n.) Makes into a general n.
(to v.) Makes into a n. agent.
Makes into a v. i. or abs.
w(i), (to v.) Makes into a v. abs.
wic(a), (to v.) Makes into v. col. pl.
(to adj.)(to n.) Makes into a n. ref. to humans.
wo , (to v.) Shoot, punch, pound, blow.
ya , (to v.) By mouth, bite, talk.
(to adj., n.) Makes into v. , meaning to speak of as such, making so with the mouth. Gla, is pos.
yu, (to v.) Pull, handle.
(to adj., n.) Makes into v. of causation. Cf. following page at the bottom for words whose meanings are altered some by one or more prefixes. They are listed thus, because with some understanding of prefixes one is able to assign to a word its more proper meaning, according to context.

pregnancy, Hokśi:-hiyukiya, v. Abort; -hiyuya; -ikpignaka, v. Be pregnant; -kaga, v. Beget; -ksuya, v. Travail, be in childbirth; -yuha, v. Give birth. Igluś'aka, v. refl. Be pregnant. Tamni, n. Womb, afterbirth. Toŋ, v. Bear: -pi, Birth; kici- , v. Bear, have a child.

prepare, v. refl. Aigluza. Piya: apikiya, v.; piic'iya, v. - self; wapikiyece śni, adv. With self well -ed. Iglusuyakel, adv. Igluwiŋyeya, v. refl. Iśitutece śni, adv. With self well -ed. Loliȟ'aŋ, v. - food. Owaŋkkaga, v. - a place. Yusu(ya), v.a. To ready; wo- , n. Preparations.

prescribe, v. Pejuta icuśi, - a medicine.
present, v. Oyaŋka, Be - in. Waciŋksapa, adj. Having presence of mind. Woḣeyaka, n. Gifts.

preserves, Śtagya, v.a. Make - .
president, n. Cf. chief.

press, Gnaśkiŋyaŋyaŋ, v.n. red. Skica: agla- , v.a.; aglu- , aka- , akigla- , apu- , apuskil, ayu- , gla- , ica- , v.; icaskice, n.; ayuśkica; iyagla- , v.n.; iyaglaskilya, v.a.; iyuśkica, v. Wring; ka- , v. - down; nakipu- , v. - together; na- ; naśkica, v. - out; opu- , v.a. - down in; oyu- , v.a. - out (juice); paipu- , v.a. - down; pakipu- , v.n. Be -ed tight together; paopu- , v.a. - down into; pa- , v. - on; paśkica, v. - out; puśkica; -haŋ, part, -ed down, close; wa- , waskita, v.a. - out with a knife; wo- , v.; yakipu- , v.a. - close together (by mouth); yukipu- , v.a. - close together. Wiyuskite, n. A press. Sli: ipa- , v.a.; ipa-ya, v.a., adv.; wa- , v.a. - out by knife. Inataŋ, v.a. Apat'a, v.a. Iyapat'o, v.n. Be cramped in: -yakel, -yela, adv. T'iŋza(s): aka- , v.n.; ana- , v.a.; aoka-ya, adv.; aoka- , v.a.; ao-ya, v.a., adv.; apa- , apu- ; a- , v.n.; na- , v. - hard (by foot); pao- , v.a. - in tight. Apauŋka, v.a. Apawiŋja, v.a. Wota, v. - against: - iyeya, v. Blow off; ahi- , v.

pressure, n. Wopat'iŋze.

pretend, (pretense). Aiic'ila, v. refl. Ecaecoŋka, ecahecoŋka, v. Iyayekiya, v. Koŋza, v. Wawaheye śni, adv. -ing.
prevaricate, v.a. Yagalgata.

prevent, Cf. obstruct. Ikuśic'iya, v. refl.; oiyayeśilya, v. - leaving. Inapteca, v.n.; iyanapta, v.a. Pajiŋ, v.: i- , v.n.; i-yaŋ, adv. Iyanica, v.n.; oiyanica, v.n. Be -ed. Iyapat'oya, v.a. Iyokiśni, v. Nikiya, v.a. Stop. Okit'eya, v.a. Pakaŋ, v.n.

previous, (former). Cf. before. Toka kiŋ hehaŋna, adv. At the first.

price, Cf. sell.
prick, Icama(e), v.n.: -ca, v.n.; -ya, adv. Pajipa(e), v.a. Sting: i- , v.a.; ipajipe, n. Pakpikpi, v. - holes in.
prickle, (sharp, knobby). Apaga, v.n.: -ya, v.a. Nasaya, adv.

priest, n. Wicaśa wakaŋ, A holy man. Wauŋyaŋpi itaŋcaŋ, n. High - . Wośnakaga, wośnapikaga, n.

print, v. Mazaagliheya.
prison, (jail). Kaśka(e), v.a. Imprison: wo- , n.; owica- , n. Waaka, n. -er of war.

<u>Prefixed Words</u> (words, roots, stems): wa- waableza etc. Cf. prefix.

ableza
acaŋkśiŋ
acaŋze
agla
aglaheya
agli
ahaŋnajiŋ
ahiŋḣpaya
ahotaŋka
aia
akaga
akaḣpa
aki
akiktoŋja
akinica
akita
aku
anagoptaŋ
anaic'ipta
anakicigoptaŋ
anakikśiŋ

anapta
anataŋ
anica
aokiyapi
apa
ape
asniyaŋ
as'iŋ
aśapa
aśluśluta
aś'aka
atoŋwaŋ
awaciŋ
awaciŋyaŋ
awaŋglaka
awaŋyaŋka
aya
ayaśkaheyela
ayaśtaŋ
ayupta
ayuta

aziltoŋ
blaska
blaya
blaza
bleca
caŋḣiŋyaŋ
caŋśilya
caŋteśica
caŋteśilya
caŋtiyokiśica
caŋtognaka
caŋtokpani
caŋzeya
cape
caśtoŋ
cekiciciya
cekiya
cet'uŋgla
cet'uŋglaya
ceya
coka

cokoŋ
cok'iŋ
conica(ka)
cosya
cutic'iŋ
ecakioŋ
ecoŋ
ekignaka
ekiya
eya
eyaku
gliyoya
gluha
gluza
gnaka
gnaśkiŋyaŋ
gnayaŋ
guguya
guya
ha
haŋpi

hiyo
hiyohi
hiyu
hocoka
hoḣpi
hośi
huḣniye
hute
Ḣa
Ḣca(Ḣca)
Ḣla(Ḣla)
Ḣna
Ḣpaŋyaŋ
Ḣugnaḣya
Ḣuḣnaḣya
Ḣwa(ka)(la)
Ḣwakiya(kel)
Ḣwaya
Ḣ'uŋt'eya
icaga
icaḣya

prize, n. Wookiye, Merit. Ok'ipe, n. A wager, what is staked.

probable, Iteyakel, adv.
probation, n. Wowiyuta^{n}pi.
probe, v.a. Pakota: pakote, n. Pazi, v.a. - into.

proclaim, v. Eyapaha; n. ; ieyapaha, v., n. Iglaota^{n}ni^n, v. refl.; wayaata^{n}ni^n, v. Make manifest.
produce, Cf. grow. Oicaḣya, v.a. Yield, make grow; woicaḣye, n.

profess, v. Waka^{n}nic'ico^{n}ze, - faith.
prolong, (protract). Wayuteha^{n}nha^{n}ka, v.
prominent, Cf. pile. Pahaya, adj. Projecting. Wocas'aya, n. Noteworthy thing: -kel, adv. -ly, very famous.

promise, v.a. Wahoya, - to: i- , v.a.; iwahokiciyapi, v. pl. Tawaci^{n}nkito^{n}nya^n, adv. Holding great promise. Waokiye, n. Yugalic'ico^{n}za, v. - under oath.

prompt, Iś'oś'oka, n. A - person; iś'oś'oya, adv. Itab, adv.

prone, Pamaglela, adv.
proof, Oblula, adj. Weather- .
prop, v.a. Paza, - up bushes (for shelter).
proper, Ececa, v.n. Be - : yu-, v.a. Make do -ly. Yusu, v.a. Make - . Yuecetu, v.a. Make - .

property, (possessions). Woha, woyuha, n.
prophet, n. Waayate, wayaata^{n}ni^n.

proposition, n. Woiwa^{n}nya^{n}nke, A fair - .
prosper, v. Ita^{n}nya^n.
protect, v.a. Awa^{n}nya^{n}nka: wo- , n. -ion.
protrude, v.n. Naglake; naglaglake s'e, adv.

proud, adj. Gu^{n}nga: -gaya, adv. Igluwa^{n}nkatuya, v. refl. Ita^n, v.n.: -pi, n.; -ta^n, v. red.; -ta^{n}npi, n.; -ta^{n}nya^n, v.n.; wita^n, v. Be - , vain: -ta^{n}nka, n. A - person; -ta^{n}nya, n. Vainglory; -ta^{n}nya^n, adv. Glorying. Iwah'a^{n}nic'ila, v. refl. Kas'ala, v. Put on airs; okas'ayakel, adv. Stu, adj.: -ic'ila, v. Be - . Wamnaic'ila, v. Be - of own: -pi, n. Pride. Yagopa, v.a. fig. Make feel - by talking.

prove, v. pos. Glasuta.
provide, (provisions). Agluha, v. pos.; aigluha, v. refl. Lol'ijicayakel, adv. Having many provisions; lol'iyuca^n, v. Be low on provisions; lol'opeto^n, v. Buy provisions. O^{n}nweya, n. Provisions; u^{n}nweya. Wagle, n. Provisions. Wiic'igni, v. - for self.

provoke, v.a. Hi^{n}nya^{n}nsya. Iwakuwa, v.a.; iwawikuwa, v.a. Kamata, v. - resistance.
prudence, Aiyaci^{n}nya^n, adv.

Prefixed Words: wa-

icaḣyapi	kabu	kaḣpa	kapa	kasna
iciya	kalu	kaḣpu	kapa^n	kasni
icu	kaga	kaḣuga	kapemni	kasota
ielgle	kagege	kaḣ'u	kapesto	kasto
iglusta^n	kagi(ya)	kaile	kapeya	kaswu
iḣpeya	kagmigma	kajaja	kapopa	kaśeca
ikceya	kagmiya^{n}nya^n	kajipa	kapota	kaśeya
ileya	kagmu^n	kajuju	kapsaka	kaśicahowaya
ipila	kahi^{n}nḣpeya	kaka^n	kapsica	kaśipa
iśkahu	kahi^{n}nta	kakca	kapsi^{n}npsi^{n}nta	kaśka
iśteca	kahoho	kaki^{n}nca	kapso^n	kaśkica
iyapat'oya	kahomni	kakiśya	kapśu^n	kaśkokpa
iyape	kahu^n(hu^{n}nza)	kakpa^n	kapta	kaśkopa
iyatagle	kaḣapa	kaksa	kaska	kaśleca
iyekiya	kaḣepa	kakśa	kaskepa	kaśloka
iyeya	kaḣla	kakśi^n	kaskica	kaśluta
iyu^{n}nga	kaḣleca	kakśija	kasleca	kaśna
kabla	kaḣliḣli	kakta^n	kasli	kaśpa
kablapi	kaḣliya	kakuka	kasloha^n	kaśtaka
kablaza	kaḣloka	ka^{n}nyeja	kasmaka	kaśta^n
kableca	kaḣniga	kaoḣpa	kasmi^{n}nya^{n}nya^n	kaśuja

prune, (pare). Caŋakaŋsmiyaŋ, v. Wakipta, v. pos. Trim own. Cf. cut.

pry, Cf. twist. Opatica, v.a.

pucker, v.a. Oyagi, Make wrinkle, fold up.

pudding, Wokija, v. Make hasty - for.

puff, Cf. bulky. Paŋja, adj. -ed up. Popo, v.n. - out, swell.

pull, Titaŋ, v. - to: aglu- , pos.; akiyu-pi, v. pl.; ayu- , v.a.; iyu- , v. - by; na- , v.a. (brace feet for). akagal, adv. Zica: ana- , v.a.; ayu- , v.a.; iglu- , v. refl. Śloka: apa- , v.a.; ayu- , v.a.; ona- , v.a. - off in; ya- , v.a. - out (with teeth); yu- , v.a. - off, out. Pśuŋ: aya- , v.a.; ayu- , v.a.; ica- , n.; kiciyu-, v. Extract for. Ayasku, v.a. Ayuguka, v.a. Ayuslohaŋ(e), v.a.: -laka, v. Ayusluta, v.a.; ayasluta, v.a. - out (with mouth). Ayuśluta, v.a. Ayuśpu, v.a.; yuśpu, v.a. - off (by hand). Ayut'iŋs, v. Gluceka, v. pos. Gluga, gluḣpa, gluḣ'u, glujiŋca, v. pos. Huyukśa, adv. Iyusna, v. - out. Ḣpa: oyu- , v.a. - down in; ya-, v.a. - down (by mouth); yuo- , v.a. - through and into. Yauŋka, v.a. - down (by mouth). Yuakaŋ, v. - out, lift out. Yuakaŋl icu, v. - up from. Yuceka, v.a. - in vain. Yugmica, v.a. - one's hair. Yujuju, v.a. - to pieces, to void. Yukikike, v.a. - over and down. Yutuka, v.a. Destroy (furs). Yuuŋzi, v.a. - backwards.

pulpit, n. Owahokoŋkiye.

pulverize, (rub, mill, make fine). Kpaŋ, adj. Fine: iyu- , v. Mill; ona- , v. - fine in; wopaŋ, v.a. Blu, adj. Fine: ka- , v. Pound fine, powder; na- , v.a. (by foot); pa- , v.a. Flatten. Katutka, v. Apawaga, v.a. (by hand).

pump, Cf. water. Mniyutaja, n.: -pi, n. -jack. Nahomni, v.a. (by foot).

punch, v.a. Awobleca, awoḣlece, awoḣloka, awoksa, awokuka, awopta, awośla, awośleca. Kpa, adj. -ed out. Woḣloka, v.a. - a hole. Owoskica, v.a. Ram in a hole. Wokaŋ, v.a. - off. Wośpuśpu, v. - to pieces.

pungent, Wokapa, n. - thing; kapaza: io- , v.n.; iyo- , v.; wo- , n. Pungency, a - thing.

punish, (correct). Pae, v.a. Inflict -ment. Teḣislolyekiya, v.a. Make suffer.

purchase, Okiciwaśakala, adj. Easily -ed for.

pure, (inviolate, undefiled). Ósteke-śni, adj. Skayakel, adv. Wakaśoteśni, adj. Clean, pure (virgin): -yaŋ, adv. Wotiyemnaśni, adj. Immaculate.

Purgatory, n. p. Wicayuskapi.

purge, v. Kajo.

Prefixed Words: wa-

kaś'aka
katata
katepa
katica
katiŋ
katka
katkuga
katkuŋza
katoto
katuka
katutka
kat'a
kat'iŋza
kauŋka
kawega
kawignuni
kawiŋja
kazaŋ
kase
kazoŋta
kceya

kibleca
kicamna
kicignaka
kicuwa
kignaka
kiksapa
kiksuya
kila
kinica
kiŋiŋ
kipajiŋ
kipika
kitaŋ
kiyuśe
kiyuśka
kiza
kokipa
kokipeya
koŋ(la)
koyagya
koyaka

kpukpa
kśija
kśu(pi)
kta
ktaŋ
kte
koŋza
kute
kuwa
k'a
k'ega
k'iŋ(kiya)(pi)
k'u
la
lolobya
lulya
makinoŋ
manoŋ(pi)
mayal
mnayaŋ
mni

mniakaśtaŋ
nablaska
nablaye
nablaza
nableca
nabu
nacaŋcaŋ
nacekceka
naceya
nagi
nagmuŋ
nagna
nagnayaŋ
naguka
nagwaka
nahiŋta
nahoho
nahomni
nahotoŋ
nahuŋhuŋza
naḣapa

naḣci
naḣeyata
naḣla
naḣlata
naḣleca
naḣloka
naḣma
naḣpa
naḣpu
naḣtagya
naḣtaka
naḣ'oŋ
najaja
najipa
najuju
nakaka
nakaŋyaŋ
nakat'iŋ
nakiḣma
nakikśiŋ
nakoka

purpose, n. Tawokoŋze, His - , influence; n. p. The Holy Spirit. Eca, adv. -ly. Wanuŋktaśni, adv.. Not -ly.

pursue, (job, follow). Kuwa, v.a. Tapa, v.a. - one; tapeya, v.a. Go after.

push, Cf. pull. Ahipani, v. Aiyotaŋic'ila, v. refl. Akiŋyeic'iya, v. Aokpazaŋ, v.a.; opazaŋ, v.a. - into, under, interlace. Aopatica, v.a. Pahomni, v.a. - around: a- , v.a. Paslohaŋ, v.a. Shove along: a- , v.a. Apauŋka, v.a. Paśloka, v.a. Shove off: a- , v.a. Pataŋ: a- , v.a.; iyopataŋ, v. Impel; -haŋ, part. -ing against; -yaŋ, adv. Patitaŋ, v.a. - against: a- , v.a.; iki- , v.a.; ik- , v. refl.; ki- , v. - with all energy. Heyata: ayu- , v.a. - back on; wa-iyeya, v., n. Ayutokaŋ, v.a. Glaya, v.a.; iglayekiya, v. Paceka, v.a. - abruptly, stagger: i- , v.a. Ipagaŋ, v.; pagapa, v.a. - off (by hand). Kakab, v. - away: pakapa, v.a.; wa- iḣpeya, v. - out of the way. Paha, v.a. Swing, - aside, oppose, reject: o- , v. - over; paoha, v.a. - into, topple in; wa- iyeya, v. - down; yuoha, v.a. - into. Pacaŋna, v.a. (strain): -l, adv. -ed out, off; wa-l iyeya, v. - to the center. Pacokab, v. - into the midst; pacokaka, v.a. - out, empty. Paececa, v.a. Guide. Paiyapat'o, v.n. Be -ed by. Pamahel, adv. -ing in: ya-iyeya, v.a. - into the mouth. Paospa, v.a. - under. Cf. submerge. Paswu, v.a. - into. Patica, v.a. Shove, - in, into. Wapaḣli, v. - into the ground, mud. Wapat'iḣpeya, v. - out of the way. Wosli, v.a. - down in, squirt.

puss, (matter). Toŋ, n.

put, (place). Cf. place. Koyaka, v. - on clothes. Okihaŋ, v. pos. - on, wear. Gnaka: oe- , n. A putting down; okici- , v.a. - for. Śtaŋ: o- , v.a. - on, in; v.n. Be put: okici- , v.t. - in; okiciyu-śtaŋ, adv. Placing one in another; oki- , v. pos. - in own; oyu- , v.a. - one into another, to cork. Ooŋpa, v. Place in.

putrid, Waḣuŋwiŋye, v. Smell - ; wicaḣuŋwiŋ, n. Purtifaction.

Prefixed Words: wa-

naksa	naśica	okicaḣniga	pagnaśkiŋyaŋ	pakiza
nakseya	naśipa	okihi(ka)(ya)	pagnayaŋ	pakota
nakśija	naśkica	ok'u	pago	pakpa
naktaŋ	naśla	oŋspe	pagoya	pakpi
nakuka	naśleca	oŋspekiya	pagweza	paksa
namna(ka)	naśloka	oŋśila	pahi(pi)	pakśija
naoḣpa	naśnija	oŋtoŋyaŋ	pahiŋl	paktaŋ
naoksa	naśośa	ośtegla	pahoho	pak'ega
naoktaŋ	naśpa	oyataŋ	pahomni	pak'eza
naot'iŋza	naśpu	oye	pahotoŋ	pamaŋ
napa	naśuja	pa	pahuŋhuŋza	pamima
napaŋ	nataka	paaglapśuŋyaŋ	paḣci	panini
napca	nataŋ	pablaska	paḣeya	paogluta
napobya	natepa	pablaya	paḣlagaŋ	paoksa
napognaka	natica	pablaza	paḣleca	paospa
napoḣya	natipa	pableca	paḣloka	paot'iŋza
napopa	natitaŋ	pablu	paḣpa	paowotaŋ
napota	natuka	pabu	paḣpu	papa
napsaka	nat'a	pacaŋcaŋ	paḣta	papaḣya
napoŋ	nawega	pacaŋnal	paḣuga	papopa
naptuja	nawiŋja	paceka	pajaja	papsaka
nasa	nica	paeze	pajiŋ	papsoŋ
naslata	nikiya	pagaŋ	pajipa	paptuja
nasleca	niyaŋ	pagapa	pajuju	papuza
nasna	noŋḣkatiyece	pageya	pajuŋ	paska
nasni	o	pagmigma	pakatiŋ	paslata
naśapa	ohola	pagmiŋyaŋyaŋ	pakca	pasleca
naśeca	okala	pamguŋ(pi)	pakiŋta	pasmaka

Prefixed Words:

wa-

pasmiŋyaŋyaŋ
pasnoŋ
pastaŋka
paśkica
paśkiśka
paśkokpa
paśleca
paśna
paśpa
paśpu
paśuja
paś'aka
pata
pataŋka
patapi
patica
pat'iḣpeya
pat'iŋza
pawaga
pawega
pawiŋja
pawiŋta
pazaŋ
pazo
pehaŋ
pemni(yaŋ)
pesto
pila
ptecela
puskepa
puspa
pustaka
pusya
putaka
saŋyaŋ
slaya
sleca
slipa
slohaŋ
slolya
soŋ
spaŋla
spayeic'iya
śaśte
śiḣtiŋ
śilḣ'aŋ
śiŋ
śipa
śloya
śnija
śniśya
śpaŋka
śpaŋkiya
śpaŋśni
śpaŋyaŋ
śtulya
śtuśteya
śuta
tage
takpe
tapa
tawat'elya
teślagkitoŋ
tka
tokapa
tokicoŋ
tokiyopeya
tokśu(pi)
totoya
tuka
tuŋgya
uŋ
uŋca(la)
wabla
wablaza
wableca
wagapa
wagna
wagṅayaŋ
wago
wagweza
waha
wahokoŋkiya
wahoya
wahuŋ
wahute(la)
waḣlagaŋ
waḣlaya
waḣleca
waḣloka
waḣpaniya
waḣ'u
wajuju
wakipajiŋ
wakoŋta
wakpaŋ
waksa
wakta(ka)
waktaŋ
wak'eza
wamna(la)
wapesto
wapota
wapsaka
wapta
waptecela
wasku
wasmiŋ
waśilkigla(ya)
waśkita
waśla
waśloka
waśpa
waśpu
watakuniśni
watepa
wat'a
wayuśna
weceya
wicekiya
wigni
wiḣpeya
wiḣ'aŋ(ka)
wiśteca
wiśtelya
witkoya
wiwahoya
wiyaciŋ
wiyaksapa
wiyape
wiyohi(ya)
wiyopekiya
wiyuŋga(pi)
wiyuta
woblaya
woblaza
wobleca
woblu
woceka
woc'o
wogna
wognaśkiŋyaŋ
wognayaŋ
wohaiyeya
wohiŋta
wohoho
wohuŋhuŋza
woḣci
woḣiŋyaŋ
woḣloka
woḣmiŋ
woḣpa
woḣtaka
wojaja
wokicaḣniga
wokpaŋ
woksa
woktaŋ
wokuka
wopaŋ
wopemni
wopota
wopsaka
wopta
wosleca
wosni
wosota
wośla
wośloka
wośna
wośpa
wośuja
woś'aka
wotakuniśni
wotiyekiya
wot'a
wot'iŋza
wowega
woyaka
yaaślaya
yablaska
yablaya
yablaza
yableca
yableza
yablu
yacaŋcaŋ
yacaśkeśkeke
yacekceka
yaceya
yacik'ala
yaciscila
yacoco
yacoza
yaececa
yaga
yagapa(pi)
yagica
yagla
yaglakiŋyaŋ
yagloka
yagmigma
yagmiyaŋ
yagnayaŋ
yahaiyeya
yahiŋta
yahoho
yahomni
yahotoŋ
yahuŋhuŋza
yaḣapa
yaḣci
yaḣepa
yaḣeyata
yaḣla
yaḣleca
yaḣloka
yaḣpa
yaḣpu
yaḣtaka
yaḣuga
yaḣugnaga
yaḣwa
yaḣ'aŋhike
yaḣ'u
yaiḣa
yaiiyowaja
yaijena
yainaḣni(ya)
yainila
yaiśteca
yajaja
yajata
yajipa
yajo
yajuju
yakaka
yakapa
yakatiŋ
yakawa
yakiza
yakokoka
yakoŋta
yakpaŋ
yakpi
yaksa
yaksapa
yakśaŋ
yakśija
yaktaŋ(yaŋ)
yakuka
yak'ega
yak'eza
yak'oga
yamima
yamna
yamnuga
yaohiŋyaŋze
yaoḣ'aŋko
yaoksa
yaoktaŋ
yaonihaŋ(yaŋ)
yaotaŋiŋ
yapa
yapemni
yapesto
yapiŋspiŋzece
yapopa
yapota
yapsaka
yapsica
yapsoŋ
yapśuŋ
yaptaŋyaŋ
yaptecela
yaptuja
yaskapa
yaskepa
yaskica
yaskita
yasku
yasleca
yaslohaŋ
yasluta
yasmiŋ(yaŋ)
yasna
yasni
yasota
yaspaya
yastaŋka

yasto
yasu
yasuta
yasuya
yaswaka
yaśapa
yaśica
yaśigla
yaśiḣtiŋ
yaśipa
yaśka
yaśkaŋśkaŋ
yaśkica
yaśkiśka
yaśkokpa
yaśkopa
yaśla
yaśloka
yaśna
yaśpa
yaśpi
yaśpu
yaśuja
yatakuniśni
yataŋ
yataŋiŋ
yataŋka
yatata
yatawaciŋhiŋ-yaŋza
yatehaŋ(haŋ)
yatepa
yatitaŋ
yatkaŋ
yatkekiya
yatko(u)ŋza
yatogtogya
yatokaŋ
yatokeca
yatuka
yat'a
yat'iŋza
yauŋka
yawa
yawakaŋ
yawaśakala
yawaśte
yawaś'aka
yawaza
yawega
yawicaka
yawicaśaśni
yawignuni
yawiŋja
yawiyakpa
yazamni
yazaŋ
yazaŋgla
yaze
yazica
yazoka
yazoŋta
yuablaya
yuaglapśuŋyaŋ
yuakiḣ'aŋ
yuakipab
yuapako
yuaśkayela
yuaślaya
yuazi
yublaska
yublaya
yublaza
yubleca
yublu
yubu
yucaŋ
yucekceka
yuceya
yucik'ala
yuciscila
yucoka(ka)
yucoya
yucoza
yuecelya
yuecetu
yueciya
yuektaśni(yaŋ)
yuga
yugaŋ
yugata
yugla
yugloka
yugmigma
yugmiyaŋyaŋ
yugmuŋ
yugna
yugnaśkiŋyaŋ
yugo
yuguka
yugweza
yuha(haka)
yuhahayela
yuhi
yuhiŋta
yuhomni
yuhuŋhuŋza
yuḣatka
yuḣepa
yuḣeyata
yuḣla
yuḣlagaŋ
yuḣlata
yuḣleca
yuḣloka
yuḣmiŋ
yuḣmuŋ
yuḣpa
yuḣpu
yuḣuga
yuḣuŋta
yuḣuŋwiŋ
yuḣ'aŋhi
yuḣ'u
yuicicahi
yuile
yuinaḣni
yuiŋyaŋka
yuiśteca
yuiyowaza
yuja
yujaka
yujiŋca
yujipa
yujuju
yujuŋ
yukakija
yukaŋ
yukapa
yukatiŋ
yukawa
yukca
yukiŋca
yukipaja
yukipehaŋ
yukiza
yukoka
yukpaŋ
yuksa
yuksapa
yukśa(la)
yukśaŋ
yukśija
yuktaŋ
yukuka
yuk'ega
yuk'eza
yuk'oga
yuk'oza
yumahel
yumaŋ
yumima
yumna
yumni
yumniga
yunajiŋ
yunaŋkeya
yuniyaśni
yuobleca
yuocikpani
yuociŋśica
yuoḣpa
yuoḣ'aŋko
yuokaḣwoka
yuokiwaŋjila
yuonihaŋ(yaŋ)
yuopteca
yuoptetu
yuoseya
yuota
yuotaŋiŋ
yuotkoŋza
yuot'iŋza
yuowotaŋ
yupaŋga
yupaŋpaŋ
yupatuja
yupcepcela
yupehaŋ
yupopa
yupota
yupowaya
yupsaka
yupsica
yupsoŋ
yupśuŋ
yupta
yuptaŋyaŋ
yuptayela
yuptecela
yuptuḣa
yuptuja
yusaŋ
yusapa
yusepa
yuska
yuskepa
yuskica
yuskita
yusku
yusleca
yuslohaŋ
yusluta
yusmiŋ
yusna
yusni
yusota
yusto(ka)
yusu
yusuta
yuswa
yuswu
yus'o
yuśa
yuśapa
yuśeca
yuśica
yuśiḣtiŋ
yuśipa
yuśka
yuśkaŋśkaŋ
yuśkehaŋ
yuśki
yuśkiśka
yuśkokpa
yuśkopa
yuśla
yuśleca
yuśloka
yuśluśluta
yuśna
yuśnaśni
yuśośa
yuśpa
yuśpi
yuśpu
yuśtaŋ(ka)
yuśuja
yuś'agya
yuś'aka
yuś'iŋś'iŋ
yuś'iŋyeya
yuta
yutaŋ
yutaŋcola
yutaŋiŋ
yutaŋka
yutaŋni(ka)
yutaŋtaŋ
yutaŋyaŋ
yuteca
yutehaŋ
yutepa
yutica
yutipa
yutitaŋ
yutkoŋza
yutkuga
yutokaŋ
yutokeca
yututa
yututka
yut'a
yut'iŋza
yuuŋka
yuwaiŋtoŋ
yuwaḣpanica
yuwaḣwala
yuwakaŋ
yuwaŋkal
yuwaśakala
yuwaśte
yuwaś'aka
yuwaś'akeśni
yuwaza
yuwega
yuwi
yuwicaka
yuwicaśaśni
yuwiŋja
yuwiŋyeya
yuwitaŋtaŋ
yuwitaya
yuwitko(ko)
yuwiyakpa

Prefixed Words: wa-

yuwoslata
yuza
yuzamni
yuzaŋ
yuze
yuzica
yuzoŋta
zilya

Prefixed Words: wa-i- which becomes: wi- wic'icage etc.

c'icage
glawa
(i)glukaŋ
(i)gni
gnu(pi)
haŋble
jicaya
jimna
kiŋca
kopa
ksapa
naḣtagye
naḣ'oŋ
najaja
nakiwizi
natake
nawizi(pi)
wahoya
waŋyaŋka
yaksapa
yanajiŋce
yape
yauŋpa(pi)
yohaŋ
yoḣi
yoḣpaya
yoḣpeya
yojaŋjaŋ
yopeya
yukcaŋ
yuŋ
yuŋga
yuśkiŋ
yuta
yuza

Prefixed Words: converted to nouns -

(Refer to People as a Group)

wica-

(a)kiḣ'aŋ
ceya
cokoŋ
gnakapi
gnaye
ka
kahiyaya
kicopi
kikcaŋpte
kini
ktepi
ktes'a
k'upi
luzahe
po
wiciśtiŋmapi*
wiciteowapi*

wico-

aie
ayuśtaŋ
bliheca
caŋlwakaŋ
caŋniye
caŋtagle
caŋtiheye
caŋtiyagleya
ekicetuye
gligle
icage
iglataŋ
inaḣni
iśtiŋme
itoŋpe
iyokiśica
iyopeic'iye
kagi(ye)
kakije
kaśke
kiciyuwaśte
kicize
kipajiŋ
kuje
mniciye
nawizi
ni
nihiŋciye
oŋwewakaŋ
śkaŋśkaŋ
śkate
ti
wicaśaśni
woglake
woyake
yutakuniśni

* wica-i- becomes: wici-

(Refer to Man)

wica-

atkuku
caje
caŋcaŋ
caŋte
caŋteoyuze
ce
ceḣpi
ceji
cepa
cesli
ciŋca
cuwita
gaŋgaŋ
hi (kage)
ho
hohu
huha
huŋku
ḣapi
ḣwa
i
iha
ksapa
leja
nape
nasu(la)
nataśloka
nite
noge
paha
pahu
paḣli
pi
poge
taŋcaŋ
wiciśta*
wicite*

wico-

caŋte
caŋteoyuze
caŋteśica
caŋtewaśte
caŋzeka
ecetu
ie
jice
jula
kaŋ
koŋze
ksapa
oŋśike
owotaŋla
suta
śice
śiḣtiŋ
ta(la)
takuniśni
takuye
tawaciŋ
teca
waciŋko
waḣwala
waśte
waś'aka
zaŋni

Prefixed Words: converting verbs to - Cf. prefix.

Verbs (of shooting etc.)
wo-

akinilya
aślaya
blaska
blaya
blaza
blu(ya)
cajeyal(ya)
ceka
ciƞ
glaka
glakiƞyaƞ
gloglo
gnaka
gnaśkiƞyaƞ
haƞ
hiƞḣpaya
hotaƞiƞ
hotoƞ
ḣaka
ḣiƞyaƞ
ḣla
ḣlagaƞ
ḣmiƞ
ḣuga
ḣ'aƞhi
ilagic'iya
ile(ya)
imagaga
itkoƞ
itoƞpeya
iyuśkiƞya
ju
jutoƞ
kaḣniga
kala
katiƞ
kibleca
kicaḣniga
kicibleca
kicic'o
kiciḣloka
kiciḣpa
kiciju
kicikpaƞ
kiciksa
kicipta
kicisni
kiciśloka
kiciśna
kiciśpa
kiciwega
kiciza
kihiƞta
kija
kikaḣniga
kiksa
kiksuyeya
kiktaƞ
kini
kinuƞkaƞ
kiƞca
kisapa
kiśla(ya)
kiśleca
kiśloka
kiśna
kiśpa
kit'a
kiya(ka)(kiya)
kpa
kpaƞ
kpi
ksa
ktaƞ
kte
kuka
k'eya
le
lota
mna
nasuƞsuƞ
ni
niya
oḣ'aƞko
oksa
ot'iƞza
pajiƞ
pemni
petoƞ
psaka
skaƞ
slohaƞ
sna
sni
sota
śpaya
śicahowaya
śitkiglaya
takuniśni
taƞiƞ
titaƞ
tkuga
tokic'oƞ
wa
waciƞyeya
waḣtelaśniya
waśagya
wot'iƞza
yaka

Nouns (substantives)
wo-

agla
agli
ahope
aḣtani
ai
aie
aiḣpeya
akage
akagege
akaḣpe
akiktoƞje
akinica
akipa
akta
aktoƞje
anagoptaƞ
anaḣma
anapta
anice
ape
asni(kiye)
aśape
atakuniśni
awaciƞ
awaƞyaƞke
ayupte
bliheca
cajeyate
caƞcaƞ
caƞḣiƞyaƞ
caƞlwaƞka
caƞniye
caƞtagle
caƞtehahayela
caƞtekaptaƞya
caƞtekiya
caƞtewaśte
caƞteiheya
caƞtkiye
caƞtognake
caƞtokpani
caƞze(ka)
cekiye
cet'uƞgla
ceye
cokoƞ
ecoƞ
ekicetu(ye)
ektoƞje
eye
gla
glakapi
gmuƞke
gnaśkiƞye
gnaye
hakakta
haƞpi
heyuƞ
hitigla
hiyaye
ḣa
ḣaka
icaƞśica
icazo
icu
ielgle
iglataƞ
igluzeze
ignu
ihakta
ihaƞble
ihaƞgye
ihaƞke
iḣa
iḣaḣa
iḣala
iḣpeye
ijajaƞ
ijica
ikope
iksape
imagaga
inaḣni
inakiwize
inape(ya)
inawizi
inihaƞ
iputake
iśtiƞme
itaƞ
itoƞpe
it'uƞgye
iwahoye
iwakta
iwapetogye
iyaksape
iyapat'oye
iyauƞpe
iyokipi
iyokiśice
iyopaśtake
iyopeye
iyotiyekiya
iyowiƞkiye
iyuƞ
iyuśkiƞ
iyutaƞke
ju(pi)
juha(la)
jutoƞ(pi)
kage
kagi(ye)
kaḣnige
kakije
kakiśye
kamna
kaslate
kasote
kaswu
kaśeya
kiciƞ
kicipasi
kicoƞze
kikcaƞpte
kiksuye
kikta
kilapi
kipajiƞ
kitaƞiƞ
kit'a
kiyuḣa
kiyuśke
kizi
kokipe
koƞ(ka)
koyake
koze
kpamni
ksape
kśije
kte
kuje
k'e
k'iƞ
lota(pi)
luzahe
mnaka
mnaye
mniciye
nagiyeye
naḣ'oƞ
na(ƞ)ke
nape
nase
nataƞ
nawizi
nihiƞciye
niya
oglake
ohitike
ohiye
ohola
oḣ'aƞko
oḣ'aƞka
okaḣnige
okihi
okitaƞiƞ
okiye

Prefixed Words: converting verbs (contin.) to Nouns.

wo-

okse
oŋspekiye
oŋśila
otaŋiŋ
oyusiŋke
ozikiye
paȟta
pakiŋte
pasnoŋ
pata
pate
petoŋ
pila(ye)

slohe
slolye
śpaye
śigla
śitkigla
śkate
takpe
taŋiŋ
waci
waciŋyaŋ
waciŋye
waciŋyuze
wahokoŋkiye

waȟtelaśni
wakoŋze
wala
wamanoŋ
wanaȟ'oŋ
wanikiye
wapetogtoŋ
wapi
wasukiye
waśpa
wawokiye
wayazaŋ
wayupike

wicake
wignu
winawizi
wiyuśkiŋ
yaśica
yataŋ
yatke
yawa
yawaśte
yukcaŋ
yuonihaŋ

yusuta
yuśice
yuśiȟtiŋ
yuśna
yuśtaŋ
yuś'iŋyaye
yutakuniśni
yutaŋiŋ
yute
yutkoŋze
yuwaśte

Prefixed Words: converting words to Verbs of -

Speaking of

ya-

ajaja
alos (fig.)
aopteca
aoptetu
apako
aślaya
ataŋiŋ
bliheca
bu
caŋzeka
ceya
cik'ala
ciscila
conala
coza
ececa
ecela
ecelya
ecetu
ecetuya
glahe(ya)
glakiŋyaŋ
gnayaŋ
gnuni
hogita
ȟapa
ȟugnaga (fig.)
ȟwa
ȟ'aŋhiya
iȟa
ijena
ikceya
ikpiska
inaȟni(ya)
inila

ipaweȟ iyeya
iśteca
iśtelya
iyowaja(śni)
iyoyaka
kakija
kaŋyela
kiyela
kokipa
konatke
kopegla
ksapa
lecakcala
lecala
lehaŋyaŋg
luzahaŋ
najiŋ
ocikpani
ocipteca
ociptetu
ogwu
oȟ'aŋko
okinihaŋ
oŋśiyakel
ota
otaŋiŋ
oteȟika
paŋpaŋla
pcecela *
pesto
pśa
suta
śica
śigla
śkaŋśkaŋ

śuśka
takuniśni(yaŋ)
taŋiŋ(yaŋ)
taŋka
taŋtaŋ
tawaciŋhiŋyaŋza
tehaŋ
tokaŋ
tokeca
t'iŋza
uŋca
waciŋko
waciŋtoŋ
waȟwaka
waȟwala
wakaŋ
waŋkal
waśakala
waśte
waś'aka
wica
wicaka
wicakeya
wicaśa(śni)
winuȟcala
wiŋyaŋ
witaya

* v.a.

Mouthing

ya-

apako
blaska
blaya
blaza
bleca
bleza
blu
caŋcaŋ
ceg iyeya
galgata
gata
ge(ge)
gmigma
gmiyaŋyaŋ
gmuŋ
hahala
hoho
huŋhuŋza (fig.)
ȟla
ȟlagaŋ
ȟmiŋ(yaŋ)
ȟmuŋ(ȟmuŋȟla)
ȟpaŋ
ikiyuta
ile
jaja
jiŋca
katiŋ(tiŋ)
kawa
kca
kipehaŋ
kśa(la)
kśaŋ
ktaŋ(ktaŋ)
ktaŋyaŋ

mima
mnumnuga
oglapśuŋ
ogmus
ot'iŋza
yapehaŋ
pemni
piza
popa
pota
powaya
pśuŋ
ptuja(ya)
puza
p'o
saŋ
ska
sla
sleca
slohaŋ
sna
sni
sota
spaya
staŋka
sto
swu
śapa
śkiśka
śkopa
ślo s'e
taŋkiŋ(yaŋ)
taŋni
tica
tkapa

Prefixed Words: converting words (contin.) to Verbs of -

Mouthing ya-	Using Teeth ya-			
tkuga	ceka	kokoka	piŋja	śla(ya)
tokaŋ	ceya	kpa	psaka	śnija
wega	coco	kpaŋ	psica	tata
wiŋśkiya	cokaka	kpi	ptecela	tepa
wiyakpa	ga	ksa	skiskita	titaŋ(yaŋ)
wosla	gweza	kśija	sku	tutka
	Ħci	kuŋtkuŋta	skuya	t'a
	Ħloka	k'ega	sli	t'aga
	Ħ'akpa	k'eza	smiŋyaŋ	wiŋja
	Ħ'aŋhike	oħloka	śiħtiŋ	
	kakiya	oksa	śkokpa	

Prefixed Words: converting words to Verbs of -

Cause

yu-

ablaya	jahaŋ	paŋga	śkokpa	waŋkala
aopteca	jaka	paŋja	śla	wasna
blaska	kaŋ	paŋpaŋ(la)	śleca	waśakala
blaya	kata	pcecela	śma	waśte
bleza	katiŋ	pe	śnija	waś'aka
blu	kca	pemni	śośa	we
caŋlwaħteśni	kiŋca	pesto	śtaśta	wega
caŋzeka	koka	piŋja	taku	wicaśa(śni)
ceħ	kpaŋ	pota	takuśni	winuħcala
cik'ala	ksa	powaya	taŋcola	wiŋyaŋ
ciscila	ksapa	psaka	taŋka(ya)	wiŋyeya
coco	kśa(la)	psica	taŋni(ka)	witaŋ
coka(ka)	kśaŋ(kiya)	pśuŋ	tawaciŋhiŋyaŋza	witaŋtaŋ
conala	kśija	ptecela	teca	witko(tko)
coza	ktaŋ	ptuja	tepa	zoŋta
ektaśni	kuka	puza	tkapa	zuzeca
gaŋgaŋla	k'eza	saŋ	tkoŋza	
gmiyaŋyaŋ	lakota	sapa	tokeca	
gmuŋ	lapa	ska(kiya)	toto(la)	
hahayela	mima	sloslo(la)	totopa	
haŋska	obleca	smismi	tuŋtuŋpa	
hoho(la)	ocikpani	sni	tuta	
hohopicaśni	ocipteca	sota	tutka	
hohoya	ocitkuŋza	staŋka	t'at'a	
hotaŋke	ocoza	sto(ya)	t'iŋza	
Ħliħli	oħlagaŋ	suta	waciŋko	
Ħloka	oko	śa	waciŋksapa	
Ħmiŋ	oŋśika	śapa	waciŋtaŋka	
Ħpaŋ	osmaka	śeca	waħpanica	
Ħwa	otaŋkaya	śica	waħwaka	
Ħ'akpa	otkoŋza	śina	waħwala	
ieska	owaŋjila	śkehaŋ(haŋ)	wakaŋ	
inila	owotaŋla	śkiśka	wanica	
itomni	pa	śkiśkeya	waŋjila	

Prefixed Words: converting words (contin.) to Verbs of -

Pulling, Pushing

yu-

aglapśuŋyaŋ
aḣwayela
ajaja
akagal
akaḣpa
akazamni
akiḣ'aŋ
akipab
akipaja
akipaś
akowapa
alosloza
aokpani
apako
asni
aśapa
aślaya
aślayela
ataŋiŋ
ataya
blaza
bleca
bliheca
bu
caŋlaśni
caŋtewaśte
caŋze
ceka
cekceka
ceya
cik'ayela
ciŋktakta
cokapa
ecelya
ecetu(ya)
gaga
glakiŋyaŋ
gloglo
gmigma
gnaśkiŋyaŋyaŋ
gnuni
gogo
howaya
huŋhuŋsya
huŋhuŋza
Ḣeyapa(ya)
Ḣla
Ḣlo
Ḣmuŋ
Ḣugnaga
Ḣuŋwiŋ
Ḣ'aŋhi
icapa
icicahi(ya)
icicawiŋ
iḣa
ijena
ikpiska
ile
inaḣni(kiya)
iŋyaŋka
iśteca
iśtogmuza
iyotag
iyowaja
jo
kakija
kawa(kiya)
kikta
kini
kinukaŋ
kiŋja
kipehaŋ
kiyela
kiza
kokela
koyaḣ'aŋ
kpi
kpukpa
k'ega
k'eḣya
leja
luzahaŋ
mna(kiya)
najiŋ(kiya)
niyaśni
ociŋśica
ociptetu
oglapśuŋ
ogmuza
oḣ'aŋko
okaḣwoka
okapota
okinihaŋ
okiwaŋjila
okiyuta
oksa
opo
opteca
otaŋiŋ
oteḣika
ot'iŋza
owaŋcaya
oweciŋhaŋ
oyaḣe
patuja
pcelyela
pehaŋ
piza
po
popa
saŋpa
scu
skica
skita
sli
sna
spaya
śigla
śilḣ'aŋ(yaŋ)
śilya
śkaŋśkaŋ
ślaya
śli(ya)
śloka
śtuta
ś'e
tahena
takiŋ
takuniśni
taŋiŋ
taŋkal icu
taŋoŋpa
taŋyaŋ
tehaŋ
tica
titaŋ(yaŋ)
tkuga
togye
tokaŋ
t'a
waciŋtoŋ
waŋkal
waŋkatu(ya)
wasla(ya)
wicaka
wilwitaya
wiŋga
witaya
wiyakpa
woslata

Note: These lists of Prefixed Words can well be made use of, at least in two ways:

1. Choose a word from a given listing. Note how it may recur under different prefix combinations. Frequently, context is built for a word by use of a prefix or a combination of them.

2. Look up in the Lakota-English section any word from the listings of Prefixed Words. One can, then, with a careful choice of prefix(es) determine and select suitable Lakota expressions of English.

Q

quadruped, n. Wahutopa

quantity, (bits, amounts). Oyuptuh'a-yakel, adv. In small -ties; oyututka-yakel, tutkatkayakel, adv. In bits. Watokelketuya, adv. In certain -ties. Yugela, n. A big - .

quarrel, (fight). Ahoyekiciyapi, n. Aigluhomni, v. refl. Akinica, v.a.: aicikinica, v.; akinilkiya, v.; aki-nilya, v.a., adv. Apakson̄lya, v.a.; apakson̄tkiciyapi, n. Ekiza, v.a. Hepa, v. Hohotela akiciyapi, n. Kapa: ai- , v.a.; i- , v.a.; i-ka, n.; i-s'a, n. Ikipajin̄, v.a. Oiglukiki-ya, v.a. Make a - . Okiciyusin̄pi, v. recip. Fall out with one another.

quarry, (pit). Oicu, oyuze, n.

quarter, (winds, heavens, powers). Ouye, n. (of the heavens). Tateouye topa, n. The four quarters of the universe; tatuye, n. A quarter, e.g. the West etc. Wajuju, v.a. - an animal.

queen, Cf. woman.
queer, adj. Oh'an̄tokeca.
quench, (stifle, ruin). Yukpa, v.a.

question, (inquire). Iyun̄ga, v. Ask a - ; wiwicayun̄gapi, wiyun̄gapi, n.; wiyun̄hya, v.a. Make inquire.

quick, (rapid). Iśin̄l, adv. Kokela, koyan̄(la), koyela, adv.; oh'an̄ko, v.n. Be - doing, handy; oh'an̄koya, adv.

quill, n. Pahin̄ (porcupine). Un̄sin̄, n. Small end of a - ; the large tail - . Wipata, v. Ornament with -s: -pi, n. -work, embroidery. Woskapi, n. -work, design.

quilt, Cf. bed. Owin̄ja popopa, n.
quit, v.n. Iyakicun̄ni: -ya, v.a.; -yan̄, adv. Iyenayan̄, v.n.

quiver, v.n. Putehniyan̄yan̄, Have lips - . Wan̄ju, n. (for arrows).

R

race, (run). Inyanka(e), v. Run: ki- , v.n.; o- , n. A - track.

rack, n. Canitokśu, howiwotka, hunkatacan.

radiate, (branch). Wogaga, v.n.; wogaya, adv. -ting.
radio, n. Ikancola mas'apapi, mazacola winaȟ'on, tatuye on winaȟ'on.

ragged, adj. Ȟ'eȟ'e, Droopy: a-ya, adv. haa- , adj.; haa-ya, adv.; -ya, adv. Woya, adv. Zazahan, adj.

railroad, (train). Mazacanku, n. Rails; a train; - petijanjan, n. Lantern; - tipi, n. Railroad car.

rain, v.n. Aglapta. Hinhan, v.n.: a- , v.n. Magaju, v.n., n.: a- , v.; a-kiya, v.a.; a-ya, v.a.; i-ya, v.a. Angaśiceca, n. Icaholhota, icahota, n. Mniicapsinpsin, n. Slashing - ; mniwanjilapapsun, v. It rains ceaselessly; mniwozan, n. Fine - ; v.n. To drizzle. Śliyela, adv. Making the sound of - . Wignunke, n. A -bow.

raise, v.a. Apaha. Ayugata(l), v.a.: -gata, v. Ayuha, v.a. Hupagluza, hupakiyuza, v. Kihiya, v. - a child, train up. Yuzan, v.a. - a curtain.

rake, v. Ayuhinhan. Hinta : ayu- , v.a. Hinte s'e, v.t.; yuhinta, v.a. - away.

ram, v. Iyopaskica, Pack in; iyopuskice, ipasminyan, n. -rod.

rancid, adj. Sewimna, sewiye.
range, Ptanśkiśka, adj. -ing about.
rank, (place, position, office). Tohe, n.

rap, (tap). Kato, v.: -han, v. (as a woodpecker).
rape, (wrestle). Kikśan, v.a. Violate: -pi, n. Kiśleya, v. Hold and feel. Wiiyaȟpaya, v. Commit - . Wikiśleyapi, n.

rascal, n. Waȟteśni t'a.
rash, Ȟanit'a, v. Be covered with - .

rather, adv. Laka(e); -laka, encl. Why don't you?
ration, (issue). Lolicupi, n.

rattle, v. Asnasna, acaȟsnasna. Ȟla, v.n.: -ȟla, n.; -ȟlaya, adv.; aka- , v.a.; ayu- , v.a.; ka-ȟla, v. Swu: ayu- , v.a.; pa-ya, v.a. (push); yu- , v.a. Hunkatawagmuha, n.; wagmuha, n. Icicaślaślayela, adv. Kaka: na- , v.a. (by foot); oyu- , v.n. - in; v.a.; iyoglagla, adv.; kagyela, adv. Kokela, v.a.; kokoka, v.n.; okaglogloka, v.; wakakoka, v. Make - ; wicakoke, n. -er; wokoka, v.a. Make - . K'oga, v.n. Lote onaȟnaȟa, v. Have a rattle in the throat. Naiyojaheyakel, adv.

ravel, v.n. Glahan; glahe, adv. Iciyuwi, v. Swahan, part. -led.
ravine, Cf. gully.

raw, (fresh). Lowitaya, adv. Sagsaka, adj. Uncooked. Śpanśni, adj.

reach, v.n. Ihunni: -kiya, v.a.; -yan; k- , v. - home, the goal. Yagle: hi- , v.n.; hi-ya, v.a., adv.; ici- , v.n.; ici-ya, adv., v.a.; i-ya, v.a., adv. Ohi, v.a. Able to - : -picaśni, v. Not able to be -ed; -ya, v.a., adv. Iyohi, v.a. Oiyahe, n. -ing the top. Zica: ao- , v.a.; aozig- , v.a.; o- , v.n. - out for (strain). Istihohiya, v., adv.; istoglukatin, v. pos.; i-stoiyohiya, adv., v.; istokatinkiya, v.a.

read, Cf. count. Yawa, v.: o- , v.a.; wa- , v.; wa-pi, n. Reading; arithmetic.

ready, Kenunic'iya, v. Get - ; kicanic'iya, kicinciya, v. Get - . Kicii-c'iya, v. Make self - ; kicinciya, v. Get self - . Winyeya, adv. Yuze, v.a. - things.

real, (really, certainly). Leceya, adv. This is so.
rear, (back). Catku, n.: -l, -ta, -tanhan, i-tanhan, adv.
reason, Cf. unconcern. Canteyukeya, adj. Taku on, n. The "why" of. Tawacinkiksuya, v. Become -able again.

rebel, Wawakipajinpi, n. -lion; wawakipajinyan, adv. -liously.
rebound, v.n. Awośtaka,

recall, Eyaś tuka, adv.
receive, Cf. get.
receptacle, n. Wognakapi
reckless, adj. Bleześni.

recline, (lay, stack). Kaituŋkab, v. Oŋpa, v.a. Place, lay; uŋpa.

recognize, Cf. find. Iyekiya, v.a. pos.: o- , n. Recognition; waw- , v.; wicit-pi s'e, adv. As if coming to - one.
reconnoiter, v. Wakcaŋyaŋ.

record, n. Wicahooyuspa, Sound -er, a sound - .

recover, (rise). Asni, v.n.: akisni, v. pos.; caŋlakisni, v.n.; caŋlasniyaŋ, v.a. Make - from sorrow; caŋl'asnikiya, v.n.; -yakel, adv. Ekicetu, v.n. pos.: -ya, v.a.; ekicicetu, v.n. Ahececa, v.n.; ahecel, adv. Blezic'iya, v. Giŋcela, adj. -ing. Kipayeȟca, v. Rise up. Okawatoŋ, v. Be recovered. Takipa, v. - what is stolen.

recreate, v. refl. Imagagaic'iya.
recruit, v. Blezic'iya.
recur, Cf. Again.

redound, v. Waayuptaŋyaŋ, - to self.
reduce, v.a. Yamniga, Shrink by chewing. Yapiśitka, v.a. - in size (by chewing).

reflexion, n. Wowiyakpa, Splendor.
refrigerate, Wapaȟlatapi, n. -tion.

refuge, Cf. shelter. Kiyonakijiŋ, v. Arrive and take - in; onakijiŋ, v.i. Take - in, behind; onakikśiŋ, onajiŋ. Onapce, n. Place of - .

refuse, v. Akiciktaśni. Glonica, glonil, v. pos.: kici- , v. - to give away. K'anajiŋ, v. - to do. Wawipila, v. (not give).

regard, v. pos. Iwaŋglaka; iwaŋic'iglaka, v. refl.
regret, v. Wokiȟiye.

reinforce, v.a. Ipatagya.
reject, Cf. refuse. Paha, v.a. Oppose, push onwards. Ȟeyata: ya- , v. (by speaking); yu- , v.a. Put back. Yaitokaŋ, v.a.

rejoice, Cf. glad. Iyuśkiŋ, v.
relapse, v.n. Oigluśkaŋ, Have a - ; onaśkaŋ; oyuśkaŋ, v. Get restless.

relative, (relation). Cf. kin. Takuya, v.a. Have for a - : wa-pi, n. -s, relationship; takukiciyapi, n.; takuye, n. A person of kin: ti- , n. Immediate -s; o- , n. Kinsfolk, brotherhood, relationship; o-ya, v. Form a relationship. Wicowe, n. Relationship, a generation; wowahecoŋ, n. Relationship, words expressing it.

release, (loose). Kiyuśka, v. - from. Kiyuśpa, v. - from (a trap); nakiciśpa, v. - from trouble.

religion, (minister, member, forms of). Cf. pray(er). Kacegu uŋ, n. A member Congregationalist. Sapuŋ, n. A Catholic priest. Skauŋ, n. An Episcopal minister. Wocekiye, n.

rely, (trust, confide). Waceya, v.a. - on.

remain, Yaŋka: ahi- , v.n.; blog- , v.n.; hi- , v.; tokena - , v. - while others move. Awiyaya, v. imp. Stay away over night. Ecayaukeca, v.n. Haŋyuŋka, v.n. Ihaŋ, v.n.; ihekiya, v. pos.; ikicihaŋ, v.; kicihaŋ, v. - for. Okapta, v.n. Be left: -pi, n. Remnants.

remember, Ksuya: i- , v.; ic'i- , v. refl.; kici- , v. Recollect for; ki- , v.a.; okiksuye, v.a., n. Waciŋki- , v. - all well.
remit, v. Kicaȟpa, - for.
remnant, (leavings). Woptuȟ'a, n.
remove, (reject). Kapoŋya, v. - rough places, to smooth. Tokaŋ: kiciyu- , v. - for; kiyu- ; yui- , v.a. - from, reject. Waikikcu, v. Take own; waikicu, v. - from by magic.

render, (rendition). Kahiyaya, v. (song).
renew, v.a. Yutelya.
rent, v. Tiyololya, - a house; woolota, Lease, -al.

repair, v.a. Gletoŋ. Piya, v.a. Mend up; adv. Well, anew: ipiye, n.; pikiya, v.t. Mend, reset, rearrange, make one's bed; piyepica, adj. Reparable.

repeal, v.a. Kiyujuju.
repeat, Iyakiglegle, adv. Yapsake śni eye, v. - again and again (saying).

repent, v. refl. Igluecetu; igluekicetu. Iyopeic'iya, v. refl.

report, adv. In the manner of a gun. Śke, v.n. It is -ed. Wakcaŋyaŋ, v. Observe and prepare and give a - . Woyake, n. An indication, a report.

represent, (delegate). Nakicijiŋ, v.a.

reprimand, (reprove, scold). Cf. speak. Owakiya, v.a. Waahoyeya, v. Wawiyopeya, v.

reprisal, Cf. vengeance.

reptiles, Cf. animal.

repute, v. refl. Oiglusica, Spoil own - .

research, n. Akitapi.

resemble, (imitate). Kigma, v.n. Owaŋgya, v.a. Imitate. Wiyaciŋpi, n. Resemblance.

reserve, v. refl. Aikpataŋ: -yaŋ, part.; apataŋ, v.a.; kicipa, v. Hold in - . Anica, v.a.; akinil.

reservoir, (tank). Mniognake, n.

reside, (live in). Ouŋyaŋ, v.n. Have residence; ouŋye, n. Home: -kiya, v.a.; -ya, v.a. Make a place home. Oyaŋke, n. A residence.

resolve, v. Akicoŋza, Make a resolution; woic'icoŋze, n. A resolution. Pagnaka, v. Have -ed upon. Coic'icoŋ, v. Tawaciŋkic'uŋ, v.n. Be resolute, obstinate: -yaŋ, adv. Resolutely; tawaciŋsuta, adj. Firm, constant: -ya, adv.

resound, v.n. Tohiŋgla. Yuiyowaza, v.a. Make - , echo.

respect, (honor, reverence, fear). Ahokipa, v. pos. Akta, adv. Caŋteelyuza, v.; waciŋkiciyuzapi, v. Have mutual regard for. Caŋtiyap'ic'iya, v. Iglawa, v. refl. Igloaya, v. Kinihaŋ, v.a. Honor: igluo- , v. pos. Ihakikta, v. pos. Taŋla, v.a. Love, honor, be patient: -ka. Wamnala, v.a. - for bravery: wa- n. One that -s.

respond, v. Woza, Start at.

rest, Asni: -kiya, v.n. Take a long - ; -ya, v.; asnisnikiya, v.i. Ataŋs'ela yaŋka, v. Ȟtaniśni, adj. Icoga, v.n. Ozi, v.n.: -ic'iya, v.n. - self; -kiya, v.n. Take a brief - ; iy- , n. Repose; okiziya, v.a. Make take a - ; -ya, v. Take a - ; -wanil, adv. Without - . Kableblesic'iya, v. - one's mind. Okiȟpaya, v.n. Remain; ooyuȟpa, n. A -ing place. Śkaŋśkaŋokile, v. Make self comfortable. Tiyoȟwaic'iya, v.

restless, adj. Oŋs'haha, Sitting -ly. Śkaŋśkaŋwaśicuŋ, n. A - person. Wanaptoŋka, woslotoŋśni.

restore, v. Kicu.

resurrection, n. Wicakini.

retract, v. pos. Gluecetu.

revenge, Cf. vengeance.

reverent, Oholaya, adv. -ly; waoholaśniyaŋ, v. Irreverently.

reverse, v. pos. Glueciya.

review, n. Woiwaŋyaŋke.

revive, v.a. Apiya.

ribbon, n. Wapaȟlate.

rich, adj. Jica: igla- , v. refl.; igla-ka, n.; i- , v.n.; wiwica- , n.; wi- , adj.; wi-ya, v. En- ; ijilya, v.a., adv.; jilya, v. Make - ; wojice, n. -es; wowi- , n. Wealth. Iwaśeca, v.n. Watoŋka, n. A - person.

ricochet, v. Awacaŋgle.

ride, v. Akaŋyaŋka. Anauŋka, v.a. Śuŋkakaŋyaŋka, n. -er; v. - horseback.

ridge, n. Blo: -aliya, adv. Ȟeyata, adv. On or to the - .

ridicule, Cf. laugh. Iȟaȟa: o- , v.a.; wow- , n.

right, (direction, perfect). Iślaya: -pataŋhaŋ, -taŋhaŋ, itaŋ-taŋhaŋ, nap-taŋhaŋ, taŋ-taŋhaŋ, taŋiśleyataŋ, adv. (direction). Ecetu: iyu- , v. Make - ; woyu- , n. A -ing; ka- , v. Make - ; lecetu, adv. This is - .

righteous, Woowotaŋla, n. -ness.

rim, n. Hugmiya ayut'iŋzela; icete, n.

ring, (sound, finger). Sna: aya- , v.a.; ayu- , v.; pa- , v.a. (push); - s'e, adv. Tinkling; -yela iyaya, v. Sound as iron. Ȟla: ayu- , v.a.; glu- , v. pos.; -yela, adv.; -ȟla, v. Rattle; na- , v.n. (telephone). Mazanapsioȟli, n. Finger - . Cf. jewelry.

rip, Mna: -haŋ, n., part.; awa- , v.a.; ika- , v.; ka- , v. - a seam; ki-haŋ, v. - off for; na- , v.a.; opa- , v.n., n.; pa- , v.a.; wa- , v.a. (by knife) Open; ya- , v.a. (by mouth); wa-yaŋ, v.a.; ana- , v.a. - open. Blaza:

awa- , v.a.; awo- , v.a.; aya- , v.a.; -haŋ, part.; okiwa- , v.a. - open. Ḣleca: aya- , v.a.; apa- , v.a.; ayu-, v.a.; haaigluḣle- , v. refl. Haakaŋhaŋheyela, adv. Haakuka, v. Okiwaśleca, v.a. - down (a log); wakicisleca, v.a. (by saw); wakisleca. Yuzahaŋ, v.a. Make a -ping sound.

ripe, Asutoŋ, v.n.; sutoŋ, v.n. -en, bear seed, fit for use: wa- , v. Get - . Aya, v.n. Gwahaŋ, part. Śtuŋka, adj. Green, not ripe, soft. Taŋcaŋtoŋ, v. Be - , full-grown.

rise, Cf. stand. Nawaŋkal, v. - upward. Woakaŋhiyuya, v.a. Make - to top.

risk, (endanger). Iyot'ognaka, v. - one's life.

river, n. Wakpa: -la, n. Creek. Kaokataŋ, adv. Over the - . Ohaŋ, n. The river's straight course.

Bad R., Wakpaśice.
Elk R., Heḣaka Wakpa. The Yellowstone R.
Fall R., Mniwoblu.
Laramie R., Maga Wakpa.
Loup R., Kuśleca Wakpa, Wiŋyaŋ Wakpala.
Missouri R., Mniśośe.
Mizpah Ck., Paŋgi Taŋkiŋkiŋyaŋ.
Niobrara tributary (southern), Naḣuga Hoḣpi Wakpala.
Pass Ck., Hokiyoḣloka Wakpala.
Platte R., Paŋkeska Wakpa.
Platte tributary, Tatetacaŋku, Waśiŋ Wakpa (South Platte).
Pumpkin Cr., Ptaŋuŋpi Wakpala.
Rosebud Cr., Oŋjiŋjiŋtka Wakpa.

road, n. Caŋku: -naptaŋ, n.; -ya, v.; makoko- , n. A fenced - ; o- , n. A street, a way; o-ya, n., adv. In the likeness of a - ; o-toŋyaŋ, adv. Forming a - ; waŋ ouŋpapi s'e o- , n. A very straight - . Hocete, n. Oiyagle, n. A - leading to. Ośkiiyaza ocaŋku, n. A - drifted in and low.

roast, Cf. fire, burn. Cok'iŋ, v.a. Pasnoŋ, pasnuŋ, v.a. - on: kici- , v. - for; kpa- , v. - own. Pelmnamnaya, v. - on a spit. Śku, v.n. Be -ed (all or part). Taka, v.a. - off (hull). Waceuŋpa, v.a.; n. One who roasts.

rob, Wakipi, n. -bery; wicakipi.

robe, n. Ptehahiŋśma, Buffalo - ; ptehiŋśmatawelaha, n. Summer - .

rock, Cf. stone. Yuptaŋptaŋ, v.a. Oscillate, vibrate back and forth: -yaŋ, v.a. Roll.

rod, Cf. hanger. Satglakiŋyaŋ, n. A drying - .

Rogation, n. p. Owoju Awacekiyapi, The - Day procession.

roll, (coil, curl, flatten; skein). Cf. turn, round, strain. Gmigma(e): ka- , v. - along; kao- , v. Make - into; oic'i-la, adv. With self -ed up; nao- , v.a.; pa- , v.a. (by hand). Gmi: ka-yayaŋ, v.a. Make - ; na-yaŋyaŋ, v.a.; pa-yaŋ, v.a. Kipeha, v. - up, fold own. Nakśa, v.a., v.n. Coil; okakśe, n. - of ribbon, cloth, thread. Ptaŋ: opa- , v. Turn, - over; pa-yaŋ, v.a. Upset; adv. -ing about; yu-ptaŋyaŋ, v.a. - over and over; yu-yaŋ, v.a. Turn, roll over; adv. Pśuŋpśuŋ: oic'i-kel, adv. -ed up; yu- , v. - into a wad. Pablaya, v.a. Spread our (dough). Pacaŋgleya hiyuya, v. - toward. Pagmuŋ, v.a. - up (by hand): -pi, n. Pawaga, v.a. Twist in the hand. Wopemnikagapi, n. A roll.

roof, n. Aokiye, awokeya, keya; keya, v. Make a - . Keiŋyaŋhaŋ, adv. -like, sloping. Ticaŋkahu, n. Beam in the peak of a gable. Tiipaslate, n. A support, pillar.

room, Kipana, v. Make - for. Ocikaŋ, adv. Roomy; okaŋ, v.n. There is - : -yaŋ, adv. Roomy. Ośuŋk'ogleśica, adj. Being no - for many. Oyaŋke, n. Tiuŋgnaga, n. The corner of a - ; tiiyokaḣmi. Tiyokalya, v. Warm a - ; tiyotateśni, n. A close, warm - . Wakipika, adj. Roomy. Waŋkaltipi, n. An upper - . Wapako, v. Make room for. Yukaŋ, v.a. Make - for: ahi- , v.; ki- , v.a. Cf. reside, house.

root, n. Hute: o- , n. Root, bottom; caŋhuta, n.; śiŋkpaŋkahu, n. Foot -s. Hutkaŋ, n.: caŋ- , n. Huokihe haŋskaska, n. Ju, v.; pajuŋ, v.a. - up (spade, pull); yajuŋ, v. - up; yujuŋ, v.a. - up by hand. Śuŋkace, n. - of calamus; śuŋkce. Tatu, n. Medicinal - . Tepa, adj. - form; tewapa, n. A

ROOTS
succulent - . Wahiŋḣeya ipiye, n. Wayaaglapśuŋyaŋ, v. - over.

Roots to words and which, in a considerable number of instances, are themselves words are listed below. Roots may be simple (a single meaningful syllable), or complex (two or more roots in composition); and both kinds of roots often used with appropriate prefix(es) and-or suffix(es).

apa
ape
asni
aś'a
bla
blaska
blaza
ble
bleca
bleza
bli
blo
blu
bu
caje
caŋ
caŋcaŋ
caŋte(l)
caŋze
capa
ce
cik'a
ciŋ
co
coka
cokoŋ
cola
coŋza
coza
cu
c'o
e
ececa
ecetu
etu
eya
ga
gaŋ
gapa
ge
gi
gla
glaka
gle
gloka
gma
gmi

gmigma
gmu
gna
gni
gnu
go
gu
gwa
ha
haha
haŋ
he
heya
hi
hiŋ
hiŋḣpa
hiŋta
hiŋyaŋze
ho
hoho
homni
hu
huŋ
huŋza
ḣa
ḣapa
ḣca
ḣci
ḣepa
ḣeya
ḣiŋ
ḣla
ḣlaga(ŋ)
ḣleca
ḣli
ḣlo
ḣma
ḣmiŋ
ḣmuŋ
ḣna
ḣni
ḣniga
ḣpa
ḣpe
ḣpi
ḣpo
ḣpu

ḣta
ḣte
ḣuga
ḣugna
ḣwa
ḣwo
ḣ'a
ḣ'aŋ
ḣ'aŋhi
ḣ'e
ḣ'oŋ
ḣ'uŋ
i
icu
ihaŋ
ihe
ile
ini
iŋ
iśta
ite
iya
ja
jaja
jaŋ
jata
ji
jica
jiŋ
jipa
jo
jola
ju
juju
ka
kaga
kaka
kaŋ
kapa
kata
katiŋ
kawa
kazo
kca
kcaŋ
kija
kiŋ

Roots Listing (contin.)

kiŋta
kiŋyaŋ
kita
kiza
ko
koŋ
koŋta
kpa
kpaŋ
kpani
kpi
kpu
ksa
ksapa
ksi(ŋ)
ksoŋta
ksu
kśa
kśaŋ
kśi
kśija
kśiŋ
kta
ktaŋ
kte
ktoŋ
ktoŋja
ku
kuja
kuka
kuŋta
kute
k'a
k'e
k'ega
k'eza
k'iŋ
k'o
k'oga
k'oza
k'u
la
lakota
lapa
le
leja
li
lipa
lo
lopa(b)
lota(l)
loza
lu
luta(l)
ma
manoŋ
maŋ
maya
mi
mima

mna
mni
mnu
mnuga
nagi
naḣ'oŋ
nape
nase
ni
nica
noge
nu
nuŋ
oŋ
oŋpa
oŋspe
oŋśi
pa
pako
pamni
pani
paŋ
paŋga
paŋja
pce
pe
peji
pemni
pesto
peta(l)
pi
pica
pika
pila
piŋja
piŋze
piza
po
poge
popa
pota(l)
powa
psa
pse
psi(ŋ)
psica
psoŋ
pśa
pśaŋ
pśiŋ
pśuŋ
pta
ptaŋ
pte
pteca
pti
pto
ptu
ptuja
pu

puta
putaga
puza
sa
saŋ
sce
scu
se
sepa
si
siŋ
siŋka
siŋte
ska
skaŋ
skapa
skepa
skica
skita
sko
sku
sla
slata
sleca
sli
slipa
slo
slol
slota(l)
sluta
sma
smaka
sme
smi
smiŋ
sna
sni
snoŋ
soŋ, suŋ
sota
spa
staŋ
sto
su
suta
swa
swe
swu
śa
śaka
śapa
śe
śeca
śi
śica
śigla
śiḣtiŋ
śina
śiŋ
śipa

Roots Listing (contin.)

śitki
śka
śkaη
śkata
śke
śki
śkica
śkiη
śkiśka
śkita
śkokpa
śkopa
śla
śleca
śli
ślo
śloka
śma
śmiη
śna
śni
śnija
śośa
śpa
śpaη
śpi
śpu
śta
śtaη
śte
śtu
śu
śuja
śwu
ś'a
ś'e
ś'iη
ś'o
ta
taka
takiη
takpa
taku
taη
taηiη
taηka
taηni
tata
te
teca
tehaη
tepa
ti
tica
tiη
tipa
titaη
tka
tko

tkoη
tku
tkuga
tkuη
togya
toka
tokaη
tokeca
tomni
toη
tu
tuja
tuka
tuta
tutka
t'a
t'aga
t'iη
t'o
t'uη
u
uη
wa
waci
waciη
waja
waη
waηka
waza
we
wega
wi
wica
wicaka
wiη
wiηja
wita
wota(l)
wotaη

ya
yaη
yaηka
yu
yuη
yupta
yuta
yute
yuza
za
zamni
zaη
ze
zi
zica
zo
zoka
zu

Cf. prefix, suffix.

rope, Cf. loop. Wikaη: tahuηsapa- , n. (horsehair); -soηpi, n. Lasso; -kaη, n. A double - . Wiyuħoηte, n. A sinew - .

rot, (decay). Kuka, adj. -ten: i- , v.n.; ikukeya, adv.; kukeya, v.a.; a- , v.n. Get -ten on. Kimaka, v.n. Poηpoη, adj. -ten, soft; puηpuη, v.n. Decay; adj. -ten. Śeca, adj. Dry, -ten.

rough, Ħa: ana- , adj.; apa-tka, adj.; apa-tkaya, adv.; -pa, adj.; Ħeośki, n. -ness; na- , v.n. Become chapped, break the surface of; pa- , v.a. Rub - ; pa-Ħa, v.n. Be - . Taja: a- , v.n.; ataś- , v.n.; taji, adj. (water). T'aga, adj. Bitter, astringent, gritty: at'aħya, v.a. Gweza: ayu- , v.a.; ka- , v. Make - ; pa- , v.a. Rub rather - ; yu- , v.a. Make - . Cica, adj.: iya- , adj. Yuħ'i: eca- , n., adj.: -ya, v. Be made - . Hiηte, adj. Ħ'akpa, adj. Icama, adj. Kaglega, v. Mark, make - . Śkiśka(e), adj.: ka- , v. Make - ; na- , v.a.; -ya, v.a., adv.; śkiśkita, adj. Pepeya, adv. With a sharp, - surface. Wicatute, n. -ness. Yuħtaη, v.a. Make - .

round, (circular). Gmiyaη, adj.: apayaη, v.a.; gmi- , adj.; -yaηla, n. Apagmoη, apagmuη, v.a. Mima, adj.: mimela, adj.; mimeyela, adv.; pa- , v.a. Make - and flat; adj. - and pointed. Gmigma, v.n.: ayu- , v.a.; gmigmela, adj.; gmigmeya, adv.; ka- , v. Make - ; pa- , v.a. Make - (by hand). Caηgleśka, adj. Icakśa, v. Pśuηka: ka- , v. Make - ; -ka, n. Tiny - things, pills. Napako, adv. -ed up. Okawiηga, v.n. Go - and - . Otosa, adj. Full, filled out, blunt. Pośla, adj. -ed off at one end. Tapoposka, n. Ball-shaped things.

round-up, (gathering). Ptemnayaηpi, n. Cf. napako.

rouse, (jog, awaken). Nani, v.a.

rout, (hew). Iyayeya, v. Skiskita, v. Mark by -ing.

row, (furrow). Caηkoye, n.: -toη, v.; -toηtoηyaη, adv. In -s. Iciyaza, adv. Ipaħlala, adv. Yuogla, adv. Lined in a - .

rowdy, n. fig. Siηtehaηska.

rub, (apply, break, crush). Apa: -coza, v.a.; -jaja, -juju, -kiŋta, -kiza, -kuka, -k'ega, -k'oza, -maŋ, -sleca, -waga, -wiŋta. Pawaga: napo- , v.a.; o- , v.a. - over and over in the hands. Pa: -cica, v.a. - together, mix up; -sepa, v.a. - off; -śla, v.a. - off, make bare; -śtuta, v.a. - with snow; -taŋiŋ, v.a. - clear, clean; -taŋiŋśni, v.n. - off, obliterate; -wiŋta, v.a.; wa-ȟatka, v. - against the grain. Kpa: i-kiŋta, v. refl.; i-k'ega, v.; i-waza, v. refl. Ipa: -kiŋja, v.; -maŋ, v.a.; -me, n.; -skica, v.; -wiŋta, v.a. Ayuhuŋta, v.a. Iyuŋ, v. Apply on: iic'- , v. refl.; ik- , v. pos. Kalapa, v. - smooth or level. Iyupaŋ, v. Break up. Puskica, v.a. - out. Yusepa, v.a. - off, deface.

rubbish, n. Watuśekśe, Dirt, sweepings.

rude, (impolite). Oȟ'aŋeciŋśniyaŋ, adj.

ruffle, (pleat, curl). Yumni: -ja, adj. -ed; ayumnimnija, v.n., n.; yumnimniśya, v.a. Curl; adv. Ȟaka, adj.; yuȟatka, v.a. Wanaśkiśkilya, v.

ruin, Takuniśni: a- , v.n.; a-yaŋ, v.a.; awo- , v.a.; ayu- , v.a.; iglu- , v. refl. Awanil, v. Ayujuju, v.a. Ayuwignuni, v.a. Ihaŋgya, v.; ihaŋgkiya, v.a. pos. Waoŋtoŋkiya, v. pos. - own. Watogya, v.a. Spoil, take vengeance.

rule, (law). Wowakoŋze, n. - of justice, a law.

rummage, v.a. Kahi; kicahi, v. - for.
rumminate, v. Wayatekoŋza.

run, Cf. flee. Iŋyaŋka, v.n.: a- , v.; huŋkpaŋkos - , v.; kaiŋyaŋg iyaye, v. Make - ; kaiŋyaŋkelaka, v. Shuffle along; o- , v.i. - about in. Napa, v. - away: anakipa, v.; a- , v.a.; k'iŋ- , v. - away with. Haŋpoȟya, adv. Icacaŋ, v.n.; ikacaŋ, v.n., v.a. Iciwotopi, v.; ikato, v.n. Kahiŋȟpeya, v. - over. Okicicuwapi, v. pl. They - after each other. Tokala iŋyaŋka, v. - with head and body bent. Yuiŋyaŋk'iŋyaŋka, v.a. Make - along.

ruse, Zomiyaŋke, adv. Using a - .
rush, Cf. grass.
rust, Ogi, n., v., adj.; agi, v.n.; iyagi, v.

rustle, (sound). Ȟapa, v.n.: ȟabȟapela, n.; icaȟabȟapela, v.n.; icicaȟab- , v. Make a -ling sound; kaȟab- , v.n.; ȟabȟabya, adv. red. Snahaŋ, adj., part. -ling. Yumnumnuga, v.a. (as the sound of corn).

S

Sacrament, n. Woecoŋwakaŋ.
Baptism, n. p. Mniakaśtaŋpi; mniaka-śtaŋ, v. a.
Eucharist, n. p. Yutapiwakaŋ.
Penance, n. p. Woglakapiwakaŋ.
Confirmation, n. p. Wicayusutapiwakaŋ.
Anointment, n. p. Wiyuŋpiwakaŋ.
Priesthood, n. p. Wicaśa Wakaŋ Kagapi.
Matrimony, n. p. Wakaŋkiciyuzapi; o-kiciyuze wakaŋ, n. Marriage.
Viaticum, n. p. Oŋweyawakaŋ.

sacred, (special). Cf. holy. Wakaŋ, adj. Cf. Wakaŋkila, v. pos. Regard own - ; wakaŋla, v.a. Reckon - .

sacrifice, Uŋyaŋ: owa- , v. - in; n. Place of - , an altar; wakici- , v. - for, offer for; waki- , v. - to, offer to; wa- , v.a. Offer - , lose: -pi, n. -es; wauŋyeya, v. Offer -es; wowauŋye, n. The gift of sacrifice. Yuśna: owa- , v. - in; n. An altar; waic'igluśna, v. refl. - self, let self fall; wigluśna, v. - self; waki- , v.a. - to, drop for; wa- , v.a. Offer - : -pi, n. ; wośna, v. Drop, offer in - ; n. An offering in - ; wośnakiya, v.a. Make to - . Htata: waic'iglu- , v. Offer - for self; waiglu- , v. Offer self in - ; wakiglu- , v. - own; wayu- , v. Offer in - , kill in - ; wayu-pi, n. A sacrifice.

sad, Aśilya, adv.; śilyela, adv.; wawiyokiśica, v. Be - . Caŋ: -ksiksizeca, adj.; -psis uŋ, v.; -śilya, v.a.; -śilyakel, adv. Caŋte:-huŋkeśniyaŋ, adv.; -mniskaŋojula, adj.; -śica, v.n., adj.; -śicaya, adv.; -śilic'iya, v.; -śilya, v.n.; -śilyakel, adv.; -yaśica, v.a.; caŋtihaŋke, adj.; o-śilya, adv.; wa-iyokiśica, adj.; wo-iyokiśice, n. -ness. Icaŋśica(1), v.n., adv.

saddle, Cf. horse. Akiŋglotaka, v. pos. Ak'iŋ, n.: caŋw- , n. Anuŋgwakicaśka, n. - bags.

Saint, n. p. Wakaŋpi: - Olakolkiciyapi, n. Communion of Saints.

sake, Oŋtaŋtaŋhaŋ, prep. For - of; taŋtaŋhaŋ, adv. For - of one.

salt, n. Cak'iglaska, Salts. Mniskuya, n.: -oyuze, n. - lake; mniskuyetoŋ, v.

salutary, adj. Nagiyuwaśte.
salute, v. Kalabiyekiya.
salvation, n. Wowanikiye; Wiconiyaŋpi, n. prop.

same, Itkoŋs, adv. Okaȟwaŋjila, n. The - form.

sand, n. Casmu: -ikacoco, n. Mniȟuha wiyuma, n. - paper.

sap, n. Śiŋ (wood).

satisfy, v. Caŋli: -caspekitoŋ, -caspekiya, -caspeya, -mna, v.; caŋticaspeya, v.n. Imna, v.n.: -haŋ(haŋ), -haŋyaŋ, -haŋyaŋkel, adv.; -ic'iya, v. refl.; -yaŋ, v.a., adv.; iwicamna, adj. Opikila, v.n. Be -ed with. Śikigla, v. Be -ed with.

save, v.a. Ataŋtoŋyaŋ. Ic'iksapa, v. Pataŋ, v. Care for, save: wa- , v. Be saving of; wa-ka, n. One who -es; wo- , n. The saving of things. Wanikiye, n. p. The Savior. Cf. live.

saw, Caŋ: -inaslelye, n. -mill; -iwakse, n.; -naslelya, v.a.; -waksa, v.; -wasleca, v.a.; -waslecapi, n. Ciŋwakse, n.; wakiksa, v. pos. Cut down. Hugmiya pepela, n. Kiwasleca, v.; ocaŋnaslece, n. A saw-mill.

say, Cf. speak. Eya, v.: keya, keciya, kekiya, v. - that; leya, leic'iya, lekiya, v. - this; tak'eya, v. - something.

scab, Hayuȟpu, v.n. Hocośpu, n. Ȟaŋ, n.: -apaha, v.n.; -ȟaŋ, adj.; -ȟaŋpi, n.; -ȟaŋyaŋ, v.a., adv. Toŋognagagya, adv. With -s.
scale, v.n. Kaȟpu, - off, fall off; naślaya, v.; powaya, v.

scalp, Iwaktegla, v.n.; iwaktegli, v.n. Paha, n. Pecokaŋ, n. - lock: -yaŋ, n. Waśpa, v.a.

scandalize, v.a. Śilwokaȟniȟya.
scar, n. Osnaze.
scarce, (hardly, slightly). Iyus'eya, adv. Kitaŋ, adv.: -eciŋyaŋ, adv.
scare, v.a. Ȟabya: a- , v. Inihaŋ: -ya, v.a.; a- , v.n.; a-yaŋ, adv. Cuwaculuza, n. Waauŋyeya, v. - away; Wanauŋgya, v. Yualos, v. Yuiyoyag, v. Get excited.

scatter, Abe: -ya, -kiya, -beya, kaya, kaiyabebeya, adv. Bleca: a-ha^n, part.; ana- , v.n.; o-ha^n, part.; o-iglu- , v. refl.; oyu- , v.a. Glegle, adj.: aca- , adj.; -ka, adj.; ici-ga, adj. Glala, v. pos.: a- , v.a.; kala, v. (seed). Akipaptapi, v. pl. Iyabya, adv. Kablesglepi s'e, adv. -ed. Oyuhi, v. - feed; oyuhi^{n}ha^n, v. Yuptuptuta, v. - in bits.

scholar, n. Wao^{n}speic'iya.
school, n. Owayawa, School, - room: gli - , gliśni - , n. Oyawa, v.a. Go to - .

scold, Cf. correct, quarrel. Oiyopeye, n. -ing. Wiicigni, v. Whip a woman.
score, v.a. Owago.

scramble, v.n. Iyaḣpaḣpaya.
scrap, (crumbs, chips, etc.). Watutka, v.a. Make crumbs, scraps; n. Wogu, n. Scraps.
scrape, v. Anawi^{n}ta. Tica, v. - off: -ha^n, part. Falling off; aoka- , v.a.; apa- , v.a.; na- , v.a. (by foot). Ki^{n}ca, adj. Scraping, cf.: ayu- , v.a.; ka- , v. - off (hair); na- , nakica, v.a. (by foot); kica- , kicica- , v. - for. Ayuwaza, v.a. K'ega, v.: ayu- , v.a.; inak'eḣya, v.; pa- , v.a. (by hand). Huha, n. -ings: ta- , n. Scraps. Kak'oga, v. - off (paint, dirt); icak'oge, n. Kaśku, v. - off (scales, corn). Nahi^{n}ta, v.a. - or wipe off. Nasepa, v. - along, clean. Nasmi^{n}ya^n, v.a. - off (by foot). Paḣlata, v.a. - along. Paḣpa, v.a. - off. Pak'eza, v.a. - smooth. Tka, v.a. - hair off. Wawaptuḣ'a, v. - off crumbs.

scratch, Cf. scrape. Ḣlata: ayu- , v.a.; igluḣla- , v. red. and refl.; na- , v.a. (with toes); onaḣlate, n.; oyu- , v.a. - in; oyuḣlate, n.; waya- , v. (with teeth); yu- , v.a. (with claws). Waza: ayu- , v.a.; ikpa- , v. refl.; naić'i- , v. - self; na- , v.a. (by foot). K'ega: ayu- , v.a.; iyu- , v.a.; iglu- , v. refl.; ikpa- , v.; naic'i- , v. - self; na- , v.a. Nak'oga, ayuk'oga, yu- , v.a. Ikpakiskija, v. refl. Iyuḣleḣlel, adv. Being -ed. Nagogo, v.n. Score; yugo, v.a. Make -es. Naic'iśnaśna, v. - self. Nawi^{n}l iyeya, v.a. Oyagi, v.a.

scream, v.n. T'ehowaya, - for fear.
screen, n. Woakeye (in gen.).
screw, Cf. nail.
scrub, v. Ipawaga.
scruple, v. Waka^{n}la s'e u^n, Be a health scrupulant.

scum, Cf. foam. Taḣto^n, v. Have - .
seal, (glue). Cf. glue. Puspa, v.a.; puspeya, v.a. Wiyaskabto^n, v.a.

seam, n. Hupeyoza^n. Okagege, n.; okayege, n. Okime, n., v.n. Join a - .

season, n. Mako^{n}cage; makasa^{n}pa, makisa^{n}pa, n. Next - , year.
Winter, n. Waniyetu.
Spring, n. Wetu; weha^n, n. Last spring; iwetu, n. Next spring; awetu, v. Be spring.
Summer, n. Bloketu, This or next summer; blokecoka^{n}ya^n, n. Mid-summer; blokeha^n, n. Last summer; abloketu, v. Have lived until summer, come summer.
Fall, n. Pta^{n}yetu, pta^{n}yela, Autumn; pti^{n}ha^n, n. Last autumn.

seasoning, n. Apaye; wapaye, n. (in gen.): -ya, v. Use for - . Aśeca, v.n. Śelya, adv. Wicahiyutapi, n. Spices, sauce: - toto, n. A salad; - zi, n. Mustard. Cf. salt; yamnumnugapi, Pepper; sugar.

seat, Cf. sit. Iyotaka, v.: ka- , v. Be -ed; oiyotake, n. Oya^{n}ke, n. Oaka^{n}ka^n, n. Bench; oaka^{n}ke, n.

secret, Cf. whisper. Naḣma(e): i- , v.a.; i-yakel, adv.; i-kiciciyapi, n.; i-ya, adv.; i-yaha^n, adv.; -kel, adv. -ly. Wawoji, v. Tell -ly.

seduce, Cf. intercourse, credulous. Inaḣma, v.a.: -^{n}pi, n. Seduction. Tawaci^{n}waśakala, adj. Credulous; tawaci^{n}pa^{n}pa^{n}la, adj. Venal. Kat'i^{n}sya, adj. Wiyukca^{n}śni, v.n. Be credulous. Yajata, v.a. Lead one to give up his good resolve.

see, (perceive). Cf. look. Wa^{n}ya^{n}ka, v.a. (perceive): iwa^{n}ya^{n}ke, n. Sight; wa^{n}glaka, v. pos. - own; wa^{n}kiciya^{n}kapi, v. recip. - each other; wa^{n}ya^{n}gkiya, v.a. Make - ; wa^{n}ya^{n}gya, v.a.

seed, n. Co, su, itka.

seek, (look). Ole, v.a. - for; okicile, v. - for; okile, v. pos.; aole, v. Akuta kuwa, v. Go after again and again. Igni, v.a. Iikiya, v. - back.

seep, (persist). Wotaŋglusasayakel, adv. -ing in. Wohiŋyaŋsyakel, adv.

seer, Cf. understand. Wokcaŋ(ka), n.

seize, Cf. capture, police. Iyaḣpaya, v.n.; iyakiḣpaya, v. pos. Iyupaga, v.a. Gather up, arrest. Wawoyuspa, v. Arrest: -pi, n. An arrest.

seldom, Cf. once.

self, (body). Iyeciŋka(la), adv. On one's own. Kihi, v. Be -supporting, befledged; oic'ihi, v. refl. Be rich and -ish. Taŋiyupse, v. Turn self to the side to see. Waciŋic'iyapi, n. -reliance. Waḣ'aŋic'ila, v. refl. Be -important: -pi, n. Pride. Wamahetuyakel, adv. By one's self. Wawipic'ila, v. refl. Think -centeredly.

sell, v.a. Ahiwiyopeya; iyopeya, v.; n. A price.

semen, n. Hiyaye.

send, v.a. Yeya, - one: iya- , v.a.; kigleya, v. - off home; ogligleya, v.a. - here and there; adv.; yekiya, v.a. Drive. Uśi, v.a. Command to come; yeśi, v.a. Command to go. Uya, v.a. Make go, start. Wahokiya, v.a. - word to; wahoya, v.a. - word for, to; promise, order.

sense, Toŋtoŋ, n. (Philosophy) That which has sensible properties: -yaŋ, adj. Visible from its properties.

sentence, (verse). Oegle, n. Wicayasupi, n. Condemnation.

separate, Abebeya, abekiya, abeya, adv. -ed. Acaglegle, adj. Akamni, v.n. Akipaptapi, v. pl.; ayukipab, adv.; gluakipab, v. pos. Glake, adj.: -keyela, -ya, -yela, adv. Kaśpa, v. (by striking); kiyuśpeya, adv. Kinuŋkaŋ, adv. Ksa, adj.: kiyukseya, adv.; ya- , yu- , adj.

serious, Śogya, adv. -ly (bad).

serve, Cf. help. Okiye: ookiye, n. A servant, assistant; ta- , n. Disciple; ta-ya, v. Have for a servant, helper. Wowilake, n. A servant, hired man.

set, Cf. place. Ogle, v.a. - in: oegle, v.a. - in; n. Paecetu, v.a. (a bone). Yaḣeyata, v. - aside (by mouth).

settle, v.n. Ayumniga. Kaskica, v. - down; kaskil, v. Naskica, v.n. Yuśtaŋ, v.a. (a question).

severe, adj. Ś'akeca, Austere, hard to deal with.

sew, (join, equipment). Kagege, v.; kayege; kicicagege, v. - for; aglagege, v.a. pos. Akiglag: -kicitoŋ, v.; -kitoŋ, v. pos.; -toŋ, v., part.; -ya, v.a. Apasisa, v.a. Stitch. Pata, v.a. Cut and - : a- , v.a.; ki- , v. Join. Mas'wicayege, n. Sewing machine. Napośtaŋ, n. Thimble. Tahiŋśpa, n. Awl: - cik'ala, n. Needle.

shade, (bower, shadow). Haŋzi: a- , v.n. Be shady; ao- , v.n.; ao-ya, v.a.; iyo- , n. Shadow; o- , o-glepi, o-zi, n. Bower; mniḣuha o- , n. Awning. Aiyohaŋsya, adv., v.a. Amaḣposaŋtagleya, adv. Silhouetted. Awakeya, v.a.

shake, Caŋ(caŋ): a- , v.n.; akiyu-pi, v. pl. They hit off together; apa- , v.a.; ayu- , v.a.; glu- , v.pos.; i- , v.n.; kiciyu- , v. - for; na- , v.n., v.a. Tremble, make - . Kaŋ: ahiyu- , v.; cuglu- , v. pos.; oka- , v.a. - into; yu- , v.a. - off. Huŋhuŋ(za,s), v.n.: -ya, v.a. Make - ; adv.; -hela, adv.; apa- , v.a.; ayu- , v.a.; glu- , v. pos.; ka- , v. Make - ; kiciyu- , v. - for; na- , v.a. Rock (by foot); pa- , v.a. (by hand); wo- , v.a. (by shooting). Apomnamna, v.a. Apoptaŋptaŋ, v.a. Hoho: ayu- , v.a.; glu- , v. pos.; yuo- , v.a. - in a tight place. Cehupaglagla, v.n. Ic'iblebleca, v. refl. Iglat'a, v. Ikoze, v. Iyokaniyaŋ, v.n. Be jarred; wani, v. (cutting), cf. cut. Kaglogloka, v. Rattle. Gna: ka- , v. - off; pa- , v.a. -off (fruit); yu- , v.a. Śkaŋ: kaśkaŋ- , v. Be shaken; na- , v.a. (by feet). Tata: na- , v.a. - off; yu- , v.a. (dust), brush off. Opawiwi s'e, adv. -ing in a mass. Yuhika, v.a. - up, arouse.

shallow, adj. Ap'eyela, kazela, puzela.

shame, (ashame). Ísteca(l), v.n.: -kiya, v.n.; -ya, v.a.; iwicaśteca, n.; wowiśtece, n.; wow-ya, v.a. Be ashamed; adv. -fully.

shape, (form). Cf. bend. Paśipa, v. Reshape.
share, v.a. Apagan. Okini, v.a. Receive a - in.

sharp, (sharpen). Yuman, v.a. -en, grind; yume, v.; a- , v.a. Pe, adj. (tools), pointed; -ya, adj., adv.; iwa- , v.; ka- , v.; ka-sto, v. Point; kazanpeya, v.a.; wa- , v. -en with; ya-sto, v.a. Make - (with teeth). Ogli: iy- , v.a., n.; mas'wiy- , n. -ener; -kiya, v.; -ya, v.a. Okagaya, v.a. Cut (by words).

shatter, v. Kaȟpaȟpa.
shave, v. Kajipa, - clean: a- , v.a.; canokajipe, canopajipe, n.; canpajipa, v. Awablayą, v.a. Wagla, v.a. - off: a- , v.a. Śla: awa- , ayu- v.a.; gla- , v. pos.; kica- , wa- , v.; putinhinica- , n. A razor; putinhinipajaja, n. A shaving brush; wakici- , v. Cut off (by knife). Ayuk'eza, v.a. Ihanceti, n. Skusku, adj. -ed off.

shear, Cf. cut, shave. Yuk'eza, v.a. Clip close.
sheath, n. Ogin, ojuha. Aokpazankiton, v.n.
shed, (fallen, drawn out). Hinska, adj. Pśun, adj.: -han, part. Dislocated; -wahan, part. Dropped out, fallen off.

shell, Gna: apa- , ayu- , pa- , v.a. Inyanha, n. Kanhe, v. - out. Pange ska, n. Large marine -s. Śku: pa- , v.a. - corn; yu- , v.a. - off; wa- , v.a. Cut from. Wogla, v.a. - off. Tuki: -ha, n.; -pśito, n. Pearl; -winunkala, n. A large - . Yagwa, v.a.

shelter, Cf. hide, proof. Napa(e): iyo- , v. Take - ; owe- , n. A place of - ; yuti- , v. Take - . Blula: o- , adj. Weather-proof; oiyo- , n. Oipeya, n. Wind, cold weather - .

shepherd, (overseer). Waawanglaka, n.

shield, (fend off, parry). Kaśeya, v. Fend off. Wahacanka, n.

shine, (brilliant, attractive). Agliheya, v.a. Aiyojanjan, v.i.: -ic'iya, v. refl.; -ya, v.a.; iyowicajanjan, n. Attraction. Ilega(ȟ), v.n.: -lega, v.n.; -ya, adv., v.a.; kalega, v. Make - ; paleȟya, v.a. Make - by.

shingle, n. Canblaska zibzipela.
shinny, Cf. ball, game.
shiver, (shake). Kacan(he), v.; yucanpi s'e, adv. -ing.

shoe, n. Hanpa, n. Moccasin: akan- , can- , n.; hankpan, n.: - oȟloka, n.; hanponaśloke, n.; hanp'onaśloke, n.; maśtecan- , n. Slippers; pso- , n. Snow- ; hanpisabye, n. - blackening.

shoot, Agleyus, v. cont. Aiglutan, v. refl. Awo: -śpa, -śpu, -blaza, -bleca, -ȟleca, -ȟpa, -ksa, -kuka, -pota, -psaka, -ptuja, -sleca, -sota, -śla, -śleca; -śloka, v.a. Wo: -gna, v.a. - off; -ȟpa, v.a. - down; -kpa, v.a. - out; -kśeca, v.a. Make keel over; -ozeze, v.a. - and let swing; -ptuja, v.a. - off a piece; -śipa, v.a. - off a protuberance. Kute, v.a.: o- , n. A shot; can- , v.n.; icute, n.; kicicute, v.a.; ki- , v. - for; wa-pi, n. A shooting. Iwopan, v. Kiwo: -ksa, v. - in two; -psaka, v. - off in; -śpa, v. - in two. Owopota, v.a. - to pieces on. Kat'iic'iya, v. - self. Kiinyeya, v.a. - an arrow. O, v.a.; oiheya, v.a. - into. Uta, v.a. Try, fire: o- , v.a. - with a gun. Slihingla, v. Fire a shot; slihingle, n. Report of a gun. Waniyaȟpeya, v.a. - arrows. Waokiya, v. Let do the -ing. Wicahmunga, v. - in, into (by magic). Yuo s'e, n. One who misses shooting (ironic).

shore, Huta: -wapa, adv.; o- , n. The water's edge; o-pa, adv. At the - ; o-henatanhan, adv. On this side of the - ; -tahenatanhan, adv. Hel, adv. Mniohuta, n. The shore. Opuze, n. Dry - , edge; puzata, adv. On - .

short, (distance, time, lack). Aśka: -hayela, adv. (time); -tula, -tuya, -tuyela, adv.; aśkinyankapila, adv. (time, distance); aśkiyankel, adv. (distance); oaśkayela, adv. Near. Otohanyan, adv. For a - distance, time; owatohanyan, adv. For a - time. Ptecela, pcecela, adj.; ocipteca, adj. -er than, not equal to; akaptecela, wakaptecela, v.a. -en. Tojela, adj. Waitebya, adv. Cut -er on one side; watepa, v.a. Cut, wear - . Wotoka, adj. Pounded off - . Iyaȟagyela, adv. Kapiŋja, v. -en (a tail). Naokpani, v.a. Be - of. Iyucaŋ, v.n. Be - of things. Katku, adj. Laking a sufficiency.

shot, n. Ouŋ, Gun load, a dose, ammunition.

shout, v.n. Ś'a: aki- , v.n.; a- , v.a.; awica- , n.; ia- , v.; iyaki- , v.; iya- , v.; iya-yapi, iya-pi, n.; wagla-pi, n. Children's -ing (over food). Aśicahowaya, v.a.; houya, hoyekiya, hoyeya, v.a.; ipaŋhoyeya, adv. Ayuceya, v.a.

shove, Cf. push. Iyeya, v.a.: -ya, v.a. Paȟeyapa, v. - aside.

show, (manifest). Pazo, v.a. Present to view: a- , v.a.; kpazo, ikpazo, v. pos. Taŋiŋ: ayao- , ayu- , v.a.; glao- , v. pos.; igluo- , iglu- , v. refl.; iyoki- , n. Owaŋyaŋke, n.: w- , n. A sight, vision.

shrink, (cringe, shrivel). Mniga: ayu-, na- , yu- , v.n. Draw up. Mniiyosnisniyapi s'e, adv. -ing (as from cold water). Napośiŋ, v.n. Shrivel up; o-po, v.n. Be shrunken. Snaŋza, snaza, snas'a, v.n. Shrivel up. Tiyokaśkapi s'e śkaŋ, v. - from one.

shrug, v. Tahuceȟkiya; tahuślikiya, v. - the shoulders.

shuck, v. Wakiciȟ'u, Cut the rind or husk away.

shuffle, v.n. Nas'os'o.

shut, (close). Aeceliyeicíya, v. refl. - self up. Kśija: awa- , v.a. - upon; awakśiś, v. cont.; kakśiśya, v. Fold, double up. Ayuȟpa, v.a. Gmuza, adj.: ayu- , v.n.; gmusya, adv.; io- , v.n., n.; iogmusya, v.a.; nao- , v.a., v.n.; o- , v.n. Naopo, v.n. (flowers).

shy, (flinch). Paoȟmiŋ, v. - from. Taŋnapa, v. - from, at, flinch.

sick, Yazaŋ, v. Feel pain: a- , iwa- , i- , v.n.; iyazi, v.; o- , v.n. Be - because; wakiyaza, v. pos. Get - for; wa-ka, v. Be - ; n. One feeling - ; yas- , v. red. - all over; -ya, v.a. Make - . Ceśloślo, v.n. Glaja(ś), v.n., adj. Ȟmuŋga, v.a. Kuja, adj.: i- , v.n.; kici- , v. Be - for; ki- , v. Have - ; kuśkoŋza, v. Pretend to be - ; o- , v.n. Be - on account of. Okit'a, v.n. Be - . Ośuŋkecalaka, n. A very - person. Tokeca, adj. Unwell. Wasazeca, n. One easily made - , one getting well.

sickness, n. Okuje, wicayazaŋ, woyazaŋ.
Ague, n. Wicacaŋcaŋ.
Cholera, n. Wicaŋakśecapi.
Consumption, n. Śap'ayapi, waśilkte; śab aya kuja, v. Have consumption.
Convulse, v. Natiŋ.
Cramps, n. Nakśecapi, nawicakśeca, nawicatipa.
Epidemic (eye), n. Iśtawicaniyaŋ.
Eye disease, n. Iśtawakaśke.
Gonorrhoea, n. Kośka, koska.
Headache, n. Natayazaŋpi.
Hemorrhage, v. Ewehiyu; pawekaluzapi, n. (nose); wekaluzapi, n. (woman's); wenapopapi, n.
Leprosy, n. Wayakayaȟ'uwicokiye.
Measles, n. Nawicaśli.
Pleurisy, n. Ipaswayazaŋ.
Pneumonia, n. Cajuŋokapoja.
Pyorrhea, n. Cakapo.
Rheumatism, n. Hohuyazaŋpi.
Scrophulus, adj. Kikika; okikiyakel, adv.
Stroke, n. Wanagiktepi.
Swelling (belly), n. Nigetaŋka aupi; (finger) śaketapa, (gland) wahiŋheya, (hoof) sikośkapi, (throat) lotepopi.
Tremor, n. Wicanaŋka.
Tuberculosis, n. Caȟuwayazaŋ, hoȟpakujapi, hoȟpawayazaŋ.
Urinate, inability to, n. Lejapiśni.
Veneral disease (woman's), n. Wikośka.

side, Anuŋg, adv. On both -s; anuŋkataŋ(haŋ), adv. On, from both -s; hoanuŋk, adv. Hoitokagataŋhaŋ, adv. Saŋni, adj. Of, on one side: -ca, adv. -ways; -la, adv. Of only one - ; hacaya, adv.; miśnasanica, adv. On my - . Houŋma, n. Icioŋb(ya), adv. Icuŋoŋb(pa), adv. Out at one - . Hutasaŋpata, hutata(henataŋhaŋ), adv. Iiślayataŋhaŋ, adv. Ikaki(ya), adv. On that - of: -yataŋhaŋ, -totaŋ, adv. Ileciya, adv. On this - of: -taŋ(haŋ), adv.; leciyataŋhaŋ, adv. Ita: -hena, -henataŋhaŋ, adv. On this side (time and place); -okśaŋ, adv. On all -s; -towapataŋhaŋ, adv. To the windward - ;

tahena, adv. (time, place): o- , adv. -taŋhaŋ, adv. From this - ; -kiya, adv. Towards one, this way. Itaŋ, adv. On the - : -anuŋk, -anuŋkataŋhaŋ, -nuŋk, adv. On both sides; -okśaŋ, adv. On all sides; taŋblas, adv. On the - ; taŋblecakiya, adv.; yuitaŋnuŋk, adv. On both -s; taŋiyupse, v. Turn -ways. Kaglala, adv. By the - of; kaglakiŋyaŋ, adv. Sticking -ways. Hepi: ka-ya, adv. Along the - ; iyotaya, adv. On this - ; ta- , adv. By the way- ; ta-ya, adv. On the - of. Kicicaic'iya, v.a. refl. Take -s with; kikcaŋpta, v.a. Kogna, adv. On that - . Opeic'iya, v. refl. - with, follow; obic'iya, v. refl. Tawośitku, n. His help, one taking his - . Kicitila, v. Side with. Cf. live.

sift, Cf. filter. Caŋ: ka- , v.; kicicacaŋ, v. - for; yu- , v.a. (sieve). Cf. lack.

sigh, v.n. Cuwiokini: -ya, v.n.
sight, Iśtableza(s), v.n.: -ya, v.a. Iyuziya, adv. In - . Toŋwe: o- , n. Eye- ; -ya, v.a. Give - to. Owaŋyaŋke, n. A - : w- , n. A show. Sabyakel, sabyela, adv. In - (far off).

sign, (mark, language). Napeoŋwoglaka, v. Use - language. Cajeoic'iwa, v. refl. - one's name. Wakta, n. Mark. Wapetokeca, n. Mark, miracle.
signal, Cf. beckon. Kosya, v.a.
signature, Wicekiye, v. Solicit -es.

silent, (still). Inila, adj.: -ya, v.a. Make still; a- , adv. Ataŋs'e, adv.: -la yaŋka, v.; ataŋs'iŋ, adv. Hohośni. Iyuśpeśni, adj. Mute. Popotkakiya, v.t. Silence one (by argument). Śuŋgnuni s'e yaŋka, v. Be - and sad.

silverware, Cf. utensil, fork.

similar, Cf. like, alike. Aiyecelya, adv. -ly. Owaŋgya, v.a. Be - to.
simmer, v.n. Nas'a.
simple, Woecetu, n. Simplicity.
simultaneous, Iyokignag, v.

sin, v. Waḣtani: -ya, v.a.; a- , v.a.; - s'a, n. Sinner; waic'iḣtani, v. refl. - against self; wakiḣtani, v. - against.

since, adv. Kapiyehaŋ, Ever - . Kohaŋś, adv. - that, so that.

sincere, (devout). Waawaciŋ, adj.
sinew, Cf. String. Takaŋ, n.

sing, (song). Lowaŋ, v.: a- , v.a.; caŋ-kiya, v. Play an instrument; eya- , v.; gloglo- , v.; gnagna- , v.; haŋ-pi, n.; ikici- , v.; i- , v.a.; ki- , v.; -pi, n. Songs, hymns; o- , n. Song. Hośiśipa, n. Word used in a playful song. H'oka, v., n. - with the drum.

single, adj. Alone, unmarried. Okinihaŋ, v.a. - out (for praise). Apatoŋyela, iciyakigle, iyabya, paoglaya, adv.

sink, (immerse, submerge). Speya: a- , v.a.; oka- , v. - into; o- , v.a. Make - . Ḣ'aŋyaŋ, Ḣ'aŋyeca, v.n. Naoḣpa, v.n. - into; naoḣpeya, v.a. Oswaswaya, part. -ing in.

sip, (suck). Yazoka, v.a. Yagopa, v.
sit, v. Iyotaka: h- , v.n.; paiyotag, adv. Down, -ting. Yaŋka, v.n. Akiglaski(ŋ), v. Akigna, v. Awajal, v. Hupaza: -gle, v. Pakśija, v.n. - down. Cf. bend.

size, Watoketuka, adv. Sizably, good -ed.

skate, n. Cah'icazo: - kic'uŋ, v.; mazacaḣ'icaza, n. -es.

skein, Cf. bunch, string. Oyaya, n.

skill, Iwayupika, v.n. Be -ed; iwayupiya, adv. Iyopteya, v. Become -ed.
skillful, adj. Aḣ'okaka; akiḣoka, n., adj. Aoḣ'aŋhaŋhaŋ(kel), adv. Awayupika, v.n.; awayupiya, adv. Ḣlaiŋśni, adv. Ksizeke, adj. Okibliheca, v.n. Be - . Śkalwayupika, adj. (at games); wopika, adj. (in making). Waḣtekeśni, adj.

skim, v. Kage, - off.
skin, n. Ha: -oyasaka, adj. With - shriveled; -pahlaya, v. Shed - ; -pasloka, v. Chafe the - ; -toŋ, v.n. Have chapped - ; -yuza, v.a.; -staŋ, adj. Dark -ned. Huka, n. The - . Haŋpsicu, n. Prepared moccasin - . Gapa: na- , v.a. (by foot); pa- , v.a. Get -ned. Ohamna, adj. Smelling of - . Oso, v. Make - open. Waaślaya, v. Wagapa, v.a. (by knife). Zapa: gla- , v. pos.; wa- , v. Cut off.

skip, v. Caḣaglapepeya; mniglapepeya,
v. Make - on water. Kaśkehaŋ, v. Make
- .

skull, Cf. bone. Pahu, n. - bone.

sky, Cf. heaven. Towaŋjila, n. Blue -.

slack, adj. Oḣtaḣta, Not tight stretched.

slander, (libel). Cf. defame. Aie: o- ,
n.; wa- s'a, n. -er; waweceyeśniśni
oie kitoŋ, v.; wico- , n. Wal'iyopeya, v.a. Waoyataŋ, v. Wawośtegla,
v. Use bad names. Wowiḣ'oiyeya, v.
- one.

slant, Cf. slope. Oḣya, adv.

slap, (strike). Kaskapa, v. Pahiḣaḣa,
v.a. - in the face.

slash, (cut, strip). Kazaza, v.a.

slate, n. Iŋyaŋ sapa.

slaughter, Optekte, n. - house.

sled, Slohaŋ(e): caŋiyu- , caŋiyuslo-
he, caŋwo- , hohukazuŋta oŋ o- kic'oŋpi, wiyu- , n.; wo- , n. A drag.

sleep, Ḣwa, adj.: -ka, adj.; -ya, v.,
adv.; -yela, adv.; a-ic'iya, v. refl.;
a-yela, adv.; ka- , v.a. Put to - ;
na- , v.a. Ahiyuŋka, v.n., v.a.; e-
yuŋka, v.a. Iśtiŋma, v.n.: a- , v.n.;
oŋśtiŋmat'a, v. - soundly. Ayugiŋ,
v.n.; ayugiic'iya, v. refl. Iyoyalal,
adv. In a manner -ing. Snicat'a, v.
Feel -y (from heat or cold).

slice, Bla: ka-pi, n.; oka- , n.;
wa- , v.a. Opasleca, v.a. Wakisku-
sku, v. pos. - off own. Wazapa, v.
(meat for drying).

slide, (slip). Slohaŋ: ka- , v. Make
- ; oka- , v.a. - in; ka-haŋ, v. -
repeatedly; na- , v.a. Make - (kick);
o- , v.n. - down; oyu- , v.a. Make -
in; v.n. Aglahaŋ, v.n. Aḣicahaŋ, v.
Śluta(l): a-ya, v.a.; aślu- , v.n.;
aya- , v.a. Caḣkazo, v. - on ice in
moccasins. Cegya, adv. Gicahe, v.n.
Slip and fall: -ya, v.a. Ikpasloka,
v. refl.

slight, v.a. Waceyeśni. Ociŋḣiŋyaŋpi,
v. recip. They feel -ed. Wakicoya,
adv. -ly.

sling, v.a. Ayuḣmiŋ. Iŋyaŋ oŋyeyapi,
n.

slip, (slide). Nasluta, v.i. - out;
naśluta, v. Śluśluta, adj. -pery,
fig., penniless; yaśluta, v.a. Let
- (from mouth); yuśluta, v.a. - out,
let - from. Nakiśna, v. pos. (feet);
naśna, v. Naicoga, v.n. - down,
loosen. Paona, v.a. - on, push on.
Tuŋtuŋpa, adj. -pery, ropy, slimy.

slit, Cf. rip. Sleca: kiwa- , v. -
in the middle (soft); okiwa- , v.a.;
pa- , v.a. Paka, v.a. Cut a - .

sliver, v.a. Ayuśuja, ayuśuśuja.

slope, n. Henake. Kaapamagle, adv.
-ing down. Oŋnaptaŋ, adj. Sideling.

sloth, n. Woślaŋkapiŋ.

slovenly, (slouchy, untidy). Cogeca,
adj. Ḣco, adj.: -ka, adj.; -ya,
-yakel, adv. Ḣlohaŋ, ḣloheca, adj.
Ḣnahaŋ, adj.; ḣnaheya, adv. Iyuhaya,
adv. Loosely. Naḣpaḣpa, v. Be - .
Naḣpiḣpi s'e, adv.

slow, Slohaŋ: a- , v.n.; a-kel, adv.;
slohe s'e, adv. -ly. Cf. crawl. Aspa-
yeic'iya, v. refl. Huŋkeśni, v.n.,
adj. Ḣpaka, adv. Ḣwayela, adv.; i-
ḣwaḣwa s'e, adv. Ḣ'aŋhi, v.n.: -ka,
n.; -kiya, adv.; -la, adj.; ka-ya,
adv. -er; na-ya, adv. Oḣ'aŋ, v.n.
Be - doing: -hi, v.n.; -slata, v.n.
Work deliberately. Wah'aŋhiya, adv.
(cut); wayuḣ'aŋhihika, n. A - person.
Icuŋsya(e), v.: -kel, adv. Not heartily; -ca, n. Iwaśte: -la, adv.; -gla,
pa-la, adv. Kilyakel, adv. -ly but
surely. Owicaḣtehaŋ, adj. Of - development. Slata, adj. Feeble, - at doing: wayu- , v. Do -ly. Śuŋk'lote,
adj. (from utter weariness). Zohela,
adv. Very -ly.

slush, (snowy). Mnicoco, adv. -y. Śloślola, n. Walolopela, n.

smack, (lips). Kipiza, v. - own. Waya-
c'o, v. - lips (eating). Yaskapa,
v.a. - lips (kissing).

small, adj. Cik'ala: -kel, adv.; cik'a-
ya, cik'ayela, adv.; ciscila, adj.;
cisciyela, adj., adv.; ka- , v.a. Cut
- ; na- , v.a. (by foot); naciscila,
v.a.; o- , adj. - within; pa- , v.a.
Rub - ; paciscila; wa- , v.a. Shave
- ; waciscila, v.a. Cut - . Aopteca,
adj. Aśuŋśiye, n. A - amount: -ce, n.

Skola: hiŋ- , adv.; ni- , adv. Very - . Hiyanuŋ, adj.

smart, Tuta: na- , v.n.; waya- , v. Make - (biting). Okapaza, v.a. Make - (as pepper does). Okibliheca, v.n. Be - in doing.

smear, Cf. glaze. Apaśluta, v.a. Siŋsiŋ, adj. Be -ed, slimed.

smell, Mna: akaŋ- , v.a.; ao- , v.a.; eca- , adj.; ha- , adj.; iji- , v.n.; nap'o- , v.a. Make - (step on); o- , v.a., n.; os'a- , adj. -ing sour, stale; śica- , adj. Bad -ing; taku- , v.n. Have - or taste. Azilkiya, aziltoŋ, v.a. Gmuŋza(s), adj.: -mna, adj. Ḣuŋwiŋ, v.n.: Ḣuiŋ, v.n.; -mna, adj.; -ya, v.a.; i- , v.n., n. Ḣwiŋ, v.n.: -mna, adj. Ḣ'a, v.n.: -mna, adj.

smile, v.n. Hiḣ'akiya, Grin.

smoke, v.n. Uŋpa (tobacco). Acaŋnumpa, v.a.; caŋnumkiya, v.a. Caŋnuŋpa, n., v.n.: - pahu, n. Pipe bowl; - siŋte, n. Pipe stem; - iglaye, n. Stem cleaner; - hahiŋ iyapehaŋpi, n. Quill-decorated pipe; hokśiśniyaŋ - , v. Send the - through the nose. Wawacaŋlilike, n. One that -es always. Śota, n., v.n.: a- , v.n.; i- , n.; o- , adj. Smoky; n. ; niya-s'e, adv. As if breathing - ; o-mna, n. Smell of - ; o- t'a, v. Suffocate from - ; o-ya, adv.; śotiyowotaŋiŋśniyaŋ, adv. Enveloped in - ; śotiyuskilya, adv.; śotoju, adj. Smoky, hazy; śotojuya, v. Fill with - ; waka- , adj. Blackened by smoke; śola śapa, v.n. Become -ed (dirty); śolkiya, v. Make - ; śolya, v. Make smoky. Zita(l), v.n.: a-ic'iya, v. refl.; a-kiya, a-toŋ, a-ya, a- , v.a.; i- , v. a.; oi- , v.n.; o-ya, v.a. Make a - . Gluskaḣciŋ, v. Kaop'ośya, v. Make - . Omnakiya, v. Give a - to.

smolder, v.n. Wazilya.

smooth, adj. (hair): aglu- , v. pos.; aka- , v.a.; ka- , v. - down; kica- , v. - for; aoka- , v.a. ; apa- , a-ya, v.a.; ayu- ; iyu- , v. - down; kiciyu- , v. - for. K'eza, adj. Beaten - : ana- , v.; apa- , aya- , ayu- , ona- , wa- , v.a. Apak'ega, v.a. K'oza(s): apa- , v.a.; ayu- , v.; -yela, adv.; pa- , v.a. Rub - ; ya- , yu- , v.a. Lapa, adj. Level: apa- , v.; pa- , v.a. - off (road); yua- , v.a. Apamaŋ, v.a. File - . Awablaya, v.a. Ayuśluśluta, v. Iyaskiska, v.n. Nakca, v.n. Be - . Onat'oza, v. Make - . Oyuślata, v. Make - , fig. corroborate. Pablaya, v.a. -en. Papsuŋpsuŋla, v. Rub - and round. Pasmiŋyaŋ, v.a. Rub or scrape - or clean. T'iŋzani, adv. -ly.

snake, n. Siŋte: -ḣla, n. Rattle - . Wagleza, n. Garden - . Waŋgleglega, n. Bull - ; waŋto, n. Blue racer. Zuzeca, n.: -kiŋyaŋpi, n. Flying - ; mnimahel - , n. Water - . Kizuzeca, v. Turn to a - .

snap, (contract, expand). Cf. splinter. Nasusuza, v. (contract).

snare, n. Igmuŋke.

snatch, v.a. Yamahe eyaya (by mouth).

sneak, v.a. Anaslata: -pi, n. Aokamna, v. Apustag, v.

sneeze, v.n. Pśa, apśa.

sniff, Cf. snivel. Pojaŋjaŋ, v. (scent).

snivel, (snuff, sniff). Paḣglajiŋca, paḣlajiŋca, v. Pogiŋjo, v. Sniff. Pośiŋ, v.n. Snuff up the nose, make faces at. T'iŋga, v.n. Grunt.

snore, v. Gopa(b): -iśtiŋma, v.; -ya, adv.

snort, v.n. Puga.

snout, n. Pute, Nose and lips.

snow, n. Wa: a- , v.n.; a-hiŋhe, v.n.; a-hiŋheya, v.a., adv.; -akata, v. Cover with - ; -gugeca, n. Crusted - ; -hiŋhe, v. It -s; -hiśnaheca, n. Soft new - ; -iśnaheca, n.; -kapopo, v. Crush (as snow); -mini, n. - water; -op'o, n. - dust; -teca, n. New - ; -woblu, v. The - flies; -zaŋzaŋ, n. Mist of - . Awosoksolya, adv. Hiŋhaŋ, v.n. Iyapa, n. - storm.

so, (long, short, high). K'uŋhehaŋyaŋ, coord. conj. - long. Lehaŋkeca, adv. - long, high, short.

soak, v.a. Ḣpaŋyaŋ: mniyo- , v. - in water. Kaḣtaŋ, v. - up, in; okaḣtaŋ, v. Kazuksugyela, adv. Sopping wet. Mniwot'a, v.n.

soap, n. Haipajaja, wipajaja.

soar, (glide, sail). Okaḣo, v.n.; okas'a, v.

sob, v.a. Ceya: -okit'a, v.; gla- , v. pos.; iglu- , v. refl. Caokit'a, v.n.; caokit'at'aya, adv.; caiglat'e, v. Ciŋktakte, v. Comniglazaŋzaŋ, v. Giŋca, v.n. Howakaŋ, v.n. Icilowaŋ, v. Ic'icaŋ, v. refl.

sober, Bleza: ki- , v.n.; o- , v.n.

society, n. Okolakiciye, League, fellowship, community. Iḣoka, Wiciŋska (Oglala military societies). Iyuptala (a society like to the Omaha Dance Society).

soft, Cf. bulky. Coco, adj.: -la, adj.; -ya, adv.; na- , v.a. Make - ; pa- , v.a. Rub - . Ḣpaŋ, adj.: gluḣpaŋ- , v. pos. Kpaŋla, adj. - and fine: kpaŋ- , adj. Hihi, adj.: -la, adj. Sloslola, adj. Turning - . Śtaka, adj. Mushy. Lopa, adj.; lolobya, v. Boil - . Ośtulya, adv. (not frozen). Paŋpaŋla, adj. Tender (skin). Paŋśpaŋja, adj. Fluffy. Pat'eca, v.a. -en (press). Wopowaya, v.a. Make - (blow). Yuḣuŋta, yuḣoŋta, v.a.: a- , v.a. Yusaka, v.a. -en (bend).

soil, Cf. dirt. Naśapa, v.a.: waa- , v. Trample. Paśica, v.a. Spoil.

solder, v.a. Apuspa: -pi, n. Aślo, v.n.: -ya, v.a. Wiyaskabye, n.
soldier, Cf. akicita, n.
sole, n. Sicuha: -toŋ, v. - a shoe. Akiglake, n.

solicit, v. Śil ecoŋ ape. Zomi, adj. -ing with deception or pretense: -ka, n. On so -ing.

some, n. Huŋḣ: -lala, adv. Taku, n. -thing: -eya, n.; takuŋl, n. -thing, anything. Enana, enagnala, adv. -times. Watohaŋl, adv. -time: i- , iwatohaŋtu, adv. Tohaŋ, adv. -time: -ḣci, -śna, adv. Tokcel, tokicel, adv. -where. Tokiyotaŋ, adv. -where (direction): -haŋ, adv. Tokśa, adv. -time, by and by. Tuktektel, adv. -times. Tuwa...eśa, pron. -one. Uŋkcaŋś, adv. By and by.

somersault, Tahujipakicuŋ, v. (on the neck).

song, Cf. sing. Olowaŋ, n. Tune, hymn. Wioweśtelowaŋpi, wioyeśtelowaŋpi, n. Night or love -s.

soon, adv. Aetulake el, aetulakeci. Aśkaŋyela, adv. Ecana, ecakcana, iyecana, adv. Ehakelakeciŋhaŋ, adv. Lecala, adv.: ka- , adv. Otehaŋyalaka, adv. A little while. Tokśa, adv. Sometime, by and by.

soot, n. Śotkazi; adj.; śolanini, n.

sore, Ḣli, v.n., n.: ḣli-(la), adj.; i- , n., adj., v.n. Ikpakiśkija, v. refl. Iśtaniyaŋ, v.: -pi, n.; iśtoḣli, adj. Kaiḣeju, adj. (riding). Katuta, adj. Naśli, v.n. Form a - . Ośtaŋhaŋ, n. A running - .

sorrow, Acaŋteśica(l), v.n.: -yakel, -ya, adv. Cuwipuskica, v.n.: -t'ekinica, v. Icakije, n. Caŋśica(e): i-pi, n.; wo- , n. Iyokiśica, v. Iyoyakeca, v.n. Be distressed.

soul, n. Hokśicaŋkiya, The spiritual seed, influence; the root of the sacred tree at the center of the nation's hoop by which it blooms. BE. BR.27.

sound, (ring). Cf. thorough. Ahotaŋ, v.a. Hotoŋ, v.: a- , v.a.; na- , v.n. Reproduce - . Aḣlo, v.n. Kaḣla, v. Kaka, adj. -ing dull: ka- , v.a.; kakoka, v. Rattle, thump; kakog, v. cont. Sna, v.n. Ring, rustle: ka- , v. Make - . Kpeya, adv. -ing; kpeyela, adv. With a loud report. Okaco, v.n. - within. Katkaŋheya, adj. Thorough.

sour, adj. Skumna, Spoiled: asuŋp-zi, n.; ośkumna, adj. Smelling badly; s'amna, adj. Smelling - . Skuya(e): ici- , adj.; o- , adj.; wi- , n. What sours things.

sow, v.a. Okala, Plant.
space, n. Oko: iy- , n. (between); -śniyaŋ, adv. Being no - ; -toŋ, v. There is a - , crack, hole; -toŋyaŋ, n. Opening, vista; adv. With free spaces; -wanilya, adv. With no - between, all over; -ya, adv. Spacing between; tiy- , adv. Between houses; tiokitahena, n. Open - in the country side; tiyokitahena, n. Cejaka, adj. Walking with legs pigeon-like.

sparce, adv. Jiyela, Thinly. Zazeca, adj. Here and there: -la, adj.; -yela, adv. Scattered. Glakeyela, adv.

spare, Akapeca, akapeya, adv. Ece cola yuha, v.; yucokala, v.a. Keep for - . Paga^n, v.a. Able to part with: -ya, v.a. Make give away; ikpaga^n, v. refl. Kpata^{n}ta^{n}kel, adv. Sparingly.

spark, (scintillate). Cf. shine. Kaḣaha, v. Curl up (flame). Ilega: na- , v. Make sparkle; nalega, v.; pa- , v. Make sparkle. Peliyaglaśyaha^n, adj. Glimmering beneath ashes. Peśnija, n. - of fire.

spatter, v.n. Nagaga. Wotica, v.n. Make - out.

speak, (utter). Cf. say, tell, defame. Iya, v.n.: -gnaśki^{n}ya^n, v.; -tą, v.a.; -yaha^n, part. Ia, v.n.: -ha^n, part.; -pi, n.; -wayapika, v. Ie: -kapi^n, v.n.; -kiya, v.a.; -ksapa, v.n.; -ska, n., v.n.; -skakiya, v.a.; -śni, v. Ioyaśka^n, v.a. Aya: -suta, v.a.; -śkaheyela, v.; -śkatuyela, v.; aglaśna, v.a. pos.; -śta^n, v.a.; aglaśta^n, v. pos.; -zamni, v.a.; -zu^{n}ta, v.a. Aia, v.a.: -pi, n.; aiekiya, v.a.; aikia, v. pos.; c- , v.
Ai: -capa(b), v.a. - against; -wa^{n}cayapi, v. pl. They - bad about each other; -kapa, v.a.; -kcapta, v. Reprove.
Eya, v.: eciya, v.a.; eic'iya, v.a.; ekiciya, v.; ekiya, v.; -hi^{n}gla, v. Burst out -ing; -hoyekiya, v.; -hoyeye, v.; - icekiye, v.; - iwahoya, v.; - iwaktaya, v.; -ke, interj. You don't say; -kico, v.; -kipa^n, v.; -kpaha, v. pos. Announce own; -śta^n, v. col. pl.; -ya, v.; eyeceleś, express. He said that long ago; eye le (ke), express. He said so; eyeya, v.a. Make say. Heya, v.; -ya, v.; heciya, v.; hehela, v. You said so; heic'iya, v.; hekiya, v.; heyekiya, v.a.; eoyaka, v.a.; ewoyaka, v.
Oglaka(e): a- , v.a.; iśnaw- , v.; iw- , v. pos.; iwoyaka, v.a.; oic'iglaka, v. - to self; woow- , n. An address. Glatokeca, v. pos. - of one as different.
Ajiji, v. Whisper about one. Ak'oka, v. - to one incessantly. Ayuḣmu^n, v.a. - without let. Iwaśicu^n, v.n. - badly. Owakiya, v.a. - to, with, harshly. Yata, v. in comp. Utter. Yugalya, v. - out to.
Ho: -akicipa, v. - for one; -bukiya, v.n. - gruffly; -ḣniya^{n}ya^n, v.n. To whimper; -ku^{n}pe śni, adv. Babbling on; -okihipicaśni, v. Unable to get a chance to - ; -śi, v. in comp. To take word, tell news.

speaker, (machine). Mazalowa^{n}kiyapi, n. Record player.

species, Cf. class.
speckle, Icigleśka, adj. -ed.
spectator, n. Wa^{n}wa^{n}ya^{n}ka, wawa^{n}ya^{n}ke.
speed, Cf. fast, swift. Oluzaha^n, n.

spend, Cf. use. Jena, adj. Having used up, sold; śena, adj. Wakasoteka, n. A -thrift. Yuwanica, v.a. - one's money. Zi^{n}lyeic'iya, v. refl. Have spent all.

spill, (pour). Kaśta^n, v. Pour: a- , v.a.; aiglaśta^n, v. refl. Pso^n, psu^n: anaic'i- , v. refl.; apa- , aya- , ayu- , v.a.; gla- , v. pos.; ka- , kica- , na- , v.a.; kpa- , naki- , v. - own; pa- , v.a.; ya- , v. (with the mouth); yu- , v.a. Kicala, v. - for (grain).

spin, Cf. twist. Kagmu^n, v. (by hand); wapagmu^{n}ke, n. A spinner. Kahomni, v.a. Kawaci, v.a. (a top); glawaci, v. pos.

spirit, (soul, shadow). Nagi(la), n. Soul: - iyaya, v.n. Yield up the - ; -niic'iya, v. Save one's soul; wa- , n. Spirit separated from the body; wa- tamakoce, n. - world; wa-tipi, n. - home; wa-ya, v. Go to the - land; wa-yata, adv. In the land of -s. Woniya, n. Life-breath, spirit: -waka^n, n. p. The Holy Spirit. Towaka^n, n. His waka^n, spirit.

spit, (foam, froth). Aglaśkica, v. pos. Śośa: ata- , v.a.; ita- , v.; ota- , v. - in; otaśośe, n. Spittoon; ta- , v. Mnitaga, n. Ohoḣpa, v.a. - into. To^{n}ikaśpa, v. Expectorate; to^{n}kaśpa, v. Wipasno^n, n. Roasting - .

spite, n. Wopasmi. Wowicaśaśni, n. Mischief.

splash, v. n. S'a. Paśkapa, v. (with hand); wayaśkapa, v. Apaśwoka, v. Push in and - .
splinter, Cf. snap. Nasuza, v.n.

split, Ja:awa-ta(l), v.a.; ka- , v. - somewhat; pa-ta, v.a. Make forked, divided; yawa- , v.a. Ka: awa- , v. a.; wa-haŋ, part. (as a quill-end); ya- , v.a. (with mouth); pakawa, v.a. Make - , insert. Sleca: awa- v.a.; awo- , ayu- , ka- , kica- , kicica- , oka- , okica- ; okiglu- , v. refl. - in middle; okina- , v.n. - open, burst open; owaslece, n.; -haŋ, part. - of itself; wakici- , v.a. Rip (by knife); wo- , v.a. (shoot); yu- , v.a. Tear. Awoȟleca, v.a. Ptuja; awo- , v.a.; pa- , v.a. Crack by working; okicaptuga, v.a. Śleca: awo- , v.a.; ka- , kica- , na- , oka- , okiwo- , pa- , wo- , v.a. Kaksa, v.a. - open, up; kicaksa, v. Kaksiȟpeya, v. Chop, sever. Kiȟ'aŋka, v.a. Naokotoŋyaŋ, adv. -ting, cracking.

spoil, Śica(l): ayu- , v.a.; ka- , v. (from striking); kiciyu- , na- , v.a.; oiglu- , v. refl. - own reputation; -ya, v.a.; wa- , v.a. (cut); wo- , v.a. (shoot). Ayukuka, v.a. Okapa, v.n. Onapiga, v.n. Ośtekaya, v.a. Deform (horse). Oya, adj. -ed. Taŋtoŋśniyaŋ, v.a. (over-cook); taŋtoŋya, v. Let - (from over-supply). Wakipi, n. A -ling. Wotuka(ka), v.a. (from shooting).

spoke, n. Huzazeca.
sponge, n. Iyuȟepe (absorber), mniiyuȟepe. Okaȟtaŋye, n.; okaȟtaŋyaŋ, v.a. Atiole, v.a.
sport, (jest). Waakicaga, v. Make - of. Wawiȟaka, n. Jester; wawiȟapi, n. -ing, making - .

spotted, adj. Glega: gle- , adj.; gleśka, adj.; pagleza, v.a. Rub to make - .
sprain, (dislocate). Hunaśte, v. - the leg. Naguka, v.a.; paguka, v. (rub). Panuŋga, v.a. Tokośtaŋ, v.n. Dislocate own.

spread, Akablaga(ȟ), v.n.; kablaga, v. - out, unfurl, - open; okabla, adj., adv.; wapabla, v. - out; kaoblagaheya, adv. Centrifugally; akablaja, v.a.; akablas(ś), v.; akablaya, v.n.; kiciyublaya, v. - out for; oyublaya, v.a. - out in. Akipsoŋwaheya, adv. -ing out into a line. Mni: a- , v.; i-taŋ, v.n., n.; ki- , v. - to dry; wa-pi, n. Fruit etc. - thinly. Ayublaya, v.a.; gluglaya, v. pos. Anableca, v.n. Gata: glu- , v. pos.; ka- , v. - out; kagal- , v. red. Kaȟtaŋyaŋ, v. Make - . Kaobleya, v. - apart; paobleya, v.a. (rub). Naȟlagaŋ, v.n. Open out, enlarge. Naowaŋcaya, v. - out. Pazica, v.a. Roll out, - out. Yaopoŋ, v. - news, rumors. Akaȟaya, v.a.

spring, (water, recoil, sprout). Cf. season. Wiwila, n.: ki- , v. Turn into a - . Minic'api, n. Naglaptuza, v.n. Recoil. Owahinape, n. A -ing up of. Uya, v.n. - up, sprout; uyekiya, v.a. Make sprout.

sprinkle, Mnimni: a- , v.a.; a-ya, ayu- , iya- , ia- , v.a.; o- , v. - into; wa- , v.; n. A sprinkler. Mniś'eś'e, v.n. Oyupsoŋpsoŋ, v. Spill.

sprout, Cf. spring. Camni, n.: a- , v.n. - on.

spy, Cf. reconnoiter. Toŋweya, n. A guide; v.n. Go as a - . Wakcaŋyeya, v.a. Make go and - .

square, Cf. edge. Katkuga, v. Cut - pieces. Katkuŋza, v. Cut off pieces. Obletoŋ, adj. - edged.
squat, (stoop). Kameyakel, adv. -ting down. Pustaka, v.n. - down.
squeal, (squeak). Kapiza, v.; pispiza, v. Kiskiza, v. Squeak. Pahotoŋ, v.a. Make - , cry out.

squeegee, v.a. Paskepa (by hand).
squeeze, v.a. Apaśli: -ya, adv. Pasli, v.a. - out. At'iŋsya, adv.; ayut'iŋza, v.a. Paokogna iyeic'iya, v. - self in. Paśkita, v.a. - out (press). Śkicahaŋ, part. -zing, pressed; waśkica, v.a. Scrape out; wośkica, v.a. - out.

squint, v. Iśtośniśkiye. Iśtakśiŋ, v.: -ka, n.; -kśiŋ, v.n.
squirt, v. Kaskepa, Press out; kaśkeb. Wosli, v.a. (push): i- , n.

stab, (stick). Cf. stick. Capa, v.a.: a- , v.a.; ai- , v.a.; cakicipa, cakipa, v. Acejiya, v.a. Stick out the tongue. Aopatica, v. Ȟloka: apa- , v.a.; caȟka- , v.; ikpa- , v. refl.; ipa- , v.a. Awaśloka, v.a.

stack, v. Okiciyuśtaŋ, Put one into another; ociyuśtaŋ, v. Be one in another. Paokiju, v. (cards).

stage-struck, (freeze). Uŋc'oŋnica, v.n. Be - .

stagger, Cf. turn. Ceka(g), v.n.: cek-ya, adv.; cek- , v.n.; ka-ya, adv. -ing; na- , v.a. Make - ; ya- iyeya, yaha iyeya, v. Turn aside with the mouth.

stain, (mark). Osiŋsiŋ, v.n. Leave a mark (tears). Oya, v.a., v.n. Sully.

stair, n. Caŋalipi; oiali, n. (house). Hokuta, adv. Down-s.

stake, Cf. pole. Paslata, v.a. Drive, set a - .

stamp, v. Iteiyaskabya, - an envelope; iteiyaskabye, n. Postage - . Nabu, v.a. (foot). Natuka, v.a. - off.

stand, (rest on). Haŋ, v.n.: a- , v.n.; ahekiya, v.n.; ahiya- , v.n.; ai- , v. col. pl. They go and - on; e- , v.n. col. pl.; eya- , v. col. pl.; i- , v.n. - in, at. Najiŋ, v.n.: -haŋ, part.; -hiyaya, v. - up; -kiya, v.a. Make - ; -yaŋ, v.; -yeyapi, v. pl. They - in a row; nakicijiŋ, v. - for; nakicijiŋka, v. - by one; nakicikśiŋ; oi- , n. Place to - ; oi-ta, n.; o- , v. - in; ayu- , v.a.; el- , v.n.; el-ya, v.a.; e- , v.n.; gli- , v. pos.; iglu- , v. refl.; i- , v.n. Rise; i-kiya, v.a.; ki- , v. Reach home and - ; kpa-k, v. Get to one's feet. Akojal(ya), adv. Apatuza, v. Ȟ'o, v.n. Ic'icaŋyaŋ, adv. Igluowotaŋla, v. refl.; paowotaŋ, v.a. - erect. Jiya, adv. -ing up, bristling. Nawosla iyeya, v. Make - up (step on). Owahe, n. Platform. Pap'oȟ'a, v.a. Make hair - (by hand). Woȟlepe s'e, adv. -ing upright.

standard, (flag, banner). Wapaha, n.: - payuktaŋ, n. (of Oglala military societies).

star, Cf. heaven. Wicaȟpi, n.: -hiŋȟpaya, n. Meteorite showers; -siŋtetoŋ, n. Comet; - śa, n. Planet.

starch, n. Mniȟuha ipatiŋ, wipatiŋ.

stare, v. Ayuta(l). Iśta: - kte nuŋs'e, adv.; -nagleśkiya, v.; -natogkiya, v.; - tolas'e ayuta, v.

start, Cf. begin, stand. Oinajiŋ, n. -ing place. Uya, v.a. Śkaŋhiŋglekiya, v. Make - up. Paalos, v. - at, from (stung). Panag, v. - at.

starve, v.n. Akiȟ'aŋ; oakiȟ'aŋ, n.

state, (condition). Ouŋ, n.: - lecala, n. The New Deal; - teca, n. The Great Society.

stay, Cf. remain. Oyuȟlagaŋ śni, v.n. (same place).

steady, Paslalyela, adv. Steadily. Ś'agyakel, adv. Woslaslate, n. One who is good and - at work.

steal, (theft). Manoŋ, v.a.: awa- , v.a.; makicinoŋ, makinoŋ, v.; -pi, n. Theft; owa- , v. - in, from; n. A thief. Paskica, v.a. (Slang) To swipe.

stealthy, Nahaha, adv. Stealthily.

steam, Cf. fog. Ip'o, n.; p'oyela, adj. -ing. Ini, v.n.: -kaga, v.n.; -opa, v.n.; -pi, n. Steam bath; -ti, n., v.n. Be in the sweat-lodge; -wokeya, n.

steep, adj. Oiyakapeya (up), oiyoȟpaya (down).

stem, n. Hucaŋ, taśpu.

step, n. Ca, One - distance: -egle, v.n. Take a - ; -eglepi, n.; -glawa, v. Count one's -s; -glegle iyutapi s'e mani, v. Make big -s; -glepi, n.; icaȟli, v. - into mud. Iyahaŋ, v.a. Kinaksa, v. Hurt the foot. Naȟli, v.n. - in mud. Oali, n. (stair).

stern, adj. Wohiŋyaŋze; hiŋyaŋza, v.n. Be - .

steward, n. Waawaŋglakiyapi.

stick, v.n. Aikoyaka(g), Cleave to: -ya, v.a. Staka: aka- , v.; aka-ya, adv.; aka-yakel, adv.; oka- , v.a. Make - on; o- , v.n. - to, on, in. Puspa: a- , v.a.; a-pi, n. Glue; apuspeya, adv.; iciya- , v.a. - together; i- , v.a.; ipuspe, n.; iya- , v.a., v.n. Glue on; iyapuspeya, v.a., adv. Skapa(b): aya- , v.n.; aya-toŋ, aya-ya, v.a.; iciya- , v.n.; iciya-ya, v.a., adv.; iya- , v.n.; iya-ya, v.a., adv.; iyaskabye, n. Paste; o-ya, adv.; o- , v.a. - to; waa- , v. - on; okaskeya, adv. -ing together lumped.

Ayuha, v.n. Caŋ, n. Wood: -ot'oza, n. A round - ; -petipiye, n.; -wipasnoŋ, n.; -wiyuze, n.; cuŋwiyawa, n. A counting - ; -jata, n.; -kujipa, n.; -kazoŋtapi, -kazuŋtapi, n. Hiyoyatake, n. That which -s between the teeth. Huŋkatacaŋnuŋpa, n. Wand (pipe like). Huŋpe, n. - for digging turnips: - okijata, n. Icapa(b), v.; icape, n. Splinter. Icaśloke, n. Pipe poker. Makiwoȟliya, v. - tight in the ground; paȟli, v.a. - in the ground. Oha, v.n. - to. Okaslata, v.n. - in (as a splinter); opaslata, v. Run into (sliver). Oya, v.n., v.a. - to: -tkapa, v.n. - on, in. Sata, n. A forked - ; satiyakaśke, n. That which ties on the sata. Tiktica, adj. -y. Tuslawayaskape s'e, adv. -ing as a leech. Yahaŋ, v.n. Be stuch with (as a splinter).

stiff, Atasaka, v.n.: iyatasaka(g), v.n.: -ya, adv. Pasuta, v.a. Make - (knead); kpasuta, v.a. -en (by kneading). Patiŋ, adj. Rigid, frozen; wotiŋ, v.n. Take a - position, be - , stand erect: -kiya, adv.; -yaŋ. T'iŋza, adj. Hard, firm: pa- , v.a. -en. Tkabya, adv. -ly. Yas'os'o, v.n. Be - from the cold.

still, Iyasni, v.n.: -ya, v.a. T'iŋzani, adv. Calmly.

sting, v.a. Pajipa, yajipa.

stingy, Apoŋpoŋyela, adv. Oȟ'aŋśica, v.n. Be - . Wateȟila, v. Be - ; n. Miser: -pi, n. Parsimony.

stink, Cf. smell. Oȟ'amna, v.n. Oniyemna, v. Have foul breath.

stir, (move, flow, propel, rummage). Kahi, v.: -hiya, v. Move; -hiyela, v. Flow. Katica, v. Onakiśośe, v. - up water (by foot). Wawakpaŋśni, adj. -ring, alert as a man.

stoke, v.a. Aoŋ, aoŋpa.

stomach, (rumminant). Tapo, n. Crop: ta- , n. Third cavity of - . Tiȟaha, n. Second cavity of - ; tiȟamnamna. Taśoka, n. Fourth cavity of - . Taśiyaka, n. Mouth of - .

stone, n. Iŋyaŋ. Icutu, n. - for grinding. Iguga, n. Ihe, n. Iȟ'e swula, n. Iswu, n.: -la, n. Kaŋgitame, n. Black shale. Wahiŋ, n. Flint waŋhi, n. Yuwipi, n. Transparent -s: - waśicuŋ, n. Power - of a dreamer.

stoop, v.a. Patuja, - over, bow down: a- , v.a.; apatuś, v. cont.; ayuki- , v.a. Apatuza, v. Paptuza, v.n. Apustag, v.: -ya, adv. Kpaoŋjiŋjiŋtka yaŋka, v. Be -ed in sorrow. Kpaśiŋśiŋ yaŋka, v. Be -ed (sorrow). Pakiŋ, v.n. Stand -ing: -yaŋ, v.n. Walk -ing; adv. Pustastaka, v. Yutuȟyela, adv. -ed.

stop, Akiyuŋka, v. col. pl. Akiti, v.n. Anapta, v.n., v.a.: -pi, part.; anapteton, v.a.; i- , v.a. Aoyutkuga, v.a. Ayuśtaŋ, v.a.: -kiya, v.a.; apa - , v.a.; o- , n. Cessation. Apat'o, v.n.: -ya, v.a. Iakicuni, v.a. Icagi, v.n. Icase, n.: -ya, v.a. Iglajata, v. refl. Igluhika, v. refl. Ikipajiŋyaŋ, adv. Kusetoŋ, v.a.; kuśeya, v.a. Oegnaka, n. Pagiŋge śni, adv. Going non- . Pątaka, v. Come to a - , - short, halt, bring to a - . Okit'eyakel, adv.

stopper, n. Iyostaŋ; iyośtaŋpi, n.; iośtaŋ(pi).

store, (lay up, business). Ju, v.a. Place, lay up. Opiye, n. Storage box: maz- , n. Tiyomnakiya, v.a. Gather and - up. Kigle, v. Lay up a - : wa- , n. A supply; wagle, n. - house, storage.

storm, v.n. Aicamna. Otkaŋ, v. Be -y. Ośiceca, n., adj. Kiȟ'aŋ, n.

story, (fable, myth). Ohuŋkakaŋ, n. Ooyake, n. -telling, narrative. Yataku, v.a. Make up a - about.

stove, n. Mazaoceti, maz'oceti; wiglioceti, n. An oil - .

straddle, (astride). Kablaśya, v. Woga, adv. Straddling, sprawling.

straight, Katiŋ, v. -en out: a-(yaŋ), v.a.; ayu- , ka- , v.a.; nakatiŋ, v.a., v.n.; nasatiŋ, v. (dying); pa- , v.a. -en out. Owotaŋla, adj.: ka- , v. Make - ; kiciyu- , v. Make - for. Pawoslata, v. Push up - . Yuotaŋ, yuowotaŋ, v. Make - . Yuzukapi s'e, adv. Moving in a - line, any direction.

strain, (roll). Jaka, v. - the eyes. Yuguka, v.a.

strap, Cf. hide. Teȟmisopi, n. Leather

strap; teḣpiwikaŋ, n. Wikaŋ, n. A packing - . Wic'iŋ, n. Meat - .

straw, Cf. grass.
streak, (stripe). Ogleza, adj. -ed.
stream, Cf. river. Wakpicagla, adv. By the side of a - ; wakpogna, adv. On the - ; wakpopta, adv. Across the - .
strength, Cf. strong. Wowaś'ake, n.

stretch, Cf. pull. Iyutaŋyaŋ, v. - out; iyutitaŋyaŋ, v. Be -ed by. Zica: kpazig- , v. - own; na- , adj. Over- ; v.a.; ya- , v.a. (by teeth); yu- , v.a. (skin). Gata(l): na- , v.n. - out the foot; yu- , v. - out (arms). Nasuŋyaŋ, adv. -ed out. Satiŋ, adj. -ed out straight. Yuglagla, v. - out, unwind. Yuguka, v.a. Draw out; yuzuka, v.a. - out from.

strike, (smite). Cf. beat. Apa, v.a. Smite. Ka: -huŋkuŋza, v. Pretend to - ; -makal iyeya, v. - down; -skapa, v. Slap, clap; -smiŋ, v. - off, make bare; -ś'aka, v. - lightly; -śtaka, v.a. Smite; o-śtaka, v.a. - in a place; o-śtake, n. Punishment; o-śpa, v.a. - off a piece; okicaśpa, v.a. Smite in two. Paha, v.a. Ready to - ; pakapa, v.a. - back, retaliate; paza, v.a. Hurt, kill; pemakiwoto, v. - the ground by hand. Waagliheya, v. (lightning). Yupuḣpuga, v. (in anger)

string, (strip). Cf. cut. Kaŋ, n. Artery. Ikaŋ, n.: -kicitoŋ, v.a.; -toŋ, -yaŋ, v.a.; he- , n. (for the hair). Oyaya, n. - of beads; oyaza, v.a., n. So, v.a. Cut into -s: so-pi, n. - cut from hide; wa- , v. Cut a - from hide.

strip, (cut, tear, divest). Kanica, v. - off clean. Kaswu, v. Cut into -s. Oyaśpaśpa, v. - off (by mouth). Smismi, smiŋyaŋ, adj. -ped clean, bare, smooth. Waka, v.a. (cut), split a quill. Yugapa, v.a. Pull off (skin). Yuka, v.a. - off. Yuso, v.a. Cut in -s; yus'o, v.a. Kiciyuśloka, v. - for (divest).

stripe, Gleza: gle- , adj. -ed; glezela, gwegweza, adj.; ka- , v.; kaglezela, v. Zuhaŋ, adj. -ed; zuheya, adv. In a -ed manner.

strive, (anxious). Kinica, v. Try to, be anxious to.

stroke, n. Maśteaglihaŋ, Sun-stroke. Oape, n. A striking. Wayuwiŋta, v. - the face.

strong, adj. Ś'aka(g): igluwa- , v. refl.; iwa- , v.n.; iwa-ya, v.a.; wa- , adj.; kawa- , v.n. Be made - ; kiciyuwa- , v. Make - for; kiwa- , adj. Having - muscles; ś'ag-, adj. Owikeśni, v.n. Be - , not fail; pawika, v.n. Be yet - , have some strength; pawiyakel, adv. Yet - . Asuta, v.n. Hupiŋyuŋ, adv.

struggle, (kick). Nagwaka, v.n. Nasuŋsuŋ, v.

stubborn, Yayaya, adv.
stubby, adj. Wamuŋta.

study, v.a. Ohaŋ.
stuff, (obstruct). Katica, v. Be -ed up. Opugi, v.a. Fill, push in: -pi, n. -ing; -toŋ, v.a. Put in -ing; -toŋyaŋ, adv. Opuḣli, v.a. - into: -yahaŋ, adj. Clogged.

stumble, (slide, slip). Kaiśuta, v. Kalektehaŋ, adv. -ling. Kaśe, v. Nagnayaŋ, v.a. Sipawakaśe, v.n.
stump, (stub). Oyaḣ'u, n. Putaŋla s'e, adv. Stubby.

stun, v. Kaitokpaza, kat'a (kill), nazaŋ (kick).

stupid, adj. Oksape woteḣi, tehaŋksape śni, tawaciŋt'at'aka.
sturdy, (hardy). **K'eze**, adj.
stutter, v. Iaouŋc'unica. Ieglaśna, v. pos.: -śna, v.n.; - s'a, n.

style, Cf. form, make.

subjuntive mood: Cf. indicative, optative. Tka, particle sign of; tkaś.

submerge, (immerse). Opaspa, v. Oyus'o, adv. -ed. Pakignuŋka, v. Push, dive under water. Pamahehe, v. Push under water repeatedly.

substitute, v.a. Heekiya; adv. Hoya, v.
successive, Ocib, adv. One after another.
such as, adj. Heca, - that; hececaka, n.; hecekcecaka, adj. Leca, adj. - this.

suck, v.a. Ayagopa; yagopa, v.a. - up, nurse. Ayazoka, v.a.; glazoka, v. pos. Aziŋ, v.a. - the breast: -kiya, v.a. Iyaskica(l), v.a.: -ya, adv. Yapa, v.: ki- , v. - for.

sudden, Cf. immediate. Hiŋgla, v.n. Wanuȟci, adv. -ly. Uŋgnahela, adv.

suffer, Cf. endure. Kakija(ś), v.n. Be afflicted: iyu- , v. Make - ; wawiyu- , v. Make - ; wicakiśya, v.; adv. In our needs.

sufficient, Icipiyela, adv.

suffix:

etu, el: (to words). Makes n. of time.

haŋ, he: (to v.). Makes participial; indicates repeated or occasional action.

haŋ, hiŋ, he: (to v.). Same as śke, They say, It is reported.

ȟci: (to words). Intensifies meaning.

ȟciŋ: (to fut. v.). Same as intensive ȟca, Very.

ka: (to v., n.). Emphasizes the word. (to words). Equivalent to śni; means also, Almost.

kel: (to adv.). Means, As it were.

kiya: (to v, etc.). Makes v. causative; makes word adv. of manner.

ko: (to v.). Means, Anxious to do.

ku: (to n. of family relatives). Makes them pos., His, hers.

la: (to words). Makes dim., or superl. (to num., dem.). Means, Only....

laka, laȟ: (to v.). Implies the question, Why don't you...?

lakel: (to v.). Makes adv. of manner.

ni: (to words). Converts to its contrary.

s'a: (to v.). Indicates frequent action; makes n. of agent.

s'e: (to words). Makes adv. of manner.

ta, ata, yata: (to n.). Makes adv. ph. At, on, to ....

taŋ: (to adv.). Develops adv.

taŋhaŋ: (to adv.). Means, From.

tu, l: (to words). Makes adv. of time.

uŋśto: (to v.). Means, All is said and done.

wapa: (to words). Develops the word with the meaning, Towards, forward (in future), upward.

ya: (to v., adj., etc.). Makes v. of cause, possession, regard.

ya, yakel, yaŋ: (to adj.). Makes adv. (to v.). Makes adv. or part.

yaŋ: (to words). Makes causative v.

yela: (to adj.). Makes adv.

yetu: euphonic etu.

(Note: pi, the common pl. form of words, as such, for v. makes them into n.)

sugar, n. Caŋhaŋpi.

suitable, Iyekicihaŋtu, v.n.

suitcase, n. Paŋśa. Cf. bag.

sulfur, n. Makazi.

summersault, Oŋziwosla, adv. Turning a - .

sun, n. Wi. Wiahinapa, v. Have the - rise on; wihinapa, n. The rising sun, the east. Wiiyaya, n. Sun-down; v. The - sets. Wiiyayuȟ, adv. In the path of the - . Wimahel iyaye, n. Setting of the - . Wiśaślayela aye, v.n. The - becomes clear and distinct. Wiyohiyaŋpa, n. The - rising.

sunshine, Cf. heaven. Omaśte, n.

supernatural, Cf. holy. Wowakaŋ, n. A - thing.

supervisor, (shepherd). Waawaŋglake, n.

supplant, (displace, rival). Paeze, v.a. Rival.

supple, adj. Psoŋpsoŋla, Lithe: -yeḷa.

supply, (provision). Waśeca, adj. Rich: -ya, adv.

support, n. Woit'iŋze.

suppress, v. Inapcapca iyeya.

surface, Gagaya, adv. On the - . Haakapa(b), adv. On the outside.

surfeit, (stuffed). Oȟaka, v.n. Be -ed.

surpass, Kapa: iya- , v.n.; iyo- , v.; kakipa, v. Excel; kapeya, v. Iyakigle, v.n.: -ya, v.a., adv.

surprise, v. Apablehiyuya. Itoŋpa(e), v.a. Be -ed, praise: itoŋic'ipa, v. refl.; itoŋkipa, v. pos.; -ya, itoŋkipeya, -yahaŋ, adv. Iyapaśtaka(g), v.n.: -ya, v.a. Iyatagle, v., adj. Ś'iŋyaya: iyu- , v. Be -ed at, frightened at; woś'iŋyeye, n. A scare; yu- , v.n. Be frightened. Nagiaktoŋśya, v.a. Uŋgnahelaya, v.a.

surrender, (yield, give up). Uŋc'oŋnica, v.a. Give up.

surround, Cf. around. Koglamnayaŋ, v.a. Restrain.

survey, v. Makaiyuta; makaiwaŋyaŋkapi, v. - on.

survive, v.n. Inapa. Ipaśloka, v.a.
suspect, v.n. T'uŋkeca, Be suspicious: i- , v.n.; t'uŋgya, v.a. Have suspicions: i- , v.a.; t'uŋkiya, v. - self; it'uŋgkiya, v.; ka- , v.a. Kenuŋyaŋ, v.

suspend, (dangle). Iyukoltkeyela, v. (on a wire). Ceśkiyutaŋ, n. Suspenders.
suspense, v. Akicoŋs, Keep in - .

swallow, v.a. Napca: a- , v. - on, after; atahnakipca, v. - one's saliva; nakicapca, v. pos.; nakipca, v.; onapce, n. Act of -ing. Tahglahota, v.; tahglaśkape, v. Choke. Yaoślog iyeya, v.a. - inadvertently.

swamp, (bog). Wiwila kapapa, n.; owiwiyela, adv. In a -y place; wiwiyela, adj. Boggy.

swarm, (throng). Pawis'e, adv. Close-packed.
sway, adj. Kcaŋkcaŋla, Very movable. Yuŋgyuŋka(haŋ), v.

sweat, (pant, give out). Cf. steam, perspire. v.n. Temni: -t'a, v.n. - profusely; -t'eyela, adv.; -yaŋ, adv. -ing; tewicamni, n. -ing.

sweep, (brush). Hiŋta: ayu- , v.a.; ka- , v. - off, out; kahiŋtu ska, v. Clear off; kicica- ; wo- , v.a., Blow away (shoot), - off. Yutaegle, v. - together.

sweet, (delicious). Skuya, adj.; skuyela, adj.; wiskuye, n. -ener. Cf. sour.

swell, (puff up, bloat, rise). Po, v.n. Puff up: a- , v.n.; na- , ka- , naka-, oka- , o- . Pogaŋ(h): na- , v.n.; ka- , naka- ; na-pi, n.; ona-ya, v.a. - out. Ipo, iwicapo, n. Kpa, v.n. Mna, v.n. Napśuŋka, n. Growth. Naśoka, v.n.

swerve, (deviate, curve). Iyukśaŋ, v. Curve off.

swift, Cf. fast. Luzahaŋ, v.n.
swim, v.n. Noŋwaŋ, nuŋwaŋ: a- , v.a.; i- , v.; ki- , v. - back (home).

swing, Cf. flap. Caŋkakiza, v.n. Gegeya, v., adv. Hohote, n. Hammock: -la, n.; -lakic'uŋ, v.n.; -lakaśka, v. Kapsaŋpsaŋ, v. Sway. Namnimni, v. red. Okazeze, v.n.; ozezeya, adv.; yazeze, v.a. Make - (by mouth). Pakoza, v.a. - back and forth. Yuwaga, v.a. - the arms (in running).

swirl, v. Okamnimni.
swish, Sliya, adv. -ing.
swivel, v. Poptaŋ, - the head.

T

table, (counter). Cf. altar. Agnawotapi, wagnawotapi, n.; wagnayutapi, waglutapi, n. (for eating); waagnaglepi, n.; wagnawopetoⁿpi, n. Store counter.

tag, (follow). Wiyuḣlagaⁿ śni, v. Have one's wife - along always.

tail, n. Situpi (bird). Siⁿte, n.; fig. A young man.
tail-wind, Itaglaḣwe, adv.: -kiya, -taⁿhaⁿ, -ya, adv.

take, v.a. Icu: ahi- , v. Ahiyaya, v.a.; eyaya, v.a.; gloeyaya, v. pos. Akinapa, v. Akiyagla, v.a.; kagla, v. - home to; waagleca, v. - home. Akśija, v.a. Eglaku, v.; eyaku, v.a.; wieyaku, v. - away a woman. Yuza, v.a. - hold of, - a wife; ekicigluza, v.; eyuza, v.a.; okiciyuze, n. Taking of one another, as in marriage. Epaḣpa, v.a.; gluḣpa, v. pos.; paḣpa, v.a. - down; wiglaḣpa, v. - down own (tent). Eyawa, v. Gloi, v. pos.; kicicai, v. - to a place for; kicigloi, v. - own to; kicigliya, v. - own to. Gluguka, v. pos. Gluḣeyapa, v. pos. Hohi, v. imp. - it. Icage, v. Igluk'o, v. Ikipemni, v. Ikpasloka, v. refl. Aya, v.: kaya, v.; ka- , v. - to, carry to. Ki, v. - from, rob: ka- , v. - home or elsewhere to; kicica- , v. - home for. Kicicagla, v. - home for. Makiglata, v. - much leave. Na, v. imp. - it; nana, v. imp. red. Ogluspa, v. pos. - hold of own. Oiglapta, v. - left-overs; okapta, v.a. - out (wages) by stages. Woze, n. The dipping out: -pi, part. Laded out; yaze, v.a. - out (by mouth). Yapa, v.a. - into the mouth (a pipe).

tale, n. Ohuⁿkakaⁿ. Cf. fable, story.

talk, Cf. speak. Kihowaya, v. - loud to. Kiyamna, v. - one out of for; oyaḣloḣloka, v. Babble; yawignuni, v. - bad, destroy (by talk). Oiglukiki, v. Gossip, backbite. Okiciciya, v. - together, court one. Śiloiepi, n. Bad - . Śilwoyaka, v. - bad of.

tall, adj. Haⁿska. Wazi s'e, adv. Very - .
tallow, n. Wasnatasaka, Hard grease. Waśiⁿkceka, n.

tan, v.a. Kpaⁿya, Dress; akpaⁿyaⁿ, v.a.
tangle, (enmesh). Iyuwiya, adv. -ed: pa- , adv. -ling; opawiwi, adv. -ed in a mass. Kaiyapehaⁿ, v. Get -ed; kaiciyapehaⁿ, adv. -ed up, folded. Oyuglaglaya, v.

tank, Cf. reservoir. Ojuminiyatke, n.

tap, v. Kalope s'e, Give a love- .
taper, (cut). Cf. wear. Katepa, v. Sli, adj. -ing: ya-tka, v.a. Make -ing (with teeth); yu-tka, v.a. Make -ing (pinch).

tardy, (slow). Śuśka, adj.
target, Cf. goal. Oweheca, n. A thrown arrow.

taste, Napiⁿ, adj. Tasty, rich: a- , v.n. Glata, v. pos. Iyuta, v. Try. Oskuya, adj. Sour; skuya, adj. Sweet; woskuye, n. Savor. Takumna, v.n. Have - or smell.

tatter, Kaⁿhaⁿ, adv. -ed: -haⁿ, adj.; kaⁿheca, adj.
tattoo, v. pos. Akito: -pi, n.; ato, v.n.

tex, (toll). Tiyopa wiśimnaye, n. - collector. Waecoⁿkiya, v. - one's strength. Waḣpaye, n. -es. Wakajujukiya, v. Impose a - .

tea, n. Caⁿkalyapi. Waḣpe, n. Leaves. Çaⁿḣlogaⁿ wakalyapi, Garden tickseed. Śeyaka, Peppermint. Cf. ceyaka. Uⁿpaⁿtawote, Smaller red-root. Waḣpeyatapi, Giant hyssop. Waḣpewaśtemna, Bergamont, (chewed). Zitkatacaⁿ, Wild tea.

teach, v. Waoⁿspekiya; waoⁿspekiye, n. A teacher.

tear, (rend). Cf. break. Akablaza, v.n. - open on. Pota: ka- , v.; kiciya- , v. - up (by mouth); oka- , v.n. (shake); aiglu- , v. refl. Hleca: kiciya- , v. - in pieces for (with mouth); kiciyu-, v. - for; na- , v.a. - a hole in, in pieces, fracture; okaḣlece, n. A rent; okina- , v.n.; ona- , v.a. - a hole; onaḣlece, n. A rent; opa- , v. - in; opaḣlece, n. A rent; oyu- , v.a. - in; oyuḣlece, n.; pa- , v.a. (push against); wo- , v.a. - through (shoot); ya- , v.a. - from (by mouth); yu- , v.a. - in pieces (by hand); aiglu- , v. refl. - own. Juju: kiciyu- , v. - down for; ya- , v.a. - down, to pieces (by mouth). Wakajuŋ, v. - up by the roots. Wopta, v. - in two. Yusleca, v.a. (by hand).

tear, (cry). Iśtamni: -gaga, adv.; -haŋpi, n.; -oślo, adv.; iśtamaniyaŋ, n. Running at the eyes.

tease, v.a. Iśkaŋyaŋ, Bring to talk by -sing. Wokikśaŋ, n. Friendly -sing between male and female. Yuhiŋhaŋ, v.a. Provoke. Yuwaza, v.a.

teem, Cf. swarm. Pawiwi, adv. -ing, in crowds.

telephone, v.a. Mazapa; omazape, n.
tell, Cf. speak. Oglaka, v. pos. - of own; oyaka, v.a. Relate, report; okiyaka, v.a. - to. Kinuŋkiciyapi, v. recip. They - each other.

temporary, Cf. short (time).
tempt, v. Iyutaŋ, Try: waw- , n. Solicitation; waw-yaŋ, v.a.; waw-ye, n. -or; wocaŋte-(ke,ye), n. -ation; wocaŋt- , n.; wow- , n. Yugekicaga, v. Hold out for. Ayuslohaŋ, v.

tender, adj. Nakiŋtkilya (meat), śtaśtayela (skin).
tension, n. Woyutitaŋ.

tent, n. Tipi, ti. Iticaga, v.; iticicaśke, n. The three main - poles. Ohiyezaptaŋ, n. A - 10 by 12 feet. Wakeya, v. Have for a - ; n. A round skin - : -ska, n. A canvas - ; -toŋ, v.a. Make a - of.

term, (terminus, setting, arrival, conclusion). Ohiyaye, n. Waceya, v.a. Be on good -s with.

terrible, (fright, brave, furious). Ohitika, v.n. Be - : -la, v.a. Consider - ; ohitilaka, n. Brave person; ohitiwaciŋ, v. Mean to be - ; wohitika, adj.

test, v.n. Ikutkuteka.
testify, v.n. Oyataŋiŋ.

thank, (glad, rejoice). Pila, v.n. Rejoice, be -ful; pikicila, v. Be glad, -ful with, for; pikila, v.n. Be -ful, glad.

that, pron. dem. He, hena; ciŋ, pron. dem. K'uŋ, k'oŋ, def. art., pron. dem. Taku, n. (relative). Kae, pron. That is he; kaeś, pron. - one; kana, pron. Those. K'eya, pron., adj. That kind. Hogna, adv. In - manner. Eyeśaŋ, express. That is he. K'eleś, he e k'eś, express. That is it!

thaw, (warm). Śtuta, adj. -ed out; v.n. Be -ed: śtulya, v.a. - out; a- , v.n.; aśtulya, v.a. Cuhaŋzi, v. imper. sing. Spaŋ, v. Soften: -la, v.

them, pron. in comp. Wica.

then, adv. Ahaŋkeya. Caś, cetu, ecaŋl. Ehaŋ, ehaŋl, ehaŋtu, ehaŋtuȟci, ehaŋtuke. Eyaś; eya śna, Every now and - . Heehaŋ, hehaŋ, hehaŋȟca, hehaŋl, hehaŋtu, hehaŋtulaȟci. Hetu, hetulaȟci; ȟcehaŋl, Just - . Icaŋl; icuŋhaŋlaȟci, Just - . Wahecel, About - .

thence, adv. Letaŋhaŋ.

there, adv. He, hel, hena, hetu, hetula, hetulaȟci. Heci, heciya, heciyotaŋ (direction). Ka, There, yonder; kaki, kakika, kakiya, kal. K'el, In that pla ce, there.

therefore, adv., conj. Ca, caŋke, caŋkeś, caŋkelaka. Hece, hecel, hececa caŋkeś, heciyataŋ; hehaŋtaŋ. Heoŋ, heoŋetaŋhaŋ. Hetaŋ, hetaŋhaŋ, On that account.

thick, (dense). Śoka(g), adj. (of solids such as cloth, wood etc.): -ya, adv.; aki-ya, adv.; aki- , adj.; a- , v.n.; o-ya, adv. -ly; o- , adj.; n. -ness; ośoke, n. -ness; wośośo s'e, adv. (lips, nose etc.). Akiś'aka, adj.; akiś'agya, adv. Growing -ly. Tiktica, adj. Stiff: ka- , v. Make - (stir); na- , v. Make - (boil, trample). Owoȟeśma, adj. - in, with. Wakipśapśa, adv. Dense.

thief, Cf. steal. Wamanoŋ s'e.

thin, adj. Atabyela (slice). Awe, v.n. Become lean. Hiȟ'ayela, adj., adv. Emaciated. Kokiwotaŋiŋ, v. Become - (clouds). Piŋśpiŋjela, adj. (hair, grass). Zaŋzaŋyela, adv. -ly covering. Zipela, adj. Fine.

think, Cf. consider. Iyukcaŋ, v. Kcama, v. defective. I thought; s'e wacaŋmi, v. I think it is so; wacaŋmi, v. defective. I thought. Kecaŋkiŋ, v. - of as, regard as. Leciŋ, keciŋ, v. - that. Waciŋ: ku- , v. - of coming home; s'e - , v. I think it is so; -kiyuza, v.a. - of; -oyuze, n. Thought or one's thinking. Kepca, v.; lepca, v. I thought this. Seca, adv. This implies, I thought so; secelaka, v.n. Have an opinion; hecetulaka. Cf. wicala. Wauŋkic'ila, v. - much of self. Śicelaka, v. - bad.

thirst, v.n. Ipuza: o- , v.n. - after; -pi, n.; -t'a, v.n.; iwicapuza, n.

this, pron. dem. Le, lena; lenakeḣciŋ, All these; lenaos, leniyos, Both of these. Lehaŋtaŋhaŋ, adv. From - ; letaŋ, adv. After - (place, time), afterwards; logna, adv. - manner.

thorough, (sound). Katkaŋheya, adv. Soundly, -ly. Kat'iŋsya, adv.

thought, n. Wowiyukcaŋ.

thrash, v. Wayablaskaska, - out in every detail.
thread, (lace). Haḣuŋta, n. Twine, cord. Iyoyaza, v. (beads etc.). Wicagege, n.
threaten, (warn). Ociŋyaŋ, v. Woinapeka, n. A threat, harm.

thresh, (trample). Cf. beat. Nakaŋ, v.a. (by foot). Wahuwataya, v. - the arms (decoy).

throttle, v. Loteogmus, lotogmus yuza.
through, (across). Pta(e): ika- , adv.; iyopte, prep.; iyo-ya, adv.; o- , adv. Across; pa- , adv. Ipaseya, ipazeya, adv. Ohaŋglela, adv. - all, - the midst of. Paja, adv. Sitomni, adv. Throughout, all over. Cf. all.

throw, Ḣpa: agla- , v. pos.; aka- , aya- , ayu- , v.a.; -haŋ, part.; -wahaŋ, part.; ikpa- , v. refl.; pa- , v.a. Buck off; yu- , v.a. - down (a load). Ḣpe: aiya-ya, v.a.; aka-toŋ, akaḣpi-ya, ei-kiya, ei-ya, gli-ya, hiŋ-ya, hiya-ya, v.a.; i-kiciciyapi, n.; i-kiciya, v.; iḣpeya, v.a.; iyaya, v.a.; iyo-ya, v.; oi-ya, oiyo-ya, v.a. - into; oyu- , n. A toss; pa-ya, v.a. - down (a load); ya-ya, v.a. - down (by mouth); yu-ya, v.a. Make - down, shake off; yuḣpi-ya, v.a. Aglaśtaŋ, v. pos. Akazamni, v.a. Akastaka, v.a.; kastaka, v. - on (as mud). Ayauŋka, v.a. Ayuḣmiŋ, v.a. Kiŋiŋ, v. - at, assail; iciŋiŋ, v.; kiciŋiŋ, v. - at own. Iḣeyatiyeya, v.a. Thrust. Iyowata, v. (rays). Kajojoyeya, v. Make whiz. Okaḣ'ol iyeya, v. - away into. Owośloka, v.t. Fling. Paiŋyaŋka, v.a. - , send through a hoop. Waŋkayeya, v. - high up. Wayaha iyeya, v. - down. Wośtepi iyeya, v. Cast down. Yuŋkaheya, v.a. - down; adv. Obliquely.

thrust, (shove). Iḣeyatiyeya, v.a. Oglaya, v. - into. Oyujuŋta, yujuŋta, v.a. - into.

thunder, n. Wakiŋyaŋ, Thunderbird (its animalistic representation): - hotoŋ, n. Thunder (sound of).

thus, (so). Hecegla, adv.; heceḣci, hecekce; hecekceca, hecekcecaka, adj.; hecekcel, hecekcetu, adv.; hecel, hecelkiya, hecelya, adv.; hecena, hecetkiya, adv.; hecetuya, v.a., adv.; lecel, adv. (manner); lecetukel, adv.; lehaŋ, adv. - far, at this place; lehaŋtu, adv. Iyecetu, v.n., adv.: -ya, adv.; -yakel, adv. Hogna, adv. That manner. Kakeca, adv. (manner); kaketu, adv. (way).

tickle, v.a. Yuś'iŋś'iŋ (under arms).

tie, v.a. Aheyuŋ, - a pack on. Kaśka, v.a.: aiya- , v.a.; aiyakaśkeya, part.; a- , aki- , v.a.; akikiglaśka, v.; glaśka, v. refl.; icaśke, n.; icaśkeya, v.a.; icicaśka, v.; icicaśkeya, adv.; ic'icaśka, v. refl.; iglaśka, v. refl.; iyaglaśka, v. pos.; iyaiglaśka, v. refl.; iya- , v.a.; iyokaśke, n.; iyokicaśka, v. - together; -piya, v.; oiya- , v.a. - into; oiyakaśke, n. Akiyuskica, v. Apaḣlata, v.a.; apaḣlate, n. Paḣta, v. Bind in, up: a- , v.a.; o- , v. - in. Ayuskita, v.a.; ayuskiskita, v.; kiciyuskita, v. - up for. Caŋiyuḣuge, v. - a tree for felling. Okikaḣa, v. - a knot; okiglaḣa, v. pos. - tight together. Yuośiŋ, v. - loosely: -yaŋ, adv. Loosely.

tight, adj. Oskica, - drawn around: oskicela, adj. Well-fitting; w- , v.a.

Pound tight. T'iŋza(e): ao- , v.n.; at'iŋsya, adv.; at'iŋsyakel, adv.; gla- , v. pos.; i- , n. A supporter; o- , v.n. Be - or fast in, be too small for; owo- , v. Pound - . Iyotitaŋla, adj. Too small.

till, v. Kicaŋyaŋ, - soil: maȟ- , v. Work the soil. Napta, v.a. Spade; yuptapta, v. - soil.

tilt, (incline, tip, slant). Uŋnaptaŋ, adj. -ed, sideling, slanted.

timber, n. Pata, Grove of trees; hiŋta, n.

time, (periods). Akigle (with num.), adv. Times; iyakigle, adv. Iyehaŋ, adv. At the - appointed: -l, -tulaȟci, -tuśni, -tuya, -wapa, adv. Okaŋśniyaŋ, adv. Having no - . Opcebyela, adv. For a short - . Otohaŋyaŋkel, adv. For some - . Takomni, adv. At any - . Tohaŋtaŋ, adv., n. For all past - ; tohaŋtuka, adv. At a certain - ; tohaŋtuke c'eyaś, adv. At any - , whenever. Wahecel, adv. About that - ; wahehaŋ, adv. In good - , about that - . Walehaŋ(l), adv. By this - ; walehaŋtu, adv. At this - .
<u>Periods</u>:
Aŋpetu, caŋ, aŋpa, Day.
Iope, Hour.
Oȟ'aŋko, Minute.
Okowaŋjila, Week.
Omaka, Year, season.
Waniyetu, Year, winter.
Wiataŋoŋmya, adv. In the afternoon.
Wicokaŋ, Noon: -yaŋ, adv.; -hiyeya, n. Afternoon; - sam iyaye, witakiŋyaŋyaŋka, n.
Wikawaŋkap'u, n. About 7-8 A.M.
Wikuciyela, n. Late afternoon.
Wikuwabya, n. About 3 P.M.
Wiwaŋkatuya, n. About 9 A.M.

timely, Iteka, v., adv.

tip, v. Paglaptus iyeya, - over. Paoŋzewosla iyeya, v. Over-turn.

tipi, tepee, (tent, lodge).
<u>Kinds</u>:
Huŋkatacaŋnum tiowapi, A tipi paintted with the form of a pipe bearing four figures on it.
Ti: -giyapi, Brown tipi.
-owa, Painted tipi.
-śayapi, Red tipi.
-woslate, Miner's tipi.
-yobleca, Square tipi.
Tipi iyokiheya, Council tipi.
Wicataŋkagapi, Specially painted - .
Wioptasabyapi, Tipi with a black circle around its outer surface.
Wiowa, A painted tipi.
Wipasabyapi, Tipi painted black on top and bottom.
Wipaśayapi, Tipi red on top and bottom.
Witiowapi, Tipi painted with the sun above the door.
Wiyapaȟica, A main tipi.
Wizi(la), An old smoky tipi.

<u>Parts</u>:
Tiislayatahaŋ, Right side of a - .
Tisaŋpatahaŋ, Wall.
Titahepiya, Middle; adv. On the wall.
Tiyepa, Door.
Wiceśka, Overlapping ends of a - ; tent-pins.
Wihuta, Lower border; wihutaśa, Lowest edge of the tipi.
Wiȟupa, Flaps of a - .
Wipa, Wind flaps.
Wipipa, Tent flaps: -ha, Vent flaps.

<u>Accessories</u>:
Tuśu, Poles.
Wahiŋpaspa, Pins; wihiŋpaspa.
Wihuta inatake, Insulation; wiluzignake.
Wiiyapaȟice, To fastenings.

Tiglujuju, v. pos. Fold up own - . Tiikceyakel, adv. In -s. Tiwohaŋ, adv. Between, among -s. Tiyepata, adv. At the - door. Tiyokiti, n. One living in his own - . Tiyoti, v. Erect a soldier's - . Wiluzignatoŋ, v. Insulate the - bottom. Wipapiya, v. Open - flaps.

tire, (fatigue). Okit'a, v.n. Be -ed: bl- , v.; blokit'eya, v.a. Watuka, adj.: i- , v.n.; ka- , v.n. (riding); tukaka, part. -ed. Kapiŋ, v. Be -ed: ecoŋ- , v. Apablaya, v.a. Aoś'agya, adv. Caŋopatiŋyaŋpi s'e, adv. -ed and stiff. Haŋt'eya, adv. Ȟ'uŋ: -kpani, v.n.; -t'a, v.n.; -t'eya, v.a.; -yaŋ, v.a. Icaśloka, adj. Istostaka, adj. Kajabjapa, v. (riding). Kśikśeya, v. Make - . Naśtaśta s'e, adv. Śtuśta(e): ka- , v. (riding); - la, adj. -ed out; -ya, v.a. Wayuȟ'aŋhica, v. - our a horse.

to, towards, adv. Aiyoptetu(l), aiyopteya. Akoitoheya, adv. Ata, suff. prep. Etkiya, hetkiya, ecetkiya, adv. Eciyapataŋhaŋ, heciyapataŋhaŋ, adv. Ektakiya, adv. El, prep. Etu, adv. Ki, prep. in comp. To, of, for. Kici, prep. in comp. To each other. Akśaŋkśaŋ, adv. To and fro. Yukiŋkiŋ, adv.

tobacco, n. Caŋli: ptegleśka - , n.p. Bull Durham tobacco; -icahiye, n.; -yatapi, -yukpaŋpi, n.; -yugmuŋpi, n. Cigar; -iyopemni, n. Cigarette; iyopemni, mniȟuha caŋnuŋpa; caŋloguha, n. - pouche; caŋtojuha, n. - bag. Caŋśaśa, n. Kiniknik. Waȟpecaŋli, n. A vine similar to wintergreen. Wowiŋye, n. Caŋli wapaȟte sece, Prayer offerings.

toe, Cf. foot. Sihu, n.; siocokaŋ, n. Middle - ; siokaza, n.; siokazuŋte, n.; sioko, n. Space between -s; sipahuŋka, n. Big - ; sipaiyokihe, n. Second - ; sipiŋkpa, n.; sipiŋkpakpala, adv. Tip- ; naslaslal adv.; siśaśte, n. Little - ; siśaśteiyokihe, n. Fourth - . Naowiŋga, v. Turn - inward. Hmiŋhmiŋ, adv. With -s outward.

together, Cf. unite. Caska, adv. suff. Eciśkaŋyaŋkel, adv. Gmuyapi s'e, adv. Icagejuya, icageya, adv.; ogejuya, adv. Among. Iyakiju(ya), adv.; kokiju, v. Come - , unite. Kaśmeyalake s'e, adv. (sit). Kawita, witakiya, witaya, witayela, adv. En masse. Okijeya, adv. Ptaptaya, adv. Collectively; ptaya adv. Sakib, adv. Both - . Wokipuskica, v.a. Drive close - .

toilet, n. Oiheya tipi, oleja (chamberpot).

tomorrow, n. Hiŋhaŋna kiŋ, kiŋhaŋ, haŋyaŋkeci.

tool, n. Wikikaŋyaŋpi, wikicaŋye, wikicaye, wowiŋyeyapi; wicage, n. Implement. Wowiŋyeya, v. Use a - .

adz, adze, Caŋicakaŋ, icakaŋ.
anvil, Mazaaglehaŋ.
arrow maker, Waŋiyukeze.
auger, Caŋiyuȟloke, caŋiyumni, wicaȟloke, makaiyuȟloke, makiyuȟloke (post-hole).
awl, Tahiŋśpa.
ax, axe, Nazoŋspe, nazuŋspe, nasoŋspe: -opetaŋka, Broad axe.
bailer, Ipaȟte.
battery, Kaŋinaśkaśkaŋ (medical).
bellows, Pelipogaŋ.
beetle (hammer), Icaśkice.
binder, Wicaśke.
brush, Wicasto, wicacice (for furs), wicaguke.
brush-breaker, Coŋwiyugoge (under-).
can-opener, Maziyuȟloke.
cement mixer, Makikacoco.
chain, Mas'icicaȟaȟa.
chisel, Maz'icakse, masicaśpe.
clamp, Wicaskice, wicaśkice.
clippers, Iwicakcaśla.
compass, Makiwaŋyaŋke.
crusher, Wicawege.
cultivator, Imaȟ'akate, makaiyuksaksa, makiyuhiŋhe.
cutter, Wicakse, wiyukse.
dash-board, Tokatahaŋ caŋblaska.
draw-knife, Caŋwicajipe.
drill, Caŋiyuhomni ciscila, maziyuhomni.
extractor, Iyuśloka.
fan, Wicalu.
file, Iyume, mas'iyume, apamaŋ, wipame, caŋipame, maz'ipame.
filter, Winaze (strainer).
flatiron, Mazablaska.
flattener, Pahiŋpabla (for quills).
gouge, Wicapote.
grappler, Wicaȟpu, wicaȟpe. Cf. hook, reach.
grinder, Wiyukpaŋ.
grindstone, Miliyuma.
hammer, Maziyapa, hohuocate, ihohucate, ihonicata, imaziyapa, wicaśkiŋ (for cherries), wakat'ozapi (stone).
harrow, Iyuhiŋhe, magicahiŋta, makinaksaksa, makiyuhiŋte, magiyuhiŋte. Cf. rake.
hayrack, Pejiitokśu.
hayrake, Pejiiyuhiŋte.
hoe, Magicamna.
hook, Mazaśkopa. Cf. grappler.
hose, Taśupa.
incisor, Wiyukeze, waŋiyugola (for arrows).
killing tool (hatchet), Wicat'e.
knife, Mila, kaŋiwapsake, miyokśijapi(pocket), wahiŋpaȟpa (fleshing).
lancet, Wicakpe, kaŋicakpe.
marking tool, Wicago.
microscope, Masiwaŋyaŋke. Cf. telescope.
mill, Onakpaŋ.
mower, Pejiinakse.
opener, Maziyuȟloke.

TOOL (contin.)
pick-axe, Makaik'e, makikaśpe.
pitch-fork, Pejiicape.
pincers, Imasoyuze, mazawoyuspa.
plane, Wicajipe.
planter, Iwoju (drill).
pliers, Mazoyuspe.
plow, Maȟiyublu, makiyublu, magiyublu; makaiyupte, makiyupte, makateca iyublu (breaking).
plow-share, Ope.
poker, Winuȟcala tacaŋpetipiye.
press, Wipaśkica.
rake, Iyuhiŋte, wiyuhiŋte, owaŋkiyuhiŋte.
reach, Iyuȟpe.
roller, Makinaskilye.
rounding tool, Waŋipame (for arrows).
saw, Wicakse, talicakse (for meat).
scissors, Iyuśla.
scraper, Iyuk'eze, wicakiŋce, wiyukiŋce; miŋska, wahiŋtka, wipaguke (for skins).
screw-jack, Mazawiyuhomni, mazawiyuwaŋkaya, maziwaŋyaŋke, maziwaŋke.
screw, nail tightener, Wicat'iŋze. Cf. wrench.
scythe, Pejiicaśla, wicaśla.
shears, Wiyuśla.
shovel, Pelicu(coal). Cf. spade.
sickle, Milakaś'iŋ, pejiicaślaope (mower), wagmezaicakse (corn).
single (double)-tree, Caŋpagmiyutitaŋ.
sledge, Wicablece.
sling, Iyuȟmuŋ.
snippers, snuffer, Iyuksa, maziyukce.
snow-plow, Waipate.
spade, Makinapte, makipapte (shovel).
spring, Wicapsice.
square, Mazawiyute (carpenter's).
strainer, Cf. filter.
syringe, Mniwosli (nozzle).
telescope, scope, field-glass, Masiwaŋyaŋke.
threshing machine, Winakaŋye, icapaŋ (combine).
trap, Maz'iyugmuŋke, mas'igmuŋke.
tree, Cf. single.
trowel, Tiicaskapi, tiakaśluta.
tweezers, Iśtaȟeyuśla.
wash-board, Wipaśkite.
wedge, Caŋicaśleca, icasleca, wicaslece.
wheel-barrow, Wipaslohaŋ.
whetstone, Miogle, miyogli(e).
wrecking-bar, Wicaȟuga.
wrench, screw-driver, drill, Maziyuhomni, wiyuhomni (wrench), wiiyuȟlate (pipe)

tooth, n. Hi: -akigle, v.; -ipajaja, n.; -ipaśpu, v. Pick the teeth; -iśta, n. Eyetooth; -maza, n.; hiŋske, n. Front, canine teeth; -onah'ayela, adv. Showing the teeth; -paśku, v. Pick the teeth; -psoŋpsoŋla, adj. Teeth being on edge; -uya, v.; -yazaŋ, v.n.; -yazaŋpi, n. -ache; -yuskablu, n.
toothpick, n. Heyotake ipaśpu.

top, n. Caŋwacikiyapi, caŋyuwacikizapi, caŋyuwacipi (toy). Hutiyagleya, adv. From - to bottom. Icitakignag, adv. On - of each other; itagnaka, v.a. Put one on - the other; itagnagye, adv.; itakignag, adv. Ipa, n. (in gen.). Piŋkpa, n. (of a tower etc.).

topple, v. Kaptuja, - over. Naituŋkab, v. - over backwards.

torch, n. Pelijaŋjaŋpi.
toss, Cf. bat. Pakapa, v.a. Paśkehaŋ, v. - aside, away.

totter, Nat'ope s'e, adv. Wohahayela, v. Make - (shoot). Wośkehaŋ, v. Make - and fall (shoot).

touch, v.a. Putaka, - the ground (by hand): a- , v.a.; aputagya, v.a., adv.; i- , v.a.; k- , v. - own; o- , v. - in. Taŋ: ayu- , v.; epa- , eyu- , v.a.; iglutaŋ- , v. refl.; iya- , kiciyu- , na- , oyu- , yu- , v. (feel). Ȟtaka: eka- , v.a.; icaȟtagya, adv., v.a.; ica- , v.n. Iglu-ś'iŋś'iŋ, v. refl. Napiśkaŋ, v.n. (evilly); napiśkaŋkiya, v.a. Caress. Pajuŋta, v.a. Yuni, v.a. Call attention.

touchwood, n. Caŋkagica, Tinder.
touchy, Wakiniya, v.n. Be - , get out of humor.
tough, (hard). Suta, adj. Durable, hardy, firm: ka- , v. Make - (by pounding). Oyataka, v.n. - eating.

toward, adv. Aitkokib, Front side. Taŋyatakiya, adv. - one.
towel, n. Itepakiŋte, itipakiŋte.
tower, n. Tiipasotka.
town, (village, city). Otoŋwahe, n.: -tu, adv. At, to - . Waśicuta, prep. n. At, to a white man's place of living; waśiyuta, n. The white people's place of living.

toy, n. Inapiśkaŋyaŋpi, winapiŋśkaye. Cik'ala skatapi, Girls' - . Cuŋkśila, - bow and arrows. Hohuyuḣmuŋpi, Bone for tossing. Ipahotoŋpi, Pop-gun. Kiŋyekiyapi, Kite. Makapte, Clay buffalo. Makaśuŋkawakaŋ, Clay horse. Napobyapi, Firecracker. Okawiŋḣela, Merry-go-round. Tatekaḣwogyapi, - to drift with the wind. Uŋḣcelapte, Cactus buffalo. Wanapoḣyapi, Balloon.

track, Cf. trail. Okaslohe, n. Okasto, adv. Leaving a - . Oye, n. (a foot, etc.): -haŋ, v. Leave -s. Oyuslohe, n.

trade, v.n. Itokiyopeya.
tradition, n. Okiciyak aupi. Wicocajeyate, n.

trail, Cf. track. Nacaŋkutoŋ, v. Make a - ; ptaŋtacaŋku, n. - of small animals. Okaslohaŋ, v.n. Leave a - (by dragging).
train, (raise). Kaoŋspe. Uŋcihiya, v.a. - to maturity.

tramp, n. Tokiiyaye s'a. Wauŋuŋka, n. Vagabond.
trample, (tread). Inablaska, v.n. Nakicija, v. - out for; nakija, v. - own; naśnija, v.a. Kill. Nakicipaŋ, v. - for; napaŋ, v.a. - out fine. Nakicisuta, v. Nawanica, v.a. Onak'oza, v.n. - on, make hard. Onasto, v. - down, make bare.

transgression, n. Wokape.
translate, Cf. interpret. Wayuieska, v.; n. An interpreter: -pi, n. Interpretation.

transport, v. Tokicikśu,
transverse, Glakiŋyaŋ, adv.

trap, v. Iyokaḣic'iya, - in one's speech. Gmuŋka, v.a. Set a - : wa- , v.; gmuŋk waciŋ, v. Think of -ping.

travel, (journey, trip). Ogligla, v.n.; oiglagya, adv. -ling in; wagligla, v. - about; wagligleca, n. A bum, one who is foot-loose. Oicimani, n. -ers; oic'imani, n. A trip. Okaḣwoka, n. A floater, a bum.

travois, n. Śuŋoŋk'oŋpa, śuŋuŋk'oŋpa, Dog or pony drag. Tuśuheyuŋpi, n. Śuŋktacaŋgleśka, n. - carriage. Initiyuktaŋ, n. - booth for a baby.

treat, v.a. Iwiśtaŋ, - well (the sick). Kiyuśe, v. Mal- one; okiḣ'aŋśuŋkeca, v.a. - badly (deprive); ośuŋg iḣpeya, v.a. Maltreat. Kuwa, v. - one.

tree, (shrub). Caŋ, n.: -glegleka, n. scattered -s; -oḣlogeca, n. Hollow - ; -oḣloka, n.; -pata, n. Clump of; -pśuŋka, n. Large -s; -skiskeya, v. Grow in thickets; -swoju, n. Grove, timber; -śabśapa oju, n. -s standing against a bank of a stream; -wojupi, n. - nursery; -ohaŋzi, n. Bower.

Kind:
apple, Taspaŋhu caŋ.
ash, Pseḣte, pseḣtiŋ caŋ (gree).
aspen, Caŋitazipa.
bass, Hiŋta.
birch, Caŋhasaŋ.
boxelder, Caŋśuśka.
brambles, Caŋpepe.
camomile, Caŋsiŋsila.
cedar, Ḣaŋte, ḣaŋteśa.
cottonwood, Caŋyaḣ'u, wagacaŋ.
dogwood, Caŋśaśa (red).
elm, P'e.
false indigo, Ziŋtkalatacaŋ.
fig, Tamnioḣpi caŋ, witaŋśnahu.
hackberry, Agugugapi caŋ, yamnumnugapi caŋ.
hawthorn, Taspaŋhu.
hickory, Caŋsuhu.
honeysuckle, Caŋiskuye, cuŋwiskuya.
ironwood, Ispaŋspaŋheca.
linden, lime, Hiŋta.
maple, Caŋhasaŋ. Cf. birch.
mulberry, Caŋska.
mushroom (tree), Caŋnakpa.
oak, Caŋsapa, ituhu, utahu; utahu caŋ, Burr oak.
poplar, Waḣciŋca.
pine, Wazi, waziCaŋ (Western).
soft-wood, Caŋkap'ojela.
spruce, Waziḣcaka(Black Hills).
sumac, Caŋzi, caŋuŋkcemna.
willow, Coḣwaŋjica , waḣpepopa caŋ, waḣpiwizilya(sand-bar).
wolf-berry, Zuzecatawote, oŋśuŋk'nasapi.

Parts:
bark, Caŋha, ha.
bud, Ciŋkpa.
resin, Caŋśiŋ.

sprout, Caŋopamna.
stump, Caŋpaksa.
top, Caŋiŋkpa.

Caŋakaŋsmiyaŋ, v. Prune. Caŋakit'a, adv. With much brush. Caŋiŋkpata, adv. At the top of a tree. Hanaȟpu-ȟpu, v. Appear ready to peel (bark, skin).

trial, n. Wakiyapi (of a case).
tribe, (clan, group). Cf. nation.
trick, (magic). Wakaŋecoŋ, v. Do -s of jugglery; wakaŋecoŋpila, v.
trickle, v. Ś'eś'e.

trifles, Cf. trinkets.
trigger, n. Inaȟpe (of a trap).
trim, (prune). Kasnasna, v. Wapta, v.a.; wakicipta, v. - off for.

trinkets, Cf. trifles. Takuku, n. Small articles: -kel, adv. Any or all sorts of things; takuśniśni, n. Tutka, n.: o- , n. Small articles, crumbs.

trip, Cf. journey. Weiglak, v. Take a camping - .
trippling, Naoksaksala s'e, adv. - along. Napsapsakela s'e, adv.

trite, Wośtepi, n. - phrases.
triumph, Cf. kill. Wakte, v.; waktukiye, v. Come in - ; n.

trot, Cf. run. Kacaŋcaŋ, v.; kacaŋglegleya, v. Stride. Nacapcapa, v.n.; yucapa, v. (horse). Yucabluzahaŋ, v. - rapidly; adj. Fast -ting.

trouble, (vex). Cf. light, make. Aigluśica, v. refl. Hniyaŋ, v.n.: -yaŋ, adj.; i-yaŋ, v.n. H'aŋȟ'aŋka, n. Iyagleic'iya, v.n. Iyotiyekiya, v. Have or find -some, hard; iyotiyeic'iya, v. refl. Nagiyeya, v.a. Tokaśniyaŋ, adv. Without - . Wayuhika, adj. -some, disturbing. Wopiŋta, part. Causing - to.

trough, n. Caŋkaśkokpapi.

truant, (stay-ahome). Kigle s'a, n. A stay-at-home. Wanajica, n. A runaway.

true, Wicaka(e), v. Be true, speak in truth: -la, v.a. Hold to be - ; -ya, adv. In truth; a- , v.n.; a-haŋ, adv.; a-ya, a-yahaŋ, a-yakel, adv.; ia- , v.n.; ia-haŋ, adv.; ie- , v.n.; ie-ya, adv.; to- , n. His truth; woya, adv. Truthfully; ya-yeȟci, adv. Making appear as - ; yu-ya, adv. Telling as - . Ehaŋuŋ, adv. Truly. Ehaś, adv. Iteśniyaŋ, adv. Itoŋ, v.n. Itukaleś, adv.

trunk, (chest). Caŋopiye, n. Storage - . Ognagnakapi, n. Chest.
trust, (confidence). Waciŋ: a- , v.a.; a-pi, n.; awakiciŋ, v.a. pos.; i-yaŋ, v.a., adv.; -kiya, v. pos. Have confidence in; -yaŋpi, n. Confidence, trustiness. Inakipa, v. pos.; inapeya, adv. Kinihaŋ, v. Have confidence in. Waceyapica, adj. -worthy. Zoŋta, adj. -worthy.

try, Cf. attempt. Wakiya, v. - a case.

tub, n. Onuŋwe, Bath- . Woijajapi, n.

tumble, v. Awocaŋgle.
tumult, n. Wawok'oya; v.n. Be -uous.

tune, (air), Oahiyaye, n.

turbid, (muddy, foggy). Śośa, adj.: ka- , v.a. Make - ; na- , v.a. Kpukpa, adj. Full of dirt, mixed up.

turn, Ptaŋ: aicaptaŋ- , v.n. Roll over and over on; aiglu-yaŋ, v. refl.; apa- , v.a.; a- , v.n.; a-yaŋ, adv.; ayuptaŋ- , ayu-yaŋ, v.a.; icaptaŋkic'uŋ, v.n.; iglu- , v. refl.; ikpa- , v. refl.; ikpa-yela, adv.; ipa- , v.; kaptaŋ- , v. - over and over; ka-ya, v. Upset; pa- , v.a. - over; wo-yaŋ, v.a. - over (shoot); ya-yaŋ, v.a. - over (by mouth). Homni: aglu- , v. col. pl.; ayu- , v.a.; yu- , v. pos.; igla- , v. refl.; iglu- , v. refl.; iglu-ya, v.a.; ito- , v.n.; kiciyu- , v. - around for; yu- , v.a. - around. Pemni: ao- , v.a.; ayu-, v.a. Gmigma: apa- , v.a.; iyu- n. A rotator. Yueciya, v.a. - inside out; a- , v.a. Egluksaŋ, ekawiŋga, v. Iglamna, v. refl. Iyaglapśiŋyaŋ, v.a.; naglapśuŋyaŋ, v. Turn bottom up; yaoglapśuŋ, v. - over; yuoglapśuŋ, v. - over; yuoglapśuŋyaŋ, adv. -ing over. Iyokawiŋga, v. - round and round; pawiŋȟya, adv. Veering from. Mni: iyu- , n. That which turns; na- , v.n. Turn back; yu- , v.a. - round; yu-mniyaŋ, adv. -ing round and round. Kataŋblablas, v. - over and over. Naȟmiŋ, v.a. - outward. Paohaha, v. - over, flip over. Waŋjitoktog, adv. By -s, one by one; uŋmatoktok, adv. Yahaiyeya, v.a. - aside, stagger. Yunake(ya), v.a. - over partly. Yuwaza, v.a. Rotate the hands (in running).

turtle, (tortoise). Cf. fish. Ke, n.: -caŋȟ'a, n.; -glezela, n. Spotted - ; -ha, n. - shell; -ȟ'aŋla, n. Small - ; -nuŋnuŋja, n. Soft-shelled - ; -pa, n. - head; -s'amna, n. Stink - ; -śkokpa, n.; -ya, n. Large - . Patkaśa, patkaśala, tatkaśa, n. Same as keglezela.

twin, n. Cekpa.
twinkle, Cf. shine.
twist, (turn, bend, pry, entangle, warp). Pemni, adj., v.n.: aya- , v.a.; ayu- , v.a.; kici- , v. - for; na- , v.n. Śkopa: aya- , v.a.; ayu- , v.a.; kaśkopa(b), v.; na- , v.a., v.n. Ayuśuja, ayuśuśuja, v.a. Gmuŋ, adj.: glu- , v. pos.; iciyu- , v.a.; iciyu-yaŋ, adv.; pa- , v.a.; kiciyu- , v. - for; kpa- , v. - own; nakici- , v. - for; naki- , v. Be -ed. Iciyumnahe s'e, adv. Iyukiŋ, v. Wrench, pry. Oglapśuŋ, v.a. pos. - off.

twitch, v.n. Naka, naŋka; ceyanaka, v.n.; iśtanaka, v.n.; inagnaka, iśtanagnaŋka, nagnaŋka, v.n.

two, Cf. number. Henayos, heniyos, henayoza, henayuza, pron. These two. Henayuzakiya, heniyozakiya, adv.

typewriter, n. Wowapiinaȟtagye; naȟtagya, v.a.; winaȟtagye, n.

U

ugly, adj. Owaŋyaŋgśica; taŋśica, adj. Deformed.

umbrella, n. Oiyohaŋzi (wagon).

unable, (impotent). Inakiŋta, v. Iyejakakeś, adv. Okikpani, v.a. Be - for, impotent, make - . Cf. able.
unaided, Akpaha, v.n. Hoikceyakel, adv.
unarmed, adj. Iyayuscola.

unbelief, n. Wacet'uŋglapi.

unchanging, Yahomnipicaśniyaŋ, adv. Unchangeably.
unclean, adj. Waśepa.
uncoil, Cf. unroll. Yaglagla, v.a. (by mouth); yuglakiya, v.a. Make - , stretch out; yuglaya, v.a.

unconcern, (no reason). Cf. proud. Kas'alakel, adv. -ed. Tokecaca, adv. -edly; tokeecaca, adv. Without specific purpose; tokecakacel, adv. For no reason. Wiŋkcekce, adv. -ed, to no purpose; wiŋkcekceya, adv.

uncover, Zamni: -mni, adj. -ed; -yahaŋ, adv. Without cover; -yaŋ, adv.; aya- , v.a.; ka- , v.a. Open; kiciyu- v. - for; ya- , v.a. (by mouth); yu-, v.a. (pull away); yu-haŋ, adv. Standing -ed. Wakaajaja, v. Lay bare; wakaaślaya, v.

undecided, adj. Waciŋjata, Hesitating; waciŋnuŋpa, adj.

under, (beneath, down). Kul, adv.; kutahaŋ, adv. Hukuta(l), adv.; hukuya, ihukul, ihukuya, adv. Ihutawab, adv. IyoȟIate, oȟIate, adv. Beneath; kaȟIate, adv. Below, undermining.

underbrush, Cf. tree. Caŋakit'a, adv. With much - . Pazaŋyaŋ, adv. With head beneath bushes (sleeping).

understand, (comprehend). Iyukcaŋ, v.; aglukcaŋ, v. pos.; iyukaŋkel, adv. Guessing. Wableza, v.n.; aic'ibleza, v. pos.; ibleza, v.n. Okaȟniga, v.a. Comprehend; okicaȟniga, okiglaȟniga, v.a.; okikaȟniga, v. - own; oglaȟniga, v. pos.; aokaȟniga, v.a. Aiśtaecelya, v.a. Aslolya, v.a. Owaciŋksapa, adj. -ing, intelligent; waciŋtoŋ, v. Have -ing.

undo, (reverse). Yuipaȟtu, v.a.

unequal, (uneven). Kpani: aoci- , adj.; kaiyo-yaŋ, adv. Unevenly; kaoci- , v. Make - ; oci- , adj. (length); wayaoyaŋ, v. Speak of as - . Ociptetu(l), adv. (length, space, time): a- , a-ya, adv.; kaocipteca, adv. Naȟ'eȟ'eyakel, adv. Unevenly. Ocihiśniśniyaŋ, adv. Unevenly spaced, - in size. Onakikiyakel, adv. Unevenly. Waŋwaŋcaśni, adj. Uneven.

unexpected, Iyapakel, adv.

unfold, (uncoil). Kagla, v. Uncoil; nagla, v.n.
unfortunate, Iksapa, v.n.
unfurl, v.a. Yublaga, Spread out.

uniform, (alike). Okiwaŋjila, adv.
unimpeded, (without obstruction, hindrance). Okawatoŋyaŋ, adv. (clear weather).
unimportant, Aȟ'eca, n. Things of minor importance.

unite, v. Ayukca. Ikoyaka(g), v.n.: -ya, v.a., adv.; icikoyagya, v.a., adv.; ic- , v.n., adj. Icipaja, adv. Iciyakaśka, v.a.; iciyaglaśka, v. pos.; iciyaiglaśkapi, v. pl. Kiyakiju, v.n.; okiju, v.n. Have a reunion. Kokiciyas'iŋ, adv. -ting, stuck together; okiciyas'iŋ, v.n. - together and flow. Kokiyuȟci, v. - two.

universals, Cf. any. Eśa, eśaś, śaś (follow the pron. they accompany).

unkempt, adj. Pehiŋtuta, Dishevelled. Poha, adj. Hair aflying; v.a. Make hair stand: -ha s'e, adv. Shaking; - s'e, adv. Bushy hair. Pśapśa s'e, adv. Disorderly, ragged, dishevelled.

unnoticed, (know). Oslolyapiśniyakel, adv. Taŋtaŋiŋśniyaŋ, adv. Wamakamaniśni, adv. Suddenly - .

unpleasant, (not to standard). Aśca, v.n.: -ya, adv. Śica(l): a-yakel, a-ya, a-yakel, adv.; oa- , adj.; oa-ya, adv. Not to standard; ośicecake, adj. Rainy.

unravel, v.a. Yuswa.
unrestrained, adj. Okiuŋśica, Hard to handle.

unroll, (untwist). Kagla, v.; kicagla, v. - for and fall out; yugla, v.a. Untwist, uncoil, stretch, unwind.

unscathed, adv. Taŋyekel, Whole, without injury.
unsettle, v.a. Yuhahala.
unsteady, adj. Ptaŋptaŋ, Rocking: -la, adj. - in mind. Apajejeya, adv.

unsubstantial, Taŋtoŋśni, v.n.: -yaŋ, adv. -ly.
unsuccessful, Wawokpani, v. Be unlucky.

untie, v.a. Ayakca; kcawahaŋ, v. Come untied. Ayugla, v.a. Śka: iyu- , v. Use to untie; na- , v.a. (by foot); v.n.; na-haŋ, part.; na-wahaŋ, part. -ed.; ya- , v.a. (by mouth); yu- , v.a. Loosen.

until, adv. Lehiŋyagleya, - this day.

untrained, (wild, skittish). Watogla, adj.

unused, Yuowiśni, v.n. Be - and thus accumulate.
unwilling, Cf. tired. Mak'eyake s'e, adv. Tauŋkaśni, v. Be - to do; t'uŋgyakel, adv. -ly. Tawat'elyeśni, v.

up, (upward, on high). Waŋka: iyu- , adv.; ka-b; ka-ka, adv. Jolted up and down, bounced. Waŋkatu(l), adv. - above: ka- , adv.; ka-wapa, adv. A little - ; pa- , adv. Upward, up high; -tkiya, adv.; waŋkatkiya, adv. Owoslal, adv. Straight up. Cf. high, height.

uphill, adv. Kaiyakapteya, waŋkaltkiya.
upright, (honest, erect). Woiyecetu, n. Honesty. Wosla, adv., adj. Erect: -haŋ, -ta, adv. On end.

uproot, v.a. Ayujuŋ, Pull out; kiciyujuŋ, v. - for. Ayupśuŋ, v.a.

upset, v.n. Iwasaza. Kaptaŋyaŋ, v.a.; naptaŋyaŋ, v.a. (by foot).
upside-down, adv. Aglapśuŋyaŋ, iyaglapśiŋyaŋ.
upstream, adv. Iŋkpata: -haŋ, -kiya, -las'e, adv. Tatowapa, adv.

urge, v.a. Pa (push). Wawiyopaśtaka, v. - on.
urine, Cf. excrete. Leja, v.a. -ate: -piśni, n. Inability to -ate; o- , v. -ate in; ta- , n.

use, v.a. Iwaśi. Uŋ, v.; nuŋ, v. You use, you have for use. Sota, adj. -ed up, gone, hazy: aglu- , v. pos.; aiglu- , v. refl.; awo- , v.a.; iglu- , v. refl.; iyu- , kiciyu- , ka- , v.a.; oka- , v. Destroy; ki- , v. - for; oki- , v.n. Be -ed up, all are gone; o- , v. col. pl. They are all gone; solya, v.a. Have -ed up. Apotahaŋ, part. Hekicinakeca, v.n. Have consumed for one. Peaglatata, v. Exhaust; wojuhaglatata, v.a. - up. Śweka, adj. Having -ed up, become "broke".

useful, adj. Tokoŋpica. Itaŋyeśni, v.n. Be useless.

utensil, (table, cooking).
dipper, Tatokahe ciŋśka (horn).
fork, Wicape, wicabwotapi (table), wicabyutapi (meat).
knife, Milapaksa(table).
ladle, Iyuze, wicaȟepa.
pitcher, Mniognake (water).
pot, Wikalye (tea, coffee).
shaker, Mniskuyaognake (salt).
sieve, Wicacaŋ, wiyucaŋ.
spoon, Ciŋśka: - cik'ala, - tukila, ptehe- . Mazakiŋska, maskiŋska, mazkiŋska, kiŋska

V

vacant, Ocokaka, v.n. Be a vacancy.
vaccinate, Cf. mark. Kago, v.; kicago, v.

vacillate, Oietatuyeyeke, adj.; tatuyeke, adj. Psaⁿpsaⁿka, adj. Easily changing views.

vain, (useless, proud, groundless). Itokaśniyaⁿ, adv. Makoskaⁿ, adv.: itu- , adv. Otaⁿla, v.n. Be - ; v.a. Be attached to. Otuḣci, adv. In - ; ituḣci, otuya, otuyaciⁿ, adv.

valley, (gulch, ravine). Cf. plain, hollow. Oblaye, n. Osmaka, n. Ravine

value, Cf. difficulty, respect. Takukiya, v.a. pos. - own. Teḣila, v.a. Love, value highly; teḣikekila, v. pos. - own; teḣikela, v.a. - much; tekiciḣila, v. Hold precious.

vanish, (turn to nothing). Kiwanice, v.

variety, n. Watokeca, - of things. Waⁿlwaⁿlwaⁿcaśniyaⁿ, adv. In great -.

varnish, n. Wiziye.

vegetable, Cf. flower, grass. Swojuha, n. Pod.
Kind:
artichoke, Paⁿgi.
bean, Omnica: makat- , Wild bean; makomnicahu, Earth bean; - taⁿkiⁿyaⁿ, Large bean.
beet, Paⁿgipepe śaśa, tiⁿpsiⁿla śaśa.
cabbage, Waḣpeyutapi.
carrot, Tiⁿpsiⁿlazizi.
corn (dried), Śpaⁿkagapi. Cf. grain.
legumen, Omnicahu.
lettuce, Waḣpeiⁿkpajiji. *
onion, Pśiⁿ: -śicamna, Wild onion; -hubloka, Poison luks.
parsley, Śahiyela tatiⁿpsiⁿla.
parsnip, Paⁿgihaⁿska.
pea, Omnicagmigmi.
potato, Blo.
raddish, Paⁿgipepe śaśa, tiⁿpsiⁿla śaśa. Cf. beet.
tomato, Uⁿjiⁿjiⁿtka.
turnip, Tiⁿpsila, tiⁿpsiⁿla skaska.

* Note: The blue lettuce, Wabluśkahiⁿśma iyececa. Cf.

vegetation, n. Watoka.

veil, n. Iteakaḣpe.

vengeance, n. Watokicoⁿpi, Retaliation; watogya, v.a. Take - on; watogyapi, n. Reprisal. Tokicic'oⁿ, v. Take - on for; tokic'uⁿ, v.a. Take revenge on.

verse, Cf. piece. Ośpe, n.
very, (extremely). Lila, liglila, lilaḣci, lilakel, adv. Iyotaⁿ, adj., adv. Most, very great. Ḣca, ḣcaḣca, ḣciⁿ, adv.; ḣcaka, adj., suff. Ḣce, adv. Ḣci, adv. Aiyuḣeya, adv. Extremely, wonderfully. Icat'a, adv. Taⁿ, prefix to adj. La, ka, laḣcaka, laḣcakaka, suffixes.

victim, Wouⁿyeya, v.a. Have for a - .
victory, n. Oohiye.

vigilant, Nagikabic'ila, v. Consider self - .

villain, n. Wicowicaśaśni.

vindicate, Wayuskapi, n. One -ed.
vine, n. Yuwi: caⁿi- , caⁿi-wi, caⁿwi- , i- , wi- , n.; o- , adj. -like.
vinegar, n. Miniskuya.

violate, v. Waḣtani (a law).
violent, Cf. much. Ośuⁿggye, adv. -ly.

virgin, n. Hokśiwiⁿla, wiⁿyaⁿ cokab ti wiⁿ, witaⁿśna uⁿ.

visible, (appear, see). Kitaⁿiⁿ, v.n.; kitaⁿiⁿśni, v. Be in- , lost for. Okopeya, adv. Seen, as though through a hole. Waⁿyaⁿgpica, adj.; owaⁿyaⁿkeśniyaⁿ, adv. Invisibly.

vision, n. Owaⁿyaⁿke; wakaⁿya wowaⁿyaⁿke, n. A sacred vision.
visit, v. Hosaⁿpata. Tilehaⁿyaⁿgya, v. Go -ing. Tiuⁿma k'el ya, v. Icimani, n.: -pi, n. Waⁿkiciyaⁿkapi, n.

vivacious, (lively, excited). Otaⁿtoⁿyaⁿ, adv. -ly.

voice, n. Ho: -bu, -gahaⁿ, -gata, -ḣapa, -piza, -taⁿka, n.; -gluwaⁿkal, adv.; -piskiya, v.a.; -ś'agya, adv.; -taⁿkakiya, adv.; -taⁿkaya, adv.
void, Yujuju, v.a.
vomit, v.a. Glepa(b): a- , v.a.; akigle- , v.n.; -kiya, v.a.; i-kiya, v.a.; igle- , v. red.; ka- , v. Make - .

vote, n. Wowapioiȟpeya.

vow, Awasuic'iya, v. Wiic'iglukcaŋ, v. Make a - . Woiglaka, v. Declare one's purpose.

v-shape , n. Yuśuŋoŋpa, as the spread of two fingers, the legs, a branching stick or tree.

W

wade, v.a. Copa(e): a- , -kiya, v.a. Waayus'o, v. - after.

wag, v. Sintonpsanpsan, sitonpsan, sintupsanpsan, situpsan. Yupsanpsan, v.a.

wage, (pay, remuneration). Wiśi, n. Remuneration: -kaĥya, adv. In lieu of wages; -ton olotapi, n. A hireling; -tonyan, adv. For wages; -yukeya, adv. For payment. Iyunwin, n. One's pay. Okamna, n. Earnings.

wagon, n. Canpagmiyanpi: cankincipagmiyan, -hugageca, - without box; -cik'ala, Buggy; - hununpa, Two-wheeled cart; canpagmiyatanka, Lumber - ; - cankahu, Underboard; - hugmiyan, Wheel; - ihupa, Pole; - ipahunhunze, Spring; - śkokpa, Box; canpagmiya ipatan, Spoke; - oaye, n. - train.

wail, (sing for). Wicakicilowan, v. Wiwakonza, v.a.

waist, Pagoptan, adv. Around the - .

wait, Ahanhepiic'iya, v. refl. Ape, v.a.: aiyape, akicipe, akipe, -kiya, gli- , hi- , iyakipe; iyakipeya, adv.; iy- , v.a.; iy-ya, v.a., adv.; ki-, v.a. - until one is home; ye- , v.a. - for, come along. Ayuhel, adv. -ing for. Glucantat'u yanka, v. Hinyanka, v.: ito-yo, v. imp.; itohiyanki yeto, v. imp. Kta, v. - for: -ka, v.; owa-, v.a. - for; waiha- , v. Make - and follow; wawiwa-ya, v. Make - for.

wake, n. Ahankiktapi (for the dead).

waken, (awaken). Hica: ayu- , v.a. - upon; aglu-, v. pos.; glu- , v. pos.; iglu- , v. refl.; oikpa- , v.n. Wake up; waka- , v. - by striking; wana- , v.a.; wayu- , v. Gica: eyu- , v.n.; ikpa- , v. refl.; ka- , kaĥica, v.; na- , v.a. (by foot); ya- , v.a. (by talk); yu- , v.a. Ayanbic'iya, v. refl. Ayanpa, v.n. Kikta, v.n.: han- , v.n. Kagopa, v. - partly. Nonĥkatiya, v. (by noise). Otuyubleza, v. - up.

walk, v. Mani: akatin- , v.n. -, moving arms sideways; a- , v.; han- , hano- , Ĥe - , Ĥtao- , i- ; o- , v. - in, according to, travel; n. ; o-yan, v. Go on a - ; o-yankel, adv. -ing; oo- , n. Sidewalk. Amakini, v. Anahaha, v.n. Ayuceka, v.a. Cahanskaska - , v. Caĥ'ali, v. - on ice. Cakazigzitkiya, v.n. Gegeic'iyela, adv. Icopa, v. - in, as in moccasins.

wallow, v.n. Paptanptan, - about. Ptemakokawaze, n. Buffalo - ; pteowaci, n.

wampum, n. Wiyokihehela.

wander, (miss, rove, roam). Nuni, v.: o- , v.n. - in; o-ya, v.a. Make - in; o-yata, adv.; wayuwig- , v. Make - . Oyumni, v. Roam.

want, (wanting). Cf. desire, insufficient.

war, (bonnet, party). Cf. dance, headdress. Zuya(e), v.n. Make - : akici- , v.; a- , a-ya, v.a.; o- , n. War, -party, an army. Okicize, n. Waktoglaka, v. pos. Tell of own - . Wayaka, n. Prisoner of - .
War Bonnets: wapaha-
iyuślohetoŋ, (with one tail).
mima, (without a tail).
okijata, (with two tails).
yuslohe, Trailer.

ward, (drive off). Ocankoze, n. A -ing off.

warm, adj. Kata(l): a-ya, v.a.; a- v.a.; ao- , v.a.; igla- , v. refl.; iyo-ya, adv. By heat; iyo- , v.n. Be - ; o-ya, v.a. Heat or - ; o-tkiya, adv. Towards a - place; peto-ic'iya, v. - self; peto-ya, v.a. - up at a fire. Coza(s), adj.: cos- , adj. red.; a-ya, adv.; a- , ai- , v.n.; ayu- , v.a.; -ic'iya, v. refl.; -ya, v.a., adv.; cos'igluza, v. pos., refl.; gla- , v. pos.; i-ya, v.a.; i- , v.n.; iglao-, v. refl.; igluocos- , v. red. refl.; iyo- , v.n.; ka- , v. (by striking); naic'io- , v. (run); o- , adj., n.; pa- , v.a. Rub - . Amaśte, v.n.: -ic'iya yanka, v.; -naptapta, n. Rays in the sun to one's self appearing on the ground's surface to be unsteady; -t'a, v.n.; -ya, adv.; -yakel, adv. T'eca, adj. Lukewarm: -ya, adv. Still - ; a- , adj.; i- , adj.; it'elya, v.a. Iśkan, v. Kas'akiya, v. - one's self.

warp, (twist). Naopo, paopo, v.n. Pemni, adj. -ed. Wapaśkopa, v. Become -ed.
wart, n. Wicośpi.

wash, Jaja: apa- , v.a.; ayu- , eiglujaja, glu- , ica- ; iglu- , v. refl.; iyu- , v. - with; ka- , v. - away; kicipa- , v. - out; kiciyu- , v. - for; kiyu- , v. - for; kpa- , v. - own; na- , v.a.; napoyu- , n. - basin; ona- , v.a. - out; oⁿiglu-pi, n. - basin; owayu- , n. - tub; wo- , v.n., n. - tub; wo-pi, n. A -ing; yu- , v.a. - clothes. Kasepa, v. - off. Mnioȟpaya, v.a. Rinse. Opsuⁿpsuⁿ, v.a. Rinse. Paśpu, wapaśpa, v.a. - out stains. Woska, v.a. - off (rain).

waste, n. Igluwaȟpanica. Inapiśkaⁿ, v.a. Oyupoⁿwaya, v. (by scattering).

watch, (attend). Awaⁿglaka, v. pos.; iwaⁿiglaka, v. Look at one's self. Waⁿyaⁿka(g): awaⁿkiciyaⁿka, v.; a- , v.a.; a-kiya, v.a.; iwaⁿkiciyaⁿka, v.; iwaⁿkiciyaⁿkapi, v. pl.; i- , v.; i-ya, adv.; kiwaⁿyaⁿk, v. - one; o-śica, adj. Hard to - . Kita: iic'icita, v.; iya- , v.a.; wa- , v. Look out. Ihakta, v.a.: -ya, v.a., adv. Iyableza, v.a. Wawaⁿke, n. -man. Wayuⁿka, v. Stand over and - .

water, n. Mni, mini.
Bodies:
mniowamniyomni, Eddy.
mniowaⁿca, Ocean, sea; mniwaⁿca.
mniskaⁿmni, Melted snow.
mniwaⁿcaokaȟmiⁿ, Bay, gulf.
mniyuśpala, Puddle.
mniyuśpaye, Pool.
mniap'eyela, Shallow.
mnicapi, Well, spring; mnioicu.

Kind:
mnicaluza, Rapid - .
mnicaśniyaⁿyaⁿla, Rippling - ; adj.
mnihiyaya, Flood - ; mniokablaya, mnitaⁿ, n., v.n.
wiwila, Spring.

Tools:
mniapaȟta, Skin bottle.
mniiwosli, Spout.
mniiyuȟlogyapi, Flume.
mniiyusli, Faucet; mniyutajapi.
mniośkokpa, Gutter.
mnipasli, Pump; mnipatajapi, mnipataje.

Miscell.:
kaiśtaminihaⁿpi, v.a. Make eyes - .
mniapaȟta, v. Bottle water.
mnic'a, v. Dig for water.
mnil, adv. In the - .
mniyapataⁿhaⁿ, adv. By the - , river.
mniyuśpaśpayela, adv. In - puddles.
mnicagla, adv. By water.
mnicaśkilyela, adv. Soaked.
mniȟ'eȟ'eyela, adv. With dripping - .

wave, Cf. drift. Taja, n. (water); adj. Rough: ka- , v. Make - ; mniakaataja, n. Kaȟwoka, v. Wave (flag). Kayeya, v.a. - a blanket. Koza, v. - a signal. Maśtenaptapta, n. - of hot air. Mnikaȟmuⁿ, n. Roar of -s. Mnikakicipehaⁿ, n. Rolling -s. Mnitate, n. -s.

waver, v. Wayahahayela, Make waver; wayahahake, n. One that makes - by biting.

wax, n. Gageca, giⁿgiⁿca, tuȟmuⁿgawigli (bees).

way, (direction). Hetkiya, katkiya, adv. That - ; letkiya, lecetkiya, adv. This - . Leciyotaⁿ, adv. In this - . Otokiyotaⁿ, n. Ocaⁿku, n. Tuktognakel, adv. In no - .

we, Cf. I.
weak, adj. Aȟtata; ahaȟtateśniyaⁿ, adv. Bleca, adv.: ble- , adj. Huⁿkeśniya, v.a.; ohuⁿkeśni, v.n. Be - . Hustaka(g), v.n. Ȟpela, adj. Ȟtata, adj.; ȟtateca, adj. Toⁿla, adj.: -s'e uⁿ, v. Be unwell. Waⁿkala, adj. Tender, easily torn or broken. Waś'agkiciya, v.a. Make - for; waś iyeya, v. Find -er; waśagkiciya, v.a.

weapon, n. Wipe.
ammunition, Ikute.
armor, Wotawe (consecrated).
arrow, Hinajiⁿ, histola, miwostake (blunt head).
arrowhead, Kehuka, kestoⁿ (barbed).
battle-axe, Caⁿmilokataⁿpi, mitahe.
bow, Icuⁿkśila (toy), itazipa; takaⁿitazipe (overlaid with sinew), takiⁿtazipa; titazipe, His bow.
bow-shot, Kiiⁿyeyapi.
bullet, Mazasu.
cap, Wahiⁿśa.
cartridge, Suto (loaded).
gun, Hutela.
gunpowder, Caȟli.

hand (wrist) guard, Napakaha.
killing tool, ikteka.
lead smelter, Mazasuiśloya.
loader (powder), Oyutaⁿwaⁿkala.
mold, Mazasuiyokaśtaⁿ (bullet).
pistol, Pahuzi (old-time).
rifle, Iwogaga, suśaśala (22-cal.).
shot-gun, Sukpaⁿla.
six-shooter, Iśakpe.
spear, Ikaⁿcola, wahukeza.
sword, Miwakaⁿ.
tomahawk, Caⁿȟpi.
trigger, Iyutaⁿ.
war-club, Caⁿnaksa, iⁿyaⁿkapemni, tahezeze (horn),
wadding, iyopuȟli.

Hitakaⁿyuwi, v. Bind an arrowhead on a shaft. Hiwajatapi, n. Arrowhead jaws. Napiⁿyuⁿ, adv. Without weapons; napiyuⁿ, adv.

wear, (clothe, spend). Icoma(i), v.a. Draw up around (clothing). Iⁿ, uⁿ, v.a. - around the shoulders; nap'iⁿ, v.a. - about the neck; uⁿkiya, v.a. Make - . Kic'uⁿ, v.a. Koyaka, v.a. - clothes. Mignaka, v. - about the loins; pegnaka, v. - in the hair; pegnagkiya, v.a. Make - in hair. Ogluⁿge, v. pos. Put on own. Ohaⁿ, v.a. - socks. Otoⁿ, v.a. Put on. Owiⁿ, v.n. - ornaments. Pośtaⁿ, v.; n. Hood, a cloak with hood. Teślaka, v. - about the head; teślagtoⁿ, v. Hloka: ona- , v.a. - holes in; ina- , opa- , v.a. Tepa, adj. Worn off: -haⁿ, part. Worn; apa- , v.a.; ateb-heyakel, adv.; a-haⁿ, part.; ayu- , v.a.; gla- , v. pos.; iyu- , v. - out; ka- , v.a.; na- , v.a., adj.; pa- , wo- , v.a. Aśpahaⁿ, part. Pota: ayu- , v.a.; ina- , kiciyu- , nakici- , v.a.; nak- , v. pos. - out one's own; na- , v. - out by foot. Hute, adj. - dull; kahute, v. - to a stump. Icaȟci, v.n. - out and come off: -ya, v.a. Inajapa, v. - our the tip of one's shoes. Inapta, v.a. - out (shoe). Inaśloka, v. - through, escape. Kaȟuⁿta , v. - out. Koⁿta: ka- , v. Fray; na- , v. - out; pa- , v. - out partly, fray; ya- , v.a. - out chewing e.g. a rope etc.; yu- , v.a. - out from handling. Kuka, adj. Worn out: ka- , v. (strike); na- , v.; pa- , v. - out handling; wanakukeca, n. One hard on moccasins. Kipacica, v. - off, out. Nasota, v.a. Use up (by feet). Taⁿnini, adj. Worn out; wakataⁿni, v. - out (strike). Yusepa, v.a. - skin.

weary, (feeble). Staka, stusta, adj. Tired out, exhausted; stusteya, adv.; v.a. Weaken. Wowatuka, n. Weariness; watuka, adj.

weather, (climate). Maśte, adj. Hot and unpleasant, rainy and damp; maśteosni, adj. Clear and cold. Otate, n. Climate.

weave, (lace, braid, plait). Opazaⁿ, v.a. Zuⁿta, adj. Woven together: ka- , kazoⁿta, v.a. Oblotopasoⁿ, v. Weave; obloyamnilasoⁿ, v.; osoⁿ, v.a. Braid; n.

web, n. Iktomi tawogmuⁿke.

wedge, Cf. tool. Kaokajayata, v. Get -ed in.

weed, Cf. flower. Iwizilye, n. Magayuśla, v. - a field; maȟ'yuśla, v. Watuśetka, n. Withered -s.

weigh, (heavy). Kaospeya, kaspeya, v. - down, weigh; kaospeyetoⁿ, kaspeyela, v. Tkeiyuta, v.a. Try, feel for weight; tkeuta, v.; otkeyute, n. A weight.

welcome, v. Cokaⁿhiyuc'iya, v. refl. Hokahe, interj.

well, Cf. water. Ominiowe, n. Dug - ; minioicu, n. Ihoeceś, adv. Just as - . Ito, adv., interj. Come, well now. Kawaśte, v. Make - , perfect. Kinaś, interj. Well then. Oigluha, v. pos. Be - off. Osutoⁿyaⁿ, adv. fig. Fairly - . Picaya, adv. Wakicoyakel, adv. - done. Ahecelya, adv. Fairly - . Oahececa, adj. Pretty - . Opiye, v.n. Make one - , mend; pikiciya, v.a. Make one - ; wapiyaȟci, adv. Soundly. Otaⁿyaⁿ, v.n. Be - ; taⁿtaⁿ, adv. Very - , nicely, good; taⁿyaⁿ, adv.; taⁿyakel, taⁿyekel, taⁿyela; taⁿyeȟci, adv. Very - ; taⁿyeni, adv. Not - . Tokecaśni, adj. Recovered, nothing the matter. Akisniyaⁿ, adv. Getting well.

wet, (moisten, soak). Cf. water. Spaya, v.n.: a- , v.n.; aya- , v.a.; ipa- , v.n.; ka- , v.a.; ki- , v. Be, become - for; naspa, v.n.; oyu- , v.a. Make - with; pa- , v.a. Make - . Staⁿka, staⁿ, adj. Moist: aya- , v.a.; ica- , v.; ka- , v. (pound); na- , v. Ayasto, v.a. Hpaⁿ: na-yaⁿ, v. Moisten;

o- , v.n. Be wet; o-kiya, v.a. Be - in; o-yaƞ, v.a. Soak; o-kiya, v.a. Splash, dabble. Totopa, adj. All -.

wheat, n. Aguyapi (bread).
wheel, n. Caƞgleśka; hugmiyaƞ, hukagmiya, n.; hulazata, icahomni, n. Kamima, v. Form a - . Akawiƞga(Ḣ), v.n. - about.

when, Cf. interrogative. Cana, caƞnahaƞ, adv. conj. Caƞ, caƞna, cana, adv., conj. Whenever. Ciƞhaƞ, kiƞhaƞ, conj. If when. C'oƞhaƞ, k'oƞhaƞ, k'uƞhaƞ, adv. (ref. to past). Ehaƞtaƞhaƞś, ehaƞtaƞś, conj. (equivalent) If. Haƞtaƞhaƞś, adv. When that is the case, i.e. .... Hececa kiƞ, adv. If so, when. Hecinahaƞ, adv. (equivalent) If so. Kinahaƞ, conj. If, when. Tohaƞ(l), adv. When, where.

where, (whence, whither). Itoki, adv. Whither: -ya, -yapa, -yapataƞhaƞ, -yataƞhaƞ, adv. Tohaƞ, tohaƞyaƞkel, adv. Tokel, adv. Somewhere, whithersoever, as: -kiyataƞhaƞ, adv. On, from what side, direction. Tokeni, adv. Whereas, as. Toki, adv. Somewhere: -yani, adv. Nowhere. Tukteni ...śni, adv. Nowhere. Tuketu ka keś, adv. Wherever.

whet, v.a. Yuḣtaƞyaƞ, Do a rough edge.
whetstone, (grindstone). Cf. tool. Izuza, n.

which, pron. Tukte e k'eyaś, Whichever, anybody: wa- , pron. (There is no relative as such.)

while, adv. Icaƞ, icuƞhaƞ. Nakenula, adv. For a short time. Ociscila, adv. For a little time.

whine, (whimper). Zaƞkel, adv. Whimpering; azaƞgzaƞka, v. Hokapsaƞpsaƞ ia, v. Kiƞja, v.n.
whip, Cf. beat. Saka: iyu- , n. Gad; ka- , v.; yu- , v.a. (snapping). Skapa: iyu- , v.; yu- , v. Crack a -. Psiƞta(e); ka- , v. Scourge, flog; wica- , n.; yupsiƞ- , v.; ica- , n. Icaḣape, n.: pte- , n. Blacksnake - .

whirl, v. Awocaƞgle. Kaomnimni, v. - around; wamniomni, n. -wind, -pool, hurricane; yumnimni, v.a., v.n. Oyupemni, v.

whiskers, Cf. hair. Pehiƞ, n.
whisper, v. Ji: o- , v.a. - about; ji- , v.; ji-lowaƞ, v. Sing lowly; ji-yahaƞ, adv. -ing; okici- , v. - to one another; wawo- , v.; wawoji- , v.; n. One who whispers.

whistle, v. Jo: a- , ajo- , v.; a-kiya, ajo-kiya, v.a.; i-kiya, v.; -lowaƞ, v. - a tune; ka- , v. (wind); ki- , v. - for. Jiƞlhiƞgla, v. (sudden). Waglaśloślo, v. (one note). Tateka s'a, v. (wind).

white man, n. Waśicuƞ: oḣ'aƞ - , n. One who makes things like a - ; cf. waśicuƞ. Lilita, n. (child's word for). Cf. man.

whittle, (scrape off). Kaptuḣ'a, v. - off.

whiz, Kiƞśyela, koƞśyela, adv. Śliyela, adv. -zing. Tum, n. -zing sound.

who, rel. pron. Tuwa...ca he, cana. Tuwekaleś, pron. -ever; tuwekeśa.
whole, (complete, round). Ogeya, adv. Just as is, the whole of it; iyugeya, adv. All of. Otoza, adv. Round and long. Walupiśni, n. Thing - , not cut; yulupśni, n. Thing intact, fresh. Yuḣtuteśni icu, v. Take the - entirely.

wicked, adj. Wicaśaśni, Mean, deceptive. Caƞtewanica, v.n. Wośiḣ'aƞ, n. -ness.

wide, (width). Blaḣa, blaga, adj. - at one end, tapering. Oglakiƞyaƞ, n.; adv.; otaƞglakiƞyaƞ, n. Width.
widow, n. Wiwazica; wicawiwazica, n. -er.

wife, Cf. woman. Wakaƞyuza, v. Take a - (as Christians do). Wiiyagleḣa, v. Tag along with one's - . Wikte, v. Be one's - . Wiƞyaƞciƞ, v. Buy a - .

wig, n. Wicapehiƞkagapi.
wild, Gnaśkiƞyaƞ, v.n. Guguhaƞ, adj. Itu, adv.; itu uƞ, v.n.; otuyauƞ, v. Be in a - state. Śkehaƞ, adj. Prancing, jumping around; śkeheca, n. An unbroken, unsteady animal.

wilderness, (desolation, desert). Makoskaŋ, n.: -l, adv. In the - ; -tu, adv. Desert-like. Tiwokitahena, n.

will, Cf. mind. Tawaciŋ, n.
willing, Caŋtiayuŋ, adv. Ciŋka, adv. Eca, ecakel, ecakeleś, adv. Ecoŋwaciŋśni, v. Be un- to do. Iyowiŋic'iya, v. Declare self - . Otawat'elya, v. Be - to; tawat'elkiya, v.a. Be - to do, suffer; tawat'elya, v.a.; witawat'elya, v. Ot'ognakel, adv. Although un- .

win, v. Ak'a. Apaksoŋlya, v.a. Glutiŋto, v. Kapa, v. Beat. Ktela, v.n. - a game. Ohikiya, v. pos. - back own. Waśagya, v.a. Beat easily. Wonate, v. Beat, excel.

wind, n. Tate(o): a-heya, i-wab, i-wal, i-wapa, i-wata, adv.; -iyumni, n. Whirl- ; -kajo, n. -storm; tatipogaŋ, n.; -yaŋpa, n. Blast of - ; v.n. Blow; -hekiya, adv. Against the - ; -heya, adv.; -wapa, adv. Up- ; -wata, adv. With the - against one. Iyokaluza, n.; adj. Breezy. Tatuyektaśniyaŋ, adv. With a cross- .

windmill, n. Mnicatomni.
window, (shutter, curtain). Ojaŋjaŋglepi, n.: - akaȟpe, n. Shutter, curtain, shade.
windpipe, n. Blobloska.

wing, n. Ape, also fin. Hupahu, icalu, n. Kiŋyaŋpi, n. The wingeds.
wink, v. Iśtakakpaŋ: -pi s'e, adv. Glakpaŋ, v. pos.
winter, n. Waniyetu: o- , n.; -okisapa, n. - with little snow; wanicokaŋyaŋ, n. Mid- ; wanihaŋ, n. Last - ; waniti, v.; wanitipi, n. - camp; waniuŋ, v. Spend the - .

wipe, (brush, scrape). Ipapuza, n. Pakiŋta(e), v.a. - dry, clean: i- , v.a., n.; ik- , v. refl.; kici- , v. - for; ki- , v. - off; k- , v. - own; nakiŋta, v.a. Brush on, off; yuwiŋta, v.a.

wise, adj. Ksapa(e): ia- , adj.; ikici- , v.; iki- , v.n.; ikiksabya, v.a., adv.; iksabya, v.a., adv.; i- , adj. Wise, prudent; oki- , v.n. Be - in regard to; to- , n. His wisdom.

wish, Cf. desire. Nuŋwe, v.n. Let it be so. Ni, particle (place after v.)

witch, Cf. shoot. Wiȟmuŋge, n. - medicine.

with, prep. Kici (one). Ob, prep. (more than one); obtu, prep.; opeya, adv.; v.a. Make go - ; aopeya, adv. Kicica, v. Be - , on one's side; kicicaya, v. Be - another; kicila, prep. Only - . Egna, prep.; agnala, adv. - so many only. Ayuȟlagaŋśni, v. Iyayustaka, v.

wither, Cf. dry. Śnija, v.: a- , v.n.; ka- , v. Make - ; na- , v.a.; śniśya, v.a. Make - ; adv. Naśeca, v.a. (by trampling); naśelya, v.a. Oyasaka, adj. -ed.

withhold, v.a. Akicinica, ipila.
within, adv. Imahetu, imaheta, imahel, imahetaŋhaŋ, imahetuyakel, timahetu, timahetaŋhaŋ, adv. Ohaŋ, prep.
without, adv. Yuhaśniyaŋ.
witness, (proclaim, testify). Waayataŋiŋ, v.; n. Woyagkiyapi, n. A - .

woman, (wife). Cf. family. Wiŋyaŋ, wi, n.: -kośkalaka, n. Young - ; siŋte-, n. fig. Young - ; -hignatoŋ, n. Married - ; -caglata, n. Women that follow men in singing at dances; -iȟpeya, v.a. Cast off a - ; -icoȟtakeśni, adj. Not having known women. Wakaŋka, n. An old - . Hokewiŋ s'e, adv. Appearing bulky, cf. Wiŋ, adj. Female (of woman, wife). Yuwiŋyaŋke s'e, adv. Being a bad - . Wiiyanajiŋce, v. Run away holding a - . Wikiśleya, v. Insult a - . Wiwoȟa, n. - living with her husband's relatives. Wiŋyaŋyatapi, n. A queen. Wiwaśteka, n. Beautiful woman. Winuȟcala, n. Old woman.

wonder, Cf. sign. Eśa, eśaś, śaś, pa rticles which being the sentence, meaning, I wonder if. Wawakaŋkaŋ, v.; n. - worker; wowaŋke, n. - to see. Wowitoŋpa, n. - to one's way of thinking.

wood, n. Caŋ: -glepi, n.; -kit'a, adv.; -blaska, n. Board; -icoga, - iyutapi, -kaga, -kagica, n.; -optuȟa, n. Chips; -wilute, -yuktaŋ, n.; cuŋȟlogeca, n.; cuŋk'iŋ, n. Load of - ; cuŋk'iŋta, n. Reserve of - .

word, (saying, speech). Cf. say. Oie, n.: -ya, v.n. Use -s; t- , n. His -s; w- , n. A saying.

work, (go, do, doing, business). Cf. occupation. Wowaśi, n. One's - , a hired man: -ya, v.a. Make - , have as a hired man. Oȟ'a^n, v.; n. Action, custom, devices: ka-ko, v. Make - fast; waȟ'a^{n}ic'iya, v. Pretend much - ; waȟ'a^{n}ka, v. Do hard - well. Kawaja, v. - at perseveringly. Eco^n, v.: o- , n. Doing of - ; o-śilya, v. a. Make one do his - badly; wo-la, v. Consider hard - ; wo-laka, n. Difficult - ; wo-ya^n, v. Do - ; n. An always busy person. Patica, v.a. - up. Toskiⁿciye, n. His doing. Wicoȟtani, n. Labor.

worse, adv. Ao^{n}śiya: -kel, adv. Kiciȟ'a^{n}ya^n, v. Fail, worsen.

worship, (ceremony). Waka^{n}kaga, v. Make waka^n or - ceremonial; waka^{n}la(ka), v.a. Yugalyapi, n. -ping. Aka^n(l)wau^{n}ya^{n}pi, n. Altar. Cf.

worthless, adj. Aśi^{n}ȟte: -yakel, adv. Ośikśicela, n. - things; śicit'e, adj. Śuśka, adj.: -ka, n. - fellow. Waȟteśni, adj. (evil). Wawaśagya, v. Render - .

wound, Cf. shoot. O, v.a.; oo, n.; opi, n. One -ed; part. -ed; oiyeye, n. (hole); tao, v.a. (shoot); taopi, n. Wound, a person -ed; part. -ed. Ocape, n. Wipemnaśni, adv. Not -ed, dead from unknown causes; wipemnaya^n, adv. -ed; wipeoȟloka, n. Wopi^{n}spi^{n}za, v. Inflict light -s.

wrap, v.a. Yuwi, - around, bind, bandage: agluwi, v. pos.; a- , v.a.; igluwi, v. refl. Aipiyaka, v.a. Iyapeha^n, v.a.; iyaic'ikpeha^n, v. refl. Pemni: aiya- , v.a.; iya- , v.a.; oki- , v. pos. - around own; o- , v.a. - in a garment. Heyu^n, v.a.: -pi, n.; o- , n. Wrapper; v.a. Opazo^{n}ta, v.a. - around, wind up in. Ou^{n}pa, v.a. Lay in and bind. Oyuskita, v.a. - up in.

wreath, (crown). Natiyuskite, n. Wateślake, n. Fillet, etc.

wrestle, v. pl. Kiśkata. Kicikśa^n, v. - with in love-play.

wriggle, (squirm). Kśa^{n}kśa^n, v.n.
wring, v.a. Yuśkica, Squeeze out; wiyuśkice, n. Press, wringer. Yuśkepa, v.a. - out.
wrinkle, (shrivel). Apija, v.n.; opijeca, adj.; piśpija, adj. -ed. Iyupiza, adj. -ed. Kakipaś, adv. Loose. Pagi^{n}gi^n, v.a. Make -es. Śi^{n}śi^n, adj. -ed; yuśi^n, v.n.; yuśi^{n}kiya, v.a.; yuśi^{n}pi, n.; yuśi^{n}ya^n, adv. Folded. Kokiya, v.a. Make - .

write, (draw, paint). Owa, v.a.: -kiya, v.a. Make - ; eya okiwa, v.; oic'iwa, v. refl. - one's self; oikwa, v. pos. - own name; okiciwa, v. - for; okiwa, v.; w-pi icage, n. Writing tool; w-pi kaga, v. Make a book; n. A clerk.

writhe, v.n. Papta^{n}pta^n (rolling over).

writing materials, n. Iyowa, iowa.
Ca^{n}wiyowa, Pencil.
Mazawiyowa, Pen.
Mniȟuha iyowa, Pen, pencil.
Mniȟuha kaka^{n}ka, Paper.
Mniȟuha ska, Paper.
Mnisapa, Ink; mnisapa ipapuza, Blotter.
Mnisapa wicazo, Penholder.

wrong, v. Śiloȟ'a^n, Do - . Toki^{n}ś, adv. Carelessly.

X (lacking)

Y

yard, n. Caŋiyutapi, hocoka.

yawn, (gape). Iyoya, v.: -ya, v.; waya- , v. Make - by talking; yaioyaya, v.a.; yaiyowa, v.a.

year, Cf. time. Iomaka, n.

yelp, (yell). Oŋześ'aś'akiya, v. Paŋpaŋ, v. (as children).

yes, adv. Haŋ, to, toś, toi (women), ho. Tokeśa, adv. - at any rate, after a while.

yesterday, n. Htalehaŋ.

yield, v. Aicaga; aicage, n.; aicaȟ, v.

yoke, n. Caŋglakiŋyaŋ.

you, pron. Niye, niyepi, niyeś, niś; niś niye, You yourself; niśnala, You alone. Ya, ni, pron. in comp. You (subject, object); ya-pi, ni-pi, pron. pl. in comp.; nic'i, pron. in comp. Yourself. Nitawa, nita, adj. Your. Nici, pron. and prep. For you; nicica, pron. and prep. With you. Niyecuȟciŋ, pron. You at any rate. Niyekaleś, pron. Even you.

young, Ojilaka, n. - of men or animals. Okihaŋ, v.a. Be -er than; okihe, v.a., adj. Cf. follow, family.

Z

zigzag, Cf. collapse, crooked. Pakśikśaŋ, adj. Crooked. Yuglakśiŋkśaŋ, adv. In a - line; yuglakśiŋkśiŋ, adj. In all kinds of ways.

APPENDIX A. Lately defined word list.

There are within the Lakota-English section of this dictionary about 900 words, noted by the sign (?). These words are uncertain in some way or other, or are simply lacking definition. They were sifted from the section and submitted to a team of Lakota people for definition. Mr. Louis and Daisy Whirlwind Horse, Sr., Mr. Frank Killsenemy, and Mr. Silas Lefthand Bull were the chief contributors. The following list is, then, submitted as a further step in refining our knowledge of words Buechel was careful to identify and transcribe for children of another year.

A

aca'je iǧlata, v. refl. To mention one's own name, give a name to one's self. Bl. KE. LHB.

aco'ḱaṫa, adv. Going too far, exceeding ordinary prudence. - imaŋkeca, as a man would say who wants more than what he gets. Bc. KE.

aglu'ḱaḱa, v. To repair one's own e.g. feathers. Same as apiic'iya. Bl. KE.

aȟ'a'yetoŋ, v. To glue, paste on e.g. color plumes on the tips of feathers on a war-bonnet; to decorate a horse for parade. LHB.

ai'glagcaŋkúya, v. To break camp for the road. Bl. KE.

aḱi'glaśke, v. To tie together. Niyeś sipa kayeś - yauŋ welo, as a man would say refusing to marry a woman. Bl. KE.

aḱi'nahaŋhaŋ, adv. Not knowing really what happened. - ia, To speak confusedly. Note: yat'iŋsyakel ia, To speak plainly. Bl. KE.

alo'wiṫaya, adv. Not well dried, as meat. Bl. KE.

ana'ḱicisoŋ, v. To cross the legs or feet; to have intercourse, as husband with wife. KE. LHB.

ana'ḱipta, v. (anapta). To bring to a stop for one.

ana'taḱiŋyece, adv. Slantedly; concealing so as to avoid something, surreptitiously. Tokiŋśkiŋś - . Bl. KE.

aŋ'ṗo wicáȟpi, express. Now the dawn of a new day. Re.

ao'glakśaŋ, v. (kakśaŋ). To come or go around; to turn or bend self in and around. KE.

a'oṫaŋȟci, adv. In the first place, before anything else; caring for a very important thing; chiefly. - taku awaciŋpi iyececa. KE. Cf. iyotaŋ.

ao'taŋiŋ, v. To approach dusk; to grow dim. KE.

apa'ha he, ph. On a low hill; fig., on the one side of the rump. When a man in a meeting moves about unnecessarily much, they say to him: Owaŋjila yaŋka yo; oŋze saŋ - s'e śkiŋnic'iyelo; thus, making one's self busy over something seems to be so described. BT. KE.

apa'ȟakayayapi, n. Something made rough or wrinkled or deformed by an injury. KE.

apa'pa, v. red. (apa). To tap one or something, as with the hand. KE.

aṗa'skiṫa, v. To press on hard. Bl. KE.

a'śląślayela, adv. Entirely open, very plainly; clearly. - waŋblake lo. KE.

aśni'yakiya, v. To tickle. Also, aśniyaŋ.

aś'a'kece, v. (aś'aka). To accumulate dirt, grease etc. Awáś'akece.

ata'tape śni, adv. Working something so as to keep it soft. Fig., - kuwa, To give no one a rest, to bother one ceaselessly. Bl. KE.

B (lacking)

C

caḣli'śniyaṅpi, n. Coal ashes. RH.KE.

caṅḣloḣ' su'ta, n. The woody sort of weeds. KE.
caṅḣloḣ' śluślúta, v. Tall slick weeds. KE.

caṅḣo'tḣa, n. A small straight shrub used for making arrows.

caṅḣa'ġiḣaḣa, n. Shavings. - wakagiṅ kte, I shall whittle the stick so as to have shaving curls intermittently. Bl. KE.

caṅ'kaiciyópteya, adv. With the wood crossed.

caṅno'pa, n. Same as caṅnuṅpa, perhaps. LHB.

caṅ peju'ta cik'ala, n. Mint: the strong form is taken from the root of the bush for making medicine (headaches); the weak is taken from the leaves to make a tea for a common drink. KE.

caṅsa'pa, n. The walnut tree.

caṅśi'huta, adj. Difficult to understand, complicated. Cf. above. Bl. KE.

caṅśiṅ'ḣaḣpu, n. Pine gum cut from oozings on the side of trees, a resin deposite chipped from pine trees for chewing. KE. Swb. Also, the downy woodpecker.

caṅte'ḣic'uṅyaṅ, adv. Willingly, at one's own risk. KE. B.H.87.3.

caṅti'ṗaṅ, n. Coot, mud hen.

caṅtḣu' sa'pela, n. Junco, chickadee.

cehu'paglagla, n. Brown thrasher, catbird.

ceḣna'ġila, n. dim. (ceḣnagi). One dressed or covered with black. - s'e ahiyaye, He passed by all dressed in black. Bl. KE.

ceḣi'caṫi, v. (ceti). To build a fire for. Cewecati. KE.

ceḣi'ṗa, v. To fry from one side then the other. KE. Nape yuptaṅptaṅ cewec'ipeḣcelo, peta kiṅ oile ecetu śni ca. Bl. -- ceḣiṗapi, n. Something fried for one. KE. Icimani - waṅji ceoṅpa yo, Roast a piece of pápa for a lonely traveler. Bl.

cikci'k'aya, adv. Spindle-like, slender. KE. Śloślola s'e hu - huokihe taṅkiṅkiṅyaṅ kaca, as is said of a person with thin legs and thick knees. Bl.

cuṅwi'yapejiji, n. Same as cuṅwiyapezizi, The yellow grape, vine or fruit. KE.

cuṅ'yapehe, n. Same as cuṅyápehe, and cuṅwiyapehe, Grapes. - puza, Raisins. KE. LHB.

D (lacking)

E

eca'icijenaya, v. To mix together. KE. Ecaicijenawaye. Bl.

eca'ic'ioṅ, v. refl. Same as ecakic'oṅ, To do for one's self. KE.

ece'e, adv., adj. Every. Omaka waṅji - ecoṅpi. KE.

ē'cela, adj. Right, correct. -- adv. ˘Once, only. Omaka waṅjila - ecoṅpi.

ece'tḣiya, adv. In some direction or other. Bl. KE.

e'cicaskaya, adv. Coming from all over. Oyate kiṅ witaya - okimniciye kta keyapelo. Bl. KE.

eciṅ'yaṅ, adv. Hardly, barely. KE. Kitaṅ - pawosla iheya yaṅke, as is said when a sick person is about to die. LB.

eha'k̇eke, adv. For the very last time. - niuŋ welo, as a woman says to a dog about to be killed. Bl. LHB.

ehaŋ'uŋ, adv. So, just so, that is so. Ya, - le Israel ciŋcapi kiŋ waŋjila yelo, Misuŋ, - toka śni. B.H.46.3; 104; 102.9. LHB. Cf. ehaŋk'uŋ.

e'huweḣwéġaŋhaŋ, v. Be inert, slothful. Toki le tuwa inaḣniyela wawaśi ca iyaye c'oŋ toke ehuweḣwegahe laka, toki iyaye taŋiŋ śni ye, i.e. he stayed away longer than he should. Bl. KE.

e'iḣpeic'iyaya, v.a. To throw self over-board, to throw out; to be thrown out. Onamniyeta eiḣpeic'imayayapelo, You let me stand alone when I had caught up with you, and then you went back. Bl. KE. LHB.

e'kekiya, v. To say of one. Hokśila kiŋ he ayaupi śni ehaŋtaŋś, waŋcakeś yaupi kte śni yelo, euŋkekiyapelo. B.H.35.5. LHB.

ē'k̇eśni, v. It seems not. hiŋhaŋna - s'e hiŋgni kta, It will be fine tomorrow. Uŋkihuŋnipi kiŋ - s'e hiŋgni kte lo, i.e. joy there will be. Bl. BT. KE. LHB. Also, to be delivered from, to get out and free without effort. KE.

e'k̇ihuŋni, v.a. To finish the course, to come to the end. Hena ewakihuŋni iyececa kiŋ, hehaŋl ake wowaśi ecoŋkoŋ kte lo. Bl. WHL.

e'ṫulak̇e kiŋ, adv. After a while, in a little while. Same as tokśa.

eye'celeś, adv. Likewise, a sortof dictum or byword. LHB.

G

ġaŋ, adj. Mussed, dishevelled. Pehiŋ nigaŋ, Your hair is mussed.

ġiya', adv. Dyed brown. Mato ciŋcala hakaktala waŋ giyeḣci yaŋkela ke'. D.116. KE.

glagle'gleġa, v.n. Be of different colors or shades. Iktomi huhá glaglegleġelo, as they say when a man tells lies. WE. KE.

glai'leġa, v. To enkindle again a fire, as in pipe smoking. Bl. WHL.

glaṗe'mni, v. To make self spin around. Bl. KE.

glesye'la, adv. Wrinkled, folded; without order or geometric line or color, as is the case in some modern art. Nige kiŋhaŋ tanasula ognake s'e - naŋke, i.e. warming himself, his niġe. Bl. KE. Swb.

gligle'kiya, adv. Doing one thing at a time. Na he icuŋhaŋ caŋnuŋpa waŋ opagipi na catku el gnakapi ca he iyataŋpi na - iyataŋpi, as in taking religiously the sweat-bath. MS.351. KE.

gligle'yakel, adv. Here and there. - omani, He walks hither and thither. - wauŋ welo, I was here and there. Bn.

gliu', v. To come to one's own home.

gliya'gli, v. To go around or about a place; to have gone and come back, esp. by another route. Na waŋna wagliyagli na wowiyuśiŋka. Note: Perhaps derived from gnayaŋ; thus, "gna" seems to be changed to"gli" and ŋ dropped for euphony.

glugwe'ze, adv. Moving fast with the hands and with the face twitching, eyes, mouth etc. as well. - iŋyaŋkelo. - mani yelo. KE.

gluk̇iŋ'yaŋ, v. To put on more speed, to accelerate. KE.

glukśe', v. To turn or do a somersault. Also, glucega. Glukśepi, They dived head-first; a dive head-first. Bl.Ke.

gluna' s'a, v. To veer in one's course, as does a struck ball when not just hit squarely, a slice or fowl curve. Bl. KE.

gluptu'za, v. refl. To bend self over, with the buttocksupward. Bl. KE.

ǧuǧu'haŋ, adj. Foolish, crazy; with no respect given. He nata - , He is foolish. ED. KE. Syn.- witko, glugluka.

ǧuǧu' kaśla', adv., adj. With hair hacked in pieces by a knife, as is sometimes done as a sign of mourning. Lila waśigla (standing mourning) na - céyahaŋ. KE.

ǧuhe'heya, v. red. (guheya). To take away from circulation. Wakpala oiŋkpa kiŋ - yuŋkelo, i.e. the starting-point of many canyons near together. Bl. KE.

ǧuhe'ya, v. Take from the course of travel somewhat, thus to produce a fanning out from an orientation point or line. Caŋku kiŋ kitaŋla - yuŋkelo, i.e. many automobile trails along a certain course which gives the appearance of windrows. Bl. WHL.

guḣ'ciŋ'cayela, adv. Perching in such wise as to avoid things and persons. - uŋyaŋpi, coming from very far. Bl. KE. Syn.- nahebyela.

gwu'la, adj. Little, small, minute. Maka akaŋl taku - , taku kpaŋla hena oyasiŋ owkiyake. Bl. KE.

H

haha'ḱe, adj. Urging to move out to another place, away. Oŋs'mahahake s'elececa, i.e. when anxious to go somewhere now. Bl. KE.

ha'kakśa, adj. Empty and folded after use. Wojuha k'oŋ - waglagli yelo, I have brought that full sack back home empty. Pagé - iḣpeyayelo, You left its belly empty, i.e. gave your horse nothing to eat all day. Bl.

haŋgla'wakel, adv. Counting the days and nights. - uŋ. Bl. WHL.

haŋgnag'ya, adv. Being aware of things, in a semi-conscious way, half-asleep. - Ḣpaya, To lie down ready to get up early. WHL. Syn.- wiŋyeya.

haŋ'iśtiŋma, v. To lie awake at night. Haŋiśtiŋme śni śkaŋ. WHL.

haŋi'yaciŋke śni, adv. Unexpectedly during the night. - wahiyelo, I came very late in the night. Bl. WHL.

haŋl iya'yapi s'e, adv. In the manner of those having been told to begone, leaving resentfully.

haŋma'nipike s'e, adv. Unusually occurring. - wauŋ kiŋ, i.e. I know absolutely nothing about it. GA.

haŋmśi'celaḣcake, adj. It being a very windy night.

haŋpi' oḱáśkeya, v. Lace a moccasin. Bl. KE.

haŋ'poḣya, adv. Losing one's way. - wanuŋwe ḣce lo, as is said of a man who runs away moving feet and arms excitedly, as if swimming. GA. KE.

haŋpśi'śica, n. An old and worn-out moccasin. - ca owakihi yelo. BT. KE.

haŋp'ṫi'ṫiŋyaŋka, n. Slippers or moccasins for use in the house. Also, haŋp'titilyaŋka. - waŋji micaga yo, Make me good shoes for use in the house. Bl. KE.

haŋya'gug, v. To spend the whole night in the cold. Nape kiŋ - imayayelo, My hands are stiff from the cold. Bl. KE.

hasaŋ'ni, n. One of a pair, team; a mate. - manice. - naȟci bluha śni. KE.

he'c̆ina, adv. (heci-na). Thus, so it is. Makataŋhaŋ wicaśa waŋ wicoȟ'aŋ waŋ awahiyaya tka hena oŋ oŋśimala yo, tuwa waŋkataŋhaŋ initaŋcaŋ - . Oŋśimala na namaȟ'oŋ yo.

he eca', pron. dem. That person there. Tuwa wiwicayuŋge ciŋ he zuya itaŋcaŋ kiŋ he wowaśi tawa kiŋ - hecoŋ. " - u welo," eya, i.e. he is now coming. KE.

he'ktapataŋ, adv. By the rear, at the rear. Si - wikaŋ k'oŋ iyakaśka; caŋke iyutitaŋ. KE.

hena'ke, pron. dem. Those there. - mak'upelo. - agla yo. KE.

hetoŋ'toŋ, adj. Brave, fearless, faces up to difficulties. Waŋ - mic'ila. Waháćaŋka taŋka wak'iŋ s'elececa, as is said by a man who suddenly gets what he always wanted and so feels greatly encouraged. Bl. Bm. KE. -- hetóŋtoŋke, n. One who is fearless. KE.

heya'pikeśni, v. pl. They think one notable. -- n. One thought not able. - k'oŋ hecoŋ. Bl. KE.

heye'ceśni, adj. Not thinking so, not informed about. - uŋ welo.

hiŋhaŋ'ke, v. To come to an end, a terminus, a close, a stop. Lehaŋyaŋ - ; kahaŋyaŋ - . Bl. KE.

hiŋ'haŋnaȟci, adv. Early in the morning. KE.

hiŋl'ȟiŋcala, n. The coot, a noisy gray water-bird. Bl.

hiŋske'kagya, v. To be ready to argue or say something in rebuttal. - iyemayelo, i.e. he says the same I did without having heard me. Bl. KE.

hoȟya'zela, n. (hogaŋ-yazela). Same as hoyázela, The kingfisher. KE.

hoka'ȟglepi, ókaȟglepi, n. Something, as a fish tackle, tied to a stake; a thing moored, tied and left floating. Fig., those come first to a big meeting and put up their tents. Bl. KE.

ho'k̇i iyokpaza, v.n. To get nowhere in using one's voice. Hoki waśte, To have a good loud voice. Cf. hokomi, below. - iyeceȟci wauŋ welo, I am unable to grasp anything. - cokaŋ wauŋ, I am bewildered. Bl. BT. KE.

hoki'toŋ, v. To holler, to sing out; to have a voice, use of one's voice. Howetoŋ, I use my voice. Ś'agya - , He has a voice to speak powerfully. HM. KE.

hoko'mi, n. The beads that were first sold to Indians in the West, at a town in Oklahoma where beads, trinkets and flannel were all first sold. Cf. Okomi, Yokomi. KE.

hokśi'uŋke, adj. Older, old enough. - eśa hecoŋ, Although old enough he did it. - śni śka hecoŋ iyececa śni. KE.

ho'waśteya, v. To produce fine sound with the voice. -- adv. Speaking with a grand voice. - waciŋksapa yo, Be clear-minded in using a fine sounding voice. KE.

hoya'zela táŋka, n. The large kingfisher. Hoyazela cik'ala, The belted kingfisher. KE.

hu'icignuniyaŋ, adv. With bones mixed together. - yuŋkapi, as is said of two friends who went on the warpath and also lie together dead. Bl. KE.

hu'ṗaza, adv. (hu-paza). With the knees bent up and feet drawn to the body. - makagle yaŋka, He sits on the ground squatting. Cf. paza.

hu'ṫawab, adv. Further down, e.g. the creek. -- húṫawabkiya, adv. In the downstream direction. KE.

huṫi'ṗak'oga, v. To scoop up taking everything along. B.H.39.3. KE.

huṫi'ṗaśpu, v. To drive away or back e.g. the enemy in battle; push away, against, cut and topple over. - iyeya. Bl. KE.

huto'kapataŋ, n. The front legs, as of an animal; but, hugmiyaŋyaŋ, Front wheels. KE.

huye', interj. (hiyu-ye). Come along. Also, hoiyé, huyá. - , hoapeśa waᶯ mini ceteta ape kahihiya nuᶯke, le uciciye, as the Indian would say when throwing out the line to catch fish. He, misuᶯ, huya, misuᶯ, Hey, say younger brother, come here, my younger brother. D. KE.

ȟaȟa'ya, v. Same as ȟ'aȟ'aya. To patter on, as sleet on a tent. Tipi kiᶯ iwaᶯkab taku ȟmuᶯ s'elececa na tipi kiᶯ - taku akalala hiyu na lila hececa. KE.

ȟaᶯi'yagnaka s'e, adv. Cautiously. - okuwa, To handle one very carefully. WE. WHL.

ȟla'ȟla iyógnaka, n. The marsh wren.

ȟpi, v. To hang down. -- adj. Hanging down. Iha - , Hanging lips. KE.

ȟpiȟpi' s'e, adv. Flapping from walking or running fast. - iᶯyaᶯka, To run, hair aflying. Wapośtaᶯ miciȟpi.

ȟpo, n. Scum that floats on the water of lakes or seas.

ȟtani', adj. Being poor. - okile, To look for slowly and carefully. Ablakela ca wicaho - ca tokiya eyaś naȟ'oᶯpi kte. Bl. WHL.

ȟ'e'ȟ'eya, adv. Running or slobbering, as does a dog's mouth after a long run. Śiyo śuᶯka s'e imniśtaᶯ - yaᶯkelaȟ. Bl. WHL. Syn. kalala s'e.

ȟ'uᶯ'yela, adv. Hardly, barely, scarcely. Kogiᶯgiᶯ naᶯkahelo; - wahiyelo. BT. WHL.

I

iča'kpaᶯ, adv. Completely crushed into small pieces. - kablebleca. Bl. WHL.

i'čanaȟ'o, v. To glance causing matter to spray; be carried away, as by the wind. WHL.

i'cana s'a, v. To ricochet or glance off.

icaᶯ'liyuha, v.n. To be set and ready with all things needed. Taku icaᶯliniyuha yelaka, winiś'oś'okelo, i.e. in good humor, hence ready to be active. Bl. WHL.

icaᶯl'śica, v.n. To be disaffected, displeased, hold hard feelings. Takuni icaᶯlśice uᶯ śni yo. Lc. KE.

ica'pcab, v.a. To pierce through. Peji to mini - he lo, i.e. drops of dew on grass as the grass comes out of the ground. Bl. KE.

ica'pepeya, adv. red. (icape). Pierced or stuck in various places. Maswiyokataᶯ - yuwaᶯkal iyeyapi. B.H.265.23. KE.

ica'ṗoǧaᶯ, n. (pogaᶯ). A sudden blowing storm. - hiyelo. - waᶯ hi, A snow storm started. Bl. KE.

ica'p'ośya, v. To make lighter, less heavy. Wapahlaya na - s'e iblabla. Bl. KE.

iča'ska, v. To eat a little lunch. - iyeya. Icask'iyewayiᶯ kte. Cik'alakel - iyeuᶯyiᶯ kte, Let us smoke, eat etc. a little in a hurry. Bl. KE.

iča'śloke, n. (kaśloke). Poker, cleaner. Caᶯnuᶯpa - , A thin stick used to press down tobacco in a burning pipe; a poker.

ica'ta, i'cat'a, adv. Very much. - iheya, To crowd together.

iča'taᶯtaᶯ, adv. Daubing along, as in painting, being smudged. - ehuᶯni yo, Rub, spread it, as glue, all over. Iwakataᶯtaᶯ. Bl. WHL.

i'ciȟloka, n. A matching suit, number; matching of bone rings, obs. - yuha, as is said of the game of dominos etc. Bl. KE. -- i'ciȟlogya, v. To follow suit.

i'cimna, v. Same as i'c'imna, To have confidence in one's self. - śni, He has no confidence in himself. B.H.74. 21.

i'cinakśiŋpi, v. pl. They stand and support, shield each other. Note: The plural ending may be put on a verb following, but that is unusual. KE.

i'cipa, v.n. To meet, to clash. Hecel iyawicapepi na ob icipapi na ob ecoŋpi. KE.

i'cipatkuȟ, v. cont. To be close together, adjacent. - yaŋkapi, They sat close together. Bl. KE. Syn.- okowanilya, icipat'iŋs.

i'cipat'iŋs, v. To push tightly together. Bl. KE. Cf. icipatuȟ.

i'cisaŋb, adv. Interruptingly. Also, i'cisam. - womayakilake, You interrupt me all the while. Bl. KE.

ici'saŋnica, v. To go to one side, be off center, out of balance. Wi - ye k'oŋ ceti yelo, tate kte lo. BT. KE. -- ici'saŋnicab, v. cont. To have made over one-half of one's way. Wanaś icisaŋnicab yapelo, They are now halfway there. KE. Bl.

i'ciťona, interrog. adj. indef. How many? in comparison to someone else's. Śuŋkawakaŋ - yuha so? How many horses has he compared to others?

i'ciyaȟlaȟ, v. To cross or lock together. Nape - iyeya, To fold the hands for prayer, crossing the fingers. Bl. KE. Cf. iciyaskabya.

ico'ȟa sapa, n. The black-billed cuckoo. Also, cepela taŋka.

ičuču, v.n. To have or take more or plenty of something. Iyacucu lakelo, blihic'iya yo, as is said encouragingly to one who is on the point of winning a race. Yakalu lakelo, iyotaŋla icu wo. Miye iwacucu kaca; eya śna wau welo, I am still active and so come now and then. Bl. KE.

i'c'imna, v. Same as icimna.

ic'i'mnikel, adv. Sprawled. - muŋkelo, I lay stretched out.

ie'slota, adj. The word should be: iye slotá, He is aware of things. Bl. LHB. Cf. slota.

igla'gleglega, v. refl. To stripe one's self with colors. KE.

iglag'yaƙe, adv. Loaded down with some of one's own luggage. - hi, To come with all one's belongings, as on a trip. WE. KE. Cf. iglaka. -- iglágyakel, adv. Same as iglagyake.

igla'ȟniga, v. To choose one's self as the object of choice. KE.

igla'oŋspe, v. refl. (kaoŋspe). To train one's self, train by one's self. Hena oŋ śuŋkawakaŋ igla oŋspepi na hena oŋ oyate icagapi kta. WHL.

igla'ṗemni, v. refl. To turn, swinging self around. Hiŋhaŋ cik'ala - śkaŋ, Littleowl spun around in haste. KE.

igla'sto, v.a. To smooth one's self or one's hair. Iwaglasto. Also, fig., to be left out, incomplete. Imaglasto tka, I almost got left out (it almost did not reach me). Bl. KE. WHL.

iglaś'yakel, adv. Sickly. WHL.

igla't'a, v. refl. To strike or pummel one's self. Caŋ oŋ - omani, i.e. to walk slowly without giving attention to anything. Bl. WHL.

igle'gleȟya, adv. With a whole assortment of things. - śkaŋ, To be busy with many things (at the same time). -- iglégleȟyakel, adv. Without clear distinction between things, in an assortment of mixed or varied things. - taku ecoŋ, Fickly to perform. - pahi, To pick up good but worthless things. Bl. WHL.

iglo'eyaya, v. To go on one's own, make one's own way. WHL.

i'gnagnaye s'e, adv. Appearing enticing, bringing one along. - aupelo, They are coming one after the other. Bl.

iǧu'ǧaot̄ila, n. The rock wren, the cliff swallow; a cliff dweller.

iha'mnapi s'e, adv. Much appealing to one's appetite. Waśpaŋka - ahimayakigle kiŋ le ibluśkiŋ. BT. Bl. WHL.

ihaŋ' iyúpta, adv. Through most of the night, through the night. - wau welo, I was acoming through the night. Bl. WHL.

ihe', v. To use sarcasm, use cutting words at one. Wayatiktil - , To find fault with others when there is no reason for it, to nag. Iwahe. LB. WHL. Cf. tikta.

ihu't̄awab, adv. and prep. Downstream beyond. WHL.

iȟe'yab, adv. Away from. Wicaśa kiŋ le ayuśtaŋ na - iyaya yo. B.H.203.8.

i'ȟtalehaŋ, adv. Day before yesterday. -- iȟtaléhaŋhaŋ, adv. red.

i'kacaŋcaŋ, n. (kacaŋcaŋ). The trot of a horse. WHL.

ik̄a'k̄eiŋ, v. To knock against and cause a slight tilt. Cf. keiŋyaŋhaŋ. WHL.

ik̄i'ȟ'aŋ, v. To cook, cook meat for. Talo - . To ka cik'ala imakiȟ'aŋ yo, as is said when a sick person wants something and so it is given him. Bl. WHL.

ik̄u'śe, v. To impede, block. Woecoŋ kiŋ le - najiŋ, He stood there impeding this work.

ik̄u't̄a, prep., adv. Below, down creek. Noŋpegnakapi - ewicoti, They camped below the scaffold.

ik'o', v. To get worried.

ile'nilyakel, adv. (ile-nica). With little enthusiasm left. - wanasapi, They went to the buffalo hunt with much despondency (there being few buffalo left). Bl.

ili't̄a, v. Be worried; take an active part, as in a game. - śkatapi opa. Ilitapi kte lo. Bl. WHL. Cf. ik'o.

imni'coyapa, v. To use for wading. Haŋp'ceyaka waŋ imnicoyapelo. Bl.WHL.

imni'ja, adj. Chuck-full of water. Ehaś - s'e cepelo, as is said of an unusually fat man or animal. Bl.

ina'jabjapa, v. red. (inajapa). To ruin completely by the wear of feet. Bl. WHL. -- inájabjabyela, adv. Going to ruin from the wear of feet. Waniśipeś śicala tanuŋka śni k'oŋ, nakeś sipa kiŋ - yaglilotake. Bl. WHL.

ina'k̄iŋlya, v.a. To rub off, as mud from the feet with a mat or rug. Fig. to borrow from. Cowiŋja akaȟpe he si - yo. Cf. Lakota section. Bl. WHL.

inaŋ'gnaŋke s'e, adv. As if moving one's lips. WHL.

ina'paŋ, v. Be packed and made hard. Caŋku kiŋ ataya - iȟpeyapi kte lo, i.e. the snow will be packed and hard. Bl. WHL.

i'nasak̄a, v. To spring and strike, as does a branch along a path when walking. Iśta caŋ inamasaka, as is said when a splinter flies into one's eye. Bl. WHL.

ipa'cica, v.t. (pacica). To mix up by rubbing on. Pehiŋ kiŋ ipacicapi s'e, as is said when a man's hair is disheveled and pressed down. Bl.

i'p̄aǧa, adv. Before dinnertime or the place of dinner. Hiŋhaŋna kiŋ waŋ cag - mauŋnipi kte lo, They will go at once in the morning before dinner. - iyuȟpapi, They rested on the way to the place for dinner. Also ipaȟe.

ip̄a'ha, v. To raise up, as a curtain; to hoist up. Wipa kiŋ - egle. D.196-7. - iyeya.

ipa'ȟna, adv. Through and through, as a needle is sent through cloth in sewing. KE. Cf. Lakota section.

ipa'śpeyuŋk, v. To be close and jolting, knocking against one another. Cf. Lakota section.

ip̄e'slet̄aŋhaŋ, adv. From the head side or end. - iyotakiŋ. B.H.271.4. -- ipeslete, adv. At the head end. - tka k'uŋ hel. B.H.109.10. WHL.

ipśiŋ'cala, adj. Like a small swallow. Ite - kaca, as they say of a man with a small and wrinkled face. Bl.

iṗu'sṫaŋ, adv. Pushing up against. - yuza, To clap up against, as a coal of fire. Bl.

isi', adv. At, on the foot. - wagluha kte, i.e. I am going to go. Na - el ite makipastoya gliḣpic'iyi na wopila eye. Sb. Pb.23.

isi'ṫuṫece, adj., adv. Lacking the necessities. Also, iśituteca. - śni u, To come well prepared, having made all preparations. LC.

iśiŋ'ḣtiŋ, v.n. Cf. iśiḣtiŋ. Bl.

iśki'śkeyece, n. Interference by one in another's talk, speech or game. WHL.

iśṗa'k̇ic'uŋyaŋ, adv. Using the elbows. - maka hewayelo. Bl. WHL.

iśpa'zihiŋ, n. A buffalo's elbow. Bl.

iśta'ḣca, v. To have obscure vision; be snow-blind. Śiyo iśtaḣcapi, i.e. on a very foggy day in spring or winter. D.21.

iśta'jotókte, v. To smoke or blind the eyes. Iśtajotomakte yelo. Bl.

iśta'natogyeya, adv. With an unnatural eye expression, as in fear or uncertainty. Wicaśayatapi kiŋ - nacaŋcaŋ. B.H.140.6. WHL.

iśṫa'saŋk̇iya, n. A side glance or snap of the eye; an eye expression of disgust. - kici uŋpi, i.e. jealousy. Bl. WHL.

iśta' wai'yojaŋjaŋ, n. Snow-glare in the eyes. Iśtawaiyomajaŋjaŋ yelo. Bl. WHL.

iśṫi'yagna, adv. Closely observing. - kuwa, To watch closely. B.H.303.3.

i'śuŋmakeci, adv. Incidentally. Also, uŋś'uŋmakeci. - he toki iyaya he? Incidentally, what became of him? WHL.

iṫa'gna, adv. Closely. - kuwa, To watch closely. Ww.

itaŋ'gluzaza, v.n. To have a feeling of fright, have a fearful scare. Itaŋmagluzaza. -- itaŋgluzazaya, v. To frighten one. Itaŋgluzazamayaya, You make me shine, glow. Bl. WHL. Bl.

itaŋ'sak t'a, v. (taŋ-saka-t'a). To be frightened to death, terrified. B.H. 280.13. WHL.

iṫaŋ'yaŋ, adv. Well, on some account. Iśtiŋme kiŋ, - kte lo. B.H.229.1.

ita'waciŋ, n. Possession of mind or property. Huŋhuŋhé mazaska - śice lo, i.e. his mind on liberal use of money, is stingy with money. BT. WHL.

ite'śnioṗa, v. To freeze the face. IS. LHB.

iṫe'zi, n. The stomach. Taku - mayazaŋ, I cannot stomach it, in dissatisfaction. Bl.

iṫi'sabye, n. Black for the face. -- v. To blacken the face with. Bl. WHL.

i'ṫok̇a, v. To be without concern for, to be alright. Etaŋś he iuŋtokapi eśa yelaka? What is that to us? B.H.259. 22;277.5. WHL.

ito'k̇ecaśni, v.n. To be unchanged, without a difference, be not one's business. B.H.305.19.

iṫo'k̇icile, v.n. (ite-ole-kici). To aim at one's face, seeking to strike. Itomiyecile yelo, You aim at my face. Bl.

iṫo'leś, interj. Really now! Supposing. - wai śni kiŋ toka kta he? Supposing I did not go, what would happen? - heya śke c'uŋ. Bl. WHL. Cf. itola.

iṫo'yuha t'e'k̇iya, v. To make or have a deadened expression on the face. Bl. WHL.

it'a', v. To die, for some reason. Bl. LHB.

it'e'nihaŋ, adj. Bothered, disturbed for some reason, so that action is impeded. - śni. Taku - ecoŋśnimayayapelo, You give me no time to do my work. - woteśni, To eat but little because one is bothered. Bl.

iwa'ciŋgnuniyaŋ, adv. Causing bewilderment, wonder, as the first sight of a giant machine's complication. Kiŋyekiyapi waŋ tima tokel kagapi kiŋ waŋyaŋkiŋ na - ayuta. Bl. WHL.

iwa'ciŋtokáŋkaŋgnagnáya, adv. With the mind not concentrating on any particular subject of idea. Ca hecel kohaŋ - omawani yelo. Bl. WHL.

iwa'ciŋyeȟci, v. To depend upon another's ability, to hold great trust, stand in great need of help. Pb.41.WHL

iwa'hukeza, n. A bayonet. Akicita num - yuhapi, Two soldiers have bayonets. - yamni yuha, He has three bayonets. B.H.95.26. WHL.

iwa'ȟwayela, adv. Gently, quietly, peacefully. Haŋkeya - glapelo, The storm clouds passed by without much noise. Bl. WHL.

iwa'kaŋyeja, adj. Poor and easily satisfied, being in distress. Taku keśa imawakaŋyeja yelo, I am satisfied with any amount, be it ever so little. Bl. Note: Teton rarely use the adj.

iwa'ktekiyagla, v.a. To cause one to go home in triumph, having taken scalps as trophies. Waniyetu amakeśakowiŋ el Scili kiŋ iwaktemakiyaglapelo. BT.

iwaŋ'jica, v.a. To control, check e.g. one's anger. Waciŋ - śni, He does not control his anger. Bl. WHL.

i'watukte, adv. From hence. Mato Śa tipi kiŋ he - el ti yelo, Red Bear lives in the house over there. BT.WHL.

iwo'hiŋyaŋsyakel, adv. In a threatening or irate manner. - wakiŋyaŋ ukiye, An awful thunderstorm is coming. Bl.

i'wokpaŋ, v.a. To crash to pieces. WHL. Bl.

i'wona s'a, n. What goes on a straight or even course but not in the desirable course, as a ball going beyond its target. - iyeyapi s'e uŋkiyayapelo, as a speedy automobile over high and low places. Bl. WHL. Cf. iwowaŋka.

i'wopsil, v. To flip off, to ricochet. Also, iwowaŋka. - wao, I struck him with a ricochet shot. Bl. WHL.

iwo'sla, adj., adv. In an upright manner. Nakpa - ikikcu, To prick up one's ears. Nakpa yuwaŋkal ikikcu. Bl. WHL.

iya' gluza, v. To have or hold for one's own protection, encouragement or support; to take back one's words. Hecelaȟci wana iyawagluzelo, Now I am well cared for (having given everything away). Bl. KE.

iya'kaŋwiŋlake s'e, adv. Speaking so as to leave the possible suggestion of a doubt about what is said. - tak'eye, He says so but I doubt it. Bl.

iya'ǩicaśka, v. To be tied or roped together. - owaheȟce, as a man says to another who is very lazy and does not want to be disturbed. Bl. KE.

iya'ǩitaŋiŋ, v. To arrive when it is yet light and things are visible and clear. - lake uŋki kiŋhaŋ waśte yelo, i.e. better to go in daylight. Aŋpetu - śni yelo, i.e. it is foggy. Bl. KE.

i'yaṗaťaŋ, adv. Pushing or shoving onto one; right up against one. - glus kat'iyewayelo, I shot it from right nearby. Bl.

iya'ṗeǩel, adv. Waiting for an opportunity, keeping careful watch. - kuwa, To watch so as to catch, wait for a chance to catch. B.H.230.11. KE.

iya'p'osp'os, n. Turbulent fog formations. - ahiyayelo, as it is said when it is very cloudy and then again clears. Bl. KE.

i'yaśka, adj. Loose-tongued. Also, iyáśka. Yuŋkaŋ hokśila kiŋ he - hokśila ic'icaga ke'. KE.

iya'śota, v. To make smoke, steam, as with one's breath. - s'e omawani, I walked about with my breath a fog in the cold weather. Bl. KE.

iya'waŋyaŋgkiciya, v. To accompany and watch over along the way. Wakaŋtaŋka taogligle waśte waŋ iawaŋyaŋgkiciyiŋ kte kiŋ he wicawala yelo. B.H.122.19. KE.

iya'yuȟǩiya, adv. Following. Wicaȟpi kiŋ he - yapi. B.H.169.18. KE.

iya'yusťaǩa, v. To bind one thing securely to another. Iyayustag heyuŋ, To tie up one thing on another. Iyayustag hemuŋ. KE.

iye'śťuka, pron. He who ought. - laka, He who did what another ought to have.

Uŋkiyeśtuka he waŋbli yeś kte yeśaŋ, i.e. was fooled inspite of his smartness. Bl. KE. Cf. Lakota section.

iyo'cosyakel, adv. With added cover on, as on the feet. - owahelo. Bl. KE. Syn.- iyowiŋhahayakel.

iyo'gluś't'eya, v. To pile up words of criticism to the point of discouraging one. Iyogluś't'emayayelo, as a man who wants to live in peace would say to another who nags him. Bl. KE.

iyo'ja, v. To amplify sound, esp. harsh sound. Tasiha taŋka waŋ iyojahe s'e ye uŋyaŋpelo, as is said when following a retreating enemy. Bl. Cf. jahaŋ.

iyo'kaŋ, adj. Open, roomy. Tipi - el caŋ wicayakaku kte lo. Bl.

iyo'ƙaskica, v. To clog, congest. Paȟli iyomakaskicelo, as is said when the nose clogs. Bl. WHL.

i'yonataŋ, v. To urge one, urge upon one; to use the foot to urge one. - mayakuwayelo, i.e. you always push me; give me time and I'll do it. Bl.

iyo'niyaŋ, adv. In the distance, faintly audible, slightly felt. Hlaȟla kiŋ - hotaŋiŋ, i.e. dimly audible because very distant. LB. WHL.

iyo'pśa s'e, adv. Like a muffled sound as of a gun-shot. -- iyópśaya, v. To be just slightly audible in the distance. -- adv. Being slightly audible. Bl. WHL.

iyo'pte, prep. Through, by way of. Miyopte śni ehaŋtaŋś, Except through me. B.H.254.22. Cf. Lakota section.

iyo'sniyaŋ, adj. Chilly, cool. Tate waŋ - uye lo; wasu hiŋhiŋ kte laka, Then the wind became chilly, so sleet might well precipitate. Bl. WHL.

iyo'ƭaŋla, v.a. To regard things such as money or property above all else. Woyuha kiŋ iyotaŋyala, You regard ownership of property above all else. Hence, to show one's pride. Pb.26.WHL.

iyo'tiƭaŋla, adj. Tightly fitted. Ogle iyomatitaŋla yelo, i.e. too small, too tight for me. Bl. WHL.

i'yot'iŋst'iŋs, v. cont. red. To take mouthful after mouthful. Wana peji kiŋ - yaślapi iyececa yelo, i.e. they choked themselves up with grass. Bl. WHL.

iyo'walya, v. To have something as an excuse. D.124. WHL. Cf. wal'iyowalya.

iyo'wamya, v.a. Same as iyoyaŋbya.

iyo'wiwila s'e, adv. As though springing water, in the likeness of a spring welling forth; fig., fatty, in appearance quite fleshy.

iyo'yaŋbya, v.a. (iyoyaŋpaya). To enlighten one. Pb.29. Cf. iyowamya.

iyu'blaȟ, v. To open, spread out well. Tipi - iyeya, To open the whole front part of a tent, i.e. to raise the walls. Yuŋkaŋ waŋna tipi kiŋ - iyeyapi. Waŋna tipi - iyeyapi waŋ eglepi.

iyu'ǧuka, v. To injure by a hard pull, to strain, sprain e.g. a tendon. Cekpa ibluguka ca hece, as a man says when a friend always wants him back. Bl. WHL.

iyu'ȟlaȟlaya, adv. Peeling or pulling off and uncovering sores or wounds, by removal of scabs and bandages. Wokoyake kiŋ coku kiŋ ekta iyaskapa keś kiyuślokapi. Hence, to open sores.WHL.

iyu'koltkeyela, adv. Hanging without touching down. - otke lo. Bl.

iyu'k'o, v. To enlarge a hole by reaming. Ibluk'o. Hi - welo. Bl. WHL.

i'yuŋƙel, adv. Travelling by foot. Hu - , On foot. KE. WHL.

iyu's'o, v. To slice a thin edge on a hide, by drawing motion. It is applied also to one who rides through water and gets wet inspite of lifting his legs. Bl. WHL. Cf. yus'o.

iyu'śiŋktiŋyaŋ, adv. Leaning one way or another. - najiŋ, To stand leaning to one side. Bl.

iyu'ślok, v. To slip off, to divest one's self e.g. of a sweater. Śina kiŋ ecela - kipi. Iyuśloka, An extractor. WHL.

iyu'śpeyeya, adv. With one having neglected to do something. - ecoŋ, To do work that somebody neglected to do. WE. WHL. KE.

iyu'śťaǩa, v. To soften, make soft, press. Cuŋwiyapehe iyuśtakapi s'e, i.e. suggesting the color purple.

iyu'wiŋśkalake s'e, express. Of anger or disgust at something said or done by another. Bl. WHL. Thus an equivalent: How frightful it is said. WHL.

J

jaja'haŋ, v. To be in need of washing. Uŋkcela heca waksiŋ na oŋ apawiŋta ca he tohiŋni jajahe śni. MS.482.

jolo'waŋwaŋ, v. To whistle e.g. a tune. - naŋke lo. Bl. WHL.

joťo'kte, v. (śoto). To suffer from smoke, be affected by smoke. Iśta jotomakte yelo, wipapiya po, i.e. the smoke makes me blind. Bl.

K

ǩaa'opťeca, v. To do a little bit; to do less. - ecoƞ, To do less than. BD. WHL.

ǩable'sglepi s'e, adv. Distinctly, clearly. - uƞ. Aƞpetu - , A clear day without mist. Tohuƞhuƞniyaƞ k'eyaś - uƞpi śni, i.e. always standing together. Bl.

kacaƞ'glegleya, v. To roll a wheel; to turn cart-wheels. Huƞpe kacaƞglegleyapi s'e iƞyaƞke lo, as is said when a man runs, making large strides. Bl. WHL.

ǩacaƞl', v. To move the heart to sadness, to gladness. Caƞte - śice. Caƞte - waśte. Thus, to sift, as flour. WHL.

ǩace'slisli, v. To walk with a bounce and a sway. - s'e mani, i.e. being weak-kneed. Bl. WHL.

ǩaci'ca, v.a. To soften and smoothen e.g. a hide, a plowed field, giving it a finishing touch with an iron tool (harrow). Wakacica. RF. Bl. WHL. Obs.

kae'tulake el, adv. ph. In a little while. Same as tokśá. - peji owayaśla kiƞ wanil aye. B.H.11.2.

ǩagmi'pi s'e, adv. As though cut all down. - yaƞkapi, They have nothing whatever left. Keye cola yaƞkapi. Bl.

ǩahe'ktaǩiya, adv. Backward. - kacekcekapi, They staggered backwards. B.H. 256.11.

ǩahiƞ'ťu ska, adv. Swept clean. - iyaya, as is said when the wind clears a place, sweeping it clear. Bl.

kahi'yaya, v. Go through a tune, sing a tune or song. Olowaƞ - , To sing a hymn, a song. Hogluwaƞkal olowaƞ - . U na waƞjila eśa, i.e. olowaƞ waƞ, at least one, uƞkicahiyayapi. D.20.

ǩa'ȟlayela, adv. Causing to ring or sound something; fig., one's full utterance being given. - iyuha oƞspeciciyelo, I have taught you all. Bl.

kaȟlo'ǧeca, adj. Poor, empty, hungry. Huƞhe - yeyele, as a woman says when a man asks for food coninuously. Owipi woteȟi. - yewayeȟcelo, as one who eats endlessly.

kaȟlu'ȟlata, adv. Hanging in abundance, drooping. - hiyu, as leaves coming out in abundance and drooping. - hiuic'iya, To stand up and talk too often. - iȟpeic'iyapi. Kaȟlúȟlul, abbrev. WE. WHL.

ǩaȟta'ǩeǩe, v. To bother, to irk. Wakaȟtakeke, i.e. my words displease him, although I said nothing bad. WHL. Bl.

kaȟya'payalake s'e, adv. Towards the front side. Wana lowaƞ kta ca - omniciye. MS.159. WHL.

kaȟyu'ȟlata, v. To make a scratch, as does a clawed creature.

kaȟ'e', v.t. To exhaust every detail, elaborate, develope. Ptepa kaȟ'epi s'e oyaka, To tell something with all its details. Bw. WHL.

kai'cisaƞnica, adv. Striking sideways, towards the side. - ahiyayelo, ecel egnaka yo, i.e. the wind etc. have blown it half off (tablecloth), so put it back on. WHL.

kai'gluwiƞyaƞ, v. To make a woman of, to become effeminate. - hiyayelo. Bl.

kai'hakteya, adv. Not as much, not fully. - s'e magaju, It rains just a few drops. Bl. WHL.

ǩai'ȟeya, adv. Drawing up behind, grouping. - aya, ahinajiƞ, To come together into groups or bunches, as is said of people or things that drift into clusters or piles. Bl.

ǩai'psilyalake s'e, adv. Keeping pace ahead of others. - iƞyaƞka, To be a little ahead of others in running; said also of the middle finger on the hand. Bl. WHL.

kai'ťececaśni, v. (ite-ececa). To change one's facial expression, as by a slap, a blow, or by a reproving remark. - iyemayayelo, as is said in fun, i.e. you make me angry. Bl. WHL.

kai'yab, adv. Without warning. Śuŋkmanitu - ihaŋ. Oyate waŋ taŋka wicoti ca - ihaŋ, Without warning, he came upon a big camp of people. D.207-8.

kai'yaǩic'ula s'e, adv. By a little more than usual amount. - mak'u śni, icewiŋś conala mak'u we, i.e. expected much but received little. - yahipi kiŋ icaŋlmawaśte. Bl. WHL.

kai'yocatka, n. Left handed performance WHL.

ǩai'yoȟpeya, adv. Down hill, downward. Bl. WHL.

kai'yoyagya, v. To shake slightly, to quiver, as do the chin or cheeks when one rides over rough roads. Kawaŋkaka iyaya ca iyoȟa kiŋ - iyeye. Tapoŋ naśkaŋ s'e iyuŋke. Bl. WHL.

kajal'ya, adv. With objects spread or stretched apart. Tiśkakaŋ - yaŋk, as is said when a lean person's neck muscles on either side protrude and form a hollow between them. Bl. WHL.

kaji'nica śni, v. To be unostensibly in want. Takuni - keś, Although not clearly in want. TH.

kaju', v.a. To uproot, as a strong wind does to trees; to break off. Tiŋpsiŋla wana hukaju, as is said in August when the stems of the wild turnip are dry and break off. A. Sb. WHL.

ǩajuŋ'he s'e, adv. Knock fast into mud. - inajiŋ, To get something mired. Bl. WHL.

ǩaǩab', v. cont. (kakapa). To knock something away from a place. - iyeya. Si - iyeya, To trip one. - iȟpeya, To strike and throw one down. LT. WHL.

kaǩi'cipapi, n. (kapa). A race, a contest. Kignuŋ - , A swimming game, as an underwater race.

ǩaǩi'ciṗehaŋ, v. To wave, form waves, in water. Mini - , Water waves. B.H. 71.12. WHL.

kakśi'kśa, adv. Tired out, as from a long ride. Leceya makakśikśelo, i.e. I am tired. Bl. KE. Cf. Lakota section.

kakśi'kśija, v. red. (kakśija). To fold up in parts, to collapse, as the knees in giving away. Bl. KE. WHL.

ǩale'calake s'e, adv. Recently. Ww. WHL.

kale'haŋyaŋk, v. To separate parts, divide away. - iyeya. B.H.249.4.

ǩama'ǩataǩiya, adv. Downward, toward the earth, ground. - uwate k'uŋ. Tate waŋ - iȟpemayelo. Bl. Also, ǩamáǩatka.

kaŋa'kalaya, adv. Very lean. - yaŋka, To be very lean, i.e. the veins being very visible and thick. Pehaŋ s'e napsu kiŋ - . Bl.

kaŋ'ȟtal, adv. With muscles relaxed, with a loss of tension. - imacu, i.e. I feel lazy. Bl. WHL.

ǩaŋi'yeyapi s'e, adv. As if without difficulties, being provided for all along the way. - ya, u, To go, come cheerfully without meeting difficulties. - oyaka, To tell well, in detail from start to finish. Bl. BE.

kaŋna'ceǧa, n. A kettle shape. - itazipa, A bow whose shape is that of a cega.

ǩaŋ'śniśnilak, v. cont. To be surprised at, not expecting one. - ataya, To meet one unexpectedly, one whom one had wanted to see. IS.

ǩaŋwiŋl' iyeya, v. To sweep or brush by, move just touching in passing.KE.

kao'heye, adj. Slanting, as in toenailing wall studs in place. WHL.

ǩao'swa, v. To slide down an incline, as dirt or sand from a river bank, or hay from a stack. WHL. - hiŋȟpaya.

ǩao'ṫeheheaŋ, adv. Afar, distant; not yet time. Nahaȟci - lakelo. Bl. WHL. Cf. kaoȟlaȟyalaka.

kao'waŋya, v. To grow, be added to. Saŋb - s'e, i.e. the story grows while it is told to others. Bl. WHL.

ǩapaŋ'yaŋ, v. (kapaŋ). To beat, pummel, soften up. - yaŋka, iyotaka yo, Make soft a spot for yourself and sit, i.e. by beating smoothe the hides etc. Bl.

kaptu'za, v. To give a blow so as to make bend forward and over, as a blow to the pit of the stomach. Bl. WHL.

ƙaski'glag, adv. Without order or system, unpatterned. - wicoti, i.e. camping together without order. Bl.

ƙaski'ska, v. To make rough or wavy by pounding.-- ƙaskiśkaska, v. red. To pound into various forms. -- ƙaskiśkaskakel, adv. Pounding into various patterns. - kagege, To work out a pattern, as for beading. - wakagege k'on wana kitanyankel wagluśtan. Bl. WHL.

ƙaswa'ka, v. To make ragged, to shred. WHL. Cf. kaza, kazazeca.

ƙaśi'kśil, adv. Ruined, spoiled, infected. - wakanpi sece. BT.

kaśni'yanyan, v. To break up, ripple, toss about. Mini - , i.e. shallow water passing over rocks. -- kaśni'yanyanla, adv. Rippling along. Mini kin - yunkelo, i.e. it rippled. Bl.

ƙaśpe'ṗilṗicaśni, adj. Solid, hard to chip; faithful to one's word. Le tuwa oie kiton k'on, as is said of a man who suddenly disappeares having said he would stay. Bl. WHL.

ƙata'kinkin, v. red. (katakin). To be shaky and staggering. Katakinkinhci wagli yelo, i.e. staggering to right and left, as if having been hit. - la s'e mawani yelo. Bl. WHL.

ƙatan'blablas, adv. On both sides of the back. - glihpeic'iya, To throw or flop self on both sides of the back, as does an itching horse. Bl. Cf. ikpaptanptan.

ƙaṫo'wotanla, adv. Struck and set upright. - kuye. Lehan wanciglak iblotaka ce, as is said when the men return from a buffalo hunt. BT.

kaṫunp', adj. Thick and sticky. Waśma iyecel unpśiś - omawani, i.e. walking through gumbo. WHL. Cf. tuntunpa.

kat'e'la, n. A long stick used by women as a drumstick, a woman drummer's drum stick. - tacancega icabu. Bl.WHL.

kaunh'ye, adj. Same as kawinhye. One hundred. Nape nupin kaská - .

ƙawa'cinksab, v. To bring about the restoral of consciousness. - iyeya. WHL.

ƙawi'lwiṫa, v. To bunch, gather in groups. Peji kin kawilwita ewagle kte, I am going to bunch the hay.WHL.

ƙayunś', adv. conj. If that is the case. The word is used by one who tells something to another who already knew but had not divulged the fact. Hecetu - oyaka tka, If it had happened so, he did not tell. WHL. Cf. B.H.115.4.

ƙaza'mnimniyela, adv. Forcing open and flapping. - tipi k'on, as is said of a tent flapping in the wind. WHL.

ƙecan'h'a, n. A turtle with an odor of wood. Bl.

ƙewo'yuspa s'e, adv. As if a turtle being dragged from mud; fig., doing the impossible. BT.

ke'ya'pi', v.n. They say. Note: Used in non-eye-witness narration. D.l.

ƙe'ye cola, adv. Entirely destitute. Also, keye cocola, kagmi s'e. - yankapi, iyayapi, They are without anything. Bl.

ke', v.n. It is said, they say. Same as śke'. D.l. Cf. below.

ƙi'camna, v. To be in the midst, be beset, surrounded with e.g. an epidemic. Wamniomni - yelo, i.e. a hurricane. Wicaśa ota - . Wecokuja okicamna el unkanpelo. Bl. WHL. -- ƙicámnayan, adv. In an overwhelming way. - ahiyaye, To pass by in large numbers. Bl.

ƙigli', v. To go straight home, to arrive home directly. Tokeya - . MW.

ƙignun', v. (kignuka). To dive. - kacicipapi, An underwater distance swimming race. Bl.

ƙihan', v. To arrive and stand. Tukte kawita unkihanpi kte lo.Bl. Cf. kiwitaya.

ƙihe', v. To make effort. - laka yo, Stick to it and keep busy. IS. WHL. Re.

ƙihpa'ya, v. To bed down; to fall down. MW. WHL.

k̇iḣ'aŋ'k̇a, v. To split, divide, break to pieces. Caŋ wakiḣ'aŋkelo, I split wood. Bl.

k̇ija'nicaśni, v. To be without capacity to be grasped or held, be elusive. - yuha yo, Try and get it even if it is impossible. Ba.

k̇ik̇i'yak̇el, adv. Not in the usual order, in a way outside the customary. - uŋ, (fig.) as is said when a married couple, or other people, do not get along well with each other. Bl. WHL. Cf. oiglukiki.

k̇ilya'kel, adv. Steadfastly, with firm determination. - ecoŋ, i.e. to do something slowly but surely. Bl. WHL.

k̇ipa'ble, v. To come to a halt, as in the course of flight, to stop and become immobile. Syn.- kipamna. Bl.WHL.

kipa'mna, v. To halt, when coming to a place of safety, as do horses or buffalo in scattered places. Bl. Cf. kipable.

kipca', v. To swallow e.g. food, saliva. Lowaciŋ ca oŋ taḣna wakipcahe lo. Bl. WHL.

k̇isiŋ'c'iya, v. refl. To groom and tidy up one's self, to ready one's self. WHL. Syn.- piic'iya.

k̇isiŋ'kṗe, v. To trick, to deceive one into doing, to solicit. Wakisiŋkpe na mak'u welo, i.e. receiving what one wanted very badly. Makisiŋkpe na uŋgnayelo. Bl. WHL.

k̇isiŋ'te, v. Same as kisiŋkpe.

kis'iŋ's'iŋ, v. To crane, jerk the head or move it up and down in quick motion. Wakis'iŋs'iŋ. Bl. WHL. Cf. kas'iŋs'iŋ, s'iŋs'iŋya.

k̇itaŋ'kognagyelaḣci, adv. Alienating one, pressing one's demands upon one. - uŋpi, as said of a disaffected couple thinking of divorce. - oyaśtaŋyelo. WHL.

k̇iṫaŋ'ṗawoslaheyelakel, adv. Reposefully. - maŋke c'oŋ nawajiŋ yelo. Bl.WHL.

k̇iṫaŋ'yelakeleś, adv. Being in a favorable attitude. - emáca. R. WHL.

k̇itoŋ'waya, v. To ooze. Tehaŋ - lo. Bl.

k̇iuŋ', v. To return to home, as a horse returns to its place on the range. Tehaŋ - na, i.e. went far away. Bl. WHL.

k̇iwaŋ'jica, adj. Not one but all. Taku - śni slolya, He understands everything thoroughly. Bl. WHL.

k̇iwa'śteśteka, v., adj. To be good to one. WHL.

k̇iye', adv. Nearby. - au wo. BT.

koġiŋ'ġiŋ, v. To nod. Tipi kiŋ iyaza caŋnuŋp gluha - omani. - naŋkahelo ḣ'uŋyela wahiyelo. BT. Cf. ogiŋgiŋ. -- koġiŋ'ġiŋkel, adv. Slow, away long. - yaŋka, To be slow, being away long. Bl. -- koġiŋ'ġiŋlag, adv. Rather slow, far away. - naŋka na hi na taku yakahe? FB.

kognag'yela, adv. Just a little. Kitaŋ - ile, It burns just a little. Bl.

k̇ohaŋ'k̇e śni, adv. Before the time comes, for the time being. Also, tokśa. - iyaye kiyelo. Bl.

koi'yayuḣk̇iya, adv. Meeting at a small angle. Also, kaiyayuḣk̇iya. - iyaya, as is said of a road leading to and into another at a narrow angle. Bl.

k̇oka'mna, v. To get, to secure. Palani - hi s'e lila owewakaŋkaŋ, as is said of a person telling lies. La.

koki'ptaŋ, v. To feel, make unsteady. Tawat'elwaye śni tka yelo; tka Lakota kiŋ komayakiptaŋpi ca heoŋ blelo. MS. 532.

koḱi'woḣci, v. To cut or tear through the skin. Kokiwowaḣci. Bl.

kośka'uŋcihikaca, v. To be or become a grandmother, as is said teasingly of a young woman not seeming to care to marry. Bl.

kpawa'ś'aka, v. pos. (pawaś'aka). To make strong and secure. WHL.

k̇u, k̇ul, n. The lower parts or things. - k'el taŋyaŋ śni, Something is wrong below, in the wagon undercarriage. Bl.

k̇uśi'ṗatoŋ, v. To support, hold up. Caŋ kuśipawatoŋ kte lo, I shall support the post. Bl.

L

laḣ, suff. (laḣca). More of (it). Waciƞlaḣ, He want still more. Huƞhe, lote waśicuƞlaḣ. Bl.

laḣca′ suff. Cf. laḣ.

le′caḳicioƞ, v.a. To do this to. Same as lecakicoƞ, lecakioƞ. Caƞ teca kiƞ el lecakicioƞpi kiƞ, tokeśke caƞ śeca ecakicioƞpi kta hwo? B.H.265.17.

lehaƞ′kalkaṫaƞhaƞ, adv. From there hence, thence, hither. Oyate - ahipi, i.e. people from other countries, foreigners. B.H.34.3.

lehaƞ′kaṫa, adv. Hither, from far away. Wicaśa - , A foreigner. B.H.27.30.

le′ja, leś, adj. Capable of holding one's urine. Bl.

le′tka, adj. Having spent all. Maletka, I am "broke"; similarly: Maƞ wegahaƞ. Bl.

lolwa′naġi, v. To give food to a spirit. - yewaye c'uƞ taƞyaƞ wiyewaye lo, If I give the spirits something to eat, then I dine well. Bl.

lolwa′zaze, adj. Being hindered from eating much, not able to eat. Bl. Syn.- lolḣwaka.

M

maġa′wapáha, n. A headdress of goose feathers. - iwekcu ktelo; and so now I go begging from door to door, i.e. tiiyaza tiole ayiƞ kte. Bl.

maḳi′paḣlala, adv. Brushing the earth, creeping along the ground; lingering along the horizon. - wakiƞyaƞ ukiye lo, i.e. storm clouds are all along the horizon and coming toward one. Bl.

maḳi′ṗastoya, adv. In a fixed, prone position on the ground. - iḣpeic'iya. B.H.215.7.

maḳi′yagle, v. To place or hold on the ground. - yuziƞ na akaƞ iḣpeic'iya, i.e. he held it (the sword) against the ground and threw himself on it. B.H.90.22.

maḳi′yeya, v. To shove aside onto the ground. Wicaśa - yuƞka, i.e. he was sick and foresaken. Bl. Cf. makóḳaḣciyela.

mako′ḳaḣciyela, adv. Floating about on the ground. - ḣpaya, i.e. nobody looks after him. Bl.

mako′p'oya, v. To raise dust. Also, makáop'oya. - upi, i.e. raised much dust while coming. Bl.

mani′ṫuḳala, n. A little guardian spirit. - siƞte onamaśloke, The manitukala's tail is running off with me, as children sing who are playing, running bout zigzag and holding a shawl up behind sailing it. Bl.

ma′niye s'e, adv. As though taking a walk. Eyiƞ nahaƞ maga śapa ca - kagle, as a woman would say teasing her brother-in-law when he leaves. Bl.

mayal′, adv. Deep in the forest. Ozuye taƞka k'uƞ - yewicaye. MS.563. WHL.

minio′pakiƞyéla, n. A water bird that flies on the water. Bl.

mini′wicagnaśka caƞ, n. The water goose-berry bush.

mi′yuġiƞġiƞ, adv. Disturbing one. Agleśka s'e - hiƞgla mani, i.e. in walking, the skin wrinkles as a lizzard's or an aged person. Bl. WHL.

mnia'li, v. To travel over the water. Caŋȟpaŋ - iŋyaŋke, i.e. moving over the water, using the wings. Bl.

mnihi'pi s'e, adv. Flooding, seeping in, as water into a house.

mniȟa'ȟa, v. To run with water. Iśta - maŋke, My eyes are running with water. Bl.

mniyo'ȟcaya, adv. Full of water, tears. Iśta - waceyakiye, i.e. with eyes full of tears. B.H.127.18.

mniyo'sniya, v. To make the water very cool, to cool water, to become cool water. Mniyosnisnikiciyapi ktelo. Hiya, mni kiŋhaŋ áp'eyela yuŋkelo, i.e. the water is shallow and the water is warm. Bl.

N

naa'k̇aȟliyeya, v. To hang out. Ceji - , To let one's tongue hang out, as do dogs in hot weather.

naa'k̇iyatagtake s'e, adv. As if the legs were crossed, in knock-kneed fashion. Ya, heyiŋ nahaŋ ka - gle, as others would say when a woman, having slandered someone goes home, i.e. she has cross-shaped legs. Bl.

nacaŋ'teśilya, adv. With yet a gluttonous feeling, or desire for more. - wipi, i.e. having eaten all one can take and being sorry for not being able to eat more. Bl.

naġi'ksap̣a, adj. Elated over one's fulfilled predictions. MF.

nagla'k̇eyeya, adv. Stretched outward, bloated, expanded. Tucuhu - wimapi yelo, i.e. to be overloaded with food so that the ribs are stretched far apart. Bl. Cf. naiŋyaŋyeya, nawizipaŋyeya.

naheb'yela, adv. On one's haunches, on one's legs folded under. - maŋke, iyotaka. - yaŋka, To be sitting with one knee bent and the other almost touching the ground and resting on this leg. RF.

naȟlal' mnióŵe, n. A spring scratched from the soil; a climbing along a cliff next to water. WHL.

naȟlo'ke s'e, adv. Noiselessly. - mani, To walk lightly, without noise. Bl. -- naȟlóȟloke s'e, adv. red.

naȟni'yela, adv. Hurriedly. -- naȟní-yeyela, adv. red. Hurrying, breaking into a run. Naȟniyeyelaȟci omani, To walk and run in turns. Bl.

naȟp̣a', v.n. To be kicked off or out. WHL. Cf. Lakota section.

naȟpi'ȟpiya, adv. Slouchy, unkempt.

naiŋl', v. To be quiet, grow silent. Wagugeca kaga ca naiŋlpica śni. As he made packed snow it was not possible for him to keep silent. Bl.

naiŋ'yaŋyeya, adv. Become like a rock, tight-packed and hard. Nige - wipi, To be filled up with food, i.e. so that the belly becomes tight and hard like a rock (iŋyaŋ). Bl. Cf. naglakeyeya, nawizipaŋyeya.

najaŋ'jaŋyelayeye, v. To be ripe and shining; to come to a mature head, as is said of a boil that is ripe. Bl.

naju'ḱaosnisni s'e, adv. As if cooling the back part of the head. - iŋyaŋka, as is said of a man who has but little hair left and it waves in the wind while he runs. Bl.

na'ḱap̄as, adv., v. To force together, gather, bring together. Mninakapas hiyuya, as is said of drops of water that appear when one has been scalded. - hiyumayelo. Mninapas hiyuye, A blister.

na'ḱap̄oḣ, v. To make swell up, come together. Mininákapoḣ hiyuya, as is said of water drops that form where one has scalded himself. Cf. nakapas, mninapas hiyuye.

nakpe'yeya, v. Lift up one's ears to hear. Noŋḣ'nakpeyemaye, I am hard of hearing, my hearing is dead. Bl.

nani'yaŋ, v. To have sore feet. Onaḣlokiŋ kte laka - ca caŋku ipaweḣ ece iŋyaŋka ciŋ yelo. Si - , The feet pain me. Si nawaniya. WHL.

nao'blel, adv. Scattered, spread out in a line. - aye s'e; kaoblagaheya, as is said of a line of soldiers spreading their line of attack.

nao'swa, v. To cut off, as from a bank or cliff. Nawaoswa. Bl. WHL.

napa'pa, v. To make bark. Waecakca nuŋkiŋ na - umayaye, You are ready to do things at will and so you get me started barking, as a father would say to his child or wife if they do wrong. - taku ecoŋ mayayapelo, i.e. you bother me unceasingly. Bl.

napḱa'wiŋc̄e s'e, adv. As if wiping or fanning something away with the hand. - śkaŋ, To steal, (slang) to swipe. Bl.

napo'glecekutepi, n. A game of skill in shooting the bow and arrow. Bl. Cf. oglecekute.

nap̄o'yublaya, v. To open the palm of the hand. Letaŋhaŋ napoyublayapi s'e yuŋka ca napeceśni waimna kiŋ kte lo, i.e. the road is now level. Bl. WHL.

napsa'psakela s'e, adv. Breaking like rope tearing apart. - mani, To walk trippling along, suggesting the sound of a rope straining and breaking. Bl. WHL.

napśi'ja, v. To ruin by stepping on. Bl. WHL.

napta'hena, adv. Forgetting. Obs. - ecamoŋ śni, I did not do it because I forgot it. RF. Cf. lotkuŋkeśni.

nasu'śtiŋca s'e, adv. As if the head were swept clean of hair, as is said of one with very little hair left, who is thin and looking ragged. Bl.

naswa', v.n. To rip, tear into fringe, to fray.

nas'iŋ'yela, adv. Stretched out. Ituŋkab - yuŋka, To lie on one's back, all stretched out.

naśa'k'oḣayeya, adv. Making a rattling sound as something grows red. - ayugal wauŋ welo, peta kiŋ, i.e. spread out hands over the stove. Bl.

naśkab'ya, v.a. To bump into.

naśkaŋ, v. To jostle, jolt. Tapoŋ - s'e iŋyaŋke, i.e. the cheeks go up and down from the jolting of the wagon. Bl.

naśka'pa, v. Bump, rub along against something, as is said of two tops which while spinning run against each other. Bl. Cf. naśkabya.

naśla'ye, adv. Peeling away, making bare. - niktepi, They bother you always. Śehaŋśtuka tuweni - nikte śni hwo? For once at last they leave you unbothered, don't they? Bl.

naśle', v. To divide, split. Cehupa namaśle kinica, My jaw tried to split me in two, as one says when chewing suddenly into something very sour. Bl.

naśu'śka, v. To make tardy; to become a worthless fellow. Tezi naśuśkayeya wimape nat'iŋsya he kapi.

natog'yeya, v. To make different, to give a strange appearance to the face etc. Iśta - yauŋ welo, i.e. you look terrified. Bl.

nawi'lwiťa s'e, adv. As if scraping together with the feet. - mani, To drag the feet over the ground as if one gathered snow together. Bl.

nawiŋ'ta, v. To clear space on the ground with the feet, scraping away things with the feet. P. WHL.

nawi'zipaŋyeya, adv. Swollen, bloated, filled up, distended. Nige - wipi, To be filled up with food, as a full bag. Bl. Cf. naglakeyeya, naiŋyaŋyeya.

nawo'holyeya, adv. Forming the shape of a tube. Ila kiŋ - matasakelo, The mouth of mine takes the shape of a tube, lips protruding, when I am stiff with cold. - po, To swell into a tube shape.

nazi'gzil, adj. Flimsy, flexible, pliant. Yuŋkaŋ taku - iwahaŋ waku, I came home then walking in something like rubbers. MS.356. WHL.

nici'caya, v. To cause to be with you. - wauŋ. Pb.6.

niȟa', n. A former time, age. Wicanike c'oŋ hehaŋ lena ocaŋku, In former times there were such things as roads. BT.

noŋȟpe'kic'uŋ, v. To have a hissing sound in the ears. - yaŋkahe c'uŋ taku waŋ onoŋȟ s'ake, While he had in his ears a strange sound, he actually was hearing something. Bl. -- noŋȟpékic'uŋśniyaŋ, adv. Without anything disturbing one's hearing; hence, not having need to use one's hands to communicate. Bl. WHL.

noŋȟwa'zaza, v. To hear only snatches of what is said. Noŋȟwamazaza tka noŋȟkatimayayelo, as a man says when asked why he is silent when others talk so much. Bl.

noŋȟwica'ȟloke s'e, adv. With ears opened. - ociciyakiŋ kte, I'll explain it to you giving ear. WHL.

noŋ'ȟ'opaya, adv. (noŋge-opaya). In or accompanying one's hearing. - yazaŋ, To have an ear-ache.

nuþiŋ'yaŋ, adv. On both sides. - zaniyaŋ okanuŋkihuŋnipi kte. B.H.124. 25. WHL.

O

oca´ȟsu, v. To be icy, be frozen in e.g. articles of clothing. Wakpala oguhan oyasin - ca oomani śice. Bl.

ocan´ku s'e, adv. Like a pathway. WHL.

ogli´ȟpaye, n. A falling down on. Owaś'ag konla taogliȟpaye lo, i.e. its fall was terrible. B.H.195.21.

ogna´la, adv. In, holding a small bit. Napognala, Only a handful.

oğu´han, n. Tracks, trail. Wakpala - oyasin ocaȟsu ca oomani śice, i.e. the roads through valleys are icy.

ohi´you, n. A port of arrival, a nesting place; home sweet home. - waśte, as is said when one comes near the place of destination not his home. Bl. KE. Cf. ogliyou.

oho´wakányankel, adv. Weeping in sorrow. - inyan on iglaśpaśpa ounye. B.H.203.6.

oȟa´ṗe, v. To overlook, not find. - taninśniyan yankelo, i.e. a man sitting between two others is overlooked. Omniciye tipi el tuweni - eśa un śni, i.e. one finds nobody at home. NP. Cf. Lakota section.

oȟla´in, v. To work loose. - manice, wanil, waśkan, I am always busy. Bl. LHB.

oȟmun´yece, v. To give attention to. Oȟmunyayece lo, You paid attention to him (when you passed him). Bl. Note: waóȟmunyece, A talkative person.

oȟpu´ȟpuya, adv. In rags, poorly dressed. - aya, as is said when a wound is healed and the skin or scab is peeling off.

oȟta´teya, adv. Being, becoming weak and languid for some reason. Ake hel asnikiyin kta iyukcan na el - ya. Yunkan el tiyopa s'e han. MS.142.

oȟ'an´wakankanyan, adv. Acting like a a wayward person; remarkable in operating. Kukuśe s'e - wakita, i.e. to see everything, for boys have clear eyes. Bl. WHL.

oȟ'e´ȟ'e, v. To be drooping, dangling. Śunka aze - s'e wahanpi waśtelake, i.e. when someone likes broth very much. KE. WHL.

oȟ'o´kpaya, v. To be sunk, ringed around with circles. Wanagi s'e iśta - , as is said when the eyes are sunk deep. Bl. WHL.

o´icoğa, n. Wood drifted ashore. WHL.

oi´c'iȟ'an, v. To do injury to one's self. Woteȟi omic'iȟ'an. Bl. WHL.

oi´c'ipa, v. To act as tributary to. Canku oic'ipe, A side road tributary to a main road. Also, oicipa. Bl.

oi´e ṗeṗeka, n. Sharp talk, bitter words. Oie pepekelaȟcak, i.e. taku eye cin oyasin canzeka ece ca heon heyapi. Bl. WHL.

oi´e waśi´cun, n. One who is a noisy and sassy person. WHL.

oi´e waśi´kśicun, n. red. (oie waśicun). One who talks without let, a garrulous person. WHL.

oi´glonica, v. To be stubborn moving out or away. B.H.165.7.

oi´kpağica, v. To awake, come awake. Hecel - na lila wiyuśkin. MS.152.

oi´kpaptanśilya, adv. Hard to roll around in, as in a bed. - mayakuwapelo, i.e. you are hard after me with your talk. - ic'iya. - tipi. Bl. WHL.

oi´kpaptanwaśteya, adv. Easy to roll from side to side in. - epelo, To say truthfully, as is said when somebody doubts a statement. Bl.

oi´nikağa, n. A sweat house; a frame building. Hihanna el - wan lila tanka ca etipi na el kagapi na hel tima iyayapi śni. MS.344,349.

o´iyapa, oi´yapa, v. To hit, beat on the side of. -- n. The hitting side. WHL.

oi´yoȟiśilya, adv. Being a sad thing to say or see. Tipi kin - he, This room, house is in great disorder. - yaceya yelo, How sad to see you weep. Bl. D.122. WHL.

oi'yopa, v.n. To be affected, to swell.

oi'yotiyek̇iya, v. To endure hard times. Oiyotiyewakiya, I am having a hard time. B.H.104.20. WHL.

o'izilya, v. To smoke in the tanning process. Itózilwayiƞ kte lo. WHL.

oji'ċaka, adj. Rich in goods etc. - ca wawicak'u we. Bl.

ok̇a'hiƞhaƞ, v. To precipitate, rain, snow etc. Wa okahiƞhe ca oye kiƞ taƞyaƞ ablespica śni, It snowed on the track so it cannot be clearly seen. Bl. WHL.

o'k̇aḣglepi, n. Cf. hokaḣglepi.

ok̇aḣ'ya, v. To set something afloat; fig. bring to birth. Śuƞkwiƞyela waƞ ciƞcokaḣya, i.e. more than one colt which one wished. Bl. WHL.

ok̇a'kseya, adv. Hard to unwind or untangle, as a rope strewn in a pile. WHL.

ok̇a'psica, v. To rise up, leap up, as water into tall waves. Hecel mini kiƞ ota - . B.H.202.17.

ok̇a'sni, v. To get cold from a draft entering in. Omakasni yelo, as is said when the wind comes in through the sleeves, etc. KE.

ok̇a'zoƞte, n. A design, pattern-work. LHB. Napokazoƞte, The ordered pattern of fingers on the hand. Nape - kiƞ napitakaha kiƞ nupiƞ iciyagleya iyakaśkapi. MS.340. Siokazoƞte, The toes.

ok̇i'capta, v.a. (okapta). To dip or deal out for one; to be left for, remain for. Hecel Chanaan makoce kiƞ he Abraham okicaptapi, Thus the land of Chanaan was left to Abraham. B.H.11. 15.

ok̇i'c'u, v. To restore, take backfor a purpose. Yu-iye kayeś iyoḣa saƞni - śni wote, i.e. he chews only on one side. Bl.

okiḣ'yaƞ, n. A bird flying, hovering about. WHL.

ok̇i'kcaƞpte, v. To seek to console, comfort for some reason. - niśicelo, as is said when while two are disputing another butts in, and then they say this to him. Bl. Cf. kikcaƞpta, kcaƞptepte.

ok̇i'liṫatoƞ, v. To make a great show of activity and enthusiasm. - śkaƞ, To work in excitement. Kaƞgi wicaśa to yo najiƞwicayapi na - . MS.526. Cf. lita śkaƞ, owilita, owolutatoƞ.

o'k̇imniciye, v. To come together. Oyate kiƞ witaya ecicaskaya - kta keyapelo. LHB. Syn.- kiwitaya, oiwitaya.

ok̇i'nica, v. To strive, attempt, try for some purpose. Bl.

ok̇iƞ'yaƞka, n. (oki-iƞyaƞka). An arena for racing; a gathering for competitive sports. Okiƞyaƞke oƞspic'iya yo. GA. KE.

ok̇i's'as'a, v. To hush or hiss one. Iśtiƞma uƞkokis'as'a, He hushed us both to sleep. Bl.

ok̇i'śilia, v. To speak entirely bad language. Bl.

okiś'yakel, adv. In the habit of being belligerent, unsociable, uncooth. - naƞke lo, as is said by a visitor who is received in silence as if he were not welcome. Bl. Syn.- ot'iƞḣyakel.

oki'wiƞja, v. To bind down thoroughly. Na wana, lel yaƞka ye, eyiƞ na pteha okise waƞ - . MS.143.

oko'mi, n. Same as hokomi. Cf. Yokomi.

o'kpaƞkpaƞ, v.n. To become crumbly. Śuƞkhiƞśa wicaḣcala s'e ite saƞ - . Bl. -- n. Crumbs, decay. WHL.

okpa'spa, v. To repress, suppress one's own reaction, i.e. actions, feelings etc. Owakpaspa. Waciƞ - , as is said of a man when he keeps silent inspite of his anger. Bl.

okpa'zaƞ, v. refl. To slip one's own in and under, to weave one's own in between things.

okpi'kpi, adj. Very small, slender, slit-like. Maká ciṅcala s'e iśta cikcik'aya, iśta - kaca, i.e. very small eyes. Bl.

o'lanuṅ s'e, adv. Almost, nearly. Bl.

o'mniyela, adv. In the manner of setting something out to dry, acting stingily. - wayatapelo, as is said when some ate sitting with others without sharing with them. Ena - ayuhel wicakuwi, as do horses in small places. BT. GA.

ona'cu, v. To be damp or chilly as to the feet. Haṅpa kiṅ onawacu welo, My moccasins are frosty inside. Bl.

ona'juju, v.n. To come apart, to go to pieces, as is said of a wagon when its wheels are broken. BT.

ona'k'eġa, v. To scratch around at or on. Ite pśuṅka waṅ onamak'ega he lo, as is said when one wants a smoke. BT. KE.

ona'mniyeta, adv. Being off on one's own way. - eiĥpeic'iyaya, To go on into a crowd somewhere, and then to return when someone else caught up with one. - eiĥpeic'imayayapelo. Bl.

ona'pceśilya, v. To be hard to swallow. Cf. Lakota section. LHB.

ona'puza, v. To dry up, evaporate. Hinu, - ca haṅpi cola wowahete, as a woman would say when all the soup had evaporated. BT.

ona'slata, v. To make one's way slowly by foot. Caṅku onaslatapi, They advance slowly, i.e. as slow horses. Bl.

ona's'amna, v. To give off a bad odor, to stink. Bl. LHB.

ona'zoṅ, ona'soṅ, v. To braid together, sew or weave. Tatamni - . Bl.

onu'niśniyaṅ, adv. Not at all wandering, to the point. Taku oyasiṅ - waehe lo, as they say to a joker. Bl.

oṅ'gluĥpe, oṅ'gloĥpe, n. One's occupation, work to be accomplished, burden to carry and dispose of. - maota, i.e. much work, but no time. MO.

oṅ'gluze, n. Things attended to, matters in hand. - maota kaca, I have much to attend to. Bc.

oṅ'gnaye, adv. Under pretense. - kaĥkaĥ ahitipelo, i.e. they arrived ahead of the others. Bl.

oṅ'naṗe watog'ya, n. Dangerous persons, i.e. those with weapons. - mazawakaṅ naiṅś mazaska bluha kte, i.e. weapons for emergency's sake so as to be prepared for anything. Bl. WHL.

oṅ'zeslohaṅ, v.n. To slide on the buttocks, as do some dogs or mules that sit and drag their rump by the front feet. WE. KE.

oo'kihi, v. To be able to be helped. - śica. Hecel le wicoĥ'aṅ kiṅ - śica. MS.489.

opa', adv. There being there. Yuṅkaṅ wakpala waṅ - caṅku ca opaya aya ewicuṅkiglegapi. Syn.- el uṅ.

oṗa'ḱiṅslasla, adv. Wiping the dirt away. Iśta kiṅ - iyewakiyelo, i.e. to rub the eyes because of dust that got in them. Bl.

oṗa'ṗiṅslasla iyeya, v. To wipe or rub clean. Iśta kiṅ - , To rub impurities out of the eyes. Bl. Note: the more correct form is opakiṅslasla.

o'ṗayeya, v. The word is doubtful. To include, to add. WHL.

oṗi'caka, v. To be good, a little better than another. Ataya coco welo, i.e. there is soft ground after the melting of the snow; oeti śicelo; hececa k'eyaś aliya ekta hinajiṅ yo, tokeś opicakelo, i.e. perhaps it is not bad after all. Bl.

opiś'yela, adv. Wrinkled up. - uṅ. Cf. piśpiś.

opi'ya, v. To tie with one, be alike; to renew, mend. BD.

opo'poya , v. Be swollen and open, as a sore or wound. B.H.10.

opśuṅ'pśuṅyela, adv. Making use of little things. - ic'ignaka po, i.e. be ready (put away just little things), for we will go soon. Bl. Also, limply.

opśuⁿ'wahe, opsuⁿ'wahe, n. Things broken off, small things like the teeth of a comb. Bl.

osaⁿ'saⁿke s'e, adv. As one who is white all over, as to hair and beard.

osiⁿ'kpekpeyakel, adv. In a sneaky way, sneaking around, snooping. - taku ecaⁿnoⁿ welo. Bl. Cf. iyupseyakel.

ospaⁿ'spaⁿheca, adv. Swelling and becoming doughy. Omaspaⁿspaⁿheca, I am thawing.

osu'ta, adj. Hard, tough. Haⁿkeke waksapi na osuta ece yuzapi s'e, as is said when a man, although little himself, has fleshy arms and legs; so too it is said of horses. Also, osute. Bl.

os'i'c'iya, Same as oziic'iya. Uⁿgnahelahci aⁿpetu waⁿji - yauⁿ welo. BT.

ośi'camna, adj. Becoming spoiled, giving off an odor. LHB.

ośo'śe, v. To become turbid, muddy, mirky. Bl.

ota'pi ka, express. You are "tops". You are the best. RE.

o'tasagya, v. To keep hard, stiff, frozen. MS.483.

oto'gmuⁿ, v. To appear kept, orderly. straight. Tipi kiⁿ - śni he, His room looks very disorderly. Bl.

oto'ketu, adv. How is it? As things go. Owicatoketu taⁿiⁿśni, It is not clear how they are, as is said when somebody did not do well and others have not cared to hear about it. WE.

o'topi ka, Same as otapi ka. The word is used by boys. - nuⁿke.

otu'tkala, adj. Only a very little of. - eśa tuweni el uⁿ śni yelo, i.e. nobody is in. Bl. KE.

ot'iⁿh'yakel, adv. Uncooth, hard, cold, unsociable. - naⁿke lo, okiśyakel naⁿke lo, as is said by a visitor who is received silently, as if he were not truly welcome. Bl.

ouⁿ'śila, adj. Showing of kindness and pity towards others. Ka wicaśa - waśte, That man is good in showing kindnesses, i.e. he is always ready to help. Bl.

owa'he, v.n. To have cooked something. Lila śkaⁿkapi ca iyowakteke ca heoⁿ owahehce, He spoke to him with harsh words, so he got "boiled".

owa'hwayakel, adv. Peacefully, quietly. B.

o'wakita, v. To look for, look about. Owakitapi s'e lemaceca, as old people say when they cannot see well anymore. Bl.

owa'nah'oⁿ, n. Hearing. Mnitate ca - śice, The waves were the reason for it being hard to hear. Bl.

owa'pahlokehaⁿ, part. Being bruised or skinned. Iśpa ha - owakihi yelo, i.e. although they bruise the skin of my elbow (held up for protection) I will carry it out. GA. -- v. To execute. WHL.

owa'pate, n. Heaped up matter, things pushed aside. -- v. To fill in a hole, to stuff. KE.

owa'sabglepi, n. A foundation, footing. Wasabglepi, A sighting pole. Tipi - , Something for a tower; a tower, a high monument. B.H.9.4.

owa'śteya, v.n. To feel good, pleasant, comfortable. KE.

owa'tohaⁿtu ka waⁿ, n. ph. Some times past. - el wokcaⁿ wicaśa ciⁿca kośkalapi eya ipi. B.H.116.1.

owe'coⁿkel, adv. With something doing or going on. Also, wóecoⁿkel. KE.

o'wehca, n. Something said or done to one. Yaowehca makihaⁿhaⁿ ye, as a woman says refusing an offer of marriage. Bl. KE.

owi'h'aⁿ, n. The being busy about many things, occupation.

owi'lita, adj. Official and cheerful in going about one's appointed work. Also, walita. - śkaⁿ, To work in good spirits. Bl. KE.

owi'p̄i, n. One filled up. - woteȟi, Trouble getting full, as is said when a person does not stop eating. Bl.KE.

owi'wila, adj. Soft, mushy, flabby, as if stored with water. - s'e uŋ, He is flabby one, as is said of a very fleshy man or animal. Bl. KE.

owo'ta, v. To drift. - aya, as is said of snow or sand etc. drifting to a certain place and heaping up. Bl. KE.

o'ya, n. One's proceeding, a start. - huŋkeśni, A slow start.

oya'ṫaŋyaŋ, v. To stick, be sticking within, so as to hold and keep. Bl. -- adv. Sticking in. Bl. KE.

oyo'pta, v. To pass or begin through something. Also, iyópta. Oyomapta. Katiŋyeya oyoptiŋ kta, i.e. will go straight through. Bl. KE.

oyu'ȟ'eȟ'eyakel, adv. Going and coming from e.g. one's work or occupation. - e ayuśtaŋ, To quit one's work, i.e. that one has done only in places, here and there and not well. KE.

oyu'ḱiḱiḱe, v.a. Same as oyukiki, To interfere with one's planned work. Omayukiki, He interrupted my work.

oyu'kśa, adv. In a little closed-in place or area. - imuŋkelo. Bl. KE.

oyu'sni, v. To cool by placing. - ewegnakiŋ kte, I shall put it away to cool, i.e. a pipe.

oyu's'o, v. To swim one's way under water. - uŋ, To be deep in water and swimming, i.e. as one does not touching the bottom. Bl.

oyu'ṫepa, v. To wear off, as by rubbing against something. Ceca kiŋ izuza oyutepe s'e, as is said of a very lean man or horse. Sicaŋ kiŋhaŋ izuza oyutepe s'e, i.e. the hips are lean as a whetstone. Bl.

ozaŋ'niyaŋkel, adv. Ambushing; being in good health. - piuŋkiyiŋ kta na uŋkiśtiŋma kte lo. Bl. WHL.

ozaŋ'yela, adv. Left visible. Ikpaȟ'ozaŋyela iŋyaŋgya, The (arrow) ran deep leaving only the notch visible. Bl.

P

p̄ablu'ḱa, v. To become crushed, routed.

p̄aġe'ya, v.a. To make flee, run away. -- adv. Troublesome, threatening. - akinajiŋ. Anuŋkataŋhaŋ upi na - najiŋpi; caŋke hehaŋl wana tokicikpapi, i.e. stood ready to charge and then they began to fight. D.267. KE.

pa'glaȟuġa, v. refl. To break, deform the head. Pawaglaȟuga. Bl.

p̄aglo'glo, v. To throttle, choke a person. WHL.

p̄agmi'ca, v. To pull one's hair. Blugmica. Wapagmica, I press the head and hair. WHL.

p̄ahi'higla, v. To pick up things on the way home. - toki ipi, i.e. went alone there and nobody else. Bl. WHL.

p̄ahi'hilag, adj., adv. Having picked or pushed one's way to. - omniciye, In a rough manner go first to a meeting. - ohimic'iye, i.e. now for once I am first. Bl. WHL.

p̄a'hiŋsḱayela, adv. By way of making manifest, disclosing, revealing, debriefing, letting go. Hena - omayakilaka waciŋ, I want you to tell me all those things you know about it. Wociŋ yahi ca cic'u; yuŋkaŋ - cic'u yaciŋ yelo. Caŋli kiŋ - uŋglasotapi, i.e. used up the last bit. - akiyagle, i.e. all the storm clouds passed by. Bl. HC. Yh.

paȟli' i'yoḱaskica, v. To clog, become stuffed, as the nose with matter. Paȟli iyomakaskica.

p̄aȟni'ȟp̄ilp̄icaśni, adj. Hardly worth wanting or choosing, worthless indeed. - wawapahi, i.e. I picked up all sorts of things, good and worthless things. Bl.

paȟwa'yaśkabya, v.a. To make one gasp from exhaustion, as from laughing. Lila iȟat'emayayapi na paȟwayaśkabmayayapelo. Bl.

paȟwa'yaśkapa, v.n. To gasp from exexhaustion, as from laughter. Paȟwayamaśkapa, i.e. the peritoneum contracting. Bl.

ṗai'ċaksa, ṗai'ċakśa, v. To carry a bed-roll over the shoulders. - eyaye. Bl. WHL.

ṗai'cisaŋnica, v. To pull to the opposite side. - iyeya. Bl. WHL.

ṗai'le, v. To rekindle a fire. - iheya yo, oteḣike, i.e. when it is cold. Bl. WHL.

ṗaiŋ'lṗica, v. To be able to bear or concentrate upon. Caŋte kiŋ - śni, i.e. cannot make an impression on him, persuade him. Bl. KE.

ṗajo', n. The common or expected trait of a thing or manner of action. Śuŋśuŋla s'e ituhu - kaca, as is said of a man whose forehead is very convex or pointed, bill-like. Bl. -- ṗajójo, n. red. Śuŋśuŋla ikpi saŋ s'e iśtaḣe - kaca, as is said of a man with heavy eyebrows. Bl. -- ṗajóḱe s'e, adv. In a manner opposite in expectation. - caŋkoze, i.e. he whips with the left hand. Bl.

ṗaḱi'gni, v. To pull home, draw behind one homeward. Hupákignipi, i.e. they tie up e.g. the two long tent-poles to the vehicle. BT.

ṗaksa' s'e, adv. Cut short in manner. - najiŋ, To stop walking, as when tired or because it is very warm. Bl. Syn.- wotoka s'e.

Pala'ni taziŋ'tkala, n. Perhaps the upland plover, a bird that lives upon the prairie; its bill about an inch long, quite gray and brown. Bl. Cf. Lakota section.

ṗale'ġa, v.a. To encourage during an intermission, as fighting between two other conflicts, or poking and stirring a fire. WHL. Thus, to threaten a fight asking foolish questions. KE.
pale'haŋyaŋk, v..To be separated from others. - yuza, He held himself apart from others. B.H.297.13.

ṗama'hel, adv. Pushing in. - iyeya, To push in.

ṗao'gla, v. To be set up or arranged in order, lined up in order. - iyeya. Bl. Cf. Lakota section.

ṗaṗo'ṫa, v.a. To pierce and open up, as with a knife. Wapepeka oŋ pa kiŋ uŋpapotapi, We disfigured his head, piercing it with thorns. Pb.27. LHB.

pa'ślayela, adv. Making bare the head. - s'e woyaka yo, i.e. tell the full truth. La. Syn.- hepaśpupi.

paśni'ja, v. To push or blow air out. Bl. LHB.

ṗatoŋ'waŋyaŋ, adv. Rubbing clear for vision. - iyeya. Iśta kiŋ - iyewakiyelo, i.e. to rub one's eyes so as to see better. - iyeyiŋ na taŋyaŋ ables waciŋ yo. Bc. Bl.

pawa'ś'aka, v. To put to a test of strength, to strengthen. WHL.

ṗawi', v. To hover, move about slowly and quietly, as a bird over carṙion or an old person who is yet able to move about. Cf. wapawi. Thus, to be old but still moving. KE.
ṗawi'cegna, n. One, e.g. a horse, that has returned to its group. - hiyuya. BT. LHB.

ṗawi'gnuni, v.a. To become unable to figure out or understand what has happened. R. Bl. LHB.

paya'pa, v. To be of the upper part of something. LHB.

ṗea'gnagkiya, v.a. To make settle upon, to put on or apply something from the outside; hence, to shine upon. Aŋpetu waŋji towaŋjica ca peagnagwicakiyiŋ kte lo, There will be a day, one all blue, to shine upon them. LP.

ṗeji'ḣota, n. The genus of five plants well known and frequently used by the Indians, all having characteristics of gray grass or sage.

ṗeji'ḣota ṗeṗe', n. A prickly herb that has but only one use and may be used only once. LHB.

ṗeji'ḣota skúya, n. One of the five kinds of gray medicinal herbs, frequently found in the Bad Lands.

ṗeji'jiji, n. The squirrel-tail or fox-tail plant. Hordeum jubatum. Ite aśniyaŋpi. Bl. #186.

p̄eji'yuskítakutépi, n. A boys' game or pastime, a game played with grass. Cf. yuskita.

peju'ta huókihetoⁿtoⁿ, n. A tall medicinal herb with many roots. It is used for sore joints. LHB.

peju'ta ȟa'ka, n. A medicinal herb having many roots, a medicinal root. KE.

peju'ta tiⁿ'psila, n. A turnip plant whose medicinal properties are used for the cure of the wounded.

peju'ta toto', n. Perhaps applied to the medicinal preparation of pejutap̄a, a plant quite common on the prairie and used for abdominal pains.

p̄eli'mnaśni, v. To be not afraid of fire, not satisfied with even extreme heat. LB. LHB.

p̄eli'yaglaśyahaⁿ, v. To keep the fire low. Peliyaglaśyahelo, i.e. the fire is glimmering under the ashes. Bl.

p̄elwi'yuśkiⁿ, v. To spit and sparkle, as does a fire when certain resinous woods are burned. - yelo. Bl.

p̄el'i'yucaⁿyaⁿkel, adv. With the fire getting low for lack of wood. - naⁿka hwo? Bl. LHB.

p̄el'ǩi'toⁿkel, adv. Absorbing the effects of fire, its warmth etc. - naⁿka hwo? i.e. staying near the fire. Bl.

p̄ilya', v. To use up, consume. Pilyapelo, i.e. they ate up all the grass. Bl.

p̄i'saⁿsaⁿ oȟ'aⁿ'ke, v. ph. To carry on with a wild idea, a dangerous and ill-considered course of thought. Note: the word is used when a man gets an idea of doing something and starts at once doing it without considering it and thinking it over first. One is said to have had pisaⁿ and died from it. Sb.

psa o'blotoⁿ, n. An edible swamp grass that has four corners to each leaf. Also, oblotoⁿtoⁿ. L. LHB.

pse, n. A very nervous water bird. Cf. Lakota section.

pśuǩe', n. Something that is deformed, crushed or twisted. Pa ca - kaca yaⁿkiⁿ na, as is said of one with a short crooked nose. Bl.

ptehi'yap̄a, v. To chase buffalo into a large bunch. WHL. La.

ptei'ciyuȟa uⁿma, n. A medicinal plant whose yellow blossoms are boiled with the fetid marigold to make tea for spitting of blood. Ti.

ptiⁿ'haⁿ, n. Last autumn. Also, ptíⁿhaⁿna. - hecoⁿpelo. HM. Bl. Note: ptaⁿyetu, Autumn, fall; haⁿ, haⁿna, seem both to refer to the night.

p̄ulki'čiⁿkel, adv. With the lips drooping. - uⁿ, To let the lips hang down, because one is displeased with something. Bl.

p̄uśǩi'ca, v.n. To be very heavily burdened. Caⁿtemaśice na cuwimapuskica mat'e. WHL. KE. -- p̄uskícat'a, v.n. To tire from suppressing one's feelings of sorrow, to suffer tension. WHL.

p̄usye'ya, v. To dry one out. Wanagoptaⁿpi c'oⁿ caka na pusyemayelo, i.e. listening with open mouth. Fig., to be dumb-struck. Bl. -- adv. In the manner of drying up. - anagoptaⁿ make. LHB.

p̄utaⁿ'yela, adv. Being cold and wrapped up in a bundle. Itoceś - mic'ignakiⁿ kte, Alright, I shall hold my tongue. Bl. LHB.

p̄ut'iⁿ'ǧela, v. To give a little grunting sound. Wakiⁿyela maku kaca - s'e yaⁿkiⁿ na, as is said of a proud, short and fleshy person. Bl.

p'o'waǩiṫa, v. To see in only a blurred and indistinct way. Iśta kiⁿ p'owakitapi s'elemaceca yelo, i.e. I do not see well, but in a blurred, foggy manner. P'owakitapi s'e wauⁿ, My vision is blurred. Bl.

S

sipa'gnagya, adv. At the tip of the toes. - eyayelo, as is said in ref. to tracks. BT. LHB.

siya'payaȟel, adv. With the feet wet or pained, hurting. - iyotiyekiye, i.e. to suffer from wet feet. Bl.

siye'mila, interj. I warn you. - , wakiⁿyaⁿ maktepi, maka niye śni śka. Sb.

siyo'natica, v. To be sticky and stinking as to the feet, to have unclean feet. Siyonawatica, My feet are stinking wet. Bl. LHB.

ska'niyaka, express. Same as śkeka, but in comp. with tuⁿweȟca. Tuⁿweȟca - , That is a lie, I doubt that very much. Bl. LHB. Note: tuⁿweȟca skaniyaka is a Wiciyela express.

skiska', n. A rough way, as a bad road. Also, a wood-duck. LHB.

skoko'gli, adj. Clear as a crystal. Taku - , i.e. I do not believe it.

slo'ta, adj. Aware of things. Slotá is the more correct form. Ieslota, One who tells the truth. Iemaslota. Bl. LHB. Cf. slolya.

sniyo'pa, adj. Frost-bitten, as might be the limbs. WE. LHB. Cf. oiyopa.

spaⁿ s'e waśte', adj. Tender and good to eat. LHB.

śaktoⁿ' s'e, adv. As if a funny sort of man. Bl. WHL.

śehaⁿ', interj. An express. of impatience. Also, śeháⁿś. It seems to mean "Good heavens!" "For heaven's sake!" RT.

He - Kola kola tatuye
Topakiya nataⁿ hiyuye
Śehaⁿ tamuⁿkaśni ye. MS.101.

śilwa'nakiȟ'oⁿ, v. To listen to something bad. Śilwanakiȟ'oⁿpi s'e inila maⁿkelhelo, i.e. I am silent. Bl.

śilwi'yauⁿpa, v. To accuse one falsely of evil. B.H.164.6.

śilye'ȟci, n. The profile of a man's face, esp. of a skinny man. - Ȟlogeca it'eyela, as is said when a man is very lean. Bl. WHL.

śiya'ka, n. A mud hen (duck). WHL.
śiyo'ka, n. The prairie chicken. WHL.

śkeca', n. An animal similar to an otter, black, and whose pelt is used for women's winter coats. Bl. R. KE.

śke', v.n. So they say, It is said. Same as śka, kéyápi', ke', all used in non-eye-witness narration. D.1.

śni'yeca, v. To fade away, reduce to nothing. Wa - , as is said when snow melts on touching the ground. Bl.

śok'iⁿ', v. To have or be in the likeness of a small but odd, humorous or absurd human appearance. Taȟca ciⁿcala s'e ite kiⁿ - laka ca yaⁿkiⁿ na, as is said of a man with a little face. LHB. -- śok'íⁿyaⁿ, v., adv. Having and unusual human appearance. Mayaślecala s'e ite - , as is said of a man with a strikingly small face. Bl.

śuⁿg'o'haⁿpi, n. Dog soup. LHB.

śuⁿ'ka naġi'ȟlo śpaⁿwa'ġeȟce, express. A dog's growling attitude makes one shiver.

śuⁿkaⁿ'yaⁿ, adv. Cheaply, after striking a bargain; shooting and missing game. Talo waⁿ - iyayelo, as is said when one fails to catch a rabbit etc. for food. Lecala taku waⁿ oye iyaya, tka - oye iyayelo, i.e. seemingly fresh tracks. Bl. LHB.

śuⁿkaⁿ'yaⁿkel, adv. Very thin, cheaply, poorly. - igluza, To have poor clothing on that does not protect. - mak'u, He gave me only a very little. Tula śuⁿkaⁿya yauⁿ welo, mato wayakita yelo, i.e. meeting one who did not notice one's coming and become afraid. Le pahiⁿ s'e - mani tka taⁿktaⁿkaya omani yelo. Bl.

śuⁿkma'niśnikiya, adv. Walking in the manner of a played-out horse. Bl.

śuⁿknoⁿ'ġekpa s'e, adv. In the manner of a stupid person, one purposely not listening. Huŋhé, wokiyakapi kiŋ el ewaciŋ śni - , as is said when a person does not listen. Roboam - wokiyakapi k'uŋ el ewaciŋ śni. B.H.103.10.

śuŋknu´nikiciyapi, n. A boys' game in losing horses. LHB.

śuŋk'i´yoṗeya, v.a. To make a poor and cheap exchange for, to give a mean price for. Śuŋk'iyopewaya. Wahaŋpi śuŋk'iyopewayelo, I paid a "pretty" price for soup (now that I have no teeth). Bl.

śuŋk'o´k̇aḣ, adv. In the form of horse, having the form of horse. - waŋjica nuŋb wicayuha, He has two horses perfectly alike. Bl.

śuŋk'o´k̇aḣwog, n. A horse that wanders all over. - uŋ ca śicelo, as is said of a horse that changes its owners very often. Bl.

śuŋ´k'oŋjiŋca, n. A horse that defecates. - s'e yusniza s'a ye, i.e. breaks wind often. Bl.

śu´śuś hiŋgla, v. To come crashing down with a loud noise. LHB. Bl.

T

taa´juŋtk'ognake, n. Cow kidney fat. Bl. WHL.

taa´k̇iḣ'aŋ, n. (taŋ-akiḣ'aŋ). A starving person or animal. - wahiyelo, i.e. come being very hungry. Bl. WHL.

tacaŋ´ḣaḣaka wapa´ha, n. A headdress made from the upper end of the buffalo's spinal column.

ṫacaŋ´k̇ohaŋhaŋke, n. The parts along the spinal column of a buffalo; fig. well ordered, straight. Oie - , as is said of a man who talks nicely, not using harsh language.

ṫace´ji ok̇áslute, n. The cutting out of a cow's tongue. Bl. LHB.

ṫace´ji su, n. Dribblings, perhaps, of the cow's tongue. LHB. Bl.

taḣ, n. Saliva, foam, lather. WHL.

ṫaḣna´, n. Running saliva. Lowaciŋ ca oŋ wakipca he lo. Bl. WHL.

takaŋ´ġi, n. The tails of the wakiŋyaŋ. - toki hilu we? yau we? as is said to a fellow who would not go with the bunch, but would want his own ways and left; but finally came back to them. Similarly: - taku yaka hwo? Bl. WHL.

ṫamna´, n. A swelling on a buffalo.

taŋglu´zaza, v. To be an awful thing, such as to be a murder. Taŋwicagluzaza s'e oyaḣ'aŋ ye. Bl. KE.

taṗe´ṫo ska, n. White spotted shoulders, as on a mature buffalo. Bt. LHB. Cf. Legend of Hiawatha.

tasu´ṫaṗahu, Cf. Lakota section, tasusu, pahu. Bl. Cf. taśúṗa.

taśu´p'okaḣmi, n. The gut cavity of a body. Bl.

ṫata´ḣpa, n. The breast of young animals; the hair drooped over the head or breast of the buffalo; the buffalo neck just behind the head. - papaya, The meat on the top of the neck. Bl. KE.

ťaťa'psiŋ, n. Buttons of fat, varied in size and adhering to the inner surface of the chorion membrane which carries the unborn calf; the sweet meat in the taniġa (pancreas) section of the buffalo cow, the most tasty part of the animal, prepared as a sausage and boiled. Bl. KE. WHL.

taťe' kaȟwógyapi, n. A little boys' toy for playing in the wind.

taťi'woǩitahena, adv. Being homeless. WHL. Cf. tiwokitahena.

tatȟa'śa, n. A small turtle. Same as the patkaśa. KE.

tā'ťu, n. Cf. Lakota section.

ťiǩi'cii, v. To visit one another. Tiwecii, timicii. Bl.

ťi'ťuťuǩa, v. To spoil or tire of visiting. - wimapi yelo, as is said in coming from other houses where one got one's fill. Bl.

ťiwo'ǩitahena, adv. Same as tatiwokitahena. Being homeless from a woman not being willing and ready to confront her own motherhood and the problems attendant upon it. Ito he hecel ecoŋpi śni kiŋhaŋ, oyate - iyotiyekiya uŋ tka yeśaŋ.

ťiya'kiȟpeca, adj. Having fallen in with one of the household because of the close environment, as is said of a young man wanting to marry a relative. HH. Cf. ómniyela.

ťiye'yaǩe, adv. In camp, as for winter. - wicayuś'iŋyeya, i.e. surprising them in their winter quarters. Bl.

tiyo'bcoǩatoŋ, v. To clear the middle by raising the pole opening the top of a tipi from within. -- n. The middle part of a tipi. Bl. KE. WHL.

ťiyo'hiyukśa, v. To remain or wander about in the house. - naŋkahe, You just sit in the tipi. Bl. WHL. LHB.

to'gmuŋ s'e, adv. Being organized but little, confusedly. - uŋ, as is said of a man who has poor property and has troubles with relatives. - yauŋ welo. Bl.

togto'ka, adv. Otherwise, another way. Caŋ kiŋ - aoŋpa, tiyoȟeyuŋka au welo, i.e. put more wood on the fire. Bl.

ťohaŋ'yaŋ śni haŋni', adv. With no measures lacking, with promptness. B.H.256.20. LHB.

ťo'kciŋkciŋka, adv. As one pleases, thoughtlesssly. - waipeyelaȟ, i.e. throws everything anywhere. Bl.

ťo'ǩeni, adv. In no wise, implying you would not suppose, of course. Cf. Lakota section.

ťokiŋ'śǩiŋś, adv. Anyway, anyhow. - anátakiŋyece. Bl. LHB.

toto'p̄ela, adj. Dripping wet, sopping wet. Hokśi - iyeniceca yelo, You act like a child, are childish. Bl.

ťukťe'haŋ, adv. At some time to come. Iśkaŋśkaŋ amayakita ye, - akiȟ'aŋ t'emayayiŋ kte, You look at me with open mouth indeed; so, while one is without food, you would make me die of hunger, thus a woman would say to grandchildren who want to eat along with her. Bl.

ťukťe' ihánkeya, adv. and adj. Where or which from the ground up, from first to last. - caŋ oteȟike kiŋ oŋ kage, One of which from the bottom up he made of the most expensive wood. B.H.60.9. Cf. tuktehaŋ.

ťukťe'kťeťaŋhaŋ, adv. From nowhere. Hecel - ceȟpi opawiŋge naiŋś wikcemna zaptaŋ naiŋś aokpaniyaŋ na wana gluśtaŋpi. MS.343-4.

ťukťena', pron. interrog. Which one of these? - Israel oyatepi tka k'uŋ otaŋiŋpi śni. LHB. WHL. B.H.119.1.

tusla', n. A blood sucker. Mni el - uŋpi. Si el - imakoyake. KE. WHL.

ťuwa'ťu, pron. Same as tuwa. - luza? Whom do you suppose you have there? LHB. WHL.

t'egna'śkiŋyaŋ s'e, adv. Franticly, in very great excitement. - ole, To look for one everywhere in utter distress. Bl.

U

uŋ'gnakaȟ, adv. Simultaneously easing one's way towards. LHB. WHL. Cf. Lakota section.

W

waa'hiŋȟpaya, v. To have something fall on one; an idiomatic express.: We were lucky ones. KE. LHB.

waa'kaŋl, adv. On, on top of the snow. - yaŋka. Bl. KE. LHB.

waa'ǩiyecetu, adj. Equal, equal in size, number, age. Waakiyeuŋcetupi. WHL.

wa'aoǩiyapi, n. A mutual planning.WHL.

waca'jeyaťapi, n. A motion, a petition. WHL. KE.

waciŋ'waśakala, v. To be poised and ready to act towards one, to be inclined e.g. to help one. Uŋgna waciŋniwaśakala ki, i.e. beware of. MS. 350. LHB.

wae'cakca, adj. Ready to do things at will, from caprice. - nuŋkiŋ na napapa umayaye, as a man would say to a child or to his wife when they do foolish things. Bl. LHB.

wae'lhiyayake, n. A friendly, not hostile person. - takuni oŋspe śni tka, i.e. wants to help but knows nothing about it. Bl. KE.

wae'lhoyeya, v. To make fun of persons. Bluskaska, yuŋkaŋ waelhoyeyiŋ kte ȟciŋ , i.e. gave him a new suit, but was ungrateful. Bl. KE.

wae'loŋoŋke, n. A careless person. KE.

wae'yeca, v. To tell or speak facts, the truth. Wicaśa waŋ - śni uŋ k'uŋ héye lo. Bl. WHL. LHB. Cf. waiece.

wa'gliukiya, v. To come home with a pack horse loaded with meat. KE.

waho'gnugnu, v. To warble, to quaver, as one's voice may do when singing; to make a certain guttural sound in singing for sacred ceremonies. WHL. LHB.

wahuŋ'cala, v. To ape, do monkeyish tricks, as some do when aping clown tricks; one who acts like a monkey, n. WHL. Cf. Lakota section. -- n. A monkey. LHB. Also, wauŋcala. WHL.

waȟ'aŋ'ksica, n. The marten. WH.

wai'ǩalelepake, n. A domineering person, one who acts as if he knows all and issues commands to everyone. Bl.

wakaŋ'kaŋ'pi, n. Spirits engaged to persons. LHB.

waǩě'za, Same as wakiza, I fight. KE. Cf. wak'eza.

waǩi'caǧa, n. Sacred ceremony. - lowaŋpi, The singing of sacred song. KE.

waǩi'cep̣a, n. A fat animal. Also, waǩicip̣a. Wamicipa. - mni woȟlecelo, as is said when just a few drops of rain fall. Heȟlogeca taŋka wakinaśleca - , as is said of a fat buffalo. Bl. BT. KE.

waǩi'cip̣a, Cf. wakicepa.

waki'janignica śni, n. Greediness. Bl. LHB.

wa'kiksu, v. To pile on, to load for one. Cf. wakśu. KE.

waki'naśleca, v. To split with the foot. WHL. Heȟlokeca taŋka - wakicepa, as is said of a fat buffalo. Bl.

waǩi'p̣a, n. Bad luck. KE. -- v. To envy one. WHL.

wa'ǩip̣a, v. To befall one. Bl. KE.

waki'scu, v. To peel. Also, wakisca. Blo - , To peel potatoes. He miye wawescu, i.e. this will be mine; let me shoot this bird, i.e. glonica. Bl. KE.

waǩi'yuwanice, adj. Deprived of property. Wakiyuwanicelaȟ, as is said when one had nothing yet received from others. Bl. KE. -- v. To squander one's holdings. KE.

waǩoŋ' s'e, adv. Forging the future beforehand, by plan. Wakoŋpi s'e naŋkapi, i.e. you are in good spirits. BT. KE. Also, like a dream.

waǩu'ni, Same as wakoŋniyaŋ. Maka óhiŋniyaŋ lila wakuniye lo, Earth always accomplishes very many things. MS.659.

wak'e'za, v. To make a mark with a sawing motion. Bl. KE. Cf. yuk'eza, wak'oga, yuk'oga.

walo'gnaka, n. A bag, a cow bladder. Cf. waloȟ'egnaka.

wama' el i, express. Cf. mă and the Lakota section.

wama'nika, n. One who visits or sees people much, but only on business; one who does not loaf. - oyamani hwo? You came alone? - agli yelo. Bl. UW.

wana'gnaⁿka, Cf. wanagnuⁿka. -- wanágnaⁿke, n. One's possession. WHL.

wana'gnuⁿka, v. To have something in one's possession. - śni s'e tak eyé, i.e. he does not tell the truth. RF. WHL.

wa'nagoptaⁿ, v. To listen, heed, as in listening to a sermon. Wanagoptaⁿpi c'oⁿ caká na pusyemayelo. Bl. WHL.

wana'p̄ičaġe, n. A feeling of self-importance, expecting to control everything and issuing commands. - yuha waciⁿ, He wants to boss everyone. LC. KE. Cf. wauⁿkeic'ila.

wao'mani, v. To travel in snow. WHL.

wap̄a'ġeyeca, v. To conquer. Pageya, To frighten into flight. -- part. Conquering. KE. Also, causing trouble to others. WHL.

wapa'ȟwuȟwu, adv. In deep snow. - waimnaⁿkelo, I am running in deep snow, i.e. falling over on my hands. Bl.KE.

wap̄aⁿ'ġeyeca, v. To make burdensome, bulky. Cf. wapageyeca.

wapa'yalake s'e, adv. As one would have expected to the top or head of. Na wana ka ekta - kupi. MS.150.

wape'gnaka, n. An Indian in full regalia and decked with a feather in his hair. KE. Also, a headdress. WHL.

wapťa'ye, n. Generic name for snake root, or for any weed. WHL.

waśiⁿ'kpe, n. The muskrat. Same as siⁿkpe. The former is Wiciyela, Yankton. KE.

waśiⁿ'kpekpeka, n. or adj. One who acts in the manner of a busy muskrat. Oȟ'aⁿ - tak tokoⁿ welo. Bl. Cf. waśiⁿkpe. -- waśíⁿkpekpeyakel, adv. In the manner of a muskrat. Wicaśa waⁿ - waículaȟcaka, i.e. he stole. Bl.

waslo'sloltkiya, v.n. To be well informed and able to speak and tell of things. KE. -- waslóslotkiyece, n. One who knows everything and is able to inform others. Bl. KE.

wa's'iⁿ, v. To look at greedily. Wawas'iⁿ. Bl. KE.

waśa'śte, n. Same as śaśte, The little finger. - wapaha. KE.

waśi'cuⁿpteole, n. (pte-ole). The American cowboy. BBB.

wa'śke, v. To present little demand for things, to offer what is not on demand. Wayaśkehelo, as is said when there is much on hand but little brought; the remark is made when in cutting what tobacco I brought I dropped some. Bl.

waślo'ślotkiya, v. To have a good memory. Cf. wasloslotkiya, wasloslotkiyece. -- waślóślotkiyece, n. One with a good memory. KE.

waśpaⁿ'kiya, v. To cook for one. KE.

waś'a'kece, v. (aś'aka). To be strong or powerful. Awaś'akece. Note: aś'áka, To be coated with. KE.

waťaⁿ'kaⁿl, adv. Trying to be wise or of some reputation. LHB.

waťaⁿ'kic'ila, v. To think self wise, or in some way great. WHL. LHB. Cf. waȟ'aⁿic'ila.

waťe'zi, n. The stomach, belly. Ituhu - ka ca yaⁿkiⁿ na, as is said when a man has a prominent balding forehead. Bl.

waťo'hantu ka waⁿ, adv. Sometime rather. B.H.12.6.

waťo'ǩiya, adv. interrog. Which side? Iwatokiya, From what direction? BT. LHB. WHL.

waṫu'kte, adv. Sometimes. - el, At times in the past, sometimes in the past. BT. KE.

wauᶯ'ke śni, v. Lit., not to stay long there; to have not right consideration or respect; to show a poor way of living. - tka heye lo, i.e. he is lying. BE. WHL.

wawa'heya śni, adj. or adv. Frank, open, not hesitating to speak out. WHL.

wawa'kiciśpaśpake, n. One who has been generous in giving away and yet sacrifices more. Bl.

wa'was'iᶯ, Cf. wás'iᶯ. Bl.

wawi'yaȟpaya, v. To make an attack for fun. T'ebleze śni - ayahilale, i.e. to wrestle for fun. Bl. WHL.

wawi'yeke s'e, adv. As one who dines upon. Śuᶯka - gliyaᶯkiᶯ kte lo, as is said of a missionary. Śuᶯkpala wowiyuśkiᶯ. Bl.

wawo'k'oyece, n. A clamor and dispersal of people, as they do in all directions on noticing a snake among them. Bl.

wawo'lhilhitika, v. To terrify; be energetic, very active. Wawolhilhitikiᶯ kte ȟciᶯ. Siᶯkpela s'e uᶯśika tka wawolhilhitikece, as is said when an old woman inspite of her helplessness cares for her husband and household. Bl. -- wawólhilhitikeca, adj. Determinedly active.

wawo'lwicayeśni uᶯ, v. To be tactful, unassuming. - yauᶯ. Bl.

wawo'pteca, adj. Sluggish, lazy. - śni, Active, energetic, well known. Wicaśa - . Pb.21. KE.

wawo'śkilya, v. To make trouble. KE.

wawo'ṫica, n. A snow drift. Bl. KE.

waya'ojigjica, v. Be quite rich in, be made rich in. Tajiyagnuᶯpa s'e - , as is said when a man desires meat. Also, to brag. WHL.

wayas'yazaᶯka, n. Ill health. -- adj. Sickly. WE. KE.

waya'tiktil, adv. Pulling with the teeth, as a dog does meat from a bone; to crush fine, grinding with the teeth; to nag others. - ihe, He nags at others. - iwaha. LB. WHL.

wayu'ȟ'iyayaka, v.n. To be inexperienced, to be a greenhorn. Wabluȟ'i-iyayaka. KE.

wayu'opeśa, n. One having respect for others. -- adj. Respectful. - śni nahaȟci ni wauᶯ, i.e. insisting on having something although one does not understand it so well. BT. KE.

wa'zaᶯzaᶯ, adv. Lying thin, as snow on the ground. -- n. A fine snow mist. WHL.

wica'laṗela, adj. Believing in one. Ite - k'el écela yelo, as they say encouragingly to a war-party. Bl. KE.

wica'paptapta iyaye ole', v. To look for a person as one goes among a throng. LHB.

wica'yaś'iᶯyaᶯyaᶯ s'e, adv. In sudden surprise, esp. in seeing something never before seen. - wawakipa. KE.

wico'ḱicamna, v. To be stirred up and going to and fro, as people in a turmoil. KE.

wi'cuᶯ śni, n. One who is incompetent to clean a house, a word applied to women. -- adj. Incompetent in women's work. La. KE. Cf. wicuᶯkeśni.

wi'gnagnaye, adv. Giving things to make others forget; giving something step by step, in a progression. - toᶯpi s'e amaupelo. Bl. KE. Cf. ignagnaye s'e.

wi'hiyala, n. The passing of the sun; the measure of clock time; the hour of the day. - tonakeca, What time is it? FN. LHB. Also, wihiyayela.

wi'naġiyeya, adv. Annoying one, as in seeking from a woman the sexual act. WHL.

wi'nap'ila, wi'nap'iᶯla, n. A species of bird.

winuȠ´kala, n. Old women. Same as winuȟcala. Bl. KE.
wi´p̣it'a, v. To gorge self. WHL.
wiwi´la tapeji´, n. The grass in and around a spring of water, about a swamp. BT. KE.

wiyag´yata, adv. At or towards the sun looking. - inaȟme s'e eyatoȠ welo, i.e. you look as it were secretly at the sun. BT.

wi´yaȟloka, v. To make an impression upon, in something. Wiblaȟloka. Cehupa wiblaȟloke śni s'elececa, i.e. made no impression on him apparently, though I told him repeatedly. Bl.

wo´caȠṫehahayela, adv. Not wholeheartedly or heart-felt. -- n. Over-sensitiveness, timidity. P. KE.

wo´caȠṫeoyuze, n. Character, mature personality; infatuation, state of having a high or low esteem or regard for a person. KE. WHL.

wo´ecoȠkel, Same as owecoȠkel.

wo´iȟaka, n. Something funny. -- v. To jest, laugh at. -- adj. Such as to cause laughter. KE. WHL.

wo´ȟlik'el, adv. (oȟli). Filthy within. -- n. Filth that is within. - ahiyaya. Bl. Also, adv. Confusedly, as in all trying to sing together. LHB.
woȟ'aȠ´yaȠkel, adv. Unnecessarily burdening esp. one's self with an extra load, charge or duty; doing things the hard way. WHL. LHB.

wo´inapiśkaȠye, n. Something to play with, a toy. Lena - ca cic'u welo. MS.356. KE.

wok̇o´k̇ipapaka, v.n. To be scared of things, be timid. - śni mani. -- wokokipapake, n. Timidity. Bl. KE.

wo´p̣ani, v. To nudge, give a signal or sign. Also, wawóp̣ani, but doubtfully wapáni. Bl. KE. WHL.

wo´slaslateke, n. That which stands erect.

wo´sukiye, n. Law. Cf. Lakota section.

wo´śikśiceke, adj. Unaware, not able to see or solve according to usual practice; troublesome. -- n. Awkwardness, ineptitude. WHL. LHB.

wo´śk̇ilya, v.a. To crush, compress with great force. Wawośkiśkeyece, wawośkilya, To make trouble. KE. WHL.

wo´ślaślateke, n. The pulling out of weeds, feathers and such like. KE.

wot'o´ġa, adj. Rasping, hackling; with point blunted. WHL.

wo´waȠk̇e, n. Something contagious; a catching or spreading things such as a disease or sickness; an admirable object, what attracts attention. KE.

wo´yuaślaye, n. Things concealed but now revealed. B.H.168.20.

wo´yuȟtani, n. Mistakes, difficulties created. Bl.

Y

yace´kceka, v. To jerk with the teeth, as a dog does to a boy, pulling him around by his clothes. WHL.

yaski´ska, v. To make teeth marks, to press together with the teeth. WHL.

yaśke´p̄a, v. To suck dry, as a calf does all the milk. KE.

yaśke´śkeke, v. To untie with the teeth. WHL.

yaśke´śkep̄a, v. To suck and spit out. KE.

Yoko´mi, n. prop. The name of a chief of the Zuni, who was also associated with the Comanche. RI. Cf. hokomi, okomi.

yugla´ǩeǩe, adj. Standing separated, somewhat in isolation. Tucuhu - hiᶯgla yauᶯ welo, i.e. you are getting thin. Bl. Also, drawing sidewise.WHL.

yugmi´yus, adv. Holding by the hair. - yupocaᶯcaᶯ, To take one by the hair and pull him to and fro. Bl. KE.

yugwa´, v. To soften by hand. Bl.

yugwo´ggwog, adv. Drawing or paddling water toward one's self. - ȟpaya, as is said of a person unable to swim but keeps himself above water by moving. Bl. KE.

yuha´ha, adv. Spreading out like a tree with many branches. Śuᶯkawakaᶯla k'oᶯ oᶯśilapica śni - yuzapi s'e nauᶯke, as is said of a played-out horse when it comes on trotting. Bl. KE.

yuha´hap̄ika, adj. Probably worth the begging. Uᶯgnahaȟci - wowaciᶯ yelo, as a hungry visitor would say who, being told there is nothing in the house thinks there is, but hidden. Bl. KE.

yuȟni´yaᶯ, v. To shake badly, quiver. Pute yuȟniyaᶯpi s'e najiᶯ yaᶯkelo, i.e. with quivering lips as from fear. Bl. KE.

yuȟta´ka, v.a. To loosen. Ehaś maka kiᶯ yuȟtakiᶯ kte s'e iᶯyaᶯkelo, as is said of a horse that holds its head down while running. Bl. LHB.

yuȟ'e´ȟ'e, adv. Tearing e.g. a cloth by twisting, tearing to shreds. WHL. -- n. Drippings, droolings, drivel.LHB.

yui´ťeśla, adv. Uncovering the face. Uᶯgna tóka śka - ciyuziᶯ na ognagna acip̄e ci. Bl. LHB.

yuka´kaǩa, v. To shake one at a time. Otutkala eśa tuweni el uᶯ śni yelo; ca tiyopa blukakakiᶯ na wagliyacu welo. Bl. KE.

yule´na, v. To make distance in a brief time, to make or anticipate a date before that on which something is expected, as the time of one's arrival. WHL. Cf. Lakota section.

yul´yul, v. cont. red. (yuta). To eat appreciatively; to eat hastily on the way. -- adv. Eating hastily along the way. Hena tokeya - waku kte lo. D.54. WHL.

yuna´p'iyeya, v. To describe a curve by one's motion. Yunap'iyeyapi sekse iᶯyaᶯkelo, as is said of a horse that runs off in a curve. Bl. KE.

yuna´ya, v. To pass something along. Yunawaya. KE.

yuna´yeya, v. To get and then give to others. KE.

yuoᶯ´jiᶯcayela, adv. Making short. - paȟta, To tie up e.g. a horse's tail. - iyaglaśka, To tuck up one's robe or dress. Bl. KE.

yuo´p̄eja śni, v. To interfere with one. Ciyuopeja śni s'elececa; to, mayaluopeja śni yelo, I do not seem to disturb you; no, you do not, come in. Bl. KE.

yuo´swa, v. To pull down with gentle force, as in pulling hay down from the top of a stack; to pull down, as sand or soil from a bank with a tool. WHL. Cf. oswahaᶯ.

yuo´waᶯcaya, v. To circulate, to spread out over an area. KE.

yuo´yaťaᶯyaᶯ, v. To stick and hold. Bl. KE. Cf. oyataᶯyaᶯ.

yup̄iŋ'p̄iŋt̄a, v. To make grow or become smaller. Yupiŋpiŋtapi s'e iŋyaŋka, as is said of little animals running. Yupiŋpiŋtapi s'e wapaha. Bl.

yupo'caŋcaŋ, v. To shake one up. Yugmiyus - , To take by the hair and shake one up to and fro. Bl. KE.

yupt̄i'nap̄eyakel, adv. Shielded, protected from; in hiding; as a protection, as in shielding one's self from the wind or in carrying a stick for frightening off animals etc. WHL.

yuswu'pi s'e, adv. As though they were running smoothly along, rustling as falling grains or leaves. Bl. Cf. Lakota section.

yuśp̄i'ka, adj. Worth buying or keeping. Iogmus - waeye eyelo. -- n. What is worth the buying or keeping. Bl. KE.

yutaŋ'ka s'e, adv. Made wide or broad. KE.

<u>WORD SOURCES</u>: The following names are of those people who assisted in the definition of the words in the above section.

BBB. Ben Black Bear.
KE. Frank KillsEnemy.
LHB. Silas Lefthand Bull.
Re. Adam Red Earth.
RI. Ruben Ironcrow.
Swb. Peter Swiftbird.
WHL. Louis and Daisy Whirlwind Horse, Sr.

A

able, Heyapikeśni, v. pl. They think one not - ; n. One so thought of. Pawi, v. To be yet - to move about.

accompany, Icinakśiŋpi, v. pl. They - one another. Nicicaya, v. To make -.

accomplish, Wapayalake s'e, adv. -ed as hoped.

accuse, Śilwiyauŋpa, v. To - one of evil.

adjacent, Icipatkuḣ, v. To be - to.

afraid, Wokokipapaka, v.n. To be -, timid.

afterwards, Etulake kiŋ, adv.

against, Ipustaŋ, adv. Pushing up - . Iyapataŋ, adv. Right up - .

age, Nika, n. A former - .

all, Kiwaŋjica, adj. Not one but - .

almost, Olanuŋ s'e, adv. Nearly.

amplify, Iyoja, v. To - sound.

anxious, Hahake, adj. - to move.

anyway, Tokiŋśkiŋś, adv.

anywhere, Tuktektetaŋhaŋ, adv. From -.

apart, Onajuju, v.n. To come - .

apply, Peagnagkiya, v.a. To - to.

arena, Okiŋyaŋka, n.

argue, Hiŋskekagya, v. To be ready to rebut, be argumentative.

arrange, Paogla, v. To - .

arrive, Iyakitaŋiŋ, v. To - in daylight. Kigli, v. To - at home. Kihaŋ, v. To - and stand.

ashes, Caḣliśniyaŋpi, n. Coal - .

assist, Wawakiciśpaśpake, n. One who helps others, as by cutting up in small pieces.

attend, Oḣmuŋyece, v. To - to.

autumn, Ptiŋhaŋ, n. Last - .

awake, Haŋiśtiŋma, v. To lie - at night. Oikpagica, v.

aware, Iyeslota, adj.

away, Iḣeyab, adv. - from.

awkward, Wośikśiceke, adj.

B

back, Kataŋblablas, adv. On both sides of the back.

backward, Kahektakiya, adv.

bag, Walognaka, n.

bald, Nasuśtiŋca s'e, adv. - ing.

balk, Oiglonica, v.

bare, Naślaye, adv. Making - . Paślayela, adv. Making - .

bark, Napapa, v. To make - .

bayonet, Iwahukeza, n.

beads, Hokomi, n. Cf.

beat, Iglat'a, v. refl. To pummel self. Oiyapa, v. To - on the side of.

bed, Kiḣpaya, v. To - down.

befall, Wákipa, v. To - one.

believing, Wicalapela, adv.

bend, Gluptuza, v. refl. To - over self. Kaptuza, v. To - with a blow.

beset, Kicamna, v. To be - , overwhelmed.

better, Opicaka, v. To be - .

bewilder, Iwaciŋgnuniyaŋ, adv. Causing -ment.

bind, Iyakicaśka, v. To - together. Iyayustaka, v. Okiwiŋja, v. To - down well.

birds:
cansinkahpu, Downy woodpecker.
cantipan, Coot.
cantku sapela, Junco.
cehupaglagla, Thrasher.
hinlhincala, Coot.
hohyazela, Kingfisher. Also, hoyazela.
Hlahla iyognaka, Marsh wren.
coka sapa, Cuckoo.
igugaotila, Cliff swallow.
ipśincala, adj. Like a small swallow.
miniopakinyela, A water bird.
okihyan, A bird that hovers.
Palani tazintkala, Upland plover.
pse, The upland plover.
winap'inla, The meadow lark.

Note: Rev. Thomas Hoffman, S.J. supplied the identification of these birds.

black, Cehnagila, n. One dressed in - . Itisabye, n. -ing used for the face.

blind, Iśtahca, v. To have poor vision. Iśtajotokte, v. To - with smoke. Iśtawaiyojanjan, n. Snow -ness.

bloat, Naglakeyeya, adv. -ed. Nawizipanyeya, adv. Swollen, distended.

blow, Kazamnimniyela, adv. -ing open, flapping.

blur, P'owakita, v. To see in a -red manner.
bone, Huicignuniyan, adv. With bones mixed together.

both, Nupinyan, adv. On - sides.
bother, Kahtakeke, v. To irk.

brag, Wayojigjica, v. To - .

break, Paksa s'e, adv. -ing off.

breast, Tatahpa, n. The - of animals; the flanks; meat left on a hide.

brown, Giya, adv. Dyed - .

bump, Naśkabya, v.a. To - . Naśkan, v. To jolt. Naśkapa, v. To - . Pajo, n. A pointed - , as a ripe pimple.

bunch, Kawilwita, v. To -.

burden, Puskica, v.n. To be -ed. Woh'anyankel, adv. Unnecessarily - ing.

Wapangeyeca, v. To make -some.

busy, Owih'an, n. The being - about.

buzzing, Nonhpekic'un, v. To have a - sound in the ears.

C

camp, Aiglagcankuya, v. To break - . Tiyeyake, adv. Encamped.

caprice, Waecakca, adj. Inclined to do from - .

care, Ongluze, n. Things attended to.
carefree, Waelononke, n. A - person, a busy-body.

cat-tail, Psa obloton, n.

cautious, Haniyagnaka s'e, adv. -ly.

center, Icisannica, v. To - . Icisannicab, v. To - half-way. Tiyobcokaton, n. The - of a tipi; v. To clear the - of the house.

ceremony, Wakicaga, n. A sacred rite.

change, Itokecaśni, v.n. To be un-ed.

cheap, Śunkanyan, adv. -ly, with little effort.

cheerful, Owilita, adj. - in doing.

chilly, Iyosniyan, adj.

choice, Watankanl, adv. Being choicely.

choke, Pagloglo, v. To - .

choose, Iglahniga, v. To - .

circulation, Guheheya, v. red. To take from - .
circumvent, Aoglakśan, v. To go around.
clash, Icipa, v.n. To meet.

clear, Patonwanyan, adv. -ing one's eyes.

clog, Pahli iyokaskica, v. To -.

close, Itagna, adv. -ly.

clown, Śakton s'e, adv. -ishly.

cold, Okasni, v. To get - .

collapse, Kakśikśija, v. red. To - .

colored, Glagleglega, v.n. To be of or changed to different colors.

come, Gliu, v. To - to one's own home. Gliyagli, v. To go and - back.

comfortable, Owaśteya, v.n. To be - .

commotion, Wawok'oyece, n. A fracas, an uproar.

compassionate, Ouŋśila, adj.

complete, Ekihuŋni, v.a. To finish.

complicated, Caŋśihuta, adj.

compress, Icipat'iŋs, v. To - . Wośkilya, v.a.

concern, Itoka, v. To be without - .

condition, Kayuŋś, adv. conj. Under such conditions.

confidence, Icimna, v.

confuse, Akinahaŋhaŋ, adv. Confusedly.

congest, Iyokaskica, v. To clog.

conglomerate, Iglegleȟya, adv. With a whole conglomeration.

conscious, Haŋgnagya, adv. Being semi- .

console, Okikcaŋpte, v. To - .

constrict, Oikpaptaŋśilya, adv. In a -ed way.

consume, Pilya, v. To - .

contagious, Wowaŋke, n. A - thing.

control, Iwaŋjica, v.a. To - anger.

convince, Painlpica, v. To be able to - .

cook, Ikiȟ'aŋ, v. To - for. Owahe, v.n. To have -ed. Waśpaŋkiya, v. To - for one.

cool, Najukaosnisni s'e, adv. As if -ing the back of the head. Oyusni, v. - by placing.

counting, Haŋglawakel, adv. - days and nights.

cover, Iyocośyakel, adv. With added - on.

cowboy, Waśicuŋpteole, n.

crackle, Naśak'oȟayeya, adv. Making -, growing red, as fire.

crane, Kis'iŋs'iŋ, v. To - .

crash, Iwokpaŋ, v.a. Śuśuś hiŋgla, v. To come -ing down.

creep, Makipaȟlala, adv. -ing along the ground.

criticize, Iyogluś't'eya, v. To - badly. Wayazazaka, v. To - .

crop, Wak'eza, v. To - .

cross, Aiglagcaŋkuya, v. To - on one's own.

crouch, Putaŋyela, adv. -ed.

crumble, Okpaŋkpaŋ, v.n. To - . -- n. Crumbs, decay.

crush, Napśija, v. To - by foot. Paśnija, v. To - . Icakpaŋ, adv. -ed.

crystalline, Skokogli, adj.

custom, Kikiyakel, adv. Not -arily.

cut, Kagmipi s'e, adv. As if - all down. Kokiwoȟci, v. To - through the skin.

D

daub, Icataŋtaŋ, adv. Smudged.

dawn, Aŋpo wicaȟpi, express. - of a new day.

day-dreaming, Iwaciŋtokaŋkaŋgnagnaya, adv.

deadened, Itoyuha t'ekiya, v. To make a - expression on the face.

decay, Okpaᶯkpaᶯ, n.

deform, Pśuke, n. Something -ed. Apaȟakayayapi, n. A -ation.
delay, Naśuśka, v. To -.

depend, Iwaciᶯyeȟci, v. To - on others

deploy, Nablel, adv. Spread out.

design, Okazoᶯte, n. A pattern.

despondent, Ilenilyakel, adv. -ly.

destination, Ohiyou, n.

destitute, Keyecola, adv. Entirely -.

die, It'a, v. To - for a reason.

difficulty, Woyuȟtani, n. A - made.
dim, Aotaᶯiᶯ, v. To grow -, dusk.
dinner, Ipaga, adv. Before - time.

direction, Ecetkiya, adv. In some -.

dirty, Aś'akece, v. To accumulate dirt, refuse, grease etc.

disaffected, Icaᶯlśica, v.n. To be -.
disapprove, Oweȟica, n. Disapproval.
disclosing, Pahiᶯskayela, adv.
dishevelled, Gaᶯ, adj.
disorder, Kaskiglag, adv. -ly.
disorganize, Togmuᶯ s'e, adv. Being -ed.
display, Okilitatoᶯ, v. To make a great -.
disrupt, Oyąkikike, v.a. To -.
distemper, Śuᶯkanagiȟlo śpaᶯwageȟce, express. To feel as a growling dog.
distinct, Kablesglepi s'e, adv. -ly.
distract, Wignagnaye, adv. -ing.
disturb, It'enihaᶯ, adj. Bothered. Miyugiᶯgiᶯ, adv. -ing one.

dive, Kignuᶯ, v. To -.
divest, Iyuślok, v. To -.
divide, Kalehaᶯyaᶯk, v. To -.

do, Ecaic'ioᶯ, v. refl. To do for self. Lecakicioᶯ, v.a. To do this. Owicoᶯkel, adv. With something doing.

domineer, Kitaᶯkognagyelaȟci, adv. -ingly.

doughy, Ospaᶯspaᶯheca, adv. Becoming -.

down, Hutawab, adv. Further down. Hutawabkiya, adv. -stream. Ihutawab, adv. and prep. -stream beyond. Ikuta, prep. and adv. -stream. Kaiyoȟpeya, adv. -ward.

dowry, Śuᶯk'iyopeya, v.a. To give a -.

draw, Yuglakeke, adj. -ing across. Yuoswa, v. To - down.

dream, Wakoᶯ s'e, adv. As a - or wish.

drift, Owota, v. To -. Wáwotica, n. A snow -; wawótica, n. A - of anything. Oicoga, n. -wood.

dripping, Totopela, adj. - wet.

drive, Hutipaśpu, v. To - back, away.

droop, Oȟ'eȟ'e, v. To -.

drumstick, Kat'ela, n.
dry, pusyeya, v. To - out.
dust, Makop'oya, v. To raise -.

E

ear, Noᶯȟwicaȟloke s'e, adv. With the ears opened.

earth, Kamakatakiya, adv. -ward.

ease, Uᶯgnakaȟ, v. To - one's way towards.
easily, Śuᶯkaᶯyaᶯkel, adv. Got cheap.

eat, Lolwazaze, adj. Not able to -. Wagliukiya, v. To bring home the "bacon", i.e. meat for food.

edible, Spaᶯ s'e waśte, adj. Easily -.

effeminate, Kaigluwiᶯyaᶯ, v. To become -.

effort, Kihe, v. To make -.

elaborate, Kaȟ'e, v.t. To -.
elate, Nagiksapa, adj. -ed.

elbow, Iśpakic'uᶯyaᶯ, adv. Using the elbows. Iśpazihiᶯ, n. A buffalo's -.

elusive, Kijanicaśni, v. To be -.

end, Hiᶯhaᶯke, v. To come to an -, to a stop.

endure, Oiyotiyekiya, v. To - .
enlarge, Yutaŋka s'e, adv. -ed.
enlighten, Iyoyaŋbya, v.a. To - .
envy, Wakípa, v. To - .

equal, Waakiyecetu, adj. - in.

erect, Woslaslateke, n. An - thing.

escort, Iyawaŋyaŋgkiciya, v. To - .

evaporate, Onapuza, v. To - .
every, Ecel, adv. and adj.
everywhere, Ecicaskaya, adv. From - .

exceed, Acokata, adv.
excuse, Iyowalya, v. To have an - .

eye, Iśtanatogyeya, adv. With an unnatural - expression. Iśtasaŋkiya, n. A snap of the - .

F

face, Iteśniopa, v. To freeze the - .

faint, Iyoniyaŋ, adv. Just audible.

fall, Ogliȟpaye, n. A - . Opśuŋwahe, n. Things, e.g. teeth, horns etc., that - out or off. Waahiŋȟpaya, v. To - on or to.

fan, Guheya, v. To - out from.

far, Kaoteheȟaŋ, adv. Distant (time).

fat, Tatapsiŋ, n. Buttons of - . Wakicepa, n. A too - animal or person.

favor, Kitaŋyelakeleś, adv. In a -able mind.

feed, Lolwanagi, v. To - the spirits.

feisty, Wawolhilhitika, v. To be - .

fill, Owapate, v. To stuff. Owipi, n. One -ed up.
filth, Woȟlik'el, adv. Filthy inside.

finally, Ehakeke, adv. The very last time.

fire, Cekicati, v. To build a - . Pelimnaśni, v. Not to fear - . Peliyaglaśyahaŋ, v. To bank a - . Pel'iyucaŋyaŋkel. adv. Lacking -wood.

Pel'kitoŋkel, adv. Having enough - .
first, Aotaŋȟci, adv. Before all else.
flap, Ȟpiȟpi s'e, adv. -ping.

flatten, Yaskiska, v. To - with the teeth.

flee, Ozaŋyela, adv. Taking to flight. Pageya, v.a. To make - .

flimsy, Nazigzil, adj.

float, Okaȟya, v.a. To - .

fly, Inasaka, v. To let -, release.

fog, Iyap'osp'os, n.

fold, Oyukśa, adv. -ing up; in a - or bend. Hakakśa, adj. -ed up. Iciyaȟlaȟ, v. To cross, lock.

follow, Iyayuȟkiya, adv. -ing.

foolish, Guguhaŋ, adj. Crazy.
foot, Isi, adv. At or on - .

forest, Mayal, adv. Deep in the - .

forget, Naptahena, adv. -ting. Pawignuni, v.a. To become -ful.

fork, Koiyayuȟkiya, adv. -ing.

form, Kaskiskaska, v. red. To - by pounding.

frank, Wawaheyaśni, adj.
frantic, T'egnaśkiŋyaŋ s'e, adv. -ly.

fray, Naswa, v.n. To - .

free, Ekeśni, v. To - self.
freeze, Otasagya, v. To - .

frighten, Itaŋgluzaza, v.n. To be -ed. Itaŋsak t'a, v.n. To be -ed to death.

front, Kaȟyapayalake s'e, adv. Toward the - .

frost-bitten, Sniyopa, adj.

fry, Cekipa, v. To - . Cekipapi, n. Something fried.

funny, Woiȟaka, n. A - thing. -- v. To jest.

future, Tukteȟaŋ, adv. In the - .

games:
napoglecekutepi, A game with bow and arrow.
pejiyuskitakutepi.
śuŋknunikiciyapi.
tatekaħwogyapi.

garrulous, Iyaśka, adv. -ly. Oie waśikśicuŋ, n. A - person.

gasp, Paħwayaśkabya, v.a. To make - .

gather, Nakpas, adv. -ing. -- v. To force together. Okimniciye, v. To come together.

glue, Aħ'ayetoŋ, v. To - .
glut, Iyot'iŋst'iŋs, v. To - . Nacaŋteśilya, adv. With a yet -tonous feeling.

go, Kigli, v. To go directly home.

good, Kiwaśteśteka, v. To be - . Śilyeħci, n. A no - thing.

goose-berry, Miniwicagnaśka caŋ, The water - .

gorge, Wipit'a, v. To - .

grab, Wawiyaħpaya, v. To attack or grip one.

grandmother, Kośkauŋcihikaca, v. To be a - .

grape, Cuŋwiyapejiji, n. Cuŋyapehe, n.
grass, Wiwila tapeji, n. Spring - .

gray, Osaŋsaŋke s'e, adv. -ing.

graze, Kaŋwiŋl iyeya, v. To brush by.

greedy, Wakijanignica śni, n. Greediness.

grimace, Natogyeya, v. To - .

groom, Iglasto, v.a. To - self. Kisiŋc'iya, v. refl. To tidy self.

ground, Makiyagle, v. To hold to the - . Makiyeya, v. To push a- . Makokaħciyela, adv. Floating about on - .

group, Kaiħeya, adv. -ing.
grow, Kaowaŋya, v. To develope.

grumble, Oie pepeka, n. Grumbling.

guardian, Manitukala, n. A little - spirit.

gum, Caŋśiŋkaħpu, n. Pine - .
gummy, Siyonatica, v. To be - .

gurgling, Yugwoggwog, adv. With a stifled sound.

gut, Taśup'okaħmi, n. A - cavity.

H

hackling, Wot'oga, adj.

hair, Gugukaśla, adv. With - hacked. Waśke, n. A - string or fastener. Yugmiyus, adv. Holding the - , by the - .

half-hearted, Wocaŋtehahayela, adv. -ly.

halt, Kipable, v. To come to a - .

hang, Hpi, v. To - down. -- adj. -ing down. Naakaħliyeya, v. To - out.

hanker, Was'iŋ, v. To - for. Wawas'iŋ, n. One who hankers.

hard, Kaśpepilpicaśni, adj. - to chip. Naiŋyaŋyeya, adv. Become rock-like. Osuta, adj. -ened.
hardly, Eciŋyaŋ, adv. Barely.

he, Iyeśtuka, pron. - who ought.

head, Ipesletaŋhaŋ, adv. From the - end.
headdress, Magawapaha, n. A - of goose feathers. Wapegnaka, n. A - of any sort.

health, Ozaŋniyaŋkel, adv. In good - .

hear, Noŋħpekic'uŋśniyaŋ, adv. With -ing unimpeded. Noŋħwazaza, v. To - only snatches. Noŋħ'opaya, adv. In one's -ing. Owanaħ'oŋ, n. What causes one to - . Śilwanakiħ'oŋ, v. To - bad said of one.

heavy, Kaħluħlata, adv. Hanging - in abundance.

heed, Wanagoptaŋ, v. To - .

help, Ookihi, v. To be able to be -ed.

hence, Iwatukte, adv. From - . Lehaⁿkalkataⁿhaⁿ, adv. Hither. Lehaⁿkata, adv. Hither.

herd, Ptehiyapa, v. To - .

here, Gligleyake, adv. - and there.

hill, Apaha he, express. fig.

hold, Ognala, adv. -ing only a bit.
hole, Okpikpi, adj. Slit-like.

holler, Hokitoⁿ, v. To use the voice.

home, Títika, v. To feel at - . Also, titutuka. Tiyohiyukśa, v. To stay indoors most of the time. Tatiwokitahena, adv. -less. Also, tiwokitahena.

horse, Śuⁿk'okaȟ, adv. -shaped. Śuⁿk'oⁿjiⁿca, n. A bob-tail - . -- adj. Rich in horses.

hundred, Kauⁿȟye, adj. One - .
hungry, Kaȟlogeca, adj.

hurried, Naȟniyela, adv. -ly.
hurt, Siyapayakel, adv. With feet -ing

hush, Okis'as'a, v.a. To - .

I

icy, Ocaȟsu, v. To be - .

ill-health, Wayasyazaⁿka, n.

imitate, Wahuⁿcala, v. To - .
impede, Ikuśe, v. To - . Kaȟiyeyapi s'e, adv. Un-ed.
impossible, Kewoyuspa s'e, adv. Doing the - .
impress, Wiyaȟloka, v. To - one.

incidentally, Iśuⁿmakeci, adv.
incite, Palega, v.a. To - .
incompetent, Wicuⁿśni, n. One - as in doing women's work.
inconsiderately, Tokciⁿkciⁿka, adv.
inexperienced, Wayuȟ'iyayaka, v.n. To be - .
infect, Kaśiksil, adv. -ed.
informed, Heyeceśni, adj. Not - about. Wasloslotkiya, v. To be well- .
injure, Oic'iȟ'aⁿ, v. To - self.

inseparable, Paȟniȟpilpicaśni, adj.
instigate, Wawośkilya, v. To - .
intercourse, Anakicisoⁿ, v. To have sexual - .
interfer, Iśkiśkeyece, n. -ence. Yopepeja śni, v. To - with.

interjections:
huyi, Come along. Also, hoiye, huya.
itoleś, Really now!
iyuwiⁿśkalake s'e, How frightful !
otapika, You are best.
siyemila, I warn you.
skaniyaka, They say.
śehaⁿ, Good heavens!

interrogatives:
icitona, adj. How many?
otoketu, adv. How is it?
tukte ihaⁿkeya, adv. Which "from the ground up"? i.e. from start to finish.
tuktena, pron. Which one of?
tuwatu, pron. Who? Same as tuwa.
watokiya, adv. Whence?

interrupt, Icisaⁿb, adv. -ing.

J

jaunt, Kaceslisli, v.

jerk, Yacekceka, v. To - with teeth.

K

keep, Yuhahapika, adj. Worth -ing.

kettle, Kaⁿnacega, n. A - shape.

kick, Naȟpa, v.n. To be -ed off, out.

kidney, Taajuⁿtk'ognake, n. - fat.

kindle, Glailega, v. - again.

knock, Kakab, v. cont. To - away.
knock-kneed, Naakiyatagtake s'e, adv. In a - manner.

L

lace, Haŋpiokaśkeya, v. To - a moccasin.

languid, Oḣtateya, adv. Becoming - .

law, Wosukiye, n.

lean, Iyuśiŋktiŋyaŋ, adv. -ing. Kaŋakalaya, adv. Very - , thin.
leave, Iglasto, v.n. To be left out.

left, Kaiyocatka, n. A -handed performance. Okicapta, v. To be - for.

leg, Hutokap̣ataŋ, n. The front legs.
leg-weary, Ṡuŋkmaniśnikiya, adv. Leg-wearied.

less, Kaaopteca, v. To do - .

lighten, Icap'ośya, v. To - .

likewise, Eyeceleś, adv.

limply, Opśuŋpśuŋyela, adv.

liniment, Tatu, n. A root used for the making of - .

lips, Inaŋgnaŋke s'e, adv. As if moving the - . Pulkiciŋkel, adv. With - drooping.

little, Kognagyela, adv. Just a - . Otutkala, adv. Tiny.

loaded, Iglagyake, adv. Also, iglagyakel, i.e. with luggage.

look, Owakita, v. To - about, examine.
loose, Oḣlaiŋ, v. To work - .
loosen, Yuḣtaka, v.a. To - .

lose, Haŋpoḣya, adv. Losing one's way.
lost, Onuniśniyaŋ, adv. Not lost.

lower, Ku, n. The - parts. Also, kul.

lunch, Icaska, v. To - .

lurk, Iyapekel, adv. -ing.

M

maniac, Oŋnapewatogya, n. A dangerous person.

marker, Owasabglepi, n. A bench - .

marriage, Tiyakitahena, adj. Throwing tent over tent, lit.; hence, wanting inter-marriage within degrees of affinity.

marshy, Owiwila, adj.

marten, Waḣ'aŋksica, n.

match, Iciḣloka, n. A pairing. Iciḣlogya, v. To - .

meanwhile, Kohaŋke śni, adv.

medicines:
pejuta huokihetoŋtoŋ, A liniment for sore joints.
pejuta ḣaka, A root.
pejuta tiŋpsila, A turnip used to treat wounds.
pejuta toto, A - for stomach pains.
pteiciyuḣa uŋma, A - for spitting of blood.

memory, Waślośloltkiya, v. To have a good - .

mend, Opiya, v. To renew, make alike.

mint, Caŋ pejuta cik'ala, n. (plant).
minute, Gwula, adj. Small.

mire, Kajuŋhe,s'e, adv. Getting -ed.
mirky, Ośośe, v. To become - .

missle, Iwona s'a, n.

mix, Ecaicijenaya, v. To - together. Ipacica, v.t. To - by rubbing.

moccasins, Haŋpśiśica, n. A worn-out pair of - . Haŋp'titiŋyaŋka, n. A pair of house - .

moderate, Kaihakteya, adv. -ly.

moist, Alowitaya, adv. Not well dried.

moor, Hokaḣglepi, n. Something -ed. Also, okaḣglepi.

more, Kaiyakic'ula s'e, adv. By a little - . Laḣ, laḣca, suff. - of it.

morning, Hiŋhaŋnaḣci, adv. Early in the - .

motion, Wacajeyatapi, n. A - made for discussion etc.

mount, Okapsica, v. To - up.

move, Kacaŋl, v. To - the heart.
moving, Glugweza, adv. - fast.

much, Icata, adv. Very - . Also, icat'a.

mud-hen, Śiyaka, n.

muffle, Iyopśa s'e, adv. -ed.

munch, Yulyul, v. To - along the way.

N

name, Acajeiglata, v. refl. To - .

near, Kiye, adv. -by.

neglect, Iyuśpeyeya, adv. Work being -ed.

night, Haŋmśicelaḣcake, adj. Being a very windy - . Haŋyagug, v. To spend the - in the cold. Ihaŋiyupta, adv. Through most of the - .

nod, Kogiŋgiŋ, v.

noiseless, Naḣloke s'e, adv. -ly.

nose, Paglaḣuga, v. refl. To break the - .

nudge, Wopani, v. To - .

O

obstructing, Wawopteca, adj.

of course, Tokeni, adv. ph.

old, Hokśiuŋke, adj. -er, - enough.

on, Waakaŋl, adv. On top.
once, Watohaŋtuka waŋ, adv. - upon a time.
only, Ecela, adv. - once.

ooze, Kitoŋwaya, v. To - .

orderly, Otogmuŋ, v. To appear - .

Tacaŋkohaŋhaŋke, n. - form.

ostentacious, Pajoke s'e, adv. In an - way.

otherwise, Togtoka, adv.

otter, Śkeca, n. An -like animal.

oval, Śok'iŋ, v. To have an - shape. Also, sok'iŋ.

overlook, Oḣape, v. To - .

P

pace, Kaipsilyalake s'e, adv. Keeping - ahead of.

pack, Inapaŋ, v. To be -ed. Pakigni, v. To - home, to carry home.

palm, Napoyublaya, v. To - .

participate, Ilita, v. To - .

path, Ocaŋku s'e, adv. Like a -way.

patter, Haḣaya, v. To - on.

peacefully, Owaḣwayakel, adv.

peel, Iyuḣlaḣlaya, adv. -ing. Wakiscu, v. To - .

perceptive, Slota, adj.

perch, Guḣ'ciŋcayela, adv. -ing.

persevere, Owapaḣlokehaŋ, part. Perseveringly.

petulant, Oie waśicuŋ, n. A - person.

pick, Pahihigla, v. To - up on the way. Pahihilag, adj. Having -ed up one's own way to.

pierce, Icapcab, v.a. To - . Icapepeya, adv. red. -ing.
plainly, Aślaślayela, adv.
plan, Waaokiyapi, n. A planning of things together.

poker, Icaśloke, n.
poor, Htani, adj. Being - , having difficulty.

possess, Wanagnaⁿka, v. To have ready. Wanagnuⁿka, v. To - . Itawaciⁿ, n. Possession.

powerful, Waś'akece, v. To be stout.

prairie-chicken, Śiyoka, n.

precipitate, Okahiⁿhaⁿ, v. To - .

precise, Igleglеȟyakеl, adv. Im-ly.

prepared, Icaⁿliyuha, v.n. To be poised. Isitutece, adj. Un- .

press, Apaskita, v. - on hard.

pretense, Oⁿgnaye, adv. Under - .

prick, Nakpeyeya, v. To - up ears.
pride, Iyotaⁿla, v.a. To show - . Wataⁿkic'ila, v. To think self great.

produce, Wakuni, v. To - .
prompt, Tohaⁿyaⁿśni haⁿni, adv. -ly.
prone, Makipastoya, adv. In a - position.

prying, Waelhiyayake, n. A - person.

pull, Pagmica, v. To - hair. Wośla-ślateke, n. The -ling out.

puncture, Papota, v.a. To - .

push, Paicisaⁿnica, v. To - away to the side. Pamahel, adv. -ing in.

Q

quaver, Wahognugnu, v. To warble.

question, Iyakaⁿwiⁿlake s'e, adv. -ingly.

quiet, Iwaȟwayela, adv. -ly, peacefully.
quiver, Yuȟniyaⁿ, v. To - .

R

race, Kakicipapi, n. A contest. Okiⁿyaⁿka, n. A racing arena.

ragged, Oȟpuȟpuya, adv. In rags.

raise, Ipaha, v. To hoist.

rash, Pisaⁿsaⁿ oȟ'aⁿke, v. To act -ly.

rattle, Yukakaka, v. To - .

ready, Wanagnaⁿka, v. To have - .
ream, Iyuk'o, v. To - .
rear, Hektapataⁿ, adv. By the - .

recent, Kalecalake s'e, adv. -ly.
recognize, Wawiyeke s'e, adv. -ing delightedly.

refuge, Wamá el i, v. To take - .

regard, Wocaⁿteoyuze, n. - for a person.

rekindle, Paile, v. To - .

relax, Kaⁿȟtal, adv. -ed.

repair, Aglukaka, v. To - .
repose, Kitaⁿpawoslaheyelakel, adv. -fully.
repress, Okpaspa, v. To - a reaction.

resent, Kaitececaśni, v. To assume a -ful face. Haⁿliyayapi s'e, adv. Leaving -fully.
respect, Wayuopeśa, n. One -ing others.
responsibility, Igloeyaya, v. To take up or go on one's own - . Oⁿgluȟpe, n.
restore, Okic'u, v. To take back.

return, Kiuⁿ, v. To - home.

revelation, Woyuaślaye, n.
revive, Kawaciⁿksab, v. To - .

rich, Ojicaka, adj. - in goods.
ricochet, Icana s'a, v. To - . Also, iwopsil, v.

ridicule, Waelhoyeya, v. To - .

right, Ecela, adj. Correct.

ripe, Najaⁿjaⁿyelayeye, v. To be - and shining.
ripple, Kaśniyaⁿyaⁿ, v. To - .

rock, Naiⁿyaⁿyeya, adv. Become hard.

roomy, Iyokaⁿ, adj.

rough, Kaskiska, v. To -en. Skiska, n. A - thing.
rout, Pabluka, v. To - .

rub, Inakiᶯlya, v.a. To - off.

ruin, Inajabjapa, v. red. To - .

S

sad, Oiyakiśilya, adv. Being a - saying or sight.

sage, Pejiȟota, n. Pejiȟota pepe, n. Prickly - . Pejiȟota skuya, n.

saliva, Taȟ, n. Foam. Taȟna, n. Running - .

sarcasm, Ihe, v. To use - , cutting words.

satisfied, Iwakaᶯyela, adj. Easily - .

savor, Ihamnapi s'e, adv. -ing.

say, Ekekiya, v. To - of one. Keyapi, v.n. They say. Ke, v.n. It is said. Śke, v.n. They say.

scarcely, H'uᶯyela, adv.

scepter, Wakeza, n. A sort of symbolic staff. Cf. wahukeza.

scoop, Hutipak'oga, v. To - .

scrape, Nawilwita s'e, adv. -ing together by foot. Nawiᶯta, v. To - .
scratch, Kaȟyuȟlata, v. To - . Onak'ega, v. To - around at.

scum, Hpo, n.

secure, Kokamna, v. To get - .

seem, Ekeśni, v. It seems not.
seep, Mnihipi s'e, adv. -ing in.

self-importance, Wanapicage, n. Feeling of - .

sensitive, Oȟ'aᶯwakaᶯkaᶯyaᶯ, adv. -ly. Waciᶯwaśakala, v. To be - .

separate, Palehaᶯyaᶯk, v. To - from, to part from.

shake, Kaiyoyagya, v. To quiver. Yuhaha, adv. Shaking up to spread out. Yupocaᶯcaᶯ, v. To - up by the hair.

shapeless, Put'iᶯgela, v. To be - and pudgy.
share, Yunaya, v. To pass to one. Yunayeya, v. To pass along to another.
shavings, Caᶯkagiȟaȟa, n.

shear, Naoswa, v. To - off.

shielded, Yuptinapeyakel, adv.

shock, Taᶯglusasa, v. To be -ed . Also, taᶯgluzaza.
shoo, Nakpawiᶯte s'e, adv. As if -ing away.
shorten, Yulena, v. To - . Yuoᶯjiᶯcayela, adv. Making short.
shoulder, Paicakśa, v. To carry over the -s. Tapetoska, n. White-spotted -s.

shred, Kaswaka, v. To - .
shrub, Caᶯȟotka, n. Small -s used for the making of arrows.

sick, Iglaśyakel, adv. -ly.

sideways, Kaicisaᶯnica, adv. Striking - .

silent, Naiᶯl, v. To grow - .

sing, Kahiyaya, v. To - through a tune.

slant, Kaoheye, adv. -ing.

slice, Iyus'o, v. To - .
slide, Kaoswa, v. To - down. Oᶯzeslohaᶯ, v.n. To - on the buttox.

slobber, H'eȟ'eya, adv. -ing.
slothful, Ehuweȟwegaᶯhaᶯ, v.n. To be inert.
slow, Kogiᶯgiᶯkel, adv. -ly.

smack, Paȟwayaśkapa, v.n. To - the lips.

smoke, Jotokte, v. To suffer from - . Oizilya, v. To - , as in tanning.

snatch, Yunap'iyeya, v. To - away.

snow, Wapaȟwuȟwu, adv. Running in crusted - . Wazaᶯzaᶯ, n. A trace of - .

so, Ehaᶯuᶯ, adv. Just so.

soft, Iyuśtaka, v. To -en. Kacica, v.a. To -en and smoothen. Kapaᶯyaᶯ, v. To -en by pummelling. Yugwa, v.

To soften by hand.

solicit, Ignagnaye s'e, adv. -ing. Kisiᥰkpe, v. To - . Kisiᥰte, v. To - . Winagiyeya, adv. Making -ations, i.e. alluring a woman, or man.

somersault, Glukśe, v. To turn a - .
sometimes, Watukte, adv.

sore, Naniyaᥰ, v. To have - feet.

sound, Kaȟlayela, adv. Causing to - .
soup, Śuᥰg'ohaᥰpi, n. Pot of dog.

sparkle, Pelwiyuśkiᥰ, v. To dance, as do flames.

speak, Okiśilia, v. To use bad language.
speed, Glukiᥰyaᥰ, v. To - up.
spent, Letka, adj.

spin, Glapemni, v. To make self - . Iglapemni, v. refl. To - one's self.
spine, Tacaᥰȟaȟaka wapaha, n. A bone used for a headdress ornament.
spirit, Wakaᥰkaᥰpi, n. The -s engaged to men.

split, Kiȟ'aᥰka, v. To - . Also, naśle. Wakinaśleca, v. To - by foot.

spoil, Kaśikśil, adv. -ed. Ośicamna, adj. Becoming -ed.

sprain, Iyuguka, v. To - .
sprawl, Icimnikel, adv. -ed. Nas'iᥰyela, adv. -ing.
spray, Icanaȟ'o, v. To - .
spread, Iyublaȟ, v. To - . Yuowaᥰcaya, v. To - out.
spring, Iyowiwila s'e, adv. As if -ing water. Naȟlal mniowe, n. A - scratched from the soil.

squander, Wakiyuwanice, v. To - .
squat, Hupaza, adv. Nahebyela, adv. On the haunches.
squirrel-tail, Pejijiji. n.

stagger, Katakiᥰkiᥰ, v. red. To - .
start, Oya, n. A - .
starve, Taakiȟ'aᥰ, n. A -ing person.
stay, Wauᥰke śni, v. To - a short time only.

steadfast, Kilyakel, adv. -ly.
steady, Kokiptaᥰ, v. To feel un- .
steam, Iyaśota, v. To - .

steps, Yupiᥰpiᥰta, v. To take short steps or movements.

stick, Katuᥰp, adj. -y. Oyataᥰyaᥰ, v. To - . Yuoyataᥰyaᥰ, v. To - in.
stingy, Omniyela, adv. Acting stingily.
stink, Onas'amna, v. To - .
stir, Wicokicamna, v. To be -red up.
stitch, Ipaȟna, adv. -ing.

stomach, Itezi, n. Watezi, n.
stop, Anakipta, v. To bring to a -.
storm, Icapogaᥰ, n. A blowing - .

stray, Pawicegna, n. A - that has returned. Śuᥰk'okaȟwog, n. A - horse.
strength, Pawaś'aka, v. To -en.
stretch, Kajalya, adv. With things spread out.
stride, Kacaᥰglegleya, v. To - .
strike, Itokicile, v.n. To try to - the face.
stripe, Iglagleglega, v. refl. To - .
stroke, Yuswupi s'e, adv. Running the hand smoothly over.
strong, Kpawaś'aka, v. pos. To make - and secure.

stupid, Śuᥰknoᥰgekpa s'e, adv. -ly.
successively, Gliglekiya, adv.
suck, Yaśkepa, v. To - dry. Yaśkeśkepa, v. To - and spit out.
sucker, Tusla, n. A blood-.

sun, Wiyagyata, adv. Towards the - .
sunk, Oȟ'okpaya, v. To be -en.

support, Iyagluza, v. To have for a - . Kuśipatoᥰ, v. To hold up.

surly, Waikalelepake, n. A - person.
surprise, Wicayuś'iᥰyaᥰyaᥰ s'e, adv. In sudden - .
surreptitiously, Anatakiᥰyece, adv.
suspend, Iyukoltkeyela, adv. -ed.

swallow, Kipca, v. To - saliva. Onapceśilya, v. To be hard to - .

sweat, Onacu, v. To be -y.
sweat-house, Oinikaga, n.
sweep, Kahiᥰtu ska, adv. Swept clean.
swell, Nakapoȟ, v. To make - . Oiyopa, v.n. To - . Opopoya, v. To be swollen. Tamna, n. A -ing.

T

tactful, Wawolwicayeśni uŋ, v. To be - .
take, Icucu, v.n. To take and have.
tap, Apapa, v.a. To - one, a thing.
team, Hasaŋni, n. A member of a - .
tear, Napsapsakela s'e, adv. -ing apart. Oyuȟ'eȟ'eyakel, adv. Slovenly. Yuȟ'eȟ'e, adv. -ing.

tense, Puskicat'a, v.n. To be - .

that, He eca, pron. dem. That person there.
there, Opa, adv. There being - .
thin, Cikcik'aya, adv. Slenderwise.
those, Henake, pron. dem.
threaten, Iwohiŋyaŋsyakel, adv. In a -ing manner.
throng, Wicapaptapta, adv. Among a - .
through, Iyopte, prep. Oyopta, v. To pass - .
throw, Eiȟpeic'iyaya, v.a. To - self over or out.
thunderbird, Takaŋgi, n. Tail feathers of the - .
thus, Hecina, adv.

tickle, Aśniyakiya, v. To - .

tie, Akiglaśke, v. To - together.
tight, Iyotitaŋla, adj. - fitting.
tilt, Ikakeiŋ, v. To knock into a - .
time, Owatohaŋtuka waŋ, n. Some times past. Wihiyala, n. A - measure.
tire, Kakśikśa, adv. Tired out.

toe, Sipagnagya, adv. To or at the tip of the toes.

tongue, Tacejiokaslute, n. - cutting. Tacejisu, n. - dribblings.
toy, Winapiśkaŋye, n.

track, Oguhaŋ, n. A trail.
train, Iglaoŋspe, v. refl. To teach.
travel, Iyuŋkel, adv. -ling by foot. Waomani, v. To - in snow.

tree, Caŋsapa, n. The Walnut - .

tributary, Oic'ipa, v. To be - to.
tricky, Osiŋkpekpeyakel, adv. In a - way.
trim, Oyus'o, v. To - off.
triumph, Iwaktekiyagla, v.a. To cause to go home in - .

trot, Ikacaŋcaŋ, n. The - of a horse.
trouble, Pageya, adv. Threatening, bullyingly, troublesome. Wapageyeca, v. To cause - .

truth, Waeyeca, v. To tell the facts.
try, Okinica, v. To strive.

tube, Nawoholyeya, adv. In the shape of a - .
tug, Wayatiktil, adv. -ging on with teeth.
turtle, Kecaŋȟ'a, n. Kewoyuspa s'e, adv. As a - dragged from the mud. Tatkaśa, n. A mud- .

U

uncooth, Okiśyakel, adv. Being - .
uncover, Yuiteśla, adv. -ing the face.

undaunted, Hetoŋtoŋ, adj. Hetoŋtoŋke, n. One who is - .

unexpected, Haŋiyaciŋke śni, adv. -ly during the night. Kaŋśniśnilak, v. cont. Not to expect one.

unkempt, Naȟpiȟpiya, adv. Slouchy.

unrestricted, Oikpaptaŋwaśteya, adv.

unsociable, Ot'iŋȟyakel, adv. Unsociably.

untangle, Okakseya, adv. Hard to - .
untie, Yaśkeśkeke, v. To - by teeth.

upper, Payapa, v. To be of the - part.
upright, Iwosla, adj. or adv. In an - manner. Katowotaŋla, adv. Knocked - .
uproot, Kaju, v.a. To - .

urge, Iyonataŋ, v. To - .
urine, Leja, leś, adj. Able to hold one's own - .

V

valuable, Yuśpika, adj. Worth buying or keeping. -- n. A - thing.

vanish, Śniyeca, v. To - .

veer, Gluna s'a, v. To - .

visible, Ozaŋyela, adv. Only a little - .

visit, Tikicii, v. To - .

voice, Hokiiyokpaza, v.n. To speak indistinctly. Howaśteya, v. To have a fine - . -- adv. Speaking well.

W

wad, Imnicoyapa, v. To use for -ding.

walk, Maniye s'e, adv. As though taking a - . Onaslata, v. To - slowly. Wamanika, n. One who likes to - .

want, Kajinica śni, v. To be apparently not in - .

warble, Wahognugnu, v. To - .
warn, Kaiyab, adv. Without -ing.
wash, Jajahaŋ, v. To be in need of -ing.

watch, Iśtiyagna, adv. Closely -ing, observing.
water, Imnija, adj. Full of - . Mniali, v. To travel over the - . Mniȟaȟa, v. To run with - . Mniyoȟcaya, adv. Full of - . Mniyosniya, v. To cool - .

wave, Kakicipehaŋ, v. To form -s.
way, Onamniyeta, adv. Being off on one's - .

wear, Oyutepa, v. To - off.
weave, Okpazaŋ, v. refl. To - one's own into. Onazoŋ, v. To - .

weed, Caŋȟloȟ suta, n. A woody sort of - . Caŋȟloȟ śluśluta, n. Tall and slick -s. Waptaye, n. A - in general.
weep, Ohowakaŋyaŋkel, adv. -ing in sorrow.

well, Itaŋyaŋ, adv.

while, Kaetulake el, adv. In a little - .
whistle, Jolowaŋwaŋ, v. To - .

willing, Caŋtekic'uŋyaŋ, adv. -ly.

wipe, Opakiŋslasla, adv. -ing the dirt away. Opapiŋslasla iyeya, v. To rub clean.

wood, Caŋkaiciyopteya, adv. With - crossed.
work, Atatape śni, adv. Keeping soft.

worry, Ik'o, v. To get worried. Ilita, v. To be worried.

wrinkled, Glesyela, adv. Opiśyela, adv. Loosely.

Y

yesterday, Iȟtalehaŋ, adv. The day before, in ref. to any given day.

Yokomi, Yokomi, n. p. A Zuni chief.

APPENDIX B. OGLALA TETON SOCIETY

(military)

Officers (12)

Pipe-bearers (2)

Drummers (2)

Lance-bearers (4)

Rattlers (2)

Whippers (2)

Witaŋśna uŋ (1)

Hunters
Warriors
Pejuta Wicaśa
Witaŋśna uŋ

(political)

Wicaśa Wakaŋ

Wicaȟcala (Naca)

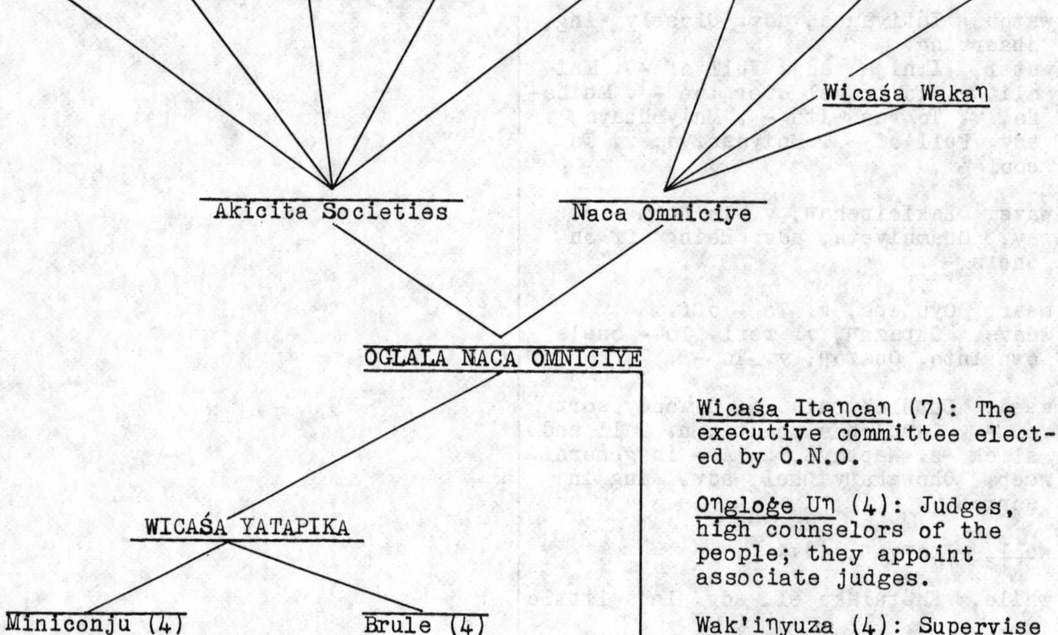

Wicaśa Itaŋcaŋ (7): The executive committee elected by O.N.O.

Oŋgloġe Uŋ (4): Judges, high counselors of the people; they appoint associate judges.

Wak'iŋyuza (4): Supervise and appoint for care of alliances, sanitation, policing.

Status: 1- Youth: accomplishments.
2- Age: maturity, wisdom.

Control Apparatus for Ambition:
1- Submerge parental ties.
2- Raise one's community interest.
3- Ascend the structure: by show of virtues.

APPENDIX C.

SIUOX NATION

Tribal and Linguistic Order

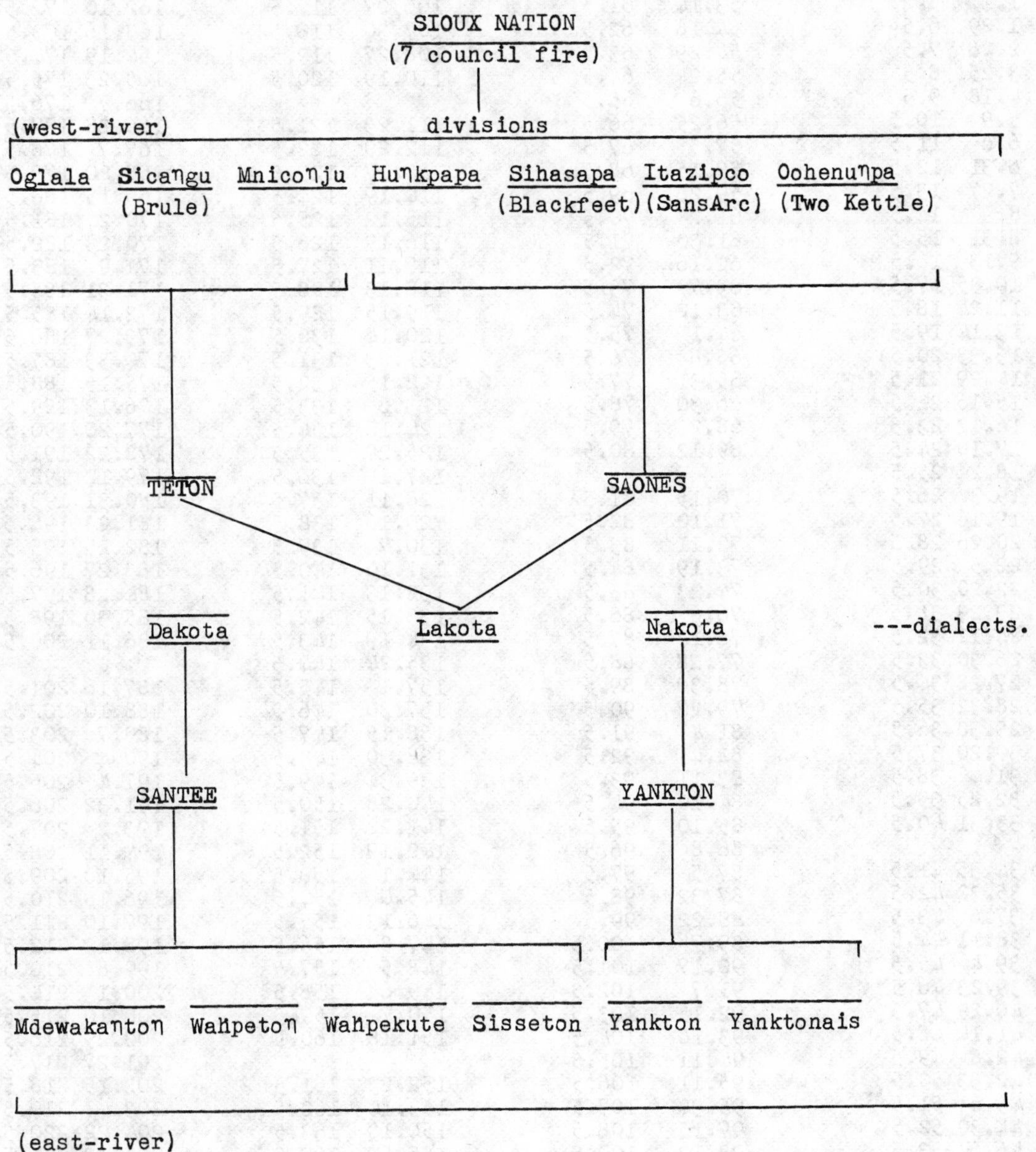

APPENDIX D.

WOWAPI WAKAŋ, Bible History, by Eugene Buechel, S.J., Benziger, 1924.
Buechel manuscript (MSS), page and line; Book, page and decimal part of page.

MSS	Book
1.1	5.2
1.29	6.5
2.26	7.5
3.25	8.5
4.18	9.5
5.9	10.5
6.6	11.5
6.31	12.5
7.27	13.5
8.9	14.5
8.31	15.5
9.13	16.5
10.35	17.5
11.24	18.5
13.14	19.5
13.33	20.5
14.29	21.5
15.16	22.5
16.12	23.5
17.10	24.5
18.2	25.5
19.3	26.5
19.16	27.5
20.26	28.5
22.5	29.5
22.20	30.5
23.23	31.5
24.12	32.5
26.30	33.5
27.28	34.5
28.32	35.5
29.30	36.5
30.20	37.5
31.4	38.5
32.25	39.5
33.31	40.5
34.35	41.5
35.32	42.5
37.6	43.5
38.11	44.5
39.4	45.5
39.23	46.5
40.29	47.5
41.14	48.5
42.8	49.5
42.33	50.5
44.6	51.5
44.30	52.5
46.6	53.5
47.4	54.5
47.20	55.5
48.18	56.5
49.10	57.5
50.20	58.5
51.16	59.5
52.31	60.5

MSS	Book
53.14	61.5
54.16	62.5
54.29	63.5
55.24	64.5
56.6	65.5
56.25	66.5
57.5	67.5
58.15	68.5
59.28	69.5
61.2	70.5
61.30	71.5
62.16	72.5
63.7	73.5
63.12	74.5
64.1	75.5
65.8	76.5
65.31	77.5
66.30	78.5
68.2	79.5
69.12	80.5
70.15	81.5
71.10	82.5
72.11	83.5
73.19	84.5
74.23	85.5
76.6	86.5
76.17	87.5
77.28	88.5
78.30	89.5
79.27	90.5
81.4	91.5
82.4	92.5
83.11	93.5
84.10	94.5
85.10	95.5
86.8	96.5
87.5	97.5
87.32	98.5
88.22	99.5
89.7	100.5
90.17	101.5
91.7	102.5
92.15	103.5
93.16	104.5
94.11	105.5
95.11	106.5
95.34	107.5
97.15	108.5
98.12	109.5
99.13	110.5
100.11	111.5
101.25	112.5
102.30	113.5
104.1	114.5
105.10	115.5
106.1	116.5

MSS	Book
106.27	117.5
107.30	118.5
108.27	119.5
110.19	120.5
111.23	121.5
112.29	122.5
113.17	123.5
114.19	124.5
115.12	125.5
116.19	126.5
117.11	127.5
118.13	128.5
119.15	129.5
120.14	130.5
121.23	131.5
122.15	132.5
123.6	133.5
124.18	134.5
125.29	135.5
127.1	136.5
128.11	137.5
129.16	138.5
130.7	139.5
131.10	140.5
132.13	141.5
133.15	142.5
134.19	143.5
135.24	144.5
137.1	145.5
137.30	146.5
138.15	147.5
138.30	148.5
139.34	149.5
140.28	150.5
141.22	151.5
142.19	152.5
144.1	153.5
145.4	154.5
146.13	155.5
147.8	156.5
148.5	157.5
149.6	158.5
150.7	159.5
151.18	160.5
152.23	161.5
153.14	162.5
154.13	163.5
155.5	164.5
155.22	165.5
156.20	166.5
157.23	167.5
158.24	168.5
159.26	169.5
160.3	170.5
160.32	171.5

MSS	Book
162.10	172.5
163.16	173.5
164.19	174.5
165.23	175.5
166.7	176.5
166.28	177.5
167.7	178.5
168.20	179.5
169.15	180.5
170.2	181.5
170.23	182.5
171.9	183.5
171.31	184.5
172.14	185.5
173.27	186.5
174.33	187.5
175.15	188.5
176.13	189.5
177.20	190.5
178.22	191.5
179.12	192.5
180.31	193.5
181.23	194.5
182.25	195.5
183.27	196.5
184.28	197.5
185.30	198.5
186.11	200.5
187.16	201.5
188.10	202.5
189.7	203.5
190.4	204.5
191.4	205.5
191.32	206.5
193.2	207.5
194.11	208.5
195.18	209.5
196.18	210.5
197.10	211.5
198.12	212.5
199.8	213.5
200.1	214.5
200.10	215.5
200.29	216.5
201.27	217.5
202.15	218.5
203.4	219.5
204.22	220.5
205.13	221.5
206.15	222.5
207.7	223.5
207.31	224.5
208.30.	225.5
210.1	226.5
211.4	227.5
212.6	228.5

Bible History ref.

MSS	Book
213.11	229.5
214.11	230.5
214.32	231.5
215.33	232.5
216.19	233.5
217.26	234.5
218.22	235.5
219.16	236.5
220.20	237.5
221.1	238.5
221.27	239.5
222.23	240.5
223.20	241.5
224.22	242.5
225.21	243.5
226.16	244.5
227.14	245.5
228.6	246.5
229.9	247.5
230.1	248.5
230.6	249.5
231.16	250.5
232.5	251.5
233.31	252.5
234.1	253.5
234.19	254.5
235.19	255.5
236.14	256.5
237.12	257.5
238.4	258.5
239.17	259.5
240.11	260.5
241.22	261.5
242.21	262.5
243.25	263.5
244.32	264.5
245.2	265.5
246.7	266.5
246.28	267.5
247.18	268.5
249.25	269.5
250.29	270.5
251.25	271.5
252.18	272.5
253.13	273.5
254.7	274.5
255.1	275.5
255.29	276.5
256.20	277.5
257.7	278.5
258.2	279.5
258.29	280.5
259.25	281.5
260.25	282.5
261.15	283.5
262.12	284.5
263.12	285.5

MSS	Book
263.15	286.5
264.24	287.5
265.14	288.5
266.1	289.5
267.7	290.5
268.9	291.5
268.34	292.5
269.15	293.5
269.32	294.5
270.17	295.5
271.31	296.5
272.13	297.5
273.11	298.5
273.32	299.5
274.20	300.5
275.20	301.5
276.12	302.5
276.25	303.5
277.10	304.5
278.4	305.5
279.11	306.5
280.12	307.5
280.21	308.5
281.24	309.5
283.3	310.5
284.8	311.5
285.14	312.5
286.3	313.5
286.26	314.5
287,21	315.5
288.7	316.5
289.2	317.5
289.23	318.5
290.27	319.5
291.27	320.5
292.23	321.5
293.15	322.5
294.15	323.5
295.20	324.5
296.16	325.5
297.7	326.5
298.11	327.5
298.19	328.5
299.31	329.5
300.20	330.5
301.18	331.5
302.17	332.5
303.5	333.5
303.28	334.5
304.20	335.5
305.26	336.5
306.17	337.5
307.7	338.3 End.

APPENDIX E. BIBLIOGRAPHY

Boas and Deloria, U. S. Government Printing Office, Washington, D. C. 1941, pp.183: Dakota Grammar.

Boas and Swanton, U. S. Government Printing Office, Bureau of Ethnology (Boas). 1911, pp. 90: Extract from Handbook of American Indian Languages, Bull. 40. Part I. Siouan Dialects, and Illustrative Sketch.

Buechel, S.J., Rev. Eugene, 1908, pp. 659: Manuscript stories and narrations (MSS).

Benziger Brothers, New York. 1924, pp. 349: Bible History in Teton Sioux. (B.H.)

St. Francis Mission. 1939, pp. 374: A Grammar of Lakota. (Gram.)

Deloria, Ella C., G. E. Steckert and Co., New York Agents. 1932, pp. 280: Dakota Texts. American Ethnological Society, Vol. XIV, ed. by Franz Boas. (D.)

Densmore, Frances, U. S. Government Printing Office, 1918, pp. 561: Bureau of American Ethnology, Bull. 61. Teton Sioux Music. (FD.)

Hunt, O.S.B., Rev. Jerome, Jos. Bering Printing Co., Cincinnati. c.1910, pp. 170: Catechism, Prayers and Instructions in Sioux.

Perrig, S.J., Rev. E., c.1902, pp. 360: Manuscript Lakota-English Dictionary. (P.)

Pilling, J. C., Government Printing Office, Bureau of Ethnology. 1887, pp. 87: Siouan Languages.

Riggs, Rev. Stephen Returns, ed. by J. O. Dorsey, U. S. Government Printing Office, 1890, pp. 665: Contribution to North American Ethnology, Vol. VII. Dakota-English Dictionary. (R.)

Walker, J. R., American Museum of Natural History, New York. 1917, pp. 221: Anthropological Papers, Vol. XVI, Part II. Sun Dance and Other Ceremonies of the Oglala Tetons. (WJR.)

Williamson, Rev. John P., American Tract Society, New York. 1902, pp. 264: English-Dakota Dictionary. (WL)

Wissler, Clark, American Museum of Natural History. 1912, pp. 99: Anthropological Papers, Vol. XI, Part I. Societies and Ceremonial Associations in the Oglala Teton.

Supplementary

Hoebel, E. Adamson, McGraw-Hill, New York. 1966, pp. 591: Anthropology: The Study of Man.

Hoijer, Harry ed., University of Chicago Press. 1958, pp. 286: Language in Culture.

Lado, Robert, University of Michigan Press. 1958, pp. 141: Linguistics Across Cultures.